International Directory of

COMPANY HISTORIES

International Directory of COMPANY HISTORIES

VOLUME 31

Editor
Tina Grant

ST. JAMES PRESS

AN IMPRINT OF THE GALE GROUP

DETROIT • NEW YORK • SAN FRANCISCO
LONDON • BOSTON • WOODBRIDGE, CT

STAFF

Tina Grant, *Editor*

Miranda H. Ferrara, *Project Manager*

Laura Standley Berger, Joann Cerrito, David J. Collins, Steve Cusack,
Nicolet V. Elert, Jamie C. FitzGerald, Kristin Hart, Laura S. Kryhoski,
Margaret Mazurkiewicz, Michael J. Tyrkus, *St. James Press Editorial Staff*

Peter M. Gareffa, *Managing Editor, St. James Press*

Library of Congress Catalog Number: 89-190943

British Library Cataloguing in Publication Data

International directory of company histories. Vol. 31
I. Tina Grant
338.7409

ISBN 1-55862-390-6

Printed in the United States of America
Published simultaneously in the United Kingdom

St. James Press is an imprint of The Gale Group

Cover photograph: Riga Stock Exchange in Latvia
(courtesy Rigas Fondu Birza)

10 9 8 7 6 5 4 3 2 1

CONTENTS

Preface . . . . page vii
List of Abbreviations ix

Company Histories

Adaptec, Inc. . . . 3
Alcan Aluminium Limited . . . 7
American Woodmark Corporation . . . 13
The Andersons, Inc. . . . 17
Associated Grocers, Incorporated . . . 22
The Associated Press . . . 27
Atlantic Richfield Company . . . 31
AutoZone, Inc. . . . 35
Avado Brands, Inc. . . . 39
The B. Manischewitz Company, LLC . . . 43
Bayou Steel Corporation . . . 47
bebe stores, inc. . . . 50
Blair Corporation . . . 53
Blockbuster Inc. . . . 56
Booker plc . . . 61
Booth Creek Ski Holdings, Inc. . . . 65
Boscov's Department Store, Inc. . . . 68
Bright Horizons Family Solutions, Inc. . . . 71
Brobeck, Phleger & Harrison, LLP . . . 74
Bunzl plc . . . 77
Candie's, Inc. . . . 81
Carolina First Corporation . . . 85
Carson, Inc. . . . 88
Casa Cuervo, S.A. de C.V. . . . 91
CEC Entertainment, Inc. . . . 94
Century Theatres, Inc. . . . 99
China Eastern Airlines Co. Ltd. . . . 102
Chinese Petroleum Corporation . . . 105
Chris-Craft Industries, Inc. . . . 109
CITGO Petroleum Corporation . . . 113
The Coastal Corporation . . . 118
Coherent, Inc. . . . 122
Colas S.A. . . . 126
Complete Business Solutions, Inc. . . . 130
Converse Inc. . . . 134
Corbis Corporation . . . 139
Dallas Semiconductor Corporation . . . 143
Data Broadcasting Corporation . . . 147
Day & Zimmermann, Inc. . . . 151
De Dietrich & Cie. . . . 156
Decora Industries, Inc. . . . 160
Dell Computer Corporation . . . 163
Dole Food Company, Inc. . . . 167
Edwards Theatres Circuit, Inc. . . . 171
Egghead.com, Inc. . . . 174
eircom plc . . . 178
Environmental Industries, Inc. . . . 182
Euromarket Designs Inc. . . . 186
Federated Department Stores, Inc. . . . 190
Fieldcrest Cannon, Inc. . . . 195
Fielmann AG . . . 201
Fifth Third Bancorp . . . 204
Florsheim Shoe Group Inc. . . . 209
Garden Fresh Restaurant Corporation . . . 213
Getty Images, Inc. . . . 216
Grameen Bank . . . 219
Greene King plc . . . 223
Green Mountain Coffee, Inc. . . . 227
Gristede's Sloan's, Inc. . . . 231
Gruma, S.A. de C.V. . . . 234
GT Interactive Software . . . 237
Hansen Natural Corporation . . . 242
Haverty Furniture Companies, Inc. . . . 246
Heidelberger Zement AG . . . 250
Henry Schein, Inc. . . . 254
Hubbell Incorporated . . . 257
I.C. Isaacs & Company . . . 260
International Rectifier Corporation . . . 263

Interscope Music Group 267
J. Baker, Inc. 270
Jennifer Convertibles, Inc. 274
Johnny Rockets Group, Inc. 277
Jos. A. Bank Clothiers, Inc. 282
Kentucky Electric Steel, Inc. 286
Kenwood Corporation 289
The King Arthur Flour Company 292
KnowledgeWare Inc. 296
Lam Research Corporation 299
Lan Chile S.A. 303
Larry Flynt Publishing Inc. 307
Lason, Inc. 311
Louisiana-Pacific Corporation 314
Lutheran Brotherhood 318
March of Dimes 322
Melaleuca Inc. 326
MIH Limited 329
Mine Safety Appliances Company 333
Monaco Coach Corporation 336
Movie Gallery, Inc. 339
Navy Exchange Service Command 342
NBTY, Inc. 346
Odwalla, Inc. 349
Oneida Ltd. 352
Pediatric Services of America, Inc. 356
Performance Food Group Company 359
Porsche AG 363
Powell Duffryn plc 367
Publix Super Markets Inc. 371
Random House Inc. 375
Redhook Ale Brewery, Inc. 381
Redrow Group plc 385
Reed Elsevier plc 388
Rotary International 395
The Rugby Group plc 398
Schibsted ASA 401
Schultz Sav-O Stores, Inc. 406
Scott Paper Company 409
Skechers U.S.A. Inc. 413
Soft Sheen Products, Inc. 416
Spirit Airlines, Inc. 419
The St. Joe Company 422
Sub-Zero Freezer Co., Inc. 426
The Talbots, Inc. 429
Tandycrafts, Inc. 433
Temple-Inland Inc. 438
TransBrasil S/A Linhas Aéreas 443
Triumph Group, Inc. 446
U.S. Cellular Corporation 449
Ultramar Diamond Shamrock Corporation . . 453
Vin & Spirit AB 458
Wildlife Conservation Society 462
Willamette Industries, Inc. 465
The Williams Companies, Inc. 469
YMCA of the USA 473
Zany Brainy, Inc. 477

Index to Companies 481
Index to Industries 649
Notes on Contributors 675

PREFACE

The St. James Press series *The International Directory of Company Histories (IDCH)* is intended for reference use by students, business people, librarians, historians, economists, investors, job candidates, and others who seek to learn more about the historical development of the world's most important companies. To date, *IDCH* has covered over 4,400 companies in 31 volumes.

Inclusion Criteria

Most companies chosen for inclusion in *IDCH* have achieved a minimum of US$50 million in annual sales and are leading influences in their industries or geographical locations. Companies may be publicly held, private, or nonprofit. State-owned companies that are important in their industries and that may operate much like public or private companies also are included. Wholly owned subsidiaries and divisions are profiled if they meet the requirements for inclusion. Entries on companies that have had major changes since they were last profiled may be selected for updating.

The *IDCH* series highlights 10% private and nonprofit companies, and features updated entries on approximately 45 companies per volume.

Entry Format

Each entry begins with the company's legal name, the address of its headquarters, its telephone, toll-free, and fax numbers, and its web site. A statement of public, private, state, or parent ownership follows. A company with a legal name in both English and the language of its headquarters country is listed by the English name, with the native-language name in parentheses.

The company's founding or earliest incorporation date, the number of employees, and the most recent available sales figures follow. Sales figures are given in local currencies with equivalents in U.S. dollars. For some private companies, sales figures are estimates and indicated by the abbreviation *est.* The entry lists the exchanges on which a company's stock is traded and its ticker symbol, as well as the company's NAIC codes.

Entries generally contain a *Company Perspectives* box which provides a short summary of the company's mission, goals, and ideals, a *Key Dates* box highlighting milestones in the company's history, lists of *Principal Subsidiaries, Principal Divisions, Principal Operating Units, Principal Competitors,* and articles for *Further Reading.*

American spelling is used throughout *IDCH*, and the word "billion" is used in its U.S. sense of one thousand million.

Sources

Entries have been compiled from publicly accessible sources both in print and on the Internet such as general and academic periodicals, books, annual reports, and material supplied by the companies themselves.

Cumulative Indexes

IDCH contains two indexes: the **Index to Companies**, which provides an alphabetical index to companies discussed in the text as well as to companies profiled, and the **Index to Industries**, which allows researchers to locate companies by their principal industry. Both indexes are cumulative and specific instructions for using them are found immediately preceding each index.

Suggestions Welcome

Comments and suggestions from users of *IDCH* on any aspect of the product as well as suggestions for companies to be included or updated are cordially invited. Please write:

The Editor
International Directory of Company Histories
St. James Press
27500 Drake Rd.
Farmington Hills, Michigan 48331-3535

ABBREVIATIONS FOR FORMS OF COMPANY INCORPORATION

A.B.	Aktiebolaget (Sweden)
A.G.	Aktiengesellschaft (Germany, Switzerland)
A.S.	Atieselskab (Denmark)
A.S.	Aksjeselskap (Denmark, Norway)
A.Ş.	Anomin Şirket (Turkey)
B.V.	Besloten Vennootschap met beperkte, Aansprakelijkheid (The Netherlands)
Co.	Company (United Kingdom, United States)
Corp.	Corporation (United States)
G.I.E.	Groupement d'Intérêt Economique (France)
GmbH	Gesellschaft mit beschränkter Haftung (Germany)
H.B.	Handelsbolaget (Sweden)
Inc.	Incorporated (United States)
KGaA	Kommanditgesellschaft auf Aktien (Germany)
K.K.	Kabushiki Kaisha (Japan)
LLC	Limited Liability Company (Middle East)
Ltd.	Limited (Canada, Japan, United Kingdom, United States)
N.V.	Naamloze Vennootschap (The Netherlands)
OY	Osakeyhtiöt (Finland)
PLC	Public Limited Company (United Kingdom)
PTY.	Proprietary (Australia, Hong Kong, South Africa)
S.A.	Société Anonyme (Belgium, France, Switzerland)
SpA	Società per Azioni (Italy)

ABBREVIATIONS FOR CURRENCY

DA	Algerian dinar	M$	Malaysian ringgit
A$	Australian dollar	Dfl	Netherlands florin
Sch	Austrian schilling	Nfl	Netherlands florin
BFr	Belgian franc	NZ$	New Zealand dollar
Cr	Brazilian cruzado	N	Nigerian naira
C$	Canadian dollar	NKr	Norwegian krone
RMB	Chinese renminbi	RO	Omani rial
DKr	Danish krone	P	Philippine peso
E£	Egyptian pound	Esc	Portuguese escudo
EUR	Euro Dollars	Ru	Russian ruble
Fmk	Finnish markka	SRls	Saudi Arabian riyal
FFr	French franc	S$	Singapore dollar
DM	German mark	R	South African rand
HK$	Hong Kong dollar	W	South Korean won
HUF	Hungarian forint	Pta	Spanish peseta
Rs	Indian rupee	SKr	Swedish krona
Rp	Indonesian rupiah	SFr	Swiss franc
IR£	Irish pound	NT$	Taiwanese dollar
L	Italian lira	B	Thai baht
¥	Japanese yen	£	United Kingdom pound
W	Korean won	$	United States dollar
KD	Kuwaiti dinar	B	Venezuelan bolivar
LuxFr	Luxembourgian franc	K	Zambian kwacha

International Directory of

COMPANY HISTORIES

Adaptec, Inc.

691 S. Milpitas Boulevard
Milpitas, California 95035
U.S.A.
Telephone: (408) 945-8600
Toll Free: (800) 934-2766
Fax: (408) 262-2533
Web site: http://www.adaptec.com

Public Company
Incorporated: 1981
Employees: 2,123
Sales: $692.4 million (1999)
Stock Exchanges: NASDAQ
Ticker Symbol: ADPT
NAIC: 33413 Semiconductor and Related Devices Manufacturing

Adaptec, Inc. is a leader in the manufacture and sale of hardware and software that allow data transfer between computers. The company has a strong share of the market for small computer system interface devices, known as SCSI (pronounced "scuzzy"). These interfaces allow data to move quickly between different computer types and allow computers to communicate with peripheral devices such as printers, scanners, disk drives, tape drives, CD-ROM drives and others. Adaptec also manufactures other technology in the general field of data movement, including advanced networking equipment and software. The firm maintains headquarters in Silicon Valley, in the town of Milpitas, California, with regional offices in Japan and Belgium. A Miami, Florida office oversees Adaptec's business in Latin America. Adaptec does not own its own manufacturing facilities, but subcontracts through vendors in Taiwan, Singapore, and elsewhere. Some of Adaptec's customers include major computer manufacturers such as IBM, Dell, Apple, and Compaq.

Beginnings in the 1980s

Adaptec was the brainchild of Laurence Boucher. Boucher had been a computer engineer at a company called Shugart Associates and at leading computer maker IBM. In 1981, at the age of 37, he left IBM to start his own company. As small computers began to get more powerful, Boucher saw a need for technology that would let them swap data with mainframe computers and other devices more quickly. The problem was known as the input/output bottleneck: very fast computers could not work to capacity if they could not get their data—from disk drives, networks, or whatever—at an acceptable speed. Eric J. Savitz, in a profile of Adaptec in the December 3, 1990 issue of *Barron's,* described the input/output bottleneck aptly as driving a sports car through Manhattan at rush hour: "Theoretically, you might be able to go 140 miles per hour, but practically, you're lucky if you reach 10 miles per hour." Boucher's company developed semiconductor chips, boards, and software that eliminated rush hour. Adaptec's technology made quick, flexible communication links between computers and their so-called peripheral devices, meaning printers, exterior drives, and other components that might be linked up to the computer.

Boucher had found a niche for a viable product, and Adaptec grew quickly. After only two years, the company had sales of more than $6 million. Management, sales, and distribution were run out of headquarters in Milpitas, California, while manufacturing and assembly of Adaptec's semiconductor chips and circuit boards were subcontracted out to factories in Singapore. The company ballooned, finding many customers among other start-up computer companies who appreciated Adaptec's cutting-edge technology. Yet this initial spurt of growth was not well managed; soon, Adaptec ran into serious financial problems. As the company was just establishing its reputation, it took all the customers it could get to achieve enough sales volume to keep going. As a result, Adaptec ended up pooling most of its sales among three companies. As these were all new ventures, and not particularly stable, this was not a wise strategy. During one disastrous quarter of 1984, all three of the companies that represented Adaptec's biggest customers ran into difficulties and decided to cancel their orders. Losing these three customers meant fully half of Adaptec's sales went down the drain. When things had been going well, the company had been casually managed, and it did not seem to matter. But in this crisis, it was clear that Adaptec needed to adopt some basic controls. The company had not been verifying shipments

Company Perspectives:

Adaptec plays a pivotal role today in satisfying the world's growing need for more data, more storage, more connectivity. The Internet revolution is increasing demand for access to information. Meanwhile, business applications are more data-intensive and mission-critical. And computers are more and more important to the way people both work and play. We provide products that support information productivity for both businesses and individuals. Our Input/Output (I/O) solutions help move data quickly and reliably into and out of all kinds of computers. Adaptec is the undisputed market leader in high-performance, high-reliability I/O. In addition, our host I/O, RAID, and software products are the preferred solutions for the fastest growing segments of the computer market: Windows NT servers, workstations, and high-end desktop PCs.

against purchase orders, and it was receiving parts it did not want and running short on essentials. The company had been running without regular production forecasts, so it was virtually impossible to clarify what parts were needed anyway. Finances were out of order, and the company was not getting paid promptly by its customers. It operated without credit checks or credit limits on customers. This sloppiness on Adaptec's part inadvertently put the company in the position of lending money to its clients—other small companies happy for the break. Early in 1984, Adaptec found itself with inventory on hand worth more than its entire sales for the 1983 fiscal year, and the firm's cash balance dwindled to only $131,000.

The company had to act quickly to avoid going under. Fortunately, Boucher recently had hired several top executives with experience working at older, established computer firms. A marketing vice-president and sales president came to Adaptec from Intel, and Boucher also hired a chief financial officer who had previously worked at an analytical instrument manufacturer in San Jose, Finnegan Corp. Whereas Boucher was an engineer with keen insight into computer technology, these managers had more business background. They worked literally day and night to turn the company around, first of all by selling off inventory. During the business day, Adaptec sold its excess parts to other area companies, and in the evening, managers attended meetings of local electronics clubs to sell off unneeded controller boards. The company leased out unused testing equipment and extracted more time to pay from its creditors. Because Adaptec did not own its own factories and manufacturing equipment, it had relatively low overhead. It managed to raise enough cash to keep going, without laying off staff. The company began to operate in a more traditional and businesslike manner. It initiated regularly scheduled executive staff meetings to fine-tune production forecasts and began running credit checks on customers and limiting customer credit. It also sought out new customers, so that it did not sell exclusively to young and high-risk companies. Adaptec soon linked up with two national electronics distributors and began selling as well to Texas Instruments, Hewlett-Packard, Sun Microsystems, and other firmly entrenched computer industry leaders.

Because of Adaptec's quick action, the 1984 crisis passed and the company was left in sound shape. In 1986 the company went public, selling its shares on the NASDAQ stock exchange. By that time, Adaptec had a customer base of more than 300 companies, and no single customer made up more than ten percent of its sales. With a more coherent business plan, growth was manageable, and the company did extremely well. Sales for fiscal 1986 rose almost 80 percent compared with the year before, reaching close to $60 million. Profits also increased significantly, more than doubling. In its crisis year, Adaptec's inventory turned over less than once, but by fiscal 1986 inventory was turning over 6.8 times a year, almost twice the industry average. The company was thinking ahead, too, spending about nine percent of its sales on research and development and bringing out scores of new products. After the company went public, founder Boucher left. He went to work starting a new company, Auspex Systems. A former IBM colleague, John G. Adler, took over the chief executive position at Adaptec.

SCSI Sales in the Late 1980s

Adaptec manufactured a wide array of microchips and subsystems that allowed computers to communicate with peripherals. One development in the late 1980s was a card that could be inserted into laser printers both to increase speed and lower costs. Adaptec also made controllers for high-capacity disk drives. Among its products, the most important by 1990 was the SCSI. Sales of SCSI and SCSI-related devices made up 70 percent of Adaptec's sales by 1990. SCSI had become more important as time passed. Originally, founder Boucher had seen the need for a device that allowed data to bypass the input/output bottleneck, the traffic jam described previously. Yet in the early 1980s, relatively few computers were powerful enough to run into this problem. But as personal computers grew more powerful, Adaptec's data flow controllers became more essential. In 1986 Apple adopted the SCSI for all of its Macintosh model computers. Several years later, IBM-compatible models were using it, and by 1989, IBM itself had made SCSI standard. Adaptec worked both ends of the market, making the adapter boards that went into computers using SCSI and the so-called protocol chips inserted into the peripheral devices that would then communicate with the host computer via SCSI. By 1990, the company had divided its manufacturing operations into three main areas. The first was systems products, which were the hard-disk controllers, local area network adapter boards, software, and SCSI host adapter boards required by computer manufacturers. The second manufacturing area was peripheral products, which meant the adapters and controller boards used by makers of equipment that networked with computers. Among the company's most prominent products in this area were its printer controller boards and hard disk controller chips. Adaptec's third division was for development products, which were components used by makers of both computers and peripherals in testing and developing new products before they went on the market. The biggest and fastest growing of these three product areas was peripherals. It made laser printer boards for the Japanese manufacturers Canon and C. Itoh, and their new printers were considered astonishingly fast. At a trade show in 1990, the company demonstrated how the Japanese printers equipped with the Adaptec card could produce in 30 seconds a complex drawing that normally would have taken 30 minutes.

Key Dates:

1981: Company founded by Laurence Boucher.
1986: Adaptec goes public.
1989: IBM adopts Adaptec's SCSI.
1995: Company gets new CEO Grant Saviers.
1997: Company's sales and stock plummet.
1999: New CEO Robert Stephens takes helm.

Changes in the Mid-1990s

Chairman John Adler stepped down in 1995 and left the chief executive position to Grant Saviers. A dozen years after its founding, Adaptec was an enviable company. It had a huge share of the market for its products, burgeoning sales, and a quite comfortable profit margin. Revenues for fiscal 1993 were more than $300 million, and net income for that year tripled from the year before, to $49 million. Its SCSI adapters were able to handle data from as many as 15 peripheral devices at once, allowing computer owners to hook up optical scanners, external hard drives, or multiple printers with great convenience. Its products were in demand, and the company had been profitable quarter after quarter. Yet in the mid-1990s, the company realized its glow might not last, and it began to look ahead to new products.

Adaptec's laser printer card business had proved unsuccessful, and by 1994 the company was no longer pursuing it. Other manufacturers had tried to get in on the computer communications device market, coming up with new technology they hoped would be better and cheaper. Competitors had come up with other devices, known by impenetrable acronyms, including IDE/ATA and ATA Packet Interface. These were different ways of doing what the SCSI did. But the looming problem for Adaptec was making its SCSI products work with voice and video applications. By 1994, voice and video components made up a very small portion of the computer market, yet it seemed to be the wave of the future. SCSI products could move large amounts of data between computers and peripherals, but the data they handled was not exactly time dependent. For voice and video, all the information had to arrive synchronously or the sound and picture would be garbled. The company poured money into research and development, devoting as much as ten percent of revenues in the mid-1990s to developing new products, particularly adaptations for voice and video.

The company also moved to shore up its product line by making acquisitions. In 1995 Adaptec acquired Power I/O, a small company founded by computer entrepreneur Robert Stephens. In 1996 Adaptec bought Cogent Data Technologies, Inc. in a transaction valued at $68 million. Cogent Data was a privately held company based in Friday Harbor, Washington, and it made a kind of adapter device known as Fast Ethernet. This was a new computer networking technology that seemed to be growing quickly. Acquiring the small company gave Adaptec entry into Fast Ethernet's markets more quickly than if it had tried to develop its own products. Two years later Adaptec tried to make another acquisition, but soon scrapped the plan. In February 1998, Adaptec offered to pay $775 million for Symbios Logic Inc., a Hyundai Electronics subsidiary based in Fort Collins, Colorado. Symbios made data storage equipment, and its 1997 sales were more than $600 million. However, a review of the merger by the Federal Trade Commission raised antitrust issues, and Adaptec backed out of the deal.

Trouble in the Late 1990s

This was a bad time for Adaptec. By 1997, the market for personal computers had slowed, and with it Adaptec's sales sank. A few years earlier, Adaptec's SCSI technology had found a place in approximately 12 percent of desktop computers. In 1997 that percentage was somewhere in the single digits. Premium chip maker Intel had incorporated technology similar to SCSI on its standard product, making Adaptec's device obsolete on Intel-powered machines. Profits slowed at Adaptec, and sales grew for fiscal 1998 only eight percent, far below the stellar rates of years earlier. The company's stock began to fall. In late 1997 it had been trading at more than $50. It bottomed out in 1998 at $8. In the summer of 1998, Adaptec's chief financial officer resigned, and shortly after, the treasurer left. When it was unable to carry through its acquisition of Symbios, the company was at a loss for a new direction, and this led to turmoil. Finally, in August 1998 Chairman and Chief Executive Grant Saviers quit. Apparently, his plan for the company was less conservative than the board wanted, and he left. The position was filled temporarily by Adaptec's founder, Laurence Boucher. Boucher had launched his third company by that time, but he came back to straighten things out at Adaptec. He announced that the company would shore up its core business, which was still the ailing SCSI. Almost immediately the firm announced layoffs in its storage systems division, and in November it sold its Peripheral Technology Solutions division to STMicroelectronics. This division made controllers for disk drives. Formerly, it had contributed as much as 25 percent of Adaptec's revenues, but that figure had fallen to about ten percent. The transaction brought Adaptec $73 million. Adaptec got out of its satellite networking business, its fibre channel business, its high-end peripheral technology business, and its external storage business. The company also cut back the amount of money it was spending on research and development.

By January 1999 the company was able to announce better than expected profits for the preceding quarter. Its quick action to cut costs and sever unprofitable product lines had shown results and demand rose again for some of its core hardware and software. Boucher continued to lead the company, while Adaptec found a new president in Robert Stephens, who had been chief operating officer since 1995.

Almost a year later, the company seemed to be returning to financial health. As the stock market continued to prosper, Adaptec's stock recovered somewhat. The company had promising new products in its so-called RAID (redundant arrays of independent disks) technology. This amalgam of hardware, software, and SCSI products was able to turn a group of disk drives into a powerful data storage unit. Adaptec also had turned itself into the leading supplier of software that let people record compact disks at home. As music from the Internet seemed to be a rapidly growing niche, the company was well positioned to take advantage of this growth. Though sales for fiscal 1999 were more than 30 percent lower than the year previous, there were signs that the company was doing better, particularly with strong fourth quarter sales and net income.

Principal Subsidiaries

Adaptec Mfg. (S) Pte. Ltd. (Singapore); Adaptec Gmbh (Germany); Adaptec Europe S.A. (Belgium); Adaptec Japan Ltd.

Principal Competitors

Hewlett-Packard; Digi International; Oak Technology.

Further Reading

''Adaptec Names CEO and Chairman,'' *Electronic News,* April 19, 1999, p. 30.

Beauchamp, Mark, ''Man the Pumps,'' *Forbes,* July 13, 1987, pp. 400–04.

DeTar, Jim, ''$73M Deal ST To Buy Adaptec Unit,'' *Electronic News,* November 30, 1998, p. 2.

Ha, K. Oanh, ''Milpita, Calif.-Based Adaptec Plans Cautious Course After CEO Quits,'' *Knight-Ridder/Tribune Business News,* August 2, 1998.

Haber, Carol, ''Adaptec Forced To Adapt to a Changing Marketplace,'' *Electronic News,* April 6, 1998, pp. 48–49.

Lashinsky, Adam, ''Silicon Street,'' *Knight-Ridder/Tribune Business News,* February 23, 1999.

Lawson, Stephen, ''Cabletron and Adaptec Buy Adapter Vendors,'' *InfoWorld,* June 10, 1996, p. 16.

Mitchell, James J., column in San Jose Mercury-News, reprinted in *Knight-Ridder/Tribune Business News,* September 3, 1995.

''Net To Significantly Exceed Expectations of Analysts,'' *Wall Street Journal,* January 7, 1999, p. A18.

Samberg, Dawson, ''In Front of the Wave,'' *Barron's,* April 2, 1990, pp. 13, 38–40.

Savitz, Eric J., ''Bruised and Battered Adaptec Attracts Interest,'' *Barron's,* August 10, 1998, p. 53.

——, ''Speed Demon,'' *Barron's,* December 3, 1990, pp. 19, 62.

Young, Jeffrey, ''Innovate or Die,'' *Forbes,* February 28, 1994, p. 106.

—A. Woodward

Alcan Aluminium Limited

1188 Sherbrooke Street West
Montreal, Quebec H3A 3G2
Canada
Telephone: (514) 8488000
Fax: (514) 8488115
Web site: http://www.alcan.com

Public Company
Incorporated: 1902 as Northern Aluminum Company Limited
Employees: 36,000
Sales: US$7.78 billion (1998)
Stock Exchanges: New York Toronto Montreal Vancouver Chicago Pacific London Paris Brussels Amsterdam Frankfurt Swiss
Ticker Symbol: AL
NAIC: 331314 Secondary Smelting and Alloying of Aluminum; 331315 Aluminum Sheet, Plate, and Foil Manufacturing; 331316 Aluminum Extruded Product Manufacturing; 331319 Other Aluminum Rolling and Drawing; 332431 Metal Can Manufacturing; 322225 Laminated Aluminum Foil Manufacturing for Flexible Packaging Uses

Alcan Aluminium Limited (Alcan) is the second-largest aluminum company in the world. Headquartered in Montreal, Canada, Alcan has operations in more than 30 countries. Alcan manufactures aluminum, with about 90 percent of revenues resulting from sales of aluminum in ingot and fabricated form. The company is the top producer of flat-rolled aluminum, the majority of which is used to make beverage cans. Alcan is involved in bauxite (aluminum ore) mining, alumina refining, aluminum smelting, and manufacturing. Among the products made by Alcan are cable and wire, automotive parts, and specialty chemicals. Alcan serves customers in an assortment of industries, including transportation, construction, electrical, and packaging. Alcan also generates hydroelectric power and is one of the biggest global recyclers of aluminum.

Advent of Aluminum in the Early 1900s

In 1899 The Pittsburgh Reduction Company later the Aluminum Company of America (Alcoa) began construction of a power plant and the first Canadian reduction works at Shawinigan Falls, Quebec. Aluminum production began two years later. This first Canadian subsidiary became known in 1902 as Northern Aluminum Company Limited.

Northern Aluminum quickly became an important player in the global aluminum markets. Aluminum was still a new metal. A commercially feasible refinement process had been discovered in 1886, but industrial applications were somewhat slow in developing. Skepticism among manufacturers forced producers toward vertical integration. Pittsburgh Reduction and its Canadian subsidiary were tireless in trying to develop aluminum markets but eventually turned to fabricating products such as cooking pots to promote the metal and broaden sales.

Demand for aluminum grew in the early years of the 20th century. Applications for the metal were found in the electrical and automotive industries. By 1914 80 percent of U.S.-made cars had aluminum crank and gear cases. Aviation, at that time a new industry, called for lightweight metals. Orville and Wilbur Wright had used aluminum in their first plane at Kitty Hawk, North Carolina.

Rapid Growth Following World War I

World War I provided new applications for aluminum. Massive quantities of the metal were employed in explosives, ammunition, and machine guns; and the Liberty V12 engine, which powered Allied planes, was one-third aluminum. Military usage absorbed 90 percent of the aluminum produced during the war years. The widespread use during the war translated into widespread acceptance by consumers after the war. Furthermore, the interruption of European aluminum shipments to North America served as a boon to Northern Aluminum after the war. In 1919 Northern alone exported 5,643 tons of Canadian aluminum to the United States compared to 2,360 for all European producers combined.

The 1920s saw fantastic growth for Northern Aluminum. In the early years of the decade, Arthur Vining Davis, head of

Company Perspectives:

Strength, growth and value are at the core of Alcan's strategic intent. We do more than make and sell aluminum—we build alliances with all our stakeholders. We also take pride in developing and delivering value-added differentiated aluminum products making Alcan the partner of choice. Strength reflects Alcan's strong financial state, its healthy debt-to-equity ratio and improved profitability. It also signifies the quality and dedication of Alcan's employees. Finally, strength together with light weight, thermal and electrical conductivity, barrier qualities, infinite recyclability and many other characteristics make aluminum . . . the material of choice. Growth is working with all our stakeholders to develop and deliver value-added, differentiated aluminum products, bringing increased value to our customers. It means continuous improvement in everything we do—earnings, technology, employee development, safety, and environmental stewardship. Growth is about looking to a new future as we enter the new millennium—fully optimizing our existing assets and aggressively pursuing opportunities to grow shareholder value. Value is the reason we're here. It is an ongoing commitment—to our shareholders, to our customers, to and by *our employees—to create value in everything we do. It also symbolizes Alcan's values—our ethics, our conduct, our reputation.*

Alcoa, became interested in two or three hydroelectric plants being proposed by U.S. tobacco magnate James B. Duke on Quebec's Saguenay River because the refinement of aluminum required vast amounts of electricity. Davis called upon A.W. Mellon, renowned financier and major stockholder in Alcoa, to help negotiate a deal with Duke. In 1925 a deal was struck. The aluminum company acquired the hydroelectric site at the so-called Lower Development, as well as water rights to the Upper Development. Duke took $16 million in preferred stock and 15 percent of the common stock of Alcoa. When Duke died three months after the deal was signed, Alcoa was given the opportunity to purchase a controlling interest in the Upper Development. Also in 1925, Northern Aluminum Company changed its name to Aluminum Company of Canada, Limited (Alcan).

These events secured the Saguenay River hydroelectric facilities, which laid the foundation for Alcan operations. Growth on the site was feverish; by 1927 the power plant on the Upper Development supplied a new 27,000 ton smelter, and the refinery neared completion. The company town of Arvida, named after Arthur Vining Davis, sprang up, and the development became the world's largest aluminum production site during World War II.

In June 1928 Alcoa, then the world's undisputed leader in aluminum, divested its foreign operations, forming a Canadian holding company called Aluminium Limited (AL). Shareholders received one share of the new company for every three shares of Alcoa stock. AL was to penetrate foreign markets and participate in international cartels away from the scrutiny of the U.S. Justice Department. Alcoa, meanwhile, would dominate the U.S. market. The Aluminum Company of Canada, Limited, became the chief operating subsidiary of AL. AL also took over all of Alcoa's other non-U.S. holdings, including Norwegian, Italian, French, and Spanish manufacturing and power concerns. Alcoa retained ownership of the power plants on the Saguenay until 1938, when AL purchased them for $35 million. Also at this time, the company moved its headquarters to Montreal from New York.

There were several reasons for the spinoff of AL from Alcoa. Alcoa's Davis felt that Alcoa's sales force neglected overseas markets in favor of the domestic market. He believed a Canadian company, with its own directors and own staff, would be in a better position to exploit international markets throughout the British Empire and elsewhere. Also, Alcoa's domination of the aluminum industry made it a frequent target of U.S. antitrust accusations. By divesting its foreign subsidiaries, Alcoa at least created the impression that it was not excluding competition from abroad. Finally, Davis was nearing retirement, and would soon be faced with choosing a successor. The choice was between his brother Edward K. Davis, and his longtime close friend and colleague, Roy Hunt. Hunt was the son of Alcoa's cofounder, Captain Alfred E. Hunt. Davis solved his problem by sending Edward Davis north to head the new international corporation.

Facing Challenges as a New Entity: 1930s–40s

As AL's first chief, Edward Davis faced some difficult challenges in the company's early years. Although not truly an infant company, AL had to redefine its approach. Formerly, the company had been a part of a vertically integrated whole. Now it was expected to compete worldwide, but it lacked the aluminum-fabrication capability to make finished products that Alcoa and the European producers had.

The Depression struck the company hard, and it was forced to borrow heavily to survive. Technical support and operating agreements with a benevolent Alcoa helped the company stay afloat. For the most part, AL did not compete with Alcoa in the U.S. market, due to a substantial U.S. tariff on imports and to the influence of Alcoa's and AL's common shareholders. As a result, AL pursued instead Asian and European markets.

Realizing it could not survive unless it integrated its operations, AL built fabricating plants in a number of countries worldwide. The growth of the automotive and aviation industries improved the position of AL. By 1937 the company was out of debt and operated profitably. Production capacity at the Arvida plant had doubled and the number of employees worldwide since 1928 had tripled. In 1937 the U.S. Justice Department filed an antitrust suit against Alcoa, Aluminium Limited, and 61 related subsidiaries and individuals. The suit called for the breakup of Alcoa and its divorce from AL. The suit alleged Alcoa and its confederates had conspired to restrain imports and to preserve its U.S. monopoly. In 1942 Alcoa and AL were cleared of the charges. The 1942 decision was appealed and was upheld on all counts except one. The appeals court opined that at the time of the original decision, Alcoa monopolized the U.S. ingot market, but that since that time new competition seemed to have evolved. The court therefore delayed further action until an assessment of the postwar industry could be made.

Key Dates:

1902: Northern Aluminum Company Limited forms.
1925: Company name changes to Aluminum Company of Canada, Limited.
1928: Aluminum Company of Canada, Limited, becomes the subsidiary of Aluminium Limited, a holding company.
1939: World War II increases demand for aluminum.
1965: A U.S. subsidiary, Alcan Aluminum Corporation, forms.
1966: Aluminium Limited is renamed Alcan Aluminium Limited.
1987: Alcan Aluminium Limited merges with its principal subsidiary, Aluminum Company of Canada, Limited.
1999: Company announces plan to merge with Pechiney S.A. and Alusuisse Lonza Group Ltd. to create the world's largest producer of aluminum.

In 1950 the court calculated that the same nine stockholders controlled 44.65 percent of AL's stock and 46.43 percent of Alcoa's stock. While the court said that the relationship between the two companies had been lawful in the past, it ordered the investors to divest the shares of one company or the other. It was the first time in history that U.S. investors had been ordered by their government to give up control of a foreign company. All of the investors except Edward Davis, who sold his Alcoa stock, sold their shares in the Canadian company. The suit remained open until 1957, when a Justice Department request for extended court supervision was denied. In the 20 years this case was open, the aluminum industry had undergone tremendous change, and AL had grown into a giant.

The late 1930s had seen demand for aluminum explode, fueled by war preparations. AL was the largest supplier within the British Empire, and Britain's demand for airplanes and other military hardware was great. During the war, the Canadian company received US$78 million in low-interest loans from the British government to expand its power and reduction facilities. In return, the additional output was earmarked for the British market. The U.S. government also offered assistance to AL; the Defense Plant Corporation, the branch of the Reconstruction Finance Corporation charged with fostering war-industries production, paid US$68 million in advance for 1.3 million pounds of aluminum. AL reportedly used the cash flow to construct another dam on the Saguenay, the Shipsaw Power Plant Number 2. The purchase agreement annoyed U.S. producers, who saw it as a boost to a potential competitor after the war. AL's contribution to the war effort was, however, paramount.

The Aluminium Limited subsidiary Alcan ended the war five times larger than it was in 1937. This expansion posed the threat of idle facilities after the war. The company's researchers worked on expanding aluminum applications in the automotive and rail transport industries.

In 1947, Nathanael V. Davis took over as CEO of AL from his father, Edward Davis. After a brief dip in aluminum consumption right after the war, consumer goods began to use the metal in quantities as never before. By 1950 the Korean War demanded a steady flow of aluminum for the military, and a shortage developed in the United States. U.S. producers increased their output, and several new competitors joined the field.

Strengthening Operations in the 1950s and 1960s

During the 1950s the United States imported 10 to 20 percent of its primary aluminum. Alcan controlled 90 percent of that import business. In 1951 the company began a $350 million expansion program, which included additions to the Quebec plants and a new hydroelectric and reduction site in British Columbia, which began operations in 1954.

In 1950, when the strong ownership ties between Alcoa and Alcan were severed, the Canadian company began to make more aggressive forays into the U.S. market. Occasionally, Alcan broke with tradition and set prices at rates lower than Alcoa; Alcoa's price leadership was followed loyally by other U.S. producers. Alcan focused on aluminum in primary-ingot form, while Alcoa, Reynolds Metal Company, and Kaiser Aluminum & Chemical Corporation dove into the semi-fabricated and fabricated products. Alcan's U.S. customers were independent fabricators, as well as Alcoa, Reynolds, and Kaiser themselves. The independents were Alcan's political allies, lobbying for low tariffs on primary aluminum.

While Alcan's exports to the United States grew in the early 1950s, market shares in other areas began to shrink. Norway and France doubled their domestic aluminum capacity, while historic importers like Germany and Japan began to develop their own industries. Although overall output increased, Alcan's percentage of world production declined from 21 percent in 1954 to 19 percent by 1960. By 1969 it had slid to 13 percent.

In 1957 Alcan's first domestic competitor, Canadian British Aluminum (CBA), was started. During the summer of 1957 a strike at Alcan's Arvida plant idled 45 percent of production capacity for four months, resulting in a loss of about 1,000 tons of aluminum production per day. Later in the year, recessionary conditions caused a global oversupply of aluminum, and Aluminium Limited's profits dipped for 1958. Sales of primary aluminum to U.S. and U.K. producers declined.

Alcan decided to bolster its fabrication efforts. In 1958 Alcan expanded fabricating operations in plants in 11 countries. The global oversupply lasted into the early 1960s, however, and as it worsened, U.S. producers slashed prices to near cost to keep plants running. Alcan slowly was being squeezed out of the U.S. market. In response, Alcan decided to build semi-fabricating plants of its own in the United States to establish stable outlets for its ingot.

In 1963 AL acquired a small U.S. metal-powders firm and an aluminum-wire and cable firm. Alcan and three of its biggest U.S. independent customers, Cerro Corporation, Scovill Manufacturing, and National Distillers & Chemical Corporation, began construction of a US$45 million hot mill in Oswego, New York, that would produce coils and aluminum plate. Alcan bought out its partners in 1965 and also acquired other sheet-fabricating plants owned by Cerro and National Distillers. A U.S. subsidiary, Alcan Aluminum Corporation, was founded in

Cleveland, Ohio, in 1965 to manage AL's U.S. fabrication concerns. The unit lost US$10.4 million in its first year but persevered. By 1967 Alcan operated 12 plants in 8 U.S. states. In 1966 Aluminium Limited was renamed Alcan Aluminium Limited, and two years later the company reorganized its corporate structure, with management divided into three groups: raw materials, smelting, and fabricating and sales.

In the late 1960s another fundamental shift occurred in Alcan Aluminium's business. Higher transportation and labor costs eroded the advantage of refining aluminum in Canada, as did the availability of cheaper power in the United States. Political developments around the globe made it advantageous for Alcan Aluminium to build primary smelters in Australia, Britain, India, Norway, and Japan. By 1972, Alcan Aluminium's foreign smelting capacity equaled that of its Canadian facilities. Alcan Aluminium had begun to develop integrated units within each country of operations.

Diversification and Continued Growth in the 1970s

Alcan Aluminium's shift toward finished products continued. In 1971 Alcan Aluminium shipped more fabricated and semi-fabricated tonnage than ingot for the first time. In 1972 Paul H. Leman took over as president of Alcan Aluminium Limited. Davis remained CEO and took on the new post of chairman. The French-Canadian Leman was the company's first president outside the Davis family. In 1975 global recession brought on by the oil crisis caused a decline in Alcan Aluminium's aluminum shipments by 16 percent worldwide. Profits took a dive as demand fell in all markets except Latin America. Alcan Aluminium continued to build plants overseas, however, adding an alumina refinery in Ireland and participating in the development of new bauxite mines in Brazil in the mid- to late 1970s.

Labor troubles caused the shutdown of four of the company's five Canadian smelters in 1976. Damage to one plant, caused by molten aluminum hardening in the pot-lines when workers cut the power, cost an estimated US$25 million. Another strike three years later had a similar effect on Alcan Aluminium's production levels. During both of these strikes other producers took advantage of the banner growth years for aluminum.

In the mid-1970s, plans to expand smelting capacity in Canada were mapped out. Uncertainty about the future of energy costs encouraged Alcan Aluminium and its Alcan subsidiary to take advantage of its own Canadian hydroelectric plants. In 1977 David Culver replaced Leman as president. The executive observed that Alcan Aluminium was the only aluminum producer in the world with the ability to expand by 30 percent without increasing its power costs. By 1978 construction on a new primary smelter in Quebec was well under way.

In July 1979 Davis stepped down as Alcan Aluminium's CEO and was replaced by Culver until 1986. Culver had joined Alcan Aluminium in 1949 and had worked his way up the sales side. He set out to bolster Alcan Aluminium's marketing efforts and strengthen the emphasis on fabricated products, eventually limiting ingot sales to 25 percent of the total. Culver initiated a new research and development push in 1980. Alcan Aluminium lagged in high-margin aerospace, automotive, and beverage container markets due to dated technology.

Expansion Amid Difficult Times in the 1980s

In the early 1980s Alcan Aluminium opened new smelters in Australia and Brazil and expanded facilities in West Germany, Britain, and Spain. The company was in a very strong financial position to face the next decade. Annual revenues had doubled since 1975 and earnings had increased eightfold. Debt was low.

Alcan Aluminium's financial strength proved a blessing when the recession of 1980 to 1982 reached the aluminum industry. Demand fell sharply. In 1982 Alcan Aluminium lost US$58 million, its first loss in 50 years. Several long-term factors came to a head in the 1980s. Increased use of scrap resulted in lower aluminum prices and new Third World producers entered the market in force. In 1960, six producers—Alcan Aluminium, Alcoa, Reynolds, Kaiser, France's Pechiney S.A., and Switzerland's Alusuisse—controlled 70 to 80 percent of the free world's aluminum market. By 1981 their share was 40 to 50 percent. More than 80 companies, double the 1960 number, produced aluminum goods worldwide, and about 30 percent of Third World producers were owned at least in part by their governments, whose interest was oriented toward full employment and acquiring hard currency rather than toward maximizing profits or maintaining supply and demand equilibrium. Another factor was increased price volatility after aluminum was listed on the London Metals Exchange in 1978. Private deals between producers and buyers became obsolete, and buyers gained tremendous advantage when the exchange price was publicized daily.

The industry would adjust to these developments but not until the latter half of the 1980s. Meanwhile, Alcan Aluminium overproduced, partly to exploit its hydroelectric power advantage while high oil prices greatly affected other producers, and partly to placate labor. In 1982 the company merged with The British Aluminium Company plc, further expanding its international markets. Profits returned in 1983 and 1984, but in 1985 Alcan Aluminium trimmed 1,100 management jobs, cutting an estimated C$40 million in costs annually. Alcan Aluminium went forward with plans to modernize its plants in Quebec, and when aluminum prices rebounded in 1985, Alcan Aluminium was better prepared to take advantage of it than any of its competitors. The company was also helped by its 1985 acquisition of most of the U.S. aluminum assets of the Atlantic Richfield Company.

In 1986 Alcan Aluminium's top managers devised a new long-term strategy to improve Alcan Aluminium's return on equity. The plan focused on technological applications of aluminum and related metals particularly in aerospace, electronics, and ceramics. Aluminum-lithium alloys were tested in Canadian and British aircraft. Composite aluminum materials also found applications in railcar and automotive assembly. Alcan Aluminium bought a gallium-purification subsidiary of Alusuisse in 1985 and planned to manufacture gallium arsenide semiconducting wafers. The company also reaffirmed its commitment to existing aluminum operations, including ingot production.

In 1987 Alcan Aluminium underwent a reorganization. Alcan Aluminium Limited, the parent company, was merged with its chief operating unit, Aluminum Company of Canada. All of the former parent's subsidiary units worldwide were transferred to the former Canadian operating unit, and the reorganized company took the name Alcan Aluminium Limited. The arrangement shed layers of management. Alcan's leaner structure and clear direction helped the company earn record profits in 1988. Alcan's net of US$931 million was more than any Canadian company had ever earned.

Streamlining Operations and Looking to the Future

With new CEO David Morton on board as Alcan entered the 1990s, the company undertook a new strategic plan as it faced a global recession. Alcan planned to divest its non-core businesses in Argentina, Brazil, and the United Kingdom, and between 1991 and 1994 the company was able to reduce its annual cost base by more than US$600 million. In 1993 a new CEO, Jacques Bougie, was appointed. Bougie already held the titles of president and chief operating officer. Alcan also carried out a year-long study of the global aluminum market and its prospects. As a result of the study, completed in mid-1993, Alcan was able to evaluate its position in the aluminum industry and establish priorities for the decade. The company made plans to focus on strategic downstream operations, expand its rolled product division internationally, reduce smelter costs as well as raw material costs, gear research and development efforts on core products and operations, and lessen overhead costs.

During the latter half of the decade Alcan continued its international expansion and focused on developing its large-scale fabricating operations. Alcan restructured its Asian holdings to strengthen its operations in Southeast Asia and China and continued to sell non-core operations, including 12 businesses in the United Kingdom and the United States in 1996, fabricating assets in Brazil and Uruguay in 1997, aluminum refining operations in Ireland and Guinea in 1998, and a chemicals operation in Canada in 1998. Alcan also reduced its holdings in recession-wracked Japan, decreasing its interest in Nippon Light Metal Company, Ltd., from 45.6 percent to 11.2 percent.

While Alcan unloaded several non-strategic businesses, the company was equally busy acquiring businesses to strengthen its core operations. In 1998 Alcan acquired a majority stake in the bauxite operations of Ghana Bauxite Company Limited and secured a majority interest (54.6 percent) in Indian Aluminium Company, Limited. Alcan also acquired a 20 percent interest in the Utkal aluminum oxide project in India. The company upped its interest in the project to 35 percent in early 1999.

Though Alcan worked tirelessly to realize its goal of being the top global producer of low-cost aluminum, poor market conditions in the late 1990s made the task all the more difficult. During 1998 aluminum prices dropped by 20 percent, forcing Alcan to curb its production of aluminum, a strategy the company first began employing in 1994 due to an industry oversupply of aluminum. Alcan also moved up its plans to close the Isle-Maligne smelter in Quebec, intending to close it by the end of 1999. Still, Alcan moved forward, anticipating future demand; construction commenced on a new US$1.6 billion smelter in Alma, Quebec, to be fully operational by the end of 2001.

Alcan's fabricated product division contributed more than 76 percent of total 1998 sales and continued to grow. Through the entire decade Alcan had invested in fabricated product operations, upgrading facilities and acquiring new businesses. In 1998 the company began expanding its rolling facilities in Brazil to meet the increasing demand of the South American can sheet market. Also that year Alcan sold a German piston business as it did not fit with Alcan's focus on rolled products fabrication. The Alcan Global Automotive Products Group continued to make inroads into the promising automotive sector, securing a ten-year supply agreement with General Motors Company. To further penetrate the automotive and distribution markets, Alcan announced plans to spend US$46 million to improve aluminum rolled sheet production facilities at the Kingston, Ontario, plant. The expansion, designed to increase production by 40 percent, was scheduled to be completed by the end of 2000.

Recycling operations grew steadily in the late 1990s, with Alcan's U.S. recycling facilities processing 31 percent of all used beverage cans recycled by Americans in 1998. The company operated 26 recycling facilities in the United Kingdom, and a plant designed to recycle used beverage cans was put into operation in Brazil in 1998.

In May 1999 Alcan further expanded its fabricated products division when it announced it would form a new aluminum rolled products company in Korea with South Korea's Taihan Electric Wire Co., Ltd. The new company would serve to meet increasing demand for can sheet products in the Asia/Pacific region, which accounted for about a third of Western World aluminum consumption in 1999. Brazil, Europe, and Asia were the fastest-growing markets for Alcan's aluminum can sheet and foil products in the late 1990s, with increased interest in aluminum in food packaging and beverage container businesses.

Alcan faced additional changes as it neared the new millennium. In spring 1999 the company restructured its operations into two primary business groups—Alcan Primary Metal Group and Alcan Global Fabrication Group. The first division was concerned with bauxite mining, alumina refining, power generation, and primary aluminum activities, while the fabrication group handled all fabrication activities, including sheet, foil, and flexible packaging, cable and extrusions, secondary metal production, and recycling operations. Though net income for the first half of 1999 was nearly $100 million lower than net income from the same period a year earlier, Alcan's fabricated products volumes reached a record high.

Alcan's biggest announcement of the decade was made in the summer of 1999 when the company revealed a proposed merger with France's Pechiney S.A. and Switzerland's Alusuisse Lonza Group Ltd. (algroup). The three companies had combined 1998 sales and operating revenues of $21.6 billion. The merger would create the largest aluminum company in the world, as well as a worldwide leader in flexible and specialty packaging. The new company, temporarily named Alcan-Pechiney-algroup (A.P.A.), would function as a Canadian company and have headquarters in Montreal, about 91,000 employees, and operations in 59 countries. It was determined that Jacques Bougie would act as CEO, and Alcan would hold a 44 percent interest, Pechiney 29 percent, and algroup 27 percent.

Principal Subsidiaries

Alcan Primary Metal Group; Alcan Global Fabrication Group; Alcan International Limited; Alcan Aluminum Corporation (U.S.); Alcan (Bermuda) Limited; Alcan Nikkei Asia Holdings Ltd.(Bermuda; 60%); Alcan Jamaica Company (West Indies); Alcan Aluminio do Brasil Ltda.(Brazil); Alcan Aluminio Pocos de Caldas S.A. (Brazil); Consorcio de Aluminio do Maranhao-Alumar (Brazil; 10%); Mineracao Rio do Norte S.A. (Brazil; 12.5%); Petrocoque S.A.-Industria e Comercio (Brazil; 25%); Ghana Bauxite Company Limited (Ghana; 80%); Compagnie des Bauxites de Guinee (Guinea; 16.8%); Alcan Deutschland GmbH (Germany); Aluminium Norf GmbH (Germany; 50%); Alcan Alluminio S.p.A. (Italy); Vigeland Metal Refinery A/S (Norway; 50%); Alcan Iberica, S.A. (Spain); Alcan Aluminium AG (Switzerland); Alcan Rorschach AG (Switzerland); Alcan Europe Limited (U.K.); British Alcan Aluminium plc (U.K.); Alcan Aluminium UK Limited (U.K.); Alcan South Pacific Pty Ltd. (Australia); Queensland Alumina Limited (Australia; 21.4%); Alcan Asia Limited (China); Alcan Asia Pacific Limited (China); Alcan Nikkei China Limited (China, 49%); Alcan Nikkei Korea Limited (China; 49%); Nonfemet International (China-Canada-Japan) Aluminium Company Limited (China; 27%); Indian Aluminium Company, Limited (India; 54.6%); Alcan Nikkei Asia Company Ltd. (Malaysia; 60%); Aluminium Company of Malaysia Berhad (Malaysia; 35.5%); Alcom Nikkei Specialty Coatings Sdn Bhd (Malaysia; 47.7%); Alcan Nikkei Thai Limited (Thailand, 46.6%); Alcan Nikkei Siam Limited (Thailand; 42%).

Principal Competitors

Alcoa Inc.

Further Reading

''Alcan's Latest Cliff Hanger'' *Forbes*, November 1, 1977.

Epstein, Gene, ''Can Alcan? Will cost cuts, better performance pull aluminum giant out of its slump?'', *Barron's,* May 31, 1999, p. 17.

Farin, Philip, and Gary G. Reibsamen, *Aluminium: Profile of an Industry*, New York: Metals Week, 1969.

From Monopoly to Competition; The Transformation of Alcoa, 1888–1986, Cambridge: Cambridge University Press, 1988.

Hight, Jack, ''Kingdom of the Saguenay: Canada's Sprawling Aluminium Giant,'' *Iron Age*, April 5, 1945.

Levy, Yvonne, *Aluminium: Past and Future*, San Francisco: Federal Reserve Bank of San Francisco, 1971.

Litvak, Isaiah Á., and Christopher J. Maule, *Alcan Aluminium Limited: A Case Study,* Toronto: Royal Commission on Corporate Concentration, 1977, 229 p.

Peltz, James F., ''Wave of Consolidation Hits Aluminum Industry,'' *Los Angeles Times,* August 12, 1999, p. C1.

Roberts, J.P., and D. McLean, *The Cape York Aluminium Companies and the Native Peoples,* Fitzroy, Victoria: International Development Action, 1976, 103 p.

Ross, Alexander, ''The Alcan Succession,'' *Canadian Business*, June 1989.

Smith, George David, and Duncan C. Campbell, *Global Mission: The Story of Alcan*, 3 Vols., Montreal: Alcan Aluminium Limited, 1985–1990.

''Why Alcan Spends So Much,'' *Business Week*, July 10, 1971.

—Thomas M. Tucker
—updated by Mariko Fujinaka

American Woodmark Corporation

3102 Shawnee Drive
Winchester, Virginia 22601-4208
U.S.A.
Telephone: (540) 665-9100
Fax: (540) 665-9176
Web site: http://www.americanwoodmark.com

Public Company
Incorporated: 1980
Employees: 3,087
Sales: $327 million (1999)
Stock Exchanges: NASDAQ
Ticker Symbol: AMWD
NAIC: 33711 Wood Kitchen Cabinet and Countertop Manufacturing

American Woodmark Corporation is one of the five largest cabinet manufacturers in the United States, specializing in custom and stock kitchen cabinets and bathroom vanities. From its headquarters in Winchester, Virginia, at the head of the Shenandoah Valley, the company operates nine manufacturing plants, in Arizona, Georgia, Kentucky, Virginia, and West Virginia, and 11 service centers around the country. It offers some 130 different cabinet lines to the remodeling and new home construction markets, with remodeling accounting for three-quarters of its 1999 sales. Its products include the brand names American Woodmark, Crestwood, Timberlake, Scots Pride, Coventry and Case, and Knapp. American Woodmark distributes its products nationally through three major channels: home centers, major builders, and independent dealer/distributors. Chairman of the Board and co-founder William F. Brandt, Jr. owns approximately 30 percent of the company.

Filling a Need for Dental Cabinets: 1951–71

The company that eventually became American Woodmark started in 1951, when a Long Island dentist, Dr. Alvin Goldhush, decided he could make better dental cabinets than those available. He named his new company Formed Laminates Inc., and he did so well that he eventually gave up dentistry. He also changed his company's name to Raygold Corp.

In 1971 Raygold caught the eye of Robert V. Hansberger, chairman of Boise Cascade Corp. Beginning in the late 1960s, Hansberger built the timber company into a conglomerate with holdings ranging from recreational vehicles to Latin American utilities. The year Boise Cascade acquired Raygold, the conglomerate's nonforest businesses accounted for $800 million or 44 percent of revenues.

By 1972, however, Hansberger's buying spree had burdened Boise Cascade with debt totaling $523.2 million and a loss that year of $170.6 million. He resigned, and John B. Fery, who had been with Boise Cascade since its founding in 1957, was named chairman.

A Division of Boise Cascade: 1971–79

Fery refocused the company on forest products, including cabinets, and sold off many of the noncore businesses over the next several years. He also implemented detailed five- and ten-year plans and took a more cautious approach to acquisitions. Between 1972 and 1978, Boise Cascade's capital spending reached $1.2 billion, as it built new facilities around the country, including a new plant and offices for its cabinet division in Winchester, Virginia, to which Raygold moved from Long Island.

In the mid-1970s, the company began to shift toward papermaking, a business that accounted for only a quarter of its pretax earnings in 1973. But the 1974–75 recession saw layoffs of mill workers as orders and prices of lumber and plywood dropped, and the company decided to refocus. In 1976, Boise Cascade bought a paper mill for $90 million, and by 1979, half of Boise Cascade's pretax profits came from its papermaking activities, as it converted and built new plants.

Starting a New Company: 1980–84

Recognizing that kitchen cabinets did not fit with Fery's "tilt toward paper," four executives of the company's cabinet division bought the division in a leveraged buyout in April

Company Perspectives:

American Woodmark is an organization of employees and shareholders who have combined their resources to pursue a common goal. What We Do. *Our common goal is to create value by providing kitchens and baths "of pride" for the American family.* Why We Do It. *We pursue this goal to earn a profit, which allows us to reward our shareholders and employees and to make a contribution to our society.* How We Do It. *Four principles guide our actions.* Customer Satisfaction: *Providing the best possible quality, service and value to the greatest number of people. Doing whatever is reasonable, and sometimes unreasonable, to make certain that each customer's needs are met each and every day.*

Integrity: *Doing what is right. Caring about the dignity and rights of each individual. Acting fairly and responsibly with all parties. Being a good citizen in the communities in which we operate.* Teamwork: *Understanding that we must all work together if we are to be successful. Realizing that each individual must contribute to the team to remain a member of the team.* Excellence: *Striving to perform every job or action in a superior way. Being innovative, seeking new and better ways to get things done. Helping all individuals to become the best that they can be in their jobs and careers.*

1980, getting financing help from General Electric Credit Corp. and Boise Cascade. They named their new company American Woodmark. William F. Brandt, Jr., who had been general manager of the division, became president and chairman. The other officers involved in the buyout were Richard A. Graber, who became marketing vice-president; Donald Mathias, operations vice-president; and Jeffrey Holcomb, vice-president of finance.

The cabinet division had brought in approximately $30 million in sales for Boise Cascade in the fiscal year ending April 1980. But it was a bad time to be launching a heavily indebted company whose business depended on a strong economy and lots of housing construction. The prime interest rate was up to 18.5 percent and housing starts had dropped to a five-year low.

The company's first two years were lean and required laying off both managerial and production staff. In 1982, however, American Woodmark's fortunes began to improve as interest rates dropped and the economy started picking up. From a loss of $697,000 for the fiscal year ending in April 1982, American Woodmark had a profit of $2.4 million in fiscal 1983, which increased to $4.1 million in fiscal 1984.

Thank Heavens for Remodeling: 1985–87

Profits dropped to $2.3 million for 1985, but were up to $5.5 million for fiscal 1986, on annual sales of $97 million. The company claimed that it was one of the five largest cabinet manufacturers in the lucrative but highly fragmented cabinet industry, with between three and four percent of the market. The industry owed much of its profitability to the growing home improvement sector of the business. In 1985, the industry as a whole sold some $2.5 billion worth of cabinets and vanities, with slightly more than half of these sold to go into new homes and the rest for remodeling. American Woodmark, however, sold 60 percent of its cabinets to the remodeling market, and the rest for new homes.

American Woodmark, which had four manufacturing plants (in Virginia, West Virginia, and Georgia) and ten distribution centers, went public in 1986, offering 1.25 million shares at $15 per share. The company itself, which sold 750,000 shares, raised $11.25 million before commissions. It used $6 million to reduce its debt to $16 million. Other proceeds went for capital spending. Company officials sold another half a million shares (for which they originally paid an average of nine cents) for $7.5 million, but retained solid control of the company.

Following the IPO, the company expanded its manufacturing facility in West Virginia and built a second plant in Georgia, 100,000 square feet in size. In fiscal 1987, the company offered 18 lines of cabinets and sales topped $100 million for the first time, reaching $116 million.

Restructuring the Company: 1988–94

By fiscal 1989, annual sales were more than $158 million and CEO Bill Brandt began a five-year restructuring program, upgrading and expanding the company's product lines, broadening its customer base, and pushing decision-making down to lower levels within the organization. Much of the efforts concentrated on increasing the speed with which American Woodmark could get its products to stores and contractors by building more assembly plants and warehouses around the country and shipping directly to the customer rather than depending heavily on independent distributors.

To implement the changes, Brandt initiated a variety of training efforts to get employees to think and work differently. According to Bob Filipczak in a 1996 article in *Training* magazine, Brandt did not have much success until he developed his "level-to-level" training. In this "peer training meets trickle-down theory" approach, Brandt himself received training in a subject and then trained the executives who reported to him. They, in turn, trained their subordinates, who continued the process. Before anyone conducted any training, however, he or she had to "model" the skills on the job, thus building accountability into the program at every level.

As part of a $34 million capital spending program, the company bought Amende Cabinetry, an Alabama-based manufacturer with $2 million in sales throughout the Southeast. With that purchase, the company operated seven manufacturing facilities and 11 regional distribution centers.

In 1990, as interest rates rose and housing starts dropped due to the 1990–91 recession, American Woodmark saw its revenues fall. The company continued its restructuring, however. During fiscal 1991, American Woodmark increased its offerings to 45 different cabinet lines, which ranged from relatively inexpensive to medium and higher priced styles. The lines all shared a common box, with the front frame (oak, maple, or cherry) and the type (low pressure laminate or wood), style, and color of cabinet door causing the price differences. The cabinets were sold under the brand names American Woodmark Cabi-

Key Dates:

1951: Dr. Alvin Goldhush founds Formed Laminates Inc. to make dental cabinets.
1971: Goldhush sells his company, now named Raygold Corp., to Boise Cascade Corp.
1980: Four Boise executives buy the cabinet division in a leveraged buyout; name new company American Woodmark Corp.
1986: American Woodmark goes public.
1989: Company restructures, expanding lines of cabinets and number of assembly plants.
1996: American Woodmark pays first quarterly cash dividend.
1999: Company buys Knapp Woodworking and breaks ground for $10 million factory.

nets, Coventry & Chase Cabinets, and Timberlake Cabinets, introduced in April 1990.

Recognizing the importance of the home remodeling sector to its business and that market's reduced dependence on interest rate fluctuations, American Woodmark focused on winning a greater share of business from the growing home improvement "superstores." Two of its customers, Builders Square, Inc. (a subsidiary of Kmart Corporation) and Home Depot, each accounted for more than ten percent of the cabinetmaker's sales. The company still had seven manufacturing plants, but had reduced the number of regional distribution centers to eight.

In fiscal 1993, four years into the restructuring plan, revenues finally began growing again, with a 22 percent jump to $167.3 million, and the company issued a special ten percent stock dividend, payable in common stock. Explained Bill Brandt, "This special dividend rewards the shareholders who have patiently stayed with us during a long and sometimes difficult period."

The following year, the company was making nearly 100 styles of stock and semicustom cabinets and vanities and had added the Crestwood and Scots Pride brand names to its offerings. Sixty percent of its $171.3 million in sales continued to go to the home remodeling business, with the remainder to new housing construction.

Creating a Growth Company: 1995–99

By fiscal 1995, sales had reached $197.4 million. In 1996 Brandt resigned as CEO, while remaining chairman. James J. "Jake" Gosa, who had been with American Woodmark since 1991, was named president and CEO. In August that year, following two quarters of record earnings and increased financial strength, the company paid its first quarterly cash dividend to shareholders. This move made it possible for those mutual funds that were required to invest in companies that paid dividends to buy shares in American Woodmark.

Sales continued to grow, topping $241 million in fiscal 1998. The company's growth mirrored that of the home center industry, with American Woodmark the leading supplier of stock cabinets to all 1,242 Home Depot and Lowe's big box outlet stores. These two chains were expected to grow their stores to 2,000 by the year 2003, and American Woodmark planned to grow with them.

The company had perfected its "just-in-time" manufacturing process, making cabinets and accessories such as spice, towel, and wine racks in its seven factories and distributing them directly to customers from the company's three assembly plants or one of its seven service centers around the country. As an example of the company's distribution proficiency, almost two-thirds of all American Woodmark cabinets sold by home centers were shipped directly to the end customer in fiscal 1999. Customers received their cabinets seven to ten days after American Woodmark got their order.

But whereas cabinets for home improvements now accounted for 70 percent of its business, American Woodmark was also a leading cabinet supplier to the new construction industry, serving seven of the Top Ten and 35 of the Top 100 home builders in the United States directly, as well as local and regional builders. It also was one of the first cabinet makers to provide improved kitchen quality and features to the prefabricated housing industry. One of the reasons builders and retailers liked American Woodmark was that the company could produce new designs and products quickly, taking a product from concept to market in less than 120 days.

The company now offered some 130 lines of framed stock cabinets, with 40 different door designs, seven colors, and four types of wood, including hickory, introduced in fiscal 1998. Its custom cabinetry included 50 door styles with 20 colors, eight glazes, and two sheens.

1999 and Beyond

During fiscal 1999, American Woodmark spent almost $22 million in capital investments, including the purchase of Knapp Woodworking, Inc. and the ground-breaking for a $10 million factory in Indiana. It needed the additional capacity. That year and into fiscal 2000, business was so good the company had to outsource some work to keep up with the demand.

With the good economy, the company expected continued growth. Even if the economy were to slacken, American Woodmark had weathered two recessions already and was confident of its ability to do so again if necessary. As an officer of the Kitchen Cabinet Manufacturers Association told Amy Joyce in a 1999 article in the *Washington Post,* "They have made some good moves being competitive, winning the bidding to get into the big [retailers]. You chalk that up to some visionary management and good implementation."

Principal Competitors

Merillat Industries; Masco; Triangle Pacific; Fortune Brands.

Further Reading

Adams, Larry, "Cabinet Industry on the Rebound," *Wood & Wood Products,* May 1992, p. 58.
"American Woodmark Breaks Ground for $10 Million Kitchen Cabinet Factory," *Associated Press,* April 15, 1999.

''American Woodmark Commences Initial Public Offering,'' *Business Wire,* July 18, 1986.
''American Woodmark Corporation Announces First Cash Dividend,'' *Business Wire,* August 22, 1996.
''Boise Cascade Corp. Plans to Sell Cabinet Division,'' *Wall Street Journal,* April 28, 1980, p. 23.
''Expansionism That Now Sticks Close to Home,'' *Business Week,* February 19, 1979, p. 54.
Filipczak, Bob, ''CEOs Who Train,'' *Training,* June 1996, p. 56.
Hinden, Stan, ''Dentist Fills Kitchen Cabinet Orders Instead of Teeth,'' *Washington Post,* September 8, 1986, p. F43.
——, ''Home Improvement Shares Show Improving Stock Values,'' *Washington Post,* November 30, 1987, p. F49.
——, ''Regional Stocks Didn't Escape Market's Battering,'' *Washington Post,* April 4, 1994, p. F29.
Joyce, Amy, ''Building on a Remodeling Boom,'' *Washington Post,* June 21, 1999, p. F9.
Knight, Jerry, ''Washington Investing,'' *Washington Post,* August 30, 1999, p. F27.
''Lowe's Turns 50,'' *National Home Center News,* October 21, 1996, p. 43.
Serwer, Andrew Evan, ''To Find Tomorrow's Hot Stocks, Go Where the Big Boys Aren't,'' *Fortune,* February 27, 1989, p. 29.
Tai, Jennifer, ''Movers & Shakers,'' *Washington Times,* August 22, 1996, p. B8.
''U.S. Wood Products Industry Enduring Severe Downturn,'' *New York Times,* April 17, 1980, p. D1.

—Ellen D. Wernick

The Andersons, Inc.

480 W. Dussel Drive
Maumee, Ohio 43537
U.S.A.
Telephone: (419) 893-5050
Fax: (419) 891-6670
Web site: http://www.andersoninc.com

Public Company
Incorporated: 1947
Employees: 3,035
Sales: $1.09 billion (1998)
Stock Exchanges: NASDAQ
Ticker Symbol: ANDE
NAIC: 115114 Postharvest Crop Activities; 311119 Other Animal Food Manufacturing; 325320 Pesticide and Other Agriculture Chemical Manufacturing; 325312 Fertilizer Manufacturing; 422510 Grain and Field Bean Wholesalers; 422990 Other Miscellaneous Non-Durable Goods Wholesalers; 441320 Tire Dealers; 444110 Home Centers; 444210 Outdoor Power Equipment Stores; 444220 Nursery and Garden Centers; 488210 Support Activities for Rail Transportation; 532411 Commercial Air, Rail, & Water Transportation Equipment Rental and Leasing

The Andersons, Inc. operates a network of closely related businesses, based in Ohio, Michigan, Indiana, and Illinois. The Agricultural Group encompasses the company's traditional area of activity—grain storage and wholesale operations. Several grain elevators serve farmers with a systemwide capacity of 80 million bushels of grain. Nine retail farm centers offer seeds and crop protection chemicals for sale, as well as soil testing, equipment rental, and other services. The Retail Group consists of six home centers in Ohio that sell building materials, housewares, specialty foods, lawn and garden supplies, pet supplies, and many other items. Products manufactured by the Processing Group include lawn fertilizer as well as consumer and industrial products utilizing corn cobs from the company's cob milling operations. The Manufacturing Group provides custom steel fabrication and rail car repair services, manages the company's rail car lease fleet, and offers rail cars for sale or trade.

Getting Off the Ground in the 1940s

Anderson's Elevator Company (AEC) experienced two business failures, in 1937 and in 1940, before establishment as a successful enterprise in 1947 as The Andersons. Harold Anderson left the National Biscuit Company (Nabisco), where he managed a flour mill in 1936, to form a grain storage and wholesale business with his father and wife. Anderson sought to attract a high volume of farmers to his grain elevator by paying higher rates for their grain. This would be made possible by transporting grain to eastern states by rail and water transportation, a less expensive alternative to the general practice of using rail only. Anderson negotiated with the Wabash Railroad for installation of railroad tracks along the elevator where long shafts transferred grain directly to the rail cars. The side track was within the proper boundaries to be included in the rate structure of the main rail line, also minimizing transportation costs.

With transportation organized, AEC began construction on a modern, concrete grain storage elevator, with the capacity to hold one million bushels of grain. The facility was located on farmland Anderson had acquired in Maumee, Ohio, near Toledo, and the farmhouse became the company office. Overworked in the final weeks of construction, a car accident in late June prevented Anderson from properly attending to the business when the company began to accept grain in July. Circumstance forced him to close the company, and AEC leased the grain elevator to Continental Grain Export Company.

After physical and emotional recuperation, Anderson sought to restart AEC in 1940. He negotiated with the Wabash Railroad to transport grain and grain products to marine vessels for $4.50 per rail car, and he built a marine transfer unit to ease movement of grain from land to lake. With low transportation costs, AEC would purchase grain by the truck load at volume prices. AEC regained control of the first grain elevator and added a second, which provided storage for an additional two million bushels of grain. Anderson contracted with Cargill, Inc. to handle 1.5 million bushels and with the Farm Bureau Cooperative Associa-

Company Perspectives:

We firmly believe that our company is a powerful vehicle through which we channel our time, talent and energy in pursuit of the fundamental goal of serving God by serving others. Through our collective action we greatly magnify the impact of our individual efforts to: Provide extraordinary service to our customers; Help each other improve; Support our communities; Increase the value of our Company.

tion to handle one million bushels. This second venture failed for a variety of reasons, including the small size of farm trucks, inadequate roads, the farmer's distrust of the new method, and lack of effective communication with customers. In addition, a dispute with the Flour, Feed, and Grain Elevator Workers Union began on August 6, 1940 and continued through the harvest season, until November 30. After heavy financial losses the company closed in 1941.

Anderson's third attempt to operate his own grain handling business began in 1946 after his sons returned from military service during World War II. In the intervening years Anderson had renewed his sense of purpose and clarified his goals toward better service to farmers. He felt certain that transporting grain from land to sea provided the greatest advantage to farmers. The mission of the new company reflected values of hard work, honesty, and service to others and the community. Committed to his dream to operate a business with his wife, daughter, and five sons, the new company was named The Andersons.

The slogan ''Farmers First'' reflected the company's commitment to assist farmers in getting their grain to the market. In 1947 The Andersons began construction on a 500,000-bushel grain storage facility with nine truck dumps to quickly serve farmers as they unloaded. To resolve previous problems of misunderstanding and distrust, the company formed an advisory board composed of local farmers and provided reports of each day's grain prices on Toledo and Fort Wayne radio stations. The Anderson family succeeded as Harold Anderson's ideas coalesced with post-WWII growth and development. The quality of roads and trucks improved, allowing farmers to travel as far as 150 miles to benefit from the higher grain prices offered by TA.

Success and Expansion in the First 25 Years

The company augmented its grain storage capacity continually, beginning with the addition of a 500,000-bushel grain elevator in 1950 and a three million-bushel storage facility in 1953. Construction on the latter attracted disdain from building trade unions, as well as attention from the national media, which labeled the project ''The Big Pour.'' Area farmers, company employees, and 225 college students worked 12 hours a day, around the clock, to complete the project in 12 days. At the new facility grain could be inspected and unloaded at the rate of 125 trucks per hour.

The Andersons endeavored to supplement the company's primary activities in ways that served the farmers. The Warehouse Market opened in 1952, offering reasonably priced seed, livestock feed, motor oil, fertilizer, and other farm supplies to farmers who would otherwise return home with empty trucks. A grain drier was added in 1952, and in 1954 construction began on a corn shelling plant. The Anderson Cob Mills Inc., officially established in 1958, sold the leftover corn cobs for use in the production of metal polishes, industrial cleaners, cosmetics, and other products. By the mid-1960s the plant grew to accommodate eight times more corn than its original volume.

After completion of the St. Lawrence Seaway in 1959 enabled more efficient water transportation to markets in Canada and eastern states, The Andersons opened the River Elevator, a 500,000-bushel grain elevator, and another marine transfer unit in Toledo on the Maumee River. The original Maumee site's 1959 grain storage capacity tripled to ten million bushels with the enhancement of 22 steel storage tanks. Capacity grew for an additional 1.5 million bushels at the River Elevator in 1964, while four express grain truck dumps added at Maumee in 1966 facilitated faster grain inspection and purchase.

The Andersons began to venture into activities on the periphery of agriculture as well. Production of lawn fertilizer began in 1959, initially mixed in a dormant concrete mixer. That business expanded with the construction of a mixing plant in 1963, a manufacturing plant in 1964, which also produced lawn herbicides and insecticides, and the addition of eight steel storage tanks in 1966. A feed mill, constructed in 1968, produced reasonably priced animal feed for domestic livestock, family pets, and zoological animals.

The Andersons added a Farm Supply Sales Office in Maumee and expanded retail operation to Toledo suburbs. The sales office was added in 1969 to better assist farmers in choosing from the wider variety of goods then available, such as building and fencing materials, various agricultural chemicals, grain bins, and other farm equipment. Supplying tires to farmers led to the opening of four tire shops at this time: Sylvania in 1969, Maumee and Oregon in 1971, and Toledo in 1973. The company opened a Garden Center in Dublin in 1967, and in Berwick and Sylvania in 1970. In 1972 the Warehouse Market moved to a larger, 155,000-square-foot building, on a 25-acre company complex across the street. Renamed the Maumee General Store and Garden Center, the store benefitted from new housing developments and drew customers from northwestern Ohio and southeastern Michigan with a wide selection and reasonable pricing.

A Second Generation Leads the Way in the Late 1960s

Under the leadership of a second generation, with John Anderson as CEO, The Andersons moved outside of northwestern Ohio for the first time in 1968. Construction began on a grain storage facility in Champaign, Illinois, which held 12.1 million bushels of grain. It was the first grain elevator in the United States to incorporate ''unit train'' stations into its design. The 100-car unit trains could transport grain farther at less expense, so when the price of oil rose in the 1970s, unit trains kept the company's costs down. The company also sought to help farmers with the cost to transport their grain by locating facilities near the farmers. In 1975 a four million-bushel storage

Key Dates:

1947: The Andersons partnership builds a grain elevator in Maumee, Ohio.
1952: Operations expand to include retail outlet Warehouse Market in Maumee.
1959: Fertilizer production begins.
1968: 12.1 million bushel grain elevator built in Champaign, Illinois.
1972: Annual sales reach nearly $200 million.
1979: Economic challenges as grain receipts peak and exports decline.
1986: Focus shifts to domestic grain production.
1996: The Andersons operations are consolidated and the company goes public on the NASDAQ.

facility at Delphi, Indiana was built to serve that corn-growing region. A General Store and a Tire Shop opened in Delphi in 1976, and a Cob Mill began to process 100,000 tons of corn annually.

High oil prices proved to be a boon to agriculture as they initiated a worldwide increase in available credit and, in turn, increased the worldwide demand for grain. The Andersons transported grain by rail and boat from Maumee to the North Atlantic ports for export, and the Champaign and Delphi facilities utilized unit trains to transport corn to ports on the Gulf of Mexico. In Maumee, grain storage capacity increased three million bushels to 17 million bushels. At the Toledo elevator the company added steel tanks with a capacity for five million bushels, bringing The Andersons's total grain storage capacity to 40 million bushels. The Andersons handled 62.1 million bushels of grain in 1970 and reached a pinnacle at 174 million bushels in 1979 as a result of the worldwide demand for grain.

Andersons continued to grow in all of its areas of business activity. In 1976 the company formed the Seed and Chemical Division, which provided agricultural chemicals, lawn and garden fertilizers, and seed for corn, wheat, soybeans, oat, barley, and rye, to suppliers in Ohio, Michigan, Indiana, Illinois, and western Pennsylvania. Construction on a new Feed Mill in Maumee was completed in 1977.

Although TA's business had always been subject to fluctuations in crop yield, changes in the 1980s compelled the company to diversify as a means to overall company stability. The availability of credit in the 1970s disintegrated in the 1980s due to the escalation of grain prices above genuine value. Farm production in the United States decreased when foreign competition prompted government policies to provide remuneration to farmers who leave some acreage dormant. The Andersons responded by placing greater emphasis on the retail businesses and on new products, and by taking a new approach to agricultural activities.

The company shifted to a system of country elevators in the early 1980s. Grain storage facilities were leased or purchased in Frankfort, and in Dunkirk, Indiana, and Findlay, Ohio, and a joint venture provided a facility in Weberville, Michigan. Construction in White Pigeon and Albion, Michigan included unit train stations that loaded grain directly from the elevators. Management agreements with grain elevators in Bunker Hill, Indiana in 1986 and in Constantine and Mendon, Michigan in 1987 further expanded The Andersons's country elevator system.

The Andersons utilized existing facilities to expand its capacity for wholesale fertilizer distribution. In Delphi fertilizer storage added in 1980 accommodated 50,000 tons, and in Champaign a facility to accommodate 35,000 tons of fertilizer was added in 1983. A 35,000-ton fertilizer storage facility as well as an Ag Products Warehouse supplemented business in Dunkirk, Indiana and in Weberville, Michigan. The Andersons added a 50,000-ton fertilizer storage facility in Toledo, and it expanded and upgraded the Maumee lawn fertilizer plant.

Retail operations expanded independently and through joint ventures. The Toledo General Store opened in 1984 and in Columbus the Brice General Store opened in 1986 and the Sawmill General Store opened in 1987. In 1988 the Woodville General Store opened in Northwood, Ohio. The company also leased Blonde's Farm Supply outlets in Litchfield and in North Adams, Michigan in 1986. Joint ventures included Tireman in Toledo in 1983 and Hubbard Feed in 1984. A joint venture with Jones Wheel Horse in 1989 took the company into the business of outdoor power equipment.

The Processing Group's enterprises comprised both consumer and industrial products in the 1980s. The Lawn Fertilizer Division adopted a more consumer-oriented marketing strategy and developed the trademarked Greensweep lawn fertilizer in 1985. Two liquid fertilizer plants acquired in Indiana provided the necessary facilities for expanded production in this division. A separate Pet Division was established in fall 1986 and expanded in 1987 when The Andersons acquired an interest in B&R, a distributor of pet products. In 1988 the company developed Slikwik Sorbents, a trademarked line of products, which utilize corn cob and synthetic ingredients for the absorption of industrial fluids and chemicals, grease, and liquid waste.

Building on Success in the 1990s

The Andersons kept pace with industry changes as the Retail Group renovated stores and added a new General Store in Lima, Ohio. The stores averaged 110,000 square feet with several distinctive departments, following the trend toward "a-store-within-a-store." New departments at these stores included Leisure Time, Home/Office products, Home Projects, Auto Care, a gourmet foods, wine, and flower store called "The Uncommon Market," and others.

The Andersons expanded into the business of rail car repair by opening the in-house repair shop, in operation for 50 years, to the other businesses. A new repair shop facility in Maumee accommodated custom steel fabrication as well as rail car repair services. The venture included a marketing office to handle the lease, purchase, and sale of rail cars.

The company's traditional agricultural business grew with the further addition of country elevators. The company purchased five storage elevators, two in Indiana, two in Ohio, and one in Michigan, as well as nine retail farm centers. In June 1996, the company leased the Rice Terminal elevator in Toledo, which served the horse racing business with TurfClub brand of bag oats. The storage facility, renamed The Anderson Reynolds Road, contained 38 storage bins, each capable of holding 2,200 to 36,5000 bushels of grain.

In November 1996 The Andersons sold its Slikwik Sorbents line of products to Sorbents Products Co. Inc. The sale included informational literature, the brand, its trademarks, and customer lists. Andersons Cob Division continued to supply corn cobs for production of the sorbents. The two companies also agreed to a non-exclusive licensing agreement for DriZorb, a line of products that sponge liquid waste in waterways and on dry land.

Organizational changes in the 1990s led to a public offering of stock in February 1996. The Andersons merged with Andersons Management Corp. to become The Andersons, Inc. (TAI). An independent appraiser placed TAI shares at $8.60, the price offered to employees. The initial stock offering priced at $15 per share, but dropped to $7.63 by the end of the year.

Competition from Home Depot, Builder's Square, and other home stores required a fresh approach in the Retail Group. Prior to the opening of a nearby Home Depot, a 10,000-square-foot indoor garden center was added to the Toledo General Store. The company reorganized all six General Stores, adjusting the sales area of each department in accordance with sales of the preceding years. Service improvements involved point-of-purchase signage and the ''We'll Load It'' program. While bulk items, such as sand and lumber, were loaded by employees, the customer carried a UPC-coded ticket to the cashier. In March 1997, the company launched a print, television, and radio advertising campaign featuring the slogan, ''For all things that you are, Andersons.'' In addition, The Andersons opened a greenhouse at the Maumee General Store.

The Andersons engaged in cooperative activities with other agricultural service companies in 1998. In March, The Andersons and Cargill, Inc. merged their grain storage businesses in Toledo. The Andersons leased two grain elevators from Cargill in Toledo and Maumee, and Cargill agreed to sell its grain to The Andersons and to make their global export network accessible to TA. As rural elevator companies have garnered a greater share of the storage market, the arrangement was expected to provide greater efficiency and revenues to both companies. With Central Soya Co., Inc., Anderson purchased DeKalb Agra Inc. of Waterloo, Indiana. The Andersons procured that company's retail farm and fertilizer assets, and Central Soya procured the grain storage and transportation facilities. In addition, in cooperation with International Raw Materials, Ltd., The Andersons formed a limited liability company that would manufacture lawn and garden fertilizers and ice melt products to markets in the northeastern United States.

In 1998 The Andersons acted to enhance all of its business areas. The Manufacturing Group added 1,000 rail cars to its fleet, increasing the number available for lease to more than 3,800 rail cars. The Retail Group evolved its marketing strategy under the idea of the ''Complete Home Store,'' which included housewares and domestic goods. Improved merchandise displays, a private label brand of paint, and wallpaper were added. The Processing Group planned to place greater emphasis on in-house product development and has been working on a proprietary cat litter using corn cobs. A stock transaction in January 1998 brought the Crop and Soil Service, Inc. retail farm stores into the Agriculture Group. The company also added six retail farm centers in Ohio, Michigan, and Indiana through either lease or purchase in 1998 and early 1999.

In March 1999 The Andersons became one of the largest producers of polyphosphate liquid agricultural fertilizer east of the Mississippi River through the purchase of a Cargill fertilizer production facility and wholesale distribution center in Seymour, Indiana. The plant, the company's fifth, offered a prime location for road and rail transportation and also brought a new product to the company—pelletized lime for soil ph balance. In June The Andersons further expanded its manufacturing capabilities for lawn and garden products with the acquisition of another facility in Montgomery, Alabama. A third generation took the lead at The Andersons as Mike Anderson, grandson of Harold Anderson, became CEO in 1999.

Principal Subsidiaries

Andersons Ag Products; Andersons Agriservices, Inc.; Andersons Grain Corp.; Crop & Soils Service, Inc.

Principal Operating Units

Retail Group; Agricultural Group; Processing Group; Manufacturing Group.

Principal Competitors

Archer Daniels Midland Company; Cenex Harvest States Cooperatives; Cargill, Inc.; Home Depot; Payless Cashways.

Further Reading

''Anderson Share Price Down, But Few Worry,'' *Toledo Blade,* December 10, 1996, p. 27.

''The Andersons Acquires Alabama Lawn Fertilizer Plant,'' *PR Newswire,* June 18, 1999.

''The Andersons Acquires Cargill's Seymour Wholesale Fertilizer Facility,'' *PR Newswire,* May 27, 1999, p. 9120.

''The Andersons, Cargill Sign Pact with Ohio Facilities,'' *Feedstuffs,* April 27 1998, p. 19.

''The Andersons, Central Soya Buy Co-Op,'' *Feedstuffs,* August 3, 1998, p. 6.

''The Andersons Expands Ag Group To Process, Bag Oats for Racehorses,'' *Milling and Baking News,* June 25, 1996, p. 17.

''The Andersons: 50 Years of Service, Growth, and Change,'' *Andersons Herald,* company publication, October 1997.

''The Andersons Going Public in 49th Year of Business,'' *Milling and Baking News,* February 20, 1996, p. 53.

''The Andersons Hones Mix; Adopts New 'Shop' Approach,'' *Discount Store News,* September 2, 1991, p. 1.

''The Andersons Is a Store for all Reasons,'' *National Home Center News,* August 9, 1999, p. 87.

''The Andersons Names New CEO,'' *National Home Center News,* January 11, 1999, p. 7.

''The Andersons—Service Still Prevails Nearly 37 Years Later,'' *Anderson Herald,* company publication, Special Issue, 1983.

''The Andersons to Acquire Farm Centers,'' *Feedstuffs,* January 26, 1998, p. 21.

''Appointments Bring Management Changes to the Andersons,'' *Do-it-Yourself Retailing,* October 16, 1996, p. 100.

''CEO Interview—Richard P. Anderson, Chairman and CEO Discusses Outlook for the Andersons,'' *Wall Street Transcript Digest,* December 15, 1997.

''Consumer Housewares Show Boosts Sales at Ohio Chain,'' *Discount Store News,* March 16, 1987, p. 55.

Keith, Natalie, ''The Andersons Celebrates Golden Anniversary,'' *National Home Center News,* August 25, 1997, p. 29.

''A Look Back,'' *Andersons Herald,* company publication, October 1987.

Newton-Doyle, Jennifer, ''The Andersons, Inc. Celebrates 50 Years of Growth,'' *Pet Product News,* November 1997, p. 8.

Schmucker, Jane, ''Cargill's Andersons to Merge Elevators,'' *Toledo Blade,* March 26, 1998, p. 38.

——, ''For Its Bond Sales, Andersons Goes Solo,'' *Toledo Blade,* July 1, 1997, p. S9.

——, ''The Andersons Quietly Ends First Year as Public Corporation,'' *Toledo Blade,* February 20, 1997, p. 38.

—Mary Tradii

Associated Grocers, Incorporated

3301 South Norfolk Street
Seattle, Washington 98118
U.S.A.
Telephone: (206) 7622100
Fax: (206) 7647731
Web site: http://www.agseattle.com

Private Company
Incorporated: 1934 as Associated Grocers Cooperative
Employees: 1,300
Sales: $1.09 billion (1998)
NAIC: 42241 General Line Grocery Wholesalers; 42242 Packaged Frozen Food Wholesalers; 42247 Meat and Meat Product Wholesalers; 42243 Dairy Product (Except Dried or Canned) Wholesalers; 42221 Drugs and Druggists' Sundries Wholesalers; 42248 Fresh Fruit and Vegetable Wholesalers.

Headquartered in Seattle, Washington, Associated Grocers, Incorporated, is a retailer-owned cooperative that distributes food products and general merchandise to about 350 independent grocery retailers in Alaska, Hawaii, Oregon, and Washington. The privately held company also serves grocers in Guam and the Pacific Rim. In addition to food and nonfood goods, Associated Grocers provides support and retail services, such as site development, electronic payment, and store decor. Included in the more than 12,000 items distributed by Associated Grocers are its own private-label brands, including Western Family, Javaworks, and Ovenworks.

Grocers Band Together in the 1930s

After the stock market crashed in 1929 and sent the U.S. economy spiraling downward, businesses that had managed to survive the tumultuous economic conditions still faced years of difficult recovery. The economic climate had still not improved by 1934 when 11 independent grocers in Seattle, Washington, banded together to form the Associated Grocers Cooperative. Although it was not the first time businesses with similar interests had created a cooperative to help stave off the harmful effects of the Depression, the formation of Associated Grocers did mark one of the first instances in which grocers united to share resources and to create an organizational structure to oversee their well-being. The eleven grocery stores, mostly smaller, street corner operations, commonly known as ''mom and pop'' stores, joined together through the assistance of Harry Henke, Jr., a corporate lawyer in Seattle. The stores also solicited the help of J.B. Rhodes, a supermarket executive working in San Francisco, to lead the newly formed cooperative.

With a starting capital of $8,325, Associated Grocers initially provided grocery products to the individual, independent stores, enabling them to compete with the larger chain stores that relied on centralized distribution centers and possessed larger reservoirs of cash. Accordingly, the cooperative provided a buffer for the independent grocers against their better-financed competition and, in effect, enabled them to pool their resources in order to survive the debilitating times. Since the cooperative was owned by the grocers, a portion of the profits earned by Associated Grocers from the sales to the grocers were returned to the grocers in the form of patronage dividends.

In its first year of operation, Associated Grocers fared well. Revenues totaled $1.27 million for the year, and the cooperative was becoming stronger as more grocery stores joined and it became better able to keep the independent grocer competitive in an industry increasingly dominated by large chain stores. Four years after its inception, in 1938, Associated Grocers constructed a 41,800-square-foot warehouse in Yakima, Washington, to complement the cooperative's warehouse in Seattle and accommodate its burgeoning clientele. The facility in Yakima, a community east of Seattle in central Washington, was established as a branch warehouse to fulfill the needs of member grocery stores near the facility. By establishing branch warehouses, Associated Grocers reduced transportation costs to stores located outside the immediate service area of its Seattle warehouse and was able to transport the merchandise in a shorter time, particularly important for the perishable products that member stores required.

When the United States entered World War II in 1941, a scarcity of some grocery products resulted, but the effects of the shortage were mitigated by Associated Grocers' ability to provide

Company Perspectives:

We will provide whatever products or services necessary to keep our customers competitive in every phase of the food business at the most competitive prices possible.

competitively priced merchandise to its customers. In addition to supplying its member stores with merchandise, the cooperative also began offering services intended to help the independent grocer's position in the marketplace. For example, Associated Grocers became one of the first wholesalers in the nation to offer retailers a complete pricing service, allowing member stores access to the prices other stores charged for products and keeping member stores apprised of competitive pricing in their market. By 1942, the cooperative had outgrown its main warehouse in Seattle, and a new warehouse was built to accommodate the cooperative's members, which by this time had increased from the original 11 stores to 260 independent grocers.

Postwar Growth and Expansion

After World War II, business accelerated, fueled by a postwar boom that increased Associated Grocers' customer base considerably. By 1952 the cooperative had 600 members, operating stores in Washington, Oregon, Alaska, and the Hawaiian islands. In addition to the warehouse in Seattle and the branch warehouse in Yakima, which had been enlarged by 11,000 square feet in 1948, the cooperative also opened nine "cash and carry" branches to supply both member and nonmember stores. Independent stores that did not belong to Associated Grocers could buy merchandise at these cash and carry outlets but did not receive the cooperative's patronage dividends. Since Associated Grocers opened for business 18 years earlier, the cooperative had returned an average of nearly $155,000 per year in patronage dividends for a total of $2.7 million. Sales now stood at $33 million, and Associated Grocers once again found itself in need of additional warehouse space as well as more modern equipment and facilities to effectively service its members.

In a much heralded event in the local press, Associated Grocers completed construction in 1952 on a $2.2 million warehouse that at once answered the increasing needs of the cooperative. Located on a 26 acre plot, the site was comprised of four buildings, including the warehouse. The warehouse featured a large loading dock to receive and dispatch merchandise to and from its fleet of trucks and 235,000 square feet of space sheltered by a nine-acre roof. Included in this large area were a series of curing rooms, to store fruit until ripened, and a separate area for frozen foods. The complex also included a building used to service and repair warehouse equipment and the cooperative's fleet of trucks, which by this time consisted of 100 trucks and trailers. Another building was devoted solely to the repair and maintenance of the tires used on the cooperative's vehicles. This distribution complex provided more than ample space to service Associated Grocers increasing membership, and additional land surrounding the new buildings offered the opportunity for the cooperative to further expand.

While the cooperative continued to expand its operations, store membership did not dramatically increase beyond the 600 stores belonging to the cooperative in 1952. Rather, growth came from an increase of services to members and in the size of the stores they operated, which in turn helped Associated Grocers realize future gains in revenues. Following the completion of the warehouse complex, a new department was created to manage drugs and sundries, and in 1953 the cooperative recorded nearly $39.5 million in sales and returned $455,417 in patronage dividends. Two years later, Associated Grocers management began looking for a way to assist its members in financing major remodeling projects and new store construction. Many wholesale grocery concerns had been assisting their members in financing new store construction recently, approximately 25 percent of the wholesale industry engaged in this activity, and Associated Grocers sought to extend the service to its members. With an initial investment of $50,000, the cooperative formed a wholly owned subsidiary named Market Finance Co. that enabled member stores to borrow the requisite funds to relocate their stores, construct new stores, or complete preapproved remodeling projects. The amount of the loans was generally limited to $50,000, for which the retailers were charged six percent simple interest. Market Finance was advanced the money from banks at a lower interest rate than charged to the retailer, with the difference between the two rates financing the subsidiary's operating expenses. Not designed to earn a profit, the subsidiary was, nevertheless, a financial success. Within two years, roughly 25 percent of the cooperative's members had applied for financing through Market Finance, amounting to over $1 million in loans.

Growing Pains Beginning in the 1960s

The addition of these services would figure prominently in the company's business strategy during the 1960s. By this time, competition from the larger, better-financed retail chains had intensified, as large supermarkets began to dominate the markets in which Associated Grocer member stores operated. Consequently, a large number of mom and pop stores were forced out of business, giving way to new stores that occupied sites as large as a city block. During this era of decline for small grocery stores, Associated Grocers increased the services it provided to its members, helping them with store decor, establishing electronic ordering systems, and supplying them with innovative packaging methods. However, these efforts were not enough to keep some of the smaller stores in business, and the cooperative's membership dwindled. By the end of the decade, the effect of these losses impelled Associated Grocers to seek new leadership.

The cooperative's new president, Bert Hambleton, was elected in 1971. Hambleton, who had spent 21 years with grocery and retailing chains in Ohio and Illinois before joining Associated Grocers, accepted the position with some reluctance. As he later recalled, "The operation was in deep trouble when I came. . . . When the board first offered me the job I turned them down because I didn't think the company was going to survive." However, under Hambleton's leadership, lasting changes were made that reinvigorated Associated Grocers' position in the wholesale industry. Throughout the cooperative's offices, computers were brought in to improve the efficiency and accuracy of all facets of operations, from the management of the warehouses to market research.

Key Dates:

1934: Eleven independent grocers form Associated Grocers Co-operative.
1938: Associated Grocers extends its reach with a warehouse in Yakima, Washington.
1952: Cooperative builds a new Seattle warehouse complex.
1955: Associated Grocers establishes subsidiary Market Finance Co.
1985: Cooperative acquires 25 Washington stores from Lucky Food Stores.
1990: Sales surpass the $1 billion mark.
1998: Associated Grocers forms joint venture with Fleming Companies Inc.

Cooperative-owned dairy and egg farms were established, creating a stable supply of dairy products for the independent grocers, and the organizational structure of the company was revamped to give its operations a configuration more characteristic of a corporation rather than a cooperative. The changes implemented by Hambleton were successful. When he assumed control of Associated Grocers, revenues were $150 million and earnings were less than $1 million. By the end of the decade, revenues had climbed to $625 million, and the dividends paid to the cooperative's members totaled $8 million.

The mounting pressure put on independent grocers continued into the 1980s, as such giants in the industry as Safeway Stores competed for customers with Associated Grocers member stores. While the cooperative had increased its market share from below 20 percent to greater than 25 percent during the 1970s, it needed to further penetrate the markets in which it operated. A supermarket development subsidiary was formed in 1981 to manage the financing and development of stores for Associated Grocers members, tasks that had clogged the cooperative's administration operations, consuming as much as 60 percent of its time. Utilizing the cooperative's computers, the subsidiary conducted site analyses and demographic studies that enabled independent stores to enter markets before other commercial and residential development. Although riskier in nature, this method proved successful in allowing Associated and its members to compete for sites with the chain store operators.

In 1985 Associated Grocers purchased 25 stores located in Washington from Lucky Food Stores, a retail chain operating in 30 states. Lucky had been unable to efficiently operate the stores from its distribution and manufacturing centers in California, so the cooperative purchased the 23 supermarkets and two discount outlets and sold the stores to independent grocers in an effort to increase the number of stores under its purview. The addition of the Lucky stores, as well as an agreement with Pacific Gamble Robinson to supply 88 grocery stores, gave Associated Grocers 406 stores. Largely due to the association with Pacific Gamble, revenues had increased by 20 percent since 1984 to reach approximately $900 million.

Later that year Associated Grocers initiated negotiations with United Retail Merchants Stores Inc., a wholesale grocery distributor operating in eastern Washington, to effect a merger. The proposed merger would join United Retail's distributing facilities with those of Associated Grocers to lend greater efficiency to the two wholesalers' purchasing and distribution operations and enable Associated Grocers to more fully utilize its warehouse space. Associated Grocers' board of directors approved the proposal, voting unanimously in favor of uniting United Retail's approximately $400 million in revenues with the cooperative's $900 million. However, United Retail backed out in early 1986. Aggressively seeking the merger, Hambleton at one point had offered to step aside if his departure would facilitate the union, but his efforts were to no avail. One month after United Retail made their announcement, Hambleton, who had been stunned by the decision, opted for early retirement and was succeeded by Donald Benson, Associated Grocers' executive vice-president of finance.

Although the collapse of the deal with United Retail in 1986 was discouraging, the year was generally good for Associated Grocers' management. Through the assistance of the cooperative, independent grocers experienced a resurgence during this time due to their new focus on customer service. Stores were now being remodeled much more frequently, the merchandise was becoming more diverse, and the stores' management began orienting their marketing and products to the residents living in proximity to the particular store. These adjustments enabled Associated Grocers to match Safeway's market share for the first time, which was a combined 72 percent for the two companies. By attempting to appeal to as many different types of customers as possible and generating more sales per square foot, Associated Grocers members increased their profits, and the cooperative, in turn, collected the rewards of a revitalized business. By 1990, Associated Grocers was the largest privately held company in Washington, and revenues surpassed the $1 billion mark.

Competition Heats Up in the 1990s

As Associated Grocers entered the 1990s, a two-month strike was effected by its workers. Increased costs resulting from the strike cut into the cooperative's earnings, which dropped from $4.2 million to $3.5 million, and the cooperative's patronage dividends fell from $14.7 million to $10.7 million. Nevertheless, Associated Grocers' performance rebounded in 1991, as the dividends climbed back up to $13.5 million, and earnings jumped to $5.2 million on revenues of $1.1 billion.

Also in the early 1990s Associated Grocers began to face increasing competition. Large supermarket chains, mini-mart stores, and discount giants such as Costco and Drug Emporium expanded into regions serviced by Associated Grocers, creating a battle for precious market share in an industry with nominal profit margins. To compete against its formidable new rivals, Associated Grocers took proactive measures; the company helped member stores remodel and modernize, expanded the product lines of its well-selling private-label brands, Western Family and Market Choice, and streamlined its delivery operations. Between early 1993 and mid-1994 Associated Grocers decreased its work force by 100 employees through attrition, and in the first half of 1994 overhead costs were reduced 0.52 percent.

Associated Grocers also planned to implement cutting-edge technology in stores to stay competitive, including electronic product pricing, which displayed prices on LCD screens attached to supermarket shelves. Associated Grocers also continued to push electronic funds transfer (EFT) services; in 1994 the company, which was the first wholesaler to adopt EFT in 1989, when the technology was still new, provided more than 180 member retailers with EFT services that covered check approval, debit card, and credit card operations. The company planned to expand its network to support 220 customers by the end of 1995 and was already providing the service to nonmember retailers.

In 1995 Associated Grocers had sales of about $1.2 billion and, based on sales, it was the largest private company in Washington. It was the sixth consecutive year Associated Grocers had attained the top ranking in *Washington CEO,* which listed the largest 150 nonpublic companies in the state annually. Despite its size, however, Associated Grocers sensed the need to take additional measures to protect the market share of its member stores. Indeed, a 1996 research project conducted by Exvere Inc. found that though the Northwest held the highest concentration of independent retailers, the figure was on the decline. The study found that 40 percent of retail grocers in Oregon, Washington, Idaho, and parts of Montana were independently owned stores, compared to a national average of 25 percent. In the western part of Washington, however, the percentage was dropping, nearing 35 percent by early 1998. The decline was attributed to expansion by large supermarket chains and a flurry of consolidation and acquisitions. For instance, Fred Meyer, Inc., became larger with its purchase of Quality Food Centers, Inc. (QFC) in 1998. The acquisition provided the chain with the top market share in the Puget Sound region and put into question Associated Grocers' role as supplier to QFC. Some industry experts estimated that Associated Grocers' sales could drop as much as 20 percent if QFC chose to stop using Associated Grocers' services.

Associated Grocers entered merger discussions with United Grocers Inc. of Milwaukee, Oregon, in spring 1997. United Grocers was also a distributor of wholesale groceries to its member retailers, serving about 390 grocers in Oregon, Washington, and California. By combining their businesses, Associated Grocers and United Grocers could gain size and clout, which would prove valuable in the fight against larger companies. Strengthening operations was especially important to United, which had suffered from declining net income since 1992. By November 1997 the two companies had agreed to establish a joint venture rather than a merger. The joint venture would provide information and distribution services to member retailers of both companies, shipping goods from the nearest warehouse to speed up delivery service. The new company was given the temporary name of Newco, and Associated Grocers' CEO and president, Donald Benson, was appointed to run the new company.

The joint venture never materialized, however, and much to United's surprise, Associated Grocers announced a joint venture with Fleming Companies Inc. in September 1998. Oklahoma City-based Fleming, the second-largest food marketing and distribution wholesaler in the United States, teamed with Associated Grocers to form AG/Fleming Northwest LLC The new company would join purchasing and distribution systems to better serve retailers in the Northwest. As part of the deal, Associated Grocers purchased Fleming's warehouse operations in Portland, which supplied 74 grocers, and two Oregon stores. Though Associated Grocers maintained that it still planned to pursue the joint venture with United, it never happened, and in the spring of 1999 United announced it would merge with Certified Grocers of California to form Unified Western Grocers.

As Associated Grocers neared the end of the 20th century, it looked toward strategic alliances and acquisitions to remain competitive in a climate increasingly filled with large, nationwide chains. In 1998 the company purchased four Stock Market grocery stores in the Puget Sound area from Fred Meyer. Also that year the cooperative signed an agreement with Jreck Subs Group, Inc. to market Georgio's Subs throughout its member group. The agreement boosted Associated Grocers offerings in the growing category of meal replacement. In October 1999 Associated Grocers extended its presence in Alaska by forming Northwest Retail Ventures, LLC with Bristol Bay Native Corporation and several Associated Grocers' members. The new venture was formed to operate six grocery stores in Alaska, three located in Anchorage, purchased from Safeway Inc. The new stores adopted the name Alaska Marketplace and combined the best that Associated Grocers had to offer—excellent customer service, pleasant shopping environments, and the finest food and nonfood goods available.

Principal Subsidiaries

Market Food Service; Market Advertising; Northwest Retail Ventures, LLC (49%); AG/Fleming Northwest LLC (50%).

Principal Competitors

Services Group of America; SUPERVALU INC.; Unified Western Grocers; The Kroger Co.; Safeway Inc.

Further Reading

"AG Is the Largest Private Firm in State," *Seattle Times,* May 21, 1993, p. C7.

"Associated Grocers Coop Fetes New Plant," *Seattle Times,* August 17, 1952, p. 48.

"Associated Grocers Is State's Top Private Firm," *Seattle Times,* March 11, 1991, p. B5.

"Associated Grocers to Buy Lucky Stores," *Seattle Times,* October 24, 1985, p. D1.

Blake, Judith, "Groceries Going All Out to Win Back Customers," *Seattle Times,* August 2, 1989, p. C1.

Dwyer, Kevin, "Billion Dollar Baby," *Washington CEO,* March 1991, pp. 28–29.

"Eleven Groups Associated in Western Area," *Seattle Times,* August 17, 1952, p. 50.

"Grocers' Coop Sets New Sales Record," *Seattle Times,* December 8, 1953, p. 35.

Hill, Jim, "Fleming, Associated Grocers Form Joint Venture," *Portland Oregonian,* September 17, 1998, p. C2.

Hopfinger, Tony, "Former Safeway Managers Reunite to Expand Smaller Chain," *Anchorage Daily News,* October 15, 1999.

Kim, Nancy J., "Associated Grocers, Big Wholesaler Align," *Puget Sound Business Journal,* December 4, 1998, p. 4.

Mahoney, Sally Gene, ''Associated Grocers May Merge with Spokane Merchant Group,'' *Seattle Times,* December 10, 1985, p. C4.
——, ''Lucky Pullout Almost Complete,'' *Seattle Times,* November 12, 1985, p. B1.
——, ''URM Calls off Merger with Associated,'' *Seattle Times,* January 8, 1986, p. D4.
Moriwaki, Lee, ''Fred Meyer's Purchase of Seattle Grocery Chain Makes Local Suppliers Anxious,'' *Seattle Times,* November 17, 1997.
''Northwest Supers Finally Cash in on ATMs,'' *Supermarket Business,* January 1985, p. 6.
Pucci, Carol, ''Bagging More Customers: Independent Grocers Alter Image to Get Growing Share of the Market,'' *Seattle Times,* December 7, 1986, p. E1.
Sharpe, Gary, ''Development Financing Grocery Company's Big Ticket,'' *Seattle Business Journal,* February 15, 1982, p. 6.
Sternman, Mike, ''NW Passage: Independents Seek to Survive,'' *Supermarket News,* March 23, 1998, p. 9.
Warren, James R., *A Century of Seattle's Business,* Bellevue, Wash.: Vernon Publications Inc., 1989.
''Wholesaler Sponsored Financing Strengthens Washington Independents,'' *Progressive Grocer,* December 1956, pp. 51–55.
Wolcott, John, ''100 Largest Private Companies: Associated Grocers Puts More Sizzle into Selling,'' *Puget Sound Business Journal,* June 24, 1994, p. 50.
Zwiebach, Elliot, ''Two Co-Ops in Northwest Agree to Form Joint Venture,'' *Supermarket News,* November 24, 1997, p. 1.

—Jeffrey L. Covell
—updated by Mariko Fujinaka

The Associated Press

50 Rockefeller Plaza
New York, New York 10020
U.S.A.
Telephone: (212) 621-1500
Toll Free: (800) 272-2551
Fax: (212) 621-5447
Web site: http://www.ap.org

Cooperative
Incorporated: 1848 as Associated Press of New York
Employees: 3,100
Sales: $494.5 million (1998)
NAIC: 51411 News Syndicates

The Associated Press (AP) describes itself as the largest newsgathering organization in the world. Organized as a non-profit cooperative, AP provides news and graphics by wire to over 1,700 member newspapers and 6,000 member television and radio stations in the United States, and 8,500 other subscribers in 110 countries around the world. To collect the news and photographs it supplies to its members, AP maintains 240 bureaus in more than 70 countries. In addition to its basic newswire, AP also offers other services including APTN, a television news agency; the 24-hour AP All News Radio service; and, on the Web, public access to news text, sound, and images via The WIRE. AP staffers have won 45 Pulitzer Prizes, 27 of them for photography.

Early Years

The Associated Press was first established in 1848, when six of the most prominent daily newspapers in New York City decided to pool their resources in order to cut costs. Representatives of the six papers—the *Journal of Commerce,* the *New York Sun,* the *Herald,* the *Courier and Enquirer,* the *Express,* and the *New York Tribune*—were able to put aside their competitive differences, and the Associated Press of New York was created. David Hale, publisher of the *Journal of Commerce,* was its first president. The purpose of the organization at the beginning was strictly a financial one. By sharing all the news that arrived by telegraph wire and dividing the expenses evenly, each member was spared the dangers of losing wire-borne information to a higher bidder.

By 1850, the group had its first paying customers, the *Philadelphia Public Ledger* and the *Baltimore Sun,* which were given access to AP dispatches for a fee, without becoming actual members of the collective. A seventh full member (another New York paper) was admitted in 1851. Over the next several years, the number of client newspapers outside of New York grew, and the AP was able to recover about half of its expenses through its sales of news to those papers. The AP kept its transmission costs in check by sending out news to each geographical area only one time. The newspapers in each area were left to distribute the news among themselves. This led to the formation of several regional associations modeled on the original AP. The Western Associated Press (WAP) was created by a group of Midwestern daily newspapers in 1862. Other groups that sprang up over the next few years were the Northwestern Associated Press, the New England Associated Press, the Philadelphia Associated Press, and the New York State Associated Press.

As the regional associations, especially the WAP, gained strength, friction developed between them and their New York parent. The Western papers felt that they were being overcharged for European news, which by the 1860s was flowing steadily to the United States by underwater telegraph cable. Concessions were made, and peace reigned for several years. Several competitors to the AP arose during the 1870s, but none were able to break the virtual monopoly the AP held on the transmission of domestic and international news by wire. The first serious rival emerged in 1882, when the United Press (UP), led by William M. Laffan of the *New York Sun,* was formed.

In 1891, Victor Lawson of the Chicago Daily News produced evidence that top executives of the AP and the UP had engaged in a secret agreement that gave the UP free access to AP News. Outraged by this revelation, the AP's Western members broke from the association, and in 1892 established the Associated Press of Illinois under the leadership of general manager Melville Stone. The New York AP quickly folded, and its original members defected to the UP. Stone then pulled off a major coup for the new AP by obtaining exclusive arrangements with three major European news agencies: Reuters in England, Havas in France, and Wolff in Germany. These con-

Company Perspectives:

The Associated Press is in the information business. Its fundamental mission is to provide state, national and international news, photos, graphics, broadcast and online services of the highest quality, reliability and objectivity to its domestic owners as economically as it can. The AP is a member-driven company. News bearing the AP logotype is expected to be accurate, balanced and informed. AP feels that unrestricted access to the sources of news is essential if those standards are to be met by the AP and other news organizations. The AP seeks no special privilege beyond free access. It believes that the more journalistic voices the world hears, the better informed it will be.

tracts put the UP in an untenable position, and by 1897, the UP had thrown in the towel. All of the New York dailies except the *Sun* and William Randolph Hearst's *Journal* were given memberships in the new AP.

1900: Dissolution of AP of Illinois; Rebirth in New York As a Cooperative

Another controversy erupted in 1898, and again Laffan of the *Sun* was involved. Laffan had set up his own agency, the Laffan News Bureau, following the collapse of the UP. When the AP discovered that one of its client papers, the *Chicago Inter Ocean,* had used Laffan copy, it sought to punish the *Inter Ocean* by cutting off its AP service. The Inter Ocean sued to block the AP from severing its service. The Illinois Supreme Court ruled in 1900 that the AP's bylaws were broad enough to make the organization akin to a public utility. The Court's decision meant that the AP must provide service to anybody who wanted it. Rather than comply with the Illinois Court's conclusion, the Associated Press of Illinois was dissolved, and the organization set up shop once again in New York. The new AP was organized under New York State law as a nonprofit membership association, with Stone continuing in his role as general manager.

By reorganizing, rather than by complying with the Illinois Supreme Court's decision, the AP was able to maintain control over who was allowed to become a member. The new AP of 1900 was a cooperative, whose members were to share their news with each other and share the costs of maintaining staff to control the flow of news among members. By 1914, the AP had about 100 member newspapers. Until 1915, AP members were prohibited from buying news from other services. By that time, there were actually two viable competitors from whom AP members could be getting additional news: the United Press Association, formed in 1907, and the International News Service, founded by Hearst in 1909. Laffan's agency, after thriving for a few years, was out of the picture by 1916.

In 1910, a young Indiana journalist named Kent Cooper approached General Manager Stone with the idea of using telephone rather than telegraph to feed news to out-of-the-way newspapers. Although this method was only put to use for a few years—due mainly to the emergence of the teletype machine in 1913—Stone was impressed, and he hired Cooper as AP's traffic chief. Cooper worked his way up to assistant general manager by 1920. A year later, Stone retired, and was succeeded by Frederick Roy Martin. Cooper replaced Martin as general manager in 1925, and he remained with the AP for a total of 41 years.

Growth Under Kent Cooper: 1925–45

It was under Cooper that the AP grew into a gigantic international news machine. From the beginning, Cooper saw countless ways to improve the organization's methods of collecting and distributing information. One of his most important moves was his ongoing battle to free the AP from its obligations to import European news by way of news agencies there—ironically, these were the same arrangements that had given the AP its decisive edge over the UP years earlier. Cooper saw that news from European agencies was often slanted in favor of their home governments. He believed that the only way for the AP to receive accurate accounts of events abroad was to use its own reporters. The AP opened bureaus in Great Britain, France, and Germany in 1929, but it took until 1934 to break free of those confining arrangements completely.

One of Cooper's most important domestic improvements was the development of state bureaus as the organization's primary operating units. Cooper also widened the AP's coverage to better reflect the public's changing interests, adding an afternoon sports service, financial information, and features. The AP's new acceptance of human interest stories, which it had historically disdained, led to the organization's first Pulitzer Prize, awarded to Kirke L. Simpson in 1922 for a series on the Unknown Soldier buried in Washington, D.C.'s Arlington Cemetery. In 1927, the AP started a news photo service, and the improved AP Wirephoto system gained approval in 1935.

In 1931, the Associated Press Managing Editors Association, a group composed of editors of AP member newspapers for the purpose of reviewing the organization's work, was formed. By 1940, AP membership had grown to more than 1,400 papers. The AP began selling its news reports to radio stations in 1940, and by 1946, radio stations were allowed to become associate AP members, without voting rights. Meanwhile, another legal skirmish forced the AP to change its bylaws concerning membership. Since 1900, the AP had generally been regarded as a private association with the right to refuse membership to any outfit it did not want to admit. When the *Chicago Sun*—a paper launched by Marshall Field in 1941 to compete with the *Tribune*—sought entry into the AP collective, it was denied membership by the publishers of the AP's member newspapers. At the *Sun*'s urging, the matter was investigated by the Justice Department, which found the AP's exclusionary rules to be in violation of federal antitrust regulations. The AP changed its rules at its next meeting, and the *Sun* became a member. As a result, since 1945 any publisher that wanted access to AP news reports could become an AP member.

Expansion of Broadcasting Operations Following World War II

World War II brought further breakthroughs in international news coverage, including the additions of transatlantic cable and radio-teletype circuits, leased land circuits in Europe, and an overseas radiophoto network. In 1946, the AP launched its World Service. Cooper retired in 1948, and was succeeded as

Key Dates:

1848: Associated Press of New York is formed to share news-gathering costs of six newspapers.
1892: AP of Illinois is founded under Melville Stone.
1900: Court-ordered reorganization; New York is reestablished as headquarters.
1927: News Photo service begins.
1929: AP opens bureaus in France, England, and Germany.
1945: Open membership in AP for all who wish to join.
1954: Associated Press Radio-Television Association is formed.
1967: Partnership with Dow Jones offers business news service.
1982: AP begins transmitting news by satellite.
1994: APTV, an international video newsgathering service, is launched.
1996: The WIRE Internet news service begins operation.

general manager by Frank J. Starzel, who had joined the AP in 1929. The organization continued to grow steadily through the 1950s under Starzel. Broadcast media began playing an increasing role in news coverage in the United States, and in 1954, the Associated Press Radio-Television Association was formed. By 1960, that subgroup was already representing over 2,000 domestic stations. Meanwhile, the AP's newspaper count had risen to nearly 1,800. In addition, about 3,500 news outlets outside of the United States were receiving AP reports.

Starzel retired in 1962, and the general manager position was assumed by Wes Gallagher, who had led the AP's World War II coverage as a reporter. By 1962, the organization had a total revenue of $44 million. Although the number of domestic newspapers subscribing to AP reports was beginning to decline, broadcast members were joining at a brisk pace. Meanwhile, advancing technology was making it easier to collect and spread news faster than ever before. Use of computers was expanded to include typesetting. Wire systems were overhauled and modernized, and a direct Teletype line connecting Moscow, London, and New York was installed. The AP also established a book division during 1963.

AP teamed with Dow Jones & Co., Inc. in 1967 to launch a new, ambitious business reporting service. The AP-Dow Jones Economic Report was an in-depth business newswire service transmitted to governments, corporations, trading firms, and other interested entities in nine European, Asian, and African countries. The following year, the same team launched the AP-Dow Jones Financial Wire, a teleprinter news service aimed primarily at stockbrokers in all of Europe's financial centers. By 1970, these services were being offered in 17 countries. Broadcast stations continued to join the AP in droves, with a total net increase of 1,224 member stations for the 1960s as a whole.

Improved Newsgathering Technology During the 1970s

Technological progress continued to improve AP services during the 1970s. One of its breakthroughs during this period was the Laserphoto news picture system, developed jointly with researchers at the Massachusetts Institute of Technology (MIT). The Laserphoto system allowed the AP to transmit photographs of a much higher quality than was previously possible to both print and broadcast members. Another new general manager, Keith Fuller, was named upon Gallagher's retirement in 1976. The following year, three new seats, bringing the total to 21, were added to the AP board of directors, in order to give AP broadcast members board representation for the first time. In 1977, the same MIT team that had developed Laserphoto broke through again with the Electronic Darkroom, a system capable of transmitting, receiving, and storing pictures in digital form.

By the early 1980s, newspapers were generating about half of AP's revenues, as new media, particularly cable television, emerged to dilute print's role in delivering news to Americans. In 1982, the organization amended its bylaws to allow the use of its news reports by member newspapers on cable systems. The AP also began developing ways of transmitting news reports via satellite. By 1984, the AP's global network included over 300 news and photo bureaus throughout the world, and it was delivering reports to 1,300 daily newspapers and 5,700 broadcast stations in the United States alone. In addition, there were 8,500 subscribers in foreign countries. Fuller retired as both president and general manager that year, and was replaced by Louis D. Boccardi, a 17-year veteran of the AP.

Under Boccardi, the AP continued to enhance its services through the rest of the 1980s. A new graphics department was added in 1985, and a year later, a transition began that made all photographs offered to member newspapers available in color. By this time, the AP's network of satellite receiving dishes had grown to 3,000. Further improvements were made on transmission speed, business coverage, and graphics over the next few years. In 1989, the organization developed a fully designed sports page that could be delivered over its GraphicsNet system. Other new services included state weather maps and a biweekly package of stories and columns aimed at senior citizens.

The AP collected revenue of $329 million in 1991. As the 1990s progressed, the organization focused on ways to make more money from nontraditional sources, such as the sale of photo technology and through its AP-Dow Jones financial services outside the United States. By early in the decade, all of the AP's photo members had the Leaf Picture Desk (a digital photo compression and transmission system) and PhotoStream (its high-speed digital photo service) in place. U.S. newspapers began to take on a more colorful look in the 1990s, and the combination of Leaf and PhotoStream was a big part of this trend.

As the 1990s continued, the AP focused on adding video news coverage to its arsenal. In 1994, the organization launched APTV, an international video newsgathering service based in London. Other developments included a 24-hour broadcasting operation, All News Radio, and the commercial sales of AP's television newsroom software, called NewsCenter. In order to remain a leader in the international newsgathering community, the AP expressed its intention to devote vast resources to research and development for the rest of the century, in recognition of the fact that technology had become perhaps the most important element in the battle for the attention of news consumers.

The year 1995 saw the introduction of AP AdSEND, a digital advertising delivery service. For a small per-use fee, advertisers could upload copy and images into an AP database, which could then be downloaded by newspapers and other users ready-to-print. The system saved both time and money for advertisers, and enabled wider and easier distribution of advertising messages. A competitor, AD/SAT, sued the AP for allegedly monopolizing the market, but the suit was dismissed and AD/SAT folded soon thereafter.

The next year the company formed a new multimedia unit which set to work creating The WIRE, AP's public news web site. The WIRE, which was also featured on many member web sites, contained text, sound, and image information, and was updated continuously. Digital technology was becoming a key part of every aspect of AP's business, particularly photography. The 1996 Super Bowl was entirely shot by the AP with digital cameras it had developed in conjunction with Eastman Kodak. The digital process saved both time and money, enabling reporters in far-flung locations to send out images instantly using only a laptop computer and modem. The AP's immense photo archive was also being digitized, allowing anyone to download a high-resolution copy from a collection of hundreds of thousands of images for a small fee.

In 1998 the AP celebrated its 150th anniversary. The company's video service was expanded during the year with the purchase of the Worldwide Television News agency from ABC. APTV was subsequently renamed APTN, or Associated Press Television News. In April 1999, 21 AP photographers shared two Pulitzer Prizes, bringing the organization's total to 45.

As the Associated Press entered the latter half of its second century in operation, it could look back on an impressive list of accomplishments in the field of newsgathering. The organization had come a long way from its early days utilizing the telegraph, but it was still engaged in the business of transmitting news via electronic media to a wide audience.

Principal Subsidiaries

La Prensa Asociada, Inc.; Press Association, Inc.; SaTellite Data Broadcast Networks, Inc.; Wide World Photos, Inc.; The Associated Press A/S (Norway); The Associated Press A/S (Denmark); The Associated Press AB (Sweden); The Associated Press (Belgium) S.A.; The Associated Press GmbH (Germany); The Associated Press, Ltd. (U.K.); The Associated Press, Ltd. (Canada); The Associated Press de Venezuela; AdSEND; AP Multimedia Services; AP Information Services; AP Telecommunications.

Principal Competitors

Agence France-Presse; Bell & Howell Company; Bloomberg L.P.; Comtex Scientific Corp.; Corbis Corporation; Dow Jones & Company, Inc.; Gannett Company, Inc.; Knight Ridder; The New York Times Company; Reuters Group PLC; The Times Mirror Company; Tribune Company; United Press International, Inc.

Further Reading

Alabiso, Vincent, ''Digital Era Dawns,'' *Editor & Publisher*, March 2, 1996, p. 8P.

Alabiso, Vincent, Tunney, Kelly Smith, and Zoeller, Chuck, *Flash!: The Associated Press Covers the World*, New York: Associated Press in association with Harry N. Abrams, 1998.

''AP in 'Healthiest Condition,' 1963—$44 Million News Year,'' *Editor & Publisher*, April 25, 1964, p. 20.

''AP Offers New Member Services,'' *Editor & Publisher*, April 29, 1989, p. 20.

''AP's Digital Darkroom Breaks New Ground,'' *Editor & Publisher*, June 11, 1977, p. 15.

''AP Upgrades,'' *Editor & Publisher*, April 30, 1994, p. 14.

''Associated Press Taps Boccardi As President and General Manager,'' *Wall Street Journal*, September 14, 1984, p. 24.

Brown, Robert U., ''Transition at AP,'' *Editor & Publisher*, April 21, 1979, p. 130.

Consoli, John, ''AP's Online Wire Making Strides,'' *Editor & Publisher*, May 3, 1997, p. 12.

——, ''Improvements at AP,'' *Editor & Publisher*, April 26, 1986, p. 20.

''Dow Jones, AP Plan International Service to Report Business News, Starting April 1,'' *Wall Street Journal*, January 23, 1967, p. 26.

Emery, Edwin, and Emery, Michael, *The Press and America*, Englewood Cliffs, N.J.: Prentice-Hall, 1977.

''Gallagher: AP Geared for 'News Explosion,' '' *Editor & Publisher*, March 21, 1970, p. 11.

Garneau, George, ''AP Archive Set to Fly,'' *Editor & Publisher*, June 22, 1996, pp. 38–39.

——, ''AP Leads Pack in Moving Ads,'' *Editor & Publisher*, May 11, 1996, pp. 22–23.

Gersh, Debra, ''State of the AP,'' *Editor & Publisher*, May 1, 1993, p. 15.

Giobbe, Dorothy, ''AP Chief Upbeat About Newspapers,'' *Editor & Publisher*, April 29, 1995, p. 12.

''Keith Fuller Chosen As A.P.'s President at Annual Meeting,'' *New York Times*, May 4, 1976, p. 14.

Kobre, Sidney, *Development of American Journalism*, Dubuque, Iowa: Wm. C. Brown Co., 1969.

Lenett, Joe, ''The Rivals . . . AP and UPI,'' *Editor & Publisher*, June 27, 1959, p. 222.

Mott, Frank Luther, *American Journalism*, New York: MacMillan, 1962.

Rathbun, Elizabeth, ''Associated Press Tackles International Video,'' *Broadcasting & Cable*, July 18, 1994, p. 44.

Rosenberg, Jim, ''AP Expands Photo Archive, Rolls Out Server,'' *Editor & Publisher*, August 1, 1998, p. 22.

Scully, Sean, ''AP Determined to Stay on Cutting Edge,'' *Broadcasting & Cable*, September 27, 1993, p. 44.

Shmanske, Stephen, ''News As a Public Good: Cooperative Ownership, Price Commitments, and the Success of the Associated Press,'' *Business History Review*, Spring 1986, p. 55.

Stein, M.L., ''AP Reports to Its Member Editors,'' *Editor & Publisher*, November 10, 1990, p. 18.

''A Strong Year for Associated Press,'' *Editor & Publisher*, May 9, 1992, p. 16.

''What's New? That's a $42 Million Question,'' *Editor & Publisher*, April 6, 1963, p. 12.

—Robert R. Jacobson
—updated by Frank Uhle

ARCO

Atlantic Richfield Company

515 South Flower Street
Los Angeles, California 90071
U.S.A.
Telephone: (213) 486-3511
Fax: (213) 486-1756
Web site: http://www.arco.com

Public Company
Incorporated: 1870 as Atlantic Refining Company
Employees: 18,400
Sales: $10.3 billion (1998)
Stock Exchanges: New York Pacific London
Ticker Symbol: ARC
NAIC: 21111 Oil and Gas Extraction; 213111 Drilling Oil and Gas Wells; 213112 Support Activities for Oil and Gas Operations; 32411 Petroleum Refineries; 48691 Pipeline Transportation of Refined Petroleum Pipelines; 22121 Natural Gas Distribution; 44711 Gasoline Stations with Convenience Stores; 44719 Other Gasoline Stations

Atlantic Richfield Company, better known as ARCO, is the seventh-largest U.S. oil company. A vertically integrated company, ARCO explores for, produces, refines, and markets crude oil, natural gas, and natural gas liquids. Although the company has operations in the North Sea, Indonesia, Russia, Venezuela, Pakistan, China, and Algeria, its largest reserves and most productive operations are in Alaska. In the lower 48 states, it is the largest marketer of gasoline in five western states, with 1,700 gasoline stations. In 1999, the company announced plans to merge with BP Amoco plc, itself created through the 1998 merger of British Petroleum and Amoco. The merger, if accomplished, would make BP Amoco the world's second largest oil and gas company.

Company Origins

ARCO's origins go back to the discrete histories of Atlantic Refining Company and Richfield Oil Corporation. In 1865, six years after Drake's Folly, the world's first oil derrick, went into operation, Charles Lockhart and his partners established the Atlantic Refining Company in Philadelphia, the first refinery in the United States. Not surprisingly, Atlantic was unable to compete successfully in the turbulent world of petroleum, and in 1874, the gigantic Standard Oil Trust swallowed up Atlantic, although the merger was kept a secret, with Atlantic retaining its name and personnel. Atlantic possessed the largest petroleum refinery in greater Philadelphia, and the company continued to grow as a subsidiary of Standard.

Atlantic's fortunes changed radically after the turn of the century. Theodore Roosevelt's trust busting was carried out faithfully by his successor, William Howard Taft. In 1911 a federal court successfully prosecuted Standard Oil, compelling it to dissolve into smaller entities, one of which was Atlantic Refining Company. Newly independent Atlantic had refineries but was dependent on others for crude oil. As a result, its president, John Wesley Van Dyke, made crude-oil self-sufficiency his goal, and under his skillful management, Atlantic increased its exploration activities.

Richfield's history is dramatically and colorfully told by its former president, Charles S. Jones, in *From the Rio Grande to the Arctic: the Story of the Richfield Oil Corporation.* Jones delves into the earliest history of Richfield, whose predecessor, the Rio Grande Oil Company, was established by a store-owner in El Paso, Texas, in 1915. Rio Grande's good fortune coincided with the heyday of Pancho Villa's raids across the border. In order to rid frontier towns like El Paso of Villa, the U.S. Army pursued Villa and his raiders deep into Mexican territory, using some 600 trucks to supply its troops. The army inadvertently became the largest consumer of Rio Grande oil at that time. From then on, the company's growth went unhindered, and its headquarters eventually shifted from Texas to California.

The Great Depression took a heavy toll on the Rio Grande Oil Company, forcing it in 1936 to reorganize and merge with other companies to become the modern Richfield Oil Corporation with Charles Jones as its president. Richfield embarked on a new era, marked by a significant oil discovery in California in 1938. Richfield consequently was well-prepared for the challenges of World War II, when the entire U.S. oil industry faced

Key Dates:

1865: Charles Lockhart establishes the Atlantic Refining Company, the first refinery in the United States.
1874: Standard Oil Trust buys Atlantic Refining.
1911: Standard Oil is broken up by federal order; Atlantic Refining is independent again.
1915: Rio Grande Oil Company is established in El Paso, Texas.
1936: Rio Grande Oil merges with other companies to become the Richfield Oil Corporation.
1957: Richfield is the first to discover oil in Alaska.
1966: Atlantic Refining and Richfield merge to form the Atlantic Richfield Company.
1977: The Alaskan pipeline opens with Atlantic Richfield as 21 percent owner.
1989: Net income reaches a record high of $1.95 billion.
1992: ARCO completes a deal to pipe gas from China to Hong Kong.
1995: ARCO purchases an eight percent stake in the Russian oil company Lukoil.
1998: ARCO sells its majority interest in ARCO Chemical Company and spins off its U.S. coal assets.
1999: Foundation laid for merger between ARCO and BP Amoco

wartime demand. A pioneer in the manufacture of high-octane aviation gasoline, Richfield increased its high-octane production in 1941–1942 by 150 percent. By 1948, according to Jones, Richfield had developed into a highly successful, well-balanced oil company.

Richfield, unlike Atlantic, continued its success in finding crude oil. In 1948 the Cuyama Valley in California yielded to Richfield huge quantities of petroleum, although insufficient to meet demand for oil. In the 1950s, Richfield's oil explorations expanded overseas but, most importantly, included an interest in Alaska.

Richfield's explorations in Alaska predated World War II, but serious prospecting did not get underway until 1955, the year California ceased being self-sufficient in oil. Richfield was the first to discover oil in Alaska, in the Swanson River area, in 1957. This discovery became the first commercial oil field in Alaska's history. Environmentalists opposed further oil exploration. This did not, however, deter Richfield from proceeding to purchase enormous tracts of federal land, laying the basis for the future ARCO's astonishing growth and prosperity.

The Philadelphia-based Atlantic Refining Company was even shorter of crude oil than was Richfield, but Atlantic's leadership was not interested in the exploration and production activities of its dynamic Dallas, Texas, branch. One Atlantic executive in Philadelphia declared he did not know what an oil well looked like and had no intention of finding out. The result of this disharmony was a palpable decline in Atlantic's profits. The company's fortunes began to turn around, however, when a former Harvard business professor, Thornton Bradshaw, became financial vice president of Atlantic in 1956. Bradshaw perceived that disunity and dependency on crude oil purchases were both undermining Atlantic's viability. The solution was a merger with another oil company.

The candidate for a merger, in 1962, was Hondo Oil & Gas Company, whose president, Robert O. Anderson, was a dynamic, multi-faceted businessman. The marriage of the two companies worked. Atlantic's strength lay in the refining of petroleum, and Hondo Oil & Gas's was in the business of finding and producing oil. With energy needs soaring in the United States, however, the new Atlantic produced at best only 50 percent of its own crude.

The 1966 Atlantic-Richfield Merger

In the mid-1960s, with Anderson as chairman and chief executive officer of Atlantic Refining Company, feelers once again went out for a partner with which to merge. This time the choice fell on oil-wealthy Richfield. The California-based company, with its vast Alaska leases, 2.5 million acres, would have had little reason to merge with eastern-based Atlantic were it not for a still-pending 1962 Department of Justice suit against Richfield. Its mergers in 1936 with Sinclair Oil Corporation and Cities Service Company was only now, nearly 30 years later, being challenged as illegal by the Justice Department on antitrust grounds. The choice for Richfield was to face possible liquidation or the divestiture of Sinclair and Cities Service, or to merge with some company untainted by monopolism. In this light, Atlantic Refining Company appeared to be ideal, especially as Robert Anderson was held in very high regard in the oil business and had turned his company into a highly profitable one.

The merger of the two oil companies took place in January 1966, forming Atlantic Richfield Company. Two years later, the biggest oil discovery in the Western Hemisphere was made in Prudhoe Bay, Alaska, with Atlantic Richfield the biggest federal leaseholder in the state. The production of this vast oil wealth would be delayed nearly a decade because of disputes with environmentalists, native Alaskans, and other oil companies with competing claims, and until the Trans-Alaska pipeline system was constructed. The stable leadership of Anderson, chairman of Atlantic Richfield until 1986, and Thornton Bradshaw, president until 1981, would resolve these difficulties and turn their company into the eighth-largest oil company in the United States, a company well equipped to face the complex challenges of the 21st century. In 1972 Atlantic Richfield moved its headquarters from New York City to Los Angeles.

The resolution of rival Alaskan interests was accelerated by the Arab oil embargo in 1973. The federal government granted permission for the construction of the much disputed pipeline, and oil flowed through it for the first time in midsummer 1977. The original estimated cost of the pipeline was $900 million. This amount had escalated to $10 billion by the time oil actually flowed through it, largely to meet environmental guidelines. This was the largest expenditure for any private undertaking in U.S. history. Despite this unimaginable cost, Atlantic Richfield, 21% owner of the pipeline, benefitted enormously. Profits soared, and by 1980 total company assets stood at $16 billion compared to $8 billion four years earlier.

The soaring profits from its Alaskan oil fields had a surprisingly sobering effect upon Atlantic Richfield's leadership, seasoned oil men who were well aware of the historic volatility of the oil market. There was a very strong consciousness, evident in Atlantic Richfield's annual reports predating even the 1973 oil embargo, that natural resources, none more than oil, were finite and that if the company were to survive and, more importantly, generate a profit, the production and refining of oil could not remain the company's main objective. The conundrum of the late 20th century—how to supply the vast U.S. energy needs in the face of oil's ultimate depletion and the country's heavy dependence on foreign crude—would be Atlantic-Richfield's chief challenge, one that would determine its fate in the decades to come.

While oil flowed through the Alaskan pipeline at a rate of nearly two million barrels a day, Atlantic Richfield was undergoing a radical restructuring that not only reflected its growth as an oil company, but as an oil company intent on branching into new products and markets. Gone, however, was the age when new products, markets, and profits were the company's sole concerns. No company could hope to survive in an environmentally conscious society without a major investment in the environment. As oil prices rocketed, therefore, so, too, did Atlantic Richfield's investment in environmental causes. As early as 1970, for instance, the company began producing lead-free gasoline. In 1972 Atlantic Richfield removed all billboard advertising, and in the same year received two awards for its conservation efforts. By 1976 total spending on conservation amounted to $400 million. Atlantic Richfield produced and marketed the first low-emissions gasoline in the United States.

A late-20th-century company could ill afford to ignore its social responsibilities, as the growing endowment of the ARCO Foundation revealed. Social responsibility, however, could neither begin nor end with siphoning off a small fraction of its oil profits to charity. ARCO also donated trees to a park, revegetated used coal-mine areas, and encouraged employees to engage in volunteer activities by releasing them from work.

Mergers and Restructurings in the 1960s-70s

In the face of its explosive growth following the opening of the Alaska pipeline, ARCO executives saw the need for a dramatic restructuring of the company. As early as 1968, the year of the Prudhoe Bay oil discovery, the company realized that it would one day have far more oil than it could refine and market. Once again merger talks began, and the partner became Sinclair Oil Corporation. Its merger with Atlantic Richfield in 1969 endowed ARCO with its biggest oil refinery, in Houston, and more importantly for the future, enabled the company to undertake a five-year, $1 billion expansion of petrochemical production.

The growth of ARCO with the completion of the pipeline in 1977 necessitated further restructuring. The aim was to decentralize into eight wholly owned companies—ARCO Alaska, ARCO Oil and Gas, ARCO Chemical, ARCO Products, ARCO Transportation, ARCO International, ARCO Coal, and ARCO Solar—and to focus on new products, apart from traditional oil and gas production. In line with this restructuring, which would be complete in 1979, ARCO merged with the Anaconda Company in 1977. Within a few years, ARCO Coal Company became a leading coal producer in the United States and the nation's number-one producer of low-sulfur coal. By the mid-1980s, under the chairmanship of Lodwrick M. Cook, a yet more radical strategy was devised to ensure profitability and a lessening dependence on oil: to divest ARCO of all marginally profitable enterprises and to drastically cut costs across the board. As a result, between 1985 and 1987, ARCO reduced its workforce by approximately 12,000 employees. The company's Philadelphia refinery was sold, along with 1,000 ARCO service stations east of the Mississippi, making "Atlantic" a name only, a reason for the increasing use of the company's acronym, ARCO.

Decentralization, concentration on areas of highest profitability, cost cutting, and diversification enabled ARCO to weather the precipitous decline in crude oil prices in 1986 and to ward off the threat of a takeover. Diversification away from traditional oil and gas production had been successful.

Besides ARCO's lucrative production of coal, success was evident in ARCO's petrochemical industry. Petrochemicals became an important facet of ARCO's business in the 1970s. In 1985 the company formed Lyondell Petrochemical Company by merging existing assets. Lyondell, a division of ARCO, increased ARCO's petrochemical capacity and moved to the forefront of petrochemical production. It became a leader in converting crude oil, for example, into feedstock. ARCO Chemical, in which ARCO had an 83.4 percent ownership interest in 1991, became the foremost producer in the world of propylene oxide, used in the manufacture of furniture foam, plastics, and detergents; and calcined coke for the manufacture of aluminum. Another creative idea turned into a successful product by Lyondell, unrelated to petrochemical production, was the WALLFRAME building system, a popular prefabricated wall system. Offering superior insulation properties, ARCO Solar represented ARCO's most radical departure from tradition. Producing energy from the sun by means of photovoltaic cells, ARCO Solar by the mid-1980s had won 45 percent of the photovoltaic market and had become the world's leading producer of photovoltaic devices. The company sold ARCO Solar because the business was not competitive on a large scale.

Increased International Activity in the 1990s

Since its inception, ARCO had expanded steadily overseas, with 25 percent of its petrochemicals exported overseas by the early 1990s, especially to Asia. In 1991 ARCO had interests in 20 foreign countries, including a petrochemical plant in southern France, significant coal-mining interests in Australia, and a highly lucrative oil-exploration venture in Indonesia.

Net income reached a record high in 1989 of $1.95 billion; however, within two years profits were almost one-third that, at $709 million. The primary culprits were lower gas prices and an economic recession, things over which ARCO had little control. To cut costs, ARCO eliminated 2,100 jobs in 1991.

As ARCO's reserves declined, it pursued several strategies to maintain its revenues over the long term. One was the purchase of proven reserves from other companies. In 1988 it purchased oil and gas properties in California from Tenneco, and in 1990 purchased properties from TXO Production in Oklahoma and from Oryx in California. Three years later,

ARCO joined with Phillips Petroleum to lease 130,000 acres near Alaska's Cook Inlet.

The company also stepped up its efforts to bring foreign reserves into production. ARCO had discovered an 85-billion-cubic-meter gas field in 1982 off the southeast coast of China, but had been unable to exploit the find. As a Chinese joint venture, the operation had to meet the Chinese regulation that it be a self-sustaining project, in effect, requiring the gas to be exported for hard currency. Finally, the operation was made feasible in 1992 when ARCO completed a deal to pipe the gas to Hong Kong for electrical power generation. ARCO held a 34.3 percent interest in the venture and managed the construction of the 480-mile Yacheng pipeline.

In 1994 Mike R. Bowlin took over as chief executive officer and the following year replaced Lodwrick M. Cook as chairman of the board. Also in 1994 ARCO finished modifying its refineries to meet EPA emission control regulations.

Acquiring interests in foreign companies was another ARCO strategy to increase its international revenues. In 1994 the company bought 9.9 percent of the Zhenhai Refining and Chemical Company in China. The following year ARCO took the risky step of purchasing an eight percent stake in Russia's top private oil company, Lukoil. The $340 million deal gave ARCO an interest in some of the largest oil reserves in the world. ARCO also worked out a joint venture with Lukoil to develop certain reserves, including several around the oil-rich Caspian Sea. However, this new relationship with Lukoil held much uncertainty. Russia's political instability and the past disappointments of Western oil companies with their investments in the country recommended a cautious outlook.

ARCO's Yacheng pipeline was completed in 1996 for $1.13 billion, under budget and two months early. As the gas from that field finally began to flow, ARCO reached an agreement with the Algerian state oil company, Sonatrach, to increase production from the Rhourde El Baguel Field, the country's second largest oil field. Estimated to have had some three billion barrels of oil at its discovery in 1962, the field was slowing in production by the mid-1990s. ARCO's experience with miscible gas technology was expected to enhance the oil recovery from the field. By the end of 1997 ARCO had increased the field's production by 17,000 barrels a day.

In 1998 ARCO sold its majority interest in ARCO Chemical Company and spun off its U.S. coal assets, leaving the company focused solely on hydrocarbon-related business.

In 1999 ARCO agreed to be acquired by BP Amoco for $26.8 billion in stock, which would make BP Amoco the world's second-largest oil and gas company. BP Amoco and ARCO planned to combine resources on Alaska's North Slope, where the two would control all oil production. The efficiencies were expected to result in significant cost reductions, including a predicted loss of about 2,000 jobs. Approved by ARCO shareholders in September 1999, the merger still had several regulatory hurdles to clear before it was finalized.

Principal Subsidiaries

ARCO Alaska, Inc.; ARCO Pipeline Company; ARCO Oil and Gas Company; ARCO International Oil and Gas Company; ARCO Products Company; ARCO Transportation Company; Vastar Resources, Inc.; Lyondell Petrochemical Company (49.9%).

Principal Competitors

BP Amoco plc; Exxon-Mobil Corporation; Royal Dutch/Shell.

Further Reading

''Alaskan Agreement Helps Clear Way for Approval of BP Amoco Deal with ARCO,'' *PR Newswire,* December 2, 1999.
''A Brief History of ARCO,'' Atlantic Richfield corporate typescript, 1989.
Cappell, Kerry, ''This Giant Sure Has a Big Appetite,'' *Business Week,* April 12, 1999, p. 34.
''Extracting Oil from the Caspian: Great Game, Awful Risks,'' *Economist,* February 15, 1997.
''From Major to Minor,'' *Economist,* May 18, 1996.
Harns, Kenneth, *The Wildcatter: A Portrait of Robert O. Anderson,* New York: Weideinfeld & Nicolson, 1987.
Jones, Charles S., *From the Rio Grande to the Arctic: The Story of the Richfield Oil Corporation,* Norman: University of Oklahoma Press, 1972.
Mack, Toni, ''Brass-Ring Time,'' *Forbes,* May 3, 1999, p. 56.
Shoenberger, Karl, ''Arco's Suprisingly Good Fortune in China,'' *Fortune,* February 5, 1996, p. 32.
''A Well-Matched Pair: Synergies Abound as BP Amoco and California's ARCO agree to a Friendly, $26.8 Billion Merger,'' *Time International,* April 12, 1999, p. 53.

—Sina Dubovoj
—updated by Susan Windisch Brown

AutoZone, Inc.

123 South Front Street
Memphis, Tennessee 38103-3607
U.S.A.
Telephone: (901) 495-6500
Fax: (901) 495-8300
Web site: http://www.autozone.com

Public Company
Incorporated: 1979 as Auto Shack
Sales: $4.12 billion (1999)
Employees: 38,500
Stock Exchanges: New York
Ticker Symbol: AZO
NAIC: 44131 Automotive Parts and Accessories Stores

The leading U.S. specialty retailer of automobile parts in the late 1990s, Memphis, Tennessee-based AutoZone, Inc., sells auto parts, maintenance items, and automotive accessories through more than 2,700 stores in 39 U.S. states and in Mexico. The retail chain offers both private-label products, including Duralast and Deutsch, and brand names. Geared primarily toward the do-it-yourself market, AutoZone also serves professional auto repair shops. AutoZone stores do not sell tires or provide repair service, but they do offer diagnostic testing for batteries, starters, and alternators. AutoZone sells heavy-duty truck parts through its subsidiary TruckPro L.P. and offers automotive diagnostic and repair software through ALLDATA Corp.

Rapid Development during the Early Years: Late 1970s–Early 1980s

Joseph R. Hyde III began working in his family's business, Malone & Hyde, Inc., immediately after graduating from college in 1968 at the age of 22. The company, a wholesale grocery business, had been founded by his grandfather in 1907. The younger Hyde expanded the family business considerably. He began with drug stores, founding Super D Drugs at age 26, and then moved on to sporting goods stores, supermarkets, and, finally, automobile parts stores.

Hyde's entry into the retail auto parts market came on July 4, 1979, when he opened his first store, named Auto Shack, in Forrest City, Arkansas. The company had 25 people on its payroll at the time. To support further expansion, Hyde opened a 12,000-square-foot warehouse in Memphis, and by the end of the first year seven more stores in Arkansas and Tennessee had made their debut.

The idea behind Auto Shack was straightforward. The company aimed to provide a wide selection of auto parts at a low price to do-it-yourselfers—what it referred to as the DIY market. In addition to these customers, the company identified a pool of potential buyers as "shade tree mechanics," that is, those who worked on other people's cars in their spare time as a source of extra income, and "buy-it-yourselfers," those who lacked the expertise to do the work themselves but who bought parts and then hired others to install them.

To serve these customers, Auto Shack sought to establish quality and expert advice from employees as a hallmark of its business plan. In addition, the company tried to locate its stores in neighborhoods where people who worked on their cars lived and to keep its stores open at hours when its customers were not otherwise occupied at work. This initially meant that many Auto Shack stores stayed open all night. Auto Shack stores were clean and bright, and the company emphasized friendly, helpful service. Company chairman Hyde himself, garbed in a company uniform with a name tag, spent a quarter of his time visiting Auto Shack stores to keep an eye on operations and to encourage employees to do their best.

In its second year of operation Auto Shack added 23 more stores, branching out into five nearby states: Alabama, Kentucky, Missouri, Mississippi, and Texas. By this time the company had started to hit its stride, and on average it would go on to open a new store every week for its first ten years in business. Before opening a new outlet, Auto Shack's research analysts spent time looking at appropriate sites. The company's intended customer base was lower- or middle-income males between the ages of 18 and 49. The company's ideal customer was a male who, both as a hobby and an economic necessity, spent a lot of time working on his car to keep it running much longer than ordinarily expected. Auto Shack estimated that the ever-rising cost of a new car, both

Company Perspectives:

We rely on innovation as our fuel for growth and let others run on imitation. We make sure the objects in our rear-view mirror aren't closer than they appear because we keep moving faster. What's more, because we're constantly fine-tuning the business, we're squeezing more horsepower out of the same fuel-efficient engine. We're experts on getting more for less. We have to be, because when the rubber hits the road, a customer with grease up to his elbows will tell you he doesn't care about anything but the right part at the right price, right now. Yes, there are other places he could go for that. But he comes to AutoZone because we give him all of that plus a level of service that helps make that tough job a little easier. So when we say we're set on customer service, we're not just yanking your timing chain. It's the foundation of our culture, and it's ours alone. It's what drives us.

in absolute dollars and as a percentage of the average family's income, was a strong incentive for a large portion of the population to enter the market for replacement auto parts.

In addition, Auto Shack took note of the business practices of other successful retailing establishments in the South, including Wal-Mart Stores, Inc., on whose corporate board Hyde sat for seven years. By selling a high volume of goods in a large number of stores serviced by central distribution centers, Auto Shack was able to keep its costs and prices low, providing the chain with a tremendous competitive advantage over smaller operations. In addition, the bright, modern, clean store interiors were a welcome contrast to the dark, grimy aura projected by some other parts outlets and by auto junkyards.

By 1981 Auto Shack had opened 45 stores, and by the following year the number was up to 74, all within its core market area. By 1982 Auto Shack's Memphis warehouse had expanded to 96,000 square feet, growth made necessary by the increasing number of Auto Shack outlets. In 1983 Auto Shack again expanded in numbers of stores, growing to 139 outlets, and in geographical scope, adding outlets in Georgia, Arizona, Illinois, and Louisiana. By the following year the number of Auto Shacks had reached 200, and openings in Florida and South Carolina pushed the company's tally of states to 13. In addition, two more distribution centers were opened to serve the increasingly far-flung Auto Shack operations. Facilities in San Antonio, Texas, and Phoenix, Arizona, raised the company's total warehouse space to 320,000 square feet.

In 1984 the leaders of Auto Shack's corporate parent, Malone & Hyde, decided that the company's stock was undervalued. To get the most value out of their properties, Hyde and his fellow executives decided to take the properties private in a leveraged buyout. To do this, they enlisted the help of the investment banking firm Kohlberg Kravis Roberts & Company (KKR), which engineered the withdrawal of Malone & Hyde from the stock market. KKR was compensated with large blocks of Auto Shack stock, in effect becoming the owner of the company.

Aggressive Growth through the Mid-1980s

Despite its new corporate status, Auto Shack continued to grow at a dramatic rate. In 1985 the company opened an additional 68 stores and moved into North Carolina. Along with its standard format, Auto Shack also inaugurated an Express Parts Service that rushed auto parts to customers who called in over a toll-free service line. In this way the company was able to offer services to parts of the country that were not yet served by an Auto Shack store.

Auto Shack took another step toward upgrading customer service in 1986 when it instituted a lifetime warranty on 42,000 separate parts it sold. The company's decision on which products to offer was closely tied to its research into what customers wanted. For some types of goods, Auto Shack stocked a wide variety of nationally known brands. Motor oil fell into this category, as surveys indicated that Auto Shack customers had a strong preference for private-label oils, being more concerned about the perception of guaranteed quality than the lowest price.

For many other goods, however, research indicated that customers simply wanted the cheapest price possible. In general, this criteria applied to more expensive car parts, where brand names were little known. Auto Shack developed its own sources for such products, eliminating the middleman and the additional costs of a distributor. In this way the company was able to offer less expensive products to its customers. On this level Auto Shack was structured like a vertically integrated business, although it had not taken on the complications of a manufacturing operation. The company's supply lines were directed by product managers, who visited factories and worked closely with suppliers to ensure quality control on various parts. The company's high volume of sales made it possible for specialized efforts like this to be efficient. In addition, Auto Shack's advertising department participated in the effort to define and upgrade products and then attempted to win new customers for them.

By 1986, as New Mexico was added, such practices had allowed Auto Shack to expand to 339 stores in 15 states. A new warehouse was also opened in Greenville, South Carolina. The company's telemarketing operation, Express Parts Service, logged its one millionth call, and an additional service, an Electronic Catalogue, was brought on-line on October 1, 1986, at the company's Bellevue store in Memphis. This database, installed throughout the company's stores, eventually grew to contain more than four million entries on parts for more than 15,000 vehicles.

Diversification and Continued Expansion in the Late 1980s and Early 1990s

In 1987 Hyde divested himself of all parts of his family business, Malone & Hyde, except Auto Shack, the fastest growing unit. For the first time Auto Shack stood alone, apart from its corporate parent. As a symbol of its new identity and to give the company's stores a more upscale image, the name was changed to AutoZone. The company announced that the new name would apply to all 390 stores.

The process of conversion began in the following year. An outlet was opened under the new name in Enid, Oklahoma,

Key Dates:

1979: Joseph R. Hyde III opens Auto Shack, a retail automobile parts store, in Arkansas.
1987: Auto Shack changes its name to AutoZone.
1989: On its tenth anniversary AutoZone opens its 500th store.
1991: AutoZone becomes a publicly traded company.
1995: The 1,000th AutoZone store opens.
1999: AutoZone expands into Mexico.

marking the company's entry into yet another state. Overall, AutoZone had 470 stores in 16 states by the end of 1988, and it served a total of 47.7 million customers in that year alone. In June 1988 the company unveiled its own line of auto products, developed by its product managers, under the trade name ADuralast. The number of AutoZone customers for these and other products rose to more than 51 million by 1989, the year of the company's tenth anniversary, and sales topped $500 million. By this time AutoZone had become the third largest American auto parts retailer. To continue to build growth, the company advertised aggressively on television, on radio (airing ads in Spanish and Navajo, as well as in English), and in newspapers.

As a symbolic gesture in 1989, AutoZone opened its 500th outlet, a store in Hobbs, New Mexico, on July 4, the date on which it had opened its first store ten years earlier. By the end of the year 14 more stores had been added, and all of the facilities were known by the company's new name. Under this name AutoZone diversified its outlets to include regular stores and superstores. The first of the larger outlets was opened in Memphis. Whereas the usual AutoZone store filled about 5,400 square feet and cost $200,000 to construct, the larger version cost about $70,000 more and stocked 5,000 additional items. More than 50 superstores had been opened by the middle of 1989, with the largest, located in New Halls Ferry, St. Louis, Missouri, boasting a 17,368-square-foot selling floor.

By 1990 AutoZone had expanded into two additional states, opening stores in Utah and Indiana, for a total of 539 outlets. The company also broke ground for a distribution center in Lafayette, Louisiana, to serve its expanded geographical operations and introduced another line of its specially manufactured items, Deutsch filters. In addition, AutoZone opened its first 8,100-square-foot prototype store in Santa Fe, New Mexico.

In April 1991 AutoZone ended its tenure as a privately held company when shares were offered for sale on the New York Stock Exchange. The 3.2 million shares offered produced a large paper profit for the company's primary owner, Kohlberg Kravis Roberts & Company. Under the structure of the stock offering, KKR retained its ownership stake in AutoZone, as investment partnerships run by KKR retained 68 percent of the company. AutoZone managers kept 16 percent of the company, and former managers retained another six percent, leaving ten percent for the public at large. With the ten percent of stock offered, AutoZone reduced its bank and mortgage debt and also invested in general company operations.

In the five months following AutoZone's stock offering, the price of the company's shares rose dramatically, fueled by enthusiasm for the company's rapid growth and financial prospects. In September 1992 KKR announced that it would sell an additional 2.3 million shares of AutoZone to the public in an effort to increase the company's financial liquidity and reduce the swings in the price of its stock.

While AutoZone's financial fate was being determined on Wall Street, the company's operations and expansion continued apace. Its fifth distribution center, in Lafayette, Louisiana, was opened in 1991, as were an additional 53 stores, including the first outlets in Colorado. Also in 1991, AutoZone introduced an electronic Store Management System that allowed prices to be bar-coded and scanned at checkout counters, thus speeding up customer transactions. In addition, the system allowed electronic credit card and check approval. It refined inventory control and automated in-store accounting procedures.

In December 1991 AutoZone held its first shareholders' meeting, at which the company was able to announce that gross revenues had increased more than 20 percent in the previous year to reach $818 million. Net income had risen to $44 million, an increase of 89 percent.

Relying on demographics indicating that the Midwest contained a large pool of blue-collar workers who repaired their own cars both as a hobby and to save money, AutoZone began to plot its expansion into this area of the country. In 1992 the company upped its number of stores to 678 and made its first move into Wisconsin. Company sales topped $1 billion for the first time, allowing the company to continue its string of store openings without going into debt. More openings were made in another Midwest state, Michigan, in 1993. To distribute products to its new customers, the company opened distribution centers in Illinois and Tennessee.

Mid- to Late 1990s: Growth through Acquisitions and New Store Openings

As AutoZone continued its rapid and aggressive expansion, its revenues continued to rise as well. Total revenues increased from $535.8 million in 1989 to $1.216 billion in 1993, and they showed no signs of slowing down. To better serve customers, AutoZone in 1994 installed Flexogram, a satellite-based system designed to customize store inventory according to local demands and to facilitate communications between store locations. The company, which opened an average of 250 new retail stores a year, including its 1,000th store in 1995, did not slow its blistering pace in the 1990s.

Although AutoZone was quickly emerging as the industry's retail leader, the market was becoming increasingly competitive, and the company believed that restricting itself to selling only auto parts would limit its potential. It was for this reason that AutoZone began to aggressively explore new businesses and opportunities, especially through acquisitions. In 1996 AutoZone expanded its consumer target to include commercial customers, such as professional automotive technicians and service stations. The company introduced a commercial program that provided credit and delivery to mechanics and technicians. Also in 1996 AutoZone purchased ALLDATA Corp., a software company that developed automotive diagnostic and repair software.

In 1997 AutoZone opened its 1,500th store, and Hyde, who had seen AutoZone grow from a single small store in Arkansas to a national retail chain, stepped down as CEO. He was replaced by then COO Johnston Adams. Shareholder KKR sold its 13 percent share in the company in 1998, and by 1999 Hyde had divested the majority of his interest in AutoZone, although he continued to serve on the board of directors.

AutoZone made several important acquisitions in fiscal year 1998, which ended August 29, 1998. In February the company bought Auto Palace, a retailer with 112 stores in six states in the northeastern United States. The purchase allowed AutoZone to move easily into a new market, and within a year all Auto Palace shops had been converted to AutoZone stores. In May the company purchased TruckPro L.P., an independent U.S. distributor of heavy-duty truck parts that had 43 stores in 14 states. The acquisition provided AutoZone with a doorway into the truck parts business, a fragmented industry with no clear leader and thus similar to the auto parts industry when AutoZone had first begun. The company planned to strengthen TruckPro's business and make it the industry leader. At the end of June, AutoZone made a third acquisition, Chief Auto Parts Inc., with 560 outlets in five states. The acquisition significantly expanded AutoZone's presence in the critical California market by increasing the number of AutoZone stores in that state to about 400, up from one store the previous year.

Although AutoZone was busily involved with acquisitions, the company still managed to open 275 new AutoZone stores during fiscal 1998. At the commencement of fiscal 1999, in October, AutoZone made yet another acquisition by purchasing 100 Express stores from The Pep Boys—Manny, Moe & Jack. In December 1998 the company opened its first international store, in Nuevo Laredo, Mexico, across the border from Texas. By the end of fiscal 1999 the company had opened five additional stores in Mexico and had remodeled and reopened 96 of the 100 Express stores as AutoZones. In addition, the company had also completed converting Chief Auto Parts stores into AutoZones, opened 167 new AutoZone stores, and opened three new TruckPro stores.

AutoZone was in strong shape as it celebrated its 20th anniversary. Sales in fiscal 1999 reached $4.12 billion, a 27 percent increase over 1998. The company planned to continue building its heavy-duty truck parts business and its commercial account division until AutoZone was the leader of both categories. The company also intended to continue seeking out new opportunities, particularly in international markets. Research by AutoZone pointed to international demand, and the company believed that international markets could support AutoZone stores comparable in number to those in the United States. In addition, to serve smaller U.S. communities that did not warrant full-size AutoZone stores, the company created a small-store prototype and planned to bring the total number of AutoZone outlets in the nation to more than 5,000.

Principal Subsidiaries

TruckPro L.P.; ALLDATA Corp.

Principal Competitors

Genuine Parts Company; The Pep Boys—Manny, Moe & Jack; Wal-Mart Stores, Inc.; Advance Holding Company; CARQUEST Corp.

Further Reading

Box, Terry, "With Texas Store Conversions Done, Auto Parts Giant Shifts Focus," *Dallas Morning News,* May 18, 1999, p. D1.

Halverson, Richard, "The Preeminent Purveyor of Parts," *Discount Store News,* December 14, 1998.

Henry, John, "AutoZone to Acquire TruckPro," *Arkansas Business,* March 9, 1998, p. 10.

Neumeier, Shelley, "AutoZone," *Fortune,* December 2, 1991.

Obermark, Jerome, "Autozone Ends '99 with Sales Up 27%," *Memphis Commercial Appeal,* September 30, 1999, p. C1.

Peltz, James F., "Overhauling Auto Parts Sales," *Los Angeles Times,* May 20, 1998, p. D1.

Tune-In Newsletters, Memphis: AutoZone, Inc., 1989–92.

—Elizabeth Rourke
—updated by Mariko Fujinaka

Avado Brands, Inc.

Hancock at Washington
Madison, Georgia 30650
U.S.A.
Telephone: (706) 342-4552
Fax: (706) 342-4057
Web site: http://www.avado.com

Public Company
Incorporated: 1986 as The MRG Company, Inc.
Employees: 20,300 (1998)
Sales: $862.7 million (1998)
Stock Exchanges: NASDAQ
Ticker Symbol: AVDO
NAIC: 722110 Full Service Restaurants

Known until 1998 as Apple South, Avado Brands, Inc. owns and operates several restaurant concepts in the United States, primarily in the upscale market between casual dining and fine dining. The company's restaurant chains include McCormick & Schmick's, which prepares more than 30 kinds of fresh seafood entrees daily, and Hops Restaurant Bar and Brewery establishments, which serve American-style food made from scratch and beer fresh brewed on-site. Avado's Don Pablo's restaurants serve authentic Mexican dishes based on the traditional recipes of Mexican ranch cooks in the 1940s. Canyon Cafes, acquired by Avado in 1997, offer a southwestern menu and atmosphere. Avado's international joint ventures include Belgo Neiuw York, which features Belgian cuisine and beer, and San Marzanno, where Neapolitan-style pizza features sauce made with tomatoes from the San Marzanno region in Italy. Avado's combined restaurant locations covered 30 states and Washington, D.C. in 1999.

Origins in Casual Restaurants Concepts

The history of Avado Brands may be traced to the 1986 founding of The MRG Company, which took the name Apple South, Inc. in 1988 through a merger with Sunburst Restaurants. As owner of Sunburst Restaurants, Tom E. DuPree, Jr., was operating six Burger King franchises and ten Hardee's franchises at the time. Moreover, DuPree's interest in full-service, casual dining led him to open an Applebee's Neighborhood Grill and Bar franchise in Greenville, South Carolina, in 1986; DuPree would eventually become one of the most successful franchisees of Applebee's restaurants; he formed Apple South to oversee the holdings. The Applebee's concept featured Mexican, Italian, and Cajun entrees, hamburgers, sandwiches, soups, and salads. Menu items ranged in price from $5.75 to $7.25 for lunch and $7.25 to $8.75 for dinner.

Under the leadership of DuPree Apple South set about opening and operating an empire of Applebee's franchises. In 1988 Apple South opened ten Applebee's restaurants in Mississippi, Tennessee, and Virginia. Another 17 units opened in 1989 in North Carolina and another 11 units opened throughout Apple South's development territory in 1990. DuPree determined store placement by researching the demographics of a potential location, including household income, age range, and retail support. Those demographics needed to sustain a 5,000-square-foot restaurant and bar with a seating capacity of approximately 160 people.

At the time of the company's initial public offering of stock in November 1991, Apple South operated 40 Applebee's franchise stores and owned development rights in 15 states, primarily in the southeastern states. Apple South retained ownership of the ten Hardee's franchises DuPree had brought with him at the founding of Apple South as well. The company offered 2.25 million shares of stock, which sold at $8.34 per share on the NASDAQ stock exchange. The proceeds were applied to debt payment and expansion of Applebee's franchises, with ten to 12 planned each year for 1992 and 1993.

After its first full year as a public company, Apple South ended 1992 with an additional 20 Applebee's restaurants in operation. The cost of opening each store averaged $1.3 million and included the purchase of real estate whenever possible. With a per-person check average at $8.50, first year sales approximately equaled opening costs. The company had added six of the franchise units through an acquisition that also included future development rights in northeastern Florida and southeastern Georgia.

Company Perspectives:

There is a point of balance in any organization that, when skillfully achieved, produces harmony. Avado Brands is the balance of innovative entrepreneurial restaurant concepts with the practical strength of effective brand management principles. Holding to our core values of honesty and integrity, best effort, and fun, Avado Brands is dedicated to moving forward with high concern for the enrichment of customers, investors, personnel, and alliance partners. That, too, we see as a carefully attended balance. It is the ongoing mission of Avado Brands to take high-growth concepts and turn them into very profitable national and international businesses. This, combined with a total commitment to the future of our entire enterprise and our company's value, will achieve the shortest distance between vision and reality.

A second public offering in March 1993 raised $41 million in equity capital for further expansion. Three-for-two stock splits in December 1992 and February 1993 allowed Apple South to offer 1.3 million shares at $16.50 per share. The company planned 15 new stores in 1993 and 20 new stores in 1994. In addition, Apple South acquired eight Applebee's franchises in northwestern Illinois, Missouri, Iowa, Minnesota, and Wisconsin, in April 1993. The $17 million cash transaction included development rights to the counties adjacent to those stores. DuPree expected to add at least 22 stores and to improve sales at existing stores in those areas.

Apple South strategically located new stores in areas where an Applebee's franchise already existed. Awareness of the existing stores provided recognition for the new stores, while the new stores acted as a promotion of the restaurant concept and increased sales at existing stores. In May 1993, Apple South opened Applebee's franchises in Louisville, Richmond, and Nashville based on this strategy. Television advertisements and promotions by Applebee's International (the franchisor) and by Apple South boosted sales as well.

Apple South ventured into an Italian restaurant concept in 1993 with the acquisition of two Gianni's Little Italy restaurants in Tampa and Winter Park, Florida. The stores provided an opportunity to develop a casual Italian restaurant concept that served as a prototype for a new chain of restaurants. Apple South changed the menu and added hand-painted murals to the interior decoration for a more authentic Italian look. The size of the original restaurants more than doubled, from 80 seats to 195 seats. By July 1994, the eighth Gianni's restaurant had opened in Charlotte and two more were planned for Knoxville and Charleston.

Apple South continued to exceed its goals for the Applebee's chain as the 100th Apple South-owned Applebee's opened in Chesapeake, Virginia, in March 1994. The company expanded in May 1994 with the purchase of another Applebee's franchisee, Apple Tenn-Flo L.P. The acquisition included nine Applebee's restaurants in Tennessee, and another under construction, as well as development rights in six states. Acquisition of Marcus Corp. added 18 restaurants to the Apple South chain with Applebee's units in Chicago, parts of Wisconsin, Minnesota, and Michigan. The $48 million transaction included development rights. Applebee's International, the franchisor, approved the acquisition, but limited Apple South to 75 new units in that market territory and to 200 additional units throughout existing Apple South franchise territory by 2000.

In September 1994, DuPree filed a proposal with the Securities and Exchange Commission for a merger between Apple South and Applebee's International. The proposal came as a surprise to Applebee's executives. While some observers regarded the situation as a hostile takeover, the filing initiated an open discussion between the two companies. The merger seemed a reasonable idea to many investment watchers and led to an increase in stock values for both companies. Apple South maintained the highest store-level profit margins, at 17 percent to 18 percent after accounting for royalties to the franchisor, than at any other Applebee's units, including those units owned and operated by Applebee's International. Negotiations to merge with Applebee's International stalled in December, however. DuPree, in an article in the December 19, 1994 *Nation's Restaurant News*, attributed the breakdown to "philosophical differences on the strategic direction and operating methods for the Applebee's concept" Other opinions attributed the collapse to differences in personal management styles.

Diversification in the Mid-1990s

Apple South continued to expand its chain of Applebee's franchises, but began to experiment with proprietary restaurant concepts as well. In April 1995 Apple South implemented changes in its Gianni's Little Italy dining concept. Renamed Tomato Rumba Pastaria Grill, the livelier format featured Rumba dancers on the weekends and the menu incorporated fun names such as Roasted Veggie Watusi, a winter vegetable dish served over penne pasta with marinara sauce. The moderately priced menu included more non-Italian selections. The first store conversions occurred in Columbia and Greenville, South Carolina, and a new store opened in each city as well. All of the 15 Gianni's Little Italy restaurants were converted by the end of 1995, and five additional Tomato Rumba stores opened.

To its chain of 170 Applebee's franchises, Apple South added two new restaurant concepts in the acquisition of DF&R Restaurants in August 1995. DF&R became a wholly owned subsidiary of Apple South and maintained separate operations involving 29 Don Pablo's Mexican Kitchen restaurants and 12 Harrigan's Grill and Bar restaurants. The plan to open 18 Don Pablo's stores created some concern as the concept competed with Rio Bravo, a Tex Mex chain owned by Applebee's International. The Don Pablo's concept attracted more families, however. By the end of 1997 the chain grew to 91 restaurants.

With other, more successful restaurant concepts drawing attention and company finances, Apple South began to close the Tomato Rumba units in the first half of 1996. The company executives learned from the experience that their talent was in their ability to expand existing concepts rather than developing their own. Although the restaurant industry's conventional wisdom proclaimed that lack of focus leads to failure for multi-concept companies, Apple South determined that high growth potential in the concepts they chose and the autonomy and talent

Key Dates:

1986: The MRG Company is formed in Georgia; Tom DuPree, Jr., begins his franchise of the Applebee's restaurants.
1988: MRG becomes Apple South, Inc., headed by DuPree.
1991: Apple South goes public.
1994: The 100th Applebee's franchise is opened.
1995: Apple South acquires Don Pablos restaurants.
1997: Apple South acquires McCormick & Schmicks, the Hops Grill & Bar, and Canyon Cafes; company announces the sale of its Applebee's franchises.
1998: Company renamed Avado Brands, Inc.

of each restaurant division would fuel its success. The company retained several of the company-owned structures from the Tomato Rumbas chain for conversion to other restaurant concepts and sought to develop its restaurant chain by acquiring restaurant chains with proven dining concepts.

In February 1997 Apple South purchased McCormick & Schmick's, a chain of 16 seafood dinner houses with locations in California, Oregon, Washington, and Colorado. In Washington, D.C., the restaurant concept operated under the name Jake's and had four additional stores planned at the time of the acquisition. Apple South planned only two new McCormick & Schmick's restaurants because of the expense of interior decoration and location for the upscale concept. In addition, the need for trained chefs and the complexity of the menu, which changed daily according to the availability of fresh seafood, required extensive forethought. The two McCormick & Schmick's stores opened in October 1997—one in Southern California and one in Northern Virginia. Three were planned for 1998, to be located in Florida, California, and Baltimore.

The day after the company announced the agreement with McCormick & Schmick's, Apple South announced that it would purchase Hops Grill and Bar, a restaurant and microbrewery with 18 units located in Florida, Colorado, and Kentucky. Each location employed its own brewmaster for handcrafting the company's signature beers and ales. The acquisition evolved when the owners of the Hops chain approached Apple South about the possible purchase of some of the Tomato Rumba structures for conversion to Hops Grill and Bar. Hops was later renamed Hops Restaurant Bar and Brewery.

The following June, Apple South acquired Canyon Cafes, Inc. The 13-unit chain of southwestern-style restaurants featured a rustic look and spicy entrees such as corn-husk barbecued salmon. *Nation's Restaurant News* named Canyon Cafes a "Hot Concept" for 1997. With locations in Arizona, California, Colorado, Georgia, Missouri, and Texas, the acquisition brought the company's total number of restaurants to 363.

Apple South's acquisitions provided mutual benefits to each company. The company increased its sales revenues, while the three new divisions benefitted from additional capital for expansion, as the acquisition transactions involved cash, stock, and debt payment. DuPree and Apple South executives had learned from some conflicts with the cofounders of Don Pablo's that each chain would operate more successfully with autonomy. The strengths the parent company offered were fiscal and administrative organization as well as chain development experience. Like DF&R, the McCormick & Schmick's, Hops, and Canyon Cafes operated as separate, autonomous entities.

Diversification into its new proprietary restaurant concepts prompted Apple South to divest other assets. The company completed the sale of its ten Hardee's franchises in May 1997. In November 1997, Apple South sold a 75 percent interest in the Harrigan's chain to Pinnacle Restaurant Group. In December 1997 the company announced its intention to divest the 264 Applebee's franchises that it owned and operated, as well as development rights in 20 states and in Washington, D.C.

The decision to sell its Applebee's franchises stemmed from Apple South's preference to pursue a variety of restaurant concepts with high growth potential in the burgeoning niche between casual dining and fine dining. The franchise agreement with Applebee's International required Apple South to open new stores on a regular basis. By selling the franchises, Apple South gained the freedom to invest available funds in its proprietary restaurant concepts, as well as to invest in concepts that might compete with Applebee's International. A conflict with Applebee's International over the alleged similarity of the Hops and Applebee's concepts played a minor role in the decision. In addition, Apple South wanted to sell the franchises before thorough saturation of the territory's development capacity, making the property more salable.

Announcement of the divestiture shocked the industry, as DuPree had spent 13 years actively pursuing new territory and expanding operations. The high-risk move resulted in a steep decline of stock values for both Apple South and Applebee's International. Although the sale of the Applebee's franchises resulted in a loss of 50 percent of the company's overall revenue, the divestiture netted $400 million, making funds available for debt payment and expansion of its proprietary restaurant chains. The process of selling the franchises and development rights resulted in 15 transactions with other franchisees and the additional sale of 33 units in Virginia to Applebee's International. Apple South offered employee bonuses to maintain the quality of the store-level staff during the transition. To reflect the transformation of the company, its name was changed to Avado Brands, Inc. in October 1998.

1998: International Enterprises

Avado Brands accessed new restaurant concepts through joint ventures with European firms. In February 1998 it acquired a 20 percent interest in England-based Belgo Group plc. BGP owned two restaurants in London that featured Belgian foods, such as fresh mussels, in appetizers and entrees, and "frites," thick slices of fried potatoes served with warm mayonnaise. Belgium had also become renowned for its wide variety of high-quality beers, another feature of the eateries. Avado and BPG invested equally in the Belgo Neiuw York in Greenwich Village, which opened at the beginning of 1999. The restaurant featured two distinct atmospheres—an exuberant bar on the first floor offered more than 100 kinds of Belgian beer, while fine dining in a contemporary setting was offered on the second floor. With the profit margin at 25 percent, Avado began to research possible locations for the Belgo concept in Boston, Chicago, San Francisco, Montreal, and Seattle. The joint venture also allowed for a future location of an Avado restaurant in Europe, likely to be the McCormick & Schmick's concept.

In a joint venture with England-based PizzaExpress plc, Avado Brands opened its first San Marzanno restaurant along Philadelphia's restaurant row on Walnut Street. PizzaExpress had been in operation for more than 35 years and owned more than 200 units in eight countries, including India, Pakistan, and Turkey. The Philadelphia eatery featured a trendy, upscale atmosphere with moderately priced, Neapolitan-style pizza, available with traditional or contemporary ingredients. First-year sales were expected to reach more than $1.5 million. Avado planned to open one or two new locations in 1999, cautiously testing the concept.

In its existing American stores Avado focused on brand quality and profit margins, as well as expansion. The company relaxed plans to expand its chain of 129 Don Pablo's Mexican Kitchens from another 30 units down to 15 planned for 1999. Plans for the 18-unit Canyon Cafe chain were reduced from eight new stores to one in 1999. Meanwhile, McCormick & Schmick's began construction on a 9,000-square-foot restaurant in Atlanta featuring an outdoor patio and a custom interior with seating for 250 people. Seafood would be flown to that location daily from the Pacific and Atlantic coasts. Hops Restaurant Bar and Brewery opened its 50th unit in March 1999, located in Newington, Connecticut. Twenty Hops restaurants planned for 1999 would be located in existing territory and in six new states—Indiana, Louisiana, Maryland, Missouri, Ohio, and Virginia. Avado completed the divestiture of the Applebee's franchises in May 1999.

Principal Subsidiaries

Belgo Group plc (20%); San Marzano Pizza Vino e Birra (50%).

Principal Divisions

Canyon Caf,; Don Pablos; Hops Restaurant, Bar, Brewery; McCormick & Schmick's Seafood.

Principal Competitors

Brinker International, Inc.; Darden Restaurants, Inc.; Carlson Restaurants Worldwide, Inc.

Further Reading

''Applebee's-Apple South Split Marks Shift in Corporate Parent-Child Relationship,'' *Nation's Restaurant News,* January 19, 1998, p. 27.

''Apple South Becomes Avado Brands,'' *Nation's Restaurant News,* October 19, 1998, p. 4.

''Apple South Opens 100th Unit,'' *Nation's Restaurant News,* March 14, 1994, p. 105.

''Apple South's DuPree Abandons Merger Quest with Applebee's,'' *Nation's Restaurant News,* December 19, 1994, p. 14.

''Avado Brands, Inc. Sheds Applebee's, Names Hall Proxy,'' *Nation's Restaurant News,* November 30, 1998, p. 4.

''Avado Completes Sale of Applebee's Division,'' *Nation's Restaurant News,* May 17, 1999, p. 3.

''Avado Scales Back Development Schedule,'' *Nation's Restaurant News,* February 1, 1999, p. 4.

''Avado to Bring Pizza Express to North America,'' *Nation's Restaurant News,* February 22, 1999, p. 4.

''A Blueprint for Success: Apple South's Head-Turning Growth Has Been Carefully Choreographed. The Next Step Is Going Beyond Franchising,'' *Restaurant Business,* November 1, 1995, p. 80.

Bolt, Ethan, ''The Exec,'' *Restaurant Business,* March 1, 1999, p. 32.

Brooks, Steve, ''Upsetting the Applecart; As DuPree and Kinsel Sell Off the Successful Applebee's, They're Taking a Big Risk on a Handful of Fledgling Chains,'' *Restaurant Business,* June 1, 1998, p. 40.

Carolino, Bill, ''Apple South Buys Hops, McCormick and Schmick's,'' *Nation's Restaurant News,* February 17, 1997, p. 1.

——, ''Apple South Grooms Gianni's Little Italy as Potential Development,'' *Nation's Restaurant News,* July 25, 1994, p. 3.

Deogun, Nikhil, ''How Apple South's Hotshot Chief Got in the Way of His Own Success,'' *Wall Street Journal,* December 14, 1994, p. S1.

Hayes, Jack, ''Apple South Fires Up Gianni's Revamp: Tomato Rumba's,'' *Nation's Restaurant News,* May 1, 1995, p. 7.

——, ''Apple South's Purchases Slices into Applebee's Territory,'' *Nation's Restaurant News,* August 11, 1997, p. 3.

Keegan, Peter O., ''Apple South Offers IPO to Fund Future Growth,'' *Nation's Restaurant News,* November 4, 1991, p. 14.

Lamm, Marcy, ''Avado Bringing Seafood Restaurant to Atlanta,'' *Atlanta Business Chronicle,* March 12, 1999, p. 10A.

Lavecchia, Gina, ''A Bit of Belgium,'' *Restaurant Hospitality,* April 1999, p. 62.

Papiernick, Richard, ''Apple South Flexes Franchise Muscle, Piques Investor Interest,'' *Nation's Restaurant News,* June 12, 1995, p. 24.

——, ''Apple South Sows Seeds for Early Applebee's Exit,'' *Nation's Restaurant News,* February 23, 1998, p. 3.

——, ''Kinsell Out at Avado, DuPree Takes Back Reins,'' *Nation's Restaurant News,* November 16, 1998, p. 1.

Roush, Chris, ''Apple South Closes Tomato Rumba's Unit,'' *Knight-Ridder/Tribune Business News,* July 30, 1996.

Ruggless, Don, ''Apple South to Acquire 13-Unit Canyon Cafes Inc. in $36M Deal,'' *Nation's Restaurant News,* June 30, 1997, p. 1.

Sweitzer, Letitia, ''Apple South Ripe for Expansion,'' *Business Atlanta,* May 1993, p. 72.

Zuber, Amy, ''Avado Brands Carves New Pie with PizzaExpress Import San Marzanno,'' *Nation's Restaurant News,* April 5, 1999, p. 11.

—Mary Tradii

The B. Manischewitz Company, LLC

One Manischewitz Plaza
Jersey City, New Jersey 07302
U.S.A.
Telephone: (201) 333-3700
Fax: (201) 333-1809
Web site: http://www.manischewitz.com

Wholly Owned Subsidiary of R.A.B. Holdings
Founded: 1888
Employees: 170
Sales: $48.8 million (1999)
NAICs: 311812 Commercial Bakeries; 311821 Cookie and Cracker Manufacturing; 311422 Specialty Canning

Since 1998, The B. Manischewitz Company, LLC, has been a subsidiary of R.A.B. Holdings, a private specialty-food company. The world's number one baker of matzo, or unleavened bread, Manischewitz also produces hundreds of other kosher foods, including baked goods, pastas, soups, gefilte fish, and borscht. It also licenses its name to other businesses producing candy, bread, seltzer, and wine. Under the Manischewitz, Horowitz Margareten, and Goodman's names, the company wholesales its products to supermarket chains, primarily in the United States and Canada. Its parent company, R.A.B. Holdings, operates Millbrook Distribution Services, which distributes a line of natural and organic foods and health and beauty care items to retail chains and stores in the East and Midwest. Historically, Manischewitz kosher products have had their greatest appeal to Jewish consumers, and until recently their fine foods have normally been offered to retail customers only on the specialty shelves of supermarkets. However, R.A.B. has taken steps to broaden the brand name's appeal by marketing some foodstuffs with wider interest under the Manischewitz label and has urged major retail outlets to shelve them in the standard sections of their stores to compete with other established, brand-name food products.

1888–1929: Rabbi Manischewitz and the Rise of Unleavened Bread

The B. Manischewitz Company traces its beginnings back to the spring of 1888, when Rabbi Dov Behr Manischewitz opened a small Matzoh bakery in Cincinnati, Ohio. He had migrated to that city in the mid-1880s, already possessing a reputation for both scholarship and piety. He had been one of the students of the famous Rabbi Israel Salanter, the Lithuanian-born spiritual leader in the *Musar* movement which stressed that piety did not require devout Jews to live reclusive lives and strove to reconcile the beliefs of traditional Judaism with the need to meet community obligations and participate in public affairs.

Rabbi Manischewitz brought with him a thorough knowledge of the sacred dietary laws of Judaism. He had been the personal shochet of the Gaon of Salant, overseeing the ritual preparation of foods in strict accordance with those laws and safeguarding their purity or kashruth. In Cincinnati he started out as a part-time peddler and shochet for the Orthodox Jews in his community, and it was largely from his spiritual concerns that he set out to make kosher unleavened or matzoh bread for Passover, first for his family and a few friends, but soon for many of the devout Jews of the city. His bakery soon evolved into a successful business, innovative and prosperous, though never inattentive to the spiritual needs of its customers.

By the end of the century, demand for his matzoh bread had become so great that Rabbi Manischewitz turned to cookie-making technology to keep up with it. An important innovator, he introduced the use of gas-fired ovens, replacing the older coal stoves being used by other Jewish bakers. The newer ovens allowed a much more careful control of the baking speed, insuring a consistent and standard quality to the bread. He also introduced portable traveling-tunnel ovens, and was the first to package his matzos for shipment to places beyond the immediate neighborhood of his bakery. He even began shipping his matzos overseas, to such diverse places as England, Japan, France, Hungary, Egypt, and New Zealand. His bright, clean bakery would become a model for future kosher bakeries, both in America and abroad.

Company Perspectives:

Deliciously different for over 100 years.

Wholly under the control of Rabbi Manischewitz and his sons through the first three decades of the 20th century, the company thrived as a private company, meeting the needs of a growing Jewish population in the United States, especially during the sacred Passover holy days.

1929–71: Good Growing Years Despite Depression and War

In 1929, the year of the great stock market debacle and the onset of the Great Depression, Manischewitz went public and began trading on the Cincinnati Stock Exchange. Because of the ongoing demand for the company's baked goods, and despite the grim economic situation in America, by the next year the company was able to build a second factory. Located in Jersey City, New Jersey, the plant quickly became the model for all new machine-made matzo bakeries world wide. Closer to a much larger Jewish population than that of Cincinnati, the new factory also made distribution of the company's product more efficient and quickly enlarged its customer base. The Manischewitz label was soon a dominant one in ethnic grocery stores and delicatessens in the larger East Coast cities. Thanks to the technology and efficiency of the New Jersey factory, in 1960 Manischewitz was able to close down the Cincinnati facility altogether.

The company also took pains to retain and expand its customer base within the Jewish community. During the 1930s and 1940s, the golden age of radio, the company also sponsored Yiddish programs—programs whose primary audience were the large Jewish immigrant population that settled in New York and other cities during the first half of the century.

In 1940 Manischewitz produced its first Tam Tam cracker. It signaled the initial departure from its line of matzo products. About the same time, in a leasing arrangement, it began marketing Monarch wines under the Manischewitz label. Monarch Wine, established in Brooklyn, New York, in 1934, had begun making sacramental wines for use on holy days, quickly replacing the homemade wines that until then filled that need. Growth in its product line encouraged the company to form the B. Manischewitz Sales Company, as distributing division of the firm. Later, Manischewitz would license other companies to use its established name, a principal example being the Canandaigua Wine Company, which for several years has made a line of kosher wines under the Manischewitz label.

Like other kosher food producers, Manischewitz found new customers in the tragic events of World War II and its aftermath. Tens of thousands of Jews arrived in America at the end of the war, many of them survivors of the Holocaust. More exiled Jews came in 1956, after the Hungarian revolt against the Soviet-backed communist dictatorship. Two years before that, in 1954, the company had acquired its processing plant, located in Vineland, New Jersey, where it produced gefilte fish, chicken soup, and borscht, three of its signature foods. It was filling a strong need of many of the new immigrants, who were putting new life in the U.S. kosher food industry. Even then, however, it was also clear that the customers of the kosher-food industry were not exclusively Jews. In America, more than half were Muslims, Seventh-day Adventists, and others who for religious or health reasons favored kosher foods.

1972–97: New Management, Acquisitions, and Sellout to Kohlberg & Co.

The five sons of Rabbi Dove Behr ran the business until the founder's grandsons took over in the 1960s. They continued to run the company until 1972, when they turned its operational reins over to a team of professional managers. However, majority ownership of the company remained with the Manischewitz family.

Further growth followed. In 1981 the company entered into a licensing agreement with Goodman's, makers and distributors of a line of matzo and matzo products. Three years later, in 1984, the company acquired various assets of Horowitz Margareten, including its name and trademark, and began marketing a line of kosher foods under that name. Its various products also became OU certified in that same year, meeting the strict standards of the Kashruth Division of the Union of Orthodox Jewish Congregations of America.

The company remained under the control of the Manischewitz heirs until January 1991, when it was purchased by Kohlberg & Co. and once again became a private company. Kohlberg appointed Donald J. Keller to the chairmanship of the reorganized company, a post he still held in 1998 when he became chairman of Vlassic International, the specialty food spin-off of Campbell Soup Company.

The new managers ran into an immediate legal problem when Manischewitz was accused of a price-fixing policy implemented during the 1980s and was fined $1 million by a federal court in New Jersey, despite the fact that the company, strictly a wholesale maker of kosher foods, had no control over what retail outlets charged for its products. However, despite the negative publicity involved, the company continued to thrive, in part because its products appealed to many health-food faddists who were looking for products low in cholesterol. In 1996 Integrated Marketing Communications claimed that the number of kosher consumers in America included about two million Jews and five million non-Jews, with a market potential that would continue to grow rapidly.

1998 and After: Purchase by R.A.B. Holdings and New Strategies

On May 1, 1998, Millbrook Distribution Services, a subsidiary of R.A.B. Enterprises, a company owned and headed by Richard A. Bernstein, the former chairman of Western Publishing, completed a purchase agreement with Kohlberg, buying Manischewitz for about $83.8 million in cash, $38.8 million in debt repayments, and $2.1 million in expenses. Millbrook, a wholesale distributor of health care, beauty care, general merchandise, and specialty food items maintains four primary

Key Dates:

1888: Rabbi Dov Behr Manischewitz starts business, baking matzo for family members and friends.
1929: Company goes public, trading on the Cincinnati Stock Exchange.
1930: Company opens second factory in Jersey City, New Jersey.
1940: Manischewitz introduces its first non-matzo product, the Tam Tam cracker.
1954: Company purchases a processing plant in Vineland, New Jersey, for the manufacture of borscht, chicken soup, and gefilte fish.
1972: Manischewitz family turns business operations over to a professional management team.
1981: In a license agreement, the company begins manufacturing and distributing Goodman's matzo and matzo products.
1984: Horowitz Margareten, an additional product line, is acquired by Manischewitz; the company becomes OU certified.
1991: Manischewitz family surrenders control of business when company is sold to Kohlberg & Co.
1998: Company is purchased by R.A.B. Holdings, Inc.

wholesale distribution centers located in Leicester, Massachusetts; Greenville, North Carolina; Harrison, Arkansas; and Ozark, Alabama. These service about 10,000 retail customers in 40 states.

Bernstein appointed Dennis M. Newnham president and CEO of R.A.B.'s new subsidiary and put in a place a new marketing strategy. This was prompted in part by quickly changing marketplace realities and promising projections, including Integrated Marketing's claim that by 2000 regular kosher consumers would grow to nine million and that another 36 million potential kosher consumers could be served by the industry. Between 1977 and 1997, the number of kosher-certified food items available in American stores had risen from 1,750 to 45,000. In 1997 sales of such items totaled $47 billion, with less than ten percent of those sales being made to people who bought the items because they were kosher-certified. With the new health-conscious, low-fat ingredients in many foods, many companies were meeting dietary and sanitary standards required for certification, eliminating, for example, animal fats from products containing dairy products. A major example was Nabisco's celebrated Oreo cookie, which qualified for certification in 1997 and within a year saw its New York-area sales increase by 160 percent. Clearly, B. Manischewitz had to undertake some bold and innovative measures or face being edged off supermarket shelves by the products of such foodstuff giants as Nabisco. The strategy, requiring the cooperation of retail outlets, called for moving the company's products from specialty-food aisle shelves onto the regular shelves. It also called for the manufacture of new products that could compete with major brands that were now meeting the requirements for kosher certification. The faith and pride in Manischewitz products was evident in Bernstein's quip that he would put the company's kosher chocolate chip biscotti up against any biscotti in the business. The problem was, said Bernstein, that the company's premium, high-quality products, didn't "get the eyeballs of Americans" because they were in the kosher department.

In many ways, the new strategy called for some risk taking. When R.A.B. acquired the company, its annual sales were just over $50 million, almost half of which were made during Passover. Its products still retained their ethnic identity, appealing largely to Jewish customers who bought them, not just for their high quality, but also because they met the specific dietary requirements of their religion. The hope was that the Manischewitz name, so long bound to high-quality foodstuffs, would help in the transition to mainstream marketing. So too would its new image, as the company began introducing such products as banana-split and rocky-road macaroons.

In late 1999 the company had the physical plant necessary to meet its full-store integration plan. The Jersey City facility was capable of baking over 600,000 lbs. of flour per week. It produced about 250 million sheets of matzo a year, making it the largest producer of matzo in the world. Also, it was developing a new line of "good for you" snacks at its Jersey City plant, where it also maintained a warehouse from which it distributed just over half of all Manischewitz products.

The Vineland, New Jersey, facility manufactured all of the company's canned and jarred products, including old, familiar favorites like gefilte fish, chicken soup, and borscht. The plant was primarily a hand-pack processing operation stressing careful attention to quality and flexibility. Workers there packed about two million pounds of fish and one million pounds of beets each year. The Vineland warehouse was responsible for slightly less than half of the distribution of Manischewitz products.

The company marketed approximately 400 stock keeping units (SKUs) and also licensed its name for additional products, the most significant of which was wine. It was also developing more products designed to compete with comparable items made by other foodstuff manufacturers. For three straight years, from 1997 through 1999, Manischewitz was the fastest-growing noodle company in the United States. Its broadening line of good tasting, healthy consumer foods had in fact made it a leading candidate among its various retail customers for full-store integration of its products, a move that one major outlet, Wal-Mart, already made. The company was giving new meaning to "Man, oh Manischewitz" as it continued its transition onto mainstream shelves.

Principal Competitors

G. Willi-Food International; The Hain Food Group, Inc.; Aron Streit, Inc.

Further Reading

Bosco, Maryellen Lo, "Stores Expanded Passover Lines, Volume," *Supermarket News*, May 11, 1998, p. 58.

Brown, Douglas, "Distributor to Buy Manischewitz for $124 Mil," *Progressive Grocer: Daily News Center*, April 20, 1998.

"Food Industry Finds Kosher Food Kosher," *Las Vegas Review-Journal*, May 31, 1998, p. 10A.

"Former Publishing Head Returns with Food Deal," *High Yield Report*, April 27, 1998, p.1.

Gahr, F.O., *Tempting Kosher Dishes: Prepared from World Famous Manischewitz's Matzo Products,* 3rd edition, Cincinnati: The B. Manischewitz Co., 1930.

"Manischewitz Sold for $125 Million," *The Record, Northern New Jersey*, October 30, 1998, Business Section, p. 1.

Nathan, Joan, *Jewish Cooking in America,* New York: Alfred A. Knopf, 1994.

Weiss, Miles, "Manischewitz Seeks Bigger Bite of Sales; Products Will Find Life beyond Kosher-Food Aisle," *St. Louis Post-Dispatch*, November 8, 1998, Business Section, p. 1.

—John W. Fiero

Bayou Steel Corporation

138 Highway 3217
LaPlace, Louisiana 70069
U.S.A.
Telephone: (504) 652-4900
Toll Free: (800) 535-7692
Fax: (504) 652-0272
Web site: http://www.bayousteel.com

Public Company
Incorporated: 1988
Employees: 580
Sales: $253.9 million (1998)
Stock Exchanges: American
Ticker Symbol: BYX
NAIC: 331111 Iron and Steel Mills; 331221 Rolled Steel Shape Manufacturing; 23591 Structural Steel Erection Contractors

Bayou Steel Corporation operates a steel "minimill" at its 287-acre site located next to the Mississippi River 35 miles north of New Orleans at LaPlace, Louisiana, where it also has its corporate headquarters. The minimill is a low-cost, steel production plant that recycles scrap steel, using electric arc furnaces to melt the raw steel, casters to process it into new billets (unfinished steel bars), and rolling mills to fabricate various bars and steel shapes from the billets, including angles, channels, flats, standard and wide-flange beams, rounds, and squares. Its products are sold, for the most part, to North American service centers in 44 states, Canada, and Mexico. These centers provide end users with steel parts used in manufacturing and construction. In addition, Bayou Steel occasionally exports both billets and steel shapes to foreign markets.

In addition to its Louisiana facility, which includes Mississippi River Recycling, Bayou Steel owns a rolling mill in Harriman, Tennessee, 37 miles to the west of Knoxville. It operates as a subsidiary, under the name Bayou Steel Corporation Tennessee. The company also maintains branch storage facilities on waterways in Chicago; Catoosa (near Tulsa), Oklahoma; and Leetsdale (near Pittsburgh), Pennsylvania.

Organization and Early Planning: 1979–80

Bayou Steel Corporation came into existence on paper in 1978 when a consortium of foreign investors, led by Voest-Alpine AG, an Austrian firm, began planning the building of a steel minimill designed to re-smelt and reprocess salvaged or scrap steel. Initial plans called for the operation to be located in Texas, in the Houston area, but in 1979 interested Louisiana businessmen convinced the group to build the $120 million facility on a 178-acre tract adjacent to the Mississippi River at La Place, in St. John Parish, north of New Orleans. Voest-Alpine, owned by the Austrian government, was to direct the building of the new plant. The site appealed to the investors because it offered easy convenient access to a waterway, railroad, and highways, and the new company incorporated in Louisiana in 1979.

The projected plans called for modeling the new facility on those operated by Voest-Alpine in Europe. The complex would include a melt shop, which would transform scrap into new steel in furnaces reaching 6,300 degrees Fahrenheit, a temperature produced by an efficient combination of electrical and oxy-fuel burners. From this re-smelting process, the liquid steel would be transported in ladles to continuous-casting machines, where it would be turned into billets, raw steel forms resembling large but rectangular telephone poles cut in 40-foot lengths. Some billets were to be sold in that form, but after the next unit came on line, the rolling mill, much of the steel would be turned into I-beams, U-beams, and various other shapes used in commercial and industrial buildings. Estimates at the time were that the minimill would produce approximately 600,000 tons of steel billets each year.

Breaking ground for the mill in that same year, 1979, the new company planned to employ abut 650 workers, many of whom were already residents of the area. Most of these would be taken from the oil production and allied industry work forces, but, since Louisiana manufactured no steel, some key personnel were to be hired from steel-producing areas in other parts of the country. Plans also called for introducing workers to the process at the new plant but then giving them four weeks of on-the-job training at the Voest-Alpine mills in Austria and a Krupp steel mill in West Germany. The new company's board

Key Dates:

1978: Company is incorporated as a jointly owned venture of Voest-Alpine, an Austrian company, and other European investors.
1981: Work is completed on the Bayou Steel minimill in La Place, Louisiana.
1986: Voest-Alpine sells its facility to R.S.R. Corp., a lead-smelting company based in Dallas, Texas.
1988: Bayou Steel is reincorporated in Delaware and goes public.
1993: Steelworkers Local 9121 begins strike against Bayou Steel on March 21.
1995: Company purchases the Tennessee Valley Steel Corporation of Harriman, Tennessee.
1996: Agreement is reached with Steelworkers Union ending 42-month strike on September 26.
1998: Merger attempt with Northwestern Steel & Wire Co. fails.

of directors was chaired by Zaki Honen, a Paris businessman and investor. Daniel O. Gloven was Bayou Steel's first president and CEO.

Startup of Operations and Ensuing Industry Slump: 1981–85

By April 1981, as the first plant shop, the melting facility, neared completion, the company had hired and begun the training of the first 100 employees of the projected work force necessary to run the operation. The melting process of scrap steel began in July of that year. Almost immediately the operation ran into some serious problems, the main one being soaring energy costs spurred by the rising cost of oil. As Gloven noted, the structure of power schedules had a punitive effect on steel producers and, nationwide, its effect was taking a grave financial toll on that industry. Relocation of Phase II, including the building of another furnace and continuous-casting machine, was considered, which would have meant the loss of about 250 jobs in the La Place area. Still, by the end of 1981, the company had hired and trained 560 workers in its projected force of 650.

Despite the relative efficiency of the Bayou Steel facility, the company could not manage a profitable operation in its early years. It lost $60 million in 1982, $46 million in 1983, and $47 million in 1984. As a result, in September of 1984 the company began laying workers off, letting 150 go and reducing the pay and benefits of the remaining employees. By 1985, by closing down one of its two melting furnaces, it had reduced its production capacity to 50 percent. The grim truth was that another year of such losses would have forced the plant to close. The situation angered the workers and caused Gloven and his personnel director, Ben Wolverton, to resign.

In fact, Bayou Steel had begun operating at the worst possible time. The high energy costs made it extremely difficult for the steel industry in the United States. It could not compete with foreign steel makers, who began flooding the American market with a cheaper product. By 1985, there was in fact serious doubt that the entire steel industry in the United States could survive the impact of the much cheaper foreign steel, even such state-of-the-art and efficient operations as that built by Voest-Alpine. Furthermore, at Bayou Steel, starting in 1984, when the move was narrowly defeated, efforts were being made to unionize the employees, a move that would inevitably escalate the company's production costs. Yet, despite the difficulties, in July of 1985 the company again fired up its second melting furnace, rehired some workers, and commenced plans to restore its full operating capacity. In May of that year it had begun to show a net operating profit. Moreover, by the summer it was in contract arrangements with LTV Corp., a Pennsylvania steel mill, which under the terms of the one-year agreement would purchase up to 17,000 tons of steel billets per month.

Sale of Company and Marginally Profitable Years: 1986–92

Faced with the uncertainty of the industry's future and workers' unrest at its mill, in 1985 Voest-Alpine undertook to pull out of the American market by selling the company. In 1986, R.S.R. Corporation, a lead-smelting firm based in Dallas and in large part owned by Howard Meyers, purchased the facility. Under the name Bayou Steel Acquisition Corporation, R.S.R. acquired all of the capital stock of the original investors for $75,343,000 and merged with the existing company. Meyers was convinced that the reprocessing of scrap steel would become the most profitable sector of the steel industry and indicated that he chose Bayou Steel because of its location, quality of its employees, and its state-of-the-art equipment.

On May 26, 1988, in Delaware, Bayou Steel was reincorporated under its current name. Thereafter it went public for the first time. It also achieved a profitable year, thanks in part to the decline in global oil prices. When recession set in, however, exacerbated in Louisiana by those falling oil prices, the company's sales once again started to slide downward. In 1992, they had dropped off by 43 percent, and the company was once more losing money.

Labor and Legal Difficulties and Purchase of Tennessee Valley Steel: 1993–96

In 1993, a crippling labor dispute led to a strike by the now-unionized workers at the LaPlace minimill. Acrimonious and litigious, it would last 42 months. Various efforts to negotiate a settlement failed, inducing the company to hire temporary workers to operate the mill at reduced capability. During the bitter strike, the unionized workers charged Bayou Steel with unfair labor practices and, in 1996, the year the strike ended, the National Labor Relations Board filed a complaint against the company for its refusal to recognize Local 9121 of the United Steelworkers of America International (USWA). The company had been fighting the strikers with countersuits and charges, including a racketeering complaint against USWA. It also sought to block unemployment compensation for the striking workers.

The dispute led to various additional legal problems for the company, including allegations that its mill violated safety standards and was emitting illegal levels of toxic flue dust. It also had to fight to maintain tax breaks it had enjoyed since first locating in Louisiana.

An agreement ending the strike finally was reached on September 23, 1996. Under its terms, the company withdrew its complaints against USWA for racketeering made to the National Labor Relations Board. In return, the union dropped its charges of unfair labor practices against the company. Contract negotiations with Local 9121, representing the La Place mill workers, involved concessions on both sides. Pension hikes, overtime and vacation pay, bonuses and health care plans were put in place for workers, but the terms also implemented a pay-for-performance program and permitted Bayou Steel to contract out. The company had to lay off about two-thirds of 310 hourly workers who had been hired to replace striking union workers.

Despite its labor and legal problems, during the strike period Bayou Steel expanded its operation, primarily in response to the fact that industry prospects were rapidly improving in the mid-1990s. By 1995, the company logged net sales of $185.8 million, up 15.5 percent from the previous year. It also negotiated a buyout of the bankrupt Tennessee Valley Steel, a minimill located in Harriman, near Knoxville, on a 198-acre site. The $30.5 million acquisition provided the company with another mill and a stocking facility on the Tennessee River. The plant, with its annual production capacity of 200,000 tons of billets, was reorganized as a subsidiary of Bayou Steel under the name Bayou Steel Corporation Tennessee (BSCT). In addition, the company created a new division, Mississippi River Recycling, which operated an automobile shredder at the main facility at LaPlace, described as "the first step in Bayou Steel's strategic plan to backward integrate into scrap processing in order to control raw material availability and to reduce cost."

Improving Prospects and Future Expectations: 1997–99

Although the steel market has remained both unpredictable and volatile, Bayou Steel has fared well since its labor and some of its legal problems were solved in 1996. The market in 1997 and 1998 was strengthened, thanks to the general health of the national economy and a growing demand for steel billets and structural shapes. For the year ending September 30, 1998, because of lower prices for scrap steel and increased sales, the company's gross profits rose to a record $40.15 million. Encouraged by the industry's health, in 1998 the company attempted a merger with Northwestern Steel & Wire Co. of Sterling, Illinois, but negotiations broke down at the eleventh hour when a final agreement over the price and concessions could not be reached.

In 1998, Bayou Steel's president and COO, Jerry Pitts, noted that the increasing demand for billets and shapes assured the company's short-term health, despite some of the company's niggling problems that have impaired production plans, including ongoing litigation over alleged violations of environmental regulations and such unanticipated difficulties as the power outages that have plagued the Louisiana operation and forced the company to purchase billets to meet demands for its structural shapes and the fire in the Tennessee bar rolling mill that in 1997 forced a brief suspension of its operations. Long-term health was less certain, however. There were too many influencing factors outside the company's control, chief among them the cost of energy and scrap steel on the global market. These were favorable for Bayou Steel in the last years of the 1990s, but they are rather mercurial and could rise to the company's disadvantage within a relatively short period of time. With its shredder operation and plans for additional ways of assuring a steady supply of scrap steel at a price under its control, however, the company was taking positive steps to reduce the impact of deep market fluctuations.

Principal Subsidiaries

Bayou Steel Corporation Tennessee (BSCT).

Principal Competitors

Birmingham Steel; Commercial Metals; Nucor.

Further Reading

Fineberg, Seth, "Bayou Still Facing Challenges," *American Metal Market,* July 7, 1996, p. 5.

Gilger, Kristin, "Bayou Steel Fires Second Furnace," *Times-Picayune* (New Orleans), July 12, 1985, Sec. B, p. 1.

——, "La. Steel Mill Being Sold to Texas Company," *Times-Picayune* (New Orleans), October 17, 1985, Sec. B, p. 1.

Hall, John, "Louisiana's First Steel Mill To Fire Up in July," *Times-Picayune* (New Orleans), April 26, 1981, Sec. 6, p. 22.

Indest, Susan D., "Bayou Steel's Hopes Rusted by Hard Times," *Times-Picayune* (New Orleans), May 5, 1985, pp. 1–2.

"La Place Steel Mill To Create 650 Jobs," *Times-Picayune* (New Orleans), January 20, 1980, Sec. 8, p. 6.

Marsh, Barri, "New Steel Plant's Big Problem Is Energy Cost," *Times-Picayune* (New Orleans), January 31, 1982, Sec. 8, p. 6.

Robertson, Scott, "NW Steel-Bayou Merger Try Dead," *American Metal Market,* April 28, 1998, p. 1.

—John W. Fiero

bebe stores, inc.

380 Valley Drive
Brisbane, California 94005
U.S.A.
Telephone: (415) 715-3900
Fax: (415) 715-3939
Web site: http://www.bebe.com

Public Company
Founded: 1976
Employees: 1,101
Sales: $201.3 million (1999)
Stock Exchanges: New York
Ticker Symbol: BEBE
NAIC: 563100 Women's Specialty Stores

The company bebe stores, inc. designs, manufactures, and sells fashionable womenswear and accessories. Named by *Business Week Magazine* as one of the fastest growing small companies in the United States in the late 1990s, bebe operates a chain of 101 boutiques in 22 states, the vast majority of which are located within upscale malls, and has as its primary customer base trend-conscious women between the ages of 18 and 35. The company offers form-fitting suits, dresses, and separates at prices competitive with such stores as Guess?, Express, and Banana Republic and presents itself as a viable option to consumers unable to afford the hefty price tag of couture. The success of bebe is due not only to its cost-effective management and production techniques, but to the entertainment industry as well; the company's designs appear regularly on such popular television shows as "Ally McBeal," "Friends," and "Beverly Hills 90210." Clothing from bebe is also seen frequently on such film and television stars as Alicia Silverstone, Jennifer Lopez, and Drew Barrymore.

The Early Years: 1976 through the 1980s

The bebe concept was founded by Manny Mashouf, a former entertainment executive who specialized in restaurant and arena management. In the mid-1970s Mashouf saw an opportunity to profit from the growing niche market of womenswear designed specifically for the younger, trend-conscious consumer, and so in 1976 he opened the first bebe store in the center of San Francisco. Mashouf chose the name bebe for his store because it encapsulated many of the images he wanted the clothing to project; the name is a play on Hamlet's famous phrase "to be or not to be" and is also Turkish for "woman" and French for "baby," which to Mashouf symbolized growth. The name (pronounced "bee-bee") was also unique for its pithy sound, representing to the customer the same sharp and youthful originality with which the company wished the clothes themselves to appear.

The store was an initial success, focusing primarily on suits for the younger, urban working woman. For its first several years, bebe remained a single boutique, only branching out in the northern California area after several years in business. Mashouf, as director of the company, was at first conservative in his approach to expansion, choosing to focus on the financial health of a handful of stores before opening new locations. The strategy worked, and the company grew slowly but steadily in the Northwest throughout the 1980s.

Part of what made bebe profitable was the company's tight control over its design and production costs; bebe manufactured all of its own products, using primarily domestically made materials and, therefore, kept its overhead lower than companies that imported wares. By designing, manufacturing, and marketing its clothing in-house, bebe benefitted not only from saving on costs, but by maintaining a firm control over the company's overall image as well. Mashouf and his design team were able to see a product through from its incipient stage of being a sketch on paper to its actual presentation on the floor, and hence gave the bebe label consistency in both quality and style. As the company's popularity grew during the 1980s so did its products, and by decade's end bebe was expanding its focus from daytime suits and other form-fitting career wear to overtly sexy cocktail dresses and separates.

National Growth: The Early 1990s

By the end of the 1980s bebe's popularity was such that the company was ready to begin competing with national chains. The stores had developed a loyal customer base who could find trendy

Company Perspectives:

The "bebe look," with the unmistakable hint of sensuality, appeals to the hip, sophisticated, and body-conscious woman who takes pride in her appearance. The bebe customer is a discriminating consumer who demands value in the form of quality at a competitive price.

looks at a fraction of the cost of more expensive lines such as Donna Karan and Ralph Lauren, and, unlike other chains such as the Gap and Banana Republic, the company made no secret of its dedication to a single niche market, that of the young, stylish woman. As the country's overall economy began to pick up and large, exclusive malls developed at a faster pace nationwide, the company had its first opportunity to grow from a successful regional chain to a nationally recognized label.

In 1994 bebe began an aggressive campaign of expansion and within a year and a half had opened 38 stores in strategically located malls across the nation. The company presented its new stores as catering directly to youthful, sexy women, with prices ranging from $30 for a simple, tight t-shirt to $150 for a flashy, short cocktail dress. The company's advertising campaign in national magazines such as *Vogue* and *Bazaar* reflected bebe's vampy, trendy image, depicting models dressed in sheer gowns and feather boas draped in seductive poses. The unique, highly sexualized image worked, and bebe's profits and name recognition soared.

The Mid-1990s: The Marriage of Fashion and Fame

One of the most important developments in the fashion industry, particularly in high fashion, was the increasingly involved relationship between individual celebrities and clothing labels in the 1990s. In couture, a celebrity could make a certain name a household word almost overnight, particularly if she wore the label to a highly publicized event such as the Academy Awards or Emmy Awards ceremonies. (Film star Michelle Pfeiffer wearing Armani to the Academy Awards ceremony is one of many examples.) For less expensive brands, which relied primarily on a mass consumer market, such exposure was considered desirable, but not entirely necessary, for increased sales. As opposed to courting celebrities with deep pockets, chain stores focused more on well-designed advertising campaigns that could reach and identify with as many consumers as possible.

In 1995, after its initial national growth, bebe took the unusual step of actively seeking out name recognition through not only its print advertising campaigns, but through celebrity exposure as well. The reasoning behind taking such a step was simple: if the label was seen on the same stars with whom bebe's primary targeted customer base could identify, the label itself would become associated with those stars, and the glamorous image those celebrities symbolized. Such an association would make the company's name almost automatically more appealing to a huge consumer base, with sales reflecting that appeal. In 1995 a phenomenally successful television show called "Melrose Place" showcased several young, attractive television stars whose distinctive wardrobes were being mimicked across the nation. In one of the show's episodes that year, its main star, Heather Locklear, wore an outfit by bebe, and thus began an indirect but potent advertising campaign for the company that was, in the long run, to prove more powerful for bebe's sales than the most artfully constructed traditional ads could ever have achieved.

After bebe's appearance on "Melrose Place" the label began showing up on other celebrities, all of whom appealed to the same sort of customer the company was trying to attract. Among them were Drew Barrymore, Alicia Silverstone, and Brooke Shields (who wore bebe on her television show "Suddenly Susan"), the models Cindy Crawford and Christy Turlington, as well as Jennifer Lopez, Madonna, and Julia Roberts. The trend of presenting labels on specific television shows continued as well, with bebe's wares making regular appearances on such shows as "Party of Five," "Beverly Hills 90210," "The Practice," and "Ally McBeal." Indeed, the relationship between clothes and entertainment in the late 1990s proved to be an increasingly vital element to a show's success: in one episode of "Ally McBeal," the entire plot line revolved around the controversial length of the skirt worn by the show's star. The skirt was by bebe, and orders for it went up around the country immediately after the program was aired.

Like any advertising campaign, the courting of a star by a clothing company had to be strategic and shrewdly planned. Bebe, in other words, was not about to send shipments to Roseanne; the young and fashionable Halle Berry, however, could have free choice of the company's inventory. This sort of planning forced bebe to know not only the sartorial preferences of its customers, but also the stars, films, and television shows they admired and wished to imitate. No longer was bebe confined to considerations specific only to the retail industry; the company had become by the late 1990s an active part of the entertainment industry as well.

Further Expansion: The Late 1990s

Unlike high fashion and bridge labels like Donna Karan or Ralph Lauren, bebe was not an innovator when it came to designs and trends. Instead, the key to the company's success was found in its ability to quickly and accurately mimic and expand upon key styles from season to season. When Karan came out with sheer, wispy dresses for one season, for instance, bebe followed with similar designs within a matter of weeks. By following up a design or trend so quickly, bebe allowed its fashion-conscious customers to keep up with the dizzying vicissitudes of the retail trade. Through imitating high fashion labels and offering its merchandise at usually less than half of what a customer would pay for more upscale names, bebe by the late 1990s had carved out an important place for itself in the growing niche market of trendy womenswear. The company had managed to make its products appealing to both the label-obsessed celebrity and the image-obsessed consumer without sacrificing quality for cost, or affordability for quality.

Another important factor in the company's growth was its "test and reorder" method, which allowed bebe to move inventory at a pace much faster than that of its competitors. According to this method, the company would at the beginning of a season ship a limited amount of a certain product to its stores.

Key Dates:

1976: Manny Mashouf opens the first bebe boutique in San Francisco.
1994: 38 new bebe stores are opened across the United States.
1998: The company goes public on the NASDAQ exchange.

If the product sold exceptionally well, the company would alter its inventory by changing its factory orders to accommodate customer demand. Bebe could do this quickly because the company, unlike many of its competitors, produced its own merchandise and thus had firmer control over both the speed with which a product was produced and the amount of product created. Considering the pace at which the trendier end of the retail market moved, the company's ''test and reorder'' philosophy became a vitally important aspect of the company's fiscal health. This process also ensured that bebe's merchandise would be constantly changing, revolving around the capricious demands of the fashion-conscious consumer, and enabled the company to keep up with trends from season to season and, in some cases, from region to region. A distinctive part of bebe's image, then, paradoxically became its chameleon-like ability to change, and change quickly, although the company never strayed far from its core devotion to snugly fitting, sexy apparel.

By the late 1990s bebe had evolved dramatically from the single, career suit-oriented boutique it had been less than two decades previously, with the company gaining enough fiscal strength from its expansion to go public in June of 1998. The company had an initial public offering of $11 a share, with 2.5 million shares sold. After the company's appearance on the stock exchange, Mashouf maintained 88 percent ownership of bebe and continued to play an active role in the company's designs and expansion as its CEO.

Bebe had always marketed itself to younger women, primarily in their twenties, but after its tremendous expansion in the 1990s the company began an attempt to appeal to an even younger age group, primarily through its offering of less expensive, logo-emblazoned shirts, sweaters, and jackets. The introduction of such merchandise not only brought in an expanded customer base, but made the company's name more visible as well. By 1998 the company was focusing on suits and dresses as its primary inventory, but also had added lingerie and more casual wear to its collections. After proving its success with a variety of apparel products, the company was noticed by several retail insiders, and thus became partners in a couple of important licensing agreements that promised to be quite lucrative for the company.

In September of 1998 bebe signed a licensing agreement with Genender International Incorporated to produce a collection of inexpensively priced but fashionable watches. Later that year the company made a similar agreement with Titan Industries to design an expansive footwear collection, which was slated to be sold in both bebe stores and upscale department stores. That year, too, bebe contracted with the well-respected eyewear company California Design Studio to produce a series of optical frames and sunglasses, with prices ranging from $50 to $150. In addition, 1998 saw bebe introduce its first on-line boutique, which proved to be an important step for the company in an increasingly technological retail trade.

By May 1999 bebe had opened 11 stores in as many weeks, and by the end of that month the company had reached a milestone of successfully operating 100 stores. Two of those stores bore international addresses, with one in Kent, England and the other in Vancouver, and the popularity of those locations inspired the company to make plans to expand into regions such as Greece, southeast Asia, and Israel.

Bebe's almost fairy tale-like success was not without risk, however: unlike the more democratic Gap or Banana Republic, bebe appealed to a highly limited customer base and frequently was criticized for its small sizing, as well as for creating clothes into which only a tiny percent of the American female population could fit. Bebe's expansion plans came off better than planned, however, and in 1999 the company had skyrocketing sales, so seeming to beat the odds against it.

Principal Competitors

Donna Karan; The Limited; Liz Claiborne.

Further Reading

''Bebe Coming to Singapore Via SSS Holding,'' *Women's Wear Daily,* August 23, 1999, p. 2.
''Bebe Stores, Inc. Enters the Eyewear Business,'' *Business Wire,* July 29, 1998, p. 07290128.
Maxwell, Alison, ''Retailers Dress TV Stars To Woo Teens,'' *Women's Wear Daily,* August 19, 1999, p. 10.
Ryan, Thomas, ''Bebe Files IPO for 2.5 Million Shares,'' *Women's Wear Daily,* April 23, 1998, p. 8.
Solnik, Claude, ''Bebe Launching New Footwear Business,'' *Footwear News,* February 1, 1999, p. 108.

—Rachel H. Martin

Blair Corporation

220 Hickory Street
Warren, Pennsylvania 16366
U.S.A.
Telephone: (814) 723-3600
Fax: (814) 726-6123

Public Company
Incorporated: 1910 as New Process Co.
Employees: 2,300
Sales: $506.8 million (1998)
NAIC: 45411 Electronic Shopping and Mail-Order Houses

Blair Corporation is a retailer of low- to mid-priced men's and women's clothing and home products. Apparel accounts for approximately 88 percent of the company's sales, with home products making up the remainder. Blair primarily sells its products via direct mail merchandising pieces, including multi-sheet, letter-style mailings and catalogs. It also operates two retail stores—one in Pennsylvania and one in Delaware—and two outlet stores in Pennsylvania. The company's products are manufactured by a number of independent suppliers, many of whom produce merchandise based on Blair's specifications. Blair receives and processes orders in its corporate offices in Warren, Pennsylvania. Orders are filled at and shipped from a nearby distribution center in Irvine, Pennsylvania.

1910–30: A Suitcase Full of Raincoats and a Good Idea

Blair Corporation was founded and built by John L. Blair, a young law student at the University of Pennsylvania. In 1910, Blair was nearing the end of his law studies when a classmate approached him with a business venture. The classmate, who had inherited a raincoat factory, wanted Blair to become the company's sales manager. Blair agreed to take a suitcase full of raincoats home with him for Easter break and consider the offer. Making sales calls at various stops on his way home, he managed to sell a single black raincoat to an undertaker he encountered in a Kane, Pennsylvania, shop. The shop owner, however, declined to carry the coats. Blair's experience convinced him that the best way to sell the coats was to market them directly to consumers. He was also convinced that the best way to reach those consumers was through the mail.

Calling his venture the New Process Rubber Company (because the raincoats had a layer of rubber between two layers of cloth), Blair borrowed $500 to print and mail advertising flyers to 10,000 undertakers across the nation. In response, he received 1,200 orders for the coats, which his classmate quickly set about producing. Soon, customers were asking Blair to offer other reasonably priced clothing items by mail. He obliged by expanding his product line, and the business grew at a rapid pace. Blair's younger brother Harold, who was still in high school, began helping out at the New Process Company on weekends.

In 1920, Blair added a small retail store to his mail-order business and made another of his brothers, Lester, its manager. The store, which was located near the company's headquarters in downtown Warren, was soon joined by another in Jamestown, New York. The direct-mail side of the business continued to grow, also. Although Blair had purchased several existing buildings in Warren to serve as warehouses, he soon discovered that more space was needed. In 1927 and 1928, a new, three-story building was added to the New Process Company's facility.

The late 1920s also marked the company's transition from a privately held company to a public one. In 1927, shares of New Process Company began trading on the American Stock Exchange. It was only the fifth company to be listed on the new exchange.

Meanwhile, the company's product line continued to expand. In addition to apparel, which was offered on a seven-day, free-trial approval basis, Blair began experimenting with a more diverse line of merchandise. Some of the items available to New Process customers in the 1920s and 1930s included electrical appliances, cameras, auto tires, motor oil, fans, healthcare products, and perfume. The company also offered a three-volume set of books, written by its own executives and entitled *The Book of Success.*

1930s–60s: Setbacks and Advances,

The advent of Depression spelled hard times for businesses all across America, and New Process was no exception. The

> ### Company Perspectives:
>
> *Providing quality products at reasonable prices, offering credit appropriately and unconditionally guaranteeing everything we sell are aspects of connecting with customers and building strong, lasting relationships with them—in essence, delivering on our promise . . . "Because Good Clothing Doesn't Have to Cost a Lot."*

generally bleak economic conditions were only made worse for the company by an October 1933 fire that destroyed many of its buildings, an estimated $500,000 loss. Blair worked tenaciously to ensure that New Process kept running, however. The company's operations resumed within ten days of the fire, and a new building was erected to house the company within a year.

From the late 1930s through the early 1950s, expansion was the watchword at New Process. Increases in sales resulted in a continuing need for more employees, more warehouse space, and more equipment. The company responded both by purchasing buildings adjacent to its property and by building additions to its existing facility. Through a series of property improvements, the New Process headquarters eventually evolved into a sprawling complex capable of handling its ever-increasing order processing and fulfillment operations. The completed plant covered almost an entire city block.

One particular expansion caught the attention of the local consumers. In 1941, the company purchased a former hardware company building, which came to be known as "the Annex," for use as a warehouse. New Process also used the Annex to hold annual warehouse sales, which gave shoppers the chance to get rock-bottom prices on closed-out and overstocked merchandise. The sales caused quite a stir, drawing thousands of people from miles away. It was not uncommon to see customers lined up for blocks outside the Annex during one of its warehouse sales. Some even camped on the sidewalk overnight to ensure a good place in line.

While expanding physically, the company also made gains in productivity by implementing new equipment. One such piece of equipment was the addressograph, a machine that used stamped metal plates to print addresses. For several decades, New Process workers had used typewriters to address each of the company's thousands of mail pieces individually, a tedious and labor-intensive task. The introduction of the addressograph near the middle of the century provided a great boost in efficiency and productivity.

The addressograph was but a humble forerunner, however, to innovations that were to come. In 1965, New Process installed its first computer system: a small IBM with auxiliary machines. In 1969, the addressograph was replaced by electronic data processing equipment. In place of the six million metal address plates—which occupied thousands of square feet of floor space—the company's entire mailing database was stored on 80 reels of EDP tape. Soon, computers were used in virtually every department at New Process, from order processing to advertising to mailing.

The 1960s also marked the passing of the company's founder and leader, John Blair, and of his brother Lester, who was then serving as vice-president and advertising manager. Upon Blair's death his son, who was also named John, assumed leadership of the New Process Company. He had previously been the company's personnel director.

1970s: A New Home for Distribution

As the 1970s got underway, New Process celebrated the mailing of its two-billionth advertising piece. The company also opened two new outlet stores—one in Warren, and one in Erie, Pennsylvania—and expanded several of its departments to accommodate the increasing number of mailings and product shipments.

In 1971, it appeared that New Process had finally outgrown its long-time home in downtown Warren. As a result, the company acquired 189 acres of land near Irvine, Pennsylvania—which was just southwest of Warren—and planned to build a new complex to house its merchandise handling operation. The 348,000-square foot distribution center opened in 1973, and soon all warehousing, shipping, and returns were being handled by the hundreds of employees located there. Customer orders were shuttled each morning from the company headquarters, which remained in Warren, to the distribution center; and an average of 48,000 orders were shipped out every day. New Process warehoused around $25 million worth of merchandise in its new complex.

The expanded warehouse and shipping facility enabled the company to once again expand its product line. It did so in 1977 with the addition of a Home Furnishings division. New products included in the line included linens, draperies, furniture covers, area rugs, and bath accessories.

The New Process Company's enhanced capacity, in combination with the expanded product line, produced dramatic growth in sales and earnings throughout the 1970s. For the years 1970 to 1974, average sales were approximately $120 million, more than twice the average for the years 1965 to 1969. Net income increased from an average of $3.3 million to an average of $8.2 million. The growth rate remained similarly high during the second part of the decade, with sales climbing to the $200 million mark and earnings averaging $9.5 million.

1985–95: Shifting to Catalogs

By the beginning of 1985, New Process Company had more than 1,800 employees and offered 1,255 different items through its mail-order operation. The company had set new records with sales of $299 million and earnings of $18.7 million. All three of its merchandise groups—women's apparel, men's apparel, and home furnishings—were showing gains in revenue and profits. It was on this high note that company president and chairman John Blair retired, leaving New Process in the hands of Murray McComas. McComas had been with the company since 1962, when he started his employment in the advertising department. Along with the change in leadership came a change in identity; in 1989, the company officially changed its name from New Process Company to Blair Corporation.

Key Dates:

1910: John L. Blair founds the New Process Company.
1920: New Process opens its first retail store.
1927: Company begins trading on the American Stock Exchange
1962: Founder John Blair dies; his son becomes president and chairman of the board.
1973: Merchandise handling operations are moved to a new distribution center in Irvine, Pennsylvania.
1989: The New Process Company changes its name to Blair Corporation
1993: Blair begins testing a catalog format for its direct-mail pieces.

In the early 1990s, Blair undertook an ambitious renovation of its headquarters. Relocating its distribution operation to the new facility in Irvine had vacated a great deal of usable space, resulting in the need for work area reconfiguration. In addition, the buildings—which Blair had occupied since 1921—needed modernization and upgrading. The renovation involved replacing most of the existing office equipment with modern workstations, making the entire building handicapped-accessible, and enlarging and remodeling the retail store section of the facility.

By 1993, Blair had built a mailing list of more than 15 million. Unlike most of its mail-order competitors, the company did not use catalogs. Instead, its letter-style mailings more closely resembled the type of flyer John Blair had originally sent out back in 1910. They generally included several individual sheets containing product information, along with a cover letter signed by the company's president. In 1993, however, Blair began testing a catalog format for its home furnishings line and other non-apparel items. Finding that the catalogs were well-received by its existing customer base, the company expanded its distribution to include potential customers. It also began creating pilot catalogs for its men's and women's apparel.

Blair released test mailings of men's apparel catalogs in July 1995 and a test batch of women's catalogs followed in January 1996. When the mailings produced promising results, the company began full mailings to both prospects and existing customers. By the end of 1996, Blair had mailed 60.3 million catalogs. That number increased to 100.7 million in 1997, and jumped to 128.2 million in 1998. As the company relied increasingly on catalogs as its marketing vehicle, its traditional letter-style mailings decreased. Between 1996 and 1998, the number of these mailings fell from 176 million to 88.5 million.

With the shift to catalog marketing came a slight shift in Blair's target demographic. The company had traditionally targeted low-to-moderate income customers who were aged 50 or older. The company believed, however, that the catalog approach enabled it to reach a younger population as well. Therefore, it redefined its customer profile as ''over 40, low-to-moderate income.'' According to Blair's 1998 annual report, its newly defined market was the fastest growing segment of the population.

Looking Ahead

Since its inception in 1910, Blair had maintained an impressive track record of surefooted, quiet growth. As the 20th century drew to a close, it appeared probable that the company would continue making gains in the coming years. One of the most significant avenues of growth was likely to be its newly expanded target market. By redefining its target age range to include 40-to-50-year-olds, Blair had opened the door to a whole new—and growing—group of consumers.

To focus advertising efforts on this group, the company planned a year 2000 launch of a new apparel catalog geared to working women. Also planned were a dress and casual men's apparel catalog and a gifts and collectibles catalog. Additional catalog releases were likely in the future as Blair continued its shift to that form of marketing. The company also had plans to focus on its Internet presence, with an eye toward joining the ranks of direct-mail companies that also offered online shopping. Blair's increased use of catalogs—and the potential use of e-commerce—was expected to result in a decrease of its letter-style mailings.

The company was also gearing up for an impending change in leadership. Blair's president, Murry McComas, planned to retire in December 1999. He was to be replaced by John Zawacki, a Blair veteran of 28 years. Zawacki was the vice-president and general manager of the company's womenswear division and a member of the board of directors.

Principal Subsidiaries

Blair Holdings, Inc.

Principal Competitors

Fingerhut Companies, Inc.; Ames Department Stores, Inc.; Brylane Inc.; Burlington Coat Factory Warehouse Corporation; J.C. Penney Company, Inc.; Kmart Corporation; Ross Stores, Inc.; Sears Roebuck and Co.; The TJX Companies, Inc.; Target Stores, Inc.; Wal-Mart Stores, Inc.

Further Reading

Anderson, Manley, ''Blair Corp. Sets Open House for Today,'' *Post-Journal* (Harrisburg, Penn.), August 26, 1995, p.5.
''Blair Corp. Opens Retail Store,'' *Post-Journal* (Harrisburg, Penn.), December 10, 1992.
Gannon, Joyce, ''Blair Enjoys Quiet Success in the Clothing Business,'' *Pittsburgh Post-Gazette*, March 26, 1991, p.2.
75th Anniversary Book, Warren, Penn.: Blair Corporation, 1985.

—Shawna Brynildssen

Blockbuster Inc.

One Blockbuster Plaza
101 Elm Street
Dallas, Texas 75270
U.S.A.
Telephone: (214) 854-3000
Toll Free: (800) 224-2677
Fax: (214) 854-4848
Web site: http://www.blockbuster.com

Public Company
Incorporated: 1982 as Cook Data Services
Employees: 37,000
Sales: $2.1 billion (1998)
Stock Exchanges: New York London
Ticker Symbol: BBI
NAIC: 53223 Video Tape and Disc Rental

Blockbuster Inc. is a leader in the field of video and video disk rental. With approximately 27 percent of the U.S. market share, Blockbuster operates about 6,500 video stores, serving more than 87 million customers in the United States, its territories, and 25 other nations. Founded in the mid-1980s as an alternative to small, local operations with limited video rental selection, the company grew quickly into a nationwide chain, with other interests in the entertainment industry as well, including music retailing. In 1994, Blockbuster became a wholly owned subsidiary of Viacom Inc., allowing Viacom the financial resources to proceed with its bid for Paramount Communications. Viacom retained total control of Blockbuster until its 1999 initial public offering of 31 million shares (about 18 percent) of Blockbuster's stock. In the late 1990s, Blockbuster faced challenges brought about by new ownership, increased competition, and a relatively soft market for videos. Nevertheless, the company has coped admirably by refocusing its efforts on its core video rental business. In 1999, Blockbuster boasted a store within a ten-minute drive of virtually every major neighborhood in the United States and strove to guarantee the availability of new video releases in most markets.

An Immediate Hit in the Mid-1980s

Blockbuster traces its history to the formation of Cook Data Services, Inc., in 1982. This company was founded by David Cook to supply computer software services to Texas's oil and gas industry. When the industry went bust, the company was left without a strong customer base. Cook was searching for another source of revenue when his wife, Sandy, a movie fan, suggested entering the video rental business.

Cook learned that the video rental field was highly fragmented. Most stores were relatively modest family operations that carried a small selection of former big hit movies. Providing a large selection of movies required a large investment of capital, since distributors typically charged approximately $70 per tape. In addition, tapes were generally not displayed, but kept behind the counter to discourage theft, and had to be fetched and laboriously signed out to the customer. Cook saw that operations could be greatly streamlined by a computerized system for inventory control and check out, something his software background prepared him to develop.

After Sandy Cook conducted several months of research into the video rental industry, David Cook sold his oil and gas software business to its managers and entered the movie rental business. In October 1985, Cook opened the first Blockbuster Video outlet in Dallas. With 8,000 tapes covering 6,500 titles, it had an inventory many times larger than that of its nearest competitor. In addition, tapes were displayed on shelves throughout the store, as in a bookstore, so that customers could pick them up and carry them to the front desk for check out. A magnetic strip on each video and sensors at the door discouraged theft. Computers were used to keep track of inventory, and a laser scanning system, which used barcodes on the tapes and on members' cards, simplified and reduced the time involved in conducting transactions.

The first Blockbuster store was an immediate hit. The Cooks discovered that the public had a much greater appetite for renting video movies than anyone had previously suspected. People were interested not just in seeing hit movies they had missed in the theaters but also in a broad variety of other features.

Company Perspectives:

The Blockbuster business model provides an advantage over other large home video chains and significant advantage over single store competitors. The key elements of this business model are to: provide a large number of copies and broad selection of movie titles; operate conveniently located and highly visible stores; offer superior and consistent customer service; optimize our pricing to local market conditions; nationally advertise and market our Blockbuster brand name and the differences between us and our competitors; use our extensive customer transaction database to effectively operate and market our business; and improve our efficiency and lower our costs through self distribution.

By summer 1986, Cook had expanded the Blockbuster concept to three additional stores. To reflect the different nature of the company, Cook Data Services became Blockbuster Entertainment Corporation in June 1986. In September, the company set out to raise money for further expansion with an initial stock offering. However, days before the sale was to take place, a financial columnist wrote a damaging article citing Cook's background in the oil industry and questioning the company's know-how in the video field. The article caused the equity offering to be canceled, and without this infusion of cash, Blockbuster began to run out of money. The company finished 1986 with a loss of $3.2 million.

In February 1987, however, Cook sold one-third of Blockbuster to a group of three investors, who were all former associates at another company, Waste Management, Inc. Wayne Huizenga had in 1972 co-founded Waste Management, which grew to be the largest garbage disposal business in the world, and served as its president and chief operating officer until 1984, when he retired. John Melk, the president of Waste Management's international division, was first to invest in a Blockbuster franchise. Joined by Donald Flynn, the chief financial officer of Waste Management, the group invested $18.6 million in Blockbuster stock.

New Management and Aggressive Expansion in the Late 1980s

With this move, Cook surrendered future control of Blockbuster, and Huizenga became the dominant voice in determining the company's future. Where Cook had envisioned growth through franchising, selling Blockbuster's name and computer system to individual entrepreneurs, Huizenga foresaw growth through company ownership of stores. In April 1987, two months after the men from Waste Management bought into Blockbuster, Cook left the company. Soon thereafter, the company's headquarters were moved to Fort Lauderdale, Florida.

By June 1987, Blockbuster owned 15 stores and franchised 20 others. With this base, Huizenga set out to transform Blockbuster into the industry's dominant player. He kept most of Cook's policies, such as store hours from ten a.m. to midnight every day; a three-day rental policy, which encouraged customers to rent more than one tape at once; and a broad selection of titles. Despite conventional wisdom that the video tape rental business was heavily dependent on hits, 70 percent of Blockbuster's rental revenues came from non-hit movies, which had the added benefit of being less expensive to purchase from distributors. In addition, Blockbuster's management decided to eschew revenue from X-rated adult films, opting instead for a family environment.

With these policies in place, Blockbuster set out on a program of aggressive expansion. The company began to buy back franchised operations with the goal of 60 percent company-owned Blockbuster outlets. In addition, Wayne Huizenga began to buy up chains of video stores that already dominated their local markets, using this as a shortcut to quick expansion. In March 1987, Blockbuster bought Southern Video Partnership as part of this policy. Two months later, it purchased Movies To Go, Inc., of St. Louis, for $14.5 million.

To support its expansion, Blockbuster established six regional offices, including a distribution center in Dallas that prepared tapes to be placed in stores. By the end of 1987, Blockbuster was operating 133 stores, and had become the country's fifth-largest video chain in terms of revenue. Sales rose from $7.4 million in 1986 to $43.2 million that year.

Blockbuster continued its ambitious expansion program in 1988. In March, the company purchased Video Library, Inc., for $6.4 million plus stock. The following month, Blockbuster made a deal with the United Cable Television Corporation (UCTC) to open 100 franchised stores over the next two-and-a-half years. In addition, UCTC purchased five percent of Blockbuster's stock for $12.25 million. By November, this stake had risen to 20 percent. With 200 stores, Blockbuster had become the largest video rental chain in the country. At the end of the year, the company's number of stores had risen to 415.

In January 1989, Blockbuster finalized its purchase of Las Vegas-based Major Video, Inc., the country's fourth-largest video rental chain, for $92.5 million. It also purchased Oklahoma Entertainment, Inc. The following month brought the purchase of Vector Video, Inc., and Video Superstores Master Limited Partnership, which, with 106 stores, had been Blockbuster's largest franchisee. By June 1989, two years after Huizenga's takeover, the company ran 700 stores. Sales had tripled, profits nearly quadrupled, and the value of the company's stock had risen sevenfold.

Despite these gains, in April 1989, Blockbuster's efforts to buy up other chains with stock suffered a setback when an analyst at a large stock brokerage issued a report condemning what he considered to be the company's misleading accounting practices. In calculating its earnings, Blockbuster spread out the costs of purchasing video store chains and building new stores over a forty-year period, and also spread out the cost of buying large numbers of hit tapes over three years, much longer than tapes retained their value. In addition, the company relied on one-time-only franchise fees for 28 percent of its revenue. Despite this criticism, Blockbuster declined to change its accounting practices, and the company's stock price eventually regained its former level.

In November 1989, Blockbuster's largest shareholder, the United Artists Entertainment Company, announced that it

Key Dates:

1985: The first Blockbuster video store opens in Dallas.
1986: Blockbuster goes public.
1987: Founder David Cook leaves the company; company headquarters move to Fort Lauderdale.
1989: Blockbuster opens its first stores in London and in Canada.
1992: Blockbuster acquires Sound Warehouse and Music Plus chains to create Blockbuster Music stores.
1994: Media giant Viacom Inc. acquires Blockbuster.
1996: Company headquarters move to Dallas.
1999: Viacom holds an initial public offering of Blockbuster shares on the New York stock exchange.

would sell its 12 percent holding in the company, having previously sold its 28 franchised Blockbuster stores, in an effort to streamline its own business holdings. Worries that the video rental industry was reaching a saturation point cast doubts on Blockbuster's ability to keep opening stores indefinitely.

Foreign Expansion and Diversification in the Early 1990s

One response to this concern was to look to markets outside the United States for growth. Accordingly, original investor John Melk was dispatched to start up a British subsidiary, with the company's first foreign store to be opened in South London called the Ritz. Blockbuster's management continued to maintain that since the video ''superstore'' concept was open for anyone to copy, it needed to grab market share as fast as possible in order to exploit its ground-breaking concept. Carrying out this philosophy, the company opened its 1,000th store before the end of 1989.

To increase business, Blockbuster embarked on a $25 million ad campaign, and also undertook joint promotions with such fast food outlets as Domino's Pizza and McDonald's. In addition, the company accelerated foreign expansion, augmenting its operations in Britain and planning for operations in Australia and the rest of Western Europe. In the United States, the chain had opened its 1,200th store by June 1990; new outlets opened at a rate of one a day.

In October 1990, Blockbuster announced plans to cooperate with Den Fujita, the company that ran McDonald's franchises in Japan, in the development and franchising of video rental stores in that country. The following month, Blockbuster made its largest acquisition to date, when it acquired Erol's, a video store chain with 200 outlets on the East Coast and in the Midwest, for $30 million, including cash, notes, and debt assumption.

Although Blockbuster continued its strong pace of new store openings in 1990, the slowing growth of the video rental industry was becoming evident. Though the company's earnings grew an astronomical 114 percent in 1988, they contracted to a still-impressive 93 percent rate of growth in 1989, followed by a rate of 48 percent in 1990. In keeping with this trend, first quarter financial results for 1991 were disappointing. Huizenga blamed the Gulf War for keeping people interested in television news instead of rented videos. In early May, Cox Communications, one of the company's franchisers, announced that it would sell all 82 of its Blockbuster stores.

Faced with a rapidly maturing industry, Blockbuster began to expand its offerings to maintain profitability. The company began to offer video game equipment and Sega Genesis video games at some of its stores. The company considered selling audio cassettes and compact disks. Blockbuster also acquired the right to market tapes of the 1992 Olympic games.

In a further effort to encourage rentals, the company launched an advertising campaign themed ''Win in a Flash,'' and made an agreement with the Showtime cable network for a joint promotion. In August 1991, Blockbuster dropped its rental price for hit movies for the first three months after their release and shortened the time they were taken out, as a further step to raise earnings. In an effort to ensure that the company would be just as good at running video stores over the long haul as it was at opening them, Blockbuster hired more senior executives with long-term experience in the retail field.

In addition to these efforts to increase earnings in the United States, Blockbuster increased its foreign efforts. Along with its operations in the United Kingdom and Japan, the company found markets in Europe, Australia, and Latin America. With 30 stores already established in Britain, Blockbuster announced in November 1991 a large expansion in that country, designed to make it the nation's number one video rental chain. Further foreign involvement came later that month, when Philips Electronics N.V., a Dutch firm, agreed to invest $66 million in the company. As a result of this partnership, Blockbuster said that it would market Philips's newly introduced interactive compact disk systems and software in its stores. Five months later, Philips purchased an additional six million shares to raise its investment to $149 million.

To streamline its corporate management, Blockbuster bought a large office building in Florida and consolidated the company's five regional offices. As Wall Street pundits continued to predict that Blockbuster's success was short-lived, and that the video rental industry would be made obsolete by new technologies, Blockbuster's systemwide sales of $1.5 billion in 1991 earned $89 million. By the end of the year, the company had opened stores in Japan, Chile, Venezuela, Puerto Rico, Spain, Australia, New Zealand, and Guam.

In further overseas expansion, Blockbuster bought Citivision plc, the largest video rental chain in Britain, for $135 million in January 1992, anticipating that this property would provide valuable exposure in the United Kingdom, and a jumping-off point for further European growth. The company hoped that, through joint ventures, international operations would contribute a quarter of revenues by 1995. With 952 stores in nine foreign countries, Blockbuster began to intensify its efforts to expand both in products and geographically.

In October 1992, Blockbuster embarked on a series of agreements that were designed to expand the company's operations beyond its core movie rental business. Blockbuster bought Music Plus and Sound Warehouse from Shamrock Holdings, a California company, for $185 million. One month later, Blockbuster entered into an agreement with the British conglomerate

Virgin Group plc to set up ''megastores'' in the United States, Europe, and Australia. In December 1992, the first such store in the United States opened in Los Angeles, the precursor to a network of stores which Huizenga envisioned not only renting videos, but also selling and renting music, computer programs, and games, and containing high-tech ''virtual reality'' entertainment arcades. The company also hoped to improve on the traditionally low profits of music retailing by adding other, more profitable products.

By 1993, the distinctive bright blue and yellow Blockbuster logo adorned more than 3,400 video stores worldwide, about one-third of them overseas. Late in January of that year, Blockbuster branched out further, paying $25 million for a one-third, controlling share in Republic Pictures, a movie and television production and distribution company based in Hollywood. Republic's most valuable asset was its film library of television shows and films, including several John Wayne movies and the hit television series ''Bonanza.'' In March 1993, Blockbuster also purchased 48.2 percent of Spelling Entertainment, a producer of popular television shows with a large library of past programs. Moreover, Blockbuster began construction of a prototype family entertainment center in Florida.

The Controversial Viacom Merger: 1994

With its ever-growing number of corporate activities, Blockbuster was committed to diversification as a means of ensuring its future in the entertainment industry in the face of the potential onslaught of new formats—video-on-demand and satellite TV—and the shift from rentals to lower-priced tapes. In September 1993, Huizenga's Blockbuster makeover hit full stride when the company proposed a $4.7 billion merger with media giant Viacom Inc..

Toward that end, Blockbuster invested heavily in Viacom, reportedly to help strengthen Viacom's bid to purchase Paramount Communications against rival QVC Network Inc. Viacom did win the war for Paramount, but the merger talks with Blockbuster stalled, and the move cost Blockbuster a great deal as Blockbuster shareholders lost confidence in the company and wondered if its investment in Viacom would pay off. By April 1994, Blockbuster's and Viacom's stock had tumbled dramatically.

Blockbuster's glory days appeared to be over. Insiders assessed that the company was suffering from dramatic changes in the industry. Specifically, with competition stiffening due to newly emerging formats, the video industry's meteoric growth began to level off. Moreover, there was trouble internally. The merger between Blockbuster and Viacom, though eventually effected, had been rough, and Viacom was reportedly depending heavily upon Blockbuster's cash to help pay its debts and have money for future investments.

In addition, leadership at Blockbuster seemed unstable. Wayne Huizenga ceded his leadership role in the company in September 1994 and was replaced as president by Steven Berrard, who focused on rapidly expanding the company during his year-and-a-half on the job. Amid legal enablements involving earlier business dealings, however, Berrard left to be succeeded by Bill Fields in March 1996. Soon thereafter, Fields was named CEO as well and during his brief tenure attempted to revitalize the company's image. Specifically, he set about transforming Blockbuster's video rental stores into whole entertainment centers, selling t-shirts, toys, snacks, books, magazines, and CDs as well as selling and renting videos. Fields also oversaw the company's move from Fort Lauderdale to Dallas to be closer to its new, centralized distribution center. He also downsized the company's workforce, paring back about one-third of its senior staff and two-thirds of its overall staff before he left for a position at Wal-Mart. In 1996, in the wake of slipping sales, Blockbuster's worth was estimated at $4.6 billion with its stock worth only 50 percent of its 1993 price. Parent Viacom's stock price was 60 percent off its former high.

New Leadership and Independence in the Late 1990s

By the time John Antioco took over in the summer of 1997, Blockbuster was floundering. New releases weren't making it to stores by their ''street date,'' and the loss of so many key people with the company's move left it stumbling in basic store operations. Cash flow for the second quarter of 1997 at Blockbuster dropped a precipitous 70 percent. As a result, the chain scaled back on expansion and moved to refocus on its core business, video rentals. In late 1997, it exited the computer business, closing its PC Upgrades stores only months after acquiring the business.

Under Antioco, the company revived its old tag line ''Make it a Blockbuster Night,'' and sought to smooth out the problems with its state-of-the-art distribution system, which allowed it to use a customer database to determine store sites and inventory based on consumer preferences. Although the company had fallen on hard times, it still controlled 25 percent of the $16 billion a year home video market. Under Antioco, the company signed ''revenue sharing'' agreements with the major Hollywood studios, making them financial partners. Now instead of paying $65 for new tapes, Blockbuster paid $4 and turned over 30 to 40 percent of the rental income to the studio. In 1998, the company boasted that it had served nearly 60 million people who rented more than 970 million movies and video games. In early 1999, it continued to expand overseas, purchasing a Hong Kong video chain, and at home with the acquisition of Denver-based Video Visions and Videoland in Oregon and Washington. The chain was making money again, and its share of the home video retail market increased to 31 percent. Still the video market was shrinking, dropping 2.6 percent in 1998 and 8.4 percent in the first half of 1999. While revenues at Blockbuster were increasing, the company was still reporting losses, of $336.6 million in 1998, for example, compared with a $318.2 million loss in 1997.

Nevertheless, Blockbuster seemed to be effecting a turnaround, when in August 1999 Viacom made an initial public offering of around 18 percent of its stock in Blockbuster, with intentions of divesting it completely. The offering raised only $465 million; clearly, investors did not take the future of Blockbuster for granted and the company needed to search for a viable business model. Toward that end, management worked on increasing Blockbuster's market share in the growing VHA/DVD tape and disk rental category. Moreover, it also made a commitment to exploring new distribution channels, such as those offered by e-commerce.

Principal Competitors

Hollywood Entertainment Corporation; Movie Gallery Inc.

Further Reading

Chakravarty, Subrata N., "Give 'Em Variety," *Forbes*, May 2, 1988, pp. 54–56.
Calonius, Erik, "Meet the King of Video," *Fortune*, June 4, 1990, p. 208.
Castle, Steven, "Wayne's World," *Robb Report*, February 1993.
Carlson, Gus, "The Next Disney," *Miami Herald*, March 14, 1993, p. 1K.
DeGeorge, Gail, "Blockbuster's Grainy Picture," *Business Week*, May 20, 1991, pp. 40–41.
——, "Call It Blockbummer," *Business Week*, May 9, 1994, p. 31.
——, "The Video King Who Won't Hit Pause," *Business Week*, January 22, 1990, pp. 47–48.
——, "They Don't Call It Blockbuster for Nothing," *Business Week*, October 19, 1992.
Engardio, Pete, and Antonio N. Fine, "Will This Video Chain Stay on Fast Forward?" *Business Week*, June 12, 1989, pp. 72–74.
Feare, Tom, "High-Tech DC; Just the Right Ticket for Blockbuster Video," *Modern Materials Handling*, October 31, 1998, p. 34.
Forest, Stephanie Anderson, "The Script Doctor Is in at Blockbuster—Again," *Business Week*, July 28, 1997, p. 101.
Govoni, Stephen J., "Blockbuster Battles the Shorts," *CFO*, December 1991.
——, "Hot Ticket," *Information Week*, August 30, 1993, p. 28.
Katel, Peter, "New Kid on the Block, Buster," *Newsweek*, January 11, 1993.
Kirchdoerffer, Ed, "Blockbuster Set to Rebuild," *Kidscreen*, October 1, 1997, p. R7.
Miller, Michael, "Coming Soon to Your Local Video Store: Big Brother," *Wall Street Journal*, December 26, 1990, p. 9.
"Not a Blockbuster Debut," *Ottawa Citizen*, August 12, 1999, p. F3.
Roberts, Johnnie L., "Chips Off the Block," *Newsweek*, February 20, 1995, p. 42.
——, "Hit the Eject Button," *Newsweek*, August 18, 1997, p. 50.
Savitz, Eric J., "An End to Fast Forward?," *Barron's*, December 11, 1989, pp. 13, 43–46.
Siklos, Richard, "Blockbuster Finally Gets It Right," *Business Week*, March 8, 1999, p. 64.
Silverman, Edward R., "Global Go-Getters," *International Business*, October 1992.
"USA/UK Blockbuster Strikes from Home Base," *Sunday Times*, November 10, 1991.
Walsh, Matt, "Rent Things," *Florida Trend*, March 1993.
Whitford, David, "The Predator's Ball Club," *M*, June 1992, pp. 80–85.

—Elizabeth Rourke
—updated by Carrie Rothburd

Booker plc

85 Buckingham Gate
London SW1E 6PD
United Kingdom
Telephone: +44-171- 411 5500
Fax: +44-171-411- 5555
Web site: http://www.booker-plc.com

Public Company
Incorporated: 1900 as Booker Brothers, McConnell & Co. Ltd.
Employees: 23,056
Sales: £6.14 billion ($9.49 billion) (1999)
Stock Exchanges: London
Ticker Symbol: U.BOK
NAIC: 42241 General Line Grocery Wholesalers

Booker plc is a leading food wholesaler and distributor in the United Kingdom, operating a network of over 180 cash-and-carry warehouses that serve retailers and caterers rather than end consumers. Though Booker controlled a far broader empire as recently as 1997— with substantial agribusiness, food service, fish processing, and literary enterprises— heavy debt and decreasing profits compelled the company to shed most of these other businesses. Leaner and more focused, Booker committed to bolstering its food distributing division in 1998. With more than a 35 percent share of the industry in the United Kingdom, Booker provides a key link between independent retailers and caterers and the manufacturing sector. Its retail customers, who number over 100,000, include independent grocers, convenience stores, and news agents, while the 300,000 caterers that rely on its cash-and-carry warehouses encompass restaurants, pubs, cafes, hotels, nursing homes, as well as independent caterers. The company also awards the annual Booker prize for fiction.

Booker's Founding and Early Enterprises

Booker's history is inextricably linked to Europe's imperialist past. When the Congress of Vienna divided the northeast coast of South America among Great Britain, the Netherlands, and France in 1815, enterprising merchants from those countries moved quickly to exploit the region's natural resources. The Booker brothers—Josias, George, and Richard—were among these entrepreneurs. Josias was first to make the trip overseas. He arrived in the British colony of Demerara (later British Guyana) in 1815 and obtained employment as a manager of a cotton plantation. Over the course of the next two decades, Josias and his brothers set up several merchant trading houses in Liverpool in anticipation of a flourishing sugar and rum trade. They capped their preparatory activities with the 1834 establishment of Booker Brothers & Co. in British Guyana and the acquisition of their first transport ship the following year. After Richard Booker died in 1838, Josias and George consolidated vertically, purchasing sugar plantations throughout British Guyana.

As is often the case in family firms, generational changes precipitated a dramatic transformation of Booker Brothers. In 1854 Josias Booker II (eldest son of Josias I) and John McConnell (who had worked as a clerk for the Bookers since 1846) created a separate new partnership called the Demerara Company. Upon the deaths of Josias I and George in 1865 and 1866, respectively, Josias II and John McConnell assumed control of all the Booker properties, including the sugar plantations and trading companies in Britain and South America. According to a 1987 essay in Milton Moskowitz's *The Global Marketplace,* the new generation ''became the principal shopkeepers of the colony,'' building a formidable trade during the late 19th century. Their ''Liverpool Line,'' established in 1887, became one of the top shipping links between South America and Europe.

After Josias II died in the early 1880s, John McConnell inherited control of Booker Bros. & Co., George Booker & Co., and his own John McConnell & Co. McConnell's sons, A.J. and F.V., took possession of the three businesses in 1890 and merged them in 1900 as Booker Brothers, McConnell & Co. Ltd. Guyanan operations had by this time expanded to include sales of food and general merchandise at the retail and wholesale levels.

The company prospered throughout the early 20th century by maintaining its concentration on the sugar and rum trade and limiting its acquisition activities to the Caribbean region. Booker McConnell made its first public stock offering in 1920

Company Perspectives:

Booker's food wholesaling business is one of the largest in the U.K., supplying more than 400,000 independent grocers, CTNs, convenience stores, and caterers. Its national network of cash and carry branches now includes many that have extensive specialist departments dedicated to the needs of caterers.

and was listed on the London Stock Exchange that same year. (The company name was shortened to Booker, McConnell Ltd. in 1968; in 1986 it would be renamed Booker plc.)

Booker Diversifies in the 1950s and 1960s

Political unrest in Guyana during the early 1950s prompted John ''Jock'' Campbell, chairman of Booker from 1952 to 1967, to diversify both geographically and commercially. Diversification became imperative after Guyana won its independence from Great Britain in 1966 and elected a Communist government. Booker was eventually compelled to sell its sugar plantations and other businesses in that country to the government. Ironically, Guyanan and other Caribbean officials asked Booker and other British sugar moguls to help manage their struggling operations in the early 1990s. Their request for management advice prompted the formation of Booker Tate, a joint venture with Tate & Lyle, in the early 1990s.

Campbell's ''hedge-building'' investments in the United Kingdom, Canada, and central Africa varied widely, from engineering to supermarketing to agricultural consulting. One of the most unusual diversifications made during this era was a division the company called ''Authors.'' This highly unusual sideline developed after the discovery of a loophole in the British tax code that allowed the conglomerate to purchase an author's copyrights, pay him or her a fat fee partly at the expense of the taxpayer, and then collect the royalties. Agatha Christie and Ian Fleming were just two of the bestselling authors in Booker's stable.

The Authors venture soon spawned another celebrated aside. According to Booker's 1994 annual report, Fleming suggested to Campbell over a game of golf that the company pump some of the millions it was earning on the backs of writers back into the literary community. Although Booker was reluctant to give the creator of the James Bond character full credit for the idea, his suggestion influenced the 1969 presentation of the first Booker McConnell Prize for Fiction (now the Booker Prize), which is bestowed upon the best novel published in Britain by a writer from the British Commonwealth. P.H. Newby's *Something to Answer For* won the first Booker Prize, which has become the most coveted and highly esteemed award in British book publishing. The recipient of the honor receives a cash award, and the status of the prize is so great that novels that are short-listed for the award often see dramatic jumps in sales.

Booker Enters Agribusiness and Food Distribution in the 1970s–80s

Booker's business focus shifted in the late 1970s and early 1980s. The company divested itself of its money-losing engineering interests, sold its last remaining import/export subsidiary, and made several acquisitions in agribusiness and food distribution. Perhaps anticipating increasing demand for low-fat, relatively low-cost sources of protein, the firm's acquisitions included poultry breeding operations and fish breeding and processing businesses during this time.

One of the company's first transitional moves came with the 1978 purchase of ten percent of International Basic Economy Corporation (IBEC). IBEC had been founded by Nelson Rockefeller and his brothers in 1947 in the hopes of profitably boosting developing countries' economies. Arbor Acres, an American producer of broiler breeder stock that had been operating since before World War II, became part of the IBEC in 1959. Arbor Acres hoped to expand its chicken breeding network from the United States to Latin America, Europe, the Middle East, and Asia. However, when IBEC's sales dropped precipitously in the late 1970s, the Rockefellers elected to liquidate. Booker helped that process along, increasing its share of IBEC to 45 percent in 1980 and a majority interest by 1985. Rodman C. Rockefeller, Nelson's son, served as chairman of Arbor Acres Farms and on Booker's board of directors into the early 1990s.

Infrequent acquisitions of fish breeders and processors in the late 1970s, 1980s, and early 1990s slowly evolved into a significant sector of Booker's business. The company bought W&F Fish Products in 1978, Atlantic Sea Products in 1987, and Marine Harvest International in 1994. By that time, Booker's annual report boasted that it was the largest specialist seafood group in the United Kingdom.

Booker also invested heavily in health foods during the 1980s. The company made at least four acquisitions in this industry in 1986 alone, and continued its buying spree in ensuing years. Health food holdings during this period included Britain's largest health food chain, Holland & Barrett; La Vie Claire, a prominent health food company in France; vitamin and nutritional supplement manufacturers in the United States and Great Britain; and several organic food producers.

During the last half of the 1980s, Booker acquired several wholesale food distributors, including E.C. Steed (1986); Copeman Ridley (1987); J. Evershed & Son (1988); Linfood Cash & Carry (1988); and County Catering Co. (1988). By the end of the decade, the company had amassed Britain's largest food wholesaling business. Its customers, which numbered in the hundreds of thousands, included independent grocers, convenience stores, and caterers. It was around this time that the company shifted its business strategy to concentrate primarily on food wholesaling and distribution to the catering trade. Booker sealed its leading position in that industry with the 1990 acquisition of Fitch Lovell plc, a leading processor and distributor of fish and other food products, for £279.7 million.

In keeping with its new focus, Booker divested several peripheral businesses during this period. In 1986, the company sold its chain of Budgen convenience stores, which had been purchased during the 1950s-era diversification. The French health food interests were divested in 1989, and those in the United Kingdom were sold in 1990 and 1991.

Booker purchased the balance of Arbor Acres' equity (ten percent) from the Rockefellers in 1991 for $22 million. Under

Key Dates:

1834: Booker Brothers & Co. is established.
1900: Booker Brothers, McConnell & Co. Ltd. is formed.
1920: Company makes its first public stock offering.
1966: Guyana wins its independence from Great Britain; this compels Booker to diversify.
1968: Company name shortened to Booker, McConnell Ltd.
1969: The first Booker Prize is awarded.
1978: Booker acquires International Basic Economy Corporation (IBEC).
1986: Company renamed Booker plc.
1994: Booker acquires Marine Harvest International.
1998: Booker commits to focusing on food distribution business.

its new management, Arbor Acres had grown to become the world's largest broiler breeding company, with customers in over 70 countries worldwide. It had emerged as the cornerstone of Booker's American agribusiness division, which also included North America's leading turkey breeder, Nicholas Turkey Breeding Farms, and CWT Farms International Inc., a producer of broiler hatching eggs.

The Early 1990s

Booker adjusted its organizational structure in the early 1990s by establishing four primary divisions: food distribution, which included wholesaling and food service; food processing, which incorporated operations producing fish and prepared foods; U.S. agribusiness, comprised of the poultry breeding operations; and U.K. agribusiness, which included salmon farming, plant breeding, sugar industry services, and forestry. Food distribution contributed about half of the company's net income in the early 1990s, while the international agribusiness and fish processing chipped in about 20 percent each.

Characterized as a "dull but worthy" company, Booker was dragged into the limelight as competition in the British supermarket industry intensified. In 1992, Booker launched its first consumer advertising campaign in support of the "Family Choice" branded products it distributed to thousands of independent grocers. These Booker clients were experiencing increased price competition from deep discounters that had entered the market to take advantage of recession-weary Brits.

Booker's sales increased steadily in the early 1990s, from £2.93 billion in 1990 to £3.72 billion in 1994. Net income increased from £49.9 million in 1990 to £59.7 million in 1993, then declined to £45.8 million in 1994. The company blamed the earnings slide on expenses related to the reorganization of the food wholesaling and food service divisions, as well as the acquisition and rationalization of Marine Harvest International, the Scotland-based salmon farming firm. Predictably, Booker Chairman Jonathan Taylor, expressed confidence that the company's reorganization would begin to pay increased dividends as Great Britain cycled out of recession in the latter part of the 1990s.

Rather than wait, however, Booker sought to remedy its slump through further acquisitions under the leadership of a new chief executive officer, Charles Bowen. In 1996, Booker purchased Nurdin & Peacock, a chain of wholesale cash and carry stores that greatly expanded Booker's food distribution network. As part of its effort to integrate the new stores, Booker launched an 18-month project to form a centralized distribution center the company named Heartland.

Restructuring the Late 1990s

Despite these measures, Booker did not emerge from its slump. Saddled by enormous debt and sinking profits, the company sold Booker Prepared Foods group, its food manufacturing division in July 1997. The enterprise, which supplied major U.K. retailers with a range of prepared food products, was bought by Prize Food Group for £57 million. Despite the revenues this transaction brought Booker, the company reported another net loss for 1997. In a unanimous decision, Booker's board of directors ousted Charles Bowen in March 1998.

Booker thereupon commenced a comprehensive review of its operations, a project which one company executive described to *AFX News* as "wide ranging and all-embracing." The process was overseen by Booker's newly appointed CEO, Alan Smith, and its chairman, Jonathon Taylor. In June 1998, the company released its findings. Committing to focusing on its food service operations, Booker pledged to rid itself of businesses outside this newly defined core competency. Booker's agribusiness ventures in the U.S. and the U.K., fish processing division, Daehnfeldt seeds business, its stake in sugar-related joint ventures, and its interest in Agatha Christie Ltd. (which held the rights to the author's work) were all slated to be sold. "We have decided that a dedicated food distribution group with a new management structure is the right way forward," Taylor proclaimed to *AFX News* on June 2, 1998.

Although Booker netted £156 million from initial sales, it was clear by November 1998 that even more cuts were necessary. Stuart Rose, who was named chief executive in October, announced that quarterly earnings were so low that Booker might breach certain covenants with its banks. In response to this announcement, Booker's stock price plummeted over 46 percent, lowering the company's market value by more than £130 million. However, by April 1999, the company had reached an agreement with its creditors. Contemporaneously, as part of an its effort to increase its cash flow, Booker sold Booker Foodservice, Recheio (its Portuguese food wholesaling joint venture), its Spanish cash-and-carry division, and Booker Wholesale Foods.

After pledging that cash-and-carry was to be the company's lifeblood, Rose and new Chairman John Napier instituted a series of measures to boost the division's sales, which had been below expectations in 1998. A sweeping efficiency program led to about 400 job cuts, and the central office strove to improve the appearance, service, and profitability of each branch store. A weekly "BlockBuster" promotion held at various branches was intended to drive sales. In addition to expanding the array of goods available at its stores, Booker committed to expanding its private label brands. Both the "Happy Shopper" line for retailers and the "Chef's Larder" products for caterers offered Booker enhanced margins.

The results of Booker's aggressive reorganizing and pruning could not be immediately determined. Though sales rose in the first months of 1999, company profits were eroded by the cost of restructuring the company. However, Booker remained optimistic about its future. As John Napier told *Dow Jones Business News*, "we look forward to a significantly better year."

Principal Subsidiaries

Booker Belmont Wholesale Limited; Booker Cash & Carry; Booker Cemasce Cash & Carry; Fletcher Smith Limited (65%).

Principal Competitors

ASDA Group Plc; J Sainsbury plc; Safeway plc; Somerfield plc; Tesco plc.

Further Reading

"Agatha Christie Helps to Bolster Booker," *Financial Times*, September 11, 1998.

Bidlake, Suzanne, "Booker Boosts Small Stores in Price War," *Marketing*, January 23, 1992, p. 6.

"Booker Buys Aquaculture Firm," *Wall Street Journal Europe*, October 24, 1994.

"Booker Fish Division Finally Goes on the Block," *Frozen and Chilled Foods*, July 1, 1998.

"Booker to Focus on Distribution Business After Strategic Review," *AFX News*, June 2, 1998.

Bykov, Dimitry, Andrei Nemzer, and Alla Latynina, "First Booker Russian Novel Prize Awarded," *Current Digest of the Post-Soviet Press*, January 13, 1993, p. 16.

"Caribbean Sugar: Come Back, Slavemasters," *Economist*, January 23, 1993, p. 83.

Jarvis, Paul, "Booker Chief Confirms Woes; Shares Plunge," *Wall Street Journal Europe*, November 11, 1998.

——, "Booker Reaches Financing Deal With Its Banks," *Wall Street Journal Europe*, April 16, 1999.

"Management-Led Team Buys Booker Food Manufacturers," *Frozen and Chilled Foods*, July 1, 1997.

Moskowitz, Milton, *The Global Marketplace*, New York: Macmillan Publishing Company, 1987.

"Radical Retailer Turning Over a New Leaf at Booker," *Financial Times*, June 6, 1998.

"So Far, So Good," *Investors Chronicle*, February 12, 1993, 21.

Wray, Richard, "Booker Says Chief Executive Bowen Was Asked to Leave," *AFX News*, March 17, 1998.

—April D. Gasbarre
—updated by Rebecca Stanfel

Booth Creek Ski Holdings, Inc.

1000 South Frontage Road West
Suite 100
Vail, Colorado 81657
U.S.A.
Telephone: (970) 476-4030
Fax: (970) 479-0291
Web site: http://boothcreek.com

Private Company
Incorporated: 1996
Employees: 6,254
Sales: $104.9 million (1998)
NAIC: 71392 Skiing Facilities

Booth Creek Ski Holdings, Inc. is the fourth largest ski resort company in North America, overseeing the operations of resorts from California to New Hampshire. Although a young company, Booth Creek boasts some of the most high profile ski resorts in the industry—including regions near Lake Tahoe and Jackson Hole, Wyoming—and is managed by industry veterans, many of whom worked in the 1980s for Vail Associates. Heading up Booth Creek is George Gillett, an entrepreneur who since the 1960s has built fortunes around businesses as diverse as meatpacking plants to the management of football teams. While Gillett's expertise in the ski industry is the hallmark of the business's success, Booth Creek is also owned and funded in part by John Hancock Mutual Life Insurance Company and the Canadian Imperial Bank of Commerce.

Antecedents of Booth Creek: 1985 through the Mid-1990s

George Gillett founded Booth Creek after intimately acquainting himself with the ski industry in the 1980s. Growing up in Racine, Wisconsin, Gillett discovered early on that his real aim in life was high finance, a discovery which led him far from his Midwestern roots.

It was perhaps Gillett's energetic career and diverse experiences that had made him so well suited for the risky ventures of the ski industry in the 1980s. In the 1960s Gillett began his business career as one of the managers of the Miami Dolphins, and by the middle of that decade he had parlayed his success with the team into an ownership of the Harlem Globetrotters, which he later sold for $3 million. With the revenue from his basketball team Gillett purchased a meatpacking plant and began buying up television stations; by the mid-1980s Gillett was the largest private owner of television stations in the country, the number of which totaled 17 in all.

It was at this point, in the mid-1980s, that Gillett became involved with the skiing industry. An avid skier, Gillett became president in 1985 of Vail Associates, the company which at the time owned the Vail ski resort in Colorado. Three years later, Gillett bought the resort outright, using revenue from his television stations to pay for the $130 million price tag.

Gillett's tactics with Vail proved him to be an aggressive, ambitious businessman: in less than a decade he turned Vail from a popular if not tremendously well known ski resort into the most successful and fashionable ski destination in the country. After becoming owner of Vail, Gillett set out to make the area desirable not only to skiers, but to those seeking general recreation as well. To that end, he developed a great deal of real estate at nearby Arrowhead and Beaver Creek, a move which, while further popularizing the sport, made him not a few enemies amongst skiing "purists."

Gillett's far reach into so many areas of business came crashing down on him at the end of the decade, when he was forced to default on almost $1 billion worth of debt. Declaring personal bankruptcy in 1991, Gillett was forced to give up not only such personal property as his 250,000-acre Oregon ranch and his $5 million car collection, but he had to cede control of Vail as well. Gillett managed, however, to save himself from complete ruin. He worked out a way by which to collect $1.5 million a year in salary from Vail's new owners, Apollo Advisors LP, which, along with some other revenue saved from his meatpacking plant, were used as seed money to start Booth Creek.

The Changing Face of Skiing: Booth Creek and its Competitors in the 1990s

After the spectacular failure of Gillett's Vail Associates, his new company, which he founded in 1996, was forced to look

Company Perspectives:

The resorts Booth Creek currently owns are friendly regional resorts whose appeal is in their proximity, unique heritage and commitment to provide exceptional guest service. Their concept rests on preserving the individuality of these gems, while establishing consistency from the standpoint of a total commitment to exceeding guests' expectations.

outside of Colorado for acquisitions and further growth. By the mid-1990s, however, competition among resorts had been reduced to a battle between only a handful of powerful national companies, each of which owned a multitude of prime skiing real estate across the country. Areas such as Vail, Aspen, and Jackson Hole were already controlled by such competitors as American Skiing Company and Vail Resorts; what was left for Booth Creek, then, were lesser known, smaller regions which attracted a more sedate, less fashionable—and therefore less wealthy—customer base.

By the 1990s the skiing industry was divided between two factions, one of which was traditional, holding on tightly to the notion that ski resorts should exist purely for the sake of skiing, and the other of which took its cue from the more expansive and commercial idea of generalized recreation, of which skiing was only a part. Exemplifying the latter, resort skiing, was the CEO of Vail Resorts, Adam Aron, who, while being the head of the largest ski company in North America, made efforts to attract every type of consumer to his locations, whether they be competitive skiers or day-tripping shoppers. Companies like Aron's, according to Bill Saporito, a writer for *Time,* were "pouring record sums into capital improvements, adding fast chair lifts and such amusements as skating rinks and snow-tubing shoots to attract more nonskiing vacationers or at least divert them while their partners, spouses and children were on the slopes."

On the opposite end of the scale was the CEO of Aspen Skiing Company, Pat O'Donnell, who held that a ski resort should cater to skiers, and to skiers only. To such purists, the idea that ski resorts should look more like Club Med than sports refuges was repugnant. Writing in *Skiing* magazine in 1997, Lee Carlson noted that the "notion of competition makes many skiing purists groan. If Vail and other resorts are going head-to-head with beach resorts and golf resorts . . . then they will have to be more like these places. To the purists, such places are for out-of-shape, conformist people, while ski areas have always been the province of athletic, free-spirited, adventurous sorts."

Gillett, in developing a strategic growth plan for Booth Creek, had to decide which route to take. Seeing the future of skiing being more tied to general recreation than the sport itself, Gillett's company, when acquiring property, chose to focus not only on the quality of slopes, but the development of real estate, golf courses, and swimming pools as well. The advantages to such a plan were many: Booth Creek's locations attracted serious skiers and novices alike, and, with the development of other amenities, the company's resorts could advertise themselves as multi-seasonal retreats.

1996–99: The Rapid Expansion of Booth Creek

By 1996 Gillett had raised over $162 million, all of which was intended to go towards acquisitions for Booth Creek. Never one to go about things prudently, Gillett began a buying spree of resorts the magnitude of which could only be accomplished by a company with a great deal of capital and connections. Once it had the financial backing, Gillett's company purchased eight resorts nationwide in less than a year, beginning in September 1996. All of the resorts purchased matched Booth Creek's strategy of finding areas close to large metropolitan cities which could supply day tripping and weekend skiers. While none of Booth Creek's purchases were of the same high profile as Vail, they were all mid-sized and had a great deal of growth potential, both in relation to slopes and housing.

In September 1996 Booth Creek purchased the Mount Cranmore ski resort, located in the northern part of New Hampshire. Mount Cranmore was a popular destination, attracting over 100,000 skiers annually, and was located not far from the Boston area. In that same month, Booth Creek bought New Hampshire's Waterville Valley resort. Both Mount Cranmore and Waterville Valley had previously been owned by Les Otten, CEO of American Skiing Company, one of Booth Creek's main competitors.

Only one week after purchasing the East Coast resorts, Booth Creek acquired a cluster of resorts from Fibreboard Corporation, a company which usually specialized not in resort operations but the production of industrial insulation. Through Fibreboard, Booth Creek became the owner of Northstar-at-Tahoe and Sierra-at-Tahoe (both of which were a half day's drive from San Francisco) and Bear Mountain, located in Southern California. Booth Creek paid about $127 million for the resorts, a price considered by many in the industry to be inflated. Still, these acquisitions were quite a boon for the young company; Tahoe had an international reputation as one of the most desirable skiing destinations in the country, while Bear Mountain was located only a few hours from both Los Angeles and San Diego, two cities in which thousands of skiers resided.

In 1997, Booth Creek continued its rapid pace, purchasing four peaks near the Seattle area: Alpental, Summit East, Summit West, and Summit Central. Called simply the Summit, the resort was one of Washington's largest and was located less than an hour's drive from Seattle. Later that year Booth Creek bought the fashionable Grand Targhee, located near the Grand Tetons and Jackson Hole, Wyoming. Known for receiving one of the highest averages of annual snowfalls in the country, Grand Targhee was also a popular summer destination, a reputation Booth Creek expanded with further development of multi-seasonal housing and activities.

Within one year Gillett's company had risen to international prominence, becoming by 1997 the fourth largest ski resort in North America. Although prevented by a no-compete clause in his personal bankruptcy filing from purchasing resorts in the state of Colorado until 1999, Gillett kept Booth Creek's headquarters in Vail and was able from that location to keep a watchful eye on skiing trends and the company's competition. That the company did so was important, as the industry in the mid- to late 1990s was facing a slow-down in revenue, even as its investors poured more

Key Dates:

1988: George Gillett purchases Vail Associates.
1991: Gillett declares personal bankruptcy and has to give up Vail.
1996: Booth Creek is founded when Gillett regroups.
1997: Booth Creek acquires eight resort properties in the span of one year, becoming the fourth largest ski resort in the country.

and more capital into slope improvements, speedier lifts, and more efficient equipment. Moreover, the competition, to say the least, was stiff. By 1997, according to *Time,* Booth Creek and three other, more powerful competitors controlled over 30 percent of the nation's 500 hundred or so resorts.

With huge companies controlling most of Booth Creek's competition, and the nationwide scattering of Booth Creek's properties, it became important for the company to find a way in which to increase customer loyalty. To that end, the company introduced two programs by which a customer could receive discounts, free lift tickets, and other specialized treatment at any of the company's locations nationwide: the "Vertical Value" program was honored at all of the company's resorts, while the "Vertical Plus" system, available at Northstar, Sierra, and Bear Mountain, gave members their own lift lines and enabled them to automatically charge food, drinks, and clothing to their accounts at any of the three resorts. "Vertical Value" and "Vertical Plus" were both examples of the way in which Booth Creek supported the notion that with customer service, combined with quality slopes, came customer loyalty. Encouraging such loyalty was important for the young company, as Booth Creek's locations were spread across the country, and, in many cases, were located near other resorts which were just as well, if not better, known.

Despite Booth Creek's phenomenal and rapid rise in the ski industry, there were some insiders who questioned the longevity of the company. During the 1980s Gillett, with his involvement in incongruous, risky ventures, had earned a reputation in the resort industry as a businessman obsessed with buying, spending, and selling. One industry expert, who in a 1997 interview with the *Denver Post* remained anonymous, questioned Gillett's ability to maintain a stable business, especially one which had grown so fast: "Why is he (Gillett) buying those ski resorts? Because they're for sale. George can't stop himself if the money is available. He's a born gambler. George will die doubling-down on something."

However, despite—or perhaps because of—Gillett's reputation for risk-taking, there were also many in the industry who recognized Gillett, and Booth Creek, as a boon to the industry. Industry executive Stacy Gardner, in the same *Denver Post* article, claimed that the company's growth plan, which centered around popularizing mid-sized resorts, was "critical to the success of the ski industry." Certainly the company's sales near the end of the decade buoyed that sentiment; in 1998 Booth Creek brought in over $104 million.

Principal Competitors

American Skiing Company; Intrawest Corp.; Vail Resorts, Inc.

Further Reading

Carlson, Lee, "Skiing Crossroads," *Skiing*, September 1997, p. 116.
"Fibreboard to Sell Resort Group," *Business Wire*, September 10, 1996.
Parker, Penny, "Gillett Buys Another One," *Denver Post*, December 31, 1996, p. C1.
——, "Sky High Comeback," *Denver Post*, February 23, 1997, p. I1.
Saporito, Bill, "King of the Hill: After an Epic Wipeout, Ski Mogul George Gillett Tackles the Slopes Again," *Time*, December 29, 1997, p. 114.
Stern, Richard L. "Bailing Out Vail," *Forbes*, May 27, 1991, p. 16.
——, "Crying All the Way to the Bank," *Forbes*, September 14, 1992, p. 24.

—Rachel H. Martin

Boscov's Department Store, Inc.

4500 Perkiomen Avenue
Reading, Pennsylvania 19606
U.S.A.
Telephone: (610) 779-2000
Fax: (610) 370-3495
Web site: http://www. boscovs.com

Private Company
Founded: 1911
Employees: 9,000
Sales: $846 million (1998)
NAIC: 45211 Department Stores

Boscov's Department Stores, Inc., operates one of the last remaining full-service department stores, featuring men's, women's, and children's apparel; shoes; jewelry; cosmetics; housewares; appliances; toys; stationery; and sporting goods. Some stores also feature travel agencies, vision and hearing centers, hair salons, pet departments, and restaurants. Twenty-five of the company's 34 stores are located in Pennsylvania; other stores are located in New Jersey, Delaware, New York, and Maryland. All stores are within a three-hour commute of the company's headquarters in Reading for easy access to its warehouses and central administrative functions. While some stores are free standing, most are in malls. Boscov's was founded by Solomon Boscov in 1911 in Reading, Pennsylvania, and is still family owned and operated. The company's popular slogan ''Have You Boscoved Today?'' appears in much of its advertising.

Meager Beginnings in 1911

Solomon Boscov emigrated to the United States in 1911 with only about $12 in his pocket. After a fruitless search for work in Washington, D.C., he traveled to Reading, Pennsylvania. In Reading Boscov could communicate better, because many inhabitants spoke Pennsylvania Dutch, which had similarities to Boscov's native Yiddish. Boscov used the little money he had to buy drygoods, which he rolled into a sack and peddled to farmers and homemakers. People liked Boscov: he was warm, honest, and had a great sense of humor. In a short time, he established a route of regular customers throughout Lancaster and Bucks counties. Boscov traveled his route on foot and did chores in exchange for lodging. He sometimes bartered merchandise for meals. Boscov made many friends along his route, who affectionately called him ''Sammy.''

Within a year, Boscov had saved enough money to buy a horse and wagon and to increase his inventory. He became a partner in a general merchandise store and eventually went into business for himself, opening a drygoods store in his family's living room at the corner of Ninth and Pike Streets in Reading. Word of Boscov's fair prices and quality merchandise spread quickly, and his business thrived. Boscov expanded only a year after opening his first store. By 1913, his store occupied all of the row houses on the street.

A Family Venture by 1954

Boscov's son Albert inherited his father's charisma and love of the deal. As a boy, he often listened while his father chatted with late-night customers and watched him cut prices for people with little money. Albert began his own sales career when he was just five, selling his used toys to neighborhood children. As he grew older, he ran errands for his father. Boscov's son-in-law Edwin Lakin joined the business in 1954 and helped him renovate and enlarge the store. After serving in the United States Navy during the Korean War, Albert moved into the family business full-time.

In 1962 Albert opened the second Boscov's, a full-service department store in suburban Reading. Albert shared his father's business philosophies: he was a hands-on manager who made friends with the customers. Albert also had a knack for advertising. He enlarged the company's newspaper ads and made them more compelling. His innovations helped quadruple the company's sales in two years.

Hard Times in the 1960s

The Boscov family endured its share of hardship in the late 1960s. In February 1967 a fire destroyed the original Boscov's at Ninth and Pike Streets. A new 60,000-square-foot store,

Company Perspectives:

Boscov's Department Store, Inc., delivers exceptional satisfaction to millions of the most discerning customers each year by blending state-of-the-art technological support with customer friendly service within a tastefully fashionable environment. Whether shopping over the web or ''just browsing'' through one of its full-line, full-service department stores, Boscov's customers are treated to a depth and breadth of inventory unlike anywhere else in the world.

As a full-service department store, we cater to all of our customers' needs by providing a range of products and services in each store unequalled in retailing today, including men's, children's, and women's apparel; shoes; jewelry; cosmetics; gifts; housewares; stationery; toys; sports equipment; and appliances. In addition, many of Boscov's stores contain special service departments such as travel agencies, hair salons, restaurants, film processing, optical and hearing centers, which serve to further enhance the company's position as a class full-service department store.

referred to as ''Boscov's East,'' was built in its place. The opening ceremony for the store was spectacular—but short. While the Boscov family was busy greeting customers, scooping ice cream, and ringing up sales at Boscov's East, the second store, Boscov's West, was burning to the ground. Fire gutted the store. The Boscovs were devastated.

Many customers shared the family's grief over the loss of their store. Calls swamped the switchboard and letters arrived in bulk from loyal customers encouraging the Boscovs to rebuild. They did. Boscov's West reopened in 1968. Solomon passed away in 1969.

Expansion and Success in the 1970s and 1980s

Boscov's spread beyond Reading in 1972 with the opening of a store in Lebanon, Pennsylvania. The Lebanon store was the first of many expansions, all within a 150-mile radius of Reading. The company proceeded to open many stores in the Mid-Atlantic region, which encompasses Pennsylvania, Delaware, Maryland, New Jersey, and New York.

Boscov's believed that utilizing the latest technology was paramount to the Company's continued success. In the mid-1970s, it developed one of the first retailing inventory management systems, which used bar-code scanning and credit-card readers to significantly reduce the transaction time of customer purchases. Such technology enhanced customer service, minimized errors, and generated accurate data for marketing and inventory purposes.

In a time when retail stores were specializing and consolidating, Boscov's decided to remain a ''true'' department store, offering everything from athletic wear to kitchen knives. Boscov put a strong emphasis on the stores' toy departments, which featured dolls, trains, books, games, and radio-controlled cars and trucks. The stores carried all the major brands and offered the company's own brands as well. Boscov hoped the stores' toy departments would make the shopping experience more enjoyable. ''Retailing should be fun. Nobody buys something only because they need it. They enjoy the fun of shopping,'' Boscov said in *Chain Store.* ''We like to give people a reason for coming to Boscov's, even when they don't want to buy anything. They enjoy themselves and hopefully we make a friend.''

The company also tried to entice customers into its stores with college courses and club meetings, which were held in its auditoriums. Boscov believed that customers would shop in the store on their way to or from their courses or meetings. He even offered a $10,000 annual award to the public relations person who scheduled the most programs in his or her store.

Because its footwear departments were a favorite among customers, Boscov's stores held many shoe sales whenever a special course or program was being offered. About 8 to 10 percent of Boscov's sales stemmed from its footwear departments, which were about 2,150 square feet. Boscov attributed the success of the stores' footwear departments to buyers Charlie and Judy Campion, who were with the company for more than 30 years. Vendors described the couple as being passionate and aggressive about their work. The Campions had nearly 100 percent control over Boscov's shoe departments and received a percent of their profits. ''They always seem to have their pulse on the business. They have a very focused market strategy that plays well in middle America,'' said Easy Spirit's Jeff Cosgrove in *Footwear News.* While the footwear departments also sold high-priced lines, the vast majority of their sales came from basic, moderately priced shoes that sold for $30 to $50. The stores' best-selling private brand was ''Charlies,'' a line named after Charlie Campion that sold for about $18 a pair.

To establish its presence in the communities surrounding its stores, the company sponsored programs such as the Boy Scouts and 4-H Clubs and raised funds for a day-care center for handicapped children and for advanced life support services for a community's ambulances. Boscov himself headed the campaign to raise $3.5 million to open the F.M. Kirby Center for the Performing Arts in Wilkes-Barre, Pennsylvania.

Boscov also developed positive relationships with his vendors. ''Retailing has become so tough. We're always fighting for better pricing. Sometimes we forget about the vendor. We're aggressively fighting for everything we can get—but we let them know that we love them,'' Boscov said in *Chain Store.*

Improvements in the 1990s

In the mid-1990s, Boscov's expanded its stores' Ready to Assemble (RTA) furniture departments. The company starting selling RTA furniture in one store in the early 1980s and it proved very successful. Soon after, Boscov's began selling RTA furniture in all of its stores. In the 1990s, RTA items became more practical and attractive, so the company decided to offer customers a larger selection. ''When we first got into the category, we were focusing on items such as television stands, carts, and entertainment pieces, which can't even compare to the fashionable and functional entertainment centers that we sell today,'' said Bill Gallagher, senior vice-president of merchandising, in *HFN.* While Boscov's sold mostly RTA entertainment centers, the stores also sold accent pieces, desks, and casual dining

Key Dates:

1911: Solomon Boscov opens the first store in Reading, Pennsylvania.
1954: Son-in-law Edwin Larkin joins the company.
1962: Son Albert opens the second Boscov's.
1967: "Boscov's East" reopens after burning down.
1968: "Boscov's West" reopens after burning down.
1972: Boscov's opens store in Lebanon, Pennsylvania.
1998: Company introduces automatic replenishing system.

furniture. RTA departments were located next to housewares, so the stores could cross-merchandise some items.

In 1998 Boscov's tested database management software that allowed it to better understand the needs of a market surrounding a particular store. The company first tested this software on its newly opened store in Albany, New York. The software extracted data such as customer information and purchasing patterns from the store and incorporated it into a geographic map. The map presented the information in easy-to-understand color-coded graphics rather than text reports. This information clearly illustrated the demographics surrounding the Albany store and allowed Boscov's to more closely tailor its store and its advertising to match the needs of its customers.

Kim Kolakowski, director of credit, promotion, and marketing, explained in *HFN* how this software helped the company's Vineland New Jersey store: "We thought we knew what the market area was. But 90 days after the store opened, we determined there were several ZIP codes that we were drawing customers from but where we had no media coverage. We realigned our advertising and had a tremendous sales lift."

Also in 1998, Boscov's implemented an automatic replenishment system, a PC-based system that automatically sent inventory information to vendors when sales were rung up. Vendors then sent replacement inventory directly to the store. With its automatic replenishment system, the store rarely ran out of merchandise, and this greatly improved customer service. For example, when a customer purchased a pair of sneakers, an electronic message was sent to the vendor, who shipped another pair. In many cases, the company was able to bypass its warehouse distribution center, which kept costs down.

With competition such as the Internet and mail-order catalogs, the retail department store business is tougher than ever. Boscov's, however, maintains a niche in one-stop shopping with a personal touch. As of 1999, Albert Boscov visited one store a week and lived by the motto "expect the unexpected." And when trouble arises, he is often first on the scene to help out. Customers have spotted him serving fudge and guiding drivers in a crowded parking lot. He was once mistaken for a cafeteria worker while serving food. The rest of Boscov's management team shares his philosophies. The Campions have taken out the trash, and Ken Larkin, vice-president of operations, directed traffic at a grand opening in Scranton, Pennsylvania. Albert Boscov's down-to-earth style has helped make his stores a success. He explained to *Chain Store:* "It's very difficult to know why people like you. But I'm glad they do."

Principal Competitors

Dayton Hudson Corporation; Federated Department Stores, Inc.; J.C. Penney Company, Inc.; Sears, Roebuck and Co.; Wal-Mart Stores, Inc.

Further Reading

"Albert R. Boscov," *Chain Store Executive with Shopping Center Age,* December 1996, p. 96.
"Albert R. Boscov," *Philadelphia Business Journal,* June 25, 1990, p. C10.
Allegrezza, Ray, "Higher Calling: Boscov's Takes RTA to the Next Level," *HFN: The Weekly Newspaper for the Home Furnishings Network,* March 11, 1996, p.13.
Berger, Jane, "Computers Automatically Order New Merchandise When Retailers Run Low," *Tribune Business News,* September 28, 1997.
"Did You Boscov Today?" *Private Placement Reporter,* February 1, 1999, p. 1.
McNally, Pamela, "Boscov's Department Store," *Footwear News,* December 6, 1993, p. 34.
Power, Denise, "An Enterprising Boscov's," *WWD,* April 15, 1998, p. 11.
——, "Boscov's Creates Information Link: Chain Aims for Easy Access to Point-of-Sale Data Via Windows," *HFN: The Weekly Newspaper for the Home Furnishings Network,* April 20, 1998, p.10.
——, "Boscov's Upgrades Store Systems," *Daily News Record,* April 15, 1998, p. 7.
——, "Boscov's Gets Graphic on Data," *HFN: The Weekly Newspaper for the Home Furnishing Network,* December 21, 1998, p. 8.
Robins, Gary, "Losing Wait: Boscov's Boosts New Accounts by Speeding Processing," *Stores,* October 1992, p. 71.
Storm, Bill, "Boscov's Gives Toys Red Carpet Treatment," *Playthings,* August 1998, p. 40.
Thilmary, Jean, "Boscov's Faster Flow of Goods," *WWD,* May 26, 1999, p. 32.

—Tracey Vasil Biscontini

Bright Horizons Family Solutions, Inc.

One Kendall Square
Building 200
Cambridge, Massachusetts 02139
U.S.A.
Telephone: (617) 577-8020
Fax: (617) 577-8967
Web site: http://www.brighthorizons.com

Public Company
Incorporated: 1998
Employees: 9,350
Sales: $209.4 million (1998)
Stock Exchanges: NASDAQ
Ticker Symbol: BFAM
NAIC: 62441 Child Day Care Services

Bright Horizons Family Solutions, Inc. is the largest provider of corporate-sponsored child-care and early education in the United States. Working with some of the nation's largest employers, the company sets up and manages work-site child-care centers. In addition to regular daily child-care, the company provides before- and after-school care for older children, emergency back-up care, summer camps, and special-event care. Bright Horizons counts among its clients 68 *Fortune* 500 companies and 45 of *Working Mother* magazine's "100 Best Companies for Working Mothers," including Citigroup, Time Warner, and Motorola. The company is expanding its services to include private and charter elementary schools and work/life consulting.

Company Origins

The origins of Bright Horizons Family Solutions date back a dozen years to the founding of two companies with remarkably similar goals and histories: Bright Horizons Inc. and Corporate Childcare Development, Inc. Both companies saw an opportunity in the growing trend of corporate-sponsored child-care. Throughout the 1980s, companies experimented with ways to attract and hold employees, particularly women. Along with an increased willingness to accommodate flexible scheduling of work hours, job sharing, and telecommuting, more and more companies were establishing work-site day care for the children of their employees. Setting up and running such a center, however, was quite outside the expertise of most companies, requiring them to learn labyrinthine government regulations and to hire and train caregivers.

Bright Horizons, Inc. was designed to provide the expertise needed to set up and manage these corporate day care centers. Founded in 1987, Bright Horizons was the brainchild of husband-and-wife team Linda Mason and Roger Brown. At the time, Brown worked as a management consultant for Bain & Company in Boston. Brown and Mason established the company in Cambridge, Massachusetts, and took advantage of the large urban hub of Boston to find clients. Its first major community service program, the Horizons Initiative, also served the greater Boston area. Beginning in 1988, it provided child-care and other services for homeless children.

Bright Horizons grew steadily, attracting *Fortune* 500 clients and expanding throughout the New England region. It worked with clients to create programs suited to each company's needs. Not only did it establish and manage onsite day care centers exclusively open to employees, it also set up corporate-sponsored centers out in communities. Enrollment at such centers was open to anyone, although employees of the sponsoring company were given enrollment priority and frequently paid lower fees. In that way, companies without enough employees to fill a center could still offer subsidized or work-site child-care. Bright Horizons also provided at certain centers emergency backup care supervised by registered nurses for parents with sick children or whose regular day care provider was ill. Bright Horizons added summer programs for older children, vacation care, and other special services designed to accommodate an employer's needs.

In 1994, six years after its founding, Bright Horizons was managing 74 day care centers for clients throughout New England and in North Carolina. Its next goal was to move outside the region and create a national presence. Within four years, it had doubled the number of its centers to 155 and was operating in 29 states and the District of Columbia. Its clients included AT&T, DuPont, IBM, Motorola, Time Warner, and Xerox, as well as 22 other *Fortune* 500 clients.

Company Perspectives:

The Bright Horizons Family Solutions mission is to provide innovative programs that help children, families, and employers work together to be their very best.

We are committed to providing the highest quality child-care, early education, and work/life solutions in the nation. We strive to: nurture each child's unique qualities and potential; support families through strong partnerships; collaborate with employers to build family friendly workplaces; create a work environment that encourages professionalism, growth, and diversity; grow a financially strong organization. We aspire to do this so successfully that we make a difference in the lives of children and families and in the communities where we live and work.

In 1997, Bright Horizons' revenues totaled $85 million, and its net income had reached $1.5 million. That year, the company went public, offering shares on the NASDAQ. The proceeds were used to further the company's expansion.

The history of Corporate Childcare Development, Inc. closely mirrored that of Bright Horizons, beginning with the company's founding in 1987, within six weeks of the founding of Bright Horizons. Corporate Childcare was conceived in the mid-1980s by Marguerite Sallee, the human services commissioner for Tennessee under Governor Lamar Alexander. Having worked in that position to encourage corporate involvement in employee child-care, Sallee saw an opportunity to build a business. When Alexander left office in 1986, Sallee sought his help in starting up a company that would manage work-site child-care centers for corporations. With funding from Alexander, Brad Martin (later chief executive officer of Saks Inc.), and Bob Keeshan (better known for his role as the television character ''Captain Kangaroo''), Sallee started Corporate Childcare Development in Nashville, Tennessee.

Corporate Childcare had a mission almost identical to that of Bright Horizons and developed very similar services, including establishment and management of work-site child-care centers, summer programs for older children, emergency child-care, and preschool and primary education. Not surprisingly, the company attracted similar clients. In 1989, Corporate Childcare began working with Marriott Management Services and was soon attracting *Fortune* 500 clients. By 1994, the company ran 38 child-care centers in 19 states. Although Corporate Childcare operated primarily in the South and Midwest, it was attempting to establish a national presence in the mid-1990s. Corporate Childcare reached that point in its expansion at the same time as Bright Horizons, resulting at that time in direct competition for national clients.

By 1997 Corporate Childcare had changed its name to CorporateFamily Solutions and was ready to go public. The initial public offering occurred just three months before Bright Horizons' IPO and generated $25 million. The company planned to use the money to finance acquisitions in flex-time consulting, corporate elementary schools, and elder care. By the end of 1997, CorporateFamily had generated revenues of $77.7 million and boasted 100 centers in 29 states and the District of Columbia. Its clients included Boeing, Citicorp, Campbell Soup, Johnson & Johnson, and Turner Broadcasting.

The 1998 Merger

After several years of battling each other for clients, Bright Horizons and CorporateFamily Solutions agreed to join forces. Their merger in 1998 created the leading provider of corporate child-care in the nation, with 250 corporate-sponsored centers and more than 8,600 employees. Given the fragmented nature of the child-care industry, the new company's nine percent share also made it one of the leading providers overall. The noncash merger was accomplished through a stock swap, in which Bright Horizons shareholders were given a very slight advantage. Linda Mason became chairman of the board, and Marguerite Sallee was named CEO. Roger Brown took over as president.

The main goal of the merger was to increase the company's national presence and name recognition. To that end, the new company was named Bright Horizons Family Solutions, Inc., making use of the solid reputations of both companies. In an industry that relies heavily on referrals, the merger combined the referral power of the companies' respective client bases. In addition, national companies have the advantage in wooing major corporations: Most large companies starting a corporate day care program want to test it with a national provider so that if they like the service, they can use the same provider to expand to other facilities around the nation.

Although many companies merged to reduce costs by eliminating overlapping employees or by making more efficient use of facilities, Bright Horizons saw few benefits on that front. The new company saw some savings, however, in combined insurance and accounting fees. More importantly, the merger meant that certain cities held clusters of company-run day care centers, an organization the company would pursue in any future expansion. Such clusters allowed Bright Horizons to conduct training for groups of centers instead of site by site and allowed centers to share substitute teacher pools.

Future Expansion in a Growing Market

Bright Horizons planned to expand primarily within the corporate market, both with its traditional services and with new services. As the benefits of work-site day care became increasingly apparent, more and more corporations moved to offer such services to their employees. In addition, companies running their own centers were frequently opting to outsource the management of their centers. Because child-care is a highly regulated enterprise, many companies found trying to master the complicated regulations for themselves an inefficient use of their time and resources. Bright Horizons saw such companies as a prime target for their services.

In addition to simply expanding their client base, Bright Horizons added new services. With 50 certified kindergartens in 1998, the company used this expertise as a springboard into elementary education. The company opened a private elementary school in Bellevue, Washington, in the fall of 1998. The elementary school grew out of a child-care center acquired by

Key Dates:

1986: Bright Horizons Inc. is founded.
1987: Corporate Childcare Development, Inc. is founded.
1997: Both companies offer shares to the public.
1998: The two companies merge to form Bright Horizons Family Solutions.

Bright Horizons in 1997. With 46 children enrolled the first year in first through fourth grade, the school used multi-age classes and team teaching. The school planned to grow with the students, adding fifth and sixth grade over the next two years. Bright Horizons was also working with corporations that wanted to establish onsite elementary schools open to employees' children or charter schools open to the community. These programs all fit with Bright Horizons goal of using its strengths in hiring and training teachers and in generating parent loyalty to expand their programs to older children.

Bright Horizons was involved in another innovative program beginning in 1998, an intergenerational center in Norwalk, Connecticut. Under One Roof, Inc. had been running a low-income elderly housing center when they decided to add a child day care facility at the same site. Bright Horizons signed on to set up and manage the child-care center. The 49 elderly residents living there in 1998 were encouraged to visit in the wing that housed the new Marvin Children's Center, with the hope that the interaction would benefit both the children and the elderly residents.

By the end of 1998, the integration of the two companies appeared to have been smoothly accomplished, and the new company was experiencing record growth. Revenues for the year rose 21 percent to $209.4 million, reflecting the addition of 29 new centers. Several new centers opened by Bright Horizons in 1998 were additional sites for existing customers, including a second site for Boeing, the sixth site for longtime customer Citigroup, and the eighth site for Motorola. According to CEO Marguerite Sallee, ''The increasing number of clients opening multiple centers across the country is confirmation that employers see real value in offering child-care at the workplace.''

In 1999 Bright Horizons added a program to make corporate-sponsored child-care easier for companies that have employees spread over several sites. The National Access Program (NAP) gave the employees at participating corporations priority placement at any Bright Horizons center nationwide that took community enrollment. Of Bright Horizons' 284 centers, 125 gave NAP participants priority over general community enrollment. Citibank, Hewlett-Packard, and Universal Studios were among the companies that used the program.

In May 1999, Bright Horizons restructured its leadership positions, following a plan established at the 1998 merger. Roger Brown stepped up as CEO, while Marguerite Sallee joined Linda Mason as co-chair. Later that year, Sallee left Bright Horizons to head another company. By mid-year, revenues had risen 18 percent to $119.4 million for the previous six months. Perhaps more importantly, net income had risen 38 percent in that period, to $4 million. A significant factor in that increase was the closing of several daycare centers that did not meet the Bright Horizons' requirements for quality education or that did not meet the company's minimum level of economic returns.

The company was also adding centers for new and existing clients at a steady pace. Bright Horizons' strategy for attracting national corporations seemed to be paying off. New customers represented a broad range of industries, from the auto industry (Subaru/SIA) to restaurant chains (Pizza Hut) to governmental agencies (International Monetary Fund).

As Bright Horizons grew, it strove to maintain its high standards for education and care: As of 1999, the company held the best record of accreditation from the National Association for the Education of Young Children (NAEYC), which published standards of excellence for child-care centers. At the time, Bright Horizons operated nearly 300 family centers for more than 200 clients, including almost 70 of the *Fortune* 500.

Principal Competitors

Aramark Corporation; KinderCare Learning Centers, Inc.; La Petite Academy.

Further Reading

Clary, Jamie, ''IPO Investing a Mixed Bag,'' *Nashville Business Journal,* December 22, 1997.
Harrison, Joan, ''Child Care Providers Are Poised for Growth,'' *Mergers & Acquisitions,* July/August 1998, pp. 51–52.
Johnson, Holly, ''Corporate Kids,'' *Boston Business Journal,* May 19, 1997.
Rehak, Judith, ''Family Time,'' *Chief Executive,* December 1997, p. 26.
''Sallee Leaves Bright Horizons,'' *Nashville Business Journal,* October 6, 1999.

—Susan Windisch Brown

Brobeck, Phleger & Harrison, LLP

1 Market Street, Spear Street Tower
San Francisco, California 94105
U.S.A.
Telephone: (415) 442-0900
Fax: (415) 442-1010
Web site: http://www.brobeck.com

Partnership
Founded: 1926
Employees: 1,635
Sales: $250.5 million (1998)
NAIC: 54111 Offices of Lawyers

Brobeck, Phleger & Harrison, LLP ranks as one of the largest law firms in the United States. Its 500-plus attorneys in ten offices work in virtually all areas of corporate and business law, from antitrust, mergers, and acquisitions to taxation, bankruptcy, real estate, and financing specialties. The firm represents over 2,000 companies, many in the chemical, computer, biotechnology, oil, gas, and healthcare industries. Although the Brobeck law firm continues to represent traditional historic clients such as Wells Fargo, Exxon, and Nike, it is one of the top law firms that emphasizes helping emerging technology firms become public corporations and grow through patenting new products or acquiring other firms. For example, two of Brobeck's high-tech clients are Cisco Systems and E*TRADE.

Origins

In 1881 Alexander F. Morrison graduated from the Hastings College of Law and then began his law practice in San Francisco. By 1910 his partnership had become known as Morrison, Dunne & Brobeck, and the firm represented many prominent California clients, including the American Trust Company, Moore Shipbuilding Company, St. Francis Hotel Company, and the Crocker, Matson, and Spreckel families.

In 1924, three years after Morrison had died, the firm of Morrison, Dunne & Brobeck split when Herman Phleger, a partner who had joined the firm in 1914, convinced other senior partners to eliminate some other partners. They locked out the fired partners, who in turn used a fire axe to break the door down to get their clients' files.

Effective January 1, 1926, the firm Brobeck, Phleger & Harrison was formed. Senior partner William I. Brobeck died the following year. Maurice E. Harrison was the other name partner, but Herman Phleger gained the clients previously represented by Brobeck and thus ran the firm for the next 45 years.

In the 1920s the firm continued to represent the Matson Navigation Company, founded in 1882 and incorporated in 1901, with Alexander Morrison as one of the incorporators. Matson became the main company providing shipping and passenger service from California to Hawaii and other Pacific ports. In the 1920s Brobeck helped Matson acquire the Moana Hotel and construct the Royal Hawaiian Hotel to serve tourists and others traveling to Hawaii. In the 1930s Brobeck attorneys assisted in the Congressional hearings that led to the Merchant Marine Act of 1936. During World War II the law firm was busy representing Matson when the federal government rented its ships for troop transport to Hawaii. In the postwar period, Brobeck continued to provide Matson with counsel on a variety of matters.

Post-World War II Practice

In the postwar era Brobeck, Phleger & Harrison, like many other growing law firms, for the first time became more formally organized. For example, the firm wrote a two-tier partnership agreement in 1953 that created general partners who managed the firm and special partners who were not involved in management but received a percentage of the firm's profits. At that time the firm included about 30 lawyers, and annual revenues remained stable at about $1.5 million. In 1961 the firm created its first lawyer recruitment program.

In the 1960s the Brobeck firm's main client in terms of fees was the El Paso Natural Gas Company. Brobeck represented El Paso in several antitrust cases and other matters.

The Brobeck firm expanded rapidly in the 1970s and beyond. In 1970 the firm brought in $4.8 million in gross revenue, with net income of $2.8 million, from the effort of its 80 lawyers

Key Dates:

1926: Firm is founded in San Francisco following the split of a predecessor firm.
1976: The firm's Los Angeles office is opened.
1980: The Palo Alto office is founded to serve Silicon Valley clients.
1987: The firm starts offices in San Diego and Orange County, California.
1990: The New York City branch is opened.
1994: Firm opens offices in Austin, Texas, and the Denver area.
1999: The Washington, D.C., office is opened.

and 184 total personnel. Although the firm's profit margins declined from 58 percent in 1970 to just 34 percent in 1989, its revenues in the same period increased to $120.1 million, with net income of $41.6 million. In 1989, Brobeck employed 1,085 total personnel, including 352 lawyers.

In the 1970s the Wells Fargo Bank, based in San Francisco, expanded into southern California and thus insisted that the Brobeck firm, its main outside counsel, do likewise. Consequently, in 1976 Brobeck opened its Los Angeles branch with three lawyers who worked closely with the Wells Fargo legal department. Eventually the Los Angeles office worked with other clients already represented by the San Francisco office, such as the Matson Navigation Company, Getty Oil Company, United Airlines, and Union Oil. Nonetheless, Wells Fargo remained the Brobeck firm's largest client in the early 1980s.

In 1980 Brobeck established its Palo Alto branch office to represent new firms in Silicon Valley, building on its earlier work for firms in the computer industry. For example, back in 1961 a Brobeck attorney had represented the founders of Signetics, an early semiconductor company. With increasing competition in the 1970s from rival corporate law firms, such as Pillsbury Madison & Sutro, Brobeck decided to expand to Palo Alto about the same time as several other law firms. Two early Brobeck clients of Brobeck's Palo Alto office were Circadian, a heart monitor developer, and the venture capital firm of Kleiner Perkins Caufield & Byers.

In 1987 Brobeck began representing Cisco Systems, then a small high-tech company with just $1.5 million in annual sales. But by 1996 Cisco's annual revenues exceeded $4 billion, and the growing firm used Brobeck's lawyers with expertise in many corporate law specialties. For example, Brobeck attorneys based mainly in Palo Alto assisted Cisco's $4.5 billion acquisition of StrataCom in 1996, at the time "the largest technology acquisition in Silicon Valley history," according to the law firm's *Memoirs*.

From the early 1970s to 1988, Brobeck attorneys helped the shareholders of the Shanghai Power Company that had been incorporated back in 1929 in Delaware to provide electricity to Shanghai, China. After the communists took over China in 1949, in 1950 the People's Republic of China seized the power company's properties. Meanwhile, the Boise Cascade Company acquired the common stock of the Shanghai Power Company. After President Nixon established diplomatic ties to the PRC, the Chinese government in 1978 agreed to pay the Foreign Claims Settlement Commission $190 million, which included $54 million to the Shanghai Power Company. With Brobeck's assistance over years of negotiations and class-action litigation, eventually power company shareholders all over the world finally received their just compensation.

Brobeck in 1983 began representing Shell Oil Company in litigation that lasted into the mid-1990s. Shell sued 350 insurance companies for cleanup costs at the Rocky Mountain Arsenal and another site. The original jury ruled against Shell, but the California Court of Appeals in 1993 in Shell Oil Company v. Winterthur reversed the jury decision, thus setting the stage for a retrial. However, The Travelers Insurance Company, the primary insurer in this case, settled out of court with Shell in 1995; soon Lloyd's and other London insurance firms, as well as the remaining U.S. insurance companies, also settled. Thus ended a landmark environmental insurance case that lasted over a decade.

To build its technology practice, Brobeck in 1987 opened a new office in San Diego with the help of 13 attorneys from the firm of Aylward, Kintz, Stiska, Wassenaar & Shannahan. In the late 1980s the area's real estate boom gave the firm the opportunity to serve clients such as La Jolla Development, Collins Development, and LandGrant Development. The San Diego branch provided legal assistance for venture capital and public offerings for companies such as Intermark and Immunetech Pharmaceuticals, later known as Dura Pharmaceuticals. Other corporate clients were Ligand Pharmaceuticals, ENCAD, Depotech, Primary Access, Applied Digital Access, and Rubio Restaurants. By 1990 the San Diego office had grown to 35 attorneys.

The law firm also started its Newport Beach, Orange County, California office in 1987 to serve high-tech and healthcare clients. By 1996 over 33 lawyers worked out of the Newport Beach office, and its clients included The Cerplex Group, ACT Networks, FileNet Corporation, Advanced Tissue Sciences, and Advanced Logic Research. In 1999 Brobeck's Newport Beach office moved to Irvine, also in Orange County.

Practice in the 1990s

In 1990 the Brobeck law firm and Boston's Hale and Dorr began a joint venture called Brobeck Hale and Dorr International (BHD) with offices in New York City and London. New York clients in the early 1990s included Robertson, Stephens & Company; North American Philips Corporation; and Oncor, Inc. Brobeck wanted to expand the New York operation and build a litigation practice, but Hale and Dorr did not agree. Thus on January 1, 1995 the New York office became a branch of just the Brobeck law firm, while the London joint venture remained in place. By the fall of 1996 the New York branch had grown to 32 lawyers and moved to a new location at 1633 Broadway.

Laterally hiring a partner and a senior associate from San Francisco's Epstein Becker & Green allowed Brobeck in 1990 to start a healthcare practice to serve hospitals, physician groups, and others in the industry. The two specialists in managed care were part of a major defection in which 11 healthcare attorneys left the Epstein law firm.

In 1993 the Brobeck law firm represented clients that raised over $3 billion in 68 offerings. It also helped 75 companies that were involved in mergers and acquisitions worth over $2 billion and counseled venture capitalists in transactions worth at least $300 million. The law firm recorded 1993 revenues of about $155 million.

After Brobeck's client Coram Healthcare Corporation moved from Orange County to Denver, it requested that the law firm establish a Colorado office. Thus in 1994 Brobeck opened a new office in Broomfield in the Denver area. In the October 7, 1994 *San Francisco Business Times*, Brobeck's Chairman John Larson said, "We are looking to become the only firm nationally that has emerging growth as its focus. That's what [is] driving this." By 1996 the Colorado office represented not only Coram but also regional clients such as LINK-VTC, Innovative Software Development, Phase-1 Molecular Toxicology, MicroOptical Devices, Optical Imaging Systems, OpenDisk Systems, and Breece Hill Technologies.

As part of Brobeck's strategy to serve innovative emerging firms, in 1994 the law firm also opened an office in Austin, Texas, to serve high-tech firms, some of whom had moved from the Silicon Valley to Austin. Clients there included Tivoli Systems, which IBM purchased in 1996 for about $750 million; Atrium Technologies, which later became DAZEL Corporation; Austin Ventures; SSM Ventures; and ichat, Inc. At first the Austin office provided initial public offering and other financial counsel for such young firms, but within a year or two it had expanded to deal with intellectual property and litigation. By 1996 Austin's approximately 900 high-tech firms gave the Brobeck law firm and its rivals plenty of opportunities to serve that expanding industry.

In the late 1990s Brobeck continued to serve a variety of local and international clients. For example, it represented the estates of Grateful Dead founder Jerry Garcia and also Larry Hillblom, founder of DHL Worldwide Express, when several parties filed claims to those inheritances. With the help of former Los Angeles mayor Tom Bradley, who joined the law firm in 1994, the firm expanded its Asian practice and also helped many Los Angeles clients who faced legal difficulties following the looting and destruction in central Los Angeles after the Rodney King trial.

With the U.S. economy booming in the 1990s, the Brobeck law firm continued its expansion. Based on number of attorneys, the *National Law Journal* ranked Brobeck, Phleger & Harrison as 40th in its November 16, 1998 listing of the nation's 250 largest law firms. Brobeck had 473 attorneys, an increase of 34 since 1997. In 1998 Brobeck reported 164 partners, 269 associates, and 40 other attorneys. The starting salary was listed as $87,000, while a few of the firms reported starting salaries over $100,000. Brobeck's main practice areas were business and technology (35 percent) and products liability (18 percent).

The *American Lawyer* in its July 1999 listing of the nation's top 100 law firms based on 1998 gross revenues ranked the Brobeck law firm as number 30. The firm reported $250.5 million in gross revenues, net operating income of $77 million, and average compensation for all partners of $545,000.

In spite of prosperity and high attorney salaries, the Brobeck firm, like other large law firms, struggled to retain its young associates. The National Association for Law Placement found that 75 percent of all associates leave their law firms before their seventh year, due sometimes to boring, unchallenging tasks, long hours, and considerable stress and anxiety. Brobeck associate Adam Epstein, for example, left the firm after three years. He eventually became an executive for Internet firms, where he made much more money but also used his legal experience to hire law firms, including Brobeck, Phleger & Harrison, as outside counsel.

Although Brobeck, Phleger & Harrison prospered in the 1990s, it faced plenty of challenges as the decade ended. For example, the Palo Alto-based firm of Wilson Sonsini Goodrich & Rosati, a key rival in helping new high-tech firms, planned to hire 170 lawyers in 2000. Many law firms had grown by consolidation, and the world's largest accounting firms hired thousands of attorneys. Some in the profession advocated multidisciplinary practices in which lawyers teamed up with other professionals, but as 1999 ended the American Bar Association still forbade such arrangements that were common in Europe.

Rapid growth in electronic commerce through Internet transactions also presented Brobeck attorneys with new ways to serve their corporate clients. The law firm itself created its own site on the World Wide Web to describe its offices and services. Unlike some law firms whose literature and web sites seldom mentioned specific clients, Brobeck openly listed many of its clients and cases. In 1996 it celebrated its 70th anniversary with the publication of the firm's *Memoirs*, evidence that it has tried to balance the firm's history and legacy with cutting-edge legal services. In any case, the Brobeck firm seemed well prepared to represent its clients in the fast-paced Information Age.

Principal Competitors

Wilson Sonsini Goodrich & Rosati; Pillsbury Madison & Sutro; Cooley Godward.

Further Reading

Levine, Daniel S., "Brobeck Expands Emerging-Growth Practice," *San Francisco Business Times*, October 7, 1994, p. 3.

Rauber, Chris, "Firm Starts Health Care Practice," *San Francisco Business Times*, September 24, 1990, p. 37.

Schmitt, Richard B., "Lawyer Finds Job Satisfaction in Cyberspace," *Salt Lake Tribune*, November 4, 1999, p. D7.

Spiegel, Hart H., editor, *Brobeck, Phleger & Harrison LLP, Attorneys at Law: Memoirs 1926–1996*, San Francisco: Brobeck, Phleger & Harrison, 1996, 144 p.

—David M. Walden

Bunzl plc

110 Park Street
London W1Y3RB
United Kingdom
Telephone: +44-171-495-4950
Fax: +44-171-495-4953
Web site: http://www.bunzl.com

Public Company
Incorporated: 1940 as Tissue Papers Ltd.
Employees: 10,000
Sales: £1.86 billion ($3.22 billion) (1998)
Stock Exchanges: London New York
Ticker Symbols: BNZL (London); BNL (New York)
NAIC: 42213 Industrial and Personal Service Paper Wholesalers; 42261 Plastics Materials and Basic Forms and Shapes Wholesalers

Bunzl plc is an international group of companies active in 220 locations in 21 countries. After a period of significant reorganization in the late 1980s and early 1990s, the company has focused its operations on four key business areas. Its largest division—Outsourcing Services—is a leading supplier of food packaging materials, disposable supplies, and cleaning products to supermarkets, caterers, and hotels in North America, Europe, and Australia. Another division, responsible for supplying cigarette filters and self-adhesive tear tape through subsidiary Filtrona International Ltd., is the world's largest provider of outsourced cigarette filters. The company's Paper Distribution division is one of the most significant fine paper merchants in the United Kingdom and Ireland. In addition, Bunzl's Plastics division provides plastic protection parts to businesses throughout the world, and is the leading U.S. extruder of custom plastic profiles used in retail, transportation, and lighting.

Bunzl's Roots

While Bunzl was set up in the United Kingdom in 1940, it was the offshoot of a much older and larger Austrian enterprise, which began in 1854 as a haberdashery business in Bratislava, Czechoslovakia, and moved to Austria in 1883. From haberdashery it moved into rag trading, and from that into textile and paper manufacturing. The firm traded as Bunzl & Biach, and was run from an early date by the Bunzl family. By 1914 the firm was well established in the textile, paper, and pulp industries, and had branches throughout the Austro-Hungarian Empire.

In the late 1920s Bunzl & Biach developed what was probably the world's first cigarette filter. It was actually invented by a Hungarian called Boris Aivaz, but as it was made from crepe paper Aivaz needed the cooperation of a paper manufacturer. The filters went into production in 1927, and over the next ten years were sold to cigarette manufacturers in 15 countries. The idea did not catch on widely, however, and cigarette filters were no more than a sideline for the firm in the 1930s.

The business, still owned and run by the Bunzl family, continued to prosper until Hitler's annexation of Austria in 1938. The Bunzls, being Jewish, had every reason to fear a Nazi takeover and had taken the precaution of moving the company's headquarters from Vienna to Switzerland two years earlier. They also had a subsidiary company in London, Bunzl & Biach (British) Ltd., which gave them an alternative base. When the Nazi government took over the company's Austrian assets, most of the family emigrated, some to Switzerland and some to the United States, but the majority to the United Kingdom.

A Wartime Move to the United Kingdom

In this new environment the family began to rebuild its business, some concentrating on textiles and some on paper. The latter group was headed by Hugo Bunzl, who had been the first to show interest in the idea of cigarette filters. In 1940, he and several colleagues founded Tissue Papers Ltd., a company manufacturing tissue and crepe paper, together with the cigarette filters, in U.K. factories. This business remained very small during the war years, with fewer than 30 employees in 1946.

Following World War II, in 1946 the Bunzl family regained control of its Austrian business, but Tissue Papers Ltd. continued to develop independently. It took on the international distribution of the Austrian company's paper products, and in 1952

Company Perspectives:

Our mission is to provide service of such excellence that customers always prefer Bunzl to be their supplier; support manufacturers who actively assist in satisfying our customers needs to the benefit of all; create a safe, satisfying, and rewarding environment for our employees by encouraging initiative, teamwork, and pride in the achievement of our business objectives; consistently achieve financial performance above both industry average and the minimum expectation of our shareholders.

changed its name to Bunzl Pulp & Paper Ltd., but continued to manufacture its own products in the United Kingdom.

Among these were cigarette filters. In the postwar period, filter-tipped cigarettes became more popular, and this side of Bunzl's business gradually expanded. In the 1940s filters were still made from paper, and the production process was a slow one. A number of chemical companies experimented with other materials and eventually Eastman Kodak came up with a superior material, cellulose acetate tow. Filters made from this material proved to be more efficient and could be produced at higher speed. Bunzl began to use this material in 1954 and the cigarette manufacturers responded by launching more filter-tipped brands.

This technical advance coincided with the first indications from medical research that cigarette smoking could be seriously harmful. The World Health Organization published one of the earliest reports on the subject in 1955. Another ten years were to pass before the link with lung cancer was conclusively proved, but from the mid-1950s filter-tipped cigarettes began to be seen as a way of reducing whatever health risk there might be.

As a result, the new filter-tipped brands started to gain market share rapidly in all the developed countries. Bunzl rose to this challenge with remarkable speed and success for a small company. In the United Kingdom it quickly stepped up its output and became virtually the sole supplier of filters to the two companies which then controlled 90 percent of the cigarette market, Imperial Tobacco and Gallaher Ltd. Both these companies had tried making their own filters but decided when the technology changed to buy their supplies from Bunzl.

American Interests and Going Public in the 1950s

In the United States, the Bunzl family set up a separate company, American Filtrona Corporation, in 1954. This company and Bunzl Pulp & Paper had shares in each other's business but neither controlled the other. Besides supplying their home markets, both established overseas subsidiaries, some wholly owned, some jointly owned, and some in partnership with local interests. In this way the Filtrona group, as it came to be called, soon became the world leader in cigarette filters. By 1964 the group was manufacturing in five European countries, the United States, Canada, South Africa, Australia, India, Brazil, and Argentina. The companies directly controlled by Bunzl Pulp & Paper increased their filter output 12-fold between 1956 and 1964.

Meanwhile, the company was expanding in other directions. Its international paper trading business was growing steadily, and it had several factories in the United Kingdom making a variety of paper and packaging products as well as filters. In the late 1950s its profits began to rise steeply, and in 1957 the company went public. Only 30 percent of the equity was released onto the market at that stage, and the Bunzl family retained control of the company for another decade.

In its first 11 years as a public company, Bunzl's profits rose uninterruptedly, from less than £1 million a year to more than £5 million, and the company became a favorite with investors. However, its growth was mainly due to the success of filter cigarettes, which was unlikely to continue at the same rate. In the United Kingdom, filter cigarettes grew from 11 percent of the market in 1959 to 70 percent in 1968, but after that their share grew more slowly. At the same time, awareness of the health risks of smoking, with or without filters, was increasing throughout the 1960s, and governments began to impose restrictions on how cigarettes could be marketed.

Bunzl suffered its first reduction in profits in 1969. Apart from the adverse market conditions it was beginning to face, the company fell under a cloud in 1967–69, when the Monopolies Commission held an inquiry into the supply of cigarette filters in the United Kingdom. This was instigated by Courtaulds, which had been supplying Bunzl with the acetate tow it needed, when Eastman Kodak and Bunzl jointly set up a factory in the United Kingdom to produce this material themselves. The commission eventually rejected Courtaulds's complaints, ruling that although Bunzl was in a monopoly position it had not abused it. Even so, the publicity was unwelcome because it drew attention to the company's vulnerability.

Against this background of assorted threats to its main profit earner, Bunzl saw that it must reduce its dependence on the cigarette market by expanding more vigorously in other directions. The company already had a foothold in the packaging market and its first thought was to develop this area. In the late 1960s, through a mixture of product development and acquisitions, Bunzl moved into the production of polythene film and bags, self-adhesive labels, tapes, and plastic tubes.

The 1970s

In 1970, a much more ambitious step was taken: Bunzl Pulp & Paper took over Bunzl & Biach, its one time big brother in Austria. The U.K. company had long been selling the paper products of the Austrian company overseas and by 1970 was the bigger of the two. This takeover increased Bunzl's sales by almost half, raised its work force to more than 7,000, and put it squarely into paper manufacturing as well as merchanting. The enlarged company was split into four divisions—filters, paper, packaging, and plastics—and for a few years profits grew strongly. In 1974, when the paper market was particularly buoyant, profits reached a peak of £4 million, of which less than half came from filters.

In the later 1970s the company found that it could not sustain this progress. Inflation continued to push up turnover, but profits did not regain their 1974 level for nine years. Taking inflation into account, there was a steep decline in real terms.

Key Dates:

1854: Bunzl & Biach, a predecessor of Bunzl, opens in 1854.
1927: Bunzl & Biach begins making cigarette filters.
1938: Hitler annexes Austria and Bunzl family flees to Britain.
1940: Hugo Bunzl founds Tissue Papers Ltd. in Britain.
1952: Tissue Papers Ltd. changes name to Bunzl Pulp & Paper Ltd.
1954: Bunzl establishes American Filtrona Corporation.
1957: Bunzl makes first public stock offering.
1970: Bunzl acquires its Austrian parent company—Bunzl & Biach.
1980: Bunzl divests Bunzl & Biach.
1984: Bunzl sells American Filtrona.
1997: Bunzl forms Bunzl Extrusion; reacquires American Filtrona; purchases Grocery Supply Systems.
1998: Bunzl acquires The Paper Company and Enitor.
1999: Bunzl acquires Provend Group plc.

The main problems were in the filter market. In the developed countries cigarette smoking was declining, and cigarette manufacturers were increasingly making their own filters. Imperial Tobacco, Bunzl's biggest single customer, began to do so in the 1970s. In less developed countries there were still growth opportunities, but Bunzl was by then struggling to maintain existing sales levels.

At the same time, the company's diversification program failed to deliver the expected benefits. The Austrian paper mills faced increasing competition from Eastern Europe and were badly in need of re-equipment. After paying interest on the debts they had accumulated, there was no surplus to swell group profits. In the United Kingdom, the plastics division successfully broke into new markets, particularly pipes for building and agricultural uses, but against that Bunzl made an ill-judged entry into the data processing business which resulted only in losses.

By 1980 it was clear that the company must find a new strategy. In that year it took the painful step of selling its Austrian paper business, which it had only owned for ten years. This sharply reduced the company's turnover and work force, but improved its financial position and opened the way to new acquisitions. At the same time G.G. Bunzl, who had headed the company since 1961, handed over the chair to Ernest Beaumont, (a Bunzl by birth, who had changed his name), and a new chief executive, James White, was brought in from outside the company.

Under the new team, Bunzl was reorganized into three divisions: filters, pulp and paper merchanting, and industrial. After the sale of Bunzl & Biach, the company's work force was down to about 4,000, the majority based in the United Kingdom, and around 70 percent of its profits were coming from the declining filter business. Of its other businesses, pulp and paper trading was the next largest contributor to profits and it was decided to develop this division. In particular, Bunzl was attracted by the growing business of distributing specialized paper and plastic products to industrial customers, such as supermarkets and airlines, as opposed to trading in bulk paper and pulp.

Rapid Expansion in the 1980s

Between 1981 and 1984 Bunzl systematically bought its way into this business, first in the United States, state by state, then in Australia. Among its more important acquisitions were Jersey Paper and the PCI/Mac-Pak Group—which entered Bunzl into the market for supplying food packaging materials to American grocery stores—and there were many others. By the end of 1984 Bunzl's sales were five times those of 1980, and profits had grown from £11 million to £28 million. More importantly, the company had finally freed itself from its long dependence on cigarette filters, which contributed less than 20 percent of profits in 1984. That year Bunzl cut its link with American Filtrona Corporation.

The success of this diversification plan led the company into what Jane Fuller, writing in the *Financial Times* on March 28, 1990, called "a headlong rush for growth." In the years 1985–87, Bunzl raised capital from two rights issues, increased borrowing, and spent some £400 million on acquisitions. Around 70 separate purchases were made. In contrast to Bunzl's previous policy, many of the acquisitions took the company into fields quite unrelated to its existing business, such as parcel distribution, graphic arts supplies, food service, and electrical equipment distribution. Between 1987 and 1990, Bunzl made a series of acquisitions that enlarged Bunzl Building Supply Inc., its U.S. building materials group, which distributed products to contractors, retailers, and industrial users. Bunzl expanded the three core divisions it had established in 1980 to five, encompassing a multitude of different products.

This policy worked well in the short term. Profits raced up from £28 million in 1984 to £86 million in 1987, and earnings per share also increased. However, problems soon emerged among the acquisitions, and by 1987 the company had started to shed some of the more troublesome ones. Most of the transportation division was sloughed off in 1988, along with other company holdings, and profits made only a small advance. In 1989, the company was back to four divisions: paper, building materials, plastics, and cigarette filters. Turnover was down by six percent, and profits slumped by 30 percent. James White, who had become chairman in 1988, came under sharp attack from shareholders and admitted in 1990 that "with the benefit of hindsight we made too many acquisitions too quickly." Unbundling some of those acquisitions in order to bolster the company's profitability remained a Bunzl priority into the 1990s.

Refocusing in the 1990s

James White left the company as a result of a management shake-up in November 1990, and David Kendall—former managing director of BP Oil and Bunzl's non-executive director since 1988—was appointed chairman. In 1991, Anthony Habgood took the helm of the company and made the divestiture of non-core operations a top priority. In his first 18 months, Bunzl sold or closed 20 businesses. In February 1992, Bunzl exited the food service sector with the sale of Bunzl Food

Service. Two months later, Bunzl rid itself of several unprofitable paper interests and in 1993 reported its first increase in profits since 1988. Not yet done, Bunzl sold its building supply arm in June 1994.

At the same time that Bunzl pruned many of its operations, it also bolstered the division that had quickly become its most profitable: outsourcing services that supplied disposable food packaging materials to supermarkets, caterers, and hotels. By 1994, this division accounted for over half of the company's profits. Supplying disposable food packaging material to supermarkets was a stable business niche, which, unlike the building materials market, was a non-cyclical and growing enterprise. Fueled in part by time-strapped Americans' appetite for ready-to-eat (or ready-to-heat) meals from supermarkets, grocery stores required an ever greater number of microwavable plastic trays, Styrofoam containers, paper napkins and cups, and bags. Consolidation in the grocery store industry also increased this market since large chains did not want to waste valuable warehouse space by filling it with disposable (and often bulky) packaging items.

Bunzl continued to expand its food packaging empire, making a number of acquisitions that further developed its outsourcing arm. In 1993, Bunzl purchased Automatic Catering Supplies and Ziff Paper, a New England distributor of paper and plastic disposables. Five paper and plastics companies were added to Bunzl's roster of operations in 1994. Three years later, Bunzl bought Grocery Supply Systems, as well as the supermarket supply business of a division of International Paper.

During its period of restructuring, Bunzl also concentrated on its cigarette filter and plastics divisions. After establishing a small U.S. filters operation in 1993, Bunzl re-acquired American Filtrona for $178 million in 1997 to help meet growing demand. As a corollary to its filter production, Bunzl also manufactured the tear tape used in cigarette and other consumer packaging, a niche it entered after purchasing P.P. Payne Companies in 1996.

Bunzl grew its plastics operations in 1997 when it added Bunzl Extrusion to its operation. In 1998 it acquired Enitor, a Netherlands-based extruder of plastic profiles. This purchase represented Bunzl's first foray into the European extrusion market. By acquiring The Paper Company in 1998, Bunzl strengthened its position as a fine paper distributor in Britain.

Perhaps the greatest indication of Bunzl's shift away from being largely a paper and cigarette company (as it had been for most of its history) occurred in 1998 when FTSE International (a joint venture between the *Financial Times* and the London Stock Exchange) listed the company in its ''Business Support Services'' sector instead of in its customary ''Paper, Packaging, and Printing'' sector. Indeed by 1998, Bunzl's outsourcing operation accounted for well over two-thirds of its sales. Emphasizing its increased presence in this area, Bunzl acquired Provend Group PLC in 1999. This strategic purchase expanded Bunzl's disposable supplies business in the United Kingdom, and also enabled Bunzl to enter into the complementary vending machine business.

Principal Subsidiaries

Filtrona International Ltd.; Bunzl Fine Papers Ltd.

Principal Divisions

Bunzl Plastics Products; Bunzl European Distribution.

Principal Competitors

Amcor Limited; Menasha Corporation; Dart Container Corporation; Rexam PLC; Jerfferson Smurfit Group plc; Sealright Co., Inc.; Sweetheart Cup Company; JPS Packaging Company; Wausau-Mosinee Paper Corporation.

Further Reading

August, Oliver, ''Bunzl to Widen Portfolio,'' *Times* (London), September 2, 1997.

''Bunzl Foodservice: After a 12.5 Percent Sales Loss, the Parent Company Calls it a Day in Foodservice,'' *ID: The Voice of Foodservice Distribution*,'' February 1, 1992.

The Bunzl Group of Companies, 1854–1954, London: Bunzl, 1954.

''Bunzl's Three-Point Acquisition Strategy Keeps Business Booming,'' *Building Supply Home Centers*, March 1, 1990.

Eadie, Alison, ''Rugby Group Buys Bunzl's U.S. Building Supplier,'' *Independent* (London), June 18, 1994.

''Habgood Sorts Out Bunzl's Bungles,'' *Daily Telegraph* (London), September 12, 1991.

Murray, Alasdair, ''Bunzl Spends Pounds 75m on Buying and Plans More,'' *Times* (London), September 3, 1996.

Stevenson, Tom, ''Bunzl Cashes in on Niche Control,'' *Independent* (London), September 5, 1995.

—John Swan
—updated by Rebecca Stanfel

Candie's, Inc.

2975 Westchester Avenue
Purchase, New York 10577
U.S.A.
Telephone: (914) 694-8600
Fax: (914) 694-8608
Web site: http://www.candies.com

Public Company
Incorporated: 1978 as Millfeld Trading Company
Employees: 93
Sales: $93 million (1998)
Stock Exchanges: NASDAQ
Ticker Symbol: CANDE
NAIC: 316213 Men's Footwear (Except Athletic) Manufacturing; 316214 Women's Footwear (Except Athletic) Manufacturing; 312219 Children's Footwear Manufacturing; 422330 Women's, Children's and Infants' Clothing & Accessories Wholesalers; 448120 Women's Clothing Stores; 53311 Trademark Licensing

Candie's, Inc., designs and markets a complete line of footwear, apparel, and accessories to young women. The Candie's trademarked line of women's products are sold in specialty stores and upscale department stores throughout the United States as well as in Canada, Brazil, New Zealand, and parts of Asia and Europe. Women's products are also available under the Bongo brand, while children's products are marketed under the Candie's and Crayons trademarks. Candie's also produces private label footwear, including men's casual shoes and sturdy boots.

Candie's Reputation Established

Candie's, Inc., took its name from the Candie's "slide," a sexy, high-heeled shoe marketed by Charles Cole, founder of El Greco, Inc. In the 1960s Cole found a way to interconnect a mesh material to produce a zipper front go-go boot, which became a favorite. Cole discovered the slide while exploring manufacturing possibilities in Italy with his son Ken (who later formed his own shoe company, Kenneth Cole Productions). Charles Cole registered the Candie's brand name in 1978, and placed it on his first order of 600 pairs of shoes.

The success of the Candie's slide followed on the heels of the movie *Grease*, in which Olivia Newton-John played the role of a naive high school girl transformed into a sexy young woman. In the final scene, wearing tight pants and high-heeled shoes similar to the Candie's style, Newton-John brought John Travolta's character to his knees. The movie made the shoe style wildly popular, and Cole filled the demand. Advertisements reflected the brash style of the footwear, including a television commercial that featured college women scampering around a dormitory in various states of undress wearing Candie's slides.

Cole used his established trade connections in the Midwest to bring the Candie's slide into the market. Specialty stores, department stores, and independent chain shoe stores were more receptive to the low price, which was a result of low-cost Italian manufacturing. Sales exploded after Macy's began to carry the brand, and better department stores followed. From 1978 to 1981, at the height of the disco craze, El Greco sold 14 million pairs of slides to women 14 to 30 years of age. Other shoe styles that El Greco made popular under the Candie's brand name included the Chrissy sneaker and Jellies, plastic sandals in bright, translucent colors.

The fate of Candie's footwear changed with new ownership. Sales declined steadily after Charles Cole sold a 60 percent majority interest in El Greco to U.K.-based Pentland Group plc in 1986. Sales dropped from a peak of $130 million in 1984 to $29 million in 1991, as the price for Candie's footwear increased and marketing for the brand steadily decreased. Neil Cole, a son of Charles Cole who had played an integral role in the success of the Candie's brand, saw an opportunity to revive it as 1970s fashions returned to the stores. Neil Cole's firm, New Retail Concepts (NRC), purchased El Greco from Pentland in June 1991. Cole then licensed the Candie's trademark to Millfeld Trading Company (MTC), which was to manufacture and market the brand.

Neil Cole and Barry Feldstein, founder and CEO of MTC, planned to reorganize MTC to make the Candie's name promi-

Key Dates:

1978: Candie's ''slide'' popular with young women.
1986: Candie's brand sold to Pentland Group plc.
1991: Neil Cole acquires Candie's brand.
1996: Jenny McCarthy featured in ad campaign.

nent. MTC purchased a 75 percent interest in El Greco from NRC with the intention of renaming the company Candie's, Inc. Neil Cole would become president and CEO of Candie's, while MTC would become a wholly owned subsidiary of Candie's under the name Millfeld. With Cole as interim president and CEO of MTC, it was decided that Millfeld would remain a public entity. MTC officially became Candie's, Inc., with a public offering of stock in February 1993. Candie's sold 1.5 million shares at $5 per share.

Candie's in the Early 1990s

Neil Cole planned a $2.5 million marketing campaign to revive the Candie's slide for launch in August 1992. Advertising outlets included television, radio, trade publications, and fashion magazines. The ads targeted the 20-year-old woman with the hope that girls as young as ten and women up to 50 years old would also be attracted to the products. The ads reflected women's increased independence 15 years after the shoe's original launch, with one television commercial featuring two women traveling across the country in scenes reminiscent of the women's adventure movie *Thelma and Louise.*

The new Candie's product line offered contemporary styles in a variety of categories, priced at $10 below competitive products. In addition to fashion shoes, the line included footwear that drew on NRC's and MTC's areas of experience: comfort, hiking, athletics, boots, vulcanized leather, and ''athleisure.'' The footwear received favorable reviews at trade shows in Las Vegas and New York, and the company received orders from specialty stores, chains, department stores, and junior store chains.

The company also extended the Candie's brand to other products for women as well as a line of footwear for children. Candie's signed licensing agreements for handbags, small leather goods, hosiery, sleepwear, hats, T-shirts, and women's apparel. A line of baby shoes, launched in February 1993, included durable outdoor ankle boots, suede fashion booties, and styles with faux jewels. A ten-year licensing agreement with Brown Group, Inc., involved the manufacture and distribution of girls' footwear. The 1994 back-to-school launch of girls' footwear included casual, outdoor, and athletic shoes, as well as a Western mid-height boot, all priced from $25 to $35. The two companies hoped to attract young mothers who remembered the Candie's brand from its heyday and wanted high-quality, fashionable footwear at a reasonable price.

Candie's sought to maximize the efficiency of its shoe production by adding other footwear brands to its operations. Candie's obtained a license to produce and distribute women's and children's footwear for the Bongo brand in 1995.

Marketing Sizzle in the 1990s

In 1996, with the company on sound financial footing, Cole orchestrated a full-scale revival of the Candie's slide through collaboration with well-known fashion designers. Targeting upscale women from 25 to 50 years of age, Candie's signed partnership agreements with four fashion designers who did not already include shoes in their collections. The designers, Betty Johnson, Nicole Miller, Anna Sui, and Vivienne Tam, created distinctively different styles. Betty Johnson designed footwear in wild colors with a hip, urban flair in thick-soled or sleek, sexy styles. Anna Sui followed classic lines, while Vivienne Tam added an Asian flair to Western classics in new fabrics. The shoes carried each of their designer's names along with the Candie's trademark.

Marketing for the designer shoes included a $1 million advertising campaign. The February issues of *Elle* and *Vogue* magazines included a five-page advertisement featuring the shoes and a photograph of the four designers, while advertisements in *Marie Claire*, *InStyle*, and *Allure* magazines featured the group picture. The designers also featured the shoes in runway fashion shows in October 1996. The project opened the doors of better department stores to the Candie's brand, including Nordstrom, May Company, Dillard's, and Federated.

Marketing to young women from 15 to 25 years of age required a different approach. A survey had shown only 30 percent of this group to be familiar with Candie's. To reach that market, the company engaged Jenny McCarthy, the former co-host of the MTV program *Singled Out.* One print ad showed McCarthy applying fingernail polish, while another showed her singing into a showerhead, scantily clad in a glittering red dress. A controversial ad featured McCarthy seated on the toilet with her underpants down at her Candie's slides. *Elle*, *Glamour*, *Allure*, and *Marie Claire* accepted the ad for their April 1997 issues; *Vogue* and *Cosmopolitan* refused to run it at all; and *Spin* ran a nude version that garnered increased sales for that issue. The $2 million advertising campaign coincided with the launch of the *Jenny McCarthy Show* on MTV.

Another $5 million marketing campaign followed in the summer of 1997. *Glamor* and *InStyle* rejected an advertisement in which McCarthy, wearing a saucy red dress, lounged on the pool table in a stuffy men's club with a roll of toilet paper stuck to the sole of her shoe. *Vogue* and *Cosmopolitan* accepted that ad, but rejected a kitchen scene in which McCarthy sat on the sink—wearing casual, ankle-high shoes—and checked out the plumber crouched under the sink with low-riding jeans exposing part of his backside.

Whatever opinions the advertisements aroused, history repeated itself as Candie's regained popularity. The high volume of sales at Macy's led the store to add a 500-square-foot Candie's shoe boutique at the front entrance of its Herald Square store in New York City. New accounts in 1997 included Foot Locker and Pacific Sunwear. Journeys specialty stores featured Candie's with a defined display area within its stores. Candie's also began to experiment with three company-owned and -operated retail stores in the New York City area. In 1997 sales rose to $93 million, which was more than double the 1996 revenues of $45 million.

International expansion came through a distribution agreement with Bata Shoe Pte. Ltd. (BSP). The agreement allowed BSP to distribute Candie's branded products, including handbags and apparel, in its 300 retail shops in Singapore and Malaysia, as well as through its distribution partnerships. BSP also hoped to open a 400- to 500-square-foot Candie's boutique in Singapore. The company reused the McCarthy advertisements in Asia, sparking demand for personal appearances.

In 1998 Candie's brought the classic slide into alignment with contemporary fashions with lower heels and a rougher, chunkier look. This time Cole selected three award-winning jewelry designers to create four styles each for the slide. Barry Kieselstein-Cord's work relied on animals and nature; Angela Cummings conveyed the impression of flowers, ocean life, and architecture; and Robert Lee Morris contributed clean, sculpted styles.

Company sponsorship of concert tours led to a partnership agreement with singer/songwriter Lisa Loeb, whose hit song "Stay" was featured in the Generation X movie *Reality Bites.* The agreement involved sponsorship of her 30-stop American tour with shoe store promotions, radio advertising, and giveaways for concert tickets and backstage passes. The tour kicked off at Macy's at Herald Square in February 1998 with a live performance in the Candie's shoe boutique. Loeb also made personal appearances for Candie's in Singapore, Malaysia, and Germany.

Candie's expanded its use of musical performers for advertising in its summer 1998 campaign. Advertisements in fashion, teen, and music magazines featured country singer Shaina Twain, rap singer Lil' Kim, and R&B singer Brandy in addition to Lisa Loeb. Some of the ads, which showed the singers performing to an atypical audience, were rejected as being too controversial. *Cosmopolitan* rejected an ad that featured Lisa Loeb holding a large pink guitar strategically placed to give the impression of nudity, in front of an audience that appeared to be wearing only spectacles. Brandy, age 19, performed in front of punk-looking senior citizens, while Shaina Twain sang to an audience of wild babies. Wearing a yellow bikini and a blonde wig, Lil' Kim danced above a crowd of nuns who looked rather apprehensive.

In addition to its international distribution in Germany, Brazil, and parts of Asia, Candie's added four international distribution agreements in August 1998. Candie's trademarked products were to be distributed by Sports Odyssee in Canada, Vanocca Industries in Hong Kong, and Platts Europe Ltd. in Switzerland. In New Zealand Hannah's began to distribute Candie's brand products in its 65 retail stores. Candie's planned to use existing advertising to appeal to consumers who made up the MTV market outside the United States.

New Products, Even Hotter Campaigns in 1999

Candie's began to expand into the jeanswear market with the acquisition of Michael Caruso & Company, maker of Bongo Jeans, in 1998. The acquisition included the Bongo brand name and related trademarks, as well as licensing agreements for children's apparel and plus-size jeanswear. Candie's entered into a 50/50 joint venture with Sweet Sportswear LLC, a subsidiary of jeans manufacturer Aztec Production International. Unzipped Apparel LLC held the licenses to produce jeans under the Bongo and Candie's trademarks. Candie's took responsibility for design, sales, marketing, and merchandise, while Sweet Sportswear took responsibility for manufacturing, distribution, operations, and administration. The company placed the Bongos line in the $20 to $30 price range and Candie's branded apparel at $30 to $50. Candie's also added its own handbags division to design and produce a line of Candie's branded purses.

With Candie's jeanswear still under development, the Bongos line of junior apparel launched in early 1999. The advertising campaign featured Jennifer Esposito, co-star of the ABC sitcom *Spin City* and the 1998 movie *I Still Know What You Did Last Summer.* Entitled "let me b," the advertisements circulated from March through June 1999 in fashion and teen magazines, targeting young women in what was known as "Generation Y," from 15 to 25 years of age.

Jeans and apparel under the Candie's trademark launched in fall 1999 in conjunction with other Candie's trademarked products. The product line included sunglasses and optical eyewear by Viva International and socks and legwear by Ben Berger LLC. Liz Claiborne Cosmetics also launched a line of Candie's and Candie's Men fragrance products. The fragrance line included perfume, soap, and body mist for young women and cologne, aftershave, and a hair-and-body-wash for young men.

Liz Claiborne Cosmetics (LCC) had approached Candie's to license the brand as a means to attract young women from Generation Y into department stores. The fifteen-year licensing agreement gave LCC rights to formulate, manufacture, and distribute fragrances and cosmetics. Due to financial difficulties at Candie's, related to its SEC filings, LCC funded the marketing campaign for the fragrance products. LCC allocated $10 million for print, television, cable television, and cooperative advertising and $10 million for promotional items such as catalogs and scented temporary tattoos.

The media campaign, entitled "Anywhere You Dare" and created by Candie's in-house marketing staff, generated controversy as some viewed the ads as too sexually provocative. Alyssa Milano, of the TV sitcom *Charmed,* starred in a print ad in which she has just opened a large medicine chest full of condoms with a bottle of Candie's fragrance on the bottom shelf. The ads tended to be banned by local television networks and magazines for teens. Several women's fashion and music magazines, as well as GQ, Details, and Maxim published the print ads, while several cable television stations, including MTV, VH-1, and Comedy Central, aired the commercials.

Just before filing for divorce, Carmen Electra and Dennis Rodman posed for several advertisements featuring the couple in ardent poses, which some media outlets refused to print. *Vogue, Vibe, Maxim, Cosmopolitan, Glamour, Jane, GQ, Penthouse,* and *Premiere* did publish them. In one ad the two lounged in satin sheets with Rodman's hand on Electra's breast, while bottles of Candie's and Candie's Men sat on a side table. The campaign included a three-page poster in *Rolling Stone,* and a billboard on Seventh Avenue in New York City. In those ads Electra sprayed Candie's fragrance down the boxer shorts of a shirtless, tatooed Rodman.

With a Web site reconstruction in progress, Candie's placed the ads on the site at www.candies.com. The Web site attracted 100,000 visitors in the first few days. The redesigned Web site launched in October. New features of the Web site involved surveys, a chat room, contests, product displays, a personality quiz, and a page with the advertisements.

New footwear in 1999 included a line of "street surfer" shoes, a cross between sandals and athletic styles based on surfer footwear. With neoprene uppers, the shoes came in such colors as yellow, lime, aqua, and periwinkle, and incorporated easy on-and-off snap buckles and buckle straps. Advertisements featured the platinum-selling country group the Dixie Chicks and Grammy-winning performer Brandy. Shown in offstage settings, the Dixie Chicks lounged in a hotel room reading Playgirl magazine and ate fast food in a limousine. Brandy sang jingles written by Ray J, her 16-year-old brother, which appealed to audiences on both MTV and Nickelodeon. The videos also played in Kids Footlocker stores.

Candie's opened two 3,000-square-foot showrooms in New York City in 1999, one for each of the Candie's and Bongo brands. Each showroom offered the full product line for its brand, including Candie's fragrances and eyewear. Monitors in the showrooms displayed Candie's television commercials and print advertisements. The location of the showrooms near other clothing showrooms, such as DKNY and Liz Claiborne, rather than near footwear showrooms, reflected the company's expanded product line.

Principal Subsidiaries

Bright Star Footwear, Ltd.; UnZipped Apparel LLC (50%).

Principal Competitors

Esprit de Corp.; Nine West Group, Inc.; Skechers U.S.A., Inc.

Further Reading

Annis, Elisa, "Designer Candie's," *Footwear News*, July 29, 1996, p. 10.

Boehning, Julie C., "Candie's Stretches Expansion Net to Asia," *Footwear News*, July 14, 1997, p. 5.

——, "Jenny McCarthy Stars in Candie's Promos," *Footwear News*, February 10, 1997, p. 22.

——, "Little Divas," *Footwear News*, March 8, 1999, p.16.

——, "Positively Shocking? Candie's Ads Are, Once Again, a Point of Contention," *Footwear News*, July 28, 1997, p. 28.

Butler, Simon. "Candie's DV8 Men's Line Taken out of Production." *Footwear News*, March 22, 1999, p. 2.

"Candie's Chickapalooza," *Footwear News*, June 5, 1998, p. 16.

"Candie's Deals for Bongo Jeans," *Footwear News*, August 31, 1998, p. 4.

"Candie's New Big Apple Digs," *Footwear News*, July 19, 1999, p. 9.

"Candie's Tries Its Hand at Bags," *Footwear News*, March 9, 1998, p. 6.

Ciampi, Thomas, "Amid Customs Probe Millfeld Ousts Prexy," *Footwear News*, March 2, 1992, p. 37.

——, "Millfeld Discontinues Most of Its Operations," *Footwear News*, May 4, 1992, p. 40.

"Cohen, Milstein, Hausfeld & Toll, P.L.L.C. Files Class Action Suit Against Candies, Inc.," *Business Wire*, June 1, 1999.

"Controversial Candie's Ads Are Just a Click Away," *Footwear News*, July 26, 1999, p. 137.

"Cosmo Shuns One of Candie's Music Ads," *Footwear News*, August 10, 1998, p. 92.

Diamond, Kerry, "Claiborne Sweet on Candie's Scents," *Women's Wear Daily*, March 26, 1999, p. 7.

——, and Alev Aktar, "Claiborne, Candie's License Deal Smells Sweet," *Women's Wear Daily*, June 24, 1998, p. 7.

D'Innocenzio, Anne, "Candie's Slates IPO Funds for Ads," *Footwear News*, March 1, 1993, p. 4.

Farnsworth, Steve, "Millfeld Files New Stock Plan for Candie's," *Footwear News*, December 28, 1992, p. 9.

"Import-Duty Query Leads to U.S. Probe of Millfeld's Ex-Aides," *Wall Street Journal*, February 25, 1992, p. A4.

Kroll, Luisa, "Like My Shoes?," *Forbes*, April 7, 1997, pp. 70–71.

"Lucky's First Foot Forward," *Women's Wear Daily*, August 22, 1996, p. 11.

Malone, Scott, "Liz Claiborne Fragrance Package Will Sweeten Candie's Name," *Footwear News*, July 27, 1998, p. 5.

"McCarthy's Back in New Candie's Campaign," *Footwear News*, February 2, 1998, p. 12.

McKay, Deirdre, "Candie's Is Getting Rugged," *Footwear News*, February 17, 1992, p. S6.

Mullins, David Philip, "Ad Ingenue," *Footwear News*, January 18, 1999, p. 21.

"NASDAQ May Delist Candie's for Failing to File 2 Reports," *Women's Wear Daily*, June 16, 1999, p. 19.

Ozzard, Janet, "Candie's Ads Butt In," *Women's Wear Daily*, July 25, 1997, p. 11.

Quick, Rebecca, "Candie's Restates Results, as SEC Probes Accounting," *Wall Street Journal*, September 23, 1999, p. B19.

Ryan, Thomas, J., "Candie's Sues Web Operator for Name Use in Porno Sales," *Footwear News*, October 6, 1997, p. 6.

Schupack, Hedda, "It's a Shoe-In," *Jewelers Circular Keystone*, June 1998, p. 194.

Seckler, Valerie, "Charles Cole," *Footwear News*, December 6, 1993, p. 39.

——, "Millfeld Agrees to Acquire El Greco's Candie's Brand," *Footwear News*, February 17, 1992, p. 2.

Sender, Isabelle, "Candie's Debuts Casual, Athletic Lines for Girls," *Footwear News*, February 1, 1993, p. 50.

——, "Candie's in Kids Pact with Brown," *Footwear News*, December 20, 1993, p. 2.

——, "Raising the "Union" Flag: Kids' Firms Roll out Strategic Alliances," *Footwear News*, February 7, 1994, p. 12.

——, "Vendors Pull out All Stops for Biz," *Footwear News*, November 13, 1995, p. 1.

Socha, Miles, "Candie's to Produce its Own Jeans Line with Bongo Purchase," *Women's Wear Daily*, August 25, 1998, p.1.

Solnik, Claude, "Candie's Fragrance Spots Found Just Too Steamy for Some TV Stations, Mags," *Footwear News*, July 19, 1999, p. 5.

——, "Candie's Hopes Rodman-Electra Ads Have That Sweet Smell of Success," *Footwear News*, August 9, 1999, p. 12.

"Sweet Success," *Footwear News*, February 9, 1998, p. 18.

"To Boldly Go Where No Shoe Has Gone Before," *Footwear News*, July 21, 1997, p. 4.

—Mary Tradii

Carolina First Corporation

102 South Main Street
Greenville, South Carolina 29601
U.S.A.
Telephone: (864) 255-7900
Toll Free: (800) 476-6400
Fax: (864) 299-6401
Web site: http://www.carolinafirst.com

Public Company
Incorporated: 1986
Employees: 900
Sales: $203.41 million (1998)
Stock Exchanges: NASDAQ
Ticker Symbol: CAFC
NAIC: 52211 Commercial Banking

As North Carolina's larger banks began to acquire South Carolina banks in the mid-1980s, Carolina First Corporation was created to fill the gap between the large and small players. Carolina First positions itself as offering the personalized attention of smaller community banks with the range of services of the larger institutions. The company has assets of $3 billion, nearly 70 offices in South Carolina and more than a dozen in Florida, and an increasing online presence.

Origins: Mid-1980s

In 1985 the South Carolina General Assembly passed legislation allowing out-of-state banks to expand into South Carolina. The next year, NCNB, which would become NationsBank, then Bank of America, bought Bankers Trust, a Columbia-based bank which had earlier been known as State Bank and Trust.

One of the bank's key executives was Senior Vice-President Mack I. Whittle, Jr., who had started his career there by rolling coins as a college student in 1969. He went to work full time after graduating from the University of South Carolina with a degree in business in 1972. Two years later, Bankers Trust bought Peoples National Bank, based in Greenville, and Whittle moved there. For the next several years he moved around the state as the fast-growing bank acquired new branches. Whittle settled in Greenville in 1982.

When NCNB bought Bankers Trust, it appeared that Whittle was slated for yet another transfer, most likely to Maryland or Florida. The prospect of uprooting his family again gave Whittle reason to seek another position. In addition, Whittle felt that the new interstate banks were not appropriately responsive to their customers, and he envisioned a better alternative.

After twenty years in business in South Carolina, Whittle had plenty of contacts to troll for support for a new, locally owned bank. Many prominent businessmen, Whittle's old clients, became stockholders or clients of the new bank, Carolina First Corp. In May 1986, Whittle hired his former secretary and rented an office. Its initial public offering in September raised $15 million, and the bank opened for business on December 18, 1986.

Carolina First's first branch office had been vacated after the merger of South Carolina National Bank and the First National Bank of South Carolina. Two years later, Carolina First moved into another property vacated by the same merger, a historic bank building in downtown Greenville dating back to 1873.

The flood of mergers in the banking business provided Carolina First with an ongoing stream of potential clients disillusioned with the increasingly impersonal nature of banking. It also provided a source of experienced employees. Nap Vandiver went to work as chairman emeritus at Carolina First after the bank he founded in 1961, Southern Bank and Trust Co., was sold to First Union, another North Carolina bank. Vandiver was in his late seventies at the time. Some of the loan officers Whittle hired brought their loyal customers with them. There appeared to be a niche just right for the new bank. By the first quarter of 1988, deposits had swelled to $95 million, up from $38 million a year earlier. Employment had increased from 20 to 30.

The bank had to be diligent in protecting its rather generic trademark as smaller, new banks sometimes adopted similar names. One was called 1st Carolina, another First Carolina. Yet another, in Myrtle Beach, called itself Carolina First.

In March 1989, Carolina First's $150 million in assets made it South Carolina's fifteenth-largest bank, and at the and of that

Company Perspectives:

Carolina First was created in 1986 with one simple, bold mission: to become a premier bank by putting customers first. After more than ten years of service, that guiding principle is more important than ever. Through our progressive and innovative approach to our customers, Carolina First delivers personable, flexible and responsive banking. Our commitment to knowing our customers and developing the right mix of services to meet their needs has always been the hallmark of Carolina First.

year Carolina First acquired Georgetown's First Federal Savings and Loan Association. The deal was made possible by new federal legislation allowing the purchase of savings and loan institutions that were not failing. That purchase and an earlier branch opened in Georgetown helped establish the bank in the fast-growing coastal region.

The Expansive Early 1990s

Local businessman Foster McKissick was named the company's first chairman. After he died in a private plane crash in 1990, William R. Timmons, Jr., succeeded him as chairman. The bank had four offices in Greenville at the time, and its executives had a goal of expanding throughout the state.

In 1991 Carolina First bought two branches of American Federal Savings Bank in Anderson, bought four First Savings Bank branches in Myrtle Beach, and opened another Greenville office. It eventually created the Carolina First Savings Bank subsidiary to manage its thrifts. The next year, the bank gained a foothold in the Midlands with the purchase of 12 Columbia branches of Republic National Bank. It bought another three branches there from Omni Savings Bank, a subsidiary of FirstFed Michigan Corp. Next on the agenda was a regional headquarters for the area. These acquisitions raised Carolina First's assets to $800 million and gave it 22 branches.

Between 1992 and 1994, Carolina First raised $48 million through preferred stock offerings. Its assets topped $1 billion in 1995. In May 1994, the goal of becoming a truly statewide bank seemed close at hand as Citadel Federal Savings and Loan was acquired. However, its attempted purchase of seven offices of another Charleston thrift, Cooper River Federal Savings Association, was thwarted by a higher bid from Columbia-based First Citizens Bank.

High-Tech Initiatives in the Mid-1990s

Carolina First's involvement with a new technology company came to be seen as both a boon for shareholders and a notorious enterprise. In 1994 Whittle and two other executives teamed Carolina First with Affinity Technology Group Inc., a Columbia-based company that was developing an ''automated loan machine'' (ALM) similar to automated teller machines. The deal gave Affinity a $200,000 loan and consulting expertise in exchange for a 20 percent share of the company. Affinity began marketing the ALMs in November 1994. In January 1996 the Carolina First board awarded the three executives ten percent of the company's Affinity stock, then worth about $580,000.

By the time of Affinity's initial public offering in April 1996, Carolina First had itself installed several ALMs around the state in places like grocery stores, with agreements in the works to place them at auto dealerships as well. Columbus, Ohio-based BancOne was also testing ALMs in West Virginia, paying Affinity a commission on loans approved. The ALMs stimulated loan business and saved employee time spent on conventionally processed loans. They spared customers what some perceived as the ordeal of meeting with a loan officer and potentially being turned down in person, and promised discrimination-proof lending. With customers already accustomed to using computerized banking technology such as ATMs, the ALMs seemed likely to be readily accepted, as Affinity president Mel Ray told the *Greenville News.* The devices were programmed to handle mortgages and other large loans, but were initially limited to amounts between $1,000 and $5,000.

Affinity offered shares to the public at $13 a share (in January, it had been valued at 88 cents a share). By May, its price hit $21 a share. The value of the shares the board had given the executives were worth $14 million. The interest in Affinity's public offering also benefited Carolina First's shareholders. The bank's stock value rose from $14 per share to $21 between November 1995 and May 1996.

Investors filed a $32 million lawsuit over the executive bonus in the fall of 1996, stating that Whittle and another Carolina First board member, Edward Sebastian, were also members of Affinity's board and most likely knew about the impending public offering that sent Affinity stock skyward. Within a year, however, the Affinity stock in question had fallen to a value of $30 million. The lawsuit also dealt with alleged improprieties related to the acquisition of Midlands National Bank in late 1994. This part of the complaint claimed that Carolina First executives had hidden large losses before the deal and asked for $24 million in damages. It alleged that Carolina First had paid too much for credit card accounts held by Republic National Bank, whose parent company had Sebastian for a CEO and chairman, then exaggerated the amortization of the payment to make its figures look better. Another lawsuit arose in September 1995 from two brothers who were officers and board members of Midlands National who claimed breach of contract. The two Midlands National lawsuits were settled in April 1997 and the Affinity lawsuit was dismissed that December.

Besides automated loan machines, the focus of Carolina First's next ten years was home banking via the Internet. It began developing this system in earnest in 1995 and began marketing it a year later after first testing it with about 90 employees who used it for their personal banking needs. In 1996 the company operated 55 offices throughout South Carolina and had acquired Blue Ridge Finance, a Greenville auto finance company. Carolina First sold most of its credit card accounts in 1997, a year that saw record levels of consumer debt and an increase in bad loan write-offs at the bank.

In 1996 Carolina First acquired forty percent of Atlanta Internet Bank. In 1997 it had a public offering of half its shares in Net.B@ank Inc., the company taking over Atlanta Internet. At the time, the online bank had attracted more than $40 million in deposits from customers in 44 states. In March 1997 the bank announced plans for a $10 million, seven-story office complex in downtown Columbia. The city of Columbia promised

Key Dates:

1986: Carolina First founded as NCNB buys Bankers Trust.
1994: Bank teams with automated loan machine pioneer Affinity Technology Group.
1996: Company invests in Atlanta Internet Bank.
1999: Carolina First enters Florida market; Bank CaroLine debuts.

$3 million to lure the bank into space vacated by Macy's and Belk's department stores years before.

Carolina First bought Resource Processing, a credit card company, early in 1998. The bank sought to expand its retail credit offerings to complement its commercial banking strengths. In February its venture capital subsidiary, CF Investment Co., made its first investment, gaining a 49 percent share of ITS Inc. in exchange for a $1.2 million line of credit. ITS was a 20-person digital document storage operation based in Greenville. The bank invested in Syneractive Marketing LLC in November 1998.

As Carolina First grew and prepared to expand outside of South Carolina, it reorganized its executive ranks, adding three new executive vice-presidents in 1998. During the year, it had bought First National Bank, Colonial Bank of South Carolina, and Poinsett Financial Corp., as well as banks in Pickens County and Camden. Carolina First had $2.7 billion in assets at the end of the year.

Finding Room in Florida in 1999

Carolina First announced plans to buy its first out-of-state bank, Citizens First National Bank, in January 1999. Whittle drew similarities between the business climate in Florida, where NationsBank Corp. had just bought Barnett Banks Inc. for $15 billion, and that in South Carolina at the time that Carolina First was founded. The purchase of Citizens First was worth about $12 million, and gave Carolina First entry into the highly lucrative Jacksonville market. Before the Citizens First deal could close, Carolina First announced that it was buying another Florida bank, Orlando-based Citrus Bank. It would also use the Citrus name for its other Florida acquisitions. Citrus had a dozen locations and assets of $300 million; Carolina First's assets were about $2.5 billion.

In late 1999 Carolina First announced plans for a $25 million disaster-proof data center in Lexington County, which was designed to give the bank transaction security in the event of a hurricane. Upon opening in 2000, the center would employ 350.

Carolina First introduced its own Internet bank, Bank CaroLine, on September 15, 1999. Bank CaroLine, officials stated, competed for a different, less ''tech-savvy'' customer than that of Net.B@ank. CaroLine Bank at first operated through Carolina First Bank, FSB, the thrift subsidiary. Before starting CaroLine, Carolina First had sought to reduce its share in Net.B@nk by giving part of its stake to a nonprofit charity, Carolina First Foundation. Carolina First then owned about nine percent of Net.B@nk, worth about $90 million.

Principal Subsidiaries

Carolina First Bank; Carolina First Mortgage Company; Carolina First Bank, F.S.B.; Citrus Bank; Blue Ridge Finance Company, Inc.; Resource Processing Group, Inc.

Principal Competitors

Bank of America; Wachovia; First Union; SunTrust Bank.

Further Reading

Alger, Alexandra, ''Carolina First Picks New Leader,'' *Greenville News,* November 14, 1990, p. D6.

Bray, Chad, ''Carolina First Merges into Florida Banking,'' *Greenville News,* March 20, 1999, p. D1.

——, ''Carolina First to Build New Technology Center,'' *Greenville News,* October 1, 1999, p. D1.

Brooks, Rick, ''South Carolina Bank Aims to Swim with the Sharks in Florida Market,'' *Wall Street Journal,* January 27, 1999, p. S4.

Chapman, Leroy, Jr., ''Bank Expands Downtown Offices,'' *The State,* March 21, 1997, pp. B1, 6.

——, ''Carolina First Builds Executive Ranks in Preparing for New Level of Growth,'' *Greenville News,* January 6, 1999, pp. D1–2.

——, ''Carolina First to Acquire Florida Bank,'' *Greenville News,* January 27, 1999, pp. D1–2.

Davidson, Paul, ''Shareholders Sue Carolina First Executives,'' *Greenville News,* November 6, 1996, p. D8.

Dietrich, R. Kevin, ''Carolina First Seeking to Broaden Net's Appeal,'' *The State,* October 7, 1999.

DuPlessis, Jim, ''Carolina First President Stresses Profits over Size,'' *Greenville News,* April 21, 1988, p. D8.

Elliott, Suzanne, ''Carolina First Looks to Fifth Branch,'' *Greenville News,* December 13, 1988, pp. C2, 7.

Keefe, Robert, ''Carolina First to Merge with Coastal S&L,'' *Greenville News,* October 21, 1989, p. C8.

Little, Loyd, ''A Banker of Many Seasons,'' *Greenville News,* March 2, 1992, pp. C1–2.

Mollenkamp, Carrick, ''Carolina First Places New Bet on the Net,'' *Wall Street Journal,* July 7, 1999, p. S1.

O'Donoghue, Ed, ''Carolina First Going Public with Internet Banking,'' *Greenville News,* July 15, 1997, p. D6.

——, ''First Suit Tossed Out,'' *Greenville News,* December 3, 1997, p. D6.

Peterson, Wayne, ''Greenville's First Bank Building Now Houses City's Newest Bank,'' *Greenville News,* March 7, 1988, pp. C1–2.

Roberts, John, ''Bank Explores Loan Machines,'' *Greenville News,* April 10, 1996, p. B12.

——, ''Bank Hopes Loan Machines Increase Lending,'' *Greenville News,* February 20, 1995, p. D4.

——, ''Carolina First Looks to Next Decade,'' *Greenville News,* April 19, 1996, p. D6.

——, ''Whittle Has Carved out Own Niche,'' *Greenville News,* June 12, 1994, pp. D1, D8–11.

——, and Paul Davidson, ''Carolina First Executives' Stock Bonus Draws Criticism,'' *Greenville News,* May 30, 1996, p. D6.

Thompson, Samantha, ''Two Financial Firms in Court Over Names,'' *Greenville News,* March 22, 1995, p. D9.

Thrower, Anne P., ''Two Carolina First Lawsuits Settled,'' *Greenville News,* April 30, 1997, p. D6.

Welling, Irvine T., IV, ''Setting up an International Banking Department,'' *Business and Economic Review,* January–March 1997, pp. 19–21.

—Frederick C. Ingram

Carson, Inc.

64 Ross Road
Savannah, Georgia 31405
U.S.A.
Telephone: (912) 651-3400
Fax: (912) 651-3471
Web site: http://www.carsonproductsco.com

Public Company
Founded: 1951 as Carson Products
Employees: 988
Sales: $150.7 million (1998)
Stock Exchanges: New York Johannesburg
Ticker Symbol: CIC
NAIC: 32562 Toilet Preparation Manufacturing; 325998 All Other Miscellaneous Chemical Product and Preparation Manufacturing

Carson, Inc. is a manufacturer of hair and skin care products specifically designed for persons of color. The company's products, which include hair relaxers and texturizers, hair color, depilatory products, and hair care maintenance products, are marketed under brand names such as Dark & Lovely, Magic Shave, Gentle Treatment, and Ultra Sheen. They are sold through mass market retailers, beauty salons, and barber shops in more than 60 countries around the world.

Forty Years of Family Ownership

Carson, Inc. was founded by a well-educated and business-savvy southern gentleman named Abram Minis. Minis, a native of Savannah, Georgia, graduated from the Harvard Business School in 1928 and returned to his hometown to become an investment counselor. His timing was not especially good; just one year into his career, the stock market collapsed, and the country was pitched headlong into the Great Depression. Minis weathered the Depression years, however, and gained a reputation as one of the best businessmen in the area. In 1951 he bought a tiny manufacturing company in Savannah that employed only five workers and produced one product. Renaming the company "Carson Products," Minis gradually built up the operation's manufacturing capabilities, added employees, and developed almost 50 new hair care products, all targeted at an African American market.

Under Minis's leadership, Carson invested heavily in research and development and became an innovator in the area of ethnic hair care products. In the early 1970s, the company became the first to introduce a line of hair color formulated specifically for black women. In 1978 it again broke new ground when it developed a hair relaxer that contained no lye. Unlike its harsher, lye-based forerunners, Carson's gentler relaxer formula reduced the chances of skin injury and hair loss.

Carson remained in the Minis family's ownership for more than 40 years. By the mid-1990s, however, the Minises were ready to get out of the hair care business. In 1994 they began accepting bids for the family business. Although a number of large companies were interested in Carson, one of its own board members managed to orchestrate a buyout.

1995: Buyout and New Leadership

Carson's new owner, Dr. Leroy Keith, was not known for his business experience. Although he had once owned some Pizza Hut franchises in South Carolina, most of his professional energies had been devoted to his position as president of Atlanta's Morehouse College. What led Keith from the ivory towers of academia into the world of business was, quite simply, Carson's potential. In the mid-1990s, the company had an 82 percent share of the ethnic hair color market, a 20 percent share of the nonprofessional hair relaxer market, and name recognition among 97 percent of African American women. An additional selling point for Keith was the overall growth potential of the ethnic hair care market. In 1995, U.S. sales of ethnic hair care products generated $1.2 billion—and were estimated to grow by five percent annually.

To buy the company, Keith obtained the backing of a Connecticut-based investment group, which helped raise $17 million in capital. The remainder of the $95 million purchase was funded through a combination of traditional bank debt, private institution funding, and promissory notes issued to the Minis family. In August of 1995, Keith finalized the Carson buyout,

Company Perspectives:

Carson has an enormous amount of heritage as a company specifically focused on African American consumers. Our world-class products have been satisfying the expectations of African American consumers for over a century. Our brands are household names among people of African descent worldwide.

becoming the company's first African American chairman and CEO. Keith immediately strengthened Carson's management team by recruiting industry veteran Joyce Roche. Roche, who had spent 19 years working for Avon, most recently as the company's vice-president of global marketing, became the company's new president.

Believing it was critical to expand the scope of Carson's market, Keith made planning for growth his first priority. Working collaboratively with 41 of his new employees, he crafted a five-point strategy that included increasing the company's share of existing markets; broadening its global presence; creating new product categories; developing a salon-exclusive product line; and acquiring production facilities and other product brands.

1996–97: Growing Pains

Before embarking on these ambitious growth plans, Carson needed to generate capital and get out from under some of the debt incurred in the leveraged buyout. Toward that end, the company's South African subsidiary, Carson Holdings Limited, sold 25 percent of its shares on the Johannesburg stock exchange in July of 1996. Three months later, Carson made its initial public offering in the United States. Together, the two offerings resulted in proceeds of slightly more than $48 million, much of which was used to pay off debt.

With a stronger balance sheet, Keith wasted no time in acting upon Carson's strategy for expansion. He quickly moved to deepen the company's presence in overseas markets by launching a major Caribbean marketing campaign. He also purchased two manufacturing facilities—one in South Africa and one in Ghana—to manufacture Carson's flagship Dark & Lovely product lines, along with smaller, region-specific lines. The company also laid the groundwork to begin producing its own cosmetics. In June of 1996, Carson invested $3 million in AM Cosmetics, Inc., a New York-based maker of cosmetic products. AM was retained to manufacture a new Dark & Lovely ethnic makeup line.

At the beginning of 1997, the company initiated an aggressive acquisition campaign, scooping up five new product lines within six months. Three of the acquisitions were made by Carson's South African subsidiary: the Nu-Me cosmetics and skin care brand, the Restore Plus hair care line, and a line of toiletries marketed under the trade name Seasilk. The two U.S. acquisitions were a line of hair styling products sold under the "Let's Jam" name and a line of nail care products sold under the brand name "Cutex." Cutex, which was a major player in the U.S. nail care market, was chosen to provide Carson an entry into the mass market.

While the company focused its efforts on expansion, the market for its ethnic hair care products was beginning to soften. Eventually, Carson fell prey to the downturn, announcing in April of 1997 that its domestic sales had fallen ten to 15 percent from those of the previous year. Citing an overall slowdown in the U.S. ethnic hair care market as the culprit, Carson warned that it was going to fall short of its sales and earnings expectations. Investor response was swift and unforgiving. The day after the company made the announcement, its stock, which had climbed to $17 a share, plummeted to $7.87.

Carson had to move quickly to minimize the damage and repair relations with investors and analysts. As a start, Keith recruited a seasoned industry pro, Robert Pierce, to become the company's chief financial officer. Pierce formerly had been the CFO for Maybelline Inc., and his industry knowledge and skills were well-respected, so Keith hoped his presence would reassure the investment community.

While working to smooth ruffled feathers and get sales and earnings back on track, Keith continued to steer Carson on a path of growth and diversification. In August 1997, the company launched its new Dark & Lovely line of cosmetics. The product line—which included lipsticks, eyeshadows, blushes, nail polish, powders, and foundations—was sold through drug stores and large department stores such as Wal-Mart and Kmart. Carson followed up the launch with a series of promotions and product line expansions designed to boost sales.

1998: Gains and Losses

The market for ethnic personal care products continued to show signs of softening throughout 1997 and into 1998, and Carson's earnings suffered accordingly. By the middle of 1998, it became apparent that the company needed something more than its current management team could provide. In June, Keith stepped down from his position as Carson's CEO and recruited Gregory Andrews to pilot the company. Andrews, who had 20 years' experience in the personal care products industry, was an executive at Colgate-Palmolive at the time. Keith explained his decision in a September 1998 interview with *Black Enterprise:* "With our aggressive acquisition strategy, we need to share the responsibilities of day-to-day operations so I can focus more on international expansion. With Gregory's background, this job was tailor made for him."

Less than a month after Andrews took over as CEO, Carson completed its most significant acquisition to date. The company purchased Johnson Products Co., Inc., a major manufacturer of personal care products for the ethnic market. The acquisition gave Carson a number of additional product lines—including Johnson's Gentle Treatment relaxer, Ultra Sheen, and Posner, one of the oldest brands in ethnic cosmetics. Immediately, Carson became the leader in five U.S. ethnic hair care categories: adult relaxer kits, hair dress/conditioners, hair color, shaving products, and comb-out/oil sheens. As part of the Johnson purchase, Carson also acquired Dermablend, Inc. Dermablend, a wholly owned subsidiary of Johnson, produced a line of corrective cosmetics that had a 40 to 50 percent ethnic consumer base.

Key Dates:

1951: Abram Minis buys Savannah-based manufacturing company and renames it Carson Products.
1995: Leroy Keith spearheads buyout of Carson.
1996: Carson makes initial public offerings on Johannesburg and New York stock exchanges.
1997: Carson acquires several product lines, including Cutex.
1998: Gregory Andrews becomes Carson's CEO; Keith stays on as chairman of the board; Carson acquires Johnson Products Co., Inc. and sells Cutex.
1999: Gregory Andrews dies while on business trip to South Africa; Malcolm Yesner is appointed CEO and president.

Carson consolidated Johnson's sales force and much of its administrative staff into its existing staff. Simultaneously, the company took measures to streamline and reduce inefficiencies in its overall operation. One such measure was the sale of its Cutex business. Citing a desire to focus more fully on the ethnic hair care market, Carson sold its Cutex line in early December, after owning it less than two years. In a second streamlining effort, Joyce Roche, who had been the company's president since 1995, resigned from her position. Greg Andrews became Carson's president as well as its CEO. ''We're trying to get our expenses in line, and, as you know, we had a really top-heavy management group,'' Andrews explained in a September 1998 interview with the *Atlanta Journal and Constitution.* ''This is as much as anything us making moves to get our costs in line with the levels of sales in the corporation.''

1999: Beginnings of a Turnaround

Carson's 1999 got off to a rocky and unforeseen start. In February, Gregory Andrews died suddenly while on a business trip in South Africa. The 47-year-old Andrews had served only eight months as the company's CEO. Stunned, Carson's board appointed Malcolm Yesner as acting CEO. Yesner, who had served previously as president of the company's international operations and as CEO of its South African subsidiary, subsequently became president and CEO on a permanent basis.

Despite the brevity of his tenure, Andrews had made some real strides toward turning Carson around. As 1999 progressed, the company began to see the fruits of his efforts. Carson had a profitable first quarter—its first in more than a year. The company also announced plans to launch a new line of hair coloring products, marketed under the name ''Dark & Lovely Diva.'' The announcement heralded the first product introduction since the 1997 launch of the Dark & Lovely cosmetics line.

The company continued its turnaround into the second and third quarters of 1999. ''Carson is clearly making progress,'' Yesner said in an October 25, 1999 press release. ''Our efforts to increase sales, improve margins, and revitalize our core brands are yielding results. We are highly enthusiastic regarding the outlook for the company.'' Investors, however, did not appear to share Yesner's optimism. The company's stock, which had fallen to $2 per share in late 1998, continued to hover in the $3 range through the third quarter of 1999.

Looking Ahead

As 1999 wound down, Carson was optimistic that it could continue making gains in its sales and earnings. The company planned to remain tightly focused on the ethnic hair market and to continue trimming expenses—including a $2.5 million reduction in annualized employee expenses.

Carson was planning several new products and promotions expected to build on the success of its two most profitable product lines, Dark & Lovely and Johnson Products. A new Dark & Lovely relaxer kit was planned for introduction in 2000. The company was also in the process of building an e-commerce website that would serve investors, retailers, and end-users of Carson products. It anticipated having the site operational by the beginning of the year 2000.

Finally, Carson planned to continue expanding rapidly in overseas markets, deepening its presence in Africa, South America, and Europe. With an estimated ten million people of color in Europe, 80 million in South America, and 230 million in Africa, the potential for growth in these markets was virtually unlimited. As of October 1999, exports accounted for only ten percent of the company's sales, but this percentage was likely to grow in the future.

Principal Subsidiaries

Carson Products Company; Carson Management Company; Johnson Products Co., Inc.; Carson Holdings Limited (South Africa); Carson Products Do Brasil; Carson UK Ltd.; Dermablend, Inc.; Carson Products (Proprietary) Limited (South Africa); Carson Products West Africa Limited (Ghana); Carson Products East Africa Limited.

Principal Competitors

Alberto-Culver Company; Revlon, Inc.; Soft Sheen Products Inc.

Further Reading

''Carson Deepens Ethnic Presence,'' *Drug Store News,* August 24, 1998, p. 13.
DeWitte, Dave, ''Savannah, Ga.-Based Ethnic Beauty-Products Firm Shifts Focus To End Skid,'' *Knight-Ridder Tribune Business News,* October 27, 1999.
Oestricher, Dwight, ''Getting All Dolled Up,'' *Black Enterprise,* October, 1997.
Poole, Shelia, ''Andrews Death Raises Concerns About Carson,'' *Atlanta Journal and Constitution,* February 28, 1999, p. F01.
——, ''President of Savannah, Ga.-Based Carson Quits in Shake-Up,'' *Atlanta Journal and Constitution,* September 19, 1998.
Puri, Shaifali, ''A Cut Above,'' *Fortune,* August 4, 1997, p. 55.
Rhea, Shawn E., ''Carson Gets a Makeover,'' *Black Enterprise,* October, 1997.

—Shawna Brynildssen

Casa Cuervo, S.A. de C.V.

Avenida Rio Churubusco 213
08400 Mexico, D.F.
Mexico
Telephone: (525) 625-4400
Fax: (525) 625-4408
Web site: http://www.cuervo.com

Wholly Owned Subsidiary of Grupo Cuervo, S.A. de C.V.
Incorporated: 1934 as Casa Tequila Cuervo, S.A.
Employees: 1,400
Sales: $400 million (1997 est.)
NAIC: 31214 Distilleries; 111998 All Other Miscellaneous Crop Farming

Casa Cuervo, S.A. de C.V. is the leading manufacturer and distributor of tequila, the best-known of the distinctive Mexican alcoholic beverages made from the sap of agave (called *maguey* in Mexico), a genus of desert plants. It is also the oldest existing producer of tequila. Casa Cuervo's tequila brands, all under the Cuervo name, rank second to Tequila Sauza in sales in Mexico but first in total because of the company's success in marketing the drink abroad. Casa Cuervo is a subsidiary of Grupo Cuervo, S.A. de C.V., a privately owned company that manufactures or imports and distributes rum, whiskey, gin, liqueurs, wines, and mixed drinks as well as tequila.

A Family Business: 1758–1940

Pulque, fermented from the sap of agave, was the only alcoholic beverage of the Aztecs. With their own wine stores in short supply, the Spanish conquerors tried the brew but found it unpalatable. When they distilled the sap, however, it yielded an acceptable spirit called mezcal. The production method that Spanish colonists passed to their descendants was to lop off the leaves of the mature agave with a long knife, leaving the 200-pound heart of the plant to be heated in a stone furnace to convert the starches of the sap into sugars. The sap then was extracted from the pulp in a mill, fermented with yeast in a tank, and distilled in a copper still.

The preferred plant species for making this spirit came to be "blue" agave—so-called for the silvery blue hue of its spiky leaves. Blue agave grew best in the state of Jalisco, particularly in the area surrounding the village of Tequila. The brew made from this plant, after being fermented, distilled twice, and aged in oak barrels, was called the "wine" of Tequila.

The family Cuervo y Montaño was the third known to have produced tequila, having founded a distillery on the hacienda deeded to José Antonio Cuervo in 1758. The Spanish government, in 1785, banned Mexican liquors to protect the home industry but ten years later recognized that this decree was ineffectual and extended to José Antonio's son José María Guadalupe Cuervo permission to produce tequila.

After his death, his son-in-law, Vicente Albino Rojas, renamed the Cuervo distillery La Rojeña. Under his management the business thrived, and the hacienda came to include three million agave plants. Rojas's son-in-law, Jesús Flores, moved the distillery to another location and was the first to bottle tequila as well as to sell it in wooden casks. Other Cuervo family members also were involved in the cultivation of agave and manufacture of tequila. (Cenobio Sauza, a Cuervo employee at this time, founded his own distillery in 1873; Tequila Sauza became Cuervo's great rival.)

By the early 1890s Cuervo family members were growing some 2.5 million to five million blue agave plants (along with other crops) on what, in 1905, totaled 10,145 hectares (about 25,000 acres). José Cuervo Labastida, who married Flores's widow, Ana González Rubio, in 1900, was the first to call the tequila produced at La Rojeña "José Cuervo." The tequila produced under this name won some international awards, including prizes given in 1907 in Madrid and 1909 in Paris. But this first tequila boom, which included the first sales of the beverage in the United States, ended in 1902–03, because of general economic hardship and dry weather. Other cited factors were adulteration with cheaper forms of alcohol and possible overproduction of the drink.

The tequila sales slump continued into the 1930s. Moreover, the land reform of this period broke up many large estates, including the hacienda San Antonio del Potrero, which covered 9,398 hectares (more than 23,000 acres) and was owned solely by Ana Gonzalez Rubio after José Cuervo Labastida died in 1921. Other such enterprises in the Tequila region were also

Key Dates:

1795: José María Guadeloupe Cuervo receives royal permission to produce tequila on his property.
1909: The firm's tequila wins an international award in Paris.
1970: The Cuervo family sells part ownership to outsiders.
1995: Cuervo introduces a $75-a-bottle premium tequila.
1997: Cuervo's output reaches 37 million liters of tequila, of which 76 percent is exported.

hard hit, so much so that the number there of agave plants—which take about a decade to mature—dropped by two-thirds.

Boom and Bust: 1940–85

The Cuervo and Sauza enterprises came to dominate the tequila industry in the 1940s, a decade that saw a second tequila boom. Tequila production doubled in the 1951–55 period, leading to a crisis of overproduction and no growth for the rest of the decade. In the 1960s and 1970s, production grew by an average of between seven to eight percent a year. Quality, however, was allowed to decline. The official standard established in 1949 required that the sugars in the beverage come 100 percent from blue agave. In 1964, however, tequila producers were allowed to obtain up to 30 percent of the sugars from other sources—such as sugarcane and honey—and in 1970, up to 48.5 percent.

Mechanized transport in the agave fields did not become the rule in the tequila industry until the 1970s. The practice of mixing agave with corn, and sometimes beans and soybeans as well, for the sake of the soil and to prevent the spread of disease, made mechanization impractical before then, and as a consequence the plants tended to grow too large. The 1970 legal revision that allowed tequila producers to obtain more sugar from other sources was due to a shortage of usable blue agave. The Cuervo and Sauza enterprises were producing 60 percent of all tequila in 1976, when a strike of both laborers and transport personnel paralyzed both firms for 20 days. The two companies then agreed to buy their agave from the union representing the strikers and to pay one percent of the value of their finished product.

Ana González Rubio died in 1934 and left her estate to a niece, Guadalupe Gallardo, who died in 1966. She left the business to her sister, Virginia Gallardo. One of Virginia's four sons, Juan Beckman (or Beckmann) Gallardo, was managing the business at this time. In 1970 the enterprise, Casa Tequila Cuervo, S.A., passed, in part, into the hands of Distribuidora Bega, S.A. de C.V., the largest bottler and distributor of alcoholic beverages in Mexico. This firm was owned in part by Grupo Kentucky Fried Chicken—the Mexican subsidiary of the U.S. company—and in part by Guadalupe Sánchez Rubio and Antonio and Diego Gutiérrez Cortina.

The part of Casa Tequila Cuervo not sold to Distribuidora Bega was shared by Juan Beckman Gallardo, his son Juan Beckman Vidal (who later succeeded his father as head of the firm), José Luis Campos, and the U.S. firm Heublein, Inc., which already held distribution rights abroad. (Kentucky Fried Chicken and Heublein merged in 1971.) This pooling of resources established a company, named Grupo Cuervo in 1979, that produced or imported and distributed a wide range of wine and spirits in Mexico, not only tequila.

Tequila Cuervo's exports increased from 300,000 liters in 1961 to 4.24 million liters in 1971, when it was exporting to 51 countries and spending $500,000 a year on advertising abroad. The company was sending the beverage overseas in 200-liter stainless steel barrels to two bottling plants in the United States (in Hartford, Connecticut and Menlo Park, California) and one each in Australia, Belgium, El Salvador, and Switzerland. (It saved on taxes by having the beverage bottled abroad rather than in Mexico.) Tequilera de Los Altos, a subsidiary, was established in 1972 to run a new distillery supplying bulk tequila exclusively to the parent company.

The severe Mexican economic crisis of the early 1980s resulted in sales of what one industry executive called the "national aperitif" dropping from 34 million liters in 1980 to 13 million in 1986. Forty percent of all tequila enterprises went out of business during this period, and Tequila Cuervo's Los Altos distillery even closed for a year. The large tequila companies suspended dividends and laid off workers. Another common measure was to cut the alcoholic content from 45 percent to 38 percent, the minimum allowed by law. The continued growth of the overseas market was the only bright spot for Cuervo, and for the tequila industry as a whole.

Relying on Export Sales: 1987–99

In 1987 Cuervo was leading Sauza in tequila production, 18 million liters to 16 millions liters, even though the latter had 65 percent of the Mexican market, because Cuervo was exporting 70 percent of its production. Nevertheless, the tequila industry as a whole was working at only 40 percent of capacity. The continued scarcity of usable agave would have been a problem if not for the fall in production. Another problem for the big producers was that cheap "pseudo" tequilas now ranked second in liquor volume in Mexico, trailing only brandy. Rum was third and "real" tequila only fourth. Bogus tequila was being produced in Europe and marketed there as tequila, despite Mexican protests.

R.J. Reynolds Industries purchased Heublein in 1986 and sold it the next year to a British company, Grand Metropolitan plc. Heublein remained the exclusive importer and marketer in the United States of José Cuervo, which in turn was the Mexican distributor for the wines and spirits of Heublein's immediate parent, International Distillers & Vintners Ltd. In 1991 Heublein's Mexican affiliate agreed to acquire a 45 percent stake in José Cuervo y Cia, S.A., which was described by a Cuervo spokesperson as a sister company of Casa Cuervo and Grupo Cuervo. The agreement also allowed International Distillers to expand Cuervo distribution worldwide. These supplies of tequila continued to be exported in bulk to avoid the 44.5 percent Mexican alcoholic beverage tax and the 15 percent value-added tax on final sales.

Grand Metropolitan was renamed Diageo plc after merging in late 1997 with Guinness plc. José Cuervo contributed more than $80 million to Diageo's gross profits that year. Grand Metropolitan had held the U.S. rights to distribute Cuervo products until 2010, but in 1998 José Cuervo challenged in court Diageo's right to continue this distribution agreement as Grand Metropolitan's successor.

Amador de Carvalho, who became director general of Grupo Cuervo in 1998, drafted a new strategic plan for the firm that, in part, called for winning back lost tequila customers. Although Casa Cuervo was the leader in production, with 37 million liters in 1997, it still ranked second in sales within Mexico to Tequila Sauza. José Cuervo had scarcely any sales presence in the Guadalajara metropolitan area, which must have been highly embarrassing to the firm since Guadalajara is the capital of the state of Jalisco, heartland of tequila. By contrast, Cuervo continued to be well ahead abroad, with half the world market. Its tequila was being sold in 85 nations. Export sales accounted for 76 percent of the company's production, which in 1998 grew to an estimated 46 million liters. Cuervo's plantations held about 40 million blue agave plants in 1999.

By this time Cuervo was upgrading its image by introducing new, expensive brands of tequila. La Reserva de la Familia, an aged tequila with all-agave sugars, introduced in 1995 and retailing in the United States for $75, sold out its first edition in weeks. In 1998 the company introduced 1800 Coleccion Añejo in a bottle made of Belgian crystal, housed in a hand-sculptured pewter decanter encased in suede and leather. This limited edition of 347 specimens was priced at $1,000 a bottle.

The José Cuervo portfolio of tequilas in 1999 consisted of Cuervo Blanco, Cuervo Oro, Cuervo Tradicional, Cuervo Añejo, and Cuervo Reserva de la Familia in the José Cuervo line; 1800 Reposado, 1800 Añejo, and 1800 Coleccion in the higher-priced 1800 line; and Plata, Reposado, Añejo, and Agavero in the highest-priced Gran Centenario line. *Reposado* indicates that tequila has been aged for at least three months in oak barrels and *añejo* that it has been aged for at least 12 months.

Principal Subsidiaries

José Cuervo International (United States).

Principal Competitors

Tequila Sauza.

Further Reading

Cáceres, Jorge A., ''A Shot Known 'Round the World,'' *Business Mexico,* November 1996, pp. 38–40.

''Grand Metropolitan PLC,'' *Wall Street Journal,* March 1, 1991, p. B4.

Jacobo, Edmundo, Matilde Luna, and Ricardo Tirado, eds., *Empresas de Mexico,* Guadalajara: University of Guadalajara, 1989.

Luna Zamora, Rogelio, *La historia del tequila, de sus regiones y sus hombres,* Mexico City: Consejo Nacional para la Cultura y las Artes, 1991.

Orellana, Margarita de, ''A Micro-History of Tequila: The Cuervo Case,'' *Artes de Mexico,* November 1994, pp. 87–89.

Preston, Julia, ''Drinking Tequila But Thinking Cognac, Maybe?,'' *New York Times,* January 4, 1996, p. D5.

Prial, Frank J., ''We'll Have the Chateau Cuervo,'' *New York Times,* March 15, 1998, Sec. 4, p. 2.

Rico Tavera, Guadalupe, ''De tequila es el tequila,'' *Expansión,* November 11, 1987, pp. 40, 44, 46–48.

——, ''Vuelto a la semilla,'' *Expansión,* December 2, 1998, pp. 71–72, 75–77.

''Tequila: el caballo de Troya,'' *Tiempo,* July 22, 1968, pp. 15–18.

Willman, John, ''Diageo in Dispute Over Tequila Deal,'' *Financial Times,* July 7, 1998, p. 25.

—Robert Halasz

CEC

entertainment, inc.

CEC Entertainment, Inc.

4441 West Airport Freeway
Irving, Texas 75062
U.S.A.
Telephone: (972) 258-8507
Fax: (972) 258-8545
Web site: http://www.chuckecheese.com

Public Company
Incorporated: 1982
Employees: 12,000
Sales: $379 million (1998)
Stock Exchanges: New York
Ticker Symbol: CEC
NAIC: 72211 Full-Service Restaurants

CEC Entertainment, Inc., formerly ShowBiz Pizza Time, Inc., is the holding company for the popular child-oriented Chuck E. Cheese restaurant and entertainment chain in the United States. Appealing primarily to families with children between the ages of two and 12, the restaurants supplement a pizza and sandwich menu with games, rides, and animated musical and comic entertainment. Stage shows feature life-sized characters, the most famous of which is Chuck E. Cheese, the chain's rodent mascot. Of these restaurants, 256 were company-operated; the other 60 were franchised.

Pizza Time Theatre Opens in 1976

The concept for the novel mixture of games, pizza, and electronic animals originated with Nolan Bushnell, the founder of Atari video games in the mid-1970s when teenagers began flocking to game arcades to test their reflexes on the latest craze—video games. The revenues generated by the quarters slotted into those games were huge, and Bushnell, who "wanted to operate and take in those quarters," came up with the idea of using the games to fill the 20 minutes customers spent waiting while their pizza order was prepared.

The Warner Corporation agreed to build one restaurant after buying Atari from Bushnell for $28 million in 1976, and the first Chuck E. Cheese's Pizza Time Theatre opened in May 1977, in San Jose, California, as a division of Atari. By banning unaccompanied teenagers and adding automated entertainers for younger children, Bushnell hoped to attract families and avoid having his pizza entertainment center turn into a teenage hangout. After a year of operation, Bushnell left Atari and bought the Pizza Time restaurant and the rights to the idea from Warner for $500,000. He then began looking for franchisees.

One person interested in such a franchise was Robert Brock, whose Dallas-based company, Brock Hotel Corp., had 1978 profits of $4.6 million. In 1979, Brock signed a co-development agreement with Bushnell to build Pizza Time restaurants and sign up franchisees in areas he knew from his Holiday Inns and their restaurants. Before the 1980 date for opening his first restaurant, however, Brock was introduced to a Florida inventor, Aaron Fechter. Fechter's company, Creative Engineering Inc., produced animated characters and singing robots for amusement parks.

Brock thought Fechter's robots were better than those used by Pizza Time and tried to get out of his contract with Bushnell. When Bushnell refused, Brock and Fechter went ahead anyway and negotiated a preliminary agreement. Early in 1980, Brock told Bushnell their agreement was canceled. Bushnell sued for breach of contract, and Brock countersued for misrepresentation. Brock and Bushnell eventually reached a legal settlement whereby Brock could use the Pizza Time Theatre concept in return for fees paid on a percentage of the annual gross revenues of the first 160 ShowBiz restaurants.

ShowBiz Pizza Place Opens in 1980

Brock opened his first ShowBiz Pizza Place in March 1980, incorporating under the name ShowBiz Pizza Time, Inc. in Kansas. The restaurant's electronic host was Billy Bob Brokali, a large bear with an ironic smile. That same year, Bushnell's Pizza Time Theatre showed a profit for the first time, and, in 1981, Bushnell took Pizza Time Theatre public. Both companies expanded quickly, building restaurants primarily in the Midwest, Southwest, and on the West Coast.

Company Perspectives:

We dedicate ourselves . . . to become the premier growth company in the entertainment and restaurant industry by operating multiple concepts with each being the Number One brand in its segment. Our concepts will be characterized by quality entertainment and food service, fun activities, while giving exceptional value and satisfaction to our customers.

Brock and Bushnell were battling for a very lucrative market. In 1981, according to a 1982 *Fortune* article, ShowBiz restaurants averaged $1.45 million in revenues and Chuck E. Cheese's Pizza Time outlets averaged $1.19 million each. This compared to average sales that year of $320,000 at PepsiCo Pizza Hut restaurants and $1.1 million at McDonald's outlets. Part of the reason for the better performance was size: the typical ShowBiz and Chuck E. Cheese's unit was between 10,500 and 11,000 square feet and could serve 400 to 500 customers per restaurant, compared to about 100 customers for most pizza chain units. The second reason for their success was the many quarters being played on the video games, which brought in over 25 percent of sales revenues. Of course, the restaurant and entertainment centers were also more expensive to build and outfit. The *Fortune* article reported that "a ShowBiz unit cost $1.25 million, including $90,000 for eight animals and their stage effects plus $200,000 for 50 video games and 30 amusement park devices for children. Pizza Time Theatres, slightly larger, cost $1.6 million each."

The two chains offered customers a similar experience, with very few distinctions other than their entertainment. Most notably, the restaurants were big and loud. An article in *Inc.* described Pizza Time Theatres as "Las Vegas casinos for kids." In the dining area, customers sat at tables, ate pizza, and watched large, wildly costumed robot animals sing and perform skits. On one of the three stages at ShowBiz, the Rock-A-Fire Explosion Band, consisting of a gorilla, a bear, a mouse, and a dog, performed songs from the 1960s to attract parents. In another room, adults had the alternative of watching soap operas on wide-screen television. At Chuck E. Cheese's Pizza Time, the big rodent led sing-alongs and cracked jokes while customers in other lounges were entertained by robotic animals resembling human entertainers such as Dolly Parton and Elvis. Above the sounds of the songs and jokes rang the bells, whistles, and shouts from the game area, at which youngsters played video and other arcade games and romped about on kiddie rides. A merchandise booth at most restaurants sold hats, T-shirts, stuffed animals, and other toys.

Despite the restaurants' popularity, there was skepticism among some financial analysts regarding their staying power, given emerging competition that offered better games and better food. But the trouble, when it came, was not from the video-game manufacturers and other companies who had opened a few competing outlets. By the mid-1980s, the video game craze was over. ShowBiz and Pizza Time Theatre began losing the teen market, and the food and other entertainment was not enough to draw new or return customers. Each company also carried large debts as a result of their rapid expansion.

ShowBiz Buys Out and Revamps Pizza Time in 1984

When Pizza Time Theatre went into bankruptcy in 1984, Brock Hotel Corp. promptly bought up its competitor's assets. But Brock soon found the two pizza chain subsidiaries were draining his company's resources. To avoid bankruptcy itself, Brock Hotel Corp. underwent a refinancing.

Between 1986 and 1988, according to *Restaurant Business*, The Hallwood Group made an equity investment in the company, receiving 14 percent ownership and control of the board of directors. Robert Brock resigned and, in 1985, Richard Frank, an experienced restaurant executive, was hired to head up the ShowBiz Pizza Time division as president and chief operating officer. In 1986, he was named chairman and chief executive officer of the restaurant division. When Frank assumed control, ShowBiz Pizza Time operated 262 restaurants: 107 Chuck E. Cheeses (30 company-owned and 77 franchised) and 155 ShowBiz units (95 company-owned and 60 franchised).

Frank began by initiating customer research, which found that although younger children liked the restaurants, their parents did not. There was too much noise, the food was mediocre, and, because there were no service personnel, parents had to order and serve themselves. Frank decided to reposition the restaurants as places to take the family and to concentrate on kids, ages two to 12, and their parents.

His strategy was to improve the food quality and make the outlets attractive to parents as well as kids. Beginning with company-owned units, ShowBiz increased the lighting, added windows, and hired service personnel to deliver the food. Restaurants reduced the number of video games, offered more rides and games for the under-12 set, and installed games of skill to attract more fathers. Moreover, the company improved the pizza and expanded the menu, installed self-serve drink stations, moved the salad bars into the middle of the room to make them more accessible, built a two foot-high wall around the toddler area and put windows in the wall between the dining area and game rooms so parents could keep an eye on their children but not hear all the noise.

Frank also implemented a new marketing approach, advertising special price deals in newspaper inserts several times a year. Television spots focused less on the animal characters and more on parents and children having fun together at the restaurant. His plan required putting money into existing outlets in addition to opening new ones. He also designed a new, smaller, 8,500 square-foot prototype, which could be built for roughly half the cost of the old format.

ShowBiz Becomes an Independent Company in 1988

In 1988, Brock Hotel Corp. changed its name to Integra-A Hotel and Restaurant Company, and spun off ShowBiz Pizza Time through a stock swap with shareholders. As reported in *Nation's Restaurant News*, for every ten shares of Integra they held, shareholders received about four shares of ShowBiz. A lawsuit arose from the Hallwood Group refinancing and ShowBiz divestiture in which plaintiffs alleged violation of Texas security laws and fraudulent transfer. Among its allegations, a group of Integra stockholders claimed that the stock options, warrants, and preferred stock they received in the refinancing

Key Dates:

1977: The Warner Corporation opens the first Chuck E. Cheese's Pizza Time Theatre in California.
1980: Brock Hotel Corp. opens the first ShowBiz Pizza Place in Kansas.
1981: Chuck E. Cheese Pizza Time Theatre goes public.
1984: Chuck E. Cheese Pizza Time Theatre enters bankruptcy; Brock Hotel Corp. buys its assets.
1988: Brock Hotel Corp. spins off ShowBiz Pizza Time.
1990: ShowBiz and Chuck E. Cheese restaurants are united under one name, Chuck E. Cheese.
1998: ShowBiz Pizza Time changes its name to CEC Enterprises.
1999: CEC Enterprises acquires the assets of the bankrupt Discovery Zone.

became worthless when ShowBiz, which by 1988 was the biggest revenue producer in Integra, was spun off to common stock holders, primarily the restaurant management and The Hallwood Group. ShowBiz maintained that the suit had no basis, and the case remained in litigation until the mid-1990s.

The independent ShowBiz also purchased Integra's Mexican dinner chain, Monterey House, with 58 restaurants. ShowBiz attempted to broaden Monterey's base of blue-collar, low-income adults by attracting more families with an expanded Tex-Mex menu, modernized furniture and brighter, lighter dining areas. However, by the end of 1989, there was no improvement in sales and the company decided to convert 26 of the units to a trendier concept, Monterey's Tex-Mex Cafes, and close the rest. In addition to Richard Frank, the new company's management team consisted of Terry Spaight, president and chief operating officer; Matthew Drennan, executive vice-president and director of operations for Monterey; and Michael Magusiak, chief financial officer.

Unification Under the Chuck E. Cheese Name in 1989

Frank's efforts to understand and please his customers appeared to be working. By the middle of 1990, after 17 quarters of increased same-store sales, the company's stock was selling at $25.25 (up from $5.25 at the beginning of 1989 when the company went public). Deciding it was necessary to create a single, stronger identity for marketing, Frank moved to unite his two pizza chains under the Chuck E. Cheese name. Within two years, the company had converted the animated characters in all its own ShowBiz restaurants to Chuck E. Cheese and his friends. It also had moved into New England and the Mid-Atlantic regions of the country and was opening 20 to 30 new outlets a year.

With an increasing employee base, ShowBiz established Chuck E. Cheese's University to train its operations and technical managers. New managers went through three weeks of hands-on training in guest relations, personnel management, food quality, and entertainment. Technical managers spent two weeks learning the basics of operating the rides, games, and animated stage shows.

Frank's strategy of reinvesting in the existing restaurant base, developing new locations, and accelerating debt repayment continued to be successful. ShowBiz reported same-store sales increases with a net income of $15.5 million on revenues of $253.1 million in 1992. However, when the company announced lower-than-expected second quarter earnings in June 1993, its stock dropped 35 percent to $18.75 a share. In a *Wall Street Journal* article appearing the Monday after the drop, the company attributed lower sales to ineffective advertising and a slowdown in unit remodeling. Analysts also pointed to the introduction and growth of new commercial indoor playgrounds at restaurants such as McDonald's, which attracted families with young children and provided the first real competition to ShowBiz's entertainment center concept.

Believing in the soundness of the Chuck E. Cheese's concept, Frank continued his customer-oriented policies, remodeling and refining existing restaurants. In 1993, smoking was banned in most of the restaurants. The company spent a year planning the change after an earlier attempt resulted in a significant drop of sales at smoke-free outlets. This time, Frank emphasized preparing customers for the change and stressing the move was being made for the kids' sakes. Parents' desire for a safe environment for their children also led to the new ''Kid Check'' child identification policy. Upon entering a restaurant, adults and children had their wrists stamped with matching invisible ink codes to show they were together. Codes were checked when an adult left the premises with a child to make sure the codes were the same.

Updating the Chuck E. Cheese Concept in the Mid-1990s

When research revealed that customers thought they were spending too much for what they got at Chuck E. Cheese's, Michael Magusiak, who was named president in 1994, began testing a value-pricing strategy. The resulting policy of having customers buy discounted game tokens when purchasing a meal, rather than at a change dispenser, allowed parents to pay for everything at one time—and actually brought in more revenues. The remodeling of units updated decor, added more game packages for older children, and new proprietary Chuck E. games for youngsters. A new play attraction, Skycrawl, was introduced as free entertainment, and the show was updated in consultation with Walt Disney Co. to include more animated characters backed by video effects. New menu items aimed at both children and their parents were also tested. These included pizzas topped with traditional kids' foods, such as french fry and hamburger pizza or macaroni and cheese pizza, as well as a southwestern chicken pizza for adults. During 1994, 22 units were upgraded and 12 more were opened, a much slower rate than in previous years. The company also restructured its management and sold its Monterey's Tex-Mex Cafes. However, it retained a 12.5 percent equity interest in River Associates, Inc., the company purchasing the Monterey's chain.

Still revenues declined from $272 million in 1993 to $268 million in 1994, and dropped again in 1995 to $264 million. Net income for that year was a mere $63,000. Despite these financial problems, ShowBiz's new policy of renovation, cautious growth, and aggressive marketing was seen by many of the company's institutional investors as the right approach for keeping the kids' market. ''They got caught in a really competitive environment and maybe started doing things a bit late, but when they realized something needed to be done, they did it,'' one analyst noted in the *Dallas Morning News*. By the mid-1990s, the remodeled restaurants were generating sales at a double-digit pace, and in shopping centers and suburbs around the country, Chuck E. Cheese continued to be a big draw.

In 1996, the company purchased the 19 Chuck E. Cheese restaurants owned by its largest franchiser, McBiz Corporation, for $2.6 million plus remodeling costs, leaving only 71 of its 315 sites still franchised. A move to remodel all of its restaurants solidified a turnaround for Chuck E. Cheese. Revenues for 1996 rebounded significantly to $294 million, while comparable store sales increased 9.8 percent and net income totaled $13.2 million.

About the time Chuck E. Cheese celebrated his 20th birthday in 1997, parent ShowBiz Pizza Time launched two other initiatives aimed at spurring growth for Chuck E. Cheese. In March, it concluded its secondary public offering of common stock, and in June, it entered into several licensing agreements to promote the Chuck E. Cheese name. The first of these agreements was with the Delicious Frookie Company to produce Chuck E. Cheese snack crackers and cookies; the second was with Street Players of Los Angeles to manufacture Chuck E. Cheese poseable figures and other toy items; and the third was with K & L Enterprises to manufacture a limited edition of Chuck E. Cheese collectible cookie jars. The year 1997 was one of record earnings for the company, which closed out its fiscal year with revenues of $350 million, net profits of $26 million, and a comparable store sales increase of almost 11 percent.

The Mouse That Roared: A Strong Showing in the Late 1990s

In 1998, ShowBiz Pizza Time tried another novel approach to increase its business, initiating a successful lottery-like incentive program among its hourly employees, issuing scratch-and-win tickets to those who exceeded sales goals for six add-on food items. The company also resumed its new store opening schedule, with 18 to 22 new units planned for the year, and ploughed almost all of its cash flow back into remodeling already existing stores. Riding the wave of the revitalizing restaurant sector, ShowBiz expanded its marketing program by underwriting children's television shows, such as ''Barney & Friends'' and ''Wishbone.''

In July 1998, ShowBiz Pizza Time changed its name to CEC Entertainment and, at the same time, moved its stock from the NASDAQ to the New York Stock Exchange. For the first six months of the year, the company's stock rose from $23 to more than $40 per share, winning it a spot among the ''Top Ten Stock Performers'' listed by *Nation's Restaurant News* in December 1998.

With the under-13 population expected to reach 56 million by 2010, CEC Entertainment implemented a five-year strategy in 1998 aimed at giving the company expansion options once it reached its U.S. saturation level, which it estimated to be at about 500 stores. Although the company's focus remained on the growth of the Chuck E. Cheese brand through the end of 1999, it began to plan the development of a casual-dining concept that, unlike Chuck E. Cheese, had its primary focus on food. The new concept's entertainment was to be geared toward older children as well as adults, while its menu was to feature a broader menu that included burgers, salads, steaks and seafood. As part of this expansion, the chain undertook to develop an animated version of Chuck E., designed to appeal to children older than seven.

In addition to concept development, CEC continued to pursue licensing items, adding frozen pizza snacks to its retail food line and introducing a line of toys in 1999. It also began to focus on small acquisitions. In December 1998, CEC acquired six more Chuck E. Cheese units from its largest franchisee. In July 1999, it acquired most of the remaining assets of the bankrupt Discovery Zone for $19 million. These included its rival's name, logo, 13 ''fun centers,'' two parcels of undeveloped real estate and the rights to seven leased properties. Discovery Zone, founded in 1989, had been the largest operator of children's indoor entertainment facilities until the early 1990s, when, like CEC, its revenues and customer counts had fallen drastically. Despite a systemwide renovation program, Discovery Zone never recovered and had twice filed for bankruptcy before CEC purchased it. CEC began plans to convert six of the units it acquired to the Chuck E. Cheese concept, putting off until later the decision of whether to operate the remaining locations or sell them.

By the late 1990s, the Chuck E. Cheese name had returned with a vengeance. The stock which had been at a low of $5 a share in 1994 now traded at $38 in May 1999. *Nation's Restaurant News* honored Richard Frank with its 1999 Golden Chain award. As Jonathan Clements wrote in *The Wall Street Journal* after an afternoon at one of the chain's outlets with his five-year-old daughter, ''as any parent knows, kids may not make money, but they sure help decide how it gets spent.'' Revenues for 1998 bore out the truth of his statement. Net income in 1998 increased to $33.7 million while revenues came in at $379 million.

Principal Operating Units

Chuck E. Cheese Restaurants.

Principal Competitors

Leaps & Bounds; McDonald's; Pizza Hut.

Further Reading

''Business Brief: ShowBiz Pizza Time Inc.: Firm To Sell Most Assets Of Monterey's Tex-Mex Line,'' *Wall Street Journal*, November 17, 1993.

Cheney, Karen, ''Kids' Chains Hit Growth Spurt,'' *Restaurants & Institutions*, April 15, 1993, pp. 12–14.

''Chuck E. Cheese: Repositioning Helped the Chain Please Parents and Young Children,'' *Restaurants & Institutions*, August 1, 1993, p. 38.

Clements, Jonathan, ''Heard on the Street: Kids Love Chuck E. Cheese's, Prompting Some To Look Beyond ShowBiz Parent's Profit Slide,'' *Wall Street Journal*, March 31, 1994, p. C4.

Coll, Steve, "When The Magic Goes," *Inc.*, October 1984, pp. 83–95.
Farrell, Kevin, "ShowBiz Pizza Time Grows Up," *Restaurant Business*, June 10, 1988, pp. 133–36.
Hamstra, Mark, "Incentives Key to Keep Staff Happy," *Nation's Restaurant News*, June 8, 1998, p. 82
Jeffrey, Don, "ShowBiz Back in Limelight After Years of Bad Reviews," *Nation's Restaurant News*, May 18, 1987, p. 246.
Jones, John A., "ShowBiz Pizza Stages a Turnaround at Chuck E. Cheese's," *Investor's Business Daily*, November 14, 1996, p. B15.
Kinkead, Gwen, "High Profits from a Weird Pizza Combination," *Fortune*, July 26, 1982, pp. 62–66.
Labate, John, "Companies to Watch: ShowBiz Pizza Time," *Fortune*, May 17, 1993, p. 102.
Marcial, Gene G., "Food-Plus-Fun Finds New Fans," *Business Week*, July 2, 1990, p. 78.
Pachuta, Michael, "CEC Entertainment Shapes Up with Shift at Chuck E. Cheese's," *Investor's Business Daily*, July 23, 1998, p. A31.
Power, William, "ShowBiz Pizza's Meltdown Has Connoisseurs Reviewing Their Lists of Trendy Restaurants," *Wall Street Journal*, June 14, 1993, p. C2.
Prewitt, Milford, "ShowBiz Parent Merges Concepts into One Big Pie," *Nation's Restaurant News*, September 10, 1990, p.12.
——, "Wall Street Cheers ShowBiz Turnaround," *Nation's Restaurant News*, June 4, 1990.
Romeo, Peter, "ShowBiz Flexes Independence in Bid to Rejuvenate," *Nation's Restaurant News*, April 3, 1989, p. 18.
——, "ShowBiz Pizza Time Tries Expansion Drive," *Nation's Restaurant News*, October 12, 1987, p. 3.
Ruggless, Ron, "New ShowBiz Prexy Shifts Focus to Refining, Remodeling," *Nation's Restaurant News*, June 20, 1994, p. 1.
Taub, Stephen, "A Noisy Decline," *Financial World*, November 30, 1983, pp. 40–43.
"That's Showbiz: Chuck E. Proves to Be Big 'Cheese' in Restaurant Turn-Around Game," *Nation's Restaurant News*, July 20, 1998, p. 53.
"This Little Family Got Its Wrists Stamped," *Restaurant Business*, October 10, 1994, p. 26.
Troy, Timothy, "Integra Board Named in Suit," *Hotel & Motel Management*, February 24, 1992, pp. 1, 42.
Woodard, Tracey Taylor, "Monterey House Goes Tex-Mex," *Nation's Restaurant News*, October 2, 1989, p. 1.
Zuber, Amy, "Chuck E. Cheese Seeks to Diversify," *Nation's Restaurant News*, March 1, 1999, p. 1
——, "Chuck E. Cheese 'Traps' Discovery Zone," *Nation's Restaurant News*, July 5, 1999, p. 1

—Ellen D. Wernick
—updated by Carrie Rothburd

Century Theatres, Inc.

150 Pelican Way
San Rafael, California 94901
U.S.A.
Telephone: (415) 448-8400
Toll Free: (877) 236-8879
Fax: (415) 448-8475
Web site: http:/www.centurytheatres.com

Private Company
Incorporated: 1940
Employees: 3,000
Sales: $300 million (1998 est.)
NAIC: 512131 Motion Picture Theaters (Except Drive-Ins); 512132 Drive-In Motion Picture Theaters

Century Theatres, Inc. is one of the top 15 motion picture exhibitors in the United States. Based for years in the West, the company has been aggressively expanding in its home territory and has been moving eastward since the mid-1990s. Century's theaters (the company spells its name with the final "e" and "r" in the word reversed) are renowned for their stadium seating, plush interiors, and state-of-the-art projection quality. The company also has earned a reputation for being a tough competitor, which on numerous occasions has resulted in legal action, either brought by rivals, the government, or Century itself. Founded in 1940 by Raymond J. Syufy, the company continues to be owned by the Syufy family, with sons Raymond W. and Joseph serving as CEO and president, respectively. Century theaters consistently report some of the top grosses nationwide for new releases.

Beginnings

Raymond Syufy was born near the end of the First World War into a family of Lebanese immigrants in Sacramento, California. Growing up in nearby Berkeley, he worked at his parents' grocery store and later attended college and law school. While there, he worked nights at a movie theater to help support himself. In 1940, at the age of 23, Syufy took charge of his own theater, the Rita in Vallejo, California.

The theater business at this time was firmly in the grip of the major film producers such as Paramount, Loew's, Inc. (MGM), and RKO, who controlled the top product offered to exhibitors. They often kept the best first-run films away from independent operators, exclusively showing them in the chains of theaters that they owned, and the U.S. Justice Department had been trying since the late 1930s to force them to open their product to others. Independent exhibitors were also in on the fight, forming trade associations and initiating lawsuits against the majors. Raymond Syufy, with his legal background, was perfectly suited to take up this cause, and he did starting in the late 1940s. A major battle for independents was won in 1949 when the Supreme Court ordered RKO and Paramount to sell off many of their theaters and separate their chains from the production and distribution ends of their companies. In 1950 the ruling was extended to Warner Brothers, Loew's, and Twentieth Century Fox. Rules also were enacted to prevent shareholders in the production/distribution businesses from gaining control over the divested theater chains.

This legal settlement enabled independent theater operators like Raymond Syufy to improve their film offerings dramatically, and the company expanded during the 1950s and 1960s, opening additional theaters as well as many drive-ins. Syufy's circuit gradually moved outward from California to Utah, Arizona, Nevada, and New Mexico. The company's buildings gained a reputation for interesting architecture, with a number of its indoor theaters featuring a domed "igloo" design. In 1968 in San Jose, California the company opened its first theater to use so-called "stadium" seats, in which each succeeding row is positioned higher than the one in front, allowing patrons an unobstructed view of the screen. By the end of the decade, Syufy Enterprises, as the company was then known, owned more drive-ins than indoor screens and was in fact one of the top drive-in chains in the world.

The movie exhibition business was often a cutthroat one, and the company continued to find itself in court over various matters. In the early 1970s Syufy filed suit against General Cinema Corp. for allegedly preventing its theaters from booking certain films. The company was itself sued by competitor American Multicinema, Inc. for alleged unfair trade practices in the late 1970s.

Company Perspectives:

It is important to know what "Century Standards" are meant to achieve. The goal we have set is to run the best-operated theaters in the country. Furthermore, all *of the theaters in the company are to meet that standard. We desire to set a standard of* excellence *against which other companies will measure their operations. The "Century Theatres Standard" consists of two components: What is seen from the perspective of our customers and what is seen from the perspective of the employees who work at the theater. Both are important to the successful operation of a theater. For our customers, the theater-going experience is more than just the film they have selected and the auditorium in which they are sitting. It commences when they open the local newspaper or call the theater recording and continues until the moment that they depart from our parking lot. We must examine every aspect of the theater operation* from the perspective of the customer.

In the mid-1980s Orion Pictures, then a major film distributor, sued the company for breach of contract for reneging on an agreement to play "The Cotton Club" in its Las Vegas multiplexes. In a rare loss for Syufy, Orion prevailed, but Syufy banned Orion product from its Las Vegas theaters for five years as a result. The court had given Orion no compensation, and the distributor ultimately lost revenues because of the affair. By 1986 Syufy Enterprises had grown to some 267 screens (including drive-ins). The closely held company did not reveal annual revenues or profits, but analysts estimated that Syufy was one of the most profitable theater chains in the United States.

Seeking To Dominate the Las Vegas Market in the 1980s

The company decided in 1981 to aggressively target the first-run film market in Las Vegas, Nevada, and that year it opened a new multiplex there, supplementing the drive-ins it already had been operating. Syufy began to consistently outbid its rivals, including Mann Theaters, Plitt Theaters, and United Artists Theaters, for the rights to show first-run titles. Within several years all of Syufy's major competitors either had sold out to the company or changed their focus to second-run releases. On the heels of lawsuits by several of these companies, in 1986 the U.S. Justice Department initiated an antitrust suit against the company, charging that it had unfairly monopolized film exhibition in Las Vegas. Although Syufy settled out of court with one of the competing theater owners, it fought back against a second one and also vigorously challenged the government's case. When the latter reached the U.S. Court of Appeals it was found for the company, which, the judge noted, had still been paying relatively high rates for films and had not charged more for tickets or concessions than it did in similar markets. Syufy retained a virtual lock on Las Vegas until the mid-1990s, when its competitors returned to the fray and opened a number of new theaters, nearly doubling the number of area screens within a year's time.

Also in the mid-1980s, Syufy expanded its holdings in the San Francisco area. The company's headquarters had long been established there, and it had opened several multiplexes and drive-ins in the Bay area over the years. In 1984 a new 8-plex was introduced, and the following year the Mountain View ten-screen theater opened on the site of the former Syufy-owned Moffet Drive-in. The Mountain View reportedly featured the largest theater lobby in the world. In 1986 Syufy purchased the 650-seat Presidio single-screen theater, an art house. The company also was continuing to open new theaters throughout its territory, such as the 12-screen Century Park 12 in Tucson, which opened in 1989 on the former site of one of its drive-ins. By 1990 Syufy Enterprises had 325 screens.

More Expansion: "1,000 Screens by 2000"

Raymond J. Syufy, the company's patriarch, passed away in the spring of 1995. His son, Raymond W., had assumed the mantle of company CEO, and several of his siblings also worked for the company. Syufy Enterprises gave way to the name Century Theatres, Inc. around this time. In late 1995 Century announced plans to expand from its then-total of 476 to nearly 700 screens and, a few months later, changed the plan to "1,000 Screens by 2000." The company, which now had some $200 million in annual revenues, estimated it would spend a comparable sum on the expansion. The plans also included upgrading all of the company's theaters that were more than ten years old. This included installing stadium seating, "love seats" (pairs of seats with no armrests in the middle), adding more screens to some smaller multiplexes, adding cafe areas and video arcades to lobbies, improving projection equipment, and the like. The company's theaters generally were considered to be a cut above most of its competitor's theaters in terms of quality.

Century was taking its cue in part from an increase in film revenues nationally, but the exhibition business also was going through a period of consolidation, with a number of regional chains being gobbled up by national ones. The company was seeking to become a national presence to keep its edge against the competition. At this time the Syufys toyed with the idea of going public, but ultimately rejected it and decided to use their own money to fund the expansion.

In 1997 Century opened its two largest theaters ever, the Century 24 in Albuquerque, New Mexico and the Century 25 in Orange, California. A major competitor, Portland, Oregon's Act III, entered Century's Las Vegas turf in the mid-1990s and the company responded by announcing plans to build a multiplex in Portland. In the late 1990s the company moved its headquarters to the San Francisco suburb San Rafael. Century also introduced a Web site that offered directions to theaters, film times and reviews, and even the option of ordering tickets online.

As the year 2000 approached, Century found that its ambitious goal of 1,000 screens was impossible to reach, with red tape of various kinds and even the El Nino weather conditions causing delays. The company still expected to reach that total, but was now giving itself at least another year. Plans were announced for the furthest expansion eastward to date, with at least one theater slated for the Chicago, Illinois market during 2000. The project, in Evanston, was to be an all-stadium seating art film multiplex, the first of its kind in the country. Three new San Francisco Bay area multiplexes, with a total of 61 screens, were also on the agenda. The company had many other projects

Key Dates:

1940: Raymond J. Syufy enters theater business with the Rita in Vallejo, California.
1940–1960: Syufy participates in lawsuits that help break stranglehold on independent exhibitors.
1960s: Syufy opens numerous drive-ins in the West, becoming a leader in this category.
1968: Stadium seating first introduced in San Jose multiplex.
1970s: Century expands its indoor theaters, builds more multiplexes.
1980s: Century becomes dominant film exhibitor in Las Vegas.
1990: Major antitrust case against Century thrown out in U.S. Court of Appeals.
1990s: Name change from Syufy Enterprises to Century Theatres.
1995: Ambitious expansion plans announced; Raymond J. Syufy passes away.

open or under way, including its first forays into Texas, South Dakota, Montana, Alaska, and Colorado.

Century's attention to detail and attractively built multiplexes were highly appealing to the public, and it ranked first in grosses among the 15 biggest theater chains, with the largest average attendance per screen in the country. The company's multiplexes typically held as many as half the positions in the list of top 15 or 20 grossing theaters nationwide for a new blockbuster film. Century offered many amenities to bring in customers, in addition to its popular stadium seating, cafés, and video arcades. Patrons could order tickets up to five days in advance from a theater, or via the Web site. Screens were large, often curved, and sound systems were all-Dolby and all-digital, with many given George Lucas's THX certification for exceptional sound. Though films were booked centrally, Century gave individual theater managers total control over day-to-day operations.

As Century neared the start of its seventh decade in business, the company had embarked upon its most ambitious undertaking ever, a move toward becoming a national presence in the film exhibition business. The company's history of assertiveness and successful expansion were strong factors in its favor, as were its dedication to quality presentation and customer service.

Principal Competitors

AMC Entertainment, Inc.; Edwards Theatres Circuit, Inc.; Pacific Theatres Corp.; Carmike Cinemas, Inc.; Loew's Cineplex Entertainment Corp.; Regal Cinemas, Inc.; United Artists Theatre Circuit, Inc.

Further Reading

Armstrong, David, ''Celluloid Dynasty: San Francisco's Syufy Family Projects Hollywood Through Century Theatres,'' *San Francisco Examiner,* February 18, 1997, p. C1.
''Century 24 Stresses Customer Service, Company CEO Says,'' *Albuquerque Journal,* May 19, 1997, p. 8.
Cling, Carol, ''Gold Coast Cuts a Deal, Links Up with Syufy Theater Circuit,'' *Las Vegas Review-Journal,* November 3, 1992, p. 5C.
Crovitz, Gordon, ''Rule of Verdict: Frantic Antitrust Ideas Are Gone with the Wind,'' *Wall Street Journal,* May 23, 1990, p. A23.
Daniels, Jeffrey, ''Syufys Bullish on Next Century,'' *Hollywood Reporter,* March 28, 1996, p. 1.
Donahue, Suzanne Mary, *American Film Distribution,* Ann Arbor, Mich.: UMI Research Press, 1987.
Mattox, Jake, ''Movie Monopoly Morphs into Big Screen Battle,'' *Las Vegas Business Press,* September 18, 1995, p. 11.
Oropreza, Lorena, ''2 Theater Chains Face Bid-Rigging Charges,'' *Los Angeles Times,* September 5, 1986, p. 4.
''Raymond Syufy, Movie Theater Pioneer,'' *San Francisco Examiner,* April 2, 1995, p. C13.
Stack, Peter, ''Larkspur Fourplex Is Sold/Festival Cinemas To Close for a Week,'' *San Francisco Chronicle,* April 15, 1998, p. E1.
Weinstein, Harvey, ''Owner of Las Vegas Movie Houses Wins Landmark Lawsuit,'' *Los Angeles Times,* May 10, 1990, p. 1.

—Frank Uhle

China Eastern Airlines Co. Ltd.

2550 Hongqiao Road
Hongqiao International Airport
Shanghai 200335
China
Telephone: (21) 6268-6268
Toll Free: (800) 200-5118
Fax: (21) 6268-8668
Web site: http://www.cea.online.sh.cn/html/enhomepage.html

Public Company
Incorporated: 1988 as China Eastern Airlines
Employees: 8,500
Sales: Y7.79 billion ($954.65 million) (1998)
Stock Exchanges: New York Hong Kong
Ticker Symbol: CEA
NAIC: 481111 Scheduled Passenger Air Transportation; 481112 Scheduled Freight Air Transportation; 481212 Nonscheduled Chartered Freight Air Transportation; 481211 Nonscheduled Chartered Passenger Air Transportation

China Eastern Air Co. Ltd. is one of China's top three airlines. One of the country's first state-owned enterprises to offer shares on the New York Stock Exchange, China Eastern remains owned for the most part by Eastern Air Group Co., the government's holding company. Since its inception in 1988, CEA has invested heavily to modernize its fleet and train its personnel to Western standards. Passenger traffic accounts for 80 percent of total revenues. The carrier operates 68 aircraft on 120 routes, from domestic flights to intercontinental voyages.

Origins

The China Civil Aviation Administration (CCAC) was formed on November 2, 1949, about a month after the creation of the People's Republic of China. CCAC was started with the scattered band of personnel and aircraft left as airlines sponsored by Chinese and American interests fled to Taiwan to escape the Communists.

CCAC was assigned responsibility for air travel in the south of China, while the Sino-Soviet Joint Stock Company (*Ren Ming Hong Kong Kun Sze* in Chinese or *Sovietsko-Kitaysko Aktsioneren Obschestvo Grazhdanskoi Aviatsii* in Russian), commonly known as SKOAGA, was responsible for northern routes. These were merged in 1954 to form the *Zhongua Ming Hong Jui* (also transliterated as *Minhaiduy*) or Chinese Civil Aviation Bureau, which had six main regional divisions based at Peking, Shanghai, Guangzhou, Shenyang, Si'an, and Wuhan. The Civil Aviation Bureau became the Civil Aviation Administration of China (CAAC) in April 1962.

At first, the CAAC was dependent on Soviet support. It operated, for the most part, Soviet-designed aircraft during the Cold War, except for a few leftover American designs and a few modern turboprops and jets bought from Great Britain in 1961. It bought more Western aircraft in the 1970s, including some British Trident jets in 1971 and ten Boeing 707s in 1972. (A few supersonic Concordes also were ordered that year but never delivered.) CAAC also bought a few smaller Australian aircraft.

By the time it was disassembled in 1984, CAAC at least had pretensions of providing Western levels of service, that is, concerning the types of aircraft used on international routes. The carrier even had bought a few Boeing 747 widebody jets, which were placed in service to Paris, San Francisco, and New York. After 25 years without a reported accident, a string of fatal crashes in the late 1970s gave impetus to modernizing the airline's operations.

In late 1984, CAAC was divided into one international carrier (Air China) and four regional airlines—Southern, Southwestern, Northwestern, and Eastern, based in Shanghai. Three others also were soon created in an atmosphere of explosive growth in air traffic. The result was unprecedented freedom of choice among passengers and unprecedented fiscal responsibility among the carriers.

Autonomous in 1988

Two of the regionals, China Southern and China Eastern, were allowed to fly abroad because of the commercial importance of their home bases, Guangzhou and Shanghai. Both soon

Company Perspectives:

China Eastern Air Co. Ltd. is a domestic large backbone airline with a passenger and cargo fleet of MD-11, A340, A300–600R, MD-82 and FK-100 etc., serving more than 100 routes to the USA, Belgium, Spain, Germany, Japan, South Korea, Thailand, Singapore, Australia, Hong Kong area and some 50 domestic points. Besides, it has a good number of representative offices both at home and abroad scattered in Europe, America, Australia, South East Asia, Hong Kong area and major Chinese cities.

developed into major airlines in their own right. They did not become officially autonomous until July 1, 1988, although they remained under the ownership of CAAC, which had authority over aircraft purchases and setting up new routes. At the time, new freedoms were sweeping the country, and small independent airlines continued to spring up until the Tiananmen Square Massacre in June 1989, which emptied Chinese airliners of foreign tourists and threatened trade with American aircraft manufacturers.

The Tiananmen crisis notwithstanding, CEA's planes usually flew full, averaging load factors of 80 percent. Its diverse fleet included Airbus Industrie A300 widebody aircraft, McDonnell Douglas MD-82s, and British Aerospace BAe 146 regional jets, which were soon sold off. CEA ordered five MD-11 tri-jet widebody transports to handle the new long-haul international routes critical to bringing in hard currency. In 1991, China Eastern carried up to 8,000 passengers a day on a total of 70 routes, including flights to several Japanese destinations and Seattle and Los Angeles in the United States. CEA employed 3,600 people at the time. Pilots and engineering personnel would remain particularly scarce for the rest of the decade.

One of the MD-11s operated as a freighter between Shanghai and Chicago. A Seattle stop was soon added and frequency increased to two flights a week. Flights to the United States ran 80 percent full and carried apparel for the most part, according to the *Journal of Commerce.* Return flights only ran at 30 percent capacity and carried items such as high-tech machinery for forwarders like Airborne Express. The beginning of passenger service on the Chicago route was delayed by late aircraft deliveries.

Annual revenues rose about 20 percent in 1992. CEA bought ten Fokker 100 regional turboprops and ordered five Airbus A340s worth $555 million. In June, CEA launched its first European route with service from Brussels, originating in Shanghai with stops in Beijing and Bahrain. A route to Madrid followed the next spring. As the world's most profitable airline, British Airways (BA) was rumored to be considering an investment in CEA. BA was building a network of global alliance partners at the time.

The China Eastern Air Group, a collection of 30 companies with operations in tourism, foodstuffs, real estate, finance, and marketing, was organized in 1993. It created the largest air transportation company in China and competed directly with the CAAC and the airlines (Air China, China Southern) still under CAAC's control. Yet another round of expansion followed the reorganization, with new McDonnell Douglas aircraft on the way and new destinations planned in Malaysia and Vietnam.

China Eastern, along with four other Chinese airlines, contracted Northwest Airlines to train its pilots in 1994. Safety concerns continued as several CEA aircraft were involved in incidents in the mid-1990s. Hijackings, disastrous crashes, and in-flight mishaps among various Chinese carriers including CEA contributed to dwindling interest in the airline's planned flotation on the New York Stock Exchange. CEA aimed to raise hard currency in the offering to finance its purchases of new Airbus and McDonnell-Douglas airliners. The new capacity was needed to keep up with China's air traffic, which grew at a rate of 25 percent per year in the mid-1990s. These planes, however, would experience low rates of utilization (about seven hours per day) and lowering load factors (about 70 percent)—representing somewhat of an excess of capacity.

CEA invested Y100 million in a new maintenance hangar and entered into a Shanghai-based wheel and brake overhaul joint venture with AlliedSignal in 1994. It also announced plans to build a second hub outside its home province (in Qingdao, the province of Shandong), the first Chinese carrier to do so. It began flying to Seoul, in the Republic of Korea, late in the year. CEA posted a profit of $76 million on revenues of $790 million in 1995. It operated 41 aircraft at the time.

1997 Public Offering

Revenues for 1996 rose ten percent to $797 million (Y7.3 billion), though after-tax profits fell about seven percent to $71.2 million (Y591 million). CEA earned more than half of its passenger revenues on international routes, although its most profitable ones, those to Hong Kong, were reclassified as domestic routes when the territory was returned to China. Cargo revenues were lagging, however. CEA operated only one dedicated freighter (Boeing, which took over McDonnell Douglas, was scheduled to convert two of CEA's MD-11 passenger airliners into freighters in 1999).

CEA hoped to raise $250 million in exchange for 35 percent of its share capital (the maximum foreign ownership allowed by Chinese law) in simultaneous offerings on the New York and Hong Kong stock exchanges in February 1997. The listing received a lackluster response, but raised $246 million nonetheless. CEA also borrowed $130 from the China Industry and Commerce Bank to help finance its new aircraft purchases, worth about $1 billion. A round of government-administered consolidation among China's other carriers was expected.

In September 1998, CEA became the first carrier from the People's Republic of China to enter a code share agreement with a U.S. airline. CEA's cooperation with American Airlines had been in the works since April 1997. A code share with a Japanese carrier, All Nippon Airways, soon followed—another first. A bilateral air services agreement between the United Kingdom and China in November 1998 raised expectations regarding the entry of British airlines into the Shanghai market. Both Virgin Atlantic Airways and British Airways expressed interest.

Key Dates:

1984: Civil Aviation Administration of China is divided into four regional airlines and one international one.
1988: China Eastern Airlines becomes officially autonomous.
1997: Thirty-five percent of equity is offered on New York and Hong Kong stock exchanges.
1998: Code share agreement with American Airlines is the first of its kind between China and the United States.

Countering the positive developments, CEA experienced serious losses resulting from the Asian economic crisis. It posted a loss of Y481 million ($58 million) for 1998 although passenger and cargo traffic were up. Revenues were Y7.79 billion. Lowered domestic airport fees and the sale of 13 MD-82s offered some hope for financial recovery. CEA traded in the jets as part of its deal to lease ten Airbus A320s from General Electric Capital Aviation Services, which had helped the carrier dispose of its Fokker 100s earlier.

CEA installed quick access recorders in its cockpits in an attempt to nip bad flying habits in the bud. After a safety audit, CEA signed a new code share agreement with Qantas, which was expected, ultimately, to increase passenger traffic 30 percent between China and Australia. Qantas was a member of the One-World global alliance that also included British Airways and American Airlines. CEA continued to seek out such partnerships.

CEA was showing a profit again by the first half of 1999. Selling planes helped, as did favorable currency markets. CEA also trimmed domestic service heavily. It anticipated completion of the new $1.6 billion Pudong International Airport near Shanghai, the largest city in the world's fastest-growing aviation market.

Principal Subsidiaries

Anhui Branch; Shandong Branch; Jianxi Branch; China Easter Jiangsu Aviation Co. Ltd.

Principal Competitors

CAAC; Cathay Pacific; Evergreen International.

Further Reading

Armbruster, William, ''Delays at McDonnell Hamper China Eastern,'' *Journal of Commerce,* May 18, 1992, p. 2B.
Bangsberg, P.T., ''China Eastern Targets Cargo,'' *Journal of Commerce,* May 1, 1997, p. 7B.
Betts, Paul, ''BA Seeks To Enter China Air Ventures,'' *Financial Times,* June 8, 1994, World Trade News Sec., p. 9.
Chau, Beverly, ''Beijing To Bend Tax Rules for Airlines,'' *South China Morning Post,* June 19, 1994, Money Sec., p. 1.
——, ''Crashes Dent Airlines' Foreign Fund-Raising Effort,'' *South China Morning Post,* June 12, 1994, Money Sec., p. 3.
Davies, R.E.G., *Airlines of Asia Since 1920,* London: Putnam, 1997.
Dobson, Chris, ''US Official Thought He Was Going To Die as Both Engines Ran Short of Fuel,'' *South China Morning Post,* May 29, 1994, p. 3.
Grindrod, Barry, ''Speculation Mounts Over BA Link-Up with Chinese Partner,'' *South China Morning Post,* February 6, 1993, p. 4.
Harding, James, and John Ridding, ''China Eastern Goes Traveling,'' *Financial Times,* Companies and Finance: Asia-Pacific, January 23, 1997, p. 25.
Hodgson, Liz, ''Turbulence Drama Claims Second Victim,'' *South China Morning Post,* April 11, 1993, p. 5.
Ionides, Nicholas, ''China Eastern Reports Dollars 58m 1998 Loss,'' *Air Transport Intelligence,* April 28, 1999.
——, ''GECAS Deal To Help China Eastern Reduce Debt,'' *Air Transport Intelligence,* April 13, 1999.
——, ''New Shanghai Airport Set To Ramp Up Operations,'' *Air Transport Intelligence,* October 6, 1999.
——, ''Virgin, China Eastern To Hold Formal Code-Share Talks,'' *Air Transport Intelligence,* November 20, 1998.
——, ''Virgin's Branson Meets China Eastern Boss Over Tie-Up,'' *Air Transport Intelligence,* November 19, 1998.
Jones, Dominic, ''Dragon To Get Bit in the Year of the Tiger,'' *Airfinance Journal,* February 1998, pp. 28–30.
——, ''The Next Step for China's Big Two,'' *Airfinance Journal,* February 1998, pp. 24–27.
Kang, William, ''Airline Hinges Growth on Pilot Quality,'' *South China Morning Post,* September 10, 1994, Business Sec., p. 1.
Kelly, Emma, ''Safety Audit Seals China Eastern/Qantas Deal,'' *Flight International,* May 12, 1999, p. 11.
Lewis, Paul, ''China Eastern To Go Public,'' *Flight International,* September 4, 1996.
''Listing Abroad May Backfire,'' *South China Morning Post,* April 17, 1994, p. 4.
Proctor, Paul, ''Upcoming Service to U.S. Fuels China Eastern Upgrade,'' *Aviation Week and Space Technology,* June 10, 1991, pp. 34–37.
Westlake, Michael, ''Flying Starts: New Chinese Carriers Replace State Monopoly,'' *Far Eastern Economic Review,* February 18, 1993, pp. 54–55.

—Frederick C. Ingram

Chinese Petroleum Corporation

83 Chung Hwa Road, Section 1
Taipei Taiwan 10031
Republic of China
Telephone: (886) 2-2361-0221
Fax: (886) 2-2331-9645
Web site: http://www.cpc.com.tw/english

State-Owned Company
Incorporated: 1946
Employees: 19,873
Sales: US$11.52 billion (1998)
NAIC: 48621 Pipeline Transportation of Natural Gas; 22121 Natural Gas Distribution; 32411 Petroleum Refineries; 42271 Petroleum Bulk Stations and Terminals; 32511 Petrochemical Manufacturing; 44719 Other Gasoline Stations

Chinese Petroleum Corporation (CPC) is a state-owned enterprise that is responsible for the Republic of China's petroleum industry. CPC is involved in many oil-related activities, including the exploration, production, storage, refining, transportation, and marketing of petroleum products in Taiwan. The company sells gasoline through about 600 CPC-owned service stations in Taiwan and also services the aviation and boating industries through its refueling stations. Scheduled to privatize by 2001, CPC worked to strengthen operations and sought strategic alliances in the late 1990s.

Civil War and the Birth of CPC in the 1940s

CPC's origins are closely allied to the Kuomintang or Nationalist Party government and the great political changes that took place in the history of the Republic of China. The Kuomintang took power on the Chinese mainland in 1928, 17 years after the last Chinese dynasty, the Qing, was replaced by the Republic of China. The SinoJapanese War began in 1937 and was superseded by World War II in which the Chinese continued to fight against the Japanese. The year 1945 saw the defeat of the Japanese and simultaneously the end of 50 years of Japanese colonial rule in Taiwan, formerly Formosa. There ensued a civil war on the Chinese mainland between the Communist Party of Mao Zedong and the Kuomintang followers under Chiang K'aishek. It was at this time that CPC was founded. When Mao finally won the civil war in 1949, 1.5 million people who supported the Kuomintang left for Taiwan and joined the six million Taiwanese already resident there. CPC also moved from Shanghai to Taiwan at this time and was charged with the important task of developing oil refining facilities, supplying energy, and promoting the petrochemical industry there.

Between 1953 and 1990, Taiwan's economy was transformed from a predominantly agricultural one to an economy based on manufacturing and service industry. The government was accused of being authoritarian and unrepresentative—martial law was in existence until 1987—but the economic development brought about was unparalleled in this part of the Far East. CPC was called upon to provide the high quality petroleum products and petrochemical feedstocks essential for Taiwan's developing industries, and its achievements undoubtedly played an important role in the economic transformation that has been brought about in the country; CPC grew to become the nation's largest enterprise. Over the years CPC's principal activities expanded to include exploration and drilling for, and production of, petroleum; the refining of crude oil and the manufacturing of petrochemicals; the storage, transportation, and marketing of petroleum products and petrochemicals; and the operation of pipelines for the provision of crude oil, natural gas, and petroleum products.

From the outset, the Taiwanese authorities played a particularly active role in the economy of the country. In 1952 the first planners of Taiwan's economic future determined that 56.6 percent of total industrial production should be in state hands. Centralized economic plans were developed and administered by the government and a substantial portion of Taiwan's heavy industry and financial institutions were assigned to the public sector. Despite the fact that the private sector invested heavily in developing industries, so much so that it gradually took over 90 percent of industry—state ownership of industrial output fell from 46.2 percent in 1952 to ten percent by 1989—key industries were to remain firmly under government control. Enter-

Company Perspectives:

With the vision to become a safe, clean, and competitive international energy conglomerate in the 21st century, CPC is persisting to provide an efficient energy service to Taiwan people by all means.

prises such as CPC, which were regarded as high risk, strategically important, liable to be monopolized, or vital to the economic development of the country were to remain part of the public sector and thus all their operations would be supervised by the Ministry of Economic Affairs.

Taiwan's energy resources were scarce in quantity, relatively inaccessible, and insufficient for domestic needs. Minor supplies of natural gas and petroleum existed, but on a limited scale, and it was CPC's task to utilize Taiwan's steadily depleting natural energy resources to their best effect and to produce an adequate supply of energy for the future.

In 1958, under central government directions, the foundations for Taiwan's now-booming petrochemical industry were laid. The petrochemical industry was to supply the basic and intermediate petrochemical raw materials to the hundreds of small industries which were to prove so vital to Taiwan's economic development. The Kaohsiung Refinery, directly owned by CPC, established plants in 1958 for the production of sulfur and sulfuric acid and these were followed by the production of benzene, toluene, and xylene in 1960 in Chiayi. From these, such products as naphtha and rubber solvents were made in order to supply the needs of the domestic market. Kaohsiung, in the south of Taiwan, was the island's largest port and principal industrial complex. It subsequently became the site of many large chemical and plastics firms and it was where CPC's major facilities were situated. It was in Kaohsiung that the first naphtha cracking plant was put into operation in 1968 as a product center for the southern petrochemical complexes.

Oil Crises in the 1970s

Petroleum, as the most popular form of energy in Taiwan, was always regarded as essential to national defense as well as to the everyday needs of industry and ordinary people. The Taiwan petroleum exploration division and the offshore petroleum exploration division were formed by CPC to explore petroleum resources in Taiwan both onshore and offshore. However, in light of the scarcity of crude oil and gas in and around the island, exploration activities were extended by CPC in 1970 to Southeast Asia, the Middle East, Africa, Australia, and South America under joint ventures with international companies and host countries. In Indonesia, CPC—under the name of OPIC (Overseas Petroleum and Investment Corporation)—worked jointly with Conoco; in the Warim Concession and in the Ecuador Amazon region, oil has been found under a joint venture with the company Conoco, Ecuador Ltd., and four other companies. Throughout the 1970s Taiwan grew ever more reliant on imported oil, in spite of the first oil price shock. The world energy crisis at this time, in conjunction with the worldwide economic recession which followed, proved to be the most testing time ever for CPC. It became essential to emphasize energy conservation and to try to diversify foreign sources of oil and other fuels. Oil had become important both as a source of energy and as a component of the country's import bill. Having leapt from 2.6 percent to 10.3 percent of the total import value between 1973 and 1979, oil imports made a further leap between 1979 and 1980 from 14.7 percent to 20.6 percent and stayed at these levels for four years. These changes were largely out of the control of the government, however, and the second oil price shock, followed by the difficult years of the early 1980s recession, gave new impetus to reduce the dependence of Taiwan on important hydrocarbons.

At the end of 1983, the Council for Economic Planning and Development approved CPC's $85 million proposal to increase oil exploration in Taiwan and abroad. CPC therefore put forward plans to sink land and offshore wells in search of both oil and geothermal resources—plans which were to be carried out with increasing vigor and expertise in subsequent years. The most important figure in CPC's history at the time, Chen Yaosheng, a chemist, was a director for CPC in the Chinese Government Procurement and Service Mission in New York in the early 1970s before being made vice president of CPC in 1978 and president in 1982. He was a key figure in leading CPC through the most difficult years since its inception—he was made chairman of the board in 1985.

It was under Chen's leadership that CPC undertook one of its most important projects to date. Taiwan's natural gas supply had been diminishing and lagging behind the rapidly increasing demand. According to CPC estimates, known reserves would be exhausted before the end of the century. The decision to import liquefied natural gas (LNG) was taken in 1979, and CPC conducted feasibility studies together with other government organizations to establish the economic effects of importing LNG. These endorsed the decision and CPC invested $800 million in the construction of an LNG receiving terminal on the coast of Yung An Hsiang in the Kaohsiung area, on reclaimed land. The terminal's purpose was to handle the transportation inland—via a 350-kilometer gas trunkline from Pingtung in the south to Keelung in the north of the island—of imported LNG for long-term household, industrial, and business consumption. It also aimed to extend the life of Taiwan's own natural gas deposits. In 1986 CPC signed an agreement to import 1.5 million tons of liquefied natural gas per year from Badak, Indonesia. The 20-year contract was signed with Pertamina, the Indonesian government-owned petroleum company, for supply starting in 1990. Market strain was also slightly alleviated by the production of natural gas from offshore wells at the end of 1986.

As part of the government's strategy of diversifying and securing reliable sources of energy supplies of crude oil for the refineries, CPC entered into long-term contracts (LTC) with politically stable oil-producing countries with the aim of maintaining constant supplies. This was in addition to its usual practice of procuring crude oils from the Middle East through major international oil companies. In 1990 36 percent of imported oil came from Saudi Arabia and 19 percent from Kuwait. However, these countries were considered by Taiwan as likely to come under the political influence of the People's Republic of China, governed from Beijing, and therefore constituted an insecure source of supply for the Republic of China, governed

Key Dates:

1946: Chinese Petroleum Corporation (CPC) forms in Shanghai.
1949: Company headquarters moves to Taiwan.
1958: CPC expands into petrochemical industry.
1968: First naphtha cracking plant put into operation.
1979: Company begins importing liquefied natural gas.
1989: CPC establishes an environmental protection division.
1990: Natural gas receiving terminal is completed.
1996: CPC begins privatization process.

from Taipei. Indeed, in 1989 Saudi Arabia announced that in accordance with the new OPEC quotas, it would be cutting shipments of crude oil to Taiwan by 40 percent. It was precisely the fear of adverse political influence on the supply of crude oil which led CPC to reduce its suppliers to those regarded as most reliable and least susceptible to political influence from Beijing.

All CPC's purchases took place on a LTC basis, never on the world spot market, and even in the event of an unanticipated additional requirement, the policy was to negotiate incremental supplies under the existing contracts rather than to turn to spot market purchases. CPC claimed that this policy proved particularly successful during the oil crisis of 1979, when major suppliers continued to deliver and even increase their deliveries to Taiwan, while other oil-buying countries suffered from cancellation of contracts and non-delivery. The Taiwanese government also effected a policy of ensuring the maintenance of a 90-day inventory for oil as a further safety net against oil shortages. The overriding concern for CPC was to meet domestic market demands, and therefore the exporting or swapping of oil products only took place when there was a surplus or when it was necessary to achieve a balance of supply or demand. In view of the steady depletion of Taiwan's few natural resources, such policies proved very important; in 1971 37 percent of the island's total energy supply was derived from indigenous resources. However, by 1983 this percentage had been reduced to only 12 percent. Authoritative sources at the time estimated that imported energy would make up 93 percent of the island's total supply by the year 2000. It was in view of this fact that CPC had to address the issue of sourcing so vigorously.

CPC's exploration activities overseas were carried out through OPIC. One of CPC's most successful overseas exploration activities was an onshore venture in Ecuador, where three oil wells of high commercial value were found. Exploration continued in the Philippines, Indonesia, Malaysia, Ecuador, Papua New Guinea, and Australia. Projects included some onshore and offshore ventures in the United States, the Etosha concession in Namibia, and the concession in Sarawak, Malaysia, where a new oil well was found.

Growing Environmental Concerns in the 1980s

One of the most pressing political issues in the 1980s in Taiwan, and one that put CPC very much in the public eye, was that of environmental pollution. Opinion polls at the time placed it as the second most important issue in the view of the populace, behind "social order" and ahead of political democratization. Taiwan's industrial growth had always been fueled by government incentives, for example tax and customs duty rebates and low interest credits. Between 1950 and 1980 the number of factories increased from 5,623 to 62,474, the fastest rate of increase being in petroleum refining and the chemical and plastics industries. Growing public awareness of the dangers of environmental pollution resulted in demonstrations and protests of an unexpectedly vociferous nature. Demonstrators managed to halt work on the fifth naphtha cracking plant in Kaohsiung, to replace the aging first and second plants, in protest at the pollution it would cause. On this occasion CPC responded by offering to build a swimming pool and hospital nearby in compensation.

More effective and direct action was demanded, and CPC responded in 1989 by setting up an environmental protection division to conduct the planning and promotion of environmental protection programs. Issues that were addressed included the reduction of pollutants from plants, mines, and stations; improved treatment of refinery waste water before discharge; efforts to reduce air pollution and increase noise control; safer disposal of solid waste; and the recovery of escaped oil vapor during transportation. CPC planned to install automatic detection and alarm systems to warn against dangerous emission of inflammable and toxic gases. CPC also paid attention to the landscaping of lands surrounding the refineries in order to minimize the negative impact of huge industrial complexes on the scenery of their locations. For every new plant CPC produced an "environmental impact statement" assessing possible adverse effects. No project could go ahead without the government's subsequent approval of these assessments. Another important aim was the provision of low sulfur fuel and unleaded and low-leaded petrol for a far more environmentally conscious public than ever before.

Competition Arises in the 1990s

The 1990s introduced many new challenges to CPC. The Republic of China faced pressure to evolve due to trends towards economic liberalization and even greater exposure to world market forces. In 1989 Taiwan entered a democratic era, bringing about drastic changes in social and political structures. Private companies were allowed to sell petroleum products, and plans to privatize state-owned monopolies and open markets to competition commenced.

In 1996 the Fair Trading Law was implemented, and not only was the domestic petroleum market opened further, but a five-year privatization program was adopted, intended to privatize CPC and other government-owned companies by June 2001.

Anticipating increasing local and foreign competition, CPC endeavored to maintain its market share and leadership position by seeking joint ventures and acquisitions. The company also worked to diversify and globalize its operations. In exploration and production, CPC continued its efforts to discover producing oil fields. In 1990 CPC acquired a stake in the Sanga Sanga Field in Indonesia, and by the end of 1998 the field had 380 oil-producing wells. At the end of 1997 CPC and Conoco, through a joint venture, began to explore offshore areas of Taiwan for petroleum resources. By May 1998 four wells had been drilled, though none appeared promising. Petroleum exploration continued in such countries as Ecuador, the United States, Venezuela, Kazakhstan, and the United Arab Emirates.

In 1998 CPC operated three refineries—the Kaohsiung Refinery, Taoyuan Refinery, and Talin Refinery—as well as three naphtha crackers. The company's crude oil purchases came primarily from the Middle East—nearly 62 percent in 1998—though CPC aimed to diversify its purchases and buy from different countries. One of CPC's more successful businesses was its petroleum product sales, particularly motor gasoline, diesel, and fuel oil, which in combination accounted for 70 percent of CPC's total sales. CPC owned and operated nearly 600 gasoline service stations in Taiwan, and the company also supplied oil to more than 1,000 privately operated service stations. Plans to modernize more than 100 existing stations and build 29 new facilities, costing NT$4.6 billion, were carried out in 1998. CPC also had significant boat refueling and aviation refueling businesses, including 36 fishing boat refueling locations along Taiwan's coast.

Demand for natural gas continued to grow in the 1990s, and 1998 natural gas sales increased 27 percent over 1997 sales. Anticipating further demand, CPC began expanding its LNG receiving terminal immediately after the terminal project was completed in 1990. The expansion project, which included extending gas trunklines and enlarging storage facilities, cost NT$19 billion and increased the handling capacity to 4.5 million tons a year by the end of 1996, up from 1.5 million tons in 1990. Another expansion project, scheduled to be completed in June 2000 and estimated to cost NT$27.8 billion, was underway in the late 1990s and included increasing the terminal's receiving capacity and installing a 226-km undersea pipeline network from Yungan to Tunghsiao. The project was designed to boost the terminal's handling capacity to 7.87 million tons of natural gas a year.

Activity for CPC increased in 1999 as the company began making preparations for privatization. Though CPC was mandated to begin privatization in 1999 and complete the process by June 2001, CPC was behind schedule, and Taiwan authorities were considering developing a new timeline. With about 19,000 employees and strong labor unions opposed to privatization, CPC faced slow going. In addition, competition in the domestic petroleum market was growing more intense, and with the full opening of the gasoline market scheduled to take place by 2002, there was no slackening expected. CPC's most formidable rival was Formosa Plastics Group (FPG), the largest manufacturer of petrochemicals in Taiwan. FPG began running an oil refinery in 1999 with plans to start mass production at the complex in early 2000.

In October 1999 CPC established its own petrochemical division with the hope of competing more effectively against FPG and announced plans to increase production of petrochemical products and to lobby for construction of a commercial harbor for shipping petrochemicals. CPC also prepared to battle FPG and its subsidiary, Formosa Petrochemical Co., in the gasoline category. In mid-1999 CPC began selling high-octane (98-octane) gasoline, promoted as being more energy efficient and better for the environment, at more than 300 service stations. Numerous stations also began to offer electronic payment services, and CPC planned to provide full e-commerce services at all its stations by the end of 1999. These efforts were made to impede the aggressive efforts of FPG to take market share from CPC. In mid-1999 FPG announced it would sell its products through the National Petroleum Co., Ltd.'s privately run chain of service stations, the second-largest chain in Taiwan after CPC.

On September 21, 1999, Taiwan suffered from the largest earthquake in its history, which resulted in the deaths of more than 2,100 citizens. CPC's operations were spared for the most part, but the Taoyuan Refinery was shut down due to lack of electrical power. A week later, however, the refinery was running at half capacity and would reach full capacity soon thereafter. Eight of CPC's service stations were also closed because of infrastructure damage. Also in September of that year CPC announced a joint venture project in the Philippines to build an oil refinery. A month later, however, CPC disclosed that it was reviewing the estimated US$600 million project. The announcement came amid increasing conflicts between Taiwan and the Philippines, primarily over air rights.

With the loss of its monopoly and complete governmental support, CPC looked to diversification and globalization of operations as it headed into the new millennium. To compete effectively in an open marketplace, CPC continued to reduce operating and production costs and to streamline operations. The company planned to look for acquisition and joint merger opportunities to boost supplies of petroleum products to Taiwan.

Principal Subsidiaries

Overseas Petroleum and Investment Corporation; China Petrochemical Development Corporation (14.1%); China American Petrochemical Co. Ltd.(25%); CPC-Shell Lubricant Co. Ltd. (49%); Dai Hai Petrol Corporation (35%; Vietnam); Qatar Fuel Additives Corp. (20%; Qatar).

Principal Competitors

Formosa Plastics Group.

Further Reading

Chang, Raymond J., *Chinese Petroleum: An Annotated Bibliography,* Boston: G.K. Hall, 1982, 204 p.

"Chinese Petroleum Launches New Unit to Face FPG Threat," *Taiwan Economic News,* August 3, 1999.

"CPC and FPG Compete in Domestic Petroleum Market," *Taiwan Economic News,* July 23, 1999.

Li, Dr K.T., *The Economic Transformation of Taiwan,* London: ShepheardWalwyn, 1988.

"Marketing in Taiwan," *Economist,* Overseas Business Reports, 1988.

"Oil Investment in Philippines in Doubt," *China News,* October 12, 1999.

"Privatization Plan Running into Problems," *China News,* October 7, 1999.

"Refinery Hindered by Outages," *China News,* September 29, 1999.

Taiwan—Country Profiles, Economist Intelligence Unit, 1990–91.

Taiwan to 1993: Politics Versus Prosperity, Economist Intelligence Unit, 1990.

—Joanne E. Cross
—updated by Mariko Fujinaka

Chris-Craft Industries, Inc.

767 Fifth Avenue
New York, New York 10153
U.S.A.
Telephone: (212) 421-0200
Fax: (212) 759-7653
Web site: http://www.chriscraft.net

Public Company
Incorporated: 1928 as National Automotive Fibers, Inc.
Employees: 1,317
Sales: $467.1 million (1998)
Stock Exchanges: New York Pacific
Ticker Symbol: CCN
NAICs: 51312 Television Broadcasting; 326199 All Other Plastics Product Manufacturing; 326113 Unsupported Plastics Film and Sheet (Except Packaging) Manufacturing

Chris-Craft Industries, Inc., is involved primarily with television broadcasting. Through its 79.96 percent ownership of subsidiary BHC Communications, Inc., and the BHC subsidiary United Television, Inc., Chris-Craft operates ten television stations across the United States. The New York-based Chris-Craft also possesses a 50 percent interest in United Paramount Network (UPN), which the company formed in 1994 with Paramount Television Group, a division of media conglomerate Viacom Inc., owner of the remaining 50 percent. Chris-Craft also operates an industrial products division, which is largely involved with the manufacture of plastic flexible film products, including water-soluble hospital laundry bags used by the health care industry. The industrial products division also services the chemical industry. Chairman and president Herbert J. Siegel, who has led the company since 1968, owns about 45 percent of Chris-Craft.

Early History Marked by Measured Growth: 1920s-1950s

The company that eventually became Chris-Craft Industries was founded in 1928 in Detroit as National Automotive Fibers, Inc. It manufactured upholstery, interior trim and carpeting, plastic products, and foam rubber for major Detroit automakers, especially Chrysler, Ford, and Studebaker-Packard. The company was successful but remained a relatively minor supplier to the automotive industry. National Automotive Fibers acquired the Montrose Chemical Company of San Francisco in the 1940s, but it nonetheless remained almost wholly dependent on the automobile, and its revenues often fluctuated wildly, reflecting the fortunes of the auto industry.

National Automotive Fibers operated during and after World War II with moderate success, but in 1956 its fortunes changed dramatically when the company lost more than $1 million on sales of $46 million. The company, however, attracted the attention of Paul V. Shields, senior partner of the Wall Street investment firm Shields & Co., who had determined that its troubles resulted from overdependence on the auto industry. Shields acquired National Automotive Fibers in a bold takeover move, trimmed it of marginally profitable products, and diversified its operations. While the sales revenues of National Automotive dropped to $23 million in 1957, profits rose to a record $1 million, and by 1960 the firm had accumulated assets of $10 million. By then the company had entered into oil and gas operations as well as television and radio broadcasting. In 1959, to emphasize its new identity as a diverse manufacturer, the company's name was changed to NAFI Corp.

Expansion into Boat Manufacturing in the 1960s

NAFI's financial health provided the means in 1960 to acquire the Chris-Craft Company, a boat manufacturer worth $50 million. Chris-Craft was privately owned by the descendants of its founders, Christopher Columbus Smith and his brother Henry. During the 1880s the Smiths were backwoodsmen in St. Clair County, Michigan, who depended on duck hunting for a living. The two brothers supplemented their incomes by acting as guides for wealthy businessmen and professionals from Detroit who vacationed in the unspoiled environment of St. Clair County. To the brothers' surprise, the tourists admired the simple, sturdy lines of the Smiths' homemade vessels, and they soon found themselves selling the boats to eager buyers. In 1884 they built a boathouse, and boatbuilding soon supplanted the hunting business.

Company Perspectives:

New technologies and media create new businesses at breathtaking speed, but uncertainty about their future creates widely disparate valuations, not only for those businesses, but for those of their seemingly mundane competitors. We remain patient during these times, and defer significant capital deployment until trends become less uncertain and we become more comfortable with valuations. We believe this approach to be the most prudent way to promote future growth in shareholder value, and it is completely consistent with our long-held management philosophy. Of course, we will continue to investigate growth and expansion opportunities, and look forward to pursuing those that make good business sense, to increase Chris-Craft's value for our shareholders, our viewers and our affiliates.

Fifteen years later business was booming in the Smith boathouse on the St. Clair River in Algonac. From simple duck boats the brothers had expanded their product line to include canoes, rowboats, and even a few sailboats. So successful were they that their business had become the town's major industry. The first gasoline-powered boat on the Great Lakes was a Smith craft, as were the fastest speedboat and the world's first hydroplane. By 1930 the boatbuilding firm was called Chris-Craft Corporation, and at the time of its acquisition by NAFI in 1960, it was the largest manufacturer of small boats in the world.

The acquisition of Chris-Craft involved a great deal of negotiation because the company's president, Harsen Smith, was opposed to the sale. Harsen's objections were rooted in his strong loyalty to the company and the desire to maintain its dynastic heritage. Harsen controlled only about 25 percent of the company, however, and the rest of the Smith family was in favor of selling. The company's valuation at approximately $50 million came as a huge surprise to the family and afforded them the opportunity to be selective in choosing a buyer.

On January 18, 1960, Joseph Flannery, who was the assistant to NAFI's Shields, happened to encounter Owen Smith, Chris-Craft's majority stockholder, at a boat show in New York. Owen indicated that he was amenable to the sale of Chris-Craft, and a series of high-level negotiations began, with the reluctant Harsen Smith the recipient of competing offers between NAFI and a rival bidder, Brunswick Corporation. Within a month of the meeting between Owen Smith and Flannery, NAFI had arranged a complicated buyout of Chris-Craft, with the sale price being $40 million. The sale was predicated on Shields's willingness to agree to a hands-off management style with Chris-Craft. The 1960s proved to be the most successful period in the boat manufacturing company's history, so successful, in fact, that in 1962 NAFI's stockholders agreed to change the company's name to Chris-Craft Industries, Inc., in order to capitalize on the division's success.

While the success of Chris-Craft's marine operations would eventually decline, the stimulus it injected into the parent company was enormous. Except for the manufacture of carpet fibers, insulation, and chemical products, virtually all identification with the old National Automotive Fibers company had disappeared. Thanks to Shields's diversification strategy, NAFI's annual revenues had long since been stabilized.

Diversification and Growth under New Leadership: 1970s and 1980s

Throughout the 1960s the Baldwin-Montrose Chemical Co., Inc., a chemical manufacturing company, had invested increasingly in Chris-Craft, and it eventually became the biggest stockholder. Herbert J. Siegel, chairman of Baldwin-Montrose, led a takeover of Chris-Craft, which was completed in 1968. Siegel then assumed the chairmanship of Chris-Craft.

In 1968 the Chris-Craft headquarters were moved from Oakland, California, where they had been since 1962, to New York. Siegel set about streamlining and reorganizing the company, which consisted of three main operations: the boat division; the fast-growing television broadcasting division, with stations in Los Angeles, Minneapolis-St. Paul, and Portland, Oregon; and the small industrial division, consisting of Montrose Chemical of California, the world's largest producer of DDT until the federal government banned it in 1972, and Chris-Craft Industrial Products, Inc. The combined sales for 1968 were $89 million.

The 1970s and 1980s saw Chris-Craft's continued expansion into television broadcasting. During the 1970s Chris-Craft invested in the Twentieth Century-Fox Film Corp., building its holdings to 19 percent of the outstanding common stock by 1980. In 1981 Chris-Craft obtained a 19.5 percent ownership of United Television, Inc. Siegel then formed BHC Communications, Inc., as a holding company for United Television. BHC owned and operated all eight of Chris-Craft's television stations and was the parent company of United Television, Inc. To further focus on expansion in broadcasting, the company sold its boat division in 1981, leasing the Chris-Craft name to the buyer.

In 1984 Warner Communications, Inc., in an attempt to avert a hostile takeover by Australian investor Rupert Murdoch, welcomed Chris-Craft's investment in the company. Siegel traded 42.5 percent of BHC for 19 percent of Warner Communications. In 1989, when Time Inc. merged with Warner Communications to form Time-Warner Inc., Chris-Craft's investment garnered $2.3 billion.

Continued Expansion into Television Broadcasting in the 1990s

In the early 1990s Chris-Craft continued to expand into television broadcasting, acquiring Pinelands, Inc., in August 1992 for $313 million. Pinelands owned WWOR-TV, an independent station that broadcast in a tristate area that included New York City, the second most important television market in the country. By 1992 the company owned and operated six independent and two network-affiliated television stations, and it had become the nation's sixth largest television broadcaster and the second largest independent television producer in the country. In addition, Chris-Craft's stations reached approximately 20 percent of the households in the United States.

Chris-Craft took a significant step in the broadcasting market in 1994 when the company announced the formation of a

Key Dates:

1928: National Automotive Fibers, Inc., is established.
1956: Paul V. Shields acquires National Automotive Fibers.
1959: National Automotive Fibers changes its name to NAFI Corp.
1960: NAFI purchases boat manufacturer Chris-Craft Company.
1962: NAFI changes its name to Chris-Craft Industries, Inc.
1968: Baldwin-Montrose Chemical Co., Inc., takes control of Chris-Craft, and Herbert J. Siegel becomes chairman.
1981: Chris-Craft sells its boat division.
1994: With Viacom Inc., the company forms United Paramount Network (UPN).
1997: Chris-Craft sells a 50 percent stake in UPN to Viacom Inc.

fifth national network—United Paramount Network—in cooperation with Viacom Inc.'s Paramount Television Group. As part of the agreement, Chris-Craft owned 100 percent of UPN, with Paramount having the option to acquire an equal share through January 15, 1997. The network, targeted toward the young male demographic group, premiered in early 1995 and offered four hours of original prime-time programming per week. The following year original programming was increased to six hours per week.

The new network severely affected Chris-Craft's revenues, and during 1995 and 1996 losses due to the costs of UPN totaled $275.6 million. Although Viacom began to share Chris-Craft's burden in early 1997, when it acquired a 50 percent interest in UPN for $160 million, losses continued to rise. In 1997 UPN losses for Chris-Craft equaled $87.4 million, and the following year the company lost $88.6 million. Despite such dismal figures, Chris-Craft's Siegel continued to support UPN and remained optimistic about the network's potential. Siegel stated in the company's 1998 annual report, ''UPN's importance to Chris-Craft as a strategic asset remains undiminished. Now in its fifth year, UPN's development, as expected, has been both expensive and uneven. Nonetheless, our commitment to the network's success is unwavering.''

UPN continued to drain Chris-Craft's resources in the late 1990s. During the 1997 season the network's ratings were so poor that UPN dropped to sixth place among the major networks. Although the network increased its original programming from three to five nights, UPN's 1998 ratings fell 39 percent from 1997. One new program that debuted in October 1998 set a record for achieving the lowest first-run broadcast rating during prime time. In early 1999 UPN rallied by introducing a new animated comedy based on the popular cartoon series ''Dilbert.'' Still, ratings for the 1998 season fell by 30 percent. Between 1995 and 1999 UPN racked up losses of more than $500 million. The network shifted its target audience from season to season, beginning with family-oriented programming, switching to programming designed to appeal to urban viewers, and then aiming for young males.

While Chris-Craft focused on its broadcast division, the industrial division carried on. With a series of improvements, including the upgrading of manufacturing equipment, the introduction of new processing control systems, and strategic capital investments, the industrial division flourished in the late 1990s. Operating income increased 77 percent over 1997 and 1998, and the division enjoyed record earnings in 1998. Increased earnings were also attributed to the streamlining of the division, as unprofitable product lines were discontinued, increasing numbers of international alliances were established, and products with lower margins were de-emphasized.

UPN's declines were somewhat offset by earnings from television stations, and Chris-Craft continued to acquire additional stations. In 1998 Chris-Craft acquired television station WHSW in Baltimore and changed its call letters to WUTB. In 1999 the company completed the acquisition of WRBW in Orlando, bringing the total number of Chris-Craft's television stations to ten. Also that year, Viacom announced plans to purchase CBS Corp. for $37 billion. Because the Federal Communications Commission (FCC) prohibited companies from owning two broadcast networks, Viacom's announcement raised questions regarding the future of Chris-Craft and Viacom's joint ownership of UPN. In Viacom and Chris-Craft's original agreement, two options for exiting the partnership had been determined—buying out the other partner or paying for what the partner had invested up to that date and providing funds for the future operation of UPN. Either option would cost Viacom substantial sums of money. Industry analysts agreed that Chris-Craft could emerge the winner and offered other possible scenarios—that Viacom might offer Chris-Craft some of its stations in exchange for severing the partnership or that Chris-Craft might sell Viacom's share to another company.

During the first half of 1999 Chris-Craft's net income dropped by nearly half compared to the same period in 1998, from $13.89 million to $7.47 million. The decline was due in large part to increased UPN losses. Undeterred, Chris-Craft continued to back UPN, expanding its prime-time schedule and developing new programs geared toward young males. A week and a half into the new 1999 season, UPN's ratings were up 20 percent from 1998 ratings, a promising start, and the network was reaching 95 percent of all U.S. households through 186 affiliates. Indeed, Chris-Craft could afford to ride out UPN's shaky and costly beginnings, for the company remained debt-free, with consolidated cash and marketable securities holdings of $1.39 billion as of mid-1999.

Principal Subsidiaries

BHC Communications, Inc. (79.96%); Chris-Craft Industrial Products, Inc.

Principal Competitors

E.I. du Pont de Nemours and Company; National Broadcasting Company, Inc.; Time Warner Inc.

Further Reading

Alexander, Keith L., ''Chris-Craft May Be Big Winner in Viacom-CBS Merger,'' *USA Today,* September 15, 1999, p. B6.

''BHC Communications (Acquires Pinelands, Inc.),'' *Wall Street Journal,* August 24, 1992, pp. B4(W), B4(E).

''FCC Clears a Chris-Craft Unit to Buy WWOR-TV,'' *New York Times,* August 20, 1992, p. D4.

Graham, Jefferson, ''Plummeting UPN Hopes for a Rebound,'' *USA Today,* October 26, 1998, p. D3.

''Little Movement in Top 25 (Chris-Craft Increased Its Reach from 11% to 18%),'' *Broadcasting & Cable,* March 22, 1993, p. 29.

''Paul V. Shields Group Acquires Control of Automotive Fibers,'' *Wall Street Journal,* September 24, 1956, p. 7.

Peers, Martin, and John R. Wilke, ''In CBS Merger with Viacom, a Wild Card,'' *Wall Street Journal,* September 9, 1999, p. B1.

Rodengen, Jeffrey L., ''The Legend of Chris-Craft,'' Fort Lauderdale: Write Stuff Syndicate, 1988, 294 pp.

Roman, Monica, and Jenny Hontz, ''Viacom Buys Equity Stake in UPN,'' *Variety,* December 9, 1996, p. 39.

—Sina Dubovoj
—updated by Mariko Fujinaka

CITGO Petroleum Corporation

1 Warren Place
6100 South Yale Avenue
Tulsa, Oklahoma 74136
U.S.A.
Telephone: (918) 495-4000
Fax: (918) 495-4511
Web site: http://www.citgo.com

Wholly Owned Subsidiary of Petróleos de Venezuela, S.A. through PDV America, Inc.
Incorporated: 1910 as Cities Service Company
Employees: 4,500
Sales: $10.91 billion (1998)
NAIC: 32411 Petroleum Refineries; 48611 Pipeline Transportation of Crude Oil; 48691 Pipeline Transportation of Refined Petroleum Products; 42272 Petroleum and Petroleum Products Wholesalers (Except Bulk Stations and Terminals)

CITGO Petroleum Corporation, owned by PDV America, Inc., an indirect, wholly owned subsidiary of Petróleos de Venezuela, S.A. (PDVSA), the national oil company of Venezuela, is involved in the refining, marketing, and transportation of numerous petroleum products, including gasoline, diesel and jet fuel, petrochemicals, asphalt, refined waxes, and lubricants. CITGO owns and operates two crude oil refineries, in Louisiana and Texas, as well as two asphalt refineries, in New Jersey and Georgia. The company owns a 42 percent share of LYONDELL-CITGO Refining Co. Ltd., a joint venture from which CITGO acquires light fuels. In the late 1990s, in addition to selling jet fuel to airlines and supplying industrial products to manufacturers, CITGO was marketing its brand of gasoline through more than 15,000 independent retail outlets in the United States.

Early Years: 1900–15

The historical origins of CITGO can be traced to the urbanization of America in the early 20th century and to a company known as Cities Service Company. A young entrepreneur, Henry L. Doherty, saw the business potential of providing adequate utility services to the expanding cities of the Midwest. Doherty was from a poor background but had taught himself engineering science and had amassed a large fortune from his own company, Henry L. Doherty & Son. The company had various activities but specialized in real estate, investments, and engineering, as well as the provision of utility services. Doherty envisioned a gigantic company wholly devoted to the provision of utility services such as gas, electricity, and transport.

In 1910 Doherty founded Cities Service Company, a holding company that earned its living from the companies whose stock it held. The company had an address in New York, but its main operations were in the West. The new company was composed of three large subsidiaries: Denver Gas and Electric, Spokane Gas and Fuel, and Empire District Electric. Each of these companies in turn possessed subsidiaries of its own. Doherty was especially interested in the supply of gas, and in the following years Cities Service expanded by buying out smaller gas utility companies throughout the nation. In 1913 alone Doherty purchased 53 utility companies, bringing together a total of 170 companies under the umbrella of Cities Service.

Oil Exploration from 1915

Because of a gas shortage experienced by its utility companies, Cities Service also engaged in gas exploration. In 1915 one of Cities Service's subsidiaries, Empire Companies, began exploring in Kansas. Geologist Charles N. Gould discovered vast quantities of oil in the town of El Dorado. Doherty realized the growing importance of oil to the U.S. economy, and he immediately organized a new Cities Service subsidiary, Empire Gas & Fuel, to take over the El Dorado operations. By 1917 Empire had more than 1,000 wells in production, and it produced over 36 million barrels in that year alone.

The discovery and expansion of the El Dorado oil fields could not have come at a better time for Cities Service. America's entry into World War I increased the demand for the precious liquid. Warfare had become increasingly mechanized, and U.S. battleships and the recently invented tanks and aircraft required large

Company Perspectives:

These Core Values are a part of every decision CITGO makes. Adherence to each of these Values will build PDVSA's trust and confidence: Safe and environmentally sound operations; Results-oriented individual and team performance; Mutually beneficial relationships with our customers and suppliers; Trust and respect among our employees; Ethical and legal business conduct; Honest and open communications, internally and externally, leading to diversity of ideas, building of consensus and dedication to the chosen course of action; Good corporate citizenship

quantities of oil for their operation. The German defeat of Russia in 1918 and its capture of the Galician and Romanian oil fields also led to an Allied shortage of oil in Europe.

Under government pressure to increase production, Cities Service developed many innovations. These included what was at the time the world's largest dehydrator, the Empire, which extracted water from oil. By 1918 El Dorado was producing more than the combined Galician and Romanian oil fields under German control and more than enough to supply the hard-pressed British convoys. By the end of the war Cities Service also operated seven refineries. Oil refining and production had become a central feature of Cities Service's operations.

Despite its increasing concentration on oil production, Cities Service also maintained its utility and service operations. By 1918 Cities Service's gas utility companies served 464,000 people in 20 states, mainly in the Midwest and Northeast. Its electric utilities served 144,000 people, and its transport operations, or so-called traction companies, carried 116 million passengers every year.

The postwar prosperity increased the demand for petroleum in the 1920s. The introduction of mass-assembly methods in automobile production reduced the price of cars to make them within the reach of the average U.S. family, and the growth in automobile ownership led to increased demands for gasoline. Also in the 1920s, Doherty played a key role in the founding of the American Petroleum Institute, in 1924. The institute attempted to coordinate prices and sought to improve efficiency in the oil production business.

Cities Service did not escape the effects of the Depression of the 1930s. In 1930 oil prices fell as low as $2.14 per barrel. Cities Service was more fortunate than other oil companies, however, since its revenues from utility services stabilized income. Already, as the 1930s began, Cities Service was supplying almost 3,000 U.S. towns with both gas and electricity. The company also began the retail marketing of petroleum products throughout the country.

Consolidation and Innovation: The 1930s–40s

During the 1930s the administration of Franklin D. Roosevelt sought to coordinate utility services in U.S. cities, since unbridled competition and company failures often led to poor service and wild price fluctuations. In 1935 the Public Utility Act was passed, enabling the U.S. government to regulate all holding companies involved in the provision of electric light, power, and gas. As part of a corporate simplification plan, holding companies were required to dispose of all but one of their public utilities. They had to begin the process in 1938 and complete it by 1940. Ultimately, Cities Service retained its oil and natural gas business but was directed to dispose of all of its utility assets.

When Doherty died in December 1939, his place was taken by W. Alton Jones, who had served Cities Service ably as vice-president. The transition in company leadership, however, was soon overshadowed by the U.S. entry into World War II. An armored division required 60,000 gallons of gasoline per day, and during the war Cities Service operated its own tanker fleet, 13 of its own ships, and 18 government oil tankers. The vital role that oil played in the conflict eased government pressure on Cities Service to sell its utilities.

Cities Service shipped oil from Texas through the Gulf of Mexico to New York. A number of Cities Service's ships were lost owing to German U-boat activity. They included the S.S. *Cities Service Empire,* which was torpedoed off the coast of Florida in February 1942. During the course of the war U-boats attacked three other Cities Service ships within sight of the U.S. coast. Jones pressed the government to construct a pipeline, arguing that "nobody ever sank a pipeline."

In June 1942 the government decided to adopt his plan, and Roosevelt appointed Jones as president of the War Emergency Pipelines (WEP). Work began on the so-called Big Inch in the summer of 1942. By August 1943 oil could be pumped from Texas to Philadelphia, thus avoiding the U-boat-infested waters of the Atlantic. During the war Cities Service also began construction of what was to be one of the world's largest oil refineries, at Lake Charles, Louisiana. The plant produced high-octane fuel for the U.S. Air Force as well as general petroleum products.

Decades of Change following World War II

After the war Cities Service continued to dispose of its utility assets, with the booming U.S. economy ensuring a good return on the sales. By 1958 all utility assets had been sold, and Cities Service had become a fully integrated oil company. With the loss of its utility business, Cities Service concentrated on oil and gas. Throughout the 1950s the company engaged in oil exploration in Louisiana and Texas. The Lake Charles refinery also played an important role in Cities Service's operations in the postwar period, and modernization of the huge refinery continued throughout the 1950s.

On March 1, 1962, Jones, on his way to meet former President Dwight D. Eisenhower, a longtime friend, was killed in an air crash near New York. A succession of company leaders followed: Burl Watson in 1962, John Burns in 1966, and Charles Mitchell in 1968. All played an important role in streamlining the company's organizational structure.

Throughout the 1960s increasing consumer sophistication and stiff competition provided an impetus for a more creative approach to retail marketing. Marketing manager Stanley Breitweiser was instrumental in devising a new brand name for

Key Dates:

1910: Henry L. Doherty establishes Cities Service Company, which supplied gas and electric utility services.
1915: Cities Service founds Empire Gas & Fuel, a subsidiary devoted to oil exploration.
1930: The company begins to market petroleum products through retail outlets.
1931: Cities Service completes the first long-distance, high-pressure natural gas pipeline system in the United States.
1958: With all utility assets sold, Cities Services focuses on oil and gas activities.
1965: Cities Service changes its brand name to CITGO.
1983: CITGO Petroleum Corporation, the refining, marketing, and transportation arm of Cities Service, is incorporated as a wholly owned subsidiary.
1983: The Southland Corporation purchases CITGO.
1986: Petróleos de Venezuela, S.A., purchases 50 percent of CITGO through its subsidiary Propernyn, B.V.
1990: Petróleos de Venezuela becomes the sole owner of CITGO.
1995: CITGO becomes the leading gasoline retailer in the United States.
1997: CITGO's prospects in the Midwest expand with Petróleos de Venezuela's purchase of UNO-VEN Company.

Cities Service's retail products. In the age of brand names such as Esso and BP, the brand name Cities Service was considered to be too large a mouthful. After 80,000 names had been put forward, CITGO was chosen as the new brand name. Along with the new name came a new gasoline, CITGO Premium.

Charles J. Waidelich, who became president in 1971, and Robert V. Sellers, who became chairman and CEO in 1972, guided the company through the turbulent 1970s. War in the Middle East between Israel and its Arab neighbors led to severe oil shortages and steep price increases. The higher prices for oil meant that the cost of offshore exploration was no longer prohibitive, which created the impetus for oil exploration in areas such as the Gulf of Mexico.

Changing Hands in the 1980s

By 1982 Cities Service had become the 19th largest oil company in the United States, but its outlook was not entirely promising. The early 1980s witnessed an upheaval in the petroleum industry. High exploration costs and a worldwide economic slump led to a rash of mergers and acquisitions. In 1981 and 1982 the business press was full of rumors concerning the fate of Cities Service. A hostile takeover threat by Mesa Petroleum was rebuffed, while negotiations for a friendly merger with Gulf Oil Corporation came to nothing. Finally, Armand Hammer, chairman of Occidental Petroleum Corporation, bought Cities Service Company for about $4.3 billion. As of December 1982, Cities Service became a wholly owned subsidiary of Occidental Petroleum.

Cities Service's refining and marketing divisions were merged into a subsidiary, known as CITGO Petroleum Corporation and incorporated as such in 1983. In the same year Occidental sold CITGO to the Southland Corporation. The sale included the Lake Charles refinery and the CITGO gasoline retailing business. By this time CITGO's wholesale business supplied gasoline to 4,000 outlets.

Southland had pioneered the development of convenience stores with its 7-Eleven outlets. In 1982 the company operated 7,300 7-Eleven stores in the United States and Canada. The company hoped to combine gasoline sales and groceries through its 7-Eleven chain, and the CITGO refinery seemed the best way to ensure a free-flowing supply of gasoline for the outlets. CITGO, however, did not live up to Southland's expectations. A nationwide overcapacity in the refining business led to increased refining costs and falling profits, and in 1984 CITGO posted a pretax loss of $50 million. In 1985 Southland cut CITGO's output by half. CITGO's president, Sam J. Susser, was replaced by former Shell Oil Company and Gulf Oil Corporation executive Ronald E. Hall.

In 1985 Hall orchestrated an internal study of CITGO's strengths and weaknesses. Two results of the study were the decisions to acquire a stable source of crude oil for CITGO's refinery and to enhance the CITGO brand name. The former goal was met in 1986 when Southland, which badly needed money to ease its own financial problems, sold 50 percent of CITGO to Propernyn, B.V., a subsidiary of PDVSA, for some $300 million. CITGO then became the operating arm of PDV America, Inc. When Southland experienced further financial losses, CITGO purchased the remaining 50 percent of its own stock for $661 million, making PDVSA the sole owner in January 1990.

Both CITGO and PDVSA benefited from the sale. Venezuela, a member of the Organization of Petroleum Exporting Countries (OPEC), was one of the world's largest oil producers. PDVSA, through its CITGO connection, found a secure market for Venezuelan crude oil, as well as access to U.S. consumers. Hall also welcomed the deal, since it secured a steady supply of crude oil and other feedstocks for its Lake Charles refinery.

Expansion in the Early 1990s

With a more stable supply, CITGO was able to embark on an aggressive expansion program to enhance the value of its brand. In 1985, 3,500 gasoline outlets carried the CITGO brand name, while by the end of 1990 the number had grown to about 10,000. Sales of gasoline to branded distributors increased 16 percent during 1990 alone. By this time the Lake Charles refinery had a rated capacity of 320,000 barrels a day, making it one of the largest such facilities in the United States.

In January 1991 PDVSA merged its other wholly owned U.S. subsidiary, Champlin Refining and Chemicals, Inc., a refiner of heavy crude oil, into CITGO. Champlin's refinery in Corpus Christi, Texas, produced high-grade gasolines, petrochemicals, and other petroleum products, and it also owned eight refined-products terminals, which brought CITGO's total to 51. Several months earlier, CITGO had purchased 50 percent of Seaview Oil Company, a Pennsylvania-based refiner and marketer. In February 1991, CITGO bought the remaining 50 percent of Seaview. Seaview's New Jersey refinery produced asphalt, naphtha, and other oils. PDVSA provided its own heavy Venezuelan crude oil to Seaview's refinery. Thus, the Seaview and Champlin mergers were in line with the company's expansion strategy.

CITGO enjoyed increasing success in the early 1990s, with net income in 1992 rising $15 million over 1991. The company continued to grow, and in 1993, with Lyondell Petrochemical Co., CITGO formed LYONDELL-CITGO Refining Co. Ltd. The terms of the joint venture included CITGO's pledge of a large sum of money for the upgrading of Lyondell's Houston refinery in order to increase its capacity for processing heavy crude, the type of oil supplied by PDVSA. In exchange CITGO acquired a minority interest in the company, with the opportunity to increase its interest to 50 percent after the completion of the upgrade.

CITGO made two key pipeline transactions in 1994 that paved the way for the company's expansion into the Midwest and central parts of the United States. It bought the southern section of ARCO Pipe Line Co.'s line, while also negotiating a transportation deal with Williams Pipe Line Co., which controlled pipelines in the upper Midwest. CITGO renamed the ARCO line Eagle Pipeline Co., which joined the LYONDELL-CITGO refinery with the Williams line. Also in 1994, CITGO purchased the CASA Pipeline, which opened up regions in southern Texas.

The aggressive expansion strategies resulted in a record year in 1994. Net income jumped 14 percent over the previous year, and CITGO had significant increases in market share. In 1989, according to the industry publication *National Petroleum News,* the company's share of total U.S. gasoline sales was 4.5 percent, which put CITGO in ninth place. In 1994 CITGO overtook third place with 8.22 percent. CITGO was also the second largest U.S. retailer of gasoline, with more than 13,000 branded retail outlets. Its marketers were satisfied with CITGO's service as well, winning the Suppliers Cup of the Petroleum Marketers Association of America four successive times. In addition, CITGO's petrochemical sales grew 77 percent in 1994, compared to 1993, and the company had an outstanding year in terms of safety. As Don Smith noted in October 1995 in *National Petroleum News,* "Citgo has outpaced and outmuscled just about every one of its refining and marketing competitors in the past five years."

Slowdown in Growth in the Mid-1990s

Credited for much of CITGO's rise to prominence was CEO Hall. When he retired in the spring of 1995, he handed the reins to Ralph S. Cunningham. Cunningham vowed to maintain Hall's strategic directions and corporate vision and said in an interview with *National Petroleum News,* "Our drive at Citgo is to be the number one refining, marketing and transportation company in the United States."

CITGO planned to spend $1.5 billion in the second half of the decade to upgrade the refineries in Corpus Christi and Lake Charles, and in 1995 the company completed the purchase of Cato Oil & Grease Co., a manufacturer of specialty petroleum products, including automotive, marine, industrial, and mining lubricants. CITGO continued to stay on its expansion track, but the company hit a number of sales snags in 1995 and 1996. Even though 1995 revenues reflected a 14 percent increase over 1994, net income declined. In 1996 revenues increased 28 percent, but net income fell 8 percent from 1995. Still, Cunningham and CITGO were undeterred. Cunningham stated that the company had performed well in light of poor refinery margins affecting the entire industry. In addition, in 1995 CITGO surpassed Texaco to become the largest gasoline retailer in the United States, adding 938 outlets and bringing its total to more than 14,000.

Several significant events occurred in 1997 for CITGO. The estimated $1.1 billion LYONDELL-CITGO refinery upgrade was completed in early 1997. The upgraded refinery became one of the most complex refineries in the United States, capable of processing more than 215,000 barrels of heavy crude oil daily. In May CITGO moved forward with its Midwest expansion when PDVSA announced its purchase of Unocal Corp.'s portion of UNO-VEN Co., a Midwest refining and marketing partnership between PDV America and Unocal. As a result, CITGO would assume operation of a refinery in Lemont, Illinois, and gain rights in UNO-VEN's Midwest marketing territory for the "76" brand, which covered 15 states and included a network of some 200 distributors who supplied approximately 2,300 independently owned retail outlets. Although suppliers were not obliged to switch to the CITGO brand, the company was confident that it could forge strong relationships with the majority of marketers.

After only two years at the helm, Cunningham resigned in mid-1997. In July, David J. Tippeconnic, formerly CEO of UNO-VEN, assumed the position. Although the company had suffered from declines in net income in 1995 and 1996, Tippeconnic voiced his confidence in CITGO, noting that parent company PDVSA had been doing extremely well since Venezuela opened up its oil business to other nations and that CITGO had the potential to become one of the top oil companies in the United States. Tippeconnic's confidence seems to have been warranted, as CITGO managed to reverse declining net income, with the figure in 1997 reaching $207 million, up from $127 million in 1996.

New Challenges in the Late 1990s

In 1998 CITGO was the top U.S. marketer of gasoline east of the Rocky Mountains. As a result of a joint venture between PDVSA and Amerada Hess Corp., which operated a refinery in St. Croix in the U.S. Virgin Islands, the company was also one of the largest refiners. By late 1998 CITGO gasoline was available at more than 15,000 retail outlets in 47 states, and in early 1999 the company launched its first major advertising campaign in an effort to enhance the CITGO brand and provide it with a stronger identity.

CITGO continued to expand its presence and to explore new opportunities. In January CITGO suggested that it was interested in selling its refinery in Illinois. Roberto Mandini, newly appointed president of PDVSA, revealed plans to focus CITGO's efforts on Latin America and the U.S. Gulf Coast and to scale down expansion in other U.S. markets. In July, however, CITGO decided to take the refinery off the market. In May 1999 CITGO formed CITGO Co. Ltd. in Dalian, China, and a few months later announced plans to build a lubricants blender there. The company also indicated interest in expanding its market in China.

The oil industry overall experienced turbulence in the late 1990s, which unavoidably affected CITGO. According to *Tulsa World,* Tippeconnic reported in early 1999 that excessive inventories of crude oil, coupled with the economic recession plaguing Pacific Rim countries, were causing energy companies to seek cost-cutting measures. Low refining margins continued to hurt oil company revenues, and CITGO's net income fell during the quarter ended June 30, 1999. The net income of $24.9 million was less than half of the net income reported for the second quarter in 1998, which reached $56.5 million. Although the outlook appeared bleak, Tippeconnic indicated that CITGO and PDVSA would continue to provide dependable and reliable service to the United States, particularly in comparison to suppliers in the Mideast, where political conditions were unpredictable.

Principal Subsidiaries

Cato Oil Inc.; CITGO Asphalt and Refining Company; Cit-Con Oil Corp.; CITGO Pipeline Co.; CITGO Co. Ltd. (China); LYONDELL-CITGO Refining Co. Ltd. (42%).

Principal Competitors

BP Amoco Corp.; Chevron Corp.; Exxon Corp.; Shell Oil Co.; Mobil Oil Corp.; Texaco Inc.

Further Reading

Brown, Wesley, "CITGO Primed, Ready for Growth," *Tulsa World,* November 9, 1997, p. E1.

Edmond, Mark, "Purchase of Uno-Ven Could Make Citgo No. 1 U.S. Gasoline Marketer," *National Petroleum News,* February 1, 1997, p. 13.

Ellis, William Donohue, "On the Oil Lands with Cities Service," Tulsa: Cities Service Oil and Gas Corporation, 1983.

Smith, Don, "Citgo's New CEO: Striving to Be Number One," *National Petroleum News,* October 1, 1995, p. 81.

Stancavage, John, "Pipeline Buy Helps Citgo Boost Market Ranking," *Tulsa World,* August 6, 1995, p. B1.

Stewart, D. R., "CITGO Leader Not Panicking," *Tulsa World,* February 4, 1999, p. 1.

—Michael Doorley
—updated by Mariko Fujinaka

The Coastal Corporation
The Energy People

The Coastal Corporation

Coastal Tower
Nine Greenway Plaza
Houston, Texas 77046
U.S.A.
Telephone: (713) 877-1400
Fax: (713) 877-6754
Web site: http://www.coastalcorp.com

Public Company
Incorporated: 1955 as Coastal States Gas Producing Company
Employees: 13,300
Sales: $7.37 billion (1998)
Stock Exchanges: New York Amsterdam Dusseldorf Frankfurt Hamburg Munich London
Ticker Symbol: CGP
NAIC: 48621 Pipeline Transportation of Natural Gas; 22121 Natural Gas Distribution; 32411 Petroleum Refineries; 42271 Petroleum Bulk Stations & Terminals; 44711 Gasoline Stations with Convenience Store

The Coastal Corporation, based in Houston with operations in several energy markets, is a Fortune 500 energy company that owns outright or through joint venture natural gas pipelines covering over 18,000 miles across the United States. The company's principal business segments consist of the gathering, processing, storage, and distribution of natural gas; oil refining and marketing; oil exploration and production; electric power production; and coal mining. With the second largest natural gas storage facilities in the United States, Coastal was handling about 13 percent of the country's total consumption of natural gas in the late 1990s. The company's ANR Pipeline subsidiary operates about 18,000 miles of domestic pipeline as well as 14 natural gas processing plants and 27 underground storage facilities. Coastal's exploration and production division, which operates primarily in the Gulf of Mexico, south Texas, and Utah, has interests in more than 3,000 wells. This segment expanded into international exploration in the 1990s. The company also owns four refineries and provides gasoline in 34 states through more than 1,500 branded retail outlets.

Rapid Development and Expansion in the 1950s and 1960s

To a great extent Coastal's success can be attributed to the dynamic leadership of founder Oscar Wyatt. Wyatt served in World War II as a bomber pilot, earned a degree in mechanical engineering from Texas A&M University, and gained experience in the oil business as a partner in Wymore Oil Company. In 1955 Wyatt founded Coastal States Gas Producing Company in Corpus Christi, Texas. Compared to the monolithic enterprise it became in later years, Coastal States began business in modest circumstances, with 68 miles of pipeline and 78 employees.

From the beginning Wyatt demonstrated an almost intuitive understanding of the energy business. His pipeline company purchased small amounts of gas from a number of producers, packaged it, and then sold it in larger volumes. Gas gathering became the company's primary business. Wyatt developed effective pipeline systems that connected both buyers and sellers and still left room for profits. Most pipeline owners set output quotas to make an oil field last for up to 20 years. Wyatt ignored this convention and generally purchased as much gas from producers as they could pump. The practice enraged other pipeline owners, but the arrangement worked to Coastal's advantage, and by 1960 revenues exceeded $17.6 million.

As the U.S. economy grew in the 1960s, dependence on energy sources, notably oil and gas, also increased, and Coastal took full advantage of the soaring demand. By the early 1960s Coastal's newly created subsidiary, LoVaca Gathering Company, supplied gas to San Antonio, Austin, Corpus Christi, and other cities in south Texas. In 1962 Coastal purchased 800 miles of crude oil pipeline from Sinclair Oil Corporation, including a major refinery in Corpus Christi with a capacity for almost 30,000 barrels of oil per day. Later, as oil refining became one of its principal activities, Coastal extended this capacity.

Much of Coastal's subsequent expansion came through takeovers—often hostile—of rival companies. Wyatt acquired a reputation as a tough business competitor and corporate raider.

Company Perspectives:

Throughout our operations, Coastal seeks to maximize the competitive advantage of our strategically integrated and diverse base of energy assets and operations; focus on core geographic areas where our assets and expertise bring unique strengths; maintain a strong balance sheet to provide the financial flexibility necessary to take advantage of rapidly emerging opportunities; allocate capital to generate growth, both long- and short-term, while sustaining a solid foundation of earnings and cash flow.

In 1968 Coastal acquired a 965-mile system from United Pipeline Company. In the same year Wyatt won control of Rio Grande Valley Gas Company. In June 1970 the company announced plans to link its west Texas natural gas reserves to the Dallas area.

Continued Expansion and Rising Controversy in the 1970s

In the early 1970s events in the Middle East overshadowed the triumphant rise of Coastal. The Arab-dominated Organization of Petroleum Exporting Countries (OPEC), by presenting a united front, began to win price increases. In 1971 OPEC cut production and raised prices by 70 percent, and by 1974 prices had quadrupled, leading to the energy crisis of the mid-1970s.

LoVaca, Coastal's pipeline subsidiary, had signed fixed-price contracts to supply cities in south Texas with natural gas. With energy prices soaring and supplies dwindling, LoVaca could not meet its contractual obligations, and at one point it cut off gas supplies to the cities of San Antonio and Austin during the winter. Wyatt then obtained regulatory permission to increase prices beyond the limits specified in the contracts.

LoVaca was the target of lawsuits by outraged customers, and the problems of the subsidiary came to haunt Coastal for years. After much wrangling, Coastal finally settled $1.6 billion in lawsuits by agreeing to spin off LoVaca. The spinoff, Valero Energy Corporation, which was formed on December 31, 1979, from LoVaca and other Coastal assets, had annual revenues of about $1 billion. The customers suing Coastal received 55 percent of Valero's stock, with the remaining split among Coastal shareholders, not including Wyatt. At the plaintiffs' insistence, he was excluded from the agreement.

Despite the impact of the energy crisis, Coastal maintained its profitability and continued to expand throughout the 1970s. Expansion was not confined to Texas. In 1973 Coastal acquired Colorado Interstate Gas Company, along with its three refineries, in a $182 million hostile bid. With the acquisition Coastal became a truly national company. In 1973 Wyatt renamed the company Coastal States Gas Corporation.

In the first half of the decade, Coastal also sought to diversify into other energy markets. In 1973 Coastal entered the coal mining field with the acquisition of Southern Utah Fuel Company. Also in 1973, with the acquisition of Union Petroleum Corporation, renamed Belcher New England, Inc., Coastal began the marketing and distribution of petroleum products. By 1975 revenues had reached $1.9 billion. Coastal's expansion continued in 1976 with the purchase of Pacific Refining Company's plant in Hercules, California, which increased Coastal's refining capacity to about 300,000 barrels per day. In 1977 Coastal acquired Miami-based Belcher Oil Company, one of the largest marketers of fuel oils in the Southeast.

Ups and Downs Amid Numerous Acquisitions in the 1980s

In 1980 Wyatt changed the company's name to Coastal Corporation, and in the same year revenues exceeded $5 billion. Yet Wyatt, in his enthusiasm to secure profits for Coastal, overstepped the law. In 1980 in Houston, Wyatt and two other oil executives pleaded guilty to criminal violations of federal crude oil pricing regulations. Wyatt and the president of Coral Petroleum were each fined $40,000 for the misdemeanors. Each company was required to refund $9 million to the U.S. Department of the Treasury, and each incurred $1 million in civil penalties.

The early 1980s witnessed a temporary setback in Coastal's successful profit record. Economic recession and an oversupply of oil and natural gas, as well as conservation by consumers, led to Coastal's first loss, which amounted to $96.4 million for the year 1981. Wyatt responded to the crisis with characteristic forcefulness. He trimmed the workforce and cut the budget, and within six months he had restored the company to profitability.

In the mid-1980s the U.S. government sought to foster competition in the natural gas industry through deregulation. The new government policy, together with falling prices, created difficulties for many energy companies. Coastal not only survived deregulation but also took full advantage of the competitive atmosphere by launching hostile takeover bids for other struggling energy companies. The mere threat of a takeover by Coastal could send the stock price of a target company soaring. In 1983, for example, Coastal's attempt to secure Texas Gas Resources failed, yet Coastal's initial investment in the company generated a total of $26.4 million in profits. Intervening companies that came to the rescue of Texas Gas Resources were forced to buy up shares held by Coastal at inflated prices. Wyatt's unsuccessful attempt to take over Houston Natural Gas in 1984 yielded a similar return of $42 million. In 1985 Wyatt set about acquiring American Natural Resources (ANR), one of the most profitable natural gas pipelines in the Midwest. Despite ANR's initial determination to stay free of Coastal's clutches, Wyatt soon pushed through an all-cash deal of $2.45 billion, which ANR shareholders could not refuse. The acquisition transformed Coastal into a major power in the U.S. gas business.

While Coastal's success and profitability drew the admiration of many in the business community, some of Coastal's activities skirted the spirit of the law. In 1987, despite sanctions prohibiting U.S. companies from dealing with Libya because of its terrorist connections, Wyatt negotiated a deal in which Libya supplied oil to Coastal's refinery in Hamburg, Germany. Wyatt's deal was legal because foreign subsidiaries of U.S. companies were exempt from U.S. regulations.

In the late 1980s Coastal took advantage of improved economic relations between the United States and the People's

Key Dates:

1955: Oscar Wyatt establishes Coastal States Gas Producing Company.
1962: Coastal buys a pipeline network and Texas refinery from Sinclair Oil Corporation.
1980: Company changes its name to The Coastal Corporation.
1987: Despite U.S. economic sanctions against Libya, CEO Wyatt negotiates a deal with Libyan dictator Muammar Qaddafi.
1993: Coastal completes construction on the Empire State Pipeline, a joint venture.
1995: Wyatt retires as CEO.

Republic of China. In 1988 Coastal concluded an agreement with China National Chemicals Import and Export Corporation (Sinochem) for joint ownership of Coastal's Pacific Refining Company. Coastal and Sinochem each held a 50 percent interest in the West Coast refiner. The agreement provided certain advantages for both sides. Sinochem obtained an opportunity to invest in the United States as well as a long-term outlet for crude oil, and Coastal secured a dependable supply of crude oil in a volatile world oil market. This joint venture represented the first investment in U.S. energy assets by China.

A key to the company's successful strategy was the continued high productivity of all Coastal employees, from unskilled workers to those in management. Coal workers employed by Coastal produced twice the industry average, and the expectations for Coastal's management staff were high. Indeed, the constant pressure for results led to a high management turnover, with Coastal's refinery business alone having five different managers between 1980 and 1989.

Steady Acquisitions and Growth in the 1990s

The U.S. government took action against Coastal's agreement with Libya in 1991 by prohibiting U.S. citizens from working for the venture. This act did not dissuade Wyatt from further deals with countries in the Middle East, however. Coastal bought large amounts of Iraqi crude in the 1980s, and prior to the commencement of the Persian Gulf War, Wyatt offered to sell Iraqi President Saddam Hussein part of the company's international marketing and refining operations. U.S. sanctions against Iraq following the war prevented Coastal from purchasing Iraqi oil, but Wyatt maintained close relations with Iraq in hopes of gaining access to the oil at some time in the future. These controversial actions did not make Wyatt a popular player in the U.S. oil industry, but he viewed the dealings as pragmatic and necessary for Coastal's business.

In 1992 Coastal shut down its refinery in Kansas when its refining and marketing division reported an operating loss of $192 million, but the company continued to grow, seeking acquisitions and joint ventures to streamline operations. In the following year, in fact, Coastal adopted an aggressive growth strategy. Through its subsidiary ANR Pipeline Company, Coastal completed construction on the Empire State Pipeline, a 156-mile line that ran from Niagara Falls to Syracuse, New York. ANR held a 50 percent interest in the pipeline, and Union Enterprises Ltd. held the remaining half. Also in 1993 the company acquired Soldier Creek Coal Co. and Sage Point Coal Co., both subsidiaries of Sun Co., Inc.

Wyatt gave up his post as CEO in 1995 but continued as chairman. David A. Arledge, the company president, became its CEO as well. In early 1995, through subsidiary Coastal Oil & Gas Corp., Coastal gained an interest in several producing fields off the coast of Louisiana from Koch Hydrocarbons, Inc. The company also acquired working interests in two dozen wells in the Utah area from Snyder Oil Corporation and bought the marketing assets of Exxon Corporation's subsidiary Esso Petrolera, S.A., located on the Caribbean island of Aruba.

In 1996 Coastal entered into discussions with Westcoast Energy Inc. to form a joint venture to market natural gas and electricity and to provide energy management services. The venture, which would create one of the largest marketers of natural gas and electricity in North America, was named Engage Energy. To procure funds for additional ventures, Coastal sold its Utah coal mining operations for approximately $610 million in late 1996. The company planned to keep its coal operations in the eastern United States.

When Wyatt stepped down as chairman in 1997, Arledge gained the additional post. In that year Coastal acquired an 11 percent interest in the 1,900-mile Alliance Pipeline, designed to move natural gas from western Canada to the Chicago region. Construction of the pipeline continued through the late 1990s. In 1999 Coastal announced plans to develop a 700-mile pipeline running from Mobile, Alabama, to Tampa Bay, Florida. The proposed Gulfstream Natural Gas System pipeline was designed to serve the growing natural gas and energy demand in Florida. It was projected that the pipeline would be completed by 2002.

In the late 1990s Coastal focused on its natural gas business. With excess reserves of crude oil and low refining margins, the global oil industry was in a state of chaos. The North American natural gas market, on the other hand, was a regional market, largely unaffected by global oil market conditions. In addition, according to Coastal, by 2010 the demand for natural gas was expected to grow considerably, from 22 trillion cubic feet to 30 trillion cubic feet per year. The company therefore chose to invest heavily in its natural gas operations, targeting the primary natural gas supply areas, which included the Gulf of Mexico, south Texas, the Rocky Mountains, and Canada. In June 1998 the company acquired additional interest in natural gas assets in Alabama, including a processing plant and a pipeline.

To bolster its exploration and production operations, Coastal upped its exploration and production budget by $100 million in 1998 and by $290 million in 1999. Coastal acquired oil and gas assets in northeastern Utah and western Colorado in late 1998. The company also acquired properties in the Texas Coastal Plain, a region that accounted for 45 percent of Coastal's net gas production in 1998. By February 1999 Coastal had seven oil rigs in operation. In the Gulf of Mexico region, Coastal built five drilling and production platforms in 1998. Coastal also sought international opportunities for its exploration and production op-

erations in the late 1990s. The company announced plans to start exploration in Australia, and in October 1998 Coastal signed a deal with Petrobras, Brazil's national oil company.

Although Coastal concentrated on boosting its natural gas operations, the company continued to implement its growth strategy in other divisions. In Coastal's electric power business, the company increased its interest in a cogeneration plant in Midland, Michigan, from 10.9 to 20.4 percent in 1998. In 1999 Coastal announced plans to build a power plant in Colorado and indicated that it had reached an agreement with the Public Service Company of Colorado regarding the purchase of power. Coastal also participated in numerous international projects. In early 1999 Coastal purchased a 24.5 percent stake in a hydroelectric plant in Panama and also began operations at its Nicaragua plant. The company acquired a 66.7 percent interest in a power plant in Bangladesh and continued work on two projects in Pakistan, which were scheduled to be operational in 1999. Coastal hoped to have its Guatemala coal-fired power plant, which began construction in 1997, operational by early 2000. In September 1999 Coastal announced that, with GENER S.A., a South American electricity company, it had purchased 50 percent of the Itabo Generation Company from the Dominican Republic. Itabo owned six thermal plants near the country's capital.

Coastal's refinery facilities expanded operations in the late 1990s as well. In July 1998 the company signed a five-year deal with PMI Comercio Internacional, S.A. de C.V., a marketing subsidiary of Mexico's national oil company, Petroleos Mexicanos, in which PMI agreed to supply crude for Coastal's refinery in Aruba. Coastal began expanding the Aruba refinery in September. In 1997 Coastal entered into discussions with Venezuela's national oil company, Petróleos de Venezuela S.A. (PDVSA), regarding a venture involving Coastal's Corpus Christi refinery facilities. Coastal's refinery in Eagle Point, New Jersey, was busy in 1998 as well. In June Coastal finalized an agreement concerning the supply of crude with Norway's state oil company, Statoil Group.

In other 1998 developments, Coastal sold or closed nearly 100 retail stores, including 64 Coastal Mart stores in the Midwest, to adhere to the company's decision to dispense with nonessential businesses. The stores continued to operate under the Coastal brand name. Coastal joined Chevron Corp. and Mobil Oil Corp. in a $200 million deal to purchase crude oil from Iraq. The agreement was part of the United Nation's oil-for-food deal, in which the proceeds of the sales would be used to purchase food and medicine for Iraqi citizens, who had suffered significantly from economic sanctions in place against Saddam Hussein since 1991. Coastal also expanded its chemical operations with a newly established ammonia plant in Oyster Creek, Texas. In its coal division Coastal progressed with plans to transform the business from a processing and marketing company to one that mined, processed, and marketed its own coal.

Although Coastal's operating revenues dropped considerably between 1996 and 1998, from $12.17 billion to $7.37 billion, the company remained confident that its business strategies would propel Coastal to success. As demand for natural gas continued to rise, Coastal's emphasis on building its natural gas business appeared to be a prudent decision. Coastal increased production of natural gas by more than 16 percent during 1998 and intended to continue expanding exploration and production operations as the company approached the year 2000. Though Coastal planned to seek international projects and joint ventures abroad, the company remained committed to pursuing opportunities in the United States.

Principal Subsidiaries

ANR Pipeline Company; ANR Alliance Pipeline Company U.S., Inc.; ANR Independence Pipeline Company; ANR Storage Company; Colorado Interstate Gas Company; Wyoming Interstate Company, Ltd.; Coastal Field Services Company; Coastal Gas International Company; Coastal Gas Marketing Company; Coastal Gas Services Company; Coastal Aux Sable Products Company; Coastal Gas Australia Pty Ltd.; Engage Energy US, L.P. (50%); Engage Energy Canada, L.P. (50%); Blue Lake Gas Storage Company (75%); Empire State Pipeline (50%); Great Lakes Gas Transmission Limited Partnership (50%); Coastal Aruba Refining Company N.V.; Coastal Refining & Marketing, Inc.; Coastal Eagle Point Oil Company; Coastal Mobile Refining Company; Coastal Refining & Marketing, Inc.; Coastal States Trading, Inc.; Coastal Canada Petroleum, Inc.; Coastal Oil & Gas Corporation; ANR Production Company; Coastal Oil & Gas USA, L.P.; CIG Exploration, Inc.; Coastal Oil & Gas Australia Pty Ltd.; Coastal Power Company; Coastal Technology, Inc.; Coastal Coal Company, LLC.

Principal Competitors

Duke Energy Corporation; The Williams Companies, Inc.; Phillips Petroleum; BP Amoco Corp.; Chevron Corp.; Exxon Corp.; Shell Oil Co.; Mobil Oil Corp.; Texaco Inc.

Further Reading

''Coastal Again Eyes Florida Market with Gulfstream Underwater Line,'' *Inside F.E.R.C.'s Gas Market Report,* March 5, 1999, p. 1.

The Coastal Corporation: Profile, Houston: Coastal Corporation, n.d.

Davis, Michael, ''Coastal-West Coast Link Wins Applause,'' *Houston Chronicle,* September 7, 1996, p. 3.

Ivanovich, David, and Chris Woodyard, ''Decision on Iraqi Oil Nears,'' *Houston Chronicle,* May 30, 1996, p. 1.

Ivey, Mark, ''The Man Who Strikes Fear in the Heart of the Oil Patch,'' *Business Week,* November 6, 1989.

Mack, Toni, ''Saddam's Pal Oscar,'' *Forbes,* December 30, 1996, p. 72.

Shook, Barbara, ''Wyatt Announces He Will Step Down, Closing Out an Era at Coastal Corp.,'' *Oil Daily,* March 26, 1997, p. 1.

Solomon, Caleb, and Allanna Sullivan, ''Strictly Texas Oil Man Wyatt Kept Ties with Iraq Despite Gulf Conflict,'' *Wall Street Journal Europe,* March 11, 1991, p. 1.

—Michael Doorley
—updated by Mariko Fujinaka

Coherent, Inc.

5100 Patrick Henry Drive
Santa Clara, California 95054
U.S.A.
Telephone: (408) 764-4000
Toll Free: (800) 527-3786
Fax: (408) 764-4800
Web site: http://www.cohr.com

Public Company
Incorporated: 1966 as Coherent Radiation
Employees: 2,261
Sales: $468.9 million (1999)
Stock Exchanges: NASDAQ
Ticker Symbol: COHR
NAIC: 335999 All Other Miscellaneous Electrical Equipment and Component Manufacturing; 334510 Electromedical and Electrotherapeutic Apparatus Manufacturing

Coherent, Inc. manufactures and sells lasers and laser-related products to the commercial, scientific, and medical markets. Coherent lasers, comprising the broadest range of products produced by any laser manufacturer, are used in a variety of applications, ranging from surgical procedures to the manufacturing of semiconductors. The company operates facilities at approximately two dozen sites in a number of foreign countries, deriving more than half its revenue from international sales. Sales and service sites are located in the United States, Mexico, Germany, the United Kingdom, France, Belgium, The Netherlands, Sweden, Hong Kong, and the Peoples Republic of China.

Origins

The invention of the laser, an acronym for ''light amplification by stimulated emission of radiation,'' represented one of the technological milestones of the 20th century. Developed at Bell Laboratories in 1958, the laser promised to ignite a technological revolution, its vast potential galvanizing the attention of scientists worldwide—one scientist in particular, physicist James Hobart. Hobart was intrigued by the possible applications for lasers, specifically the use of lasers in factory settings. He envisioned lasers performing tasks such as cutting and welding metal, but was unable to convince management at his place of employment, Spectra-Physics, Inc., to pursue the development of industrial lasers. Determined to see his ideas manifested, Hobart enlisted the help of five other individuals and started his own company.

Coherent was founded in May 1966, when Hobart was in his early 30s. The company's start was modest, backed by the $10,000 Hobart and his associates were able to come up with for Coherent's start-up capital. With limited financial resources, the founders established company headquarters in the Palo Alto, California home of Eugene Watson, a former sales and marketing manager for Spectra-Physics. Initially, the most pressing need was for a 220-volt outlet to power the laser they intended to build, which forced Coherent's brain trust to build the laser in a laundry room, the only place in Watson's house with a suitable outlet. Next to a washer and dryer, Hobart and his colleagues began building Coherent's first product during the summer of 1966, using a piece of a rain gutter as one of the key components of their prototype industrial laser. Despite the somewhat crude methods of their homespun efforts, the entrepreneurs achieved remarkable results swiftly, compensating for their lack of resources with ingenuity. Four months after the company was founded, Coherent unveiled its first laser at the Westcon trade show, a precision instrument that had shed its rain gutter vestiges and evolved into a shiny, telescope-like device. More important than aesthetics, manufacturers were interested in Coherent's first product.

The laser Coherent built during the summer of 1966 was the first carbon dioxide laser available commercially. The power output of the company's first product set a precedent, forcing Coherent to develop a power meter capable of measuring its power. The power meter became the company's second product, a device that continued to garner sales 30 years later. In the fall of 1966, however, the primary focus was on selling the laser. Boeing Co. was the first company to order a Coherent laser. Hobart performed the installation of the laser himself in January 1967, inadvertently burning a hole through a sport coat

Company Perspectives:

Coherent's mission is to focus on laser product innovations. Leveraging its competitive strengths in laser technology development, new product applications, engineering R&D and manufacturing expertise, Coherent is dedicated to customer satisfaction, quality and service. Coherent's mission is to continue its tradition of providing medical, scientific, commercial and OEM customers with cost effective laser products that provide performance breakthroughs and application innovations. Coherent's goals are to serve its customers, employees and stockholders. Specific goals include providing: customers with innovative products, superb technology, total quality, support and satisfaction; employees with a challenging, fulfilling place to work while expanding their skills and horizons; stockholders with consistent returns on equity capital and long-term growth in sales and earnings.

hanging on a chair during the process. Hobart paid to replace the sport coat and, after the initial foible, secured Coherent's first satisfied customer.

Market Diversification in the 1970s–80s

After receiving capital from the Rockefeller family, Coherent converted to public ownership in 1970. The company developed a family of industrial lasers to complement its first product, diversifying from there into medical and scientific markets, where applications for lasers were in abundance. As the years passed, Coherent's commitment to research and development spawned a diverse range of lasers, stretching from small, argon green lasers for use in eye surgery to invisible carbon dioxide lasers developed to cut metal. Coherent lasers were used to repair herniated discs, to study biological and semiconductor processes, and to light walls of water at Disneyland. The applications were manifold, developed by a highly regarded and expansive research and development team. ''Coherent has more Ph.D.s on staff than most competitors have employees,'' remarked an industry analyst to *California Business* in 1992. The dedication to developing new types of lasers to address ever-expanding needs bolstered Coherent's stature. With lasers developed and marketed for industrial, scientific, and medical markets, the company ranked as the largest independent laser maker in the world by the early 1980s. The company's elite industry position, however, did not guarantee a commensurate standing in financial matters.

Despite a full roster of laser products, and despite its impressive intellectual talent, Coherent did not boast a financial stature that was reflective of its global dominance in a significant technological sector. Lasers had failed to produce the kind of investor returns and swelling financial figures typical of other major technological breakthroughs, such as computers, semiconductors, and fiber optics. Part of Coherent's problem, which became more evident as the 1980s progressed, was that lasers had become relatively easy to develop. As the technology underpinning their development matured, lasers took on the market characteristics of commodity items, particularly lasers used in compact disc players and telephone lines. To produce lasers for medical applications, relatively little start-up capital was required, eliminating what otherwise would have served as a formidable obstacle barring entry to start-up companies. Accordingly, the number of Coherent's competitors proliferated, weakening the company's market position. Beyond external pressures, Coherent also suffered from internal difficulties, perhaps the most deleterious source of the company's problems during the 1980s.

Early 1980s Joint Venture Creates Crisis

By the late 1980s, a number of industry observers had begun to brand Coherent as an underachiever, hailing the company's potential yet deriding its financial performance. In 1990, Coherent was tagged by *Forbes* as ''Laser Laggard'' and by *California Business* as ''A Lagging Laser Maker,'' unflattering appellations that drew their source from analysts who watched the global leader in lasers stumble financially. One of the chief and most enduring internal problems stemmed from an early 1980s joint venture with General Electric Co. The subsidiary created through the joint venture was Sturidge, Massachusetts-based Coherent General Inc. Shortly after its formation, Coherent General prematurely introduced an industrial laser that suffered from profound problems. In the aftermath, Coherent's reputation, which had been steadily cultivated since the early days in Watson's laundry room, was seriously tarnished. Equally troubling, Coherent lost its market lead to Siemens. The aftershocks of the laser's flop reverberated outward: some of Coherent's customers in the machine tool business realized that making lasers to punch holes, cut metals, and weld materials could be done internally. As Coherent lost market share to its closest rival and to its own customers, other problems unrelated to Coherent General's miscue emerged.

Looking back at the troubled 1980s, Terry McGoldrick, director of operations of Coherent Laser Group, part of the company's scientific unit, succinctly summarized Coherent's mistakes. ''Inability to perform was our basic problem,'' he conceded to *California Business* in February 1990. The company inadequately dealt with corporate functions revolving around quality, delivery, and service. In 1986, for instance, McGoldrick estimated that only 13 percent of Coherent's deliveries were on time. Financially, the company was struggling, losing $2.3 million in 1987, another $1.3 million in 1988, and, after posting a profit of $8.9 million in 1989, registering a loss of $449,000 in 1990. As a consequence, Coherent's market value plummeted from $200 million in 1985 to $90 million by 1990, punctuating the sweeping problems affecting the company.

Hobart Spearheads Revival in the Early 1990s

In the years leading up to Coherent's downward spiral, Hobart had delegated management responsibilities to others while he devoted his energies to developing the company's lasers. As Coherent's problems magnified, Hobart emerged from the laboratory to assume a leading role in the company's management, taking on the responsibilities of chief executive officer in August 1988. His first objective was to restructure Coherent's nonscientific units, namely, the company's medical/surgical and industrial units. As the reorganization of the nonscientific units was under way, Hobart used the company's

Key Dates:

1966: The first commercial carbon dioxide laser is developed.
1970: Initial public offering of stock is completed.
1977: Coherent Radiation is renamed Coherent, Inc.
1990: Extensive employee training programs are implemented.
1992: Headquarters are relocated from Palo Alto to Santa Clara.

scientific laser group as a testing ground for a multifaceted improvement program patterned after the methods employed by Japanese manufacturers. Employees were trained in the Just In Time (JIT) system of limited delivery, Statistical Process Control (SPC), and Continuous Process Improvement (CPI) manufacturing, all of which stressed an organization-wide commitment to quality and efficiency. The scientific laser group was the first to benefit from the JIT, SPC, and CPI training programs. In 1989 the unit's production output was 20 percent greater than in 1987, an increase achieved with 30 percent fewer employees. Further, the percentage of product defects was cut in half, and 90 percent of deliveries were made on time. The drastic improvements prompted an extension of the training programs to other Coherent divisions, proving instrumental to the company's turnaround as it entered the 1990s.

Although Coherent ranked as one of the top five industrial laser makers, the business unit continued to produce disappointing financial results as the 1990s began. The strength of the company was in medical and scientific lasers, where Coherent ranked as the market leader in each category. Hobart, presiding as chairman and chief executive officer, pinned the company's future on the development of a greater lead in the medical market. During the early 1990s, Coherent derived 40 percent of its sales from medical lasers, but Hobart hoped to derive at least half of the company's sales from medical lasers by the mid-1990s, a feat to be accomplished by investing heavily in research and development. In 1991 the company spent more than $26 million on research and development, which led to the introduction of more than 34 new products in a two-year span. In all, the company manufactured and sold more than 1,000 different laser products through 22 production, sales, and service sites worldwide.

With the troubles of the late 1980s behind it, Coherent looked toward the 1990s as its opportunity to realize the rewards of its potential. In a sense, the beginning of the decade represented a fresh start, a new beginning that would be led from new corporate headquarters. In 1992 the company paid $7.5 million for a 200,000-square-foot building in Santa Clara, moving Coherent away from its long-time base in Palo Alto. By the time of the move, Hobart's efforts to cultivate efficiency and greater attention to customer service and quality had produced encouraging results, aided in part by the divestiture of Coherent General in 1993. At the company's manufacturing facility in Auburn, California, productivity had increased 60 percent between 1990 and 1994, while overhead costs had been reduced by 58 percent. The implementation of the JIT, CPI, and SPC programs, coupled with a concerted focus on medical and scientific laser products, was enabling Coherent to break free at last from the constraints that held annual sales at $200 million. The company was growing, evidenced by the expansion of its Auburn plant by 57 percent in 1996. The 105,000-square-foot plant, which had garnered national awards for its operating efficiency, was augmented by an adjacent 60,000-square-foot building, half of which was set aside for future expansion.

The need for extra manufacturing space had been necessitated, in part, by two acquisitions completed in 1995, which helped fuel robust increases in Coherent's revenue volume. In October, Coherent acquired the diode laser operation of Applied Laser Systems, a Medford, Oregon firm whose technology was sought after by companies involved in manufacturing medical instruments, alignment, and inspections systems. The following month, Coherent purchased the laser optics division of ATx Telecom Systems Inc., which developed coating processes for lenses and mirrors used in the development of solid-state lasers. Both of the acquisitions were folded in Coherent's Auburn facility, thus creating the need for additional space. Prior to the acquisitions, Coherent's annual revenue volume had begun to swell, after years of languishing at $200 million. In 1994, sales reached $215 million; by the end of the company's fiscal 1995 year, concluded in September before the Applied Laser and ATx acquisitions were completed, sales shot upward to $285 million. Perhaps more important, profits for 1995 amounted to $19.3 million, helping to erase the memories of successive annual losses during the late 1980s.

In July 1996, Bernard J. Couillaud, formerly vice-president and general manager of Coherent Laser Group, was named president and chief executive officer. Hobart's departure in 1997 positioned Couillaud as Coherent's senior executive. Against the backdrop of the managerial changes, the company completed two notable acquisitions that formed a new business segment. In July 1995, Coherent acquired the laser diode operations of Uniphase Corporation. In December 1996, the company purchased 80 percent of Tutcore OY, Ltd., a Tampere, Finland-based company that ranked as the leading manufacturer of aluminum-free semiconductor wafers used to manufacture laser diodes. These two acquisitions were organized as a separate business group in August 1997 known as the Coherent Semiconductor Group.

During the late 1990s, Coherent demonstrated the consistent performance of an industry leader. In November 1997, Coherent signed a partnership agreement with Palomar Medical Technologies, Inc. for laser-based hair removal systems. The partnership agreement led to the April 1999 acquisition of Palomar's subsidiary, Star Medical Technologies, Inc., a $65 million transaction that strengthened Coherent's technology in commercial and medical markets. Sales by the end of the company's fiscal year in September 1999 reached $468.9 million, a 14 percent gain from the previous year's total that was outshined by a 40 percent increase in net income, which rose to $22.6 million. Considering Coherent's role as a pioneer in laser development, which had inculcated a commitment to substantial annual investments in research and development, the company appeared well-equipped to produce similar financial growth in the years ahead. Further, Coherent offered a broader range of laser products than any of its competitors, fueling expectations that the company would continue to rank as an industry leader in the 21st century.

Principal Subsidiaries

Coherent Auburn Group; Coherent Laser Group; Coherent Medical Group; Coherent Semiconductor Group; Coherent Lambda Physik (Germany; 80%).

Principal Competitors

ThermoTrex Corporation; Trex Medical Corporation; Cymer, Inc.

Further Reading

Aragon, Lawrence, ''Laundry Room Was Birthplace for Laser Giant,'' *Business Journal,* September 21, 1992, p. 1.

Barlas, Pete, ''A Coherent Strategy: Not in Vain Has Firm Zapped Veins,'' *Business Journal,* February 10, 1997, p. 1.

Cook, Dan, ''Coherent: A Lagging Laser Maker Commits to Quality,'' *California Business,* February 1990, p. 16.

Larson, Mark, ''Coherent Expands Auburn Laser Plant for Growing Staff,'' *Business Journal Serving Greater Sacramento,* February 26, 1996, p. 2.

Slutsker, Gary, ''Laser Laggard,'' *Forbes,* March 5, 1990, p. 138.

''This Lasermaker Could Beam Big Profits Your Way,'' *Money,* August 1993, p. 50.

—Jeffrey L. Covell

Colas S.A.

7, place Rene Clair
92653 Boulogne-Billancourt Cedex
France
Telephone: (33) 1 47 61 75 00
Fax: (33) 1 47 61 76 00
Web site: http://www.colas.fr

Public Company
Incorporated: 1929 as Société Routière Colas
Employees: 42,000
Sales: FFr 29.5 billion (US $5.12 billion) (1998)
Stock Exchanges: Paris
Ticker Symbol: Colas
NAIC: 23411 Highway and Street Construction

France's Colas S.A. is the world's leading road construction and road infrastructure maintenance company, with operations in more than 45 countries employing more than 42,000 worldwide, with some 90,000 projects completed worldwide. Colas not only builds and maintains roads, airport runways and surfaces, parking lots, and parking garage surfaces, the company also produces the raw materials for its roads. Each year Colas produces more than 49 million metric tons of aggregates used for road construction, as well as nearly 36 million metric tons of asphalt mix. Colas is also the world's number two leading producer of bitumen emulsions for road surfacing, producing 1.18 million tons, to place it behind the United States' Koch. Historically active in France and the former French colonies, which together represent more than 62 percent of the company's annual sales, Colas also has built a strong presence in North America (18 percent of annual sales) and in the rest of Europe (15 percent of sales). Whereas road construction and maintenance and sales of road materials together produced 85 percent of Colas's sales in 1998, the company is also active in pipes and mains and other civil engineering projects and in road signs and other traffic signs, as well as highway management, through a 12 percent participation in French Autoroute concessionaire Cofiroute. Colas has targeted acquisitions for its continued growth; nonetheless, in the traditionally locally oriented road construction industry, the company's subsidiaries retain a large degree of autonomy. In most cases, management of new acquisitions remain in place and under the same company name. Led by CEO Alain Dupont, Colas has seen its revenues more than triple in the years between 1987 and 1998. Trading on the Paris stock exchange, the company is 57 percent owned by French construction and telecom giant Bouygues.

Surfacing in the 1920s

''Société Routière Colas'' was formed in May 1929 to exploit a patent for a new type of road surfacing material—the first usable bituminous emulsion. Originally called Cold Spray, this method of surfacing roads was considered revolutionary and quickly became the basis of the modern roadway. Cold Spray was invented at the beginning of the 1920s by Hugh Allan Mackay and George Samuel Illay in England, receiving a patent in 1922. By then, Mackay had formed his own company, Asphalt Cold Mix Limited, to exploit the patent in the United Kingdom. The pair, however, sought to license their emulsion procedure overseas.

Cold Spray was soon brought to the attention of Alexandre Giros, one of France's most prominent construction and road building figures, who arranged an agreement with Mackay to give the Sociètè Générale d'Entreprises (SGE) the exclusive rights to the Cold Spray patent in France. Testing of the product began in 1924, at first as Suresnes, then along the route between Bayonne and Biarritz, and finally in the then-French colonies Algeria and Tunisia. By then, however, other emulsions began to appear, often as counterfeits under the Cold Spray. In 1924, therefore, the product's name was changed to ''Colas,'' as an abbreviation of Cold Asphalt.

Colas operated as a division of the SGE through the end of the decade, achieving great success. By 1925, the emulsion technique had its first application on a runway, serving to pave the airfield at Monthléry. Colas also found a strong market beyond France, finding sales in Romania, Algeria, Polond and Tunisia. Steady demand led to increased production needs. In 1926 the SGE opened a new Colas production facility at Grand-Couronne; two years later, the SGE added five more

Company Perspectives:

To maintain the pace of growth set over the past ten years, Colas is developing its international network through a strategy of external expansion which focuses on regions offering high growth potential.

production facilities, at Alger, Bergerac, Lyon, Montluçon and Port St.-Louis-du-Rhône.

By then, however, the huge demand for the Colas product and paving method outpaced the SGE's ability to finance the division's growth. In 1929, then, the SGE sought a partnership with the Anglo-Dutch petroleum giant Shell. The company Société Routière Colas was set up as a joint venture between two Shell subsidiaries, the U.K.-based Colas Flintkote and the Netherlands-based Nederlandsch Indisch Industrie Maatschappij, and the SGE, with each of the three entities holding equal parts of the new subsidiary. Société Routière Colas operated in France and France's colonial possessions; at the same time, Shell developed other Colas companies around the world, linked by a central research facility operated by the London-based company Colas Products. Alexandre Giros and Georges Mathieu took the lead of the French operation. Giros served as the company's first president, but Colas's major growth came under the guidance of Georges Mathieu, who served as president from 1932 to 1948.

Société Routière Colas started official operations at an inauspicious time: the stock market crash of 1929 plunged the world into a decade-long depression. Yet Colas nevertheless achieved strong growth during this time. Where roads had previously been paved in expensive concrete or tar, the Colas procedure proved more durable, safer, and less expensive and faster to apply, in that it could be used even during the rain. France's road network, in large part damaged during the First World War, was in dire need of repair and development. Despite a shortage of funds, the government invested heavily in the country's road network. Colas quickly extended its operations across all of France; by the end of the decade the company also had moved into the country's colonial possessions, opening subsidiary operations in Algeria, Morocco, and other French African possessions, while also reaching the French Antilles.

Part of Colas's success was Mathieu's early decision to extend operations beyond simply manufacturing asphalt and emulsions. At the same time, Mathieu was credited with creating a separate Colas company culture and winning more and more autonomy from its investors. Under Mathieu's leadership, Colas began to take over its own research and development needs, financing this activity through its own profits. Generating these profits was a series of new products, including Colas 50 and Colasmix, a cold-bitumen-based concrete emulsion introduced in 1929; the concentrated Colas 60 and Colas 65; a freeze-resistant emulsion, Colas Hiver (winter); and Colsol Normal, an emulsion useful for the stabilization of sand-based roadways, particularly useful in the company's colonial markets.

By the end of the 1930s, Colas had diversified successfully to provide a full range of roadwork services, from raw materials, to materials transport, to road construction itself. Colas also was aided by its association with Shell, which had built a strong presence in France during the same period. Shell decided to reinvest Colas's profits into growing the emulsion company's infrastructure. This strategy, which enabled Colas's capital nearly to double its worth by the mid-1930s, also provoked the departure of the SGE from the Colas shareholding, as the SGE sought to recoup its investment in the face of the difficult economic climate.

By the end of the 1930s, Colas had expanded to a full-scale operation, with 19 factories in France and seven more factories in Algeria, Morocco, Senegal, and Martinique. The years leading up to the Second World War, with the rapid buildup of Europe's militaries, the adoption of new mobile military tactics (in contrast to the previous war's reliance on fixed trenches), as well as the introduction of the airplane at the heart of the armed forces, encouraged the rapid deployment of extensive road networks and airports with runways capable of serving the larger and faster airplanes. Colas found its road and surfacing products in high demand.

The outbreak of the Second World War nearly ended the company's existence, however, as France capitulated to the Nazi forces. As a subsidiary of the Anglo-Dutch Shell, Colas was classified as an enemy possession and, therefore, was taken over by the German invader. Deprived of raw materials, Colas's activities ground to a standstill.

Postwar Growth

Mathieu regained his position as Colas's president after the Liberation. Rebuilding the company's fortunes, however, fell to Mathieu's successor, Henry Forien, named CEO at the beginning of January 1948. Forien, who served as CEO for more than ten years, succeeded in recapturing Colas's position as the leading French roadwork company, ahead of such long-term rivals as Sacer and others. Forien quickly added new production units, including a new French bitumen processing facility and three new factories to the company's colonial operations. Forien also worked to boost the company's presence in the colonies, especially in northern Africa. To develop its overseas operations, Colas transformed what had previously been branch offices into full-fledged subsidiary operations, beginning with the creation of Colas du Maroc in 1949, followed by Colas d'Algérie in 1950, and the acquisition of Société d'Entreprises de Routes en Algérie, based in Oran. The company's reinforced presence in northern Africa brought strong revenue growth and profits, encouraging Colas to expand its Antilles operations, where the company was awarded contracts for constructing the Guadeloupe and Martinique airports.

During the 1950s, the company diversified its activities to protect itself against the market fluctuations that had been hampering its growth. The company turned to road construction, increasing its presence in this area especially with the participation in the construction of the country's first high-speed "autoroutes" freeway network. The company also stepped up its activities in airport runway construction, taking on the newly developed NATO alliance as a major client, building NATO airstrips in Luxeuil-Saint-Saveur, Lure-Malbouhans, and Haute Saône, as well as airstrips in Turkey.

Key Dates:

1922: "Cold Spray" road surfacing method receives patent.
1929: Société Routière Colas is founded to exploit Cold Spray patent in France.
1949: Colas du Maroc is created.
1950: Colas d'Algérie is formed; Société d'Entreprises de Routes en Algérie, based in Oran, is acquired.
1958: Company acquired by Société Parisienne Raveau-Cartier.
1961: Public listing on Paris stock exchange.
1965: Acquisitions of Arboroute (Belgium), Fabit Ltd. and Modern Paving (Canada).
1966: U.S. subsidiary in Vermont is established.
1993: Sacer of France is acquired.
1997: Screg of France is acquired.

Another important development was the establishment of Société Routière Colas's own research and development department, entirely independent from Shell and the rest of the network of international Colas companies. During the early years of the 1950s, Colas developed several new products, in particular that of a new cationic emulsion, which enabled the use of silicates, and the acid emulsions Colacid R series and Colacid E series. In the middle of the decade, the company rolled out a series of anionic emulsions—Colaster A, Colaster B, Colsol HP, and Colsol ST. The company also developed its own homogenizing machine, which was capable of topping 12 tons of emulsion per hour.

By the end of the 1950s, Société Routière Colas had come a long way toward independence from its primary shareholder, Shell. The last step was taken at the end of the decade, when Shell turned the majority of its shares in Colas to the Société Parisienne Raveau-Cartier. Georges Raveau had been active in North Africa before the outbreak of the Second World War, where he operated a fuel distribution network. During the war, Raveau had used his network to support the Allied cause and, in the process, aided Shell as well. After the war, Shell rewarded Raveau with a majority shareholding in Colas; Shell's participation was reduced to 15 percent, with an additional eight percent held by banking house Worms & Cie.

World Leader in the 1990s

In 1959 the sudden death of Henry Forien placed Georges Raveau at the head of Société Routière Colas, a position he retained until 1973. Raveau greatly expanded the company, particularly with extensive investments in research and development. Colas quickly established a world leadership position in a number of areas, especially that of emulsions. New products, such as Colmat and Colflex gave Colas new market successes. The company's importance in the development of road surfacing and road building technologies was recognized, too, by a growing collaboration between Colas and the French department of roads and bridges. This collaboration eventually grew to give Colas more or less a monopoly in the French road materials market.

Raveau eyed greater growth during the 1960s. In 1961 Colas went to the market, listing on the Paris stock exchange. The company also began a policy of external growth, primarily through acquisitions. This policy soon established Colas as a globally operating company.

During the 1960s and 1970s, Colas expanded its operations in Africa, increasing its presence in what were now the former French colonies, particularly with greater activity in Tunisia, the creation of subsidiaries in Martinique and Guadaloupe, and the creation of separate subsidiaries for Cameroon, the Ivory Coast, and Mali, while spreading the company's operations throughout the so-called "Zone Franc" of Africa. In the mid-1960s, the company also began expanding beyond the French-speaking countries, opening operations in Nigeria and Kenya. Back home, Colas began expanding into other European countries, starting with Germany, where the company acquired a number of local companies, including J.J. Ipendorf A.G.

Colas's policy of expansion through acquisition began during this time. At the same time, Colas developed its policy of maintaining its network of subsidiaries as more or less autonomous, locally based companies. From Germany, Colas quickly expanded into other European countries, including Belgium, Spain, and Switzerland. The company also entered North America, beginning operations in Mexico.

Colas continued to grow steadily in France as well, making a number of strategic acquisitions, including those of the Compagnie Lyonnaise des Goudrons de Bitumes; France-Route; Routes Modernes; Compagnie Métropolitaine de Asphaltes; and Maison Devaux. Overseas, the company's acquisition trail gave it Arboroute in Belgium, in 1965, and Canadian companies Fabit Ltd. and Modern Paving. The Canadian purchases led to the company's entry into the United States market in 1967, when the company established a subsidiary in Vermont. By the end of the decade, Colas was particularly active in the New England region, where it became involved in the construction of a number of the region's freeways and highways.

Colas's international growth took the forefront into the 1980s, even as the company maintained its leading position in its traditional French and French African bases. During the 1980s, Colas found new ownership, as the French construction giant Bouygues entered the company's capital, building a solid 57 percent share. At this time, Colas was grouped under the Société d'Investissement de Travaux Publics (SITP), a partnership between Bouygues (66.6 percent) and Colas's longtime shareholder, Shell (33 percent). The SITP structure enabled Colas to buy up the various Shell-backed "Colas" subsidiaries around the world; by the end of the decade, the French Colas remained the sole Colas, and the world's leading road builder.

In its position in the SITP, Colas, which posted revenues of FFr 8.5 billion in 1987, found itself together with two of its principal French rivals, the companies Screg and Sacer, both of which were also Bouygues subsidiaries. In the 1990s, however, Colas and Bouygues embarked on a consolidation drive: in 1992 Colas took over the operations of the smaller Sacer, boosting Colas's revenues to FFr 16.5 billion for 1993. A similar move was undertaken in 1997, when Colas took over the

Screg operations. By 1999, Colas's revenues of FFr 29.5 billion, for net income of more than FFr 500 million, gave it the leadership position in the worldwide road construction market. With an annual investment program of more than FFr 1.5 billion per year, Colas, which pledged to continue investing in and upgrading its industrial base, also saw a long smooth road ahead of potential acquisitions in the unconsolidated road construction industry.

Principal Subsidiaries

SPAC (France); Sacer S.A. (France); Screg (S.A.); Carrières Roy (France; 49.98%); Cofiroute (France; 16.66%); Colas Martinique; Colas Guadeloupe; Colas de Nouvelle-Calédonie; Colas GmbH (Austria); Colas Bauchemie GmbH (Germany); Jouret (Belgium); Colas Danmark A/S; Valtatie Oy (Finland; 50%); Colas Ltd. (UK); I,C,B Emulsions (Ireland); Eszakkö (Hungary); Strada Sp. Zo.o. (Poland; 50.90%); Sorocam (Romania; 51%); Colas S.A. (Switzerland); Sintra Ltee (Canada); Barrett P.M. Inc. (US); Colas Inc. (US); Reeves Construction Company (US); Sloan Construction Company (US); Sully-Miller Construction Company (US); Routière Colas de Côte-d'Ivoire; Routière Colas de Gabon (89.89); Colas du Maroc; Colas Emulsions (Morocco; 95.66%); Wasco (Indonesia; 50%); Thai Slurry Seal Co. Ltd. (Thailand; 49.65%); Raycol Asphalt Co. Ltd. (Thailand; 38.98%); Hincol (India; 29.99%).

Principal Competitors

Eiffage; Ferrovial; FCC; Societe Generale d'Entreprises; Granite Construction; Italcementi; Jean Lefebvre; Lafarge SA; Peter Kiewit Sons; RMC Group; Skanska; Suez Lyonnaise des Eaux; Tarmac.

Further Reading

Barjonet, Claude, "Colas veut doubler en cinq ans a l'international," *Les Echos,* May 22, 1997, p. 13.

Bauer, Anne, "Colas lance une OPE-OPA sur Sacer," *Les Echos,* November 16, 1992, p. 11.

—— "Colas poursuit sa route sans encombre," *Les Echos,* April 2, 1999, p. 14.

—M.L. Cohen

Complete Business Solutions, Inc.

32605 West Twelve Mile Road
Farmington Hills, Michigan 48334-3339
U.S.A.
Telephone: (248) 488-2088
Fax: (248) 488-2089
Web site: http://www.cbsinc.com

Public Company
Incorporated: 1985
Employees: 4,800
Sales: $376.6 million (1998)
Stock Exchanges: NASDAQ
Ticker Symbol: CBSI
NAIC: 541511 Custom Computer Programming Services

Founded in 1985 as a contract programming firm, Complete Business Solutions, Inc. (CBSI) has grown through a series of strategic acquisitions into a leading provider of information technology (IT) services. The company's 1997 initial public offering (IPO) was one of Wall Street's most successful, with the value of the newly issued shares rising an incredible 262 percent within nine months. By 1999 CBSI had about 500 customers, with 70 percent of them mid-range companies with revenues of $500 million to $4 billion. Other major clients included the Big Three automakers General Motors, Ford Motor Co., and Chrysler Corporation, and several state governments.

Good Clients Help New Firm Grow: 1985–90

CBSI was founded in 1985 as a contract programming firm by Rajendra Vattikuti, a native of India. After earning a bachelor's degree in India, he graduated from Detroit's Wayne State University with master's degrees in electrical and computer engineering. From 1983 to 1985 he was a management information systems project leader for Chrysler Corporation. Chrysler was one of CBSI's first clients, providing the firm with $200,000 in revenues in 1985. By 1996 Chrysler would account for $7.5 million of CBSI's revenue.

The firm started with 20 employees and earned $432,000 in revenues in 1985. Initially, CBSI hired out computer consultants to clients as needed. In the 1980s many firms were cutting back on their internal computer departments and hiring outside consultants to develop software and solve information problems. CBSI was called in, typically, when a company experienced some type of computer problem. CBSI's consultants would fix it and remain available for follow-up service as needed.

Another early customer was a Belgian banking network firm called Swift, which had offices in Washington, D.C. Swift did interbank networking for about 3,000 banks. When its system needed an overhaul, it called in CBSI. Vattikuti told the *Detroit News,* "We grew to 50 people on that account. It was a good cash cow for us." Swift paid in advance and helped CBSI avoid going into debt.

In 1990 Vattikuti noted that 70 percent of CBSI's business was repeat business. The company tried to provide "a total long-term solution" to each customer's problem, not just sell them some software. Its biggest clients included the Big Three automakers (General Motors, Ford, and Chrysler), as well as the state of Michigan. By 1990 the firm had grown to more than 300 employees. Revenues for 1989 were $18 million, a five-year compound growth rate of 92 percent. The firm had established regional offices in Chicago, Dallas, San Jose, and Connecticut. In April 1990 it opened an office in London, England.

Developing into a Computer Consulting Firm in the 1990s

CBSI was relatively unknown until the Y2K problem brought increased recognition to a lot of information technology (IT) companies. During the 1990s CBSI developed into a computer consulting firm that helped companies apply new technology to gain a competitive edge. CBSI's growth during the 1990s would far outpace Vattikuti's 1990 prediction that sales would reach $120 million by 2000.

In 1991 CBSI opened an off-shore service center in India to tap the expertise of Indian computer programmers and technical people. The service center gave CBSI access to computer programmers at wage levels lower than those in the United States and provided the company with a 24-hour work force. CBSI's global presence would be a positive factor in its later acquisition of smaller Information Technology (IT) service

Company Perspectives:

Our goal is to become the preferred single-source provider of IT [Information Technology] services to an expanding base of clients by establishing teams that quickly and cost-effectively provide industry-based IT applications solutions.

companies. CBSI later opened a second service center in India and in 1999 established another off-shore service center in the Philippine Islands.

In 1992 CSBI gained another major client, grocery retailer Spartan Stores Inc. It provided CBSI with $200,000 in revenue in its first year; by 1996 the account had grown to $4 million. CBSI had grown to about 600 employees in 1993. It kept supervisors to a minimum, with only one layer of management between the CEO and the lowest-level consultant. It created a loyal group of managers by providing training to encourage entrepreneurship and leadership.

Revenues continued to grow steadily in the first half of the decade without any significant acquisitions. Revenues increased from $32.4 million in 1992 to $83.2 million in 1996. About 15 percent of the company's business came from automotive companies. Other clients included Spartan Stores Inc., insurance provider UNUM Ltd., the state of Nevada, and Citibank. Helping clients with Y2K computer problems accounted for just eight percent of CBSI's revenues in 1996, or about $6.6 million.

Aggressive Growth Fueled by Initial Public Offering: 1997–99

In March 1997 CBSI went public at $12 a share. The IPO generated $25.7 million, some of which would be used to grow the company through acquisitions. The debt-free company was in good financial shape. Filings with the SEC revealed that the company enjoyed a 30 percent annual revenue growth for the previous five years as a private company. At the time of the IPO CBSI had 1,500 employees, 500 of them overseas including 450 in India, and 1,000 in the United States including 350 in Michigan.

During 1997 the company's stock rode a wave of Wall Street enthusiasm for companies that fixed Y2K computer problems. For the second quarter of 1997 it led all 85 Detroit-area stocks tracked by *Crain's Detroit Business* with a 154 percent gain to $24.75 a share, up from a low of $8.37 in mid-March due to a general decline in the market. The company filed for a secondary stock offering in August 1997 for an additional 2.25 million shares. It was operating in six major areas: contract programming, re-engineering, client-server development, packaged software implementation, information technology consulting, and application maintenance.

CBSI completed the first of four strategic acquisitions in November 1997, when it acquired Synergy Software Inc. of Schaumberg, Illinois, for $31.2 million of stock. CBSI stock was trading at $34.50 a share. Synergy Software provided computer training, installation, and maintenance. It also provided Y2K consulting services. Synergy was founded in 1989 by Carl DePaolis and Louis Borders as a spin-off of the information technology division of Borders Books and Music.

CBSI expected to transform Synergy into a regional center serving Chicago and Milwaukee. Vattikuti hoped the acquisition would help the company attract more highly skilled computer professionals, which were in short supply. The acquisition marked the beginning of CBSI's strategy to grow through acquisitions, mergers, and business combinations. It added about 100 employees. For 1997 CBSI reported revenues of $123.8 million.

CBSI's second major acquisition took place in January 1998, when it acquired C.W. Costello & Associates Inc. of Connecticut for $72.7 million in stock. For 1997 Costello had revenues of $70.2 million and a net loss of $1.9 million. The acquisition added about 700 IT professionals to the company.

In March 1998 CBSI paid a two-for-one stock dividend. The company's first quarter earnings report of $.16 a share beat Wall Street's expectations of $.12 a share. Prior to the stock split CBSI shares were trading in the $65 range. At the time of the split, company employees other than Vattikuti owned six percent of the company.

CBSI was gaining recognition from Wall Street as a premier IT company for several reasons. It was able to recruit and retain scarce software programmers by developing a team environment. It also was able to buy smaller IT service companies and merge their staffs into its own. The acquisitions allowed CBSI to expand its service delivery capabilities to include on-site, off-site, and off-shore service—whatever the client preferred.

At the time of the stock split in March 1998 about 20 percent of the company's 2,000 employees worldwide were engaged in correcting Y2K problems in computer code. A typical client may have thousands of programs involving five to 15 million lines of code. Each project could take 16–18 months. CBSI was debugging programs for about 45 clients throughout the United States, including Chrysler Corporation, Ford Motor Co., and the state of Michigan.

In July 1998 CBSI acquired Claremont Technology Group Inc. of Beaverton, Oregon, for some $285 million in stock. Claremont was a leading IT systems integration firm with large and mid-sized corporations and state governments as clients. It was especially strong in enterprise resource planning (ERP) software implementation and client-server technology, two important areas for CBSI. Claremont strengthened CBSI's presence on the West Coast and added more than 600 employees. It also had 16 domestic offices and overseas offices in Canada and Australia.

In December 1998 CBSI made its fourth major acquisition. It acquired Sudbury River Consulting Group for $5 million plus potential future consideration. Sudbury River Consulting Group had recently moved to Providence, Rhode Island, in July 1997, where CBSI's northeast operations center was located. Following the acquisition, CBSI's 135-person Providence staff and Sudbury's 53-person office were consolidated in a new 30,000-square-foot office space in the Foundry complex in Providence. Sudbury was known for its expertise in providing enterprise resource planning, an information technology useful for just-in-time manufacturers.

Key Dates:

1985: Complete Business Solutions is founded in the suburbs of Detroit by Rajendra Vattikuti.
1987: CBSI goes public.
1990: London office is opened.
1998: Major acquisitions include C.W. Costello & Associates Inc.; Claremont Technology Group Inc.; Sudbury River Consulting Group.

For 1998 CBSI's financial results reflected the recent mergers and acquisitions involving Synergy Software Inc., C.W. Costello & Associates Inc., and Claremont Technology Group Inc. Revenues rose 37 percent from $275.3 million in 1997 (restated to reflect recent acquisitions) to $376.6 million in 1998. Net income, however, decreased 21 percent from $8.4 million in 1997 to $6.7 million in 1998, with both figures reflecting the recent mergers. The lower net income was attributed to $28.3 million in merger costs and other one-time expenses.

The company's revenue growth was due to its offering a broader range of services, especially services related to emerging technologies such as data warehousing, electronic commerce, and network services. Chairman Raj Vattikuti said, "Our clients continued to rely on CBSI as an extension of their IT departments and to outsource a broad range of IT services." As a result of the company's recent acquisitions, it was able to offer a broader array of services.

Outlook: Beyond the 20th Century

In February 1999 CBSI completed a secondary stock offering of 5.4 million shares of common stock at $31 per share, including 2.1 million newly issued shares. Net proceeds to the company were approximately $60 million. During the first part of 1999 CBSI's stock was trading at lower prices, as was that of other information technology companies. Between January and May CBSI's stock lost about a third of its value. It peaked on January 4 at $33.87 a share and was down to $15.44 in April. Investors were concerned about the transition from Y2K consulting to other services.

After recovering somewhat, CBSI's stock dropped to $16.37 a share in June 1999 after a negative report that three of CBSI's off-shore India contracts, each valued at $1 to $2 million, would be delayed, causing CBSI to lower its revenue forecast for the second half of 1999. CBSI noted that the long-term contracts had been replaced with 22 short-term electronic commerce projects worth about $250,000 each.

During the first two months of 1999 CBSI signed 247 new contracts worth more than $70 million. About 37 percent involved electronic commerce and emerging technologies. One $5 million contract was signed with Unum Business Solutions Inc., a Portland, Maine-based insurance provider, to provide two years' worth of maintenance, development, and support services. CBSI also signed a contract to develop a Web site for Medsite.com, a New York e-commerce site for physicians.

CBSI planned to replace the lost Y2K revenue by focusing on building small computer networks, redoing older computer systems, and developing Internet commerce. These three new lines associated with emerging technologies accounted for 30 percent of revenue. Y2K revenues for CBSI peaked at 19 percent of the company's revenues in the third quarter of 1998. Employees who had been involved in Y2K projects were receiving training to develop their Internet software writing skills.

As CBSI replaced its Y2K consulting business with information technology consulting and emerging technologies, its operating margins doubled to 12.4 percent over two quarters. These new areas included e-commerce, Internet services, software development and maintenance, applications management, and data warehousing. They represented higher margin businesses than Y2K consulting. Another source of revenue came from the company's offshore development centers in India and the Philippines, which accounted for ten percent of the company's revenues in 1998, up from five percent in 1997.

Although CBSI and other IT firms remained under pressure from Wall Street to demonstrate that they can replace Y2K-related revenue, CBSI demonstrated that it could broaden its services through successful acquisitions of other IT firms. Its acquisitions provided CBSI with a broader range of services and strengthened its expertise, and the company had sufficient financial resources to take advantage of new acquisition opportunities in the future. Its customer base of about 500 customers, with 70 percent of them mid-range companies with revenues of $500 million to $4 billion, were likely to continue to utilize CBSI's skills in such areas as electronic commerce, emerging technologies, enterprise consulting, and IT planning. CBSI also had launched an aggressive marketing campaign to attract new customers.

Principal Competitors

IBM; Andersen Consulting; Electronic Data Systems Corp.; Perot Systems Corp.; Cap Gemini S.A.

Further Reading

Brennan, Mike, "Complete Business Solutions Inc. to Buy Illinois Company," *Knight-Ridder/Tribune Business News,* November 22, 1997.
——, "Farmington Hills, Mich.-Based Tech Consultant's Stock Plummets," *Knight-Ridder/Tribune Business News,* June 1, 1999.
Bridgeforth, Arthur, Jr., "High-Tech Firms Find a Life Outside the Auto Industry," *Crain's Detroit Business,* July 7, 1997, p. M19.
——, "Market Didn't Give Complete Picture," *Crain's Detroit Business,* May 12, 1997, p. 4.
Garland, Russell, "Providence, R.I., Software Firm Buys Crosstown Consulting Group," *Knight-Ridder/Tribune Business News,* December 23, 1998.
Henderson, Tom, "Computer Firm Raises $45 Million," *Detroit News,* March 4, 1999, p. 4B.
"Hot Growth Companies," *Business Week,* June 1, 1998.
Kachadourian, Gail, "Complete Biz Stock Falls After Report," *Crain's Detroit Business,* June 7, 1999, p. 21.
Mercer, Tenisha, "Looking Beyond 2000," *Crain's Detroit Business,* August 18, 1997, p. 2.
——, "Y2K Transition Watched: CBSI Redirecting to New Technology Work," *Crain's Detroit Business,* April 12, 1999, p. 2.

Michaels, Philip, ''Taking on More Complex Systems Projects,'' *Investor's Business Daily,* July 7, 1999.

''Michigan Info Technology Firm Approves 2-for-1 Stock Split,'' *Knight-Ridder/Tribune Business News,* February 22, 1998.

Oboler, Leon, ''From Grand Rapids to India and Back,'' *U.S. Distribution Journal,* January-February 1998, p. 34.

''Programmer Says Year 2000 Bug Work Tedious, Repetitive But Rewarding,'' *Knight-Ridder/Tribune Business News,* March 6, 1998.

Roush, Matt, ''Tech Stocks Lead Pack in Quarter,'' *Crain's Detroit Business,* July 14, 1997, p. 3.

Schlagheck, Carol, ''SWAT Team Strategies Prove Effective for CBSI,'' *Michigan Business,* May 1990, p. 34.

Walton, Christopher, ''Michigan's CBSI Cashes in on Year 2000 Computer Problem,'' *Knight-Ridder/Tribune Business News,* June 19, 1997.

Wernle, Bradford, ''9 Entrepreneurial Firms Showing Survival Instincts,'' *Crain's Detroit Business,* July 12, 1993, p. 12.

Yamada, Ken, ''Winning It All,'' *Solutions Integrator,* August 1998.

—David P. Bianco

Converse Inc.

One Fordham Road
North Reading, Massachusetts 01864-2619
U.S.A.
Telephone: (978) 664-1100
Fax: (978) 664-7472
Web site: http://www.converse.com

Public Company
Incorporated: 1908 as Converse Rubber Company
Employees: 2,658
Sales: $308 million (1998)
Stock Exchanges: New York
Ticker Symbol: CVE
NAIC: 31621 Footwear Manufacturing

Converse Inc. is the largest manufacturer of athletic footwear in the United States, producing approximately 8.4 million pairs of shoes domestically in 1998. It owns and operates a manufacturing facility in Lumberton, North Carolina, where it produces the majority of its athletic originals, and leases manufacturing plants in Mission, Texas and Reynosa, Mexico. The Converse All-Star basketball shoe was the first in the athletic footwear industry, and by the early 1990s, more than 500 million pairs, in more than 56 colors and styles, had been sold in more than 90 countries worldwide. In addition, the company has diversified into varied rubber products, sports apparel, and full lines of athletic shoes for tennis, cross-training, team sports, running, walking, and children's recreation.

From Basketball Shoe Innovator to Market Leader in the Early 20th Century

The origins of Converse Inc. date back to 1908, when Marquis M. Converse founded the Converse Rubber Company in Malden, Massachusetts with a capital investment of $250,000. Converse had gained extensive retail experience as a general manager of one of Boston's largest department stores and at Beacon Falls Rubber Shoe Co. He started his own firm after Beacon was absorbed by U.S. Rubber, and, within a year of its founding, the Converse Rubber Company had integrated 350 employees into a full-production team in a new plant. By 1910, the company had expanded its plant to produce 4,000 pairs of boots and rubbers daily.

The young company experienced a dramatic increase in sales after its 1917 introduction of the Converse canvas All Star, one of the world's first basketball shoes. The game of basketball was then in its infancy, having been invented by James Naismith in 1891 at the International Young Men's Christian Association Training School. All Star's rapid success was spurred by the reputation and marketing savvy of basketball star Charles "Chuck" H. Taylor, who joined the Converse sales force in 1921 to become the brand's first player endorser. In a town outside of Columbus, Indiana, Taylor had graduated from high school to a career in basketball. After playing for barnstorming basketball teams, including the Buffalo Germans and the Akron Firestones, Taylor joined Converse's Chicago sales office in 1921. He traveled around the country selling the shoe and promoting basketball in clinics. In 1968, a year before his death, Taylor was inducted into the Naismith Memorial Hall of Fame.

The original Converse Rubber Company soared beyond the scope of its 1908 designs until 1929 when it fell into bankruptcy. Control of the company then passed on to Mitchell B. Kaufman, who had been president of Hodgman Rubber Company since 1925. After Kaufman's untimely death a year later, his successor, Albert Wechsler, operated the company for the Kaufman estate until 1933, when a depressed economy and reduced profits prompted yet another change in command.

The 1933 purchase of the company by the Stone family began a 39-year period of family ownership during which time Converse became a market leader. After providing protective footwear, special-purpose boots, parkas, and other equipment for the American Armed Services during World War II, the Stones concentrated on rapid growth in a civilian market. In 1946 the company's Granite State Division in New Hampshire began operating two large plants. In 1953 Converse established the Coastal Footwear Corporation in Canovanas, Puerto Rico. Converse brand lines were further expanded with the 1961 acquisition of the Tyer Rubber Company and the 1964 acquisition of the Hodgman brand of sporting goods equipment. The company also opened a new factory in Presque Isle, Maine in

Company Perspectives:

The Company's marketing strategy is centered on the Converse All Star brand, which is positioned as the American performance brand with authentic sports heritage. The company believes that there are significant opportunities to build the brand, which commands high consumer awareness generated by reason of its 91-year history. The company's consumer research has become an integral part of its product development, advertising campaigns and in-store point of purchase materials.

1967 and purchased the Bristol manufacturing company in Rhode Island in 1969.

Expansion and Increased Competition in the 1970s

By the early 1970s, Converse had diversified beyond footwear to provide numerous industries—textile, plastic, automotive, paper, paper converting, photocopying, and leather processing—with products ranging from hockey pucks to teethguards, sports and industrial boots, and rubber compounds for specific applications. Sales were delegated to three separate divisions: Sporting Goods, Footwear, and Industrial.

The Stone family dynasty ended its reign in 1972, when Converse was purchased by the Eltra Corporation. That same year, the footwear division of B.F. Goodrich Co. was acquired, adding a modern manufacturing plant in Lumberton, North Carolina and a large distribution center in Charlotte, North Carolina, which remained the hub for Converse distribution as the company continued to expand.

By the late 1970s, factors, including increased foreign competition, soaring labor and overhead costs, and a weak domestic economy, forced the company to pare down operations, consolidate, and increase efficiency. The Hodgman line was sold, and the Malden and Andover plants were closed, followed by the Granite State Division. Sales divisions, which had traditionally been divided between sporting goods and footwear, were consolidated into one team.

Converse changed hands once again in 1979. Under the ownership of Allied Corporation, the brand would achieve unprecedented sales and profits. In 1982, however, the giant chemical conglomerate underwent a restructuring and moved out of the consumer products business. Although Converse produced 12 million pairs of sports shoes a year and had become the leader in basketball footwear, Allied put the company up for sale.

Through the combined efforts of a group of senior managers, Converse spun off from its parent to become a privately owned and operated entity. The group, led by Richard B. Loynd, president of Allied's Eltra Corporation, of which Converse was part, and John P. O'Neil, Converse president, negotiated the purchase of the Converse division from Allied for approximately $100 million. By 1983, Converse stock was available on the NASDAQ national market.

Facing the growing pressure of foreign imports, Converse moved to develop its export business to international markets. In 1984 the company signed separate agreements with Moon-Star Chemical Corp., Mizuno Corp., and Zett Corp. to handle the manufacture, distribution, and sale of Converse footwear in Japan. With the opening of an office and warehouse in Osaka in 1984 and plans to develop new shoes specifically for the Japanese market, Converse anticipated that "within three years, it [would] be a leader in the distribution of athletic footwear in Japan," according to company president John P. O'Neil. Between 1987 and 1988, Converse's international business increased by more than 60 percent. One driving force behind such growth was the building of direct company operations in key European, Asian, and North American locations, in addition to licensed distributors in more than 90 countries worldwide.

The Beginnings of a Full-Line Athletic Shoe Operation in the 1980s

Converse also faced competition from other domestic shoe companies. Since the early 1970s, the introduction of high-performance, leather athletic shoes strained Converse's leading position with its simple, canvas classic. By January 1986, the *New York Times* reported that "Nike of Beaverton, Ore., maker of Air Jordan basketball shoes, appears to be outrunning such competitors as Reebok International Ltd., Converse Inc. and Hyde Athletic Industries."

Consequently, Converse diversified to become a full-line athletic shoe operation. By the mid-1980s, Converse running shoes had become a popular item. Sales of tennis shoes, including the popular Jimmy Connors leather model, increased 400 percent in 1983 alone. By the 1990s, the Converse brand was associated not only with the famous Chuck Taylor All Star line, but with other fashion canvas shoes and footwear for all major sports played by all age groups.

To ensure continued development of innovative and well-designed footwear, Converse invested in an advanced technologies lab staffed by a 70-member research and development team. Upon its completion in the early 1980s, it was one of only two in-house, biomechanical footwear labs in the country. The facility included work stations equipped with powerful computers, robots, and testing systems.

In addition to designing the most effective shoes possible, Converse enhanced its reputation by sponsoring major basketball organizations and events worldwide. Converse was the first company named the official shoe of the National Basketball Association. Valid from 1995, its contract granted the company permission to use the NBA name in all advertising and promotions and to manufacture shoes with logos of NBA teams or other affiliations. Converse also supplied merchandise to cheerleaders and ball retrievers throughout the league.

Converse was also a sponsor of USA Basketball beginning with its inception in 1975. The Colorado Springs-based group was responsible for selecting national teams to represent the country in various international competitions and served as a class A member of the United States Olympic Committee. After 1977, Converse was contracted as the official shoe of USA Basketball, which agreed to "use its best efforts to outfit players in Converse shoes," according to Jeffrey Orridge, assistant executive director for corporate and legal affairs for the sports

Key Dates:

1908: The company is founded as Converse Rubber Co.
1917: Converse introduces the All Star, one of the world's first basketball shoes.
1929: Converse Rubber Co. falls into bankruptcy.
1972: Converse is purchased by the Eltra Corporation and acquires the footwear division of B.F. Goodrich Co.
1979: Allied Corporation purchases Converse.
1982: Allied Corporation sells Converse to a group of its senior managers.
1983: Converse stock becomes available on the NASDAQ national market.
1984: The company signs agreements with Moon-Star Chemical Corp., Mizuno Corp., and Zett Corp. to handle the manufacture, distribution, and sale of Converse footwear in Japan.
1985: The company is named the official shoe of the National Basketball Association.
1986: Converse is acquired by Interco Incorporated.
1994: Converse is spun off from Interco in November.
1999: Converse introduces the He:01 shoe.

group, in a September 1992 article in *The American Lawyer.* That agreement later caused legal conflicts, as USA Basketball team members including Michael Jordan held contracts with competing shoe companies such as Nike. Requiring players to wear Converse shoes introduced ethical and legal problems that had to be carefully resolved.

With the globalization of basketball, Converse increased its overseas contacts. In 1988 the company signed a sponsorship for the World Association of Basketball Coaches (WABC), located in Rome, Italy, and responsible for more than 50 clinics worldwide. In February 1990, the company began a five-year, seven-figure contract as the sponsor of the Federation Internationale de Basketball (FIBA). Founded in 1932 and based in Munich, Germany, FIBA included 176 member countries and approximately 119 million registered players. Its competitions included the European Championship Club Cup Final and the European Championship for both men and women.

Converse also made a presence at the Olympic Games. Though the company had provided Olympic footwear every year since 1936, in 1984 it became the first footwear supplier ever chosen to officially represent the games. The honor was not cheap: Converse paid the Los Angeles Olympic Organizing Committee (LAOCC) \$4 million and spent an additional \$3.5 million for national television advertising. Total promotional costs approached the \$10 million mark.

New and Innovative Marketing Strategies in the 1990s

Ever since Chuck Taylor served as its first player endorser, Converse has continued to promote its footwear through high-profile sports celebrities and athletes. By 1990, the brand had contracted endorsements with more than 14 pros representing 11 different teams across the United States. In addition, company statistics showed that 21 percent of all professional basketball players wore Converse shoes.

In the case of basketball endorser Earvin ''Magic'' Johnson, Converse received more publicity than it may have bargained for. In 1979 Johnson was enlisted as an official company endorser until 1994. By the late 1980s, Johnson showed dissatisfaction with the deal, which placed him in the top income echelon of Converse endorsers, but yielded less than those of other top endorsers with other leading brands. After Converse filed suit against the player for failing to comply with his long-term endorsement contract in 1987, matters were resolved temporarily.

When Johnson won the NBA's most valuable player award, Converse created a 30-second highlight piece of his best moves in the NBA tournament filmed in slow motion to the accompaniment of ''Amazing Grace.'' In 1990 the brand allotted a quarter of its \$40 million advertising campaign to launch its Magic Johnson footwear and apparel line. After the player announced that he had tested HIV positive in the winter of 1991, Converse aired a \$1 million public service campaign called ''Magic's Athletes Against AIDS.'' Yet, in 1992 old friction resumed with Johnson's public statements that Converse marketing was outdated and that he was terminating his contract before the official date. ''Converse as a company is stuck in the '60s and '70s. They think the Chuck Taylor sneaker days are still here,'' Johnson told reporters in Monte Carlo after the U.S. basketball team practiced for the Olympics. ''I've been trying to get out for years.''

Despite Johnson's criticism, Converse moved into the late 1980s and early 1990s with new and innovative marketing strategies aimed at regaining lost market share. In 1985 the brand paired two rival coaches—Denny Crum from the University of Louisville Cardinals and Joe B. Hall of the University of Kentucky Wildcats—on one poster to promote the Converse brand. Other promotional strategies included free trial shoes at the 1985 Sports & Runners Expo in Boston; environmental sponsorship of the Windstar Foundation of Snowmass, Colorado; and sponsorship of the Hoop-It-Up three-on-three basketball tour, bringing the game of American streetball to 13 European cities and to youth groups at home.

In the late 1980s, Converse stressed advertising and promotional campaigns to compete with such brands as Nike, Reebok, L.A. Gear, and Keds. Even under the financial strain of its bankrupt parent, Converse garnered an effective creative team at its New York agency, Ingalls Quinn and Johnson, which developed a hit campaign featuring NBA Rookie of the Year Larry Johnson dressed up as his basketball-playing ''grandmama.'' In her new, light Converses, the ad proclaimed, grandmama could blow by you ''faster than a passing thought. She'll eat point guards for lunch and pick her teeth with a power forward.''

In October 1986, Converse was acquired by Interco Incorporated, a broad-based manufacturer and retailer of consumer products and services primarily in the areas of footwear and furniture products. Citing doubt regarding Interco's future profitability, Standard & Poor's placed the company on CreditWatch. Nevertheless, Converse announced record sales for fiscal 1987, breaking the \$315 million barrier and representing a 36 percent increase over 1986.

In January 1991, however, Standard & Poor's doubts proved justified. Interco filed for relief under Chapter 11 of the federal bankruptcy laws. Until it emerged from bankruptcy proceedings in the autumn of 1992, support for rapidly slipping Converse brands was limited to a dangerously low budget. Apollo Investment Fund, led by former Drexel Burnham Lambert dealmaker Leon Black, wound up with 60 percent of the company's stock.

Interco's 1992 financial restructuring, however, freed up new funds for Converse investments and marketing plans. In June of that year, Converse's advertising team at Ingalls startled Madison Avenue by pulling up stakes and moving across town to Houston, Effler & Partners Inc. The $25 million Converse account followed along one day later. Houston took off with a new generation of ads to sell new shoes. In 1993 Converse introduced its Run 'N' Gun, featuring a patented React cushioning device with a combination of gas and gel built into the heel to absorb shock and provide additional maneuvering control. After some critics objected to the shoe's name as too violent, Converse changed it to Run 'N' Slam.

Houston also designed a 30-second television spot featuring Kevin "KJ" Johnson of the Phoenix Suns, with music by pop group En Vogue. The spots primarily targeted cable channels such as the Black Entertainment Network and MTV. In another 1993 award-winning campaign for the new AeroJam shoe, the agency again played off Larry Johnson's "grandmama" theme. While grandmama performed staggering jumps and dunks in her AeroJams, Johnson narrated: "There was an old lady who lived in a shoe. . . . And that shoe let her do things that no man could do."

These and other aggressive promotional programs began to pay off for Interco's shoe business. Footwear group sales by Florsheim and Converse for the second quarter of 1993 were $162.1 million compared with $146.2 million in the same period of the previous year. In 1994, however, despite record revenues of $437 million, increased profits of $17.6 million, and the success of Converse's Jack Purcell racquet sports shoe, Interco Inc. decided to sell its Converse subsidiary. It was spun off in November 1994.

Diversification into the Apparel Business in 1995

Diversification followed for the once-again independent company. In 1995 it entered into a licensing deal with Shalom Children's Wear to manufacture infants' and toddlers' sporting goods apparel. It also purchased Apex One Inc., a designer and marketer of sports-related footwear and apparel that also made products under license with professional sports teams, leagues, and institutions of higher education. Following the acquisition of Apex, Converse launched an "integrated head-to-toe apparel program" of coordinated outfits bearing the colors of top college teams. The universities of Arkansas and Kentucky were the first to take to the court in Converse garb and matching sneakers.

But the second half of 1995 unfolded in a fiasco for Converse, with layoffs, leaky shoes, and trouble at its new subsidiary. In June, it announced the cutback of 200 jobs at its Lumberton plant; in August, just 85 days after its Apex One acquisition, it decided to close down that business given unexpectedly slow orders and high costs in the face of a soft apparel market. In fact, the undercapitalized Apex, which had long had trouble making orders, no longer had the trust of most retailers, despite its affiliation with Converse. Converse eventually won $25.6 million in settlement from Apex for misrepresentation, but the episode hurt Converse, which was having financial troubles of its own—an operating loss of $8.4 million in the second quarter—and in September, it moved to indefinitely suspend operations at its Mission, Texas factory. In October and November, it laid off two more rounds of employees, and in December, just when it looked as if Converse was getting back on track with the decision to eliminate its outdoor, running, walking, tennis, and football product lines, its RAW Energy and RAW power basketball shoes literally sprang a leak, and the company was faced with the embarrassment and recall of 400,000 pairs of shoes. By year's end, Converse posted a loss of $71.7 million, compared with profits of $17.6 million in 1994.

New Management and the Retro Trend in the Late 1990s

Looking to regain momentum in 1996, Converse hired Glenn N. Rupp, former head of Wilson Sporting Goods Co., to replace Gib Ford, who retired as chief executive in that year. Rupp believed Converse should play to its strength as one of the few shoe companies with sizable domestic production facilities. Exploiting the marketability of the "Made in the U.S.A." label, Rupp's goal was to decrease the time it took for an order to be filled from six to only a few weeks. Together with President Michael "Mickey" Bell, who would resign abruptly in August 1996, Rupp undertook a restructuring of the nation's No. 5 athletic shoe company.

Fortunately, for Converse, "retro" was in, and the company undertook its biggest campaign ever aimed at recapturing the glory of its past. Its All Star 2000, a leatherized update of its traditional basketball show, which featured an old-fashioned Chuck Taylor All Star patch, began selling at a rapid clip in 1997. In the wake of this success, Converse made plans to market the Dr. J 2000 basketball shoe and the All Star 91, or Dennis Rodman shoe, in spring 1997 in time for the NBA's 50th anniversary. The company entered into deals with Rodman, Latrell Sprewell, Larry Johnson, and ABL star Theresa Edwards (40 percent of Chuck Taylor high tops were purchased by women) to help market its updated old shoe designs. In addition, Converse initiated a licensing agreement with A4 of Los Angeles to produce its Star 91 line of apparel and footwear, as well as two other men's apparel lines. The idea was to leverage the company's history as a long-time staple among professional athletes and to play up the emotional ties people had to the Converse brand.

Unfortunately, by the end of 1997, people had shifted from wearing basketball sneakers and other athletic shoes to what the industry called "brown shoes"—work boots, hiking shoes, and casual footwear in brown or black. Converse slipped to sixth place in its industry, posting a $5 million loss despite record sales of $450 million and an increase in revenues, while throughout the sector inventories bloated and sales showed signs of going flat. In early 1998, Converse cut more jobs and changed its marketing strategy, instituting its new "Stay true" campaign, designed to appeal to 12- to 18-year-old athletes and featuring younger players at the start of their careers. The campaign was at least in part a reaction to the embarrassment brought upon the company by Rodman and Sprewell, whose behavior on and off court was no longer something with which the company wanted to be associated. The company also continued to promote its athletic originals, its Chuck Taylor and Jack Purcell shoes.

Converse continued to struggle throughout 1998, at which point it moved to reduce its heavy reliance on its basketball category and to institute other footwear categories, such as men's and women's athletic originals and action sports. Rupp's goals for the year included marketing the retro look, expanding the supply of children's lines, pursuing a larger share of women's and girl's athletic shoes, and garnering a significant portion of sales in its new action sports category—gear for boarding and eco-training. Still the company's market share slipped further, from 3.6 percent in 1997 to 2.3 percent in 1998, and revenues for the year dropped about 30 percent to $308 million despite an increase in action sports sales.

The company's strategy for 1999 was likewise broad. With sales outside of the United States now close to 50 percent of net revenues, Converse formed Converse Canada and assigned the new division exclusive distribution and license rights for footwear, apparel, hats, and bags in Canada. It also continued to promote its athletic originals in Japan, where they were a huge success, and its skate casual shoes in Europe. Back home, it instituted a new approach to its children's product market, focusing on colorful and imaginative footwear designed specifically for children and partnering with OddzOn, Inc., marketers of Koosh sports toys. It also introduced a women's line of athletic originals in the spring of 1999.

Drawing upon the fruits of the $6.5 million, $8.8 million, and $7.7 million it spent on research and development in 1996, 1997, and 1998, respectively, Converse introduced a new shoe technology in 1999: He:01, a helium gas-cushioned shoe and the company's first technological innovation since the early 1990s. To better market its products, it partnered with pro basketball hopeful and recording artist, Master P, on a line of sneakers to complement its joint No Limit apparel, the All Star MP. It also signed a licensing agreement with Genender International design to manufacture and market a line of Converse clocks and watches. In this way, despite the ongoing layoffs and losses that continued to plague Converse into the first half 1999, the company aimed to position itself to take advantage of the anticipated improvement in industry conditions.

Principal Divisions

Converse Canada.

Principal Competitors

Adidas; Fila; Nike; L.A. Gear; Keds; Reebok.

Further Reading

Barboza, David, "To Build Basketball Sneaker Sales, Converse Tries a Novel Double Team," *New York Times,* March 26, 1997, p. D3.

Bidlake, Suzanne, "Converse Steps Away from Plan To Launch Across Europe; Athletic Footwear Manufacturer," *Marketing Publications Ltd.* (England), April 19, 1990, p. 2.

Carter, Leon H., "Timeout; Bird Won't Fly from Converse," *Newsday,* July 26, 1992, p. 19.

"Converse Aims at Again Being a Men's Wear All-Star," *DNR,* August 18, 1997, p. 90.

"Converse and 'Grandmama' Hoop-It-Up for the First Time in Boston," *PR Newswire,* July 16, 1993.

"Converse Basketball Goes Global with NBA Stars," *PR Newswire,* July 7, 1993.

"Converse Seizes 100 Pairs on N.C. Fakes, Goes to Court," *Footwear News,* August 13, 1984, p. 20.

"Converse Signs Mizuno, Zett and Moon-Star for Japanese Sales and Distribution," *Business Wire,* January 26, 1984.

"Courting the Female Athlete," *Women's Wear Daily Fairchild 100 Supplement,* November 1997, p. 44.

Farley, Maggie, "The $25 Million Heist; Ingalls' Biggest Ad Account Gets Away," *Boston Globe,* July 12, 1992, p. 45.

Farley, Maggie, and Bob Ryan, "Magic Kicking Converse," *Boston Globe,* July 23, 1992, p. 45.

"Interco Files for Chapter 11 Reorganization," *PR Newswire,* January 25, 1991.

Jankowski, Dianna, "Boston Expo Crowd Belies Running's Decline," *Footwear News,* April 22, 1985.

Krupa, Gregg, "Chucks Go Hip-Hop," *Boston Globe,* March 10, 1999, p. C1.

Lee, Sharon, "Converse Shoots for Fashion," *Footwear News,* March 5, 1990, p. 34.

Maremont, Mark, "How Converse Got Its Laces All Tangled," *Business Week,* September 4, 1995, p. 17.

Palmer, Thomas, "If Converse Can't Pay, Will Its Stars Leave?," *Boston Globe,* March 9, 1991, p. 15.

Rattray, Jim, "Converse Sues Magic Johnson," *United Press International,* December 4, 1987.

Reidy, Chris, "A Shift in Fashion Gives Sneaker Sales the Slip," *Boston Globe,* February 6, 1998, p. C1.

Rifkin, Glenn, "The Machines of a New Sole," *New York Times,* February 10, 1993, p. D7.

"Spreading the Action; Converse Betting on Magic Ads—$10 million Worth," *Footwear News,* February 12, 1990, p. 106.

Vartan, Vartanig G., "A Brisk Pace Is Set by Nike," *New York Times,* January 21, 1986, p. D12.

Wessling, Jack, "Converse Improves Productivity," *Footwear News,* February 13, 1984, p. 126.

——, "Converse Inks Big Name in College Basketball," *Footwear News,* January 21, 1985, p. 33.

Yerton, Stewart, "Dream Job with the Dream Team," *American Lawyer,* September, 1992, p. 40.

—Kerstan Cohen
—updated by Carrie Rothburd

Corbis Corporation

15395 Southeast 30th Place, Suite 300
Bellevue, Washington 98007
U.S.A.
Telephone: (425) 641-4505
Toll Free: (800) 260-0444
Fax: (425) 643-9740
Web site: http://www.corbis.com

Private Company
Incorporated: 1989 as Interactive Home Systems
Employees: 550
Sales: $30 million (1998 est.)
NAIC: 51331 Wired Telecommunications Carriers; 514191 On-Line Information Services

Corbis Corporation provides digital images to professional and nonprofessional customers through a handful of Web sites, licensing its collection to users for personal use and for reproduction in a variety of print and electronic media. Corbis controls the rights to 65 million images, which the company scans into digital form for display and purchase on the Internet. Included within the company's vast holdings are images from a number of highly regarded collections, including the National Gallery of London, the State Hermitage Museum in St. Petersburg, Russia, and the Bettmann Archive, and from several renowned photographers, such as Ansel Adams and Jack Moebes. The range of the company's visual content attempts to encompass the breadth of civilization, containing everything from reproductions of cave drawings to contemporary celebrity photographs. Corbis operates offices in Seattle, New York City, Los Angeles, San Diego, and Paris.

Origins

Corbis began its business life with an objective significantly different from what its posture during the late 1990s suggested. The company was founded in 1989 as Interactive Home Systems, a company personally funded by Microsoft founder and chairman, Bill Gates. At its formation, Interactive Home Systems presented itself to the corporate world as an art-licensing company, an enterprise whose strategy, not surprisingly, hinged on electronic technology, the realm of Gates's mastery. Gates envisioned a system that could deliver the great art works of human history into consumers' homes, and he formed Interactive Home Systems as the company that eventually would beam the paintings of famous artists via technology that had yet to be developed. Interactive television was suggested as a way to deliver the content, but as the development of the ultimate conduit was under way, Gates's privately held company busied itself with its first order of business. Before the technology was in place to provide home delivery of the world's art treasures on display screens, the content itself had to be obtained. Accordingly, Interactive Home Systems, bankrolled by Gates's growing fortunes, began acquiring the rights to the content that technology would supply later to the public.

The company embarked on a campaign of acquiring the electronic rights to artwork from a number of famous collections, securing nonexclusive digital rights to personal collections and those held by museums. Exhibiting the fear of monopolistic control evoked by Gates's advances in the software industry, observers watched Interactive Home acquire collections from the National Gallery of London, the Library of Congress, the Sakamoto Archive, the Philadelphia Museum of Art, and the State Hermitage Museum in St. Petersburg, Russia. The company's acquisitions covered the gamut of artistic work, ranging from the Barnes Foundation, which controlled paintings by Renoir, Cézanne, and Matisse, to the archive of the Massachusetts Institute of Technology's School of Architecture and Planning. Having purchased the digital rights to thousands of images for digital conversion, Interactive Home awaited the technology that could deliver its newly acquired content to the public. The wait promised to be a long one: acceptable technology had not yet emerged.

Strategic Change in 1994 Leads to Bettmann Archive Acquisition in 1995

In 1994—the same year Gates acquired the Codex Leicester, Leonardo da Vinci's notebook, for $30.8 million—five fruitless years of waiting for a widespread technological revolution had proved sufficient to provoke a change in strategy. A new man-

Key Dates:

1989: Microsoft founder Bill Gates forms Interactive Home Systems.
1995: The Bettmann Archive is acquired, dramatically increasing the company's visual content collection.
1996: Exclusive rights to 40,000 Ansel Adams photographs are obtained.
1997: New management leads Corbis to greater presence on the Internet.
1998: Digital Stock Corp. and Westlight are acquired, greatly increasing content available to professional customers.
1999: France-based Sygma is acquired, adding 40 million images to Corbis's content collection.

agement team was put in place, as the pursuit of developing technology became a secondary concern. Of primary importance was cataloging, indexing, and acquiring further image collections. The change in priorities reflected a shift from the company's roots as an art-licensing concern toward a new corporate objective: assembling the most comprehensive digital photographic archive in the world. Along with the altered business focus came a new name for the Gates-sponsored company. Interactive Home Systems was abandoned as the company's corporate banner, replaced by Continuum Productions, which, as the company struggled to find direction, was dropped in favor of Corbis Corporation, adopted in 1995.

The name Corbis, Latin for ''woven basket,'' signaled the company's intention to develop into a formidable repository of digital content. By October 1995, there was little doubt that the company was pursuing such an objective, its intentions made clear with the purchase of the Bettmann Archive. Acquired from the Kraus Organization for a reported $25 million, the Bettmann Archive represented the life's work of Otto Bettmann, the son of a German-Jewish surgeon who began collecting discarded medical illustrations from his father's wastebasket at the age of 12. Bettmann's penchant for gathering miscellanea was unleashed at the Berlin State Arts Museum, where he worked as a curator of rare books. Bettmann photographed everything he could get his hands on, snapping images of photographs, illustrations, lithographs, and old prints with his Leica camera. In 1935, he left Nazi Germany, fleeing to the United States with two steamer trunks containing the core of all of the material he had collected during the previous two decades. Bettmann moved to New York City, where he resumed collecting photographs and other images and turned his pastime into a business. For a fee, material from Bettmann's ever-growing collection was available for one-time use, an opportunity that publishers, educators, scholars, advertising agencies, and movie and television studios took advantage of, paying Bettmann licensing fees ranging from $50 to $3,000. Bettmann sold his archive in 1981 to a small publishing firm who continued to add to the collection as Bettmann had done ceaselessly since 1915.

Prior to acquiring the Bettmann Archive, Corbis controlled roughly 500,000 images, a total that would increase exponentially when the Bettmann drawings, artworks, news photographs, and other illustrations were added to the company's portfolio. In all the Bettmann Archive contained 16 million images, ranging from Mathew Brady's Civil War pictures to photographs of Rosa Parks's symbolic bus ride, making Corbis the largest supplier of stock photography in the world. Douglas Rowan, Corbis's chief executive officer, was elated. For a company that had been somewhat rudderless, the acquisition of the Bettmann Archive provided clear direction, instilling Rowan with sufficient confidence to declare, ''We want to capture the entire human experience throughout history,'' as quoted in the December 11, 1995 issue of *Fortune* magazine. The company immediately began the arduous task of scanning the Bettmann material for digital distribution to a broad range of print and electronic media publishers, a process that Bettmann, in his early 90s at the time of the acquisition, applauded. In an interview with *Time* magazine, Bettmann revealed that he was delighted ''to have seen my original acorn nourished and cultivated into a formidable digitized oak.''

In the wake of the Bettmann Archive acquisition, Corbis pressed forward with actualizing the lofty ambition articulated by Rowan. In 1996 the company acquired the exclusive rights to approximately 40,000 images photographed by renowned wilderness photographer Ansel Adams. The Ansel Adams acquisition was coupled with a licensing agreement signed by Corbis with the Mariners' Museum in Newport News, Virginia, which controlled 650,000 photographic images. By 1997, however, the confidence and direction engendered by the Bettmann Archive acquisition had begun to fade. The company continued to grapple with problems stemming from its business focus and how to make money from whichever focus it chose. The significance of the problems reached a critical point when Bill Gates intervened and demanded that further fundamental changes needed to be made.

Reevaluation of Strategy in 1997

Corbis was a singular company, financially sponsored by the world's wealthiest individual and charged with turning a vision of the future into reality. The company had failed to provide electronic home delivery of great art works to the public; eight years after its founding the only system capable of such a feat was installed in Bill Gates's mansion. More pressing, and more relevant during the late 1990s, was the fact that Corbis lacked the ability to turn a profit. In 1997 revenues covered only one-third of the company's costs, a situation made more depressing by the prediction of Corbis executives that profitability for the company was still five to seven years away. Aside from licensing the images from its collections, Corbis generated revenue from the CD-ROM titles it published, a market the company had entered as a way to utilize its growing visual content. Corbis had earned critical acclaim for its software, publishing award-winning titles such as *A Passion for Art: Renoir, Cézanne, Matisse, and Dr. Barnes,* compiled from the Barnes Foundation collection, and *Leonardo da Vinci,* which showcased the Codex Leicester. But critical success did not necessarily translate to financial success. Although sales of CD-ROM games and educational software were increasing in excess of 20 percent annually, the market was a difficult one in which to make money. Of the more than 5,000 titles produced annually, only four percent produced a profit. Corbis could not count itself among the profitable few. Gates voiced his displeasure in the summer of 1997. At roughly the same time, Rowan resigned, frustrated by Corbis's lack of strategic direction. The situation called for yet another approach to achieving success with visual content, an approach that had to resolve the company's problems with marketing its esteemed imagery.

Following the departure of Rowan, Corbis's leadership devolved to a jointly held office of the president. Steven Davis, a lawyer specializing in intellectual property, and Anthony Rojas, an accountant picked to oversee operations, were named as co-presidents of the firm. Davis and Rojas immediately scuttled the company's CD-ROM business and fixed their sights on the Internet, where Corbis would act as a digital curator, providing all types of visual content through digital technologies to professionals and consumers alike. As the pair set out, the company had scanned one million images into digital form and cataloged them in an extensive database. Structurally, Corbis comprised The Corbis Collection, containing the main body of the company's content, and Corbis Images, the image-licensing division geared for professional customers. The late 1990s would be spent fleshing out the content of these two segments, adding other subdivisions of content, and pressing ahead with the daunting task of converting the continuously growing collection of material to digital form.

Corbis's image-licensing division benefited from significant acquisitions completed in 1998 that underscored the company's commitment to electronic commerce and ignited impressive revenue growth. In February, the company acquired Digital Stock Corp., a leading supplier of royalty-free images. As opposed to traditional licensing agreements that allowed a customer to use an image once in a particular medium, royalty-free transactions allowed the customers to use an image in any medium for an indefinite period. The acquisition of Digital Stock ushered Corbis into the royalty-free niche of the visual content industry, which was expected to be a high-growth market in the digital age. Organized as an operating division of Corbis's image-licensing business, Digital Stock broadened Corbis's customer base substantially, adding advertising, graphic design, corporate communication, multimedia, and Web site design customers. In May, Corbis followed up on the acquisition of Digital Stock by purchasing Westlight, founded by a National Geographic photographer whose collection of commercial images contained more than three million photographs. In July, another division was added to Corbis Images when the company acquired Outline Press Syndicate, Inc., the leading supplier of celebrity portrait photography. Renamed Corbis Outline, the company syndicated studio portraits and candid photographs of actors, musicians, athletes, politicians, business leaders, scientists, and other celebrities and provided the images for sale to a broad range of national magazines. In 1998 the company also added to the Corbis Collection, which by the end of the year comprised 25 million images, with more than 1.4 million available on-line. In April, Corbis signed a nonexclusive agreement to license and to distribute the work of photojournalist John G. Moebes, renowned for his photographs of the civil rights movement.

The acquisitions completed in 1998 were a large part of the reason Corbis executives could celebrate an occasion not often celebrated by company officials: the release of financial information. The most encouraging financial figures were recorded by the company's image-licensing division, which recorded explosive growth between 1997 and 1998. Corbis Images' sales increased 200 percent, led by a 278 percent increase in digital sales. Also contributing to the growth in sales was a number of technological improvements that professional customers could use to obtain digital images. Search filters had been added to a newly designed interface at the division's Web site, http://www.corbisimages.com., allowing customers to use more than 170,000 catalogued terms to aid their search for a particular image. Further, the division began employing new server technology, which accelerated access to the 1.4 million images that had been converted to digital form. For the remainder of the collection, Corbis Images offered scan-on-demand service.

Strengthening the professional segment of Corbis's business occupied much of the company's attention in 1998, but the consumer side was not ignored. In December 1998, concurrent with the on-line release of certain images from the Ansel Adams collection, Corbis launched the Corbis Store, an online fine art and photography shopping center for the general public. At http://store.corbis.com, customers were provided access to more than 1,000 prints, posters, and Digital Picture Packs, which included images for personal use. The launch of the Corbis Store was followed by a more ambitious offering to consumers when the company, touting itself as "the Place for Pictures on the Internet," offered consumers the opportunity to purchase and download images form the Corbis Collection. Debuting in April 1999, the Corbis Picture Experience, http://search.corbis.com, allowed consumers to browse and license more than 350,000 images for their personal use. Included in the electronic offering were images covering a variety of content categories, such as historical, contemporary, fine art, and celebrity images, available for $3 per download.

As Corbis prepared for the future, it exited the 1990s on a positive note. The encouraging financial performance of 1998 was equaled during the first quarter of 1999, as sales increased more than 200 percent over the total registered during the first quarter of 1998. To fuel further confidence at company headquarters, traffic at the company's image-licensing Web site increased 273 percent between March 1998 and March 1999, and membership during the period increased 94 percent. The robust growth rates of 1998 and 1999 demonstrated what had eluded the company throughout much of its history: that the strategy in place was working. To build on the momentum achieved during the last years of the 1990s, further acquisitions of visual content were expected in the decade ahead, as the company endeavored to supply the full spectrum of visual needs on the Internet. Evidence of the company's insatiable appetite for content marked its exit from the 1990s, when Corbis completed the largest acquisition in its history. In June 1999, the company acquired Sygma, the largest news photography agency in the world. Organized as a division of Corbis Images, the France-based company, renamed Corbis Sygma, added an astounding 40 million additional images to the company's collection, expanding Corbis's portfolio beyond 65 million images. In the years ahead, Corbis's content collection promised to grow further, as the company pressed forward with its goal of creating a one-stop source for all image needs.

Principal Subsidiaries

Corbis Productions; Corbis Images.

Principal Divisions

Corbis Images; Corbis Sygma; Corbis Outline; Corbis.com.

Principal Competitors

Getty Images, Inc.; The Associated Press; Dorling Kindersley plc.; Time Warner Inc.

Further Reading

Birnbaum, Jesse, ''Gates Snaps Top Pix,'' *Time,* October 23, 1995, p. 107.

''Business,'' *Time,* October 23, 1995, p. 32.

Failing, Patricia, ''Brave New World,'' *ARTnews,* October 1996, p. 114.

''Gates-Owned Corbis Corp. Buys the Bettmann Archives,'' *Publishers Weekly,* October 16, 1995, p. 14.

Hafner, Katie, ''Picture This,'' *Newsweek,* June 24, 1996, p. 88.

Koselka, Rita, ''Tasteful. Unprofitable. Microsoft?,'' *Forbes,* November 3, 1997, p. 46.

Lieber, Ronald B., ''Picture This: Bill Gates Dominating the Wide World of Digital Content,'' *Fortune,* December 11, 1995, p. 38.

''My Information at Your Fingertips,'' *PC Week,* October 30, 1995, p. E3.

Ransdell, Eric, ''There's a da Vinci in My PC,'' *U.S. News & World Report,* January 13, 1997, p. 46.

Rupley, Sebastian, ''The Digital Curator: Bill Gates Expands Electronic Art Collection,'' *PC Magazine,* December 19, 1995, p. 29.

''Virtual Vacations,'' *PC Magazine,* September 1, 1998, p. 9.

Wildstrom, Stephen H., ''A CD-ROM To Make Leonardo Smile,'' *Business Week,* December 2, 1996, p. 26.

—Jeffrey L. Covell

Dallas Semiconductor Corporation

4401 South Beltwood Parkway
Dallas, Texas 7524-43292
U.S.A.
Telephone: (972) 371-4000
Fax: (972) 371-3715
Web site: http://www.dalsemi.com

Public Company
Incorporated: 1984
Employees: 1,530
Sales: $342.6 million (1998)
Stock Exchanges: New York
Ticker Symbol: DS
NAIC: 334413 Semiconductor and Related Device Manufacturing

Dallas Semiconductor Corporation designs, manufactures, and markets a wide variety of semiconductors and semiconductor-based subsystems used in computers and other electronic equipment. Its product mix is one of the most diversified in the market, with some 350 proprietary base products and more than 2,000 variations. The company sells its components directly to manufacturers of personal computers, industrial controls, automatic identification devices, telecommunications equipment, and scientific and medical equipment, among others. With more than 15,000 customers worldwide—including Compaq, Hewlett Packard, IBM, Intel, Lucent, Motorola, Nortel, and Sony—Dallas Semiconductor enjoys one of the more balanced customer mixes in the semiconductor industry. These factors have helped it successfully navigate the volatile semiconductor market, posting record sales every year until 1998, when industry conditions caused a drop in sales. That year sales totaled $342.6 million, with a net income of $55.4 million.

Founding, Mid-1980s

The continued success of Dallas Semiconductor is perhaps the product of a lesson well learned. Dallas Semiconductor was established in 1984 by C. Vincent Prothro (chairman, chief executive officer, and president) and several of his former colleagues from the Mostek Corp. From 1977 to 1982, Prothro had served as president and then chief executive of Mostek, a subsidiary of United Technologies, a company that pioneered the development of random access memory chips. In 1980 Mostek was an incredibly profitable firm. It was one of the few manufacturers of a random access memory chip, known as a DRAM, that had quickly become a standard component in personal computers and other electronic products. In 1981 Mostek enjoyed 55 percent of the world market and $360 million in sales. The following year, however, sales plummeted by $160 million to $200 million. One year later, sales were even more dismal.

During the early 1980s, a number of competitors in Asia and the United States had developed less expensive ways of making a chip capable of performing the same function as Mostek's. ''With almost no warning, we went from having a wonderful time to being in great jeopardy,'' Prothro told *Investor's Business Daily* in 1993. The semiconductor war was on, and the market became treacherous. One of Mostek's problems was that it hadn't diversified either its product line or its customer base: 70 percent of its sales were of the same product, split between five customers.

In 1983 Prothro left Mostek and with a number of partners formed Southwest Enterprise Associates, a high technology venture capital fund. The following year, Dallas Semiconductor was established as Prothro and Southwest Enterprise joined forces with Dr. Chao C. Mai and Michael L. Bolan, former Mostek executives, and John W. Smith, Jr., a venture capitalist who assumed the duties of president, chief executive officer, and chief operating officer.

Product and Market Diversification, 1984–87

The founders recognized the need for a strategy that would prevent the company from relying on a single market, product, customer, or technology. ''The semiconductor industry long ago learned to make the same product cheaply,'' Bolan told *Fortune* in 1985. ''Our goal is to make unique products cheaply.'' Its strategy was to address specific client needs, develop a solution, and then later adapt the solution to fit other client needs.

Company Perspectives:

Dallas Semiconductor Corporation designs, manufactures, and markets electronic chips and chip-based subsystems. The Company continually invests in multiple, non-commodity products using advanced technologies to reach diverse markets and customers. Founded in 1984, Dallas Semiconductor's strategy has resulted in diversified revenues, balanced end-markets, and a global customer base.

One of the primary ways Dallas Semiconductor sought to do this was to allow clients to customize chips at a very late stage in the production process. Known as ''late definition technology,'' the process used ion implants, lasers, or embedded lithium to etch chips according to precise customer specifications. This process gave Dallas Semiconductor a great deal of flexibility in adapting to changes in the marketplace and also provided the foundation for the company's versatile product mix. ''All the major developments in the industry have been decided by the marketplace, not by planning,'' Bolan said in 1985, adding that ''Our cardinal promise is not to fall in love with any one product.''

Another innovation was a product whose origins could be traced to Mostek: the pairing of lithium batteries—a small, long-lasting battery found in wristwatches—with a random access memory chip called a complementary metal oxide semiconductor or CMOS. CMOS chips were used to power individual software programs and were popular because data could be added to or erased from them at will. Their main drawback, however, was that whenever the power supply was cut from the chip, all stored data was erased from the chip's memory. With this new product, known as nonvolatile RAM, the lithium battery would continue to supply power when electricity failed, allowing the chip to be powered continuously for over ten years. The development was essential for lifesaving medical equipment and for cash registers or banking systems that keep running totals of deposits and other transactions.

By March 1985 Dallas Semiconductor had regional sales offices in Philadelphia, Indianapolis, and Phoenix, and had begun filling orders for a series of nonvolatile RAM it had developed based on the lithium battery technology. The company also introduced a line of electronic chips based on the same technology that prevented software theft. The product consisted of a key containing an integrated circuit coupled with a lithium battery and a corresponding socket inserted into the computer. Software manufacturers could encode the key's circuit to match a code in the software package, and only when the user inserted the key in the socket could he or she use the program. Although theft was one of the primary concerns of software manufacturers, this product was not as successful as the nonvolatile RAM, most likely because software buyers were reluctant to purchase and install the socket.

In its first year of operation, Dallas Semiconductor posted sales of approximately $3 million, slightly below its projected figure of $3.5 million. In 1986 the company received $10.8 million in a second round of capitalization, a move that increased its total capitalization to $32.2 million. Construction continued on the company's fabrication plant, which had already grown to 65,000 square feet. By late 1986 the company had introduced a line of application-specific telecommunications products, primarily T1 circuits capable of supporting a high volume of voice and data transmission.

Continuous Growth as a Public Company, 1987–97

In 1987 the three-year-old Dallas Semiconductor went public on the New York Stock Exchange at $9 per share. The initial public offering brought in an estimated $30 million, which was funneled into research and development. This led to the creation of ''one conductor semiconductor technology'' which, when coupled with the company's other technologies, formed the basis of Dallas Semiconductor's automatic identification systems and Touch Memory chips. In 1987 the company also introduced a line of highly successful computer clocks, a simple self-powered component added to computers that could keep time for ten years, regardless of whether the machine was turned on. One version was even capable of ''waking a computer up'' to perform a specific task and then shutting it down after the task was completed. Dallas Semiconductor quickly became the market leader in computer clocks, a position it continued to hold throughout the 1990s.

In its first four years of business, Dallas Semiconductor's annual sales increased almost tenfold to $30.6 million, and net income grew to $2.6 million. Sales jumped in 1989 to $58 million, while net income grew to $9.9 million. All income was fueled back into operations under the conservative directorship of Prothro, who had begun assuming many of the executive duties held by Smith. In 1989 Smith retired and Prothro assumed position of chairman, chief executive officer, and president of the company.

In 1991 Dallas Semiconductor borrowed a concept from Post-It Notes and introduced an innovative line of data storage and retrieval systems called Touch Memory. The system consisted of a memory chip stored in a stainless steel case about the size of a nickel. On the back of the case was a band of adhesive that allowed the chip to be attached to anything from goods moving through a factory to employee identification tags. Data could be stored in and retrieved from the chip using a simple metal probe linked to a handheld computing device, personal computer, or factory controller. Because the chips could be updated at will, they were more flexible than bar codes or printed tags; because they were small, they could be placed just about anywhere.

Dallas Semiconductor soon began customizing this system for a variety of different applications. In 1993 the U.S. Postal Service purchased the system to monitor drop box mail collection and to provide carriers with an efficient means of reporting on the condition of the postal box. Ryder Systems Inc., operator of a nationwide truck rental service, purchased more than 1,000 systems of Touch Memory in 1994, which it attached to rental trucks and used to store maintenance records. Another variation of the system was used to replace the punch cards that farm workers used to count the number of bushels each farmer picked. This system allowed farm owners to track each worker's daily harvest more efficiently and simplified payroll procedures. However, according to the *Wall Street Journal,* it

Key Dates:

1984: Company founded by former employees of Mostek Corporation.
1986: Introduces line of telecommunications-specific products.
1987: Goes public on the New York Stock Exchange.
1991: Introduces Touch Memory system.
1994: Doubles production capacity with a new manufacturing facility.
1995: Declares first dividend.

also caused concern among farm workers unions, due to the possibility that the ''system would allow farm owners to track workers from job to job, in effect keeping a record of their employment history.''

By 1993 Dallas Semiconductor had developed more than 170 base products in 14 different categories. Its core products included telecommunications and timekeeping systems, nonvolatile RAM, automatic identification systems, and microcontrollers. ''Individually none of the products are showstoppers,'' an analyst told *Investor's Business Daily* that year, ''but collectively they provide nice growth and better than average earnings.'' Net sales totaled $156.8 million to more than 8,000 customers. For 75 percent of those customers, Dallas Semiconductor was the product's sole supplier.

The company continued to pour its earnings into research and development, creating novel applications for existing technology and building a new wafer fabrication facility that doubled the company's production capacity in 1994. In 1993 Dallas Semiconductor was nominated for *EDN Magazine*'s ''Innovation of the Year'' award for a high-speed microcontroller that was three times faster than existing micros. Touch Memory continued to show promise as the company introduced an Emissions Memory Tag, which allowed chemical companies to monitor emissions for compliance with the 1994 Clean Air Act. The company also successfully transferred its digital technology to create the first digital thermometer that could be read directly by a computer. And in 1994 the company introduced a microchip said to prevent even the best computer hacker from entering corporate systems. Called Dallas SignOn, the chip used the same technology as hotel security cards and was allegedly 100 percent tamperproof. In 1994 overall sales grew for the fifth consecutive year, to $181.4 million, although sales in some core products began to slow as their markets matured.

In just ten years, Dallas Semiconductor's sales had grown from $3 million to more than $180 million. In the mid-1990s, the company made the *Forbes* list of the 200 best small companies in America, and its future seemed healthy. This was largely attributable to Prothro, known as a ''cost-conscious manager who is focused on the bottom line and gets by with moderate resources.'' Prothro's management style was perhaps best characterized by the company's efficient use of existing technology and its steady, measured growth. The company had $75 million in reserve that would serve it well if the semiconductor market were to take a sudden turn for the worse. But more importantly, it had a diversified line of products which it sold to an equally diverse customer base in a variety of markets.

As further proof of its growing financial strength, Dallas Semiconductor declared its first dividend ($0.025 per share) in the first quarter of 1995. Future plans included efforts to expand its markets in Europe and Asia, and to increase growth through acquisition. In 1994 the company proposed a merger with RF Monolithics Inc., a manufacturer of remote and wireless technologies. However, RFM was in the process of going public, and the deal was never consummated. Most likely this was due to Prothro's concern with the bottom line. ''When we put this company together, we wanted it to be self-funding, not a giant consumer of cash,'' Prothro told *Investor's Business Daily* in 1994, adding, ''We'll take the slower growth path if we can become more profitable as a result.''

Annual revenues continued to grow, reaching $233 million for 1995, $288 million for 1996, and $368.2 million in 1997 before falling back in 1998 to $342.6 million, a drop largely attributable to weak market conditions. It was the first drop in sales revenue in the company's history. During this period the company's diverse product mix and avoidance of commodity products gave it a stability unusual for the semiconductor industry. Its stock did not rise as fast as the overall industry, but when there was a downturn, it did not lose as much value, either. In May 1997 insiders at the company sold between 44 percent and 86 percent of their actionable holdings following a surge in the stock price after a strong first quarter. At the beginning of 1998 there was more significant insider selling, despite analysts' predictions for a strong 1998. In September 1999 the company adopted a Shareholders' Rights Plan to discourage a hostile takeover; the plan would go into effect whenever a person or group acquired 15 percent or more of the firm's common stock or announced a tender offer to do so.

About half of the company's production was exported outside the United States, with 30 percent going to Asia and 20 percent to Europe. Although it had a presence in 40 countries, all manufacturing was done in Dallas. The company invested a record $60.5 million in 1996 in added fabrication and test equipment, facilities, and design automation tools. Its facilities took up 40 acres.

It was around this time that Dallas Semiconductor began developing its line of iButton branded automatic information products. These were products that could be attached to an object or carried by a person and that identified the user and held relevant information. In 1996 Dallas Semiconductor came out with a wearable security chip called the Cryptographic iButton, which was expected to provide a solution to ensuring the identity of Internet users, especially mobile ones. The product included a processor, true time clock, random number generator, arithmetic accelerator, and 8KB of SRAM. The first generation of the product was originally introduced in 1992 as a memory device that electronically stored cash and was used in Turkey and other countries to pay fares on the transit system. The new product—a ''computer on a chip''—functioned as a security device by positively authenticating an individual to a server-computer or to another person through possession of the button and a personal identification number (PIN). One of its first applications was through the U.S. Postal Service (USPS), which distributed it to customers using postage meters. By 1999 Dallas Semiconductor had shipped more than 30 million portable data carriers under its iButton brand for a wide range of applications, from the labeling of printer cartridges to physical access control keys for Federal Reserve Bank vaults.

Dallas Semiconductor continued to work with the USPS, and in 1998 the company provided a postal-security device for the first Internet electronic-stamp delivery system, which was developed by E-Stamp Corporation. Beta testing of the system was approved by the U.S. Postal Service on March 31, 1998. The system allowed users to purchase and download electronic stamps to an electronic postal-security device attached to their computer's parallel port. The device protected and kept track of remaining postage. E-Stamp provided Windows-based software to interact with the device and print the stamps.

The postal-security device was a new version of the Crypto iButton, with an 8051-compatabile multiprocessor, a real-time clock, 32KB of ROM, 6KB of nonvolatile RAM, and an exponential accelerator for integers up to 1024 bytes. The electronics were packaged in a heavy-duty, stainless-steel housing with tamper-detection circuitry that immediately erased critical data when there was an intrusion.

In August 1999 the USPS and Dallas Semiconductor jointly announced that the cryptographic iButton had successfully completed laboratory testing under the direction of the National Institute of Standards and Technology (NIST). The testing was a prerequisite for the iButton's role in an Internet-based system for issuing electronic postage on home computers and printers. The USPS referred to these electronic stamps as Information Based Indicia and called the iButton a Postal Security Device (PSD). Dallas Semiconductor planned to deliver an adapter for use with Microsoft's release of Windows 2000 as well as a Java-powered version.

Also in 1999 Dallas Semiconductor introduced a variation on the iButton called the Thermochron iButton, a reusable time- and temperature-logging device. It could monitor data in two ways concurrently, one by recording the temperature and date, and the other by recording the frequency of thermal events.

Commitment to Conservative Growth: 1999

Another manufacturing expansion took place in early 1999 when the company opened a new automated manufacturing facility to produce its proprietary 1-Wire chips in packages no bigger than the chip itself. The chip employed a unique solder bump that enabled it to merge bi-directional digital communication and power into one signal plus a ground return. The minimalist chip was designed to save space in portable and other space-constrained applications.

Dallas Semiconductor's strategy of investing in non-commodity products for diverse markets and customers has served it well. Its largest customer accounts for less than five percent of the company's total sales, and its top 25 customers account for less than 30 percent of total sales. The firm's 350 base products and their variations are grouped into seven major product categories, giving the company a basis for stable growth that is unusual in the semiconductor industry. After sales declined to a low point in the third quarter of 1998, they have risen steadily for three consecutive quarters. As the company prepared to announce results for the third quarter of 1999, its stock was trading at a 52-week high.

Principal Competitors

Analog Devices; National Semiconductor; Rockwell International; Microchip Technology; STMicroelectronics; Texas Instruments.

Further Reading

Bruner, Richard, "Dallas Semi Thrives on Diversification," *Electronic News,* April 7, 1997, p. 24.

Cohen, Sarah, "Dallas Semi Unveils Wearable Security Chip," *Electronic News,* October 14, 1996, p. 22.

"Crypto iButton Validated as a Postal Security Device: U.S. Postal Service Now Accepts Computer-Made Stamps as Postage," *Business Wire,* August 9, 1999.

"Dallas Semiconductor," *CDA-Investnet Insiders' Chronicle,* May 19, 1997, p. 3.

"Dallas Semiconductor," *CDA-Investnet Insiders' Chronicle,* February 16, 1998, p. 13.

"Dallas Semiconductor Corporation Announces Adoption of Stockholder Rights Plan," *PR Newswire,* September 10, 1999.

"Dallas Poses Merger with RF Monolithics," *Electronic News,* July 25, 1994, p. 12.

"Dallas Shows Touch Memory for Chemicals," *Electronic News,* August 22, 1994, p. 46.

Deagon, Brian, "Dallas Semiconductor's Prothro: Making a Mark with Lots of Products, a Little Humor," *Investor's Business Daily,* July 8, 1993.

Hayes, Thomas C., "A Chip Maker Shuns Big Markets and Finds Growth in Small Places," *New York Times,* February 5, 1993, p. 4C.

Lineback, J. Robert, "Product Diversity Helps Dallas Semi Avoid Chip-Market Problems," *Electronic Business Buyer,* June 1994, p. 56.

Machrone, Bill, "Got the Decoder Ring and the Message," *PC Week,* October 28, 1996, p. 73.

"Monitor Time and Temperature," *Industry Week,* July 19, 1999, p. 16.

Newport, John Paul, Jr., "A Maker of Chips That Won't Forget," *Fortune,* June 10, 1985, p. 106.

"One-Wire Chips Come in Smallest Package Ever," *Electronic Design,* January 25, 1999, p. 25.

Rampey, Jennifer, "Benchmarq Squares Off against Dallas Semi," *Dallas Business Journal,* January 5, 1996, p. 3.

——, "Investors: Top Execs Overpaid," *Dallas Business Journal,* September 20, 1996, p. 1.

Ristelhueber, Robert, "Identification Systems: New Techniques Tighten Keyless-Entry Security," *Electronic Business Buyer,* August 1995, p. 37.

Teresko, John, "Jewelry for the Information Age," *Industry Week,* September 18, 1995, p. 49.

"There's Always a First Time," *Electronic News,* January 18, 1999, p. 48.

Wade, Will, "A Clock Chip Solves Year 2000 Problem," *Electronic News,* January 19, 1998, p. 6.

Webb, Warren, "Electronic Stamps Lick Internet Security," *EDN,* August 3, 1998, p. 44.

—Maura Troester
—updated by David P. Bianco

Data Broadcasting Corporation

3490 Clubhouse Drive #I-2
Jackson, Wyoming 83001
U.S.A.
Telephone: (307) 733-9742
Fax: (307) 733-4935
Web site: http//:www.dbc.com

Public Company
Incorporated: 1992
Employees: 756
Sales: $108.3 million (1999)
Stock Exchanges: NASDAQ
Ticker Symbol: DBCC
NAIC: 514191 Online Information Access Services

Data Broadcasting Corporation provides financial information services to private investors, financial institutions, and the professional investment community via FM transmission, cable, satellite broadcast, and the Internet. Specifically, the company provides real-time and delayed time stock quotes, bond values, futures, and options data for both domestic and international markets. The company also provides analysis in the form of news and commentary, fundamental data (such as 52 week highs and lows), historical data, foreign currency exchange rates, portfolio management, and advanced charting. Data Broadcasting's information services are packaged and marketed according to the technological capabilities and needs of each subscriber. Many of these services provide access to online trading.

Origins in an Early 1990s Bankruptcy

Data Broadcasting emerged as an autonomous company during the Chapter 11 bankruptcy proceedings of the Financial News Network, Inc. (FNN) in 1991. Among FNN's holdings at the time was a division specializing in real-time stock market data for individual investors. The Signal and QuoTrek brand stock quote services had been developed in 1982 by a company called Dataspeed. In 1984, Dataspeed's technology was acquired and folded into Lotus Development Corp, which created a new subsidiary called Lotus Information Network Corporation, or LINC. In 1990, FNN, a cable television network specializing in financial news, acquired LINC. By the following year, however, FNN was on the verge of disaster, with its top executive reportedly facing charges of bank fraud.

Hoping to salvage what they could from the failed company, FNN's creditors contacted noted turnaround artist Allan Tessler, who brought in his friend, a former head of Columbia Pictures and Twentieth Century Fox Films, Alan Hirschfield, to help sell off and reorganize FNN's holdings.

Tessler and Hirschfield pared away most of FNN's holdings, including the Learning Channel, which they sold to TCI's Discovery Channel. They kept FNN's successful data services company, Data Broadcasting. This division, which included the Signal and QuoTrek brand services for private investors, became a new entity, Data Broadcasting Corp. (DBC), incorporated in 1992. While the company's Signal service relayed information from the New York, NASDAQ, and American stock exchanges to desktop computers via cable or satellite, QuoTrek, a hand-held wireless receiver, allowed subscribers to receive stock information via FM transmission.

Although they had no intentions of acquiring a company when they went to help FNN out, Tessler and Hirschfield ended up buying Data Broadcasting, paying $1 million each for what was then a 25 percent interest in the public company. They distributed the remainder of its stock to FNN's creditors and former shareholders. Next, they moved the company's headquarters to Hirschfield's home town of Jackson Hole, Wyoming, presumably so that they could pursue their interests in skiing and fishing in the resort area.

New Management Builds the Company

The relatively small investment Tessler and Hirschfield made in Data Broadcasting paid off handsomely. The Signal real-time stock quote service, in particular, proved a solid business activity for DBC, becoming a leading source of stock quotes and related information due to its higher degree of compatibility between available analytic software packages for desktop computers and the Signal data feed, received through an external decoder box. The satellite relay gave private traders

Key Dates:

1992: Data Broadcasting is incorporated.
1994: Company acquires Capital Management Sciences.
1995: DBC enters into Internet-based information delivery.
1996: The DBC Online Trading Center is launched.
1998: Company begins expanding services for professional investors.

essentially the same service that brokerage firms and financial institutions received, but at much lower cost. Also, the pricing structure allowed subscribers to receive and pay only for the information they wanted. Enhancements to Signal included subscriptions to news and advisory services, and a custom Autolist function for active futures and options. With the financial data services providing the foundation for the company's activities, DBC attained first year revenues of $14.8 million, and a profit of $927,000.

DBC applied its data service technology to sports through a partnership with DataSport in 1992. Using QuoTrek as a format, the two companies created SporTrax to provide continuously updated scores of sporting events and other sports news via DBC's FM transmission network. DBC purchased DataSport in 1994. With the acquisition of Computer Sports World in 1995, DBC added historical sports information and Race Trax, which provided handicapping information for horse racing and other sports.

As its primary focus, however, DBC sought to enhance its financial data with complementary information relevant to investment decision-making. In 1994 DBC acquired Capital Management Sciences (CMS), a profitable private company best known for its BondEdge Internet-based service. The 1995 acquisition of competitor Broadcast International, Inc. (BII) included CheckRite International, a check verification company, and InStore Satellite Network, a provider of private satellite communications and services.

DBC launched an Internet website in 1995, initiating its entry in Internet-based information delivery. New software technology enabled the translation of satellite delivered information into DBC's website, providing stock quotes on a 15-minute delay. In addition to free delayed-time stock quotes, as well as financial and sports news, DBC's website included an overview of DBC's services, and free software which could be downloaded for desktop computer reception of the Signal data feed.

In conjunction with the website, DBC launched Brand Label Quotes, which offered stock quotes, on a 15 minute delay, to other information services on the Internet. DBC's 30 partnership agreements for the service involved Microsoft Network (MSN), Silicon Investor, and Business Wire in the United States, AsiaOne in Singapore, MoneyWorld in the United Kingdom, and The Electronic Mail & Guardian in South Africa. By mid-1996 DBC's website had received more than two million "hits" a day. The reliability of DBC's stock information attracted new partners from diverse information-oriented companies to the Brand Label Quotes service. *U.S. News and World Report* and the *Washington Post* began to use the service, as did Charles Schwab & Co., which provided the market information to its active investors via its new PC-based, electronic stock trading system.

Delivery and Content Improvements: 1996–97

DBC facilitated PC-based financial analysis with the release of Signal for Windows 1.2 in January 1996. In addition to real time and delayed time stock charting capabilities, the software featured a stock quote window from which subscribers viewed the latest stock price, the day's high and low price, bid and ask information, and volume traded for over 100,000 stocks on all major domestic stock exchanges. Moreover, Signal for Windows provided real time stock data at a much lower cost than previously available. DBC also updated its QuoTrek service, including foreign currency exchange rates and bond data.

DBC complemented its financial information with new content and new services. Its CMS division introduced BondVu, an Internet-based, real time data service which covered over 900,000 domestic, fixed-income securities, and other bond-related information. DBC signed an agreement with Internet Financial Network (IFN), developer and owner of a software which provided access to the U.S. Securities and Exchange Commission's (SEC) Electronic Data Gathering Analysis and Retrieval system (EDGAR). The software transferred the information to the Internet within seconds after a company filed a form with the SEC on EDGAR. The agreement gave DBC exclusive Internet access to the SEC filings through IFN and also gave DBC the option to obtain a majority interest in IFN.

In April 1996 the company launched DBC MarketWatch, an Internet information service available on a subscription basis. MarketWatch data services included real time stock quotes, historical data, SEC filings, and direct Internet links to online brokerage firms. Targeted for individual investors, the $29.95 monthly rate included fees to the stock exchanges required to obtain real-time data. DBC also handled subscriber registration to the stock exchanges.

A partnership with Telesphere added stock market information for over 100 international stock and commodities exchanges to DBC's online data services. For the first time private investors were given access to exchanges in the United Kingdom, Germany, France, Japan, the Far East, and Latin America.

DBC expanded on its sports and gaming information services in 1996, acquiring odds maker Las Vegas Sports Consultants, as well as Instant Odds Network, the exclusive real time provider of betting odds through electronic transmission from six major Las Vegas casinos. The electronic products aligned with those companies were SportSignal, and Casino Instant Odds, respectively.

DBC sought to become a complete provider of investment related services to the individual investor with the launch of its online Trading Center. The Trading Center would give DBC's customers ready access to online brokerage firms through direct Internet links. E-TRADE Securities, which offered 24 hour, online stock trading services, was the first Internet brokerage firm to link to DBC's Trading Center. Later associates included CompuTrade and Charles Schwab.

DBC next expanded its information content to include government, agriculture, and business. Addition of legal and political information services came through the November 1996 acquisition of the Federal News Service (FNS). FNS provided transcripts from U.S. and Russian government proceedings, such as hearings, briefings, and press conferences, to over 200 customers, including governments, corporations, news organizations, lobbyists, and lawyers. In early 1997 DBC launched the AgCast Network, which offered agricultural data services to subscribers via satellite, on television, or through a computer receiver. AgCast provided commodities and futures pricing for agricultural products in the United States and worldwide, as well as news, weather, and agricultural information.

New technology allowed DBC to advance its Signal brand of market information services. In February 1997 the company released Signal for Windows 2.0 which enabled a desktop or laptop computer to receive information directly from DBC's private broadcast network via satellite, FM transmission, or cable.

DBC entered the market for professional investors with Signal I-Net, designed for small and mid-sized investment brokerage firms. Signal I-Net provided a wide array of market information via satellite, FM transmission, or cable. Launched in April 1997, Signal I-Net provided a wide array of market information.

Internet-Based Information Delivery Accelerates in 1997

DBC designed StockEdge and StockEdge Online specifically for the private investor. Launched within a few months of each other in mid-1997, the services allowed their subscribers to monitor a maximum of 50 stocks through a customized scrolling ticker. Both StockEdge services provided quotes from the New York, Nasdaq, and the American stock exchanges, as well as bid and ask information. DBC delivered StockEdge through its Signal broadcast network, and StockEdge Online via the Internet. These services offered many of the same features as Signal services, such as custom news alerts and real time portfolio value update, but with limited capabilities which enabled a lower fee more attractive to individuals.

In December 1997 DBC entered into a joint venture with CBS to improve its web-based financial information service, MarketWatch. Renamed CBS MarketWatch, CBS' involvement added a team of journalists, editors, and producers, as well as a marketing staff, while DBC provided the technological infrastructure. CBS MarketWatch targeted the mass consumer market for financial information.

DBC's success in 1997 was reflected in four Reader's Choice Awards from *Stocks and Commodities Magazine.* DBC won first place for, ''Best Real-Time Data,'' the fourth year in a row, for, ''Best Futures Data,'' and, ''Best Options Data.'' BII's BMI MarketCenter won in the, ''Best Professional Trading Platform,'' category.

Two of the DBC's subsidiaries, DBC West and CMS merged in 1997 for the purpose of providing Internet-based financial information services to institutional investors, such as banks, and mid- to large-sized investment brokerage companies. The new entity, DBCMS, introduced InSite in early 1998, as the professional community began to recognize the accuracy and speed of Internet-delivered market information. InSite utilized the best of Windows and Internet technologies to create a market information service often available only at great expense through such competitors as Bloomberg and Reuters. InSite combined existing services with newly available information. In addition to Signal, BondVu, and stock-related financial news, InSite provided futures and options information, foreign currency exchange, and analytic functions, such as the capacity to chart a company's stock price history.

DBC's transition to Internet-based subscription resulted in a net loss in fiscal year ended June 30, 1998. The loss of $4.8 million contrasted to a net income of $18.3 million in fiscal 1997. The company expected sales to rebound as the number of Internet customers continued to climb.

Expansion of Reach and Content in 1998

DBC's strategy at this time involved expanding the breadth of its content and divestiture of non-information services. The divestiture of CheckRite closed in May 1998, for $15.5 million, while DBC waited for a buyer for InStore Satellite. In September 1998 DBC acquired ADP Global Treasury Information Services (GTIS). Renamed GTIS Corporation, the acquisition extended DBC's reach into institutional markets and expanded the information content available to private investors.

DBC expanded the scope of StockEdge Online and Signal Online customer access through partnerships with stock brokerage firms. Trend Trader LLC offered the services to its customers free of charge, and, in exchange, allowed DBC's customers to order stock purchases through its Electronic Order Delivery System. Most brokerage firms simply offered the services at a discount, as did Ameritrade Holding Corp., Freeman Welwood, Birchtree Financial, and others. Global Link Securities offered StockEdge Online and Signal Online on its SuperTrade services in English, German, and Chinese. DBC extended its Brand Label Quotes service to Signal Online. Private label versions included Jack Carl Futures, Columbia Asset Management, and several others. Partnerships with brokerage firms helped DBC reach a milestone of 10,000 subscribers to Signal Online in February 1999.

DBC and CBS made an initial public offering (IPO) for MarketWatch.com in January 1999. DBC had experienced losses of $600,000 in MarketWatch.com for fiscal 1998, and expected those losses to continue. With the expected success of the IPO, DBC's stock almost tripled in late 1998. The IPO set a stock price at $17, but it quickly rose to $130 per share by the end of the first day, a 474 percent increase. As with many Internet companies, however, the stock value was associated more with potential than actual value, and the stock stabilized in the $70 to $80 range. CBS and DBC each retained 38% ownership in the company.

In May 1999 DBC launched eSignal, a total trading package which combined StockEdge and Signal in one service and gave subscribers the capability to trade stock online. The improvement attracted several online brokerage firms to DBC's Brand Label Quotes, including U.S. Securities and Futures Corp., Farr

Financial, and Crown Futures, Inc. The new eSignal service automatically transferred to all subscribers of Signal Online. New subscribers to eSignal grew 100 percent in the last six months of fiscal year-ended June 30, 1999, and increased DBC's Internet customer base to over 15,000.

New software, launched in fall 1999, offered several improvements to traders. With MetaStock Professional 7.0, DataOnDemand allowed access to current and historical price data without having to perform several tedious functions before a chart could be created. A user simply entered a ticker symbol to view a particular type of chart. New capabilities included pager and email alerts for buy and sell requests, easier access to the user-created templates, and the ability to create a personal daily index like the Dow. DBC's eSignal 5.2 added after-hours trading, while Autolink simplified information access for specific stocks. A stock symbol entered into the quote window automatically transferred to analytic charts, options, Nasdaq Level II, news, and research functions, saving the user several tedious steps.

As it neared a new millennium DBC was upgrading the technology it used to provide financial services. The company chose Compaq's Alpha Servers to power its data feed to ensure continued timeliness as DBC expected the number of traders to grow and projected the number of stock transactions to increase dramatically.

Principal Subsidiaries

Broadcast International, Inc.; Capital Management Sciences, Inc.; Casino Instant Odds, Inc.; MarketWatch.com (38%); Datasport, Inc.; GTIS Corporation; Las Vegas Sports Consultants, Inc.

Principal Divisions

AgCast; Capital Management Sciences; DBC Europe (U.K.); DBC West; DBC Sports; Federal News Service; Global Treasury Information Services.

Principal Competitors

Bloomberg L.P., Bridge Information Systems, Inc.; Dow Jones and Company, Inc., Reuters Group plc.

Further Reading

Beer, Matt, "There's Something About Larry: MarketWatch Founder's Journey from Ink-Stained Wretch to On-Line Media Mogul," *San Francisco Examiner*, January 24, 1999, p. B1.

"Data Broadcasting and Jack Carl Team Up to Provide Brand-Labeled Internet Service," *PR Newswire*, November 13, 1998.

"Data Broadcasting Corp.: Signal Provides the Right Stuff for Your Trading Needs," *Futures* (Cedar Falls, Iowa), July 15, 1992, p. 12.

"Data Broadcasting is Spinning a Web," *Business Wire*, January 11, 1999, p. 57.

"DBC's Signal Online Service Surpasses 10,000 Subscribers." *Electronic Information Report*, April 9, 1999.

Gianturco, Michael. "Picking the Best Stock-Quote Service," *Forbes*, April 7, 1997, p. S27.

Gilpin, Kenneth, N., "Internet Stock Rockets 474% in Initial Offer," *Wall Street Journal*, January 19, 1999, p. C1.

Helenius, Tanya, "DBC to Sell Stake in CBS MarketWatch," *Wall Street & Technology*, November 1998, p. 58.

Lubove, Seth, "The Golden Years," *Forbes*, November 18, 1996, p. 130.

"Microsoft Picks Firm to Be On-Line Services Provider," *Wall Street Journal,* June 14, 1995, p. B5.

"Technology for DBC Holds Promise of New Services, Markets," *Mobile Data Report*, April 8, 1996.

Webb, Andy, "Second-Tier Data Suppliers Raise the Bar," *Wall Street & Technology*, March 1999, p. 32.

Wilcox, JoAnn, "Beaming Information," *Successful Farming*, November 1997, p. 53.

Woods, Bob, "Data Broadcasting to Focus on Net Delivery on Financial Info," *Newsbytes*, November 8, 1997.

—Mary Tradii

Day & Zimmermann, Inc.

1818 Market Street
Philadelphia, Pennsylvania 19103
U.S.A.
Telephone: (215) 299-8000
Fax: (215) 299-8208
Web site: http://www.dayzim.com

Private Company
Incorporated: 1916
Employees: 16,500
Sales: $1.08 billion (1998)
NAIC: 54133 Engineering Services; 56111 Office Administrative Services; 541611 Administrative Management and General Management Consulting Services; 23331 Manufacturing and Industrial Building Construction; 23332 Commercial and Institutional Building Construction; 54131 Architectural Services

Day & Zimmermann, Inc., a private, family-run company headquartered in Philadelphia, provides technical, engineering, and management consulting services, as well as construction services, to a wide range of clients, both in the United States and in other countries. With some 20 operating units, Day & Zimmermann offers such services as project and program management, security, travel, technical staffing and temporary personnel, and property appraisal. The company has a long history of working with U.S. government agencies, including the Departments of Defense and Energy. Other clients have included public utility companies, health care facilities, financial institutions, and various private companies. The firm frequently establishes offices dedicated to serving individual clients, including an office in Charlotte, North Carolina, that serves Du Pont and an engineering office in Orlando, Florida, that serves Lucent Technologies. The company has completed projects in more than 75 countries worldwide.

Early History and Growth: 1901–20

Day & Zimmermann traced its ancestry to two companies: Dodge & Day, founded in 1901, and the H.L. Yoh Company, founded in 1940. In 1901 two young men just out of college joined forces to start their own company. Charles Day, an electrical engineer, and Kern Dodge, a mechanical engineer, formed Dodge & Day and were hired to modernize machine tool drives for LinkBelt Engineering Company of Philadelphia. The following year, Jeansville Iron Works hired the young firm to help update its facilities by converting belt-driven machine tools to motor-driven ones, designing power plant steam heating and electrical systems, and supervising the installation of machine foundations and equipment. In 1903 Dodge & Day won a contract from Westinghouse Electric and Manufacturing Company to evaluate new equipment. In 1905 Dodge & Day added an architectural department and construction force. By the following year the firm needed more work space and moved from its offices at the LinkBelt Engineering Company to facilities in downtown Philadelphia.

The company continued to grow, expanding its services to include electric railway engineering and construction and expanding its territory to include North Carolina as well as its home base of Pennsylvania. John Zimmermann, a former classmate of Day, joined the firm in 1907, bringing expertise in finance and operations, and in 1910 the firm's name was changed to Dodge, Day & Zimmermann. The company's history of contracting its services with the U.S. government began during this time when the government hired the firm to evaluate efficiency at naval yards. In 1912 Dodge resigned, and the company's name was changed to Day & Zimmermann, under which it was incorporated in 1916.

As U.S. involvement in World War I became inevitable, Day & Zimmermann's services were in demand to help companies prepare to convert their facilities to wartime production. Day also became a member of the Council of National Defense, which was formed to advise the government on the mobilization of U.S. resources in the event of war. The United States entered World War I in April 1917, and in the following year Day & Zimmermann took over the design, engineering, and construction supervision of the army's giant quartermaster terminal in Philadelphia.

The 1920s through World War II

Another project Day & Zimmermann took on in Philadelphia during this time had to be postponed until the end of the war. The city had hired the firm to build the 685-foot Bensalem Bridge, an

Company Perspectives:

At Day and Zimmermann our success is built on our values. . . . We will create a work environment that protects the health and SAFETY of our employees, our clients and the public. We conduct our business with absolute INTEGRITY and all of us are accountable for our own decisions and actions. We believe a total commitment to QUALITY is essential to client and employee satisfaction. We believe PROFIT is the healthy and constructive reward for individual and corporate effort. We value GROWTH that is strategic because it is critical to creating opportunities for our employees and ensuring the Company's long term success. Our employees belong to a FAMILY at home and a team at work, and are of most value at work if they are able to balance their personal and professional lives. We will be active members of a larger COMMUNITY, corporately and professionally, and will support deserving cultural, civic and charitable organizations, and professional societies that guard the standards of and advance our business practices.

important part of the proposed traffic network. The war interrupted construction, and by the time work was resumed, inflation had doubled the cost of labor and materials. Nevertheless, Day & Zimmermann fulfilled the terms of its original contract, completing the construction and absorbing immense losses that nearly bankrupted the company. The firm eventually recovered and continued to accept new work from the city, and the Day & Zimmermann name appeared on many bond issues proposed by the city for engineering and construction projects.

In the late 1920s Day & Zimmermann formed Penn Central Light & Power and the Municipal Service Company as umbrella organizations under which to operate electric utilities and rail transportation services in the eastern part of the United States. When Zimmermann became president of United Gas Improvement Company, the state's largest utility company, he brought Day & Zimmermann under its umbrella, and thus for a short time Day & Zimmermann became a subsidiary. This arrangement lasted only a year, however. In 1928 W. Findlay Downs and Nicholas Roosevelt bought Day & Zimmermann back from United Gas Improvement and reestablished it as an independent, privately held company that offered consulting, engineering, and management services.

Day & Zimmermann weathered the 1929 stock market crash and the following Great Depression largely because of its involvement in utility projects, including the construction of electric transmission lines to support rural electrification following the completion of Boulder Dam.

By the late 1930s the U.S. economy was recovering, and the threat of another world war was imminent. Day & Zimmermann designed and built a 1.5-million-square-foot aluminum reclamation area in Cressona, Pennsylvania, which it operated during World War II to produce artillery for the U.S. Navy. Other wartime contracts included the design and construction of the Iowa Ordinance Plant, which was built in a record 11 months and operated by Day & Zimmermann during the war years. During the peak production years of the war, the company employed 18,000 men and women.

Expansion and a Change in Ownership: 1950s-60s

In 1951 the company began its operation of the Lone Star Army Ammunition Plant in Texarkana, Texas. The plant encompassed 16,000 acres, contained more than 900 buildings, and was served by 160 miles of roads, 40 miles of railroad, 90 miles of electrical distribution service, 45 miles of water mains, and 25 miles of sewers. Day & Zimmermann continued to operate the plant for more than 40 years, and in 1965 the plant was awarded a presidential citation for making an outstanding contribution to improvements in economy and operations.

During the 1950s Day & Zimmermann undertook projects throughout the United States and in other countries, including a feasibility study of Lincoln Center in New York City and a survey of electrical power requirements in the Republic of Vietnam. By the end of the decade Day & Zimmermann was operating four major departments: reports, industrial engineering, management service, and engineering design and construction.

In 1961 Day & Zimmermann was acquired by the engineering firm H.L. Yoh Company for about $2.5 million, creating one of the largest technical firms of its kind in the United States, with 3,300 employees. The H.L. Yoh Company had been founded in 1940 by Harold L. Yoh for the purpose of war production and training. Yoh was the son of Ohio farmers whose ancestors had emigrated from Holland in the 1700s. Upon graduation from the Wharton School in 1929, he became a partner in a tool design firm. After 11 years he formed the company that bore his name, and largely because of his determination, the firm grew quickly. By 1953 the engineering division employed more than 500 engineers, draftspeople, architects, and industrial planners.

Upon acquiring Day & Zimmermann, Yoh decided to retain the name of the larger company, with H.L. Yoh Company becoming a subsidiary. In the four years following Yoh's acquisition, the company more than doubled in size, employing over 8,000 people involved in evaluation, planning, engineering, construction, ordnance development, and management. Day & Zimmermann continued to do substantial work for the U.S. military. In 1967, at the request of the navy, the company provided engineering, procurement, and construction services for two airfields in Thailand to support U.S. operations in Southeast Asia. The next year, the company completed modernization projects at the naval shipyards in Philadelphia and in Portsmouth, Virginia.

Vigorous Growth in the 1970s and 1980s

The 1970s brought further expansion. Day & Zimmermann opened the Kansas Division to operate the U.S. Army's munitions plant in that state. Moreover, the company acquired the Cole-Layer-Trumble Company, one of the largest mass appraisal companies, and MDC, which became part of Day & Zimmermann's infrastructure services division. Also during this time, Day & Zimmermann was hired as the construction inspector for the $50-million Veterans' Stadium complex in Philadelphia.

Key Dates:

1901: Charles Day and Kern Dodge form Dodge & Day.
1907: John Zimmermann joins Dodge & Day.
1912: Dodge leaves firm, and company name is changed to Day & Zimmermann.
1916: Day & Zimmermann is incorporated.
1927: The company diversifies into electric utility services.
1951: Day & Zimmermann begins operation of the Lone Star Army Ammunition Plant.
1961: H. L. Yoh Company acquires Day & Zimmermann.
1975: Harold L. Yoh retires and sells Day & Zimmermann to his son, Harold L. "Spike" Yoh, Jr.
1998: Ownership of Day & Zimmermann shifts to Spike Yoh's children.

Further projects included conducting a property valuation of the railroad system of Penn Central Transportation Company when it declared bankruptcy; the project, which resulted in a $2.1 billion valuation, continued until the early 1980s. Under contract with the U.S. Railway Association, Day & Zimmermann developed a system plan for the government-sponsored ConRail. After serving as project manager for a new airport terminal in Charlotte, North Carolina, the company played a key role as master contractor in the three-year modernization program for the U.S. Postal Service and supervised more than 300 architectural and engineering firms throughout the eastern region of the postal system.

The 1970s also brought a change of ownership. Yoh, who had run Day & Zimmermann after his company acquired it in 1961, retired and sold the firm to his son, Harold L. "Spike" Yoh, Jr., who had worked with his father since 1958. The son and five other executives offered $16 million for the company, outbidding two other investor groups. Upon his retirement from the firm, the senior Yoh moved to Florida, where he bought a restaurant and where in 1976, a year after selling Day & Zimmermann, he died.

Growth through acquisition and internal expansion continued into the 1980s. In a joint venture with the Frank E. Basil Company, the Day & Zimmermann/Basil Corporation began operating the Hawthorne Plant, an army facility in Nevada. Located on 236 square miles and featuring more than 2,800 buildings, the plant represented the largest ammunition storage depot in the world, housing 400,000 tons of ammunition. In the early 1990s, with the end of the cold war, Day & Zimmermann personnel would also become responsible for demilitarizing much of the munitions stockpiled at the Hawthorne Plant.

In the 1980s Day & Zimmermann helped to staff a Du Pont office and provided further management through its Day Engineering division. The acquisition of SEACOR in 1982 gave the company the marine engineering skills to serve naval and commercial ship operators. Acquisitions later in the decade included the Wagner Group, Delta Associates, NPS Energy Services and NPS, Inc., Aquidneck Data Company, and Barry Services.

In 1983 the company's property appraisal services were retained by the state of West Virginia for a statewide property revaluation. A year later, Day & Zimmermann introduced Landisc, a new technique for mass real estate appraisal that utilized both computer and laser video technology to create a property image useful to tax assessors, police and fire departments, and real estate offices. Other services in this area included analysis of hardware and software needs of clients, training, disaster planning, off-site backup storage, and computer time-sharing, as well as public education programs to support assessors as they conducted revaluations.

Innovation and Sustained Growth in the Early 1990s

At the onset of the 1990s, Day & Zimmermann restructured itself, forming D&Z, Inc., to coordinate efforts in engineering, design, construction, operation, and maintenance, and SEACOR Services, Inc., to manage international and base support projects. During this time Day & Zimmermann provided a wide range of services to foreign and domestic military, industrial, and municipal clients. The younger Yoh continued to head the company, and as his fellow investors from the 1975 buyout retired and sold their interests to him, he became the principal owner. The company was eventually owned by Yoh and by one other executive, who held less than a ten percent interest.

Because Day & Zimmermann's roots were in pioneering engineering techniques, the company continued to modernize engineering processes in the 1990s. Engineers helped manufacturers incorporate statistical process controls, computer-integrated manufacturing techniques, and vision-capable robotics in order to streamline the production process. The company also designed air circulation and filtration systems to meet stringent requirements for contamination control in the manufacture of foods, beverages, and health care products. Despite cuts in defense spending, Day & Zimmermann continued to contract for work with the U.S. military and its allies. The company was involved in demilitarizing and destroying obsolete weaponry, making conventional ammunition items from primers and detonators to fully assembled bombs and missiles, and providing clients in a number of countries with consulting services in setting up manufacturing systems.

With governments at all levels taking a serious look at the condition of the U.S. infrastructure, Day & Zimmermann looked forward to continued growth by providing services for the expansion of roads, railroads, bridges, water and sewer works, and airports. For more than 50 years Day & Zimmermann had served as a consulting engineer on water and sewer projects, with its services including construction management support and direct contact operations. The company was also a leading consultant on airport construction, having worked for more than 90 airports or airline clients. Its services included noise abatement studies, economic analyses, and environmental impact statements.

In rail transportation the company provided systems integration services and assistance with improvements to control systems and equipment. The company also developed a program management oversight concept for the Urban Mass Transportation Administration to help its staff evaluate major transit projects and determine the efficiency of their use of federal grant money.

The growing concern for the environment in the United States also fueled growth at Day & Zimmermann in the early 1990s. The company worked on technology for plastics recycling, often in conjunction with state, county, and municipal governments, in order to reduce the amount of solid waste taken to landfills. Furthermore, the company worked with Rutgers University to turn waste products into carpet, containers, construction materials, and automotive parts. In 1993 Day & Zimmermann sold its subsidiary Day Products Inc., which operated a plastic bottle recycling facility in New Jersey, to Wellman Inc., the largest plastics recycler in the nation at the time.

Acquisitions and Partnerships in the Mid-1990s

As Day & Zimmermann headed into the latter half of the 1990s, it moved to meet new challenges and to grow, a key component to the firm's success, according to Yoh. The company's interest in growth through acquisitions and mutually beneficial partnerships was not unique, however. An October 1995 article in *Engineering News-Record* reported that many U.S. companies involved in engineering, architecture, and construction sought to expand through acquisitions rather than internal growth. As the article noted, "Acquisition mania is being driven by the globalization of markets as firms seek geographic diversity, new market segments and large-sized public projects." The article also indicated that a survey of some 500 executives in construction and design firms revealed that approximately 95 percent planned to seek partnerships.

In late 1994 Day & Zimmermann acquired Spartan Constructors, Inc., an Atlanta-based industrial contracting firm. Day & Zimmermann announced that Spartan's construction resources and hands-on abilities would complement its own strengths in engineering and construction management. As part of Day & Zimmermann, Spartan, which had previously worked on small and medium-sized projects, would possess the financial resources to take on larger projects. A year later Day & Zimmermann formed a partnership between its Day & Zimmermann Information Solutions (DZIS) subsidiary, which handled information technology systems and services, and Documentum, Inc., a document management vendor. The partnership was formed to provide business solutions for clients in the power and utility industries. Another partnership was announced in January 1996, pairing DZIS with Fulcrum Technologies Inc., a provider of information-retrieval software. The alliance allowed DZIS to integrate Fulcrum products with other technologies, including Documentum's, to provide clients with customized business solutions.

Day & Zimmermann formed yet another alliance in February 1996 when it announced a three-year agreement with AlliedSignal Inc., a manufacturer of chemicals and industrial fibers. Day & Zimmermann agreed to assist in the design of production lines at four AlliedSignal facilities, which made polyester fiber, carpet fiber, bullet-proof vests, and chemicals. Day & Zimmermann's expertise in the fiber industry—the firm's clients included AlliedSignal rivals Du Pont and Monsanto Co.—convinced AlliedSignal to form a partnership with the firm. In June, Day & Zimmermann formed a partnership with Environmental Science & Engineering Inc. to form an environmental cleanup company providing construction and consulting services.

In the mid-1990s some of Day & Zimmermann's attention was diverted from acquisitions and joint ventures as it worked to resolve issues surrounding the Alamodome, a sports arena in San Antonio, Texas, for which it had provided project management services in the early 1990s. The Alamodome, financed through a voter-approved tax increase and completed in May 1993, was built on the grounds of a former industrial site. The soil was later discovered to be contaminated, giving rise to allegations that appropriate environmental assessment procedures had been ignored in order to speed construction and keep costs down. Although the Metropolitan Transit Authority (VIA) had been responsible for the preparation of the site, Day & Zimmermann found itself in the middle of numerous lawsuits, including a civil lawsuit filed by the city of San Antonio in 1994. The lawsuit against Day & Zimmermann, Alamo Iron Works, which had sold VIA the site, and two environmental consulting firms sought to recoup about $16 million, the amount the city expected to spend cleaning up the soil. The case was settled out of court in 1996.

Significant Changes and Continued Expansion for the New Millennium

Day & Zimmermann experienced a significant transition in the late 1990s as ownership shifted from the younger Yoh to his children. Spike Yoh, who had seen the firm's sales grow from $100 million to nearly $1.1 billion from 1976 to 1998, stepped down as president, handing over the role to his son Hal Yoh, who also took over as CEO and chairman in early 1999. After bidding against two public companies, Hal was given the opportunity to buy the company from his father. Spike Yoh and a minority shareholder sold their shares of Day & Zimmermann to the children and company in the late 1990s.

The transition in ownership did not stop Day & Zimmermann from its aggressive growth plan, and the company continued to grow and to take on new partnerships and major projects. In late 1998, for instance, the firm progressed with its international expansion by forming a joint venture with M + W Sander, a subsidiary of Jenoptik AG, to build the world's largest insulin plant in Frankfurt, Germany. In the United States the company signed a five-year contract with the Hanford nuclear plant in Washington State to provide security and other services, bringing its total U.S. Department of Energy security projects to three. In April 1999 Day & Zimmermann acquired The Mason Company, a private firm that provided manufacturing, engineering, base operations, and security services to the federal government, primarily under the name Mason & Hanger. Mason was merged with Day & Zimmermann's Government Systems Group, which provided services, including manufacturing, storing, and demilitarizing ammunition and weapons, to the U.S. Department of Defense and to other governments. It was believed that the acquisition would boost Day & Zimmermann's sales to $1.5 billion a year and increase its number of employees to about 22,000.

Word that Day & Zimmermann planned to sell subsidiary D&Z Infrastructure Inc., which handled infrastructure and airport construction, began to spread in early 1999. This would be a departure from its acquisition strategy, but it was rumored that the company planned to sell the business to Daniel, Mann, Johnson & Mendenhall, a design and construction company serving the airport market, in order to help fund the purchase of Spike Yoh's shares. Although Day & Zimmermann declined to confirm the reports in February, in June it was announced that the division had been sold to AECOM Technology Corporation, which also owned Daniel, Mann, Johnson & Mendenhall.

In May 1999 Day & Zimmermann announced plans to grow further by investing in its core businesses, particularly in its engineering and construction division, Day & Zimmermann International, Inc. (DZII). The firm intended to position DZII as an innovative, technologically advanced firm offering speed and flexibility to customers. The company also reported that, while it would continue to seek new alliances, it would focus on building stronger relationships with existing clients as well. In June the firm reported that NPS Energy Services was being raised to full business group status, indicating an interest in expanding its operations, which involved working with fossil and nuclear power facilities. The company then set the stage for increased international growth by establishing an office in Manchester, England, in August 1999. The office was established to service Du Pont facilities but also served as a base for Day & Zimmermann's European expansion.

By late 1999 Day & Zimmermann had five operating groups offering a wide range of services—Day & Zimmermann International, Inc.; Day & Zimmermann LLC; H.L. Yoh Group; NPS Energy Services, Inc.; and Day & Zimmermann Mason & Hanger—and serving to meet client needs in a rapidly changing culture. With the third generation of the Yoh family firmly in control of the business, the firm intended to continue growing and expanding its services, fortifying its operations, and increasing its competitive edge as it entered the 21st century.

Principal Subsidiaries

D&Z Construction Services; Transportation Construction Services, Inc.; Day & Zimmermann Construction, Inc.; Life Sciences International; Process & Industrial Division; D&Z Microelectronics; Barclay Travel Agency; Cole-Layer-Trumble Company; Protection Technology; Day & Zimmermann Services; Day & Zimmermann Hawthorne Corporation; Kansas Division; Lone Star Division; Munitions Technologies Division; DZIC-Contract Labor Administration Services; Day & Zimmermann Information Solutions; H.L. Yoh Company LLC; NPS Energy Services, Inc.

Principal Operating Units

Day & Zimmermann International, Inc.; Day & Zimmermann LLC; Day & Zimmermann Mason & Hanger; H.L. Yoh Group; NPS Energy Services, Inc.

Principal Competitors

Bechtel Group, Inc.; Fluor Corporation; Foster Wheeler Corporation.

Further Reading

Binzen, Peter, ''This Family Firm Has Grown Up a Lot, but It's Not Done Yet,'' *Philadelphia Inquirer,* January 6, 1992, p. D3.

Brooke, Bob, ''Day & Zimmermann's Enduring Dynasty,'' *Philadelphia Business Journal,* May 29, 1998, p. B3.

A History of Quality and Excellence, Philadelphia: Day & Zimmermann, Inc., 1993.

Korman, Richard, ''D&Z May Sell Airport Unit to DMJM,'' *Engineering News-Record,* February 15, 1999, p. 10.

Lobsenz, George, ''Day & Zimmermann Buys DOE Pantex Operator,'' *Energy Daily,* April 19, 1999.

Powers, Mary Buckner, ''Circling the Wagons at Alamodome,'' *Engineering News-Record,* March 21, 1994, p. 8.

Schriener, Judy, and William J. Angelo, ''Big Firms Are Getting Bigger on the Bones of the Small,'' *Engineering News-Record,* October 23, 1995, p. 26.

—Wendy J. Stein
—updated by Mariko Fujinaka

De Dietrich & Cie.

23 rue de Bitche
67110 Niederbronn les Bains, Alsace
France
Telephone: (33) 3 88 80 26 00
Fax: (33) 3 88 80 26 99
Web site: http://www.dedietrich.fr/

Public Company
Incorporated: 1684
Employees: 5,085
Sales: FFr 3.96 billion (US $660 million) (1998)
Stock Exchanges: Paris
Ticker Symbol: DIET
NAIC: 33241 Power Boiler and Heat Exchanger Manufacturing; 33242 Metal Tank (Heavy Gauge) Manufacturing; 33651 Railroad Rolling Stock Manufacturing

After more than 300 years in operation in France's Alsace region, on the German border, De Dietrich & Cie. qualifies as one of Europe's oldest firms. One secret to the company's survival has been the De Dietrich family's devotion to location, rather than to any one single product line. After producing railroads, home appliances, and even automobiles, the De Dietrich of the turn of the century operates in three major areas. The company's De Dietrich Thermique division produces a range of standing cast iron boilers and furnaces, as well as hot-water tanks, wall-mounted boilers, burners, radiators, and control equipment. De Dietrich Thermique is Europe's second largest producer of cast iron boilers and furnaces and contributed 43 percent of the company's total sales in 1998. Cogifer, the company's railroads subsidiary, is Europe's leading provider of fixed railroad and other rail-guided installations, offering turnkey new railroad design and installation, as well as signaling, switching, safety, and other equipment and maintenance services for rail-guided systems ranging from tramways to high-speed train lines. Representing 44 percent of De Dietrich's total sales, Cogifer provides equipment and services throughout Europe, with subsidiary operations in eight countries. The third segment of De Dietrich's operations is De Dietrich Chemical, the world's second largest manufacturer of glass-lined steel equipment for the pharmaceuticals and chemicals industries. Operating on a global scale, with subsidiary operations in Brazil, China, Japan, Spain, South Africa, and the United States, De Dietrich Glass-Lined Equipment produces a range of reactors, columns, agitators, and storage tanks, providing 13 percent of the company's annual sales. This division was boosted with the January 1999 acquisition of Switzerland's Rosenmund-Guèdu, a world-leading provider of downstream filtration and separation equipment. In 1998, De Dietrich's annual sales reached FFr 3.96 billion (approximately US $660 million). In that year, the company sold off its remaining shares in its former De Dietrich Ferroviaire holding; the company also sold off its forestry division, including one of the Alsace region's largest forestry holdings. De Dietrich remains controlled by the founding De Dietrich family, who hold 35 percent of the company's shares.

The Founding of a Dynasty in the 17th Century

The De Dietrich family's involvement with the political and economic life of Strasbourg and the Alsace region began in the 16th century when Demange Didier, 12 years old and from a well-to-do Protestant family near Nancy in the Lorraine, fled the persecution against the Protestants led by the Duke of Lorraine. Didier arrived in Strasbourg in 1561, where he gained a position in the commercial business of Nicolas de Turckheim. Didier changed his name to the more Germanic form Dietrich and soon became a leading figure of Strasbourg society. Dietrich's son Jean went into business for himself; Jean Dietrich's son Dominique became mayor of Strasbourg in 1660. When the Alsace region was annexed to France by King Louis XIV in 1681, Dominique Dietrich led negotiations to guarantee the region's Protestants freedom to practice their religion. Four years later, however, Louis XIV sought to break the influence of Protestantism on the region, calling upon a number of notable Protestants, including Dominique Dietrich, to renounce their faith. Dietrich's refusal led to his forced exile.

The Dietrich family, however, remained in the region, continuing their merchant activities. At the same time the family sought a means to preserve their social and economic standing, while

Company Perspectives:

Since De Dietrich was founded in 1684 in a valley north of Strasbourg in the northeast of France, the Group has remained closely devoted to its region of origin which lies, today, at the geographic and economic heart of Europe.

also searching for a means to gain the return of Dominique Dietrich. In 1684, Dominique Dietrich's son Jean Dietrich II purchased a 20 percent share of an iron works in Jaegerthal, itself built in 1602. Although mostly in ruins, the iron works would provide the basis of the family's future fortune and remain in operation for more than 200 years. In 1685, Jean II decided to buy up the remaining 80 percent of the iron works and invested in restoring and refitting its forge and other equipment, including the addition of a high furnace. Jean II quickly turned his iron works toward service of the king and began supplying weapons for the French army on the eastern front. In this way, Jean II hoped to gain favor for his exiled father and to improve the condition of Strasbourg's Protestant community in general. Serving the monarchy provided a way for the Dietrich family to avoid persecution in the Catholic-dominated France.

In addition to manufacturing arms and equipment for the French army, the Dietrichs turned their commercial experience to the royal benefit. The family also branched out into banking. When Jean II died in 1740, the industrial side of the family business was taken over by his son, Jean-Daniel. The family's banking arm was placed under the guidance of grandson Jean III, whose marriage into the Hermanny banking family gave the family a prominent position in the French financial world. In this way, the Dietrich family became indispensable for financing the War of Austrian Succession from 1741 to 1748 and the Seven Years' War, which began in 1756.

Such service to the king was not without its rewards. In 1761 the Dietrich family was granted noble standing, both by the French king and by the German emperor. As such, the Dietrichs were given the right to add "de" (of) to the family name. Nobility had two immediate effects on the family business. First, the De Dietrichs were obliged to exit from banking, as this profession was considered unseemly for a member of the nobility. Second, the family was granted the right to own land—a right given only to the nobility. As such, the De Dietrich family acquired vast sections of Alsatian forest land and, therefore, a ready supply of the lumber fuel necessary for the Jaegerthal iron works.

Assuring lumber supply became a driving force behind the De Dietrichs' business growth. Unable to purchase the land surrounding the Jaegerthal works because of a dispute with another family, the De Dietrichs established four new smithies, at Niederbronn, Reichshoffen, Rothau, and Rauschendwasswer, after purchasing the land. Before long, the De Dietrichs had become the single largest landowners in the Alsace region. By then, Jean III, departing from the typical role of noble landholders and iron works owners, had taken an active role in the company's forge operations. By the dawn of the French Revolution, the De Dietrich works employed more than 1,000 workers.

19th Century Industrialist

The De Dietrichs did not have long to enjoy the privileges of nobility. The Revolution threatened the family with ruin. Philippe-Frédéric Dietrich, son of Jean III and mayor of Strasbourg, was guillotined by Robespierre in 1793. Broken, Jean III died a year later. Leadership of the family's iron works was taken over by Jean-Albert-Frédéric, the 20-year-old son of Philippe-Frédéric. Jean-Albert Dietrich fought to maintain the company's operations, succeeding in keeping the family's control over the iron works. Yet Jean-Albert died in 1806, at the age of 33. After more than 100 years as an important influence in French society, the De Dietrich family appeared set to fade into obscurity.

Jean-Albert left behind a widow, four children, and an iron works in debt. But Amélie de Dietrich was determined to keep the family's business in operation. Her first move was to sell off the business's money-losing units, including the Rothau forges, returning the focus of operations to the Jaegerthal works. There, she pointed the company toward its future direction, extending beyond the manufacture of weapons to the production of the industrial machinery necessary for the dawning Industrial Age. Before long, the company's name had changed, to Veuve (widow) de Dietrich & Fils. Aided by Napoleon Bonaparte, who restored much of the family's landholdings, the family rebuilt itself into one of the region's most prominent independent businesses.

The De Dietrich forges were transformed into true factories; by the time of Amélie de Dietrich's death in 1855, the company operated six factories and were award-winning producers of wrought iron and steel products ranging from ornamental railings to bridges. In 1850, the company produced its first wood-burning stove, launching the company into a product range that remained a company hallmark for nearly 150 years. Nevertheless, cast iron and forged iron became less important to the company as it increased its participation in mechanical products and, especially, took a leading role in building the country's railroad system. After the death of Amélie de Dietrich, her sons took over operations and continued building the company, focusing its manufacturing arm more and more on the manufacture of railroad and railroad equipment.

The German annexation of Alsace-Lorraine in 1870 once again threatened the company's existence. Whereas most of the region's industrialists chose to abandon the region to rebuild their businesses within the newly declared French borders, De Dietrich decided to remain. Its determination to remain loyal to its Alsatian origins came to mark the company more than any single product line. In Germany, the company was all but excluded from its chief product line, that of manufacturing for railroads. To succeed in the German marketplace, the company quickly adapted its product offerings, developing an extensive line of consumer goods, including heating stoves and equipment, cooking stoves, wood furniture, enameled cast iron and other cast iron products, such as bathtubs. An early interest in chemical equipment brought the company to begin production of distilling equipment as well. This period marked the beginning of De Dietrich as a diversified group with a geographic focus—that of its Alsace base. While continuing to exploit its forest lands, De Dietrich also branched out into a more unlikely area—trout farming.

Key Dates:

1561: Demange Didier arrives in Strasbourg.
1684: Jean Dietrich II purchases Jaegerthal iron works.
1761: Dietrich family receives noble status.
1806: Amélie de Dietrich takes over operations.
1850: First wood-burning stove produced by De Dietrich.
1898: Production of Dietrich-Bollee automobile.
1902: Production of De Dietrich-Bugatti automobile.
1904: De Dietrch exits from automobile manufacturing.
1974: Company is listed on the Paris Stock Exchange.
1992: Exit from home appliance manufacturing.
1999: Company acquires Rosenmund, a filters and filter-dryer manufacturer, and the boiler manufacturing operations of Schäfer of Germany.

Into the 21st Century

The company continued to expand on its diversified product range in the 1880s when a new form of transportation began to attract the attention of the public. De Dietrich was one of the first manufacturers of the new motor vehicles, and one of the few industrialists to turn production to the new product line. Led by Eugène de Dietrich, the company's automobile division picked up speed toward the turn of the century, after the company acquired a patent from Amédé Bollée. The company's Bollée-based automobile won the first international automobile race, the Paris-Amsterdam race of 1898. The boost in reputation brought orders from throughout Europe, and the company soon found itself with a waiting list of some 20 months. At the same time, the company opened a Berlin office, its first move beyond the Alsace region. De Dietrich's automobiles continued to win races and to prove remarkably hardy, crossing some 3,000 kilometers from Paris to St. Petersburg in just a matter of weeks.

De Dietrich's automobile adventure was to be short-lived, however. In 1902, De Dietrich hired a young engineer from Italy, who had already built his first car. Ettore Bugatti began designing for De Dietrich, producing the first De Dietrich-Bugatti the following year. But manufacturing automobiles—and keeping up with the steadily increasing pace of technical innovations—required too much capital for the De Dietrich company and, in 1904, the company produced its last automobile. Instead, De Dietrich entered the new century focused on mechanical construction and engineering, farm equipment, urban railway equipment and systems, and household appliances. The company also entered the young chemicals industry, supplying equipment to chemical and pharmaceutical laboratories.

The diversity of De Dietrich's product offerings enabled it to survive the most turbulent periods of the new century. By the end of the First World War, De Dietrich found itself once again on French soil, as the defeated Germans were forced to cede the Alsace-Lorraine region to France. In the Depression years, De Dietrich's diversified products helped buffer it against the collapse of many of its markets. During this time, the company's operations were taken over by five De Dietrich cousins, each of whom took an interest in a particular product area. In this way, De Dietrich's product divisions developed into de facto subsidiary operations.

De Dietrich's Electromenager (household appliance) division achieved great popularity with the French consumer in the second half of the century as the company continued producing heaters and heating equipment as well as ovens and ranges for the kitchen, including the first French-branded built-in stove in the late 1960s. During this time, Gilbert de Dietrich, who had joined the company in 1957, took over as head of the company, helping to unify the company's product strategy.

De Dietrich continued to build in four primary areas: home appliances; equipment for the chemicals industry, with a growing focus on glass-lined steel and iron tanks; railroad and railway equipment; and boiler tanks and other industrial heating equipment. The company also continued its activities in the forestry and lumber markets, because of its extensive landholdings. To fund growth, particularly beyond France and across most of Europe, De Dietrich went public in 1974. Nevertheless, the De Dietrich family remained the company's primary shareholder.

By the end of the 1980s, however, De Dietrich faced into the beginning of a new economic recession, which would last through the first half of the 1990s throughout most of Europe. Fearing hostile takeover attempts, the company reduced its market capitalization, buying back shares, while transferring other shares to a "friendly" shareholder group led by the Duval-Fleury family; together the two families controlled more than 55 percent of the company's shares and voting rights. Meanwhile, De Dietrich's appliance sales had stagnated. Despite contributing nearly FFr 1 billion to the company's annual sales, the division was judged too small to compete against the international giants, such as Whirlpool or Bosch. In 1991, therefore, De Dietrich announced that it had formed a joint venture with France's Thomson Electronics to form the Thomson Electromenager partnership. De Dietrich tranferred its home appliance operations to the joint venture, in exchange for 51 percent control of the partnership.

The deepening recession, however, forced De Dietrich to exit the home appliance market altogether in 1992. Instead, De Dietrich now sought to concentrate its activities where it had achieved market leadership. As such, its Cogifer railway systems division, its De Dietrich Thermique division, and its De Dietrich Chemical Equipment division became the company's three-pronged strategy for continued growth into the new century. After helping define the new strategy, Gilbert de Dietrich stepped down from the company's leadership in 1996, replaced by new CEO Regis Bello. At the end of 1998, the company sold its remaining shares of its De Dietrich Ferroviaire railroad construction subsidiary to France's Alstom Transports. At the same time, De Dietrich exited the forestry business, selling off its vast forest lands. Meanwhile, the company began boosting its three core divisions. In January 1999, the company extended its Chemical Equipment Division with the purchase of Switzerland's Rosenmund, whose leading position in the filters and filter-dryers market provided a means for the company to extend its sales downstream in the chemical and pharmaceuticals equipment market. In July 1999, the company boosted its Thermal division with the acquisition of the boiler-manufacturing operations of Schäfer, of Germany.

Principal Subsidiaries

De Dietrich Thermique; De Dietrich Equipment Chimique; Cogifer S.A.; De Dietrich Heiztechnik (Germany); De Dietrich

Heiztechnik (Austria); De Dietrich Technika Grzewcza (Poland; 85%); Serv'Elite; Oertli Thermique; Pacific S.A.; De Dietrich USA; De Dietrich Singapore; De Dietrich do Brasil; Nihon Dietrich (Japan); DDG Glasslining (South Africa; 40%); Rosenmund VTA (Switzerland); Cogifer T.F.; Cogifer Americas (USA); Teijo (Finland); Redelokken (Norway); Kihn (Luxembourg; 89.2%); Futrifer (Portugal; 61%); Amurrio (Spain; 50%).

Principal Competitors

Robbins & Myers.

Further Reading

Chabert, Patrick, ''De Dietrich fait de la résistance,'' *Les Echos,* April 30, 1992, p. 6.

——, ''De Dietrich quitte l'électroménager au profit de Thomson,'' *Les Echos,* October 16, 1992, p. 13.

''De Dietrich,'' *Les Echos,* February 2, 1999.

Hennion, Blandine, ''Alliance française originale,'' *Les Echos,* May 29, 1991, p. 11.

—M.L. Cohen

Decora Industries, Inc.

One Mill Street
Fort Edward, New York 12828
U.S.A.
Telephone: (518) 747-0681
Fax: (518) 747-5089
Web site: http://www.decoraind.com

Public Company
Incorporated: 1983 as Utilitech, Inc.
Employees: 926
Sales: $176.6 million (fiscal 1999)
Stock Exchanges: NASDAQ
Ticker Symbol: DECO
NAIC: 32611 Unsupported Plastics Film and Sheet (Except Packaging) Manufacturing; 32613 Laminated Plastics Plate, Sheet and Shape Manufacturing; 42183 Industrial Machinery and Equipment Wholesalers; 42261 Plastics Materials and Base Forms and Shapes Wholesalers

Decora Industries, Inc. is the world leader in the development, manufacture, and sales of consumer decorative products under the brand names Con-Tact in the United States and d-c-fix internationally for its self-adhesive surface coverings. It also manufactures and markets specialty industrial and commercial products. The company has production plants in Fort Edward, New York—also the site of corporate headquarters—and Weissbach, Germany.

Con-Tact Manufacturer: 1952–90

Decora Corp. got its start in 1945 and introduced the decorative vinyl self-adhesive covering it patented as Con-Tact in 1952. This was actually a film: printed, surface-treated, and specially adhesive-coated, then laminated in a paper backing. The marketing and distribution of this product, manufactured at Decora's plant in Fort Edward, was licensed to United Merchants & Manufacturers, Inc. (UM&M), a large vertically integrated firm that specialized in textiles and placed the product in the Comark Plastics Division of Cohn-Hall-Marx Co., a UM&M subsidiary. By the end of fiscal 1956 (ended June 30, 1956), Con-Tact was available in 22 colors and was being used as a wall and floor covering as well as a shelf liner. By 1960 Con-Tact was billed as the world's largest-selling self-adhesive decorative plastic.

UM&M purchased Decora Corp. in 1959 and began producing other specialized vinyl products in Fort Edward, especially the self-adhesive product trademarked as Kwik-Kover and a fabric known as ''Comark'' Patent Vinyl. Nylon multicolored flocked, foil, and printed Con-Tact designs, featuring more depth and texture, were introduced in the late 1960s. By 1970 the Con-Tact name had been licensed to several producers outside the United States. UM&M was calling it the world's most popular do-it-yourself home decorating aid, available in more than 200 patterns, washable, and easily applied to any surface. A chrome line was added in 1971. The Decora plant was enlarged, and new machinery was added.

The Arab oil embargo of 1973 interrupted the vinyl supplies needed by UM&M's Comark Plastics Division, since vinyl was produced from petrochemical raw materials. The Decora plant also sustained a seven-week strike. Despite these setbacks, Con-Tact commercials were introduced on daytime television over more than 200 CBS stations and affiliates. During fiscal 1975 the plastics division introduced a second generation of Con-Tact employing A-21, an innovative adhesive system permitting the product to be lifted and repositioned as it was being applied.

UM&M subsequently fell into bankruptcy and, to become solvent again, sold many of its operations. In 1981 it sold the Con-Tact brand name and some inventory to Carlan Inc., a company based in Stamford, Connecticut. Before the year had ended, however, Carlan had been acquired by Rubbermaid Inc. Rubbermaid introduced a totally new marketing program for Con-Tact, which, a company executive told a *Wall Street Journal* reporter in 1982, had a stodgy image as ''something for 40- and 50-year-olds to hide something, like a burned countertop.'' By contast, Rubbermaid began trying to market Con-Tact to younger consumers, particularly upscale, two-income families, as a ''self-expression,'' do-it-yourself product. A television ad urged viewers to ''Brighten up a wall that's smart, even make a piece of art. Go from practical to whimsical.''

Company Perspectives:

Our market and product strategy is to increase sales in the well established markets, such as the U.S. and Europe, through better product merchandising, improved consumer communication and broader consumer awareness, while opening up new regions worldwide with the entire Con-Tact and d-c-fix product range.

Based in Statesville, North Carolina, Rubbermaid Specialty Products Inc. was established in 1983 by combining the shelf liner business of the company's Home Products Division with Con-Tact. The operation remained part of the Home Products Division. By the end of 1983 Rubbermaid had introduced 31 new patterns and colors to replace what it called ''outdated designs.'' Eight more patterns and colors were introduced in 1984 and nine in 1985. In 1986, 29 new Con-Tact patterns were introduced, including Chalkboard, Gro-Chart, and Christmas patterns. The following year, Con-Tact introduced Letter Perfect, a lettering system featuring peel-off self-adhesive letters and numbers. In 1988 it introduced abstract patterns and became part of Rubbermaid's Housewares Products Division, headquartered in Wooster, Ohio.

A Broader Role in the 1990s

UM&M, which still owned and operated Con-Tact's Fort Edward production facility as its Decora division, sold the 230,000-foot plant in 1990 to Utilitech, Inc. In recent years Decora had been expanding its business into other areas of pressure-sensitive materials, including specialty tapes, roll-label stock, and siliconized release paper. Nevertheless, in fiscal 1991 (ended March 31, 1991), 87 percent of the $35.5 million in revenue earned by Decora Manufacturing Inc.—a subsidiary of Utilitech—came from its role as exclusive manufacturer of Con-Tact. In fiscal 1992 Con-Tact accounted for 96 percent of the Fort Edward operation's revenue of $40.8 million.

After Los Angeles-based Utilitech sold its Yorkville Industries Inc. lighting products subsidiary in 1992, it changed its name to Decora Industries, Inc. and moved its headquarters to Fort Edward. The manufacturing plant's operations became virtually the sole business of Decora Industries when it discontinued ComTel Inc., its telecommunications equipment manufacturing subsidiary, in 1994. By the end of 1992 Decora also was developing Wearlon, a new anticorrosive polymer used on the backing paper of Con-Tact sheets and based on its patented and proprietary A-21 and A-23 water-based adhesive systems.

Decora expanded its relationship with Rubbermaid in 1995, when the two companies signed a four-year agreement consolidating at Fort Edward manufacturing processes related to the Rubbermaid decorative covering business currently housed in Statesville. A Decora executive said the company had been fabricating certain Rubbermaid-marketed products—including Fibercraft wall coverings and Foam Cushion shelf liner as well as Con-Tact adhesives—in Fort Edward, then sending them to Statesville to be cut into consumer-sized rolls and packaged. These final two steps were now moved to Fort Edward. Decora also had by this time negotiated a licensing and technology development agreement with B.F. Goodrich Co. for its Wearlon line of specialty coatings.

In 1997 Decora expanded its operations significantly by acquiring a 73 percent interest in Konrad Hornschuch AG, one of the world's largest independent manufacturers and marketers of consumer self-adhesive products, including d-c-fix, developed in 1957 and similar to Con-Tact. Hornschuch also was manufacturing decorative and functional films for use by original equipment manufacturers in the automotive, building, furniture, handbag, shoe, and interior decoration markets. Decora paid $35.2 million for this German acquisition, which raised its sales from $41.1 million in fiscal 1997 to $98.4 million in fiscal 1998. Net income dropped from $3.6 million to $2.7 million, however. By the end of fiscal 1999 Decora had raised its share of Hornschuch to about 90 percent.

The relationship with Rubbermaid came to an end in 1998, when Decora purchased the company's Decorative Coverings Group for $55.1 million, with another $2.5 million held in escrow for payment depending on 1998 results. This Rubbermaid division had revenues of $70 million in 1997. Over the years, Decora had sold 90 percent of the Con-Tact it produced to Rubbermaid, but it had recently been adversely affected by a nine percent fall in Rubbermaid's decorative coverings sales in 1997 and by the company's decision to adopt a just-in-time inventory system. The acquisition consisted of, in addition to the Con-Tact product line, Rubbermaid's Shelf Liner light-adhesive line and Grip Line nonadhesive covering line, the latter being manufactured by a third party pursuant to the terms of an exclusive manufacturing agreement.

After the Rubbermaid acquisition, Decora established a sales office in the Cleveland area and began meeting with large domestic retailers such as Target Stores, Wal-Mart Stores, and Kmart, to assure them that Decora could distribute the acquired products without Rubbermaid's help. Company officials also indicated that they wanted to increase sales in nonhousewares sectors, such as arts, crafts, stationery, and do-it-yourself repairs. Specifically, the company was seeking greater exposure in Home Depot stores for refurbishing cabinets, counters, and windows.

With the Rubbermaid addition, Decora's net sales nearly doubled, to $176.6 million in fiscal 1999. After an extraordinary charge of $2 million, it registered net income of $1.7 million for the year. The company's long-term obligations came to $164.7 million at the end of the fiscal year, compared with only $18.8 million two years earlier.

In 1999 Decora acquired the assets of EtchArt Inc. of Orlando, Florida, manufacturer and marketer of ''Wallpaper for Windows,'' a line of glass coverings to give windows the appearance of etched glass. EtchArt products were being sold mainly through do-it-yourself channels of distribution, including home and decorating center retailers and mail order catalogs.

Decora, which in 1998 had implemented a 1-to-5 reverse stock split to raise its share price and increase its appeal to institutional investors, bought back warrants held by a Textron Inc. trust in 1999 for stock and cash valued at about $3 million.

Key Dates:

1945: Formation of Decora Corp.
1952: Development of Con-Tact self-adhesive covering.
1959: Sale of Decora to United Merchants & Manufacturers, Inc.
1981: Rubbermaid Inc. buys Con-Tact name and marketing rights.
1988: United Merchants sells Decora to Utilitech, Inc.
1992: Utilitech changes its name to Decora Industries.
1997: Decora purchases majority stake in Konrad Hornschuch AG.
1998: Decora buys Rubbermaid's Decorative Coverings Group.

This reduced Textron's holdings, counting warrants, in Decora from 19.4 percent to 3.5 percent.

Decora Industries in Fiscal 1999

The United States accounted for 37 percent of Decora's revenues in fiscal 1999, with Germany accounting for 29 percent and the rest of the world for the remaining 34 percent. Consumer products represented 69 percent of Decora's revenues. These branded, self-adhesive decorative and surface coverings were being marketed primarily under the Con-Tact and d-c-fix names for a wide range of applications, including shelf lining, glass covering, furniture and door repair and resurfacing, arts and crafts, and general surface protection.

Con-Tact was the leader in the U.S. consumer self-adhesive decorative market and was being sold primarily in the housewares departments of mass merchandisers in roll form, with a wide range of finishes, including functional coatings, printed patterns, solid colors, and clear and textured films. In its shelving category, Decora also was selling Con-Tact brand Shelf Liner and Grip Liner product lines, also as decorative and functional covering materials. Hornschuch's consumer decorative coverings d-c-fix products had been sold historically through the hardware and do-it-yourself markets rather than as housewares. Germany accounted for about one-third of d-c-fix's sales in fiscal 1999, with the remainder primarily in other parts of Europe, the Far East, and the Middle East.

Decora's commercial and industrial products accounted for the remaining 31 percent of net sales in fiscal 1999. In the United States, the company was marketing a range of proprietary industrial coatings under the Wearlon brand name for a range of specialized applications and various other industrial products, including commercial laminating, coating, and printing services and a line of high-quality hazardous marking tapes sold under the Cobra brand name. Hornschuch's industrial business was more important, accounting for 49 percent of its net sales in fiscal 1999. Most of these sales were of films processed specifically for the fashion, automotive, and laminate markets, with the former including synthetic leathers and other materials used in the manufacture of shoes, upholsteries, and handbags under the brand name Skai.

In addition to its owned plant and corporate headquarters in Fort Edward, Decora was leasing a small manufacturing/office facility in Longwood, Florida and an office facility in North Ridgeville, Ohio. Hornschuch owned a million-square-foot manufacturing and office facility in Weissbach, Germany.

Principal Subsidiaries

Decora, Incorporated; Decora Industries Deutschland GmbH (Germany, including about 90 percent of Konrad Hornschuch AG).

Principal Competitors

American Biltrite Inc.; Avery Dennison Corp.; Minnesota Mining & Manufacturing Co.

Further Reading

"Buyout To Bring Orlando, Fla., Glass Coverings Firm to European Market," *Knight-Ridder/Tribune Business News,* April 19, 1999 (on General Business File ASAP database).
"Decora Industries, Inc.," *Wall Street Journal,* August 12, 1999, p. A4.
Farrell, Michael, "Debt Restructuring Clears Way for Focus on New Products," *Capital District Business Review,* December 14, 1992, p. 4.
——, "Rubbermaid Deal To Bring Work to Decora Plant," *Capital District Business Review,* May 8, 1995, p. 16.
Neiman, Janet, "New Structure Poured for Rubbermaid Push," *Advertising Age,* November 9, 1981, pp. 4, 90.
Springer, Neil, "Decora's Latest Deal Designed To Increase Shelf Space," *Capital District Business Review,* April 6, 1998, p. 16.
"Utilitech, Inc.," *Barron's,* February 5, 1990, p. 78.
Wood, Sylvia, "Decora Industries Puts Its Destiny in Its Own Hands," *Albany Times Union,* October 25, 1998, p. S5.
Yao, Margaret, "Rubbermaid Reaches for Greater Glamour in World Beyond Dustpans and Drainers," *Wall Street Journal,* June 9, 1982, p. 56.

—Robert Halasz

Dell Computer Corporation

1 Dell Way
Round Rock, Texas 78682-2244
U.S.A.
Telephone: (512) 338-4400
Toll Free: (800) 472-3355
Fax: (512) 728-3653
Web site: http://www.dell.com

Public Company
Incorporated: 1984
Employees: 29,300
Sales: $18.24 billion (1999)
Stock Exchanges: NASDAQ
Ticker Symbol: DELL
NAIC: 334111 Electronic Computer Manufacturing

The largest direct-sale computer vendor in the world, Dell Computer Corporation sells desktop personal computers, notebook computers, network servers, and a variety of computer peripherals and software. The manufacturer sells its equipment directly to consumers, largely businesses and government agencies, through its toll-free number and its web site. Dell also sells workstations, network servers, and high-end storage products. Founder Michael Dell holds 14 percent of the company and continues to run the company as CEO.

Early History

Dell was founded by Michael Dell, who started selling personal computers out of his dorm room as a freshman at the University of Texas in Austin. Dell bought parts wholesale, assembled them into clones of IBM computers, and sold them by mail order to customers who did not want to pay the higher prices charged by computer stores. The scheme was an instant success. He was soon grossing $80,000 a month, and in 1984 he dropped out of school to found Dell Computer.

At the time, the PC industry was dominated by such large firms as IBM, while smaller, lesser known mail order firms sold IBM clones at a steep discount. Dell used low-cost direct marketing to undersell the better known computers being sold through such high-overhead dealer networks. Dell placed ads in computer magazines, gearing his merchandise to buyers who were sophisticated enough to recognize high quality merchandise at low prices. Customers placed orders to Dell by dialing a toll-free number. As a result of these methods, Dell's computers became the top brand name in the direct mail market.

Dell achieved sales of $6 million its first full year in business, approaching $40 million the next year. Dell hired former investment banker E. Lee Walker as president in 1986 to help deal with his firm's explosive growth. By 1987 Dell held a dominant position in the mail-order market, but it was clear that the firm had to move beyond mail order if it was to continue growing. To accomplish this goal the firm needed a larger professional management staff, and Dell hired a group of marketing executives from Tandy Corp., another maker of low-cost PCs. The group built a sales force able to market to large corporations and put together a network of value-added resellers, who assembled packages of computer components to sell in specialized markets.

The Tandy team soon helped raise gross margins to 31 percent, up from 23 percent a year earlier. Rather than merely undercutting the prices of competitors, they set prices in relation to the firm's costs. The new marketing department soon ran into trouble with Michael Dell, however. Battles erupted over advertising budgets and the number of salespeople required for corporations and resellers. While Dell believed that the new team did not understand direct selling and was trying to create a traditional marketing department with an overly large sales force, the Tandy group alleged that Dell lacked the patience to wait for the sales force to pay off. By early 1988, most of the Tandy group had resigned or been forced out.

Regardless, the firm continued growing rapidly, opening a London office that sold $4 million worth of computers during one month in 1988. Dell also formed a Canadian subsidiary. Early in 1988 the firm formed various divisions to raise its profile among corporate, government, and educational buyers. With reported sales of $159 million in 1987, the firm went public during this time, selling 3.5 million shares at $8.50 a share.

Company Perspectives:

Dell's mission is to be the most successful computer company in the world at delivering the best customer experience in markets we serve. In doing so, Dell will meet customer expectations of: highest quality; leading technology; competitive pricing; individual and company accountability; best-in-class service and support; flexible customization capability; superior corporate citizenship; financial stability.

Increased Competition in the Late 1980s

The firm faced several challenges, however. Announcing their own clone of IBM's new PS/2 computer system well before it was actually ready, Dell later had trouble reproducing important aspects of the PS/2's architecture, and the computers were delayed significantly, embarrassing the young company. Furthermore, Dell faced competition from several Japanese manufacturers, which were offering IBM clones at low prices. Further, having had trouble meeting demand, Dell used money raised from its stock offering to expand capacity and warehouse space, leaving the company with little cash. When it overestimated demand during the fourth quarter of 1988, the firm suddenly had no cash and warehouses full of unsold computers.

Dell responded to the increasing competition by increasing the level of technical sophistication in its computers. Half of its 1988 sales came from PCs using the Intel Corp.'s 80386 microprocessor, the most powerful PC chip at the time, and the company began producing file servers using the sophisticated Unix operating system. Dell also hired computer scientist Glenn Henry away from IBM to work on product development. Scrapping the company's first attempts at cloning IBM's PS/2, Henry initiated new plans for producing clones. Henry built Dell's research and development staff from almost nothing to 150 engineers, who began working on ways to combine the function of several chips onto one chip. When Intel released its 486 microprocessor, Dell began speeding to market the computers that could use it. Another of Henry's goals was high-quality graphics, which required better monitors and special circuit boards. By mid-1989 Dell had finished initial attempts at graphics hardware, giving it inroads into the higher end of the PC market.

Despite these advances, Dell still had a research and development budget of $7 million, compared with the hundreds of millions spent by larger competitors like IBM. Dell's share of the PC market was only 1.8 percent, but it was still growing rapidly. U.S. sales for 1989 reached $257.8 million, while sales in Britain increased to $40 million and a branch in western Germany realized the break-even point.

Dell considered itself as much a marketing company as a hardware company, and its sales staff played an important role in its successes. Dell's sales personnel trained for six weeks or more before taking their seats at the phonebanks, and, along with their managers, they held weekly meetings to discuss customer complaints and possible solutions. In addition to fielding questions and taking orders, sales staff were trained to promote products. They helped buyers customize orders, selling them more memory or built-in modems. Orders were then sent to Dell's nearby factory where they were filled within five days. The telemarketing system also allowed Dell to compile information on its customers, helping the firm spot opportunities and mistakes far more quickly than most other PC companies.

In 1990 Dell set up subsidiaries in Italy and France and began selling some computers through large computer stores, whose high-volume, low-margin strategy complemented Dell's established operations. The firm was making important corporate inroads as well, developing client/server computing systems with Andersen Consulting, for example, and introducing powerful servers using the Unix operating system. As a result, 40 percent of Dell's $546 million in 1990 sales came from the corporate world, up from 15 percent in 1987. Dell became the sixth largest PC maker in the United States—up from number 22 in 1989—and retained a staff of 2,100. Furthermore, the company's emphasis on customer satisfaction paid off, as it was rated number one in J.D. Powers & Associates' first survey of PC customer satisfaction.

That year, however, Dell manufactured too many memory chips and was forced to abandon a project to start a line of workstations. As a result, 1990 profits fell 65 percent to $5 million, despite the doubling of the firm's sales.

Price Wars in the Early 1990s

Also during this time, the traditional PC market channels were in flux. With a recession dampening sales, PC makers engaged in a furious price war that resulted in slumping profits nearly across the board. Compaq, IBM, and Apple all had profit declines or were forced to lay off employees. Furthermore, Compaq filed a lawsuit against Dell, which it eventually won, claiming that Dell's advertising made defamatory statements against Compaq. Nevertheless, the economic recession actually benefitted Dell. While customers had less money, they still needed PCs, and they purchased Dell's inexpensive but technologically innovative IBM clones in record numbers. Consequently, annual sales shot up toward $1 billion.

In the early 1990s, notebook-sized computers were the fastest growing segment of the PC market, and Dell devoted resources to producing its first notebook model, which it released in 1991. The following year it introduced a full-color notebook model and also marketed PCs using Intel's fast 486 microchip.

As the PC wars continued, Compaq, which had been a higher priced manufacturer stressing its quality engineering, repositioned itself to take on Dell, releasing a low-end PC priced at just $899 and improving its customer services. The new competition affected Dell's margins, forcing it to cut its computer prices by up to $1,400 to keep its market share. Dell could afford such steep price cuts because its operating costs were only 18 percent of revenues, compared with Compaq's 36 percent. The competition also forced Dell away from its attempts to stress its engineering. Dell executives began speaking of computers as consumer products like appliances, downplaying the importance of technology. Reflecting this increased stress on marketing, Dell began selling a catalogue of computer peripherals and software made by other companies; it soon

Key Dates:

1984: Michael Dell founds Dell Computer Corporation.
1988: Company goes public with 3.5 million shares of company stock.
1991: Dell introduces its first notebook PC.
1993: Dell establishes subsidiaries in Australia and Japan.
1996: Company begins selling over the Internet.
1997: Dell introduces a line of workstations.

expanded into fax machines and compact discs. Dell's database, containing information on the buying habits of over 750,000 of its customers, was instrumental in this effort.

Toward the end of 1992 Dell's product line experienced technological difficulties, particularly in the notebook market. In 1993 quality problems forced the firm to cancel a series of notebook computers before they were even introduced, causing a $20 million charge against earnings. The firm was projected to hold a 3.5 percent share of the PC market in 1993, but Digital Equipment Corporation, whose focus was minicomputers, nevertheless topped Dell as the biggest computer mail order company. To fight back against Compaq's inexpensive PC line, Dell introduced its Dimensions by Dell line of low-cost PCs. Sales for the year reached $2 billion, and Dell made a second, $148 million stock offering.

During the early 1990s Dell also attempted a foray into retail marketing, the most popular venue with individual consumers. In 1990 Dell placed its products in Soft Warehouse Superstores (later renamed CompUSA) and in 1991 they moved into Staples, a discount office supply chain. Dell agreed to allow the stores to sell the products at mail-order prices, a policy that soon caused Dell a lot of grief. The value of existing computers on store shelves plummeted whenever Dell offered a new computer through its direct sales, and Dell had to compensate retailers for that loss. With its direct sales channel, Dell had never had inventories of old computers that it could not sell, because each of those computers was made specifically to fill a consumer's order. Dell abandoned the retail market in 1994.

With price wars continuing, Dell cut prices again in early 1993 and extended the period of its warranty. However, increased competition and technical errors had hurt Dell, and despite growing sales, the firm announced a quarterly loss in excess of $75 million in 1993, its first loss ever. Dell attributed many of the problems to internal difficulties caused by its incredible growth. It responded by writing down PCs based on aging technology and restructuring its notebook division and European operations.

Like most of its competitors, Dell was hurt by an industry-wide consolidation taking place in the early 1990s. The consolidation also offered opportunity, however, as Dell fought to win market share from companies going out of business. Dell moved aggressively into markets outside of the United States, including Latin America, where Xerox began to sell Dell computers in 1992. By 1993, 36 percent of Dell's sales were abroad. That year, Dell entered the Asia-Pacific region by establishing subsidiaries in Australia and Japan.

Late 1990s Expansion

After a loss of $36 million in 1994, Dell rebounded spectacularly, reporting profits of $149 million in 1995. That year, the company introduced Pentium-based notebook computers and a popular dual-processor PC. The company grew by almost 50 percent that year and the next, raising its market share to approximately four percent and entering the company into the ranks of the top-five computer sellers in the world.

Expansion continued on many fronts in 1996. Dell introduced a line of network servers and was soon the fastest-growing company in that sector. The company also opened a manufacturing facility in Penang, Malaysia. The most important development that year, however, was Dell's expansion into selling directly to consumers over the Internet. Within three years, Dell was selling $30 million a day over the Internet, which would come to account for 40 percent of the company's overall revenue. Dell achieved enviable efficiencies using the Internet to coordinate the orders of consumers with its own orders of parts from suppliers. The company's web site also provided technical support and allowed consumers to track their orders from manufacturing through delivery.

Dell continued its exponential growth in 1997 and 1998, reaching profits of $944 million in 1998. The company introduced new products and services, including a line of workstations, a leasing program for individual consumers, and a line of storage products. Dell also expanded its manufacturing facilities in the United States and in Europe. In 1998 it established a production and customer center in Xiamen, China, raising the number of its overseas plants to three. By the time Dell sold its ten-millionth computer in 1997, it was a close fourth behind IBM, Hewlett-Packard, and Compaq in the computer industry. By mid-1998, it had captured nine percent of the market and the number two spot.

Following on the success of its direct sales over the Internet, Dell opened an online superstore of computer-related products in 1999. Gigabuys.com offered low-priced computer hardware, software, and peripherals from various companies in the industry, although Dell continued to sell its own products at www.dell.com. The company also expanded its Internet offerings in 1999 with Dellnet, an Internet access service for Dell customers.

Although Dell had faced competition from numerous small companies imitating Dell's direct-selling strategy, it encountered stiffer competition in the late 1990s from the big players in the industry. Compaq, for example, began selling a new line of personal computers over the phone and through its web site. While Dell's growth showed some signs of slowing in 1999, few doubted that Dell would continue to maintain a lead position in the industry, given its hit combination of direct sales and made-to-order merchandise.

Principal Divisions

Dell Americas; Dell Asia Pacific; Dell Japan; Dell Europe, Middle East, Africa.

Principal Competitors

Compaq Computer Corporation; Gateway, Inc.; Hewlett-Packard Company; International Business Machines Corporation (IBM).

Further Reading

"Dell Computer: Selling PCs Like Bananas," *Economist,* October 5, 1996.

Forest, Stephanie Anderson, "PC Slump? What PC Slump?," *Business Week,* July 1, 1991, p. 66.

Jones, Kathryn, "Bad News for Dell Computer," *New York Times,* July 15, 1993, p. C3.

Kelly, Kevin, "Dell Computer Hits the Drawing Board," *Business Week,* April 24, 1989, p. 138.

——, "Michael Dell: The Enfant Terrible of Personal Computers," *Business Week,* June 13, 1988, p. 61.

Pope, Kyle, "For Compaq and Dell Accent Is on Personal in the Computer Wars," *Wall Street Journal,* July 2, 1993, p. A1.

"Personal Computers: Didn't Delliver," *Economist,* February 20, 1999.

"You'll Never Walk Alone," *Economist,* June 26, 1999.

—Scott M. Lewis
—updated by Susan Windisch Brown

Dole Food Company, Inc.

31355 Oak Crest Drive
Westlake Village, California 91361
U.S.A.
Telephone: (818) 879-6600
Fax: (818) 879-6615
Web site: http://www.dole.com

Public Company
Incorporated: 1894 as Castle & Cooke Co., Inc.
Employees: 53,500
Sales: $4.42 billion (1998)
Stock Exchanges: New York Pacific
Ticker Symbol: DOL
NAIC: 111336 Fruit & Tree Nut Combination Farming; 111339 Other Noncitrus Fruit Farming; 111219 Other Vegetable (Except Potato) and Melon Farming; 11131 Orange Groves; 11132 Citrus (Except Orange) Groves; 111331 Apple Orchards; 31152 Ice Cream and Frozen Dessert Manufacturing; 311421 Fruit & Vegetable Canning; 311423 Dried and Dehydrated Food Manufacturing; 311411 Frozen Fruit, Juice, and Vegetable Manufacturing; 311911 Roasted Nuts and Peanut Butter Manufacturing; 42248 Fresh Fruit and Vegetable Wholesalers; 42249 Other Grocery and Related Products Wholesalers; 111422 Floriculture Production

Best known for making pineapple available across the globe, Dole Food Company, Inc., is the world's largest producer and distributor of fresh fruits and vegetables. Dole entered the fresh flower category in 1998 through four major acquisitions that also made it the world's largest grower of flowers. In addition, the company produces dried fruits and nuts, canned fruits, and packaged fresh vegetables and salad mixes, the fastest-growing supermarket segment in the late 1990s. Dole's worldwide operations span more than 90 countries.

Company Origins

The company that eventually became Dole Food Company, Inc., was established in Hawaii in 1851 by Samuel Northrup Castle and Amos Starr Cooke. Cooke and Castle set up business to sell wholesale goods, and in 1858 the pair entered the food business, investing in Hawaii's sugar industry. The business continued to grow, and in 1894 the company was incorporated as Castle & Cooke Co., Inc. A few years later, James Drummond Dole, a 21-year-old graduate of Harvard, arrived in Hawaii. With degrees in business and horticulture and a keen interest in farming, Dole hoped to make a living by growing the exotic pineapple. His cousin, Sanford B. Dole, an influential politician who became governor of the newly acquired territory of Hawaii, encouraged James's ambition to market pineapple commercially.

By 1901 James Dole had acquired 60 acres of land 18 miles north of Honolulu, in Wahiawa, and had formed the Hawaiian Pineapple Company. His groves of smooth Cayenne pineapples were ready to be harvested two years later. Rather than trying to export the fresh fruit, Dole decided to market his pineapple in cans. He established a cannery near the pineapple groves, which allowed him to achieve the best results by canning soon after the ripened produce was harvested. The Hawaiian Pineapple Company packaged and marketed nearly 2,000 cases of canned pineapple in 1903.

Two years later Dole was shipping 25,000 cases of canned pineapple. The company's success was facilitated by a new railroad constructed between Wahiawa and Honolulu, and the availability of ample, cheap labor allowed the company to keep its costs low. In addition, Dole persuaded the American Can Company to establish a manufacturing plant next to his cannery. For Dole this eliminated the expense of importing cans from the mainland and allowed vast quantities of pineapple to be processed quickly and cheaply. The company's increasing supply, however, required a corresponding growth in demand, but few Americans outside those living on the California coast had ever seen, much less tasted, a pineapple. Thus, the company's existing market was approaching saturation.

The Mainstreaming of Pineapple in the United States: 1910–30

In 1911 engineer Henry Ginaca, an employee of the Hawaiian Pineapple Company, invented a machine capable of pro-

Company Perspectives:

The Dole brand means high quality, nutritious, delicious, fresh and packaged food products. Dole will continue to meet customers' expectations by consistently providing products that meet the highest standard in the food industry—the Dole Standard. For Dole, anything less is unacceptable. Dole's dedication to quality is a worldwide commitment solidly backed by: comprehensive programs for food safety; scientific pest management programs; stringent quality control measures; state-of-the-art production and transportation technologies; nutrition education to help the public understand the benefits of eating 5–9 servings of fruits and vegetables a day. Dole is a founding member of the national 5 A Day For Better Health Program and is the leader in developing technology-based nutrition education programs for children; continuous improvement through research and innovation; dedication to the safety of our workers, communities and the environment.

cessing 100 pineapple cylinders a minute. Such production facilities enabled the company to market its produce across a large portion of the United States. Developing a successful marketing strategy became a high priority for the company during this time, particularly important if Dole was to attain his goal of making pineapple available throughout the country.

Together with several smaller companies that were also involved in the processing of pineapple, Dole financed an advertising blitz in magazines and newspapers on the mainland, promoting canned pineapple products under exotic, foreign brand names such as Ukelele and Outrigger. As a result, demand increased significantly. Toward the end of World War I, in 1918, Dole's Hawaiian Pineapple Company was producing one million cases annually and had gained a reputation as the largest processor of pineapples in the world. During this time Dole purchased more land in order to expand his business and in 1922 purchased the island of Lanai for a pineapple plantation. To finance the purchase, Dole sold a third interest in his company to Waialua Agricultural Company, which was a division of Castle & Cooke. By the mid-1920s Castle & Cooke had evolved into a Hawaiian real estate and land development company.

Surplus supply in the 1920s compelled Dole and other pineapple growers to pool their resources to mount an even bigger national advertising campaign. Using the new medium of radio, the company aired advertising using slogans such as "It Cuts with a Spoon like a Peach" and "You Can Thank Jim Dole for Canned Pineapples." As a result, sales and profits increased dramatically.

New Products and Continued Growth: 1930–70

With the onset of the Great Depression, the company's sales declined, and its advertising budget was depleted. The introduction of a new product, pineapple juice, was unsuccessful when the company could not promote it. In the first nine months of 1932, Hawaiian Pineapple lost more than $5 million, and the principal stockholders, Castle & Cooke, took over Dole's company by acquiring an additional 21 percent. Thereafter the Hawaiian Pineapple Company became Castle & Cooke's principal business, and beginning in 1933 the Dole name was affixed to the company's products.

The new owners managed to reverse the downward trend of the Hawaiian Pineapple Company. With greater financial resources at its disposal, the company launched a major advertising campaign for pineapple juice, boosting sales and putting the company back on a profitable footing by 1936. Sales of pineapple juice were also facilitated by the end of Prohibition, as the company promoted pineapple juice as a mixer for liquors, particularly gin.

The company continued to report healthy profits over the next two decades. By the 1950s Americans were spending more on food than the people of any nation on earth, and food companies were quickly expanding their markets to accommodate demand. In 1961, three years after the death of James Dole, Castle & Cooke purchased the remainder of Hawaiian Pineapple. Dole products retained the Dole name because of its strong brand image.

Castle & Cooke introduced several new pineapple products during the 1950s and 1960s, including both fresh and canned pineapple processed in chunks and slices or crushed, in addition to expanding its markets to include citrus fruits, macadamia nuts, vegetables, and even tuna. Particularly noteworthy was Castle & Cooke's entrance into the banana business. The company established pineapple and banana farms in the Philippines in 1963 to serve markets in East Asia. A year later the company bought 55 percent of the Standard Fruit & Steamship Company, one of the largest U.S. producers and importers of bananas. In 1968 Castle & Cooke bought the remainder of Standard Fruit.

Given the tremendous diversification of Dole products, advertising became critical to ensuring the company's dominance in the marketplace. In order to capitalize on public recognition of the Dole brand name, Castle & Cooke decided to use it on the labels of several of its non-pineapple food products. In addition, television became an important medium for the company's advertising, and by the 1960s James Dole's dream of making pineapple as familiar as apples and oranges had been realized.

Expansion and Sustained Success in the 1970s and 1980s

During the 1970s Dole continued to diversify and grow. In 1972 Standard Fruit's bananas began carrying the Dole label, and in the same year all food activities except sugar were organized into a single division—Castle & Cooke Foods. The company branched into mushrooms in 1973 with the acquisition of West Foods, Inc., the biggest producer of mushrooms in the western United States. Also in 1973 Castle & Cooke became the nation's leading banana producer, adding two large banana plantations to its roster. In addition, the company took advantage of the increasing demand for nutritious foods, advertising its products as healthy additions to the diets of adults and children.

Despite the company's accelerated growth, Castle & Cooke suffered financial setbacks in the early 1980s. The company was heavily in debt and had barely escaped two hostile takeover attempts. Its problems were largely resolved when it merged with Flexi-Van Corporation, a business that leased transporta-

Key Dates:

1851: Castle and Cooke obtain licenses to sell wholesale products in Hawaii.
1858: Castle and Cooke enter the food business with an investment in Hawaii's sugar industry.
1894: Castle & Cooke Co. is incorporated.
1901: James Dole begins growing pineapple and incorporates his company as the Hawaiian Pineapple Company.
1932: Castle & Cooke acquires a 21 percent ownership of Hawaiian Pineapple Company.
1961: Castle & Cooke and the Hawaiian Pineapple Company merge.
1964: Castle & Cooke enters the banana business.
1986: The Dole brand enjoys a worldwide recognition rate of 98 percent.
1991: Castle & Cooke changes its name to Dole Food Company, Inc.
1996: Dole pioneers packaged fresh salad mixes.
1998: Dole enters the fresh flower industry.

tion equipment, in 1985. Flexi-Van's owner, David H. Murdock, became the chairman and CEO of Castle & Cooke, and the company continued to expand and build equity in the Dole brand.

In 1986 Dole's logo was redesigned. The resulting yellow sunburst logo was intended to convey quality, freshness, and wholesomeness. The Dole brand name came to be used to promote additional products as Dole Fresh Fruit operations extended its line to include table grapes, strawberries, nuts, raisins, cherries, and strawberries. In 1988 Dole introduced a new line of dried fruits and nuts. The following year, Dole Fresh Vegetables began marketing produce under the Dole name, dropping the Bud of California name it had been using since 1978, and the company purchased two apple growers in Washington State. By the late 1980s Dole had a global recognition factor of 98 percent.

Innovation in the 1990s

In the early 1990s Dole launched a major multimedia advertising campaign accompanied by the slogan "How'd You Do Your Dole Today?" The campaign was designed to encourage consumers to eat more vegetables and fruits, including pineapple, regularly. As a result of its effective advertising, Dole maintained the largest market share of pineapples and bananas in North America. The company also continued its tradition of diversification and innovation, introducing a line of packaged fresh vegetable products in 1990. The convenience of precut vegetables and salads appealed to consumers and soon became the fastest-growing division in grocery stores.

In 1991, under the direction of Murdock, Castle & Cooke's stockholders voted to use the Dole name to represent all of the company's fruit and vegetable operations, reorganizing under the name Dole Food Company, Inc. The Castle & Cooke name was retained solely for the company's real estate business, which became a subsidiary of Dole Food Company. In the early 1990s ice cream bars were added to the list of Dole products. The company also retained interests in beer processing in Honduras, sugar refining in Hawaii, and tropical flower marketing in the Philippines. In addition to the individual consumer, Dole's market expanded to include other food processors, who used Dole products as ingredients.

Dole began to expand more aggressively into international markets in the 1990s. While Dole products had the leading market share in the United States, Canada, Mexico, and Japan, the company began to gain a significant share of the European market. In 1989 a division of Dole Food Company was established in London, poised to take advantage of imminent changes in the integrated European market. Dole's international growth strategy included expansion into eastern Europe, South Korea, and the Middle East. In 1992 Dole bought SAMICA, a dried fruits and nuts firm in Europe, and in 1994 acquired an interest in Jamaica Fruit Distributors. A year later the company purchased the New Zealand operations of Chiquita Brands International, Inc. Dole's international expansion continued in 1996 with the purchase of Pascual Hermanos, the largest grower of fruit and vegetables in Spain, and in 1998 with the acquisition of 60 percent of SABA Trading AB, a Swedish importer and distributor of fruits and vegetables. Dole also established operations in South Africa following the deregulation of that country's fresh fruit industry.

In 1995 Dole sold its juice and beverage business, except for pineapple juice, to the Seagram Co. Ltd., which planned to market the juices under its Tropicana brand. In the same year Dole separated its food and real estate business, and Castle & Cooke began to operate independently of Dole as a real estate development firm. Dole was thus focusing solely on its operations as a producer and distributor of food products. By the end of 1995 the company served more than 90 countries, and its product line included more than 170 food products.

Taking advantage of the growing interest in packaged fresh produce, Dole introduced packaged salad mixes in 1996 and set off a major trend. Dole's salad operations plant in Soledad, California, received *Food Engineering Magazine*'s Plant of the Year Award in 1996 for its design quality. The salad business grew rapidly, and Dole founded a processing plant in Ohio to service states in the Midwest and the East. Plans for new salad products were implemented to ensure continued growth through the new millennium. The company also established a salad plant in Japan in 1998 to introduce the packaged product to Japanese consumers.

To further diversify its product line, Dole entered the fresh flower market through several acquisitions in 1998. The company bought Sunburst Farms, Inc., the largest U.S. importer and marketer of fresh cut flowers, as well as Finesse Farms, an importer and marketer of roses, Four Farmers, Inc., a bouquet company, and CCI Farms, a Miami-based producer, importer, and marketer of fresh-cut flowers. Dole hoped that its new flower division would generate revenues of more than $200 million a year in the United States, which, with sales of about $7 billion, was the largest floral market in the world. The floral industry's growth was attributed in large part to the increased availability of fresh-cut flowers in supermarkets, an arena in which Dole already held a commanding position.

Although the company moved forward in its acquisitions and innovations in 1998, Dole faced numerous challenges, some presented by unpredictable weather conditions and others by unstable economic conditions in key markets. The economic crisis afflicting East Asia significantly affected Dole, as the Asian market had played an important role in Dole's growth in the 1990s. Russia accounted for about eight percent of the global banana business, and when the Russian economy collapsed in late 1998, Dole lost an important market for its bananas. Farming was adversely affected by El Niño weather patterns, which generated unpredictable and uncommon weather, including heavy rains in California, flooding in Ecuador, and drought in the Philippines and Thailand. In October, Hurricane Mitch wreaked havoc on Dole operations in Honduras, resulting in $160 million in damages. In December a severe freeze in California destroyed most of the state's citrus crops, with Dole taking a $20 million charge for losses. As a result of these events, net income declined in 1998 to $12 million, down from $160 million in 1997.

Despite Dole's struggles in 1998, the company prepared to continue as the world's largest producer and marketer of fresh fruits, vegetables, and flowers. Dole Fresh Vegetables attained record sales in 1998, and by mid-1999 Dole's share of the fresh-cut salad category was 33.3 percent. Canned pineapple continued to be one of Dole's strongest performers, with a leading market share of 45 percent. In the first half of 1999 revenues climbed 15 percent over sales during the same period in 1998, boosted by the acquisition of flower businesses and the investment in SABA Trading AB. Weak banana pricing affected sales in North America and Europe, however, and Dole's net income for the first half of the year, ending June 19, 1999, was considerably lower than for the same period in 1998.

Principal Subsidiaries

Dole Fresh Fruit Company; Dole Fresh Vegetables; Dole Packaged Foods; Royal Packing Co.; CCI Farms; Finesse Farms; Four Farmers Inc.; Sunburst Farms Inc.; Beebe Orchard Co.; Wells & Wade Fruit Co.; SABA Trading AB (60%; Sweden).

Principal Operating Units

Dole North America; Dole Latin America; Dole Asia; Dole Europe.

Principal Competitors

Chiquita Brands International, Inc.; Fresh Del Monte Produce Inc.; Fyffes plc.

Further Reading

Booth, Jason, "Not a Fruitful Year at Dole As Banana Prices Plummet," *Los Angeles Business Journal,* November 2, 1998, p. 50.

Dole, Richard, and Elizabeth Dole Porteus, *The Story of James Dole,* Aiea, Hawaii: Island Heritage Publishing, 1999, 120 pp.

Facts On: Dole Fresh Pineapple, Westlake Village, Calif.: Dole Food Company, Inc., 1992.

Fairclough, Gordon, and Darren McDermott, "Fruit of Labor: The Banana Business Is Rotten, So Why Do People Fight over It?," *Wall Street Journal,* August 9, 1999, p. A1.

The History of Dole, Westlake Village, Calif.: Dole Food Company, Inc., 1992.

Koeppel, Dan, "Dole Wants the Whole Produce Aisle: Branded Fruits and Vegetables Are Turning the Nation's Supermarkets into Dole Country," *Adweek's Marketing Week,* October 22, 1990, p. 20.

Kravetz, Stacy, "Retailing: King of Pineapples Tiptoes to Tulips for Faster Growth," *Wall Street Journal,* July 6, 1998, p. A17.

Lynch, Russ, "Dole Net Slips on Banana Woes," *Honolulu Star-Bulletin,* November 6, 1998, p. B1.

Petruno, Tom, "Why Dole Offers More Than Just a Bit of Appeal," *Los Angeles Times,* October 11, 1991, p. D3.

Taylor, Frank J., Earl M. Welty, and David W. Eyre, *From Land and Sea: The Story of Castle & Cooke of Hawaii,* San Francisco: Chronicle Books, 1976, 288 pp.

Zwein, Jason, "Pineapples, Anyone? (Dole Food Operations)," *Forbes,* November 27, 1989, p. 286.

—Sina Dubovoj
—updated by Mariko Fujinaka

Edwards Theatres Circuit, Inc.

300 Newport Center Drive
Newport Beach, California 92660
U.S.A.
Telephone: (949) 640-4600
Fax: (949) 721-7170
Web site: http://www.edwardscinemas.com

Private Company
Incorporated: 1930
Employees: 3,100
Sales: $300 million (1998)
NAIC: 512131 Motion Picture Theaters (Except Drive-Ins)

Edwards Theatres Circuit, Inc. owns and operates approximately 90 motion picture theaters with more than 725 screens. Almost all of the theaters are located in southern California, where the company was founded and is headquartered. Since 1997, however, Edwards has been expanding across California state lines, opening four theaters in Idaho and one in Houston, Texas. Since its inception in 1930, the company has been family owned and managed.

Depression Era Beginnings: 1930–50

James Edwards, founder of Edwards Theatres Circuit, bought his first movie theater in 1930—a single-screen cinema in Monterey Park, California, which cost him $1,000. The middle of the Great Depression may not have seemed like the most opportune time to start a business—especially a business that relied entirely on consumers' disposable income. To the tenacious 23-year-old Edwards, however, the leanness of the times was no deterrent. Willing to do whatever was necessary, he and his wife essentially ran the business by themselves, manning the ticket booth, screening the movies, and cleaning up the theater after shows. Even operating on a shoestring, however, the Edwards' fledgling business was not always solvent; the couple had to postpone payroll more than once when money was especially tight.

Despite poor economic conditions, Edwards had chosen an exciting time to enter the theater business. Hollywood's motion picture industry was just then coming into its heyday—what would later be called its ''golden age.'' The new ''talkie'' films, which had been introduced four years earlier, had almost completely replaced the earlier, silent movies. And movie stars like Errol Flynn, Greta Garbo, Gary Cooper, Mae West, and Gloria Swanson were filling the silver screen with glamour, mystery, romance, and adventure.

Through persistence and hard work, Edwards managed to parlay his Monterey Park theater into a small chain of ten screens. In 1939 he created what some consider to be the first movie multiplex by buying the building next to his theater in Alhambra, California and installing a second screen. Eventually, he and two partners started another theater circuit, which grew to include 80 screens.

Newport Beach Circuit: 1950–80

In the 1950s, a health scare sent Edwards into early retirement. Selling his interest in the theater chain, he and his family moved to Newport Beach, California—an oceanside town in Orange County, just south of Los Angeles. Health concerns notwithstanding, the retirement lifestyle did not suit Edwards; within two years of moving to Newport Beach, he was back in the theater business. Deciding to start a new circuit, Edwards began opening movie theaters in Orange County.

In the years Edwards was building his new chain, Orange County itself was undergoing a period of intense growth. One of the main catalysts of this growth was the Santa Ana Freeway. The freeway, which opened in 1954, provided a direct, convenient route between Los Angeles and the Orange County cities of Anaheim and Santa Ana. With a commute to L.A. made feasible, thousands of Los Angeles residents poured into Orange County in search of more affordable housing. Edwards realized the potential inherent in the population boom, and he set about filling the high-growth region with movie theaters. By the end of the 1970s, Edwards Theatres had almost 50 screens in more than 20 Orange County locations.

In his theaters, Edwards strove to provide the best that the industry had to offer. Believing that going to the movies should be a rich, exciting experience, he was careful to create theaters

Company Perspectives:

It is all part of our philosophy that we are providing a total entertainment experience. We want our guests to feel comfortable to return again and again, whether it is to watch a movie, or to enjoy being out among their neighbors.

that were both comfortable and visually appealing. Edwards also fought to give his moviegoers the latest in entertainment and motion picture technology. In the 1960s, he went to bat for Orange County, persuading Hollywood execs that his theaters should offer first-run movies. Until that time, area residents had to drive into Los Angeles to see the newest shows.

Rapid Growth: 1980 to Mid-1990s

Throughout the 1980s, Edwards continued to add to his theater empire in southern California and, especially, to strengthen his presence in Orange County. Toward the latter part of the decade, the company launched a $48 million program of expansion to add 117 screens to its growing collection. As the company established more cinemas in more Orange County cities, many of the area's residents came to view ''Edwards'' as synonymous with ''movie theater.''

Edwards Theatres was not alone in its building frenzy; theater owners all across America were rushing to open cinemas. Much of this building boom was spurred by the shopping malls that were popping up both in urban and suburban areas all over the country. As the number of shopping centers grew, so did the number of movie theaters, which were often built directly into the mall proper. Many of these mall cinemas were multiplexes—theaters that had up to six screens. Between 1980 and 1990, the number of theater screens in the United States grew from 17,590 to 23,689—a 35 percent increase.

By the beginning of the 1990s, the glut of theaters had begun to create a saturated market. Movie attendance had not kept pace with the increase in screens, and several theater owners were beginning to lose money on theaters in heavily screened areas. Many chains put the brakes on their expansion efforts—but Edwards was not among them. The company continued building the theaters to which it had committed, believing the new cinemas would succeed by virtue of being in high-growth areas that were ''under-screened.''

As it turned out, the slowdown in the theater business was only temporary. Within just a few years, another building boom was under way. In fact, theater chains were building theaters that were bigger than ever. The multiplexes that had become so common during the 1980s were giving way to a new industry concept: the megaplex. A megaplex was generally defined as a theater with 16 or more movie screens. Like multiplexes, they were typically located near shopping malls, but were not always attached to the malls themselves. The megaplexes were able to offer customers more movie choices, often including foreign language and art house films typically unavailable in mainstream theaters. By showing the same movie on several screens, they also were able to offer moviegoers more start times and a better chance of getting a seat. Most megaplexes also tended to run movies much longer than the three or four weeks common in smaller theaters.

Edwards Theatres jumped on the megaplex bandwagon in a big way. By the mid-1990s, the company had grown to include 425 screens, 207 of which were in Orange County. An estimated 25 million moviegoers visited Edwards' cinemas in a year's time. With earnings of $18 million on revenues of $170 million, it was one of the most profitable theater chains in the United States. In 1996 Edwards took the industry's ''bigger is better'' trend to a new level by building a $27 million, state-of-the-art megaplex in Irvine, California. The 158,000-square-foot Irvine theater contained 21 screens and seated 6,000—making it the largest theater complex in the nation.

Like many megaplexes, the Edwards Spectrum 21 offered sloping stadium seating designed to improve sight lines, more leg room, digital sound, and larger-than-normal screens. But Edwards went beyond mere comfort in designing its new complex. In keeping with James Edwards' desire to make moviegoing an ''event,'' the theater exuded glamour and luxury. From its modern, high-ceilinged lobby to its soft seats to the flavored coffees and fresh-made pizza available at the concession stand, the Edwards 21 offered moviegoers a treat for the senses.

In addition to being the largest theater in the nation, Edwards' Irvine project was also the first commercial movie complex on the West Coast to include a 3-D sight-and-sound IMAX theater. IMAX was an innovative type of theater that used giant screens and three-dimensional sound and imaging to give moviegoers a ''larger-than-life'' viewing experience.

With the theater industry still buzzing about the new Irvine theater, Edwards announced plans to build another impressive megaplex. The new complex, located in Ontario, California, contained 21 traditional movie screens and an IMAX and was similar in design to the Edwards 21. The Ontario theater attracted an extra share of attention by its location. The theater was built just a few hundred feet away from a competitor's brand new megaplex. The two cinemas, which opened within weeks of each other, gave moviegoers a total of 52 screens from which to choose.

Beyond California: 1997

Since its slight lag in the late 1980s and early 1990s, the theater industry's rush to build more and bigger cinemas had not abated. Between 1996 and 1997, the nation's screen count increased by seven percent—bringing the total number of screens to 29,731. The building furor was especially pronounced in southern California, where the number of movie screens was increasing by approximately 11 percent annually.

Although Edwards was not one to shy away from head-to-head competition, he realized that his core market—Orange County—was very close to being overscreened. To grow, the company needed to find less saturated markets. So for the first time in its 67-year history, Edwards Theatres ventured away from its home turf.

The company's search for likely markets took it first to Idaho. Edwards began negotiations with a developer who was erecting a mall in Boise, on the state's busiest freeway inter-

Key Dates:

1930: James Edwards buys his first theater in Monterey Park, California.
1939: Edwards opens what some consider to be the first multiplex theater in Alhambra, California.
1950s: After a heart attack, Edwards sells his interest in the theater chain and retires in Newport Beach, California.
1960s: Coming out of retirement, Edwards starts a new theater circuit, targeting locations in Orange County.
1996: Edwards Theatres builds what is then the nation's largest megaplex movie theater in Irvine, California.
1997: The Edwards Boise 21 opens in Boise, Idaho—the first Edwards outside California. James Edwards dies at the age of 90.
1999: Edwards opens a megaplex in Houston, making Texas the third state to have an Edwards.

change. One of four theater companies vying to anchor the mall, Edwards won the coveted spot and began planning another of its sumptuous 21-screen megaplexes. Meanwhile, the company also began looking at locations in Texas, Arkansas, and the Washington, DC area.

Edwards' Boise 21 opened in December of 1997—just in time for the holiday movie rush. The 106,000-square-foot theater contained 4,500 seats and featured wall-to-wall screens, state-of-the-art digital sound, ten indoor box offices, a 100-foot concession counter, and two satellite concession stands at each end of the building. The theater was such a success that it surpassed the company's expectations. Within 60 days of opening, the complex sold 600,000 tickets, generated the 14th highest sales of the movie ''Titanic'' in the nation, and quickly became one of Edwards top-earning theaters. Encouraged by these results, Edwards quickly set about adding a 280-seat 3-D IMAX theater to the Boise location. The company also agreed to work with the Boise mall developer to build cinemas in shopping malls planned for Little Rock, Arkansas, and in Idaho Falls and Nampa, Idaho.

Bigger Still: 1999

The next non-California Edwards Theater to open was in Houston, Texas. As if to prove the assertion that ''everything's bigger in Texas,'' the company's Houston complex contained more screens than any of its earlier theaters. Calling the $26 million, two-story megaplex a ''Grand Palace design,'' Edwards implied that it would duplicate the new theater concept elsewhere. ''Houston residents will be the first to enjoy our most spectacular design to date,'' James Edwards III said in an October 1999 press release. ''Just stepping into the 11,000-square-foot lobby with its stone and mosaics, its plasma and flat television monitors, will allow our guests to begin their premiere theatre experience.'' The theater also boasted nine hand-painted murals depicting classic Hollywood scenes and stars, four full-service concession stands, and an attached, multilevel parking garage with automated ticket outlets at its entrances.

After establishing beachheads in Idaho and Texas, Edwards wasted no time in further penetrating its new markets. By the time the Houston Grand Palace opened on October 22, 1999, the company was already working on a second 24-screen theater in Houston, which was scheduled to open by Christmas. By the middle of November 1999, Edwards had opened two additional Idaho theaters located in Idaho Falls and Nampa. The two new cinemas were more modest than the Boise project, each containing only 14 screens.

Coming Soon to a Theater Near You

As the end of the 20th century approached, it appeared that Edwards Theatres would continue to grow at a rapid pace. The company had two projects planned for Arkansas—a 21-screen theater in North Little Rock and a similar theater in Fayetteville. Also in the planning stage were two megaplexes to be located in the Washington, DC vicinity.

It seemed likely that as Edwards grew, it would continue to expand outward from its southern California base, seeking regions that were less heavily screened. It also seemed probable that the company would increasingly focus on what it was best known for—huge, upscale megaplexes that sought to pamper moviegoers in every way possible.

Principal Competitors

AMC Entertainment Inc.; Loews Cineplex Entertainment Corporation; Regal Cinemas, Inc.; WestStar Cinemas, Inc.

Further Reading

Green, Tom, ''Screen-Happy Theater Owners Leap from Multiplexes to Megaplexes,'' *USA Today,* August 7, 1996, p. 07D.
Johnson, Greg, ''Family Business Faces Growth Challenge,'' *Los Angeles Times,* April 27, 1997, p. A-32.
——, ''Marquee Performer: James Edwards Still Battling Big Theater Chains at Age 88,'' *Los Angeles Times,* November 12, 1995, p. 3.
La Franco, Robert, ''My Megaplex Is Bigger Than Your Megaplex,'' *Forbes,* February 24, 1997, p. 50.
Lippman, John, ''Hollywood Pulls Curtain Down on Theater Chains Entertainment,'' *Los Angeles Times,* September 15, 1991, p. 1.
McNary, Dave, ''With Megaplexes, Industry Sits Back and Enjoys Show,'' *Minneapolis Star Tribune,* December 30, 1996, p. 05D.
Mines, Cynthia, ''SCW Profile: Boise Silences the Critics,'' *Shopping Center World,* December 1, 1998.

—Shawna Brynildssen

Egghead.com, Inc.

1350 Willow Road
Suite 100
Menlo Park, California 94025
U.S.A.
Telephone: (650) 470-2400
Fax: (650) 473-6990
Web site: http://www.egghead.com

Public Company
Incorporated: 1988
Employees: 200
Sales: $207.8 million (1998)
Stock Exchanges: NASDAQ
Ticker Symbol: EGGS
NAIC: 45411 Electronic Shopping and Mail-Order Houses

Egghead.com, Inc. is a leading Internet-based discount retailer of computer hardware, software, peripherals, and accessories. For most of its history, the company operated a chain of specialty retail stores under the name Egghead, Inc. However, increased competition from mass merchandisers and consumer electronics ''superstores'' eroded Egghead's sales and profits during the 1990s and forced the company to re-evaluate its strategy. In 1998, Egghead made the bold decision to close its ''bricks and mortar'' retail operation. After re-christening itself Egghead.com, the company opted to sell its products primarily through the Internet, as well as by phone and catalogue. In addition to running its eponymous web site—Egghead.com—the company also operates an Internet auction site (www.surplusauction.com) and re-sells computer hardware, software, and accessories at its off-price web warehouse (www.surplusdirect.com). Moreover, Egghead.com owns a 25 percent stake in Elekom Corporation, which creates electronic commerce applications. In 1999, Egghead.com's Internet empire expanded again when the company merged with on-line auctioneer Onsale Inc.

A Consumer-Oriented Software Company is Founded

Victor D. Alhadeff founded Egghead in 1984. Alhadeff had been involved in an oil and gas limited partnership until a drop in prices drove him out of business in 1983. Shopping for software later that year he found that salespeople at computer stores spoke in technical jargon that often confused the average customer. Alhadeff had sold shoes while in college, and with this retail experience, he decided that he could sell software far more effectively using traditional customer-friendly methods.

Using $50,000 of his own money along with $1 million from local investors—including Paul Allen, a co-founder of Microsoft Corp.—Alhadeff opened his first Egghead store in Bellevue, Washington. From the beginning, Egghead made an effort to make computer software less intimidating to the average consumer, projecting a warm image through the store mascot, a cartoon character named Professor Egghead. Salespeople received intensive training in order to become familiar with a wide range of software and explain it in simple terms. Egghead carried a wide range of software, as many as 1,300 titles, while its warehouse maintained a further 1,000. Customers were allowed to take software home for a 30-day trial period, and stores had up to four computers available for in-store demonstrations. Furthermore, Egghead featured extremely low prices, sometimes 40 percent off the list price.

With its unique approach to software retailing, Egghead's sales rose quickly, and it soon was adding new stores. Corporate customers accounted for a major percentage of Egghead's sales, and the company established a large direct-sales force in 1985. Soon it was selling to Fortune 500 companies like IBM and Boeing. Despite its growth, Egghead kept its costs down, investing its savings in new stores. The firm's quick growth attracted attention and investor interest. Some investors were cautious, however, due to a controversy surrounding the bankruptcy of Alhadeff's previous company, against which several investors filed suit claiming Alhadeff had misled them about the company's finances.

Rapid Growth in the Late-1980s

In 1987, Egghead prepared to go public. The offering was called off at the last minute, however, when the U.S. stock market fell dramatically in October of that year. Alhadeff instead raised $25 million in credit from the U.S. Bank of Wash-

Company Perspectives:

We receive more than 7 million customer visits per month. Each customer has a unique set of needs and budgets. To accommodate our diverse customer base, Egghead offers a variety of services and benefits.

ington, and several million more from private investors, including Prudential Venture Capital, for a total of $47 million in venture capital invested in Egghead. Egghead's sales came to $77.5 million in 1987, nearly doubling sales of the previous year. Perhaps more importantly, the firm had profits of $2 million, after losing nearly $1 million in 1985 and 1986. However, in the rapidly changing computer industry, the firm faced new competitors. B. Dalton Books was expanding its Software Etc. division, which had over 100 boutiques, many of them in the bookstores, and Babbages Inc., carrying similar merchandise, doubled its stores in 1987 to 58.

By early 1988, Egghead operated 107 stores in 13 cities and maintained $40 million of software inventory. In June 1988, Egghead finally went public, with an initial offering of 3.6 million shares at prices above 50 times the firm's 1987 earnings. Egghead used nearly $24 million raised in the offering to add about 100 new stores and put the rest into working capital. In one nine-month period, 64 new Egghead stores were opened as the chain tried to saturate the market before it was filled by competitors. As a result of this growth, Egghead stores and corporate sales staff accounted for about ten percent of U.S. software sales in 1988.

Despite annual sales climbing toward $350 million, however, profits declined due to the swiftness of expansion. In addition to opening the new stores, Egghead added 60 salespeople to the direct sales staff of 132. That meant an addition of 1,600 total employees in one year, and new salespeople required extensive training. As a result, the firm's administrative and selling costs doubled in a year and its operating margins sunk from 4.5 percent in 1988 to about 3.7 percent in 1989. Egghead tried to obtain maximum profits from its low margins by getting volume discounts from software manufacturers. That meant increasing inventory, however, which was both expensive and risky in an increasingly unstable software market.

This tumult lead to two straight years of losses for Egghead, and the company was forced to close 29 stores to cut costs. With large volumes of software flowing quickly through its warehouses, control over Egghead's inventory system slipped and theft increased. In 1989, in the midst of this period, Alhadeff hired Stuart Sloan and Matthew Griffin to help turn around the company. Sloan, who became chief executive officer, had a background on Wall Street, where he had led the leveraged buyout of Quality Food Centers Inc. in 1986. Griffin, who replaced Alhadeff as chairman, had made millions in real estate. The two put internal controls into effect that made each store manager responsible for the performance of his or her store. Retail store managers were sent monthly profit-and-loss statements for their stores, while district managers were sent statements for their areas. Furthermore, Sloan and Griffen refocused company efforts on selling software directly to corporate customers, who accounted for 60 percent of sales. The moves strengthened Egghead's bottom line.

During this time, however, a new rival was emerging: chains of computer superstores that matched or beat the prices of Egghead's software and also sold computer hardware. Egghead responded by strengthening its promotional machinery. When Microsoft's MS-DOS 5 operating system came out, Egghead promoted it extensively, and sold it for $39.99, which was 60 percent lower than the $99.95 list price. Seeking to take advantage of its higher level of customer service, Egghead invested $3 million into training its sales experts. It also added 300 items to the store's inventory, increasing the selection in the average store to 1,600 items.

The Early 1990s

Egghead was profitable again by 1990, with sales of $519 million and profits of $15.4 million. However, a growing recession was affecting the sale of personal computers as well as PC software, and computer superstores were becoming more popular. Furthermore, hardware manufacturers were beginning to offer free software with hardware purchases, circumventing software retailers altogether. As software became more standardized and easier to use, Egghead's customer service became a less significant advantage, and other retail outlets, such as bookstores and office supply stores, began to stock software. Attempting to boost sales, Egghead began promoting and licensing business applications by Computer Associates, the country's second largest software firm. It signed a $3.5 million contract with SalePoint Systems to shift its point-of-sales (POS) software to IBM's OS/2 operating system. The POS system linked the firm's stores, distribution centers, and headquarters. Most software products were bar coded by version when the firm received them, helping its sales and distribution.

By the end of 1991, the firm had 205 stores in 20 states and sales of $665 million. It remained profitable, with earnings of $15.7 million. As Egghead continued to expand rapidly, opening 12 stores and closing two during the first quarter of 1992, earnings again declined. Furthermore, the company made a costly error when it overstocked Microsoft's new Windows 3.1 software, predicting heavy demand that never appeared, in part because several computer manufacturers had already loaded the program onto their hardware as an added feature. Egghead fought back with an aggressive marketing campaign and planned to open between 20 and 40 stores by the summer of 1993.

Software industry price wars intensified during 1992, driving margins still lower, and Egghead brought in a new management team in early 1993. Timothy E. Turnpaugh, previously vice-chairman and operations manager at Seafirst Bank in Seattle, became president and chief executive. Griffin, who had resigned the year before, was replaced by Richard P. Cooley, a director and retired chairman at Seafirst.

Egghead's problems could not be solved simply by changing management. As fierce competition continued to batter the company's bottom line, Egghead's earnings for the fiscal year of 1993 plummeted 56 percent from 1992. In the wake of these dismal reports, Egghead once again brought in new leadership.

Key Dates:

1984: Victor Alhadeff founds Egghead.
1988: Egghead makes its first public stock offering.
1995: Egghead creates the Elekom Unit.
1997: Egghead acquires Surplus Software and spins off Elekom into an independent company.
1998: Egghead closes its retail stores and concentrates on Internet business.
1999: Egghead merges with Onsale Inc.

Turnpaugh was named chairman in July 1993, while Terence Strom, the former chief of electronics retailer Best Buy Co., was chosen as Egghead's new president.

Strom quickly trimmed the company's workforce and led Egghead into the rapidly growing catalogue sector with the purchase of the mail-order business, Mac's Place. He also cut software prices by five percent in an effort to make Egghead more competitive with electronics superstores. Although cheaper software prices drove Egghead's sales for fiscal 1994, the company's profits suffered as a result. Upon reporting a net loss of $500,000 for the year, Turnpaugh resigned. Strom and former Egghead vice-chairman Ronald Erickson jointly assumed leadership of the company.

The Mid-1990s

Since Egghead's boutique software stores continued to lose sales to one-stop-shopping superstores such as Fry's Electronics, Strom stewarded the company through a major shift in strategy. In July 1995, Egghead announced that it would open larger stores more akin to its giant competitors. While the typical Egghead outlet was only about 2,000 square feet, Strom planned to build 10,000 square foot stores that would now offer computers and peripherals to go along with the software that had been the company's traditional focus. That same year, Egghead formed Elekom, which concentrated on business-to-business electronic transactions.

Though 1995 proved to be a successful year for Egghead—due in part to brisk sales of Microsoft's newly launched Windows 95—Egghead's profits sunk once again in 1996. Egghead had shed its direct sales unit, depriving it of the revenue generated by software sales to corporate, government, and education clients. Moreover, the transition to larger-format stores had proved costly, and the company reported a net loss of nearly $11 million. In January 1997, Strom announced his resignation, and George Orban, a long-time Egghead board member, took the reigns of the troubled company.

In an effort to improve Egghead's profitability, Orban closed nearly half of the company's 158 stores and pulled out of a number of markets altogether. According to the February 24, 1997, edition of *PC Week*, Orban believed that Egghead had ''expanded into too many geographic markets—more than it could afford to advertise and distribute in.'' At the same time that Orban decreased Egghead's retail presence, he poured money into the company's Internet business, which had begun to sell software directly to customers over the world wide web in November of 1996. ''This business is in its infancy, but it is showing promising growth and consumer acceptance,'' Orban told the *Washington Post* on February 1, 1997.

In May 1997, Egghead further bolstered its on-line operations by acquiring Surplus Software, which sold computer hardware and software directly to consumers through catalogues and the Internet. This purchase marked a diversification of Egghead's business plan. Previously, the company had simply aimed to supply the latest software at the high end of the retail market. However, with Surplus Software, Egghead entered the ''off market'' sector of the industry. Consumers of ''off market'' products were less interested in the newest generation of program and more so in obtaining outdated but still functional products at lower prices. Through Surplus Software, Egghead purchased ''distressed inventories'' (outdated products or overstock) from manufacturers and resold them to consumers over the Internet. By November 1997, Egghead had three Internet sites operational. In addition to selling discount computer products on its Surplus Direct web site (www.surplusdirect.com), Egghead also launched a consumer auction web site (www.surplusauction.com), whereby consumers made bids on refurbished or off-price technology products. The company's flagship web site (www.egghead.com) offered a range of hardware, software, and accessories. At the same time, Egghead spun off its Elekom division into an independent company, albeit one in which it retained a 25 percent stake.

A New Focus Emerges in 1998

While Egghead's ''bricks and mortar'' retail sales remained weak in 1997, its Internet business thrived. Between the first and third quarters of the 1997 fiscal year, traffic at Egghead.com increased from 600,000 to over six million customers. Recognizing which direction offered it a better chance at future profitability, Egghead made the bold decision in January of 1998 to close its remaining 85 retail stores and become exclusively an Internet business. To reinforce this new direction, the company changed its name to Egghead.com. ''We decided on the Internet, which is growing much more rapidly than the retail channels,'' Orban told the surprised *Spokesman Review* on January 29, 1998. By shuttering its retail operation, Egghead stood to reap substantial savings. In addition to reducing its workforce by 800 employees, the company also was freed from both leasing and construction costs. Moreover, distribution expenses would be only a fraction of what they were, since the individual Internet customer—not the company—paid merchandise shipping costs. Even more promising for Egghead was the potential profits e-commerce offered. Industry insiders predicted that Internet sales in computer hardware and software products would grow from $2 billion in 1998 to $11 billion in 2000.

While market analysts applauded Egghead.com's brave move, the company's transition to an Internet-only operation was fraught with challenges. ''We expect to invest heavily in marketing and technology and therefore expect to incur substantial operating losses in the foreseeable future,'' Orban announced to the *Spokesman Review* on May 6, 1998. To develop its Internet presence, Egghead.com entered into several alliances with major Internet portals. For instance, in February 1998, Egghead.com became the premier computer and software merchant on Yahoo! Internet guide. Its efforts were successful.

Egghead's three web sites collectively ranked sixth among major Internet commerce sites as measured by Media Matrix in May 1998.

Although Egghead.com reported significant losses in fiscal 1998 and 1999 ($50.2 million and $34.4 million, respectively), the company's outlook was positive. As the *Portland Oregonian* explained, ''in the developing e-commerce world, the bottom line [was] replaced with new performance indicators,'' in which Egghead.com ''scored well.'' The company's inventory costs had plummeted as expected from $100 million to about $14 million. With over 40,000 products for sale, Egghead.com enjoyed seven million customer visits per month.

Demonstrating its continued desire to strengthen its position in the on-line market, Egghead.com merged with a leading cyber auctioneer in November, 1999. This new partner, Onsale Inc., sold a variety of computer hardware and software products, as well as vacation packages, consumer electronics, and fitness equipment. Onsale's AtCost site was rolled into the Egghead.com site, while Surplus Auction and Surplus Direct were moved to Onsale's auction area. With the merger, Egghead.com had the size and strength to leverage better prices from its providers. Even more promising was the fact that Egghead.com could cease its price war with Onsale (which had undermined both companies' profits) and could compete more effectively with the likes of Gateway Computer and Buy.Com. Egghead.com moved its headquarters to Onsale's offices in Menlo Park, California. Orban was named chairman of the new company, while Onsale CEO Jerry Kaplan became president of Egghead.com.

Principal Subsidiaries

Surplus Software; Elekom Corp.(25%).

Principal Competitors

Beyond.com Corporation; BID.COM International Inc.; CNET, Inc.; CompUSA Inc.; Cyberian Outpost, Inc.; Dell Computer Corporation; Micro Warehouse, Inc.; Multiple Zones International, Inc.

Further Reading

Bjorhus, Jennifer, ''Vancouver, Washington-Based Egghead Completes Its Rebirth,'' *Portland Oregonian*, May 25, 1999.

Fryer, Alex, ''Egghead Hopes Acquisition Will Repair Cracks,'' *Seattle Times*, May 1, 1997.

Grant, Lorrie, ''Egghead.com, Onsale Link for On-line Computer Sales,'' *USA Today*, July 15, 1999.

Guglielmo, Connie, ''He's Unscrambling Egghead,'' *PC Week*, February 24, 1997.

Haines, Thomas, ''Egghead Will Move from Storefronts to Cyberspace,'' *Seattle Times*, January 28, 1998.

Hafner, Katherine M., ''Selling Software High and Low: Two Winning Formulas,'' *Business Week*, February 29, 1988.

Hutheesing, Nikhil, ''Last Chance For a Software Vendor,'' *Forbes*, June 15, 1998.

Jerenski, Laura, ''Soft in the Head?,'' *Forbes*, March 6, 1989.

Muller, Joan, ''Trailblazing Life on Line,'' *Boston Globe*, March 13, 1998.

Murphey, Michael, ''Egghead Cuts Stake in Elekom,'' *Spokesman Review*, November 13, 1997.

——, ''Egghead Lays Foundation for Comeback,'' *Spokesman Review*, August 10, 1997.

——, ''Egghead Takes Crack at Web Company,'' *Spokesman Review*, January 29, 1998.

Norr, Henry, ''Egghead Whips Up a $400 Million Deal with Onsale,'' *San Francisco Chronicle*, July 15, 1999.

''Over Easy,'' *The Economist*, October 3, 1992.

Segal, David, ''Free-Falling Egghead Grasps at New Cost-Cutting Measures,'' *Washington Post*, February 1, 1997.

Scholl, Jaye, ''Scramble for Egghead,'' *Barron's*, May 16, 1988.

Solmon, Christopher, ''Egghead to Shut 77 Stores, Cut Staff,'' *Seattle Times*, January 31, 1997.

Timmerman, Luke, ''Egghead Loss Totals $35 Million,'' *Spokesman Review*, May 6, 1998.

Yang, Dori Jones, and Stephanie Anderson Forest, ''Egghead Scrambles Back,'' *Business Week*, July 29, 1991.

—Scott M. Lewis
—updated by Rebecca Stanfel

eircom plc

114 St. Stephen's Green West
Dublin 2
Ireland
Telephone: +353-1-671-4444
Fax: +353-1-671-6916
Web site: http://www.eircom.com

Public Company
Incorporated: 1984
Employees: 12,163
Sales: EUR 1.82 billion ($1.85 billion) (1999)
Stock Exchanges: Irish London New York
Ticker Symbol: EIR
NAIC: 51333 Telecommunications Resellers

Formerly known as Telecom Eireann, Irish telecommunications company eircom plc took its current name when it made its first public stock offering in 1999. The company faces a host of challenges as it negotiates the newly-deregulated Irish communications market; once a protected state-owned phone monopoly, eircom now confronts private competitors for the first time. However, the company seems to be flourishing in its new environment. In addition to operating 1.5 million phone lines, eircom's Eircell division provides mobile phone service to over 645,000 customers. eircom also offers Internet access and a variety of advanced voice, data, and multimedia services. The company's origins are thoroughly rooted in the development of British telecommunications, owing to British domination of Ireland throughout the 19th and early 20th centuries. Ireland has come forth from Britain's shadow to become an industrial force in Europe. As a crucial component in Ireland's industrial infrastructure, telecommunications has grown immeasurably in value. Telecom Eireann—and now eircom plc—has been at the forefront of that growth.

Telephone Systems Emerge in Ireland

The establishment of telephonic communications in Ireland in the late 1800s closely followed the demise of what had been the dominant electronic medium of the day, telegraphy. Ireland's first commercial telegraph was established by the English & Irish Magnetic Telegraph Company in 1851, linking Galway and Dublin along railway lines. The following year a submarine link was built, connecting Dublin to the English network at Holyhead, Wales.

Private ownership of telegraph systems, however, left vast areas of Ireland unserved because they were not profitable. In 1870 the British Post Office took control of the national telegraph system in an effort to spread the technology throughout Ireland, and operated at a substantial loss. Ireland, however, was the last "stepping stone" for transatlantic cables linking Europe with the United States. Important stations were established at Valentia, Ballingskelligs, and Waterville, providing direct connections between England and Germany and Nova Scotia.

Soon after Alexander Graham Bell invented the telephone in 1876, he demonstrated the device in England. The Post Office subsequently won permission to operate a telephone network under license from Bell, whose English company merged with Thomas Edison's in 1880 to form United Telephone.

Britain's Post Office understood immediately what effect the telephone would have on its telegraph monopoly and petitioned the government to allow it to take control of United Telephone. The Treasury Department, however, shocked by the projected costs of expanding the network, did not believe it was the government's place to run a telephone service. Eventually, the Post Office's involvement was limited merely to collecting licensing fees from United.

While this battle was being fought, United constructed its first exchange in Ireland, switching five lines in Dublin. So few calls were handled by this office that the switchboard operator, a young boy, frequently went off to play marbles out of boredom. The following year, the office was expanded to 20 lines and an operator was hired.

Shareholders grew impatient with United Telephone when their investments failed to show immediate returns. In 1882, acting upon shareholder discomfort, the newly formed Telephone Company of Ireland negotiated a takeover of United Telephone's Irish operations. Subsequent growth continued to

Company Perspectives:

eircom's strategic objective is to strengthen its position as the principal provider of telecommunications services to Ireland and to become the recognized provider of selected services in the extended home market of Great Britain and Northern Ireland, as well as in other locations where eircom has existing customers or traffic.

be slow. By 1888 the Dublin office and three sub-exchanges handled only 500 customers. In addition, all lines were single-wire systems that used the earth as part of its circuit. This allowed virtually anyone with even the most rudimentary equipment to eavesdrop on conversations. Thus, the practice of "rubbernecking" became a serious impediment to sales.

National Telephone: 1893–1914

In 1893 the company's backers lost faith in the company and agreed to sell the operation to National Telephone, an English concern that had previously taken over United Telephone. National attacked the privacy problem decisively by ordering a massive reconstruction program to install wires in pairs.

While the Post Office negotiated free passage rights along railway lines in Ireland, development of an intercity trunk system continued to proceed slowly because expenditures were opposed at every turn by the Treasury Department. Still, by 1900 the company managed to construct 56 exchanges in the country, principally in Dublin and southern and western Ireland. Railway companies became avid users of telephone service because it was cheaper and faster than the telegraph.

By virtue of its unusual arrangement with the government, National Telephone lived in continual fear of being taken over by the Post Office, whose intentions were clear. Only the Treasury Department kept the Post Office from acting on its ambitions. But as the profitability of telephony became ever more apparent, Treasury opposition subsided.

Finally, in 1905, the Post Office won an order to assume control of National Telephone when that company's charter expired in 1911. But when the takeover was completed in 1912, the network, which included 150 exchanges in Ireland, was saddled with widespread equipment shortages and six years of disrepair.

The War Years

When World War I began in 1914, virtually all work on the telephone network ground to a halt. Only military telephony received any funding and materials. In addition, because they were strategic targets, many of the submarine cables came under attack and were disabled.

As the war drew to a close in 1918, an Anglo-Irish conflict and civil war for independence from Britain erupted. The domestic telephone network was frequently targeted during the hostilities, and many exchanges were destroyed and miles of cable were knocked out. In 1922, as the conflict came to an end, a new Irish government appointed a Department of Posts & Telegraphs (P&T) to assume control of the telephone network and develop telecommunications in Ireland. Construction of the network resumed in 1924. Part of the rebuilding plan called for the establishment of an automated Strowger-type switching system in Dublin, and the assignment of five-digit telephone numbers. These switches, which eliminated the need for a switchboard operator, were installed in 1927.

The worldwide economic depression of the 1930s hit the fragile Irish economy with brutal force, causing demand for new telephones to dry up. This hardship was followed by the emerging European war some years later. As during World War I, all civilian construction in the network was suspended in favor of military communications. After the fall of France in 1940, the P&T was called upon to wire 84 lookout posts at strategic points around Ireland where German warships could be observed or, worse, where invasion might be expected.

Despite the tremendous destruction the war caused in England, France, and Germany, Ireland emerged from the war mostly unscathed. The telephone network P&T built for the military, which included miles of new trunks, was subsequently converted to civilian use.

Postwar Expansion through the 1970s

The huge demand for telephones after the war, coupled with P&T's conversion to underground cable systems, left P&T with virtually no available transmission facilities. As a result, when Dublin's tram system was eliminated after the war, P&T purchased the line's underground duct network for telephone cables. As part of a wider government-backed expansion plan, P&T also resolved to improve trunk service, increase subscribership from 31,000 to 100,000, and expand all operator services to 24-hours.

Despite several obstacles, continued demand for telephone service enabled the company to exceed all these goals. In 1957 P&T installed the first of its crossbar switches, which were easier to maintain than the Strowger step switches. The company began phasing out switchboards in remote areas in favor of automated switches.

P&T surveys during this time revealed low levels of usage in the network due to limited applications of the local call rate. Most calls, it was discovered, required expensive trunk connections. In 1958 the company invited G.J. Kamerbeek, an engineer with the Dutch Post Office, to propose a new rate structure for P&T. While this required extensive re-engineering of the network, it established wider local call zones. This change, as well as other pricing reforms, succeeded in raising Irish telephone subscriptions to levels comparable with other European countries.

The company began to experiment with new transmission mediums. Just as aerial cable had proven no match for Ireland's seasonal ice and wind, buried cable soon lost its appeal because of the high cost of boring trenches. In 1961 P&T installed its first microwave system, linking Althone and Galway.

The company also made other efforts to increase the number of subscribers, including reclassifying Ireland's thousand of

Key Dates:

1876: Alexander Graham Bell invents the telephone.
1880: United Telephone is formed in England, overseeing Great Britain's telephone lines.
1882: Telephone Company of Ireland takes over United Telephone's Irish operations.
1893: Britain's new National Telephone Co. steps in to oversee and improve Irish telecommunications.
1911: British Post Office assumes control of National Telephone.
1922: New Irish government gives its Department of Posts & Telegraphs (P&T) responsibility for developing country's phone service.
1978: The Dargan Report reveals that Irish telephone system is in need of an overhaul.
1979: Telecom Eireann is formed.
1983: Telecom Eireann formally takes charge of Ireland's phone service.
1993: First private competitor to Telecom Eireann receives operating license.
1999: Telcom Eireann becomes a public company; changes name to eircom plc.

farms as residences, thus enabling farmers to avoid high rental rates for business telephones. In addition, the ambitious Rural Automisation Programme provided for the construction of new crossbar switching facilities, for the first time, outside of rural post office facilities.

As late as 1974, a year after Ireland gained admission to the European Economic Community, all calls to and from the Continent continued to be switched through London. While this was mainly an engineering consequence of years of British domination over Ireland, the time had arrived for Ireland to declare its independence, at least in the area of international telephony. That year P&T installed its first international crossbar in Dublin, greatly facilitating call traffic with other European countries and North America.

However, during this time P&T stumbled in several areas. A series of industrial actions, including worker strikes, and a growing inability on the part of management to address these problems, led to a severe drop in service quality. Almost weekly, national and provincial newspapers berated the company for its poor service.

The 1980s: Dargan Report Calls for Telecom Reorganization

In 1978 the government, fearing that Ireland's telephone system was once again falling behind those of its European neighbors, commissioned a Posts and Telecommunications Review group to study the situation. The following year the group issued what became known as the Dargan Report. The study's conclusions were bleak, stating that the Irish telecommunications system was failing to keep pace with Ireland's growing economy and its customers' expectations. Urgent action was deemed necessary to avoid a crisis.

The Dargan Report recommended that P&T be separated from the civil postal system and reorganized as a state-owned company. The report specified that the new company should be operated according to modern business principles, emphasizing marketing, customer service, and high returns on equity.

In July 1979 the Irish Parliament agreed to split P&T into two entities, a postal service called An Post and a telephone company called Bord Telecom Eireann. The telephone company was given a IR£650 million development budget as part of a five-year program to construct as many as 500 new buildings, double subscriptions, drastically increase the number of trunk lines, and improve customer service. At the end of the five-year program, the Postal and Telecommunications Services Act of 1983 authorized Telecom Eireann to take formal control of Ireland's telecommunications system.

The new company benefitted tremendously from a far-sighted decision made by P&T leadership some years earlier to begin the transition to digital switches, which were faster and more efficient than the mechanical switches previously used. As a result, the new company encountered none of the difficulties experienced by other European telephone companies in converting to the new system.

When Telecom Eireann took over the national system on January 1, 1984, only 309 manual exchanges remained. The last of these older switches was replaced in 1987. At last, the entire network was standardized and digital. By 1991 Telecom Eireann would service its one millionth customer.

The 1990s and Beyond

In order to keep pace with other communications systems in the world, Telecom Eireann devoted tremendous resources to the development of new technologies, including satellite transmission and national fiber optic networks. After launching Eircell, a national cellular phone network, Telecom Eireann introduced Eirpage, a large paging operation produced in conjunction with Motorola. Also in the early 1990s, Telecom Eireann worked to bring ISDN capabilities to the network and to establish an integrated broadband communications network in Europe by 1995.

While Telecom Eireann shared many characteristics with other independent enterprises, its board was appointed by its one and only shareholder, the Irish government. Moreover, Telecom Eireann faced virtually no competition. This state of affairs was soon to change. A gradual opening of the Irish communications market occurred in 1992 when the year-old Estat Telecom Group plc began lobbying the government for a license to operate, which it obtained in 1993.

The impetus towards privatization began in 1991 and gained force as the decade advanced. As Ireland's economy emerged in the era of global commerce, telecommunications became an essential factor in economic success. Critics argued that a private industry was necessary for further economic expansion—to lower costs and facilitate the introduction of new cutting-edge services. The analysts contended that, while Telecom Eireann had brought Ireland to the verge of an economic boom, only a free market would ensure continued prosperity. Ireland also received pressure from the European Union which mandated that its member nations phase out phone monopolies by 2000. Although Ireland and Italy were given more time to implement these changes, the deadline still loomed. In 1998 the Irish government announced that complete deregulation of the telecommunications industry would occur in 2000.

Ireland's economy boomed without deregulation. As the fastest-growing economy in Europe, Ireland garnered scores of corporate investors, eager to establish their operations on the island. After Microsoft Corp. selected Ireland as the new headquarters for its European division, the company proceeded vigorously to lobby the Irish government to deregulate telecommunications ahead of schedule. Government regulators acquiesced to the demands of big business and declared that Telecom Eireann would go public in July 1999.

To underscore the significance of this event on its corporate identity, Telecom Eireann changed its name to eircom plc. The initial public stock offering was a rousing success. The Irish government had sold its entire 50.1 percent stake in the company because of demand for shares. To help bolster employee dedication to eircom, 14.9 percent of the company was reserved in an Employee Share Ownership Plan.

Netherlands's KPN and Sweden's Telia AB jointly held a 35 percent stake in eircom, and Telia and Norway's Telenor were poised to merge and form a massive Scandinavian carrier with $10 billion in annual revenue. Like these and others of its European counterparts, eircom set its sights on expansion. The company first sought to extend its reach across Great Britain. In October 1998 the company launched Telecom Ireland, which strove to penetrate Northern Ireland. One year later, eircom acquired a 30 percent stake in Viasec, a provider of e-mail security solutions.

Since eircom faced competition in its domestic markets, the company strove to bolster its image by touting its newest services and slashing its rates. eircom introduced a slew of services, such as a ''Circle of Friends'' discount and Caller Display. The strategy paid off. For the financial year that ended April 1, 1999, eircom reported a growing customer base— both for its fixed line services and Eircell's mobile communications.

Principal Subsidiaries

Eircell Ltd.; Irish Telecommunications Investments plc.; eircom Ireland Ltd.; Eirtrade Services Ltd.; eircom Ireland International Ltd.; eircom PhoneWatch Ltd.; Eirpage Ltd.; Indigo Services Group Ltd.; TNI (Telecom) Ltd.; eircom Retail Ltd.; Atlas Communications (UK) Ltd.; Lan Communications Ltd.; Local Ireland Ltd. (86%); Golden Pages Ltd. (63%); Trinity Commerce Ltd. (51%).

Principal Competitors

Estat Telecom Group plc; Cable & Wireless plc; MCI WorldCom, Inc.; British Telecommunications plc; NTL Inc.

Further Reading

Marks, Debra, ''Irish Government to Sell Its Entire Stake in Telecom Eireann,'' *Wall Street Journal Europe,* June 14, 1999.

——, ''Irish Stocks Seen Gaining After Debut,'' *Wall Street Journal Europe,* July 14, 1999.

Naik, Gautam, ''Telecom Eireann Plans IPO for 1999,'' *Wall Street Journal Europe*, March 27, 1998.

Telecom Eireann, 1991.

''Telephone Explosion Broadens Market,'' *Irish Times*, January 3, 1998.

—John Simley
—updated by Rebecca Stanfel

Environmental Industries, Inc.

24121 Ventura Boulevard
Calabasas, California 91302
U.S.A.
Telephone: (818) 223-8500
Fax: (818) 223-8142
Web site: http://www.envind.com

Private Company
Incorporated: 1949 as Valley Crest Landscape Nurseries, Inc.
Employees: 5,500
Sales: $500 million (1999 est.)
NAIC: 111421 Nursery and Tree Production; 56173 Landscaping Services; 54132 Landscape Architectural Services

Originating as a retail landscape nursery in southern California, Environmental Industries, Inc. (EII) is the largest full-service site development, landscape and horticultural services contractor in the United States. Its clients include landscape architects, developers, general contractors, property managers, and public agencies.

Over the years the company, which is owned by the Sperber family, developed a reputation for being able to handle big contracts on schedule. National contracts have included Walt Disney Co.'s Animal Kingdom in Orlando, Florida; the Getty Museum in Los Angeles; the Mercedes-Benz corporate campus in Alabama; the Denver International Airport; and the 1996 Summer Olympic venues in Atlanta, Georgia, among others.

EII has five operating divisions and a growing nationwide network of service centers and branch offices. Environmental Care, Inc. (ECI) provides landscape maintenance and renovation, irrigation and water management, and tree care services. Valley Crest offers site development, landscape construction, irrigation installation, and concrete/water-theming. Valley Crest Tree Co. specializes in specimen tree growing, relocation, preservation, and wholesale nursery production. Environmental Golf is a one-stop source and expert in complete golf course construction, renovation, maintenance, and management. U.S. Lawns is a landscape maintenance franchise company.

From Retail Nursery to Landscape Business: 1949–60

In 1949 Burton S. Sperber and his father opened Valley Crest Landscape Nurseries, Inc., in North Hollywood, California. With just a few hundred dollars, an old pickup truck, and a dream, they planned to make a living with the nursery while developing a small landscape business. They hoped to take advantage of the post-World War II boom in new home construction that was taking place in the San Fernando Valley. After Burton Sperber obtained his Landscape Architect's and Engineering and Landscape Contractor's licenses, the company began doing landscape design and construction on apartment projects, industrial and commercial projects, and model home developments. The company developed a strong reputation in the home-building market for its on-time completions. It also began building golf courses in the 1950s.

In 1959 the company name was changed to Valley Crest Landscape, Inc. Focusing on landscape work, its fleet of poppy red trucks became a familiar sight throughout the new subdivisions in southern California. By the end of the 1950s the company was an industry leader in the landscape and landscape maintenance business, with contracts from California's school system and work on the state's growing highway system.

By 1960 Valley Crest had landscaped more than 100 schools in the Los Angeles area and was recognized for its expertise in landscaping parks, hillsides, and golf courses, as well as for landscaping thousands of homes throughout California. It was also one of the first landscape companies to do landscape work on freeways in California and later landscaped freeways in Arizona, Colorado, Georgia, Florida, Illinois, Washington, and Nevada.

Multiple Operating Units in the 1960s

In 1961 the company established a tree-growing nursery called Valley Crest Tree Company. It was considered a major

Company Perspectives:

Welcome to Environmental Industries, Inc., the nation's largest full-service landscape, site development, and horticultural services contractor. Building and maintaining landmark projects for 50 years, we offer a complete range of services through our five operating divisions. See why more landscape architects, developers, general contractors, property managers and public agencies continue to choose Environmental Industries, Inc. by browsing our division Web sites. The seamless integration of our divisions streamlines production and reduces costs while our philosophy to meet and exceed client expectations ensures high quality and customer satisfaction. Environmental Industries, Inc.'s network of service centers and branch offices continues to grow nationwide as an expanding family of companies.

innovation in the wholesale nursery business to grow large specimen trees for major landscape projects, when other nurseries were primarily growing only one- and five-gallon trees and shrubs. Valley Crest Tree Company opened on three acres of land in Sepulveda, California, under the operating leadership of Burt's brother, Stuart Sperber. Under his leadership Valley Crest Tree Company developed high standards in moving large specimen trees and became known for its expertise in moving trees of any size.

In 1964 Valley Crest expanded by opening an office in Santa Ana, California, to serve the Orange County market. In 1966 it moved into the northern California market and began work on a multimillion-dollar landscape project, Rossmoor Leisure World, one of the largest retirement communities in the United States.

By 1965 Valley Crest had established branch operations throughout the United States. Its operations were connected by a computerized information system that provided support and information to its branch offices and facilitated the expansion of services.

New Organizational Structure: 1970–90s

In 1969, Environmental Industries, Inc. (EII) was formed for the purpose of consolidating ownership of the firm's multiple operating units. With the formation of EII, the company was reorganized into three operating divisions. Landscape maintenance services were consolidated into a new division of EII called Environmental Care, Inc. (ECI) in 1970. The company's other divisions were Valley Crest, headed by Burt Sperber's son, Richard A. Sperber, and Valley Crest Tree Co., headed by Burt's brother, Stuart Sperber. Together the company's three divisions provided a range of landscape and site development services.

Environmental Care was originally established with only two major landscape contracts in northern and southern California. In 1980 Bruce K. Wilson was appointed president of ECI. Within three years he expanded the division's operations by developing ten new branches, including offices in the East Bay area of San Francisco, Riverside, Palm Springs, San Diego, Houston, and Denver, and opened new markets in Florida and Georgia.

ECI distinguished itself by offering a broad range of landscape maintenance services. In addition to exterior landscape maintenance, it offered professional arborist services, irrigation and water management programs, interiorscapes, and sports turf maintenance. ECI could claim not only to maintain the value of its clients' landscape assets, but also to help them appreciate over time through year-round full maintenance programs for shrubs, groundcovers, seasonal color rotation, tree pruning, and water management.

Valley Crest focused on landscape and site construction. It became the largest landscape and site construction company in the United States. Working in any location in the United States, its services included site construction, landscape construction, irrigation installation, specialty concrete, water features and theming, golf course construction, natural and artificial sports fields, wetlands restoration, landfills, and gas recovery systems.

Valley Crest Tree Company focused on tree moving and growing. It was eventually organized into three divisions. The Specimen Contracting Division offered tree preservation and relocation services. It supplied, relocated, and procured specimen trees and operated worldwide from its offices in San Fernando, near Los Angeles. The Specimen Tree Division maintained an inventory of a wide variety of larger and rare specimen trees for use by developers, landscape architects, and landscape contractors. It specialized in unusual and distinctive trees not usually available from ordinary stock. The Nursery Division operated on more than 1,200 acres, with five growing facilities and four offices throughout California. It produced plant material, mainly specimen trees and shrubs, in container sizes ranging from one gallon to 72-inch boxes. It kept an inventory level of around two million items.

Two related companies operated as part of Valley Crest Tree. Environmental Landscape Products, Inc. provided plant materials for the interiorscape industry from its base in Orange County, California. Its greenhouse stocks commonly used materials as well as imported items from Florida and Hawaii. A related company, Garden Art International, specialized in Italian terra cotta pottery, hand-carved Italian limestone, cast iron pieces, and a variety of garden statuary, fountains, benches, and pedestals. It replicated existing pieces, created new products, and offered a line of finishes to customize each project.

Expanded Landscape Maintenance and Golf Course Construction in the 1990s

Environmental Golf was established in 1990 as a separate subsidiary. Previously, EII had been building golf courses through its subsidiary company, Valley Crest Landscape. Environmental Golf, though, would focus exclusively on building golf courses.

Environmental Golf maintained private and public golf courses throughout the country. It assumed all of the maintenance operating costs and the risk of maintaining its clients'

Key Dates:

1949: Burton S. Sperber and his father open Valley Crest Landscape Nurseries, Inc., in North Hollywood, California.
1954: Burt Sperber obtains his Landscape Architect license.
1959: Company is renamed Valley Crest Landscape, Inc.
1961: Valley Crest Tree Co. is opened on three acres of land.
1966: Expands into Northern California market.
1969: Environmental Industries, Inc. is formed to consolidate multiple operating units.
1970: Environmental Care Inc. is formed to consolidate landscape maintenance services.
1990: Environmental Golf is formed to consolidate golf course construction and maintenance.
1996: Environmental Industries acquires U.S. Lawns.
1999: Company celebrates its 50th anniversary.

golf courses. The company employed Class A level golf course superintendents and more than 1,500 horticultural technicians and owned more than 800 pieces of advanced turf equipment.

In addition to building and maintaining golf courses, Environmental Golf also owned and operated several courses. In 1999 it completed a cluster of five golf courses in southern California that it called California Classics. The five courses were Glenn Annie Golf Club and Sandpiper Golf Course in Santa Barbara, The Links at RiverLakes Ranch in Bakersfield, Sterling Hills Golf Club in Camarillo, and Westridge Golf Club in La Habra. Environmental Golf expected to enjoy many strategic advantages from owning and managing this cluster of championship courses. The final course, The Links at RiverLakes Ranch, opened Labor Day weekend in 1999.

The firm's landscape maintenance division, Environmental Care, Inc., grew steadily. By the end of the 1990s ECI was bringing in revenues in excess of $100 million and had 2,500 employees nationwide. Its national network of regional offices and service and operation centers were located throughout the Sunbelt and Southeast in California, Nevada, Arizona, Colorado, Texas, Georgia, North Carolina, and Florida.

In 1996 ECI acquired U.S. Lawns, a rapidly growing lawn and landscape franchise organization based in Orlando, Florida. Its franchises extend coast-to-coast, primarily in the East, South, and Southeast from Maryland to Florida, Ohio to Texas, and also in California, Idaho, and Utah. U.S. Lawns (www.uslawns.com) was founded in Orlando, Florida, in 1986, as a landscape maintenance franchise company. Its network of franchises consisted of company-owned and operator-owned businesses. The company provided guidance, training, and support to its family of franchises through operations facilities that served as training hubs. A typical U.S. Lawn franchisee was encouraged to take on a wide range of landscape maintenance projects, including commercial and industrial centers, shopping malls, retail facilities, multifamily residential communities, homeowner associations, theme parks, civic centers, and so on. As of 1999 there were 46 U.S. Lawns franchises and company stores operating in 15 states.

Continuing Commitment to Community Service and Environmentally Friendly Practices into the 21st Century

As Valley Crest Landscape grew and developed into Environmental Industries Inc., it became the nation's largest landscape corporation with more than 5,500 employees and $450 million in sales. Throughout its history the company had pioneered environmentally friendly landscaping and site development. It received numerous awards and recognition, starting in the early 1950s, including honors from American Nurserymen, California Landscape Contractors, Colorado Landscape Architects, American Society of Landscape Architects, Sargent Shriver, Lady Bird Johnson, National Arborist Association, International Society of Arboriculture, Los Angeles Beautiful, and Grand Awards from the Associated Landscape Contractors of America.

As part of its community service commitment, the firm provided hundreds of scholarships annually to colleges and universities for students in landscape architecture and horticulture programs. Many of the scholarship recipients specialized in ornamental horticulture, irrigation technology, environmental resource management, and arbor science. EII and its operating divisions also supported agricultural education as corporate sponsors of the National Future Farmers of America Foundations and contributed to FFA's National Landscape and Nursery Career Development Event. EII also provided support to the Associated Landscape Contractors of America and its programs.

Other corporate support was directed to community medical services, housing, and education. As part of its 50th anniversary celebration in 1999, EII was building and donating "Pocket Parks" in impoverished areas where there was a need for more parks to help preserve those communities.

The company was also a committed partner with the State of California's Integrated Waste Management Board to promote grass recycling and green resource management. It actively supported integrated landscape management programs to promote the efficient use of natural resources.

Through its operating divisions, Environmental Industries, Inc. was a vertically integrated landscape industry leader. It had the resources to handle several major projects simultaneously anywhere in the United States. The firm owned the industry's largest equipment fleet, and its network of branch locations enabled it to staff, manage, and complete projects to the highest standards on a local basis.

For the future, the company expected to use its vast resources to remain healthy and competitive. The company was likely to remain private and under the capable direction of the Sperber family. The firm boasted an experienced management team, and its employees demonstrated a great deal of loyalty to the family-controlled company. To quote Burt Sperber, "Our business is all about building nature, making things grow, making things last, and nurturing them for generations to come."

Principal Divisions

Environmental Care, Inc.; Valley Crest; Valley Crest Tree Co.; Environmental Golf; U.S. Lawns.

Principal Competitors

Tru-Green/LandCare; The Brickman Group.

Further Reading

''Calabasas Company Forms Golf Subsidiary,'' *Los Angeles Business Journal,* June 11, 1990, p. 25.

''50 Years of Creating Living Art: Entrepreneurial Seeds Grow into Landscape Industry Giant,'' company history, Environmental Industries Inc., 1999.

Lubove, Seth, ''Green Begets Green,'' *Forbes,* December 14, 1998, p. 142.

—David P. Bianco

Crate&Barrel

Euromarket Designs Inc.

725 Landwehr Road
Northbrook, Illinois 60062
U.S.A.
Telephone: (847) 272-2888
Toll Free: (800) 967-6696
Fax: (847) 272-5276
Web site: http://www.crateandbarrel.com

Private Company
Incorporated: 1962
Employees: 4,200
Sales: $530 million (1998 est.)
NAIC: 44211 Furniture Stores; 442299 All Other Home Furnishings Stores; 45322 Gift, Novelty, and Souvenir Shops; 45411 Electronic Shopping and Mail-Order Houses

Euromarket Designs Inc. is the official corporate name for the famous Crate and Barrel retail chain of contemporary home furnishings and housewares. In 1999, Crate and Barrel had more than 80 stores in 17 markets in the United States. Based in the Chicago suburb of Northbrook, Illinois, Crate and Barrel is considered a trendsetter in style and retail display, and about one-third of store merchandise is exclusive to Crate and Barrel. The company also offers its wide range of products through a mail-order catalog sent to more than ten million homes across the nation. Mail-order accounts for about ten percent of total company sales, and the fast-growing furniture division contributes nearly 30 percent of Crate and Barrel's revenues.

Innovative Roots in the 1960s

Crate and Barrel was founded in 1962 by Gordon and Carole Segal. Gordon Segal had recently graduated from Northwestern University and was working as a real estate agent, while Carole was a schoolteacher. According to company lore, Gordon was inspired to open a store while doing the dishes at home one day. While he stood admiring the beauty of the piece of imported German china dripping in his hand, Segal mulled the fact that reasonably priced but classy items for the kitchen were not readily available to the Chicago consumer. With the St. Lawrence Seaway newly opened, the Segals got the idea to have European goods shipped straight to Chicago, where they could be sold directly to the public. In this way, importers and wholesalers could be bypassed, allowing the fledgling merchants to keep prices in check. With their life savings of $12,000, plus $5,000 borrowed from Gordon's father, a successful Chicago restaurateur and caterer, the Segals went into business in spite of their complete lack of experience in either importing or retailing.

The first Crate and Barrel store was opened in a former elevator factory in Old Town, an area of Chicago in the process of gentrification. The store was put together in a mere two weeks. By opening day, Crate and Barrel consisted mainly of a big room, one employee, and a bunch of merchandise. Even the cash register had not yet arrived. With no tables or display cases available, the goods, mainly plates, glassware, and cookware, were stacked on overturned packing crates and barrels. From the necessity of the company's humble beginning came the chain's now household name. The Segals' inexperience showed in the first few months of operation. In the first month, the store sold $8,000 worth of merchandise. The following month, however, this figure was cut in half. Sales fell by 50 percent again the month after that.

As customers began to discover Crate and Barrel, the Segals became interested in a broader range of products. In 1964 they took their first European buying trip in order to make direct contact with the independent and often small craftspeople and manufacturers that would serve as the sources of their merchandise for years to come. Another key to the company's early survival was Gordon Segal's ability to concoct unique and advantageous leasing agreements with landlords. For example, in 1965, as the first Crate and Barrel was thriving in the Old Town location, the company found itself faced with the possibility of losing its lease. Segal was able to patch together a deal with the landlord in which Crate and Barrel would build a new home and rent it back from the landlord. Under the agreement, Crate and Barrel would then purchase the building in 15 years. The year 1965 also marked the departure of Carole Segal from the operation. The driving force in the company's early stylistic innovations, Carole left to attend graduate business courses, as

Company Perspectives:

At Crate and Barrel, our motto is "stay humble and stay nervous." We continually challenge ourselves to avoid getting too comfortable. Taking risks and anticipating trends helps us stay a step ahead in the marketplace—it's a tremendous outlet for the creativity of everyone here, and keeps us all on our toes. We like new ideas, and we keep evolving with the times, which makes it fun to come to work.

well as study gourmet cooking. In 1979 she started a store of her own called Foodstuffs, a high-end food store with a merchandising approach similar to that of Crate and Barrel.

In 1966 Segal and Lon Habkirk, a designer who would remain affiliated with the company for at least 20 more years, traveled to Boston to study a store called Design Research. Design Research, the creation of architect Ben Thompson, dealt in imported housewares and furniture. In Design Research Segal saw the clean, modern, Eurolook that he sought for his store, and was heavily influenced by Thompson's unorthodox retail approach. Design Research, however, sold expensive and rare items and had trouble turning a profit in spite of a high dollar per square foot sales ratio. Segal realized that Crate and Barrel had to focus more on keeping prices lower through volume buying. His goal was to keep prices 30 to 40 percent lower than similar merchandise at other retail outlets by keeping profit margins low and importing goods directly from the manufacturer.

By 1968 Crate and Barrel had annual sales of around $500,000. That year a second store was opened at the Plaza del Lago shopping center in Wilmette, an upscale suburb of Chicago. As the company grew, Crate and Barrel began to face the problem of developing a reliable management team in an industry with traditionally low pay and high employee turnover. Segal's solution was to hire young college graduates into sales positions with the explicit goal of eventually moving them into management roles. Segal also aimed to create an environment conducive to keeping employees around, partly by expanding only to cities that were hospitable to workers, avoiding rough-and-tumble markets like New York. This strategy paid off handsomely in employee loyalty. In 1970, for instance, a core of new staff members was brought on board. Fifteen years later, nearly two-thirds of this group held senior executive positions with the company.

Expansion and Growing Recognition: 1970s–80s

Oak Brook, another affluent Chicago suburb, became home to Crate and Barrel's third store in 1971. By the middle of the 1970s, the chain was beginning to receive widespread attention for its unique marketing style and the quality of its wares. This attention was boosted by the 1975 opening of a new store at a highly visible location on Michigan Avenue in Chicago. Over the course of the next few years, Crate and Barrel began its nationwide expansion, propelled by its sterling reputation among the growing class of young adults with money to spend, otherwise known as "yuppies." The first non-Chicago markets into which the chain expanded were Boston and Dallas, and the stores were usually placed in upscale malls. Soon thereafter, San Francisco and Washington, D.C., were added to the list. In 1981 Crate and Barrel tried its hand at retail furniture sales for the first time. One of the company's Boston stores was converted into a furniture outlet at that time. This Boston location was used as a test subject as Segal considered the possibility of expanding further into furniture retailing. This allowed Segal to experiment with different approaches and product lines without risking a heavy commitment to the furniture business. Ten years later, furniture sales were contributing about one-fifth of the company's revenue.

In 1983 Crate and Barrel raised $7 million through Harris Bank industrial revenue bonds to finance a new 136,000-square-foot complex in Northbrook, Illinois, another suburb of Chicago. The complex would house the corporate headquarters and a central warehouse. The chain had grown to 17 stores by 1985. That year, these stores generated about $50 million in sales and employed 600 workers (twice as many during peak periods). Revenue was growing at a rate of 20 percent a year. The merchandise sold at Crate and Barrel stores across the United States was supplied by about 350 different manufacturers, many of them small independents. Of these, 250 were located overseas. In addition, the company had developed a vibrant mail-order operation, which by this time was processing about 3,000 pieces each day.

In the middle part of the 1980s, Crate and Barrel found that the tastes of its customers had become somewhat more expensive. This was most apparent in the furniture operations. When the company first began to sell furniture, the emphasis was on glass, chrome, and black leather, in keeping with the clean, basic look of its tabletop merchandise. It soon became clear that its young, relatively affluent constituency wanted more classic, comfortable furniture and was willing to pay higher prices for it. This trend away from sleek and toward warm then seeped into the kitchen, where the demand for painted dinnerware and hand-decorated glassware began to increase. Meanwhile the catalog business continued to thrive. Although the mail-order operation was costly to run (50,000 orders a year were required just to break even), direct mail had the helpful side effect of boosting in-store sales. In fact, sales at the stores generally grew by as much as 20 percent during a month that immediately followed a catalog mailing.

Crate and Barrel doubled its sales over the next few years, passing the $100 million mark in 1989. By this time the chain was 27 stores in size. Los Angeles and Houston had been added to the carefully selected group of markets into which Crate and Barrel had ventured. The company's second furniture store was launched in 1989, this time on home turf, as an extension of its Plaza del Lago store in Wilmette, Illinois. The Wilmette furniture store was an immediate hit, generating $1,000 in sales per square foot, triple what was considered good in an industry that was in the midst of a lengthy slump. The success of the Wilmette furniture operation led to the announcement later that year of a second planned furniture outlet in the Chicago area, this one an expansion of the chain's Oakbrook Center accessories location.

Conservative Growth in the Early 1990s

In 1990, with sales at about $150 million, Crate and Barrel opened a new flagship store on a ritzy stretch of Michigan

Key Dates:

1962: First Crate and Barrel store opens in Chicago, Illinois.
1967: Mail-order service commences.
1977: Crate and Barrel expands beyond Chicago with two stores in Boston.
1981: Crate and Barrel starts selling furniture in addition to housewares.
1989: Sales surpass the $100 million mark.
1990: Company opens flagship store on Michigan Avenue in Chicago.
1995: Crate and Barrel enters New York market.
1998: Company partners with Otto Versand GmbH & Co. of Germany, the biggest mail-order company in the world.
1999: Crate and Barrel web site is launched.

Avenue in Chicago. The building was designed by John Buenz, whose firm (Solomon Cordwell Buenz & Associates) had been designing Crate and Barrel stores since 1976. The exterior of the four-story, 45,000-square-foot structure showed lots of glass and metal, reflecting the clean, modern feel of the standard Crate and Barrel interior. Two floors of the new outlet were to be devoted to furniture. This was a bold move, in light of the fact that furniture had not been sold successfully on this pricey stretch of Michigan Avenue for many years, including failed attempts by such well-known retailers as John M. Smyth and Marshall Field's. That year also marked the closing of the oldest operating Crate and Barrel store, the 5,000-square-foot outlet on Wells that had opened in 1965 just down the street from the original Old Town store. This store was replaced by a new 10,000-square-foot location about a mile away, to be used primarily as an outlet for end-of-season and closeout merchandise.

By the early 1990s, Crate and Barrel had tapped into the Minneapolis and San Diego markets with new store locations. Four new stores were added in 1991, bringing the chain's total to 34. The company had more than 1,000 employees by this time. Merchandise sold at the various Crate and Barrel stores came from at least 25 different countries, although most of the furniture was manufactured in the United States. In 1992, the company entered the Florida market for the first time, opening stores in Palm Beach Gardens and Boca Raton. Sales at Crate and Barrel reached $170 million that year.

Full Speed into the 21st Century

By the mid-1990s Crate and Barrel had about 60 stores scattered across the United States, triple its size since the mid-1980s. The detail-oriented Segal, now in his mid-50s, continued to have his hands in every aspect of Crate and Barrel. In the spring of 1995 Crate and Barrel entered the New York market by unveiling a store on expensive Madison Avenue in Manhattan. The Manhattan store, at about 55,000 square feet, was nearly twice the size of Chicago's Michigan Avenue flagship store and offered furniture and housewares. Crate and Barrel intended to make a splash and boost its image with the Manhattan store. "We wanted to open a store that had some meaning," Segal told *Chief Executive.* "Most retailers are somewhat egomaniacal," Segal continued. "It's because you're competitive by nature—you're constantly trying to make a more important statement." Crate and Barrel followed up the Manhattan opening with two new stores in shopping malls in the greater New York area.

Although 1995 had been a poor year for the retail industry overall, Crate and Barrel saw a four percent increase in sales. In early 1996 the traditionally conservative Crate and Barrel began to step up its expansion efforts and announced plans to double its revenues in the next five years. Segal relinquished the role of president, giving the position to longtime employee Barbara Turf, in order to concentrate on accelerating Crate and Barrel's growth. The chain particularly hoped to expand its furniture business, which contributed about $70 million a year to store sales. Though Crate and Barrel had been selling furniture since 1981, only eight stores offered furniture in early 1996. Plans to open three additional furniture stores in 1996 were in place, however, and the company hoped to expand into uncharted territory as well.

To fuel Crate and Barrel's growth, the company sold a majority interest to Otto Versand GmbH & Co. in early 1998. Based in Hamburg, Germany, privately held Versand was the largest mail-order company in the world, the parent of about 100 companies, all operating autonomously. Crate and Barrel needed outside assistance to remain competitive in the marketplace, which was becoming increasingly filled with vendors similar to Crate and Barrel. The retailer planned to increase its store openings from about four to six new stores a year to about eight to ten, and the company also intended to continue opening larger-scale, flagship stores in major urban markets. Segal explained in the *Wall Street Journal,* "The whole marketplace is more dynamic and aggressive. . . . You have just got to grow, and our only choices were to go public or find a strategic partner." Segal chose not to go public because, as he told *Fortune,* "I've talked to too many people who are public who say that if you don't have to do it—don't!" Segal also explained that the priority for Crate and Barrel was not to be the largest chain but to be the best, and this was not usually a goal adopted by public companies. The deal with Versand allowed Crate and Barrel to implement its plans to increase its presence from 17 U.S. markets to 30 within five years and to grow its catalog operations, which accounted for about eight percent of sales at the time of Versand's purchase. Crate and Barrel also planned to boost its store numbers to 150 within five years. The partnership was also beneficial to Versand, which picked up a popular company with, according to *Fortune,* revenues growing at a rate of 18 percent a year.

With a boost to its finances as a result of the Versand partnership and a healthy economy stimulating retail sales, Crate and Barrel continued its successful path. In the summer of 1998 the company opened a new, 47,000-square-foot home furnishings store in Chicago. The store had many "firsts," including a fresh-flower market and a coffee shop. The home store featured furniture and accessories placed in homelike settings to provide customers with furnishing ideas and decorating possibilities. The new Crate and Barrel continued the chain's recent trend of moving outside of shopping malls; Segal believed convenience was the key to motivating busy shoppers—shoppers too busy to wander around malls. Also in 1998 Crate and Barrel finished construction of a national distribution center in Naperville, Illinois. The company planned to move its catalog operations into the facility in 1999. Crate and Barrel also announced plans to build a new, 110,000-square-foot headquarters in Northbrook. Scheduled to be completed in late 2000, the company said it would move about 200 staff members to the new facility in early 2001. The new headquarters was designed to facilitate the growing staff, which was expected to swell to more than 400 employees over the course of five years.

In 1999 Crate and Barrel's mail-order operations experienced significant growth, thanks in large part to Versand's influence. Versand hired consultants to help Crate and Barrel's mail-order business, and annual catalog sales grew more than 20 percent, from $33 million in 1997 to $40 million in 1998. Crate and Barrel hoped mail-order sales would grow to eventually account for 12 to 15 percent of total sales. In May Crate and Barrel unveiled its e-commerce web site, which allowed online shoppers to make purchases around the clock.

In early 2000 Crate and Barrel planned to open a new store, called CB2, offering basic housewares at lower prices than those found at the increasingly upscale Crate and Barrel stores. CB2 stores, at about half the size of a standard Crate and Barrel, would enable the company to open more stores in more markets, such as college towns. While Crate and Barrel stores had a development period of about three to four years, CB2 stores would require less time and less money to launch. CB2 was also designed to lure customers seeking more affordable items, such as those offered by Crate and Barrel when it first opened its doors in the 1960s.

With revenues increasing steadily and the popularity of Crate and Barrel growing as rapidly as store expansions, the company seemed poised to vault energetically and successfully into the new millennium. More than 80 stores served shoppers across the United States in 1999, and the company announced an interest in expanding internationally in 2000 or 2001. There appeared little reason to doubt that Crate and Barrel could not succeed.

Principal Competitors

Bed Bath & Beyond Inc.; Pier 1 Imports; Williams-Sonoma Inc.'s Pottery Barn; Target Stores; IKEA; Cost Plus Inc.

Further Reading

Barnhart, Bill, and Sallie Gaines, "Fewer Fish in the Barrel?," *Chicago Tribune,* December 5, 1984, sec. 7, p. 1.

Berner, Robert, "Crate & Barrel Sells a Majority Stake to German Mail-Order Firm Versand," *Wall Street Journal,* February 13, 1998, p. B20.

Burton, Jonathan, "King of the House," *Chief Executive,* November 1, 1995, p. 20.

Carroll, Margaret, "Segals Create Barrel of Fun While Selling," *Chicago Tribune,* February 12, 1986, sec. 3, pp. 1–2.

Chandler, Susan, "Crate & Barrel Designs Smaller Store for Shoppers on Budgets," *Chicago Tribune,* September 18, 1999.

——, "New Competition Rearranges the Furniture Business," *Seattle Times,* March 27, 1999, p. E4.

Collins, Lisa, "Crate Expectations Fuel Furniture Push," *Crain's Chicago Business,* April 22, 1990, p. 1.

——, "Crate Gets Respect; A Customer at a Time," *Crain's Chicago Business,* November 26, 1990, p. 20.

Gapp, Paul, "Made to Order," *Chicago Tribune,* October 21, 1990, sec. 13, p. 14.

George, Melissa, "Uberdeal Has Crate Over Otto's Barrel: A Look at Price Segal Will Pay for Euro-Giant's Cash," *Crain's Chicago Business,* February 16, 1998, p. 1.

Greenberg, Herb, "Why Would You Want to Go Public?" *Fortune,* May 24, 1999, p. 324f.

Gruber, William, "Crate and Barrel Plans for Florida and More," *Chicago Tribune*, July 22, 1991, sec. 4, p. 2.

Kahn, Joseph P., "On Display," *Inc.,* November, 1985, pp. 110–22.

McNamara, Michael D., "Crate and Barrel Set to Launch Furniture Store in Chi. Area," *HFD*, April 10, 1989, p. 20.

Miller, Paul, "Following Otto's Lead," *Catalog Age,* March 15, 1999, p. 10.

Morrell, Lisa, "Crate Has Blueprint for Returning to Roots: Going After Low-Cost Housewares Set," *Crain's Chicago Business,* November 16, 1998, p. 4.

Palmeri, Christopher, "Stanley, This Is What I Want to Do," *Forbes*, January 20, 1992, pp. 90–92.

Podmolik, Mary Ellen, "Expansion for Crate & Barrel," *Chicago Sun-Times,* February 1, 1996, p. 39.

Schmitt, Anne, "Crate and Barrel Plans New Northbrook Headquarters," *Chicago Daily Herald,* November 24, 1998, p. 1.

Strangenes, Sharon, "The Gambler," *Chicago Tribune,* August 26, 1990, sec. 15, p. 1.

Tisch, Carol, "Crate & Barrel Plans Home Store Rollout; Opens Prototype for Expanded Format in Chicago," *HFN The Weekly Newspaper for the Home Furnishing Network,* June 15, 1998, p. 1.

—Robert R. Jacobson
—updated by Mariko Fujinaka

Federated
DEPARTMENT STORES, INC.

Federated Department Stores, Inc.

7 West 7th Street
Cincinnati, Ohio 45202
U.S.A.
Telephone: (513) 579-7000
Fax: (513) 579-7555
Web site: http://www.federated-fds.com

Public Company
Incorporated: 1929
Employees: 118,800
Sales: $15.83 billion (1998)
Stock Exchanges: New York
Ticker Symbol: FD
NAIC: 45211 Department Stores; 45411 Electronic Shopping and Mail-Order Houses

With over 400 department stores in 33 states and a burgeoning direct-to-customer retail business, Federated Department Stores, Inc. is one of the largest retail store operators in the nation. Its department store divisions include some of the most venerable names in the industry: Macy's East, Macy's West, Rich's/Lazarus/Goldsmith's, Bloomingdale's, Burdines, The Bon Marché, and Stern's. Recognizing the success of catalogue retailers and Internet merchants, Federated has more recently aimed to build a competitive direct-to-consumer division. After launching Macys.Com and Macy's By Mail, Federated subsequently acquired Fingerhut Companies, Inc., a leader in catalogue and e-commerce.

Prosperity During the 1930s

Federated Department Stores, Inc. was incorporated in Columbus, Ohio, in 1929 as a holding company for F&R Lazarus & Company, its subsidiary Shillito's, and Abraham & Straus department stores. The Federated group was formed and led by Fred Lazarus, Jr., whose eponymous company was the dominant retail store in Columbus. F&R Lazarus was created by Fred's grandfather, Simon. The elder Lazarus, a Jewish refugee who fled religious persecution in Germany, founded the men's clothing store in 1851. Shillito's, a Cincinnati-based store acquired by F&R Lazarus in 1928, was founded in 1830. While Shillito's was the oldest store west of the Allegheny Mountains, it ranked only fourth among Cincinnati stores at the time it was purchased by Lazarus. Shillito's sales grew by over 50 percent during its first year under the management of the Lazarus family, and within a decade, the store had regained the top spot in its urban market. The other founding member of Federated, Abraham & Straus (A&S), was founded in 1865 in Brooklyn, New York. It would grow to become the group's sales and profits leader by the mid-20th century.

Bloomingdale's joined the Federated group in 1930, a year after Federated was organized. This revered name in retail had been founded in 1872 by Lyman and Joseph Bloomingdale on New York's east side. Although the brothers had chosen an area of the city that was underdeveloped at the time, Bloomingdale's reputation for carrying unique merchandise brought more and more patrons to the store. The department store carried European imports as early as 1886 and quickly became a leader in home furnishings.

During the 1930s, Fred Lazarus, Jr., earned a reputation for innovation that made his family "the first name in retail," according to a 1961 *Forbes* article. In the late 1920s, "Mr. Fred" instituted an administrative division of labor that placed department managers in charge of buying and selling all of the merchandise in their particular department. This brought a spirit of entrepreneurship to the individual departments in each store. In 1934, Lazarus revolutionized retail clothing sales when he adopted a French merchandising technique in which apparel was arranged according to size, rather than by color, price, or brand. The system became an industry standard. In 1939, Mr. Fred was a key figure in convincing President Roosevelt to move the Thanksgiving holiday to the fourth Thursday of November. The calendar change extended the Christmas shopping season, giving retailers more time to sell at their busiest time of year.

Federated stores helped their customers during the Great Depression by extending credit and establishing a reputation for community involvement in times of crisis. The Federated organization helped support its divisions throughout the Great Depression by sharing their risks and benefits. The loosely defined

Company Perspectives:

Federated clearly recognizes that the customer is paramount, and that all actions and strategies must be directed toward providing an enhanced merchandise offering and better service to targeted customers through dynamic department stores and direct-to-customer retail formats. Aggressive implementation of the company's strategies, as well as careful and thorough planning, will provide Federated's department stores with an important competitive edge. Federated is committed to open and honest communications with employees, shareholders, vendors, customers, analysts, and the news media. The company seeks to be proactive in sharing information and in keeping these key stakeholder groups up-to-date on important and material developments. At Federated Department Stores our greatest strength lies in the skill, judgment, and talent of our people. Every day a production of enormous magnitude takes place on our selling floors and behind the scenes, where our people bring the company's strategic goals to life. Our priority on attracting, retaining, and growing the most talented people in the retail industry has been and will continue to be our greatest advantage.

coalition worked so well that, by the end of World War II, the holding company was making more money than it could profitably reinvest in existing stores.

Federated's Postwar Expansion

By the end of the war, Federated had reached a turning point. Faced with increasingly fierce competition from suburban shopping centers, the company had to decide whether to dissolve itself or form a central organization geared towards expansion. Chairperson Fred Lazarus, Jr., whose chain had contributed substantially to the success of Federated, pushed for a stronger organization, which he achieved in June 1945. Federated's main office was moved to Cincinnati, and the central management team worked to capture a leading role in the retail revolution of the postwar era. Although the holding company's leadership took a more aggressive role in corporate administration after 1945, divisional autonomy remained a hallmark of the Federated organization for decades.

Federated ''boomed'' along with the postwar population of the 1950s through expansion and acquisition. In 1956, Burdines, of Miami, became a division of Federated through an exchange of common stock. Rikes' and Goldsmith's, the largest department stores in Dayton, Ohio, and Memphis, Tennessee, respectively, were purchased in 1959. Over the course of the decade, sales at Federated's 50 main stores and 32 branches increased over 100 percent, and the group became the United States' largest and most profitable department store company. Its members included the most prestigious department store chains in almost any given metropolitan area: Foley's of Houston, Sanger's in Dallas, and Filene's of Boston. The haute couture reputation of Federated's stores carried a high price, which translated into the high profit margins that accounted for much of the corporation's success.

Growth continued in the 1960s: by mid-decade, Federated's annual sales topped the $1 billion mark. Sales increased 250 percent from 1960 to 1970, reaching $2 billion by 1970. Ralph Lazarus succeeded his father, Fred Lazarus, Jr., as chair and chief executive officer of Federated in 1967. He had worked his way up through the corporate ranks, from salesperson to general merchandise manager, vice-president for publicity, executive vice-president, and finally president by 1957. In 1965, Federated purchased Bullock's and I. Magnin, two upscale department stores based in California. As a result of the antitrust concerns this acquisition generated, Federated was forced to enter into a consent decree with the Federal Trade Commission that prohibited the company from acquiring any more department stores until 1970.

Venturing into New Territory

Since Federated's expansion by acquisition was limited, Ralph Lazarus led Federated into the supermarket industry in 1968 with the purchase of Ralph's Industries, a West Coast supermarket chain that served upper-income markets. The chain had 65 stores that were accounting for ten percent of Federated's total sales by the end of the decade. Federated also entered the mass merchandising segment during the 1960s, with the creation of Gold Circle discount stores in 1968. The small Gold Circle chain totaled five stores in Columbus and Dayton at the end of the decade.

However, Federated's success was not uninterrupted. In 1971, the group sold its Fedway chain to a competitor, Dillard Department Stores, for $6 million in cash. Fedway had been created in 1951 to take advantage of southward population shifts. Its stores represented a new direction for Federated, a move into the small, but burgeoning markets of the ''sunbelt'': Texas, Arizona, and southern California. Fedway peaked in the mid-1960s with 11 stores and over $30 million in annual sales. After that point, the chain was overcome by larger, more experienced retailers including Sears & Roebuck, Montgomery Ward, and J.C. Penney. By the time it was liquidated, Fedway's sales volume had dwindled to $13 million, and the chain had shrunk to six stores.

Acquisitions of the 1970s

The Federated chain continued to expand in the 1970s. Net income increased from $91.1 million in 1970 to $277.7 million in 1979, and sales nearly tripled during that time to $6.3 billion. The growth was stimulated by a $2.2 billion acquisition spree that almost doubled the group's number of stores to over 350 units. This growth was doubly astonishing in light of punishing recessions that cycled throughout the decade. Part of Federated's enduring success stemmed from the fact that most of its upper-class clientele was not as badly affected by economic downturns as working class shoppers.

The group made a pivotal acquisition in 1976 when the purchase of Rich's Inc. gave it a foothold in southeastern retail. The $157 million stock swap gave Federated control of the 109-year-old, Atlanta-based institution with its 11 department stores, three Rich's II boutiques, and 11 Richway discount stores in Atlanta, Birmingham, Alabama, and Charlotte, North

Key Dates:

1851: F&R Lazarus men's clothing store is founded by Fred Lazarus.
1929: Federated Department stores is launched as a holding company for F&R Lazarus, Shillito's, and Abraham & Strauss department stores.
1930: Bloomingdale's enters the Federated group.
1956: Federated acquires Burdines department stores.
1988: Federated is acquired by Campeau Corporation.
1989: Campeau files for bankruptcy and a major reorganization ensues.
1992: Federated emerges from bankruptcy protection.
1994: Federated acquires R.H. Macy & Co.
1995: Federated acquires Broadway Stores, Inc.
1999: Federated acquires Fingerhut Companies, Inc.

Carolina. From this installed base, Federated hoped to expand its operations throughout the South.

Federated also expanded its established chains more aggressively. In 1976, Bloomingdale's opened its first full-line store outside the New York market, in a suburb of Washington, D.C. Bullock's, I. Magnin, Burdine's, and other divisions were also planning regional and cross-country branches far from their traditional metropolitan markets. For example, Bullock's, based in Los Angeles, moved into Arizona in 1977. I. Magnin planned to add five new stores and go national between 1976 and 1980. Filene's, a Boston store, moved into New Hampshire, and Cincinnati-based Shillito's had three stores in Kentucky by 1977. New stores were built 20 percent smaller than usual to squeeze more profits from less space. Federated's tradition of divisional autonomy gave way to more centralized supervision.

Unsuccessful Efforts in the 1970s and 1980s

But Federated's growth was countered by troubled divisions throughout the 1970s. In the early years of the decade, Federated's biggest unit and dollar producer, the original Abraham & Straus store in Brooklyn, pulled the entire A&S division down. Some of the division's problems were out of its control, like a demographic shift that eroded its traditionally affluent customer base. As middle-class Brooklyners escaped to the suburbs, they were replaced by an impoverished population with little interest in A&S's pricey merchandise. Many of the new residents were also drawn to a large regional mall located just a few miles away. Furthermore, the chain's management had neglected its 100-year-old, 1.5 million-square-foot Brooklyn store. By 1973, both sales and profits at A&S had leveled off, and two years later, A&S's pretax profits slid a disturbing 45 percent. The chain launched a comprehensive remodeling effort in an attempt to recapture its middle-income shoppers.

Ralph's, the 98-unit Los Angeles-based supermarket chain, faltered throughout most of the decade as well, as management made a lukewarm commitment to that competitive industry. Although Ralph's was recognized as one of the country's most productive, enterprising food stores, it fell victim to costly price wars in California in 1976 and 1977. The grocery chain eventually withdrew to its home region, closing 18 stores after failing in northern California.

Federated's long-running attempts to diversify into mass merchandising, which began in the 1960s, reaped uninspiring results in the 1970s. Gold Circle, which was projected to grow into a 200-unit upscale discounter, had only 42 units by 1981. It had run into trouble after it expanded into California with seven stores in 1976 and 1977. Prior to the expansion, the chain had been limited to Cleveland, Columbus, Cincinnati, and Rochester, New York. High startup costs and no profits in the western units disappointed Federated officials, who had underestimated the competition that came from Kmart and Target. By the end of the decade, Gold Circle was slated to retreat from the California market entirely.

Two industry trends also threatened Federated's dominant position in retail. Specialty stores started to broaden their appeal, attracting increasingly more upscale shoppers. At the same time, Sears, J.C. Penney, and other mass merchandisers were enhancing their stores to attract more affluent shoppers. Federated felt the squeeze between these two forces: the company's 1979 profits stayed level at $179.9 million, even though sales had increased ten percent to $5.4 billion.

When Howard Goldfeder was elevated from president to CEO, succeeding Ralph Lazarus in 1981, he set demanding return-on-investment quotas as a prerequisite for further expansion. Furthermore, he instituted seven new strategies to induce Federated to retake its position as a retail innovator. These included: enlarging market share through more aggressive promotions and deeper inventories; renovating key units in major markets; expanding department stores into the high-growth sunbelt; cultivating new divisions; ensuring lower management turnover; repositioning and expanding Ralph's supermarkets; and disposing of or merging less profitable units.

Nevertheless, some industry analysts criticized Federated, and especially Goldfeder, for attempting to dominate too many segments of the retail industry. While rivals Dayton-Hudson and R.H. Macy's limited their focus to either mass merchandising or upscale retail, Federated spread its investments and profit margins among a wide range of concepts. As the decade wore on, Federated's return-on-equity stagnated, and its stock price dwindled. By the late 1980s, the company was ripe for a hostile takeover; it was not strong enough to command a high stock price, yet it was not weak enough to be beyond help.

Tough Times for Federated

In 1988 Federated was acquired by Campeau Corporation. Subsequently, Federated's Bullock's and I. Magnin divisions were sold to competitor R.H. Macy, and the Foley's and Filene's divisions were sold to other retailers. Furthermore, the headquarters of Allied Stores Corporation was moved from New York to Cincinnati to be consolidated with Federated. Allied had been founded in 1935 to succeed Hahn Department Stores, Inc., a holding company that managed Boston's Jordan Marsh stores, among others. Allied had been instrumental in the establishment of the United States' first regional shopping center in 1950, and had acquired the Stern Brothers and Block's department stores over the course of its history.

Campeau Corporation's Robert Campeau had acquired Allied for $3.6 billion in a 1986 hostile, debt-financed takeover. Then he borrowed $6.5 billion—97 percent of the purchase price—to buy Federated in 1988. Campeau had scheduled his 1989 debt payments according to profit projections of $740 million. However, Federated only made $372 million that year, and Campeau's creditors clamored for the $627 million that was due them. On January 15, Federated and Allied filed the second largest nonbank bankruptcy on record and entered the largest, most complex restructuring in the retail trade.

During the course of the two-year reorganization, Federated and Allied merged and cut all ties with Campeau Corporation. More than 40 stores were liquidated. Federated traded $8.2 billion in debt for $850 million in cash, plus $2.8 billion in new debt and 92 million shares of new stock valued at $2.3 billion. Over $2 billion of the debt was forgiven, but the new Federated was still stuck with $3.5 billion of debt on its balance sheet. The new entity boasted 220 department stores in 26 states and annual sales of about $7 billion. A new CEO, Allen Questrom, led the reorganization. He had been instrumental in the turnaround of Federated's troubled Rich's division in the 1980s and was hailed as one of the top leaders in retailing during the 1990s.

Together with Federated President James A. Zimmerman, Questrom instituted cost-cutting measures that benefited Federated and its customers in the first months after the reorganization. SABRE, a data processing system, and FACS, the credit services operation, helped centralize sales, credit, and inventory tracking while promoting economies of scale. The merger of the background operations of Abraham & Straus and Jordan Marsh saved Federated $25 million per year without disrupting either chain's image. Part of the savings realized by these measures was passed on to the choosier shopper of the 1990s. Some industry observers cited Questrom's commitment to GMROI (gross margin return on investment), a new, but reliable performance measurement for department stores, as another reason for high confidence in the new Federated.

Federated's Resurgence in the 1990s

Buoyed by these improved perceptions of the company, Federated made one of Wall Street's largest initial public offerings of 1992 within months of emerging from bankruptcy. The group had planned to offer 40 million shares and use the proceeds to prepay a chunk of its long-term debt, but was pleasantly surprised when applications for 50 million shares poured in, enabling the company to generate more than $500 million. In 1992, Federated prepaid almost $1 billion of its debt. During the first six months of 1993, the company was able to retire $355 million of its most expensive bonded debt. The interest savings permitted Federated to increase its 1993–96 budget for store renovations and openings by $461 million to $1.2 billion.

In 1994, Federated embarked on a series of acquisitions. Consolidation offered Federated a number of benefits as the department store industry encountered intense competition from both discount merchandisers such as Wal-Mart and specialty retailers like The Gap. "There are certain economies of scale that size gives you," a retail analyst explained to the *Tribune Review*. By purchasing the Joseph Horne Co. of Pittsburgh in 1994, Federated added ten Pennsylvania stores to its Lazarus division. Federated made a more substantial acquisition in December 1994, when it bought erstwhile rival R.H. Macy & Co. With this development, Federated became the largest department store company in the United States. But the company was not finished. In 1995, Federated purchased the 82-store Broadway Stores, Inc., which included Broadway, Emporium, and Weinstock's department stores. The Broadway acquisition, given that chain's strength on the West Coast, afforded Federated with much desired access to that part of the country—particularly the markets of populous and prosperous California.

Smoothly incorporating these diverse additions into the Federated fold presented its own challenges. As the *Commercial Appeal* explained, for Federated to benefit from its buying spree, it had to "trim costs and use its enormous buying clout to pare expenses and boost earnings." In an effort to integrate Macy's operations with its own, Federated launched its Federated Logistics Division in 1994, in an effort to coordinate distribution facilities and functions in the United States. Federated then consolidated its A&S/Jordan Marsh division into Macy's East—creating a single 89-store division stretching across 15 eastern states. On the opposite side of the country, Federated folded its Bullock's stores into a new Macy's West division. Shortly thereafter, Federated dissolved the I. Magnin chain, converting some of the 13 I. Magnin stores into Macy's or Bullock's, and selling off the rest. In 1995, Macy's followed suit by consolidating Rich's/Goldsmith's and Lazarus into a single operating unit—Rich's/Lazarus's/Goldsmith's. After acquiring the Broadway Stores empire, Federated converted 56 of those stores to the Macy's nameplate. Five others were slated to become Bloomingdale's, which represented the first time that upscale department store had ventured into California. In 1996, the Jordan Marsh stores in the Northeast (already administered under the Macy's East division) were renamed Macy's.

Despite its bevy of new stores, Federated still needed to concentrate on boosting sales. In an effort to distinguish its stores from those of its competitors, Federated focused on developing its own brands of clothing and other merchandise, including Alfani, I.N.C., Charter Club, and Tools of the Trade. Since private brands essentially cut out all middlemen, Federated was able to generate higher profit margins on these in-house lines. Moreover, private labels could draw customers to Federated stores. According to Gannett News Service, labels such as Charter Club "built customer loyalty because they can only come back to [the store] for that brand." Federated rapidly expanded its Federated Merchandising Group, which was responsible for designing, manufacturing, and marketing all its private labels. At the same time, Federated bolstered the presence of its unique brands by creating catchy vendor shops within its department stores. In 1997 alone, Federated built over 680 of these sub-units, which served to leverage its private labels.

While Federated worked to lure customers into its diverse department stores, the company also acknowledged that commerce was evolving, as Internet sales rose exponentially each year. Analysts forecast that by 2003, total Internet sales would exceed $108 billion. Like its competitors, Federated was "faced with a growing force of shoppers who opt to point and click to make their purchases from home rather than step inside a store," as the *Newark Star-Ledger* noted. Moreover, younger consumers—who were in the process of building life-long loyalties to stores—were more likely to embrace Internet shopping. To adapt to these tectonic shifts, Federated launched Macys.Com in 1996. This online retail venue allowed Internet-savvy consumers to purchase many of the same items found in Macy's department stores. In 1998, Federated also introduced Macy's By Mail, a catalogue business.

James M. Zimmerman—who had replaced Allen Questrom as Federated's chairman and chief executive officer in 1997—led the company to acquire Fingerhut Companies, Inc. for $1.5 billion in 1999. Federated planned to exploit Fingerhut's considerable expertise in direct-to-customer and Internet retailing. In addition to its position as the second largest catalogue retailer in the United States, Fingerhut owned Arizona Mail Order (a catalogue apparel retailer), Bedford Fair Industries, Inc. (a women's apparel catalogue retailer), Figi's (a food and gift catalog company), and Popular Club (a membership-based cataloguer of general merchandise). Because Fingerhut had pioneered database marketing—and still maintained information on 30 million customers—Federated hoped to use its acquisition as a springboard into the realm of direct-to-customer retail. As the *Cincinnati Courier* noted, ''Fingerhut provide[d] a platform for [Federated] to learn the e-commerce side of the business.''

Federated's numerous acquisitions, consolidations, and strategy shifts proved tremendously successful. Sales increased from $8.31 billion in 1994 to $15.83 billion in 1998. As consumer confidence levels surged to a 30-year high in 1999, Federated's sales in both its department stores and its direct-to-consumer operations were brisk.

Principal Subsidiaries

Fingerhut Companies, Inc.; Arizona Mail Order Inc.; Old Pueblo Traders; Figi's Inc.; FreeShop.com.

Principal Divisions

Macy's East; Macy's West; Rich's/Lazarus/Goldsmith's; Bloomingdale's By Mail, Ltd.; Burdines; The Bon Marché; Stern's; Federated Logistics and Operations; Federated Merchandising Group; Federated Systems Group; Financial and Credit Services; Federated Direct.

Principal Competitors

The May Department Store Company; Neiman Marcus, Inc.; Saks Incorporated; Dayton-Hudson Corporation; Nordstrom, Inc.; Dillard's, Inc.

Further Reading

''Bloomingdale's Celebrates a Century,'' *Stores,* November 1972, p. 10.

Chakravarty, Subrata N., ''Federated Chooses Not to Choose,'' *Forbes,* April 8, 1985, pp. 82, 86–87.

Churchill, Mike, ''Department Store Chain Placed on the Selling Block,'' *Tribune Review,* April 20, 1994.

Cobleign, Ira U., ''Federated Department Stores, Inc.'' *Commercial and Financial Chronicle,* July 31, 1969, p. 393.

''Earnings: Wal-Mart Profits Up; Macy Buy Weakens Federated,'' *Commercial Appeal,* March 1, 1995.

''Fadeout for Fedway,'' *Dun's,* October 1971, p. 60.

''Federated: Blue Chip Retailer,'' *Financial World,* March 22, 1972, p. 6.

''Federated's Push to Improve Profitability,'' *Business Week,* July 6, 1981, pp. 44–46.

''Federated: The Most Happy Retailer Grows Faster and Better,'' *Business Week,* October 18, 1976, pp. 74–77, 80.

Feinberg, Phyllis, ''Federated Finesses Recession,'' *Commercial and Financial Chronicle,* October 27, 1957, pp. 1, 3.

''The First Family of Retailing,'' *Forbes,* March 15, 1961, pp. 19–22.

Frazier, Mya, ''Federated's James Zimmerman Knows the Web Holds Promise, But Not at the Expense of Today,'' *Cincinnati Courier,* October 18, 1999.

Jereski, Laura, ''Damn the Torpedoes,'' *Forbes,* June 10, 1991, p. 66.

Klokis, Holly, ''Retailing's Grande Dame: Cloaked in New Strategies,'' *Chain Store Age Executive,* March 1985, pp. 18–20.

Loomis, Carol J., ''The Biggest, Looniest Deal Ever,'' *Fortune,* June 18, 1990, pp. 48–72.

Moin, David, ''Acquisitions Digested, Federated Takes Aim at Top Spot in Profits,'' *Women's Wear Daily,* May 19, 1997.

Nolan, John, ''Macy's Parent Gets a Finger on the E-Tail Pulse,'' *Newark Star-Ledger,* February 12, 1999.

''Optimism at Federated,'' *New York Times,* May 24, 1993, p. D3.

Power, Gavin, ''Federated Will Dump the Emporium Name,'' *San Francisco Chronicle,* August 16, 1995.

Quick, Rebecca, ''Federated Department Stores Net Rises 45 %,'' *Wall Street Journal,* May 13, 1999.

——, ''Federated Department Stores Profit Jumps 27 % As Shopping Spree Goes On,'' *Wall Street Journal,* August 12, 1999.

''Ralph Lazarus of Federated,'' *Stores,* January 1974, pp. 2–3.

Reda, Susan, ''Staying in Tune: Allen Questrom, Chairman and CEO, Federated Dept. Stores,'' *Stores,* September 1992, pp. 18–24.

Rosenberg, Hillary, ''Life Among the Ruins,'' *Institutional Investor,* June 1990, pp. 92–94+.

Silverman, Edward, ''Shareholders OK Federated Merger Deal,'' *Newsday,* November 30, 1994.

''A Southern Bastion Falls to Federated,'' *Business Week,* July 26, 1976, pp. 43–44.

''This Peacock Won't Be Tomorrow's Feather Duster,'' *Forbes,* June 15, 1957, pp. 24–33.

''Where 'Beautiful People' Find Fashion,'' *Business Week,* September 2, 1972, pp. 44, 45.

Zinn, Laura, and Michele Galen, ''Short Chapter, Happy Ending,'' *Business Week,* February 10, 1992, pp. 126–27.

—April S. Dougal
—updated by Rebecca Stanfel

Fieldcrest Cannon, Inc.

Pillowtex Corporation
4111 Mint Way
Dallas, Texas 75237
U.S.A.
Telephone: (214) 333-3225
Fax: (214) 333-6016
Web site: http://www.pillowtex.com

Brand Name and Assets Acquired by Pillowtex Corporation
Incorporated: 1953 as Fieldcrest Mills, Inc.
Dissolved: 1997
Final Sales: $1.1 billion (1996)
NAIC: 31321 Broadwoven Fabric Mills; 314129 Other Household Textile Product Mills

Prior to its acquisition by Pillowtex Corporation in 1997, Fieldcrest Cannon, Inc. was a leading producer of towels, bed sheets, bath accessories, bath rugs, and furniture coverings. Formed by the union of Fieldcrest Mills and Cannon Mills in 1986, the giant home textile company sold its products under an array of brand names, including Cannon, Fieldcrest, Monticello, Royal Velvet, St. Mary's, and Caldwell. After enduring a difficult period during the early 1990s, Fieldcrest Cannon regrouped and made several important acquisitions. However, in 1996, the company was over-extended and sold its blanket-manufacturing operations to Dallas-based Pillowtex, which then acquired the remainder of Fieldcrest Cannon the following year. Although Fieldcrest Cannon was wholly subsumed into Pillowtex—and ceased to exist as a corporate entity thereafter—Pillowtex remained committed to maintaining Fieldcrest Cannon's strong brand names.

The History of Fieldcrest Mills

The early histories of both Fieldcrest Mills and Cannon Mills center on determined industrialists. Fieldcrest started with aspiring empire-builder, Benjamin Franklin Mebane, who launched an ambitious plan to open one mill a year on and around 600 acres of land he had purchased in Spray, North Carolina, in 1893. By 1905 he owned six mills in the area, renamed Eden (after a surveyor's comment that it resembled the garden of Eden). Mebane had gone to Chicago retailer Marshall Field for help in financing his plan, and after Mebane started having trouble repaying his debt, Field decided to take over. By 1910 Field had gained voting control of Mebane's Spray Water Power & Land Co. and had installed new managers; by 1912 the takeover was complete and the company had become a subsidiary of Marshall Field & Co. Field invested in improvements and expansion projects for the subsidiary, which was renamed the Thread Mills Company. In 1916 the company acquired a 1,600-acre site near Martinsville, Virginia, for a huck (flat weave) and terry towel plant and employee housing; the facility in the newly created community of Fieldale, started operation in 1919. It would continue operating into the 1990s.

In 1935 the mills were reorganized. Previously part of Marshall Field's wholesale division, they became part of the manufacturing division, and sales departments distributed their products nationally at both wholesale and retail levels.

During World War II shortages hampered the mills' ability to meet consumer demand. Nevertheless, they did produce a variety of goods for the armed services, including silk cartridge cloth, camouflage net, parachute cloth, and mosquito netting. In 1947 the division's name was changed to Fieldcrest Mills, to clearly identify them with the nationally advertised products that it manufactured.

By 1953 Marshall Field & Co. was eager to expand its stores, especially in the emerging suburban landscape. To raise enough capital, the company sold its mill operations (including its carpet mills, which manufactured the well-respected Karastan brand of carpets) to Amoskeag Co. Fieldcrest Mills, Inc., was incorporated in September of that year; its sales were $39 million.

Amoskeag Co., an investment trust based in Boston, also owned the Bangor & Aroostoock Railroad in Maine and various real estate and mining interests. Amoskeag, in turn, was controlled by the Dumaine trust, a family trust organized by F.C. Dumaine, Sr., a textile mill baron who had become the head of Amoskeag in 1905. Upon his death in 1951 stewardship

Key Dates:

1888: Cannon Mills is founded.
1898: Benjamin Franklin Mebane builds mills in North Carolina.
1910: Thread Mills Co. (unit of Marshall Field) takes over Mebane's operation.
1935: Thread Mills renamed Fieldcrest Mills.
1953: Fieldcrest is sold to Amoskeag Company.
1962: Fieldcrest becomes a public company.
1986: Fieldcrest Mills acquires Cannon Mills; company renamed Fieldcrest Cannon.
1993: Unsolicited buyout offer from Springs Industries threatens Fieldcrest Cannon.
1994: Fieldcrest Cannon acquires Amoskeag.
1997: Fieldcrest Cannon is acquired by Pillowtex Corporation.

for the trust passed to his son F.C. Dumaine, Jr., who had started working for Amoskeag in 1922. By 1961 sales had reached $77 million, and the following year Fieldcrest became a publicly owned company, with Amoskeag holding about 40 percent of the stock. In 1967 Fieldcrest was listed on the New York Stock Exchange.

Fieldcrest grew through the mid-1960s via a series of acquisitions and improvements, and by 1967 those costs totaled $82.3 million. At that time the Fieldcrest division, which produced blankets, bedspreads, sheets, and towels, comprised 65 percent of the company's sales, while the Karastan division, which produced Karastan and Laurelcrest carpets, contributed 20 percent. Sales that year were $175.3 million.

Fieldcrest produced goods under its own name as well as private labels, with customers Sears, Roebuck & Co. and J.C. Penney accounting for almost 15 percent of total sales. Fieldcrest's strength came from strong showing of its medium- and upper-priced lines, which made up almost two-thirds of total sales. These lines, carrying the Fieldcrest label, appeared primarily in department stores; its Royal Velvet towels, introduced in 1954, were known for their luxury. The lower priced St. Marys brand was sold through mass merchandisers.

The 20th anniversary of Fieldcrest Mills, Inc., in 1973, saw sales reach $290 million and annual growth since 1961. By 1977 volume had grown to $417 million. Profits had generally followed this upward trend as well. During this time, Fieldcrest tried to meet the growing consumer demand for more fashionable styles for bed and bath products, entering the "designer" sweepstakes. In 1976 it introduced its first designer line, the Halston collection, and the following year a Geoffrey Beene line was introduced, as well as the Carleton Varney line for the St Marys brand. The market responded favorably, and Fieldcrest saw a 43 percent gain in its bed and bath products in 1976–77. Carpet sales also increased, due to a boom in housing as well as an aggressive promotional program and a successful entry in the contract carpeting market. Halston rugs were introduced in 1977.

That year the company formed a 50 percent joint venture with the Bank of Ireland and P.J. Carroll & Co. Ltd.—Fieldcrest Ireland, Ltd.—to build and operate a Fieldcrest towel plant in Kelkenney, Ireland, in an attempt to penetrate the European market.

Profits crested at $24.8 million on sales of $517.7 million in 1979. Thereafter profits began to slide, falling to $10.4 million in 1982 on sales of $492 million. The recession had affected the company's performance, but other mills proved able to sustain earnings during that period. Market analysts pointed to ill-conceived and expensive expansion attempts; Fieldcrest had spent $100 million expanding or updating its facilities between 1978 and 1981. Furthermore, Fieldcrest had responded to a surge in blanket sales in 1977 and 1978 due to unusually cold winters and high energy costs by modernizing its blanket mill in Eden for $40 million, but blanket sales had begun declining after 1978. The plant in Ireland closed in 1982 after high inflation in that country priced the towels out of the European market, and Fieldcrest lost $8 million.

Most troubling for Fieldcrest were attempts by other manufacturers to encroach upon its ensconced and lucrative position at the head of the premium towel market. Fieldcrest had decided aggressively to expand its St. Marys line, and this triggered attempts by J.P. Stevens, West Point-Pepperell, and most notably Cannon Mills to move into the upper end of the market as well. Cannon added a Royal Touch towel to its Royal Family line that directly competed with Fieldcrest's Royal Velvet. Fieldcrest found itself defending its territory at the top, where the profits were highest, while trying to advance farther at the other end of the market. As the recession took hold, rounds of discounting began and inventory was reduced.

Amoskeag Co., whose earnings were largely sustained by those of Fieldcrest, grew concerned, and in 1982 the chief executive of Amoskeag, Joseph Ely II, was brought in to head Fieldcrest, for which he had served as a board member since 1976. In December of that year, Fieldcrest wrote off its half of a Canadian joint venture, Crossley Karastan Carpet Mills, Ltd., which had lost $1.2 million in 1981.

Soon thereafter, Fieldcrest shifted its marketing strategy. Instead of trying to increase profits through high volume of its lower end products, it sought to broaden its range of items built around the Fieldcrest name. By reemphasizing the Fieldcrest lines, which it had neglected to update while the effort had been on the designer lines, the company chose to retain profits and avoid price cuts at the expense of expanding its market share. Fieldcrest was the only towelmaker that continued to use its name solely with its premium products; Cannon Mills, for example, sewed its name into all of its towels, regardless of the price category. Fieldcrest promised department stores carrying its line that they had the protected use of its name, thereby hoping to seal their loyalty and expand its carriage trade. Fieldcrest also hoped to grow its private-brand business, of which Sears was its biggest customer, contributing $75 million in sales in 1983.

In 1986 Fieldcrest took the bold step of acquiring Cannon Mills, which it purchased for $321 million. With that acquisition, Fieldcrest, which became Fieldcrest Cannon, Inc., gained 12,900 employees, 12 plants, and 14 sales offices, thus doubling its size and becoming the country's fifth largest publicly held textile company.

The History of Cannon Mills, Co.

Towards the end of the 19th century, James William Cannon, a 35-year old partner and manager of a general store, became intrigued with the textile business and decided to open a cotton mill. He raised $75,000 and built a mill in Concord, North Carolina, which started business in 1887 as the Cannon Manufacturing Company. Cannon also managed the plant. He evidently brought some knowledge of the retail business with him when he decided to put his name on the fabric that his mill manufactured, reasoning that sales could only increase if customers could ask for a product by name. The popularity of ''Cannon cloth'' spread throughout the south, and thus the Cannon retailing philosophy was born.

Realizing that the South had no towel manufacturing plants, Cannon opened a mill that produced huck towels in 1894 and another mill that made terry towels four years later. In 1906 Cannon bought a 600-acre parcel of land, previously a cotton plantation, and started developing the community that became Kannapolis. The mills there started operation in 1908 and were able to produce more towels than any other group of mills, due in part to automatic terry looms. The mills also produced a variety of ''gray goods'' such as cotton cloth and woman's hosiery.

By 1916 Cannon had decided to try to market as well as manufacture his products, and so a new sales force, Cannon Mills, Inc., was established in New York City. James Cannon died in 1921 at which time he controlled 12 mills with over 15,000 employees and an estimated $40 million in annual sales. Kannapolis was considered a ''model mill city,'' and its mills could turn out 300,000 towels daily. His youngest son, Charles Cannon, who had quit college at the age of 19 to start work in his father's mills and had become a vice-president at the age of 23, became the company's president.

Charles ''Mr. Charlie'' Cannon ran the company for the next 50 years. Under his stewardship, Cannon Mills maintained its dominant position in the U.S. towel market, regularly producing half of all towels purchased. It also carried one-fifth of the sheeting business. Much of Cannon Mills' success was due to the very high efficiency of its mills, which were virtually all within a 20-mile radius of one another, affording close supervision; only a few steps separated the back door of the CEO's office from Plant No. 1. The company's production was vertically integrated, from the spinning of the cotton to the finished product.

In 1923 Cannon had the Cannon name sewn into all of its towels, becoming the first company to do so. By unabashedly identifying with what had been seen as purely a ''commodity'' product, Cannon was to develop an intense brand loyalty among consumers, who came to identify the Cannon name with affordability and quality. Cannon, unlike other mills, used its name on its top-of-the line goods as well as its more affordably priced items. Most of Cannon Mills' products were distributed through mass merchandisers.

Cannon's tenure was marked by an entrenched fiscal conservatism. He made no effort to diversify, eschewing the idea of growth for growth's sake. While Cannon was in control, the company did not acquire any long-term debt. Furthermore, Cannon's reign over Kannapolis—which remained unincorporated—also reflected his paternalistic style. Kannapolis had no mayor, town council, or legal charter. Cannon Mills paid for the community's police and fire services and was responsible for its water and sewerage system, trash collection, and street maintenance. It also owned approximately 1,600 houses that were rented to mill employees. Moreover, Cannon owned virtually all the property within the one-square-mile business district. Later, in the 1930s, Charlie Cannon returned from a business trip to Williamsburg so impressed by its colonial architecture that he had facades for the business district constructed to mimic their colonial style, and downtown Kannapolis was thus transformed into a Georgian village. A massive sign on the edge of town, lighted by 1,800 bulbs and visible from the highway and the railroad, proclaimed that Cannon Mills was the ''World's Largest Manufacturer of Towels.'' (After World War II, the sign was altered to read ''Leading Manufacturer of Towels'' and updated with neon.)

In 1927 Charlie Cannon brought his company to the New York Stock Exchange, becoming the first southern mill owner to do so. The following year he consolidated the mills into a single entity, the Cannon Mills Co.

In the 1930s Cannon Mills started manufacturing sheets. For many years Charlie Cannon resisted turning out sheets in anything but white. Over time they became more colorful, but prints were disdained, except for one featuring a tightly closed rosebud introduced in 1953. ''It took another 13 years to get that rosebud opened,'' a marketing vice-president told *Forbes.*

In 1962 Cannon Mills was removed from the New York Stock Exchange, when Charlie Cannon refused to solicit proxies from all of the company's shareholders, preferring to solicit only those who held voting stock. Cannon felt the required disclosure of information was intrusive and unnecessary. At that time the Cannon family and relatives held 40 percent of the voting stock and 27 percent of the total stock.

Charlie Cannon died in 1971 after suffering a heart attack at his office. At that time, Cannon Mills owned 17 plants and employed 24,000 workers, making it the largest employer in the Carolinas. The population of Kannapolis was 36,000, ten percent of which lived in company housing. Sales in 1971 reached $323 million. Cannon left no long-term debt and over $60 million in cash and marketable securities. The Cannon name was recognized by a remarkable 90 percent of consumers. However, growth had been very slow; in the five years prior to Cannon's death, sales figures had increased only two percent a year.

The neon sign remained unlit after Cannon died, but Cannon Mills stock soared on Wall Street as investors believed that new management would fully take advantage of the company's cash-rich, debt-free position. Nevertheless, Charlie Cannon's hand-picked successor, Don Holt, continued his mentor's policies of neither diversifying nor broadening its market appeal. As other mills were bringing in well-known designers to update their look, Cannon continued to resist. ''We have the Cannon name. We don't need designers' names,'' the president of Cannon's merchandising subsidiary told *Forbes* in 1972.

For much of the 1970s Cannon was able to hold onto its share of the towel market, although its sales growth barely matched the rate of inflation and was far outstripped by its competitors. In 1975 its earnings were less than those of 1965,

$2.66 a share, although its sales volume had grown 42 percent since that year to $395 million. A new chairperson, Harold Hornaday, was installed, who conceded to *Forbes* that "the times require that Cannon be more market oriented." Nonetheless, Hornaday hesitated to change strategies as its share of the sheet market dropped from 20 to 15 percent. Sales in 1979 reached $609 million. In that year, Cannon was reinstated to the New York Stock Exchange, having given voting rights to all public shareholders and begun publishing more detailed annual reports. Hornaday, however, was asked to leave in October 1980 after several embarrassing missteps led to Cannon's first money-losing quarter in over a decade.

Cannon attempted vigorously to catch up with its competitors, under the youthful leadership of its next chairperson, Otto Stolz. The company diversified into the manufacture of various items for kitchen and bath, including mats and rugs. Luxury fabric designer Robin Roberts was also hired to create a fashionable and upscale line of sheets and towels. Cannon had difficulty changing its old-fashioned image, however, and its share of the towel market fell to below 35 percent.

Cannon Mills was to experience dramatic change in 1982, after David Murdock, a self-made millionaire and takeover artist from California, disclosed his intention of acquiring the company. Charlie Cannon's son William was the first to sell, and the other trustees followed his example. After the $413 million leveraged buyout, Murdock took the company private.

Murdock set out to reshape the way Cannon did business. As other mills were reporting slowing growth or declines, Murdock sought to increase Cannon's sales by updating the company with a glamorous and trendy image. The design department was doubled in size, its manager released, and most of the existing towels and sheets discontinued. The Japanese designer Issey Miyake and the Swedish designer Katja were hired to create their own lines. A racy advertising campaign was launched featuring various celebrities between Cannon sheets with the tag line "Two of the most famous names in America sleep together." Towels were marketed at all price levels, including a line that competed directly with Fieldcrest's Royal Velvet. Efforts were also made to expand profits at the mass merchandisers; to that end, an agreement was signed with the producers of the nighttime soap opera *Dynasty* to produce a Dynasty collection, patterned after the sets used on the show.

Murdock quickly invested $200 million in upgrading mill equipment. Furthermore, he immediately laid off several hundred employees; mill workers who lived in company-owned homes were informed they would have to buy their houses or leave. And Murdock spent $30 million to raze businesses, move homes, build a highway, and refurbish the Georgian business district so as to turn it into "Cannon Village," a factory-outlet shopping mall.

Despite Murdock's attempts to invigorate Cannon with splashy designs and heavy advertising, Cannon continued to lose money. The import-battered market had led to further layoffs (reaching 3,000), the closing of three mills, and a $31 million drop in exports. Under these conditions, the Amalgamated Clothing & Textile Workers Union (ACTWU) attempted to organize Cannon employees, which culminated in a vote in October 1985. The union had failed previously, most recently in 1974 in a 44 to 56 percent vote. Murdock, by that time seeking a buyer for Cannon, fought the union in a venomous campaign in which he jetted frequently into Kannapolis, touring the factories and shaking hands with virtually all of the company's 10,000 employees. The movement to unionize was defeated in a 37 to 63 percent vote.

Several months later, in January 1986, Murdock sold approximately 75 percent of Cannon Mills to Fieldcrest Mills for $321 million. He retained the real estate holdings, which included most of the commercial real estate in downtown Kannapolis, worth approximately $100 million, as well as several other mills. The sale to Fieldcrest did not mark the end of Murdock's involvement with Cannon or the union, however. Murdock had also left Kannapolis with around $25 million from the Cannon pension fund, which had been terminated shortly before the sale was consummated. In October 1986 the ACTWU filed suit, charging that Murdock had mishandled the funds and thus violated his fiduciary duties as a trustee of the plan.

The point of contention was Murdock's use of the funds while he was battling for control of Occidental Petroleum. Murdock had started acquiring Occidental stock in 1981. In February 1982 he was elected as a director of that company under conditions which barred him from acquiring more than five percent of its stock. Late in that year the Cannon pension fund began to purchase Occidental stock, which by 1984 accounted for 7.8 percent of the fund's holding. In 1984 Occidental repurchased its stock from Murdock-controlled entities—including the Cannon pension fund—with a $60 million premium attached. After the fund was terminated late in 1985, the fund's excess assets—including the profits from the Occidental deal—were folded back into Murdock's other entities. The union's suit charged that Murdock had used the funds to either "greenmail" or take over Occidental, as opposed to managing the funds for its participants and beneficiaries, and that he had used the funds similarly in actions against Kaiser Cement. The case was settled out of court in 1989 for a reported $1 million.

Upon the liquidation of the pension plan, Murdock invested the funds with Executive Life Insurance of California. The company, which had invested heavily in junk bonds underwritten by Michael Milken of Drexel Burnham Lambert during the 1980s, suffered sharp losses after the junk bond industry collapsed in 1990. In April 1991 state regulators seized its assets, and monthly pension payments were cut by 30 percent. In August, Murdock announced he would "personally pay all Cannon retirees the full amount of reduction they suffered." The payments were to be in the form of personal checks and were to compensate for the shortfall from May 1 to September 30, when full payments were to resume.

Fieldcrest Cannon is Formed

The acquisition by Fieldcrest of Cannon catapulted the company to the number one position in the towel and blanket market and the number three spot in the sheet market. Observers wondered how Fieldcrest and Cannon, two textile powerhouses with very different market strategies, would work together, especially on the retail floor. The erstwhile rivals' various lines seemed poised to continue to compete against each other for market share and counterspace. Fieldcrest's flagship brand still prevailed in the department stores, where Cannon's Royal Family line vied against it. Cannon was the number one brand with discounters, where Fieldcrest's St. Marys always placed behind Cannon's Monticello line. There were tactical differences as well. Fieldcrest had chosen to not expand its market share to avoid price cuts, while Cannon had elected to cut prices to generate sales. Fieldcrest executives felt that it was best to keep the lines separate to hold onto precious counterspace as the retail industry consolidated. Fieldcrest had also quickly moved out some of Cannon's management team, replacing them with Fieldcrest staffers. Some observers felt that Fieldcrest lost much-needed experience with high-volume, low-margin mass merchandising.

Less than one year after the purchase of Cannon, Fieldcrest bought Bigelow-Sanford, Inc., a manufacturer of residential and industrial contract carpeting. Bigelow-Sanford had been purchased by a group of its executives in 1981, who in turn sold it to Fieldcrest Cannon in December 1986 for $129 million—$4 million in cash and 460,727 shares of Fieldcrest common stock. After the acquisition, Fieldcrest Cannon merged Bigelow-Sanford with its Karastan division and dismissed the Bigelow-Sanford executives. Soon thereafter, DuPont introduced its Stainmaster fiber, which was enormously popular but proved to be very difficult to dye into the carpet colors that consumers wanted. Lacking knowledgeable staff at the top of its carpet operations and still heavily in debt from its acquisitions, Fieldcrest Cannon committed to big capital outlays in an attempt to master the process.

In 1987 Fieldcrest Cannon lost $3.7 million on sales of $1.4 billion, and much of the loss was attributed to problems with Bigelow-Sanford. By 1988 Fieldcrest Cannon announced that it wanted out of the carpet business altogether and was looking for a buyer. Profits rebounded to $11.3 million that year and reached $23.4 million in 1989. However, 1990's economic downturn exacerbated internal problems, and the company posted a $38 million loss on $1.24 billion in sales. The company's stock value, which had peaked in 1986 at $43, dropped to below six dollars per share.

Restructuring and Takeover Threats in the 1990s

Several analysts pointed to Chairperson Ely as directly responsible for the troubles at Fieldcrest Cannon. They cited an overly rapid expansion financed with heavy debt commitments, the exorbitant price paid for Cannon, ill-timed cotton purchases, and difficulties with Bigelow-Sanford. Moreover, critics reasoned that Ely had been able to remain at Fieldcrest Cannon as long as he had by virtue of his position as treasurer of the Dumaine trust, holding ultimate power over an elderly board on which remained several members from F.C. Dumaine, Sr.'s, era.

After Ely was forced out, Fieldcrest Cannon underwent a series of cost-cutting measures in 1990 under its new chairperson, James Fitzgibbons, which included reducing its workforce by 1,700, discontinuing its unprofitable automatic blanket operations, and unloading inventory. Unable to find a buyer for its rug and carpet division, the company consolidated those operations and was able to turn a profit in 1991. That year Fieldcrest Cannon as a whole was able to claim $3.2 million in profit, although sales were reported at $1.21 billion, less than those of 1990. Income in 1992 exceeded that of the previous year, aided by lower cotton prices and higher sales. In mid-1992 the company refinanced its loan agreements, reducing its interest payments. Nevertheless, Fieldcrest Cannon had experienced lower sales from 1988 to 1992, largely because of a decline in carpet and rug sales from $371.1 million in 1988 to $235.5 million in 1992. Total sales in 1992 were $1.22 billion.

In January 1993 Amoskeag announced that it was considering selling off its shares of Fieldcrest Cannon, disclosing that the Dumaine trust was reviewing its own investment in Amoskeag. At that time the Dumaine trust owned approximately 76 percent of the voting power of the equity of Amoskeag, and Amoskeag controlled about 80 percent of the voting stock and 30 percent of the equity of Fieldcrest Cannon. Some of the trust's beneficiaries had criticized the trust's management, but the Dumaine heirs had no say in the management of the trust unless Amoskeag failed to provide a dividend, which was largely furnished by Fieldcrest Cannon. Long-simmering dissension and rivalry ruptured into several legal battles attempting to break the trust, each of which ultimately failed.

The ownership issue came to a head again in May 1993 when one of Fieldcrest Cannon's chief competitors, Springs Industries, Inc., offered to purchase the company for $330 million. The unsolicited bid came at an especially bad time. With its new management in place since 1990, Fieldcrest Cannon was "turning around nicely," according to the *Daily News Record.* Earlier in the year, Fieldcrest Cannon had obtained the lucrative manufacturing and distribution operations for Caldwell, Canada's leading towel brand. Though Fitzgibbons tersely met Springs's takeover bid with the warning that "Fieldcrest Cannon is not for sale," rumors flew about the possible acquisition.

Fieldcrest Cannon's apparent weakness emboldened others to try to make inroads. Various competitors hungrily eyed the company, including Bibb Co., which made its own unsolicited offer for a controlling interest in the company. At the same time, the Amalgamated Clothing and Textile Workers sensed an opportunity to once again approach Fieldcrest Cannon workers and sent representatives to the company's mills in Rowan and Cabarrus, North Carolina, to attempt to unionize employees.

In the face of these challenges, Fieldcrest Cannon finally was able to divest its carpet and rug business in June 1993. The company raised over $140 million with the sale of the division—including the Bigelow and Karastan brands—to Mohawk Industries Inc. Fitzgibbons announced that Fieldcrest Cannon would thereafter focus on its core bed and bath operations. Springs's acquisition efforts continued, with a proposal to purchase Amoskeag, an offer the Dumaine trust rejected. Fieldcrest Cannon finally put an end to all acquisition efforts when it purchased Amoskeag—its largest shareholder—in August 1993 for $137.6 million.

After withstanding this period of turbulence, Fieldcrest Cannon turned to new ventures. In 1994 the company entered the bath fashions market, debuting a line of shower curtains and bath ceramics. That same year, the company signed on as the official supplier of bedding and towels for the 1996 Summer Olympic Games in Atlanta. In 1995 it acquired Sure Fit, a division of UTC Holdings. Sure Fit was the leading producer of furniture coverings, especially slip covers. Fieldcrest Cannon swiftly converted Sure Fit's "Decor Express" and "Homescapes" to its own recognizable Cannon, Cannon Royal Family, and Fieldcrest labels.

Yet 1996 proved to be another difficult year for the company. Though Fieldcrest Cannon's sales reached $1.09 billion, profits flagged at $1.1 million. In an effort to reign in costs, the company closed a number of manufacturing facilities, including a towel-weaving plant, a towel-yarn plant, and two sheeting-yarn plants. The company also sold its blanket-manufacturing operations for $30 million to Pillowtex Corporation, a firm which made pillows, sheets, and blankets under the Ralph Lauren, Disney, and Martha Stewart labels.

Pillowtex happened to be eager to gain access to the bath textile market. On September 11, 1997 it acquired the remainder of Fieldcrest Cannon's assets for $400 million. Fieldcrest Cannon's operations and assets were folded into Pillowtex, and Pillowtex's chairman and chief executive officer pledged to cut costs at its new facilities by $30 million. In keeping with this goal, he fired 20 percent of Fieldcrest Canon's salaried employees, six days before Christmas. Pillowtex then shed two Fieldcrest Cannon home furnishing fabrics plants in 1998, and closed a factory that made decorative bedding as well.

Though Pillowtex had abruptly reduced Fieldcrest Cannon's workforce, it had no similar desire to decimate the company's roster of brands. Cannon, Fieldcrest, Charisma, and Royal Velvet were the industry's most recognizable labels, and Pillowtex stood to gain from their popularity. In 1998, Pillowtex resolved to expand the brand names into new product lines to boost sales. Although Fieldcrest Cannon had ceased to exist as a company, its name remained valuable to Pillowtex.

Further Reading

Ames, Elizabeth, and Marc Frons, "There Are Two David Murdocks—and Both Are Used to Getting Their Way," *Business Week*, January 28, 1985, pp. 88–90.

"Amoskeag May Sell Its Majority Stake in Fieldcrest," *Wall Street Journal*, January 29, 1993.

Anreder, Steven S., and David A. Hoddeson, "Fieldcrest Mills Spins Stylish Profits Pattern," *Barron's*, June 3, 1968.

Bodipo-Memba, Alejandro, "Bed-and-Bath Products Maker Pillowtex, Fieldcrest Cannon to Merge," *Dow Jones Online News*, January 11, 1997.

Burck, Charles G., "Reveille at Cannon Mills," *Fortune*, January 26, 1981, pp. 68–76.

Campanella, Frank W., "Fieldcrest Mills Enjoys Smart Advance in Profits," *Barron's*, December 11, 1978, pp. 44–45.

Chernoff, Joel, "Union Charges Misuse of Assets," *Pensions & Investment Age*, October 13, 1986, p. 1.

Clune, Ray, "Union Vote in Dispute at Fieldcrest Cannon," *Daily News Record*, August 23, 1991.

Coletti, Richard J., "Fieldcrest: Stains on the Carpet," *Financial World*, October 18, 1988, p. 16.

Deogun, Nikhil, "Fieldcrest to Buy Its Largest Holder, Amoskeag, Ending Efforts for Control," *Wall Street Journal*, August 16, 1993.

Emory, Thomas Jr., "Auction for Fieldcrest Cannon," *Wall Street Journal*, July 23, 1993.

Engardio, Pete, "Why David Murdock Is So Afraid of a Union," *Business Week*, October 14, 1985, p. 43.

Feldman, Amy, "Changing the Sheets," *Forbes*, February, 1992.

"Fieldcrest Buys 80% of Cannon," *Textile World*, January 1986, pp. 22–23.

"Fieldcrest Cannon Will Stay in the Carpet Biz," *Textile World*, January 1989, p. 28.

"Fieldcrest: Profit-Blazing Un-Textile Firm," *Textile World*, June 1979, pp. 53–118.

"Fieldcrest: Saving Its Name for a Luxury Image," *Business Week*, January 9, 1984, pp. 112–13.

Hackney, Holt, "Fieldcrest Cannon: Turnaround at Last?," *Financial World*, April 16, 1991.

Heins, John, "...'I Just Make Ideas Happen'," *Forbes*, October 26, 1987, pp. 33–35.

Hughes, Bill, "Speculation About New Bidders for Fieldcrest Cannon," *Spartanburg (South Carolina) Herald-Journal*, June 5, 1993.

Hussey, Allan F., "Capital Gains: Heavy Outlays Pull Fieldcrest Out of Earnings Slump," *Barron's*, January 23, 1984, pp. 54–55.

Jaffe, Thomas, "One Rude Awakening," *Forbes*, October 25, 1982, p. 116.

Jenkins, J., "Barony in Carolina: The Town that Towels Built," *Nation*, May 12, 1956, pp. 405–07.

Lappen, Alyssa A., "Thank You, Mr. Ely," *Forbes*, December 12, 1988, pp. 100–02.

"Living in the Past," *Forbes*, June 1, 1975, pp. 46–47.

Leonhardt, David, "Amoskeag's Major Holder Rejects Offer," *Boston Globe*, June 19, 1993.

MacIntosh, Jeane, "Full Cannon Pensions Set," *Home Furnishings Daily*, August 19, 1991.

Marcial, Gene G., "White Sale at Fieldcrest Cannon," *Business Week*, March 19, 1990, p. 107.

Nowell, Paul, "Fieldcrest Cannon Rejects Buyout Bid," *Associated Press*, May 27, 1993.

"The Passing of Mr. Charlie," *Forbes*, July 15, 1972, pp. 22–24.

Peckenham, Nancy, "Out in the Cold at Cannon Mills," *Nation*, September 16, 1991, pp. 298–302.

Saunders, Dero A., "Frederic Dumaine: Upstreaming the Profits," *Forbes*, July 13, 1987, pp. 258–62.

"Sleeping with the Stars Pays Off for Cannon," *Business Week*, September 24, 1984, pp. 67–68.

"Springs Makes Bid to Take Over Fieldcrest Cannon, Which Says 'No Sale'," *Daily News Record*, May 28, 1993.

Tasini, Jonathan, "Playing with Pension Funds: What's the Limit?," *Business Week*, November 12, 1986, p. 89.

Troy, Colleen, "Leading Separate Lives," *Home Furnishings Daily*, November 16, 1987, p. 1.

Wheelan, Joe, "Pillowtex Acquiring Fieldcrest Cannon for $400 Million," *Associated Press*, September 11, 1997.

—C. L. Collins
—updated by Rebecca Stanfel

Fielmann AG

Weidestrasse 118a
D-22083 Hamburg
Germany
Telephone: (49)(40) 270-760
Fax: (49)(40) 270-763-99
Web site: http://www.fielmann.de

Public Company
Incorporated: 1972
Employees: 6,950
Sales: DM 1.11 billion ($568.66 million) (1998)
Stock Exchanges: Frankfurt/Main
Ticker Symbol: FIE3
NAIC: 44613 Optical Goods Stores; 339115 Ophthalmic Goods Manufacturing

Fielmann AG, based in Germany, is Europe's largest optician; more than every third pair of eyeglasses sold in Germany in 1998 carried a Fielmann label. Fielmann operates and franchises eye care retail businesses which sell vision aids of all kinds, including eyeglasses, frames and lenses, sunglasses, contact lenses, and optical accessories. More than four million eyeglasses per year are sold at the group's 451 branches, some of which are Fielmann Supercenters, in Germany, Switzerland, and Austria, each of which is managed by a certified optician. Fielmann is also a leading producer and vendor of frames for the optical industry and wholesale trade with operations in Germany and France. Further afield, Fielmann frames are also sold in Holland and Denmark, and the company operates lens grinding facilities in Minsk, Belarus, and the Ukraine, as well as through a joint venture in Hong Kong. Moreover, Fielmann holds shares in Italian, French, and Japanese frame manufacturing companies.

1972: The Founder and His First Shop

Günther Fielmann, the founder of Fielmann AG, was born in 1939 in a small village in Northern Germany. As a young boy Fielmann dreamed of becoming an adventurer and revolutionary; he didn't know yet that he would truly revolutionize a whole industry as an innovative business leader. Upon graduating from high school, Fielmann wanted to become a photographer, but his father insisted on something more down to earth, suggesting he consider a career as an optician, which was also connected with light and lenses.

Fielmann later recalled that as an apprentice optician, he had a hard time getting used to organized workdays and the demands of his exacting boss. However, a newly hired optician's aide fostered Fielmann's advancement, and at the end of his apprenticeship he was awarded the highest grade possible and the title of optician's aide. During this time, Fielmann also worked as a freelance photographer for a Hamburg daily newspaper, but he eventually decided to forgo photography in order to get his master optician's certificate.

While attending professional school in Berlin, Fielmann made his living selling used cars, honing his business instincts all the while. Once he gained qualification as a state-certified optician, Fielmann traveled the world, working as an optician and salesman in Europe, the Middle and Far East, and North America. At Bausch & Lomb in Rochester, New York, he studied modern American management and marketing.

In 1972 23-year old Fielmann borrowed the money he needed to open his first store in Cuxhaven, a town in Northern Germany. At that time, opticians enjoyed a fairly secure life in Germany. Traditionally, prices for eyeglasses were kept high by opticians who charged their customers between 200 and 1,000 percent of the purchasing price, using anonymously distributed calculation guidelines throughout the industry. People without the means to afford decent and fashionable eyeglasses had the ''choice'' between three frame styles each for women and men, and just two styles for children, all completely covered by German health insurance and all utilitarian and unattractive. Fielmann, who had to wear eyeglasses from the time he was 16, felt that people with low incomes were being discriminated against and decided to change this situation. From the very beginning he offered a variety of prescription glasses with plastic or metal frames for significantly lower prices. Instead of pulling different models out of hidden boxes as generations of opticians had before him, he presented all available frames

Company Perspectives:

Fielmann acquired market leadership with the motto 'You are the customer.' Strictly customer-orientated thinking sent Fielmann to the top. Short-term profit maximization always takes a back seat to long-term business success at Fielmann. The employees of Fielmann learn to see themselves in the customer. They serve the customer as they would like to be served themselves. Fielmann staff do not suffer under the pressure of having to talk customers into buying expensive spectacles. They have the satisfying job of finding the optimum solution for each customer, independent of the price. With the result that 13 million Germans are currently wearing spectacles from Fielmann. Fielmann has repeatedly introduced totally new, consumer-friendly benefits to the sector. With its fair prices, extensive assortment, many years of guarantee, the above-average service and friendly advice, Fielmann has taken over market leadership in the German optical industry.

openly in his store and let his customers choose them freely. In 1977 Fielmann introduced another industry novelty: a two-year warranty on his eyeglasses, including the models for children, and the warranty was later extended to three years.

1981: A Special Deal

By 1981 there were about 30 Fielmann-owned stores in Germany, and eyeglasses at Fielmann's were much cheaper than anywhere else. Economies of scale more than made up for the losses caused by lower prices. Fielmann eliminated wholesalers wherever possible and simply sold more eyeglasses than his competitors, which in turn allowed him to buy lenses and frames in bulk from Italy, France, Spain, England, the United States, and Japan.

Next, in the presence of Germany's Federal Minister of Employment, Fielmann signed a contract with the local branch of the Allgemeine Ortskrankenkasse (AOK), a German national health insurance carrier in Northern Germany. Under the contract, Fielmann agreed to provide 90 different plastic and metal frames for eyeglasses in 640 variations for top quality prescription glasses without charging more than the amount for which AOK would reimburse its customers. If Fielmann's earlier activities were warning signals for Germany's opticians, then this was their wake up call. With a wave of delivery boycotts, advertising campaigns, threats to Fielmann employees, and several dozen lawsuits, the industry tried to stop a man who seemed bent on destroying the basis of their lucrative business. Fielmann was disturbed by this wave of hostility, but refused to give up. Only two years after the first contract with the AOK was signed, Fielmann's business consisted of 76 shops with 800 employees and 177 trainees, each of them with its own profit center. Some of them were managed by independent opticians who decided to run their businesses under the Fielmann brand concept.

In 1982 and 1983 Fielmann opened two flagship optical centers in Northern Germany. The first one in Kiel offered a variety of 7,000 brand-name and designer frames, a range unprecedented in Europe. The new store included the first Fielmann light gallery, where the works of holography artists with an international reputation were exhibited. The second Fielmann megastore, which opened in 1993 in Hamburg, was according to company literature the biggest optical center in the world at that time. It included a second holography gallery and a museum for eyeglasses. In the following years Fielmann also introduced new product innovations. In 1984 the Fielmann money-back guarantee was introduced. Since Fielmann's advertising was mainly based on the unbeatable low prices, Fielmann customers who found a pair of brand-name eyeglasses cheaper in another store could get their money back from Fielmann. Three years later, all non-prescription Fielmann eyeglasses were also automatically insured against breakage, loss, and theft for 12 months.

By 1988 Fielmann was the single largest employer in the optical industry, and with over 500 trainees it was also the largest provider of training for professionals in the field. However, proper training was not the sole motivation for Fielmann employees. More than 70 percent of them were also Fielmann shareholders. In addition to Fielmann's activities in promoting holography, the company also spent significant amounts of money for environmental protection. In 1986 Fielmann founded an initiative to plant a tree for every staff member each year, a tradition that has been honored every year since.

1989: Fielmann Goes East

In 1989 the German government passed new legislation that shook the whole optical industry. The new Health Reform Act significantly reduced government subsidies for the rates that national health insurers paid opticians for prescription glasses. In reaction many German opticians were forced to increase their rates. Fielmann stores, however, continued to offer prescription glasses at no extra charge, constantly improving their quality at the same time. Fielmann's corrosion-proof and non-fading frames, for example, were the first to pass the test for DIN 58199, a new product quality standard.

The fall of the Berlin Wall gave a boost to the stagnant optical market in Germany. In 1990 Fielmann negotiated a contract with the former East German social security administration to provide prescription eyeglasses and three-year warranty without extra charge to Germans from the former GDR. Within a few weeks, more than 30,000 East Germans owned Fielmann eyeglasses. By 1992, Fielmann also employed more opticians and support staff in the new eastern states of Germany than any other business in the industry.

In 1992, a brand-new production facility for Fielmann eyeglasses was set up in Rathenow, about 80 miles from Berlin. Rathenow had a long tradition of making eyeglasses and a well trained supply of opticians and lens crafters. The new factory, with a production capacity of 200,000 acetate frames a year, was equipped with state-of the art technology in order to react more quickly to fashion trends than competitors. Fielmann's plan to quickly penetrate the new East German market worked well. While other German opticians saw their sales drop by 15 to 20 percent in the first half of 1993, Fielmann's revenues went up by 20 percent. When the capacity of the Rathenow factory

Key Dates:

1972: Günther Fielmann opens his first optical retail store.
1981: First contract with a national health insurance signed.
1982: First Fielmann superstore opened in Kiel.
1994: Fielmann goes public.
1995: Fielmann acquires Pro-optic, Switzerland's third largest optician.
1997: Sales reach DM 1 billion for the first time.

reached its limit, Fielmann took over another frame production facility in Osterburg in the East German state of Saxony-Anhalt and entered a joint venture for lens grinding in Belarus' capital Minsk. Fielmann's investment amounted to about DM 155 million and created about 1,500 new jobs. By 1993, one out of four East Germans were wearing Fielmann glasses. The number of Fielmann stores all over Germany had reached 273. Because an old schoolmate of Fielmann's, optician Jörg Ruhnke, did business in Berlin, Fielmann stayed out of the Berlin market until later, when Ruhnke died.

1994: Fielmann Goes Public and Keeps Expanding

On June 17, 1994, Fielmann's business became a public enterprise. In the German stock market's most successful initial public offering (IPO) that year, Fielmann raised DM 105 million. In the same year Fielmann purchased Rathenow Optische Werke, the top East German producer of eyeglasses, including its well recognized brand name ROW. By the end of 1994, every third pair of eyeglasses in Germany were sold in one of the 296 Fielmann stores. In the second half of the 1990s Fielmann systematically developed the facilities in Rathenow into a high-tech manufacturing center with facilities for frame production, galvanizing and coloring, lens crafting, and a factory outlet. About 1.5 million silicate and plastic lenses were manufactured in the Rathenow lens grinding facility in 1998. Two other lens grinding joint ventures were set up in Belarus and the Ukraine. Because all steps of the eyeglass manufacturing process were concentrated in Rathenow, that city also became Fielmann's central training location for employees, whose numbers rose from about 5,850 in 1994 to over 7,960 in 1998.

Beginning in 1995 Fielmann concentrated on expanding into Southern Germany, Switzerland, and Austria. That year Fielmann acquired Pro-optik AG, Switzerland's third largest optician, headquartered in Basel. While the sales of eyeglasses in Switzerland grew into double digits, German health care reform led to another downturn of the German optical retail business. As of January 1, 1997, federal subsidies for prescription eyeglass frames were abolished. Günther Fielmann, a strong believer in the welfare state, had presented a proposal to the German government, showing how to save the expected DM 300 million without abolishing the subsidies, through more efficient organization and rationalization. While Fielmann's proposal did meet with some approval, the government eventually decided to stick with its original bill. In the aftermath, sales of the German optical industry dropped again by 15 percent in 1997 and stabilized at that level in the year after. Fielmann managed to limit its drop in sales to only five percent and returned to two-digit growth figures thereafter.

By mid-1999 there were 451 Fielmann branches, four of them in Austria and 12 in Switzerland. For the new millennium, Fielmann planned to open more Fielmann superstores, with their selection of 10,000 frames, as well as more outlets in large West European cities. Other growth markets Fielmann chose to focus on included sunglasses, contact lenses, and eyeglasses designed for people working with computers. Fielmann and his management team had ambitious goals; by expanding into those new markets they were aiming at DM 2.5 billion in revenues by 2010.

After 25 years, Fielmann was still very active in his company's operations, creating many frames out of material he chose himself, as well as contributing slogans and ideas to the company's aggressive advertising campaigns. According to some analysts, one of the key questions for the company's future was whether Fielmann would be able to give up his role as the patriarch of a family enterprise in order to make Fielmann AG over into a truly international group of companies. Chances are, he will. Much to the disappointment of his financial controller, Fielmann began spending increasing amounts of time at his organic farm and ranch near Hamburg as the century drew to a close.

Principal Subsidiaries

Fielmann AG (Switzerland); Fielmann Augenoptik AG (Germany); Fielmann-BelOMO Minsk GmbH (Belorus); Fielmann GmbH Wien (Austria); Fielmann-Optic GmbH (Germany); Louvre AG (Switzerland); MBV Modebrillenvertrieb GmbH (Germany); Optic Ladenbau Planungs- und Beratungsgesellschaft mbH; OTR Oberflächentechnik GbmH (Germany); Pro-Optik AG (Switzerland); RA-Optik (Ukraine); Rathenower Optik GmbH (Germany); Rathenower Optische Werke GmbH (Germany).

Principal Competitors

Pearle Opticiens.

Further Reading

''Fielmanns viele Gesichter,'' *Stern*, November 9, 1989.

Graf, Monika, ''Hüter der Bebrillten,'' *Profit*, May 22, 1998.

Grubbe, Peter, and Johanna Müller, ''Günther Fielmann im Gespräch'' (radio interview), *Norddeutscher Rundfunk*, broadcast November 24, 1983.

Hübner, Hannelore, ''Brillenkönig und kobauer,'' *Neues Deutschland*, September 18, 1993.

Koenen, Krisztina, ''Günther Fielmann hat eine verschlafene Branche aufgerüttelt und sich viele Feinde gemacht,'' *Frankfurter Allgemeine Magazin*, August 15, 1997, p. 7.

Nagel, Wolfgang, ''Günther Fielmann,'' *Manager Magazin*, October 1989.

—Evelyn Hauser

Fifth Third Bancorp

38 Fountain Square Plaza
Fifth Third Center
Cincinnati, Ohio 45263
U.S.A.
Telephone: (513) 579-5300
Toll Free: (800) 972-3030
Fax: (513) 579-6020
Web site: http://www.53.com

Public Company
Incorporated: 1908 as The Fifth Third National Bank of Cincinnati
Employees: 8,761
Total Assets: $38 billion (1998)
Stock Exchanges: NASDAQ
Ticker Symbol: FITB
NAIC: 52211 Commercial Banking; 52221 Credit Card Issuing; 52219 Other Depository Credit Intermediation; 551111 Office of Bank Holding Companies; 52231 Mortgage and Nonmortgage Loan Brokers; 52393 Investment Advice

Based in Cincinnati, Ohio, Fifth Third Bancorp is a holding company that operates 12 banking affiliates, managed autonomously, with more than 495 banking locations in Ohio, Kentucky, Indiana, Arizona, Florida, and Michigan. Fifth Third also services its customers through more than 100 Bank Mart locations, found in Kroger grocery stores and TOPS Friendly Markets, which provide banking services seven days a week with extended hours. Fifth Third offers retail banking services, including checking and savings accounts, residential mortgages, and consumer loans, as well as services for the commercial business customer, such as business loans, leasing services, and advisory assistance. Subsidiary Midwest Payment Systems provides credit card and transaction processing services to financial institutions across the nation. Fifth Third also offers brokerage and financial services and equipment leasing financing through subsidiaries Fifth Third Securities, Inc. and Fifth Third Leasing Company.

Pioneer of the National Banking System: 1860–1920

Fifth Third Bancorp traces its history to the mid-19th-century formulation of America's national banking system. Although national banks had existed in the United States since the late 18th century, a lack of consensus on the advantages of a national currency prevented the federal government from establishing a unified currency structure. Rampant inflation during the Civil War, however, prompted the 1863 ratification of the Federal Banking Act, thereby creating a uniform, government-backed national currency to replace the diverse currencies issued by state banks and other firms. That same year, a group of influential Cincinnati businessmen led by A.L. Mowry applied for and received one of the first national bank charters. Their institution, Cincinnati's Third National Bank, opened in a Masonic Temple later that year under a 20-year charter.

The firm that would become Fifth Third Bancorp evolved and grew through dozens of mergers over the ensuing decades. When the Third National Bank acquired the Bank of the Ohio Valley in 1871, the *Cincinnati Enquirer* hailed the union as "one of the best managed banks in Ohio." The superlative descriptions continued when Third National was recapitalized in 1882 at $1.6 million, the highest-asset bank in the state.

The Panic of 1907 brought a run on banks and the first substantial banking and currency reform since the Civil War. Fearful of widespread bank failures, the federal government ordered the consolidation of several big-city banks to shore up weaker institutions. As a result, Third National merged with Fifth National to form The Fifth Third National Bank of Cincinnati, with a capitalization of $2.5 million and $12.1 million in deposits, in 1908. Fifth Third's 1910 acquisition of two other local banks—American National Bank and S. Kuhn & Sons—increased its capital to $3 million.

The Federal Reserve Act of 1913 organized a regional system of 12 Federal Reserve banks that were capitalized with contributions from national banks in each region. The legislation required each national bank to deposit three percent of its capital and surplus into its regional Federal Reserve bank. These moves helped inspire confidence in the national banks, thus preventing panics and runs on banks. The Federal Reserve

Company Perspectives:

Each time we pass another milestone of consistent earnings growth, I am often asked "how we do it" or "how can we continue." All I can say is that the only thing that has remained constant at Fifth Third over the past 25 years is our simple focus on a few basics—hard work, aggressive selling, teamwork, disciplined expense control and strong credit quality. Quite simply, our employees think like owners. They consistently find a way to "out-hustle" the competition and execute better. Fifth Third is obviously much larger than 25 years ago, but we constantly strive to keep ourselves "small" by pushing accountability farther down in the organization and giving more individual managers the opportunity to grow their own business' bottom line.

—George A. Schaefer, Jr., President/CEO

Act also gave the federal government more control over the United States' money supply, made commercial credit available, and discouraged venturesome banking practices. Although bankers initially resisted its creation, the Federal Reserve laid the groundwork for the country's modern banking system.

Branching Out: 1920s–40s

Another bank industry consolidation followed World War I. The 1919 affiliation with Union Savings Bank and Trust Company, a state-chartered bank, brought several changes to Fifth Third's operations. Affiliation with a state bank permitted Fifth Third to circumvent the stricture against national banks' establishment of branches. Before the end of the year, Fifth Third assumed control of the assets of several local banks, including Market National Bank, Security Savings Bank and Safe Deposit Company, Mohawk State Bank, and Walnut Hills Savings Bank. It operated these institutions as branch offices.

Although the 1920s were marked by increased governmental supervision and general economic prosperity, many U.S. banks remained weak. The situation gave Fifth Third the opportunity to continue to grow through the acquisition of four local banks. Fifth Third consolidated with the Union Trust Company to form the Fifth Third Union Trust Company in 1927. The advent of the Great Depression in 1929 intensified this activity somewhat, because Fifth Third was one of the stronger banks in the Cincinnati area. Fifth Third assumed control of three banks from 1930 to 1933.

The Great Depression also brought increased regulation of the banking industry, including expansion of the Federal Reserve Board's powers and the establishment of the Federal Deposit Insurance Corporation (FDIC). The economic crisis also spawned a plethora of federal and state legislation restricting interstate retail banking. Strong popular and governmental reaction to the Great Depression helped make banking one of the most regulated segments of U.S. industry (and inspired the *Economist* to call the American system "one of the world's wackiest banking systems" in 1988). These barriers effectively restricted Fifth Third's growth through acquisition until after World War II.

Diversification into Personal and Commercial Banking: 1950s–70s

Distanced from the Great Depression by the trauma of global war, U.S. banks began to cautiously expand their operations to include a broader range of financial services, especially in the field of retail or personal banking, in the postwar era. Under the direction of G. Carlton Hill from 1955 to 1963, Fifth Third began to formulate its focus on retail or consumer banking. For example, the company established a travel department to issue travelers checks and plan tours. These activities intensified during the presidency of Bill Rowe, who was the son of 1930s-era Fifth Third leader John J. Rowe. Over the course of the 1960s, the bank instituted a program of internal expansion with an emphasis on convenience and personal service. Advertising featuring the company's 5/3 shield logo promoted Fifth Third's many suburban locations and extended hours. During the 1970s, the bank shifted its lending emphasis from commercial or business loans to consumer credit. In 1973, Fifth Third hired Johnny Bench, famed catcher for the Cincinnati Reds baseball team, as spokesman. It adopted the long-running slogan, "The only bank you'll ever need" the same year.

"Back office" changes supported the bank's growth and profitability. Fifth Third, which had booted up its first computer in 1960, initiated home banking services and JEANIE automated teller machines (ATMs) in the 1970s. The institution's home banking system, which could be accessed via the average touchtone phone, was uniquely user-friendly. These electronic services formed the basis of what would become Fifth Third's Midwest Payment Services department. Later in the decade, the bank offered its automated services to other banks and corporate clients. By the early 1990s, Midwest Payment Services maintained automated teller machines and electronic cash registers for more than 1,000 clients. This lucrative business niche contributed one-third of the bank's annual income in the early 1990s.

The 1975 creation of a bank holding company, Fifth Third Bancorp, enabled the institution to sidestep some of the most rigorous state banking regulations. This new corporate entity was not technically a bank and thus was exempt from laws that prohibited cross-county branching. By 1976 Fifth Third included 37 banking offices.

Aggressive Growth and Increased Acquisitions: 1980s

The further liberalization of Ohio banking laws in the early 1980s expanded both the types of products banks were permitted to offer and the geographic reach they were allowed to attain. Strictures against growth outside the home bank's county were first to fall. Barriers to interstate branching continued to deteriorate in the early 1980s. In September 1985, federal and state banking regulations changed dramatically, freeing Ohio's banks to enter into agreements with banking organizations outside the state. Fifth Third became Ohio's first holding company to take advantage of the new legislation when it acquired American National Bank in Newport, Kentucky, just across the Ohio River, later that year. Fifth Third's roster of branches increased by 125 percent over the course of the 1980s, and it expanded its reach from a single Ohio county to an interstate bank.

Much of this vigorous growth was inspired by a new corporate leader, Clement L. Buenger, who took the helm of Fifth Third in

Key Dates:

1863: The Third National Bank forms in Cincinnati, Ohio.
1908: The Third National Bank merges with The Fifth National Bank to form The Fifth Third National Bank of Cincinnati.
1927: Company merges with The Union Trust Company and establishes The Fifth Third Union Trust Company.
1969: Fifth Third Union Trust company is renamed Fifth Third Bank.
1975: Fifth Third Bancorp incorporates.
1998: Company completes two largest acquisitions to date—CitFed Bancorp, Inc., and State Savings Company; celebrates its 25th consecutive year of increased earnings.

1981. Buenger, who was called ''one of the best acts in the business'' in a 1991 *Fortune* article, brought his background in life insurance sales to the bank. The new president transformed the bank's corporate culture through innovative incentive programs and personal example. Whereas some Fifth Third offices were only open from 10:00 a.m. to 2:00 p.m., Buenger worked ten to 12-hour days and expected many of his managers to do the same. The president (who later became CEO and chairman) even made cold calls on prospective clients. One incentive program, the ''Shoe Leather Award,'' evolved from his passion for earning new business. A new pair of designer shoes was awarded to each month's best cold caller. In fact, all employees could earn sales incentives: *Fortune* noted in 1991 that the bank ''already had several secretaries worth $500,000.''

Fifth Third's focus on consumer banking and safe lending helped the bank avoid the real estate loans, Third World debt, and leveraged buyout problems that troubled many financial institutions during the 1980s. The ''banking bust'' that followed led *Fortune* to call the early 1990s ''the hardest times for bankers since the Great Depression'' in November 1991.

George Schaefer, Jr., took Fifth Third's reins in 1989 at the age of 44. Schaefer was trained in engineering, but when a hoped for job designing a nuclear power plant fell through in 1969, he entered the bank's management trainee program. Some industry observers predicted that the new leader would be stymied, both by the shadow of his predecessor and by the difficult banking environment. But while literally hundreds of banks failed each year in the late 1980s and early 1990s, Fifth Third continued its outstanding performance and was even able to benefit from the misfortune of others by inexpensively acquiring dozens of new outlets. This allowed the bank to slowly expand its sphere of influence, yet maintain shareholder value.

Continued Growth in the Early 1990s

In 1992 Fifth Third proposed a merger with Star Banc Corp. that would have unified the two largest Cincinnati-based financial institutions. Star had not grown as fast as Fifth Third, but its recent record of continued growth made it an enticing acquisition target. The alliance was viewed by many analysts and investors as a good deal for both banks—Fifth Third made a generous offer of $42 per share, which amounted to more than twice Star's book value. But when CEO Schaefer prematurely publicized the heretofore private proposition, Star's longtime president, Oliver Waddell, balked, and the target's board unanimously rejected the offer.

Shunned by Star, Schaefer returned to Fifth Third's previous course of growth through relatively small acquisitions. Then, in 1994, the bank made two significant purchases: the 45-office Cumberland Federal Bancorporation in Kentucky, which had $1.1 billion in assets; and Falls Financial Inc. in northeastern Ohio, a company with $581 million in assets. The Cumberland acquisition became Fifth Third Bank of Kentucky, Louisville, and the Falls purchase was merged with Fifth Third Bank, Northeastern Ohio. According to the company's 1994 annual report, these two acquisitions contributed to the largest one-year increase in assets—22 percent—in the institution's history. The purchases also made Fifth Third the preeminent operator of supermarket bank locations in the United States, with 81 full-service locations.

Rapid Expansion Through Acquisitions in the Mid- to Late 1990s

Fifth Third moved aggressively through the second half of the decade, building upon its 20 consecutive years of increased earnings. To remain competitive and to assure continued growth and strong earnings, the company stepped up its acquisition efforts and began to pursue new businesses, including mortgage brokering and investment services, and new territories. In mid-1995, for instance, Fifth Third acquired Bank of Naples, Florida, and increased its assets in the Florida region, which Fifth Third first entered in 1989. Other acquisitions Fifth Third made in 1995 included Mutual Federal Savings Bank in Dayton, Ohio; Bank One Lebanon; PNC Bank's Dayton division; and seven offices of Bank One, Cincinnati. The PNC purchase, which included 12 offices, increased Fifth Third's banking centers in the Dayton area to 30, making it the fourth largest financial establishment in the region.

In the following years the firm continued to follow its strategy to increase market share in the Midwest by acquiring small businesses. Fifth Third made three acquisitions in 1996: the Ohio branch of 1st Nationwide Bank, the Ohio operations of First Chicago NBD Bank, and Kentucky Enterprise Bancorp, Inc., located in northern Kentucky. Four acquisitions were made the following year, all in Fifth Third's familiar Midwest region. In June, Fifth Third purchased Gateway Leasing Corporation for $2.2 million, and a month later it bought Suburban Bancorporation, Inc., a savings and loan holding company. Fifth Third also acquired Heartland Capital Management Inc., a money managing company in Indiana, and Great Lakes National Bank Ohio, with eight branches in Ohio, in 1997.

Fifth Third found substantial support from industry analysts, who regarded the company's stock as reliable and profitable. From 1993 to 1998, according to the *Wall Street Journal,* Fifth Third's annual revenue increased 15.9 percent, about three points better than the industry average. To continue its streak of increased earnings, Fifth Third in 1998 branched into new business arenas and made some major acquisitions. To start out 1998, Fifth

Third announced it would acquire CitFed Bancorp Inc. of Dayton and its subsidiary Citizens Federal Bank FSB for $661 million in stock. CitFed had 35 offices in Ohio. The acquisition, completed in June, created the largest bank in Dayton and boosted its market share there to 28 percent. Fifth Third's market share in its hometown of Cincinnati was 22.7 percent.

Also at the beginning of 1998 Fifth Third announced plans to buy State Savings Co. of Columbus, which would create the fourth largest bank in Columbus, and The Ohio Company, a brokerage and investment management firm with 49 offices in Ohio and four additional states. Fifth Third expanded into another new business field when it acquired W. Lyman Case & Company, a commercial mortgage banking company with headquarters in Columbus. Also that year Fifth Third bought State Savings Company and its subsidiaries, State Savings Bank, Century Bank, and State Savings Bank, FSB, which provided Fifth Third access to a new territory—Arizona. Four offices of Bank One were acquired as well, boosting Fifth Third's presence in southern Ohio. Fifth Third celebrated its 25th consecutive year of increased revenues at the end of 1998 and had increased the number of its branches from 35 to 468.

The year 1999 showed no signs of slowdown for Fifth Third. CEO Schaefer revealed in the *Cincinnati Business Courier* that he planned to continue expanding through acquisitions. "I see more opportunity for us now than at any point in the last 25 years," said Schaefer. "We continue to pick up market share in every market." The company completed the acquisition of Enterprise Federal Bancorp Inc., one of the biggest thrifts in the Cincinnati area. The purchase, estimated at $96.4 million, provided Fifth Third with 11 additional branches in greater Cincinnati. Fifth Third also acquired Ashland Bankshares, Inc. and subsidiary Bank of Ashland, both based in Kentucky. The $80 million purchase gave Fifth Third four more branches, as well as $160 million in assets. Fifth Third also began to implement plans to expand further into Florida and acquired South Florida Bank Holding Corp. in June, adding another four branches to its Florida roster. Additional expansion into the Cleveland, Ohio, area came with the acquisition of Emerald Financial Corp. for $204 million. Fifth Third also acquired Cleveland-based Emerald Financial Corp. and its subsidiary, Strongsville Savings Bank.

Fifth Third further strengthened its commercial banking services by acquiring Vanguard Financial Corporation, a commercial mortgage banking firm, in July 1999. Fifth Third merged Vanguard with previously acquired W. Lyman Case and created Fifth Third Real Estate Capital Markets Company. Prior to the purchases, Fifth Third offered three-year commercial real estate financing, which meant loans had to be renegotiated every three years. With the acquisitions, however, Fifth Third was able to provide long-term financing, thus better serving the business client.

In mid-1999 Fifth Third made its largest acquisition to date when it announced it would purchase CNB Bancshares Inc., the biggest independent bank holding company in Indiana. The $2.4 billion purchase propelled Fifth Third deeper into Indiana and made Fifth Third the third largest bank in Indiana, as well as the 28th biggest bank in the nation. CNB was the parent company of Civitas Bank and had 145 banking offices and $7.2 billion in assets. The CNB purchase also provided Fifth Third with an entry into insurance sales. Fifth Third quickly followed up the CNB purchase with another significant acquisition. Increasing its presence in the Indianapolis area, Fifth Third bought Peoples Bank & Trust Co. for $228 million. The buy moved Fifth Third from sixth place to fourth in the Indianapolis market, with a market share of about seven percent. Peoples had nine Indianapolis offices.

As Fifth Third approached the 21st century, it appeared poised and ready for continued growth. CEO Schaefer told the *Cincinnati Business Courier* that Fifth Third was ready to undertake additional billion-dollar deals and move away from smaller, million-dollar acquisitions. After accomplishing 12 deals, amounting to nearly $5 billion in a mere 16 months, Fifth Third was certainly on a fast track. In 1999 Fifth Third received the top ranking from Salomon Smith Barney in its Top 50 Bank Annual for the eighth consecutive year. Banks were rated according to profitability, operating efficiency, asset quality, capital strength, and operating growth. Its Midwest Payment Systems data processing subsidiary saw net income increase 34 percent in 1998 over 1997, and in mid-1999 the subsidiary's profits were already up 37 percent from the previous year. Fifth Third's net income for the first half of 1999 was up 21 percent compared to the same period a year earlier. Reporter Geert De Lombaerde declared in the *Cincinnati Business Courier,* "Fifth Third is in the midst of a metamorphosis. It is no longer primarily a commercial bank—40 percent of revenues comes from fees—or just a strong performer in the middle-of-the-road Midwest. It is on the cusp of becoming a sizable national player."

Principal Subsidiaries

Fifth Third Securities, Inc.; Fifth Third Leasing Company; Midwest Payment Systems, Inc.; Heartland Capital Management Inc.; Fifth Third Bank; Fifth Third Bank, Indiana; Fifth Third Bank, Central Ohio; Fifth Third Bank, Northeastern Ohio; Fifth Third Bank, Northwestern Ohio; Fifth Third Bank, Western Ohio; Fifth Third Bank, Ohio Valley; Fifth Third Bank, Southwest, FSB; Fifth Third Bank, Butler County; Fifth Third Real Estate Capital Markets Company; Fifth Third Bank, Florida; Fifth Third Bank, Kentucky, Inc.; Fifth Third Bank, Northern Kentucky, Inc.; Fifth Third Bank of Central Kentucky, NA; Fifth Third Company; Fifth Third Trust Co. & Savings Bank, FSB; Fifth Third Community Development Company; Fifth Third Investment Company.

Principal Competitors

BANK ONE CORPORATION; Huntington Bancshares Incorporated; PNC Bank Corp.

Further Reading

Barnes, Jon, "Fifth Third Bancorp Expanding in Ohio, Data-Processing Field," *Investor's Business Daily,* November 18, 1998, p. B20.

Bennett, Robert A., "How to Earn 1.6% on Assets," *United States Banker*, January 1992, pp. 20–27.

Buenger, Clement L., *Fifth Third Bank: The Only Bank You'll Ever Need,* New York: Newcomen Society of the United States, 1991.

De Lombaerde, Geert, "Acquisitions Continue to Fuel Fifth Third's Growth," *Cincinnati Business Courier,* April 9, 1999, p. 30.

——, "Fast Times at Fifth Third," *Cincinnati Business Courier,* August 6, 1999, p. 1.

''Fifth Third Drops Offer to Buy Star Banc Corp.,'' *American Banker,* July 1, 1992, p. 1.

''Fifth Third, the 'Charlie Hustle' of Banking,'' *United States Banker,* April 1995, p. 24.

Fraust, Bart, ''Fifth Third to Enter Kentucky: Becomes 1st Ohio Holding Company to Acquire Out-of-State Bank,'' *American Banker,* July 31, 1985, p. 3.

Klinkermann, Steve, et al., ''Fifth Third's Schaefer: Hard Work, Expense Control and the Secrets to Success,'' *American Banker,* December 19, 1994, p. 16.

Larkin, Patrick, ''Fifth Third Expanding Its Reach,'' *Cincinnati Post,* June 9, 1999, p. C5.

Murray, Matt, ''Fifth Third Bancorp Is First on Experts' List Of Bank Stocks Due to High Revenue Growth,'' *Wall Street Journal,* January 13, 1998, p. C4.

Pare, Terence P., ''Bankers Who Beat the Bust,'' *Fortune,* November 4, 1991, p. 159.

Peale, Cliff, ''Merger Proposal Came Too Quickly for Star,'' *Cincinnati Business Courier,* May 4, 1992, p. 3.

Piggott, Charles, ''The World's Best Banks: The Americans Bounce Back,'' *Euromoney,* August 1994, pp. 68–72.

Pramik, Mike, ''Fifth Third Looms Larger,'' *Columbus Dispatch,* July 17, 1999, p. C1.

''The Safest and Soundest of the Big Banks,'' *United States Banker,* July 1992, pp. 19–25.

Slater, Robert Bruce, ''Banking's Cincinnati Kid,'' *Bankers Monthly,* January 1993, p. 14.

—April D. Gasbarre
—updated by Mariko Fujinaka

Florsheim Shoe Group Inc.

200 North LaSalle Street
Chicago, Illinois 60601-1014
U.S.A.
Telephone: (312) 458-2500
Fax: (312) 458-7470
Web site: http://www.florsheim.com

Public Company
Incorporated: 1892 as Florsheim & Company
Employees: 2,037
Sales: $244.8 million (1998)
Stock Exchanges: NASDAQ
Ticker Symbol: FLSC
NAIC: 3143 Men's Footwear, Except Athletic

Florsheim Shoe Group Inc. manufactures and sells one of the world's best-known brands of men's dress shoes. These brands—Florsheim Imperial, FLS, @ease, and Florsheim Comfortech—were complemented by the debut of a line of Florsheim golf shoes. In 1997, Florsheim secured several lucrative licensing agreements, and since then has produced John Deere work boots (for Deere & Co.) and Joseph Abboud dress shoes (for upscale designer Joseph Abboud). In addition to operating 350 company-operated stores, Florsheim sells it shoes at over 6,000 department and specialty stores. Two investment groups run by Leon Black own over 67 percent of the company.

Founding of a Family Business

The company was launched under the name Florsheim & Co. in 1892. Milton Florsheim, the company's founder, sought to produce high quality men's dress shoes at a moderate price, and he opened his first factory in Chicago. The first Florsheim shoes were made by Milton and his father, Sigmund Florsheim. Florsheim's distribution system was established in the company's infancy. The company provided support for entrepreneurs who wished to set up stores that would sell Florsheim shoes retail. In this way, Florsheim shoes began to go on sale in small towns throughout the United States.

Florsheim expanded its distribution system in the early part of the 20th century. Wholesale distribution was set up in several metropolitan areas. Company-owned retail outlets were also established in several cities. These stores were large enough to display and sell the entire line of Florsheim shoes and became the company's flagship operations. In 1929, the company began manufacturing women's shoes. By 1930, there were five Florsheim factories in Chicago. The shoes were sold through 71 retail outlets, either wholly or partly owned by the company, as well as through nearly 9,000 dealers not directly affiliated with the manufacturer. The company had 2,500 employees by this time.

After approaching $3 million in net income in 1929, Florsheim, like most companies dependent on retail sales, was hurt badly by the onset of the Great Depression. By 1931, the company's net income had shrunk to $717,000. As the Depression eased up somewhat in the second half of the 1930s, net income hovered around the $1 million mark, and sales began slowly to climb once again, reaching $9.4 million in 1940.

Despite its size, Florsheim was still very much a family operation in the 1930s. Aside from Milton Florsheim, the company's two highest ranking officers in 1930 were his sons, Irving and Harold, who had joined the business in 1914 and 1920, respectively, after graduating from Cornell University. Two other Florsheims, Louis and Felix, also sat on the board of directors. In addition to its business successes, the Florsheim family was also prominent in the art world, both as patrons and artists. Helen Florsheim, Irving's wife, had a distinguished career as a sculptor. In 1936, Milton Florsheim died and was replaced as head of Florsheim Shoe by Irving. Sales at Florsheim stalled once again in the mid-1940s, hovering around $17 million. In 1946, Irving Florsheim ascended to the position of chairperson, leaving the company's presidency to his brother Harold.

Acquisition by Interco

By 1949, Florsheim's sales were $25.3 million. At that time, there were 82 wholly or partly owned Florsheim retail outlets, and another 4,500 unaffiliated stores that sold Florsheim shoes. The bulk of Florsheim's manufacturing was still taking place at the company's Chicago plants, principally the original facility

Company Perspectives:

Over the years, Florsheim innovation has continued, and the partnership has flourished. Committing considerable resources to research and development, the company has produced a continuous flow of product and distribution breakthroughs. These include significant new footwear design and manufacturing processes, as well as the pioneering use of new systems to make the selling of our shoes much more efficient.

Using advanced electronic technology, we've recently created the unique ''Florsheim Express Shop'' which allows our retail partners to place the entire Florsheim stock line at their customer's fingertips.

Through strong ideas like this, we will continue to forge even closer partnerships with our loyal dealers. In addition, we will continue to deepen our understanding of our customers' lifestyles and needs. Our ongoing research into improved comfort and fit will expand. Our unparalleled selection of styles and sizes will grow. And our commitment to quality will never falter. Because even with all our success, we have never, and will never, change the fundamentals upon which Milton Florsheim established his company.

near Chicago's Loop and two others on the northwest side of the city. In 1953, Florsheim was purchased by International Shoe Company (now called Interco), the largest shoe manufacturer in the world, for about $21 million. Three years later, Florsheim's status was changed from that of a subsidiary to a division of Interco. Florsheim was still run autonomously, however, with Harold Florsheim in charge of the division.

Florsheim quickly became International's most important unit. In fact, in its first decade as part of International, Florsheim thrived, increasing its sales nearly every year, while the parent company struggled for the most part. Between 1953 and 1963, Florsheim's sales doubled. By the end of that period, Florsheim was contributing an impressive 58 percent of International's earnings, while generating only about a quarter of its sales. Florsheim was the overwhelming leader among producers of better shoes for men (with prices of at least $20 per pair), controlling over 70 percent of that market. The company's success had much to do with Harold Florsheim's marketing innovations, as well as with the company's wise refusal to dilute its line with cheaper shoes, which could increase sales but would also trim its profit ratios.

A Period of Expansion

Florsheim's operations were again expanded in the mid-1960s. Facilities at Cape Girardeau, Missouri, were enlarged, and, in 1966, 39 new company-owned retail outlets were added, bringing the total number of stores to 238, while the number of outside dealers selling Florsheim shoes reached 5,000. Furthermore, a new Florsheim plant was opened in Anna, Illinois, and soon thereafter one of that facility's units was converted for the additional production of women's shoes, which were sold through Interco's Thayer-McNeil chain of retail stores. Harold Florsheim became company chairperson in 1966. He held this position until his retirement three years later, and remained active in the company for several years before his death in 1987.

In 1971, two new Florsheim manufacturing facilities were launched, bringing the company's total to 14. Retail stores run by the company sold about 25 percent of the shoes produced in these plants. By the end of that year, there were 546 Florsheim outlets, and, of these, 75 were Thayer-McNeil Shoe Salons, where Florsheim's women's line was sold. The following year, 36 more stores were added, including seven Thayer-McNeils. However, later in the 1970s, Florsheim began to phase out its production of women's shoes. Although the company continued to operate its Thayer-McNeil stores, wholesale women's operations were cut out completely, and all outside retail accounts for women's shoes were discontinued.

Developments in the 1980s

During this time, an influx of imported shoes began to cripple the U.S. shoe industry. By 1978, the number of American workers in the industry was cut in half to 30,000. Furthermore, between 1980 and 1985, the share of imported men's shoes sold in the United States rose from 44 to 70 percent. As a response to this trend, Florsheim shifted more of its production to foreign countries, where labor was considerably less expensive. About 200 people were put out of work in 1986, when Florsheim closed its Poplar Bluff, Missouri, factory, a plant that had been in operation for 40 years. Despite this industrywide downturn, Florsheim reintroduced women's shoes to its product line in 1986.

In 1985, Ronald Mueller took over as head of Florsheim. Mueller had worked for the company since 1951, when, at age 15, he was employed as an assistant window dresser. Under Mueller, Florsheim began to experiment with an electronic retailing system called the Florsheim Express Shop. The Express Shop was an interactive computerized system allowing stores to order shoes through a terminal connected to the warehouse at the company's Chicago headquarters, which maintained an inventory of 1.5 million pairs of shoes. The system allowed the customer to view the shoes on a video monitor, and to select any style or size in the 250-style Florsheim line. The buyer then received the shoes via UPS within a week. The test placements of the Express Shop were a clear-cut success. By mid-1987, the terminals were in place at 200 stores.

By the beginning of 1988, 336 Florsheim Express Shops were in operation in 16 states, and the company set a goal of maintaining a total of 2,000 Express Shops. Stores with the terminals installed generally showed increases of 15 to 33 percent in sales. During that year, Interco consolidated its International Shoe Company division into Florsheim, moving its operations into Florsheim's Chicago headquarters. Toward the end of the 1980s, there were actually fewer Florsheim stores, about 250 total, but these stores garnered more sales. This was partly due to a broadening of the Florsheim line to include casual and athletic shoes for the first time in the company's history, including the Florsheim Comfortech line, which incorporated elements of athletic and walking shoes into a dress shoe design. Many stores that had to supplement their inventories with lower-priced casual shoes were now able to carry stock com-

Key Dates:

1892: Milton Florsheim founds Florsheim & Co.
1936: Irving Florsheim succeeds Milton at the helm of the company.
1953: Florsheim is acquired by International Shoe Company (now InterCo).
1966: Harold Florsheim is named chairman of the company.
1987: Ronald Mueller heads the company.
1990: Florsheim boutiques open in Sears stores.
1991: InterCo files for bankruptcy.
1994: InterCo spins off Florsheim into a separate public company.
1995: Mueller is replaced by Charles Campbell.
1996: Company name is changed to Florsheim Group Inc.

posed entirely of Florsheim products. In 1989, Florsheim stores that carried the company's comfort shoe line showed a ten percent increase in sales over the stores that did not.

Meanwhile, Florsheim continued to cut its production costs by moving more of its manufacturing overseas. Between 1986 and 1989, the portion of the company's shoes made in the United States shrank from 80 to less than 50 percent. In 1988 and 1989, nine Florsheim and International Shoe Co. factories in the United States were shut down, leaving only four domestic facilities in operation, all located in Missouri and southern Illinois. In 1990, the company began developing a franchising program, in which smaller stores were opened under franchise agreements in secondary markets (initially Council Bluffs, Iowa, and Clarksville, Tennessee), while the company continued to operate its own stores in the major market areas. Florsheim also began to withdraw from its leased shoe department arrangements in other stores due to their unimpressive sales volume.

Around this time, testing was begun on in-store sales at some well established chains, particularly Kuppenheimer's discount men's clothing stores and Sears, Roebuck & Co. outlets. The Sears test was a huge success, and in 1990, the company announced that Florsheim footwear boutiques would be opened at 100 Sears locations, replacing the regular men's shoe departments of stores in Chicago, Detroit, Milwaukee, southern California, New Jersey, New York, and Connecticut. The boutiques would include electronic Express Shop kiosks, which by this time numbered over 500 nationwide.

The 1990s

In 1991, Interco filed for Chapter 11 bankruptcy. Interco had been starved for cash since fighting off a 1988 takeover attempt by the Rales brothers through their private investment firm, City Capital Associates. That battle saddled Interco with a debt of $1.9 billion, which it sought to reduce by selling off or liquidating most of its holdings. Florsheim was one of the few parts of Interco left intact. In spite of Interco's problems, Florsheim remained active in the early 1990s. Two new shoe styles were introduced in 1991. One of them, the Bantam Walking Shoe, was an attempt to tap into the popular walking shoe market that had long been dominated by such brands as Rockport and Reebok. The Florsheim Comfortech Imperial was a new spin on Florsheim's traditional top-of-the-line Imperial, adding its patented Flor-Flex cushioning and heel padding.

A joint venture was also launched in 1991 with a Mexican investor to sell Florsheim shoes in Mexico. Although this project was reasonably successful, it too was sold off the following year by the cash-poor parent company. Florsheim made another international move in 1991, establishing a wholly owned subsidiary in Italy, the company's most important European market. That year, the company focused on sales abroad, and was able to increase its exports by 35 percent. Domestically, the alliance with Sears continued to pay off handsomely. A presence in such a widespread chain helped Florsheim increase its market share significantly. The arrangement also helped Sears, which benefited from the presence of products with a reputation for high quality in its stores.

Although dress shoes remained Florsheim's principal product in the early 1990s, an overall shrinkage of the U.S. market for dress shoes prompted the company to focus more on casual footwear. Florsheim courted younger buyers in its attempt to beef up sales, unveiling a new, more modern, brass plate logo to replace its longstanding shield logo. Furthermore, the company hired popular sports commentator John Madden to endorse Florsheim shoes in media spots, a move which resulted in increased sales for the Comfortech line. The share of Florsheim's sales contributed by Comfortech (which sold an estimated one million pairs) grew from less than five percent to 23 percent in the four-year period ending in 1992.

Interco emerged from bankruptcy in 1992. Leo Black's Apollo Investment Fund, which had advised the company during its financial reorganization, gained a majority stake in Interco. In 1994 Interco, which sought to focus on its furniture operations, spun off its two successful shoe divisions—Florsheim and Converse—into publicly held companies. Mueller was slated to head Florsheim.

The young company concentrated on boosting its sales. Since dress shoes continued to lose ground to casual and dress-casual shoes in the competitive footwear market, Florsheim made it a top priority to expand its product line beyond its standard wing tips. "The new design reflects our expanded product line," Mueller told *Retail Store Image*. Gone were the dark stores that resembled exclusive men's clubs more than shoe shops. Instead Florsheim brightened up its outlets and dressed its salespeople in hipper, more casual outfits.

Florsheim's bold tactics to broaden its customer base grew more aggressive after Mueller retired in 1995 and was replaced as chairman and CEO by Charles Campbell. "We need to diversify product," Campbell declared in an interview with *Dow Jones Investor Network* shortly after taking the company's helm. He noted, "Florsheim has got the image of 'my father is Florsheim.' My father's dress shoe. If you look in our stores, we're somewhat intimidating towards a younger consumer." After changing the company's name in 1996 to the Florsheim Group Inc., Campbell launched a bevy of sub-brands in 1996 and 1997 that were designed to target men of different ages and income levels than the 48-year old businessman who typically bought Florsheim. The @ease brand, a casual shoe priced below $50 and aimed at younger consumers, debuted, as did FLS, a dress-casual offering, and Florsheim Imperial, a less expensive dress shoe. Florsheim also introduced Frogs, a line of golf shoes that targeted its original older and wealthier customers. Such sub-branding protected Florsheim from diluting its highly respected core brand with its new additions. The company's efforts proved effective. In 1996 Florsheim reported a profit of about $2 million, a substantial improvement over its net loss of $4.8 million in 1995.

In a further bid to broaden its appeal, Florsheim finalized licensing deals in 1996, and in 1997 released its John Deere work boots and Joseph Abboud dress shoes. In 1998, the company opened a new chain of stores called @ease that catered to men from 20 to 35 to distance itself from its stodgier connotations. To increase traffic in both its Florsheim and @ease retail outlets, the company began offering rivals' shoes, including Timberland and Doc Martens.

Apart from the launching of its @ease stores, Florsheim deemphasized its retail ventures. The company closed 15 of its 92 factory outlet stores and 20 of its Florsheim stores in 1998. At the same time, Florsheim strove to build its wholesale operations. After forging a relationship with J.C. Penney in 1998, Florsheim installed its kiosks in over 400 Penney branches. The company also focused on bolstering international sales.

Turbulent times were ahead, however. Sales for 1998 disappointed investors, and the bankruptcy of two of Florsheim's biggest customers, Chernin's Shoe Corp. and the Shoe Corporation of America, eroded Florsheim's 1999 profits. In May 1999, a former assistant to Campbell sued the company for Campbell's alleged sexual misconduct. After the case was settled, Florsheim continued to focus on increasing its presence in the non-athletic shoe market.

Principal Competitors

Bally Management Ltd.; Berkshire Hathaway Inc.; Brown Shoe Company Inc.; Kenneth Cole Productions, Inc.; Nike, Inc.; Phillips-Van Heusen Corporation; Reebok International Ltd.; The Timberland Company; Wolverine World Wide, Inc.

Further Reading

George, Melissa, ''Slimmer Florsheim Steps Up Wholesale Focus,'' *Crain's Chicago Business*, June 15, 1998.

Goldenburg, Jane, ''Casuals, Athletic Lines Add to Florsheim Punch,'' *Footwear News*, January 9, 1989, p. 1.

——, ''Florsheim Puts Thumbs Up for Video Buying System,'' *Footwear News*, January 11, 1988, p. 10.

Gruber, William, ''Florsheim Success Work of 'Sole' Man,'' *Chicago Tribune*, April 6, 1987, sec. 4, p. 4.

Howard, Tammi, ''Florsheim Mulls Reentry into Women's Wholesale,'' *Footwear News*, March 25, 1985, p.1.

''Interco: Making Big Strides,'' *Financial World*, February 9, 1972, p. 5.

''Interco Strides Toward Third Successive Peak,'' *Barron's*, April 17, 1967, p. 29.

Lassiter, Dawn, ''Harold Florsheim Dies at 87; Industry Pioneer,'' *Footwear News*, February 9, 1987, p. 2.

Lazarus, George, ''Florsheim Sees Good Fit in Franchising Venture,'' *Chicago Tribune*, February 6, 1990, sec. 3, p. 4.

Musgrove, Matt, ''Stepping into the Next Century,'' *Retail Store Image*, January 1, 1994.

''Nepotism: Good & Bad,'' *Forbes*, July 15, 1964, pp. 32–33.

Patterson, Greg, ''Charles Campbell: Chairman, CEO, President of Florsheim Shoe,'' *Dow Jones Investor Network*, November 28, 1995.

Randle, Wilma, ''Florsheim Works to Capture Heart and Sole of Younger Men,'' *Chicago Tribune*, August 6, 1990, sec. 4, p. 1.

Rooney, Ellen, ''Florsheim Grows Beyond Dress Shoe Foundation,'' *Footwear News*, August 31, 1992, p. 2.

——, ''Florsheim, Sears Team Up with Boutique Operations,'' *Footwear News,* September 10, 1990, p. 4.

Schechter, Dara, ''Florsheim, Converse at Interco Still,'' *Footwear News*, January 16, 1989, p. 1.

Schmeltzer, John, ''Florsheim Steps Forward While Parent Company Treads Water,'' *Chicago Tribune*, May 4, 1992, sec. 4, p. 1.

Waterman, Phil, ''Interco Strides Toward Ninth Straight Peak Year,'' *Barron's*, February 21, 1972, pp. 26–28.

Wessling, Jack, ''Florsheim Expanding Its Electronic Retailing,'' *Footwear News*, June 29, 1987, p. 2.

——, ''Int'l Shoe Name May Be Dropped,'' *Footwear News*, March 21, 1988, p. 1.

—Robert R. Jacobson
—updated by Rebecca Stanfel

Garden Fresh Restaurant Corporation

17180 Bernardo Center Drive
San Diego, California 92128
U.S.A.
Telephone: (619) 675-1600
Fax: (619) 675-1616

Public Company
Incorporated: 1995 as Souplantation Incorporated
Employees: 3,955
Sales: $132 million (1999)
Stock Exchanges: NASDAQ
Ticker Symbol: LTUS
NAIC: 722211 Limited-Service Restaurants

Garden Fresh Restaurant Corporation is one of the fastest growing restaurant chains in southern California. Started in the late 1970s, Garden Fresh offers buffet style dining with an emphasis on fresh salads, homemade breads and pastries, and soups made from scratch. Garden Fresh operates 61 restaurants under the names Souplantation and Sweet Tomatoes, and has locations primarily in the western and southern regions of the country. Much of the company's success is due to the rapidly growing market of health-conscious fast-food dining, as well as to Garden Fresh's strategic growth plan. Besides Souplantation and Sweet Tomatoes, Garden Fresh also owns and operates a takeout deli called Ladles, located in southern California.

A Fresh Idea: 1978–Late 1980s

Garden Fresh, originally founded as Souplantation Incorporated, was started in 1978 by Michael Mack, a San Diego businessman who, while possessing little background in the restaurant industry, saw great potential in the development of a fast-food chain with a health-conscious twist. Souplantation presented itself from the beginning as an affordable, healthy alternative to other chains, with prices kept well below the cost of a more traditional restaurant meal. It was not only low prices which initially drew customers to the business: Souplantation also offered a tremendous variety of condiments, vegetables, soups, and breads, all of which were laid out on two long buffet tables. During the time Souplantation was founded, ''all-you-can-eat'' buffets were becoming increasingly popular, and the restaurant took advantage of this trend by offering its own version: for a fixed price, a customer could without limit choose as many meals as he or she desired, with the added incentive that, unlike more traditional buffet restaurants, what was being offered was beneficial to the customer's health.

The idea took off, and Souplantation in the 1980s began to grow rapidly in the San Diego area. The restaurants featured two buffet tables of approximately 55 feet in length located at the center of an open dining area. The company's attempt at uniformity in its look and quality was necessary to establish customer recognition and loyalty, especially as other, similar chains began to establish themselves during the course of the decade.

Competition became increasingly intense in the 1980s, as what the local San Diego papers referred to as the ''soup-n-salad'' wars began to heat up in southern California. California consumers were among the first in the nation to popularize health food trends and, with that region's notoriously frenetic lifestyle, it was natural for that trend to be tied to fast-food and takeout restaurants. By the middle of the decade, San Diego had three chains competing against one another, with each offering similar fare at similar prices. The companies Soup Exchange, Fresh Choice, and Souplantation found themselves in a neck and neck battle for customers, and had to find some way in which to distinguish themselves from one another.

In response to the threat of Soup Exchange, a regional franchise, and Fresh Choice, Souplantation tightened its focus on its menu selections, concentrating primarily on salads and soup. While Fresh Choice and Soup Exchange experimented with other menus and pricing systems, Souplantation kept its fare and price packages simple and uniform. The company maintained such basic simplicity in its menu in an effort to refrain from confusing customers, with the notion that reliability and quality would win out over novelty. The strategy proved sound, as Fresh Choice's stock began to tumble at the end of the decade, and Soup Exchange, after revamping its image several times, saw its sales plummet.

While its two competitors struggled, Souplantation began to expand rapidly during the last few years of the 1980s. By 1987,

Company Perspectives:

Since the opening of its first Souplantation in 1978 in San Diego, California, Garden Fresh Restaurant Corporation has expanded to 61 salad buffet restaurants with locations in Southern California, where they are known as Souplantation, and in Northern California and ten other states, where they are known as Sweet Tomatoes. Differing in name only, the restaurants are known for their abundance of fresh, great tasting salad selections, soups, bakery items, pastas and desserts in a self-serve format, set in a casual dining atmosphere.

the company's sites had a healthy average of 700 to 1,200 customers a day, with each paying between $5.00 to $7.00 for a meal. The chain grew throughout the southern California area and by 1990 had over two dozen sites in operation. In a spurt of tremendous expansion, Souplantation opened 11 new restaurants in just under 13 months, a period of growth which was ultimately to prove too much of a financial and managerial burden on the young company. Just after its rapid expansion, the company's sales began to falter, falling prey to unexpectedly high overhead and a system of management poorly equipped to handle so many sites at one time.

In 1990 the company took the drastic step of bringing in a new CEO who would have enough experience and understanding of the restaurant industry to turn the company around. After an extensive search, Souplantation finally brought in industry veteran John Bifone, an executive who had in the past year turned the 160-unit chain of Bojangles restaurants from a doomed company losing $9 million a year to one that was back in the black by over $1 million in 1989. Bifone had positive instincts about the company's future, saying to the *San Diego Business Journal* soon after taking over that "What I really liked about the business was that I thought the Souplantation concept was a brilliantly positioned concept for the '90s and the turn of the century."

Immediately upon taking the helm of Souplantation, Bifone began to systematically alter some of the more glaring problems at the company. First, he increased the company's focus on making its locations more uniform in appearance and quality. During the company's expansion at the end of the 1980s, some of its sites had, due to poor or misguided management, grown sloppy in their appearance and menu preparation. Bifone solved this issue by instituting a new training program whereby all Souplantation employees were given instruction over everything from food presentation to sanitation, with the most important emphasis being quality control and keeping each Souplantation location similar to the others.

Besides the new training program, Bifone also slowed the company's growth, choosing instead to focus on the quality and increased sales of the existing restaurants. Most drastically, Bifone convinced the company to change the name of some of the restaurants to Sweet Tomatoes, particularly those which were being introduced outside the San Diego area. The name Souplantation, Bifone felt, was too similar in sound to Soup Exchange, and did not emphasize enough the chain's focus on salads and other products.

1990–95: National Expansion

Bifone's efforts to renew Souplantation were successful, and within less than two years the company was ready to begin further expansion, this time with a focus on national growth. The company, unlike some of its competitors, particularly those which were franchises, renewed and maintained tight control over its quality and menus. In addition, because of its service structure the company had much lower labor costs—between 16 and 19 percent of its sales—than that of other, more traditional restaurants.

The concept behind Souplantation held the company in good stead as well: Richard Martin, writing for *Nation's Restaurant News,* stated that "The relative ease with which salad and soup bar offerings can be modified to suit changing taste trends is seen as a fundamental advantage enjoyed by a food-bar based concept." In other words, because Souplantation offered such perennial basics as salad, soup, and bread, it could easily adapt to changing fashions in cuisine and culture, regardless of region or time.

When Souplantation first expanded into regions other than the company's home base of southern California it chose areas which were naturally compatible to the restaurant's image and menu, namely regions in which agriculture flourished and healthy lifestyles were popular. In the early 1990s, Souplantation opened several new restaurants in Arizona and Florida, all of which operated under the name Sweet Tomatoes. Arizona and Florida were both states in which the products necessary for the company were easily attained at relatively low cost, and, because of the high population of retirees in the regions, buffet style restaurants had a history of healthy sales.

The early 1990s saw Souplantation not only mitigate successfully the risks it took during the company's rapid expansion during the previous decade, but begin to grow again as well, and this time with a more strategic, conservative agenda. Within a few years, the company penetrated markets in Utah, Texas, New Mexico, and, by the middle of the decade, made a bid for southern consumers in Georgia. The company's sales were doing so well that the business found it necessary to change locations in 1993, moving to a more spacious office space in the San Diego area which would allow for the hiring of more employees and further expansion.

1995–99: Going Public and Continued National Growth

In May 1995 Souplantation went public with a listing on the NASDAQ. The company made the decision to go public in order to both reduce debt, much of which it had accrued during its expansion and restructuring in the early 1990s, and use the profit gained from stock sales to prepare for further expansion across the country. Just before Souplantation's IPO, the company changed its name to Garden Fresh Restaurant Corporation, but maintained the names Souplantation and Sweet Tomatoes for its restaurants.

Key Dates:

1978: Souplantation is founded.
1990: Company adds the name Sweet Tomatoes to its restaurants.
1995: Initial public offering.
1999: Garden Fresh launches the Ladles takeout deli concept.

In 1996 Garden Fresh trumped its faltering competitors, experiencing a 74 percent increase in profits. Despite devastating floods in southern California the previous year, which had caused the price of lettuce and other salad products to skyrocket, Garden Fresh maintained its steady climb in sales, and managed to continue to keep the cost of its menu well below the $10 mark. In August 1996, Garden Fresh opened another restaurant in Florida, and had a record opening day guest count of over 1,500 customers, a tremendous amount of traffic for a 7,500-square-foot restaurant.

The middle years of the 1990s saw Garden Fresh develop into a truly national company: by 1997, almost 40 percent of the company's growth was due to restaurant openings in states other than California, with many of the locations centered in the western part of the country. In 1998, Garden Fresh had a total of 56 restaurants, spread from throughout the Southwest all the way to the eastern regions of the country, and had sales totaling over $110 million. Garden Fresh's focus on healthy, convenient food was paying off, especially as consumer trends in the 1990s continued to lean towards low-fat, high-fiber fare. In 1998, Garden Fresh also opened four new locations in Atlanta, Houston, Vancouver, and Portland, the latter of which represented a new territory for the company.

Because the company utilized a steady, strategic growth plan, Garden Fresh's sales continued to meet or exceed the company's projections, and were able to answer to much of the managerial and structural overhead costs run up by expansion. The company's stability, even in the face of rapid expansion, was also in evidence when, in the summer of 1999, a hurricane disrupted the opening of three new Sweet Tomatoes sites on the East Coast. Although the dates had to be set back because of damage done to the buildings, the openings went ahead as planned.

Century's End: Experimenting with a New Niche Market

Garden Fresh had proved its success in the buffet business, and the company saw in that success another opportunity to develop a new market, what the company called its "takery" concept. The "takery" idea—a combination of "takeout" and "bakery"—made use of Garden Fresh's reputation for serving freshly made food which could be enjoyed on the run. In July 1999 Garden Fresh opened its first "takery" in Encinitas, California. Calling it Ladles, the store offered pre-packaged soups, salads, and freshly made breads to go. The company based the idea on both the success of its own chain and the inspiration of gourmet New York delis such as Dean & DeLuca and Balducci's. Ladles was not a sit-down buffet like Sweet Tomatoes and Souplantation, and instead was presented as a healthy, gourmet alternative to meals cooked at home. Ladles' prices, because all the meals were prepackaged and had a gourmet twist, were slightly higher than those of either Sweet Tomatoes or Souplantation, averaging just around $10 for a full meal.

By 1999 Garden Fresh was operating 61 restaurants across the nation and had plans to continue expanding on an average of 12 restaurants a year. With that year's sales over $132 million, and trends in the restaurant industry increasingly tending towards the company's favor, Garden Fresh's future appeared bright.

Principal Competitors

Buffets, Inc.; Fresh Choice, Inc.; Furr's Supermarkets, Inc.; Bishop's.

Further Reading

Core, Richard, "Garden Fresh Finds Salad Days Again," *San Diego Business Journal*, February 8, 1993, p. 8.

"Garden Fresh Ends Fiscal '98 with Gains in Sales," *Nation's Restaurant News*, December 7, 1998, p. 12.

"Garden Fresh Opens Seventh Florida Restaurant to Record Opening Day Attendance," *PR Newswire*, August 5, 1996, p. 0805

Liddle, Alan, "Garden Fresh Optimistic About Return of 'Salad' Days," *Nation's Restaurant News*, March 24, 1997, p. 11.

Martin, Richard, "California Sprouts Soup-n-Salad Wars," *Nation's Restaurant News*, August 17, 1987, p. 1.

——, "Souplantation Parent Garden Fresh Going Public to Pay Debts, Expand," *Nation's Restaurant News*, May 1, 1995, p. 3.

Spector, Amy, "Garden Fresh Launches Ladles 'Takery' Concept," *Nation's Restaurant News*, August 2, 1999, p. 4.

—Rachel H. Martin

Getty Images, Inc.

2101 Fourth Avenue, Suite 500
Seattle, Washington 98121
U.S.A.
Telephone: (206) 695-3400
Fax: (206) 695-3401
Web site: http://www.getty-images.com

Public Company
Incorporated: 1995 as Getty Communications plc
Employees: 1,345
Sales: $185.1 million (1998)
Stock Exchanges: NASDAQ
Ticker Symbol: GETTY
NAIC: 51412 Libraries and Archives; 51331 Wired Telecommunications Carriers

Getty Images, Inc. is the largest provider of visual content in the world, controlling more than 60 million still images and more than 30,000 hours of footage. Getty's content ranges from contemporary to archival material, grouped within branded collections that include: Tony Stone Images, a contemporary stock photography provider; Hulton Getty, one of the two largest privately owned collections of archival photography; Allsport, a leading sports photography brand; PhotoDisc, a pioneer in royalty-free stock photography and electronic delivery; Liaison Agency, specializing in news-oriented images; and Energy Film Library, a leading supplier of stock footage. Getty marketed its visual content through catalogs and through a handful of Web sites, maintaining its contact with customers through a worldwide network of sales offices and agents in 67 countries.

Origins

Fittingly, the occasion of Getty's birth as a visual content provider occurred through an acquisition, one of many to follow in the years ahead. On March 14, 1995, the company commenced operations when founders Mark Getty, a descendant of Jean Paul Getty, the multibillionaire business executive, and Jonathan Klein completed their first acquisition, purchasing Tony Stone Images. Tony Stone was regarded as one of the world's leading providers of contemporary stock photography, owning a body of images, highlighted by a tightly edited core collection called the Dupe Master Collection, of more than one million photographs. With $42 million in sales for the year preceding its acquisition by Getty and Klein, Tony Stone became the foundation of the newly formed company, inaugurating its bid to become the preeminent provider of visual content. To reach such heights, Getty and Klein planned to be consolidators in the fragmented visual content industry, a strategy that required the founders to assess acquisition opportunities constantly. Their search was not restricted to contemporary stock photography, but encompassed a range of formats and subject matters, stretching from contemporary and archival stills and footage, to news, current affairs, features, and celebrity material. It was a plan predicated on acquisitions, something the company did with enthusiasm during the latter half of the 1990s as it added to its portfolio of images by the millions.

A year passed after the acquisition of Tony Stone Images before Getty acquired its next major collection. In April 1996, the company purchased Hulton Deutsch, one of the world's largest privately owned collections of archival photography. Renamed Hulton Getty, the collection included vintage prints taken by the photography industry's pioneers and images from throughout the world portraying significant events and people during the 19th and 20th centuries. Divided into 300 separate collections comprising approximately 15 million images, Hulton Getty drew the majority of its customers from the United Kingdom—primarily professional customers such as magazine, news, and book publishers. Tony Stone attracted similar users, but the collection also was used by advertising and design agencies, travel companies, and poster and calendar manufacturers. For those customers interested in either collection, Getty offered the material through a network of international sales offices in the traditional manner. Catalogues were sent to interested parties, who then selected the specific images they wanted to use, for which privilege they paid a sizable fee to Getty. As customers perused the collection catalogues, however, Getty, along with other companies in its industry, was preparing for a new era in the visual content industry. The digitization of photographs, which then could be displayed on Web pages, promised to expedite the selection and buying process for traditional customers and, potentially, spark demand among the general public. Accordingly, Getty estab-

Company Perspectives:

Our imagery is used in the broad spectrum of applications. There is a good chance that the next time you see a television commercial, read an annual report, glance at a poster, visit a website, or choose a greetings card, the image that catches your eye will have been supplied by us. Getty Images thrives in this dynamic and fast-moving industry because we are obsessed with providing the highest quality imagery capable of multiple sales; our customer service; our strong brand names; and our worldwide distribution network. We will capitalize on these key strengths to grow our existing business and to acquire complementary businesses in the future.

lished in-house departments charged with digitizing the images in each of its major collections.

For Getty, success in the visual content industry hinged on the geographic reach of the company and the breadth and depth of its images and footage. Displaying images on Web pages would greatly aid the company's attempt to reach as many customers as possible, but, with or without the advantages of electronic technology, Getty's marketing efforts depended on a group of strategically placed sales offices. Headquartered in London, Getty maintained sales offices in Boston, Chicago, Los Angeles, New York, Seattle, Toronto, Paris, Munich, Hamburg, and Vienna, while serving markets in other regions through agent licensees in 20 countries. Through this sales network, the company supplied the visual content demands of an international customer base, striving to offer as comprehensive a selection of imagery as its acquisitive efforts yielded. Like a retail superstore, Getty strove to be a one-stop destination for anyone interested in any form of visual content, which meant its management was continually either acquiring content or in search of acquiring content to flesh out the company's selections.

Stock Offering in 1996 Enables Future Acquisitions

One month after the purchase of Hulton Deutsch, Getty struck again, acquiring Fabulous Footage, a leading North American provider of contemporary stock footage. With content in three major categories—contemporary stills, archival stills, and contemporary footage—Getty represented enough of a presence in the visual content industry by mid-1996 to attract the attention of investors. The company presented itself to the investing public in July 1996, completing an initial public offering on the NASDAQ Exchange that raised the cash needed to fuel its acquisition campaign. The company's next move on the acquisition front bolstered its control over distribution in Europe. In November 1996, Getty purchased World View, the exclusive licensee of Tony Stone images in Holland, Belgium, Sweden, and Denmark. Based in Amsterdam, World View had served as a licensee for Tony Stone since 1987. Its acquisition by Getty represented part of the company's strategy to have wholly owned offices in major markets rather than operating through agents.

By the end of 1996—the first full year of operation—Getty's sales totaled $85 million and its net income stood at $2.7 million. The company's annual financial totals would increase significantly as new collections were added and as new segments of the visual content market were penetrated, which the company accomplished in November 1997 when it made its first foray into photojournalism. The entry into photojournalism came through the purchase of the Liaison Agency, a New York-based photography agency regarded as one of the world's leading suppliers of news material. Founded in 1966, Liaison possessed a library containing several million images of major news and entertainment events, stocked by the company's global network of photojournalists. Through its own connections and through a production and distribution agreement with France-based Gamma Presse Images SA, Liaison had contracts with roughly 750 photojournalists spread throughout the world. Magazine, book, and multimedia publishers ranked as the company's primary customers, who were serviced by Liaison agents in more than 50 countries. Liaison, which was organized as a subsidiary named Gamma Liaison, Inc., added yet another dimension to Getty's collection of images, giving the company news content it previously lacked and bolstering its selection in existing categories. Liaison, through a division called Liaison International, operated a contemporary stock photography business, which represented more than 250 renowned photographers. Another complementary aspect of Liaison's business was its corporate assignment division, which provided corporate clients with images for annual reports, company magazines, and corporate brochures.

With the additions to its content, Getty stood as a serious contender for supremacy in the visual content industry. One by one, the company had methodically enriched its image and footage collection, building on the contemporary stock photography of the Tony Stone collection by adding archival photography, contemporary stock footage, and news-oriented photography in successive order. By 1997, Getty was ready to unveil a new way to market its growing collection, a signal moment in the company's history that coincided with the formation of a development partnership with computer giant IBM. In April 1997, Getty and IBM began working together to create a digital image distribution system based on IBM's Digital Library watermarking system, which enabled a digital image to be visually identified as belonging to a copyright holder without detracting from the image's visual appeal. Concurrently, Getty launched ''Hulton Getty On-Line,'' a Web site containing selected images from the Hulton Getty collection. Initially, several thousand of the 15 million images within the collection were put on display, the first stage of a plan that called for 500,000 archival images to be online by the end of 1998.

Getty's foray into electronic commerce promised to mark a new era in the company's short history. No longer restricted to requesting catalogues, customers could examine and select images via the Internet, expediting the selection process substantially. Once their selection was made, customers contacted their nearest Getty sales office to license the rights to their selection and subsequently received a copy of the image suitable for reproduction in a variety of digital and analogue formats. The ease of online systems touched off excitement throughout the visual content industry, prompting providers to marshal their efforts toward the development of digital catalogues tailored for Web site display. Getty, which had been attempting to be the leading supplier of visual content in the world since its inception, added the objective of becoming the leading provider of visual content on the Internet. Toward this end, the company made rapid progress in 1997, shouldering past rivals by maintaining its posture as an aggressive acquirer.

Key Dates:

1995: Getty Communications is formed through acquisition of Tony Stone Images.
1996: Company debuts on the NASDAQ Exchange.
1997: The launch of "Hulton Getty On-Line" ushers company into electronic commerce.
1998: Getty Communications and PhotoDisc, Inc. merge, creating Getty Images, Inc.
1999: The Image Bank is acquired for $183 million.

In July 1997, Getty completed two important acquisitions. First, the company purchased the photographic work of Slim Aarons, regarded as one of the world's leading photojournalists. Aarons's photographs, which had appeared in a variety of national magazines in the United States, included portraits of politicians, entertainers, and his perspective of American society, capturing "a bygone world with a mischievous eye," according to Mark Getty in the press release announcing the acquisition. One week later, the company purchased Energy Film Library, greatly increasing the content of its footage collection. Energy, whose customers included advertising companies, feature film producers, and industrial clients, controlled a library containing 3,500 hours of footage, the majority of which had been mastered to digital imagery for online search and distribution. The acquisition represented a major step toward Getty's goal of amassing the largest collection of moving imagery in the world, adding one of the two leading companies in the stock footage industry to its existing Fabulous Footage collection.

1998 Merger with PhotoDisc

Getty's next move on the acquisition front led to profound changes, creating a new company and eventually prompting the relocation of headquarters away from London. In September 1997, Getty agreed to a union with PhotoDisc Inc., the leading royalty-free digital stock photography provider and the largest provider of imagery on the Internet. Traditionally, the royalty fee paid by customers entitled them to use an image for a limited time in a particular medium, but royalty-free providers sold images on a flat-fee basis, allowing the customer to use the image in any media without any time constraints. PhotoDisc, a pioneer in the royalty-free concept, represented an enormous addition to the content owned by Getty, creating a new company called Getty Images in February 1998 that drew its senior executives from both companies. Mark Torrance, the founder of PhotoDisc, became co-chairman of the new company, serving alongside co-chairman Mark Getty, while Klein assumed the responsibilities of chief executive officer, the same position he had held for Getty Communications.

As the details of the merger agreement between Getty and PhotoDisc were being finalized, another acquisition was announced. In February 1998, the company acquired Allsport plc., a sports photography agency whose photographers captured images from sports events throughout the world. Getty planned to distribute Allsport's current photographs and the agency's archive of four million edited images through its global network of sales offices and to distribute the images digitally on the Internet. After the absorption of Allsport and the completion of the merger between Getty Communications and PhotoDisc, the company ranked as the largest visual content provider in the world, registering $185 million in revenue at the end of 1998. Growth had come quickly, fueled through acquisitions that saw Getty complete a three-year climb to the top of its industry. Leadership, in terms of revenue, was a position Getty intended to maintain, an objective that called for the continued enhancement of the company's content collection and a concerted exploration of marketing opportunities in the digital age. As the 1990s drew to a close, Getty proved its rapid rise within the industry had not bred complacency. The company ended the decade decisively, setting the stage for its growth at the dawn of the 21st century.

In March 1999, Getty announced it was relocating its headquarters from London to the United States, where the majority of the company's revenue was collected. Seattle was selected as the new hub for the global organization, situating the company in the same city occupied by its closest rival, Corbis Corporation, spawned from the fortunes of Microsoft founder, Bill Gates. The move from London to Seattle reflected Getty's commitment to the potential of electronic commerce. "Because of the importance of technology, which is completely transforming our industry," Klein told the *Puget Sound Business Journal* in May 1999, "we wanted to be close to that expertise." The move to Seattle was expected to be completed before the end of 1999, but as the transition was taking place, the company announced the largest acquisition in its history. In September 1999, Getty revealed it was purchasing The Image Bank from Eastman Kodak Co. for $183 million. With 70 sales offices in 40 countries, The Image Bank owned significant contemporary and archival photography and film footage, representing the work of more than 1,500 photographers and more than 200 cinematographers. With the inclusion of The Image Bank's content into the disparate collections owned by Getty, the company's foundation for the 21st century was set, but was sure to increase as further acquisitions were completed in the years ahead. Controlling more than 60 million still images and more than 30,000 hours of footage, Getty promised to be an industry leader in the future.

Principal Subsidiaries

PhotoDisc, Inc.; Allsport Photographic plc; Carlton Communications BV.

Principal Competitors

Corbis Corporation; Eastman Kodak Company; United News & Media.

Further Reading

"Getty Images Teams with RealNetworks to Bring World-Class Images and Footage to Streaming Media Users," *PR Newswire,* September 14, 1999.

"Getty Images to Buy Image Bank," *United Press International,* September 22, 1999.

Goldstein, Alan, "Seattle-Based Getty Images Buys Photo, Video Collection from Eastman Kodak," *Knight-Ridder/Tribune Business News,* September 22, 1999.

Tice, Carol, "Stock Central: Seattle Is Now a Photo Capital," *Puget Sound Business Journal,* May 7, 1999, p. 1.

—Jeffrey L. Covell

Grameen Bank

Mirpur Two
Dhaka 1216
Bangladesh
Telephone: +880 (2) 801-138
Fax: +880 (2) 803-559
Web site: http://www.grameen.com

Private State-Owned Company
Incorporated: 1983
Employees: 13,000
Total Assets: $100 million (1998 est.)
NAIC: Commercial Banking; 513322 Cellular and Other Wireless Telecommunications

Grameen Bank founder Muhammad Yunus pioneered the concept of ''micro-credit''—minuscule loans to the very poor. The bank currently lends more than $500 million a year with a repayment rate of better than 97 percent (although critics have reported that some borrowers merely take out additional loans to meet their repayment schedules). Its Group Savings Funds have assets of $186 million. Grameen Bank operates 1,100 branches in half of Bangladesh's nearly 80,000 villages. The program has been successfully replicated in dozens of countries, including the Philippines, Malaysia, Vietnam, South Africa, and Bolivia. It has also been applied to inner city and rural poverty in rich nations in North America and Europe.

Origins

Muhammad Yunus was born in 1940 to a successful Muslim jeweler's family in Chittagong, then a part of colonial India. While teaching at a local college in the early 1960s, he noticed a need for a packaging plant in eastern Pakistan and established one with the help of his father and a loan from the state.

In 1965, Yunus left to study at the University of Colorado and Vanderbilt University under a Fulbright Scholarship. While teaching at Middle Tennessee State University in 1971, the War of Liberation broke out in eastern Pakistan, and Yunus lobbied for the Bengali cause in Washington, D.C.

Yunus returned home to the newly formed country of Bangladesh in 1972. Soon he was heading the economics department at Chittagong University. While there, the plight of the poor in the nearby village of Jobra distressed Yunus greatly as famine enveloped the country. With the help of his students, he surveyed the economic situation of the villagers and organized a project to plant higher yielding varieties of rice.

Such agrarian reforms required some financial and political finesse and stirred up considerable controversy. Yunus espoused the view that, as hunger and malnutrition limited a person's freedom of thought and action, so too was credit itself—access to economic resources—a basic human right. He developed a distrust of governmental and non-governmental aid programs whose funds, usually due to greed or infighting somewhere along the line, simply did not reach the society's very poorest members.

These people, Yunus found, existed in a cycle of debt, at the mercy of moneylenders charging ten percent interest a week and usurious traders. A person would borrow money for raw materials, work all day, then sell their handiwork back to the trader for a profit of only two cents. In 1976, Yunus had one of his students tally a list of villagers trapped in such situations. She came up with 42 names, who together needed less than US$27.00 to break out of the cycle and set out in business for themselves. Yunus loaned them the money himself.

The professor's attempts to get traditional banks to lend to poor people who had no collateral met with solid resistance. However, he was able to arrange for such a loan from the Janata Bank after months of wrangling and signing himself as guarantor. With this money, the Grameen Project (literally, ''of the village'') was launched in January 1977.

Yunus then set out to develop a lending methodology that would work for his impoverished clients. Rather than have a large lump sum payment at the end of the loan period, he structured the loans with minuscule daily payments in order to detect problems early and to increase borrowers' confidence. This was soon changed to weekly payments to reduce the accounting load. The term of the loans was set at one year.

Company Perspectives:

Grameen Bank (GB) has reversed conventional banking practice by removing the need for collateral and created a banking system based on mutual trust, accountability, participation and creativity. GB provides credit to the poorest of the poor in rural Bangladesh, without any collateral. At GB, credit is a cost effective weapon to fight poverty and it serves as a catalyst in the overall development of socioeconomic conditions of the poor who have been kept outside the banking orbit on the grounds that they are poor and hence not bankable. Professor Muhammad Yunus, the founder of ''Grameen Bank'' and its Managing Director, reasoned that if financial resources can be made available to the poor people on terms and conditions that are appropriate and reasonable, ''these millions of small people with their millions of small pursuits can add up to create the biggest development wonder.''

Another unique feature was the group of five that prospective borrowers had to organize. All the members would be collectively responsible for each individual's loan. Besides peer pressure, the groups were also a source of mutual support, and a large reason Grameen would be able to boast repayment rates in excess of 97 percent. Five percent of each loan went into a group fund that served as a kind of insurance.

The groups helped Grameen overcome its greatest source of resistance among the borrowers—*purdah,* or the set of Muslim practices relating to a woman's purity. (Although its clientele was evenly mixed at first, the bank soon began to loan more to females, who spent more of their profits on family needs rather than personal desires.) A rigid interpretation of these codes kept women indoors, out of sight of neighbors. In addition, many were afraid to handle money, traditionally the province of the husband. Grameen was able to help these women work within their own homes, more in harmony with *purdah* than other forms of employment. However, Grameen Bank would have to be vigilant against the practice of ''pipelining,'' or turning over loans to the husbands for unauthorized uses.

After operating through the Janata Bank for a year, Yunus in 1978 struck up an arrangement with the Bangladesh Krishi (Agriculture) Bank which freed him from having to personally sign for every single loan (the program had under 500 borrowers at the time). The Krishi Bank also hired a few of Yunus's students, giving them their first salary for this work.

The program was expanded through 25 branches of the Central Bank in 1979. Yunus took a leave of absence to oversee operations in Tangail, in the country's center. He stepped into a lawless, desperate place but the bank continued to grow. Grameen disbursed $13.4 million in loans in 1981 and $23.9 million the next year, when it had 28,000 members.

In order to prove to skeptics the bank did not run merely through the personal charisma of Yunus, its ambitious expansion plan covered five districts isolated from each other. The plan was financed by the Central Bank and a $3.4 million loan from the International Fund for Agricultural Development. Grameen was able to borrow from the government at a two percent annual interest rate. It charged borrowers 20 percent a year simple interest, paying the principal off first. This resulted in an effective ten to 12 percent annual rate, according to Grameen workers.

Independent in 1983

Grameen was made its own, independent bank in 1983. Yunus served as the government-appointed managing director. Eventually, his position was changed so that he answered to the board of directors; however, the chairman remained a government appointee. The government's ownership was also gradually reduced from an initial 60/40 majority to 25 percent, which it held with its Somali Bank and the Bangladesh Krishi Bank. The other 75 percent (by 1993, 88 percent) was owned by the bank's members themselves. Bank headquarters were moved to Dhaka's financial district.

Against typical institutional resistance, it started a fund for modest housing loans in 1984, which provided ten-year loans in the $125 to $300 range for basic shelters. The way the bank interacted with its members developed as well. Its expectations were reflected in four resolutions adopted at a 1980 workshop which by 1984 had become the bank's famous ''Sixteen Decisions.'' These ranged from abstractions—promising to follow the principles of ''discipline, unity, courage, and hard work''—to practical mandates—''We shall not live in dilapidated houses. . . . We shall grow vegetables all the year round.'' Also included was a statement against the dowry system.

By the mid-1980s, the Grameen program had garnered international attention and various attempts to replicate it were being made in other undeveloped countries such as Malaysia and the Philippines. Grameen started its own replication program through the Grameen Trust, initially funded by the MacArthur Foundation. At home, it took over a fisheries project from the Bangladesh government.

Other Grameen-inspired programs began to address poverty in the United States from urban Chicago to Sioux and Cherokee reservations. Bill Clinton, then governor of Arkansas, asked Yunus to help set up a similar program in his home state in 1986. The Clintons remained avid supporters of the Grameen Bank. Yunus traveled to the United States in 1987 to testify before a Congressional committee; this resulted in extensive media coverage. Two years later, ''Sixty Minutes'' dispatched a crew to Bangladesh to report on the bank's success.

Trying Times in 1991

In 1991, a newly democratic government in Bangladesh made it a policy to forgive all government loans of less than 5,000 Bangladesh Takas or $125. As Grameen Bank was not on the government payroll, it could not forgive its micro-loans and survive, making it unable to share the same windfall with the very poor who made up its own clientele. A horrific cyclone in April 1991 also set back the bank's efforts considerably.

Key Dates:

1976: Professor Muhammad Yunus begins micro-credit experiment by loaning $27 to 42 villagers in need.
1977: The Janata Bank loans Yunus money to start the Grameen Project.
1983: Grameen Bank created as its own official entity; relocates headquarters from Chittagong to Dhaka.
1987: U.S. visit by Yunus garners extensive support and media coverage.
1991: Bank's worst year complicated by horrific cyclone.
1998: Bank reaches $2 billion in total loans disbursed; seeks outside support after severe flooding.

In 1993, Grameen organized a cooperative, Grameen Uddog (Initiatives), to help desperately poor local weavers sell their goods on the international market. The weavers produced a unique fabric, Grameen Check, which the group pitched in Europe and North America.

By the mid-1990s, Grameen was lending US$500 million a year. Its 1,000 branches served two million borrowers—more than nine in ten of them women—in 35,000 villages. It had 11,000 employees and instituted a pension program for them. The value of its cumulative loans reached US$1 billion in 1996 and US$2 billion in 1998.

Grameen diversified the types of loans it made. Among its new interests, hand-powered wells and loans to support the enterprises of Grameen members' immediate relatives. There were also seasonal agricultural loans and lease-to-own agreements for equipment and livestock. The bank also posited a new goal for itself: making each of its branches free of poverty, as defined by benchmarks such as having adequate food and access to clean water and latrines.

Most rural villages in Bangladesh lacked electricity and in 1997, Bangladesh had only one phone for every 300 people. Communicating with distant relatives required the use of a messenger and an inordinate expenditure of time. A unique solution was proposed to help the poor communicate, bypassing the infrastructure of land phone lines. GrameenPhone, a four member, for-profit consortium 51 percent owned by Norway's Telenor, became one of Bangladesh's three cellular phone providers in 1997. The nonprofit Grameen Telecom unit bought its airtime for resale to village "telephone ladies," who in turn sold their neighbors access to their own cellular phones, bought with Grameen loans. To power these phones in rural areas, Grameen Shakti was formed to develop solar energy sources. Two other offshoots of the phone program, Grameen Cybernet and Grameen Communications, offered Internet services on a for-profit and nonprofit basis, respectively.

The high cost of healthcare remained one of the Grameen Bank's biggest concerns, it being one force that could totally wipe out the progress any one borrower made. A health program was set up to provide health insurance at a very low cost (less than $5 per year). Retirement funds were also organized around the profitable Grameen businesses, managed by the Grameen Securities Management Company.

Natural forces also offered up potent problems. In 1998, flooding destroyed the shelters of half the bank's borrowers and left Yunus scrambling for outside financial support. The momentum of the micro-credit concept continued nevertheless. In the spring of 1999, the Soros Economic Development Fund gave Grameen Telecom a $10.6 million loan to place a cell phone in each of 50,000 villages. As the Grameen Foundation USA established Project Enterprise Peer Lending programs in Harlem and Brooklyn, a launch party for Professor Yunus's new book at the United Nations' New York headquarters drew numerous celebrities.

Principal Subsidiaries

Grameen Trust; Grameen Motsho (Fisheries) Foundation; Grameen Uddog; Grameen Telecom; GrameenPhone (35%); Grameen Shakti (Energy); Grameen Cybernet Ltd.; Grameen Communications; Grameen Securities Management Company; Grameen Foundation USA; Grameen Shamogree (Products); Grameen Kalyan (Welfare).

Principal Competitors

World Bank.

Further Reading

Auwal, Mohammad A., "Promoting Microcapitalism in the Service of the Poor: The Grameen Model and Its Cross-Cultural Adaptation," *Journal of Business Communication*, January 1996, pp. 27–49.

Bernasek, Alexandra, and James Ronald Stanfield, "The Grameen Bank As Progressive Institutional Adjustment," *Journal of Economic Issues*, June 1997, pp. 359–66.

Bornstein, David, *The Price of a Dream: The Story of the Grameen Bank and the Idea That Is Helping the Poor to Change Their Lives,* New York: Simon & Schuster, 1996.

"Community Banking: Group Power," *Economist,* September 10, 1994, pp. 93–94.

Counts, Alex, *Give Us Credit: How Muhammad Yunus's Micro-Lending Revolution Is Empowering Women from Bangladesh to Chicago,* New York: Times Books, 1996.

Currie, Antony, "Small Lenders Count Too," *Euromoney,* July 1996, p. 20.

Dichter, Thomas, Review of *Give Us Credit* by Alex Counts and *Women at the Center* by Helen Todd, *Finance and Development*, September 1997, pp. 52–54.

Hashemi, Syed M., Sidney Ruther Schuler, and Ann P. Ripley, "Rural Credit Programs and Women's Empowerment in Bangladesh," *World Development*, April 1996, pp. 635–53.

Jolis, Alan, "The Good Banker," *Independent,* Sunday supplement, May 5, 1996.

Jordan, Miriam, "It Takes a Cell Phone—A New Nokia Transforms a Village in Bangladesh," *Wall Street Journal,* June 25, 1999, p. B1.

Kamaluddin, S., "Lender with a Mission," *Far Eastern Economic Review,* March 18, 1993, pp. 38, 40.

Margolis, Judy, "When a Little Money Goes a Long Way," *Canadian Banker,* January/February 1996, pp. 26–30.

"Microlending: From Tiny Acorns," Review of *Banker to the Poor* by Muhammad Yunus and Alan Jolis, *Economist,* December 12, 1998.

Power, Carol, "Banker to Poor Makes Big Impact with Small Loans," *Irish Times,* June 25, 1999, p. 54.

Rahman, Aminur, "Micro-Credit Initiatives for Equitable and Sustainable Development: Who Pays?" *World Development*, January 1999, pp. 67–82.

Taub, Richard P., "Making the Adaptation Across Cultures and Societies: A Report on an Attempt to Clone the Grameen Bank in Southern Arkansas," *Journal of Developmental Entrepreneurship*, Summer 1998, pp. 53–69.

Todd, Helen, *Women at the Center: Grameen Bank Borrowers After One Decade,* Boulder, Colo.: Westview Press, 1996.

Wahid, Abu, "The Grameen Bank and Women in Bangladesh," *Challenge,* September/October 1999, pp. 94–101.

Yaron, Jacob, "Successful Rural Finance Institutions," *Finance and Development,* March 1994, pp. 32–35.

Yunus, Muhammad, and Alan Jolis, *Banker to the Poor: Micro-Lending and the Battle Against World Poverty,* New York: PublicAffairs, 1999.

—Frederick C. Ingram

Greene King plc

Westgate Brewery
Bury St Edmunds
Suffolk
IP331QT
United Kingdom
Telephone: +44-1284-763-222
Fax: +44-1284-706-502

Public Company
Founded: 1799
Employees: 6,431
Sales: £292.6 million ($472.7 million) (1998)
Stock Exchanges: London
Ticker Symbol: GNKL
NAIC: 422810 Beer and Ale Wholesalers; 722110 Full Service Restaurants

Located in eastern England, Greene King plc maintains a tradition of brewing beer in Bury St. Edmunds, Suffolk, which began sometime before 1086. The dark, heavy Strong Suffolk Vintage Beer is aged in oak barrels for two years and mixed with fresh ale before it is sold. Greene King brews a variety of ales that reflect changing tastes in beers, as well as a variety of seasonal and special occasion ales. In addition to its brewery, Greene King is also involved in the lease and management of more than 1,600 pubs under the name Greene King Pub Partners. This licensing arrangement, called "tied estate," results in pubs with a variety of atmospheres depending on their location, customer base, facilities, and proprietor. Greene King Pub Company oversees company-owned and -operated pubs. These businesses included Hungry Horse branded pubs, which offer food, Greene King cask ale and other drinks, darts, skittles, and big screen television. Community Pubs are traditional pubs with an emphasis on beer. Town Locals tend to attract local residents, while Circuit Bars, located in commercial districts, attract a lunch crowd from area businesses and young singles in the evenings. Greene King Inns included traditional pubs, hotels, and golf courses.

The Greene Brewery in its Early Days

Nineteen-year-old Benjamin Greene arrived in Bury St. Edmund in 1799 ready to found his own brewery, having completed his brewer training at the Whitbread Brewery in London. He moved into the former house of Abbot Reve, the town's last Abbot, and began to establish himself in East Anglia, an area known for its malting barley. In 1805 Benjamin Greene and William Buck, a 60-year-old yarn maker, formed a partnership to purchase Wright's Brewery, which had already been in operation in Westgate since around 1700.

The brewery completed its first batches of ale, porter, and "old beer" in June 1806. The Beer Act of 1830 prompted the brewery's first surge of growth. Since 1550, licensing of inns, taverns, and alehouses had been controlled by local magistrates. The Beer Act opened up the beer trade by allowing anyone who applied for a license and paid the two-guinea fee to brew and sell beer.

When Parliament approved the Act, 51,000 establishments were involved in the sale of beer; by 1838 an additional 46,000 beer houses had opened for business. The impact of the Beer Act on Greene Brewery was immediate, as beer sales rose 50 percent in the first year after the Act was passed; however, competition among breweries increased as well. The company was unusual for an East Anglian brewer in that in 1833 the company had only one "tied" public house, a pub the company leased to a tenant who sold Greene beer exclusively.

By the mid-1830s, the brewery still produced less than 2,000 barrels of its strong Suffolk beer annually. It wasn't until Edward Greene, son of Benjamin Greene, took over that the company began to reap the advantages of the "free trade" in beer.

In 1836, at the age of 21, Edward acquired the brewery from his father. Edward effectively capitalized on the construction of railroads in the 1840s, using the railroads to expand the company's distribution network throughout East Anglia. Edward began brewing a lighter, less intoxicating version of the popular Burton India bitter ale. When he passed away in 1891, his obituary enthused, "He was one of the first country brewers to discover that beer need not be vile, black, turgid stuff." Greene

Company Perspectives:

Our objective for our bicentenary year and into the millennium is to become the leading pub retailer-brewer, in terms of profitability and market share, in the south of England.

sold Burton ale, which was originally an expensive brew, at the low price of a shilling per gallon, and, as the obituary said, "made a fortune."

The company's growth necessitated expansion of its brewing facilities. In 1845 Greene built a new malt house, where the first step in making beer took place. Wet barley was spread on the floor and allowed to sprout. Roasting the barley stopped germination and produced malt. In 1854 the company razed Abbot Reve's house to expand the brewery again. In 1851 Greene had employed 18 men and three boys. The number of employees doubled with the 1854 expansion, while annual production increased to 20,000 barrels, with each barrel holding 288 pints. As beer consumption increased and the British brewing industry boomed, Greene beers continued to grow in popularity. By 1870 the company's barrelage increased to 40,000.

Greene expanded its sales network by employing sales agents in Bury, Haverhill, Stowmarket, and Sutton, and by establishing two company-owned stores in London and Wolverhampton. Its tied estate of public houses grew by 90 pubs between 1868 and 1887.

Change and Adaption at the Turn of the 20th Century

In 1887 the company merged with another Bury St. Edmunds brewer, Frederick King, to form Greene, King and Sons, Ltd. (GKS). Founded in 1765 as Maulkin's Maltings, the brewery was purchased by Frederick King in 1852. King found keen competition in Greene, however, which was more firmly established by mid-century. The merger, which was prompted by the Greene Brewery, meant that the two companies no longer competed with each other. The new company remained under private ownership, with shares divided among the two owners and three family members involved in the business, as various challenges affected brewers throughout the United Kingdom.

After two decades of steady growth, beer consumption began to decline. In addition, the British government imposed restrictions on brewer ownership of tied houses in the 1880s and 1890s, which resulted in an increase in the cost of purchasing a pub. In the early 1890s GKS paid £550 to £4,000 for pub properties, which was approximately two-thirds more than the same properties would have cost ten years earlier. The brewery maintained financial stability by accounting for profit on a per-barrel basis and by working to reduce costs each year at every phase of production. Dividends ranged between eight and ten percent.

Government policy continued to affect the company as temperance gained favor in the late 1800s. The brewing industry supported the Licensing Act of 1904, because it provided compensation for pubs that closed when magistrates revoked their licenses. GKS mitigated losses by closing pubs with lower sales or profits when its number of licenses was reduced. GKS became one of the largest brewers in East Anglia by 1903, with sales peaking at 75,378 barrels.

New technology, such as pasteurization and refrigeration, helped GKS adapt to changes in drinking habits. Customers visited public houses less often due to temperance propaganda, which stigmatized pubs, but frequently purchased beer to take home, so the availability of pasteurized bottled beer became more important. GKS bottled 5,045 barrels of beer annually by 1913.

Brewing through World Wars

During World War I, government controls on raw materials and the military service of company employees led to a nationwide decrease in beer production. At GKS production declined 23 percent, from 74,142 barrels in 1914 to 58,568 barrels in 1918. Retail prices on beer doubled, however, and brewer profits exceeded the wartime rate of inflation. This allowed GKS to acquire three breweries in 1917: Clarke's in Bury St. Edmund, Oliver's in Sudbury, and Christmas in Haverhill. The acquisitions added 128 pubs to the company's tied estate, for a total of 460 by the end of the war.

The years between the two world wars were a period of financial growth despite the poor economic conditions. GKS became publicly owned in 1926, but its stock remained largely under family control. GKS acquired the Baily & Tubbut Penton Brewery in Cambridge, along with 48 pubs, in 1925, and the Rayments Brewery in Furneux Pelham, with 35 pubs, in 1928. Beer duties in 1930 and 1931, combined with the effects of the Great Depression, sent per capita beer consumption down to less than half of pre-World War I levels. Prompted by the temperance movement, which sought to upgrade the atmosphere of public houses, GKS actively improved its pubs at this time.

World War II brought both prosperity and difficulty to GKS. Beer consumption increased during the war, resulting in a 60 percent increase in sales for GKS. The British government did not restrict beer production in terms of quantity produced, but it did regulate the "gravity" or density of the wort in water during fermentation, which determined the alcohol level of the beer produced. GKS experienced difficulty in maintaining the required low gravities. The war also created shortages in labor, containers, and grain. After the war, conditions were difficult for brewers. High duties persisted, while the worldwide food shortage of 1946 resulted in reductions in the amount of grain that was allocated for brewing beer. Great Britain imposed restrictions on production and reduced the average gravity of beer by ten percent. Beer duties went down in the late 1940s and early 1950s, but the British economy remained unstable until the mid-1950s.

Growth and Identity in the Postwar Era

As a small regional brewer, GKS found itself a target for aggressive merger overtures by larger brewers in the late 1950s. GKS sought to make the company less desirable for acquisition by making acquisitions of its own. The company purchased J.C. Mauldon & Sons in 1958; Simpson's Brewery in Baldock, with 130 pubs, in 1959; and the Wells and Winch Brewery in Biggleswade, with 287 pubs, in 1961. E.P. Taylor and Bass

Key Dates:

1806: Benjamin Greene and William Buck purchase a brewery at Westgate.
1836: Edward Greene acquires company from father.
1887: Company merges with F.W. King Brewery.
1903: Sales peak at 75,378 barrels of beer.
1928: Company oversees more than 540 licensed pubs.
1951: Abbot Ale is introduced.
1962: Takeover protection achieved through trade agreement with Guinness.
1996: The Magic Pub is acquired.

Charrington acquired an 11.2 percent interest in GKS with the potential for proposing a takeover bid. GKS sought protection under Guinness, which offered to preserve the independence of smaller brewers by purchasing sufficient stock. Guinness did not interfere with management of the company, but a trade agreement allowed the sale of Harp lager and Draught Guinness in GKS tenant pubs. Although the British brewing industry experienced a steady increase in sales during the 1960s and 1970s, revenues at public houses declined due to competition from other types of establishments, such as clubs, as well as increased concern about drinking and driving, which frequently led consumers to imbibe at home. In the early 1960s GKS counted more than 900 pubs in its tied estate, which shrank to 730 pubs in 1981. Though GKS rebounded to 776 pubs in 1985, by the end of that decade approximately 50 percent of the company's sales existed in the "free trade," or wholesale business not associated with its tenants. The public's interest in a wider variety of beverages prompted investments in soft drink and liquor companies and in a chain of Thomas Peatling retail wine stores.

As a purveyor of traditional cask ale, GKS benefitted from renewed interest in the English tradition of cask-conditioned beer. New technology in brewing and beer storage led larger brewing companies to condition beer before bottling, and prompted the formation of a new consumer group in the 1970s—Campaign for Real Ale (CAMRA)—that encouraged support for traditional brewing methods. Cask-conditioned beer utilized "finings," which settled the remnants of yeast to the bottom of the cask to yield a clear beer at the tap. Brewery-conditioned beer was chilled and filtered, had carbon dioxide added, and was pasteurized before being packaged in kegs or bottles to prevent the beer from spoiling. Cask ale involved special handling. A tapped cask needed to "breathe" for 24 hours to allow the residual yeast to settle. Once opened, the cask ale had to be consumed within three days. With consolidation of breweries and the growth of national brands, only a few regional brewers maintained this tradition.

Entering the 1990s as Greene King plc

With its new status as a public limited company, Greene King engaged in new strategies for growth in the 1990s. These strategies included expansion of company-owned and -managed pubs, expansion into the south of England and elsewhere, brand development, and improvements in tied pubs.

Greene King became the second-largest regional brewery in May 1990 with the purchase of 87 retail pubs from Allied Lyons. The acquisition expanded its trade network in England's southern counties, and also expanded its network of company-owned and -managed pubs. The acquisition of 44 retail pubs from Bass in September 1992 increased the number of company-managed pubs to 194. A recession in the early 1990s effected East Anglia more than other areas of England. With about two-thirds of its distribution in East Anglia, Greene King endured in part on the strength of its expansion in southern England. A new sales outlet opened in Camberly in 1994, and a new warehouse opened in Hampshire in 1995. While the East Anglian beer market declined seven percent, sales at GKS declined only one percent.

Retail brands King's Fayre and Ale Cafe also boosted profits in 1995 and 1996. Brand development and advertising became more important in the highly competitive environment, and Greene King implemented several creative promotions. In one promotion at participating tenant pubs a customer rolled dice that carried the logos of Greene King IPA, Abbot Ale, and Rayment the Brewer for a glass of one of the brands. Following consumer demand for premium bottle beers, Greene King began to bottle Abbot Ale for test marketing in early 1993. The company planned to develop Abbot Ale as a national brand. In 1995 Greene King introduced four seasonal ales under character-based brands, beginning with the winter brew Black Baron, a full-bodied, dark red beer, and followed in 1996 with The Sorcerer, an amber ale for spring. The King's Champion, a light ale for summer, was personified by a blond knight, while The Mad Judge for autumn featured a cranberry flavor.

Expansion in all areas of its business led the company to restructure into three major divisions: Greene King Pub Partners encompassed the pubs that the company leased to individual tenants; Greene King Pub Company covered company-owned and -operated pubs; and Brewing and Brands was responsible for oversight of the brewery, sales and distribution, and brand development.

The company divested its investments in other beverages, including the sale of 21 Thomas Peatling wine stores in 1996. The company also sold its 29 percent interest in Moorland Brewery. In 1996 Greene King acquired The Magic Pub, a 277-unit chain with locations in London and southern England. The chain included 47 Hungry Horse pub-restaurants and 21 Country Inns. With the acquisition the company's revenues increased, as did the chain's profit margins.

The acquisition of The Magic Pub fit the company's strategy to balance tenanted pubs with free trade establishments. Greene King began to divest tenanted pubs that functioned poorly, and changed tenants to free trade establishments when appropriate. In 1998 Greene King converted 35 managed pubs to the Hungry Horse brand. Greene King also offered specialized management assistance to tenants to improve their profitability. Acquisition of Beards of Sussex added nine managed pubs and 24 tied pubs, while the purchase of 165 pubs from Wolverhampton & Dudley added 63 managed pubs and 102 tenanted pubs in southern England and southeast Midlands.

In 1997 the shrinking market for cask-conditioned ale prompted Greene King and three other traditional brewers to develop the Cask Marque, "For pubs which serve the perfect pint." Pubs that had proved their ability to properly handle cask ale, through unannounced checks on temperature and presentation, were acknowledged with plaques, certificates, and advertising materials. Greene King continued to develop new brands, such as Greene King XS Smooth, which attempted to satisfy the public demand for smooth ale, and Green King Triumph, a blonde beer with four different types of hops. The acquisition of Morland Brewery in August 1999 added two popular brands, Ruddles and Old Speckled Hen, as well as 400 pubs to the company's holdings. Greene King celebrated its 200th anniversary with 1799 Special Bicentennial Ale, brewed with English-grown hops and barley.

Principal Operating Units

Greene King Pub Company; Greene King Brewing and Brands; Greene King Pub Partners.

Principal Competitors

Bass; Scottish & Newcastle; Whitbread.

Further Reading

"Abbot Ale Gets Bottled Up," *Super Marketing*, June 4, 1993, p. 40.

Blackwell, David, "Beard Growth for Greene King," *Financial Times*, July 1, 1998, p. 26.

——, "Greene King Takes over Magic Pub," *Financial Times*, June 19, 1996, p. 25.

——, "Greene King to Close Maltings," *Financial Times,* October 15, 1998, p. 29.

——, "Magic Casts Its Spell on Greene King," *Financial Times*, December 6, 1997, p. 16.

——, "Retail Side Helps Greene King to 16% Advance," *Financial Times*, June 19, 1996, p. 28.

"Brewer Limits the Damage from Beer," *Financial Times*, December 13, 1993, p. 23.

Burt, Tim, "Greene King Static at 20.4m Pound Sterling," *Financial Times*, July 8, 1994, p. 20.

Fry, Andy, "Greene King Widens Realm," *Marketing*, May 10, 1990, p. 5.

Gourvish, T.R., and R.G. Wilson, *The British Brewing Industry 1830–1980,* Cambridge, England: Cambridge University Press, 1994.

"Greene King," *Investors Chronicle*, December 17, 1993, p. 54.

"Greene King Appoints CKT to Launch Irish 'Hybrid' Ale," *Marketing Week*, May 17, 1996, p. 13.

"Greene King Back to Basics After Failure of Morland Takeover," *Guardian*, July 29, 1992, p. 10.

Brewing Fine Ales Since 1799, Greene King plc, 1999.

"Greene King plc Offer to Buy Magic Pub Would Give It 1,139 Pubs," *Wall Street Journal*, June 19, 1996.

Jackson, Tony, and Christopher Price, "Whitbread Sells Holdings in Regional Brewers," *Financial Times*, March 11, 1994, p. 19.

"£182m Morland Deal Fuels Greene King Marketing Rejig," *Marketing Week*, August 12, 1999, p. 9.

Mazur, Laura, "Brewing a Storm," *Management Today*, June 1989, p. 48.

"McCann Nets L2.5m Greene King Rands in Centralisation," *Marketing Week*, March 5, 1998, p. 13.

McKenzie, Sophie, "Pump Action," *Marketing Week*, September 8, 1995, pp. 60–63.

Oram, Roderick, "Greene King 13% Ahead at 11m Pounds Sterling," *Financial Times*, December 12, 1995, p. 26.

——, "Greene King Ahead to 22m Pounds Sterling," *Financial Times*, July 14, 1995, p. 19.

——, "Greene King Benefits from Magic Spell," *Financial Times*, December 12, 1996, p. 25.

——, "Greene King Sells Morland Stake," *Financial Times*, September 7, 1994, p. 24.

——, "Improved Beer Sales Volumes Help Greene King to 10.7m Pounds Sterling," *Financial Times*, December 16, 1994, p. 24.

Rawstorne, Philip, "A Fight to the Bitter End," *Financial Times*, July 24, 1992, p. 23.

——, "Greene King Below Expectations at 9.6m Pounds Sterling," *Financial Times*, December 14, 1993, p. 20.

Tieman, Ross, "Greene King Aided by Magic's Spell," *Financial Times*, June 26, 1997, p. 36.

"UK: Morland to Sell to Greene King," *Daily Telegraph*, June 5, 1998, p. 29.

"UK: Offer for Marston Pubs from Greene King," *Daily Telegraph*, December 24, 1998, p. 21.

"UK: Wolves Finally Captures Marston," *Daily Telegraph*, February 5, 1999, p. 29.

—Mary Tradii

Green Mountain Coffee, Inc.

33 Coffee Lane
Waterbury, Vermont 05676-1529
U.S.A.
Telephone: (802) 244-5436
Toll Free: (800) 545-2326
Fax: (802) 244-5436
Web site: http://www.GreenMountainCoffee.com

Public Company
Incorporated: 1981 as Green Mountain Coffee Roasters, Inc.
Employees: 400
Sales: $55.8 million (1998)
Stock Exchanges: NASDAQ
Ticker Symbol: GMCR
NAIC: 31192 Coffee and Tea Manufacturing

Green Mountain Coffee, Inc. is the holding company for a rapidly growing roaster of specialty coffee. Green Mountain Coffee Roasters, Inc.'s 5,000 wholesale customers—grocery stores, conveniences stores, restaurants, and places of work—are located mostly in the Northeast, but sales territories extend to Arizona and Florida. Based in Vermont, the company has aimed to expand internationally, to England, Turkey, Canada, the Caribbean, and the Pacific Rim. It also has invested in an online store, while closing or selling its retail stores in 1998.

Hazy Origins

The prehistory of Green Mountain Coffee, Inc. is shrouded in smoke—marijuana smoke. In 1971 company founder Robert Stiller had helped launch E-Z Wider, a maker of rolling papers. E-Z Wider offered smokers wider papers, so they did not have to lick and splice two papers together to make bigger joints. As the high flying days of the 1970s came to a close, Stiller and his partner Burton Rubin sold the company to English tobacconeer Rizla for $6.2 million.

Then, one day while lounging at a Vermont ski resort, Stiller found a cup of coffee so good that he bought the company. At the time, Green Mountain was a small specialty store, begun in 1981, that sold to the public and a few restaurants. Stiller bought out the owners, prospective snowbirds, for $200,000. The couple went to Florida to start another coffee business.

The specialty coffee industry had been growing at a seven to ten percent clip a year since the late 1960s. Still, Stiller discovered that competition was keener in coffee than in cigarette papers. Green Mountain floundered for four years, competing at the highest end of the market: prized arabica beans (versus the lower quality robusta variety). Although he turned a profit on retail sales, Stiller had a hard time convincing restaurants to pay premium prices. Eventually, however, his company's coffee would be served at some of the Northeast's finest restaurants.

Free samples, distributed through such charitable organizations as the Kiwanis club, helped spark demand. The company was making money by 1985. Advertising in gourmet magazines helped build a mail order business. Promotions continued with high-end products like Muesli cereal.

Stiller convinced a doubtful convenience store owner to let him sell coffee there, competing with Dunkin' Donuts across the street. Attention to details not only kept the sales flowing, it increased traffic to the gas station. Stiller took this to the next level, placing Green Mountain coffee in Mobil Corporation's 1,000 stores nationwide. Green Mountain similarly segued an opportunity to sell cups of fresh coffee at a supermarket chain into shelf placement.

Getting Earthy in 1989

In 1989 Green Mountain Coffee Roasters formed an environmental committee to steer it on conservation issues. The company cut its refuse in half through a recycling program and switched to oxygen-whitened filters, deemed less hazardous than standard bleached filters. It began selling these Green Mountain Earth Friendly Filters to the public soon after. In 1990 Green Mountain introduced Rain Forest Nut flavored coffee to sponsor the cause of rain forest preservation. It divvied ten percent of net profits between Conservation International and The Rainforest Alliance.

Company Perspectives:

In the beautiful mountains of Vermont, where time is measured more by the change in seasons than the tick of a clock, and where a faster way of doing things is not always a better way, you'll find the home of Green Mountain Coffee Roasters. At Green Mountain Coffee, we are dedicated to providing the richest aroma and flavor, for the highest quality coffee experience. We travel the globe to purchase the finest coffees, small batch roast them to peak flavor, and vacuum package them fresh for your enjoyment. We take our time . . . and taking our time has its own reward . . . perfect coffee.

Stiller focused on streamlining operations and applying contemporary principles of quality manufacturing. He invested in a $30,000 computerized roaster at the company's store in Winooski, Vermont. The company began a database management program to keep beans moving in clients' stores. In the fiscal year 1991, Green Mountain boasted seven retail outlets, plus a thousand wholesale clients. Sales were $11 million, producing profits of $200,000.

Going Public in 1993

Serving 2,400 wholesale accounts, Green Mountain had sales of about $10 million in 1993. The holding company Green Mountain Coffee, Inc. was formed and an initial public offering was completed in September. Green Mountain opened its ninth store, in Waterbury, Vermont, in December. It was selling 80 varieties of coffee, roasting 25 different types of arabica beans.

A link-up with a large New England food service distributor helped solidify Green Mountain's position among restaurants and institutions. Jordan's Food Corporation, based in Maine, reported that it had been fielding customer requests for the brand. Wholesale continued to account for most of Green Mountain's business, although its retail chain then operated in Vermont, New Hampshire, Maine, Connecticut, and upstate New York.

Green Mountain continued to tout its environmental consciousness. In 1994 it joined the national BuyRecycled! Alliance. Aside from using paper with recycled content for its letterhead and invoices, the company reduced its roasting emissions. Its Stewardship line of coffee declaimed "respect for the land and workers." These beans came from specially inspected farms in Mexico, Hawaii, Peru, Guatemala, and Sumatra. Locally, the company sponsored "Dr. Trash," who lectured children about environmental responsibility. (Another interesting mascot was "The Green Mountain Coffee Buster," who became something of a celebrity for serving rush hour Boston commuters five-second cups of coffee.) The company also gave away its bean chaff and burlap bags to gardeners.

Social causes were supported as well. Apart from standard charities like the United Way, the Salvation Army, and the Red Cross, Coffee Kids Conservation International worked to improve living conditions for children in coffee-producing areas. Customers were invited to contribute through coin drops and the sale of gift boxes.

Exporting in 1994

Green Mountain began exporting to Canada and Taiwan in 1994. This brought in revenues of $80,000 the first year. Frosts in Brazil, where Green Mountain did not buy coffee, sent the worldwide price of coffee up, prompting the company to raise its own prices by 30 percent. Sales for 1994 were about $22 million; the company lost nearly $3 million. The next year produced an income of $179,000 on sales of $34 million.

Green Mountain Coffee Roasters became the launch customer for sophisticated, Window-based roasting control software developed by Praxis Werke, Inc. in New Jersey. In addition to providing unprecedented consistency, the software also promised reduced costs and greater safety.

In 1996 Green Mountain sponsored a study of the comparative economic benefits of traditional shaded coffee growing systems with full-sun systems. Traditionally, coffee plants were raised in the shade of trees. New sun-resistant hybrids offered higher yields but were more reliant on synthetic pesticides and fertilizers.

The company announced an assault on national supermarket chains in June 1996. By the end of the year, its retail stores had increased to 12, in Vermont, Connecticut, Illinois, Maine, Massachusetts, New Hampshire, and New York. Its wholesale clients by then included Weight Watchers International and the L.L. Bean Catalog.

Business Express was one of the first airlines to offer Green Mountain coffee. By October 1996, Green Mountain Coffee was also being served on more than a hundred Delta Express flights per day. Enthusiastic Delta Shuttle customers helped Green Mountain land the Delta Express contract. The next month, Amtrack added the brew, putting it in the cups of even more commuters. While two million passengers flew Delta Express each year, eleven million rode Amtrack's Northeast trains. Midway Airlines added Green Mountain Coffee in 1997. The carrier's reputation for customer satisfaction enhanced the roaster's own reputation.

Green Mountain started 1997 in a big way. It signed up as exclusive supplier to The Coffee Station, Inc. The retailer had only been in business since 1994 but already operated the largest specialty coffee stores in the United States: its two locations in New York's World Trade Center served more than 7,500 customers a day. The Coffee Store operated 25 other locations in downtown areas in Los Angeles, Atlanta, Charlotte, and Seattle. The agreement brought the Green Mountain brand to one million consumers.

NASDAQ in 1997

In March 1997, Green Mountain's shares began trading on the Nasdaq National Market System, instead of the SmallCap Market System and the Boston Stock Exchange. Green Mountain's 1996 income qualified it for the listing. The company earned $1.26 million on revenues of $38.35 million for the fiscal year ending September 28. Sales had increased 145 percent during the three previous years.

Key Dates:

1981: Robert Stiller purchases the Green Mountain coffee store in Vermont.
1985: Green Mountain Coffee turns a profit.
1989: Employees form an environmental steering committee.
1991: Company installs $30,000 computerized roaster.
1993: Green Mountain holds initial public offering.
1994: First exports shipped to Canada and Taiwan.
1997: Shares listed on NASDAQ.
1998: Company closes its retail stores; secure ordering is added to its web site.

In 1997 the growing company licensed PeopleSoft software for manufacturing and accounting applications. The cost of implementing the new system was reported as about $1.5 million. A year later, Green Mountain reported good results. The company's IT personnel praised the new efficiency it brought to communicating with suppliers and distribution centers. Bar coding and online inventory tracking were two key features speeding the process. Electronic data interchange (ETI) also was becoming a prerequisite for doing business with large customers such as grocery chains.

Green Mountain struck a deal with office supplies discounter Staples Inc. in May 1997. This put the coffee in 600 office superstores throughout North America and in the Staples mail order catalog and marked a major step into penetrating the office coffee market. The company revamped its packaging, beckoning patrons to ''Sip and relax—you're on Green Mountain time.''

In September 1997, Green Mountain made another significant move into the office market by teaming with Poland Spring Natural Spring Water Co. (a subsidiary of the Perrier Group of America). Poland Spring's existing distribution network brought Green Mountain Coffee to thousands of offices in the Northeast. In the first year of the five-year agreement, Green Mountain expected to ship more than one million pounds of coffee through this channel. Coffee and bottled water were the fastest growing categories in the beverage industry. Although a regional brand, Poland Spring sold more bottled water than anyone else in the country. Poland Spring's sales were $248 million in 1996.

Exiting Retail in 1998

According to Stiller, Green Mountain remained passionate about its social and environmental responsibilities. In April 1998, as one of its Earth Day tie-ins, the company introduced ''bird-friendly'' coffees grown without synthetic fertilizers or pesticides. It expanded its support of its Coffee Kids microlending projects in Mexico.

With wholesale trade booming, Green Mountain announced plans to leave retail entirely in May 1998. The company kept its mail order business operational, devoting energy to its new consumer online business, which, although it accounted for only a fraction of sales, was deemed promising because of the unprecedented convenience it offered customers. Sales through www.GreenMountainCoffee.com increased fivefold within four months of the introduction of secure online ordering in 1998. Green Mountain aimed to have 30 percent of its 5,000 resellers order online by 2000. The company promoted the site on www.CNN.com.

Green Mountain distributed its first corporate gifts catalog in the fall of 1998. Businesses had long turned to the company to remember their clients, vendors, and friends at the holidays. The catalog offered volume discounts on gift baskets, mugs, and Vermont products. It also introduced filtered hospitality packs for in-room coffee service at hotels. The company continued to use brewed cups as a tool to introduce itself to new customers.

The American Skiing Company picked Green Mountain coffee for its resorts in November 1998. The group operated nine resorts that had more than five million visits per year; the coffee was to be served at its six eastern resorts during the first winter of the five-year contract. Maine-based American Skiing was the largest alpine ski, snowboard, and golf resorts operator in the United States. It had previously served Starbucks coffee.

In late 1998, Mobil Corporation's On the Run shops became the first national convenience store chain to offer certified organic coffee. To match the pace of hurried shoppers, espresso-based drinks were not offered, only brewed, to-go cups of coffee. In addition, since most households did not own coffee grinders, whole beans were not sold either. The program brought Green Mountain certified organic coffee to 283 stores in the United States and more than 300 abroad.

International Expansion in 1999

About 70 percent of coffee was purchased in supermarkets, making this segment a key priority for future growth, as Stiller reported to shareholders in 1999. In the previous year, Green Mountain had been able to expand its supermarket distribution from 180 to more than 500 stores. Stop & Shop and Shaws were two chains that had added Green Mountain coffee.

Another area for growth was the overseas market, particularly Great Britain. Green Mountain teamed with the Scottish company Banana Brothers to open outlets offering juice, soup, and coffee. The first debuted in Glasgow in September 1999. An additional 12 outlets were planned. It was hoped the soup and juice offerings would encourage customers to linger in the stores. Green Mountain also was developing mobile coffee bars for shopping centers and examining acquisition targets. Exports were worth about $500,000 a year at the time.

In September 1998, Green Mountain had begun buying back about $500,000 of its shares, feeling they were undervalued. In the five years prior, the company averaged a growth rate of 30 percent a year, with international sales nearly doubling.

Principal Subsidiaries

Green Mountain Coffee Roasters, Inc.

Principal Competitors

Starbucks; Kraft Foods; Proctor & Gamble.

Further Reading

"Fill'er Up with Gas and Organic Coffee," *Specialty Coffee Retailer,* December 1998, p. 8.

Grover, Mary Beth, "Hippie Redux," *Forbes,* December 9, 1991, pp. 326, 328.

Jacobs, April, "Business Process Software Pays Off," *Computerworld,* August 31, 1998, pp. 33–37.

Sinanoglu, Elif, "Wake Up and Smell the $5 French Roast," *Money,* November 1994, p. 223.

"US Coffee Giant Lifts Lid on Joint Venture Chain," *LeisureWeek,* August 12, 1999, p. 4.

—Frederick C. Ingram

Gristede's Sloan's, Inc.

823 11th Avenue
New York, New York 10019-3535
U.S.A.
Telephone: (212) 956-5770
Fax: (212) 247-4509

Public Company
Incorporated: 1913 as Gristede Brothers, Inc.
Employees: 1,323
Sales: $157.5 million (1998)
Stock Exchanges: American Boston
Ticker Symbol: GRI
NAIC: 42241 General Line Grocery Wholesalers; 42248 Fresh Fruit & Vegetable Wholesalers; 44511 Supermarkets & Other Grocery (Except Convenience) Stores; 446199 All Other Health & Personal Care Stores; 551112 Offices of Other Holding Companies

Gristede's Sloan's, Inc., composed of two once distinct supermarket chains, is a holding corporation that owns and operates 40 supermarkets in the New York City metropolitan area, including 35 in Manhattan. Twenty-nine were operating under the Gristede's name and 11 under the Sloan's name at the end of 1998, but all were scheduled to be under the Gristede's name at the end of 1999. The company also owns and operates a warehouse that supplies these supermarkets with groceries and fresh produce and sells wholesale fresh produce to third parties. Gristede's Sloan's is 91 percent owned or controlled by John A. Catsimatidis, sole owner of Red Apple Group, Inc., a private holding company.

Gristede Brothers: 1891–1987

Charles Gristede and his brother Diedrich came to the United States from Germany in 1888, found work in grocery stores, and in 1891 opened a tiny gaslit store at 42nd Street and Second Avenue in Manhattan. This site was then far uptown from the central shopping area but close to housewives who walked or rode in private carriages to the store. A second store opened in Harlem—then a middle-class white neighborhood—in 1896. The business flourished and expanded, reaching suburban Westchester County in 1920 and Connecticut in 1926. Gristede Brothers also opened a wine and liquor store in Manhattan in 1933. When Charles Gristede died in 1948, the chain consisted of 141 stores in Manhattan, the Bronx, Westchester, and Connecticut. In 1956 it opened its first Long Island store, in Garden City.

In Manhattan, Gristede Brothers remained concentrated on the more affluent East Side, where it specialized in personal service and gourmet items and charged premium prices. It shipped items to customers around the world, including, for example, a Greek who wanted melons sent to him in Paris by air freight. The company had annual sales of about $60 million and 115 stores in all—including six liquor stores in Connecticut—when it was sold in 1968 to The Southland Corporation, owner of the 7-Eleven convenience store chain, for Southland stock valued at $11.5 million.

Southland retained the prior Gristede Brothers management and for more than a decade left the chain to its own devices. In 1977 Gristede's consisted of 120 stores, mostly ranging in size from 6,000 to 11,000 square feet and carrying 7,000 to 8,000 gourmet items, including size 23 grapefruit—about the size of a large cantaloupe—strawberries picked in California only 36 hours earlier, large Idaho potatoes already wrapped in tin foil, quiche Lorraine, and Beluga caviar.

By the early 1980s, however, Gristede's, as well as other supermarket chains with outlets in New York City, was reeling from a number of adverse conditions, including the small size of the stores, the high cost of delivery in the city, escalating rents, and competition from gourmet shops and specialty food stores. In 1980 the chain still consisted of 100 outlets, including 24 Charles & Co. sandwich shops, but by 1983, when Gristede's fell into the red, there were only 84. During 1983–84 Gristede's concentrated its operations in Manhattan, closing 36 stores and its warehouse. In 1985 there were 18 conventional supermarkets; 17 generally smaller service stores featuring telephone ordering, home delivery, and charge accounts; ten Charles & Co. sandwich shops and one gourmet shop; and one liquor store. Sales came to about $105 million in 1985.

Key Dates:

1891: Charles and Diedrich Gristede open their first store.
1956: Max Sloan opens his first supermarket.
1968: Gristede Brothers is sold to The Southland Corporation.
1986: Southland sells Gristede's to Red Apple Co.
1993: Red Apple completes the purchase of Sloan's begun in 1991.
1997: The two chains are combined as Gristede's Sloan's, Inc.

Southland sold the Gristede's and Charles & Co. stores to Red Apple Co. in 1986 for an estimated $50 million. Red Apple, owned by John A. Catsimatidis and operating in the Bronx as well as Manhattan, now became the largest supermarket chain in New York City. Gristede's and Red Apple remained distinct, however. Red Apple had completed 14 Gristede's remodels by the fall of 1987, including adding in-store delicatessens, bakeries, salad bars, hot takeout foods, and upscale cheese, prime-meat, and seafood sections. The Charles & Co. stores were closed.

Sloan's Supermarkets: 1956–97

Born in the Bronx and reared by foster families after his mother died, Max Sloan left school after the eighth grade to sell fruit and vegetables from a pushcart. A small vegetable and fruit store he opened in 1940 with $500 grew into the Orange Grove chain. Sloan and his partner, Lou Meyer, also ran a wholesale produce operation supplying fruits and vegetables to many grocery stores in Manhattan and the Bronx. They entered the supermarket business in 1956 with two Manhattan stores. There were 25 Sloan Supermarket Stores—mostly on Manhattan's West Side—in 1973, when the chain purchased seven more from Bohack Corp. By this time Sloan had annual sales of $42 million.

Meyer died in 1969, and Sloan retired in 1977. His successor was a son-in-law, Jules Rose. By 1982 the 42-store Sloan's Supermarkets Inc. chain had estimated sales of $150 million a year. Its viability, Rose said, rested on seeking to market items with the greatest profit margin, such as meat, frozen items, produce, and gourmet foods. The city's consumer affairs agency had consistently listed Sloan's as one of the most expensive food chains in Manhattan. Sloan's success also rested on careful monitoring of the borough's ethnically diverse clientele. A store on the Lower East Side, for example, had a large line of Goya-brand products for Hispanics and kosher products for Orthodox Jews. Another, close to the United Nations, had full international foods sections. Located in a high-income area, it also had a higher proportion of frozen food and dairy products sales and included health and natural foods sections.

Sloan's Supermarkets had 38 stores in early 1990, when it was first reported on the auction block. Cynthia Rigg of *Crain's New York Business* wrote, "Over the past decade Sloan's reputation for quality has fallen dramatically. The privately held chain has done little to upgrade its stores while [its competitors] have undertaken extensive expansion and modernization programs." She also reported that industry sources said the four principals of Sloan's were "often at loggerheads, which stymies decision making." Despite its problems, Sloan's was said to hold a 20 percent share of Manhattan's grocery business.

After selling three stores to various companies in 1990, Sloan's Supermarkets sold 21 more to Red Apple during 1991–92. One observer explained to Richard Turcsik of *Supermarket News,* "Gristede is definitely considered upscale. Sloan's is somewhere in between and Red Apple is considered low-end. By keeping the Sloan's name, Red Apple will be able to service all three segments of the customer base from one distributor." The acquisition had its hazards, however, because three of Sloan's owners were, in 1993, being charged with fraudulently redeeming at least $3.5 million of discount coupons clipped from newspapers, an action that threatened 15 of the acquired units with forfeiture to the federal government. The three Sloan's partners—Rose, Max Sloan's other son-in-law, and Meyer's son—eventually went to jail.

Despite these problems, Red Apple bought the remaining 11 Sloan's supermarkets—ten in Manhattan and one in Brooklyn—in 1993 for $8.8 million plus certain accounts payable. This purchase was not assigned to Red Apple itself but to Designcraft, Inc., a publicly owned shell corporation whose main stockholder was Catsimatidis. Following the sale the federal government agreed to withdraw all claims against Sloan's Supermarkets. Designcraft then took the Sloan's Supermarkets name and continued operations under Red Apple Group management.

This transaction raised the number of supermarket stores in the New York area controlled by Red Apple to 75. In 1994 the Federal Trade Commission filed a complaint, seeking the sale of ten Red Apple-controlled stores in four Manhattan neighborhoods because of possible anticompetitive effects, such as higher food prices and lower quality and selection. Supermarkets under the Red Apple, Gristede's, and Sloan's names were serving 37 percent of Manhattan's food shoppers on a regular basis, according to a survey. Catsimatidis agreed later in 1994 to divest six stores in order to settle the complaint. In 1997, however, he and three of his firms agreed to pay a $600,000 penalty for failing to comply with the FTC order. Only one of the stores had been divested, according to the agency.

The Red Apple name virtually disappeared during this period, its outlets sold to Rite Aid Corporation or converted to Gristede's or Sloan's supermarkets. Sloan's acquired three more supermarkets from a subsidiary of Red Apple Group in 1995 for $5 million plus the cost of inventory. It also opened an additional supermarket and a Brooklyn health and beauty aids store in 1996.

Gristede's Sloan's: 1997–99

In 1997 Sloan's Supermarkets acquired 19 Gristede's and 10 Sloan's supermarkets, plus a produce distribution center, from Red Apple for $36 million worth of stock plus the assumption of $4 million in debt. The company was then renamed Gristede's Sloan's, Inc. During fiscal 1998 (the year ended November 30, 1998), Gristede's Sloan's acquired another supermarket from an affiliate of Catsimatidis and remodeled ten stores at a cost of $10 million. The company also closed four stores and combined two adjacent ones into a single store.

Company sales came to $157.5 million, with a net loss of $288,339. Gristede's Sloan's had a long-term debt of $21.6 million at the end of the fiscal year. Catsimatidis, the chief executive officer, owned or controlled 91 percent of the company in February 1999.

Of the 40 Gristede's Sloan's stores in 1998, 35 were in Manhattan, one was in Brooklyn, three were in Westchester County, and one was on Long Island. They ranged from 3,200 to 23,000 square feet in selling space, with an average of 9,000, and were all leased. City Produce Operating Corp., on leased premises in the Bronx, was a warehouse operation supplying the company's supermarkets with groceries and fresh produce and selling fresh produce wholesale to third parties.

Gristede's Sloan's supermarkets were offering broad lines of merchandise, including nationally and regionally advertised brands and private-label and generic brands. Their food items included fresh meats, produce, dry groceries, dairy products, baked goods, poultry and fish, fresh fruits and vegetables, frozen foods, delicatessen items, and gourmet foods. Nonfood items included cigarettes, soaps, paper products, and health and beauty aids. The company also was operating an in-store pharmacy in one of its supermarkets. Check-cashing services were available to qualified customers, and groceries were being delivered to apartments for a small fee. The stores were open 16 hours a day, seven days a week, and on holidays. At least one was open around the clock.

Gristede's Sloan's was planning to remodel 12 more stores in fiscal 1999 and to open two new stores and four in-store pharmacies. Of the 11 stores operating under the Sloan's name, four had been converted to Gristede's by May 1999, when the company announced that the remaining seven would also take the Gristede's name by the end of the year. Catsimatidis told *Supermarket News* that the Gristede's banner "is a better name, with better marketing potential."

Principal Subsidiaries

City Produce Operating Corp.; Gristede's Operating Corp.; Namdor Inc.; RAS Operating Corp.; SAC Operating Corp.

Principal Competitors

Associated Food Stores Inc.; C Town Supermarkets; D'Agostino Supermarkets, Inc.; The Great Atlantic & Pacific Tea Company Inc. (for A & P Food Stores and The Food Emporium); Key Food Stores Co-operative Inc.

Further Reading

"Charles Gristede, Grocer 77, Is Dead," *New York Times,* October 31, 1948, p. 88.
Clark, Chapin, "Ex-CEO of Sloan's Begins Prison Sentence," *SN/Supermarket News,* March 9, 1998, pp. 1, 73.
Collins, Glenn, "Red Apple to Sell up to 20 Stores," *New York Times,* November 30, 1994, p. D3.
Finklea, Robert W., "The Gristede's Link in Southland's Chain," *New York Times,* July 17, 1977, Sec. 3, p. 3.
"Gristede's Flag Will Fly Over Remaining Sloan's," *SN/Supermarket News,* May 3, 1999, p. 8.
"Holders Approve Purchase of Stores from Chairman," *Wall Street Journal,* October 31, 1997, p. B4.
Nagle, James J., "Gristede-Southland Merger Set," *New York Times,* October 16, 1968, pp. 59, 64.
Pace, Eric, "Max Sloan, 83, Whose Pushcart Grew into a Supermarket Chain," *New York Times,* August 7, 1995, p. B10.
Paikert, Charles, "Jules Rose: Manhattan's Food Market Maven," *Chain Store Age Executive,* January 1982, pp. 48, 55–56, 59.
Reckert, Clare M., "Bohack Sells 7 Units," *New York Times,* August 14, 1973, pp. 43, 47.
Rigg, Cynthia, "At Sloan's, the Specials for Investors Are Stakes," *Crain's New York Business,* December 6, 1993, p. 4.
——, "Fraud Case Threatens Sloan Sale," *Crain's New York Business,* March 22, 1993, pp. 3, 36.
Schmitt, Eric, "Red Apple Buying Gristedes," *New York Times,* February 6, 1986, p. D4.
Tanner, Ronald, "How Jules Rose Nourishes His Broadway Baby," *Progressive Grocer,* February 1983, pp. 105, 108, 110, 112.
Turcsik, Richard, "Red Apple Starts Sloan's Store Buyout," *Supermarket News,* July 2, 1991, pp. 1, 34.
"Washington Briefs," *Supermarket Business,* February 1997, p. 9.

—Robert Halasz

Gruma, S.A. de C.V.

Calzada del Valle 407 Oriente
66220 San Pedro, Garza Garcia, Nuevo León
Mexico
Telephone: (528) 399-3300
Toll Free: (800) 424-7862
Fax: (528) 335-9935
Web site: http://www.gruma.com

Public Company
Incorporated: 1971
Employees: 12,384
Sales: 13.77 billion pesos ($1.39 billion) (1998)
Stock Exchanges: Mexico City New York
Ticker Symbol: GMK
NAIC: 115114 Postharvest Crop Activities; 311211 Flour Milling; 311812 Commercial Bakeries; 31183 Tortilla Manufacturing; 311919 Other Snack Food Manufacturing; 333294 Food Product Machinery Manufacturing; 551112 Offices of Other Holding Companies

Gruma, S.A. de C.V. is perhaps best known as the holding company for a Mexican food conglomerate, Grupo Industrial Maseca S.A. de C.V. (Gimsa), and its proprietary brand of Maseca corn tortillas. Through 71 percent-owned Gimsa, Gruma is the world's leading producer of corn flour and corn tortillas. Gruma Corp., the parent firm's wholly owned U.S. subsidiary, makes the same products plus snack foods and bakery products. A smaller Central American subsidiary also makes and sells the same products, and another Mexican subsidiary produces and markets both tortillas and bread. Gruma is 22-percent owned by the U.S. conglomerate Archer-Midland-Daniels Co. (ADM), and a joint venture with ADM performs milling of wheat flour in both the United States and Mexico. Gruma's founder, Roberto González Barrera, and other family members own about two-thirds of Gruma's stock.

A Dry Process for Making Tortillas: 1949–89

The humble tortilla—essentially a corn pancake that also doubles as a sandwich-like wrapper for a variety of fillings—is a staple of the Mexican diet. For at least 1,000 years the making of tortillas involved husking ears of corn, boiling the kernels in water to which lime has been added, and then forming a patty of the wet dough and placing it in a flat earthenware pan for frying. Unfortunately, the traditional tortilla becomes stale a mere four or five hours after frying.

In 1949 Roberto M. González and his son, Roberto González Barrera, established a plant producing 15 tons of corn flour a month in Cerralvo, a community in the state of Nuevo León. Only 18 at the time, González Barrera had dropped out of school at 11 and was a traveling salesman for Mexico's largest industrial enterprise, Petroleos Mexicanos (Pemex) before going into business for himself. After years in the corn flour business, during which they researched and tested new technologies, González Barrera and his associate Manuel Jesús Rubio took out a patent, in 1965, on an improved tortilla apparatus and production method. At the beginning of 1971 González's enterprise consisted of seven plants. Although widely known as Maseca (''dry dough'') for the brand name of its product, the company's name was Gruma (an acronym for Grupo Maseca).

The Maseca process of preparing the raw material for a tortilla consisted of boiling corn for 30 minutes, drying the kernels instantly by injections of hot air, and milling them into flour prior to humidifying the product into a mass suitable for making tortillas. This had certain advantages over the traditional wet dough prepared by thousands of small shops as well as millions of homemakers. Not only was the Maseca product more sanitary and uniform in quality, it had a longer shelf line. Moreover, Gruma's machines were better than the ones already in existence, which made only 30 to 40 tortillas per minute. Gruma's machines were not only faster, they used less water and fuel per tortilla and made 20 percent more tortillas per kilogram of corn.

Gruma collaborated with research groups in the design of plant and equipment processes and products. Elektra Good Machinery Co. began making the machines in 1976 and also was responsible for roasting, frying, packing, mixing, and cutting. Enrichment of Maseca corn flour with vitamins and proteins began in the 1970s at the San José, Costa Rica, tortilla plant Gruma had established in 1971. The largest such facility in the world, the plant also converted soy meal to protein.

According to the Mexican weekly *Proceso,* González Barrera enjoyed political support from General Bonifacio Sali-

Company Perspectives:

Gruma is committed to achieving dynamic, long-term profitable growth by leading the field in the production, marketing and distribution of high-quality basic food products and flours made from corn and wheat, maintaining its principal focus on corn flour and tortillas. Our operations will be supported by efficient manufacturing and marketing systems, including mass distribution, where profitable.

nas Leal, a governor of Nuevo León, and Raúl Salinas Lozano, minister of trade and industry from 1958 to 1964, who extended loans and special permits during this period. However, González later told Jorge Monjaras of the Mexican business magazine *Expansión* that he was handicapped by heavy government regulation of the tortilla industry. ''One couldn't just open a mill,'' he complained, adding ''One had to obtain permission, and production was limited by a quota. Similarly, one couldn't just open a tortilla shop anywhere. A certain number of inhabitants were required for each store.'' Selling the product directly to homes was forbidden. Existing artisinal tortilla producers stifled potential competition through these means, with the help of allies in the nation's ruling Institutional Revolutionary party.

In spite of these restraints, Gruma was 46th in size among reporting Mexican companies in 1979, with sales of 4.16 billion pesos ($183.9 million), compared to 1.65 billion pesos ($72.2 million) in 1977. By this time its annual production was 750,000 tons of flour. Gruma also opened its first U.S. plant in 1976 and began marketing tortillas, tortilla chips, and taco shells on the West Coast under the Mission Foods name. Automatic International Corp. was Gruma's research and development company in the United States, while Asesoria de Empresas S.A. was the Mexican subsidiary established in 1979 to provide the others with technical, financial, commercial, and administrative assistance. There were 16 affiliated companies in 1978 and a total of 8,500 employees. The 12 plants in Mexico included one that produced air conditioners.

Giant Strides Forward: 1990–95

The main Mexican subsidiary, Grupo Industrial Maseca, S.A.(Gimsa) tripled in sales in real terms between 1987 and 1989 and became a public subsidiary in 1990, selling 15 percent of its shares and using the proceeds to add three more plants. Another seven percent of the company was quickly sold in two secondary offerings. The three new plants raised Gimsa's production from 1.2 million to 1.65 million tons of flour. By the end of the year Gimsa held 61 percent of the Mexican market for industrialized corn flour. However, 73 percent of the nation's tortillas still were being made by the traditional wet-dough method.

Gruma was at this time a privately owned conglomerate of 80 companies engaged in a host of activities, including the fabrication of machinery for the food sector, the development of technology for the corn industry, and the Mexican operation of fast-food restaurants chains such as Burger Boy and Pizza Hut. It had also opened a tortilla plant in Honduras in 1987.

Gruma became a public company in 1992, and its shares began trading on the Mexican stock exchange in 1994. González Barrera became director in 1992 of the Banco Mercantil del Norte (Banorte), which was privatized after a decade in government hands. Gruma acquired ten percent of the bank's shares. The company discontinued its operations in the fast-food restaurant business in 1994.

Of Gruma's 1990 sales of about $800 million, $220 million were in the United States. In 1991 Gruma Corp., the U.S. subsidiary, was operating 12 plants in five states. By 1994 Gruma Corp. accounted for almost 40 percent of the parent company's revenue. Sales consisted of corn flour, tortillas, snack foods, and bakery products sold under the brand names Mission and Guerrero. Mission, a more upscale brand, made packaged tortillas and served institutional customers such as Taco Bell, which was buying one-third of its taco shells. (Guerrero Foods, a Los Angeles-based company, had been purchased by Gruma in 1988.)

Still, González Barrera was not satisfied with the results his firm had achieved in the United States. ''In that country there's lots of discrimination,'' he told an *Expansión* reporter in 1994. ''We struggle to win the confidence of supermarkets, to prove that we're as good as other suppliers,'' he added.

In Mexico, Gruma benefitted greatly from support by Carlos Salinas de Gortari, who was president from 1988 to 1994. In 1990 the Mexican government committed itself to promoting the substitution of corn flour for dough in the production of tortillas. Conasupo, the government agency that distributed basic foods, resolved that the following year, in any part of Mexico where new corn-flour plants were built, it would phase out its program of supplying millers of corn for traditionally made tortillas with cheap corn. If the millers paid the higher market price, the ministry of commerce said it wouldn't let them pass on the higher price to consumers. Furthermore, according to a 1996 *New York Times* article, millers who still refused to convert corn to flour received strictly limited amounts of Conasupo's worst corn. Seven thousand Mexican tortilla-making shops closed between 1993 and 1995.

At the same time, government subsidies to Gruma grew. According to *Proceso,* between 1989 and 1992 producers of corn received subsidies of more than $7 billion. Because Gimsa and other millers were the ones who had to pay the growers the government-guaranteed price of corn—higher than the international market price—and were required to sell to tortilla producers at a fixed price, they went to the government for the difference as a rebate, which in 1992 represented about 35 percent of Gimsa's 1.93 billion pesos ($492.6 million) in revenue. This subsidy grew to 43 percent of Gimsa's revenue in 1994. Practically the only flour-making alternative to Gimsa was Miconsa, a poorly run public enterprise that was later privatized. By this time Gonzalez was a billionaire; his net worth was estimated at $1.7 billion in 1997.

To *Proceso* and other critics of the Mexican government and ruling party, the tortilla policy was a prime examples of *amiguismo*—the Mexican version of crony capitalism. González Barrera had come to the aid of Raúl Salinas Lozano—father of the president—when he fell into disgrace in the 1970s. Moreover, he was related by marriage to Carlos Hank González, secretary of agriculture in the Salinas administration. In 1996, after the end of Salinas' term in office, the Mexican government

Key Dates:

1949: Roberto González Barrera and his father open a corn-flour plant.
1971: Gruma establishes the world's largest tortilla factory.
1976: The company's first plant in the United States is opened.
1992: Gruma goes public.
1996: Archer-Daniels-Midland buys a 22 percent stake in Gruma.

imposed quotas on sales of subsidized corn in order to combat fraud and waste. Corn subsidies and tortilla price controls were phased out during 1998 and eliminated at the end of the year.

Alliance with Archer-Daniels-Midland: 1996–98

U.S.-based Archer-Daniels-Midland Co.(ADM) purchased a 22 percent stake in Gruma for $258 million in 1996. The transaction also established two joint ventures. One, 80-percent owned by Gruma—already the largest corn-flour producer in the United States—combined the U.S. corn-flour operations of both companies, representing about 25 percent of the U.S. market. Gruma Corp. was already running the biggest tortilla factory in the world in the Los Angeles area, with the capability of making 800,000 tortillas an hour.

The other joint venture, 60 percent controlled by Gruma, involved two new wheat-flour mills that ADM had opened in Mexico. The alliance with ADM gave Gruma the technology and financial backing to break into Mexico's $1.5-billion-a-year wheat-flour and bread market, dominated by Grupo Bimbo, S.A. de C.V., which held about 95 percent of the nation's packaged-bread market. By the fall of 1997, Molinera de México, S.A. de C.V., the name of this joint venture, had acquired three more mills and two wheat-flour brands and was scheduled to provide the flour for a bread plant to open in Monterrey.

Gruma Corp. had sales of 6.62 billion pesos (about $670 million) in 1998, with 12 tortilla plants and five corn-flour plants in the United States. The company held 83 percent of the U.S. corn-flour market under the Maseca label and 24 percent of the tortilla market under the Mission and Guerrero labels. At the beginning of 1999 it acquired four more tortilla-producing plants.

Gimsa had 18 corn-flour plants in Mexico in 1998. The parent company's sales from this 71 percent owned subsidiary came to 5.07 billion pesos (about $512.7 million). The corn-flour industry had a 47 percent market share in the production of tortillas in Mexico (excluding self-production), of which Gimsa's share came to 69 percent. Gimsa also opened a tortilla factory in Birmingham, England, in 1997, expecting $30 million in sales that year from all over Europe.

Gruma Centro America had five corn-flour plants and five other plants in 1998, including a bread factory and two bakeries opened in San José, Costa Rica, in 1995. Products included packaged bread and tortillas, tortilla chips, and pastries as well as corn flour. Sales in 1998 came to slightly more than 1 billion pesos (about $101 million). In 1999 Gruma purchased the Venezuelan operations of International Multifoods Corp., including facilities producing wheat and corn flour, for $74.5 million.

Molinas de México, the parent company's 60 percent owned joint venture, had seven wheat-flour mills, nine percent of the Mexican wheat-flour market, and 1998 sales of 791 million pesos (about $80 million). Productos y Distribuidora Azteca, manufacturer and marketer of packaged corn and wheat tortillas under the Mision label—introduced in 1994—and bread under the Breddy brand, had three tortilla plants and one bread plant. (Gruma claimed in 1999 to have captured a 12 percent share of the bread market in northern Mexico with the Breddy brand.) The Gruma empire also included tortilla machines and related equipment sold to supermarkets.

Principal Subsidiaries

Gruma Centro America, S.A.; Gruma Corporation (United States); Grupo Financiero Banorte, S.A. de C.V. (10 percent); Grupo Industrial Maseca, S.A. de C.V. (70.6 percent); Molinera de México, S.A. de C.V. (60%); Productos y Distribuidora Azteca, S.A. de C.V.

Principal Competitors

Grupo Bimbo, S.A. de C.V.; Grupo Minsa, S.A.; Tyson Foods Corp.

Further Reading

Black, Thomas, ''Tortilla Plan Rolled Up for Now,'' *Houston Chronicle,* January 2, 1998, pp. 1C, 6C.

DePalma, Anthony, ''How a Tortilla Empire Was Built on Favoritism,'' *New York Times,* February 15, 1996, pp. A1, A12.

Duffy, Tim, ''Mexico Tortilla Deregulation Doesn't Boost Sales,'' *Wall Street Journal,* January 8, 1999.

Duggan, Patrice, ''Tortilla Technology,'' *Forbes,* April 29, 1992, p. 48.

''Gruma to Compete with Bimbo in Mexico's Bread Market,'' *Milling & Baking News,* September 30, 1997, p. 14.

''Grupo Maseca: En el principio sola era maíz,'' *Expansión,* December 12, 1979, pp. 65–68.

Guadarrama H., José de Jesús, ''Maseca, un 'taco de alta technologia','' *El financiero,* November 4, 1997, p. 30.

Jacquez, Antonio, ''La riqueza de Roberto González Barrera,'' *Proceso,* February 19, 1996, pp. 14–18, 20–21.

Kilman, Scott, and Joel Millman, ''ADM, Showing New Interest in Mexico, Agrees to Buy 22% Stake in Gruma SA,'' *Wall Street Journal,* August 23, 1966, p. C15.

Millman, Joel, ''Mexican Baker Turns Up the Heat on Rivals,'' *Wall Street Journal,* August 27, 1999, p. A7.

——, ''Mexican Tortilla Firms Stage U.S. Bake-Off,'' *Wall Street Journal,* May 10, 1996, p. A6.

Moffett, Matt, ''Mexico's Campaign to Modernize Sparks Battle Over Tortillas,'' *Wall Street Journal,* September 9, 1993, pp. A1, A14.

Monjaras Moreno, Jorge, ''La modernización de la tortilla,'' *Expansión,* February 20, 1991, pp. 46–48, 51.

——, ''Roberto González Barrera: El hombre de *Expansión,*'' *Expansión,* January 12, 1994, pp. 32–33, 35, 37, 40.

—Robert Halasz

GT Interactive Software

417 Fifth Avenue
New York, New York 10016
U.S.A.
Telephone: (212) 726-6500
Fax: (212) 679-3424
Web site: http://www.gtinteractive.com

Public Company
Incorporated: 1993
Employees: 1,693
Sales: $572.3 million (1999)
Stock Exchanges: NASDAQ
Ticker Symbol: GTIS
NAIC: 42143 Computer and Computer Peripheral Equipment and Software Wholesalers; 511210 Software Publishers; 514191 On-Line Information Services

GT Interactive Software is a major publisher and distributor of entertainment software for PC and Macintosh computers, including CD-ROM, and for game system consoles manufactured by Nintendo and Sony. The company provides software for entertainment and ''edutainment,'' including value-priced offerings, to mass merchants such as Kmart, Wal-mart, and Target, and to more than 20,000 specialty retail stores. GT Interactive publishes and distributes worldwide software from its seven in-house development studios, as well as for associated development companies. The company also distributes to mass merchants in the United States software developed and published by other companies.

Company Origins

GT Interactive Software (GTIS) began as a division of GoodTimes Entertainment, a private company owned by three brothers, Joseph, Stanley, and Kenneth Cayre. The business success of the Cayre brothers has been attributed to their ability to identify opportunities early. In the 1970s they started a record company that produced and distributed Latin music before the major record labels recognized the potential of that market. In the 1980s, when movie videos were retail priced at $40 to $90 each, the Cayre brothers found obscure movies that did not require royalty payments and reproduced them for retail sale at $9.99. GoodTimes Entertainment offered the videos to Wal-Mart for $7.00 each wholesale, including shipping costs as well as return shipping costs for unsold merchandise, and arranged with Wal-Mart to lease shelf space for the videos near the front of their stores. GoodTimes' revenue reached $3 million the first year. When the movie studios realized that they could achieve high volume sales by pricing new movie releases at $19.95, the Cayre brothers began looking for new business opportunities.

GTIS was born in 1993 when Ronald Chaimowitz, a former competitor in the Latin music business as well as a former employee at GoodTimes, happened to call the Cayres to propose that they publish and distribute computer game software. Chaimowitz suggested replication of the same sales concept used in the music and video business: obtain prime retail shelf space to attract software developers. GoodTimes owned a rack-jobbing company that monitored video inventory by a satellite-linked computer system and stocked videos with a staff of 500 field personnel. Chaimowitz proposed that this rack-jobbing system could be applied to interactive computer games as well.

The Cayre brothers hired Chaimowitz as CEO and President. In his first major action, Chaimowitz attained the rights to publish ''Wolfenstein 3D,'' developed by id Software. The sales of the wartime adventure game had waned, but GTIS sold more than 100,000 units by using the jobber system to distribute the computer games. GTIS achieved a sizable presence in the computer game software market in 1994 after Wal-Mart approached the company to supply and manage its software displays. First-year revenues at GTIS reached $10.3 million.

The successful sale of ''Wolfenstein 3D'' led id Software to give GTIS the publishing rights to its ''Doom'' series of computer games. Prior to the October 10, 1994 release of ''Doom II: Hell on Earth,'' GTIS had obtained preorders for more than 250,000 units. Available on PC floppy disc or CD-ROM, ''Doom II'' was the sequel to a free, online shareware computer game, and an eager audience awaited the greater firepower and

Company Perspectives:

GT Interactive is a high performance corporation for a high performance world.

higher resolution graphics that the new software offered. The action of these games was ''first-person,'' viewed by the player from the perspective of the action hero. In ''Doom II'' the action was viewed through a marine who has returned to Earth to find it captive to demons, monsters, and mutants from Hell. GTIS rated ''Doom II'' for mature audiences as it contained animation of violence, blood, and gore. A record breaker, more than 500,000 copies of the game sold in the first four months of distribution.

With its reputation as an effective software distributor established, GTIS sought to publish and distribute worldwide a variety of software for computers and game consoles. In an exclusive partnership with Williams Entertainment, GTIS would develop and distribute computer software games such as, ''Troy Aikman Football,'' an interactive guide to the NFL, and ''Fun and Games,'' multimedia activities for kids. Their first joint production was a high speed go-kart race game, ''Super Karts.'' Players chose from 16 race tracks worldwide, each with its particular hazards, such as ice on the track in Russia. As with many computer games, a second player could compete on the same computer or through a network connection.

GTIS ventured into children's ''edutainment'' software in February 1995 through a contract with Big Tuna New Media. Mercer Mayer, award-winning author of children's stories, approached GTIS to publish and distribute his stories in both computer and game system platforms. The first release, ''Just Me and My Dad,'' followed the characters through a camping experience, with fishing, ghost stories, and a starry nighttime sky. Designed for three- to eight-year-old children, the story could be watched like a movie, be read by Little Critter and other characters, or be approached interactively by using a mouse to click on certain pictures for sound and movement. The storyline included lessons for children, such as respect for others and prevention of forest fires.

GTIS approached expansion through various means, beginning with the acquisition of Slash Corporation in June 1995. GTIS entered into a joint venture with Softbank, Japan's largest distributor of software and related products, and Roadshow Entertainment PTY of Australia, which allowed GTIS to market software titles in those countries. Distribution in Japan began with the Playstation console version of the ''Doom'' series. In Australia the ''HEXEN'' series of action-adventure games was distributed for Windows 95 compatibility. At the end of 1995, GoodTimes took GTIS public as a separate company and raised $150 million, which it planned to use to grow through acquisitions of game software companies.

GTIS on Its Own in 1996

GTIS began 1996 improving its marketing techniques. GTIS placed 20 electronic kiosks in Wal-Mart stores as a new avenue to promote more than 2,000 PC and CD-ROM game titles. The interactive kiosks allowed customers to preview new software and to order software through an electronic connection to GTIS headquarters in New York City. In addition, GTIS developed a display of low-cost software, value-priced at less than $20. These displays were set up at 700 Wal-Mart stores and 600 Kmart stores.

GTIS expanded its base of distribution through numerous agreements with software development companies and mass merchandisers. In February GTIS signed an agreement to supply its line of computer games to 600 Target stores. GTIS agreed to administer point-of-sale replenishment, electronic data invoicing, and a purchase ordering system. In March 1996, GTIS signed an agreement with Graphix Zone and Star Press (which were in the process of merging under Graphix Zone) to distribute their line of entertainment CD-ROMs and software to Wal-Mart, Kmart, Sam's Club, and Target. Star Press produced travel and health software, while Graphix Zone produced such music titles as ''Bob Dylan: Highway 61 Interactive'' on CD-ROM. GTIS purchased 800,000 shares of Graphix Zone common stock.

GTIS maintained its business alliance with id Software. The two companies signed an agreement for GTIS to publish and distribute worldwide ''Quake,'' a new 3D action game and ''Beyond Heretic,'' the second part of a complex fantasy game trilogy. In this game the player chose a character—either a fighter, a cleric, or a mage—which determined how challenges were handled as he traveled through swamps, ice castles, and other scenes.

New distribution agreements with game developers followed in April 1996. GTIS expanded in the global market in an agreement with Scavenger, Inc., which published a variety of PC video games, including ''Into the Shadow,'' a fantasy adventure, and ''Scorcher,'' a futuristic race. CyberSites gave GTIS the rights to publish ''SPQR,'' an Internet mystery game set in Ancient Rome. The intriguing story line and high quality graphics attracted GTIS to this product.

Six months after becoming a public company, GTIS began to expand with acquisitions and investments. GTIS's investment in Mirage, an entertainment software development company in England, involved an agreement to publish multiple titles. Investment in software developer Off World Entertainment included the option to convert preferred stock to 50 percent common stock equity. Acquisition of the WizardWorks Group added low-cost entertainment software to GTIS's publication stock.

The acquisition of Humongous Entertainment, Inc. expanded the company's publication of children's software. In exchange for four million shares of stock, a $76 million value, GTIS acquired all of the stock for Humongous Entertainment, Inc. Humongous published software for children with hand-animated characters, such as Putt-Putt, a friendly purple car, Freddi Fish, and Buzzy the Knowledge Bug. Humongous had received positive reviews and had a loyal customer base, but had not adequately reached its potential market.

The acquisition of Candel Inc., parent company of FormGen Inc., brought a best-selling interactive computer game to GTIS's distribution list, ''Duke Nukem 3D,'' released in July

Key Dates:

1994: Release of software game "Doom II: Hell on Earth" establishes company presence.
1995: Public offering of stock raises $150 million.
1996: Best-seller Duke Nukem 3D released.
1998: Acquisition of OneZero Media, Inc.
1999: Thomas Heyman of Walt Disney Store named CEO.

1996. With 28 playing levels, the game featured a media editor that allowed players to create additional levels of play and to share them with others. Other features included detailed 3D graphics that provided realistic animation, ten new weapons, such as the laser trip mine, and a working subway system. *PC Magazine* (July 1996) described this adults only title as, "the most technically impressive first-person action game on the market." The software offered parents the option of a password lock that eliminated scenes with nudity, adult language, and profanity.

When GTIS acquired Warner Interactive Entertainment, the European subsidiary of Warner Music Group, the company gained access to software markets in France, Germany, and Australia, as well as a staff of software developers. Based in Manchester, England, the staff included artists, graphic designers, and programmers.

In April 1997, Wal-Mart decided that it would purchase some entertainment software directly from the publishers rather than GTIS. These publishers were CUC International, Electronic Arts, Inc., and LucasArts Entertainment Company. GTIS would continue to handle 85 percent of Wal-Mart's software merchandise. The loss amounted to less than five percent of revenue; in terms of 1996 sales of $365.5 million that loss would mean $20 million in lost revenue. With constricted profit margins the move was not unexpected. The strength of GTIS laid in its ability to sell direct to mass merchandisers such as Wal-Mart and Kmart and direct sales of its own published products to Toys 'R' Us and other retail chains. To compensate for the loss at Wal-Mart, GTIS expanded the software assortment distributed to Kmart stores and, in other areas, GTIS reduced the assortment from 40 to 50 titles down to 30 to 35 of the better selling titles.

GTIS also planned to expand in the publishing aspect of the business. In June 1997 it purchased SingleTrac Entertainment Technologies, which would become the company's first in-house developer of entertainment software for computer and game system platforms. An agreement with MTV gave GTIS the rights to publish software games that feature Beavis and Butt-head, as well as Aeon Flux, animations owned by MTV.

Business Ventures Fruitful in 1997

Previous business activities began to bear fruit for GTIS by mid-1997. "Abe's Oddysee" by OddWorld Inhabitants introduced a new genre in game software with A.L.I.V.E., Aware Life forms in Virtual Entertainment. Released for the PlayStation game system and Windows 95, the game featured realistic character portrayals, including displays of emotion such as fear, happiness, and frustration. The choices characters make when facing ethical dilemmas affect the outcome of the game, while GameSpeak allows a character to learn the Odd-World languages. A breakthrough in video graphics, the motion picture-like animation did not have the normal disruption in the graphics sequence between player and computer playback. GTIS and OddWorld launched a $10 million campaign that included television and print advertising, an Internet preview, in-store promotions, and joint promotions with Sony and MTV. Upon release 500,000 units were shipped worldwide, available in English, Spanish, French, Italian, and German.

A year after its acquisition, sales of children's software at Humongous doubled to $20 million, and Humongous entered the top five in children's software development. Humongous used their signature characters to create a line of children's products, stuffed animals, puzzles, bedspreads, and clothing, with the hope that these characters would endure for years to come. An animated television show was put into development as well. New game products included the division's first educational software, "Big Thinkers," and the "Spy Fox" game.

Humongous added a new adult entertainment division, Cave Dog Entertainment. The company issued the real-time strategy game, "Total Annihilation," in December 1997, its first software publication. In the final conflict of a 4,000-year struggle, the storyline setting encompassed a wide variety of terrains in fine detail, such as ice planets, desert valleys, and mechanical worlds.

Other 1997 releases included Fantasy Football Smarts by WizardWorks. The game encompassed all aspects of football, such as coaching and management of football teams, with an infinite number of leagues, divisions, and teams possible. The "Youngblood" game was based on the best-selling comic books by Rob Liefeld. In addition, in 1997, Los Angeles Dodgers 1997 All-Star player Mike Piazza signed on as the headline pitcher in the arcade style baseball video game, "StrikeZone." The "Deer Hunter" computer game secured a place at the top of the value-priced entertainment software market for several months.

Continued Expansion in 1998

In December 1997 GTIS launched the Affiliate Label program, which offered exclusive sales and distribution to more than 40,000 retailers worldwide as well as marketing consultation. Highlights of distribution through GTIS included electronic data invoicing and same-day replenishment. Empire Interactive was the first company to affiliate. Palladium Interactive joined the program in April 1998, adding children's entertainment and genealogy software to GTIS stock. Australia-based Beam International Ltd. joined in June 1998. SmartCode Interactive, maker of a variety of hand-held electronic organizers, some with Internet and e-mail capacity, affiliated with GTIS in July 1998. Sega PC and Segasoft joined in December 1998.

GTIS ventured into different aspects of the entertainment media in 1998. In February GTIS entered into an agreement with Threshold Entertainment and 3D Realms to transform the Duke Nukem game series into motion picture, television, and home video media. An agreement with Mercury Records provided a soundtrack for the ''Rogue Trip'' game featuring platinum sellers The Mighty Mighty Bosstones and other artists.

Humongous captured a five-year, exclusive partnership to produce and distribute CD-ROMs based on Nickelodeon's ''Blue's Clues,'' the highly acclaimed television show for preschool children. ''Blue's ABC Time Activities'' and ''Blue's Birthday Adventure'' were released in 1998.

GTIS obtained publishing rights to Scholastic Entertainment's Animorphs, based on storylines from more than 15 million books and a television show on Nickelodeon. Animorphs is the story of five teenagers who must use ingenuity rather than brawn in their mission to save the earth from aliens. The global agreement gave GTIS exclusive, multi-title publishing rights to PC and game console software as well as new add-on and playing level packs.

GTIS bolstered in-house publishing with the launch of Bootprint Entertainment in November 1998. Bootprint's first project was to develop a proprietary engine for an action/strategy PC game expected to be released in 2000. In December GTIS acquired England-based Reflections Interactive, bringing in-house software development staff to more than 230 programmers, graphic designers, and artists.

In November 1998 GTIS announced the acquisition of OneZero Media, Inc. (OZM) for $15 million in stock. GTIS would benefit from the Internet ''portal'' market provided by OZM, which has had exclusive rights to operate the entertainment zone of Alta Vista, an Internet search engine. The company produced the Wild Wild Web Internet site, which provided information on entertainment—music, movies, and television. The Wild Wild Web television show, which discussed Internet topics, was renewed for its third season in January 1999 in 148 syndicates. OZM has generated advertising revenue from e-bay, Compaq, Web TV, and CD Now. GTIS hoped OZM would provide new opportunities for on-line sales, as the company's own web site, www.gtinteractive.com, has generated only one percent of direct sales.

New Leadership Challenges in 1999

The ever widening scope of GTIS business and continual losses required new leadership. Thomas Heyman became the new chairman and CEO in February 1999, bringing with him experience at the Walt Disney Store, which he turned from a million dollar operation into a billion dollar worldwide operation. John Baker IV, from competitor Activision, was named president and COO. The two confronted a number of financial challenges at GTIS. An ambitious software development schedule resulted in the late shipment of new games. Although revenue for the fiscal year ending March 31, 1999 was $57.3 million, the company experienced a net loss of $71 million. Another setback came in May 1999 when Wal-Mart opted to purchase software titles directly from Microsoft and Activision. The change was estimated to result in a loss of $50 million in revenue for GTIS.

Heyman and Baker took a number of steps to realign the company's finances. GTIS decided to lay off 35 percent of its staff, primarily at its distribution center in New Jersey. The 192,000-square-foot center was closed in April 1999, and an independent contractor was hired to handle distribution, Arnold Logistics in Lancaster, Pennsylvania. GTIS hired the Bear Stearns Company to examine options such as a sale or recapitalization to bring the company's finances into alignment. In addition, the company planned a relocation from New York City to Los Angeles.

The good news in 1999 involved several awards for GTIS published software. At the World Animation Celebration, ''Abe's Oddysee'' won Best Director for CD-ROM Games and took second place for Best Animation for CD-ROM Games. ''Unreal,'' by Epic MegaGames and Digital Extremes, listed among the top ten best-selling games in 1998 and won more than 20 industry awards, including the 1999 Codie Award for Best New Arcade/Action Software Game, given by the Software and Information Industry Association. With a new level of power in computer graphics engines, ''Unreal'' players traversed an alien world environment with a variety of exotic scenery and outdoor panoramas while trying to free the native people from a race of reptilian monsters. Another publishing agreement followed for ''Unreal Tournament'' and a sequel to ''Unreal.''

Business as usual continued at GTIS in 1999, beginning with the acquisition of Legend Entertainment, adding to in-house software development. GTIS entered into a global agreement with IMS Properties to publish and distribute interactive software. All teams and drivers for the Indianapolis 500, the Indy Racing League, Indianapolis Motor Speedway as well as sequels, add-on, and level packs were included in the deal. Significant game releases in 1999 included ''Duke Nukem: Zero Hour'' for the Nintendo 64 game console. Humongous Entertainment released two ''Blue's Clues'' video games, ''Blue's 123 Activities'' and ''Blue's Treasure Hunt'' for CD-ROM.

Principal Subsidiaries

Bootprint Entertainment; Candel, Inc.; Cave Dog Entertainment; FormGen, Inc.; G.T. Interactive Software France S.A.; G.T. Interactive Entertainment Company Germany GmbH; G.T. Interactive Entertainment (Europe) Limited; Humongous Entertainment, Inc.; Legend Entertainment, Inc.; Premier European Promotional Limited; OneZero Media, Inc,; SingleTrac Entertainment Technologies; WizardWorks Group, Inc.; Wizardworks (UK) Limited.

Principal Competitors

Activision, Inc.; CUC International; Disney Interactive; Electronic Arts Inc.; Mattel, Inc.; Microsoft Corp.; Sierra On-Line, Inc.

Further Reading

Delaney, John, ''Doom II,'' *PC Magazine,* January 10, 1995, p. 370.

——, ''Hexen: Beyond Heretic,'' *PC Magazine,* February 6, 1996, p. 364.

Eng, Paul M., ''Lots of Doom But No Gloom,'' *Business Week,* September 2, 1996, p. 74.

Garcia, Erica, ''New York-Based Video Game Maker To Cut 35 Percent of Work Force,'' *Knight-Ridder Business News,* April 8, 1999.

Gillen, Marilyn A., "Retailers Await Their Impending 'Doom'; Game Sequel Preorders Hit Quarter-Million Mark," *Billboard,* July 16, 1994, p. 60.

——, "A Year of Firsts for Vid-Game Market," *Billboard,* January 7, 1995, p. 77.

"GT Gets Rights to #D Game, Quake," *HFN-The Weekly Newspaper for the Home Furnishings Network,* January 22, 1996, p. 101.

"GT Hits Bull's-Eye with Target," *HFN-The Weekly Newspaper for the Home Furnishings Network,* February 19, 1996, p. 89.

"GT Interactive Goes Boom with 'Doom,' " *Billboard,* October 29, 1994, p. 76.

"GT Interactive Leaves the Nest," *Billboard,* January 21, 1995, p. 52.

"GT Interactive Moves," *Television Digest,* July 7, 1997, p. 13.

"GT Interactive Software Signed a Deal with MTV Last Week To Publish Several Software Titles Using MTV Animation Properties," *Broadcasting and Cable,* June 23, 1997, p. 97.

"GT Interactive to Bring Internet Game to CD-ROM," *HFN-The Weekly Newspaper for the Home Furnishings Network,* April 22, 1996, p. 168.

"GT Nabs Warner Interactive," *Billboard,* December 7, 1996, p. 62.

"GT to Add Two Makers' Software," *HFN-The Weekly Newspaper for the Home Furnishings Network,* March 25, 1996, p. 53.

Herz, J.C., "On 'Deer Hunter's' Trail, Rivals and a Spoof," *New York Times,* December 17, 1998, p. G4.

McKay, Martha, "Hundreds to Lose Jobs at Computer-Game Firm's Edison, NJ Warehouse," *Knight-Ridder Business News,* August 5, 1999.

Mooney, Shane, "Real-Time Roundup," *PC Magazine,* December 2, 1997, p. 516.

"PC Software Selection Changing," *Television Digest,* July 7, 1997, p. 12.

Ryan, Michael, "Duke Nukem 3D: Atomic Edition," *PC Magazine,* September 9, 1997, p. 372.

——, "The Next Big Thing: This Action Game Shouldn't Be Compared with Quake: It's in a Category by Itself," *PC Magazine,* September 1, 1998, p. 338.

——, "Quake," *PC Magazine,* September 9, 1997, p. 379.

——, "Shall We Play a Game?," *PC Magazine,* July 1996, p. 451.

Trachtenberg, Jeffrey, "GT Interactive Buys Third Software Firm in Two Week Period," *Wall Street Journal,* July 11, 1996, p. B7.

Trainman, Steve, "GTI/RED Meld Music, Game Industries with 'Nukem' Album," *Billboard,* May 15, 1999, p. 65.

Upbin, Bruce, "Scholars of Shelf Space," *Forbes,* October 21, 1996, p. 210.

"Video for Us All," *PC Week,* July 22, 1996, p. A6.

—Mary Tradii

Hansen Natural Corporation

2380 Railroad Street, Suite 101
Corona, California 92880-5471
U.S.A.
Telephone: (909) 739-6200
Fax: (909) 739-6210
Web site: http://www.hansens.com

Public Company
Incorporated: 1990
Employees: 50
Sales: $53.87 million (1998)
Stock Exchanges: NASDAQ
Ticker Symbol: HANS
NAIC: 312111 Soft Drink Manufacturing

A descendant of a venerable California juice maker, Hansen Natural Corporation went from bankruptcy case to NASDAQ darling by focusing on innovation in the beverage marketplace. A new line of smoothies helped get the company regain profitability after some losses in the mid-1990s. Since then, Hansen Natural has pioneered the functional beverage category, the fastest growing segment of the industry, in the United States. All of Hansen Natural Corporation's operations were carried out through its sole subsidiary, Hansen Beverage Company.

A Sunny Beginning

''Hansen's Fruit and Vegetable Juices'' first appeared in southern California in 1935. Assisted by his three sons, Hubert Hansen started the business in Los Angeles selling fresh, unpasteurized fruit juices. Hollywood film studios provided his first clients. That company became Hansen's Juices, later known as The Fresh Juice Company of California, Inc. The plant it opened in Los Angeles in 1946 was used until operations were moved to a new plant in Azusa, California in 1993.

This company's fresh juice line included orange, carrot, apple, strawberry, and banana juices, as well as blends. By this time, Hansen's Juices was firmly established in the West and was shipped to the East Coast and Hawaii as well. Some of its 35,000 gallons of juice produced per week was marketed by an Illinois company, and some was shipped overseas, reported the *Los Angeles Times.*

One of Hubert Hansen's grandsons, Tim Hansen, formed his own, separate fruit juice business in 1977: Hansen Foods, Inc. He obtained a license to use the family name as a trademark. The new company, also based in Los Angeles, specialized in pasteurized, shelf-stable juices, particularly apple. It was known for innovation in combining flavors as well as in marketing. Hansen Foods branched out into Hansen's Natural Sodas in 1978. These featured all natural ingredients.

Hansen's sales reached an estimated $50 million in the mid-1980s. Sales failed, however, to climb sufficiently to repay financing for a new factory, and the company filed for bankruptcy in 1988. California CoPackers Corporation (d/b/a/ Hansen Beverage Company), based in Hawaii, subsequently acquired the Hansen's brand name in January 1990.

Annual sales reached $13.7 million that year and rose to $17.1 million the next. Hansen, always known for using cans, introduced its first glass bottle in the summer of 1991. At this time, Harold C. Taber, Jr. was serving as president and CEO of the company, then based in Brea, California.

Hansen Natural Corporation Created in 1992

An investment group including Rodney Sacks, who would become CEO, bought the money-losing company on July 27, 1992. The investors felt that the brand's longevity and name recognition would be worth banking on and that its niche was just opening up in the market. Aside from Sacks, a corporate lawyer from South Africa, other new management talent included Taber, a 27-year Coca-Cola veteran. Investors included British industrialist Hilton H. Schlosberg, who became vice-chairman and president, and friends and family members. Hansen Natural Corporation went public at the same time, listing on NASDAQ. The company soon seemed to evidence a turnaround. Revenues reached $21.3 million in 1992.

Company Perspectives:

The mission of Hansen Beverage Company is to satisfy consumers' needs for superior quality and great tasting, healthy natural beverages. Our beverages will be positioned as an upscale brand and will be marketed at a premium to competitive mainstream products. In fulfilling this mission, Hansen's will be guided by the following values: Superior Quality. *Quality is the cornerstone of the Company's activities, and will never be compromised. Consumers should always be able to trust the superior quality and taste of our products, and have their families consume them with full confidence.* Natural Beverages. *Hansen's products will always be free of preservatives, artificial flavors and colors. They will also have minimal, if any, sodium and, in general, will be without added caffeine. Caffeine may be added to certain functional drinks, where caffeine may be useful, i.e. to help accelerate the metabolism by the body of certain nutrients.* Our Customers. *We are in business because of our customers. We are committed to establishing and maintaining a profitable partnership with our customers by providing high quality products, superior service, and effective promotional support for our brands.* Continuous Quest for Excellence. *We are determined to be the best, both as a company and as individuals. We will never be satisfied with our current performance—no matter how good it is—and will continually strive to seek improvement, unparalleled excellence in our products and new opportunities for business growth.* Respect for the Individual. *Our people are our most valued asset and are critical to our success; we will recognize and respect their rights, dignity, opinions and individuality. Our people will not tolerate mediocrity.* Uncompromising Integrity. *We set high ethical and moral standards. We will never engage in or support any act that is unethical, illegal or inappropriate.* Continuous Growth. *We continually strive for growth opportunities to expand our markets and our product range with new and, where possible, different beverages, without compromising the excellence of our existing operations.*

Hansen employed about a dozen people at the time. Since Tropicana had acquired the Hansen factory in the bankruptcy, the company now outsourced most of its operations, even turning to flavor consultants for new formulations. Independent companies blended the drinks and shipped it to independent bottlers.

Pint-sized, bottled iced teas, lemonades, and juice drinks came out in the early 1990s. These competed in the "New Age" drink category, which also included alternatives to traditional cola drinks such as flavored water and iced tea. What defined the category was the public perception of these drinks as relatively healthy. Hansen's heritage was perceived as particularly healthy. Its labeling began to proclaim, for example, "California's original clear natural soda."

Industry leaders such as Coca-Cola and Pepsi fought for a share of this segment, the fastest growing part of the $50 billion a year soft drink market. Coca-Cola introduced Nordic Mist, and Pepsi offered Crystal Pepsi as an alternative. Snapple's drinks quickly came to dominate this $1 billion category. It sold $232 million worth of iced tea in 1992. Its advertising and marketing budget that year—$30 million—exceeded Hansen's total revenues, noted the *Los Angeles Times.* Some analysts, however, believed that Hansen's long-term interests were best served by a focus on keeping costs down. They felt that the company was less likely to "crash and burn" in the event of a price war. Hansen embarked on a major expansion into the Midwest in 1993, introducing a multiserve, 23-ounce glass bottle to its packaging mix.

New Age drinks were faddish and in July 1994 Hansen introduced a line specially branded to appeal to young consumers. Equator drinks initially debuted in Southern California. They came in 16-ounce cans (a 24-ounce version also was tried) wrapped in environmentally conscious imagery and copy. By not packaging the drinks in glass bottles, they could be sold in more locations, such as gyms and swimming pools where risk of breakage might be considered a hazard. To capture the loyalty of younger consumers, the traditional Hansen's brand, which was identified with older drinkers, was not featured on the packaging. The first flavors were Blue Raspberry Creation Iced Tea, Cosmic Mango Iced Tea, Black Cherry Eclipse Lemonade, Heavenly Strawberry Banana Juice Cocktail, and Guava Berry Earthshine Juice Cocktail. A portion of the proceeds from each can sold went to Earth Day USA.

A "Smoothie" Return to Profitability in 1996

Hansen Natural lost nearly $3 million in 1994 and 1995 ($1.4 million in the latter). The debut of its Smoothie drinks late in 1995 carried high hopes. They proved to be a lifesaver. In their first nine months on the shelves, the Smoothie line brought in one-third of the company's revenues; one in every five cases sold contained Smoothies. Hansen Natural was able to report income of $357,000 in 1996.

Smoothies were available in 11.5-ounce cans and 11.5-ounce glass bottles. Though inspired by the smoothies found in fresh juice bars, Hansen's were not formulated as thick so that they could be bottled. Some smoothies had herbal additives ginseng and taurine, a meat-derived amino acid featured in many Asian "energy" drinks. Radically redesigned packaging helped Hansen's products stand out on store shelves. Smoothies were sold in distinctive fluted bottles.

The smoothies were more than a new product. They signaled a new innovative spirit at the company, Sacks told the *Business Press/California.* Previous national product launches had failed since they were too similar to what Snapple already had in stores—that is, iced tea, lemonade, and juice cocktails.

Another shot in the arm, Hansen's "functionals" came out in early 1997. This category was defined as drinks bought primarily for health benefits. They typically included extra vitamins. This trend had already been established in Europe, where they first caught the attention of Sacks. Similar, often syrupy concoctions had been popular in Asia for more than 30 years and constituted a $3 billion market there.

Key Dates:

1935: Hubert Hansen and sons begin selling juice in Los Angeles.
1977: Founder's grandson Tim Hansen establishes fast-growing Hansen Foods, Inc.
1988: Hansen Foods succumbs to debt load in Chapter 11.
1992: Rodney Sacks and others acquire company, list Hansen Natural Corporation on NASDAQ.
1996: After two years of losses, company again posts a profit.
1997: "Functionals" line energizes Hansen's sales and share price.
1998: Company relocates to Corona, California, from Anaheim.

Hansen's energy drinks were lightly carbonated. They were packaged in skinny 8.2-ounce cans, offering a more manageable serving for an energy drink. Each can retailed for about $2, whereas sodas cost 60 cents. They offered "an immediate boost whenever you need it the most." Part of the pitch was naming the drinks not for their flavoring, but for the benefits they touted. An anti-oxidant ("anti-ox") variety fought aging. Yet another pitched "stamina." Finally, "D-Stress" was intended to enable the drinker to relax.

Some wondered whether the U.S. Food and Drug Administration would eventually regulate this category more strictly, but since the drinks were marketed as food, not as drugs promising any specific medicinal benefits, they fell out of that agency's purview. Hansen labeled the amounts of different herbs and additives in its drinks to enhance its credibility and to advise people with allergies. Although the company always had avoided adding caffeine to its drinks, and even formulated its iced tea to be decaffeinated, it was added to some of the functional drinks for the purposes of stimulating metabolism.

Bullfighting in 1997 and Beyond

Hansen had ventured into Great Britain in 1994, but found the market unwelcoming. It also failed to differentiate its products sufficiently. Its subsidiary there, Hansen Beverage Company (UK) Limited, stopped operating at the end of 1997. Back home, Hansen faced some competition on its own turf from Red Bull, an Austrian company that virtually owned the $500 million European market for functional drinks. Speaking to a local newspaper, Sacks characterized Red Bull as a one-product company.

Another advantage credited to Hansen was that its drinks tasted comparatively good. The company also had an established distribution network. Hansen pitched its functional drinks heavily, giving out free samples and setting up literature centers in grocery stores. Convenience stores and liquor stores were among the first to sell the new beverage, but they were soon joined by a variety of retailers. The "new" Hansen received much praise from analysts for finding its own niche on the "cutting edge" rather than competing directly with the larger players.

In 1997, three-quarters of the company's sales came from California. The success of the functionals line helped Hansen sell more of its other products out of state. Earnings were $1.3 million on revenues of $43 million. The next year, functional drinks accounted for a quarter of Hansen's sales of $54 million, and the company's earnings doubled. Within a year of the introduction of the functionals line, the company's share price nearly quadrupled, to $6. The nutrient-enhanced beverage category of New Age drinks increased more than fourfold in 1998.

Hansen Natural relocated from Anaheim to Corona, California in January 1998. Its headquarters and warehouse shared a 65,000-square-foot building. It was developing the DynaJuice blended fruit drink, which contained 15 vitamins and minerals. This was first in a line of "Healthy Start" products for supermarket chains.

In April 1999, Brio Industries Inc. of British Columbia agreed to market Hansen's products throughout Canada. More than 18,000 venues were to be offered opportunities to sell the drinks. Because of the vastness of territory and its lack of name recognition up north, Hansen planned to introduce its products gradually there. The company had worked previously with a small Toronto-based distributor. As Canadian law forbade adding any type of vitamins to drinks, some reformulations were in order.

Revenues were expected to reach $64 million in 1999. Hansen had signed distribution agreements with Dr. Pepper and 7-Up and secured a national product introduction through 7-Eleven convenience stores. The company was planning to bring out a nutritional boxed drink for children as well as a "super smoothie." Also forthcoming were Signature Soda gourmet carbonated drinks made with cane sugar and clover honey. Sacks sought to differentiate the brand on nutrition, not taste. "What we're trying to do is sell people something that's honest—something that will do something for their bodies," he told one California business journal.

Principal Subsidiaries

Hansen Beverage Company.

Principal Competitors

Red Bull North America; Triarc Group; The Coca-Cola Company; PepsiCo, Inc.

Further Reading

Ascenzi, Joseph, "Hansen Inks Deal To Pop into Canada," *Business Press/California,* April 26, 1999, p. 1.
——, "Hansen Natural Squeezes Profits from Fruit-Based Health Drinks," *Business Press/California,* June 22, 1998, p. 17.
Berkman, Leslie, "Pick-Me-Up for the Bottom Line: Beverages That Claim To Energize (or Tranquilize) the Drinker Have Boosted Sales and Profits at Hansen Natural of Corona," *Press-Enterprise,* September 6, 1998, p. H1.
"Corona, California Beverage Maker Aims To Take 'Energy' Drinks Nationwide," *Press-Enterprise,* September 6, 1998.

''Drinking to Your Health—Literally,'' *Convenience Store News,* July 12, 1999.

''Hansen Hoping for a Smoothie Ride,'' *Orange County Register,* May 5, 1996.

Jabbonsky, Larry, ''What the Heck Is a New Age Beverage?,'' *Beverage World,* September 1991, p. 42.

Johnson, Greg, ''Juice or Soda, Company's Assets Increasingly Liquid,'' *Los Angeles Times,* Bus. Sec., June 1, 1993, p. D8.

——, ''Liquid Assets: Hansen Natural Corp. in Anaheim Seeks To Expand Its Market,'' *Los Angeles Times,* Bus. Sec., May 28, 1993, p. D1.

Khermouch, Gerry, and Theresa Howard, ''Herbal Elixirs Creating a Buzz, But May Also Awaken Feds, Execs Worry,'' *Brandweek,* November 2, 1998, pp. 8–9.

Sfiligoj, Eric, ''Hansen's Branches Out Beyond California by Mixing Its Packages To Match All Tastes,'' *Beverage World,* September 30, 1993, p. 18.

——, ''It's Bad to Be a Fad, Figures Taber, So Hansen's Is No Age, Not New Age,'' *Beverage World,* December 31, 1994, p. 1.

——, ''Rail-ly Quick Change,'' *Beverage World,* October 1993, p. 80.

Trager, Cara, ''Stirring Up Soft Drinks,'' *Beverage World,* September 1991, p. 48.

—Frederick C. Ingram

HAVERTYS
FURNITURE

Haverty Furniture Companies, Inc.

866 West Peachtree Street N.W.
Atlanta, Georgia 30308
U.S.A.
Telephone: (404) 881-1911
Toll Free: (800) 535-1885
Fax: (404) 870-9424
Web site: http://www.havertys.com

Public Company
Incorporated: 1885 as Haverty Furniture Company
Employees: 3,286
Sales: $540.30 million
Stock Exchanges: New York
Ticker Symbol: HVT
NAIC: 44211 Furniture Stores

Haverty Furniture Companies, Inc. is a leading furniture retailer in the south and central United States, with approximately 100 stores in 14 states. Havertys, as the company is known, targets the middle to upper-middle income market, eschewing high-pressure sales tactics and deep discounts in favor of quality merchandise, friendly customer service, and quick delivery of goods. The company also operates its own credit service. In 1998 Havertys reached an agreement with Furniture Brands International, the number two U.S. maker of residential furniture, to prominently feature its brands chainwide in exchange for improved access to that company's products. Havertys also has been on a campaign of expansion, adding or relocating as many as ten stores per year, sometimes through purchases of smaller retailers.

Beginnings

Havertys was founded in 1885 by J.J. Haverty and his brother Michael in Atlanta, Georgia. As young children they had seen the city burned during the Civil War and had endured the privations of the postwar years. As they grew to adulthood they also had watched Atlanta's inhabitants begin to rebuild. Believing in the city's potential, the brothers used $600 of J.J.'s money and an equal amount in borrowed capital to open a furniture store. The first 12 months were not an overwhelming success, with only some $6,000 in revenue, but by the third year the new company had grown enough to move to a larger location.

In 1889 J.J. and Michael Haverty entered a partnership with the owner of a neighboring furniture store, Amos G. Rhodes, forming the Rhodes-Haverty Furniture Company. Both stores liquidated their inventories prior to the new venture so that they could start fresh, and a new building was constructed to house the enterprise. The company issued 200 shares of stock, which the three partners split. In these early days sales were often made by men who canvassed neighborhoods carrying photographs of the various styles of furniture that were available, which included the full residential line from bedroom sets to parlor chairs. The company offered the popular option of purchasing on the installment plan, as well as free delivery. Illustrated newspaper advertisements also were used to promote the company's wares.

A year and a half after the Rhodes-Haverty store opened, J.J. Haverty decided to move westward to St. Louis with his family and go into business there. His first new store opened in 1891, and he soon bought interest in a number of smaller showrooms in outlying areas. In 1894 he returned to Atlanta and, with Rhodes and Peyton A. Snook, opened a new store in the former National Hotel building. Other stores soon followed in Waco and Dallas, Texas. In 1898 this partnership was dissolved, however, and Haverty and Rhodes opened yet another Atlanta store, later adding other locations around the South. By 1908 the company boasted 17 outlets.

J.J. Haverty's son Clarence, who started in the business sweeping floors, had risen to a leadership position by 1908. The ambitious young man, now 27, sought to take more control of the company's destiny, and a friendly split with Amos Rhodes was arranged. All but one of the company's stores was divided by the two senior partners through a series of coin tosses. The main Atlanta location was purchased outright by the Havertys, and the business took back its original name of Haverty Furniture Company. The company's nine stores were located in Atlanta and Savannah, Georgia; Memphis, Tennessee; and Dallas, Fort Worth, and Houston, Texas. Once again 200 ownership shares were distributed, this time among various Haverty family members.

Company Perspectives:

Throughout its history, Havertys has sought to provide home furnishings to the homemaker, together with a financial service to ease the purchase of those home furnishings. Haverty Furniture Companies, Inc. is organized to make a fair profit for its stockholders, together with a steady enhancement of invested capital. Profitable management requires a well trained, experienced and harmonious team. To attract, develop, and hold a good operating team requires sound personnel practices, together with adequate wages that encourage individual productivity. Successful management in today's complex economy requires professional techniques of management, research and development, and continual advance planning. The company will periodically draw long range plans, and annually review and update those plans. The company encourages training to improve understanding, competence, and productivity at every level. Special emphasis will be continually exercised toward identifying, encouraging, and training potential management personnel. The company must provide its product and services in a manner that will attract an increasing number of customers and their repeat business. Therefore, dealing fairly with customers in a courteous and thoughtful manner is a basic policy of the company.

Following the split with Rhodes, the company began to expand, opening stores in Birmingham, Alabama and Charleston and Columbia, South Carolina by 1916. Havertys also moved its Atlanta headquarters to a larger six-story building in 1924. A newspaper advertising section announcing the new location stated, ''Our policy will be the same as we have maintained throughout our history—complete stocks, expertly selected, priced as low as our tremendous Buying Power and conservative merchandising will permit. Every article in our store is marked in Plain Figures. Our well known liberal credit system with terms to suit you applies to everything. A discount of 10 percent will be allowed for cash.'' Offering a complete tour of the store, the ad went on to note, ''You will not be asked to buy anything unless you indicate that you are definitely interested.'' The company continued to offer free delivery, as it had done from the beginning, and maintained a fleet of trucks painted ''Haverty blue'' for this purpose.

Other Haverty Furniture stores were opened in the mid-1920s in Little Rock, Arkansas; Chattanooga, Tennessee; Charlotte, North Carolina; Greenville, South Carolina; and New Orleans, Louisiana. Also during this period, J.J. Haverty and Amos Rhodes formed another partnership, this time to erect the Rhodes-Haverty Building, which would remain Atlanta's tallest structure until 1955.

Initial Public Stock Offering in 1929

In the late 1920s the company decided to take advantage of the booming stock market and go public. Haverty Furniture at this time was owned by 17 separate stockholder corporations, and these were consolidated at the same time that 100,000 shares of preferred stock in the newly named Haverty Furniture Companies, Inc. were issued. J.J. Haverty retained 25,000 shares, and 75,000 were purchased for resale by Hambleton & Co. of Baltimore. The stock sale took place on October 1, 1929, and four weeks later the market crashed. Haverty stock dropped from $20 to $5 per share, and Hambleton went bankrupt. Despite this calamity, Havertys had no debt, and business remained steady enough for the company to weather the crisis. New locations were even opened in 1930, in Winston-Salem, North Carolina, and in 1931, in Jacksonville, Florida. The company had 23 locations by this year.

The Depression saw Havertys experience larger than usual amounts of product returns and credit defaults, as well as lower overall sales, and losses were posted for 1931, 1932, and 1933. In the wake of President Franklin D. Roosevelt's efforts toward economic recovery, however, the company made a return to profitability in 1934. Clarence Haverty, who had been running the business for many years, was officially named president in 1938, at which time J.J. Haverty became chairman of the company's board. In October of 1939, just short of his 81st birthday, founder J.J. Haverty passed away.

In December 1941 the United States entered World War II, and the company faced a reduction in revenues brought on by the rationing of materials used in furniture production. Profits dropped for 1942 and slipped further the following year, before rebounding slightly in 1944. When the war ended, pent-up demand for consumer goods caused sales to surge, and the company took advantage of the booming economy to remodel its older stores, also opening new locations in Shreveport, Louisiana; Richmond, Virginia; and Augusta, Georgia. Havertys' annual sales of $6 million in 1945 nearly doubled for 1946, topping $11 million. Clarence Haverty's son Rawson, who had returned from war service a major, assumed the position of corporate secretary.

Havertys continued to prosper during the 1950s, with new locations added in Alabama, Virginia, Arkansas, and Florida. Clarence Haverty stepped down as president in 1955 at the age of 73, and Rawson took on the role. By 1960, the year of the company's 75th anniversary, Havertys had 42 stores in ten states and annual sales of more than $22 million. That year also saw the passing of Clarence Haverty at the age of 79. In 1961 Havertys made a major expansion move by purchasing ten National Biederman stores in the Houston, Texas area, giving them the Haverty name. Additional stores also were opened in Charlotte and Jacksonville.

By the end of the 1960s, retail trends were changing. Suburban malls were luring shoppers away from downtown businesses, and Havertys began to adapt, moving its main Atlanta location from downtown to the area of the popular Lenox Square mall. Over the next several years other downtown stores also were closed in Roanoke, Virginia; Chattanooga, Tennessee; and Birmingham, Alabama. The company's structure was decentralized during this period as well, with regional managers appointed to oversee stores in Florida, the Mid-South, the Carolina/Virginia area, and the Western region. A downturn in sales had occurred during the early 1970s, but by 1973 the company was again growing, with revenues of $52 million and profits of $1.9 million.

Key Dates:

1885: First store opened by J.J. Haverty and his brother Michael.
1889: Partnership with Amos G. Rhodes to form Rhodes-Haverty Furniture.
1908: J.J. Haverty and son Clarence split with Rhodes and re-establish Haverty Furniture Co.
1929: Company goes public as Haverty Furniture Companies, Inc.
1938: Clarence Haverty named president of Havertys.
1955: Clarence Haverty's son Rawson becomes company president.
1979: Sales top $100 million.
1984: J.J. Haverty's grandson, Frank McGaughey, Jr., becomes president.
1994: John E. Slater is named president and CEO.
1998: Marketing agreement forged with Furniture Brands, International; stock moves to New York Stock Exchange.
1999: 100th store opened.

1979: $100 Million in Sales

In the mid-1970s Havertys management set a goal of $100 million in sales for 1980, and the company's growth was such that revenues topped that mark a year early. In 1984 CEO Rawson Haverty stepped down as president, taking the role of board chairman. Company veteran and J.J. Haverty's grandson Frank McGaughey, Jr. was tapped as his replacement. In 1986 the company closed its last downtown Atlanta store, although it still remained the area's largest furniture retailer, with locations distributed throughout the metropolitan area. The company also recapitalized and created two classes of stock, leaving the Haverty family and other management personnel with control of about a third of the voting shares.

In the late 1980s Havertys began to embark upon a comprehensive revitalization program, upgrading most of the company's stores over the next decade. Enhanced lighting and display areas were the primary improvements, with some stores also being expanded in size. The changes were intended to appeal to a more upscale clientele, while continuing to retain the company's traditional middle-income customers. A new, more aggressive expansion strategy was also in place, with five to ten new stores opening per year, in some cases as replacements for smaller outlets. In 1990 a new regional distribution center also came on line in Jacksonville, Mississippi.

Despite a relatively weak year in 1991, sales for Havertys continued an upward trajectory during the early 1990s, with revenues reaching $322 million by 1993. Net income was $9.7 million, double that of the previous year. The company reached an agreement with mid- to high-end furniture maker Thomasville Furniture Industries, Inc. to prominently feature that company's products in many Haverty stores. Havertys also opened a prototype store in Naples, Florida in late 1992 that solely featured Thomasville merchandise; three more such stores were added over the next year. The company had made the alliance to gain better access to the manufacturer's products, as customers were increasingly seeking out top brand names like Thomasville.

In 1994 Frank McGaughey stepped down, and John E. Slater was named president and CEO. Slater had joined the company in 1956 and was serving as its chief operating officer. Havertys now owned 90 stores. Nearly three-fourths of sales were made via the company's own credit program, and this provided it with another consistent source of income. In contrast to the problems experienced in this area by many lower-priced furniture stores, Havertys had an insignificant default rate of less than one percent of sales. The company began to rethink its distribution of furniture to stores at this time and implemented a ''Just In Time'' system. This made better use of Havertys' five regional warehouses, which were linked with computers to the retail locations. Truckloads of furniture could be sent from a regional center to stores for final delivery so quickly that large backstocks no longer needed to be maintained in each city, thus reducing storage costs.

Continued Growth and New Manufacturer Alliances in the Late 1990s

In the late 1990s Havertys continued to grow, with 1997 seeing the company purchase its first two locations in Kentucky, replace eight smaller outlets with seven larger ones, and open a new store in the Dallas distribution center. Sales for the year hit $490 million, both on the growth in revenues from new locations and on rising same-store sales figures. The year also saw Havertys' credit operations more centrally consolidated, which cut administrative costs and improved efficiency.

Early in 1998 the company announced a strategic alliance with Thomasville's parent company Furniture Brands International, the number two manufacturer of furniture in the United States. Havertys agreed to allocate as much as half of its display space chainwide to products manufactured by Furniture Brands, which also owned names such as Broyhill and Action/Lane. This agreement allowed the company to put the popular Thomasville line in all of its stores, which it had not been able to do previously. Furniture Brands pledged to improve delivery times for Havertys and also to design some pieces for exclusive sale in the company's stores. In August of 1998 Havertys' stock listing moved from the NASDAQ exchange to the more prestigious New York Stock Exchange.

The company formed another alliance with a major manufacturer in 1999, announcing an agreement with La-Z-Boy Inc. to take over an existing La-Z-Boy store in Memphis and possibly open a second store in the area. Other new Havertys openings were planned that would take the company's holdings to more than 100 stores by year's end.

As it approached its 115th year in business, Haverty Furniture Companies could look back on a long history of growth and prosperity. Boasting a continuous string of annual profits since the Second World War, a seasoned management team, new strategic manufacturer alliances, and a successful program of expansion and store renovations, the company's prospects for a long and healthy future looked bright.

Principal Subsidiaries

Havertys Capital, Inc.; Havertys Credit Services, Inc.; Havertys Enterprises, Inc.

Principal Competitors

Ethan Allen Interiors, Inc.; Heilig-Meyers Co.; Levitz Furniture, Inc.; J.C. Penney Company, Inc.; The Rowe Companies; Sears, Roebuck and Co.

Further Reading

Boyd, Terry, ''Haverty Furniture to Open at Two Ex-Herelinger's Sites,'' *Business First of Louisville,* January 27, 1997.

Haverty Furniture Companies, Inc., 1985.

Deogun, Nikhil, ''Heard in the Southeast: Some Believe Haverty Furniture Is Neglected Stock Worth Polishing,'' *Wall Street Journal,* October 26, 1994, p. S2.

''Haverty Furniture Cos. Proposes Measures To Thwart Takeovers,'' *Wall Street Journal,* April 1, 1986.

''Haverty Furniture Finds Cushy Spot on Wall Street,'' *Atlanta Business Chronicle,* July 10, 1998, p. 4A.

''John Slater CEO and Dennis Fink CFO of Haverty Furniture'' (interview), *Dow Jones Investor Network,* September 11, 1996.

Liscio, John, ''Here's Haverty: All Spruced Up and Ready To Grow,'' *Barron's,* April 20, 1987.

Marks, Robert, ''Haverty: More Stores, Some for Thomasville,'' *HFD—The Weekly Home Furnishings Newspaper,* April 26, 1993, p. 16.

''Slater To Become Haverty's President,'' *HFD—The Weekly Home Furnishings Newspaper,* February 14, 1994, p. 6.

Switzer, Liz, ''Haverty, Vendor Partner: Furniture Brands' Goods to Fill Up to Half the Stores,'' *HFN—The Weekly Newspaper for the Home Furnishing Network,* February 16, 1998, p. 10.

Winokur, Leslie, ''John Slater CEO & Dennis Fink CFO of Haverty Furniture'' (interview), *Dow Jones Investor Network,* April 17, 1995.

Wray, Kimberley, ''Havertys Formula: Drive Down Inventory,'' *HFN—The Weekly Newspaper for the Home Furnishing Network,* August 17, 1998, p. 68.

—Frank Uhle

Heidelberger Zement AG

Berliner Strasse 6
D-69120 Heidelberg
Germany
Telephone: (49)(6221) 481-227
Fax: (49)(6221) 481-203
Web site: http://www.hzag.de

Public Company
Incorporated: 1873 as Portland-Cement-Werk, Heidelberg, Schifferdecker & Söhne OHG
Employees: 24,311
Sales: DM 7.65 billion ($3.91 billion) (1998)
Stock Exchanges: Frankfurt/Main
Ticker Symbol: HEI
NAIC: 32731 Cement Manufacturing; 32732 Ready-Mix Concrete Manufacturing; 327331 Concrete Block and Brick Manufacturing; 32739 Other Concrete Product Manufacturing; 327122 Ceramic Wall and Floor Tile Manufacturing; 322221 Coated and Laminated Packaging Paper and Plastics Film Manufacturing; 333993 Packaging Machinery Manufacturing; 484121 General Freight Trucking, Long-Distance, Truckload

Heidelberger Zement AG is one of the world's five largest producers of construction materials. Its main product lines include standard and specialty cements, concrete products, limestone and lime products, building chemicals, dry mortar, special gypsums, sand lime bricks, and insulation materials. The company also offers specialty products and services for the construction of waste dumps and for the immobilization of toxic materials, as well as logistics services. While about one-third of its total sales are generated in Germany, Heidelberger Zement is active in Central and Western Europe, North America, and Asia. The company's export and trade activities in over 30 countries are executed by a subsidiary, Netherlands-based HC Trading B.V.

Trainee Becomes Company Leader in 1873

Heidelberger Zement has its roots in two areas: the rich sources of limestone near the German town of Heidelberg and the entrepreneural spirit of Johann Philipp Schifferdecker, a young brewer from a small village. The struggling man moved to Eastern Prussia where he opened a brewery in Königsberg and made a fortune with it. In 1872 he sold his brewery and returned to Heidelberg where his son Paul began studying chemistry. Encouraged by the success of a nearby cement manufacturing plant in Mannheim, he decided to invest in this promising building material. In January 1873 Schifferdecker acquired the remainder of the bankrupt cement factory Bergheimer Mühle on the shores of the Neckar River near Heidelberg. That same year the work started on the transformation of the existing mills into a water-powered cement production facility. Schifferdecker, his son, Dr. Paul Schifferdecker, and his son-in-law, lawyer Rudolf Heubach, became shareholders in the newly founded Portland-Cement-Werk, Heidelberg, Schifferdecker & Söhne OHG.

The first year of cement production was a disaster. The raw material used contained too much magnesium, and at the end of 1875 the Schifferdecker company reported a significant loss. However, the following year the company leased another limestone mine which provided raw material of better quality. Local farmers broke up the raw limestone at the edge of their fields, loaded it onto horse-drawn coaches and brought it to the cement factory. Three years later the company was able to acquire the land outright and employed independent mining professionals to collect the limestone, which was then shipped, again by the farmers, to the factory about four miles away. The cement was loaded into barrels and shipped to the local train station. At that time, cement was sold in drugstores where it was taken out of the bins and filled into little paper bags.

In 1883 the company built a railroad to transport the raw material to the factory. The track cut through the land of over 600 farmers, and the Schifferdecker company had to reach a contractual agreement with each of them. In 1888 a second factory, the ''Cementwarenfabrik,'' was built for manufacturing goods made of cement. It supplied building materials for large construction projects such as bridges, tunnels, harbors, and sewer systems in the German states of Bavaria, Baden, Würtemberg, and Prussia, as well as Amsterdam in the Netherlands. The independent Schifferdecker enterprise existed for 15 years. However, the death of the company's founder in 1888 marked the end of the era. The following year the company became a public enterprise and was

Company Perspectives:

Environmental precaution measures accompany the entire production process: main areas are the conservation of raw materials, air purification, the recultivation of quarries as well as the reduction of primary energy consumption by utilization of waste materials from other branches of industry. The high German environmental standards represent a yardstick for all our international locations.

renamed ''Portland-Cementwerk Heidelberg, vormals Schifferdecker & Söhne.'' Schifferdecker's heirs became the company's shareholders. On February 4, 1895, a fire devastated the wooden factory buildings; only the steam engines and ovens escaped with minor damage.

The Early Years of Expansion until 1913

Instead of giving up, Schifferdecker's descendants started from scratch. A new cement factory, the most modern of its kind at that time, was built in the German town of Leimen. All the necessary machinery for breaking, drying, and milling the stones, as well as the shipping offices were located in one large hall, which was approximately 500 meters long and 60 meters wide. In the beginning, the work in the quarries proved difficult and time-consuming. However, Portland-Cementwerk Heidelberg soon invested in better equipment which eliminated not only many back-breaking jobs but also significantly increased productivity.

Due to radical technological progress, the numbers of employees kept decreasing over the following years. In 1898, 1,100 employees produced 100,000 tons of cement at the Leimen plant. Only five years later, 130,000 tons were produced by 910 employees. By around 1900, the company boasted machines capable of measuring the quality of the produced concrete as well as a factory laboratory. Moreover, the tracks of the municipal electrical trams around Heidelberg were used to transport raw materials. Other technological improvements included the use of pneumatic drills for limestone mining, dust filters for the revolving ovens, and an automated packing department where cement was weighed, filled in sacks, and loaded onto about 120 railroad wagons a day.

The construction boom at the turn of the century provided a tremendous boost for the cement business, and the Portland-Cementwerk Heidelberg started expanding. Step by step the company acquired shares in brick factories, gypsum mines and cement-producing plants in Southern Germany. On June 5, 1901 the Portland-Cementwerk Heidelberg, vormals Schifferdecker & Söhne merged with the Mannheimer Portland-Cement-Fabrik AG, a competitor founded by Carl Dietzsch in 1860. The new Portland-Cementwerke Heidelberg und Mannheim AG was headquartered in Heidelberg. Two years later the cement factory in Mannheim was closed and the production transferred to a plant in Weisenau which also belonged to Mannheimer and to the Leimen plant. In 1913, many important buildings around the world were being built with Heidelberg-Mannheimer cement. The Military Academy in West Point, the Home Office Building in Philadelphia, and several buildings in New York City's Manhattan were among them.

The Turmoil of War, Inflation, and Depression

When World War I began in 1914, most construction activities in Germany were cancelled or postponed, as were Heidelberg-Mannheimer's plans to purchase a stake in a Brazilian cement enterprise. Because of the sudden drop in demand and shortages in coal supply, all plants were running well below their capacity, and in 1915 production in the smaller facilities was stopped completely. In one location, equipment was used to produce foodstuff for animals and fertilizers instead, a change which lasted until 1921. Between 1916 and 1923, the entire cement industry was run by the German government.

After the war was over, European construction markets remained depressed. On August 24, 1918 Portland-Cementwerke Heidelberg und Mannheim merged again with a public company in southern Germany, the Stuttgarter Immobilien- und Bau-Geschäft AG. Stuttgarter's owned two brick plants, four cement factories with a capacity of 180,000 tons per year, and holdings on two other cement factories. The Treaty of Versailles required that Allied troops occupy the Saarland, German territory west of the Rhine River, so that all of the new Portland-Cementwerke Heidelberg-Mannheim-Stuttgart AG holdings except one were cut off from coal supplies which came mainly from the occupied coal mines. Consequently, all facilities except the cement factory in Weisenau had to be shut down temporarily.

This was not the end of the turmoil. In the aftermath of World War I, under the weight of Germany's heavy financial obligations, the government began printing more money, and the German economy was thrown into hyperinflation. One year before the currency crisis reached its peak, prices for cement were 765 times higher than they had been in 1914. In 1923 the company's balance sheet was a mere formality. Profits totaled over 22,890 trillion Marks. After the end of the hyperinflation, all company figures were revised to conform to the new German currency, the Reichsmark. Beginning in 1926, almost all factories of the Portland-Cementwerke Heidelberg-Mannheim-Stuttgart AG were once again in operation.

The year 1927 marked the beginning of a three-year investment rally. With a total investment of RM8.1 million, all of the company's production facilities were electrified. However, two years later a worldwide economic depression rose on the horizon. All of Heidelberger's factories were shut down during the winters of 1929–30 and 1930–31, and the cement output shipped dropped by almost two-thirds from 897,000 tons in 1927 to 304,000 tons in 1932.

World War II and a New Beginning

Between 1935 and 1938 all factories of the Portland-Cementwerke Heidelberg-Mannheim-Stuttgart AG underwent another technological overhaul. Almost RM12 million were spent to boost productivity and expand capacities. (During this time, wooden barrels were replaced by paper sacks for shipping cement.) In 1936 cement shipments reach the total of one million tons for the first time. The next important step in expansion followed two years later. After renaming the company once again, this time to Portland-Zementwerke Heidelberg AG, an agreement with the Portland-Cementfabrik Blaubeuren Gebr. Spohn AG in which the Heidelberger Zementwerke already held 42,82 percent, sealed its financial and organizational dependence on Heidelberg. Heidel-

Key Dates:

1873: Johann Schifferdecker sets up a water-powered cement production facility near Heidelberg.
1889: Company reincorporated and named Portland-Cementwerk Heidelberg.
1901: Merger creates Portland-Cementwerke Heidelberg und Mannheim AG.
1916: German government takes over the country's cement industry.
1918: Merger with Stuttgarter Immobilien- und Bau-Geschäft AG.
1926: Return to normal operations and recovery from postwar economic turmoil.
1940: By law, all German cement factories are enrolled in a newly founded trade organization, the Deutsche Zementverband.
1965: Heidelberger Zement's total annual shipments reach six million tons.
1977: Pennsylvania-based Lehigh Portland Cement Company is acquired.
1989: First shares in an Eastern European cement factory purchased in Hungary.
1997: International expansion includes acquisitions in China, Turkey, and Bulgaria.

berg's share increased to 88.9 percent while two positions on the Advisory Board were taken by members of the Spohn family. The lucrative Blaubeuren-based company with a high output of high-quality cement opened the door to the booming highway construction market. The output reached 1.5 million tons by 1938.

After the Nazis won political power in Germany, Dr. Erhard Schott, one of Heidelberger Zement's top managers and director of the Leimen factory, was forced to resign because of his "distant attitude" toward the Nazi regime. One year after World War II had started, the Reichswirtschaftsministerium, Germany's national economy ministry, passed a law that automatically enrolled all German cement factories in a newly founded trade organization, the Deutsche Zementverband. During the war, the cement industry was highly regulated by the German government. After Germany's surrender, Allied troops occupied the partly-destroyed cement factories which were managed until 1948 by three trustees. One of them was Dr. Erhard Schott.

The years of reconstruction after World War II guaranteed that Heidelberger Zement's order books would be full. This new era in Heidelberger Zement's history was accompanied by the introduction of various new products. Loose cement was shipped in special silo vehicles. New gypsum products included different plaster mixtures and prefabricated walls. With compost from a newly established compost factory, Heidelberger Zement reclaimed quarries that had been closed down. Beginning in the late 1950s the company supported a new technology—finished wet concrete that was shipped in special vehicles with revolving metal containers (cement trucks). By 1960 almost half of the company's concrete was shipped as premixed concrete. In 1963 the Leimen factory alone produced one million tons of cement, and two years later Heidelberger Zement's total shipments reached six million tons.

Heidelberger Becomes International Enterprise in 1970s

In 1971 a computer was utilized for the first time at a Heidelberger Zement facility to manage and control raw material processing. In 1970 Heidelberger Zement started producing chemicals that were added to concrete to change its characteristics. From the mid-1970s on, those concrete additives and other building chemicals were marketed under the brand name "Addiment."

The first oil crisis in 1974 caused an economic recession, and construction activities dropped significantly. As a result, Heidelberger Zement's cement shipments decreased by 15 percent in comparison to 1973. After the second wave of the oil crisis in 1978, the company decided to invest heavily in technology based on coal instead of oil. The conversion had been completed by 1981, a changeover which cost the company approximately DM 100 million. At the same time facilities for burning old tires were set up as an alternative energy source.

In 1971 a new executive took over as speaker of Heidelberger Zement's Executive Board—Peter Schumacher—and under his leadership the company became an international enterprise. In 1977 Heidelberger Zement took over Allentown, Pennsylvania-based Lehigh Portland Cement Company, which was founded in 1897 by General Harry Clay Trexler and five businessman from Allentown. At the time of the takeover, Lehigh operated five cement factories with a total capacity of 2.7 million tons. To oversee its American subsidiary, the German parent created Heidelberg Cement, Inc. In the year of this groundbreaking deal, Peter Schuhmacher became CEO of the company, and in 1978 the company's name was changed to Heidelberger Zement AG.

The 1980s began with another deal in the United States. Heidelberger Zement, Inc. purchased US Steel Corporation's cement division, Atlas Cement Company, with seven cement production facilities. As a result, Lehigh expanded to operate operate 15 factories and employ 2,678 people. In 1984 Heidelberger Zement founded Addiment Inc., headquartered in Doraville, Georgia, to market its building chemicals product line in the United States.

New Products and New Markets after 1985

A significant drop in sales in the mid-1980s required the reduction of overcapacities. Heidelberger Zement's strategy was aimed at cost reduction, concentration, product diversification, and international expansion. Three new programs, one a company-wide energy cost reduction program, one to streamline the company's product divisions, and one to consolidate production locations, were implemented in the late 1980s. Addiment Italia s.r.l., headquartered in Casale Monferrato, was founded together with Italian cement manufacturer Fratelli Buzzi to produce and market concrete additives for the Italian market. The takeover of the French packaging producer Seraic S.A. strengthened Heidelberger Zement's plastics, print, and paper division. The newly founded Heidelberger Baustofftechnik GmbH bundled the company's activities in building chemicals, including "Addiment" and "Sealcrete" product lines. In 1991 Heidelberger Zement together with gas concrete manufacturer Hebel took over the French company Siporex,

S.A., market leader for gas concrete in the Paris and Avignon/Nimes regions. Moreover, the unexpected breakdown of the eastern European Bloc opened promising opportunities for long-term growth.

The privatization of the Hungarian cement industry made it possible for Heidelberger Zement to acquire shares in three Hungarian cement factories. In Czechoslovakia, the company purchased a 40-percent share in Pragocement, a government-owned company that operated a large cement factory in Radotin near Prague. A second 40-percent share was acquired in the Czech cement manufacturer Kralodvorska Cementarna a.s. Other acquisitions in Eastern European countries included facilities in Kroatia and Poland.

The fall of the Berlin Wall also opened new markets right at Heidelberger Zement's own front door, and this would prompt a major shift in the company strategy. Instead of product diversification, Heidelberger Zement aimed at concentrating its activities in the building materials markets. New production facilities for mortars, plasters, limestone, ready-mixed concrete, and concrete products were built in the East German states Saxony, Thuringia and Mecklenburg-Vorpommern. In 1993 Heidelberger Zement's subsidiary for plastics took over a processing facility for agricultural products and transformed into a modern insulation materials production facility.

A New Dimension of Growth Begins in 1993

The end of 1993 was a milestone in the history of Heidelberger Zement. On December 21 the company acquired a 42.4 percent majority stake in the Belgian S.A. Cimenteries CBR from Société Generale de Belgique for approximately DM 1.1 billion. The CBR group was a perfect match for Heidelberger Zement. Both companies were about the same size and complemented each other in product range and geographical outreach. CBR operated 19 cement manufacturing plants in Belgium, the Netherlands, the Czech Republic, Poland, the United States, and Canada, with a total capacity of 17 million tons. The first consolidation of the CBR group in 1994 catapulted Heidelberger Zement to a new high. Some 24,000 Heidelberger Zement employees sold 27 million tons of cement in 15 countries around the world, generating a total of DM 6.3 billion in sales and profits of DM 362 million.

Because of the ongoing internationalization of the Heidelberger Zement group, the organizational structure was focused on four regions: Central Europe West, particularly Germany; Western Europe; Central Europe East; and North America. Activities in each of the regions were divided into three units: cement, concrete, and building materials. As one of the first German public companies, Heidelberger Zement began using International Accounting Standards in 1994; this was the last important corporate achievement of energetic CEO Peter Schuhmacher, who retired from his job after 18 years.

Heidelberger Zement's new CEO Rolf Hülstrunk continued the company's strategy of aggressive international expansion. All activities of Lehigh and CBR in North America, including 12 cement factories, more than 150 pre-mixed concrete production facilities, 58 locations for building chemicals, and 40 other building materials production plants, were bundled in the newly founded holding company CBR-HCI Construction Materials Corporation based in Allentown, Pennsylvania. In 1995 CBR acquired a five percent share in China Cement Century Limited, a company that owned three cement factories with a total capacity of 2.6 million tons in the Southern Chinese province Guangdong. In January 1996 CBR purchased a 97.7 percent stake in Canakkale Cimento Sanayii A.S., Turkey's leading cement producer based in Istanbul. In the same year HC Trading B.V. was founded in Istanbul in order to exclusively coordinate and execute all export and trade activities of the whole Heidelberger Zement Group. In mid-1997 Heidelberger Zement entered the Bulgarian market by acquiring from the Bulgarian government a majority share in two cement factories there. In 1999 Heidelberger Zement announced that it was planning to purchase a majority stake in Scancern AB, a Swedish cement company which was the market leader in Scandinavia and the Baltic countries and the number two company in Great Britain, and production facilities in Africa and Bangladesh. If the transaction was approved by the European Commission, Heidelberger Zement was poised to become the third largest cement manufacturer in the world.

Principal Subsidiaries

Baustoffwerke Wittmer + Klee GmbH; Heidelberger Bauchemie GmbH; Heidelberger Baustoffwerke GmbH; Vulkan Verwaltungs-und Beteiligungsgesellschaft mbH; Schmitt & Weitz Baustoffwerke GmbH; WIKA-Beton GmbH&Co. KG (73.9%); ZEAG Zementwerk Lauffen-Elektrizitätswerk Heilbronn AG (27.4%); Anneliese Zementwerke AG (41.4%); Portland-Zementwerk Gebr. Wiesböck&Co. GmbH (32.3%); CBR-HCI Construction Materials Corporation (United States); Lehigh Portland Cement Co. (United States); ENCI N.V. (Netherlands); HC Trading B.V. (Netherlands); Südbayer Duna-Drava Cement-es Meszmüvek Kft.(Hungary; 50%); S.A. Cimenteries CBR (Belgium; 52.5%); Vicat S.A. (France; 35%); ZCW Gorazdze S.A. (Poland; 82.9%); Akcansa Cimento Sanayi ve Ticaret A.S. (Turkey; 39.7%); China Century Cement Ltd. (China; 30%); Cementowina Strzelce Opolskie S.A.(Poland; 93.4%) Ceskomoravsky Cement a.s. (Czech Republic; 86.5%)

Principal Competitors

Holderbank Financiere Glaris Ltd.; Lafarge S.A.; RMC Group plc.

Further Reading

Dauscher, Karin, "Am Neckar betrat Heidelzement den Weg zum Weltmarkt," *Rheinpfalz*, June 18, 1998.

Fassbender, Ernest, Nigel Meeks and Crispin Wright, "Heidelberger Zement gets stuck in," *Acquisitions Monthly*, February 1994, p. 46.

Hof, Thorsten, "Vom Gesellen zum Firmenchef," *Mannheimer Morgen*, June 18, 1998.

"Heidelberger Zement," *World Cement*, September 1998, p. 30.

"Investment and Innovation at Heidelberger Zement," *World Cement*, September 1999, p. 30.

Schollmaier, Christiane, "Heidelzement mischt seit 125 Jahren ganz vorn in der Branche mit," *Mannheimer Morgen*, June 18, 1998.

—Evelyn Hauser

Henry Schein, Inc.

135 Duryea Road
Melville, New York 11747
U.S.A.
Telephone: (516) 843-5500
Toll Free: (877) 299-1135
Fax: (516) 843-5658
Web site: http://www.henryschein.com

Public Company
Incorporated: 1992
Employees: 6,000
Sales: $1.92 billion
Stock Exchanges: NASDAQ
Ticker Symbol: HSIC
NAIC: 42145 Medical, Dental and Hospital Equipment and Supplies Wholesalers; 45411 Electronic Shopping and Mail-Order Houses; 51121 Software Publishing

Henry Schein, Inc. is the largest distributor of health care products and services to office-based health care practitioners in the combined North American and European markets. The company sells products and services to more than 300,000 customers. These are mainly dentists and dental laboratories but also include physicians, veterinarians, and institutions. Through its catalogs and other direct sales and marketing programs, Schein offers its customers a broad product selection in excess of 60,000 stockkeeping units in North America and about 55,000 in Europe. It also offers certain other products and services, chiefly practice management software systems for North American dentists.

Henry Schein to 1990

Henry Schein, a pharmacist, with his wife, Esther, founded his eponymous company in 1932 as a corner drugstore in the Woodside community of New York City's borough of Queens. In 1962 he moved the store to a larger location in Flushing, Queens. Soon after, he also started offering supplies to doctors, and perhaps dentists as well, by mail order. In 1964 a federal prosecutor filed a criminal complaint against Schein, who was charged with selling bottles containing counterfeit Dexedrine capsules to three out-of-state pharmacies. Schein also was charged with illegally selling amphetamine, barbiturate, and penicillin tablets to an undercover federal agent.

The mail order operation, which was intended to address a need not met by sales representatives, apparently suffered no such problems. ''It was in the 1970s that things really took off,'' Chief Executive Officer Stanley Bergman told Susan Konig of the *New York Times* in 1996. ''That's when the Schein family discovered the dental market. There were around 3,000 dental distributors back then. But they sold products at relatively high prices and with relatively poor service. So the Scheins decided to put together catalogues which would offer them at lower prices and have them ready for immediate delivery. That was a pretty new concept at the time.''

Henry Schein sold his retail store in the mid-1970s to become a full-time distributor of medical and dental supplies and generic drugs. By the late 1970s his company had annual sales of about $40 million. Within a decade, the company was dominant in its field and by 1988 controlled more than 40 percent of the mail order market for dental supplies. The firm moved in 1979 from Queens to a 100,000-square-foot facility in suburban Port Washington, Long Island.

After Schein's son Jacob, a Wall Street attorney, joined the company in 1980, it began automating distribution. In the mid-1980s the firm introduced two interactive methods to enable dentists to file orders for supplies at any time of day or night, either by telephone or computer. It also issued one of the first affinity credit cards and, in 1988, developed a frequent-buyer program at a time when such incentives were confined to airlines.

During this period Schein, which had purchased a Connecticut pill producer in 1970, also became an important manufacturer and distributor of generic drugs. In 1985 it formed a subsidiary, Schein Pharmaceutical, Inc., to serve retail and hospital pharmacies. This company was offering more than 1,500 prescription and over-the-counter drugs and vitamin products through a network of franchised wholesalers. The prescription drugs were being produced for the most part by another Schein subsidiary, Danbury Phamacal Inc., and the over-the-counter drugs and vitamins were being supplied by a number of vendors. In 1992 Schein Holdings, Inc.,

Company Perspectives:

The company's mission is to be the worldwide leader in providing the quality and value in products and services for our healthcare customers.

the parent of Henry Schein, Inc. and Schein Pharmaceutical, spun off the latter as an independent company.

By this time Schein was being run by Bergman, who became chief executive officer after Jacob Schein's premature death from cancer in 1989. Henry Schein had died in 1987. (Esther Schein, who also had been active in management, died in 1992. Jacob's brother Marvin became head of the company's dental equipment division in 1995, after it purchased Schein Dental Equipment Corp., a separate company that had been founded by Marvin Schein.)

Broadening Its Scope: 1990–95

According to Bergman, Henry Schein was barely profitable when he took charge. "In the early 80's, our competitors started copying us," he recalled to Konig. "They came out with catalogues, they started discounting their products and improving their service, and the bottom line was we started looking just like them. We had to differentiate ourselves again in the dental world, and we did it with value-added services." These services included selling computer products to dentists and offering them financial products.

Another way that Henry Schein differentiated itself from its competitors was to start focusing on European markets in 1990, when it opened its first foreign subsidiary, in The Netherlands. By mid-1991 the company had established three more such foreign operations—in England, Germany, and Spain. It also had begun selling through a distributor to Mexico and it launched its first catalog directed to the Canadian market. Schein was now receiving orders from 70 countries.

In the United States, some 160 telemarketing representatives at Schein's Woodbury, Long Island office were responding to more than 1.5 million calls a year from doctors, dentists, and veterinarians. Computer-telephone integration, installed in 1992, allowed agents to send a computer profile, simultaneously with the call, to the first available agent. This enabled the company to cut an average of 17 seconds each from incoming calls—a significant saving when considering the volume of calls. By collecting data on the items ordered by a particular account, as well as the frequency of the orders, the profile enabled Schein representatives to anticipate which products the customer might need and to make further suggestions.

Schein's reliance on catalogs and telemarketing rather than salespeople was allowing it to price its products five to ten percent lower than its competitors, according to a securities analyst, but in 1993 the company added 200 field sales consultants to take face-to-face orders from health professionals. In 1996 the company opened a 25,000-square-foot retail outlet near Miami International Airport to cater to the Caribbean and Latin American health care markets. Some 5,000 to 6,000 of its more than 50,000 items were available for purchase on the spot.

Schein's annual sales grew from $236.3 million in 1990 to $415.7 million in 1993. Of this total, the North American Dental Group accounted for 40 percent (and 20 percent of the total U.S. dental supplies market). The Diversified Healthcare Group, established in the 1980s to market products to general practitioners, pediatricians, podiatrists, and other nondentist health care professionals, accounted for almost one-third. The International Group accounted for less than 20 percent of company revenues. The Professional Services Group, Schein's newest division, had developed the leading software package for dental office management and another program for complying with safety regulations. This group also was selling and configuring computer hardware, repairing dental equipment, conducting continuing education, and providing some financial services to dentists.

By late 1994 Schein was selling products in more than 140 countries. The firm also was forming alliances with professional organizations and some other companies. The Diversified Healthcare Group, for example, had taken a 50.1 percent share of Universal Footcare Products Inc., a joint venture with Chicago Medical Equipment Co. to market products to health maintenance organizations and more than 9,500 podiatrists. An agreement with the American Medical Association enabled the group's member physicians to receive discounts on Schein's catalog roster of 18,000 medical supply products. Schein then formed a partnership with the U.S. Army under which it became the prime vendor for the army's more than 100 dental clinics in the United States.

Acquisition-Fueled Growth: 1996–99

Schein went public in November 1995, raising $72.5 million from its initial public offering at $16 a share. In July 1996 it raised an additional $124.1 million by selling more stock at $35 a share. Some of the proceeds were used to retire debt, but much of it was reserved for the company's continuing acquisitions program. By the fall of 1996 Schein had acquired 40 regional dental, medical, and veterinarian supply companies over the past five years, including 14 in 1996 alone with combined annual revenue of $100 million. Schein's strategy for integrating its acquisitions—usually made for stock rather than cash—was to deploy a team that spent 10 to 12 weeks evaluating the new company's products and shedding those that did not fit with Schein's own goods, plus integrating the acquired company's customer list with Schein's own and contacting new customers with marketing materials. Schein often retained the acquired firm's sales force but generally eliminated its warehouse operations.

In March 1997 Schein purchased Micro Bio-Medics Inc., a company with $150 million in annual revenues that was expected to double Schein's sales to physicians. Three months later it entered into a joint venture by acquiring a majority interest in the dental division of a regional health care group with operations in Australia and Auckland, New Zealand. In the United States, 65 percent of all dentists and 30 percent of all physicians were Schein customers, according to an investment analyst firm.

Later in 1997 the company, which had ranked second in the U.S. dental distribution industry, became the world's largest distributor of dental equipment and supplies by purchasing the third largest U.S. firm in its field, Sullivan Dental Products Inc., for stock valued at $318 million. Tim Sullivan stayed on as president of the Wisconsin-based company, which was renamed

Key Dates:

1932: Henry Schein opens a drugstore in New York City.
Mid-1960s: Schein adds a mail-order operation.
1979: Schein moves its headquarters to Long Island.
1990: Schein establishes its first European subsidiary.
1992: Schein spins off its drugs and vitamins business.
1995: Schein becomes a publicly owned company.
1997: By the end of this year Schein's roster of acquired companies has reached 67 in six years.

Sullivan-Schein Dental Products Inc. In all, Schein's 24 acquisitions in 1997 had aggregate net sales of about $558.6 million in 1996 and enabled it to reach net sales of $1.52 billion in 1997. The company lost $1 million, however.

In 1998 Schein acquired five more companies. The biggest of these was H. Meer Dental Supply Co., a Michigan-based dental distributor with 1997 sales of about $180 million that was purchased for stock valued at $145.5 million. During the same year, however, Schein sold Marus Dental International, its dental equipment manufacturing operation. In early 1999 the company acquired General Injectibles and Vaccines, Inc., a direct marketer of vaccines and other injectible products with 1998 sales of about $120 million. It also purchased the international dental, medical, and veterinary health care distribution businesses of German-based Heiland Holding GmbH., which had 1998 sales of about $130 million.

Schein had, in 1994, moved its headquarters and telemarketing office to a three-story leased building in Melville, accepting financial and tax incentives from the state of New York, Suffolk County, and Long Island Lighting Co. to remain on the island. The company sold its Port Washington warehouse in 1998, with the intention of moving the operation to a larger leased space in Denver, Pennsylvania. Of its eight warehouses, three were in the United States and five in Europe. Schein also was leasing space in nine other countries.

Including its acquisitions, Schein had net sales of $1.92 billion in 1998 and net income of $16.3 million. The dental group accounted for 56 percent of the total; medical, for 27 percent; international, for 12 percent; and the veterinary and technology groups for about equal shares of the remaining five percent. Sales under the Henry Schein private label (manufactured by third parties or affiliated HS Pharmaceutical, Inc.) accounted for 8.6 percent of the total. The company's total debt at the end of the year was $209.5 million. In April 1999 Bergman held or controlled more than 15 percent of the stock.

Schein was selling products to more than 75 percent of the estimated 100,000 dental practitioners in the United States in 1998. It distributed more than 12.5 million pieces of direct marketing materials, such as catalogs, flyers, and order stuffers to about 600,000 office-based health care practitioners. The number of its stock-keeping units now exceeded 60,000 in North America and came to about 55,000 in Europe and about 22,000 in Australia. The company also sold more than 28,000 dental practice management software systems, more than any of its competitors. It estimated that about 99 percent of all orders in the United States and Canada received before 7:00 p.m. and 4:00 p.m., respectively, were shipped on the same day the order was received and that about 99 percent were received within two days. The number of its telesales personnel had reached about 700 and its field sales consultants amounted to about 1,100.

Principal Subsidiaries

Henry Schein UK Holdings Ltd.; Henry Schein Van den Braak, B.V. (Netherlands); Zahn Holdings, Inc.

Principal Operating Units

International Group; Management Technologies Group; Medical Group; North American Dental Group.

Principal Competitors

Allegiance Corp.; Owens & Minor Inc.; Patterson Dental Co.; World Med Inc.

Further Reading

Anderson, David, ''Millions of Fake Dexedrine Pills Sold,'' *New York Times,* August 29, 1964, p. 11.
Anderson, Jim, ''CTI Enhances Customer Service for Healthcare Marketer,'' *Telemarketing,* May 1993, pp. 74–75.
Bernstein, James, ''Nassau Loses Big Employer to Suffolk,'' *Newsday,* November 5, 1993, p. 61.
Chevan, Harry, ''Henry Schein,'' *Catalog Age,* April 1994, p. 63.
Gallun, Alby, ''Sullivan Dental Acquisition Shines Through,'' *Business Journal-Milwaukee,* October 30, 1998, p. 7.
Joshi, Pradnya, ''Shopping Spree,'' *Newsday,* July 7, 1997, pp. C6–C7.
Kiley, Kathleen, ''A Healthy Schein,'' *Catalog Age,* October 15, 1996, p. 5.
Konig, Susan, ''From Small Beginnings to a Company with Millions in Sales,'' *New York Times,* June 30, 1996, Sec. 13 (Long Island), p. 2.
LaFemina, Lorraine, ''Henry Schein Shines as New IPO,'' *LI Business News,* February 26, 1996, p. 3.
Miller, Susan R., ''Filling a Medical Cavity,'' *South Florida Business Journal,* October 4, 1996, p. 3 and continuation.
''New Schein Subsidiary To Serve Pharmacies,'' *Drug Topics,* June 17, 1985, p. 40.
Oberndorf, Shannon, ''Associating with Strategic Partners,'' *Catalog Age,* March 1995, p. 65.
——, ''Henry Schein, That Is . . . ,'' *Catalog Age,* March 1997, p. 72.
'' 'Scheining' Overseas,'' *Catalog Age,* July 1991, p. 8.
Somerville, Janice, ''Pair of Foot Care Companies Merges into Universal Force,'' *Crain's Chicago Business,* October 31, 1994, p. 28.
Unger, Michael, ''Schein's Biggest Buy Yet,'' *Newsday,* August 5, 1997, p. A36.
Wax, Alan J., ''Melville Firm Plans Warehouse Closing,'' *Newsday,* December 19, 1997, p. A64.

—Robert Halasz

Hubbell Incorporated

584 Derby Milford Road
Orange, Connecticut 06477
U.S.A.
Telephone: (203) 799-4100
Fax: (203) 799-4205
Web site: http://www.hubbell.com

Public Company
Incorporated: 1905 as Harvey Hubbell Incorporated
Employees: 10,600
Sales: $1.42 billion (1998)
Stock Exchanges: New York
Ticker Symbol: HUBB
NAIC: 335931 Current-Carrying Wiring Device Manufacturing; 35121 Residential Lighting Fixture Manufacturing

Hubbell Incorporated produces electrical and electronic items for commercial, industrial, utility, and telecommunications uses. With over 23 manufacturing divisions and several global subsidiaries, Hubbell produces such items as lighting fixtures, outlet boxes, wire and cable, and insulators and surge arrestors. For many decades, Hubbell maintained a modest and unassuming profile, manufacturing the important products invented by its founder, Harvey Hubbell II; one correspondent for *Forbes* admonished his readers in 1977 that "unless you are reading this on safari, there is probably a Harvey Hubbell invention within six feet of you right now." The company had remained strongly focused on such products until the 1960s, when it embarked on a diversification program. While non-consumer electrical products remain its core business, the company has also gained footholds in the manufacture of telecommunications equipment and high voltage cables.

The Early Years

Hubbell bears the name of inventor and businessman Harvey Hubbell II. Born in Connecticut in 1859, he graduated from high school and began working for companies that manufactured marine engines and printing machinery. During this time, he accumulated several ideas for new inventions, and in 1888 he set out on his own, opening a small manufacturing facility in Bridgeport, Connecticut. Hubbell's first product was taken from his own patent for a paper roll holder with a toothed blade for use in stores that sold wrapping paper. This cutter stand became a tremendous success; it was a common feature of retail stores that used wrapping paper in the early 1900s and remained in wide use into the late 20th century.

Hubbell also designed and built a series of new and improved machine tools during his early years in business. In the early 1890s, he began to consider the opportunities presented by Edison's new electric light bulb, and the fruits of his work would secure both the future of his company and his place in history. On a visit to New York City, Hubbell happened upon a penny arcade, featuring several electrically operated games which, although popular with customers, caused maintenance headaches. Every day, the janitor had to detach each of the power supply wires for the games from separate terminals in the wall so that he could move them and sweep the floor underneath. After he was done, he faced the tedious task of reconnecting the wires, making sure that each one went into the proper terminal—the consequence of not doing so being a short circuit. Watching the janitor gave Hubbell the idea for an electrical plug in which the wires were permanently attached in their proper sequence, so that devices could be easily detached and reattached to their power sources. Hubbell built a prototype, which he tested with the help of the janitor, and later patented it. The two-pronged electrical plug that became standard for electrical appliances is a direct descendant of this innovation. In 1896 Hubbell patented a light bulb socket with an on/off pull chain, another invention in use to this day.

In 1901 Hubbell published a 12-page catalogue that listed 63 electrical products of his company's manufacture, and four years later he incorporated his enterprise as Harvey Hubbell, Incorporated. In 1909 the company began constructing a four-floor factory and office building that would become the first building in New England made of reinforced concrete.

As electricity became the power source of choice in the United States, Hubbell's company did its best to keep up. Its

Company Perspectives:

Hubbell Incorporated's commitment to the industry; diversification of product and market; a continuing tradition of quality; partnership with the independent electrical distributor; and the experience of accomplishment in research and development have forged Hubbell's exceptional records of growth. The same comprehensive corporate capability will expand Hubbell's growth in the commercial, telecommunications, lighting, utility, industrial, and consumer markets of the future.

1917 catalogue was 100 pages long and listed over 1,000 electrical products, including 277 different types and sizes of light bulb sockets. One important product was a toggle light switch, which Hubbell had invented to replace the old two-button switch. A line of 288 heavy-duty ''Presturn'' products marked the company's entry into industrial electrical products. In the 1920s, the company produced a line of low-voltage devices for use by farmers who had not tapped into higher-voltage urban electrical grids. Also during this time, Hubbell developed a device that locked streetlamp and household light bulbs firmly in place, filling a need in cities where new trolley cars were producing vibrations that loosened bulbs and caused them to fall out of their sockets.

Harvey Hubbell died in 1927 and was succeeded as president of the company by his son, Harvey Hubbell III. The 26-year-old Hubbell had been trained as an electrical engineer and was already at work for the family firm. Under Harvey Hubbell III, the company went public in 1936, a timely move considering that, during the later years of the Great Depression, some employees occasionally had to accept company stock in lieu of pay. He also proved his business acumen by establishing a network of independent distributors to help market and disseminate the company's products, a system that would help offset the low profile that the company has traditionally kept.

During World War II, much of the company's capacity was devoted to manufacturing electrical components for the military, including battery-charging systems for the M-4 Sherman tank. Hubbell also opened a plant in Lexington, Kentucky, in part to meet demand for its military products and also because its original factory in Connecticut was considered vulnerable to air attack.

Postwar Expansion and Diversification

After the war, Harvey Hubbell Inc. shifted its focus back to making products for the civilian economy. It custom designed and produced electrical devices for the luxury ocean liner *United States,* which was launched in 1952 and required electrical wiring that would resist the corrosive effects of salt air while fitting into narrow stateroom partitions. At the end of the 1950s, the company began to ponder the benefits of diversification. Until that point, Hubbell had always been a conservative company with a reputation for making high quality products that sold for higher than average prices. Its narrow range of products, however, limited opportunities for growth and left it vulnerable to cyclical ups and downs. Even with its strong desire to diversify, however, Hubbell chose its targets carefully and did not stray far from its field of expertise. In 1962 it acquired Kellems, a Connecticut-based manufacturer of mesh grips, cord connectors, and wire management products. In 1963 it bought Grelco, an English company that made industrial controls, the California-based Shalda Lighting, and the Chicago-based Ralco Manufacturing. Hubbell later merged Grelco into its British subsidiary, Harvey Hubbell Limited. In 1966 Hubbell purchased Euclid Electric, which it later renamed Hubbell Industrial Controls. The following year, Harvey Hubbell Limited acquired Watford Electric & Manufacturing, solidifying its presence as a producer of industrial controls in Great Britain.

Continued Growth in the 1970s and 1980s

Harvey Hubbell III died in 1968 and was succeeded as CEO by George Weppler, who became the first non-Hubbell to run the company in its 80 years of existence. Under Weppler, the pace of Hubbell's acquisition campaign was maintained. In 1969 the company acquired Kerite, a Connecticut-based manufacturer of high voltage electrical cables used mainly by utility companies and railroads. The next year, it acquired Steber Lighting to augment its light fixtures business. In 1972 Hubbell entered the telecommunications equipment field when it purchased Pulse Communications, a Virginia-based manufacturer of voice and data signal processing components. Also that year Hubbell acquired Southern Industrial Diecasting. Moreover, the company established a presence in South America with its Brazilian subsidiary, Harvey Hubbell do Brasil, after acquiring H.K. Porter do Brasil in 1973 and Metal-Arte Industrias Sao Paolo in 1974.

Weppler was succeeded by Robert Dixon in 1975. Dixon had spent 12 years studying electrical and mechanical engineering in night school and was a firm believer in Hubbell's odyssey through diversification and expansion. ''If we had stayed only in the wiring business, our numbers would look better but we wouldn't be as strong,'' he told a *Forbes* correspondent in 1982, adding that ''I even question whether we'd still be independent.'' Under Dixon, Hubbell acquired Hermetic Refrigeration, a Phoenix-based re-manufacturer of air conditioning compressors, in 1976. In 1978 it purchased Ohio Brass, which made insulation and surge arrestor for high voltage electrical equipment, as well as mining equipment. In 1981 the company spun off Harvey Hubbell do Brasil, and picked up Arrestor, an American manufacturer of switch, junction, and outlet boxes and electrical fittings.

By this time, Hubbell's diversifications had produced mixed results. On the one hand, the company's original wiring and light fixture business accounted for a disproportionate share of profits into the 1980s, a sign that acquired companies were not proving terribly lucrative despite the fact that Hubbell had made few outright missteps. On the other hand, Hubbell generated record profits every year from 1961 to 1983. In 1961, the company posted a relatively modest $22 million in sales; by 1981 sales had reached $445.8 million. Robert Dixon retired as CEO in 1983 and was succeeded by Fred Dusto, who presided over the final acquisitions of Hubbell's long spree: Miller Lighting and Killark Electric Manufacturing, both purchased in 1985. In 1986 the company shortened its name to its current form.

Key Dates:

1901: Harvey Hubbell publishes his first catalogue.
1905: Harvey Hubbell, Incorporated is established.
1909: Company builds its first factory.
1927: Harvey Hubbell dies and is succeeded at helm of company by Harvey III.
1968: George Weppler chairs the company and quickens Hubbell's pace of acquisitions.
1972: Hubbell enters the telecommunications equipment field.
1986: Harvey Hubbell Inc. shortens its name to its current form.

The 1990s

Dusto retired in 1987 and was succeeded by George Ratcliffe, who had once served as the company's chief counsel. Under Ratcliffe, Hubbell spent aggressively on upgrading and automating its capital equipment as well as on research and development. This reinvestment produced profit margins higher than those of its competitors during the 1980s, as the company was able to cut labor costs and also sell innovative products that commanded relatively high returns. Hubbell also made further acquisitions during this time. In 1991 it purchased Westinghouse's Bryant Electric division, which made wiring devices for industrial applications. In 1993 Hubbell acquired Hipotronics, a manufacturer of high-voltage cables, test and measurement equipment, and E.M. Weigmann and Co., Inc., a manufacturer of industrial enclosures.

Hubbell continued to add to its roster of companies those that performed well in its core lighting operations. Recognizing that electricity's central role would not be diminished in the coming years, Hubbell's electrical equipment empire spanned across the globe and across applications. Because no alternative power source even remotely threatened to challenge electricity, Hubbell's strategy was sound, as its acquisitions provided for stable long-term growth.

In March 1994, Hubbell purchased A.B. Chance Industries, a powerful presence in the electrical utility sector with a number of products such as overhead and underground distribution switches, fuses, cutouts, insulators, and safety equipment. Hubbell's next acquisition was in 1996, when it bought Gleason Reel Corp., an industrial-grade electrical cable producer. In September 1997, Hubbell acquired Namar/Wirecon, a leading producer of self-contained electrical switches and receptacle tools used in the manufacture of pre-fabricated housing and recreational vehicles. Buoyed by its new operations, Hubbell's sales soared from $832.4 million in 1994 to $1.38 billion in 1997. Even more impressive was the company's profits which increased from $66.3 million in 1993 to $130.3 million in 1997.

The year 1998 witnessed several key acquisitions. On November 17, Hubbell announced its impending purchase of Sterner Lighting, a designer and manufacturer of specification-grade outdoor lighting fixtures, as well as custom lighting products. Sterner's wares could often be found in indoor sports arenas. This producer of light fixtures for corrosive and hazardous locations, complemented Hubbell's existing businesses. Sales kept rising through 1998, as Hubbell achieved over $169 million in profit.

At the close of the century, Hubbell's four key divisions remained centered on lighting and its application in a variety of spheres. With manufacturing facilities in Canada, Mexico, Puerto Rico, Singapore, the United Kingdom, and the United States, Hubbell had grown considerably beyond its humble origins. Joint ventures in Germany, South America, and Taiwan, as well as sales offices in Asia, Mexico, and the Middle East, rounded out Hubbell's far-flung operations.

Although Harvey Hubbell II is not widely remembered today, his inventions were instrumental in facilitating and disseminating the pioneering work of more famous inventors such as Edison and Westinghouse. Similarly, the company that Hubbell founded has labored for over a century without widespread recognition for the company's name or products. Nevertheless, the success of its products, which people use and rely upon daily, signaled profitable years ahead for Hubbell.

Principal Subsidiaries

A.B. Chance Co., Inc.; Gleason Reel Corp.; Hipotronics, Inc.; Hubbell Premise Wiring, Inc.; Hubbell Canada Inc.; The Kerite Co.; Killark Electric Manufacturing Co.; The Ohio Brass Co.; Hubbell Lighting, Inc.; Hubbell Industrial Controls, Inc.; RACO, Inc.

Principal Competitors

Cooper Industries, Inc.; Graybar Electric Company; Rexel, Inc; Anixter International Inc.

Further Reading

''Analysts' Ratings: Electric Components,'' *Professional Investor Report,* April 25, 1997.
Chandler, Douglas, ''Hubbell Lighting Buys Sterner Lighting,'' *Electrical Wholesaling,* December 30, 1998.
''Crossed Currents,'' *Forbes,* July 5, 1982.
Hannon, Kerry, ''Live Wire,'' *Forbes,* November 14, 1988.
''Harvey Hubbell, Harvey Hubbell,'' *Forbes,* August 1, 1977.
''Hubbell Announces Acquisition Agreement,'' *Business Wire,* November 18, 1998.
''Hubbell Inc.,'' *Milwaukee Journal Sentinel,* February 1, 1996, Bus. Sec.
Second Century of Solutions, Orange, Conn.: Hubbell Incorporated, 1988.
''Wall St. Roundup: Hubbell, Inc,: *Wall Street Transcripts,* February 6, 1995.

—Douglas Sun
—updated by Rebecca Stanfel

I.C. Isaacs & Company

3840 Bank Street
Baltimore, Maryland 21224
U.S.A.
Telephone: (410) 342-8200
Fax: (410) 276-4087
Web site: http://www.icisaacs.com

Public Company
Incorporated: 1913
Employees: 450
Sales: $113.7 million (1998)
Stock Exchanges: NASDAQ
Ticker Symbol: ISAC
NAIC: 315224 Men's and Boys' Cut and Sew Trouser, Slack, and Jean Manufacturing; 315239 Women's and Girls' Cut and Sew Other Outerwear Manufacturing

I.C. Isaacs & Company manufactures and sells sportswear for men, women, and children under the licensed labels Boss, Girbaud, and Beverly Hills Polo Club, as well as producing clothing under its own labels I.C. Isaacs, Lord Isaacs, Pizazz, and UBX. The company's labels are sold at hundreds of specialty and department stores across the United States, as well as in Puerto Rico and Europe. After growing steadily during the 1980s and 1990s, I.C. Isaacs has been financially troubled since going public in late 1997.

Early Beginnings, 1913 to 1980s

I.C. Isaacs was founded in 1913 by Isaac C. Isaacs and his family. Located in Baltimore, Maryland, the company was established to cater to the local horse racing industry, focusing its manufacturing on riding britches, jodhpurs, and shirts. The merchandise was produced in two company-owned factories in Mississippi. By keeping design and production under tight control, I.C. Isaacs was able to maintain the highest standards of quality. The company remained family owned and operated, with a narrow focus on riding gear, for decades. I.C. Isaacs enjoyed steady success, with its reach limited to the close-knit racing community of Maryland and other parts of the South, until the early 1980s.

National Growth, 1980s and 1990s

In 1984 I.C. Isaacs was purchased by outside investors who were interested in utilizing the company's name and manufacturing plants to extend the business into the broader and more lucrative world of general men's and women's apparel. Soon after the buyout, I.C. Isaacs began producing inexpensive men's and women's sportswear under an eponymous label. The brand sold well locally, and was within a few years picked up by the national chain J.C. Penney.

The new management hoped to make its mark on the national apparel industry by developing popular and profitable brand names. In addition to building up its own label, the company set out to license other brands with strong name recognition. Boss was a high-profile menswear collection featuring casual sportswear as well as dress jackets and suits. The label was sold at such national department stores as Macy's and J.C. Penney, and, with appeal for both older and young consumers, was considered a sound, stable investment. The Boss line continued to sell well under I.C. Isaacs, and the company began generating enough revenue to consider further acquisitions.

Soon after the acquisition of Boss, I.C. Isaacs licensed Beverly Hills Polo Club, a casual sportswear line for men and women that was sold primarily through J.C. Penney. The Beverly Hills Polo Club brand sold for slightly less than the Boss label, and, because it produced both men's and women's apparel, appealed to a broader range of consumers. Like Boss, Beverly Hills Polo Club was consistently profitable, and by the middle of the decade I.C. Isaacs was on its way to becoming a national contender in the apparel industry.

During this time I.C. Isaacs introduced two other collections of its own: Lord Isaacs, a menswear line, and Pizazz, a juniors' collections. Because the company was growing so quickly during the late 1980s and early 1990s, I.C. Isaacs had to turn to other companies for manufacturing. Within a decade after the

Company Perspectives:

I.C. Isaacs & Company, Inc., is a designer, manufacturer, and marketer of branded sportswear based in New York City and Baltimore. The company offers full lines of sportswear for men and women under the Marithe and Francois Girbaud brand in the United States and Puerto Rico; for young men, women, and boys under the Boss brand in the United States and Puerto Rico; and for men and boys under the Beverly Hills Polo Club brand in the United States, Puerto Rico, and Europe. The company also markets women's pants and jeans under various other company-owned brand names and under third-party private labels.

company's 1984 buyout, more than 70 percent of the company's merchandise was being produced by outside manufacturers, including denim factories in Mexico. However, the company continued to utilize its two Mississippi factories to produce the I.C. Isaacs line.

By the mid-1990s I.C. Isaacs was growing rapidly, with sales rising into the hundreds of millions. Between 1992 and 1997, sales rose at an average rate of 30 percent a year. In 1996 the national chain store J.C Penney was the company's biggest customer, accounting for 13 percent of total revenue. I.C. Isaacs had risen within a decade from a small family-owned business to a company of national prominence.

The Acquisition of Girbaud and Faltering Sales, Late 1990s

In 1996 the company's most popular line was Boss, which accounted for more than 72 percent of sales. The Beverly Hills Polo Club label was growing quickly at that time as well, with sales jumping by 83 percent in 1995 and by 102 percent in 1996. As a result of this tremendous growth, the company's owners decided to take it public in 1997. Under the guidance of CEO Robert Arnot, I.C. Isaacs debuted on the NASDAQ stock exchange with an initial public offering of $10 a share. The company sold 3.8 million shares, raising $38 million.

In 1997 I.C. Isaacs also made one of its most important acquisitions, purchasing the license to Girbaud sportswear and jeans from VF Corporation. Girbaud, a French label, appealed to younger men and women, and had helped to make designer denim and sportswear chic in the late 1980s and early 1990s. Interest in the brand waned in the middle of the decade, however, as ''grunge'' fashion supplanted designer labels, and Girbaud's sales in the United States fell.

I.C. Isaacs focused on regaining the brand's popularity, looking to other successful U.S. denim companies for inspiration. Soon the company was producing cargo fatigue pants and slouchy denim jeans under the Girbaud brand, establishing the label as a purveyor of hip urbanwear that would appeal to buyers of Calvin Klein, Donna Karan, or the more traditional Levi's. Although the Girbaud acquisition was a bit risky, within a year the label was showing strong sales and was being offered in more than 370 stores nationwide.

Nevertheless, the fortunes of the company as a whole began to decline soon after I.C. Isaacs went public. The company's shares, after a brief initial rise, began a steady decrease in value, and finally bottomed out at $1.88 per share in 1999. With the exception of the Girbaud label, which was selling well, all of the company's brands were decreasing in sales.

Restructuring and Relaunching I.C. Isaacs, 1998–99

In November 1998 I.C. Isaacs announced a major restructuring plan that was designed to streamline production, cut unnecessary costs, and reduce the amount of overhead the company had developed during its decade-long growth spurt. In hopes of revitalizing its brands, I.C. Isaacs also planned to streamline the Boss label's junior line for boys in order to focus on guaranteed successes like jeans, discontinue Beverly Hills Polo Club women's sportswear, and refocus on Beverly Hills Polo Club sportswear for boys and men.

More drastically, the company discontinued most of its I.C. Isaacs women's sportswear and closed one of its oldest plants, in Carthage, Mississippi. The company cut its advertising budget as well, but spared the campaign for Girbaud, which was selling strongly. In a final step to streamline the company, I.C. Isaacs repurchased about $4 million of the company's common stock. By reducing the inventory and styles of labels that were not readily recognizable to the consumer, such as the I.C. Isaacs brand, and focusing on the growth of Boss and Girbaud, the company hoped to renew its profitability and gain a larger, more fashion-conscious consumer base. In the words of President Jerry Lear, speaking to the *Baltimore Business Journal* in 1998, ''Our brands speak for the company, and that suits me fine. That's much more preferable to people knowing who I.C. Isaacs is and not giving a damn about our brands.''

With that in mind, in 1999 I.C. Isaacs named retail insider Danny Gladstone president of Girbaud. Gladstone had formerly been president of sales for Calvin Klein's highly successful CK line, and was well equipped to lead I.C. Isaacs toward its goal of making Girbaud a household name. At the time of Gladstone's hiring, the label was being sold in almost 600 stores; within a year, that number had increased to nearly 900.

In September 1999 the company launched a new label called Urban Expedition, or UBX, a line of sportswear which, while having some similarity to the company's Boss and Beverly Hills Polo Club lines, overtly appealed to younger consumers who identified more with ''streetwear'' than sportswear. The collection included baggy jeans, t-shirts, and jackets, and was targeted at consumers interested in hip-hop and urbanwear. The company hired the hip-hop artist Rakim to promote the line. According to CEO Arnot, speaking to *PR Newswire* in September 1999, ''The launch of Urban Expedition gives us the opportunity to capitalize on what we do best, providing style-conscious customers with cutting-edge fashions. By offering up-scale streetwear collections under a fresh new brand, we have an opportunity to capture a share of the audience who appreciates fashion-forward urban styling.'' I.C. Isaacs had taken a new turn indeed, using such trendy phrases ''urban

Key Dates:

1913: Isaac C. Isaacs founds I.C. Isaacs.
1984: Bought out by investors.
1990: Purchases its first license to a clothing label, the nationally known Boss.
1997: Goes public and purchases the Girbaud license.
1998: Announces a sweeping restructuring plan.

styling'' and ''streetwear'' to present the company as modern, fashionable, and competitive.

Principal Competitors

Levi Strauss & Co.; Fubu; Tommy Hilfiger Corporation; Guess, Inc.

Further Reading

Curan, Catherine, ''Isaacs Hopes to Cut Loss by Keying on Sportswear,'' *Women's Wear Daily,* November 30, 1998, p. 12.

''Gladstone Is New President of I.C. Isaacs' Girbaud Unit,'' *Women's Wear Daily,* January 26, 1999, p. 15.

''I.C. Isaacs & Company Reports Third Quarter 1998 Results and Announces Restructuring Plan,'' *PR Newswire,* November 11, 1998.

''I.C. Isaacs to Launch Urban Expedition Sportswear Brand,'' *PR Newswire,* September 23, 1999.

''Isaacs' Net Loss in Period: $9.5 Million,'' *Women's Wear Daily,* April 7, 1999, p. 12.

Karpovich, Todd, ''Newly Public I.C. Isaacs Sees Stock Plunge,'' *Baltimore Business Journal,* July 24, 1998, v. 16, p. 1.

Owens, Jennifer, ''I.C. Isaacs Sells 3.8 Million Shares at $10 in IPO,'' *Daily News Record,* December 24, 1997, p. 2.

Spevack, Rachel, ''I.C. Isaacs New Licensee for Girbaud Men's; VF Corp. Giving Up,'' *Daily News Record,* November 7, 1997, p. 1A.

Stipe, Suzanne, ''Maker of Boss Jeans Plots out New Course,'' *Baltimore Business Journal,* August 14, 1998, p. 12.

—Rachel H. Martin

International Rectifier Corporation

233 Kansas Street
El Segundo, California 90245
U.S.A.
Telephone: (310) 726-8000
Fax: (310) 332-3332
Web site: http://www.irf.com

Public Company
Incorporated: 1947
Employees: 4,495
Sales: $545.4 million (1999)
Stock Exchanges: New York Pacific Philadelphia
Ticker Symbol: IRF
NAIC: 334413 Semiconductor and Related Device Manufacturing

International Rectifier Corporation (IR) is the oldest independent power semiconductor manufacturer in the world. IR's products, protected by hundreds of patents, control the direction and flow of electrical current, a necessity for manufacturers of myriad electronics products. The company develops, manufactures, and sells control integrated circuits, diodes, rectifiers, and its signature product, HEXFET power MOSFET switches. More than half of IR's sales are to customers in Asia and Europe. The company operates production facilities in China, India, Italy, Mexico, the United Kingdom, and the United States.

Post-World War II Origins

An offshoot of the fast-growing aerospace industry in the Los Angeles area during the 1940s was the rise of attendant semiconductor manufacturers. IR was there from the start, founded on August 9, 1947 by Leon Lidow and his son Eric. Eric Lidow, who would control the company for the next half-century, was born in Vilnius, Lithuania. He attended the Technical University of Berlin, where he earned a degree in electrical engineering in 1937, the same year he immigrated to the United States. In 1940 he co-founded and served as general manager of Selenium Corporation of America, which was acquired by Sperry Corporation in 1944. Lidow stayed on after the acquisition, serving as vice-president of engineering until teaming up with his father to form IR. The Lidows created IR to put to use advanced processes they had developed for manufacturing selenium rectifiers, which converted alternating electrical current to direct electrical current. Their technology, formally employed on IR's August 9 founding date, was pioneering, predating the development of the transistor by more than four months.

IR started with six employees in an unincorporated area of Los Angeles, marking the beginning of the company's continuous efforts to produce devices with increasingly higher power ratings and superior reliability characteristics. The company's business revolved around controlling the flow and direction of electricity, an engineering feat of fundamental importance in the vast world of electronics, enabling appliances, automobiles, computers, and thousands of other devices, components, and systems to function. To switch and condition electricity, manufacturers relied on power semiconductors, using diodes, rectifiers, transistors, and other devices to make their products operate. IR, with its foundation resting on commercial semiconductor processes and devices based on selenium (a nonmetallic element), emerged as an early leader in the industry. At its start, the company manufactured rectifiers, diodes, and transistors for sale to domestic customers, but quickly demonstrated its talent for developing superior technology and its ambition to expand its presence outside the U.S. market.

From selenium, IR made the technological leap to germanium-based systems, introducing germanium rectifiers in November 1954. Three years later, the company's tenth anniversary was marked by the formation of International Rectifier Corp., Japan Ltd., representing the company's first foray into international expansion. In September 1958, Eric Lidow took IR public, completing an initial public offering of stock that preceded the establishment of the company's second foreign subsidiary, IR, Great Britain Ltd., in December 1958. One year later, Lidow drew the semiconductor industry's attention by besting his germanium rectifiers with the September 1959 introduction of the first silicon rectifier, which, facilitated by the company's previous international expansion, made IR the first company to introduce silicon technology to Japan.

Company Perspectives:

International Rectifier (IR) provides enabling technologies for products that work smarter, run cooler, and raise the world's productivity-per-watt. The world's largest industry is electronics, and over the long term, global demand for power electronics makes IR's role more important and our contribution more valuable. IR is powering the next generation of servers and computers, cars, satellites, and home appliances. We set performance and architecture standards for power electronics across a broad spectrum, and we're lengthening our competitive lead.

An acknowledged force in the semiconductor industry, Lidow's company proceeded to accumulate an impressive list of technological achievements as it extended its global reach. In 1960, after introducing solar cells two years earlier, IR produced the world's first solar-powered automobile. One year later, the company commenced operations in Italy, followed by the establishment of subsidiaries in India in 1965, Canada in 1966, and Mexico in 1973.

Against the backdrop of IR's geographic expansion, the company's leading role in the technological development of power semiconductors produced disparate financial results. For IR, being the pioneer of widely used technology did not necessarily guarantee long-term financial success, which, as a publicly traded company, was an all-important objective. For instance, based in large part on the company's achievements as a pioneer in silicon control rectifiers, IR's stock swelled to $31 per share in 1966. By 1969, after the company's competitors had successfully jumped on the silicon bandwagon, IR's shares plummeted below $12. The company's technological achievements were exemplary, but, frustrating for Lidow, IR's financial reputation was not. Despite the dozens of pioneering patents held by the company, it began to falter by the 1970s, perceived by investors and industry observers as an organization suffering from stagnation. As the prospect of an industry pioneer withering on the vine began to emerge, the next generation of Lidows was exhibiting talents that soon would breathe new life into IR.

Lidow Sons Begin To Exert Influence in the 1970s

Eric Lidow's two sons, Alexander and Derek, possessed exceptional minds. Alexander, two years younger than Derek, built a photoelectric cell at the age of eight, but, nevertheless, was overshadowed by his older brother when the two boys were in their teens. Derek graduated from Beverly Hills High School at age 16, setting an example Alexander was unable to match. Alexander did not conclude his studies at Beverly Hills High School until the usual age of 18, which fueled a rivalry between the two brothers that would endure for the next 30 years. ''I couldn't let him do better than me,'' Alexander told a *Forbes* reporter in September 1995, but, for Alexander, matching the academic pace of his brother would prove to be a difficult endeavor. Derek graduated from Princeton summa cum laude at the age of 20, then earned a Stanford Ph.D. in two years. Alexander earned an undergraduate degree in physics from California Institute of Technology in three years and was awarded his Ph.D. in applied physics from Stanford, like his brother, at age 22. In terms of the ongoing rivalry between the Lidow brothers, the race against one another in the academic world had produced no clear winner. IR would serve as the next proving ground, setting the stage for a brotherly battle that had a profound effect on their father's company. For Alexander, who had suffered the indignity of spending four years in high school, redemption would be found.

Derek and Alexander concluded their academic careers in 1975 and 1977, respectively, joining IR at roughly the same time the semiconductor industry was undergoing a dynamic change in technology. For years, the job of converting alternating current into direct current had been performed by bipolar transistors, but the electronics industry had struck upon a substitute for bipolars in many applications: power MOSFETs. MOSFETs, an acronym for metal oxide semiconductor field effect transistor, were more efficient, faster, and smaller than bipolars, threatening to replace the world market for bipolars, which was valued at roughly $1 billion. The potential for MOSFETs was vast, representing a critical area of development for a specialized power semiconductor manufacturer like IR. Not coincidentally, Alexander Lidow had experimented with the technology surrounding MOSFETs while pursuing his academic work at Stanford. His discoveries signaled the beginning of a new era for IR.

In 1976, one year before he was awarded his Ph.D., Alexander began working on an advanced MOSFET with promising capabilities. The early development of his chip, which broke up electrical current into smaller, more usable units, impressed his father, persuading the IR chairman to give his son $100,000 worth of equipment and the aid of one engineer for further development of the chip, dubbed HEXFET because of its hexagonal shape. HEXFET was under development for production by the time Alexander left Stanford, but the price to make HEXFETs a commercial reality was severe. IR accumulated massive debt: ''We bet the company, bet again, and borrowed to bet some more on HEXFET,'' Alexander recalled in a September 11, 1995 interview with *Forbes.* Alexander lobbied his father to shelve IR's existing businesses and concentrate fully on HEXFET chips. ''The company had plateaued and was struggling,'' Alexander reflected in his interview with *Forbes.* ''From my perspective, International Rectifier had nowhere to go.'' Derek disagreed, convinced that if the company invested everything in HEXFET its future existence could be in peril. The brotherly rivalry transmogrified into a feud, but plans went ahead for the commercial debut of HEXFET as long-term debt soared to 88 percent of IR's capitalization.

The HEXFET power MOSFET was introduced in June 1979, marking the market entry of what would become IR's mainstay product. By 1983, when sales amounted to $127 million, the rewards of the commitment to HEXFET chips were evident. IR controlled more than half of the fast-growing market for power MOSFETs, maintaining a 12- to 18-month lead over rivals such as Motorola, Hitachi, RCA, and Siliconix. Wall Street was impressed, evinced by a dramatic rise in the company's stock value from $7 per share at the start of the 1980s to more than $40 per share by 1983. The debt incurred from the headlong push into commercializing HEXFETs, however, had not disappeared. In 1983 IR's debt stood at 57 percent of its

Key Dates:

1947: Leon Lidow and his son, Eric, form International Rectifier Corporation.
1958: Company offers shares of stock for public trading.
1959: Company introduces the first silicon controlled rectifier.
1979: HEXFET power MOSFET is introduced.
1987: Production at HEXFET America commences.
1992: After splitting the company three years earlier, control over all operations is unified.
1995: Alexander and Derek Lidow are appointed co-chief executive officers.
1999: Alexander Lidow is named sole chief executive officer.

capitalization and would soon increase as the company prepared to build the most automated semiconductor manufacturing plant in the nation. The $82 million plant, called HEXFET America, engulfed the company further into debt, but as with the initial investment in Alexander's hexagonal chip, the potential rewards were convincing. The new plant would enable IR to manufacture HEXFETs in one continuous process, cutting production costs in half and increasing the yearly output per worker to $350,000, or more than double the industry average. The financial hurdles were cleared and HEXFET America, located in Temecula, California, commenced production in April 1987. Behind the scenes, however, the tug and pull between Eric Lidow's two sons tempered the celebratory unveiling of the new plant. The IR chief executive officer and chairman was determined to resolve the problem.

Fraternal Rift Divides IR in 1989

By the end of the 1980s, the constant bickering between Alexander and Derek over corporate strategy, which had persisted for roughly a decade-and-a-half, had forced Eric Lidow to take action. In 1989 he divided the company in two, giving Alexander control over IR's newer businesses and giving Derek command of the company's older business lines. "I felt both were right," the senior Lidow explained to *Forbes* in 1995, "and both were willing to accept responsibility for their ideas." What appeared as a natural solution to a nagging problem, however, quickly developed into a more pernicious problem. Separated, Alexander and Derek built contrary business groups that were inherently at odds with each other, symbolized by the adoption of computer systems that could not communicate with each other. Further, the split spawned a host of corporate redundancies, with Alexander and Derek operating distinct administrative staffs and sales and marketing departments, creating a tangle of operations that ultimately enveloped IR's customers, who found themselves suffering as a consequence of the Lidow brothers' inability to work together. Eric Lidow, in his late 70s as IR stumbled into the 1990s, looked for another solution.

In 1992 Eric Lidow went to the heart of the problem and hired J. Mitchell Perry, a Palo Alto psychologist. With therapy as the recourse, the process of mending the differences between the brothers began—a difficult process that aimed to resolve a lifetime of issues. Eventually, the relationship improved, opening the lines of communication between Alexander and Derek. Before the end of 1992, they agreed to reunite their halves of the company, which, sparked by the new spirit of conciliation, led to a new product, the electric power conversion chipset. For decades, the company had sold components piecemeal, rather than combining components—the newer products governed by Alexander and the older products governed by Derek—to create a more comprehensive product. Alexander explained to *Forbes* in 1995: "The minute we got together and compared the things we were doing, it became clear all these [components] worked together synergistically in the process of converting electricity into refined energy." The combined chipset, far smaller and far more inexpensive than separate components, was expected to generate half of IR's sales by the end of the 1990s. Before its promising future materialized, however, there was already cause to celebrate. The reunited brothers and a unified IR produced encouraging results. By 1995, debt had been whittled down to 12 percent of capitalization, sales were up to $429 million, a 30 percent gain from the previous year's total, and earnings reached $39 million, double the total recorded in 1994.

Late 1990s: A Roller Coaster Ride

After three years of watching his sons work together, Eric Lidow was convinced the familial squabbles of the past were over. In 1995 he named his sons co-chief executive officers, with Alexander in charge of manufacturing and technology development and Derek in charge of marketing, computer systems, and strategic planning. Initially, the company's financial performance continued to impress. Revenues slipped past the half-billion-dollar mark for the first time in 1996, rising to $576.8 million, while earnings continued to increase exponentially, swelling to $66.5 million. The following year, however, the company's financial results were negatively affected by oversupply and the costs incurred from restructuring the organization. The 1997 restructuring, aimed at improving efficiency, involved revaluing assets, consolidating administrative and service departments, reducing payroll, and relocating manufacturing operations, among other actions. Restructuring led to a one-time charge of $75 million, contributing significantly to the net loss of $43.2 million registered for the year. Despite the loss, IR expanded manufacturing capacity, confident that it would ultimately gain a substantial return on its investment. Expansion of the Temecula facility was announced in 1997, followed by the disclosure in 1998 of plans to build a $40 million manufacturing plant in Swansea, Wales. As the decade drew to a close, there remained one final chapter in the fraternal story that dominated IR's history, recasting the company for the 21st century.

In May 1999, IR announced it was eliminating one of its chief executive officer positions to pass the powers of joint control to a single individual. Alexander was named the company's sole chief executive officer; Derek, in June 1999, resigned from his post to pursue other interests, although he continued to serve as a member of IR's board of directors. Derek's statement regarding his departure, as quoted in the May 17, 1999 issue of *Electronic News,* explained the move and touched on IR's orientation for the future: "The co-CEO structure played a key role in executing a successful transition through periods of unprecedented demand, volatile market conditions, intense competition, and rapidly developing technology. IR is well positioned with an excellent strategy and exciting new products in an improving marketplace. The board of directors, Alex, and I all feel a single-CEO structure helps IR to achieve its long-range objectives.''

Principal Subsidiaries

HEXFET America; Rectificadores Internacionales S.A. de C.V. (Mexico); International Rectifier Company Great Britain, Ltd.; International Rectifier Corporation Italiana, S.p.A. (Italy).

Principal Competitors

STMicroelectronics N.V.; National Semiconductor Corporation; Samsung Group; Siliconix Incorporated.

Further Reading

Crider, Jeff, ''Chip Maker International Rectifier of California Says Profits to Decline,'' *Knight-Ridder/Tribune Business News,* September 13, 1996.

——, ''El Segundo, Calif-Based International Rectifier Plans Temecula Expansion,'' *Knight-Ridder/Tribune Business News,* December 6, 1997.

——, ''International Rectifier Adding to Temecula, Calif.,'' *Knight-Ridder/Tribune Business News,* November 17, 1995.

Flores, J.C., ''Semiconductor Industry in L.A. Finds Survival in Niche Markets,'' *Los Angeles Business Journal,* March 26, 1990, p. 10.

Haber, Carol, ''IR Settles Suits,'' *Electronic News,* January 11, 1999, p. 10.

''International Rectifier Posts Net Loss,'' *Knight-Ridder/Tribune Business News,* July 18, 1997.

''Int'l Rectifier Adopts New Single CEO Structure: Alex Lidow Named to Top Position; Derek Lidow Steps Down,'' *Electronic News,* May 17, 1999, p. 14.

''IR Sets $40M Plant in Wales,'' *Electronic News,* October 5, 1998, p. 46.

''My Brother, My Rival,'' *Forbes,* September 11, 1995, p. 134.

Paris, Ellen, ''Hot Again,'' *Forbes,* November 21, 1983, p. 332.

''Profits Up for California's International Rectifier,'' *Knight-Ridder/Tribune Business News,* April 15, 1996.

—Jeffrey L. Covell

Interscope Music Group

10900 Wilshire Boulevard
Los Angeles, California 90024
U.S.A.
Telephone: (310) 208-6547
Fax: (310) 208-7817
Web site: http://www.interscoperecords.com

Division of Universal Music Group
Incorporated: 1990 as Interscope Records
Employees: 150
Sales: $260 million (1999)
NAIC: 51222 Integrated Record Production/Distribution

Interscope Music Group, with its Interscope Records label, is one of the most successful and controversial record companies in the music industry. Founded in 1990 by veteran music producer Jimmy Iovine and Ted Field, one of the heirs to the Marshall Field fortune, Interscope produces and distributes such musical stars as Primus, the Wallflowers, Dr. Dre, Marilyn Manson, and Nine Inch Nails. In addition to producing its own artists, Interscope has also been involved with the distribution of other, smaller industry labels, most notoriously that of Death Row Records, a high-profile West Coast rap label. After being initially funded by Time Warner, Interscope is now owned in part by Universal Music Group (previously MCA Records), which is a part of the Seagram Company. Interscope specializes in producing the sort of music of which other, more traditional companies are wary; hard-core, gangsta' rap, alternative fringe rock, and the sub-genre known as Goth are all a part of the company's roster.

Interscope's Beginnings: 1990–96

In an industry famous for its eccentric, iconoclastic characters, Interscope co-founder Ted Field upon first glance might seem an anomaly. Born into the Chicago area Marshall Field family, Field was slated from childhood to follow in the family's footsteps, first attending prestigious private schools, then running the family fortune, which included the Marshall Fields department stores and the *Chicago Sun Times.* From his childhood, however, Field proved himself to be a rebel and risk-taker. After spending much of his adolescence in Alaska, Field moved from school to school, finally becoming involved in race car driving and, later, fund-raising for the Democratic Party. In 1984, after a less than harmonious period of negotiation with his brother, Field inherited over $200 million from the family fortune and within a couple of years had settled permanently in California, where he developed an interest in film production.

It was during this time that Field met music producer Jimmy Iovine, and, using $15 million of Field's own inheritance, the two together founded Interscope Records in 1990. At the same time he started his record company, Field also founded Interscope Communications, a film production company which eventually produced such film hits as "Three Men and a Baby," and the thriller "The Hand that Rocked the Cradle."

Besides Field's abundance of financial resources, Interscope had another advantage from its inception: the expertise and reputation of Jimmy Iovine. Iovine had been involved in the music industry for several years and had been a producer for acts as various as the New York-based singer Patti Smith to the phenomenally successful pop band U2. Between Iovine's inside influence and Field's high-profile financing, it wasn't difficult for Interscope to find further backing, both in the form of monetary support and publicity, in Time Warner, a huge company which was involved in all aspects of the entertainment and communications industries. Time Warner's music production division saw in Interscope an opportunity to share in profits from music which the publicly owned company could not otherwise overtly touch.

Shortly after the establishment of Interscope, a small rap label called Death Row Records was started by former professional football player Marion "Suge" Knight. In 1992, Death Row produced Dr. Dre's "The Chronic," a rap album filled with explicit, violent lyrics, the nature of which were to set the standard for gangsta' rap for years to come. Although Death Row had successfully produced "The Chronic," the company could not find a distributor for the album, as most well-established labels found the contents too controversial. Seeing profit in controversy, however, Interscope stepped in and agreed

Key Dates:

1990: Interscope founded by Ted Field and Jimmy Iovine.
1992: Company has its first breakthrough with Dr. Dre's "The Chronic."
1995: Time Warner sells its 50 percent of Interscope back to the company.
1996: Edgar Bronfman's Seagram Co. buys that percentage at a great profit to Interscope.
1998: Interscope breaks its ties with Death Row Records.
1999: Geffen and A&M record labels are folded into Interscope operations, following Seagram's purchase of PolyGram Records.

to distribute the album, thus establishing an intimate partnership with Death Row. Interscope's gamble proved a success; "The Chronic" was one of the biggest albums of the decade, selling almost four million copies, and helped to make the company a real contender in the music industry.

"The Chronic" helped establish a new genre of music, and gangsta' rap in the early 1990s became one of the most popular forms of hip-hop, its appeal crossing cultural, economic, and racial barriers. Death Row's Dr. Dre pioneered gangsta' rap, and other Death Row artists, all of whom were distributed by Interscope, were not far behind: the rap artists Snoop Doggy Dogg, Tha' Dogg Pound, and Tupac Shakur were all part of the label's roster during the 1990s, and they all sold millions of albums.

Soon after the distribution of "The Chronic," Interscope began producing other artists as well, focusing particularly on hard-core alternative music, such as that of the bands Nine Inch Nails and Primus. The popularity of Nine Inch Nails allowed the band to create in conjunction with Interscope a small, alternative rock label called Nothing Records, which Interscope distributed. Interscope not only focused on fringe sub-genres, however. The company also produced the mainstream pop band No Doubt, which Interscope distributed in partnership with Trauma Records, and which brought in millions in revenue for the company.

The Politics of Music: Interscope in the Mid-1990s

By 1995 Interscope had well established itself as a renegade company willing to take on artists, no matter how outrageous or controversial, that other labels would not touch. While its reputation had garnered a great deal of profit for the company—well into the hundreds of millions by 1995—it had also in turn put Interscope in a high-profile position which, given the political climate of the time, came at a cost to the company's stability.

Indeed, almost from the company's inception it had been subject to political upbraiding of the most public sort. In 1992, after Interscope produced and distributed Tupac Shakur's "2Pacalypse Now," an album which would later be blamed in part, by some, for police shootings in Texas. At the time, Vice-President Dan Quayle announced to the press that "There is absolutely no reason for a record like this to be published by a responsible corporation. Today I am suggesting that the Time Warner subsidiary Interscope Records withdraw this record. It has no place in our society." The album, which brought Interscope millions of dollars, however, continued to help the company garner stature and financial gain.

Had Interscope not been half-owned by the corporate giant Time Warner, a company which had to answer to both the financial and moral concerns of its shareholders, it might not have found itself in the middle of an increasingly mercurial and divided public debate in the middle of the decade. However, that is exactly what happened to the company in 1995, when a political activist named C. Delores Tucker, head of the National Political Congress of Black Women, bought a few shares of Time Warner stock. In September of that year, Tucker attended a shareholder's meeting in New York, and there, with several members of the press in front of her and conservative leader William Bennett by her side, she made a 15-minute speech denouncing Time Warner's involvement in the production of gangsta' rap, taking pains to point out the corporation's ownership of the notorious Interscope.

Tucker placed Time Warner's part-ownership of Interscope at the heart of an increasingly heated battle, the climax of which occurred later that same year when Interscope announced its intentions to release the much-hyped album by Tha' Dogg Pound called "Dogg Food." The album was rumored to be filled with lyrics of extreme violence and misogyny, and Tucker made it her personal—and political—mission to prevent the album's release. Time Warner grew increasingly uncomfortable under such highly-publicized negative limelight, particularly when the prominent conservative politician Bob Dole became involved, calling the music Time Warner was producing "nightmares of depravity."

Time Warner could not censor what Interscope chose to produce without breaking a legal contract signed by the two companies. If Interscope opted to release "Dogg Food," it could do so with or without Time Warner's blessing. Interscope did release "Dogg Food," and in doing so forced Time Warner's hand; the latter bowed out of its 50 percent stake in Interscope at the end of the year, despite the fact that the company was bringing in tremendous amounts of revenue. Time Warner sold its part in Interscope back to the company for a little over $100 million, a price considered by many in the industry to be well below what the growing company was worth.

Tucker declared a political and moral triumph upon hearing of the sale, claiming that "It's a great victory for our children and America's future, and it does show me that Time Warner does have a corporate soul." Some of the artists at Interscope, however, were just as happy to be free of the mainstream influences of Time Warner. Dr. Dre, speaking to *U.S. News & World Report,* said that Interscope's new independence was "going to be a great coup for Interscope because they can make more money. And I won't have to deal with Papa Warner."

Dr. Dre was right. Interscope continued to not only survive, but thrive. In 1996 the company had songs at the top four spots on Billboard's charts, an unmatched record established in 1976, 20 years earlier, by Columbia records. The company was flourishing in genres spanning the gamut of popular music and was successfully involved in the distribution of such lucrative labels as Death Row and Nothing Records. While Tucker may have felt Time Warner's capitulation to public pressure was a moral victory, the sale did nothing to slow or censor the proliferation of music from Interscope's controversial artists. Other companies, too, saw more profit than risk in Interscope, and four months after the company bought back Time Warner's 50 percent interest in Interscope, it sold that same stake to MCA Records for just over $200 million, netting a $100 million profit for the company.

MCA had recently been bought out by Edgar Bronfman's Seagram empire, and the CEO was eager to turn MCA into a powerful force in the pop music industry. With the 50 percent acquisition of Interscope, MCA became the fourth largest record company in the business, helping the aging company become up-to-date on current musical trends. Bronfman, however, was wary of the furor created over Interscope's involvement with Death Row and maintained a right to refrain from supporting the release of material deemed too controversial or subversive by MCA standards, a clause Time Warner had lacked with Interscope.

Severing Ties and Expanding Appeal: Interscope in the Late 1990s

In 1997, *Newsweek* claimed that "In a business where finding a successful act is about as easy as spotting a necktie at the Grammy Awards, Interscope has assembled an unmatched array of alternative-rock and urban-music hit makers." However, in that same article, founder Ted Field confessed that, due to the scandal surrounding Interscope's distribution of Death Row and the controversial lyrics of some of its other stars, particularly Marilyn Manson, he could no longer even donate money to the Democratic Party, of which he had been a longtime supporter and fund-raiser. His company had simply become too hot, both socially and politically.

Field's new partner was quick to notice this, especially when Death Row's head, Marion Knight, was sent to jail for nine years on assault charges. MCA—renamed Universal Records—pressured Interscope to drop its contracts with the besieged Death Row. Not only had Knight been jailed, but Tupac Shakur, Death Row's most lucrative star, had been gunned down in a gang-land style shooting the year before, and there were questions over ownership of the prolific star's estate. Finally, in 1998, Interscope acquiesced to Universal's request, and the company cut its ties with one of its most profitable labels, a move which earned Interscope not a little bad press in the rap community.

Interscope had also come to loggerheads with Trauma Records, which was involved in the production of the popular band No Doubt. In 1997, the two companies settled out of court, with Trauma Records receiving recording rights to the band as well as an additional $3 to $5 million from Interscope. Thus, the late 1990s brought even more challenging times to Interscope, with sales dipping and the company losing some of its more bankable artists. However, with sales still well over $200 million in 1998, the company could hardly have been said to be in dire straits.

After cutting ties with Death Row, Interscope continued to expand its roster, most notably developing a focus on the increasingly popular Christian bands which appealed to a crossover secular audience. In 1999 the same company that had delivered "The Chronic" to gansta' rap enthusiasts produced an album from the Christian children's choir "God's Property," with impressive financial results. As Interscope moved toward a new millennium, it was joined by popular record labels Geffen and A&M, when Bronfman and the Seagram Co. acquired the holdings of PolyGram Records early in 1999. Under the auspices of the newly created Universal Music Group (UMG), Interscope management expected that the remaining 50 percent stake in Interscope would be acquired by UMG. Despite its new corporate structure, the company continued to attract the kind of controversy and publicity on which it was founded. In the spring of 1999, for example, Interscope executive Steve Stoute was involved in a melee in Interscope's New York offices which landed him in the hospital and his alleged attacker, Sean "Puffy" Combs from rival Bad Boy Entertainment, in jail on charges of second degree assault and criminal mischief. In July of that year, the company named a new senior vice-president: Fred Durst, lead singer from the band "Limp Bizkit."

Principal Competitors

Def Jam Records; Bad Boy Entertainment; Priority Records; Arista Records.

Further Reading

Branch, Shelly, "Goodbye, Gangsta'," *Fortune*, July 7, 1997, p. 40.

Geier, Thom, "Trying to Avoid a Bad Rap: Time Warner Moves to Unload its Stake in Interscope Records," *U.S. News & World Report*, August 21, 1995, p. 48.

"MCA Reaches $200 Million Agreement to Purchase Half of Interscope Records," *Jet*, February 12, 1996, p. 64.

Morris, Chris, "Quayle's 2Pac/Interscope Attack Puts New Heat on Time Warner," *Billboard*, October 3, 1992, p. 5.

Roberts, Johnnie L., "Field Marshall: The Man Behind Gangsta' Rap is Mild-Mannered, Old-Money and into Politics. Is Interscope Records' Ted Field a Menace to Society?," *Newsweek*, February 10, 1997, p. 44.

Rosen, Craig, "Dr. Dre Solo Album Going Out through Interscope," *Billboard*, December 12, 1992, p. 9.

——, "Interscope Reaches Crossroads with Trauma Split, Death Row Uncertainty," *Billboard*, September 13, 1997, p. 10.

"Time Warner Sells its Rap Division Back to Interscope Records," *Jet*, October 16, 1995, p. 61.

Willman, Chris, "Unleash Tha' Dogg?," *Entertainment Weekly*, September 8, 1995, p. 10.

—Rachel H. Martin

J.Baker, Inc.

J. Baker, Inc.

555 Turnpike Street
Canton, Massachusetts 02021
U.S.A.
Telephone: (781) 828-9300
Fax: (781) 821-0614
Web site: http://www.thinkbig.com

Public Company
Founded: 1985 as Shoecliff Corp.
Employees: 6,154
Sales: $584.3 million (1999)
Stock Exchanges: NASDAQ
Ticker Symbol: JBAK
NAIC: 44811 Men's Clothing Stores; 45411 Electronic Shopping and Mail-Order Houses

J. Baker, Inc., is the leading U.S. retailer of clothing and footwear for the men's big and tall market, which comprises some 16 million consumers. As of October 1999, the company operated 450 Casual Male Big & Tall stores, over 90 REPP Big & Tall stores, some 50 REPP Premier stores, the REPP By Mail catalog, and the ThinkBig.com e-commerce site. In addition, its Work 'n Gear division operated 65 retail stores, selling uniforms, healthcare clothing, and utility workwear in 13 states in the Northeast and Midwest. Through its JBI Footwear division, J. Baker is the largest independent operator of self-service licensed footwear departments in discount department stores, operating 866 units.

Early Days: 1920s–1960s

Jacob Baker launched his eponymous business in 1925 or 1927—accounts differ—selling his shoes wholesale to mom-and-pop stores from the rear of his brother's shoe factory in Spencer, Massachusetts. After Jacob's death, the company was taken over by his son Sherman, who soon began selling shoes at retail. As Sherman Baker told David Mehegan of the *Boston Globe*, "A couple of women from Springfield stopped by and asked if they could buy some shoes. We sold them some shoes and they came back with their friends. They'd wait in the alley for hours, and they'd take away 25 pairs of shoes." The company's retail business grew, operating with a small markup and heavy volume.

In 1953 Sherman took J. Baker in a new direction that would eventually become its main source of revenue: operating shoe departments in discount department stores. Under such arrangements, a mass merchandiser hired J. Baker to provide shoes, display racks and staff. In return, the store received a fixed percentage of revenues and did not have to worry about ordering and inventory. In 1958 J. Baker's one-year-old neighbor, Ames Department Stores Inc., licensed the company to run that chain's shoe departments, and as Ames grew, so did J. Baker.

Part of National Shoes: 1968–84

By 1968, Sherman Baker was looking to expand. To raise the money he needed, he sold J. Baker to National Shoes, a chain of full-service shoe stores controlled by the Siegel family. However, National's stores were in urban neighborhoods, not in the suburban malls that were experiencing dramatic growth, and the company was soon losing money. Although Baker became president of National in 1970, the Siegel family remained involved in the decision making. For ten years J. Baker carried the company, offsetting losses from the National stores with revenues from its licensed shoe departments.

In 1980 National's creditors forced both the parent and its subsidiary into bankruptcy. At the time, National Shoe had 210 retail stores, including Delton, A.S. Beck, Joffrey, and National. J. Baker had 237 leased shoe departments. Sherman Baker brought the company out of Chapter 11 protection in 1982, in large part because his suppliers agreed to continue shipping merchandise on extended credit terms. Two years later Baker sold 114 of National's store leases to Butler Shoe Corp. at a large profit, providing enough case to pay off the creditors.

A New J. Baker Inc.: 1985–87

As the stripped-down company regained its financial footing, Baker wanted to buy out the Siegels. With Baker, financier Thomas Lee, and a partnership of the Bass brothers of Fort Worth each taking a one-third equity interest, Baker created

Key Dates:

1920s: Jacob Baker begins a wholesale shoe business.
1940: Sherman Baker joins his father's business.
1953: First licensing agreement with department store.
1968: J. Baker sold to National Shoe, Inc.
1980: National and J. Baker declare bankruptcy.
1985: Sherman Baker buys National Shoe, renaming it J. Baker, Inc.; opens first Parade of Shoes store
1986: J. Baker, Inc. goes public.
1991: Company diversifies into clothing for large-size men.
1993: Company expands retail shoe division with acquisitions.
1997: Retail shoe operations are sold off.
1999: Repp Ltd. Big and Tall and Repp Ltd. by Mail are acquired.

Shoecliff Corp., which acquired National and its subsidiary in 1985 through a cost merger at a price of some $31.6 million. The new entity, J. Baker, Inc., was a private company headquartered in the Boston neighborhood of Readville. The transaction was the first in a series for Sherman Baker, who went on to buy successful divisions of other bankrupt companies.

Soon after taking control, Baker started the company's own retail operation, the Parade of Shoes chain of discount shoe stores in New England. These self-service stores charged one price ($13.88) for any pair of women's shoes, with a high percentage of the shoes being leather and most with familiar brand names. J. Baker was joining a discounting movement in the industry that had mushroomed following an oversupply of shoes the year before. Sales for the company's first fiscal year, which ended February 1, 1986, were $116.7 million.

In 1986 J. Baker went public. At the time, the company owned 29 Parade of Shoes retail stores, leased and operated shoe departments in 400 stores in 18 states, and supplied shoes at wholesale to 207 more stores in two other chains. Parade of Shoes operated on the same low-margin/high-volume principle Baker had first used in the early 1940s. The sales volume at the retail stores was among the industry's highest, averaging $250 per square foot compared to the industry's average of between $150 and $200. The chain did very little advertising, depending instead on word-of-mouth to generate sales. The company's revenues for the year grew to $167.8 million

Growing the Shoe Business: 1987–89

With both the retail and licensing divisions of the company generating cash, Sherman Baker announced that the company was considering buying freestanding stores and had already made a bid for Morse Shoe, which eventually went private in a leveraged buyout. Prices at Parade of Shoes rose to $15.88, to offset increases in the cost of imported shoes, and the chain expanded into New York and New Jersey.

In 1987 the company started its second discount chain, Step In Shoes. These self-service stores specialized in low-cost shoes for the entire family. According to a 1998 *Forbes* article, the establishment of the new chain was a defensive move to keep May Department Store's discount shoe division from gaining ground in New England. By the end of the year the new chain had five stores and Parade of Shoes had grown to 83 locations. Baker then turned his attention to his wholesale and licensing businesses. During 1988 wholesale customers increased to 607 stores with nine chains, and the number of licensed shoe departments operated by J. Baker grew to 598 in 23 discount department store chains.

The year 1989 was one of significant change. The company bought Boston-based Spencer Shoe, which operated 190 leased footwear departments in discount stores in the Northeast, for about $4.5 million in stock. Then Ames Department Stores Inc. replaced its usual five- or six-year licenses with a 20-year lease agreement for J. Baker to operate the shoe departments in all the Ames stores as well as the 315 Zayre stores Ames had just purchased. Between these two events, Sherman Baker selected his designated successor, bringing Jerry Socol, who had been chairman and chief executive of Filene's, to the company as president. Socol soon took on CEO responsibilities as well, while Baker remained chairman. J. Baker ended the year with sales of $399 million and was named the best small company in America by Forbes.

Adding Clothes to the Mix: 1990–91

In 1990, the *Boston Globe* estimated, one out of every 25 pairs of shoes sold in the United States was sold by J. Baker. Parade of Shoes, now with 125 stores, was growing by about 35 percent a year. The wholesale division reached 118 discount stores. In the licensing area, the company signed a deal with discounter Rose's Stores Inc. to operate shoe departments in all 260 Rose's locations. This brought the number of licensed shoe departments to 1,513. Almost at the same time, however, Ames Department Stores filed for Chapter 11 protection, and eventually closed 231 of its 692 stores. The bankruptcy cost J. Baker about $20 million in lost sales.

According to the *Boston Globe*, J. Baker had only two serious competitors in the licensing/wholesaling businesses, Morse Shoe and Meldisco, a division of Melville Corp. Even though the two biggest discounters, Kmart and Wal-Mart, had long-term arrangements for their shoe departments, analysts estimated there were 2,500 other discount stores with shoe departments for J. Baker to pursue. In October the company surprised the analysts by announcing that it would buy Massachusetts-based Casual Male Corp.'s chain of 190 big and tall men's clothing stores, which was the only division still operated by the bankrupt company. The chain concentrated on moderately priced casual clothing and accessories for men who were taller than 6 feet 2 inches or with waist sizes of 40 to 66 inches. Most of the stores were in the Northeast, but the chain spread as far as Minnesota and Texas. The purchase, while following Baker's habit of buying successful divisions of bankrupt companies, also fit Socol's preferred strategy of focusing on specialty retailers with strong niches. The price was just $7.2 million to Casual Male Corp.'s creditors over two years. In its first year as part of J. Baker, Casual Male Big & Tall's operating profits were double that amount.

The move to diversify was important, as the company's licensed shoe department business dropped significantly with the Ames bankruptcy and store closings and the announcement by Rose's Stores that they would be closing 25 locations. The 141-store Parade of Shoes chain was also feeling the effects of a weak economy, and at about this time, the company closed its Step In Shoe chain. A year later the company continued its apparel diversification with the purchase of WearGuard's 29-store retail chain, adding work clothes and medical uniforms to its specialty niches. The 40-year old family-owned company founded to sell work clothes to gas station owners had grown to become a leader in catalog sales of work clothes. Under the deal, which cost about $5.5 million in stock, J. Baker acquired the inventory and leases of the stores and a license to use the WearGuard name.

More Shoe Purchases: 1992–94

Despite the move into apparel, selling shoes was still the company's main business. During 1992 the company turned around its flagging Parade of Shoes chain, with annual sales per store jumping from $100,000 in 1991 to $525,000 in 1992. ''You get a warm fuzzy feeling when you look at what they've done with Parade of Shoes,'' one analyst told *Footwear News* in a 1993 article. The winning strategy was to shift from brand names to upgrading the quality of its unbranded leather shoes, increasing prices to $19.98 a pair, and improving the stores' appearance.

In December the company announced it was buying the bankrupt Morse Shoe Inc. for a stock swap worth $58 million, beating out May Department Stores in the process. Morse was the company's nearest competitor in leased shoe departments, and the purchase bought J. Baker the national 480-store Fayva chain, more licensed shoe departments, and a new headquarters in Canton, Massachusetts. In December Ames emerged from bankruptcy and continued to use J. Baker to operate its shoe departments. Revenues for the year reached $532 million with earnings of $11 million.

In 1993 sales jumped 73 percent, to $919 million. Early in the year, the company changed the name of its work clothes chain to Work 'n Gear when WearGuard Corp. terminated the licensing agreement it had with J. Baker, citing ''disagreements over royalties and value,'' according to the *Patriot Ledger*. In November, the company bought Ohio-based Tishkoff Enterprises Inc., the parent of Shoe Corp. of America (SCOA), which operated shoe outlets in upscale department stores. J. Baker paid $1.9 million in stock and cash for SCOA, which had sales of $40 million, and gained entry into a new segment of the licensed footwear department business.

But the news that year was not all good. Sherman Baker agreed to pay $713,000 to settle SEC charges that he sold company stock before the announcement of the closing of Ames stores caused the stock price to drop. And the company lost a patent infringement suit over a plastic device that tied pairs of shoes together, eventually paying $4.1 million in damages.

Attempts to Counter Market Weaknesses: 1995–96

Over the next two years, the company continued to expand the Casual Male Big & Tall chain, which accounted for over half of the company's revenues. It added stores, began operating shoe departments in Today's Man stores, and initiated catalog sales. At the same time, things were going poorly in the footwear business. Throughout the industry, over 1,500 shoe stores closed during the winter of 1995–96. Existing Parade of Shoes stores had modest but continuing declines in sales. In September 1995 the company decided to liquidate its Fayva chain, blaming competition from discounters Wal-Mart, Kmart, and Payless ShoeSource and the poor retail environment.

In 1996 the company put SCOA on the market and tried to turn around the slumping Parade of Shoes chain. Company officials and analysts agreed that the chain had alienated its core customer base of working women by introducing young, hip fashions and moving from strip malls to urban locations. Despite efforts to refocus the chain, Parade of Shoes lost money for the year.

Profits in the licensed department division were also declining as discount department stores, including customers Jamesway and Bradlees, sought bankruptcy court protection. In September Jerry Socol left the company. Chief Financial Officer Alan Weinstein was named acting president and CEO, and later took on the positions permanently. At the end of Socol's eight-year tenure, J. Baker operated 1,032 licensed footwear departments in discount department stores, 450 licensed footwear departments in semi-service and full-service department and specialty apparel stores, 200 Parade of Shoes stores, 427 Casual Male Big & Tall stores, and 66 Work 'n Gear stores.

Footwear Restructuring: 1997–98

During 1997 and 1998, the company completed the restructuring of its footwear division. In March 1997 it finalized the sale of its Shoe Corporation of America division to division executives and the Parade of Shoes division to Payless ShoeSource, Inc., the largest family footwear retailer in the country. It also downsized its licensed-department business and renamed it JBI Footwear.

In its apparel business, the company opened its first Rx Uniforms stores, hoping to cash in on (or create) a niche market for pastel hospital scrubs. The healthcare wear had started as a small department in the Work 'n Gear shops, and grew into a ''store-within-a-store.'' As a company official explained in a 1998 *Boston Globe* article, demand by nurses grew with relaxed dress codes in hospitals and the cut in uniform subsidiaries by health maintenance organizations. Television shows *ER* and *Chicago Hope* also contributed to the acceptance of non-white hospital wear. The company designed a new store format, with Work 'n Gear and Rx Uniforms each having its own doorway and exterior sign.

ThinkBig.com: 1999

In May 1999 J. Baker bought the profitable Repp Ltd. Big & Tall and Repp Ltd. by Mail divisions of the bankrupt shoe and apparel retailer Edison Brothers Stores, Inc., for $31.7 million. The purchase added 133 retail locations in the Midwest and West as well as a catalog business. The traditional clothing in the upscale REPP Ltd. stores also gave J. Baker access to the more affluent customers in the men's big and tall market. Later in the year the company announced retail formats for the discount end of the market (B&T Factory Store, an outlet chain) and for designer collections (REPP Premier Big & Tall).

J. Baker's consolidation as the heavyweight retailer in the big and tall men's market occurred as that $5.5 billion industry was growing at a rate of 11 percent. While still maintaining a major presence in the footwear departments of mass merchandisers, the company appeared to have successfully moved away from its exclusive reliance on selling shoes.

Principal Operating Divisions

Casual Male Big & Tall; Repp Big & Tall; Work 'n Gear; JBI Footwear.

Principal Competitors

J.C. Penney; Sears; Wal-Mart; Kmart; Target; Wearguard/ARAMARK; Life Uniform.

Further Reading

''AC Case in U.S. Sets Year 2000 Milestone,'' *Management Consultant International*, February 1999, p. 5.

Berner, Robert, ''The Secret Success: Little-Known Firm Takes Big Strides,'' *Patriot Ledger*, March 26, 1994, p. 21.

——, ''ARA Group Buys WearGuard,'' *Patriot Ledger*, February 27, 1992.

Biddle, Frederic M., ''J. Baker Wins Battle over Morse Shoe,'' *Boston Globe*, December 11, 1992, p. 77.

——, ''J. Baker Chief to Pay $713,000,'' *Boston Globe*, October 28, 1993, p. 35.

——, ''J. Baker Buys Ohio Shoe Firm,'' *Boston Globe*, November 23, 1993, p. 40.

Busche, Linda, ''J. Baker Has Room to Run, Pros Say,'' *USA Today*, May 13, 1993, p. 3B.

''Casual Male Plans Major Expansion,'' *DNR*, June 7, 1995, p. 1.

Chmielewski, Dawn, ''Shoe Chain Grows in New Direction,'' *Patriot Ledger*, March 28, 1996, p. 30.

''Discounters Upgrading in Many Areas,'' *Footwear News*, April 25, 1988, p. 1.

Galambos, Ellen, ''WearGuard Tells Stores to Stop Using Name,'' *Patriot Ledger*, January 30, 1993.

''J. Baker Acquisition, Realignment of Key Divisions Put It in $1 Billion Club,'' *Footwear News*, May 3, 1993, p. 2.

''J. Baker, Inc., Completes Acquisition,'' *Daily News Record*, October 1, 1991, p. 19.

''J. Baker, Inc., Announces Settlement of Litigation,'' *Business Wire*, October 1, 1997.

''J. Baker Lands New Outlet,'' *Boston Globe*, March 17, 1990, p. 15.

Jankowski, Dianna, ''Baker Offering Is $14 a Share,'' *Footwear News*, June 9, 1986, p. 2.

——, ''Baker to Expand Plant to Keep up with Growth, *Footwear News*, November 24, 1986, p. 59.

Kindleberger, Richard, ''J. Baker Agrees to Takeover of Casual Male,'' *Boston Globe*, October 19, 1990, p. 74.

King, Ralph, Jr., ''The Basses Get Richer,'' *Forbes*, February 8, 1988, p. 84.

Lewis, Diane E., ''J. Baker Chief Executive Jerry Socol Quits,'' *Boston Globe*, September 13, 1996, p. C1.

Lunt, Dean, ''J. Baker Continues to Sell off Shoe Units,'' *Patriot Ledger*, January 15, 1997, p. 8.

Mehegan, David, ''Jerry Socol's Big Hit in Shoes,'' *Boston Globe*, March 21, 1989, p. 33.

——, ''Hyde Park Retailer Blends Experience, Execution to Top Rivals,'' April 9, 1990, p. 18.

Pulda, Ellen, ''Baker Eyes Acquisition of Free Standing Stores, *Footwear News*, June 22, 1987, p. 4.

Reidy, Chris, ''Fall from Fayva,'' *Boston Globe*, September 7, 1995, p. 63.

——, ''J. Baker, Inventor Each Claim a Win in Patent Suit,'' *Boston Globe*, June 14, 1996, p. 38.

——, ''J. Baker Yearning to be 'Category Killer',,'' *Boston Globe*, September 8, 1998, p. E1.

——, ''J. Baker Plans Outlet Featuring Brand Names,'' *Boston Globe*, July 20, 1999, p. D9.

Tedeschi, Mark, ''Baker Reacts to Setbacks with Expansion Agenda,'' *Footwear News*, November 26, 1990, p. 2.

—Ellen D. Wernick

Jennifer Convertibles, Inc.

419 Crossways Park Drive
Woodbury, New York 11797
U.S.A.
Telephone: (516) 496-1900
Fax: (516) 496-8380
Web site: http://www.jenniferfurniture.com

Public Company
Incorporated: 1976
Employees: 440
Sales: $111 million (1998)
Stock Exchanges: OTC
Ticker Symbol: JENN
NAIC: 5712

Jennifer Convertibles, Inc. is one of the fastest growing specialty retail stores in the United States. As a specialty retailer, the company's stores focus on selling a complete line of sofabeds as well as companion pieces, including chairs, recliners, and loveseats, all priced to appeal to a broad range of consumers. Each of the stores has a kiosk which sells mattresses, and Jennifer Convertibles stores are well-known as the largest dealers of Sealy sofabeds across the United States. At the end of fiscal 1998, the company reported that it operated 153 stores, including 46 Jennifer Convertible stores, 32 Jennifer Leather stores, two Jennifer Living Room stores, and 73 licensed Jennifer Convertible stores. The firm's Leather Stores concentrate on the retail sale of living room furniture made of leather, while its Living Room Stores focus on the sale of a broad range of sofabeds and furniture also marketed in the company's other stores. The company's headquarters are situated in Woodbury, New York, but its stores are located primarily on the Eastern seaboard, Florida, and around the Chicago metropolitan area.

Early History

Jennifer Convertibles, Inc. was founded in 1975 by three enterprising businessmen who knew they could offer a better product at a lower price. Harley Greenfield, Fred Love, and Ed Seidner were all friends who worked as manufacturing representatives for furniture companies during the early part of the 1970s. As they began to talk more and more about striking out on their own, the three men engaged in late night strategy sessions as to what market niche they could best meet. Well acquainted with all of the various furniture lines within the industry, Greenfield, Love, and Seidner finally decided to focus on the sale of sofabeds. The three men were convinced that, due to the changing demographics within large cities where many young people lived in small spaces, selling sofabeds would be easy since there was a strong desire to use such small space as efficiently as possible. Furthermore, by selling sofabeds exclusively, they hoped to take advantage of the specialty merchandising trend that was sweeping across the industry, keep start-up costs within an affordable limit, and attract manufacturers by ordering large volumes. Having decided what business to engage in, the three men then put their heads together and searched for a name. They finally agreed upon naming their business after Fred Love's daughter, who also happened to be Harley Greenfield's niece. Thus Jennifer Convertibles, Inc. was born.

The first item on the new owners' agenda was to come up with a detailed and workable marketing strategy that would enable Jennifer Convertibles to compete with the large number of retail department stores and other specialty stores that carried various lines of sofabeds. Greenfield, Love, and Seidner decided to focus on the image of the company's store as the cornerstone of a comprehensive marketing strategy. Accordingly, all stores were designed to display merchandise in model room settings, with each store similar to the next one in layout, carpeting, and use of lighting to emphasize both sofabeds and other furniture alike. The owners decided to display a wide variety of sofabeds and companion pieces of furniture and accessories such as lamps and tables and carpeting. By focusing on the image of company stores in this way, the owners hoped to distinguish themselves from their competitors in an attempt to attract a wider range of people from various socioeconomic classes, especially since their line of sofabeds sold for between $299 and $2,200.

Throughout the late 1970s and early 1980s, Jennifer Convertibles attracted far more people than the traditional retail stores and specialty stores that sold their sofabeds to niche markets. Not

Key Dates:

1975: Jennifer Convertibles, Inc. opens its first retail store in New York City.
1989: Company reports $35 million in revenues.
1990: Company expands into Florida.
1991: Licensee operation is initiated in Chicago metropolitan area.
1995: The Securities and Exchange Commission announces formal inquiry into the firm.
1998: The SEC does not recommend legal action against Jennifer Convertibles and its ownership; company reports $111 million in sales.

surprisingly, Greenfield, Love, and Seidner discovered that they were right after all, namely, that price was one of their best weapons to use against competitors. Soon the company was not only selling merchandise made by brand name manufacturers, but was also offering merchandise at its stores under the "Jennifer" brand name for sofabeds. The average sofabed cost $400, which was significantly less than any other chain retail store and specialty store price. In addition, the company implemented an aggressive and rather expensive advertising campaign during the early 1980s. The owners hired an in-house staff of advertising executives and gave them the freedom to devise a marketing campaign that would attract more customers to company stores. Within a short period of time, the in-house advertising staff had created both print and television ads that were highly successful. The print campaign during this time featured a sofabed or loveseat with the tagline, "The largest selection of $400 sofabeds," and a prominent display of the price. Advertising in the *New York Times Magazine,* among other prestigious publications, gave the company a high level of visibility and resulted in a growing number of customers.

By the end of fiscal 1987, Jennifer Convertibles reported revenues of approximately $5 million. The company had grown from one retail store to 18 privately owned stores in just over ten years. Most of the stores were located in the New York metropolitan area, but plans had already been laid to expand the company's operations up and down the East Coast. When Jennifer Convertibles finally got the necessary capital from an initial public offering of stock near the end of the fiscal year, management was ready to take advantage of the opportunity to implement its long awaited expansion program, and within a very short time the firm reported a total of 47 stores operating from Washington, D.C., to the upper reaches of New England. By the end of fiscal 1988, Jennifer Convertibles reported sales of over $15 million. Most importantly, as the first stores opened began to reap the rewards of the constant image building emphasized by the owners, the increasing number of customers helped to push sales and revenues sky high. By the end of fiscal 1989, the company reported revenues of $35 million for the year.

The 1990s

By 1990, Jennifer Convertibles was widely regarded as one of the fastest growing retail specialty stores within the United States. The company counted over 65 convertible-sofa stores located throughout the Northeast, with much publicized plans to continue its expansion strategy. But the owners, especially Harley Greenfield, recognized that the sofabed market had changed dramatically in the 15 years since Jennifer Convertibles was founded. At first, Jennifer Convertibles marketed its merchandise to a broad socioeconomic range of the population that lived primarily in high-rise apartment buildings. In fact, every time Greenfield passed by an apartment complex he used to wonder how many potential sofabed customers lived in the building. But as the cost of living in apartment buildings increased significantly during the decade of the 1980s, many younger families began relocating to the immediate suburbs or so-called bedroom communities, while many older people who were retired moved to smaller homes in the Southwest and Southeast.

Although the company maintained its commitment to market sofabeds to a broad socioeconomic range of the population living in apartments located primarily within large metropolitan areas, Greenfield came to the realization that the firm's expansion strategy had to branch out to include both the suburban and retirement communities. With the $1.5 billion sofabed market continuing to grow at a dramatic rate, Jennifer Convertibles clearly did not want to be beaten by its competitors. Consequently, at the beginning of 1990 the company announced plans to expand into six carefully chosen markets, including Florida. Florida was specifically chosen as an expansion site due to the fact that many retirees live or own second homes in the state and, of course, have many uses for the kinds of merchandise sold by Jennifer Convertibles. At approximately the same time, management at the firm announced that it had reached an agreement to license 20 Jennifer Convertible stores in the greater Chicago metropolitan area. The agreement, concluded in 1991, was the first of its kind for the specialty retailer, and provided the company with exposure to the growing sofabed market in the Midwest.

In 1993, Jennifer Convertibles announced both to the public and company shareholders that it was embarking upon an experiment to expand the current sofabed operation. This experiment, according to Greenfield, involved opening brand new retail stores that sold regular furniture and accessories. These stores were to be divided into two retail groups, including one called Elegant Living, and the other called Jennifer Leather. Elegant Living stores would specialize in upholstered living room furniture, while Jennifer Leather would specialize in upscale leather furniture and accessories. Owned by licensees who paid a two percent royalty on sales, the first stores opened their doors for business during the same year on Long Island. Greenfield was confident that the two new types of retail stores under the Jennifer Convertibles umbrella would be lucrative, since he pointed to ample evidence that suggested the market for regular sofas was approximately four times larger than that of sofabeds, while the market for leather furniture was about equal to that of sofabeds. In addition, it was the owners hope that both the Elegant Living stores and the Jennifer Leather stores could expand across the United States.

At the end of fiscal 1993, Jennifer Convertibles seemed to be on the edge of one of the most impressive success stories in American business. Sales continued to increase, more and more stores were added to the company's licensee operations, and the firm's marketing campaign indicated that even greater revenues were on the horizon. Then, suddenly, the company's momentum came to a grinding halt. Although sales and royalties were up significantly during the autumn of 1994, the company reported a serious loss for the entirety of the year. Consequently, the firm's stock price dropped precipitously, from $15⅞ to $3⅛ after the report was made public. After shareholder lawsuits were filed against the company, the Securities and Exchange Commission announced that it was conducting an informal inquiry into the financial records and business dealings of Jennifer Convertibles with an affiliated private business named Jara Enterprises, Inc. Jara Enterprises was also founded by Greenfield, Love, and Seidner. The company helped Jennifer Convertibles to select store sites and arrange limited partnerships for Jennifer stores that were about to be opened. Jara provided these services to Jennifer on a contractual basis and for clearly stated fees. A former member of the board of directors, Michael Colnes, accused Greenfield, Love, and Seidner of numerous examples of misconduct, including undisclosed transactions, self-dealing, and providing misleading information to the board of directors at Jennifer Convertibles. In May 1995, the Securities and Exchange Commission upgraded its inquiry from an informal investigation to a formal investigation.

Shedding the Past, Facing the Future

After years of examining the financial records of both Jennifer Convertibles and Jara Enterprises, Inc., the Securities and Exchange Commission ended its investigation in October 1998 without recommending any enforcement or legal action. As a result, all the class actions that had been brought against the company were settled in a federal district court of New York. Under the terms of the settlement, certain individuals were to receive approximately $7 million in cash and nearly $400,000 in preferred stock. Although the company continued to grow during the years of investigation and lawsuits, nonetheless, the firm's stock price was affected by the cloud of unfavorable publicity and by the prospect of an uncertain future. Yet once the announcement was made by the Securities and Exchange Commission not to recommend legal action, Jennifer Convertibles entered upon a period of revitalization and renewal. Revenues began to slowly increase, and management's strategy of expanding the number of Jennifer stores into new geographical locations progressed gradually but smoothly.

With its legal problems over, and the accompanying publicity no longer at the forefront of management's concern, Jennifer Convertibles was beginning to recover the momentum it had created during the early 1990s. The company had made a concerted effort to renew its expansion strategy into both Florida and the Midwest, especially around the Chicago metropolitan area. Harley J. Greenfield, still CEO, was confident that the company had weathered its worst storm, and that Jennifer Convertibles would now enhance its image as one of the largest retailers of sofabeds in the United States.

Principal Competitors

Haverty Furniture; Heilig-Meyers, Inc.; IKEA; Macy's Department Store; Dayton-Hudson, Inc.

Further Reading

Ariane, Sains, "Jennifer Convertibles Looks Hard at Who Sleeps Where and Why," *AdWeek's Marketing Week,* August 28, 1989, p. 26.

"Jennifer Convertibles Inc.," *Wall Street Journal,* January 11, 1993, p. A9A(E).

"Jennifer Convertibles Rebuts Claims by a Former Director," *Wall Street Journal,* April 11, 1995, p. B4(E).

"Judge Approves Settlement of Suits Against Company," *Wall Street Journal,* December 1, 1998, p. B11(E).

LaFemina, Lorraine, "Inquiry into Jennifer Convertibles," *Business News,* January 9, 1995, p. 3.

"Probe Begun in May 1995 by the SEC Is Terminated," *Wall Street Journal,* October 13, 1998, p. A6(E).

"S.E.C. Inquiry on Jennifer," *New York Times,* December, 15, 1994, p. D6(L).

"Twenty Licensed Jennifer Units Due in Chicago," *Weekly Home Furnishings Newspaper,* July 29, 1991, p. 6.

—Thomas Derdak

Johnny Rockets Group, Inc.

15635 Alton Parkway, Suite 350
Irvine, California 92718
U.S.A.
Telephone: (949) 789-7575
Fax: (949) 789-7588
Web site: http://www.johnnyrockets.com

Private Company
Incorporated: 1986
Employees: 2,600
Sales: $115 million (1999 est.)
NAIC: 722110 Full Service Restaurants

Johnny Rockets Group, Inc.'s restaurants offer American nostalgia with a menu of basic American food, served in a 1940s-style diner complete with an open chrome kitchen, a chrome and black formica counter, red vinyl seats, and counter-top jukeboxes that play old tunes for a nickel. The restaurants' signature items are its four hamburgers: "The Original," a hand-shaped hamburger; "The Double," with two patties, cheddar cheese, and a special sauce; "#12," with cheddar cheese and "red, red sauce"; and "St. Louis," with bacon, Swiss cheese, and "St. Louis" sauce. The balance of the menu consists of a few "classic" sandwiches, such as a BLT, a hot dog/chili dog, "American Fries," chili, and few other items. Malts and shakes are hand-dipped and come with an extra serving on the side in the mixing canister, just like the old diners used to do. Beverages include Coca-Cola flavored with cherry, chocolate, or vanilla. Apple pie, baked fresh on the premises, is available with ice cream or Tillamook cheddar cheese and is served with a small paper American flag.

A Company Founded on a Dream

Ronn Teitelbaum founded Johnny Rockets in 1986, at the age of 46, after selling his successful, Beverly Hills-based chain of fine men's clothing stores. Though he had no experience in the restaurant business, it had been his dream to own and operate a 1940s-style diner. Teitelbaum's restaurant reflected the nostalgia he felt for his own childhood memories of the 1940s, such as the friendliness and the cleanliness of old-time diners, but his idea also coincided with a surge in "retro" dining concepts.

Teitelbaum took a year and a half to plan his first Johnny Rockets burger and malt shop, using the same attention to detail that he gave to his men's clothing business. Teitelbaum sought to recreate the hamburger of his childhood memories. He cooked hamburgers with a number of seasoning combinations until he found the right flavor. A favorite employee story exemplified the extremes Teitelbaum took to attain perfection in every detail. After Teitelbaum had eaten a delicious tuna fish sandwich at a Los Angeles restaurant, he returned to the restaurant with a flashlight after hours and looked in the dumpster for an empty tuna can to see which brand the company used.

Teitelbaum's $250,000 restaurant project encompassed an 844-square-foot malt shop with 20 red vinyl stools. Skeptical friends and restaurant business consultants thought that the small-scale concept could not succeed. They assumed that peak meal times would require too long of wait and that the shop could not maintain an adequate level of business during slow business hours, between lunch and dinner, and late at night. In addition, the high-fat menu, with hamburgers, fried potatoes, and ice cream shakes, did not fit the stereotype of the Californian's preference for salad and pasta.

The moment Johnny Rockets opened on chic Melrose Avenue in Los Angeles, customers filled the restaurant, and a line of 30 customers formed at the door. The wait staff, dressed in white, 1940s-style "soda jerk" uniforms, mixed malts on 30-year-old spindle mixers (which required frequent repair) and supplied nickels to customers to play the vintage countertop jukeboxes. Instead of using a machine that would squeeze the juices from the fresh ground beef, kitchen staff hand-patted hamburgers and cooked them to order. The burgers were served wrapped in paper on a cardboard plate. Outside the restaurant, above the smooth white exterior, a 1940s-style logo blazed, "Johnny Rockets," in yellow neon on a red and blue lighted background. On its first day of business, June 6, 1987, Johnny Rockets stayed open until 5:00 a.m. to serve all of the day's customers.

Attracting a panoply of Los Angeles residents of all ages, the restaurant sustained a continuous flow of customers in the days

Company Perspectives:

Johnny Rockets maintains a dedication to the integrity, high standards, and ongoing attention to detail that has become its hallmark. Reasonable prices, snappy, happy service, and a simple menu of nostalgic favorites—that's the winning combination that keeps our guests coming back time and time again.

that followed. Business hours spanned from 11:00 a.m. to 12:00 midnight except Fridays and Saturdays, when the shop stayed open until 2:00 a.m. The high turnover cycled at approximately every 30 minutes. Johnny Rockets served 600 to 700 customers per day, involving around 19 percent takeout sales. With customers spending more than $5.00 each, revenues reached $1 million the first year.

Within the first year of operation Johnny Rockets grew into a small chain with franchises and company-owned stores. In the Los Angeles area, restaurants opened in Westwood, Sherman Oaks, and Beverly Hills. Franchises in Atlanta and San Francisco resulted when interested parties approached Johnny Rockets to license the concept. Johnny Rockets restaurants also opened in Minneapolis and Chicago. In an article in the October 24, 1988 *Nation's Restaurant News,* Teitelbaum attributed the success of Johnny Rockets to his own inexperience in the restaurant business, stating, "I didn't know it was impossible to do over $1 million in 20 seats. I didn't know people wouldn't line up at midnight for a hamburger, fries, and a malt."

With intentions to further expand the chain Teitelbaum sought to protect the Johnny Rockets trade dress. The company won the first of its trademark-related cases in New York in August 1989. Despite the objections of Teitelbaum, the Johnny Rock-it bar and grill opened in New York City in early 1989. Teitelbaum contended that the value of the Johnny Rockets name was undermined, and he supported that view with the deposition of a prospective franchisee reluctant to open a Johnny Rockets restaurant in New York because of concern that the similar name would cause confusion. Trademark infringement precedents helped win a federal injunction that prevented the lounge from using "Johnny" or "rock" in its new name. The company also filed suit against Suzy Q's diners in Winnipeg, Manitoba for trade dress violation.

Johnny Rockets expanded internationally, capitalizing on the appeal of American popular culture abroad. Teitelbaum used a business connection from his clothing business to open a Johnny Rockets restaurant in Tokyo in September 1989. City Centre Restaurants, which operated a variety of casual dining chains in London, opened a Johnny Rockets there in 1990. In addition, a prospective franchisee approached the company to open a Johnny Rockets in Melbourne, Australia, which went into development at this time. By June 1992 the company had expanded to 28 stores in the chain, with six company-owned units and 22 franchises.

The Johnny Rockets dining concept found many believers, including Lloyd Sugarman. Originally senior vice-president of Johnny Rockets, Sugarman acquired ownership of the first San Francisco restaurant, a 42-stool location in the Marina, as well as franchise rights to the San Francisco Bay area. Sugarman boosted growth in northern California with two new shops in the summer of 1992, while negotiations for locations in San Jose, Santa Rosa, and Fisherman's Wharf in San Francisco progressed.

Sugarman attained the Fisherman's Wharf location with some difficulty, but it would set a significant precedent for the company. The city of San Francisco did not allow fast food restaurants at Fisherman's Wharf, in an effort to retain the historical integrity of the area. The city did allow a Johnny Rockets malt shop, however, as cooked-to-order hamburgers and made-to-order shakes differed from fast food restaurants, which precooked sandwiches to be available upon request and dispensed premixed shakes. The issue defined the market niche that Johnny Rockets occupied, between fast food and casual dining restaurants. That niche served customers who had grown weary of fast food, who wanted full service and an inexpensive, fresh-cooked meal. Johnny Rockets accommodated that customer base with quick food preparation, but further distinguished itself with wait people who were known to suddenly break into song and dance routines using ketchup bottles as microphones. Johnny Rockets' wait staff learned as many as nine dance routines, to such old songs on the countertop jukeboxes as "Great Balls of Fire" and "Respect."

Expansion and Leadership Changes in the 1990s

In mid-1992 the company opened a new burger and malt shop every three to four weeks. The chain expanded in Southern California with new stores in Encino and Agora Hills in August 1992. New franchises opened around the United States, in Miami; Baltimore; Scottsdale, Arizona; Sunriver, Oregon; and Burlington, Massachusetts. Unit-level sales averaged $850,000 annually with only 20 to 26 seats. Expansion of the chain required experienced leadership in franchise development, and Ray Cabana, formerly of Taco Bell and Kentucky Fried Chicken, became president in June 1992. Teitelbaum remained chairman and CEO.

Growth at Johnny Rockets meant the company confronted challenges to its identity. Teitelbaum set a new precedent for the Mexican government's acknowledgement of international franchise law after an imitation of Johnny Rockets appeared in Cancun, Mexico. The company won the case and government officials shut the place down at gunpoint, just in time for the debut of Johnny Rockets in Mexico City in April 1993. Another situation occurred two days before the grand opening of a Johnny Rockets restaurant at West Edmonton Mall, the world's largest shopping mall at that time, in Alberta, Canada. McDonald's of Canada obtained an injunction to prevent the opening. The agreement between McDonald's and the mall owner, Triple Five, stated that no other fast food restaurant in the Phase II area could serve hamburgers, except in the food court. Johnny Rockets used the Fisherman's Wharf store as an example of the company's identity as a full-service restaurant. In June an Alberta Court dismissed the argument by McDonald's of Canada, which identified Johnny Rockets as a fast food restaurant, and lifted the injunction.

Teitelbaum's ambitions to expand the Johnny Rockets chain prompted negotiations with Carpenter Investment and Develop-

Key Dates:

1987: First shop opens on Melrose Avenue in Los Angeles.
1989: Period of rapid expansion ensues, including a Johnny Rockets in Tokyo.
1995: New ownership by Carpenter Investment and Development Corporation.
1998: 100th Johnny Rockets unit opened in The Georgetown area of Washington, D.C.
1999: Michael Shumsky named CEO.

ment Corporation (CIDC), whose primary activities involved hotel and shopping center development. CIDC would aid the growth of Johnny Rockets with its knowledge of city centers and shopping malls, as well as its affiliations with shopping malls and with the Hilton and Hyatt hotels. In June 1994 CIDC agreed to acquire a majority interest in Johnny Rockets International, as the company was called then. Internal disputes at Johnny Rockets slowed the transition to CDIC ownership, however. Rockets Holding Inc., which formed to handle the acquisition, had to negotiate separate terms of sale with Teitelbaum and Alfred M. Bloch, another majority stock owner.

In the immediate interim Johnny Rockets continued to grow and succeed. When Johnny Rockets won the 1994 Golden Chain award from *Nation's Restaurant News,* the company encompassed 63 units including five in Australia, three in Mexico, and one each in Japan, England, and Canada. Customer checks averaged $6.50 per person. Rare changes to the menu involved the addition of a peanut butter and jelly sandwich to the children's menu and the addition of a vegetarian burger, the "Streamliner," to the regular menu. In April 1995 Johnny Rockets signed an agreement to place a restaurant on the main floor of the casino at the Hilton Casino Resort in Reno, Nevada. The menu included breakfast to accommodate all night and early morning gamblers. Internationally, new stores opened in Kuwait and in the United Arab Emirates in 1995.

CIDC completed its acquisition of Johnny Rockets in November 1995 and named the new company Johnny Rockets Group (JRG). JRG held a 95 percent ownership, with the balance owned by Teitelbaum and a group of small investors. The majority investors included Patricof & Company Ventures, Inc. of New York with $12.5 million invested, General Motors Pension Fund with $10 million, Center Partners of New York with $6 million, as well as CSK Ventures, Tokyo, and CIDC. A total investment of $44 million involved $25.6 million paid to previous investors, $12 million for expansion, and $4.4 million to acquire five franchises.

New ownership was followed by a time of turbulent changes in leadership. With the formation of JRG, Teitelbaum remained on the board of directors and became the company's creative consultant. JRG hired Jeffrey Campbell, former CEO and chairman of Burger King, as the new CEO. Cabana retained the title of CEO, although he reported to Campbell until he eventually resigned. Campbell resigned in July 1996 because of disagreements over strategy, in regard to the pace of development of new stores, and management, in regard to whether to franchise or open company-owned units. Glen Hemmerle became president of JRG in February 1997. He brought retail experience with Pearle Vision, Crown Books, and Athletes Foot, but no restaurant experience. Hemmerle's strong customer orientation led to the addition of a hot fudge sundae, lemonade, and a hot dog/chili dog to the menu.

Hemmerle became president during a surge in expansion. The earlier internal disputes slowed long-term growth, with only two restaurant openings from 1995 until February 1997, compared with 20 restaurants from mid-1994 into 1995. In addition, some restaurants closed, such as the Sherman Oaks, California store, because of the 1994 earthquake, and the Laguna Beach, California store, because of the 1997 floods. Some stores in Australia closed as well, because of poor locations chosen by subfranchisees. Finally, in February 1997 JRG opened four new malt shops, in Miami, Boston, Memphis, and Birmingham.

JRG opened a total of 14 stores in 1997 and 1998 with the assistance of $15 million in venture capital that the company received in spring 1997. JRG sought to develop company-owned stores in three kinds of locations: neighborhood outlets that would attract local residents, unusual locations like the casino at the Reno Hilton, and high-traffic shopping areas. The company preferred mall locations near movie theaters, because it combined two distinctly American inventions—the diner and the movies. New stores in 1998 included openings at Providence Place Mall in Rhode Island and at Downtown Plaza Mall in Sacramento, a 2,200-square-foot store next to the movie theaters. In October 1998 JRG opened its 100th unit, in historic Georgetown in Washington, D.C. In addition, after four years in development, a Johnny Rockets opened in Beirut, Lebanon. The restaurant's interior was constructed in London, shipped to Lebanon, and snapped together at the site. The interior could be relocated if necessary.

In May 1999 Hemmerle suddenly resigned, and JRG immediately replaced him with Michael Shumsky, former president of Sonic Restaurants, a 2,000-unit drive-in restaurant based in Oklahoma City. JRG chose Shumsky because of the similarity of the Johnny Rockets and Sonic restaurant concepts and Shumsky's experience in franchise development. Shumsky would provide needed leadership, as JRG had decided to grow through franchises rather than through company ownership, as well as stability, with Shumsky's agreement to a five-year contract.

Strategy and Identity in Focus in 1999

Shumsky intended to focus on brand development, store-level operations, and market development. Though same store sales increased six percent during the fiscal year ended May 2, 1999, systemwide sales showed lower than expected revenues as some larger stores did not attain the same customer appeal as small, intimate stores. In addition, Shumsky found that JRG did not have a store prototype, and he planned to develop one based on the smaller units, which seated from 20 to 65 customers. New stores would be located in areas where Johnny Rockets malt shops already existed, mainly California, Florida, and New York, at an average cost of $575,000. Shumsky prepared JRG for new development with two new positions, regional vice-presidents of the eastern and western United States. Shumsky hired Pamela Britton, from Cinnabon, for the east, and Barry Cook, from Sonic Restaurants, for the west.

To sharpen Johnny Rockets brand identity, an art program was embarked upon. David Willardson, known for his posters for the movies ''American Graffiti'' and ''Raiders of the Lost Ark,'' produced ten oil paintings that featured Johnny Rockets' signature menu items, as well as its logo. The paintings then replaced some of the older pictures that hung at Johnny Rockets restaurants.

JRG cooperated with Warner Brothers in a movie promotion for the animated feature film, ''The Iron Giant,'' during the summer of 1999. The storyline of the movie centered on a single mother employed as a wait person at a 1950s-style malt shop. For the first three weeks after the movie's release, Johnny Rockets wait staff gave a comic book or cassette tape to each child customer. The promotion involved the sale of Johnny Rockets promotional items at Warner Brothers retail outlets, including t-shirts, sweatshirts, and caps with the Johnny Rockets logo in embroidery. A compact disc of old tunes from Johnny Rockets' jukeboxes, such as ''Stand By Me'' and ''Under the Boardwalk,'' was also among the company's promotional items.

With more than 120 restaurants in 25 states, Washington, D.C., and seven countries, JRG's plans for expansion in late 1999 involved 35 new units. Johnny Rockets' franchisee in Mexico opened a new store in Cancun in August and planned another for that city. In November 1999 Johnny Rockets became the first branded restaurant chain to be located on a passenger cruise ship. An agreement with Royal Caribbean International placed a 259-seat Johnny Rockets malt shop on the pool deck of its new cruise ship, Voyager of the Seas.

Principal Competitors

Dave and Buster's; Hard Rock Cafe; Ruby's Diner.

Further Reading

Acle Chasko, Ana, and Raul Ruberia, ''At Johnny Rockets, Entertainment Costs a Nickel,'' *Miami Herald,* December 11, 1994, p. 4.

Apodaca, Patricia, ''Venture Capital Financing Nearly Doubles,'' *Los Angeles Times,* September 17, 1997, p. 10D.

Ballon, Marc, ''Johnny Rockets Names Shumsky as New CEO,'' *Los Angeles Times,* May 27, 1999, p. 6C.

Barnes, Tom, and Dan Fitzpatrick, ''Pittsburgh Unveils Plans for Retail Development at Heart of City,'' *Knight-Ridder/Tribune Business News,* October 5, 1999, p. OKRB992780FF.

Battaglia, Andy, ''Johnny Rockets's Success Takes Off; Chain Launches 100th Unit,'' *Nation's Restaurant News,* October 12, 1998, p. 102.

Beck, David, L., ''Johnny Rockets Knows Its Burgers,'' *San Jose Mercury News,* September 29, 1995, p. 53.

''Campbell Resigns Johnny Rockets Prexy, CEO Posts,'' *Nation's Restaurant News,* August 5, 1996, p. 156.

Correa, Tracy, ''Fresno, Calif, Shopping Center To Add Restaurants, Retailers,'' *Knight-Ridder/Tribune Business News,* August 18, 1999, p. OKRB9923007F.

''Corrections'' (to February 24, 1997 article), *Nation's Restaurant News,* March 24, 1997, p. 4.

Durman, Paul, ''City Centre Beats Second-Half Blues,'' *Independent* (London), April 10, 1991, p. 25.

Glover, Kara, ''Investor Group Acquires Johnny Rockets,'' *Los Angeles Business Journal,* November 6, 1995, p. 10.

Greenberg, Herb, ''What's Mickey Drexler Doing When He's Not Running Gap? He's Got His Mind and Lots of Money on Johnny Rockets,'' *San Francisco Chronicle,* September 6, 1996, p. E1.

Hardesty, Greg, ''Irvine, Calif.-Based Johnny Rockets Embarks on New Marketing Campaign,'' *Knight-Ridder/Tribune Business News,* June 18, 1999, p. OKRB991690B5.

——, ''Retro-Look Restaurant Chain Changes Leadership at Key Stage,'' *Knight-Ridder/Tribune Business News,* May 25, 1999, p. OKRB99145115.

Hernandez, Greg, ''Johnny Rockets To Drop Art Used in Rival Ruby's Chain,'' *Los Angeles Times,* June 23, 1999, p. 6C.

''Investors Finalize Majority Buyout of Johnny Rockets,'' *Nation's Restaurant News,* November 6, 1995, p. 2.

''Johnny Rockets Adds Operations VPS,'' *Supermarket News,* September 6, 1999, p. 30.

''Johnny Rockets Debuts in Hilton,'' *Nation's Restaurant News,* April 3, 1995, p. 11.

''The Johnny Rockets Group, Inc. Appoints Two New VPs of Operations for East and West Coasts,'' *PR Newswire,* July 30, 1999, p. 2590.

''Johnny Rockets Investor Ignites Unit Expansion,'' *Nation's Restaurant News,* June 20, 1994, p. 2.

''Johnny Rockets Launches Cruise Ship Restaurant,'' *Nation's Restaurant News,* September 13, 1999, p. 60.

Johnson, Greg, ''Noshing on Nostalgia Is Big with Consumers and Developers,'' *Los Angeles Times,* February 4, 1996, p. 1.

Lipson, Larry, ''Dine Beat: New links in Chains,'' *Los Angeles Daily News,* July 10, 1992, p. L45.

Lockwood Tooher, Nora, ''Proposed Providence, RI, Mall Announces Names of Its Restaurants,'' *Knight-Ridder/Tribune Business News,* April 29, 1998, p. OKRB98119116.

Loyie, Florence, ''Johnny Rockets Restaurant Finally Blasts Off; Diner Rockin' at West Edmonton Mall After Court Lifts Injunction Sought by McDonald's,'' *Edmonton Journal,* July 16, 1993, p. B3.

Martin, Richard, ''Diner Days Add to Nostalgia Craze,'' *Nation's Restaurant News,* August 29, 1988, p. F11.

——, ''Hot Johnny Rockets Lifts Off; Newest Entry in Rock 'n' Roll Diner Revival,'' *Nation's Restaurant News,* February 2, 1987, p. 1.

——, ''Johnny Rockets Founder Sues To Oust Prexy, Break Sale Block,'' *Nation's Restaurant News,* October 10, 1994, p. 2.

——, ''Johnny Rockets Names Taco Bell/KFC Vet Prexy,'' *Nation's Restaurant News,* June 29, 1992, p. 3.

——, ''Johnny Rockets Taps Retail Vet Hemmerle as President,'' *Nation's Restaurant News,* February 24, 1997, p. 3.

——, ''Johnny Rockets Wins NY Copycat Injunction,'' *Nation's Restaurant News,* August 21, 1989, p. 3.

——, ''McDonald's Scrubs Johnny Rockets' Canadian Launch,'' *Nation's Restaurant News,* May 10, 1993, p. 11.

——, ''Rockets' Kingpin Oust Teitelbaum; Boardroom Shakeup Rocks Chain,'' *Nation's Restaurant News,* November 7, 1994, p. 1.

——, ''Ronn Teitelbaum: Riding on His Own Set of Rules,'' *Nation's Restaurant News,* September 19, 1994, p. 178.

Mehegan, Sean, ''From Burger King to Rockets' Man,'' *Restaurant Business,* March 1, 1996, p. 118.

Montgomery, Christine, ''Take Rockets Back in Time: Food, Decor from the 1950s,'' *Washington Times,* April 8, 1999, p. 6.

''The Old Fashioned Corner Malt Shop Comes of Age,'' *San Francisco Chronicle,* June 24 1992, p. B3.

Rogers, David K., ''Gap Store Among Tenants for Planned St. Petersburg, Fla. Downtown Plaza,'' *Knight-Ridder/Tribune Business News,* June 3, 1999, p. OKRB9915415A.

Sigo, Shelly, ''Comedy Club Owners Consider Ybor Close to Camelot,'' *Tampa Bay Business Journal,* August 27, 1999, p. 4.

Slater, Pam, ''Johnny Rockets Off with Sacramento, Calif., Hamburger Restaurant,'' *Knight-Ridder/Tribune Business News,* April 28, 1998, p. OKRB9811910A.

——, ''Nostalgic Eatery Rockets into Town Malt-Era Throwback for Downtown Plaza,'' *Sacramento Bee,* November 7, 1997, p. G1.

Spector, Amy, ''Johnny Rockets Taps Shumsky To Succeed Hemmerle as CEO,'' *Nation's Restaurant News,* June 7, 1999, p. 4.

Tannenbaum, Jeffrey A., ''Hamburger Chain Hopes Buyout Will Hasten Growth,'' *Wall Street Journal,* January 12, 1996, p. 12.

Telberg, Rick, ''Guts, Determination Key to Success as Restaurateur,'' *Nation's Restaurant News,* October 24, 1988, p. F46.

—Mary Tradii

Jos. A. Bank Clothiers, Inc.

500 Hanover Pike
Hampstead, Maryland 21074
U.S.A.
Telephone: (410) 239-2700
Toll Free: (800) 285-2265
Fax: (410) 239-5700
Web site: http://www.josbank.com

Public Company
Incorporated: 1945
Employees: 1,150
Sales: $187.16 million (1998)
Stock Exchanges: NASDAQ
Ticker Symbol: JOSB
NAIC: 44811 Men's Clothing Stores

Jos. A. Bank Clothiers, Inc., is a retailer of men's formal and casual wear with over 100 stores, mostly located in the Eastern and Midwestern United States. The company also sells through catalogs and via the Internet. Bank only sells the company's own branded lines of clothing, which are priced 20 to 30 percent lower than goods of comparable quality offered by competitors like Brooks Brothers and Polo. Since coming close to bankruptcy in the late 1980s following a leveraged buyout (LBO), Banks has been fine-tuning its marketing and expanding its retail locations with successful results.

Beginnings

Jos. A. Bank traces its origins to the end of the nineteenth century, when Lithuanian immigrant Charles Bank opened a small tailor shop in Baltimore, Maryland. In 1898 his grandson Joseph A. Bank joined the firm, which had evolved into a trouser manufacturing company. Joseph, who had started working at the age of 11 as a cloth cutter, had become a salesman over the next decade, and in 1912 he married Anna Hartz, a saleswoman for a rival company. He then joined forces with his new mother-in-law to form L. Hartz and Bank, which manufactured and suits in the Baltimore area and sold them at wholesale.

The company continued in this form over the next several decades, in 1940 purchasing a building in Baltimore to house its offices, showroom, cutting, and shipping departments. In 1945 Joseph Bank and his son Howard bought out the Hartz family interest, renaming the company Joseph A. Bank Clothiers. At this time the Banks decided to focus on making clothing for businessmen, in an ''understated, conservative'' style, as there was a shortage of men's formal wear following World War II.

Bank's move into retailing took place when Howard Bank began selling the company's suits out of the factory, initially hanging them for display on a pipe rack, as legend has it. Interest in retail sales was sparked, and the company reached an agreement with a store named Louie's in Washington, D.C., to market the company's goods. Out-of-town customers had also begun writing to request cloth swatches and to order clothes, and in 1960 a catalog was introduced to allow sales over a wider geographical area. The company continued to manufacture men's clothing for the wholesale market as well.

Beginning in the late 1960s more retail outlets were opened, with the location of catalog customers often giving the company an idea about where to open a new store. Bank's line of clothing continued to feature men's suits, which were well-manufactured and conservative in design. In 1977 the company branched out into women's professional clothing, introducing a line of skirts and suits.

Sale to Quaker Oats

In 1981 the Bank family, enticed by an offer of some $20 million, sold Jos. A. Bank to the Quaker Oats Company. At this time the company had 11 stores and several manufacturing facilities. Leonard Ginsberg, who had been with the company for a number of years, was retained as president. Under Quaker, Bank embarked on a campaign of expansion, opening 20 more locations within the next five years. Annual sales reached a peak of $112 million by 1986. Quaker, however, decided to get out of retailing and concentrate on its core strengths of food products and toys, and sold Jos. A. Bank and two other chains it owned in December of that year. Bank was purchased for $105 million in a leveraged buyout by a group that included McKinley Hold-

Company Perspectives:

Maximizing our opportunities within each of our four distribution channels, we are positioned to increase our profitability by opening new stores, increasing catalog sales, expanding corporate sales, and growing Internet sales. As styles and shopping preferences change in the years to come, we are well prepared to meet the demands of a dynamic marketplace and a highly diversified customer base. We are eagerly anticipating the possibilities of the coming century as we integrate all channels of distribution—enhancing the consistency of our message and the compatibility of selling channels for our customers. By supporting all channels of distribution and using each channel to educate our customers about the others, we will secure our position as a dominant men's clothing retailer for the 21st century.

ings, Eli S. Jacobs, and Bank management. Much of the financing came from Drexel Burnham Lambert.

Over the next several years Bank began to experience difficulties from both the debt generated by the LBO and soft sales from a weakening retail environment. In addition, the workplace was changing. The less formal style of the baby boom generation, which was moving into management, and the growing numbers of workers in computer industry, with its casual ethos, led increasing numbers of companies to relax their dress codes.

In 1988 CEO Leonard Ginsberg retired and was succeeded by David Waters, a veteran of Brooks Brothers and other major retailers. The company was still performing poorly, and losses continued to mount. In May 1989 Bank was restructured, and the company's lenders were given new bond notes and stock shares in exchange for accepting a delayed payment plan. McKinley Holdings, Jacobs, and Bank company management all essentially wrote off their investments, with one insider telling Warfield's that the purchase price had been $20 million too high. Bank reported a loss of $48 million for the year.

1990: Bank Nears Bankruptcy

In early 1990 the company's board proposed to the bondholders that they exchange their bonds for equity in Jos. A. Bank. The offer was rejected, and shortly afterward a number of senior managers left the company, including CEO Waters. Bank was now on the verge of bankruptcy, and the board sought out a crisis management company, The Finley Group, for help. Timothy Finley, founder and president of that company, agreed to take the reins of Bank and try to get it back on its feet.

Timothy Finley, age 47, had been an accountant for Cannon Mills and Deloitte, Haskins & Sells before founding his crisis management firm in 1985. One of his team of eight associates would take charge of failing companies, and, in a period typically ranging from 6 to 18 months, either nurse them back to health or liquidate their assets. Finley was known for his quick decision making, which he sometimes characterized with the motto, ''Ready, Fire, Aim.'' After examining Bank's situation, he came to the conclusion that its problems were not merely caused by the debt load of some $70 million, but by a loss of overall purpose and some bad marketing decisions. Though the company had always stood for quality at a fair price, it had recently been upgrading its stores into elegant, plush showrooms that gave customers the impression that the clothing cost more than it actually did. There were also production problems within Bank's factories, as well as other issues.

After taking charge, Finley quickly let 250 employees go, and also tried once more to renegotiate with the company's lenders. In 1991 an agreement was reached in which they took an equity stake in Bank in exchange for their bonds. As part of this arrangement, Finley agreed to stay on for three years, something he had never done before. To address the company's image and marketing problems, he hired Henry ''Chick'' Schwartz to serve as president and oversee merchandising. Schwartz, who had many years of clothing industry experience, set about lowering prices and adding more contemporary flair to the suits. The company also began to run national advertisements to build brand awareness outside of its Baltimore stronghold. Plans were soon being made to open additional stores in Florida, and move or upgrade others in Philadelphia, St. Louis, and Louisville, Kentucky.

In the summer of 1991, Bank moved its corporate headquarters from Owings Mills, Maryland, to its distribution warehouse in Hampstead, and instituted a new computer system for stores that enabled improved gathering of data on customer preferences. In the fall, the company introduced its own credit card, with General Electric Credit handling the operation of this service. Bank stores, which had featured other brand names along with Bank-made products, began to drop all but the company's own lines from the shelves.

In 1992 Bank opened a prototype store in Oak Brook, Illinois, which featured a modified ''Shaker'' look, as opposed to the fancier, upscale style that had been introduced in the late 1980s. The chain soon had the new design in five other stores of the 43 it owned, with more to follow. The cost of the simplified interior was half that of the more luxurious style it was replacing. For 1992 Bank reported sales of nearly $150 million and profits of close to $3 million, its first time in the black since 1989. In 1993 the company began to expand more aggressively, opening 11 more stores over the year in widespread locations including Kansas, Connecticut, and Texas.

Initial Public Offering Follows Return to Profitability

With its financial situation now stabilized and a renewed emphasis on growth, the company's management went to Wall Street to secure more capital for expansion. In May 1994 an initial public offering of two million shares of stock was made on the NASDAQ exchange, with an additional million shares sold by the lenders who had become part owners in 1991. The response from investors was mixed, with prices lower than expected, and the value of the stock declined over the following months.

The company kept refining its approach. Plans were made to open a small number of catalog stores in towns where full showrooms were not warranted, but which had shown a good response from customers ordering by mail. These 1,100-square-foot outlets displayed the company's wares but did not stock

Key Dates:

1905: Jos. A. Bank's grandfather Charles Bank formally establishes his clothing business.
1912: Joseph A. Bank forms L. Hartz and Bank Co. with his mother-in-law.
1945: Joseph and Howard Bank buy out Hartz's interest, company renamed Joseph A. Bank.
1950s: Company enters retailing at its Baltimore factory then at a Washington, D.C., store.
1960: Bank begins catalog sales.
1977: Women's clothing line introduced.
1981: Bank family sells company to Quaker Oat Co.
1986: Leveraged buyout by McKinley Investments and others.
1990: Bank, nearly bankrupt, hires Timothy Finley as crisis manager/CEO.
1994: Company goes public.
1995: Women's clothing dropped.

merchandise for sale. Customers could try on the styles and have their purchases shipped to them via overnight delivery. Catalog stores were opened in locations such as Portland, Maine; Bedford, New Hampshire; and Montgomery, Alabama. Bank was also considering introducing specialty catalogs that featured only certain types of clothing, such as ties or sportswear. The company was accelerating its development of the latter category for its stores to meet the demand brought on by "casual Fridays" in the business world. Availability of big and tall sizes was also being expanded.

In September 1994 Bank opened its first store in New York City, on the corner of 46th Street and Madison Avenue, just blocks from the flagship stores of many of its major competitors. The 9,000-square-foot showroom was expected to do as much as $8 million in business the first year. Radio advertisements for the new location featured the tag line, "There's no status in overpaying." The company's expansion plans had begun slowing down, however, and Bank announced that it would be opening fewer stores than previously expected so it could concentrate more on its catalog, which accounted for about 15 percent of sales. The catalog, which had been a useful source of information on where to open new stores, was also serving as a trend-spotter. Items such as vests, which showed sudden surges of catalog orders, were highlighted in stores with good results.

In early 1995 Chick Schwartz stepped down as president, and Finley added that job to his other duties. Several months later, in May, the company announced that it was dropping women's clothes from its lineup by year's end. Men's casual wear was expected to fill the space in stores, in a new department to be named Joe's Casuals. Bank's casual clothing was being purchased from outside suppliers, as was its women's line, rather than manufactured in its Baltimore and Hampstead, Maryland, plants.

In late 1995 Bank officials announced the closing of the Hampstead sewing factory and the loss of 100 jobs, as well as several store closings. The period since the stock offering had been a tough one, with national clothing sales declining and casual workplace trends increasing. The company reported losses for fiscal 1995 of $13.2 million, two-thirds of which were restructuring costs.

Sportswear Sales Spur Growth in the Late 1990s

1996 saw a turnaround in sales, however, with the expanded sportswear offerings doing particularly well, and the company managed a slim profit of $300,000. Bank had found a replacement for Chick Schwartz in Frank Tworecke, formerly of Merry-Go-Round stores, who was named president in September. The company also reached an agreement with golf pro David Leadbetter to feature his casual wear line in Bank stores.

In 1997 the company resumed its expansion, opening ten stores within a 12-month period. New locations were often added in existing markets so the company could get better bang for its advertising dollar. In February 1998 Bank announced it was selling its sole remaining factory, becoming the last major U.S. men's formal wear maker to leave this end of the business. M.S. Pietrafesa LP, the buyer, announced it would continue to operate the plant to produce clothing for Bank as well as other customers. Numbers for fiscal 1997 delivered more good news, with $2.5 million in profits reported on $172 million in sales.

In 1998 the company introduced a Web site where customers could order clothing, and additional stores were also opened. Over 100 were in business by year's end, located in 28 states and Washington, D.C. Ten were franchise outlets, while the rest were company-owned. Bank also established a Corporate Sales division, which sold monogrammed clothing and other products directly to businesses for use as gifts or as employee uniforms. In May 1999 Timothy Finley stepped down after nearly nine years as CEO. He was widely credited with saving Bank from the scrap heap.

Having weathered the crisis years that followed its leveraged buyout, as well as the change to more casual styles of business wear, Jos. A. Bank appeared to be back on solid ground. Under Timothy Finley the company had examined its operations from the ground up and had made significant improvements in many areas. As it neared the end of its first century in business, the company was in the best health it had been in over a decade, and looked ripe for continued growth.

Principal Subsidiaries

Joseph A. Bank Manufacturing Co., Inc.; National Tailoring Services, Inc.

Principal Competitors

Brooks Brothers; Dillard's, Inc.; Federated Department Stores, Inc.; Hartmarx Corporation; Land's End, Inc.; The May Department Stores Company; The Men's Wearhouse, Inc.; Nordstrom, Inc.; Phillips-Van Heusen Corp.; Polo Ralph Lauren Corp.; S&K Famous Brands, Inc.

Further Reading

Ariano, Alexis, "Jos. A. Bank Joins Ranks of Retailers Capitalizing on Online Shopping Growth," *Daily Record (Baltimore)*, February 1, 1999, p. 7A.

Bowie, Liz, ''A Seamless Commitment,'' *Baltimore Sun*, March 30, 1997, p. 1F.

D'Innocenzio, Anne, ''Finley's Bailout Plan: Re-Define Bank's Image,'' *Daily News Record*, March 28, 1991, p. 2.

Hall, Jessica, ''Bank's Fashions a Turnaround,'' *Daily Record*, March 22, 1994, p. 1.

——, ''Jos. A. Bank Public Offering Falls Far Short of Projections,'' *Daily Record*, May 4, 1994.

Hancock, Jay, ''Jos. A. Bank Adopts a More 'Casual' Approach,'' *Baltimore Sun*, December 1, 1994, p. 9C.

——, ''Jos. A. Bank Alters Line, Management,'' *Baltimore Sun*, March 16, 1995, p. 13D.

——, ''Jos. A. Bank: On the Mend,'' *Baltimore Sun*, May 22, 1994, p. 1D.

Hinden, Stan, ''Jos. A. Bank Clothiers Seeks a Suitable New Look,'' *Washington Post*, March 28, 1994, p. F29.

Krieger, Dale, ''Hanging by a Thread,'' *Warfield's*, February 1, 1991, p. 38.

Mayer, Caroline E., ''Bank Clothiers Is Fashioning Expansion Plans,'' *Washington Post*, April 11, 1988, p. F05.

Mirabella, Lorraine, ''Clothier Loses the Man Who Mended It,'' *Baltimore Sun*, May 22, 1999, p. 12C.

——, ''Jos. A. Bank Bets on Corporate Casual,'' *Baltimore Sun*, September 21, 1999, p. 1C.

——, ''Jos. A. Bank Sells a Plant, Ends an Era,'' *Baltimore Sun*, February 19, 1998, p. 1C.

Murray, Shanon D., ''Clothier Sells 2 Operations in City,'' *Baltimore Sun*, April 22, 1998, p. 1D.

Owens, Jennifer, ''You Can Take It to the Bank; Jos. A. Bank CEO Tim Finley Has Strong Growth Plans,'' *Daily News Record*, September 8, 1997, p. 7.

Palmieri, Jean E., ''Putting Jos. A. Bank Back in the Black,'' *Daily News Record*, December 27, 1993, p. 4.

——, ''The First Bank of New York: Jos. A. Bank Opens Its First New York Retail Store Today,'' *Daily News Record*, September 1, 1994, p. 8.

Pressler, Margaret Webb, ''Jos. Bank Suits up to Win in Retailing Fray,'' *Washington Post*, April 26, 1996, p. F05.

Singletary, Michelle, ''Jos. Bank Pins Turnaround Hopes on Ad Campaign,'' *Baltimore Evening Sun*, March 18, 1991, p. B1.

Sundius, Ann, ''Interview With the Chairman of Jos. A. Bank Clothiers from the Wall Street Forum Institutional Investor Conference'' [transcript], *MSNBC Private Financial Network*, June 24, 1997.

Wilson, Marianne, ''Jos. A. Bank Sharpens Image,'' *Chain Store Age Executive with Shopping Center Age*, October 1, 1992, p. 86.

—Frank Uhle

Kentucky Electric Steel, Inc.

U.S. Route 60 West
P.O. Box 3500
Ashland, Kentucky 41105
U.S.A.
Telephone: (606) 929-1222
Fax: (606) 929-1261

Public Company
Incorporated: 1963 as Kentucky Electric Steel Corporation
Employees: 421
Sales: $109.5 million (1998)
Stock Exchanges: NASDAQ
Ticker Symbol: KESI
NAIC: 331111 Iron and Steel Mills

Kentucky Electric Steel, Inc. is a steel minimill that melts scrap and turns it into bar flats. The bar flats, which are produced to a variety of specifications, are of two basic types: special bar quality (SBQ) and merchant bar quality (MBQ). Sales of SBQ bar flats account for approximately 80 percent of the company's total sales. These bars, which are manufactured in more than 2,600 varieties, conform to precise customer-ordered specifications in order to ensure that the customer's end product meets performance requirements. The remainder of Kentucky Electric's sales come from MBQ bar flats, which are used for more generic applications, such as metal buildings.

Kentucky Electric Steel's bar flats are used in a number of niche markets in the United States, Canada, Mexico, South America, and England. The majority of its sales are made to manufacturers of the leaf-spring suspensions used in trucks, trailers, minivans, and sport utility vehicles. Other major customers include steel service centers, truck trailer producers, and cold drawn bar converters—companies that draw steel bars through cutting dies to create bars of a specific tolerance.

1960s: From Scrap Yard to Minimill

Kentucky Electric Steel was formed by the Mansbach family, of Ashland, Kentucky—a small community in the northeastern part of the state near the Ohio border. The Mansbach's original business was a scrap metal yard. In 1963, however, the family decided to expand its scrap operation. Forming Kentucky Electric Steel Corporation, they began constructing a steel minimill.

The Mansbachs' decision to enter the steelmaking business was a timely one. Since 1960, minimills had been claiming an increasingly large share of the total domestic steel output. The smaller minimills, which made their steel from melted scrap, had several advantages over the large integrated steel makers, which produced steel by melting and processing iron ore. Operating on a much smaller scale and offering far fewer products, minimills had lower labor costs and higher productivity then the big steel makers.

Construction of the Kentucky Electric mill was completed in 1964; in 1965 the company began manufacturing its first products—steel rounds. The original mill was a fairly small operation. All the metal was melted in a single 20-ton electric arc furnace, and the molten metal was then poured into individual molds in order to shape it. After cooling, the metal ingots were run through a one-stand rolling mill, which compressed and refined them. The rolling mill was operated by workers called "tongmen," who fed the ingots through, then pulled them out, turned them, and sent them back through again. Once they had been rolled, they were sawed, stacked by hand, and banded as finished product.

In 1968, Kentucky Electric expanded its melting capacity by adding a second 20-ton electric arc furnace. It also added a baghouse—an air-pollution control device that captured particulate from waste combustion gases in filter bags. Even more significantly, the company began planning to install a two-strand continuous caster. The continuous caster cast molten steel into continuous strands, replacing the process of pouring the metal into molds. The new caster allowed the company to offer more flexibility in the lengths of its products.

The next item on the list of upgrades was the rolling mill. The company's improvements to the rolling mill meant that the bars no longer had to be hand-fed, cutting down on labor and greatly enhancing efficiency. With its new equipment and expanded capabilities, Kentucky Electric was able to add MBQ

Company Perspectives:

Our mission is to be a world class bar mill, world class in product quality and customer service.

flat bars to its product line. Although the company was successful, in the late 1960s the Mansbachs sold it to a California-based conglomerate.

1970s: New Products, Facility Upgrades

In the late 1970s, Kentucky Electric's new owners decided to begin production of SBQ flat bars. Producing SBQ bars was a much more involved process than producing MBQ bars or any of the mill's other products. To produce SBQ flat bars, the mill had to be able to add a variety of alloys to the metal to make different grades of steel. It also had to have a variety of specialized equipment in order to assure precision in the product's dimensions and chemistry.

The decision to expand into SBQ flat bars led to a $30 million improvement program, which the company called ''Project '80.'' Some of the Project '80 upgrades included the addition of a third strand to the continuous caster, two new 50-ton electric arc furnaces, and new mill stands to expand and complete the finishing mill. The project also called for a quality control testing facility, complete with state-of-the-art spectographic computer-controlled equipment. The addition of new process-control computers expanded the mill's metallurgical capabilities and maintained tighter tolerances.

In the years following Kentucky Electric's completion of Project '80, the company continued to upgrade the mill in a piecemeal fashion. Several new pieces of equipment were installed, which further improved efficiency and enabled greater precision in production. In addition, the company purchased 40 acres of land adjoining its existing facility, in preparation for anticipated future growth.

1980s: Ownership Change

The early and mid-1980s were difficult times for U.S steelmakers. High labor costs, overcapacity, and competition from imports had combined to depress profits industrywide. In addition, the U.S. was seeing a sharp decrease in the use of steel altogether; between 1978 and 1985, domestic consumption of rod and bar steel dropped by 20 percent. Although steel minimills had for years been able to operate more profitably than large integrated mills, by the mid-1980s they, too, were feeling the effects of the soft market. Unable to remain profitable, many began closing down.

Kentucky Electric Steel was no exception. In January 1985, the company's parent, Triton Group Ltd., discontinued operation of the mill—and a few months later, announced that it was closing the operation permanently. In an August 2, 1985 press release, Triton's President and CEO Ralph Briscoe said that conditions in the domestic steel industry had put Kentucky Electric in a non-competitive condition. He also announced that Triton was seeking a buyer for the mill.

A year later, Triton found its buyer. A group of four former managers of a steel mill in Newport, Kentucky, purchased the closed-down minimill for $7.3 million. Kentucky Electric was the second such mill acquired by the four partners. In 1981, they had banded together to acquire Newport Steel Works—their former employer—after its owner shut it down. After acquiring Kentucky Electric, the partners formed a holding company, NS Group, for its subsidiaries.

The company's new owners proved adept at turning around troubled steel mills. After absorbing $1.9 million in start-up costs to get operations up and running again, NS Group managed to return the mill to profitability within a year. In the first three quarters of 1987, Kentucky Electric's steel bars produced a $9 million profit on sales of $61.3 million. NS Group's earnings mounted throughout 1987, and in March 1988, the company went public. Its IPO generated $46 million—almost $10 million more than it had anticipated.

1990s: Independence

In the early 1990s, the NS Group's fortunes reversed. The company posted losses in 1991, 1992, and 1993, and accrued substantial debt. In 1993, attempting to improve its financial situation, NS decided to spin off its Kentucky Electric subsidiary as a public company. The new company, Kentucky Electric Steel, Inc., was capitalized in an initial public offering on October 6, 1993, and began trading on the NASDAQ under the ticker symbol KESI. At the time of its spinoff, Kentucky Electric had sales of approximately $90 million, net earnings of $5.5 million, and around 450 employees.

A year after becoming an independent company, Kentucky Electric initiated an ambitious $26 million capital improvements program designed to greatly expand the plant's capacity and modernize its operations. The program, called ''Project '94,'' was divided into two phases.

Phase I, which was completed in 1995, boosted capacity in several aspects of the company's steelmaking process. A fourth strand was added to the melt shop's continuous caster, increasing its casting capabilities to approximately 400,000 tons. A new billet transfer line allowed the mill to transport larger-sized bars to storage, and new rolling mill equipment enabled the completion of 400,000 tons of finished products. Project '94 also provided a new cooling bed that was 2.7 times larger than the previous one, and a new shear with a 54-inch cut and a 1,000-ton capacity. The previous shear had a 36-inch cut and a 400-ton capacity. Not only did the improvements allow KESI to produce *more* product, but they also allowed it to expand the size range of its bars. Before Project '94, the company was able to produce bars up to two inches in thickness and eight inches in width; after the project's completion, it was capable of making bars up to three inches thick and 12 inches wide. KESI hoped that its expanded product size ranges would serve to both enlarge the company's share of existing markets and enable it to enter new ones.

With the new equipment in place, the mill was able to finish more product in its rolling operation than it could produce in its melting shop. The company took steps to remedy that imbalance in Phase II of Project '94, which involved the installation of a ladle metallurgy station. The ladle metallurgy station,

Key Dates:

1964: The Mansbach family opens Kentucky Electric Steel Corporation.
1968: The Mansbachs sell Kentucky Electric to a California-based conglomerate.
1980: Kentucky Electric embarks on Project '80, a $30 million upgrade program.
1985: Unable to remain profitable in adverse market conditions, Kentucky Electric is shut down.
1986: Kentucky Electric is purchased by Newport, Kentucky-based NS Group.
1993: NS Group spins off Kentucky Electric as a public company.
1994: Kentucky Electric begins Project '94, another capital improvements program designed to enhance capacity and product line.

which began start-up operations in the fourth quarter of 1996, was the step between melting the metal and pouring it into the continuous caster. In the station, the molten steel was mixed with a variety of alloys to make different grades of steel—a process that had previously taken place in the electric arc furnaces. By removing the refining cycle from the furnace, the ladle metallurgy station reduced the amount of furnace time, thereby allowing more steel to move through the melt shop in a shorter period. The station also made for cleaner, more homogenous steel, and increased the number of grades that the mill could produce. The company sold 225,800 tons of finished goods in 1996, which amounted to 87 percent of its production capacity. Earnings were $58,000, on sales of $98.3 million.

In 1997, KESI inadvertently melted some radioactive scrap in its furnaces. The error caused a 12-day shutdown in its melt shop operations while a contractor tested and cleaned the mill's ductwork and baghouse. The company lost another ten days of production that same year, when the melt shop was shut down for caster superstructure repairs. The shutdowns hurt the company's financial performance. Its sales for 1997 decreased by $3.6 million from 1996's level—and it posted a net loss of $2.6 million.

In 1998, Kentucky Electric finally saw the fruits of its Project '94 labor. As productivity in the rolling and finishing operations improved through the year, the company set records in output. Sales for the year were up by almost 16 percent over 1997, and net income was $1.5 million. The productivity gains made in the company's finishing operation, however, meant that its melt shop remained unable to keep up. While the rolling and finishing facility could output approximately 400,000 tons of product annually, the melt shop's capacity was only around 300,000.

1999 and Beyond

One of Kentucky Electric's main goals for the future was to balance its overall capacity in both melting and finishing operations at around 400,000 tons. This, obviously, meant increasing the capacity of the melt shop. Toward that end, the company had begun testing a method of adding chemical energy to the electric arc furnaces. It was also planning an overhaul of both its furnaces and a replacement of some of its melt shop equipment. The company believed that the improvements, along with the increased energy to the electric arc furnaces, would increase the melt shop's output—thereby allowing the plant as a whole to operate at its full capacity.

Much of the company's future performance, however, hinged on conditions in the U.S. steel market. As 1999 drew to a close, domestic steelmakers faced heavy competition from lower-priced imports, which were claiming an increasingly large share of the U.S. market. The flood of cheap steel from foreign producers had driven down steel prices, hurt the industry's bottom line, and caused the loss of thousands of jobs. Kentucky Electric, like many steel mills, posted losses in the first half of 1999.

It appeared possible that the import situation would be ameliorated somewhat, however. Following a series of dumping charges against foreign steelmakers, the U.S. Commerce Department and International Trade Commission ordered punitive tariffs on several steel firms' imports. The government also signed agreements with Russia and Brazil that limited their steel imports and set price levels in exchange for a suspension of dumping tariffs. Those actions, and similar ones, were likely to prove beneficial to Kentucky Electric's business, as well as to the domestic steel industry in general.

Principal Subsidiaries

KESI Finance Company.

Principal Competitors

AK Steel Holding Corporation; AmeriSteel Corporation; Bethlehem Steel Corporation; Birmingham Steel Corporation; Cargill, Incorporated; Commercial Metals Company; Nucor Corporation; The LTV Corporation; Steel Dynamics, Inc.; Steel of West Virginia, Inc.; USX-U.S. Steel Group; WHX Corporation.

Further Reading

Hershberg, Ben, "Despite Steel's Woes, NS Group Forges Ahead," *Louisville Courier-Journal,* December 26, 1988, p. 10B.
Russell, Mark, "Steel Minimills Face Difficult Times," *Wall Street Journal,* September 4, 1985.
Rohan, Thomas, "Minimill Miracle Workers," *Industry Week,* October 16, 1989, p. 31.

—Shawna Brynildssen

KENWOOD

Kenwood Corporation

14-6 Dogenzaka 1-chome, Shibuya-ku
Tokyo 150-8501
Japan
Telephone: 011 81 3 5457-7111
Fax: 011 81 3 5457-7110
Web site: http://www.kenwoodcorp.com

Public Company
Incorporated: 1946 as Kasuga Radio Company
Employees: 2,600
Sales: US$2.6 billion (1999)
Stock Exchanges: Tokyo
NAIC: 42162 Electrical Appliances, Television, and Radio Set Wholesalers; 33431 Audio and Video Equipment Manufacturing

Kenwood Corporation is one of Japan's largest and most successful consumer-oriented electronics companies. The firm designs, manufactures, and markets a broad range of electronic consumer products for markets around the world, including such high-technology items as amplifiers, speakers, home and automotive audio products, receivers, CD players, cassette decks, high-end personal computer components, cellular phones, oscilloscopes, and mobile radios. Most of the firm's revenues come from the sale of audio equipment and products, but Kenwood's entry into new markets such as meteorological satellite receivers is garnering more and more revenue with each passing year. The company's brand name electronics products are among the most popular in the United States, and much of the firm's success can be attributed to the well-managed Kenwood USA Corporation subsidiary located in Long Beach, California. In addition to its U.S. presence, Kenwood also has manufacturing facilities and sales offices in numerous countries around the world.

Early History

Incorporated as Kasuga Radio Company in 1946, a young group of entrepreneurs had decided to take advantage of the growing market for postwar consumer products. Since much of Japan had been destroyed by the effects of World War II, the nation was eager and ready to re-create its national economy. One of the worldwide burgeoning markets included electronic equipment, so the Kasuga Radio Company was established in Nagano, Japan, to manufacture sophisticated high-fidelity electronic components and amateur radio equipment. Within a short time, the company was one of the leading electronic consumer products companies in the nation, and in 1949 Kasuga Radio Company made a major leap in technology-intensive manufacturing when it introduced the very first high-frequency transformer.

Throughout the 1950s, the company continued to develop innovative products for the electronic consumer products industry. Once again, in 1957, engineers at the company achieved a major innovative breakthrough in research with the development and manufacture of the first FM tuner in Japan. At approximately the same time, the company also began producing a wide range of precision test and measuring instruments, including such items as oscilloscopes, voltometers, and regulated DC power supplies. In order to reflect the values and efficiency of a modern company, management decided to change the name of the firm to Trio-Kenwood Corporation.

Fortunately, as the national economy of Japan expanded, Trio-Kenwood rode the wave of continuing economic prosperity and expansion. By the time the 1960s arrived, the company was poised to shift its operations from a national to an international focus. Having already completed a comprehensive strategic plan for expansion in the late 1950s, company management took its first step in 1963 with the establishment of Kenwood Electronics, Inc. in Los Angeles, California. The company was formed as a distributorship and began to market and sell Trio products under the exclusive brand name of Kenwood. The first Japanese firm operating in the United States under its own name, Kenwood within a few years would catapult to the top of the rapidly expanding consumer electronics market in the United States. At the same time, the company established major production and marketing subsidiaries in France, Belgium, Italy, West Germany, Canada, the United Kingdom, Australia, Hong Kong, and Singapore. By the mid-1960s, Trio-Kenwood was mass producing audio, communications, and test equip-

Company Perspectives:

Our goal is to create a lively, challenging corporate culture in which employees are proud to work. In terms of the company's philosophy, this translates into three corporate objectives: to have a vital, active organization; to take risks and meet new challenges; and to have a company that employees will find attractive.

ment around the world. By 1969, the firm had grown so large that it was listed on the First Section of the Tokyo Stock Exchange, and began selling shares of stock to the public.

As Trio-Kenwood expanded overseas, its engineering department continued to design and develop some of the most important electronic components within the industry. During the early 1960s, the company designed and manufactured a solid state amplifier, the first of its kind in Japan. This development signaled a major change within the electronics industry from the use of vacuum tubes to the widespread use of transistors. During the mid-1960s, the firm produced the world's first fully solid state amplifier, and very soon thereafter it began to eclipse the traditional tube amplifiers that had held a stranglehold on the electronics market for years.

Growth and Expansion

The decade of the 1970s was the best for the company in its history. Sales continued to increase, resulting in higher profits and more valuable stock prices. Trio-Kenwood's facilities around the world were manufacturing electronic consumer products at a dizzying pace. By the mid-1970s, Kenwood Corporation in the United States had captured over 70 percent of the amateur radio market in the country. What drove the company forward, however, was the innovative and creative genius of the engineers in its research and development department. In 1976, Trio-Kenwood introduced the first DC amplifier made in Japan and the first amplifier with dual power sources. In 1977, the company manufactured a 40-watt receiver that sold for less than $300, thus breaking a pricing milestone within the industry. Over the following two years, this model of receiver outsold all the other models on the international market. Also in 1977, Trio-Kenwood designed and manufactured both the direct-drive power amplifier, and a concrete turntable base which was widely regarded as eliminating mechanical and acoustical feedback.

During the late 1970s, company engineers did not rest on the achievements made in the mid-1970s. In 1978 alone, Trio-Kenwood designed, manufactured, and patented Hi Speed amplifiers that reacted almost instantaneously to high frequency inputs, patented a Pulse Count Detector tuner that significantly reduced FM distortion, and introduced Variable Bandwidth Tuning that narrowed the I.F. pass band. Not surprisingly, the efforts of the engineers within the research and development department did not go unrewarded that year. The company captured every major award for FM tuners in 1978, as well as having its KD-500 turntable named the best of its class. The year 1979 was just as productive. Trio-Kenwood introduced the first amplifier with multiple stage power sources, and the first Liquid Crystal Display, which was the very first microprocessor controlled hand-held radio of its kind within the growing field of electronic communications. During the same year, the company began to use non-magnetic material for manufacturing its large line of amplifiers and tuners, intending to diminish magnetic fields and distortions.

In the early 1980s, management committed Kenwood to developing car audio products both in Japan and in the United States. The company planned to market its car audio systems and component parts through auto accessories dealers, and this could not have been a better decision. From the beginning of its introduction of car audio products, such as its cassette deck receivers which were the first in the industry to offer automatic noise reduction and an automatic broadcast sensor system, sales skyrocketed. Before long the company was garnering even more awards from various design and engineering competitions. At the same time, Trio-Kenwood engineers were busy developing the world's first Audio/Visual amplifier and system, which had no competition for a full three years after its introduction in 1981. One year later, Trio-Kenwood made another leap into the future with the introduction and shipment of its first VCR.

The rest of the 1980s consisted of an impressive listing of company innovations within the consumer electronics industry. In 1982, the company introduced and sold its first CD player, and later that year the firm introduced the first solid state HF transceiver that was manufactured with a built-in antenna tuner. In another major breakthrough in 1983, Trio-Kenwood designed and manufactured the very first car stereo that included 24 presets. During the same year, the company also brought out its first land mobile radios. One of the most popular and lucrative products conceived by the engineering team was the first car stereo with a "Theft Prevention Chassis" that was designed to slide in and out of a automobile's dash board, thus breaking all electrical connections, include that of the antenna, but with no lasting, ill effects on the quality of sound or performance of the stereo.

In 1985, Trio-Kenwood introduced the first satellite receiving system, which brought significant attention to the company's research in advanced electronics technology. During the same year, company engineers designed and produced a new VIG-DLD circuit; the first car audio speaker to employ a honeycombed linear plane diaphragm in its design and manufacture; the very first car audio system that featured automatic volume reduction; and the company's first CD player designed and made specifically for the car, featuring a unique suspension that minimized road shock as much as possible. One year later, management at the company decided to change the firm's name in order to reflect a streamlined, efficient organization. Kenwood Corporation became the formal name of the firm and was also used for its brand name products.

By the late 1980s, Kenwood began to reap the rewards of its high-quality electronic products. In 1988 alone, Kenwood won awards for the best mobile security system, the best car CD player, the best cassette, the best tuner, the best amplifier, and the best equalizer. Throughout these years, the company's engineering and research department invariably won various design and engineering awards from a myriad number of associations, publications, consumer groups, and industry competitions.

Key Dates:

1946: Kasuga Radio Company is established in Nagano, Japan.
1955: Company plants in Tokyo are mass-producing audio, communications, and test equipment.
1957: Kasuga Radio Company changes its name to Trio-Kenwood Corporation.
1963: Kenwood USA Corporation is established in California.
1968: Listing on the First Section of the Tokyo Stock Exchange.
1980: Audio products for the car are sold in both America and Japan.
1983: Company introduces its first compact disc player.
1985: Satellite receivers are first marketed in the United States.
1986: Company changes its name from Trio-Kenwood to Kenwood Corporation.
1996: Kenwood revises marketing strategy and focuses on high-end segment of the market.

Perhaps even more important for the company, however, was the implementation of an aggressive overseas expansion strategy. Sales offices were established throughout Europe, with the larger operations in France and Belgium, while the offices already established in the United States and Canada moved to more spacious locations.

The 1990s and Beyond

During the 1990s, management at Kenwood continued to engage in an aggressive overseas expansion that had started a decade earlier. In 1993, the company entered into a joint agreement with a government firm located in Shanghai, China, to make compact component systems. In addition, management decided to open new offices in three of the major Chinese cities along the coast. The early 1990s also saw Kenwood expand rapidly in Israel, and by 1992 the company reported sales of over $10 million in that country. This success convinced Kenwood to introduce a series of innovative kitchen appliances for the following two years. In 1995, Kenwood acquired Ariete, a major Italian designer and manufacturer of upscale consumer appliances such as food processors, irons, and espresso machines. In 1996, the company announced that it would expand its existing manufacturing facility in Malaysia, near Johor, in order to double its production capacity for such items as home and car audio products, while at the same time Kenwood's U.S. subsidiary announced that it had finalized an agreement to establish a car audio manufacturing facility in Juarez, Mexico, to produce car amplifiers.

Although Kenwood had garnered a large share of the electronics consumer market by the mid- 1990s, competition was fierce, and there seemed no way for consumers themselves to distinguish the products of one company from another. In light of this development within the industry, management at Kenwood took it upon itself to implement a new marketing strategy to differentiate the company's home electronics products from competitors'. Consequently, Kenwood began to focus on the design and manufacture of new product lines. As a result, by the late 1990s the company had focused on the high-end segment of the market, and introduced such products as touch-screen remote control, home-theater sound features, and a new tuner that cost $2,800.

By most accounts, competition within the electronic consumer products industry was likely to grow increasingly intense. Yet Kenwood had a history of introducing innovative designs in a wide variety of product lines. As long as the engineering and research department at the company continued to introduce highly unique designs, it was very likely that Kenwood would remain one of the leaders in the industry.

Principal Subsidiaries

Linear Italiana, S.P.A.; Sofradore Trio-Kenwood (S.D.K.) S.A.

Principal Competitors

Samsung Electronics Co., Ltd.; Sony Corporation; Matsushita Electric Works, Ltd.; Aiwa Company Ltd.; Philips Electronics N.V.

Further Reading

''An Audio Revamp: Kenwood Pumping Up the High End,'' *Weekly Newspaper for the Home Furnishing Network,* January 22, 1996, p. 81.
Blackwell, David, ''Kenwood Likely to Win Vote,'' *Financial Times,* December 16, 1996, p. 12.
——, ''Kenwood to Close Its Main UK Factory,'' *Financial Times,* June 8, 1999, p. 24.
''Kenwood,'' *Television Digest,* August 30, 1993, p. 16.
''Kenwood Success in Israel,'' *Israel Business Today,* June 25, 1993, p. 8.
''Kenwood Will Expand Existing Production Base in Malaysia,'' *Television Digest,* January 2, 1995, p. 13.
Olenick, Doug, ''Kenwood's A-V Moves to Stage 3,'' *Weekly Newspaper for the Home Furnishing Network,* November 13, 1995, p. 73.
——, ''Surround Sound Chip Licenses,'' *Weekly Newspaper for the Home Furnishing Network,* October 2, 1995, p. 75.
Ryan, Ken, ''Kenwood's Spring Surprises,'' *Weekly Newspaper for the Home Furnishing Network,* March 8, 1993, p. 49.
''Seen and Heard,'' *Weekly Newspaper for the Home Furnishing Network,* January 2, 1995, p. 36.

—Thomas Derdak

The King Arthur Flour Company

P.O. Box 1010
Norwich, Vermont 05055
U.S.A.
Telephone: (802) 649-3881
Toll Free: (800) 827-6836
Fax: (802) 649-3323
Web site: http://www.kingarthurflour.com

Private Company
Incorporated: 1904 as Sands, Taylor & Wood Co.
Employees: 120
Sales: $22 million (1999)
NAIC: 311211 Flour Milling; 45411 Electronic Shopping and Mail-Order Houses

The King Arthur Flour Company celebrates its 210th anniversary in the year 2000. Founded in Boston, it is America's oldest flour company and the earliest food company in New England. The King Arthur Flour Company is the fifth-fastest-growing company in Vermont, as measured by its five-year employee growth, according to *Vermont Business Magazine.* The company is the number one seller of whole-wheat flour in New England, where it commands more than 80 percent of that market. The company's main product, King Arthur Flour, is a premium flour that outsells all other combined brands in New England by four to one. For many years this flour was available only in New England, but it is now sold in supermarkets throughout the Northeast and in select markets across the United States. It also is available nationwide by mail order from the company's *Baker's Catalogue* and from the company's web site. The team-managed company operates as four closely related divisions: a flour division, a bakery, a mail-order and on-line catalogue, and a retail store. As its slogan—"Never Bleached, Never Bromated"—implies, King Arthur Flour is a natural food containing no chemicals.

1790–1896: Postwar Troubles and Creation of a Premium Flour

The company's origins go back to 1790, seven years after the end of the American Revolutionary War and a year after the inauguration of George Washington. While the war prompted a boycott of English products, American colonists kept a taste for fine English flour. When the war ended and trade was resumed, Henry Wood—under the name of Henry Wood & Son—was one of the commission merchants (wholesalers or distributors) who distributed the flour brought by English ships to the Long Wharf in Boston's harbor. At the end of the 18th century, bread was still a basic dietary item for New Englanders, who ate much more bread than people do today, and Henry's company thrived.

In 1838 Henry Wood and a partner, George J. Cook, bought a flour company named Richards and Co. Two years later they were joined by salesman John Low Sands, who was the first of five generations of Sands to lead the company. As the years went by, deaths and departures from Richards and Co. brought in new partners and, consequently, changes to the company's name. By 1895 the company was owned in a limited co-partnership by Orin E. Sands (youngest son of John Low Sands), Mark C.Taylor, and George E. Wood. The company—renamed Sands, Taylor & Wood Co. (ST&W)—was incorporated on July 1, 1904, and kept that name for 95 years.

Freed from England, the colonists prospered as they resumed trading and shipping. Soon, however, the booming economy caused inflated land values and speculation. Furthermore, the climate of uncertainty and suspicion that followed the end of the Civil War contributed to a financial panic in New York in 1873. John Sands and his two sons, Benjamin and Orin, safeguarded the flour company's reputation for honesty and promoted its flour by pioneering advertisements in Boston streetcars.

When famine spread throughout Russia in 1891, demand drove wheat prices up and standards of quality deteriorated. Meanwhile, ST&W conducted many costly experiments to produce flour of the highest quality. When the company tried to find a name for this high-quality flour, George E. Wood recalled his reaction to a musical production titled *King Arthur and the Knights of the Round Table*. He had been impressed by how the legendary King Arthur defended and upheld the ideals of strength, purity, and honesty. These were precisely the ideals that George held for his company, where he felt a strong corporate structure was represented by honest salesmen, high standards assured quality products, and the new unbleached and unbromated flour was to be sold to all dealers at the same fair

Company Perspectives:

The most important things in business are confidence in the integrity of the men who manage it and the merchandise offered its patrons. This business was built on honor by its founders and will be so maintained. We seek wider knowledge, greater enthusiasm, more friendliness.

price. ST&W did not allow merchants to do any price-cutting and guaranteed the quality of each purchase.

King Arthur Flour was introduced at the Boston Food Fair in October 1896. The display at the fair was built to represent a castle, and, according to the *Boston Post* of November 14, 1896, ''a horseman clad in glittering armor and armed cap-a-pie [from head to foot]'' carried a standard bearing the words *King Arthur Flour* as he rode a black horse through the streets of Boston. The newspaper went on to say: ''the inference is obvious—that as King Arthur was a champion without fear and above reproach, so is King Arthur Flour the peerless champion of modern civilization.''

Early 20th-Century Events and the Flour Market

To assure the quality of King Arthur Flour, ST&W had to contend with a number of difficulties, including distance from agricultural centers, weather, world events, advances in technology, and government regulations. Initially, King Arthur Flour was made of only hard, red, spring wheat from Minnesota and Canada. This high-protein wheat produced more gluten, which absorbed moisture better, made yeast-baked goods rise better, and kept baked goods fresher for a longer time. Wheat crops, however, were very vulnerable to vagaries of the weather: hot, dry spells caused deterioration and diseases such as black rust. Nevertheless, ST&W continued to safeguard the quality of its flour, even if that meant paying premium prices for the best grade of wheat.

Henry Ford's invention of the farm tractor in 1915 helped farmers to raise more wheat, but the quality wheat on which ST&W depended was very expensive and in short supply because of exports to U.S. troops and to the European countries involved in World War I. By 1917 sales of King Arthur Flour had dropped 50 percent from sales in 1914, when the war began. At this time, ST&W was still selling wheat flour, rye flour, oatmeal, cornmeal, rice flour, and even soybean meal, among other products made from 13 different kinds of grains—products that were reminders of the company's origin as a wholesale distributor.

During the war, new technology and mass production changed the way business was conducted, and an era of prosperity created further divisions between rich and poor. After serving in the war, Donald Sands returned to work as general manager for his father, Frank E. Sands, who had helped in the early marketing of King Arthur Flour and been named president of the company in 1917. In 1922 demand for flour in the retail market had dropped—in 1914 housewives baked 60 percent of the bread consumed, as opposed to only 25 percent after the war—so ST&W began concentrating on its bakery business, which helped to increase sales.

In the 1930s, however, ST&W struggled to remain in business because of Congress's attempt to stabilize the economy by passing laws—such as the 1933 Agricultural Adjustment Act and the Farm Credit Act—that increased the price of available hard wheat. Furthermore, the U.S. Department of Agriculture established a processing tax for manufacturing wheat into flour. This tax was expected to yield about $150 million a year, part of which was to be given to the wheat growers who promised to reduce their wheat acreage. Historian Whitney Sands pointed out that when the tax was lifted, ''all the money collected as taxes had to be returned to the customers, mostly bakeries. Refunds were made at a great loss to ST&W, and it is generally believed that it was Donald's frustration over the situation that killed him'' at the age of 41. He was succeeded as general manager by his younger brother, Walter E. Sands.

Walter followed up on Donald's earlier suggestion for introducing King Arthur Flour to New York stores and established the King Arthur Coffee business in Boston. The company also began to sell King Arthur Wheat Germ and King Arthur Tea. Several other products appeared on the market during the next decade: King Arthur Biscuit Mix, King Arthur Farin-O-Gram, and King Arthur Whole Wheat Shreds. These products, relatively inexpensive and high in nutritional value, appealed to consumers in the throes of economic depression.

1944–66: More Inhibiting Legislation, Continuing Decline of Flour Sales

In 1944 Walter Sands was elected ST&W president; by 1963 his two sons, Frank E. Sands II and Robert Graham Sands, were helping to lead the company. During World War II and its aftermath, Walter was very vocal about the subsidy the government paid farmers and the high prices millers had to pay for wheat. In a 1944 article he wrote that ''The wheat subsidy [for the farmers] has changed our industry from a healthy American enterprise into a zombie of bureaucracy.'' He predicted that flour would become harder and harder to obtain because wheat was being used for feed and for making alcohol instead of being stored to take care of European needs after the war.

Walter's forecast proved to be accurate when, at the end of the war, many flour mills were shut down because wheat was being shipped to Europe in order to implement the United Nations' Refugee Relief Act—designed to feed the millions of people left homeless after World War II—and the Marshall Plan for funding the rebuilding of Europe. The price of wheat soared and supplies dried up. During these years of economic recession, wheat shortages, and government intervention, Walter kept the company free of debt and maintained its professional salesmanship. By 1963 ST&W held only six percent market share but upheld its high standards of quality even when it became necessary to notify customers that shortages of quality wheat prevented the company from filling any more orders.

As the radio grew in popularity, ST&W was quick to use that medium for promotion. In 1931 a company-sponsored radio show starring Marjorie Mills was broadcast in Massachusetts, Maine, Connecticut, and Rhode Island. Listeners were invited to write in for purchase warrants that allowed them to receive free five-pound bags of flour. During the 1940s, Mills also began to make personal appearances in grocery stores. Later,

Key Dates:

1790: Henry Wood & Co. is established to market English flour.
1838: Henry Wood & Co. acquires and merges into Richards and Co.
1840: John Low Sands joins Richards and Co. as a flour salesman.
1896: King Arthur Flour is introduced at the Boston Food Fair.
1904: Sands, Taylor & Wood Co. (ST&W) is incorporated.
1917: Frank Edgar Sands is named ST&W president.
1933: The Agricultural Adjustment Act, the Farm Credit Act, and the processing tax threaten ST&W's viability.
1944: Walter Edgar Sands becomes ST&W president.
1967: Frank E. Sands II becomes president, launches a decade of acquisitions, and introduces new products, including stone-ground whole wheat flour.
1984: Frank E. Sands II moves company headquarters to Norwich, Vermont, and restructures the company.
1990: ST&W introduces a mail-order catalog: *The Baker's Catalogue.*
1996: ST&W establishes an employee stock-ownership plan.
1999: ST&W changes its name to The King Arthur Flour Company.

Bert Porter—an ST&W employee—gave live demonstrations of bread baking.

By the 1960s, home baking was rapidly decreasing and retail sales of flour were declining. ST&W then adopted a two-pronged marketing strategy: increase consumer awareness of the nutritional benefits of baking with King Arthur Flour and expand wholesale relationships with bakers. Attentive to the American public's growing awareness of additives to foods and of the differences between natural and processed foods, ST&W's advertisements emphasized ''the high protein and lack of bromate that were exclusive to King Arthur Flour'' because, true to its slogan, it was ''Never Bleached, Never Bromated.'' The process for bleaching flour includes benzoyl peroxide—an ingredient in acne medicine—and chlorine dioxide, the principal ingredient in laundry bleach. Potassium bromate, recognized as a carcinogen, has been outlawed in Europe, Japan, Canada, and California. The wholesale division expanded rapidly and branched into sales of all the bakery products.

1967 and Beyond: Expansion and Restructure

In 1967 Frank E. Sands II was named president. The company leased the Wayside Inn Grist Mill (made famous by Longfellow's *Tales of the Wayside Inn)* in Sudbury, Massachusetts, and began to sell stone-ground whole wheat flour. Frank then launched a series of acquisitions that made ST&W the largest New England distributor of bakery supplies, including practically every ingredient bakers use; the company also sold pie fillings, jams, jellies, flavorings, and ice cream toppings. Within ten years ST&W sales shot up to $45 million, and the number of employees rose from 20 to 150. However, when interest rates rose in the late 1970s, the company found it almost impossible to pay off its expansion debt. Frank Sands sold off the bakery supply business and the new acquisitions, resolved a large part of the debt, and decided to restructure the company into one operation: the sale of family flour. Over the years, ST&W had moved its headquarters from Boston to other cities in Massachusetts. In 1984 Frank relocated company headquarters to Norwich, Vermont.

From its narrow focus, the company gradually expanded its geographic reach and developed new products. In 1990 demand for King Arthur Flour from outside ST&W's New England market led to the publication of a mail-order catalog under the title *The Baker's Catalogue.* Baking enthusiasts responded quickly to this catalog, which was little more than a pamphlet about various kinds of flour. Then ST&W increased the number of available mail-order items to include professional-quality baking equipment and ingredients (such as whole grains and seeds, specialty flours, spices, dried fruits, and natural sweeteners). In 1998 *The Baker's Catalogue* was mailed to some 3.5 million people and accounted for $10 million in sales. By 1999, the brightly illustrated monthly catalog featured seasonal recipes and more than 600 items, including hard-to-find baking supplies, accessories, and extracts. In 1992 ST&W opened the King Arthur Flour Baker's Store in Norwich, offering all the items in the mail-order catalog as well as locally produced teas, jams, and other Vermont specialties.

In 1993 ST&W introduced a white whole-wheat flour made from a new variety of hard white winter wheat. This flour contained 100 percent of the wheat berry and was a lighter, sweeter-tasting flour especially suited to most baked goods calling for all-purpose flour. Bakeries could buy this flour—as well as Queen Guinevere Cake Flour, Sir Lancelot High-Gluten Flour, and Round Table Pastry Flour—in 50- and 100-pound bags. In 1995, in response to the growing popularity of bread machines, ST&W launched King Arthur Special for Machines Bread Flour. This flour was made from a high-protein hard, red spring wheat and was especially milled for machine-kneaded, yeast-baked goods; it was ideal for use in bread machines, food processors, and heavy-duty mixers. In 1996 the Sands Family established an employee stock-ownership plan.

In addition to selling a variety of flours, baking equipment, and supplies, ST&W was interested in educating future home bakers and perpetuating traditional American baking. In 1992 the company inaugurated the ''Life Skills Bread Baking Program'' for 900 middle-school students in Dayville, Connecticut. Since then, more than 40,000 students across the country have learned how to make basic hearth bread. Michael Jubinsky, who served for more than 20 years at ST&W as a culinary arts instructor and expert bread baker, traveled with a team to conduct baking demonstrations for adults. Regular classes and demonstrations were also held at the company's store in Norwich.

On the Threshold of the 21st Century

On July 1, 1999, ST&W changed its name to The King Arthur Flour Company, thereby emphasizing the name of its main product, the flour that since 1896 was ''Never Bleached, Never Bromated.'' Late that year the company made all its products available electronically by placing *The Baker's Cata-*

logue on the company's Web site, where it was expected to generate nearly a million dollars in sales over the next 12 months. Although industry-wide flour sales had declined slightly, The King Arthur Flour Company's increased geographic distribution and catalog sales helped increase sales from $5.2 million in 1990 to $22 million in fiscal year 1999.

Principal Competitors

General Mills, Inc.; The Pillsbury Company.

Further Reading

Duroni, Charlene, ''Free Classes: Interest in Bread Baking Is on the Rise,'' *Lancaster New Era* (Pennsylvania), February 24, 1999, pp. C1–2.

Hedbor, Eloise Roberts, ''Food Business Is Big Business in Vermont,'' *Vermont Business Magazine*, January 1, 1999, p. 42.

Horner, Cassie, ''The Baker's Hotline,'' *Rutland Herald* (Vermont), September 26, 1999, p. 4.

Sands, Brinna, *The King Arthur Flour 200th Anniversary Cookbook*, Woodstock, Vermont: Countryman Press, 1992.

Sands, Whitney, *Sands, Taylor & Wood Company: The Oldest Flour Company in America*, Norwich, Vermont: The King Arthur Flour Company (archives), 1987.

Swartz, Jerry, ''Baking with the Fall Harvest,'' *The Call* (Woonsocket, Rhode Island), September 22, 1999, pp. D1–2.

—Gloria A. Lemieux

KnowledgeWare®

KnowledgeWare Inc.

Sterling Software, Inc.
Suite 1200
300 Crescent Court
Dallas, Texas 75201
U.S.A.
Telephone: 214-981-1000
Fax: 214-981-1215
Web site: http://www.sterling.com

Assets Acquired by Sterling Software in 1994
Incorporated: 1979 as Database Design, Inc.
Dissolved: 1994
Final Sales: $132.5 million (1994)
NAIC: 51121 Software Publishers

Acquired and absorbed by Sterling Software, Inc. in 1994, KnowledgeWare Inc. built its reputation as a leading developer of computer-aided software engineering, or CASE, tools. Much more complex than word processing programs, CASE systems are used by computer professionals for the development of applications ranging from payroll to financial management. CASE tools can also be used to customize, modify, or speed up existing programs. As a result, they can greatly increase the efficiency of computer systems and the profitability of the companies that use them. KnowledgeWare's Application Development Workbench (ADW) was used by over 4,000 companies, and became the industry standard. After making a series of rapid acquisitions in an effort to regain its position, KnowledgeWare was left cash-strapped with sagging revenues, and it was then swallowed up by Sterling Software.

Young Company Finds a Business Niche

KnowledgeWare was founded by James Martin in Ann Arbor, Michigan, in 1979. The company, originally called Database Design, Inc., began operations relatively early in the history of software engineering. Computers at that time were generally large, expensive, and slow, and the market for software programs was limited to corporate and institutional customers.

The company's original line of business was consulting, offering client companies logical data modeling services, as well as two software packages, called Information Planner and Data Designer, which were introduced in 1982. These systems used graphics tools organized around an instruction repository, referred to as an encyclopedia.

Database Design also developed a DOS-based system modeling package in conjunction with the accounting consultancy Ernst & Young. This product, called Information Engineering Workbench, or IEW, enabled programmers to quickly and easily build customized programs to handle a variety of specialized financial management tasks. Gradually the company built up a clientele. To better reflect its graduation from consulting into software engineering, Database Design changed its name to KnowledgeWare.

Expansion in the 1980s

During this period, Minnesota Vikings quarterback Fran Tarkenton was wrapping up his distinguished career in professional football and beginning a new career as a public speaker. The articulate athlete began giving motivational speeches before employees of corporations, and his colorful and surprisingly effective message for building teamwork inspired greater enthusiasm and raised productivity. During his tours of the corporate circuit, Tarkenton discovered that many companies were crippled to a great extent by the inadequate state of their computer systems. This prompted him to hire a team of programming experts in order to market the additional services of management consulting and troubleshooting for companies with unstable or poorly managed computer systems. Tarkenton named his enterprise Tarkenton Software, Inc., and the new company soon began marketing a COBOL code generator product developed by his engineers. Tarkenton made it clear that his role at the company was that of productivity consultant, not programmer. Nevertheless, some executives dismissed his company as the whim of a retired athlete who didn't even understand the business he was in.

In 1985 Tarkenton decided to merge his small enterprise with a firm that was better established in the market. He soon discovered James Martin's KnowledgeWare, whose software "workbenches" were in great demand. In turn, Tarkenton Software's Gamma code generator provided the back-end coding and testing component that KnowledgeWare needed to enhance its own product line.

Key Dates:

1979: James Martin founds Database Design, Inc. (later renamed KnowledgeWare).
1985: Fran Tarkenton's Tarkenton Software, Inc. merges with KnowledgeWare.
1988: KnowledgeWare introduces its IEW/Construction Workstation.
1989: IBM purchases an 8.7 percent stake in KnowledgeWare; KnowledgeWare launches its Application Development Workbench (ADW) program.
1994: KnowledgeWare is acquired by Sterling Software, Inc.

When the two firms combined operations later that year, KnowledgeWare adopted Tarkenton's Atlanta headquarters as its new home. Tarkenton eventually retired from productivity consulting and became a senior executive at KnowledgeWare, representing the company to clients that included DuPont and Grumman. This enabled Martin to devote his full attention to the engineering group.

The company's IEW software product walked programmers through a series of customized functions, allowing them to choose individual command sequences and quickly customize a complete, error-free, and often highly complex computer program. These CASE programs contained options developed directly from customer requests, often specifically articulated by system operators.

KnowledgeWare quickly established a powerful reputation in the industry. Large companies with thousands of employees and increasingly complex accounting needs found CASE programs essential to maintaining financial order. Furthermore, they appreciated the flexibility of the programs, which could be tailored to the companies' own needs.

In 1988 KnowledgeWare introduced its first desktop-based code generator, called IEW/Construction Workstation. The system enabled customers to analyze business requirements, design new applications, and write new code for mainframes, using only a personal computer.

Hundreds of new clients were drawn to KnowledgeWare, including Caterpillar and Martin Marietta. These clients each paid more than $200,000 for multiple copies of KnowledgeWare's CASE workbench. KnowledgeWare also sparked the interest of IBM, which saw KnowledgeWare as a potentially lucrative business partner as well as a catalyst for sales of its own products. Since KnowledgeWare's popular CASE programs were run on IBM computers, the company, it was hoped, would inspire customers to purchase or retain IBM computers.

KnowledgeWare was the largest and fastest growing CASE company in the market, and IBM—which produced its own CASE programs—was determined to latch on to the company and ally its product line with KnowledgeWare's. In August 1989 IBM purchased an 8.7 percent stake in KnowledgeWare for $10.5 million, which helped preserve IBM's position in the market.

With such a powerful vote of confidence, KnowledgeWare became popular on Wall Street. The company seized the opportunity by launching a public offering of 1.7 million shares, representing 15 percent of the company. The sale generated $20 million. Tarkenton personally sold 150,000 shares, netting $1.9 million.

A month after IBM's investment in KnowledgeWare, the latter company's programs were incorporated into IBM's AD/Cycle mainframe CASE product. A few months later, KnowledgeWare introduced its Application Development Workbench, or ADW, program, which garnered the "analysts choice" award from *PC Week* magazine. At the time, ADW was the only CASE system that was compatible with IBM's popular new OS/2 system. IBM customers who wanted to use ADW first had to upgrade their systems to OS/2, providing IBM with the increased sales it had hoped for.

Challenges in the 1990s

In 1990, KnowledgeWare doubled its sales over the previous year to $92.3 million, representing a four-year growth rate of 1,700 percent. Profits rose by 54 percent, to $9.8 million. On paper, IBM's investment in KnowledgeWare was a smashing success.

However, the partnership was derailed later that year when KnowledgeWare introduced a new software product called ADW/MVS. This system used a repository that closely resembled one under development by IBM. Rather than risk incurring a lawsuit from IBM, KnowledgeWare pulled ADW/MVS out of distribution. However, IBM's similar software system, AD/Cycle, met with flat sales and, while the losses did not have a profound effect on IBM, KnowledgeWare had bet its entire future on a projected steady stream of revenue from ADW/MVS. The failure of this product put other joint marketing arrangements with IBM into disarray, denying the company an important sales channel. Furthermore, these failures amplified doubts about KnowledgeWare's other products.

Nevertheless, by March 1991, total sales of ADW reached 25,000, while sales of IEW reached 34,000. Despite its trouble with IBM, KnowledgeWare posted a profit of $5.3 million on sales of $40.3 million during the fourth quarter of 1991. These results were augmented by the company's introduction of the RAD Workstation, Documentation Workstation, and a Japanese-language version of ADW.

KnowledgeWare's fiscal health appeared sound, especially when its dominance in the mainframe programming market was analyzed. However, scores of investors and industry analysts failed to recognize the flaw in KnowledgeWare's seemingly rosy future. Aided by the sharper vision of hindsight, *The Wall Street Journal* succinctly explained the situation in an article in its June 3, 1994 edition: "mainframes had already begun to disappear, replaced by more nimble networks of personal computers." Caught off guard, KnowledgeWare had virtually no product in which to compete in this emerging "client-server" sector.

In an effort to remedy this situation, KnowledgeWare embarked on a series of acquisitions in 1991. In January the company took over UDM Technology, a processing tool designer. In May the company added Quinsoft, and in August it acquired Language Technology. Soon thereafter, Tarkenton announced that KnowledgeWare would attempt to buy out IntelliCorp.

Tarkenton's acquisition campaign was aimed at maintaining the company's earlier sales growth and beefing up its product line. However, KnowledgeWare's president Terri McGowan and financial director Don Ellis reportedly advised against further expansion. Tarkenton, fearing that McGowan and Ellis had become overly cautious, asked for their resignations in September and proceeded with the business of acquiring IntelliCorp.

The bid for IntelliCorp failed, however, as KnowledgeWare announced bleak financial results for 1991. With a deficit of $4.9 million and sales down by ten percent, the company was unable to counteract some of the negative effects of both its acquisitions and the nationwide economic downturn. Furthermore, the company faced increased competition from Texas Instruments, whose Information Engineering Facility CASE program reportedly worked more smoothly than KnowledgeWare's IEW and ADW.

During this time, KnowledgeWare stock plummeted from $43 to $19 a share. When it was revealed that some of the company's senior executives, including Tarkenton, had cashed in lucrative stock options only months before their decline in value, a lawsuit was filed charging that the management team had profited at the expense of shareholders. The court found that Tarkenton and the others were protected by a new Securities and Exchange Commission (SEC) rule allowing investors to sell their options at the time that they were awarded. However, while the executives were cleared of charges of impropriety, the incident proved to be a public relations disaster.

Nevertheless, Tarkenton's acquisitions succeeded in giving KnowledgeWare a toe-hold in the client/server market. The technologies assembled through the purchases enabled KnowledgeWare to develop a new product, the Legacy Workstation, and the subsequent roll-out of Construction Workstation-GUI bolstered KnowledgeWare's position. With the takeover of Viewpoint Systems, Computer and Engineering Consultants, Ltd., and Matesys Mathematics, Knowledgeware moved even further into client/server operations. Matesys' ObjectView program was especially important to KnowledgeWare.

By January 1992 KnowledgeWare had reversed its losses, in part due to a massive layoff of employees. Still, sales in the second quarter again fell, this time to $1.3 million, down 57 percent from the previous year. During this time, *ComputerWorld* magazine reported that Flashpoint, the company's first product in the client/server market, was inferior to that of rival Powersoft Corp.'s PowerBuilder.

In an effort to remain competitive, KnowledgeWare instituted additional efficiency measures. To improve service and support, KnowledgeWare formed an Application Development Solution Services division and expanded its distribution channels to include systems integrators. Furthermore, the company established an international presence by taking over Ernst & Young's CASE distribution operation in Europe and setting up an international sales division. KnowledgeWare also acquired Ernst & Young's CASE business in Australia in December 1993.

For a time, it appeared as though KnowledgeWare had weathered the storm of plummeting sales and would emerge unscathed. In October 1993 the company reported better-than-anticipated profits for the second straight quarter, and an article in the February 14, 1994 *ComputerWorld* lauded KnowledgeWare for being "on the cutting edge of client/server software development," as the company released more positive results for the third consecutive quarter.

Despite these indications of success, however, KnowledgeWare was in deep trouble. Though Tarkenton optimistically declared to the June 3, 1994 *Wall Street Journal* that "we like our position and think we're in great shape to go forward," the opposite was true. KnowledgeWare's spate of acquisitions had left the company with a negative cash flow. Moreover, ObjectView and its other client/server products never regained the sizable client base that had flocked to its earlier ADW software.

The bottom fell out in July 1994 when the company reported a third quarter loss of $25.8 million. In response, KnowledgeWare laid off 240 people—one quarter of its workforce—in a bid to lower expenses. In August, Sterling Software—a Dallas-based software company that managed data processing center operations and was successful in network management—offered $143 million to acquire KnowledgeWare, which would thereafter conduct business as Sterling. Tarkenton was invited to serve on Sterling's board of directors. "We see tremendous opportunity for Sterling and predict excellent growth," a Sterling spokesperson told *Advertising Age.*

KnowledgeWare did not enter the Sterling fold quietly, however. In January 1995 several former KnowledgeWare shareholders sued Tarkenton and other executives for securities fraud and breach of contract. The investors alleged that Tarkenton had deliberately misrepresented KnowledgeWare's earnings between November 3, 1993 and August 29, 1994. Sterling was forced to allocate $15 million for legal fees, and court costs negatively impacted Sterling's 1995 revenue. Nevertheless, Sterling did successfully integrate KnowledgeWare into its growing roster of acquisitions. Tarkenton remained on Sterling's board until 1997.

Further Reading

"A Football Star Scores in One of Software's Hottest Games," *Business Week*, November 20, 1989, p. A138.

Ballou, Melinda-Carol, "KnowledgeWare Rides Road To Discovery," *ComputerWorld,* February 14, 1994.

"IBM to Purchase Stake in Firm," *Electronic News*, August 24, 1989, p. 6

"KnowledgeWare: A Worst-CASE Scenario?," *Information Week*, February 17, 1992, p. 30.

"KnowledgeWare Executive Biographies," Company Document, October 1992.

"KnowledgeWare to Buy Client/Server Firm," *ComputerWorld*, January 25, 1993, p. 15.

O'Brien, Timothy, "KnowledgeWare's Tarkenton Scrambles to Survive," *Wall Street Journal*, June 3, 1994.

O'Brien, Timothy, "What Did KnowledgeWare's Know, and When Did it Know It?," *Wall Street Journal*, September 9, 1994.

"Pressure Weighs on KnowledgeWare," *ComputerWorld*, March 2, 1992, p. 53.

"Tarkenton Turns Computer Jock," *Fortune*, September 24, 1990, p. 211.

Welch, Mary, "KnowledgeWare is now Sterling," *Advertising Age,* August 29, 1994.

—John Simley
—updated by Rebecca Stanfel

Lam Research Corporation

4650 Cushing Parkway
Fremont, California 94538
U.S.A.
Telephone: (510) 659-0200
Fax: (510) 572-6454
Web site: http://www.lamrc.com

Public Company
Incorporated: 1980
Employees: 3,300
Sales: $648 million (1999)
Stock Exchanges: NASDAQ
Ticker Symbol: LRCX
NAIC: 333295 Semiconductor Machinery Manufacturing

Lam Research Corporation is a leading supplier of manufacturing equipment to the global semiconductor industry. The company invents and produces chip-making machinery in two key areas: etching machines, which cut minuscule circuitry patterns onto silicon wafers; and chemical mechanical planarization (CMP) cleaning systems, which clean and remove particles from the surface of semiconductors. Lam's patented etching technology—Transformer Coupled Plasma—provided chipmakers with a high level of detail etching at a low cost, and solidified Lam's position in the industry.

David Lam Forms Lam Research in 1980

Lam Research was originally the brainchild of David Lam, a highly intelligent and restless player in the high-tech hotbed known as Silicon Valley. The son of Chinese refugees, Lam graduated from a Hong Kong high school and received a scholarship to study at the University of Toronto. He majored in physics and engineering and, at age 24, enrolled in Massachusetts Institute of Technology to study nuclear engineering. Because of a lack of funding for nuclear programs, Lam instead received a doctorate in chemical engineering with an emphasis in plasma, a specialty that would benefit him in the semiconductor industry.

Lam took a job in the early 1970s at Texas Instruments working with emerging semiconductor plasma technology. The semiconductor industry was still young; Bell Laboratories had only introduced the solid-state transistor in 1947, and a significant demand for chips had not emerged until the 1960s. Importantly, Intel Corp.'s introduction of the memory integrated circuit in 1971 spawned a plethora of opportunities in the U.S. semiconductor industry. True to his restless nature, Lam switched jobs several times during the 1970s, working for Xerox, Hewlett Packard, and finally as a salesman for Plasma-Therm.

Lam left Plasma-Therm in 1980 to form Lam Research Corp. With a loan from his mother, he developed plans to build his own prototype plasma-etching system, a technology used in the semiconductor, or chip, manufacturing process. Chipmaking entails a four-step procedure: 1)deposition of thin film on a (usually silicon) wafer; 2) impurity doping, when impurities are introduced that control conductivity; 3) lithographic patterning, which creates the geometric features and layout of the circuit; and 4) etching, which removes the film coating material to reveal the layout patterned in the lithographic process.

Lam used the start-up money from his mother to market his idea to venture capitalists. Citing his mastery of cutting-edge plasma-etching technology and a decade of sales and management experience, Lam was able to attract $800,000 in capital during his first year. Amazingly, by 1983 Lam Research was selling chip manufacturing systems and was sustaining a steady cash flow. ''David had a great combination of skills in putting the company together, and he was always able to come up with financing in times of adversity,'' recalled Tom Nicoletti, Lam's chief financial officer during the mid-1980s, in a June 1990 issue of *San Francisco Business Times.* ''He was outstanding in position and strategy, and he had an intuitive understanding of the industry,'' Nicoletti added.

Although Lam Research outshone many of its competitors during the early 1980s, its success was also attributable to the vast increase in semiconductor sales during the decade. Despite huge gains by Japanese companies during the 1980s that seriously weakened U.S. dominance of the global market, sales of chip manufacturing equipment grew strongly because of flour-

Company Perspectives:

Lam Research is dedicated to the success of our customers by being the world class provider of innovative productivity solutions to the semiconductor industry.

ishing demand. Besides the massive personal computer market, chips were being integrated into products ranging from automobiles and stereos to dishwashers and telephones. Lam Research leveraged the demand growth by offering cutting-edge products and service.

Lam went public in 1984, garnering a hefty $20 million from the sale of stock. However, he was still not content staying in one place for any length of time. Just five years after founding the company that bore his name, Lam walked away from the highly successful venture to accept a position with Link Technologies; he would soon shift gears completely, trying his hand at developing computer software. The company, however, remained in excellent hands. In fact, the unprecedented growth that Lam Research would achieve in the coming decade would be a testament to the depth and proficiency of the management team that built a strong foundation for Lam Research.

The semiconductor manufacturing equipment industry fell on relatively rough times during the middle and late 1980s. Although demand for chip-making equipment continued to increase, U.S. producers experienced continuously rising pressure from efficient Japanese firms that were dominating the market for high-volume, commodity like chip manufacturing systems. Japan increased its share of the world chip machine market from almost nothing in the late 1970s to nearly 50 percent by the late 1980s—U.S. producers supplied the remainder of demand. As a result, U.S. suppliers regrouped during the late 1980s by boosting productivity and concentrating on the development of high-volume, proprietary manufacturing technologies that they believed would benefit them in the 1990s.

Lam Research managed to prosper during the turbulent late 1980s by focusing on technological innovation, global expansion, market penetration, quality, and customer service. Its technological strength was achieved through heavy spending on research and development, which averaged about ten percent of revenues, and the cultivation of a forward-thinking development team. Importantly, it broadened its product focus to include deposition equipment, another high growth segment in the service equipment industry. Of particular note was the development of the breakthrough Integrity system, a chemical vapor deposition (CVD) system which integrated several manufacturing steps into a single process, thereby reducing production time and costs. Unveiled in 1990, the system won the *R&D Magazine* top product innovation award in 1991.

Expansion During the Late 1980s and Early 1990s

Lam's strategy of global expansion during the late 1980s and early 1990s emphasized the Pacific Rim and Europe. Since selling its first systems to Asian buyers in 1983, Lam had pursued a strategy of global growth, garnering about 50 percent of its revenues from overseas sales by the early 1990s. Of importance was its success in Japan. Lam entered a partnership with Japan's Sumitomo Metal Industries, Ltd. (SMI) in 1987 to help its renowned Rainbow etch product line in Japan. The two companies eventually stepped up joint research and marketing efforts. Lam opened its Lam Technology Center, a wholly owned subsidiary, near Tokyo in 1991 to support its increased activities in that region.

Thinking ahead, Lam management had long been pursuing growth in smaller markets, such as Taiwan and Korea. In fact, Lam had concentrated on Taiwan since the mid-1980s but had also opened customer support centers throughout Europe, Japan, the United States, and several Asian countries. By the early 1990s, Lam had a strong foothold in such burgeoning markets as Korea, Singapore, and Taiwan, and it was beginning to set its sights on growing demand in Malaysia, China, Israel, and several other emerging markets. By the early 1990s, Lam was engaged in, or considering, the establishment of development/demonstration or production facilities in Japan, Korea, Taiwan, and several other markets.

In addition to technological leadership and global expansion, Lam's insistence on quality and customer satisfaction bolstered its bottom line during the late 1980s and early 1990s. Its accomplishments in this area were evidenced by its attainment of the coveted VLSI Research Top Ten Award nine years in a row after the award's inception in 1988. VLSI Research Inc. bestowed the award on only ten recipients after surveying 35,000 equipment users worldwide. The award is based primarily on customer satisfaction and product quality. "Lam's philosophy has always been to deliver equipment that works and to take responsibility for keeping it operating at optimum performance," said Dan Hutcheson, president of VLSI, adding "It is this philosophy that has led to Lam's obvious success in customer satisfaction."

Astounding Profits in the Early 1990s

Lam was able to parlay its competencies into solid profit and revenue gains by the early 1990s, despite a global recession that had stumped many of its competitors. In 1991, in fact, Lam earned $6.1 million from $144 million in sales, 44 percent of which came from overseas shipments; however, this followed a loss of $5.8 million in 1990. Earnings topped $10 million from 1992 sales of $171 million, though, as the industry began to emerge from its doldrums. In addition to the improved economy, Lam and its U.S. counterparts were benefitting from a general revival in the competitiveness of the U.S. semiconductor equipment industry. Initiatives of the middle and late 1980s began to pay off as U.S. producers increased productivity and took the lead in important new technologies.

As of a result of steady growth, Lam's workforce swelled to about 1,500 by the early 1990s, shadowing a rise in its production capacity. To house its growing operations, Lam announced plans in 1991 to expand its facilities by 58,000 square feet. It was already using more than 150,000 square feet and had the option of expanding onto a 50,000-square-foot parcel adjacent to its new location. In addition, in 1992 Lam applied for a 71,000-square-foot space in Korea, on which it planned to build an assembly plant. Reflecting its optimism, Lam also requested

Key Dates:

1980: David Lam founds Lam Research Corporation.
1984: Lam research makes its first public stock offering.
1985: David Lam leaves Lam Research.
1990: Lam Research introduces its Integrity system.
1992: Company debuts its Transformer Coupled Plasma (TCP) technology.
1994: Lam Research receives grant from United States Display Consortium.
1997: Lam Research merges with OnTrak Systems, Inc.

permission in its application to eventually expand the plant to as much as ten times that size.

Lam's success during the early 1990s was the direct result of its savvy management team, a collection of thinkers and doers gathered from all corners of the industry. For example, in 1992, David Lam transferred his responsibilities, becoming chief scientist, and Roger Emerick was recruited in as president to grow the company further. Dennis Key served as vice-president of domestic sales before assuming leadership of global sales in 1992. Key brought more than 20 years of industry experience to his new post. Augmenting Key's efforts was Way Tu, head of Lam's Asian operations. Tu had been with Lam since 1983. Prior to that, the Stanford graduate had served a four-year stint with a leading semiconductor producer. Key, Tu, and other noted industry talents reported to chip-making veteran Roger Emerick, chief executive officer of the company.

Research, development, and marketing efforts implemented by Lam's talented management group during the 1980s also began to bear fruit in the early 1990s, as the company introduced breakthrough etch and deposition technologies that were expected to reap big profits throughout the 1990s. After unveiling its Integrity CVD system in 1990, Lam launched its TCP 9400 polysilicon etch system, which was the first product to integrate Lam's patented Transformer Coupled Plasma (TCP) technology that it introduced in May 1992. The second product in the series was the TCP 9600 metal etch system. The new TCP systems utilized advanced plasma-etch technology that was expected to allow greater production efficiency, chip quality, and chip uniformity.

In 1993, Lam released several products based on next generation technologies. The two new TCP products generated $33 million in sales in less than one year. Lam also introduced its new Epic system, a high-density CVD system offering capabilities no other system was capable of providing. These new products were helping the company start to achieve its stated goal of becoming a strong player in the deposition market. Management cited this goal as imperative to its survival in the increasingly integrated industry. ''We are not doing this just to become a giant company,'' Emerick explained in the January 28, 1994, issue of *San Francisco Business Times.*

Because of its product introductions and sales growth in established product lines, Lam increased its sales 55 percent in fiscal 1993 to an impressive $265 million. Net income, moreover, rose 99 percent to nearly $19 million. The company achieved the rank of the leading manufacturer of etching equipment and grew to become the fourth-largest producer of semiconductor equipment. ''This has been a banner year for Lam,'' Emerick declared in Lam's year-end results, posted on *Business Wire* on August 10, 1993. ''We have benefitted from the semiconductor industry's strong growth in recent months, as well as from the market share gains made over the last several years,'' Emerick wrote.

Buoyed by these escalating profits, Lam expanded its operations in 1994. The deal was the second of its type in the history of semiconductor fabrication industry. In addition to dedicating about 15 percent of its annual sales to research an development, Lam received a $6.7 million grant from the United States Display Consortium (USDC) in June 1994 to develop new etching devices for the manufacture of flat-panel screen displays. Flat-panel screens were used in a variety of applications, including notebook personal computers and display screens in cockpits and video phones. While demand for flat-panel displays was growing quickly—and was expected to increase even more by the end of the century—Japanese companies controlled over 95 percent of the market in 1993. Lam sought to gain entry into this lucrative area.

The company grew physically to accommodate its new ventures as well. In 1994, Lam announced that it would hire 400 workers and build a new sales and service office in San Jose, California. Moreover, Lam planned to expand its existing offices in Massachusetts and Phoenix, as well as open additional offices in Austin, Texas, and Vancouver, Washington. The construction of a new manufacturing facility in Korea was also slated for 1995. 1994 profits doubled, and sales climbed 86 percent to break $493 million.

A Turbulent Industry in the Late 1990s

As semiconductors played a greater role in more everyday products, such as cars and televisions, the entire industry expanded dramatically, growing 77 percent in 1995. Anticipating continued growth, Lam aimed to hire an additional 1,500 workers between December 1995 and July 1997. These plans were interrupted, however, when the semiconductor market slumped badly in 1996, due in large part to declining personal computer sales. Chip manufacturers postponed building new factories, and since Lam stocked such factories, its sales fell. In response, Lam laid off over 500 employees in August 1996.

The industry rebounded quickly from this downturn, and Lam made a significant acquisition in March, 1997 when it merged with OnTrak Systems Inc., a chip equipment manufacturer that specialized in chemical mechanical planarization (CMP) cleaning. With OnTrak's expertise in CMP—which involved cleaning the silicon wafer precisely so that multiple interconnected levels could be added—Lam could offer its clients a wider range of equipment and services. An additional consequence of the acquisition was that OnTrak's chairman and chief executive officer, James Bagley, assumed the helm at Lam.

Successful product launches augmented Lam's most recent acquisition. In 1996 Lam's grant from USDC came to fruition with its debut of Continuum, the company's etch equipment designed to manufacture flat panel displays. *Industry Week* magazine named the equipment one of the year's "Top 25 Technologies." In 1997, Lam introduced two new etching systems, the TCP 9100 oxide etch and the TCP 9600PTX metal etch. The company's CVD technologies continued to advance, as well.

However, another downturn in the semiconductor market, coupled with a financial collapse in several Asian nations, crippled Lam's sales. The company reported a net loss of $33.6 million in 1997. The following year brought additional bad news. In February 1998, Lam was forced to lay off 14 percent of its workforce. A scant four months later 20 percent of its global workforce was cut, and 500 more employees lost their jobs in November. After consolidating its California manufacturing operations, Lam closed its plants in South Korea and Massachusetts. Moreover, the company abandoned its CVD business. The result of this massive restructuring was a net loss of $145 million in 1998.

The company was undeterred. In an effort to return to profitability, Lam refocused on its etching and CMP operations in 1999. Despite its many setbacks, its future looked positive. The semiconductor industry was notoriously cyclical. Lam had weathered the storm and remained the fourth-largest producer of chip-making technologies.

Principal Subsidiaries

OnTrak Systems, Inc.

Principal Competitors

AlliedSignal Inc.; ASM International N.V.; Canon Inc.; Ebara Corporation; Genus, Inc.; Hitachi, Ltd.; Tokyo Electron Limited; Trikon Technologies, Inc.

Further Reading

Barry, David, and James S. Goldman, "Lam Research Inks Deal with Devcon Principals," *Business Journal-San Jose,* October 28, 1991, p. 3.

Carlsen, Clifford, "David Lam's Career Path Winds to Presidential Commission Spot," *San Francisco Business Times,* June 18, 1990, p. 12.

——, "Lam Breaks Away from the Flock," *San Francisco Business Times,* January 28, 1994, Sec. 2, p. 5A.

——, "Lam to Open Asian Offices," *San Francisco Business Times,* March 20, 1992, p. 4.

Evenhuis, Henk, "Lam Reports Year-End Results; Record Revenues and Profits for Third Straight Year," *Business Wire,* August 10, 1993.

Goldman, James S., "Chip Boom to Boost Suppliers in '93," *Business Journal—San Jose,* p. 1.

Hardy, Quentin, "Lam Research to Merge with OnTrak in Stock Swap," *Wall Street Journal,* March 25, 1997.

Hayes, Mary, "Applied and Lam May Build in Korea," *Business Journal—San Jose,* April 26, 1993, p. 1.

——, "Lam Research Jumping into Flat-Panel Display Equipment," *Business Journal-San Jose,* September 20, 1993, p. 5.

"Lam Attains Number One Position in Worldwide Dry Etch Market," *Business Wire,* January 26, 1991.

"Lam Gets Flat-Panel Grant Awarded," *San Jose Mercury News,* June 23, 1994.

"Lam Launches Breakthrough Etch Technology," *Business Wire,* May 11, 1992.

"Lam Research Clinches $60 Million Sale," *Oakland Tribune* (California), May 6, 1994.

"Lam To Hire 1500 Locally," *San Jose Mercury-News,* December 14, 1995.

McLennan, Karen, and Carolyn Schwartz, "Lam Opens Technology Center in Japan; Names Vice President to Head New Operation," *Business Wire,* June 4, 1991.

"Lam Listed Among World's 10 Best; Receives VLSI Research Award for Third Year Running," *Business Wire,* May 21, 1991.

Takahashi, Dean, "Chip Equipment Makers' Gathering Won't Be a Picnic," *Wall Street Journal,* July 13, 1998.

——, "Makers of Chip Equipment Feel Pain of Slow-Down," *Wall Street Journal,* August 14, 1996.

—Dave Mote
—updated by Rebecca Stanfel

Lan Chile S.A.

Avenida Americo Vespucio 901
Renca
Estado 10
Santiago de Chile
Chile
Telephone: (2) 687-2525
Toll Free: (800) 735-5526
Fax: (2) 687-2483
Web site: http://www.lanchile.cl

Public Company
Incorporated: 1929 as Línea Aeropostal Santiago-Arica
Employees: 8,100
Sales: $1.08 billion (1998)
Stock Exchanges: New York
Ticker Symbol: LFL
NAIC: 481111 Scheduled Passenger Air Transportation; 481112 Scheduled Freight Air Transportation; 481212 Nonscheduled Chartered Freight Air Transportation; 481211 Nonscheduled Chartered Passenger Air Transportation

Four million passengers a year fly Lan Chile S.A., or LanChile as it has been styling itself since the mid-1990s. After surviving decades of the most precarious financial situations, the carrier has been transformed under the leadership of the Cueto family, which had previously demonstrated its air cargo expertise as operators of Fast Air. A new alliance with American Airlines and the Oneworld system ensures LanChile a dominant position in the fastest growing aviation market at the dawn of the millennium.

Air Force Origins

Comandante Arturo Merino Benitez, founder of the National Air Force and Chile's first General del Aire, created Línea Aeropostal Santiago-Arica in 1929. Its first duty was to fly the mail and some passengers between Santiago and Arica, on the Peruvian border, with de Havilland Gipsy Moth aircraft (although small and light, the Gypsy Moth's impressive altitude records sold it with the Chilean authorities). The next year the Chilean Air Force supplied the airline with three larger Ford Trimotors. It flew 95,000 passenger miles (762 passengers) its first year.

At that time, PANAGRA, the joint venture between Pan American Airways and the W.R. Grace shipping company, had just started its mail service from Panama. So influential was W.R. Grace that PANAGRA continued to operate in what would have otherwise been a monopoly for the Chilean state carrier. Línea Aeropostal had been connected to the routes of Aéropostale, the French mail carrier. The French government withdrew support for that enterprise, however, in 1931.

The airline was made its own agency separate from the Air Force in 1932, taking simply the name "Línea Aérea Nacional" or LAN for short. LAN received exclusive cabotage privileges within Chile—that is, the right to carry passengers between points within the country.

The late 1930s saw a proliferation of LAN's routes. Its routes had covered about 1,000 miles since it was founded, but after 1935 the figures were closer to 2,000 and 3,000 miles. These were subsequently pared back. After losing money for four years, LAN reached earnings of about $39,000 on revenues of $509,000 in 1940. At the time fares amounted to about nine cents per mile. Mail and subsidies accounted for 71 percent of revenues, up sharply from 42 percent the year before. In 1941, LAN posted $300,000 in profits on revenues of $661,000. The number of passenger-miles flown also had increased handsomely, from 2,160,000 to 3,490,000.

After experimenting with different aircraft on various routes, LAN bought three Junkers Ju-86 cargo planes in 1938. The German design was fast but lacked range. Its parts supply chain was cut off by WWII, so LAN switched to U.S.-made Lockheed aircraft. Fares were reduced after the changeover to these newer planes, resulting in a more than tenfold increase in passenger journeys between 1940 (2,600) and 1945 (27,000). With these numbers, the company felt safe in expanding its route structure again. After the war, LAN flew its first international route, to Buenos Aires. It shared this route with FAMA,

Company Perspectives:

LanChile is now flying the world's skies spreading the unique and gentle spirit of the South of the World, through its friendly and modern service. Renowned for it abundant hospitality, LanChile mirrors the nature of our warm and friendly people, their hospitality and warmth. The identity of LanChile captures the colors, the textures, the sounds and the aromas representative of the vast Chilean landscape with a personality that offers a friendly and cordial service typical of the Chilean people. Our new service-oriented philosophy is the result of a reinforcement of our traditional values in a fresh and modern way. LanChile, the airline of Chile, seeks to match the quality and service standards of our international competitors in order to compete in the global market. We aim to offer you the best of both worlds—the warmth and hospitality of our people together with a modern, efficient and professional approach.

an Argentine carrier. LAN then finally began flying Santiago-Punta Arenas with a DC-3.

Postwar Competition

The Chilean government allowed new international airlines to operate in its skies beginning in 1953. Two local upstarts, Compañía Nacional de Turismo Aéreo (CINTA) and ALA, Sociedad de Transportes Aéreos, challenged LAN and PANAGRA with fares sometimes cheaper by half. The two new entrants effectively created a new market of budget travelers to Cuba and the United States. By 1957, however, they had merged. A new company, LADECO, took over their routes. It catered to copper mining interests, hence its full name, "Linea Aerea del Cobre, Ltda." CINTA-ALA continued flying until the 1959 revolution in Cuba and declared bankruptcy two years later.

The Chilean state carrier adopted the appellation "LAN-Chile" as its route network expanded across South America. With new Douglas DC-6 aircraft, it reached Miami in August 1958. LAN had, in December 1956, sent a plane to Antarctica, where Chile claimed territory. The network expanded westward as well. LAN Chile began service to Easter Island, making that remote and unique destination accessible as never before. Tahiti was added in 1968. LAN stretched across the Atlantic in 1970, reaching Madrid, Paris, and Frankfurt. Secondhand Boeing 707 and 727 jets were becoming the mainstays of its fleet. The Boeing 707 allowed nonstop Lima-New York service beginning in 1968. Fiji became the new westernmost destination in 1974.

In 1964, Eric Campaña had been brought in as executive vice-president to try to make LAN profitable. He succeeded, not only in that but in formalizing the airline's role as a state carrier. These improvements were not continued into the next decade, however.

Turning Left and Right in the 1970s

The election of Dr. Salvador Allende, a Marxist, to power in 1970 brought about a political realignment of Chile through which LAN Chile had to navigate with some finesse. It reinitiated, briefly, service to Madrid via Havana in 1971. Cuba was then Chile's newfound friend in the western hemisphere. The airline also felt political pressure to buy Soviet Ilyushin Il-62 jets, a prospect management dreaded, because of the aircraft's substandard performance, unreliability, and the distance over which replacement parts would have to be shipped. LAN Chile was able to avoid buying any of them, in spite of government urging. The nationalization of a copper mine resulted in LAN Chile's New York facilities being seized by the U.S. government and service to that city stopped for a few days.

Operationally, the carrier had to deal with cut fares and a doubled work force of 4,000. The airline nevertheless was able to make some significant achievements during Allende's reign, such as doubling the number of European flights. It investigated routes to Australia and flew its first charter to Sydney in September 1973 on an innovative Great Circle route (France would have been unlikely to grant it more landing rights in Tahiti at the time). This was not developed into scheduled service, however, because of the lack of a reliable alternate landing field.

Allende was assassinated on September 11, 1973, opening the way for the Pinochet regime. Several of the small air freight companies that had been closed down began operating again, if only briefly. Several new domestic airlines also were formed. The preferential exchange rate that had kept LAN afloat during the Allende years was abolished, forcing the carrier into debt. It halved its work force again but was left with considerable severance payments. LAN was able, though, to develop its western South America network, and it added a nonstop Santiago-Miami flight in November 1977.

The government's new "open skies" policy exposed LAN Chile to unprecedented competition beginning in 1979. Its domestic market share was consumed by LADECO after that carrier's new owners, Grupo Cruzat, invested heavily in modernizing it. For the first time, LADECO had begun competing on LAN Chile's own routes, controlling a majority (63 percent) of the domestic market by 1980. Before deregulation, LAN Chile had a 70 to 80 percent share.

LAN was still hindered by government bureaucracy. It could take months to gain permission to buy an aircraft. It also was stuck with extremely generous pilot contracts. By 1983, the airline was in a very precarious position, owing $60 million to banks even after government transfers of $165 million. The airline was virtually bankrupt.

Drastic action was necessary. Under the leadership of company president Patricio Sepulveda, LAN Chile was closed down in 1984. A new LAN was started up, free of old debts and labor agreements. Employment was halved; many former workers became suppliers on a contractual basis. Management also was restructured. In exchange for the old LAN's $56 million debt, the Chilean government held 98.7 percent of the new LAN through its CORFO holding company. CORFO (Corporación de Fomento de la Producción) also paid about $11 million in other obligations.

Lan Chile moved quickly to regain market share. It invested in new Boeing 767s and increased its routes and flight frequencies, particularly to the United States and Argentina. It controlled nearly half the domestic market in 1986. (Annual sales

Key Dates:

1929: Línea Aeropostal Santiago-Arica is created to fly mail and passengers.
1932: Airline is separated from Air Force, taking name "Línea Aérea Nacional."
1946: LAN flies first international route, to Buenos Aires.
1958: Route network reaches Miami.
1964: New management is brought in to reverse financial decline.
1970: New leftist administration of Dr. Salvador Allende radically changes carrier's operating environment.
1979: Chilean government deregulates its skies.
1984: LAN Chile is restructured, begins vigorous campaign to recapture lost market share.
1989: Government sells 51 percent of LAN Chile to private investors.
1994: LAN Chile becomes 100 percent privately owned.
1995: LADECO, Chile's next-largest carrier, is acquired.
1997: Shares are offered publicly on local market and New York Stock Exchange.

were about $145 million, up from $18 million in 1984 and $33 million in 1985.) Meanwhile, its rival, LADECO, had declared bankruptcy, been taken over by the state, and then again transferred to private owners. The idea of privatizing Lan Chile also had begun to take shape.

Privatization in 1989

Originally, the Pinochet government had considered selling about 30 percent of Lan Chile to private investors. It first sold about 16 percent at a low share price to LAN's workers in 1988. A subsequent offering of 32.7 percent of the airline failed to attract enough qualified bidders. A majority offering finally succeeded, and in September 1989 ICAROSAN bought a 51 percent interest in the company. ICAROSAN was a local investment group led by Guillermo Carey that had previously owned 12.5 percent of LADECO.

Carey had backing from SAS (Scandinavian Airline System), and within a year of the purchase that carrier had itself invested $25 million for a 30 percent share of Lan Chile. SAS had aspirations of becoming a global "megacarrier" and recently had been frustrated in its attempts to acquire Aerolíneas Argentinas. It did not finalize the deal to become the largest stockholder, however, until a few days after President Patricio Aylwin took office in December 1989. An April 1990 stock offering left ICAROSAN and SAS with an even larger percent share of the company (16.6 percent and 41.2 percent, respectively).

With the new capital and some new debt, Lan Chile invested in a $550 million fleet renewal program, leasing or buying new state-of-the-art Boeing 767s for international routes and British Aerospace BAe 146 jets with which it expanded its domestic network. Employment rose 50 percent as well.

The result was a disaster. Lan Chile had ordered far too many planes, at a commitment of $48 million per year. The Persian Gulf crisis drove up the price of jet fuel, a major expenditure for any airline. By the end of 1990, SAS had ousted Carey and set about attempting to unload as many planes as it could.

The Cueto family, which owned cargo carrier Fast Air, gained a controlling share of Lan Chile in 1994, with Enrique Cueto becoming chief executive. Cueto, former CEO at Fast Air, surrounded himself with the best managers he could find and set out to renegotiate the carrier's aircraft leases (some with "outrageous terms"). In the future, the airline would prefer to own more of its planes. Standardization of the long-range fleet around the Boeing 767 was a priority.

Buoyed by a recovering economy and atmosphere of political reform, Lan Chile again found profitability in the mid-1990s, posting income of $5.7 million, $24.5 million, and $38.3 million in 1994, 1995, and 1996. The cargo sector provided the most immediate opportunities, and the passenger market grew rapidly in the next few years.

In 1994, Lan Chile bought Fast Air, a 16-year-old, two-plane cargo line specializing in the Miami-Santiago route. The next year, after some sophisticated antitrust maneuvering, Lan Chile also took over the next largest airline in Chile, LADECO, which operated about 20 airliners at the time of the takeover. One condition of the purchase was that the carriers continue to operate separately. LADECO continued to have difficulty posting a profit after the acquisition.

LanChile (as it was dubbed by then) was reorganized in April 1997, floating some 30 percent of its shares on the local stock market. A subsequent $100 million offering was launched on the New York Stock Exchange, making LanChile the first Latin American airline listed there. Investor worries connected to the Asian financial crisis, however, conspired to produce somewhat disheartening results. Only $135 million was raised, half what was expected. In September 1997, the carrier signed into an alliance with American Airlines, but would have to wait a couple of years for U.S. government approval to fully realize its partnership.

LanChile agreed to purchase 20 Airbus A320 short-haul jets in February 1998. The Airbus consortium was bidding against Boeing and offered more beneficial financing. LanChile actually had participated in an arrangement with TACA and TAM, airlines of El Salvador and Brazil, that gave the group a volume discount commensurate with Airbus's second largest order ever.

The late 1990s was a period of incredible growth—more than 30 percent a year. Cueto stressed that he was not after growth for its own sake, but was more interested in profits. High levels of service was a means to that end. LanChile invested $30 million in implementing a corporate image program to reflect its commitment to becoming a world-class carrier. A new office complex in Santiago was opened about the same time.

The entrance of Continental into the U.S.-Chile market dampened LanChile's income in 1998; however, its cargo operations continued to be highly successful. LanChile was the largest freight carrier in Miami, where it had relocated its cargo operations in 1996 and spent $50 million on new facilities. One area of fantastic passenger traffic growth was Peru, which also signed an open skies agreement with Chile.

While negotiating for an open skies agreement, signed in early 1999, the Chilean government pressured the United States for approval to a code sharing arrangement between LanChile and American Airlines. The alliance gave the two airlines dominance of both the Chile-U.S. market and Miami and led to Lan Chile's inclusion in the global Oneworld system, which included American, British Airways, Cathay Pacific, Canadian Airlines, Quantas, Finnair, and Iberia.

Principal Subsidiaries

Lancourier; LanChile Cargo; Fast Air.

Principal Competitors

Continental; United Air Lines; Aerolíneas Argentinas; VARIG.

Further Reading

Acton, Kyrl, ''All in a Day's Work: Kyrl Acton,'' *Airfinance Journal,* May 1999, p. 44.

''Alliance Adds to the Gloss,'' *Business Yearbook 1999—10th Anniversary* (supplement to *Airfinance Journal*), 1999, pp. 10–11.

Burden, William A.M., *The Struggle for Airways in Latin America,* New York: Council on Foreign Relations, 1943, Arno Press, 1977.

Cameron, Doug, ''Everything That Rises Must Converge,'' *Airfinance Journal,* April 1996, p. 26.

Constance, Paul, ''US Threatens Sanctions in Chile,'' *Aviation Week and Space Technology,* November 22, 1993, p. 83.

Davies, R.E.G., *Airlines of Latin America Since 1919,* Washington, DC: Smithsonian Institution, 1984.

''Lan Chile Equity Sale Hit by Asian Fall-Out,'' *Euroweek,* November 7, 1997, p. 8.

Lennane, Alexandra, and Enrique Cueto, ''Size Is Not Everything,'' *A Guide to Latin America* (supplement to *Airfinance Journal,*) October 1998, pp. 26–28.

Lima, Edvaldo Pereira, ''LanChile's FAA-Certified Base,'' *Air Transport World,* March 1992, pp. 101–02.

——, ''Prospering Under Privatization,'' *Air Transport World,* February 1992, pp. 102–04.

——, ''South American Spirit,'' *Air Transport World,* March 1999, pp. 41–44.

——, ''The Third Private Life,'' *Air Transport World,* June 1994, pp. 193–95.

Magnusson, Michael, *Latin Glory: Airlines of Latin America,* Osceola, Wis.: Motorbooks International, 1995.

Paredes-Molina, Ricardo, and Ravi Ramamurti, ''Ownership and Competition in Chile's Airline Industry,'' *Privatizing Monopolies: Lessons from the Telecommunications and Transport Sectors in Latin America,* edited by Ravi Ramamurti, Baltimore and London: Johns Hopkins University, 1996, pp. 177–202.

Marray, Michael, ''Back from the Cold,'' *Airfinance Journal,* June 1997, pp. 26–28.

——, ''Lan Chile Stutters in US,'' *Airfinance Journal,* December 1997, p. 20.

Ott, James, ''Chile Is Selling Its Remaining Interest in LanChile Airlines,'' *Aviation Week and Space Technology,* January 22, 1990, pp. 94–95.

Torres, Craig, ''Chilean Airline Plays Political Hardball—LAN Is Bargaining Chip in Proposed Air Pact with US,'' *Wall Street Journal,* December 18, 1998, p. A12.

—Frederick C. Ingram

Larry Flynt Publishing Inc.

8484 Wilshire Boulevard, Suite 900
Beverly Hills, California 90211
U.S.A.
Telephone: (323) 651-5400
Fax: (323) 651-3525

Private Company
Incorporated: 1976
Employees: 300
Sales: $135 million (1998 est.)
NAIC: 51112 Periodical Publishers; 7812 Motion Picture and Video Tape Production

Larry Flynt Publishing Inc. (LFP) is a privately held publishing company that produces approximately 30 magazines. The company's oldest and best known publication is *Hustler*, an adult entertainment men's magazine with a circulation of around 750,000. Although many of LFP's other magazines are similar in nature to *Hustler*, the company also produces several more mainstream periodicals. Approximately 60 percent of the company's revenues derive from magazine sales. The remainder of the income is generated by several by-subscription websites and a Hustler store in Hollywood, which carries adult books, magazines, and products.

1960s: Bar Beginnings

The history of Larry Flynt Publishing is, in many ways, inextricable from the history of its colorful, controversial founder and president, Larry Flynt. Flynt was born in 1942 into less-than-idyllic conditions. Poverty, isolation, and alcoholism were the most pervasive characteristics of his home life and his tiny Kentucky community. Flynt dropped out of school in the ninth grade to join the Army but was discharged a year later due to low scores on a general education test. Not easily dissuaded, he then enlisted in the Navy. Flynt was more successful in his second enlistment, eventually becoming a radar technician on an aircraft carrier.

When discharged from the Navy in 1964, Flynt moved to Dayton, Ohio, and began working at two manufacturing jobs. In 1965, with $1,800 in savings, he made a down payment on a bar in one of Dayton's working-class neighborhoods. Naming his establishment Hillbilly Haven, Flynt began his first experiment with niche marketing. By setting up horseshoe stakes and picnic tables, and deliberately targeting a rowdy, hard-drinking, and often violent clientele, he exponentially increased the bar's sales in just a few months. By the end of 1965, Flynt was able to buy a second bar, and, the following year, a third. Both were similar in approach and customer base to Hillbilly Haven.

Flynt's fourth bar, named Whatever's Right, was a departure from his earlier ventures. Striving for a more elegant atmosphere, the club featured a dance floor, popular music, and a collection of attractive ''hostesses'' whose job was to dance with the patrons. The dancing hostesses were a huge success, and the club soon inspired several local imitations. In 1968, Flynt took his hostess idea one step further. Reasoning that if fully clothed girls resulted in good drink sales, semi-clothed girls would result in *great* drink sales, he opened Dayton's first go-go club: the Hustler Club.

When the Hustler Club proved to be a money-maker, Flynt decided to get out of the working-class bar business and focus more on his ''upscale'' clubs. Selling his first two bars, he began opening a string of Hustler Clubs across Ohio—in Cincinnati, Columbus, Cleveland, Toledo, and Akron. By early 1973, he had eight clubs and approximately 300 employees.

1970–75: Becoming a Publisher

Flynt's first foray into the publishing industry was an entertainment newspaper called *Bachelor's Beat*. The publication, which was in part a PR piece for the Hustler Clubs, lasted for two years and never made a profit. Flynt sold it at the beginning of the 1970s. In 1972, Flynt again tried his hand at publishing when he began producing a monthly newsletter for Hustler Club members. The publication, a modest four-page single-fold, contained short news and feature articles on various Hustler Club dancers. The newsletter was an immediate hit with readers, and Flynt soon received calls urging him to expand it. For the third issue of the *Hustler Newsletter*, he did so, upping the size to eight pages and abbreviating the name to simply *Hustler*. The

Key Dates:

1965: Larry Flynt opens his first bar in Dayton, Ohio.
1968: Flynt opens Dayton's first go-go bar, The Hustler Club.
1972: The Hustler Club begins publishing a monthly newsletter for its members.
1974: The first issue of *Hustler Magazine* is published.
1976: Flynt founds Larry Flynt Publishing Inc.; he is tried in Cincinnati on charges of obscenity, pandering, and organized crime, and convicted on all counts.
1978: Flynt survives an assassination attempt that leaves him paralyzed from the waist down.
1984: Televangelist Jerry Falwell sues Flynt over *Hustler* ad parody featuring Falwell; Flynt is found guilty on one of the charges.
1986: Larry Flynt Publishing begins producing other magazines, including some mainstream titles.
1988: The Supreme Court overturns Flynt's conviction in the Falwell case.
1998: Flynt arrested in Cincinnati on 15 counts of obscenity and corruption; he takes out ad in *Washington Post,* offering payment for evidence of illicit sexual relations involving high-ranking politicians.
1999: Flynt settles Cincinnati case with plea bargain.

newsletter remained highly popular and continued to expand in size. By August 1973, it contained 32 pages.

In late 1973, Flynt merged his newsletter with a national magazine called *Gallery,* which was published by Ron Fenton. Billing *Gallery* as the ''new official publication of the Hustler Clubs,'' Flynt and Fenton co-published three issues. Before they could go further, however, their distribution company foreclosed on the venture, effectively shutting down production. The shutdown of *Gallery* did not discourage Fenton and Flynt, and soon they were back in business. In May 1974, Fenton suggested they team up to develop a new national men's magazine, and Flynt agreed. After securing a distribution company, however, the would-be publishers were faced with the problem of raising enough money to produce the first few issues. Flynt solved the dilemma by temporarily diverting his employees' withholding tax.

Like Flynt's earlier newsletter, the new publication was called *Hustler*. It debuted in July of 1974—to less than rave reviews. In his autobiography, *An Unseemly Man*, Flynt describes the first issue as a mess: ''a high school version of *Playboy* with a little *Penthouse* thrown in.'' Upon seeing it, Fenton immediately bailed out of the operation.

While Flynt scrambled to produce the next few issues on his own, he gradually developed a vision of what he wanted the magazine to be. Eschewing the soft-focus photography and picture-perfect models of most popular men's magazines, he chose for *Hustler* a cruder, more explicit look. For models, Flynt sought what he termed ''real women,'' which included those with obvious imperfections and anomalies. He also showed more of his models than was generally accepted, becoming the first mass-circulation magazine to show full female genitalia. Flynt aimed for a similar level of single-minded explicitness in the magazine's editorial content. ''The question I had to face right away was whether the magazine ought to include lifestyle issues, movie reviews, and interviews with mainstream figures,'' he wrote in *An Unseemly Man.* ''My instinct was to try something different. It seemed to me that if the theme and focus of a magazine is sex, then its whole content ought to serve that purpose,'' he noted.

A year into publishing *Hustler*, Flynt knew that he had hit on the right formula for success. By April, the magazine was grossing more than $500,000 per issue. By June, with publishing profits far surpassing those of the Hustler Clubs, Flynt decided to get out of the bar business. For better or for worse, he had become a publisher.

1976–80: In Trouble

From the start, *Hustler* provoked a great deal of public outrage. Not only were its photographs more graphic than those of its competitors, but its bitingly satiric and often vulgar cartoons and features offended virtually everyone. The magazine was to land Flynt in numerous legal battles on charges of everything from obscenity to libel.

Flynt's first major court case was tried in 1976 in Cincinnati, Ohio. He was charged with pandering, obscenity, and organized crime, and was convicted on all three counts. Filing an appeal, Flynt's attorneys got him released on bond, and he returned to Columbus to run *Hustler*. As it turned out, the trial publicity had been good for business. Sales of the magazine had reached an all-time high of 2.7 million copies monthly.

In early 1978, while his Cincinnati appeal was still pending, obscenity charges were filed against Flynt and *Hustler* in Lawrenceville, Georgia. While in Lawrenceville for the trial, the controversial publisher was gunned down outside the courthouse. Shot twice in the abdomen, Flynt barely survived. He was left paralyzed from the waist down and in blinding pain.

When released from the hospital, Flynt immediately moved *Hustler* to Beverly Hills. By that time, however, he had developed a debilitating addiction to painkillers. Disinterested in and unable to run *Hustler*, he left the business mostly in the hands of his staff. Meanwhile, he contended with a series of legal battles. Although his Cincinnati conviction had been overturned on appeal, there was still a long list of individuals who had been offended by *Hustler*, and hence a long list of lawsuits. With his personality altered by both pain and painkillers, Flynt's courtroom behavior grew increasingly bizarre. Eventually, he was sentenced to 15 months in a federal psychiatric prison. Five-and-a-half months into his sentence, however, that ruling too was overturned, and Flynt was released.

1980–96: Media Scourge, Media Darling

By the early 1980s, *Hustler* was once again at the center of a public maelstrom. In 1983, the magazine ran a parody of an ad that featured the Reverend Jerry Falwell, a well-known televangelist. The parody, which mimicked a popular liquor advertisement, featured a picture of Falwell and a fabricated ''interview'' with him in which he discussed having sex with his mother. In 1984, Falwell filed a $45 million lawsuit against *Hustler* and Flynt, claiming libel and emotional distress. The jury found Flynt not guilty on the charge of libel but guilty on the charge of emotional distress. Although his lawyers immediately filed an appeal, the verdict was upheld by the Court of Appeals for the Fourth Circuit. Flynt's legal team then petitioned for a review of the case by the U.S. Supreme Court and was granted the review. In the midst of much media attention and public outcry, the Supreme Court ruled in favor of Flynt, reversing the earlier decision.

While Flynt was fighting his very public court battle, his business was quietly growing into new areas. The market for men's magazines softened somewhat in the 1980s, leaving Larry Flynt Publishing in need of new income streams. As a result, the company expanded to include adult video production and a collection of Internet sites, including a by-subscription online version of *Hustler*.

LFP also began testing the water in the mainstream publishing market, launching a series of new special-interest magazines with such unobjectionable titles as *Camera & Darkroom Photography, PC Laptop Computers*, and *Maternity Fashion & Beauty*. To accommodate its expansion, the company moved into a new, larger headquarters on the famed Wilshire Boulevard in Beverly Hills.

Flynt and *Hustler* were immortalized by Hollywood in 1997, with the motion picture ''The People vs. Larry Flynt.'' The movie, which offered a somewhat sanitized version of Flynt's ascension, was nominated for several Oscars. It also put Flynt squarely back where he liked to be: in the spotlight.

1997: Back to Ohio

Although Flynt's 1977 conviction in Cincinnati had been overturned, the case had essentially managed to drive *Hustler* out of town. For the 20 years after the trial, almost all Cincinnati area retailers refused to carry the magazine for fear of being prosecuted. In 1997, Flynt decided it was time to change all that. ''I've always felt that Cincinnati was unfinished business,'' he said in an April 1997 interview with *The Cincinnati Enquirer*, adding, ''I just think it's ridiculous after all these years that the magazine is not being sold there when similar ones are. It's not the content; it's the name.''

Flynt believed that the best way to resolve his ''unfinished business'' was to be indicted again and win an acquittal. In a calculated attempt to provoke authorities and get arrested, he stationed himself on a street corner in downtown Cincinnati and began handing out copies of *Hustler* to the crowd that quickly gathered. Although the stunt garnered a great deal of attention, it did not result in an arrest.

It was not in Flynt's nature to give up easily. When he failed to get his day in court by distributing *Hustler* on the street, he upped the stakes by opening an adult bookstore. Located in the heart of downtown Cincinnati, the store—Hustler Books, Magazines and Gifts—opened its doors in October 1997. Although there was some debate about zoning violations, no arrests were made. In the first part of 1998, however, the Hustler store finally prodded the city into action by adding hard-core adult videos to its product mix. Flynt was indicted on 15 obscenity and corruption charges, including pandering obscenity, conspiracy, and disseminating matter harmful to juveniles. All of the charges were linked to the store's sale of adult videos.

The trial, originally set for January 1999, was delayed until May and then ended in a surprising plea bargain before jury selection was even complete. Flynt agreed to have Hustler News and Gifts, Inc., the FLP subsidiary that operated the Cincinnati store, become the defendant in the case and plead guilty to two counts of pandering obscenity. Under the terms of the agreement, Flynt agreed to remove all pornographic materials from the Hustler store and to stop distributing hard-core pornography anywhere in the county. The prosecutor agreed to drop the remaining 13 obscenity charges. Explaining his decision to plead out, Flynt said that the deal was a victory for *Hustler*. ''They gave us what we wanted,'' he said in a May 12, 1999 interview with *Court TV Online*. ''When I originally returned to Cincinnati, it was to get my *Hustler* magazine distributed in Hamilton County. If prosecutors had told me that *Hustler* had to go, we would still be up there picking a jury.''

While Flynt was in the thick of his second Cincinnati arrest, the whole nation was focused on a much larger sex-related issue. U.S. President Bill Clinton was embroiled in a very public scandal involving White House intern Monica Lewinsky. Accused of perjuring himself during questioning about Lewinsky, Clinton faced both personal humiliation and political disaster. Flynt jumped into the fray by taking out a full-page ad in the *Washington Post* that offered $1 million for evidence of illicit sexual relations involving members of Congress or senior government officials. Receiving some 2,000 responses, Flynt hired investigators to look into the ones that seemed credible and worthwhile. Eventually, the stories were compiled in a special publication called *The Flynt Report*. In addition to keeping Flynt's name in the news, the dirt-digging tactic managed to topple at least one politician. Republican House Speaker-elect Bob Livingston resigned from office after Flynt's investigators discovered he'd had a series of extra-marital affairs.

Looking Ahead

In late 1998, Flynt opened Hustler Hollywood, an upscale combination of sex shop and coffee bar located in West Hollywood. The store was to serve as a prototype and flagship for a whole chain of stores, to be located in major cities nationwide. Although no other locations had been officially announced, Flynt was reputed to be considering Atlanta, Miami, and Las Vegas for his next such ventures.

As LFP prepared to usher out the 20th century, the advent of the Internet and cable television had caused a decline in its magazine sales, a trend which was unlikely to reverse. Together, the company's 31 periodicals had a monthly circulation of between 2.5 and 3 million. This was a far cry from the 1970s, when *Hustler* alone sold that many copies each month. With magazine sales softening, Flynt planned to rely more heavily on Internet sites and adult videos to generate revenue.

Principal Subsidiaries

Hustler News and Gifts Inc.

Principal Competitors

Bertelsmann AG; General Media International, Inc.; The Hearst Corporation; Playboy Enterprises, Inc.; The Times Mirror Company.

Further Reading

Delguzzi, Kristen, ''Flynt Hawks *Hustler* Today,'' *Cincinnati Enquirer,* May 14, 1997.

DiFilippo, Dana, ''Flynt's Focus is on Videos,'' *Cincinnati Enquirer,* February 19, 1998.

Flynt, Larry, *An Unseemly Man*, Los Angeles: Dove Books, 1996, 265 p.

Hentoff, Nat, ''Larry Flynt's Famous Victory,'' *Village Voice*, April 1, 1997, p. 22.

Horn, Dan, ''Cincinnati vs. Flynt: The Sequel,'' *Cincinnati Enquirer*, May 2, 1999.

——, ''Inside the World of Larry Flynt,'' *Cincinnati Post*, April 25, 1998.

Kipnis, Laura, ''It's a Wonderful Life: *Hustler* Publisher Larry Flynt's Long, Strange Journey from Hillbilly to Entrepreneur to First Amendment Hero,'' *Village Voice*, December 31, 1996, p. 37.

Ramos, Steve, ''The Redemption of Larry Flynt,'' *CityBeat*, January 9–15, 1997, p.1.

Robinson, Bryan, ''Plea Deal Reached in Larry Flynt Obscenity Trial,'' *Court TV Online*, May 12, 1999.

Rosin, Hanna, ''Hustler,'' *New Republic*, January 6, 1997, p. 20.

Shepard, Alicia, ''Gatekeepers Without Gates,'' *American Journalism Review,* March 1999, p. 22.

—Shawna Brynildssen

Lason, Inc.

1305 Stephenson Highway
Troy, Michigan 48083
U.S.A.
Telephone: (248) 597-5800
Fax: (248) 597-5761
Web site: http://www.lason.com

Public Company
Incorporated: 1985 as Lason Systems Inc.
Employees: 13,000
Sales: $279.8 million (1998)
Stock Exchanges: NASDAQ
Ticker Symbol: LSON
NAIC: 514191 On-Line Information Services; 541513 Computer Facilities Management Services

Lason, Inc.'s core business is the provision of information management services, including document and data capture, data management through electronic storage and retrieval, and output of information digitally or in print. After operating as a private company for about ten years, Lason went public in 1996. From 1997 to 1999 it pursued an aggressive acquisitions program that transformed the company into one of the leading international providers of information management services. As of late 1999 the company had more than 85 multifunctional imaging and data capture centers—all linked via satellite—and was operating more than 100 facility management sites located on customers' premises. It had operations in 30 states, and in the United Kingdom, Canada, Mexico, India, Mauritius, and the Caribbean.

A Private, Regional Company: 1985–96

Lason Systems, Inc., a Michigan corporation and the predecessor to Lason, Inc., was formed in 1985 through a management buyout of the direct mail division of McKesson Corporation's 3PM subsidiary. The company operated for the next decade primarily as a regional direct mail services firm.

In January 1995 the firm was recapitalized. It became a Delaware corporation, and the name was changed to Lason, Inc. in August 1996. In October 1996 the company went public. The 3.45 million-share initial public offering resulted in net proceeds to the company of $53 million, which were used primarily to repay outstanding credit debts and to redeem shares held by the company's largest shareholder. After the company went public, Chairman, Chief Executive Officer, and President Gary L. Monroe led Lason on an acquisitions spree designed to transform the company from a small regional firm in Michigan into a national electronic document force positioned to go global. These acquisitions, which began in June 1995 before the company went public, were accelerated to expand the company geographically into the Northeast, West, and Midwest. Monroe formerly ran Eastman Kodak Co.'s $300-million-a-year imaging business before joining Lason.

Expansion Through Acquisitions: 1997–99

Lason accelerated its acquisition program in 1997. An August 1997 stock offering of 2.5 million shares raised $58 million, which was used primarily to repay long-term debt the company had incurred to finance its previous acquisitions. Among the major acquisitions for 1997 were Churchill Communications Corporation for $9 million in cash and stock; Automated Enterprises Inc. for about $6.5 million in cash and stock; Image Conversion Systems Inc. for $20 million in cash and stock; Spectrum Document Services, Inc., for about $3.5 million; and VIP Imaging Inc. for $18.5 million in cash and stock. Lason also made several other acquisitions during the year for another $13 million.

Net revenues for 1997 increased 72 percent to $120.3 million, up from $69.9 million in 1996. Approximately $39.3 million of the increase in revenues was due to acquisitions and about $11.1 million from internal growth. Output processing accounted for $8.5 million of the firm's internal growth in 1997, with print on demand services contributing an additional $3 million in revenue and computer-output-to-laser-disk services adding some $2 million. These increases were offset by decreases in revenues from discontinued services. For 1997 gross profit increased to $39.5 million, up from $22.4 million in 1996, while net income increased from $3.7 million in 1996 to $9.1 million in 1997.

Company Perspectives:

It takes more than new technology to manage the explosion in document growth. Lason specialists focus on providing customers with strategic information solutions that translate into improved productivity and a better bottom line. It's a value proposition that makes Lason and its employees a valuable part of their customer's team.

In 1998 another stock offering of 2.9 million shares raised nearly $130 million. Lason completed 16 acquisitions in 1998, expanding the company's operations to 27 states and five countries. The large number of acquisitions reflected the consolidation that was taking place in the information management and direct marketing services industries.

In early 1998 Lason acquired Racom Information Technologies and API Systems, which were its two largest acquisitions to date and included its first international acquisition. It paid $26 million in cash and stock for Racom's parent company, Southern Microfilm Associates, Inc., and $25.3 million in cash and stock for API Systems. Another major acquisition was Consolidated Reprographics for $41.7 million in cash and stock. Other significant acquisitions included Lonestar Southwest Mailing Services, Inc. for $7 million, and City Microfilm, Inc. for $11.9 million.

During the year Lason acquired Quality Mailing & Fulfillment Services, Inc. of Detroit, Michigan. Quality had $4.6 million in 1997 sales. The acquisition gave Lason new fulfillment services capabilities, involving the assembly of multiple documents in a packet for mailing. Lason had outsourced its fulfillment services previously.

Lason added more international capabilities when it acquired Digital Imaging & Technologies Inc of Anaheim, California, a provider of image and data management services with operations in Mexico, Barbados, and Grenada. Lason paid $12.2 million for the company, which had 1997 revenues of $16 million.

Revenues for 1998 increased 132 percent to $279.8 million, and net income rose 101 percent to $18.2 million. The firm had an internal growth rate of 18 percent for the year and estimated that about 80 percent of 1998 revenues were from existing businesses.

In January 1999 Lason strengthened its management team by appointing John Messinger as president and chief operating officer (COO). Gary Monroe remained as chairman of the board and chief executive officer (CEO) after giving up his presidency. Messinger had joined Lason in 1997 after his company was acquired by Lason.

Lason's acquisition of Vetri Systems, Inc., a leading provider of electronic media services such as media-to-media conversions, HTML conversions for the Internet, and forms processing, also was completed in January 1999.

In March 1999 Lason acquired the London, England-based M-R Group plc, a firm that specialized in document and data management, in a deal valued at $145 million. For fiscal 1998 M-R had revenues of $76 million and had been increasing its revenues by 18 to 20 percent a year. It was Lason's largest acquisition to date. M-R's clients included the British government, major banks in Germany and England, and international oil companies. According to one analyst, the M-R acquisition made Lason the largest information management company in the world.

The M-R acquisition also added another 1,000 employees to Lason's work force of 8,000 and gave it additional offices in New York, Atlanta, Washington, and San Francisco. About 20 percent of M-R's business was in the United States and 80 percent in the United Kingdom.

In March 1999 Lason acquired Cover-All Computer Holdings, Inc., which had four operating locations in the greater Toronto, Ontario area and annual revenues of $13 million. The acquisition doubled Lason's revenue base in Canada. With 120 employees, Cover-All was a leading independent provider of data management and output processing services for the insurance, financial, utilities, and commercial markets.

In April 1999 Lason announced that it would acquire Redmond Technologies Inc., based in Richmond, Virginia. Redmond was a small information technology consulting firm that specialized in network and systems integration consulting services. It had about 20 employees. The acquisition strengthened Lason's capabilities in systems integration. In May Lason acquired another firm specializing in systems integration, MSCI Inc., that also offered imaging and scanning services. Based in Illinois, MSCI had 1998 revenues of $12 million. It was a leading provider of imaging services and systems integration for financial and commercial customers in the greater Chicago and St. Louis markets.

From March 25 to April 16, Lason's stock dropped from $55.37 a share to a low of $32 before rebounding to around $40 a share. With the pending M-R acquisition dependent on Lason's stock price, Lason revised the terms of its offer and increased the number of Lason shares that M-R stockholders would receive. M-R stockholders were to vote on the acquisition at M-R's June 7 annual meeting, where they overwhelmingly approved the merger. The merger was approved subsequently by the High Court of England and Wales.

During the year Lason introduced a new service, Lason Statement Express, which would allow customers to electronically distribute statements and process the subsequent electronic payments. The new service was linked to Visions, Lason's electronic document storage and retrieval service that allowed customers to maintain an interactive database of past statements for archive and customer service applications. Electronic bill presentment services were seen as expanding dramatically in the future.

In May 1999 Lason acquired Crest Information Technologies Inc., with headquarters in Cedar Rapids, Iowa and operations in Des Moines, Iowa, and Sioux Falls, South Dakota. With $15 million in annual revenues, Crest became the centerpiece of Lason's Midwest region. Crest president Jay Johnson was also named president of Lason's Midwest region. Crest provided imaging services along with data storage and retrieval.

Key Dates:

1985: Lason is founded in Michigan as a direct mail operation.
1996: Lason goes public and positions itself to become a national presence in information management.
1998: Sales reach almost $280 million.

That month Lason also acquired Marketing Associates, Inc., based in Bloomfield Hills, Michigan. With $11 million in annual revenues, Marketing Associates specialized in database management services primarily for commercial customers.

In August Lason acquired Addressing Services Co. Inc. (ASCO), based in East Hartford, Connecticut. The independent provider of business communications and output processing services had $15 million in annual revenues. The acquisition strengthened Lason's presence in the Northeast and New York metropolitan region.

Lason clearly was committed to its acquisition strategy, which was built on providing, on a regional basis, integrated information management services in three core areas: image and data capture, data management, and output processing. To finance its acquisition program, Lason in 1998 raised nearly $131 million through a stock offering and expanded its credit facility to $200 million.

After three solid years characterized by numerous acquisitions and revenue growth, Lason was perceived as a medium-sized player in its industry in early 1999. Some analysts felt that Lason had to become even bigger and dominate its market sector. That level of dominance was reached with the 1999 acquisition of the London, England-based M-R Group plc, which gave the company its first European operation and added substantially to its revenue base. Combined with other acquisitions made during 1999, Lason's revenues were expected to surpass the $500 million mark in 1999. For the year 2000, Lason was positioned to become a worldwide leading information management company.

Principal Subsidiaries

Lason Canada Co.

Principal Competitors

First Data Corp.; FYI Inc.; IKON Office Solutions Inc.; Pitney Bowes Inc.; Xerox Corp; IBM Corp.; EDS.

Further Reading

Brennan, Mike, "Troy, Mich.-Based Electronic Storage Firm Strives To Be Powerhouse," *Knight-Ridder/Tribune Business News,* February 25, 1999.

Herzog, Boaz, "Lason Nets Record Deals," *Detroit Free Press,* October 13, 1999, p. E2.

Leffal, J., "Michigan Company To Buy Richmond, Va-Based Technology Consulting Firm," *Knight-Ridder/Tribune Business News,* April 8, 1999.

Mercer, Tenisha, "Lason Deal Teetering: Stock Swing Could Kill M-R Group Purchase," *Crain's Detroit Business,* May 10, 1999, p. 2.

——, "Lason Wraps Up Deal for Calif. Company," *Crain's Detroit Business,* November 30, 1998, p. 1.

——, "Purchase Makes Lason Info-Management Giant," *Crain's Detroit Business,* March 29, 1999, p. 4.

Pryweller, Joseph, "When Size Matters: Industry Consolidation Forces Sale of Small Mail Service," *Crain's Detroit Business,* June 22, 1998, p. 3.

—David P. Bianco

Louisiana-Pacific®
Helping the forest work for people.®

Louisiana-Pacific Corporation

111 Southwest Fifth Avenue
Portland, Oregon 97204
U.S.A.
Telephone: (503) 221-0800
Fax: (503) 796-0204
Web site: http://www.lpcorp.com

Public Company
Incorporated: 1972
Employees: 10,000
Sales: $2.29 billion (1998)
Stock Exchanges: New York
Ticker Symbol: LPX
NAIC: 321113 Sawmills; 321212 Softwood Veneer and Plywood Manufacturing; 321213 Engineered Wood Member (Except Truss) Manufacturing; 321219 Reconstituted Wood Product Manufacturing

A leading manufacturer and marketer of building and lumber products, Louisiana-Pacific Corporation (L-P) revolutionized the industry by inventing alternatives to plywood and solid wood building products. Instead of relying on larger, more expensive old-growth timber, L-P found ways to make structural building products from small-diameter, fast-growing trees. L-P pioneered the use of oriented strand board (OSB)—a reconstituted plywood substitute made by pressing wood wafers together. OSB is the basis for many of L-P's structural building products, including the company's line of Visual Precision roof and wall sheathing, its SmartSystem wood siding and exterior panels, and its Top Notch T & G flooring. L-P also manufacturers industrial wood products, such as hardboard and medium density fiberboard, which are used by furniture and cabinet makers. Furthermore, along with wood products such as LPI joists and laminated veneer lumber, the company also produces Cocoon cellulose insulation. Plywood and pulp manufacturing round out L-P's operations. The company controls over 950,000 acres of timberland, and owns plants in 29 states, as well as in Canada and Ireland.

Forming a New Company

Louisiana-Pacific was formed in July 1972 when the Georgia-Pacific Corporation spun off the wholly owned subsidiary. Afer Georgia-Pacific had acquired 16 small firms in the southern United States, the Federal Trade Commission (FTC) accused the company of becoming a monopolist in the softwood plywood industry. As part of its settlement with the FTC, Georgia-Pacific agreed to divest 20 percent of its assets. William H. Hunt, a vice-chairman at Georgia-Pacific, was selected as Louisiana-Pacific's first chairman. In 1974 Harry A. Merlo, who had been chief executive officer of L-P since its foundation, succeeded Hunt as chairman while remaining CEO.

Prior to the official spinoff of L-P, Georgia-Pacific had transferred several of its operations to L-P ownership, including its Samoa, Ukiah, Intermountain, Weather-Seal, and Southern divisions, as well as its 50 percent investments in Alaska's Ketchikan Pulp Company; Ketchikan Spruce Mills, Inc.; and Ketchikan International Sales Company. However, Georgia-Pacific had kept most of its low-cost timber reserves and the bulk of its tree farms for itself. Thus the newly independent L-P had to "scramble for raw materials," particularly timber, as the July 29, 1990 *Portland Oregonian* explained.

This proved to be an especially difficult task as timber shortages wracked the entire industry. Overcutting, Japanese demand for logs, and pressure on the U.S. Forest Service to tighten harvesting restrictions on large trees caused prices to soar. To make matters worse, L-P lost 26,000 acres of prime old-growth timberland when the U.S. government appropriated the property to expand the Redwood National Park in northern California.

Merlo strove to shepherd the company through its early difficulties. L-P acquired several lumber companies in California, Oregon, Montana, Washington, Missouri, and Alabama, and in 1976 it purchased the Fibreboard Corporation, a manufacturer of products used in making furniture and cabinets. In 1979, the company bought fifteen building-material centers in southern California from Lone Star Industries, which provided L-P with much needed distribution centers.

Company Perspectives:

We are creating a new Louisiana-Pacific: customer-driven, with a strong technology base, staffed by skilled and well-trained people whose capabilities and efforts are aimed at building the best, most cost-efficient manufacturer and marketer of building products in North America.

A Breakthrough Product

To ensure its long-term success, however, L-P would need to compensate for its comparative dearth of southern pine and Douglas fir timber, as well as lumber production. To address this shortfall, L-P turned its attention to the development of wood products derived from less-expensive and faster-growing trees, such as cottonwood and aspen. As Merlo told the *Portland Oregonian* in 1990, "we recognized that the days of making wood products from big trees were numbered for both economic and environmental reasons." In the late 1970s, the company began manufacturing OSB by slicing logs into wafers, mixing the wafers with resin, and then pressing them into sheets. First introduced under the trade name Waferwood (later re-christened Inner-Seal), this new product line revolutionized the construction industry by offering a less expensive, stronger alternative to plywood sheathing and sub-flooring. After opening its first Inner-Seal mill in 1980, L-P advertised the product as "the smart man's plywood."

Expansion During the 1980s

L-P's OSB products protected the company from the vicissitudes of the timber market. Buoyed by this success, the company soon expanded its line of products made from reconstituted wood to include I-beams for floor joists and rafters. These structural beams used half as much lumber as their solid wood counterparts, yet were stronger and lighter. L-P also introduced a concrete form of Inner-Seal, and in 1985 began to market Inner-Seal siding for the exterior of homes. Driven by these breakthroughs, a housing boom, and a thriving remodeling and repair business that increased demand for its specialty building products, L-P's sales grew 50 percent between 1980 and 1988, according to the *Portland Oregonian*. During the same period, its profits increased 400 percent. Moreover, OSB products accounted for an escalating portion of the company's total sales. Only six percent of sales in 1980, the Inner-Seal line by 1990 amounted to almost 30 percent of total sales volume. L-P's sales of lumber—once the mainstay of the building industry—decreased from 53 to 30 percent over the same period.

L-P made a number of acquisitions to strengthen its position. In 1986, the company purchased Kirby Forest Industries and the California properties of Timber Realization Company. From these transactions, L-P gained almost 830,000 acres of timberland, which helped balance the land taken in 1978 for Redwood National Park. (L-P received a final payment of $440 million from the government for this land in 1988.) In 1990, L-P bought Weather Guard Inc., a manufacturer of housing insulation made from recycled newsprint, as well as MiTek Wood Products, a North Carolina-based producer of laminated veneer lumber and engineered wood I-beams.

The company also continued to invent new alternatives to existing building materials. In 1990, L-P completed its first factory to make FiberBond, a wallboard. Furthermore, FiberBond held nails better than other wallboard and could be used as sheathing. Merlo was ecstatic about his company's breakthrough. FiberBond "is the most exciting product line that we have embarked upon in our short history," he crowed to the *Portland Oregonian* in July 1990.

The Early 1990s

During 1990, however, sales and profits in the company's softwood lumber, plywood, and building products areas slumped due to weakening demand. This situation was attributed to an economic downturn, increasing concerns over the U.S. federal budget deficit, and fears about the unsettled global geopolitical environment. The construction industry suffered because of bankers' reluctance to finance new projects and consumers' decisions to delay home purchases. Housing starts for 1990 fell to 1.19 million, the lowest level since 1982 and down 13.3 percent from 1989. L-P responded to these developments by curtailing production at many of its plants and increasing exports of its specialty building products.

The pulp market also experienced slowing growth in 1990. After a four-year period of rapidly rising prices, pulp manufacturers then faced eroding profit margins due to worldwide economic problems and larger than normal inventories. Although L-P saw its own pulp sales and profits peak in mid-1989 and expected only a minor recovery in 1991, the company continued to operate three pulp manufacturing mills. One mill supplied paper pulp to non-integrated paper producers. A second mill produced dissolving pulp for manufacturers of rayon and cellophane products. The third and newest pulp mill, using a bleached chemi-thermo mechanical pump process, revolutionized pulp production by eliminating the use of chlorine and operated in a completely closed system without discharge into neighboring water supplies. This mill marketed its output to manufacturers of printing and writing papers.

L-P was able to rebound smartly from the downturn of 1990. While its competitors struggled in the face of dwindling timber supplies, L-P enjoyed record sales in 1992, 1993, and 1994. According to the *Spokane Journal of Business*, "L-P [was] flourishing because it had vigorously developed alternatives to dimensional lumber and plywood." Indeed, Merlo told the *Wall Street Journal* that "technology"—not old-growth timber resources—"had proven to be [the company's] lifeblood." Profits for 1992 were up 216 percent from the previous year, and in 1994, the company achieved an all-time high of $3.04 billion in sales. By that year, only one-third of L-P's sales came from dimensional lumber—the studs and solid wood joists that frame houses—while over half its revenue came from OSB products, and another 20 percent from engineered wood products and pulp.

Key Dates:

1972: Louisiana-Pacific is spun off from Georgia-Pacific.
1974: Harry Merlo is named Louisiana-Pacific's first chairman.
1978: Louisiana-Pacific acquires Fibreboard Corporation; U.S. government acquires a portion of Louisiana-Pacific's timberlands to form Redwood National Park in California.
1985: Louisiana-Pacific begins marketing its Oriented Strand Board (OSB) as an exterior siding.
1990: Lawsuits relating to defective OSB exterior siding begin.
1996: Mark Suwyn replaces Merlo as chairman and CEO.
1998: Louisiana-Pacific acquires ABT Building Products as part of its effort to focus on the building products market.

Lawsuits, Threatening Louisiana-Pacific's Future

Despite its many achievements, L-P encountered a number of serious obstacles in the 1990s. Foremost among these were lawsuits pertaining to its simulated cedar Inner-Seal exterior siding. Many homeowners alleged that Inner-Seal siding, which carried a 25-year warranty, began to rot prematurely—discoloring, disintegrating, and even growing fungi. Class-action suits brought by various collections of homeowners as well as the attorney general of Minnesota, were filed. Although L-P admitted to no wrongdoing, the company moved quickly to settle the cases. At the close of 1991, L-P had paid over $22 million to settle OSB claims, and between 1993 and 1994, the company paid out an additional $14 million. In 1996, L-P committed at least $275 million to a settlement with 800,000 homeowners who had used the Inner-Seal siding.

L-P's woes did not end there, however. In 1996, L-P paid $65 million to settle a class-action lawsuit filed the previous year by L-P shareholders who alleged that the company had ''violated securities laws by failing to disclose that the company's oriented-strand boards were defective,'' as the *Portland Oregonian* reported on December 5, 1996. It was the largest securities settlement in Oregon history. Also that year, the company settled a 1993 sexual harassment suit against Merlo. Moreover, the state of Colorado brought a 56-count indictment against L-P in 1995, charging fraud and environmental violations at its plant in Montrose, Colorado. The same year, L-P's eight-person board ''lost confidence in the ability of Merlo and his top two lieutenants to steer the *Fortune* 500 company,'' declared the August 4, 1995, edition of the *Portland Oregonian.* Merlo resigned and was replaced as chairman and CEO by Mark Suwyn, a former executive at International Paper.

Rebuilding in the Late 1990s

Under this new leadership, L-P began the difficult task of regrouping. The year 1995 had been particularly difficult, one in which the company endured a net loss of $51.7 million. The market for building products had sunk as an influx of Canadian lumber had flooded the United States. High interest rates and poor weather (which affected home building) only exacerbated L-P's problems. Even more dangerous to L-P, however, was the inauguration of several rival OSB mills. As OSB increasingly replaced plywood as a basic construction material, Inner-Seal became less a specialty item exclusively made by L-P and more of a building commodity.

Faced with these new threats, Suwyn implemented a multi-dimensional plan for recovery. First, the company strove to eliminate unprofitable operations. In 1996, L-P closed the Ketchikan Paper Company, as well as 22 plants and mills. More closings followed in 1997 and 1998, and the company sold off a number of additional operations, including the Weather-Seal door and window division in 1998. All told, L-P sold over $875 million of assets during the three-year period. ''The assets sales will do two things for us,'' Suwyn told *Business Wire.* ''They will provide us with additional financial flexibility to grow the company and allow us to focus all our management attention on becoming the premier supplier of building materials.''

Suwyn also concentrated on developing L-P's specialty products lines. As its past innovations had become industry standards (and were imitated by numerous competitors), it was essential for L-P to launch new products that would give the company an edge over its rivals. To further this goal, L-P engaged in a series of targeted acquisitions. In 1996, L-P purchased Associated Chemists, a key supplier of specialty coatings to the wood products industry, as well as GreenStone Industries, a manufacturer of cellulose insulation, and Tecton Laminates Corp., a producer of laminated veneer lumber and wood I-joists used in the construction industry. Two years later, L-P acquired ABT Building Products Corporation, a transaction it heralded as a way ''to expand its specialty products lines and complement its low-cost commodity building products,'' according to the *Wall Street Journal.* In 1999, L-P purchased Evans Forest Products Ltd., a Canadian manufacturer of engineered wood and lumber products.

L-P did more than simply buy other companies, however. In 1997 L-P unveiled its state-of-the-art Advanced Technology Center, which provided the company with the facilities to conceive, test, and improve new offerings. L-P soon introduced a bevy of new product systems, including Smart Start siding, TechShield energy efficient structural panels, TopNotch flooring, and Cocoon insulation. L-P's 1998 introduction of its Visual Precision Sheathing was lauded by the construction industry. Voted the year's top product by *Prodealer*, the sheathing also was named the best new product by *Today's Homeowner* magazine.

A final prong of L-P's rebuilding efforts involved improving operations. In 1996, the company instituted an intensive employee training course—*Rapid Change Technologies*—designed to enhance workers' communication skills and to empower them to accept new ideas with ease. To increase productivity, L-P utilized *Business Process Improvement* technology to make its OSB mills more efficient. L-P also sought to bolster the company's relationship with large and national home center chains, such as Home Depot and Lowes. These ''superstores'' represented the fastest-growing segment of the building industry.

The outcome of L-P's vigorous reorganization was not immediately evident. Sales for 1996 were 13 percent lower than in 1995, and resulted in a net yearly loss of $200.7 million. Although the company again operated at a net loss of $101.8 million in 1997, executives remained optimistic.

In 1998, L-P returned once more to profitability, achieving $12.8 million of net profit from $2.29 billion in sales. Reinforced by a strong housing market, a booming economy, operational improvements, and greater numbers of specialty products, Louisiana-Pacific's future looked bright.

Principal Subsidiaries

ABT Building Products Corporation; ABT Canada Limited; Associated Chemists, Inc.; CP Investment Corp.; GreenStone Industries, Inc.; Louisiana-Pacific Canada, Ltd.; Louisiana-Pacific Chile SA; Louisiana-Pacific Coillte Ireland Limited; Louisiana-Pacific de Mexico, SA de CV; Louisiana-Pacific de Venezuela, CA; Louisiana-Pacific Polymers, Inc.; Louisiana-Pacific Timber Company, L-P Redwood, LLC; New Waverly Transportation, Inc.

Principal Competitors

Georgia-Pacific Group; Boise-Cascade Corporation; International Paper Company; Weyerhaeuser Company; MacMillan Bloedel Limited; Champion International Corporation; Potlatch Corporation; Rayonier Inc.

Further Reading

''Judge OKs Millions for L-P Investors,'' *Portland Oregonian,* December 5, 1996.

Kadera, Jim, ''New Ideas, New Products at Louisiana-Pacific,'' *Portland Oregonian*, July 29, 1990.

Levine, Jonathon, ''Finally, the Lumber Giants Are Almost Out of the Woods,'' *Business Week*, September 16, 1985.

''Louisiana-Pacific Corp.: Accord Set for Acquisition of ABT Building Products,'' *Wall Street Journal*, January 20, 1999.

''Louisiana-Pacific Earnings Up More Than 300 Percent,'' *Associated Press*, January 27, 1993.

''Louisiana-Pacific Net Increased 58% As Sales Rose 13% for 3rd Period,'' *Wall Street Journal*, October 18, 1984.

''Louisiana-Pacific to Restructure,'' *Do-It-Yourself Retailing*, December 1, 1997.

''More Class Actions Against Louisiana-Pacific,'' *National Law Journal*, June 26, 1995.

''Profits: Forest Products Firms Expect Recovery to Continue,'' *Wall Street Journal*, May 9, 1983.

''Profits: Wood Products Sales Slump, Paper and Pulp Steady,'' *Wall Street Journal*, February 10, 1982.

Read, Paul, ''Louisiana-Pacific Flourishes Despite Industry's Tough Times,'' *Spokane Journal of Business*, April 28, 1994.

Woodward, Steve, ''Vintage Merlo,'' *Portland Oregonian*, August 4, 1995.

—Joan Harpham and Sandy Schustef
—updated by Rebecca Stanfel

Serving through Stewardship

LUTHERAN BROTHERHOOD
625 Fourth Avenue South Minneapolis, Minnesota 55415

Lutheran Brotherhood

625 Fourth Avenue South
Minneapolis, Minnesota 55415
U.S.A.
Telephone: (612) 340-7000
Toll free: (800) 990-6290
Fax: (612) 340-6897
Web site: http://www.lutheranbrotherhood.com

Private Company
Incorporated: 1917 as Luther Union
Employees: 2,648
Sales: $1,693 million (1998)
NAIC: 524113 Direct Life Insurance Carriers

Lutheran Brotherhood is the second-largest fraternal benefit society in the United States. It provides a variety of financial services to members of the Lutheran faith and their families. Lutheran Brotherhood offers life insurance, health insurance, and property and casualty insurance to its members, and operates mutual funds, annuities, retirement plans, and other financial services. The company runs a bank, the LB Community Bank and Trust, which offers traditional banking services both to Lutheran Brotherhood members and to the general public. The company also runs a network of financial programs to aid Lutheran charitable organizations. It provides matching funds for these charities, offers scholarships and loans, and helps congregations meet financial goals through services such as arranging electronic transfer of funds from members to their church collection plates. Lutheran Brotherhood also funds and manages a wide range of community service projects. The company is the major sponsor behind a national initiative to foster positive behavior in teens called Healthy Communities, Healthy Youth. In the late 1990s Lutheran Brotherhood had more than $19 billion in consolidated assets, and more than one million members.

Early History

Lutheran Brotherhood began in 1917 as an aid society for members of the Norwegian Lutheran Church of America. Norwegian Lutherans in the United States had belonged to three different church organizations, called synods, that held longstanding theological differences. In June 1917 the three synods held a massive convention in St. Paul, Minnesota, and agreed to merge into a unified church body. Thousands of delegates attended the historic meeting, and thousands of other Norwegian-Americans observed the proceedings and celebrated the new church, the Norwegian Lutheran Church of America. Prominent members of the unification convention were Jacob Preus, state insurance commissioner for Minnesota, and Herman Ekern, a Chicago attorney and one-time insurance commissioner for Wisconsin. These men were concerned that many Norwegian Lutherans felt that the Bible forbade them to buy insurance. Norwegian Lutherans commonly interpreted several verses from the New Testament, including Matthew 6:34, ''Take therefore no thought for the morrow: for the morrow shall take thought for the things of itself,'' as meaning that insurance was not sanctioned by the Bible. As a result, not only were Norwegian Lutheran church buildings of the time typically not insured, but church members who took out life insurance were shunned. Many church members therefore took out insurance secretly, or else joined secret societies and lodges that gave insurance benefits. Ekern and Preus were worried that as more Norwegian Lutherans left their rural communities and moved to big cities, more church members would be left without even the benefit of the informal aid delivered by friends and neighbors in a crisis. Legitimate insurance was desperately needed by the Lutheran community. Ekern and Preus dared to raise this volatile issue at the unification convention. They were given the go-ahead to begin a mutual aid society. This was to be a non-profit corporation open to church members. Its stated goals were very broad, and included fostering patriotism and providing proper entertainment and amusements for its membership. But its articles of incorporation also spelled out that the aid society would pay out benefits in case of death, disability, or sickness. The society was named Luther Union, with Ekern and Preus as directors and the Reverend Thore Eggen as president. Within a year, it had over 500 applicants, and it received its Minnesota life insurance license in September 1918.

The concept of the mutual aid society dated back to shortly after the Civil War in America. Little commercial or government insurance was available to working people at the time. Many

Company Perspectives:

The mission of Lutheran Brotherhood is to work together to provide financial security for members and to serve Lutherans, their congregations, institutions, and communities.

workers participated in fraternal societies, which were generally social clubs for people in a particular field, such as railroad workers or mill workers. These fraternal societies gradually began offering insurance benefits, with all the members chipping in a certain amount for the surviving family if a member died. Most life insurance in the United States was issued by these fraternal benefit societies by the turn of the century.

Despite Luther Union's initial success in signing up members for its life insurance benefits, the Norwegian Lutheran Church was still apparently uncomfortable with the idea of the mutual aid society. Luther Union issued a report on its activities to the church in 1919, but the report was not officially recognized. This was the end of Luther Union's legal ties to the Norwegian Lutheran Church. Luther Union solicited help from a broader organization, the Lutheran Brotherhood of America, or LBA. The Lutheran Brotherhood had been formed in 1917 to provide for the comfort and spiritual life of Lutherans in the armed services. It had grown quickly to approximately 60,000 members, and it brought together Lutherans of many different synods. Luther Union made a formal agreement with the LBA in 1920 to become the group's insurance auxiliary, open to all Lutherans. It gained national exposure through advertising in the LBA newsletter, as well as some financial backing. Luther Union decided at that point to change its name to Lutheran Brotherhood. This was somewhat confusing, as it was still a distinct entity from the Lutheran Brotherhood of America. This became a troubling issue. Lutheran Brotherhood grew slowly, making only slight gains in membership through the mid-1920s. Some members and employees suggested changing the name again, to make it clear that Lutheran Brotherhood was not the LBA, and that any Lutheran, whether in the LBA or not, was eligible for its insurance. Lutheran Brotherhood's board declined to change the name, but by 1927 the point was moot, as the LBA dissolved.

By the mid-1920s, Lutheran Brotherhood had around 350 sales representatives. They recruited members mostly from rural areas of the Midwest. It was not an easy job, and most of the Brotherhood's salesmen worked part-time, selling insurance as a sideline. Others were dedicated travelers, visiting far-flung small towns and persuading first the Lutheran minister, then the congregation, of the benefits of life insurance. The salesmen encountered strong resistance to the idea of insurance because of the long-held beliefs of Norwegian Lutherans, so Lutheran Brotherhood began publishing a magazine in 1924, aimed principally at gaining the trust of members and prospective members. Entitled *The Bond,* the magazine used many strategies to win converts to insurance. It profiled church leaders who worked with Lutheran Brotherhood, ran articles from salesmen who were ministers first, insurance brokers second, and even reached out to children with essays describing how nice Lutheran Brotherhood's directors were. *The Bond* also took the opportunity to proclaim Lutheran Brotherhood's financial soundness. It declared that its healthy-living Lutheran members had a low mortality rate, and printed tables demonstrating that the death benefits the society paid out far outweighed the premiums paid by the deceased.

Through the Great Depression

The stock market crash of October 1929 destroyed many businesses, but Lutheran Brotherhood was not immediately affected. Its membership continued to grow, and in 1930 its total insurance in force grew by approximately $6 million, to reach nearly $37 million. The total assets of the society stood at almost $2.5 million in that year. But because of the shakiness of the American economy, investing those assets became quite risky. So in 1931 Lutheran Brotherhood hired an investment manager for the first time. Harold Ingvaldson took the position, and he initiated a lending program. Lutheran Brotherhood began writing mortgages, mostly for its members' single-family homes, family farms, or Lutheran churches. By the end of the decade, the society had issued over 1,400 loans, worth around $5.5 million. Despite the lean times, Lutheran Brotherhood continued to find new recruits. In 1937 the society had 48,500 members, and over $61 million of insurance in force. Most of its members were found in the Midwest, but the Brotherhood gradually widened out, reaching farmers in Pennsylvania and extending loans to clients in California and Florida. Though the bulk of the society's members lived in rural communities, by the mid-1940s it had penetrated into Chicago, which became a ripe picking ground for new members.

Lutheran Brotherhood was quietly and conservatively managed, and it blossomed through the 1940s from a small regional insurance company to a major player. By the end of the decade, the society's assets had grown to approximately $65 million, and it had about $366 million of insurance in force. Its president was still Herman Ekern, who had been one of the original instigators of the fraternal benefit society and who had taken over from Reverend Eggen in 1929. But at the end of the 1940s, younger executives at the society began agitating for certain practical changes. Lutheran Brotherhood was using an actuarial table called the American Experience Table, which was based on mortality rates from the early 1940s. Ekern was opposed to using a more modern and accurate table, and finally he resigned over the issue. He left the society in 1951, and a new era at Lutheran Brotherhood began.

Growth and Modernization in the 1950s and 1960s

Lutheran Brotherhood's new president was a Minneapolis lawyer named Carl Granrud. He had served on the board of directors since 1940. One of his first acts was to draft plans for a new corporate headquarters. The society had previously rented space in a downtown Minneapolis office building, but Granrud wanted it to have a grand building of its own. This was erected between 1955 and 1956, and it became known as "the green building," a Minneapolis landmark.

Granrud also pushed Lutheran Brotherhood to build a national presence. Though it was well-known in the Midwest, even selling insurance in rural Pennsylvania had been difficult because its name was not recognized. Lutheran Brotherhood

Key Dates:

1917: Luther Union founded.
1920: Name changed to Lutheran Brotherhood.
1929: Herman Ekern becomes president.
1962: Lutheran Brotherhood first issues health insurance.
1969: Debuts its first mutual fund.
1980: Clair Strommen assumes presidency.
1998: Brotherhood buys a Minneapolis thrift.

hired a Minneapolis advertising agency, who convinced the society that advertising only in Lutheran publications meant that it missed many prospective members. The society began taking out ads in secular magazines for the first time, advertising in popular mass-market journals like *Life* and *Reader's Digest.* By the early 1960s, Lutheran Brotherhood's advertising had expanded to include billboards across the country, much print advertising, and even radio commercials. In 1955 the society produced a filmstrip giving the history of Lutheran Brotherhood and clearly explaining benefits. Long a conservative organization, Lutheran Brotherhood found itself on the cutting edge of multi-media selling. It was one of the first insurance companies to use a filmstrip.

The society also embraced technology. Lutheran Brotherhood worked with two IBM computers, which ran a program to analyze how much insurance a prospect needed. Few other insurance companies at the time were computerized. By the late 1950s, the society had grown to over 300,000 members, and close to $850 million of insurance in force.

Lutheran Brotherhood began offering health insurance in 1962. Later in the decade, it began investigating offering its own mutual fund. Mutual funds pooled the savings of many small investors, and skilled managers guided the funds so that returns were generally high. This kind of investment had an advantage over life insurance because its benefits rose as the stock market rose, while life insurance offered a fixed amount. With inflation, the relative value of the life insurance benefit might dwindle. Lutheran Brotherhood made careful study of the mutual fund field, and then began offering its own Lutheran Brotherhood Fund in 1969. It did this through two new subsidiaries, Lutheran Brotherhood Securities Corp. and the Lutheran Brotherhood Research Corp. Lutheran Brotherhood's mutual funds became very popular with members. The first fund attracted nearly $12 million in its initial investment period, much more than management had hoped for. Through the 1970s, the society added several more funds, tailored to different needs.

Change in the 1980s

The success of Lutheran Brotherhood's mutual funds was one indication of the change that was overtaking the insurance industry. Previously, life insurance was seen as a safe investment that could be used as guaranteed retirement income. But rising inflation made life insurance a less comfortable plan. Growth in the insurance industry slowed as consumers preferred to put money in other types of investment plans. And policy holders also found they could borrow against the cash value of their life insurance policies and invest that money at higher rates. Lutheran Brotherhood began to find its assets depleted by its members' borrowing. The society found a new president, Clair Strommen, in 1980, and Strommen moved quickly to force Lutheran Brotherhood to be more productive and competitive. First, Strommen introduced new insurance products and overhauled old ones to make sure the society was offering competitive rates. The society worked to improve the education and training of its field force, and sought to stem the declining productivity of many of its older general agents. The general agents were responsible for recruiting and training the district representatives who worked the field selling policies. By the early 1980s, many of these general agents were nearing retirement age, and their productivity was not as high as it had been. Between 1980 and 1985, more than two-thirds of Lutheran Brotherhood's general agencies changed leadership, as agents retired, resigned, or took new posts. But the changes had results, as the amount of insurance in force actually doubled between 1980 and 1987, from around $10 billion to over $20 billion.

The society also continued to bring in new technology. In 1986 Lutheran Brotherhood began issuing its agents laptop computers outfitted with sophisticated software. The software was able to produce graphics such as graphs and pie charts, so sales people could easily demonstrate values to prospective clients. It also hooked its sales force up to the home office via e-mail. Lutheran Brotherhood was in the forefront of this type of technology in the insurance industry.

Challenges in the 1990s

By 1990, Lutheran Brotherhood had spent about $10 million on computers, software, and training for its sales force. Life insurance accounted for about 75 percent of the society's sales at that time. It had approximately one million members, and $26 billion of insurance in force. As a non-profit organization, its excess earnings went to its charitable projects, and so it was not society policy to shower its sales force with expensive gadgets. But the investment in laptops had concrete results. The society first deployed laptops at the end of 1986, and then made a significant upgrade in hardware and software in 1990. Life insurance sales rose by 35 percent in the four months after the new laptops were introduced compared to the same period a year earlier, an increase attributed to the better features of its new machines.

The Brotherhood's mutual funds also prospered in the 1990s. While the whole field of mutual funds grew, Lutheran Brotherhood continued to market exclusively to Lutherans. Its family of funds grew to six by the mid-1990s, with its oldest, the Lutheran Brotherhood Fund, holding $525 million in assets by 1994. This fund had a proud record, with growth over 13 percent annually over the five years preceding 1994. Another fund, the Lutheran Brotherhood Opportunity Growth Fund, was singled out in *Barron's* in 1996 for its stellar performance.

The society continued to introduce new products for its Lutheran membership, including a disability policy that paid out a person's regular church donations along with an income benefit if a claimant became disabled. It also pioneered a unique tool in 1998 called Simply Giving. This allowed members to make donations to their churches through an automated electronic payment plan. This helped churches receive consistent donations, and made the process easier for churchgoers. Lutheran Brotherhood designed this first-ever program, and made it available free of charge to Lutheran churches. The Brotherhood also began offering regular banking services to its members in 1998. It spent $3.5 million to buy a small Minneapolis thrift called Metro Community Bank. This was to serve the Minneapolis community as well as the Lutheran Brotherhood members at large, who had access to the bank through the Internet. The bank's services included checking accounts, home mortgages, certificates of deposit, and trust services.

By the end of the 1990s, Lutheran Brotherhood was rated as a very stable, solid, and consistent provider of financial services. Its particular strength was its customer loyalty. Standard & Poor's continued to rate the society AA+ in 1999, based on its strong niche market and the low policy lapse rate of its dedicated customer base. At the same time, another credit rating company, Duff & Phelps, brought the Brotherhood's rating down from AAA to AA+. Though both raters affirmed the society's very strong financial position, the outlook for Lutheran Brotherhood seemed to be growing more dim. While the loyalty of its Lutheran members was of signal importance, the Lutheran market was not growing, and its members were on average older than the general population. Yet the Brotherhood had shown repeatedly that it could overcome obstacles to growth, and it had adapted many times to changes in the industry.

Principal Subsidiaries

Lutheran Brotherhood Financial Corporation.

Principal Competitors

Aid Association for Lutherans; Aetna; Prudential.

Further Reading

Calian, Sara, ''These Fund Investors Look to a Higher Power,'' *Wall Street Journal,* January 7, 1994, p. R10.

Hakala Associates, Inc., *A Common Bond: The Story of Lutheran Brotherhood,* Minneapolis: Lutheran Brotherhood, 1989.

Jones, David C., ''Fraternal's Producers Go High Tech,'' *National Underwriter,* November 2, 1987, pp. 10–11.

Lampman, Jane, ''The Electronic Collection Plate,'' *Christian Science Monitor,* August 5, 1999, p. 14.

Lutton, Laura Pavlenko, ''Lutherans-Only Insurer Buying Minneapolis Thrift to Offer Banking Products,'' *American Banker,* July 8, 1998, p. 9.

Pompili, Tony, ''Non-Profit Insurer Bets on Lap-Tops for Better Field Position,'' *PC Week,* October 20, 1987, p. C4.

''S&P Affirms Lutheran Brotherhood 'AA+' Rating,'' *PR Newswire,* July 27, 1999, p. 9995.

Skillings, Jonathan, ''Laptop Upgrade Answer to Productivity Prayers,'' *PC Week,* December 3, 1990, p. 17.

Ward, Sandra, ''Lutheran Fund Rates Hosannas,'' *Barron's,* September 9, 1996, pp. 43–44.

—A. Woodward

March of Dimes

1275 Mamaroneck Avenue
White Plains, New York 10605
U.S.A.
Telephone: (914) 428-7100
Fax: (914) 428-8203
Web site: http://www.modimes.org

Not-For-Profit Foundation
Incorporated: 1938
Employees: 225
Sales: $181.3 million (1998)
NAIC: 813212 Voluntary Health Organizations

The March of Dimes is one of the most successful and well-known nonprofit foundations in the United States. It was founded to fight polio, and after the disease was controlled by the invention of a vaccine, the March of Dimes turned its efforts to eradicating birth defects. The foundation funds research, giving grants to hundreds of scientists annually at a cost of more than $20 million. It organizes fundraising events to promote awareness and bring in cash for its programs, and it helps run community services and educational projects. The March of Dimes is responsible for backing major scientific breakthroughs in genetics and prenatal health. The organization has been highly effective in advocating for women's and children's health, for example working through its volunteers to pass legislation guaranteeing women a minimum hospital stay of 48 hours after giving birth to a baby. The March of Dimes also sponsors public awareness campaigns, such as its work in the late 1990s to encourage women of childbearing age to consume folic acid to help prevent birth defects. The roster of esteemed scientists the March of Dimes has supported through grants includes ten winners of the Nobel Prize. Among these laureates are some of the most famous names in medicine, including Linus Pauling, who discovered the relationship between molecular structure and human diseases, and James Watson, the discoverer of the structure of DNA. The March of Dimes is organized into more than 90 local chapters, overseen by a national office.

Polio Strikes in 1916

The March of Dimes began as an organization to combat a baffling and fearsome disease, polio. The sickness caused an inflammation of the spinal cord that could leave its victims unable to move arms, legs, or even lungs. Although isolated outbreaks had been noted since the middle of the 19th century, it was not until 1916 that it became serious enough even to be given a name. The first devastating outbreak of polio in the United States came in the summer of 1916. It began in New York City and spread to neighboring states, striking mainly children. The cause of the outbreak was completely unknown. It began with a few cases in June, and by August almost 9,000 people had come down with the ravaging illness. The epidemic spread, finally covering 26 states, causing 6,000 deaths out of a total of some 27,000 cases. It had lasted approximately six months. Because most of the victims were less than five years old, the disease was called infantile paralysis and given the scientific name poliomyelitis, which means inflammation of the anterior spinal cord.

Most of the victims of the outbreak survived, but many had withered limbs, for which there was no acceptable treatment or therapy. Few facilities existed for the care of such disabled people, and since the cause of the disease was unknown, families who had been visited by it were subject to prejudice that they had brought it on themselves through lack of hygiene. Many outbreaks of polio followed the 1916 epidemic, devastating communities. Though most of polio's victims were young children, it also struck older people. In 1921 Franklin Delano Roosevelt, former Under-Secretary of the Navy, one-time Democratic vice-presidential candidate, and one of the leading lights of the Democratic party, became ill. On August 10 he went to bed fatigued. Two days later, his legs were paralyzed. He had polio, and he never walked unassisted again.

Roosevelt spent the next seven years trying to cure his paralysis. He was a wealthy and influential man, and he used his money on all the available treatments, from massage to stimulation with electrical currents. In 1924 he visited a spa in Georgia called Warm Springs to bathe in its naturally heated waters. Warm Springs was a resort for well-to-do Americans, but Roosevelt's fame attracted other polio victims to the spa, and it soon

Company Perspectives:

The mission of the March of Dimes is to improve the health of babies by preventing birth defects and infant mortality. The March of Dimes carries out this mission through programs of research, community services, education and advocacy.

transformed into a therapeutic center for people trying to recover from paralysis. The waters actually did nothing to cure the paralysis and muscle atrophy, but Roosevelt was able to exercise his other muscles in the warm pools so that he had the strength to support himself on crutches or on someone's arm. He purchased Warm Springs in 1926, spending what was estimated as half his personal fortune to do so. Two years later he ran for governor of New York, and in 1932 he was elected to his first term as president.

When the nation's most famous polio victim returned to public office, he left the running of Warm Springs to his law partner, Basil O'Connor. The spa was terribly expensive to keep up, and O'Connor helped Roosevelt transform it into a nonprofit foundation for polio victims. Its new name was the Georgia Warm Springs Foundation. O'Connor began raising money from wealthy patients and their families and used these funds to help other less well-off polio sufferers. Warm Springs was soon joined by a sister foundation, the National Foundation for Infantile Paralysis. After Roosevelt became president, O'Connor used his fame as the key to fundraising. Beginning in 1935, the National Foundation inaugurated a series of fundraising balls in the month of January, pegged to fall near Roosevelt's birthday. In its first year, 6,000 balls were held across the country, and the Foundation raised close to $800,000. The money went both to patient care at Warm Springs and to funding research into the cause and prevention of poliomyelitis.

Roosevelt's Foundation from the 1930s to the 1950s

By 1938, the January balls were in decline, bringing in less and less money each year, and a new kind of promotion was needed. That year the name March of Dimes was coined by the vaudeville entertainer Eddie Cantor, who was a leading fundraiser both for the Democratic party and for the National Foundation's balls. The phrase was a play on the "March of Time," a popular series of newsreels. The implication of Cantor's phrase was that even a dime was of use in the fight against polio. Cantor and other entertainment world luminaries stumped for the March of Dimes campaign, urging people to send dimes to the White House. President Roosevelt established the March of Dimes foundation in January of 1938. This name was tagged onto the National Foundation's, effectively revitalizing that organization. The March of Dimes immediately began issuing research grants, giving scholarships to doctors and nurses, and providing equipment for laboratories and hospitals. The nonprofit foundation was desperately needed, because there was little government funding for medical research, no public health insurance, and little private health insurance. The March of Dimes bought iron lungs, crutches, and laboratory equipment as well as trucks to transport it in, so all that was needed could be moved quickly to regions in the midst of an outbreak. National headquarters were in Basil O'Connor's Wall Street law office, and local chapters sprang up across the country. Much fundraising was done by Hollywood stars and other popular idols. Mickey Rooney and Elvis Presley made March of Dimes fundraising appeals, as well as actresses Lucille Ball, Zsa Zsa Gabor, and Helen Hayes, among others. But the local chapters effectively raised money without star power. The March of Dimes called on ordinary people to contribute just a little money. One tactic was to go to movie theaters, stop the film in the middle, turn up the lights, and pass out a collection can. March of Dimes collection cans were placed on store counters, and people filled them with change. Children mailed in dimes on special cards.

Much of the credit for enlisting the middle class into the March of Dimes is attributed to Elaine Whitelaw. A wealthy New York society woman, Whitelaw made her career out of raising money. She first became a fundraiser during the Spanish Civil War, when she raised money for the Loyalists. During World War II, she worked with the National War Fund. In 1943 President Roosevelt appointed Whitelaw to head the national women's committee of the March of Dimes. She moved in high society circles, dining with politicians, writers, and artists. Nevertheless, Whitelaw understood that polio was an issue that touched every ordinary woman with children. She orchestrated the campaigns that had such mass appeal, and she was key to the enormous success of the organization.

Whitelaw arrived at the March of Dimes during World War II, when many men were off in the armed forces. The organization began to concentrate even more on polio as a women's issue, and more women fundraisers came into the foundation. One innovation was the poster child campaign, which began in 1946. The March of Dimes Poster Child was meant to look happy and attractive, though leg braces or some other symptom of disability was evident. These children were far from pathetic, and it was a vision of disability that had not been seen in the United States before. The image of the vibrant, though crippled, child projected hope for recovery and inspired people to give money to the foundation. Another campaign of the 1940s that was enacted all across the country was the porchlight campaign. Local chapters organized marches and told people in the community to turn their porchlights on if they wanted the marchers to stop by and collect.

The March of Dimes put its money into a variety of programs. The foundation set up more than a dozen respirator centers around the country, where doctors, physical therapists, and other health professionals worked with polio patients who had been confined to respirators. They aimed to get the patients back to breathing on their own. As this was not always possible, the March of Dimes also invested in new respirator technology so that some patients could be cared for at home. The foundation also funded rehabilitation centers, for long-term care of polio victims. In addition, the March of Dimes directly funded doctors and scientists working on curing polio. In 1949, the foundation chose Dr. Jonas Salk to lead its research efforts. By 1951, the March of Dimes had spent $1 million to support a number of scientists who finally identified all three types of polio virus. In 1953, Dr. Salk announced that a vaccine for polio was feasible, and the next year the March of Dimes organized and funded the

Key Dates:

1938: March of Dimes is founded by President Roosevelt.
1954: March of Dimes mobilizes huge field trial for polio vaccine.
1955: Jonas Salk's polio vaccine is found safe and effective.
1958: Organization changes focus to prevention of birth defects.
1976: First Gourmet Gala fundraiser.
1982: Babies & You campaign begins.
1998: Birth Defects Prevention Act passes with March of Dimes support.

first field trials of the vaccine. A total of 1,830,000 schoolchildren participated in the vaccine trial, and this was called the largest peacetime mobilization of volunteers in the nation's history. The organization had put $9 million toward production of the vaccine, before it was proved safe and effective. If something had gone wrong, that money would have been gambled away. But in 1955, the Salk vaccine was declared effective. Mass inoculation began, and the fear of polio quickly died away.

Changing Gears After the Salk Vaccine: The Late 1950s Through the 1970s

The March of Dimes campaign to fight polio had been a remarkable victory. The organization had worked on all fronts, responding to the emergency of local outbreaks, funding and arranging long-term care for victims, mobilizing awareness, and paying for the research that led to the vaccine. After 1955, the impetus that had led people to give money to the foundation ebbed away, and the March of Dimes was in something of a quandary. It still had debts owing to its massive spending on the vaccine, but people were not willing to be stopped in the middle of a movie for a disease that could now be easily prevented. In 1958, the organization came up with a new mission. Its work on polio mostly behind it, the March of Dimes turned to another burning issue of infant health: birth defects. At the time, the term birth defects was not in use. Parents of a baby who was born with a debilitating condition were often not given any explanation for what affected their child. The numbers or percentages of babies born with these conditions were not known, and the diseases that affected children at birth were mostly mysteries. The March of Dimes put its volunteer and fundraising organization to work in this new area. The foundation brought together scientists from diverse specialties to work together on birth defects, and as with polio, the March of Dimes had quick and concrete results. In 1961, research the March of Dimes had funded led to the development of the PKU test, which can identify and prevent some forms of mental retardation. In 1968, the organization funded the first successful bone marrow transplant used to correct a birth defect.

But birth defects had many causes, so this issue was not as focused as the fight against polio had been. Eventually, medical researchers identified approximately 3,000 distinct disorders causing birth defects. Some of these were genetic diseases, some were disorders caused by conditions in utero, and others were caused by problems with the birth itself, such as a child being born prematurely. The March of Dimes continued to use many of the techniques it had deployed during its polio campaign to raise funds to combat birth defects. The foundation used celebrities to lead fundraising and appealed to ordinary women with a variety of local events such as marches and store promotions. Elaine Whitelaw still led fundraising for the organization. She used her particular personal panache to launch glamorous events that raised hundreds of thousands of dollars for the charity. One exceedingly successful fundraiser was a fashion show, and another was the Gourmet Gala. The first Gourmet Gala was held in 1976. Hundreds of guests paid regal amounts to the March of Dimes to eat dinners prepared by celebrities and judged by cooking experts. With the money raised, the organization helped make possible many signal advances in the treatment of birth defects. Researchers it funded found in 1973 that alcohol consumption can affect fetal development. The organization also funded the first in utero treatment for a birth defect that year. The foundation had a far-reaching effect on hospital policy when it began working for the development of a regional system of neonatal intensive care units in the mid-1970s.

Broad Goals in the 1980s and 1990s

Education and outreach became a vital part of the March of Dimes agenda once it began work with birth defects, since some conditions turned out to be preventable. Researchers it funded had found that alcohol and drug use by the mother can influence fetal development, and other scientists had made many advances in treating birth defects before the babies were born. March of Dimes-funded doctors had perfected some in utero surgical techniques, and other researchers had discovered ways to diagnose certain birth defects prenatally. Good prenatal care was essential if doctors were to find preventable problems before birth. So in 1982 the foundation launched a public awareness campaign called ''Babies & You,'' which brought prenatal education into the workplace. This was followed by several other education campaigns in the 1990s. In 1994, the organization began a program to educate women of childbearing age on the value of taking folic acid supplements, since this can prevent some particular birth defects. That same year, the March of Dimes did something of a follow-up to Babies & You, aimed more succinctly at employers and their pocketbooks. The organization put out a book entitled *Healthy Babies, Healthy Business,* which detailed to employers the cost to them of poor birth outcomes among their employees' children. It stressed the importance of prenatal care and gave tips to employers on how to make it easier for their workers to obtain the care they needed.

At the same time, March of Dimes funded research that led to impressive results. In 1985, research sponsored by the organization led to a new method to treat respiratory distress syndrome in infants. Four years later, a doctor funded by the foundation performed the first in utero surgery to repair a diaphragmatic hernia in an unborn child. In addition, scientists backed by the March of Dimes made a number of significant advances in the 1990s in identifying the genes responsible for particular syndromes.

The March of Dimes was also influential in getting legislation passed in the 1990s that benefited mothers and children. In

1996, the organization's volunteers were very visible in the fight to get the Mothers' and Newborns' Health Protection Act passed. This legislation guaranteed mothers a minimum hospital stay of 48 hours after delivery, ending the practice of some hospitals and insurers to send new mothers home as soon after the birth as possible. The next year, the organization was again influential in getting the State Children's Health Insurance Program passed. This legislation ensured health insurance coverage for an estimated five million children. In 1998, March of Dimes volunteer workers helped bring about the Birth Defects Prevention Act, which established a national network for monitoring birth defects.

By 1998, the March of Dimes was composed of more than 90 local chapters, with approximately three million volunteers contributing to its work. Its revenue had grown to more than $181 million. A total of 75 percent of this went to its programs, with the remainder spent on fundraising costs, management, and general expenses. The March of Dimes set aside money that year for a six-year research program. It planned to invest more than $11 million over the six years in research into methods to deliver healthy genes to patients needing gene therapy. The organization planned to spend another $3.8 million over the same period on research into the causes of premature birth. The March of Dimes also launched a new, massive public health campaign beginning in 1998 and expected to last three years. This was a $10 million effort to get the word out about the benefits of folic acid. The foundation had been working on this since the mid-1990s, and the latest campaign was an intensification of that effort. The foundation also gave out $20.5 million in grants in 1998, awarded to 300 scientists. With a lot of vital work left to do, the March of Dimes seemed to be thriving as the century came to a close, expanding its revenue and attracting a growing number of volunteers.

Further Reading

Carey, Joseph, ''New Insight into Genes: Now the Payoff,'' *U.S. News & World Report,* August 6, 1984, p. 57.

Clune, Ray, ''A Stroke of Generosity,'' *Daily News Record,* October 12, 1995, p. 4.

''Coke Campaign Involves March of Dimes, Coleco,'' *Wall Street Journal,* August 24, 1984, p. 14.

''March of Dimes Still Leading the Fight for Healthy Babies After 50 Years,'' *American Baby,* May 1988, pp. 16–19.

Noble, Barbara Presley, ''A Guide to Lower Health Care Costs,'' *New York Times,* January 4, 1994, p. F25.

O'Neill, Molly, ''Elaine Whitelaw, 77, March of Dimes Backer, Dies,'' *New York Times,* December 17, 1992, p. B22.

——, ''Learning To Turn Dimes into Millions,'' *New York Times,* October 17, 1990, pp. C1, C7.

Seavey, Nina Gilden, Jane S. Smith, and Paul Wagner, *A Paralyzing Fear: The Triumph Over Polio in America,* New York: TV Books, 1998.

—A. Woodward

Melaleuca, Inc.

Melaleuca Inc.

3910 South Yellowstone Highway
Idaho Falls, Idaho 83402
U.S.A.
Telephone: (208) 522-0700
Toll Free: (800) 282-3000
Fax: (208) 528-2090
Web site: http://www.melaleuca.com

Private Company
Incorporated: 1985
Employees: 1,300
Sales: $300 million (1998 est.)
NAICs: 325411 Medicinal and Botanical Manufacturing

Melaleuca, Inc. is perhaps best known for its role in the herbal renaissance of the late 20th century as a producer of personal care products that feature the melaleuca oil from an Australian plant purported to contain healing benefits. In fact, the company manufactures and sells over 100 nutritional, personal care, and home cleaning products. Since its products are sold by a self-employed sales force, the company provides an opportunity for a home-based business, one of the major trends in the Information Age. Outside of its base in the United States, Melaleuca makes its products available in three foreign markets: Canada, Taiwan, and Japan.

An Ancient Healing Plant

Long before Melaleuca, Inc. was founded, Australian Aborigines realized the healing properties of the *Melaleuca alternifolia* tree found in the land down under. Aborigines, especially the Bundjalung, used the plant to treat insect bits and heal wounds.

Captain James Cook, the first European to discover Australia, noticed that some Aborigines boiled the plant's leaves to make a tea, so he coined the commonly used term Tea Tree. In the early 1920s Dr. A.R. Penfold of the Sydney Technological Museum used laboratory tests to document for the first time that the Tea Tree oil was effective in treating burns, insect bites, fungal and bacterial infections, and other skin problems. Some used the plant for so many applications that they called it a ''first-aid kit in a bottle,'' reflected in the fact that Australian soldiers in World War II carried Melaleuca oil in their first-aid kits.

However, few people outside Australia knew about this plant. Moreover, after World War II, the widespread use of antibiotics caused many to forget or ignore such natural remedies. Then in 1982 an American named Roger Ball first learned about the plant during a visit to Australia. He returned to his hometown of Idaho Falls, Idaho, where he told his brother Allen Ball about his discovery. Tests performed on the plant by the Ball's small lab, B&V Technology, indicated that it had antiseptic and other therapeutic traits without major side effects.

The First Melaleuca Company is Formed

Next, Roger and Allen Ball located an Australian ranch owner who claimed to control 80 percent of all the tea trees in the world. The Ball brothers invested in a 50 percent ownership of the ranch and soon started a firm called Oil of Melaleuca, Inc. based on multilevel marketing (MLM) of their unique products. According to Idaho state government records, Oil of Melaleuca, Inc. was incorporated under Idaho law in 1984.

The Ball brothers needed an experienced person to run the new business, especially since the firm's sales had grown to $90,000 a month within its first five months of operation. For that job, they tapped their friend Frank VanderSloot. A 1973 graduate from Brigham Young University with a B.S. degree in business management, VanderSloot at the time lived in Vancouver, Washington, where he served as a regional vice-president at Cox Communications. Skeptical at first, VanderSloot eventually decided to take the challenge; he moved to Idaho Falls, where the Ball brothers gave him control of the firm's management.

Within a few months VanderSloot realized that, despite its rapidly increasing sales, the company had major problems. Melaleuca's early distributors had been required to purchase and sell many expensive starter kits. This resulted in some angry distributors who had invested significant funds and then could not get unload the pricey starter kits. Moreover, this practice of ''front-loading'' was illegal. In addition, some original Oil of Melaleuca products had caused some adverse side effects and had to be taken off the market. Another problem was

Company Perspectives:

Melaleuca, Inc.'s mission is enhancing the lives of those we touch by helping people reach their goals.

that some Melaleuca literature had exaggerated the benefits of melaleuca oil, and company literature with claims not backed by Food and Drug Administration (FDA) studies had to be removed. Finally, management learned that the firm's Australian rancher had only about five percent of the world's tea trees, not the 80 percent he had claimed earlier.

Thus the Ball brothers and Frank VanderSloot shut down Oil of Melaleuca, Inc. after its initial profits turned into huge financial losses. However, not longer afterwards the three men decided to start a new firm with better planning and products. On August 19, 1985, according to Idaho state records, Melaleuca, Inc. was incorporated under Idaho law with Frank VanderSloot as president.

A New Melaleuca Inc. in 1985

VanderSloot set about making sure that the new firm resolved or avoided all together the problems that had plagued the earlier venture, Oil of Melaleuca. First, he implemented a program called Consumer Direct Marketing, in which customers ordered products described in catalogs via a toll-free number. Products were sent direct to the consumers' homes, while Melaleuca sales persons received a commission on all direct sales. Melaleuca distributors could also recruit other distributors and make a commission on sales of their recruits. In this way, Melaleuca was regarded as a multi-level marketing (MLM) company akin to Amway Corporation, though VanderSloot and management maintained that it employed a more sound and successful strategy than most MLMs.

In spite of several changes, VanderSloot admitted in an article in the March 24, 1996 *Idaho Falls Post Register* that "People find it hard to separate us from the original organization." In any case, the new firm continued to grow. Sales grew steadily, from $0.3 million in 1985 to $1.2 million in 1986, $2.6 million in 1987, $11.6 million in 1988, and $17 million in 1989.

The 1990s began on a positive note when *Inc.* magazine included Melaleuca on its list of the nation's 500 fastest growing private firms. Melaleuca would remain on that list for the next four years in a row. In 1991 the U.S. Chamber of Commerce honored Melaleuca with its Blue Chip Enterprise Award. In spite of a poor economy, Melaleuca's sales increased from $29 million in 1990 to $105 million in 1991. The firm in 1991 prospered from the efforts of over 100,000 independent sales persons and also the company's 900 plus workers at its Idaho Falls, Pocatello, and Rexburg plants. In 1993 the company opened its new manufacturing plant in Knoxville, Tennessee, to meet the growing need from consumers in the East. By 1997 the Knoxville plant would total 170,000 square feet.

Melaleuca's success during this time relied on the efforts of its many distributors, who began as Marketing Executives and could progress to higher levels as they recruited others and built a sales organization. Unlike some other direct marketing firms, Melaleuca published statistics on the annual income of its various distributor levels. At the entry level, Marketing Executives in 1996 averaged $93.17 in annual income, with a maximum of $1,228.48. Melaleuca's top sales persons, called Executive Directors, reportedly averaged $131,818.58 in annual income in 1996, with a maximum at that level of $862,871.13.

Melaleuca's most successful sales person at the time was Russell Paley of Teaneck, New Jersey. Paley began as a Melaleuca Marketing Executive in 1991, after a career with Nu Skin Enterprises, a large multilevel marketing firm in Provo, Utah. By 1996 Paley's sales organization for Melaleuca included about 6,500 persons, and it was reported in the March 24, 1996 *Idaho Falls Post Register* that his organization accounted for sales of $218,000 in the month of January 1996 alone.

According to papers filed with the Idaho state government, B&V Technology, Inc., then headed by Frank VanderSloot as president, Allen Ball as secretary, and Roger Wright and Harold Ball as directors, merged with Melaleuca, Inc. on December 30, 1993. The following year, Melaleuca became an international firm when it commenced sales in Canada through a separate firm called Melaleuca of Canada. Canadian product labels, catalogs, and sales materials were printed in both English and French. The following year the company expanded into Argentina, and later it moved into Taiwan and Japan.

Expanding Product Lines and Incentives in the 1990s

In the 1990s Melaleuca made alliances with other companies in order to provide new products and services to its customers. For example, in 1994 the company signed an agreement with MCI for long-distance and other communication services. By August 1999 hundreds of thousands of the company's Preferred Customers used MCI-provided MelaCom Long Distance that saved them up to 30 percent on long-distance telephone calls. Moreover, the Melaleuca Visa card, requiring no annual fee, allowed the firm's marketing executives to earn base points whenever customers in their groups used the credit cards. In addition, Melaleuca Executive Travel offered discounts on airline, hotel, and other travel expenses. President/CEO VanderSloot in the August 1999 *Leadership in Action* claimed that "Melaleuca Executive Travel has grown to one of the largest travel agencies in the world."

News of the so-called French Paradox helped lead to new Melaleuca products by the end of the decade. Specifically, the Paradox involved the fact that although the French consumed high rates of lard and butter and had higher blood pressures and cholesterol levels than Americans, they had only one-third the number of heart attacks. Research suggested that the red wine consumed by the French contained flavonoids, a natural substance that helped reduce blood clots and thus prevent heart attacks. So in 1995 Melaleuca teamed up with Dr. John Folts to develop a supplement based on flavonoids. Other firms began offering flavonoid supplements as well, but Melaleuca's research indicated flavonoids in those supplements were incompletely absorbed by the body. After two years, Melaleuca and Folts found a way to combine flavonoid extracts with enzymes as a means to increase the body's absorption of the flavonoids.

This breakthrough led to Melaleuca's 1997 introduction of ProVexCV, a trademarked flavonoid supplement available to the firm's sales force. Folts presented his bioflavonoid research

Key Dates:

1982: Roger Ball learns about melaleuca oil during a visit to Australia.
1984: Oil of Melaleuca, Inc. is incorporated in Idaho and later fails.
1985: Melaleuca, Inc. is incorporated in Idaho and headed by Frank L. VanderSloot.
1989: Vitality Pak, a vitamin packet, is introduced.
1990: Company is included on the *Inc.* magazine list of the 500 fastest growing private companies.
1993: Company opens its manufacturing plant in Knoxville, Tennessee.
1993: Vitality for Life nutritional supplements are introduced.
1994: Company begins selling its products in Canada, its first international market.
1997: Dietary supplement Provex CV is introduced; sales begin in Taiwan.
1998: Operations begin in Japan.

at two meetings in 1997 and 1998, but Melaleuca President VanderSloot cautioned against much publicity until Folts had actually published his research results. Nonetheless, the company was quite excited about the future possibilities of its new patent-protected product, especially in light of the fact that heart disease was the nation's main cause of death.

At the firm's 1999 annual convention, Melaleuca announced another new partnership that promised a new line of products for consumers and new business opportunities for Melaleuca distributors. VanderSloot explained the partnership in the firm's August 1999 *Leadership in Action:* "One of the highlights of this year was when Nicole Miller, one of the world's foremost fashion designers, decided to have Melaleuca market her prestigious line of skin care products for women. Nicole had many options. Her elite line of women's fashion clothing is carried in the most prestigious department and women's fashion stores. She could have chosen any or all of those stores to carry her products. But she did not. She chose Melaleuca! That says a lot for how the world is beginning to see us."

The Nicole Miller Skin Care line included cleansing and makeup removal items, moisturizing lotions, eye gels, lipstick, and other cosmetics. Many Nicole Miller products featured vitamins and herbal ingredients, as did the Freshen Balancing Toner with extracts from horse chestnut, ginkgo biloba, cranberry, and grape seed. The alliance between Melaleuca and Nicole Miller was a significant move for both firms and also one more example of how more companies were turning to multilevel or direct marketing to increase their distribution opportunities.

Former Melaleuca employee Richard M. Barry published a favorable account on the history and development of Melaleuca in 1999 entitled *Built on Solid Principles: The Melaleuca Story.* Barry and his wife Tina had joined Melaleuca in 1991 and worked part-time as Melaleuca distributors before deciding to concentrate on an enterprise of their own, RM Barry Publications. Barry's account of Melaleuca cited numerous Melaleuca magazines and other company sources, though Melaleuca, Inc. did not authorize its writing or publication.

In addition to previously mentioned products, Melaleuca sold toothpaste, mouthwash, other dental care products, soaps, bath oils, and various deodorants , colognes, fragrances, shampoos, and other hair care and personal care items for men and women. Melaleuca oil was found in antifungal creme, acne medication, and an antibiotic ointment. The company also sold the trademarked CounterAct family of products such as Ibuprofen and various items for pain and cold relief. Its EcoSense line included MelaPower Laundry Detergent and other clothes cleaning products, plus other household cleaners. Its nutritional products line featured vitamin, mineral, and herbal supplements with names such as ProstAvan for prostate health, Luminex for emotional stability, EstrAval to provide relief for symptoms of menopause, and various energy bars and weight management products.

By late 1999 Melaleuca was prospering in the United States, Canada, Japan, and Taiwan, but it was in the process of closing its Argentina operations, while looking at various other international markets for future expansion. The company reported having only a one percent market share, so it had plenty of room to grow. As part of the herbal or natural products movement, which accounted for $12 billion in consumer spending in 1997, Melaleuca seemed well positioned for continued growth.

Principal Divisions

Melaleuca of Canada; Melaleuca of Taiwan; Melaleuca of Japan; B&V Technology.

Principal Competitors

Amway Corporation; Avon Products, Inc.; Mary Kay Corporation; Nu Skin Enterprises Inc.; The Sunrider Corporation.

Further Reading

Barry, Richard M., *Built on Solid Principles: The Melaleuca Story,* Littleton, Colo.: RM Barry Publications, 1999.
Cates, Nancy D., "Tea Tree Oil: Australian for Skin Health," *Better Nutrition*, August 1997, p. 50.
Cornwall, Warren, "Bonneville County, Idaho, Residents Object to Melaleuca Inc. Move," *Knight-Ridder/Tribune Business News*, March 26, 1997.
Englert, Stuart, "Melaleuca Succeeds in Hard Times," *Idaho Falls Post Register*, April 26, 1992.
Greenwald, John, "Herbal Healing," *Time*, November 23, 1998, pp. 58–67.
Menser, Paul, "Melaleuca Expands into Far East Market," *Idaho Falls Post Register*, September 24, 1996.
Menser, Paul, "Melaleuca Teams with Fashion Line," *Idaho Falls Post Register*, August 18, 1999.
Menser, Paul, "Booming Melaleuca Grows Out of a Shady Past into a Jobs Bonanza," *Idaho Falls Post Register*, March 24, 1996.
Menser, Paul, "Melaleuca Inks $100 Million MCI Pact, Expands Exports," *Idaho Falls Post Register*, May 16, 1996, p. B5.
Wimborne, Margaret, "Melaleuca Soars into National Spotlight," *Idaho Falls Post Register*, April 28, 1991.

—David M. Walden

MIH Limited

MIH Limited

Jupiterstraat 13-15
2132 HC Hoofddorp
The Netherlands
Telephone: +31 23556 2860
Fax: +31 23556 2880
Web site: http://www.mih.com

Public Company
Incorporated: 1991
Employees: 3,352
Sales: $610.1 million (1999)
Stock Exchanges: NASDAQ Amsterdam
Ticker Symbol: MIHL
NAIC: 51321 Cable Networks; 51334 Satellite Telecommunications

MIH Limited (MIHL) operates pay-television services internationally in three regions: Africa, the Mediterranean, and Asia. It provides analog and digital service in Africa and Asia and is awaiting legislative approval to add digital service to its analog service in the Mediterranean. The firm's strategy emphasizes being the leading supplier of pay-television services, obtaining exclusive programming, improving customer care, and offering new services and technology. In each market it serves—South Africa, the rest of sub-Saharan Africa, Greece, Cyprus, and Thailand—MIHL is the leading pay-television operator. In most of its markets MIHL has exclusive pay-television rights to transmit premium movies, major sporting events, and popular children's programming.

In addition, MIHL provides a comprehensive package of technology products and support services through Mindport, its technology division, to pay-media operators worldwide. Mindport's customers include leading international pay-media companies as well as the company's own pay-television businesses. Mindport is focused on the pay-media industry's evolution from analog to digital transmission as well as on interactive and Internet services. Since 1997 MIHL also has been involved in providing Internet services in South Africa, where it developed and spun off M-Web Holdings Ltd. as the country's leading Internet service provider.

Operation of Pay-Television Services: 1986–91

MIH Limited was incorporated on July 26, 1991 in the British Virgin Islands and its corporate offices are in The Netherlands, but the company was first established in 1986 as M-Net Ltd., a television platform operator in South Africa. M-Net Ltd. was formed by several large South African media companies and was South Africa's first ever pay-television service provider. Its license to broadcast was first obtained on October 17, 1985, from the South African Minister of Posts and Telecommunications.

In 1990 M-Net was publicly listed in South Africa on the Johannesburg Stock Exchange (JSE). The next year MIHL was incorporated in the British Virgin Islands. Its principal activity was the operation of pay-television services. In 1991 MIHL acquired FilmNet, a leading pay-television operator in Europe serving the Benelux countries of Belgium, The Netherlands, and Luxembourg, and Scandinavia.

Expansion and Reorganization: 1992–95

In 1992 the company entered the cellular telephone business when it joined a consortium that obtained the second GSM cellular license ever awarded in South Africa. Through the consortium it owned a one-quarter interest in the cellular telephone operator, Mobile Telephone Networks Holdings (Proprietary) Ltd. (MTN), and subsequently increased its ownership to slightly more than one-third. In 1995 MTN was spun off as a new corporation, M-Cell Ltd., which was listed publicly on the Johannesburg Stock Exchange.

In October 1993 a new company, MIH Holdings (MIHH), was split from M-Net Ltd. MIHH would include M-Net's subscriber management, signal distribution, and cellular telephone businesses as well as its holding in FilmNet. M-Net continued to hold other corporate operations and provide pay-television programming. MIHH retained a controlling interest in M-Net, which eventually focused on providing premium film channels for MIHL's pay-television subsidiary in Africa, MultiChoice Africa (MCA).

Company Perspectives:

The world of communications has become one of the fastest-changing environments, filled with daily challenges to its players. It has become a world where innovation and dedication have become invaluable tools for success. Since our inception in 1986, we have risen to this challenge and have evolved from a television platform operator to a global electronic media company with television platform operations spanning more than 40 countries and a global technology group providing interactive media-related software solutions to many of the world's electronic television operations.

Pay-Television Services in Europe, Africa, and the Middle East: 1995–97

In 1995 MIHH merged its global pay-television operations with those of Richemont S.A. to form a new venture called NetHold B.V., which MIHH held through MIHL. From 1995 to March 31, 1997, MIHL's main activity was its 50 percent share in NetHold, which had pay-television operations in Africa, Greece, Cyprus, the Middle East, the Benelux and Scandinavian countries, and Italy. The company's pay-television service in Greece and Cyprus began in 1994 and was operated through its subsidiary, NetMed Hellas.

In March 1997 MIHL and Richemont merged most of NetHold with Canal+, the French-based pay-television operator, in a deal that valued NetHold at $1.8 billion. MIHL retained NetHold's African, Mediterranean, and Middle East pay-television businesses, acquired 49 percent of Irdeto, a provider of conditional access and encryption technology services, and received an interest in Canal+. MIHL later acquired the remainder of Irdeto from Canal+ in January 1998, and Irdeto became part of MIHL's Mindport division. MIHL subsequently sold its interest in Canal+ to fund expansion in Asia.

Reorganization and Expansion into Asia and Internet Services: 1997–99

Effective March 31, 1997, MIHL sold its interest in NetHold to Canal+ in exchange for a five percent share in Canal+ and all of NetHold's pay-television businesses in Africa, Greece, Cyprus, and the Middle East. MIHL realized a gain of $540 million on the sale of its interest in NetHold. Subsequently, MIHL paid $17.7 million in cash to Canal+ for a 49 percent share in Irdeto.

During fiscal 1998 (ending March 31) MIHL sold its shares in Canal+ for $262 million, resulting in a gain of $3 million. Then the company began to expand in Asia, develop an Internet service in South Africa, and diversify into other related areas.

In 1997 MIHL began purchasing an interest in its Thai pay-television joint venture, United Broadcasting Corporation Public Company Ltd. (UBC), then known as International Broadcasting Corporation Public Company Ltd. (IBC). UBC was founded in 1985. In 1989 UBC entered into a joint venture with Mass Communications Organization of Thailand (MCOT), one of two primary media regulators in Thailand, to provide subscription television service. Under subsequent amendments, UBC was allowed to provide subscription service to the whole of Thailand, using satellite to provide a direct-to-home service to the entire country, cable in the provincial areas, and other services as permitted.

MIHL gradually increased its ownership interest in UBC and its subsidiaries. During fiscal 1998 MIHL invested an additional $17.7 million in UBC. Following IBC's merger with UTV Cable Network Public Co. in February 1998 to form UBC, MIHL's interest in the new merged entity was 17.3 percent. MIHL's shares in UBC were pledged as security for a revolving credit facility. MIHL's principal investment partner in UBC was Telecom Holding Company Ltd., which owned about 41 percent of UBC. During fiscal 1999 MIHL increased its interest in UBC from 17.3 percent to 27.8 percent for a consideration of $67 million. MIHL expected to exercise options to increase its interest in UBC to 31.1 percent.

UBC's pay-television business consisted of a digital satellite service, a cable television service, signal transmission and distribution, and the production of pay-television channels featuring movies, drama, educational programming, news, and sports. MIHL conducted its development operations in Asia through an office in Hong Kong.

MIHL contributed its acquired Internet businesses to the start-up of a South African Internet service provider, M-Web Holdings Ltd. (M-Web), in 1997. M-Web was created through a series of transactions, with MIHL contributing its Internet-related businesses to the new entity, M-Web Holdings Ltd., and subsequently capitalizing it with a special dividend to MIH Holdings. During 1997 MIHL had acquired several Internet-related businesses in South Africa for about $21.5 million. These were sold on October 1, 1997, to M-Web Holdings Ltd., for $20.5 million. M-Web's shares were linked to those of MIHH on the Johannesburg Stock Exchange in South Africa. By December 31, 1998, M-Web was the leading Internet service provider in South Africa, with nearly 127,000 subscribers.

MIHL also was expanding more into technology. In 1997 it began investing in OpenTV, Inc., a California-based company that produced operating systems for interactive television. MIHL started with a 44.5 percent interest, which it acquired in January 1998 for $15.5 million, and increased it to 80.1 percent in March 1999 through a transaction with Thomson Consumer Electronics Inc.

In January 1998 MIHL acquired the remaining 51 percent of Irdeto for $11 million in cash. As part of MIHL's Mindport division, Irdeto Access provided conditional access systems for both analog and digital broadcasting platforms. Its products were installed in more than 3.6 million decoders on more than 25 broadcasting platforms. Its clients included, for the most part, television platform operators, but it was developing applications for data broadcasters and other information providers. A new product, M-Crypt, was launched during fiscal 1999 (ending March 31) for smaller pay-media operators.

In other activities MultiChoice Africa (Proprietary) Ltd. (MCA), an indirect subsidiary of MIHL, transferred 28 million shares of Electronic Media Network Ltd./SuperSport Interna-

Key Dates:

1986: M-Net Ltd., a television platform operator in South Africa, is established.
1990: M-Net goes public on the Johannesburg Stock Exchange.
1991: MIH Ltd. (MIHL) is incorporated in the British Virgin Islands.
1993: MIH Holdings (MIHH) is split from M-Net Ltd.
1995: MIHH merges its global pay-television operations with those of Richmont S.A. to form NetHold B.V., of which MIHL owns 50 percent.
1997: NetHold merges with Canal+, and MIHL acquires NetHold's African, Mediterranean, and Middle East pay-television businesses; MIHL forms a Thai pay-television joint venture, UBC, and begins investing in OpenTV, Inc.
1998: MIHL acquires TV/COM International Inc., a San Diego-based pay-technology company.
1999: MIHL becomes a publicly listed company on the NASDAQ and the Amsterdam exchanges.

tional Holdings Ltd. (M-Net/SuperSport) to the Pluthuma Futhi share scheme to promote black empowerment in April 1998. MIHL received a consideration of $22 million. MCA retained a 19.8 percent interest in M-Net/SuperSport. SuperSport provided premium pay-television sports coverage for all of Africa. It became a separately listed company on the Johannesburg Stock Exchange in early 1998.

During fiscal 1999 MIHL acquired TV/COM International Inc., a San Diego-based pay-technology company, for $14.5 million and added it to its Mindport division. The acquisition gave Mindport greater intellectual property rights to technology it used as well as a basis for penetrating the U.S. market.

Following the close of its fiscal year on March 31, 1999, MIHL became a publicly listed company on NASDAQ and the Amsterdam Stock Exchange in April. The company's initial public offering (IPO) raised $187.8 million before expenses through the sale of nine million Class A ordinary shares. A substantial portion of the proceeds were earmarked to finance acquisitions of pay-television services, Internet services, interactive television services, and pay-media technology businesses in different countries. Following the IPO, MIH Holdings continued to retain effective voting control over MIHL through its ownership of the company's Class B ordinary shares.

For fiscal 1999 ending March 31, MIHL reported net revenues of $610.1 million, up from $501.5 million in fiscal 1998. It reported an operating loss of $44 million and a net loss of $68.8 million for fiscal 1999.

Simultaneously with its IPO, MIHL increased its ownership of OpenTV by acquiring Thomson Consumer Electronics Inc.'s entire interest in OpenTV in exchange for MIHL Class A Ordinary shares, which were issued when MIHL went public. MIHL then sold a portion of its interest in OpenTV to Sun Microsystems for $9 million in cash. Following the sale to Sun, MIHL had an 80.1 percent ownership interest in OpenTV, and Sun owned the remaining 19.9 percent. In June 1999 Sun's chief strategy officer, William J. Raduchel, accepted an invitation to join MIHL's board of directors.

OpenTV provided operating systems, development tools, applications, and related technical services for interactive television. The OpenTV system can be downloaded from a pay-television provider directly into each viewer's decoder. The system works with a wide range of decoder configurations and conditional access systems. It has been used to generate electronic program guides, simple gaming concepts, home shopping and virtual weather channels, as well as a variety of pull-down menus to enhance broadcasting programs.

OpenTV delivered its operating system for interactive television to BskyB, which launched its service in the United Kingdom in October 1998. By March 1999, when MIHL became an 80 percent owner of OpenTV, its operating system already was deployed in more than two million decoders, and the OpenTV operating system software was licensed to 22 manufacturers of digital receivers worldwide.

Outlook

MIHL's businesses were focused in two areas, technology and the operation of television platforms in different countries. Its technology assets were grouped in the company's Mindport division, which provided technology solutions to media companies worldwide for interactive television operating systems, subscriber management, conditional access, and other pay-media applications. MIHL had plans to transform Mindport from a division into a subsidiary as a holding company for all of the company's technology assets.

In the technology area, Mindport and OpenTV have strengthened their positions and were poised for clients to roll out new services during the coming year. Television platforms were experiencing significant change, especially the partial integration of television platforms with the Internet through interactive television applications. Mindport technology was chosen by the Chinese state broadcaster, CCTV, for use in its new satellite service, CBSat, which was established to broadcast eight channels to rural areas not receiving broadcast signals. The service was successfully launched in January 1999, and MIHL expected that the trial system would be expanded and additional integrated receiver decoders would be ordered.

Other Mindport operating units included Mindport Integrated Business Systems, which provided subscriber management products to clients in 27 countries, including third-party companies as well as MIHL companies; Mindport STB, which produced digital and analog decoders; Mindport Media Commerce Technologies, the content management unit that produced a software system for all of a platform operator's programming and scheduling operations; and Mindport Solutions, which offered business consulting and systems integration services to pay-television providers.

MIHL also operated television platforms in Africa, the Mediterranean region, and Asia, through various direct and indirect subsidiary companies, joint ventures, and associated companies. These included MultiChoice Africa (MCA), MultiChoice Middle East, MultiChoice Egypt, NetMed Hellas, MIH Asia, and UBC. During fiscal 1999 MultiChoice Africa launched a new division, International Gaming Networks (IGN), to penetrate the relatively new sports betting market in South Africa.

During fiscal 1999 the overall subscriber base serviced by MIHL increased to more than 1.9 million subscriber households. MCA had a subscriber base of nearly 1.3 million households in more than 40 countries across Africa and adjacent islands. The company continued to experience a trend of analog subscribers migrating to digital platforms.

In Greece and Cyprus, regulatory problems delayed the launch of a digital business. MIHL expected, however, to have a license awarded and to launch its digital satellite service in early 2000s through its subsidiary, MultiChoice Hellas.

In Thailand, the subscriber base grew to 300,000 households following the merger of IBC and Cable Network Public Company (UTV) to form UBC. MIHL intended to focus on developing television platform and online Internet service opportunities in Southeast Asia and China.

Principal Subsidiaries

MultiChoice Africa (South Africa); MultiChoice Middle East (Dubai); MultiChoice Egypt; NetMed Hellas (Greece); MIH Asia (Hong Kong); United Broadcasting Corporation Public Company Ltd. (Thailand); TV/COM International Inc.; OpenTV, Inc.; Irdeto Access (France); Electronic Media Network Ltd. (South Africa); SuperSport International Holdings Ltd. (South Africa).

Principal Divisions

Mindport.

Principal Competitors

MediaHighway; Enhanced TV; Power TV; NCI; WebTV; MediaGuard; ViaAccess; NDS; NagraVision.

Further Reading

''Bill Raduchel of Sun Microsystems To Join MIH Limited Board,'' *PR Newswire,* June 17, 1999.

''France's Canal+ Does $1.8 Billion Merger Deal with Rival NetHold,'' *Broadcasting & Cable,* September 16, 1996, p. 59.

''MIH Increases Stake in OpenTV,'' *PR Newswire,* April 7, 1999.

''MIH Limited: Thomson Multimedia Takes Equity Stake,'' *PR Newswire,* April 7, 1999.

''MIH Prospectus,'' Merrill Lynch & Co. and Donaldson, Lufkin & Jenrette, April 13, 1999.

—David P. Bianco

Mine Safety Appliances Company

121 Gamma Drive
P.O. Box 426
Pittsburgh, Pennsylvania 15238
U.S.A.
Telephone: (412) 967-3000
Fax: (412) 967-3460
Web site: http://www.MSAnet.com

Public Company
Incorporated: 1914
Employees: 4,200
Sales: $494 million (1998)
Stock Exchanges: NASDAQ
Ticker Symbol: MNES
NAIC: 339113 Helmets (Except Athletic), Safety, Manufacturing; 339115 Ophthalmic Goods Manufacturing; 33999 All Other Miscellaneous Manufacturing

Mine Safety Appliances Company (MSA) is one of the world's largest designers and manufacturers of equipment that protects both the safety and the health of workers in a variety of hazardous occupations around the world, including such industries as general manufacturing, fire service, construction, power generation, transportation, aerospace, asbestos abatement, petroleum, hazardous materials and waste cleanup, and mining. Personal protective equipment includes such items as eye and face, head, and body protectors, and respiratory protective equipment such as air-supplied, air-purifying containers. The company also designs and makes a wide range of instruments that monitor and analyze industrial processes and workplace environments. From its beginnings in the early part of the 20th century to the turn of the new millennium, MSA has expanded from a small local firm into an organization that markets its products in over 140 countries around the world.

Early History

Mine Safety Appliances was founded in 1914 by the Deike Family in Pittsburgh, Pennsylvania, to provide helmets and other safety devices to the men who worked in the coal mines of Pennsylvania and beyond. The company remained quite small for nearly 20 years, and was built from nothing into a solid concern within a generation of the firm's first day of business. As with most company histories, however, it is the person who takes the initial product or business idea and develops it into a worldwide success story that deserves the focus of attention. The person at Mine Safety who fits this description is John T. Ryan, Jr.

John T. Ryan, Jr., was born in 1912 in the city of Pittsburgh, Pennsylvania. His father, John T. Ryan, attended the School of Mines at Pennsylvania State University, concentrating in the Mining Engineering, Metallurgy, and Geology programs, one of the best programs in the entire area. When he was old enough, John, Jr., was sent to the same school where he studied the same subjects. While he was attending the School of Mines, however, John, Jr., had already become acquainted with the Mine Safety company since his father worked there for a number of years. After he graduated in 1934 with a degree in mining engineering, John, Jr., saved his money and then applied to and was accepted in the M.B.A. program at Harvard University.

After Ryan graduated from Harvard in 1936 with an M.B.A., he began to work as an employee at Mine Safety Appliances Company. Luckily, the Ryan family was not hard hit by the economic hardships of the Great Depression, which drove numerous individuals into bankruptcy, and signaled the collapse of what many people regarded as stable businesses and corporations. Throughout the latter half of the 1930s, John, Jr., found steady employment in the midst of economic insecurity, and was able to focus on learning all of the company's operations, from the design and manufacture of protective mining helmets to the accounting methods used in the annual financial reports. As he became more familiar with the firm, he was promoted quickly, and proved himself an energetic and talented manager.

When he was promoted to General Manager of Mine Safety Appliances in 1940, the company was at a crossroads in its historical development. Many of the upper management executives at the firm remained committed to the product line that had brought Mine Safety to the secure and stable financial position it found itself in at the time. But some of the more influential individuals of the upper management at the company, and the

Company Perspectives:

That men and women may work in safety and that they, their families and their communities may live in health throughout the world, our mission is to be the leading innovator and provider of quality safety and instrumental products, services and specialty chemicals that protect and improve health, safety and the environment.

founding members of the Deike family itself, clearly recognized the changing nature of the mining industry, and the potential effects that a war would have on the manufacturing industry in the United States. This view was shared by Ryan and many of his coworkers. Amid acrimonious and sometimes bitter disagreement, Ryan was promoted to general manager of the company with the imperative to expand its product line and its operations. Rather than focusing on the word ''Mine'' in the company name, Ryan focused on the word ''Safety'' and set a new course for the firm that would ultimately make it one of the most successful multinational corporations within the personal safety products industry.

World War II and the Postwar Era

During World War II, as General Manager Ryan directed the company into a broader product line. No longer an exclusive manufacturer of mining helmets, the company began to design and make firemen helmets, construction helmets, and a wide array of protective headgear for different manufacturing sectors in the U.S. economy, such as the steel and the paper and pulp industries. Orders from companies who had received government contracts for the production of tanks, aircraft, and battleships, and that needed protective helmets and eyewear for their employees, streamed into the firm. Revenues increased, more employees were hired, and the product line continued to expand. By the end of World War II in the summer of 1945, Mine Safety Appliances Company was looking forward to a very lucrative postwar era.

Ryan was made executive vice-president of the company in 1948, and from that time onward he virtually traveled the globe to expand his firm's presence. Ryan was committed to an aggressive expansion strategy that included extensive personal travel to developing countries. Wherever his journey led him, he tried to position his organization not only as a supplier of high quality products, but of products that would enable men and women to work in safety whatever their chosen profession. Immediately before World War II, Ryan had personally directed and arranged for Mine Safety Appliances Company to expand into Canada, Australia, and South Africa. Although his plans to continue the firm's strategic expansion program were delayed during the war, the first initiative he undertook after the war's end was the establishment of Mine Safety Appliances Company (Britain) in Glasgow, Scotland. The formation of this operation in the United Kingdom gave the company its initial foothold in Europe, a move that would become enormously important in the future.

As Ryan's leadership ability grew more evident to everyone associated with MSA, as the company came to be known, it was a foregone conclusion that when the position of president became available he would be the only man to fill the job. In 1953, Ryan was named president of the company, and continued his aggressive worldwide expansion program. The next destination on his travel itinerary included Mexico; by the mid-1950s MSA was operating a profitable enterprise just south of the Mexico-American border. With sales offices and manufacturing facilities established throughout North America, Ryan decided to use the remainder of the decade to consolidate the company's gains, including the increasing share of a growing worldwide market for personal safety products. However, although this period was devoted to a thoroughgoing examination and improvement of the company's administrative and organizational operations, Ryan did not lose sight of his overall expansion program. In fact, much of this time was used in planning for the next stage of the company's expansion into mainland Europe.

In 1958, Ryan spearheaded the negotiations that led to purchasing Auergesellschaft Gmbh, an innovative firm first established in 1892 that invented the gas mantle which was used to light the streets of Berlin for many years. Ryan viewed the acquisition as the cornerstone of MSA's future operations throughout Europe, in spite of the fact that many experts advised him not to acquire a company in Berlin, a city at the time surrounded by the communist regime of East Germany and isolated from the West. At the height of the Cold War in 1961, when the Berlin Wall was built by the Soviets and the city itself appeared to be the focalpoint if a war started, Ryan stood firm and refused to sell or move the company. His German employees never forgot the courage and steadfast resolve showed by Ryan during this time, and he was ever after honored as a hero in Berlin.

Continuing Growth and Expansion

After the Cold War had somewhat dissipated during the late 1960s, Ryan once again provided personal direction to the company's operational development in France, Italy, Spain, and The Netherlands. By the end of the 1960s, Ryan had added strategic acquisitions in Sweden and Switzerland that would ultimately enhance MSA's presence and market position across Europe. From the beginning of his career at the company, Ryan held the vision that men and women should be provided with equipment that protected their safety while they worked. Ryan's genius as a businessman was to see that such protective products were not only supplied in traditional developed countries, but in nations that most business leaders had previously all but ignored. This vision led Ryan to promote the interests of MSA in such diverse and remote countries as India, Peru, Chile, and Zimbabwe. In addition, just as the company had also supplied U.S. industrial markets, Ryan pushed it toward ''emerging markets'' in Brazil, Japan, the Middle East, and Singapore. Fully cognizant of the logistical difficulties and the cultural problems surrounding startups in exotic and remote locations, Ryan thought it well worth the trade off to gain early access to markets where MSA could participate before the arrival of its competitors.

By the beginning of the 1990s, MSA was a highly successful multinational company. As always, Ryan was at the head of his company's forays into China, Eastern Europe, and post-communist Russia. He was a major influence in setting up

Key Dates:

1914: Mine Safety Appliances Company is founded by the Deike Family.
1939: MSA expands into Canada, Australia, and South Africa.
1946: Mine Safety Appliance Company (Britain) is established.
1953: John T. Ryan, Jr., becomes president of MSA.
1990: Ryan retires as chairman of the board.
1993: MSA expands into former communist Eastern Europe and Russia.
1997: John T. Ryan III becomes CEO.

subsidiary WUXI-MSA in China, and personally led the negotiations that established MSA in both Russia and Hungary. The impressive scope of Ryan's international vision, and his personal commitment to forging international business ventures for the company cannot be underestimated. Throughout the second half of his career, from about 1960 onward, approximately one-third of the firm's total sales came from overseas markets, a remarkable achievement made years before what most companies aspire to today. Although Ryan's international vision was to provide personal safety equipment for people on the job throughout the world, the effect of his efforts was extremely practical, namely, that MSA's international diversity protected it from unexpected swings in the economies and markets of specific geographical markets around the world. This resulted in a strong and stable company, one that was readily able to weather the vicissitudes of a changing global economy.

When John T. Ryan, Jr., died in 1996, he was widely mourned throughout the world by people from many diverse cultures and backgrounds. He was replaced by one of his own grandsons, John Ryan III. Although Ryan III was a relatively young man when he assumed control of the company, he had been well trained by his grandfather and senior executives in the company for a number of years. Wisely, Ryan III continued his grandfather's policy of international development, and strongly supported the idea that each MSA affiliate, no matter where it operated, maintain close relations to the local community and act as a leading advocate of the safety product movement in its own country. By the end of the 1990s, MSA reported more than 30 principle operating facilities throughout the world, and the firm's products were being sold in over 140 nations. MSA appeared well-positioned for continued growth and expansion into the next millennium. The firm's organizational structure was decentralized so that regional managers could either act on their own initiative or react quickly to changes in the marketplace. In addition, the company's research and development department was one of the best and most innovative in the industry, and would undoubtedly continue to introduce new personal safety equipment products in the years to come.

Principal Subsidiaries

MSA International, Inc.; Better Breathing, Inc.; Rose Manufacturing Company; Callery Chemical; Compañia MSA de Argentina S.A.; MSA Pty. Ltd. (Australia); MSA-Auer Sicherheitstechnik Vertriebs GmbH (Austria); MSA Belgium NV; MSA do Brasil Ltda. (Brazil); MSA Canada; MSA de Chile Ltda.; WUXI-MSA Safety Equipment Co., Ltd. (China); MSA de France; MSA-Auer Safety Technology (Hungary); MSA Italiana SpA (Italy); MSA Japan Ltd.; MSA de Mexico S.A. de C.V.; MSA Nederland B.B. (The Netherlands); MSA del Peru S.A.; MSA-Auer Polska Sp.z.o.o.; MSA (Britain) Ltd. (Scotland); MSA S.E. Asia Pte. Ltd. (Singapore); MSA Africa (Pty.) Ltd.; MSA Española S.A. (Spain); AB Tegma (Sweden); Aritron Instrument A.G. (Switzerland); Auergesellschaft GmbH (Germany); MSA Zimbabwe (Pvt.) Ltd.

Principal Competitors

Pfeiffer Vacuum Products, Inc.

Further Reading

Androshick, Julie, ''Kaboom!,'' *Forbes,* November 18, 1996, p. 18.
Hierbaum, John, ''SCSRs-MSA Puts a Higher Level of Protection in a Smaller Package,'' *Coal Age,* February 1997, p. 48.
Lott, Ethan, ''Mine Safety Tackles Retail Market with NFL Hard Hats,'' *Pittsburgh Business Times,* March 5, 1999, p. 14.
''Mine Safety Appliances Company,'' *Wall Street Journal,* March 4, 1993, p. B7(E).
''Mine Safety Appliances Company,'' *Wall Street Journal,* February 11, 1997, p. C16(E).
''SCSR Technology Can Help Save Lives Underground,'' *Engineering and Mining Journal,* February 1996, p. WW55.

—Thomas Derdak

MONACO

Monaco Coach Corporation

91320 Industrial Way
Coburg, Oregon 97408
U.S.A.
Telephone: (541) 686-8011
Toll Free: (800) 634-0855
Fax: (541) 302-3800
Web site: http://www.monaco-online.com

Public Company
Incorporated: 1968 as Caribou Manufacturing Company
Employees: 3,050
Sales: $595 million (1998)
Stock Exchanges: New York
Ticker Symbol: MNC
NAIC: 336213 Motor Home Manufacturing

Monaco Coach Corporation is one of the leading manufacturers of premium motor coaches and towable recreational vehicles. The company's motor coaches are a bit more expensive than its competitors, ranging from $60,000 to $750,000, while the firm's towable recreational vehicles are typically priced between $15,000 to $70,000. What makes the higher-priced Monaco coaches so attractive to prospective customers, according to the company, is their impeccable performance and unparalleled accommodations. The company's products include the high-end Royale Coach model, priced between $550,000 and $750,000, as well as the Signature Series, Executive, Navigator, Dynasty, Imperial Windsor, Endeavor-Diesel, Endeavor-Gasoline, and the Vacationer, all from 30 to 45 feet long and with engines of up to 500 horsepower. The company's towable recreational vehicles are some of the most luxurious ever designed, including such brand name products as televisions from Sony and Quasar, microwave ovens from General Electric, stoves from KitchenAid, and fully automated DSS (satellite) systems. With its headquarters located in the quiet town of Coburg, Oregon, the company sells its product line though an extensive network of independent dealerships across the United States.

Early History

Monaco Coach Corporation grew out of Caribou Manufacturing Company. In 1968, Ray Mehaffey and his wife and children, along with some other friends, decided to change their lifestyle and move from Orange County, California, to Junction City, Oregon. The plan was to relocate to a more sedate and quiet part of the country and start their own business. Mehaffey and his friends focused on manufacturing campers for the growing outdoor recreation market, and opened for business in December 1968. The firm was dubbed Caribou Manufacturing Company, and the strategy was to initiate manufacturing after the start of the new year. Mehaffey and his management team planned the manufacturing schedule to include one camper a day to begin with, and then increase the amount to five campers per day once the company had achieved its full production capacity. The first campers produced by the company cost approximately $2,100, depending upon which of the 11 sizes a customer chose and which individualized floor plan was ordered.

When the company open its doors in 1968, little did the three friends realize that their operation would expand rapidly. Initially, the production facility at Caribou Manufacturing Company was quite small, and the firm had contracted only one exclusive dealer. Yet by the summer of 1971, the company required larger manufacturing space, and so the entire firm was moved to 325 East First Street where it remained for over 25 years. In fact, the owners had much to be proud of—Caribou Manufacturing Company had designed and produced approximately 1,000 high-quality campers, with many of them including individualized floor plans. Most impressive was the company's rapidly growing sales distribution network, which included almost 30 dealers over a large five state region in the Pacific Northwest.

Although flush with the feeling of success, the three owners were taking nothing for granted. All of them were well aware of the highly competitive nature of their industry, and it was of paramount importance to them to introduce new and improved products. Searching for a new design, the owners of Caribou decided to design and manufacture a mini-motor home called the Monaco. Having established a reputation for including deluxe features and accommodations in all of its previously built campers, the Monaco was also designed for comfort and luxury. The mini-motor home soon became the best selling mini-motor home across the United States, and sales for the company began to increase steadily. From its introduction in October 1971 through

Company Perspectives:

At Monaco, we strive to match or exceed our owners' expectations. Before any recreational vehicle is shipped, it must pass rigorous quality assurance checks at each step of the process. Our owners expect this, and their satisfaction is the ultimate measure of success. Our goal of designing and manufacturing a world-class motorhome is only half of the equation. The ultimate key to our continued success is satisfying customers. We devote much of our time listening to our owners at rallies, on caravans, and in our plants and service centers. We're not afraid to ask them what they think, and they're certainly not afraid to tell us. We listen and the owners keep coming back.

February 1972, Caribou Manufacturing Company sold hundreds of the Monaco mini-motor homes. One of the added benefits for the firm was the expansion of its dealer network from 30 to over 40 participants in less than a six-month period.

Unfortunately, the energy crisis during the early and mid-1970s brought the company's growth and development to a sudden halt. As OPEC tightened its grip on the price of oil, the increase in costs for gasoline across the United States jolted consumers into a heightened state of awareness about the country's dependence on foreign oil and started a movement toward fuel conservation. Almost overnight consumers were more inclined to purchase automobiles that gave them more miles to the gallon than ever before. The trend away from big motor-homes and campers was a part of this movement as well, and sales at the company began to plummet. In response, Caribou Manufacturing Company produced a mini-model pickup camper in 1974, but the energy crisis had its effect on the firm, and the owners were just managing to keep sales high enough to remain in business.

Change and Transition

Although many other recreational vehicle manufacturers were unable to survive the effects of the energy crisis, Caribou Manufacturing Company had produced a desirable product, and was managed well enough, to survive. Yet the owners seemed overwhelmed by the challenges facing them, and decided to sell their holdings in the company for $15 million to Brian Obie, the mayor of Eugene, Oregon. A well-known and highly successful businessman in the area, Obie was the president of his own company, Obie Communications, which functioned as a holding company for a radio station in Eugene called KUGN, and Obie Outdoor Advertising. Ray Mehaffey, still wanting to participate in the firm he had founded, became one of the vice-presidents.

Under Obie's leadership, Caribou Manufacturing Company focused exclusively on the production of motor homes while giving up the entire product line of campers. As Obie provided some investment capital for the company to expand, in May 1976 production increased from seven to eight motor homes per day. In addition, Obie's contacts within the advertising industry and his ability to market the company's products through his own advertising company were invaluable. Soon sales were on the increase, with more and more orders arriving each day. By February 1977, the company's daily production of motor homes had increased to 16 units, over 200 people were employed by the firm, and its current facilities required almost double the space to continue the expansion program. At the same time, Obie decided that the company needed a new name to reflect its new image and developing product line, so he changed the company's name to Monaco Motor Home, Inc.

Ray Obie had a vision for the company that he purchased, and he was just beginning to implement that vision during the late 1970s and early 1980s. With its focus now on the manufacture of a line of motor homes that included sophisticated brand name appliances, luxurious accommodations, and finely tooled craftsmanship, Monaco Motor Homes was on its way to increasing sales and profitability. More and more new models were introduced during this period, while the company's dealer network expanded across the United States. One of the turning points for the firm occurred in 1984 when Obie decided to purchase the Roadmaster Chassis Division of the Chrysler Corporation. This single acquisition provided Monaco with the personnel and resources to begin designing and manufacturing highly innovative chassis for the motor homes it was now introducing at a rapid pace.

As the company grew, plans for expanding manufacturing facilities were announced in July 1984. Although Monaco would remain at its present location, the total plant size would be increased to 110,000 square feet. Such an increase in production capacity necessitated an increase in the number of employees as well, from 310 in 1984 to 450 by the end of 1985. Monaco motor homes were being sold for between $60,000 and $95,000, with the Crown Royale model sold for between $195,000 and $220,000. There was only one Crown Royale model manufactured each week, and the company soon had a backlog of orders. The company's Cavalier model was sold for between $49,000 and $60,000, but unlike the Crown Royale, it was manufactured at a rate of one per day. Increasing the company's manufacturing capacities enabled Monaco to bump production of the Crown Royale to one per day and the Cavalier to between two and four per day. As a result, the completed expansion of the firm's manufacturing facilities led to a dramatic jump in annual earnings, from $30 million in 1984 to $50 million by the end of 1985.

Along with the successful growth of the company, and its increasing revenues, came the interest from people who wanted to purchase Monaco. In 1987, Ray Obie finally decided to sell the firm to Bill Warrick and a number of his investment associates, including Kay Toolson. Immediately after the conclusion of the acquisition agreement, Warrick became chairman of the board, while Toolson was chosen as president. The company was renamed Monaco Coach Corporation and the management team implemented a comprehensive assessment of the firm's product line. When the assessment was finished, Toolson decided to rework many of the company's products. In 1988, the Crown Royale was totally redesigned, with the first rear engine Roadmaster chassis, and introduced during the autumn of that year. In late 1989, the company introduced the 1990 model of the Crown Royale Signature series, with a completely redesigned semi-monocoque chassis. Similarly, the 1991 Dynasty was introduced in the autumn of 1990. In 1991, Monaco Coach Company purchased both the Diplomat and the Executive product lines and necessary tooling for their manufacture. Thus the product line that was to make the company successful and

Key Dates:

1968: Caribou Manufacturing Company opens for business.
1974: Mayor of Coburg, Oregon, purchases company.
1977: Name is changed to Monaco Coach Corporation.
1984: Acquires Roadmaster Chassis Division of Chrysler Corporation.
1987: Warrick Industries, Inc. purchases Monaco.
1991: New manufacturing plant opens in Elkhart, Indiana.
1993: Management buyout of Warren Industries.
1996: Acquires Holiday Rambler Division of Harley-Davidson.
1998: Sales reach $595 million.

famous during the decade of the 1990s had been put together by new management. With such an attractive product line, the company was soon besieged with orders, and decided to expand its operations by opening a manufacturing and sales facility in Elkhart, Indiana. The once small company started by three friends in a quaint little town nestled in the Pacific Northwest had grown into a national corporation that was the undisputed leader of the market for coaches above $100,000.

The 1990s and Beyond

From 1988 to 1992, on the strength of its product line, sales for Monaco Coach company skyrocketed $64 million, an increase of 372 percent during that four-year span. Led by Kay Toolson, along with eight additional company managers and a small number of investors from outside the firm, management bought out Warrick Industries in March 1993 for a little over $25 million. In the autumn of that year, the company announced its initial stock offering and sought to raise approximately $18 million to pay off its outstanding loans and pursue an expansion program. After the buyout and the successful IPO, Toolson became chairman and CEO. Under the sure hand of Toolson, who had extensive experience in the recreational vehicle industry before arriving at Monaco, revenues at the company jumped to $150 million by the end of fiscal 1995.

With Monaco motor homes developing into some of the most successful offerings within the recreational vehicle industry, Toolson decided to acquire the Holiday Rambler Division of Harley-Davidson in order to secure an even larger share of the market. Holiday Rambler manufactured mobile homes in the $65,000 to $125,000 range, with both front gasoline and diesel engines. With a loyal customer base, Holiday Rambler was the RV of choice for most of middle-class America. Moreover, with Holiday Rambler's manufacturing facility located in Waukarusa, Indiana, just down the road from Elkhart, the combination of the two firms' product lines was a natural fit.

Under astute management, Monaco Coach Company developed during its 30-year history into one of the best run firms in the nation. By the end of fiscal 1998, sales had increased to $595 million, with hundreds of vehicles sold every year. Although competition was quite intense within the recreational vehicle industry, Monaco Coach Company had both the managerial skills and the resources to continue its uninterrupted story of success.

Principal Subsidiaries

Royale Coach of Monaco, Inc.; MCC Acquisition Corporation.

Principal Competitors

Fleetwood Enterprises, Inc.; Airstream, Inc.; Hanmar Motor Corporation; National RV, Inc.; Coachman Industries, Inc.; Rexhall Industries, Inc.

Further Reading

Ashley, Bob, "The ARI Connection," *RV Business,* September 1998, p. 21.
Goldenberg, Sherman, "FMCA Convention Showcases '99 Debuts," *RV Business,* October 1998, p. 14.
Hymen, Michelle, "Monaco Offers Stock," *Register-Guard,* March 8, 1993, p. 1B.
Kisiel, Ralph, "Monaco Coach Purchases Harley's Holiday Rambler," *Automotive News,* January 29, 1996, p. 14.
Kronemyer, Bob, "National, Monaco, Fleetwood Were Top Investments," *RV Business,* April 1998, p. 24.
"Monaco Celebrates a Quarter Century of Family and Success," *Monaco Lifestyles,* Fall 1993, p. 12.
Sharma, Katherine, "Rainy Start Can't Dampen FMCA Show's Motorhome Debuts," *RV Business,* May 1993, p. 7.

—Thomas Derdak

Movie Gallery, Inc.

739 West Main Street
Dothan, Alabama 36301
U.S.A.
Telephone: (717) 677-2108
Fax: (717) 794-4688
Web site: http://www.moviegallery.com

Public Company
Incorporated: 1985
Employees: 7,000
Sales: $267.6 million (1998)
Stock Exchanges: NASDAQ
Ticker Symbol: MOVI
NAIC: 53223 Video Tape and Disc Rental

Movie Gallery, Inc., is the nation's third-largest video store operator. The Dothan, Alabama-based company owns over 900 video stores and franchises about 90 more. Movie Gallery stores are located mainly in small towns in rural areas—areas too small to attract video store giants Blockbuster and Hollywood Entertainment. Movie Gallery stores are stocked with 3,000 to 10,000 films and 150 to 750 Sony, SEGA, and Nintendo video games. The company's stores also sell blank cassettes, VCR cleaning equipment, movie memorabilia, and snacks. Some stores sell DVDs (digital video discs). The company operates video stores in 29 states, mainly in the Southeast and Midwest. Movie Gallery also sells merchandise such as new and used video films, video games, and gift items via its web site, www.moviegallery.com. Cofounder, Chairman, and CEO Joseph T. Malugan owns 20 percent of the company; cofounder and President H. Harrison Parrish also owns 20 percent.

A Risky Endeavor in 1985

When Joseph T. Malugan and H. Harrison Parrish decided to go into the video rental business in the mid-1980s, many people thought they were making a big mistake. At that time, the video industry was new, and no one was sure whether people would eventually tire of renting movies. ''In the early years, there was not a lot of confidence in the video business,'' Malugan, a tax attorney-turned-investor, explained in the *Knight-Ridder/Tribune Business News.* ''There was some fear it would be a fad.''

However, Malugen and Harrison believed video rentals were an inexpensive form of entertainment that was here to stay. They sub-franchised a small Orlando video store chain that was having financial problems. The two friends began operating video specialty stores in Alabama and the Florida panhandle through their subsidiary M.G.A. Inc. (Movie Gallery of Alabama).

The first Movie Gallery stores were successful and the video industry as a whole was thriving. Malugen and Harrison rapidly expanded the company, buying out small ''mom-and-pop'' stores in rural areas. By June 1987, Movie Gallery owned five stores and franchised 45 more. The following year the company began to consolidate the franchises into company-owned stores. In 1992 Malugan and Harrison acquired the rights to the company's name—Movie Gallery. By 1994 Movie Gallery had 73 stores with sales over $12 million. To raise money and pay off debt, Movie Gallery went public in 1994. The company sold three million shares at $14 each to raise approximately $35 million.

Trouble in the Mid-1990s

The mid-1990s was a tough time for video store operators. Customers became frustrated when they were unable to rent popular new releases because video stores had only a few copies. Many were turning to pay-per-view channels and watching HBO and Cinemax instead of renting videos. The Summer Olympics in 1996 and delays in Nintendo's new N64 platform hurt video store sales further. At the same time, Movie Gallery was also experiencing difficulties of its own. It had recently acquired the New England-based Home Vision Entertainment Inc. for $32 million in stock. However, slumping sales that year made purchasing the 55-store chain difficult. After the acquisition, the company struggled to convert its many new stores into Movie Gallery formats. Industry experts feared Movie Gallery had grown too big too fast—in just two-and-a-half years, the company had expanded its portfolio from 97 stores to a staggering 863 stores. New point-of-sale equipment added to the company's expenses. In July 1996 former shareholders from Home Vision a complaint against Movie Gallery in the United

Key Dates:

1985: Cofounders Joseph T. Malugan and H. Harrison Parrish sub-franchise a small Orlando video chain.
1988: Movie Gallery begins to consolidate its franchises into company-owned stores.
1992: The company acquires the rights to the Movie Gallery name.
1994: Movie Gallery goes public.
1996: The company purchases Home Vision video chain.
1997: Robert Sirkis is hired as chief operating officer and Will Guerrette as senior vice-president of sales and marketing.
1999: The company launches an e-commerce site and purchases 88 stores from BlowOut Entertainment, Inc.

States District Court for the District of Maine citing breach of contract. They sued for more than $7 million in damages.

Reorganization in the Late 1990s

After much deliberation, Movie Gallery executives decided to halt the company's expansion and concentrate on internal operations—a decision that proved to be wise. Movie Gallery passed up a chance to buy the struggling Moovies Inc. video chain. The company closed 50 stores and laid off 15 percent of its staff. In just a few years, it reduced its debt from $80 million to $42 million.

In an effort to boost sales, Movie Gallery decentralized its operations. It allowed regional managers to make decisions regarding the design and management of individual stores, so the stores would be more carefully targeted toward the local customer base. It added large magazine racks to most of its stores and began selling snacks such as pizza. The company increased the its copy-depth, the number of copies of videos per store, through revenue-sharing plans with movie studios. The company also upgraded some its stores, adding new signs and fixtures, and greatly expanded its selection of videos that were for sale. The company diversified its selections of for-sale videos to include classics and children's products as well as new releases. The company hoped this new selection would increase customer traffic and stimulate rental sales. Around the same time, Movie Gallery stores became some of the first to offer DVDs. The company began selling DVDs in 25 of its stores in the Dallas and Virginia areas.

In 1997 Movie Gallery announced a joint venture with Hollywood Partners, Inc., in which it would feature in-store promotions for the movie *The Lost World: Jurassic Park.* The partnership was part of an aggressive campaign in which *Lost World* products would be sold in Movie Gallery stores. Included in the promotion was popcorn packaged in bold, brightly colored T-Rex collector tins decorated with the Lost World logo.

The company also made some managerial changes in 1997. Malugan and Harrison hired Robert Sirkis as chief operating officer. Sirkis was the former chief executive officer at Boston Chicken (Boston Markets) and a former vice-president at Pizza Hut. Before hiring Sirkis, Harrison had served as chief operating officer for Movie Gallery. Also in 1997, former Home Vision executive Will Guerrette joined the company as senior vice-president of sales and marketing.

With its internal operations on sound footing and new management to handle the company's day-to-day operations, Malugan and Harrison felt it was time to refocus their efforts on expanding the company. While the Home Vision purchase had been difficult, it had opened new markets for Movie Gallery. Before the purchase, the company had acquired stores mainly in the Southeast. However, with the Home Vision purchase, it had branched out into New England. While Movie Gallery intended to continue buying out stores in rural areas away from markets dominated by Blockbuster and Hollywood, the company felt it was time to expand into other areas of the country. ''We think we're well-positioned to expand across the United States, now, which is different from our previous view,'' Malugan said in *Video Store.* Industry experts agreed that Movie Gallery was well established and ready to expand. Its conservative approach during difficult times had spared it the serious financial problems some of its competitors faced. Furthermore, because its stores were much smaller than video superstores such as Blockbuster, the company's overhead was lower, enabling it to secure substantial credit for expansion. In March 1998 the company received more good news: a judge ruled in favor of Movie Gallery and against Home Vision Entertainment Inc.

Back on Track in 1999

By 1999, Movie Gallery was back on the buying track—it had 900 stores and planned to continue acquiring new ones. The company signed 75 new leases and planned to open 30 to 35 more stores. Using some of the proceeds from its initial public offering, Movie Gallery invested over $1 million in launching an e-commerce site, www.moviegallery.com. The company believed the site would offer its rural customers products not available in its stores, and it also hoped the site would allow it to tap into a new, urban market. To set themselves apart from competitors, Movie Gallery offered a wide variety of merchandise on its web site. Customers could purchase previously viewed movies at discounted rates as well as items like Pokémon videos and Sega games, which were in great demand.

''You have to realize that many of our customers have no Blockbuster, Barnes and Noble, or even a Wal-Mart within miles of their homes,'' Will Guerrette, Movie Gallery senior vice-president of sales and marketing explained in *Video Store.* ''That gives us a unique position to offer them more than videos, DVDs, and music.'' Movie Gallery planned to eventually offer telecommunication products and services via its Web site.

A Blowout in 1999

In May 1999, Movie Gallery acquired 88 stores from BlowOut Entertainment Inc., which had filed for Chapter 11 protection in March. BlowOut had video rental outlets located mainly in Wal-Mart stores and Kmart superstores. Movie Gallery paid $2.4 million for BlowOut's stores, which had generated $18 million in sales. While some in the industry considered the move risky, Malugen felt Movie Gallery was in a position to make the stores thrive. He explained in *Supermarket News* that the buyout ''represents a substantial growth opportunity for

Movie Gallery with limited risk. As the only major video specialty store operator that focuses primarily on operating in small-town markets, we have developed a significant expertise in managing stores that are relatively small by industry standards.'' Movie Gallery invested $250,000 in the BlowOut stores to boost their inventories. The company also hired a design consultant to give the stores a new look.

In April 1999 Movie Gallery signed a deal with TransWorld Entertainment chains to test FastTake video kiosks in its stores to give customers background information on thousands of videos. In September of the same year, the company repurchased about eight percent or 13.4 million outstanding shares of its stock in an effort to protect the company and its stock price.

With the industry trending toward consolidation and facing strong competition from pay-per-view channels, the video rental business is tougher than ever. In the first quarter of 1999, Movie Gallery posted a net income of $1.8 million and was utilizing its positive cash flow to reduce its debt. While the company lacked the high sales of giants Blockbuster and Hollywood Entertainment, it felt its niche as a ''rural video rental specialist'' would be secure for many years to come.

Principal Subsidiaries

MGA Inc.

Principal Competitors

Blockbuster, Inc.; Hastings Entertainment Inc.; Hollywood Entertainment Corporation; Video Update Inc.

Further Reading

Alaimo, Dan, ''Blowout Sells Leased Departments to Movie Gallery,'' *Supermarket News,* April 5, 1999, p. 5.

Armoudian, Greg, ''Market Drop Pulls Video Stocks to Record Lows,'' *Video Store,* November 2, 1997, p. 1.

Armoudian, Maria, ''Movie Gallery Breaks out of Southeast, Eyes Nation,'' *Video Store,* June 16, 1996, p. 1.

——, ''Movie Gallery Cuts Staff, Slows Its Acquisition Pace,'' *Video Store,* October 27, 1996, p. 1.

——, ''Movie Gallery Decentralizes Operations, Gets into Audio,'' *Video Store,* March 23, 1997, p. 1.

——, ''Movie Gallery Still Searching for a Silver Lining,'' *Video Store,* February 23, 1997, p. 8.

——, ''Movie Gallery Will Get a Makeover, Inside and Out,'' *Video Store,* May 25, 1997, p. 1.

Brass, Kevin, ''Movie Gallery Selling DVD at Slow Clip; Player Sales Hit Seasonal Lull,'' *Video Store,* June 29, 1997, p. 8.

——, ''Slow and Steady Movie Gallery Deserves a Nod,'' *Video Store,* September 26, 1999, p. 16.

Fisher, Tracy, ''Movie Gallery Expected Loss, Decline in Same-Store Revenues,'' *Video Store,* August 24, 1997, p. 10.

McDonald, Owen, ''Public Video Chains Weather Transitional Year,'' *Video Store,* January 3, 1999, p. 1.

''Movie Gallery,'' *Video Store,* May 9, 1999, p. 36.

''Movie Gallery Cuts Staff, Slows Its Acquisition Pace,'' *Video Store,* October 27, 1996, p. 1.

''Movie Gallery Wins Jury Verdict in Litigation with Certain Former Home Vision Shareholders,'' *Business Wire,* March 19, 1998.

''News Briefs,'' *Video Store,* April 18, 1999, p. 10

Poole, Shelia, M., ''Georgia Video Rental Company Foresaw More than a Fad in Mid-1980s,'' *Knight-Ridder/Tribune Business News,* June 15, 1995.

Sporich, Brett, ''Moody's Blues,'' *Video Store,* June 27, 1999, p. 1.

——, ''Movie Gallery Executives Say It's Back on Track and Ready to Grow,'' *Video Store,* August 8, 1999, p. 7.

——, ''Movie Gallery Last Week Announced Plans to Launch an E-Commerce Web Site,'' *Video Store,* May 9, 1999, p. 6.

''Video Stores Get Thumbs Down from Investors,'' *Indianapolis Business Journal,* September 29, 1997, p. 33A.

—Tracey Vasil Biscontini

Navy Exchange Service Command

3280 Virginia Beach Boulevard
Virginia Beach, Virginia 23452-5724
U.S.A.
Telephone: (757) 463-6200
Toll Free: (800) NAV-EXCH; (800) 628-3924
Fax: (757) 631-3659
Web site: http://www.navy-nex.com

State-Owned Company
Incorporated: 1946 as the Navy Ship's Store Office
Employees: 20,000
Sales: $1.79 billion (1997)
NAIC: 45211 Department Stores

The Navy Exchange Service Command (NEXCOM) operates various types of retail outlets for the benefits of Naval personnel, retirees, and their families. Some of its stores' sales volumes are quite high—the Pearl Harbor exchange brings in more than $125 million a year—and the system produces comparable profits to its civilian retail counterparts. However, NEXCOM disburses most of these to Morale, Welfare, and Recreation programs. About a quarter of its exchanges produce little or no profits but are kept open for the benefit of military personnel stationed in remote areas. In January 1998, the system had 116 Navy Exchanges, 207 Ship Stores, 112 Uniform Centers, and 38 Navy Lodges.

Origins

Before onboard stores were established, the only shopping opportunities for sailors on U.S. Navy ships came from bumboats—small local vessels peddling sundry overpriced merchandise. In 1896, the first unofficial canteen was created on the USS *Indiana* to sell beer. As the ships traveled, paymasters sometimes neglected to pay the canteens' vendors, resulting in something of an image problem for the Navy.

The Naval Appropriations Act of March 3, 1909, authorized the first official, nonprofit ships stores and commissaries. Although subsequent legislation outlawed bumboating, a collection of enterprising tradesmen began offering sailors personal services such as haircuts and shoe repair through something known as the ships service. This soon developed into alternate retail outlets as well. In 1923, ships service stores were sanctioned and made the responsibility of the Bureau of Navigation, later called the Bureau of Naval Personnel. The official ships stores remained under the Bureau of Supplies and Accounts.

Space became scarce as the Navy expanded between the wars. In 1943, a ship store and a ship service store were combined aboard the USS *Boston* under the direction of the Bureau of Supplies and Accounts, a pattern later followed on all ships with supply officers. Service stores on land remained in the hands of individual commanding officers, however.

In 1945, a committee was created to design a centralized system of retail outlets. Captain Wheelock H. Bingham, later president of R.H. Macy & Co., headed the group, which recommended bringing the land-based retail activities under the control of the Bureau of Supplies and Accounts. The Navy Ship's Store Office (NSSO), precursor of the Navy Exchange System, was created on April 1, 1946 to manage these stores.

NSSO's first headquarters was located at 116 E. 16th Street in New York City but it soon moved to Brooklyn. Its staff numbered about 90; the first officer in charge was Captain T.L. Becknell, Jr. NSSO's mission comprised two parts: providing quality goods and services at low cost and supporting welfare and recreation funds with its profits. In 1949, NSSO received authority to manage ship stores afloat. The same year, the Philbin Committee made several important recommendations: ships service stores were to be renamed Navy Exchanges and limits were placed on pricing and merchandise selection. For example, the exchanges were to carry two brands of chewing gum and cigarettes. Forbidden were furs, vacuum cleaners, and power tools, among other things.

Innovations in the 1950s

In 1950, NSSO assumed control of the exchanges of the Military Sea Transportation Service (MSTS), whose vessels carried military personnel, their families, and immigrants. MSTS had 60 exchanges on ships and four at major seaports.

Company Perspectives:

From enlistment through retirement, throughout their careers and throughout the years, we have been there for our Sailors, and we are here today. With 123 Navy Exchanges, 218 Ships Stores, 112 uniform shops and 42 Navy Lodges, we continue to serve the worldwide Navy Community.

We are where our customers are in Bahrain; in Keflavik, Iceland; in Guantanamo Bay, Cuba; and on the high seas. For 50 years, our quality of life mission has included operating in remote locations, providing quality merchandise at a savings and distributing a large percentage of our profits to Morale, Welfare and Recreation funds.

A West Coast branch was established in Oakland in August 1952. NSSO created a Commissary Store Division in 1955. Its low-cost supermarkets and the branch stores it managed became immediately popular with military families.

As the number of customers declined with postwar demobilization, a number of innovations sought to make the stores more inviting and convenient. Self service was added; previously, clerks had assembled orders. NSSO's mobile canteens delivered temporary food service to recreational events. NSSO even set up a store in Antarctica to supply Admiral Byrd's Antarctic expedition.

By its tenth anniversary in 1956, NSSO had had more than $2 billion in total revenues, $126 million of which was given to welfare and recreation programs. Beginning in 1958, the types of stores operated were reduced to two. All stores selling groceries became commissaries; those without, exchanges. The next year, NSSO acquired one of the first Remington Rand UNIVAC computers for handling its considerable accounting functions.

Automation During the 1960s

On the first day of 1960, NSSO took over the Naval Uniform Shop, a centralized, made-to-measure operation. It began stocking Navy Exchanges with officers' and chiefs' uniforms. Enlisted men's clubs came under NSSO control in 1961. NSSO also sponsored movie theaters and an overseas entertainment circuit. It started its Navy Guest House Program, aimed at remedying a shortage of temporary housing, in 1964. Edward E. Carlson, who would lead both Westin Hotels and United Airlines, was a distinguished advisor to the Navy Lodge program.

After reducing the number of nonfood items carried and expanding their assortment of kosher foods, larger commissaries installed Robot XI computers to automate inventory management in 1967. Meanwhile, management of Navy Exchanges was streamlined and refined. Payroll began to be processed centrally. An award-winning training film was coproduced with the Eastman Kodak Co. in 1967.

A Navy Exchange Service Center patterned after commercial retailers' supply depots opened in 1969 in San Diego. That year, the Yokosuka exchange began distributing a mail-order catalog to personnel in Vietnam. NSSO soon sold all its exchanges there to the Army Air Force Exchange Service. In 1969, the Bureau of Naval Personnel launched the Navy Lodge Program, which would double NSSO's temporary lodging capacity. After a period of new construction on facilities in Virginia, Guam, and California, the Guantanamo Bay Navy Exchange burned to the ground in 1969. Facilities in Brooklyn, New York, and Glenview, Illinois, were also lost to fire.

NSSO's annual revenues exceeded $1 billion at the time, making the organization one of the top 25 retailers in the United States. Navy Exchanges accounted for $706 million of revenues. One declining area of sales was the operation of MSTS Exchanges, as more service families chose airliners over military surface vessels. MSTS was renamed the Military Sealift Command in 1970. NSSO ended the decade with its own new name: Navy Resale System Office (NRSO).

Further Developments: 1970s

Navy Exchange gas stations had to cope with worldwide fuel shortages in the early 1970s, though they were limited in the savings they could offer patrons by the Federal Energy Administration. The system's hair salons evolved beyond the traditional barber shop and commissaries began selling health and beauty products for the first time. NRSO introduced fast food through delis, pizza parlors, and ice cream shops. Dependent support ships brought retailing to fleets separated from permanent exchanges.

As consolidated procurement exercised NRSO's buying power, retail outlets experimented with the popular shop-within-a-shop department store concept. The Standard Automated Accounting and Merchandising System (SAAMS), unveiled in 1975, and electronic cash register systems provided a new level of efficiency overall.

Systemwide employment reached 31,000 in the 1970s. Legislation brought wages and working conditions for many Navy Exchange personnel more in line with those in the private sector. This and cost of living increases significantly raised payroll expenses. Inflation raised wholesale prices; however, both exchanges and commissaries maintained a policy of not marking up items already on the sales floor.

Authority for enlisted clubs was transferred to the agency responsible for messes in 1977. Entertainment offered at the clubs had become increasingly sophisticated before the transition. Food represented a more significant component of club sales. By 1977, the Navy Exchanges had assumed control of all retail uniform stores from the Naval Uniform Shop, which retained its mail-order operation. Uniforms themselves had undergone a few changes. A new, short-lived enlisted uniform appeared in 1972, and maternity uniforms arrived in 1978. Video games were instantly popular when first installed on ships in 1979. NRSO was again renamed in 1979, becoming the Navy Resale and Services Support Office (NAVRESSO).

Private Labels and Joint Agreements: 1980s

Due to rising property costs as well as crime rates, NAVRESSO moved its headquarters from Brooklyn to Staten Island in 1981. NAVRESSO's scope of operations continued to

Key Dates:

1896: First canteen is established on the USS *Indiana.*
1909: Naval Appropriations Act authorizes first official ships stores and commissaries.
1946: Navy Ship's Store Office is created.
1952: NSSO forms West Coast branch.
1960: NSSO takes over Naval Uniform shop.
1984: McDonald's signs agreement to build franchise restaurants at Navy bases around the world.
1991: Commissaries are transferred from NEXCOM to new Defense Commissary Agency.
1993: NEXCOM relocates to Virginia Beach.

expand during the decade. It assumed responsibility for school lunch programs of dependent children overseas in 1980.

The Navy Resale System and AAFES merged their mail-order catalogs in 1981. The next year, NAVRESSO introduced its own private label program. The Navy Exchange brand offered commonly used items at a discount. The Harbor View line of men's and women's clothing was introduced in the mid-1980s. Other products followed, including health and beauty products and Harborware cookware.

In 1984, McDonald's signed an agreement with NAVRESSO to open 75 restaurants at Navy bases around the world. In return for the concession, the restaurants' independent owners agreed to pay royalties to the Navy Exchange program. Vie de France Corp., a bakery chain, entered into a similar agreement in 1986. The Navy Lodge program was expanded in the mid-1980s, gaining a central toll-free reservation center.

Legislation in 1987 transferred more of the responsibility for the Navy's Morale, Welfare and Recreation Fund from Congress to NAVRESSO, which simultaneously received authority to manage liquor stores and various coin-operated concessions such as pay phones. Naval reservists were granted limited shopping privileges that year. NAVRESSO also instituted a policy of garnishing wages for bad checks.

The 1990s, Preparing for the Future

Commissaries boasted three times the sales per square foot of civilian supermarkets. More civilian managers were being hired as Navy expansion plans drew their personnel. However, management of all military commissaries was turned over to the new Defense Commissary Agency in 1991. Several large Navy Exchanges were also lost due to base closings, and several facilities in the Pacific were damaged by storms.

NAVRESSO was renamed the Navy Exchange Service Command (NEXCOM) in June 1991. With mounting competitive pressures from private sector retailers and outdated equipment, NEXCOM had begun the process of consolidating its supply offices and cutting personnel. It relocated from New York to Virginia Beach in 1993 to help save costs. The Ship's Stores Program moved to Norfolk, Virginia, in 1993.

Next, NEXCOM focused on updating and streamlining its data processing. Buying, distribution, and other functions were more centralized as well. NEXCOM consolidated six warehouses into a new distribution center in Chino, California. Business process reengineering accompanied these improvements. Updating these systems required a $64 million investment.

The first NEX Video stores, a cooperative enterprise with AAFES, appeared in 1992. A bulk-packaged warehouse concept similar to Sam's Club—NEX Club—was tried for a couple of years in Alameda, California. NEXCOM was more successful with its fast-food brands. Within a couple of years, the Mr. Roberts in-house hot dog franchise went from a couple of weenie carts in Puerto Rico to a foodservice unit with annual sales of more than $1.5 million. The Pizza Galley, another in-house franchise, also exceeded $1 million in sales that year. The use of food vending machines was stepped up in 1993 with the introduction of AAROs, or automated auxiliary retail outlets.

Subway, Dunkin' Donuts, and Taco Bell were among the well-known restaurant franchises setting up shop on base. McDonald's renewed its contract in 1994. One manager reported that the name brands doubled foodservice sales at retail stores. An Applebee's restaurant opened at Naval Station Norfolk in March 1998.

Although the Navy's active duty population shrank by 15 percent between 1992 and 1994, exchange sales fell less than three percent. Private label brands proliferated, including Sea Soda, Andrea's Closet and New Crew apparel for young men and women, Bristol House men's clothing, and Elysian Fields lingerie. In 1994, Congress gave the system control of federally owned Stars and Stripes bookstores overseas. Sailors at sea eagerly welcomed the telephones, ATMs, and American Greeting Card machines that were installed in Ship's Stores in the mid-1990s. These stores accounted for $70 million of NEXCOM's total sales.

NEXCOM continued to add new types of ventures. The first Navy Exchange optometry clinic opened in Norfolk in 1995. AT&T signed a comprehensive, worldwide contract in December 1995, covering all types of telecommunications services. The ten-year license provided for pay phones, phones in dorms and Navy Lodges, and calling cards. Discover Card parent company Novus issued the NEXCOM-sanctioned Bravo and Private Issue credit cards in 1995.

In the late 1990s, NEXCOM unveiled the Basic Concepts private label line, which attempted to meet customers' needs for low-cost apparel. Navy Exchanges also retailed their own line of children's school uniforms. Apparel and accessories accounted for more than 20 percent of NEXCOM's revenues.

NEXCOM operated 123 Navy Exchanges, 218 ships stores, 112 uniform shops, and 42 Navy Lodges at the time of its 50th anniversary in 1996. It had disbursed nearly $2 billion to Morale Welfare and Recreation funds. This also marked the 100th year since the founding of the first canteen on the USS *Indiana.* Total NEXCOM revenues were $1.79 billion in 1997. Navy Exchange contributed $1.66 billion. Navy Lodges had billings of $39.8 million while Ship's Stores and onboard vending sales brought in $16.9 million.

Principal Divisions

Navy Exchanges; Navy Lodges; Ship's Stores.

Principal Competitors

Wal-Mart Stores, Inc.; Kmart Corporation.

Further Reading

''For NEXCOM, a New Network That's Really, Really Secure,'' *Chain Store Age Executive with Shopping Center Age,* July 1995, p. 38.

Pellet, Jennifer, ''Storing the Seven Seas,'' *Discount Merchandiser,* June 1995, p. 28.

Ratliff, Duke, ''NEXCOM Merges Distribution,'' *Discount Merchandiser,* April 1996, p. 23.

Ross, Jacqueline, *Fifty Years of Serving You: 1946–1996,* Virginia Beach, Va.: Navy Exchange Service Command, 1996.

Stankevich, Debby Garbato, ''Branding the Burger,'' *Discount Merchandiser,* September 1997, pp. 78–81.

——, ''Seas of Green,'' *Discount Merchandiser,* February 1999, pp. 88–90.

—Frederick C. Ingram

NBTY, Inc.

89 Orville Drive
Bohemia, New York 11716
U.S.A.
Telephone: (516) 567-9500
Toll Free: (877) 426-8689
Fax: (516) 563-1180

Public Company
Incorporated: 1971 as Nature's Bounty, Inc.
Employees: 3,000
Sales: $572.1 million (fiscal 1998)
Stock Exchanges: NASDAQ
Ticker Symbol: NBTY
NAIC: 325411 Medicine and Botanical Manufacturing; 42221 Drugs, Drug Proprietaries and Druggists' Sundries Wholesalers; 446191 Food (Health) Supplement Stores; 45411 Electronic Shopping and Mail-Order Houses

NBTY, Inc. is a manufacturer and marketer of nutritional supplements. It sells more than 900 products, consisting of vitamins and other nutritional supplements such as minerals, amino acids, and herbs. The company's branded products are sold by mail order under the Puritan's Pride and Nutritional Headquarters brand names. NBTY owns a retail chain, Vitamin World, in the United States, and another, Holland & Barrett, in the United Kingdom. It also sells products through independent and chain pharmacies, supermarkets, health food stores, and wholesalers under the Nature's Bounty, Natural Wealth, American Health, and Good 'N Natural brand names.

Nature's Bounty Through 1990

NBTY began its existence in 1971 as Nature's Bounty, Inc., a subsidiary of Arco Pharmaceuticals, Inc., a company founded by Arthur Rudolph in 1960. Rudolph served as chairman and chief executive officer of Arco from its inception. In 1974 Arco and Nature's Bounty established a joint venture in manufacturing, Starlen Labs, Ltd., to produce pills, tablets, and other powdered and liquid vitamins and food supplements sold by the company. In 1977 the company purchased its previously leased building in Bohemia, New York. Arco Pharmaceuticals had net sales of $10.85 million in 1978 and $16.1 million in 1979 and net income was $273,000 and $720,000, respectively.

Nature's Bounty, which made its initial public offering of stock in 1972, acquired Arco Pharmaceuticals at the beginning of 1980, and Starlen became a division of the company, manufacturing, in 1984, 90 percent of the products sold by the company. Nature's Bounty was, in that year, marketing products under the Nature's Bounty label through sales representatives and also to independent and chain drug stores and chain department stores. The company also marketed products under a private label specified by the customer and products under the Puritan's Pride name by mail order, soliciting in general circulation newspapers and magazines and mailing a quarterly catalog. In addition, it was marketing its Nature's Bounty products in 74 Vitamin World kiosks located in enclosed malls and shopping centers in 14 states. This retail chain also served as a marketing aid, enabling the company to keep aware of what customers wanted.

Nature's Bounty also began a joint marketing program with Spiegel, Inc. in 1982, preparing a special mail order catalog of its products under the brand name Arco with Spiegel's endorsement. Similar programs were initiated with Lane Bryant, Inc., Montgomery Ward Enterprises, Inc., and Sears, Roebuck & Co., under the brand names Natural Wealth and Puritan's Pride. The catalogs were mailed directly by Nature's Bounty to customers of each participating retailer and received orders directly from such customers.

The products sold by Nature's Bounty were a full range of vitamin products, including vitamins A through E in varying potencies and combinations. In addition, it was offering minerals such as bone meal, calcium lactate, magnesium, and zinc. Its food supplements consisted of such items as antacid-digestant, bee pollen, brewers yeast, KLB6 and ultra-KLB6, and protein powder. In addition, it carried a personal care line that included a cocoa-butter cleansing bar, E-cream, E-oil, E-soap herb-oil shampoo, and lip salve. In all, more than 300 hundred products were being offered to customers. The company had record net sales of $36.3 million in 1984 but lost $550,000 after having earned net income of more than $1 million in each of the two previous years.

Company Perspectives:

Nurtured by the strength and endurance of its earliest roots, NBTY continues to branch out to meet the evolving needs of our ever-expanding marketplace. Thirty years later, we remain firmly committed to our original mission. . . . To deliver the highest quality nutritional supplements with the best value to our customers.

In 1986 Nature's Bounty purchased U.S. Nutrition Co., Inc., a company founded by Arthur Rudolph's son Scott in 1977, for about $4.2 million in stock. This company was selling vitamins, food supplements, skin care items, and pet products under its own name to about 110,000 mail order customers. Scott Rudolph then succeeded his father as president of Nature's Bounty. Also in 1986, Nature's Bounty purchased Hudson Pharmaceutical Corp., a privately held marketer of vitamins and over-the-counter drugs. That year the company added Hudson and Vitamin World to its roster of brand names.

Nature's Bounty dropped its arrangement with Montgomery Ward in 1986 and with Sears, Roebuck in 1988, the year Spiegel merged with Nature's Bounty's own mail order program. The company began selling its products in supermarkets in 1988. The following year it purchased General Nutrition Corp.'s mail order unit for $7 million in cash and notes, thereby roughly doubling its mail order business. Nature's Bounty added Good'N Natural to its brand list in 1989 and began selling its products to health food stores in 1990. By this time the Vitamin World retail chain had shrunk to only 38 kiosks in eight states. The company's Bohemia facilities had expanded nearly eightfold, however, since 1977, to 260,000 square feet. Net sales reached $70.8 million in fiscal 1990 (ended September 30, 1990), and net income was $723,000.

Like many other marketers of vitamins and nutritional supplements, Nature's Bounty was periodically locked in conflict with the U.S. Food and Drug Administration. In 1987 the FDA advised the company that its nasally administered vitamin B12 gel, called Ener-B, was a drug and thus illegal to market without the agency's approval. In 1989 the company, as a distributor, was involved in a recall of L-Tryptophan, a Japanese-made amino acid used to treat insomnia that was linked to a rare blood disorder and resulted in a number of deaths.

Company Growth in the 1990s

The acquisition of Sturdee Co., Sturdee Health Products, Inc., and Biorganic Brands, Inc. in 1991 for about $4.2 million allowed Nature's Bounty to add Sturdee Health Products and Biorganic Brands to its mail order product lines. A $5 million remodeling program enabled the company's Bohemia facilities to reach 355,000 square feet in 1992 and to boost output to five million vitamin tablets an hour and 3.2 billion tablets a year. That year Nature's Bounty acquired Beautiful Visions Inc. for $4.8 million. The company now claimed to be the largest publicly owned vitamin supplier in the United States.

Nature's Bounty's focus remained on marketing as well as manufacturing; for example, the company was offering a range of support services to the retailers who stocked its products. A company executive told a *Drug Topics* reporter, "There's fierce competition for shelf space. We make sure our space is really producing per linear foot. We will recommend that drugstores add or even take products off the shelf. For example, fish liver oils don't sell as well now, so we might suggest they add garlic oil, which is selling well." He called the Vitamin World stores "a gold mine of information. We stock lots of brands, not just our own, to get an idea of what's selling and what's not selling. We ask lots of questions and we try out new packaging and tablets with different coatings, shapes, and sizes."

The Nature's Bounty line, still the company's leading brand in 1992, was being distributed to drug wholesalers and drugstore chains across the United States. The Hudson brand, found in independent drugstores and including more than 50 over-the-counter drug products, was the largest direct-service full-line vitamin brand in the United States. The Natural Wealth product line was being sold in supermarkets, and the American Health and Good'N Natural brands were being marketed to health food stores. Private-label agreements had been established with many retail chains, including Genovese, Osco, and Rock Bottom. By 1993 the company also was offering personal care products, including shampoos, soaps, cosmetics, skin creams, fresheners, and lotions, under the Beautiful Visions name at discount prices.

In 1993 Nature's Bounty acquired Prime Natural Health Laboratories, a private distributor of vitamins and health and beauty aids to chain drug stores, for $5 million. It also added a plant in Holbrook, New York, for cosmetics production, and a leased facility in Carson, California. Also that year, Arthur Rudolph, who had yielded his position as chief executive officer in fiscal 1992, resigned as chairman of the company and sold his holdings, which consisted of about one-third of the common stock. Nature's Bounty was reaching a potential three million mail order customers in 1993 through eight-times-a-year issues of two catalogs, Puritan's Pride and Beautiful Visions (which was sold in 1995). The Vitamin World chain resumed growth after falling to a low of 31 outlets in 1994. Company net income reached a peak of $9.8 million in fiscal 1993 on net sales of $138.4 million.

The U.S. Postal Service filed false advertising charges against Nature's Bounty in 1990, charging that its Puritan's Pride catalog contained illegal health-related claims for 19 products and adding that it did "not mean to imply that all of Nature's Bounty's other advertisements are true." The following year the company agreed to either discontinue or modify its statements for these products. In 1994 General Nutrition agreed to pay $2.4 million to settle a deceptive-advertising claim by the Federal Trade Commission that involved products manufactured by, among others, Nature's Bounty. According to a security analyst, the company lost sales and profits after a 1994 *New England Journal of Medicine* article challenged the benefits of taking Vitamin A and beta-carotene supplements.

Nature's Bounty was Long Island's largest publicly owned vitamin and health food company by 1995, when it changed its name to NBTY, Inc., after the letters of its stock symbol, to separate the corporate name from the Nature's Bounty product line. By this time the company's Bohemia complex occupied 35 acres near the entrance to MacArthur Airport. In late 1995 NBTY secured a package of tax exemptions and abatements to

Key Dates:

1971: Founded as Nature's Bounty, Inc.
1980: Acquired its parent, Arco Pharmaceuticals, Inc.
1992: Claims to be the largest publicly owned vitamin supplier in the nation.
1995: Changes its name to NBTY, Inc.
1997: Purchases the British vitamin and health food retail chain Holland & Barrett.

stay in Bohemia rather than move to Georgia and also began making plans to build a new manufacturing plant on 62 acres in Bayport. After completion, this facility became one of the nation's largest manufacturing facilities for the soft gelatin capsules used as a delivery system for liquid vitamins and other supplements.

Following disappointing profit performances in fiscal 1994 and 1995—in part due to the poor performance of the company's cosmetics products—NBTY had record net income of $13.4 million on sales of $194.4 million in fiscal 1996, which was attributed in part to refocusing on mail order sales. By purchasing the Holland & Barrett vitamin and health food chain in 1997, NBTY became the largest retailer of vitamins and health foods in the United Kingdom. NBTY paid $168.8 million in cash to secure this 410-store chain, which had been in business since 1920 and had sales of £90.6 million (about $145 million) and operating profits of £7.8 million (about $12.5 million) in 1996.

By this time NBTY had raised the number of its Vitamin World outlets to 110, with plans to add 80 more in 1998 and reach 500 stores in the next three years. In 1999 NBTY joined Phar-More Inc., a deep-discount drug chain, in selling vitamins and other nutritional supplements over the Internet on a page linked to Phar-More's web site. NBTY's net sales reached $572.1 million in fiscal 1998. Net income of $38.8 million was a record for the third consecutive year, despite sharply higher interest expenses of $16.5 million because of the company's increasing debt incurred for the Holland & Barrett and other acquisitions. In 1997 NBTY paid $8 million in cash and stock to settle a three-year-old class action suit in which shareholders alleged that the company artificially inflated sales, improperly capitalized costs, and overstated inventory and accounts receivable.

NBTY in 1998

NBTY's Vitamin World retail chain had reached 230 outlets in 40 states and the territory of Guam by the end of fiscal 1998. Holland & Barrett, which derived 40 percent of its sales from food products rather than vitamins, minerals, and other nutritional supplements, had 415 locations. The Nature's Bounty brand was being sold to drugstore chains and drug wholesalers.

A full line of products to supermarket chains and wholesalers was available under the Natural Wealth brand. Sales to health food stores were under the Good'N Natural brand and to health food wholesalers under the American Health brand. Direct-mail sales, including personal care items, were under the Puritan's Pride and Nutrition Headquarters brands. NBTY had expanded sales of various products to many countries throughout Europe, Asia, and Latin America.

In addition to its facilities in Bohemia, Holbrook, and Bayport, NBTY had leased warehouse space in Reno, Nevada, and Southampton, England. Holland & Barrett was leasing headquarters and warehouse and distribution space in Hinckley, United Kingdom. NBTY had long-term debt of $173.3 million at the end of fiscal 1998. Scott Rudolph owned 16.7 percent of the common stock and Arthur Rudolph owned three percent in December 1998.

Principal Subsidiaries

American Health, Inc.; Arco Pharmaceuticals, Inc.; Beautiful Visions, New York Corp.; Fountain Publishing, Inc.; Good'N Natural Nutrition Corp.; Herbal Harvest, Inc.; Holland & Barrett Holdings Ltd. (United Kingdom); The Hudson Corp.; Natural Wealth Nutrition Corp.; Nature's Bounty, Inc.; Nature's Bounty Manufacturing Corp.; Omni Vitamin & Nutrition Corp.; Prime Natural Health Laboratories, Inc.; Puritan's Pride, Inc.; Specialized Manufacturing and Marketing Corp.; United Vitamin Manufacturing Corp.; Vitamin World, Inc.; Vitamin World Ltd.

Principal Operating Units

Capsuleworks; Good 'N Natural; Vitamin World.

Principal Competitors

Nature's Sunshine Products Inc.; Rexall Sundown Inc.; TwinLaboratories Inc.

Further Reading

Ansberry, Clare, "General Nutrition Corp. Discusses Sale of Mail Order Unit to Nature's Bounty," *Wall Street Journal,* February 22, 1989, p. B8.
"Medical Wonders That Ain't," *Catalog Age,* August 1991, p. 7.
Moore, Elizabeth, and Michael Unger, "Vitamin Maker To Expand on LI," *Newsday,* December 14, 1995, pp. A55, A57.
"NBTY To Settle 1994 Lawsuit," *Wall Street Journal,* October 24, 1997, p. B15.
"Phar-More, NBTY To Sell Vitamins on the Internet," *Chain Drug Review,* February 15, 1999, pp. 1, 4.
Talley, Karen, "Nature's Bounty Spends $5-M on Improvements," *Long Island Business News,* July 13, 1992, p. 1.
Ukens, Carol, "Nature's Bounty Working To Make America Healthier," *Drug Topics,* July 20, 1992, pp. 74, 76.
Unger, Michael, "Bohemia's 24-Hour-a-Day Vitamin Plant," *Newsday,* May 23, 1994, p. C5.
——, "Call Them Vitamin NBTY," *Newsday,* April 8, 1995, p. A15.
——, "NBTY Completes Purchase of UK Health Food Chain," *Newsday,* August 9, 1997, p. A23.
——, "Strong Sales for NBTY; More Stores To Open," *Newsday,* November 13, 1997, p. A60.
Wax, Alan J., "False Advertising by LI Firm Alleged," *Newsday,* November 15, 1990, p. 49.

—Robert Halasz

Odwalla, Inc.

120 Stone Pine Road
Half Moon Bay, California 94019
U.S.A.
Telephone: (650) 726-1888
Toll Free: (800) 639-2552
Fax: (650) 726-4441
Web site: http://www.odwalla.com

Public Company
Incorporated: 1985
Employees: 500
Sales: $59.09 million (1998)
Stock Exchanges: NASDAQ
Ticker Symbol: ODWA
NAIC: 311421 Fruit and Vegetable Canning; 312112 Bottled Water Manufacturing

Youthful, hip, and fresh, Odwalla, Inc. went from backyard juicer to big business faster than you can say ''Strawberry C Monster.'' While an *E. coli* scandal in 1996 squelched its explosive growth, the company's openness in response to the crisis, won it kudos and it remains today one of the country's leading brands of fresh juice. Other popular varieties of its ''Juice for Humans'' include Mango Tango, Femme Vitale, and Serious Ginseng. In 1997 Odwalla converted most of its delivery trucks to run on compressed natural gas, for which it won a Clean Air Award from the American Lung Association.

Orange Juicing Origins

In 1980, 25-year-old George Steltenpohl and two fellow musicians, Gerry Percy and Bonnie Bassett, were in Santa Cruz casting about for ways to make money without much capital. They also wanted to contribute something positive to their community. A business guidebook gave them the idea of selling fruit juices and thus Odwalla was launched in a shed in Steltenpohl's backyard in September 1980.

The company's name came from a character in an Art Ensemble of Chicago song-poem called ''Illistrum.'' Odwalla delivered the ''people of the sun'' from the ''gray haze.'' The group set out to do the same with a secondhand, $225 juicer and a 1968 Volkswagen van. Local restaurants were the first clients for the fresh-squeezed orange juice.

Business was brisk. The company was incorporated in California in September 1985. It expanded into San Francisco in 1988. Steltenpohl, who earned a degree in environmental science from Stanford University, attributed Odwalla's success to the fact that consumers were becoming more quality-conscious in general. In fruit drinks, this translated to the taste, nutrients, and enzymes available only in nonpasteurized, fresh juice. This utter reliance on fresh produce left the company somewhat at the whim of nature, though, and subject to unexpected losses.

In 1992, *Inc.* magazine reported on the pride and passion that rallied its 80 employees around the product. The company kept workers informed about the juices' nutritional benefits and involved them in taste testing and product naming. A pint of juice (two for drivers) was part of the daily salary. The company marketed about 20 different types of juices at the time, which sold for about $1.50 to $2.00 a pint.

Into the IPO Zone in 1993

Steltenpohl aimed for more than simple enthusiasm through empowerment. ''If you can take wage earners and instill an entrepreneurial drive, that translates into much greater productivity,'' he told *Nation's Business.* People were essentially trained to manage themselves, he said. Employees could also design their own jobs to an extent. Corporate headquarters a couple of blocks from the surf in Davenport, California also was considered a motivator.

Odwalla operated 35 delivery trucks in 1993, when sales were about $13 million a year. It invested in state-of-the-art hand-held computers for its drivers, who served as de facto PR reps as they escorted the juice along the ''cold chain'' to the ''O-Zone''—the company's distinctive in-store coolers.

The company launched its initial public offering (IPO) in December 1993, when it had slightly less than 200 employees. The RvR Securities (''risk-versus-reward'') arm of San Francisco investment bank Hambrecht & Quist Inc. had begun investing in the company in 1992, acquiring a 16 percent stake.

Company Perspectives:

Odwalla has strived to make and deliver great products while nurturing our relationships with humans and the environment. Our beacon phrase, "Nourishing the Body Whole," reflects a fundamental value of caring for all the communities that are touched by our business.

The group was impressed by Odwalla's strong customer loyalty and its distribution network. Soon after the IPO, the company expanded into the Pacific Northwest via the acquisition of Dharma Juice. It then bought Just Squeezed, based in Denver.

In 1994, Odwalla moved production to a renovated plant in Dinuba, California surrounded by produce fields. It moved its corporate headquarters to Half Moon Bay, California the next year. Odwalla by then dominated Northern California's fresh juice sales, holding half the market. Its products were sold in 1,400 locations.

Odwalla began selling bottled water in the mid-1990s. It was supplied by Idaho's Trinity Springs, whose aquifer held water carbon dated from the Stone Age, 16,000 years ago. This new line was very much the opposite of its highly perishable, unpasteurized fruit drinks. Water did not require refrigeration and could be sold in more outlets, offering a distinctive growth opportunity.

Revenues for fiscal year 1996 were $59.2 million. Odwalla supplied 4,000 locations in seven states (California, Colorado, Nevada, New Mexico, Oregon, Texas, and Washington) and British Columbia. Its largest customer was the Safeway grocery chain. The natural foods market was growing at a rate of 25 percent a year. Steltenpohl estimated that the company would reach $100 million in sales around 1999. He and co-CEO Stephen Williamson told shareholders: "Our objective, our passion, is to lead the fresh beverage revolution." It spent heavily to get on Texas shelves in October 1996. Odwalla was on the verge of becoming a national brand.

1996: Disaster and Mitigation

As part of its sanitation process, the company cleaned its fruit with a phosphoric acid wash and whirling brushes. But this failed in October 1996. An outbreak of food poisoning caused by *E. coli* 0157:H7 killed a toddler in Denver and sickened 66 other people in the West, and the problem was traced to Odwalla apple juice. Pure apple juice accounted for a tenth of the company's revenues; it also was used in blended drinks, which accounted for a majority of its business.

Investigators speculated that Odwalla may have been sent fallen apples (or "grounders") that had come into contact with animal feces (the bug lives primarily in the digestive tract of cattle). Or it may have come from carrots harvested from the earth. The *Seattle Times* reported that Odwalla's sanitation was substandard in the week the tainted juice was produced.

Odwalla officials stated that they believed this strain of *E. coli,* only discovered in 1982, could not survive in cooled, acidic apple juice. The microbe appeared to be evolving. Steltenpohl pointed out that it also could be spread on fresh lettuce. Even minuscule amounts of the germ could spread infection. This was the same virulent pathogen that in 1993 had killed three people in Washington State who had eaten insufficiently cooked hamburgers at the Jack-in-the-Box chain.

Odwalla responded by recalling its juices containing apples or carrots, which were processed on the same line. It offered to pay medical bills for consumers who the juice made ill. The public relations problem was serious. As Steltenpohl later told *Forbes,* "Children's health problems are ranked as the worst thing that can happen to a company." Damage control took many forms. Aside from holding press conferences and setting up an 800 number hotline, Odwalla used the Internet to disseminate information about the health problem and Odwalla's response to it. Edelman Public Relations had a web site devoted to the crisis running on the same day Odwalla received word of the contamination. The site received 20,000 hits in the first two days. Links to authorities like the Centers for Disease Control helped firm Odwalla's credibility.

Odwalla's stock fell 40 percent. It would not be considered an attractive takeover candidate by the major fruit juice brands. Its brand name was damaged. There were also numerous lawsuits, which the company faced with $27 million worth of insurance and $10 million in cash. (The Jack-in-the-Box *E. coli* lawsuits of 1993 cost Foodmaker $56 million in legal costs.) Most of the suits were settled within a year. Sales fell 90 percent in the immediate wake of the crisis. Odwalla laid off ten percent of its 650 workers by December 1996 and posted a loss of $11.3 million for the fiscal year ending February 28, 1997. In December Odwalla announced plans to flash-pasteurize its apple juice.

The crisis affected not just Odwalla; grocery store chains dropped other fresh juice producers as well. Growers across the country grappled with the issue of pasteurization as the FDA considered making it mandatory. Most felt that the process destroyed the freshness with which they differentiated their offerings, in addition to adding another set of costs. Some growers in the Apple Hill area of California were among the first to implement a 23-point quality assurance plan that, among other things, forbade the use of "grounders," or fallen apples. These guidelines were referred to as Hazardous Analysis Critical Control Point (HACCP) rules.

Fresh juice accounted for only two percent of the total juice market in the United States. Some producers resented attempts by Odwalla, the media, and government to deflect criticism to the industry as a whole. "Let's not lose track of the real issue," one told the *San Mateo Times,* "Odwalla got animal poop on its apples and failed to wash it off." According to FDA statistics, the fresh juice industry overall reported only 447 illnesses (including the one fatality) for more than 500 million servings between 1993 and 1996. Nevertheless, the agency required juice marketers to label the following warning on fresh apple juice beginning in September 1998 (and all other fruit and vegetable juices by November): "WARNING: This product has not been pasteurized and, therefore, may contain harmful bacteria which can cause serious illness in children, the elderly, and persons with weakened immune systems." Juice produced to the HACCP standard was exempt from the labeling requirement. The fresh juice industry naturally railed against the labeling, believing it would scare away consumers. They

Key Dates:

1980: Odwalla begins juicing in Santa Cruz.
1994: First shipments delivered outside of California.
1996: *E. coli* outbreak traced to company's apple juice.
1998: Odwalla returns to profitability.

complained that it was ''more aggressive'' than that required even on raw pork.

Although Odwalla's openness in the face of the crisis was commended by many, the company received the highest food injury penalty ever in what was reportedly the country's first criminal conviction in a food poisoning case. It was levied a $1.5 million fine after it pled guilty to 16 counts of delivering adulterated food products into interstate commerce, a misdemeanor. At Odwalla's suggestion, one-sixth of the fine was earmarked for the Safe Tables Our Priority charity and to researchers at the University of Maryland and Penn State University. Fortunately, the resolution of this case made Odwalla stock safe again for institutional investors, who owned about 28 percent of the company before the crisis. That would fall to a low of four percent in 1998.

Rebuilding in 1997–98

Product offerings proliferated as the company pulled out all the stops to win back consumers. A new type of liquid lunch debuted in May 1997. Odwalla's Future Shake, designed to appeal to a younger market than that of nutrient-fortified Ensure, was marketed as a ''drinkable feast'' made from ''real food'' like oats, almonds, soy, banana, and mango. No diet drink (one pint contained 12 grams of fat), it offered a lunchtime alternative to fried fast food. These were offered in Inner Chai, Dutch Chocolate, and Café Latte flavors. Odwalla introduced an energy bar, its first solid product, in September 1998. This entered the company in a $900-million-a-year market. There was also a new line of ''Nutritionals'' enhanced with proteins, herbs, vitamins, and fruits. Redesigned packaging appeared in September 1999. The new bottles featured bolder graphics and a sturdier cap but held slightly less juice. Odwalla also introduced pasteurized versions of its citrus drinks.

Odwalla announced that it was again profitable by the third quarter of 1997–98, posting a profit of $140,000 versus the previous year's $1.8 million loss for the period. Analysts reckoned there was still life left in its brand name. The company continued to expand geographically, entering Philadelphia and Washington, D.C. markets. This expansion was soon followed by entry into markets of Chicago, Detroit, Minneapolis, and Phoenix. Analysts felt it wise for the company to get a toehold in these new markets before someone else did, even if it came at the expense of bottom line profits. Odwalla's revenues were up 12 percent in 1998, to $59.1 million.

''Odwalla is in the business of providing easy access to great-tasting nourishment,'' CEO Stephen Williamson told the *Wall Street Journal.* It *was* still in business—sales were on track to reach $67 million in 1999, a rise of more than 12 percent. Nevertheless, a net loss was projected. One analyst estimated that the company would have been a $150 million-a-year, national business were it not for the *E. coli* incident.

Principal Competitors

Just Squeezed; Tropicana; Minute Maid; Nantucket Nectars; Naked Juice (Chiquita Brands); Fresh Samantha's.

Further Reading

Bianchi, Alessandra, ''Best Love of Product: True Believers,'' *Inc.,* July 1993, p. 72.
De Lisser, Eleena, ''FDA Is Putting the Squeeze on Makers of Fresh Juice—New Warning Labels Are Sparking Safety Concerns Among Customers,'' *Wall Street Journal,* September 22, 1998, B2.
Evan, Thomas J., ''Odwalla,'' *Public Relations Quarterly,* Summer 1999, pp. 15–17.
Fryer, A.P., ''Fresh Fears: The Odwalla Crisis Has Put a Hard Squeeze on Local Makers of Fresh Juice,'' *Puget Sound Business Journal,* November 8, 1996, p. 1.
Groves, M., ''Firm Might Stop Making Apple Juice,'' *Los Angeles Times,* November 12, 1996, p. D2.
——, ''Juice Left in Odwalla: Company Posts Loss, But Sales and Cash Up Despite Recall,'' *Los Angeles Times,* January 8, 1997, p. D1.
Isaacs, Marc, ''The Fresh Juice Industry: An Industry in Transition?,'' *Beverage Industry,* August 1998, p. 29.
Joyce, Andee, ''Odwalla's Pickup Line of the Future: How About a Meal with that Shake?,'' *Beverage World,* September 30–October 31, 1997, p. 17.
Kaufman, Steven B., ''Freshness by the Bottle,'' *Nation's Business,* February 1994, p. 14.
King, W., ''How Sleuths Traced Source of E. coli to Odwalla Juice,'' *Seattle Times,* October 31, 1996, p. A1.
——, ''Odwalla's E. coli Error: Acid,'' *Seattle Times,* November 3, 1996, p. A1.
Kokmen, L., ''Odwalla Can Learn from Jack-in-the-Box—Eatery Chain Showed What Not To Do, Experts Say,'' *Seattle Times,* November 7, 1996, p. A21.
Lifsher, Marc, ''Apple Growers Revamp to Reassure Wary Public,'' *Wall Street Journal,* September 17, 1997, p. CA1.
Martinelli, Kathleen A., and William Briggs, ''Integrating Public Relations and Legal Responses During a Crisis: The Case of Odwalla, Inc.,'' *Public Relations Review,* Winter 1998, pp. 443–60.
Masters, Greg, ''All Juiced Up,'' *Discount Merchandiser,* July 1999, pp. 107, 109ff.
Moore, Brenda L., ''Time May Be Right to Take Bite of Odwalla,'' *Wall Street Journal,* August 19, 1998, p. CA1.
Postlewaite, Kimbra, ''Comeback in a Bottle,'' *Beverage Industry,* March 1999.
Rapaport, Richard, ''PR Finds a Cool New Tool,'' *Technology's 100 Richest* (supplement to *Forbes*), October 6, 1997, pp. 101–08.
Rice, Eric, ''Local Investors Bullish on Odwalla's Future,'' *Half Moon Bay Review,* July 8, 1998, p. 10A.
Richards, Bill, ''Odwalla's Contaminated Apple Juice Blamed for E. coli Outbreak in Seattle,'' *Wall Street Journal,* November 1, 1996, p. B3.
——, ''Odwalla's Woes Are a Lesson for Natural-Food Industry—FDA Seeks Tighter Quality Controls as E. coli Outbreak Raises Concerns,'' *Wall Street Journal,* November 4, 1996, p. B4.
Thomsen, Steven R., and Bret Rawson, ''Purifying a Tainted Corporate Image: Odwalla's Response to an E. coli Poisoning,'' *Public Relations Quarterly,* Fall 1998, pp. 35–46.
Veverka, Mark, ''Odwalla Still Faces Some Problems That Could Make It a Risky Bet,'' *Wall Street Journal,* December 4, 1996, p. CA2.
Wyatt, Edward A., ''H&Q Lite,'' *Barron's,* September 5, 1994, p. 19.

—Frederick C. Ingram

ONEIDA®

Oneida Ltd.

163-181 Kenwood Avenue
Oneida, New York 13421
U.S.A.
Telephone: (315) 361-3000
Fax: (315) 361-3658
Web site: http://www.oneida.com

Public Company
Incorporated: 1880 as Oneida Community, Limited
Employees: 5,010
Sales: $465.9 million (1998)
Stock Exchanges: New York
Ticker Symbol: OCQ
NAIC: 332211 Cutlery and Flatware (Except Precious) Manufacturing; 327112 Vitreous China, Fine Earthenware, and Other Pottery Product Manufacturing; 327215 Glass Product Manufacturing Made of Purchased Glass

Oneida Ltd. is the world's largest stainless steel and silver-plated flatware maker, serving both the consumer and food service markets. Its operations in the United States, Canada, Mexico, the United Kingdom, and Italy manufacture and market sterling, silver-plated, and stainless flatware, as well as china dinnerware and hollowware (coffee sets and trays). Oneida also markets crystal products and gift items and licenses its name to makers of linens, cookware, and utensils. Under its wholly owned subsidiary, Kenwood Silver Company, Inc., Oneida runs more than 60 Oneida Factory Stores. Established as a utopian community in the mid-19th century, the company has maintained a strong reputation for quality.

Company Roots in a Utopian Community

The Oneida Community was founded by John Humphrey Noyes in upstate New York in 1848. The Community practiced Noyes's theology of Perfectionism—a form of Christianity rooted in the two basic tenets of self-perfection and communalism. In addition to abolishing private property, the Oneida Community raised children communally and espoused ''complex marriage,'' in which monogamous marriages were discouraged.

This communal child care system enabled the Oneida women, as well as the men, to take part in the Community's manufacturing of animal traps, chains, silk items, and silver knives, forks, and spoons, which it sold to the outside world to sustain itself. Soon the Oneida Community developed a reputation not just for the unconventional lifestyle of its members, but also for the quality of its goods. For instance, the Newhouse trap was invented by a founding member of the Community and was known around the world.

The Oneida Community survived longer than most other 19th century utopian societies, in part because of the solvency of its businesses. Indeed, Oneida members continued to live and work together until the late 1870s. But prosperity did not shield the organization from conflict, and in 1879 the Community split into two factions. Unable to resolve their differences, the members voted to transform the group's businesses into a joint stock company, the Oneida Community, Limited, which would be owned and operated by former members of the society. The Community was valued at $600,000 and shares were distributed according to each member's original contribution and length of service. The stock was divided among 226 men, women, and children, the majority of whom received shares worth between $2,000 and $4,999. The progressive nature of the new company was reflected in, among other things, the selection of a woman (Harriet Joslyn) to be superintendent of the silk mill and a member of the board of directors.

During the 15 years following Oneida's reorganization, the company's financial standing deteriorated. A severe depression in the 1890s, inadequate leadership, and emigration from the community plagued the new company. Some have speculated that the failure of the utopian community contributed to demoralization of the worker/stockholders, further eroding the company's prospects for success.

Oneida Enters the Industrial Age

But in January 1894, Pierrepont Burt (P.B.) Noyes, the son of Oneida's charismatic founder, rejoined the company after working as an Oneida wholesaler in ''The World,'' as many Oneidans

> **Company Perspectives:**
>
> *Our goal is to profitably and ethically satisfy our customers' needs in a manner that enhances the welfare of our stockholders, our employees, and the communities in which we reside.*

referred to the broader society outside their community. At only 23 years old, Noyes replaced an uncle on Oneida's board of directors. His experience outside the Community enabled him to see and criticize weaknesses that threatened the company's viability. Within two months Noyes led a proxy fight to oust directors who clung to old-fashioned business strategies. Nearly 24,000 shares were voted, and Noyes's side won by just 16 shares. Noyes was offered the position of superintendent at Oneida's Niagara Falls Plant and soon raised the operation's standards of quality to their former high levels. In 1899 the company announced what were then the largest profits in its history and paid its stockholders a dividend of seven percent.

By the time he reached the age of 30, Noyes had attained de facto control of Oneida. The board nominated him to the newly created post of general manager with authority to oversee all of the company's divisions—canning and manufacturing of tableware, traps, chains, and silk thread. Noyes's rise to prominence at Oneida helped bring the company into the industrial world of the 20th century. Previously, Oneida had relied on its managers' creativity, thrift, and diligence, as well as the excellent reputation of its products, to succeed in the competitive marketplace. Noyes introduced the new production methods, competitive strategies, large-scale distribution methods, and promotional efforts that were beginning to typify American industry. In 1904 Oneida began to place heavy emphasis on marketing and brand recognition, increasing its promotion budget from $5,000 to $30,000 per year. Noyes financed this move by diverting profits from the trap business (that would otherwise have been used to expand trap manufacturing), which he saw as a dying enterprise.

From that time on, even during the Great Depression, advertising remained an essential aspect of Oneida's operations. Early marketing campaigns established many of the features that would characterize Oneida's advertising for decades to come. The print ads typically appeared in widely circulated women's magazines. Rather than describe all of its tableware at length, Oneida used most of its advertising space for a picture of one or two pieces of silver plate, which it often associated visually with someone or something attractive. Oneida was also one of the first companies to employ celebrity spokespeople to promote its products. Ten years before the practice was widely accepted, Oneida commissioned Irene Castle—a famous dancer and fashion plate—to promote the Community's wares.

Despite Noyes's aggressive efforts to gain control of Oneida, he still sought to preserve the communal harmony and idealism on which the Community was founded. Managers who lost positions on the board of directors retained positions within the company, and many grew to respect the new management. In addition, a private community built around the company (called Kenwood) gave Oneida a sense of family that remained strong through the early decades of the 20th century; well into the 1920s, descendants of the original Oneidans held almost 90 percent of company stock. Noyes sought to make Oneida and the community of Kenwood ''modern utopias'' by increasing wages, improving work conditions, providing welfare and recreational benefits, and improving the physical environs of Kenwood.

By appealing to their sense of ambition, Noyes attracted children of Oneidans who had left the Community in favor of college education and careers in ''The World.'' Instead of touting the Community's old doctrine of Perfectionism, Noyes advocated a ''modern utopia'' based on intellectual challenge, reasonable pay, and self-improvement. The company's inventiveness and cooperation between labor and management have distinguished Oneida throughout its history. Indeed, the company's silverware operations have yet to suffer a work stoppage due to a labor dispute.

The company's enlightened attitude was reflected in other ways as well. In 1904 Noyes proposed voluntary salary reductions for management when the company encountered financial difficulties. In 1914 all salaried personnel took a ten percent pay cut, which remained in effect until early 1916. In 1921 larger cuts were necessary—Noyes reduced his own salary by half, the directors took 33 percent cuts, and other officials took smaller cuts corresponding to their salaries. The Great Depression necessitated similar sacrifices.

In a further effort to strengthen its financial position, Oneida sold its chain business in 1912, liquidated its silk industry holdings the following year, when man-made substitutes for silk were invented. The company's canning business was discontinued in 1915 because it was unable to compete with large-scale modern production methods. But the consolidations enabled Oneida to open its first international factory, in Niagara Falls, Ontario, in 1916.

Changes from World War I to World War II

Noyes resigned from the general managership in 1917 to let a younger generation into Oneida's management. Three months after he resigned, the United States entered World War I. Oneida assisted the war effort by producing ammunition clips, lead-plated gas shells, and combat knives. The company also served as the principal source of a wide range of surgical instruments used in military hospitals. In 1919 Noyes returned briefly to Oneida after working with the U.S. government's Fuel Administration. He later played a role in the post-World War I Peace Conference and the Rhineland Commission, which decided the particulars of the Allied occupation of Germany.

Amid financial crisis in 1921, Noyes resumed the general managership of Oneida. After steering the company through that predicament, he bequeathed the position of general manager to his son-in-law, Miles E. Robertson, in 1926. But Noyes retained both the post of president and de facto control of the company. Oneida's trap business was sold in 1925, which left the company entirely dependent on its silverware business.

In 1935 the company's name was changed to Oneida Ltd. to differentiate tableware produced by Oneida from that of lower quality subsidiaries of the company, such as Wm. A. Rogers. The name change also signaled a new era at Oneida. Noyes ceded control of the company to Miles Robertson, although he did not formally hand over the presidency until 1950. Robertson

Key Dates:

1848: John Humphrey Noyes founds the Oneida Community.
1880: Oneida Community, Limited is incorporated.
1894: Pierrepont Burt Noyes joins Oneida's board of directors and institutes major changes.
1904: Oneida dedicates greater attention to marketing and brand recognition.
1935: Company's name is changed to Oneida Ltd.
1977: Oneida acquires Camden Wire Co., Inc in an effort to diversify.
1998: Oneida sells Camden Wire and seeks to become a complete tableware company. Oneida also purchases a number of tableware companies to augment its existing products.
1999: Oneida successfully avoids an unsolicited buyout from Libbey Inc.

was known for his ''toughness'': despite the rigors of the Great Depression, Oneida made a profit in 1933, when no other company in the silverware industry could. By this time, Oneida had subsidiaries in Canada and Great Britain.

Beginning in the 1930s, Oneida became less community-oriented and more like a typical corporation with few family ties and less of a social-utopian bent. By 1930, 33 percent of the board of directors were not from the Community. Robertson aggressively began to recruit new employees from ''The World.'' Even Noyes's ideological influence gave way to more worldly viewpoints in the late 1930s. Whereas Oneida's management had once sought personal satisfaction over personal wealth, the arrival of greater numbers of ''outsiders'' inevitably altered these values. As competition for quality personnel escalated and the company grew more segregated from the Community, management salaries increased to match prevailing wages in the industry.

World War II brought about other changes at Oneida as well. The company's contribution to the war effort included production of silverware for the Army and Navy and surgical instruments for military hospitals. Oneida also manufactured products for the battlefield, including rifle sights, parachute releases, hand grenades, shells, survival guns, bayonets, aircraft fuel tanks, and chemical bombs. The company even purchased a separate factory in Canastota, New York, which produced army trucks, aircraft survival kits, and jet engine parts. That plant stayed in operation for several years after the war.

The 1950s and 1960s

Although the Oneida of the 1950s had accepted the wage scales of the outside world, it continued to operate by Noyes's principle that management should take salary cuts during difficult financial periods. The employees of the 1950s had changed along with the times, however, and a 1957 cut in directors' salaries was perceived by employees not as a demonstration of management's vested interest in the welfare of the company, but as a drastic measure indicating impending financial disaster.

The directors restored their pay, but Oneida continued to be plagued by financial problems through 1960, when the company posted its first annual deficit. That same year Pierrepont Trowbridge (''Pete'') Noyes replaced his father as company president. Oneida had trouble adjusting to the loss of government orders that had supplemented silverware sales during World War II and the Korean War. The work force declined from a high of 3,800 in 1949 to 2,000 in 1960. Oneida responded by developing additional product lines, reorganizing production, and introducing new advertising and marketing strategies. By the end of the decade, the work force had grown to more than 3,000 employees.

During the 1960s, Oneida began to focus more on stainless steel flatware, instead of on the more expensive and prestigious silver-plated and sterling flatware that had previously been its hallmark. Technological breakthroughs in the late 1960s allowed Oneida to introduce the first ornate stainless flatware that had a decorative pierced pattern similar to sterling and silver plate. With these more attractive and formal patterns, stainless flatware gained a place in the silver departments of fine department stores. Because stainless was easier to care for and was far less expensive than sterling and silver plate, this new flatware sold briskly, sparking a recovery that led Oneida into a new era of growth.

Efforts To Expand in the 1970s and 1980s

In 1977 Oneida moved to diversify its interests through the purchase of the Camden Wire Co., Inc.—one of the principal U.S. manufacturers of industrial wire products. One year later Oneida acquired Rena-Ware, a cookware manufacturer that operated in 34 countries and generated the majority of sales outside the United States. That year the company also got a new president, John Marcellus, Jr., who had joined Oneida in 1946. Pete Noyes continued as chairman until 1981, when Marcellus assumed that position as well.

By 1983, the company sold more than half of all flatware purchased in the United States. To broaden its penetration of the overall tableware market, Oneida purchased other companies, such as Buffalo China Inc., one of the nation's largest volume producers of commercial chinaware, and Webster-Wilcox, a producer of expensive hollowware. In 1984 the company bought D.J. Tableware, which manufactured high-quality flatware, hollowware, and china for the food service industry. Oneida also began to market a line of crystal stemware and gift ware in the mid-1980s.

Tough Times for Oneida During the Early 1980s

The recession of the early 1980s, however, eroded Oneida's profits. Primarily a consumer products company (industrial wire sales only constituted 24 percent of Oneida's profits in the mid-1980s and less than 30 percent in 1991), Oneida suffered more than expected. In 1982 alone, the company's earnings plummeted 65 percent. The company's problems were exacerbated when Japanese and other importers flooded American housewares departments with inexpensive flatware. Although it initially attempted to ignore this new threat by touting the superiority of its merchandise, Oneida's market share dropped precipitously to 39 percent in 1986. Between 1985 and 1986, the company laid off workers and lost more than $1 million.

In the late 1980s, Oneida instituted sweeping changes to both its management and its business strategies in a bid to return the company to its former preeminence. John Marcellus retired in 1986 and William Matthews was named chairman and CEO. Samuel Lanzafame, the former head of the Camden Wire subsidiary, was appointed president. Because Lanzafame had made Camden Wire Oneida's most profitable division, the board hoped that he could do the same with the parent company.

Oneida strove to recapture the market for lower-end, less expensive flatware that it had lost to import competition. Lanzafame worked to enhance Oneida's economies of scale and placed a renewed emphasis on the company's high-volume lines. He also sought to boost the capacity of Oneida's two flatware plants. The company began importing more inexpensive flatware to market under its name until it could bring its own factories up to speed to produce lower-quality (but higher-volume) merchandise.

Matthews, the new chairman of the board, undertook cost-cutting measures as well. He sold off the company's fleet of limousines and its corporate jet, and then trimmed the management staff by 15 percent. He also encouraged worker loyalty by offering an Employee Stock Option Plan in 1987 that put 15 percent of the company's stock in the employees' hands. Late in the decade, he oversaw the investment of more than $26 million for plant improvements, including computer design and manufacturing systems, plant consolidation, and machinery upgrades. By the end of the 1980s, Oneida had regained its 52 percent share of the flatware market. Lanzafame resigned as president in 1989, and Gary Moreau became president in 1991, holding that position until his 1995 resignation. In 1996 Peter Kallet was named president and chief operating officer, joining Matthews at the helm of the company. Kallet had a strong background in sales, marketing, product, and purchasing departments.

Becoming a Tableware Powerhouse in the 1990s

During the mid-1990s, Oneida revamped its strategy once more and attempted to build itself into a complete tableware products company. In 1997 Oneida sold off its Camden Wire subsidiary, which no longer conformed to the company's focus. Oneida also made a number of acquisitions that were intended to increase the company's scope. In 1996, following a year of record sales, Oneida purchased THC Systems, Inc., the parent company of Rego China. "This truly rounds out the selection of food service china we can offer, giving us a great array of products," Matthews told the *Buffalo News*. The following year, Oneida acquired Encore Promotions, a marketer of grocery store redemption programs, which the company hoped to use to market flatware, dinnerware, cookware, cutlery, towels, and linen. Also in 1997, Oneida gained exclusive rights to distribute Schott-Zwiesel crystal. In 1998 the company bolstered its international presence in the tableware market when it purchased the Italian manufacturer of flatware and hollowware, Table Top Engineering and Design, as well as two Australian tableware leaders, Stanley Rogers & Son and Westminster China. That same year, Oneida entered into an agreement to become the exclusive marketer and distributor of products from CALP, an Italian crystal producer.

Oneida's spate of acquisitions pushed corporate earnings down 31 percent in 1998, forcing the company to shed 95 jobs. The additional costs Oneida incurred in introducing its new lines were only made worse by the collapse of Asian economies and the overall weakness of the U.S. dollar. In 1999 Oneida closed its original factory in Niagara Falls, Ontario, and planned to cut more jobs. In April 1999, Libbey Inc., a leading glassware manufacturer, made an unsolicited bid to acquire Oneida. Oneida successfully rebuffed the offer and sought to restructure its operations to reduce expenses.

In 1999 the company's sales and profits rose, indicating that the difficult cuts had paid off. Oneida's future looked bright, as the company enjoyed an unparalleled brand reputation in the housewares industry. A 1995 survey had revealed that consumers thought first of Oneida when queried about stainless steel flatware. Throughout the economic, social, and political changes that Oneida endured during its 150-year history, its reputation for excellence remained untarnished.

Principal Subsidiaries

Oneida Canada Limited; Oneida Mexicana, S.A.; Kenwood Silver Company, Inc.; Buffalo China, Inc.; D.J. Tableware, Inc.; Oneida International, Inc. (88%); Sant' Andrea S.r.l.; Oneida Silversmiths, U.K.; THC Systems, Inc. (Dba Rego China); Encore Promotions, Inc.

Principal Competitors

Mikasa, Inc.; Reed & Barton Silversmiths; Waterford Wedgwood plc; Brown-Forman Corporation; Corning Incorporated.

Further Reading

Carden, Maren L., *Oneida: Utopian Community to Modern Corporation*, Baltimore: The Johns Hopkins Press, 1969.

Cohn, Lynne M., "Flatware Market May Be Regaining Its Luster," *American Metal Market*, June 14, 1993.

Fish, Mike, "Oneida Ltd. Earnings Jump 20% in Third Quarter," *Syracuse Post-Standard*, November 22, 1995.

Kates, William, "Communal Roots Lie at Heart of Oneida Ltd.'s Success," *Buffalo News*, May 28, 1996.

McGough, Robert, "Too Much of a Good Thing," *Forbes*, November 17, 1986, pp. 68–70.

Niedt, Bob, "Oneida To Buy China Company," *Syracuse Post-Standard*, August 30, 1996.

"Oneida Ltd.: Plan To Eliminate 200 Jobs Is Part of Expanded Cuts," *Wall Street Journal*, April 1, 1999.

"Oneida: Profit Drops, Sales Gain," *HFN: The Weekly Newspaper for the Home Furnishing Network*, September 21, 1998.

"Oneida Resisting Libbey Buyout," *Albany Times Union*, May 6, 1999.

Robertson, Constance, "The Oneida Community," Oneida Ltd., 1985.

Rosen, Daniel, "Big-Time Plugs on Small-Company Budgets," *Sales & Marketing Management*, December 1990, pp. 48–54.

Sutor-Terrero, Ruthanne, "Oneida: Making Stainless Shine," *Financial World*, July 25, 1989, p. 14.

Taub, Stephen, "First a Strikeout, Now a Triple Play," *Financial World*, August 31, 1983, pp. 34–35.

—April S. Dougal
—updated by Rebecca Stanfel

Pediatric Services of America, Inc.

310 Technology Parkway
Norcross, Georgia 30092
U.S.A.
Telephone: (770) 441-1580
Toll Free: (800) 950-1580
Fax: (770) 263-9340
Web site: http://www.psakids.com

Public Company
Incorporated: 1989
Employees: 5,000
Sales: $302.5 million (1998)
Stock Exchanges: NASDAQ
Ticker Symbol: PSAI
NAIC: 62161 Home Health Care Services

Pediatric Services of America, Inc. (PSA) provides home medical care to pediatric patients through more than 110 branch offices scattered across 28 states and the District of Columbia. PSA focuses on providing medical care to infants suffering from respiratory problems, but the company also provides nursing, pharmacy, and infusion therapy services. Based in Norcross, Georgia, PSA is headed by Joseph D. Sansone, who presided as chairman, chief executive officer, and president.

Origins

Prior to founding PSA, Sansone accumulated the experience he would need to create an industry leader in pediatric home care. His career path in the years immediately preceding PSA's formation included two years as a senior executive of a subsidiary owned by American Medical International, Inc. The subsidiary, comprising a division of American Medical that specialized in durable medical equipment sales and rentals, was AMI Home Health Equipment Centers. Sansone served as vice-president of the subsidiary between 1985 and 1987, leaving in September 1987 to join Macon, Georgia-based Charter Medical Corporation. At Charter Medical, Sansone was given responsibility to head a Charter Medical subsidiary named Ambulatory Services of America, a geriatric care provider that would become the foundation of PSA. Sansone, in his position as president of Ambulatory Services, was granted considerable control over the Charter Medical subsidiary, enough to entirely transform the orientation of the company. He moved Ambulatory Services away from its traditional business of caring for the elderly, a segment of the health care industry deemed overpopulated, and pushed the company headlong into another health care industry niche: the home care of pediatric patients.

At first blush, the strategy behind the shift in markets was sound. The United States was inundated with health care providers for the elderly and bereft of pediatric home care providers. As outside observers looked deeper into Ambulatory Services' dramatic change in focus, the prudence of Sansone's decision became clearer. At the time, insurance companies, the primary payors of health care costs, were desperately seeking to reduce their payments. With hospital stays reaching upwards of $3,000 per day, home care as a means to meet the medical needs of patients of all ages was more cost-effective than institutional care. For pediatric care, the savings realized by the payors generally increased. Children suffering from bronchopulmonary dysplasia, congenital heart defects, cystic fibrosis, hemophilia, and a host of other serious medical problems required medical attention for years, rather than weeks. Accordingly, the fragile medical condition of pediatric patients, exacerbated by their age, predicated the financial argument for home care, a business that was relatively unexploited during the late 1980s. Beyond the financial benefits, pediatric home care also was an attractive alternative for parents of pediatric patients and for the patients themselves, both of whom preferred, when the situation allowed it, to remain at home rather than at a hospital. Such were the motivations behind Sansone's redirection of Ambulatory Services' market focus, but as it soon became apparent, Sansone desired more than to lead a Charter Medical subsidiary toward greater success.

1989 Leveraged Buyout

After two years spent transforming Ambulatory Services into a pediatric home care specialist, Sansone proposed to buy the subsidiary from Charter Medical. He enlisted the help of a bank

Company Perspectives:

PSA offers a coordinated approach to home healthcare. This approach provides the most technically advanced nursing, respiratory, durable medical equipment, and infusion therapy services to our patients while enhancing communication among physicians, case managers, third party payors, and family.

and two venture capital concerns and completed a leveraged buyout of Ambulatory Services in 1989, renaming the enterprise Pediatric Services of America. Initially, his intent was to concentrate on premature births, which constituted ten percent of the four million babies born each year in the United States. ''I thought,'' Sansone explained to *Forbes* magazine in April 1998, ''why not let preemies go home instead of sitting in the ICU while Mom stares through the window?'' By positioning PSA as a specialist in pediatric home care, Sansone stood to gain from favorable industry conditions, namely, the absence of any dominant pediatric home care concerns operating on a national basis. The industry was populated by a large number of local and regional concerns, each restricted to competing for control of a relatively small market. The few nationally oriented pediatric home care providers were divisions within broader-based health care companies, whose efforts to penetrate the pediatric market represented only a facet of their overall operating strategy. Sansone theorized that a company committed specifically to providing pediatric home care through a network of national offices could dominate the industry, a theory to be made manifest by his development of PSA into a national leader.

Before the process of building PSA into a national force began, Sansone took time to ensure that the company's administrative functions were working properly. Otherwise formidable health care companies, boasting deep and broad market presence, had fallen victim to administrative inefficiencies, unable to maintain profitability amid the tangle of paperwork involved in providing medical services and receiving payment from third-party payors. Sansone was careful to avoid the dangers of lackadaisically tracking patient services and recouping costs from insurance companies and other payors, particularly so after gaining full control over the former Ambulatory Services subsidiary. He discovered in 1989 that the company suffered from woeful bookkeeping, its profitability hobbled by accounts receivable that stretched into months rather than weeks. To fix the problems and establish a sturdy administrative foundation to support the company's future growth, Sansone hired a skilled chief financial officer and spent two years computerizing billing and collection procedures. The commitment to improving internal efficiencies paid off, significantly reducing the duration of accounts receivable and helping PSA transform into a profitable enterprise.

1994 Debut as a Publicly Traded Company

PSA's development into a national pediatric home care specialist did not begin in earnest until several years after its billing and collecting methods were honed for profitability. The geographic reach of the company began to extend after it completed its initial public offering (IPO) and converted to a public ownership. The IPO was completed in 1994, when PSA's $13.6 million stock offering debuted on the NASDAQ Exchange. With the proceeds gained from the stock offering, Sansone was able to act upon the expansion strategy he had devised. His strategy for growth depended heavily on acquiring the legions of local and regional operators who constituted the overwhelming majority of the pediatric home care industry, but also included partnerships with health care providers, particularly the largest providers. Instances of PSA's partnership agreements included a deal completed in 1995 with 15 OrNda hospitals in southern California and three agreements reached in 1996. In May 1996, PSA formed a joint venture company named PSA Home HealthCare L.P. with Miami Children's Hospital, operator of a 268-bed facility. Later in 1996, PSA began providing comprehensive health care services to pediatric patients of New Jersey-based Hackensack University Medical Center. The company also signed a subcontract agreement in 1996 with Columbia/HCA Healthcare Corp.'s home health care division in Houston. According to the terms of the agreement, PSA supplied home nursing services, medical equipment, and intravenous therapy to children discharged from roughly 20 hospitals in the Houston area.

In an August 19, 1996 PSA press release, Sansone described the company's decision to seek partnerships as being ''complementary to our acquisition strategy,'' adding, ''they are worth it with the big players.'' The focus for PSA's growth, however, which was intended to spur its maturation into a national pediatric home care company, was on acquisitions. A fragmented industry, such as the pediatric home care industry, represented fertile ground for an aggressive acquirer to stake its claim on national leadership, an objective hotly pursued by Sansone. At the time of the IPO, PSA operated 41 offices in 12 states, generating $46 million in annual revenue. With the proceeds from the IPO and a secondary offering of stock in 1996 that raised an additional $23 million, the company's stature grew significantly and swiftly. Between the 1994 IPO and 1997, the number of PSA locations tripled, fueling a fourfold increase in annual sales. By mid-1997, with $200 million in annual sales, the company operated at 123 locations spread across 25 states, having greatly increased its geographic reach through the acquisition of pediatric care providers and related companies. Generally, the acquisitions completed by PSA were relatively small, as Sansone targeted local and regional care providers, medical equipment suppliers, and pharmacies.

1996 Diversification

As PSA's pediatric home care business expanded robustly, ranking as the largest in the country by 1997, Sansone ushered the company into a new business area. In February 1996, PSA entered the paramedical testing business through the acquisition of Premier Medical Services. Serving more than 1,000 insurance companies and corporate customers, Premier provided a variety of services, including collecting blood and urine samples, taking health histories, and performing electrocardiogram physical examinations. The foray into the paramedical testing field was strengthened considerably nearly two years later when the company purchased Physical Measurements Information (PMI), an acquisition that made PSA the third-largest provider of paramedical testing services in the country. Acquired from

Key Dates:

1989: Sansone leads leveraged buyout of Ambulatory Service of America, Inc.
1991: PSA completes sweeping program aimed at improving billing and collection services.
1994: Initial stock offering touches off aggressive acquisition campaign.
1996: PSA enters paramedical testing services business.

ChoicePoint Services, Inc. for $21 million, PMI dispatched nurses to perform physical examinations on individuals outside an institutional setting, frequently conducting the examination at the individual's workplace. Like Premier, PMI served the health and life insurance industries. Its inclusion under PSA's corporate umbrella significantly expanded the scale of Sansone's paramedical testing services business, placing PSA on the approved provider list for more than 200 new insurance company customers and greatly extending the company's geographic reach.

As part of the PMI acquisition, PSA also acquired an advanced computer software system under development by ChoicePoint. Called the PMI System and renamed by PSA as the SOLAR System, the software was designed for entering orders, scheduling examinations, and providing status reports, serving as an electronic communications link between PSA and its insurance company clients. The purchase of the Solar System reflected Sansone's commitment to improving PSA's administrative functions, following up on the pervasive changes he implemented between 1989 and 1991 with the company's billing and collection procedures. Several months before he acquired the PMI System, Sansone had invested $1.4 million on a new computerized billing system, dubbed the Encore System. The Encore System, which was integrated with the Solar System, was an automated patient accounting system. As well as performing billing and collection services, the Encore System provided each of the PSA's health care branch offices with immediate access to patient information, strengthening the company's ability to track the status of patient accounts.

As PSA added a new facet to its business and bolstered the administrative underbelly of its operations, the expansion of its mainstay business progressed without disruption. By the beginning of 1998, Sansone had acquired 38 pediatric care companies since the 1994 IPO, adding facilities to care for premature infants to the purchased properties. The additions included the purchase in May 1997 of Home Vitality Inc., an Illinois-based home care pharmacy that served the greater Chicago area. In July 1997, PSA acquired Special Medical Services, a Minnesota-based home health equipment services company. Two months later, the company purchased Home Health Nursing, a Vermont-based nursing agency, as well as two Florida companies: Individual Development Services, Inc., a day treatment center for children with special medical needs; and Medical Services Providers Inc., a medical equipment and home pharmacy supplier. The five acquisitions completed between May and September of 1997 represented a cross section of the acquisition campaign launched in 1994, indicative of the pace and geographic diversity of Sansone's acquisitive activities. Assessed separately, the acquisitions did not significantly add to PSA's revenue volume—most of the companies acquired only generated $1 million or $2 million in sales—but each contributed meaningfully to PSA's geographic coverage and to the comprehensiveness of the company's medical services. Although the company's services focused on respiratory problems suffered by infants, PSA's patients ranged from teenagers with leukemia who required home infusions of antibiotics to one instance in which a pair of conjoined twins required antibiotic infusions prior to separation surgery.

As PSA planned for the future, further acquisitions were expected. According to Sansone's calculations, the pediatric segment represented one-sixth of the $40-billion-in-sales home care market, or a $6 to $7 billion business. Acquisitions were expected to fuel the company's expansion, but as the 1990s drew to a close, PSA announced a significant divestiture. In August 1999, the company revealed that it was selling its paramedical testing division to Hooper Holmes Inc. Once completed, the divestiture would strip the company of roughly $90 million in annual revenue, but the proceeds from the sale would give Sansone the funding to further develop PSA's medical services business, an objective the company promised to pursue as it moved past its tenth anniversary.

Principal Competitors

Apria Healthcare Group, Inc.; Coram Healthcare Corporation; ChoicePoint Inc.; RoTech Medical Corporation; American HomePatient, Inc.

Further Reading

Grover, Mary Beth, "Healthy Choice," *Forbes,* April 20, 1998, p. 68.
Luke, Robert, "The Atlanta Journal and Constitution Insider Trading Column," *Knight-Ridder/Tribune Business News,* August 23, 1998, p. OKRB9823511F.
Meltzer, Mark, "PSA Provides Home Care to Seriously Sick Children," *Atlanta Business Chronicle,* July 21, 1997, p. 3.
"PSA Expands," *Atlanta Business Chronicle,* August 19, 1996, p. 2.

—Jeffrey L. Covell

Performance Food Group Company

6800 Paragon Place, Suite 500
Richmond, Virginia 23230
U.S.A.
Telephone: (804) 285-7340
Fax: (804) 285-5360
Web site: http://www.pfgc.com

Public Company
Incorporated: 1987 as Pocahontas Food Group
Employees: 3,200
Sales: $1.62 billion (1998)
Stock Exchanges: NASDAQ
Ticker Symbol: PFGC
NAIC: 42241 General Line Grocery Wholesalers

Performance Food Group Company (PFG) distributes food and food-related products to institutional customers, such as hotels, schools, and health care facilities, and to restaurants, primarily casual dining restaurant chains and fast food chains. PFG also operates a pre-cut produce division that distributes produce to fast food chains and controls two distributor buying groups, Pocahontas Foods USA and Affiliated Paper Companies, Inc. Together, the company's operating companies distribute more than 25,000 products to approximately 20,000 customers in the southern, southwestern, central, and northeastern United States.

Origins

During the mid-1980s, the U.S. food distribution industry was in flux. With increasing frequency, the larger members of the industry were acquiring smaller distributors, hoping to take advantage of a highly fragmented industry by swallowing up as many companies as feasible and secure a greater share of the market. Two industry participants who were watching the consolidation surrounding them—and growing increasingly anxious—were Robert Sledd and Michael Gray. Sledd was president of Taylor & Sledd, a family food marketing company that owned a distributor buying group named Pocahontas Foods USA. Gray served as president of Pocahontas Foods USA. As the two executives surveyed the developments affecting their industry, noting that in one energetic fit Kraft Foodservice had acquired eight of the 50 largest distributors in the country in 1986 alone, they grew alarmed. "There was a lot of consolidation going on in the industry at the time," Sledd reflected in September 1998 in the periodical *ID,* "and we were looking for ways to protect our distributor base from being acquired." Sledd and Gray decided to ward off predator companies by merging several companies together under the corporate shield of a holding company, an entity that would enable them eventually to go public and pursue their own aggressive growth strategy. They named the holding company Pocahontas Food Group, under which Pocahontas Foods USA, the distributor group, would operate as a wholly owned subsidiary. Deciding upon a name was the easy part of the solution, but to make Pocahontas Food Group more than a mere façade, Sledd and Gray needed distributors willing to operate beneath their corporate umbrella. Sledd and Gray faced the difficult challenge of convincing distributors that their best interests would be served with the newly christened Pocahontas Food Group rather than with established distributor conglomerates.

To turn Pocahontas Food Group into a reality, Sledd and Gray approached three Pocahontas Foods USA members in 1987. As they discovered, their fears of potentially losing a portion of their distributor base were not unfounded. Caro Produce and Institutional Foods, a family-run distribution company based in Houma, Louisiana, had an offer from a suitor. I. Feldman Co., based in Washington, D.C., had been approached as well. Lebanon, Tennessee-based K.O. Lester Co. was entertaining a bid from a larger concern. Sledd and Gray asked each distributor to ally itself with the newly formed Pocahontas Food Group, promising that each would be allowed to retain its management. The two executives also argued that, as part of a greater whole, each distributor would benefit from the advantages of a larger capital base. For evidence to support the implied threat that the Pocahontas Foods USA distributors risked losing control of their companies, Sledd and Gray could point to ample cases within the industry. Frequently, the acquiring companies replaced family and other long-time executives with their own employees, effecting what was referred to as a "new broom." The fear of being swept aside after being

Company Perspectives:

Performance Food Group serves an integral role in the movement of food from the nation's farms to our dining tables. At the heart of the company's success is a focus on delivering exceptional customer service throughout its operations.

acquired may have struck a chord with the management of Caro Produce, I. Feldman, and K.O. Lester, but the prospect of risking their businesses in a new venture was less enticing. I. Feldman opted to accept an offer to sell to the fast growing Kraft Foodservice. Kenneth O. Lester, head of the eponymic distributor, balked at Sledd and Gray's proposal, while he weighed the merits of an offer by Kraft Foodservice. The fledgling consortium appeared destined for failure, but Jerry Caro, head of Caro Produce, decided to take the risk and ally his company with Pocahontas Food Group. Caro's decision represented a seminal moment in Pocahontas Food Group's history, its importance not lost on Sledd. "If Jerry hadn't taken that step," Sledd remarked to *ID* in September 1998, "there would be no PFG (Performance Food Group) today."

First Acquisition Campaign Launched During the Late 1980s

Although Pocahontas Food Group did not get off to a roaring start, the company did have a founding distributor company, the $67-million-in-sales Caro Produce, and a founding chairman, Jerry Caro. The holding company's constituency would soon increase, however. Before the end of 1987, the company completed its first acquisition, purchasing a distributor based in Gainesville, Florida named Hi Neighbor Wholesale. The acquisition was subsequently renamed Pocahontas Foodservice. Kenneth O. Lester, meanwhile, was still considering Kraft Foodservice's offer, but by July 1988 he had decided to bring his $58-million-in-sales company into the Pocahontas Food Group fold. After the acquisition of his company, Lester took over as chairman of Pocahontas Food Group and Caro took on the title of vice-chairman, concurrent with the relocation of corporate headquarters from Richmond, Virginia to Nashville, Tennessee.

As the company set out to pursue its own growth strategy, two decisions made during its first few months of existence were intrinsic to its later success. First was the decision in 1988 to create an employee stock ownership plan that gave the companies operating within the holding company an ownership stake in Pocahontas Food Group. With a personal stake in the holding company's fortunes, the managers of the subsidiary companies adopted an entrepreneurial approach to running their businesses, infusing the entire organization with a healthy combination of ambitious drive and accountability. The second decision, which complemented the employee stock ownership plan, centered on the corporate structure of Pocahontas Food Group. "When we were formed," Sledd explained in September 1998 to *ID*, "there were two ways we could go: decentralized or centralized." The company chose to operate in a decentralized manner, preferring to let the distributors manage their businesses as independent subsidiaries. "We didn't believe that by sitting in some ivory tower we would make better decisions than the guys in the operating companies," Sledd continued, "so we gave them a lot of autonomy to run their business." Decentralized management and an employee stock ownership plan bred the entrepreneurial spirit Sledd and Gray wanted to cultivate, giving Pocahontas Food Group the corporate culture it needed to succeed.

Pocahontas Food Group had the mindset of a successful organization from the start, but during the late 1980s its progress was constrained by a glaring shortcoming. Pocahontas Food Group lacked sufficient financial resources to embark on an aggressive acquisition spree, forcing its senior executives to develop an initial strategy for growth that conformed to the realities of the company's financial might. The company had to restrict its purchases to a limited number of acquisitions and it could entertain the acquisition of only troubled companies that subsequently could be turned into profitable enterprises. Accordingly, Pocahontas Food Group earned its initial recognition as a turnaround artist, applying its restorative touch to the companies it acquired after Kenneth O. Lester assumed the chairmanship. In 1989 the company acquired Hale Brothers, a Morristown, Tennessee-based distributor, followed by the acquisition of Tampa, Florida-based B&R Foods in 1991 and New Orleans-based Loubat-L. Frank, Inc. the following year.

Although the company was unable to burst from the starting block with a spate of acquisitions, the purchases it did make served as tangible evidence of its talents. Sound management had led to the revitalization of the acquired properties and to impressive financial growth, to which the company could point when it offered itself to the investing public. Sales in 1992 were up more than 20 percent to $325 million and profits rose 25 percent, reaching $51 million. The rising financial totals provided the record of accomplishment Pocahontas Food Group needed for its initial public offering (IPO), a debut to be made under a new corporate banner. In 1992 the company changed its name to Performance Food Group (PFG). The company's performance during the first half of 1993—highlighted by a 15 percent increase in sales—provided the final impetus for PFG's bid to become a public concern. The company filed with the Securities and Exchange Commission for the sale of 2.075 million shares at $14 per share, structuring its IPO to raise $20.4 million.

1993 IPO Fuels Expansion

The August 1993 IPO on the NASDAQ Exchange raised exactly what PFG had been hoping for, enabling the company to reduce its debt and to secure the financial wherewithal to assume a more ambitious and aggressive acquisitive posture. Before the company renewed its acquisition campaign, however, it suffered through a difficult 1994. PFG was beset by operational inefficiencies late in the year, a difficult period that company officials shrugged aside by attributing the problems to "growing pains." A more disruptive blow occurred at the end of 1994, when the company lost its leader. Lester died of a massive heart attack in December, causing a sudden management shake-up. Sledd retained his title as chief executive officer, but moved from his position as president to assume the chairmanship. Gray, meanwhile, took over as president and chief operating officer.

Following the tragedy that affected the company's progress in 1994, PFG entered 1995 ready to acquire, but the second

Key Dates:

1987: Founding distributor, Caro Produce and Institutional Foods, is acquired.
1988: K.O. Lester Co. is acquired; Kenneth O. Lester is named chairman.
1993: Performance Food Group debuts on the NASDAQ Exchange.
1998: Acquisitions and internal growth lift sales to $1.6 billion, a more than threefold increase in three years.

phase of the company's acquisition campaign followed a strategy different from the first. Forced to acquire only ailing companies during the late 1980s and early 1990s, PFG reversed its criteria during the latter half of the 1990s, buoyed by its newfound financial strength. "We don't have time to do turnarounds now," Sledd declared to *ID,* auguring an ambitious start to the second half of the decade. In 1995, when headquarters were relocated back to Richmond, the company acquired Milton's Foodservice, based outside of Atlanta, and Cannon Foodservice, a distributor based in Asheville, North Carolina. The year these two acquisitions were completed also marked the last year Caro Produce and K.O. Lester reported their revenue independently. When the sales generated by the two subsidiaries became part of PFG's annual financial statement, the result was a prolific jump in the holding company's stature. In 1995 the company did not appear on the list of the 50 largest distributors in the country, as ranked by *ID.* In 1996 PFG catapulted to the number nine position, propelled by its $664 million sales volume.

Ranking as one of the industry's elite by the mid-1990s, PFG earned its lofty position by recording consistent and energetic growth during the decade. Sales more than doubled between 1990 and 1995, in large part because of the growth recorded by PFG's two largest customers, casual-dining chains Cracker Barrel and Outback Steakhouse. Together, the two restaurant chains accounted for approximately 35 percent of PFG's total sales. For these two chains, PFG supplied everything from steaks to the sugar packets on the tables, part of the company's customized division that distributed goods exclusively to large chains. During the first half of the 1990s, the customized division registered annual growth of more than 30 percent, with the majority of the increase in sales occurring when Outback Steakhouse became a PFG customer in 1993. Cracker Barrel had been a customer since the early days of Pocahontas Food Group (Lester had served as a director of the company from 1970 to 1986). The company's other major operating segment was its broadline division—so named because of the broad selection of goods it distributed—which averaged annual sales growth of eight percent during the first half of the 1990s. PFG's broadline division served more than 9,000 customers, supplying food and related products to particular outlets operated by Wendy's, Subway, McDonald's, Kentucky Fried Chicken, Burger King, and Taco Bell, as well as to institutional customers, such as hospitals, schools, nursing homes, and hotels. Two other smaller divisions operated under PFG's auspices, a pre-cut produce division that distributed lettuce and other produce to fast food restaurants and a merchandising services division. The merchandising services division comprised Pocahontas Foods USA, the buying unit for small, independent distributors. The subsidiary purchased more than 18,000 products, charging a fee to the 140 distributors it served for its buying services. Although the subsidiary accounted for less than one percent of PFG's revenue, it served a vital role as a provider of marketing and computer assistance services to its parent company and, by virtue of its association with independent distributors, figured as a useful go-between for acquisitions.

Combined, PFG's four divisions distributed more than 15,000 food and food-related products to more than 13,000 customers, but despite the company breadth and reach, there was ample room for further growth. The food distribution industry remained highly fragmented, with the ten largest concerns in the country controlling roughly 20 percent of the $125 billion in sales up for grabs each year. Beneath the short list of the industry's largest companies were more than 3,000 distributors who averaged well below $100 million in sales, providing PFG with legions of acquisition candidates from which to choose. Efforts to achieve growth through internal means—the company was in search of adding a third major restaurant chain to its fast growing customized division—were pursued, but during the late 1990s acquisitions figured heavily in PFG's growth strategy. Sledd was aiming to increase revenue to $1.5 billion or $2 billion by the end of the 1990s.

A second offering of stock was completed in March 1996 to fuel the company's acquisition campaign during the late 1990s, a buying binge that began in late 1996 when PFG acquired McLane Foodservice, a distributor to fast food chains, such as Kentucky Fried Chicken, Dairy Queen, and Dunkin' Donuts, and to vending customers. The acquisition of McLane increased PFG's annual sales by more than 20 percent, touching off an era in the company's history that saw its revenue increase exponentially. In 1997 the company completed acquisitions that pushed sales toward Sledd's projected total, purchasing W.J. Powell Company, Central Florida Finer Foods, Inc., Tenneva Foodservice, Inc., and AFI Food Service Distributors. By the end of 1997, sales towered at $1.2 billion, nearly doubling in two years' time.

As PFG prepared for the 21st century, the company was positioned as a formidable force in its industry, having achieved remarkable growth during its first decade of business. Moving past its tenth anniversary, PFG continued to add to the depth of its operations, acquiring Virginia Food Service Group, a $45 million distributor, in 1998. In 1998 the company also acquired Affiliated Paper Companies, Inc., a privately owned marketing organization that served as a paper and sanitation supplies buyer for independent distributors. In one of its last transactions in the 1990s, PFG nearly doubled the size of its pre-cut produce business with the August 1999 acquisition of Dixon Tom-A-Toe Cos. Inc. Based in Atlanta, Dixon processed fresh-cut produce, generating approximately $60 million in sales a year. As the company looked ahead, further acquisitions were in the offing. According to 1997 figures, 55 percent of the industry's $141 billion in annual sales was controlled by distributors one-tenth PFG's size, presenting the company with numerous opportunities to secure greater market share in the years ahead.

Principal Subsidiaries

Kenneth O. Lester Company, Inc.; Hale Brothers/Summit, Inc.; Milton's Foodservice, Inc.; Performance Food Group of Texas, LP; W.J. Powell Company, Inc.; AFI Food Service Distributors, Inc.; Virginia Foodservice Group, Inc.; Affiliated Paper Companies, Inc.; B&R Foods.

Principal Competitors

AmeriServe; SYSCO Corp.; U.S. Foodservice.

Further Reading

''Acquisitions: Reaching Out and Folding In,'' *ID: The Voice of Foodservice Distribution,* September 1998, p. 49.

Gilligan, Gregory J., ''Richmond, Va.-Based Food Company Buys Paper Supplies Buyer,'' *Knight-Ridder/Tribune Business News,* June 3, 1998, p. OKRB981540B7.

——, ''Richmond, Va.-Based Performance Food Group Wants Bigger Piece of Market,'' *Knight-Ridder/Tribune Business News,* January 9, 1996, p. 1090040.

''Great Performances,'' *ID: The Voice of Foodservice Distribution,* September 1998, p. 40.

''Ken Lester, PFG Chairman, Dead at 60,'' *ID: The Voice of Foodservice Distribution,* February 1995, p. 31.

Perkins, Caroline, ''Behind the Headlines at PFG,'' *ID: The Voice of Foodservice Distribution,* September 1998, p. 13.

''PFG Promotes Two to Exec.,'' *Nation's Restaurant News,* February 27, 1995, p. 50.

''PFG To Go Public in Bid To Reduce Debt, Enhance Opportunities for Growth,'' *ID: The Voice of Foodservice Distribution,* September 1, 1993, p. 19.

''PFG Will Expand 2 Distribution Centers,'' *Nation's Restaurant News,* February 7, 1994, p. 48.

''Pocahontas Foods USA: The Benefits Are Mutual,'' *ID: The Voice of Foodservice Distribution,* September 1998, p. 50.

Stern, William, ''Nonperformance?,'' *Forbes,* January 17, 1994, p. 128.

—Jeffrey L. Covell

Porsche AG

70432 Stuttgart
Germany
Telephone: 49-711-911-0
Fax: 49-711-911-5777
Web site: http://www.porsche.com

Public Company
Incorporated: 1931 as Dr. Ing. h. c. F. Porsche AG
Employees: 8,151
Sales: DM 4.9 billion (1998)
Stock Exchanges: Frankfurt
NAIC: 336111 Automobile Manufacturing; 42111 Automobile and Other Motor Vehicle Wholesalers

Porsche AG is legendary for its innovative and beautiful automobile designs. The Porsche 911, first manufactured in 1964, quickly became one of the world's most famous and most recognizable automobiles. The company has also been on the cutting edge of automotive engineering and technology, using the sports car racing circuit to develop and improve products renowned for their high performance and outstanding handling. It is not surprising that Porsche has recorded more victories than any other automobile manufacturer in such classics as the 24-hour LeMans and the 24-hour Daytona races. In 1997 the company successfully introduced the Boxster, a newly designed, lower priced sports car. Plans to design and manufacture a suburban utility vehicle in conjunction with Volkswagen were announced in 1998.

Early Years

The founder of the company, Dr. Ferdinand Porsche, was born in Bohemia and studied mechanical engineering in Vienna. In 1923 he traveled to Stuttgart, Germany, and by 1930 the ambitious young man had established his own engineering and design firm there under the name Dr. Ing. h. c. F. Porsche KG. The new firm garnered a reputation for innovative car designs, and when Adolf Hitler came to power in Germany, he summoned Ferdinand Porsche to meet with him, requesting that he find a solution to some of the technical difficulties that were delaying production of the ''Volkswagen,'' or people's car. The famous Volkswagen design had been created in Porsche's office, and as early as 1935 Porsche had designed a special sports version of the car. The Nazi regime initially rejected his application to produce the sporting version, but during the late 1930s Hitler himself approved a contract with Porsche to design a car for the 1939 Auto-Union Grand Prix, a famous motor race from Berlin to Rome.

Porsche's idea for a racing car was based on expanding the capacity of the utilitarian Volkswagen engine by using different valves and cylinder heads and by including a new system known as fuel injection. The car also included a significantly enlarged wheelbase and a unique aerodynamic body design. Although three prototypes of the car were built in early 1939, the beginning of World War II in September of that year led to cancellation of the race and halted further development of the Porsche car. During the war years, the well-known engineer remained in Germany while continuing to work on Hitler's Volkswagen project. On various occasions, he also gave Hitler advice on how to increase the production of military equipment used by the German armed services. At the end of the war, Dr. Porsche was imprisoned in France for a short time because of his association with Adolf Hitler and the Nazi regime.

1948: First Production-Line Porsches

After World War II, the Porsche design firm relocated to Gmund in Kärnten, Austria, and survived primarily by repairing and servicing different kinds of automobiles. By 1946, however, the Porsche design team was working on various sports and racing car designs. Ferdinand Porsche's son, Ferry Porsche, Jr., insisted on conducting market research in order to determine whether people were willing to buy an expensive, handmade, high performance sports car. Ferry approached a circle of well-to-do Swiss financiers who agreed to fund production. Working from the basic design model of a Volkswagen Beetle, the company created a lightweight sports car, and the Porsche design office became an automobile factory. The prototype of the Porsche sports car was on the road by March 1948, and small-scale production was initiated by the end of the year. The Gmund plant manufactured five handmade Porsche cars a month, each with a single aluminum body hand-beaten for hours over a wooden rig by a master craftsman of the art.

Company Perspectives:

The first sports car bearing the Porsche name rolled out of a small test workshop in Gmund, Austria in June 1948. Back then, none of its founding fathers could have imagined the success story that more than one million descendants of this ''Porsche Number One'' have written in the five decades since then. It is from this tradition that we draw the energy to face the challenges of the future. As we understand ourselves (and as countless people throughout the world perceive us), today, Porsche is a mature and vigorous company. Over the past fifty years, it has become the absolute definition of sports-car driving. What is more: despite the zeal for mergers that the large carmakers have displayed recently, we remain thoroughly convinced that the world's smallest independent volume-production automobile manufacturer has the potency and skill to maintain its independence in the future as well. This conviction is not mere hubris; it is based on the certainty that our company is distinguished by a different and very special kind of logic. Porsche is a vital piece of counterevidence that disproves the commonly held theory that a small company can only survive if carried along on the shoulders of a giant. We do not consider size alone, or size at any price, to be a desirable goal; our philosophy is aimed at keeping the company efficient and flexible, both for today and for tomorrow, in all areas.

Also near the end of 1948, Porsche signed an important agreement with Volkswagenwerk which allowed Porsche to use the larger company's service organization throughout Germany and Austria. In addition, a short time later Porsche moved its growing car production facilities from Gmund to Stuttgart, and occupied the Zuffenhausen factory recently vacated by American occupation forces. This move provided the company with more space and the ability to manufacture more cars. In early 1950 the first Porsche 356 rolled off the Stuttgart production line. By March 1951 the company had manufactured its 500th car, and, a short six months later, the 1,000th Porsche sports car was delivered. Ferdinand Porsche died that year, having seen his vision come to fruition. More than 200 workmen were hammering out handmade Porsche sports cars, and the company's reputation was growing rapidly. Porsche customers included film and radio stars, as well as financiers and shipping magnates. In a tragic accident, the American film idol James Dean was killed while driving a Porsche Spyder.

By 1952 customers and distributors were frequently requesting a trademark or symbol to adorn the hoods of their automobiles. Dr. Ferry Porsche designed an emblem including both the coat of arms of Stuttgart and the coat of arms of Württemberg, along with the Porsche name. The emblem first appeared in 1953 on the steering wheel hub of a Porsche 356 and has remained unchanged to the present time.

1956: 10,000th Porsche Built

The Porsche company celebrated its Silver Anniversary in March 1956 by unveiling the 10,000th Porsche car to leave the production line. In the mid- and late 1950s, nearly 70 percent of all Porsche cars manufactured were exported to eager customers abroad, and between 1954 and 1956 Porsche cars won over 400 international motor races. As the car's popularity continued to increase, different Porsche 356 models were developed, including the 356A and 356B.

In 1960 the company expanded both its physical plant and the number of its employees: a new sales department, service shop, spare parts center, and car delivery department were added, and more than 1,250 factory and office workers helped increase production. Porsche was determined to guard its reputation for reliability and high performance, assigning nearly one of every five workers to quality control. In December 1960 the company produced 39,774 cars, and each of them had earned four quality control certificates, including a certificate for the engine, transmission, general vehicle examination, and measurements. For the fiscal year 1960, Porsche reported revenues totaling DM 108 million.

Introduction of the Porsche 911

During the early 1960s, the 356 Porsche remained similar in design to the Volkswagen Beetle and continued to incorporate many of its predecessor's parts. Dr. Ferry Porsche and his management team decided that it was time for an entirely new Porsche design, one that did not rely heavily on the Volkswagen Beetle. They considered designing a four-seat sedan, but ultimately decided to remain with a two-seat sports car. A low waistline and expanded glass areas gave the new design a more elegant look, and the air-cooled flat engine remained situated in the rear of the car. With many other additions, the unique Type 911 Porsche was introduced in 1964 at a list price of DM 21,000. One year later, the last Porsche 356 model left the factory after almost 20 years of increasing sales. With a total production of 76,302, the Porsche 356 series had made the company famous throughout the world. New Porsche models such as the 912, 924, and 928 soon followed.

Until the 1970s, Porsche KG was under the joint ownership of the Porsche and Piech families, headed by Dr. Ferry Porsche and his sister, Louise Piech, who also owned Porsche Konstruktionen AG in Salzburg, Austria. Dr. Ferry Porsche was still head of the design office, while his two nephews, Ferdinand and Michael Piech, worked in administration. In 1971 revenues reached DM 900 million, and the family decided that the company was growing so rapidly that it needed a thorough reorganization. As a result, the family incorporated its holdings into a single organization with administration centralized in Stuttgart. Dr. Ferry Porsche and his sister presided over an expanded board of directors, and Dr. Ernst Fuhrmann was hired as president of the company. In 1973 the firm went public and became a joint stock company under the name Porsche AG.

During the mid- and late 1970s, Porsche AG committed itself to large-scale research and development in fields related to automotive design and production. Prompted by requests from the German government and numerous private companies, Porsche technicians began expanding their research in engine development to include metrology and vibrations, metal processing, plastics, and welding and bonding techniques. The company opened a Development Center in Weissach, outside of Stuttgart, at a cost of DM 80 million, to test cars and different

Key Dates:

1931: Dr. Ferdinand Porsche establishes his design firm; at the subsequent request of Hitler, Porsche designs the Volkswagen ''Beetle.''
1948: Manufacturing begins under Porsche nameplate.
1951: Death of Dr. Ferdinand Porsche; his son ''Ferry,'' Jr., continues to run company.
1956: Porsche builds its 10,000th automobile.
1964: Introduction of the Model 911.
1973: Porsche goes public.
1992: Sales slowdown; company cuts costs under new CEO Wendelin Wiedeking.
1996: The lower-priced Boxster is introduced; demand outpaces production.
1998: Ferry Porsche dies; company celebrates 50th anniversary; joint SUV venture is announced.

types of cross-country vehicles. Nearly 4,000 employees worked directly on research and development projects, and data compiled by Porsche was used to fight air pollution and improve auto safety. Porsche's Development Center garnered such a stellar reputation for its auto engineering design that even Rolls Royce and competitor Mercedes-Benz contracted the company for design work.

The Growing Export Market: 1970s–80s

During the 1970s, Japan developed into one of Porsche's most important foreign markets. Although Porsche sold only 97 cars in Japan in 1970, the repeal of Japanese import restrictions led to a significant sales increase, with sales of Porsche cars jumping from 122 in 1973 to nearly 500 in 1976. By 1978 Porsche was selling more than 900 cars in Japan, nearly the same number sold in the United Kingdom and Switzerland. These sales figures were even more impressive when the costs of transport and modifications required by Japanese import law were figured into the price of the cars. A Porsche 930 Turbo, for example, which sold for DM 78,800 in Germany in 1980, was priced at DM 148,000 in Japan.

The 1980s were boom years for Porsche AG. Despite a change in management upon Ernst Fuhrmann's retirement, the company increased production and revenues continued to soar: in fiscal 1981, revenues reached DM 1.5 billion. Of all the cars manufactured in Stuttgart, a total of 70 percent were exported, with the United States accounting for nearly 40 percent of the company's total sales. This successful trend continued throughout the decade: in 1986, for example, Porsche sold a total of 49,976 sports cars, including more than 60 percent to U.S. customers. Models such as the 924, 944, and 928 were introduced during the late 1980s and—along with the 911, perhaps the most popular sports car ever built—contributed to Porsche's seemingly endless string of production successes. By the end of the decade, the United States had developed into Porsche's most important market.

During the 1990s, however, the market collapsed. From its peak of 30,471 sports cars sold in the United States in 1986, Porsche's U.S. sales amounted to only 4,400 by 1991. Unfortunately, the slide continued. One year later, worldwide sales for the company dropped to 23,060 units, with only 4,133 cars sold in the United States. Some automotive industry analysts blamed a slowdown in the U.S. economy and its negative impact on car imports, while others pointed to the ever increasing prices for Porsche cars, from $40,000 to $100,000, and growing competition from other sports car manufacturers such as Mazda and Jaguar. A steady loss of top management in the early 1990s exacerbated a deteriorating situation.

The Mid-1990s: A New CEO and a Porsche Revival

In order to reduce costs and increase efficiency, in 1992 the Porsche and Piech families hired Wendelin Wiedeking, an engineering and manufacturing expert, as chief executive. Wiedeking immediately eliminated overtime for company employees and convinced a majority of them to reduce their daily working hours. He also brought in a team of Japanese consultants who greatly streamlined manufacturing operations and implemented ''just in time'' parts procurement. Addressing weaknesses in the company's product lineup, Wiedeking initiated an updated version of the Porsche 911 and made plans to introduce a new two-seater sports car with a completely original design and shape. In order to make it more attractive to U.S. customers, he promised that Porsche would sell the car at a list price of less than $40,000. The Boxster, as it was named, entered production in 1996. The new mid-engine car was an instant success, with the entire first year's production run sold out in advance. Porsche, after three years in the red, had broken even in 1995 and turned a profit in 1996. The company also discontinued production of its front-engine models 928, 944, and 968 during this recovery period.

In March 1998, at the age of 88, Ferry Porsche died, just two months before his company celebrated its golden anniversary. During this year Porsche also announced it would be forming a joint venture with Volkswagen to build suburban utility vehicles (SUVs), with an anticipated production date of 2002. Sales of the company's cars in the United States had climbed back to 18,200 for fiscal 1998, with total sales of vehicles worldwide topping 38,000. The company reported profits of DM 324.4 million on sales of DM 4.9 billion for the fiscal year. The popular Boxsters continued to be sold out in advance, and the company announced the introduction of a more powerful 3.2 liter, 252 horsepower version for the fall of 1999.

As one of the few remaining small, independent automobile manufacturers, Porsche AG hoped to remain competitive in a volatile industry. The Porsche and the Piech families had the financial resources to weather periods of economic difficulty, as well as an unwavering commitment to the survival of Porsche AG as an independent sports car manufacturer.

Principal Subsidiaries

Karosseriewerk Porsche GmbH; Porsche Classic GmbH; Porsche Financial Services GmbH; Porsche Financial Services Japan K.K. (Japan); Porsche Zentrum Hoppegarten GmbH; Porsche Consulting GmbH; Porsche Engineering Services GmbH; PIKS Porsche-Information-Kommunikation-Services GmbH; Porsche Cars Great Britain, Ltd. (U.K.); Enfina S.p.A.

(Italy); Porsche Italia S.p.A. (Italy; 60%); Porsche Cars Australia Pty. Ltd. (Australia); Porsche International Financing plc. (Ireland); Porsche Financial Management Services Ltd. (Ireland); Porsche Japan K.K. (Japan); PPF Holding AG (Switzerland); Porsche Enterprises, Inc. (96.3%); Porsche Espana S.A. (Spain).

Principal Competitors

Bayerische Motoren Werke AG; DaimlerChrysler AG; Fiat S.p.A.; Ford Motor Company; General Motors Corp.; Honda Motor Co. Ltd.; Mazda Motor Corp.; Mitsubishi Group; Nissan Motor Co. Ltd.; PSA Peugeot Citroen S.A.; Renault S.A.; Saab Automobile AB; Volkswagen AG.

Further Reading

Boshen, Lothar, *The Porsche Book*, New York: Arco, 1984.

Carreyrou, John, ''Porsche Is Upbeat on Sales Despite Bearish Factors,'' *Wall Street Journal Europe*, October 1, 1998, p. 9.

Coleman, Brian, ''Porsche Posts Record Sales As It Keeps a Rosy Outlook,'' *Wall Street Journal Europe*, December 4, 1998, p. 3.

Csere, Csaba, ''Bittersweet Times for the Porsche Faithful,'' *Car & Driver*, July 1, 1998, p. 11.

Feast, Richard, ''Porsche's Near-Death Experience: New Models and Processes Lead Company's Resurrection,'' *Automotive Industries*, September, 1996, pp. 95–96.

Flint, Jerry, ''Porsche Turns,'' *Forbes*, February 1, 1993, p. 104.

Fong, Diana, ''A Family Affair,'' *Forbes*, April 27, 1992, p. 43.

Griffiths, John, and Parkes, Christopher, ''Porsche Manoeuvres for Space,'' *Financial Times (London)*, March 29, 1994, p. 28.

Israel, Beatrix, ''Porsche Turns 50 Without Ferry,'' *Automotive News Europe*, July 6, 1998, p. 21.

Jensen, Christopher, and Sherman, Don, ''The Porsche Process,'' *Automotive Industries,* November 1997, pp. 88–90.

''Life in the Fast Lane,'' *Economist,* November 6, 1993, p. 84.

Machan, Dyan, ''Salvation in Stuttgart,'' *Forbes,* September 11, 1995, pp. 154–55.

''Professor Dr. Ferdinand Porsche: He Put the Porsche Name on Cars, and on the Map,'' AutoWeek, April 6, 1998, p. 20.

Womack, James P., and Jones, Daniel T., ''How Porsche Revived Itself,'' *Detroit News,* December 8, 1996, p. D1.

—Thomas Derdak
—updated by Frank Uhle

Powell Duffryn plc

Powell Duffryn House
London Road
Bracknell, Berkshire
RG12 2AQ
United Kingdom
Telephone: (44) 134-466-6800
Fax: (44) 134-466-6801
Web site: http://www.powellduffryn.co.uk

Public Company
Incorporated: 1864 as Powell Duffryn Steam Coal Company
Employees: 5,000
Sales: £409.1 million ($1.2 billion) (1998)
Stock Exchanges: London
Ticker Symbol: PDUF.L
NAIC: 48831 Port and Harbor Operations; 49311 General Warehousing and Storage; 33391 Pump and Compressor Manufacturing

Once nearly synonymous with the Welsh coal mining industry, Powell Duffryn plc has transformed itself into a two-pronged industrial manufacturing and services group. The company's main activities are in port operations and related cargo and shipping services, as well as in specialized engineering and manufacturing of marine equipment, including pump room and engine room equipment, industrial compressors, combustion systems, and waste disposal containers and systems. Powell Duffryn's Port Operations division includes Tees and Hartlepool port, in the northeast of England, the country's fourth largest port with annual output of 50 million tons; Humberside Sea & Land Services, offering stevedoring, warehousing, and other port services; shipping services through the company's Cory Brothers Shipping subsidiary; and more than 650,000 square feet of warehousing and wharf facilities. On the engineering side, Powell Duffryn's primary subsidiaries include Hamworthy KSE, a leading manufacturer of ship equipment, such as pump room systems and other liquid cargo systems, equipment for the roll-on roll-off market, and compressors, waste management, sewage treatment, high-performance rudders, and other systems for offshore and marine-based vessels and platforms. After a thorough restructuring in the 1990s, which saw the shedding of some 16 subsidiaries in just four years, Powell Duffryn has begun to look for acquisitions to boost its core activities. After paying Kvaerner ASA pounds 34 million for its Kvaerner Ships Equipment (KSE) in December 1998, Powell Duffryn indicated that it hoped to acquire new port operations to expand that side of its business as well.

Coal Tyrant of the 19th Century?

The death of his father left Thomas Powell, when he was less than 14 years old, in charge of running the family's modest Newport, Monmouthshire timber yard. That business, however, barely provided for Powell and his mother, and Powell began looking for other sources of income. Born in 1779, Powell was quick to realize that the introduction of new steam-driven engines and machinery would bring a rising demand for a more efficient and powerful fuel source. Although scarcely in use at the time, coal was to become the power source of the Industrial Revolution. Powell recognized that the coal-rich Welsh valleys offered an opportunity for a vast fortune. Over the decade, Powell, and the company he founded, profoundly transformed the South Wales area from, for the most part, rural, agricultural, and pasture lands, into what one source described as a countryside where "ravaged valleys were bestrode by giant bridges, great waterways and railways, and roaring towns with brutalised and degraded inhabitants."

In 1810, Powell purchased a small piece of land at Llanhilleth from which he meant to dig coal. He hired a couple of helpers, but Powell himself worked alongside them to dig out what became Powell's first colliery. In this way Powell gained firsthand mining experience, which, however, provided little comfort to workers in the later Powell coal empire.

Between 1810 and 1830, Powell expanded his holdings, opening collieries in Blackwood, Gelligaer, and other locations. Yet Powell was still ahead of his time. Although gaining, use of coal remained limited in the early years of the 19th century. Lack of demand for his coal nearly forced Powell into bankruptcy. But Powell persevered and continued to bring more and

Company Perspectives:

Powell Duffryn is an industrial group engaged in Ports and Engineering. We aim to provide high quality services and products for our customers, challenging opportunities for employees and sustained growth for shareholders.

more coal seams in the Newport area and surrounding valleys under his control.

By 1825, Powell's efforts began to pay off. The use of steam-drive engines was becoming more commonplace and with the rapid development of industry came the explosive growth in coal demand. Welsh coal quickly earned a reputation for its excellent quality; in addition, the region's midwestern location gave it access to a large swath of the United Kingdom. Located near the River Severn and with access to the canal system linking much of England, Powell's coal found easy shipment. Increases in canal traffic, as coal-driven barges became commonplace, added to the drive in coal demand. The construction of the United Kingdom's railway system and the developing importance of the steam-driven locomotive also contributed to the development of Powell's business.

By 1830, Powell was considered a successful businessman. But he was soon to become more than this. By the end of that decade, Powell joined the ranks of an exclusive few. The Industrial Revolution had brought a new breed of men to the forefront of society. Known to some as tycoons and to others as tyrants, these men controlled the fuel and materials that served as the backbone of the Industrial Revolution. Some, like Powell, became infamous for their unscrupulous pursuit of wealth and power.

In 1834, Powell's business was aided by the repeal of the export tax that had been in place on shipments of coal west of the River Holmes. The repeal of this tax—which had protected the northern England coal owners—opened this area to Welsh coal, and to Powell. By undercutting prices and vaunting the quality of Welsh coal, Powell succeeded in winning a strong share of the northern market, sending his coal to Liverpool, which, in turn, provided the launch site for entering the international coal trade.

Moving his coal now took on a greater importance for Powell, and in the 1830s and 1840s Powell began building his own fleet of barges and other vessels. The next step was to join in the building of a railway line linking Newport with the rest of the United Kingdom. Powell contributed some BP 20,000 to what was to become the Taft Vale Railway. Yet Powell, in a dispute for control of the railway (and for better pricing for his own shipments), nearly caused the young railway to fold. By then, Powell was more than 60 years old and a member of what became known as the Industrial Aristocracy. But Powell's greatest success was still to come. In 1842, Powell opened a vast new mine in Tirffounder, in the Aberdere Valley; the following year, he opened a four-foot seam in Mountain Ash. These new mines, joined by a number of others in the Aberdere and nearby valleys, boosted Powell to the status of the world's largest coal producer.

By the late 1840s, Powell's empire consisted of a number of companies, including Powell & Son, Thos Powell & Sons, Powell and Prothero, Thomas Powell Bank Merchant and Powell's Duffryn (which means ''valley'' in Welsh) Company, reflecting the company's various mining, transportation, and financial interests. Powell also was entering a period of social upheaval, brought on in part by Powell's treatment of his workers and the often unsafe working environments of his mining operations. By the mid-19th century, the coal mining industry saw the first workers' strikes—and Powell was at the forefront in devising strike-breaking methods.

The strike movement took on greater influence, while industrialists countered with still more hardened employment policies. A series of explosions rocked Powell's operations in the 1850s, due in part to a lack of safety measures. Then, in 1858, the coal owners, with Powell at the lead, decided to cut back miners' wages by 15 percent. The workers went on strike, bringing the industry to a near standstill. Powell introduced scab labor, bringing in English labor to replace the striking Welsh miners. At last, the miners had no choice but to return to work, if they did not want to lose their jobs entirely. For their efforts, their wages were cut back an additional five percent.

Coal Leader for the 20th Century

By the 1860s, the elderly Powell recognized that the coal industry was changing to a corporate, rather than personality-driven business; shortly before his death in 1863, Powell negotiated a merger of his coal holdings with those of Sir George Elliot. The merged operations, completed by Powell's sons after their father's death, were formed under the name Powell Duffryn Steam Coal Company. The new company's first year of operations, with an initial capitalization of BP 500,000, produced 400,000 tons from its eight collieries.

Powell Duffryn prepared to enter into its period of greatest growth. The next 50 years also were to prove the most turbulent, with several devastating strikes, economic depressions, many mining disasters, and a world war providing frequent interruptions. Yet, Powell Duffryn was often as not able to profit from the adversity affecting the coal industry in general. During the period leading to the First World War, Powell Duffryn made a number of acquisitions—both of existing collieries and of land in which the company sank new coal pits—from other financially troubled coal mining operations, extending the company's annual coal output to four million tons. Part of the increase in coal production also came from the company's constant incorporation of new mining technologies, such as coal-cutting machinery, which was especially useful in older mines, and electrical power, which the company began incorporating—and producing—in 1904.

The outbreak of the First World War saw the loss of many of Powell Duffryn's export markets. The period also was marked by an extreme labor shortage and growing government control over an industry that was vital to the country's economic and military efforts. Nonetheless, Powell Duffryn was able to continue its expansion, opening a French subsidiary shortly before the war and, following the war, forming a shipping partnership with Stephenson Clarke and Company, in 1920, called Maris Export & Trading Company Ltd. Powell Duffryn's entry into

Key Dates:

1810: Thomas Powell digs his first mine.
1864: Powell Duffryn Steam Coal Company formed.
1913: Launch of French coal distribution subsidiary.
1928: Acquisition of Stephenson and Clarke.
1935: Merger with Welsh Associated Collieries Ltd. to form Powell Duffryn Associated Collieries Ltd.
1946: Nationalization of U.K. coal industry.
1962: Acquisition of Hamworthy Engineering Ltd.
1988: Rationalization of business; sale of shipping division.
1992: Purchase of Tees and Hartlepool port.
1996: Restructuring and sale of fuel and chemical storage subsidiaries.
1998: Sale of UK Petroleum Products subsidiary and exit from fuel industry; acquisition of Kvaerner Ships Engineering.

the shipping industry—consolidated in 1928 with its acquisition of Stephenson Clarke itself—was to serve it in good stead in coming years.

In the meantime, as the United Kingdom suffered through economic hardships in the postwar years, Powell Duffryn continued to grow—leading the way to a consolidation of the Welsh coal industry. During the 1920s, Powell Duffryn made several significant acquisitions, including that of the Rhymney Iron Company, with seven collieries; the 1925 acquisition of the money-losing Windsor Colliery (restored to profitability two years after the acquisition by Powell Duffryn); and the 1928 purchases of ten collieries and related equipment and properties from Lewis Morthyr, the Great Western Colliery Company, and the Nantgawr Colliery. At the same time, the company continued sinking its own collieries, including the partnership mine Taff Morthyr, with an annual output reaching one million tons, and the sinking of three new Powell Duffryn pits with a combined output of more than two million tons. The Stephenson Clarke acquisition, made in 1928, placed Powell Duffryn as the United Kingdom's largest coal distributor, with not only its own fleet of barges and other vessels, but also the country's largest private fleet of railroad wagons.

Powell Duffryn's biggest expansion came in the 1930s. In 1935, Powell Duffryn merged its operations with those of Welsh Associated Collieries Ltd.; formed in 1930, Welsh Associated combined the coal output and distribution activities of 34 collieries. The merger with Powell Duffryn, forming P.D. Associated Collieries Ltd., gave the company an annual output of more than 20 million tons. It also gave the company another subsidiary interest, that of Cambrian Wagon Works Ltd., a wagon-building and repairs business that provided the basis for a third Powell Duffryn interest, after mining and shipping—later to be known as Powell Duffryn Engineering Ltd.

Powell Duffryn continued to make acquisitions in the years leading up to the outbreak of the Second World War. By then, the company's output had topped 21 million tons per year, representing more than a third of the total South Wales coal output. At the same time, the company's resources, estimated at more than 1.7 billion tons, gave the company reason to look forward to the postwar period. During the war, the company's engineering resources, under the Rhymney Iron Company subsidiary, expanded to fulfill military orders, including aircraft bomber doors and hulls. The acquisition of Cory Bros & Co. Ltd. in 1942 not only gave the company 12 additional collieries, but also 53 coaling stations located worldwide. This acquisition launched the company into a new market, that of fuel storage and distribution.

By the end of the Second World War, Powell Duffryn had achieved the number one ranking among the world's largest coal producers. Yet, at the beginning of 1947, the company ran headlong into the Coal Industry Nationalisation Act. Overnight, Powell Duffryn saw the loss of its core business. The compensation agreement with the government took nearly ten years to work out; in 1955, the government paid a little less than BP 16 million to the company for its loss of assets.

Regrouping for the 21st Century

Powell Duffryn was forced back on its former side-businesses. The company developed a multi-pronged approach, boosting its engineering, fuel storage and distribution, and shipping divisions by a series of acquisitions. Among these was the acquisition of Hamworthy Engineering Ltd., in 1962, which brought the company a major position as a maker of fuel, combustion, and pumping systems. Powell Duffryn also expanded its Stephenson Clarke shipping and railroad subsidiary.

The new Powell Duffryn had regained some of its footing lost to the coal industry nationalization (which, with the dwindling importance of coal as a fuel source, might have been a blessing in disguise). By the 1970s, while still on a far smaller scale than its prewar position, the company had achieved a strong share in each of its new markets, and strong profits. This made the company an attractive takeover target during the 1980s. The company was able to shake off a takeover attempt by the Hansen Trust in 1984, retaining its independence.

Yet the economic crisis of the late 1980s and the growing burden of environmental regulations led the company to restructure its operations for the 1990s. Faced with the increasing cost of upgrading its shipping and railroad fleet and of refitting its bulk liquid storage facilities to meet stricter environmental standards, Powell Duffryn decided to exit these businesses and restructure around a new core of shipping services, engineering, and, with the acquisition of the Tees and Hartlepool port in 1992, port operations.

After selling off the Stephenson Clarke shipping subsidiary, the company began paring away its other divisions, shutting down its money-losing railroad engineering arm in 1993 and 1994 and then turning to its fuel and chemical storage division in the second half of the decade. Between 1996 and 1998, Powell Duffryn sold or closed some 14 subsidiaries and related operations, including its Savannah, Georgia and Bayonne, New Jersey chemical storage terminals in 1996; its Eurogas liquefied heating fuel distribution subsidiary in 1997; and its National Pump subsidiary in 1998. The sale of its UK Petroleum Products subsidiary in that same year ended nearly 200 years of involvement in the United Kingdom's fuel market.

The purchase of Tees and Hartlepool gave the company operating control of the nation's fourth busiest port, a strong base around which Powell Duffryn began to expand its port, storage, and shipping services efforts. By 1998, the company acknowledged its interest in adding to its port holdings, as the primarily government-owned British ports prepared to undergo a privatization effort at the beginning of the next century. Powell Duffryn also significantly expanded its engineering division—focused mainly on marine products—with the BP 34 million purchase of Kvaerner Ships Equipment from the Swedish shipping giant in December 1998.

Principal Subsidiaries

Air Compressor Products Inc. (USA); Belliss & Morcom Ltd. (UK); Eagle Compressors Inc. (USA); Geesink BV (The Netherlands); Hamworthy Combustion Engineering Ltd. (UK); Hamworthy Heating Ltd. (UK); Hamworthy Compressor Group (UK); Hamworthy Canada Ltd.; Hamworthy Compressor Systems Ltd. (UK); Hamworthy Marine Ltd. (UK); Hamworthy Marine Technology Ltd. (UK); Hamworthy Pumps and Compressors Ltd. (UK); Humberside Holdings Ltd. (UK); H&L Garages Ltd. (UK); Humberside Sea & Land Services Ltd. (UK); JIP Kugleventiler (Denmark); Peabody Engineering Corporation (USA); Powell Duffryn Shipping Ltd. (UK); Powell Duffryn Storage Ltd. (UK); Svanehoj International A/S (Denmark); Tees and Hartlepool Port Authority Ltd. (UK).

Principal Competitors

Associated British Ports; Mersey Docks and Harbour Company; Peninsular and Oriental.

Further Reading

Cave, Andrew, "Powell Sell-Off Raises Pounds 13.5m," *Daily Telegraph,* November 27, 1997.

Cole, Robert, "Powell Challenges Dividends Review," *Independent,* June 3, 1994, p. 34.

Osborne, Alistair, "Powell Duffryn Has Pounds 150m to Spend," *Daily Telegraph,* June 5, 1998.

"New-Look Powell Pays Higher Dividend," *Daily Telegraph,* May 27, 1999.

Powell Duffryn Corporate Profile, Bracknell: Powell Duffryn plc, 1999.

"The Powell Duffryn Story," Bracknell: Powell Duffryn plc, 1999.

—M.L. Cohen

Publix Super Markets Inc.

1936 George Jenkins Boulevard
Lakeland, Florida 33801
U.S.A.
Telephone: (941) 688-1188
Fax: (941) 284-5532

Private Company
Incorporated: 1930
Employees: 117,000
Sales: $12.06 billion (1998)
NAIC: 44511 Supermarkets and Other Grocery (Except Convenience) Stores

Publix Super Markets Inc. stands as one of the top seven chains of supermarkets in the United States as measured by sales volume and number of stores. It is the largest employee-owned supermarket; its current and former employees own about 85 percent of the business. The rest of the company is owned by its officers and directors, many of whom are members of the Jenkins family. Most of the chain's more than 600 stores are in Florida, but the company also does business in Georgia, Alabama, and South Carolina.

A Commitment to Service During the Great Depression

Publix was founded in 1930 by George W. Jenkins, the son of a rural Georgia grocer. Jenkins moved to Winter Haven, Florida, in 1927 and took a job as a stock clerk at the local Piggly Wiggly. He became the store's manager six weeks later at the age of 17. At 20, he borrowed less than $2,000 and started his own 27-by-65-foot grocery store across the street with five employees. The store earned $500 its first year, in the midst of the Great Depression. By 1935, Jenkins owned five stores.

Jenkins was one of the first in the grocery business to stress customer service and high-quality goods. While most of his competitors focused on price and productivity, the signs on the front of the Publix store read, "Where shopping is a pleasure," reflecting the firm's early belief in the importance of customer satisfaction. Jenkins also stressed employee satisfaction, promoting almost entirely from within, and giving his workers a large amount of control over the section of the store in which they worked.

By 1940, Jenkins had an additional 18 Publix stores, some of which he acquired from the small All-American chain in 1939. In 1940, Jenkins also opened his first supermarket, an 11,000-square-foot space with a paved parking lot, air conditioning, wide aisles, electric doors, and frozen-food cases. The aesthetics and features of Jenkins's superstore were unusual for American grocery stores during the Depression, reflecting the founder's attempt to make shopping an enjoyable experience. By 1950, 22 Publix supermarkets had been opened, with total chain sales of $12.1 million.

In 1949, R. William Schroter stepped in to head up Publix's own one-person advertising department, employing local freelancers. The department eventually grew into the W.M. Zemp & Associates advertising firm in St. Petersburg. Publix advertised heavily in newspapers, but avoided the weekly circulars used by many supermarkets.

In the early 1950s, Publix began giving out S&H Green Stamps, handing shoppers a fixed number of stamps per dollar spent, which they could then redeem for discounted merchandise. The resulting sales increase far exceeded the cost of the stamp program, and Publix quickly became the largest vendor of S&H stamps in the country. Jenkins liked the stamps because he believed that they encouraged store loyalty as well as thrifty habits. In the late 1950s, Publix began to sell stock to its employees.

Steady Growth Throughout the 1960s and 1970s

Publix's success in less developed parts of Florida encouraged Jenkins to move into the lucrative, but highly competitive, Miami market in 1959. In 1963, the firm opened a warehouse to service the growing number of supermarkets it was opening there. The state of Florida itself contributed to the chain's expansion as it became one of the fastest-growing states in the country. Fueled partly by its move to Miami, Publix grew to 114 stores in 1965, with sales of $262.9 million, and 157 stores, with sales of $465.7 million in 1970. In 1974, the firm opened a 200,000-square-foot warehouse in Jacksonville to supply Publix stores between Jacksonville and Tallahassee.

Company Perspectives:

The Publix guarantee to never knowingly disappoint customers is legendary in the industry. The purpose of the guarantee remains to satisfy the customer. The ongoing mission of Publix Super Markets is to operate the best stores possible. We believe the key to that is dedicated and responsible employees, called associates. Publix is dedicated to the dignity, value and employment security of its associates. We treat each other as family and treat our company as a prized possession because we own it.

Publix management kept a careful eye on lifestyle trends. By 1966, as more women began to work and more people remained single, stores shifted from one small frozen-food display case to large, upright cases with glass doors. Frozen-food sales continued to grow, and Publix added more freezers and devoted more attention to their stocking, keeping brand name products together rather than sorting by food type. The firm identified and responded to food trends such as yogurt and frozen pizza earlier than most of its rivals. In setting up shelves, dairy cases, and freezers, it was careful to keep ease of shopping its top priority, while also displaying high-margin items at eye level and making certain that products were arranged in a way that facilitated quick restocking.

In the early 1970s, with a wave of discount stores taking hold in Florida, Publix opened its own discount chain called Food World. In 1976, Publix introduced in-store photofinishing, giving away a roll of film or an extra set of prints with each roll it developed. Within ten years, the firm accounted for 12 percent of the total photofinishing business in its marketing area and had 24 discount stores.

In 1979, the company reached nearly $2 billion in sales and had 234 stores and 26,000 employees. It was the 11th largest chain in national sales and had an after-tax net averaging 1.7 percent, far ahead of most of its rivals. Publix was the leading grocery chain in Daytona Beach, Palm Beach, and St. Petersburg, where it had 30.6 percent of the market. It was the second largest chain in the Miami area, with 26 percent of the market. All Publix stores were similar inside and had in-store delis and bakeries. Publix supermarkets also took advantage of technology, using the second largest number of price scanners of any business in the United States.

Publix's skilled marketing and use of up-to-date technology had contributed to its success, but so had the stability of its workforce. The firm had never experienced a strike, lockout, or layoff; it had the lowest employee turnover of any large chain. This was attributed to employment policies that included a profit-sharing plan that distributed 20 percent of net profits at each store to that store's full-time workers; a retirement plan funded by 15 percent of pre-tax profits; and the policy of promoting from within the company. Employees were also given more responsibility than at most large chains.

The Move to Superstores in the 1980s

By 1980, Publix had a strong presence throughout the state of Florida, with the exception of the panhandle. Its operations were divided into three divisions: the Jacksonville division, which covered the northern third of the state; the Miami division, which covered the eastern coast south of Brevard County; and the Lakeland division, which covered the rest of the state. The company headquarters were located in Lakeland, where a 425,000-square-foot grocery warehouse stored a three-week supply of goods.

Publix spent about 0.75 percent of sales on advertising, amounting to about $15 million in 1980. Newspaper ads accounted for 68 percent of the advertising budget, television 24 percent, and radio, which aimed to reach younger Floridians, five percent. In-store merchandising displays, accounting for the remainder, were highly theatrical and changed weekly. They were created by employees without direction from the Publix central office since Jenkins believed that store managers best knew what would work in their own territories.

The 1980s brought considerable change to Publix. One of the first changes was automatic teller machines, which Publix began installing before many banks did. The firm was also the first supermarket chain to install bar-code scanners in every store. Jenkins had always refused to open his stores on Sunday, but in 1982, losing market share to stores that did, he relented. In 1984, Joe Blanton, who had been president for ten years, died, and was replaced by Mark Hollis. Hollis began with Publix in 1946 as a bag boy at age 12 and had worked as a stock clerk and a produce and store manager. In 1985, all but three of the discount Food Worlds were closed, unable to give workers a percentage of their store's profits and turn a profit for Publix. Sales for the entire chain in 1985 reached $3.2 billion, up from $2.8 billion in 1983, making Publix the ninth largest grocery chain by sales.

Superstores, with 30,000 square feet or more, were another 1980s innovation. After competitors successfully began to rely upon them, Publix began opening its own superstores of up to 39,000 square feet each. Most were located in shopping malls where customers could shop for goods other than food as well. In the 1980s, when Publix's competitors opened combination stores where customers could fill prescriptions in addition to buying groceries, Publix followed suit, opening its first combination store in Orlando in 1986. The 55,000-square-foot, upscale space combined a grocery store with gourmet food and deli and bakery sections, as well as hardware and toy departments and the firm's first pharmacy. The combination stores included a one-hour photo department, a counter where cameras and small electronics were sold, and an expanded cosmetics, health, and beauty aids section. The stores were intended to appeal to younger, professional, two-income families, and their sites were carefully selected with an eye on demographics. Publix quickly opened two more Publix Food & Pharmacy stores in Tampa, one in Tamarac, near Fort Lauderdale, and three more in other parts of Florida. The firm also remodeled and expanded old supermarkets and opened new ones. Publix opened 28 stores in 1986 and more than 30 in 1987, often choosing sites in advance of Florida's population explosion.

A String of Legal Woes in the 1990s

To help support these new stores, Publix doubled the size of the Lakeland warehouse to 440,000 square feet, and planned a

Key Dates:

1930: Publix is founded by George W. Jenkins in Winter Haven, Florida.
1940: Jenkins closes his first two stores and opens the first Publix supermarket.
1956: Publix records it first million-dollar profit; the company opens a 125,000-square-foot warehouse and headquarters in Lakeland, Florida.
1959: First Miami Publix supermarket opens.
1964: Publix opens its 100th store in Winter Haven, Florida.
1974: The chain captures $1 billion in sales and opens a 200,000-square-foot warehouse in Jacksonville.
1990: Howard M. Jenkins succeeds George W. Jenkins as CEO.
1994: Three million-square-foot distribution/warehouse/diary processing facility opens in Atlanta.
1995: Publix is named a *Fortune* 500 company; eight women bring a class-action suit against Publix.
1996: George Jenkins dies.

660,000-square-foot perishables warehouse near Fort Lauderdale. To increase flexibility in merchandising and marketing, Publix dropped S&H Green Stamps in the Lakeland and Jacksonville divisions in June 1987. In 1989, Publix again tried a new technology when it began moving toward automatic checkout machines with machines that allowed customers to scan their own groceries, then pay a central cashier.

In January 1990, after suffering a stroke, George Jenkins retired as chairman and chief executive of Publix and became chairman emeritus. He was succeeded by his son, Howard M. Jenkins, who was 38 years old. As with many Publix executives, the younger Jenkins had begun at the retail level and worked his way up through the company's ranks. At the time of the leadership change, Publix ranked as the 21st largest retailer in the United States, with 370 stores, 60,000 employees, and profits of $128.5 million on sales of $5.38 billion. Late in 1990, it announced plans to build a 48,000-square-foot store in Kingsland, Georgia, about 80 miles south of Savannah, and plans for a second store in a Savannah shopping mall soon followed. In August 1991, with 384 stores, the firm announced that it was looking for sites in Atlanta. It opened its first store in Georgia in 1992 and began aggressively to build in and around Atlanta. By 1994, Publix had snapped up 10.1 percent of the market, trailing only Kroger and Winn-Dixie, whose market shares nonetheless dropped as a result of Publix's performance. By 1995, Publix had constructed a three million-square-foot distribution center in Lawrenceville and a milk processing plant. Its 34 Atlanta stores, all built from the ground up, offered features unknown to its Florida counterparts, such as freshly grilled fajitas and stir-fry dishes in a 100-seat dining area.

Publix was named as one of the top ten companies to work for in the nation by the 1993 edition of *The 100 Best Companies to Work for in America*. However, the timing of this honor was somewhat ironic, as the company was then in the throes of racial- and gender-bias charges with several groups. The chain had been picketed by the United Food and Commercial Workers union since its entry into Georgia for allegedly racial- and gender-biased employment and promotion practices. In 1992, a coalition of labor, feminist, Hispanic, and African American rights groups began threatening to boycott Publix supermarkets if the company did not place more women and minorities in management jobs by 1994. Their position was based on a survey revealing that women held fewer than two percent, African Americans fewer than three percent, and Hispanics fewer than four percent of the store's top management positions. In 1993, the Equal Employment Opportunity Commission asked the U.S. District Court in Miami to force Publix to turn over employment data for an investigation into sex bias charges. That same year, Publix agreed to pay a $500,000 fine after the Labor Department found minors working too many hours and during prohibited times in 11 Publix stores.

The year 1994 saw temporary respite from Publix's legal woes. By 1994, stores in Georgia and South Carolina were contributing to sales growth, and sales reached $8.66 billion, up 16 percent from 1993. In 1995, Publix, now the seventh largest supermarket chain in the nation, also introduced a smaller sized, 27,000-square-foot store in Tampa, Florida. At half the size of most new Publix supermarkets, this downscaled version of Publix's megastore offered neither a pharmacy nor health and beauty aids department, and fewer dry goods to provide space to the deli, bakery, and perishable goods sections. Instead its focus was on prepackaged deli items in response to the new consumer demand for prepared foods. The company also opened its Atlanta Division distribution facility and began to introduce full-service banks located in its stores.

Yet despite such advances, sluggish gains in profits and sales bespoke a difficult year for Publix. Accompanying a general downturn in retailing, sales increased only eight percent to total almost $9.4 billion in 1994. However, Publix added a net total of about 50 stores that year to reach the 500-store mark, and the chain was rated number two, behind Kroger, in the Atlanta market with 31 stores and 14 percent of sales. The company made the *Fortune* 500 list in 1995 and became the seventh largest-volume supermarket chain in the nation.

However, the chain's legal woes were resurrected in 1995 when eight women sued that Publix clustered women in cashier, delicatessen, and bakery jobs, denying them promotions and equal pay to men. Late in 1995, the U.S. Equal Opportunity Commission joined in the discrimination lawsuit, and in March 1996, a judge ruled to allow the case to proceed as a class-action suit, expanding the field of possible litigants to 120,000 current or former workers and making it the largest sex discrimination case in U.S. history. A second class-action suit was filed in Miami several months later by a firm representing women who worked in the company's administrative offices, warehouses, and plants. In addition, a former employee accused Publix of coding job applications to denote race, gender, and disabilities and work safety inspectors targeted Publix as the Florida company with the most workers' compensation claims.

Publix's growth still continued unabated. By 1996, it had captured 18 percent of the Atlanta market. Its sales for the year totaled $10 billion, an impressive 9.5 percent increase over 1995. However, the settlement in January 1997 of the first of its class-action suits for $81.5 million, the fourth largest such settlement in U.S. history, took a huge chunk out of the company's earnings. In addition, it agreed to pay a $3.5 million fine to the EEOC over accusations that it had denied blacks job opportunities.

Before the company had the chance to recover, a third high-profile class-action suit was filed. Despite the fact that the company had earlier signed an agreement with the Southern Christian Leadership Conference setting specific goals on hiring, training, and promoting more minority workers, and had opened three stores in predominantly black neighborhoods in 1996, early in 1997, a group representing 50,000 blacks, who had worked for Publix since 1993, claimed that the chain systematically denied equal hiring and promotion opportunities to blacks and created a hostile work environment for minorities.

Still Publix remained a favorite among customers. A *Consumer Reports* article in 1997 ranked it as tied for the highest overall score in terms of shopping experience. It placed above average for checkout speed, meat, deli, and produce, and average on price. The younger Jenkins had successfully wed Publix's longstanding commitment to customer service to advances in technology. Throughout 1998 and 1999, the chain held to its practice of building 40 or more stores a year. In 1998, it pulled in $12 billion in sales and $378 million in profits. In 1999, the company completed a new corporate headquarters in Polk County, Florida.

Principal Competitors

Albertson's Inc.; The Kroger Company; Winn-Dixie Stores, Inc.

Further Reading

Albright, Mark, ''Magistrate: Publix Racial Bias Suit Should Widen,'' *St. Petersburg Times*, June 17, 1998, p. 1E.

——, ''Publix Faces New Bias Lawsuit,'' *St. Petersburg Times*, April 3, 1997, p.1E.

——, ''Suit Is Just One of Chain's Legal Woes,'' *St. Petersburg Times*, January 11, 1998, p. 2H.

——, ''Union, Publix Exchange Charges on Meat Labels,'' *St. Petersburg Times*, December 20, 1995, p. 1E.

Backman, Lisa, ''Marching into Atlanta,'' *Tampa Tribune*,'' May 22, 1995, p. 8.

Dietrich, Robert, Linsen, Mary Ann, et al, ''Publix, Where Pleasure Is Profitable,'' *Progressive Grocer*, September, 1980.

Bork, Robert H., Jr., ''Call Him Old-Fashioned,'' *Forbes*, August 26, 1985.

Elson, Joel, ''Publix and the New Florida Market,'' *Supermarket News*, April 20, 1987.

Harris, Nicole, ''Revolt at the Deli Counter,'' *Business Week*, April 1, 1996, p. 32.

Myerson, Allen R., ''Supermarket Chain to Pay $81 Million to Settle a Bias Suit,'' *New York Times*, January 25, 1997, p.1.

Power, Paul, Jr., ''Publix Sex Bias Case Inches Closer to Closure,'' *Tampa Tribune*, May 23, 1997, p. 1.

''Publix Enters National Rankings for Size and Quality,'' *PR Newswire*, January 18, 1996.

''Publix Settles Suit Claiming Applications Were Coded,'' *St. Petersburg Times*, April 17, 1996, p.6E.

Zweibach, Elliot, ''George Jenkins Named Chairman Emeritus at Publix,'' *Supermarket News*, January 8, 1990.

—Scott Lewis
—updated by Carrie Rothburd

RANDOM HOUSE, INC.

Random House Inc.

201 East 50th Street
New York, New York 10022
U.S.A.
Telephone: (212) 751-2600
Fax: (212) 572-8700

Wholly Owned Subsidiary of Bertelsmann AG
Incorporated: 1925
Employees: Not Available.
Sales: $1.6 billion (1999 est.)
NAIC: 51113 Book Publishers

Random House Inc. was already the largest general trade book publisher in the English-speaking world when it was acquired by German entertainment and publishing conglomerate Bertelsmann AG in 1998 and merged with Bantam Doubleday Dell (BDD), which Bertelsmann already owned. The new publishing entity continued with the name of its senior partner, Random House Inc., and had estimated worldwide sales of $1.6 billion in fiscal 1999 ending June 30.

Modern Library Provides a Solid Foundation: 1925–30

When Bennett A. Cerf and Donald S. Klopfer decided to rename their joint publishing venture Random House Inc. (RH) in 1927, its pedigree was already well established. The 27-year-old Cerf and his 23-year-old partner had purchased the 109-volume Modern Library line in 1925 for $215,000 from the Boni & Liveright publishing firm in New York. Since 1923, Cerf had worked at Boni & Liveright as a vice-president (replacing Richard L. Simon, who left to form a joint venture with M. Lincoln Schuster), and he had become increasingly aware of the series' value and potential. When Horace Liveright's financial problems grew untenable and forced him to sell the seven-year-old Modern Library, Cerf and Klopfer jumped at the opportunity.

Inspired by Everyman's Library, founded in 1905 by Londoners Joseph Malaby Dent and Ernest Rhys, Modern Library already was considered a classic in its time. Cerf and Klopfer replaced the company's logo with a leaping torch-bearer designed by Lucian Bernhard, bound the books in cloth instead of the original navy lambskin, and recouped their initial investment within two years. The partners soon changed the company's name to "Random House" to reflect their intention of publishing a wide array of fiction and nonfiction without limitations, literally "at random."

Extravagances Cut During Depression: The 1930s

In 1931, Cerf and Klopfer created the Modern Library Giants, "a collection of the most significant and thought-provoking books in modern literature," as a sibling series of longer classics, like Leo Tolstoy's *War and Peace* and Victor Hugo's *Les Miserables.* The partners also produced a few "deluxe" editions, like the Rockwell Kent illustrated version of Voltaire's *Candide* and a lavish version of Mark Twain's *Adventures of Tom Sawyer.* These indulgences were discontinued when the Depression took a firm hold of the economy in the 1930s.

Moving into less expensive trade books, Cerf immediately set out to sign up the day's literati, including playwright Eugene O'Neill and poet Robinson Jeffers. Cerf also flew overseas to secure U.S. publishing rights to James Joyce's *Ulysses.* When his unexpurgated copy of the book was seized by customs as "obscene" material upon his return, Cerf and attorney Morris Ernst gained international acclaim by taking the case to court. On December 6, 1933, Judge John Woolsey issued a decision with historic implications by upholding Cerf's right not only to possess the book, but also to publish an uncensored version of *Ulysses* in America. Cerf's precedent-setting crusade made Random House a household word, and the Modern Library's *Ulysses* was published in 1934.

In 1936, RH purchased Robinson Smith & Robert Haas, Inc. and netted several prominent authors in the process, including Isak Dinesen, William Faulkner, Edgar Snow, and Jean de Brunhoff. The acquisition of de Brunhoff, creator of the popular Babar series, proved both timely and prescient, as RH expanded into children's books.

Domestic and International Expansion: The 1940s and 1950s

After World War II ended, RH sought both domestic and international expansion, beginning with the establishment of

Company Perspectives:

Random House Inc., founded in 1925, is the world's largest English-language general trade book publisher. It includes an array of prestigious imprints that publish some of the foremost writers of our time—in hardcover, trade paperback, mass market paperback, audio, multimedia, and other formats.

Random House Canada and the development of a college books division in 1944. In 1947, after years of research and at a cost of more than $500,000, RH published the *American College Dictionary,* the first of its many reference books. Continuing in this vein but directing its efforts toward children, RH's think tank initiated a series of Landmark Books about legendary Americans in 1950. Written by famous authors like Pearl S. Buck, C.S. Forester, and John Gunther, the line was expanded in 1953 to cover historic world events and leaders.

RH's children's division published a picture book in 1957 called *The Cat in the Hat* by Dr. Seuss (Theodor Geisel). Simple and silly, the book was so successful it was reprinted in 1958 as the first of a new line christened ''Beginner Books.'' The series enjoyed huge success, becoming an enduring favorite for new readers and remaining a staple of libraries and bookstores to this day. The same year, RH hired Saxe Commins as its editor-in-chief. ''With Mr. Commins's counsel and Mr. Cerf's instincts,'' Alden Whitman of the *New York Times* observed, ''Random House began to grow into one of the giants of the books business.''

Rapid Expansion After Initial Public Offering: The 1960s

In 1959, RH went public with an offering of more than 220,000 shares at $11.25 each, with Cerf selling about a third of his stock (he kept 200,000 shares). Much of the proceeds went into rapid expansion, beginning with the 1960 acquisition of Alfred A. Knopf for about $3 million. In Knopf, RH gained one of the nation's most distinguished and respected publishers. Cerf assured the new subsidiary complete editorial independence, and he and Knopf forged a close alliance, both professionally and personally, that endured for decades. RH's second major acquisition was textbook producer L.W. Singer, which was followed by Helen and Kurt Wolff's brainchild, the 19-year-old Pantheon Books, in 1961. Andre Schiffrin was named editor-in-chief of Pantheon in 1963 at the age of 28.

Changes in Ownership, Editorial Leadership: 1965–73

In 1965 the first of several significant events affecting RH's future occurred. In a curious role reversal, the acquisitive RH was purchased by Radio Corporation of America (RCA). Cerf became chairman of the board following the sale, and he relinquished the presidency to protege Robert L. Bernstein the next year. Though the buyout was one ''of mingled sadness and joy'' for Cerf, he was pleased with RH's record earnings and happy to end the company's independence ''in a blaze of glory.'' In 1966 one of the company's crowning achievements came to fruition—the unabridged, 2,059-page *Random House Dictionary of the English Language,* which took more than ten years to research and compile at an estimated cost of $3 million, was published. It sold significantly more than 500,000 copies within the next five years.

The changing of the guard was nearly complete in 1969, when RH moved from the old Villard House on Madison Avenue—a historic landmark located behind St. Patrick's Cathedral—to the company's current location at 201 East 50th Street. Cerf stepped down as chairman the following year, with his longtime friend and colleague Klopfer taking over. Cerf remained at RH as a senior editor until his death in 1971, at age 73. Called ''a glorious amalgam of pragmatist and leprechaun'' by John Daly, former host of *What's My Line?*—a television game show on which Cerf had been a panelist for 16 years—the RH founder was a popular man whose funeral was a veritable who's who of the publishing and show business worlds. ''I wonder,'' Eudora Welty mused, ''if anyone else of such manifold achievements in the publishing world could ever have so many friends.''

With Bernstein and Klopfer running the ship, RH continued to flourish. In 1971 the Modern Library exceeded 400 titles and sold 50 million books. The 1973 acquisition of mass marketer Ballantine Books added considerably to RH's paperback audience.

Decade of Extraordinary Growth: The 1980s

In 1980 RH was again the object of a takeover, this time by Advance Publications, Inc., part of the Newhouse family's vast holdings, which purchased the publisher from RCA for $70 million. The next decade was one of extraordinary growth, marked by the 1982 purchase of Fawcett Books, the 1983 founding of Villard Books, and the 1984 acquisition of Times Books from the New York Times Company. In 1985 RH launched its AudioBooks division, drawing on the company's extensive backlist to create abridged and unabridged cassette recordings.

RH continued to expand its reach with the 1986 purchase of Fodor's Travel Guides and the 1987 acquisition of Chatto, Virago, Bodley Head & Jonathan Cape, Ltd., a prestigious British publishing group. ''With companies like Bantam and Simon & Schuster becoming more involved overseas, we had a feeling we should do something ourselves,'' Bernstein told *Publishers Weekly.* As with previous mergers, the companies remained autonomous but also stood to benefit immensely from the alliance for subsidiary rights and other negotiations. Also in 1987, RH's renowned Pantheon Books and the newly acquired Schocken Books were merged editorially.

The following year, RH once again expanded its holdings by acquiring the large, respected Crown Publishing Group, comprised of Crown Books, Clarkson N. Potter, Inc., Harmony Books, and the Outlet Book Company. In 1989 the company experienced its second changing of the guard when Bernstein departed RH after 23 years. His replacement as president, chairman, and CEO was Alberto Vitale, former head of rival Bantam Doubleday Dell (BDD).

Key Dates:

1925: Co-founders Bennett Cerf and Donald Klopfer acquire Modern Library.
1927: Company is renamed Random House Inc.
1934: Random House publishes James Joyce's *Ulysses.*
1944: Company establishes Random House Canada and college books division.
1947: Company publishes *American College Dictionary,* the firm's first reference book.
1950: Landmark Books series for children is introduced.
1957: First Dr. Seuss book, *The Cat in the Hat,* is published.
1959: Random House goes public.
1960: Company acquires Alfred A. Knopf.
1965: Random House is acquired by Radio Corporation of America (RCA).
1966: *Random House Dictionary of the English Language* is published.
1971: Co-founder Bennett Cerf dies.
1973: Random House Acquires Ballantine Books.
1980: Company is acquired by Advance Publications and becomes part of the Newhouse family's media empire.
1986: Fodor's Travel Guides is acquired.
1988: Crown Publishing Group is acquired.
1989: Alberto Vitale becomes president, chairman, and CEO of Random House.
1989: Random House U.K. is established.
1997: Random House U.K. acquires adult trade division of Reed Books.
1998: Random House is acquired by German conglomerate Bertelsmann AG.

Among Vitale's immediate concerns were trimming the fat and overhauling RH's operations. In addition, Vitale focused RH on the 21st century by diversifying into the burgeoning electronic field and developing multimedia products. This year also saw further U.K. expansion with the acquisition of Century Hutchinson, Ltd., which along with the Chatto, Virago, Bodley Head and Cape group became Random House UK, with subsidiaries in Australia, New Zealand, and South Africa.

In his continuing efforts to streamline the company, Vitale set his sights on the ailing Pantheon Books. Since Bernstein—one of Pantheon's most ardent supporters—was gone, the industry was rife with rumors of the imprint's imminent dissolution. Andre Schiffrin, Pantheon's directional force for 28 years, resigned in 1990 after refusing to go along with Vitale's cost-cutting measures. His departure stirred up a storm of controversy, as Studs Terkel (Pantheon's best-selling author), E.L. Doctorow, Barbara Ehrenreich, Kurt Vonnegut, and 350 others staged a demonstration in front of RH's offices, while another 300 writers signed a letter of protest on Pantheon's behalf. In response, Vitale told *Publishers Weekly,* "I want to most emphatically reaffirm Random House's commitment to maintaining Pantheon's position as one of our most prestigious imprints and to insuring its continuity and success in the future." Vitale soon hired Erroll McDonald—who had criticized the demonstrators in an op-ed piece for the *New York Times*—as the new executive editor of Pantheon, and the imprint continued with a smaller staff and fewer projected titles.

In 1992 Vitale raided his former employer's legions to hire William Wright, who became his righthand man as RH's executive vice-president and chief operating officer. Also during this year, RH founded two new imprints under the Ballantine group's umbrella: One World, to produce culturally diverse originals and reprints in hardcover and trade paperback; and Moorings, to publish hardcover and trade paperbacks with a Christian, devotional, or inspirational leaning.

Yet 1992's biggest news was the renaissance of the Modern Library, with the reintroduction of 27 volumes, complete with new bindings and reset pages, to celebrate the series' 75th anniversary. Simultaneously, those at Knopf put the finishing touches on the revival of Everyman's Library, the long dormant hardcover classics once published by Dutton that were the original model for RH's own Modern Library series. Though there was some concern about competition, Jane Friedman, president of RH Audio, posited, "Would we have been any happier if some other publisher had brought out Everyman's?"

Once again solidifying assets and looking for more, Vitale engineered the purchase of BDD's Bantam Electronic Publishing in 1993. The move was intended to beef up RH's own electronic division, or as Vitale told *Publishers Weekly,* "to create more critical mass in a field that, while evolving, is here to stay." As proof of his commitment, Vitale formed RH's New Media Division to "identify and pursue multimedia opportunities" and installed Randi Benton as its president.

In addition, RH formed several joint ventures in 1993, including one to distribute the National Geographic Society's books; a second with Brøderbund to create and market story-based multimedia software for children; and another between RH's Electronic Publishing division and Prentice Hall to produce and market a line of computer-oriented books under the newly established imprint of HewlettPackard Press.

RH continued its trend of acquisition and reorganization in 1994 and 1995. Its investment in Worldview Systems Corporation, a San Francisco-based provider of electronic destination information, enabled RH's Fodor's subsidiary to launch Fodor's Worldview Travel Update (FWTU), a service that provided buyers of Fodor's travel guides with updated information sent electronically or via fax or mail.

That year RH also entered into an agreement with Kiplinger Washington Editors to publish books on personal finance and other business topics under a new imprint, Times Business Books. RH Value Publishing introduced a new adult trade imprint, Park Lane Press, which also would publish children's titles in addition to titles on cooking, gardening, history, and illustrated gift books. Other RHVP imprints included Gramercy, Wings, Crescent, and Glorya Hale Books. RH acquired a 20 percent interest in *The Princeton Review.* The investment enabled *The Princeton Review* to double its output of book titles from 60 to 120 by the end of 1997. RH already was publishing *The Princeton Review's* books and distributing its software to the book market.

With ownership of electronic rights becoming a contentious issue between authors and publishers, RH discovered in 1993 that it did not own the electronic rights to Theodor Geisel's Dr. Seuss books. RH was able to negotiate with representatives from Geisel's estate and acquire the multimedia rights to Dr. Seuss. More significantly, it changed the wording in its author contracts and added tough clauses regarding electronic and other rights not yet defined. The William Morris Agency, angry over the new contract language, refused to do business with RH for about a year before softening its stance. Julia Child, a longtime Knopf author, parted ways with Knopf in a dispute over electronic rights.

In 1996 RH withdrew from the annual American Booksellers Association (ABA) convention, after the ABA filed a lawsuit against RH charging RH with illegally providing discounts to chain bookstores. After a federal judge refused to dismiss the ABA's lawsuit, RH and the ABA reached an out-of-court settlement in November 1996. Under the agreement RH admitted no wrongdoing and would not reimburse the ABA's legal fees. RH agreed to abide by a ten-year consent decree that required RH to abide by its principles on pricing and promotional allowances. Any changes must be made available to all customers. The ABA had accused RH of offering selective discounts to the larger chain bookstores at the expense of smaller independent booksellers.

The publisher also received negative publicity in 1996 when it unsuccessfully attempted to reclaim a $1.3 million advance paid to author Joan Collins, in large part because her contract contained a clause saying RH would accept the manuscript regardless of its quality. The decision to sue Collins was attributed to RH's feisty chairman and CEO, 62-year-old Alberto Vitale. Vitale also was feuding with the ABA over its lawsuit and with several top literary agencies over RH's insistence on purchasing all electronic rights to its books.

Philip Pfeffer became RH's new president and COO in 1996, replacing William Wright and reporting to Vitale. Pfeffer was formerly chairman and CEO of the Ingram Distribution Group. In 1997 RH established a new division, RH Client Services, to expand its sales and distribution systems. Gilbert Perlman was named president of the division. RH was distributing books for about 30 other publishers and sought to expand its distribution business. Distribution was seen as an area with significant growth potential.

In 1997 RH established a new children's book imprint, Knopf Paperbacks, with 14 titles drawn from the Knopf and Crown lists. The imprint was established to create a more focused literary identity, with new covers and designs for backlist and reissued titles. In addition, the Juvenile and Merchandise Group was renamed Children's Publishing in an effort to clarify its publishing program.

The RH Information Group, with Walter Weintz as group president, was formed within the company's trade publishing group in 1997.

It contained three nonfiction publishing units—Times Books, Princeton Review, and Reference and Information Publishing. Also that year Random House U.K. acquired the adult trade division of Reed Books, making it England's leading fiction publisher. The acquisition included the lists of William Heinemann, Methuen, and Secker & Warburg.

Ann Godoff was promoted to editor-in-chief and executive vice-president in the trade group. She joined RH in 1991, became vice-president and associate editorial director in 1994, and editorial director in 1995. At the end of 1997 Harold Evans, head of RH's trade publishing group, left to become editorial director and vice-chairman of Mortimer Zuckerman's publications, which included *U.S. News and World Report, New York Daily News, Atlantic Monthly,* and *Fast Company.* Ann Godoff replaced Evans as president of the trade group, while retaining her titles of editor-in-chief, executive vice-president, and member of the executive committee.

Period of Transition Under Bertelsmann: 1998–99

In 1998 RH was acquired by privately held German publishing and entertainment conglomerate Bertelsmann AG for anywhere from $1.2 to $2 billion. Bertelsmann already owned American publisher Bantam Doubleday Dell (BDD). Bertelsmann was known for its marketing savvy, and RH for the quality of its publications. Bertelsmann ran the largest book club business in the world and had acquired publishers in Germany, France, England, Spain, and the United States.

RH and BDD were expected to dominate the best-seller lists in the United States. For 1997 the two publishers had a combined total of 69 hardcover and 69 paperback titles on *Publishers Weekly's* best-seller lists, or about a third of all hardcover best-sellers and half of the best-selling paperbacks. After the merger RH would have 20 to 23 percent of the trade publishing market, but only about seven percent of total U.S. book sales.

The announcement on March 23, 1998 took the American trade publishing industry by surprise. Merger talks had been held over several months in secret between Thomas Middelhoff, Bertelsmann's next CEO, and Si Newhouse, head of RH's parent company Advance Publications. Since both Bertelsmann and Advance were private companies, no financial details concerning the merger were given. *Publishers Weekly,* the book industry trade publication, estimated Bertelsmann would pay about $1.4 billion for RH.

Following the merger, BDD and RH would operate under the name of the senior partner, Random House Inc., with estimated annual sales of $1.8 billion, almost double its nearest rivals, Penguin Putnam and Simon & Schuster. The head of the combined U.S. publishers would be Peter Olson, chairman and CEO of Bertelsmann's North American operations. Alberto Vitale became chairman of a newly created supervisory board that would serve as an advisory board but have no operating responsibilities for RH.

In April 1998 the U.S. Department of Justice filed suit to block the acquisition. Authors and agents, represented by the Authors Guild and the Association of Authors' Representatives, sent a complaint about the merger to the U.S. Federal Trade Commission (FTC). The complaint claimed that the new Random House would control more than 36 percent of the U.S. adult trade book market, not including textbooks and professional books. Agents and authors were concerned about access to publishers for new and established authors. Bertelsmann pegged the new RH market share at 10.9 percent, including mass market paperbacks and book club sales.

In June the FTC approved the acquisition, and the transaction was completed by July 1, 1998, the start of Bertelsmann's fiscal year. Olson named Erik Engstrom, former head of BDD North America, as president and chief operating officer of the new Random House. Addressing concerns over whether the many RH imprints would continue to bid independently for books—something that BDD imprints were not allowed to do under Bertelsmann—Olson circulated a statement to the company's employees worldwide indicating that Bertelsmann would support "continuity of editorial autonomy of each of the publishing divisions and imprints of BDD and Random House."

With new ownership RH's organizational structure began to change. In October three new publishing groups were formed: 1) RH Children's Media Group, consisting of all the book publishing imprints, video publishing, multimedia activities, outside joint ventures, and third-party distribution arrangements of the previous BDD Books for Young Readers and the RH Children's Publishing divisions; 2) RH Audio Publishing Group; and 3) RH Diversified Publishing Group, which included RH Value Publishing and RH Large Print.

In March 1999 the RH sales force was reorganized into three sales groups, with the Ballantine sales group eliminated. One of the new sales divisions included Ballantine, Bantam, Broadway, Dell, and Doubleday imprints. The children's sales division was expanded significantly to sell titles from all of the company's children's publishing divisions. The RH trade sales division was left, in large part, unchanged, representing books from Crown, Knopf, RH trade publishing, RH information, and Fodor's adult books, as well as audios and large-print titles.

Following repeated statements that distribution was no longer a priority at RH, Gilbert Perlman and a group of RH executives agreed to purchase RH's distribution division and form a new company, Client Distribution Services, Inc. Operations of the new company were expected to begin in September 1999.

The realignment of RH's adult publishing began in May 1999 with the formation of four new publishing groups. The most significant were the formation of the Doubleday Broadway Publishing Group and the Bantam Dell Publishing Group, the latter uniting two paperback giants under one roof. Carole Baron, president and publisher of Dell for 18 years, left the company effective June 30. In addition, Anchor Books joined Vintage in the Knopf Publishing Group to form a new trade paperback unit. A new Doubleday Religious Publishing division also was established, which would include RH's WaterBrook religious imprint. All affected imprints were to retain their distinct editorial identities.

In July 1999 RH acquired Listening Library Inc., a Connecticut-based publisher of unabridged audio titles for children. Listening Library would become the children's audio imprint of the RH Audio Publishing Group. Founded in 1955, Listening Library was a pioneer in creating unabridged audio titles for the trade market and later focused on children's literary titles.

For fiscal 1999 ending June 30, RH had estimated worldwide sales in excess of $1.6 billion, with 80 percent of sales coming in North America. RH Chairman Peter Olson noted that the company was able to maintain the distinction of its publishing programs and imprints even as it reorganized. The company was receiving the same number of submissions from agents as in the past, and different imprints continued to compete for the same title as long as another publisher was also bidding for the book. Olson also noted that he had increased the level at which an editor could make an offer to an author before seeking corporate approval.

After acquiring RH in 1998, Bertelsmann took a decentralized approach to managing its American publishing property. It gave editors freedom to sign authors and publishers the freedom to run their own publishing programs. Centralization was limited to support services and back-office functions. RH's management was given wide latitude in running the company, and Bertelsmann executives were more interested in long-term results than results for a single year.

Concerns for the future centered on expanding and refocusing the company's distribution center in Westminster, Maryland, which took on inventory from BDD's warehouse in Illinois and Ballantine's distribution center in Tennessee. Another ongoing concern was RH's ability to continue to attract top authors and publishing talent, especially in non-editorial areas such as operations and information systems.

Principal Divisions

The Ballantine Publishing Group; Bantam Books; Broadway Books; The Crown Publishing Group; Dell; Doubleday; The Knopf Publishing Group; Random House Audio Publishing Group; Random House Children's Media Group; The Random House Information Group; The Random House Trade Publishing Group; Random House Diversified Publishing Group; Fodor's Travel Publications; Random House New Media; Random House Direct Marketing; Random House International; Random House UK (England).

Principal Competitors

Penguin Putnam USA; Simon & Schuster Inc.; HarperCollins Publishers; Time Warner Inc.; Hearst Corporation.

Further Reading

Alter, Jonathan, "The Rumble at Random House," *Newsweek,* October 26, 1987, p. 62.

Alterman, Eric, "Random Violence," *The Nation,* April 13, 1998, p. 5.

Baker, John F., "BDD/Random Merger Gets Extra Scrutiny in Washington," *Publishers Weekly,* May 11, 1998, p. 13.

——, "Bertelsmann's Buy of Random Completed," *Publishers Weekly,* July 6, 1998, p. 12.

Baker, John F., and Jim Milliot, "Bertelsmann to Buy Random House," *Publishers Weekly,* March 30, 1998, p. 10.

Baker, John F., and Nora Rawlinson, "BDD Culture Won't Necessarily Prevail at Random," *Publishers Weekly,* April 6, 1998, p. 12.

Cerf, Bennett, *At Random: The Reminisces of Bennett Cerf,* New York: Random House, 1977.

Giles, Jeff, and Ray Sawhill, "A Brand-New Chapter," *Newsweek,* April 6, 1998, p. 39.

Maughan, Shannon, "Random House Acquires Listening Library," *Publishers Weekly,* July 12, 1999, p. 11.

Milliot, Jim, "Court Denies RH Move to Dismiss ABA Lawsuit," *Publishers Weekly,* August 19, 1996, p. 11.

——, "Random House and ABA Settle Antitrust Lawsuit," *Publishers Weekly,* November 25, 1996, p. 10.

——, "Random House Creates Three New Publishing Groups," *Publishers Weekly,* October 12, 1998, p. 11.

——, "Random House Forms New Adult Publishing Groups," *Publishers Weekly,* May 31, 1999, p. 18.

——, "RH Has Widespread Gains in Transition Year," *Publishers Weekly,* August 9, 1999, p. 198.

Milliot, Jim, and Herbert R. Lottman, "U.S. Is Now No. 1 Market for Bertelsmann," *Publishers Weekly,* September 28, 1998, p. 10.

Milliot, Jim, and John F. Baker, "A Problem with Market Share and Antitrust?," *Publishers Weekly,* March 30, 1998, p. 12.

Model, F. Peter, "A Volvo, Not a Caddy: The Modern Library's Second Coming," *Wilson Library Bulletin,* December 1992, pp. 66–68.

Mutter, John, "Del Rey Creates 'Cybercommunity'," *Publishers Weekly,* December 19, 1994, pp. 18–19.

"Random and Prentice Hall Sign Joint Deal with HewlettPackard," *Publishers Weekly,* March 15, 1993, p. 9.

"Random, CTW Form New Imprint," *Publishers Weekly,* March 2, 1998, p. 16.

"Random Thoughts: Who Wants to Be in Book Publishing? Bertelsmann, Because of a Revolution in the Business That It Is Bringing About," *Economist,* March 28, 1998, p. 58.

"Random, Wiley in Business Book Deals," *Publishers Weekly,* April 10, 1995, p. 9.

Raymont, Henry, "Cerf Rites Draw Friends of 'Two Worlds'," *New York Times,* September 1, 1971, p. 40.

Reilly, Patrick M., "Godoff Named Editorial Chief at Random House," *Wall Street Journal,* January 13, 1995, p. B2.

Reuter, Madalynne, "After the UnRandom Showdown," *Publishers Weekly,* October 30, 1987, p. 11.

Richardson, Jean, "Reed Buy Makes Random House U.K. a Formidable Fiction House," *Publishers Weekly,* February 10, 1997, p. 14.

Shapiro, Laura, "Publisher at the Barricades," *Newsweek,* March 19, 1990, p. 71.

"RH Buys Stake in Princeton Review," *Publishers Weekly,* July 17, 1995, p. 121.

Turner, Richard, "Wild About Harry: Buzzing About Evans," *Newsweek,* December 8, 1997, p. 76.

Wexler, Diane Patrick, "Random House Tries Online Bookselling," *Publishers Weekly,* May 12, 1997, p. 18.

—Taryn Benbow-Pfalzgraf
—updated by David P. Bianco

Redhook Ale Brewery, Inc.

3400 Phinney Avenue North
Seattle, Washington 98103
U.S.A
Telephone: (206) 548-8000
Fax: (206) 548-1305
Web site: http://www.redhook.com

Public Company
Incorporated: 1982
Employees: 202
Sales: $32.6 million (1998)
Stock Exchanges: NASDAQ
Ticker Symbol: HOOK
NAIC: 31212 Breweries

Redhook Ale Brewery, Inc. brews nonpasteurized, European-style beer for sale to commercial establishments and retail locations in 48 states. Redhook's year-round labels include Redhook E.S.B., Redhook India Pale Ale, Redhook Hefe-Weizen, Blackhook Porter, and Double Black Stout, which are complemented by seasonal selections that include Winterhook, Redhook Blonde Ale, and Redhook Nut Brown Ale. Redhook's popularity in Seattle led to the distribution of the brand into neighboring western states, before a 1994 distribution and equity partnership agreement with Anheuser Busch, Inc. fueled its expansion nationally. The company's product line is led by Redhook E.S.B., which accounts for more than 60 percent of total sales. Brewing operations comprise two facilities, one in Woodinville, Washington, and another in Portsmouth, New Hampshire, which had a combined production capacity of 350,000 barrels a year by the end of 1998.

Origins

Redhook was the inspiration of Gordon Bowker. At the beginning of the 1980s, Bowker was determined to start his own brewery, convinced that the growing import beer market could support a domestic brewer of high-quality beers. One of Bowker's first tasks in getting his start-up enterprise up and running was finding the individual to run the brewery. He drew up a list of candidates, but the search did not take long. The list was a short one, containing one name: Paul Shipman. At the time, Shipman was working as a marketing analyst for the Chateau Ste. Michelle Winery, his first job after earning an MBA at the University of Virginia in 1978. Shipman was loquacious and beguiling, renowned for hour-long stories and a deceptive intellect. Often, Shipman failed to impress at first blush but his outward naiveté belied an incisive mind, leading his boss at Chateau Ste. Michelle to describe him as "the Columbo of the business world," according to the *Business Journal-Portland.* Although Shipman had spent only a limited time at Chateau Ste. Michelle, his accomplishments had made a strong impression on Bowker, who was able to see through the young executive's veneer and perceive a bright and tireless worker. Shipman agreed to join Bowker in 1981, becoming the president and co-founder of the radical Redhook Ale Brewery.

Redhook earned its maverick status by virtue of its early emergence as a microbrewery, a foreign concept in the domestic beer industry during the early 1980s. When Bowker set out to enlist the financial help of investors, his second inquiry prompted a response that typified the mindset of the early 1980s: "Breweries don't start up," the investor chided Bowker, "they shut down." Undeterred by the prevailing opinion that they would fail, Bowker and Shipman succeeded in securing the capital to start their company, incorporating Redhook in May 1981.

1984 Introduction of Ballard Bitter Sparks Growth

Bowker and Shipman established the company's offices in Seattle, choosing the location because the Pacific Northwest had the highest per capita draft beer consumption in the United States. A small, 5,000-square-foot brewery was built in Ballard, a Scandinavian enclave of Seattle that offered the light industrial facilities needed for brewing and a community steeped in European traditions, including the centuries-old tradition of craft brewing. After developing a recipe similar to spicy Belgian ales, the company introduced its inaugural beer on August 11, 1982, when the first pint of Redhook Ale was sold in Seattle. Referred to as "banana beer," Redhook Ale attracted a small number of devout fans, but it did not attract legions of beer drinkers, limiting the brewery's sales to less than 1,000 barrels during its first year of

Company Perspectives:

A well-built chair serves as a chair in the best way. It appeals to the eye. It serves a nobler purpose than just being a place to sit. Well-builtness isn't the material used; oak, beech, metal or some form of extruded plastic. It may be how those materials support the sitter when he is sitting, but just as important is how that chair looks from across the room. We know people who are well-built not just that they are physically strong or cut a handsome figure, but that they embody proportion and grace that goes beyond appearances. A well-built person has mental balance, personality and style. A well-built business will always make money. But inside of that business are people who feel accomplished. In that well-builtness is a generous, human enterprise serving a range of needs. A well-built movie or play has three acts, a beginning, middle and end. But more than that it makes you feel something far deeper than admiration for the skill of the author. Well-builtness is in the craft of things. Sturdiness, honesty and proportion create a psychological sense of well-being. A sense that you are in good hands. Heft. Click. Touch and feel. Warmth. Pleasure. Satisfaction. Ahhhh! We don't always have the exact right word to describe what we mean when we say something is well built. But we do have a beer. It's called Redhook.

operation, 2,000 barrels below capacity. A second selection called Blackhook Porter debuted the following year, but like Redhook Ale, the brand only established a small following. Bowker and Shipman needed a beer that could transform their fledgling brewery into a burgeoning enterprise, and they produced such a beer in 1984. The introduction of Ballard Bitter marked a seminal moment in Redhook's history, giving the company its first widely popular brand. Seattleites began seeking out establishments that served Ballard Bitter, pushing Redhook's brewery to capacity. Within a few short years, Bowker and Shipman were forced to expand; the company's brewery could no longer meet the demand for Ballard Bitter.

For their next brewery, the Redhook founders wanted to build a state-of-the-art facility that would give them the most technically advanced craft brewery in North America. A German company was hired to design and build the company's new and much larger brewery, which was located in the Fremont neighborhood of Seattle. For the site of the new brewery, the company obtained a trolley car barn used by the defunct Seattle Electric Railway, a 26,000-square-foot building that housed the new brewery and Redhook's new brewpub, the Trolleyman. The brewery commenced production in 1989, starting with an annual capacity of 30,000 barrels. The new brewing operations and the adjoining brewpub served as a showcase for the newly prominent company, evidence of Shipman's belief that a true microbrewer should offer brewery tours and an on-site premises where the public could sample the brewery's offerings.

With a facility five times larger than the original operation in Ballard and a beer embraced by a growing audience, Redhook closed the 1980s by cementing its reputation as an unmitigated success story in the microbrewery industry. The company began selling beer in northern California in 1989, helping to fuel sales growth that led to a 55 percent gain in revenues for the year. Shipman, the promoter and architect of Redhook's growth, showed no signs of complacency as he ushered the company into the 1990s. In March 1990, he announced plans for another new brewery with four times the production capacity of the Fremont brewery, which had been in operation for only a year and a half. The 150,000-barrel-capacity plant, slated to be built somewhere in western Washington, was expected to be used to produce lower-priced beers than the company's microbrews, pitting Redhook against super-premium brands such as Michelob and Henry Weinhard's. The bold plan to take on much larger competitors never materialized as planned, however. Details involving the financing and the specific site for the new brewery were expected to be announced by the end of 1990, but the entire expansion project was shelved before the end of the year, its progress halted by uncertain market conditions. Shipman scotched plans for the $18 million brewery when it became apparent that the parent company of the largest regional brand, Rainier, was mired in profound financial difficulties. Rainier's parent company, G. Heileman Brewing Co. Inc., filed for bankruptcy in January 1991, provoking wariness in the investment community Shipman planned to solicit for the brewery's financing. Shipman decided to forestall plans for the big brewery, but he was determined to one day press forward with his original plan, declaring to the *Puget Sound Business Journal* in March 1991 that building a second brewery "is still my mission."

Entering the 1990s, Redhook stood poised to reap the rewards of a microbrew revolution. No longer hard-to-find curiosities, domestic craft beers were the preferred choice of a growing number of beer drinkers during the 1990s. Although Shipman had checked his effort to build a second brewery at the start of the decade, Redhook enjoyed an otherwise progressive start to its second decade of business. Underpinned by the increasing consumption of microbrews, Redhook's sales grew explosively during the first half of the decade, averaging annual increases of nearly 50 percent. The burgeoning growth of the craft beer market further invigorated Shipman's desire for another brewery, presenting the company's ambitious chief executive with an irrepressible opportunity to seize a greater share of an expanding market. Financing the project, however, remained a troublesome task, particularly during the economically recessive early 1990s, but Shipman moved forward with the preparations for Redhook's future expansion. A private placement was completed in 1993, raising $10 million for the company. Also in 1993, a site for a new brewery was obtained in Woodinville, Washington, a suburb of Seattle, and production capacity at the Fremont brewery was increased to 75,000 barrels. Shipman also adopted a methodical approach to Redhook's future debut as a public company. In 1992, he began gearing the company for an initial public offering (IPO), implementing a pervasive program that touched on all aspects of the company's activities. Employees involved with legal, financial, brewing, marketing, and trademark functions of Redhook's operation began preparing on a daily basis for the company's IPO, a preparatory process that went so far as to tailor the company's telephone system for the eventual public debut. By the beginning of the mid-1990s, Redhook was amply prepared for an expansive conclusion to the 1990s, a period in the company's history that was touched off by several landmark developments between 1994 and 1995.

Key Dates:

1982: First pint of Redhook Ale is sold in Seattle on August 11.
1989: Fremont brewery and adjoining pub, the Trolleyman, are opened.
1994: Anheuser Busch and Redhook sign a distribution and equity partnership agreement.
1995: Redhook debuts on the NASDAQ Stock Exchange.
1996: Portsmouth, New Hampshire brewery begins operation, Redhook's first facility outside the Pacific Northwest.
1998: Distribution of Redhook covers 48 states; Fremont brewery is shuttered.

1994 Partnership with Anheuser Busch Fuels National Expansion

Redhook's competitors and industry observers were served notice of a new era in the craft brewing industry by an announcement in June 1994. Anheuser Busch, Inc., the self-proclaimed "king of beers" and the world's largest brewer, announced that it had reached a distributorship and equity partnership agreement with Redhook. For Jim Koch, founder of Redhook's rival, Boston Beer Co., nothing would ever be the same again. In response to the news that Anheuser Busch had purchased a 25 percent stake in Redhook in exchange for distributing Redhook labels nationwide, Koch told *Inc.* magazine in June 1994, "That was no press release; it was a declaration of war. What it means is that the cozy fraternal days of the microbrewery business are over." Koch marked the end of the era by derisively referring to Redhook as "Budhook," an appellation meant to relate the cynicism surrounding the partnership of a craft brewer with a mass production giant. For his part, Shipman responded by referring to Boston Beer Co.'s flagship brand Sam Adams as "Scam Adams," because Boston Beer Co., without a brewery of its own, contracted all production out to contract brewers.

Beyond the name calling, the agreement was profoundly important to the actualization of Shipman's plans. By his own admission, the company's growth had been constrained by a lack of capacity in 1994, but with the cash from the Anheuser Busch deal Shipman was able to accelerate his expansion plans. Construction of the company's Woodinville brewery was nearly completed by the time the Anheuser Busch partnership was announced, with limited production of 60,000 barrels beginning in September 1994. Shipman had waited four years for a second brewery, but he would not have to wait long for the third addition to the company's portfolio. In January 1995, coming off $15 million in sales for the previous year, Redhook announced plans for a third brewery—the company's first facility located outside the Pacific Northwest. For a location, Shipman chose Portsmouth, New Hampshire, where construction began on 250,000-barrel brewery and 6,000-square-foot pub. In preparation for the construction of the $25 million facility, Redhook began shipping draft beer to taverns in the Boston area in November 1994 and began selling bottled beer in retail locations in January 1995. According to the company's calculations, the brewery in Portsmouth, which was scheduled to be completed by early 1996, would enable Redhook to reach roughly 40 percent of the country's population and it would make the company the largest specialty beer maker in New England. Production began in October 1996, starting with a 100,000-barrel capacity. The addition of a brewery on the East Coast, coupled with the distribution agreement with Anheuser Busch, gave Redhook the ability to develop into a national force, but Shipman's efforts to expand did not end in Portsmouth. Concurrent with the construction of the Portsmouth facility, the Woodinville brewery was expanded, inching toward the brewery's production capacity of 250,000 barrels annually.

Redhook entered the mid-1990s as a growing giant in an industry niche previously populated by small, local concerns. Technically, the company that had started as one of the pioneers of the microbrew industry was no longer a microbrewery. According to industry standards, microbreweries produced 15,000 barrels or less a year, a production level Redhook had exceeded years earlier. The company had promoted itself to a regional specialty brewer, a designation applicable to brewers of between 15,000 and one million barrels annually. Shipman showed no signs of nostalgia for Redhook's former industry status. Having realized his mission of building a second brewery and quickly adding a third brewery, Shipman next turned his attention to fulfilling the objective he had been working toward for the previous three years. By mid-1995, Redhook's lengthy preparations for an IPO were over. With the proceeds gained from the IPO, the company planned to pay for the Portsmouth facility and finance its transformation from a regional brewer into a national brewer. Shipman planned to sell 26 percent of the company to the public, hoping to garner between $13 and $15 per share. Anheuser Busch, wishing to maintain its 25 percent stake in the company, invested an additional $9.2 million through a private placement, which, together with the proceeds from the IPO, would give Shipman nearly $50 million to funnel toward Redhook's expansion. During the August 1995 IPO, investors demonstrated greater exuberance than expected, attracted by Redhook's annual revenue growth of nearly 50 percent during the 1990s. The stock debuted at $17 per share and quickly shot upward in value before settling at $32 per share a week later.

With the IPO completed and production capacity increased significantly, attention turned to rolling out the stable of Redhook brands to a national audience: The time had come to put the Anheuser Busch distribution agreement to work. Prior to the Anheuser Busch partnership, Redhook distributed its beers in eight western states; by 1995, the company's bottled and draft beers were available in 19 states nationwide. In 1996, efforts to broaden the company's geographic reach were intensified, leading to the release of Redhook brands in 15 new states. Of the half-dozen beer styles produced by the company, none was more important than Redhook E.S.B. (Extra Special Bitter), born from the company's first successful brand, Ballard Bitter. The flagship brand accounted for more than half of the company's total sales, by far outdistancing the contributions of the company's other major labels, which included Redhook India Pale Ale, Blackhook Porter, Nut Brown Ale, Redhook Rye, and a coffee-flavored beer introduced in late 1995, Double Black Stout. Supporting these year-round offerings was an ever-changing selection of seasonal beers, which, as in the case of Redhook Rye, occasionally became part of the company's primary roster of beers. Of the seasonal variety, two promising beers made their debut in 1997, Winterhook and Redhook Blonde Ale. The distribution of these beers to a significantly larger customer base led to a considerable rise in sales by the end of 1996, as 1995's total of $28 million swelled to nearly $40 million after the energetic push into new markets. After 1996, however, sales dipped for two successive years, as Redhook grappled with stiff competition from a plethora of new craft brewers.

As Redhook exited the 1990s, it stood strongly positioned as one of the few craft breweries supported by a national network of distributors. By the end of 1998, penetration into new markets had extended the company's geographic reach into 48 states, a charge led by the signature Redhook E.S.B. brand, which accounted for 62 percent of sales at the end of the 1990s. Despite the company's prominent position, the craft brewing industry was becoming increasingly competitive, as the number of specialty brewers, microbreweries, and brewpubs proliferated during the latter half of the 1990s. To combat the pressures of mounting competition, Redhook management decided in 1999 to invest in media advertising, something the company had not done to any great extent previously. The company also was exploring new areas for revenue growth. In 1999, Redhook introduced Doubleblack Barbecue Sauce, made with the brewery's Double Black Stout and Starbucks coffee, which initially was sold in the company's pubs and in selected retail locations in Seattle. As the company prepared for the 21st century, it did so without one of its breweries. In January 1998, production was significantly reduced at the Fremont brewery before being abandoned entirely several months later. The decision to close the brewery left Redhook with production capacity of 350,000 barrels annually, but as the company galvanized its national recognition, the room to increase production at the Woodinville and Portsmouth breweries promised to be utilized in the years ahead.

Principal Competitors

Anchor Brewing; Boston Beer Co.; Bridgeport Brewery; Hart Brewing Co.

Further Reading

''A-B Closes Pact for Redhook Partnership,'' *Nation's Restaurant News,* December 5, 1994, p. 64.

Baker, M. Sharon, ''Captain Redhook,'' *Business Journal-Portland,* March 1, 1996, p. 10.

——, ''Redhook Eyes an IPO To Tap Frothy Stock Market,'' *Puget Sound Business Journal,* May 19, 1995, p. 1.

——, ''Redhook IPO Won't Slake Anheuser Busch's Thirst,'' *Puget Sound Business Journal,* July 14, 1995, p. 7.

——, ''Redhook Will Build Brewery in the Northeast,'' *Puget Sound Business Journal,* January 6, 1995, p. 1.

''Brewed Awakening,'' *Inc.,* October 1994, p. 11.

Denne, Lorianne, ''Red Hook's Ambitious Expansion Scheme Is Placed in Hold for Now,'' *Puget Sound Business Journal,* March 18, 1991, p. 8.

''Leap of Faith,'' *Restaurants & Institutions,* March 15, 1999, p. 17.

Turcsik, Richard, ''Microbrews Getting Larger: Manufacturer Outlook,'' *Supermarket News,* May 29, 1995, p. 14A.

—Jeffrey L. Covell

Redrow Group plc

Redrow House
St. David's Park
Flintshire CH5 3PW
United Kingdom
Telephone: (44) 1244 520 044
Fax: (44) 1244 520 720
Web site: http://www.redrow.co.uk

Public Company
Incorporated: 1974
Employees: 1091
Sales: £341.6 million ($512.4 million) (1999)
Stock Exchanges: London
Ticker Symbol: RDW
NAIC: 23321 Single Family Housing Construction; 23311 Land Subdivision and Development; 23332 Commercial and Institutional Building Construction

Flintshire-based Redrow Group plc is one of the United Kingdom's largest home builders and developers. In fiscal 1999, the company completed more than 3,100 homes, for an average selling price of more than £106,000. Many of Redrow's homes, which hit chiefly the suburban middle-to-upper income brackets, sell at prices ranging up to £400,000 or more. Redrow's operations are structured into three primary divisions: Homes, Land, and Commercial. Redrow's home real estate sales are grouped under two main subsidiaries: the mid- to high-end Redrow Homes, and its Heritage brand, which, with more than 2,500 completions per year, at an average selling price of £112,900, comprises the bulk of the company's home sales; and Harwood Homes, lower-priced homes, townhomes, and apartment structures targeted primarily at the first-home-buying urban market, with average selling prices of less than £64,000. Despite its smaller size, Harwood Homes represents the company's fastest growing sales division; in the late 1990s, the company has been rolling out the Harwood brand across England and into Scotland. The company's Land division holds an essential position in the company's future growth. Redrow's ''land bank'' of more than 12,000 development lots gives the company an approximately four-year supply of buildable land, providing a buffer against sudden rises in land prices. Redrow's policy of purchasing forward land and guiding those purchases through a government-led approval process, rather than buying land at market prices, has enabled the company to keep land costs low, at less than 18 percent of housing sales prices. In 1999, Redrow held more than 27,000 plots of forward land. Redrow's third division, Commercial, builds and sells commercial properties, including office buildings, executive parks, restaurants, and retail centers. Redrow Commercial represents only four percent of the company's sales; however, in January 1999 the company paid £34 million for a proposed mixed home and commercial site, expected to boost the Commercial division's share in the company's total revenues. Redrow continues to be guided by founder and chairman Steve Morgan; day-to-day operations, however, are led by longtime partner Paul Pedley, who was named company CEO in 1999.

Modest Beginnings in the 1970s

Steve Morgan most likely had no idea that the modest Northwest England firm he founded in the early 1970s was to grow into one of the United Kingdom's leading real estate developers and that he himself would become one of England's richest businessmen. In 1974, at the age of 21, Morgan took a £5,000 loan from his father and opened a civil engineering firm. Operating at first from a small bungalow in the town of Rhyl, in Cheshire, Morgan focused on local trench-digging and pipe-laying projects. The location of one of his earliest projects—on Redwood and Harrow drives—contracted to provide his company's name. (This project also provided the name to Morgan's later Harwood Homes division.)

From its earliest pipe-laying projects, Redrow expanded into providing general construction contracting services. By 1978, Redrow added full-scale building contracting to its projects. The following year, the company moved to more spacious quarters in Denhigh, North Wales, where it built its own offices and plant yard. The company's growth enabled to it to expand its building contracting beyond its home base to cover the Cheshire region and to enter Merseyside. Redrow also was taking on larger and larger projects. In 1980, the company signed to perform its first £1 million contract, at Presthaven Sands, in Prestatyn.

Key Dates:

1974: Redrow is founded by Steve Morgan.
1978: Company expands into building contracting.
1980: Redrow achieves its first million-pound contract.
1982: Redrow Homes development subsidiary is formed.
1983: Construction of ''Heritage'' homes begins.
1994: Public listing on London Stock Exchange.
1996: Redrow enters the Scottish market.
1999: Paul Pedley named CEO of Redrow.

A dip in the building market in the 1980s encouraged Morgan to take Redrow into a new direction. In 1982, Morgan formed the Redrow Homes subsidiary and began construction of the company's first private homes. Initially targeted at the more modestly priced housing brackets, Redrow quickly turned its ambitions to a higher—and more profitable—end. In 1983, the company began construction of the first of its ''Heritage'' homes, targeted at the mid-priced and luxury housing markets.

The company expanded quickly during the next five years, spreading its activities to cover more and more of England, and particularly the booming South East region around London. By 1985, Redrow had entered three of the country's most important building markets, the Midlands, the South East, and the South West, and had built up a particularly strong land bank in the South East. The company grew so quickly that Morgan was forced to hire a righthand man, taking on Paul Pedley to assist in the company's expansion during the soaring real estate climate of the mid-1980s.

The company expanded both internally, through land purchases, and externally, with the acquisition of other developers, notably the 1987 acquisition of Whelmar Homes, bringing the company into Lancashire. At the same time, Redrow entered the commercial real estate market, forming its Commercial division for construction of office complexes and industrial parks, as well as fast food and other restaurant and retail structures. By then, also, the company's building contracting and civil engineering projects had taken a clear back seat to its home building programs.

Then, in early 1988, Morgan and Pedley sold off nearly all of the company's South East land bank—just in time to see the British housing market crash. Morgan received a great deal of attention for his foresight and probably prevented the company from going under in the difficult real estate climate—called the worst building market in England since the Second World War—that lasted until well into the next decade.

Rebuilding in the 1990s

Whereas Redrow's South East competitors found themselves saddled with huge parcels of suddenly worthless land, Redrow had escaped the region with its pockets full. Nonetheless, overbuilding in the 1980s, coupled with a slump into an extended recession, itself compounded by the outbreak of the Persian Gulf War, put a virtual halt to new building construction. Redrow continued to operate in its Northwest regional base, including building a new headquarters in Flintshire in 1990, but the building recession soon spread throughout the United Kingdom. By 1991, with few new projects on hand, Morgan placed day-to-day operations of the company into the hands of Paul Pedley and took off with his family on a six-month backpacking tour of the world. Named managing director, Pedley led Redrow into new territories, establishing Redrow in the South Wales and Yorkshire regions.

The company's acquisition of Costain Homes in 1993, for which it paid £25 million, announced Morgan and Pedley's belief that the South East building market was soon to pick up again. The Costain Homes acquisition gave Redrow a new foothold in the region, while its other regional operations also were beginning to rebuild. By the end of 1993, the company had completed more than 1,200 homes, for a total turnover of £111 million. The company, however, prepared to expand still more—within two years, Redrow nearly doubled its annual sales.

Fueling the company's growth was its decision to take Redrow public in 1994. Despite building market uncertainties, which led to a lower-than-expected initial share price, the public offering nonetheless made Morgan one of the United Kingdom's richest businessmen, as he reduced his ownership in the company from 98 percent to 60 percent. The public offering enabled Redrow to build up extensive land banks not only in the Northwestern regions, but in the South East as well. Much of the company's land bank took the form of forward land purchases, that is, land that had not yet received any development approval, rather than purchases of more expensive market-ready lands, which would have exposed the company to greater risks of price fluctuations.

At mid-decade, Redrow turned its new construction focus to the Northwestern region. At the same time, it sought to profit from new government ''brownfield'' incentives. To preserve the country's rural or ''greenfield'' environment, the British government instead sought to encourage builders and prospective homeowners to construct on urban land converted from former industrial and other commercial uses. Redrow developed a new division, Harwood Homes, for its brownfield projects, offering new homes—mostly attached homes and townhouses—at an average of half the price of its Heritage line of homes. The Harwood line was initially targeted at the young urban professional market, with smaller home designs; its success, however, prompted the company to roll out new models to accommodate the needs of larger families. Originally operating in the Northwest, the Harwood division quickly rolled out on a national scale, as well as taking Redrow into Scotland for the first time.

Despite a construction dip in 1996, the United Kingdom pulled out of the recession in the mid-1990s, sparking a rising demand for new construction. By 1997, Redrow was completing more than 2,600 houses per year. In that year, also, the company bought a 140-acre parcel in Dunfermline, Scotland, which, capable of supporting up to 1,600 homes, was Redrow's largest development to date. Meanwhile, Morgan became even richer, when he sold off an additional 25 percent of his control of the company, reducing his shareholding to just 35 percent of Redrow's total stock.

By the end of 1997, Redrow had readied the launch of the redesigned Heritage line. Dubbed the New Heritage Range, and offering some 42 different home models, the new line was highly successful, winning a number of the country's most prominent housing awards. The New Heritage line also transformed the company's image: with sales in the south topping those in the north for the first time in the company's history, Redrow was no longer ''merely'' a Northwest home builder, but a truly national British builder. By the end of the company's June 1999 fiscal year, revenues had swelled to £342 million, for pretax earnings of £56 million. As a recognition of his role in helping to build the company into one of the United Kingdom's leading home builders, Paul Pedley was name CEO. The company had already made a number of prominent land purchases, including the January 1999 purchase of four land sites from British chemical giant ICI for £34.5 million. This purchase, together with the company's extensive land bank, ensured plenty of Redrow developments for the start of the new century.

Principal Subsidiaries

Redrow Homes Limited; Redrow Homes (Jersey) Limited; Harwood Homes; Redrow Commercial Developments Limited; Redrow Group Services Limited; Poche Interior Design Limited.

Principal Competitors

Barratt Developments; Bryant Group; Beazer Group; Centex; Bellway; George Wimpey; Berkeley Group; John Laing; Bovis Homes; Persimmon; British Land Company; Westbury; Brixton Estate; Wilson Bowden.

Further Reading

Cave, Andrew, ''Redrow Cuts Exposure to London Values,'' *Daily Telegraph,* August 18, 1997.

Jagger, Suzy, ''Redrow Poised To Finalise Pounds 34.5m ICI Land Bank Deal,'' *Daily Telegraph,* January 11, 1999.

''Redrow Builds on Growth in the South-East,'' *Financial Times,* September 15, 1999.

''Redrow Founder To Cut Stake,'' *Financial Times,* March 11, 1997, p. 20.

''Redrow Is on Firm Foundations,'' *Independent,* September 15, 1999, p. 21.

Stevenson, Tom, ''Redrow May Have Homed in Too Late,'' *Independent,* April 29, 1994, p. 32.

——, ''Redrow Shaves Pounds 25m Off Float Forecast,'' *Independent,* April 13, 1994, p. 33.

—M.L. Cohen

REED ELSEVIER

Reed Elsevier plc

25 Victoria Street
London SW1H0EX
United Kingdom
Telephone: (44) 171 222-8420
Fax: (44) 171 227-5799
Web site: http://www.reed-elsevier.com

Joint Venture of Elsevier N.V. and Reed International plc
Incorporated: 1880 as Uitgeversmaatschappij Elsevier; 1903 as Albert E. Reed & Company Ltd.
Employees: 26,100
Sales: £3.16 billion ($5.29 billion) (1998)
NAIC: 51112 Periodical Publishers; 51111 Newspaper Publishers; 5114 Database and Directory Publishers; 51113 Book Publishers; 511199 All Other Publishers

Reed Elsevier plc is the joint venture of London-based Reed International plc and Netherlands-based Elsevier N.V. The company is a leading publisher and information provider with principal operations in Europe and North America. Reed Elsevier focuses on scientific, professional, and business publishing and publishes about 1,200 scientific and trade journals and magazines, including a medical journal, *The Lancet.* The company's business division produces magazines, including *Variety* and *Publishers Weekly,* through subsidiary Cahners Business Information. Reed Elsevier also owns information service provider LEXIS-NEXIS. In the late 1990s, Reed Elsevier was focusing on expanding its electronic publishing operations to remain competitive in the rapidly changing publishing industry.

The History of Elsevier N.V.

Elsevier was founded as Uitgeversmaatschappij Elsevier in Rotterdam in 1880 by a group of five Dutch booksellers and publishers, led by Jacobus George Robbers. They took the company name and imprint from the publishing house of the Elsevier family, which had flourished between the late 16th and early 18th centuries. After the company moved its headquarters to Amsterdam in 1887, its early success depended on publishing a literary journal, Dutch versions of the then-popular novels of Jules Verne, and the *Winkler Prins* encyclopedia, which became the Dutch equivalent of the *Britannica.*

Elsevier first ventured into scientific publishing in the late 1930s, and then, after World War II, diversified its range, publishing trade journals and consumer magazines but chiefly building up its reputation as publisher of a number of scientific journals in English, starting in 1947 with *Biochimica et Biophysica Acta (BBA).* Elsevier Science Publishers then expanded further by acquiring other companies in the same field, such as the North Holland Publishing Company—founded in 1931, acquired in 1970—and Excerpta Medica, acquired in 1971.

For Elsevier "scientific" had the wider meaning common on the continent of Europe of "academic," rather than the narrower Anglo-American definition. Thus, while the company was the world's leading publisher in the life sciences, and issued journals covering the whole range of the natural sciences, it also published journals on history, law, economics, and statistics, as well as engineering and technology. A measure of the company's prestige was that by 1990 its publications had included work by the winners of 62 Nobel prizes, of which 29 were for physiology or medicine. More crucially, perhaps, its leading journals maintained this prestige by a rigorous process of peer review. In the case of *Brain Research*, for example, this meant that half of the articles submitted were rejected, and only four percent were published unaltered.

Elsevier merged with the newspaper group Nederlandse Dagbladunie N.V. early in 1979. This merger brought ownership of the national newspapers *NRC Handelsblad* and *Algemeen Dagblad,* which by the late 1980s had a combined circulation of nearly 650,000; three regional newspapers; and several local newspapers, including free advertisement-based papers. The enlarged group was reorganized under the newly founded holding company Elsevier N.V.

Elsevier's strategy beginning in 1980 was to concentrate on the English-language market, both by developing its existing output further and by acquiring new American subsidiaries, which had been organized into two groups. Elsevier Information Systems Inc. comprised three subsidiaries. The Congressio-

Company Perspectives:

Our priority will be to develop our products in tune with our customers' needs, and our success will be based upon quality products and information services at appropriate prices. In each of these businesses, we must strike the right balance between building our services in electronic media and optimising the performance of our traditional print activities.

nal Information Service (CIS), based in Bethesda, Maryland, was Elsevier's first American acquisition, in 1979. CIS issued information from American and international government sources and archive material on scholarly subjects, on microfiche and microfilm. The Greenwood Publishing Group, based in Westport, Connecticut, specialized in reference works and books on the humanities, business, and law, and included the Praeger, Bergin & Garvey, and Auburn House imprints. Elsevier Realty Information, Inc. (ERI), of Bethesda, Maryland, was an amalgamation of Redi and Damar, two companies acquired in 1988. It distributed information on property to professional customers and published real estate maps of most major cities in the United States.

Elsevier Business Press group consisted of four subsidiaries. The Springhouse Corporation of Springhouse, Pennsylvania, acquired in 1988, published a range of journals, books, and videotapes for healthcare and education professionals and small and medium-sized businesses. Delta Communications of Chicago specialized in magazines for various industries, such as *Modern Metals* and *Packaging Digest.* Gordon Publications of Morris Plains, New Jersey, acquired in 1985, issued nearly 20 product news publications. Finally, the Excerpta Medica International group, based in Princeton, New Jersey, as successor to the Excerpta Medica company acquired in 1971, published the highly successful Excerpta Medica Database (EMbase), which was an annual compilation of abstracts of more than 300,000 items of medical literature, as well as other publications on medicine.

In 1985 Elsevier expanded into the flourishing business of educational courses and materials, in the Netherlands and in Belgium, through its subsidiary Elsevier Opleidingen (Elsevier Training Institutes). Its other European operations comprised the Pan European Publishing Company (Pepco) of Brussels, which issued product news tabloids in English; Misset Publishers, based in Doetinchem, which led the Dutch market for trade journals; Bonaventura of Amsterdam, which published the weekly news magazine *Elsevier* and many other periodicals; and Argus of Amsterdam, publisher of the *Grote Winkler Prins* encyclopedia and other Dutch-language reference books.

Not all of Elsevier's attempts at expansion were successful. The group began a long campaign to take over Kluwer, which was then the third-largest publisher in the Netherlands, in 1987. Kluwer, which had a similar range to Elsevier's, but preferred to develop its Dutch market, resisted the attempt, even when Elsevier lowered its sights to trying for 49 percent of its rival's shares. In order to finance this operation Elsevier itself had to issue new shares, which were bought mainly by the British media magnate Robert Maxwell, who ended up with a holding of nine percent in Elsevier. The next step was a merger between Kluwer and its main shareholder, Wolters Samsom, to form Wolters Kluwer, which temporarily took Elsevier's place as the second-largest Dutch publisher. Eventually Elsevier ended up with 28 percent of Wolters Kluwer. It sold these shares in 1990, yet announced that it had not abandoned the idea of an eventual merger with Wolters Kluwer.

In 1988 Elsevier formed a publishing alliance with Pearson plc, a publishing conglomerate based in London, which owned the *Financial Times*, Viking Penguin, Longman, and several other media companies. Also in 1988 Elsevier successfully resisted a takeover bid by Maxwell Communication Corporation, the holding company owned and operated by Robert Maxwell. By 1991 Pearson owned 22.5 percent of Elsevier shares, while Elsevier held 8.8 percent of Pearson's equity. In April 1990 the two groups announced that they would not proceed with any further moves toward merging because of the legal and fiscal problems such moves would bring. In March 1991 Pearson sold all of its Elsevier shares to the merchant bank Goldman, Sachs, which was to sell them on to other investment institutions. One month later Elsevier decided to sell its holdings in Pearson in its turn.

Dagbladunie, Elsevier's newspaper subsidiary, was to have merged with a rival group, Perscombinatie, until negotiations were abandoned in 1989. The same year saw strikes by printers and journalists at the *Algemeen Dagblad*, which led to a slight fall in the paper's circulation. In 1990, however, both of the national newspapers in the subsidiary significantly increased their circulation, taking readers away from their rivals, while the three regional newspapers improved their advertising revenue. The decision to invest in extra color printing capacity, to come into operation by 1995, represented a vote of confidence in the future of all five titles.

Like other companies which have been successful in one sector of the media, Elsevier started to cross into other sectors. The group owned 50 percent of the film financing partnership Elsevier Vendex Film CV—perhaps best known for producing Peter Greenaway's recent films—and in 1990 it bought 19 percent of RTLVéeronique, a company based in Luxembourg, which produced television programs for satellite broadcast.

Between 1984 and 1990 Elsevier's net income quadrupled as its directors carried out a policy of shifting resources away from less international, less specialized, and less profitable areas, such as consumer magazines, toward the heights of international, specialized, and very profitable scientific publishing, for which the market tended not to be much affected by the ups and downs of the wider economy. In 1989 alone, for example, Elsevier Science Publishers added another 30 titles to its list of periodicals, most of them acquired rather than newly launched. As a result of these and other ventures Elsevier's net profits reached Dfl 500 million in 1990.

In 1991 Elsevier added to its list of subsidiaries the biggest single acquisition it had ever made, the British scientific publisher Pergamon Press, which it intended to maintain separately from Elsevier Science Publishers. Elsevier paid £440 million for Pergamon, most of which went to its founder, Robert

Key Dates:

1880: Five Dutch booksellers form Uitgeversmaatschappij Elsevier, a publishing company.
1894: Reed International, a paper manufacturer, forms in the United Kingdom.
1903: Reed incorporates as Albert E. Reed & Company Ltd.
1963: The *Daily Mirror* and *Sunday Pictorial* companies become the International Publishing Corporation.
1970: International Publishing Corporation and Reed merge to become Reed International.
1979: Elsevier merges with Nederlandse Dagbladunie N.V., a newspaper group, and forms Elsevier N.V.
1979: Elsevier acquires Congressional Information Service.
1987: Reed acquires Octopus Publishing, its largest publishing acquisition to date.
1991: Elsevier purchases Pergamon Press in its largest acquisition to date.
1993: Reed Elsevier joint venture forms.
1994: Company acquires LEXIS-NEXIS, a premier information services provider.
1998: Reed Elsevier acquires Matthew Bender & Company, Inc., a legal information provider.

Maxwell, the man who had tried to buy Elsevier itself only three years before. Maxwell had created Pergamon Press in 1951 on the basis of his connections with the German scientific publisher Springer Verlag and then built it up into a major rival to Elsevier Science Publishers.

The Elsevier group, immensely profitable as it was in the early 1990s, was not without problems. The record of failure of its attempts to merge with or take over its large rivals, other than Pergamon, somewhat offset the success even of its largest acquisition. Whatever less specialized publications it chose to retain were subject to suffer from economic recession and competition from rival media groups seeking to build up strength for the European single market. Those areas of Elsevier's Dutch-language activities which depended on advertising revenue—especially newspapers and general-interest magazines—might also have been adversely affected by competition from commercial television, which reached the Netherlands at the end of 1989.

The History of Reed International

The beginnings of Reed International date to 1894, when Albert Reed bought Upper Tovil paper mill at Maidstone, Kent. He was then 48 and already successful in paper manufacturing. After going into the paper business as a boy he had become a manager, and then part owner, of a number of paper mills in different parts of the country, but Upper Tovil was the first that was entirely his. It had been badly damaged in a fire when he bought it, so he was able to install new machinery before reopening it.

Over the years Reed had experimented with different materials and machinery to produce types of paper suitable for the halftone blocks that were then being introduced. At his new mill he specialized in these papers and soon built up a good trade with the publishers of illustrated magazines. Within two years he had more than 100 employees and had installed a new machine. When Upper Tovil had been expanded to its limit, Reed bought other mills, owning seven by 1903. In that year the business was incorporated as Albert E. Reed & Company Ltd., to enable more capital to be raised.

One of the firm's best customers in its early days was the publishing business of Harmsworth Brothers. This connection chiefly fueled Reed's growth from 1904 onward. Alfred and Harold Harmsworth, shortly to become Lord Northcliffe and Lord Rothermere, respectively, had built up the most dynamic publishing business in London. Only 15 years after launching their first magazine, *Answers*, they controlled a string of magazines and newspapers, including the successful *Daily Mail.* They had one failure, however, a new paper aimed at women, called the *Daily Mirror.* To save it they decided to relaunch it in 1904 for a general readership as an all-picture paper, using a new grade of fine newsprint introduced by Reed. In this form the *Daily Mirror* became a success, and the Reed paper business grew with it. By the outbreak of World War I in 1914, the *Daily Mirror* was the largest-selling daily newspaper in the world, and Reed was supplying the newsprint not only for that but also for several national newspapers. The company took over more paper mills in the United Kingdom and invested in pulp mills in Norway and in Newfoundland, Canada.

World War I put a temporary stop to Reed's growth. Supplies of pulp from Scandinavia were cut off, newspapers became smaller, and Reed was forced to close some of its mills. At the same time the Newfoundland venture proved uneconomical. Reed sold it to his friends, the Harmsworths, who were developing their own pulp mill nearby. Soon after World War I another financial crisis was precipitated by Albert Reed's death in 1920. His twin sons, Ralph and Percy, were determined to carry on the business, but a large sum had to be found to pay the duty on their father's estate and, in any case, some members of the family wanted to turn their shares into cash. Once again, the Reeds turned to their largest customer. Lord Northcliffe had died, but Lord Rothermere agreed to buy a large block of shares in Reed, through the *Daily Mirror* and *Sunday Pictorial* companies, which he now controlled. The Reed brothers still had voting control, but Rothermere's holding of around 40 percent of the equity rendered him a major influence in its affairs. He seems to have made little use of this influence, having had many other business commitments, but half a century later this shareholding was to change the nature of Reed's business.

The Reed brothers began to implement the plan for the company that their father had conceived during the war. This was to sell their remaining overseas operations and most of their U.K. mills and concentrate their resources on a single, modern plant, using the largest machines available. In this way they hoped to undercut all competition. A site was selected at Aylesford, a few miles downriver from Tovil, and the new mill began production in 1922.

The new strategy worked well. Despite the Depression the Aylesford plant was steadily expanded and, by 1939, was the largest of its kind of Europe. Newsprint remained the company's chief product, but from 1929 onward Reed also made kraft paper from which it produced corrugated board and paper sacks. With these new products the company captured a large share of the packaging market.

During World War II production had to be drastically reduced because of lack of pulp and did not regain prewar levels until 1950. The next few years were a boom period for Reed. The company added to its newsprint and kraft manufacturing capacity, expanded into new forms of packaging, entered the paper tissue market in a joint venture with Kimberly-Clark, and invested some of its profits in pulp mills overseas. Within seven years Reed's work force doubled to 14,000.

In the late 1950s, however, conditions changed for the worse. First the government put an end to the price-fixing arrangements that Reed had with other paper manufacturers, and then to the tariffs that had shielded the U.K. paper industry from Scandinavian competition. This latter change was the result of U.K. membership in the European Free Trade Area and was to be introduced over several years, but its implications were clear from 1959. Without the tariffs, newsprint and kraft made from imported pulp would be unable to compete with Scandinavian products. Reed would have to make major changes.

It was unfortunate that the company had to face this crisis with a relatively untried management. Sir Ralph Reed had retired in 1954, ending the era of family control, and his most able colleague, Clifford Sheldon, had died a few years earlier. Both the new chairman and managing director came from outside the paper industry. They took prompt steps to reduce the company's dependence on imported pulp but could not prevent a slide in profits. In 1960 the company's largest shareholder decided to intervene.

This was no longer Lord Rothermere, who had sold his shares in the *Daily Mirror* in the 1930s, but a new group that had been created from the nucleus of the *Mirror*. The latter paper and the *Sunday Pictorial* had declined in the 1920s under Rothermere's ownership but had recovered under his successors. In the late 1930s a new team led by Guy Bartholomew and including Cecil King, a nephew of Lords Northcliffe and Rothermere, had completely restyled the two papers. Now they were aimed at younger, working class readers. Through a mixture of populist style and radical campaigning on social issues, they captured most of this market during the unsettled war years and increased their hold on it in the more prosperous times that followed. The combined circulation of both papers rose from around one million in the 1930s to more than five million in the 1960s.

From the large profits that flowed from this success, Cecil King, who became chairman in 1951, began to build a broad-ranging publishing group. It bought further newspapers, in Scotland and abroad, and a stake in one of the first commercial television companies in the United Kingdom, Associated TV, which proved to be highly lucrative. King next turned his attention to magazines. In 1958 he bought Amalgamated Press, the magazine group founded by his uncles, then Associated Iliffe Press, and finally Odhams Press. This included newspapers as well as the Odhams, Newnes, and Hulton magazine groups. When the Mirror and Pictorial companies became the International Publishing Corporation (IPC) in 1963, it was by far the largest publishing group in the United Kingdom. It had four mass circulation newspapers, all of the leading women's magazines, a host of specialized magazines and directories, and no less than 25 printing plants.

Through this period of upheaval the *Mirror* and *Pictorial* companies had held on to their shares in Reed, which they saw as a substantial asset, to be protected and developed. When its future began to look uncertain, King obtained voting control of Reed by transferring to it all of the pulp and paper mills owned by Mirror and Pictorial. In 1963, while retaining the chairmanship of IPC, he made himself chairman of Reed and installed one of his senior managers, Don Ryder, as managing director.

Don Ryder was a former financial journalist who had shown a flair for management. Under his vigorous lead, Reed expanded and diversified. Its success in packaging and its growing overseas interests had already reduced its dependence on the U.K. newsprint and kraft business, and Ryder speeded up this process by a series of takeovers. First he bought companies in other branches of the paper and packaging industry. Then in 1965 he successfully bid for The Wall Paper Manufacturers (WPM), a large but sleepy company that then had a virtual monopoly of the wallpaper market in the United Kingdom. It also included a paint business and Sanderson fabrics. In the same year, Reed bought Polycell Holdings, which made Polyfilla and other decorating products. With these brands Reed acquired instant dominance of the fast-growing do-it-yourself market. Then, through further takeovers, Ryder took Reed into bathroom equipment and other building products. By 1970 the company could be described as a conglomerate. Its work force had grown to 56,000. The enlargement of its share capital had freed it from IPC's control, and its market value had risen well above that of IPC.

Meanwhile, IPC had run into difficulties. The worst of these concerned the *Daily Herald,* a Labour Party newspaper owned jointly by Odhams and the trade unions, which lost money steadily. IPC persuaded the trade unions to relinquish their share and relaunched the paper as the *Sun*. This was no more successful and was finally sold to Rupert Murdoch at a very low price. In addition, there were serious losses on the printing side of IPC. Many of the works it had acquired in its takeovers were found to be obsolete and had to be closed down or modernized at further cost.

Finally, King's activities created a problem. Instead of tackling the company's financial difficulties, he became increasingly preoccupied with politics. The *Daily Mirror* had helped to get the Labour government elected in 1964, and afterward King felt that it should listen to his views. When it did not, he turned on Labour with irrational fury. In 1968, on the front page of the *Daily Mirror,* King demanded the prime minister's resignation. King's colleagues at IPC felt that he was misusing the paper's power and forced him to resign.

King was succeeded by Hugh Cudlipp, a brilliant editor but a poor businessman. Afterward, he admitted that his chairmanship of IPC was "uninspired." The company's decline continued and takeover rumors began. As IPC still owned 27 percent of Reed, and Ryder could not allow it to fall into unfriendly hands, he and Cudlipp agreed in 1970 that Reed should take over IPC.

The combined company was named Reed International, incorporating art of IPC's name, and its turnover made it the 30th largest U.K. company. Its work force numbered 85,000, and its business spanned more markets than at any time before or since. Reed's position in most of these markets, however, was far from secure.

The U.K. paper business was still contracting, and Reed had to close down some operations in the 1970s. Its Canadian pulp and paper business was only intermittently profitable. The printing business inherited from IPC continued to lose money, even after the older plant was closed, and Reed failed to deal with its overmanning. WPM faced increasingly tough competition in wall coverings and saw its market share steadily erode. Newspaper circulations in the United Kingdom were declining and all of IPC's nationals lost ground. It was the *Sun's* recovery under Murdoch that hit the *Mirror* hardest.

In the early 1970s Ryder kept profits moving upward, by rationalizing in the weaker areas and increasing investment in the stronger ones. Indeed, his reputation as a manager was so impressive that at the end of 1974 he was plucked from Reed by the government to head its new National Enterprise Board. His successor, Alex Jarratt, continued to implement Ryder's policy, but it was no longer working. In 1975–76 the company's profits fell by more than 50 percent, and in the next few years made only a partial recovery.

Only in 1978 did the company recognize that the expansion policy initiated by Ryder had failed in the long run. Turnover had grown tenfold in his 11-year reign, but profits had grown much more slowly, and the outlook was poor. Jarratt decided to dispose of its unprofitable parts. Most of the overseas subsidiaries were sold, and the work force was reduced to 60,000. Nevertheless, 1980–81 saw another halving of profits, and another round of cutbacks began, this time mainly in the U.K. paper division.

In 1982 a new chief executive was appointed, Leslie Carpenter, who had come up through the magazine division of the company. The next annual report pointed out that 60 percent of the company's trading profit was coming from the 40 percent of its turnover that lay in publishing. From that time onward, new investment was concentrated in this area. Local newspaper chains were acquired in the United Kingdom, together with publishing and exhibition companies in the United States, where the Cahners subsidiary, a magazine publisher wholly owned since 1977, was thriving.

At this time the company's publishing activities still included U.K. national newspapers. Despite the introduction of photo-composition, these were far less profitable than the magazines. In 1984 Reed decided to float them as a separate company. ''National newspapers do not sit easily in a large commercial corporation,'' said Carpenter. The move was forestalled by a takeover bid for the newspaper group, which was accepted. This was from Robert Maxwell, who had already bought the Odhams gravure printing works from Reed.

Reed was thus left with a flourishing magazine business on both sides of the Atlantic and a miscellany of less profitable manufacturing businesses—the much-reduced paper and packaging division, as well as paints and building products. During Carpenter's time as chief executive there were further disposals in the manufacturing area, and the final moves to abandon manufacturing were made under his successor, Peter Davis, who became chief executive in 1986.

The most significant change came in 1987. In that year the paints and do-it-yourself division was sold, and Octopus Publishing was bought. Octopus, which cost Reed £540 million, was the largest publishing business the company had acquired since IPC. It was a diversified international publishing group with a major presence in mass market nonfiction books, fiction and general trade books, children's books, educational books at both the primary and secondary level, and in business and technical books, and greatly increased Reed's strength in these areas. Its founder, Paul Hamlyn, moved to Reed with the business and became the company's largest non-corporate shareholder.

Paper and packaging, for so long Reed's sole business, was the last of the manufacturing divisions to go. It was bought in 1988 by its own management, taking the name Reedpack, and two years later was sold again to a Swedish company, Svenska Cellulosa. Reed also sold its North American paper group to Daishowa Paper Manufacturing Co., Ltd. in 1988.

With Reed now a purely publishing concern, Davis quickly moved to bolster the company's position through acquisitions. In 1989 Reed purchased the U.K. consumer magazine *TV Times*. Later that same year, £535.4 million was spent to buy the Travel Information Group, a U.S. travel guide producer, from the News Corporation. The following year Reed enlarged its presence in the area of legal publishing with the purchase of the American firm Martindale-Hubbell. Martindale-Hubbell was subsequently merged into Reed's existing legal publisher, R.R. Bowker, and complemented Butterworths, the legal publisher in the United Kingdom, also owned by Reed. In 1991 Marquis Who's Who, publisher of biographical directories, and the National Register Publishing Co., publisher of business directories, were purchased from the Macmillan directory division for $145 million.

Davis became chairman of Reed in 1990. By the following year, thanks to Davis's acquisitions, Reed had grown to become the third-largest publisher in Europe, trailing only Germany's Bertelsmann and France's Hachette. Although 1991 sales were only slightly higher than sales when Davis took over, profits had increased from £100 million to £251 million.

The Reed Elsevier Joint Venture: 1993

In 1992 Davis made his boldest move yet by engineering a merger with the Dutch publisher Elsevier N.V., which was then the world's leading publisher of scientific journals. At the start of 1993, Reed International and Elsevier were transformed into holding companies, each holding equalized stakes in the joint venture. To reflect Reed's larger capitalization, Reed gained a 5.8 percent stake in Elsevier. Both companies held a 50 percent stake in the newly formed Reed Elsevier plc, which became the parent company for all of Reed's and Elsevier's publishing businesses. Also newly created was Elsevier Reed Finance B.V., which became the parent company for the companies' financing and treasury companies. Reed International held 46 percent of Elsevier Reed Finance, and Elsevier held 54 percent. The Reed Elsevier joint venture immediately vaulted into the list of the top ten publishing companies in the world, with combined annual revenue of $4.5 billion.

However, tensions between the Anglo and Dutch partners surfaced following the agreement, and though Reed Elsevier existed as a joint venture, Reed International and Elsevier did not formally merge. The most noteworthy dispute came in 1994 when Davis resigned in a power struggle won by the Dutch. Initially, Davis served as co-chairman of Reed Elsevier, along with Pierre Vinken, who was also chairman of Elsevier. Davis was slated to become sole chairman when Vinken retired in 1995. But the Dutch pushed for a collective style of leadership whereby the four-person executive committee (two from Reed, two from Elsevier) would manage collectively. When the board voted for the Dutch approach, Davis resigned and was succeeded as Reed International chairman by the second-in-command, Ian Irvine.

Meanwhile, Reed Elsevier concluded several significant acquisitions. In 1993 Official Airline Guides was bought from the bankrupt Maxwell for $425 million. The American market was targeted next. First, both Reed International and Elsevier had their stock placed on the New York Stock Exchange. Later that year, Reed Elsevier took a huge plunge into the online publishing world by acquiring LEXIS-NEXIS, which offered a number of online information services in the legal, news, and business fields, from Mead Corp. for $1.5 billion. The purchase instantly doubled the amount of Reed Elsevier revenue derived from electronic publishing from ten to 20 percent.

Strengthening and Focusing Core Operations: 1995 and Beyond

By 1995 Reed Elsevier was operating in four main publishing segments: scientific, professional, business, and consumer. The consumer segment, which included magazines, newspapers, and books, was the most troublesome of these and did not fit well with the other three segments. That year Reed Elsevier decided to divest of non-core businesses to focus on building its scientific, business, and professional divisions. As a result, newspaper businesses in the Netherlands and the United Kingdom and consumer magazines in the United States and the Netherlands were sold in five separate transactions for $1.1 billion in late 1995. Reed Elsevier also announced plans to sell its consumer book publishing business, which the company eventually completed in 1998 when it sold IPC Magazines, the U.K. magazine publishing arm.

Reed Elsevier's scientific division provided information on the life sciences, chemistry, and physical sciences and was a global leader in the scientific publishing category. To maintain its leadership position, Reed Elsevier adopted an aggressive acquisition strategy and focused on internal growth as well. In 1997 the company purchased MDL Information Systems, Inc., a U.S. software systems and information database developer geared toward the scientific community, and the following year made several journal acquisitions, including the *American Journal of Ophthalmology* and *MAGMA,* the journal of the European Society for Magnetic Resonance in Medicine and Biology. The purchase of JAI Press/Ablex Publishing boosted Reed Elsevier's offerings in the ''soft'' sciences, which included social sciences, business, and economics. Reed Elsevier also acquired the Beilstein Database, an online database of about eight million chemical structures, in 1998, allowing the company to better serve science specialists.

In 1998 Reed Elsevier launched *ScienceDirect,* an online scientific database that contained nearly 400,000 scientific articles from more than 1,000 journals. The company also introduced a number of new titles, including such specialized journals as *Materials Science,* which focused on semiconductor processing, *Ocean Modelling,* a journal covering ocean and atmospheric data management, *Environmental Science and Policy,* and *Integrative Medicine,* which offered the latest developments in alternative and conventional medicine. In Europe Reed Elsevier launched *EMCALL,* an electronic service that linked drug companies with medical experts.

Reed Elsevier worked to further enhance its offerings in the legal category, particularly in order to transform LEXIS-NEXIS into a full-service provider in the legal information market. Reed Elsevier formed a joint venture with Times Mirror Company in 1996 to own and manage Shepard's Company, a U.S. legal citation business. A year later Reed Elsevier acquired Tolley Publishing Company, a British publisher of legal and tax publications, and formed LEXIS-NEXIS Europe to serve European markets. In 1998 the company used the proceeds from the sale of the consumer books division to acquire Matthew Bender & Company Inc., a U.S. publisher of legal information, for $1.65 billion. The firm also acquired the remaining 50 percent interest in Shepard's from Times Mirror.

LEXIS-NEXIS continued to refine its services in the late 1990s to maintain its dominance in the highly competitive online information services category. LEXIS Online, which handled legal information, implemented improvements and new features to its web browser product, *LEXIS-NEXIS Xchange.* NEXIS Online, the business arm, launched *LEXIS-NEXIS Universe,* a web browser product geared toward the business market. Other online services launched in the legal field in 1998 included *lawyers.com,* a service that linked small law firms with prospective clients, and *Butterworth Direct,* an online legal information service in the U.K.

Reed Elsevier's business group published a wide array of business magazines, newspapers, and directories and also provided online services and organized international events. Demand in the business information industry continued to grow, and Reed Elsevier's strategy was to provide specialized products and information to strengthen and expand its reach. In 1997 the company acquired Chilton Business Group, a U.S. business information publishing company, for US$447 million. Included in the purchase were Chilton's research division, which provided research services to U.S. companies, Chilton's exhibitions group, and the trade magazines division, which included 39 titles. Chilton was merged with Reed Elsevier's Cahners Publishing Company to form Cahners Business Information. The purchase boosted Cahners' trade magazine offerings to more than 130.

In the late 1990s the business group extended its reach in various sectors. For example, in 1998 Cahners introduced *Home*

Accents Today and *Kids Today* to enhance the company's products in the retail furnishing market, which included *Furniture Today* and *Home Textiles Today.* The business division also continued to develop its electronic publishing operations in order to provide a growing number of titles through electronic delivery, a fast-growing medium. One web site, *Manufacturing Marketplace,* for instance, signed up more than 150,000 registered users in a year. Reed Elsevier's exhibition group showed strong growth as well, though demand in Asia fell as a result of poor economic conditions. In 1998 the exhibition division launched 26 new shows and signed on several new events, including the Cannes Boat Show and two golf equipment events from the Professional Golfers Association of America.

Though Reed Elsevier demonstrated tireless activity since its founding in 1993, the company did not face an entirely smooth road as it endeavored to streamline and strengthen operations. In 1997 the company revealed a proposed merger with Wolters Kluwer N.V., renewing Elsevier's old interest in acquiring the Dutch publisher. One year later, however, the company announced that merger talks had been abandoned because the companies were unable to reach mutually agreeable terms. Poor market conditions in the late 1990s affected some of Reed Elsevier's operations, and the rapid changes and volatility of the publishing and information services markets continued to provide challenges. The company was determined to rise to the challenges, however, and planned to continue growing and increase profitability through acquisitions, internal growth, and innovation. To further prepare for the future, Reed Elsevier abandoned its collective management structure in 1998 and opted to appoint a single CEO. Crispin Davis formally became the company's new CEO in September 1999, as well as the CEO of Reed International plc and chairman of the executive board of Elsevier N.V.

Principal Divisions

Scientific; Professional; Business.

Principal Operating Units

Elsevier Reed Finance BV (The Netherlands); Reed Elsevier Legal Division; Butterworths; Cahners Business Information (United States); Cahners Travel Group (United States); Editions du Juris-Classeur (France); Editions Scientifiques et Médicales (France); Elsevier Business Information (The Netherlands); Elsevier Opleidingen (The Netherlands); Elsevier Science (The Netherlands); Elsevier Science); Elsevier Science Inc. (United States); LEXIS-NEXIS (United States); Matthew Bender (United States); OAG Worldwide; Reed Business Information; Reed Educational & Professional Publishing; Reed Exhibition Companies; Springhouse Corporation (United States); Excerpta Medica Communications; MDL Information Systems, Inc.; LEXIS Law Publishing; Shepard's Company; Martindale-Hubbell; Congressional Information Services; REZsolutions, Inc. (United States; 67%); Tolley Publishing; Dott. A. Giuffre Editore (Italy; 40%); Verlag Orac (Austria); Stämpfli Verlag (Switzerland; 40%); Wydawnictwa Prawnicze PWN (Poland; 50%).

Principal Competitors

Reuters Group plc; The Thomson Corporation; Wolters Kluwer N.V.

Further Reading

Bannon, Lisa, and Kimberley A. Strassel, ''Reed Elsevier to Buy Two Units of Times Mirror,'' *Wall Street Journal,* April 28, 1998, p. A3.

''A Bigger, Better? Reed and Elsevier,'' *Economist,* September 19, 1992, p. 83.

Blackhurst, Chris, ''Dinosaur's New Lease on Life,'' *Management Today,* January 1992, p. 12.

Blankenhorn, Dana, ''Reed Elsevier Press On; New Name Close,'' *Business Marketing,* February 1, 1998, p. 2.

Chapters from Our History, London: Reed International, 1990.

DuBois, Martin, and Janet Guyon, ''Britain's Reed Agrees to Merge with Elsevier'', *Wall Street Journal,* September 18, 1992, pp. A2, A7.

Evans, Richard, ''Playing House: After Nearly Three Years, Reed and Elsevier Still Haven't Consummated Their Marriage,'' *Financial World,* August 1, 1995, p. 37.

Hayes, John R., ''The Internet's First Victim?,'' *Forbes,* December 18, 1995, p. 200.

Hochwald, Lambeth, ''Reed Elsevier: The Dancing Elephant,'' *Folio: The Magazine for Magazine Management,* September 1, 1994, p. 58.

House, Richard, ''A Marriage for the '90s,'' *Institutional Investor,* February 1993, p. 99.

Hudson, Richard L., ''Reed Elsevier Enters Big Leagues of OnLine Services,'' *Wall Street Journal,* October 6, 1994, p. B4.

Marcom, John Jr., ''Down to Earth, Mostly,'' *Forbes,* October 29, 1990, pp. 57, 61.

Pope, Kyle, ''Reed Elsevier May Use Its Cash Hoard on Acquisitions, Possibly in the U.S.,'' *Wall Street Journal,* March 14, 1996, p. A15.

Prokesch, Steven, ''Britain's Low-Profile Publishing Giant: Reed International, Big in America, Treads Carefully as It Grows,'' *New York Times,* February 9, 1992, p. F5.

Reed International: Developments in a Company History, 1960–1974, London: Reed International, 1980.

Skeel, Shirley, ''Reed All About It,'' *Management Today,* October 1992, p. 62.

Steinmetz, Greg, and Raju Narisetti, ''Reed Elsevier Wins Bidding for Lexis/Nexis,'' *Wall Street Journal,* October 5, 1994, pp. A3, A11.

Strassel, Kimberley A., ''Reed Elsevier's CEO Search Hurts Stock,'' *Wall Street Journal Europe,* April 8, 1999, p. 13.

Sykes, Philip, *Albert Reed and the Creation of a Paper Business, 1860–1960,* London: Reed International, 1980.

''Which Way Will Davis Drive Reed?'', *Media Week,* July 30, 1999, p. 12.

Yates, Andrew, ''Corporate Profile: Reed This and Weep,'' *Independent* (London), June 16, 1999, p. 3.

—Patrick Heenan and John Swan
—updated by Mariko Fujinaka

Rotary International

Rotary International

One Rotary Center
1560 Sherman Avenue
Evanston, Illinois 60201
U.S.A.
Telephone: (847) 866-3000
Fax: (847) 866-9732
Web site: http://www.rotary.org

Not-for-Profit Service Organization
Founded: 1905
Employees: 400
Donations: $172 million (1998)
NAIC: 81341 Civic and Social Organizations

Rotary International is one of the largest not-for-profit service organizations in the world, with more than one million members actively participating in thousands of local clubs spread across 161 countries around the world. From its headquarters in Evanston, Illinois, Rotary International provides its members with the opportunity to address such issues as AIDS, homelessness, polio, lack of education, hunger, and other national and international problems. Rotary International Foundation contributes nearly $100 million every year toward humanitarian programs in which Rotary members participate and voluntarily raise funds. More than any other membership organization throughout the United States, the members of Rotary International have been able to claim that they put ''Service Above Self.''

Early History

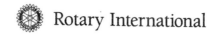

The founder of Rotary International, Paul Harris, grew up in the small town of Wallingford, Vermont, attended law school, traveled extensively after he graduated, and then journeyed in 1899 to the city of Chicago to establish a law practice of his own. Unfortunately, Harris found it difficult to find either clients or friends in the large metropolis, and he slowly began to realize that success in business went hand-in-hand with the ability to cultivate a network of the city's social elite. As his law practice struggled to establish itself, Harris came upon the idea of forming a club whose members would be businessmen in much the same circumstance as his own. By meeting once a week to have lunch and develop a fellowship among themselves, Harris also intended for the men to trade or do business with each other, thereby forming both a social and a business network at the same time. The first meeting, held in 1905, was an immediate success and the Rotary Club, named because of the rotating meetings held from office to office of the members, was off to a grand beginning.

What was unique about the Rotary Club was that Paul Harris had modeled it, not on the organization and professionalism that one found at the highest levels of the corporate sector and in the boardrooms of the most successful firms in Chicago, but on the spirit and boosterism of small businessmen who banded together for the benefit of their community and for their individual gain. Harris's ingenious adaptation of this spirit and boosterism that he found in small businessmen throughout Chicago was to argue that it was the common pursuit of one's own individual benefit that ultimately served as a foundation for a community club. In keeping with this vision, the Rotary Club stressed a jaunty informality at its meetings, where members would loudly greet each other with backslapping familiarity and anyone who said ''Mister'' or ''Sir'' was fined immediately for breaking club rules.

Within a short time, however, members of the club who originally thought it beneficial to do business or trade within the membership began to chafe at the unremitting pressure to trade only with other members of the Rotary Club. When some members began to resign, and when other businessmen balked at joining the Chicago Rotary Club, Harris came up with a brilliant idea.

He de-emphasized the backslapping business networking of the club and began emphasizing the notion of public improvement as one of the main activities of membership. Thus the Chicago Rotary Club teamed up with the Chicago Association of Commerce to fund and arrange for construction of the first public toilets in the city's burgeoning business district. By 1910, at the first annual Rotary national convention, Harris was able to persuade the majority of delegates to de-emphasize business dealings among the membership while at the same time wholeheartedly concentrating on a ''spirit of fellowship.'' When a Chicago Rotarian named Arthur Sheldon, who gave the banquet address at the first annual convention, ended his speech with the phrase, ''he

Company Perspectives:

The object of Rotary is to encourage and foster the ideal of service as a basis of worthy enterprise and, in particular, to encourage and foster: 1. The development of acquaintance as an opportunity for service; 2. High ethical standards in business and professions; the recognition of the worthiness of all useful occupations; and the dignifying by each Rotarian of his occupation as an opportunity to serve society; 3. The application of the ideal of service by every Rotarian to his personal, business and community life; 4. The advancement of international understanding, good will, and peace throughout a world fellowship of business and professional men united in the ideal of service.

profits most who serves best,'' the entire audience burst into roars of approval, and soon thereafter the phrase was voted the official slogan of the Rotary Club. From this time forward, Harris and his fellow Rotarians pursued programs that focused on community service and business ethics.

By 1910, Rotary was growing by leaps and bounds, with clubs organized in San Francisco, New York City, Boston, and the first international club established in Winnipeg, Canada. Soon, new clubs were operating in London, Dublin, Belfast, and Glasgow. The name was formally changed to ''International Association of Rotary Clubs'' in 1912, and one year later the organization embarked on its first full-scale relief effort, the collection of donations from all the clubs, both those based in the United States and those in other nations, to assist flood victims within the states of Indiana and Ohio, where flooding had left thousands of people hungry and without homes. With the advent of World War I in 1914 in Europe, Rotary Clubs throughout Ireland and England provided services to soldiers at home and at the front, including raising combat battalions, organizing special constabulary companies, and entertaining wounded soldiers. When the United States entered World War I in 1917, Rotary Clubs across the country jumped into action by mobilizing school boys for farm work, organizing Liberty Loan drives, and implementing highly effective campaigns for food, books, and tobacco for use by those men who recently had entered army training camps.

Expansion, War, and Recovery: 1920s–50s

By the end of World War I in November 1918, Rotary had granted charter number 500 to the Rotary Club of Fremont, Nebraska, and by 1921 the organization counted more than 1,000 clubs worldwide. The following year, the organization changed its name from ''International Association of Rotary Clubs'' to ''Rotary International.'' Throughout the 1920s, Rotary continued raising money from clubs around the globe for disaster relief, including thousands of dollars donated to the Rotary Club of Tokyo for the destruction caused by a devastating earthquake. During the decade, expansion continued uninterrupted with new clubs starting in such diverse countries as Guatemala, Portugal, Sweden, Pakistan, Korea, Greece, and a host of others. By 1929, there were more than 3,000 chartered Rotary Clubs, with membership amounting to more than 100,000.

With the onset of the worldwide depression in the autumn of 1929, most national economies were severely affected. This economic effect was seen in the loss of nearly 20 Rotary Clubs, which disbanded because of lack of funding and the personal financial troubles of its respective members. Yet this loss was more than offset by the continued expansion of Rotary Clubs throughout the world, including new charters for clubs in Lebanon, Kenya, Siam, Algeria, Hong Kong, Iceland, Tunisia, the Fiji Islands, Syria, Venezuela, and The Netherlands. But storms on the horizon caused by the Nazi rise to power in Germany resulted in the disbanding of almost all of the Rotary Clubs in Germany and, later, in Austria and Italy. In contrast, the clubs throughout the United Kingdom braced themselves and organized for the coming onslaught of World War II. Rotary Clubs across Britain provided funds to take care of refugees from Eastern and Western Europe and for food parcels to be sent to Allied prisoners-of-war in Germany. Near the end of the war, Rotary Clubs in Sweden and Finland implemented projects to take care of thousands upon thousands of children orphaned by the hostilities during the international conflagration.

The postwar years was a time of unprecedented growth for Rotary International. The organization held its first international conference in 1948 in Rio de Janeiro, Brazil, with members from all over the world in attendance. Rotary Clubs were established once again in Germany and Japan, as well as in other countries such as Tanganyika, Macao, and North Borneo. Thousands and thousands of food packages were sent to Rotarian families living in war-devastated areas, while Rotary International continued its tradition of raising money from clubs around the world to meet the needs of disadvantaged people. The first Rotary Foundation Fellowships, created in memory of founder Paul Harris, who died in 1947, were granted to 18 students for the 1947–48 school year. By the mid-1950s, total contributions to the Rotary Foundation exceeded $5 million, and Rotary's membership in North America alone amounted to nearly 270,000 individuals. Rotary's North American membership continued to increase slowly during the late 1950s and early 1960s, but Rotary International, like all service clubs in the United States, was about to experience a new era.

Change and Transition: The 1960s–90s

As the decade of the 1960s unfolded, club members throughout the United States began to observe the growing racial disturbances, student unrest, and political dissatisfaction with alarm, since these events were shattering the national consensus that Rotary Clubs had supported for such a lengthy period of time. In trying to renew the commitment to personal, nonpolitical interaction, however, the deep divisions caused by the civil rights movement, the Vietnam war, the shift in sexual morality, and a changing economy prevented Rotary Clubs in the United States from bridging both generational and cultural rifts. As a result of these trends, Rotary International began to emphasize and promote world community service more strongly. Rather than emphasizing home-town solutions to local problems, the Rotary membership began thinking of itself as world members and made a commitment to provide resources wherever it was most needed around the world.

During this period in its development, Rotary International slowly expanded its membership to include both African-

Key Dates:

1905: First Rotary meeting is held in Chicago.
1910: First national Rotary convention is held.
1922: The name Rotary International is adopted among the organizations more than 1,000 chapters worldwide.
1948: First international convention is held in Rio de Janeiro.
1953: Rotary headquarters moves to Evanston, Illinois.
1960s–70s: Organization's focus broadens to include such global issues as poverty and hunger relief.
1987: U.S. Supreme Court rules that all male service organizations must accept women as members.
1998: Rotary International includes more than 29,000 clubs in 161 countries.

Americans and women. As the civil rights movement gained momentum, more and more African-Americans were allowed to join Rotary Clubs throughout the United States. Previous to the 1960s and 1970s, individual Rotarians had argued that the inclusion of African-Americans would disrupt the camaraderie of white businessmen. The admittance of women members in Rotary Clubs was delayed even longer. It was not until the U.S. Supreme Court ruled in 1987 that all-male service organizations had to accept women as members that Rotary International opened its doors. From that time onward, women have joined Rotary Clubs throughout the world and have been at the forefront of the organization's efforts to provide necessary resources to disadvantaged people. By the mid-1990s, nearly 20 percent of the organization's entire membership was composed of women. In 1996 Rotary International reported that the number of clubs with women presidents grew 50 percent during that year, amounting to more than 1,700 female presidents of local clubs within the organization.

The participation of women in Rotary International has resulted in clubs across the world giving more attention to and raising more funds for women's issues, especially domestic violence, education for young girls and women in developing countries, and the need for basic health care for poor women and children around the globe. In fact, by the middle and late 1990s, Rotary International and its not-for-profit foundation were at the forefront of addressing many health care and educational issues, such as AIDS in Sub-Saharan Africa, polio vaccination and immunizations in Africa and Asia, and the lack of education provided most girls of primary school age in Latin America. With this kind of active intervention, Rotary International was able to attract 70,000 brand new members in fiscal 1996, an impressive number considering the organization was able to sign up barely more than 15,000 members the previous year.

At the end of fiscal 1998, Rotary International counted more than 29,000 clubs in 161 countries, with new Rotary Clubs springing up throughout the former Soviet Union and Eastern Block countries.

Rotary International had approximately 1.2 million members worldwide, and donations amounted to slightly more than $170 million by the end of fiscal 1998. If Rotary International can maintain its membership list and can continue to encourage the members of Rotary Clubs throughout the world that they can make a difference in the lives of people less fortunate than themselves, then Paul Harris's idea of the businessman's involvement in community affairs will be more successful than he ever envisioned.

Further Reading

Charles, Jeffrey, *Service Clubs in American Society: Rotary, Kiwanis, and Lions,* Urbana, Ill.: University of Illinois Press, 1993.

Harriman, Jarvis, *The Man from the Hills: A Biography of Leland Davidson Case,* Oklahoma City, Okla.: Westerners International, 1994.

Harris, Paul P., *My Road to Rotary,* Chicago, Ill.: A. Kroch, 1948.

——, *This Rotarian Age,* Chicago, Ill.: Rotary International, 1935.

Nicholl, David Shelley, *The Golden Wheel: The Story of Rotary, 1905 to the Present,* Plymouth, Mass.: MacDonald & Evans, 1984.

Rotary International, 1955.

International Association of Rotary Clubs, 1998.

Wolf, Alan M., "Gearing Up for Growth, Rotary Woos Women, Targets Finances," *Crain's Chicago Business,* September 9, 1996, p. 26.

—Thomas Derdak

The Rugby Group plc

Crown House
Rugby
Warwickshire
CV21 2DT
United Kingdom
Telephone: 44(0)1788 542666
Fax: 44(0)1788 540256
Web site: www.rugbygroup.co.uk

Public Company
Incorporated: 1925 as Rugby Portland Cement Company Ltd.
Employees: 10,000
Sales: £1.02 billion ($1.69 billion) (1998)
Stock Exchanges: London
Ticker Symbol: RBY.L
NAIC: 32731 Cement Manufacturing

The Rugby Group plc is one of the United Kingdom's largest producers of cement and related products, such as lime and fuel ash. After an extensive late 1990s restructuring effort, Rugby has stripped back to these core products, shedding its joinery (windows, sashes, doors, and stairs) division and U.S.-based building products distribution business. The streamlined Rugby Group now consists of Rugby Cement, Ash Resources Ltd., and Lytag Ltd. in the United Kingdom; Cockburn-Adelaide Cement in Australia, the leading cement producer in that country; a 34.4 percent stake in Cementownia Chelm, in Poland, with an option to increase its shareholding to 75 percent; and the Rugby Jamaica Lime and Minerals. In total, the Rugby Group processes nearly seven million tons of cement per year; with nearly three million tons produced in the United Kingdom, Rugby ranks in the country's top three cement makers. Meanwhile, the company has jettisoned its joinery division, which included John Carr and Boulton & Paul Ltd., sold to Jeld-Wen, of Oregon, in 1999 for $135 million; the Netherlands-based group of joinery operations, including Zeeland Kozijnen, Van Bruchem Deurenfabriek, Ge-Ka Fenster & Türen GmbH (in Germany), and De Vries Trappen; and Stegbar, the company's Australian joinery arm. In November 1999, Rugby also agreed to sell its U.S.-based distribution business to its Huttig Building Products, which in turn is to be spun off as an independent company from parent Crane Co. The selloff of these interests cut out some 70 percent of the Rugby Group's annual sales, but only 40 percent of its net earnings. As part of its reorganization, Rugby has begun looking to make acquisitions to boost its cement production operations. However, the company has also suggested that it might itself be a takeover candidate at the start of the new century.

Cementing the 19th Century

The Rugby Group began as a small family business in the early decades of the 19th century. Taking its name from its Rugby, Warwickshire location, the family-run company opened its first cement processing works in 1825. The company took advantage of the growing market for cement during the Industrial Revolution; as with many of its competitors, however, the quality of the cement produced tended to vary widely, depending on the proportions of the ingredients used. By the turn of the century, the thriving company began to initiate stricter quality controls, especially with the adoption of the so-called Portland cement method. This process was stepped up in 1925, when, after 100 years of existence, the company formally incorporated as the Rugby Portland Cement Company.

The next milestone in the company's history came with the appointment of Sir Halford Reddish as the company's managing director in 1935. Reddish was chiefly responsible for building Rugby Cement into a full-fledged corporation, expanding operations beyond its Warwickshire base by adding larger production capacity and a more extensive quarry base and acquiring complementary operations. The times were right for cement, particularly with the introduction of steel-reinforced and other, stronger cement types. As construction turned from brick to cement and steel, the Rugby Cement company was able to grow into one of the United Kingdom's largest cement producers.

In the postwar years and resulting building boom, Rugby continued to prosper. By the mid-1950s, the company sought further expansion internationally. In 1955, Rugby founded its Cockburn Cement Ltd. subsidiary, in Perth, Australia.

Key Dates:

1825: Company founded as family business in Rugby, Warwickshire.
1925: Incorporated as Rugby Portland Cement Company Ltd.
1935: Sir Halford Reddish is named Managing Director; he expands company on national scale.
1955: Cockburn Cement is established in Perth, Australia.
1984: Rugby acquires Addison Corporation of Atlanta, Georgia, to enter joinery industry.
1997: Rugby acquires Cementownia Chelm, in Poland.
1999: Merger of Cockburn Cement with Adelaide Brighton Cement (Australia).

Cockburn grew to become one of that country's largest cement and lime producers, gradually adding new kilns across the country, including its sixth kiln, brought into operation in 1997.

By the late 1980s, Rugby had branched out from its Portland cement base at the beginning of the century to offer a wide variety of cement types, including sulfate-resistant cements, cements for the offshore oil well industry, quick-drying cements, and others. In 1987, Rugby acquired Ash Resources Ltd., which produced the cement extender product, pulverized fuel ash, using byproducts from coal-based power generation facilities. In 1996, Rugby added to the division's product versatility with the acquisition of Lytag Ltd., a producer of lightweight aggregates, sports surfaces, and other lightweight cement products.

Diversifying in the 1980s

The cement industry's vulnerability to the cyclical construction industry led Rugby to look for ways to shore up its earnings during economic downswings. At the same time, the company eyed entry into the vast U.S. construction market. Rugby achieved both of these objectives when it bought the Addison Corporation, based in Atlanta, Georgia, in 1984. Addison brought Rugby into the joinery business, that is, the manufacture of doors, windows, staircases, and related products. In this way, Rugby's newest operations remained linked to its construction industry base, but diversified enough to withstand the cyclical downturns of its industry.

Rugby quickly followed the Addison acquisition with a series of smaller acquisitions that enabled the company to solidify its U.S. position. Rugby also imported the new joinery operations to its U.K. home, with the 1985 acquisition of the John Carr Group. This acquisition formed the basis of what became the Rugby Group's Joinery division in the 1990s. Meanwhile, Rugby continued to seek new acquisitions to boost its newest product line. In 1988, the company expanded onto continental Europe, purchasing the first of several Dutch and German joinery businesses, including the wooden windows companies Zeeland Kozijnen, Kuin Kozijnen, and Limburg Kozijnen; wooden door manufacturers Van Bruchem Deurenfabriek, Kegro Deuren, and Tinga Deuren; and staircase maker De Vries Trappen, among others. These companies were formed into Rugby's European Joinery Division in 1988.

In that same year, Rugby took its joinery business to Australia as well, buying up Melbourne-based Stegbar Pty Ltd. Stegbar had been founded in 1946 for the manufacture of wooden clock cases. By the end of the 1950s, however, Stegbar had expanded through much of Australia, adding new wood products, including joinery products, before going public in 1965. Stegbar continued its expansion as a Rugby subsidiary, maintaining a position as one of the leading joinery products manufacturers in Australia, with a network of manufacturing facilities and display rooms.

By the 1990s, joinery products had become Rugby's largest revenue producer. Rugby continued to build this division, increasing its European operations through more acquisitions, mostly in The Netherlands, while also expanding its operations in the United States. The U.S. operations were brought under more central control with the formation of the company's Rugby Building Products division. In addition to joinery, Rugby Building Products took on a role as a distributor for building materials and industrial building products to the construction industry, while also operating millwork facilities. In 1994, Rugby Building Products took a leap into the big leagues, with the US $61 million purchase of the building supplies division of Bunzl Inc., as that company turned toward plastics and paper-related manufacturing. The Bunzl purchase made Rugby one of the largest building products suppliers in the United States.

Streamlining for the 21st Century

The severe downturn in the worldwide construction industry, beginning with the 1988 crash in the building market, after years of overbuilding, and compounded by a slip into the long recession of the early 1990s, not only gave Rugby a number of acquisition opportunities, but also left it with a heavy debt burden. Meanwhile, the joinery division was facing added pressure. While Rugby's joinery products continued to rely largely on wood and wood materials, the construction industry had begun increasingly to adopt new PVC-based products. Rugby moved to counter this threat in 1995, buying up the United States' Pioneer Plastics Corporation, which gave Rugby an extensive line of high-quality plastic laminates and entry into the plastics construction materials market. The company also tried to shore up its joinery operations by acquiring money-losing British rival Boulton & Paul in 1997. Rugby attempted to revive the flagging Boulton & Paul, closing some of its production facilities, eliminating some 750 jobs, and placing the new acquisitions under its John Carr division with the newly created Rugby Joinery UK subsidiary. The growth of PVC in the construction industry, however, particularly the increasing adoption of PVC beyond the replacement products market into the new construction market, traditionally the preserve for wooden joinery products, placed too much strain on the company's books.

Meanwhile, a new slump in the construction industry, starting in 1995, forced Rugby to cut back on its cement operations, where the company closed two plants and dropped some 20 percent of its work force. At the same time, the company faced the retirement of the company's former chairman and the resignation of its CEO. By 1997 the new management team of Robin Gourley, chairman, and Peter Johnson, CEO, were forced to restructure the struggling company, burdened with debt and unable to build the critical mass it needed to meet the growing competition. Johnson decided to jettison any subsidiary operation unable to meet a targeted 20 percent return on assets by 1999. At the same time, the company hoped to build a war chest to place it in position to add to its core cement products division.

By November 1999, Johnson had transformed the Rugby Group from a diversified building products company to a streamlined manufacturer of cement and cement products. Pioneer Plastics was sold off in 1998. In April 1999, the company sold off its United Kingdom and Australian joinery operations, including John Carr, Boulton & Paul, and Stegbar, to the U.S.-owned Jeld-Wen, based in Oregon, for US $135 million—a price that was reportedly $100 million less than the company had hoped to receive. That sale was followed by the announcement in October 1999 of the company's agreement to sell its U.S.-based construction products and distribution businesses to Huttig Door & Sash, the Crane Co. subsidiary set to be spun off as the independent company Huttig Building Products at the same time. As part of the deal, Rugby retained a 32 percent ownership position in Huttig, making it the new U.S. building products giant's largest single shareholder.

On the more constructive side, Rugby continued to shore up its cement operations. In 1997, the company moved its cement business into the continental European market for the first time, with the purchase of slightly more than 34 percent of Cementownia Chelm, in Poland. The purchase price of BP 60.5 million gave Rugby the option to acquire up to 75 percent of Cementownia, one of Poland's largest cement makers, with an annual production of more than two million tons. In Australia, Rugby took the unusual move of merging its Cockburn cement operations with those of rival Adelaide Brighton Cement. Rugby retained a 55 percent controlling position in the newly merged company, which took on the name of Cockburn-Adelaide Cement.

These moves not only gave the Rugby Group a vastly streamlined organization and product line, but also a war chest worth more than BP 500 million. Rugby immediately signaled its interest in adding to its cement operations through acquisitions. A possible takeover target was British rival Castle Cement, which appeared likely to be put on the block by Norway's Scancem, as that company prepared to dismantle much of its operations before the end of the century. If Rugby managed to acquire Castle, it might achieve the mass necessary to maintain independent operations. Yet the question remained whether Rugby intended to continue nearly 175 years of history. In November 1999, the company announced that it had been approached about the possibility of being acquired. While no names were mentioned, the approach was expected to take the form of a formal buyout offer with the beginning of the new century.

Principal Subsidiaries

Cementownia Chelm (Poland; 34.3%); Cockburn-Adelaide Cement (Australia; 55%); Rugby Cement (UK); Ash Resource Ltd. (UK); Lytag Ltd. (UK); Rugby Jamaica Lime and Minerals (Jamaica).

Principal Competitors

Aggregate Industries; Blue Circle Industries; Cemex; Ciments Français; CRH; Franz Haniel; Hanson; Heidelberger Zement; Holderbank; Lafarge SA; RMC Group; Saint-Gobain.

Further Reading

Anderson, Simon, "Rugby Falls After Building Delays," *Daily Telegraph,* September 22, 1999.

——, "Rugby Group Has a Try To Convert," *Daily Telegraph,* July 20, 1999.

Andrew, Clark, "Rugby Ready to Kick Businesses into Touch," *Daily Telegraph,* September 23, 1997.

"Crane Co. Aims To Buy Rugby," *Times Union,* October 21, 1999.

Levi, Jim, "Rugby Group Cements Two More Deals," *Daily Telegraph,* March 31, 1999.

Potter, Ben, "Rugby's Delights May Trigger Bidding Scrum," *Daily Telegraph,* March 31, 1999.

"Rugby Group Cements Two More Deals," *European Report,* April 10, 1999.

"Rugby Receives Approach, May Lead to Offer," *Reuters,* November 1, 1999.

"Rugby Ready to spend Pounds 500m War Chest," *Daily Telegraph,* October 21, 1999.

—M.L. Cohen

Schibsted ASA

Postboks 1178 Sentrum
0107 Oslo
Norway
Telephone: (+47) 23 10 66 00
Fax: (+47) 23 10 66 01
Web site: http://www.schibsted.no

Public Company
Incorporated: 1992
Employees: 2,780
Sales: NKr 6.6 billion ($845 million) (1998)
Stock Exchanges: Oslo
NAIC: 51111 Newspaper Publishers; 51112 Periodical Publishers; 51312 Television Broadcasting; 51411 News Syndicates; 51211 Motion Picture and Video Production

After operating for more than 100 years as a family-owned newspaper business, Schibsted ASA was incorporated in 1992 as the parent company of The Schibsted Group. The firm is organized into three segments: newspapers, television and film, and multimedia. While it is involved in a broad range of media, Schibsted continues to be strongest in the newspaper field, where its subsidiary Schibsted Print Media AS owns Norway's two largest newspapers, *VG* and *Aftenposten,* as well as Sweden's *Aftonbladet,* the largest newspaper in Scandinavia, and two national newspapers in Estonia, among other holdings. The company also owns newspaper printing plants in Norway, Sweden, and Estonia.

Schibsted's television and film subsidiary, Schibsted TV and Film AS, owns one-third of TV 2, the largest commercial television company in Norway, which it helped found in 1991. Schibsted is also involved in television and film production in Norway, Denmark, and Sweden, through its subsidiary Metronome Film & Television AB. In 1998 Schibsted's production group, which is headquartered in Stockholm, became the largest independent producer of television films and commercials in Scandinavia.

Through Sandrew Metronome AB, a 50–50 joint venture with Swedish film company Anders Sandrews Stiftelse formed in 1998, Schibsted buys and distributes films, distributes videos, manages cinemas, and sells films to television companies. Sandrew Metronome is one of three companies that dominate the market for film rights and distribution in Scandinavia.

Schibsted Multimedia AS is the holding company for Schibsted's interests in the Internet, media surveillance, book publishing, and photo and news agencies. In 1997 Schibsted became a partner in Scandinavia Online AS, which is jointly owned by Schibsted and the state-owned telecommunications company Telenor. Scandinavia Online has become the leading point of entry for the Internet in Norway and Scandinavia.

Background to 1860

The name Schibsted came to Norway from Denmark in the 1750s. Schibsted ASA can trace its roots to founder Christian Michael Schibsted (1812–78), who grew up in humble circumstances and entered an orphanage in Norway's capital, then called Christiania, when he was nine. The orphanage, called Christiania Opfostingsanstalt, operated a book printing business and published the newspaper *Christiania Intelligentssedler.* Christian M. Schibsted received training there as a typesetter and printer and learned about running a newspaper.

As a young adult he worked for several of the capital's printing companies. In 1839 he joined a book printing company run by Johan J. Krohn. In 1843 Schibsted took over the company and ran it as its sole proprietor. At first he printed mainly brochures and small books. Then in 1849 he was contracted to print a recently launched satirical magazine called *Krydseren,* which translates as *The Cruiser.* The magazine became successful, and after first appearing as a monthly, became a weekly. From 1855 it was published as a liberal daily newspaper under the name *Aftenbladet.*

New Venture Becomes a Success, 1860–85

In 1859 Bjornstjerne Bjornson (1832–1910) became the editor of *Aftenbladet* and published a song in the newspaper that became Norway's national anthem. Bjornson's strong political

Company Perspectives:

Schibsted will achieve future growth and value creation as a focused Norwegian and international media company. Schibsted's ambition is to become Scandinavia's leading media company through being the preferred supplier of content to readers, viewers, and advertisers, irrespective of their choice of media.

views alienated many of the newspaper's readers, and it was sold by its editors to another printer in 1860. To replace the lost income, Schibsted launched his own newspaper, *Christiania Adresseblad.* By the end of 1860 the paper was renamed *Aftenposten.* It would eventually become Norway's leading newspaper.

Aftenposten began as a small newssheet of four to six pages. During its first ten years it became financially self-sufficient through modest growth in circulation and advertising. Its growth paralleled that of the capital and Norway's population, as well as the modernization of Norwegian society. It was also helped by the rise of towns and cities, which were gradually becoming larger, and by more efficient means of communication such as railways and the telegraph. By 1876 Schibsted was able to purchase property in the center of Christiania and buy a new printing press.

Upon Schibsted's death in 1878, the newspaper was inherited by his son, Amandus Schibsted (1849–1913), who was a gifted journalist as well as strong business manager. He pioneered modern ways of news reporting and developed *Aftenposten* into a broadly based newspaper for a wide readership. When its rival *Aftenbladet* ceased publication in 1881, *Aftenposten* picked up many of its subscribers and some of its staff.

The mid-1880s witnessed an increase in the capital's population as well as its economic activities, both of which led to an expanded market for newspapers. Faster presses were making it possible to print more copies of larger editions, while quicker access to the news made the papers more topical. With improved distribution, they reached a larger audience. It was also a time of political struggle, especially concerning the union of Norway and Sweden. Modern political parties began to appear, and newspapers generally took sides. Neutral at first, *Aftenposten* took a conservative stance. The political struggles culminated in 1884 when Norway established a parliamentary system of government.

Aftenposten's chief competitor at the time was *Morgenbladet,* a morning newspaper. When *Morgenbladet* launched an evening edition in 1885, *Aftenposten,* which was traditionally an evening paper, launched its own morning edition the next day. The burden of appearing twice daily nearly broke both newspapers, but they carried on the struggle.

Modernization, 1885–1905

By 1885 *Aftenposten* was well established in Kristiania, as the capital was named from 1877 until becoming Oslo in 1924, as a newspaper for the middle class. In 1886 a new press, the first rotary press in Norway, was installed. Amandus Schibsted was a dynamic leader, and the paper attracted well-known and highly respected writers. By 1901 *Aftenposten* had overtaken *Morgenbladet* with a circulation of 13,730.

Becoming a National Newspaper, 1905–13

The union between Norway and Sweden was dissolved in 1905. It was around this time that *Aftenposten* became allied with the conservative party Hoire, as an independent supporter, not a party organ. The newspaper would remain allied with the conservatives until the 1960s, when it declared itself independent of any political party.

With the help of improved technology, new presses, and faster communications, *Aftenposten* became a national newspaper. Its network of correspondents supplied news from all parts of Norway. The paper was one of the first in Norway to use photography, air transport, and radio in reporting the news. Norway's newspapers operated under intense and at times rough competition. New papers were launched, trade unions fought their employers, advertising price wars were common, and editors regularly traded insults and carried on feuds. Still, the press gradually embarked on a process of cooperation, and in 1910 the Norwegian Press Association was formed. That year a very popular newspaper, *Tidens Tegn,* was launched in the capital and soon became *Aftenposten*'s most serious challenger. Coverage of Arctic and Antarctic exploration was popular, and both papers sought rights to Norwegian explorer Roald Amundsen's conquest of the South Pole in 1911.

The Newspaper Business through Two World Wars, 1913–1970s

When Amandus Schibsted died in 1913, *Aftenposten* was a highly respected, hard-hitting modern newspaper. His wife, Thrine (1849–1933), inherited the paper and remained its proprietor until her death. They had two daughters, Hildur (1879–1944) and Gudrun (1861–1966), both of whom married. Hildur's daughter, Margrete Lindboe, married Leif Nagell-Erichsen (1901–66), and Gudrun's daughter, Cathrine Huitfeldt, married Hans J. Riddervold (1901–80). Both Nagell-Erichsen and Riddervold became members of *Aftenposten*'s board of directors, and in 1939 they were appointed business managers of the newspaper.

In 1935 Chr. Schibsteds Forlag, the original printing business established by Christian Schibsted, became an active book publisher when *Aftenposten* acquired the rights to publish a new annual reference book, *Hvem, Hva, Hvor,* which translates as *Who, What, Where.* Through the development of different handbooks, Chr. Schibsteds Forlag became a highly reputable publisher of handbooks on Norway. It later expanded its line to include best-sellers and high-quality illustrated books on various subjects.

Norway was occupied by German forces during World War II, and *Aftenposten*'s printing capacity was requisitioned to produce the German occupation newspaper, *Deutsche Zeitung in Norwegen,* and other publications. *Aftenposten* was published

Key Dates:

1843: Christian Michael Schibsted first takes over a book printing company.
1860: *Aftenposten* founded.
1935: Chr. Schibsteds Forlag begins publishing reference books.
1966: *Aftenposten* takes over operations of *VG.*
1992: Schibsted goes public.
1995: Company establishes Hugin AS and acquires Oslonett AS, later called Schibsted Nett.
1996: Schibsted acquires 49.99 percent of the stock of *Aftonbladet*
1997: Schibsted becomes a partner with in Scandinavia Online AS.

during the war under control of Nasjonal Samling, or National Unity, the collaborationist political party run by Vidkun Quisling, who formed a puppet administration during the war.

After World War II conditions in Norway gradually returned to normal, and the development of *Aftenposten* was resumed. At the time of its centenary in 1960, the paper was Norway's largest and leading newspaper. In 1966 it took over the operations of another newspaper, *Verdens Gang,* which translates as *The Way of the World. Verdens Gang,* or *VG* as it became known, was started in 1945 by a group from a wartime resistance movement headed by Chr. A.R. Christensen. It soon developed financial and technical problems, and *Aftenposten* took over technical production of the paper and then the company itself. As part of the takeover agreement, the two newspapers would continue to compete for readers and advertising and only cooperate in other areas, in an arrangement similar to a joint operating agreement (JOA) in the United States. In addition, the editors of *Aftenposten* committed to keeping *VG* independent from all political parties.

Tinius Nagell-Erichsen, born 1934 as son of Margrete and Leif Nagell-Erichsen, became business manager of *VG.* He then served as managing director of *Aftenposten* from 1970 until 1985. In the mid-1970s the owners of *Aftenposten* and *VG* established The Schibsted Group, a precursor to the present Schibsted corporation, as a holding company for the two newspapers. It was headed by Hans H. Riddervold (1928–80), the son of Cathrine and Hans J. Riddervold.

During the 1970s *VG* grew into a leading national newspaper. Its editorial staff was improved and enlarged, it changed from a broadsheet to a tabloid format, and it was consciously developed as a newstand, rather than a subscription, paper. In 1972 *VG* passed its main competitor, the liberal daily *Dagbladet,* to become Norway's second-largest daily newspaper behind *Aftenposten.* After building up a nationwide distribution network and taking on the role of a national newspaper, *VG* surpassed *Aftenposten* and in June 1981 became Norway's largest circulation newspaper. As publishers of Norway's two leading newspapers, Schibsted's proprietors assumed a new role within the newspaper industry and in Norwegian society. As part of a modernization program, they built a new printing plant in Oslo in 1977.

Competitive and Organizational Changes, 1980s and 1990s

Several factors affected the stable ownership of newspapers in Norway in the 1980s and 1990s. Toward the end of the 1970s and early 1980s certain interest groups began a systematic acquisition of newspaper shares. At the same time television was becoming the dominant news and entertainment medium. In 1986 The Schibsted Group, through *VG,* took over the newspaper *Tromso,* published in northern Norway. It was later sold to another northern newspaper, *Harstad Tidende.* Schibsted also launched a local newspaper for Oslo, called *Osloavisen,* on March 1, 1988, but it was closed down on November 5.

In 1990 *VG* and *Aftenposten* both began publishing Sunday editions after an absence of several decades. *VG* also began investing in related media properties. The takeover of the film laboratory Laboratorie-Service AS in 1986 in cooperation with Filmteknik AB of Stockholm marked Schibsted's first entry into the film business.

In 1988 Schibsted began reorganizing from a family-owned business to a joint-stock company. Subsidiaries were formed and the corporation Schibsted ASA was established. Tinius Nagell-Erichsen was named chairman of the corporate board of directors, and Kjell Aamot, the former managing director of *VG,* became CEO. The corporation went public on the Oslo Stock Exchange in 1992.

Recent Developments: Newspapers, 1990s

In May 1996 Schibsted acquired 49.99 percent of the total stock and 100 percent of the common stock of *Aftonbladet,* Sweden's and Scandinavia's largest daily newspaper. The Swedish Federation of Trade Unions owned the remainder of *Aftonbladet*'s stock. The evening newspaper surpassed Sweden's *Expressen* in circulation in October 1996. It can trace its history to 1830, when it was founded by the liberal Lars Johan Hierta. In August 1994 it became the first Swedish daily newspaper to appear on the Internet. In 1998 Schibsted acquired a 74 percent interest in Sweden's morning newspaper, *Svenska Dagbladet.*

Schibsted established the Eesti Meedia group in 1998 after acquiring Estonia's largest newspaper, *Postimees.* It also acquired the country's fourth-largest newspaper, *Sonumilhet.* With a staff of about 1,000, Eesti Meedia publishes nine magazines, has interests in the printing business, and has holdings in five local newspapers, in addition to publishing *Postimees* and *Sonumilhet.*

In November 1998 a new printing plant began operating at Nydalen in Oslo. It was built with an investment of NKr 1.4 billion ($179 million) and printed 4.5 million newspapers per week.

In April 1999 Schibsted launched a free newspaper, *Avis 1,* which is delivered twice a week by *Aftenposten*'s carriers to households in the Oslo area that do not subscribe to *Aftenposten. Aftenposten* subscribers can also request delivery of *Avis 1,* which has a circulation of some 200,000.

Schibsted has a one-third minority interest in *Adresseavisen,* Norway's fifth-largest newspaper and the dominant regional newspaper in Central Norway. It is published in Trondheim, the hub of central Norway. In addition, the *Adresseavisen* group has interests in six wholly or partly owned local newspapers as well as local television stations and an advertising agency. *Adresseavisen* can trace its history to 1767, when it was established by royal charter. Schibsted also has a one-third minority interest in *Stavenger Aftenblad,* the major newspaper published in southwestern Norway. It is Norway's sixth-largest newspaper by circulation and third largest by advertising volume. It was founded in 1893 and also owns a local television station.

Schibsted has a one-fourth ownership interest in *Faedrelandsvennen,* a regional newspaper for the south of Norway. It is by far southern Norway's largest media company, with a staff of 200 and seven branch offices. The newspaper first appeared in 1875. Other regional and local newspapers in which Schibsted has an interest include *Harstad Tidende,* the fourth-largest newspaper in northern Norway; *Bergens Tidende,* western Norway's major newspaper; and *Asker og Bærums Budstikke,* the local newspaper for Asker and Bærum, western suburbs of Oslo.

Also falling within the holding company Schibsted Print Media AS are Norway's national news agency, Norsk Telegrambryå, in which Schibsted has a 21 percent interest, and Scanpix Scandinavia AB, a holding company for Schibsted's Scandinavian picture agencies Scanpix Norway AS and Scanpix Sweden AB.

Recent Developments: Television and Film, 1990s

Schibsted became Norway's leading corporation in television and film in the 1990s. In addition to co-founding and holding a one-third ownership interest in TV 2, Norway's first nationwide commercial television channel, it also owns 86 percent of the Estonian television channel Kanal 2. Schibsted's television and film interests are organized under the holding company Schibsted TV & Film AS. They are grouped into three main divisions: television channels, operated by Schibsted Broadcast AS; television and film production, operated by Metronome Film and Television AB; and rights and distribution, operated by Sandrew Metronome AB.

Recent Developments: Multimedia, 1990s

On September 1, 1995, Schibsted acquired Oslonett AS, which had been formed in 1991 to provide services in connection with the Internet, e-mail, Unix, and Wide Area Networks for business users. In 1995 Oslonett changed its name to Schibsted Nett, which subsequently developed into a leading Internet supplier in Norway. By December 1996 it had 50,000 private access customers. Then, on January 1, 1997, Schibsted became a partner with the state-owned telecommunications company Telenor in Scandinavia Online AS. Telenor acquired all of Schibsted Nett's access customers and agreed to provide the technical link-up with the Internet. Scandinavia Online AS is jointly owned by Schibsted, which holds a 65 percent interest, and Telenor, which owns the remaining 35 percent. Scandinavia Online built content services with other partners and has become the leading point of entry for the Internet in Norway and Scandinavia.

In spring 1995 Schibsted established Hugin AS to provide financial products and services to large Norwegian companies. That summer Hugin launched its first product, an annual reports CD-ROM. By the end of the year Hugin Online was launched. It was one of the first commercial Internet services in Norway. Hugin Online gathers financial information for listed companies and offers a text service over the Internet. It also has a separate service in which unlisted companies can publish their financial information. Hugin AS also offers other services aimed primarily at the finance departments of large Norwegian companies.

Other multimedia ventures include the book publisher Chr. Schibsteds Forlag AS, which traces its roots to the original printing business of Christian Schibsteds. Imedia Norge AS surveys a wide range of media for clients who are interested in what is written and said about them in the media. SMS Publishing AS, based in Stockholm, is a holding company for Headhunter AB, which publishes the weekly magazine *Headhunter* for free distribution to passengers on domestic flights in Sweden, and for Svenska Forlaget live & ledarskap AB, a medium-sized publishing company that specializes in leadership seminars and runs a book club for business executives.

Schibsted established Dine Penger AS in the late 1990s to take over the activities of the publishing company Dine Pengers Forlag AS and its operating subsidiary, which publishes the personal finance magazine *Dine Penger (Your Money).* Its circulation nearly equals the combined circulation of its two chief rivals. Finally, Schibsted's multimedia photo agency, Scan-Foto AS, is a major supplier of feature and news photos from Norway and around the world.

Outlook

Schibsted has operated profitably since it became publicly traded in 1992. Revenues and profits increased at a steady pace from 1993 through 1997, but 1998 was a difficult year for the company financially. It was involved in several acquisitions and took a one-time restructuring charge in the fourth quarter. While revenues rose from 5.4 billion NKr in 1997 to 6.7 billion NKr in 1998, net profit decreased significantly from 488 million NKr in 1997 to 166 million NKr in 1998. The company's stock fell from a high around 150 NKr in 1998 to around 82 NKr at the end of the year, and its stock continued to trade between 82 and 110 NKr for most of 1999. Some 85 percent of Schibsted's revenues come from its newspaper group, and approximately 11 percent from television and film. While its multimedia division shows the fastest rate of revenue growth, it has operated at a loss for the past two years.

Principal Subsidiaries

Schibsted Print Media AS (Norway); Aftenposten AS (Norway); Verdens Gang AS (Norway); Aftonbladet Hierta AB (Sweden); Handelsbolaget Svenska Dagbladets AB & Co. (Sweden); AS Eesti Media (Estonia); Gratisavisen AS (Norway); Scanpix Scandinavia AB (Sweden); Schibsted TV &

Film AS (Norway); Metronome Film & Television AB (Sweden); Schibsted Broadcast AS (Norway); Sandrew Metronome AB (Sweden); Schibsted Multimedia AS (Norway); Scandinavia Online AS (Norway); Hugin AS (Norway); Chr. Schibsteds Forlag AS (Norway); Scan-Foto AS (Norway).

Principal Competitors

Axel Springer Verlag AG; News Corporation Limited; Bertelsmann AG.

Further Reading

Edmunds, Marlene, ''Film Giant Forms in Norway,'' *Variety,* January 19, 1998, p. 29.

——, ''Mergers Make Sense: Publishing Companies Focus on Vertical Integration,'' *Variety,* February 9, 1998, p. 61.

—David P. Bianco

SCHULTZ SAV-O STORES, INC.
PIGGLY WIGGLY SUPERMARKETS

Schultz Sav-O Stores, Inc.

2215 Union Avenue
P.O. Box 419
Sheboygan, Wisconsin 53082
U.S.A.
Telephone: (920) 457-4433
Fax (920) 208-5180
Web site: http://www.shopthepig.com

Public Company
Incorporated: 1912 as The Schultz Brothers Company Wholesale Grocers
Employees: 1,700
Sales: $484.9 million (1998)
Stock Exchanges: NASDAQ
Ticker Symbol: SAVO
NAIC: 42241 General Line Grocery Wholesalers; 42242 Packaged Frozen Food Wholesalers; 42243 Dairy Product (Except Dried or Canned) Wholesalers; 42247 Meat and Meat Product Wholesalers; 42248 Fresh Fruit and Vegetable Wholesalers; 44511 Supermarkets and Other Grocery (Except Convenience) Stores

Schultz Sav-O Stores, Inc., distributes food and other grocery items through 69 franchised and 18 corporate retail supermarkets, which operate under the trade name ''Piggly Wiggly.'' All of Schultz's stores are located in eastern Wisconsin and northeastern Illinois, but the company also has marketing rights to all of Wisconsin, additional counties in Illinois, and portions of Michigan, Minnesota, and Iowa. Schultz serves as a wholesaler to its corporate-owned and franchised Piggly Wiggly stores, as well as to a number of independent food retailers in its market area.

The company distributes grocery, dairy, produce, and frozen food products from its distribution and warehouse center in Sheboygan, Wisconsin. Fresh and processed meat and deli products are provided by a third-party distribution center in Milwaukee. Through contracts with a number of third-party vendors, Schultz also bottles and distributes its own line of carbonated soft drinks, fruit drinks, and water under the trade name ''Springtime.''

1911–50: The Schultz Brothers Meet Piggly Wiggly

The predecessor to Schultz Sav-O Stores was formed in 1911, when three brothers in Wisconsin teamed up to become a wholesale grocery distributorship. The brothers, Herman, Arthur, and Oscar Schultz, first called their new enterprise ''The Schultz Brothers Company,'' but soon changed the name to the more descriptive ''Schultz Brothers Company Wholesale Grocers.''

The brothers began by distributing nationally branded nonperishable products to local grocers. By 1928, they had developed their own brands—Schultz's Finest and Pine Hills—which they distributed along with the other, national brands. In 1946 the Schultzes expanded their wholesale operation to include fresh produce and frozen food products, adding a new building to their original facility to accommodate the expansion.

Three years later, Schultz Brothers entered into an agreement with the Tennessee-based Piggly Wiggly Corporation. The agreement, which gave the company the right to franchise the Piggly Wiggly name in Wisconsin, was to greatly influence the course of the business. Piggly Wiggly had been founded in Memphis in 1916 as an innovative ''self-serve'' grocery store. In most grocery stores of that era, shoppers did not select items from the shelf themselves. Rather, they gave their orders to a clerk, who then retrieved the specified items for them. In a radical departure from this method, Piggly Wiggly let the shoppers do the shopping. Customers carried baskets around the store, choosing items from the open shelves, then taking their purchases to the check-out stand to pay for them. Despite dire forecasts of failure, the new model was a success. Soon, Piggly Wiggly began granting franchises to independently owned grocery retailers in other counties and states who wanted to use the concept and the name.

Schultz Brothers, however, was not just another franchisee. Rather, it was a Piggly Wiggly regional franchiser, able to grant franchise rights to individual supermarket owners within the designated geographic territory. The company granted its first

Company Perspectives:

Our mission is to be the premier food distribution organization to our defined market to achieve optimum results for both our customers and the corporation by providing exceptional customer service through a highly efficient distribution network.

Piggly Wiggly franchises in Sturgeon Bay, Manitowac, Green Bay, and Kaukauna, Wisconsin. A year later, in the early 1950s, Schultz opened its first corporate-owned Piggly Wiggly in Sheboygan.

1950s–80s: Expansion on Multiple Fronts

By 1954, the Schultz operation had expanded in terms of both franchised and corporate-owned stores. To enable its stores to offer a line of lower-priced, private-label products, the company became a member of Topco Associates, Inc. Topco was a large purchasing cooperative that had been formed in the 1940s by several grocery retailers and wholesalers who wanted to combine their purchasing power and take advantage of economies of scale. Membership in the cooperative allowed Schultz to purchase and retail several lower-priced Topco brands, including the Food Club, Top Crest, and Top Care product lines. The company was also able to buy store and warehouse equipment and supplies at bulk-purchasing prices.

In 1957, to support its growing chain of supermarkets, Schultz Brothers purchased 16 acres of land and a warehouse facility in Sheboygan, Wisconsin. The Sheboygan purchase was, over the years, to evolve into a 364,000-square foot headquarters and distribution center. A few years later, in 1962, Schultz made the transition to public ownership. At that time its name was changed to "Schultz Sav-O Stores, Inc."

In the early 1970s, Schultz opened a small bottling operation within its Sheboygan warehouse facility and began bottling soft drinks, juices, and water under the trade name "Springtime." The bottling business supplied product to Schultz's franchised and corporate-owned Piggly Wiggly stores, as well as to independent supermarkets. Eventually, Schultz also began bottling soft drinks for various regional beverage distributors on a contract basis.

After 70 years of operating solely within Wisconsin, in 1982 the company purchased franchising rights for an expanded territory that included designated areas of Michigan and Illinois. Schultz soon crossed its southern border, expanding into Illinois. The company followed the same strategy in its new territory that it had followed since its inception: avoiding major urban areas and carving out a market niche in small to mid-sized cities. The company's stores themselves were scaled to fit these smaller communities: ranging in size from 8,340 to 47,000 square feet, the average Schultz Piggly Wiggly was approximately 25,000 square feet. By comparison, the huge superstores that were proliferating in the larger metropolitan areas often sprawled over more than 40,000 square feet. By keeping store size modest and catering to smaller communities, Schultz was able to avoid head-on competition with these retail giants.

Early 1990s: Fewer Corporate-Owned Stores

By the beginning of the 1990s, Schultz had grown into an 86-store chain, with more than one-third of the units corporate-owned. Sales were hovering around $480 million, with earnings approximately $2.5 million. The new decade brought a slowdown in the inflation of food prices. Whereas the 1980s had seen annual price increases of six to eight percent, the rate slowed to two to three percent in the 1990s. This meant that grocery retailers were unable to justify raising their product prices, which hurt their bottom lines.

Faced with this difficult retail environment, Schultz sought to trim costs by shedding several of its corporate-owned stores. According to Schultz board member Bernard Kubale, wholesaling product to franchisees was more economically viable for the company than running its own retail locations. "Cost cutting can be done more efficiently by franchisers," he was quoted as saying in *the Business Journal Serving Greater Milwaukee.* In 1993 the company closed one corporate store and converted four others into franchise operations. Between 1994 and 1996, two more company-owned stores were closed, and two others sold to franchisees. By the end of 1996, Schultz operated only 18 corporate-owned stores, with dramatically improved results: although the company's sales declined, its profits more than doubled between 1991 and 1995.

Mid-1990s: Focus on Marketing

In the mid-1990s, Schultz focused its attention on an aggressive marketing campaign designed to attract new shoppers and build customer loyalty. The program provided customers with an electronically read "Preferred Club Card" that, when scanned at the checkout, registered automatic price reductions on monthly and weekly store specials. The Preferred Club Card, which was valid in any Piggly Wiggly supermarket in any location, also served as identification for cashing checks and renting videos. Schultz provided additional savings to customers by aligning its Club Card system with a national marketing program operated by an outside company. Each time a Card Club customer made purchases at a Piggly Wiggly, the computer system used the UPC information from their purchases to identify related items that might interest the customer and print manufacturers' coupons for those items right at the store checkout. Schultz's card program was a progressive one, especially for a smaller supermarket chain. At the time of the program rollout, only 25 percent of all U.S. supermarkets had similar systems.

Schultz got underway with its electronic card system in 1995, installing it in 11 of its stores. By the end of 1996, 50 of the company's locations were using the system, and the remainder were up and running by the end of 1997. The card program was bolstered by a single, corporate-coordinated "Shop the Pig" advertising campaign that included weekly newspaper inserts, outdoor billboards, and radio and television spots. In 1996 Schultz unveiled its Web site, which offered location and contact information, weekly specials, contests, recipes, and product information.

The card program, in tandem with the ad campaign, proved an almost immediate success. Sales for 1996 increased 3.2 percent over the previous year—the first such increase since

Key Dates:

1911: Herman, Arthur, and Oscar Schultz form a wholesale grocery distributorship.
1949: Company enters into franchise agreement with Piggly Wiggly Corporation.
1954: Schultz Brothers Company becomes a member of Topco Associates, Inc.
1962: Company is incorporated as Schultz Sav-O Stores, Inc., and goes public.
1982: Company expands its Piggly Wiggly franchise territory to include select counties in Illinois and Michigan.
1995: The Piggly Wiggly Preferred Club Card marketing program is implemented.
1998: Company expands its franchise territory to include portions of Iowa and Minnesota, as well as more counties in Michigan, Illinois, and Wisconsin.

Schultz began selling off its corporate-owned stores in 1993. 1997 sales also showed improvement, climbing 4.2 percent over the previous year. Earnings also continued to increase, growing more than 30 percent between 1995 and 1997.

Another of Schultz's major initiatives in the mid-1990s involved upgrading and expanding the produce sections of its distribution center. In a multi-million dollar renovation, the company installed controlled atmosphere areas that created optimum storage environments for all types of produce and ensured that "fresh" foods were truly fresh when they reached their destination. These improvements at the wholesale level were echoed by similar upgrades at the retail level. Schultz began to focus on expanding the "fresh" areas of its stores, offering wider selections of fresh fruit, vegetables, meats, and bakery and deli goods. The company also began placing greater advertising emphasis on its fresh departments.

Becoming more focused on building and marketing the Piggly Wiggly brand, Schultz decided to outsource the bottling of its Springtime beverages. In mid-1997 the company shut down its bottling operation, and production of the beverage line was outsourced to several other vendors.

Late 1990s: Building up the Wholesale Business

As the 1990s drew to a close, Schultz was committed to developing its wholesale business by attracting new franchisees. The company marketed itself to potential franchisees as a "virtual chain," meaning that although stores were operated by different owners, each store received the advertising, administrative support, and purchasing power usually associated with corporate-owned stores.

In the summer of 1998, Schultz significantly enhanced its franchise growth potential by negotiating a territory expansion agreement with the Piggly Wiggly Company . Under the terms of the agreement, Schultz acquired the right to franchise or open corporate Piggly Wiggly stores in the 31 Wisconsin counties not already in its operating area. The agreement also included rights to 5 counties in southeastern Minnesota, 18 counties in eastern Iowa, 9 counties in Michigan's Upper Peninsula, and 13 additional counties in northern Illinois. The expansion gave Schultz the chance to establish a presence in 128 counties in five states. "We are very excited about gaining this additional area to expand our successful Piggly Wiggly program with either corporate or independent franchise units," Schultz CEO James Dickelman said in a June 8, 1998, press release. "We believe this will afford us many opportunities to expand our store base through a combination of new store construction, acquisition of existing stores, or conversion of stores from other wholesale programs."

Another strategy Schultz used to bulk up its wholesale business was investing in major expansions at several of its franchise locations. By increasing the selling space of stores that were performing well, the company sought to increase the amount of product those franchises purchased from the wholesale operation.

Sales and earnings continued to show modest but steady gains. In 1998 the company posted a 2.5 percent increase in sales and an 11.5 percent hike in earnings. At the midpoint of 1999, the company's sales were up by 2.3 percent over the first two quarters of 1998. Before-tax earnings were up 3.5 percent.

Looking at the Future

As Schultz prepared for the new millennium, the company planned to increase its traditionally conservative growth rate. "Clearly, our challenge is to grow this company faster than we've been able to do historically," Dickelman said in an address at the company's 1999 annual meeting. In addition to growing by opening or acquiring new Piggly Wiggly stores, the company intended to actively seek out more independent grocery retailers as customers for its wholesale operation.

Principal Subsidiaries

PW Trucking, Inc.

Principal Competitors

Albertson's, Inc.; Copps Corporation; Cub Foods Stores; Fleming Companies, Inc.; Kmart Corporation; Kohls Food Stores; Nash Finch Company; ShopKo Stores, Inc.; Supervalu Inc.; Wal-Mart Stores, Inc.

Further Reading

Chandler, Kurt, "Shopping the Pig: Schultz Selling Stores," *Business Journal Serving Greater Milwaukee*, July 27, 1996, p. 21.
Daykin, Tom, "Schultz Sav-O Stores Looks toward Expansion," *Milwaukee Journal Sentinel*, May 13, 1999.
"Schultz Sav-O Stores, Inc.: The Pig Story," http://www.shopthepig.com/tales/history.html

—Shawna Brynildssen

Scott Paper Company

Kimberly-Clark Corporation
351 Phelps Drive
Irving, Texas 75038
U.S.A.
Telephone: (972) 281-1200
Fax: (972) 281-1435
Web site: http://www.kimberly-clark.com

Assets acquired by Kimberly-Clark in 1995
Incorporated: 1922
Dissolved: 1995
Final Sales: $3.6 billion (1994)
NAIC: 322291 Sanitary Paper Product Manufacturing

Until its acquisition by the Kimberly-Clark Corporation, Scott Paper Company was a global consumer products company and the world's leading manufacturer of tissue products such as toilet tissue, paper towels, and paper napkins. Scott had an arsenal of well-known brands and dominated the American market for mid-ranged tissue paper and paper towels with its ScotTowels and ScotTissue products. Other Scott offerings included facial tissues, baby wipes, paper towels, napkins, tablecloths, plates, and plastic cutlery and cups. The company also operated the S.D. Warren Company as a wholly owned subsidiary until 1994, when it sold this leading producer of lightweight and heavy-weight coated papers. After Al Dunlap took the helm of the company in 1994, Scott shed some $2 billion worth of assets and laid off one-third of its global workforce. Although Scott ceased to exist as a corporate entity upon merging with Kimberly-Clark, its new parent company maintained many of Scott's brands.

Scott Paper Company Launched in 1879

Scott Paper Company was founded by brothers E. Irvin Scott and Clarence R. Scott in Philadelphia, Pennsylvania, in the fall of 1879. Scott originally produced ''coarse'' paper goods such as bags and wrapping paper. By the late 19th century, however, the introduction of domestic bathroom plumbing created a market for a new product, toilet tissue. Scott soon began tissue production, though Victorian mores prevented the company from launching an effective advertising campaign, so Scott sold various grades of tissue to private dealers who marketed the tissue under 2,000 individual brand names.

At the turn of the 20th century, Irvin Scott's son Arthur Hoyt Scott urged the company to begin marketing toilet tissue under its own label. He established a company philosophy that characterized Scott's marketing style well into the 1960s. Arthur's idea was to make only a few high-quality products, to sell them at as low a cost as possible, and to keep them in the public eye with high-profile advertising.

In 1902, the company made its first acquisition, purchasing the private label Waldorf from one of its customers. The oldest name-brand toilet tissue in the United States, Waldorf continued to be sold in U.S. grocery stores into the 1980s and was one of the few consumer products that had been available since the turn of the century.

In 1907, Scott introduced the paper towel. The invention was supposedly inspired by a Philadelphia school teacher who thought it unsanitary for her pupils to share the same cloth towel day after day. Whatever its origins, the paper towel, together with toilet tissue, formed the backbone of Scott's business.

A Long Period of Prosperity

As the demand for consumer paper products rose steadily, Scott hired innovative engineers to upgrade its papermaking technology. With the introduction of new machines in its Chester, Pennsylvania, plant in the early 1920s, Scott became the world's largest and most technologically advanced tissue manufacturer. In order to guarantee its growing success, Scott saw that it would be wise to acquire control of its sources of raw materials. When Thomas McCabe became president of the company in 1927, he began Scott's long-term acquisition of mills, machines, and timberland with the 1927 purchase of a Nova Scotia, Canada, pulp mill and its attendant timber holdings.

Despite the stock market crash and the Great Depression, Scott's plant was operating at full tilt in 1930; not one employee was laid off, and company sales were as high as ever. This was

Key Dates:

1879: Scott Paper Company is founded.
1907: Scott begins producing paper towels.
1915: Company goes public.
1957: Procter & Gamble promotes Puffs tissues and White Cloud toilet tissue, stealing market share from Scott.
1967: Scott diversifies operations through purchase of S.D. Warren.
1976: Scott introduces Cottonelle toilet tissue.
1993: Scott reports its all-time worst yearly net loss.
1994: Al Dunlap assumes position of Scott as chairman and CEO; announces plans to fire nearly 11,000 workers.
1995: Scott absorbed by rival Kimberly-Clark.

partly because the economic climate did not affect consumption of Scott products, and partly because Scott was the largest advertiser in its industry. As a result of its unimpeded success, Scott was able to continue its acquisition program. In 1936, it joined with The Mead Corporation to form Brunswick Pulp & Paper Company, which built and operated a pulp mill in Georgia to supply both Mead and Scott.

During World War II, Scott continued to prosper despite paper shortages. Scott's aggressive acquisition program continued during the 1940s and 1950s; the company bought mills in Fort Edward, New York, and in Marinette and Oconto Falls, Wisconsin. By 1948, Scott's sales approached $75 million. During the 1950s, Scott merged with Southview Pulp Company and Hollingsworth & Whitney Company, which provided substantial timberlands and pulp and papermaking facilities in Everett, Washington; Mobile, Alabama; and Winslow, Maine.

Throughout the 1950s, Scott's Scottie tissues and Scotkins napkins dominated the home paper products market with little competition except from Kleenex, made by Kimberly-Clark. By 1955, Scott had a 38 percent share of the sanitary-paper business, its closest competitor taking only 11 percent. During the late 1950s, Scott led the U.S. paper industry in profits and growth despite the fact that it introduced only two new products—a plastic wrap and a sanitary napkin—between 1955 and 1961. Much of the company's success lay in its impressive product research and development. Bringing out few new products, the company focused on careful development and elaborate advertising. This was the basic strategy that Arthur Scott had prescribed at the turn of the century.

New Competitors Enter the Market in the 1950s and 1960s

Scott's success could also be attributed to its virtual monopoly of its market, which began to erode with Procter & Gamble's entry into the home paper products market. Primarily a soap maker, Procter & Gamble (P&G) in 1957 acquired Charmin Paper Mills, a regional producer of facial and toilet tissues and paper towels and napkins. P&G aggressively promoted Charmin's Puffs facial tissue and White Cloud toilet tissue in their traditional market area, the north central states. By 1961, these brands began edging out Scott products in that region. Nevertheless, in 1961 Scott was the most profitable paper company in the United States in terms of profit margin and return on investment, and was not greatly disturbed by P&G's regional success. In a conservative response, Scott refused to use promotional coupons and price deals, opting instead to reduce the price of its products. With its entry, however, P&G had opened up the sanitary-paper market; by 1966, Scott had five major competitors. In addition, supermarket chains began selling their own low-cost private-brand tissues. Scott responded mildly, introducing new colors and styles for its already established product lines.

Heavy competition eventually led the company to use one of its most innovative promotional gimmicks: the launch of the paper dress. Scott had developed its Dura-Weve paper fabric with the intention of marketing disposable medical products such as linens, towels, and wipes, but in 1966 it also sold 50,000 disposable dresses for $1.25 each in grocery stores to promote its new colored tissues. While the fashion fad came and went, the development of paper fabric gave rise to such modern conveniences as P&G's Pampers, the first completely disposable paper-plastic laminated diapers. Scott's own disposable diaper, introduced in 1969, was never a commercial success.

Diversification in the 1970s and 1980s

Believing that its philosophy of specializing in just a few products was becoming outmoded, Scott also began to diversify. McCabe made Scott's first non-paper acquisition in 1965—Plastic Coating Corporation of Holyoke, Massachusetts, and its subsidiary, Tecnifax Corporation. Plastic Coating allowed itself to be bought by Scott to finance a major expansion of its coating plants. Plastic Coating needed to expand to meet the needs of its two largest customers, Polaroid and SCM Corporation. However, following the expansion, Polaroid failed to grow as expected, and SCM built its own coating plant. Moreover, the Tecnifax subsidiary, which made visual education aids, lost its profitability when the government cut back on educational funding in the late 1960s.

In 1967, Scott purchased S.D. Warren, a maker of fine book papers. Within a few years, Warren's profits were eaten up by the general advertising recession and the government cuts in educational funding, which reduced the textbook market. Brown Jordan, a maker of casual furniture, was purchased in 1968, as were two manufacturers of audio-visual aids. By 1969, Scott's sales reached their highest to that date, yet its return on equity was only 12 percent.

McCabe retired as chairman in 1969, and president and CEO Harrison Dunning took over as chairman of the board. Dunning decentralized Scott's management by instituting profit centers, and designating brand managers with responsibility for the research, manufacture, sales, advertising, and earnings of their respective products. This delegation of power cleared the decision-making bottleneck that had plagued Scott, as did Dunning's three-man president's office in which he worked with president Charles Dickey and vice-chairman Paul C. Baldwin. All three men were empowered to make a decision on any issue at any time.

By 1970, Scott's competitors in the toilet tissue market had increased to 11, and in facial tissue to seven. Both markets were fully mature, growing at about two percent annually. Between the erosion of their market share and unprofitable acquisitions costing nearly $200 million, Scott was faltering badly. Its earnings fell 18 percent by the end of 1970, at which point return on equity was down to 9.5 percent. To make matters worse, in 1971 P&G began national marketing of its Charmin toilet tissue, advertising for which soon made Charmin the most popular bathroom tissue.

Dunning's office of the chairman, as it had become, was broken up in 1971, as middle managers called for more leadership from the top. In 1972, Charles Dickey was appointed chairman. During the next five years Scott saw heavy outlays of cash—more than $700 million. More than $100 million was spent on meeting new government requirements for pollution control, and the rest went toward new plants and equipment. Business began to recover slowly with the 1976 introduction of Cotonelle, Scott's answer to Charmin. Scott's aging facilities kept production costs high, however, and by the early 1980s another capital-spending program was required to upgrade its plants and expand capacity. In one effort to raise money for the $1.6 billion, five-year spending program, Scott sold $102 million of new common stock to Canadian-based Brascan, Ltd., raising that holding company's share in Scott to 20.5 percent. Brascan agreed not to increase its holdings in Scott to more than 25 percent before 1986.

Philip E. Lippincott took over as CEO in 1983. Lippincott, who had initiated the spending program in 1981, began to reap its benefits. Profits increased 51 percent in 1984, rising to $187 million, while sales rose five percent to $2.8 billion. Scott promptly bought out Brascan, taking on a $300 million debt but eliminating any threat of takeover.

Lippincott eliminated extraneous staff and instituted an incentive program in which the top 600 people at Scott were remunerated partly according to their contribution to profits. Although most decisions at Scott traditionally came from the Philadelphia headquarters, Lippincott invested lower-level managers with more decision-making power, hoping commitment would increase if corporate strategy were developed organically rather than handed down from above. At the same time, Scott decreased its production costs by using scrap wood and wastes produced by the pulping process as fuel for its mills. In Maine, energy costs were reduced from $140 to $40 per ton of paper. A new system for transporting raw materials at the Mobile, Alabama, plant saved the company about $25 million a year in freight and inventory expenses.

The 1980s and Global Expansion

The 1980s brought a welcome spurt of growth for Scott's coated paper subsidiary, S.D. Warren. Although Warren had long been a market leader, high production costs made its profits mediocre. In 1982, Scott built Warren a new machine to produce lighter-weight papers, anticipating an increase in medium-weight paper consumption. Since other companies had predicted a decrease in demand because of the proliferation of cable television and other media, Warren was able to profit from the burgeoning market for catalog and magazine papers while its competitors were caught unprepared. As a result, Warren was responsible for 45 percent of Scott's profits in 1984, and continued to contribute at least a healthy 25 percent of total profits annually.

A full 50 percent of Scott's profits still came from toilet and facial tissue and paper towels. In the early 1980s, Scott finally found its niche in the market. While its Cottonelle toilet tissue and Viva paper towels still competed with P&G's top-quality brands, ScotTissue and ScotTowels lay claim to the title of midrange or value brands, leaving the higher end of the market to P&G and the lower end to store brands and cheaper labels. Scott's market share stabilized at 25 percent, down from its one-time peak of 50 percent but still a respectable share.

The U.S. home tissue products market remained virtually stagnant and glutted with competitors. To capitalize on its strength, Scott had to seek new venues for selling its traditional products. Scott began selling tissue products to commercial buyers such as restaurant chains and public facilities, but the real opportunities for growth lay in overseas markets. In 1982, Scott's international operations had a loss of $39 million, down from a profit of $40 million the year before. By 1986, however, Scott had rebounded and was the dominant player in Western Europe, with sales of $750 million. Anticipating the integration of the European Common Market in 1992, Scott bought out its European partners in the late 1980s so that it would not have to share its future profits, and Lippincott instituted a three-year, $250 million expansion program for Scott's European facilities.

Scott Worldwide was formed in 1987, to operate in Europe, Latin America, and the Far East. Scott planned to penetrate the latter two markets more forcefully once the European market matured. Still the world's largest producer of personal tissue products, in the early 1990s Scott concentrated on transforming itself from a U.S. company with foreign interests to a truly international company, controlling its operations on a local level rather than from its U.S. headquarters in Philadelphia. Always a specialist, Scott continued to acquire related operations such as Texstyrene Corporation, a maker of styrofoam cups, but the company primarily aimed to expand its worldwide markets rather than to diversify its product lines radically.

Difficult Times in the Early 1990s

Confident in the upgrades the company had made to its production facilities and Scott's stable market share, Lippincott led Scott to expand its capacity in 1990. This decision would prove to be disastrous. According to one observer in the *Guardian*, 1990 marked the "beginning of one of the tissue industry's worst downturns." A slew of new competitors coupled with rampant overproduction drove down prices for Scott's core brands.

Beginning in 1990, Lippincott undertook three major corporate restructurings with the goal of boosting flagging profits. Scott pledged to focus on its successful personal care products business and began to sell off operations outside this realm. In 1991, for instance, Scott divested its substantial share in the Japanese joint venture Sanyo Scott Company Ltd. and the proceeds were used to reduce mounting debt. Despite Lippincott's efforts, Scott's profits fell from $302.1 million in 1989 to

$117.6 million in 1993. *Financial World* proclaimed that Scott "hasn't been able to do anything right for the past several years." In 1994, with the announcement that pre-tax earnings had plummeted 61 percent since 1989 and that sales had remained flat, Lippincott instituted his final restructuring and announced that Scott would lay of 8,300 workers—about 25 percent of its workforce.

Lippincott left the company in 1994, and Scott recruited its first outsider to replace him. After building his reputation for reducing operations, cutting workforces, and dumping all but the most profitable divisions, Scott's new Chairman and Chief Executive Officer Al Dunlap had earned the less than affectionate moniker "Chainsaw Al." Despite the trail of unemployment he left in his wake, Dunlap was revered for his ability to return flailing companies to profitability and, more importantly, to raise share prices.

Dunlap immediately got down to business at Scott. He "has people jumping up and down. He is asking for all kinds of justification reports, analyses of what businesses the company should be in," a Scott executive told *Delaney Informed Communications* on May 30, 1994. After filling top management positions with like-minded colleagues, Dunlap put S.D. Warren on the sales block. Although Warren had become the clear-cut leader in its field, the subsidiary did not conform with Dunlap's vision of a streamlined Scott with interests primarily in tissue paper.

In August 1994, Scott announced it would fire 10,500 workers to save an estimated $400 million each year. Dunlap closed Scott's older, more costly, manufacturing plants; reduced warehouses from 60 to 19; and sold off the company's printing and writing paper production operations, Mexican joint ventures, health care and foodservice operations, as well as its energy operations. In his first nine months as CEO, Dunlap divested over $2 billion worth of assets. Scott's share price rose from $37.35 to $84.62—an increase of 225 percent in 18 months. Scott reported a $200 million profit in 1994, compared to the net loss of $277 million recorded in 1993.

1995 Takeover by Kimberly-Clark

Many analysts had speculated that Dunlap's underlying goal was to make Scott an attractive acquisition target. Such suspicions were fueled in July 1995 when Wayne Sanders, the chairman and CEO of Kimberly-Clark, confirmed that Kimberly-Clark and Scott had signed a merger agreement. The deal, which would create a $13 billion consumer products behemoth, offered Kimberly-Clark clear advantages. Kimberly-Clark could use Scott's dominance in the tissue sector, especially in the crucial mid-level segment, as part of its bid to overtake Procter & Gamble. Moreover, Scott had a powerful European division, with best-selling brands such as the U.K.'s Andrex. Kimberly-Clark, on the other hand, had not been as successful in entering European markets. The merger was finalized on December 12, 1995.

After the merger was complete, an "Integration Team" formulated a plan to unite the two companies' manufacturing operations, product lines, and workforces. More layoffs were enacted, and Scott's headquarters, as well as some office facilities, were closed. Kimberly-Clark stockholders outnumbered those of Scott in the new corporate entity, so the unified company bore the Kimberly-Clark name, and all Scott assets were subsumed within Kimberly-Clark. Nevertheless, Kimberly-Clark kept alive most Scott brands. Not only were Scott's brands the best-selling in the world, but by retaining their cachet with consumers, Kimberly-Clark could also lay claim to Scott's rich and storied legacy.

Further Reading

Harrington, Jeff, "Kimberly, Scott Talking Merger," *Cincinnati Enquirer,* June 24, 1995.

Irvine, Martha, "Scott CEO Names Ex-Colleagues to Fill Senior Positions," *Wall Street Journal*, June 2, 1994.

"Judgment Day," *Delaney Informed Communications,* May 30, 1994.

Saporito, Bill, "Scott Isn't Lumbering Anymore," *Fortune*, September 30, 1985.

"Scott Paper Raises Lay-Off Target," *Financial Post*, August 4, 1994.

"Scott Sells Shares in Japanese Business," *Associated Press*, November 21, 1991.

Sparks, Debra, "Ming the Merciless," *Financial World*, June 21, 1994.

Spector, Robert, *Shared Values: A History of Kimberly-Clark*, Lyme, Conn.: Greenwich Publishing Group, 1997, 238 p.

Tran, Mark, "Ax to Fall on Scott Paper Jobs," *Guardian*, August 4, 1994.

Usborne, David, "Merger Could Create US Paper Colossus," *Independent* (London), June 24, 1995.

Zweig, Phillip L., "Doing a Geographic," *Financial World*, July 12, 1988.

—Elaine Belsito
—updated by Rebecca Stanfel

Skechers U.S.A. Inc.

228 Manhattan Beach Boulevard, #200
Manhattan Beach, California 90266
U.S.A.
Telephone: (310) 318-3100
Fax: (310) 318-5019
Web site: http://www.skechers.com

Public Company
Incorporated: 1992
Employees: 863
Sales: $372.7 million (1998)
Stock Exchanges: New York
Ticker Symbol: SKX
NAIC: 316213 Men's Footwear (Except Athletic) Manufacturing; 316214 Women's Footwear (Except Athletic) Manufacturing

Founded in 1992, Skechers U.S.A. Inc. is one of the fastest growing footwear companies in the United States, focusing on trendy, casual styles aimed primarily at men and women from the ages of 19 to 40. With 1998 sales at almost $400 million, the company designs and markets more than 900 different styles of shoes, which are sold in major department stores such as Macy's and Nordstrom as well as in 38 of the company's own freestanding boutiques. Skechers's shoes are produced overseas at factories in China, Mexico, Brazil, and Romania, which allows the company to keep the prices of its designs below those of its competitors, and are designed to appeal to younger, active, fashion-conscious consumers. Skechers devotes much of its creative energy and revenue to flashy, highly visible ad campaigns—a strategy that has helped the company grow within a matter of years to a multimillion dollar business.

The Company's Beginnings: The Early 1990s

In 1990 the hottest selling shoe brand among young American women was called L.A. Gear, a label created and owned by a veteran of the retail industry named Robert Greenberg. Founded in 1983, L.A. Gear by 1990 was grossing more than $900 million in sales and, with its neon tennis shoes and overtly feminine image, seemed to be an unstoppable and unique presence within the industry. After a series of missteps, however, L.A. Gear took a sudden turn for the worse, and by 1992 Robert Greenberg, along with his son Michael, found himself without a job, forced out of the company he helped to create.

Greenberg was no stranger to the unpredictable vicissitudes of the retail trade, however: The executive began his career in the 1960s selling wigs to beauty shops in Boston and by the next decade he had moved on to importing designer jeans to sell at the department stores Filene's and Jordan Marsh. At the end of the 1970s Greenberg moved to Los Angeles, where he founded a chain of roller skate stores, his first entré into the footwear industry. His first big break came in 1982, when Greenberg licensed the image of the film character E.T. to appear on shoelaces—a move that netted him $3 million in less than two months. This success gave him lasting clout and recognition within the retail trade, and it was with that revenue that Greenberg founded L.A. Gear.

After Greenberg's departure from L.A. Gear in 1992, he immediately founded Skechers. Originally intended to be a distributor of Dr. Martens shoes, a British label made by R. Griggs Ltd., Greenberg within a year began to focus on designing and marketing his own brand. Utilizing the experience he gained through L.A. Gear, Greenberg began marketing Skechers primarily to young, hip consumers, although unlike L.A. Gear the focus was this time not on women's athletic wear but on casual, stylish street shoes for men. In addition, although Nike had a firm hold on men's athletic wear, there was no large, well established company against which Skechers had to compete in the market for men's street shoes, and this provided Greenberg the opportunity to help create and support a new and burgeoning niche market.

Aside from being the largest distributor for Dr. Martens shoes, Skechers in 1992 also owned and marketed the labels Cross Colours, a brand that helped put urbanwear on the retail map, as well as Karl Kani and So. . . . L.A. Although all three of these labels were successful, by 1993 Greenberg saw more financial opportunity in the development of his own label, and so he began consolidating his fiscal and creative resources to

Company Perspectives:

The Company's objective is to become a leading source of contemporary casual and active footwear while ensuring the longevity of both the Company and the Skechers brand name through controlled, well managed growth. The Company strives to achieve this objective by developing and offering a balanced assortment of basic and fashionable merchandise across a wide spectrum of product categories and styles, while maintaining a diversified, low-cost sourcing base and controlling the growth of its distribution channels.

focus on Skechers. As a result, the labels Karl Kani and So. . . . L.A. were discontinued by 1995; Cross Colours was discontinued not long after that and was sold a few years later.

Within a year of Skechers's signing of a licensing agreement with R. Griggs Ltd., the makers of Dr. Martens shoes, the two companies had a falling out, with Skechers accusing R. Griggs of failing to deliver on orders for its increasingly popular merchandise. Skechers filed a complaint against R. Griggs for breach of contract, and a complicated array of countersuits ensued. By 1993, only one year after the two companies had formed a partnership, Skechers no longer served as a distributor for the Dr. Martens brand and had to rely on its own label for survival.

Skechers U.S.A. had its first big break under its own label in 1993, with the introduction of a design known as the ''Chrome Dome.'' Appealing to both sexes, this shoe was an urban street boot that reflected the increasing popularity of the ''grunge'' look among younger consumers: the ''Chrome Dome'' shoe was made to look well-worn and scuffed at the heel—much like the stone-washed, pre-torn jeans that were so popular at the time—and presented an image of tough androgyny. The ''Chrome Dome'' design proved Skechers to be a company well aware of the quickly changing trends among young consumers, and the label soon was picked up by such stores as Foleys and Nordstrom.

Expansion: The Middle to Late 1990s

By 1995 the two-year-old Skechers was a vibrant, growing company, reflecting the many years of retail expertise of the company's CEO Robert Greenberg as well as that of the company's president, Greenberg's son Michael. In March of that year Skechers was ready to branch out, and it signed licensing agreements with the companies Genova Incorporated and Signal/American to produce casual boys' and menswear. Created under the Skechers label, the clothes were intended to appeal to the same customers who bought the company's shoes, with an emphasis on style, wearability, and comfort. The clothes, primarily fleece tops, t-shirts, and jeans, were sold at major national department stores and were produced both overseas and domestically by Genova and Signal/American.

Two years later, in 1997, Skechers was doing well enough to expand its customer base to overseas markets. That year, the company began selling its footwear in Southeast Asia, where most of Skechers's products were made, and in Eastern Europe. Because the company kept a watchful eye on the trends of the youth market, the label sold well internationally from the beginning and by 1998 accounted for 15 percent of the company's sales.

By 1998, only six years after the company's inception, Skechers had 2,200 accounts, including Genesco Federated, the May Company, Dayton-Hudson, Dillard's, Nordstrom, Woolworth Corporation, Foot Action, and Finish Line. The company also had opened more than 30 of its own stores, though it continued to focus on accounts with national department stores for the majority of its revenue. That year, demand for Skechers's products was so high the company made the unusual decision to stop opening new accounts altogether, choosing instead to focus on the expansion and quality control of existing accounts. Although the company already had begun to make its mark in women's footwear, the company at this time began to aggressively expand its womenswear line, producing funky, high platform sandals and boots that appealed to teenagers and young, urban women. With the company's new emphasis on women's shoes, as well as its introduction of a children's line, its design team increased output from 600 styles of shoes to 900 in the span of only one year.

In April 1998 Skechers revealed plans that would place the company in direct competition with such footwear powerhouses as Nike and Reebok. In an aggressive move, the company rented a 54,000-square-foot exhibit space at the World Congress Center in Atlanta, which had been occupied previously by Nike. Promising a new focus on athletic footwear, Skechers utilized that space to showcase a flashy, hip image influenced in equal measure by hip-hop, urbanwear, and sports. The exhibit space occupied by Skechers was the largest space at the Center, and the Skechers image was a ubiquitous presence at that year's trade show. The company spent $2 million on light shows, dancers, and models wearing new Skechers designs, as well as video screens flashing picture after picture of the Skechers logo. Interestingly, Nike was nowhere to be seen that year, indicating to some in the industry that there was a shift in emphasis in athletic wear from performance-based shoes to designs that concerned themselves more with style and appearance. Indeed, while Skechers began to produce more athletic shoes, the company made no secret of the fact that it did so not with athletics in mind so much as the fact that athletic shoes were becoming more popular as streetwear.

By decade's end Skechers had skyrocketed to a conspicuous prominence within the footwear industry, producing hundreds of casual and trendy styles for men, women, and children. In September of 1998 the company was successful enough for Macy's to offer the label its own space within the national department store's central New York location. While other, less prominent labels had to compete in Macy's shoe department side by side, the Skechers brand was presented in its own small boutique, giving the company a status usually reserved for such brands as Coach and Fendi.

While the trajectory of Skechers's sales arched continually upward, the company did have to face some unforeseen problems: with such increased prominence and popularity came copycat labels and designs, the nature of which threatened both the Skechers image and the company's revenue. Along with the company's initial difficulties with R. Griggs—a battle that

Key Dates:

1992: Skechers is founded.
1993: Skechers develops its first successful shoe, the "Chrome Dome."
1998: Skechers enters the field of athletic footwear, taking over Nike's space at the Atlanta trade show.
1999: Skechers goes public.

continued into the late 1990s—Skechers in 1998 also filed two complaints against the labels Candies and Payless Shoe Source for copying original Skechers designs. By approaching the protection of its label and designs with such aggressive, proactive tactics, Skechers made it clear that it was not only willing to play an innovative role in the retail industry, but was also capable of fighting to keep that role.

Marketing Know-How: Skechers at Millennium's End

An element intrinsic to the success and rapid growth of the Skechers label was the company's marketing strategy, which was designed in large part by Robert and Michael Greenberg, the father-and-son team behind Skechers. In an interview in *Footwear News,* Michael Greenberg told Simon Butler, "If we spent a billion dollars a year in marketing, it wouldn't be overkill. There's no limit to creating brand awareness." It is that sentiment that drove the Skechers philosophy, both in terms of marketing and design, from the company's beginning. After decades in the apparel industry, the elder Greenberg was aware that, regardless of the quality or originality of a product, without the right image and ad campaign to sell that product a company would never survive in the relentlessly competitive world of retail. Indeed, a common utterance used by both Greenbergs was the laconic mantra, "Unseen, untold, unsold," a phrase that underscores well the aggressive marketing of the Skechers label.

Aside from using the typical media of print ads in fashion magazines and men's periodicals and, a few years after the company's start, television, Skechers also availed itself of some rather experimental forms of marketing. After the company's success in 1998 at the Atlanta trade show, where Skechers turned the exhibition into more of a nightclub than an exhibit space, the label formed a partnership with Nordstrom and Sprint to develop a promotion aimed directly at teenagers. In 1999, using the phrase, "Skechers hooks you up from head to toe," the company offered a free phone card (compliments of Sprint) worth 15 minutes of air time with purchase of any of Skechers shoes from Nordstrom. The promotion, which was followed later that year with a similar offer of a free Motorola pager with purchase, reflected the extent to which the company was willing to go to maintain its appeal to younger consumers. The partnership between those companies and Skechers also emphasized the way in which the retail industry, particularly labels devoted to trend-conscious customers, was increasingly melding itself to the world of technology.

In spring of 1999, ever aware of its customer base's changing tastes, Skechers launched a dressier, high-fashion line of men's shoes called Skechers Collection. The line, priced slightly higher than Skechers's more casual styles, was designed to appeal to young, professional but fashion-conscious men, and was slated to be sold through Skechers's high-end accounts, such as Nordstrom, Macy's, and Foleys.

In June 1999 Skechers was doing well enough to go public, with an initial public offering of seven million shares costing $11 each. The IPO raised more than $88 million for the company, with the Greenbergs continuing to own more than 60 percent of the company. After going public the company continued to do well and was able to increase its name recognition through larger, more expansive ad campaigns, the budgets of which required more than 20 percent of Skechers's revenue. In an industry notorious for its high turnover and fiercely competitive environment, Skechers's skyrocketing success has caused some in the trade to speculate over how long such growth can last. With the retail-savvy Greenbergs managing everything from the company's marketing to its design, however, the Skechers label was by decade's end becoming a formidable and stable force within the footwear industry.

Principal Competitors

Nike, Inc.; R. Griggs Ltd.; The Timberland Company.

Further Reading

Butler, Simon, "Family Matters," *Footwear News,* October 13, 1998, p. 10.

Ebenkamp, Becky, "Skechers Dials Up Teens Via Spring, Nordstrom," *Brandweek,* January 18, 1999, p. 8.

Heiderstadt, Donna, "Robert Greenberg Still Shifting Gears," *Footwear News,* October 4, 1993, p. 4.

Malone, Scott, "Skechers Takes Candies to Court in Piracy Charge," *Footwear News,* June 29, 1998, p. 4.

McAllister, Robert, "Michael Greenberg Distributing Dr. Martens Line," *Footwear News,* December 7, 1992, p. 17.

McKinney, Melonee, "Super Show Kicks Up Its Heels: Young Men's Sports Apparel Gets Inspiration From Footwear," *Daily News Record,* February 15, 1999, p. 8.

Melville, Greg, "Skechers Takes Over Nike Super Show Site," *Footwear News,* April 13, 1998, p. 2.

Solnik, Claude, "S Is for Success," *Footwear News,* December 7, 1998, p. 28.

Taub, Daniel, "Former L.A. Gear Chief Puts on New Shoe," *Los Angeles Business Journal,* August 10, 1998, p. 3.

Wertheim, Jon, "Nike, Shmike: Little-Known Skechers Enters the Sneaker Wars," *Sports Illustrated,* February 22, 1999, p. R6.

—Rachel H. Martin

Soft Sheen Products, Inc.

1000 East 87th Street
Chicago, Illinois 60619
U.S.A.
Telephone: (773) 978-0700
Fax: (773) 978-2297

Wholly Owned Subsidiary of L'Oreal, S.A.
Founded: 1964
Employees: 400
Sales: $94.5 million (1997)
NAIC: 32562 Toilet Preparation Manufacturing; 325998 All Other Miscellaneous Chemical Product and Preparation Manufacturing

Soft Sheen Products Inc. is the top U.S. producer of ethnic hair care products. Its 200-plus products include shampoos, conditioners, relaxers, perms, and gels. They are marketed under various brand names, including Alternatives, Baby Love, Care Free Curl, Frizz Free, as well as Sportin' Waves, Wave Nouveau, and Optimum Care. The company sells its products to salons, beauty supply houses, and such retailers as drug stores and department stores. In fact, retailers account for approximately 75 percent of its sales, and salons for 20 percent. Soft Sheen markets its products in several countries, including Africa, Brazil, and the Caribbean, as well as in the United States.

1964–85: Tapping an Untapped Market

Soft Sheen was founded in 1964, in the basement of a home on the south side of Chicago. Its founders, Edward and Bettiann Gardner, began the business when they became aware that there was a decided lack of hair care products formulated for people of color. Hair care companies of that time catered almost exclusively to the Caucasian market, and non-Caucasians essentially had to make do with products that were not chemically designed for their hair. The pioneering Gardners saw the opportunity to offer better products to people of color and, taking matters into their own hands, began experimenting with shampoo and pomade ''recipes.''

Testing various mixtures on their children, the Gardners developed several products that were specifically formulated to address the needs of African Americans. Two of the company's early products were Soft Sheen Hair & Scalp Conditioner and Miss Cool Five Minute Fast Set, a quick-setting lotion that eliminated the need for sleeping in rollers. Consumer interest in the products was not overwhelming but was enough to keep the Gardners plugging away at their slowly growing business.

Everything changed in 1979, however, when Soft Sheen introduced a new product called Care Free Curl. Care Free Curl was a solution that dramatically reduced the amount of time it took to relax hair—from almost eight hours to only two. The innovative product was a phenomenal success. Soft Sheen built on that success by launching a full line of Care Free Curl products, including shampoos, conditioners, gels, and sprays, that were sold both in salons and in drugstores. The company also began selling its products in foreign markets. The popularity of Care Free Curl drove revenues up at an almost unbelievable pace, from $500,000 in 1979 to $55 million by 1982.

Soft Sheen scored another success in the late 1980s, when it introduced Optimum Care, a relaxer kit that allowed salon stylists to straighten and condition hair at the same time. Conditioning was particularly important to preserve the health of black hair, which tended to dry out under the stress of styling and chemical processing. The gentle, conditioning Optimum Care quickly became the industry's best-selling relaxer.

Soft Sheen's already exponential sales growth got a further boost in the 1980s from the widespread vogue of the ''Jheri-curl'' hairstyle. Popularized by recording artist Michael Jackson, the wet-looking, loosely curled style required a whole host of hair care products to achieve and maintain. The increased consumer use of gels, sprays, and moisturizers, in tandem with the continued sales growth of the Care Free Curl and Optimum Care lines, elevated Soft Sheen's sales to $87.2 million in 1989.

Mid-1980s–90s: Second-Generation Gardner Leadership

In the middle of Soft Sheen's astonishing growth spurt, Edward and Bettiann Gardner turned the company's presidency

Key Dates:

1964: Gary and Bettiann Gardner begin Soft Sheen in the basement of their home.
1979: Soft Sheen introduces Care Free Curl, causing revenues to increase dramatically.
1985: Gary Gardner becomes president and CEO of Soft Sheen.
1996: Gary Gardner resigns, and is replaced by his sister, Terri Gardner.
1998: Soft Sheen is acquired by L'Oreal S.A.

over to their oldest son, Gary. The 27-year-old Gary Gardner had been involved with Soft Sheen since its earliest days, when he and his siblings helped their parents by filling shampoo bottles. What he faced as the newly appointed president, however, was less a matter of getting a fledgling company off the ground and more a matter of controlling a business that was growing too fast. "We grew so fast, we were afraid the franchise would be taken away from us," Gardner said in a February 1991 interview with *USA Today.*

To ensure that the company did not outgrow its capabilities, Gardner deliberately decelerated. He reduced employment 27 percent, to 620 employees, between 1984 and 1988 by not replacing workers who left. He also cut operational costs, in an effort to boost profits. As it turned out, Gardner's slowing-down tactics were timely. In the late 1980s, the ethnic hair care market began to soften, with overall industry growth slowing to around three percent a year. The slowdown was largely due to a consumer trend toward shorter and drier hairstyles, which required fewer styling products.

In 1987, Soft Sheen moved to compensate for diminishing domestic sales by expanding its presence in overseas markets. It acquired 66 percent of Dyke and Dryden, Ltd., a London-based manufacturer of ethnic hair care products and the largest black-owned business in Europe. Dyke and Dryden distributed its products in the United Kingdom and in Africa, giving Soft Sheen solid entry into a market of approximately 440 million potential customers. The company expected its global expansion to drive sales up to $150 million by the middle of the 1990s.

Despite such optimistic predictions, Soft Sheen did not have great success in penetrating foreign markets, and domestic sales continued to make up the great bulk of its revenues. Unfortunately, the domestic market for ethnic hair care products remained in its slump, with hairstyles still tending toward a more natural, less time-intensive look. The overall slowdown in sales was compounded by increased competition within the industry. More and more, large cosmetics firms were looking for a share of the ethnic market by adding their own ethnic product lines or acquiring smaller black hair-care companies. These industry giants, with their vast distribution networks and their huge marketing budgets, were formidable competitors.

In addition to battling the soft market and growing competition, Soft Sheen was also struggling with internal problems. Its distribution system was inefficient and slow, with orders taking ten days to be filled. The company had also lagged in product development, not introducing a major new product for more than two years. These operational shortcomings, along with adverse market conditions, put the brakes on Soft Sheen's sales growth. In 1994, the company posted only a .6 percent increase over 1993 sales. 1995 sales were about $94 million, considerably short of Gardner's expectations.

Mid-1990s: Leadership Shakeup

By the middle of 1995, Soft Sheen's stalled growth led the Gardners to begin questioning the wisest course of action for the company's future. In May, the family hired a financial advisory firm to review Soft Sheen's options, prompting a flurry of rumors that the company was for sale. Although there was no change in ownership, the company's decision-making process *did* result in a change in leadership.

In early 1996, Gary Gardner resigned from his post as Soft Sheen president. Simultaneously, his wife Denise resigned from her position as vice-president of marketing. Although the company gave no official reason for the resignations, industry insiders speculated that they were due to disagreement over Soft Sheen's future course. Disagreement or no, Gary Gardner retained his seat on the board of directors, while the company installed his sister, Terri Gardner, as interim president and CEO. Terri had previously served as Soft Sheen's executive vice-president of advertising, as well as president of Brainstorm Communications, the company's ad agency.

Soft Sheen's plan was to conduct a search for a new president from outside the family and thereby begin transitioning the Gardners into a purely ownership role. Their interim leader Terri Gardner, however, was no mere figurehead. Upon assuming her position, she almost immediately began making significant changes in the company's operations. One of her first moves was to purge Soft Sheen's product line of unprofitable products and package sizes, eliminating 40 of the company's 250 SKUs. Another of her initiatives involved restructuring and consolidating the company's warehouse operations, a move that increased on-time shipments and improved service levels. Impressed with Terri Gardner's leadership abilities, the Soft Sheen board of directors asked her to fill the president and CEO positions on a permanent basis. She agreed in March 1996.

Meanwhile, Gardner continued giving Soft Sheen a makeover, with many of her efforts focused on improving customer relations. She developed new packaging options that helped retailers better manage their inventories, and upgraded the company's computer system to facilitate electronic customer communication. She also hired a third-party company to maintain inventory and positioning of Soft Sheen's products in retail stores. To boost sales, she doubled the company's advertising budget, and began developing new television commercials.

Gardner also took steps to revive the company's languishing product development department, hiring a new vice-president of science and technology. In a November 1996 interview with *Drug Store News*, she promised that consumers would see new Soft Sheen products in the stores in the first quarter of 1997. "This past year, we took some time to tend to our operations and our physical plant to make sure that we were efficient," she said, adding, "For 1997, we will have some major new product introductions. We will introduce items that will grow every category we compete in, from hair color through relaxers, styling aids, conditioners, and wave products.''

She made good on her promise. By May 1997, Soft Sheen had released two new lines, Mizani and Hair Werks, that were designed exclusively for use in salons. Another major product introduction soon followed. In the fall of 1997, the company launched Alternatives, a line of relaxers and styling products designed for younger women who varied their hairstyles from day to day. Targeting these ''Generation Y'' consumers—which research showed to be an underserved segment of the market—Soft Sheen went for an innovative, fresh look and feel in its product packaging and ad copy. The product itself offered styling flexibility and a unique ''moisture retention complex'' that conditioned the hair and protected it from heat styling and chemical processing applications.

1998–99: Acquisition by L'Oreal

Soft Sheen finished 1997 with sales of $94.5 million. only a slight increase over 1996, despite new product introductions and improvements in operational efficiency. Once again, the Gardners started thinking about selling their 33-year-old business. Early in 1998, they began talks with French-owned cosmetics company, L'Oreal S.A. L'Oreal—which operated in 150 countries and had a collection of brands that included Maybelline, Redkin, and Lancôme—needed a portal to the ethnic market.

In early July 1998, Soft Sheen announced that it had agreed to be acquired by L'Oreal's New York-based U.S. subsidiary, Cosmair Inc. Although the company refused to release the price of the acquisition, industry analysts estimated it at more than $160 million. Under the terms of the agreement, Terri Gardner remained on as president of the Soft Sheen division and also became a member of Cosmair's executive committee. In a September 1998 interview with *Black Enterprise*, Gardner explained the company's decision to join L'Oreal. ''We saw a strategic partner with muscle through which we could fulfill our vision for the company,'' she said. ''Going forward, this opportunity will magnify Soft Sheen's success on multiple levels,'' she observed.

Once the Soft Sheen acquisition was complete, L'Oreal began strategizing how to best grow its new subsidiary and expand its beachhead in the ethnic market. The answer seemed to lie, first, in research and development. In July 1998, L'Oreal announced that it planned to open a specialized research and development center in Chicago dedicated to ethnic products, the only such R&D center in the world. Soft Sheen's research and development staff were to be included as part of the new facility. L'Oreal, which had a reputation for heavy investment in research and development, expected its new Chicago center to be operational by the year 2001.

Meanwhile, Soft Sheen continued to introduce new products. In early 1999, the company unveiled Frizz Free, an anti-frizzing product that contained conditioners and oils to combat dryness and damage. Frizz Free was the first frizz control product made specifically for ethnic women by an ethnic hair-care products company.

Looking to the Future

With the backing of L'Oreal, it was expected that Soft Sheen would grow rapidly in the coming years. The planned research and development center was almost certain to result in substantial innovations in ethnic hair care products and a steady flow of new product introductions. The company's presence in overseas markets was also likely to increase, supported by L'Oreal's vast global reach.

Principal Subsidiaries

Dyke & Dryden, Ltd. (U.K.; 66%); Soft Sheen Products, Ltd. (Jamaica); Soft Sheen International.

Principal Competitors

Alberto-Culver Company; Carson Inc.; Massimo Enterprises Inc.; Revlon, Inc.

Further Reading

Brucato, Patricia, ''Sit Back and Relax (Ethnic Hair Care Products),'' *Soap-Cosmetics-Chemical Specialties,* May 1, 1997, p. 34.

Cleaver, Joanne, ''Soft Sheen CEO Gives Family Company a Whole New Look,'' *Crain's Chicago Business*, January 6, 1997, p. 4.

Fetterman, Mindy, ''Soft Sheen Carefully Plots Course: Africa is Next for Hair-Care Firm,'' *USA Today*, February 28, 1991, p. 8B.

''Gary Gardner Resigns as President of Soft Sheen,'' *Jet,* February 19, 1996, p. 8.

Parks, Liz, ''L'Oreal, With New Soft Sheen Division, Plans Record-Setting Ethnic R&D,'' *Drug Store News*, August 24, 1998, p. 13.

——, ''Shaping the Soft Sheen of Tomorrow,'' *Drug Store News*, November 18, 1996, p. 27.

Shakespeare, Tonia, ''Is Soft Sheen Products Being Sold?,'' *Black Enterprise*, September 1995, p. 16.

Smith, Eric L., ''Gardner Out as Soft Sheen President,'' *Black Enterprise, May 1996,* p. 24.

—Shawna Brynildssen

Spirit Airlines, Inc.

2800 Executive Way
Miramar, Florida 33025
U.S.A.
Telephone: (954) 447-7965
Toll Free: (800) 772-7117
Fax: (954) 447-7979
Web site: http://www.spiritair.com

Private Company
Incorporated: 1980
Employees: 1,400
Sales: $130.6 million (1998 est.)
NAIC: 481111 Scheduled Passenger Air Transportation

Travel Agent magazine calls Spirit Airlines, Inc. ''the most successful small carrier you've never heard of.'' The carrier's raison d'etre is ferrying northerners to hot vacation spots for less. It attracts travelers with low, low fares and is known for filling planes better than anyone else—load factors typically average more than 80 percent. In 1998, more than two and a half million people flew Spirit, one of the few budget start-ups to see a second decade. Its 20 aircraft fly to 14 cities with 50 flights a day.

High-Rolling Origins

Commercial aviation is inherently risky, so it is appropriate that the venture that lead to the birth of Spirit Airlines involved rolling the dice. Ned Homfeld had once considered designing racing yachts for a living. Instead, he started Ground Air Transfer, a surface transportation company specializing in delivering critical parts for automotive manufacturers. In 1983, he was asked to help finance a tour operator that he renamed Charter One. It hired turboprop aircraft for gambling trips from Chicago to Atlantic City, which it soon began serving from Boston, Detroit, and Providence.

Flights to Florida became the next focus as gambling became more commonplace in other states. The Bahamas became a destination in 1984, first served from Boston and then from Chicago and Detroit as well. San Juan and Las Vegas were added in a couple of years.

To better control its destiny, Charter One began leasing two planes of its own in 1990, Convair 580 turboprops. The demise of the original Midway Airlines brought down the prices for used aircraft. The company bought four DC-9 aircraft, allowing it to launch twice-daily service between Detroit and Atlantic City as Spirit Airlines.

Spirit's background as tour operator gave it a predisposition to filling as many seats as possible. It employed 120 at the time and carried 150,000 passengers. By 1993, annual revenues were almost $21 million. The carrier flew more than 275,000 people that year. Phenomenal growth continued the next year; sales were $56 million with 683,000 passengers.

The early 1990s were a period of consolidation among airlines. A global recession and the repercussions of the Persian Gulf War made it nearly impossible for even established carriers to post a profit. Making things easier for the new start-ups were readily available aircraft and personnel that had been employed by Pan Am, Eastern, or Midway before their demise. Spirit also was able to obtain cheaper, nonunion labor.

Major airlines could still make it very difficult for low-cost airlines to get a toehold in their hubs. In 1994, Spirit attempted to buy two gates at Detroit Metropolitan Wayne County Airport from US Airways for $950,000. But they were sold to Northwest Airlines, which resold them to Trans World Airlines, according to the *Wall Street Journal.* Spirit was able to buy a hangar at Detroit Metropolitan Wayne County Airport from Delta Airlines in 1995, which it used to perform its own maintenance. Northwest Airlines also had been eyeing the hangar.

Spirit's low-cost strategy axed some traditional amenities, such as frequent flyer miles and in-flight meals. Tickets were also nonrefundable. Spirit introduced ''Freedom Fare'' service from Detroit to New England beginning in December 1995. The first once-daily flights, to Philadelphia, featured fares as low as $49 one way. The next February, Boston was added, beginning at $69 one way. A month later, Spirit announced service to

Company Perspectives:

Our mission is: to provide a safe, customer oriented, market responsive air transportation product; to provide the highest level of customer service offering prompt, efficient and friendly service; to provide the best valued products for the most competitive prices; to be an easy company to do business with; to respect our fellow employees and acknowledge the power of teamwork; to be a company in which our staff experiences a friendly environment and enjoys being a part of Spirit's family. A place where work can be fun; to consistently strive to improve what we do and how we do it.

Myrtle Beach, South Carolina, which boasted plenty of golf courses—one of Spirit's prerequisites for leisure destinations.

Spirit's Annus Terribilis: 1996

In the spring of 1996, Comair Holdings Inc. announced plans to buy Spirit Airlines for $20 million. It had considered investing in Spirit since 1994. The deal, however, never materialized. By this time, Spirit was flying ten DC-9s, five of which it owned. It had 500 employees, a fifth of them seasonal. Revenues were about $60 million per year, with profits of $3 to $4 million. Comair, regional carrier for Delta Airlines, was looking for opportunities among start-ups with low-cost labor, while Spirit sought a ''big brother'' to help it along amidst increased competition.

Comair backed out of the deal, ostensibly because of another start-up's accident in the Everglades. The May 1996 ValuJet crash stigmatized virtually all budget carriers in the United States. Spirit sent out thousands of postcards assuring its customers of the safety of its planes. A ''Catch the Spirit'' media campaign was launched at the end of 1996, pitching Spirit's perfect safety record to family travelers. The $2 million promotion used radio and TV advertising and billboards and involved painting the company's jets with a new logo.

Spirit had sales of $63 million in 1996, when it carried more than 750,000 passengers and had about 700 employees. These were respectable results, as the price of jet fuel rose 25 percent, necessitating an increase in fares. Overall sales fell only moderately in the winter of 1996–97, and many other start-ups failed. Still, Spirit posted its only annual loss in 1996.

Spirit was driven out of the Detroit-Philadelphia market by Northwest, which matched its fares and added more seats after the ValuJet crash. A couple of months after Spirit abandoned the route, Northwest raised fares to their previous levels, giving rise to charges of predatory pricing that the Justice Department and Department of Transportation took very seriously, spurring talk of possible ''reregulation'' in the industry. (Reno Air levied similar charges against Northwest's tactics on its Detroit-Reno route.)

Spirit's planes soon filled up again. The airline began flying some of Sun Jet Inc.'s routes out of New Jersey after the Florida charter carrier declared bankruptcy in June 1997. Reservations and marketing company World Technology Systems had been using both Sun Jet and Spirit to fly its tours, the latter in partnership with charter operator Myrtle Beach Jet Express, based in Atlanta.

Spirit's partnership with Jet Express was dissolved amid name calling and finger pointing in August 1997. A Jet Express spokesman pointed to Spirit's poor performance, and Homfeld called attention to the questionable finances of its rival, which owed the city of Myrtle Beach $770,000. When Jet Express pulled out of the market two years later, *Sun News* business writer David Wren claimed Spirit was to blame for its demise as it had copied its service and marketing plan. He noted that in 1995, before Jet Express started, ''Myrtle Beach International was a sleepy airport with little air service—especially low cost air service—to speak of.''

Homfeld moved to Miami in November 1997. That city and four others in Florida (as well as Atlantic City, New Jersey) were soon wooing Spirit Airlines, then looking for a new place to locate its headquarters, reservations center, and maintenance base. Spirit was planning to relocate its administrative staff of 50 by the summer's end and had plans to create another 500 jobs within three years.

Spirit began to replace its DC-9s with larger MD-80s in the fall of 1997 as it vied for a slot at New York City's La Guardia International Airport. A few months later, Spirit Airlines Vice-Chairman Mark Kahan testified before the U.S. Senate Subcommittee on Transportation regarding the Northwest anticompetitiveness matter.

As an impending pilots' strike at Northwest Airlines loomed nearer in late summer 1998, Spirit stepped up service in the areas where it had competed against its giant rival. As its reservation calls peaked, Spirit rerouted two of its DC-9s and acquired an MD-80 from another airline to increase capacity.

Spirit Airlines had $131 million in revenues in 1998 and expected $235 million the next year. Profits were $6.7 million. Spirit's fleet had grown to 20 aircraft. Although it had increased its seating capacity by 50 percent, it posted the industry's highest load factor for the year, 76.4 percent. It carried 1.4 million passengers that year, a nearly 80 percent increase over 1997, and had 1,000 employees. Spirit had more than tripled its advertising budget to $7 million in 1998.

Detroit Metropolitan Wayne County Airport, which had embarked upon a $1.8 billion expansion project, announced plans to build six temporary gates in February 1999. Two were to be assigned to Spirit and the other four to Southwest Airlines, which had also had to borrow gates. Spirit was spending $1.3 million a year at $250 to $400 a turn to rent spare gates from other carriers, according to the *Wall Street Journal.* Lack of gates had contributed to Spirit's spotty service record, as sometimes passengers would be kept on the tarmac for up to an hour while a plane bargained for a place to park. Spirit operated more than two dozen flights a day out of Detroit.

A New Home in 1999

The company relocated its headquarters to the Fort Lauderdale area after months of being courted by various cities. Fort Lauderdale was already home to Spirit's tour company. Miami

Key Dates:

1983: Ned Homfeld becomes involved with Charter One, ferrying gamblers to Atlantic City.
1990: Company begins leasing its own planes.
1992: Scheduled service begins under the name Spirit Airlines.
1996: ValuJet crash and Northwest Airlines pricing conspire to produce Spirit's only money-losing year.
1999: Headquarters moved from Michigan to Florida.

soon was ruled out, as it was crowded and not even one of Spirit's destinations. State tax incentives worth up to $1.65 million had been offered the carrier in an attempt to land it at Southwest Florida International Airport in Lee County. In March 1999, however, Spirit chose Miramar, near Fort Lauderdale in Broward County. This would ultimately bring 500 high-paying jobs (with an average annual salary of $35,000) to the area. In April, 25 administrative employees were the first to relocate to a temporary home at Fort Lauderdale-Hollywood International Airport. They were scheduled to be followed by flight training, finance, and accounting personnel in November upon completion of the company's office building. An additional reservations facility also was planned for the area. The total state/county incentive package was worth $2 million in cash and tax cuts.

At the same time, Horry County, South Carolina was trying to convince Spirit to build a heavy maintenance facility at its Myrtle Beach International Airport, which also would bring hundreds of jobs. Spirit accounted for a quarter of the airport's traffic. Interestingly, Spirit's employment at Detroit was expected to increase following the relocation of its headquarters. Spirit became a signatory carrier there, giving it more of a voice regarding airport expansion projects and assuring it of gate space until 2008. It still had to wait months before completion of its two temporary gates, however.

With the opening of casinos in Michigan, Spirit suspended service between Detroit and Atlantic City. Having successfully expanded into New York, it added Los Angeles in June 1999, viewing it as a leisure market. The red-eye flight allowed Spirit to increase utilization without adding aircraft, Homfeld told *Air Transport World.* Spirit's new headquarters opened in November 1999, and the carrier expected to post $235 million in revenues for the year.

Principal Subsidiaries

Spirit Tours.

Principal Competitors

Northwest Airlines; US Airways.

Further Reading

Baertlein, Lisa, "And the Winner Is. . . ," *Miami Daily Business Review,* February 17, 1999, p. A1.

Clancy, Carole, "Miramar's Spirit Airlines Upgrades its Fleet, Has Big Plans," *South Florida Business Journal,* May 17, 1999.

Cordle, Ina Paiva, "Broward County, Fla. Cities Woo Spirit Airlines," *Miami Herald,* November 4, 1998.

——, "Miami-Dade County Tries To Land Detroit-Based Discount Airline," *Miami Herald,* April 4, 1998.

——, "Spirit Airlines To Expand Fort Lauderdale, Fla. Service," *Miami Herald,* March 18, 1999.

Flint, Perry, "Spirit(ed) Bottom Feeder," *Air Transport World,* May 1999, pp. 63–66.

Fricker, Daniel G., "Small Carriers Hope To Step into Void If Northwest Airlines Strikes," *Detroit Free Press,* August 26, 1998.

Gallagher, John, "A Nice Niche for Spirit," *Detroit Free Press,* September 16, 1999, pp. 1C–2C.

——, "Discount Airline To Move Base from Michigan to Florida," *Detroit Free Press,* March 18, 1999.

Grant, Elaine X., "A Neat Little Airline," *Travel Agent,* September 28, 1998.

Homfeld, Ned, "Entrepreneurs Only," Interview by Lauren Theirry, CNNfn, May 10, 1999.

Ingersoll, Bruce, "Flexible Flier: Gateless in Detroit, Low-Fare Spirit Docks at Rivals' Convenience—Big Airlines' Lock on Leases for Ground Facilities Is Challenge to Newcomers—The Daily Struggle for Space," *Wall Street Journal,* July 12, 1999, p. A1.

Kayal, Michele, "Washington Comment," *Journal of Commerce,* March 31, 1997, p. 7.

Keough, Caroline, and Ina Paiva Cordle, "Spirit Airlines To Build Headquarters in Miramar, Fla.," *Miami Herald,* March 16, 1999.

Kosdrosky, Terry, "Metro Airport Infused with Spirit Until 2008," *Crain's Detroit Business,* August 16, 1999, p. 28.

Lovelace, Craig S., "Spirit Airlines Considers Maintenance Facility in Myrtle Beach, S.C.," *Sun News,* March 18, 1999.

Muellner, Alexis, "Cushman Team Got into the Spirit of the Deal," *South Florida Business Journal,* October 25, 1999.

Ott, James, "Comair Adds Spirit Air," *Aviation Week and Space Technology,* April 1, 1996, p. 14.

Rothman, Andrea, Gail DeGeorge, and Eric Schine, "The Season of Upstart Startups," *Business Week,* August 31, 1992, p. 68.

"Spirit Airlines Is Rising on the Wings of Travel Agent Bookings," *Travel Trade,* February 15, 1999.

Stopa, Marsha, "Predatory Pricing? Small Airlines Are Taking on the Majors," *Crain's Detroit Business,* March 16, 1998, p. 1.

——, "Spirit Battles Back After ValuJet Crash," *Crain's Detroit Business,* April 14, 1997, p. 3.

——, "Spirit Picks Up Bankrupt Sun Jet's Flights," *Crain's Detroit Business,* June 23, 1997, p. 3.

Wren, David, "David Wren Column," *Sun News,* July 4, 1999.

——, "Spirit, Jet Express Step Up Competition in Myrtle Beach, S.C.," *Sun News,* January 6, 1998.

Zellner, Wendy, "How Northwest Gives Competition a Bad Name," *Business Week,* March 16, 1998, p. 34.

—Frederick C. Ingram

The St. Joe Company

duPont Center
1650 Prudential Drive, Suite 400
Jacksonville, Florida 32207
U.S.A.
Telephone: (904) 396-6600
Fax: (904) 396-4042
Web site: http://www.joe.com

Public Company
Incorporated: 1936 as St. Joe Paper Co.
Employees: 2,100
Sales: $392.2 million (1998)
Stock Exchanges: New York
Ticker Symbol: JOE
NAIC: 23311 Land Subdivision and Land Development; 53121 Offices of Real Estate Agents and Brokers; 531311 Residential Property Managers; 531312 Nonresidential Property Managers; 53112 Lessors of Nonresidential Buildings (Except Miniwarehouses); 482111 Line-Haul Railroads; 11311 Timber Tract Operations

The St. Joe Company is one of the largest real estate operating companies in the Southeast. It is also the largest private landowner in Florida, with more than 1.1 million acres located across the Panhandle and along the state's eastern coast. Using its massive land holdings, the company develops both residential and commercial properties. Its majority-owned residential development subsidiary, Arvida Company L.P., builds planned residential, retirement, and resort communities. The St. Joe Commercial Group is the company's commercial development subsidiary, which builds corporate office space. Both Arvida and The St. Joe Commercial Group also have real estate brokerage components. The brokerage services arm of Arvida is Arvida Realty Services, the fifth-largest real estate brokerage firm in the nation. The Commercial Group's real estate services component is Advantis. Advantis provides brokerage, corporate real estate financial management, representation services, and tenant construction through more than 500 agents. St. Joe is also a major owner of rail, timber, and sugar assets which it is currently in the process of selling off in order to focus on real estate development.

St. Joe Beginnings: A Family Rebel and a Fortune in Real Estate

The St. Joe Company can trace its roots back to the duPonts, one of America's legendary entrepreneurial families. The duPonts built their fortune by manufacturing and marketing explosives, such as gunpowder, dynamite, and nitroglycerine, before diversifying into paints, plastics, and dyes. The St. Joe Company was founded by a rebellious family member, Alfred Irenee duPont, who decided to take his money out of the family business and put it elsewhere. Having started as a laborer in the duPont gunpowder-manufacturing company, Alfred eventually became the company's president. A colorful character and a nonconformist, he had a propensity for unconventional behavior. In 1921 the 57-year-old Alfred married a woman who was in her mid-thirties, scandalizing the staid Delaware society and causing something of an uproar.

In 1926 he again startled both his peers and his family by leaving Delaware altogether. The reason behind his sudden departure was his cousin, Pierre duPont. Pierre, who had just become Delaware's tax commissioner, intended to make the wealthy pay more in taxes. Alfred, who couldn't tolerate the thought of Pierre going over his personal finances, was determined to move his money matters safely out of his cousin's grasp. Taking his young wife, Jessie Ball, and his assets, duPont went south to Jacksonville, Florida.

Florida was just then in the throes of economic collapse. A hurricane had wreaked havoc on the Miami area, and real estate prices were spiraling downward. DuPont took advantage of the depressed market, buying up large tracts of land for just a few dollars per acre. His long-range goal was to open a paper company.

Shortly after he moved to Florida, duPont commissioned his wife's brother, Edward Ball, to locate and acquire good investment properties. Ball moved aggressively, purchasing hundreds of thousands of acres of land, as well as various banks and

Company Perspectives:

St. Joe is one company, yet it operates as if it were two. The first St. Joe is focused on opening its abundant storehouse of value. The second St. Joe is a real estate operating company. Making new places. And building relationships with people where they live, work, and play.

companies that had fallen into financial trouble. In 1933 a single transaction added 240,000 acres in northwest Florida to the duPont holdings. This particular transaction included two railroads, some phone companies, a land development company, a port terminal, and a sawmill. It also included almost the entire the gulf town of Port St. Joe.

1935–97: Sleepy Years

DuPont died in 1935, leaving the majority of his assets in a trust for his wife and appointing Edward Ball as head of his business conglomerate. His longstanding dream of opening a paper mill was finally realized when the executors of his estate formed the St. Joe Paper Company in Port St. Joe, Florida, in the late 1930s. Ball continued to aggressively add to the company's holdings, purchasing a number of corrugated cardboard box plants, a sugar company, and a controlling interest in the Florida East Coast Railway Company, which ran from Jacksonville to Key West. In addition, Ball kept building St. Joe's already-impressive land holdings. Beginning in the 1940s, the company began purchasing large tracts of timberland and using the timber to provide the pulp for paper products. By the 1970s, St. Joe's pulp and paper operation was one of the largest in the nation.

Ball ran St. Joe Paper until his death in 1981, and amassed enough real estate during his tenure to make the company the largest private landowner in Florida. Upon Ball's death, control of St. Joe remained with the Alfred I. duPont Testamentary Trust, which owned well over half of the company. The trust's beneficiary was the Nemours Foundation, an organization that operated children's clinics throughout Florida and Delaware, and a children's hospital in Wilmington, Delaware.

The 15 years following Ball's death were relatively uneventful. The managers who followed him did little with St. Joe's enormous land holdings, its various businesses, or its cash reserves. Although the company was profitable, it was far from being as profitable as it could be, and in the early 1990s, representatives of the duPont trust, Florida officials, and outside investors began to demand that the company produce more income. In response, the highly diversified St. Joe began to narrow its focus. Determining that its greatest potential lay in its vast land holdings, the conglomerate began the process of remaking itself as a real estate company.

The first step in the transformation process was to begin selling off holdings that fell outside the realm of real estate development. In April 1996 the company sold the stock of its telecommunications company, St. Joe Communications, as well as its interests in three cellular limited partnerships. The next businesses on the block were the company's namesake, the Port St. Joe paper mill, and its cardboard container plants, which were sold in May 1996. With the divestiture of its paper operations, the St. Joe Paper Company changed its name to the St. Joe Corporation.

1997: Peter Rummell Takes the Helm

More significant than the change in name was a change in leadership. In January 1997, after a nationwide search, the St. Joe board appointed Peter S. Rummell as the company's new CEO. The 51-year-old Rummell was a seasoned real estate veteran. He had begun his real estate career in 1971, developing Hilton Head Island, South Carolina, and Amelia Island, Florida, for the Sea Pines Company. In 1977 he took a managerial position with the Boca Raton-based Arvida Co., one of Florida's best-known residential community builders. He left Florida for New York in 1983, joining the Rockefeller Center Management Corp. Then, two years later, he became president of the Disney Development Company. At Disney, Rummell was charged with developing thousands of acres of land in Florida and elsewhere that were owned by the entertainment giant.

Rummell had plenty of raw material to work with in his new position at St. Joe. The company owned 1.1 million acres of land—located mostly in northwestern Florida—and had half of a billion dollars in cash and securities, with no debt. He also had plenty of autonomy: his mandate was simply to develop the company's land holdings in whatever ways he thought would improve earnings. Rummell recognized the unique nature of his new assignment. "I don't know of anyone who has been given an almost $3 billion market capitalization, $500 million in cash, no debt, and almost six million feet of built and leased inventory, and been told to go make something happen," he was quoted as saying in an April 1998 article in *Fortune* magazine.

One of Rummell's first moves was to replace most of the company's existing managers with a team of his own choosing. For his second-in-command, the company's president and chief operating officer, Rummell recruited Charles Ledsinger, Jr., the former CFO of Harrahs Entertainment. He also brought two former Disney execs on board as senior managers.

Rummell's strategy was to focus on all four segments of real estate: residential, commercial/industrial, resort, and entertainment. In his first year as CEO, he made headway in all four segments. Building up its commercial/industrial segment, the company formed a joint venture with the Orlando, Florida-based CNL Group, a large, privately held real estate finance and development company. The partnership was created to acquire commercial property and develop single and multi-tenant office buildings and industrial space in the central Florida area. The commercial group also purchased a one-third interest in the Miami-based Codina Group, Inc., a commercial/industrial developer in southern Florida. The company began planning new resorts for the state's Gulf Coast and purchased a golf course development company.

St. Joe Commercial also began planning for the development of several parcels of land that it owned through a 54 percent interest in Florida East Coast Industries (FECI). FECI and its subsidiaries, which owned and operated two railroads and more than 15,400 acres of undeveloped land, which was

Key Dates:

1926: Alfred I. duPont moves his assets from Delaware to Florida.
1933: DuPont purchases 240,000 acres in northwest Florida, including almost all of the town of Port St. Joe.
1935: DuPont dies, leaving his holdings to his wife and a charitable trust. DuPont's brother-in-law, Edward Ball, assumes control of the duPont business.
1936: Executors of the Alfred I. duPont trust form the St. Joe Paper Co.
1981: Edward Ball dies.
1997: Peter Rummell becomes CEO.
1999: Company announces plans to sell off much of its timberlands.

mostly located adjacent to the railroads. St. Joe planned to develop the FECI-owned land into office and industrial parks.

St. Joe's residential division also made an important move in 1997 by acquiring a 74 percent interest in the Arvida Company. In addition to being one of Rummell's former employers, Arvida was one of Florida's best-known residential community developers.

Rummell launched St. Joe's entertainment division by partnering with the National Football League to develop a chain of interactive entertainment centers for U.S. cities that had NFL franchises. The company also purchased a one-third interest in a Seattle-based company that produced interactive games for club settings.

While it was moving to establish itself as a real estate development power, St. Joe was also quietly disposing of holdings that no longer fit into its plan. Late in 1997, the company agreed to sell its sugar operation—a 50,000-acre sugarcane plantation in the Everglades—to the federal government for $133.5 million. The company's decision to sell to the government stemmed, in part, from a desire to protect the Everglades from destruction.

1998–99: Rapid Growth

The rapid pace St. Joe set in 1997 only increased over the next two years, on all four of the company's identified real estate fronts. Progress was especially noteworthy in the area of residential community development. St. Joe targeted several thousand acres of its Panhandle land holdings for residential development, and initiated construction in 1998. Rather than build traditional subdivisions, the company opted to create master-planned communities—actual small towns, complete with shopping, dining, and entertainment within walking distance of the homes. The planned community concept was a familiar one to Rummell, who had been a key player in the development of Disney's innovative planned community, Celebration, Florida.

Two of St. Joe's projects that best exemplified this mixed-use development approach were Seagrove, a development in Northwest Florida's Walton County, and Southwood, a town planned for a 3,000-acre tract of land outside Tallahassee. Seagrove, which was modeled after a neighboring community named Seaside, was to be a 498-acre development, with 1,140 housing units, a resort hotel, retail space, and a beach club. Plans for Southwood included areas designated for office, commercial, and institutional use, a golf course, several parks, and a town center, as well as low-, medium-, and high-density residential zones. By the end of 1997, St. Joe had 23 communities in various stages of planning and development, including Seagrove and Southwood.

The residential arm of St. Joe also made an important move that allowed it to broaden the range of real estate services it offered. In July 1998 the company purchased Prudential Florida Realty Services, the largest real estate brokerage, sales, and services company in Florida. Renamed Arvida Realty Services, the subsidiary began handling residential sales, title and mortgage services, rentals, and marketing for the company through its 80 offices in south and central Florida.

On the commercial/industrial side of the business, St. Joe spread its geographic reach to include the rapidly developing triangle extending between Miami, Dallas, and Washington, D.C. The company entered this new territory by means of a single acquisition: the Virginia-based Goodman Segar Hogan Hoffler, L.P., one of the Southeast's largest commercial real estate firms. The Goodman Segar purchase, which was completed in September 1998, gave St. Joe a presence in such major Southeastern cities as Atlanta, Georgia; Raleigh and Durham, North Carolina; Richmond and Norfolk, Virginia; and Washington, D.C. The company also formed partnerships with two other out-of-state developers to develop commercial properties in Georgia and Texas.

In December 1998 St. Joe Commercial expanded again with the purchase of Florida Real Estate Advisors (FREA), a commercial real estate services company based in Tampa. The company combined its newly acquired Goodman Segar and FREA subsidiaries to form a commercial real estate services firm. The firm, christened Advantis, was one of the Southeast's largest, with more than 500 employees managing more than 30 million square feet of commercial and industrial space.

The company also looked for ways to improve profits from its transportation holdings. In early 1998 St. Joe's FECI subsidiary signed an agreement with Qwest, Inc., a fiber-optic company, to allow Qwest to install fiber-optic cable along FECI's railway tracks. It was speculated that contract could generate as much as $5 million in new revenue. FECI also began negotiations that would allow Amtrak to run passenger trains on its rails.

While ramping up its real estate business, St. Joe simultaneously prepared to shed another of its non-development-related assets. In March 1999 the company announced that it would sell up to 800,000 of its 1 million acres of timberland. To make the land a feasible purchase for more bidders, St. Joe planned to auction it off in 100,000-acre parcels instead of in its entirety.

Developing the Future

In Peter Rummell's first two years as CEO, St. Joe made enormous strides toward transforming itself. As of March 1999, St. Joe's residential division had 23 communities and resorts in various stages of planning and development, mostly located in northwest Florida. When fully built, the company's in-progress projects were expected to contain up to 19,500 housing and resort units.

St. Joe's commercial group, in part through Florida East Coast Industries, owned and managed more than six million square feet of rentable commercial and industrial space and had an additional 2.2 million square feet in planning and construction. The company planned to start work on yet another three million square feet of commercial space during the remainder of 1999.

In the summer of 1999, the company suspended its plans to auction off its forest holdings, citing a soft timber market as the reason. ''Market conditions have weakened since we initiated the timberland auction process largely due to mill closures, low pulp prices, and competition from three million acres of timberlands offered for sale across the region,'' Rummell said in a July 22, 1999, press release. ''The economic cycles of the pulp and paper industry are well documented. St. Joe can and will be a disciplined seller in this highly cyclical marketplace.'' The company anticipated resuming the auction process when market conditions improved.

Principal Subsidiaries

Arvida/JMB Partners, L.P. (26%); Arvida Realty Services; Codina Group, Inc. (33%); Deerfield Park, L.L.C. (61%); ENTROS, Inc. (44%); Florida East Coast Industries, Inc. (54%); St. Joe/Arvida Company, L.P. (74%); St. Joe/CNL Realty Group, Ltd. (50%); St. Joe Commercial Property Service, Inc.; St. Joe Timberland Company: WBP One, L.P. (50%).

Principal Competitors

Ampace Corporation; Bluegreen Corporation; CSX Corporation; Del Webb Corporation; Gables Residential Trust; Legend Properties, Inc.; Lennar Corporation; Norfolk Southern Corporation.

Further Reading

Faircloth, Anne, ''Land Rush,'' *Fortune*, April 27, 1998.

Faris, Mark, ''St. Joe Builds Southern Power,'' *Commercial Property News*, July 1, 1999, p. 1.

Finotti, John, ''A Million Acres,'' *Florida Trend*, August 1998, p. 34.

Frantz, Douglas, ''A Land Giant Is Stirring: Will Florida Ever Be the Same?'' *New York Times,* April 12, 1998, Sec. 3, pp. 1–12.

Kaczor, Bill, ''St. Joe Has Big Plans for the Panhandle,'' *Tallahassee Democrat*, July 5, 1999, p. 1C.

Snyder, Jack, ''Power to Reshape Florida Will Rest with 1 Company,'' *Orlando Sentinel*, July 4, 1999, p. A1.

Webb, Bailey, ''Jacksonville's The St. Joe Co. Positioned to Shake Things up in Southeastern Markets,'' *National Real Estate Investor*, February 1999.

Word, Ron, ''The St. Joe Co. Looks to Reinvent Itself,'' *Tallahassee Democrat,* July 4, 1999, p. 9C.

—Shawna Brynildssen

Sub-Zero Freezer Co., Inc.

4717 Hammersley Road
Madison, Wisconsin 53711
U.S.A.
Telephone: (608) 271-2233
Toll Free: (800) 444-7820
Fax: (608) 270-3339

Private Company
Incorporated: 1945
Employees: 500
Sales: $100 million (1998 est.)
NAIC: 335222 Refrigerator and Home Freezer Manufacturing

Sub-Zero Freezer Co., Inc., is the leading manufacturer of built-in refrigerators, which can be fronted with cabinetry to blend in with any kitchen décor. Sub-Zero initiated the ''built-in'' trend in home appliances and once held a virtual monopoly in the category. Priced at thousands of dollars above most other refrigerators, with as much as 50 percent of the work on each product done by hand, Sub-Zeros are marketed to America's wealthiest households and are found in the homes of many celebrities. While most of the company's customers are on the East Coast, the West Coast, and in the Sun Belt, Sub-Zero also has international distributors, with a concentration of customers in the Middle East. The company is privately held by the family of founder Westye Bakke. In addition to refrigerators, Sub-Zero also manufactures freezers and a line of wine storage products.

Early Years

Westye Bakke was born on a farm near Rice Lake, Wisconsin, one of ten children. Shortly before World War I, Bakke and his brother Oscar went into business together selling a winterized motorcycle they had invented. The motorcycle, which had a ski on its front wheel so it could go through deep snow, was purchased by Canada's Northwest Royal Mounted police and by other customers as far away as Russia. In addition to their motorcycle business, the brothers also ran a livery service for doctors; however, when it became apparent that there wasn't enough money in the combined enterprises to support two families, Westye ceded the business to Oscar and moved to Madison in 1926. He began working as a refrigerator salesman, first for Frigidaire, and later for York, an industrial refrigeration company.

Not satisfied with selling someone else's refrigerators, in 1943 Bakke built a home deep-freeze, a product that was not commercially available at the time. He applied for a permit from the War Production Board to make freezers, and then returned to his native Rice Lake with $2,000 in savings to begin producing freezers on a small scale. His Rice Lake factory was in an abandoned potato machinery, and in 1945 he opened a plant in Madison. The building was a converted two-car garage which could barely accommodate Bakke and two employees. When it rained, they had to close down, because it got too wet inside. The firm turned out about three freezers a day.

Sub-Zero incorporated in 1945, and began making many specialty freezers, with Bakke capitalizing on his extensive contacts in the refrigeration industry to secure orders. Bakke's son Lawrence ''Bud'' Bakke joined the company in 1948 after graduating from the University of Wisconsin with a degree in mechanical and agricultural engineering, and his expertise allowed the company to move beyond its usual markets. When General Electric, Westinghouse, and other major appliance manufacturers moved into the home freezer market, the tiny firm lost its competitive advantage, so Sub-Zero concentrated instead on specialty freezers and refrigerators for commercial use. Sub-Zero became known as a firm with particular know-how in low-temperature refrigeration. It worked on projects including simulators for the Air Force to test rocket engines in conditions of high altitude and low temperatures. Sub-Zero did work for the Atomic Energy Commission, the Argonne National Laboratory, and scores of university science laboratories with specialized refrigeration needs. Sub-Zero contributed to the modernization of the animal breeding industry with innovative equipment designed for handling frozen bull semen. Sales gradually increased, and the company plowed most of its profits back into the business, allowing it to expand its facilities several times. By 1972 Sub-Zero had moved into a 100,000 square-foot facility in Madison and employed about 100 people.

Company Perspectives:

Welcome to Sub-Zero. We make the ultimate built-in, integrated, and undercounter refrigerators and freezers, and the ultimate wine storage. Hidden refrigerators is an idea we invented; it's an idea we continue to define. For hundreds of designers and hundreds of thousands of homeowners, a kitchen is neither right nor complete without a Sub-Zero.

New Direction in the 1970s

Westye Bakke died in 1973, and the leadership of the company passed to his son. Sales stood at about $2.5 million annually. Most top executives at Sub-Zero had been promoted from inside the company, but the year before the founder's death, the company reorganized and hired experienced managers from elsewhere in the industry. The firm divided into four units: sales and marketing; finance; engineering; and manufacturing. Sub-Zero hired an executive from another firm to head quality control, and brought in a kitchen design expert with 20 years' experience to head its new marketing division.

Through the 1960s, Sub-Zero had been primarily dedicated to commercial refrigeration, but had had some small success building units for family homes. In 1953 a friend of Westye Bakke's who lived in a Milwaukee suburb asked the company to build him a refrigerator that would blend into his kitchen cabinetry, and Sub-Zero responded with a special refrigerator that was only 24 inches deep, just the size of the standard kitchen cabinet. This slim unit that didn't look like a refrigerator was the design that was to make the company famous. One other company, Michigan-based Revco, had made similar refrigerators, but their units were difficult to service and plagued with technical problems. Revco declined by the 1960s, leaving Sub-Zero the only American manufacturer of this type of appliance, and word of mouth soon built up the company's reputation. By the early 1970s, the company was focused almost exclusively on its retail business. Several factors seem to have occurred at once to invigorate Sub-Zero. The reorganization of the company, with a new emphasis on professional marketing, happened just as the Sun Belt of the Southwestern United States was beginning to explode with new housing, especially for affluent buyers. President Bud Bakke gave television celebrity Dinah Shore a Sub-Zero to use on the cooking segment of her show, providing exposure that set the Sub-Zero on the road to being the refrigerator of the stars. The list of celebrities who owned Sub-Zeros began to grow, and before long, the Sub-Zero was the highest status appliance a home kitchen could boast. The Sub-Zero was considered to be an exceptionally high-quality machine, with two compressors—one for the refrigerator and one for the freezer—and patented door and shelving systems. The refrigerators were finished at the factory with a simple white coat of paint, but customers paneled them to match their kitchen cabinets or ornamented them with etchings, murals, or mirrors. This made the Sub-Zero unique: there was no other refrigerator, no matter how costly or technologically advanced, that didn't look like a refrigerator. Designers and architects loved the Sub-Zero because it was not a big, ugly metal box.

By 1982, the company was firmly entrenched as the leader in luxury refrigerators. It was called variously the ''Rolls-Royce of refrigerators,'' the ''Ferrari of refrigerators,'' and other appellations that pronounced it the necessary choice of the very wealthy. Sub-Zero's customers were found mainly in the top five or six percent of American households in terms of wealth. Johnny Carson owned several Sub-Zeros, as did Bob Hope and Danny Thomas. Politicians too adored the Sub-Zero: Richard Nixon and Henry Kissinger each had one. As many as eight yacht manufacturers used Sub-Zero as their refrigeration equipment supplier. In the early 1980s the company had more than 50 distributors, who sold principally on the East Coast, in Southern California, and in Texas. Sub-Zero also had several overseas distributors, with a cluster in the wealthy countries of the Middle East. Sub-Zero's sales were around $25 million in 1980, and by 1985 they stood at $50 million. In the mid-1980s, a Sub-Zero cost around $3,000, which was about $2,000 more than the top-of-the-line Amana refrigerator. In fact, the Sub-Zero was in a class by itself, and in its market niche, price was not a consideration. In terms of total refrigerator market share, Sub-Zero took up only one to two percent. The company was very small compared to other makers such as General Electric and Amana, but it was quite profitable. Envious manufacturers attempted to imitate Sub-Zero. By the mid-1980s, Whirlpool was introducing a similar product, and Sears introduced a built-in refrigerator made for it by Sanyo. But Sub-Zero's president, Homer Price, noted in a March 3, 1986, *Business Week* profile of the company that ''None of our customers would set foot in a Sears store.'' Sub-Zeros belonged with the class of people that had limos and private planes, and competition from mainstream brands didn't seem to be a problem.

Challenges in the 1990s

By 1990, sales at Sub-Zero had surpassed $100 million. The majority of its sales—65 percent—still came from the East and West Coasts. The typical Sub-Zero customer was a 45- to 50-year-old college-educated professional with a salary of at least $100,000 and a home worth at least $400,000. While the 1980s had been a period of conspicuous consumption, by the early 1990s spending had declined, and Sub-Zero struggled to maintain a steady growth rate. The company intensified its marketing and public relations, giving top kitchen designers Sub-Zeros so the machines could be photographed for articles in upscale magazines like *Architectural Digest* and *Town & Country*. Nevertheless, sales slowed in the early 1990s. The company's factories had to shut down in February 1991 as the start of the Persian Gulf War hurt its sales, and workers were laid off again in April. To shore up sales, the company offered rebates. The firm also took good care of its dealers, spending $3 million to $4 million on a trip to Europe for 500 dealers, who were the essential link between the company and the architects and builders who recommended the product to homeowners. Despite its best efforts, by the mid-1990s, Sub-Zero was no longer the only high-end refrigerator, as General Electric and Whirlpool had managed to position products to appeal to Sub-Zero's market. At the same time, Sub-Zero retained a sprawling 70 percent of the upscale refrigerator market, and its sales were still growing at twice the pace of the refrigerator market overall.

Attempting to expand the product line, the company developed smaller refrigerators, some the size of cabinet drawers,

Key Dates:

1943: Westye Bakke builds his prototype freezer.
1945: Sub-Zero incorporates in Madison.
1953: Company sells its first built-in refrigerator.
1972: Firm reorganizes, hires outside executives.
1973: Bud Bakke becomes president.
1980: Sales reach $50 million.
1990: James Bakke, founder's grandson, becomes president.

which could be employed around the kitchen or in other rooms. Michael Jordan, star of the Chicago Bulls basketball team, had 13 installed in his mansion. The company expanded its facilities in 1993, building a new 60,000-square-foot building next to its Madison headquarters. Sub-Zero employed roughly 600 people, with about 400 in Wisconsin and the remainder at a second plant in Phoenix, Arizona. While the company had grown dramatically in sales and expanded its manufacturing facilities several times, it had not significantly modernized the basic construction of its products. About 50 percent of the assembly work on each Sub-Zero was still done by hand.

In order to maintain its edge with consumers, Sub-Zero began using data from focus groups in the late 1990s. These groups helped tell the company's designers what features people considered most valuable in their refrigerators, and what features should be enhanced. As a result of this customer input, in 1998 Sub-Zero released a new series, the 600, with more feature options. The 600s used advanced microprocessors that adjusted the temperature setting inside the unit and employed ''fuzzy logic'' to make changes based on the temperature in the room and how often the refrigerator door was opened. The electronic processor also ran a self-checking program and could instruct service technicians in making repairs. Some units offered a Sabbath mode, that allowed the refrigerator to be programmed to perform certain chores for Jewish customers who abstained from work on the Sabbath.

The company began building a huge warehouse near Madison in 1998. The 200,000-square-foot building was split between a distribution center and new manufacturing facilities. By that time, Sub-Zero was making 30 different models of refrigerators, and it anticipated further growth. The company had been looking for a line extension for some time (though President James Bakke remarked in an April 8, 1996, article in *Forbes* that the Sub-Zero name just didn't work on a stove). In early 1999 the company introduced wine storage and cooling units. To prepare for more production, Sub-Zero acquired more land in Phoenix, near its earlier site, and also made plans to add to its Madison headquarters.

Principal Competitors

General Electric; Whirlpool.

Further Reading

Arndt, Michael, ''Sub-Zero Keeps its Cool in Upscale Appliance Market,'' *Wisconsin State Journal,* March 31, 1996, p. 4E.
''Cool!'' *Forbes,* April 8, 1996, p. 98.
Deveny, Kathleen, ''Sub-Zero Isn't Trembling over a Little Competition,'' *Business Week,* March 3, 1986, p. 118.
Langill, Ellen D., *Sub-Zero at Fifty: A History of the Sub-Zero Freezer Company, Inc.,* Madison, Wisconsin: Sub-Zero Freezer Company, 1995.
Milano, Mike, ''Sub-Zero: A Chilling Effect,'' *HFN,* June 14, 1999, p. 34.
Newhouse, John, ''Sub-Zero Freezer Co. Is Doing as Well under Son as under Dad,'' *Wisconsin State Journal,* October 8, 1972.
Parkins, Al, ''Sub-Zero—Best Business Secret Around,'' *Capital Times* (Madison, Wisconsin), August 17, 1982, p. 4.
''Sub-Zero Heats Up 600 Line; Presents Fresh Designs, Materials, Features and Functions,'' *HFN,* March 23, 1998, p. 60.
Stevens, Amy, ''Will Millionaires' Toys Reach Masses?,'' *Wall Street Journal,* March 14, 1997, p. B6.
Treleven, Ed, ''Appliance Maker Fortunes Vary,'' *Wisconsin State Journal,* February 23, 1992.

—A. Woodward

IT'S A CLASSIC

The Talbots, Inc.

175 Beal Street
Hingham, Massachusetts 02043-1586
U.S.A.
Telephone: (781) 749-7600
Toll Free: (800) 825-2687
Fax: (781) 741-7734
Web site: http://www.Talbots.com

Public Company
Incorporated: 1947
Employees: 8,600
Sales: $1.14 billion
Stock Exchanges: New York
Ticker Symbol: TLB
NAIC: 44812 Women's Clothing Stores; 45411 Electronic Shopping and Mail-Order Houses

The Talbots, Inc. is a leading niche retailer of women's apparel and related products, with more than 600 stores and a catalog operation. The company got its start in New England in 1947 and remained a small regional chain for nearly 30 years before it was purchased by General Mills, which undertook its nationwide expansion. In the late 1980s, Talbots was sold to a Japanese retail conglomerate, which funded further growth for the company. In the 1990s, Talbots expanded both its product offerings and its geographical scope as it began to open stores overseas.

Starting a Tradition in Hingham, Massachusetts in the 1940s

Talbots was founded in 1947 by Rudolf and Nancy Talbot. The couple inherited a store in Hingham, Massachusetts, a suburb of Boston, from Rudolf's father and named it "The Talbots." Over time, the company became known simply as Talbots. The couple stocked their store with classic women's apparel. In their first year in business, sales totaled $18,000. During their second year in business, the Talbots branched out from in-store retailing and launched a catalog operation. After buying a list of subscribers to *The New Yorker* magazine, they distributed 3,000 black-and-white fliers featuring illustrations of Talbots clothing to these potential customers.

By 1950, the Talbots' business had outgrown its first location, and it moved to a two-story colonial frame house that had been built in the 17th century in Hingham. The first floor was given over to sales, and the second floor was converted into office space. The front door of this building was lacquered a bright red, and this architectural touch later became a hallmark of the Talbots chain. Five years after the expansion, Talbots opened its first branch store, in Duxbury, Massachusetts, a town south of Hingham. In the following years, stores also were opened in Lenox, Massachusetts; Hamden, Connecticut; and Avon, Connecticut.

Throughout the social and cultural upheavals of the 1960s, Talbots maintained its focus on classic styles and traditional clothing for an affluent, well-educated customer. By the end of the decade, the company's growth in store number and size, along with expanding catalog sales, necessitated larger facilities. In 1970 Talbots moved its business headquarters and mail-order operations to a new location in Hingham. By this time, the company's staff had grown to include 71 employees, who worked in the five New England Talbots stores.

Expansion Under General Mills Through the 1980s

By 1973, the original black-and-white Talbots brochure had evolved into four yearly full-color catalogs, which, combined with the company's five retail outlets, brought in $8 million in annual revenues. This success attracted the attention of larger companies, and, that year, the Talbots sold their chain of stores to consumer goods giant General Mills.

After purchasing the chain, General Mills began a program of limited regional expansion. Over the next seven years, Talbots opened eight new stores in locations throughout New England. In 1980 the company moved outside New England for the first time, inaugurating outlets in New York, Pennsylvania, and Delaware. With these new locations, Talbots's payroll swelled to include 800 people. Also in 1980, Talbots established a toll-free telephone number to make it easier for cus-

Company Perspectives:

Talbots has a long-standing commitment to serving both its customer and the community in which she resides. This synergy between customer and community service is best summarized by the Company's credo, ''Do What is Right for the Customer.''

tomers to order from its catalog. The company also expanded its headquarters facility from 80,000 to 200,000 square feet.

Throughout the 1980s, with a heavy infusion of funds from General Mills, Talbots expanded its chain of stores dramatically. The company grew from fewer than 20 stores to 126 stores in just eight years. With each new store that it opened, Talbots implemented its retailing strategy. The company strove to give all of its outlets the residential feel of the company's original 17th-century Hingham home. Interiors were decorated with maple floors and wainscoting, and walls were hung with traditional botanical and equestrian prints, to simulate the atmosphere of a gracious English home. In addition, each store was fitted with a bright red door and, wherever possible, matching red awnings over the windows.

In 1984 Talbots expanded the range of its merchandise offerings when it introduced clothing in petite sizes in both its stores and catalog. In this way, the company hoped to tap into the sizable market of women who needed professional and sophisticated clothing in smaller sizes. The following year, Talbots expanded its efforts in this area, opening a Talbots Petites store in Cambridge, Massachusetts.

By 1988, Talbots had expanded its primary store concept to 25 states, and the company was taking in $350 million annually in sales. Of those revenues, 40 percent were derived from catalog sales. The company's 24 annual glossy and colorful brochures were distributed to 70 million customers throughout the world. To better serve catalog customers, Talbots opened a new catalog fulfillment and merchandise distribution center in Lakeville, Massachusetts, in January 1988. The 555,000-square-foot facility processed an average of 20,000 items a day and was capable of completing two-and-a-half times as many during peak periods, such as the holiday shopping season.

Refocusing Operations in the Late 1980s as Part of the ÆON Group

At the start of 1988, General Mills announced that it was divesting itself of its clothing retail operations, to concentrate fully on its food-related businesses. Talbots's corporate parent put it up for sale along with Eddie Bauer, Inc., an outdoor clothing company that also maintained catalog operations. Although industry observers were hesitant about General Mills' asking price of $250 million for each chain and also were concerned about difficulties in the mail-order business overall, several companies indicated interest in purchasing Talbots, among them Sears, Roebuck & Company and Spiegel, Inc., another women's clothing cataloger.

Ultimately, however, General Mills sold the chain to the Jusco Group, a leading Japanese retailer that was the core company of the ÆON Group. ÆON brought together approximately 150 different international retail properties, led by Jusco, a major chain of Japanese department stores. Jusco purchased Talbots for $350 million in June 1988. At the time of this sale, Talbots also acquired a data processing center in Tampa, Florida, owned by General Mills, and Arnold B. Zetcher, a seasoned retail executive, became CEO.

Talbots's new owner planned to use the company as a first step toward American retailing operations and also hoped to successfully expand the Talbots concept in Japan. Although Talbots's president had resigned when General Mills announced that it was selling the chain, its second-in-command remained, and Jusco put him in charge of running its new purchase.

Talbots's rapid expansion had left it with some problems in its operation. At the catalog sales telemarketing center, frequent computer breakdowns forced employees to write out orders by hand, a cumbersome process. In addition, customers often had difficulty getting through on the phone. Moreover, systems in Talbots's stores also needed improvements. For instance, employees had no way of monitoring stock at stores to recommend that customers seek certain items at other locations. Jusco spent $50 million implementing new computer systems in an effort to fix these and other problems.

In addition, Talbots refocused its merchandise offerings. Rather than rely on other clothing manufacturers' labels for 75 percent of its merchandise, the company decided to rely almost exclusively on its own private label. In this way, it was able to keep more of the money it made on clothing and also was able to maintain strict control over the quality of the clothes it sold. Under this new program, 95 percent of the clothes sold in Talbots stores carried the Talbots label.

Talbots also decided to emphasize its retail outlets over its catalog operations. Under this strategy, the company began to use its catalog primarily as a market indicator of the most potentially profitable parts of the country. Once mail-order sales were running at $100,00 to $150,000 within a given zip code, a store located in that area would draw $1 million to $1.5 million in annual sales, while only cutting catalog sales by 25 percent. With this in mind, Talbots set out to open a large number of stores in areas across the nation. In addition, Talbots embarked on a multifaceted program to expand beyond women's clothing into other related lines of merchandise. This facility augmented the operations at the company's original Hingham, Massachusetts telemarketing location.

At the same time, Talbots also inaugurated its first overseas operation, establishing Talbots International Retailing Limited, Inc., in Hong Kong. This office was responsible for overseeing manufacture of many Talbots private-label products in the Far East, including quality control, design, and testing. It also provided a communications link between the company's Asian manufacturers and its American Product Development and Merchandising offices.

In July 1989, Talbots introduced a catalog devoted entirely to children's clothing called ''Talbots Kids.'' With this line of

Key Dates:

1947: Talbots is founded with one store in Hingham, Massachusetts.
1948: Talbots launches its direct mail catalog business.
1950: Talbots moves to its landmark house with the red door.
1970: Corporate offices move to 175 Beal Street.
1973: General Mills acquires Talbots.
1980: Talbots expands beyond New England.
1988: General Mills sells Talbots, which joins the Tokyo-based ÆON Group.
1989: International sourcing operation opens in Hong Kong.
1990: Talbots introduces its Talbots Kids stores and Talbots Petites line.
1991: First Talbots store opens in Canada.
1993: Talbots is listed on the New York Stock Exchange.
1994: Talbots opens its first European store outside London.
1995: The Talbots Babies line is introduced and Talbots Accessories & Shoes is opened.
1997: The company's 50th anniversary is marked by $1 billion in total company sales.
1998: The "Talbots Woman" is introduced for large-sized women.

goods, the company hoped to capitalize on the brand loyalty of mothers who bought Talbots merchandise for themselves, hoping they would also want to do so for their children. When the Talbots Kids catalog proved successful, the company went on to open the first two Talbots Kids stores, in Westport, Connecticut and in Charlotte, North Carolina. These stores were placed next to existing Talbots stores, to make a block of stores carrying the Talbots line. The children's stores featured bright colors, whimsical fixtures, and fun children's furniture. About 80 percent of the goods they offered carried the Talbots brand name.

As Talbots made the transition from the ownership of General Mills to ÆON and tried to retool itself for further growth in the 1990s, the company experienced several challenges. In 1990, for instance, Talbots introduced clothing in more trendy, less traditional colors, stocking stores with blouses and skirts in avocado and gold, rather than the traditional navy blue and red. Customers were less than pleased with this development, and operating profits dropped by 40 percent, as the chain suffered a loss for the year of $7 million. In response to these poor results, Talbots returned to its more traditional styles, and the chain's sales soon began to recover.

In November 1990, Talbots also branched out into its first nonclothing line of merchandise, when it began to market "Talbots," a white floral perfume. The company offered the scent in five different forms, including lotion, powder, and gel. By the end of 1990, Talbots had also begun to roll out the expansion of its Talbots Petites stores, opening locations next to previously established Talbots outlets. Further extension of Talbots's line of products came in July 1991, when the company began to offer underwear and sleepwear through its fall catalog. This line was designed to compete with the market that Victoria's Secret had pioneered, but in a more traditional vein.

International Expansion in the 1990s

Also that year, Talbots launched its first international subsidiary, creating Talbots Canada, Inc., headquartered in Toronto. In September 1991, the first Canadian Talbots stores opened in three separate Toronto locations. Seven Talbots stores already had been opened in Japan, but these were directly owned by the company's Japanese parent and thus were not run by the American subsidiary. By the end of the year, Talbots ran 240 stores of its own, 43 of which had been opened in the preceding 12 months. Overall, Talbots sales from these locations and its catalog operation, which made up one-third of the whole, totaled more than $500 million.

Part of Talbots's strategy for maintaining its profitability was to resist the lure of constant discounting to pump up sales. The company conducted four annual markdowns and otherwise sold all merchandise at full price. In addition, Talbots benefited from a strong demand for its traditionally styled clothing among those who rejected other emerging fashion trends, including grunge and the baby-doll look, from the rest of the fashion industry.

Talbots continued its strong showing in 1992. The company began to team up with other niche retailers, such as the Gap, to open stores in mini-malls, which offered lower rents than larger suburban malls. In addition, the company pushed forward with its policy of clustering the different stores in its line, Talbots Kids and Talbots Petites, for greater selling power.

In October 1992, Talbots introduced a new member of its retail family, when freestanding Talbots Intimates stores were opened in Austin, Texas; St. Louis, Missouri; and Troy, Michigan. In addition, the company opened in-store boutiques in existing outlets in Boston; Chicago; Pittsford, New York; and Short Hills, New Jersey. Each of these locations was designed to look like a New England summer cottage, with lots of light and whitewashed wood. The stores offered perfume, books, and an assortment of gifts, as well as lingerie and sleepwear. About half of the merchandise carried the Talbots label, a percentage lower than that of the company's other operations. Talbots Intimates goods also were offered through a separate catalog.

By the end of 1992, Talbots sales had increased 23 percent over the 12-month period, to reach $642 million, and the company continued to open new stores at a brisk pace. In May 1993, Talbots opened a Midwest flagship store on Michigan Avenue in Chicago. With its location in a popular shopping area, the outlet was expected to become the company's highest grossing store. In addition, Talbots moved forward with its Canadian expansion, opening four new stores in the fall of 1993, in Ottawa and Vancouver, British Columbia.

In September 1993, Talbots's Japanese parent announced that it would sell shares in the company to the public. The initial public offering of 11 million shares, which took place in November 1993, reaped $242 million, with ÆON Group retaining 67 percent ownership in the company. In the first day of trading, the company's stock proved to be extremely popular with investors, and its price quickly rose by 20 percent, as buyers responded favorably to Talbots's strong brand name and image.

With the money from the sale of stock, Talbots paid off some debts and repurchased some trademark rights from ÆON's European arm.

At the time of its sale to the public, Talbots had grown to comprise 313 stores in 44 states, which included eight Talbots Surplus stores, where the company sold outdated merchandise at discounted prices. By the end of 1993, Talbots sales had risen to $737 million, a gain of 15 percent. The company's net income also rose, to $35 million. Overall, earnings had grown sevenfold since the start of the 1990s. At the end of 1994, the company's first full year as a public entity, net income was $54.5 million on net sales of $879.6 million.

In April 1994, Talbots opened three more stores in Canada and announced plans for a major push into Europe. Anticipating that its current rate of growth—approximately 50 new stores in the United States each year—would saturate the market within seven years, the company turned to foreign shores for future growth. On the basis of its strong success in Canada, Talbots chose England as its next target, and in September 1994, the company opened a test store in a London suburb. Pending the results from the London store, Talbots planned to open 30 stores in the United Kingdom and 170 stores in other parts of Europe and Mexico.

Concurrent with its expansion overseas, Talbots also sought to expand its market at home. In response to customer demand, it introduced two new retail concepts in 1995, Talbots Babies and Talbots Accessories & Shoes. Of its 65 new stores in 1995, five were separate shoe and accessory stores.

Product lines were not the only thing to see change at Talbots in the late 1990s. Talbots entered a new merchandise field when it began distributing a catalog focusing on shoes and accessories. In the same way that it had previously used other catalogs to test the market for children's clothing and lingerie, Talbots hoped in this way to fine-tune its entry into yet another retail category. Yet, despite breaking the $1 billion mark in sales in 1997, Talbots faced a two-year softening of sales at its 600-odd stores. Revenues had grown only 3.9 percent in 1996, a fraction of the 23 percent gain posted in 1992. Earnings rose just two percent to reach $63.6 million, a small gain compared with the 55 percent posted in 1994. In 1996 the company was cited for buying goods from manufacturers that had flouted the nation's wage and hour laws. To counter the slump in the industry and head off any negative publicity, the company responded by changing its focus with its 1997 spring-summer line to more casual clothes aimed at a younger, less "traditional" customer.

The result was disastrous; the new line bombed so badly, Talbots was forced to take steep markdowns. Sales and stock price slumped, and Talbots beat a quick return to the classics as profits dropped from $63.6 million in 1996 to $5.84 million in 1997. It contracted with Arnold Communications to develop an ad campaign, the company's largest and most comprehensive effort in its 50-year history, that stressed the personality of the Talbots woman by showing her in different, "real" situations and settings. Arnold also modified the company slogan from "Talbots is the classics" to "It's a classic" in an attempt to contemporize the company's image, to update it in a way that attracted new customers while not, as before, alienating the old.

But signs persisted that Talbots's growth machinery was tiring. Even as it stepped up its print campaign, the company hit a 52-week low on the New York Stock Exchange. In early 1998, Talbots reported flat sales and greatly reduced income for fiscal 1997. Still the company and analysts were optimistic about its future. Under a new merchandising team, headed by Mark Shulman, Talbots instituted plans to open another 35 stores in 1998 and launch both a new catalog and retail operations aimed at full-figured women. Talbots also planned to open a prototyped Talbots Woman store in St. Louis as well as departments in seven established stores, to showcase its plus-size clothing line.

By late 1998, Talbots appeared to be regaining sales momentum. Third-quarter earnings for the year exceeded expectations, and company stock was once again trading close to its 52-week high. The company put preventive measures in place, such as lower inventory levels, but by mid-1999, Talbots felt confident enough to experiment again, this time with a plan to launch an e-commerce site in the fall. With a still-solid base of loyal customers, a trusted brand name, and a commitment to woo back those it had lost, Talbots appeared well situated to prosper in the years to come.

Principal Subsidiaries

Talbots Canada, Inc.

Principal Competitors

Ann Taylor; Federated; May.

Further Reading

Barmash, Isidore, "General Mills To Pick Bids for Two Units," *New York Times,* May 10, 1988.

Biddle, Frederic M., "Talbots: Master of Nice Retailing," *Boston Sunday Globe,* August 2, 1992.

Fallon, James, "Talbots Revs Up Expansion Plans in Europe," *Women's Wear Daily,* June 23, 1994.

Feldman, Amy, "Basics for the Nineties," *Forbes,* May 9, 1994.

Neale, Stacy, "Talbots Inc. Is Set To Try on Europe for Size," *Boston Business Journal,* May 20–26, 1994.

Reidy, Chris, "Updating the Classic," *Boston Globe,* September 12, 1997, p. C2.

——, "Dressed for Success," *Boston Globe,* August 24, 1995, p. 69.

Schmeltzer, John, "Talbots Has Red-Letter Day on Michigan Ave.," *Chicago Tribune,* May 15, 1993.

Symonds, William, "Talbots Drops the 'Funkier Stuff,' " *Business Week,* October 6, 1997, p. 164.

—Elizabeth Rourke
—updated by Carrie Rothburd

Tandycrafts, Inc.

1400 Everman Parkway
Fort Worth, Texas 76140
U.S.A.
Telephone: (817) 551-9600
Fax: (817) 551-9795
Web site: http://www.tandycrafts.com

Public Company
Incorporated: 1975
Employees: 2,800
Sales: $194.7 million (1999)
Stock Exchanges: New York
Ticker Symbol: TAC
NAIC: 315223 Men's & Boys' Cut and Sew Shirt Manufacturing; 323113 Commercial Screen Printing; 339999 All Other Miscellaneous Manufacturing; 421920 Toy and Hobby Goods and Supplies Wholesalers; 422110 Furniture Stores; 453210 Office Supply and Stationery Stores; 455110 Electronic Shopping and Mail-Order Houses; 511191 Greeting Card Publishers

Tandycrafts, Inc. manufactures and distributes consumer goods in four distinctive areas. Frames and Wall Decor, Tandycrafts' largest and most profitable division, manufactures picture and art frames, mirrors, and wall art as well as greeting cards and inspirational gift items. The Novelties and Promotional division produces a number of promotional goods for political campaigns, nonprofit organizations, national sports teams, and tourist businesses. The Office Supplies division includes the Save-On Office Supplies chain of retail stores. The leathercraft business endures under the Leather and Crafts division, now a direct-to-customer business that is conducted by mail order catalog and an Internet site.

A Small ''Shoe-findings'' Storefront Established in 1919

Tandycrafts, Inc. started in a small storefront in downtown Forth Worth, Texas as Hinckley-Tandy Leather Company. The company sold ''shoe-findings,'' leather shoe laces, shoe soles, and leather and rubber heels, and other items to shoe repair shops. Company founders Dave Tandy and Norton Hinckley met while working in the shoe-findings department of a Dallas leather company. When the two started their own business in 1919 they discovered that they had complementary talents. Tandy, being more outgoing, sold to shops outside the Forth Worth area, while Hinckley focused on local sales. As business grew, Tandy supervised the sales and marketing area of the business and Hinckley managed internal business such as buying inventory. With a Texas oil boom in progress, the Hinckley-Tandy Leather Company did well in its first decade, moving to a larger storefront in 1923 and opening a branch in Beaumont in 1927.

The historical events of the following decades proved to be both difficult and beneficial to the company. The Depression forced the closure of the Beaumont branch, but negotiations with suppliers to extend payment of invoices over a year's time saved the company. During this period Dave Tandy spoke to business groups on optimism in sales and psychology in marketing. To shoe repair shops he recommended that signs reading, ''Shoes Repaired While You Wait,'' be changed to, ''Shoes Repaired While You Rest.''

The oversupply of inventory during the Depression gave way to a shortage of supplies during World War II when the military used most of the leather available, creating a shortage of leather for civilian use. Dave Tandy pursued leathercraft supply business as a sideline when his son Charles reported that military hospitals provided leathercraft programs for the recreation and rehabilitation of injured military personnel. The hospitals required specialty leathers for crafting belts, billfolds, and purses.

When Charles Tandy joined the company after the war, he brought great ambitions. He already had experience producing and selling products in a variety of leather-related businesses from the age of ten, when Charles taught school friends how to make belts from the leather scraps he sold them from his father's business. Charles assisted in expansion of Hinckley-Tandy to branches in Amarillo, Dallas, Houston, Albuquerque, and southern Oklahoma. In addition to shoe-findings, the company sold leather uppers to custom boot makers and began a mail order business, issuing catalogs to individuals as well as

Key Dates:

1919: Hinckley-Tandy Leather Company founded.
1947: Charles Tandy joins company.
1950: Dave and Charles Tandy form Tandy Leather Company.
1955: Merger with American Hide and Leather Company.
1960: Company renamed The Tandy Corporation.
1975: Tandycrafts, Inc. established as a separate company.
1999: Tandy Leather stores close.

shoe repair shops. Charles Tandy's ambitions went beyond these improvements, however; Charles envisioned a national chain of retail leathercraft stores.

The Tandys' attraction to the leathercraft supply business led to a division in the Hinckley-Tandy Leather Company. After the company suffered a loss in 1949, despite higher sales than in 1948, the Board of Directors divided the business into two departments to determine where profit or loss originated. Each department had its own bookkeeping system, inventory, employees, and physical space. Hinckley oversaw the shoe-findings department, and the Tandys oversaw the leather uppers department. The official split in the company occurred in spring 1950. The Tandys purchased the Fort Worth, Houston, Amarillo, and Albuquerque operations from Hinckley, and Hinckley purchased the Dallas operations from the Tandys. The Tandy Leather Company (TLC) was established in May 1950 and moved to an uptown location.

Leathercraft Popularity in the 1950s

The Tandys quickly expanded their business. TLC's first catalog included eight pages of products. Most business came from institutions, such as prisons, youth summer camps, and youth organizations, but the number of individual leathercrafters grew as well. Leathercraft stores opened in El Paso and San Antonio, areas where a minimum of 1,000 catalog customers already existed. Acquisition of the Cardat Leather Goods company expanded the line of business to finished leather goods, such as purses, watchbands, and billfolds. The first year in business, TLC obtained a 100 percent return on investment.

The company grew based on the location of catalog sales customers. Stores that opened in North Carolina and Georgia in 1951 served nearby prisons where leathercraft programs offered inmates productive activity and income from sales to other inmates. New stores opened in Beaumont, Salt Lake City, Los Angeles, and Omaha. Each store also served the catalog customers in its area. Part of the Tandy strategy was to locate stores just off main business avenues, such as Mission Street in San Francisco and Olive Street in St. Louis. The company's product line expanded to prepackaged kits, hides, tools, instruction books, and a wider variety of precut leather.

Charles Tandy paid close attention to profitability and the potential for future growth. As a tax shelter, each store incorporated separately. To sustain sales incentive, the Tandys required store managers to own a 25 percent interest in the store and provided loans, averaging $2,500, toward that end. Dave Tandy also co-signed loans so that administrative staff in Forth Worth could invest in the stores. Charles was particularly adamant with employees to buy stock with their year-end bonus checks. As the company succeeded, no one regretted the inducement. With a bold and charismatic personality, Charles successfully employed a mix of humor and pressure to provoke store managers to improve sales.

TLC furthered expansion with the acquisition of New Jersey-based American Handicrafts Company. The company sold a variety of art supplies, and leathercraft supplies comprised 25 percent of the business. The business, which included two stores and a large mail order business, neared bankruptcy when TLC purchased it for $90,000 in 1952. By 1954 TLC began to open stores around the country.

The company's first big success involved a kit for baby moccasins, which included precut white lambskin. The kit sold for 50 cents a pair through two-inch advertisements in *Ladies Home Journal, Good Housekeeping,* and *Work Basket* magazines. With 50 to 100 of the advertisements running simultaneously, TLC sold more than three million pairs over five years. By 1954 the company catalog had grown to 68 pages and the mail order business reached one million customers. Four factories served 67 retail stores in 36 states and the territory of Hawaii.

1955: Risky Business Going Public

The death of Dave Tandy of a heart attack in 1954 resulted in financial challenges for TLC related in part to inheritance taxes. In addition, employee stock owners did not know the value of their ownership, especially given the different levels of ownership in different stores. Charles Tandy sought to resolve these issues and became determined to list the company on the New York Stock Exchange. TLC was too small, however. To resolve that problem, Charles sought a merger with a company already listed. Charles made an agreement with the insolvent American Hide and Leather Company (AHLC) of Boston.

TLC's agreement with AHLC risked control of the company. The agreement allowed AHLC to acquire TLC for $2.3 million in promissory notes with no interest and no cash up front. Basically, TLC gave AHLC the money to buy TLC, as AHLC could make payments to TLC based on TLC's earnings over a ten-year period. TLC stockholders had the option to buy 500,000 shares of stock at $4 per share during the first four years. After Charles obtained stockholder consent, the agreement was signed in October 1955, and TLC was renamed Tandy Industries, Inc. (TII), a wholly owned subsidiary of AHLC, with Charles as president.

Although Charles and two other TII executives became members of the Board of AHLC, majority control of TII's earnings remained in the hands of original AHLC directors. Charles willingly risked ownership of the company because TII earnings would not be taxable for five years because of tax regulations on net loss, which AHLC insolvency secured. Charles also believed that he could turn AHLC into a profitable company. Trouble ensued when AHLC began to use TII earnings to acquire poorly performing businesses in a variety of industries. AHLC changed its name to General American Industries (GAI) in December 1956 and two TII executives were replaced on the Board with people from two of those companies. Profits from TII and Tex Tan, a Western leather goods manufacturer acquired that year, covered the losses of the other companies in the conglomerate and prevented Charles from expanding the leathercraft business. Charles tried to stop the shifting of his company's earnings to insolvent companies.

As struggles for power among the Board's newest members intensified, Charles prepared for a stockholder proxy fight over Board membership. With GAI stock valued at $3.00 to $3.50 per share, lower than TII's stock option agreement, Charles exercised that option at a loss. He requested that all store managers maximize their credit line to purchase the stock and also received financial assistance from his wife and other family members. A business associate persuaded a foreign investor to remain neutral. With a win in the proxy vote assured, negotiations at the November 1959 Board meeting settled the matter and gave TII five of the nine Board seats.

Under the new Board the three recently acquired subsidiaries were sold at a loss, and GAI returned to the business of leather goods. In 1960 Charles relocated GAI to Fort Worth and renamed it the Tandy Corporation, with TAN as the exchange symbol. Stock sold at $4.00 per share, but by the end of 1961 stock rose to more than $11.00 per share. In 1961 Tandy acquired Cleveland Crafts Inc., which operated educational and craft supply stores in New York City, Los Angeles, and Nashville, as well as Cleveland. Other acquisitions included the May and Corral Sportswear of Oklahoma, Merribee Needlearts, the Electronic Crafts Division of Swieco Inc., and Toys for Men, Ltd. A successful new product at this time was a saddle kit sold to YMCA summer camps; the children put the saddle together for use at the camp.

Charles experimented with a new retail concept, the Tandy Craft and Hobby Mart, which opened in Fort Worth in November 1961. The 18,000-square-foot space sold a variety of hobby and craft products within 35 different shops, selling more than 50,000 different items for more than 50 crafts and hobbies, including Electronic Crafts, which sold do-it-yourself stereo kits. The Mart included pet, gourmet food, and record stores. The market was anchored by a Tandy Leather store and an American Handicraft store. Similar marts opened in Dallas in November 1962 and in San Antonio in September 1963. By that time the company had grown to more than 140 retail stores in 100 cities.

Diversification in the 1960s included a variety of retail businesses. Cost Plus, renamed Pier 1 Imports, an importer of household goods, required a different type of management than leathercraft, with a longer lead buying time. The company's employees purchased the company from Tandy in 1966. Charles was best known for turning Radio Shack, electronic equipment stores, into a household name. Although that company became a major focus of Charles's attention, Tandy Leather continued to grow to more than 350 retail stores in the mid-1970s.

Tandycrafts on Its Own in 1975

By 1975 it became clear that the Tandy Corporation would need to be divided into three separate companies. Two new companies formed were Tandy Brands and Tandycrafts, Inc. Tandycrafts encompassed the Tandy Leather Company, American Handicrafts, *Decorating and Crafts* magazine, Color Tile, Magee, Merribee Needlearts, Woodie Taylor Vending, Automated Custom Food Services, Stafford-Lowdon, and Bona Allen. Tandycrafts received $6 million from the Tandy Corporation and was listed on the stock exchange at $13.00 per share. John Wilson, former president of the Tandy Corporation, became president, CEO, and a Board Director of Tandycrafts.

As a separate company Tandycrafts redirected operations. Tandycrafts divided further when Stafford-Lowdon, a printing operation, and Color Tile became separate companies, in May 1976, and in March 1979, respectively. The company discontinued Merribee Needlearts and American Handicrafts in 1982 and eventually sold or discontinued other companies as well.

The market for leathercraft goods began to shrink by the 1980s. The lower birth rate meant than the size of a primary customer base—youth groups and summer camp programs—folded. In addition, schools no longer taught handicrafts at previous levels. By May 1991, Tandy Leather Company operated 187 retail stores. The company continued to pursue the wholesale leather goods business with the purchase of western apparel and accessory companies, the Nocona Belt Company and Two-Gether Leather in 1992, and Prestige Leather Creations in 1993.

Tandycrafts ventured into the business of Christian bookstores with the acquisition of the chain of 34 Joshua's Christian Bookstores in 1986. That business would be supplemented by the acquisition of J-Mar Associates, which produced inspirational gifts sold in Christian bookstores. The acquisitions of the Mustard Seed chain of five bookstores in Denver in December 1993; Lord's Vineyard, Inc., a 15,000-square-foot store in Colorado Springs, in April 1994; and the Christian Outlet of Phoenix in May 1995, added to the Joshua's Christian Bookstores chain. The stores sold an even mix of gifts, Christian music, and motivational books.

Realignment in the 1990s

In the 1990s Tandycrafts dabbled in a number of business ventures before it settled into four areas of vertically integrated manufacturing, wholesale, and retail concepts. Tandycrafts sought to build on the strength of its frames and wall art businesses. Magee Company, a manufacturer of steel and wood picture frames acquired by the Tandy Corporation in 1968, was one of the top suppliers of frames to retail stores with distribution to mass merchants such as Wal-Mart and Venture. In November 1993, Tandycrafts acquired Impulse Designs, a manufacturer of framed wall art that also distributed to mass merchants with a wider and higher price range, from $10 to $100 retail. Hermitage Fine Arts specialized in an upscale market of specialty and department stores.

Tandycrafts also pursued novelty and licensed product companies in the 1990s. David James Manufacturing and Brand Name Apparel were acquired in the fall of 1992. TAG Express, licensed by the NFL, NBA, NHL, Major League Baseball, U.S. Soccer League, and all major colleges to produce bumper stickers, key tags, pennants, and similar products, was purchased in

September 1993. The acquisition of Birdlegs provided a similar product line in souvenir t-shirts, sweatshirts, and related products bearing screen-printed resort and location names for vacation travelers. Rivertown Button, acquired in April 1994, produced buttons, posters, and similar promotional items for political campaigns, nonprofit organizations, schools, and businesses. The company also purchased College Flags and Manufacturing Co. Inc. in September 1994.

Tandycrafts began to reorganize in 1995, to consolidate and prune company operations by forming four new operating divisions and selling unrelated or unprofitable businesses. The Novelties and Promotional division included Rivertown Button and Licensed Lifestyles, the latter being a consolidation of TAG Express, Birdlegs, and College Flags. Most assets of Brand Name Apparel were sold, and David James Manufacturing closed. The Leather and Crafts division included Tandy Leather and Crafts and Tandy Wholesale International. A slowdown in the sales of Western clothing led to the sale of Prestige Leather Creations in 1996 and Nocona Belt Company in 1999.

The Office Supplies division consisted of Save-On Office Supplies stores. The chain consisted of seven stores when it was purchased in 1991, and eight more stores opened within the first year. To improve sales, Tandycrafts added office furniture, facsimile machines, and computer-related products to its inventory and hired outside sales representatives to increase awareness of the stores. The chain had grown to more than 40 stores in 11 states, primarily in the South and Midwest, in 1999.

The Frames and Wall Decor division encompassed the three frame and art companies under Pinnacle Art and Frame and J-Mar Associates. Sales and marketing for Magee and Impulse Designs were combined because of their similar retail outlets. The Impulse Designs plant in Van Nuys, California relocated to Durango, in northern Mexico, where a new, state-of-the art factory opened in July 1999. Administration, design, and other office staff were transferred to Fort Worth. After intensive market research, J-Mar Associates launched a new product line of greeting cards and gift items designed for women. Trademarked, "By the way," packets of five products—a greeting card, sachet, note pad, refrigerator magnet, and bookmark—eased gift-giving. The relationship-oriented themes included Family, Friendship, and Encouragement.

Other actions to streamline the company included the sale of Cargo Furniture to management and employees in January 1997. The company was forced to buy back the company in June 1999 when Cargo defaulted on a loan guaranteed by Tandycrafts. The company planned to transform the unprofitable stores to the more successful Cargo Collection concept, which offered a wider variety of furniture styles and home accessories. Cargo products were available on the Internet at www.cargohome.com and through a national network of representatives to commercial accounts. The Joshua's Christian Bookstores chain was sold in April 1998.

The leathercraft business had continued to shrink in the 1990s. By 1991 only 187 Tandy Leather stores remained open. A temporary surge in sales occurred in the late 1980s and early 1990s when clothing and home decorations in the Southwestern style became popular, but by 1995 a permanent decline in sales had begun. In October 1998 the company opened a Craft Your World store in Fort Worth as a pilot project for a new retail concept. The product line included home decorations, gift items, and a wide variety of craft supplies. A workshop area was designed to attract youth groups and individuals to a variety of weekly craft classes. After the new concept failed, in large part because of poor store locations, Tandycrafts decided to close the remaining Tandy Leather stores, 122 stores in 41 states, as well as its manufacturing plant.

The company shifted to direct-to-customer distribution through mail order catalog and Internet sales. Since stores filled catalog orders from nearby customers, a 70,000-square-foot facility opened in Fort Worth to stock inventory and fill customer orders. The company launched an Internet site at www.tandycrafts.com in March 1999, with 400 items available, including leathercrafting kits, tools, books, and patterns. More than 2,000 products would become available, as well as a chat room, and a craft resource guide would be implemented over time. The company continued to sell wholesale leather goods to existing craft stores as well as through more than 100 dealers around the world.

Principal Subsidiaries

Cargo Furniture and Accents, Inc.; J-Mar Associates, Inc.; Licensed Lifestyles Inc.; Pinnacle Art and Frame; Sav-On Discount Office Supplies; Tandy Leather Company; Tandy Wholesale International.

Principal Competitors

Office Depot; Interior, Inc.; National Picture and Frame.

Further Reading

"Cargo Employees Paid $4.2 M To Acquire Chain from Parent," *Furniture-Today,* March 10, 1997, p. 33.

"Change of Plans," *Chain Store Age Executive with Shopping Center Age,* May 1999, p. 259.

Farman, Irvin, *Tandy's Money Machine,* Chicago: The Mobium Press, 1992.

Halkias, Maria, "Fort Worth, Texas-Based Tandycrafts to Close Leather Stores," *Knight-Ridder/Tribune Business News,* January 8, 1999.

Harris, Jim, "Storming the Market: Magee Co. of Pocahontas a Division of Hot Stock Tandycrafts Inc.," *Arkansas Business,* February 8, 1993, p. 22.

Kehoe, Ann-Margaret, "Frame Fusion: Tandycrafts to Combine Divisions," *HFN—The Weekly Newspaper for the Home Furnishings Network,* October 13, 1997, p. 77.

"Mexican President Zedillo Celebrates Opening of New Tandycrafts Frames Facility in Durango," *PR Newswire,* July 9, 1999.

Milliot, Jim, "Family Christian Stores to Acquire Joshua Stores," *Publishers Weekly,* April 27, 1998, p. 11.

Netherly, Ross, "Pruning Makes Tandycrafts Ready for Growth," *Dallas Business Journal,* January 29, 1993, p. 37.

——, "Tandycrafts Stock for the Thick-Skinned Only," *Dallas Business Journal,* April 29, 1994, p. 37.

Reed, Dan, "Fort Worth, Texas-Based Tandycrafts to Move Pinnacle Facility to Mexico," *Knight-Ridder/Tribune Business News,* June 14, 1999.

Scott, Dave, "Sleeper Stock Has Yet to Rouse Wall Street," *Dallas Business Journal,* May 1, 1992, p. B1.

''Tandycrafts Acquires Wall Art Company,'' *HFD—The Weekly Home Furnishings Newspaper,* January 17, 1994, p. 31.

''Tandycrafts Buys Christian Store Chain,'' *Publishers Weekly,* January 10, 1994, p. 12.

''Tandycrafts Forms Division for Licensed Products,'' *Fort Worth Star-Telegram,* June 8, 1996, p. C2.

''Tandycrafts, Inc. Approves $2 Million Stock Repurchase Program,'' *PR Newswire,* September 2, 1998.

''Tandycrafts, Inc. Opens First Craft Your World Stores,'' *PR Newswire,* October 19, 1998, p. 4148.

Wren, Worth, Jr., ''Fort Worth, Texas-Based Tandycrafts Buys Back Furniture Chain,'' *Knight-Ridder/Tribune Business News,* June 23, 1999.

—Mary Tradii

Temple-Inland Inc.

303 South Temple Drive
Diboll, Texas 75941
U.S.A.
Telephone: (409) 829-5511
Fax: (409) 829-1537
Web site: http://www.templeinland.com

Public Company
Incorporated: 1983
Employees: 15,700
Sales: $3.74 billion (1998)
Stock Exchanges: New York Pacific
Ticker Symbol: TIN
NAIC: 32213 Paperboard Mills; 322211 Corrugated and Solid Fiber Box Manufacturing; 321113 Sawmills; 321211 Hardwood Veneer and Plywood Manufacturing; 321212 Softwood Veneer and Plywood Manufacturing; 321219 Reconstituted Wood Product Manufacturing; 52212 Savings Institutions; 52231 Mortgage and Nonmortgage Loan Brokers

Temple-Inland Inc. is a holding company with operations in paper, packaging, building materials, and financial services. Based in Texas, Temple-Inland owns or operates about 2.2 million acres of timberland located in Alabama, Georgia, Louisiana, and Texas. The lands provided Temple-Inland with 61 percent of the fiber needed for its wood operations. Through subsidiary Inland Paperboard and Packaging, Inc., the company manufactures such goods as container board, corrugated containers, and bleached paperboard. Temple-Inland's building products operations produce such materials as lumber, plywood, particle board, medium-density fiberboard (MDF), gypsum wallboard, and fiber-cement siding. The financial services division provides savings accounts, mortgage loans, insurance services, and real estate development services.

Early Years in Texas: 1890s–1940s

What would become Temple-Inland Inc. began in 1893, when Thomas Louis Latane Temple, Sr., founded Southern Pine Lumber Company on 7,000 acres of East Texas, Angelina County, timberland. Temple built the town of Diboll around his company, and by 1894 the first sawmill was operating, cutting 50,000 board feet of old growth timber each day. During the next few years, Southern Pine Lumber Company continued to expand its operations in Diboll. In 1903 the company built its second sawmill and in 1907 created a hardwood mill. In 1910, Temple Lumber Company was formed and established operations in Hemphill and Pineland, both in Sabine County, Texas.

In 1934 Thomas Temple died, leaving his son Arthur with 200,000 acres of land and a company that was $2 billion dollars in debt. Three years later the Hemphill sawmill was destroyed by fire, and Temple Lumber Company operations moved to a smaller mill in Pineland. Recovery was on the way, however.

During these early years and through the housing boom following World War II, Southern Pine Lumber primarily produced basic lumber products, both hardwood and pine, for the construction and furniture industries. By the 1950s technology offered new directions and opportunity for growth. Southern Pine Lumber Company began converting chips, sawdust, and shavings into panel products. In subsequent years, the company pioneered the production of southern pine plywood, particle board, gypsum wallboard, and other building materials.

Growth Spurt in the 1950s and 1960s

Credit for substantial growth in the 1950s was due to the aggressive leadership of the grandson of Thomas Temple, Arthur Temple, who took over in 1951. Under his direction, the company used technological advances in the forest industry to expand the company's production and reduce its debt. In 1954 Southern Pine Lumber built a new plant in Diboll for fiberboard production, using wood waste and whole pine chips to make asphalt-coated insulation sheathing. Southern Pine Lumber of Diboll and Temple Lumber of Pineland merged in 1956, taking Southern Pine Lumber's name.

In 1962 Southern Pine Lumber purchased the controlling interest in Lumbermen's Investment Corporation of Austin, Texas, a mortgage-banking and real estate development company that became a wholly owned subsidiary in the early 1970s.

Company Perspectives:

Temple-Inland's extensive forest holdings are invaluable, not just as a renewable fiber source, but as an integral and long-term part of America's landscape. Equipped with decades of forestry experience and the most advanced technology available, the company has the ability to double pine fiber on its more intensively managed lands over a growing cycle. The key will be to continue balancing society's demand for wood and paper products with the need to perpetuate the diversity of the forest.

In 1963 gypsum wallboard production began with the purchase of Texas Gypsum, of Dallas, that also became a wholly owned subsidiary of the company. That same year, Southern Pine Lumber set up a joint venture with United States Plywood Corporation to build a $3 million plywood-sheathing plant at Diboll. The plant, supplied with raw material from 400,000 acres of Southern Pine Lumber's timberland, was designed for producing plywood for sheathing, rock decking, sub-flooring, and industrial uses. After several successful years of operating the plant as a joint venture, the company bought out United States Plywood.

In 1963 Southern Pine Lumber Company changed its name to Temple Industries, Inc., and built a pilot plant in Pineland to make particle board from sawdust and shavings. After 70 years of business, the company's land holdings had grown to more than 450,000 acres. In 1964 Temple Industries expanded into financial services, including mortgage banking and insurance.

In 1966 the company built a stud mill at Pineland. In 1969 it rebuilt the Diboll sawmill a year after it was destroyed by fire and, also that year, acquired two beverage-case plants in Chattanooga, Tennessee, and Dallas. Two new wholly owned subsidiaries joined Temple Industries in 1969. Sabine Investment Company of Texas, Inc. was formed, and Temple Associates, Inc. was acquired.

Continued Growth and Ownership Change in the 1970s

The 1970s were even more significant for the company, beginning with the production of medium-density siding and the expansion of the fiberboard operation. Temple Industries formed Creative Homes, Inc., in Diboll, to build mobile and modular homes for approximately four years. In 1971 the company built a new particle board plant in Diboll, and in 1972 acquired AFCO Industries, Inc., manufacturer of do-it-yourself consumer products. That same year Temple's West Memphis, Tennessee, gypsum operation began production.

The decade, however, was defined by the events of 1973: Time Inc. acquired Temple Industries and merged it with its Eastex Pulp and Paper Company subsidiary to form Temple-Eastex Incorporated. Eastex Pulp and Paper had been founded in the early 1950s by Time and Houston Oil Company, as East Texas Pulp and Paper. Houston Oil's 670,000 acres of southern pine and hardwood provided raw material for the new paper mill, opened at Evadale, Texas, in 1954. Time had purchased Houston Oil's 50 percent ownership in 1956, thus acquiring the 670,000 acres of timberland.

When Time created Temple-Eastex, magazines were providing only about one-fourth of Time's sales, and Time officials decided to expand the company's more profitable forest products business. Both companies were looking to diversify; Time's underperforming stock made it vulnerable to takeover. Temple met with Eastex president R.M. (Mike) Buckley, and the arrangements were made. Time bought Temple Industries for stock, and the Temples became Time's largest outside shareholders.

Temple-Eastex produced lumber and other building materials, in addition to paperboard used for household paper products. In 1974 Temple-Eastex opened a new particle board plant in Thomson, Georgia, and a new plywood plant in Pineland, Texas. In 1975 the stud mill at Pineland was automated, and all operations except plywood and studs were phased out. That same year Temple-Eastex installed an innovative process for bleaching of pulp, required for white paper products, in the Evadale mill, as part of an expansion in kraft pulp capacity. The $55 million Temple-Eastex expansion boosted Evadale production by 17 percent. The company stayed busy during the late 1970s with openings, closings, purchases, and moves. A wood molasses plant was built in Diboll in 1977 to use the wood sugars found in the waste water from fiber products. The following year a $100 million capital improvement was begun at Evadale to further enhance operations there. In 1978, Arthur Temple became vice-chairman of Time and served in that position until 1983. In 1979 Temple-Eastex moved into new corporate offices in Diboll, while the nearby plywood operation was closed permanently.

Going Solo in the 1980s

The 1980s started off smoothly with some improvements at the Diboll mill. In 1980 a plastic-foam operation was put on line to manufacture urethane for rigid-foam insulation, and the company's newest and largest wood-fired boiler began operation. A new chip mill and log processing operation was constructed in 1982 in Pineland to supply chips to Evadale, plywood and stud logs to Pineland, and fuel for all other operations. In 1982, however, the company was fined $40,000 by the Texas Air Control Board for violating state particulate rate and opacity standards. In addition to the fine, the Evadale kraft pulp and paper mill was required to install two electrostatic precipitators.

In 1983, ten years after acquiring Temple Industries, Time decided to spin off the company's forest products operations into a separate company, again as an antitakeover measure. Time distributed 90 percent of the common stock in the newly formed company, Temple-Inland Inc., to its shareholders. Time also agreed to sell the balance of its holdings within five years after the spinoff.

Temple-Inland, which was then comprised of Temple-Eastex, Inland Container Corporation, and several other operations, offered a wide range of products, including plywood, fiberboard, lumber, particle board, gypsum, rigid foam board, and wall paneling. The building products division operates five retail stores in Texas and one in Louisiana. Temple-Inland also

Key Dates:

1893: Southern Pine Lumber Company forms in Texas.
1910: Temple Lumber Company forms.
1956: Temple Lumber and Southern Pine merge. New company retains the Southern Pine Lumber Company name.
1963: Southern Pine is renamed Temple Industries, Inc.
1973: Time Inc. acquires Temple Industries and merges it with Eastex Pulp and Paper Company; resultant company is named Temple-Eastex Incorporated.
1978: Time Inc. purchases Inland Container Corporation.
1983: Time divests its forest products companies and creates a separate company, Temple-Inland Inc., made up of Temple-Eastex Incorporated, Inland Container Corporation, and several other operations.
1988: Temple-Eastex changes its name to Temple-Inland Forest Products Corporation.
1988: Temple-Inland expands its financial services operations with the purchase of three Texas savings and loans. Temple-Inland combines the three into Guaranty Federal Savings Bank.
1992: Subsidiaries Kilgore Federal Savings and Loan Association and Guaranty Federal Savings Bank merge to form Guaranty Federal Bank, F.S.B.

has successful financial services operations, offering mortgage banking, real estate development, and insurance. The company's heaviest volume, however, came from its container and container board segment, which accounted for 59 percent of the company's earnings in 1989. This segment ranked fifth in container board production in the United States and third among the country's 800 corrugated box producers in 1990.

Inland Container Corporation, a fully integrated packaging company, made corrugated boxes and other containers at its six paper mills. The company got its start in 1918 when Herman C. Krannert started Anderson Box Company in Anderson, Indiana, to make ventilated corrugated boxes for the shipment of chickens. By 1925 he moved to Indianapolis, Indiana, and opened the first Inland Box Company plant the following year. The company acquired a second plant in Middletown, Ohio, in 1929, and in 1930 was reincorporated as Inland Container Corporation. By 1946 Inland Container had grown into a multi-plant box maker but was relying entirely on outside sources for its paper supply. Later that year, through a joint venture with The Mead Corporation, Georgia Kraft Company, half of which was owned by Inland Container, was formed, and construction of a new liner board mill was begun at Macon, Georgia. Georgia Kraft owned approximately one million acres of timberland in Georgia and Alabama and operated three liner board mills with five machines, as well as plywood and lumber mills.

In 1958 Inland Container acquired a majority of the outstanding stock of General Box Corporation, which, when combined with shares previously held, gave Inland Container more than 50 percent control of that company. This acquisition led to an antitrust charge in 1960 by the Federal Trade Commission (FTC) against Inland Container for its purchase of shares of General Box's Louisville, Kentucky, plant. Inland Container was ordered to sell the corrugated shipping container plant that it had acquired from General Box.

In the late 1960s, Inland Container further integrated its operations with construction of a corrugating-medium mill in Tennessee, which began operations in 1970. In 1978 Time paid $272 million to buy Inland Container. Other operating divisions of Inland Container marketed packaging materials for the agricultural, horticultural, and poultry industries, and manufactured and marketed paper and reinforced box tapes.

Following the 1983 spinoff, Temple-Inland incorporated Inland Container and Temple-Eastex. Temple-Inland adopted the same aggressive stance as its subsidiaries had in previous years. The Temple family was still in control of the company, although it had been expanded, diversified, and modernized since Thomas Temple began operations in 1894. During its first year of business, the subsidiary Temple-Eastex purchased Elmendorf Board of Claremont, New Hampshire, a manufacturer of oriented-strand board (OSB). The next year, the company acquired National Fidelity Life Insurance Company of Kansas for $28 million with an eye to expanding its financial services group. In December 1987, Temple-Inland Financial Services acquired Kilgore Federal Savings and Loan Association in Texas for $10 million.

In 1986 Temple-Inland purchased a liner board mill, three box manufacturing plants, a short line railroad, and approximately 260,000 acres of timberland in east Texas and Louisiana at a cost of about $220 million, from Owens-Illinois, a Toledo, Ohio-based packaging company. The mill, in Orange, Texas, greatly increased the company's capacity for production of liner board. The mill and timberland were also valuable because of their proximity to Temple-Inland's other facilities. That same year, Temple-Eastex announced construction of a $30 million wood-converting facility in Buna, Texas. The facility was intended as a high-tech sawmill and lowcost residue provider to paper mills in the Texas cities of Evadale and Orange.

In 1988 Temple-Eastex Incorporated changed its name to Temple-Inland Forest Products Corporation. That same year Georgia Kraft Company was dissolved and its assets divided between Temple-Inland and Mead. Temple-Inland acquired the Rome, Georgia, liner board mills, a sawmill in Rome, and more than 400,000 acres of timberland.

The big news of 1988, however, was the purchase of three insolvent Texas savings and loans. Temple-Inland, along with Trammell Crow and Mason Best Company, bought Delta Savings Association of Texas, in Alvin; Guaranty Federal Savings & Loan Association of Dallas; and First Federal Savings & Loan Association of Austin. The three institutions were combined into one, Guaranty Federal Savings Bank, operating in Dallas, of which Temple-Inland had an 80 percent interest. Temple-Inland's initial outlay was $75 million, and the company committed to contribute another $50 million by January 1991. Temple-Inland was hoping for future payoffs. Purchase of the institutions was a low-risk investment that complemented the company's plans for growth in its financial services group.

In 1989 Temple-Inland was deemed "the most undervalued paper stock on the Big Board" by *Business Week*, May 22,

1989. The company was described as having superb leadership but stock that failed to reflect Temple-Inland's rapid growth. The following year, Temple-Inland sold its Great American Reserve Insurance Company, using the $10 million profit from the sale to bolster Guaranty Federal's capital to expand its home-mortgage lending and consumer banking services. Also in 1990, the company started a new sawmill in DeQuincy, Louisiana, which produced chips for the Evadale and Orange mills, as well as 100 million board feet of lumber annually. In 1991 the company expanded and upgraded its recycled liner board mill in Ontario, California.

Diversification and Growth through Acquisitions in the Early 1990s

Demand for paper products was consistent during the late 1980s and early 1990s, and the demand for liner board for corrugated boxes continued to increase. Containers and container board sales accounted for more than one-half of the company's profits. The smaller, but highly profitable bleached-pulp-and-paperboard division had seen a rise in demand. This division was one of the company's strongest segments, with bleached paperboard being used for many products, including paper cups and paper plates.

In 1991 Arthur Temple, Jr., retired, and Clifford Grum was appointed chairman and CEO. Grum was the first chairman with no ties to the Temple family. Grum announced that Temple-Inland would focus on new technology, including synthetic paper products such as heat-resistant microwave containers, in the 1990s. He predicted that synthetic paper would play an increasingly important role in the future of the industry. Temple-Inland sought to expand its paper operations, and the company acquired Rand-Whitney Packaging in 1994. The following year the company's Latin America presence grew with the opening of a box plant in Chile and a corrugated container sheet facility in Mexico.

Temple-Inland's financial services division grew steadily through the early 1990s, aided by a string of strategic acquisitions. In 1991 the company purchased Capitol Mortgage Bankers, Inc., and the following year its subsidiaries, Guaranty Federal Savings Bank and Kilgore Federal Savings and Loan Association, merged its operations and formed Guaranty Federal Bank, F.S.B. Guaranty bought all of the outstanding stock of AFB in 1993 and acquired the First Saving Bank of San Antonio in 1994 for about $42 million.

Changing Market Conditions in the Late 1990s

Paper market conditions worsened in the late 1990s, and worldwide demand declined, spurring Temple-Inland to restructure its paper products division in 1998. Operating earnings for the paper group were $113 million in 1996, but in 1997 they dropped to a loss of $39 million. Despite poor market conditions, Temple-Inland began operating two new corrugated packaging facilities in 1997, one in Ohio and the other in Mexico. Also that year the company sold the operating assets of Temple-Inland Food Service Corporation, a subsidiary, and closed a box plant in Pennsylvania.

In 1998 the paper group opted for a more decentralized structure in the hope of becoming more competitive. The company set a goal of increasing its paper division earnings by $150 million, despite a continued dreary outlook for paper markets. Temple-Inland closed corrugated packaging facilities in Newark, California, because they were considered noncompetitive and outdated, and sold the Rexford Paper Company, determined to be a non-core asset. Paperboard production was curbed to balance inventory levels. Temple-Inland also added new plants in 1998—two new sheet plants, located in Tennessee and Virginia, began operations. In 1998 operating earnings fared better than 1997, reaching $32.5 million. The improvement was attributed to an increase in the average prices for corrugated packaging and paperboard; box prices fell 19 percent in 1996, dropped an average of 11 percent in 1997, and improved in 1998, with box prices averaging seven percent higher than 1997 prices.

In 1999 Temple-Inland and Caraustar Industries, Inc., entered into an agreement to form Premier Boxboard Limited LLC, which would operate a Temple-Inland-owned mill in Indiana. Plans to convert the container board mill to one able to produce lightweight gypsum facing paper commenced immediately. The company also sold its bleached paperboard facility in Evadale, Texas, to Westvaco Corp. that year. To better serve customers in Mexico, Temple-Inland planned to open a new sheet plant in Guadalajara, Mexico, in early 2000.

The building products group enjoyed growth and profitability in the late 1990s despite tumbling lumber markets. Though average lumber prices fell ten percent in 1998, increases in U.S. housing starts and the strong U.S. economy deflected losses. In addition, Temple-Inland began to diversify and moved more aggressively into the composite panel market to provide alternatives to traditional lumber. In 1996, as part of a joint venture with Caraustar, Temple-Inland purchased a wallboard facility and a gypsum quarry in Texas. Under the terms of the agreement of the joint venture, named Standard Gypsum L.L.C., Temple-Inland agreed to manage and operate the two facilities, while Caraustar would provide gypsum paperboard supplies.

To meet increasing demand for medium-density fiberboard (MDF) and offset declines in lumber prices in the late 1990s, Temple-Inland acquired two MDF plants from MacMillan Bloedel Limited for about $106 million in 1998. The plants, located in Pennsylvania and Ontario, Canada, complemented the company's particle board operations, as many particle board customers also used MDF. Temple-Inland continued to strengthen its gypsum wallboard and fiber-cement operations to facilitate rapidly growing construction markets, completing a fiber-cement plant in Texas and progressing with the construction of a gypsum wallboard plant in Tennessee during 1998. Temple-Inland also streamlined its building products operations by implementing modernization plans; the company renovated its Diboll, Texas, mill, modernized its Buna, Texas, sawmill, and converted its Pineland, Texas, sawmill to manufacture lumber rather than plywood.

Temple-Inland's financial services division achieved record earnings in the late 1990s and continued its growth strategy. In 1997 Temple-Inland bought California Financial Holding Company, the parent company of Stockton Savings Bank F.S.B. of Stockton, California. Two years later the company acquired HF Bancorp, Inc., the parent company of Hemet Federal Savings and Loan Association, for $120 million. The purchase greatly expanded Guaranty Federal Bank's geographic reach and strengthened its operations in the Southern California region.

Though mortgage loan rates were at record lows in the late 1990s, the low rates resulted in high numbers of new mortgage originations. To capitalize on the highly active mortgage market, Temple-Inland acquired Western Cities Mortgage Corporation for $11.5 million in 1996, and a year later the company purchased Knutson Mortgage Corporation for approximately $14.6 million. Temple-Inland's mortgage operations, which served primarily single-family home buyers through 78 offices, saw production volumes nearly double from 1997 to 1998.

Despite uncertain market conditions, Temple-Inland remained committed to improving operations and revenues. The company planned to take advantage of promising markets, such as the MDF and gypsum wallboard segments, and to divest of non-strategic operations. With a diverse offering of paper and building products, access to more than two million acres of timberland, and financial services that included more than 135 Guaranty Federal Bank branches in Texas and California, Temple-Inland seemed poised to head into the 21st century.

Principal Subsidiaries

Inland Paperboard and Packaging, Inc.; Temple-Inland Forest Products Corporation; Temple-Inland Financial Services Inc.; Guaranty Federal Bank, F.S.B.; Temple-Inland Mortgage Corporation.

Principal Competitors

International Paper Company; Smurfit-Stone Container Corporation; The Mead Corporation; Georgia-Pacific Corporation; Weyerhaeuser Company.

Further Reading

Antosh, Nelson, ''Temple-Inland Agrees to Buy California Thrift,'' *Houston Chronicle,* December 10, 1996, p. 2.

Chipello, Christopher J., ''All-Star Analysts 199 Survey: Paper & Forest Products,'' *Wall Street Journal,* June 29, 1999, p. R12.

''Chronology of Temple-Inland Operations,'' Diboll, Tex.: Temple-Inland, 1990.

Jennings, Diane, ''Emotional Investment: E. Texas Town Finds Century-Old Ties to Lumber Giant are Slowly Eroding,'' *Dallas Morning News,* May 12, 1996, p. A1.

''A Proud Tradition,'' Diboll, Tex.: Temple-Inland, 1984.

''Temple-Inland Urged to Hire Consultant,'' *Dallas Morning News,* March 27, 1999, p. F3.

''Westvaco to Acquire Paperboard Facility,'' *Wall Street Journal,* October 5, 1999, p. B13.

—Leslie C. Halpern
—updated by Mariko Fujinaka

TransBrasil S/A Linhas Aéreas

Rua General Pantaleao Telles 40
BR 04355-040 Sao Paulo/SP
Brazil
Telephone: (11) 532-4600
Toll Free: (800) 872-3153
Fax: (11) 533-4983
Web site: http://www.transbrasil.com.br

Public Company
Incorporated: 1955 as Sadia S.A. Transportes Aéreos
Employees: 4,600
Sales: $750 million (1998)
Stock Exchanges: Rio de Janiero
Ticker Symbol: TRLA
NAIC: 481111 Scheduled Passenger Air Transportation; 481112 Scheduled Freight Air Transportation; 481212 Nonscheduled Chartered Freight Air Transportation; 481211 Nonscheduled Chartered Passenger Air Transportation

TransBrasil S/A Linhas Aéreas, Brazil's third-largest airline, flies about three million passengers a year. In spite of impressive growth, it has suffered through harsh recessions and cut-throat fare wars that have made a merger between it and the three other major Brazilian carriers likely.

Origins

The company's origins lie in the 1950s, when a meatpacker 1,000 kilometers away from his prime market in the days before refrigerated trucks had an aviation buff for a son, factors that combined to engender a new air cargo service. Attilio Fontana owned the Sadia Concordia Group in Santa Catarina. In 1953 the company relied on trucks to carry frozen beef to Sao Paulo, a three-and-a-half day ordeal over terrible roads that involved cooling stops along the way. Fontana's son Omar flew part-time for Panair do Brasil (in addition to working for his father, going to law school, composing music, and playing piano). He persuaded his father to lease one of the carrier's DC-3s, which sat parked on weekends, in order to ship the meat to market in two and a half hours. *Pelo ar para seu lar*—"from the air to your lair"—became the company's catchy new slogan.

The next year, over the objections of his father, the younger Fontana convinced the Sadia board to buy a DC-3 from Panair do Brasil. It was heavily utilized, logging fifteen hours a day in three round trips. Maintaining the plane at its home base in Joaçaba was a primitive affair, with fuel poured out of barrels. Although more modern facilities and cheaper fuel were available in Sao Paulo, at the other end of the line, the operation was hit by heavy tariffs in maintaining the private plane. In addition, VARIG (Viaçao Aérea Rio-Grandense) refused to let the company use its radio facilities.

These factors prompted Omar Fontana to fly in the face of the established airlines of Brazil and start his own. Sadia S.A. Transportes Aéreos was created on January 5, 1955, and began flying charters the next year. Scheduled service began on March 16, 1956, on a Sao Paulo-Joaçaba-Videira-Florianópolis route. The company had seventeen employees and three aircraft (two DC-3s and a C-46). The cargo business helped keep the flights profitable, whatever the passenger turnout, and the route system soon expanded. In 1957 Sadia was flying beef to feed the workers building the new capital of Brasilia. Later that year, the new carrier entered a cooperation agreement with REAL, an established national carrier. In exchange for 50 percent of its shares, Sadia received four aircraft, allowing it to stretch its routes to Rio de Janeiro and Porto Alegre. Omar Fontanta became of vice-president of REAL. He bought his shares back in 1961, however, when VARIG took over REAL.

Sadia bought Transportes Aéreos Salvador in 1962. Its five aircraft allowed expansion to the northeast, bringing the number of destinations served past fifty. Another auspicious development in the 1960s was the National Integration Network (*Rede de Integraçao,* or RIN), a government subsidy aimed at developing feeder routes in the face of increasing aircraft costs.

A New Name in 1972

Sadia became known as Transbrasil S.A. Linhas Aéreas in July 1972. At the same time, employees were offered shares in

Company Perspectives:

TransBrasil operates the youngest fleet in Latin America, and one of the youngest in the whole world, 6.8 years. This means more passenger comfort and safer operations. Our fleet consists exclusively of the WideBoeing 767–200/300ER and Boeing 737 in the 300 and 400 versions, the most advanced aircraft today. One of TransBrasil's characteristics is that our main aircraft is the WideBoeing 767, which ensures a very comfortable travel for our passengers due to its spacious cabin. But passengers are not the only ones who benefit from our young fleet. The environment is also thankful: TransBrasil's aircraft are less noisy and pollute less.

the company through the Transbrasil Foundation. New red, yellow, and blue livery symbolic of Brazil's natural resources began adorning the planes. The next year, along with Transportes Aéreos Regionais S.A. (TAM), Transbrasil began flying the Embraer EMB-110 turboprop, the first commercial aircraft produced in Brazil. Transbrasil had been operating the British BAC 1-11 jet since 1970, and became the largest operator of Boeing 727s in Latin America by 1978. In 1983, Transbrasil began operating the state-of-the-art Boeing 767, a widebody, twin-engine jet. A few years later, it bought updated versions of the smaller Boeing 737.

Except for a few charter flights, Transbrasil was excluded from serving the international market. This placed it at a particular disadvantage, as it had to pay for aircraft in hard currency but could only take in income in *cruzeiros.* Toward the end of the decade, Transbrasil and VASP (Viaçao Aérea de Sao Paulo) intensified their campaign to break the monopoly given VARIG by the government. They met with some success. VASP, owned by the state of Sao Paulo, began making scheduled flights to Aruba in 1989.

However, before Transbrasil could win international routes, it had to rectify its financial situation—it was $120 million in debt, thanks to an economic reform program (*Plano Cruzado*) that froze fares while allowing its costs to rise. Transbrasil began selling off planes in order to survive. (So did VASP, which owed $520 million.) It also laid off 800 employees and borrowed $40 million from the government.

A long-running legal dispute unfolded. The governor of the State of Sao Paulo proposed merging Transbrasil with VASP. When Transbrasil failed to make its first payment on its $40 million, two-year loan, the Air Ministry installed Brig. Josué Mil-Homens as president of Transbrasil. Within a few months Fontana had sued Mil-Homens for mismanagement, and a shareholders meeting selected new administrators. The government intervened, again placing Mil-Homens in charge. Fontana appealed to the Supreme High Court. A proposed joint power-sharing agreement was scuttled by a group of pilots who preferred the government administrator, Mil-Homens, who had meanwhile committed Transbrasil to the purchase of several new aircraft.

Meanwhile, the carrier also cast about for a foreign investor, which stimulated much controversy within the Brazilian aviation community, particularly as Transbrasil's focus was on domestic routes. At the time, Fontana owned 35 percent of the company and served as the president of the Transbrasil Foundation, which owned 49 percent. In the midst of this confusion, on September 1, 1989, Transbrasil began scheduled service to Orlando. Mil-Homens favored cutting this route to save costs.

New Freedom in the 1990s

Wagner Canhedo bought VASP, Brazil's largest airline after VARIG, from the State of Sao Paulo in September 1990. Number three Transbrasil entered a wide-ranging, 10-year agreement with VASP in April 1991 that had the potential of saving the two airlines $7 million a month. Still, Transbrasil officials felt that Canhedo's investments were putting too much capacity in the market. Further, a new entrant, Air Brasil, was about to take wing.

Aviation Week and Space Technology cataloged Transbrasil's advantages in 1991. It had grown to employ 4,800 and operated a rather new fleet of 23 aircraft. It had recently given Brasilia and Washington, D.C., their first non-stop connection, which saved passengers eight hours of flying time. It was planning special ecological tour packages to Manaus, in the heart of the Amazon, to appeal to North Americans and Europeans. However, these plusses could not outpace Brazil's runaway inflation and a global recession, and Transbrasil lost $91 million in 1991. It only owned three planes of its own and owed $270 million—most to the Brazilian government. In 1992 Brazil's nine airlines asked the government for a $2.2 billion low-interest loan, which was refused. Banks were charging 40 percent interest at the time.

TransBrasil lost $45 million in 1993 on sales of $422 million. By the second half of 1994, the Brazilian's government's *Plano Real* had introduced some stability to the economy, and the airline showed every sign of a promising recovery. In 1994 it posted a $34 million profit on sales of $562 million. However, one survey at the time found Brazilian airline productivity to be less than half of that in America.

The Fontana family owned about three-quarters of Transbrasil in 1995, increased from the less than fifty percent share Fontana held during the crisis of the late 1980s. The airline's fleet comprised 29 aircraft, all made by Boeing. However, it canceled an order for three Boeing 777s—part of Fontana's hardball fleet rationalization tactics. The carrier aimed to own two-thirds of its aircraft by 2000.

The domestic market accounted for about 75 percent of sales. In July 1995 Transbrasil formed a regional carrier, Interbrasil Star Airlines. Cargo, operating through the Aerobrasil subsidiary, accounted for 15 percent of revenue. The carrier teamed with Evergreen Airlines for Boeing 747 freight service to and from New York and Miami, soon adding Hong Kong.

Finding international partners was a critical focus of Transbrasil's survival strategy in the mid-1990s. The airline began flying to Vienna in 1993 and had ambitious plans stretching as far as Beijing and Moscow, both to be served via Europe. Trans World Airlines joined Transbrasil in a code share agreement in 1996. Transbrasil also began leasing a Boeing 767 from TWA. Delta Air Lines signed its own code share accord in the fall of

Key Dates:

1953: Omar Fontana suggests his father's meatpacking company fly beef to market in a rented plane.
1955: Sadia S.A. Transportes Aéreos is founded.
1963: Creation of National Integration Network helps subsidize Transbrasil as a feeder airline.
1972: Transbrasil name is adopted.
1988: Brazilian government installs its own administrator after the airline misses a loan payment.
1994: Newly stabilized currency helps carrier again post a profit.
1998: Brazilian aviation market deregulated, increasing likelihood of eventual merger.

1997. The *Economist* noted that from Sao Paulo, it was cheaper to fly to Miami than to north-east Brazil.

The Brazilian commercial aviation market was radically deregulated in January 1998. Airlines began slashing fares, which filled planes with record numbers of travelers. TAM had meanwhile grown from a small air taxi operator to a serious, low-cost threat to Brazil's top three—and on TransBrasil's home turf. It had carved itself a 16 percent market share and partnered with American Airlines, the region's strongest international operator. VARIG had also grown leaner and more competitive and had joined the formidable Star Alliance. Brazilian *reals* were devalued in January 1999. The resulting increases in costs had the country's air carriers cutting international routes. By this time, all four major U.S. airlines were flying to Brazil.

Antitrust regulators, anxious about the foreign domination of faltering domestic industries, gave their blessing to the same consolidation in the airline industry that had restructured brewing and maritime industries. VARIG had a 41 percent market share, while VASP and TransBrasil each held about 16 percent. In October 1999, Andrea Calabi, president of Brazil's National Development Bank (BNDES), announced definite plans for the country's four major carriers (VARIG, VASP, TAM, and TransBrasil) to merge. In the meantime, TransBrasil faced the new millennium with a new corporate logo, a new capital letter in its name, and a new director/president, Paulo Enrique Coco.

Principal Subsidiaries

AeroBrasil; InterBrasil Star Airlines.

Principal Competitors

VARIG (Viaçao Aérea Rio-Grandense); VASP (Viaçao Aérea de Sao Paulo); Transportes Aéreos Regionais S.A. (TAM); American Airlines; United Air Lines.

Further Reading

"Brazilian Airlines: As Free as a Bird," *Economist,* May 9, 1998, p. 64.

Bruce, James, "Brazilian Airlines Weigh Merger, Privatization," *Journal of Commerce,* October 20, 1987, p. 5B.

——, "Transbrasil Plan for Rescuer Gets Strafed on the Ground," *Journal of Commerce,* November 10, 1988, p. 5B.

Cordle, Ina Paiva, "Transbrasil Airlines Takes off with Flying Colors," *Miami Herald,* December 8, 1997.

Davies, R.E.G., *Airlines of Latin America Since 1919,* London: Putnam, 1984.

Fotos, Christopher P., "Brazilian Reforms to Give Airlines New Era of Freedom," *Aviation Week and Space Technology,* November 11, 1991, pp. 36–37.

Fritsch, Peter, "Brazil's Four Major Airlines Weigh Merging into Two; Government Shifts, Supports Creating Tougher Rivals," *Wall Street Journal,* August 11, 1999, p. A13.

——, "Brazilian Carriers Plunge into First Fare War as Deregulation Ignites Ferocious Competition," *Wall Street Journal,* May 12, 1998, p. A15.

Kamm, Thomas, "Brazil's Airlines Seek Government Loan; Rejection Could Mean Industry Shakeout," *Wall Street Journal,* March 6, 1992, p. A6.

Lima, Edvaldo Pereira, "Transbrasil's Instinct for Survival," *Air Transport World,* September 1992, pp. 74–76.

Moorman, Robert W., "Tenacious Transbrasil," *Air Transport World,* November 1995, pp. 89–92.

Ogier, Thierry, "Air Carriers Facing a Shakeout," *Journal of Commerce,* August 26, 1999, p. 15.

——, "Country's Four Domestic Carriers to Merge; Customers Are Apprehensive" *Journal of Commerce,* October 20, 1999, p. 4.

Pessoa, Lenildo Tabosa, *História Da Aviaçao Comercial Brasileira,* Sao Paulo: Editora Rios, 1989.

"Transbrasil Expands International Service," *Aviation Week and Space Technology,* November 11, 1991, pp. 50–51.

"VASP and Transbrasil Discuss Union to Form Brazil's Biggest Airline," *Wall Street Journal,* April 2, 1992, p. A8.

—Frederick C. Ingram

Triumph Group, Inc.

Four Glenhardie Corporate Center
1255 Drummers Lane, Suite 200
Wayne, Pennsylvania 19087
U.S.A.
Telephone: (610) 975-0420
Fax: (610) 975-0563
Web site: http://www.triumphgrp.com

Public Company
Incorporated: 1993 as Triumph Group Inc.
Employees: 2,600
Sales: $400.11 million (1999)
Stock Exchanges: New York
Ticker Symbol: TGI
NAIC: 336413 Other Aircraft Parts and Auxiliary Equipment Manufacturing

Triumph Group, Inc., was formed out of the Alco Diversified Services division of Alco Standard Corporation. Most of its companies produce or repair aircraft components. Triumph takes a two-pronged approach to weathering the severe cycles of the aviation industry. During boom years, the group's part-making companies fare well supplying original equipment manufacturers. In down times, airlines fly older planes longer, which boosts business at Triumph's overhaul and repair facilities. Clients include Boeing (the largest), Gulfstream, Bombardier, Southwest Airlines, and United Air Lines. Commercial aircraft account for 70 percent of the company's business.

Amalgamated Origins

By the late-1980s, Alco Standard Corporation executives were looking for ways to focus the conglomeration on its core operations: paper distribution, office products, and food service. Office products were the fastest-growing segment, the one that the corporation would focus on.

In July 1986, Alco announced plans to sell its distribution businesses. A sale of the Triumph Group was also under consideration at the time. The Triumph Group specialized in aerospace, an industry subject to heavy ups and downs. The group earned $14.9 million on sales of $118.3 million in the fiscal year 1987, while its corporate parent had total revenues of $3.63 billion. In the early 1990s, the Triumph Group's earnings lagged behind those of Alco's Office Products division, which saw a 35 percent increase in profits in the fiscal year 1991, while the paper distribution subsidiary saw earnings fall 15 percent.

The Triumph Group was also a force in the domestic steel industry. Its customers were becoming more demanding in terms of quality and communication. They were also turning over more value-added functions to steel suppliers and reducing the numbers of vendors they worked with. Computerization added a new level of sophistication to the buying process. Triumph President Richard C. Ill joined other steel executives in calling for a Multilateral Steel Agreement to bring order to a domestic market subject to trade wars and floods of cheap imports.

Alco Standard formed a new operating group out of the 11 companies that made up the Triumph Group, as well as two paper-converting companies and the Aerospace Technologies subsidiary. Known as Alco Diversified Services, the new entity had revenues of $340 million. Ill, a longtime Alco veteran who had been president of the Triumph Group, was named president of Alco Diversified Services.

Alco Standard sold its food division in 1991. In October 1992, the corporation announced it would sell Alco Diversified Services to a management group and buy a 49.9 percent share of a German office products distributor, IMM Office Systems Holding GmbH, based in Munich. A management-led investment group, Triumph Group Inc., took over Alco Diversified Services in a leveraged buyout in July 1993. The deal was reportedly worth $85 million. Citicorp Venture Capital invested $26 million. Besides aviation repair and overhaul, the 13 companies in the group performed industrial machining, and paper and steel converting. The companies had annual sales of $227 million and employed 1,450 people in 22 sites around the United States. Aviation accounted for $60 million of total sales. The Triumph Group was headquartered in Wayne, Pennsylvania.

Defense cutbacks in the early 1990s tested the group. Triumph divested the struggling Otto Konigslow Manufacturing

Company Perspectives:

"Everything Has to Be Right." Triumph Group, Inc., knows that everything has to work together. We provide a full range of products and services to the aviation industry, with a consistently high level of quality and service. Our companies design, engineer, manufacture, repair, overhaul, and distribute aircraft components for a broad spectrum of the aviation industry on a worldwide basis. We have been providing creative, cost-effective solutions to the best in the business for years.

Co. in 1995, which it sold to two of its managers. After the sale, Konigslow, which manufactured aerospace components, was eligible for preferential treatment under federal bidding practices as a small, minority-owned, disadvantaged company. Sales were $3 million a year, down from an early 1980s peak of $6 million.

Taking Off in the Mid-1990s

The commercial aviation business took off in the mid-1990s. Annual sales increased from $200 million to $300 million in just three years. Ill projected reaching the $500 million mark by 1999. The group posted a profit of $9.7 million in 1996. This was fueled by unprecedented demand for airline capacity. Boeing was making more than forty jets a month to try to satisfy a record backlog. Pressure to keep production resulted in Boeing both using more outsourcing and reducing its number of suppliers.

Triumph had about 1,500 employees and annual sales of more than $300 million. Just nine people worked at corporate headquarters, however, due to the group's highly decentralized approach. Seven of the companies were involved in specialty metal products; the other six, aviation. The latter group supplied original equipment manufacturers and overhauled and repaired commercial aircraft.

In the mid-1990s, the aviation businesses accounted for two-thirds of Triumph's annual revenues. Corporate managers invested heavily in acquiring new companies for the profitable aviation division. They aimed to increase profit by 20 percent a year, half of this by acquisition. The new companies generally extended Triumph's technical expertise or product lines, making the group more compelling when bidding for large contracts. The purchases also tended to extend its customer base. The group generally left the managers of the acquired companies to their own devices, and was known for not raiding assets or laying off workers. Acquisitions included Air Lab, a Seattle company specializing in cockpit repairs, purchased in the fall of 1995. The Teleflex Inc. controls business was bought in January 1996 and renamed Triumph Controls. It had annual sales of $35 million and 150 workers. Another range-extending acquisition was K-T Corp., which formed aluminum fuselage panels for Boeing 777s.

Divestitures were also used to focus the group. Triumph's largest holding, Quality Park Products Inc., in St. Paul, Minnesota, made envelopes. The company had brought in $100 million in revenues but was decidedly out of step with the group's aviation-centered growth strategy. It was sold in March 1996 for $27.4 million. Although profitable, Triumph was highly leveraged and needed more cash to expand. A public offering in October 1996 raised more than $50 million.

The group announced it was selling its Air Lab Division to the American subsidiary of Sextant Avionique S.A. in July 1997. Triumph's A. Biederman instrument subsidiary simultaneously entered into a five-year agreement to service and market the French company's products. The Air Lab acquisition extended Sextant Avionique's U.S. franchise into nearly all areas of its product line. Triumph bought Hydro-Mill Co., a California aircraft part manufacturing and repair business, in September 1997. This added about $30 million a year to Triumph's net sales and broadened its product line. Hydro-Mill had lacked the capital to make the necessary upgrades to win orders from Boeing.

Still Strong in the Late 1990s

DV Industries, a metal finishing company, and DG Industries, Inc., a machining company, were acquired in autumn 1998. Triumph made its first foray into Europe in December 1998, when it acquired the British firm Chase Aerospace Limited. The company serviced auxiliary power units (APUs) and other equipment for the commercial aviation industry. It was expected to contribute $6 million per year to Triumph's revenues. Although Triumph usually highly valued the goodwill associated with existing company names, it announced it was renaming this acquisition to Triumph Air Repair (Europe) Limited. Soon afterward, Triumph bought Hartford Tool and Die Co., Inc., a maker of engine parts.

At the same time, falling share prices prompted a stock buyback. Ill allayed concerns about projected declines in Boeing's aircraft production. He stated that downturns in the manufacturer's larger aircraft programs were to be offset by more work on next generation 737s. Soon afterward, Boeing awarded Triumph Air Repair its largest contract ever, a one year, $7.4 million agreement to service APUs and line replaceable units for Air Force KC-10 tankers. With Boeing's eight annual options to renew, the deal had the potential of increasing to a value of more than $67 million. Boeing had acquired McDonnell Douglas, the original maker of the KC-10, an aerial refueling version of the DC-10 airliner. Most of Triumph Air Group's work had been related to Boeing 727s and 737s.

The group acquired aggressively, continuing its strategy of becoming a comprehensive MRO provider. It bought four companies in 1998 alone. In early 1999, its aviation subsidiaries numbered 18. Triumph had total group sales of $400 million for the year ending March 31, 1999. Net profits were about $33 million and employees numbered more than 2,000, including 15 at headquarters.

Triumph bought a maker of oversized aircraft components in May 1999. Ralee Engineering Co., based in City of Industry, California, gave the group the capability of producing virtually all of a commercial aircraft's structural parts. Ralee had revenues of about $20 million a year.

Operating profits for the aviation group were up by nearly half in fiscal year 1999, to $58.6 million. Net sales increased

Key Dates:

1986: Alco Standard Corporation executives consider selling Triumph Group.
1993: Triumph Group spun off from Alco Standard in a leveraged management buyout.
1996: IPO raises $50 million.
1998: Triumph enters European market through purchase of Chase Aerospace Limited.

36 percent to $328.6 million. Triumph had acquired six businesses during this period, and invested $20 million in its existing ones. Triumph's manufacturing divisions produced honeycomb flight control surfaces, control systems, and machined metal parts. About half of the Triumph Group's revenues were derived from aircraft maintenance. Its divisions serviced virtually every commercial aircraft system except for cabins, main landing gears, radios, and engines, or the heaviest of maintenance checks. The maintenance, repair, and overhaul (MRO) market was valued at $25 billion. The world commercial airliner fleet had doubled in size in the previous twenty years. The Federal Aviation Administration ordered airlines to bring aircraft to ''Stage III'' compliance by the end of 1999—essentially vectoring more planes towards overhauls.

Principal Subsidiaries

A. Biederman, Inc.; Advanced Materials Technologies, Inc.; Aerospace Technologies, Inc.; DG Industries, Inc.; DV Industries; Frisby Aerospace; Great Western Steel; HTD Aerospace, Inc.; Hydro-Mill Co.; JDC Company; K-T Corporation; Kilroy Steel, Inc.; Kilroy Structural Steel; L.A. Gauge Co., Inc.; Lamar Electro-Air Corporation; Northwest Industries; Nu-Tech Industries, Inc.; Ralee Engineering Corp.; Special Processes of Arizona, Inc.; Stolper-Fabralloy Co. LLC; Triumph Air Repair; Triumph Controls, Inc.

Principal Operating Divisions

Aviation Group; Metals Group.

Principal Competitors

AAR Corp.; Aviation Sales Co.

Further Reading

''Alco Standard in Triumph Spin-Off Plan,'' *Financial Times,* December 14, 1987, p. 26.

Belden, Tom, ''Profits Soar on the Wings (and Other Parts) of Planes,'' *Philadelphia Inquirer,* March 29, 1998, pp. C1, C9.

Binzen, Peter, ''Watching the Pennies and Making Things Grow at Triumph,'' *Philadelphia Inquirer,* March 4, 1996, p. C3.

Breskin, Ira, ''Triumph Group Inc.,'' *Investor's Business Daily,* December 20, 1996, p. A4.

''CEO Interview: Richard C. Ill,'' *Wall Street Transcript,* October 1998.

Cook, Brian M., ''Steel Service Centers: No More Warehouses,'' *Industry Week,* February 3, 1992, p. 36.

Kjelgaard, Chris, ''KC-10 APU/LRU Award Is Triumph's Biggest-Ever Contract,'' *Air Transport Intelligence,* December 15, 1998.

Lamb, Michele R., ''New Flat-Rolled Capacity Implications on Service Centers,'' *Metal/Center News,* June 1995, p. 40.

Leder, Michelle, ''In Aviation, the Bargains May Be in the Hangars,'' *New York Times,* February 28, 1999.

Leibs, Anthony, ''Aerospace Aftermarket M&A Blasts Off,'' *Mergers and Acquisitions Report,* April 12, 1999.

Marino, Joe, ''Only an MSA Will Bring Order,'' *Metal/Center News,* June 1994, p. 44.

Much, Marilyn, ''Blue Skies: Triumph Group Keeping Busy as Aircraft Production Soars,'' *Investor's Business Daily,* February 18, 1998.

Prizinsky, David, ''Smaller Should Be Better,'' *Crain's Cleveland Business,* May 15, 1995, p. 5.

Proulx, Jim, ''Overhaul & Maintenance MRO Guide Part II: Triumph Tacks Name to Established Winners,'' *Overhaul & Maintenance,* Fall 1998, pp. 103–105.

Turner, David L., ''Alco Investing in German Firm, Selling Division,'' *Philadelphia Inquirer,* October 6, 1992, p. F1.

Velocci, Anthony L., Jr., ''Market Focus,'' *Aviation Week & Space Technology,* August 24, 1998, p. 11.

——, ''Primes Pledge to Cut Excessive Audits,'' *Aviation Week & Space Technology,* September 13, 1999, pp. 77–78.

—Frederick C. Ingram

U.S. Cellular Corporation

8410 West Bryn Mawr Avenue
Suite 700
Chicago, Illinois 60631
U.S.A.
Telephone: (312) 399-8900
Fax: (312) 399-8936
Web site: http://www.uscellular.com

Public Company
Incorporated: 1983 as United States Cellular Corporation
Employees: 4,800
Sales: $1.16 billion (1998)
Stock Exchanges: American
Ticker Symbol: USM
NAIC: 513322 Radiotelephone Communications

U.S. Cellular Corporation, the 11th largest wireless telephone company in the United States, acquires, operates, and invests in cellular systems through the country. As one of the fastest-growing communications companies in the industry, U.S. Cellular owns cellular interests in over 183 markets, and serves more than two million customers. Through acquisitions and exchanges with other cellular companies, U.S. Cellular seeks to consolidate its diverse franchises into geographic clusters, mostly in upper New England, the Mid-Atlantic states, the Midwest, the Northwest, and the South. In 1983 the company was founded as United States Cellular Corporation—the cellular communications division of Telephone and Data Systems, Inc. (TDS), an independent telephone holding company based in Chicago. Still largely controlled by TDS, U.S. Cellular took its current name in 1999.

U.S. Cellular's Origins

TDS was established in 1968 by Chicago entrepreneur LeRoy T. Carlson who, over a period of years, assembled a small rural telephone conglomerate consisting of 50 independent companies. TDS realized tremendous economies through centralized purchasing and system standardization. The policy of collecting companies in adjacent areas, along with consistent growth in rural areas, amplified these benefits.

By 1982 TDS had invested heavily in cable television services, operating 16 individual cable companies. The diversification was spurred by fear that cable companies might one day usurp traditional telephone companies by offering their own telephone services. At the time, cable companies were unwilling to develop telephone services out of their own fear that such a move would provide justification for the huge Bell companies to storm into the cable television industry.

Cellular communication, still in its embryonic stages, was beginning to emerge as a much more serious and immediate threat to the business of wireline telephone companies. One of the first companies to recognize this was TDS, whose senior management quickly devised plans to establish its own cellular communications franchises. There was no shortage of companies willing to compete for licenses to provide cellular service. Start-up costs were high, but economies of scale were extremely impressive, particularly in metropolitan areas. The Federal Communications Commission (FCC), which granted the licenses, established a bidding process for the 30 most populous market service areas (MSAs), and proclaimed that only two companies would be licensed to compete in each one. The first license was reserved for the local wireline company (most often a Bell company), while the second would be awarded to another bidder.

The FCC was monumentally ill-prepared to handle the deluge of applications it received. While TDS applied for a license to serve Indianapolis, a fierce turf battle erupted throughout the industry. Because MSAs often covered several different wireline franchises, dozens of perplexing questions arose over the FCC's as-yet-unofficial definitions. The commission finally asked its vast pool of applicants to hammer out their own partnership agreements prior to requesting a license. As a result, TDS opted to abandon its bid for Indianapolis in favor of a five percent stake in the hugely profitable Los Angeles MSA. Because it was obliged to provide detailed engineering and market surveys, TDS poured $250,000 into its first application. By the time the second set of 30 MSAs was put up for grabs, however, the company had become experienced in such matters, and soon the average application cost fell below $10,000.

Company Perspectives:

United States Cellular exists to provide quality wireless communications services for our customers and to rapidly grow our customer base, revenue, and profits. The Company is committed to professional growth for our associates and good corporate citizenship in the communities we serve.

No longer able to support its growing activities in the cellular industry by itself, TDS created a separate subsidiary called United States Cellular Corporation (USCC). The new company began operations on December 23, 1983, with Rudy Hornacek, a TDS executive, as its president.

The FCC's call for prearranged agreements among applicants eliminated years of comparative studies and appeals processes. It also emboldened the larger, predominantly metropolitan Bell companies into running roughshod over smaller companies. Such cavalier disregard for companies such as USCC hit a nerve with LeRoy Carlson. He took such an aggressive position in negotiations that larger companies were forced to make room for USCC. One bemused representative complained that Carlson did not realize how small his company really was. As the process rambled on, the public grew more vocal and critical of the FCC's seemingly endless formalities. Finally, the commission decided to award remaining licenses through a series of lotteries.

In a separate agreement signed by the Bell companies, TDS, and other independents, TDS was allowed to operate cellular networks in Knoxville and Tulsa. In October 1984, before the FCC formally granted the licenses, USCC began to assemble its management team. This team was responsible for the selection of cell sites, construction of towers, installation of operating systems, establishment of business offices, and staffing. Accordingly, USCC moved its operations out of TDS headquarters and into a new building in Park Ridge, near Chicago's O'Hare Airport.

By March 1985 the senior management of TDS had become convinced that the cellular industry was poised for tremendous growth. The company decided to make the development of its cellular unit a major priority. In order to be a more serious bidder, the company needed access to greater investment funding. Rather than raising the necessary financing through additional debt or selling additional shares to an equity partner, TDS elected to abandon the cable television market and devote the proceeds of the sales of its systems to USCC. In addition, funding that was earmarked for the development of new cable systems was diverted to cellular investments.

TDS decided to concentrate on the cellular industry, at the expense of cable television, because cellular promised considerably higher growth and rates of return. Moreover, cellular communications posed a greater threat to TDS's established wireline services than cable, since the technologies needed to provide telephone service over cable systems had not been developed. TDS disposed of its cable operations during 1985, and sold its last system in November 1986.

Expansion in the 1980s

USCC's Knoxville system commenced in June 1985, and its Tulsa system went on line in August. Meanwhile, the Los Angeles system, which was activated the previous year, turned its first profit in October. That year, the company filed applications for five of the nation's largest markets, and applications for 70 more in smaller markets. The licenses for smaller MSAs were important because they covered areas adjacent to larger existing systems or formed corridors along heavily traveled highway routes. USCC's goal of combining adjacent markets into clusters was essential. Clusters allowed USCC to offer its customers large areas around their homes where they could use their phones without incurring extra charges (''roaming charges'') by entering into another service carrier's territory. Moreover, USCC's clusters enabled the company to ''capture economies of scale in system operations, marketing, and consumer service functions,'' Donald Nelson explained to the November 16, 1992, *Wall Street Journal.*

In addition to the two MSAs USCC operated in 1986, the company was a minority partner in an additional nine. The following year, it completed eight more cellular networks, including systems in Peoria, Des Moines, and Poughkeepsie. To meet the company's growing organizational demands, USCC established five operating regions in 1987, including a Midwest Region headquartered in Davenport, Iowa; a Southeast Region in Knoxville; a Southwest Region in Tulsa; and a North Central Region located in Minneapolis. That year, Don Nelson, head of operations at USCC, succeeded Hornacek as president of the company and took on the title of CEO as well.

In an effort to derive additional revenue from its systems, USCC negotiated numerous roaming agreements with other cellular providers, which allowed customers to continue calls even if they strayed outside their provider's service area. In addition, the company began implementation of enhanced ''vertical'' services, such as voicemail and information services. By 1987 USCC had been recognized as a formidable player in the cellular communications industry. Clearly in a position to win additional licenses, the company had exhausted its credit lines and would be unable to maintain its growth without a sizable issue of equity capital. The company therefore sold 6.2 percent of its capital stock to Coditel, a Belgian cable television company, for $10 million.

U.S. Cellular: Going Public

Late in the summer of 1987, USCC planned a public stock offering to raise additional capital. While the company was preparing its prospectus and working with the Securities and Exchange Commission to make the offering, the stock market took an enormous plunge. The date, October 19, became known as Black Monday. The Dow Jones Industrial Index fell by more than 500 points, to about 1700 points. The collapse of confidence in the markets not only torpedoed USCC's prospective share offering, it ruined public offerings of at least three other cellular companies. The company finally went forward with its public share offering on May 4, 1988. Three million shares were distributed, mostly in the United States, at $15 per share, and the company was listed on the American Stock Exchange. The share offering diluted TDS's control of USCC to just over 80 percent.

Key Dates:

1968: Telephone and Data Systems, Inc. (TDS) is founded by LeRoy Carlson.
1983: TDS establishes United States Cellular Corporation (USCC) as a subsidiary.
1985: USCC makes its first public stock offering.
1993: USCC reports its first profit.
1997: USCC acquires key cellular markets from BellSouth.
1999: United States Cellular changes name to U.S. Cellular and adopts a new logo.

By December 1988, USCC was active in 31 MSAs, including Wichita, Atlantic City, and Columbia, Missouri. This rapid growth forced the company to move out of its Park Ridge offices and into a larger facility in Chicago. Bolstering its identity in the increasingly crowded industry, USCC adopted a new logo and promotional materials that included the no-nonsense tag line "Mobile Telephone Network."

To augment its growth in the market, USCC began issuing additional blocks of shares. During one 18-month period, the number of USCC shares increased by 61 percent. TDS maintained its ownership in USCC at 82.3 percent. Due to the high start-up costs associated with cellular systems, investments in new franchises had severely hampered TDS's earnings potential. USCC was a constant drain to TDS, but these investments were necessary to ensure that USCC had a good position in the industry. If the company did not invest in new systems while they were available, it risked losing opportunities to build the enterprise.

When the cellular market had been exhausted of the most desirable franchises, the market value of existing licenses began to climb. In fact, USCC bought into the market at relatively low prices. Later, the value of its cellular properties climbed so dramatically that if it were to sell the licenses it had acquired, it would realize a tremendous gain.

After USCC secured the necessary licenses and completed the establishment of new networks, it prepared to collect on its substantial investments. A portion of the earnings from these operations was channeled back toward the servicing or retirement of debt and the settlement of obligations to TDS. A second, but rapidly growing portion of USCC's operating income was distributed to its shareholders, the largest of which was TDS. As a result, TDS began collecting an increasingly large dividend from USCC, which registered a 58 percent increase in subscribers, to 182,500, in 1992. TDS used its share of the earnings to retire its own debt and finance new investment opportunities, including additional wireline franchises.

Rapid Expansion in the 1990s

Between 1989 and 1992, USCC expanded from interests in 33 cellular systems to 129. Forty percent of this growth occurred in areas where TDS had a presence in the wireline market, or through settlements with other companies. The remaining licenses were acquired directly through acquisitions of licenses awarded to TDS and other companies.

As the supply of available cellular licenses continued to dwindle, and the prices increased, USCC was faced with the possibility of actually making money. As the investment stage of the company's development drew near an end, positive cash flow was likely to follow. The primary beneficiary of this profitability would be TDS, whose shares were favored over those of USCC because its business was more thoroughly diversified. In 1993 USCC had interests in 193 cellular systems, 129 of which it had a hand in managing. Of that number, the company maintained a majority interest in 91 franchises.

To sustain its astounding growth rates, USCC began to deepen its distribution channels in 1992. The first cellular phone users had been primarily in the business sector, but, as the cellular market boomed—and the cost of service dropped substantially—increasingly more consumers wanted cell phones for everyday use. To address the needs of this burgeoning group of potential cellular phone customers, USCC opened several retail stores in 1992. Instead of relying solely on its direct sales team, which had catered to business clients, USCC converted some of its office locations into walk-in stores where consumers could purchase a cellular phone and service. By 1995, USCC had over 100 such retail outlets, from which it derived 24 percent of its sales. The same year, the company signed an agreement with Wal-Mart to set up kiosks in 80 Wal-Mart stores, further expanding USCC's ability to reach consumers directly.

USCC continued to pursue its strategy of growing its cellular markets in ever expanding clusters. As Donald Nelson told the *Wall Street Journal* on May 3, 1993, "the number one thing our customers want is a wider area in which they can make their wireless telephone calls. The wider that area is, the happier they are. That's our concentration, growth of the system. . . ." In 1993, USCC acquired access to ten additional markets, and in 1995 signed an agreement with ALLTELL Mobile Communications, Inc., in which USCC exchanged operating interests and expanded its clusters in West Virginia, Virginia, Missouri, and Oklahoma. Furthermore, USCC conducted three asset exchanges with Centennial Cellular Corp. in March 1995 to bolster its clusters in Virginia, North Carolina, and Iowa. USCC's subscriber base rose 66 percent in 1995 alone. In February 1996, USCC followed these acquisitions with another exchange—this time with Sprint Cellular—for the controlling interests of cellular markets in Ohio and Kansas.

From this transaction, USCC strengthened its clusters in the Milwaukee and Madison, Wisconsin, markets. All told, USCC gained 3.9 million population equivalents from its trade with BellSouth. In 1998, USCC added key markets in Wisconsin and North Carolina and, in 1999, negotiated with GTE Wireless, Inc. to obtain two critical markets in North Carolina.

Despite its many recent additions, USCC remained committed to serving medium and small markets. The choice was a wise one. While many of its competitors encountered flagging sales, USCC's subscriber growth rate in 1996 was 56 percent. In January 1997, USCC added its one millionth customer, marking a doubling of its customer base in two years. Moreover, as the May 11, 1997, *Chicago Tribune* noted, USCC had a distinct advantage over its rivals because its ''markets ha[d not] attracted the competitors flocking to larger markets like Chicago and Los Angeles.''

USCC did experience fierce competition in other venues, however, especially as personal communications services (PCS) grew rapidly. PCS, a sort of low-power radio service that could be used for telephone calls, won over a number of cellular customers with lower airtime rates, no contracts, and extra services, according to *Radio Communications Report.* Like many other players in the wireless industry, USCC focused on adding new customers, as well as on keeping current subscribers. One way USCC strove to do so was by offering new services. For example, in September 1997, USCC inaugurated its TalkTracker service, a pre-pay option that appealed particularly to consumers who wanted maximum convenience without having to sign a contract or worry about incurring charges. Moreover, USCC strove to lower per unit costs, and began a digital conversion plan in 1997. By the end of 1998, digital service was available to 28 percent of USCC's customers in 11 clusters.

In addition to keeping its technology and service options current, USCC also used branding and advertising to keep customers aware of the company and the benefits it could provide. In May 1999, USCC changed its name to U.S. Cellular and debuted a stylish new logo. The company continued to heavily tout its 1998 advertising tag line, ''The Way People Talk Around Here.'' As Donald Nelson explained in a 1999 press release, ''it's extremely important that we promote our brand image as much as we do our products and services.'' The company also participated in many local and national community programs to maintain visibility. In addition to a national domestic violence prevention program, S.A.F.E. (Stop Abuse From Existing), U.S. Cellular led an effort to provide free long distance telephone calls to homeless people during the holidays (H.O.P.E.) and to support neighborhood watch efforts (C.A.L.L.)

Although new competitors in the wireless communications market proliferated, U.S. Cellular's future looked positive. In 1988, the company increased its customer base by 28 percent. *Fortune* magazine included U.S. Cellular in its list of the fastest-growing companies.

Principal Subsidiaries

Aerial Communications Inc.; US Link Inc.; Suttle Press Inc; TDS Computing Svc. Inc.; TDS Telecom Inc.

Principal Competitors

ALLTELL Corporation; American Cellular Corporation; AT&T Corp.; Bell Atlantic Corporation; General Wireless, Inc.; GTE Corporation; MCI WorldCom, Inc.; Nextel Communications, Inc.; SBC Communications Inc.; Sprint Corporation; U S West, Inc.; Vodafone AirTouch Plc.

Further Reading

August, K. C., *TDS: The First Twenty Years,* Madison, Wis.: Telephone and Data Systems, Inc., 1989.

Beckman, Kristen, ''Cellular Growth Begins to Slow, But Market Not Mature Yet,'' *Radio Communications Report*, May 18, 1998.

Carter-Lome, Maxine, ''Company Profile,'' *Cellular Marketing*, January 1, 1995.

''Cellular Providers Score Big Gains on Top and Bottom Lines,'' *Wireless Business and Finance*, August 3, 1994.

''Cellular Subscribers, Revenues Continue Upward Trend,'' *Mobile Phone News*, April 24, 1995.

''CEO Interview: United States Cellular Corporation,'' *Wall Street Journal*, November 16, 1992.

''CEO Interview: United States Cellular Corporation,'' *Wall Street Journal*, May 3, 1993.

''Chicago Company Gains Control of Cellular One,'' *Wisconsin State Journal*, February 6, 1997.

''Chicago's Top 100 Companies: United States Cellular Corp.,'' *Chicago Tribune*, May 11, 1997

''Company Watch,'' *Financial World,* September 15, 1992, pp. 12–13.

''Growth Slows, Companies Strive to Keep Churn, Theft Down,'' *Mobile Phone News*, August 19, 1996.

''TDS,'' *Telephone News,* April 14, 1985, p. 8; September 9, 1989, p. 1.

''U.S. Cellular' 1997 Growth Comes in at 59 Percent,'' *Wireless Today*, January 28, 1998.

—John Simley
—updated by Rebecca Stanfel

ULTRAMAR DIAMOND SHAMROCK
C O R P O R A T I O N

Ultramar Diamond Shamrock Corporation

6000 North Loop 1604 West
San Antonio, Texas 78249
U.S.A.
Telephone: (210) 592-2000
Fax: (210) 592-2054
Web site: http://www.udscorp.com

Public Company
Incorporated: 1910 as Diamond Alkali Company
Employees: 24,000
Sales: $11.14 billion (1998)
Stock Exchanges: New York Montreal
Ticker Symbol: UDS ULR
NAIC: 32411 Petroleum Refineries; 48691 Pipeline Transportation of Refined Petroleum Products; 48621 Pipeline Transportation of Natural Gas; 454311 Heating Oil Dealers; 42271 Petroleum Bulk Stations and Terminals; 44711 Gasoline Stations with Convenience Store; 32511 Petrochemical Manufacturing

Ultramar Diamond Shamrock Corporation (UDS), based in San Antonio, Texas, is the second largest independent oil refining and marketing company in the United States. UDS, which was formed in late 1996 through the merger of Ultramar Corporation and Diamond Shamrock, Inc., owns seven refineries, located in California, Texas, Oklahoma, Colorado, Michigan, and Quebec, Canada. The refineries have a combined capacity of 685,000 barrels per day. The company also owns some 6,000 retail gasoline and convenience store outlets in the United States and Canada. The majority of the gasoline stations are branded Diamond Shamrock, Ultramar, Beacon, or Total. UDS also operates petrochemical and home heating oil businesses.

Beginnings Rooted in Glassmaking: 1910–45

In 1910 a group of Pittsburgh businessmen associated with the glass industry formed the Diamond Alkali Company to produce soda ash, a basic raw material of glass manufacturing. Diamond Alkali was incorporated in West Virginia in March of that year, with the company's headquarters established in Pittsburgh. The new corporation was capitalized at $1.2 million, with most of the funds going toward the construction of a soda ash plant in Painesville, Ohio.

After World War I began, the demand for canning glass increased, and Diamond Alkali found a niche in the market. At about the same time Diamond Alkali began marketing increasing quantities of its soda ash for laundry preparations, baking soda, water softeners, paper and pulp production solutions, and textile processing. By 1915 Diamond's ability to produce soda ash exceeded customer demand, and the company began using soda ash and limestone to produce caustic soda. This development opened new markets in lye, soap, detergents, and, eventually, rayon and cellophane. In 1918 Diamond began making bicarbonate of soda. A short time later the company's product line was expanded beyond the basic alkalis of soda ash, caustic soda, and bichromates. In 1920 Diamond opened a second plant in Cincinnati to produce silicate of soda by combining soda ash with sand.

The company expanded its product line again in 1925 when the Painesville plant began to manufacture calcium carbonates, cement, and coke. A sludge by-product of soda ash was treated to make the calcium carbonate, marketed as an agent to give paint smoothness, speed dry printers' inks, and add physical properties to rubber and plastic products. In 1929 the company began making caustic soda through the new process of electrolysis of salt, a method of running brine through electricity. Two by-products formed from the process, chlorine and pure hydrogen, also were marketed. Chlorine was sold to the water purification industry and also was used in the manufacture of dry cleaning solvents. The hydrogen was used for hydrochloric acid production, welding fuel, food oil hardening, electric lamp production, and ammonia production.

Diamond began a modest research program in 1936 that resulted in the production of magnesium oxide. After World War II began, magnesium became an important component for incendiary bombs, and Diamond was selected by the United States to operate one of 12 government-owned magnesium plants. Diamond's first research laboratory was established in

Company Perspectives:

Be the Best—Win and Grow. Focus on our customers; produce and provide quality products and services.

Improve everything we do; create opportunities out of change; control costs; and outperform competition. Encourage each employee's participation and ideas; communicate openly and honestly; value, respect, and develop every employee. Be safe; ethical; responsible and protective of the environment; have fun; and take pride in our work.

1942 by Raymond F. Evans, son of Diamond founder T.R. Evans. He became general manager of the company the following year.

By 1944 Diamond was operating three plants constructed through Defense Plant Corporation funds, including the magnesium plant, a calcium hypochlorite plant, and a synthetic catalyst plant under joint lease with the M.W. Kellogg Company. Before the war concluded, Diamond acquired Emeryville Chemical Company, a West Coast manufacturer of silicate of soda.

Rapid Diversification Following World War II

After 1945 Diamond's focus turned to a program of selling unprofitable assets, simplifying corporate structure, and modernizing, expanding, and adding plants. During the late 1940s several new plants opened, including a chlorine and caustic soda plant, a magnesium oxide plant, a silicate plant, and an electrochemical plant. Diamond signed five-year lease agreements with the U.S. government for chlorine and caustic soda plants at the U.S. Army chemical corps arsenal at Edgewood, Maryland, and at Pine Bluff, Arkansas. Detergent plants were established in Dallas and Painesville and at Emeryville, California.

Around 1947 the government lifted price controls imposed during the war, and Evans, appointed company president in 1947, directed Diamond's first price hike in nine years, seeking to reverse a wartime downward trend in earnings. A year later Diamond moved its headquarters from Pittsburgh to Cleveland, closer to its central operations in Painesville. Sales passed the $50 million mark for the first time in that year, but they slumped in 1949 due in part to a two-month strike that cost the company about $750,000 in net earnings. Diamond boosted its bichromate production with the acquisition of the Martin Dennis Company, operator of two New Jersey plants. With export sales on the rise, in 1949 Diamond formed an exports sales division that included Martin Dennis.

By 1950 Diamond's first phase of postwar expansion and diversification was nearly complete, with the company's assets having grown to include 12 different plants producing more than 100 different chemicals. In mid-1950, after the United States entered the Korean War, the demand for Diamond's products increased. The war also spurred the U.S. government to reactivate the Painesville magnesium plant that Diamond had operated during World War II, and the company was again charged with operating the facility, forfeiting any profit.

During the first half of the 1950s, Diamond embarked on its second phase of postwar growth by implementing diversification, geographical expansion, and modernization programs that helped it gain entry into the organic and agricultural chemicals, plastics, and chromic acid fields. In the fall of 1950 Diamond acquired the chromic acid business of E.I. du Pont de Nemours and Company. One year later Diamond purchased Kolker Chemical Works, Inc., a manufacturer and distributor of organic insecticides and agricultural chemicals, including DDT. In 1953 Diamond Alkali began producing polyvinyl chloride, a product used in the manufacture of plastic articles, and perchloroethylene, a product used in metal cleaning and dry cleaning. That same year Diamond acquired Belle Alkali Company, a producer of chemicals used in the manufacture of silicone resins, solvents, and drugs.

Evans became company chairman in 1954, and John A. Sargent, executive vice-president, became president. In the same year Diamond created an exploratory research department to assist in strategic planning. Diamond continued its geographical diversification in early 1955 with the acquisition of a 51 percent interest in Diamond Black Leaf Company, an agricultural chemicals firm with plants in Virginia, Alabama, Kentucky, and Texas. Two years later Diamond Black Leaf became a wholly owned subsidiary.

In 1955 Diamond acquired a government-owned chlorine and caustic soda plant at Muscle Shoals, Alabama, for $15 million. That same year the company passed the $100 million sales mark for the first time, logging $110 million in revenue. While sales were increasing, Diamond's name recognition outside the chemical industry lagged, and in 1956 Diamond joined a number of chemical companies adopting new trademarks. The former ''alkali'' enclosed in a horizontal diamond was replaced by a vertical diamond surrounded by a curved letter ''d.'' In 1957 Sargent resigned, and Evans assumed the additional duties of president.

Diamond's growth continued in the 1960s. In 1960 Bessemer Limestone & Cement Company, an operator of a cement plant and limestone quarries, was merged into Diamond. Diamond also acquired Harte & Company, a producer of vinyl film and sheeting that served the plastics industry, and Chemical Process Company, a producer of chemicals used for water purification, pharmaceuticals, and polyester resins. In 1961 Diamond joined three foreign firms in building a $15 million electrolytic caustic chlorine plant in Brazil, the largest in South America, to produce fertilizer chemicals. The following year Diamond and a French firm, Prosim, S.A., formed the joint venture company Dia Prosim, S.A., to manufacture water treatment chemicals at a new plant in Mobile, Alabama.

Arthur B. Tillman, who had worked his way through the ranks from division manager to company vice-president, was named president in 1966. In 1967 Diamond merged with Nopco Chemical Company, a New Jersey producer of a wide range of inorganic and organic chemicals. Also that year, Diamond acquired the polypropylene resin and film plants of Alamo Industries, boosting its foothold in the plastics market.

Expansion into the Oil Industry and Continued Diversification: Late 1960s–70s

In the summer of 1967 Diamond laid the foundation for expansion into the petrochemicals field by merging with

Key Dates:

1910: Diamond Alkali Company is formed to produce chemicals for the glass industry.
1936: Company begins the production of magnesium oxide, used in the manufacture of incendiary bombs.
1967: Diamond merges with Shamrock Oil and Gas Company to form Diamond Shamrock Corporation.
1983: Diamond Shamrock merges with Natomas Company and gains oil and gas wells in Canada, Indonesia, and the North Sea.
1987: Restructuring leads to the formation of Diamond Shamrock R&M, Inc., an independent oil refining and marketing company.
1989: Company enters the petrochemicals industry.
1990: Company's name is changed to Diamond Shamrock, Inc.
1996: Diamond Shamrock Corporation and Ultramar Corporation merge to form Ultramar Diamond Shamrock Corporation.

Shamrock Oil and Gas Company to form Diamond Shamrock CorporationUltramar Diamond Shamrock Corporation[/idx] (Diamond). The merger combined Diamond Alkali's chemical assets with Shamrock Oil's production interests in oil, gas, and petrochemical fertilizers and its marketing assets, which included a chain of service stations.

Evans was named chairman of the new corporation, and James A. Hughes, a former Diamond Alkali vice-chairman, became president. C.A. Cash, former Shamrock president, became executive vice-president and president of the new subsidiary Diamond Shamrock Oil and Gas Company, while Tillman also was named executive vice-president of the corporation and president of the new subsidiary Diamond Shamrock Chemical Company. J.H. Dunn, former Shamrock chairman, was named chairman of the executive committee of the board.

In 1968 Diamond Shamrock sold its Bessemer Cement division to Louisville Cement Co. for $20 million to comply with a Federal Trade Commission ruling to divest itself of the unit. One-quarter of Diamond Shamrock's sales that year came from oil and gas, with the remainder of its revenues coming from a mix of commodity chemicals, plastics, specialty chemicals, and agricultural chemicals. The mix changed in 1969 after Diamond acquired Taylor-Evans Seed Company, a producer of farming seeds with international marketing operations, and Pickland Mather & Company, a leading supplier of raw materials to the steel industry, with interests in iron ore mining, mineral management, and ocean shipping vessels.

Diamond's oil exploration activities during the early 1970s focused in large part on the Gulf of Mexico, Gulf of Alaska, North Sea, and Texas Panhandle, while production centered on domestic drilling in the West and Southwest. In 1971 Diamond Shamrock's growing interest in the fields of animal health and veterinary medicine led to the purchase of BioToxicological Research Laboratories, which was engaged in chemical research related to agriculture and animal health. The following year Diamond acquired American Chocolate & Citrus Company of St. Louis, a provider of flavorings, fruit drink bases, and food processes to commercial dairies. Three years later Hughes retired, and Cash was named chairman. William H. Bricker, who had joined the company in 1969 as a vice-president overseeing agricultural chemicals, was named president. In 1976 he was named chief executive officer.

Diamond's specialty chemical operations continued to grow during the late 1970s. The company expanded its foothold in the commercial baking market when it bought three Philadelphia-based providers of baking supplies: Federal Yeast Corporation, Gold Star Foods Company, and Bakery Products Inc. Diamond also acquired the animal health business of Shell Chemical Company and expanded its existing vinyl chloride and potassium carbonate plants.

Diamond continued to build on a growing oil and gas foundation, with the area of exploration more than doubling between 1972 and 1977 to more than 2.5 million acres, while oil production increased more than 60 percent. In 1977 Diamond announced plans to construct a $25 million catalytic cracking unit at its McKee refinery near Dumas, Texas, to meet federal regulations calling for increased production of unleaded gasoline. The following year Diamond acquired a 21 percent stake in Sigmor Corporation of San Antonio for $28 million and then sold Sigmor $19 million in service station properties, a majority of which carried the Shamrock brand.

After Cash retired in 1979, Bricker assumed the additional duties of chairman and moved to make Diamond a major energy company. That same year Diamond acquired Falcon Seaboard Inc., a Houston-based producer of steam coal for $250 million. In a move that prompted Evans to resign as a director, Bricker relocated the company's headquarters from Cleveland to Dallas to follow its growing energy interests in the Southwest. Reflecting the change in Diamond Shamrock's focus, the 1979 annual report noted that the ''energy, technology and chemicals'' company had more than quadrupled during the decade.

Consolidation and Increasing Challenges in the Early 1980s

Diamond Shamrock entered the 1980s with a new president, Allan J. Tomlinson, a former executive vice-president in charge of the company's international and technology unit. In 1980 Diamond announced a slate of divisions targeted for divestiture, including plastics, metal coatings, domestic polymers, food-related products, animal nutrition, and medical products.

While courting buyers for its chemical assets, in 1980 Diamond turned its acquisition goals toward coal. The company paid $30 million for undeveloped coal reserves and then formed a coal marketing subsidiary. In 1981, in a second major expansion move into coal, Diamond purchased Amherst Coal Company for $220 million and then reached an agreement with the French government to provide steam coal for power generation. Diamond posted record earnings in 1981 of $230 million on $3.4 billion in sales.

In 1982, after having spent $161 million for drilling rights in Alaska's Beaufort Sea, earnings dropped by roughly $150 million because of recessionary conditions and falling energy prices. J.L. Jackson, former president of Diamond's coal unit, was named corporation president in 1983. Diamond continued seeking buyers for its weak chemical assets, and the company expanded its divestiture slate to include its water conditioning and process chemical divisions. Diamond permanently laid off 500 workers in 1983 but still reported a $60 million loss due to tax write-offs on a dry hole in the Beaufort Sea. Diamond's most expensive move of 1983 was its $1.2 billion stock swap in the merger with Natomas Company. The merger gave Diamond oil and gas operations in Indonesia, a geothermal energy business, and wells producing oil in the North Sea, Canada, and the United States.

Diamond's involvement with the defoliant Agent Orange in the mid-1960s affected the company in 1984. In March 1984 Diamond agreed to spend $412 million to clean up contaminants at a New Jersey plant where it had produced the defoliant for use during the Vietnam War. Two months later Diamond was one of seven chemical companies that agreed to a settlement to compensate Vietnam War veterans for injuries claimed to be associated with exposure to dioxin, a toxic substance used in Agent Orange. Although Diamond Shamrock produced only five percent of the Agent Orange used in the Vietnam War, the company's chemical compound contained the highest concentration of dioxin. In the settlement Diamond agreed to contribute $21.6 million to a compensation fund.

Turbulent Times in the Late 1980s

In 1985 Bricker tentatively agreed to sell Diamond for $28 a share to Occidental Petroleum Corporation but then withdrew the offer. The scrapped deal drew takeover speculation, and Diamond announced a restructuring to fend off possible hostile maneuvers. Included in the restructuring was the formation of a master limited partnership, Diamond Shamrock Offshore Partners Ltd., to hold the company's oil and gas assets in the Gulf of Mexico. Diamond also announced $810 million in write-offs, in large part due to its Indonesian properties, and said that it would repurchase about six percent of its stock.

In 1986 the company announced that it would eliminate 600 more jobs, sell its chemical and coal operations, and increase its oil and natural gas reserves. Jackson resigned a few months after the announcement. Later that year, Diamond's chemical business was sold to Occidental Petroleum for $850 million. With Diamond retrenching, in December 1986 Texas oilman T. Boone Pickens, who controlled the oil firm Mesa Limited Partnership, offered $2 billion for Diamond in a securities exchange. The offer was dropped a few weeks later, after Diamond had rejected the bid and filed suit against Pickens.

A second bid from Pickens in early 1987 prompted Diamond to announce its third restructuring in two years. Bricker, in his last move as chairman, had the company split in two to form a production and exploration company, named Maxus Energy Corporation, and an independent refining and marketing company, which kept the Diamond Shamrock name and became Diamond Shamrock R&M, Inc., to be based in San Antonio. Roger R. Hemminghaus, who had been running Diamond's refining business for two years, was named president. Assets for the new company included $1.6 billion in sales; two Texas refineries in McKee and Three Rivers; a natural gas processing plant; 4,000 miles of pipeline; 2,000 branded stations in 12 states; 550 company-operated retail stores in Texas, Colorado, and Louisiana; a lube oil blending and automotive accessories distribution company; and a liquid propane gas underground storage facility in Mont Belvieu, Texas, with a capacity of 30 million barrels. The new Diamond Shamrock went public in 1987.

Hemminghaus announced that Diamond Shamrock R&M would sell its more remote assets and concentrate on marketing operations in the Southwest. In 1988 the company began expanding its refinery and pipeline capacity and bolstering its retail presence. In the same year construction began on a $25 million hydrocracker unit for its McKee refinery, and Diamond purchased 80 Texas gasoline stations. In 1989 the company also established a development and new ventures department to identify related businesses in fields where it had expertise. Profits soared from $1.6 million in 1987 to $53.5 million in 1988, while stock prices nearly doubled to $28. Diamond formed the subsidiary, Diamond Shamrock Natural Gas Marketing Company, and then purchased two companies, Merit Tank Testing, Inc., which provided environmental testing for underground petroleum storage, and Petro/Chem Environmental Services, Inc., which marketed petroleum-related environmental services. The two were merged under the Petro/Chem name in 1989.

In 1989 Diamond entered the petrochemicals business and became a 33 percent partner in a propane-propylene operation in Mont Belvieu. Diamond's Mont Belvieu underground storage facility became the world's largest that year with the acquisition of XRAL Storage and Terminaling Company, which raised the company's capacity to 50 million barrels. Diamond also acquired a telephone services company and formed the subsidiary North American InTeleCom, Inc., a firm that was based in San Antonio and that provided operator-assisted services for correctional facilities and that managed private pay telephones, including those at many of Diamond's retail outlets.

Continued Changes and Challenges in the 1990s

In 1990 the company name was changed to Diamond Shamrock, Inc., and the company completed projects to pave the way for growth in the new decade, including major refinery additions, pipeline expansions, and the addition of some 40 new retail outlets. To increase its presence in the retail gasoline market in the Southwest, Diamond purchased 661 National Convenience Stores in Texas for $260 million in 1995. Also in 1995 Argentine oil company YPF purchased Maxus, Diamond's exploration and production business.

A major change occurred in December 1996 when Diamond merged with Ultramar Corporation to form Ultramar Diamond Shamrock Corporation (UDS). Ultramar had been founded in 1935 as Ultramar Exploration Co. Ltd., a company focused on developing oil fields in Venezuela. Beginning in the 1950s the company's operations spread into Canada, the United States, and Europe, and by 1975 Ultramar's assets included more than 1,000 retail gas stations in eastern Canada. The state of the oil industry in the 1980s created problems for Ultramar, however, and in 1991 the British oil firm LASMO purchased Ultramar in a hostile takeover. The following year LASMO spun off Ultramar's refining and marketing operations in North America as Ultramar Corporation.

The newly formed Ultramar Diamond Shamrock bought Total Petroleum (North America) Ltd. in September 1997, adding three refineries, in Oklahoma, Michigan, and Colorado, and some 2,000 gas stations in the central United States to Ultramar's operations. The merger and the acquisition resulted in increased net income for the company in 1997. Net income was $154.8 million, up significantly from 1996, but it amounted to a loss of $35.9 million.

In June 1998, with the hope of improving profitability and operating efficiencies, the company adopted a major restructuring plan. The plan included the sale or closure of more than 300 convenience stores, the cutting of more than 450 jobs, and the reorganization of some pipeline and refinery operations. The company planned to record a one-time pretax charge of $130 million for the quarter ended June 30, 1998, because of the restructuring. UDS president and COO Jean Gaulin voiced his support of the plan in a prepared statement and said, ''The restructuring will reduce costs and increase our customer focus. . . . The initiatives we are announcing today [June 9, 1998] will dramatically improve our operating performance and help us achieve our objectives for market leadership and higher return on capital employed.'' In the second half of 1998 UDS began to carry out its plan, selling or closing 65 convenience stores and eliminating nearly 200 employee positions. At the beginning of 1999 UDS announced plans to cut all nonessential and underperforming jobs and programs, which resulted in the almost immediate termination of 300 employees, including six vice-presidents. The layoffs raised the total job cuts to more than 1,300 since the merger that had created UDS in 1996.

UDS's improvement strategy included seeking beneficial joint ventures, and in July 1998 the company announced that it had reached a definitive agreement with utilities provider PG&E Corporation to manage UDS's energy services. The $2 billion, seven-year energy alliance was intended to assist UDS in reducing its energy costs. In September UDS formed Diamond-Koch L.L.C. with Koch Hydrocarbon Company, Koch Pipeline Company, L.P., and Koch Chemical Company, a division and subsidiaries of Koch Industries, Inc., respectively. The joint venture added several pipeline segments and a natural gas liquids fractionator to UDS's petrochemical assets.

Several attempts by UDS to streamline its operations in the wake of declining crude oil prices were foiled. In early 1998 the company signed an agreement with Petro-Canada to form a joint venture in which UDS's Canadian and northern U.S. operations would be combined with Petro-Canada's. When the Competition Bureau of Canada raised concerns regarding the venture, UDS terminated the project in June 1998. In October UDS entered into discussions with Phillips Petroleum Co. about the tentative formation of a refining and marketing joint venture. The North American venture was to include the operating assets of UDS and the North American refining, marketing, and transportation operations of Phillips. Unable to reach agreeable terms, however, the deal was terminated in March 1999. In another setback, UDS announced plans to close its refinery in Alma, Michigan, in October 1999. The refinery had been offered for sale, but no buyer materialized. UDS did, however, locate a buyer for its retail stores, terminals, and pipelines located in Michigan when it agreed to sell the operations to Marathon Ashland Petroleum L.L.C.

Despite the setbacks presented by the low refinery margins in the oil business and the failed mergers and ventures, UDS believed that its restructuring strategy would help modernize the company, eventually leading to increased productivity and success. The company experienced an upward trend as it headed toward the new millennium; in the second quarter of 1999, ended June 30, net income reached $48.4 million, a marked improvement over the same period in 1998, when UDS had reported a net loss of $52.6 million. CEO Gaulin, who replaced Hemminghaus at the beginning of 1999 when the latter retired, announced at the 1999 company shareholders' meeting, ''Looking forward, we are focused on three objectives; continue to grow earnings per share, improve our competitive position, and further strengthen our balance sheet. . . . In summary, it is imperative that we have a clear goal—and we have it. We must successfully execute the goal—we have, and we are.''

Principal Subsidiaries

Autotronic Systems, Inc.; Diamond-Koch L.L.C. (50%); D.S.E. Pipeline Company; Diamond Shamrock Pipeline Company; Diamond Shamrock Refining Company, L.P.; Diamond Shamrock Refining and Marketing Company; Emerald Corporation; Emerald Pipe Line Corporation; Kempco Petroleum Company; National Convenience Stores Incorporated; Sigmor Corporation; Sigmore Pipeline Company; The Shamrock Pipe Line Corporation; Ultramar Ltd.; West Emerald Pipe Line Corporation.

Principal Competitors

BP Amoco Corp.; Exxon Corp.; 7-11, Inc.

Further Reading

Atterbury, Paul, and Julia MacKenzie, *A Golden Adventure: The First 50 Years of Ultramar,* London: Hartwood Press, 1985.

Bricker, William H., *Partners by Choice and Fortune: The Story of Diamond Shamrock,* Princeton, N.J.: Princeton University Press, 1977.

Johnston, David, ''Phillips, UDS Call Off U.S. Downstream JV,'' *Platt's Oilgram News,* March 23, 1999, p. 1.

Lee, Steve H., ''Ultramar To Acquire Total Petroleum,'' *Dallas Morning News,* April 16, 1997, p. D2.

Mason, Todd, and G. David Wallace, ''The Downfall of a CEO: The Inside Story of Bill Bricker's Reign at Diamond Shamrock,'' *Business Week,* February 16, 1987.

Norman, James, ''Phillips, UDS Join in U.S. Refining Venture,'' *Platt's Oilgram News,* October 9, 1998, p. 1.

''Petro-Canada, UDS Form Joint Venture,'' *National Petroleum News,* February 1, 1998, p. 22.

Spencer, Starr, ''UDS Sells Michigan Retail, To Shut Refinery,'' *Platt's Oilgram News,* May 25, 1999, p. 1.

''Ultramar Diamond Shamrock Hires PG&E To Manage All Its Power and Gas Supplies,'' *Industrial Energy Bulletin,* March 20, 1998, p. 1.

''Ultramar, Diamond Shamrock Merge 'Unique,' '' *National Petroleum News,* November 1, 1996, p. 19.

''Ultramar Diamond Shamrock Restructures Operations,'' *National Petroleum News,* July 1, 1998, p. 13.

Zipf, Peter, ''Ultramar Diamond's Plan Targets Lagging Returns,'' *Platt's Oilgram News,* November 19, 1997, p. 1.

—Roger W. Rouland
—updated by Mariko Fujinaka

Vin & Spirit AB

Box 47319
Formansvägen 19
S-100 74 Stockholm
Sweden
Telephone: (46) 8-744 70 00
Fax: (46) 8-645 60 15
Web site: http://www.vinspirit.se

State-Owned Company
Incorporated: 1917
Employees: 698
Sales: SKr 3.48 billion ($416.27 million) (1998)
NAIC: 31214 Distilleries

Government-owned Vin & Spirit AB (V&S) lost its monopoly on the production, wholesale, export, and import of alcoholic beverages in Sweden in 1995. Yet V&S, which is grouped under the country's Ministry of Finance, remains Sweden's largest producer, exporter, and importer of alcoholic beverages and has achieved worldwide recognition with the success of its Absolut vodka brand, the world's number six biggest-selling alcoholic beverage brand. After the end of the liquor monopoly, which was taken down upon Sweden's entry into the European Union, V&S was forced to restructure its operations, cutting staff and streamlining its product positioning. As such, the company now operates in two primary divisions, as its name implies: Wine and Spirits. The company's wine division handles the company's own wine brands, ranging from ''bag-in-a-box'' wines to high-quality imports, including imported wine from V&S-owned Domaine Rabiega vineyards in Provence, in the south of France. A total of 75 percent of the company's wine sales are provided by its own brands. V&S's brands account for more than 25 percent of all wine sold by the Swedish retail alcohol monopoly, Systembolaget. At sales of 32.4 million liters per year, wine remains the smaller part of V&S's total annual sales volume of 98.1 million liters. The largest part goes to the company's Spirits division, which itself is divided into two subsidiary operations: The Absolut Company, responsible for the company's world-renowned vodka product—and its single largest-selling brand—and Reimersholms, which produces and markets spirits chiefly for the Swedish market. In all, spirits sales reached 64.4 million liters. Absolut vodka alone represented 53 million liters of this total, with sales in 125 countries. The United States, however, with more than 32 million liters of Absolut sold in 1998, remains the brand's single biggest market. Other V&S spirits brands include Renat Brännvin, Grönstedts cognac, Reimersholms Aquavit, and Explorer and Kron vodkas. These other brands helped V&S win the coveted ''Distiller of the Year'' award from the coveted International Wine & Spirits Competition of 1998. In that year, the company recorded sales of nearly SKr 3.48 billion, with net earnings of more than SKr 861.5 million.

Swedish-Style Prohibition in the 20th Century

Concern over the negative impact of alcoholic beverage consumption on health and society inspired a number of prohibition movements around the world. In the year surrounding the First World War, a number of countries enacted prohibition policies, beginning with Iceland, where alcohol was banned in 1912, and reaching Norway in 1916, Finland in 1919, and the United States in 1922. Sweden, too, weighed the possibility of prohibiting sales of alcohol, taking a vote in 1922. By then, however, the country had already enacted a strict rationing system, called the Bratt System, after its developer Dr. Ivar Bratt. Under that system, which was introduced in Stockholm in 1914 and expanded throughout the country in 1919, not only were restaurants and taverns placed on strict licensing procedures—with veto rights given to local governments—but individuals, too, were granted the right to purchase only as much alcohol as they were deemed able to afford to buy. The immediate effect of the Bratt system was to limit alcohol sales among the country's female and poor populations. The Bratt system introduced a sort of ''bank book'' for alcohol purchases, which each citizen was required to present before being allowed to purchase any alcoholic beverage. At the same time, retail sales were placed under the Systembolaget monopoly, which continued to control all retail alcoholic beverage sales through the end of the century.

Company Perspectives:

There is a growing need to change the conditions for players in the Swedish market. Also, continued integration of markets in Europe demands innovative thinking and development, for the businesses and within them. V&S is working to adapt to this scenario, where growth, flexibility, focus and control of key stages in processes acquire great importance.

The referendum vote on prohibition was taken in 1922. The prohibitionists lost that battle by a slim margin—with 50.7 percent of the population voting against—the Bratt system, however, remained in effect and was not abolished until 1955. The failure of the prohibition referendum had saved the existence of a relatively young organization. Vin & Spirit had been set up in 1917 as the government-run monopoly on the production and importation of all beverages with alcoholic content greater than 2.8 percent. V&S's monopoly extended over the entire spectrum of alcohol production, exportation, and importation, as well as wholesale distribution and distribution to the Systembolaget retail monopoly. As such V&S took over production of many of Sweden's most popular and revered names in spirits, such as Reimersholms' Renat Brandvin, introduced in 1877; OP Anderson, introduced in 1891; the world-famous Grönstedt line of cognacs, established in 1846; and Absolut Rent Brännvin, introduced in 1879.

V&S's monopoly gave it little need or incentive to engage in marketing campaigns to its captive audience. Attached to the Ministry of Finance, the liquor monopoly functioned not only as a tax collector, but also as a source of revenues for the Swedish government. V&S nonetheless had to take into account the tastes of the Swedish consumer, adapting its products accordingly. As such, the company introduced a new vodka brand in 1959, Explorer, which was highly popular among drinkers in a country where vodka was the number one preferred spirits type.

That vodka was also the biggest-selling category of spirits worldwide had not escaped the attention of V&S's president, Lars Lindmark, in the 1970s. Sweden was hardly recognized by the world's vodka lovers as a producer of vodka. Yet the country had been producing its own ''bränvin'' (literally, ''burnt wine'') since the 15th century. Attributed various medicinal properties, this spirits type was generally sold by pharmacies, in the typical pharmaceutical bottles of the day; it also found other uses, however, specifically in the making of gunpowder. Even as the Swedish consumer was discovering other, more recreational properties of spirits, the first alcohol restrictions were enacted to ensure the supply of distilled alcohol for the Swedish military. Nonetheless, by the 17th century, the Swedish vodka had become the country's most popular type of alcoholic beverage.

Production centered around the country's southern regions, particularly the Skane region, which accounted for half of the country's production. Regional clashes tended to restrict distribution, however, as cities sought to control the production and sale of vodka in the areas under their control. As such, the city of Stockholm, for example, enacted its own vodka monopoly that barred distribution of vodkas produced outside of the city. Despite these restrictions, in the 19th century, the Swedish kingdom saw the rise of a new kind of nobility: the ''King of Vodka,'' Lars Olsson Smith.

Smith had started his career as a child—by the age of ten, he had already achieved success as a businessman, and by the age of 15 he had already amassed a personal fortune. Smith had developed a new type of vodka, produced using a distillation method dubbed ''rectification,'' which permitted the production of a purer vodka. Smith's grain-based vodka, which was introduced in 1879, was not only smoother, it tasted better, according to many. Called ''Absolut Rent Bränvin'' (''absolutely pure vodka''), this new brand enabled Smith to gain control of more than one-third of the country's total vodka production.

While Smith's Absolut production was located on the island of Reimersholme, outside of Stockholm, Smith quickly began buying out other distillers in the southern Skane region. At the same time Smith went to battle with the Stockholm liquor monopoly, refusing to apply for a permit to sell his vodka within the city, but instead setting up a retail store next to his Reimersholme distillery. Meanwhile, Smith declared war on the many inferior-quality vodkas then available, even stirring up labor union boycotts against the inferior vodkas and their distributors.

By the turn of the century, Absolut Rent Bränvin had helped Smith become one of the country's wealthiest citizens. Smith also began exporting his vodka, achieving still greater success. Nonetheless, a born entrepreneur, Smith was also prone to losing his fortune, only to rebuild it and lose it again. Finally, by the time of his death in 1913, Smith was bankrupt. When the Swedish Wine and Spirits Monopoly was formed, Absolut Rent Bränvin came under its aegis. The brand remained popular in its homeland, but was quickly forgotten overseas.

A Worldwide Marketing Success Story by the 1990s

By the 1990s, Smith's Absolut brand was once again at the top of its field—Absolut had become the world's sixth largest-selling spirits brand. When Lars Lindmark took over the presidency of the V&S monopoly in the 1970s, he began looking for ways to improve sales, specifically through exports. With the approach of the 100th anniversary of the vodka created by Lars Olsson Smith, Lindmark saw an opportunity not only to mark that occasion, but also to re-introduce to the world a fine vodka. Lindmark chose the United States as his first export market, given that the United States was one of the world's largest single consumers of vodka.

Lindmark recognized that, as president of a monopoly, he had little experience in the marketing methods needed to create an international brand. Lindmark began assembling a marketing team, hiring not only a Swedish design team, but also advertising experts in the United States. Before the vodka had even been given a name, the team went to work on its packaging, eventually settling on the now famous bottle, inspired by the original pharmaceutical bottles in which Swedish vodka had long ago

Key Dates:

1846: Vin & Spirit's oldest brand name, Grönstedt cognacs, is established.
1877: Renat Brandvin is introduced.
1879: The brand Absolut Rent Brännvin (absolutely pure vodka) is created.
1914: Creation of Bratt alcohol rationing system.
1917: Establishment of Vin & Spirit, the Swedish national wine and spirit monopoly.
1955: Abolishment of Sweden's Bratt system.
1959: Launch of Explorer brand vodka.
1979: U.S. launch of Absolut brand vodka.
1985: Andy Warhol designs first in Absolut Art bottle series.
1995: Loss of Swedish spirit and wine monopoly.
1998: Launch of Kron vodka brand in Poland; launch of Sundsvall super premium vodka brand in United States.
1998: Vin & Spirit is named Distiller of the Year at the International Wine and Spirit Competition.

been sold. Other aspects of the bottle came into shape, such as the use of low-lead-content sand to increase the bottle's clarity—the better to show off the purity of the vodka itself. Instead of attaching labels to the bottle, the team decided to engrave the lettering directly onto the bottle. By the time it came to give the vodka a name, the team—inspired by the bottle's vintage design—decided to go back to the vodka's origins as Absolut Rent Bränvin, translated into English for the international export market. Trademark restrictions in the United States, however, made it impossible to use the words "absolute" or "pure" in the vodka's name. Instead, the marketing team dropped the "e" from absolute, which had the effect of enhancing the vodka's Swedish origins. To reinforce this connection still further, the team added the words "Country of Sweden."

Absolut was first introduced to the Boston market in 1979; in that year, the vodka won an award for best packaging design. Yet Absolut's march to become the U.S. market's—and the world's—biggest vodka brand really began in 1981. In that year, the vodka's U.S.-based advertising team, Geoff Hayes and Graham Turner of TBWA, introduced one of the era's most successful advertising campaigns. The first Absolut ad, called "Absolut Perfection," established the look of what remained an Absolut standard through the 1990s. With its play on words and graphic puns (the ad featured the bottle wearing a halo) the Absolut Perfection ad sparked a series of ads, all of which featured the tagline "Absolut Something dot," topping 1,000 in number by the end of the 1990s.

The ads not only captured the attention of consumers, who quickly made Absolut one of the United States' biggest sellers. By 1982, it had taken over the number two spot and, by 1985, it had beat out its prime Russian competitor to lead U.S. vodka sales. That year, also, saw the first of what was to become the world renowned Absolut Art series, when Andy Warhol was commissioned to design an Absolut ad. The list of artists who contributed to the Absolut Art series soon read as a who's who of the 1980s and 1990s art world, with names like Keith Haring, Edward Ruscha, Kenny Scharf, Arman—more than 350 artists in all. In the late 1980s and especially in the 1990s, Absolut's marketing effort branched out to include designers such as Donna Karan and photographers such as Helmut Newton, and has even moved into cinema, producing preview advertisements for motion picture audiences.

With the United States and Canadian markets conquered, V&S turned its Absolut juggernaut toward the rest of the world. In the 1990s, V&S began rolling out Absolut to its European neighbors, entering the United Kingdom, Germany, France, and others, tailoring its campaign to each country's audience. New country launches typically drew on the company's stock of "basic" ads, including the original Absolut Perfection ad, before becoming country-specific in terms of cultural icons and references.

The success of Absolut encouraged V&S as it prepared to face a new challenge. Sweden's admission to the European Community meant that it was forced to abolish its liquor and wine monopoly. The loss of V&S's monopoly occurred in 1995; a direct result was the shutting down of its Stockholm production facility and the closing of its Provinum Distribution subsidiary. The company also faced into the onslaught of direct domestic competition for the first time since its formation in 1917. Nonetheless, buoyed by the experience gained with Absolut's international success and by the success of the V&S 500-strong catalog of spirits and wine brands, V&S remained confident of retaining at least a 50 percent share of alcohol and wine production, importation, and exportation in Sweden. At the same time, the company prepared other international moves, including the creation of a new vodka brand, Kron, specifically for the Polish market. That country, the world's number two market for vodka sales, required that vodka sold in the country be produced domestically. In keeping with this restriction, V&S established a joint venture production facility in Poland. In the late 1990s, V&S sought further expansion in the North American market, introducing its aquavit—a popular Swedish spirit—brands to the U.S. market. Not all of V&S's expansion moves were successful. The company's entry into the vast Russian vodka market, the world's largest, met with relative indifference, as the Russian consumer remained committed to their domestic brands.

In the second half of the decade, V&S began restructuring its operations, grouping its operations into two major categories, Wine and Spirits, with the latter being organized into two principal subsidiaries: The Absolut Company and Reimersholms. At the same time the company centralized most administrative and financial functions. Although V&S saw the inevitable erosion of its Swedish market share, it nevertheless posted strong revenues and earnings, while retaining a 55 percent share of all Systembolaget sales. V&S also continued rolling out new products, such as the Sundsvall "super premium" vodka, launched in 1998. In that year, the company was awarded international recognition for the high quality of its spirits range, winning the coveted "Distiller of the Year" award at the prestigious International Wine and Spirit Competition.

Principal Subsidiaries

The Absolut Company; V&S Domaine Rabiega (France); Amfora Vinhus AB; Vin&Spiritsällskapet; Vin & Spirithistoriska Museet.

Principal Competitors

The Seagram Company Ltd.; Grand Metropolitan plc.

Further Reading

Beck, Ernest, ''Western Vodka Makers Come Up Dry in Russia,'' *Denver Rocky Mountain News,* January 25, 1998, p. 52.

Carter, Meg, ''The Drink Is Distilled, So Is the Message,'' *Independent on Sunday,* September 29, 1996, p. 9.

Rothenberg, Randall, ''Absolut Madness,'' *Esquire,* October 1, 1996, p. 68.

Sutton, Henry, ''Absolutely in the Spirit of Art's Sake,'' *European,* October 28, 1994, p. 21.

—M.L. Cohen

Wildlife Conservation Society

2300 Southern Boulevard
Bronx, New York 10460
U.S.A.
Telephone: (718) 220-5197
Fax: (718) 220-2685
Web site: http://www.wcs.org

Not-for-Profit Organization
Incorporated: 1895 as the New York Zoological Society
Employees: 750
Sales: $78.42 million (1998)
NAIC: 813312 Environment, Conservation and Wildlife Organizations; 71213 Zoos and Botanical Gardens

The Wildlife Conservation Society (WCS) is an organization dedicated to saving wildlife and natural environments; in 1999 it boasted about 85,000 members and 140,000 subscribers to its *Wildlife Conservation* magazine. The Society employs 60 full-time conservationists and over 70 research and conservation fellows, who conduct hundreds of field studies throughout the world. WCS also lobbies for international legislation to protect wildlife and works to increase the public's awareness of the dangers faced as a result of natural resource destruction. WCS highlights this awareness at its urban centers in New York, which include the Bronx Zoo, the New York Aquarium, and the Central Park, Queens, and Prospect Park Wildlife Centers. The Bronx Zoo is the largest urban zoo in the United States and home to about 6,500 animals. More than four million people visited the Society's zoos in 1997, half of them school children.

Eminent Origins

WCS traces its history to the family of venerable environmental groups that sprang up in the late 1800s as a response to the large-scale clearing of American wilderness. Only three other major private conservation organizations in the United States predated WCS: Audubon Society (1886), Sierra Club (1890), and Boone and Crockett Club (1887).

Attorney Madison Grant is credited with the idea of creating a zoological park in New York City. Theodore Roosevelt, as president of the Boone and Crockett Club, itself created to save game animals from extinction, helped sponsor the enterprise. The New York Zoological Society was chartered in 1895, with an aim to create a wildlife preserve in New York City to foster an appreciation of the natural world among the populace. It also aimed to be a kind of Noah's Ark, to shelter representatives of species facing extinction. In 1897 it commissioned its first field study, on the effects of hunting on the Alaskan fur seal population.

In 1906, William T. Hornaday, previously chief taxidermist at the Smithsonian Institution, was named as the first director of the New York Zoological Park (which became known as the Bronx Zoo), a position he would hold for 30 years. Hornaday was an ardent conservationist and helped introduce legislation to protect ducks, bison, fur seals, and other species endangered by overhunting. Hornaday selected the site for the world's largest zoo, which opened on November 8, 1899. Although New York City provided $425,000 to the Society's building fund for construction of the zoo, prominent citizens such as J.P. Morgan, Andrew Carnegie, and John D. Rockefeller contributed an additional $250,000 in start-up capital. Moreover, about 1,000 $10-a-year memberships were issued. Moreover, in 1902, the Society gained management of the New York Aquarium, founded in Manhattan in 1896, from the city's government.

The Society's field studies proved valuable from the onset. The findings from the Society's first field study, conducted by Andrew J. Stone, led to the Alaskan Game Act of 1902. Eminent biologist William Beebe embarked upon a massive survey of Asian pheasants in 1909, covering 50,000 miles during his studies. Seven years later, Beebe would be tapped to head up the Society's first Tropical Research Station in British Guiana.

Closer to home, the Bronx Zoo became an important center for animal preservation and study. It was the first zoo to hire a full-time veterinarian and would establish the first modern animal hospital in 1916. In addition, William Hornaday led the Society to help open three bison reserves in the Midwest, beginning with the Wichita Mountains Forest Reserve in Oklahoma, which was started in 1907 with 15 bison supplied by the Bronx Zoo.

Company Perspectives:

The Wildlife Conservation Society's mission is to save wildlife, to teach ecology, and to inspire care for nature.

In 1913, the Society published Hornaday's *Our Vanishing Wildlife,* a book that would profoundly influence public policy in the United States, helping establish legislation to spare migratory birds from hunting. Moreover, the Society helped form the Save-the-Redwoods League in 1918 to protect that species in California. Aiming to inspire an appreciation of ecological diversity through observation of wildlife in captivity, the Society founded the first formal zoo education program in 1929. Moreover, its commitment to conservation escalated as it fought to save the white rhinoceros from government-sponsored slaughter in South Africa. The New York Aquarium and Bronx Zoo proved popular diversions during the Great Depression, allowing the Society to continue to fund field studies and to enhance its facilities.

A Broadening Society Focus: The 1940s–70s

Although the New York Aquarium in Battery Park closed its doors in 1940 when construction on the Brooklyn-Battery Tunnel commenced, the Bronx Zoo was thriving. At this time, the Society received new leadership. Fairfield Osborn and Laurance S. Rockefeller, named Society president and board chairman, respectively, in 1940, would oversee a long period of growth. Under Osborn and Rockefeller, the Society broadened the scope of its mission, building on Hornaday's concern for animal species by emphasizing global responsibility for the environment as well.

The zoo's next projects focused on the creation of natural environment exhibits. An innovative, open habitat known as African Plains was installed at the Bronx Zoo in 1941, a savanna environment recreated for zebras, antelopes, and other grazing animals and birds, with lions kept apart on an island on the other side of a moat. One year after the installation of the Bronx Zoo's first Children's Zoo in 1941, a Farm-in-the-Zoo was opened as well with a similar educational mission.

The Society's global conservation concerns were discussed in the Society-sponsored book *Our Plundered Planet,* published in 1948. Also that year, the Society established a division devoted to conservation issues, which would become the Conservation Foundation. Moreover, the Society began backing the operation of a research station at Wyoming's Jackson Hole Wildlife Park. Research would become a hallmark of the modern WCS. Other projects included supporting the work of Olaus and Margaret Murie, who did exploratory studies in Alaska, leading to the creation of the Arctic National Wildlife Refuge.

In 1957, the Society celebrated the opening of a new aquarium on Coney Island. The city and the Society had agreed to share the expense of building the new facility, which had been many years in the planning stages.

Financial support for the Society, its causes, and its facilities continued to gain momentum, as generous donations were received from wealthy philanthropists, corporations, and general membership drives. In the 1960s, the Society was able to establish funds for several of its efforts, including the African Wildlife Fund, which supported studies and preservation projects in Kenya, Zaire, and Uganda, and a general fund for new and improved zoo exhibits. In 1964, a newly renovated Aquatic Bird House reopened to the public at the Bronx Zoo, 65 years after its original debut. Other new zoo exhibits and facilities followed, notably the World of Birds in 1972. Like African Plains, the new additions sought to recreate as faithfully as possible the residents' natural living conditions.

The Society's commitment to the study of wildlife continued during this time. Field biologists backed by the Society focused on seabirds, African elephants, humpback whales, primates populations, and tropical rainforests. At the Bronx Zoo, scientists studied social behavior among animals with the aim of improving breeding success; for some species, this represented the last chance before extinction.

Renovations in the 1980s and a New Name in the 1990s

In 1980 the City of New York turned to the Society for help in renovating three aging municipal zoos. The Central Park, Queens, and Prospect Park Wildlife Centers opened under Society management between 1988 and 1993. The three zoos focused, respectively, on tropical, temperate, and polar habitats; North American habitats; and children's exhibits. The Society also implemented an active outreach program in city schools during this time.

A cooperative effort among zoos and aquariums in breeding endangered species was initiated by Society President William Conway. It was known as the American Zoo and Aquarium Association Species Survival Plan. Politically, the Society remained active as well, helping sponsor legislation in New York to curb the trade of exotic birds.

To better reflect its role in saving wildlife across the world, and not just as the operator of a New York zoo, the New York Zoological Society became known as the Wildlife Conservation Society (WCS) in 1993. By this time, WCS was funding studies and developing nature preserves in Brazil, Tibet, Zaire, Papua New Guinea, and the Congo. The protected acreage established by WCS during the 1990s amounted to an area the size of California.

Among its many notable successes in the 1990s was in establishing its historic Paseo Pantera (Path of the Panther) program in 1994, which united the Central American nations in preserving a corridor of tropical habitat where panthers and other large wildcats resided. WCS also launched the Global Tiger Campaign to protect the species by preserving its prey and educating Asian consumers about the illegal tiger trade. Moreover, in 1998, a WCS biologist uncovered a new deer species in Burma, known as the leaf deer among locals in the remote Himalayan region. By this time, the conservationist's art had expanded to include comprehensive medical care, elaborate breeding programs, and genetic engineering in some cases. Closer to home, WCS continued to study amphibians in the Great Swamp north of New York City.

WCS had expanded its global conservation efforts into more than 50 countries by the late 1990s, reaching even into the demilitarized zone (DMZ) between North and South Korea, where land mines and barbed wire from the Korean War had kept developers out of the habitat of tigers and cranes. Political conflict complicated WCS's efforts in Rwanda, Congo, and the Democratic Republic of Congo (formerly Zaire). WCS planned to open a six-and-a-half acre exhibit called Congo Gorilla Forest at the Bronx Zoo to raise public awareness for that area's unique, dense rain forest. WCS also planned to give zoo visitors the option of earmarking their admission fee for a particular field project.

In addition to preserving wildlife at home and abroad, WCS sought to educate the public, particularly children, about the importance of conservation. Toward that end, a new Children's Zoo was opened in 1997, and WCS even began educational programs for schoolchildren in Papua New Guinea and in China. WCS hoped to engender in future generations an appreciation for wildlife, and in June 1998 it held its second Pan American Congress on the Conservation of Wildlife through Education. Interestingly, the conference was conducted entirely on the Internet, using chat rooms for live chats with important figures in the conservation business as well as electronic bulletin boards for posting important papers on a variety of subjects.

In 1998 WCS reported an operating deficit of about $24,000, a relatively small amount that WCS attributed in its annual report to a "three-year trend bringing operating revenue and expenditures in line with one another." WCS stressed that visitors to the zoos, aquarium, and parks contributed 36 percent of the Society's revenues and that those facilities were all experiencing healthy sales. The WCS operating budget included about $19 million in funding from the City of New York, and an additional $2 million from Federal funding for conservation and education programs. The remainder of WCS's 1998 revenues of $78 million was generated through contributions, investment income, grants, and subscriptions to the Society's publication *Wildlife Conservation.*

Further Reading

Goddard, Donald L., ed., *Saving Wildlife: A Century of Conservation,* New York: Harry N. Abrams, 1995.

—Frederick C. Ingram

Willamette
Industries, Inc.

Willamette Industries, Inc.

1300 S.W. Fifth Avenue
Portland, Oregon 97201
U.S.A.
Telephone: (503) 227-5581
Fax: (503) 273-5603
Web site: http://www.wii.com

Public Company
Incorporated: 1906 as Willamette Valley Lumber Company
Employees: 14,000
Sales: $3.7 billion (1998)
Stock Exchanges: New York
Ticker Symbol: WLL
NAIC: 322121 Paper (Except Newsprint) Mills; 322211 Corrugated and Solid Fiber Box Manufacturing; 322222 Coated and Laminated Paper Manufacturing; 32211 Pulp Mills; 321113 Sawmills; 321211 Hardwood Veneer and Plywood Manufacturing; 321212 Softwood Veneer and Plywood Manufacturing; 321219 Reconstituted Wood Product Manufacturing

Willamette Industries, Inc., headquartered in Portland, Oregon, is a medium-sized, diversified forest-products company. The company owns and operates more than 100 manufacturing facilities in 23 U.S. states, as well as in Ireland, France, and Mexico. Willamette pursues two primary lines of business—paper products, both white and brown, and building materials. Among the products offered by Willamette are pulp, fine paper, paper bags, corrugated containers, kraft linerboard, business forms, cut sheet paper, inks, lumber, plywood, particleboard, medium-density fiberboard (MDF), oriented-strand board (OSB), I-joists, and laminated beams. The company owns or manages about 1.7 million acres of timberland, mostly in the Pacific Northwest and the South, which supply nearly 60 percent of its lumber requirements.

A Mix of Controversy and Success: 1900s-20s

Willamette Industries, Inc., was first organized in 1906 in Dallas, Oregon, as the Willamette Valley Lumber Company. The company consisted of a sawmill, a small railroad, some logging equipment, and 1,200 acres of timberland. A pair of entrepeneurs, Louis and George Gerlinger, father and son, were two of the partners in the original corporation. The Gerlinger family would retain an interest in Willamette into the 1990s when the company's chief executive officer and president was William Swindells, grandson of George Gerlinger.

The company grew enormously in its first 15 years. The original corporation, including timberland, mill, and equipment, had been founded with $50,000. In 1920 a half-interest in the company was offered for sale for $375,000. Net assets of the company were valued at $1.5 million at that time. The original sawmill had been expanded and improved, and the Gerlingers had built a planing mill and drying kilns. The company owned more than 11,000 acres of timberland, containing more than 334 million board feet of timber.

Some of the company's early prosperity, like that of other lumber companies in the Pacific Northwest, was due to a tremendous demand for timber following the United States's entry into World War I. Because the army needed spruce to build military aircraft, Pacific Northwest lumber companies were able to sell as much spruce as they could cut. Willamette benefitted, although the company also suffered from the labor agitation that racked the industry.

Lumber workers in Oregon, Washington, and Idaho were strong supporters of the Industrial Workers of the World (IWW), a socialist labor union whose members were known as Wobblies. With much of the work force off to war and lumber production running at full capacity, many longstanding labor grievances were brought to a crisis point in 1917. Long hours, low pay, and unhealthy working conditions were the main points of contention. In the summer of 1917 the IWW organized a general strike throughout the Pacific Northwestern lumber industry. In July 1917 a large grain elevator in Klamath Falls, Oregon, burned to the ground; the fire was attributed to IWW arson. A fire at Willamette's Balderee camp created more than $200,000 in damages and was thought to have been set by Wobblie provocateurs. This fire put a temporary stop to all logging in the county, and arson hysteria swept the area. The allegations of arson were never substantiated, although the

> **Company Perspectives:**
>
> *One of Willamette's strengths is its ability to make products literally from the ground up, assuring customers of quality and reliability at reasonable prices.*

governor of Oregon sent a special military force to the area to investigate.

Eventually the federal government stepped in, taking an unprecedented step to ensure continued production of lumber for the war effort. In November 1917, the government instituted the first federally sponsored labor union: the Loyal Legion of Loggers and Lumbermen. The Four L's, as it came to be called, worked quickly to recruit members from the IWW. Workers took a loyalty oath, swearing to faithfully support their company to produce logs and lumber for the construction of army planes and ships. The new union then wrested reforms from management. Workers were granted an eight-hour day, and improvements in living conditions followed. Never before or since had the federal government acted as a union organizer, but it seemed to be the only way to get the stumbling timber industry back on its feet. Throughout the war, Willamette's George Gerlinger served on the Loyal Legion's central committee. Recognizing the great contribution the Loyal Legion had made to labor relations, Gerlinger helped convince the industry to keep the union on after the war was over.

Early Innovation in the 1930s

Willamette achieved a competitive edge early on by finding ways to utilize timber products ignored by other companies. Up to the 1940s, for example, hemlock was considered an unusable species of tree. Willamette's timber lands, however, were almost 30 percent hemlock, and the company found many uses for this wood, marketing the wood for ladders, refrigerators, and door moldings. In 1932 Willamette started selling its waste hemlock chips for papermaking. Chips that could not be sold were burned to produce power. Willamette's policy was to sell or use everything it cut, and this efficiency helped the company through the lean years of the Great Depression. The Willamette mill ran double shifts throughout the Depression, closing down only once because of lack of logs. Many larger lumber companies were much harder hit.

To stimulate the economy, President Franklin D. Roosevelt instituted the National Industrial Recovery Act (NIRA) in 1933, which called for regulation of prices and set production quotas for the lumber industry. Large companies wanted to hold production down in order to boost prices, so Willamete was ordered to shut down its second shift. Willamette's president, George Gerlinger, protested the quota to the National Recovery Administration in Washington, D.C., but his appeals were turned down. Willamette was forced to comply with the code, and 250 workers were laid off. Willamette's management, however, saw that while it could be forced to limit hours at its Dallas mill, the Lumber Code did not prevent the opening of new mills. Thus, the week after Gerlinger's appeal was denied by a federal court judge, Gerlinger announced that within the month Willamette would open a small log mill, for which he rehired laid off workers.

Gerlinger's son-in-law, William Swindells, bought an interest in Willamette in 1930 and began to learn the business. In 1935 Willamette bought the nearby Corvallis Lumber Company, and Swindells was named manager of this new venture. Willamette bought close to 10,000 acres of timberland in 1938 and acquired almost 4,000 more the next year. Despite a crippling fire in 1940, by the time the United States entered World War II, Willamette was again ready to produce as much timber as the government could buy for military ships and planes. When George Gerlinger died in 1948, Swindells took over as president. He continued the course of growth embarked on by Gerlinger.

Diversification and Steady Growth After World War II

After World War II, Willamette began to diversify. The company acquired a substantial interest in the Santiam Lumber Company in 1950. Willamette and Santiam set about to make a business out of selling their waste wood chips. In 1954 the two companies formed a third, the Western Kraft Corporation, which built a paper mill to process the chips for use in kraft paper. Willamette acquired the Western Veneer and Plywood Company in 1952. Another subsidiary of Willamette was the Western Corrugated Box Company, formed in 1955. A venture into another wastewood product, particleboard, yielded the Wood Fiberboard Company in 1959. By the end of the 1950s, Willamette Valley Lumber Company had developed a solid base of timberlands and a network of related companies that processed every part of the tree.

These related companies continued to expand in the following decade. Paper, bag, and plywood mills were opened in the South and West. By 1967 it became clear that a merger of Willamette's subsidiaries and joint ventures into one large company would yield substantial savings in taxes and management costs. On March 3, 1967, five companies—Willamette Valley Lumber Company, Santiam Lumber Company, Wood Fiberboard Company, Western Veneer and Plywood Company, and Dallas Lumber and Supply Company-merged into one entity. The new company took the neutral name Columbia Forest Products, but it was changed a few weeks later to the present name, Willamette Industries, Inc. The Western Kraft Corporation became an 80-percent-owned subsidiary of the new company, until its outstanding shares were purchased in 1970. It too merged with the parent Willamette in 1973.

William Swindells, Sr., was named president of the new company; Gene Knudson, a forester with Willamette since 1949, executive vice-president; and two of Swindells's sons, William, Jr., and George, were vice-presidents. The newly consolidated Willamette Industries surprised Wall Street with its success. In the ten years following the merger, Willamette's sales more than tripled, from $114 million in 1967 to $420 million in 1975. In 1972 Willamette acquired Hunt Lumber Company in a stock swap. In 1976 the company's 444,000 acres of timberland still represented a fraction of the land its competitors owned, yet Willamette was consistently one of the most profitable corporations in the forest products industry. Its man-

Key Dates:

- **1906:** Willamette Valley Lumber Company is formed in Dallas, Oregon.
- **1954:** Willamette and Santiam Lumber Company establish the Western Kraft Corporation.
- **1967:** Merger creates Willamette Industries, Inc.
- **1973:** Western Kraft merges with Willamette.
- **1983:** Willamette reaches annual sales of more than $1 billion.
- **1996:** Company acquires Cavenham timberlands for $950 million and also expands overseas in Ireland.

agement was expert at keeping costs down, and the company had achieved an excellent balance between its lumber and paper divisions. In general, paper and lumber run in opposite business cycles; that is, when building products are in high demand, paper products fall into a lull, and vice versa. As Willamette was spread evenly in both wood and paper, the company experienced relatively stable growth. Industry observers noted that Willamette enjoyed one of the most balanced mixes of paper and building materials in the entire forest products field during the post-merger decade.

Willamette Industries made a major acquisition in 1980, purchasing the Woodard-Walker Lumber Company in northern Louisiana for $85 million, giving Willamette two new plywood plants and approximately 50,000 more acres of timberland. The company then owned a total of more than 550,000 more acres of timber. Aware that worldwide resources were waning, Willamette increased attention to its longstanding policy of careful and efficient management of its trees.

The only significant lag in Willamette's steady growth since the late 1960s was caused by antitrust litigation. In 1972 plywood buyers brought a class action suit against more than 50 plywood producers, including Willamette. The suit charged producers with conspiring to fix freight rates. In 1978 a jury found Willamette, Weyerhauser, and Georgia-Pacific guilty of billing their plywood customers as if the product had been shipped form the Pacific Northwest, even though the transaction might involve buyers in Mississippi and sellers in Louisiana. The case dragged through several appeals until in 1982 Willamette agreed to pay a $29 million settlement. Earnings from operations were low in 1982, and with payment of the settlement, the company sustained its first loss in 75 years.

William Swindells, Sr., retired in 1976. Gene Knudson then became chairman and chief executive officer. William Swindells, Jr., took over leadership of the company in 1980. He was promoted to president and chief operations officer when Knudson made plans to retire.

New Challenges in the 1980s and Early 1990s

Throughout Willamette's history, the company attempted to provide stable employment for its work force. Even during the Great Depression the Willamette mill closed down only once. In the 1980s, however, labor relations grew more strained. Several strikes hit Willamette mills in the Pacific Northwest and in the South. As demand for forest products lessened worldwide, many Pacific Northwest lumber companies had to cut production. Willamette workers in Oregon struck in 1986 and 1988 but eventually settled for contracts that reduced average hourly wages.

Several Willamette sawmills closed in 1989 and 1990. Political decisions restricting timber supply and the limited availability of quality softwood and hardwood logs led to the shutdown of mills in Sweet Home, Oregon; Moncure, North Carolina; and Chester, South Carolina. Meanwhile, the company began to build vertically integrated operations in North Carolina and South Carolina in 1987. The company also continued to grow in non-hardwood areas. A new hardwood-and-softwood-mix finepaper mill in Marlboro County, South Carolina, opened in 1990, and the company began construction of a MDF plant at the same location. Willamette also made some acquisitions in 1990, including fine-papers manufacturer Pentech Papers, Inc., of Pennsylvania. The following year Willamette bought Bohemia, Inc., which had plants in Oregon that processed wood and made laminated beams, among other wood products. Bohemia also owned more than 45,000 acres of timberland in Oregon. Also in 1991 a new plant to make corrugated containers in the Houston, Texas, area was completed. Willamette's sales exceeded $2 billion that busy year.

In 1992 Willamette further boosted its presence in the corrugated products business by acquiring 11 corrugated container facilities from Boise Cascade. The plants were all located east of the Rockies—in Alabama, Arkansas, Colorado, Illinois, Indiana, Kentucky, Minnesota, North Carolina, and Tennessee. Willamette opened an MDF plant in South Carolina and a fine paper converting facility in Pennsylvania in 1992 as well.

By the early 1990s Willamette had grown into a significant player in the forest products industry. When Willamette Industries formed in 1967, the business operated 30 plants in six states. In 1992, as Willamette celebrated its 25th anniversary, the company had three times as many facilities and had expanded both geographically and in its product lines.

Continued Growth and Diversification: 1995 and Beyond

Willamette continued to hone its operations and grow steadily as it moved toward the new millennium. When the company made acquisitions, it chose them carefully, focusing on companies that would strengthen Willamette's existing operations in white paper, brown paper, and building materials. The company also grew through building additional facilities and updating existing plants. To maximize capital, Willamette did its own engineering and contracting when building, which was uncommon in the forest products industry. Also during the 1990s the company had to face growing environmental concerns and restrictions over the logging of the Pacific Northwest's public timberlands. These issues prompted Willamette to begin securing private lands and to expand in the East, which had less stringent regulations.

In 1995 new CEO Steven Rogel came on board when William Swindells retired. Under Rogel, Willamette acquired a paper mill in Tennessee from Mead and modernized its Campti, Louisiana, plant by adding a new linerboard machine. The following year the company made a major acquisition when it bought 1.1 million acres of timberland in the Pacific Northwest and the South from Cavenham Forest Industries, part of British conglomerate Hanson plc. Willamette paid $950 million for the Cavenham lands, and the purchase made Willamette the largest private landowner in Oregon. The company eventually sold about half of the land to others, keeeping more than 500,000 acres.

Looking for opportunities abroad, Willamette acquired a fiberboard plant in Clonmel, Ireland, in 1996 for $61.5 million. The following year the company purchased an interest in Corrugados La Colmena, S.A. de C.V., a corrugated box manufacturer in Mexico. In 1998 Willamette continued its European expansion with the purchase of MDF plant MDF D'Aquitaine, located in Morcenx, France. The acquisition allowed Willamette to better serve European customers and further penetrate the European market.

Improvements to existing facilities and new plants strengthened Willamette's operations in the late 1990s. 1998 volumes in the corrugated container division grew eight percent over 1997 volumes, a solid gain compared to the industry growth average of one percent. A new cut sheet plant in Brownsville, Tennessee, began operating in 1998, resulting in an increase in cut sheet production, and a second machine was added to the Hawesville, Kentucky, paper mill, boosting fine paper production and making Willamette the fourth-largest producer of uncoated free sheet. The company's business forms division, which consisted of six plants in six states, made 21 percent of the U.S. production of continuous forms bond during 1998. Willamette also manufactured 12 percent of the nation's paper bags through four plants in four states. Of Willamette's sales in 1998, brown paper product sales accounted for 37 percent, and white paper products represented 29 percent.

The building materials division grew as well, supported by the opening of a sawmill in Louisiana, which increased lumber production; the expansion of a laminated veneer lumber (LVL) facility in Oregon; and the completion of an engineered wood products facility in Simsboro, Louisiana, designed to make LVL and I-joists. The company planned to offer a comprehensive array of engineered wood products to serve the wide-ranging needs of customers, and in 1998 Willamette made 22 percent of the nation's supply of MDF. Through its European plants, Willamette made seven percent of Europe's production of MDF. Plywood production, however, did not fare as well, as a fire resulted in a six-month closure of a Zwolle, Louisiana, plywood plant in 1998, and a plywood plant in Taylor, Louisiana, was closed in mid-1997. Willamette sold 117,000 acres of timberland in southwestern Washington State to Cathlamet Timber Company for $234 million in 1998 as well, land that had been part of the Cavenham purchase. The company planned to pare down outstanding debt with the proceeds from the sale.

Much to the surprise of Willamette management, CEO Rogel left the company after only two years in order to become CEO at competitor Weyerhaeuser Company, based in Washington. Duane McDougall was named as Rogel's successor. Overall, Willamette did quite well in 1998, with sales up 5.7 percent from 1997 and net income up 22 percent. Early in 1999 Willamette announced plans to build a new cut sheet converting facility in the Midwest. The new plant would allow the company to better meet increased demand for cut sheet products. Willamette also planned to build a new $85 million particleboard plant in South Carolina. Construction was scheduled to commence in 2000. An additional acquisition in Europe was finalized in 1999 as well, when Willamette purchased Darbo, S.A., a particleboard manufacturer located in Linxe, France. Although some observers characterized Willamette's growth as cautious, the company demonstrated few signs of slowing down in the next century.

Principal Subsidiaries

Willamette Timber Company, Inc.; Wimer Logging Co.

Principal Competitors

Boise Cascade Corporation; International Paper Company; Smurfit-Stone Container Corporation; The Mead Corporation; Georgia-Pacific Corporation; Weyerhaeuser Company.

Further Reading

Bernton, Hal and Jonathan Brinckman, "The Future of Oregon's Forests," *Portland Oregonian,* September 27, 1998, p. A1.

Bernton, Hal, "Willamette Industries Takes Cautious Path to Success," *Portland Oregonian,* June 22, 1997, p. R18.

Dunn, Catherine Baldwin, "Making the Most of the Best: A History of Willamette Industries, Inc.," Portland, Oregon: Willamette Industries, 1994.

Kerfoot, Kevin, "Willamette Industries Acquires Cavenham Properties," *Kentucky Manufacturer,* May 1, 1996, p. 11.

Leeson, Fred, "Willamette Considers Sustainable Forestry Audit," *Portland Oregonian,* April 21, 1999, p. F1.

——, "Willamette Industries CEO Didn't Calculate Lofty Climb," *Portland Oregonian,* March 21, 1999, p. B1.

—Angela Woodward
—updated by Mariko Fujinaka

The Williams Companies, Inc.

One Williams Center
Tulsa, Oklahoma 74172
U.S.A.
Telephone: (918) 588-2000
Fax: (918) 588-2296
Web site: http://www.williams.com

Public Company
Incorporated: 1908 as The Williams Brothers Corporation
Employees: 21,011
Sales: $7.66 billion (1998)
Stock Exchanges: New York Pacific
Ticker Symbol: WMB
NAIC: 48691 Pipeline Transportation of Refined Petroleum Pipelines; 22121 Natural Gas Distribution; 32411 Petroleum Refineries; 44512 Convenience Stores; 51331 Wired Telecommunications Carriers; 51334 Satellite Telecommunications

The Williams Companies, Inc., is the largest interstate natural gas supplier in the United States. Rivaling its pipeline network in importance is its communications network: The Williams Communications Group, 86 percent owned by the parent company, offers wholesale long distance service. Its subsidiaries include Global Access, an audio- and videoconferencing service, and Vyvx, a transmission service for broadcast and cable networks. With the purchase of MAPCO in 1998, Williams also entered the refining business and the convenience store market.

Company Origins

Williams traces its history to 1908, when brothers S. Miller Williams, Jr. and David R. Williams were working for a construction contractor who had an order to pave sidewalks in Fort Smith, Arkansas. The contractor pulled out when funding for the project was delayed, but the Williams brothers decided to take care of the job themselves. They stayed in the construction business after the Fort Smith job, making their headquarters in that city and working under the name The Williams Brothers Corporation. Eventually, they established steel pipeline construction as their specialty, and in 1924 they moved to Tulsa, Oklahoma, in the heart of oil and gas country.

Williams Brothers remained a family-run business, small and privately held, for the next 25 years. Although the company maintained its headquarters in Tulsa, the petroleum and natural gas industries were not its only customers. When Miller and David's nephew, John H. Williams, joined the firm just after the bombing of Pearl Harbor, his first job was to help lay a water line for the U.S. Navy between Homestead and Key West in Florida.

In 1949 the Williams brothers decided to sell the company to their nephew John and his brother Charles, David Williams, Jr., David's son, and six middle managers. The new owners reincorporated under the name Williams Brothers Company, with initial capitalization of $25,000, and bought the old Williams Brothers's construction equipment for $3 million in debt. John Williams, who put up $5,000, was named president and CEO. Although only 30 years old, he had led an unusual and varied life. Born and raised in Havana, where his father was a distributor for a number of U.S. companies, he did not learn English until he was five years old. His uncles paid his expenses at Yale, from which he received a degree in engineering in 1940. In 1942, during World War II, he left Williams Brothers to join the navy. He returned to the family firm in 1946.

The new Williams Brothers' first job ended with unfortunate results. The company had received a $7.5 million contract to build a pipeline from Baton Rouge, Louisiana to Greensboro, North Carolina, but flooding caused by unusually heavy rains damaged the company's equipment, and the company actually lost $800,000 on the job. Within five years, however, it had made enough money to pay off its initial debt. In 1957, with a net worth of $8 million, it went public.

By the early 1960s Williams Brothers had established itself as a leader in its field, but a severe slump in the demand for new pipelines threatened its profitability. In 1963 the company lost $4 million on its domestic operations, and only strong overseas business limited its overall net loss to $500,000.

Company Perspectives:

We believe in many things—and they're not just related to the bottom line. We believe in giving employees the freedom and initiative to do their jobs. In taking chances. Celebrating diversity. Holding true to a set of solid, respectable values. And we strongly believe in being an active member of the communities in which we live. We're proud of our employees and their substantial volunteer work, and we do all we can to support and extend their efforts to make a difference.

Diversification and Expansion in the 1960s and 1970s

John Williams saw his first big opportunity to diversify in 1965, when he spotted an article in the *Wall Street Journal,* announcing that Great Lakes Pipe Line Company was for sale. Great Lakes Pipe Line had been founded in 1930 by a consortium of eight U.S. oil companies—Continental Oil Company, Sunray DX Oil Company, Skelly Oil Company, Texaco, Union Oil Company of California, Sinclair Oil, Cities Service, and Phillips Petroleum—to service the Midwest. A recent federal consent decree limiting Great Lakes's profit to seven percent convinced the owners that their resources were better spent elsewhere. The Williamses, for their part, believed that they could run the pipeline better than the oil companies, and Williams Brothers was one of the first parties to offer a bid. It was the only one left standing when the dust settled.

The Great Lakes pipeline network was the longest in the United States, consisting of 6,228 miles of pipe and 20 terminals. Its purchase price was $287.6 million. Williams Brothers' net worth in 1965 was $27 million. In lining up the financing for the deal, the company had to borrow almost the entire amount, making it a leveraged buyout (LBO) that would be audacious even by the standards of the LBO mania that would grip Wall Street 20 years later. Williams Brothers paid only $1.6 million of its own cash for Great Lakes Pipe Line.

The Great Lakes Pipe Line deal left Williams Brothers with a high debt-equity ratio, 89 percent (it would shoot up to 160 percent by 1970), but this did not deter John Williams from seeking new avenues for growth and diversification. In 1969, in a stock swap, the company acquired Edgcomb Steel Company, which processed and distributed metal products in the East and Midwest. At the same time, Williams Brothers began to look into the fertilizer business as another possibility. Fertilizer manufacturers were then suffering from low demand and oversupply, and the Williamses wanted to buy into the business while such companies were cheap.

In 1971 the company acquired The Suburban Companies, a liquid propane gas retailer. It also bought Colonial Insurance Company, a move that John Williams would later call his worst acquisition; uncharacteristically, the company had not secured a competent insurance executive ahead of time to take charge of Colonial, and it floundered as a result. It was sold off in 1974. Williams Brothers had become a diversified enterprise, and in May 1971 it recognized that fact by changing its name to Williams Companies.

In 1971 the company finally bagged a fertilizer company when it acquired Gulf Oil Corporation's agrichemical operations for $60 million. The next year, it added Agrico Chemical Company, Continental Oil Company's fertilizer subsidiary, for $140 million and merged the two operations under the Agrico name. John Williams then brought in his friend Kenneth Lundberg, CEO of major farm cooperative CF Industries, to head Agrico. The timing of these two acquisitions could scarcely have been better. Fertilizer prices turned up almost immediately. In 1974 Williams as a whole posted $950 million in sales—up from $235 million in 1970—and more than half of that figure was supplied by Agrico.

The company formed a new subsidiary in 1974, Williams Exploration Company, and branched out into the business of drilling for and producing oil and natural gas. Such operations were meant not only to generate profits for the parent company, but also feedstock for Agrico's manufacturing activity. In 1976 Williams joined with Newmont Mining Corporation, Bechtel Group, Boeing Company, Fluor Corporation, and Equitable Life Assurance Society to buy Peabody Coal from Kennecott Corporation, coming away with a 27.5 percent share. Also that year, the company sold its Williams International Group subsidiary, which had been formed in 1972 to take charge of its original pipeline construction operations. It was sold to an employee group, thus cutting Williams's tie to its old core business.

New Leadership in the Late 1970s

Signs of trouble began appearing at about this time as fertilizer prices dropped. Williams's earnings plunged as a result. Nonetheless, the company acquired Rainbow Resources in 1977, a Wyoming oil and gas exploration concern, for $40 million, and spent another $40 million expanding its pipeline network. When John Williams retired as chairman and CEO in 1978 at the age of 59, he left the relatively small family business that he had founded in 1949 as a conglomerate with sales of more than $1 billion and assets of almost $2 billion.

He was succeeded by Joseph Williams, David Williams, Jr.'s 45-year-old brother. Williams became a more conservative company, concentrating on the steady profits generated by its pipeline operations and shedding less dependable businesses. In 1979 it sold its Williams Energy subsidiary, which consisted of what used to be The Suburban Companies, to Penn Central Corporation for $57 million.

At about the same time, Agrico's financial performance was mercurial. The subsidiary posted a record profit of $175.5 million in 1980 only to plummet to a loss of $30.3 million in 1982, following a sharp drop in the demand for fertilizer. As a result, Williams's profits dropped from $57 million in 1981 to $34 million in 1982. In 1983 Agrico sold its entire retail operation to a management group for $51.7 million and a 40 percent stake in the new company, Crop Production Services, Inc. The relatively stable pipeline business looked more attractive, and that same year Williams acquired two natural gas pipelines: Northwest Pipeline, which served the West Coast, and Northwest Central, which was located in the Midwest.

Key Dates:

1908: Brothers S. Miller Williams, Jr. and David R. Williams begin their construction business with an order to pave sidewalks.
1924: Williams Brothers Corporation moves to Tulsa, Oklahoma.
1949: The Williams brothers sell the company to a group led by their nephew John Williams.
1965: Williams purchases the Great Lakes Pipe Line Company for $287.6 million.
1971: The company acquires Gulf Oil Corporation's agrichemical operations.
1972: The company buys Agrico Chemical Company.
1994: Williams sells its subsidiary WilTel for $2.5 billion.
1999: Subsidiary Williams Communications Group goes public.

By the middle of the decade, Joe Williams had concluded that his company needed a major restructuring to cut its dependence on commodity-based operations whose revenues were as unstable as the prices of those commodities. In 1984 Williams divested Edgcomb Metals, selling it to a management group. The next year, it embarked on a new venture. It established a subsidiary, Williams Telecommunications (WilTel), to run a fiber-optic cable network that would be installed inside abandoned steel pipelines.

The restructuring continued in 1986 when Williams sold all of Williams Exploration's assets to the U.S. subsidiaries of two Belgian oil companies, Petrofina and Cometra Oil. The reorganization ended in 1987, when the company sold its stake in Peabody Coal to consortium partner Newmont Mining for $320 million and divested Agrico by selling it to Freeport-McMoRan Resource Partners for $350 million. Also in 1987, Joe Williams added "The" to the company's name.

At the same time, The Williams Companies, Inc. showed that it was serious about the telecommunications business. In 1987 Williams acquired LDX NET, Inc., which owned a 1,295-mile-long fiber-optic network. In 1989 WilTel became the fourth largest fiber-optic telecommunications company in the United States when it acquired another fiber-optics concern, LIGHTNET, and added 4,500 miles to its system. This gave Williams a total of more than 11,000 miles over fiber-optic cable, transmitting signals from New England to the Pacific coast.

Wall Street approved of the new, leaner version of The Williams Companies and its name surfaced more than once in the late 1980s as an attractive takeover candidate. No takeover bid ever surfaced, however.

Throughout the middle to late 1980s, Williams had been building on to its natural gas pipelines. In a joint venture with Tenneco, the company created the Kern River Pipeline, significantly adding to its network of pipelines. In 1991 Williams completed the project. Other ventures in the early 1990s included the creation of WilTech, a digital video business that used WilTel's fiber-optic network to transmit video.

In 1994 Joseph Williams retired and Keith Bailey was named chairman. Bailey's first big move was to accept an offer from LDDS Communications to buy WilTel for $2.5 billion. The all-cash sale, which was completed early in 1995, gave the Williams Companies ample return on the $700 million it had invested to develop WilTel.

Expansion in Communications and Pipelines in the Mid-1990s

The sale of WilTel did not indicate the company's abandonment of the communications industry. Williams retained possession of one of the 12 strands of fiber in the pipe, over which it continued to develop WilTech, its digital video venture. Also in 1995, Williams acquired ICG Wireless Services, which gave a boost to WilTech by allowing it to connect satellite transmission of video with its fiber-optic network. The move quickly paid off: In 1996, WilTech won a multimillion contract from Time Warner to interconnect its cable and broadcasting companies.

Williams used the cash from the WilTel deal to purchase Transcontinental Gas Pipe Line Corp. (Transco) in 1995. The $3 billion deal added 16,000 miles of natural gas pipeline to Williams' network and made Williams the nation's largest interstate natural gas supplier. The following year, the company spent $205 million to buy out Tenneco's 50 percent share of the Kern River pipeline. At a time when many companies were selling their government-regulated pipelines and diversifying, Williams was expanding its pipeline network, betting that the trend toward less utility regulation would soon reach the pipeline business.

The Williams Companies made several other purchases in 1995 and 1996, including Pekin Energy, the nation's second largest ethanol manufacturer, and Cycle-Sat, Winnebago Industries' telecommunications services company. The following year, Williams Communications Group joined with Northern Telecom to create Williams Communications Solutions, a provider of voice, data, and video equipment.

By the late 1990s Williams was well into rebuilding its telecommunications business, which it had organized into the Williams Communications Group. In addition to Williams Communications Solutions, the group included WilTech, the video transmission service, which had been renamed Vyvx and was thriving on its contracts with major broadcast and cable networks. Williams squeezed more use out of its one fiber-optic strand from the WilTel network by creating Global Access, which furnished video- and audioconferencing to businesses.

Perhaps the most important development for the Williams Communications Group was the termination in 1998 of Williams' noncompetition agreement with WorldCom (signed at the sale of WilTel). Now free to reenter the long distance telephone service business, Williams began rebuilding its fiber-optic network and signed a deal with U.S. West Communications. By 1999, the network had grown to 19,500 miles in service, with an additional 13,500 expected to round out connections to 125 cities by the end of 2000.

Williams entered additional new markets in 1998 with its purchase of MAPCO, a leading U.S. propane seller. The $3 billion purchase not only expanded Williams' pipeline network, it added two refineries, 250 convenience stores, and two data and information management companies to Williams' stable of businesses.

In October 1999, Williams sent its Communications Group public, offering 29.6 million shares over the New York Stock Exchange. Williams held on to 86 percent of the business, with seven percent going in the IPO and seven percent being sold to SBC Communications, Intel Corporation, and Telefonos de Mexico (TELMEX). The private placements assured Williams Communications Group of business: SCG invested $425 million and agreed to use WCG as its preferred provider for long distance and data; Intel invested $200 million and chose WCG to provide transport for Web-hosting service centers; TELMEX invested $100 million and agreed to connect its long distance fiber-optic network with WCG.

Principal Subsidiaries

Thermogas; Mid-America Pipeline Company; MAPCO Express; Williams Express; Northwest Pipeline Corp.; Williams Production Co.; Williams Field Services Co.; Williams Western Pipeline Co.; Williams Natural Gas Co.; Williams Energy Co.; Williams Pipe Line Co.

Principal Operating Units

Williams Communications; Energy Services; Gas Pipeline.

Principal Competitors

Enron Corp.; El Paso Energy; AT&T; MCI Worldcom, Inc.

Further Reading

''The Best Defense . . . ,'' *Forbes,* November 15, 1977.

''Building a Winning Management Team,'' *Nation's Business,* April 1976.

Palmeri, Christopher, ''Arbitrage,'' *Forbes,* January 16, 1995, p. 45.

Ransdell, Eric, ''Rolling Out the Future: Williams Moves from Oil Pipelines to a Cutting-Edge fiber-Optic Network,'' *U.S. News & World Report,* August 12, 1996, p. 47.

''SBC Makes a Long-Distance Deal,'' *Business Week,* February 22, 1999.

''Sleeper,'' *Forbes,* May 2, 1988, p. 146.

''Williams: A Shelter from Inflation's Cost Is Caving In,'' *Business Week,* August 1, 1983.

—Douglas Sun
—updated by Susan Windisch Brown

YMCA of the USA

101 North Wacker Drive
Chicago, Illinois 60606
U.S.A.
Telephone: (312) 977-0031
Toll Free: (800) 872-9622
Fax: (312) 977-9063
Web site: http://www.ymca.net

Not-for-Profit Organization
Founded: 1844
Employees: 30,000
Sales: $3.13 billion (1998)
NAIC: 81341 Civic and Social Organizations

The YMCA of the USA is a not-for-profit, charitable organization offering various services to local, independent YMCAs throughout America. It provides assistance in many areas, including accounting, financing, purchasing, and programming. It is currently organized into six major groups: (1) the Association Advancement Group, which handles communications, marketing, advertising, public policy, and media and corporate relations; (2) the International Group, which oversees the integration of international education into current YMCA programs and such international activities as emergency and development assistance, training events, and conferences; (3) the Knowledge Management Group, which is responsible for disseminating knowledge, conducting research, and maintaining computer and other technological services; (4) the Leadership Development Group, which is responsible for human resources, staff training and development, and such matters as national YMCA employee benefits; (5) the Membership and Program Development Group, which helps develop and support programs, membership, volunteer enlistment and training, and purchasing; and (6) the Organizational and Management Consulting Group, which provides consulting services for the individual Ys across the United States. The national organization also staffs four Field offices and supports eighteen MRCs (Management Resource Centers). It is through the Clusters that individual Ys have input at the national level. Each elects two members to its section Field committee. The four Field committees in turn elect thirty members, or three-fifths, of the National Board. The other twenty members include the immediate past chair and nineteen persons elected by the Board.

Through its elaborate infrastructure and centralized administration, the YMCA of the USA assures that 2,227 individual YMCAs in America offer programs and services to the public that are consistent in quality and variety, but it does not micro manage the operations of any of the Ys, all of which are administered at the area and branch levels and maintain a high degree of autonomy. Of the total number of Ys in America, 1,260 are branches of the 967 units that are formal members of the national organization.

The services and programs of YMCAs in America have an impressive range, appealing to all age groups, as is suggested by the current slogan of the Ys: ''We build strong kids, strong families, strong communities.'' They include health and fitness programs, day camps, childcare, youth sports, job and GED training, mentoring, counseling for abuse victims, international exchanges, and substance-abuse prevention—an aggregate of programs developed over the long history of the YMCA. The individual YMCAs also belong to the World Alliance of YMCAs, consisting of independent Ys from about 130 countries.

1844–1900: Founding and Expansion into an International Movement

The Young Men's Christian Association was founded on June 6,1844, in London, England. Its prime mover was George Williams, a draper (a cloth and dry goods salesman) who had migrated to London from a rural section of the country to seek work. At the time, the Industrial Revolution was still condemning many urban dwellers to abysmal working and slum-like living conditions, to lives, in short, of unrelieved gloom and despair. Like all the working-class sections of the rapidly overcrowding industrialized cities of England in that era, much of London was a virtual cesspool, with streets overrun with pickpockets, thieves, murderous thugs, prostitutes, beggars, drunks, and destitute and abandoned children, the conditions that Charles Dickens exposed in such novels as *Oliver Twist* (1837–39) and *Hard Times* (1854).

Company Perspectives:

The YMCA's mission is to put Christian principles into practice through programs that build healthy spirit, mind and body for all. The effect of the national system is not measured by the number of conference reports, newsletters or phone calls we handle. It is counted by the number of lives changed through what we do—the lives of the 16 million people served by YMCAs, the lives of the 57,000 volunteers who govern YMCAs nationwide, and the lives of the hundreds of thousands of staff members and volunteers who carry out the work of their associations.

Williams and some fellow drapers sought to help alleviate the gloom of the city working class by providing Christian fellowship, prayer, and bible study as an alternative to the squalor of the streets. Their efforts were very successful, and the movement quickly spread. By 1851, there were 24 Ys in Great Britain, with a total membership of 27,000, and by late in that same year the movement had spread to North America, first to Canada, and then to the United States, where, in Boston, the first YMCA was founded on December 29th, under the tutelage of a lay missionary and retired sea captain named Thomas Sullivan. As it did in Europe, the YMCA quickly took hold in the United States and sprang up in various seaboard cities.

In 1854 the first international convention was held in Paris. By that time there were almost 400 Ys in seven countries, having a combined membership of 30,369. Because it cut across class, sex, race, and denominational barriers that usually segregated various social and ethnic groups during the Victorian Age, the movement was almost unique. So was its social aim of ameliorating the plight of the destitute.

The rapid growth of the YMCA in the United States was temporarily reversed during the Civil War, when Y memberships were reduced by two-thirds. Nevertheless, the Y's in the Union states played an important role as the U.S. Christian Commission, which was formed to assist both soldiers and prisoners of war. A necessary rebuilding took place after the war. The number of Ys at war's end had been reduced to 59, but four years later had grown by an additional 600. In the aftermath of the war, the prestigious New York YMCA had proclaimed a fourfold mission: "The improvement of the spiritual, mental, social, and physical condition of young men."

It was not until the 1880s that the YMCAs began erecting buildings that needed full-time staff members, replacing the volunteers that had formerly run the Ys. By that time, large auditoriums, swimming pools, gymnasiums, and bowling alleys were included in the large urban Ys, as were dormitories or residences that allowed members to lodge in the Ys for one or more nights. It was in the gyms of the YMCA that both basketball and volleyball began their evolution into important indoor sports. The residences remained until the late 1950s, providing income for the various, proliferating YMCA activities, including boys' work programs, summer camps, special classes featuring such activities as exercise drills using dumbbells, medicine balls, and Indian clubs, and social activities for young adults.

In 1894 George Williams was knighted by England's Queen Victoria for his great contributions to the welfare of his fellow citizens. Before his death in 1905, he had seen his YMCA grow into the premier, worldwide organization of its kind. A bit earlier, in 1899, Dwight L. Moody had died, marking an end to formative period in the YMCA's development in the United States. An influential lay evangelist and national leader, Moody oversaw the growth of both national and international voluntary and missionary work and was the dominant force in the organization.

1901–29: Continued Growth and Wartime Services

By the end of the century, the fourfold purpose advanced by the New York Y had been revamped into a triangle: spirit, mind, and body. For the next half century, the leading figure in the YMCA was John Mott, who, like Moody, was also a lay evangelist. As Moody had, Mott served long periods as a staff member, paid for his professional services.

When the United States entered World War I in 1917, Mott initiated the move to place YMCA volunteers and paid workers at the service of the country, operating the canteens at military camps at home and in France. The organization also raised funds for other military projects, and also took on war relief aid for both prisoners of war and refugees. In the war's aftermath, it eased the plight of African American soldiers returning to their Southern, segregated communities, and it also supervised laborers in Europe brought from China to clear areas devastated by the horrific trench warfare. The YMCA also used residual funds from its war-effort fund raising to finance a decade of new building, to foster its outreach to small communities, and to develop YMCA trade schools and colleges.

1929–40: Surviving the Great Depression and Helping the Destitute

Even before the infamous Black Tuesday that ushered in the Great Depression in 1929, many of the YMCAs were already involved in helping the poor. Unemployment had been worsening before the stock market crash, and in 1928 these associations began using direct relief to alleviate the plight of those out of work. Less emphasis was given to such things as Bible classes, which saw enrollment drop by 60 percent between 1929 and 1933. By that year, when the New Deal programs of Franklin D. Roosevelt had begun providing government relief, the YMCA and other private nonprofit organizations were able to direct their attention to surviving. Many of the local YMCAs had suffered from a significant loss of income, many up to 50 percent. That caused some necessary self-scrutiny, as did pressure exerted by militant student YMCAs, which wanted the movement to become more involved in the socioeconomic difficulties facing the nation. The result was that the YMCA entered partnerships with various welfare agencies. Engaged in joint community projects, the association stressed that both character-building and social-amelioration activities were its responsibility in such unfortunate times. In addition to the traditional physical and mental health activities, Ys across America offered both educational and vocational training as well as medical assistance.

Key Dates:

1844: YMCA is founded in London by George Williams.
1851: First Y established in the United States, in Boston.
1854: First international convention is held in Paris.
1917: YMCAs begin canteen and war-relief work.
1944: YMCA youth secretaries adopt the "four fronts" of youth work.
1945: With the end of World War II, women's membership in YMCA begins rapid expansion.
1958: Association initiates Building for Brotherhood for renovations of old facilities and building of new Ys.
1983: The Y formalizes childcare services.

1941–79: World War II and New Peacetime Challenges and Changes

As it had in the first World War, in the second global conflict the YMCA served both the nation and, internationally, the victims of the war. It helped create the USO (United Service Organization) for servicemen and servicewomen and worked with refugees and displaced families. The YMCA of the USA, then known as the Nation Council of YMCAs, also collaborated with YMCAs in thirty-six other countries to aid prisoners of war.

However, with peace and the onset of the Cold War, the YMCA faced new challenges. World War II had prompted a growing sense of women's opportunities outside the home, and by the end of it 62 percent of the nation's Ys were admitting women. In 1944 YMCA youth secretaries had adopted what became known as the "four fronts" of youth work: Y-Indian Guides (a father-son program) and three boys' clubs (Gra-Y, Junior Hi-Y, and Hi-Y). These, originally for boys alone, would eventually serve as models for similar clubs for girls and, finally, for gender-integrated clubs. There was still an emphasis on youth, but the gradual shift from young Christian men to the entire family, without any gender, sectarian, or racial restrictions, was underway and would not be reversed.

In the next decade, the YMCA undertook a program to refurbish some of its facilities and build new ones. In 1958, with Canadian Ys, under the rubric "Buildings for Brotherhood," the Y raised $55 million to renovate or build almost 100 buildings at home and abroad. After the war, many old YMCAs in the inner cities had been abandoned as demographic changes shifted America's rapidly growing citizenry into suburbia, forcing the YMCAs to relocate or dissolve through membership attrition.

During the social and cultural upheaval of 1960s and early 1970s, exacerbated by the Vietnam War, the YMCA faced new challenges. It was charged by its National General Secretary James Bunting to discover new ways to remain both viable and relevant or face possible dissolution. In some parts of the country, certain programs, like the four-fronts youth programs, were already dying for lack of interest. With the support of the YMCA of the USA and federal aid, community Ys redoubled their outreach efforts, offering some new programs, but when the federal aid was withdrawn, many Ys faced financial problems. The organization was also subjected to some aggressive criticism, both at home and abroad, something difficult for many of its associates to countenance. However, starting around 1975, thanks to a growing health consciousness in America, there was a resurgence of interest in physical training programs and facilities of the Ys.

1980–2000: Revamping the YMCA's Image and Redefining Its Mission

The new health consciousness and the rapid increase of families in which both parents or a single parent are employed prompted a new period of growth and program changes in the 1980s. Responding to community needs, local Ys began updating both their facilities and their equipment, becoming family health and fitness centers on a par with many of the burgeoning private health clubs. In 1983 Ys also began formalizing childcare services for working parents, a service that had been provided for years. It quickly became an important source of income for the association.

Starting in 1984, the refurbishing and updating of the Ys brought them under the scrutiny of federal and local tax authorities. Why, the various agencies asked, were Ys tax exempt when they seemed no different in kind than privately owned health clubs and spas? By 1992, when the query lost its steam, the matter had been raised in 40 states, and although the investigation had no effect on the YMCA's non-profit status, it did prompt a reexamination of the organization's mission and programs, the first such reappraisal undertaken since the 1930s.

The last decade of the century found the nation's Ys in good health, with a stabilized array of income resources, an increase in both clients and volunteers, and an impressive spread of programs reflecting the movement's sensitivity to social change. Also, the organization's self-scrutiny and re-evaluation begun in 1980s gave the Ys, in their own words, "a new appreciation both for their mission as community service agencies and for the Judeo-Christian values that lie at the heart of the movement." According to the organization, "during the 1980s and '90s, the ideas of 'values clarification' were slowly replaced by ideas of 'character.' " Much of the concern in the national leadership of the YMCA has been directed to the moral laxity and relativism and disruption of the family that seemed to be eroding traditional values in which the YMCA itself was firmly rooted. The result was the formulation of four "core values" (caring, honesty, respect, and responsibility), part of an "asset-based approach" to solving social problems through developing character and instilling a sense of civic virtue in the nation's youth. In collaboration with The Search Institute, the YMCA of the USA studied the issue and turned its findings into practical results, measures to enhance family and youth "assets" that would serve as shields against irresponsibility and unhealthy or negative behavior. Clearly, it is through this sort of continuing self-appraisal and redefinition of its mission in response to social change that the YMCA will continue to thrive.

Principal Subsidiaries

Three Aches Limited.

Further Reading

Hopkins, Charles Howard, *History of the Y.M.C.A. in North America.* New York: Association Press, 1951.

——, *John R. Mott, 1865–1955: A Biography,* Grand Rapids, Michigan: Eerdmans, 1979.

Macleod, David I., *Building Character in the American Boy: The Boy Scouts, YMCA, and Their Forerunners, 1870–1920,* Madison: University of Wisconsin Press, 1983.

Mjagkij, Nina, and Margaret Spratt, eds., *Men and Women Adrift: The YMCA and the YWCA in the City*, New York: New York University Press, 1997.

Simpson, Elizabeth, "YMCA Director to Give Advice to Strengthen Nation's Families," *Virginian-Pilot and Ledger-Star, Norfolk, Virginia,* January 21, 1999, Local Sec., p. 1.

Zald, Mayer N., *Organizational Change: The Political Economy of the YMCA,* Chicago: University of Chicago Press, 1970.

—John W. Fiero

Zany Brainy, Inc.

2520 Renaissance Boulevard
King of Prussia, Pennsylvania 19406
U.S.A.
Telephone: (610) 278-7800
Fax: (608) 849-3614
Web site: http://www.zanybrainy.com

Public Company
Founded: 1991
Employees: 2,000
Sales: $168.5 million (1998)
Stock Exchanges: NASDAQ
Ticker Symbol: ZANY
NAIC: 45112 Hobby, Toy, and Game Stores

Zany Brainy, Inc., is the first educational multimedia superstore for children. Zany Brainy's 100-plus stores in 26 states are stocked with over 20,000 educational toys such as science kits, puzzles, and learning games. Using the slogan ''a zillion neat things for kids,'' Zany Brainy markets toys that are nontoxic, nonviolent, multicultural, and gender-neutral. The company designs its stores to be as much fun as the toys within them. Each store has brightly colored walls; plush carpeting; aisles large enough for kids, adults, and strollers; comfortable, kid-sized couches; and a video theater. Each of the toys in a Zany Brainy store is on display, so parents and children can try it out before they buy it. Specially trained ''kidsultants'' enthusiastically help customers. Stores are divided into areas with different themes, such as ''Bright Star'' and ''Let's Pretend.'' The company is dedicated to developing positive relationships with the communities in which its stores are located. Zany Brainy donates a portion of the proceeds from each new store's grand opening to a local charity, such as a zoo or science center. At 10,000 square feet, Zany Brainy stores are much smaller than toy superstores such as Toys 'R Us. Most Zany Brainy stores are located in strip malls in the Northeast, Southeast, Midwest, and California. Zany Brainy founder David Schlessinger owns approximately four percent of the company.

A Brainy Idea

When he was only 18, David Schlessinger purchased a bookstore in downtown Philadelphia. He paid for the store with money he had saved from summer jobs and gifts and had borrowed from his younger brother and sister. Schlessinger called the store Encore Books. In just a few years, Encore books became one of the largest retail bookstore chains in the United States. Eventually, however, Schlessinger grew tired of the bookstore business and wanted to pursue other interests, including starting a family. In 1984 Schlessinger sold a controlling stake in Encore Books to Rite Aid; in 1986, he sold his remaining shares and left the company entirely.

After his departure from Encore, the 31-year-old Schlessinger spent a lot of time with his nieces and nephews. Schlessinger became frustrated when he tried to buy creative, fun toys from which they could learn. He found that most creative toys were only available through mail order catalogs or were sold in cramped stores with small selections, poor service, and high prices. Schlessinger researched the educational toy market, but couldn't find any chains that specialized in the kind of toys he thought were good for kids.

Schlessinger envisioned a toy store that sold high-quality, safe, educational toys at affordable prices, which was also attractive, cleverly stocked, and ''kid friendly'' with knowledgeable and friendly sales associates. In late 1991 Schlessinger launched Zany Brainy, Inc., the first store of this kind, under the parent company Children's Concept.

The First Zany Brainy, 1991

The first Zany Brainy store, located in Wynnewood, Pennsylvania, a suburb of Philadelphia, opened its doors just two days after the birth of Schlessinger's son on December 1, 1991. The store was 6,000 square feet and stocked with more than 15,000 toys, including wood knob puzzles that teach letters, numbers, and geography, telescopes, globes, and archeological tools. All of the toys in the store were on display so children could play with them. Kids could watch videos in the Zany Showtime Theater and play computer games on kiosks in the store. Sales associates called ''kidsultants'' answered parents'

Company Perspectives:

Zany Brainy, Inc., provides the best merchandise for children at the right price. We seek interactive products that encourage a sense of wonder and stimulate creativity. Our stores have everything kids need for creative play—with over 20,000 books, toys, electronic learning games, creative crafts, science kits, software and teacher resources. It's a kind of ''kid-rific'' collection of the most innovative and exciting children's products on the market today, including many items not found anywhere else. We are also committed to developing and maintaining strong relationships with the local communities our stores serve. We regularly invite local theaters, museums, and other cultural groups to host in-store events.

questions. Zany Brainy scheduled special events and programs such as book signings, miniconcerts, and software demonstrations. The store became actively involved in the community. It donated a portion of its opening day sales to the Columbus Zoo's 1996 Zoo Fund and invited the zoo officials, local theater groups, and museum officials to give presentations at the store.

The first Zany Brainy was a great success. By 1993, the company had opened a second store in Wynnewood. By 1994, it had expanded outside of the Philadelphia area and opened stores in Atlanta, New York City, and Washington, D.C. Zany Brainy had 32 stores by 1995.

Tough Competition in the Mid-1990s

Zany Brainy's success generated some tough competition. Stores similar to Zany Brainy were opened, such as the New York-based Noodle Kidoodle. Right Start and Sesame Street opened retail outlets in the King of Prussia mall, which was only miles from the company's Wynnewood headquarters. Large toy superstores, such as Toys 'R Us, Inc., created departments similar to Zany Brainy's stores. In 1994 Toys 'R Us tested educational software in five of its Philadelphia-area stores, and then greatly increased the number of software titles and educational products in all of its stores.

Retail toy stores were also engaged in a price war that made competing even more difficult. Many retailers that were either emerging from Chapter 11 bankruptcy or trying to avoid it launched discount and going-out-of-business sales and cut prices far below average. Like many toy stores, Zany Brainy was losing money.

In an effort to get the company back on track, Schlessinger hired a new senior management team. He hoped his management team would handle Zainy Brainy's day-to-day operations, so he could focus on the company's future growth. Howard Ross, a partner in the company's accounting firm, commented on Schlessinger's decision in the *Philadelphia Business Journal*. ''While people may try to copy the concept, I take comfort in the fact that David is working on the second or third version of Zany Brainy while every one else is trying to figure out the first,'' he said.

In 1996 Schlessinger hired Keith C. Spurgeon as CEO. Spurgeon had a strong background in retail. Most recently he had served as Toys 'R Us vice-president for Asia and Australia. The company believed expansion was the key to future success. In 1997 Zany Brainy opened nine more stores, including its first West Coast stores, in Thousand Oaks, Torrance, and San Diego, California. During its rapid expansion, the company took care to promote from within: two regional managers and all district managers were former kidsultants, and many Zany Brainy customers were hired as kidsultants. ''They love the Zany Brainy experience as shoppers, so it is easy for them to transition into a sales role,'' Surgeon explained. ''I know of no other retail company that is as mission-driven as ours. We really strive to maintain our position as the expert resource for our customers. Our kidsultants build trusting relationships with customers through their credibility. They can talk confidently to customers of any age.''

Zany Brainy also tried to maintain its competitive edge in a number of other ways. The company added a limited assortment of its own branded products to the toys already offered in its stores. Zany Brainy's products included chess and checker sets and a new cooking category with recipes and basic cooking implements. With the cooking category, children could prepare dishes such as holiday candy, fudge, pasta, and pizza. The store maintained its specialized advertising, which was almost all direct mail. Issues of ''Zany Zone'' were distributed to customers monthly, and the company published a 52-page holiday gift guide. Some Zany Brainy items were also sold on QVC.

Despite its struggles, Zany Brainy was recognized for its contributions to the retail toy industry. Its many honors included the 1998 Independent Retailer of the Year award from the National Retail Federation and the 1998 First Award for Store Promotion from *Playthings Magazine*. In 1998 Spurgeon replaced Schlessinger as chairman of the company. That summer Schlessinger resigned from Zany Brainy's board of directors to spend more time with his family.

Going Public in 1999

To pay off its debt and raise money for expansion, Zany Brainy went public in June 1999, under the symbol ZANY on the NASDAQ exchange. The company sold a total of 6.1 million shares at $10 per share to raise approximately $34 million. Schlessinger sold 1.2 million of his own shares during the IPO and decided to remain with the company only as an investor. During the same year, Zany Brainy relocated its headquarters from Wynnewood to King of Prussia, Pennsylvania, and opened a new distribution center. The company also changed the name of its parent company from Children Concepts to Zany Brainy, Inc.

Zany Brainy opened its 100th store on September 24, 1999, in Bridgewater, New Jersey. To celebrate the milestone, the company scheduled ten days of special events in each of its stores and raffled off a $10,000 U.S. savings bond to be used toward a college education. ''Our 100th store opening provides us with a platform to reinforce our dedication to the development and education of children,'' Spurgeon said in *Business Wire*.

Key Dates:

1991: Founder David Schlessinger opens the first Zany Brainy store in Wynnewood, Pennsylvania.
1993: Schlessinger opens a second store in Wynnewood.
1994: The company expands outside of the Philadelphia area and into other states.
1996: Schlessinger hires Keith C. Spurgeon as CEO.
1997: Zany Brainy opens its first West Coast stores.
1999: The company goes public and launches an e-commerce Web site.

In October 1999, Zany Brainy announced a joint venture with the Vermont Teddy Bear Company . In an effort to combine the nation's largest teddy bear manufacturer and Zany Brainy's interactive philosophy, the two companies designed a ''Make-a-Friend-for-Life'' kiosk and set it up in a Zany Brainy store in Marlton, New Jersey. Using the kiosk, called the ''Huffin' Puffin' machine,'' customers selected a ''fat free'' teddy bear and everything they needed to assemble the bear, including its outfits and accessories. For about $20, a customer could assemble his or her own personal bear onsite in about twenty minutes. A ''certified official'' recorded the bear's time of birth on a birth certificate.

Around the same time, Zany Brainy launched its web site, www.zanybrainy.com. The site was a joint venture between Zany Brainy and Online Retail Partners (ORP), a company that provided Zany Brainy with the marketing and technical expertise it needed to launch the site. The web site offered customers a large selection of high-quality toys similar to those found in Zany Brainy stores.

A Bright Future

In 1999 Zany Brainy planned to continue its aggressive expansion. ''Every new store opening is a testament to our commitment to bring Zany Brainy to children and adults in the community and give parents hands-on access to a unique merchandise assortment that combines learning, discovery, and fun,'' Surgeon said in a company press release.

The company hoped to expand into new areas including Denver, Minneapolis, and Salt Lake City and strengthen its presence in the West Coast.

Principal Competitors

Barnes & Noble, Inc.; Borders Group, Inc.; CompUSA, Inc.; Consolidated Stores Corporation; eToys Inc.; FAO Schwarz; Noodle Kidoodle Inc.; Sears, Roebuck and Co.; SmarterKids .com Inc.; Target Stores, Inc.; Toys 'R Us, Inc.; Wal-Mart Stores, Inc.; World of Science, Inc.

Further Reading

Ahles, Andrea, ''Wynnewood, Pa., Toy Retailer Outlines Details of Stock Offering,'' *Knight-Ridder/Tribune Business News,* May 4, 1999.

Hollreiser, Eric, ''Zany Brainy Storming Ahead to Keep Its Edge,'' *Philadelphia Business Journal,* December 8, 1995, p.1.

Kaufman, Leslie, ''Beyond the 'Big Box','' *Newsweek,* November 30, 1998, p. 46.

Massingill, Teena, ''Northern California Toy Retailers Fall on Hard Times,'' *Knight-Ridder/Tribune Business News,* April 21, 1999.

Milliot, Jim, ''Zany Brainy Hopes to Raise $37 Million in Public Offering,'' *Publishers Weekly,* May 24, 1999, p. 12.

Mutter, John, ''Zany Brainy Sets Sights on Chicago,'' *Publishers Weekly,* August 7, 1995.

Sekhri, Rajiv, ''High-End Retails Heads Here,'' *Business Courier Serving Cincinnati,* January 15, 1999, p. 3.

''The Vermont Teddy Bear Company and Zany Brainy Sign Exclusive Agreement to Roll Out Bear Making Facilities,'' *PR Newswire,* September 13, 1999.

''Zany Brainy Reaches 100th Store Milestone,'' *Business Wire,* September 21, 1999.

—Tracey Vasil Biscontini

INDEX TO COMPANIES

Index to Companies

Listings in this index are arranged in alphabetical order under the company name. Company names beginning with a letter or proper name such as Eli Lilly & Co. will be found under the first letter of the company name. Definite articles (The, Le, La) are ignored for alphabetical purposes as are forms of incorporation that precede the company name (AB, NV). Company names printed in bold type have full, historical essays on the page numbers appearing in bold. Updates to entries that appeared in earlier volumes are signified by the notation **(upd.)**. Company names in light type are references within an essay to that company, not full historical essays. This index is cumulative with volume numbers printed in bold type.

A & A Die Casting Company, **25** 312
A and A Limousine Renting, Inc., **26** 62
A & C Black Ltd., **7** 165
A&E. *See* Arts & Entertainment Network.
A&E Plastics, **12** 377
A. & J. McKenna, **13** 295
A&K Petroleum Company. *See* Kerr-McGee Corporation.
A & M Instrument Co., **9** 323
A&M Records, **23** 389
A&N Foods Co., **II** 553
A&P. *See* Great Atlantic & Pacific Tea Company, Inc.
A&P Water and Sewer Supplies, Inc., **6** 487
A. and T. McKenna Brass and Copper Works, **13** 295
A & W Brands, Inc., **II** 595; **25 3–5**
A.A. Housman & Co., **II** 424; **13** 340
A.A. Mathews. *See* CRSS Inc.
A. Ahlström Oy, **IV** 276–77
A.B. Chance Industries Co., Inc., **II** 20; **31** 259
A.B.Dick Company, **II** 25; **28 6–8**
A.B. Hemmings, Ltd., **13** 51
A.B. Leasing Corp., **13** 111–12
A-B Nippondenso, **III** 593
A-BEC Mobility, **11** 487
A.C. Delco, **26** 347, 349
A.C. Nielsen Company, **IV** 605; **13 3–5**
A.C. Moore Arts & Crafts, Inc., **30 3–5**
A.C. Wickman, **13** 296
A.D. International (Australia) Pty. Ltd., **10** 272
A. Dager & Co., **I** 404
A. Dunkelsbuhler & Co., **IV** 20–21, 65; **7** 122
A/E/C/ Systems International, **27** 362
A.E. Fitkin & Company, **6** 592–93
A.E. Gutman, **16** 486
A.E. LePage, **II** 457
A.E. Lottes, **29** 86
A.G. Becker, **II** 259–60; **11** 318; **20** 260
A.G. Edwards, Inc., **8 3–5**; **19** 502
A.G. Industries, Inc., **7** 24
A.G. Morris, **12** 427
A.G. Spalding & Bros., Inc., **I** 428–29; **24** 402–03
A.G. Stanley Ltd., **V** 17, 19; **24** 75
A. Gettelman, Co., **I** 269
A. Goertz and Co., **IV** 91
A.H. Belo Corporation, **IV** 605; **10 3–5**; **28** 367, 369; **30 13–17 (upd.)**
A.H. Robins Co., **10** 70; **12** 188; **16** 438
A. Hirsh & Son, **30** 408
A.I. Credit Corp., **III** 196
A.J. Caley and Son. Ltd., **II** 569
A.J. Oster Co., **III** 681
A. Johnson & Co. *See* Axel Johnson Group.
A.L. Laboratories Inc., **12** 3
A.L. Pharma Inc., **12 3–5**
A. Lambert International Inc., **16** 80
A.M. Castle & Co., **25 6–8**
A.M. Collins Manufacturing Co., **IV** 286
A.O. Smith Corporation, **11 3–6**; **24** 499
A.O. Smith Data Systems, **7** 139; **22** 181
A-1 Steak Sauce Co., **I** 259
A-1 Supply, **10** 375
A.P. Green Refractories, **22** 285
A.R. Pechiney, **IV** 173
A. Roger Perretti, **II** 484
A.S. Abell Co., **IV** 678
A.S. Aloe, **III** 443
A.S. Cameron Steam Pump Works, **III** 525
A/S Titan, **III** 418
A.S. Watson & Company, **18** 254
A.S. Yakovlev Design Bureau, **15 3–6**
A. Schilling & Company. *See* McCormick & Company, Incorporated.
A. Schulman, Inc., **8 6–8**
A. Sulka & Co., **29** 457
A.T. Cross Company, **17 3–5**
A-T-O Inc. *See* Figgie International, Inc.
A.V. Roe & Co., **I** 50, 81; **III** 508; **24** 85
A.W. Bain Holdings, **III** 523
A.W. Shaw Co., **IV** 635
A.W. Sijthoff, **14** 555
A-Z International Companies, **III** 569; **20** 361
AA Development Corp., **I** 91
AA Distributors, **22** 14
AA Energy Corp., **I** 91
AAA Development Corp., **17** 238
Aachener und Münchener Feuer-Versicherungs-Gesellschaft, **III** 376
Aachener und Münchener Gruppe, **III** 349–50
Aachener Union, **II** 385
AAE Ahaus Alstatter Eisenbahn Holding AG, **25** 171
AAF-McQuay Incorporated, **26 3–5**
Aalborg, **6** 367
Aansworth Shirt Makers, **8** 406
AAON, Inc., **22 3–6**
AAR Corp., **III** 687; **IV** 60; **28 3–5**
Aargauische Portlandcement-Fabrik Holderbank-Wildegg, **III** 701
Aaron Brothers, Inc., **17** 320, 322
Aaron Rents, Inc., **14 3–5**
AARP, **27 3–5**
Aasche Transportation, **27** 404
Aastrom Biosciences, Inc., **13** 161
AAV Cos., **13** 48
Aavant Health Management Group, Inc., **11** 394
Aavid Thermal Technologies, Inc., **29 3–6**
AB Capital & Investment Corporation, **23** 381
AB-PT. *See* American Broadcasting-Paramount Theatres, Inc.
ABA. *See* Aktiebolaget Aerotransport.
Abacus Fund, Inc., **II** 445; **22** 405
ABACUS International Holdings Ltd., **26** 429
Abana Pharmaceuticals, **24** 257
Abar Staffing, **25** 434
ABB ASEA Brown Boveri Ltd., **II 1–4**, 13; **III** 427, 466, 631–32; **IV** 66, 109, 204, 300; **15** 483; **22 7–12 (upd.)**, 64, 288; **28** 39
ABB Hafo AB. *See* Mitel Corp.
Abba Seafood AB, **18** 396
Abbatoir St.-Valerien Inc., **II** 652

Abbey Business Consultants, **14** 36
Abbey Home Entertainment, **23** 391
Abbey Life Group PLC, **II** 309
Abbey Medical, Inc., **11** 486; **13** 366–67
Abbey National PLC, 10 6–8
Abbey Rents, **II** 572
Abbey Road Building Society, **10** 6–7
Abbott Laboratories, I 619–21, 686, 690, 705; **II** 539; **10** 70, 78, 126; **11 7–9 (upd.)**, 91, 494; **12** 4; **14** 98, 389; **22** 75; **25** 55
Abbott, Proctor & Paine, **II** 445; **22** 405
ABC Appliance, Inc., 10 9–11
ABC Carpet & Home Co. Inc., 26 6–8
ABC, Inc., **I** 463–64; **II** 89, 129–33, 151, 156, 170, 173; **III** 188, 214, 251–52; **6** 157–59, 164; **11** 197–98; **17** 150; **XVIII** 65; **19** 201; **21** 25; **24** 516–17. *See also* Capital Cities/ABC Inc.
ABC Markets, **17** 558
ABC Rail Products Corporation, 18 3–5
ABC Records, **II** 144
ABC Supply Co., Inc., 22 13–16
ABC Treadco, **19** 455
ABD Securities Corp., **II** 239, 283
ABECOR. *See* Associated Banks of Europe Corp.
Abercom Holdings, **IV** 92
Abercrombie & Fitch Co., **V** 116; **15 7–9**; **17** 369; **25** 90
Aberthaw Cement, **III** 671
Abex Aerospace, **III** 512
Abex Corp., **I** 456; **10** 553; **18** 3
Abex Friction Products, **III** 512
ABF. *See* Associated British Foods PLC.
ABF Freight System, Inc., **16** 39–41
ABI. *See* American Furniture Company, Inc.
Abigail Adams National Bancorp, Inc., 23 3–5
Abington Shoe Company. *See* The Timberland Company.
Abitibi-Consolidated, Inc., 25 9–13 (upd.); **26** 445
Abitibi-Price Inc., IV 245–47, 721; **9** 391
Abko Realty Inc., **IV** 449
ABM Industries Incorporated, 25 14–16 (upd.). *See also* American Building Maintenance Industries Inc.
ABN. *See* Algemene Bank Nederland N.V.
Above The Belt, Inc., **16** 37
ABR Foods, **II** 466
Abraham & Straus, **V** 168; **8** 443; **9** 209; **31** 192
Abraham Schaaffhausenscher Bankverein, **IV** 104
Abrams Industries Inc., 23 6–8
Abri Bank Bern, **II** 378
Absolut Company, **31** 458, 460
Abu Dhabi National Oil Company, IV 363–64, 476
Abu Qir Fertilizer and Chemical Industries Co., **IV** 413
AC Design Inc., **22** 196
ACA Corporation, **25** 368
Academic Press, **IV** 622–23
Academy Sports & Outdoors, 27 6–8
Acadia Entities, **24** 456
Acadia Investors, **23** 99
Acadia Partners, **21** 92
Access Dynamics Inc., **17** 255
Access Graphics Technology Inc., **13** 128
Access Technology, **6** 225
Accessory Network Group, Inc., **8** 219
Accident and Casualty Insurance Co., **III** 230–31
Acclaim Entertainment Inc., 13 115; **24 3–8**, 538
ACCO World Corporation, 7 3–5; **12** 264
Accor SA, 10 12–14; **13** 364; **27 9–12 (upd.)**
Accord Energy, **18** 367
Accountants on Call, **6** 10
Accounting and Tabulating Corporation of Great Britain, **6** 240
Acctex Information Systems, **17** 468
Accuralite Company, **10** 492
Accurate Forming Co., **III** 643
Accuride Corp., **IV** 179
Accuscan, Inc., **14** 380
Ace Comb Company, **12** 216
Ace Electric Co., **I** 156
Ace Hardware Corporation, 12 6–8; **22** 258; **30** 168
Ace Medical Company, **30** 164
Ace Novelty Company, **26** 374
Ace Refrigeration Ltd., **I** 315; **25** 81
Acer Inc., 6 244; **10** 257; **16 3–6**
Acer Sertek, **24** 31
Aceros Fortuna S.A. de C.V., **13** 141
ACF Industries, **30** 282
Acheson Graphite Corp, **I** 399; **9** 517
ACI Holdings Inc., **I** 91; **28** 24
ACI Ltd., **29** 478
Aciéries de Ploërmel, **16** 514
Aciéries et Minières de la Sambre, **IV** 52
Aciéries Réunies de Burbach-Eich-Dudelange S.A. *See* ARBED S.A.
Acker Drill Company, **26** 70
Ackerley Communications, Inc., 9 3–5
Acklin Stamping Company, **8** 515
ACLC. *See* Allegheny County Light Company.
ACLI Government Securities Inc., **II** 422
ACM. *See* Advanced Custom Molders, Inc.
Acme Boot, **I** 440–41
Acme Brick Company, **19** 231–32
Acme Can Co., **I** 601; **13** 188
Acme Carton Co., **IV** 333
Acme Corrugated Cases, **IV** 258
Acme Cotton Products, **13** 366
Acme Fast Freight Inc., **27** 473
Acme Market. *See* American Stores Company.
Acme Newspictures, **25** 507
Acme Quality Paint Co., **III** 744
Acme Quilting Co., Inc., **19** 304
Acme Road Machinery, **21** 502
Acme Screw Products, **14** 181
Acme-Cleveland Corp., I 531; **13 6–8**
Acme-Delta Company, **11** 411
ACMI, **21** 118–19
Acorn Computer, **III** 145
Acorn Financial Corp., **15** 328
Acoustics Development Corporation, **6** 313
Acova S.A., **26** 4
Acquired Systems Enhancement Corporation, **24** 31
ACR. *See* American Capital and Research Corp.
AcroMed Corporation, **30** 164
Act III Theatres, **25** 453
Actava Group, **14** 332
Action, **6** 393
Action Furniture by Lane, **17** 183
Action Performance Companies, Inc., 27 13–15
Action Temporary Services, **29** 273
Activenture Corporation, **16** 253
Activision, **24** 3
Acton Bolt Ltd., **IV** 658
Acumos, **11** 57
Acuson Corporation, 9 7; **10 15–17**
ACX Technologies, **13** 11
Acxiom Corp., **6** 14; **18** 170
Ad Astra Aero, **I** 121
AD-AM Gas Company, **11** 28
Adage Systems International, Inc., **19** 438
Adam, Meldrum & Anderson Company (AM&A), **16** 61–62
Adam Opel AG, 7 6–8; **11** 549; **18** 125; **21 3–7 (upd.)**
Adams Childrenswear, **V** 177
Adams Express Co., **II** 380–81, 395–96; **10** 59–60; **12** 533
Adams Industries, **19** 414
Adams/Cates Company, **21** 257
Adanac General Insurance Company, **13** 63
Adaptec, Inc., 11 56; **31 3–6**
Adaptive Data Systems, **25** 531
Adar Associates, Inc. *See* Scientific-Atlanta, Inc.
ADC of Greater Kansas City, Inc., **22** 443
ADC Telecommunications, Inc., 10 18–21; **30 6–9 (upd.)**
Adco Products, **I** 374
Addison Corporation, **31** 399
Addison Structural Services, Inc., **26** 433
Addison Wesley, **IV** 659
Addressograph-Multigraph, **11** 494
Adecco, **26** 240
Adelphi Pharmaceutical Manufacturing Co., **I** 496
Adelphia Communications Corp., 17 6–8
Ademco. *See* Alarm Device Manufacturing Company.
Adger Assuranceselskab, **III** 310
Adhere Paper Co., **IV** 252; **17** 29
ADI Group Limited. *See* AHL Services, Inc.
Adia S.A., 6 9–11; **9** 327
Adiainvest S.A., **6** 9, 11
Adidas AG, 8 392–93; **13** 513; **14 6–9**; **17** 244; **22** 202; **23** 472, 474; **25** 205, 207
Adirondack Industries, **24** 403
Adjusters Auto Rental Inc. **16** 380
Adler, **23** 219
Adler and Shaykin, **III** 56; **11** 556–57
Adler Line. *See* Transatlantische Dampfschiffahrts Gesellschaft.
Adley Express, **14** 567
ADM. *See* Archer-Daniels-Midland Co.
Admiral Co., **II** 86; **III** 573
Admiral Cruise Lines, **6** 368; **27** 91
Adnan Dabbagh, **6** 115
ADNOC. *See* Abu Dhabi National Oil Company.
Adobe Systems Incorporated, 10 22–24; **15** 149; **20** 46, 237
Adolph Coors Company, I 236–38, 255, 273; **13 9–11 (upd.)**; **18** 72; **26** 303, 306
Adolphe Lafont, **17** 210
Adonis Radio Corp., **9** 320
Adorence, **16** 482
ADP, Inc., **18** 297
Adria Produtos Alimenticos, Ltd., **12** 411
Adria Steamship Company, **6** 425
Adrian Hope and Company, **14** 46
Adriatico Banco d'Assicurazione, **III** 206, 345–46

Adrienne Vittadini, **15** 291
Adsega, **II** 677
Adstaff Associates, Ltd., **26** 240
ADT Ltd., **26** 410; **28** 486
ADT Security Systems, Inc., **12 9–11**
Adtel, Inc., **10** 358
Adtran Inc., **22 17–20**
ADtranz. *See* ABB ASEA Brown Boveri Ltd.
Advacel, **18** 20
Advance Chemical Company, **25** 15
Advance Foundry, **14** 42
Advance Publications Inc., **IV 581–84**; **13** 178, 180, 429; **19 3–7 (upd.)**; **31** 376, 378
Advance Transformer Co., **13** 397
Advance-Rumely Thresher Co., **13** 16
Advanced Casino Systems Corporation, **21** 277
Advanced Communications Engineering. *See* Scientific-Atlanta, Inc.
Advanced Custom Molders, Inc., **17** 533
Advanced Data Management Group S.A., **23** 212
Advanced Entertainment Group, **10** 286
Advanced Fiberoptic Technologies, **30** 267
Advanced Gravis, **28** 244
Advanced Logic Research, Inc., **27** 169
Advanced Marine Enterprises, Inc., **18** 370
Advanced Marketing Solutions, Inc., **24** 354
Advanced Medical Technologies, **III** 512
Advanced Metal Technologies Inc., **17** 234
Advanced Metallurgy, Inc., **29** 460
Advanced Micro Devices, Inc., **6 215–17**; **9** 115; **10** 367; **11** 308; **16** 316; **18** 18–19, 382; **19** 312; **20** 175; **30 10–12 (upd.)**
Advanced MobilComm, **10** 432
Advanced Structures, Inc., **18** 163
Advanced System Applications, **11** 395
Advanced Technology Laboratories, Inc., **9 6–8**
Advanced Telecommunications Corporation, **8** 311
Advanced Web Technologies, **22** 357
Advanstar Communications, **27** 361
ADVANTA Corp., **8 9–11**; **11** 123
Advantage Company, **8** 311; **27** 306
The Advantage Group, Inc., **25** 185–86
Advantage Health Plans, Inc., **11** 379
Advantage Health Systems, Inc., **25** 383
Advantage Insurers, Inc., **25** 185, 187
Advantica Restaurant Group, Inc., **27 16–19 (upd.)**; **29** 150
Advent Corporation, **22** 97
Advertising Unlimited, Inc., **10** 461
Advo, Inc., **6 12–14**
AEA. *See* United Kingdom Atomic Energy Authority.
AEA Investors Inc., **II** 628; **13** 97; **22** 169, 171; **28** 380; **30** 328
AEG A.G., **I** 151, 193, **409–11**; **II** 12, 119, 279; **III** 466, 479; **IV** 167; **6** 489; IX 11; **14** 169; **15** 142; **22** 28; **23** 495
Aegis Group plc, **6 15–16**
Aegis Insurance Co., **III** 273
AEGON N.V., **III 177–79**, 201, 273
AEL Ventures Ltd., **9** 512
Aeneas Venture Corp., **26** 502
AEON Group, **V** 96–99; **11** 498–99; **31** 430–31
AEP. *See* American Electric Power Company.
AEP Industries, Inc., **22** 95
AEP-Span, **8** 546
Aer Lingus, **6** 59; **12** 367–68
Aerial Communications Inc., **31** 452
Aeritalia, **I** 51, 74–75, 467; **24** 86
Aero Engines, **9** 418
Aero International (Regional) SAS, **24** 88
Aero International Inc., **14** 43
Aero Mayflower Transit Company. *See* Mayflower Group Inc.
Aero O/Y, **6** 87–88
Aero-Coupling Corp., **III** 641
Aero-Portuguesa, **6** 125
Aeroflot—Russian International Airlines, **29 7–10 (upd.)**
Aeroflot Soviet Airlines, **I** 105, 110, 118; **6 57–59**; **14** 73; **27** 475
Aerojet, **8** 206, 208
Aerojet-General Corp., **9** 266
Aerolíneas Argentinas, **I** 107; **6** 97
Aeroméxico, **20** 168
Aeroquip Corporation, **III** 640–42; **V** 255; **16 7–9**; **19** 508
Aerospace Avionics, **III** 509
The Aérospatiale Group, **I** 41–42, 46, 50, 74, 94; **7 9–12**; **12** 190–91; **14** 72; **21 8–11 (upd.)**; **24** 84–86, 88–89; **26** 179
The AES Corporation, **10 25–27**; **13 12–15 (upd.)**; **24** 359
Aetna, Inc., **20** 59; **21 12–16 (upd.)**, 95; **22** 139, 142–43; **30** 364
Aetna Life and Casualty Company, **II** 170–71, 319; **III** 78, **180–82**, 209, 223, 226, 236, 254, 296, 298, 305, 313, 329, 389; **IV** 123, 703; **10** 75–76; **12** 367; **15** 26; **17** 324; **23** 135
Aetna National Bank, **13** 466
Aetna Oil Co., **IV** 373
AFC. *See* America's Favorite Chicken Company, Inc.
AFCO Industries, Inc., **III** 241; **IV** 341
Afcol, **I** 289; **24** 449–50
AFE Ltd., **IV** 241
Affiliated Enterprises Inc., **I** 114
Affiliated Music Publishing, **22** 193
Affiliated Paper Companies, Inc., **31** 359, 361
Affiliated Products Inc., **I** 622
Affiliated Publications, Inc., **6** 323; **7 13–16**; **19** 285
Affordable Inns, **13** 364
AFG Industries Inc., **I** 483; **9** 248
AFIA, **22** 143
Afianzadora Insurgentes Serfin, **19** 190
AFL. *See* American Football League.
AFLAC Inc., **10 28–30 (upd.)**. *See also* American Family Corporation.
AFP. *See* Australian Forest Products.
AFRA Enterprises Inc., **26** 102
African and European Investment, **IV** 96
African Coasters, **IV** 91
African Explosive and Chemical Industries, **IV** 22
AFT. *See* Advanced Fiberoptic Technologies.
AFW Fabric Corp., **16** 124
AG Communication Systems Corporation, **15** 194
AG&E. *See* American Electric Power Company.
Ag-Chem Equipment Company, Inc., **17 9–11**
AGA, **I** 358
Agan Chemical Manufacturers Ltd., **25** 266–67
Agar Manufacturing Company, **8** 2
Agatha Christie Ltd., **31** 63 67
AGCO Corp., **13 16–18**
AGEL&P. *See* Albuquerque Gas, Electric Light and Power Company.
Agence France Presse, **IV** 670
Agency, **6** 393
Agency Rent-A-Car, **16** 379
AGF, **III** 185; **27** 515
AGFA, **I** 310–11
Agfa-Ansco Corporation, **I** 337–38; **22** 225–27
Agfa-Gevaert, **III** 487; **18** 50, 184–86; **26** 540–41
Aggregate Industries, **28** 451
Agiba Petroleum, **IV** 414
Agip SpA, **IV** 419–21, 454, 466, 472–74, 498; **12** 153
AGLP, **IV** 618
AGO, **III** 177, 179, 273, 310
Agor Manufacturing Co., **IV** 286
AGRAN, **IV** 505
AGRANA, **27** 436, 439
AgriBank FCB, **8** 489
Agrico Chemical Company, **IV** 82, 84, 576; **7** 188; **31** 470
Agricole de Roquefort et Maria Grimal, **23** 219
Agricultural Insurance Co., **III** 191
Agricultural Minerals and Chemicals Inc., **IV** 84; **13** 504
Agrifan, **II** 355
Agrifull, **22** 380
Agrigenetics, Inc., **I** 361. *See also* Mycogen Corporation.
Agrippina Versicherungs AG, **III** 403, 412
Agrobios S.A., **23** 172
Agroferm Hungarian Japanese Fermentation Industry, **III** 43
AGTL. *See* Alberta Gas Trunk Line Company, Ltd.
Agua Pura Water Company, **24** 467
Aguila (Mexican Eagle) Oil Co. Ltd., **IV** 657
Agway, Inc., **7 17–18**; **19** 250; **21 17–19 (upd.)**
AHL Services, Inc., **26** 149; **27 20–23**
Ahmanson
Ahold. *See* Koninklijke Ahold NV.
AHP. *See* American Home Products.
AHS. *See* American Hospital Supply Corporation.
AHSC Holdings Corp., **III** 9–10
Ahtna AGA Security, Inc., **14** 541
AI Automotive, **24** 204
AIC. *See* Allied Import Company.
AICA, **16** 421
Aichi Bank, **II** 373
Aichi Kogyo Co., **III** 415
Aichi Steel Works, **III** 637
Aid Auto, **18** 144
Aida Corporation, **11** 504
AIG. *See* American International Group, Inc.
AIGlobal, **III** 197
Aiken Stores, Inc., **14** 92
Aikenhead's Home Improvement Warehouse, **18** 240; **26** 306
Aikoku Sekiyu, **IV** 554
AIM Create Co., Ltd., **V** 127
Ainsworth National, **14** 528

Air & Water Technologies Corporation, 6 441–42
Air BP, **7** 141
Air Brasil, **6** 134; **29** 496
Air Canada, 6 60–62, 101; **12** 192; **23 9–12 (upd.)**; **29** 302
Air Compak, **12** 182
Air de Cologne, **27** 474
Air Express International Corporation, 13 19–20
Air France, **I** 93–94, 104, 110, 120; **II** 163; **6** 69, 373; **8** 313; **12** 190; **24** 86; **27** 26. *See also* Groupe Air France *and* Societe Air France.
Air Inter. *See* Groupe Air France.
Air La Carte Inc., **13** 48
Air Lanka Catering Services Ltd., **6** 123–24; **27** 464
Air Liberté, **6** 208
Air Micronesia, **I** 97; **21** 142
Air Midwest, Inc., **11** 299
Air New Zealand Limited, 14 10–12; **24** 399–400; **27** 475
Air Nippon Co., Ltd., **6** 70
Air Pacific, **24** 396, 400
Air Products and Chemicals, Inc., I 297–99, 315, 358, 674; **10 31–33 (upd.)**; **11** 403; **14** 125
Air Russia, **24** 400
Air Southwest Co. *See* Southwest Airlines Co.
Air Spec, Inc., **III** 643
Air-India Limited, 6 63–64; **27 24–26 (upd.)**
Airborne Accessories, **II** 81
Airborne Freight Corp., 6 345–47 345; **13** 19; **14** 517; **18** 177
Airbus Industrie, **6** 74; **7** 9–11, 504; **9** 418; **10** 164; **13** 356; **21** 8; **24** 84–89. *See also* G.I.E. Airbus Industrie.
AirCal, **I** 91
Airco, **25** 81–82; **26** 94
Aircraft Marine Products, **II** 7; **14** 26
Aircraft Modular Products, **30** 73
Aircraft Services International, **I** 449
Aircraft Transport & Travel Ltd., **I** 92
Aircraft Turbine Center, Inc., **28** 3
Airex Corporation, **16** 337
Airguard Industries, Inc., **17** 104, 106
Airlease International, **II** 422
Airlink, **24** 396
Airmark Plastics Corp., **18** 497–98
Airmec-AEI Ltd., **II** 81
Airpax Electronics, Inc., **13** 398
Airport Ground Service Co., **I** 104, 106
Airshop Ltd., **25** 246
Airstream, **II** 468
Airtel, **IV** 640
AirTouch Communications, 10 118; **11 10–12**
Airtours Plc, II 164; **27 27–29**, 90, 92
AirTran Holdings, Inc., 22 21–23; **28** 266
AirWair Ltd., **23** 399, 401–02
AirWays Corporation. *See* AirTran Holdings, Inc.
Airways Housing Trust Ltd., **I** 95
Airwick Industries, **II** 567
Aisin Seiki Co., Ltd., III 415–16; **14** 64
Aitken, Inc., **26** 433
AITS. *See* American International Travel Service.
Aiuruoca, **25** 85
Aiwa Co., Ltd., 28 360; **30 18–20**
Ajax, **6** 349
Ajax Iron Works, **II** 16
Ajinomoto Co., Inc., II 463–64, 475; **III** 705; **28 9–11 (upd.)**
Ajman Cement, **III** 760
AJS Auto Parts Inc., **15** 246
AK Steel Holding Corporation, 19 8–9
Akane Securities Co. Ltd., **II** 443
Akashic Memories, **11** 234
Akemi, **17** 310; **24** 160
AKH Co. Inc., **20** 63
Akin, Gump, Strauss, Hauer & Feld, **18** 366
AKO Bank, **II** 378
Akro-Mills Inc., **19** 277–78
Akron Brass Manufacturing Co., **9** 419
Akron Corp., **IV** 290
Akroyd & Smithers, **14** 419
Akseli Gallen-Kallela, **IV** 314
Aktiebolaget Aerotransport, **I** 119
Aktiebolaget Electrolux, 22 24–28 (upd.). *See also* Electrolux Group
Aktiebolaget SKF, III 622–25; **IV** 203
Aktiengesellschaft für Berg- und Hüttenbetriebe, **IV** 201
Aktiengesellschaft für Maschinenpapier-Zellstoff-Fabrikation, **IV** 323
Aktiv Placering A.B., **II** 352
AKU. *See* Akzo Nobel N.V.
Akzo Nobel N.V., I 674; **II** 572; **III** 44; **13 21–23**, 545; **14** 27; **15** 436; **16** 69, 462; **21** 466
Al Copeland Enterprises, Inc., **7** 26–28
Alaadin Middle East-Ersan, **IV** 564
Alabama Bancorp., **17** 152
Alabama Gas Corporation, **21** 207–08
Alabama Shipyards Inc., **21** 39–40
Alabaster Co., **III** 762
Aladdin Industries, **16** 487
Aladdin Mills Inc., **19** 276
Aladdin's Castle, **III** 430, 431
Alagasco, **21** 207–08
Alais et Camargue, **IV** 173
Alamac Knit Fabrics, Inc., **16** 533–34; **21** 192
Alamito Company, **6** 590
Alamo Engine Company, **8** 514
Alamo Rent A Car, Inc., 6 348–50; **24 9–12 (upd.)**; **25** 93; **26** 409
Alania, **24** 88
ALANTEC Corporation, **25** 162
Alarm Device Manufacturing Company, **9** 413–15
Alaron Inc., **16** 357
Alascom, **6** 325–28; **26** 358
Alaska Air Group, Inc., 6 65–67; **11** 50; **29 11–14 (upd.)**
Alaska Co., **III** 439
Alaska Commercial Company, **12** 363
Alaska Hydro-Train, **6** 382; **9** 510
Alaska Junk Co., **19** 380
Alaska Natural Gas Transportation System, **V** 673, 683
Alaska Pulp Co., **IV** 284, 297, 321
Alaska Steel Co., **19** 381
Alatas Mammoet, **26** 279
Alba Foods, **III** 619–20; **27** 197
Alba-Waldensian, Inc., 30 21–23
Albany and Susquehanna Railroad, **II** 329
Albany Assurance Co., Ltd., **III** 293
Albany Cheese, **23** 219
Albany Felt Company. *See* Albany International Corp.
Albany International Corp., 8 12–14
Albemarle Paper Co., **I** 334–35; **10** 289
Albers Brothers Milling Co., **II** 487
Albert E. Reed & Co. Ltd. *See* Reed International PLC.
Albert Heijn NV, **II** 641–42
Albert Nipon, Inc., **8** 323
Albert Willcox & Co., **14** 278
Alberta Distillers, **I** 377
Alberta Energy Company Ltd., 16 10–12
Alberta Gas Trunk Line Company, Ltd., **V** 673–74
Alberta Sulphate Ltd., **IV** 165
Alberto, **II** 641–42
Alberto-Culver Company, 8 15–17
Albertson's Inc., II 601–03, 604–05, 637; **7 19–22 (upd.)**; **8** 474; **15** 178, 480; **16** 249; **18** 8; **22** 38; **27** 247, 290, 292; **30 24–28 (upd.)**
Albi Enterprises, **III** 24
Albion Industries, Inc., **16** 357
Albion Reid Proprietary, **III** 673
Albright & Friel, **I** 313; **10** 154
Albright & Wilson Ltd., **I** 527; **IV** 165; **12** 351; **16** 461
Albuquerque Gas & Electric Company. *See* Public Service Company of New Mexico.
Albuquerque Gas, Electric Light and Power Company, **6** 561–62
Albury Brickworks, **III** 673
Alcan Aluminium Limited, II 415; **IV 9–13**, 14, 59, 154–55; **9** 512; **14** 35; **31 7–12 (upd.)**
Alcantara and Sores, **II** 582
Alcatel Alsthom Compagnie Générale d'Electricité, II 13, 69, 117; **6** 304; **7** 9; **9 9–11**, 32; **11** 59, 198; **15** 125; **17** 353; **18** 155; **19** 164, 166; **21** 233
Alchem Capital Corp., **8** 141, 143
Alchem Plastics, **19** 414
Alco Capital Group, Inc., **27** 288
Alco Health Services Corporation, III 9–10
Alco Hydro-Aeroplane, **I** 64
Alco Office Products Inc., **24** 362
Alco Standard Corporation, I 412–13; **III** 9; **9** 261; **16** 473–74
ALCO Trade Show Services, **26** 102
Alcoa. *See* Aluminum Company of America.
Alcon Laboratories, **II** 547; **7** 382; **10** 46, 48; **30** 30–31
Alcudia, **IV** 528
Alden Merrell Corporation, **23** 169
Aldermac Mines Ltd., **IV** 164
Aldi Group, 11 240; **13 24–26**; **17** 125
Aldine Press, **10** 34
Aldrich Chemical Co., **I** 690
Aldus Corporation, 10 34–36
Aldwarke Main & Car House Collieries, **I** 573
Alenia, **7** 9, 11
Alert Management Systems Inc., **12** 380
Alessio Tubi, **IV** 228
Alestra, **19** 12
Alex & Ivy, **10** 166–68
Alex Lee Inc., 18 6–9
Alexander & Alexander Services Inc., III 280; **10 37–39**; **13** 476; **22** 318
Alexander & Baldwin, Inc., I 417; **10 40–42**; **24** 32; **29** 307
Alexander and Lord, **13** 482
Alexander Grant & Co., **I** 481, 656

Alexander Hamilton Life Insurance Co., **II** 420; **29** 256
Alexander Howden Group, **III** 280; **10** 38–39; **22** 318
Alexander Martin Co., **I** 374
Alexander Smith, Inc., **19** 275
Alexander's Inc., **10** 282; **12** 221; **26** 111
Alexander-Schroder Lumber Company, **18** 514
Alexis Lichine, **III** 43
Alfa Romeo, **I** 163, 167; **11** 102, 104, 139, 205; **13 27–29**, 218–19
Alfa, S.A. de C.V., **II** 262; **11** 386; **19 10–12**
Alfa Trading Company, **23** 358
Alfa-Laval AB, **III 417–21**; **IV** 203; **8** 376
Alfalfa's Markets, **19** 500–02
Alfinal, **III** 420
Alfred A. Knopf, Inc., **13** 428, 429; **31** 376–79
Alfred Bullows & Sons, Ltd., **21** 64
Alfred Dunhill Limited, **19** 369; **27** 487–89
Alfred Hickman Ltd., **III** 751
Alfred Marks Bureau, Ltd., **6** 9–10
Alfred Nobel & Co., **III** 693
Alfred Teves, **I** 193
Alfried Krupp von Bohlen und Halbach Foundation, **IV** 89
ALG. *See* Arkla, Inc.
Alga, **24** 83
Algemeen Burgerlijk Pensioenfonds, **26** 421
Algemeene Bankvereeniging en Volksbank van Leuven, **II** 304
Algemeene Friesche, **III** 177–79
N.V. Algemeene Maatschappij tot Exploitatie van Verzekeringsmaatschappijen, **III** 199
Algemeene Maatschappij van Levensverzekering en Lijfrente, **III** 178
Algemeene Maatschappij voor Nijverheidskrediet, **II** 304–05
Algemeene Nederlandsche Maatschappij ter begunstiging van de Volksvlijt, **II** 294
Algemene Bank Nederland N.V., **II 183–84**, 185, 239, 527; **III** 200
Algo Group Inc., **24 13–15**
Algoma Steel Corp., **IV** 74; **8** 544–45; **24** 143
Algonquin Energy, Inc., **6** 487
Algonquin Gas Transmission Company, **6** 486; **14** 124–26
Alidata, **6** 69
Aligro Inc., **II** 664
Alimenta (USA), Inc., **17** 207
Alimentana S.A., **II** 547
Alimondo, **17** 505
Alitalia–Linee Aeree Italiana, S.p.A., **I** 110, 466–67; **6** 96, **68–69**; **24** 311; **29 15–17 (upd.)**
Alken, **II** 474
Oy Alkoholiliike Ab, **IV** 469
Alkor-Oerlikon Plastic GmbH, **7** 141
All American Airways. *See* USAir Group, Inc.
All American Communications Inc., **20 3–7**; **25** 138
All American Gourmet Co., **12** 178, 199
All American Sports Co., **22** 458–59
All British Escarpment Company LTD, **25** 430
All Nippon Airways Company Limited, **I** 106, 493; **6 70–71** 118, 427; **16** 168; **24** 326
All Woods, Inc., **18** 514
Allami Biztosito, **III** 209; **15** 30
Allcom, **16** 392
Allders International, **III** 502
Alleanza & Unione Mediterranea, **III** 208
Alleanza-Securitas-Esperia, **III** 208
Alleghany Corporation, **II** 398; **IV** 180–81; **10 43–45**; **19** 319; **22** 494
Allegheny Airlines. *See* USAir Group, Inc. *and* US Airways Group, Inc.
Allegheny Beverage Corp., **7** 472–73
Allegheny County Light Company, **6** 483–84
Allegheny International, Inc., **III** 732; **8** 545; **9** 484; **22** 3, 436
Allegheny Ludlum Corporation, **I** 307; **II** 402; **8 18–20**; **9** 484; **21** 489
Allegheny Power System, Inc., **V 543–45**
Allegheny Steel and Iron Company, **9** 484
Allegiance Life Insurance Company, **22** 268
Allegis, Inc. *See* United Airlines.
Allegmeine Transpotmittel Aktiengesellschaft, **6** 394; **25** 169
Allegretti & Co., **22** 26
Allen & Co., **I** 512, 701; **II** 136; **12** 496; **13** 366; **25** 270
Allen & Ginter, **12** 108
Allen & Hanbury's, **I** 640
Allen Tank Ltd., **21** 499
Allen's Convenience Stores, Inc., **17** 170
Allen-Bradley Co., **I** 80; **II** 110; **III** 593; **11** 429–30; **17** 478; **22** 373; **23** 211
Allen-Liversidge Ltd., **I** 315; **25** 80
Allergan, Inc., **10 46–49**; **23** 196; **30 29–33 (upd.)**
Allforms Packaging Corp., **13** 442
Allgemeine Deutsche Creditanstalt, **II** 211, 238, 383; **12** 536
Allgemeine Eisenbahn-Versicherungs-Gesellschaft, **III** 399
Allgemeine Elektricitäts-Gesellschaft. *See* AEG A.G.
Allgemeine Rentenstalt Lebens- und Rentenversicherung, **II** 258
Allgemeine Schweizerische Uhrenindustrie, **26** 480
Allgemeine Versicherungs-Gesellschaft Helvetia, **III** 375
Alliance Agro-Alimentaires S.A., **II** 577
Alliance Amusement Company, **10** 319
Alliance Assurance Co., **III** 369–73
Alliance Brothers, **V** 356
Alliance Capital Management Corp., **22** 189
Alliance Entertainment Corp., **17 12–14**
Alliance Gaming Corp., **15** 539; **24** 36
Alliance Insurance Co., **III** 224
Alliance Manufacturing Co., **13** 397
Alliance Marine, **III** 373
Alliance Mortgage Co., **I** 610
Alliance Packaging, **13** 443
Alliance Paper Group, **IV** 316
Alliance Tire and Rubber Co., **II** 47; **25** 267
AllianceWare, Inc., **16** 321
Alliant Techsystems Inc., **8 21–23**; **30 34–37 (upd.)**
Allianz AG Holding, **I** 411, 426; **II** 239, 257, 279–80; **III 183–86**, 200, 250, 252, 299–301, 347–48, 373, 377, 393; **IV** 222; **14** 169–70; **15 10–14 (upd.)**
Allibert, **III** 614
Allied Bakeries Ltd., **II** 465–66; **13** 52–53
Allied Breweries Ltd., **I** 215; **III** 105; **IV** 712
Allied Chemical, **I** 310, 332, 351–52; **8** 526; **9** 521–22; **13** 76; **22** 5. *See also* General Chemical Corp.
Allied Chemical & Dye Corp., **I** 414; **7** 262; **9** 154; **22** 29
Allied Color Industries, **8** 347
Allied Communications Group, **18** 77; **22** 297
Allied Construction Products, **17** 384
Allied Container Corp., **IV** 345
Allied Corporation, **I** 68, 141, 143, 414, 534; **III** 118, 511; **6** 599; **7** 356; **9** 134; **11** 435; **24** 164; **25** 224; **31** 135. *See also* AlliedSignal Inc.
Allied Crude Vegetable Oil Refining Co., **II** 398; **10** 62
Allied Distributing Co., **12** 106
Allied Domecq PLC, **24** 220; **29 18–20**, 85
Allied Dunbar, **I** 427
Allied Engineering Co., **8** 177
Allied Fibers, **19** 275
Allied Food Markets, **II** 662
Allied Gas Company, **6** 529
Allied Grape Growers, **I** 261
Allied Health and Scientific Products Company, **8** 215
Allied Healthcare Products, Inc., **24 16–19**
Allied Holdings, Inc., **24** 411
Allied Import Company, **V** 96
Allied Irish Banks, plc, **16 13–15**
Allied Maintenance Corp., **I** 514
Allied Mills, Inc., **10** 249; **13** 186
Allied Oil Co., **IV** 373
Allied Overseas Trading Ltd., **I** 216
Allied Plywood Corporation, **12** 397
Allied Polymer Group, **I** 429
Allied Products Corporation, **21 20–22**
Allied Radio, **19** 310
Allied Safety, Inc., **V** 215
Allied Shoe Corp., **22** 213
Allied Signal Engines, **9 12–15**
Allied Steel and Conveyors, **18** 493
Allied Steel and Wire Ltd., **III** 495
Allied Stores Corporation, **II** 350, 611–12; **V** 25–28; **9** 211; **10** 282; **13** 43; **15** 94, 274; **16** 60; **22** 110; **23** 59–60; **25** 249; **31** 192
Allied Structural Steel Company, **10** 44
Allied Supermarkets, Inc., **7** 570; **28** 511
Allied Suppliers, **II** 609
Allied Telephone Company. *See* Alltel Corporation.
Allied Tin Box Makers Ltd., **I** 604
Allied Towers Merchants Ltd., **II** 649
Allied Van Lines Inc., **6** 412, 414; **14** 37
Allied Vintners, **I** 215
Allied-Lyons plc, **I 215–16**, 258, 264, 438; **IV** 721; **9** 100, 391; **10** 170; **13** 258; **21** 228, 323; **29** 18, 84
Allied-Signal Corp., **I** 85, 141, 143, **414–16**; **III** 511–12; **V** 605; **6** 599–600; **9** 519; **11** 435, 444; **13** 227; **16** 436; **17** 20; **21** 200, 396–97
AlliedSignal Inc., **22 29–32 (upd.)**; **29** 408; **31** 154

Allis Chalmers Corporation, **I** 163; **II** 98, 121; **III** 543–44; **9** 17; **11** 104; **12** 545; **13** 16–17, 563; **14** 446; **21** 502–03; **22** 380
Allis-Gleaner Corp. *See* AGCO Corp.
Allison Engine Company, **21** 436
Allison Engineering Company. *See* Rolls-Royce Allison.
Allison Gas Turbine Division, 9 16–19, 417; **10** 537; **11** 473
Allmanna Svenska Elektriska Aktiebolaget. *See* ABB ASEA Brown Boveri Ltd.
Allmänna Telefonaktiebolaget L.M. Ericsson, **V** 334
Allnatt London & Guildhall Properties, **IV** 724
Allnet, **10** 19
Allo Pro, **III** 633
Allor Leasing Corp., **9** 323
Allou Health & Beauty Care, Inc., 28 12–14
Alloy & Stainless, Inc., **IV** 228
Alloys Unlimited, **II** 82
Allserve Inc., **25** 367
Allsport plc., **31** 216, 218
The Allstate Corporation, **I** 23; **III** 231–32, 259, 294; **V** 180, 182; **6** 12; **10 50–52**; **13** 539; **18** 475; **21** 96–97; **22** 495; **23** 286–87; **25** 155; **27 30–33 (upd.)**; **29** 397
Alltel Corporation, 6 299–301; **16** 318; **20** 440
Alltrans Group, **27** 472
Alltrista Corporation, 30 38–41
Allwaste, Inc., 18 10–13
Almac Electronics Corporation, **10** 113
Almac's Inc., **17** 558–59
Almaden Vineyards, **I** 377–78; **13** 134
Almanij. *See* Algemeene Maatschappij voor Nijverheidskrediet.
Almay, Inc., **III** 54
Almeida Banking House. *See* Banco Bradesco S.A.
Almours Security Co., **IV** 311; **19** 266
Almys, **24** 461
Aloe Vera of America, **17** 187
Aloha Airlines, Incorporated, **I** 97; **9** 271–72; **21** 142; **22** 251; **24 20–22**
Alp Sport Sandals, **22** 173
Alpen-Elektrowerke Aktiengesellschaft, **IV** 230
Alpex Computer Corp., **III** 157
Alpex, S.A. de C.V., **19** 12
Alpha Beta Co., **II** 605, 625, 653; **17** 559
Alpha Engineering Group, Inc., **16** 259–60
Alpha Healthcare Ltd., **25** 455
Alpha Technical Systems, **19** 279
Alphanumeric Publication Systems, Inc., **26** 518
Alphonse Allard Inc., **II** 652
Alpina Versicherungs-Aktiengesellschaft, **III** 412
Alpine, **IV** 234
Alpine Electronics, Inc., II 5; **13 30–31**
Alpine Lace Brands, Inc., 18 14–16
Alpine Securities Corporation, **22** 5
Alpre, **19** 192
Alps Electric Co., Ltd., II 5–6; **13** 30
Alric Packing, **II** 466
Alsen-Breitenbury, **III** 702
ALSO Holding AG, **29** 419, 422
Alsons Corp., **III** 571; **20** 362
Alsthom, **II** 12
Alsthom-Atlantique, **9** 9
Alta Dena, **25** 83, 85
Alta Electric Company, **25** 15
Alta Gold Co., **IV** 76
ALTA Health Strategies, Inc., **11** 113
Alta Holidays Ltd., **I** 95
Altamil Corp., **IV** 137
Altana AG, **23** 498
Alte Leipziger, **III** 242
Altec Electronics, **I** 489–90
ALTEC International, **21** 107–09
Altenburg & Gooding, **22** 428
Altera Corporation, 18 17–20
Alternate Postal Delivery, **6** 14
Alternative Youth Services, Inc., **29** 399–400
Altex, **19** 192–93
Althoff KG, **V** 101
Althouse Chemical Company, **9** 153
Althus Corp, **I** 361
Altman Weil Pensa, **29** 237
Alton & Eastern Railroad Company, **6** 504
Alton Box Board Co., **IV** 295; **19** 225
Altos Computer Systems, **6** 279; **10** 362
Altos Hornos de Mexico SA de CV, **13** 144; **19** 220
Altron Incorporated, 20 8–10
Aluar. *See* Aluminios Argentinos.
Aluma Systems Corp., **9** 512; **22** 14
Alumax Inc., **I** 508; **III** 758; **IV** 18–19; **8** 505–06; **22** 286
Alumina Partners of Jamaica, **IV** 123
Aluminate Sales Corp, **I** 373
Aluminio de Galicia, **IV** 174
Aluminios Argentinos, **26** 433
Aluminium Co. of London, **IV** 69
L'Aluminium Francais, **IV** 173
Aluminium Ltd., **IV** 9–11, 14, 153
Aluminium Plant and Vessel Co., **III** 419
Aluminium-Oxid Stade GmbH, **IV** 231
Aluminum Can Co., **I** 607
Aluminum Company of America, **I** 373, 599; **II** 315, 402, 422; **III** 490–91, 613; **IV** 9–12, **14–16**, 56, 59, 121–22, 131, 173, 703; **6** 39; **12** 346; **19** 240, 292; **20 11–14 (upd.)**; **22** 455
Aluminum Company of Canada Ltd., **II** 345; **IV** 10–12, 154
Aluminum Cooking Utensil Co., **IV** 14
Aluminum Forge Co., **IV** 137
Aluminum Norf GmbH, **IV** 231
Aluminum of Korea, **III** 516
Aluminum Rolling Mills, **17** 280
Aluminum Sales Corporation, **12** 346
Aluminum Seating Corp., **I** 201
Alun Cathcart, **6** 357
Alup-Kompressoren Pressorun, **III** 570; **20** 361
Alupak, A.G., **12** 377
Alusaf, **IV** 92
Alusuisse,
Alusuisse Lonza Group Ltd.,**IV** 12; **31** 11
Alva Jams Pty., **I** 437
Alvic Group, **20** 363
Alyeska Pipeline Service Co., **IV** 522, 571; **14** 542; **24** 521
Alyeska Seafoods Co., **II** 578
ALZA Corporation, 10 53–55
Alzwerke GmbH, **IV** 230
AM Acquisition Inc., **8** 559–60
AM Cosmetics, Inc., **31** 89
Am-Par Records, **II** 129
Am-Safe, Inc., **16** 357
AM-TEX Corp., Inc., **12** 443
Amagasaki Co., **I** 492; **24** 325
Amagasaki Spinners Ltd., **V** 387
Amagasaki Steel Co., Ltd., **IV** 130
Amalgamaize Co., **14** 18
Amalgamated Chemicals, Ltd., **IV** 401
Amalgamated Dental International, **10** 271–72
Amalgamated Distilled Products, **II** 609
Amalgamated Press, **IV** 666; **7** 244, 342; **17** 397
Amalgamated Roadstone Corp., **III** 752; **28** 449
Amalgamated Sugar Co., **14** 18; **19** 467–68
Amalgamated Weatherware, **IV** 696
Amana, **18** 226
Amana Refrigeration, **II** 86; **11** 413
Amaray International Corporation, **12** 264
Amarillo Railcar Services, **6** 580
Amarin Plastics, **IV** 290
AMAX Inc., I 508; **III** 687; **IV 17–19**, 46, 139, 171, 239, 387; **6** 148; **12** 244; **22** 106, 286
Amazon.com, Inc., 25 17–19; **27** 517; **30** 70
Amazôna Mineracao SA, **IV** 56
Ambac Industries, **I** 85
AmBase Corp., **III** 264
Amber's Stores, Inc., **17** 360
Amblin Entertainment, 21 23–27
Ambrose Shardlow, **III** 494
AMC Entertainment Inc., 12 12–14; **14** 87; **21** 362; **23** 126
AMCA International Corporation, **7** 513; **8** 545; **10** 329; **23** 299
Amcell. *See* American Cellular Network.
Amchem Products Inc., **I** 666
AMCO, Inc., **13** 159
Amcor Limited, IV 248–50; **19 13–16 (upd.)**
Amcraft Building Products Co., Inc., **22** 15
AMD. *See* Advanced Micro Devices, Inc.
Amdahl Corporation, III 109–11, 140; **6** 272; **12** 238; **13** 202; **14 13–16 (upd.)**; **16** 194, 225–26; **22** 293; **25** 87
AME Finanziaria, **IV** 587; **19** 19
AMEC, **I** 568
Amedco, **6** 295
Amer Group Ltd., **24** 530
Amer Sport, **22** 202
Amerada Hess Corporation, IV 365–67, 400, 454, 522, 571, 658; **11** 353; **21 28–31 (upd.)**; **24** 521
Amerco, 6 351–52
Ameri-Kart Corp., **19** 277, 279
America Japan Sheet Glass Co., **III** 714
America Latina Companhia de Seguros, **III** 289
America Online, Inc., 10 56–58, 237; **13** 147; **15** 54, 265, 321; **18** 24; **19** 41; **22** 52, 519, 522; **26 16–20 (upd.)**; **27** 20, 106, 301, 430, 517–18; **29** 143, 227. *See also* CompuServe Interactive Services, Inc.
America Publishing Company, **18** 213
America Today, **13** 545
America Unplugged, **18** 77
America West Airlines, 6 72–74, 121
American & Efird, Inc., **12** 501; **23** 260
American Agricultural Chemical Co., **IV** 401
American Air Conditioning, **25** 15
American Air Filter, **26** 3–4
American Airlines, I 30–31, 48, 71, **89–91**, 97, 106, 115, 118, 124–26, 130,

132, 512, 530; **III** 102; **6** 60, 81, **75–77 (upd.)**, 121, 129–31; **9** 271–72; **10** 163; **11** 279; **12** 190, 192, 379, 381, 487, **13** 173; **14** 73; **16** 146; **18** 73; **21** 141, 143; **24** 21, 399–400; **25** 90–91, 403, 421–22; **26** 427–28, 441; **31** 103, 306. *See also* AMR Corporation.
American Alliance Co., **III** 191
American Allsafe Co., **8** 386
American Amusements, Inc., **III** 430
American Appliance Co., **II** 85; **11** 411
American Arithmometer Company. *See* Burroughs Corporation.
American Asiatic Underwriters, **III** 195
American Association of Retired Persons, **9** 348. *See also* AARP.
American Automar Inc., **12** 29
American Automated, **11** 111
American Automobile Insurance Co., **III** 251
American Aviation and General Insurance Co., **III** 230
American Aviation Manufacturing Corp., **15** 246
American Avitron Inc, **I** 481
American Bakeries Company, **12** 275–76
American Bancorp, **11** 295
American Bancshares, Inc., **11** 457
American Bank, **9** 474–75
American Bank Note, **IV** 599
American Bank of Vicksburg, **14** 41
American Bankcorp, Inc., **8** 188
American Banker/Bond Buyer, **8** 526
American Banknote Corporation, 30 42–45
American Barge and Towing Company, **11** 194
American Beauty Cover Company, **12** 472
American Beef Packers, Inc., **16** 473
American Beet Sugar Company, **11** 13–14
American Bell Telephone Company, **V** 259; **14** 336
American Beryllium Co., Inc., **9** 323
American Beverage Corp., **II** 528
American Biltrite Inc., 16 16–18; **18** 116, 118
American Biodyne Inc., **9** 348
American Biomedical Corporation, **11** 333
American Biscuit Co., **II** 542
American Box Board Company, **12** 376
American Box Co., **IV** 137
American Brake Shoe and Foundry Company, **I** 456. *See also* ABC Rail Products Corporation.
American Brands, Inc., II 468, 477; **IV** 251; **V 395–97**, 398–99, 405; **7** 3–4; **9** 408; **12** 87, 344; **14** 95, 271–72; **16** 108, 110, 242; **19** 168–69. *See also* Fortune Brands, Inc.
American Bridge Co., **II** 330; **IV** 572; **7** 549
American Broadcasting Co., **25** 418. *See also* ABC, Inc. *and* Capital Cities/ABC Inc.
American Builders & Contractors Supply Co. *See* ABC Supply Co., Inc.
American Builders, Inc., **8** 436
American Building Maintenance Industries, Inc., 6 17–19. *See also* ABM Industries Incorporated.
American Bus Lines Inc., **24** 118
American Business Information, Inc., 18 21–25
American Business Interiors. *See* American Furniture Company, Inc.
American Business Products, Inc., 20 15–17
American Cable Systems, Inc. *See* Comcast Corporation.
American Cablesystems, **7** 99
American Cafe, **I** 547
American Can Co., **IV** 36, 290; **8** 476; **10** 130; **11** 29, 197; **12** 408; **13** 255; **15** 127–28; **17** 106; **22** 210; **23** 98. *See also* Primerica Corp.
The American Cancer Society, 24 23–25
American Capital and Research Corp., **28** 201
American Car & Foundry Inc., **21** 503
American Carbide Corporation, **7** 584
American Cash Register Co., **III** 150; **6** 264
American Casualty Co., **III** 230–31, 404
American Casualty Co. of Dallas, **III** 203
American Cellular Network, **7** 91; **24** 122
American Cellulose and Chemical Manufacturing Co., **I** 317
American Cement Co. *See* Giant Cement Holding, Inc.
American Central Insurance Co., **III** 241
American Cereal Co., **II** 558; **12** 409
American Chicle Co., **I** 711; **21** 54
American Chocolate & Citrus Co., **IV** 409
American Chrome, **III** 699
American Classic Voyages Company, 22 340, **27 34–37**
American Clay Forming Company, **8** 178
American Clip Company, **7** 3
American Coin Merchandising, Inc., 28 15–17
American Colloid Co., 13 32–35
American Commercial Bank, **II** 336
American Commercial Lines Inc., **22** 164, 166–67
American Commonwealths Power Corporation, **6** 579
American Community Grocers, **II** 670
American Computer Systems. *See* American Software Inc.
American Continental Insurance Co., **III** 191–92
American Cotton Cooperative Association, **17** 207
American Cotton Oil Co., **II** 497
American Council on Education, **12** 141
American Courier Express, Inc., **24** 126
American Crayon Company, **12** 115
American Credit Corporation, **II** 236; **20** 59
American Crystal Sugar Company, 7 377; **11 13–15**
American Cyanamid, I 300–02, 619; **III** 22; **IV** 345, 552; **8 24–26 (upd.)**; **10** 269; **11** 494; **13** 231–32; **14** 254, 256; **16** 68; **22** 147; **27** 115–16
American Dairy Queen Corporation, **10** 373
American Data Technology, Inc., **11** 111
American Distilling Co., **I** 226; **10** 180–81
American District Telegraph Co., **III** 644; **12** 9
American Diversified Foods, Inc., **14** 351
American Drew, Inc., **12** 301
American Drug Company, **13** 367
American Eagle Airlines, Inc., **28** 22
American Eagle Fire Insurance Co., **III** 240–41
American Eagle Outfitters, Inc., 14 427; **24 26–28**; **25** 121
American Education Press, **10** 479
American Electric Company, **II** 27; **12** 193; **22** 10
American Electric Power Company, II 3; **IV** 181; **V 546–49**; **6** 449, 524; **11** 516
American Empire Insurance Co., **III** 191
American Emulsions Co., **8** 455
American Encaustic Tiling Co., **22** 170
American Envelope Co., **III** 40; **16** 303; **28** 251
American Equipment Co., **I** 571
American Export Steamship Lines, **I** 89
American Express Company, I 26–27, 480, 614; **II** 108, 176, 309, 380–82, **395–99**, 450–52, 544; **III** 251–52, 319, 340, 389; **IV** 637, 721; **6** 206–07, 409; **8** 118; **9** 335, 343, 391, 468–69, 538; **10** 44–45, **59–64 (upd.)**; **11** 41, 416–17, 532; **12** 533; **14** 106; **15** 50; **18** 60, 112, 516, 543; **21** 97, 127; **23** 229; **26** 516
American Factors, Ltd. *See* Amfac/JMB Hawaii L.L.C.
American Family Corporation, III 187–89. *See also* AFLAC Inc.
American Family Publishers, **23** 393–94
American Feldmühle Corp., **II** 51; **21** 330
American Filtrona Corp., **IV** 260–61
American Finance Systems, **II** 349
American Financial Corporation, II 596; **III 190–92**, 221; **8** 537; **9** 452; **18** 549
American First National Supermarkets, **16** 313
American Fitness Centers, **25** 40
American Flange, **30** 397
American Flavor & Fragrance Company, **9** 154
American Flyer Trains, **16** 336–37
American Food Management, **6** 45
American Football League, **29** 346
American Fore Group, **III** 241–42
American Foreign Insurance Association, **III** 223, 226. *See also* AFIA.
American Forest Products Co., **IV** 282; **9** 260
American Fructose Corp., **14** 18–19
American Fur Company, **25** 220
American Furniture Company, Inc., 12 300; **21 32–34**
American Gage Co., **I** 472
American Gas & Electric. *See* American Electric Power Company.
American Gasoline Co., **IV** 540
American General Capital Corp., **I** 614
American General Corporation, III 193–94; **10 65–67 (upd.)**; **11** 16
American General Finance Corp., 11 16–17
American General Life Insurance Company, **6** 294
American Graphics, **23** 100
American Greetings Corporation, 7 23–25; **12** 207–08; **15** 507; **16** 256; **21** 426–28; **22 33–36 (upd.)**
American Grinder and Manufacturing Company, **9** 26
American Hardware & Supply Company. *See* TruServ Corporation.
American Harvester, **II** 262
American Hawaii Cruises, **27** 34
American Health & Life Insurance Company, **27** 47
American Heritage Savings, **II** 420

American Hoechst Corporation. *See* Hoechst Celanese Corporation.
American Hoist & Derrick Co., **8** 544
American Home Assurance Co., **III** 196–97
American Home Assurance Co. of New York, **III** 203
American Home Products, I 527, **622–24**, 631, 676–77, 696, 700; **III** 18, 36, 444; **8** 282–83; **10 68–70 (upd.)**, 528; **11** 35; **15** 64–65; **16** 191, 438; **21** 466; **24** 288; **25** 477
American Home Publishing Co., Inc., **14** 460
American Home Shield, **6** 46; **23** 428, 430
American Home Video, **9** 186
American Homestar Corporation, 18 26–29
American Homeware Inc., **15** 501
American Honda Motor Co., **I** 174; **10** 352
American Hospital Association, **10** 159
American Hospital Supply Co., **I** 627, 629; **III** 80; **10** 141–43; **11** 459, 486; **19** 103; **21** 118; **30** 496
American Hydron, **13** 366; **25** 55
American I.G. Chemical Corporation. *See* GAF Corporation.
American Impacts Corporation, **8** 464
American Improved Cements. *See* Giant Cement Holding, Inc.
American Independent Oil Co., **IV** 522, 537. *See also* Aminoil, Inc.
American Industrial Manufacturing Co., **I** 481
American Information Services, Inc., **11** 111
American Institutional Products, Inc., **18** 246
American Instrument Co., **I** 628; **13** 233
American Insurance Agency, **III** 191, 352
American Insurance Co., **III** 251
American International Airways, Inc., **17** 318; **22** 311
American International Group, Inc., II 422; **III 195–98**, 200; **6** 349; **10** 39; **11** 532–33; **15 15–19 (upd.)**; **18** 159
American International Travel Service, **6** 367; **27** 90
American Iron and Steel Manufacturing Co., **IV** 35; **7** 48
American Isuzu Motors, Inc. *See* Isuzu Motors, Ltd.
American Italian Pasta Company, 27 38–40
American Janitor Service, **25** 15
American Jet Industries, **7** 205
American Ka-Ro, **8** 476
American Knitting Mills of Miami, Inc., **22** 213
American La-France, **10** 296
American Laboratories, **III** 73
American Land Cruiser Company. *See* Cruise America Inc.
American Learning Corporation, **7** 168
American Life Insurance Co., **III** 195–96
American Light and Traction. *See* MCN Corporation.
American Lightwave Systems, Inc., **10** 19
American Limestone Co., **IV** 33
American Limousine Corp., **26** 62
American Linseed Co, **II** 497
American Machine and Foundry Co., **II** 7; **III** 443; **7** 211–13; **11** 397; **25** 197
American Machine and Metals, **9** 23
American Machinist Press, **IV** 634
American Magnesium Products Co., **I** 404
American Maize-Products Co., 14 17–20; **23** 464
American Management Systems, Inc., 11 18–20
American Manufacturers Mutual Insurance Co., **III** 269, 271; **15** 257
American Materials & Technologies Corporation, **27** 117
American Media, Inc., 27 41–44
American Medical International, Inc., III 73–75, 79; **14** 232
American Medical Optics, **25** 55
American Medical Services, **II** 679–80; **14** 209
American Medicorp, Inc., **III** 81; **6** 191; **14** 432; **24** 230
American Melamine, **27** 317
American Merchandising Associates Inc., **14** 411
American Merchants Union Express Co., **II** 396
American Metal Climax, Inc. *See* AMAX.
American Metal Co. Ltd. *See* AMAX.
American Metal Products Company. *See* Lear Seating Corporation.
American Metal Products Corp., **I** 481
American Metals and Alloys, Inc., **19** 432
American Metals Corp., **III** 569; **20** 361
American Micro Devices, Inc., **16** 549
American Microsystems, **I** 193
American Milk Products Corp., **II** 487
The American Mineral Spirits Company, **8** 99–100
American Motorists Insurance Co., **III** 269, 271; **15** 257
American Motors Corp., I 135–37, 145, 152, 190; **II** 60, 313; **III** 543; **6** 27, 50; **8** 373; **10** 262, 264; **18** 493; **26** 403
American Movie Classics Co., **II** 161
American Multi-Cinema. *See* AMC Entertainment Inc.
American National Bank, **13** 221–22
American National Bank and Trust Co., **II** 286
American National Can Co., **III** 536; **IV** 173, 175; **26** 230
American National Corp., **II** 286
American National Fire Insurance Co., **III** 191
American National General Agencies Inc., **III** 221; **14** 109
American National Insurance Company, 8 27–29; **27 45–48 (upd.)**
American Natural Resources Co., **I** 678; **IV** 395; **13** 416
American Natural Snacks Inc., **29** 480
American Newspaper Publishers Association, **6** 13
American of Philadelphia, **III** 234
American Oil Co., **IV** 369–70; **7** 101; **14** 22
American Olean Tile Company, **III** 424; **22** 48, 170
American Optical Co., **I** 711–12; **III** 607; **7** 436
American Overseas Airlines, **12** 380
American Overseas Holdings, **III** 350
American Pad & Paper Company, 20 18–21
American Paging, **9** 494–96
American Paper Box Company, **12** 376
American Patriot Insurance, **22** 15
American Payment Systems, Inc., **21** 514
American Petrofina, Inc., **IV** 498; **7** 179–80; **19** 11
American Pfauter, **24** 186
American Phone Centers, Inc., **21** 135
American Photographic Group, **III** 475; **7** 161
American Physicians Service Group, Inc., **6** 45; **23** 430
American Platinum Works, **IV** 78
American Postage Meter Co., **III** 156
American Potash and Chemical Corporation, **IV** 95, 446; **22** 302
American Power & Light Co., **6** 545, 596–97; **12** 542
American Power Conversion Corporation, 24 29–31
American Premier Underwriters, Inc., 10 71–74
American Prepaid Professional Services, Inc. *See* CompDent Corporation.
American President Companies Ltd., III 512; **6 353–55**
American Printing House for the Blind, 26 13–15
American Protective Mutual Insurance Co. Against Burglary, **III** 230
American Publishing Co., **IV** 597; **24** 222
American Pure Oil Co., **IV** 497
American Radiator & Standard Sanitary Corp., **III** 663–64
American Railway Express Co., **II** 382, 397; **10** 61
American Railway Publishing Co., **IV** 634
American Re Corporation, III 182; **10 75–77**
American Record Corp., **II** 132
American Recreation Company Holdings, Inc., **16** 53
American Ref-Fuel, **V** 751
American Refrigeration Products S.A, **7** 429
American Republic Assurance Co., **III** 332
American Research and Development Corp., **II** 85; **III** 132; **6** 233; **19** 103
American Residential Mortgage Corporation, 8 30–31
American Resorts Group, **III** 103
American Rice, Inc., **17** 161–62
American River Transportation Co., **I** 421; **11** 23
American Robot Corp., **III** 461
American Rolling Mill Co., **IV** 28; **8** 176–77
American Royalty Trust Co., **IV** 84; **7** 188
American Rug Craftsmen, **19** 275
American RX Pharmacy, **III** 73
American Safety Equipment Corp., **IV** 136
American Safety Razor Company, III 27–29; **20 22–24**
American Saint-Gobain, **16** 121
American Sales Book Co., Ltd., **IV** 644
American Salt Co., **12** 199
American Satellite Co., **6** 279; **15** 195
American Savings & Loan, **10** 117
American Savings Bank, **9** 276; **17** 528, 531
American Sealants Company. *See* Loctite Corporation.
American Seating Co., **I** 447; **21** 33
American Seaway Foods, Inc, **9** 451
American Service Corporation, **19** 223
American Sheet Steel Co., **IV** 572; **7** 549
American Shipbuilding, **18** 318

American Skiing Company, **28 18–21**; **31** 67, 229
American Sky Broadcasting, **27** 305
American Smelting and Refining Co., **IV** 31–33
The American Society of Composers, Authors and Publishers (ASCAP), **29 21–24**
American Software Inc., **22** 214; **25 20–22**
American Southern Insurance Co., **17** 196
American Standard Companies Inc., **30 46–50 (upd.)**
American Standard Inc., **III** 437, **663–65**; **19** 455; **22** 4, 6; **28** 486
American States Insurance Co., **III** 276
American Steamship Company, **6** 394–95; **25** 168, 170
American Steel & Wire Co., **I** 355; **IV** 572; **7** 549; **13** 97–98
American Steel Foundries, **7** 29–30
American Stock Exchange, **10** 416–17
American Stores Company, **II 604–06**; **12** 63, 333; **13** 395; **17** 559; **18** 89; **22 37–40 (upd.)**; **25** 297; **27** 290–92; **30** 24, 26–27
American Sugar Refining Company. *See* Domino Sugar Corporation.
American Sumatra Tobacco Corp., **15** 138
American Surety Co., **26** 486
American Systems Technologies, Inc., **18** 5
American Teaching Aids Inc., **19** 405
American Technical Services Company. *See* American Building Maintenance Industries, Inc. *and* ABM Industries Incorporated.
American Telephone and Telegraph Company. *See* AT&T.
American Television and Communications Corp., **I** 534–35; **II** 161; **IV** 596, 675; **7** 528–30; **18** 65
American Textile Co., **III** 571; **20** 362
American Thermos Bottle Company. *See* Thermos Company.
American Tile Supply Company, **19** 233
American Tin Plate Co., **IV** 572; **7** 549
American Tissue Company, **29** 136
American Title Insurance, **III** 242
American Tobacco Co., **I** 12–14, 28, 37, 425; **V** 395–97, 399, 408–09, 417–18, 600; **14** 77, 79; **15** 137–38; **16** 242; **18** 416; **27** 128–29. *See also* American Brands Inc., B.A.T. Industries PLC., *and* Fortune Brands, Inc.
American Tool & Machinery, **III** 420
American Tool Company, **13** 563
American Totalisator Corporation, **10** 319–20
American Tourister, Inc., **10** 350; **13** 451, 453; **16 19–21**
American Tractor Corporation, **10** 379
American Trading and Production Corporation, **7** 101
American Transport Lines, **6** 384
American Trust and Savings Bank, **II** 261
American Trust Co., **II** 336, 382; **12** 535
American Twist Drill Co., **23** 82
American Ultramar Ltd., **IV** 567
American VIP Limousine, Inc., **26** 62
American Viscose Corp. *See* Avisco.
American Water Works Company, **V** 543–44; **6 443–45**; **26** 451
American Window Glass, **16** 120
American Wood Reduction Company, **14** 174
American Woodmark Corporation, **31 13–16**
American Woolen, **I** 529
American Yard Products, **22** 26, 28
American Yearbook Company, **7** 255; **25** 252
American-Marietta Corp., **I** 68, 405
American-Palestine Trading Corp., **II** 205–06
American-South African Investment Co. Ltd., **IV** 79
American-Strevell Inc., **II** 625
Americana Entertainment Group, Inc., **19** 435
Americana Foods, Inc., **17** 474–75
Americana Healthcare Corp., **15** 522
Americana Hotel, **12** 316
America's Favorite Chicken Company, Inc., **7 26–28**
AmeriFirst Bank, **11** 258
Amerifirst Federal Savings, **10** 340
AmeriGas Partners, L.P., **12** 498
AmeriGas Propane, Inc., **12** 500
Amerihost Properties, Inc., **30 51–53**
Amerimark Inc., **II** 682
Amerisystems, **8** 328
Ameritech Corporation, **V 265–68**; **6** 248; **7** 118; **10** 431; **11** 382; **12** 137; **14** 252–53, 257, 259–61, 364; **15** 197; **18 30–34 (upd.)**; **25** 499
Ameritech Illinois. *See* Illinois Bell Telephone Company.
Ameritrust Corporation, **9** 476
Ameriwood Industries International Corp., **17 15–17**
Amerock Corp., **13** 41
Amerotron, **I** 529
Amersil Co., **IV** 78
Ames Department Stores, Inc., **V** 197–98; **9 20–22**; **10** 497; **15** 88; **19** 449; **30 54–57 (upd.)**
AMETEK, Inc., **9 23–25**; **12** 88
N.V. Amev, **III 199–202**
Amey Roadstone Corp., **III** 503; **7** 209
AMF Bowling, Inc., **19** 312; **23** 450
Amfac Inc., **I 417–18**, 566; **IV** 703; **10** 42; **23** 320
Amfac/JMB Hawaii L.L.C., **24 32–35 (upd.)**
Amfas, **III** 310
Amgen, Inc., **I** 266; **8** 216–17; **10 78–81**; **13** 240; **14** 255; **21** 320; **30 58–61 (upd.)**
Amherst Coal Co., **IV** 410; **7** 309
AMI. *See* Advanced Metallurgy, Inc.
Amiga Corporation, **7** 96
Aminoil, Inc., **IV** 523. *See also* American Independent Oil Co.
AMISA, **IV** 136
Amisys Managed Care Information Systems, **16** 94
Amitron S.A., **10** 113
Amity Leather Products Company. *See* AR Accessories Group, Inc.
AMK Corporation, **II** 595; **7** 85; **21** 111
Amkor, **23** 17
Amling Co., **25** 89
Ammirati Puris Lintas, **14** 316; **22** 294
Ammo-Phos, **I** 300; **8** 24
L'Ammoniac Sarro-Lorrain S.a.r.l., **IV** 197
Amoco Corporation, **I** 516, 202; **II** 376; **III** 611; **IV 368–71**, 412, 424–25, 453, 525; **7** 107, 443; **10** 83–84; **11** 441; **12** 18; **14 21–25 (upd.)**, 494; **18** 365; **19** 297; **26** 369
Amoseas, **IV** 453–54
Amoskeag Company, **6** 356; **8 32–33**; **9** 213–14, 217; **22** 54; **31** 199
Amot Controls Corporation, **15** 404
AMP, Inc., **II 7–8**; **11** 319; **13** 344; **14 26–28 (upd.)**; **17** 274; **22** 542; **28** 486
Ampad Holding Corporation. *See* American Pad & Paper Company.
AMPAL. *See* American-Palestine Trading Corp.
AMPCO Auto Parks, Inc. *See* American Building Maintenance Industries, Inc. *and* ABM Industries Incorporated.
AMPEP, **III** 625
Ampex Corporation, **III** 549; **6** 272; **17 18–20**
Ampol Petroleum Ltd., **III** 729; **27** 473
Ampro, **25** 504–05
AMR Corporation, **I** 90–91; **6** 76; **8** 315; **22** 252; **26** 427–28; **28 22–26 (upd.)**; **29** 409
AMR Information Services, **9** 95
Amram's Distributing Limited, **12** 425
AMRE, **III** 211
AMREP Corporation, **I** 563; **21 35–37**; **24** 78
Amro. *See* Amsterdam-Rotterdam Bank N.V.
AMS Trading Co., **III** 112
Amsco International, **29** 450
AmSouth Bancorporation, **12 15–17**
Amstar Corp., **14** 18
Amstar Sugar Corporation, **II** 582; **7** 466–67; **26** 122
Amsted Industries Incorporated, **7 29–31**
Amstel Brewery, **I** 257
Amsterdam-Rotterdam Bank N.V., **II** 184, **185–86**, 279, 295, 319; **III** 200; **14** 169; **17** 324
Amstrad plc, **III 112–14**
AMT. *See* American Materials & Technologies Corporation.
Amtech. *See* American Building Maintenance Industries, Inc. *and* ABM Industries Incorporated.
Amtech Systems Corporation, **11** 65; **27** 405
Amtel, Inc., **8** 545; **10** 136
Amtliches Bayerisches Reisebüro, **II** 163
Amtorg, **13** 365
Amtrak, **II** 2; **10** 73; **19** 141; **26** 440. *See also* National Railroad Passenger Corporation.
AmTrans. *See* American Transport Lines.
Amvent Inc., **25** 120
Amway Corporation, **III 11–14**; **13 36–39 (upd.)**; **17** 186; **18** 67, 164; **20** 435; **23** 509; **29** 493; **30 62–66 (upd.)**; **31** 327
Amylum, **II** 582
ANA Enterprises, Ltd., **6** 70
Anacomp, Inc., **11** 19
Anaconda Aluminum, **11** 38
Anaconda Co., **III** 644; **IV** 33, 376; **7** 261–63
Anaconda-Jurden Associates, **8** 415
Anadarko Petroleum Corporation, **10 82–84**
Anadex, Inc., **18** 435–36
Anaheim Imaging, **19** 336

Analog Devices, Inc., **10 85–87**; **18** 20; **19** 67
Analogic Corporation, **23 13–16**
Analytic Sciences Corporation, **10 88–90**; **13** 417
Anam Group, **21** 239; **23 17–19**
Anamax Mining Co., **IV** 33
AnAmo Co., **IV** 458
Anarad, Inc., **18** 515
ANB Bank, **I** 55
Anchor Bancorp, Inc., **10 91–93**
Anchor Brake Shoe, **18** 5
Anchor Cable, **III** 433
Anchor Corporation, **12** 525
Anchor Gaming, **24 36–39**
Anchor Hocking Glassware, **I** 609–10; **13 40–42**; **14** 483; **26** 353
Anchor Motor Freight, Inc., **12** 309–10
Anchor National Financial Services, Inc., **11** 482
Anchor National Life Insurance Company, **11** 482
Anchor Oil and Gas Co., **IV** 521
Anchor Records, **II** 130
Ancienne Mutuelle, **III** 210
Anders Wilhelmsen & Co., **22** 471
Andersen Corporation, **9** 344; **10 94–95**; **11** 305; **22** 346
Andersen Worldwide, **29 25–28 (upd.)**
Anderson & Kerr Drilling Co., **IV** 445
Anderson and Campbell, **II** 479
Anderson Box Co., **IV** 342; **8** 267
Anderson Clayton & Co., **II** 560; **12** 411
Anderson, Greenwood & Co., **11** 225–26
Anderson Testing Company, Inc., **6** 441
The Andersons, Inc., **31 17–21**
Anderton, **III** 624
Andes Candies, **II** 520–21
Andian National Corp. Ltd., **IV** 415–16
André Courrèges, **III** 47; **8** 342–43
Andreas Christ, **26** 243
Andreas Stihl, **16 22–24**
Andrew Corporation, **10 96–98**
Andrew Jergens Co., **III** 38; **25** 56
Andrew Weir & Co., **III** 273
Andrews, Clark & Company, **IV** 426; **7** 169
Andrews Group, Inc., **10** 402
Andrews Office Supply and Equipment Co., **25** 500
Andritz AG, **27** 269
Anfor, **IV** 249–50
Angele Ghigi, **II** 475
Angelica Corporation, **15 20–22**
Angelo's Supermarkets, Inc., **II** 674
ANGI Ltd., **11** 28
Angle Steel, **25** 261
Anglo American Corporation of South Africa Limited, **I** 289, 423; **IV 20–23**, 56–57, 64–68, 79–80, 90, 92, 94–96, 118–20, 191, 239–40; **7** 121–23, 125; **16 25–30 (upd.)**, 292; **21** 211, 354; **22** 233; **28** 88, 93
Anglo American Paper Co., **IV** 286
Anglo Company, Ltd., **9** 363
Anglo Energy, Ltd., **9** 364
Anglo Mexican Petroleum Co. Ltd., **IV** 657
Anglo-American Chewing Gum Ltd., **II** 569
Anglo-American Clays Corp., **III** 691; **IV** 346
Anglo-American Oil Company Limited, **IV** 427; **7** 170
Anglo-American Telegraph Company Ltd., **IV** 668; **25** 98
Anglo-Belge, **II** 474
Anglo-Canadian, **III** 704
Anglo-Canadian Mining & Refining, **IV** 110
Anglo-Canadian Telephone Company of Montreal. *See* British Columbia Telephone Company.
Anglo-Celtic Watch Company, **25** 430
Anglo-Dutch Unilever group, **9** 317
Anglo-Egyptian D.C.O., **II** 236
Anglo-Egyptian Oilfields, **IV** 412, 414
Anglo-Elementar-Versicherungs-AG, **III** 185
Anglo-Huronian Ltd., **IV** 164
Anglo-Iranian Oil Co., **IV** 379, 419, 435, 450, 466, 559; **7** 57, 141; **21** 81
Anglo-Lautaro Nitrate Corporation, **9** 363
Anglo-Palestine Co., **II** 204
Anglo-Persian Oil Co., **IV** 363, 378–79, 381, 429, 450, 466, 515, 524, 531, 557–59; **7** 56–57, 140; **21** 80–81
Anglo-Swiss Condensed Milk Co., **II** 545
Anglo-Thai Corp., **III** 523
Anglo-Transvaal Consolidated, **IV** 534
Anglovaal Industries Ltd., **20** 263
Angus Hill Holdings, **IV** 249
Anheuser-Busch Company, Inc., **I** 32, **217–19**, 236–37, 254–55, 258, 265, 269–70, 290–91, 598; **IV** 624; **6** 20–21, 48; **9** 100; **10 99–101 (upd.)**, 130; **11** 421; **12** 337–38; **13** 5, 10, 258, 366; **15** 429; **17** 256; **18** 65, 70, 72–73, 499, 501; **19** 221, 223; **21** 229, 319–20; **22** 421; **23** 403; **25** 281–82, 368; **26** 432; **29** 84–85; **29** 218; **31** 381, 383
ANIC Gela, **IV** 421
Anikem, **I** 374
Anitec Image Technology Corp., **IV** 287; **15** 229
Ann Taylor Stores Corporation, **V** 26–27; **13 43–45**; **15** 9; **25** 120–22
Annabelle's, **II** 480–81; **26** 57
Anne Klein & Co., **15** 145–46; **24** 299
Anneplas, **25** 464
Annuaries Marcotte Ltd., **10** 461
Anocout Engineering Co., **23** 82
Anonima Infortunia, **III** 208
ANR Pipeline Co., **17 21–23**; **31** 119
Ansa Software, **9** 81
Ansaldo, **II** 191
Ansbacher-Siegle Corp., **13** 460
Anschütz & Co. GmbH, **III** 446
Anschutz Corp., **12 18–20**
Anschütz-Kaempfe, **III** 446
Ansell, **I** 215
Ansell Rubber Company, **10** 445
Anselmo L. Morvillo S.A., **19** 336
Ansett Airlines, **6** 73; **14** 11; **27** 475
Ansett Australia, **24** 398, 400; **26** 113
Ansett Transport Industries Limited, **V** 523–25; **27** 473
Ansonia Brass and Battery Co., **IV** 176–77
Ansonia Manufacturing Co., **IV** 176
Ant Nachrichtentechnik GmbH., **I** 411
Anta Corporation, **6** 188; **25** 308
Antar group, **IV** 544, 546
Antares Alliance Group, **14** 15
Antares Electronics, Inc., **10** 257
Ante Corp., **22** 222
ANTEX. *See* American National Life Insurance Company of Texas.
Anthem Electronics, Inc., **13 46–47**; **17** 276
Anthem P&C Holdings, **15** 257
Anthes Imperial Ltd., **I** 274; **26** 304
Anthes Industries Inc., **9** 512
Anthony Industries Inc. *See* K2 Inc.
Anthony Stumpf Publishing Company, **10** 460
Anthropologie, **14** 524–25
Antillaase Bank-Unie N.V., **II** 184
Antique Street Lamps, **19** 212
ANTK Tupolev. *See* Aviacionny Nauchno-Tehnicheskii Komplex im. A.N. Tupoleva.
Antoine Saladin, **III** 675
Antwerp Co., **IV** 497
ANZ. *See* Australia and New Zealand Banking Group Ltd.
ANZ Securities, **24** 400
Anzon Ltd., **III** 681
AOE Plastic GmbH, **7** 141
Aoki Corporation, **9** 547, 549; **29** 508
AOL. *See* America Online, Inc.
Aon Corporation, **III 203–05**; **22** 495
AP. *See* The Associated Press.
AP Bank, Ltd., **13** 439
AP Support Services, **25** 13
AP&L. *See* American Power & Light Co.
AP-Dow Jones/Telerate Company, **10** 277
APAC, Inc., **IV** 374
Apache Corp., **10 102–04**; **11** 28; **18** 366
Apache Energy Ltd., **25** 471
APACHE Medical Systems, Inc., **16** 94
Apartment Furniture Rental, **26** 102
Apex, **17** 363
Apex Financial Corp., **8** 10
Apex One Inc., **31** 137
Apex Smelting Co., **IV** 18
APH. *See* American Printing House for the Blind.
Apita, **V** 210
APL. *See* American President Companies Ltd.
APL Corporation, **9** 346
Aplex Industries, Inc., **26** 363
Apline Guild, **12** 173
Aplix, **19** 477
APM Ltd., **IV** 248–49
Apogee Enterprises, Inc., **8 34–36**; **22** 347
Apollo Advisors L.P., **16** 37; **26** 500, 502
Apollo Apparel Partners, L.P., **12** 431
Apollo Computer, **III** 143; **6** 238; **9** 471; **11** 284
Apollo Group, Inc., **24 40–42**
Apollo Heating & Air Conditioning Inc., **15** 411
Apollo Investment Fund, **31** 211
Apollo Ski Partners LP of New York, **11** 543, 545
Apollo Technologies, **I** 332
Apotekarnes Droghandel A.B., **I** 664–65
Apothekernes Laboratorium A.S., **12** 3–5
Appalachian Computer Services, **11** 112
Appalachian Travel Services, Inc., **25** 185, 187
Applause Inc., **17** 461; **24 43–46**
Apple Computer, Inc., **II** 6, 62, 103, 107, 124; **III** 114, **115–16**, 121, 125, 149, 172; **6 218–20 (upd.)**, 222, 225, 231, 244, 248, 254–58, 260, 289; **8** 138; **9** 166, 170–71, 368, 464; **10** 22–23, 34, 57, 233, 235, 404, 458–59, 518–19; **11** 45, 50, 57, 62, 490; **12** 139, 183, 335,

449, 455, 470; **13** 90, 388, 482; **16** 195, 367–68, 372, 417–18; **18** 93, 511, 521; **20** 31; **21** 391; **23** 209; **24** 370; **25** 299–300, 348, 530–31; **28** 244–45
Apple Container Corp., **III** 536; **26** 230
Apple South, Inc., **21** 362. *See also* Avado Brands, Inc.
Applebee's International Inc., 14 29–31; **19** 258; **20** 159; **21** 362; **31** 40
Appleton & Cox, **III** 242
Appleton Papers, **I** 426
Appleton Wire Works Corp., **8** 13
Appliance Buyers Credit Corp., **III** 653
Les Applications du Roulement, **III** 623
Applied Beverage Systems Ltd., **21** 339
Applied Bioscience International, Inc., 10 105–07
Applied Color Systems, **III** 424
Applied Communications, Inc., **6** 280; **11** 151; **25** 496; **29** 477–79
Applied Data Research, Inc., **6** 225; **18** 31–32
Applied Digital Data Systems Inc., **II** 83; **9** 514
Applied Engineering Services, Inc. *See* The AES Corporation.
Applied Films Laboratory Inc., **12** 121
Applied Industrial Materials Corporation, **22** 544, 547
Applied Komatsu Technology, Inc., **10** 109
Applied Laser Systems, **31** 124
Applied Learning International, **IV** 680
Applied Materials, Inc., 10 108–09; 18 382–84
Applied Network Technology, Inc., **25** 162
Applied Power, Inc., 9 26–28
Applied Programming Technologies, Inc., **12** 61
Applied Solar Energy, **8** 26
Applied Technology Corp., **11** 87
Applied Thermal Technologies, Inc., **29** 5
Approvisionnement Atlantique, **II** 652
Appryl, **I** 303
Aprilia SpA, 17 24–26
APS. *See* Arizona Public Service Company.
APS Healthcare, **17** 166, 168
Apura GmbH, **IV** 325
APUTCO, **6** 383
Aqua Glass, **III** 570; **20** 362
Aqua Pure Water Co., **III** 21
Aqua-Chem, Inc., **I** 234; **10** 227
Aquafin N.V., **12** 443
Aquarium Supply Co., **12** 230
Aquarius Group, **6** 207
Aquila, **IV** 486
Aquila Energy Corp., **6** 593
Aquitaine. *See* Société Nationale des Petroles d'Aquitaine.
AR Accessories Group, Inc., 23 20–22
AR-TIK Systems, Inc., **10** 372
ARA Services, II 607–08; **21** 507; **25** 181
Arab Contractors, **III** 753
Arab Japanese Insurance Co., **III** 296
Arab Petroleum Pipeline Co., **IV** 412
Arabian American Oil Co., **I** 570; **IV** 386, 429, 464–65, 512, 536–39, 552, 553, 559; **7** 172, 352; **14** 492–93. *See also* Saudi Arabian Oil Co.
Arabian Gulf Oil Co., **IV** 454
Arabian Investment Banking Corp., **15** 94; **26** 53
Arabian Oil Co., **IV** 451
Aral, **IV** 487
Aramark Corporation, 13 48–50; **16** 228; **21** 114–15
Aramco. *See* Arabian American Oil Co. *and* Saudi Arabian Oil Company.
Aramis Inc., **30** 191
Arapuã. *See* Lojas Arapuã S.A.
Aratex Inc., **13** 49
Aratsu Sekiyu, **IV** 554
ARBED S.A., IV 24–27, 53; **22 41–45 (upd.);** **26** 83
Arbitron Corp., **III** 128; **10** 255, 359; **13** 5
Arbor Acres, **13** 103
Arbor Drugs Inc., 12 21–23
Arbor International, **18** 542
Arbor Living Centers Inc., **6** 478
Arbuthnot & Co., **III** 522
Arby's Inc., II 614; **8** 536–37; **14 32–34,** 351
ARC. *See* American Rug Craftsmen.
ARC International Corporation, **27** 57
ARC Ltd., **III** 501
ARC Materials Corp., **III** 688
ARC Propulsion, **13** 462
Arcadia Company, **14** 138
Arcadia Group plc, 28 27–30 (upd.), 95–96
Arcadia Partners, **17** 321
Arcadian Corporation, **18** 433; **27** 317–18
Arcadian Marine Service, Inc., **6** 530
Arcadis NV, 26 21–24
Arcata Corporation, **12** 413
Arcata National Corp., **9** 305
Arcelik, **I** 478
Arch Mineral Corporation, IV 374; **7 32–34**
Archbold Ladder Co., **12** 433
Archer Drug, **III** 10
Archer Management Services Inc., **24** 360
Archer-Daniels-Midland Co., I 419–21; **IV** 373; **7** 432–33;, 241 **8** 53; **11 21–23 (upd.);** **17** 207; **22** 85, 426; **23** 384; **25** 241; **31** 234
Archers Gilles & Co., **II** 187
Archway Cookies, Inc., 29 29–31
ARCO. *See* Atlantic Richfield Company.
ARCO Chemical Company, IV 376–77, 456–57; **10 110–11**
ARCO Comfort Products Co., **26** 4
Arco Electronics, **9** 323
Arco Pharmaceuticals, Inc., **31** 346
Arco Societa Per L'Industria Elettrotecnica, **II** 82
Arcon Corporation, **26** 287
Arctco, Inc., 12 400–01; **16 31–34**
Arctic, **III** 479
Arctic Alaska Fisheries Corporation, **14** 515
ARD. *See* American Research & Development.
Ardal og Sunndal Verk AS, **10** 439
Arden Group, Inc., 29 32–35
Ardent Computer Corp., **III** 553
Ardent Risk Services, Inc. *See* General Re Corporation.
Areal Technologies, **III** 715
Argbeit-Gemeinschaft Lurgi und Ruhrchemie, **IV** 534
Argentine National Bank, **14** 46
Argo Communications Corporation, **6** 300
Argon Medical, **12** 327
Argonaut, **I** 523–24; **10** 520–22
Argos, **I** 426; **22** 72
Argosy Gaming Company, 21 38–41
Argosy Group LP, **27** 197
Argus Chemical Co., **I** 405
Argus Corp., **IV** 22, 272, 611
Argus Energy, **7** 538
Argus Motor Company, **16** 7
Argyle Television Inc., **19** 204
Argyll Group PLC, I 241; **II 609–10,** 656; **12** 152–53; **24** 418
Aria Communications, Inc. *See* Ascend Communications, Inc.
Ariel Capital Management, **28** 421
Aries Technology, **25** 305
Aris Industries, Inc., 15 275; **16 35–38**
Aristech Chemical Corp., **12** 342
Arizona Airways, **22** 219
Arizona Copper Co., **IV** 177
Arizona Edison Co., **6** 545
Arizona Growth Capital, Inc., **18** 513
AriZona Iced Tea. *See* Ferolito, Vultaggio & Sons.
Arizona One, **24** 455
Arizona Public Service Company, **6** 545–47; **19** 376, 412; **26** 359; **28** 425–26
Arizona Refrigeration Supplies, **14** 297–98
Arjo Wiggins Appleton, **13** 458; **27** 513
Ark Restaurants Corp., 20 25–27
Ark Securities Co., **II** 233
Arkady Co., Ltd., **I** 421; **11** 23
Arkansas Best Corporation, 16 39–41; **19** 455
Arkansas Breeders, **II** 585
Arkansas Chemicals Inc., **I** 341
Arkansas Louisiana Gas Company. *See* Arkla, Inc.
Arkansas Power & Light, **V** 618
Arkay Computer, **6** 224
ARKE, **II** 164
Arkia, **23** 184, 186–87
Arkla, Inc., V 550–51; **11** 441
Arlesey Lime and Portland Cement Co., **III** 669
Arlington Corporation, **6** 295
Arlington Motor Holdings, **II** 587
Arlington Securities plc, **24** 84, 87–89
Arlon, Inc., **28** 42, 45
Armaturindistri, **III** 569
Armco Inc., III 259, 721; **IV 28–30,** 125, 171; **10** 448; **11** 5, 255; **12** 353; **19** 8; **26** 407; **30** 282–83
Armin Corp., **III** 645
Armin Poly Film Corp., **III** 645
Armitage Shanks, **III** 671
Armor All Products Corp., 12 333; **15** 507; **16 42–44;** **22** 148; **26** 349
Armor Elevator, **11** 5
Armor Holdings, Inc., 27 49–51
Armour & Company, **8** 144; **12** 198; **13** 21, 506; **23** 173
Armour Food Co., **I** 449–50, 452; **II** 494, 518; **12** 81, 370; **13** 270
Armour Pharmaceutical Co., **III** 56
Armour-Dial, **I** 14; **8** 144; **23** 173–74
Armstrong Advertising Co., **I** 36
Armstrong Air Conditioning Inc. *See* Lennox International Inc.
Armstrong Autoparts, **III** 495
Armstrong Communications, **IV** 640
Armstrong Cork Co., **18** 118
Armstrong Nurseries, **I** 272
Armstrong Rees Ederer Inc., **IV** 290
Armstrong Tire Co., **15** 355
Armstrong, Whitworth & Co. Ltd., **I** 50; **III** 508; **IV** 257; **24** 85

Armstrong World Industries, Inc., III 422–24; **9** 466; **12** 474–75; **22 46–50 (upd.)**, 170–71; **26** 507
Armstrong-Siddeley Co., **III** 508
Armtek, **7** 297
Army Cooperative Fire Insurance Company, **10** 541
Army Ordnance, **19** 430
Army Signal Corps Laboratories, **10** 96
Arndale, **IV** 696
Arno Press, **IV** 648; **19** 285
Arnold Communications, **25** 381
Arnold Electric Company, **17** 213
Arnold Foods Co., **II** 498
Arnold, Schwinn & Company. *See* Schwinn Cycle and Fitness L.P.
Arnold Thomas Co., **9** 411
Arnoldo Mondadori Editore S.p.A., IV 585–88, 675; **19 17–21 (upd.)**
Arnotts Ltd., **II** 481; **26** 57–59
Aro Corp., **III** 527; **14** 477, 508; **15** 225
Aromat Corporation, **III** 710; **7** 303
Aromatic Industries, **18** 69
Arpet Petroleum, **III** 740; **IV** 550
Arpic, **III** 426
Arrosto Coffee Company, **25** 263
Arrow Electronics, Inc., 10 112–14; **13** 47; **19** 310–11, 313; **29** 414; **30** 175
Arrow Food Distributor, **II** 675
Arrow Furniture Co., **21** 32
Arrow Oil Co., **IV** 401
Arrow Oil Tools, **III** 570; **20** 360
Arrow Pump Co., **I** 185
Arrow Shirt Co., **24** 384
Arrow Specialty Company, **III** 570; **20** 360
Arrowhead Mills Inc., **27** 197–98
Arrowsmith & Silver, **I** 428
Arsam Investment Co., **26** 261
A.B. Arsenalen, **II** 352
The Art Institute of Chicago, 29 36–38
Art Van Furniture, Inc., 28 31–33
Artec, **III** 420; **12** 297
Artech Digital Entertainments, Inc., **15** 133
Artek Systems Corporation, **13** 194
Artémis Group, **27** 513
Artesian Manufacturing and Bottling Company, **9** 177
Artex Enterprises, **7** 256; **25** 167, 253
Arthur Andersen & Company, Société Coopérative, III 143; **6** 244; **10 115–17**, 174; **16** 92; **25** 358; **29** 392. *See also* Andersen Worldwide.
Arthur D. Little, **IV** 494; **10** 139, 174–75
Arthur Ovens Motor Freight Co., **6** 371
Arthur Rank Organisation, **25** 328
Arthur Tappan & Co., **IV** 604
Arthur Young & Company, **IV** 119; **10** 386; **19** 311. *See also* Ernst & Young.
Artisan Life Insurance Cooperative, **24** 104
Artisoft, Inc., **18** 143
Artists & Writers Press, Inc., **13** 560
ArtMold Products Corporation, **26** 342
Arts & Entertainment Network, **IV** 627; **19** 204
Arvey Corp., **IV** 287
Arvida Corp., **IV** 703
Arvin Industries, Inc., 8 37–40
ASAB, **III** 480
Asahi Breweries, Ltd., I 220–21, 282, 520; **13** 454; **20 28–30 (upd.)**; **21** 230, 319–20; **26** 456
Asahi Chemical Industry Co., **I** 221; **III** 760; **IV** 326
Asahi Corporation, **16** 84
Asahi Glass Company, Limited, I 363; **III 666–68**; **11** 234–35
Asahi Kasei Industry Co. Ltd., **IV** 476
Asahi Komag Co., Ltd., **11** 234
Asahi Kyoei Co., **I** 221
Asahi Manufacturing, **III** 592
Asahi Milk Products, **II** 538
Asahi National Broadcasting Company, Ltd., 9 29–31
Asahi Oil, **IV** 542
Asahi Real Estate Facilities Co., Ltd., **6** 427
Asahi Seiko, **III** 595
Asahi Shimbun, **9** 29–30
Asahi Trust & Banking, **II** 323
Asano Group, **III** 718
Asanté Technologies, Inc., 20 31–33
ASARCO Incorporated, I 142; **IV 31–34**
ASB Agency, Inc., **10** 92
Asbury Associates Inc., **22** 354–55
Asbury Group, **26** 501
ASCAP. *See* The American Society of Composers, Authors and Publishers.
Ascend Communications, Inc., 24 47–51
Aschaffenburger Zellstoffwerke AG, **IV** 323–24
ASCO Healthcare, Inc., **18** 195–97
Asco Products, Inc., **22** 413
Ascom AG, 9 32–34; **15** 125
Ascometal, **IV** 227
Ascotts, **19** 122
ASD, **IV** 228
ASDA Group plc, II 611–12, 513, 629; **11** 240; **28 34–36 (upd.)**
ASEA AB. *See* ABB ASEA Brown Boveri Ltd.
Asean Bintulu Fertilizer, **IV** 518
Asepak Corp., **16** 339
A.B. Asesores Bursatiles, **III** 197–98; **15** 18
ASF. *See* American Steel Foundries.
Asgrow Florida Company, **13** 503
Asgrow Seed Co., **29** 435
Ash Company, **10** 271
Ash Resources Ltd., **31** 398–99
Ashbourne PLC, **25** 455
Ashitaka Rinsan Kogyo, **IV** 269
Ashland Inc., 19 22–25; **27** 316, 318
Ashland Iron and Mining Co., **IV** 28
Ashland Oil, Inc., I 420; **IV** 71, 198, 366, **372–74**, 472, 658; **7** 32–33; **8** 99; **9** 108; **11** 22; **18** 279
Ashton Joint Venture, **IV** 60, 67
Ashton Mining, **IV** 60
Ashton-Tate Corporation, **9** 81–82; **10** 504–05
Ashworth, Inc., 26 25–28
Asia Life Insurance Co., **III** 195–96
Asia Oil Co., Ltd., **IV** 404, 476
Asia Television, **IV** 718
Asia Terminals Ltd., **IV** 718
Asian Football Confederation, **27** 150
Asiana, **24** 400
Asiatic Petroleum Co., **IV** 434, 530
ASICS Corp., **24** 404
Asil çelik, **I** 479
ASK Group, Inc., 9 35–37; **25** 34
Ask Mr. Foster Agency, **22** 127; **26** 308
Asland SA, **III** 705, 740
Aso Cement, **III** 705
Aspect Telecommunications Corporation, 16 392–93; **22 51–53**
Aspen Imaging International, Inc., **17** 384
Aspen Mountain Gas Co., **6** 568
Aspen Skiing Company, II 170; **15 23–26**, 234
Aspen Systems, **14** 555
Asplundh Tree Expert Co., 20 34–36
Assam Co. Ltd., **III** 522–23
Assam Oil Co., **IV** 441, 483–84
Asset Management Company, **25** 86
Asset Marketing Inc. *See* Commercial Financial Services, Inc.
L'Assicuratrice Italiana, **III** 346–47
Assicurazioni Generali SpA, II 192; **III 206–09**, 211, 296, 298; **14** 85; **15 27–31 (upd.)**
Associate Venture Investors, **16** 418
Associated Anglo-Atlantic Corp., **III** 670
Associated Aviation Underwriters, **III** 220
Associated Banks of Europe Corp., **II** 184, 239
Associated Biscuit Co., **II** 631
Associated Book Publishers, **8** 527
Associated Bowater Industries, **IV** 258
Associated Brewing Co., **I** 254
Associated British Foods PLC, II 465–66, 565, 609; **11** 526; **13 51–53 (upd.)**; **24** 475
Associated British Maltsters, **II** 500
Associated British Picture Corporation, **I** 531; **II** 157; **22** 193
Associated City Investment Trust, **IV** 696
Associated Communications Companies, **7** 78; **23** 479
Associated Container Transportation, **23** 161
Associated Cooperative Investment Trust Ltd., **IV** 696
Associated Dairies Ltd., **II** 611
Associated Dry Goods Corp., **V** 134; **12** 54–55; **24** 298
Associated Electrical Industries, Ltd., **II** 25; **III** 502
Associated Employers General Agency, **III** 248
Associated Estates Realty Corporation, 25 23–25
Associated Fire Marine Insurance Co., **26** 486
Associated Food Holdings Ltd., **II** 628
Associated Fresh Foods, **II** 611–12
Associated Fuel Pump Systems Corp., **III** 593
Associated Gas & Electric Company, **V** 621, 629–30; **6** 534; **14** 124
Associated Gas Services, Inc., **11** 28
Associated Grocers, Incorporated, 9 38–40; **19** 301; **31 22–26 (upd.)**
Associated Grocers of Arizona, **II** 625
Associated Grocers of Colorado, **II** 670
The Associated Group, **10** 45
Associated Hospital Service of New York, **III** 245–46
Associated Iliffe Press, **IV** 666; **17** 397
Associated Indemnity Co., **III** 251
Associated Inns and Restaurants Company of America, **14** 106; **25** 309; **26** 459
Associated Insurance Cos., **III** 194
Associated International Insurance Co. *See* Gryphon Holdings, Inc.
Associated Lead Manufacturers Ltd., **III** 679, 680–81
Associated London Properties, **IV** 705
Associated Madison Insurance, **I** 614
Associated Merchandisers, Inc., **27** 246
Associated Merchandising Corp., **16** 215

Associated Milk Producers, Inc., 11 24–26
Associated National Insurance of Australia, **III** 309
Associated Natural Gas Corporation, 11 27–28
Associated Newspapers, **IV** 686; **19** 118, 120
Associated Octel Company Limited, **10** 290
Associated Oil Co., **IV** 460
Associated Pipeline Contractors, **III** 559
Associated Piping & Engineering Corp., **III** 535
Associated Portland Cement Manufacturers (1900) Ltd., **III** 669–71
The Associated Press, IV 629, 669–70; **7** 158; **10** 277; **13 54–56**; **25** 506; **31 27–30 (upd.)**
Associated Publishing Company, **19** 201
Associated Pulp & Paper Mills, **IV** 328
Associated Sales Agency, **16** 389
Associated Spring Co., **III** 581; **13** 73
Associated Stationers, **14** 521, 523
Associated Television, **7** 78
Associated Timber Exporters of British Columbia Ltd., **IV** 307
Associated TV, **IV** 666; **17** 397
Associates First Capital Corporation, **22** 207
Associates Investment Co., **I** 452
Assubel, **III** 273
Assurances du Groupe de Paris, **III** 211
Assurances Generales de France, **III** 351; **27** 513
AST Holding Corp., **III** 663, 665
AST Research, Inc., 9 41–43; **10** 459, 518–19; **12** 470; **18** 260
Asta Pharma AG, **IV** 71
Asta Werke AG, **IV** 71
Astech, **18** 370
Asteroid, **IV** 97
Astley & Pearce, **10** 277
Aston Brooke Software, **14** 392
Astor Holdings Inc., **22** 32
Astor Trust Co., **II** 229
Astra AB, I 625–26, 635, 651; **11** 290; **20 37–40 (upd.)**
Astra Resources, **12** 543
Astrolac, **IV** 498
Astrotech, **11** 429
Astrum International Corp., **12** 88; **13** 453; **16** 20–21
Asylum Life Assurance Co., **III** 371
Asylum Records, **23** 33; **26** 150
Asymetrix, **6** 259
AT&E Corp., **17** 430
AT&T Bell Laboratories, Inc., 13 57–59; **22** 17
AT&T Corp., I 462; **II** 13, 54, 61, 66, 80, 88, 120, 125, 252, 403, 430–31, 448; **III** 99, 110–11, 130, 145, 149, 160, 162, 167, 246, 282; **IV** 95, 287; **V 259–64**, 265–68, 269, 272–75, 302–04, 308–12, 318–19, 326–30, 334–36, 339, 341–342, 344–346; **6** 267, 299, 306–07, 326–27, 338–40; **7** 88, 118–19, 146, 288–89, 333; **8** 310–11; **9** 32, 43, 106–07, 138, 320, 321, 344, 478–80, 495, 514; **10** 19, 58, 87, 97, 175, 202–03, 277–78, 286, 431, 433, 455–57; **11** 10, 59, 91, 183, 185, 196, 198, 302, 395, 500–01; **12** 9, 135–36, 162, 544; **13** 212–13, 326, 402, 448; **14** 15, 95, 251–53, 257–61, 318, 336–37, 345, 347, 354, 363–64; **15** 125–26, 228, 455; **16** 223, 318, 368, 467; **18** 30, 32, 74, 76, 111–12, 155, 164–65, 368, 516–18, 569–70; **19** 12, 41; **20** 34, 313; **21** 70, 200–01, 514; **22** 51; **23** 135; **25** 100, 256, 301, 495–99; **26** 187, 225, 431, 520; **27** 363; **28** 242; **29** 59, **39–45 (upd.)**; **30** 99, 339
AT&T Istel Ltd., 14 35–36
Ataka & Co., **I** 433; **II** 361
Atari Corporation, II 176; **III** 587; **IV** 676; **6** 244; **7** 395–96; **9 44–47**; **10** 284, 482, 485; **13** 472; **23 23–26 (upd.)**; **28** 319
ATAS International, **26** 527, 530
ATC, **III** 760; **13** 280
Atchison Castings Corp., **24** 144
Atchison, Topeka and Santa Fe Railroad, **V** 507–08; **12** 19–20; **27** 86
ATCO Ltd., **13** 132
ATD Group, **10** 113
ATE Investment, **6** 449
Atelier de Construction Electrique de Delle, **9** 9
ATEQ Corp., **III** 533
Atex, **III** 476; **7** 162; **10** 34
ATH AG, **IV** 221
Atha Tool Co., **III** 627
Athalon Products, Ltd., **10** 181; **12** 313
Athena Assurances, **27** 513, 515
Athenia Steel Co., **13** 369
Athens National Bank, **III** 190
Athens Piraeus Electricity Co., **IV** 658
Athern, **16** 337
Athlete's Foot, **29** 186
Athletic Attic, **19** 230
Athletic Shoe Company, **17** 243
Athletic Textile Company, Inc., **13** 532
Athletic X-Press, **14** 293
Athol Machine Co., **13** 301
ATI, **IV** 651; **7** 390
Atlalait, **19** 50
Atlanta Gas Light Company, 6 446–48; **23 27–30 (upd.)**
Atlanta National Bank, **16** 521
Atlanta Paper Co., **IV** 311; **19** 267
Atlantic & Pacific Tea Company (A&P). *See* Great Atlantic & Pacific Tea Company, Inc.
Atlantic Acceptance Corporation, **7** 95
Atlantic Aircraft Corp., **I** 34; **17** 197
Atlantic American Corp., **23** 413
Atlantic Auto Finance Corp. *See* United Auto Group, Inc.
Atlantic Cement Co., **III** 671
Atlantic Coast Carton Company, **19** 77
Atlantic Coast Line Railroad Company. *See* CSX Corporation.
Atlantic Computers, **14** 35
Atlantic Container Lines Ltd., **23** 161
Atlantic Energy, Inc., 6 449–50
The Atlantic Group, 23 31–33
Atlantic Gulf and Caribbean Airways, **I** 115
Atlantic Import, **I** 285
Atlantic Mills, **27** 188
Atlantic Precision Instrument Company, **13** 234
Atlantic Precision Works, **9** 72
Atlantic Records, **II** 176; **18** 458; **26** 150
Atlantic Refining Co., **III** 497; **III** 498; **IV** 375–76, 456, 504, 566, 570; **24** 520–21
Atlantic Research Corp., **13** 462
Atlantic Richfield Company, I 452; **II** 90, 425; **III** 740; **IV 375–77**, 379, 435, 454, 456–57, 467, 494, 522, 536, 571; **7** 57, 108, 537–38, 558–59; **8** 184, 416; **10** 110; **13** 13, 341; **19** 175; **24** 521, 524; **26** 4, 372; **31 31–34 (upd.)**
Atlantic Sea Products, **13** 103
The Atlantic Seaboard Dispatch. *See* GATX.
Atlantic Securities Ltd., **II** 223; **III** 98
Atlantic Southeast, **26** 439
Atlantic Southern Properties, Inc., **6** 449–50
Atlantic Surety Co., **III** 396
Atlantic Transport Company, **19** 198
Atlantic Wholesalers, **II** 631
Atlantic-Union Oil, **IV** 570; **24** 520
Atlantis Group, Inc., **17** 16; **19** 50, 390
Atlantis Ltd., **II** 566
Atlantis Resort and Casino. *See* Sun International Hotels Limited.
Atlas Assurance Co., **III** 370
Atlas Cement Company, **31** 252
Atlas Chemical Industries, **I** 353
Atlas Copco AB, III 425–27, 480; **IV** 203; **28 37–41 (upd.)**
Atlas Corp., **I** 58, 512; **10** 316
Atlas Eléctrica S.A., **22** 27
Atlas Hotels, Inc., **V** 164
Atlas Petroleum Ltd., **IV** 449
Atlas Plastics, **19** 414
Atlas Powder Company, **I** 343–44; **22** 260
Atlas Shipping, **I** 285
Atlas Steel Works, **I** 572
Atlas Steels, **IV** 191
Atlas Supply Co., **IV** 369
Atlas Tag & Label, **9** 72
Atlas Van Lines, Inc., 14 37–39
Atlas Ventures, **25** 96
Atlas Works, **I** 531
Atlas-Werke AG, **IV** 88
Atle Byrnestad, **6** 368; **27** 92
Atmel Corporation, 17 32–34; **19** 313
Atmos Lebensmitteltechnik, **III** 420
Atmospherix Ltd. *See* Blyth Industries, Inc.
ATO Chimie, **I** 303; **IV** 560
Atochem S.A., I 303–04, 676; **IV** 525, 547; **7** 484–85
AtoHaas Americas, **26** 425
Atom-Energi, **II** 2; **22** 9
ATR, **7** 9, 11
ATS. *See* Magasins Armand Thiéry et Sigrand.
ATT Microelectrica España, **V** 339
Attachmate Corp., **11** 520
Atvidabergs Industrier, **25** 463
Atwater McMillian. *See* St. Paul Companies, Inc.
Atwood Resources Inc., **17** 372
ATx Telecom Systems Inc., **31** 124
Au Bon Marché, **26** 160
Au Bon Pain Co., Inc., 18 35–38
Au Printemps S.A., V 9–11; **17** 124. *See also* Pinault-Printemps-Redoute S.A.
Aubrey G. Lanston Co., **II** 301
Auchan, **10** 205; **23** 230; **27** 94
Audi, **I** 202; **IV** 570
Audio Development Company, **10** 18
Audio King Corporation, 24 52–54
Audio/Video Affiliates, Inc., **10** 468–69
Audiotronic Holdings, **III** 112
Audits & Surveys Worldwide Inc., **28** 501, 504
Aufina Bank, **II** 378

Aug. Stenman A.B., **III** 493
Aughton Group, **II** 466
Augsburger Aktienbank, **III** 377
Auguri Mondadori S.p.A., **IV** 586
August Max Woman, **V** 207–08
August Schell's Brewing Co., **22** 421
August Thyssen-Hütte AG, **IV** 221–22
Auguste Metz et Cie, **IV** 24
Aunor Gold Mines, Ltd., **IV** 164
Aunt Fanny's Bakery, **7** 429
Aurora Foods, **26** 384
Aurora Products, **II** 543
Aurora Systems, Inc., **21** 135
Ausilio Generale di Sicurezza, **III** 206
Ausimont N.V., **8** 271
Ausplay, **13** 319
AUSSAT Ltd., **6** 341
Aussedat-Rey, **IV** 288; **23** 366, 368
The Austin Company, 8 41–44
Austin Industries, **25** 402
Austin Motor Company, **I** 183; **III** 554; **7** 458
Austin Nichols, **I** 248, 261, 280–81
Austin Rover, **14** 321
Austin-Morris, **III** 494
Austral Waste Products, **IV** 248
Australasian Paper and Pulp Co. Ltd., **IV** 248
Australasian Sugar Co., **III** 686
Australasian United Steam Navigation Co., **III** 522
Australia and New Zealand Banking Group Ltd., II 187–90
Australia Gilt Co. Group, **II** 422
Australia National Bank, Limited, **10** 170
Australian Airlines, **6** 91, 112; **24** 399–400; **27** 475
Australian and Kandos Cement (Holdings) Ltd., **III** 687, 728; **28** 83
Australian and Overseas Telecommunications Corporation, **6** 341–42
Australian Associated Press, **IV** 669
Australian Automotive Air, Pty. Ltd., **III** 593
Australian Blue Asbestos, **III** 687
Australian Consolidated Investments, Limited, **10** 170
Australian Consolidated Press, **27** 42
Australian Forest Products, **I** 438–39
Australian Guarantee Corp. Ltd., **II** 389–90
Australian Gypsum Industries, **III** 673
Australian Iron & Steel Company, **IV** 45; **22** 105
Australian Metal Co., **IV** 139
Australian Mutual Provident Society, **IV** 61, 697
Australian Paper Co., **IV** 248
Australian Petroleum Pty. Ltd., **25** 471
Australian Tankerships Pty. Ltd., **25** 471
Australian Telecommunications Corporation, **6** 342
Australian United Corp., **II** 389
Australian Window Glass, **III** 726
Austrian Airlines, **27** 26
Austrian Industries, **IV** 485, 486
Austrian National Bank, **IV** 230
Austro-Americana, **6** 425
Austro-Daimler, **I** 138, 206; **11** 31
Authentic Fitness Corp., 16 511; **20 41–43**
Auto Avio Costruzione, **13** 219
Auto Coil Springs, **III** 581
Auto Ordnance Corporation, **19** 430–31
Auto Parts Wholesale, **26** 348
Auto Shack. *See* AutoZone, Inc.
Auto Strop Safety Razor Co., **III** 27–28
Auto Union, **I** 150
Auto Value Associates, Inc., 25 26–28
Auto-Flo Corp., **III** 569; **20** 360
Auto-Trol Technology, **14** 15
Autodesk, Inc., 10 118–20
Autogrill, **24** 195
Autolite, **I** 29, 142; **III** 555
Autologic Information International, Inc., 20 44–46; **26** 518–20
Automat, **II** 614
Automated Building Components, **III** 735
Automated Communications, Inc., **8** 311
Automated Design Systems, **25** 348
Automated Loss Prevention Systems, **11** 445
Automated Security (Holdings) PLC, **11** 444
Automated Wagering Systems, **III** 128
Automatic Data Processing, Inc., III 117–19; **9 48–51 (upd.)**, 125, 173; **21** 69
Automatic Fire Alarm Co., **III** 644
Automatic Manufacturing Corporation, **10** 319
Automatic Payrolls, Inc., **III** 117
Automatic Retailers of America, Inc., **II** 607; **13** 48
Automatic Sprinkler Corp. of America. *See* Figgie International, Inc.
Automatic Telephone & Electric, **II** 81
Automatic Toll Systems, **19** 111
Automatic Vaudeville Arcades Co., **II** 154
Automobile Insurance Co., **III** 181–82
Automobiles Citroen, I 162, 188; **III** 676; **IV** 722; **V** 237; **7 35–38**; **11** 103; **16** 121, 420
Automobili Lamborghini S.p.A., 13 60–62, 219
Automotive Components Group Worldwide, **10** 325
Automotive Diagnostics, **10** 492
Automotive Group. *See* Lear Seating Corporation.
Automotive Industries Holding Inc., **16** 323
AutoNation USA. *See* Republic Industries, Inc.
Autonet, **6** 435
Autophon AG, **9** 32
Autotote Corporation, 20 47–49
AutoTrol Technology, **III** 111
AUTOWORKS Holdings, Inc., **24** 205
AutoZone, Inc., 9 52–54; **26** 348; **31 35–38 (upd.)**
Avado Brands, Inc., 31 39–42
Avana Group, **II** 565
Avantel, **27** 304
Avco. *See* Aviation Corp. of the Americas.
Avco Financial Services Inc., 13 63–65
Avco National Bank, **II** 420
Avecor Cardiovascular Inc., **8** 347; **22** 360
Aveda Corporation, 24 55–57
Avendt Group, Inc., **IV** 137
Avenir, **III** 393
Avenor Inc., **25** 13
Avery Dennison Corporation, IV 251–54; **15** 229, 401; **17 27–31 (upd.)**, 445
Avesta Steel Works Co., **I** 553–54
Avfuel, **11** 538
Avgain Marine A/S, **7** 40
Avia Group International, Inc., **V** 376–77; **26** 397–99
Aviacion y Comercio, **6** 95–96
Aviacionny Nauchno-Tehnicheskii Komplex im. A.N. Tupoleva, 24 58–60
AVIACO. *See* Aviacion y Comercio.
Aviation Corp. of the Americas, **I** 48, 78, 89, 115, 530; **III** 66; **6** 75; **9** 497–99; **10** 163; **11** 261, 427; **12** 379, 383; **13** 64
Aviation Inventory Management Co., **28** 5
Aviation Power Supply, **II** 16
Aviation Services West, Inc. *See* Scenic Airlines, Inc.
Avion Coach Corporation, **I** 76; **III** 484; **11** 363; **22** 206
Avions Marcel Dassault-Breguet Aviation, I 44–46; **7** 11; **7** 205; **8** 314. *See also* Groupe Dassault Aviation SA.
Avis, Inc., I 30, 446, 463; **II** 468; **III** 502; **IV** 370; **6** 348–49, **356–58**, 392–93; **8** 33; **9** 284; **10** 419; **11** 198; **16** 379–80; **22** 524
Avis Rent A Car, Inc., 22 54–57 (upd.); **24** 9; **25** 93, 143, 420–22
Avisco, **I** 317, 365, 442–43; **V** 359; **17** 117
Avisun Corp., **IV** 371
Avnet Electronics Supply Co., **19** 311, 313
Avnet Inc., 9 55–57; **10** 112–13; **13** 47
Avon Products, Inc., III 13, **15–16**, 62; **8** 329; **9** 331; **11** 282, 366; **12** 314, 435; **13** 38; **14** 501–02; **17** 186; **19 26–29 (upd.)**, 253; **21** 49, 51; **25** 292; 456; **27** 429; **30** 64, 308–09
Avon Publications, Inc., **IV** 627; **19** 201, 204
Avon Rubber plc, **23** 146
Avoncraft Construction Co., **I** 512
Avondale Industries, Inc., I 512–14; **7 39–41**
Avondale Mills, Inc., **8** 558–60; **9** 466
Avondown Properties Ltd., **IV** 711
Avro. *See* A.V. Roe & Company.
AVS, **III** 200
Avtex Fibers Inc., **I** 443; **11** 134
AVX Corporation, **21** 329, 331
AWA Defence Industries (AWADI). *See* British Aerospace Defence Industries.
Award Foods, **II** 528
Awesome Transportation, Inc., **22** 549
AXA Colonia Konzern AG, III 209, **210–12**; **15** 30; **21** 147: **27 52–55**
Axel Johnson Group, I 553–55
Axel Springer Verlag AG, IV 589–91; **20 50–53 (upd.)**; **23** 86
Axelrod Foods, **II** 528
Axon Systems Inc., **7** 336
Ayco Corp., **II** 398; **10** 62
Aydin Corp., 19 30–32
Ayerst, **I** 623
Ayr-Way Stores, **27** 452
AYS. *See* Alternative Youth Services, Inc.
Ayshire Collieries, **IV** 18
Azcon Corporation, 23 34–36
Azerty, **25** 13
Azienda Generale Italiana Petroli. *See* Agip SpA.
Azienda Nazionale Idrogenazione Combustibili, **IV** 419–22
AZL Resources, **7** 538
Aznar International, **14** 225
Azon Limited, **22** 282
AZP Group Inc., **6** 546
Aztar Corporation, 13 66–68

Azteca, **18** 211, 213
Azuma Leather Co. Ltd., **V** 380
Azuma Shiki Manufacturing, **IV** 326
Azusa Valley Savings Bank, **II** 382

B & K Steel Fabrications, Inc., **26** 432
B & O. *See* Baltimore and Ohio Railroad.
B&Q plc, **V** 106, 108; **24** 266, 269–70
B&S. *See* Binney & Smith Inc.
B&W Diesel, **III** 513
B.A.T. Industries PLC, 14 77; **16** 242; **22 70–73 (upd.); 25** 154–56; **29** 196
B. B. & R. Knight Brothers, **8** 200; **25** 164
B.B. Foods, **13** 244
B-Bar-B Corp., **16** 340
B.C. Rail Telecommunications, **6** 311
B.C. Sugar, **II** 664
B.C. Ziegler and Co. *See* The Ziegler Companies, Inc.
B. Dalton Bookseller Inc., 10 136; **13** 545; **16** 160; **18** 136; **25 29–31; 30** 68
B-E Holdings, **17** 60
B/E Aerospace, Inc., 30 72–74
B.F. Ehlers, **I** 417; **24** 32
B.F. Goodrich Co. *See* The BFGoodrich Company.
B.F. Walker, Inc., **11** 354
B.I.C. America, **17** 15, 17
B.J.'s Wholesale, **12** 335
The B. Manischewitz Company, LLC, 31 43–46
B. Perini & Sons, Inc., **8** 418
B.R. Simmons, **III** 527
B.S. Bull & Company. *See* Supervalu Inc.
B. Stroh Brewing Co., **I** 290
B.T.I. Chemicals Ltd., **I** 313; **10** 154
B Ticino, **21** 350
B.V. Tabak Export & Import Compagnie, **12** 109
BA. *See* British Airways.
BAA plc, 10 121–23; 29 509, 511
Bålforsens Kraft AB, **28** 444
Baan Company, 25 32–34; 26 496, 498
Babbage's, Inc., 10 124–25
Babcock & Wilcox Co., **III** 465–66, 516, 559–60; **V** 621; **23** 199
Baby Furniture and Toy Supermarket, **V** 203
Baby Superstore, Inc., 15 32–34
Babybird Co., Ltd., **V** 150
Babyliss, S.A., **17** 110
BAC. *See* Barclays American Corp. *and* British Aircraft Corporation.
Bacardi Limited, 18 39–42
Baccarat, 23 241; **24 61–63; 27** 421, 423
Bache & Company, **III** 340; **8** 349
Bachman Foods, **15** 139
Bachman Holdings, Inc., **14** 165
Bachman's Inc., 22 58–60; 24 513
Bachrach Advertising, **6** 40
Back Bay Restaurant Group, Inc., 20 54–56
Backer & Spielvogel, **I** 33; **12** 168; **14** 48–49; **22** 296
Backroom Systems Group, **II** 317
Bacon & Matheson Drop Forge Co., **I** 185
Bacova Guild, Ltd., **17** 76
Bad Boy Entertainment, **31** 269
Baddour, Inc. *See* Fred's, Inc.
Badger Co., **II** 86
Badger Illuminating Company, **6** 601
Badger Meter, Inc., 22 61–65
Badger Paint and Hardware Stores, **II** 419
Badger Paper Mills, Inc., 15 35–37
Badin-Defforey, **27** 93
Badische Analin & Soda Fabrik A.G., **I** 305
BAe. *See* British Aerospace plc.
BAFS. *See* Bangkok Aviation Fuel Services Ltd.
Bahia de San Francisco Television, **IV** 621
Bailey, Banks & Biddle, **16** 559
Bailey Controls, **III** 560
Bain & Co., **III** 429; **9** 343; **21** 143
Bain Capital, Inc., **14** 244–45; **16** 466; **20** 18; **24** 456, 482; **25** 254; **26** 184
Baird, **7** 235, 237
Bairnco Corporation, 28 42–45
BÅKAB. *See* Bålforsens Kraft AB.
Bakelite Corp., **I** 399; **9** 517; **13** 231
Baker and Botts, L.L.P., 28 46–49
Baker & Co., **IV** 78
Baker & Crane, **II** 318; **17** 323
Baker & McKenzie, 10 126–28
Baker & Taylor, Inc., I 548; **16 45–47**
Baker Casing Shoe Co., **III** 429
Baker Cummins Pharmaceuticals Inc., **11** 208
Baker Extract Co., **27** 299
Baker Hughes Incorporated, III 428–29; 11 513; **22 66–69 (upd.); 25** 74
Baker Industries, Inc., **III** 440; **8** 476; **13** 124
Baker International Corp., **III** 428–29
Baker Oil Tools. *See* Baker Hughes Incorporated.
Baker-Raulang Co., **13** 385
Bakers Best Snack Food Corporation, **24** 241
Bakers Square. *See* VICORP Restaurants, Inc.
Bakersfield Savings and Loan, **10** 339
Bakery Products Inc., **IV** 410
Balair Ltd., **I** 122
Balco, Inc., **7** 479–80; **27** 415
Balcor Co., **II** 398; **IV** 703
Balcor, Inc., **10** 62
Baldor Electric Company, 21 42–44
Baldwin Filters, Inc., **17** 104
Baldwin Hardware Manufacturing Co., **III** 570; **20** 361
Baldwin Piano & Organ Company, 16 201; **18 43–46**
Baldwin Rubber Industries, **13** 79
Baldwin Technology Company, Inc., 25 35–39
Baldwin-Ehret-Hill Inc., **28** 42
Baldwin-Montrose Chemical Co., Inc., **31** 110
Baldwin-United Corp., **III** 254, 293
Baldwins Ltd., **III** 494
Bålforsens Kraft AB, **IV** 339–40; **28** 444
Balfour Beatty Construction Ltd., **III** 433–34; **13** 206
Balfour Company, L.G., **19** 451–52
Balikpapan Forest Industries, **I** 504
Ball & Young Adhesives, **9** 92
Ball Corporation, I 597–98; 10 129–31 (upd.); 13 254, 256; **15** 129; **16** 123; **30** 38
The Ball Ground Reps, Inc., **26** 257
Ball Industries, Inc., **26** 539
Ball Stalker Inc., **14** 4
Ball-Bartoe Aircraft Corp., **I** 598; **10** 130
Ballantine & Sons Ltd., **I** 263
Ballantine Beer, **6** 27
Ballantine Books, **13** 429; **31** 376–77, 379
Ballantyne of Omaha, Inc., 27 56–58
Ballard & Ballard Co., **II** 555
Ballard Medical Products, 21 45–48
Ballast Nedam Group, **24** 87–88
Balli Group plc, **26** 527, 530
Bally Entertainment Corp., **19** 205, 207
Bally Gaming International, **15** 539
Bally Manufacturing Corporation, III 430–32; 6 210; **10** 375, 482; **12** 107; **15** 538–39; **17** 316–17, 443
Bally Total Fitness Holding Corp., 25 40–42
AB Baltic, **III** 418–19
Baltic Cable, **15** 521
Baltica, **27** 54
Baltimar Overseas Limited, **25** 469
Baltimore & Ohio Railroad, **I** 584; **II** 329. *See also* CSX Corporation.
Baltimore Aircoil Company, **7** 30–31
Baltimore Gas and Electric Company, V 552–54; 11 388; **25 43–46 (upd.)**
Baltimore Paper Box Company, **8** 102
Baltino Foods, **13** 383
Balzaretti-Modigliani, **III** 676; **16** 121
Bamberger's of New Jersey, **V** 169; **8** 443
Banamex, **22** 285; **23** 170. *See also* Banco Nacional de Mexico.
Banana Boat Holding Corp., **15** 359
Banana Brothers, **31** 229
Banana Republic Inc., V 61–62; **18** 193–94; **25 47–49; 31** 51–52
Banc One Corporation, 9 475; **10 132–34; 11** 181
Banca Brasiliana Italo-Belga, **II** 270
Banca Coloniale di Credito, **II** 271
Banca Commerciale Italiana SpA, I 368, 465, 467; **II 191–93**, 242, 271, 278, 295, 319; **III** 207–08, 347; **17** 324
BancA Corp., **11** 305
Banca d'America e d'Italia, **II** 280
Banca Dalmata di Sconto, **II** 271
Banca de Gottardo, **II** 361
Banca di Genova, **II** 270
Banca Internazionale Lombarda, **II** 192
Banca Italiana di Sconto, **II** 191
Banca Italo-Cinese, **II** 270
Banca Italo-Viennese, **II** 270
Banca Jacquet e Hijos, **II** 196
Banca Luis Roy Sobrino, **II** 196
Banca Nazionale de Lavoro, **II** 239
Banca Nazionale dell'Agricoltura, **II** 272
Banca Nazionale di Credito, **II** 271
Banca Serfin. *See* Grupo Financiero Serfin, S.A.
Banca Unione di Credito, **II** 270
Bancard Systems, **24** 395
BancFinancial Services Corporation, **25** 187
BancItaly Corp., **II** 226–27, 288, 536; **13** 528
BancMortgage Financial Corp., **25** 185, 187
Banco Aleman-Panameno, **II** 521
Banco Aliança S.A., **19** 34
Banco Azteca, **19** 189
Banco Bilbao Vizcaya, S.A., II 194–96
Banco Bradesco S.A., 13 69–71; 19 33
Banco Capitalizador de Monterrey, **19** 189
Banco Central, II 197–98; III 394; **IV** 397
Banco Central de Crédito. *See* Banco Itaú.
Banco Chemical (Portugal) S.A. *See* Chemical Banking Corp.
Banco Comercial, **19** 188
Banco da América, **19** 34

Banco de Londres, Mexico y Sudamerica. *See* Grupo Financiero Serfin, S.A.
Banco de Mexico, **19** 189
Banco del Norte, **19** 189
Banco di Roma, **I** 465, 467; **II** 191, 257, 271
Banco di Santo Spirito, **I** 467
Banco do Brasil S.A., II 199–200
Banco Español de Credito, **II** 195, 198; **IV** 160
Banco Espírito Santo e Comercial de Lisboa S.A., 15 38–40
Banco Federal de Crédito. *See* Banco Itaú.
Banco Frances y Brasiliero, **19** 34
Banco Industrial de Bilbao, **II** 195
Banco Industrial de Monterrey, **19** 189
Banco Italo-Belga, **II** 270, 271
Banco Italo-Egiziano, **II** 271
Banco Itaú S.A., 19 33–35
Banco Nacional de Cuba, **II** 345
Banco Nacional de Mexico, **9** 333; **19** 188, 193
Banco Pinto de Mahalhãhes, **19** 34
Banco Popolar, **III** 348; **6** 97
Banco Português do Brasil S.A., **19** 34
Banco Santander, **III** 271, 294; **15** 257
Banco Sul Americano S.A., **19** 34
Banco Trento & Bolanzo, **II** 240
Banco União Comercial, **19** 34
Banco Vascongado, **II** 196
BancOhio National Bank in Columbus, **9** 475
Bancomer, **19** 12
Bancorp Leasing, Inc., **14** 529
BancorpSouth, Inc., **14** 40–41
Bancroft Racket Co., **III** 24
BancSystems Association Inc., **9** 475, 476
Bandag, Inc., 19 36–38, 454–56
Bandai America Inc., **23** 388; **25** 488
Banesto. *See* Banco Español de Credito.
Banexi, **II** 233
Bangkok Airport Hotel, **6** 123–24
Bangkok Aviation Fuel Services Ltd., **6** 123–24
Bangladesh Krishi Bank, **31** 220
Bangor and Aroostook Railroad Company, **8** 33
Bangor Mills, **13** 169
Bangor Punta Alegre Sugar Corp., **30** 425
Bangor Punta Corp., **I** 452, 482; **II** 403
Banister Continental Corp. *See* BFC Construction Corporation.
Bank Austria AG, 23 37–39
Bank Brussels Lambert, II 201–03, 295, 407
Bank Bumiputra, **IV** 519
Bank Central Asia, **18** 181
Bank CIC-Union Européenne A.G., **II** 272
Bank du Louvre, **27** 423
Bank Européene de Credità Moyen Terme, **II** 319; **17** 324
Bank for International Settlements, **II** 368
Bank für Elektrische Unternehmungen. *See* Elektrowatt AG.
Bank für Gemeinwirtschaft, **II** 239
Bank Hapoalim B.M., II 204–06; **25** 266, 268
Bank Hofmann, **21** 146–47
Bank Leu, **I** 252; **21** 146–47
Bank Leumi Le-Israel, **25** 268
Bank of Adelaide, **II** 189
Bank of America, **I** 536–37; **II** 226–28, 252–55, 280, 288–89, 347, 382; **III** 218; **6** 385; **8** 94–95; **9** 50, 123–24, 333, 536; **12** 106, 466; **13** 69; **14** 170; **18** 516; **22** 542; **25** 432; **26** 486. *See also* BankAmerica Corporation.
Bank of America National Trust and Savings Assoc. (NT & SA), **I** 536; **II** 227, 288; **13** 528. *See also* BankAmerica Corporation.
Bank of Antwerp, **IV** 497
Bank of Asheville, **II** 336
Bank of Australasia, **II** 187–89
The Bank of Bishop and Co., Ltd., **11** 114
Bank of Boston Corporation, II 207–09; **7** 114; **12** 31; **13** 467; **14** 90
Bank of Brandywine Valley, **25** 542
Bank of Britain, **14** 46–47
Bank of British Columbia, **II** 244, 298
Bank of British Honduras, **II** 344
Bank of British North America, **II** 220
Bank of California, **II** 322, 490. *See also* Union Bank of California.
Bank of Canada, **II** 210, 376
Bank of Central and South America, **II** 344
Bank of Chicago, **III** 270
Bank of China, **II** 298
Bank of Chosen, **II** 338
Bank of Commerce, **II** 331
Bank of Delaware, **25** 542
Bank of England, **II** 217, 235–36, 306–07, 318–19, 333–34, 357, 421–22, 427–28; **III** 234, 280; **IV** 119, 366, 382, 705, 711; **10** 8, 336; **14** 45–46; **17** 324–25
Bank of Finland, **III** 648
Bank of France, **II** 232, 264–65, 354; **III** 391
Bank of Hamilton, **II** 244
Bank of Hindustan, **IV** 699
Bank of Ireland, **16** 13–14; **19** 198
Bank of Israel, **II** 206
Bank of Italy, **I** 536; **II** 192, 226, 271–72, 288; **III** 209, 347; **8** 45
The Bank of Jacksonville, **9** 58
Bank of Japan, **I** 519; **II** 291, 325
Bank of Kobe, **II** 371
Bank of Lee County, **14** 40
Bank of Liverpool, **II** 236
Bank of London and South America, **II** 308
Bank of Manhattan Co., **II** 247–48
Bank of Mexico Ltd., **19** 188
The Bank of Milwaukee, **14** 529
Bank of Mississippi, Inc., 14 40–41
Bank of Montreal, II 210–12, 231, 375; **26** 304
Bank of Nettleton, **14** 40
Bank of New Brunswick, **II** 221
Bank of New England Corporation, II 213–15; **9** 229
Bank of New Orleans, **11** 106
Bank of New Queensland, **II** 188
Bank of New South Wales, **II** 188–89, 388–90
Bank of New York Company, Inc., II 192, **216–19**, 247
Bank of North Mississippi, **14** 41
Bank of Nova Scotia, II 220–23, 345; **IV** 644
Bank of Oklahoma, **22** 4
Bank of Ontario, **II** 210
Bank of Osaka, **II** 360
Bank of Ottawa, **II** 221
Bank of Pasadena, **II** 382
Bank of Queensland, **II** 188
The Bank of Scotland. *See* The Governor and Company of the Bank of Scotland.
Bank of Sherman, **14** 40
Bank of Spain, **II** 194, 197
Bank of the Ohio Valley, **13** 221
Bank of the People, **II** 210
Bank of the United States, **II** 207, 216, 247
Bank of the West, **II** 233
Bank of Tokyo, Ltd., II 224–25, 276, 301, 341, 358; **IV** 151; **12** 138; **16** 496, 498; **24** 358
Bank of Tokyo-Mitsubishi Ltd., 15 41–43 (upd.), 431; **26** 454, 457
Bank of Toronto, **II** 375–76
Bank of Tupelo, **14** 40
Bank of Upper Canada, **II** 210
Bank of Wales, **10** 336, 338
Bank of Western Australia, **II** 187
Bank of Winterthur, **II** 378
Bank Powszechny Depozytowy, **IV** 119
Bank voor Handel en Nijverheid, **II** 304
Bank-R Systems Inc., **18** 517
BankAmerica Corporation, II 226–28, 436; **8 45–48 (upd.)**, 295, 469, 471; **13** 69; **17** 546; **18** 518; **25** 187; **26** 65. *See also* Bank of America *and* Bank of America National Trust and Savings Assoc.
BankCard America, Inc., **24** 394
Bankers and Shippers Insurance Co., **III** 389
Bankers Co., **II** 230
Bankers Corporation, **14** 473
Bankers Investment, **II** 349
Bankers Life and Casualty Co., **10** 247; **16** 207
Bankers Life Co., **III** 328–30
Bankers National Bank, **II** 261
Bankers National Life Insurance Co., **II** 182; **10** 246
Bankers Trust New York Corporation, I 601; **II** 211, **229–31**, 330, 339; **III** 84–86; **10** 425; **11** 416; **12** 165, 209; **13** 188, 466; **17** 559; **19** 34; **22** 102; **25** 268; 317
Bankhaus IG Herstatt, **II** 242
BankVermont Corp., **II** 208
Banner Aerospace, Inc., 14 42–44
Banner Industries, **21** 431
Banner International, **13** 20
Banner Life Insurance Company, **III** 273; **24** 284
Banque Belge et Internationale en Egypte, **II** 295
Banque Belge pour l'Etranger, **II** 294
Banque Belgo-Zairoise, **II** 294
Banque Bruxelles Lambert. *See* Bank Brussels Lambert.
Banque Commerciale du Maroc, **II** 272
Banque Commerciale-Basle, **II** 270
Banque d'Anvers/Bank van Antwerpen, **II** 294–95
Banque de Bruxelles, **II** 201–02, 239
Banque de Credit et de Depot des Pays Bas, **II** 259
Banque de France, **14** 45–46
Banque de l'Indochine et de Suez, **II** 259
Banque de l'Union Européenne, **II** 94
Banque de l'Union Parisienne, **II** 270; **IV** 497, 557
Banque de la Construction et les Travaux Public, **II** 319; **17** 324
Banque de la Société Générale de Belgique, **II** 294–95
Banque de Louvain, **II** 202

Banque de Paris et des Pays-Bas, **II** 136, 259; **10** 346; **19** 188–89
Banque de Reports et de Depots, **II** 201
Banque du Congo Belge, **II** 294
Banque Européenne pour l'Amerique Latine, **II** 294
Banque Française et Espagnol en Paris, **II** 196
Banque Francaise pour le Commerce et l'Industrie, **II** 232, 270
Banque Génerale des Pays Roumains, **II** 270
Banque Générale du Luxembourg, **II** 294
Banque Indosuez, **II** 429
Banque Internationale à Luxembourg, **II** 239
Banque Internationale de Bruxelles, **II** 201–02
Banque Italo-Belge, **II** 294
Banque Italo-Francaise de Credit, **II** 271
Banque Lambert, **II** 201–02
Banque Nationale de Paris S.A., II 232–34, 239; **III** 201, 392–94; **9** 148; **13** 203; **15** 309; **19** 51
Banque Nationale Pour le Commerce et l'Industrie, **II** 232–33
Banque Nordique du Commerce, **II** 366
Banque Orea, **II** 378
Banque Paribas, **II** 192, 260; **IV** 295; **19** 225
Banque Rothschild, **IV** 107
Banque Sino-Belge, **II** 294
Banque Stern, **II** 369
La Banque Suisse et Française. *See* Crédit Commercial de France.
Banque Transatlantique, **II** 271
Banque Worms, **III** 393; **27** 514
Banquet Foods Corp., **II** 90, 494; **12** 81
Banta Corporation, 12 24–26; **19** 333
Bantam Ball Bearing Company, **13** 522
Bantam Books, Inc., **III** 190–91
Bantam Doubleday Dell Publishing Group, **IV** 594; **13** 429; **15** 51; **27** 222; **31** 375–76, 378
Banyan Systems Inc., 25 50–52
Banyu Pharmaceutical Co., **I** 651; **11** 290
Baoshan Iron and Steel, **19** 220
BAP of New York, Inc., **15** 246
BAPCO, **III** 745
Bar Technologies, Inc., **26** 408
Barat. *See* Barclays PLC.
Barber Dental Supply Inc., **19** 291
Barber-Greene, **21** 502
Barberet & Blanc, **I** 677
Barcel, **19** 192
Barclay Furniture Co., **12** 300
Barclay Group, **I** 335; **10** 290
Barclays Business Credit, **13** 468
Barclays PLC, I 604–05; **II** 202, 204, **235–37**, 239, 244, 308, 319, 333, 383, 422, 429; **III** 516; **IV** 23, 722; **7** 332–33; **8** 118; **11** 29–30; **17** 324–25; **20 57–60 (upd.)**; **25** 101; **28** 167
BarclaysAmerican Mortgage Corporation, 11 29–30
Barco Manufacturing Co., **16** 8; **26** 541
Barcolo Manufacturing, **15** 103; **26** 100
Barden Cablevision, **IV** 640; **26** 273
Bareco Products, **15** 352
Barefoot Inc., **23** 428, 431
Bari Shoes, Inc., **22** 213
Barilla G. e R. Fratelli S.p.A., 17 35–37
Barings PLC, III 699; **14 45–47**
Barker & Dobson, **II** 629
Barker and Company, Ltd., **13** 286
Barlow Rand Ltd., I 288–89, **422–24**; **IV** 22, 96
Barlow Specialty Advertising, Inc., **26** 341
Barmer Bankverein, **II** 238, 241
Barnato Brothers, **IV** 21, 65; **7** 122
Barnes & Noble, Inc., 10 135–37; **12** 172; **13** 494, 545; **14** 61–62; **15** 62; **16** 160; **17** 524; **23** 370; **25** 17, 29–30; **30 67–71 (upd.)**
Barnes Group, **III** 581
Barnes-Hind, **III** 56, 727
Barnett Banks, Inc., 9 58–60
Barnett Brass & Copper Inc., **9** 543
Barnett Inc., 28 50–52
Barnetts, Hoares, Hanbury and Lloyds, **II** 306
Barney's, Inc., 27 330; **28 53–55**
Barnstead/Thermolyne Corporation, **14** 479–80
Baroid, **19** 467–68
Barr & Stroud Ltd., **III** 727
Barr Laboratories, Inc., 26 29–31
Barranquilla Investments, **II** 138; **24** 193
Barratt Developments plc, I 556–57
Barret Fitch North, **II** 445; **22** 405
Barrett Burston, **I** 437
Barrett Business Services, Inc., 16 48–50
The Barrett Co., **I** 414–15; **18** 116; **22** 29
Barricini Foods Inc., **27** 197
Barris Industries, Inc., **23** 225
Barry & Co., **III** 522
Barry Callebaut AG, 29 46–48
Barry Wright Corporation, **9** 27
Barry's Jewelers. *See* Samuels Jewelers Incorporated.
Barsab Investment Trust. *See* South African Breweries Ltd.
Barsotti's, Inc., **6** 146
Bart Starr, **12** 284
Barth Smelting Corp., **I** 513
Barton & Ludwig, Inc., **21** 96
Barton Beers, Ltd., **29** 219
Barton Brands, **I** 227; **II** 609; **10** 181
Barton, Duer & Koch, **IV** 282; **9** 261
Barton Incorporated, **13** 134; **24** 140
Bartow Food Company, **25** 332
Barwig Medizinische Systeme. *See* OEC Medical Systems, Inc.
BASF Aktiengesellschaft, I 275, **305–08**, 309, 319, 346–47, 632, 638; **II** 554; **IV** 70–71; **13** 75; **14** 308; **16** 462; **18 47–51 (upd.)**, 186, 234; **21** 544; **24** 75; **26** 305, 368; **27** 22; **28** 194
Basic American Retirement Communities, **III** 103
Basic Resources, Inc., **V** 725
Basics, **14** 295
BASIS Information Technologies, Inc., **11** 112–13, 132
Baskin-Robbins Ice Cream Co., **I** 215; **7** 128, 372; **17** 474–75; **25** 366; **29** 18
Basle A.G., **I** 632–33, 671–72; **8** 108–09
Basle Air Transport, **I** 121
Basler Bankverein, **II** 368
Bass & Co., **I** 142
Bass Brewers Ltd., **15** 441; **29** 85
Bass Brothers Enterprises Inc., **28** 107
Bass Charington, **29** 84
Bass PLC, I 222–24; **III** 94–95; **9** 99, 425–26; **15 44–47 (upd.)**; **16** 263; **23** 482; **24** 194
Bassett Boat Company, **30** 303
Bassett Foods, **II** 478
Bassett Furniture Industries, Inc., 18 52–55; **19** 275
Bassett-Walker Inc., **V** 390–91; **17** 512
Bassins Food Chain, **II** 649
BAT. *See* British-American Tobacco Co., Ltd.
BAT Industries plc, I 425–27, 605; **II** 628; **III** 66, 185, 522; **9** 312; **23** 427; **30** 273
Bataafsche Petroleum Maatschappij, **V** 658
Batavia Wine Company, **13** 134
Batchelors Ltd., **I** 315; **25** 81
Bateaux Parisiens, **29** 442
Bateman Eichler Hill Richards, **III** 270
Bates, **16** 545
Bates & Robins, **II** 318; **17** 323
Bates Chemical Company, **9** 154
Bates Manufacturing Company, **10** 314
Bates Worldwide, Inc., 14 48–51; **26** 500
Batesville Casket Company, **10** 349–50
Bath & Body Works, **11** 41; **24** 237
Bath Industries Inc., **18** 117–18
Bath Iron Works Corporation, 12 27–29
Bathurst Bank, **II** 187
Baton Rouge Gas Light Company. *See* Gulf States Utilities Company.
Battelle Laboratories, **25** 260
Battelle Memorial Institute, Inc., 6 288; **10 138–40**
Batten Barton Durstine & Osborn, **I** 25, 28–31, 33; **16** 70
Battle Creek Food Company, **14** 557–58
Battle Creek Toasted Corn Flake Co., **II** 523; **13** 291
Battle Mountain Gold Company, IV 490; **23 40–42**
Battlefield Equipment Rentals, **21** 499, 501
BATUS Inc., **9** 312; **18** 136; **30** 273
Bauborg, **I** 560–61
Baudhuin-Anderson Company, **8** 553
Bauer Audio Visual, Inc., **24** 96
Bauer Publishing Group, 7 42–43; **20** 53
Baume & Mercier, **27** 487, 489
Bausch & Lomb Inc., III 446; **7 44–47**; **10** 46–47; **13** 365–66; **25** 22, **53–57 (upd.)**, 183; **30** 30
Bavarian Brewing Limited, **25** 280
Bavarian Railway, **II** 241
Bavarian Specialty Foods, **13** 383
Baxter Estates, **II** 649
Baxter International Inc., I 627–29; **9** 346; **10 141–43 (upd.)**, 198–99; **11** 459–60; **12** 325; **18** 469; **22** 361; **25** 82; **26** 433
Baxter Travenol, **21** 119; **24** 75
The Bay, **16** 216
Bay Area Review Course, Inc., **IV** 623
Bay Cities Transportation Company, **6** 382
Bay City, **21** 502
Bay City Cash Way Company, **V** 222; **25** 534
Bay Colony Life Insurance Co., **III** 254
Bay Harbour Management L.C., **28** 55
Bay Networks, **20** 33, 69; **26** 276
Bay Petroleum, **I** 526
Bay Ridge Savings Bank, **10** 91
Bay Shipbuilding Corporation, **18** 320
Bay State Glass Co., **III** 683
Bay State Iron Manufacturing Co., **13** 16
Bay State Tap and Die Company, **13** 7
Bay West Paper Corporation. *See* Mosinee Paper Corporation.
BayBanks, Inc., 12 30–32

Bayer A.G., **I** 305–06, **309–11**, 319, 346–47, 350; **II** 279; **12** 364; **13 75–77 (upd.)**; **14** 169; **16** 439; **18** 47, 49, 51, 234; **21** 544; **22** 225
Bayer S.p.A., **8** 179
Bayerische Aluminium AG, **IV** 230
Bayerische Hypotheken- und Wechsel-Bank AG, **II 238–40**, 241–42; **IV** 323
Bayerische Kraftwerke AG, **IV** 229–30
Bayerische Landesbank, **II** 257–58, 280; **14** 170
Bayerische Motoren Werke A.G., **I** 73, 75, **138–40**, 198; **II** 5; **III** 543, 556, 591; **11 31–33 (upd.)**; **13** 30; **17** 25; **21** 441; **27** 20, 203
Bayerische Rückversicherung AG, **III** 377
Bayerische Rumpler Werke, **I** 73
Bayerische Stickstoff-Werke AG, **IV** 229–30
Bayerische Vereinsbank A.G., **II** 239–40, **241–43**; **III** 401
Bayerische Versicherungsbank, **II** 238; **III** 377
Bayerische Wagnisbeteiligung GmbH, **27** 192
Bayerische Wasserkraftwerke Aktiengesellschaft, **IV** 231
Bayerische Zellstoff, **IV** 325
Bayernwerk AG, **IV** 231–32, 323; **V 555–58**, 698–700; **23 43–47 (upd.)**
Bayliner Marine Corporation, **22** 116
Bayou Boeuf Fabricators, **III** 559
Bayou Steel Corporation, **IV** 234; **31 47–49**
Bayside National Bank, **II** 230
Baystate Corporation, **12** 30
Baytree Investors Inc., **15** 87
Bayview, **III** 673
Bazaar & Novelty. *See* Stuart Entertainment Inc.
Bazar de l'Hotel de Ville, **19** 308
BBC. *See* British Broadcasting Corp.
BBC Brown, Boveri Ltd. *See* ABB ASEA Brown Boveri Ltd.
BBDO. *See* Batten Barton Durstine & Osborn.
BBDO Worldwide Network, **22** 394
BBME. *See* British Bank of the Middle East.
BBN Corp., **19 39–42**
BBO & Co., **14** 433
BC Development, **16** 481
BC TEL. *See* British Columbia Telephone Company.
BCal. *See* British Caledonian Airways.
BCC, **24** 266, 270
BCE, Inc., **V 269–71**; **6** 307; **7** 333; **12** 413; **18** 32
BCI. *See* Banca Commerciale Italiana SpA.
BCP Corporation, **16** 228–29
BCPA. *See* British Commonwealth Pacific Airways.
BDB. *See* British Digital Broadcasting plc.
BDB Corp., **10** 136
BDDP. *See* Wells Rich Greene BDDP.
Beach Patrol Inc., **29** 181
BeachviLime Ltd., **IV** 74; **24** 143, 144
Beacon Communications Group, **23** 135
Beacon Manufacturing Company, **I** 377; **19** 304–05
Beacon Oil, **IV** 566
Beacon Participations, **III** 98
Beacon Publishing Co., **IV** 629
Beall-Ladymon, Inc., **24** 458
Bealls, **24** 456
Beamach Group Ltd., **17** 182–83
Beaman Corporation, **16** 96; **25** 390
Bean Fiberglass Inc., **15** 247
Bear Automotive Service Equipment Company, **10** 494
Bear Creek Corporation, **12** 444–45
Bear Stearns Companies, Inc., **II 400–01**, 450; **10 144–45 (upd.)**, 382; **20** 313; **24** 272
Beard & Stone Electric Co., **I** 451
Bearings, Inc., **I** 158–59; **13 78–80**
Beasley Industries, Inc., **19** 125–26
Beatrice Company, **I** 353; 440–41; **II 467–69**, 475; **III** 118, 437; **6** 357; **9** 318; **12** 82, 87, 93; **13** 162–63, 452; **14** 149–50; **15** 213–14, 358; **16** 160, 396; **19** 290; **24** 273; **26** 476, 494; **28** 475. *See also* TLC Beatrice International Holdings, Inc.
Beatrice Foods, **21** 322–24, 507, 545; **25** 277–78
Beauharnois Power Company, **6** 502
Beaulieu of America, **19** 276
Beaulieu Winery, **I** 260
Beaumont-Bennett Group, **6** 27
Beauté Prestige International S.A. *See* Shiseido Company Limited.
BeautiControl Cosmetics, Inc., **21 49–52**
Beauty Biz Inc., **18** 230
Beaver Lumber Company Limited, **I** 274; **26** 303, 305–06
Beazer Homes USA, Inc., **17 38–41**
Beazer Plc., **7** 209
bebe stores, inc., **31 50–52**
BEC Group Inc., **22** 35
Bechtel Group, Inc., **I 558–59**, 563; **III** 248; **IV** 171, 576; **6** 148–49, 556; **13** 13; **24 64–67 (upd.)**; **25** 402; **26** 220
Beck & Gregg Hardware Co., **9** 253
Becker Drill, Inc., **19** 247
Becker Group of Germany, **26** 231
Becker Paribas Futures, **II** 445; **22** 406
Becker Warburg Paribas, **II** 259
Beckett Papers, **23 48–50**
Beckley-Cardy Co., **IV** 623–24
Beckman Coulter, Inc., **22 74–77**
Beckman Instruments, Inc., **I** 694; **14 52–54**; **16** 94
Becton, Dickinson & Company, **I 630–31**; **IV** 550; **9** 96; **11 34–36 (upd.)**; **25** 82
Bed Bath & Beyond Inc., **13 81–83**; **14** 61; **18** 239; **24** 292
Bedcovers, Inc., **19** 304
Beddor Companies, **12** 25
Bedford Chemical, **8** 177
Bedford-Stuyvesant Restoration Corp., **II** 673
Bee Chemicals, **I** 372
Bee Discount, **26** 476
Bee Gee Shoe Corporation, **10** 281
Bee Gee Shrimp, **I** 473
Beech Aircraft Corporation, **II** 87; **8 49–52**, 313; **11** 411, 413; **27** 98
Beech Holdings Corp., **9** 94
Beech-Nut Nutrition Corporation, **I** 695; **II** 489; **21 53–56**
Beecham Group PLC, **I** 626, 640, 668; **II** 331, 543; **III** 18, 65–66; **9** 264; **14** 53; **16** 438
Beechwood Insurance Agency, Inc., **14** 472
Beeck-Feinkost GmbH, **26** 59
Beerman Stores, Inc., **10** 281
Beghin Say S.A., **II** 540
Behr-Manning Company, **8** 396
Behringwerke AG, **14** 255
Beiersdorf AG, **29 49–53**
Beijerinvest Group, **I** 210
Beijing Contact Lens Ltd., **25** 56
Beijing Dentsu, **16** 168
Beijing Liyuan Co., **22** 487
Beijing Machinery and Equipment Corp., **II** 442
Beijing Yanshan Petrochemical Company, **22** 263
Beirao, Pinto, Silva and Co. *See* Banco Espírito Santo e Comercial de Lisboa S.A.
Bejam Group PLC, **II** 678
Beker Industries, **IV** 84
Bekins Company, **15 48–50**; **26** 197
Bel. *See* Fromageries Bel.
Bel, **25** 83–84
Bel Air Markets, **14** 397
Belairbus, **I** 42; **12** 191
Belcher New England, Inc., **IV** 394
Belcher Oil Co., **IV** 394
Belco, **23** 219
Belden Inc., **II** 16; **19 43–45**
Beldis, **23** 219
Beldoch Industries Corp., **17** 137–38
Belfast Banking Co., **II** 318; **17** 323
Belgacom, **6 302–04**
Belgian De Vaderlandsche, **III** 309
Belgian Rapid Access to Information Network Services, **6** 304
Belgian Société Internationale Forestière et Minière, **IV** 65
Belglas, **16** 420
Belgo Group plc, **31** 41
Belgochim, **IV** 499
Belize Sugar Industries, **II** 582
Belk Stores Services, Inc., **V 12–13**; **19 46–48 (upd.)**
Bell (Quarry and Concrete), **III** 674
Bell Aerospace, **I** 530; **24** 442
Bell Aircraft Company, **I** 529; **11** 267; **13** 267
Bell and Howell Company, **I** 463; **IV** 642; **9** 33, **61–64**; **11** 197; **14** 569; **15** 71; **29 54–58 (upd.)**, 159
Bell Atlantic Corporation, **V 272–74**; **9** 171; **10** 232, 456; **11** 59, 87, 274; **12** 137; **13** 399; **18** 33; **25 58–62 (upd.)**, 91, 497; **27** 22, 365
Bell Canada Enterprises Inc. *See* BCE, Inc.
Bell Canada International, Inc., **V** 269, 308–09; **6 305–08**; **12** 413; **21** 308; **25** 102
Bell Communications Research, **13** 58; **25** 496
Bell Fibre Products, **12** 377
Bell Helmets Inc., **22** 458
Bell Industries, **13** 47; **18** 498; **19** 311
Bell Laboratories, **II** 33, 60–61, 101, 112; **V** 259–64; **8** 157; **9** 171; **10** 108; **11** 327, 500–01; **12** 61; **14** 52, 281–82; **23** 181; **29** 41, 44. *See also* AT&T Bell Labroatories, Inc.
Bell Mountain Partnership, Ltd., **15** 26
Bell Pharmacal Labs, **12** 387
Bell Resources, **I** 437–38; **III** 729; **10** 170; **27** 473
Bell Sports Corporation, **16 51–53**
Bell System, **II** 72, 230; **6** 338–40; **7** 99, 333; **11** 500; **16** 392–93

Bell Telephone Company, **I** 409; **6** 332, 334
Bell Telephone Company of Pennsylvania, **I** 585
Bell Telephone Manufacturing, **II** 13
Bell's Asbestos and Engineering, **I** 428
Bell-Northern Research, Ltd., **V** 269–71; **15** 131
Bellcore. *See* Bell Communications Research.
Belle Alkali Co., **IV** 409; **7** 308
Belledune Fertilizer Ltd., **IV** 165
Bellefonte Insurance Co., **IV** 29
Bellemead Development Corp., **III** 220; **14** 108
Bellofram Corp., **14** 43
BellSouth Corporation, **V 276–78**; **9** 171, 321; **10** 431, 501; **15** 197; **18** 23, 74, 76; **19** 254–55; **22** 19; **27** 20; **29 59–62 (upd.)**
Belmin Systems, **14** 36
Belmont Electronics, **II** 85–86; **11** 412
Belmont Plaza, **12** 316
Belmont Savings and Loan, **10** 339
Belmont Springs Water Company, Inc., **I** 234; **10** 227
Belo Corporation. *See* A.H. Belo Corporation
Beloit Corporation, **8** 243; **14 55–57**
Beloit Tool Company. *See* Regal-Beloit Corporation.
Beloit Woodlands, **10** 380
Belridge Oil Co., **IV** 541
Belzer Group, **IV** 198–99
Bemis Company, Inc., **8 53–55**; **26** 43
Bemrose group, **IV** 650
Ben & Jerry's Homemade, Inc., **10 146–48**; **17** 139–41
Ben Franklin Retail Stores, Inc. *See* FoxMeyer Health Corporation.
Ben Franklin Savings & Trust, **10** 117
Ben Hill Griffin, **III** 53
Ben Johnson & Co. Ltd., **IV** 661
Ben Line, **6** 398
Ben Myerson Candy Co., Inc., **26** 468
Ben Venue Laboratories, **16** 439
Bendicks, **I** 592
Bendix Corporation, **I** 68, **141–43**, 154, 166, 192, 416; **II** 33; **III** 166, 555; **7** 356; **8** 545; **9** 16–17; **10** 260, 279; **11** 138; **13** 356–57; **15** 284; **17** 564; **21** 416; **22** 31
Beneficial Corporation, **II** 236; **8 56–58**, 117; **10** 490
Beneficial Finance Company, **27** 428–29
Beneficial National Bank USA, **II** 286
Beneficial Standard Life, **10** 247
Benefit Consultants, Inc., **16** 145
Benesse Corporation, **13** 91, 93
Benetton Group S.p.A., **8** 171; **10 149–52**; **15** 369; **18** 193; **25** 56
Bengal Iron and Steel Co., **IV** 205–06
Benihana, Inc., **18 56–59**
Benjamin Allen & Co., **IV** 660
Benjamin Moore and Co., **13 84–87**
Benlox Holdings PLC, **16** 465
Benn Bros. plc, **IV** 687
Bennett Biscuit Co., **II** 543
Bennett Industries, Inc., **17** 371–73
Bennett's Smokehouse and Saloon, **19** 122; **29** 201
Bennigan's, **II** 556–57; **7** 336; **12** 373; **13** 408; **19** 286; **25** 181
Bensdorp, **29** 47
Benson & Hedges, Ltd., **V** 398–99; **15** 137; **19** 171
Benson Wholesale Co., **II** 624
Bentley Laboratories, **22** 360
Bentley Mills, Inc., **8** 272
Bentley Motor Ltd., **I** 194; **21** 435
Bentley Systems, **6** 247
Benton & Bowles, **I** 33; **6** 20, 22
Benton International, Inc., **29** 376
Benwood Iron Works, **17** 355
Benxi Iron and Steel Corp., **IV** 167
Benzina, **IV** 487
Benzinol, **IV** 487
N.V. Benzit. *See* N.V. Gemeenschappelijk Benzit van Aandeelen Philips Gloeilampenfabriken.
Berec Group, **III** 502; **7** 208
Beresford International plc, **24** 335; **27** 159
Berg Manufacturing Sales Co., **I** 156
Berg- und Metallbank, **IV** 139–40
Bergdorf Goodman, **I** 246; **V** 30–31; **25** 177
Bergedorfer Eisenwerk, **III** 417–20
Bergen Bank, **II** 352
Bergen Brunswig Corporation, **I** 413; **V 14–16**, 152; **13 88–90 (upd.)**; **18** 97
Berger Associates, Inc., **26** 233
Berger, Jenson and Nicholson, **I** 347; **18** 236
Berger Manufacturing Company, **26** 405
Bergische-Markische Bank, **II** 278
Berglen, **III** 570; **20** 362
Bergmann & Co., **II** 27
Bergstrom Paper Company, **8** 413
Bergswerksgesellschaft Hibernia, **I** 349; **IV** 194
Bergvik & Ala, **IV** 336, 338–39
Beringer Wine Estates Holdings, Inc., **22 78–81**
Berisford International plc, **19** 492, 494
Berjaya Group, **22** 464–65
Berkeley Computers, **III** 109; **14** 13
Berkey Photo Inc., **I** 447; **III** 475
Berkley Dean & Co., **15** 525
Berkline Corp., **17** 183; **20** 363
Berkshire Hathaway Inc., **III** 29, **213–15**; **12** 435–36, 554–55; **18 60–63 (upd.)**; **29** 191; **30** 411
Berkshire International, **V** 390–91; **17** 512
Berkshire Partners, **10** 393
Berleca Ltd., **9** 395
Berlex Laboratories, **I** 682; **10** 214
Berli Jucker, **18** 180–82
Berlin Exchange, **I** 409
Berlin Göring-Werke, **IV** 233
Berliner Bank, **II** 256
Berliner Bankverein, **II** 278
Berliner Handels- und Frankfurter Bank, **II** 242
Berliner Union, **I** 409
Berlinische Bodengesellschaft, **I** 560
Berlitz International, Inc., **IV** 643; **7** 286, 312; **13 91–93**
Berman Brothers Fur Co., **21** 525
Berman Buckskin, **21** 525
Bernard Chaus, Inc., **27 59–61**
Bernardin Ltd., **30** 39
Bernheim-Meyer: A l'Innovation. *See* GIB Group.
Berni Inns, **I** 247
Bernie Schulman's, **12** 132
Bernstein Macauley, Inc., **II** 450
Berrios Enterprises, **14** 236
Berry Bearing Company, **9** 254
Berry Industries, **III** 628
Berry Plastics Corporation, **21 57–59**
Bert L. Smokler & Company, **11** 257
Bertea Corp., **III** 603
Bertelsmann AG, **IV 592–94**, 614–15; **10** 196; **15 51–54 (upd.)**; **17** 399; **19** 285; **22** 194; **26** 19, 43; **30** 67, 70; **31** 375, 378
Bertolini's Authentic Trattorias, **30** 329
Bertram & Graf Gmbh, **28** 45
Bertron Griscom & Company, **V** 641
Bertucci's Inc., **16 54–56**, 447
Berwind Corp., **14** 18
Beryl Corp., **26** 149
Beryllium Resources, **14** 80
Berzelius Metallhütten Gesellschaft, **IV** 141
Berzelius Umwelt-Service, **III** 625; **IV** 141
Besi, **26** 498
Besnier SA, **19 49–51**; **23** 217, 219; **24** 444–45; **25** 83, 85
Bess Mfg., **8** 510
Bessemer Capital Partners L.P., **15** 505
Bessemer Gas Engine Co., **II** 15; **20** 163
Bessemer Limestone & Cement Co., **IV** 409; **31** 454
Bessemer Steamship, **IV** 572; **7** 549
Besser Vibrapac, **III** 673
Best Apparel, **V** 156
Best Buy Co., Inc., **9 65–66**; **10** 305; **17** 489; **18** 532–33; **19** 362; **23 51–53 (upd.)**; **24** 52, 502; **29** 120, 123; **30** 464, 466
Best Fabric Outlets, **16** 198
Best Holding Corporation. *See* Arkansas Best Corporation.
Best Manufacturing, **15** 490
Best Power, **24** 29
Best Products Inc., **19** 396–97
Best Western, **14** 106; **25** 308
Bestfoods, **II** 496–97; **22 82–86 (upd.)**
Bestline Products, **17** 227
Bestop Inc., **16** 184
Bestwall Gypsum Co., **IV** 281; **9** 259
Bestway Distribution Services, Inc., **24** 126
Bestway Transportation, **14** 505
Beswick, **II** 17
BET Holdings, Inc., **18 64–66**; **22** 224; **25** 213
Beta West Properties, **25** 496–97
Bethesda Research Laboratories, Inc., **I** 321; **17** 287, 289
Bethlehem Steel Corporation, **IV 35–37**, 228, 572–73; **6** 540; **7 48–51 (upd.)**, 447, 549–50; **11** 65; **12** 354; **13** 97, 157; **18** 378; **22** 285; **23** 305; **25** 45; **26** 405; **27 62–66 (upd.)**
Beton Union, **III** 738
Better Communications, **IV** 597
Betz Laboratories, Inc., **I 312–13**; **10 153–55 (upd.)**; **15** 536
Bevan and Wedd Durlacher Morduant & Co., **II** 237
Beveridge-Marvellum Company, **8** 483
Beverly Enterprises, Inc., **III 76–77**, 80; **14** 242; **16 57–59 (upd.)**; **25** 309
Beverly Hills Savings, **II** 420
Beverly Pest Control, **25** 15
Bevis Custom Furniture, Inc., **12** 263
Bevrachtingskantoor, **26** 280
Bezeq, **25** 266
BFC Construction Corporation, **25 63–65**

The BFGoodrich Company, **I** 28, 428, 440; **II** 414; **III** 118, 443; **V 231–33**; **8** 80–81, 290; **9** 12, 96, 133; **10** 438; **11** 158; **19 52–55 (upd.)**; **20** 260, 262; **21** 260; **22** 114; **23** 170; **25** 70; **30** 158; **31** 135
BFI. *See* Browning-Ferris Industries, Inc.
BFP Holdings Corp. *See* Big Flower Press Holdings, Inc.
BG Freight Line Holding B.V., **30** 318
BG plc, **29** 104
BG&E. *See* Baltimore Gas and Electric Company.
BGC Finance, **II** 420
BGJ Enterprises, Inc. *See* Brown Printing Company.
BH Acquisition Corporation, **22** 439
Bharat Coking Coal Ltd., **IV** 48–49
Bharat Petroleum Ltd., **IV** 441
Bharti Telecom, **16** 84
BHC Communications, Inc., **9** 119; **26 32–34**; **31** 109
BHP. *See* Broken Hill Proprietary Company Ltd.
BHP Steel of Australia, **18** 380
Bhs plc, **16** 466; **17 42–44**, 334–35
BHV. *See* Bazar de l'Hotel de Ville.
Bi-Lo Inc., **II** 641; **V** 35; **16** 313
Biacore International AB, **25** 377
Bianchi, **13** 27
Bibb Co., **31** 199
BIC Corporation, **III** 29; **8 59–61**; **20** 23; **23 54–57 (upd.)**
BICC PLC, **III 433–34**; **11** 520
BICE Med Grille, **16** 447
Bicoastal Corporation, **II 9–11**
Bidermann Industries, **22** 122
Biederman & Company, **14** 160
Bieffe, **16** 52
Bienfaisance, **III** 391
Bierbrauerei Wilhelm Remmer, **9** 86
Biesemeyer Manufacturing Corporation, **26** 363
Biffa Waste Services Ltd. *See* Severn Trent PLC.
Big B, Inc., **17 45–47**
Big Bear Stores Co., **13 94–96**
Big Boy, **III** 102–03
Big 5 Sporting Goods, **12** 477
Big Flower Press Holdings, Inc., **21 60–62**
Big Foot Cattle Co., **14** 537
Big Horn Mining Co., **8** 423
Big M, **8** 409–10
Big O Tires, Inc., **20 61–63**
Big Rivers Electric Corporation, **11 37–39**
Big Three Industries, **I** 358
Big V Supermarkets, Inc., **25 66–68**
Big Y Foods, Inc., **23** 169
Bigelow-Sanford, Inc., **31** 199
Bike Athletics, **23** 449
BIL. *See* Brierley Investments.
Bilbao Insurance Group, **III** 200
Bilfinger & Berger Bau A.G., **I 560–61**
Bill France Racing, **19** 222
Billboard Publications, Inc., **7** 15
Billerud, **IV** 336
Billing Concepts Corp., **26 35–38**
Billiton International, **IV** 56, 532; **22** 237
Bill's Casino, **9** 426
Biltwell Company, **8** 249
Bimar Foods Inc., **19** 192
Bimbo Bakeries USA, **29** 341
Binder Hamlyn, **IV** 685
Binderline Development, Inc., **22** 175
Bindley Western Industries, Inc., **9 67–69**
Bing Crosby Productions, **IV** 595
Binghamton Container Company, **8** 102
Bingo King. *See* Stuart Entertainment Inc.
Binks Sames Corporation, **21 63–66**
Binney & Smith Inc., **II** 525; **IV** 621; **13** 293; **25 69–72**
Binnie & Partners, **22** 89
Binny & Co. Ltd., **III** 522
Binter Canarias, **6** 97
Bio/Dynamics, Inc., **10** 105, 107
Bio Synthetics, Inc., **21** 386
Bio-Clinic, **11** 486–87
Bio-Toxicological Research Laboratories, **IV** 409
Biofermin Pharmaceutical, **I** 704
Biogen Inc., **I** 638, 685; **8** 210; **14 58–60**
Bioindustrias, **19** 475
Biokyowa, **III** 43
Biological Research, **III** 443
Biological Technology Corp., **IV** 252; **17** 29
Biomedical Reference Laboratories of North Carolina, **11** 424
Biomega Corp., **18** 422
Biomet, Inc., **10 156–58**
Bionaire, Inc., **19** 360
BioSensor A.B., **I** 665
Biotechnica International, **I** 286
Bioteknik-Gruppen, **I** 665
Bioter S.A., **III** 420
Bioter-Biona, S.A., **II** 493
Biotherm, **III** 47
Bird & Sons, **22** 14
Bird Corporation, **19 56–58**
Birdsall, Inc., **6** 529, 531
Bireley's, **22** 515
Birfield Ltd., **III** 494
Birkbeck, **10** 6
Birkenstock Footprint Sandals, Inc., **12 33–35**
Birmingham & Midland Bank. *See* Midland Bank plc.
Birmingham Joint Stock Bank, **II** 307
Birmingham Screw Co., **III** 493
Birmingham Slag Company, **7** 572–73, 575
Birmingham Steel Corporation, **13 97–98**; **18** 379–80; **19** 380
Birra Moretti, **25** 281–82
Birtman Electric Co., **III** 653; **12** 548
Biscayne Bank. *See* Banco Espírito Santo e Comercial de Lisboa S.A.
Biscayne Federal Savings and Loan Association, **11** 481
Biscuiterie Nantaise, **II** 502; **10** 323
Biscuits Belin, **II** 543
Biscuits Delacre, **II** 480; **26** 56
Biscuits Gondolo, **II** 543
Bishop & Babcock Manufacturing Co., **II** 41
Bishop & Co. Savings Bank, **11** 114
Bishop National Bank of Hawaii, **11** 114
Bishopsgate Insurance, **III** 200
BISSELL, Inc., **9 70–72**; **30 75–78**
Bit Software, Inc., **12** 62
Bits & Pieces, **26** 439
Bitumax Proprietary, **III** 672
Bitumen & Oil Refineries (Australia) Ltd., **III** 672–73
BIZ Enterprises, **23** 390
Bizmark, **13** 176
BizMart, **6** 244–45; **8** 404–05
BJ Services Company, **15** 534, 536; **25 73–75**
BJ's Wholesale Club, **12** 221; **13** 547–49
BJK&E. *See* Bozell Worldwide Inc.
Björknäs Nya Sågverks, **IV** 338
BK Tag, **28** 157
BKW, **IV** 229
BL Ltd., **I** 175; **10** 354
BL Systems. *See* AT&T Istel Ltd.
The Black & Decker Corporation, **I** 667; **III 435–37**, 628, 665; **8** 332, 349; **15** 417–18; **16** 384; **17** 215; **20 64–68 (upd.)**; **22** 334
Black & Veatch LLP, **22 87–90**
Black Arrow Leasing, **II** 138; **24** 193
Black Box Corporation, **20 69–71**
Black Clawson Company, **24** 478
Black Entertainment Television. *See* BET Holdings, Inc.
Black Flag Co., **I** 622
Black Hawk Broadcasting Group, **III** 188; **10** 29
Black Hills Corporation, **20 72–74**
Black Spread Eagle, **II** 235
Blackburn Group, **III** 508; **24** 85
Blackhawk, **9** 26
Blackhorse Agencies, **II** 309
Blackmer Pump Co., **III** 468
Blackstone Capital Partners L.P., **V** 223; **6** 378; **17** 366
The Blackstone Group, **II** 434, 444; **IV** 718; **11** 177, 179; **13** 170; **17** 238, 443; **22** 404, 416; **26** 408
Blackstone Hotel Acquisition Co., **24** 195
Blaine Construction Company, **8** 546
Blair and Co., **II** 227
Blair Corporation, **25 76–78**; **31 53–55**
Blair Paving, **III** 674
Blair Radio, **6** 33
Blakiston Co., **IV** 636
Blane Products, **I** 403
Blatz Breweries, **I** 254
Blaupunkt-Werke, **I** 192–93
BLC Insurance Co., **III** 330
BLD Europe, **16** 168
Bleichröder, **II** 191
Blendax, **III** 53; **8** 434; **26** 384
Blessings Corp., **14** 550; **19 59–61**
Blimpie International, Inc., **15 55–57**; **17** 501
Bliss Manufacturing Co., **17** 234–35
Blitz-Weinhart Brewing, **18** 71–72
Blochman Lawrence Goldfree, **I** 697
Block Drug Company, Inc., **6** 26; **8 62–64**; **27 67–70 (upd.)**
Block Financial Corporation, **17** 265; **29** 227
Block Management, **29** 226
Block Medical, Inc., **10** 351
Blockbuster Entertainment Corporation, **II** 161; **IV** 597; **9 73–75**, 361; **11** 556–58; **12** 43, 515; **13** 494; **18** 64, 66; **19** 417; **22** 161–62; **23** 88, 503; **25** 208–10, 222; **26** 409; **28** 296; **29** 504
Blockbuster Inc., **31 56–60 (upd.)**, 339–40
Blockson Chemical, **I** 380; **13** 379
Bloedel, Stewart & Welch, **IV** 306–07
Blohm & Voss, **I** 74
Bloomberg L.P., **18** 24; **21 67–71**

Bloomingdale's Inc., **I** 90; **III** 63; **IV** 651, 703; **9** 209, 393; **10** 487; **12** **36–38**, 307, 403–04; **16** 328; **23** 210; **25** 257; **31** 190
Blount International, Inc., **I** 563; **12** **39–41**; **24** 78; **26** 117, 119, 363
BLT Ventures, **25** 270
Blue Arrow PLC, **II** 334–35; **9** 327; **30** 300
Blue Bell Creameries L.P., **30** **79–81**
Blue Bell, Inc., **V** 390–91; **12** 205; **17** 512
Blue Chip Stamps, **III** 213–14; **30** 412
Blue Circle Industries PLC, **III** **669–71**, 702
Blue Cross and Blue Shield Association, **10** **159–61**; **14** 84
Blue Cross and Blue Shield Mutual of Northern Ohio, **12** 176
Blue Cross and Blue Shield of Colorado, **11** 175
Blue Cross and Blue Shield of Greater New York, **III** 245, 246
Blue Cross and Blue Shield of Ohio, **15** 114
Blue Cross Blue Shield of Michigan, **12** 22
Blue Cross of California, **25** 525
Blue Cross of Northeastern New York, **III** 245–46
Blue Diamond Growers, **28** **56–58**
Blue Funnel Line, **I** 521; **6** 415–17
Blue Line Distributing, **7** 278–79
Blue Metal Industries, **III** 687; **28** 82
Blue Mountain Arts, Inc., **IV** 621; **29** **63–66**
Blue Ribbon Beef Pack, Inc., **II** 515–16
Blue Ribbon Sports. *See* Nike, Inc.
Blue Ridge Grocery Co., **II** 625
Blue Ridge Lumber Ltd., **16** 11
Blue Shield of California, **25** 527
Blue Tee Corporation, **23** 34, 36
Blue Water Food Service, **13** 244
Bluebird Inc., **10** 443
Bluffton Grocery Co., **II** 668
Blumberg Communications Inc., **24** 96
Blunt Ellis & Loewi, **III** 270
Blyth and Co., **I** 537; **13** 448, 529
Blyth Eastman Dillon & Company, **II** 445; **22** 405–06
Blyth Industries, Inc., **18** **67–69**
Blyth Merrill Lynch, **II** 448
Blythe Colours BV, **IV** 119
BMC Industries, Inc., **6** 275; **17** **48–51**
BMC Software Inc., **14** 391
BMG/Music, **IV** 594; **15** 51
BMI. *See* Broadcast Music Inc.
BMI Ltd., **III** 673
BMI Systems Inc., **12** 174
BMO Corp., **III** 209
BMW. *See* Bayerische Motoren Werke.
BNA. *See* Banca Nazionale dell'Agricoltura *or* Bureau of National Affairs, Inc.
BNCI. *See* Banque Nationale Pour le Commerce et l'Industrie.
BNE. *See* Bank of New England Corp.
BNG, Inc., **19** 487
BNP. *See* Banque Nationale de Paris S.A.
BNS Acquisitions, **26** 247
BOAC. *See* British Overseas Airways Corp.
Boardwalk Regency, **6** 201
Boart and Hard Metals, **IV** 22
Boart Longyear Company, **26** **39–42**, 69
Boase Massimi Pollitt, **6** 48
Boatmen's Bancshares Inc., **15** **58–60**
Bob Evans Farms, Inc., **9** **76–79**; **10** 259
Bobbie Brooks Inc., **17** 384
Bobbs-Merrill, **11** 198
Bobingen A.G., **I** 347
Bobro Products. *See* BWP Distributors.
BOC Group plc, **I** **314–16**, 358; **11** 402; **12** 500; **25** **79–82 (upd.)**
Bochumer Verein für Gusstahlfabrikation, **IV** 88
Bock Bearing Co., **8** 530
Bodcaw Co., **IV** 287; **15** 228
Boddington, **21** 247
Bodegas, **8** 556
Bodeker Drug Company, **16** 399
The Body Shop International PLC, **11** **40–42**
The Boeing Company, **I** 41–43, **47–49**, 50, 55–56, 58, 61, 67–68, 70–72, 74, 77, 82, 84–85, 90, 92–93, 96–97, 100, 102, 104–05, 108, 111–13, 116, 121–22, 126, 128, 130, 195, 489–90, 511, 530; **II** 7, 32–33, 62, 442; **III** 512, 539; **IV** 171, 576; **6** 68, 96, 130, 327; **7** 11, 456, 504; **8** 81, 313, 315; **9** 12, 18, 128, 194, 206, 232, 396, 416–17, 458–60, 498; **10** **162–65 (upd.)**, 262, 316, 369, 536; **11** 164, 267, 277–79, 363, 427; **12** 180, 190–91, 380; **13** 356–58; **21** 140, 143, 436; **24** 21, 84, 85–86, 88–89, 442; **25** 34, 224, 430–31; **26** 117; **28** 195, 225
Boeke & Huidekooper, **III** 417
Boerenbond, **II** 304
Boettcher & Co., **III** 271
Bofors Nobel Inc., **9** 380–81; **13** 22
Bogen Company, **15** 213
Bohemia, Inc., **13** **99–101**; **31** 467
Bohm-Allen Jewelry, **12** 112
Böhme-Fettchemie, Chenmitz, **III** 32
Bohn Aluminum & Brass, **10** 439
Boise Cascade Corporation, **I** 142; **III** 499, 648, 664; **IV** **255–56**, 333; **6** 577; **7** 356; **8** **65–67 (upd.)**, 477; **15** 229; **16** 510; **19** 269, 445–46; **22** 154; **31** 13
Bokaro Steel Ltd., **IV** 206
Bolands Ltd., **II** 649
Bolar Pharmaceutical Co., **16** 529
Boley G.m.b.H., **21** 123
Boliden Mining, **II** 366
Bolinder-Munktell, **I** 209; **II** 366
Bolitho Bank, **II** 235
Bölkow GmbH, **I** 74
Bolles & Houghton, **10** 355
The Bolsa Chica Company, **8** 300
Bolt, Beranek & Newman Inc., **26** 520
BOMAG, **8** 544, 546
Bombardier, Inc., **12** 400–01; **16** 78; **25** 423; **27** 281, 284
The Bombay Company, Inc., **III** 581; **10** **166–68**; **27** 429
Bon Appetit, **II** 656
The Bon Marché, Inc., **V** 25; **9** 209; **19** 88, 306, 309; **23** **58–60**; **26** 158, 160
Bon Secours Health System, Inc., **24** **68–71**
The Bon-Ton Stores, Inc., **16** **60–62**
Bonanza, **7** 336; **10** 331; **15** 361–63
Bonanza Steakhouse, **17** 320
Bonaventura, **IV** 611
Bonaventure Liquor Store Co., **I** 284
Bond Brewing International, **23** 405
Bond Corporation Holdings Limited, **I** 253, 255; **10** **169–71**
Bondex International, **8** 456
Bonduel Pickling Co. Inc., **25** 517
Bongrain SA, **19** 50; **23** 217, 219; **25** **83–85**
Boni & Liveright, **13** 428
Bonifiche Siele, **II** 272
Bonimart, **II** 649
Bonneville International Corporation, **29** **67–70**; **30** 15
Bontrager Bicycles, **16** 495
Bonwit Teller, **13** 43; **17** 43
Book-of-the-Month Club, Inc., **IV** 661, 675; **7** 529; **13** **105–07**
Booker plc, **13** **102–04**; **31** **61–64 (upd.)**
Booker Tate, **13** 102
Booklink Technologies, **26** 19
Bookmasters, **10** 136
Books-A-Million, Inc., **14** **61–62**; **16** 161
Bookstop, **10** 136
Boole & Babbage, Inc., **25** **86–88**
Booth Bay, Ltd., **16** 37
Booth Creek Ski Holdings, Inc., **31** **65–67**
Booth Fisheries, **II** 571
Booth, Inc., **II** 420
Booth Leasing, **I** 449
Booth-Kelly Lumber Co., **IV** 281; **9** 259
Bootprint Entertainment, **31** 240
The Boots Company PLC, **I** 640, 668, 708; **II** 650; **V** **17–19**; **8** 548; **19** 122; **24** **72–76 (upd.)**
Boots Pharmaceuticals, **18** 51
Booz Allen & Hamilton Inc., **10** **172–75**
Boral Limited, **III** **672–74**
Borax Holdings, **IV** 191
Bordas, **IV** 615
Borden Cabinet Corporation, **12** 296
Borden, Inc., **II** **470–73**, 486, 498, 538, 545; **IV** 569; **7** 127, 129, 380; **11** 173; **15** 490; **16** 43; **17** 56; **22** 84, **91–96 (upd.)**; **24** 273, 288, 520; **27** 38, 40, 316, 318
Border Fine Arts, **11** 95
Borders Group, Inc., **9** 361; **10** 137; **15** **61–62**; **17** 522; **18** 286; **25** 17
Borders Inc., **30** 69
Borders, Perrin and Norrander, **23** 480
Borealis A/S, **30** 205
Borg Instruments, **23** 494
Borg-Warner Automotive, Inc., **14** **63–66**; **23** 171
Borg-Warner Corporation, **I** 193, 339, 393; **III** 428, **438–41**; **14** 63, 357; **22** 228; **25** 74, 253
Borg-Warner Security Corporation, **13** 123–25; **14** 63, 65, 541
Borland International, Inc., **6** 255–56; **9** **80–82**; **10** 237, 509, 519, 558; **15** 492; **25** 300–01, 349
Borman's, Inc., **II** 638; **16** 249
Borneo Airways. *See* Malaysian Airlines System BHD.
Borneo Co., **III** 523
Borregaard Osterreich AG, **18** 395
Borror Corporation. *See* Dominion Homes, Inc.
Borsheim's, **III** 215; **18** 60
Borun Bros., **12** 477
Bosanquet, Salt and Co., **II** 306
Bosch. *See* Robert Bosch GmbH.
Boschert, **III** 434
Boscov's Department Store, Inc., **31** **68–70**
Bose Corporation, **II** 35; **13** **108–10**; **22** 97

Bosendorfer, L., Klavierfabrik, A.G., **12** 297
Bosert Industrial Supply, Inc., **V** 215
Boso Condensed Milk, **II** 538
Bostich, **III** 628
Boston Acoustics, Inc., 22 97–99
Boston and Maine Corporation, **16** 350
Boston Beer Company, 18 70–73; 22 422; **31** 383
Boston Brewing Company, **18** 502
Boston Casualty Co., **III** 203
Boston Celtics Limited Partnership, 14 67–69
Boston Chicken, Inc., 12 42–44; 23 266; **29** 170, 172
Boston Co., **II** 451–52
Boston Consulting Group, **I** 532; **9** 343; **18** 70; **22** 193
Boston Corp., **25** 66
Boston Distributors, **9** 453
Boston Edison Company, 12 45–47
Boston Educational Research, **27** 373
Boston Fruit Co., **II** 595
Boston Garden Arena Corporation, **14** 67
Boston Gas Company, **6** 486–88
Boston Globe, **7** 13–16
Boston Herald, **7** 15
Boston Industries Corp., **III** 735
Boston Marine Insurance Co., **III** 242
Boston National Bank, **13** 465
Boston News Bureau, **IV** 601
Boston Overseas Financial Corp., **II** 208
Boston Popcorn Co., **27** 197–98
Boston Properties, Inc., 22 100–02
Boston Ventures Limited Partnership, **17** 444; **27** 41, 393
Boston Whaler, Inc., **V** 376–77; **10** 215–16; **26** 398
Bostrom Seating, Inc., **23** 306
BOTAS, **IV** 563
Botsford Ketchum, Inc., **6** 40
Botswana General Insurance Company, **22** 495
Botto, Rossner, Horne & Messinger, **6** 40
Bottu, **II** 475
Bougainville Copper Pty., **IV** 60–61
Boulder Creek Steaks & Saloon, **16** 447
Boulder Natural Gas Company, **19** 411
Boulet Dru DuPuy Petit Group. *See* Wells Rich Greene BDDP.
Boulevard Bancorp, **12** 165
Boulton & Paul Ltd., **31** 398–400
Boundary Gas, **6** 457
Boundary Healthcare, **12** 327
Bouquet, **V** 114
Bourdon, **19** 49
Bourjois, **12** 57
Boussois Souchon Neuvesel, **II** 474; **III** 677; **16** 121–22
Bouygues S.A., I 562–64; 13 206; **23** 475–76; **24 77–80 (upd.)**; **31** 126, 128
Bouzan Mines Ltd., **IV** 164
Bovaird Seyfang Manufacturing Co., **III** 471
Bovis Ltd., **I** 588
Bow Bangles, **17** 101, 103
Bowater PLC, III 501–02; **IV 257–59**; **7** 208; **8** 483–84; **25** 13; **30** 229
Bower Roller Bearing Company. *See* Federal-Mogul Corporation.
Bowery and East River National Bank, **II** 226
Bowery Savings Bank, **II** 182; **9** 173
Bowes Co., **II** 631
Bowman Gum, Inc., **13** 520
Bowmar Instruments, **II** 113; **11** 506
Bowne & Co., Inc., 18 331–32; **23 61–64**
Box Innards Inc., **13** 442
Box Office Attraction Co., **II** 169
BoxCrow Cement Company, **8** 259
The Boyds Collection, Ltd., 29 71–73
Boyer Brothers, Inc., **14** 17–18
Boyer's International, Inc., **20** 83
Boykin Enterprises, **IV** 136
Boyles Bros. Drilling Company. *See* Christensen Boyles Corporation.
Boys Market, **17** 558–59
Boz, **IV** 697–98
Bozel Électrométallurgie, **IV** 174
Bozell, Jacobs, Kenyon, and Eckhardt Inc. *See* True North Communications Inc.
Bozell Worldwide Inc., 25 89–91
Bozkurt, **27** 188
Bozzuto's, Inc., 13 111–12
BP. *See* British Petroleum Company PLC.
BP Amoco plc, **31** 31, 34
BPB, **III** 736
BPD, **13** 356
BPI Communications, Inc., **7** 15; **19** 285; **27** 500
BR. *See* British Rail.
Braas, **III** 734, 736
Brabant, **III** 199, 201
Brabazon, **III** 555
Brach and Brock Confections, Inc., 15 63–65; **29** 47
Brad Foote Gear Works, **18** 453
Bradbury Agnew and Co., **IV** 686
Braden Manufacturing, **23** 299–301
Bradford District Bank, **II** 333
Bradford Exchange Ltd. Inc., **21** 269
Bradford Insulation Group, **III** 687
Bradford Pennine, **III** 373
Bradlees Discount Department Store Company, II 666–67; **12 48–50**; **24** 461
Bradley Lumber Company, **8** 430
Bradley Producing Corp., **IV** 459
Bradstreet Co., **IV** 604–05; **19** 133
Braegen Corp., **13** 127
Bragussa, **IV** 71
BRAINS. *See* Belgian Rapid Access to Information Network Services.
Bramalea Ltd., 9 83–85; **10** 530–31
Brambles Industries, **III** 494–95
Brambles Ltd., **24** 400
Bramco, **III** 600
Bramwell Gates, **II** 586
Bran & Lübbe, **III** 420
Brand Companies, Inc., **9** 110; **11** 436
Branded Restaurant Group, Inc., **12** 372
Brandeis & Sons, **19** 511
Brandenburgische Motorenwerke, **I** 138
Brandywine Insurance Agency, Inc., **25** 540
Brandywine Iron Works and Nail Factory, **14** 323
Brandywine Valley Railroad Co., **14** 324
Braniff Airlines, **I** 97, 489, 548; **II** 445; **6** 50, 119–20; **16** 274; **17** 504; **21** 142; **22** 406
Branigar Organization, Inc., **IV** 345
Brascade Resources, **IV** 308
Brascan Ltd., **II** 456; **IV** 165, 330; **25** 281
Braspetro, **IV** 454, 501–02
Brass Craft Manufacturing Co., **III** 570; **20** 361
Brasseries Kronenbourg, **II** 474–75
Braswell Motor Freight, **14** 567
Braud & Faucheux. *See* Manitou BF S.A.
Brauerei Beck & Co., 9 86–87
Braun, **III** 29; **17** 214–15; **26** 335
Braunkohlenwerk Golpa-Jessnitz AG, **IV** 230
Brazilian Central Bank, **IV** 56
Brazos Gas Compressing, **7** 345
Brazos Sportswear, Inc., 23 65–67
Breakstone Bros., Inc., **II** 533
Breakthrough Software, **10** 507
Breckenridge-Remy, **18** 216
Breco Holding Company, **17** 558, 561
Bredel Exploitatie B.V., **8** 546
Bredell Paint Co., **III** 745
Bredero's Bouwbedrijf of Utrecht, **IV** 707–08, 724
BREED Technologies, Inc., **22** 31
Breedband NV, **IV** 133
Brega Petroleum Marketing Co., **IV** 453, 455
Breguet Aviation, **I** 44; **24** 86
Breitenburger Cementfabrik, **III** 701
Bremner Biscuit Co., **II** 562; **13** 426
Brenco Inc., **16** 514
Brenda Mines Ltd., **7** 399
Brennan College Services, **12** 173
Brenntag AG, 8 68–69, 496; **23 68–70 (upd.)**, **23** 453–54
Brentano's, **7** 286
Breslube Enterprises, **8** 464
Brewster Lines, **6** 410
Breyers Ice Cream Co. *See* Good Humor-Breyers.
BRI Bar Review Institute, Inc., **IV** 623; **12** 224
BRI International, **21** 425
Brian Mills, **V** 118
Briarpatch, Inc., **12** 109
Brickwood Breweries, **I** 294
Bricorama, **23** 231
Bridas S.A., **24** 522
Bridel, **19** 49–50; **25** 85
Bridge Oil Ltd., **I** 438
Bridge Technology, Inc., **10** 395
Bridgeman Creameries, **II** 536
Bridgeport Brass, **I** 377
Bridgeport Machines, Inc., 17 52–54
Bridgestone Corporation, V 234–35; **15** 355; **20** 262; **21 72–75 (upd.)**
Bridgestone Liquefied Gas, **IV** 364
Bridgestone/Firestone, **19** 454, 456
Bridgeway Plan for Health, **6** 186
Bridgford Company, **13** 382
Bridgford Foods Corporation, 27 71–73
Brier Hill, **IV** 114
Brierly Investment Limited, **19** 156; **24** 399
Briggs & Stratton Corporation, III 597; **8 70–73**; **27 74–78 (upd.)**
Briggs and Lundy Lumber Cos., **14** 18
Brigham's Inc., **15** 71
Bright Horizons Family Solutions, Inc., 31 71–73
Bright of America Inc., **12** 426
Bright Star Technologies, **13** 92; **15** 455
Brighter Vision Learning Adventures, **29** 470, 472
Brighton & Hove Bus and Coach Company, **28** 155–56
Brighton Federal Savings and Loan Assoc., **II** 420
Brightpoint, Inc., 18 74–77
Brightwork Development Inc., **25** 348
Briker, **23** 231

Brillion Iron Works Inc., **23** 306
Brimsdown Lead Co., **III** 680
Brin's Oxygen Company Limited. *See* BOC Group plc.
Brinco Ltd., **II** 211
Brink's, Inc., **IV** 180–82; **19** 319
Brinker International, Inc., **10 176–78**; **18** 438
BRIntec, **III** 434
Brinton Carpets, **III** 423
BRIO AB, **24 81–83**
Brio Technology, **25** 97
Brisbane Gas Co., **III** 673
Bristol Aeroplane, **I** 50, 197; **10** 261; **24** 85
Bristol Gaming Corporation, **21** 298
Bristol Hotel Company, **23 71–73**
Bristol PLC, **IV** 83
Bristol-BTR, **I** 429
Bristol-Erickson, **13** 297
Bristol-Myers Squibb Company, **I** 26, 30, 37, 301, 696, 700, 703; **III 17–19**, 36, 67; **IV** 272; **6** 27; **7** 255; **8** 210, 282–83; **9 88–91 (upd.)**; **10** 70; **11** 289; **12** 126–27; **16** 438; **21** 546; **25** 91, 253, 365
Bristol-Siddeley, Ltd., **I** 50; **24** 85
Britannia Airways, **8** 525–26
Britannia Security Group PLC, **12** 10
Britannica Software, **7** 168
Britches of Georgetowne, **10** 215–16
BRITE. *See* Granada Group PLC.
Brite Voice Systems, Inc., **20 75–78**
British & Commonwealth Shipping Company, **10** 277
British Aerospace plc, **I** 42, 46, **50–53**, 55, 74, 83, 132, 532; **III** 458, 507; **V** 339; **7** 9, 11, 458–59; **8** 315; **9** 499; **11** 413; **12** 191; **14** 36; **18** 125; **21** 8, 443; **24 84–90 (upd.)**; **27** 474
British Airways plc, **I** 34, 83, **92–95**, 109; **IV** 658; **6** 60, 78–79, 118, 132; **14 70–74 (upd.)**; **18** 80; **22** 52; **24** 86, 311, 396, 399–400; **26** 115; **27** 20–21, 466; **28** 25, 508; **31** 103
British Aluminium, Ltd., **II** 422; **IV** 15
British American Cosmetics, **I** 427
British American Insurance Co., **III** 350
British American Nickel, **IV** 110
British American Tobacco. *See* B.A.T. Industries PLC.
British and Dominion Film Corp., **II** 157
British and Foreign Marine, **III** 350
British and Foreign Steam Navigation Company, **23** 160
British and French Bank, **II** 232–33
British and North American Royal Mail Steam Packet Company. *See* Cunard Line Ltd.
British Bank of North America, **II** 210
British Bank of the Middle East, **II** 298
British Borneo Timber Co., **III** 699
British Broadcasting Corporation Ltd., **III** 163; **IV** 651; **7 52–55**; **21 76–79 (upd.)**; **24** 192
British Caledonian Airways, **I** 94–95; **6** 79
British Can Co., **I** 604
British Car Auctions, **14** 321
British Celanese Ltd., **I** 317
British Cellulose and Chemical Manufacturing Co., **I** 317
British Chrome, **III** 699
British Coal Corporation, **IV 38–40**
British Columbia Forest Products Ltd., **IV** 279; **19** 155
British Columbia Packers, **II** 631–32
British Columbia Resources Investment Corp., **IV** 308
British Columbia Telephone Company, **IV** 308; **6 309–11**
British Commonwealth Insurance, **III** 273
British Commonwealth Pacific Airways, **6** 110; **24** 398
British Continental Airlines, **I** 92
British Credit Trust, **10** 443
British Digital Broadcasting plc, **24** 192, 194
British Dyestuffs Corp., **I** 351
British Dynamite Co., **I** 351
British Energy Group, **19** 391
British Engine, **III** 350
British European Airways, **I** 93, 466
British Executive and General Aviation, **I** 50; **24** 85
British Fuels, **III** 735
British Gas plc, **II** 260; **V 559–63**; **6** 478–79; **11** 97; **18** 365–67. *See also* Centrica plc.
British Gauge and Instrument Company, **13** 234
British General, **III** 234
British General Post Office, **25** 99–100
British Goodrich Tyre Co., **I** 428
British Home Stores PLC. *See* Storehouse PLC.
British Hovercraft Corp., **I** 120
British Independent Television Enterprises Ltd. *See* Granada Group PLC.
British India and Queensland Agency Co. Ltd., **III** 522
British India Steam Navigation Co., **III** 521–22
British Industrial Solvents Ltd., **IV** 70
British Industry, **III** 335
British Insulated and Helsby Cables Ltd., **III** 433–34
British Interactive Broadcasting Ltd., **20** 79
British Isles Transport Co. Ltd., **II** 564
British Land Company, **10** 6
British Leyland Motor Corporation, **I** 175, 186; **III** 516, 523; **13** 286–87; **14** 35–36
British Linen Bank, **10** 336
British Marine Air Navigation, **I** 92
British Metal Corp., **IV** 140, 164
British Motor Corporation, **III** 555; **7** 459; **13** 286
British Motor Holdings, **7** 459
British National Films Ltd., **II** 157
British National Oil Corp., **IV** 40
British Newfoundland Corporation, **6** 502
British Nuclear Fuels PLC, **I** 573; **6 451–54**; **13** 458
British Nylon Spinners (BNS), **17** 118
British Overseas Airways Corp., **I** 51, 93, 120–21; **III** 522; **6** 78–79, 100, 110, 112, 117; **14** 71; **24** 86, 397
British Oxygen Co. *See* BOC Group.
The British Petroleum Company plc, **I** 241, 303; **II** 449, 563; **IV** 61, 280, 363–64, **378–80**, 381–82, 412–13, 450–54, 456, 466, 472, 486, 497–99, 505, 515, 524–25, 531–32, 557; **6** 304; **7 56–59 (upd.)**, 140–41, 332–33, 516, 559; **9** 490, 519; **11** 538; **13** 449; **14** 317; **16** 394, 461–62; **19** 155, 391; **21 80–84 (upd.)**, 352; **25** 101; **26** 366, 369; **30** 86, 88
British Plasterboard, **III** 734
British Portland Cement Manufacturers, **III** 669–70
British Printing and Communications Corp., **IV** 623–24, 642; **7** 312; **12** 224
British Prudential Assurance Co., **III** 335
British Rail, **III** 509; **V** 421–24; **10** 122; **27** 474
British Railways, **6** 413
British Railways Board, **V 421–24**
British Road Services, **6** 413
British Royal Insurance Co., Ltd., **III** 242
British Satellite Broadcasting, **10** 170
British Shoe Corporation, **V** 178
British Sky Broadcasting Group Plc, **20 79–81**; **24** 192, 194
British South Africa Co., **IV** 23, 94
British South American Airways, **I** 93
British South American Corporation, **6** 95
British Steel Brickworks, **III** 501; **7** 207
British Steel plc, **III** 494–95; **IV** 40, **41–43**, 128; **17** 481; **19 62–65 (upd.)**, 391; **24** 302
British Sugar plc, **II** 514, 581–82; **13** 53
British Tabulating Machine Company, **6** 240
British Telecommunications plc, **I** 83, 330; **II** 82; **V 279–82**; **6** 323; **7** 332–33; **8** 153; **9** 32; **11** 59, 185, 547; **15 66–70 (upd.)**, 131; **16** 468; **18** 155, 345; **20** 81; **21** 233; **24** 370; **25** 101–02, 301; **27** 304; **29** 44
British Thermoplastics and Rubber. *See* BTR plc.
British Timken Ltd., **8** 530
British Trimmings Ltd., **29** 133
British Twin Disc Ltd., **21** 504
British Tyre and Rubber Co., **I** 428
British United Airways, **I** 94
British Vita PLC, **9 92–93**; **19** 413–15
British World Airlines Ltd., **18 78–80**
British Zaire Diamond Distributors Ltd., **IV** 67
British-American Tobacco Co., Ltd., **V** 396, 401–02, 417; **9** 312; **29** 194–95
Britoil, **IV** 380; **21** 82
Britt Airways, **I** 118
Britt Lumber Co., Inc., **8** 348
Brittains Bricks, **III** 673
Brittania Sportswear, **16** 509
BritWill Healthcare Corp., **25** 504
BRK Brands, Inc., **28** 134
BRK Electronics, **9** 414
Bro-Well, **17** 56
Broad, Inc., **11** 482
Broad River Power Company, **6** 575
Broadcast Music Inc., **23 74–77**; **29** 22–23
Broadcast Technology Systems, Inc., **13** 398
Broadcom Eireann Research, **7** 510
Broadcort Capital Corp., **13** 342
The Broadmoor Hotel, **30 82–85**
BroadPark, **II** 415
BroadVision Inc., **18** 543
Broadway & Seymour Inc., **17** 264; **18** 112
Broadway Stores, Inc., **31** 193
Broadway-Hale Stores, Inc., **12** 356
Brobeck, Phleger & Harrison, LLP, **31 74–76**
Brock Candy Company. *See* Brach and Brock Confections, Inc.
Brock Hotel Corp., **13** 472–73; **31** 94
Brock Residence Inn, **9** 426

Brockway Glass Co., **I** 524; **15** 128
Brockway Standard Holdings Corporation. *See* BWAY Corporation.
Broderbund Software, Inc., **10** 285; **13** **113–16**; **25** 118; **29** **74–78 (upd.)**
Broederlijke Liefdebeurs, **III** 177
Broken Hill Proprietary Company Ltd., **I** 437–39; **II** 30; **III** 494; **IV** **44–47**, 58, 61, 171, 484; **10** 170; **21** 227; **22** **103–08 (upd.)**; **26** 248
The Bronfman Group, **6** 161, 163; **23** 124–25
Bronson Pharmaceuticals, **24** 257
Brooke Group Ltd., **15** **71–73**
Brooke Partners L.P., **11** 275
Brookfield Athletic Shoe Company, **17** 244
Brooklyn Flint Glass Co., **III** 683
Brooklyn Trust Co., **II** 312
Brooklyn Union Gas, **6** **455–57**; **27** 264–66
Brooks Brothers Inc., **V** 26–27; **13** 43; **22** **109–12**; **24** 313, 316
Brooks Fashion, **29** 164
Brooks Fiber Properties, Inc., **27** 301, 307
Brooks, Harvey & Company, Inc., **II** 431; **16** 376
Brooks Shoe Manufacturing Co., **16** 546
Brooks, Shoobridge and Co., **III** 669
Brooks-Scanlon Lumber Co., **IV** 306
Brookshire Grocery Company, **16** **63–66**
Brookstone, Inc., **II** 560; **12** 411; **18** **81–83**
Brookville Telephone Company, **6** 300
Brookwood Health Services, **III** 73
Brother Industries, Ltd., **13** 478; **14** **75–76**
Brother International, **23** 212
Brothers Foods, **18** 7
Brothers Gourmet Coffees, Inc., **20** **82–85**
Brotherton Chemicals, **29** 113
Broughton Foods Co., **17** **55–57**
Brown & Bigelow, **27** 193
Brown & Dureau Ltd., **IV** 248–49; **19** 14
Brown & Haley, **23** **78–80**
Brown & Root, Inc., **III** 498–99, 559; **13** **117–19**; **25** 190–91
Brown & Sharpe Manufacturing Co., **23** **81–84**
Brown and Williamson Tobacco Corporation, **I** 426; **14** **77–79**; **15** 72; **22** 72–73
Brown Bibby & Gregory, **I** 605
Brown Boveri. *See* BBC Brown Boveri.
Brown Co., **I** 452; **IV** 289
Brown Corp., **IV** 286
Brown Drug, **III** 9
Brown Foundation, **III** 498
Brown Group, Inc., **V** **351–53**; **9** 192; **10** 282; **16** 198; **20** **86–89 (upd.)**
Brown Instrument Co., **II** 41
Brown Jordan Co., **12** 301
Brown Oil Tools, **III** 428
Brown Paper Mill Co., **I** 380; **13** 379
Brown Printing Company, **26** **43–45**
Brown Shipbuilding Company. *See* Brown & Root, Inc.
Brown Shoe Co., **V** 351–52; **14** 294
Brown-Forman Corporation, **I** **225–27**; **III** 286; **10** **179–82 (upd.)**; **12** 313; **18** 69
Brown-Service Insurance Company, **9** 507
Brown-Shipley Ltd., **II** 425; **13** 341
Browne & Nolan Ltd., **IV** 294; **19** 225
Browning Manufacturing, **II** 19
Browning Telephone Corp., **14** 258
Browning-Ferris Industries, Inc., **V** **749–53**; **8** 562; **10** 33; **17** 552; **18** 10; **20** **90–93 (upd.)**; **23** 491
Broyhill Furniture Industries, Inc., **III** 528, 530; **10** **183–85**; **12** 308
BRS Ltd., **6** 412–13
Bruce's Furniture Stores, **14** 235
Bruckmann, Rosser, Sherill & Co., **27** 247
Bruegger's Bagel Bakery, **29** 171
Brufina, **II** 201–02
Brugman, **27** 502
Brummer Seal Company, **14** 64
Brunner Mond and Co., **I** 351
Bruno's Inc., **7** **60–62**; **13** 404, 406; **23** 261; **26** **46–48 (upd.)**
Brunswick Corporation, **III** **442–44**, 599; **9** 67, 119; **10** 262; **17** 453; **21** 291; **22** **113–17 (upd.)**, 118; **30** 303
Brunswick Pulp & Paper Co., **IV** 282, 311, 329; **9** 260; **19** 266
The Brush Electric Light Company, **11** 387; **25** 44
Brush Electrical Machines, **III** 507–09
Brush Moore Newspaper, Inc., **8** 527
Brush Wellman Inc., **14** **80–82**
Bryan Bros. Packing, **II** 572
Bryant Heater Co., **III** 471
Bryce & Co., **I** 547
Bryce Brothers, **12** 313
Bryce Grace & Co., **I** 547
Brylane Inc., **29** 106–07
Brymbo Steel Works, **III** 494
Bryn Mawr Stereo & Video, **30** 465
Brynwood Partners, **13** 19
BSB, **IV** 653; **7** 392
BSC (Industry) Ltd., **IV** 42
BSkyB, **IV** 653; **7** 392; **29** 369, 371
BSN. *See* Danone.
BSN Groupe S.A., **II** **474–75**, 544; **22** 458; **23** 448
BSR, **II** 82
BT. *See* British Telecommunications, plc.
BTI Services, **9** 59
BTM. *See* British Tabulating Machine Company.
BTR Dunlop Holdings, Inc., **21** 432
BTR plc, **I** **428–30**; **III** 185, 727; **8** 397; **24** 88
BTR Siebe plc, **27** **79–81**
Buchanan, **I** 239–40
Buchanan Electric Steel Company, **8** 114
Buckaroo International. *See* Bugle Boy Industries, Inc.
Buckeye Business Products Inc., **17** 384
Buckeye Tractor Ditcher, **21** 502
Buckeye Union Casualty Co., **III** 242
Buckhorn, Inc., **19** 277–78
Buckingham Corp., **I** 440, 468
The Buckle, Inc., **18** **84–86**
Buckler Broadcast Group, **IV** 597
Buckley/DeCerchio New York, **25** 180
Bucyrus Blades, Inc., **14** 81
Bucyrus International, Inc., **17** **58–61**
Bucyrus-Erie Company, **7** 513
Budapest Bank, **16** 14
The Budd Company, **III** 568; **IV** 222; **8** **74–76**; **20** 359
Buderus AG, **III** 692, 694–95
Budget Group, Inc., **25** **92–94**
Budget Rent a Car Corporation, **I** 537; **6** 348–49, 393; **9** **94–95**; **13** 529; **22** 524; **24** 12, 409; **25** 143
Budgetel Inn. *See* Marcus Corporation.
Budweiser, **18** 70
Budweiser Japan Co., **21** 320
Buena Vista Distribution, **II** 172; **6** 174; **30** 487
Buffalo Forge Company, **7** 70–71
Buffalo Insurance Co., **III** 208
Buffalo Mining Co., **IV** 181
Buffalo News, **18** 60
Buffalo Paperboard, **19** 78
Buffalo-Springfield, **21** 502
Buffets, Inc., **10** **186–87**; **22** 465
Buffett Partnership, Ltd., **III** 213
Bugaboo Creek Steak House Inc., **19** 342
Bugatti Industries, **14** 321
Bugle Boy Industries, Inc., **18** **87–88**
Buick Motor Co., **I** 171; **III** 438; **8** 74; **10** 325
Builders Emporium, **13** 169; **25** 535
Builders Square, **V** 112; **9** 400; **12** 345, 385; **14** 61; **16** 210; **31** 20
Building Products of Canada Limited, **25** 232
Buitoni SpA, **II** 548; **17** 36
Bulgari S.p.A., **20** **94–97**
Bulgarian Oil Co., **IV** 454
Bulgheroni SpA, **27** 105
Bulkships, **27** 473
Bull. *See* Compagnie des Machines Bull S.A.
Bull HN Information Systems, **III** 122–23
Bull Motors, **11** 5
Bull Run Corp., **24** 404
Bull S.A., **III** 122–23
Bull Tractor Company, **7** 534; **16** 178; **26** 492
Bull-GE, **III** 123
Bull-Zenith, **25** 531
Bulldog Computer Products, **10** 519
Bullock's, **III** 63; **31** 191
Bulolo Gold Dredging, **IV** 95
Bulova Corporation, **I** 488; **II** 101; **III** 454–55; **12** 316–17, 453; **13** **120–22**; **14** 501; **21** 121–22
Bumble Bee Seafoods, Inc., **II** 491, 508, 557; **24** 114
Bumkor-Ramo Corp., **I** 539
Bunawerke Hüls GmbH., **I** 350
Bundy Corporation, **17** **62–65**, 480
Bunker Ramo Info Systems, **III** 118
Bunte Candy, **12** 427
Bunzl plc, **IV** **260–62**; **12** 264; **31** **77–80 (upd.)**
Buquet, **19** 49
Burbank Aircraft Supply, Inc., **14** 42–43
Burberrys Ltd., **V** 68; **10** 122; **17** **66–68**; **19** 181
Burda Holding GmbH. & Co., **20** 53; **23** **85–89**
Burdines, **9** 209; **31** 192
Bureau de Recherches de Pétrole, **IV** 544–46, 559–60; **7** 481–83; **21** 203–04
The Bureau of National Affairs, Inc., **23** **90–93**
Burelle S.A., **23** **94–96**
Burger and Aschenbrenner, **16** 486
Burger Boy Food-A-Rama, **8** 564
Burger Chef, **II** 532
Burger King Corporation, **I** 21, 278; **II** 556–57, **613–15**, 647; **7** 316; **8** 564; **9** 178; **10** 122; **12** 43, 553; **13** 408–09; **14** 25, 32, 212, 214, 452; **16** 95–97, 396; **17** **69–72 (upd.)**, 501; **18** 437; **21** 25, 362; **23** 505; **24** 140–41; **25** 228; **26** 284

Burgess, Anderson & Tate Inc., **25** 500
Bürhle, **17** 36
Burhmann-Tetterode, **22** 154
Burke Scaffolding Co., **9** 512
BURLE Industries Inc., **11** 444
Burlesdon Brick Co., **III** 734
Burlington Coat Factory Warehouse Corporation, 10 188–89
Burlington Homes of New England, **14** 138
Burlington Industries, Inc., **V** 118, **354–55**; **8** 234; **9** 231; **12** 501; **17** **73–76 (upd.)**, 304–05; **19** 275
Burlington Mills Corporation, **12** 117–18
Burlington Motor Holdings, **30** 114
Burlington Northern, Inc., **IV** 182; **V** **425–28**; **10** 190–91; **11** 315; **12** 145, 278
Burlington Northern Santa Fe Corporation, 27 82–89 (upd.); **28** 495
Burlington Resources Inc., **10 190–92**; **11** 135; **12** 144
Burmah Castrol PLC, **IV** 378, **381–84**, 440–41, 483–84, 531; **7** 56; **15** 246; **21** 80; **30 86–91 (upd.)**
Burmeister & Wain, **III** 417–18
Burn & Co., **IV** 205
Burn Standard Co. Ltd., **IV** 484
Burnards, **II** 677
Burndy, **19** 166
Burnham and Co., **II** 407–08; **6** 599; **8** 388
Burns & Wilcox Ltd., **6** 290
Burns Companies, **III** 569; **20** 360
Burns Fry Ltd., **II** 349
Burns International Security Services, **III** 440; **13 123–25**
Burns Philp & Company Limited, **21** 496–98
Burns-Alton Corp., **21** 154–55
Burnup & Sims, Inc., **19** 254; **26** 324
Burpee & Co. *See* W. Atlee Burpee & Co.
Burr & Co., **II** 424; **13** 340
Burr-Brown Corporation, **19 66–68**
Burrill & Housman, **II** 424; **13** 340
Burris Industries, **14** 303
Burroughs Corp., **I** 142, 478; **III** 132, 148–49, 152, 165–66; **6** 233, 266, 281–83; **18** 386, 542. *See also* Unisys Corporation.
Burroughs Mfg. Co., **16** 321
Burroughs Wellcome & Co., **I** 713; **8** 216
Burrows, Marsh & McLennan, **III** 282
Burrups Ltd., **18** 331, 333
Burry, **II** 560; **12** 410
Bursley & Co., **II** 668
Burt Claster Enterprises, **III** 505
Burthy China Clays, **III** 690
Burton Group plc, **V 20–22**. *See also* Arcadia Group plc.
Burton J. Vincent, Chesley & Co., **III** 271
Burton, Parsons and Co. Inc., **II** 547
Burton Retail, **V** 21
Burton Rubber Processing, **8** 347
Burton Snowboards Inc., **22 118–20**, 460
Burton-Furber Co., **IV** 180
Burtons Gold Medal Biscuits Limited, **II** 466; **13** 53
Burwell Brick, **14** 248
Bury Group, **II** 581
Bush Boake Allen Inc., **IV** 346; **30 92–94**
Bush Hog, **21** 20–22
Bush Industries, Inc., **20 98–100**
Bush Terminal Company, **15** 138
Business Communications Group, Inc. *See* Caribiner International, Inc.
Business Depot, Limited, **10** 498
Business Expansion Capital Corp., **12** 42
Business Express Airlines, Inc., **28** 22
Business Information Technology, Inc., **18** 112
Business Men's Assurance Company of America, **III** 209; **13** 476; **14 83–85**; **15** 30
Business Objects S.A., **25 95–97**
Business Resources Corp., **23** 489, 491
Business Science Computing, **14** 36
Business Software Association, **10** 35
Business Software Technology, **10** 394
Business Wire, **25** 240
Businessland Inc., **III** 153; **6** 267; **10** 235; **13** 175–76, 277, 482
Busse Broadcasting Corporation, **7** 200; **24** 199
Büssing Automobilwerke AG, **IV** 201
Buster Brown, **V** 351–52
BUT S.A., **24** 266, 270
Butano, **IV** 528
Butler Bros., **21** 96
Butler Cox PLC, **6** 229
Butler Group, Inc., **30** 310–11
Butler Manufacturing Co., **12 51–53**
Butler Shoes, **16** 560
Butterfield & Swire. *See* Swire Pacific Ltd.
Butterfield, Wasson & Co., **II** 380, 395; **10** 59; **12** 533
Butterick Co., Inc., **23 97–99**
Butterley Company, **III** 501; **7** 207
Butterworth & Co. (Publishers) Ltd., **IV** 641; **7** 311; **17** 398
Buttrey Food & Drug Stores Co., **18 89–91**
Butz Thermo-Electric Regulator Co., **II** 40; **12** 246
Buxton, **III** 28; **23** 21
Buzzard Electrical & Plumbing Supply, **9** 399; **16** 186
BVA Investment Corp., **11** 446–47
BVD, **25** 166
BWAY Corporation, **24 91–93**
BWP Distributors, **29** 86, 88
Byerly's, Inc. *See* Lund Food Holdings, Inc.
Byers Machines, **21** 502
Byrnes Long Island Motor Cargo, Inc., **6** 370
Byron Jackson, **III** 428, 439. *See also* BJ Services Company.
Byron Weston Company, **26** 105
Bytrex, Inc., **III** 643

C&A Brenninkmeyer KG, **V 23–24**
C&E Software, **10** 507
C.&E. Cooper Co., **II** 14
C & G Systems, **19** 442
C.&G. Cooper Company, **II** 14; **20** 162
C & H Distributors, Inc., **27** 177
C & O. *See* Chesapeake and Ohio Railway.
C&R Clothiers, **17** 313
C&S Bank, **10** 425–26
C&S/Sovran Corporation, **10** 425–27; **18** 518; **26** 453
C.A. Pillsbury and Co., **II** 555
C.A. Reed Co., **IV** 353; **19** 498
C.A.S. Sports Agency Inc., **22** 460, 462
C.A. Swanson & Sons. *See* Vlasic Foods International Inc.
C. Bechstein, **III** 657
C. Brewer, **I** 417; **24** 32
C.D. Haupt, **IV** 296; **19** 226
C.D. Kenny Co., **II** 571
C.D. Magirus AG, **III** 541
C.E. Chappell & Sons, Inc., **16** 61–62
C.E.T. *See* Club Européen du Tourisme.
C.F. Burns and Son, Inc., **21** 154
C.F. Hathaway Company, **12** 522
C.F. Mueller Co., **I** 497–98; **12** 332
C.F. Orvis Company. *See* The Orvis Company, Inc.
C. Francis, Son and Co., **III** 669
C.G. Conn, **7** 286
C.H. Dexter & Co., **I** 320
C.H. Heist Corporation, **24 111–13**
C.H. Knorr Company, **II** 497; **22** 83
C.H. Masland & Sons. *See* Masland Corporation.
C.H. Musselman Co., **7** 429
C.H. Robinson, Inc., **8** 379–80; **11** **43–44**; **23** 357
C-I-L, Inc., **III** 745; **13** 470
C. Itoh & Co., **I 431–33**, 492, 510; **II** 273, 292, 361, 442, 679; **IV** 269, 326, 516, 543; **7** 529; **10** 500; **17** 124; **24** 324–25; **26** 456
C.J. Devine, **II** 425
C.J. Lawrence, Morgan Grenfell Inc., **II** 429
C.J. Smith and Sons, **11** 3
C.L. Bencard, **III** 66
C. Lee Cook Co., **III** 467
C.M. Aikman & Co., **13** 168
C.M. Armstrong, Inc., **14** 17
C.M. Barnes Company, **10** 135
C.M. Page, **14** 112
C.O. Lovette Company, **6** 370
C.O.M.B. Company, **18** 131–33
C/P Utility Services Company, **14** 138
C.P.U., Inc., **18** 111–12
C.R. Anthony Company, **24** 458
C.R. Bard Inc., **IV** 287; **9 96–98**; **22** 360–61
C.R. Eggs, Inc., **25** 332
C. Reichenbach'sche Maschinenfabrik, **III** 561
C. Rowbotham & Sons, **III** 740
C.S. Rolls & Co., **I** 194
C.T. Bowring, **III** 280, 283; **22** 318
C-Tec Corp. *See* Commonwealth Telephone Enterprises, Inc.
C.V. Buchan & Co., **I** 567
C.V. Gebroeders Pel, **7** 429
C.V. Mosby Co., **IV** 677–78
C.W. Acquisitions, **27** 288
C.W. Costello & Associates Inc., **31** 131
C.W. Holt & Co., **III** 450
C.W. Zumbiel Company, **11** 422
C. Wuppesahl & Co. Assekuranzmakler, **25** 538
CAA. *See* Creative Artists Agency.
Cabela's Inc., **26 49–51**
Cable & Wireless HKT, **30 95–98 (upd.)**. *See also* Hong Kong Telecomminications Ltd.
Cable and Wireless plc, **IV** 695; **V** **283–86**; **7** 332–33; **11** 547; **15** 69, 521; **17** 419; **18** 253; **25 98–102 (upd.)**; **26** 332; **27** 307
Cable Communications Operations, Inc., **6** 313
Cable London, **25** 497
Cable Management Advertising Control System, **25** 497
Cable News Network, **II** 166–68; **6** 171–73; **9** 30; **12** 546

Cablec Corp., **III** 433–34
Cableform, **I** 592
Cabletron Systems, Inc., 10 193–94; 10 511; **20** 8; **24** 183; **26** 276
Cablevision Systems Corporation, 7 63–65; 18 211; **30 99–103 (upd.)**
Cabot, Cabot & Forbes, **22** 100
Cabot Corporation, 8 77–79; 29 79–82 (upd.)
Cabot Medical Corporation, **21** 117, 119
Cabot Noble Inc., **18** 503, 507
Cabot-Morgan Real Estate Co., **16** 159
Cabrera Vulcan Shoe Corp., **22** 213
Cache Incorporated, 30 104–06
CACI International Inc., 21 85–87
Cacique, **24** 237
Cadadia, **II** 641–42
Cadbury Schweppes PLC, I 25–26, 220, 288; **II 476–78**, 510, 512, 592; **III** 554; **6** 51–52; **9** 178; **15** 221; **22** 513; **25** 3, 5
CADCAM Technology Inc., **22** 196
Caddell Construction Company, **12** 41
Cademartori, **23** 219
Cadence Design Systems, Inc., 6 247; **10** 118; **11 45–48**, 285, 490–91; **24** 235
Cadence Industries Corporation, **10** 401–02
Cadet Uniform Services Ltd., **21** 116
Cadillac Automobile Co., **I** 171; **10** 325
Cadillac Fairview Corp., **IV** 703
Cadillac Plastic, **8** 347
Cadisys Corporation, **10** 119
Cadmus Communications Corporation, 16 531; **23 100–03**
Cadoricin, **III** 47
CAE Systems Inc., **8** 519
Caere Corporation, 20 101–03
Caesar-Wollheim-Gruppe, **IV** 197
Caesars World, Inc., 6 199–202; 17 318
Caf'Casino, **12** 152
Café Grand Mère, **II** 520
Caffarel, **27** 105
CAFO, **III** 241
Cagiva Group, **17** 24; **30** 172
Cagle's, Inc., 20 104–07
Cahners Publishing, **IV** 667; **12** 561; **17** 398; **22** 442
CAI Corp., **12** 79
Cailler, **II** 546
Cain Chemical, **IV** 481
Cains Marcelle Potato Chips Inc., **15** 139
Caisse Commericale de Bruxelles, **II** 270
Caisse de dépôt et placement du Quebec, **II** 664
Caisse des Dépôts, **6** 206
Caisse National de Crédit Agricole, **II** 264–66
Caisse Nationale de Crédit Agricole, **15** 38–39
Caja General de Depositos, **II** 194
Cajun Bayou Distributors and Management, Inc., **19** 301
Cajun Electric Power Cooperative, Inc., **21** 470
Cal Circuit Abco Inc., **13** 387
CAL Corporation, **21** 199, 201
Cal-Dive International Inc., **25** 104–05
Cal-Van Tools. *See* Chemi-Trol Chemical Co.
Cal/Ink, **13** 228
Cala, **17** 558
Calais Railroad Company, **16** 348
Calcined Coke Corp., **IV** 402
Calcitherm Group, **24** 144
Calco, **I** 300–01
CalComp Inc., 13 126–29
Calculating-Tabulating-Recording Company. *See* International Business Machines Corporation.
Calcutta & Burmah Steam Navigation Co., **III** 521
Caldbeck Macgregor & Co., **III** 523
Calder Race Course, Inc., **29** 118
Caldor Inc., 12 54–56, 508; **30** 57
Caledonian Airways. *See* British Caledonian Airways.
Caledonian Bank, **10** 337
Caledonian Paper plc, **IV** 302
Calédonickel, **IV** 107
Calgary Power Company. *See* TransAlta Utilities Corporation.
Calgene, Inc., **29** 330
Calgon Corporation, **6** 27; **16** 387
Calgon Water Management, **15** 154
California Arabian Standard Oil Co., **IV** 536, 552
California Automated Design, Inc., **11** 284
California Bank, **II** 289
California Charter Inc., **24** 118
California Cheese, **24** 444
California Computer Products, Inc. *See* CalComp Inc.
California Cooler Inc., **I** 227, 244; **10** 181
California Dental Supply Co., **19** 289
California Design Studio, **31** 52
California Federal Bank, **22** 275
California First, **II** 358
California Fruit Growers Exchange. *See* Sunkist Growers, Inc.
California Ink Company, **13** 227
California Institute of Technology, **9** 367
California Insurance Co., **III** 234
California Oilfields, Ltd., **IV** 531, 540
California Pacific, **22** 172
California Perfume Co., **III** 15
California Petroleum Co., **IV** 551–52
California Pizza Kitchen Inc., 15 74–76
California Plant Protection, **9** 408
California Portland Cement Co., **III** 718; **19** 69
California Pro Sports Inc., **24** 404
California Slim, **27** 197
California Steel Industries, **IV** 125
California Telephone and Light, **II** 490
California Test Bureau, **IV** 636
California Texas Oil Co., **III** 672
California Tile, **III** 673
California Woodfiber Corp., **IV** 266
California-Western States Life Insurance Co., **III** 193–94
Caligen, **9** 92
Caligor. *See* Henry Schein Medical.
Call-Chronicle Newspapers, Inc., **IV** 678
Callaghan & Company, **8** 526
Callard and Bowser, **II** 594
Callaway Golf Company, 15 77–79; 16 109; **19** 430, 432; **23** 267, 474
Callaway Wines, **I** 264
Callebaut, **II** 520–21
Callender's Cable and Construction Co. Ltd., **III** 433–34
Calloway's Nursery Inc., **12** 200
Calma, **II** 30; **12** 196
Calmar Co., **12** 127
CalMat Co., III 718; **19 69–72**
Calmic Ltd., **I** 715
Calor Group, **IV** 383
Caloric Corp., **II** 86
Calpine Corp., **IV** 84
Calsil Ltd., **III** 674
Caltex Petroleum Corporation, II 53; **III** 672; **IV** 397, 434, 440–41, 479, 484, 492, 519, 527, 536, 545–46, 552, 560, 562, 718; **7** 483; **19 73–75; 21** 204; **25** 471
Calumatic Group, **25** 82
Calumet & Arizona Mining Co., **IV** 177
Calumet Electric Company, **6** 532
Calvert & Co., **I** 293
Calvert Insurance Co. *See* Gryphon Holdings, Inc.
Calvin Bullock Ltd., **I** 472
Calvin Klein, Inc., 9 203; **22 121–24; 25** 258; **27** 329
Camargo Foods, **12** 531
CamBar. *See* Cameron & Barkley Company.
Camber Corporation, **25** 405
Cambex, **12** 147–48
Cambrex Corporation, 16 67–69
Cambria Steel Company, **IV** 35; **7** 48
Cambrian Wagon Works Ltd., **31** 369
Cambridge Applied Nutrition Toxicology and Biosciences Ltd., **10** 105
Cambridge Biotech Corp., **13** 241
Cambridge Electric Co., **14** 124, 126
Cambridge Gas Co., **14** 124
Cambridge Interactive Systems Ltd., **10** 241
Cambridge Steam Corp., **14** 124
Camco Inc., **IV** 658
Camden Wire Co., Inc., **7** 408; **31** 354–55
CAMECO, **IV** 436
Camelot Barthropp Ltd., **26** 62
Camelot Music, Inc., 26 52–54
Cameron & Barkley Company, 13 79; **28 59–61**
Cameron Ashley Inc., **19** 57
Cameron Iron Works, **II** 17
Cameron Oil Co., **IV** 365
Cameron-Brown Company, **10** 298
CAMI Automotive, **III** 581
Camintonn, **9** 41–42
Camp Manufacturing Co., **IV** 345; **8** 102
Campbell Box & Tag Co., **IV** 333
Campbell Cereal Company. *See* Malt-O-Meal Company.
Campbell, Cowperthwait & Co., **17** 498
Campbell Hausfeld. *See* Scott Fetzer Company.
Campbell Industries, Inc., **11** 534
Campbell Soup Company, I 21, 26, 31, 599, 601; **II 479–81**, 508, 684; **7 66–69 (upd.)**, 340; **10** 382; **11** 172; **18** 58; **25** 516; **26 55–59 (upd.)**
Campbell Taggart, Inc., **I** 219; **19** 135–36, 191
Campbell-Ewald Co., **I** 16–17
Campbell-Mithun-Esty, Inc., 13 516; **16 70–72**
Campeau Corporation, IV 721; **V 25–28; 9** 209, 211, 391; **12** 36–37; **13** 43; **15** 94; **17** 560; **22** 110; **23** 60; **31** 192
Campo Electronics, Appliances & Computers, Inc., 16 73–75
Campo Lindo, **25** 85
Campofrio Alimentacion, S.A., **18** 247
CAMPSA. *See* Compañia Arrendataria del Monopolio de Petróleos Sociedad Anónima.
Campus Services, Inc., **12** 173
Canada & Dominion Sugar Co., **II** 581
Canada Cable & Wire Company, **9** 11

Canada Cement, **III** 704–05
Canada Cup, **IV** 290
Canada Development Corp., **IV** 252; **17** 29
Canada Dry, **I** 281
Canada, Limited, **24** 143
Canada Packers Inc., II 482–85
Canada Safeway Ltd., **II** 650, 654
Canada Surety Co., **26** 486
Canada Trust. *See* CT Financial Services Inc.
Canada Tungsten Mining Corp., Ltd., **IV** 18
Canada Wire & Cable Company, Ltd., **IV** 164–65; **7** 397–99
Canadair, Inc., **I** 58; **7** 205; **13** 358; **16 76–78**
Canadian Ad-Check Services Inc., **26** 270
Canadian Airlines International Ltd., **6** 61–62, 101; **12** 192; **23** 10; **24** 400
Canadian Bank of Commerce, **II** 244–45
Canadian British Aluminum, **IV** 11
Canadian Cellucotton Products Ltd., **III** 40; **16** 302
Canadian Copper, **IV** 110
Canadian Copper Refiners, Ltd., **IV** 164
Canadian Dominion Steel and Coal Corp., **III** 508
Canadian Eastern Finance, **IV** 693
Canadian Fina Oil, **IV** 498
Canadian Football League, **12** 457
Canadian Forest Products, **IV** 270
Canadian Fuel Marketers, **IV** 566
Canadian General Electric Co., **8** 544–45
Canadian Government Merchant Marine, **6** 360–61
Canadian Gridoil Ltd., **IV** 373
Canadian Imperial Bank of Commerce, **II 244–46**; **IV** 693; **7** 26–28; **10** 8
Canadian Industrial Alcohol Company Limited, **14** 141
Canadian International Paper Co., **IV** 286–87; **15** 228
Canadian Keyes Fibre Company, Limited of Nova Scotia, **9** 305
Canadian National Railway System, **I** 284; **6 359–62**; **12** 278–79; **22** 444; **23** 10
Canadian Odeon Theatres, **6** 161; **23** 123
Canadian Overseas Telecommunications Corporation, **25** 100
Canadian Pacific Enterprises, **III** 611
Canadian Pacific Limited, **V 429–31**; **8** 544–46
Canadian Pacific Railway, **I** 573; **II** 210, 220, 344; **III** 260; **IV** 272, 308, 437; **6** 359–60; **25** 230
Canadian Packing Co. Ltd., **II** 482
Canadian Petrofina, **IV** 498
Canadian Radio-Television and Telecommunications Commission, **6** 309
Canadian Telephones and Supplies, **6** 310
Canadian Tire Corporation, Limited, **25** 144
Canadian Transport Co., **IV** 308
Canadian Utilities Limited, **13 130–32**
Canadian Vickers, **16** 76
Canal Bank, **11** 105
Canal Electric Co., **14** 125–26
Canal Plus, **III** 48; **7** 392; **10 195–97**, 345, 347; **23** 476; **29** 369, 371; **31** 330
CanalSatellite, **29** 369, 371
CanAmera Foods, **7** 82
Canandaigua Wine Company, Inc., **13 133–35**
Cananwill, **III** 344
Canary Wharf Group Plc, **30 107–09**
Candie's, Inc., **31 81–84**
Candle Corporation of America. *See* Blyth Industries, Inc.
Candy SpA, **22** 350
Canfor Corp., **IV** 321; **17** 540
Cannell Communications, **25** 418
Cannon Assurance Ltd., **III** 276
Cannon Mills, Co., **9** 214–16
Cannondale Corporation, **16** 494; **21 88–90**; **26** 183, 412
Canon Inc., **I** 494; **II** 103, 292; **III 120–21**, 143, 172, 575, 583–84; **6** 238, 289; **9** 251; **10** 23; **13** 482; **15** 150; **18 92–95 (upd.)**, 186, 341–42, 383, 386–87; **24** 324; **26** 213
Canpet Exploration Ltd., **IV** 566
Canpotex Ltd., **18** 432
Canrad-Hanovia, **27** 57
Cans Inc., **I** 607
Canstar Sports Inc., **15** 396–97; **16 79–81**
Canteen Corp., **I** 127; **II** 679–80; **12** 489; **13** 321
Cantel Corp., **11** 184; **18** 32; **20** 76; **30** 388
Canton Chemical, **I** 323; **8** 147
Canton Railway Corp., **IV** 718
Cantor Fitzgerald Securities Corporation, **10** 276–78
Canyon Cafes, **31** 41
Cap Rock Electric Cooperative, **6** 580
CAPCO. *See* Central Area Power Coordination Group *or* Custom Academic Publishing Company.
Capcom Co., **7** 396
Cape and Vineyard Electric Co., **14** 124–25
Cape Cod-Cricket Lane, Inc., **8** 289
Cape Horn Methanol, **III** 512
Cape May Light and Power Company, **6** 449
Cape PLC, **22** 49
Cape Wine and Distillers, **I** 289
Capehart-Farnsworth, **I** 463; **11** 197
Capex, **6** 224
AB Capital & Investment Corporation, **6** 108; **23** 381
Capital Advisors, Inc., **22** 4
Capital Airlines, **I** 128; **III** 102; **6** 128
Capital and Counties Bank, **II** 307; **IV** 91
Capital Bank N.A., **16** 162
Capital Cities/ABC Inc., **II 129–31**; **III** 214; **IV** 608–09, 613, 652; **11** 331; **15** 464; **18** 60, 62–63, 329; **30** 490. *See also* ABC, Inc.
Capital Concrete Pipe Company, **14** 250
Capital Controls Co., Inc. *See* Severn Trent PLC.
Capital Distributing Co., **21** 37
Capital Financial Services, **III** 242
Capital Grille, **19** 342
Capital Group, **26** 187
Capital Holding Corporation, **III 216–19**
Capital Life Insurance Company, **11** 482–83
Capital Management Services. *See* CB Commercial Real Estate Services Group, Inc.
Capital One, **18** 535
Capital Trust Corp., **17** 498
Capital-Gazette Communications, Inc., **12** 302
Capitol Film + TV International, **IV** 591
Capitol Films, **25** 270
Capitol Pack, Inc., **13** 350
Capitol Printing Ink Company, **13** 227–28
Capitol Publishing, **13** 560
Capitol Radio Engineering Institute, **IV** 636
Capitol Records, **22** 192–93
Capitol-EMI, **I** 531–32; **11** 557
Capper Pass, **IV** 191
Capseals, Ltd., **8** 476
CapStar Hotel Company, **21 91–93**
Capsugel, **I** 712
Car-lac Electronic Industrial Sales Inc., **9** 420
Car-X, **10** 415
Caracas Petroleum Sociedad Anónima, **IV** 565–66
Caradon plc, **18** 561; **20 108–12 (upd.)**
Carando Foods, **7** 174–75
Carat Group, **6** 15–16
Caratti Sports, Ltd., **26** 184
Caraustar Industries, Inc., **19 76–78**
Caravali, **13** 493–94
Caravelle Foods, **21** 500
Carbide Router Co., **III** 436
Carbis China Clay & Brick Co., **III** 690
Carbocol, **IV** 417
Carboline Co., **8** 455
CarboMedics, **11** 458–60
Carbon Research Laboratories, **9** 517
La Carbonique, **23** 217, 219
Carborundum Company, **III** 610; **15 80–82**
Cardàpio, **29** 444
Cardboard Containers, **IV** 249
Cardem Insurance Co., **III** 767; **22** 546
Cardiac Pacemakers, Inc., **I** 646; **11** 90; **11** 458; **22** 361
Cardinal Distributors Ltd., **II** 663
Cardinal Health, Inc., **18 96–98**
Cardiotronics Systems, Inc., **21** 47
Cardon-Phonocraft Company, **18** 492
Care Advantage, Inc., **25** 383
Care Group, **22** 276
CareerCom Corp., **25** 253
CareerStaff Unlimited Inc., **25** 455
Caremark International Inc., **10** 143, **198–200**
Carenes, SA, **12** 377
CarePlus, **6** 42
CareUnit, Inc., **15** 123
Carey Canada Inc., **III** 766; **22** 546
Carey International, Inc., **26 60–63**
Carey Straw Mill, **12** 376
Carey-McFall Corp., **V** 379; **19** 421
S.A. CARFUEL, **12** 152
Cargill, Inc., **II** 494, 517, **616–18**; **11** 92; **13 136–38 (upd.)**, 186, 351; **18** 378, 380; **21** 290, 500; **22** 85, 426; **25** 332; **31** 17, 20
Cargill Trust Co., **13** 467
Cargo Express, **16** 198
Cargo Furniture, **31** 436
CARGOSUR, **6** 96
Carhartt, Inc., **30 110–12**
Cariani Sausage Co., **II** 518
Caribair, **I** 102
Caribbean Chemicals S.A., **I** 512
Caribe Co., **II** 493
Caribe Shoe Corp., **III** 529
Caribiner International, Inc., **24 94–97**
Cariboo Pulp & Paper Co., **IV** 269
Caribou Coffee Company, Inc., **28 62–65**

Carintusa Inc., **8** 271
CARIPLO, **III** 347
Carisam International Corp., **29** 511
Carita S.A., **III** 63; **22** 487
Caritas Foundation, **22** 411, 413
Carl Byoir & Associates, **I** 14
Carl Karcher Enterprises, Inc., **19** 435
Carl Marks & Co., **11** 260–61
Carl's Superstores, **9** 452
Carl-Zeiss-Stiftung, III 445–47, 583
Carlan, **III** 614
Carless Lubricants, **IV** 451
Carleton Financial Computations Inc., **II** 317
Carlin Gold Mining Company, **7** 386–87
Carling O'Keefe Ltd., **I** 218, 229, 254, 269, 438–39; **7** 183; **12** 337; **26** 305
Carlingford, **II** 298
Carlisle Companies Incorporated, 8 80–82
Carlisle Memory Products, **14** 535
Carlo Erba S.p.A., **I** 635
Carlon, **13** 304–06
Carlova, Inc., **21** 54
Carlsberg A/S, I 247; **9 99–101**; **29 83–85 (upd.)**
Carlson Companies, Inc., 6 363–66; **22 125–29 (upd.)**; **26** 147, 439–40; **27** 9, 11; **29** 200
Carlton and United Breweries Ltd., I 228–29, 437–39; **7** 182–83
Carlton Communications plc, 15 83–85; **23** 111, 113; **24** 194
Carlton Investments L.P., **22** 514
The Carlyle Group, **11** 364; **14** 43; **16** 47; **21** 97; **30** 472
CarMax, **26** 410; **29** 120, 123
Carmeda AB, **10** 439
Carmichael Lynch Inc., 28 66–68
Carmike Cinemas, Inc., 14 86–88; **21** 362
Carnation Company, I 269; **II 486–89**, 518, 548; **7** 339, 383, 429; **10** 382; **12** 337; **28** 311
Carnaud Basse-Indre, **IV** 228
Carnaud-Metalbox, **13** 190; **20** 111
Carnegie Brothers & Co., Ltd., **9** 407
Carnegie Foundation for the Advancement of Teaching, **12** 141
Carnegie Steel Co., **II** 330; **IV** 572; **7** 549
Carnival Corporation, 27 90–92 (upd.)
Carnival Cruise Lines, Inc., 6 367–68; **21** 106; **22** 444–46, 470; **27** 27
Caro Produce and Institutional Foods, **31** 359–61
Carol Moberg, Inc., **6** 40
Carol's Shoe Corp., **22** 213
Carol-Braugh-Robinson Co., **II** 624
Carolco Pictures Inc., **III** 48; **10** 196
Carolina Biological Supply, **11** 424
Carolina Coach Co., **13** 397–98
Carolina Coin Caterers Corporation, **10** 222
Carolina Energies, Inc., **6** 576
Carolina First Corporation, 31 85–87
Carolina First National, **II** 336
Carolina Freight Corporation, 6 369–72
Carolina Paper Board Corporation. *See* Caraustar Industries, Inc.
Carolina Power & Light Company, V 564–66; **23 104–07 (upd.)**
Carolina Telephone and Telegraph Company, 10 201–03
Carolinas Capital Funds Group, **29** 132
Carolinas-Virginia Nuclear Power Association, **27** 130
Carpenter Investment and Development Corporation, **31** 279
Carpenter Paper Co., **IV** 282; **9** 261
Carpenter Technology Corporation, 13 139–41
CarpetMAX, **25** 320
Carpets International Plc., **8** 270–71
CARQUEST Corporation, 26 348; **29 86–89**
Carr Fowler, **III** 673
Carr's of Carlisle, **I** 604; **II** 594
Carr-Gottstein Foods Co., 17 77–80
Carr-Lowrey Glass Co., **13** 40
Carr-Union Line, **6** 397
Carrabba's Italian Grill, **12** 373–75
Carrefour SA, II 628; **8** 404–05; **10 204–06**; **12** 153; **19** 98, 309; **21** 225; **23** 230–32; 246–47, 364; **24** 475; **27** 207, **93–96 (upd.)**
Carreras, Limited, **V** 411–12; **19** 367–69
Carrier Corporation, I 85; **III** 329; **7 70–73**; **13** 507; **22** 6; **26** 4; **29** 216
Carroll County Electric Company, **6** 511
Carroll Reed Ski Shops, Inc., **10** 215
Carroll's Foods, **7** 477; **22** 368
Carrows, **27** 16, 19
Carry Machine Supply, Inc., **18** 513
Carson, Inc., 31 88–90
Carson Pirie Scott & Company, II 669; **9** 142; **15 86–88**; **19** 324, 511–12
Carson Water Company, **19** 411
Carte Blanche, **9** 335
CarTemps USA. *See* Republic Industries, Inc.
Carter & Co., **IV** 644
Carter Automotive Co., **I** 159
Carter, Berlind, Potoma & Weill, **II** 450
Carter Hawley Hale Stores, I 246; **V 29–32**; **8** 160; **12** 356; **15** 88; **16** 466; **17** 43, 523; **18** 488; **25** 177
Carter Holt Harvey Ltd., **IV** 280; **15** 229; **19** 155
Carter Oil Company, **IV** 171; **11** 353
Carter-Wallace, Inc., 6 27; **8 83–86**
Carteret Savings Bank, **III** 263–64; **10** 340
Carterphone, **22** 17
Cartier, **27** 329, 487–89
Cartier Monde, IV 93; **V** 411, 413; **29 90–92**
Cartier Refined Sugars Ltd., **II** 662–63
Cartiera F.A. Marsoni, **IV** 587
Cartiere Ascoli Piceno, **IV** 586
Cartiers Superfoods, **II** 678
Cartillon Importers, Ltd., **6** 48
Carver Pump Co., **19** 36
Carworth Inc., **I** 630; **11** 34
Cary-Davis Tug and Barge Company. *See* Puget Sound Tug and Barge Company.
CASA. *See* Construcciones Aeronautics S.A.
Casa Bancária Almeida e Companhia. *See* Banco Bradesco S.A.
Casa Bonita, **II** 587
Casa Cuervo, S.A. de C.V., 31 91–93
Casa Ley, S.A. de C.V., **24** 416
Casablanca Records, **23** 390
Casarotto Security, **24** 510
Cascade Communications Corp., **16** 468; **20** 8; **24** 50
Cascade Fertilizers Ltd., **25** 232
Cascade Fiber, **13** 99
Cascade Lumber Co., **IV** 255; **8** 65
Cascade Natural Gas Corporation, 6 568; **9 102–04**
Cascade Steel Rolling Mills, Inc., **19** 380–81
CasChem, Inc. *See* Cambrex Corporation.
Casco Northern Bank, 14 89–91
Case Manufacturing Corp., **I** 512
Case, Pomeroy & Co., Inc., **IV** 76
Case Technologies, Inc., **11** 504
Casein Co. of America, **II** 471
Casey's General Stores, Inc., 19 79–81
Cash America International, Inc., 20 113–15
Cash Wise Foods and Liquor, **30** 133
Casino, **10** 205; **23** 231; **26** 160; **27** 93–94
Casino. *See* Etablissements Economiques de Casino Guichard, Perrachon et Cie, S.C.A.
Casino Frozen Foods, Inc., **16** 453
Casino S.A., **22** 515
Casino USA, **16** 452
Casinos International Inc., **21** 300
Casio Computer Co., Ltd., III 448–49, 455; **IV** 599; **10** 57; **16 82–84 (upd.)**; **21** 123; **26** 18
Cassa Generale Ungherese di Risparmio, **III** 207
Cassady Broiler Co., **II** 585
Cassatt, **II** 424
Cassco Ice & Cold Storage, Inc., **21** 534–35
CAST Inc., **18** 20
Cast-Matic Corporation, **16** 475
Castex, **13** 501
Castings, Inc., **29** 98
Castle & Cooke, Inc., I 417; **II 490–92**; **9** 175–76; **10** 40; **20 116–19 (upd.)**; **24** 32, 115. *See also* Dole Food Company, Inc.
Castle Brewery, **I** 287
Castle Cement, **31** 400
Castle Communications plc, **17** 13
Castle Rock Pictures, **23** 392
Castle Rubber Co., **17** 371
Castle Tretheway Mines Ltd., **IV** 164
Castlemaine Tooheys, **10** 169–70
Castorama. *See* Groupe Castorama-Dubois Investissements.
Castro Convertibles. *See* Krause's Furniture, Inc.
Castrol Ltd., **IV** 382–83
Castrorama, **10** 205; **27** 95
Casual Corner, **V** 207–08; **25** 121
Catalina Marketing Corporation, 18 99–102
Catalogue Marketing, Inc., **17** 232
Catalyst Telecom, **29** 414–15
Catamaran Cruisers, **29** 442
Catamount Petroleum Corp., **17** 121
CATCO. *See* Crowley All Terrain Corporation.
Catellus Development Corporation, 24 98–101; **27** 88
Caterair International Corporation, **16** 396
Caterpillar Inc., I 147, 181, 186, 422; **III 450–53**, 458, 463, 545–46; **9** 310; **10** 274, 377, 381, 429; **11** 473; **12** 90; **13** 513; **15 89–93 (upd.)**, 225; **16** 180, 309–10; **18** 125; **19** 293; **21** 173, 499–501, 503; **22** 542
Cathay Insurance Co., **III** 221; **14** 109
Cathay Pacific Airways Limited, I 522; **II** 298; **6** 71, **78–80**; **16** 480–81; **18** 114–15

Catherines Stores Corporation, 15 94–97
Cathodic Protection Services Co., **14** 325
Catholic Order of Foresters, 24 102–05
Cato Corporation, 14 92–94
Cato Oil and Grease Company, **IV** 446; **22** 302
Catteau S.A., **24** 475
Cattleman's, Inc., 20 120–22
Cattybrook Brick Company, **14** 249
CATV, **10** 319
Caudill Rowlett Scott. *See* CRSS Inc.
Caudle Engraving, **12** 471
CAV, **III** 554–55
Cavallo Pipeline Company, **11** 441
Cavedon Chemical Co., **I** 341
Cavendish International Holdings, **IV** 695
Cavendish Land, **III** 273
Cavenham Ltd., **7** 202–03; **28** 163
Caves Altovisto, **22** 344
Caves de Roquefort, **19** 51; **24** 445
Cawoods Holdings, **III** 735
Caxton Holdings, **IV** 641
CB Commercial Real Estate Services Group, Inc., 21 94–98
CB&I, **7** 76–77
CB&Q. *See* Chicago, Burlington and Quincy Railroad Company.
CB&T. *See* Synovus Financial Corp.
CBC Film Sales Co., **II** 135
CBI Industries, Inc., 7 74–77; **22** 228
CBM Realty Corp., **III** 643
CBN Cable Network, **13** 279–81
CBN Satellite Services, **13** 279
CBR-HCI Construction Materials Corp., **31** 253
CBRL Group, **29** 292
CBS Corporation, 28 69–73 (upd.); **30** 269, 272
CBS Inc., I 29, 488; **II** 61, 89, 102–03, 129–31, **132–34**, 136, 152, 166–67; **III** 55, 188; **IV** 605, 623, 652, 675, 703; **6 157–60 (upd.)**; **11** 327; **12** 75, 561; **16** 201–02; **17** 150, 182; **19** 210, 426, 428; **21** 24; **24** 516–17; **25** 330, 418; **26** 102
CBS Musical Instruments, **16** 201–02
CBS Records, **II** 103, 134, 177; **6** 159; **22** 194; **23** 33; **28** 419
CBSI. *See* Complete Business Solutions, Inc.
CBT Corp., **II** 213–14
CBWL-Hayden Stone, **II** 450
CC Soft Drinks Ltd., **I** 248
cc:Mail, Inc., **25** 300
CCA. *See* Container Corporation of America *and* Corrections Corporation of America.
CCAir Inc., **11** 300
CCC Franchising Corporation. *See* Primedex Health Systems, Inc.
CCG. *See* The Clark Construction Group, Inc.
CCH Computax, **7** 93–94
CCH Inc., 7 93; **14 95–97**
CCI Asia-Pacific Ltd., **27** 362
CCI Electronique, **10** 113
CCL Industries, Ltd., **15** 129
CCM Sport Maska, Inc., **15** 396
CCP Insurance, Inc., **10** 248
CCS Automation Systems Inc., **I** 124
CCT. *See* Crowley Caribbean Transport.
CD Titles, Inc., **22** 409
CDC. *See* Canada Development Corporation *or* Control Data Corporation.
CdF-Chimie, **I** 303; **IV** 174, 198, 525
CDG Books Canada Inc., **27** 224
CDI. *See* Centre de Dechets Industriels Group.
CDI Corporation, 6 139–41
CDMS. *See* Credit and Data Marketing Services.
CDR. *See* Consortium de Realisation.
CDR International, **13** 228
CDS Holding Corp., **22** 475
CDW Computer Centers, Inc., 16 85–87
CDX Audio Development, Inc., **18** 208
CE-Minerals, **IV** 109
CEAG AG, **23** 498
Ceat Ltd., **III** 434; **20** 263
CEC Entertainment, Inc., 31 94–98 (upd.)
Ceco Doors, **8** 544–46
Ceco Industries, Inc. *See* Robertson-Ceco Corporation.
CECOS International, Inc., **V** 750
Cedar Engineering, **III** 126
Cedar Fair, L.P., 22 130–32
Cedarapids, Inc., **11** 413
Cedec S.A., **14** 43
Cederroth International AB, **8** 17
CEDIS, **12** 153
Cegedur, **IV** 174
CEIR, **10** 255
Celadon Group Inc., 30 113–16
Celanese Corp., I 317–19, 347; **19** 192. *See also* Hoechst Celanese Corporation.
Celebrity Entertainment, Inc., **27** 43
Celebrity, Inc., 22 133–35, 472
Celeron Corporation, **20** 258, 262–63
Celestial Farms, **13** 383
Celestial Seasonings, Inc., II 534; **16 88–91**
Celfor Tool Company. *See* Clark Equipment Company.
Celite Corporation, **III** 706; **7** 291; **10** 43, 45
Cella Italian Wines, **10** 181
CellAccess Technology, Inc., **25** 162
Cellnet Data Systems, **11** 547; **22** 65
Cellonit-Gesellschaft Dreyfus & Cie., **I** 317
Cellstar Corporation, **18** 74
Cellu-Products Co., **14** 430
Cellular America, **6** 300
Cellular One, **9** 321
CellularVision, **13** 399
Cellulosa d'Italia, **IV** 272
Cellulose & Chemical Manufacturing Co., **I** 317
Cellulose & Specialties, **8** 434
Cellulose du Pin, **III** 677, 704; **16** 121–22; **19** 226–27
Celotex Corporation, **III** 766–67; **22** 545
Celsius Energy Company, **6** 569
Celtex **I** 388–89. *See also* Pricel.
Cementia, **III** 705
Cementos Portland Moctezuma, **21** 261
Cementownia Chelm, **31** 398, 400
Cemex SA de CV, 20 123–26
Cemij, **IV** 132
Cemp Investments Ltd., **16** 79–80
Cemsto, **13** 545
CenCall Communications, **10** 433
Cenco, Inc., **6** 188; **10** 262–63; **25** 308
Cencor, **25** 432
Cenex Cooperative, **21** 342
Cenex Inc., **II** 536; **19** 160
Cengas, **6** 313
Centel Corporation, 6 312–15, 593; **9** 106, 480; **10** 203; **14** 258; **16** 318; **17** 7
Center Rental & Sales Inc., **28** 387
Centerior Energy Corporation, V 567–68
Centerra Corporation, **24** 79
Centertel, **18** 33
Centex Corporation, 8 87–89, 461; **11** 302; **23** 327; **29 93–96 (upd.)**
Centocor Inc., 14 98–100
CentraBank, **II** 337; **10** 426
Central Alloy Steel Corporation. *See* Republic Engineered Steels, Inc.
Central and South West Corporation, V 569–70; **21** 197–98
Central Area Power Coordination Group, **V** 677
Central Arizona Light & Power Company, **6** 545
Central Asia Gas Pipeline Ltd, **24** 522
Central Bancorp of Cincinnati, **II** 342
Central Bank for Railway Securities, **II** 281
Central Bank of Italy, **II** 403
Central Bank of London, **II** 318; **17** 323
Central Bank of Oman, **IV** 516
Central Bank of Scotland, **10** 337
Central Coalfields Ltd., **IV** 48–49
Central Computer Systems Inc., **11** 65
Central Covenants, **II** 222
Central Detallista, S.A. de C.V., **12** 154; **16** 453
Central Electric & Gas Company. *See* Centel Corporation.
Central Electric and Telephone Company, Inc. *See* Centel Corporation.
Central Elevator Co., **19** 111
Central Fiber Products Company, **12** 376
Central Finance Corporation of Canada, **II** 418; **21** 282
Central Florida Press, **23** 101
Central Foam Corp., **I** 481, 563; **16** 322
Central Garden & Pet Company, 23 108–10
Central Hankyu Ltd., **V** 71
Central Hardware, **III** 530
Central Hudson Gas And Electricity Corporation, 6 458–60
Central Illinois Public Service Company. *See* CIPSCO Inc.
Central Independent Television, 7 78–80; **15** 84; **23 111–14 (upd.)**
Central India Spinning, Weaving and Manufacturing Co., **IV** 217
Central Indiana Power Company, **6** 556
Central Investment Corp., **12** 184
Central Japan Heavy Industries, **III** 578–79; **7** 348
Central Maine Power, 6 461–64; **14** 126
Central Maloney Transformer, **I** 434
Central Mining and Investment Corp., **IV** 23, 79, 95–96, 524, 565
Central National Bank, **9** 475
Central National Bank & Trust Co., **13** 467
Central National Life Insurance Co., **III** 463; **21** 174
Central Nebraska Packing, **10** 250
Central Newspapers, Inc., 10 207–09
Central Pacific Railroad, **II** 381; **13** 372
Central Park Bank of Buffalo, **11** 108
Central Parking Corporation, 18 103–05
Central Penn National Corp., **11** 295
Central Planning & Design Institute, **IV** 48
Central Point Software, **10** 509

Central Public Service Corporation, **6** 447; **23** 28
Central Public Utility Corp., **13** 397
Central Research Laboratories, **22** 194
Central Savings and Loan, **10** 339
Central Solvents & Chemicals Company, **8** 100
Central Songs, **22** 193
Central Soya Company, Inc., 7 81–83; 31 20
Central Sprinkler Corporation, 29 97–99
Central States Indemnity, **18** 62
Central Supply Company. *See* Granite Rock Company.
Central Telephone & Utilities Corporation. *See* Centel Corporation.
Central Terminal Company, **6** 504
Central Textile, **16** 36
Central Transformer, **I** 434
Central Trust Co., **II** 313; **11** 110
Central Union Telephone Company, **14** 251, 257
Central Union Trust Co. of New York, **II** 313
Central West Public Service Company. *See* Centel Corporation.
Centralab Inc., **13** 398
Centrale Verzorgingsdienst Cotrans N.V., **12** 443
Centran Corp., **9** 475
Centre de Dechets Industriels Group, **IV** 296; **19** 226
Centre Lait, **II** 577
Centre Partners Management LLC, **18** 355; **24** 482
Centrica plc, 29 100–05 (upd.)
Centron DPL Company, Inc., **25** 171
Centronics Corp., **16** 192
Centros Commerciales Pryca, **23** 246, 248
Centrum Communications Inc., **11** 520
CenTrust Federal Savings, **10** 340
Centura Software, **10** 244
Centurion Brick, **14** 250
Century Bakery. *See* Dawn Food Products, Inc.
Century Bank, **II** 312
Century Brewing Company. *See* Rainier Brewing Company.
Century Cellular Network, Inc., **18** 74
Century Communications Corp., 10 210–12
Century Data Systems, Inc., **13** 127
Century Electric Company, **13** 273
Century Finance, **25** 432
Century Hutchinson, Ltd., **13** 429
Century Manufacturing Company, **26** 363
Century Papers, Inc., **16** 387
Century Savings Assoc. of Kansas, **II** 420
Century Telephone Enterprises, Inc., 9 105–07
Century Theatres, Inc., 31 99–101
Century Tool Co., **III** 569; **20** 360
Century 21 Real Estate, **I** 127; **II** 679; **III** 293; **11** 292; **12** 489; **21** 97; **25** 444
CEPAM, **21** 438
CEPCO. *See* Chugoku Electric Power Company Inc.
CEPSA. *See* Compañia Española de Petroleos S.A.
Cera Trading Co., **III** 756
Ceramesh, **11** 361
Ceramic Art Company, **12** 312
Ceramic Supply Company, **8** 177
Cerberus Limited, **6** 490
Cereal Industries, **II** 466
Cereal Packaging, Ltd., **13** 294
Cereal Partners Worldwide, **10** 324; **13** 294
Cerebos, **II** 565
Cerex, **IV** 290
Ceridian Corporation, **10** 257
Cermalloy, **IV** 100
Cerner Corporation, 16 92–94
Cerro Corp., **IV** 11, 136
Cerro de Pasco Corp., **IV** 33
Cerro Metal Products Company, **16** 357
CertainTeed Corp., **III** 677–78, 621, 762; **16** 8, 121–22; **19** 58
Certanium Alloys and Research Co., **9** 419
Certified Grocers of Florida, Inc., **15** 139
Certified Laboratories, **8** 385
Certified TV and Appliance Company, **9** 120
Certus International Corp., **10** 509
Cerus, **23** 492
Cerveceria Cuahtémoc Moctezuma, **25** 281
Cerveceria Cuauhtemoc, **19** 10
Cerveceria Moctezuma, **23** 170
Cerveceria Polar, I 230–31
Cessna Aircraft Company, III 512; **8** 49–51, **90–93**, 313–14; **26** 117; **27 97–101 (upd.)**
Cetelem S.A., 21 99–102
Cetus Corp., **I** 637; **III** 53; **7** 427; **10** 78, 214
CF AirFreight, **6** 390; **25** 149
CF Braun, **13** 119
CF Holding Corporation, **12** 71
CF Industries, **IV** 576
CF&I Steel Corporation, **8** 135
CFC Investment Company, **16** 104
CFM. *See* Compagnie Française du Méthane.
CFP. *See* Compagnie Française des Pétroles.
CFS Continental, Inc., **II** 675; **26** 504
CG&E. *See* Cincinnati Gas & Electric Company.
CGCT, **I** 563
CGE. *See* Alcatel Alsthom.
CGM. *See* Compagnie Générale Maritime.
CGR-MeV, **III** 635
Chace Precision Metals, Inc., **29** 460–61
Chaco Energy Corporation, **V** 724–25
Chadwick's of Boston, Ltd., V 197–98; **27** 348; **29 106–08**
Chalet Suisse International, Inc., **13** 362
Chalk's International Airlines, **12** 420
Challenge Corp. Ltd. *See* Fletcher Challenge Ltd.
Challenger Airlines, **22** 219
Challenger Minerals Inc., **9** 267
Chamberlain Group, Ltd., **23** 82
Chambers Corporation, **8** 298; **17** 548–49
Chambosse Brokerage Co., **29** 33
Champ Industries, Inc., **22** 15
Champion Engineering Co., **III** 582
Champion Enterprises, Inc., 17 81–84; 22 207
Champion, Inc., **8** 459; **12** 457
Champion Industries, Inc., 28 74–76
Champion International Corporation, III 215; **IV 263–65**, 334; **12** 130; **15** 229; **18** 62; **20 127–30 (upd.)**; **22** 352; **26** 444
Champion Modular Restaurant Company, Inc. *See* Checkers Drive-Up Restaurants Inc.
Champion Products Inc., **27** 194
Champion Spark Plug Co., **II** 17; **III** 593
Champion Valley Farms, **II** 480; **26** 56
Champlin Petroleum Company, **10** 83
Champps Americana, **27** 480–82
Champs Sports, **14** 293, 295
Chance Bros., **III** 724–27
Chance Vought Aircraft Co., **I** 67–68, 84–85, 489–91
Chancellor Media Corporation, 23 294; **24 106–10**
Chancery Law Publishing Ltd., **17** 272
Chanco Medical Industries, **III** 73
Chandeleur Homes, Inc., **17** 83
The Chandris Group, **11** 377
Chanel, 12 57–59; 23 241
Channel Master Corporation, **II** 91; **15** 134
Channel One Communications Corp., **22** 442
Channel Tunnel Group, **13** 206
Chansam Investments, **23** 388
Chantex Inc., **18** 519
Chantiers de l'Atlantique, **9** 9
Chaparral Steel Co., 8 522–24; **13 142–44; 18** 379; **19** 380
Chapman Printing Company. *See* Champion Industries, Inc.
Chapman Valve Manufacturing Company, **8** 135
Chappel Music, **23** 389
Charan Industries Inc., **18** 519
Charan Toy Co., Inc., **18** 519
Chargeurs International, 6 373–75, 379; **20** 79; **21 103–06 (upd.)**; **29** 369, 371
Charise Charles Ltd., **9** 68
Charisma Communications, **6** 323
Charles A. Eaton Co., **III** 24
Charles B. Perkins Co., **II** 667; **24** 461
Charles Barker, plc, **25** 91
Charles D. Burnes Co., Inc. *See* The Holson Burnes Group, Inc.
Charles Hobson, **6** 27
Charles Huston & Sons, **14** 323
Charles Luckman Assoc., **I** 513
Charles of the Ritz Group Ltd., **I** 695–97; **III** 56; **23** 237
Charles Pfizer Co., **I** 96
Charles Phillips & Co. Ltd., **II** 677
Charles R. McCormick Lumber Company, **12** 407
Charles River Laboratory, **25** 55
The Charles Schwab Corporation, II 228; **8 94–96**; **18** 552; **22** 52; **26 64–67 (upd.)**
Charles Scribner's Sons, **7** 166
Charleston Consolidated Railway, Gas and Electric Company, **6** 574
Charlestown Foundry, **III** 690
Charley Brothers, **II** 669
Charley's Eating & Drinking Saloon, **20** 54
Charlie Browns, **24** 269–70
Charmin Paper Co., **III** 52; **IV** 329; **8** 433; **26** 383
Charming Shoppes, Inc., 8 97–98
Charrington & Co., **I** 223
Chart House Enterprises, Inc., II 556, 613–14; **17** 70, 71, **85–88**
Chart Industries, Inc., 21 107–09
Charter Bank, **II** 348
Charter Club, **9** 315
Charter Consolidated, **IV** 23, 119–20; **16** 293
Charter Corp., **III** 254; **14** 460
Charter Golf, Inc. *See* Ashworth, Inc.

Charter Medical Corporation, **31** 356
Charter National Life Insurance Company, **11** 261
Charter Oil Co., **II** 620; **12** 240
Charter Security Life Insurance Cos., **III** 293
Chartered Bank, **II** 357
Chartered Co. of British New Guinea, **III** 698
Chartered Mercantile Bank of India, London and China, **II** 298
Charterhouse Japhet, **24** 269
Charterhouse Petroleum, **IV** 499
Chartwell Associates, **III** 16; **9** 331
Chartwell Land plc, **V 106**; **24** 266, 269
Chas. A. Stevens & Co., **IV** 660
Chas. H. Tompkins Co., **16** 285–86
Chase & Sanborn, **II** 544
Chase Corp., **II** 402
Chase Drier & Chemical Co., **8** 177
Chase, Harris, Forbes, **II** 402
The Chase Manhattan Corporation, I 123, 334, 451; **II** 202, 227, **247–49**, 256–57, 262, 286, 317, 385, 397, 402; **III** 104, 248; **IV** 33; **6** 52; **9** 124; **10** 61; **13 145–48 (upd.)**, 476; **14** 48, 103; **15** 38–39; **16** 460; **17** 498; **23** 482
Chase National Bank, **25** 114
Chastain-Roberts Company, **II** 669; **18** 504
Chaston Medical & Surgical Products, **13** 366
Chateau Cheese Co. Ltd., **II** 471
Chateau Grower Winery Co., **II** 575
Chateau St. Jean, **22** 80
Chateau Souverain, **22** 80
Chateaux St. Jacques, **24** 307
Chatfield & Woods Co., **IV** 311; **19** 267
Chatfield Paper Co., **IV** 282; **9** 261
Chatham and Phenix National Bank of New York, **II** 312
Chatham Bank, **II** 312
Chatillon. *See* John Chatillon & Sons Inc.
Chattanooga Gas Company, Inc., **6** 577
Chattanooga Gas Light Company, **6** 448; **23** 30
Chattanooga Medicine Company. *See* Chattem, Inc.
Chattem, Inc., 17 89–92
Chatto, Virago, Bodley Head & Jonathan Cape, Ltd., **13** 429; **31** 376
Chaux et Ciments de Lafarge et du Teil, **III** 703–04
Chaux et Ciments du Maroc, **III** 703
Check Point Software Technologies Ltd., **20** 238
Checker Holding, **10** 370
Checker Motors Corp., **10** 369
Checkers Drive-Up Restaurants Inc., 14 452; **16 95–98**
CheckFree Corporation, **22** 522
The Cheesecake Factory Inc., 17 93–96
Chef Boyardee, **10** 70
Chef Francisco, **13** 383
Chef Pierre, **II** 572
Chef's Orchard Airline Caterers Inc., **I** 513
Chef-Boy-Ar-Dee Quality Foods Inc., **I** 622
Cheil Sugar Co., **I** 515
Cheil Wool Textile Co., **I** 515
Chelan Power Company, **6** 596
Chelsea GCA Realty, Inc., **27** 401
Chelsea Milling Company, 29 109–11
Chem-Nuclear Systems, Inc., **9** 109–10
Chemap, **III** 420
Chemcentral Corporation, 8 99–101
Chemcut, **I** 682
Chemdal Corp., **13** 34
Chemed Corporation, 13 149–50; **15** 409–11; **16** 386–87
Chemetron Process Equipment, Inc., **8** 545
Chemex Pharmaceuticals, Inc., **8** 63; **27** 69
ChemFirst, Inc., **27** 316
Chemgrout, **26** 42
Chemi-Trol Chemical Co., 16 99–101
Chemical Banking Corporation, II 234, **250–52**, 254; **9** 124, 361; **12** 15, 31; **13** 49, 147, 411; **14 101–04 (upd.)**; **15** 39; **21** 138; **26** 453
Chemical Coatings Co., **I** 321
Chemical Process Co., **IV** 409; **7** 308
Chemical Products Company, **13** 295
Chemical Specialties Inc., **I** 512
Chemical Waste Management, Inc., V 753; **9 108–10**; **11** 435–36
Chemie Linz, **16** 439
Chemins de fer de Paris à Lyon et à la Méditerranée, **6** 424
Chemins de fer du Midi, **6** 425
Chemins de Fer Fédéraux, **V** 519
Chemisch-Pharmazeutische AG, **IV** 70
Chemische Fabrik auf Actien, **I** 681
Chemische Fabrik Friesheim Elektron AG, **IV** 229
Chemische Fabrik vormals Sandoz, **I** 671
Chemische Fabrik Wesseling AG, **IV** 70–71
Chemische Werke Hüls GmbH. *See* Hüls A.G.
Chemise Lacoste, **9** 157
ChemLawn, **13** 199; **23** 428, 431
Chemmar Associates, Inc., **8** 271
Chemonics Industries–Fire-Trol, **17** 161–62
Chemonics International–Consulting, **17** 161–62
Chempump, **8** 135
Chemurgic Corporation, **6** 148
Chemway Corp., **III** 423
Cheney Bigelow Wire Works, **13** 370
Cheplin Laboratories, **III** 17
Cherokee Inc., 18 106–09
Cherokee Insurance Co., **I** 153; **10** 265
Cherry Company Ltd., **I** 266; **21** 319
Cherry Hill Cheese, **7** 429
Cherry-Burrell Process Equipment, **8** 544–45
Cherry-Levis Co., **26** 172
Chesapeake and Ohio Railroad, **II** 329; **V** 438–40; **10** 43; **13** 372. *See also* CSX Corporation.
Chesapeake Corporation, 8 102–04; **10** 540; **25** 44; **30 117–20 (upd.)**
Chesebrough-Pond's USA, Inc., II 590; **7** 544; **8 105–07**; **9** 319; **17** 224–25; **22** 123
Cheshire Wholefoods, **II** 528
Chester Engineers, **10** 412
Chester G. Luby, **I** 183
Chester Oil Co., **IV** 368
Cheung Kong (Holdings) Limited, I 470; **IV 693–95**; **18** 252; **20 131–34 (upd.)**; **23** 278, 280. *See also* Hutchison Whampoa Ltd.
Chevrolet, **V** 494; **9** 17; **19** 221, 223; **21** 153; **26** 500
Chevron Corporation, II 143; **IV** 367, **385–87**, 452, 464, 466, 479, 484, 490, 523, 531, 536, 539, 563, 721; **9** 391; **10** 119; **12** 20; **17** 121–22; **18** 365, 367; **19** 73, 75, **82–85 (upd.)**; **25** 444; **29** 385
Chevron U.K. Ltd., **15** 352
Chevy Chase Savings Bank, **13** 439
Chevy's Mexican Restaurants, **27** 226
ChexSystems, **22** 181
Cheyenne Software, Inc., 12 60–62; **25** 348–49
CHF. *See* Chase, Harris, Forbes.
Chi-Chi's Inc., 13 151–53; **14** 195; **25** 181
Chiat/Day Inc. Advertising, 9 438; **11 49–52**
Chiba Riverment and Cement, **III** 760
Chibu Electric Power Company, Incorporated, V 571–73
Chic by H.I.S, Inc., 20 135–37
Chicago & Calumet Terminal Railroad, **IV** 368
Chicago and Alton Railroad, **I** 456
Chicago and North Western Holdings Corporation, I 440; **6 376–78**
Chicago and Southern Airlines Inc., **I** 100; **6** 81
Chicago Bears, **IV** 703
Chicago Bridge & Iron Company, **7** 74–77
Chicago Burlington and Quincy Railroad, **III** 282; **V** 425–28
Chicago Chemical Co., **I** 373; **12** 346
Chicago Corp., **I** 526
Chicago Cubs, **IV** 682–83
Chicago Cutlery, **16** 234
Chicago Directory Co., **IV** 660–61
Chicago Edison, **IV** 169
Chicago Flexible Shaft Company, **9** 484
Chicago Heater Company, Inc., **8** 135
Chicago Magnet Wire Corp., **13** 397
Chicago Medical Equipment Co., **31** 255
Chicago Motor Club, **10** 126
Chicago Musical Instrument Company, **16** 238
Chicago Pacific Corp., **I** 530; **III** 573; **12** 251; **22** 349; **23** 244
Chicago Pneumatic Tool Co., **III** 427, 452; **7** 480; **21** 502; **26** 41; **28** 40
Chicago Radio Laboratory, **II** 123
Chicago Rawhide Manufacturing Company, **8** 462–63
Chicago Rock Island and Peoria Railway Co., **I** 558
Chicago Rollerskate, **15** 395
Chicago Screw Co., **12** 344
Chicago Shipbuilding Company, **18** 318
Chicago Steel Works, **IV** 113
Chicago Sun-Times Distribution Systems, **6** 14
Chicago Times, **11** 251
Chicago Title and Trust Co., **III** 276; **10** 43–45
Chicago Tribune. *See* Tribune Company.
Chick-fil-A Inc., 23 115–18
Chicken of the Sea International, 24 114–16 (upd.)
Chicopee Manufacturing Corp., **III** 35
Chief Auto Parts, **II** 661
Chieftain Development Company, Ltd., **16** 11
Chiers-Chatillon-Neuves Maisons, **IV** 227
Chilcott Laboratories Inc., **I** 710–11
Child World Inc., **13** 166; **18** 524
Childers Products Co., **21** 108
Children's Book-of-the-Month Club, **13** 105
Children's Palace, **13** 166

Children's Record Guild, **13** 105
Children's Television Workshop, **12** 495; **13** 560
Children's World Learning Centers, **II** 608; **V** 17, 19; **13** 48; **24** 75
Chiles Offshore Corporation, 9 111–13
Chili's Grill & Bar, **10** 331; **12** 373–74; **19** 258; **20** 159
Chillicothe Co., **IV** 310; **19** 266
Chilton Corp., **III** 440; **25** 239; **27** 361
Chiminter, **III** 48
Chimio, **I** 669–70; **8** 451–52
China Airlines, **6** 71
China Borneo Co., **III** 698
China Canada Investment and Development Co., **II** 457
China Coast, **10** 322, 324; **16** 156, 158
China Communications System Company, Inc. (Chinacom), **18** 34
China Development Corporation, **16** 4
China Eastern Airlines Co. Ltd., 31 102–04
China Electric, **II** 67
China Foreign Transportation Corporation, **6** 386
China Industries Co., **II** 325
China International Capital Corp., **16** 377
China International Trade and Investment Corporation, **II** 442; **IV** 695; **6** 80; **18** 113, 253; **19** 156; **25** 101. *See also* CITIC Pacific Ltd.
China Light & Power, **6** 499; **23** 278–80
China Mutual Steam Navigation Company Ltd., **6** 416
China National Automotive Industry Import and Export Corp., **III** 581
China National Aviation Corp., **I** 96; **18** 115; **21** 140
China National Cereals, Oils & Foodstuffs Import and Export Corporation, **24** 359
China National Chemicals Import and Export Corp., **IV** 395; **31** 120
China National Heavy Duty Truck Corporation, **21** 274
China National Machinery Import and Export Corporation, **8** 279
China National Petroleum Corp. (SINOPEC), **18** 483
China Navigation Co., **I** 521; **16** 479–80
China Orient Leasing Co., **II** 442
China Resources (Shenyang) Snowflake Brewery Co., **21** 320
China Southern, **31** 102
China Zhouyang Fishery Co. Ltd., **II** 578
Chinese Electronics Import and Export Corp., **I** 535
Chinese Metallurgical Import and Export Corp., **IV** 61
Chinese Petroleum Corporation, IV 388–90, 493, 519; **31 105–108 (upd.)**
Chinese Steel Corp., **IV** 184
The Chinet Company, **30** 397
Chino Mines Co., **IV** 179
Chinon Industries, **III** 477; **7** 163
Chipcom, **16** 392
Chippewa Shoe, **19** 232
CHIPS and Technologies, Inc., **6** 217; **9 114–17**
Chiquita Brands International, Inc., **II** 595–96; **III** 28; **7 84–86**; **21 110–13 (upd.)**
Chiro Tool Manufacturing Corp., **III** 629
Chiron Corporation, **7** 427; **10 213–14**; **25** 56
Chisso Chemical, **II** 301
Chiswick Products, **II** 566
Chita Oil Co., **IV** 476
Chitaka Foods International, **24** 365
Chivers, **II** 477
Chiyoda Bank, **I** 503; **II** 321
Chiyoda Chemical, **I** 433
Chiyoda Fire and Marine, **III** 404
Chiyoda Kogaku Seiko Kabushiki Kaisha, **III** 574–75
Chiyoda Konpo Kogyo Co. Ltd., **V** 536
Chiyoda Mutual, **II** 374
Chloé Chimie, **I** 303
Chloride S.A., **I** 423
Choay, **I** 676–77
Chock Full o'Nuts Corp., 17 97–100; **20** 83
Chocoladefabriken Lindt & Sprüngli AG, 27 102–05; **30** 220
Chocolat Ibled S.A., **II** 569
Chocolat Poulait, **II** 478
Chocolat-Menier S.A., **II** 569
Chogoku Kogyo, **II** 325
Choice Hotels International Inc., **6** 187, 189; **14 105–07**; **25** 309–10; **26** 460
ChoiceCare Corporation, **24** 231
ChoicePoint Services, Inc., **31** 358
Chorlton Metal Co., **I** 531
Chorus Line Corp.,
Chorus Line Corporation, 25 247; **30 121–23**
Chosen Sekiyu, **IV** 554
Chotin Transportation Co., **6** 487
Chouinard Equipment. *See* Lost Arrow Inc.
Chow Tai Fook Jewellery Co., **IV** 717
Chris-Craft Industries, Inc., **II** 176, 403; **III** 599–600; **9 118–19**; **26** 32; **31 109–112 (upd.)**
Christal Radio, **6** 33
Christensen Boyles Corporation, 19 247; **26 68–71**
Christensen Company, **8** 397
Christiaensen, **26** 160
Christian Bourgois, **IV** 614–15
Christian Broadcasting Network, **13** 279
Christian Dior S.A., **I** 272; **19 86–88**; **23** 237, 242
Christie, Mitchell & Mitchell, **7** 344
Christie's International plc, 15 98–101
Christopher Charters, Inc. *See* Kitty Hawk, Inc.
Chromalloy American Corp., **13** 461
Chromalloy Gas Turbine Corp., **13** 462
Chromatic Color, **13** 227–28
Chromcraft Revington, Inc., 15 102–05; **26** 100
The Chronicle Publishing Company, Inc., 23 119–22
Chronimed Inc., 26 72–75
Chronoservice, **27** 475
Chrysalis Records, **22** 194
Chrysler Corporation, **I** 10, 17, 28, 38, 59, 79, 136, **144–45**, 152, 162–63, 172, 178, 182, 188, 190, 207, 420, 504, 516, 525, 540; **II** 5, 313, 403, 448; **III** 439, 517, 544, 568, 591, 607, 637–38; **IV** 22, 449, 676, 703; **7** 205, 233, 461; **8** 74–75, 315, 505–07; **9** 118, 349–51, 472; **10** 174, 198, 264–65, 290, 317, 353, 430; **11 53–55 (upd.)**, 103–04, 429; **13** 28–29, 61, 448, 501, 555; **14** 321, 367, 457; **16** 184, 322, 484; **17** 184; **18** 173–74, 308, 493; **20** 359–60; **22** 52, 55, 175, 330; **23** 352–54; **25** 89–91, 93, 142–44, 329; **26** 403, 501; **31** 130
CH2M Hill Ltd., 22 136–38
Chu Ito & Co., **IV** 476
Chubb Corporation, **II** 84; **III** 190, **220–22**, 368; **11** 481; **14 108–10 (upd.)**; **29** 256
Chubu Electric Power Co., **IV** 492
Chuck E. Cheese, **13** 472–74; **31** 94
Chugai Pharmaceutical Company, **8** 215–16; **10** 79
Chugai Shogyo Shimposha, **IV** 654–55
Chugoku Electric Power Company Inc., V 574–76
Chunghwa Picture Tubes, **23** 469
Chuo Trust & Banking Co. *See* Yasuda Trust and Banking Company, Limited.
Church & Dwight Co., Inc., 29 112–15
Church and Tower Group, **19** 254
Church, Goodman, and Donnelley, **IV** 660
Church's Fried Chicken, Inc., **I** 260; **7** 26–28; **15** 345; **23** 468
Churchill Downs Incorporated, 29 116–19
Churchill Insurance Co. Ltd., **III** 404
Churny Co. Inc., **II** 534
Cianbro Corporation, 14 111–13
Cianchette Brothers, Inc. *See* Cianbro Corporation.
Ciba-Geigy Ltd., **I** 625, **632–34**, 671, 690, 701; **III** 55; **IV** 288; **8** 63, **108–11 (upd.)**, 376–77; **9** 153, 441; **10** 53–54, 213; **15** 229; **18** 51; **21** 386; **23** 195–96; **25** 55; **27** 69; **28** 193, 195; **30** 327
CIBC. *See* Canadian Imperial Bank of Commerce.
CIBC Wood Gundy Securities Corp., **24** 482
Ciber, Inc., 18 110–12
Ciby 2000, **24** 79
CICI, **11** 184
CIDLA, **IV** 504–06
Cie Continental d'Importation, **10** 249
Cie des Lampes, **9** 9
Cie Générale d'Electro-Ceramique, **9** 9
Cie. Generale des Eaux S.A., **24** 327
Cifra, S.A. de C.V., **8** 556; **12 63–65**; **26** 524
Cigarrera La Moderna, **21** 260; **22** 73
Cigarros la Tabacelera Mexicana (Cigatam), **21** 259
CIGNA Corporation, **III** 197, **223–27**, 389; **10** 30; **11** 243; **22 139–44 (upd.)**, 269
CIGWELD, **19** 442
Cii-HB, **III** 123, 678; **16** 122
Cilag-Chemie, **III** 35–36; **8** 282
Cilbarco, **II** 25
Cilva Holdings PLC, **6** 358
Cima, **14** 224–25
Cimarron Utilities Company, **6** 580
CIMCO Ltd., **21** 499–501
Cimenteries CBR S.A., **23** 325, 327
Ciments d'Obourg, **III** 701
Ciments de Chalkis Portland Artificiels, **III** 701
Ciments de Champagnole, **III** 702
Ciments de l'Adour, **III** 702
Ciments Lafarge France, **III** 704
Ciments Lafarge Quebec, **III** 704
Cimos, **7** 37
Cincinnati Bell, Inc., 6 316–18; **29** 250, 252
Cincinnati Chemical Works, **I** 633

Cincinnati Electronics Corp., **II** 25
Cincinnati Financial Corporation, 16 102–04
Cincinnati Gas & Electric Company, 6 465–68, 481–82
Cincinnati Milacron Inc., 12 66–69
Cincom Systems Inc., 15 106–08
Cineamerica, **IV** 676
Cinecentrum, **IV** 591
Cinema International Corp., **II** 149
Cinemark, **21** 362; **23** 125
Cinemax, **IV** 675; **7** 222–24, 528–29; **23** 276
Cineplex Odeon Corporation, II 145, **6 161–63**; **14** 87; **23 123–26 (upd.)**
Cinnabon Inc., 13 435–37; **23 127–29**
Cintas Corporation, 16 228; **21 114–16**, 507; **30** 455
Cintel, **II** 158
Cintra. *See* Corporacion Internacional de Aviacion, S.A. de C.V.
Cipal-Parc Astérix, **27** 10
Ciprial S.A., **27** 260
CIPSCO Inc., 6 469–72, 505–06
Circa Pharmaceuticals, **16** 529
Circle A Ginger Ale Company, **9** 177
Circle International, Inc., **17** 216
The Circle K Company, II 619–20; V 210; **7** 113–14, 372, 374; **20 138–40 (upd.)**; **25** 125; **26** 447
Circle Plastics, **9** 323
Circon Corporation, 21 117–20
Circuit City Stores, Inc., 9 65–66, **120–22**; **10** 235, 305–06, 334–35, 468–69; **12** 335; **14** 61; **15** 215; **16** 73, 75; **17** 489; **18** 533; **19** 362; **23** 51–53, 363; **24** 52, 502; **26** 410; **29 120–24 (upd.)**; **30** 464–65
Circus Circus Enterprises, Inc., 6 201, **203–05**; **19** 377, 379
Circus Knie, **29** 126
Circus World, **16** 389–90
Cirque du Soleil Inc., 29 125–28
Cirrus Logic, Incorporated, 9 334; **11 56–57**; **25** 117
Cisco Systems, Inc., 11 58–60, 520; **13** 482; **16** 468; **19** 310; **20** 8, 33, 69, 237; **25** 499; **26** 276–77
Cise, **24** 79
CIT Alcatel, **9** 9–10
CIT Financial Corp., **II** 90, 313; **8** 117; **12** 207
CIT Group/Business Credit, Inc., **13** 446
CIT Group/Commercial Services, **13** 536
Citadel General, **III** 404
Citadel, Inc., **27** 46
CitFed Bancorp, Inc., 16 105–07
CITGO Petroleum Corporation, II 660–61; **IV 391–93**, 508; **7** 491; **31 113–117 (upd.)**
Citibanc Group, Inc., **11** 456
Citibank, **II** 227, 230, 248, 250–51, 253–55, 331, 350, 358, 415; **III** 243, 340; **6** 51; **9** 124; **10** 150; **11** 418; **13** 146; **14** 101; **23** 3–4, 482; **25** 180, 542. *See also* Citigroup Inc
CITIC Pacific Ltd., 16 481; **18 113–15**; **20** 134. *See also* China International Trade and Investment Corporation.
Citicasters Inc., **23** 293–94
Citicorp, II 214, **253–55**, 268, 275, 319, 331, 361, 398, 411, 445; **III** 10, 220, 397; **7** 212–13; **8** 196; **9 123–26 (upd.)**, 441; **10** 463, 469; **11** 140; **12** 30, 310, 334; **13** 535; **14** 103, 108, 235; **15** 94, 146, 281; **17** 324, 559; **21** 69, 145; **22** 169, 406; **25** 198, 542
Cities Service Company, **IV** 376, 391–92, 481, 575; **12** 542; **22** 172
Citifor, **19** 156
Citigroup Inc., 30 124–28 (upd.)
Citinet. *See* Hongkong Telecommunications Ltd.
Citivision PLC, **9** 75
Citizen Watch Co., Ltd., III 454–56, 549; **13** 121–22; **21 121–24 (upd.)**; **23** 212
Citizen's Electric Light & Power Company, **V** 641
Citizen's Federal Savings Bank, **10** 93
Citizen's Fidelity Corp., **II** 342
Citizen's Industrial Bank, **14** 529
Citizens and Southern Bank, **II** 337; **10** 426
Citizens Bank, **11** 105
Citizens Bank of Hamilton, **9** 475
Citizens Bank of Savannah, **10** 426
Citizens Building & Loan Association, **14** 191
Citizens Federal Savings and Loan Association, **9** 476
Citizens Financial Group, **12** 422
Citizens Gas Co., **6** 529
Citizens Gas Fuel Company. *See* MCN Corporation.
Citizens Gas Light Co., **6** 455
Citizens Gas Supply Corporation, **6** 527
Citizens Mutual Savings Bank, **17** 529–30
Citizens National Bank, **II** 251; **13** 466; **25** 114
Citizens National Gas Company, **6** 527
Citizens Saving and Trust Company, **17** 356
Citizens Savings & Loan Association, **9** 173
Citizens Savings and Loan Society. *See* Citizens Mutual Savings Bank.
Citizens Telephone Company, **14** 257–58
Citizens Trust Co., **II** 312
Citizens Utilities Company, 7 87–89
Citizens' Savings and Loan, **10** 339
Citroën. *See* Automobiles Citroen *and* PSA Peugeot Citroen S.A.
City and St. James, **III** 501
City and Suburban Telegraph Association and Telephonic Exchange, **6** 316–17
City and Village Automobile Insurance Co., **III** 363
City Auto Stamping Co., **I** 201
City Bank Farmers' Trust Co., **II** 254; **9** 124
City Bank of New York, **II** 250, 253
City Brewery, **I** 253
City Capital Associates, **31** 211
City Centre Properties Ltd., **IV** 705–06
City Finance Company, **10** 340; **11** 261
City Ice Delivery, Ltd., **II** 660
City Investing Co., **III** 263; **IV** 721; **9** 391; **13** 363
City Light and Traction Company, **6** 593
City Light and Water Company, **6** 579
City Market Inc., **12** 112
City Mutual Life Assurance Society, **III** 672–73
City National Bank of Baton Rouge, **11** 107
City National Leasing, **II** 457
City of London Real Property Co. Ltd., **IV** 706
City of Seattle Water Department, **12** 443
The City Post Publishing Corp., **12** 359
City Products Corp., **II** 419
City Public Service, 6 473–75
City Savings, **10** 340
City Stores Company, **16** 207
Cityhome Corp., **III** 263
Civic Drugs, **12** 21
Civic Parking LLC, **18** 105
Civil & Civic Pty. Ltd., **IV** 707–08; **17** 286
Civil Aviation Administration of China, **31** 102
Civil Service Employees Insurance Co., **III** 214
CKE Restaurants, Inc., 19 89–93, 433, 435; **25** 389; **27** 19; **29** 203
CKS Inc., **23** 479
Clabir Corp., **12** 199
Claeys, **22** 379–80
Claire's Stores, Inc., 17 101–03; **18** 411
Clairol, **III** 17–18; **17** 110
Clairton Steel Co., **IV** 572; **7** 550
Clal Electronic Industries Ltd., **24** 429
Clal Group, **18** 154
CLAM Petroleum, **7** 282
Clancy Paul Inc., **13** 276
Clapp-Eastham Company. *See* GenRad, Inc.
Clara Candy, **15** 65
Clarcor Inc., 17 104–07
Claremont Technology Group Inc., **31** 131
Clares Equipment Co., **I** 252
Clariden Bank, **21** 146–47
Claridge Group, **25** 266, 268
Clarion Hotels and Resorts, **25** 309
Clark & Co., **IV** 301
Clark & McKenney Hardware Co. *See* Clarcor Inc.
Clark & Rockefeller, **IV** 426
Clark Bros. Co., **III** 471
The Clark Construction Group, Inc., 8 112–13
Clark, Dietz & Associates-Engineers. *See* CRSS Inc.
Clark Equipment Company, I 153; **7** 513–14; **8 114–16**; **10** 265; **13** 500; **15** 226
Clark Estates Inc., **8** 13
Clark Filter, Inc., **17** 104
Clark Materials Handling Company, **7** 514
Clark Motor Co., **I** 158; **10** 292
Clark-Schwebel, Inc., **28** 195
Clarkins, Inc., **16** 35–36
Clarkson International Tools, **I** 531
CLASSA. *See* Compañia de Líneas Aéreas Subvencionadas S.A.
Claudel Roustand Galac, **19** 50
Claussen Pickle Co., **12** 371
Clayton & Dubilier, **III** 25
Clayton Brown Holding Company, **15** 232
Clayton Dubilier & Rice Inc., **25** 501; **29** 408
Clayton Homes Incorporated, 13 154–55
Clayton-Marcus Co., **12** 300
Clayton/National Courier Systems, Inc., **24** 126
CLE. *See* Compagnie Laitière Européenne.
Clean Window Remodelings Co., **III** 757
Cleanaway Ltd., **III** 495
Cleancoal Terminal, **7** 582, 584

Clear Channel Communications, Inc., 23 130–32, 294; **25** 418; **27** 278
Clear Shield Inc., **17** 157, 159
Clearing Inc., **III** 514
Clearwater Tissue Mills, Inc., **8** 430
Clef, **IV** 125
Clemente Capital Inc., **25** 542
Clements Energy, Inc., **7** 376
Cleo Inc., **12** 207–09
Le Clerc, **21** 225–26
Cletrac Corp., **IV** 366
Cleve-Co Jig Boring Co., **23** 82
Cleveland and Western Coal Company, **7** 369
Cleveland Electric Illuminating Company. *See* Centerior Energy Theodor.
Cleveland Fabric Centers, Inc. *See* Fabri-Centers of America Inc.
Cleveland Grinding Machine Co., **23** 82
Cleveland Iron Mining Company. *See* Cleveland-Cliffs Inc.
Cleveland Oil Co., **I** 341
Cleveland Paper Co., **IV** 311; **19** 267
Cleveland Pneumatic Co., **I** 457; **III** 512
Cleveland Precision Instruments, Inc., **23** 82
Cleveland Twist Drill Company. *See* Acme-Cleveland Corp.
Cleveland-Cliffs Inc., 13 156–58; **17** 355
Clevepak Corporation, **8** 229; **13** 442
Clevite Corporation, **14** 207
CLF Research, **16** 202
Click Messenger Service, Inc., **24** 126
Clifford & Wills, **12** 280–81
Cliffs Corporation, **13** 157; **27** 224
Climax Molybdenum Co., **IV** 17–19
Clinchfield Coal Corp., **IV** 180–81; **19** 320
Clinical Assays, **I** 628
Clinical Partners, Inc., **26** 74
Clinical Pathology Facility, Inc., **26** 391
Clinical Science Research Ltd., **10** 106
Clinique Laboratories, Inc., **30** 191
Clinton Pharmaceutical Co., **III** 17
Clipper Group, **12** 439
Clipper, Inc., **IV** 597
Clipper Manufacturing Company, **7** 3
Clipper Seafoods, **II** 587
La Cloche d'Or, **25** 85
The Clorox Company, III 20–22, 52; **8** 433; **22 145–48 (upd.)**, 436; **26** 383
The Clothestime, Inc., 20 141–44
Clouterie et Tréfilerie des Flandres, **IV** 25–26
Clover Leaf Creamery, **II** 528
Clover Milk Products Co., **II** 575
Clovis Water Co., **6** 580
CLSI Inc., **15** 372
Club Aurrera, **8** 556
Club Corporation of America, **26** 27
Club de Hockey Canadien Inc., **26** 305
Club Européen du Tourisme, **6** 207
Club Méditerranée S.A., I 286; **6 206–08**; **21 125–28 (upd.)**; **27** 10
Clubhôtel, **6** 207
Cluett Corporation, **22** 133
Cluett, Peabody & Co., Inc., **II** 414; **8** 567–68
Clyde Iron Works, **8** 545
Clydebank Engineering & Shipbuilding Co., **I** 573
Clydesdale Group, **19** 390
Clyne Maxon Agency, **I** 29
CM Industries, **I** 676
CM&M Equilease, **7** 344
CMB Acier, **IV** 228
CMB Packaging, **8** 477
CME. *See* Campbell-Mithun-Esty, Inc.
CMI International, Inc., **27** 202, 204
CML Group, Inc., 10 215–18; **22** 382, 536
CMP Media Inc., 26 76–80; **28** 504
CMP Properties Inc., **15** 122
CMS Energy Corporation, IV 23; **V 577–79**; **8** 466; **14 114–16 (upd.)**
CMS Healthcare, **29** 412
CMT Enterprises, Inc., **22** 249
CN. *See* Canadian National Railway System.
CNA Financial Corporation, I 488; **III 228–32**, 339; **12** 317
CNA Health Plans, **III** 84
CNB Bancshares Inc., **31** 207
CNBC, Inc., **28** 298
CNC Holding Corp., **13** 166
CNCA. *See* Caisse National de Crédit Agricole.
CNEP. *See* Comptoir National d'Escompte de Paris.
CNF Transportation. *See* Consolidated Freightways Corporation.
CNG. *See* Consolidated Natural Gas Company.
CNN. *See* Cable News Network.
CNP. *See* Compagnie Nationale à Portefeuille.
CNS, Inc., 20 145–47
Co-Axial Systems Engineering Co., **IV** 677
Co-Counsel, Inc., **29** 364
Co. Luxemburgeoise de Banque S.A., **II** 282
Co. of London Insurers, **III** 369
Co-Steel International Ltd., **8** 523–24; **13** 142–43; **24** 144
Coach Leatherware, 10 219–21; **12** 559
Coach Specialties Co. *See* Fleetwood Enterprises, Inc.
Coach USA, Inc., 24 117–19; **30** 431, 433
Coachmen, **21** 153
Coal India Limited, IV 48–50
Coalport, **12** 528
Coast American Corporation, **13** 216
Coast Consolidators, Inc., **14** 505
Coast to Coast Hardware. *See* TruServ Corporation.
Coast-to-Coast Stores, **II** 419; **12** 8
Coastal Coca-Cola Bottling Co., **10** 223
Coastal Container Line Inc., **30** 318
Coastal Corporation, IV 366, **394–95**; **7** 553–54; **31 118–121 (upd.)**
Coastal Lumber, S.A., **18** 514
Coastal States Corporation, **11** 481
Coastal States Life Insurance Company, **11** 482
Coastal Valley Canning Co., **I** 260
CoastAmerica Corp., **13** 176
Coates/Lorilleux, **14** 308
Coating Products, Inc., **III** 643
Coats Viyella Plc, V 356–58
CoBank. *See* National Bank for Cooperatives.
Cobb & Branham, **14** 257
Cobb, Inc., **II** 585; **14** 515
COBE Laboratories, Inc., 13 159–61; **22** 360
Cobham plc, 30 129–32
Coborn's, Inc., 30 133–35
Cobra Electronics Corporation, 14 117–19
Cobra Golf Inc., 16 108–10; **23** 474
Cobra Ventilation Products, **22** 229
Coburn Optical Industries, **III** 56
Coburn Vision Care, **III** 727
Coca-Cola Bottling Co. Consolidated, II 170, 468; **10 222–24**; **15** 299
Coca-Cola Bottling Company of Northern New England, Inc., **21** 319
The Coca-Cola Company, I 17, **232–35**, 244, 248, 278–79, 286, 289, 440, 457; **II** 103, 136–37, 477–78; **III** 215; **IV** 297; **6** 20–21, 30; **7** 155, 383, 466; **8** 399; **9** 86, 177; **10** 130, 222–23, **225–28 (upd.)**; **11** 421, 450–51; **12** 74; **13** 284; **14** 18, 453; **15** 428; **16** 480–81; **17** 207; **18** 60, 62–63, 68, 467–68; **19** 391; **21** 337–39, 401; **23** 418–20; **24** 516; **25** 183; **27** 21, 150; **28** 271, 473; **29** 85; **31** 243
Coca-Cola Enterprises, Inc., 10 223; **13 162–64**; **23** 455–57
Cochrane Corporation, **8** 135
Cochrane Foil Co., **15** 128
Cockburn-Adelaide Cement, **31** 398, 400
Cockerill Sambre Group, IV 26–27, **51–53**; **22** 44; **26 81–84 (upd.)**
Coco's, **I** 547; **27** 16, 19
Codec, **19** 328
Codex Corp., **II** 61
Codville Distributors Ltd., **II** 649
Coeur d'Alene Mines Corporation, 20 148–51
Cofica, **21** 99
COFINA, **III** 347
COFIRED, **IV** 108
Cofitel SA, **25** 466
Coflexip S.A., 25 103–05
Cofroma, **23** 219
Cogéma, **IV** 108
COGEMA Canada, **IV** 436
Cogent Data Technologies, Inc., **31** 5
Cogentrix Energy, Inc., 10 229–31
Cogetex, **14** 225
Cogifer, S.A., **18** 4; **31** 156, 158
Cognex Corp., **22** 373
CogniSeis Development, Inc., **18** 513, 515
Cognitive Solutions, Inc., **18** 140
Cognos Corp., **11** 78; **25** 97
Cohasset Savings Bank, **13** 468
Coherent, Inc., 31 122–25
Cohn-Hall-Marx Co. *See* United Merchants & Manufacturers, Inc.
Coils Plus, Inc., **22** 4
Coinamatic Laundry Equipment, **II** 650
Coinmach Laundry Corporation, 20 152–54
Coktel Vision, **15** 455
Colas S.A., 31 126–29
Colbert Television Sales, **9** 306
Colchester Car Auctions, **II** 587
Cold Spring Granite Company, 16 111–14
Coldwater Creek Inc., 21 129–31
Coldwell Banker, **IV** 715, 727; **V** 180, 182; **11** 292; **12** 97; **18** 475, 478; **27** 32. *See also* CB Commercial Real Estate Services Group, Inc.
Cole & Weber Inc., **I** 27
Cole National Corporation, 13 165–67, 391
Cole's Craft Showcase, **13** 166
Coleco Industries, Inc., **III** 506; **18** 520; **21** 375
Coleman & Co., **II** 230

The Coleman Company, Inc., III 485; **9 127–29**; **22** 207; **26** 119; **28** 135, 247; **30 136–39 (upd.)**
Coleman Outdoor Products Inc., **21** 293
Colemans Ltd., **11** 241
Coles Book Stores Ltd., **7** 486, 488–89
Coles Express Inc., 15 109–11
Coles Myer Ltd., V 33–35; **18** 286; **20 155–58 (upd.)**
Colex Data, **14** 556
Colgate-Palmolive Company, I 260; **II** 672; **III 23–26**; **IV** 285; **9** 291; **11** 219, 317; **14 120–23 (upd.)**, 279; **17** 106; **25** 365; **27** 212–13, 390
Colgens, **22** 193
Collabra Software Inc., **15** 322
College Construction Loan Insurance Assoc., **II** 455; **25** 427
College Entrance Examination Board, **12** 141
College Survival, Inc., **10** 357
Collegiate Arlington Sports Inc., **II** 652
Collett Dickinson Pearce International Group, **I** 33; **16** 168
Collins & Aikman Corporation, I 483; **13 168–70**; **25** 535
Collins Radio Co., **III** 136; **11** 429
Colo-Macco. *See* CRSS Inc.
Cologne Re. *See* General Re Corporation *or* Kölnische Rückversicherungs-Gesellschaft AG.
Cologne Reinsurance Co., **III** 273, 299
Colombia Graphophone Company, **22** 192
Colombo, **25** 84
Colonia, **III** 273, 394
Colonia Versicherung Aktiengesellschaft. *See* AXA Colonia Konzern AG.
Colonial & General, **III** 359–60
Colonial Air Transport, **I** 89, 115; **12** 379
Colonial Airlines, **I** 102
Colonial Bancorp, **II** 208
Colonial Bank, **II** 236
Colonial Candle of Cape Cod, **18** 69
Colonial Container, **8** 359
Colonial Food Stores, **7** 373
Colonial Healthcare Supply Co., **13** 90
Colonial Insurance Co., **IV** 575–76
Colonial Life Assurance Co., **III** 359
Colonial Life Insurance Co. of America, **III** 220–21; **14** 108–09
Colonial Life Insurance Company, **11** 481
Colonial National Bank, **8** 9
Colonial National Leasing, Inc., **8** 9
Colonial Packaging Corporation, **12** 150
Colonial Penn Group Insurance Co., **11** 262; **27** 4
Colonial Penn Life Insurance Co., **V** 624
Colonial Rubber Works, **8** 347
Colonial Stores, **II** 397
Colonial Sugar Refining Co. Ltd. *See* CSR Limited.
Colony Capital, Inc., **27** 201
Colony Communications, **7** 99
Colony Gift Corporation, Ltd., **18** 67, 69
Color Corporation of America, **8** 553
Color Me Mine, **25** 263
Color Tile, **31** 435
Color-Box, Inc., **8** 103
Colorado Belle Casino, **6** 204
Colorado Cooler Co., **I** 292
Colorado Electric Company. *See* Public Service Company of Colorado.
Colorado Fuel & Iron (CF&I), **14** 369
Colorado Gaming & Entertainment Co., **21** 335
Colorado Gathering & Processing Corporation, **11** 27
Colorado Interstate Gas Co., **IV** 394
Colorado National Bank, **12** 165
Colorcraft, **I** 447
Colorfoto Inc., **I** 447
Colossal Pictures, **10** 286
Colson Co., **III** 96; **IV** 135–36
Colt, **19** 430–31
Colt Industries Inc., I 434–36, 482, 524; **III** 435
Colt Pistol Factory, **9** 416
Colt's Manufacturing Company, Inc., 12 70–72
Coltec Industries Inc., **30** 158
Columbia Brewery, **25** 281
Columbia Broadcasting System. *See* CBS Corporation.
Columbia Chemical Co. *See* PPG Industries, Inc.
Columbia Electric Street Railway, Light and Power Company, **6** 575
Columbia Forest Products, **IV** 358
Columbia Gas & Electric Company, **6** 466. *See also* Columbia Gas System, Inc.
Columbia Gas Light Company, **6** 574
Columbia Gas of New York, Inc., **6** 536
The Columbia Gas System, Inc., V 580–82; **16 115–18 (upd.)**
Columbia Gas Transmission Corporation, **6** 467
Columbia General Life Insurance Company of Indiana, **11** 378
Columbia Hat Company, **19** 94
Columbia House, **IV** 676
Columbia Insurance Co., **III** 214
Columbia News Service, **II** 132
Columbia Paper Co., **IV** 311; **19** 266
Columbia Pictures Entertainment, Inc., II 103, 134, **135–37**, 170, 234, 619; **IV** 675; **10** 227; **12** 73, 455; **21** 360; **22** 193; **25** 139; **28** 71. *See also* Columbia TriStar Motion Pictures Companies.
Columbia Railroad, Gas and Electric Company, **6** 575
Columbia Records, **II** 132; **16** 201; **26** 150
Columbia River Packers, **II** 491
Columbia Savings & Loan, **II** 144
Columbia Sportswear Company, 19 94–96
Columbia Steamship Company, **17** 356
Columbia Steel Co., **IV** 28, 573; **7** 550
Columbia Transportation Co., **17** 357
Columbia TriStar Motion Pictures Companies, 12 73–76 (upd.); **28** 71. *See also* Columbia Pictures Entertainment, Inc.
Columbia TriStar Television Distribution, **17** 149
Columbia/HCA Healthcare Corporation, 13 90; **15 112–14**; **22** 409–10; **27** 356
Columbian Carbon Company, **25** 70–71
Columbian Chemicals Co., **IV** 179; **28** 352, 356
Columbian Peanut Co., **I** 421; **11** 23
Columbus & Southern Ohio Electric Company (CSO), **6** 467, 481–82
Columbus Bank & Trust. *See* Synovus Financial Corp.
Columbus Realty Trust, **26** 378
Columbus Savings and Loan Society, **I** 536; **13** 528
Columbus-Milpar, **I** 544
Colwell Systems, **19** 291; **22** 181
Com Ed. *See* Commonwealth Edison.
Com-Link 21, Inc., **8** 310
Comair Holdings Inc., 13 171–73; **31** 420
Comalco Fabricators (Hong Kong) Ltd., **III** 758
Comalco Ltd., **IV** 59–61, 122, 191
Comark, **24** 316; **25** 417–18
Comat Services Pte. Ltd., **10** 514
Comau, **I** 163
Combibloc Inc., **16** 339
Combined American Insurance Co. of Dallas, **III** 203
Combined Casualty Co. of Philadelphia, **III** 203
Combined Communications Corp., **II** 619; **IV** 612; **7** 191
Combined Insurance Co. of America, **III** 203–04
Combined International Corp., **III** 203–04
Combined Mutual Casualty Co. of Chicago, **III** 203
Combined Properties, Inc., **16** 160
Combined Registry Co., **III** 203
Combustion Engineering Group, **22** 11; **25** 534
Combustiveis Industriais e Domésticos. *See* CIDLA.
Comcast Corporation, 7 90–92; **9** 428; **10** 432–33; **17** 148; **22** 162; **24 120–24 (upd.)**; **27** 342, 344
ComCore Semiconductor, Inc., **26** 330
Comdata, **19** 160
Comdial Corporation, 21 132–35
Comdisco, Inc., 9 130–32; **11** 47, 86, 484, 490
Comdor Flugdienst GmbH., **I** 111
Comer Motor Express, **6** 370
Comerco, **III** 21; **22** 147
Comet, **II** 139; **V** 106–09; **24** 194, 266, 269–70
Cometra Oil, **IV** 576
ComFed Bancorp, **11** 29
Comfort Inns, **21** 362
Comforto GmbH, **8** 252
Cominco Fertilizers Ltd., **IV** 75, 141; **13** 503
Cominco Ltd., **16** 364; **27** 455
Comision Federal de Electricidad de Mexico (CFE), **21** 196–97
Comitato Interministrale per la Ricostruzione, **I** 465
Comm-Quip, **6** 313
CommAir. *See* American Building Maintenance Industries, Inc.
Commander Foods, **8** 409
Commander-Larabee Co., **I** 419; **25** 242
Commemorative Brands Inc., **19** 453
Commentry, **III** 676; **16** 120
Commerce and Industry Insurance Co., **III** 196, 203
Commerce Clearing House, Inc., 7 93–94. *See also* CCH Inc.
Commerce Group, **III** 393
Commerce Union, **10** 426
Commercial & General Life Assurance Co., **III** 371
Commercial Air Conditioning of Northern California, **25** 15
Commercial Air Lines, Inc., **23** 380
Commercial Alliance Corp. of New York, **II** 289

Commercial Aseguradora Suizo Americana, S.A., **III** 243
Commercial Assurance, **III** 359
Commercial Bank of Australia Ltd., **II** 189, 319, 388–89; **17** 324
Commercial Bank of London, **II** 334
Commercial Bank of Tasmania, **II** 188
Commercial Banking Co. of Sydney, **II** 187–89
Commercial Bureau (Australia) Pty., **I** 438
Commercial Chemical Company, **16** 99
Commercial Credit Company, III 127–28; 8 117–19; 10 255–56; **15** 464
Commercial Exchange Bank, **II** 254; **9** 124
Commercial Federal Corporation, 12 77–79
Commercial Filters Corp., **I** 512
Commercial Financial Services, Inc., 26 85–89
Commercial Insurance Co. of Newark, **III** 242
Commercial Life, **III** 243
Commercial Life Assurance Co. of Canada, **III** 309
Commercial Metals Company, 15 115–17
Commercial Motor Freight, Inc., **14** 42
Commercial National Bank, **II** 261; **10** 425
Commercial National Bank & Trust Co., **II** 230
Commercial National Bank of Charlotte, **II** 336
Commercial Realty Services Group, **21** 257
Commercial Ship Repair Co., **I** 185
Commercial Union plc, II 272, 308; **III** 185, **233–35**, 350, 373; **IV** 711
Commerzbank A.G., II 239, 242, **256–58**, 280, 282, 385; **IV** 222; **9** 283; **14** 170
Commerzfilm, **IV** 591
CommLink Corp., **17** 264
Commodity Credit Corp., **11** 24
Commodore Corporation, **8** 229
Commodore International, Ltd., II 6; **III** 112; **6** 243–44; **7 95–97**, 532; **9** 46; **10** 56, 284; **23** 25; **26** 16
Commonwealth & Southern Corporation, **V** 676
Commonwealth Aluminium Corp., Ltd. *See* Comalco Ltd.
Commonwealth Bank, **II** 188, 389
Commonwealth Board Mills, **IV** 248
Commonwealth Edison, II 28, 425; **III** 653; **IV** 169; **V 583–85**; **6** 505, 529, 531; **12** 548; **13** 341; **15** 422
Commonwealth Energy System, 14 124–26
Commonwealth Hospitality Ltd., **III** 95
Commonwealth Industrial Gases, **25** 82
Commonwealth Industries, **III** 569; **11** 536; **20** 360
Commonwealth Insurance Co., **III** 264
Commonwealth Land Title Insurance Co., **III** 343
Commonwealth Life and Accident Insurance Company, **27** 46–47
Commonwealth Life Insurance Co., **III** 216–19
Commonwealth Limousine Services, Ltd., **26** 62
Commonwealth Mortgage Assurance Co., **III** 344
Commonwealth National Financial Corp., **II** 316
Commonwealth Oil Refining Company, **II** 402; **7** 517
Commonwealth Power Railway and Light Company, **14** 134
Commonwealth Southern Corporation, **14** 134
Commonwealth Telephone Enterprises, Inc., 25 106–08
Commtron, Inc., **V** 14, 16; **11** 195; **13** 90
Communication Services Ltd. *See* Hongkong Telecommunications Ltd.
Communications and Systems Specialists, **18** 370
Communications Consultants, Inc., **16** 393
Communications Corp. of America, **25** 418
Communications Data Services, Inc., **IV** 627; **19** 204
Communications Industries Inc., **25** 496
Communications Network Consultants, **29** 400
Communications Properties, Inc., **IV** 677
Communications Solutions Inc., **11** 520
Communications Technology Corp. (CTC), **13** 7–8
Communicorp, **III** 188; **10** 29
Community Direct, Inc., **7** 16
Community HealthCare Services, **6** 182
Community Hospital of San Gabriel, **6** 149
Community Medical Care, Inc., **III** 245
Community National Bank, **9** 474
Community Power & Light Company, **6** 579–80
Community Psychiatric Centers, 15 118–20
Community Public Service Company, **6** 514
Community Savings and Loan, **II** 317
Comnet Corporation, **9** 347
Comp-U-Card of America, Inc. *See* CUC International Inc.
Compac Corp., **11** 535
Compactom, **I** 588
Compagnia di Assicurazioni, **III** 345
Compagnia di Genova, **III** 347
Compagnia di Participazioni Assicurative ed Industriali S.p.A., **24** 341
Compagnie Auxilaire de Navigation, **IV** 558
Compagnie Bancaire, **II** 259; **21** 99–100
Compagnie Belge pour l'industrie, **II** 202
Compagnie Continentale, **I** 409–10
Compagnie d'Assurances Générales, **III** 391
Compagnie d'assurances Mutuelles contre l'incendie dans les départements de la Seine Inférieure et de l'Eure, **III** 210
Compagnie d'Investissements de Paris, **II** 233
Compagnie de Compteurs, **III** 617; **17** 418
Compagnie de Five-Lille, **IV** 469
Compagnie de Mokta, **IV** 107–08
Compagnie de Navigation Mixte, **III** 185
Compagnie de Reassurance Nord-Atlantique, **III** 276
Compagnie de Recherche et d'Exploitation du Pétrole du Sahara, **IV** 545; **21** 203
Compagnie de Saint-Gobain S.A., II 117, 474–75; **III 675–78**, 704; **8** 395, 397; **15** 80; **16 119–23 (upd.)**; **19** 58, 226; **21** 222; **26** 446
Compagnie de Transport Aerien, **I** 122
Compagnie des Cristalleries de Baccarat. *See* Baccarat.
Compagnie des Machines Bull S.A., II 40, 42, 70, 125; **III 122–23**, 154; **IV** 600; **12** 139; **13** 574; **25** 33. *See also* Groupe Bull.
Compagnie des Messageries Maritimes, **6** 379
Compagnie des Produits Chimiques et Électrométallurgiques d'Alais, Froges et Camargue, **IV** 173–74
Compagnie du Midi, **III** 209, 211
Compagnie du Nord, **IV** 108
Compagnie Européenne de Publication, **IV** 614–15
Compagnie Financier Richemont AG, **19** 367, 369–70
Compagnie Financiere Alcatel, **9** 10
Compagnie Financière Belge des Pétroles. *See* PetroFina S.A.
Compagnie Financière de Paribas, II 192, **259–60**; **III** 185; **21** 99; **27** 138
Compagnie Financière de Richemont AG, **29** 90
Compagnie Financière de Suez, **III** 394
Compagnie Financiere du Groupe Victoire, **27** 54
Compagnie Financière Richemont AG, **27** 487; **29** 91–92
Compagnie Française Chaufour Investissement, **27** 100
Compagnie Française de Distribution en Afrique, **IV** 559
Compagnie Française de Manutention, **27** 295
Compagnie Française de Raffinage, **IV** 558–60
Compagnie Française des Lubricants, **I** 341
Compagnie Française des Minerais d'Uranium, **IV** 108
Compagnie Française des Mines de Diamants du Cap, **IV** 64; **7** 121
Compagnie Française des Pétroles. *See* TOTAL S.A.
Compagnie Française des Produits d'Orangina, **I** 281
Compagnie Française du Méthane, **V** 626
Compagnie Française Thomson-Houston, **I** 357; **II** 116
Compagnie Fromagère de la Vallée de l'Ance, **25** 84
Compagnie Générale d'Électricité, I 193; **II 12–13**, 25; **IV** 174, 615; **9** 9–10
Compagnie Generale de Cartons Ondules, **IV** 296; **19** 226
Compagnie Generale de Radiologie, **II** 117
Compagnie Generale de Telegraphie Sans Fils, **II** 116
Compagnie Générale des Eaux, **V** 632–33; **6** 441
Compagnie Générale des Établissements Michelin, V 236–39; **19** 508
Compagnie Générale Maritime et Financière, 6 379–81
Compagnie Industriali Riunite S.p.A., **IV** 587–88
Compagnie Industrielle de Matérials de Manutention, **27** 296
Compagnie Industrielle des Fillers. *See* L'Entreprise Jean Lefebvre.
Compagnie Internationale de l'Informatique, **III** 123
Compagnie Internationale Express, **25** 120
Compagnie Internationale Pirelli S.A., **V** 249
Compagnie Laitière Européenne, **25** 83, 85

Compagnie Luxembourgeoise de Télédiffusion, **15** 54
Compagnie Nationale à Portefeuille, **29** 48
Compagnie Nationale de Navigation, **27** 515
Compagnie Navale Des Pétroles, **IV** 558
Compagnie Parisienne de Garantie, **III** 211
Compagnie Pneumatique Commerciale, **III** 426
Compagnie Tunisienne de Ressorts a Lames, **III** 581
Companhia Brasileira de Aluminio, **IV** 55
Companhia Brasileira de Mineracão e Siderugica, **IV** 54
Companhia de Celulose do Caima, **14** 250
Companhia de Diamantes de Angola, **IV** 21
Companhia de Minerales y Metales, **IV** 139
Companhia de Pesquisas Mineras de Angola, **IV** 65; **7** 122
Companhia de Seguros Argos Fluminense, **III** 221
Companhia de Seguros Tranquilidade Vida, S.A. *See* Banco Espírito Santo e Comercial de Lisboa S.A.
Companhia Siderúrgica de Tubarao, **IV** 125
Companhia Siderúrgica Mannesmann S.A., **III** 565–66
Companhia Siderúrgica Nacional, **II** 199
Companhia Uniao Fabril, **IV** 505
Companhia Vale do Rio Doce, IV 54–57
Compañia Arrendataria del Monopolio de Petróleos Sociedad Anónima, **IV** 396–97, 527–29
Compañia de Investigacion y Exploitaciones Petrolifera, **IV** 397
Compañia de Líneas Aéreas Subvencionadas S.A., **6** 95
Compañia Española de Petroleos S.A., IV 396–98, 527
Compania Fresnillo, **22** 286
Compania General de Aceptaciones. *See* Financiera Aceptaciones.
Compania Hulera Euzkadi, **21** 260; **23** 170
Compañia Mexicana de Transportación Aérea, **20** 167
Compania Minera de Penoles. *See* Industrias Penoles, S.A. de C.V.
Compañia Minera La India, **IV** 164
Compania Minera Las Torres, **22** 286
Compañia Nacional Minera Petrólia del Táchira, **IV** 507
Compania Siderurgica Huachipato, **24** 209
Compañía Telefónica Nacional de España S.A., **V** 337
Compaq Computer Corporation, II 45; **III** 114, **124–25; 6** 217, **221–23 (upd.)**, 230–31, 235, 243–44; **9** 42–43, 166, 170–71, 472; **10** 87, 232–33, 366, 459, 518–19; **12** 61, 183, 335, 470; **13** 388, 483; **16** 4, 196, 367–68; **17** 274; **21** 123, 391; **22** 288; **25** 184, 239, 498, 531; **26 90–93 (upd.)**; **27** 365; **28** 191; **29** 439; **30** 12
Compart, **24** 341
Compass Airlines, **27** 475
Compass Design Automation, **16** 520
Compass Group, plc, **6** 193; **24** 194; **27** 482
CompDent Corporation, 22 149–51
Compeda, Ltd., **10** 240
Competence ApS, **26** 240
Competition Tire East/West, **V** 494; **19** 292
Competrol Ltd., **22** 189
Compex, **II** 233
CompHealth Inc., 25 109–12
Complete Business Solutions, Inc., 31 130–33
Completion Bond Co., **26** 487
Components Agents Ltd., **10** 113
Composite Craft Inc., **I** 387
Composite Research & Management Co., **17** 528, 530
Comprehensive Care Corporation, 15 121–23
Comprehensive Resources Corp., **IV** 83
Compressed Industrial Gases, **I** 297
Compression Labs Inc., **10** 456; **16** 392, 394; **27** 365
Compressor Controls Corporation, **15** 404
Comptoir d'Escompte de Mulhouse, **II** 232
Comptoir des Textiles Artificielles, **I** 122, 388–89
Comptoir Général de la Photographie. *See* Gaumont SA.
Comptoir Métallurgique Luxembourgeois, **IV** 25
Comptoir National d'Escompte de Paris, **II** 232–33, 270
Comptoirs Modernes S.A., 19 97–99
Compton Communications, **I** 33
Compton Foods, **II** 675
Compton's MultiMedia Publishing Group, Inc., **7** 165
Compton's New Media, Inc., **7** 168
Compu-Notes, Inc., **22** 413
CompuAdd Computer Corporation, 11 61–63
CompuChem Corporation, **11** 425
CompuCom Systems, Inc., 10 232–34, 474; **13** 176
Compugraphic, **III** 168; **6** 284
Compumech Technologies, **19** 312
Compumotor, **III** 603
CompuPharm, Inc., **14** 210
CompUSA, Inc., 10 235–36; 11 63
CompuServe Incorporated, 9 268–70; **10 237–39; 12** 562; **13** 147; **15** 265; **16** 467, 508; **26** 16; **29** 224, 226–27. *See also* America Online, Inc.
CompuServe Interactive Services, Inc., 27 106, **106–08 (upd.)**, 301, 307. *See also* America Online, Inc.
Computax, **6** 227–28
Computer Associates International, Inc., 6 224–26; 10 394; **12** 62; **14** 392; **27** 492
Computer City, **12** 470
The Computer Company, **11** 112
Computer Consoles Inc., **III** 164
Computer Data Systems, Inc., 14 127–29
The Computer Department, Ltd., **10** 89
Computer Depot, **6** 243
Computer Discount Corporation. *See* Comdisco, Inc.
Computer
Computer Engineering Associates, **25** 303Dynamics, Inc., **6** 10
Computer Factory, Inc., **13** 176
Computer Learning Centers, Inc., 26 94–96
Computer Network, **20** 237
Computer Peripheral Manufacturers Association, **13** 127
Computer Plaza K.K., **IV** 542–43
Computer Power, **6** 301
Computer Renaissance, Inc., **18** 207–8
Computer Research Corp., **III** 151; **6** 265
Computer Resources Management, Inc., **26** 36
Computer Sciences Corporation, 6 25, **227–29; 13** 462; **15** 474; **18** 370
Computer Shoppe, **V** 191–92
Computer Systems and Applications, **12** 442
Computer Systems Division (CDS), **13** 201
Computer Terminal Corporation, **11** 67–68
ComputerCity, **10** 235
ComputerCraft, **27** 163
Computerized Lodging Systems, Inc., **11** 275
ComputerLand Corp., 6 243; **9** 116; **10** 233, 563; **12** 335; **13 174–76**, 277
Computervision Corporation, 6 246–47; **7** 498; **10 240–42; 11** 275; **13** 201; **24** 234
Computing Scale Company of America. *See* International Business Machines Corporation.
Computing-Tabulating-Recording Co., **III** 147
Compuware Corporation, 10 243–45; 30 140–43 (upd.)
CompX International, Inc., **19** 466, 468
Comsat Corporation, II 425; **12** 19; **13** 341; **23 133–36; 28** 241; **29** 42
Comshare Inc., 23 137–39
Comstock Canada, **9** 301
Comtel Electronics, Inc., **22** 409
Comverse Technology, Inc., 15 124–26
Comviq GSM AB, **26** 331–33
Con Ed. *See* Consolidated Edison of New York, Inc.
Con-Ferro Paint and Varnish Company, **8** 553
ConAgra, Inc., II 493–95, 517, 585; **7** 432, 525; **8** 53, 499–500; **12 80–82 (upd.)**; **13** 138, 294, 350, 352; **14** 515; **17** 56, 240–41; **18** 247, 290; **21** 290; **23** 320; **25** 243, 278; **26** 172, 174
Conahay & Lyon, **6** 27
Conair Corp., 16 539; **17 108–10; 24** 131; **25** 56
Concept, Inc., **23** 154
Concert Communications Company, **15** 69; **27** 304–05
Concession Air, **16** 446
Concord Fabrics, Inc., 16 124–26
Concord International, **II** 298
Concord Watch Company, S.A., **28** 291
Concorde Hotels, **27** 421
Concordia, **IV** 497
Concrete Industries (Monier) Ltd., **III** 735
Concurrent Logic, **17** 34
The Condé Nast Publications Inc., IV 583–84; **13 177–81; 19** 5; **23** 98
Condor Systems Inc., **15** 530
Cone Communications, **25** 258
Cone Mills Corporation, 8 120–22
Conelectron, **13** 398
Conestoga National Bank, **II** 316
Confectionaire, **25** 283
Confederacion Norte-Centromericana y del Caribe de Futbol, **27** 150
Confederacion Sudamericana de Futbol, **27** 150
Confederation Africaine de Football, **27** 150
Confederation Freezers, **21** 501

Confederation of Engineering Industry, **IV** 484
Confidata Corporation, **11** 111
Confindustria, **I** 162
Confiserie-Group Hofbauer, **27** 105
Congas Engineering Canada Ltd., **6** 478
Congoleum Corp., **12** 28; **16** 18; **18 116–19**
Congress Financial Corp., **13** 305–06; **19** 108; **27** 276
Congressional Information Services, **IV** 610
Conic, **9** 324
Conifer Group, **II** 214
Conill Corp., **II** 261
Coniston Partners, **I** 130; **II** 680; **III** 29; **6** 130; **10** 302
CONNA Corp., **7** 113; **25** 125
Connect Group Corporation, **28** 242
Connecticut Bank and Trust Co., **II** 213–14
Connecticut General Corporation. *See* CIGNA Corporation.
Connecticut Health Enterprises Network, **22** 425
Connecticut Light and Power Co., **13 182–84**; **21** 514
Connecticut Mutual Life Insurance Company, **III** 225, **236–38**, 254, 285
Connecticut National Bank, **13** 467
Connecticut River Banking Company, **13** 467
Connecticut Telephone Company. *See* Southern New England Telecommunications Corporation.
Connecticut Trust and Safe Deposit Co., **II** 213
Connecticut Yankee Atomic Power Company, **21** 513
Connecting Point of America, **6** 244
The Connection Group, Inc., **26** 257
Connectix Corporation, **28** 245
The Connell Company, **29 129–31**
Conner Corp., **15** 327
Conner Peripherals, Inc., **6 230–32**; **10** 403, 459, 463–64, 519; **11** 56, 234; **18** 260
Connie Lee. *See* College Construction Loan Insurance Assoc.
Connolly Data Systems, **11** 66
Connolly Tool and Machine Company, **21** 215
Connors Brothers, **II** 631–32
Connors Steel Co., **15** 116
Conoco Inc., **I** 286, 329, 346, 402–04; **II** 376; **IV** 365, 382, 389, **399–402**, 413, 429, 454, 476; **6** 539; **7** 346, 559; **8** 152, 154, 556; **11** 97, 400; **16 127–32 (upd.)**; **18** 366; **21** 29; **26** 125, 127
Conorada Petroleum Corp., **IV** 365, 400
Conover Furniture Company, **10** 183
ConQuest Telecommunication Services Inc., **16** 319
Conquistador Films, **25** 270
Conrad International Hotels, **III** 91–93
Conrail Inc., **22** 167, 376. *See also* Consolidated Rail Corporation.
Conran Associates, **17** 43
Conrock Co., **19** 70
Conseco Inc., **10 246–48**; **15** 257
Consgold. *See* Consolidated Gold Fields of South Africa Ltd. *and* Consolidated Gold Fields PLC.
Conshu Holdings, **24** 450
Conso International Corporation, **29 132–34**
Consolidated Aircraft Corporation, **9** 16, 497
Consolidated Aluminum Corp., **IV** 178
Consolidated Asset Management Company, Inc., **25** 204
Consolidated Brands Inc., **14** 18
Consolidated Cable Utilities, **6** 313
Consolidated Cement Corp., **III** 704
Consolidated Cigar Holdings, Inc., **I** 452–53; **15** 137–38; **27** 139–40; **28** 247
Consolidated Coal Co., **IV** 82, 170–71
Consolidated Coin Caterers Corporation, **10** 222
Consolidated Controls, **I** 155
Consolidated Converting Co., **19** 109
Consolidated Copper Corp., **13** 503
Consolidated Delivery & Logistics, Inc., **24 125–28**
Consolidated Denison Mines Ltd., **8** 418
Consolidated Diamond Mines of South-West Africa Ltd., **IV** 21, 65–67; **7** 122–25; **16** 26
Consolidated Distillers Ltd., **I** 263
Consolidated Edison Company of New York, Inc., **I** 28; **V 586–89**; **6** 456
Consolidated Electric & Gas, **6** 447; **23** 28
Consolidated Electric Supply Inc., **15** 385
Consolidated Electronics Industries Corp. (Conelco), **13** 397–98
Consolidated Foods Corp., **II** 571–73, 584; **III** 480; **12** 159, 494; **22** 27; **29** 132
Consolidated Freightways Corporation, **V 432–34**; **6** 280, 388; **12** 278, 309; **13** 19; **14** 567; **21 136–39 (upd.)**; **25** 148–50
Consolidated Gas Company. *See* Baltimore Gas and Electric Company.
Consolidated Gold Fields of South Africa Ltd., **IV** 94, 96, 118, 565, 566
Consolidated Gold Fields PLC, **II** 422; **III** 501, 503; **IV** 23, 67, 94, 97, 171; **7** 125, 209, 387
Consolidated Grocers Corp., **II** 571
Consolidated Insurances of Australia, **III** 347
Consolidated Marketing, Inc., **IV** 282; **9** 261
Consolidated Mines Selection Co., **IV** 20, 23
Consolidated Mining and Smelting Co., **IV** 75
Consolidated National Life Insurance Co., **10** 246
Consolidated Natural Gas Company, **V 590–91**; **19 100–02 (upd.)**
Consolidated Oatmeal Co., **II** 558
Consolidated Papers, Inc., **8 123–25**; **11** 311; **26** 363
Consolidated Power & Light Company, **6** 580
Consolidated Power & Telephone Company, **11** 342
Consolidated Press Holdings, **8** 551
Consolidated Products, Inc., **14 130–32**, 352
Consolidated Rail Corporation, **II** 449; **V 435–37**, 485; **10** 44; **12** 278; **13** 449; **14** 324; **29** 360. *See also* Conrail Inc.
Consolidated Rand-Transvaal Mining Group, **IV** 90; **22** 233
Consolidated Rock Products Co., **19** 69
Consolidated Specialty Restaurants, Inc., **14** 131–32
Consolidated Steel, **I** 558; **IV** 570; **24** 520
Consolidated Stores Corp., **13** 543; **29** 311
Consolidated Temperature Controlling Co., **II** 40; **12** 246
Consolidated Theaters, Inc., **14** 87
Consolidated Tire Company, **20** 258
Consolidated Trust Inc., **22** 540
Consolidated Tyre Services Ltd., **IV** 241
Consolidated Vultee, **II** 7, 32
Consolidated Zinc Corp., **IV** 58–59, 122, 189, 191
Consolidated-Bathurst Inc., **IV** 246–47, 334; **25** 11; **26** 445
Consolidation Coal Co., **IV** 401; **8** 154, 346–47
Consortium de Realisation, **25** 329
Consortium De Realization SAS, **23** 392
Consoweld Corporation, **8** 124
Constar International Inc., **8** 562; **13** 190
Constellation, **III** 335
Constellation Energy Corporation, **24** 29
Constellation Enterprises Inc., **25** 46
Constellation Insurance Co., **III** 191–92
Constinsouza, **25** 174
Construcciones Aeronauticas S.A., **I** 41–42; **7** 9; **12** 190; **24** 88
Construcciones y Contratas, **II** 198
Construction DJL Inc., **23** 332–33
Construtora Moderna SARL, **IV** 505
Consul Restaurant Corp., **13** 152
Consumer Access Limited, **24** 95
Consumer Products Company, **30** 39
Consumer Value Stores, **V** 136–37; **9** 67; **18** 199; **24** 290
Consumer's Gas Co., **I** 264
Consumers Cooperative Association, **7** 174
Consumers Distributing Co. Ltd., **II** 649, 652–53
Consumers Electric Light and Power, **6** 582
The Consumers Gas Company Ltd., **6 476–79**
Consumers Mutual Gas Light Company. *See* Baltimore Gas and Electric Company.
Consumers Power Co., **V** 577–79, 593–94; **14** 114–15, **133–36**
Consumers Public Power District, **29** 352
Consumers Union, **26 97–99**
Consumers Water Company, **14 137–39**
Contact Software International Inc., **10** 509
Contadina, **II** 488–89
Container Corporation of America, **IV** 295, 465; **V** 147; **7** 353; **8** 476; **19** 225; **26** 446
Container Transport International, **III** 344
Containers Packaging, **IV** 249
Contaminant Recovery Systems, Inc., **18** 162
Conte S.A., **12** 262
Contech, **10** 493
Contel Corporation, **II** 117; **V** 294–98; **6** 323; **13** 212; **14** 259; **15** 192
Contempo Associates, **14** 105; **25** 307
Contempo Casuals, Inc. *See* The Wet Seal, Inc.
Contemporary Books, **22** 522
Contex Graphics Systems Inc., **24** 428
Contherm Corp., **III** 420
Conti-Carriers & Terminals Inc., **22** 167
ContiCommodity Services, Inc., **10** 250–51
Continental AG, **9** 248; **15** 355

Continental Airlines, Inc., I 96–98, 103, 118, 123–24, 129–30; **6** 52, 61, 105, 120–21, 129–30; **12** 381; **20** 84, 262; **21 140–43 (upd.)**; **22** 80, 220; **25** 420, 423; **26** 439–40
Continental Aktiengesellschaft, V 240–43, 250–51, 256; **8** 212–14; **19** 508
Continental American Life Insurance Company, **7** 102
Continental Assurance Co., **III** 228–30
Continental Baking Co., **I** 463–64; **II** 562–63; **7** 320–21; **11** 198; **12** 276; **13** 427; **19** 192; **27** 309–10
Continental Bancor, **II** 248
Continental Bank and Trust Co., **II** 251; **14** 102
Continental Bank Corporation, I 526; **II** 261–63, 285, 289, 348; **IV** 702
Continental Bio-Clinical Laboratories, **26** 391
Continental Blacks Inc., **I** 403
Continental Cablevision, Inc., 7 98–100; **17** 148; **19** 201
Continental Can Co., Inc., I 597; **II** 34, 414; **III** 471; **10** 130; **13** 255; **15 127–30**; **24** 428; **26** 117, 449
Continental Carbon Co., **I** 403–05; **II** 53; **IV** 401
Continental Care Group, **10** 252–53
Continental Casualty Co., **III** 196, 228–32; **16** 204
Continental Cities Corp., **III** 344
Continental Corporation, III 230, **239–44**, 273; **10** 561; **12** 318; **15** 30
Continental Cos., **III** 248
Continental Divide Insurance Co., **III** 214
Continental Electronics Corporation, **18** 513–14
Continental Emsco, **24** 305
Continental Equipment Company, **13** 225
Continental Express, **11** 299
Continental Fiber Drum, **8** 476
Continental Gas & Electric Corporation, **6** 511
Continental General Tire Corp., 23 140–42
Continental Grain Company, 10 249–51; **13 185–87 (upd.)**; **30** 353, 355
Continental Group Co., I 599–600, 601–02, 604–05, 607–09, 612–13, 615; **IV** 334; **8** 175, 424; **17** 106
Continental Gummi-Werke Aktiengesellschaft, **V** 241; **9** 248
Continental Hair Products, Inc. *See* Conair Corp.
Continental Health Affiliates, **17** 307
Continental Homes, **26** 291
Continental Illinois Corp. *See* Continental Bank Corporation.
Continental Illinois Venture Co., **IV** 702
Continental Insurance Co., **III** 239–42, 372–73, 386
Continental Insurance Cos. of New York, **III** 230
Continental Investment Corporation, **9** 507; **12** 463; **22** 541
Continental Life Insurance Co., **III** 225
Continental Medical Systems, Inc., 10 252–54; **11** 282; **14** 233; **25** 111
Continental Milling Company, **10** 250
Continental Motors Corp., **I** 199, 524–25; **10** 521–22
Continental Mutual Savings Bank, **17** 529
Continental National American Group, **III** 230, 404
Continental National Bank, **II** 261; **11** 119
Continental Oil Co., **IV** 39, 365, 382, 399–401, 476, 517, 575–76
Continental Packaging Inc., **13** 255
Continental Plastic Containers, Inc., **25** 512
Continental Radio, **IV** 607
Continental Reinsurance, **11** 533
Continental Research Corporation, **22** 541
Continental Restaurant Systems, **12** 510
Continental Risk Services, **III** 243
Continental Savouries, **II** 500
Continental Scale Works, **14** 229–30
Continental Securities Corporation, **II** 444; **22** 404
Continental Telephone Company, **V** 296–97; **9** 494–95; **11** 500; **15** 195
Continental Wood Preservers, Inc., **12** 397
Continental-Caoutchouc und Gutta-Percha Compagnie, **V** 240
Continental-Emsco, **I** 490–91
Continental-National Group, **III** 230
Continentale Allgemeine, **III** 347
ContinueCare Corporation, **25** 41
Contran Corporation, **19** 467
Contrans Acquisitions, Inc., **14** 38
Contred Ltd., **20** 263
Control Data Corporation, **17** 49; **19** 110, 513–15; **25** 496; **30** 338
Control Data Systems, Inc., III 118, **126–28**, 129, 131, 149, 152, 165; **6** 228, 252, 266; **8** 117–18, 467; **10 255–57**, 359, 458–59; **11** 469; **16** 137
Controladora PROSA, **18** 516, 518
Controlled Materials and Equipment Transportation, **29** 354
Controlonics Corporation, **13** 195
Controls Company of America, **9** 67
Controlware GmbH, **22** 53
Convair, **I** 82, 121, 123, 126, 131; **II** 33; **9** 18, 498; **13** 357
Convenient Food Mart Inc., **7** 114; **25** 125
Convergent Technologies, **III** 166; **6** 283; **11** 519
Converse Inc., III 528–29; **V** 376; **9 133–36**, 234; **12** 308; **31 134–138 (upd.)**, 211
Conway Computer Group, **18** 370
Conwest Exploration Company Ltd., **16** 10, 12
Conycon. *See* Construcciones y Contratas.
Conzinc Riotinto of Australia. *See* CRA Limited.
Cook Data Services, Inc., **9** 73
Cook Industrial Coatings, **I** 307
Cook Standard Tool Co., **13** 369
Cook United, **V** 172
Cooke Engineering Company, **13** 194
The Cooker Restaurant Corporation, 20 159–61
Cooking and Crafts Club, **13** 106
Cookson Group plc, III 679–82; **16** 290
Coolerator, **I** 463
Coolidge Mutual Savings Bank, **17** 529
Cooper Cameron Corporation, 20 162–66 (upd.)
Cooper Canada Ltd., **16** 80
Cooper Industries, Inc., II 14–17; **14** 564; **19** 43, 45, 140; **30** 266
Cooper Laboratories, **I** 667, 682
Cooper LaserSonics Inc., **IV** 100
Cooper McDougall & Robertson Ltd., **I** 715
Cooper Tire & Rubber Company, 8 126–28; **23 143–46 (upd.)**
Cooper's, Inc., **12** 283
Cooper-Weymouth, **10** 412
Cooperative Grange League Federation Exchange, **7** 17
Coopers & Lybrand, 9 137–38; **12** 391; **25** 383. *See also* PricewaterhouseCoopers.
CooperVision, **7** 46; **25** 55
Coordinated Caribbean Transport. *See* Crowley Caribbean Transport.
Coors Company. *See* Adolph Coors Company.
Coorsh and Bittner, **7** 430
Coos Bay Lumber Co., **IV** 281; **9** 259
Coosa River Newsprint Co., **III** 40; **16** 303
Coote & Jurgenson, **14** 64
Cooymans, **I** 281
Copart Inc., 23 147–49, 285, 287
Copeland Corp., **II** 20
Copeman Ridley, **13** 103
Copland Brewing Co., **I** 268; **25** 280
Copley Pharmaceuticals Inc., **13** 264
The Copley Press, Inc., 23 150–52
Copley Real Estate Advisors, **III** 313
Copolymer Corporation, **9** 242
Copper Queen Consolidated Mining Co., **IV** 176–77
Copper Range Company, **IV** 76; **7** 281–82
Copperweld Steel Co., **IV** 108–09, 237
Copycat Ltd., **8** 383
Cora Verlag, **IV** 590
Coral Drilling, **I** 570
Coral Leisure Group, **I** 248
Coral Petroleum, **IV** 395
Corbett Enterprises Inc., **13** 270
Corbis Corporation, 31 139–42
Corby Distilleries Limited, 14 140–42
Corco. *See* Commonwealth Oil Refining Company.
Corco, Inc. *See* Liqui-Box Corporation.
Corcoran & Riggs. *See* Riggs National Corporation.
Cordiant plc. *See* Saatchi & Saatchi plc.
Cordis Corp., 19 103–05
Cordon & Gotch, **IV** 619
Cordon Bleu, **II** 609
Cordovan Corp., **IV** 608
Core Laboratories Inc., **I** 486; **11** 265
Corel Corporation, 15 131–33
CoreStates Financial Corp, 17 111–15
Corfuerte S.A. de C.V., **23** 171
Corimon, **12** 218
Corinthian Broadcast Corporation, **IV** 605; **10** 4
Cormetech, **III** 685
Corn Exchange Bank, **II** 316
Corn Exchange Bank Trust Co., **II** 251; **14** 102
Corn Exchange National Bank, **II** 261
Corn Products Company. *See* Bestfoods.
Corn Sweetners Inc., **I** 421; **11** 23
Cornelia Insurance Agency. *See* Advantage Insurers, Inc.
Cornell Corrections, **28** 255
Cornerstone Direct Marketing, **8** 385–86
Cornerstone Title Company, **8** 461
Cornhill Insurance Co., **I** 429; **III** 185, 385
Cornhusker Casualty Co., **III** 213
Corning Asahi Video Products Co., **III** 667
Corning Clinical Laboratories, **26** 390–92
Corning Consumer Products Company, **27** 288

Corning Incorporated, **I** 609; **III** 434, 667, **683–85**, 720–21; **8** 468; **11** 334; **13** 398; **22** 454; **25** 254; **30** 151–52
Coronado Corp., **II** 112
Coronet Industries, Inc., **II** 90; **14** 436
Corp. d'acquisition Socanav-Caisse Inc., **II** 664
Corp. of Lloyd's, **III** 278–79
Corporacion Estatal Petrolera Ecuatoriana, **IV** 510–11
Corporación Internacional de Aviación, S.A. de C.V. (Cintra), **20 167–69**
Corporación Moctezuma, **21** 261
Corporacion Siderurgica Integral, **22** 44
Corporación Venezolana de Petroleo, **IV** 507
Corporate Childcare Development, Inc. *See* Bright Horizons Family Solutions, Inc.
Corporate Express, Inc., **22 152–55**, 531
Corporate Microsystems, Inc., **10** 395
Corporate Partners, **12** 391
Corporate Software Inc., **9 139–41**
CorporateFamily Solutions. *See* Bright Horizons Family Solutions, Inc.
Corporation for Public Broadcasting, **14 143–45**
Corporation Trust Co. *See* CCH Inc.
Corpoven, **IV** 508
Corrado Passera, **IV** 588
Corral Midwest, Inc., **10** 333
Correctional Services Corporation, **30 144–46**
Corrections Corporation of America, **23 153–55**; **28** 255
Corrigan's, **16** 559
Corrigan-McKinney Steel Company, **13** 157
Corroon & Black. *See* Willis Corroon Group Plc.
Corrpro Companies, Inc., **20 170–73**
Corrugated Paper, **IV** 249
CORT Business Services Corporation, **26 100–02**
El Corte Inglés Group, **26 128–31 (upd.)**
Cortec Corporation, **14** 430
Corvallis Lumber Co., **IV** 358
Cory Bros & Co. Ltd., **31** 367, 369
Cory Corp., **II** 511
Cory Food Services, Inc., **II** 608
Cory Orchard and Turf. *See* Chemi-Trol Chemical Co.
Cosco Pacific, **20** 313
Cosden Petroleum Corp., **IV** 498; **26** 367
Cosgrove & Co., **III** 283
Cosmair Inc., **III** 47–48; **8 129–32**, 342–44; **12** 404; **31** 418
The Cosmetic Center, Inc., **22 156–58**
Cosmetic Technology International, Inc., **22** 409
Cosmo Oil Co., Ltd., **IV 403–04**
Cosmopolitan Productions, **IV** 626; **19** 203
Cosorzio Interprovinciale Vini, **10** 181
Cost Plus, Inc., **12** 393; **27 109–11**
Costa Apple Products, **II** 480; **26** 57
Costa Cruise Lines, **27** 29, 90, 92
Costa e Ribeiro Ltd., **IV** 504
Costain Civil Engineering Ltd., **III** 495; **13** 206
Costain Homes, **31** 386
Costco Wholesale Corporation, **V 36**; **10** 206; **11** 240; **14** 393–95; **15** 470; **25** 235; **27** 95
Costruzioni Meccaniche Nazionalia, **13** 218
Côte d'Or, **II** 521
Cott Beverage Corporation, **9** 291
Cottees General Foods, **II** 477
Cotter & Company, **V 37–38**; **12** 8. *See also* TruServ Corporation.
Cotter Corporation, **29** 488
Cotton Producers Association. *See* Gold Kist Inc.
Coty, **I** 662
Coudert Brothers, **30 147–50**
Coulter Corporation. *See* Beckman Coulter, Inc.
Counselor Co., **14** 230
Country Fresh, Inc., **26** 449
Country Kitchen Foods, **III** 21
Country Kitchen International, **22** 127
Country Music Television, **11** 153
Country Poultry, Inc., **II** 494
Country Seat Stores, Inc., **15** 87
Country Store of Concord, Inc., **10** 216
Countrywide Credit Industries, Inc., **16 133–36**
County Bank, **II** 333
County Catering Co., **13** 103
County Data Corporation, **18** 24
County Fire Insurance Co., **III** 191
County Market, **II** 670
County NatWest, **II** 334–35
County Perfumery, **III** 65
County Seat Stores Inc., **II** 669; **9 142–43**
County Trust Co., **II** 230
Cour des Comptes, **II** 233
Courage Brewing Group., **I** 229, 438–39; **III** 503
Courcoux-Bouvet, **II** 260
Courrèges Parfums, **III** 48; **8** 343
The Courseware Developers, **11** 19
Court Courier Systems, Inc., **24** 126
Court House Square, **10** 44
Courtaulds plc, **I** 321; **IV** 261, 670; **V** 356–57, **359–61**; **12** 103; **17 116–19 (upd.)**
Courtney Wines International, **II** 477
Courtot Investments, **II** 222
Courtyard by Marriott, **9** 427
Cousins Mortgage and Equity Investments, **12** 393
Coutts & Co., **II** 333–34
Couvrette & Provost Ltd., **II** 651
Covance Inc., **30 151–53**
Covantage, **11** 379
Covenant Life Insurance, **III** 314
Coventry Climax Engines, Ltd., **13** 286
Coventry Co., **III** 213
Coventry Corporation, **17** 166, 168
Coventry Machinists Company, **7** 458
Coventry Ordnance Works, **I** 573
Coventry Union Banking Co., **II** 318; **17** 323
Covidea, **II** 252
Coville Inc., **16** 353
Cow & Gate Ltd., **II** 586–87
Cowham Engineering, **III** 704
Cowles Media Company, **IV** 613, 648; **7** 191; **19** 285; **23 156–58**; 344
Cox & Co., **II** 236, 307–08
Cox Enterprises, Inc., **IV** 246, **595–97**; **6** 32; **7** 327; **9** 74; **17** 148; **22 159–63 (upd.)**; **24** 120; **30** 217
Cox Medical Enterprises, Inc., **21** 47
Cox Newsprint, Inc., **25** 11
Cox Woodlands Company, **25** 11
Coz Chemical Co., **21** 20, 22
CP. *See* Canadian Pacific Limited.
CP Air, **6** 60–61
CP National, **6** 300; **19** 412
CP/AAON. *See* AAON, Inc.
CPC International Inc., **II** 463, **496–98**; **27** 40. *See also* Bestfoods.
CPL. *See* Carolina Power & Light Company.
CRA Limited, **IV 58–61**, 67, 192; **7** 124. *See also* Rio Tinto plc.
Crabtree Electricals, **III** 503; **7** 210
Cracker Barrel Old Country Store, Inc., **9** 78; **10 258–59**; **29** 292
Craft House Corp., **8** 456
Craig Bit Company, **13** 297
Crain Communications, Inc., **12 83–86**
Cramer Electronics, **10** 112
Cranberry Canners, Inc. *See* Ocean Spray Cranberries, Inc.
Crane & Co., Inc., **26 103–06**; **30** 42
Crane Co., **8 133–36**, 179; **24** 332; **30 154–58 (upd.)**
Crane Packing Company, **19** 311
Crane Supply Company, **8** 135
Cranston Mills, **13** 168
Crate and Barrel, **9 144–46**; **27** 429. *See also* Euromarket Designs Inc
Cravath, Swaine & Moore, **27** 325
Craven Tasker Ltd., **I** 573–74
Crawford and Watson, **IV** 278
Crawford Gosho Co., Ltd., **IV** 442
Crawford Group, Inc., **17** 372
Crawford Supply Company, **6** 392
Cray Research, Inc., **III** 126, 128, **129–31**; **10** 256; **16 137–40 (upd.)**; **21** 391; **22** 428; **29** 440
Crazy Eddie Inc., **23** 373
CRD Total France, **IV** 560
Cream City Railway Company, **6** 601
Cream of Wheat Corp., **II** 543; **22** 427
Creamola Food Products, **II** 569
Creasy Co., **II** 682
Creative Artists Agency, **10** 228; **22** 297; **23** 512, 514
Creative BioMolecules, Inc., **29** 454
Creative Concepts in Advertising, **27** 194
Creative Displays, Inc., **27** 279
Creative Engineering Inc., **13** 472
Creative Food 'N Fun Co., **14** 29
Creative Forming, Inc., **8** 562
Creative Homes, Inc., **IV** 341
Creative Integration and Design Inc., **20** 146
Creative Technologies Corp., **15** 401
Credit & Risk Management Associates, Inc., **18** 170
Credit Acceptance Corporation, **18 120–22**
Crédit Agricole, **II 264–66**, 355; **19** 51
Credit and Data Marketing Services, **V** 118
Credit Clearing House, **IV** 605
Crédit Commercial de France, **25** 173
Credit du Nord, **II** 260
Crédit Foncier, **II** 264
Crédit Général de Belgique, **II** 304
Credit Immobilier, **7** 538
Crédit Liégiois, **II** 270
Crédit Lyonnais, **II** 242, 257, 354; **6** 396; **7** 12; **9 147–49**; **19** 34, 51, 166; **21** 226; **25** 170, 329
Credit Mobilier, **II** 294
Crédit National S.A., **9 150–52**
Credit Service Exchange, **6** 24
Credit Suisse First Boston. *See* Financière Crédit Suisse-First Boston.

Crédit Suisse Group, II 267–69, 369–70, 378–79, 402–04; **21 144–47 (upd.)**. *See also* Schweizerische Kreditanstalt.
Creditanstalt-Bankverein, **II** 242, 295
CrediThrift Financial, **11** 16
Credithrift Financial of Indiana, **III** 194
Credito de la Union Minera, **II** 194
Credito Italiano, I 368, 465, 567; **II** 191, **270–72**; **III** 347
Credito Minero y Mercantil, S.A., **22** 285
Credito Provincial Hipotecario, **19** 189
Cree Research, Inc., **13** 399
Crellin Holding, Inc., **8** 477
Crellin Plastics, **8** 13
Crenlo Corp., **16** 180
Creole Petroleum Corporation, **IV** 428; **7** 171
Crescendo Productions, **6** 27
Crescent Box & Printing Co., **13** 442
Crescent Chemical, **I** 374
Crescent Niagara Corp., **II** 16
Crescent Real Estate Equities Company, **25** 454
Crescent Software Inc., **15** 373
Crescent Vert Company, Ltd., **II** 51; **21** 330
Crescent Washing Machine Company, **8** 298
Crescott, Inc., **15** 501
Cressbrook Dairy Co., **II** 546
Cressey Dockham & Co., **II** 682
Crest Fruit Co., **17** 458
Crest Ridge Homes, Inc., **17** 83
Crest Service Company, **9** 364
Crestbrook Forest Industries Ltd., **IV** 285
Crestmont Financial Corporation, **14** 472
Creusot-Loire, **II** 93–94; **19** 166
Crevettes du Cameroun, **13** 244
Crimson Associates L.P., **26** 48
Criterion Casualty Company, **10** 312
Criterion Life Insurance Company, **10** 311
Critikon, Inc., **III** 36
Crocker National Bank, **II** 226, 317, 319, 383; **13** 535; **17** 324–25
Crocker National Corporation, **12** 536
Crockett Container Corporation, **8** 268
Croda International Ltd., **IV** 383
Croitex S.A., **26** 374
Crompton & Knowles Corp., I 633; **9 153–55**
Crop Production Services, Inc., **IV** 576
Crosby Enterprises, **17** 19
Croscill Home Fashions, **8** 510
Crosfield, Lampard & Co., **III** 696
Cross & Trecker Corporation, **10** 330
Cross Country Group, **25** 358
Cross Creek Apparel, Inc., **30** 400
Cross Pointe Paper Corporation, **26** 363
Cross-Continent Auto Retailers, **26** 501
Cross/Tessitore & Associates, **16** 259
Crossair, **I** 121
Crosse and Blackwell, **II** 547
Crossett Lumber Co., **IV** 281; **9** 259
Crossland Capital Corp., **III** 293
Crossley Motors, Ltd., **13** 285
Crothall, **6** 44
Crothers Properties, Ltd., **21** 500
Crouse-Hinds Co., **II** 16; **19** 45
Crow Catchpole, **III** 752; **28** 448
Crowell Publishing Company, **19** 266
Crowell-Collier Publishing Company, **IV** 310; **7** 286
Crowley Foods, Inc., **II** 528
Crowley Maritime Corporation, 6 382–84; **9** 510–11; **28 77–80 (upd.)**
Crowley, Milner & Company, 19 106–08
Crown Advertising Agency. *See* King Kullen Grocery Co., Inc.
Crown Aluminum, **I** 544
Crown America Corp., **13** 393
Crown Books Corporation, 14 61; **16** 159–61; **21 148–50**
Crown Can Co., **I** 601
Crown Center Redevelopment Corp., **IV** 621
Crown Central Petroleum Corporation, 7 101–03
Crown, Cork & Seal Company, Inc., I 601–03; **13 188–90 (upd.)**; **15** 129; **17** 106; **24** 264; **30** 475
Crown Courier Systems, Inc., **24** 126
Crown Crafts, Inc., 16 141–43
Crown Drugs, **II** 673
Crown Equipment Corporation, 15 134–36
Crown Forest Industries, **IV** 279; **19** 155
Crown Life Insurance Company, **III** 261; **6** 181–82
Crown Oil and Refining Company, **7** 101
Crown Packaging, **19** 155
Crown Publishing Group, **IV** 584; **13** 429; **31** 376, 379
Crown Radio, **17** 123–24
Crown Vantage Inc., 29 135–37
Crown Zellerbach Corporation, **IV** 290, 345; **8** 261; **22** 210; **24** 247
Crownx Inc., **6** 181–82
Crowson and Son Ltd., **23** 219
CRSS Inc., 6 142–44; **23** 491
CRTC. *See* Canadian Radio-Television and Telecommunications Commission.
Crucible Steel, **I** 434–35
Crude Oil Pipe Line Co., **IV** 400
Cruden Investments Pty Ltd., **IV** 651; **7** 390
Cruise America Inc., 21 151–53
Cruise Associates, **22** 471
Crum & Forster Holdings, Inc., **II** 448; **III** 172; **6** 290; **13** 448; **26** 546
Crump E & S, **6** 290
Crump Inc., **I** 584
Crush International, **II** 478; **III** 53
Crushed Stone Sales Ltd., **IV** 241
Cruzan Rum Distillery, Ltd., **27** 478
Cruzcampo, **18** 501
Cruzeiro do Sul Airlines, **6** 133
Cryenco Sciences Inc., **21** 109
Cryomedics Inc., **I** 667
Crystal Brands, Inc., 9 156–58; **12** 431
Crystal Oil Co., **IV** 180, 548
CS Crable Sportswear Inc., **23** 66
CS First Boston Inc., II 269, **402–04**; **III** 289; **12** 209; **21** 146. *See also* First Boston Corp.
CS Holding. *See* Credit Suisse Group.
CS Life, **21** 146–47
CSA Press, **IV** 661
CSC. *See* Computer Sciences Corporation.
CSC Industries, Inc., **IV** 63
CSE Corp., **III** 214
CSFB. *See* Financière Crédit Suisse-First Boston *and* Credit Suisse Group.
CSK, **10** 482
CSO. *See* Columbus & Southern Ohio Electric Company.
CSR Limited, III 686–88, 728, 735–36; **IV** 46; **22** 106; **28 81–84 (upd.)**
CST Office Products, **15** 36
CSX Corporation, V 438–40, 485; **6** 340; **9** 59; **13** 462; **22 164–68 (upd.)**; **29** 360–61
CSY Agri-Processing, **7** 81–82
CT Financial Services Inc., **V** 401–02
CT&T. *See* Carolina Telephone and Telegraph Company.
CTA. *See* Comptoir des Textiles Artificielles.
CTG, Inc., 11 64–66
CTI. *See* Cosmetic Technology International, Inc.
CTNE, **I** 462
CTR. *See* International Business Machines Corporation.
CTS Corp., **19** 104
CTX Mortgage Company, **8** 88
Cub Foods, **II** 669–70; **14** 411; **17** 302; **18** 505; **22** 327
Cuban American Nickel Co., **IV** 82; **7** 186
Cuban American Oil Company, **8** 348
Cuban Telephone Co., **I** 462–63
Cuban-American Manganese Corp., **IV** 81; **7** 186
Cubic Corporation, 19 109–11
Cubitts Nigeria, **III** 753
CUC International Inc., 16 144–46
Cuckler Steel Span Co., **I** 481
Cudahy Corp., **12** 199
Cuisinart Corporation, 17 110; **24 129–32**
Culbro Corporation, 14 19; **15 137–39**
Culinary Foods, Inc., **14** 516
Cullen/Frost Bankers, Inc., 25 113–16
Culligan International Company, I 373; **II** 468; **12 87–88**, 346; **16** 20
Cullinet Software Corporation, **6** 225; **14** 390; **15** 108
Cullman Bros. *See* Culbro Corporation.
Cullum Companies, **II** 670
Culp, Inc., 29 138–40
Culter Industries, Inc., **22** 353
Cumberland Farms, Inc., 17 120–22; **26** 450
Cumberland Federal Bancorporation, **13** 223; **31** 206
Cumberland Newspapers, **IV** 650; **7** 389
Cumberland Packing Corporation, 26 107–09
Cumberland Paper Board Mills Ltd., **IV** 248
Cumberland Pipeline Co., **IV** 372
Cumberland Property Investment Trust Ltd., **IV** 711
Cummins Engine Co., Inc., I 146–48, 186; **III** 545; **IV** 252; **10** 273–74; **12 89–92 (upd.)**; **16** 297; **17** 29; **19** 293; **21** 503; **26** 256
Cumo Sports, **16** 109
CUNA Mutual Insurance Group, **11** 495
Cunard Line Ltd., I 573; **23 159–62**; **27** 90, 92
Cuno Kourten, **13** 353
Cupples Products Co., **IV** 15
Current, Inc., **7** 137, 139; **22** 181
Currys Group PLC, **V** 49; **19** 123
Cursenir, **I** 280
Curtice-Burns Foods, Inc., 7 17–18, **104–06**; **21** 18, **154–57 (upd.)**
Curtin & Pease/Peneco, **27** 361
Curtis Circulation Co., **IV** 619
Curtis Homes, **22** 127
Curtis Industries, **13** 165

Curtis 1000 Inc. *See* American Business Products, Inc.
Curtis Squire Inc., **18** 455
Curtiss Candy Co., **II** 544
Curtiss-Wright Corporation, **I** 524; **III** 464; **7** 263; **8** 49; **9** 14, 244, 341, 417; **10 260–63**; **11** 427; **21** 174; **23** 340
Curver Group, **III** 614
Curver-Rubbermaid, **III** 615
Cushman Motor Works, **III** 598
Custom Academic Publishing Company, **12** 174
Custom Chrome, Inc., **16 147–49**
Custom Electronics, Inc., **9** 120
Custom Expressions, Inc., **7** 24; **22** 35
Custom Hoists, Inc., **17** 458
Custom Metal Products, Inc., **III** 643
Custom Organics, **8** 464
Custom Primers, **17** 288
Custom Products Inc., **III** 643
Custom Publishing Group, **27** 361
Custom Technologies Corp., **19** 152
Custom Thermoform, **24** 512
Custom Transportation Services, Inc., **26** 62
Customized Transportation Inc., **22** 164, 167
AB Custos, **25** 464
Cutler-Hammer Inc., **I** 155; **III** 644–45
Cutter & Buck Inc., **27 112–14**
Cutter Laboratories, **I** 310
Cutter Precision Metals, Inc., **25** 7
CVE Corporation, Inc., **24** 395
CVI Incorporated, **21** 108
CVL Inc., **II** 457
CVN Companies, **9** 218
CVS. *See* Consumer Value Stores.
CWM. *See* Chemical Waste Management, Inc.
CWT Farms International Inc., **13** 103
Cyber Communications Inc., **16** 168
CyberCash Inc., **18** 541, 543
Cybermedia, Inc., **25 117–19**, 349
Cybernet Electronics Corp., **II** 51; **21** 330
Cybernex, **10** 463
CyberSource Corp., **26** 441
CYBERTEK Corporation, **11** 395
CyberTel, **IV** 596–97
Cycle & Carriage Ltd., **20** 313
Cycle Video Inc., **7** 590
Cyclo Chemical Corp., **I** 627
Cyclo Getriebebau Lorenz Braren GmbH, **III** 634
Cyclone Co. of Australia, **III** 673
Cyclops Corporation, **10** 45; **13** 157
Cygna Energy Services, **13** 367
Cygne Designs, Inc., **25 120–23**
Cymbal Co., Ltd., **V** 150
Cynosure Inc., **11** 88
Cyphernetics Corp., **III** 118
Cypress Amax Minerals Co., **13** 158; **22** 285–86
Cypress Insurance Co., **III** 214
Cypress Semiconductor Corporation, **6** 216; **18** 17, 383; **20 174–76**
Cyprus Amax Minerals Company, **21 158–61**
Cyprus Minerals Company, **7 107–09**
Cyrix Corp., **10** 367; **26** 329
Cyrk Inc., **19 112–14**; **21** 516
Cytec Industries Inc., **27 115–17**

D&D Enterprises, Inc., **24** 96
D&F Industries, Inc., **17** 227
D&K Wholesale Drug, Inc., **14 146–48**
D&N Systems, Inc., **10** 505
D&O Inc., **17** 363
D & P Studios, **II** 157
D&W Computer Stores, **13** 176
D & W Food Stores, Inc., **8** 482; **27** 314
D.B. Kaplan's, **26** 263
D.B. Marron & Company, **II** 445; **22** 406
D.C. Heath & Co., **II** 86; **11** 413
D.C. National Bancorp, **10** 426
D. Connelly Boiler Company, **6** 145
D. de Ricci-G. Selnet et Associes, **28** 141
d.e.m.o., **28** 345
D.E. Makepeace Co., **IV** 78
D.E. Shaw, **25** 17
D.E. Winebrenner Co., **7** 429
D.G. Calhoun, **12** 112
D. Hald & Co., **III** 417
D.K. Gold, **17** 138
D.L. Saslow Co., **19** 290
D.M. Nacional, **23** 170
D.M. Osborne Co., **III** 650
D.R. Horton Inc., **25** 217; **26** 291
D.W. Mikesell Co. *See* Mike-Sell's Inc.
Da Gama Textiles Company, **24** 450
Dabney, Morgan & Co., **II** 329
Dade Reagents Inc., **19** 103
Dade Wholesale Products, **6** 199
DADG. *See* Deutsch-Australische Dampfschiffs-Gesellschaft.
Dae Won Kang Up Co., **III** 581
Daejin Shipping Company, **6** 98; **27** 271
Daesung Heavy Industries, **I** 516
Daewoo Group, **I** 516; **II** 53; **III 457–59**, 749; **12** 211; **18 123–27 (upd.)**; **30** 185
DAF, **I** 186; **III** 543; **7** 566–67
Daffy's Inc., **26 110–12**
NV Dagblad De Telegraaf. *See* N.V. Holdingmaatschappij De Telegraaf.
Dage-Bell, **II** 86
Dagincourt. *See* Compagnie de Saint-Gobain S.A.
D'Agostino Supermarkets Inc., **19 115–17**
Dagsbladunie, **IV** 611
Dahl Manufacturing, Inc., **17** 106
Dahlberg, Inc., **18** 207–08
Dahlgren, **I** 677
Dahlonega Equipment and Supply Company, **12** 377
Dai Nippon. *See also listings under* Dainippon.
Dai Nippon Brewery Co., **I** 220, 282; **21** 319
Dai Nippon Ink and Chemicals, **I** 303
Dai Nippon Mujin, **II** 371
Dai Nippon Printing Co., Ltd., **IV 598–600**, 631, 679–80
Dai Nippon X-ray Inc., **II** 75
Dai Nippon Yuben Kai, **IV** 631–32
Dai-Ichi. *See also listings under* Daiichi.
Dai-Ichi Bank, **I** 507, 511; **IV** 148
Dai-Ichi Kangyo Bank Ltd., **II 273–75**, 325–26, 360–61, 374; **III** 188
Dai-Ichi Mokko Co., **III** 758
Dai-Ichi Mutual Life Insurance Co., **II** 118; **III** 277, 401; **25** 289; **26** 511
Daido Boeki, **24** 325
Daido Spring Co., **III** 580
Daido Steel Co., Ltd., **IV 62–63**
Daido Trading, **I** 432, 492; **24** 324
The Daiei, Inc., **V** 11, **39–40**; **17 123–25 (upd.)**; **18** 186, 285; **19** 308
Daignault Rolland, **24** 404
Daihatsu Motor Company, Ltd., **7 110–12**; **21 162–64 (upd.)**
Daiichi. *See also listings under* Dai-Ichi.
Daiichi Atomic Power Industry Group, **II** 22
Daiichi Bussan Kaisha Ltd., **I** 505, 507
Daiichi Fire, **III** 405
Daijugo Bank, **I** 507
Daiken Company. *See* Marubeni Corporation.
Daikin Industries, Ltd., **III 460–61**
Daikyo Oil Co., Ltd., **IV** 403–04, 476
Dailey & Associates, **I** 16
Daily Chronicle Investment Group, **IV** 685
Daily Mail and General Trust plc, **19 118–20**
Daily Mirror, **IV** 665–66; **17** 397
Daily Press Inc., **IV** 684; **22** 522
Daimaru, **V 41–42**, 130
Daimler Airway, **I** 92
Daimler-Benz Aerospace AG, **16 150–52**; **24** 84
Daimler-Benz AG, **I** 27, 138, **149–51**, 186–87, 192, 194, 198, 411, 549; **II** 257, 279–80, 283; **III** 495, 523, 562, 563, 695, 750; **7** 219; **10** 261, 274; **11** 31; **12** 192, 342; **13** 30, 286, 414; **14** 169; **15 140–44 (upd.)**; **20** 312–13; **22** 11; **26** 481, 498
Dain Bosworth Inc., **15** 231–33, 486
Daina Seikosha, **III** 620
Daini-Denden Incorporated, **12** 136–37
Daini-Denden Kikaku Company, Ltd., **II** 51. *See also* DDI Corporation.
Dainippon. *See also listings under* Dai-Nippon.
Dainippon Celluloid Company, **I** 509; **III** 486; **18** 183
Dainippon Ink & Chemicals, Inc., **IV** 397; **10** 466–67; **13** 308, 461; **17** 363; **28** 194
Dainippon Shurui, **III** 42
Dainippon Spinning Company, **V** 387
Daio Paper Corporation, **IV 266–67**, 269
Dairy Farm Ice and Cold Storage Co., **IV** 700
Dairy Farm Management Services Ltd., **I** 471; **20** 312
Dairy Fresh, Inc., **26** 449
Dairy Maid Products Cooperative, **II** 536
Dairy Mart Convenience Stores, Inc., **7 113–15**; **17** 501; **25 124–27 (upd.)**
Dairy Queen National Development Company, **10** 372
Dairy Supply Co., **II** 586; **III** 418, 420
Dairyland Food Laboratories, **I** 677
Dairymen, Inc., **11** 24
Daishowa Paper Manufacturing Co., Ltd. **II** 361; **IV 268–70**, 326, 667; **17** 398
Daisy Systems Corp., **11** 46, 284–85, 489
Daisy/Cadnetix Inc., **6** 248; **24** 235
Daisytek International Corporation, **18 128–30**
Daiwa Bank, Ltd., **II 276–77**, 347, 438; **26** 457
Daiwa Securities Company, Limited, **II** 276, 300, **405–06**, 434; **9** 377
Daka, Inc. *See* Unique Casual Restaurants, Inc.
Dakin Inc., **24** 44
Dakota Power Company, **6** 580; **20** 73
Dakotah Mills, **8** 558–59; **16** 353
Daksoft, Inc., **20** 74

Dal-Tile International Inc., 22 46, 49, **169–71**
Dalberg Co., **II** 61
Dale Carnegie Training, Inc., 28 85–87
Dale Electronics, **21** 519
Daleville & Middletown Telephone Company, **14** 258
Dalfort Corp., **15** 281
Dalgety PLC, II 499–500; **III** 21; **12** 411; **22** 147; **27** 258, 260. *See also* PIC International Group PLC
Dalian, **14** 556
Dalian Cement Factory, **III** 718
Dalian International Nordic Tire Co., **20** 263
D'Allaird's, **24** 315–16
Dallas Airmotive, **II** 16
Dallas Ceramic Co. *See* Dal-Tile International Inc.
Dallas Lumber and Supply Co., **IV** 358
Dallas Power & Light Company, **V** 724
Dallas Semiconductor Corporation, 13 191–93; 31 143–46 (upd.)
Dallas Southland Ice Co., **II** 660
Dallas-Fort Worth Suburban Newspapers, Inc., **10** 3
Daltex General Agency, Inc., **25** 115
Damar, **IV** 610
Damark International, Inc., 18 131–34
Damart, **25** 523
Dameron-Pierson Co., **25** 500
Dames & Moore, Inc., 25 128–31
Dammann Asphalt, **III** 673
Damodar Valley Corp., **IV** 49
Damon, **21** 153
Damon Clinical Laboratories Inc., **26** 392
Damon Corporation, **11** 334
Dan's Supreme, **24** 528
Dana Alexander Inc., **27** 197
Dana Corporation, I 152–53; 10 264–66 (upd.); **23** 170–71
Dana Design Ltd., **16** 297
Danaher Corporation, 7 116–17
Danair A/S, **I** 120
Danapak Holding Ltd., **11** 422
Danat-Bank, **I** 138
Danbury Phamacal Inc., **31** 254
Dancer Fitzgerald Sample, **I** 33; **23** 505
Daniel Industries, Inc., 16 153–55
Daniel International Corp., **I** 570–71; **8** 192
Daniel P. Creed Co., Inc., **8** 386
Daniel's Jewelers, **16** 559
Danieli & C. Officine Meccaniche, **13** 98
Daniels Linseed Co., **I** 419
Daniels Packaging, **12** 25
Daniels Pharmaceuticals, Inc., **24** 257
Danish Aalborg, **27** 91
Danish Almindelinge Brand-Assurance-Compagni, **III** 299
Danley Machine Corp., **I** 514
Danner Shoe Manufacturing Co., **18** 300
Dannon Co., Inc., II 468, 474–75; **14 149–51**
Danone, **25** 85
Danray, **12** 135
Dansk Bioprotein, **IV** 406–07
Dansk International Designs Ltd., **10** 179, 181; **12** 313
Dansk Metal and Armaturindistri, **III** 569; **20** 361
Dansk Rejsebureau, **I** 120
Danskin, Inc., 12 93–95; **15** 358
Danville Resources, Inc., **13** 502
Danzas Group, V 441–43
DAP, Inc., **III** 66; **12** 7; **18** 549
Dara Michelle, **17** 101–03
D'Arcy Masius Benton & Bowles, Inc., I 233–34; **6 20–22**; **10** 226–27; **26** 187; **28** 137
Darden Restaurants, Inc., 16 156–58
Darigold, Inc., 9 159–61
Darling and Hodgson, **IV** 91
Darling, Brown & Sharpe. *See* Brown & Sharpe Manufacturing Co.
Darmstadter, **II** 282
Darracq, **7** 6
Darrell J. Sekin Transport Co., **17** 218
Dart & Kraft Financial Corp., **II** 534; **III** 610–11; **7** 276; **12** 310; **14** 547
Dart Group Corporation, II 645, 656, 667, 674; **12** 49; **15** 270; **16 159–62**; **21** 148; **23** 370; **24** 418; **27** 158
Dart Industries, **II** 533–34; **III** 610; **9** 179–80. *See also* Premark International Inc.
Dart Transit Co., **13** 550
Dart Truck Co., **I** 185
Dartex, **18** 434
Darty S.A., 27 118–20
Darvel Realty Trust, **14** 126
Darya-Varia Laboratoria, **18** 182
DASA. *See* Daimler-Benz Aerospace AG *or* Deutsche Aerospace Airbus.
Dashwood Industries, **19** 446
Dassault Aviation SA, **21** 11
Dassault Systèmes S.A., 25 132–34; **26** 179. *See also* Groupe Dassault Aviation SA.
Dassault-Breguet. *See* Avions Marcel Dassault-Breguet Aviation.
Dassler, **14** 6
Dastek Inc., **10** 464; **11** 234–35
DAT GmbH, **10** 514
Dat Jidosha Seizo Co., **I** 183
Data Acquisition Systems, Inc., **16** 300
Data Architects, **14** 318
Data Base Management Inc., **11** 19
Data Broadcasting Corporation, 31 147–50
Data Business Forms, **IV** 640
Data Card Corp., **IV** 680
Data Corp., **IV** 311; **19** 267
Data Documents, **III** 157
Data Force Inc., **11** 65
Data General Corporation, II 208; **III** 124, 133; **6** 221, 234; **8 137–40**; **9** 297; **10** 499; **12** 162; **13** 201; **16** 418; **20** 8
Data One Corporation, **11** 111
Data Preparation, Inc., **11** 112
Data Printer, Inc., **18** 435
Data Resources, Inc., **IV** 637
Data Specialties Inc. *See* Zebra Technologies Corporation.
Data Structures Inc., **11** 65
Data Systems Technology, **11** 57
Data Technology Corp., **18** 510
Data 3 Systems, **9** 36
Data-Beam Corp., **25** 301
Datac plc, **18** 140
Datachecker Systems, **II** 64–65; **III** 164; **11** 150
Datacraft Corp., **II** 38
DataFocus, Inc., **18** 112
Datamatic Corp., **II** 41, 86; **12** 247
Datapoint Corporation, 11 67–70
Datapro Research Corp., **IV** 637
Dataquest Inc., **10** 558; **21** 235, 237; **22** 51; **25** 347
Datas Incorporated, **I** 99; **6** 81
Dataset Communications Inc., **23** 100
Datastream International Ltd., **IV** 605; **10** 89; **13** 417
DataTimes Corporation, **29** 58
Datavision Inc., **11** 444
Datec, **22** 17
Datext, **IV** 596–97
Datran, **11** 468
Datsun. *See* Nissan Motor Company, Ltd.
Datteln, **IV** 141
Datura Corp., **14** 391
Dauphin Deposit Corporation, 14 152–54
Dauphin Distribution Services. *See* Exel Logistics Ltd.
Daut + Rietz and Connectors Pontarlier, **19** 166
Davenport & Walter, **III** 765
Davenport Mammoet Heavy Transport Inc., **26** 280
The Davey Tree Expert Company, 11 71–73
David B. Smith & Company, **13** 243
David Berg & Co., **14** 537
David Brown & Son. *See* Brown & Sharpe Manufacturing Co.
David Brown, Ltd., **10** 380
David Clark, **30** 357
David Crystal, Inc., **II** 502; **9** 156; **10** 323
The David J. Joseph Company, 14 155–56; **19** 380
David Sandeman Group, **I** 592
David Sassoon & Co., **II** 296
David Williams and Partners, **6** 40
David's Supermarkets, **17** 180
Davidson & Associates, **16** 146
Davidson & Leigh, **21** 94
Davidson Automatic Merchandising Co. Inc., **II** 607
Davidson Brothers Co., **19** 510
Davies, William Ltd., **II** 482
Davis & Geck, **I** 301; **27** 115
Davis & Henderson Ltd., **IV** 640
Davis Coal & Coke Co., **IV** 180
Davis Estates, **I** 592
Davis Manufacturing Company, **10** 380
Davis Vision, Inc., **27** 209
Davis Wholesale Company, **9** 20
Davis-Standard Company, **9** 154
Davison Chemical Corp., **IV** 190
Davlyn Industries, Inc., **22** 487
Davox Corporation, **18** 31
Davy Bamag GmbH, **IV** 142
Davy McKee AG, **IV** 142
DAW Technologies, Inc., 25 135–37
Dawe's Laboratories, Inc., **12** 3
Dawn Food Products, Inc., 17 126–28
Dawnay Day, **III** 501
Dawson Mills, **II** 536
Day & Zimmermann Inc., 6 579; **9 162–64; 31 151–155 (upd.)**
Day Brite Lighting, **II** 19
Day International, **8** 347
Day Runner, Inc., 14 157–58
Day-Glo Color Corp., **8** 456
Day-Lee Meats, **II** 550
Day-N-Nite, **II** 620
Daybridge Learning Centers, **13** 49
Daybridge/Children's World, **13** 299
Dayco Products, **7** 297

Days Inns of America, Inc., **III** 344; **11** 178; **13** 362, 364; **21** 362
Daystar International Inc., **11** 44
Daystrom, **III** 617; **17** 418
Daytex, Inc., **II** 669; **18** 505
Dayton Engineering Laboratories, **I** 171; **9** 416; **10** 325
Dayton Flexible Products Co., **I** 627
Dayton Hudson Corporation, **V 43–44**; **8** 35; **9** 360; **10** 136, 391–93, 409–10, 515–16; **13** 330; **14** 376; **16** 176, 559; **18** 108, **135–37 (upd.)**; **22** 59
Dayton Power & Light Company, **6** 467, 480–82
Dayton Walther Corp., **III** 650, 652
Daytron Mortgage Systems, **11** 485
Dazey Corp., **16** 384
DB. *See* Deutsche Bundesbahn.
DBA Holdings, Inc., **18** 24
DBMS Inc., **14** 390
DC Comics Inc., **25 138–41**
DCA Advertising, **16** 168
DCA Food Industries, **II** 554; **27** 258–60, 299
DCL BioMedical, Inc., **11** 333
DCMS Holdings Inc., **7** 114; **25** 125
DDB Needham Worldwide, **14 159–61**; **22** 394
DDI Corporation, **7 118–20**; **13** 482; **21** 330–31
De Beers Consolidated Mines Limited / De Beers Centenary AG, **I** 107; **IV** 20–21, 23, 60, **64–68**, 79, 94; **7 121–26 (upd.)**; **16** 25–26, 29; **21** 345–46; **28 88–94 (upd.)**
De Bono Industries, **24** 443
De Dietrich & Cie., **31 156–59**
De Grenswisselkantoren NV, **III** 201
De Groote Bossche, **III** 200
de Havilland Aircraft Co., **I** 82, 92–93, 104, 195; **III** 507–08; **7** 11
de Havilland Holdings, Ltd., **24** 85–86
De La Rue PLC, **10 267–69**
De Laurentiis Entertainment Group, **III** 84; **25** 317
De Laval Turbine Company, **III** 418–20; **7** 236–37
De Leuw, Cather & Company, **8** 416
De Nederlandse Bank, **IV** 132
De Ster 1905 NV, **III** 200
De Tomaso Industries, **11** 104
De Trey Gesellchaft, **10** 271
De Vito/Verdi, **26** 111
De Walt, **III** 436
de Wendel, **IV** 226–27
De-sta-Co., **III** 468
DEA Group, **23** 83
Dealer Equipment and Services, **10** 492
Dean & Barry Co., **8** 455
Dean Foods Company, **7 127–29**; **17** 56; **21** 157, **165–68 (upd.)**; **26** 447; **29** 434
Dean Witter, Discover & Co., **II** 445; **IV** 186; **V** 180, 182; **7** 213; **12 96–98**; **18** 475; **21** 97; **22** 405–07
Dean-Dempsy Corp., **IV** 334
Death Row Records, **27 121–23**
Deb Shops, Inc., **16 163–65**
DeBartolo Realty Corp., **27** 401
Debenhams Plc, **V** 20–22; **28** 29–30, **95–97**
Debis, **26** 498
DeBoles Nutritional Foods Inc., **27** 197–98
Debron Investments Plc., **8** 271
DEC. *See* Digital Equipment Corp.
Decafin SpA, **26** 278, 280
Decca Record Company Ltd., **II** 81, 83, 144; **23** 389
Decision Base Resources, **6** 14
Decision Systems Israel Ltd. (DSI), **21** 239
DecisionQuest, Inc., **25** 130
Decker, Howell & Co., **26** 451
Deckers Outdoor Corporation, **22 172–74**
Deco Industries, Inc., **18** 5
Decoflex Ltd., **IV** 645
Decolletage S.A. St.-Maurice, **14** 27
Decora Industries, Inc., **31 160–62**
Dee and Cee Toy Co., **25** 312
Dee Corporation plc, **I** 549; **II** 628–29, 642; **24** 269
Deeks McBride, **III** 704
Deep Oil Technology, **I** 570
Deep Rock Oil Company. *See* Kerr-McGee Corporation.
Deep Rock Water Co., **III** 21
DeepFlex Production Partners, L.P., **21** 171
Deepsea Ventures, Inc., **IV** 152; **24** 358
DeepTech International Inc., **21 169–71**
Deepwater Light and Power Company, **6** 449
Deer Park Spring Water Co., **III** 21
Deere & Company, **I** 181, 527; **III 462–64**, 651; **10** 377–78, 380, 429; **11** 472; **13** 16–17, 267; **16** 179; **17** 533; **21 172–76 (upd.)**; **22** 542; **26** 492
Deering Harvesting Machinery Company. *See* Navistar.
Deering Milliken & Co. *See* Milliken & Co.
Def Jam Records, Inc., **23** 389, 391; **31** 269
Defense Plant Corp., **IV** 10, 408
Defense Technology Corporation of America, **27** 50
Defiance, Inc., **22 175–78**
Deft Software, Inc., **10** 505
DEG. *See* Deutsche Edison Gesellschaft.
Degussa Group, **I** 303; **IV 69–72**, 118
Deinhard, **I** 281
DeKalb AgResearch Inc., **9** 411
Dekalb Energy Company, **18** 366
DeKalb Farmers Market, **23** 263–64
DeKalb Genetics Corporation, **17 129–31**; **29** 330
DeKalb Office Supply, **25** 500
Del Laboratories, Inc., **28 98–100**
Del Mar Avionics, **26** 491
Del Monte Corporation, **II** 595; **7 130–32**; **12** 439; **14** 287; **25** 234
Del Monte Foods Company, **23 163–66 (upd.)**
Del Webb Corporation, **14 162–64**; **17** 186–87; **19** 377–78; **26** 291
Del-Rey Petroleum, **I** 526
Delafield, Harvey, Tabrell, Inc., **17** 498
Delafield Industries, **12** 418
Delagrange, **I** 635
Delaware and Hudson Railway Company, **16** 350
Delaware Charter Guarantee & Trust Co., **III** 330
Delaware Guarantee and Trust Co. *See* Wilmington Trust Company.
Delaware Lackawanna & Western, **I** 584
Delaware Management Holdings, **III** 386
Delaware North Companies Incorporated, **7 133–36**
Delbard, **I** 272
Delchamps, Inc., **II** 638; **27** 247
Delco Electronics, **II** 32–35; **III** 151; **6** 265; **25** 223–24
Delhaize Freres & Cie, **II** 626; **15** 176
Delhaize Frères-Le-Lion, **27** 94
Delhi Gas Pipeline Corporation, **7** 551
Delhi International Oil Corp., **III** 687; **28** 83
Deli Universal, **13** 545
dELiA*s Inc., **29 141–44**
Delicious Foods, **13** 383
Delimaatschappij, **13** 545
Dell Computer Corporation, **9 165–66**; **10** 309, 459; **11** 62; **16** 5, 196; **24** 31; **25** 254; **27** 168; **31 163–166 (upd.)**
Dell Distributing, **25** 483
Dell Publishing Co., **13** 560
Dellwood Elevator Co., **I** 419
Delmar Chemicals Ltd., **II** 484
Delmar Paper Box Co., **IV** 333
Delmarva Properties, Inc., **8** 103; **30** 118
Delmonico Foods Inc., **II** 511
Delmonico International, **II** 101
Deloitte & Touche, **9 167–69**, 423; **24** 29
Deloitte Touche Tohmatsu International, **29 145–48 (upd.)**
DeLong Engineering Co., **III** 558
DeLorean Motor Co., **10** 117; **14** 321
Delphax, **IV** 252; **17** 29
Delphi, **22** 52; **25** 223
Delprat, **IV** 58
Delta & Pine Land Co., **21** 386
Delta Acceptance Corporation Limited, **13** 63
Delta Air Lines Inc., **I** 29, 91, 97, **99–100**, 102, 106, 120, 132; **6** 61, **81–83 (upd.)**, 117, 131–32, 383; **12** 149, 381; **13** 171–72; **14** 73; **21** 141, 143; **22** 22; **25** 420, 422–23; **26** 439; **27** 20, 409
Delta Biologicals S.r.l., **11** 208
Delta Biotechnology Ltd., **25** 82
Delta Communications, **IV** 610
Delta Education, **29** 470, 472
Delta Faucet Co., **III** 568–69
Delta International Machinery Corp., **26** 361–63
Delta Lloyd, **III** 235
Delta Manufacturing, **II** 85
Delta Motors, **III** 580
Delta Pride Catfish Inc., **18** 247
Delta Queen Steamboat Company, **27** 34–35
Delta Resources Inc., **26** 519
Delta Savings Assoc. of Texas, **IV** 343
Delta Steamship Lines, **9** 425–26
Delta Woodside Industries, Inc., **8 141–43**; **17** 329; **30 159–61 (upd.)**
Deltak Corp., **23** 300
Deluxe Corporation, **7 137–39**; **19** 291; **22 179–82 (upd.)**
Deluxe Data, **18** 518
DeLuxe Laboratories, **IV** 652
Deluxe Upholstering Ltd., **14** 303
Delvag Luftürsicherungs A.G., **I** 111
Demag AG, **II** 22; **III** 566; **IV** 206
Demerara Company, **13** 102
Deminex, **IV** 413, 424
Deming Company, **8** 135
Demka, **IV** 132–33
Demko, **30** 469
DeMoulas / Market Basket Inc., **23 167–69**
Dempsey & Siders Agency, **III** 190

Den Fujita, **9** 74
Den Norske Bank, **22** 275
Den norske Creditbank, **II** 366
Den Norske Stats Oljeselskap AS, IV 405–07, 486
Den-Tal-Ez, **I** 702
Denain-Nord-Est-Longwy, **IV** 227
DenAmerica Corporation, 29 149–51
Denault Ltd., **II** 651
Denison Corp., **III** 628
Denison Mines, Ltd., **12** 198
Denker & Goodwin, **17** 498
Denki Seikosho, **IV** 62
Denney-Reyburn, **8** 360
Dennison Manufacturing Company. *See* Avery Dennison Corporation.
Denny's Restaurants Inc., **II** 680; **III** 103; **V** 88–89; **12** 511; **13** 526; **27** 16–18
Denshi Media Services, **IV** 680
Dent & Co., **II** 296
Dental Capital Corp., **19** 290
Dental Research, **25** 56
DentiCare, Inc., **22** 149
Dentons Green Brewery, **21** 246
Dentsply International Inc., 10 270–72
Dentsu Inc., I 9–11, 36, 38; **6** 29; **9** 30; **13** 204; **16 166–69 (upd.)**; **25** 91
Denver & Rio Grande Railroad, **12** 18–19
Denver Chemical Company, **8** 84
Denver Gas & Electric Company. *See* Public Service Company of Colorado.
DEP Corporation, 20 177–80
Department 56, Inc., 14 165–67; **22** 59
Department Stores International, **I** 426; **22** 72
Deposit Guaranty Corporation, 17 132–35
Deposito and Administratie Bank, **II** 185
Depositors National Bank of Durham, **II** 336
DePree Company, **17** 90–91
DePuy, Inc., 10 156–57; **30 162–65**
Der Anker, **III** 177
Derby Commercial Bank, **II** 318; **17** 323
Derby Outdoor, **27** 280
Derbyshire Stone and William Briggs, **III** 752
Deritend Computers, **14** 36
Dermablend, Inc., **31** 89
Deruluft, **6** 57
Derwent Publications, **8** 526
Des Moines Electric Light Company, **6** 504
DESA Industries, **8** 545
Desc, S.A. de C.V., 23 170–72
Deseret Management Corporation, **29** 67
Deseret National Bank, **11** 118
Deseret Pharmaceutical Company, **21** 45
Desert Partners, **III** 763
Design Craft Ltd., **IV** 640
Design-Center Southwest, **19** 411
Designcraft Inc. *See* Sloan's Supermarkets Inc.
Designer Holdings Ltd., 20 181–84; **22** 123
Desmarais Frères, **IV** 557, 559
DeSoto, Inc., **8** 553; **13** 471
Desoutter Brothers plc, **III** 427; **28** 40
Destec Energy, Inc., 12 99–101
Det Danske/Norske Luftartselskab, **I** 119
Detroit Aircraft Corp., **I** 64; **11** 266
Detroit Automobile Co., **I** 164
Detroit Ball Bearing Co., **13** 78
Detroit Chemical Coatings, **8** 553
Detroit City Gas Company. *See* MCN Corporation.
Detroit Copper Co., **IV** 176–77
Detroit Diesel Corporation, V 494–95; **9** 18; **10 273–75**; **11** 471; **12** 90–91; **18** 308; **19** 292–94; **21** 503
The Detroit Edison Company, I 164; **V 592–95**; **7** 377–78; **11** 136; **14** 135; **18** 320. *See also* DTE Energy Co.
Detroit Fire & Marine Insurance Co., **III** 191
Detroit Gear and Machine Co., **III** 439
Detroit Radiator Co., **III** 663
Detroit Red Wings, **7** 278–79; **24** 293
Detroit Steel Products Co., Inc., **IV** 136; **13** 157; **16** 357
Detroit Tigers, **24** 293
Detroit Toledo & Ironton Railroad, **I** 165
Detroit Vapor Stove Co., **III** 439
Detroit-Graphite Company, **8** 553
Detrola, **II** 60
Deutsch Erdol A.G., **IV** 552
Deutsch Shea & Evans Inc., **I** 15
Deutsch-Australische Dampfschiffs-Gesellschaft, **6** 398
Deutsch-Luxembergische Bergwerks und Hütten AG, **I** 542; **IV** 105
Deutsch-Österreichische Mannesmannröhren-Werke Aktiengesellschaft, **III** 564–65
Deutsch-Skandinavische Bank, **II** 352
Deutsche Aerospace Airbus, **I** 41–42; **7** 9, 11; **12** 190–91; **21** 8
Deutsche Allgemeine Versicherungs-Aktiengesellschaft, **III** 412
Deutsche Anlagen Leasing GmbH, **II** 386
Deutsche BA, **14** 73; **24** 400; **26** 115
Deutsche Babcock AG, II 386; **III 465–66**
Deutsche Bank A.G., I 151, 409, 549; **II** 98, 191, 239, 241–42, 256–58, **278–80**, 281–82, 295, 319, 385, 427, 429; **III** 154–55, 692, 695; **IV** 91, 141, 229, 232, 378, 557; **V** 241–42; **14 168–71 (upd.)**; **15** 13; **16** 364–65; **17** 324; **21** 147
Deutsche BP Aktiengesellschaft, 7 140–43
Deutsche Bundepost Telekom, V 287–90; **18** 155
Deutsche Bundesbahn, V 444–47; **6** 424–26
Deutsche Edelstahlwerke AG, **IV** 222
Deutsche Edison Gesellschaft, **I** 409–10
Deutsche Erdol Aktiengesellschaft, **7** 140
Deutsche Gold-und Silber-Scheideanstalt vormals Roessler, **IV** 69, 118, 139
Deutsche Grammophon Gesellschaft, **23** 389
Deutsche Hydrierwerke, **III** 32
Deutsche Industriewerke AG, **IV** 230
Deutsche Kreditbank, **14** 170
Deutsche Länderbank, **II** 379
Deutsche Lufthansa Aktiengesellschaft, I 94, **110–11**, 120; **6** 59–60, 69, 95–96, 386; **12** 191; **25** 159; **26 113–16 (upd.)**; **27** 465
Deutsche Marathon Petroleum, **IV** 487
Deutsche Mineralöl-Explorationsgesellschaft mbH, **IV** 197
Deutsche Nippon Seiko, **III** 589
Deutsche Petroleum-Verkaufsgesellschaft mbH, **7** 140
Deutsche Post AG, 29 152–58
Deutsche Reichsbahn. *See* Deutsche Bundesbahn.
Deutsche Schiff-und Maschinenbau Aktiengesellschaft "Deschimag," **IV** 87
Deutsche Shell, **7** 140
Deutsche Spezialglas AG, **III** 446
Deutsche Strassen und Lokalbahn A.G., **I** 410
Deutsche Telekom, **18** 155; **25** 102
Deutsche Texaco, **V** 709
Deutsche Union, **III** 693–94
Deutsche Union-Bank, **II** 278
Deutsche Wagnisfinanzierung, **II** 258
Deutsche Werke AG, **IV** 230
Deutsche-Asiatische Bank, **II** 238, 256
Deutsche-Nalco-Chemie GmbH., **I** 373
Deutscher Aero Lloyd, **I** 110
Deutscher Automobil Schutz Allgemeine Rechtsschutz-Versicherung AG, **III** 400
Deutscher Kommunal-Verlag Dr. Naujoks & Behrendt, **14** 556
Deutsches Reisebüro DeR, **II** 163
Deutz AG, **III** 541
Deutz Farm Equipment, **13** 17
Deutz-Allis, **III** 544. *See also* AGCO Corp.
Devcon Corporation, **III** 519; **22** 282
Developer's Mortgage Corp., **16** 347
Development Finance Corp., **II** 189
Devenish, **21** 247
DeVilbiss Company, **8** 230
DeVilbiss Health Care, Inc., **11** 488
Deville, **27** 421
Devoe & Raynolds Co., **12** 217
Devoke Company, **18** 362
Devon Energy Corporation, **22** 304
DeVry Incorporated, 9 63; **29** 56, **159–61**
Dewars Brothers, **I** 239–40
Dewey & Almy Chemical Co., **I** 548
The Dexter Corporation, I 320–22; **12 102–04 (upd.)**; **17** 287
Dexter Shoe, **18** 60, 63
DFS Dorland Worldwide, **I** 35
DFW Printing Company, **10** 3
DG&E. *See* Denver Gas & Electric Company.
DH Compounding, **8** 347
DH Technology, Inc., 18 138–40
Dharma Juice, **31** 350
DHI Corp., **II** 680
DHJ Industries, Inc., **12** 118
DHL Worldwide Express, 6 385–87; **18** 177, 316; **24 133–36 (upd.)**; **26** 441; **27** 471, 475; **29** 152
Di Giorgio Corp., II 602; **12 105–07**; **24** 528–29
Di-Rite Company, **11** 534
Dia Prosim, S.A., **IV** 409
Diageo plc, 24 137–41 (upd.); **25** 411; **29** 19; **31** 92
Diagnostic Health Corporation, **14** 233
Diagnostic Imaging Services, Inc., **25** 384
Diagnostics Pasteur, **I** 677
The Dial Corp., 8 144–46; **23 173–75 (upd.)**; **29** 114
Dial Home Shopping Ltd., **28** 30
Dial-Net Inc., **27** 306
Dialight Corp., **13** 397–98
Dialog Information Services, Inc., **IV** 630
Dialogic Corporation, 18 141–43
Diamandis Communications Inc., **IV** 619, 678
Diamang, **IV** 65, 67
Diamedix, **11** 207
Diamond Communications, **10** 288

Diamond Corporation Ltd., **IV** 21, 66–67; **7** 123
Diamond Electronics, **24** 510
Diamond Fields Resources Inc., **27** 457
Diamond Head Resources, Inc. *See* AAON, Inc.
Diamond International Corp., **IV** 290, 295; **13** 254–55; **19** 225; **26** 446
Diamond M Offshore Inc., **12** 318
Diamond Match Company, **14** 163
Diamond Oil Co., **IV** 548
Diamond Park Fine Jewelers, **16** 559
Diamond Rug & Carpet Mills, **19** 276
Diamond Savings & Loan, **II** 420
Diamond Shamrock Corporation, IV 408–11, 481; **7** 34, 308–099, 345; **13** 118; **19** 177. *See also* Ultramar Diamond Shamrock Corporation.
Diamond Trading Company, **IV** 66–67; **7** 123
Diamond Walnut Growers, **7** 496–97
Diamond-Star Motors Corporation, **9** 349–51
Dianatel, **18** 143
Diasonics Ultrasound, Inc., **27** 355
Dibrell Brothers, Incorporated, 12 108–10; **13** 492
dick clark productions, inc., 16 170–73
Dick Simon Trucking, Inc. *See* Simon Transporation Services Inc.
Dickerman, **8** 366
Dickson Forest Products, Inc., **15** 305
Dickstein Partners, L.P., **13** 261
Dictaphone Corp., **III** 157
Didier Lamarthe, **17** 210
Didier Werke AG, **IV** 232
Diebold, Incorporated, 7 144–46; **22 183–87 (upd.)**
Diehl Manufacturing Co., **II** 9
Diemakers Inc., **IV** 443
Diesel United Co., **III** 533
AB Diesels Motorer, **III** 425–26
Diet Center, **10** 383
Dieter Hein Co., **14** 537
Dieterich Standard Corp., **III** 468
Dietrich & Cie. *See* De Dietrich & Cie.
Dietrich Corp., **II** 512; **15** 221
Dietrich's Bakeries, **II** 631
DiFeo Automotive Group, **26** 500–01
DiFranza Williamson, **6** 40
DIG Acquisition Corp., **12** 107
Digi International Inc., 9 170–72; **20** 237
Digicom, **22** 17
DiGiorgio Corporation, **25** 421
Digital Audio Disk Corp., **II** 103
Digital City, Inc., **22** 522
Digital Data Systems Company, **11** 408
Digital Devices, Inc., **III** 643
Digital Directory Assistance, **18** 24
Digital Equipment Corporation, II 8, 62, 108; **III** 118, 128, **132–35**, 142, 149, 166; **6** 225, **233–36 (upd.)**, 237–38, 242, 246–47, 279, 287; **8** 137–39, 519; **9** 35, 43, 57, 166, 170–71, 514; **10** 22–23, 34, 86, 242, 361, 463, 477; **11** 46, 86–88, 274, 491, 518–19; **12** 147, 162, 470; **13** 127, 202, 482; **14** 318; **15** 108; **16** 394, 418; **18** 143, 345; **19** 310; **21** 123; **25** 499; **26** 90, 93
Digital Marketing, Inc., **22** 357
Digital Research in Electronic Acoustics and Music S.A., **17** 34
Digitech, **19** 414
Diligent Engine Co., **III** 342
Dill & Collins, **IV** 311; **19** 266
Dill Enterprises, Inc., **14** 18
Dillard Department Stores, Inc., V 45–47; **10** 488; **11** 349; **12** 64; **13** 544–45; **16 174–77 (upd.)**, 559; **19** 48, 324; **27** 61
Dillard Paper Company, 11 74–76
Dillingham Corp., I 565–66
Dillingham Holdings Inc., **9** 511
Dillon Companies Inc., II 645; **12 111–13**; **15** 267; **22** 194
Dillon Paper, **IV** 288
Dillon, Read, and Co., Inc., **I** 144, 559; **III** 151, 389; **6** 265; **11** 53; **20** 259; **24** 66
Dime Banking and Loan Association of Rochester, **10** 91
Dime Savings Bank of New York, F.S.B., 9 173–74
Dimeling, Schrieber & Park, **11** 63
Dimeric Development Corporation, **14** 392
DIMON Inc., 12 110; **27 124–27**
Dinamica, S.A., **19** 12
Dine S.A., **23** 170–72
Diners Club, **II** 397; **6** 62; **9** 335; **10** 61
Dinner Bell Foods, Inc., **11** 93
de Dion, **III** 523
Dirección General de Correos y Telecomunicaciónes, **V** 337
Dirección Nacional de los Yacimientos Petrolíferos Fiscales, **IV** 577–78
Direct Container Lines, **14** 505
Direct Friends, **25** 91
Direct Line, **12** 422
Direct Mail Services Pty. Ltd., **10** 461
Direct Marketing Technology Inc., **19** 184
Direct Spanish Telegraph Co., **I** 428
Direction Générale des Télécommunications, **V** 471
DirectLine Insurance, **22** 52
Directorate General of Telecommunications, 7 147–49
DirecTV, **21** 70
Dirr's Gold Seal Meats, **6** 199
Disc Go Round, **18** 207, 209
Disc Manufacturing, Inc., **15** 378
Disclosure, Inc., **18** 24
Disco SA, **V** 11; **19** 308–09
Discol SA, **V** 11; **19** 308
Disconto-Gesellschaft, **II** 238, 279
Discount Auto Parts, Inc., 18 144–46; **26** 348
Discount Bank, **II** 205
Discount Corporation, **12** 565
Discount Drug Mart, Inc., 14 172–73
Discount Investment Corporation Ltd., **24** 429
Discount Labels, Inc., **20** 15
Discount Tire Co., **19** 294; **20** 263
Discover, **9** 335; **12** 97
Discovery Toys, Inc., **19** 28
Discovery Zone, **31** 97
DiscoVision Associates, **III** 605
Discreet Logic Inc., 20 185–87
Disctronics, Ltd., **15** 380
Disney Channel, **6** 174–75; **13** 280
Disney Co. *See* The Walt Disney Company.
Disney Studios, **II** 408; **6** 174, 176
Disneyland, **6** 175
Disneyland Paris. *See* Euro Disneyland SCA.
Dispatch Communications, **10** 432
Display Components Inc., **II** 110; **17** 479
Displayco Midwest Inc., **8** 103
Disposable Hospital Products, **I** 627
Distillers and Cattle Feeders Trust, **I** 376
Distillers Co. plc, I 239–41, 252, 263, 284–85; **II** 429, 609–10; **IV** 70
Distillers Securities, **I** 376
Distinctive Printing and Packaging Co., **8** 103
Distinctive Software Inc., **10** 285
Distribuidora Bega, S.A. de C.V., **31** 92
Distribution Centers Incorporated. *See* Exel Logistics Ltd.
Distribution Services, Inc., **10** 287
Distribution Solutions International, Inc., **24** 126
District Bank, **II** 333
District Cablevision, **II** 160
District News Co., **II** 607
Distrigas, **IV** 425
DITAS, **IV** 563
Ditzler Color Co., **III** 732
DIVAL, **III** 347
Divani & Divani. *See* Industrie Natuzzi S.p.A.
Divco-Wayne Corp., **17** 82
DIVE!, **26** 264
Diversey Corp., **I** 275, 333; **13** 150, 199; **26** 305–06
Diversified Agency Services, **I** 32
Diversified Foods Inc., **25** 179
Diversified Retailing Co., **III** 214
Diversified Services, **9** 95
Diversifoods Inc., **II** 556; **13** 408
Dixie Airline, **25** 420
Dixie Bearings, Inc., **13** 78
Dixie Carriers, Inc., **18** 277
Dixie Container Corporation, **12** 377
The Dixie Group, Inc., 20 188–90
Dixie Hi-Fi, **9** 120–21
Dixie Home Stores, **II** 683
Dixie Paper, **I** 612–14
Dixie Power & Light Company, **6** 514
Dixie Yarns, Inc., **9** 466; **19** 305
Dixie-Narco Inc., **III** 573; **22** 349
Dixieland Food Stores, **II** 624
Dixon Industries, Inc., 26 117–19
Dixon Ticonderoga Company, 12 114–16
Dixons Group plc, II 139; **V 48–50**; **9** 65; **10** 45, 306; **19 121–24 (upd.)**; **23** 52; **24** 194, 269–70
DIY Home Warehouse, **16** 210
DJ Moldings Corp., **18** 276
Djedi Holding SA, **23** 242
DKB. *See* Dai-Ichi Kangyo Bank Ltd.
DLC. *See* Duquesne Light Company.
DLJ. *See* Donaldson, Lufkin & Jenrette.
DLJ Merchant Banking Partners II, **21** 188
DM Associates Limited Partnership, **25** 127
DMA, **18** 510
DMB&B. *See* D'Arcy Masius Benton & Bowles.
DMP Mineralöl Petrochemie GmbH, **IV** 487
DNAX Research Institute, **I** 685; **14** 424
DNEL-Usinor, **IV** 227
DNN Galvanizing Limited Partnership, **24** 144
DNP DENMARK A/S, **IV** 600
Do It All, **24** 75
Do it Best Corporation, 30 166–70
Dobbs House, **21** 54
Dobbs Houses Inc., **I** 696–97; **15** 87
Dobrolet, **6** 57
Doctors' Hospital, **6** 191

Documentation Resources, **11** 65
DOD Electronics Corp., **15** 215
Dodd, Mead & Co., **14** 498
Dodge & Day. *See* Day & Zimmermann, Inc.
Dodge Corp., **I** 144; **8** 74; **11** 53
The Dodge Group, **11** 78
Dodge Manufacturing Company, **9** 440
Dodge Motor Company, **20** 259
Doduco Corporation, **29** 460–61
Dodwell & Co., **III** 523
Doe Run Company, **12** 244
Dofasco Inc., IV 73–74; 24 142–44 (upd.)
Doherty Clifford Steers & Sherfield Inc., **I** 31
Doherty, Mann & Olshan. *See* Wells Rich Greene BDDP.
Dolby Laboratories Inc., 20 191–93
Dole Food Company, Inc., I 565; **II** 491–92; **9 175–76**; **20** 116; **31 167–170 (upd.)**
Dolland & Aitchison Group, **V** 399
Dollar Bills, Inc. *See* Dollar Tree Stores, Inc.
Dollar General, **26** 533
Dollar Rent A Car, **6** 349; **24** 10
Dollar Steamship Lines, **6** 353
Dollar Thrifty Automotive Group, Inc., 25 92, **142–45**
Dollar Tree Stores, Inc., 16 161; **23 176–78**
Dollfus Mieg & Cie. *See* Groupe DMC.
Dolphin Book Club, **13** 106
Dom Perignon, **25** 258
Domain Technology, **6** 231
Domaine Chandon, **I** 272
Dombrico, Inc., **8** 545
Domco Industries, **19** 407
Dome Laboratories, **I** 654
Dome Petroleum, Ltd., **II** 222, 245, 262, 376; **IV** 371, 401, 494; **12** 364
Domestic Electric Co., **III** 435
Domestic Operating Co., **III** 36
Dominick International Corp., **12** 131
Dominick's Finer Foods, **9** 451; **13** 25, 516; **17** 558, 560–61
Dominion Bank, **II** 375–76
Dominion Bridge Company, Limited, **8** 544
Dominion Cellular, **6** 322
Dominion Dairies, **7** 429
Dominion Engineering Works Ltd., **8** 544
Dominion Far East Line, **I** 469; **20** 311
Dominion Foils Ltd., **17** 280
Dominion Foundries and Steel, Ltd., **IV** 73–74
Dominion Hoist & Shovel Co., **8** 544
Dominion Homes, Inc., 19 125–27
Dominion Industries Ltd., **15** 229
Dominion Life Assurance Co., **III** 276
Dominion Mushroom Co., **II** 649–50
Dominion Ornamental, **III** 641
Dominion Paper Box Co. Ltd., **IV** 645
Dominion Resources, Inc., V 591, **596–99**
Dominion Securities, **II** 345; **21** 447
Dominion Steel Castings Company, Ltd. *See* Dofasco Inc.
Dominion Stores Ltd., **II** 650, 652
Dominion Tar & Chemical Co. Ltd., **IV** 271–72
Dominion Terminal Associates, **IV** 171; **7** 582, 584
Dominion Textile Inc., V 355; **8** 559–60; **12 117–19**
Domino Sugar Corporation, 26 120–22
Domino Supermarkets, **24** 528
Domino's Pizza, Inc., 7 150–53; **9** 74; **12** 123; **15** 344, 346; **16** 447; **21 177–81 (upd.)**; **22** 353; **24** 295; **25** 179–80, 227–28; **26** 177
Domtar Inc., IV 271–73, 308
Don Baxter Intravenous Products Co., **I** 627
Don's Foods, Inc., **26** 164
Donac Company, **V** 681
Donald L. Bren Co., **IV** 287
Donaldson Co. Inc., 16 178–81
Donaldson, Lufkin & Jenrette, Inc., II 422, 451; **III** 247–48; **9** 115, 142, 360–61; **18** 68; **22 188–91**; **26** 348
Donaldson's Department Stores, **15** 274
Doncaster Newspapers Ltd., **IV** 686
Dong-A Motor, **III** 749
Dong-Myung Industrial Co. Ltd., **II** 540
Dongbang Life Insurance Co., **I** 515
Dongguan Shilong Kyocera Optics Co., Ltd., **21** 331
Dongil Frozen Foods Co., **II** 553
Dongsu Industrial Company, **III** 516; **7** 232
Donn, Inc., **18** 162
Donna Karan Company, 15 145–47; **24** 299; **25** 294, 523
Donnelley, Gassette & Loyd, **IV** 660
Donnellon McCarthy Inc., **12** 184
Donnelly Corporation, 12 120–22; **26** 154
Donnkenny, Inc., 17 136–38
Donohue Inc., **12** 412
Donohue Meehan Publishing Co., **27** 362
Donruss Leaf Inc., **19** 386
Donzi Marine Corp., **III** 600
Dooner Laboratories, **I** 667
Door-to-Door, **6** 14
Dorado Beach Development Inc., **I** 103
Dordrecht, **III** 177–78
Dorenbecher Properties, **19** 381
Doric Corp., **19** 290
Dorling Kindersley Holdings plc, 20 194–96
Dorman Long & Co. Ltd., **IV** 658
Dorman's, Inc., **27** 291
Dorney Park, **22** 130
Dornier, **I** 46, 74, 151; **15** 142
Dorothy Hamill International, **13** 279, 281
Dorothy Perkins, **V** 21
Dortmunder Union, **II** 240; **IV** 103, 105
Doskocil Companies, Inc., 12 123–25. *See also* Foodbrands America, Inc.
Double A Products Co., **23** 82–83
Doubleday Book Shops, Inc., **10** 136; **25** 31; **30** 68
Doubleday-Dell, **IV** 594, 636
Doubletree Corporation, 21 182–85
Douglas & Lomason Company, 16 182–85
Douglas Aircraft Co., **I** 48, 70, 76, 96, 104, 195; **II** 32, 425; **III** 601; **9** 12, 18, 206; **10** 163; **13** 48, 341; **16** 77; **21** 141; **24** 375
Douglas Oil Co., **IV** 401
Douglas-Dahlin Co., **I** 158–59
Doulton Glass Industries Ltd., **IV** 659
Douwe Egberts, **II** 572
Dove International, **7** 299–300
Dover Corporation, III 467–69; **28 101–05 (upd.)**
Dovrat Shrem, **15** 470
Dow Chemical Co., I 323–25, 334, 341–42, 360, 370–71, 708; **II** 440, 457; **III** 617, 760; **IV** 83, 417; **8 147–50 (upd.)**, 153, 261–62, 548; **9** 328–29, 500-501; **10** 289; **11** 271; **12** 99–100, 254, 364; **14** 114, 217; **16** 99; **17** 418; **18** 279; **21** 387; **28** 411
Dow Corning, **II** 54; **III** 683, 685
Dow Jones & Company, Inc., IV 601–03, 654, 656, 670, 678; **7** 99; **10** 276–78, 407; **13** 55; **15** 335–36; **19 128–31 (upd.)**, 204; **21** 68–70; **23** 157
Dow Jones Telerate, Inc., 10 276–78
DOW Stereo/Video Inc., **30** 466
Dowdings Ltd., **IV** 349
DowElanco, **21** 385, 387
Dowell Australia Ltd., **III** 674
Dowell Schlumberger. *See* Schlumberger Limited.
Dowidat GmbH, **IV** 197
Dowlais Iron Co., **III** 493
Down River International, Inc., **15** 188
Downe Communications, Inc., **14** 460
Downingtown Paper Company, **8** 476
Downyflake Foods, **7** 429
Dowty Aerospace, **17** 480
Doyle Dane Bernbach, **I** 9, 20, 28, 30–31, 33, 37, 206; **11** 549; **14** 159; **22** 396
DP&L. *See* Dayton Power & Light Company.
DPCE, **II** 139; **24** 194
DPF, Inc., **12** 275
DPL Inc., 6 480–82
DQE, 6 483–85
DR Holdings, Inc., **10** 242
Dr. Gerhard Mann Pharma, **25** 56
Dr. Ing he F. Porsche GmbH, **13** 413–14
Dr. Martens, **23** 399, 401
Dr. Miles' Medical Co., **I** 653
Dr Pepper/7Up Companies, Inc., I 245; **II** 477; **9 177–78**
Dr. Richter & Co., **IV** 70
Dr. Solomon's Software Ltd., **25** 349
Dr. Tigges-Fahrten, **II** 163–64
Drackett Professional Products, III 17; **12 126–28**
DraftDirect Worldwide, **22** 297
Draftline Engineering Co., **22** 175
Dragados y Construcciones S.A., **II** 198
Dragon, **III** 391
Dragon International, **18** 87
Dragonair, **16** 481; **18** 114. *See also* Hong Kong Dragon Airlines.
The Drake, **12** 316
Drake Bakeries, **II** 562
Drake Beam Morin, Inc., **IV** 623
Drake Steel Supply Co., **19** 343
Drallos Potato Company, **25** 332
Draper & Kramer, **IV** 724
Draper Corporation, **14** 219; **15** 384
Drathen Co., **I** 220
Dravo Corp., **6** 143
Draw-Tite, Inc., **11** 535
Drayton Corp., **II** 319; **17** 324
DreamWorks SKG Studio, **17** 72; **21** 23, 26; **26** 150, 188
Dreher Breweries, **24** 450
Dresdner Bank A.G., I 411; **II** 191, 238–39, 241–42, 256–57, 279–80, **281–83**, 385; **III** 201, 289, 401; **IV** 141; **14** 169–70; **15** 13

Dresdner Feuer-Versicherungs-Gesellschaft, **III** 376
The Dress Barn, Inc., 24 145–46
Dresser Industries, Inc., I 486; **III** 429, **470–73**; 499, 527, 545–46; **12** 539; **14** 325; **15** 225–26, 468; **16** 310; **18** 219; **24** 208; **25** 188, 191
Dresser Power, **6** 555
Drew Graphics, Inc., **13** 227–28
Drew Industries Inc., 28 106–08
Drewry Photocolor, **I** 447
Drexel Burnham Lambert Incorporated, II 167, 329–30, **407–09**, 482; **III** 10, 253, 254–55, 531, 721; **IV** 334; **6** 210–11; **7** 305; **8** 327, 349, 388–90, 568; **9** 346; **12** 229; **13** 169, 299, 449; **14** 43; **15** 71, 281, 464; **16** 535, 561; **20** 415; **22** 55, 189; **24** 273; **25** 313. *See also* New Street Capital Inc.
Drexel Heritage Furnishings Inc., III 571; **11** 534; **12 129–31**; **20** 362
Dreyer's Grand Ice Cream, Inc., 10 147–48; **17 139–41**; **30** 81
Dreyfus Interstate Development Corp., **11** 257
DRI. *See* Dominion Resources, Inc.
Dribeck Importers Inc., **9** 87
Drip In Irrigation, **26** 494
Drott Manufacturing Company, **10** 379
Drouot Group, **III** 211
DRS Investment Group, **27** 370
Drug City, **II** 649
Drug Emporium, Inc., 12 132–34, 477
Drug House, **III** 9
Drug, Inc., **III** 17
Drummond Lighterage. *See* Puget Sound Tug and Barge Company.
Drummonds' Bank, **12** 422
Druout, **I** 563; **24** 78
Dry Milks Inc., **I** 248
DryClean U.S.A., **14** 25
Dryden and Co., **III** 340
Drypers Corporation, 18 147–49
Drysdale Government Securities, **10** 117
DSC Communications Corporation, 9 170; **12 135–37**
DSL Group Ltd., **27** 49
DSM Melamine America, **27** 316–18
DSM N.V., I 326–27; **III** 614; **15** 229
DST Systems Inc., **6** 400–02; **26** 233
DTAG. *See* Dollar Thrifty Automotive Group, Inc.
DTE Energy Company, 20 197–201 (upd.)
Du Bouzet, **II** 233
Du Mont Company, **8** 517
Du Pont. *See* E.I. du Pont de Nemours & Co.
Du Pont Fabricators, **III** 559
Du Pont Glore Forgan, Inc., **III** 137
Du Pont Photomask, **IV** 600
Duane Reade Holding Corp., 21 186–88
Dublin and London Steam Packet Company, **V** 490
DuBois Chemicals Division, **13** 149–50; **22** 188; **26** 306
Ducatel-Duval, **II** 369
Ducati Motor Holding S.p.A., 17 24; **30 171–73**
Duck Head Apparel Company, Inc., **8** 141–43; **30** 159
Ducks Unlimited, **28** 306
Duckwall-ALCO Stores, Inc., 24 147–49
Duco Ltd., **25** 104–05
Ducommun Incorporated, 30 174–76
Ducon Group, **II** 81
Dudley Stationery Ltd., **25** 501
Duff Bros., **III** 9–10
Duffy Meats, **27** 259
Duffy-Mott, **II** 477
Duke Energy Corporation, 27 128–31 (upd.)
Duke Energy Field Services, Inc., **24** 379
Duke Power Company, V 600–02
Dumes SA, **13** 206
Dumez, **V** 655–57
Dumont Broadcasting Corporation, **7** 335
The Dun & Bradstreet Corporation, I 540; **IV 604–05**, 643, 661; **8** 526; **9** 505; **10** 4, 358; **13** 3–4; **19 132–34 (upd.)**
Dun & Bradstreet Software Services Inc., 11 77–79
Dunbar-Stark Drillings, Inc., **19** 247
Duncan Foods Corp., **I** 234; **10** 227
Duncan, Sherman & Co., **II** 329
Duncanson & Holt, Inc., **13** 539
Dundee Acquisition Corp., **19** 421
Dundee Cement Co., **III** 702; **8** 258–59
Dunfey Brothers Capital Group, **12** 368
Dunfey Hotels Corporation, **12** 367
Dunhams Stores Corporation, **V** 111
Dunhill Holdings, **IV** 93; **V** 411
Dunkin' Donuts, **II** 619; **21** 323; **29** 18–19
Dunlop Coflexip Umbilicals Ltd. *See* Duco Ltd.
Dunlop Holdings, **I** 429; **III** 697; **V** 250, 252–53
Dunlop Ltd., **25** 104
Dunn Bros., **28** 63
Dunn Manufacturing Company, **25** 74
Dunn Paper Co., **IV** 290
Dunning Industries, **12** 109
Dunoyer. *See* Compagnie de Saint-Gobain S.A.
Dunwoodie Manufacturing Co., **17** 136
Duo-Bed Corp., **14** 435
Dupey Enterprises, Inc., **17** 320
Dupil-Color, Inc., **III** 745
Duplainville Transport, **19** 333–34
Duplex Products, Inc., 17 142–44, 445
Dupol, **III** 614
Dupont. *See* E.I. du Pont de Nemours & Company.
Dupont Chamber Works, **6** 449
Duquesne Light Company, **6** 483–84
Duquesne Systems, **10** 394
Dura Convertible Systems, **13** 170
Dura Corp., **I** 476
Dura-Vent, **III** 468
Duracell International Inc., 9 179–81; **12** 559; **13** 433; **17** 31; **24** 274
Durametallic, 17 147; **21 189–91**
Durand & Huguenin, **I** 672
Durango-Mapimi Mining Co., **22** 284
Duray, Inc., **12** 215
Durban Breweries and Distillers, **I** 287
Durham Chemicals Distributors Ltd., **III** 699
Durham Raw Materials Ltd., **III** 699
Duriron Company Inc., 17 145–47; **21** 189, 191
Durkee Famous Foods, **II** 567; **7** 314; **8** 222; **17** 106; **27** 297
Durr-Fillauer Medical Inc., **13** 90; **18** 97
Dutch Boy, **II** 649; **III** 745; **10** 434–35
Dutch Crude Oil Company. *See* Nederlandse Aardolie Maatschappij.
Dutch East Indies Post, Telegraph and Telephone Service, **II** 67
Dutch Nuts Chocoladefabriek B.V., **II** 569
Dutch Pantry, **II** 497
Dutch State Mines. *See* DSM N.V.
Dutchland Farms, **25** 124
Dutton Brewery, **I** 294
Duttons Ltd., **24** 267
Duty Free International, Inc., 11 80–82. *See also* World Duty Free Americas, Inc.
Duval Corp., **IV** 489–90; **7** 280; **25** 461
DWG Corporation. *See* Triarc Companies, Inc.
Dyckerhoff, **III** 738
Dyersburg Corporation, 21 192–95
Dyke and Dryden, Ltd., **31** 417
Dylex Limited, 29 162–65
Dymed Corporation. *See* Palomar Medical Technologies, Inc.
Dynaco Corporation, **III** 643; **22** 409
DynaMark, Inc., **18** 168, 170, 516, 518
Dynamatic Corp., **I** 154
Dynamem Corporation, **22** 409
Dynamic Capital Corp., **16** 80
Dynamic Controls, **11** 202
Dynamic Microprocessor Associated Inc., **10** 508
Dynamit Nobel AG, **III** 692–95; **16** 364; **18** 559
Dynamix, **15** 455
Dynapar, **7** 116–17
Dynascan AK, **14** 118
Dynasty Footwear, Ltd., **18** 88
Dynatech Corporation, 13 194–96
Dynatron/Bondo Corporation, **8** 456
Dynell Electronics, **I** 85
Dyno Industrier AS, **13** 555
Dyonics Inc., **I** 667
DYR, **I** 38; **16** 167

E. & B. Carpet Mills, **III** 423
E&B Company, **9** 72
E&B Marine, Inc., **17** 542–43
E & H Utility Sales Inc., **6** 487
E. & J. Gallo Winery, I 27, **242–44**, 260; **7 154–56 (upd.)**; **15** 391; **28 109–11 (upd.)**, 223
E&M Laboratories, **18** 514
E & S Retail Ltd. *See* Powerhouse.
E! Entertainment Television Inc., 17 148–50; **24** 120, 123
E*Trade Group, Inc., 20 206–08
E.A. Miller, Inc., **II** 494
E.A. Pierce & Co., **II** 424; **13** 340
E.A. Stearns & Co., **III** 627
E.B. Badger Co., **11** 413
E.B. Eddy Forest Products, **II** 631
E.C. Snodgrass Company, **14** 112
E.C. Steed, **13** 103
E. de Trey & Sons, **10** 270–71
E.F. Hutton Group, **I** 402; **II** 399, 450–51; **8** 139; **9** 469; **10** 63
E.F. Hutton LBO, **24** 148
E. Gluck Trading Co., **III** 645
E.H. Bindley & Company, **9** 67
E.I. du Pont de Nemours & Company, I 21, 28, 305, 317–19, 323, **328–30**, 334, 337–38, 343–44, 346–48, 351–53, 365, 377, 379, 383, 402–03, 545, 548, 675; **III** 21; **IV** 69, 78, 263, 371, 399, 401–02, 409, 481, 599; **V** 360; **7** 546; **8 151–54 (upd.)**, 485; **9** 154, 216, 352, 466; **10** 289; **11** 432; **12** 68, 365,

416–17; **13** 21, 124; **16** 127, 130, 201, 439, 461–62; **19** 11, 223; **21** 544; **22** 147, 260, 405; **24** 111, 388; **25** 152, 540; **26 123–27 (upd.)**
E.J. Brach & Sons, **II** 521. *See also* Brach and Brock Confections, Inc.
E.J. Longyear Company. *See* Boart Longyear Company.
E. Katz Special Advertising Agency. *See* Katz Communications, Inc.
E.L. Phillips and Company, **V** 652–53
E.M. Warburg Pincus & Co., **7** 305; **13** 176; **16** 319; **25** 313; **29** 262
E. Missel GmbH, **20** 363
E.N.V. Engineering, **I** 154
E.R. Squibb, **I** 695; **21** 54–55
E. Rabinowe & Co., Inc., **13** 367
E.S. Friedman & Co., **II** 241
E.S. International Holding S.A. *See* Banco Espírito Santo e Comercial de Lisboa S.A.
E-Systems, Inc., **I** 490; **9 182–85**
E-II Holdings Inc., **II** 468; **9** 449; **12** 87. *See also* Astrum International Corp.
E.W. Bliss, **I** 452
E.W. Oakes & Co. Ltd., **IV** 118
The E.W. Scripps Company, **IV 606–09**; **7 157–59 (upd.)**; **24** 122; **25** 507; **28 122–26 (upd.)**
E.W.T. Mayer Ltd., **III** 681
E-Z Haul, **24** 409
E-Z Serve Corporation, **15** 270; **17 169–71**
Eagle Airways Ltd., **23** 161
Eagle Credit Corp., **10** 248
Eagle Family Foods, Inc., **22** 95
Eagle Floor Care, Inc., **13** 501
Eagle Gaming, L.P., **16** 263
Eagle Hardware & Garden, Inc., **9** 399; **16 186–89**; **17** 539–40
Eagle Industries Inc., **8** 230; **22** 282; **25** 536
Eagle Managed Care Corp., **19** 354, 357
Eagle Oil Transport Co. Ltd., **IV** 657
Eagle Plastics, **19** 414
Eagle Printing Co. Ltd., **IV** 295; **19** 225
Eagle Snacks Inc., **I** 219
Eagle Square Manufacturing Co., **III** 627
Eagle Star Insurance Co., **I** 426–27; **III** 185, 200
Eagle Supermarket, **II** 571
Eagle Thrifty Drug, **14** 397
Eagle Travel Ltd., **IV** 241
Eagle-Lion Films, **II** 147; **25** 328
Eagle-Picher Industries, Inc., **8 155–58**; **23 179–83 (upd.)**
Early American Insurance Co., **22** 230
Earth Resources Company, **IV** 459; **17** 320
Earth Wise, Inc., **16** 90
Earth's Best, **21** 56
EAS. *See* Executive Aircraft Services.
Easco Hand Tools, Inc., **7** 117
Eason Oil Company, **6** 578; **11** 198
East African External Communications Limited, **25** 100
East Chicago Iron and Forge Co., **IV** 113
East Hartford Trust Co., **13** 467
East India Co., **I** 468; **III** 521, 696; **IV** 48; **20** 309
East Japan Heavy Industries, **III** 578–79; **7** 348
East Japan Railway Company, **V 448–50**
East Midlands Electricity, **V** 605
The East New York Savings Bank, **11** 108–09
East of Scotland, **III** 359
East Texas Pulp and Paper Co., **IV** 342, 674; **7** 528
East-West Airlines, **27** 475
East-West Federal Bank, **16** 484
Easter Enterprises, **8** 380; **23** 358
Easterday Supply Company, **25** 15
Eastern Air Group Co., **31** 102
Eastern Airlines, **I** 41, 66, 78, 90, 98–99, **101–03**, 116, 118, 123–25; **III** 102; **6** 73, 81–82, 104–05; **8** 416; **9** 17–18, 80; **11** 268, 427; **12** 191, 487; **21** 142, 143; **23** 483; **26** 339, 439
Eastern Associated Coal Corp., **6** 487
Eastern Australia Airlines, **24** 396
Eastern Aviation Group, **23** 408
Eastern Bank, **II** 357
Eastern Carolina Bottling Company, **10** 223
Eastern Coal Corp., **IV** 181
Eastern Coalfields Ltd., **IV** 48–49
Eastern Corp., **IV** 703
Eastern Electricity, **13** 485
Eastern Enterprises, **IV** 171; **6 486–88**
Eastern Gas and Fuel Associates, **I** 354; **IV** 171
Eastern Indiana Gas Corporation, **6** 466
Eastern Kansas Utilities, **6** 511
Eastern Machine Screw Products Co., **13** 7
Eastern Market Beef Processing Corp., **20** 120
Eastern Operating Co., **III** 23
Eastern Pine Sales Corporation, **13** 249
Eastern Software Distributors, Inc., **16** 125
Eastern States Farmers Exchange, **7** 17
Eastern Telegraph Company, **V** 283–84; **25** 99–100
Eastern Texas Electric. *See* Gulf States Utilities Company.
Eastern Tool Co., **IV** 249
Eastern Torpedo Company, **25** 74
Eastern Wisconsin Power, **6** 604
Eastern Wisconsin Railway and Light Company, **6** 601
Eastex Pulp and Paper Co., **IV** 341–42
Eastman Chemical Company, **14 174–75**; **25** 22
Eastman Christensen Company, **22** 68
Eastman Kodak Company, **I** 19, 30, 90, 323, 337–38, 690; **II** 103; **III** 171–72, **474–77**, 486–88, 547–48, 550, 584, 607–09; **IV** 260–61; **6** 288–89; **7 160–64 (upd.)**, 436–38; **8** 376–77; **9** 62, 231; **10** 24; **12** 342; **14** 174–75, 534; **16** 168, 449; **18** 184–86, 342, 510; **25** 153; **29** 370
Eastman Radio, **6** 33
Eastmaque Gold Mines, Ltd., **7** 356
Eastover Mining, **27** 130
Eastpak, Inc., **30** 138
Eatco, Inc., **15** 246
Eaton Axle Co., **I** 154
Eaton, Cole & Burnham Company, **8** 134
Eaton Corporation, **I 154–55**, 186; **III** 645; **10 279–80 (upd.)**; **12** 547; **27** 100
Eaton Vance Corporation, **18 150–53**
Eavey Co., **II** 668
Ebamsa, **II** 474
EBASCO. *See* Electric Bond and Share Company.
Ebasco Services, **III** 499; **V** 612; **IV** 255–56
EBC Amro Ltd., **II** 186
Eberhard Faber, **12** 115
Eberhard Foods, **8** 482
EBIC. *See* European Banks' International Co.
Ebiex S.A., **25** 312
EBS. *See* Electric Bond & Share Company *or* Electronic Bookshelf.
EBSCO Industries, Inc., **17 151–53**
EC Comics, **25** 139
EC Erdolchemie GmbH, **7** 141
ECC Group plc, **III 689–91**. *See also* English China Clays plc.
Echigoya Saburobei Shoten, **IV** 292
Echlin Inc., **I 156–57**; **11 83–85 (upd.)**; **15** 310
Echo Bay Mines Ltd., **IV 75–77**; **23** 40
Les Echos, **IV** 659
EchoStar Communications Corporation, **18** 355; **27** 307
ECI Telecom Ltd., **18 154–56**
Eckerd Corporation, **9 186–87**; **18** 272; **24** 263
Eckert-Mauchly Corp., **III** 166
Ecko Products, **I** 527
Ecko-Ensign Design, **I** 531
ECL, **16** 238
Eclipse Candles, Ltd., **18** 67, 69
Eclipse Machine Co., **I** 141
Eclipse Telecommunications, Inc., **29** 252
Eco Hotels, **14** 107
Ecolab Inc., **I 331–33**; **13 197–200 (upd.)**; **26** 306
Econo Lodges of America, **25** 309
Econo-Travel Corporation, **13** 362
Economist Group, **15** 265
Economy Book Store, **10** 135
Economy Fire & Casualty, **22** 495
Economy Grocery Stores Company. *See* The Stop & Shop Companies, Inc.
Ecopetrol. *See* Empresa Colombiana de Petróleos.
EcoSystems Software, Inc., **10** 245; **30** 142
EcoWater Systems, Inc., **16** 357
ECS S.A, **12 138–40**
Ecusta Corporation, **8** 414
Edah, **13** 544–45
Eddie Bauer Inc., **II** 503; **V** 160; **9 188–90**; **9** 316; **10** 324, 489, 491; **11** 498; **15** 339; **25** 48; **27** 427, 429–30; **29** 278
Eddy Bakeries, Inc., **12** 198
Eddy Paper Co., **II** 631
Edeka Zentrale A.G., **II 621–23**
Edelstahlwerke Buderus AG, **III** 695
Edenhall Group, **III** 673
Edenton Cotton Mills, **12** 503
EDF. *See* Electricité de France.
Edgars, **I** 289
Edgcomb Metals, **IV** 575–76; **31** 470–71
Edge Research, **25** 301
Edgell Communications Inc., **IV** 624
Edgewater Hotel and Casino, **6** 204–05
EDI, **26** 441
Edina Realty Inc., **13** 348
Edison Brothers Stores, Inc., **9 191–93**; **17** 369, 409
Edison Electric Appliance Co., **II** 28; **12** 194
Edison Electric Co., **I** 368; **II** 330; **III** 433; **6** 572
Edison Electric Illuminating Co., **II** 402; **6** 595, 601; **14** 124

Edison Electric Illuminating Company of Boston, **12** 45
Edison Electric Light & Power, **6** 510
Edison Electric Light Co., **II** 27; **6** 565, 595; **11** 387; **12** 193
Edison General Electric Co., **II** 27, 120, 278; **12** 193; **14** 168; **26** 451
Edison Machine Works, **II** 27
Edison Phonograph, **III** 443
Editions Albert Premier, **IV** 614
Editions Bernard Grasset, **IV** 618
Editions Dalloz, **IV** 615
Editions Jean-Baptiste Baillière, **25** 285
Editions Nathan, **IV** 615
Editions Ramsay, **25** 174
Editorial Centro de Estudios Ramón Areces, S.A., **V** 52; **26** 130
Editorial Televisa, **18** 211, 213; **23** 417
Editoriale L'Espresso, **IV** 586–87
Editoriale Le Gazzette, **IV** 587
EdK. *See* Edeka Zentrale A.G.
Edmark Corporation, 14 176–78
Edmonton City Bakery, **II** 631
Edogawa Oil Co., **IV** 403
EdoWater Systems, Inc., **IV** 137
Edper Equities, **II** 456
EDS. *See* Electronic Data Systems Corporation.
Education Association Mutual Assurance Company. *See* Horace Mann Educators Corporation.
Education Funds, Inc., **II** 419
Education Systems Corporation, **7** 256; **25** 253
Educational & Recreational Services, Inc., **II** 607
Educational Credit Corporation, **8** 10
Educational Publishing Corporation, **22** 519, 522
Educational Supply Company, **7** 255; **25** 252
Educational Testing Service, 12 141–43
EduQuest, **6** 245
Edward Ford Plate Glass Co., **III** 640–41, 731
Edward J. DeBartolo Corporation, V 116; **8 159–62**
Edward Jones, 30 177–79
Edward Lloyd Ltd., **IV** 258
Edward P. Allis Company, **13** 16
Edward Smith & Company, **8** 553
Edwards & Jones, **11** 360
Edwards Dunlop & Co. Ltd., **IV** 249
Edwards Food Warehouse, **II** 642
Edwards George and Co., **III** 283
Edwards Industries, **IV** 256
Edwards Theatres Circuit, Inc., 31 171–73
Edwardstone Partners, **14** 377
EEC Environmental, Inc., **16** 259
Eerste Nederlandsche, **III** 177–79
Eff Laboratories, **I** 622
Effectenbank, **II** 268; **21** 145
EFM Media Management, **23** 294
Efnadruck GmbH, **IV** 325
Efrat Future Technology Ltd. *See* Comverse Technology, Inc.
EG&G Incorporated, 8 163–65; **18** 219; **22** 410; **29 166–69 (upd.)**
EGAM, **IV** 422
Egerton Hubbard & Co., **IV** 274
Egghead Inc., 9 194–95; **10** 284
Egghead.com, Inc., 31 174–177 (upd.)
EGPC. *See* Egyptian General Petroleum Corporation.
EGUZKIA-NHK, **III** 581
EgyptAir, I 107; **6 84–86**; **27 132–35 (upd.)**
Egyptian General Petroleum Corporation, IV 412–14
EHAPE Einheitspreis Handels Gesellschaft mbH. *See* Kaufhalle AG.
Eidgenössische Bank, **II** 378
Eidgenössische Versicherungs-Aktien-Gesellschaft, **III** 403
Eiffage, 27 136–38
Eiffel Construction Metallique, **27** 138
800-JR Cigar, Inc., 27 139–41
84 Lumber Company, 9 196–97
Eildon Electronics Ltd., **15** 385
EIMCO, **I** 512
Einstein/Noah Bagel Corporation, 29 170–73
eircom plc, 31 178–181 (upd.)
EIS Automotive Corp., **III** 603
Eisai Company, **13** 77
Eisen-und Stahlwerk Haspe AG, **IV** 126
Eisen-und Stahlwerk Hoesch, **IV** 103
Eisenhower Mining Co., **IV** 33
EKA AB, **I** 330; **8** 153
Eka Nobel AB, **9** 380
Ekco Group, Inc., 12 377; **16 190–93**
El Al Israel Airlines Ltd., I 30; **23 184–87**
El Camino Resources International, Inc., 11 86–88
El Chico Restaurants, Inc., 19 135–38
El Corte Inglés, S.A., V 51–53; **26 128–31 (upd.)**
El Dorado Investment Company, **6** 546–47
El Paso & Southwestern Railroad, **IV** 177
El Paso Electric Company, 21 196–98
El Paso Healthcare System, Ltd., **15** 112
El Paso Natural Gas Company, 10 190; **11** 28; **12 144–46**; **19** 411; **27** 86
El Pollo Loco, **II** 680; **27** 16–18
El Taco, **7** 505
El-Mel-Parts Ltd., **21** 499
ELAN, **IV** 486
Elan Corp. plc, **10** 54
Elan Ski Company, **22** 483
Elano Corporation, 14 179–81
Elcat Company, **17** 91
Elco Corporation, **21** 329, 331
Elco Industries Inc., **22** 282
Elco Motor Yacht, **I** 57
Elda Trading Co., **II** 48; **25** 267
Elder Dempster Line, **6** 416–17
Elder Smith Goldsbrough Mort Ltd., **21** 227
Elder's Insurance Co., **III** 370
Elder-Beerman Stores Corporation, 10 281–83; **19** 362
Elders IXL Ltd., I 216, 228–29, 264, **437–39**, 592–93; **7** 182–83; **21** 227; **26** 305; **28** 201
Elders Keep, **13** 440
Eldorado Gold Corporation, **22** 237
ele Corporation, **23** 251
Electra Corp., **III** 569; **20** 361–62
Electra/Midland Corp., **13** 398
Electralab Electronics Corp., **III** 643
Electric Boat Co., **I** 57–59, 527; **II** 7; **10** 315
Electric Bond & Share Company, **V** 564–65; **6** 596
Electric Clearinghouse, Inc., **18** 365, 367
Electric Energy, Inc., **6** 470, 505
Electric Fuels Corp., **V** 621; **23** 200
Electric Heat Regulator Co., **II** 40; **12** 246
Electric Iron and Steel, **IV** 162
Electric Light and Power Company, **6** 483
Electric Light Company of Atlantic City. *See* Atlantic Energy, Inc.
Electric Thermostat Co., **II** 40; **12** 246
Electrical Lamp Service Co. *See* EMI Group plc.
Electricité de France, I 303; **V** 603–05, 626–28
Electro Dynamics Corp., **I** 57, 484; **11** 263
Electro Metallurgical Co., **I** 400; **9** 517; **11** 402
Electro Refractories and Abrasives Company, **8** 178
Electro String Instrument Corporation, **16** 201
Electro-Alkaline Company. *See* The Clorox Company.
Electro-Chemische Fabrik Natrium GmbH, **IV** 69–70
Electro-Flo, Inc., **9** 27
Electro-Mechanical Research, **III** 617; **17** 417
Electro-Motive Engineering Company, **10** 273
Electro-Nite International N.V., **IV** 100
Electro-Optical Systems, **III** 172; **6** 289
Electrobel, **II** 202
ElectroData Corp., **III** 165; **6** 281
Electrolux Group, II 69, 572; **III** 420, **478–81**; **IV** 338; **6** 69; **11** 439; **12** 158–59, 250; **13** 562, 564; **17** 353; **21** 383. *See also* Aktiebolaget Electrolux.
Electromagnetic Sciences Inc., 21 199–201
Electromedics, **11** 460
Electronic Arts Inc., 10 284–86; **13** 115; **29** 76
Electronic Banking Systems, **9** 173
Electronic Book Technologies, Inc., **26** 216 **29** 427
Electronic Data Systems Corporation, I 172; **II** 65; **III 136–38**, 326; **6** 226; **9** 36; **10** 325, 327; **11** 62, 123, 131; **13** 482; **14** 15, 318; **22** 266; **27** 380; **28 112–16 (upd.)**; **241**; **29** 375. *See also* Perot Systems Corporation.
Electronic Engineering Co., **16** 393
Electronic Rentals Group PLC, **II** 139; **24** 194
Electronic Tool Company, **16** 100
Electronics Corp. of Israel Ltd. *See* ECI Telecom Ltd.
Electronics for Imaging, Inc., 15 148–50
Electrorail, **II** 93; **18** 472
Electrowatt Ltd., **21** 146–47
Electrowerke AG, **IV** 230
Elekom, **31** 176
Elektra Records, **III** 480; **23** 33
Elektriska Aktiebolaget. *See* ABB Asea Brown Boveri Ltd.
Elektrizitäts-Gesellschaft Laufenburg, **6** 490
Elektrizitätswerk Wesertal GmbH, **30** 206
Elektrizitätswerk Westfalen AG, **V** 744
ElektroHelios, **III** 479; **22** 26
Elektromekaniska AB, **III** 478
Elektromekano, **II** 1
Elektrowatt AG, 6 489–91
Eleme Petrochemicals Co., **IV** 473
Eletson Corp., **13** 374

Elettra Broadcasting Corporation, **14** 509
Elettrofinanziaria Spa, **9** 152
Eleventh National Bank, **II** 373
Elf Aquitaine SA, **21 202–06 (upd.)**; **23** 236, 238; **24** 494; **25** 104; **26** 369, 425. *See also* Société Nationale Elf Aquitaine.
Elgin Blenders, Inc., **7** 128
Elgin Exploration, Inc., **19** 247; **26** 70
Eli Lilly & Co., **I** 637, **645–47**, 666, 679, 687, 701; **III** 18–19, 60–61; **8** 168, 209; **9** 89–90; **10** 535; **11** 9, **89–91 (upd.)**, 458, 460; **12** 187, 278, 333; **14** 99–100, 259; **17** 437; **18** 420, 422; **19** 105; **21** 387; **26** 31
Eli Witt Company, **15** 137, 139
Elias Brothers Restaurants, **III** 103
Elit Circuits Inc., **I** 330; **8** 153
Elite Microelectronics, **9** 116
Elite Sewing Machine Manufacturing Co., **III** 415
Elizabeth Arden Co., **I** 646, **III** 48; **8 166–68**, 344; **9** 201–02, 428, 449; **11** 90; **12** 314; **30** 188
Eljer Industries, Inc., **II** 420; **24 150–52**
Elk River Resources, Inc., **IV** 550
Elka, **III** 54
Elke Corporation, **10** 514
Elko-Lamoille Power Company, **11** 343
Ellenville Electric Company, **6** 459
Ellesse International S.p.A., **V** 376; **26** 397–98
Ellett Brothers, Inc., **17 154–56**
Ellington Recycling Center, **12** 377
Elliott Automation, **II** 25; **6** 241; **13** 225
Elliott Bay Design Group, **22** 276
Elliott Paint and Varnish, **8** 553
Ellis Adding-Typewriter Co., **III** 151; **6** 265
Ellis Banks, **II** 336
Ellis, Chafflin & Co. *See* Mead Corporation.
Ellis Paperboard Products Inc., **13** 442
Ellis Park Race Course, **29** 118
Ellos A.B., **II** 640
ELMA Electronic, **III** 632
Elmendorf Board, **IV** 343
Elmer's Products, Inc. *See* Borden, Inc.
Elphinstone, **21** 501
Elrick & Lavidge, **6** 24
Elrick Industries, Inc., **19** 278
Elscint Ltd., **20 202–05**
Elsevier NV, **IV 610–11**, 643, 659; **7** 244; **14** 555–56; **17** 396, 399
Elsi, **II** 86
ELTO Outboard Motor Co., **III** 597
Eltra Corporation, **I** 416, 524; **22** 31; **31** 135
Elwerath, **IV** 485
Elyria Telephone Company, **6** 299
Email Ltd., **III** 672–73
Emballage, **III** 704
Embankment Trust Ltd., **IV** 659
Embassy Book Co., Ltd., **IV** 635
Embassy Hotel Group, **I** 216; **9** 426
Embassy Suites, **9** 425; **24** 253
Embers America Restaurants, **30 180–82**
Embraer, **25** 422
Embry-Riddle, **I** 89
EMC Corporation, **12 147–49**; **20** 8
EMC Technology Services, Inc., **30** 469
Emco, **III** 569; **20** 361
EMD, **27** 21
Emerald Coast Water Co., **III** 21
Emerald Technology, Inc., **10** 97
Emerson Drug, **I** 711
Emerson Electric Co., **II 18–21**, 92; **III** 625; **8** 298; **12** 248; **13** 225; **14** 357; **15** 405–06; **21** 43; **22** 64; **25** 530
Emerson Foote, Inc., **25** 90
Emerson Radio Corp., **30 183–86**
Emerson-Brantingham Company, **10** 378
Emery Air Freight Corporation, **6** 345–46, 386, **388–91**; **18** 177. *See also* Emery Worldwide Airlines, Inc.
Emery Group, **I** 377; **III** 33
Emery Worldwide Airlines, Inc., **21** 139; **25 146–50 (upd.)**
Emeryville Chemical Co., **IV** 408
Emge Packing Co., Inc., **11 92–93**
Emhart Corp., **III** 437; **8** 332; **20** 67
EMI Group plc, **I** 531; **6** 240; **22 192–95 (upd.)**; **24** 485; **26** 188, 314. *See also* Thorne EMI plc.
Emirates, **24** 400
Empain, **18** 472; **19** 165
Empain-Schneider, **II** 93
Empaques de Carton Titan, **19** 10–11
Empex Hose, **19** 37
Empire Blue Cross and Blue Shield, **III 245–46**; **6** 195
Empire Brewery, **I** 253
Empire Co., **II** 653
Empire Cos., **IV** 391
Empire District Electric, **IV** 391
Empire Family Restaurants Inc., **15** 362
Empire Gas & Fuel, **IV** 391
Empire Hanna Coal Co., Ltd., **8** 346
Empire Inc., **II** 682
Empire Life and Accident Insurance Co., **III** 217
Empire National Bank, **II** 218
Empire of America, **11** 110
Empire Pencil, **III** 505
Empire Savings, Building & Loan Association, **8** 424
Empire State Group, **IV** 612
Empire State Petroleum, **IV** 374
Empire State Pickling Company, **21** 155
Empire Stores, **19** 309
Empire Trust Co., **II** 218
Employee Solutions, Inc., **18 157–60**
Employers' Liability Assurance, **III** 235
Employer's Overload, **25** 432
Employers Reinsurance Corp., **II** 31; **12** 197
Empresa Brasileira de Aeronautica, S.A., **15** 73
Empresa Colombiana de Petróleos, **IV 415–18**
Empresa Nacional de Electridad, **I** 459
Empresa Nacional del Petroleo, **IV** 528
Empresa Nacional Electrica de Cordoba, **V** 607
Empresa Nacional Hidro-Electrica del Ribagorzana, **I** 459; **V** 607
Empresa Nacional Hulleras del Norte, **I** 460
Empresas Frisco, **21** 259
Empresas La Moderna, **21** 413; **29** 435
Empresas Tolteca, **20** 123
Emprise Corporation, **7** 134–35
EMS Technologies, Inc., **21** 199, 201; **22** 173
Ems-Chemi, **III** 760
Enagas, **IV** 528
ENCAD, Incorporated, **25 151–53**
ENCASO, **IV** 528
ENCI, **IV** 132
Encore Computer Corporation, **13 201–02**
Encore Distributors Inc., **17** 12–13
Encryption Technology Corporation, **23** 102
Encyclopedia Britannica, Inc., **7 165–68**; **12** 435, 554–55; **16** 252
Endata, Inc., **11** 112
ENDESA Group, **V 606–08**
Endevco Inc., **11** 28
Endiama, **IV** 67
Endicott Trust Company, **11** 110
Endo Vascular Technologies, Inc., **11** 460
Endovations, Inc., **21** 47
ENECO. *See* Empresa Nacional Electrica de Cordoba.
ENEL. *See* Ente Nazionale per l'Energia Elettrica.
Enerchange LLC, **18** 366
Enercon, Inc., **6** 25
Energen Corporation, **6** 583; **21 207–09**
Energie-Verwaltungs-Gesellschaft, **V** 746
Energieversorgung Ostbayern AG, **23** 47
Energizer, **9** 180
Energy Absorption Systems, Inc., **15** 378
Energy Biosystems Corp., **15** 352
Energy Coatings Co., **14** 325
Energy Corp. of Louisiana, **V** 619
Energy Film Library, **31** 216, 218
The Energy Group, **26** 359
Energy Increments Inc., **19** 411
Energy National, Inc., **27** 485
Energy Resources, **27** 216
Energy Steel Corporation, **19** 472
Energy Systems Group, Inc., **13** 489
Energy Transportation Systems, Inc., **27** 88
Energyline Systems, **26** 5
EnergyOne, **19** 487
Enerplus Resources, **21** 500
Enesco Corporation, **11 94–96**; **15** 475, 477–78
Engelhard Corporation, **II** 54; **IV** 23, **78–80**; **16** 28; **21 210–14 (upd.)**
Engen, **IV** 93; **22** 236
Engineered Polymers Co., **I** 202
Engineering Co. of Nigeria, **IV** 473
Engineering Company, **9** 16
Engineering for the Petroleum and Process Industries, **IV** 414
Engineering Plastics, Ltd., **8** 377
Engineering Research Associates, **III** 126, 129
Engineers & Fabricators, Inc., **18** 513
England Corsair Furniture, **14** 302
Englander Co., **I** 400
Engles Management Corp., **26** 448
English China Clays plc, **III** 689–91; **15 151–54 (upd.)**
English Condensed Milk Co., **II** 545
English Electric Co., **I** 50; **II** 25, 81; **6** 241; **24** 85
English Mercantile & General Insurance Co., **III** 376
English Property Corp., **IV** 712
English, Scottish and Australian Bank Ltd., **II** 187–89
Engraph, Inc., **12 150–51**
Enhanced Services Billing, Inc. *See* Billing Concepts Corp.
ENHER. *See* Empresa Nacional Hidro-Electrica del Ribagorzana.
ENI. *See* Ente Nazionale Idrocarburi.
ENIEPSA, **IV** 528
Enimont, **IV** 422, 525

Ennia, **III** 177, 179, 310
Ennis Business Forms, Inc., **21 215–17**
Eno Proprietaries, **III** 65
Enocell Oy, **IV** 277
The Enoch F. Bills Co., **25** 365
Enogex, Inc., **6** 539–40
Enova Corporation. *See* Sempra Energy.
ENPAC Corporation, **18** 162
Enpetrol, **IV** 528
Enquirer/Star Group, Inc., **10 287–88**; **12** 358. *See also* American Media, Inc.
Enron Corporation, **III** 197; **V** 609–10; **6** 457, 593; **18** 365; **19 139–41**, 162, 487; **27** 266
Enseco, **III** 684
Enserch Corp., **V 611–13**
Ensidesa, **I** 460
Ensign Oil Company, **9** 490
Enskilda S.A., **II** 352–53
Enso-Gutzeit Oy, **IV 274–77**; **17** 539
ENSTAR Corporation, **IV** 567; **11** 441
Enstar Group Inc., **13** 299
Ensys Environmental Products, Inc., **10** 107
ENTASA, **IV** 528
Ente Gestione Aziende Minerarie, **I** 466
Ente Nazionale di Energia Elettrica, **I** 466
Ente Nazionale Idrocarburi, **I** 369; **IV** 412, **419–22**, 424, 453, 466, 470, 486, 546; **V** 614–17
Ente Nazionale per l'Energia Elettrica, **V 614–17**
Entenmann's, **I** 246, 712; **10** 551
Entergy Corp., **V 618–20**; **6** 496–97
Enterprise Development Company, **15** 413
Enterprise Electronics Corporation, **18** 513–15
Enterprise Federal Savings & Loan, **21** 524
Enterprise Integration Technologies, **18** 541
Enterprise Leasing, **6 392–93**
Enterprise Metals Pty. Ltd., **IV** 61
Enterprise Oil plc, **11 97–99**
Enterprise Rent-A-Car, **16** 380
Enterra Corp., **25** 546
Entertainment Publications, **16** 146
Entertainment UK, **24** 266, 269
Entertainment Zone, Inc., **15** 212
Entex Information Services, **24** 29
Entity Software, **11** 469
Entrada Industries Incorporated, **6** 568–69; **26** 387
Entré Computer Centers, **6** 243–44; **13** 175
Entremont, **I** 676
Entreprise de Recherches et d'Activités Pétrolières, **IV** 453, 467, 544, 560; **7** 481, 483–84
Entreprise Nationale Sonatrach, **IV 423–25**; **V** 626, 692; **10** 83–84; **12** 145
Entrex, Inc., **III** 154
Entrust Financial Corp., **16** 347
Envergure, **27** 421
Envirex, **11** 361
Envirodrill Services, Inc., **19** 247
Envirodyne Industries, Inc., **17 157–60**
EnviroLease, Inc., **25** 171
ENVIRON International Corporation, **10** 106
Environmental Defense Fund, **9** 305
Environmental Industries, Inc., **31 182–85**
Environmental Planning & Research. *See* CRSS Inc.
Environmental Research and Technology, Inc., **23** 135
Environmental Systems Corporation, **9** 109
Environmental Testing and Certification Corporation, **10** 106–07
Environmentals Incorporated. *See* Angelica Corporation.
Envirosciences Pty. Ltd., **16** 260
Envision Corporation, **24** 96
Enwright Environmental Consulting Laboratories, **9** 110
Enzyme Bio-Systems, Ltd., **21** 386
Enzyme Technologies Corp., **I** 342; **14** 217
Eon Productions, **II** 147; **25** 328
Eon Systems, **III** 143; **6** 238
l'Epargne, **12** 152
EPE Technologies, **18** 473
EPI Group Limited, **26** 137
Les Epiceries Presto Limitée, **II** 651
Epiphone, **16** 238–39
Epoch Systems Inc., **9** 140; **12** 149
Eppler, Guerin & Turner, Inc., **III** 330
Eppley, **III** 99
Epsilon Trading Corporation, **6** 81
Epson, **18** 386–87, 435
Equator Bank, **II** 298
Equicor Group Ltd., **29** 343
EQUICOR-Equitable HCA Corp., **III** 80, 226
Equifax, Inc., **6 23–25**; **25** 182, 358; **28 117–21 (upd.)**
Equilink Licensing Group, **22** 458
EquiStar Hotel Investors L.P. *See* CapStar Hotel Co.
Equitable Bancorporation, **12** 329
Equitable Equipment Company, **7** 540
Equitable Life Assurance Society of the United States, **II** 330; **III** 80, 229, 237, **247–49**, 274, 289, 291, 305–06, 316, 329, 359; **IV** 171, 576, 711; **6** 23; **13** 539; **19** 324, 511; **22** 188–90; **23** 370, 482; **27** 46
Equitable Resources, Inc., **6 492–94**
Equitable Trust Co., **II** 247, 397; **10** 61
Equitas, **22** 315
Equitec Financial Group, **11** 483
Equitex Inc., **16** 431
Equity & Law, **III** 211
Equity Corp. Tasman, **III** 735
Equity Corporation, **6** 599
Equity Group Investment, Inc., **22** 339
Equity Marketing, Inc., **26 136–38**
Equity Title Services Company, **13** 348
Equivalent Company, **12** 421
Equus Capital Corp., **23** 65
Equus II Inc., **18** 11
Eramet, **IV** 108
ERAP. *See* Entreprise de Recherches et d'Activités Pétrolières.
Erasco Group, **II** 556; **26** 58
EraSoft Technologies, **27** 492
ERCO Systems Group, **16** 461–63
Erdal, **II** 572
Erdölsproduktions-Gesellschaft AG, **IV** 485
Erftwerk AG, **IV** 229
Ericson Yachts, **10** 215
Ericssan, AB, **11** 501
Ericsson, **9** 32–33; **11** 196; **17** 33, 353; **18** 74. *See also* L.M. Ericsson.
Eridania Beghin-Say, S.A., **14** 17, 19
Erie and Pennyslvania, **I** 584
Erie County Bank, **9** 474
Erie Railroad, **I** 584; **II** 329; **IV** 180
Erie Scientific Company, **14** 479–80
Eritsusha, **IV** 326
ERKA. *See* Reichs Kredit-Gesellschaft mbH.
ERLY Industries Inc., **17 161–62**
Ernest Oppenheimer and Sons, **IV** 21, 79
Ernst & Young, **I** 412; **9 198–200**, 309, 311; **10** 115; **25** 358; **29 174–77 (upd.)**, 236, 392
Erol's, **9** 74; **11** 556
ERPI, **7** 167
Ersco Corporation, **17** 310; **24** 160
Erste Allgemeine, **III** 207–08
Erving Distributor Products Co., **IV** 282; **9** 260
Erving Healthcare, **13** 150
Erwin Wasey & Co., **I** 17, 22
Erzbergbau Salzgitter AG, **IV** 201
ES&A. *See* English, Scottish and Australian Bank Ltd.
Esanda, **II** 189
Esaote Biomedica, **29** 298
ESB Inc., **IV** 112; **18** 488
Esbjerg Thermoplast, **9** 92
Escada AG, **14** 467
Escalade, Incorporated, **19 142–44**
Escambia Chemicals, **I** 298
Escan, **22** 354
Escanaba Paper Co., **IV** 311; **19** 266
Escaut et Meuse, **IV** 227
Escher Wyss, **III** 539, 632
Eschweiler Bergwerks-Verein AG, **IV** 25–26, 193
ESCO Electronics Corporation, **17** 246, 248; **24** 425
Esco Trading, **10** 482
Escoffier Ltd., **I** 259
Escotel Mobile Communications, **18** 180
Esdon de Castro, **8** 137
ESE Sports Co. Ltd., **V** 376; **26** 397
ESGM. *See* Elder Smith Goldsbrough Mort.
ESI Energy, Inc., **V** 623–24
Eskay Screw Corporation, **11** 536
Eskilstuna Separator, **III** 419
Eskimo Pie Corporation, **21 218–20**
Esmark, Inc., **I** 441; **II** 448, 468–69; **6** 357; **12** 93; **13** 448; **15** 357; **19** 290; **22** 55, 513
Esperance-Longdoz, **IV** 51–52
Espírito Santo. *See* Banco Espírito Santo e Comercial de Lisboa S.A.
ESPN Inc., **II** 131; **IV** 627; **19** 201, 204; **24** 516
Esprit de Corp., **8 169–72**; **29 178–82 (upd.)**
La Espuela Oil Company, Ltd., **IV** 81–82; **7** 186
Esquire Education Group, **12** 173
Esquire Inc., **I** 453; **IV** 672; **13** 178; **19** 405
ESS Technology, Inc., **22 196–98**
Essanelle Salon Co., **18** 455
Essantee Theatres, Inc., **14** 86
Essef Corporation, **18 161–63**
Esselte Pendaflex Corporation, **11 100–01**
Essence Communications, Inc., **24 153–55**
Essener Reisebüro, **II** 164
Essex International Ltd., **19** 452
Essex Outfitters Inc., **9** 394
Essilor International, **18** 392; **21 221–23**
Esso Petroleum, **I** 52; **II** 628; **III** 673; **IV** 46, 276, 397, 421, 423, 432–33, 439, 441, 454, 470, 484, 486, 517–19, 531,

555, 563; **7** 140, 171; **11** 97; **13** 558; **22** 106; **24** 86; **25** 229, 231–32. *See also* Imperial Oil Limited *and* Standard Oil Company of New Jersey.
Estat Telecom Group plc, **31** 180
Estech, Inc., **19** 290
Estee Corp., **27** 197
The Estée Lauder Companies Inc., **30** **187–91 (upd.)**
Estée Lauder Inc., **I** 696; **III** 56; **8** 131; **9** **201–04**; **11** 41; **24** 55
Estel N.V., **IV** 105, 133
Esterline Technologies Corp., **15** **155–57**
Eston Chemical, **6** 148
Estronicks, Inc., **19** 290
ETA Systems, Inc., **10** 256–57
Etablissement Mesnel, **I** 202
Etablissement Poulenc-Frères, **I** 388
Etablissements Badin-Defforey, **19** 98
Etablissements Braud. *See* Manitou BF S.A.
Etablissements Economiques du Casino Guichard, Perrachon et ie, S.C.A., **12** **152–54**; **16** 452
Etablissements Pierre Lemonnier S.A., **II** 532
Etablissements Robert Ouvrie S.A., **22** 436
Eteq Microsystems, **9** 116
Ethan Allen Interiors, Inc., **III** 530–31; **10** 184; **12** 307; **12** **155–57**
Ethical Personal Care Products, Ltd., **17** 108
Ethicon, Inc., **III** 35; **8** 281; **10** 213; **23** **188–90**
Ethyl Corp., **I** **334–36**, 342; **IV** 289; **10** **289–91 (upd.)**; **14** 217
Etienne Aigner, **14** 224
Etimex Kunstoffwerke GmbH, **7** 141
L'Etoile, **II** 139
Etos, **II** 641
ETPM Entrêpose, **IV** 468
Euclid, **I** 147; **12** 90
Euclid Chemical Co., **8** 455–56
Euclid Crane & Hoist Co., **13** 385
Euralux, **III** 209
Eurasbank, **II** 279–80; **14** 169
The Eureka Company, **III** 478, 480; **12** **158–60**; **15** 416; **22** 26. *See also* White Consolidated Industries Inc.
Eureka Insurance Co., **III** 343
Eureka Specialty Printing, **IV** 253; **17** 30
Eureka Technology, **18** 20
Eureka Tent & Awning Co., **III** 59
Eureka X-Ray Tube, Inc., **10** 272
Euris, **22** 365
Euro Disneyland SCA, **6** 174, 176; **20** **209–12**
Euro RSCG Worldwide S.A., **10** 345, 347; **13** **203–05**; **16** 168
Euro-Pacific Finance, **II** 389
Eurobel, **II** 139; **III** 200; **24** 193
Eurobrokers Investment Corp., **II** 457
Eurocan Pulp & Paper Co. Ltd., **III** 648; **IV** 276, 300
Eurocard France, **II** 265
Eurocom S.A. *See* Euro RSCG Worldwide S.A.
Eurocopter SA, **7** 9, 11; **21** 8
EuroDollar Rent A Car. *See* Republic Industries, Inc.
Eurofighter Jagdflugzeug GmbH, **24** 84
Eurofilter Airfilters Ltd., **17** 106
Eurogroup, **V** 65
Euroimpex, **18** 163
Euromarché SA, **10** 205; **19** 308–09; **23** 231; **27** 94–95
Euromarket Designs Inc., **9** 144; **31** **186–189 (upd.)**
Euromarket Designs Inc.,
Euromissile Dynamics Group, **7** 9; **24** 84
Euromoney Publications, **19** 118, 120
Euronda, **IV** 296; **19** 226
Euronova S.R.L., **15** 340
Europa Discount Sud-Ouest, **23** 248
Europa Metalli, **IV** 174
Europaischen Tanklager- und Transport AG, **7** 141
Europcar Chauffeur Drive U.K. International, **26** 62
Europcar International Corporation, Limited, **25** 142, 144, **27** 9, 11
Europcar Interrent, **10** 419
Europe Computer Systems. *See* ECS S.A.
Europe Craft Imports, Inc., **16** 37
European and African Investments Ltd., **IV** 21
European Banking Co., **II** 186
European Banks' International Co., **II** 184–86, 295
European Coal and Steel, **II** 402
European Gas Turbines, **13** 356
European Investment Bank, **6** 97
European Periodicals, Publicity and Advertising Corp., **IV** 641; **7** 311
European Petroleum Co., **IV** 562
European Retail Alliance (ERA), **12** 152–53
European Silicon Structures, **17** 34
European Software Company, **25** 87
European-American Bank & Trust Company, **14** 169
European-American Banking Corp., **II** 279, 295
Europeia, **III** 403
Europemballage, **I** 600
Europene du Zirconium (Cezus), **21** 491
Europensiones, **III** 348
Eurosar S.A., **25** 455
Eurotec, **IV** 128
Eurotech BV, **25** 101
Eurotechnique, **III** 678; **16** 122
Eurotunnel PLC, **13** **206–08**
Eurovida, **III** 348
Euthenics Systems Corp., **14** 334
EVA Airways Corporation, **13** 211
Evaluation Associates, Inc., **III** 306
Evan Picone, **III** 55
Evans, **V** 21
Evans & Sutherland Computer Corporation, **19** **145–49**
Evans, Inc., **30** **192–94**
Evans Products Co., **13** 249–50, 550
Evans Rents, **26** 101
Evans-Aristocrat Industries, **III** 570; **20** 361
Evansville Veneer and Lumber Co., **12** 296
Eve of Roma, **III** 28
Evelyn Haddon, **IV** 91
Evelyn Wood, Inc., **7** 165, 168
Evence Coppée, **III** 704–05
Evenflo Companies, Inc., **19** 144
Evening News Association, **IV** 612; **7** 191
Ever Ready Label Corp., **IV** 253; **17** 30
Ever Ready Ltd., **7** 209; **9** 179–80; **30** 231
Everan Capital Corp., **15** 257
Everest & Jennings, **11** 200
Everett Pulp & Paper Company, **17** 440
Everex Systems, Inc., **12** 162; **16** **194–96**
Everfresh Beverages Inc., **26** 326
Evergenius, **13** 210
Evergreen Healthcare, Inc., **14** 210
Evergreen Marine Corporation Taiwan Ltd., **13** **209–11**
Evergreen Media Corporation, **24** 106
Evergreen Resources, Inc., **11** 28
Everlaurel, **13** 210
Everready Battery Co., **13** 433
Eversharp, **III** 28
Everyday Learning Corporation, **22** 519, 522
Everything for the Office, **22** 154
Everything Yogurt, **25** 180
Everything's A Dollar Inc. (EAD), **13** 541–43
Evian, **6** 47, 49
Evinrude Motor Co., **III** 597–99
Evinrude Outboard Motor Company, **27** 75
Evinrude-ELTO, **III** 597
Ewell Industries, **III** 739
Ewo Breweries, **I** 469; **20** 311
Ex-Cell-O Corp., **IV** 297
Ex-Lax Inc., **15** 138–39
Exabyte Corporation, **12** **161–63**; **26** 256
Exacta, **III** 122
Exar Corp., **14** **182–84**
Exatec A/S, **10** 113
Excaliber, **6** 205
EXCEL Communications Inc., **18** **164–67**
Excel Corporation, **11** 92–93; **13** 138, 351
Excel Mining Systems, Inc., **13** 98
Excelsior Life Insurance Co., **III** 182; **21** 14
Excelsior Printing Company, **26** 105
Excerpta Medica International, **IV** 610
Exchange & Discount Bank, **II** 318; **17** 323
Exchange Bank of Yarmouth, **II** 210
Exchange Oil & Gas Corp., **IV** 282; **9** 260
Excite, Inc., **22** 519; **27** 517
Exco International, **10** 277
Execu-Fit Health Programs, **11** 379
Executive Aircraft Services, **27** 21
Executive Airlines, Inc., **28** 22
Executive Fund Life Insurance Company, **27** 47
Executive Gallery, Inc., **12** 264
Executive Income Life Insurance Co., **10** 246
Executive Life Insurance Co., **III** 253–55; **11** 483
Executive Systems, Inc., **11** 18
Executone Information Systems, Inc., **13** **212–14**; **15** 195
ExecuTrain. *See* International Data Group, Inc.
Executrans, Inc., **21** 96
Exel Logistics Ltd., **6** 412, 414
Exel Ltd., **13** 150
Exeter Oil Co., **IV** 550
Exide Electronics Group, Inc., **9** 10; **20** **213–15**; **24** 29
Exmark Manufacturing Company, Inc., **26** 494
Exors. of James Mills, **III** 493
Expeditors International of Washington Inc., **17** **163–65**
Expercom, **6** 303
Experian Inc., **28** 120
Experience, **III** 359
Exploitasi Tambang Minyak Sumatra Utara, **IV** 492

Explorer Motor Home Corp., **16** 296
Explosive Fabricators Corp., **III** 643
Export & Domestic Can Co., **15** 127
Export-Import Bank, **IV** 33, 184
Express Airlines, Inc., **28** 266
Express Baggage Reclaim Services Limited, **27** 21
Express Foods Inc, **I** 247–48
Express Newspapers plc, **IV** 687; **28** 503
Express Rent-a-Tire, Ltd., **20** 113
Express Scripts Incorporated, 17 166–68
Expression Homes, **22** 205, 207
Extel Corp., **II** 142; **III** 269–70
Extel Financial Ltd., **IV** 687
Extendicare Health Services, Inc., III 81; **6 181–83**
Extracorporeal Medical Specialties, **III** 36
Extron International Inc., **16** 538
Exxon Corporation, I 16–17, 360, 364; **II** 16, 62, 431, 451; **IV** 171, 363, 365, 403, 406, **426–30**, 431–33, 437–38, 454, 466, 506, 508, 512, 515, 522, 537–39, 554; **V** 605; **7 169–73 (upd.)**, 230, 538, 559; **9** 440–41; **11** 353; **14** 24–25, 291, 494; **12** 348; **16** 489, 548; **20** 262; **23** 317; **25** 229–30; **26** 102, 369; **27** 217
Eye Masters Ltd., **23** 329
Eyeful Home Co., **III** 758
Eyelab, **II** 560; **12** 411
EZ Paintr Corporation, **9** 374
EZPor Corporation, **12** 377

F. & F. Koenigkramer Company, **10** 272
F&G International Insurance, **III** 397
F. & J. Heinz, **II** 507
F & J Meat Packers, Inc., **22** 548–49
F & M Distributors, **12** 132
F. & M. Schaefer Brewing Corporation, **I** 253, 291, **III** 137; **18** 500
F & M Scientific Corp., **III** 142; **6** 237
F & R Builders, Inc., **11** 257
F.A. Computer Technologies, Inc., **12** 60
F.A. Ensign Company, **6** 38
F.A.I. Insurances, **III** 729
F.A.O. Schwarz, **I** 548
F. Atkins & Co., **I** 604
F.B. McFarren, Ltd., **21** 499–500
F.E. Compton Company, **7** 167
F. Egger Co., **22** 49
F.F. Dalley Co., **II** 497
F.F. Publishing and Broadsystem Ltd., **IV** 652; **7** 392
F.H. Tomkins Buckle Company Ltd., **11** 525
F. Hoffmann-La Roche & Co. A.G., I 637, 640, **642–44**, 657, 685, 693, 710; **7** 427; **9** 264; **10** 80, 549; **11** 424–25; **14** 406
F.J. Walker Ltd., **I** 438
F.K.I. Babcock, **III** 466
F. Kanematsu & Co., Ltd. *See* Kanematsu Corporation.
F.L. Industries Inc., **I** 481, 483
F.L. Moseley Co., **III** 142; **6** 237
F.N. Burt Co., **IV** 644
F. Perkins, **III** 651–52
F.S. Smithers, **II** 445; **22** 405
F.W. Dodge Corp., **IV** 636–37
F.W. Means & Company, **11** 337
F.W. Sickles Company, **10** 319
F.W. Williams Holdings, **III** 728
F.W. Woolworth & Co. Ltd. *See* Kingfisher plc.
F.W. Woolworth Co. *See* Woolworth Corporation.
F.X. Matt Brewing Co., **18** 72
Fab Industries, Inc., 27 142–44
Fab 9, **26** 431
Fab-Asia, Inc., **22** 354–55
Fabco Automotive Corp., **23** 306; **27** 203
Fabergé, Inc., **II** 590; **III** 48; **8** 168, 344; **11** 90
Fabri-Centers of America Inc., 15 329; **16 197–99**; **18** 223
Fabrica de Cemento El Melan, **III** 671
Facchin Foods Co., **I** 457
Facit, **III** 480; **22** 26
Facts on File, Inc., **14** 96–97; **22** 443
Fafnir Bearing Company, **13** 523
FAG Kugelfischer, **11** 84
Fagersta, **II** 366; **IV** 203
Fahr AG, **III** 543
Fahrzeugwerke Eisenach, **I** 138
FAI, **III** 545–46
Failsafe, **14** 35
Fair, Isaac and Company, 18 168–71, 516, 518
Fairbanks Morse Co., **I** 158, 434–35; **10** 292; **12** 71
Fairchild Aircraft, Inc., 9 205–08, 460; **11** 278
Fairchild Camera and Instrument Corp., **II** 50, 63; **III** 110, 141, 455, 618; **6** 261–62; **7** 531; **10** 108; **11** 503; **13** 323–24; **14** 14; **17** 418; **21** 122, 330; **26** 327
Fairchild Communications Service, **8** 328
Fairchild Industries, **I** 71, 198; **11** 438; **14** 43; **15** 195
Fairchild Semiconductor Corporation, **II** 44–45, 63–65; **III** 115; **6** 215, 247; **10** 365–66; **16** 332; **24** 235
Fairclough Construction Group plc, I 567–68
Fairey Industries Ltd., **IV** 659
Fairfax, **IV** 650
Fairfield Manufacturing Co., **14** 43
Fairfield Publishing, **13** 165
Fairmont Foods Co., **7** 430; **15** 139
Fairmont Insurance Co., **26** 487
Fairmount Glass Company, **8** 267
Fairport Machine Shop, Inc., **17** 357
Fairway Marketing Group, Inc., **24** 394
Falcon Oil Co., **IV** 396
Falcon Seaboard Inc., **II** 86; **IV** 410; **7** 309
Falconbridge, Ltd., **IV** 165–66
Falconbridge Nickel Mines Ltd., **IV** 111
Falconet Corp., **I** 45
Falley's, Inc., **17** 558, 560–61
Fallon McElligott Inc., 22 199–201
Falls Financial Inc., **13** 223; **31** 206
Falls National Bank of Niagara Falls, **11** 108
Falls Rubber Company, **8** 126
FAME Plastics, Inc., **18** 162
Family Bookstores, **24** 548
Family Channel. *See* International Family Entertainment Inc.
Family Dollar Stores, Inc., 13 215–17
Family Golf Centers, Inc., 29 183–85
Family Health Program, **6** 184
Family Life Insurance Co., **II** 425; **13** 341
Family Mart Company, **V** 188
Family Restaurants, Inc., **14** 194
Family Steak Houses of Florida, Inc., **15** 420
Famosa Bakery, **II** 543
Famous Amos Chocolate Chip Cookie Corporation, **27** 332
Famous Atlantic Fish Company, **20** 54
Famous Players-Lasky Corp., **I** 451; **II** 154; **6** 161–62; **23** 123
FAN, **13** 370
Fannie Mae. *See* Federal National Mortgage Association.
Fansteel Inc., 19 150–52
Fantastic Sam's, **26** 476
Fantle's Drug Stores, **16** 160
Fantus Co., **IV** 605
Fanuc Ltd., III 482–83; **17 172–74 (upd.)**
Fanzz, **29** 282
Faprena, **25** 85
Far East Airlines, **6** 70
Far East Machinery Co., **III** 581
Far Eastern Air Transport, Inc., **23** 380
Far West Restaurants, **I** 547
Faraday National Corporation, **10** 269
Farah Incorporated, 24 156–58
Farben. *See* I.G. Farbenindustrie AG.
Farbenfabriken Bayer A.G., **I** 309
Farberware, Inc., **27** 287–88
Farbwerke Hoechst A.G., **I** 346–47; **IV** 486; **13** 262
Farine Lactée Henri Nestlé, **II** 545
Farinon Corp., **II** 38
Farley Candy Co., **15** 190
Farley Industries, **25** 166
Farley Northwest Industries Inc., I 440–41
Farm Credit Bank of St. Louis, **8** 489
Farm Credit Bank of St. Paul, **8** 489–90
Farm Electric Services Ltd., **6** 586
Farm Fresh Foods, **25** 332
Farm Power Laboratory, **6** 565
Farmer Jack, **16** 247
Farmers and Mechanics Bank of Georgetown, **13** 439
Farmers and Merchants Bank, **II** 349
Farmers Bank of Delaware, **II** 315–16
Farmers Insurance Group of Companies, 23 286; **25 154–56**; **29** 397
Farmers' Loan and Trust Co., **II** 254; **9** 124
Farmers National Bank & Trust Co., **9** 474
Farmers Regional Cooperative, **II** 536
Farmland Foods, Inc., IV 474; **7** 17, **7 174–75**
Farnam Cheshire Lime Co., **III** 763
Farrar, Straus and Giroux Inc., IV 622, 624; **12** 223, 225; **15 158–60**
FASC. *See* First Analysis Securities Corporation.
Fasco Consumer Products, **19** 360
Fasco Industries, **III** 509; **13** 369
Faserwerke Hüls GmbH., **I** 350
Fashion Bar, Inc., **24** 457
Fashion Bug, **8** 97
Fashion Co., **II** 503; **10** 324
Fasquelle, **IV** 618
Fasson. *See* Avery Dennison Corporation.
Fast Air, **31** 305
Fast Fare, **7** 102
Fastenal Company, 14 185–87
Fata European Group, **IV** 187; **19** 348
Fateco Förlag, **14** 556
FATS, Inc., **27** 156, 158
Fatum, **III** 308
Faugere et Jutheau, **III** 283
Faulkner, Dawkins & Sullivan, **II** 450
Fauquet, **25** 85

Favorite Plastics, **19** 414
Fawcett Books, **13** 429
Fay's Inc., 17 175–77
Fayette Tubular Products, **7** 116–17
Fayva, **13** 359–61
Fazoli's Systems, Inc., **13** 321; **27 145–47**
FB&T Corporation, **14** 154
FBC. *See* First Boston Corp.
FBO. *See* Film Booking Office of America.
FC Holdings, Inc., **26** 363
FCBC, **IV** 174
FCC. *See* Federal Communications Commission.
FCC National Bank, **II** 286
FCI. *See* Framatome SA.
FDIC. *See* Federal Deposit Insurance Corp.
Fearn International, **II** 525; **13** 293
Feather Fine, **27** 361
Featherlite Inc., **28 127–29**
Feature Enterprises Inc., **19** 452
Fechheimer Bros. Co., **III** 215; **18** 60, 62
Fedders Corp., **18 172–75**
Federal Barge Lines, **6** 487
Federal Bearing and Bushing, **I** 158–59
Federal Bicycle Corporation of America, **11** 3
Federal Cartridge, **26** 363
Federal Coca-Cola Bottling Co., **10** 222
Federal Communications Commission, **6** 164–65; **9** 321
Federal Deposit Insurance Corp., **II** 261–62, 285, 337; **12** 30, 79
Federal Electric, **I** 463; **III** 653
Federal Express Corporation, **II** 620; **V 451–53**; **6** 345–46, 385–86, 389; **12** 180, 192; **13** 19; **14** 517; **17** 504–05; **18** 315–17, 368, 370; **24** 22, 133; **25** 148; **26** 441; **27** 20, 22, 471, 475. *See also* FedEx Corporation.
Federal Home Life Insurance Co., **III** 263; **IV** 623
Federal Home Loan Bank, **II** 182
Federal Home Loan Mortgage Corp., **18** 168; **25** 427
Federal Insurance Co., **III** 220–21; **14** 108–109
Federal Lead Co., **IV** 32
Federal Light and Traction Company, **6** 561–62
Federal Mining and Smelting Co., **IV** 32
Federal National Mortgage Association, **II 410–11**; **18** 168; **25** 427
Federal Pacific Electric, **II** 121; **9** 440
Federal Packaging and Partition Co., **8** 476
Federal Packaging Corp., **19** 78
Federal Paper Board Company, Inc., **I** 524; **8 173–75**; **15** 229
Federal Paper Mills, **IV** 248
Federal Power, **18** 473
Federal Reserve Bank of New York, **21** 68
Federal Savings and Loan Insurance Corp., **16** 346
Federal Signal Corp., **10 295–97**
Federal Steel Co., **II** 330; **IV** 572; **7** 549
Federal Trade Commission, **6** 260; **9** 370
Federal Yeast Corp., **IV** 410
Federal-Mogul Corporation, **I 158–60**; **III** 596; **10 292–94 (upd.)**; **26 139–43 (upd.)**
Federale Mynbou, **IV** 90–93
Federated Department Stores Inc., **IV** 703; **V** 25–28; **9 209–12**; **10** 282; **11** 349; **12** 37, 523; **13** 43, 260; **15** 88; **16** 61, 206; **17** 560; **18** 523; **22** 406; **23** 60; **27** 346–48; **30** 379; **31 190–194 (upd.)**
Federated Development Company, **8** 349
Federated Metals Corp., **IV** 32
Federated Publications, **IV** 612; **7** 191
Federated Timbers, **I** 422
Fédération Internationale de Football Association, **27 148–51**
Federation Nationale d'Achats des Cadres. *See* FNAC.
FedEx Corporation, **18** 128, **176–79 (upd.)**, 535
Fedmart, **V** 162
FEE Technology, **29** 461–62
Feed-Rite Controls, Inc., **16** 270
Feffer & Simons, **16** 46
Feikes & Sohn KG, **IV** 325
Feinblech-Contiglühe, **IV** 103
Felco. *See* Farmers Regional Cooperative.
Feldmühle Nobel AG, **II** 50–51; **III 692–95**; **IV** 142, 325, 337; **21** 330
Felixstowe Ltd., **18** 254
Fellowes Manufacturing Company, **28 130–32**
Felten & Guilleaume, **IV** 25
Femsa, **19** 473. *See also* Formento Económico Mexicano, S.A. de C.V.
Femtech, **8** 513
Fendel Schiffahrts-Aktiengesellschaft, **6** 426
Fender Musical Instruments Company, **16 200–02**
Fenestra Inc., **IV** 136
Fenicia Group, **22** 320
Fenn, Wright & Manson, **25** 121–22
Fenner & Beane, **II** 424
Fenton Hill American Limited, **29** 510
Fenwal Laboratories, **I** 627; **10** 141
Ferembal S.A., **25** 512
Ferfin, **24** 341
Fergus Brush Electric Company, **18** 402
Ferguson Machine Co., **8** 135
Ferguson Manufacturing Company, **25** 164
Ferguson Radio Corp., **I** 531–32
Ferienreise GmbH., **II** 164
Fermentaciones Mexicanas, **III** 43
Fernando Roqué, **6** 404; **26** 243
Ferngas, **IV** 486
Ferolito, Vultaggio & Sons, **27 152–55**
Ferranti Business Communications, **20** 75
Ferranti Ltd., **II** 81; **6** 240
Ferrari S.p.A., **I** 162; **11** 103; **13 218–20**
Ferrier Hodgson, **10** 170
Ferro Corporation, **III** 536; **8 176–79**; **9** 10; **26** 230
Ferro Engineering Co., **17** 357
Ferroxcube Corp. of America, **13** 397
Ferrum Inc., **24** 144
Ferruzzi Agricola Finanziario, **I** 369; **7** 81–83
Ferruzzi Finanziaria S.p.A., **24** 341
Fesca, **III** 417–18
Fetzer Vineyards, **10** 182
FHP International Corporation, **6 184–86**; **17** 166, 168
Fianzas Monterrey, **19** 189
Fiat S.p.A., **I** 154, 157, **161–63**, 459–60, 466, 479; **II** 280; **III** 206, 543, 591; **IV** 420; **9** 10; **11 102–04 (upd.)**, 139; **13** 17, 27–29, 218–20; **16** 322; **17** 24; **22** 379–81
Fibamex, **17** 106
Fiber Chemical Corporation, **7** 308
Fiberglas Canada, **III** 722
Fiberite, Inc., **27** 117; **28** 195
Fibermux Corporation, **10** 19; **30** 7
Fibic Corp., **18** 118
Fibre Containers, **IV** 249
Fibreboard Corporation, **IV** 304; **12** 318; **14** 110; **16 203–05**
FibreChem, Inc., **8** 347
Fibro Tambor, S.A. de C.V., **8** 476
Fichtel & Sachs AG, **III** 566; **14** 328
Fidata Corp., **II** 317
Fidelco Capital Group, **10** 420
Fidelio Software GmbH, **18** 335, 337
Fidelity and Casualty Co. of New York, **III** 242
Fidelity and Guaranty Life Insurance Co., **III** 396–97
Fidelity Federal Savings and Loan, **II** 420
Fidelity Fire Insurance Co., **III** 240
Fidelity Insurance of Canada, **III** 396–97
Fidelity Investments Inc., **II 412–13**; **III** 588; **8** 194; **9** 239; **14 188–90 (upd.)**; **18** 552; **19** 113; **21** 147; **22** 52. *See also* FMR Corp.
Fidelity Life Association, **III** 269
Fidelity Mutual Insurance Co., **III** 231
Fidelity National Life Insurance Co., **III** 191
Fidelity National Title, **19** 92
Fidelity Oil Group, **7** 324
Fidelity Title and Trust Co., **II** 315
Fidelity Trust Co., **II** 230
Fidelity Union Life Insurance Co., **III** 185
Fidelity-Phenix Fire Insurance Co., **III** 240–42
Fidenas Investment Ltd., **30** 185
Fides Holding, **21** 146
Field Corporation, **18** 355
Field Enterprises Educational Corporation, **16** 252; **26** 15
Field Enterprises, Inc., **IV** 672; **12** 554; **19** 404
Field Group plc, **30** 120
Field Limited Partnership, **22** 441
Field Oy, **10** 113
Fieldale Farms Corporation, **23 191–93**; **25** 185–86
Fieldcrest Cannon, Inc., **8** 32–33; **9 213–17**; **16** 535; **19** 276, 305; **31 195–200 (upd.)**
Fieldstone Cabinetry, **III** 571; **20** 362
Fielmann AG, **31 201–03**
FIFA. *See* Fédération Internationale de Football Association.
Fifteen Oil, **I** 526
Fifth Generation Systems Inc., **10** 509
Fifth Third Bancorp, **II** 291; **9** 475; **11** 466; **13 221–23**; **31 204–208 (upd.)**
50-Off Stores, **23** 177. *See also* LOT$OFF Corporation.
Figgie International Inc., **7 176–78**; **24** 403–04
Figi's Inc., **9** 218, 220
Fil-Mag Group, **29** 461
Fila Holding S.p.A., **20 216–18**
Filene's, **V** 132, 134
Filergie S.A., **15** 355
Filipacchi Medias S.A. *See* Hachette Filipacchi Medias S.A.
Filiz Lastex, S.A., **15** 386
Filles S.A. de C.V., **7** 115; **25** 126
Film Booking Office of America, **II** 88
Films for the Humanities, Inc., **22** 441
Filter Queen-Canada, **17** 234
Filtertek, Inc., **24** 425

Filtrol Corp., **IV** 123
Filtrona International Ltd., **31** 77
Filtros Baldwin de Mexico, **17** 106
Filtros Continental, **17** 106
Fimaser, **21** 101
Fimestic, **21** 101
Fin. Comit SpA, **II** 192
FINA, Inc., 7 179–81; **26** 368
Financial Computer Services, Inc., **11** 111
Financial Corp. of Indonesia, **II** 257
Financial Data Services, Inc., **11** 111
Financial Investment Corp. of Asia, **III** 197
Financial Network Marketing Company, **11** 482
Financial News Ltd., **IV** 658
Financial News Network, Inc., **25** 507; **31** 147
Financial Security Assurance Inc., **III** 765; **25** 497
Financial Services Corp., **III** 306–07
Financial Services Corporation of Michigan, **11** 163
Financial Systems, Inc., **11** 111
Financial Technologies International, **17** 497
Financiera Aceptaciones, **19** 189
Financière Crédit Suisse-First Boston, **II** 268, 402–04
Financiere de Suez, **II** 295
Financière Saint Dominique, **9** 151–52
FinansSkandic A.B., **II** 352–53
Finast. *See* First National Supermarkets, Inc.
Fincantieri, **I** 466–67
Find-A-Home Service, Inc., **21** 96
Findomestic, **21** 101
Findus, **II** 547; **25** 85
Fine Art Developments Ltd., **15** 340
Fine Fare, **II** 465, 609, 628–29
Fine Fragrances, **22** 213
Finelettrica, **I** 465–66
Finevest Services Inc., **15** 526
Fingerhut Companies, Inc., I 613; **V** 148; **9 218–20**; **15** 401; **18** 133; **31** 190
Fininvest Group, **IV** 587–88
The Finish Line, Inc., 29 186–88
FinishMaster, Inc., 17 310–11; **24 159–61**
Finland Wood Co., **IV** 275
Finlay Enterprises, Inc., 16 206–08
Finlay Forest Industries, **IV** 297
Finmare, **I** 465, 467
Finmeccanica S.p.A., **II** 86; **13** 28; **23** 83
Finnair Oy, I 120; **6 87–89**; **25 157–60 (upd.)**
Finnforest Oy, **IV** 316
Finnigan Corporation, **11** 513
Finnish Cable Works, **II** 69; **17** 352
Finnish Fiberboard Ltd., **IV** 302
Oy Finnish Peroxides Ab, **IV** 300
Finnish Rubber Works, **II** 69; **17** 352
Oy Finnlines Ltd., **IV** 276
Finsa, **II** 196
FinSer Capital Corporation, **17** 262
Finservizi SpA, **II** 192
Finsider, **I** 465–66; **IV** 125
Firan Motor Coach, Inc., **17** 83
Fire Association of Philadelphia, **III** 342–43
Firearms Training Systems, Inc., 27 156–58
Fireman's Fund Insurance Company, I 418; **II** 398, 457; **III** 214, **250–52**, 263; **10** 62
Firemen's Insurance Co. of Newark, **III** 241–42
Firestone Tire and Rubber Co., **III** 440, 697; **V** 234–35; **8** 80; **9** 247; **15** 355; **17** 182; **18** 320; **20** 259–62; **21** 73–74
Firma Hamburger Kaffee-Import-Geschäft Emil Tengelmann. *See* Tengelmann Group.
The First, **10** 340
First Acadiana National Bank, **11** 107
First Alert, Inc., 28 133–35
First American Bank Corporation, **8** 188
First American Media, Inc., **24** 199
First American National Bank, **19** 378
First American National Bank-Eastern, **11** 111
First Analysis Securities Corporation, **22** 5
First and Merchants, **10** 426
First Atlanta Corporation, **16** 523
First Atlantic Capital, Ltd., **28** 340, 342
First Bancard, Inc., **11** 106
First BanCorporation, **13** 467
First Bank and Trust of Mechanicsburg, **II** 342
First Bank of Savannah, **16** 522
First Bank of the United States, **II** 213, 253
First Bank System Inc., 11 130; **12 164–66**; **13** 347–48; **24** 393
First Boston Corp., **II** 208, 257, 267–69, 402–04, 406–07, 426, 434, 441; **9** 378, 386; **12** 439; **13** 152, 342; **21** 145–46. *See also* CSFB.
First Brands Corporation, 8 180–82; **16** 44
First Capital Financial, **8** 229
First Carolina Investors Inc., **17** 357
First Chicago Corporation, II 284–87
First Chicago Venture Capital, **24** 516
First City Bank of Rosemead, **II** 348
First Colony Farms, **II** 584
First Colony Life Insurance, **I** 334–35; **10** 290
First Commerce Bancshares, Inc., 15 161–63
First Commerce Corporation, 11 105–07
First Commercial Savings and Loan, **10** 340
First Consumers National Bank, **10** 491; **27** 429
First Dallas, Ltd., **II** 415
First Data Corporation, 10 63; **18** 516–18, 537; **24** 393 **30 195–98 (upd.)**
First Data Management Company of Oklahoma City, **11** 112
First Delaware Life Insurance Co., **III** 254
First Deposit Corp., **III** 218–19
First Empire State Corporation, 11 108–10
First Engine and Boiler Insurance Co. Ltd., **III** 406
First Executive Corporation, III 253–55
First Federal Savings & Loan Assoc., **IV** 343; **9** 173
First Federal Savings and Loan Association of Crisp County, **10** 92
First Federal Savings and Loan Association of Hamburg, **10** 91
First Federal Savings and Loan Association of Fort Myers, **9** 476
First Federal Savings and Loan Association of Kalamazoo, **9** 482
First Federal Savings Bank of Brunswick, **10** 92
First Fidelity Bank, N.A., New Jersey, 9 221–23
First Fidelity Bank of Rockville, **13** 440
First Financial Management Corporation, 11 111–13; **18** 542; **25** 183; **30** 195
First Florida Banks, **9** 59
First Hawaiian, Inc., 11 114–16
First Health, **III** 373
FIRST HEALTH Strategies, **11** 113
First Healthcare, **14** 242
First Heights, fsa, **8** 437
First Hospital Corp., **15** 122
First Industrial Corp., **II** 41
First Insurance Agency, Inc., **17** 527
First Insurance Co. of Hawaii, **III** 191, 242
First International Trust, **IV** 91
First Interstate Bancorp, II 228, **288–90**; **8** 295; **9** 334; **17** 546
First Investment Advisors, **11** 106
First Investors Management Corp., **11** 106
First Jersey National Bank, **II** 334
First Liberty Financial Corporation, **11** 457
First Line Insurance Services, Inc., **8** 436
First Madison Bank, **14** 192
First Maryland Bancorp, **16** 14
First Mid America, **II** 445; **22** 406
First Mississippi Corporation, 8 183–86. *See also* ChemFirst, Inc.
First Mississippi National, **14** 41
First National Bank, **10** 298; **13** 467
First National Bank (Revere), **II** 208
First National Bank and Trust Company, **22** 4
First National Bank and Trust Company of Kalamazoo, **8** 187–88
First National Bank and Trust of Oklahoma City, **II** 289
First National Bank in Albuquerque, **11** 119
First National Bank of Akron, **9** 475
First National Bank of Allentown, **11** 296
First National Bank of Atlanta, **16** 522
First National Bank of Azusa, **II** 382
First National Bank of Boston, **II** 207–08, 402; **12** 310; **13** 446
First National Bank of Carrollton, **9** 475
First National Bank of Chicago, **II** 242, 257, 284–87; **III** 96–97; **IV** 135–36
First National Bank of Commerce, **11** 106
First National Bank of Harrington, Delaware. *See* J.C. Penny National Bank.
First National Bank of Hartford, **13** 466
First National Bank of Hawaii, **11** 114
First National Bank of Highland, **11** 109
First National Bank of Houma, **21** 522
The First National Bank of Lafayette, **11** 107
The First National Bank of Lake Charles, **11** 107
First National Bank of Lake City, **II** 336; **10** 425
First National Bank of Mexico, New York, **II** 231
First National Bank of Minneapolis, **22** 426–27
First National Bank of New York, **II** 254, 330
First National Bank of Raleigh, **II** 336

First National Bank of Salt Lake, **11** 118
First National Bank of Seattle, **8** 469–70
First National Bank of York, **II** 317
First National Bankshares, Inc., **21** 524
First National Boston Corp., **II** 208
First National Casualty Co., **III** 203
First National City Bank, **9** 124; **16** 13
First National City Bank of New York, **II** 254; **9** 124
First National City Corp., **III** 220–21
First National Holding Corporation, **16** 522
First National Insurance Co., **III** 352
First National Life Insurance Co., **III** 218
First National Supermarkets, Inc., **II** 641–42; **9** 452
First Nationwide Bank, 8 30; **14 191–93**
First Nationwide Financial Corp., **I** 167; **11** 139
First Nationwide Holdings Inc., **28** 246
First New England Bankshares Corp., **13** 467
First Nitrogen, Inc., **8** 184
First of America Bank Corporation, 8 187–89
First of America Bank-Monroe, **9** 476
First of Boston, **II** 402–03
First Omni Bank NA, **16** 14; **18** 518
First Pacific Company Limited, 18 180–82
First Penn-Pacific Life Insurance Co., **III** 276
First Pick Stores, **12** 458
First Railroad and Banking Company, **11** 111
First Republic Bank of Texas, **II** 336
First Republic Corp., **III** 383; **14** 483
First RepublicBank Corporation, **II** 337; **10** 425–26
First Savings and Loan, **10** 339
First Seattle Dexter Horton National Bank, **8** 470
First Security Corporation, 11 117–19
First Signature Bank and Trust Co., **III** 268
1st State Bank & Trust, **9** 474
First SunAmerican Life Insurance Company, **11** 482
First Team Sports, Inc., 15 396–97; **22 202–04**
First Tennessee National Corporation, 11 120–21
First Texas Pharmaceuticals, **I** 678
First Trust and Savings Bank, **II** 284
First Trust Bank, **16** 14
First Union Corporation, 10 298–300; **24** 482
First Union Trust and Savings Bank, **II** 284–85; **11** 126; **22** 52
First United Financial Services Inc., **II** 286
First USA, Inc., 11 122–24
First USA Paymentech, **24** 393
First Virginia Banks, Inc., 11 125–26
First Westchester National Bank of New Rochelle, **II** 236
First Western Bank and Trust Co., **II** 289
First Women's Bank of New York, **23** 3
First Worth Corporation, **19** 232
Firstamerica Bancorporation, **II** 288–89
Firstar Corporation, 11 127–29
FirstBancorp., **13** 467
FirstMiss, Inc., **8** 185
Firth Carpet, **19** 275
Fischbach & Moore, **III** 535
Fischbach Corp., **III** 198; **8** 536–37
FISCOT, **10** 337
Fiserv Inc., 11 130–32
Fisher & Company, **9** 16
Fisher Body Company, **I** 171; **10** 325
Fisher Broadcasting Co., **15** 164
Fisher Companies, Inc., 15 164–66
Fisher Controls International, Inc., 13 224–26; 15 405, 407; **29** 330
Fisher Corp., **II** 92
Fisher Foods, Inc., **II** 602; **9** 451, 452; **13** 237
Fisher Marine, **III** 444; **22** 116
Fisher Nut, **14** 275
Fisher Scientific International Inc., III 511–12; **24 162–66; 25** 260
Fisher-Camuto Corp., **14** 441
Fisher-Price Inc., II 559–60; **12 167–69,** 410–11; **13** 317; **25** 314, 380
Fishers Agricultural Holdings, **II** 466
Fishers Nutrition, **II** 466
Fishers Seed and Grain, **II** 466
Fishery Department of Tamura Kisen Co., **II** 552
Fisk Telephone Systems, **6** 313
Fisons plc, 9 224–27; 23 194–97 (upd.)
Fitch Lovell PLC, **13** 103
Fitchburg Daily News Co., **IV** 581
Fitchell and Sachs, **III** 495
Fitel, **III** 491
Fitzsimmons Stores Inc., **16** 452
Fitzwilton Public Limited Company, **12** 529
Five Bros. Inc., **19** 456
Five Star Entertainment Inc., **28** 241
FKM Advertising, **27** 280
FL Industries Holdings, Inc., **11** 516
Flachglass A.G., **II** 474
Flagship Resources, **22** 495
Flagstar Companies, Inc., 10 301–03; 29 150. *See also* Advantica Restaurant Group, Inc.
Flair Corporation, **18** 467
Flair Fold, **25** 11
Flanagan McAdam Resources Inc., **IV** 76
Flapdoodles, **15** 291
Flatbush Gas Co., **6** 455–56
Flatiron Mandolin Company, **16** 239
Flatow, Moore, Bryan, and Fairburn, **21** 33
Fleck Controls, Inc., **26** 361, 363
Fleer Corporation, 10 402; **13** 519; **15 167–69; 19** 386
Fleet Call, Inc., **10** 431–32
Fleet Financial Group, Inc., IV 687; **9 228–30; 12** 31; **13** 468; **18** 535
Fleet Holdings, **28** 503
Fleetway, **7** 244
Fleetwood Enterprises, Inc., III 484–85; 13 155; **17** 83; **21** 153; **22 205–08 (upd.)**
Fleischmann Co., **II** 544; **7** 367
Fleischmann Malting Co., **I** 420–21; **11** 22
Fleming Companies, Inc., II 624–25, 671; **7** 450; **12** 107, 125; **13** 335–37; **17 178–81 (upd.); 18** 506–07; **23** 407; **24** 529; **26** 449; **28** 152, 154; **31** 25
Fleming Foodservice, **26** 504
Fleming Machine Co., **III** 435
Fleming-Wilson Co., **II** 624
Fletcher Challenge Ltd., III 687; **IV** 250, **278–80; 19 153–57 (upd.); 25** 12
Fleuve Noir, **IV** 614
Flex Elektrowerkzeuge GmbH, **26** 363
Flex Interim, **16** 421
Flex-O-Lite, **14** 325
Flexi-Van Corporations, **II** 492; **20** 118
Flexible Packaging, **I** 605
Flexsteel Industries Inc., 15 170–72
Flextronics Inc., **12** 451
Flexys, **16** 462
FLGI Holding Company, **10** 321
Flick Industrial Group, **II** 280, 283; **III** 692–95
Flight One Logistics, Inc., **22** 311
Flight Refuelling Limited. *See* Cobham plc.
Flight Transportation Co., **II** 408
FlightSafety International, Inc., 9 231–33; 29 189–92 (upd.)
Flint and Walling Water Systems, **III**.570; **20** 362
Flint Eaton & Co., **I** 627
Flint Ink Corporation, 13 227–29
Floral City Furniture Company, **14** 302–03
Flori Roberts, Inc., **11** 208
Florida Cypress Gardens, Inc., **IV** 623
Florida Distillers Company, **27** 479
Florida East Coast Railway Company, **8** 486–87; **12** 278
Florida Frozen Foods, **13** 244
Florida Gas Co., **15** 129
Florida Gas Transmission Company, **6** 578
Florida National Banks of Florida, Inc., **II** 252
Florida Presbyterian College, **9** 187
Florida Progress Corp., V 621–22; 23 198–200 (upd.)
Florida Rock Industries Inc., **23** 326
Florida Steel Corp., **14** 156
Florida Telephone Company, **6** 323
FloridaGulf Airlines, **11** 300
Florimex Verwaltungsgesellschaft mbH, **12** 109
Florists' Transworld Delivery, Inc., 28 136–38
Florsheim Shoe Group Inc., III 528–29; **9** 135, **234–36; 12** 308; **16** 546; **31 209–212 (upd.)**
Flow Laboratories, **14** 98
Flow Measurement, **26** 293
Flower Gate Inc., **I** 266; **21** 320
Flower Time, Inc., **12** 179, 200
Flowers Industries, Inc., 12 170–71; 29 340
Floyd West & Co., **6** 290
Fluent, Inc., **29** 4–6
Fluf N'Stuf, Inc., **12** 425
Fluke Corporation, 15 173–75
Fluor Corporation, I 569–71, 586; **III** 248; **IV** 171, 533, 535, 576; **6** 148–49; **8 190–93 (upd.); 12** 244; **26** 220, 433
The Fluorocarbon Company. *See* Furon Company.
Flushing Federal Savings & Loan Association, **16** 346
Flushing National Bank, **II** 230
Flying J Inc., 19 158–60
Flying Tiger Line, **V** 452; **6** 388; **25** 146
Flymo, **III** 478, 480; **22** 26
FMC Corp., I 442–44, 679; **II** 513; **11 133–35 (upd.); 14** 457; **22** 415; **30** 471
FMR Corp., II 412; **8 194–96; 14** 188; **22** 413; **30** 331
FMXI, Inc. *See* Foamex International Inc.
FN Life Insurance Co., **III** 192
FN Manufacturing Co., **12** 71
FNAC, 21 224–26; 26 160
FNC Comercio, **III** 221
FNCB. *See* First National City Bank of New York.

FNMA. *See* Federal National Mortgage Association.
FNN. *See* Financial News Network.
Foamex International Inc., 17 182–85; 26 500
Focal Surgery, Inc., **27** 355
Focke-Wulf, **III** 641; **16** 7
Fodens Ltd., **I** 186
Fodor's Travel Guides, **13** 429
Fokker. *See* N.V. Koninklijke Nederlandse Vliegtuigenfabriek Fokker.
Fokker Aircraft Corporation of America, **9** 16
Fokker-VFW, **I** 41–42; **12** 191
Foley & Lardner, 28 139–42
Folgers, **III** 52
Folland Aircraft, **I** 50; **III** 508; **24** 85
Follett Corporation, 12 172–74; 16 47
Follis DeVito Verdi. *See* De Vito/Verdi.
Fomento de Valores, S.A. de C.V., **23** 170
Fomento Economico Mexicano, S.A. de C.V. *See* Femsa.
Fondiaria Group, **III** 351
Fonditalia Management, **III** 347
Font & Vaamonde, **6** 27
Font Vella, **II** 474
FONTAC, **II** 73
Fontana Asphalt, **III** 674
Food City, **II** 649–50
Food Fair, **19** 480
Food 4 Less Supermarkets, Inc., **II** 624; **17** 558–61
Food Giant, **II** 670
Food Ingredients Technologies, **25** 367
Food Investments Ltd., **II** 465
Food King, **20** 306
Food Lion, Inc., II 626–27; 7 450; **15 176–78 (upd.)**, 270; **18** 8; **21** 508
Food Machinery Corp. *See* FMC Corp.
Food Marketing Corp., **II** 668; **18** 504
Food Town Inc., **II** 626–27
Food World, **26** 46; **31** 372
Foodarama Supermarkets, Inc., 28 143–45
FoodBrands America, Inc., 21 290; **22** 510; **23 201–04.** *See also* Doskocil Companies, Inc.
FoodLand Distributors, **II** 625, 645, 682
Foodmaker, Inc., II 562; **13** 152, 426; **14 194–96**
Foodstuffs, **9** 144
Foodtown, **II** 626; **V** 35; **15** 177; **24** 528
Foodways National, Inc., **12** 531; **13** 383
Foot Locker, **V** 226; **14** 293–95
Footaction. *See* Footstar, Incorporated.
Foote Cone & Belding Communications Inc., I 12–15, 28, 34; **11** 51; **13** 517; **22** 395; **25** 90–91. *See also* True North Communications Inc.
Foote Mineral Company, **7** 386–87
Footquarters, **14** 293, 295
Footstar, Incorporated, 24 167–69
Forages et Exploitations Pétrolières. *See* Forex.
Forbes Inc., 30 199–201
Ford Motor Company, I 10, 14, 20–21, 136, 142, 145, 152, 154–55, 162–63, **164–68**, 172, 183, 186, 201, 203–04, 280, 297, 337, 354, 423, 478, 484, 540, 693; **II** 7–8, 33, 60, 86, 143, 415; **III** 58, 259, 283, 439, 452, 495, 515, 555, 568, 591, 603, 637–38, 651, 725; **IV** 22, 187, 597, 722; **6** 27, 51; **7** 377, 461, 520–21; **8** 70, 74–75, 117, 372–73, 375, 505–06; **9** 94, 118, 126, 190, 283–84, 325, 341–43; **10** 32, 241, 260, 264–65, 279–80, 290, 353, 407, 430, 460, 465; **11** 53–54, 103–04, **136–40 (upd.)**, 263, 326, 339, 350, 528–29; **12** 68, 91, 294, 311; **13** 28, 219, 285, 287, 345, 555; **14** 191–92; **15** 91, 171, 513, 515; **16** 321–22; **17** 183, 303–04; **18** 112, 308, 319; **19** 11, 125, 221, 223, 482, 484; **20** 359; **21** 153, 200, 503; **22** 175, 380–81; **23** 143, 339–41, 434; **24** 12; **25** 90, 93, 142–43, 224, 226, 358; **26** 176, 452, 501; **27** 20, 202; **29** 265
Ford Motor Company, S.A. de C.V., 20 219–21
Ford New Holland, Inc. *See* New Holland N.V.
Ford Transport Co., **I** 112; **6** 103
Fordyce Lumber Co., **IV** 281; **9** 259
FORE Systems, Inc., 25 161–63
Forefront Communications, **22** 194
Foreman State Banks, **II** 285
Foremost Dairy of California, **I** 496–97
Foremost Warehouse Corp., **14** 372
Foremost-McKesson Inc., **I** 496–97, **III** 10; **11** 211; **12** 332
Forenza, **V** 116
Forest City Auto Parts, **23** 491
Forest City Enterprises, Inc., 16 209–11
Forest City Ratner Companies, **17** 318
Forest E. Olson, Inc., **21** 96
Forest Laboratories, Inc., 11 141–43
Forest Oil Corporation, 19 161–63
Forest Products, **III** 645
Forestry Corporation of New Zealand, **19** 156
Företagsfinans, **25** 464
Forethought Group, Inc., **10** 350
Forever Living Products International Inc., 17 186–88
Forex Chemical Corp., **I** 341; **14** 216; **17** 418
Forex-Neptune, **III** 617
Forge Books. *See* Tom Doherty Associates Inc.
Forges d'Eich–Le Gallais, Metz et Cie, **IV** 24; **22** 42
Forges de la Providence, **IV** 52
Formento Económico Mexicano, S.A. de C.V., **25** 279, 281
Formica Corporation, 10 269; **13 230–32**
Forming Technology Co., **III** 569; **20** 361
Formonix, **20** 101
Formosa Plastics Corporation, 11 159; **14 197–99; 16** 194, 196
Formosa Plastics Group, **31** 108
Formosa Springs, **I** 269; **12** 337
Formularios y Procedimientos Moore, **IV** 645
Formule 1, **13** 364; **27** 10
Forney Fiber Company, **8** 475
Forsakrings A.B. Volvia, **I** 20
Forstmann Little & Co., **I** 446, 483; **II** 478, 544; **III** 56; **7** 206; **10** 321; **12** 344, 562; **14** 166; **16** 322; **19** 372–73, 432; **22** 32, 60; **30** 426
Fort Associates, **I** 418
Fort Bend Utilities Company, **12** 269
Fort Dummer Mills, **III** 213
Fort Garry Brewery, **26** 304
Fort Howard Corporation, 8 197–99; 15 305; **22** 209. *See also* Fort James Corporation.
Fort James Corporation, 22 209–12 (upd.); 29 136
Fort Mill Manufacturing Co., **V** 378
Fort William Power Co., **IV** 246; **25** 10
Forte Plc, **15** 46; **16** 446; **24** 195; **29** 443
Forte's Holdings Ltd., **III** 104–05
Fortis, Inc., 15 179–82
Fortum Corporation, 30 202–07 (upd.)
Fortun Foods, **26** 59
Fortuna Coffee Co., **I** 451
Fortune Brands, Inc., 19 168; **29 193–97 (upd.)**
Fortune Enterprises, **12** 60
Fortunoff Fine Jewelry and Silverware Inc., 26 144–46
Forum Cafeterias, **19** 299–300
Forum Hotels, **I** 248
Foseco plc, **IV** 383
Foss Maritime Co., **9** 509, 511
Fossil, Inc., 17 189–91
Foster & Kleiser, **7** 335; **14** 331
Foster & Marshall, **II** 398; **10** 62
Foster and Braithwaite, **III** 697
Foster Forbes, **16** 123
Foster Grant, **I** 670; **II** 595–96; **12** 214
Foster Management Co., **11** 366–67
Foster Medical Corp., **III** 16; **11** 282
Foster Sand & Gravel, **14** 112
Foster Wheeler Corporation, I 82; **6 145–47; 23 205–08 (upd.); 25** 82
Foster's Brewing Group Ltd., 7 182–84; 21 227–30 (upd.); 26 303, 305–06
Fotomat Corp., **III** 549
Fougerolle, **27** 136, 138
Foundation Computer Systems, Inc., **13** 201
Foundation Fieldbus, **22** 373
Foundation Health Corporation, 11 174; **12 175–77**
Founders Equity Inc., **14** 235
Founders of American Investment Corp., **15** 247
Fountain Powerboats Industries, Inc., 28 146–48
Four Seasons Hotels Inc., II 531; **9 237–38; 29 198–200 (upd.)**
Four Seasons Nursing Centers, Inc., **6** 188; **25** 308
Four Winds, **21** 153
Four Winns, **III** 600
Four-Phase Systems, Inc., **II** 61; **11** 327
Fournier Furniture, Inc., **12** 301
4P, **30** 396–98
Fourth Financial Corporation, 11 144–46; 15 60
Foussard Associates, **I** 333
Fowler Road Construction Proprietary, **III** 672
Fowler-Waring Cables Co., **III** 162
Fox & Jacobs, **8** 87
Fox Broadcasting Co., **II** 156; **IV** 608, 652; **7** 391–92; **9** 428; **21** 25, 360; **24** 517; **25** 174, 417–18
Fox Children's Network, **21** 26
Fox Family Worldwide, Inc., 24 170–72
Fox Film Corp., **II** 146–47, 154–55, 169; **25** 327–28
Fox, Fowler & Co., **II** 307
Fox Glacier Mints Ltd., **II** 569
Fox Grocery Co., **II** 682
Fox, Inc., **12** 359; **25** 490
Fox Network, **29** 426
Fox Paper Company, **8** 102
Fox Photo, **III** 475; **7** 161

Fox-Vliet Drug Company, **16** 212
Foxboro Company, **13 233–35**; **27** 81
FoxMeyer Health Corporation, **V** 152–53; **8** 55; **16 212–14**
Foxmoor, **29** 163
Foxx Hy-Reach, **28** 387
FP&L. *See* Florida Power & Light Co.
FPK LLC, **26** 343
FPL Group, Inc., **V 623–25**
FR Corp., **18** 340
Fram Corp., **I** 142, 567
Framatome SA, **9** 10; **19 164–67**
Framingham Electric Company, **12** 45
France Cables et Radio, **6** 303
France 5, **6** 374; **21** 105
France Quick, **12** 152; **26** 160–61; **27** 10
France Telecom Group, **V 291–93**, 471; **9** 32; **14** 489; **18** 33; **21 231–34 (upd.)**; **25** 96, 102
France-Loisirs, **IV** 615–16, 619
Franchise Associates, Inc., **17** 238
Franchise Business Systems, Inc., **18** 207
Franchise Finance Corp. of America, **19** 159
Francis H. Leggett & Co., **24** 527
Franco-Américaine de Constructions Atomiques, **19** 165
Franco-American Food Co., **I** 428; **II** 479
Frank & Hirsch, **III** 608
Frank & Schulte GmbH, **8** 496
Frank Dry Goods Company, **9** 121
Frank H. Nott Inc., **14** 156
Frank J. Rooney, Inc., **8** 87
Frank Schaffer Publications, **19** 405; **29** 470, 472
Frank's Nursery & Crafts, Inc., **12 178–79**, 198–200
Fränkel & Selz, **II** 239
Frankenberry, Laughlin & Constable, **9** 393
Frankford-Quaker Grocery Co., **II** 625
Frankfort Oil Co., **I** 285
Frankfurter Allgemeine Versicherungs-AG, **III** 184
Franklin Assurances, **III** 211
Franklin Baker's Coconut, **II** 531
Franklin Brass Manufacturing Company, **20** 363
Franklin Container Corp., **IV** 312; **19** 267
Franklin Corp., **14** 130
Franklin Electronic Publishers, Inc., **23 209–13**
Franklin Life Insurance Co., **III** 242–43; **V** 397; **29** 195
Franklin Mint, **IV** 676; **9** 428
Franklin National Bank, **9** 536
Franklin Plastics, **19** 414
Franklin Quest Co., **11 147–49**
Franklin Rayon Yarn Dyeing Corp., **I** 529
Franklin Research & Development, **11** 41
Franklin Resources, Inc., **9 239–40**
Franklin Sports, Inc., **17** 243
Franklin Steamship Corp., **8** 346
Franks Chemical Products Inc., **I** 405
Frans Maas Beheer BV, **14** 568
Franz and Frieder Burda, **IV** 661
Franz Foods, Inc., **II** 584
Franz Ströher AG, **III** 68–69
Fraser & Chalmers, **13** 16
Fraser Cos. Ltd., **IV** 165
Fratelli Manzoli, **IV** 585
Fratelli Treves, **IV** 585
Fraternal Assurance Society of America, **III** 274
Fray Data International, **14** 319
Fre Kote Inc., **I** 321
Frears, **II** 543
Fred Campbell Auto Supply, **26** 347
Fred Harvey Hotels, **I** 417
Fred Meyer, Inc., **II** 669; **V 54–56**; **18** 505; **20 222–25 (upd.)**
Fred S. James and Co., **III** 280; **I** 537; **22** 318
Fred Sammons Co., **9** 72
Fred Sammons Company of Chicago, **30** 77
Fred Sands Realtors, **IV** 727
Fred Schmid Appliance & T.V. Co., Inc., **10** 305; **18** 532
The Fred W. Albrecht Grocery Co., **13 236–38**
Fred's, Inc., **23 214–16**
Freddie Mac. *See* Federal Home Loan Mortgage Corporation.
Fredelle, **14** 295
Frederick & Nelson, **17** 462
Frederick Atkins Inc., **16 215–17**
Frederick Bayer & Company, **22** 225
Frederick Gas Company, **19** 487
Frederick Manufacturing Corporation, **26** 119
Frederick Miller Brewing Co., **I** 269
Frederick's of Hollywood Inc., **16 218–20**; **25** 521
Free-lance Uitzendburo, **26** 240
Freeborn Farms, **13** 244
Freedom Technology, **11** 486
Freedom-Valvoline Oil Co., **IV** 373; **19** 23
Freeman, Spogli & Co., **17** 366; **18** 90
Freemans, **V** 177
Freeport-McMoran Inc., **IV 81–84**; **7 185–89 (upd.)**; **16** 29; **23** 40
Freezer House, **II** 398; **10** 62
Freezer Queen Foods, Inc., **21** 509
Freezer Shirt Corporation, **8** 406
Freiberger Papierfabrik, **IV** 323
Freight Car Services, Inc., **23** 306
Freight Outlet, **17** 297
Freightliner, **I** 150; **6** 413
FreightMaster, **III** 498
Frejlack Ice Cream Co., **II** 646; **7** 317
Fremlin Breweries, **I** 294
Fremont Butter and Egg Co., **II** 467
Fremont Canning Company, **7** 196
Fremont Group, **21** 97
Fremont Investors, **30** 268
Fremont Partners, **24** 265
Fremont Savings Bank, **9** 474–75
French and Richards & Co., **I** 692
French Bank of California, **II** 233
French Fragrances, Inc., **22 213–15**
French Kier, **I** 568
French Petrofina, **IV** 497
French Quarter Coffee Co., **27** 480–81
Frequency Sources Inc., **9** 324
Fresenius Ag, **22** 360
Fresh America Corporation, **20 226–28**
Fresh Choice, Inc., **20 229–32**
Fresh Fields, **19** 501
Fresh Foods, Inc., **25** 391; **29 201–03**
Fresh Start Bakeries, **26** 58
Freshbake Foods Group PLC, **II** 481; **7** 68; **25** 518; **26** 57
Fretter, Inc., **9** 65; **10** 9–10, **304–06**, 502; **19** 124; **23** 52
Frialco, **IV** 165
Frictiontech Inc., **11** 84
Friday's Front Row Sports Grill, **22** 128
Friden, Inc., **II** 10; **30** 418
Fridy-Gauker & Fridy, **I** 313; **10** 154
Fried. Krupp AG Hoesch-Krupp. *See* Thyssen Krupp AG.
Fried. Krupp GmbH, **II** 257; **IV** 60, **85–89**, 104, 128, 203, 206, 222, 234
Friedman's Inc., **29 204–06**
Friedrich Flick Industrial Corp., **I** 548; **III** 692
Friedrich Roessler Söhne, **IV** 69
Friedrichshütte, **III** 694
Friendly Hotels PLC, **14** 107
Friendly Ice Cream Corp., **II** 511–12; **15** 221; **30 208–10**
Friesch-Groningsche Hypotheekbank, **III** 179
Frigidaire Home Products, **III** 572; **13** 564; **19** 361; **22** 28, **216–18**, 349
Frigo, **II** 587
Friguia, **IV** 165
Frisby P.M.C. Incorporated, **16** 475
Frisdranken Industries Winters B.V., **22** 515
Frisia Group, **IV** 197–98
Frito-Lay Company, **I** 219, 278–79; **III** 136; **22** 95
Fritz Companies, Inc., **12 180–82**
Fritz Thyssen Stiftung, **IV** 222
Fritz W. Glitsch and Sons, Inc. *See* Glitsch International, Inc.
Fritzsche Dodge and Ollcott, **I** 307
Froebel-Kan, **IV** 679
Frolic, **16** 545
Fromagerie d'Illoud. *See* Bongrain SA.
La Fromagerie du Velay, **25** 85
Fromagerie Paul Renard, **25** 85
Fromageries Bel, **II** 518; **6** 47; **19** 51; **23 217–19**
Fromageries des Chaumes, **25** 84
Fromarsac, **25** 84
Frome Broken Hill Co., **IV** 59
Fromm & Sichel, **I** 285
Frontec, **13** 132
Frontenac Co., **24** 45
Frontier Airlines, Inc., **I** 97–98, 103, 118, 124, 129–30; **6** 129; **11** 298; **21** 141–42; **22 219–21**; **25** 421; **26** 439–40
Frontier Corp., **16 221–23**; **18** 164
Frontier Electronics, **19** 311
Frontier Expeditors, Inc., **12** 363
Frontier Oil Co., **IV** 373
Frontier Pacific Insurance Company, **21** 263
Frosch Touristik, **27** 29
Frost National Bank. *See* Cullen/Frost Bankers, Inc.
Frozen Food Express Industries, Inc., **20 233–35**; **27** 404
Fru-Con Corp., **I** 561
Fruehauf Corp., **I 169–70**, 480; **II** 425; **III** 652; **7** 259–60, 513–14; **13** 341; **27** 202–03, 251
Fruit of the Loom, Inc., **8 200–02**; **16** 535; **25 164–67 (upd.)**
Fry's Diecastings, **III** 681
Fry's Food Stores, **12** 112
Fry's Metal Foundries, **III** 681
Frye Copy Systems, **6** 599
Frymaster Corporation, **27 159–62**
FSA Corporation, **25** 349
FSI International, Inc., **17 192–94**. *See also* FlightSafety International, Inc.
FSP. *See* Frank Schaffer Publications.
FTD, **26** 344
F3 Software Corp., **15** 474

FTP Software, Inc., 20 236–38
Fubu, 29 207–09
Fuddruckers, **27** 480–82
Fuel Pipeline Transportation Ltd., **6** 123–24; **27** 464
Fuel Resources Development Co., **6** 558–59
Fuel Resources Inc., **6** 457
FuelMaker Corporation, **6** 569
Fuji, **18** 94, 342, 511
Fuji Bank, Ltd., I 494; **II 291–93,** 360–61, 391, 422, 459, 554; **III** 405, 408–09; **17** 556–57; **24** 324; **26** 455
Fuji Electric Co., Ltd., II 22–23, 98, 103; **III** 139; **13** 356; **18** 511; **22** 373
Fuji Gen-Gakki, **16** 202
Fuji Heavy Industries, **I** 207; **III** 581; **9** 294; **12** 400; **13** 499–501; **23** 290
Fuji Iron & Steel Co., Ltd., **I** 493; **II** 300; **IV** 130, 157, 212; **17** 349–50; **24** 325
Fuji Kaolin Co., **III** 691
Fuji Paper, **IV** 320
Fuji Photo Film Co., Ltd., III 172, 476, **486–89,** 549–50; **6** 289; **7** 162; **18** 94, **183–87 (upd.),** 341–42
Fuji Seito, **I** 511
Fuji Television, **7** 249; **9** 29
Fuji Xerox. *See* Xerox Corporation.
Fuji Yoshiten Co., **IV** 292
Fujian Hualong Carburetor, **13** 555
Fujikoshi Kozai, **III** 595
Fujimoto Bill Broker & Securities Co., **II** 405
Fujisawa Pharmaceutical Co., I 635–36; III 47; **8** 343
Fujita Airways, **6** 70
Fujitsu Limited, I 455, 541; **II** 22–23, 56, 68, 73, 274; **III** 109–11, 130, **139–41,** 164, 482; **V** 339; **6** 217, 240–42; **10** 238; **11** 308, 542; **13** 482; **14** 13–15, 512; **16** 139, **224–27 (upd.); 17** 172; **21** 390; **27** 107
Fujitsu Takamisawa, **28** 131
Fujitsu-ICL Systems Inc., 11 150–51
Fujiyi Confectionery Co., **II** 569
Fukuin Electric Works, Ltd., **III** 604
Fukuin Shokai Denki Seisakusho, **III** 604
Fukuju Fire, **III** 384
Fukuoka Paper Co., Ltd., **IV** 285
Fukutake Publishing Co., Ltd., **13** 91, 93
Ful-O-Pep, **10** 250
Fulbright Jaworski & Reavis McGrath, **22** 4
Fulcrum Communications, **10** 19
The Fulfillment Corporation of America, **21** 37
Fulham Brothers, **13** 244
Fullbright & Jaworski, **28** 48
Fuller Brush Co., **II** 572; **15** 475–76, 78
Fuller Co., **6** 395–96; **25** 169–70
Fuller Manufacturing Company **I** 154. *See also* H.B. Fuller Company.
Fulton Bank, **14** 40
Fulton Co., **III** 569; **20** 361
Fulton Insurance Co., **III** 463; **21** 173
Fulton Manufacturing Co., **11** 535
Fulton Municipal Gas Company, **6** 455
Fulton Performance Products, Inc., **11** 535
Funai-Amstrad, **III** 113
Funco, Inc., 20 239–41
Fund American Cos., **III** 251–52
Fundimensions, **16** 337
Funk & Wagnalls, **IV** 605; **22** 441
Funk Software Inc., **6** 255; **25** 299
Funnel Cake Factory, **24** 241
Fuqua Enterprises, Inc., 17 195–98
Fuqua Industries Inc., I 445–47, 452; **8** 545; **12** 251; **14** 86
Furalco, **IV** 15
Furnishings International Inc., **20** 359, 363
Furniture Brands International, **31** 246, 248
The Furniture Center, Inc., **14** 236
Furon Company, 28 149–51
Furr's Supermarkets, Inc., II 601; **28 152–54**
Furst Group, **17** 106
Furukawa Electric Co., Ltd., II 22; **III** 139, **490–92; IV** 15, 26, 153; **15** 514; **22** 44
Fusi Denki, **II** 98
Fuso Marine Insurance Co., **III** 367
Fuso Metal Industries, **IV** 212
Futagi Co., Ltd., **V** 96
Futronix Corporation, **17** 276
Future Diagnostics, Inc., **25** 384
Future Graphics, **18** 387
Future Now, Inc., 6 245; **12 183–85**
Fuyo Group, **II** 274, 291–93, 391–92, 554
FWD Corporation, **7** 513

G&G Shops, Inc., **8** 425–26
G & H Products, **III** 419
G&K Services, Inc., 16 228–30; 21 115
G&L Albu, **IV** 90
G&L Inc., **16** 202
G&R Pasta Co., Inc., **II** 512
G. and T. Earle, **III** 669, 670
G.A. Serlachius Oy, **IV** 314–15
G.B. Lewis Company, **8** 359
G. Bruss GmbH and Co. KG, **26** 141
G.C.E. International Inc., **III** 96–97
G.C. Murphy Company, **9** 21
G.C. Smith, **I** 423
G.D. Searle & Company, I 365–66, **686–89; III** 47, 53; **8** 343, 398, 434; **9** 356–57; **10** 54; **12 186–89 (upd.); 16** 527; **26** 108, 383; **29** 331; **29** 331
G. Felsenthal & Sons, **17** 106
G.H. Bass & Co., **15** 406; **24** 383
G.H. Besselaar Associates, **30** 151
G.H. Rinck NV, **V** 49; **19** 122–23
G.H. Wetterau & Sons Grocery Co., **II** 681
G. Heileman Brewing Co., I 253–55, 270; **10** 169–70; **12** 338; **18** 501; **23** 403, 405
G.I.E. Airbus Industrie, I
G.I. Joe's, Inc., 30 221–23 41–43, 49–52, 55–56, 70, 72, 74–76, 107, 111, 116, 121; **9** 458, 460; **11** 279, 363; **12 190–92 (upd.)**
G-III Apparel Group, Ltd., 22 222–24
G.J. Coles & Coy. Ltd., **20** 155
G.L. Kelty & Co., **13** 168
G.L. Rexroth GmbH, **III** 566
G.M. Pfaff AG, **30** 419–20
G.P. Group, **12** 358
G.P. Putnam's Sons, **II** 144
G.R. Foods, Inc. *See* Ground Round, Inc.
G.R. Herberger's, **19** 324–25
G.R. Kinney Corporation, **V** 226, 352; **14** 293; **20** 88
G. Riedel Kälte- und Klimatechnik, **III** 420
G.S. Blodgett Corporation, 15 183–85; 22 350
G.S. Capital Partners II L.P. *See* Goldman, Sachs & Company.
G. Washington Coffee Refining Co., **I** 622
Gabelli Asset Management Inc., 13 561; **30 211–14**
Gable House Properties, **II** 141
Gabriel Industries, **II** 532
GAC. *See* The Goodyear Tire & Rubber Company.
GAC Corp., **II** 182; **III** 592
GAC Holdings L.P., **7** 204; **28** 164
Gadzooks, Inc., 18 188–90
GAF, I 337–40, 524–25, 549; **II** 378; **III** 440; **8** 180; **9** 518; **18** 215; **22** 14, **225–29 (upd.); 25** 464
Gage Marketing Group, 26 147–49; 27 21
Gagliardi Brothers, **13** 383
Gail Borden, Jr., and Company. *See* Borden, Inc.
Gain Technology, Inc., **10** 505
Gaines Dog Food Co., **II** 531
Gainsborough Craftsmen Ltd., **II** 569
Gainsco, Inc., 22 230–32
Gair Paper Co., **I** 599
Galas Harland, S.A., **17** 266, 268
Galavision, Inc., **24** 515–17
Galaxy Carpet Mills Inc., **19** 276
Galaxy Energies Inc., **11** 28
Galbreath Escott, **16** 474
Gale Research Inc., **8** 526; **23** 440
Galen Health Care, **15** 112
Galen Laboratories, **13** 160
Galerías Preciados, **26** 130
Galeries Lafayette S.A., V 57–59; 23 220–23 (upd.)
Galesburg Coulter Disc Co., **III** 439–40
Galey & Lord, Inc., 20 242–45
Gallagher Limited, **29** 195
Gallaher Limited, IV 260; **V 398–400; 19 168–71 (upd.)**
Gallatin Bank, **II** 312
Gallatin Steel Company, **18** 380; **24** 144
Galletas, **II** 543
Gallimard, **IV** 618
Gallo Winery. *See* E. & J. Gallo Winery.
Gallop Johnson & Neuman, L.C., **26** 348
Galoob Toys. *See* Lewis Galoob Toys Inc.
Galor, **I** 676
GALP, **IV** 505
Galvanizing Co., **IV** 159
Galveston *Daily News*, **10** 3
Galvin Manufacturing Corp., **II** 60; **11** 326
GALVSTAR, L.P., **26** 530
Gamble-Skogmo Inc., **13** 169; **25** 535
Gambrinus Co., **29** 219
Gambro Engstrom AB, **13** 159–61, 327–28
Gamesa, **II** 544; **19** 192
GameTime, Inc., **19** 387; **27** 370–71
GAMI. *See* Great American Management and Investment, Inc.
Gamlestaden, **9** 381–82
Gamlestadens Fabriker, **III** 622
Gamma Capital Corp., **24** 3
Gammalink, **18** 143
Gander Mountain, Inc., 20 246–48
Gang-Nail Systems, **III** 735
Gannett Co., Inc., III 159; **IV 612–13,** 629–30; **7 190–92 (upd.); 9** 3; **18** 63; **23** 157–58, 293; **24** 224; **25** 371; **30 215–17 (upd.)**
Gannett Supply, **17** 282
Gantos, Inc., 17 199–201
The Gap, Inc., V 60–62; 9 142, 360; **11** 499; **18 191–94 (upd.); 24** 27; **25** 47–48; **31** 51–52
GAR Holdings, **19** 78

Garamond Press, **23** 100
Garan, Inc., **16 231–33**
Garantie Mutuelle des Fonctionnaires, **21** 225
Garden Botanika, **11** 41
Garden Escape, **26** 441
Garden Fresh Restaurant Corporation, **31 213–15**
Garden of Eatin' Inc., **27** 198
Garden Ridge Corporation, **27 163–65**
Garden State BancShares, Inc., **14** 472
Garden State Life Insurance Company, **10** 312; **27** 47–48
Gardener's Eden, **17** 548–49
Gardenia, **II** 587
Gardner & Harvey Container Corporation, **8** 267
Gardner Advertising. *See* Wells Rich Green BDDP.
Gardner Cryogenics, **13** 140
Gardner Merchant Ltd., **III** 104; **11** 325; **29** 442–44
Gardner Rubber Co. *See* Tillotson Corp.
Gardner-Denver Co., **II** 16
Garelick Farms, Inc., **26** 449
Garfield Weston, **13** 51
Garfinckel, Brooks Brothers, Miller & Rhodes, Inc., **15** 94; **22** 110
Garlock, **I** 435
Garnier, **III** 47
A.B. Garnisonen, **II** 352
Garrard Engineering, **II** 82
Garrett, **9** 18; **11** 472
Garrett & Company, **27** 326
Garrett AiResearch, **9** 18
Garrett Poultry Co., **II** 584; **14** 514
Garrett-Buchanan, **I** 412
Garrick Investment Holdings Ltd., **16** 293
Garrido y Compania, Inc., **26** 448
Gart Sports Company, **24 173–75**
Gartner Group, Inc., **21 235–37**; **25** 22
Gartrell White, **II** 465
Garuda Indonesia, **I** 107; **6 90–91**
Gary Fisher Mountain Bike Company, **16** 494
Gary Industries, **7** 4
Gary-Wheaton Corp., **II** 286
Gary-Williams Energy Corporation, **19** 177
Gas Authority of India Ltd., **IV** 484
Gas Corp. of Queensland, **III** 673
Gas Energy Inc., **6** 457
Gas Group, **III** 673
Gas Light and Coke Company. *See* British Gas plc.
Gas Light Company. *See* Baltimore Gas and Electric Company.
Gas Machinery Co., **I** 412
Gas Service Company, **6** 593; **12** 542
Gas Supply Co., **III** 672
Gas Tech, Inc., **11** 513
Gas Utilities Company, **6** 471
Gaston Paper Stock Co., Inc., **8** 476
Gasunie. *See* N.V. Nederlandse Gasunie.
GATC. *See* General American Tank Car Company.
Gate City Company, **6** 446
The Gates Corporation, **9 241–43**
Gates Distribution Company, **12** 60
Gates Radio Co., **II** 37
Gates Rubber, **26** 349
Gates/FA Distributing Inc., **29** 413–14
Gateway Books, **14** 61
Gateway Corporation Ltd., **II** 612, **628–30**, 638, 642; **10** 442; **16** 249; **25** 119
Gateway Foodmarkets Ltd., **II** 628; **13** 26
Gateway, Inc., **27 166–69 (upd.)**
Gateway 2000, Inc., **10 307–09**; **11** 240; **22** 99; **24** 31; **25** 531
Gatliff Coal Co., **6** 583
Gatwick Handling, **28** 157
GATX, **6 394–96**; **25 168–71 (upd.)**
Gaumont SA, **II** 157–58; **25 172–75**; **29** 369–71
Gauntlet Developments, **IV** 724
Gavilan Computer Corp., **III** 124; **6** 221
Gaya Motor, P.T. **23** 290
Gaylord Container Corporation, **8 203–05**; **24** 92
Gaylord Entertainment Company, **11 152–54**
Gaymer Group, **25** 82
Gaz de France, **IV** 425; **V 626–28**
Gazelle Graphics Systems, **28** 244
Gazprom, **18** 50; **30** 205
GB Foods Inc., **19** 92
GB Papers, **IV** 290
GB s.a. *See* GIB Group.
GB Stores, Inc., **14** 427
GB-Inno-BM, **II** 658; **V** 63
GBL, **IV** 499
GC Companies, Inc., **25 176–78**
GCFC. *See* General Cinema Finance Co.
GD Express Worldwide, **27** 472, 475; **30** 463
GDE Systems, Inc., **17** 492
GDF. *See* Gaz de France.
GDS, **29** 412
GE. *See* General Electric Company.
GE Aircraft Engines, **9 244–46**
GE Capital Corporation, **29** 428, 430
GE Capital Services, **27** 276
GE SeaCo SRL, **29** 428, 431
GEA AG, **27 170–74**
Geant Casino, **12** 152
Gearhart Industries Inc., **III** 499; **15** 467
Gearmatic, **I** 185
Gebrüder Kiessel GmbH, **IV** 197
Gebrüder Sulzer Aktiengesellschaft. *See* Sulzer Brothers Limited.
Gebrüder Volkart, **III** 402
Gebrueder Ahle GmbH, **III** 581
GEC. *See* General Electric Company.
GECO, **III** 618; **17** 419
Geco Mines Ltd., **IV** 165; **7** 398
Geer Drug, **III** 9–10
Geffen Records Inc., **21** 26; **23** 33; **26 150–52**
GEGC, **III** 434
GEHE AG, **27 175–78**
Gehl Company, **19 172–74**
GEICO Corporation, **III** 214, 248, 252, 273, 448; **10 310–12**; **18** 60, 61, 63
Gelatin Products Co., **I** 678
Gelco Express, **18** 177
Gelco Truck Services, **19** 293
Gellatly, Hankey and Sewell, **III** 521
Gelsenberg AG, **IV** 454; **7** 141
Gelsenkirchener Bergwerks AG, **I** 542; **IV** 194
Gelson's, **29** 32
Gem State Utilities, **6** 325, 328
GEMA Gesellschaft für Maschinen- und Apparatebau mbH, **IV** 198
Gemco, **17** 366
Gemcolite Company, **8** 178
N.V. Gemeenschappelijk Benzit van Aandeelen Philips Gloeilampenfabriken, **II** 79; **13** 396
Gemeinhardt Co., **16** 201
Gemey, **III** 47
Gemina, **I** 369
Gemini Computers, **III** 109; **14** 13
Gemini Group Limited Partnership, **23** 10
Gemini Industries, **17** 215
GemPlus, **18** 543
Genbel Investments Ltd., **IV** 92
GenCare Health Systems, **17** 166–67
Gencor Ltd., **I** 423; **IV 90–93**, 95; **22 233–37 (upd.)**
GenCorp Inc., **8** 206–08; **9 247–49**; **13** 381
Gendex Corp., **10** 270, 272
Gene Reid Drilling, **IV** 480
Gene Upton Co., **13** 166
Genender International Incorporated, **31** 52
Genentech Inc., **I** 628, **637–38**; **III** 43; **8 209–11 (upd.)**, 216–17; **10** 78, 80, 142, 199; **17** 289; **29** 386; **30** 164
General Accident plc, **III 256–57**, 350
General America Corp., **III** 352–53
General American Oil Co., **IV** 523
General American Tank Car Company. *See* GATX Corporation.
General Aniline and Film Corporation. *See* GAF Corporation.
General Aquatics, Inc., **16** 297
General Artificial Silk Co., **IV** 310; **19** 265
General Atlantic Partners, **25** 34; **26** 94
General Automotive Parts Corp., **I** 62; **9** 254
General Aviation Corp., **I** 54; **9** 16
General Battery Corp., **I** 440–41
General Binding Corporation, **10 313–14**
General Box Corp., **IV** 342
General Brewing Corp, **I** 269
General Bussan Kaisha, Ltd., **IV** 431–32, 555
General Cable Co., **IV** 32; **7** 288; **8** 367; **18** 549
General Casualty Co., **III** 258, 343, 352, 404
General Chemical Corp., **I** 414; **22** 29, 115, 193, 349, 541; **29** 114
General Chocolate, **II** 521
General Cigar Co., Inc. *See* Culbro Corporation.
General Cigar Holdings, Inc., **27** 139–40
General Cinema Corporation, **I 245–46**; **II** 478; **IV** 624; **12** 12–13, 226, 356; **14** 87; **19** 362; **26** 468; **27** 481
General Cinema Finance Co., **II** 157–58
General Cinema Theaters. *See* GC Companies, Inc.
General Co. for Life Insurance and Superannuation, **III** 309
General Corporation, **9** 173
General Credit Ltd., **II** 389
General Crude Oil Co., **II** 403; **IV** 287; **15** 228
General DataComm Industries, Inc., **14 200–02**
General Diaper Corporation, **14** 550
General Dynamics Corporation, **I** 55, **57–60**, 62, 71, 74, 77, 482, 525, 527, 597; **6** 79, 229; **7** 520; **8** 51, 92, 315, 338; **9** 206, 323, 417–18, 498; **10 315–18 (upd.)**, 522, 527; **11** 67, 165, 269, 278, 364; **13** 374; **16** 77–78; **18** 62, 554; **27** 100; **30** 471

General Electric Capital Corp., **15** 257, 282; **19** 190
General Electric Company, **I** 41, 52, 82–85, 195, 321, 454, 478, 532, 534, 537; **II** 2, 16, 19, 22, 24, **27–31**, 38–39, 41, 56, 58–59, 66, 82, 86, 88–90, 98–99, 116–17, 119–21, 143, 151–52, 330, 349, 431, 604; **III** 16, 110, 122–23, 132, 149, 152, 154, 170–71, 340, 437, 440, 443, 475, 483, 502, 526, 572–73, 614, 655; **IV** 66, 203, 287, 596, 675; **V** 564; **6** 13, 27, 32, 164–66, 240, 261, 266, 288, 452, 517; **7** 123, 125, 161, 456, 520, 532; **8** 157, 262, 332, 377; **9** 14–18, 27, 128, 162, 244, 246, 352–53, 417–18, 439, 514; **10** 16, 241, 536–37; **11** 46, 313, 318, 422, 472, 490; **12** 68, 190, **193–97 (upd.)**, 237, 247, 250, 252, 484, 544–45, 550; **13** 30, 124, 326, 396, 398, 501, 529, 554, 563–64; **15** 196, 228, 285, 380, 403, 467; **17** 149, 173, 272; **18** 228, 369; **19** 110, 164–66, 210, 335; **20** 8, 152; **22** 37, 218, 406; **23** 104–05, 181; **26** 371; **28** 4–5, 8, 298; **30** 490; **31** 123
General Electric Company, PLC, **I** 411, 423; **II** 3, 12, **24–26**, 31, 58, 72, 80–83; **III** 509; **9** 9–10; **13** 356; **20** 290; **24** 87
General Electric Credit Corporation, **19** 293; **20** 42
General Electric Railcar Wheel and Parts Services Corporation, **18** 4
General Electric Venture Capital Corporation, **9** 140; **10** 108
General Electronics Co., **III** 160
General Elevator Corporation, **25** 15
General Europea S.A., **V** 607
General Export Iron and Metals Company, **15** 116
General Felt Industries Inc., **I** 202; **14** 300; **17** 182–83
General Film Distributors Ltd., **II** 157
General Finance Corp., **II** 419; **III** 194, 232; **11** 16
General Finance Service Corp., **11** 447
General Fire and Casualty, **I** 449
General Fire Extinguisher Co. *See* Grinnell Corp.
General Foods Corp., **I** 26, 36, 608, 712; **II** 414, 463, 477, 497, 502, 525, 530–34, 557, 569; **III** 66; **V** 407; **7** 272–74; **10** 323, 551; **12** 167, 372; **13** 293; **18** 416, 419; **25** 517; **26** 251
General Foods, Ltd., **7** 577
General Furniture Leasing. *See* CORT Business Services Corporation.
General Gas Co., **IV** 432
General Glass Corporation, **13** 40
General Growth Properties, **III** 248
General Health Services, **III** 79
General Host Corporation, **7** 372; **12** 178–79, **198–200**, 275; **15** 362; **17** 230–31
General Housewares Corporation, **16** **234–36**; **18** 69
General Instrument Corporation, **II** 5, 112, 160; **10** **319–21**; **17** 33
General Insurance Co. of America, **III** 352–53
General Jones Processed Food, **I** 438
General Learning Corp., **IV** 675; **7** 528
General Leisure, **16** 33
General Life Insurance Co. of America, **III** 353
General Medical Corp., **18** 469
General Merchandise Company, **V** 91
General Merchandise Services, Inc., **15** 480
General Milk Co., **II** 487; **7** 429
General Milk Products of Canada Ltd., **II** 586
General Mills, Inc., **II** 493, **501–03**, 525, 556, 576, 684; **III** 505; **7** 547; **8** 53–54; **9** 156, 189–90, 291; **10** 177, **322–24 (upd.)**; **11** 15, 497–98; **12** 80, 167–68, 275; **13** 244, 293–94, 408, 516; **15** 189; **16** 71, 156–58, 337; **18** 225, 523; **22** 337–38; **25** 90, 241, 243, 253; **30** 286; **31** 429–31
General Mining and Finance Corporation. *See* Gencor Ltd.
General Mortgage and Credit Corp., **II** 256
General Motors Acceptance Corporation, **21** 146; **22** 55
General Motors Corporation, **I** 10, 14, 16–17, 54, 58, 78–80, 85, 101–02, 125, 136, 141, 144–45, 147, 154–55, 162–63, 165–67, **171–73**, 181, 183, 186–87, 203, 205–06, 280, 328–29, 334–35, 360, 448, 464, 481–82, 529, 540; **II** 2, 5, 15, 32–35, 268, 431, 608; **III** 55, 136–38, 292, 442, 458, 482–83, 536, 555, 563, 581, 590–91, 637–38, 640–42, 760; **6** 140, 256, 336, 356, 358; **7** 6–8, 427, 461–64, 513, 565, 567, 599; **8** 151–52, 505–07; **9** 16–18, 36, 283, 293–95, 341, 343, 344, 439, 487–89; **10** 198, 232, 262, 264, 273–74, 279–80, 288–89, **325–27 (upd.)**, 419–20, 429, 460, 537; **11** 5, 29, 53, 103–04, 137–39, 339, 350, 427–29, 437–39, 471–72, 528, 530; **12** 90, 160, 309, 311, 487; **13** 109, 124, 179, 344–45, 357; **14** 321, 458; **15** 171; **16** 321–22, 436, 484; **17** 173, 184, 304; **18** 125–26, 168, 308; **19** 293–94, 482, 484; **21** 3, 6, 444; **22** 13, 169, 175, 216; **23** 267–69, 288–91, 340, 459–61; **24** 29; **25** 142–43, 149, 223–24, 300; **26** 23; **27** 203; **28** 114; **29** 375, 407–08
General Nucleonics Corp., **III** 643
General Nutrition Companies, Inc., **11** **155–57**; **24** 480; **29** **210–14 (upd.)**; **31** 347
General Office Products Co., **25** 500
General Packing Service, Inc., **19** 78
General Parts Inc., **29** 86
General Petroleum and Mineral Organization of Saudi Arabia, **IV** 537–39
General Petroleum Corp., **IV** 412, 431, 464; **7** 352
General Physics Corporation, **13** 367
General Portland Cement Co., **III** 704–05; **17** 497
General Portland Inc., **28** 229
General Precision Equipment Corp., **II** 10; **30** 418
General Printing and Paper, **II** 624–25
General Printing Ink Corp. *See* Sequa Corp.
General Property Trust, **IV** 708
General Public Utilities Corporation, **V** **629–31**; **6** 484, 534, 579–80; **11** 388; **20** 73
General Radio Company. *See* GenRad, Inc.
General Railway Signal Company. *See* General Signal Corporation.
General Re Corporation, **III** **258–59**, 276; **24** **176–78 (upd.)**
General Rent A Car, **6** 349; **25** 142–43
General Research Corp., **14** 98
General Seafoods Corp., **II** 531
General Sekiyu K.K., **IV** **431–33**, 555; **16** 490
General Signal Corporation, **III** 645; **9** **250–52**; **11** 232
General Spring Products, **16** 321
General Steel Industries Inc., **14** 324
General Supermarkets, **II** 673
General Telephone and Electronics Corp., **II** 47; **V** 295, 345–46; **13** 398; **19** 40; **25** 267
General Telephone Corporation, **V** 294–95; **9** 478, 494
General Time Corporation, **16** 483
General Tire, Inc., **8** 206–08, **212–14**; **9** 247–48; **20** 260, 262; **22** 219
General Transistor Corporation, **10** 319
General Utilities Company, **6** 555
Generale Bank, **II** **294–95**
Genérale Biscuit S.A., **II** 475
Générale de Mécanique Aéronautique, **I** 46
Générale des Eaux Group, **V** **632–34**; **21** 226
Generale du Jouet, **16** 428
Générale Occidentale, **II** 475; **IV** 614–15
Generali. *See* Assicurazioni Generali.
GenerComit Gestione SpA, **II** 192
Genesco Inc., **14** 501; **17** **202–06**; **27** 59
Genesee & Wyoming Inc., **27** **179–81**
Genesee Brewing Co., **18** 72
Genesee Iron Works. *See* Wickes Inc.
Genesis, **II** 176–77
Genesis Health Ventures, Inc., **18** **195–97**; **25** 310
Genetic Systems Corp., **I** 654; **III** 18
Genetics Institute, Inc., **8** **215–18**; **10** 70, 78–80
Geneva Metal Wheel Company, **20** 261
Geneva Pharmaceuticals, Inc., **8** 549; **22** 37, 40
Geneva Rubber Co., **17** 373
Geneva Steel, **7** **193–95**
Genex Corp., **I** 355–56; **26** 246
GENIX, **V** 152
Genix Group. *See* MCN Corporation.
Genossenschaftsbank Edeka, **II** 621–22
Genovese Drug Stores, Inc., **18** **198–200**; **21** 187
Genpack Corporation, **21** 58
GenRad, Inc., **24** **179–83**
GenSet, **19** 442
Genstar, **22** 14; **23** 327
Genstar Gypsum Products Co., **IV** 273
Genstar Stone Products Co., **III** 735; **15** 154
Gentex Corporation, **12** 121–22; **26** **153–57**
Gentex Optics, **17** 50; **18** 392
GenTrac, **24** 257
Gentry Associates, Inc., **14** 378
Gentry International, **I** 497
Genuine Parts Company, **9** **253–55**
Genung's, **II** 673
Genus, **18** 382–83
Genzyme Corporation, **13** **239–42**
Geo Space Corporation, **18** 513
GEO Specialty Chemicals, Inc., **27** 117
Geo. W. Wheelwright Co., **IV** 311; **19** 266
Geodynamics Oil & Gas Inc., **IV** 83
Geographics, Inc., **25** 183

Geomarine Systems, **11** 202
The Geon Company, **11 158–61**
Geon Industries, Inc. *See* Johnston Industries, Inc.
Geophysical Service, Inc., **II** 112; **III** 499–500; **IV** 365
GeoQuest Systems Inc., **17** 419
Georesources, Inc., **19** 247
George A. Hormel and Company, **II 504–06**; **7** 547; **12** 123–24; **18** 244. *See also* Hormel Foods Corporation.
George A. Touche & Co., **9** 167
George Batten Co., **I** 28
George Booker & Co., **13** 102
George Fischer, Ltd., **III** 638
George H. Dentler & Sons, **7** 429
The George Hyman Construction Company, **8** 112–13; **25** 403
George J. Ball, Inc., **27** 507
George K. Baum & Company, **25** 433
George K. Smith & Co., **I** 692
George Kent, **II** 3; **22** 10
George Newnes Company, **IV** 641; **7** 244
George Peabody & Co., **II** 329, 427
George R. Newell Company. *See* Supervalu Inc.
George R. Rich Manufacturing Company. *See* Clark Equipment Company.
George Smith Financial Corporation, **21** 257
George W. Neare & Co., **III** 224
George Weston Limited, **II** 465, **631–32**, 649; **13** 51
George Wimpey PLC, **12 201–03**; **28** 450
Georges Renault SA, **III** 427; **28** 40
Georgetown Group, Inc., **26** 187
Georgetown Steel Corp., **IV** 228
Georgia Carpet Outlets, **25** 320
Georgia Cotton Producers Association. *See* Gold Kist Inc.
Georgia Credit Exchange, **6** 24
Georgia Federal Bank, **I** 447; **11** 112–13; **30** 196
Georgia Gulf Corporation, **IV** 282; **9 256–58**, 260
Georgia Hardwood Lumber Co., **IV** 281; **9** 259
Georgia International Life Insurance Co., **III** 218
Georgia Kraft Co., **IV** 312, 342–43; **8** 267–68; **19** 268
Georgia Natural Gas Corporation, **6** 447–48
Georgia Power & Light Co., **V** 621; **6** 447, 537; **23** 28; **27** 20
Georgia Railway and Electric Company, **6** 446–47; **23** 28
Georgia-Pacific Corporation, **IV 281–83**, 288, 304, 345, 358; **9** 256–58, **259–62 (upd.)**; **12** 19, 377; **15** 229; **22** 415, 489; **31** 314
Georgie Pie, **V** 35
GeoScience Corporation, **18** 515
Geosource Inc., **III** 182; **21** 14; **22** 189
Geotec Boyles Brothers, S.A., **19** 247
Geotek Communications Inc., **21 238–40**
Geothermal Resources International, **11** 271
Geoworks Corporation, **25** 509
Geraghty & Miller Inc., **26** 23
Gérard, **25** 84
Gerber Products Company, **II** 481; **III** 19; **7 196–98**, 547; **9** 90; **11** 173; **21** 53–55, **241–44 (upd)**; **25** 366
Gerber Scientific, Inc., **12 204–06**
Gerbes Super Markets, Inc., **12** 112
Geren Associates. *See* CRSS Inc.
Geriatrics Inc., **13** 49
Gerling of Cologne, **III** 695
Germaine Monteil Cosmetiques Corp., **I** 426; **III** 56
German Cargo Service GmbH., **I** 111
German Mills American Oatmeal Factory, **II** 558; **12** 409
German-American Car Company. *See* GATX.
German-American Securities, **II** 283
Germania Refining Co., **IV** 488–89
Germplasm Resource Management, **III** 740
Gerresheimer Glas AG, **II** 386; **IV** 232
Gerrity Oil & Gas Corporation, **11** 28; **24** 379–80
Gervais Danone, **II** 474
GESA. *See* General Europea S.A.
Gesbancaya, **II** 196
Gesellschaft für Chemische Industrie im Basel, **I** 632
Gesellschaft für den Bau von Untergrundbahnen, **I** 410
Gesellschaft für Linde's Eisenmachinen, **I** 581
Gesellschaft für Markt- und Kühlhallen, **I** 581
Gesparal, **III** 47; **8** 342
Gestettner, **II** 159
Gestione Pubblicitaria Editoriale, **IV** 586
Getty Images, Inc., **31 216–18**
Getty Oil Co., **II** 448; **IV** 367, 423, 429, 461, 479, 488, 490, 551, 553; **6** 457; **8** 526; **11** 27; **13** 448; **17** 501; **18** 488; **27** 216
Getz Corp., **IV** 137
Geyser Peak Winery, **I** 291
Geysers Geothermal Co., **IV** 84, 523; **7** 188
GFS. *See* Gordon Food Service Inc.
GFS Realty Inc., **II** 633
GHH, **II** 257
GHI, **28** 155, 157
Ghirardelli Chocolate Company, **24** 480; **27** 105; **30 218–20**
GI Communications, **10** 321
GI Export Corp. *See* Johnston Industries, Inc.
GIAG, **16** 122
Gianni Versace SpA, **22 238–40**
Giant Bicycle Inc., **19** 384
Giant Cement Holding, Inc., **23 224–26**
Giant Eagle, Inc., **12** 390–91; **13** 237
Giant Food Inc., **II 633–35**, 656; **13** 282, 284; **15** 532; **16** 313; **22 241–44 (upd.)**; **24** 462
Giant Industries, Inc., **19 175–77**
Giant Resources, **III** 729
Giant Stores, Inc., **7** 113; **25** 124
Giant TC, Inc. *See* Campo Electronics, Appliances & Computers, Inc.
Giant Tire & Rubber Company, **8** 126
Giant Video Corporation, **29** 503
Giant Wholesale, **II** 625
GIB Group, **V 63–66**; **22** 478; **23** 231; **26 158–62 (upd.)**
Gibbons, Green, van Amerongen Ltd., **II** 605; **9** 94; **12** 28; **19** 360
Gibbs Automatic Molding Co., **III** 569; **20** 360
Gibbs Construction, **25** 404
GIBCO Corp., **I** 321; **17** 287, 289
Gibraltar Casualty Co., **III** 340
Gibraltar Financial Corp., **III** 270–71
Gibson Greetings, Inc., **7** 24; **12 207–10**; **16** 256; **21** 426–28; **22** 34–35
Gibson Guitar Corp., **16 237–40**
Gibson McDonald Furniture Co., **14** 236
GIC. *See* The Goodyear Tire & Rubber Company.
Giddings & Lewis, Inc., **8** 545–46; **10 328–30**; **23** 299; **28** 455
Giftmaster Inc., **26** 439–40
Gil-Wel Manufacturing Company, **17** 440
Gilbert & John Greenall Limited, **21** 246
Gilbert Lane Personnel, Inc., **9** 326
Gilbert-Ash Ltd., **I** 588
Gilde-Verlag, **IV** 590
Gilde-Versicherung AG, **III** 400
Gildon Metal Enterprises, **7** 96
Gilkey Bros. *See* Puget Sound Tug and Barge Company.
Gill and Duffus, **II** 500
Gill Industries, **II** 161
Gill Interprovincial Lines, **27** 473
Gillett Holdings, Inc., **7 199–201**; **11** 543, 545
The Gillette Company, **III 27–30**, 114, 215; **IV** 722; **8** 59–60; **9** 381, 413; **17** 104–05; **18** 60, 62, 215, 228; **20 249–53 (upd.)**; **23** 54–57; **26** 334; **28** 247
Gilliam Furniture Inc., **12** 475
Gilliam Manufacturing Co., **8** 530
Gilman & Co., **III** 523
Gilman Fanfold Corp., Ltd., **IV** 644
Gilmore Brother's, **I** 707
Gilmore Steel Corporation. *See* Oregon Steel Mills, Inc.
Gilroy Foods, **27** 299
Giltspur, **II** 587
Gimbel Brothers, Inc. *See* Saks Holdings, Inc.
Gimbel's Department Store, **I** 426–27; **8** 59; **22** 72
Gindick Productions, **6** 28
Ginn & Co., **IV** 672; **19** 405
Ginnie Mae. *See* Government National Mortgage Association.
Gino's, **III** 103
Gino's East, **21** 362
Ginsber Beer Group, **15** 47
Giorgio Beverly Hills, Inc., **26** 384
Giorgio, Inc., **III** 16; **19** 28
Girard Bank, **II** 315–16
Girbaud, **17** 513; **31** 261
Girling, **III** 556
Giro Sport Designs, **16** 53
Girod, **19** 50
Girsa S.A., **23** 170
Girvin, Inc., **16** 297
Gist-Brocades Co., **III** 53; **26** 384
The Gitano Group, Inc., **8 219–21**; **20** 136 **25** 167
GJM International Ltd., **25** 121–22
GK Technologies Incorporated, **10** 547
GKH Partners, **29** 295
GKN plc, **III 493–96**, 554, 556
Glaceries de Saint-Roch, **III** 677; **16** 121
Glaces de Boussois, **II** 474–75
Glacier Park Co., **10** 191
Gladieux Corp., **III** 103
Glamar Group plc, **14** 224
Glamor Shops, Inc., **14** 93
Glasrock Home Health Care, **I** 316; **25** 81
Glass Containers Corp., **I** 609–10
Glass Fibres Ltd., **III** 726

GlasTec, **II** 420
Glatfelter Wood Pulp Company, **8** 413
Glaverbel, **III** 667
Glaxo Holdings plc, I 639–41, 643, 668, 675, 693; **III** 66; **6** 346; **9 263–65 (upd.)**; **10** 551; **11** 173; **20** 39; **26** 31
Gleason Corporation, 24 184–87
Glen & Co, **I** 453
Glen Alden Corp., **15** 247
Glen Cove Mutual Insurance Co., **III** 269
Glen Iris Bricks, **III** 673
Glen Line, **6** 416
Glen-Gery Corporation, **14** 249
Glencairn Ltd., **25** 418
Glendale Federal Savings, **IV** 29
The Glenlyte Group, **29** 469
Glenlyte Thomas Group LLC, **29** 466
Glenn Advertising Agency, **25** 90
Glenn Pleass Holdings Pty. Ltd., **21** 339
Glens Falls Insurance Co., **III** 242
GLF-Eastern States Association, **7** 17
The Glidden Company, I 353; **8 222–24**; **21** 545
Glimcher Co., **26** 262
Glitsch International, Inc., **6** 146; **23** 206, 208
Global Access, **31** 469
Global Apparel Sourcing Ltd., **22** 223
Global Energy Group, **II** 345
Global Engineering Company, **9** 266
Global Interactive Communications Corporation, **28** 242
Global Marine Inc., 9 266–67; **11** 87
Global Natural Resources, **II** 401; **10** 145
Global Transport Organization, **6** 383
GlobalCom Telecommunications, Inc., **24** 122
GlobaLex, **28** 141
Globe & Rutgers Insurance Co., **III** 195–96
Globe Co. **I** 201
Globe Electric Co., **III** 536
Globe Feather & Down, **19** 304
Globe Files Co., **I** 201
Globe Grain and Milling Co., **II** 555
Globe Industries, **I** 540
Globe Insurance Co., **III** 350
Globe Life Insurance Co., **III** 187; **10** 28
Globe National Bank, **II** 261
Globe Newspaper Co., **7** 15
Globe Petroleum Ltd., **IV** 401
Globe Steel Abrasive Co., **17** 371
Globe Telegraph and Trust Company, **25** 99
Globe-Union, **III** 536; **26** 229
Globe-Wernicke Co., **I** 201
Globetrotter Communications, **7** 199
Globo, **18** 211
Gloria Jean's Gourmet Coffees, **20** 83
La Gloria Oil and Gas Company, **7** 102
Gloria Separator GmbH Berlin, **III** 418
Glosser Brothers, **13** 394
Gloster Aircraft, **I** 50; **III** 508; **24** 85
Gloucester Cold Storage and Warehouse Company, **13** 243
Glovatorium, **III** 152; **6** 266; **30** 339
Glycomed Inc., **13** 241
Glyn, Mills and Co., **II** 308; **12** 422
GM. *See* General Motors Corp.
GM Hughes Electronics Corporation, II 32–36; **10** 325. *See also* Hughes Electronics Corporation.
GMARA, **II** 608
GMFanuc Robotics, **III** 482–83
GMR Properties, **21** 257
GNB International Battery Group, **10** 445
GND Holdings Corp., **7** 204; **28** 164
GNMA. *See* Government National Mortgage Association.
The Go-Ahead Group Plc, 28 155–57
Goal Systems International Inc., **10** 394
Godfather's Pizza Incorporated, II 556–57; **11** 50; **12** 123; **14** 351; **17** 86; **25 179–81**
Godfrey Co., **II** 625
Godfrey L. Cabot, Inc., **8** 77
Godiva Chocolatier, **II** 480; **26** 56
Godo Shusei, **III** 42
Godsell, **10** 277
Godtfred Kristiansen, **13** 310–11
Goebel & Wetterau Grocery Co., **II** 681
Goelitz Confectionary. *See* Herman Goelitz, Inc.
Goering Werke, **II** 282
Göhner AG, **6** 491
Gokey Company, **10** 216; **28** 339
Gold Bond Stamp Company, **6** 363–64; **22** 125
Gold Crust Bakeries, **II** 465
Gold Dust Corp., **II** 497
Gold Exploration and Mining Co. Limited Partnership, **13** 503
Gold Fields of South Africa Ltd., I 423; **IV** 91, **94–97**
Gold Kist Inc., 7 432; **17 207–09**; **26 166–68**
Gold Lance Inc., **19** 451–52
Gold Lion, **20** 263
Gold Seal, **II** 567
Gold Star Foods Co., **IV** 410
Gold's Gym Enterprises, **25** 450
Goldblatt Bros., **IV** 135
Goldblatt's Department Stores, **15** 240–42
Golden, **III** 47
Golden Belt Manufacturing Co., 16 241–43
Golden Books Family Entertainment, Inc., 28 158–61
Golden Circle Financial Services, **15** 328
Golden Corral Corporation, 10 331–33
Golden Eagle Exploration, **IV** 566–67
Golden Enterprises, Inc., 26 163–65
Golden Gate Airlines, **25** 421
Golden Grain Company, **30** 219
Golden Grain Macaroni Co., **II** 560; **12** 411
Golden Hope Rubber Estate, **III** 697, 699
Golden Nugget, Inc. *See* Mirage Resorts, Incorporated.
Golden Partners, **10** 333
Golden Peanut Company, **17** 207
Golden Poultry Company, **26** 168
Golden Press, Inc., **13** 559–61
Golden Sea Produce, **10** 439
Golden Skillet, **10** 373
Golden State Bank, **II** 348
Golden State Newsprint Co. Inc., **IV** 296; **19** 226; **23** 225
Golden State Sanwa Bank, **II** 348
Golden Tulip International, **I** 109
Golden West Homes, **15** 328
Golden Wonder, **II** 500; **III** 503
Golden Youth, **17** 227
Goldenberg Group, Inc., **12** 396
Goldenlay Eggs, **II** 500
Goldfield Corp., **12** 198
Goldfine's Inc., **16** 36
Goldkuhl & Broström, **III** 419
Goldline Laboratories Inc., **11** 208
Goldman, Sachs & Co., II 11, 268, 326, 361, **414–16**, 432, 434, 448; **III** 80, 531; **IV** 611; **9** 378, 441; **10** 423; **12** 405; **13** 95, 448, 554; **15** 397; **16** 195; **20 254–57 (upd.)**, 258; **21** 146; **22** 427–28; **26** 456; **27** 317; **29** 508
Goldome Savings Bank, **11** 110; **17** 488
Goldsbrough Mort & Co., **I** 437
Goldsmith's, **9** 209
Goldstar Co., Ltd., II 5, 53–54; **III** 517; **7** 233; **12 211–13**; **13** 213; **30** 184
Goldwell, **III** 38
Goldwyn Films. *See* Metro-Goldwyn-Mayer Inc.
Golf Day, **22** 517
The Golub Corporation, 26 169–71
Gomoljak, **14** 250
Good Foods, Inc., **II** 497
The Good Guys!, Inc., 10 334–35; **30 224–27 (upd.)**
The Good Humor-Breyers Ice Cream Company, II 533; **14 203–05**; **15** 222; **17** 140–41
Good Natural Café, **27** 481
Good Times, Inc., **8** 303
Good Vibrations, Inc., **28** 345
Good Weather International Inc., **III** 221; **14** 109
Goodbody & Company, **II** 425; **13** 341; **22** 428
Goodbody James Capel, **16** 14
Goodby, Berlin & Silverstein, **10** 484
Goodebodies, **11** 41
Gooderham and Worts, **I** 216, 263–64
Goodlass, Wall & Co., **III** 680–81
Goodman Bros. Mfg. Co., **14** 436
Goodman Fielder, Wattie's, Ltd., **II** 565; **7** 577
GoodMark Foods, Inc., 26 172–74
Goodrich Oil Co., **IV** 365
Goodrich, Tew and Company, **V** 231
Goodrich Tire Company, **V** 240–41; **6** 27
Goodson Newspaper Group, **29** 262
GoodTimes Entertainment, **31** 238
Goodwill Industries International, Inc., 15 511; **16 244–46**
Goodwin & Co., **12** 108
Goodwin, Dannenbaum, Littman & Wingfield, **16** 72
Goody Products, Inc., 12 214–16
Goody's Family Clothing, Inc., 20 265–67
The Goodyear Tire & Rubber Company, I 21; **II** 304; **III** 452; **V 244–48**; **8** 81, 291–92, 339; **9** 324; **10** 445; **15** 91; **16** 474; **19** 221, 223, 455; **20 259–64 (upd.)**; **21** 72–74
Gordon A. Freisen, International, **III** 73
Gordon B. Miller & Co., **7** 256; **25** 254
Gordon Capital Corp., **II** 245
Gordon Food Service Inc., 8 225–27
Gordon Investment Corp., **II** 245
Gordon Jewelry Corporation, **16** 559, 561
Gordon Manufacturing Co., **11** 256
Gordon Publications, **IV** 610
Gordon-Van Cheese Company, **8** 225
Gordy Company, **26** 314
Gore Newspapers Company, **IV** 683; **22** 521
Gorges Foodservice, Inc., **14** 516
Gorham Silver, **12** 313
Gorilla Sports Club, **25** 42
Gorman Eckert & Co., **27** 299

The Gorman-Rupp Company, **18 201–03**
Gormully & Jeffrey, **IV** 660
Gorton's, **II** 502; **10** 323; **13 243–44**
The Gosho Co. *See* Kanematsu Corporation.
Gotaas-Larsen Shipping Corp., **6** 368; **27** 91
Götabanken, **II** 303, 353
Göteborgs Handelsbank, **II** 351
Göteborgs Handelskompani, **III** 425
Gothenburg Light & Power Company, **6** 580
Gothenburg Tramways Co., **II** 1
Gott Corp., **III** 614; **21** 293
Gottschalks, Inc., **18 204–06**; **26** 130
Goulard and Olena, **I** 412
Gould Electronics, Inc., **III** 745; **11** 45; **13** 127, 201; **14 206–08**; **21** 43
Goulding Industries Ltd., **IV** 295; **19** 225
Goulds Pumps Inc., **24 188–91**
Gourmet Award Foods, **29** 480–81
Gourmet Foods, **II** 528
Government Bond Department, **9** 369
Government Employees Insurance Company. *See* GEICO Corporation.
Government National Mortgage Assoc., **II** 410
Governor and Company of Adventurers of England. *See* Hudson's Bay Company.
The Governor and Company of the Bank of Scotland, **II** 422; **III** 360; **V** 166; **10 336–38**
Goya Foods Inc., **22 245–47**; **24** 516
GP Group Acquisition Limited Partnership, **10** 288; **27** 41–42
GPE. *See* General Precision Equipment Corporation.
GPI. *See* General Parts Inc.
GPS Pool Supply, **29** 34
GPT, **15** 125
GPU. *See* General Public Utilities Corporation.
GPU, Inc., **27 182–85 (upd.)**
Graber Industries, Inc., **V** 379; **19** 421
Grace. *See* W.R. Grace & Co.
Grace Drilling Company, **9** 365
Grace-Sierra Horticultural Products Co., **22** 475
Graco Inc., **19 178–80**
Gradco Systems, Inc., **6** 290
Gradiaz, Annis & Co., **15** 138
Gradmann & Holler, **III** 283
Graef & Schmidt, **III** 54
Graf, **23** 219
Graf Bertel Dominique/New York, **6** 48
Graficas e Instrumentos S.A., **13** 234
Graftek Press, Inc., **26** 44
Graham Brothers, **27** 267, 269
Graham Container Corp., **8** 477
Graham Page, **III** 568; **20** 359
Grahams Builders Merchants, **I** 429
Gralla, **IV** 687
Grameen Bank, **31 219–22**
Gramercy Pictures, **23** 391
Gramophone Company, **22** 192
Grampian Electricity Supply Company, **13** 457
Gran Central Corporation, **8** 487
Granada Group PLC, **II** 70, **138–40**; **17** 353; **24 192–95 (upd.)**, 269; **25** 270
Granada Royale Hometels, **9** 426
Granaria Holdings B.V., **23** 183
GranCare, Inc., **14 209–11**; **25** 310
Grand Bazaar Innovations Bon Marché, **13** 284; **26** 159–60
Grand Casinos, Inc., **20 268–70**; **21** 526; **25** 386
Grand Department Store, **19** 510
Grand Hotel Krasnapolsky N.V., **23 227–29**
Grand Magasin de Nouveautés Fournier d'Annecy, **27** 93
Grand Metropolitan plc, **I 247–49**, 259, 261; **II** 555–57, 565, 608, 613–15; **9** 99; **13** 391, 407, 409; **14 212–15 (upd.)**; **15** 72; **17** 69, 71; **20** 452; **21** 401; **26** 58. *See also* Diageo plc.
Grand Rapids Carpet Sweeper Company, **9** 70
Grand Rapids Gas Light Company. *See* MCN Corporation.
Grand Rapids Wholesale Grocery Company, **8** 481
Grand Trunk Corp., **6** 359–61
Grand Union Company, **II** 637, 662; **7 202–04**; **8** 410; **13** 394; **16** 249; **28 162–65 (upd.)**
Grand Valley Gas Company, **11** 28
Grandes Superficies S.A., **23** 247
Grandmet USA, **I** 248
Les Grands Magasins Au Bon Marché, **26** 159–60
Grands Magasins L. Tietz, **V** 103
Grandy's, **15** 345
Granger Associates, **12** 136
Gränges, **III** 480; **22** 27
Granite City Steel Company, **12** 353
Granite Furniture Co., **14** 235
Granite Rock Company, **26 175–78**
Grant Oil Tool Co., **III** 569; **20** 361
Grant Street National Bank, **II** 317
Grantham, Mayo, Van Otterloo & Co. LLC, **24** 407
GranTree, **14** 4
Graphic Controls Corp., **IV** 678
Graphic Industries Inc., **25 182–84**
Graphic Research, Inc., **13** 344–45
Graphic Services, **III** 166; **6** 282
Graphics Systems Software, **III** 169; **6** 285; **8** 519
Graphite Oil Product Co., **I** 360
Graphix Zone, **31** 238
Grass Valley Group, **8** 518, 520
Grasselli Chemical Company, **22** 225
Grasselli Dyestuffs Corp., **I** 337
Grasset, **IV** 617–18
Grattan Plc, **V** 160; **29** 356
The Graver Company, **16** 357
Gray Communications Systems, Inc., **24 196–200**
Gray Dawes & Co., **III** 522–23
Gray Drug Stores, **III** 745
Gray Dunn and Co., **II** 569
Gray Line, **24** 118
Gray, Seifert and Co., **10** 44
Grayarc, **III** 157
Grayrock Capital, **I** 275
Grays Harbor Mutual Savings Bank, **17** 530
Greaseater, Ltd., **8** 463–64
Great Alaska Tobacco Co., **17** 80
Great American Bagel and Coffee Co., **27** 482
Great American Broadcasting Inc., **18** 65–66; **22** 131; **23** 257–58
Great American Cookie Company. *See* Mrs. Fields' Original Cookies, Inc.
Great American Entertainment Company, **13** 279
Great American First Savings Bank of San Diego, **II** 420
Great American Life Insurance Co., **III** 190–92
Great American Lines Inc., **12** 29
Great American Management and Investment, Inc., **8 228–31**
Great American Reserve Insurance Co., **IV** 343; **10** 247
Great American Restaurants, **13** 321
The Great Atlantic & Pacific Tea Company, Inc., **II 636–38**, 629, 655–56, 666; **13** 25, 127, 237; **15** 259; **16** 63–64, **247–50 (upd.)**; **17** 106; **18** 6; **19** 479–80; **24** 417; **26** 463
Great Bagel and Coffee Co., **27** 480–81
Great Beam Co., **III** 690
Great Eastern Railway, **6** 424
Great 5¢ Store, **V** 224
Great Halviggan, **III** 690
Great Lakes Bancorp, **8 232–33**
Great Lakes Bankgroup, **II** 457
Great Lakes Carbon Corporation, **12** 99
Great Lakes Chemical Corp., **I 341–42**; **8** 262; **14 216–18 (upd.)**
Great Lakes Corp., **IV** 136
Great Lakes Pipe Line Co., **IV** 400, 575; **31** 470
Great Lakes Steel Corp., **IV** 236; **8** 346; **12** 352; **26** 528
Great Lakes Window, Inc., **12** 397
Great Land Seafoods, Inc., **II** 553
Great Northern, **III** 282
Great Northern Import Co., **I** 292
Great Northern Nekoosa Corp., **IV** 282–83, 300; **9** 260–61
Great Northern Railway Company, **6** 596
Great Plains Transportation, **18** 226
Great Shoshone & Twin Falls Water Power Company, **12** 265
The Great Universal Stores plc, **V 67–69**; **15** 83; **17** 66, 68; **19 181–84 (upd.)**
The Great Western Auction House & Clothing Store, **19** 261
Great Western Billiard Manufactory, **III** 442
Great Western Financial Corporation, **10 339–41**
Great Western Foam Co., **17** 182
Great Western Railway, **III** 272
Great World Foods, Inc., **17** 93
Great-West Lifeco Inc., **III 260–61**; **21** 447
Greatamerica Corp., **I** 489; **10** 419; **24** 303
Greater All American Markets, **II** 601; **7** 19
Greater New York Film Rental Co., **II** 169
Greater Washington Investments, Inc., **15** 248
Greb Industries Ltd., **16** 79, 545
Grebner GmbH, **26** 21
Greeley Beef Plant, **13** 350
Green Acquisition Co., **18** 107
Green Bay Food Company, **7** 127
Green Capital Investors L.P., **23** 413–14
Green Cross K.K., **I** 665
Green Giant, **II** 556; **13** 408; **14** 212, 214; **24** 140–41
Green Island Cement (Holdings) Ltd. Group, **IV** 694–95
Green Line Investor Services, **18** 553

Green Mountain Coffee, Inc., 31 227–30
Green Power & Light Company. *See* UtiliCorp United Inc.
Green River Electric Corporation, **11** 37
Green Thumb, **II** 562
Green Tree Financial Corporation, 11 162–63
The Greenalls Group PLC, 21 245–47
The Greenbrier Companies, 19 185–87
Greene King plc, 31 223–26
Greenfield Healthy Foods, **26** 58
Greenfield Industries Inc., **13** 8
Greenleaf Corp., **IV** 203
Greenman Brothers Inc. *See* Noodle Kidoodle.
GreenPoint Financial Corp., 28 166–68
Greensboro Life Insurance Company, **11** 213
Greenville Insulating Board Corp., **III** 763
Greenville Tube Corporation, **21** 108
Greenwell Montagu Gilt-Edged, **II** 319; **17** 325
Greenwich Associates, **19** 117
Greenwich Capital Markets, **II** 311
Greenwood Mills, Inc., 14 219–21
Greenwood Publishing Group, **IV** 610
Greenwood Trust Company, **18** 478
Gregg Publishing Co., **IV** 636
Greif Bros. Corporation, 15 186–88
Grenfell and Colegrave Ltd., **II** 245
Gresham Insurance Company Limited, **24** 285
Gresham Life Assurance, **III** 200, 272–73
GretagMacbeth Holdings AG, **18** 291
Grey Advertising, Inc., I 175, 623; **6 26–28**; **10** 69; **14** 150; **22** 396; **25** 166, 381
Grey United Stores, **II** 666
Greyhound Corp., I 448–50; **II** 445; **6** 27; **8** 144–45; **10** 72; **12** 199; **16** 349; **22** 406, 427; **23** 173–74; **27** 480
Greyhound Temporary Services, **25** 432
Greylock Mills, **III** 213
GRiD Systems Corp., **II** 107
Griesheim Elektron, **IV** 140
Grieveson, Grant and Co., **II** 422–23
Griffin and Sons, **II** 543
Griffin Bacal, **25** 381
Griffin Pipe Products Co., **7** 30–31
Griffin Wheel Company, **7** 29–30
Griffon Cutlery Corp., **13** 166
Grigg, Elliot & Co., **14** 555
Grimes Aerospace, **22** 32
Grindlays Bank, **II** 189
Gringoir/Broussard, **II** 556
Grinnell Corp., III 643–45; **11** 198; **13 245–47**
Grip Printing & Publishing Co., **IV** 644
Grisewood & Dempsey, **IV** 616
Grist Mill Company, 15 189–91; **22** 338
Gristede Brothers, **23** 407; **24** 528–29
Gristede's Sloan's, Inc., 31 231–33
GRM Industries Inc., **15** 247–48
Grocer Publishing Co., **IV** 638
Grocery Store Products Co., **III** 21
Grocery Warehouse, **II** 602
Groen Manufacturing, **III** 468
Grogan-Cochran Land Company, **7** 345
Grolier Inc., IV 619; **16 251–54**
Groot-Noordhollandsche, **III** 177–79
Groovy Beverages, **II** 477
Gross Brothers Laundry. *See* G&K Services, Inc.
Gross Townsend Frank Hoffman, **6** 28
Grosset & Dunlap, Inc., **II** 144; **III** 190–91
Grosskraftwerk Franken AG, **23** 47
Grossman's Inc., 13 248–50
Grossmith Agricultural Industries, **II** 500
Grosvenor Marketing Co., **II** 465
Groton Victory Yard, **I** 661
Ground Round, Inc., 21 248–51
Ground Services Inc., **13** 49
Group Hospitalization and Medical Services, **10** 161
Group Lotus, **13** 357
Group Schneider S.A., **20** 214
Groupe AB, **19** 204
Groupe AG, **III** 201–02
Groupe Air France, 6 92–94. *See also* Air France *and* Societe Air France.
Groupe Ancienne Mutuelle, **III** 210–11
Groupe André, 17 210–12
Groupe Barthelmey, **III** 373
Groupe Bisset, **24** 510
Groupe Bruxelles Lambert, **26** 368
Groupe Bull, **10** 563–64; **12** 246; **21** 391. *See also* Compagnie des Machines Bull.
Groupe Casino. *See* Etablissements Economiques de Casino Guichard, Perrachon et Cie, S.C.A.
Groupe Castorama-Dubois Investissements, 23 230–32
Groupe Danone, **14** 150
Le Groupe Darty, **24** 266, 270
Groupe Dassault Aviation SA, 26 179–82 (upd.)
Groupe de la Cité, IV 614–16, 617
Groupe de la Financière d'Angers, **IV** 108
Groupe DMC (Dollfus Mieg & Cie), 27 186–88
Groupe Jean Didier, **12** 413
Groupe Lagardère S.A., **15** 293; **21** 265, 267
Groupe Legris Industries, 23 233–35
Groupe Les Echos, 25 283–85
Groupe Pinault-Printemps-Redoute, **19** 306, 309; **21** 224, 226
Groupe Promodès S.A., 19 326–28
Groupe Rothschild, **22** 365
Groupe Rougier SA, 21 438–40
Groupe Salvat, **IV** 619
Groupe Sidel S.A., 21 252–55
Groupe Victoire, **III** 394
Groupe Vidéotron Ltée., 20 271–73
Groupe Yves Saint Laurent, 23 236–39
Groupe-SEB, **25** 394
Groupement des Exploitants Pétroliers, **IV** 545
Groupement Laitier du Perche, **19** 50
Groux Beverage Corporation, **11** 451
Grove Manufacturing Co., **I** 476–77; **9** 393
Grow Biz International, Inc., 18 207–10
Grow Group Inc., 12 217–19, 387–88
Growing Healthy Inc., **27** 197
Growmark, **I** 421; **11** 23
Growth International, Inc., **17** 371
Grubb & Ellis Company, 21 256–58
Gruene Apotheke, **I** 681
Gruma, S.A. de C.V., 19 192; **31 234–36**
Grumman Corp., I 58–59, **61–63**, 67–68, 78, 84, 490, 511; **7** 205; **8** 51; **9** 17, 206–07, 417, 460; **10** 316–17, 536; **11 164–67 (upd.)**, 363–65, 428; **15** 285; **28** 169
Grün & Bilfinger A.G., **I** 560–61
Grundig AG, I 411; **II** 80, 117; **13** 402–03; **15** 514; **27 189–92**
Grundig Data Scanner GmbH, **12** 162
Grunenthal, **I** 240
Gruner + Jahr AG & Co., **IV** 590, 593; **7** 245; **15** 51; **20** 53; **22** 442; **23** 85
Gruntal & Co., L.L.C., III 263; **20 274–76**
Gruntal Financial Corp., **III** 264
Grupo Acerero del Norte, **22** 286
Grupo Bimbo, S.A. de C.V., **31** 236
Grupo Cabal S.A., **23** 166
Grupo Carso, S.A. de C.V., 14 489; **21 259–61**
Grupo Corvi S.A. de C.V., **7** 115; **25** 126
Grupo Cuervo, S.A. de C.V., **31** 91–92
Grupo de Ingenieria Ecologica, **16** 260
Grupo Financiero Banamex-Accival, **27** 304
Grupo Financiero Inbursa, **21** 259
Grupo Financiero Serfin, S.A., 19 188–90, 474
Grupo Herdez S.A., **18** 247
Grupo Hermes, **24** 359
Grupo Industrial Alfa, S.A. *See* Alfa, S.A. de C.V.
Grupo Industrial Bimbo, 19 191–93; **29** 338
Grupo Industrial Maseca S.A. de C.V. (Gimsa). *See* Gruma, S.A. de C.V.
Grupo Irsa, **23** 171
Grupo Modelo, S.A. de C.V., 29 218–20
Grupo Nacional Provincial, **22** 285
Grupo Protexa, **16** 210
Grupo Pulsar. *See* Pulsar Internacional S.A.
Grupo Quan, **19** 192–93
Grupo Televisa, S.A., 9 429; **18 211–14**; **19** 10; **24** 515–17
Grupo Tudor, **IV** 471
Grupo Zeta, **IV** 652–53; **7** 392
Gruppo GFT, **22** 123
Gruppo IRI, **V** 325–27
Gryphon Development, **24** 237
Gryphon Holdings, Inc., 21 262–64
GSG&T, **6** 495
GSI. *See* Geophysical Service, Inc.
GSI Acquisition Co. L.P., **17** 488
GSR, Inc., **17** 338
GSU. *See* Gulf States Utilities Company.
GT Bicycles, 26 183–85, 412
GT Interactive Software, 19 405; **31 237–41**
GTE Corporation, II 38, 47, 80; **III** 475; **V 294–98**; **9** 49, 171, 478–80; **10** 19, 97, 431; **11** 500; **14** 259, 433; **15 192–97 (upd.)**; **18** 74, 111, 543; **22** 19; **25** 20–21, 91; **26** 520; **27** 302, 305. *See also* British Columbia Telephone Company.
GTECH Holdings, Inc., **27** 381
GTI Corporation, **29** 461–62
GTM-Entrepose, **23** 332
GTO. *See* Global Transport Organization.
GTS Duratek, Inc., **13** 367–68
Guangzhou M. C. Packaging, **10** 130
Guaranty Bank & Trust Company, **13** 440
Guaranty Federal Bank, F.S.B., **31** 441
Guaranty Federal Savings & Loan Assoc., **IV** 343
Guaranty Properties Ltd., **11** 258
Guaranty Savings and Loan, **10** 339
Guaranty Trust,
Guaranty Trust Co., **II** 329–32, 428; **IV** 20; **16** 25; **22** 110
Guardian, **III** 721
Guardian Bank, **13** 468

Guardian Federal Savings and Loan Association, **10** 91
Guardian Mortgage Company, **8** 460
Guardian National Bank, **I** 165; **11** 137
Guardian Refrigerator Company. *See* Frigidaire Home Products.
Guardian Royal Exchange Plc, **III** 350; **11 168–70**
Gubor Schokoladen, **15** 221
Guccio Gucci, S.p.A., **12** 281; **15 198–200**; **27** 329
GUD Holdings, Ltd., **17** 106
Guelph Dolime, **IV** 74
Guerlain, **23 240–42**
Guernsey Banking Co., **II** 333
Guess, Inc., **15 201–03**; **17** 466; **23** 309; **24** 157; **27** 329
Guest, Keen and Nettlefolds plc. *See* GKN plc.
Guest Supply, Inc., **18 215–17**
Gueyraud et Fils Cadet, **III** 703
Guidant Corp., **30** 316
Guild Press, Inc., **13** 559
Guild Wineries, **13** 134
Guilford Industries, **8** 270–72
Guilford Mills Inc., **8 234–36**
Guilford of Maine, Inc., **29** 246
Guilford Transportation Industries, Inc., **16** 348, 350
Guinness Overseas Ltd., **25** 281
Guinness Peat, **10** 277
Guinness plc, **I** 239, 241, **250–52**, 268, 272, 282; **II** 428–29, 610; **9** 100, 449; **10** 399; **13** 454; **18** 62, 501; **29** 84. *See also* Diageo plc.
Guitar Center, Inc., **29 221–23**
Gujarat State Fertilizer Co., **III** 513
Gulco Industries, Inc., **11** 194
Güldner Aschaffenburg, **I** 582
Gulf + Western Inc., **I** 418, **451–53**, 540; **II** 147, 154–56, 177; **III** 642, 745; **IV** 289, 672; **7** 64; **10** 482; **13** 121, 169, 470; **22** 210; **24** 33; **25** 328, 535
Gulf + Western Industries, **22** 122. *See also* Paramount Communications.
Gulf Air, **6** 63; **27** 25
Gulf Canada Ltd., **I** 216, 262, 264; **IV** 495, 721; **6** 478; **9** 391; **13** 557–58
Gulf Caribbean Marine Lines, **6** 383
Gulf Coast Sportswear Inc., **23** 65
Gulf Energy Development, **22** 107
Gulf Engineering Co. Ltd., **IV** 131
Gulf Exploration Co., **IV** 454
Gulf Marine & Maintenance Offshore Service Company, **22** 276
Gulf Mobile and Northern Railroad, **I** 456
Gulf Mobile and Ohio Railroad, **I** 456; **11** 187
Gulf of Suez Petroleum Co., **IV** 412–14
Gulf Oil Chemical Co., **13** 502
Gulf Oil Corp., **I** 37, 584; **II** 315, 402, 408, 448; **III** 225, 231, 259, 497; **IV** 198, 287, 385–87, 392, 421, 450–51, 466, 470, 472–73, 476, 484, 508, 510, 512, 531, 538, 565, 570, 576; **17** 121–22; **21** 494; **24** 521; **25** 444
Gulf Plains Corp., **III** 471
Gulf Public Service Company, **6** 580
Gulf Resources & Chemical Corp., **15** 464
Gulf States Paper, **IV** 345
Gulf States Steel, **I** 491
Gulf States Utilities Company, **6 495–97**; **12** 99
Gulf United Corp., **III** 194
Gulfstream Aerospace Corporation, **7 205–06**; **13** 358; **24** 465; **28 169–72 (upd.)**
Gulfstream Banks, **II** 336
Gulfwind Marine USA, **30** 303
Gulistan Holdings Inc., **28** 219
Gulton Industries Inc., **7** 297; **19** 31
Gummi Werke, **I** 208
Gump's, **7** 286
Gunder & Associates, **12** 553
Gunderson, Inc. *See* The Greenbrier Companies.
Gunfred Group, **I** 387
Gunite Corporation, **23** 306
The Gunlocke Company, **12** 299; **13** 269; **23 243–45**
Gunnite, **27** 203
Gunns Ltd., **II** 482
Gunpowder Trust, **I** 379; **13** 379
Gunter Wulff Automaten, **III** 430
Gunther, S.A., **8** 477
Gupta, **15** 492
Gurneys, Birkbeck, Barclay & Buxton, **II** 235
Gusswerk Paul Saalmann & Sohne, **I** 582
Gustav Schickendanz KG, **V** 165
Gustavus A. Pfeiffer & Co., **I** 710
Gustin-Bacon Group, **16** 8
Gutehoffnungshütte Aktienverein AG, **III** 561, 563; **IV** 104, 201
Guthrie Balfour, **II** 499–500
Gutta Percha Co., **I** 428
Gutteridge, Haskins & Davey, **22** 138
Gutzeit. *See* W. Gutzeit & Co.
Guy Carpenter & Co., **III** 282
Guy Motors, **13** 286
Guy Salmon Service, Ltd., **6** 349
Guyenne et Gascogne, **23 246–48**
GW Utilities Ltd., **I** 264; **6** 478
Gwathmey Siegel & Associates Architects LLC, **II** 424; **13** 340; **26 186–88**
Gymboree Corporation, **15 204–06**
Gynecare Inc., **23** 190
Gynetics, Inc., **26** 31
Gypsum, Lime, & Alabastine Canada Ltd., **IV** 271

H&D. *See* Hinde & Dauch Paper Company.
H&H Craft & Floral, **17** 322
H & H Plastics Co., **25** 312
H & R Block, Incorporated, **9 268–70**; **25** 434; **27** 106, 307; **29 224–28 (upd.)**
H.A. Job, **II** 587
H. and D.H. Brooks & Co. *See* Brooks Brothers Inc.
H.B. Claflin Company, **V** 139
H.B. Fenn and Company Ltd., **25** 485
H.B. Fuller Company, **8 237–40**
H.B. Nickerson & Sons Ltd., **14** 339
H.B. Reese Candy Co., **II** 511
H.B. Tuttle and Company, **17** 355
H.B. Viney Company, Inc., **11** 211
H. Berlind Inc., **16** 388
H.C. Christians Co., **II** 536
H.C. Frick Coke Co., **IV** 573; **7** 550
H.C. Petersen & Co., **III** 417
H.C. Prange Co., **19** 511–12
H Curry & Sons. *See* Currys Group PLC.
H.D. Lee Company, Inc. *See* Lee Apparel Company, Inc.
H.D. Pochin & Co., **III** 690
H. Douglas Barclay, **8** 296
H.E. Butt Grocery Co., **13 251–53**
H.E. Moss and Company Tankers Ltd., **23** 161
H.F. Ahmanson & Company, **II 181–82**; **10 342–44 (upd.)**; **28** 167
H. Fairweather and Co., **I** 592
H.G. Anderson Equipment Corporation, **6** 441
H.H. Brown Shoe Company, **18** 60, **18** 62
H.H. Cutler Company, **17** 513
H.H. Robertson, Inc., **19** 366
H.H. West Co., **25** 501
H. Hackfeld & Co., **I** 417
H. Hamilton Pty, Ltd., **III** 420
H.I.G. Capital L.L.C., **30** 235
H.I. Rowntree and Co., **II** 568
H.J. Green, **II** 556
H.J. Heinz Company, **I** 30–31, 605, 612; **II** 414, 480, 450, **507–09**, 547; **III** 21; **7** 382, 448, 576, 578; **8** 499; **10** 151; **11 171–73 (upd.)**; **12** 411, 529, 531–32; **13** 383; **21** 55, 500–01; **22** 147; **25** 517; **27** 197–98
H.J. Justin & Sons. *See* Justin Industries, Inc.
H.K. Ferguson Company, **7** 355
H.K. Porter Company, Inc., **19** 152
H.L. Green Company, Inc., **9** 448
H.L. Judd Co., **III** 628
H.L. Yoh Company. *See* Day & Zimmerman, Inc.
H. Lewis and Sons, **14** 294
H.M. Byllesby & Company, Inc., **6** 539
H.M. Goush Co., **IV** 677–78
H.M. Spalding Electric Light Plant, **6** 592
H. Miller & Sons, Inc., **11** 258
H N Norton Co., **11** 208
H.O. Houghton & Company, **10** 355
H.P. Foods, **II** 475
H.P. Hood, **7** 17–18
H.P. Smith Paper Co., **IV** 290
H.R. MacMillan Export Co., **IV** 306–08
H. Reeve Angel & Co., **IV** 300
H. Salt Fish and Chips, **13** 320
H.T. Cherry Company, **12** 376
H.V. McKay Proprietary, **III** 651
H.W. Heidmann, **I** 542
H.W. Johns Manufacturing Co., **III** 663, 706–08; **7** 291
H.W. Madison Co., **11** 211
H.W.S. Solutions, **21** 37
H.W. Wilson Company, **17** 152; **23** 440
H. Williams and Co., Ltd., **II** 678
Ha-Lo Industries, Inc., **27 193–95**
Häagen-Dazs, **II** 556–57, 631; **10** 147; **14** 212, 214; **19** 116; **24** 140, 141
Haake-Beck Brauerei AG, **9** 86
Haas, Baruch & Co. *See* Smart & Final, Inc.
Haas Corp., **I** 481
Haas Publishing Companies, Inc., **22** 442
Haas Wheat & Partners, **15** 357
Habersham Bancorp, **25 185–87**
Habirshaw Cable and Wire Corp., **IV** 177
Habitat/Mothercare PLC. *See* Storehouse PLC.
Hach Co., **14** 309; **18 218–21**
Hachette Filipacchi Medias S.A., **21 265–67**
Hachette S.A., **IV** 614–15, **617–19**, 675; **10** 288; **11** 293; **12** 359; **16** 253–54; **17** 399; **21** 266; **22** 441–42; **23** 476. *See also* Matra-Hachette S.A.
Hachmeister, Inc., **II** 508; **11** 172

Hacker-Pschorr Brau, **II** 242
Hadco Corporation, 24 201–03
Hadleigh-Crowther, **I** 715
Haemocell, **11** 476
Haemonetics Corporation, 20 277–79
Hafez Insurance Co., **III** 242
Hagemeyer, **18** 180–82
Haggar Corporation, 19 194–96; 24 158
Haggie, **IV** 91
Hahn Automotive Warehouse, Inc., 24 204–06
Hahn Department Stores. *See* Allied Stores Corp.
Hahn, Inc., **17** 9
Haile Mines, Inc., **12** 253
Hain Food Group, Inc., I 514; **27 196–98**
Hainaut-Sambre, **IV** 52
A.B. Hakon Swenson, **II** 639
Hakuhodo, Inc., 6 29–31, 48–49; **16** 167
Hakunetsusha & Company, **12** 483
HAL Inc., 6 104; **9 271–73.** *See also* Hawaiian Airlines, Inc.
Halcon International, **IV** 456
Hale and Dorr, **31** 75
Haleko Hanseatisches Lebensmittel Kontor GmbH, **29** 500
Halewood, **21** 246
Halfords Ltd., **IV** 17, 19, 382–83; **24** 75
Halifax Banking Co., **II** 220
Halifax Timber, **I** 335
Hall & Levine Agency, **I** 14
Hall and Co., **III** 737
Hall and Ham River, **III** 739
Hall Bros. Co., **IV** 620–21; **7** 23
Hall Containers, **III** 739
Hall-Mark Electronics, **23** 490
Hallamore Manufacturing Co., **I** 481
La Halle aux Chaussures, **17** 210
Haller, Raymond & Brown, Inc., **II** 10
Halliburton Company, II 112; **III** 473, **497–500,** 617; **11** 505; **13** 118–19; **17** 417; **25 188–92 (upd.)**
Hallivet China Clay Co., **III** 690
Hallmark Cards, Inc., IV 620–21; 7 23–25; **12** 207, 209; **16 255–57 (upd.),** 427; **18** 67, 69, 213; **21** 426–28; **22** 33, 36; **24** 44, 516–17; **25** 69, 71, 368; **28** 160; **29** 64
Hallmark Chemical Corp., **8** 386
Hallmark Investment Corp., **21** 92
Halo Lighting, **30** 266
Haloid Company. *See* Xerox Corporation.
Halsam Company, **25** 380
Halsey, Stuart & Co., **II** 431; **III** 276
Halstead Industries, **26** 4
Halter Marine, **22** 276
Hamada Printing Press, **IV** 326
Hamashbir Lata'asiya, **II** 47; **25** 267
Hambrecht & Quist Group, **10** 463, 504; **26** 66; **27** 447; **31** 349
Hambro American Bank & Trust Co., **11** 109
Hambro Life Assurance Ltd., **I** 426; **III** 339
Hambros Bank, **II** 422; **16** 14; **27** 474
Hamburg-Amerikanische-Packetfahrt-Actien-Gesellschaft, **6** 397–98
Hamburg Banco, **II** 351
Hamburg-Amerika, **I** 542
Hamburger Flugzeubau GmbH., **I** 74
Hamelin Group, Inc., **19** 415
Hamer Hammer Service, Inc., **11** 523
Hamersley Holdings, **IV** 59–61
Hamil Textiles Ltd. *See* Algo Group Inc.
Hamilton Aero Manufacturing, **I** 47, 84; **10** 162
Hamilton Beach/Proctor-Silex Inc., 7 369–70; **16** 384; **17 213–15; 24** 435
Hamilton Blast Furnace Co., **IV** 208
Hamilton Brown Shoe Co., **III** 528
Hamilton Group Limited, **15** 478
Hamilton Industries, Inc., **25** 261
Hamilton Malleable Iron Co., **IV** 73; **24** 142
Hamilton National Bank, **13** 465
Hamilton Oil Corp., **IV** 47; **22** 107
Hamilton Standard, **9** 417
Hamilton Steel and Iron Co., **IV** 208
Hamilton/Hall-Mark, **19** 313
Hamish Hamilton, **IV** 659; **8** 526
Hammacher Schlemmer & Company, 21 268–70; 26 439–40
Hammamatsu Commerce Bank, **II** 291
Hammarplast, **13** 493
Hammarsforsens Kraft, **IV** 339
Hammerich & Lesser, **IV** 589
Hammermill Paper Co., **IV** 287; **15** 229; **23** 48–49
Hammers Plastic Recycling, **6** 441
Hammerson Property Investment and Development Corporation PLC, IV 696–98; 26 420
Hammery Furniture Company, **14** 302–03
Hamming-Whitman Publishing Co., **13** 559
Hammond Corp., **IV** 136
Hammond Lumber Co., **IV** 281; **9** 259
Hammond's, **II** 556
Hammonton Electric Light Company, **6** 449
Hamomag AG, **III** 546
Hampton Industries, Inc., 20 280–82
Hampton Inns, **9** 425–26
Hampton Roads Food, Inc., **25** 389
Hamworthy Engineering Ltd., **31** 367, 369
Han Kook Fertilizer Co., **I** 516
Hanbury, Taylor, Lloyd and Bowman, **II** 306
Hancock Fabrics, Inc., 16 197–99; **18 222–24**
Hancock Holding Company, 15 207–09
Hancock Jaffe Laboratories, **11** 460
Hancock Park Associates. *See* Leslie's Poolmart, Inc.
Hancock Textile Co., Inc., **27** 291
Hand in Hand, **III** 234
Handelsbank of Basel, **III** 375
Handelsfinanz Bank of Geneva, **II** 319; **17** 324
Handelsmaatschappij Montan N.V., **IV** 127
Handelsunion AG, **IV** 222
Handleman Company, 15 210–12
Handley Page Transport Ltd., **I** 50, 92–93; **24** 85
Handy & Harman, 23 249–52
Handy Andy Home Improvement Centers, Inc., **16** 210; **26** 160–61
Handy Dan, **V** 75
Hanes Corp., **II** 572–73; **8** 202, 288; **15** 436; **25** 166
Hanes Holding Company, **11** 256
Hang Chong, **18** 114
Hang Seng Bank, **II** 298; **IV** 717
Haniel & Cie. GmbH, **27** 175
Hanil Development Company, **6** 98
Hanjin Group, **6** 98; **27** 271–72
Hankook Tyre Manufacturing Company, **V** 255–56; **19** 508
Hankuk Glass Industry Co., **III** 715
Hankyu Corporation, V 454–56; 23 253–56 (upd.)
Hankyu Department Stores, Inc., V 70–71
Hanley Brick, **14** 250
Hanmi Citizen Precision Industry, **III** 455
Hanna Iron Ore Co., **IV** 236; **26** 528
Hanna Mining Co., **8** 346–47
Hanna Ore Mining Company, **12** 352
Hanna-Barbera Cartoons Inc., 7 306; **18** 65; **23 257–59,** 387; **25** 313
Hannaford Bros. Co., 12 220–22
Hannen Brauerei GmbH, **9** 100
Hannifin Corp., **III** 602
Hannoversche Bank, **II** 278
Hanover Bank, **II** 312–13
Hanover House, Inc., **24** 154
Hanovia Co., **IV** 78
Hanrstoffe-und Düngemittelwerk Saar-Lothringen GmbH, **IV** 197
Hans Grohe, **III** 570; **20** 362
Hansa Linie, **26** 279–80
Hanseco Reinsurance Co., **III** 343
Hansen Natural Corporation, 31 242–45
Hanson PLC, I 438, 475, 477; **II** 319; **III 501–03,** 506; **IV** 23, 94, 97, 169, 171, 173, 290; **7 207–10 (upd.); 8** 224; **13** 478–79; **17** 39–40, 325; **18** 548; **21** 545; **22** 211; **23** 296–97; **24** 152; **27** 287–88; **30 228–32 (upd.),** 441
Hansvedt Industries Inc., **25** 195
Hapag-Lloyd Ag, 6 397–99
Happy Air Exchangers Ltd., **21** 499
Happy Eater Ltd., **III** 106
Happy Kids Inc., 30 233–35
Haralambos Beverage Corporation, **11** 451
Harald Quant Group, **III** 377
Harbert Corporation, 13 98; **14 222–23**
Harbison-Walker Refractories Company, III 472; **24 207–09**
Harbor Tug and Barge Co., **6** 382
Harborlite Corporation, **10** 45
Harbour Group, **24** 16
Harcourt Brace and Co., IV 622; **12 223–26**
Harcourt Brace Jovanovich, Inc., II 133–34; **III** 118; **IV 622–24,** 642, 672; **7** 312; **12** 224; **13** 106; **14** 177; **19** 404; **25** 177
Harcourt General, Inc., 12 226; **20 283–87 (upd.); 25** 178
Harcros Chemical Group, **III** 699
Harcros Investment Trust Ltd., **III** 698–99
Hard Rock Cafe International, Inc., 12 227–29; 25 387; **27** 201
Hardee's Food Systems Inc., **II** 679; **7** 430; **8** 564; **9** 178; **15** 345; **16** 95; **19** 93; **23** 505; **27** 16–18
Hardin Stockton, **21** 96
Harding Lawson Associates Group, Inc., 16 258–60
Hardinge Inc., 25 193–95
Hardison & Stewart Oil, **IV** 569; **24** 519
Hardman Inc., **III** 699
Hardware Wholesalers Inc., **12** 8. *See also* Do it Best Corporation.
Hardwick Stove Company, **III** 573; **22** 349
Hardy Spicer, **III** 595
Harima Shipbuilding & Engineering Co., Ltd., **I** 511, 534; **III** 513, 533; **12** 484
Harima Zosenjo, Ltd., **IV** 129
Harken Energy Corporation, **17** 169–70
Harland and Wolff Holdings plc, 19 197–200

Harlem Globetrotters, **7** 199, 335
Harlequin Enterprises Ltd., **IV** 587, 590, 617, 619, 672; **19** 405; **29** 470–71, 473
Harley-Davidson, Inc., **III** 658; **7 211–14**; **13** 513; **16** 147–49; **21** 153; **23** 299–301; **25** 22, **196–200 (upd.)**
Harlow Metal Co. Ltd., **IV** 119
Harman International Industries Inc., **15 213–15**
Harmon Industries, Inc., **25 201–04**
Harmon Publishing Company, **12** 231
Harmsworth Brothers, **17** 396
Harmsworth Publishing, **19** 118, 120
Harnischfeger Industries, Inc., **I** 186; **8 241–44**; **14** 56; **26** 355
Harold A. Wilson & Co., **I** 405
Harold's Stores, Inc., **22 248–50**
Harp Lager Ltd., **15** 442
Harper Group Inc., **12** 180; **13** 20; **17 216–19**
Harper House, Inc. *See* Day Runner, Inc.
Harper Robinson and Company, **17** 163
HarperCollins Publishers, **IV** 652; **7** 389, 391; **14** 555–56; **15 216–18**; **23** 156, 210; **24** 546
Harpers, Inc., **12** 298
Harpo Entertainment Group, **28 173–75**; **30** 270
Harrah's Entertainment, Inc., **9** 425–27; **16 261–63**; **27** 200
Harrell International, **III** 21; **22** 146
Harriman Co., **IV** 310; **19** 266
Harriman, Ripley and Co., **II** 407
Harris Abattoir Co., **II** 482
Harris Adacom Corporation B.V., **21** 239
Harris Bankcorp, **II** 211
Harris Corporation, **II 37–39**; **11** 46, 286, 490; **20 288–92 (upd.)**; **27** 364
Harris Daishowa (Australia) Pty., Ltd., **IV** 268
Harris Financial, Inc., **11** 482
Harris Laboratories, **II** 483; **14** 549
Harris Manufacturing Company, **25** 464
Harris Microwave Semiconductors, **14** 417
Harris Oil Company, **17** 170
Harris Pharmaceuticals Ltd., **11** 208
Harris Publications, **13** 179
Harris Queensway, **24** 269
Harris Teeter Inc., **23 260–62**
Harris Transducer Corporation, **10** 319
Harris-Emery Co., **19** 510
Harrisburg National Bank and Trust Co., **II** 315–16
Harrison & Sons (Hanley) Ltd., **III** 681
Harrisons & Crosfield plc, **III 696–700**
Harrods, **21** 353
Harrow Stores Ltd., **II** 677
Harry F. Allsman Co., **III** 558
Harry Ferguson Co., **III** 651
Harry N. Abrams, Inc., **IV** 677; **17** 486
Harry's Farmers Market Inc., **23 263–66**
Harry's Premium Snacks, **27** 197
Harsah Ceramics, **25** 267
Harsco Corporation, **8 245–47**; **11** 135; **30** 471
Harshaw Chemical Company, **9** 154; **17** 363
Harshaw/Filtrol Partnership, **IV** 80
Hart Glass Manufacturing, **III** 423
Hart Press, **12** 25
Hart, Schaffner & Marx, **8** 248–49
Hart Son and Co., **I** 592
Harte & Co., **IV** 409; **7** 308
Harte-Hanks Communications, Inc., **17 220–22**
Harter Bank & Trust, **9** 474–75
Hartford Container Company, **8** 359
Hartford Electric Light Co., **13** 183
Hartford Fire Insurance, **11** 198
Hartford Insurance Group, **I** 463–64; **22** 428
Hartford Machine Screw Co., **12** 344
Hartford National Bank and Trust Co., **13** 396
Hartford National Corporation, **13** 464, 466–67
Hartford Trust Co., **II** 213
Hartley's, **II** 477
Hartmann & Braun, **III** 566
Hartmann Fibre, **12** 377
Hartmann Luggage, **12** 313
Hartmarx Corporation, **8 248–50**; **25** 258
The Hartstone Group plc, **14 224–26**
The Hartz Mountain Corporation, **12 230–32**
Harvard Private Capital Group Inc., **26** 500, 502
Harvard Sports, Inc., **19** 144
Harvard Table Tennis, Inc., **19** 143–44
Harvard Ventures, **25** 358
Harvest Day, **27** 291
Harvest International, **III** 201
Harvestore, **11** 5
Harvey Aluminum Inc., **I** 68; **22** 188
Harvey Benjamin Fuller, **8** 237–38
Harvey Group, **19** 312
Harvey Hotel Corporation, **23** 71, 73
Harvey Lumber and Supply Co., **III** 559
Harveys Casino Resorts, **27 199–201**
Harwood Homes, **31** 386
Harza Engineering Company, **14 227–28**
Hasbro, Inc., **III 504–06**; **IV** 676; **7** 305, 529; **12** 168–69, 495; **13** 561; **16 264–68 (upd.)**; **17** 243; **18** 520–21; **21** 375; **25** 313, 380–81, 487–89; **28** 159
Haslemere Estates, **26** 420
Hasler Holding AG, **9** 32
Hassenfeld Brothers Inc., **III** 504
Hasten Bancorp, **11** 371
Hastings Entertainment, Inc., **29 229–31**
Hastings Filters, Inc., **17** 104
Hastings Manufacturing Company, **17** 106
Hatch Grinding, **29** 86, 88
Hatersley & Davidson, **16** 80
Hatfield Jewelers, **30** 408
Hathaway Manfacturing Co., **III** 213
Hathaway Shirt Co., **I** 25–26
Hattori Seiko Co., Ltd. *See* Seiko Corporation.
Hausted, Inc., **29** 451
Havas, SA, **IV** 616; **10** 195–96, **345–48**; **13** 203–04
Haven Automation International, **III** 420
Haverty Furniture Companies, Inc., **31 246–49**
Haviland Candy Co., **15** 325
Hawaii National Bank, **11** 114
Hawaiian Airlines Inc., **9** 271–73; **22 251–53 (upd.)**; **24** 20–22; **26** 339. *See also* HAL Inc.
Hawaiian Dredging & Construction Co., **I** 565–66
Hawaiian Electric Industries, Inc., **9 274–77**
Hawaiian Fertilizer Co., **II** 490
Hawaiian Pineapple Co., **II** 491
Hawaiian Tug & Barge, **9** 276
Hawaiian Tuna Packers, **II** 491
Hawker Siddeley Group Public Limited Company, **I** 41–42, 50, 71, 470; **III 507–10**; **8** 51; **12** 190; **20** 311; **24** 85–86
Hawkeye Cablevision, **II** 161
Hawkins Chemical, Inc., **16 269–72**
Hawley & Hazel Chemical Co., **III** 25
Hawley Group Limited, **12** 10
Hawley Products, **16** 20
Haworth Inc., **8 251–52**; **27** 434
Hawthorn Company, **8** 287
Hawthorn-Mellody, **I** 446; **11** 25
Hawthorne Appliance and Electronics, **10** 9–11
Haxton Foods Inc., **21** 155
Hay Group, **I** 33
Hayakawa Electrical Industries, **II** 95–96
Hayakawa Metal Industrial Laboratory, **II** 95; **12** 447
Hayaku Zenjiro, **III** 408
Hayama Oil, **IV** 542
Hayashi Kane Shoten, **II** 578
Hayashikane Shoten K.K., **II** 578
Hayden Clinton National Bank, **11** 180
Hayden Publications, **27** 499
Hayden Stone, **II** 450; **9** 468
Hayes Conyngham & Robinson, **24** 75
Hayes Corporation, **24 210–14**
Hayes Industries Inc., **16** 7
Hayes Lemmerz International, Inc., **27 202–04**
Hayes Microcomputer Products, **9** 515
Hayes Wheel Company, **7** 258
Hayne, Miller & Swearingen, Inc., **22** 202
Hays Petroleum Services, **IV** 451
Hays Plc, **27 205–07**
Hazard, **I** 328
HAZCO International, Inc., **9** 110
Hazel Bishop, **III** 55
Hazel-Atlas Glass Co., **I** 599; **15** 128
Hazelden Foundation, **28 176–79**
Hazell Sun Ltd., **IV** 642; **7** 312
Hazeltine, Inc., **II** 20
Hazlenut Growers of Oregon, **7** 496–97
Hazleton Laboratories Corp., **30** 151
HBO. *See* Home Box Office Inc.
HCA Management Co., **III** 79
HCA Psychiatric Co., **III** 79
HCI Holdings, **I** 264
HCL America, **10** 505
HCL Sybase, **10** 505
HCR Manor Care, **25** 306, 310
HCS Technology, **26** 496–97
HDM Worldwide Direct, **13** 204; **16** 168
HDR Inc., **I** 563
HDS. *See* Heartland Express, Inc.
Head Sportswear International, **15** 368; **16** 296–97
Headrick Outdoor, **27** 280
Heads and Threads, **10** 43
Heal's, **13** 307
Heald Machine Co., **12** 67
Healey & Baker, **IV** 705
Health & Tennis Corp., **III** 431; **25** 40
Health and Diet Group, **29** 212
Health Care & Retirement Corporation, **III** 79; **22 254–56**; **25** 306, 310
Health Care International, **13** 328
Health Maintenance Organization of Pennsylvania. *See* U.S. Healthcare, Inc.
Health Maintenance Organizations, **I** 545
Health Management Center West, **17** 559

Health O Meter Products Inc., **14 229–31**; **15** 307
Health Plan of America, **11** 379
Health Plan of Virginia, **III** 389
Health Products Inc., **I** 387
Health Risk Management, Inc., **24 215–17**
Health Services, Inc., **10** 160
Health Systems International, Inc., **11 174–76**; **25** 527
Health Way, Inc., **II** 538
Health-Mor Inc. *See* HMI Industries.
HealthAmerica Corp., **III** 84
Healthcare, L.L.C., **29** 412
HealthCare USA, **III** 84, 86
HealthCo International, Inc., **19** 290
Healthdyne, Inc., **17** 306–09; **25** 82
Healthmagic, Inc., **29** 412
Healthshares L.L.C, **18** 370
Healthsource Inc., **22** 143
HealthSouth Rehabilitation Corporation, **14 232–34**; **25** 111
Healthtex, Inc., **17 223–25**, 513
HealthTrust, **III** 80; **15** 112
Healthy Choice, **12** 531
The Hearst Corporation, **IV** 582, 596, 608, **625–27**; **12** 358–59; **19 201–204 (upd.)**; **21** 404; **22** 161
Hearthstone Insurance Co. of Massachusetts, **III** 203
Heartland Building Products, **II** 582
Heartland Components, **III** 519; **22** 282
Heartland Express, Inc., **13** 550–51; **18 225–27**
Heartstream Inc., **18** 423
Heat Transfer Pty. Ltd., **III** 420
Heatcraft Inc., **8** 320–22
Heath Co., **II** 124; **13** 573
Heath Steele Mines Ltd., **IV** 18
Heatilator Inc., **13** 269
Heavy Duty Parts, Inc., **19** 37
Hebrew National Kosher Foods, **III** 24
Hechinger Company, **12 233–36**; **28** 51
Hecker-H-O Co., **II** 497
Heckett Technology Services Inc., **8** 246–47
Heckler & Koch GmbH, **24** 88
Hecla Mining Company, **17** 363; **20** 149, **293–96**
Heco Envelope Co., **IV** 282; **9** 261
Heekin Can Inc., **10** 130; **13 254–56**
HEFCO, **17** 106
Hefei Rongshida Group Corporation, **22** 350
HEI Investment Corp., **9** 276
HEICO Corporation, **15** 380; **30 236–38**
Heidelberg, **III** 701
Heidelberger Zement AG, **23** 325–26; **31 250–53**
Heidelburger Drueck, **III** 301
Heidemij. *See* Arcadis NV.
Heidi Bakery, **II** 633
Heidrick & Struggles International, Inc., **14** 464; **28 180–82**
Heights of Texas, fsb, **8** 437
Heil Company, **28** 103
Heil-Quaker Corp., **III** 654
Heileman Brewing Co. *See* G. Heileman Brewing Co.
Heilig-Meyers Co., **14 235–37**; **23** 412, 414
Heim-Plan Unternehmensgruppe, **25** 455
Heimstatt Bauspar AG, **III** 401
Heineken N.V., **I** 219, **256–58**, 266, 288; **II** 642; **13 257–59 (upd.)**; **14** 35; **17** 256; **18** 72; **21** 319; **25** 21–22; **26** 305
Heinkel Co., **I** 74
Heinrich Bauer North America, **7** 42–43
Heinrich Bauer Verlag, **23** 85–86
Heinrich Koppers GmbH, **IV** 89
Heinrich Lanz, **III** 463; **21** 173
Heinz Co. *See* H.J. Heinz Company.
Heinz Deichert KG, **11** 95
Heinz Italia S.p.A., **15** 221
Heisers Inc., **I** 185
Heisey Glasswork Company, **19** 210
Heiwa Sogo Bank, **II** 326, 361
Heizer Corp., **III** 109–11; **14** 13–15
HEL&P. *See* Houston Electric Light & Power Company.
Helados La Menorquina S.A., **22** 515
Helemano Co., **II** 491
Helen of Troy Corporation, **18 228–30**
Helen's Arts & Crafts, **17** 321
Helena Rubenstein, Inc., **III** 24, 48; **8** 343–44; **9** 201–02; **14** 121; **30** 188
Helene Curtis Industries, Inc., **I** 403; **8 253–54**; **18** 217; **22** 487; **28 183–85 (upd.)**
Helix Biocore, **11** 458
Hellefors Jernverk, **III** 623
Heller Financial, Inc., **7** 213; **16** 37; **25** 198
Hellman, Haas & Co. *See* Smart & Final, Inc.
Hellschreiber, **IV** 669
Helly Hansen ASA, **18** 396; **25 205–07**
Helme Products, Inc., **15** 139
Helmerich & Payne, Inc., **18 231–33**
Helmsley Enterprises, Inc., **9 278–80**
Helmut Delhey, **6** 428
Helmuth Hardekopf Bunker GmbH, **7** 141
Help-U-Sell, Inc., **III** 304
Helvetia General, **III** 376
Helvetia Milk Condensing Co., **II** 486; **7** 428
Helvetia Schweizerische Feuerversicherungs-Gesellschaft St. Gallen, **III** 375
Hely Group, **IV** 294; **19** 225
Helzberg's Diamond Shops, **18** 60, 63
Hemelinger Aktienbrauerei, **9** 86
Hemex, **11** 458
Hemlo Gold Mines Inc., **9 281–82**; **23** 40, 42
Hemma, **IV** 616
A.B. Hemmings, Ltd., **II** 465
Henderson's Industries, **III** 581
Henderson-Union Electric Cooperative, **11** 37
Henijean & Cie, **III** 283
Henkel KGaA, **III** 21, **31–34**, 45; **IV** 70; **9** 382; **13** 197, 199; **22** 145, 257; **30** 291
Henkel Manco Inc., **22 257–59**
Henley Drilling Company, **9** 364
The Henley Group, Inc., **I** 416; **III 511–12**; **6** 599–600; **9** 298; **11** 435; **12** 325; **17** 20
Hennes & Mauritz AB, **29 232–34**
Hennessy Company, **19** 272
Henney Motor Company, **12** 159
Henredon Furniture Industries, **III** 571; **11** 534; **20** 362
Henri Bendel Inc., **17** 203–04
Henry Broderick, Inc., **21** 96
Henry Denny & Sons, **27** 259
Henry Grant & Co., **I** 604
Henry Holt & Co., **IV** 622–23; **13** 105; **27** 223
Henry I. Siegel Co., **20** 136
Henry J. Kaiser Company, Ltd., **28** 200
Henry J. Tully Corporation, **13** 531
The Henry Jones Co-op Ltd., **7** 577
Henry Jones Foods, **I** 437–38, 592; **7** 182; **11** 212
Henry L. Doherty & Company, **IV** 391; **12** 542
Henry Lee Company, **16** 451, 453
Henry, Leonard & Thomas Inc., **9** 533
Henry Meadows, Ltd., **13** 286
Henry Pratt Company, **7** 30–31
Henry S. King & Co., **II** 307
Henry S. Miller Companies, **21** 257
Henry Schein, Inc., **29** 298; **31 254–56**
Henry Tate & Sons, **II** 580
Henry Telfer, **II** 513
Henry Waugh Ltd., **I** 469; **20** 311
Henry Willis & Co. *See* Willis Corroon Group Plc.
Henthy Realty Co., **III** 190
HEPCO. *See* Hokkaido Electric Power Company Inc.
Her Majesty's Stationery Office, **7 215–18**
Heraeus Holding GmbH, **IV 98–100**, 118
Herald and Weekly Times, **IV** 650, 652; **7** 389, 391
Herald Publishing Company, **12** 150
Heralds of Liberty, **9** 506
Herbalife International, Inc., **17 226–29**; **18** 164
Herbert Clough Inc., **24** 176
Herbert W. Davis & Co., **III** 344
Herco Technology, **IV** 680
Hercofina, **IV** 499
Hercules Filter, **III** 419
Hercules Inc., **I 343–45**, 347; **III** 241; **19** 11; **22 260–63 (upd.)**; **28** 195; **30** 36
Hercules Nut Corp., **II** 593
Hercules Offshore Drilling, **28** 347–48
Hereford Paper and Allied Products Ltd., **14** 430
Herff Jones, **II** 488; **25** 254
Heritage Bankcorp, **9** 482
Heritage Communications, **II** 160–61
Heritage Federal Savings and Loan Association of Huntington, **10** 92
Heritage House of America Inc., **III** 81
Heritage Life Assurance, **III** 248
Heritage Media Group, **25** 418
Heritage National Health Plan, **III** 464
Heritage Springfield, **14** 245
Herman Goelitz, Inc., **28 186–88**
Herman Miller, Inc., **8** 251–52, **255–57**
Herman's World of Sports, **I** 548; **II** 628–29; **15** 470; **16** 457
Hermann Pfauter Group, **24** 186
Hermannshütte, **IV** 103, 105
Hermes Kreditversicherungsbank, **III** 300
Hermès S.A., **14 238–40**
Herrburger Brooks P.L.C., **12** 297
Herrick, Waddell & Reed. *See* Waddell & Reed, Inc.
Herring-Hall-Marvin Safe Co. of Hamilton, Ohio, **7** 145
Hersey Products, Inc., **III** 645
Hershey Bank, **II** 342
Hershey Foods Corporation, **I** 26–27; **II** 478, 508, **510–12**, 569; **7** 300; **11** 15; **12** 480–81; **15** 63–64, **219–22 (upd.)**, 323; **27** 38–40; **30** 208–09

Hertel AG, **13** 297
Hertford Industrial Estates, **IV** 724
Hertie Waren- und Kaufhaus GmbH, V 72–74; **19** 234, 237
Herts & Beds Petroleum Co., **IV** 566
Herts Pharmaceuticals, **17** 450
The Hertz Corporation, **I** 130; **II** 90; **6** 52, 129, 348–50, 356–57, 392–93; **V** 494; **9 283–85**; **10** 419; **11** 494; **16** 379; **21** 151; **22** 54, 56, 524; **24** 9, 409; **25** 143
Hertz-Penske Leasing. *See* Penske Corporation.
Hervillier, **27** 188
Hespeler Hockey Inc., **22** 204
Hess Department Stores Inc., **16** 61–62; **19** 323–24
Hess Oil & Chemical Corp., **IV** 366
Hessische Berg- und Hüttenwerke AG, **III** 695
Hessische Landesbank, **II** 385–86
Hessische Ludwigs-Eisenbahn-Gesellschaft, **6** 424
Hesston Corporation, **13** 17; **22** 380
Hetteen Hoist & Derrick. *See* Polaris Industries Inc.
Heublein Inc., **I** 226, 246, 249, **259–61**, 281; **7** 266–67; **10** 180; **14** 214; **21** 314–15; **24** 140; **25** 177; **31** 92
Heuer. *See* TAG Heuer International SA.
Heuga Holdings B.V., **8** 271
Hewitt & Tuttle, **IV** 426; **17** 355–56
Hewitt Motor Company, **I** 177; **22** 329
Hewlett-Packard Company, **II** 62; **III** 116, **142–43**; **6** 219–20, 225, **237–39 (upd.)**, 244, 248, 278–79, 304; **8** 139, 467; **9** 7, 35–36, 57, 115, 471; **10** 15, 34, 86, 232, 257, 363, 404, 459, 464, 499, 501; **11** 46, 234, 274, 284, 382, 491, 518; **12** 61, 147, 162, 183, 470; **13** 128, 326, 501; **14** 354; **15** 125; **16** 5, 139–40, 299, 301, 367, 394, 550; **18** 386–87, 434, 436, 571; **19** 515; **20** 8; **25** 96, 118, 151–53, 499, 531; **26** 177, 520; **27** 221; **28 189–92 (upd.)**
Hexalon, **26** 420
Hexatec Polymers, **III** 742
Hexcel Corporation, **11** 475; **27** 50; **28 193–95**
Heyden Newport Chemical Corp., **I** 526
Heyer-Schulte, **26** 286
HFC. *See* Household Finance Corporation.
HFS Inc., **21** 97; **22** 54, 56
HG Hawker Engineering Co. Ltd., **III** 508
HGCC. *See* Hysol Grafil Composite Components Co.
HI. *See* Houston Industries Incorporated.
Hi Tech Consignments, **18** 208
Hi-Bred Corn Company, **9** 410
Hi-Lo Automotive, Inc., **26** 348–49
Hi-Mirror Co., **III** 715
Hi-Tek Polymers, Inc., **8** 554
Hibbett Sporting Goods, Inc., **26 189–91**
Hibbing Transportation, **I** 448
Hibernia & Shamrock-Bergwerksgesellschaft zu Berlin, **I** 542–43
Hibernia Bank, **18** 181
Hibernian Banking Assoc., **II** 261
Hickman Coward & Wattles, **24** 444
Hickory Farms, Inc., **12** 178, 199; **17 230–32**
Hickorycraft, **III** 571; **20** 362
Hicks & Greist, **6** 40
Hicks & Haas, **II** 478
Hicks, Muse, Tate & Furst, Inc., **24** 106; **30** 220
Hicksgas Gifford, Inc., **6** 529
Hidden Creek Industries, Inc., **16** 397; **24** 498
HiFi Buys, **30** 465
Higginson et Hanckar, **IV** 107
Higgs & Young Inc., **I** 412
High Point Chemical Corp., **III** 38
High Retail System Co., Ltd., **V** 195
Highgate Hotels, Inc., **21** 93
Highland Container Co., **IV** 345
Highland Superstores, **9** 65–66; **10** 9–10, 304–05, 468; **23** 51–52
Highland Telephone Company, **6** 334
Highlands Insurance Co., **III** 498
Highmark Inc., **I** 109; **27 208–11**
Highveld Steel and Vanadium Corp., **IV** 22
Higo Bank, **II** 291
Hilbun Poultry, **10** 250
Hilco Technologies, **III** 143; **6** 238
Hildebrandt International, **29 235–38**
Hilex Poly Co., Inc., **8** 477
Hill & Knowlton Inc. *See* WPP Group PLC.
Hill Publishing Co., **IV** 634
Hill Stores, **II** 683
Hill's Pet Nutrition, Inc., **14** 123; **26** 207; **27 212–14**, 390
Hill-Rom Company, **10** 349–50
Hillard Oil and Gas Company, Inc., **11** 523
Hillards, PLC, **II** 678
Hillenbrand Industries, Inc., **6** 295; **10 349–51**; **16** 20
Hiller Aircraft Company, **9** 205
Hiller Group, **14** 286
Hillerich & Bradsby Co., **24** 403
The Hillhaven Corporation, **III** 76, 87–88; **6** 188; **14 241–43**; **16** 57, 515, 517; **25** 307, 456
Hillin Oil, **IV** 658
Hillman, **I** 183
Hills & Dales Railway Co. *See* Dayton Power & Light Company.
Hills Brothers Inc., **II** 548; **7** 383; **28** 311
Hills Pet Products, **III** 25
Hills Stores Company, **11** 228; **13 260–61**; **21** 459; **30** 57
Hillsborough Holdings Corporation. *See* Walter Industries, Inc.
Hillsdale Machine & Tool Company, **8** 514
Hillsdown Holdings, PLC, **II 513–14**; **24 218–21 (upd.)**; **28** 490
Hillshire Farm, **II** 572
Hillside Industries Inc., **18** 118
Hilo Electric Light Company, **9** 276
Hilton, Anderson and Co., **III** 669
Hilton Athletic Apparel, **16** 296–97
Hilton Gravel, **III** 670
Hilton Hotels Corporation, **II** 208; **III 91–93**, 98–99, 102; **IV** 703; **6** 201, 210; **9** 95, 426; **19 205–08 (upd.)**; **21** 91, 93, 182, 333, 363; **23** 482; **27** 10
Hilton International Co., **6** 385; **12** 489
Himley Brick, **14** 248
Himolene, Inc., **8** 181
Hinde & Dauch Ltd., **IV** 272
Hinde & Dauch Paper Company, **19** 496
Hindell's Dairy Farmers Ltd., **II** 611–12
Hinds, Hayden & Eldredge, **10** 135
Hindustan Petroleum Corp. Ltd., **IV** 441
Hindustan Shipyard, **IV** 484
Hindustan Steel Ltd., **IV** 205–07
Hino Motors, Ltd., **7 219–21**; **21** 163, **271–74 (upd.)**; **23** 288
Hinode Life Insurance Co., Ltd., **II** 360; **III** 365
Hinomaru Truck Co., **6** 428
HIP Health Plan, **22** 425
Hip Hing Construction, **IV** 717
Hipercor, S.A., **V** 52; **26** 129
Hiram Walker Resources Ltd., **I** 216, **262–64**; **IV** 721; **6** 478; **9** 391; **18** 41
Hiram Walker-Consumers' Home Ltd. *See* Consumers' Gas Company Ltd.
Hiram Walker-Gooderham & Worts Ltd., **29** 18
Hire-Purchase Company, **16** 13
Hiroshima Yakult Co., **25** 449
The Hirsh Company, **17** 279
Hirth-Krause Company. *See* Wolverine World Wide Inc.
Hirz, **25** 85
Hispanica de Petroleos, **IV** 424, 527, 546
Hispano Aviacion, **I** 74
HISPANOBRAS, **IV** 55
Hispanoil. *See* Hispanica de Petroleos.
Hispeed Tools, **I** 573
Hisshin-DCA foods, **II** 554
History Book Club, **13** 105–06
Hit, **II** 164
Hit or Miss, **V** 197–98
Hitachi, Ltd., **I 454–55**, 494, 534; **II** 5, 30, 59, 64–65, 68, 70, 73, 75, 114, 273–74, 292–91; **III** 130, 140, 143, 464, 482; **IV** 101; **6** 238, 262; **7** 425; **9** 297; **11** 45, 308, 507; **12 237–39 (upd.)**, 484; **14** 201; **16** 139; **17** 353, 556; **18** 383; **19** 11; **21** 174–75, 390; **23** 53; **24** 324
Hitachi Metals, Ltd., **IV 101–02**
Hitachi Zosen Corporation, **III 513–14**; **8** 449
Hitchiner Manufacturing Co., Inc., **23 267–70**
Hitco, **III** 721–22
Hjalmar Blomqvist A.B., **II** 639
HL&P. *See* Houston Lighting and Power Company.
HLH Products, **7** 229
HMI Industries, Inc., **17 233–35**
HMO-PA. *See* U.S. Healthcare, Inc.
HMT Technology Corp., **IV** 102
HMV, **I** 531
Hoan Products Ltd. *See* Lifetime Hoan Corporation.
Hoare Govett Ltd., **II** 349
Hobart Corporation, **II** 534; **III** 610–11, 654; **7** 276; **12** 549; **22** 282, 353
Hobart Manufacturing Company, **8** 298
Hobbes Manufacturing, **I** 169–70
Hobby Lobby Stores Inc., **17** 360
Hobson, Bates & Partners, Ltd., **14** 48
Hochschild, Kohn Department Stores, **II** 673
Hochtief AG, **14** 298; **17** 376; **24** 88
Hocking Glass Company, **13** 40
Hoden Oil, **IV** 478
Hodenpyl-Walbridge & Company, **14** 134
Hodgart Consulting. *See* Hildebrandt International.
Hodgkin, Barnett, Pease, Spence & Co., **II** 307
Hoechst AG, **I** 305–06, 309, 317, **346–48**, 605, 632, 669–70; **IV** 451; **8** 262, 451–53; **13** 75, 262–64; **18** 47, 49, 51, **234–37 (upd.)**, 401; **21** 544; **22** 32; **25** 376

Hoechst Celanese Corporation, **8** 562; **11** 436; **12** 118; **13** 118, **262–65**; **22** 278; **24** 151; **26** 108
Hoeganaes Corporation, **8** 274–75
Hoerner Waldorf Corp., **IV** 264; **20** 129
Hoesch AG, **IV 103–06**, 128, 133, 195, 228, 232, 323
Hoffman Enclosures Inc., **26** 361, 363
Hoffmann-La Roche & Co. *See* F. Hoffmann-La Roche & Co.
Hoffritz, **27** 288
Högbo Stål & Jernwerks, **IV** 202
Högforsin Tehdas Osakeyhtiö, **IV** 300
Hojalata y Laminas S.A., **19** 10
Hokkaido Butter Co., **II** 575
Hokkaido Colonial Bank, **II** 310
Hokkaido Dairy Cooperative, **II** 574
Hokkaido Dairy Farm Assoc., **II** 538
Hokkaido Electric Power Company Inc., **V 635–37**
Hokkaido Forwarding, **6** 428
Hokkaido Rakuno Kosha Co., **II** 574
Hokkaido Takushoku Bank, **II** 300
Hokoku Cement, **III** 713
Hokoku Fire, **III** 384
Hokuetsu Paper Manufacturing, **IV** 327
Hokuriku Electric Power Company, **V 638–40**
Hokusin Kai, **IV** 475
Hokuyo Sangyo Co., Ltd., **IV** 285
Holbrook Grocery Co., **II** 682
Holcroft & Company, **7** 521
Hold Everything, **17** 548–50
Holden Group, **II** 457
Holderbank Financière Glaris Ltd., **III 701–02**; **8** 258–59, 456
Holdernam Inc., **8** 258–59
N.V. Holdingmaatschappij De Telegraaf, **23 271–73**
Holec Control Systems, **26** 496
Holga, Inc., **13** 269
Holgate Toys, **25** 379–80
Holiday Corp., **16** 263; **22** 418
Holiday Inns, Inc., **I** 224; **III 94–95**, 99–100; **6** 383; **9** 425–26; **10** 12; **11** 178, 242; **13** 362; **14** 106; **15** 44, 46; **16** 262; **18** 216; **21** 361–62; **23** 71; **24** 253; **25** 386; **27** 21. *See also* The Promus Cos., Inc.
Holiday Magic, Inc., **17** 227
Holiday Mart, **17** 124
Holiday Rambler Corporation, **7** 213; **25** 198
Holiday RV Superstores, Incorporated, **26 192–95**
Holland & Barrett, **13** 103; **31** 346, 348
Holland America Line, **6** 367–68; **26** 279; **27** 90–91
Holland Casino, **23** 229
Holland Electro B.V., **17** 234
Holland Hannen and Cubitts, **III** 753
Holland House, **I** 377–78
Holland Motor Express, **14** 505
Holland van 1859, **III** 200
Hollandsche Bank-Unie, **II** 184–85
Hollandse Signaalapparaten, **13** 402
Holley Carburetor, **I** 434
Hollinger International Inc., **24 222–25**
Hollingsworth & Whitney Co., **IV** 329
Hollostone, **III** 673
Holly Corporation, **12 240–42**
Holly Farms Corp., **II** 585; **7** 422–24; **14** 515; **23** 376–77
Holly Sugar Company. *See* Imperial Holly Corporation.
Hollywood Casino Corporation, **21 275–77**
Hollywood Entertainment Corporation, **25 208–10**; **29** 504; **31** 339
Hollywood Park, Inc., **20 297–300**
Hollywood Park Race Track, **29** 118
Hollywood Pictures, **II** 174; **30** 487
Hollywood Records, **6** 176
Holme Roberts & Owen LLP, **28 196–99**
Holmen Hygiene, **IV** 315
Holmen S.A., **IV** 325
Holmens Bruk, **IV** 317–18
Holmes Electric Protective Co., **III** 644
Holmes International. *See* Miller Industries, Inc.
Holmsund & Kramfors, **IV** 338
Holnam Inc., **III** 702; **8 258–60**
Holophane Corporation, **19 209–12**
Holson Burnes Group, Inc., **14 244–45**
Holt Manufacturing Co., **III** 450–51
Holt, Rinehart and Winston, Inc., **IV** 623–24; **12** 224
Holthouse Furniture Corp., **14** 236
Holvick Corp., **11** 65
Holvis AG, **15** 229
Holyman Sally Ltd., **29** 431
Holyoke Food Mart Inc., **19** 480
Holzer and Co., **III** 569; **20** 361
Holzverkohlungs-Industrie AG, **IV** 70
Homart Development, **V** 182
Home & Automobile Insurance Co., **III** 214
Home Box Office Inc., **II** 134, 136, 166–67, 176–77; **IV** 675; **7 222–24**, 528–29; **10** 196; **12** 75; **18** 65; **23 274–77 (upd.)**, 500; **25** 498; **28** 71
Home Builders Supply, Inc. *See* Scotty's, Inc.
Home Centers of America, Inc., **18** 286
Home Charm Group PLC, **II** 141
The Home Depot, Inc., **V 75–76**; **9** 400; **10** 235; **11** 384–86; **12** 7, 235, 345, 385; **13** 250, 548; **16** 187–88, 457; **17** 366; **18 238–40 (upd.)**; **19** 248, 250; **21** 356, 358; **22** 477; **23** 232; **26** 306; **27** 416, 481; **31** 20
Home Entertainment of Texas, Inc., **30** 466
Home Furnace Co., **I** 481
Home Insurance Company, **I** 440; **III 262–64**
Home Interiors, **15** 475, 477
Home Nutritional Services, **17** 308
Home Office Reference Laboratory, Inc., **22** 266
Home Oil Company Ltd., **I** 264; **6** 477–78
Home Products Corp., **18** 492
Home Properties Co., Inc., **21** 95
Home Quarters Warehouse, Inc., **12** 233, 235
Home Savings of America, **II** 181–82; **10** 342–43; **16** 346; **28** 167
Home Shopping Network, Inc., **V 77–78**; **9** 428; **18** 76; **24** 517; **25 211–15 (upd.)**; **26** 441
Home Telephone and Telegraph Company, **10** 201
Home Telephone Company. *See* Rochester Telephone Corporation.
Home Vision Entertainment Inc., **31** 339–40
Homebase, **II** 658; **13** 547–48
HomeClub Inc., **13** 547–48; **16** 187; **17** 366
Homécourt, **IV** 226
HomeFed Bank, **10** 340
Homelite, **21** 175
Homemade Ice Cream Company, **10** 371
Homemakers Furniture. *See* John M. Smyth Co.
Homer McKee Advertising, **I** 22
Homes By Oakwood, Inc., **15** 328
Homestake Mining Company, **IV** 18, 76; **12 243–45**; **20** 72; **27** 456
HomeTown Buffet, Inc., **19** 435; **22** 465
Homette Corporation, **30** 423
Homewood Stores Co., **IV** 573; **7** 550
Homewood Suites, **9** 425–26
Hominal Developments Inc., **9** 512
Hon Industries Inc., **13 266–69**; **23** 243–45
Honam Oil Refinery, **II** 53
Honcho Real Estate, **IV** 225; **24** 489
Honda Giken Kogyo Kabushiki Kaisha. *See* Honda Motor Company Limited.
Honda Motor Company Limited, **I** 9–10, 32, **174–76**, 184, 193; **II** 5; **III** 495, 517, 536, 603, 657–58, 667; **IV** 443; **7** 212–13, 459; **8** 71–72; **9** 294, 340–42; **10 352–54 (upd.)**; **11** 33, 49–50, 352; **12** 122, 401; **13** 30; **16** 167; **17** 25; **21** 153; **23** 289–90, 338, 340; **25** 197–99; **27** 76; **29 239–42 (upd.)**
Hondo Oil & Gas Co., **IV** 375–76
Honeywell Inc., **I** 63; **II** 30, **40–43**, 54, 68; **III** 122–23, 149, 152, 165, 535, 548–49, 732; **6** 266, 281, 283, 314; **8** 21; **9** 171, 324; **11** 198, 265; **12 246–49 (upd.)**; **13** 234, 499; **17** 33; **18** 341; **22** 373, 436; **23** 471; **29** 464; **30** 34
Hong Kong Aircraft Engineering Co., **I** 522; **6** 79; **16** 480
Hong Kong Airways, **6** 78–79; **16** 480
Hong Kong and Kowloon Wharf and Godown Co., **I** 470; **IV** 699
Hong Kong Dragon Airlines, **18** 114
Hong Kong Industrial Co., Ltd., **25** 312
Hong Kong Island Line Co., **IV** 718
Hong Kong Mass Transit Railway Corp., **19** 111
Hong Kong Resort Co., **IV** 718
Hong Kong Telecommunications Ltd., **IV** 700; **V** 285–86; **6 319–21**; **18** 114; **25** 101–02. *See also* Cable & Wireless HKT.
Hong Leong Corp., **III** 718
Hong Leong Group Malaysia, **26** 3, 5
Hongkong & Kowloon Wharf & Godown Company, **20** 312
Hongkong and Shanghai Banking Corporation Limited, **II** 257, **296–99**, 320, 358; **III** 289; **17** 325; **18** 253; **25** 12. *See also* HSBC Holdings plc.
Hongkong Electric Company Ltd., **6 498–500**; **20** 134
Hongkong Electric Holdings Ltd., **23 278–81 (upd.)**
Hongkong Land Holdings Ltd., **I** 470–71; **IV 699–701**; **6** 498–99; **20** 312–13; **23** 280
Honig-Copper & Harrington, **I** 14
Honjo Copper Smeltery, **III** 490
Honolua Plantation Land Company, Inc., **29** 308
Honolulu Oil, **II** 491
Honolulu Sugar Refining Co., **II** 490

Honshu Paper Co., Ltd., **IV** 268, **284–85**, 292, 297, 321, 326
Hood Rubber Company, **15** 488–89
Hood Sailmakers, Inc., **10** 215
Hoogovens. *See* Koninklijke Nederlandsche Hoogovens en Staalfabricken NV.
Hooiberg, **I** 256
Hook's Drug Stores, **9** 67
Hooker Chemical, **IV** 481
Hooker Corp., **19** 324
Hooker Furniture Corp. *See* Bassett Furniture Industries, Inc.
Hooker Petroleum, **IV** 264
Hooper Holmes, Inc., **22 264–67**
Hoosier Park L.P., **29** 118
Hooters of America, Inc., **18 241–43**
Hoover Ball and Bearing Co., **III** 589
The Hoover Company, **II** 7; **III** 478; **12** 158, **250–52**; **15** 416, 418; **21** 383; **30** 75, 78
Hoover Group Inc., **18** 11
Hoover Industrial, **III** 536; **26** 230
Hoover Treated Wood Products, Inc., **12** 396
Hoover-NSK Bearings, **III** 589
Hopkinton LNG Corp., **14** 126
Hopper Soliday and Co. Inc., **14** 154
Hops Restaurant Bar and Brewery, **31** 41
Hopwood & Company, **22** 427
Horace Mann Educators Corporation, **22 268–70**
Horizon Air Industries, Inc. *See* Alaska Air Group, Inc.
Horizon Bancorp, **II** 252; **14** 103
Horizon Corporation, **8** 348
Horizon Group Inc., **27** 221
Horizon Healthcare Corporation, **25** 456
Horizon Holidays, **14** 36
Horizon Industries, **19** 275
Horizon Organic Dairy Inc., **26** 447
Horizon Travel Group, **8** 527
Horizon/CMS Healthcare Corp., **25** 111, 457
Horizons Laitiers, **25** 85
Hormel Foods Corporation, **18 244–47 (upd.)**. *See also* George A. Hormel and Company.
Horn & Hardart, **II** 614
Horn Silver Mines Co., **IV** 83; **7** 187
Horn Venture Partners, **22** 464
Hornblower & Co., **II** 450
Hornbrook, Inc., **14** 112
Horne's, **I** 449; **16** 62
Hornsberg Land Co., **I** 553
Horst Breuer GmbH, **20** 363
Horst Salons Inc., **24** 56
Horten, **II** 622
Horton Homes, Inc., **25 216–18**
Hospital Corporation of America, **II** 331; **III 78–80**; **15** 112; **23** 153; **27** 237
Hospital Cost Consultants, **11** 113
Hospital Products, Inc., **10** 534
Hospital Service Association of Pittsburgh, **III** 325
Hospitality Franchise Systems, Inc., **11 177–79**; **14** 106; **17** 236
Hospitality Worldwide Services, Inc., **26 196–98**
Hosposable Products, Inc. *See* Wyant Corporation.
Host Communications Inc., **24** 404
Host Marriott Corporation, **21** 366
Host Marriott Services Corp., **III** 103; **16** 446; **17** 95
Hot 'n Now, **16** 96–97
Hot Dog Construction Co., **12** 372
Hot Sam Co., **12** 179, 199. *See also* Mrs. Fields' Original Cookies, Inc.
Hot Shoppes Inc., **III** 102
Hotchkiss-Brandt, **II** 116
Hoteiya, **V** 209–10
Hotel Corporation of America, **16** 337
Hotel Corporation of India, **27** 26
Hotel Properties Ltd., **30** 107
Hotel Scandinavia K/S, **I** 120
Houdry Chemicals, **I** 298
Houghton Mifflin Company, **10 355–57**; **26** 215
Houlihan's Restaurant Group, **25** 546
Housatonic Power Co., **13** 182
House and Land Syndicate, **IV** 710
House of Fabrics, Inc., **16** 197–98; **18** 223; **21 278–80**
House of Fraser Plc., **21** 353
House of Miniatures, **12** 264
House of Windsor, Inc., **9** 533
Household International, Inc., **I** 31; **II 417–20**, 605; **7** 569–70; **8** 117; **10** 419; **16** 487–88; **21 281–86 (upd.)**; **22** 38, 542; **24** 152
Household Products Inc., **I** 622; **10** 68
Household Rental Systems, **17** 234
Housing Development Finance Corporation, **20** 313
Housmex Inc., **23** 171
Houston, Effler & Partners Inc., **9** 135
Houston General Insurance, **III** 248
Houston Industries Incorporated, **V 641–44**; **7** 376
Houston International Teleport, Inc., **11** 184
Houston Natural Gas Corp., **IV** 395; **V** 610
Houston Oil & Minerals Corp., **11** 440–41
Houston Oil Co., **IV** 342, 674
Hoveringham Group, **III** 753; **28** 450
Hoving Corp., **14** 501
Hovis-McDougall Co., **II** 565
Hovnanian Enterprises, Inc., **29 243–45**
Howaldtswerke-Deutsche Werft AG, **IV** 201
Howard B. Stark Candy Co., **15** 325
Howard Flint Ink Company, **13** 227
Howard H. Sweet & Son, Inc., **14** 502
Howard Hughes Medical Institute, **II** 33, 35
Howard Hughes Properties, Ltd., **17** 317
Howard Humphreys, **13** 119
Howard Johnson International, Inc., **III** 94, 102–03; **6** 27; **7** 266; **11** 177–78; **15** 36; **16** 156; **17 236–39**; **25** 309
Howard Printing Co., **III** 188; **10** 29
Howard Research and Development Corporation, **15** 412, 414
Howard Smith Paper Mills Ltd., **IV** 271–72
Howden. *See* Alexander Howden Group.
Howdy Company, **9** 177
Howe & Fant, Inc., **23** 82
Howe and Brainbridge Inc., **I** 321
Howe Sound Co., **12** 253
Howe Sound Inc., **IV** 174
Howe Sound Pulp and Paper Ltd., **IV** 321
Howmedica, **29** 455
Howmet Corporation, **12 IV** 174; **253–55**; **22** 506
Hoya Corp., **III** 715
Hoyt Archery Company, **10** 216
HQ Office International, **8** 405; **23** 364
HRB Business Services, **29** 227
Hrubitz Oil Company, **12** 244
HSBC Holdings plc, **12 256–58**; **17** 323, 325–26; **26 199–204 (upd.)**
HSN Inc., **25** 411
HTH, **12** 464
HTM Goedkoop, **26** 278–79
H2O Plus, **11** 41
Hua Bei Oxygen, **25** 82
Huaneng Raw Material Corp., **III** 718
Hub Group, **26** 533
Hub Services, Inc., **18** 366
Hubbard Air Transport, **10** 162
Hubbard, Baker & Rice, **10** 126
Hubbard Broadcasting Inc., **24 226–28**
Hubbard Construction Co., **23** 332
Hubbard, Westervelt & Motteley, **II** 425; **13** 341
Hubbell Incorporated, **9 286–87**; **31 257–259 (upd.)**
Hubinger Co., **II** 508; **11** 172
Huck Manufacturing Company, **22** 506
Huddart Parker, **III** 672
Hudepohl-Schoenling Brewing Co., **18** 72
Hudnut, **I** 710
Hudson Automobile Company, **18** 492
The Hudson Bay Mining and Smelting Company, Limited, **12 259–61**; **13** 502–03; **16** 29
Hudson Engineering Corp., **III** 559
Hudson Foods Inc., **13 270–72**
Hudson Housewares Corp., **16** 389
Hudson Motor Car Co., **I** 135, 158; **III** 568; **10** 292; **20** 359
Hudson Packaging & Paper Co., **IV** 257
Hudson Pharmaceutical Corp., **31** 347
Hudson River Railroad, **II** 396
Hudson River Rubber Company, **V** 231
Hudson Scott & Sons, **I** 604
Hudson Software, **13** 481
Hudson Underground Telephone Company, **6** 299
Hudson's. *See* Dayton Hudson Corporation.
Hudson's Bay Company, **I** 284; **IV** 400–01, 437; **V 79–81**; **6** 359; **8** 525; **12** 361; **25 219–22 (upd.)**, 230
Hue International, **8** 324
Hueppe Duscha, **III** 571; **20** 362
Huff Daland Dusters, **I** 99; **6** 81
Huffco, **IV** 492
Huffman Manufacturing Company, **7** 225–26
Huffy Bicycles Co., **19** 383
Huffy Corporation, **7 225–27**; **26** 184, 412; **30 239–42 (upd.)**
Hugerot, **19** 50
Hugh O'Neill Auto Co., **12** 309
Hughes Air West, **25** 421
Hughes Aircraft Corporation, **I** 172, 484, 539; **III** 428, 539; **7** 426–27; **9** 409; **10** 327; **11** 263, 540; **13** 356, 398; **15** 528, 530; **21** 201; **23** 134; **24** 442; **25** 86, 223; **30** 175. *See also* GM Hughes Electronics Corporation.
Hughes Communications, Inc., **13** 398; **18** 211
Hughes Corp., **18** 535
Hughes Electric Heating Co., **II** 28; **12** 194
Hughes Electronics Corporation, **25 223–25**
Hughes Helicopter, **26** 431
Hughes Markets, Inc., **22 271–73**
Hughes Network Systems Inc., **21** 239
Hughes Properties, Inc., **17** 317

Hughes Supply, Inc., 14 246–47
Hughes Television Network, **11** 184
Hughes Tool Co., **I** 126; **II** 32; **12** 488; **15** 467; **25** 74. *See also* Baker Hughes Incorporated.
Hugo Neu Corporation, **19** 381–82
Hugo Stinnes GmbH, **I** 542; **8** 69, 494–95
Huguenot Fenal, **IV** 108
Huhtamaki, **30** 396, 398
Hüls A.G., I 349–50; 25 82
Hulton, **17** 397
Hulton Getty, **31** 216–17
Humana Inc., III 79, **81–83; 6** 28, 191–92, 279; **15** 113; **24 229–32 (upd.)**
Humanetics Corporation, **29** 213
Humason Manufacturing Co., **III** 628
Humber, **I** 197
Humberside Sea & Land Services, **31** 367
Humble Oil & Refining Company, **III** 497; **IV** 373, 428; **7** 171; **13** 118; **14** 291. *See also* Exxon.
Humboldt-Deutz-Motoren AG, **III** 541–42, 543; **IV** 126
Hummel, **II** 163–64
Hummingbird, **18** 313
Humongous Entertainment, Inc., **31** 238–40
Humphrey Instruments, **I** 693
Humphrey's Estate and Finance, **IV** 700
Humphreys & Glasgow Ltd., **V** 612
Hunco Ltd., **IV** 640; **26** 273
Hungária Biztositó, **III** 185
Hungarian-Soviet Civil Air Transport Joint Stock Company. *See* Malæv Plc.
Hungarotex, **V** 166
Hungry Howie's Pizza and Subs, Inc., 25 226–28
Hunt Consolidated, Inc., 27 215–18 (upd.)
Hunt Lumber Co., **IV** 358
Hunt Manufacturing Company, 12 262–64
Hunt Oil Company, IV 367, 453–54; **7 228–30**, 378. *See also* Hunt Consolidated, Inc.
Hunt-Wesson, Inc., 17 240–42; 25 278
Hunter Engineering Co., **IV** 18
Hunter Fan Company, 13 273–75
Hunter-Douglas, **8** 235
Hunter-Hayes Elevator Co., **III** 467
Hunters' Foods, **II** 500
Hunting Aircraft, **I** 50; **24** 85
Huntington Bancshares Inc., 11 180–82
Huntley and Palmer Foods, **II** 544
Huntley Boorne & Stevens, **I** 604
Huntsman Chemical Corporation, 8 261–63; 9 305
Hupp Motor Car Company, **III** 601; **8** 74; **10** 261
Hurd & Houghton, **10** 355
Hurlburt Paper Co., **IV** 311; **19** 267
Huron Steel Company, Inc., **16** 357
Huse Food Group, **14** 352
Husky Oil Ltd., **IV** 454, 695; **V** 673–75; **18** 253–54; **19** 159
Husqvarna Forest & Garden Company, **III** 480; **13** 564; **22** 26–27
Hussmann Corporation, **I** 457–58; **7** 429–30; **10** 554; **13** 268; **22** 353–54
Hutcheson & Grundy, **29** 286
Hutchinson Technology Incorporated, 18 248–51
Hutchinson Wholesale Grocery Co., **II** 624
Hutchinson-Mapa, **IV** 560
Hutchison, **I** 470
Hutchison Microtel, **11** 548
Hutchison Whampoa Ltd., IV 694–95; **18** 114, **252–55; 20** 131, 312–13; **25** 101
Huth Manufacturing Corporation, **10** 414
Hüttenwerk Oberhausen AG, **IV** 222
Hüttenwerk Salzgitter AG, **IV** 201
Huttig Building Products, **31** 398, 400
Huttig Sash & Door Company, **8** 135
Hutton, E.F. *See* E.F. Hutton.
Huyck Corp., **I** 429
Hvide Marine Incorporated, 22 274–76
HWI. *See* Hardware Wholesalers, Inc.
Hy-Form Products, Inc., **22** 175
Hyatt Corporation, II 442; **III** 92, **96–97; 9** 426; **16 273–75 (upd.); 22** 101; **23** 482
Hyatt Legal Services, **20** 435; **29** 226
Hyatt Medical Enterprises, **III** 73
Hyatt Roller Bearing Co., **I** 171–72; **9** 17; **10** 326
Hybridtech, **III** 18
Hyde Athletic Industries, Inc., 17 243–45
Hyde Company, A.L., **7** 116–17
Hydra Computer Systems, Inc., **13** 201
Hydraulic Brake Co., **I** 141
Hydro Carbide Corp., **19** 152
Hydro Electric, **19** 389–90
Hydro Med Sciences, **13** 367
Hydro-Aire Incorporated, **8** 135
Hydro-Carbon Light Company, **9** 127
Hydro-Electric Power Commission of Ontario, **6** 541; **9** 461
Hydro-Quebéc, 6 501–03
Hydrocarbon Services of Nigeria Co., **IV** 473
Hydroponic Chemical Co., **III** 28
Hydrox Corp., **II** 533
Hyer Boot, **19** 232
Hygeia Sciences, Inc., **8** 85, 512
Hygienic Ice Co., **IV** 722
Hygrade Containers Ltd., **IV** 286
Hygrade Foods, **III** 502; **7** 208; **14** 536
Hyland Laboratories, **I** 627
Hylsa. *See* Hojalata y Laminas S.A.
Hyosung Group, **III** 749
Hyper Shoppes, Inc., **II** 670; **18** 507
Hypercom Corporation, 27 219–21
Hyperion Press, **6** 176
Hyperion Software Corporation, 22 277–79
Hypermart USA, **8** 555–56
Hyplains Beef, **7** 175
Hypo-Bank. *See* Bayerische Hypotheken- und Wechsel-Bank AG.
Hypobaruk, **III** 348
Hyponex Corp., **22** 475
Hypro Engineering Inc., **I** 481
Hysol Corp., **I** 321; **12** 103
Hyster Company, 17 246–48
Hyster-Yale Materials Handling, Inc., **I** 424; **7** 369–71
Hystron Fibers Inc., **I** 347
Hyundai Group, I 207, 516; **II** 53–54, 122; **III** 457–59, **515–17; 7 231–34 (upd.); 9** 350; **10** 404; **12** 211, 546; **13** 280, 293–94; **18** 124; **23** 353; **25** 469; **29** 264, 266

I Can't Believe It's Yogurt, Inc., **17** 474
I. Appel, **30** 23
I.C.H. Corp., **I** 528
I.C. Isaacs & Company, 31 260–62
I.C. Johnson and Co., **III** 669
I.D. Systems, Inc., **11** 444
I-DIKA Milan SRL, **12** 182
I. Feldman Co., **31** 359
I.G. Farbenindustrie AG, **I** 305–06, 309–11, 337, 346–53, 619, 632–33, 698–99; **II** 257; **III** 677, 694; **IV** 111, 485; **8** 108–09; **11** 7; **13** 75–76, 262; **16** 121; **18** 47; **21** 544; **22** 225–26; **26** 452. *See also* BASF A.G. *and* Bayer A.G. *and* Hoechst A.G.
I.J. Stokes Corp., **I** 383
I.M. Pei & Associates, **I** 580; **III** 267
I.M. Singer and Co., **II** 9
I. Magnin Inc., **8** 444; **15** 86; **24** 422; **30** 383; **31** 191, 193
I.N. Kote, **IV** 116; **19** 219
I.N. Tek, **IV** 116; **19** 219
I.R. Maxwell & Co. Ltd., **IV** 641; **7** 311
I-T-E Circuit Breaker, **II** 121
I-X Corp., **22** 416
IAM/Environmental, **18** 11
Iams Company, 26 205–07; 27 213
IBANCO, **26** 515
IBC Holdings Corporation, **12** 276
Iberdrola, **V** 608
Iberia Líneas Aéreas De España S.A., I 110; **6 95–97**
Ibero-Amerika Bank, **II** 521
Iberswiss Catering, **6** 96
Ibex Engineering Co., **III** 420
IBH Holding AG, **7** 513
IBJ. *See* The Industrial Bank of Japan Ltd.
IBM. *See* International Business Machines Corporation.
IBP, Inc., II 515–17; 7 525; **21 287–90 (upd.); 23** 201
IBS Conversions Inc., **27** 492
Ibstock plc, III 735; **14 248–50**
IC Industries Inc., I 456–58; III 512; **7** 430; **10** 414, 553; **18** 3; **22** 197. *See also* Whitman Corporation.
ICA AB, II 639–40
ICA Mortgage Corporation, **8** 30
ICA Technologies, Ltd., **III** 533
Icarus Consulting AG, **29** 376
ICE, **I** 333
ICEE-USA, **24** 240
ICF Kaiser International, Inc., 28 200–04
ICH Corporation, **19** 468
Ichikoh Industries Ltd., **26** 154
ICI. *See* Imperial Chemical Industries plc.
ICI Canada, **22** 436
ICL plc, II 65, 81; **III** 141, 164; **6 240–42; 11** 150; **16** 226
ICM Mortgage Corporation, **8** 436
ICOA Life Insurance, **III** 253
Icon International, **24** 445
Icot Corp., **18** 543
ICS. *See* International Care Services.
ICS, **26** 119
ICX, **IV** 136
ID, Inc., **9** 193
id Software, **31** 237–38
Idaho Frozen Foods, **II** 572–73
Idaho Power Company, 12 265–67
IDB Communications Group, Inc., 11 183–85; 20 48; **27** 301, 307
IDC, **25** 101
Ide Megumi, **III** 549
Ideal Basic Industries, **III** 701–02; **8** 258–59; **12** 18
Ideal Corp., **III** 602; **23** 335

Ideal Loisirs Group, **23** 388
Idemitso Petrochemicals, **8** 153
Idemitsu Kosan K.K., **II** 361; **IV 434–36**, 476, 519
Identification Business, Inc., **18** 140
IDEXX Laboratories, Inc., **23 282–84**
IDG Books Worldwide, Inc., **27 222–24**. *See also* International Data Group, Inc.
IDG Communications, Inc, **7** 238
IDG World Expo Corporation, **7** 239
IDI, **22** 365
IDO. *See* Nippon Idou Tsushin.
IDS Ltd., **22** 76
IEL. *See* Industrial Equity Ltd.
IFC Disposables, Inc., **30** 496–98
IFI, **I** 161–62; **III** 347
Ifil, **27** 515
IFM, **25** 85
IFS Industries, **6** 294
IG Farben. *See* I.G. Farbenindustrie AG.
IG Holdings, **27** 430
IGA, **II** 624, 649, 668, 681–82; **7** 451; **15** 479; **18** 6, 9; **25** 234
Iggesund Bruk, **IV** 317–18
Igloo Products Corp., **21 291–93**; **22** 116
IGT-International, **10** 375–76
IGT-North America, **10** 375
IHI, **I** 534
IHI Granitech Corp., **III** 533
IHOP Corporation, **17 249–51**; **19** 435, 455
Iida & Co., **I** 493; **24** 325
IinteCom, **III** 169
IIS, **26** 441
IISCO-Ujjain Pipe and Foundry Co. Ltd., **IV** 206
IK Coach, Ltd., **23** 290
IKEA Group, **V 82–84**
IKEA International A/S, **26** 161, **208–11 (upd.)**
Il Fornaio (America) Corporation, **27 225–28**
Il Giornale, **13** 493
Ilaco, **26** 22
Illco Toy Co. USA, **12** 496
Illinois Bell Telephone Company, **IV** 660; **14 251–53**; **18** 30
Illinois Central Corporation, **I** 456, 584; **8** 410; **10** 553; **11 186–89**
Illinois Glass Co., **I** 609
Illinois Merchants Trust Co., **II** 261
Illinois National Bank & Trust Co., **III** 213–14
Illinois Power Company, **6** 470, **504–07**
Illinois Steel Co., **IV** 572; **7** 549; **8** 114
Illinois Terminal Company, **6** 504
Illinois Tool Works Inc., **III 518–20**; **22 280–83 (upd.)**
Illinois Traction Company, **6** 504
Illinois Trust and Savings Bank, **II** 261
Illinova Energy Partners, **27** 247
Ilmor Engineering of Great Britain, **V** 494
Ilse-Bergbau AG, **IV** 229–30
Ilselder Hütte, **IV** 201
Ilwaco Telephone and Telegraph Company. *See* Pacific Telecom, Inc.
Ilyushin, **24** 60
IMA Bancard, Inc., **24** 395
IMA Holdings Corp., **III** 73–74
Imabari, **25** 469
Image Business Systems Corp., **11** 66
Image Industries, Inc., **25** 320–21
Image Technologies Corporation, **12** 264
Imageline Inc., **25** 348
Imaging Technologies, **25** 183
Imaje, S.A., **28** 104
IMall Inc., **26** 441
Imasa Group, **IV** 34
Imasco Limited, **I** 514; **II** 605; **V 401–02**
Imation Corporation, **20 301–04**. *See also* Minnesota Mining & Manufacturing Company.
Imatran Voima Oy, **IV** 469. *See also* Fortum Corporation
Imax Corporation, **21** 362; **28 205–08**
IMC Drilling Mud, **III** 499
IMC Fertilizer Group, Inc., **8 264–66**
Imcera Group, Inc., **8** 264, 266
IMED Corp., **I** 712; **III** 511–12; **10** 551
Imetal S.A., **IV 107–09**
IMG. *See* International Management Group.
IMI plc, **III** 593; **9 288–89**; **29** 364
Imigest Fondo Imicapital, **III** 347
Imlo, **26** 22
Immersion Corporation, **28** 245
Immunex Corporation, **8** 26; **14 254–56**
Immuno Serums, Inc., **V** 174–75
Immuno Therapeutics, Inc., **25** 382
Imo Industries Inc., **7 235–37**; **27 229–32 (upd.)**
IMO Ltd., **III** 539
Impala Platinum Holdings, **IV** 91–93
Imperial Airways. *See* British Overseas Airways Corporation.
Imperial and International Communications Limited, **25** 100
Imperial Bank of Canada, **II** 244–45
Imperial Bank of Persia, **II** 298
Imperial British East Africa Co., **III** 522
Imperial Business Forms, **9** 72
Imperial Chemical Industries plc, **I** 303, **351–53**, 374, 605, 633; **II** 448, 565; **III** 522, 667, 677, 680, 745; **IV** 38, 110, 698; **7** 209; **8** 179, 222, 224; **9** 154, 288; **10** 436; **11** 97, 361; **12** 347; **13** 448, 470; **16** 121; **17** 118; **18** 50; **21** 544
Imperial Feather Company, **19** 304
Imperial Fire Co., **III** 373
Imperial Goonbarrow, **III** 690
Imperial Group Ltd., **II** 513; **III** 503; **7** 209; **17** 238
Imperial Holly Corporation, **12 268–70**
Imperial Japanese Government Steel Works, **17** 349–50
Imperial Life Co., **III** 288, 373
Imperial Marine Insurance Co., **III** 384, 405–06
Imperial Metal Industries Ltd. *See* IMI plc.
Imperial Oil Limited, **IV** 428, **437–39**, 494; **25 229–33 (upd.)**
Imperial Outdoor, **27** 280
Imperial Packing Co. *See* Beech-Nut Nutrition Corp.
Imperial Paper, **13** 169
Imperial Pneumatic Tool Co., **III** 525
Imperial Premium Finance, **III** 264
Imperial Savings Association, **8** 30–31
Imperial Smelting Corp., **IV** 58
Imperial Sports, **19** 230
Imperial Sugar Company. *See* Imperial Holly Corporation.
Imperial Tobacco Company, **I** 425–26, 605; **IV** 260; **V** 401. *See also* B.A.T. Industries PLC.
Imported Auto Parts, Inc., **15** 246
Impressions Software, **15** 455
Imprimis, **8** 467
Impulse, **9** 122
Impulse Designs, **31** 435–36
Imreg, **10** 473–74
IMRS. *See* Hyperion Software Corporation.
IMS International, Inc., **10** 105
In Focus Systems, Inc., **22 287–90**
In Home Health, Inc., **25** 306, 309–10
In-N-Out Burger, **19 213–15**
In-Sink-Erator, **II** 19
INA Corporation, **II** 403; **III** 79, 208, 223–25, 226; **11** 481; **22** 269. *See also* CIGNA Corporation.
INA Wälzlager Schaeffler, **III** 595
INA-Naftaplin, **IV** 454
Inabata & Co., **I** 398
InaCom Corporation, **13** 176, **276–78**; **19** 471
Incasso Bank, **II** 185
Incentive Group, **27** 269
Inchcape PLC, **II** 233; **III 521–24**; **16 276–80 (upd.)**
Incheon Iron & Steel Co., **III** 516
Inchon Heavy Industrial Corp., **IV** 183
Inco Limited, **IV** 75, 78, **110–12**
INCO-Banco Indústria e Comércio de Santa Catarina, **13** 70
Incola, S.A., **II** 471; **22** 93
InControl Inc., **11** 460
Incredible Universe, **12** 470; **17** 489
Ind Coope, **I** 215
Indemnité, **III** 391
Indemnity Insurance Company. *See* CIGNA Corporation.
Indentimat Corp., **14** 542
Independent Breweries Company, **9** 178
Independent Exhibitions Ltd., **27** 362
Independent Grocers Alliance. *See* IGA.
Independent Lock Co., **13** 166
Independent Metal Products Co., **I** 169
Independent Oil & Gas Co., **IV** 521
Independent Petrochemical, **14** 461
Independent Power Generators, **V** 605
Independent Stave Company, **28** 223
Independent Torpedo Company, **25** 73
Independent Warehouses, Inc., **IV** 180
India Exotics, Inc., **22** 133
India General Steam Navigation and Railway Co., **III** 522
India Life Assurance Co., **III** 359
India Rubber, Gutta Percha & Telegraph Works Co., **I** 428
Indian, **7** 211; **25** 196
Indian Airlines Corporation. *See* Air-India.
Indian Archery and Toy Corp., **19** 142–43
Indian Iron & Steel Co. Ltd., **IV** 49, 205–07
Indian Oil Corporation Ltd., **IV 440–41**, 483
Indian Point Farm Supply, Inc., **IV** 458–59
Indiana Bearings, Inc., **13** 78
Indiana Bell Telephone Company, Incorporated, **14 257–61**; **18** 30
Indiana Board and Filler Company, **12** 376
Indiana Electric Corporation, **6** 555
Indiana Energy, Inc., **27 233–36**
Indiana Gaming Company, **21** 40
Indiana Gas & Water Company, **6** 556
Indiana Group, **I** 378
Indiana Oil Purchasing Co., **IV** 370
Indiana Parts and Warehouse, **29** 86, 88
Indiana Power Company, **6** 555
Indiana Refining Co., **IV** 552
Indiana Tube Co., **23** 250
Indianapolis Air Pump Company, **8** 37

Indianapolis Brush Electric Light & Power Company, **6** 508
Indianapolis Cablevision, **6** 508–09
Indianapolis Light and Power Company, **6** 508
Indianapolis Motor Speedway Company, **9** 16
Indianapolis Power & Light Company, **6** 508–09
Indianapolis Pump and Tube Company, **8** 37
Indianhead Truck Lines, **6** 371
Indigo NV, **26 212–14**, 540–41
Indo-Asahi Glass Co., Ltd., **III** 667
Indo-China Steam Navigation Co., **I** 469; **20** 311
Indola Cosmetics B.V., **8** 16
Indonesia Petroleum Co., **IV** 516
Indresco, Inc., **22** 285
Induban, **II** 196
Indura SA Industria Y Commercio, **25** 82
Industri Kapital, **27** 269
Industria Gelati Sammontana, **II** 575
Industria Metalgrafica, **I** 231
Industria Raffinazione Oli Minerali, **IV** 419
Industrial & Trade Shows of Canada, **IV** 639
Industrial Acceptance Bank, **I** 337
Industrial Air Products, **19** 380–81
Industrial Air Tool, **28** 387
Industrial Bancorp, **9** 229
Industrial Bank of Japan, Ltd., **II 300–01**, 310–11, 338, 369, 433, 459; **17** 121
Industrial Bank of Scotland, **10** 337
Industrial Bio-Test Laboratories, **I** 374, 702
Industrial Cartonera, **IV** 295; **19** 226
Industrial Chemical and Equipment, **16** 271
Industrial Circuits, **IV** 680
Industrial Computer Corp., **11** 78
Industrial Development Corp., **IV** 22, 92, 534
Industrial Development Corp. of Zambia Ltd., **IV** 239–41
Industrial Engineering, **III** 598
Industrial Engineering Associates, Inc., **II** 112
Industrial Equity Ltd., **I** 438; **17** 357
Industrial Fuel Supply Co., **I** 569
Industrial Gas Equipment Co., **I** 297
Industrial Gases Lagos, **25** 82
Industrial Instrument Company. *See* Foxboro Company.
Industrial Light & Magic, **12** 322
Industrial Mutual Insurance, **III** 264
Industrial National Bank, **9** 229
Industrial Powder Coatings, Inc., **16** 475
Industrial Publishing Company, **9** 413; **27** 361
Industrial Reorganization Corp., **III** 502, 556
Industrial Resources, **6** 144
Industrial Shows of America, **27** 362
Industrial Tectonics Corp., **18** 276
Industrial Trade & Consumer Shows Inc., **IV** 639; **26** 272
Industrial Trust Co. of Wilmington, **25** 540
Industrial Trust Company, **9** 228
Industrial Vehicles Corp. B.V., **III** 543–44
Industrias Nacobre, **21** 259
Industrias Negromex, **23** 170
Industrias Penoles, S.A. de C.V., **22 284–86**
Industrias Resistol S.A., **23** 170–71
Industrias y Confecciones, S.A. **V** 51; **26** 129
Industrie Natuzzi S.p.A., **18 256–58**
Industrie Regionale du Bâtiment, **IV** 108
Industrie-Aktiengesellschaft, **IV** 201
Industriegas GmbH., **I** 581
Les Industries Ling, **13** 443
Industriforvaltnings AB Kinnevik, **26** 331–33
Industrionics Control, Inc., **III** 643
Industrivärden, **II** 366
Induyco. *See* Industrias y Confecciones, S.A.
Indy Lighting, **30** 266
Inelco Peripheriques, **10** 459
Inespo, **16** 322
Inexco Oil Co., **7** 282
Infinity Broadcasting Corporation, **11 190–92**; **22** 97; **23** 510; **28** 72
INFLEX, S.A., **8** 247
Inflight Sales Group Limited, **11** 82; **29** 511
InfoAsia, **28** 241
Infobase Services, **6** 14
Infonet Services Corporation, **6** 303; **27** 304
Infoplan, **14** 36
Informatics General Corporation, **III** 248; **11** 468; **25** 86
Informatics Legal Systems, **III** 169; **6** 285
Information Access Company, **12** 560–62; **17 252–55**
Information and Communication Group, **14** 555
Information Associates Inc., **11** 78
Information Builders, Inc., **14** 16; **22 291–93**
Information Consulting Group, **9** 345
Information, Dissemination and Retrieval Inc., **IV** 670
Information International. *See* Autologic Information International, Inc.
Information Management Reporting Services. *See* Hyperion Software Corporation.
Information Management Science Associates, Inc., **13** 174
Information Please LLC, **26** 216
Information Resources, Inc., **10 358–60**; **13** 4; **25** 366
Information Unlimited Software, **6** 224
Informix Corporation, **10 361–64**, 505; **30 243–46 (upd.)**
Infoseek Corporation, **27** 517; **30** 490
InfoSoft International, Inc. *See* Inso Corporation.
Infotechnology Inc., **25** 507–08
Infrasud, **I** 466
Infun, S.A., **23** 269
ING, B.V., **14** 45, 47
Ing. C. Olivetti & C., S.p.A., **III** 122, **144–46**, 549, 678; **10** 499; **16** 122; **25** 33
Ingalls Quinn and Johnson, **9** 135
Ingalls Shipbuilding, Inc., **I** 485; **11** 264–65; **12** 28, **271–73**
Ingear, **10** 216
Ingersoll-Rand Company, **III** 473, **525–27**; **10** 262; **13** 27, 523; **15** 187, **223–26 (upd.)**; **22** 542
Ingka Holding B.V. *See* IKEA International A/S.
Ingleby Enterprises Inc. *See* Caribiner International, Inc.
Inglenook Vineyards, **13** 134
Ingles Markets, Inc., **20 305–08**
Inglis Ltd., **III** 654; **12** 549
Ingram Book Group, **30** 70
Ingram Corp. Ltd., **III** 559; **IV** 249
Ingram Industries, Inc., **10** 518–19; **11 193–95**; **13** 90, 482
Ingram Micro Corporation, **24** 29
AB Ingredients, **II** 466
Ingredients Technology Corp., **9** 154
Ingres Corporation, **9** 36–37; **25** 87
Ingwerson and Co., **II** 356
INH. *See* Instituto Nacional de Hidrocarboros.
Inhalation Therapy Services, **III** 73
INI. *See* Instituto Nacional de Industria.
Inland Container Corporation, **IV** 311, 341–42, 675; **7** 528; **8 267–69**; **19** 267
Inland Motors Corporation, **18** 291
Inland Paperboard and Packaging, Inc., **31** 438
Inland Pollution Control, **9** 110
Inland Specialty Chemical Corp., **I** 342; **14** 217
Inland Steel Industries, Inc., **II** 403; **IV 113–16**, 158, 703; **7** 447; **13** 157; **15** 249–50; **17** 351; **19** 9, **216–20 (upd.)**, 311, 381; **23** 35; **30** 254
Inland Valley, **23** 321
Inmac, Inc., **16** 373
Inmos Ltd., **I** 532; **11** 307; **29** 323
InnerCity Foods Joint Venture Company, **16** 97
Inno-BM, **26** 158, 161
Inno-France. *See* Societe des Grandes Entreprises de Distribution, Inno-France.
Innova International Corporation, **26** 333
Innovacom, **25** 96
Innovation, **26** 158
Innovative Marketing Systems. *See* Bloomberg L.P.
Innovative Pork Concepts, **7** 82
Innovative Products & Peripherals Corporation, **14** 379
Innovative Software Inc., **10** 362
Innovative Sports Systems, Inc., **15** 396
Innovex Ltd., **21** 425
Inns and Co., **III** 734
Innwerk AG, **IV** 229
Inoue Electric Manufacturing Co., **II** 75–76
Inpaco, **16** 340
Inpacsa, **19** 226
Input/Output, Inc., **11** 538
INS. *See* International News Service.
Insalaco Markets Inc., **13** 394
INSCO, **III** 242
Inserra Supermarkets, **25 234–36**
Insight Enterprises, Inc., **18 259–61**
Insilco Corporation, **I** 473; **12** 472; **16 281–83**; **23** 212
Insley Manufacturing Co., **8** 545
Inso Corporation, **26 215–19**
Inspiration Resources Corporation, **12** 260; **13** 502–03
Inspirations PLC, **22** 129
Insta-Care Holdings Inc., **16** 59
Insta-Care Pharmacy Services, **9** 186
Instant Interiors Corporation, **26** 102
Instant Milk Co., **II** 488
Instapak Corporation, **14** 429
Institut de Sérothérapie Hémopoiétique, **I** 669
Institut für Gemeinwohl, **IV** 139

Institut Merieux, **I** 389
Institut Ronchese, **I** 676
Institute de Development Industriel, **19** 87
Institute for Professional Development, **24** 40
Institute for Scientific Information, **8** 525, 528
Institution Food House. *See* Alex Lee Inc.
Institutional Financing Services, **23** 491
Instituto Nacional de Hidrocarboros, **IV** 528
Instituto Nacional de Industria, I 459–61; **V** 606–07; **6** 95–96
Instituto per la Ricostruzione Industriale, **V** 614
Instone Airline, **I** 92
Instromet International, **22** 65
Instrumentarium Corp., **13** 328; **25** 82
Instrumentation Laboratory Inc., **III** 511–12; **22** 75
Instrumentation Scientifique de Laboratoire, S.A., **15** 404
Insulite Co. of Finland, **IV** 275
Insurance Auto Auctions, Inc., **23** 148, **285–87**
Insurance Co. against Fire Damage, **III** 308
Insurance Co. of Scotland, **III** 358
Insurance Co. of the State of Pennsylvania, **III** 196
Insurance Company of North America. *See* CIGNA Corporation.
Insurance Corp. of Ireland (Life), **III** 335
Insurance Partners L.P., **15** 257
Intabex Holdings Worldwide, S.A., **27** 126
Intalco Aluminum Corp., **12** 254
Intamin, **17** 443
INTEC, **6** 428
InteCom Inc., **6** 285
Integon Corp., **IV** 374
Integra-A Hotel and Restaurant Company, **13** 473
Integral Corporation, **14** 381; **23** 446
Integrated Business Information Services, **13** 5
Integrated Computer Systems. *See* Learning Tree International Inc.
Integrated Data Services Co., **IV** 473
Integrated Genetics, **I** 638; **8** 210; **13** 239
Integrated Health Services, Inc., **11** 282
Integrated Medical Systems Inc., **12** 333
Integrated Resources, Inc., **11** 483; **16** 54; **19** 393
Integrated Silicon Solutions, Inc., **18** 20
Integrated Software Systems Corporation, **6** 224; **11** 469
Integrated Systems Operations. *See* Xerox Corporation.
Integrated Systems Solutions Corp., **9** 284; **11** 395; **17** 264
Integrated Technology, Inc., **6** 279
Integrated Telecom Technologies, **14** 417
Integrity Life Insurance, **III** 249
Intel Corporation, II 44–46, 62, 64; **III** 115, 125, 455; **6** 215–17, 222, 231, 233, 235, 257; **9** 42–43, 57, 114–15, 165–66; **10 365–67 (upd.)**, 477; **11** 62, 308, 328, 490, 503, 518, 520; **12** 61, 449; **13** 47; **16** 139–40, 146, 394; **17** 32–33; **18** 18, 260; **19** 310, 312; **20** 69, 175; **21** 36, 122; **22** 542; **24** 233, 236, 371; **25** 418, 498; **26** 91, 432; **27** 365–66; **30** 10
Intelcom Support Services, Inc., **14** 334
Intelicom Solutions Corp., **6** 229
IntelliCorp, **9** 310; **31** 298
Intelligent Electronics, Inc., **6 243–45**; **12** 184; **13** 176, 277
Intelligent Software Ltd., **26** 275
Intellimetrics Instrument Corporation, **16** 93
Inter American Aviation, Inc. *See* SkyWest, Inc.
Inter IKEA Systems B.V., **V** 82
Inter Island Telephone, **6** 326, 328
Inter State Telephone, **6** 338
Inter Techniek, **16** 421
Inter-American Development Bank, **IV** 55
Inter-American Satellite Television Network, **7** 391
Inter-City Gas Ltd., **III** 654; **19** 159
Inter-City Western Bakeries Ltd., **II** 631
Inter-City Wholesale Electric Inc., **15** 385
Inter-Comm Telephone, Inc., **8** 310
Inter-Island Airways, Ltd., **22** 251; **24** 20
Inter-Island Steam Navigation Co. *See* Hawaiian Airlines.
Inter-Mountain Telephone Co., **V** 344
Inter-Ocean Corporation, **16** 103
Inter-Regional Financial Group, Inc., **15 231–33**
Interactive Computer Design, Inc., **23** 489, 491
Interactive Systems, **7** 500
Interamericana de Talleras SA de CV, **10** 415
Interbake Foods, **II** 631
InterBold, **7** 146; **11** 151
Interbrás, **IV** 503
Interbrew S.A., **16** 397; **17 256–58**; **25** 279, 282; **26** 306
Interchemical Corp., **13** 460
Intercity Food Services, Inc., **II** 663
Interco Incorporated, **III 528–31**; **9** 133, 135, 192, 234–35; **10** 184; **12** 156, 306–08; **22** 49; **29** 294; **31** 136–37, 210
Intercolonial, **6** 360
Intercomi, **II** 233
Intercontinental Apparel, **8** 249
Intercontinental Breweries, **I** 289
Intercontinental Hotels, **I** 248–49
Intercontinental Mortgage Company, **8** 436
Intercontinental Rubber Co., **II** 112
Intercontinentale, **III** 404
Intercord, **22** 194
Intercostal Steel Corp., **13** 97
Interdesign, **16** 421
Interedi-Cosmopolitan, **III** 47
Interessen Gemeinschaft Farbenwerke. *See* I.G. Farbenindustrie AG.
Interface Group, **13** 483
Interface, Inc., **8 270–72**; **18** 112; **29 246–49 (upd.)**
Interferon Sciences, Inc., **13** 366–67
Interfinancial, **III** 200
InterFirst Bankcorp, Inc., **9** 482
Interfood Ltd., **II** 520–21, 540
Interglas S.A., **22** 515
Intergram, Inc., **27** 21
Intergraph Corporation, **6 246–49**; **10** 257; **24 233–36 (upd.)**
Interhandel, **I** 337–38; **II** 378; **22** 226
INTERIM Services, Inc., **9** 268, 270; **25** 434; **29** 224, 227
Interlabor, **16** 420–21
The Interlake Corporation, **8 273–75**
Interlake Steamship Company, **15** 302
Intermagnetics General Corp., **9** 10
Intermark, Inc., **12** 394
Intermec Corporation, **29** 414
Intermed, **I** 429
Intermedia, **25** 499
Intermedics, **III** 633; **11** 458–59; **12** 325–26
Intermedics Intraocular Inc., **I** 665
Intermoda, **V** 166
Intermountain Broadcasting and Television Corp., **IV** 674
Intermountain Health Care, Inc., **27 237–40**
International Aero Engines, **9** 418
International Agricultural Corporation, **8** 264–65
International Air Service Co., **24** 21
International Assurance Co., **III** 195
International Bank, **II** 261
International Bank of Japan, **17** 122
International Bank of Moscow, **II** 242
International Banking Corp., **II** 253; **9** 123
International Banking Technologies, Inc., **11** 113
International Basic Economy Corporation, **13** 103
International Beauty Supply, Ltd. *See* L.L. Knickerbocker Co., Inc.
International Brewing Holdings Pty., **21** 229
International Business Directories, Inc., **26** 484
International Business Machines Corporation, **I** 26, 455, 523, 534, 541; **II** 6, 8, 10, 42, 44–45, 56, 62, 68, 70, 73, 86, 99, 107, 113, 134, 159, 211, 274, 326, 379, 397, 432, 440; **III** 9, 109–11, 113–18, 121–28, 130, 132–34, 136, 139–43, 145, **147–49**, 151–52, 154–55, 157, 165–72, 200, 246, 313, 319, 326, 458, 475, 549, 618, 685; **IV** 443, 711; **6** 51, 218–25, 233–35, 237, 240–42, 244–48, **250–53 (upd.)**, 254–60, 262, 265, 269–71, 275–77, 279, 281–89, 320, 324, 346, 390, 428; **7** 145–46, 161; **8** 138–39, 466–67; **9** 36, 41–42, 48, 50, 114–15, 131, 139, 165–66, 170–71, 184, 194, 284, 296–97, 310, 327, 463–64; **10** 19, 22–24, 58, 119, 125, 161, 194, 232, 237, 243–44, 255–56, 309, 361–62, 366–67, 394, 456, 463, 474, 500–01, 505, 510, 512–13, 518–19, 542; **11** 19, 45, 50, 59, 61–62, 64–65, 68, 86–88, 150, 273–74, 285, 364, 395, 469, 485, 491, 494, 506, 519; **12** 61, 138–39, 147–49, 161–62, 183, 204, 238, 278, 335, 442, 450, 469–70, 484; **13** 47, 127, 174, 214, 326, 345, 387–88, 403, 482; **14** 13–15, 106, 268–69, 318, 354, 391, 401, 432–33, 446, 533; **15** 106, 440, 454–55, 491–92; **16** 4, 94, 140, 224–26, 301, 367–68, 372; **17** 353, 418, 532–34; **18** 94, 110, 112, 162, 250, 292, 305–07, 344, 434–36; **19** 41, 110, 310, 312, 437; **20** 237, 313; **21** 86, 391; **22** 17; **23** 135, 138, 209, 470; **24** 234; **25** 20–21, 34, 86–87, 96, 133–34, 149, 298–301, 356, 358, 530–32; **26** 90, 187, 275–76, 427, 429, 441, 540, 542; **27** 365; **28** 112, 189; **29** 375, 414; **30 247–51 (upd.)**, 140, 300, 337–38; **31** 217
International Care Services, **6** 182
International Cellucotton Products Co., **III** 40; **16** 302–03
International Cementers Inc., **25** 74

International Commercial Bank, **II** 257
International Communication Materials, Inc., **18** 387
International Computers. *See* ICL plc.
International Controls Corporation, 10 368–70
International Corona Corporation, **12** 244
International Credit Card Business Assoc., **II** 436
International Dairy Queen, Inc., **7** 266; **10 371–74**
International Data Group, Inc., **7 238–40**; **12** 561; **25 237–40 (upd.)**; **27** 222
International Development Bank, **IV** 417
International Digital Communications, Inc., **6** 327
International Distillers & Vintners Ltd., **31** 92
International Egyptian Oil Co., **IV** 412
International Engineering Company, Inc., **7** 355
International Epicure, **12** 280
International Equities Corp., **III** 98
International Factoring Corp., **II** 436
International Factors, Limited, **II** 208
International Family Entertainment Inc., **13 279–81**
International Finance Corp., **19** 192
International Flavors & Fragrances Inc., **9 290–92**
International Foods, **II** 468
International Game Technology, **10 375–76**; **24** 37 **25** 313
International Graphics Corp., **IV** 645
International Group, **13** 277
International Harvester Co., **III** 473, 650, 651; **10** 264, 280, 378, 380, 528; **13** 16; **17** 158; **22** 380. *See also* Navistar International Corporation.
International Healthcare, **III** 197
International House of Pancakes. *See* IHOP Corporation.
International Hydron, **10** 47; **13** 367
International Imaging Limited, **29** 58
International Income Property, **IV** 708
International Industries, **17** 249
International Learning Systems Corp. Ltd., **IV** 641–42; **7** 311
International Lease Finance Corp., **III** 198; **6** 67
International Light Metals Corp., **IV** 163
International MacGregor, **27** 269
International Management Group, **18 262–65**
International Marine Oil Co., **IV** 363
International Marine Services, **22** 276
International Match, **12** 463
International Mercantile Marine Co., **II** 330
International Milling. *See* International Multifoods Corporation.
International Mineral & Chemical, Inc., **8** 265–66
International Minerals and Chemical Corporation, **19** 253
International Multifoods Corporation, **II** 493; **7 241–43**; **12** 80, 125; **14** 515; **21** 289; **23** 203; **25 241–44 (upd.)**; **28** 238
International Music Co., **16** 202
International News Service, **IV** 626–27; **19** 203; **25** 507
International Nickel Co. of Canada, Ltd., **III** 677; **IV** 78, 110–12
International Nickel Corporation, **16** 122; **18** 488
International Nutrition Laboratories, **14** 558
International Organization of Consumers Unions, **26** 98
International Pacific Corp., **II** 389
International Paper Company, **I** 27; **II** 208, 403; **III** 693, 764; **IV** 16, 245, **286–88**, 289, 326; **8** 267; **11** 76, 311; **15 227–30 (upd.)**; **16** 349; **17** 446; **23** 48–49, 366, 368; **25** 9; **26** 444; **30** 92, 94
International Parts Corporation, **10** 414
International Permalite, **22** 229
International Petroleum Co., Ltd., **IV** 415–16, 438, 478; **25** 230
International Petroleum Corp., **IV** 454, 484
International Playtex, Inc., **12** 93
International Proteins Corporation, **21** 248
International Publishing Corp., **IV** 641, 666–67; **7** 343; **17** 397; **23** 350
International Raw Materials, Ltd., **31** 20
International Rectifier Corporation, **31 263–66**
International Roofing Company, **22** 13–14
International Sealants Corporation, **8** 333
International Shipholding Corporation, Inc., **27 241–44**
International Shoe Co., **III** 528–30
International Silver Company, **I** 30; **12** 472; **14** 482–83
International Specialty Products, Inc., **22** 225, 228–29
International Speedway Corporation, **19 221–23**
International Standard Electric, **II** 66–68
International Stores, **I** 427
International Supply Consortium, **13** 79
International Talent Group, **25** 281
International Talent Management, Inc. *See* Motown Records Company L.P.
International Telcell Group, **7** 336
International Telephone & Telegraph Corporation, **I** 434, 446, **462–64**, 544; **II** 13, 66, 68, 86, 130, 331; **III** 98–99, 162–64, 166, 644–45, 684; **V** 334–35, 337–38; **6** 356; **8** 157; **9** 10–11, 324; **10** 19, 44, 301; **11 196–99 (upd.)**, 337, 516; **12** 18; **13** 246; **14** 332, 488; **19** 131, 205, 208; **22** 55; **25** 100, 432
International Television Corporation Entertainment Group, **23** 391
International Terminal Operation Co., **I** 513
International Thomson Organization Ltd., **23** 92
International Time Recording Company. *See* International Business Machines Corporation.
International Trust and Investment Corp., **II** 577
International Trust Co., **II** 207
International Utilities Corp., **IV** 75–76; **6** 444
International Western Electric Co., **I** 462; **II** 66; **III** 162; **11** 196
International Wind Systems, **6** 581
International Wine & Spirits Ltd., **9** 533
International Wire Works Corp., **8** 13
International Wireless Inc., **21** 261
Internationale Industriële Beleggung Maatschappij Amsterdam BV, **IV** 128
Internationale Nederlanden Group, **24** 88
Internet Shopping Network, **26** 441
InterNorth, Inc., **II** 16; **V** 610
Interocean Management Corp., **9** 509–11
Interpac Belgium, **6** 303
Interprovincial Pipe Line Ltd., **I** 264; **IV** 439; **25** 231
The Interpublic Group of Companies, Inc., **I 16–18**, 31, 36; **6** 53; **14** 315; **16** 70, 72, 167; **20** 5; **22 294–97 (upd.)**; **23** 478; **28** 66–67
InterRedec, Inc., **17** 196
Interscience, **17** 271
Interscope Communications, Inc., **23** 389, 391; **27** 121
Interscope Music Group, **31 267–69**
Intersec, Inc., **27** 21
Intersil Inc., **II** 30; **12** 196; **16** 358
Interstate & Ocean Transport, **6** 577
Interstate Bag, **I** 335
Interstate Bakeries Corporation, **7** 320; **12 274–76**; **27** 310
Interstate Brick Company, **6** 568–69
Interstate Electric Manufacturing Company. *See* McGraw Electric Company.
Interstate Finance Corp., **11** 16
Interstate Financial Corporation, **9** 475
Interstate Iron and Steel Company. *See* Republic Engineered Steels, Inc.
Interstate Logos, Inc., **27** 278
Interstate Paint Distributors, Inc., **13** 367
Interstate Power Company, **6** 555, 605; **18** 404
Interstate Public Service Company, **6** 555
Interstate Stores Inc., **V** 203; **15** 469; **18** 522
Interstate Supply Company. *See* McGraw Electric Company.
Interstate United Corporation, **II** 679; **III** 502; **13** 435
Intertec Publishing Corp., **22** 441
Interturbine Holland, **19** 150
Intertype Corp., **II** 37
Interunfall, **III** 346
Intervideo TV Productions-A.B., **II** 640
Intervision Express, **24** 510
Interweb, **IV** 661
InterWest Partners, **16** 418
Intimate Brands, Inc., **24 237–39'** **29** 357
Intrac Handelsgesellschaft mbH, **7** 142
Intradal, **II** 572
Intraph South Africa Ltd., **6** 247
IntraWest Bank, **II** 289
The Intrawest Corporation, **15 234–36**; **31** 67
Intrepid Corporation, **16** 493
IntroGene B.V., **13** 241
Intuit Inc., **13** 147; **14 262–64**; **23** 457
Invacare Corporation, **11 200–02**, 486
Invenex Laboratories, **17** 287
Invento Products Corporation, **21** 269
Invep S.p.A., **10** 150
Inveresk Paper Co., **III** 693; **IV** 685
Invergordon Distillers, **III** 509
Inversale, **9** 92
INVESCO MIM Management Limited, **21** 397
Invesgen S.A., **26** 129
InvestCorp International, **15** 200; **24** 195, 420; **25** 205, 207
Investcorp S.A. *See* Arabian Investment Banking Corp.
Investimentos Itaú S.A., **19** 33
Investors Bank and Trust Company, **18** 152

Investors Diversified Services, Inc., **II** 398; **6** 199; **8** 348–49; **10** 43–45, 59, 62; **21** 305; **25** 248
Investors Group, **III** 261
Investors Management Corp., **10** 331
Investors Overseas Services, **10** 368–69
Investrónica S.A., **26** 129
Invista Capital Management, **III** 330
Iolab Corp., **III** 36
Iomega Corporation, **18** 509–10; **21 294–97**
Ionpure Technologies Corporation, **6** 486–88
Iowa Beef Packers, **21** 287
Iowa Beef Processors, **II** 516–17; **IV** 481–82; **13** 351
Iowa Manufacturing, **II** 86
Iowa Mold Tooling Co., Inc., **16** 475
Iowa Public Service Company, **6** 524–25
IP Gas Supply Company, **6** 506
IP Services, Inc., **IV** 597
IP Timberlands Ltd., **IV** 288
IP&L. *See* Illinois Power & Light Corporation.
Ipalco Enterprises, Inc., 6 508–09
IPC. *See* International Publishing Corp.
IPC Communications, Inc., **15** 196
IPC Magazines Limited, **IV** 650; **7 244–47**
IPEC Holdings Ltd., **27** 474–75
Ipko-Amcor, **14** 225
IPSOA Editore, **14** 555
IPSOS, S.A., **24** 355
IQUE, Inc., **21** 194
Iran Air, **6** 101
Iran Pan American Oil Co., **IV** 466
Iranian Oil Exploration and Producing Co., **IV** 466–67
Iraq Petroleum Co., **IV** 363, 386, 429, 450, 464, 558–60
Irby-Gilliland Company, **9** 127
Irdeto, **31** 330
IRI. *See* Instituto per la Ricostruzione Industriale.
Iris Associates, Inc., **25** 299, 301
IRIS Holding Co., **III** 347
Irish Life Assurance Company, **16** 14
Irish Paper Sacks Ltd., **IV** 295; **19** 225
Irish Sugar Co., **II** 508
Iron and Steel Corp., **IV** 22, 41, 92, 533–34
Iron and Steel Press Company, **27** 360
Iron Cliffs Mining Company, **13** 156
Iron Mountain Forge, **13** 319
Iron Ore Company of Canada, **8** 347
Iroquois Gas Corporation, **6** 526
Irvin Feld & Kenneth Feld Productions, Inc., **15 237–39**
Irving Bank Corp., **II** 192
Irving Tanning Company, **17** 195
Irving Trust Coompany, **II** 257; **22** 55
Irvington Smelting, **IV** 78
Irwin Lehrhoff Associates, **11** 366
Irwin Toy Limited, **14 265–67**
Isabela Shoe Corporation, **13** 360
Isagro S.p.A., **26** 425
Iscor. *See* Iron and Steel Corporation.
Isetan Company Limited, **V 85–87**; **28** 54
Iseya Tanji Drapery, **V** 85
Ishikawajima-Harima Heavy Industries Co., Ltd., **I** 508, 511, 534; **II** 274; **III 532–33**; **9** 293; **12** 484
Ishizaki Honten, **III** 715
Isis Distributed Systems, Inc., **10** 501
Island Air, **24** 22
Island Equipment Co., **19** 381
Island Holiday, **I** 417
Island Pictures Corp., **23** 389
Island Records, **23** 389
Islands Restaurants, **17** 85–87
Isolite Insulating Products Co., **III** 714
Isosceles PLC, **II** 628–29; **24** 270
Isotec Communications Incorporated, **13** 213
Isover, **III** 676; **16** 121
Ispat International N.V., **30 252–54**
ISS International Service System, Inc., **8** 271
Istanbul Fertilizer Industry, **IV** 563
Istante Vesa s.r.l., **22** 239
Istituto per la Ricostruzione Industriale S.p.A., **I** 207, 459, **465–67**; **II** 191–92, 270–71; **IV** 419; **11 203–06**; **13** 28, 218
Isuzu Motors, Ltd., **II** 274; **III** 581, 593; **7** 8, 219; **9 293–95**; **10** 354; **23 288–91 (upd.)**
Isuzu Motors of Japan, **21** 6
IT Group, **28** 203
IT International, **V** 255
Itabira Iron Ore Co. Ltd., **IV** 54
ITABRASCO, **IV** 55
Italcarta, **IV** 339
Italcementi, **IV** 420
Italianni's, **22** 128
Italiatour, **6** 69
Italmobiliare, **III** 347
Italstate. *See* Societa per la Infrastrutture e l'Assetto del Territoria.
Italtel, **V** 326–27
Italware, **27** 94
Itaú. *See* Banco Itaú S.A.
Itaú Winterthur Seguradura S.A., **III** 404
Itaúsa. *See* Investimentos Itaú S.A.
Itek Corp., **I** 486; **11** 265
Itel Corporation, **II** 64; **III** 512; **6** 262, 354; **9** 49, **296–99**; **15** 107; **22** 339; **26** 328, 519
Items International Airwalk Inc., **17 259–61**
Ithaca Gas & Electric. *See* New York State Electric and Gas.
ITI Education Corporation, **29** 472
ITM International, **IV** 239
Ito Carnation Co., **II** 518
Ito Food Processing Co., **II** 518
Ito Gofuku Co. Ltd., **V** 129
Ito Meat Processing Co., **II** 518
Ito Processed Food Co., **II** 518
Ito-Yokado Co., Ltd., **II** 661; **V 88–89**
Itochu and Renown, Inc., **12** 281
Itochu Corporation, **19** 9
Itochu of Japan, **14** 550
Itoh. *See* C. Itoh & Co.
Itoham Foods Inc., **II 518–19**
Itokin, **III** 48
Itoman & Co., **26** 456
ITT, **21** 200; **24** 188, 405; **30** 101. *See also* International Telephone and Telegraph Corporation.
ITT Sheraton Corporation, **III 98–101**; **23** 484
ITT World Directories, **27** 498, 500
iTurf Inc., **29** 142–43
ITW. *See* Illinois Tool Works Inc.
ITW Devcon, **12** 7
IU International, **23** 40
IURA Edition, **14** 556
IV Therapy Associates, **16** 440
IVAC Corp., **I** 646; **11** 90
IVACO Industries Inc., **11** 207
Ivanhoe, Inc., **II** 662, 664
IVAX Corporation, **11 207–09**
Iveco, **I** 148; **12** 91
Ives Trains, **16** 336
Iwai & Co., **I** 492, 509–10; **IV** 151; **24** 325, 358
Iwata Air Compressor, **III** 427
IXC Communications, Inc., **29 250–52**
IYG Holding Company of Japan, **7** 492
The IZOD Gant Corporation, **24** 385
Izod Lacoste, **II** 502–03; **9** 156–57; **10** 324
Izumi Fudosan, **IV** 726
Izumiya, **V** 477

J&E Davy, **16** 14
J&G Meakin, **12** 529
J&J Colman, **II** 566
J&J Corrugated Box Corp., **IV** 282; **9** 261
J & J Snack Foods Corporation, **24 240–42**
J&L Industrial Supply, **13** 297
J&L Steel. *See* Jones & Laughlin Steel Corp.
J&R Electronics Inc., **26 224–26**
J. & W. Seligman and Co., **17** 498
J.A. Baldwin Manufacturing Company, **17** 106
J.A. Jones, Inc., **16 284–86**; **17** 377
J. Aron & Co., **II** 415
J.B. Hudson & Son, **18** 136
J.B. Hunt Transport Services Inc., **12 277–79**; **15** 440; **26** 533
J.B. Lippincott & Company, **IV** 652; **14** 554–56
J.B. McLean Publishing Co., Ltd., **IV** 638
J.B. Williams Company, **III** 66; **8** 63
J.B. Wolters Publishing Company, **14** 554
J. Baker, Inc., **13** 361; **31 270–73**
J. Beres & Son, **24** 444–45
J Bibby & Sons, **I** 424
J Bibby Agriculture Limited, **13** 53
J. Bulova Company. *See* Bulova Corporation.
J. Byrons, **9** 186
J.C. Baxter Co., **15** 501
J.C. Hillary's, **20** 54
J.C. Penney Company, Inc., **I** 516; **V 90–92**; **6** 336; **8** 288, 555; **9** 156, 210, 213, 219, 346–94; **10** 409, 490; **11** 349; **12** 111, 431, 522; **14** 62; **16** 37, 327–28; **17** 124, 175, 177, 366, 460; **18** 108, 136, 168, 200, **269–73 (upd.)**, 373, 478; **19** 300; **21** 24, 527; **25** 91, 254, 368; **26** 161; **27** 346, 429; **31** 260–61
J. Crew Group Inc., **12 280–82**; **25** 48
J.D. Bassett Manufacturing Co. *See* Bassett Furniture Industries, Inc.
J.D. Edwards & Company, **14 268–70**
J.D. Powers & Associates, **9** 166
J.E. Baxter Co., **I** 429
J.E. Nolan, **11** 486
J.E. Sirrine. *See* CRSS Inc.
J.E. Smith Box & Printing Co., **13** 441
J. Edward Connelly Associates, Inc., **22** 438
J. Evershed & Son, **13** 103
J.F. Corporation, **V** 87
J.F. Lauman and Co., **II** 681
J. Fielding & Co., **IV** 249
J.G. McMullen Dredging Co., **III** 558

J. Gadsden Paper Products, **IV** 249
J. George Leyner Engineering Works Co., **III** 525–26
J.H. Heafner Co., **20** 263
J.H. Stone & Sons, **IV** 332
J.H. Whitney & Company, **9** 250
J. Homestock. *See* R.H. Macy & Co.
J.I. Case Company, **I** 148, 527; **III** 651; **10 377–81**; **13** 17; **22** 380
J.K. Armsby Co., **7** 130–31
J.K. Starley and Company Ltd, **7** 458
J.L. Clark, Inc. *See* Clarcor Inc.
J.L. Hudson Company. *See* Dayton Hudson Corporation.
J.L. Kraft & Bros. Co., **II** 532
J.L. Shiely Co., **III** 691
J.L. Wright Company, **25** 379
J. Levin & Co., Inc., **13** 367
J. Lyons & Co., **I** 215
J.M. Brunswick & Brothers, **III** 442
J.M. Douglas & Company Limited, **14** 141
J.M. Horton Ice Cream Co., **II** 471
J.M. Jones Co., **II** 668; **18** 504
J.M. Kohler Sons Company, **7** 269
The J.M. Smucker Company, **11 210–12**
J.M. Tull Metals Co., Inc., **IV** 116; **15** 250; **19** 219
J. Mandelbaum & Sons, **19** 510
J-Mar Associates, **31** 435–36
J-Mass, **IV** 289
J. Muirhead Ltd., **I** 315; **25** 81
J.P. Heilwell Industries, **II** 420
J.P. Morgan & Co. Incorporated, **II** 281, **329–32**, 407, 419, 427–28, 430–31, 441; **III** 237, 245, 380; **IV** 20, 180, 400; **9** 386; **11** 421; **12** 165; **13** 13; **16** 25, 375; **19** 190; **26** 66, 500; **30 261–65 (upd.)**
J.P. Stevens Inc., **8** 234; **12** 404; **16** 533–35; **17** 75; **19** 420; **27** 468–69; **28** 218
J.P. Wood, **II** 587
J.R. Brown & Sharpe. *See* Brown & Sharpe Manufacturing Co.
J.R. Geigy S.A., **I** 632–33, 635, 671; **8** 108–10
J.R. Parkington Co., **I** 280
J.R. Simplot Company, **16 287–89**; **21** 508; **26** 309
J.R. Wyllie & Sons, **I** 437
J. Ray McDermott & Co., **III** 558–59
J.S. Fry & Sons, **II** 476
J.S. Morgan & Co., **II** 329, 427
J Sainsbury plc, **II 657–59**, 677–78; **10** 442; **11** 239, 241; **13 282–84 (upd.)**; **17** 42; **21** 335; **22** 241
J. Sanders & Sons, **IV** 711
J. Sears & Company, **V** 177
J. Spiegel and Company. *See* Spiegel, Inc.
J.T. Wing and Co., **I** 158
J.U. Dickson Sawmill Inc. *See* Dickson Forest Products, Inc.
J.W. Bateson, **8** 87
J.W. Buderus and Sons, **III** 694
J.W. Charles Financial Services Inc., **25** 542
J.W. Foster and Sons, Inc. *See* Reebok International Ltd.
J.W. Higman & Co., **III** 690
J.W. Spear, **25** 314
J.W. Wassall Ltd. *See* Wassall PLC.
J. Walter Thompson Co., **I** 9, 17, 25, 37, 251, 354, 623; **10** 69; **11** 51; **12** 168; **16** 167
J. Weingarten Inc., **7** 203; **28** 163
J. Wiss & Sons Co., **II** 16
J.Z. Sales Corp., **16** 36
J. Zinmeister Co., **II** 682
Jacintoport Corporation, **7** 281
Jack Daniel Distillery, **10** 180
Jack Eckerd Corp., **16** 160; **19** 467
Jack Frain Enterprises, **16** 471
Jack Henry and Associates, Inc., **17 262–65**
Jack Houston Exploration Company, **7** 345
Jack in the Box, Inc. *See* Foodmaster, Inc.
Jack Schwartz Shoes, Inc., **18 266–68**
Jackpot Enterprises Inc., **21 298–300**; **24** 36
Jackson & Curtis, **II** 444; **22** 405
Jackson Box Co., **IV** 311; **19** 267
Jackson Cushion Spring Co., **13** 397
Jackson Ice Cream Co., **12** 112
Jackson Marine Corp., **III** 499
Jackson Mercantile Co. *See* Jitney-Jungle Stores of America, Inc.
Jackson National Life Insurance Company, **III** 335–36; **8 276–77**
Jackson Purchase Electric Cooperative Corporation, **11** 37
Jacksonville Shipyards, **I** 170
Jaco Electronics, Inc., **19** 311; **30 255–57**
Jacob Holm & Sons A/S, **22** 263
Jacob Leinenkugel Brewing Company, **12** 338; **28 209–11**
Jacobs Brake Manufacturing Company, **7** 116–17
Jacobs Engineering Group Inc., **6 148–50**; **26 220–23 (upd.)**
Jacobs Suchard (AG), **II 520–22**, 540, 569; **15** 64; **29** 46–47
Jacobson Stores Inc., **21 301–03**
Jacoby & Meyers, **20** 435
Jacor Communications, Inc., **6** 33; **23 292–95**; **24** 108; **27** 339
Jacques Borel International, **II** 641; **10** 12
Jacques Fath Perfumes, **III** 47
Jacuzzi Inc., **7** 207, 209; **23 296–98**
Jade Accessories, **14** 224
Jade KK, **25** 349
Jadepoint, **18** 79–80
JAF Pampryl, **I** 281
Jafra Cosmetics, **15** 475, 477
Jagenberg AG, **9** 445–46; **14** 57
Jaguar Cars, Ltd., **III** 439, 495; **11** 140; **13** 28, 219, **285–87**, 414
JAI Parabolic Spring Ltd., **III** 582
JAIX Leasing Company, **23** 306
Ab Jakobstads Cellulosa-Pietarsaaren Selluloosa Oy, **IV** 302
JAL. *See* Japan Air Lines.
Jalate Inc., **25 245–47**
Jaluzot & Cie. *See* Pinault-Printemps-Redoute S.A.
Jamaica Gas Light Co., **6** 455
Jamaica Plain Trust Co., **II** 207
Jamaica Water Supply Company. *See* JWP Inc.
JAMCO, **III** 589
James A. Ryder Transportation (Jartran), **V** 505
James Bay Development Corporation, **6** 502
James Beam Distilling Co., **I** 226; **10** 180
James Burn/American, Inc., **17** 458
James C. Heintz Company, **19** 278
James Ericson, **III** 324
James Felt Realty, Inc., **21** 257
James Fison and Sons. *See* Fisons plc.
James Fleming, **II** 500
James G. Fast Company. *See* Angelica Corporation.
James Gulliver Associates, **II** 609
James Hardie Industries Limited, **IV** 249; **26** 494
James Hartley & Son, **III** 724
James Heekin and Company, **13** 254
James Lyne Hancock Ltd., **I** 428
James Magee & Sons Ltd., **IV** 294; **19** 224
James McNaughton Ltd., **IV** 325
James O. Welch Co., **II** 543
James Publishing Group, **17** 272
James R. Osgood & Company, **10** 356
James River Corporation of Virginia, **IV 289–91**; **8** 483; **22** 209; **29** 136. *See also* Fort James Corporation.
James Stedman Ltd., **II** 569
James Talcott, Inc., **11** 260–61
James Thompson, **IV** 22
James Wholesale Company, **18** 7
James Wrigley & Sons, **IV** 257
Jamestown Publishers, **22** 522
Jamesway Corporation, **IV** 136; **13** 261; **23** 177
Jamie Scott, Inc., **27** 348
Jamieson & Co., **22** 428
Jamna Auto Industries Pvt. Ltd., **III** 581
Jämsänkoski Oy, **IV** 347
Jan Bell Marketing Inc., **24** 335
Janata Bank, **31** 219
Jane Jones Enterprises, **16** 422
Jane's Information Group, **8** 525
Janesville Electric, **6** 604
Janet Frazer, **V** 118
Janson Publications, **22** 522
N.V. Janssen M&L, **17** 147
Janssen Pharmaceutica, **III** 36; **8** 282
Janssen-Kyowa, **III** 43
JANT Pty. Ltd., **IV** 285
Jantzen Inc., **V** 391; **17** 513
Janus Capital Corporation, **6** 401–02; **26** 233
Japan Acoustics, **II** 118
Japan Advertising Ltd., **16** 166
Japan Air Filter Co., Ltd., **III** 634
Japan Air Lines Co., **I 104–06**; **6** 70–71, 118, 123, 386, 427; **24** 399–400; **27** 464
Japan Brewery. *See* Kirin Brewery Company, Limited.
Japan Broadcasting Corporation, **I** 586; **II** 66, 101, 118; **7 248–50**; **9** 31
Japan-California Bank, **II** 274
Japan Commerce Bank, **II** 291
Japan Copper Manufacturing Co., **II** 104; **IV** 211
Japan Cotton Co., **IV** 150; **24** 357
Japan Creative Tours Co., **I** 106
Japan Credit Bureau, **II** 348
Japan Dairy Products, **II** 538
Japan Day & Night Bank, **II** 292
Japan Development Bank, **II** 300, 403
Japan Dyestuff Manufacturing Co., **I** 397
Japan Elanco Company, Ltd., **17** 437
Japan Electricity Generation and Transmission Company (JEGTCO), **V** 574
Japan Energy Corporation, **13** 202; **14** 206, 208
Japan Food Corporation, **14** 288
Japan International Bank, **II** 292
Japan International Liquor, **I** 220

Japan Iron & Steel Co., Ltd., **IV** 157; **17** 349–50
Japan Leasing Corporation, **8 278–80**; **11** 87
Japan Medico, **25** 431
Japan National Oil Corp., **IV** 516
Japan National Railway, **V** 448–50; **6** 70
Japan Oil Development Co., **IV** 364
Japan Petroleum Development Corp., **IV** 461
Japan Petroleum Exploration Co., **IV** 516
Japan Pulp and Paper Company Limited, **IV 292–93**, 680
Japan Reconstruction Finance Bank, **II** 300
Japan Special Steel Co., Ltd., **IV** 63
Japan Steel Manufacturing Co., **IV** 211
Japan Steel Works, **I** 508
Japan Telecom, **7** 118; **13** 482
Japan Telegraphic Communication Company (Nihon Denpo-Tsushin Sha), **16** 166
Japan Tobacco Incorporated, **V 403–04**; **30** 387
Japan Trust Bank, **II** 292
Japan Try Co., **III** 758
Japanese and Asian Development Bank, **IV** 518
Japanese Electronic Computer Co., **III** 140
Japanese Enterprise Co., **IV** 728
Japanese National Railway, **I** 579; **III** 491
Japanese Victor Co., **II** 118
Japex Oman Co., **IV** 516
Japonica Partners, **9** 485
Jara Enterprises, Inc., **31** 276
Jarcho Brothers Inc., **I** 513
Jardinay Manufacturing Corp., **24** 335
Jardine Matheson Holdings Limited, **I 468–71**, 521–22, 577, 592; **II** 296; **IV** 189, 699–700; **16** 479–80; **18** 114; **20 309–14 (upd.)**
Jartran Inc., **V** 505; **24** 410
Järvenpään Kotelo Oy, **IV** 315
Jas, Hennessy & Co., **I** 272
Jas. I. Miller Co., **13** 491
JASCO Products, **III** 581
Jason Incorporated, **23 299–301**
Jasper Corporation, **III** 767; **22** 546. *See also* Kimball International, Inc.
JAT, **27** 475
Jato, **II** 652
Jauch & Hübener, **14** 279
Java Software, **30** 453
Java-China-Japan Line, **6** 403–04; **26** 242
Javelin Software Corporation, **10** 359
Javex Co., **IV** 272
Jax, **9** 452
Jay Cooke and Co., **III** 237; **9** 370
Jay Jacobs, Inc., **15 243–45**
Jay's Washateria, Inc., **7** 372
Jay-Ro Services, **III** 419
Jayco Inc., **13 288–90**
Jaywoth Industries, **III** 673
JBL, **22** 97
JCB, **14** 321
JCJL. *See* Java-China-Japan Line.
JD Wetherspoon plc, **30 258–60**
Jean Lassale, **III** 619–20; **17** 430
Jean Lincet, **19** 50
Jean Nate, **I** 695
Jean Pagées et Fils, **III** 420
Jean Prouvost, **IV** 618
Jean-Jacques, **19** 50
Jeanmarie Creations, Inc., **18** 67, 69
Jeanne Piaubert, **III** 47
Jefferies Group, Inc., **25 248–51**
Jefferson Chemical Co., **IV** 552
Jefferson Fire Insurance Co., **III** 239
Jefferson National Life Group, **10** 247
Jefferson Smurfit Group plc, **IV 294–96**; **16** 122; **19 224–27 (upd.)**. *See also* Smurfit-Stone Container Corporation.
Jefferson Standard Life Insurance, **11** 213–14
Jefferson Ward, **12** 48–49
Jefferson Warrior Railroad Company, **III** 767; **22** 546
Jefferson-Pilot Corporation, **11 213–15**; **29 253–56 (upd.)**
Jeffery Sons & Co. Ltd., **IV** 711
Jeffrey Galion, **III** 472
JEGTCO. *See* Japan Electricity Generation and Transmission Company (JEGTCO).
Jell-O Co., **II** 531
Jem Development, **17** 233
Jenaer Glaswerk Schott & Genossen, **III** 445, 447
Jenn-Air Corporation, **III** 573; **22** 349
Jennie-O Foods, **II** 506
Jennifer Convertibles, Inc., **31 274–76**
Jenny Craig, Inc., **10 382–84**; **12** 531; **29 257–60 (upd.)**
Jeno's, **13** 516; **26** 436
Jensen Salsbery, **I** 715
Jenson, Woodward & Lozier, Inc., **21** 96
JEORA Co., **IV** 564
Jeppesen Sanderson, Inc., **IV** 677; **17** 486
Jepson Corporation, **8** 230
Jeri-Jo Knitwear, Inc., **27** 346, 348
Jerome Increase Case Machinery Company. *See* J.I. Case Company.
Jerrico Inc., **27** 145
Jerrold Corporation, **10** 319–20
Jerry Bassin Inc., **17** 12–14
Jerry's Famous Deli Inc., **24 243–45**
Jerry's Restaurants, **13** 320
Jersey Central Power & Light Company, **27** 182
Jersey Paper, **IV** 261
Jersey Standard. *See* Standard Oil Co. of New Jersey.
Jervis B. Webb Company, **24 246–49**
Jesse Jones Sausage Co. *See* GoodMark Foods, Inc.
Jesse L. Lasky Feature Play Co., **II** 154
Jessup & Moore Paper Co., **IV** 351; **19** 495
Jet America Airlines, **I** 100; **6** 67, 82
Jet Capital Corp., **I** 123
Jet Petroleum, Ltd., **IV** 401
Jet Research Center, **III** 498
Jet Set Corporation, **18** 513
Jetway Systems, **III** 512
Jeumont-Industrie, **II** 93
Jeumont-Schneider Industries, **II** 93–94; **9** 10; **18** 473
Jewel Companies, Inc., **II** 605; **6** 531; **12** 63; **18** 89; **22** 38; **26** 476; **27** 291
Jewel Food Stores, **7** 127–28; **13** 25
Jewell Ridge Coal Corp., **IV** 181
JFD-Encino, **24** 243
JG Industries, Inc., **15 240–42**
Jheri Redding Products, Inc., **17** 108
Jiamusi Combine Harvester Factory, **21** 175
JIB Group plc, **20** 313
Jiffee Chemical Corporation, **III** 21; **22** 146
Jiffy Auto Rental, **16** 380
Jiffy Convenience Stores, **II** 627
Jiffy Lube International, Inc., **IV** 490; **21** 541; **24** 339; **25** 443–45
Jiffy Mixes, **29** 109–10
Jiffy Packaging, **14** 430
Jiji, **16** 166
Jim Beam Brands Co., **14 271–73**; **29** 196
Jim Cole Enterprises, Inc., **19** 247
The Jim Henson Company, **23 302–04**
Jim Walter Corporation. *See* Walter Industries, Inc.
Jim Walter Papers, **IV** 282; **9** 261
Jitney-Jungle Stores of America, Inc., **27 245–48**
Jitsugyo no Nihon-sha, **IV** 631
Jitsuyo Jidosha Seizo Co., **I** 183
JLA Credit, **8** 279
JMB Internacionale S.A., **25** 121
JMB Realty Corporation, **IV 702–03**. *See also* Amfac/JMB Hawaii L.L.C.
Jno. H. Swisher & Son. *See* Swisher International Group Inc.
JNR. *See* Japan National Railway.
Jo-Ann Fabrics and Crafts, **16** 197
Jo-Gal Shoe Company, Inc., **13** 360
Joanna Cotton Mills, **14** 220
Joannes Brothers, **II** 668
Jobete Music. *See* Motown Records Company L.P.
JobWorks Agency, Inc., **16** 50
Jockey International, Inc., **12 283–85**
Joe Alexander Press, **12** 472
Joe B. Hughes, **III** 498
Joe's American Bar & Grill, **20** 54
Joe's Crab Shack, **15** 279
Joh. Parviaisen Tehtaat Oy, **IV** 276
Johann Jakob Rieter & Co., **III** 402
Johannesburg Consolidated Investment Co. Ltd., **IV** 21–22, 118; **16** 293
John A. Frye Company, **V** 376; **8** 16; **26** 397–98
John A. Pratt and Associates, **22** 181
John Alden Life Insurance, **10** 340
John B. Sanfilippo & Son, Inc., **14 274–76**
John Bean Spray Pump Co., **I** 442
John Blair & Company, **6** 13
John Brown plc, **I 572–74**
John Bull, **II** 550
John Carr Group, **31** 398–400
John Chatillon & Sons Inc., **29** 460
John Crane International, **17** 480
John Crosland Company, **8** 88
John de Kuyper and Son, **I** 377
John Deere. *See* Deere & Company.
John F. Jelke Company, **9** 318
John F. Murray Co., **I** 623; **10** 69
John Fairfax Holdings Limited, **7 251–54**
John Gardner Catering, **III** 104
John Govett & Co., **II** 349
John Gund Brewing Co., **I** 253
John H. Harland Company, **17 266–69**
John H.R. Molson & Bros. *See* The Molson Companies Limited.
John Hancock Mutual Life Insurance Company, **III 265–68**, 291, 313, 332, 400; **IV** 283; **13** 530; **25** 528
John Hill and Son, **II** 569
John Holroyd & Co. of Great Britain, **7** 236
John L. Wortham & Son Agency, **III** 193

John Labatt Ltd., **I** 267; **II** 582; **8** 399; **16** 397; **17** 256–57. *See also* Labatt Brewing Company Limited.
John Laing plc, **I 575–76**, 588
John Lewis Partnership plc, **V 93–95**; **13** 307
John Lucas Co., **III** 745
John Lysaght, **III** 493–95
John M. Hart Company, **9** 304
John M. Smyth Co., **15** 282
John Macfarlane and Sons, **II** 593
John Mackintosh and Sons, **II** 568–69
John McConnell & Co., **13** 102
John McLean and Sons Ltd., **III** 753
John Morrell and Co., **II** 595–96; **21** 111
John Nicholls & Co., **III** 690
The John Nuveen Company, **III** 356; **21 304–06**; **22** 492, 494–95
John Oster Manufacturing Company. *See* Sunbeam-Oster.
John Paul Mitchell Systems, **24 250–52**
John Pew & Company, **13** 243
John Q. Hammons Hotels, Inc., **24 253–55**
John R. Figg, Inc., **II** 681
John Rogers Co., **9** 253
John Sands, **22** 35
John Schroeder Lumber Company, **25** 379
John Sexton & Co., **26** 503
John Strange Paper Company, **8** 358
John Swire & Sons Ltd. *See* Swire Pacific Ltd.
John Walker & Sons, **I** 239–40
John Wanamaker, **22** 110
John Wiley & Sons, Inc., **17 270–72**
John Williams, **III** 691
John Wyeth & Bro., **I** 713
John Yokley Company, **11** 194
John Zink Company, **22** 3–4; **25** 403
Johnny Rockets Group, Inc., **31 277–81**
Johns Manville Corporation, **19** 211–12
Johns Perry, **III** 673
Johns-Manville Corp., **III** 708; **7** 293; **11** 420
Johnsen, Jorgensen and Wettre, **14** 249
Johnson. *See* Axel Johnson Group.
Johnson & Higgins, **14 277–80**
Johnson & Johnson, **I** 301; **II** 582; **III** 18, **35–37**; **IV** 285, 722; **7** 45–46; **8 281–83 (upd.)**, 399, 511–12; **9** 89–90; **10** 47, 69, 78, 80, 534–35; **11** 200; **12** 186; **15** 357–58, 360; **16** 168, 440; **17** 104–05, 340, 342–43, 533; **18** 216; **19** 103, 105; **20** 8; **22** 257; **23** 188; **25** 55–56; **30** 162
Johnson and Patan, **III** 671
Johnson and Sons Smelting Works Ltd., **IV** 119
Johnson Brothers, **12** 528
Johnson, Carruthers & Rand Shoe Co., **III** 528
Johnson Controls, Inc., **III 534–37**; **13** 398; **16** 184, 322; **26 227–32 (upd.)**
Johnson Diversified, Inc., **III** 59
Johnson Matthey PLC, **II** 390; **IV** 23, **117–20**; **16** 28, **290–94 (upd.)**, 439
Johnson Motor Co., **III** 597–99
Johnson Products Co., Inc., **11** 208; **31** 89
Johnson Publishing Company, Inc., **27** 361; **28 212–14**
Johnson Systems, **6** 224
Johnson Wax. *See* S.C. Johnson & Son, Inc.
Johnson Worldwide Associates, Inc., **24** 530; **28 215–17**, 412
Johnston Coca-Cola Bottling Company of Chattanooga, **13** 163–64
Johnston Evans & Co., **IV** 704
Johnston Foil Co., **IV** 18
Johnston Harvester Co., **III** 650
Johnston Industries, Inc., **15 246–48**
Johnstown America Industries, Inc., **23 305–07**
Johnstown Sanitary Dairy, **13** 393
Jointless Rim Ltd., **I** 428
Jokisch, **II** 556
Jonathan Backhouse & Co., **II** 235
Jonathan Logan Inc., **13** 536
Jonell Shoe Manufacturing Corporation, **13** 360
Jones & Babson, Inc., **14** 85
Jones & Johnson, **14** 277
Jones & Laughlin Steel Corp., **I** 463, 489–91; **IV** 228; **11** 197
Jones Apparel Group, Inc., **11 216–18**; **27** 60; **30** 310–11
Jones Brothers Tea Co., **7** 202
Jones Environmental, **11** 361
Jones Financial Companies, L.P. *See* Edward Jones.
Jones Intercable, Inc., **14** 260; **17** 7; **21 307–09**; **24** 123; **25** 212
Jones Janitor Service, **25** 15
Jones Medical Industries, Inc., **24 256–58**
Jones Motor Co., **10** 44
Jones-Rodolfo Corp. *See* Cutter & Buck, Inc.
Jonker Fris, **II** 571
Jonkoping & Vulcan, **12** 462
Jordache Enterprises, Inc., **15** 201–02; **23 308–10**
The Jordan Co., **11** 261; **16** 149
Jordan Marsh, **III** 608; **V** 26; **9** 209
Jordan Valley Electric Cooperative, **12** 265
Jos. A. Bank Clothiers, Inc., **II** 560; **12** 411; **31 282–85**
Josef Meys, **III** 418
Joseph Bellamy and Sons Ltd., **II** 569
Joseph Campbell Company. *See* Campbell Soup Company.
Joseph Crosfield, **III** 31
Joseph E. Seagram & Sons Inc., **I** 266, 285; **21** 319
Joseph Garneau Co., **I** 226; **10** 180
Joseph Leavitt Corporation, **9** 20
Joseph Littlejohn & Levy, **27** 204
Joseph Lucas & Son, **III** 554–56
Joseph Lumber Company, **25** 379
Joseph Magnin, **I** 417–18; **17** 124
Joseph Malecki Corp., **24** 444–45
Joseph Nathan & Co., **I** 629–40
Joseph Rank Limited, **II** 564
Joseph Schlitz Brewing Company, **25** 281
Joseph T. Ryerson & Son, Inc., **IV** 114; **15 249–51**; **19** 217, 381
Josephson International, **27** 392
Joshin Denki, **13** 481
Joshu Railway Company, **6** 431
Joshua's Christian Bookstores, **31** 435–36
Josiah Wedgwood and Sons Limited. *See* Waterford Wedgewood Holdings PLC.
Jostens, Inc., **7 255–57**; **25 252–55 (upd.)**
Journal Register Company, **29 261–63**
Journey's End Corporation, **14** 107
Jovan, **III** 66
Jove Publications, Inc., **II** 144; **IV** 623; **12** 224
Jovi, **II** 652
Joy Manufacturing, **III** 526
Joy Planning Co., **III** 533
Joy Technologies Inc., **II** 17; **26** 70
Joyce International, Inc., **16** 68
JP Foodservice Inc., **24** 445
JP Household Supply Co. Ltd., **IV** 293
JP Information Center Co., Ltd., **IV** 293
JP Planning Co. Ltd., **IV** 293
JPC Co., **IV** 155
JPF Holdings, Inc. *See* U.S. Foodservice.
JPS Automotive L.P., **17** 182–84
JPS Textile Group, Inc., **28 218–20**
JPT Publishing, **8** 528
JT Aquisitions, **II** 661
JTL Corporation, **13** 162–63
JTN Acquisition Corp., **19** 233
JTS Corporation, **23** 23, 26
Jude Hanbury, **I** 294
Judel Glassware Co., Inc., **14** 502
Judson Dunaway Corp., **12** 127
Judson Steel Corp., **13** 97
Jugend & Volk, **14** 556
Jugo Bank, **II** 325
Juice Bowl Products, **II** 480–81; **26** 57
Juice Works, **26** 57
Jujamycn, **24** 439
Jujo Paper Co., Ltd., **IV** 268, 284–85, 292–93, **297–98**, 321, 326, 328, 356
Julius Berger-Bauboag A.G., **I** 560–61
Julius Garfinckel & Co., Inc., **22** 110
Jumping-Jacks Shoes, Inc., **17** 390
Jung-Pumpen, **III** 570; **20** 361
Junghans Uhren, **10** 152
Junkers Luftverkehr, **I** 110, 197; **6** 87–88
Juno Lighting, Inc., **30 266–68**
Juovo Pignone, **13** 356
Jupiter National, **15** 247–48; **19** 166
Jurgens, **II** 588–89
Jurgensen's, **17** 558
Jurgovan & Blair, **III** 197
Juristförlaget, **14** 556
Jusco Car Life Company, **23** 290
JUSCO Co., Ltd., **V 96–99**; **11** 498
Jusco Group, **31** 430
Just For Feet, Inc., **19 228–30**
Just Squeezed, **31** 350
Just Toys, Inc., **29** 476
Justin Industries, Inc., **19 231–33**
JVC. *See* Victor Company of Japan, Ltd.
JW Aluminum Company, **22** 544
JWP Inc., **9 300–02**; **13** 176
JWT Group Inc., **I** 9, **19–21**, 23; **6** 53. *See also* WPP Group plc.
Jylhävaara, **IV** 348
JZC. *See* John Zink Company.

K&B Inc., **12 286–88**; **17** 244
K&F Manufacturing. *See* Fender Musical Instruments.
K & G Men's Center, Inc., **21 310–12**
K&K Insurance Group, **26** 487
K&K Toys, Inc., **23** 176
K&L, **6** 48
K&M Associates, **16** 18
K & R Warehouse Corporation, **9** 20
K-C Aviation, **III** 41; **16** 304
K-Graphics Inc., **16** 306
K-Group, **27** 261
K-H Corporation, **7** 260
K-Swiss, **22** 173
K-tel International, Inc., **21 325–28**

K-III Holdings. *See* Primedia Inc.
K.C.C. Holding Co., **III** 192
K.F. Kline Co., **7** 145; **22** 184
K.H. Wheel Company, **27** 202
K. Hattori & Co., Ltd., **III** 454–55, 619–20. *See also* Seiko Corporation.
k.k. Staatsbahnen, **6** 419
K Line. *See* Kawasaki Kisen Kaisha, Ltd.
K.O. Lester Co., **31** 359, 361
K.W. Muth Company, **17** 305
KA Teletech, **27** 365
Ka Wah AMEV Insurance, **III** 200–01
Kabelvision AB, **26** 331–33
Kable News Company. *See* AMREP Corporation.
Kable Printing Co., **13** 559
Kaduna Refining and Petrochemicals Co., **IV** 473
Kaepa, **16** 546
Kaestner & Hecht Co., **II** 120
Kafte Inc., **28** 63
Kaga Forwarding Co., **6** 428
Kagami Crystal Works, **III** 714
Kagle Home Health Care, **11** 282
Kagoshima Central Research Laboratory, **21** 330
Kahan and Lessin, **II** 624–25
Kahn's Meats, **II** 572
Kai Tak Land Investment Co., **IV** 717
Kaiser + Kraft GmbH, **27** 175
Kaiser Aluminum & Chemical Corporation, **IV** 11–12, 15, 59–60, **121–23**, 191; **6** 148; **12** 377; **8** 348, 350; **22** 455. *See also* ICF Kaiser International, Inc.
Kaiser Cement, **III** 501, 760; **IV** 272
Kaiser Company, **6** 184
Kaiser Engineering, **IV** 218
Kaiser Industries, **III** 760
Kaiser Packaging, **12** 377
Kaiser Permanente Corp., **6** 279; **12** 175; **24** 231; **25** 434, 527
Kaiser Steel, **IV** 59
Kaiser's Kaffee Geschäft AG, **27** 461
Kaizosha, **IV** 632
Kajaani Oy, **II** 302; **IV** 350
Kajima Corp., I 577–78
Kal Kan Foods, Inc., 22 298–300
Kalamazoo Paper Co., **IV** 281; **9** 259
Kalbfleish, **I** 300
Kaldveer & Associates, **14** 228
Kalitta Group, **22** 311
Kalua Koi Corporation, **7** 281
Kalumburu Joint Venture, **IV** 67
Kamaishi, **IV** 157; **17** 349
Kaman Corp., 12 289–92; **16** 202
Kamewa Group, **27** 494, 496
Kaminski/Engles Capital Corp. *See* Suiza Foods Corporation.
Kamioka Mining & Smelting Co., Ltd., **IV** 145, 148
Kammer Valves, A.G., **17** 147
Kanagawa Bank, **II** 291
Kanda Shokai, **16** 202
Kanders Florida Holdings, Inc., **27** 50
Kane Financial Corp., **III** 231
Kane Foods, **III** 43
Kane Freight Lines, **6** 370
Kane-Miller Corp., **12** 106
Kanebo Spinning Inc., **IV** 442
Kanegafuchi Shoji, **IV** 225
Kanematsu Corporation, **IV 442–44**; **24 259–62 (upd.)**
Kangaroo. *See* Seino Transportation Company, Ltd.
Kangol Ltd., **IV** 136
Kangyo Bank, **II** 300, 310, 361
Kanhym, **IV** 91–92
Kanoldt, **24** 75
Kansai Electric Power Co., Inc., **IV** 492; **V 645–48**
Kansai Seiyu Ltd., **V** 188
Kansai Sogo Bank, **II** 361
Kansallis-Osake-Pankki, **II** 242, **302–03**, 366; **IV** 349
Kansas City Power & Light Company, **6 510–12**, 592; **12** 541–42
Kansas City Securities Corporation, **22** 541
Kansas City Southern Industries, Inc., **6 400–02**; **26 233–36 (upd.)**; **29** 333
Kansas City White Goods Company. *See* Angelica Corporation.
Kansas Fire & Casualty Co., **III** 214
Kansas Power Company, **6** 312
Kansas Public Service Company, **12** 541
Kansas Utilities Company, **6** 580
Kanto Steel Co., Ltd., **IV** 63
Kanzaki Paper Manufacturing Co., **IV** 285, 293
Kao Corporation, **III 38–39**, 48; **16** 168; **20 315–17 (upd.)**
Kaohsiung Refinery, **IV** 388
Kaolin Australia Pty Ltd., **III** 691
Kapalua Land Company, Ltd., **29** 307–08
Kaplan Educational Centers, **12** 143
Kapy, **II** 139; **24** 194
Karafuto Industry, **IV** 320
Karan Co. *See* Donna Karan Company.
Karastan Bigelow, **19** 276
Karg'sche Familienstiftung, **V** 73
Karmelkorn Shoppes, Inc., **10** 371, 373
Karstadt Aktiengesellschaft, **V 100–02**; **19 234–37 (upd.)**
Kasado Dockyard, **III** 760
Kasai Securities, **II** 434
Kasco Corporation, **28** 42, 45
Kaset Rojananil, **6** 123
Kash n' Karry Food Stores, Inc., **20 318–20**
Kasmarov, **9** 18
Kaspare Cohn Commercial & Savings Bank. *See* Union Bank of California.
Kast Metals, **III** 452; **15** 92
Kasuga Radio Company. *See* Kenwood Corporation.
Kat-Em International Inc., **16** 125
Katalco, **I** 374
Kataoka Electric Co., **II** 5
Katelise Group, **III** 739–40
Katharine Gibbs Schools Inc., **22** 442
Kathleen Investment (Australia) Ltd., **III** 729
Kathy's Ranch Markets, **19** 500–01
Katies, **V** 35
Kativo Chemical Industries Ltd., **8** 239
Katy Industries Inc., **I 472–74**; **14** 483–84; **16** 282
Katz Communications, Inc., **6 32–34**
Katz Drug, **II** 604
Katz Media Group Inc., **24** 108
Kauffman-Lattimer, **III** 9–10
Kaufhalle AG, **V** 104; **23** 311
Kaufhof Holding AG, **II** 257; **V 103–05**
Kaufhof Warenhaus AG, **23 311–14 (upd.)**
Kaufman and Broad Home Corporation, **8 284–86**; **11** 481–83
Kaufmann Department Stores, Inc., **V** 132–33; **6** 243; **19** 262
Kaukaan Tehdas Osakeyhtiö, **IV** 301
Oy Kaukas Ab, **IV** 300–02; **19** 462
Kaukauna Cheese Inc., **23** 217, 219
Kauppaosakeyhtiö Kymmene Aktiebolag, **IV** 299
Kauppiaitten Oy, **8** 293
Kautex Werke Reinold Hagen AG, **IV** 128
Kautex-Bayern GmbH, **IV** 128
Kautex-Ostfriedland GmbH, **IV** 128
Kawachi Bank, **II** 361; **26** 455
Kawamata, **11** 350
Kawasaki Denki Seizo, **II** 22
Kawasaki Heavy Industries, Ltd., **I** 75; **II** 273–74; **III** 482, 513, 516, **538–40**, 756; **IV** 124; **7** 232; **8** 72; **23** 290
Kawasaki Kisen Kaisha, Ltd., **V 457–60**
Kawasaki Steel Corporation, **I** 432; **II** 274; **III** 539, 760; **IV** 30, **124–25**, 154, 212–13; **13** 324; **19** 8
Kawashimaya Shoten Inc. Ltd., **II** 433
Kawecki Berylco Industries, **8** 78
Kawneer GmbH., **IV** 18
Kawsmouth Electric Light Company. *See* Kansas City Power & Light Company.
Kay County Gas Co., **IV** 399
Kay Home Products, **17** 372
Kay's Drive-In Food Service, **II** 619
Kay-Bee Toy Stores, **V** 137; **15 252–53**; **16** 389–90
Kaydon Corporation, **18 274–76**
Kayex, **9** 251
Kaynar Manufacturing Company, **8** 366
Kayser Aluminum & Chemicals, **8** 229
Kayser Roth Corp., **8** 288; **22** 122
Kaysersberg, S.A., **IV** 290
KBLCOM Incorporated, **V** 644
KC. *See* Kenneth Cole Productions, Inc.
KC Holdings, Inc., **11** 229–30
KCI Konecranes International, **27** 269
KCPL. *See* Kansas City Power & Light Company.
KCS Industries, **12** 25–26
KCSI. *See* Kansas City Southern Industries, Inc.
KCSR. *See* Kansas City Southern Railway.
KD Manitou, Inc. *See* Manitou BF S.A.
KDT Industries, Inc., **9** 20
Keebler Co., **II** 594
Keefe Manufacturing Courtesy Coffee Company, **6** 392
Keegan Management Co., **27** 274
Keen, Robinson and Co., **II** 566
Keene Packaging Co., **28** 43
KEG Productions Ltd., **IV** 640; **26** 272
Keihan JUSCO, **V** 96
Keil Chemical Company, **8** 178
Keio Teito Electric Railway Company, **V 461–62**
Keisei Electric Railway, **II** 301
Keith Prowse Music Publishing, **22** 193
Keith-Albee-Orpheum, **II** 88
Keithley Instruments Inc., **16 299–301**
Keller-Dorian Graveurs, S.A., **17** 458
Kelley & Partners, Ltd., **14** 130
Kellock, **10** 336
Kellogg Company, **I** 22–23; **II** 463, 502–03, **523–26**, 530, 560; **10** 323–24; **12** 411; **13** 3, **291–94 (upd.)**; **15** 189; **18** 65, 225–26; **22** 336, 338; **25** 90; **27** 39; **29** 30, 110
Kellwood Company, **V** 181–82; **8 287–89**
Kelly & Associates, **III** 306

Kelly & Cohen, **10** 468
Kelly, Douglas and Co., **II** 631
Kelly Nason, Inc., **13** 203
Kelly Services, Inc., 6 35–37, 140; **9** 326; **16** 48; **25** 356, 432; **26 237–40 (upd.)**
The Kelly-Springfield Tire Company, 8 290–92; **20** 260, 263
Kelsey-Hayes Group of Companies, I 170; **III** 650, 652; **7 258–60**; **27 249–52 (upd.)**
Kelso & Co., **III** 663, 665; **12** 436; **19** 455; **21** 490; **30** 48–49
Kelty Pack, Inc., **10** 215
Kelvinator Inc., **17** 487
KemaNobel, **9** 380–81; **13** 22
Kemet Corp., 14 281–83
Kemi Oy, **IV** 316
Kemira, Inc., **III** 760; **6** 152
Kemp's Biscuits Limited, **II** 594
Kemper Corporation, III 269–71, 339; **15 254–58 (upd.)**; **22** 495
Kemper Financial Services, **26** 234
Kemper Motorenfabrik, **I** 197
Kemper Snowboards, **22** 460
Kemperco Inc., **III** 269–70
Kempinski Group, **II** 258
Kemps Biscuits, **II** 594
Ken-L-Ration, **II** 559
Kendall International, Inc., I 529; **III** 24–25; **IV** 288; **11 219–21**; **14** 121; **15** 229; **28** 486
Kendall-Jackson Winery, Ltd., 28 111, **221–23**
Kenetech Corporation, 11 222–24
Kennametal, Inc., IV 203; **13 295–97**
Kennecott Corporation, III 248; **IV** 33–34, 79, 170–71, 179, 192, 288, 576; **7 261–64**; **10** 262, 448; **12** 244; **27 253–57 (upd.)**
Kennedy Automatic Products Co., **16** 8
Kenner, **II** 502; **10** 323; **12** 168
Kenner Parker Toys, Inc., **II** 503; **9** 156; **10** 324; **14** 266; **16** 337; **25** 488–89
Kenneth Cole Productions, Inc., 22 223; **25 256–58**
Kenneth O. Lester, Inc., **21** 508
Kenny Rogers' Roasters, **22** 464; **29** 342, 344
Kenroy International, Inc., **13** 274
Kent Drugs Ltd., **II** 640, 650
Kent Electronics Corporation, 17 273–76
Kent Fire, **III** 350
Kent-Moore Corp., **I** 200; **10** 492–93
Kentland-Elkhorn Coal Corp., **IV** 181
Kentrox Industries, **30** 7
Kentucky Bonded Funeral Co., **III** 217
Kentucky Electric Steel, Inc., 31 286–88
Kentucky Fried Chicken, **I** 260–61; **II** 533; **III** 78, 104, 106; **6** 200; **7** 26–28, 433; **8** 563; **12** 42; **13** 336; **16** 97; **18** 8, 538; **19** 92; **21** 361; **22** 464; **23** 384, 504. *See also* KFC Corporation.
Kentucky Institution for the Education of the Blind. *See* American Printing House for the Blind.
Kentucky Utilities Company, 6 513–15; **11** 37, 236–38
Kenway, **I** 155
Kenwood Corporation, I 532; **19** 360; **23** 53; **31 289–91**
Kenwood Silver Company, Inc., **31** 352
Kenworth Motor Truck Corp., **I** 185–86; **26** 354
Kenyon & Eckhardt Advertising Agency, **25** 89–91
Kenyon Corp., **18** 276
Kenyon Sons and Craven Ltd., **II** 593–94
Kenzo, **25** 122
Keo Cutters, Inc., **III** 569; **20** 360
KEPCO. *See* Kyushu Electric Power Company Inc.
Kerlick, Switzer & Johnson, **6** 48
Kerlyn Oil Co., **IV** 445–46
Kern County Land Co., **I** 527; **10** 379, 527
Kernite SA, **8** 386
Kernkraftwerke Lippe-Ems, **V** 747
Kernridge Oil Co., **IV** 541
Kerr Concrete Pipe Company, **14** 250
Kerr Corporation, **14** 481
Kerr Group Inc., III 423; **10** 130; **22** 48; **24 263–65**; **30** 39
Kerr-Addison Mines Ltd., **IV** 165
Kerr-McGee Corporation, IV 445–47; **13** 118; **22 301–04 (upd.)**
Kerry Group plc, 27 258–60
Kerry Properties Limited, 22 305–08; **24** 388
Keski-Suomen Tukkukauppa Oy, **8** 293
Kesko Ltd (Kesko Oy), 8 293–94; **27 261–63 (upd.)**
Ketchikan International Sales Co., **IV** 304
Ketchikan Paper Company, **31** 316
Ketchikan Pulp Co., **IV** 304
Ketchum Communications Inc., 6 38–40
Ketner and Milner Stores, **II** 683
Kettle Chip Company, **26** 58
Kettle Restaurants, Inc., **29** 149
Keumkang Co., **III** 515; **7** 231
Kewanee Public Service Company, **6** 505
Kewaunee Scientific Corporation, 25 259–62
Key Computer Laboratories, Inc., **14** 15
Key Industries, Inc., **26** 342
Key Markets, **II** 628
Key Pharmaceuticals, Inc., **11** 207
Key Tronic Corporation, 14 284–86
KeyCorp, 8 295–97; **11** 110; **14** 90
Keyes Fibre Company, 9 303–05
KeySpan Energy Co., 27 264–66
Keystone Aircraft, **I** 61; **11** 164
Keystone Consolidated Industries, Inc., **19** 467
Keystone Custodian Fund, **IV** 458
Keystone Foods Corporation, **10** 443
Keystone Franklin, Inc., **III** 570; **9** 543; **20** 362
Keystone Frozen Foods, **17** 536
Keystone Gas Co., **IV** 548
Keystone Health Plan West, Inc., **27** 211
Keystone Insurance and Investment Co., **12** 564
Keystone International, Inc., 11 225–27; **28** 486
Keystone Life Insurance Co., **III** 389
Keystone Paint and Varnish, **8** 553
Keystone Pipe and Supply Co., **IV** 136
Keystone Portland Cement Co., **23** 225
Keystone Savings and Loan, **II** 420
Keystone Tube Inc., **25** 8
Keytronics, **18** 541
KFC Corporation, 7 265–68; **10** 450; **21 313–17 (upd.)**; **23** 115, 117, 153. *See also* Kentuckey Fried Chicken.
Khalda Petroleum Co., **IV** 413
KHBB, **16** 72
KHD AG. *See* Klöckner-Humboldt-Deutz AG.
KHD Konzern, III 541–44
KHL. *See* Koninklijke Hollandsche Lloyd.
Kholberg, Kravis & Roberts, **13** 453
Kia Motors Corporation, I 167; **12 293–95**; **29 264–67 (upd.)**
Kidd, Kamm & Co., **21** 482
Kidde Inc., I 475–76; **III** 503; **7** 209; **23** 297
Kidder, Peabody & Co., **II** 31, 207, 430; **IV** 84; **7** 310; **12** 197; **13** 465–67, 534; **16** 322; **22** 406
Kidder Press Co., **IV** 644
Kiddie Products, Inc., **24** 413
Kids "R" Us, **V** 203–05; **9** 394
Kids Foot Locker, **14** 293, 295
Kidston Mines, **I** 438
Kiekhaefer Corporation, **III** 443; **22** 115
Kien, **13** 545
Kienzle Apparate GmbH, **III** 566
Kierulff Electronics, **10** 113
Kieser Verlag, **14** 555
Kiewit Diversified Group Inc., **11** 301
Kiewit-Murdock Investment Corp., **15** 129
Kijkshop/Best-Sellers, **13** 545
Kikkoman Corporation, I 9; **14 287–89**
Kilburn & Co., **III** 522
Kilgo Motor Express, **6** 370
Kilgore Ceramics, **III** 671
Kilgore Federal Savings and Loan Assoc., **IV** 343
Killington, Ltd., **28** 21
Kilpatrick's Department Store, **19** 511
Kilsby Tubesupply, **I** 570
Kimball International, Inc., 12 296–98
Kimbell Inc., **II** 684
Kimberley Central Mining Co., **IV** 64; **7** 121
Kimberly-Clark Corporation, I 14, 413; **III** 36, **40–41**; **IV** 249, 254, 297–98, 329, 648, 665; **8** 282; **15** 357; **16 302–05 (upd.)**; **17** 30, 397; **18** 147–49; **19** 14, 284, 478; **22** 209
Kimco Realty Corporation, 11 228–30
Kincaid Furniture Company, **14** 302–03
Kinden Corporation, **7** 303
KinderCare Learning Centers, Inc., 13 298–300
Kinear Moodie, **III** 753
Kineret Acquisition Corp. *See* Hain Food Group, Inc.
Kinetic Concepts, Inc., 20 321–23
King & Spalding, 23 315–18
The King Arthur Flour Company, 31 292–95
King Bearing, Inc., **13** 79
King Cullen, **II** 644
King Features Syndicate, **IV** 626; **19** 201, 203–04
King Folding Box Co., **13** 441
King Fook Gold and Jewellery Co., **IV** 717
King Hickory, **17** 183
King Kullen Grocery Co., Inc., 15 259–61; **19** 481; **24** 528
King Ranch, Inc., 14 290–92
King Soopers Inc., **12** 112–13
King World Productions, Inc., 9 306–08; **28** 174; **30 269–72 (upd.)**
King's Lynn Glass, **12** 528
King-Seeley, **II** 419; **16** 487
Kingbird Media Group LLC, **26** 80
Kingfisher plc, V 106–09; **10** 498; **19** 123; **24 266–71 (upd.)**; **27** 118, 120; **28** 34, 36
Kings, **24** 528

Kings County Lighting Company, **6** 456
Kings County Research Laboratories, **11** 424
Kings Mills, Inc., **13** 532
Kings Super Markets, **24** 313, 316
Kingsford Corporation, **III** 21; **22** 146
Kingsin Line, **6** 397
Kingsport Pulp Corp., **IV** 310; **19** 266
Kingston Technology Corporation, 20 324–26
Kinki Nippon Railway Company Ltd., V 463–65
Kinko's Inc., 12 174; **16 306–08; 18** 363–64
Kinnevik, **IV** 203–04
Kinney Corporation, **23** 32; **24** 373
Kinney National Service Inc., **II** 176; **IV** 672; **19** 404; **25** 140
Kinney Services, **6** 293
Kinney Shoe Corp., V 226; **11** 349; **14 293–95**
Kinney Tobacco Co., **12** 108
Kinoshita Sansho Steel Co., **I** 508
Kinpo Electronic, **23** 212
Kinross, **IV** 92
Kinson Resources Inc., **27** 38
Kintec Corp., **10** 97
Kirby. *See* Scott Fetzer Company.
Kirby Corporation, 18 277–79; 22 275
Kirby Forest Industries, **IV** 305
Kirch Group, **10** 196
Kirchner, Moore, and Co., **II** 408
Kirin Brewery Company, Limited, I 220, 258, **265–66**, 282; **10** 78, 80; **13** 258, 454; **20** 28; **21 318–21 (upd.)**
Kirk Stieff Company, **10** 181; **12** 313
Kirkland Messina, Inc., **19** 392, 394
Kirkstall Forge Engineering, **III** 494
Kirsch Co., **II** 16
Kirschner Manufacturing Co., **16** 296
Kishimoto & Co., **I** 432, 492; **24** 325
Kishimoto Shoten Co., Ltd., **IV** 168
Kistler, Lesh & Co., **III** 528
Kit Manufacturing Co., 18 280–82
Kita Consolidated, Ltd., **16** 142
Kita Karafunto Oil Co., **IV** 475
Kita Nippon Paper Co., **IV** 321
Kitagawa & Co. Ltd., **IV** 442
Kitchell Corporation, 14 296–98
KitchenAid, III 611, 653–54; **8 298–99**
Kitchenbell, **III** 43
Kitchens of Sara Lee, **II** 571–73
Kittery Electric Light Co., **14** 124
Kittinger, **10** 324
Kitty Hawk, Inc., 22 309–11
Kiwi International Airlines Inc., 20 327–29
Kiwi Packaging, **IV** 250
Kiwi Polish Co., **15** 507
KJJ. *See* Klaus J. Jacobs Holdings.
Kjøbenhavns Bandelsbank, **II** 366
KJPCL. *See* Royal Interocean Lines.
KKK Shipping, **II** 274
KKR. *See* Kohlberg Kravis Roberts & Co.
KLA Instruments Corporation, 11 231–33; 20 8
Klaus J. Jacobs Holdings, **29** 46–47
KLC/New City Televentures, **25** 269
Klein Bicycles, **16** 495
Kleiner, Perkins, Caufield & Byers, **I** 637; **6** 278; **10** 15, 504; **14** 263; **16** 418; **27** 447
Kleinwort Benson Group PLC, II 379, **421–23; IV** 191; **22** 55
Kline Manufacturing, **II** 16
KLLM Transport Services, **27** 404
KLM Royal Dutch Airlines, **26** 33924 311, 396–97; **27** 474; **29** 15, 17. *See also* Koninklijke Luftvaart Maatschappij N.V.
Klöckner-Humboldt-Deutz AG, **I** 542; **III** 541–44; **IV** 126–27; **13** 16–17
Klöckner-Werke AG, IV 43, 60, **126–28**, 201; **19** 64
Klondike, **14** 205
Klopman International, **12** 118
Kloth-Senking, **IV** 201
Kluwer Publishers, **IV** 611; **14** 555
Klynveld Main Goerdeler, **10** 387
Klynveld Peat Marwick Goerdeler. *See* KPMG Worldwide.
KM&G. *See* Ketchum Communications Inc.
Kmart Canada Co., **25** 222
Kmart Corporation, I 516; **V** 35, **110–12; 6** 13; **7** 61, 444; **9** 361, 400, 482; **10** 137, 410, 490, 497, 515–16; **12** 48, 54–55, 430, 477–78, 507–08; **13** 42, 260–61, 274, 317–18, 444, 446; **14** 192, 394; **15** 61–62, 210–11, 330–31, 470; **16** 35–37, 61, 187, 210, 447, 457; **17** 297, 460–61, 523–24; **18** 137, **283–87 (upd.)**, 477; **19** 511; **20** 155–56; **21** 73; **22** 258, 328; **23** 210, 329; **24** 322–23; **25** 121; **26** 348, 524; **27** 313, 429, 451, 481
KMC Enterprises, Inc., **27** 274
KMP Holdings, **I** 531
KN. *See* Kühne & Nagel Group.
Kna-Shoe Manufacturing Company, **14** 302
Knape & Vogt Manufacturing Company, 17 277–79
Knapp & Tubbs, **III** 423
Knapp Communications Corporation, **II** 656; **13** 180; **24** 418
Knapp-Monarch, **12** 251
Knauf, **III** 721, 736
KNI Retail A/S, **12** 363
Knickerbocker Toy Co., **III** 505
Knickerbocker Trust Company, **13** 465
Knife River Coal Mining Company, **7** 322–25
Knight Paper Co., **III** 766; **22** 545
Knight-Ridder, Inc., III 190; **IV** 597, 613, **628–30**, 670; **6** 323; **7** 191, 327; **10** 407; **15 262–66 (upd.)**; **18** 323; **30** 216
Knightsbridge Partners, **26** 476
KNILM, **24** 397
Knoff-Bremse, **I** 138
Knogo Corp., **11** 444
Knoll Group Inc., I 202; **14 299–301**
Knoll Pharmaceutical, **I** 682
Knomark, **III** 55
Knorr Co. *See* C.H. Knorr Co.
Knorr Foods Co., Ltd., **28** 10
Knorr-Bremse, **11** 31
Knott, **III** 98
Knott's Berry Farm, 18 288–90; 22 130
Knowledge Systems Concepts, **11** 469
KnowledgeWare Inc., 9 309–11; 27 491; **31 296–298 (upd.)**
Knox Reeves Advertising Agency, **25** 90
Knoxville Paper Box Co., Inc., **13** 442
KNSM. *See* Koninklijke Nederlandsche Stoomboot Maatschappij.
Knudsen & Sons, Inc., **11** 211
Knudsen Foods, **27** 330
Knutange, **IV** 226
Knutson Construction, **25** 331
Kobacker Co., **18** 414–15
Kobayashi Tomijiro Shoten, **III** 44
Kobe Shipbuilding & Engine Works, **II** 57
Kobe Steel, Ltd., I 511; **II** 274; **IV** 16, **129–31**, 212–13; **8** 242; **11** 234–35; **13** 297; **19 238–41 (upd.)**
Kobelco America Inc., **19** 241
Kobelco Middle East, **IV** 131
Kobold. *See* Vorwerk & Co.
Kobrand Corporation, **24** 308
Koç Holdings A.S., I 167, **478–80; 11** 139; **27** 188
Koch Enterprises, Inc., 29 215–17
Koch Industries, Inc., IV 448–49; 20 330–32 (upd.); **21** 108; **22** 3
Koch-Light Laboratories, **13** 239
Kockos Brothers, Inc., **II** 624
Kodak. *See* Eastman Kodak Company.
Kodansha Ltd., IV 631–33
Ködel & Böhn GmbH, **III** 543
Koehring Company, **8** 545; **23** 299
Koehring Cranes & Excavators, **7** 513
Koei Real Estate Ltd., **V** 195
Koenig Plastics Co., **19** 414
Kohl's Corporation, 9 312–13; 22 72; **30 273–75 (upd.)**
Kohl's Food Stores, Inc., **I** 426–27; **16** 247, 249
Kohlberg Kravis Roberts & Co., I 566, 609–11; **II** 370, 452, 468, 544, 645, 654, 656, 667; **III** 263, 765–67; **IV** 642–43; **V** 55–56, 408, 410, 415; **6** 357; **7** 130, 132, 200; **9** 53, 180, 230, 469, 522; **10** 75–77, 302; **12** 559; **13** 163, 166, 363; **14** 42; **15** 270; **17** 471; **18** 3; **19** 493; **22** 55, 91, 441, 513, 544; **23** 163; **24** 92, **272–74**, 416, 418; **25** 11, 278; **26** 46, 48, 352; **27** 11; **28** 389, 475; **30** 386
Kohler Bros., **IV** 91
Kohler Company, 7 269–71; 10 119; **24** 150
Kohler Mix Specialties, Inc., **25** 333
Kohner Brothers, **II** 531
Koholyt AG, **III** 693
Koike Shoten, **II** 458
Kojiro Matsukata, **V** 457–58
Kokkola Chemicals Oy, **17** 362–63
Kokomo Gas and Fuel Company, **6** 533
Kokuei Paper Co., Ltd., **IV** 327
Kokura Sekiyu Co. Ltd., **IV** 554
Kokura Steel Manufacturing Co., Ltd., **IV** 212
Kokusai Kisen, **V** 457–58
Kokusaku Kiko Co., Ltd., **IV** 327
Kokusaku Pulp Co., **IV** 327
Kolb-Lena, **25** 85
Kolbenschmidt, **IV** 141
Kolker Chemical Works, Inc., **IV** 409; **7** 308
The Koll Company, 8 300–02; 21 97; **25** 449
Kollmorgen Corporation, 18 291–94
Kölnische Rückversicherungs-Gesellschaft AG, **24** 178
Komag, Inc., 11 234–35
Komatsu Ltd., III 453, 473, **545–46; 15** 92; **16 309–11 (upd.)**
Kommanditgesellschaft S. Elkan & Co., **IV** 140
Kommunale Energie-Beteiligungsgesellschaft, **V** 746
Kompro Computer Leasing, **II** 457
Konan Camera Institute, **III** 487

Kone Corporation, **27 267–70**
Kongl. Elektriska Telegraf-Verket, **V** 331
Kongo Bearing Co., **III** 595
Konica Corporation, **III 547–50**; **30 276–81 (upd.)**
Koninklijke Ahold N.V., **II 641–42**; **12** 152–53; **16 312–14 (upd.)**
Koninklijke Bols Wessanen, N.V., **29** 480–81
Koninklijke Distilleerderijen der Erven Lucas Böls, **I** 226
Koninklijke Hoogovens NV, **26** 527, 530
Koninklijke Java-China Paketvaart Lijnen. *See* Royal Interocean Lines.
Koninklijke KPN N.V. *See* Royal KPN N.V.
Koninklijke Luchtvaart Maatschappij N.V., **I** 55, **107–09**, 119, 121; **6** 95, 105, 109–10; **14** 73; **28 224–27 (upd.)**
Koninklijke Nederlandsche Hoogovens en Staalfabrieken NV, **IV** 105, 123, **132–34**
Koninklijke Nederlandsche Maatschappig Tot Exploitatie van Petroleumbronnen in Nederlandsch-indie, **IV** 530
Koninklijke Nederlandsche Petroleum Maatschappij, **IV** 491
Koninklijke Nederlandsche Stoomboot Maatschappij, **26** 241
N.V. Koninklijke Nederlandse Vliegtuigenfabriek Fokker, **I** 46, **54–56**, 75, 82, 107, 115, 121–22; **28 327–30 (upd.)**
Koninklijke Nedlloyd Groep N.V., **6 403–05**
Koninklijke Nedlloyd N.V., **26 241–44 (upd.)**
Koninklijke Paketvaart Maatschappij, **26** 242
Koninklijke PTT Nederland NV, **V 299–301**; **27** 471–72, 475
Koninklijke Van Ommeren, **22** 275
Koninklijke Wessanen N.V., **II 527–29**
Koninklijke West-Indische Maildienst, **26** 242
Koniphoto Corp., **III** 548
Konishi Honten, **III** 547
Konishi Pharmaceutical, **I** 704
Konishiroku Honten Co., Ltd., **III** 487, 547–49
Konoike Bank, **II** 347
Konrad Hornschuch AG, **31** 161–62
Koo Koo Roo, Inc., **25 263–65**
Koopman & Co., **III** 419
Koor Industries Ltd., **II 47–49**; **22** 501; **25 266–68 (upd.)**
Koors Perry & Associates, Inc., **24** 95
Koortrade, **II** 48
Kop-Coat, Inc., **8** 456
Kopin Corp., **13** 399
Köpings Mekaniska Verkstad, **26** 10
Koppel Steel, **26** 407
Koppens Machinenfabriek, **III** 420
Kopper United, **I** 354
Koppers Inc., **I** 199, **354–56**; **III** 645, 735; **6** 486; **17** 38–39
Koppers Industries, Inc., **26 245–48 (upd.)**
Koracorp Industries Inc., **16** 327
Korbel, **I** 226
Korea Automotive Fuel Systems Ltd., **13** 555
Korea Automotive Motor Corp., **16** 436
Korea Development Leasing Corp., **II** 442
Korea Steel Co., **III** 459
Korea Telecommunications Co, **I** 516
Korean Air Lines Co. Ltd., **II** 442; **6 98–99**; **24** 443; **27 271–73 (upd.)**
Korean Development Bank, **III** 459
Korean Tungsten Mining Co., **IV** 183
Kori Kollo Corp., **23** 41
Koro Corp., **19** 414
Korrekt Gebäudereinigung, **16** 420
KorrVu, **14** 430
Kortbetalning Servo A.B., **II** 353
Kortgruppen Eurocard-Köpkort A.B., **II** 353
Korvettes, E.J., **14** 426
Koryeo Industrial Development Co., **III** 516; **7** 232
Koryo Fire and Marine Insurance Co., **III** 747
Kosset Carpets, Ltd., **9** 467
Kotobukiya Co., Ltd., **V 113–14**
Kowa Metal Manufacturing Co., **III** 758
Koyo Seiko, **III** 595–96, 623–24
KPM. *See* Koninklijke Paketvaart Maatschappij.
KPMG International, **29** 176
KPMG Worldwide, **7** 266; **10** 115, **385–87**
KPN. *See* Koninklijke PTT Nederland N.V.
KPR Holdings Inc., **23** 203
Kraft Foods, Inc., **II** 129, **530–34**, 556; **V** 407; **III** 610; **7 272–77 (upd.)**, 339, 433, 547; **8** 399, 499; **9** 180, 290, 318; **11** 15; **12** 372, 532; **13** 408, 515, 517; **14** 204; **16** 88, 90; **17** 56; **18** 67, 246, 416, 419; **19** 51; **22** 82, 85; **23** 219, 384; **25** 366, 517; **26** 249, 251; **28** 479
Kraft Foodservice, **26** 504; **31** 359–60
Kraft Jacobs Suchard AG, **26 249–52 (upd.)**
Kraft-Versicherungs-AG, **III** 183
Kraftco Corporation, **II** 533; **14** 204
KraftMaid Cabinetry, Inc., **20** 363
Kraftwerk Union, **I** 411; **III** 466
Kragen Auto Supply Co., **27** 291
Kramer, **III** 48
Krämer & Grebe, **III** 420
Kramer Guitar, **29** 222
Kramer Machine and Engineering Company, **26** 117
Krames Communications Co., **22** 441, 443
Kransco, **25** 314
Krasnapolsky Restaurant and Wintergarden Company Ltd., **23** 228
Krause's Furniture, Inc., **27 274–77**
Krauss-Maffei AG, **I** 75; **II** 242; **III** 566, 695; **14** 328
Kravco, **III** 248
Kredietbank N.V., **II** 295, **304–05**
Kreditanstalt für Wiederaufbau, **IV** 231–32; **29 268–72**
Kreft, **III** 480; **22** 26
Kreher Steel Co., **25** 8
Krelitz Industries, Inc., **14** 147
Krema Hollywood Chewing Gum Co. S.A., **II** 532
Kremers-Urban, **I** 667
Kresge Foundation, **V** 110
Kreuger & Toll, **IV** 338; **12** 462–63
Kreymborg, **13** 544–45
Kriegschemikalien AG, **IV** 229
Kriegsmetall AG, **IV** 229
Kriegswollbedarfs AG, **IV** 229
Krislex Knits, Inc., **8** 235
Krispy Kitchens, Inc., **II** 584
Krispy Kreme Doughnut Corporation, **21 322–24**
Kroeze, **25** 82
The Kroger Company, **II** 605, 632, **643–45**, 682; **III** 218; **6** 364; **7** 61; **12** 111–13; **13** 25, 237, 395; **15** 259, **267–70 (upd.)**, 449; **16** 63–64; **18** 6; **21** 323, 508; **22** 37, 126; **24** 416; **25** 234; **28** 512; **30** 24, 27
Krohn-Fechheimer Shoe Company, **V** 207
Krones A.G., **I** 266; **21** 319
Kronos, Inc., **18 295–97**; **19** 468
Krovtex, **8** 80
Kroy Tanning Company, **17** 195
Krueger Insurance Company, **21** 257
Kruger Inc., **17 280–82**
Krumbhaar Chemical Inc., **14** 308
Krupp, **17** 214; **22** 364. *See also* Fried. Krupp GmbH *and* Thyssen Krupp AG.
Krupp Widia GmbH, **12** 66
KSSU Group, **I** 107–08, 120–21
KT Contract Services, **24** 118
KTR. *See* Keio Teito Electric Railway Company.
K2 Inc., **16 295–98**; **22** 481, 483; **23** 474
KU Energy Corporation, **6** 513, 515; **11 236–38**
Kubota Corporation, **I** 494; **III 551–53**; **10** 404; **12** 91, 161; **21** 385–86; **24** 324
Kubota, Gonshiro. *See* Gonshiro Oode.
Kuhara Mining Co., **IV** 475
Kuhlman Corporation, **20 333–35**
Kuhlmann, **III** 677; **IV** 174; **16** 121
Kühn + Bayer, **24** 165
Kuhn Loeb, **II** 402–03
Kühne & Nagel International AG, **V 466–69**
Kuitu Oy, **IV** 348
KUK, **III** 577, 712
Kukje Group, **III** 458
Kulka Smith Inc., **13** 398
Kulmobelwerk G.H. Walb and Co., **I** 581
Kum-Kleen Products, **IV** 252; **17** 29
Kumagai Gumi Co., **I 579–80**
Kumsung Companies, **III** 747–48
Kunkel Industries, **19** 143
Kunst und Technik Verlag, **IV** 590
Kuo International Ltd., **I** 566
Kuok Group, **28** 84
The Kuppenheimer Company, **8** 248–50
Kureha Chemical Industry, **I** 675
Kureha Spinning, **24** 325
Kureha Textiles, **I** 432, 492
Kurosawa Construction Co., Ltd., **IV** 155
Kurose, **III** 420
Kurt Möller Verlag, **7** 42
Kurushima Dockyard, **II** 339
The Kushner-Locke Company, **25 269–71**
Kuusankoski Aktiebolag, **IV** 299
Kuwait Airways, **27** 135
Kuwait Investment Office, **II** 198; **IV** 380, 452; **27** 206
Kuwait Petroleum Corporation, **IV** 364, **450–52**, 567; **18** 234
Kvaerner ASA, **20** 313; **31** 367, 370
KW, Inc. *See* Coca-Cola Bottling Company of Northern New England, Inc.
Kwaishinsha Motor Car Works, **I** 183
Kwik Save Group plc, **11 239–41**; **13** 26
Kwik Shop, Inc., **12** 112
Kwikasair Ltd., **27** 473
KWIM. *See* Koninklijke West-Indische Maildienst.

KWV, **I** 289
Kygnus Sekiyu K.K., **IV** 555
Kymi Paper Mills Ltd., **IV** 302
Kymmene Corporation, **IV** 276–77, **299–303**, 337
Kyocera Corporation, **II 50–52**; **III** 693; **7** 118; **21 329–32 (upd.)**
Kyodo, **16** 166
Kyodo Dieworks Thailand Co., **III** 758
Kyodo Gyogyo Kaisha, Limited, **II** 552
Kyodo Kako, **IV** 680
Kyodo Kokusan K.K., **21** 271
Kyodo Oil Co. Ltd., **IV** 476
Kyodo Securities Co., Ltd., **II** 433
Kyodo Unyu Kaisha, **I** 502–03, 506; **IV** 713; **V** 481
Kyoei Mutual Fire and Marine Insurance Co., **III** 273
Kyoritsu Pharmaceutical Industry Co., **I** 667
Kyosai Trust Co. *See* Yasuda Trust and Banking Company, Limited.
Kyoto Bank, **II** 291
Kyoto Ceramic Co., Ltd. *See* Kyocera Corporation.
Kyoto Ouchi Bank, **II** 292
Kyowa Hakko Kogyo Co., Ltd., **III 42–43**
Kyusha Refining Co., **IV** 403
Kyushu Electric Power Company Inc., **IV** 492; **V 649–51**; **17** 349
Kyushu Oil Refinery Co. Ltd., **IV** 434
Kywan Petroleum Ltd., **13** 556
KYZ International, **9** 427
KZO, **13** 21

L & G, **27** 291
L. & H. Sales Co., **16** 389
L&W Supply Corp., **III** 764
L.A. Darling Co., **IV** 135–36; **16** 357
L.A. Gear, Inc., **8 303–06**; **11** 349; **31** 413
L.A. Mex. *See* Checkers Drive-Up Restaurants Inc.
L.A. T Sportswear, Inc., **26 257–59**
L.B. DeLong, **III** 558
L. Bamberger & Co., **V** 169; **8** 443
L. Bosendorfer Klavierfabrik, A.G., **12** 297
L.C. Bassford, **III** 653
L.D. Canocéan, **25** 104
The L.D. Caulk Company, **10** 271
L. Fish, **14** 236
L.G. Balfour Company, **12** 472; **19** 451–52
L. Greif & Bro. Inc., **17** 203–05
L. Grossman and Sons. *See* Grossman's Inc.
L.H. Parke Co., **II** 571
L.J. Knowles & Bros., **9** 153
L.J. Melody & Co., **21** 97
L.K. Liggett Company, **24** 74
L. Kellenberger & Co. AG, **25** 194
L.L. Bean, Inc., **9** 190, 316; **10 388–90**; **12** 280; **19** 333; **21** 131; **22** 173; **25** 48, 206; **29** 278
The L.L. Knickerbocker Co., Inc., **25 272–75**
L. Luria & Son, Inc., **19 242–44**
L.M. Electronics, **I** 489
L.M. Ericsson, **I** 462; **II** 1, 70, 81–82, 365; **III** 479–80; **11** 46, 439; **14** 488
L-N Glass Co., **III** 715
L-N Safety Glass, **III** 715
L-O-F Glass Co. *See* Libbey-Owens-Ford Glass Co.
L. Prang & Co., **12** 207
L.S. DuBois Son and Co., **III** 10
L.S. Starrett Co., **13 301–03**
L. Straus and Sons, **V** 168
L.W. Hammerson & Co., **IV** 696
L.W. Pierce Co., Inc. *See* Pierce Leahy Corporation.
L.W. Singer, **13** 429
La Banque Suisse et Française. *See* Crédit Commercial de France.
La Barge Mirrors, **III** 571; **20** 362
La Cerus, **IV** 615
La Choy Food Products Inc., **II** 467–68; **17** 241; **25 276–78**
La Cinq, **IV** 619
La Cloche d'Or, **25** 85
La Concorde, **III** 208
La Crosse Telephone Corporation, **9** 106
La Cruz del Campo S.A., **9** 100
La Favorita Bakery, **II** 543
La Fromagerie du Velay, **25** 85
La Halle aux Chaussures, **17** 210
La India Co., **II** 532
La Oroya, **22** 286
La Petite Academy, **13** 299
La Quinta Inns, Inc., **11 242–44**; **21** 362
La Redoute S.A., **19** 306, 309
La Rinascente, **12** 153
La Ruche Meridionale, **12** 153
La Societe Anonyme Francaise Holophane, **19** 211
La Vie Claire, **13** 103
La-Ru Truck Rental Company, Inc., **16** 386
La-Z-Boy Chair Company, **14 302–04**; **31** 248
Laakirchen, **IV** 339–40; **28** 445
LAB. *See* Lloyd Aereo de Bolivia.
LaBakelite S.A., **I** 387
Labatt Brewing Company Limited, **I 267–68**; **18** 72; **25 279–82 (upd.)**; **26** 303, 306
Labaz, **I** 676; **IV** 546
Labelcraft, Inc., **8** 360
LaBelle Iron Works, **7** 586
Labor für Impulstechnik, **III** 154
Labor Ready, Inc., **29 273–75**
Laboratoire Michel Robilliard, **IV** 546
Laboratoire Roger Bellon, **I** 389
Laboratoires d'Anglas, **III** 47
Laboratoires Goupil, **III** 48
Laboratoires Roche Posay, **III** 48
Laboratoires Ruby d'Anglas, **III** 48
Laboratorios Grossman, **III** 55
Laboratorios Liade S.A., **24** 75
Laboratory for Electronics, **III** 168; **6** 284
LaBour Pump, **I** 473
LaBow, Haynes Co., **III** 270
Lachine Rapids Hydraulic and Land Company, **6** 501
Lackawanna Steel & Ordnance Co., **IV** 35, 114; **7** 48
Laclede Steel Company, **15 271–73**
Lacombe Electric. *See* Public Service Company of Colorado.
Lacquer Products Co., **I** 321
LaCrosse Footwear, Inc., **18 298–301**
Lacto Ibérica, **23** 219
Lactos, **25** 85
Lacy Diversified Industries, Ltd., **24** 159–61
Ladbroke Group PLC, **II** 139, **141–42**; **19** 208; **21 333–36 (upd.)**; **24** 194
Ladd and Tilton, **14** 527–28
LADD Furniture, Inc., **12 299–301**; **23** 244
Ladd Petroleum Corp., **II** 30
LADECO, **6** 97; **31** 304
Ladenburg, Thalmann & Co. Inc., **17** 346
Ladenso, **IV** 277
Ladish Co., Inc., **30 282–84**
Lady Foot Locker, **V** 226; **14** 293, 295
Lady Lee, **27** 291
Laerdal Medical, **18** 423
Lafarge Coppée S.A., **III** 702, **703–05**, 736; **8** 258; **10** 422–23; **23** 333
Lafarge Corporation, **24** 332; **28 228–31**
Lafayette Manufacturing Co., **12** 296
Lafayette Radio Electronics Corporation, **9** 121–22
Laflin & Rand Powder Co., **I** 328; **III** 525
LAG&E. *See* Los Angeles Gas and Electric Company.
LaGard Inc., **20** 363
Lagardère Groupe SCA, **16** 254; **24** 84, 88
Lagoven, **IV** 508
Laidlaw Transportation, Inc., **6** 410
Laing, **IV** 696
Laing's Properties Ltd., **I** 575
L'Air Liquide, **I** 303, **357–59**; **11** 402
Laitaatsillan Konepaja, **IV** 275
Laiterie Centrale Krompholtz, **25** 84
Laiterie de la Vallée du Dropt, **25** 84
Laiterie Ekabe, **19** 50
SA Laiterie Walhorn Molkerel, **19** 50
Laiteries Prairies de l'Orne, **19** 50
Lake Arrowhead Development Co., **IV** 255
Lake Central Airlines, **I** 131; **6** 131
Lake Erie Screw Corp., **11** 534, 536
Lake Odessa Machine Products, **18** 494
Lake Superior Consolidated Mines Company, **IV** 572; **7** 549; **17** 355–56
Lake Superior Paper Industries, **26** 363
Lakeland Fire and Casualty Co., **III** 213
Läkemedels-Industri Föreningen, **I** 664
Laker Airways, **I** 94; **6** 79; **24** 399
Lakeside Laboratories, **III** 24
The Lakeside Publishing and Printing Co., **IV** 660
Lakestone Systems, Inc., **11** 469
Lam Research Corporation, **IV** 213; **11 245–47**; **18** 383; **31 299–302 (upd.)**
Lamar Advertising Company, **27 278–80**
Lamb Technicon Corp., **I** 486
Lamb Weston, Inc., **I** 417; **23 319–21**; **24** 33–34
Lambert Brothers, Inc., **7** 573
Lambert Brussels Financial Corporation, **II** 407; **11** 532
Lambert Kay Company, **8** 84
Lambert Pharmacal Co., **I** 710–11; **III** 28
Lamborghini. *See* Automobili Lamborghini S.p.A.
Lamkin Brothers, Inc., **8** 386
Lamons Metal Gasket Co., **III** 570; **11** 535; **20** 361
Lamontagne Ltd., **II** 651
Lamonts Apparel, Inc., **15 274–76**
Lampadaires Feralux, Inc., **19** 472
Lamson & Sessions Co., **13 304–06**
Lamson Bros., **II** 451
Lamson Corporation, **7** 145
Lamson Industries Ltd., **IV** 645
Lamson Store Service Co., **IV** 644
Lan Chile S.A., **31 303–06**
Lanca, **14** 224
Lancashire, **III** 350
Lancaster Caramel Co., **II** 510

Lancaster Colony Corporation, 8 307–09
Lancaster Cork Works, **III** 422
Lancaster Financial Ltd., **14** 472
Lancaster National Bank, **9** 475
Lancaster Press, **23** 102
Lance, Inc., 14 305–07
Lancel, **27** 487, 489
Lancer Corporation, 21 337–39
Lanchester Motor Company, Ltd., **13** 286
Lancia, **I** 162; **11** 102
Lancôme, **III** 46–48; **8** 342
Land O'Lakes, Inc., II 535–37; **7** 339; **13** 351; **21 340–43 (upd.)**
Land Securities PLC, IV 704–06
Land-O-Sun Dairies, L.L.C., **26** 449
Land-Wheelwright Laboratories, **III** 607; **7** 436
Lander Alarm Co., **III** 740
Lander Company, **21** 54
Länderbank, **II** 282
Landesbank für Westfalen Girozentrale, Münster, **II** 385
Landis International, Inc., **10** 105–06
Landmark Banks, **10** 426
Landmark Communications, Inc., 12 302–05; **22** 442
Landmark Financial Services Inc., **11** 447
Landmark Target Media, **IV** 597
Landmark Union Trust, **18** 517
Landoll, Inc., **22** 522
Landor Associates, **I** 94
Landry's Seafood Restaurants, Inc., 15 277–79
Lands' End, Inc., 9 314–16; **12** 280; **16** 37; **19** 333; **26** 439; **27** 374, 429; **29 276–79 (upd.)**
Landstar, **26** 533
Lane Bryant, **V** 115–16
The Lane Co., Inc., III 528, 530; **12 306–08**
Lane Drug Company, **12** 132
Lane, Piper, and Jaffray, Inc. *See* Piper Jaffray Companies.
Lane Processing Inc., **II** 585
Lane Publishing Co., **IV** 676; **7** 529
Lane Rossi, **IV** 421
Laneco, Inc., **II** 682
Lang Exploratory Drilling, **26** 42
Langdon Rieder Corp., **21** 97
Lange International S.A., **15** 462
Lange, Maxwell & Springer, **IV** 641; **7** 311
Langford Labs, **8** 25
Lanier Business Products, Inc., **II** 39; **8** 407; **20** 290
Lanman Companies, Inc., **23** 101
Lannet Data Communications Ltd., **18** 345–46; **26** 275–77
Lano Corp., **I** 446
Lansi-Suomen Osake-Pankki, **II** 303
Lanson Pere et Fils, **II** 475
Lantic Industries, Inc., **II** 664
Lanvin, **I** 696; **III** 48; **8** 343
LAPE. *See* Líneas Aéreas Postales Españolas.
LaPine Technology, **II** 51; **21** 331
Laporte Industries Ltd., **I** 303; **IV** 300
Lapp, **8** 229
Lara, **19** 192
Larami Corp., **14** 486
Lareco, **26** 22
Largo Entertainment, **25** 329
Laroche Navarron, **I** 703
Larousse Group, **IV** 614–15
Larrowe Milling Co., **II** 501; **10** 322
Larry Flynt Publishing Inc., 31 307–10
Larry H. Miller Group, 29 280–83
Larsen & Toubro, **IV** 484
Larsen Company, **7** 128
Larson Lumber Co., **IV** 306
Larwin Group, **III** 231
Las Vegas Gas Company, **19** 411
LaSalle Machine Tool, Inc., **13** 7–8
LaSalle National Bank, **II** 184
LaSalle Steel Corporation, **28** 314
LaSalles & Koch Co., **8** 443
Lasco Shipping Co., **19** 380
Laser Tech Color, **21** 60
Lasercharge Pty Ltd, **18** 130
LaserSoft, **24** 349
Oy Läskelä Ab, **IV** 300
Lasky's, **II** 141; **24** 269
Lasmo, **IV** 455, 499
Lason, Inc., 31 311–13
Latitude Communications, **22** 52
Latrobe Brewing Co., **25** 281
Latrobe Steel Company, **8** 529–31
Lattice Semiconductor Corp., 16 315–17
Lauder Chemical, **17** 363
Laura Ashley Holdings plc, 13 307–09
Laura Scudder's, **7** 429
Laurentien Hotel Co., **III** 99
Lauson Engine Company, **8** 515
LaVista Equipment Supply Co., **14** 545
Lavold, **16** 421
Law Life Assurance Society, **III** 372
Lawn Boy Inc., **7** 535–36; **8** 72; **26** 494
Lawrence Manufacturing Co., **III** 526
Lawrence Warehouse Co., **II** 397–98; **10** 62
Lawrenceburg Gas Company, **6** 466
The Lawson Co., **7** 113; **25** 125
Lawson Milk, **II** 572
Lawter International Inc., 14 308–10; **18** 220
Lawyers Cooperative, **8** 527–28
Lawyers Trust Co., **II** 230
Layne & Bowler Pump, **11** 5
Layne Christensen Company, 19 245–47; **26** 71
Layton Homes Corporation, **30** 423
Lazard Freres & Co., **II** 268, 402, 422; **IV** 23, 79, 658–59; **6** 356; **7** 287, 446; **10** 399; **12** 165, 391, 547, 562; **21** 145
Lazare Kaplan International Inc., 21 344–47
LBO Holdings, **15** 459
LBS Communications, **6** 28
LCI International, Inc., 16 318–20
LCP Hotels. *See* CapStar Hotel Co.
LDDS WorldCom, Inc., **16** 467–68
LDDS-Metro Communications, Inc., 8 310–12
LDI. *See* Lacy Diversified Industries, Ltd.
LDS Health Services Corporation, **27** 237
LDX NET, Inc., **IV** 576
Le Bon Marché. *See* Bon Marché.
Le Brun and Sons, **III** 291
Le Buffet System-Gastronomie, **V** 74
Le Clerc, **21** 225–26
Le Courviour S.A., **10** 351
Le Rocher, Compagnie de Reassurance, **III** 340
Lea & Perrins, **II** 475
Lea County Gas Co., **6** 580
Lea Lumber & Plywood Co., **12** 300
Lea Manufacturing, **23** 299
Leach McMicking, **13** 274
Lead Industries Group Ltd., **III** 681; **IV** 108
Leadership Housing Inc., **IV** 136
Leaf River Forest Products Inc., **IV** 282, 300; **9** 261
Leahy & Co. *See* Pierce Leahy Corporation.
Leamington Priors & Warwickshire Banking Co., **II** 318; **17** 323
Lean Cuisine, **12** 531
Lear Corporation, **17** 303, 305
Lear Inc., **II** 61; **8** 49, 51
Lear Romec Corp., **8** 135
Lear Seating Corporation, 16 321–23
Lear Siegler Holdings Corporation, **25** 431
Lear Siegler Inc., I 481–83; **III** 581; **8** 313; **13** 169, 358, 398; **19** 371–72; **30** 426
Learjet Inc., 8 313–16; **9** 242; **27 281–85 (upd.)**
The Learning Company Inc., 24 275–78, 480; **29** 74, 77
Learning Tree International Inc., 24 279–82
LeaRonal, Inc., 23 322–24
Leasco Data Processing Equipment Corp., **III** 342–44; **IV** 641–42; **7** 311
Lease International SA, **6** 358
Leaseway Personnel Corp., **18** 159
Leaseway Transportation Corp., V 494; **12 309–11**; **19** 293
Leatherback Industries, **22** 229
LeBoeuf, Lamb, Greene & MacRae, L.L.P., 29 284–86
Lebr Associates Inc., **25** 246
Lech Brewery, **24** 450
Lechmere Inc., 10 391–93
Lechters, Inc., 11 248–50
Leclerc, **12** 153
Lectorum Publications, **29** 426
Lederle Laboratories, **I** 300–02, 657, 684; **8** 24–25; **14** 254, 256, 423; **27** 115
Lederle Standard Products, **26** 29
Lee Ackerman Investment Company, **18** 513
Lee Apparel Company, Inc., 8 317–19; **17** 512, 514
Lee Brands, **II** 500
Lee Company, **V** 390–92
Lee Enterprises, Incorporated, 11 251–53
Lee Hecht Harrison, **6** 10
Lee International, **24** 373
Lee National Corporation, **26** 234
Lee Optical, **13** 390
Lee Rubber and Tire Corp., **16** 8
Lee Telephone Company, **6** 313
Lee Way Holding Co., **14** 42
Lee Way Motor Freight, **I** 278
Leeann Chin, Inc., 30 285–88
Leeds & County Bank, **II** 318; **17** 323
Leeds & Northrup Co., **III** 644–45; **28** 484
Lees Carpets, **17** 76
Leewards Creative Crafts Inc., **17** 322
Lefeldt, **III** 417, 418
Lefrak Organization Inc., 8 357; **26 260–62**
Legacy Homes Ltd., **26** 290
Legal & General Group plc, III 272–73; **IV** 705, 712; **24 283–85 (upd.)**; **30** 494
Legal Technologies, Inc., **15** 378
Legault and Masse, **II** 664
Legent Corporation, 10 394–96; **14** 392

Legetojsfabrikken LEGO Billund A/S. *See* Lego A/S.
Legg, Mason & Co., **11** 493
Leggett & Platt, Incorporated, **9** 93; **11 254–56**
Leggett Stores Inc., **19** 48
Lego A/S, **12** 495; **13 310–13**
Legrand SA, **21 348–50**
Lehigh Portland Cement Company, **23 325–27**; **31** 252
Lehigh Railroad, **III** 258
Lehman Brothers, **I** 78, 125, 484; **II** 192, 259, 398, 448, 450–51; **6** 199; **10** 62–63; **11** 263–64; **13** 448; **14** 145; **22** 445; **25** 301
Lehman Merchant Bank Partners, **19** 324
Lehmer Company. *See* Centel Corporation.
Lehn & Fink, **I** 699
Lehnkering AG, **IV** 140
Lehrman Bros., **III** 419
Lehser Communications, Inc., **15** 265
Leigh-Mardon Security Group, **30** 44
Leighton Holdings Ltd., **19** 402
Leinenkugel Brewing Company. *See* Jacob Leinenkugel Brewing Company.
Leisure Lodges, **III** 76
Leisure System Inc., **12** 359
Leitz, **III** 583–84
LeMaster Litho Supply, **13** 228
Lemmerz Holding GmbH, **27** 202, 204
Lempereur, **13** 297
Lena Goldfields Ltd., **IV** 94
Lenc-Smith, **III** 430
Lend Lease Corporation Limited, **IV 707–09**; **17 283–86 (upd.)**
Lending Textiles, **29** 132
Lenel Systems International Inc., **24** 510
Lennar Corporation, **11 257–59**
Lennon's, **II** 628
Lennox Industries, Inc., **22** 6
Lennox International Inc., **8 320–22**; **28 232–36 (upd.)**
Lenoir Furniture Corporation, **10** 183
Lenox, Inc., **I** 227; **10** 179, 181; **12 312–13**; **18** 69
Lens, Inc., **30** 267–68
LensCrafters Inc., **V** 207–08; **13** 391; **17** 294; **23 328–30**
Lentheric, **I** 426
L'Entreprise Jean Lefebvre, **23 331–33**
Leo, **I** 665
Leo Burnett Company, Inc., **I 22–24**, 25, 31, 37; **11** 51, 212; **12** 439; **20 336–39 (upd.)**
Léon Gaumont et Cie. *See* Gaumont SA.
Leonard Bernstein Music Publishing Company, **23** 391
Leonard Development Group, **10** 508
Leonard Express, Inc., **6** 371
Leonard Green & Partners LP, **12** 477–78; **24** 173
Leonard Machinery Corp., **16** 124
Leonard Parker Company, **26** 196
Leonard Silver, **14** 482
Leonardo Editore, **IV** 587
Leonberger Bausparkasse, **II** 258
Lepco Co., **III** 596
Leprino Foods Company, **28 237–39**
Lern, Inc., **II** 420
Lerner Plastics, **9** 323
Lerner Stores, **V** 116
Leroy-Merlin, **23** 230
Les Chantiers de l'Atlantique, **II** 13
Les Echos. *See* Groupe Les Echos.
Les Grands Magasins Au Bon Marché: Etablissements Vaxelaire-Claes, **26** 159–60
Les Industries Ling, **13** 443
Les Papeteries du Limousin, **19** 227
L'Escaut, **III** 335
Lesco Inc., **19 248–50**
The Leslie Fay Companies, Inc., **8 323–25**
Leslie Paper, **IV** 288
Leslie's Poolmart, Inc., **18 302–04**
Lesser-Goldman, **II** 18
Lester B. Knight & Associates, **II** 19
Lester Ink and Coatings Company, **13** 228
Lestrem Group, **IV** 296; **19** 226
Let op Uw Einde, **III** 199
Leucadia National Corporation, **6** 396; **11**; **25** 170 **260–62**
Leuna-Werke AG, **7** 142
Level Five Research, Inc., **22** 292
N.V. Levensverzekering Maatschappji Utrecht, **III** 199–200
Lever Brothers Company, **I** 17, 21, 26, 30, 333; **II** 497, 588–89; **III** 31; **7** 542–43, 545; **9** 291, **317–19**; **13** 199; **14** 314
Levi Strauss & Co., **I** 15; **II** 634, 669; **V** 60–61, **362–65**; **9** 142; **12** 430; **16 324–28 (upd.)**, 509, 511; **17** 512; **18** 191–92; **19** 196; **23** 422; **24** 158; **25** 47
Leviathan Gas Pipeline Company, **21** 171
Levine, Huntley, Vick & Beaver, **6** 28
Levitt & Sons, **IV** 728
Levitt Corp., **21** 471
Levitt Homes, **I** 464; **11** 198
Levitt Industries, **17** 331
Levitt Investment Company, **26** 102
Levitz Furniture Inc., **15 280–82**; **23** 412, 414
Levtex Hotel Ventures, **21** 363
Levy Bakery Goods, **I** 30
Levy Restaurants L.P., **26 263–65**
Lew Liberbaum & Co., **27** 197
The Lewin Group, Inc., **21** 425
Lewis and Marks, **IV** 21–22, 96; **16** 27
Lewis Batting Company, **11** 219
Lewis Construction, **IV** 22
Lewis Galoob Toys Inc., **16 329–31**
Lewis Grocer Co., **II** 669; **18** 504
Lewis Refrigeration Company, **21** 500
Lewis's, **V** 178
Lewis's Bank, **II** 308
Lewis-Howe Co., **III** 56
Lex Electronics, **10** 113
Lex Service plc, **19** 312
Lexecon, Inc., **26** 187
Lexington Broadcast Services, **6** 27
Lexington Furniture Industries, **III** 571; **20** 362
Lexington Ice Company, **6** 514
Lexington Insurance Co., **III** 197
Lexington Utilities Company, **6** 514; **11** 237
LEXIS-NEXIS, **17** 399; **18** 542; **21** 70; **31** 388, 393
Lexitron, **II** 87
Lexmark International, Inc., **9** 116; **10** 519; **18 305–07**; **30** 250
Leybold AG, **IV** 71
Leyland and Birmingham Rubber Co., **I** 429
Leyland Motor Corporation, **7** 459
LFC Financial, **10** 339
LFC Holdings Corp. *See* Levitz Furniture Inc.
LFE Corp., **7** 297
LG Chemical Ltd., **26** 425
LG Electronics Inc., **13** 572, 575
LG Group, **18** 124
LG&E Energy Corp., **6 516–18**; **18** 366–67
Lhomme S.A., **8** 477
Liaison Agency, **31** 216–17
Liaoyang Automotive Spring Factory, **III** 581
Libbey-Owens-Ford Company, **I** 609; **III** 640–42, 707, 714–15, 725–26, 731; **IV** 421; **7** 292; **16** 7–9; **22** 434; **23** 83; **26** 353; **31** 355
Libby, **II** 547; **7** 382
Libby McNeil & Libby Inc., **II** 489
Libeltex, **9** 92
Liber, **14** 556
Liberty Bank of Buffalo, **9** 229
Liberty Brokerage Investment Company, **10** 278
Liberty Can and Sign Company, **17** 105–06
The Liberty Corporation, **22 312–14**
Liberty Gauge Company, **17** 213
Liberty Hardware Manufacturing Corporation, **20** 363
Liberty House, **I** 417–18
Liberty Life, **IV** 91, 97
Liberty Media Corporation, **18** 66; **19** 282; **25** 214
Liberty Mexicana, **III** 415
Liberty Mutual Insurance Group, **I** 28; **11** 379
Liberty Mutual Savings Bank, **17** 530
Liberty National Bank, **II** 229
Liberty National Insurance Holding Company. *See* Torchmark Corporation.
Liberty National Life Insurance Co., **III** 217; **9** 506–07
Liberty Natural Gas Co., **11** 441
Liberty Software, Inc., **17** 264
Liberty's, **13** 307
Libra Bank Ltd., **II** 271
Librairie de Jacques-Francois Brétif, **IV** 617
Librairie Fayard, **IV** 618
Librairie Générale Francaise, **IV** 618
Librairie Larousse, **IV** 614–16
Librairie Louis Hachette, **IV** 617–18
Librairie Nathan, **IV** 614, 616
Librairie Victor Lecou, **IV** 617
Libyan Arab Airline, **6** 85
Libyan Arab Foreign Bank, **IV** 454
Libyan National Oil Corporation, **IV 453–55**
Libyan-Turkish Engineering and Consultancy Corp., **IV** 563
Lidköpings Mekaniska Verkstad AB, **III** 623
Lieberman Enterprises, **24** 349
Liebert Corp., **II** 20
Life and Casualty Insurance Co. of Tennessee, **III** 193
Life Assoc. of Scotland, **III** 310
Life Fitness Inc., **III** 431
Life Insurance Co. of Georgia, **III** 310
Life Insurance Co. of Scotland, **III** 358
Life Insurance Co. of Virginia, **III** 204
Life Insurance Securities, Ltd., **III** 288
Life Investors International Ltd., **III** 179; **12** 199

Life of Eire, **III** 273
Life Retail Stores. *See* Angelica Corporation.
Life Savers Corp., **II** 129, 544; **7** 367; **21** 54
Life Science Research, Inc., **10** 105–07
Life Technologies, Inc., **I** 321; **12** 103; **17** **287–89**
Life Uniform Shops. *See* Angelica Corporation.
Lifecycle, Inc., **III** 431; **25** 40
LifeLink, **11** 378
Lifemark Corp., **III** 74; **14** 232
LIFETIME, **IV** 627; **19** 204
Lifetime Corp., **29** 363–64
Lifetime Foam Products, Inc., **12** 439
Lifetime Hoan Corporation, **27** **286–89**
Lift Parts Manufacturing, **I** 157
Ligand Pharmaceutical, **10** 48
Liggett & Meyers, **V** 396, 405, 417–18; **18** 416; **29** 195
Liggett Group Inc., **I** 248; **7** 105; **14** 213; **15** 71; **16** 242
Light & Power Company, **12** 265
Light Corrugated Box Co., **IV** 332
Light Savers U.S.A., Inc. *See* Hospitality Worldwide Services, Inc.
Light-Servicos de Eletricidade S.A., **II** 456
Lightel Inc., **6** 311
Lighthouse, Ltd., **24** 95
Lighting Corp. of America, **I** 476
LIGHTNET, **IV** 576
Lightwell Co., **III** 634
Lignum Oil Co., **IV** 658
LILCO. *See* Long Island Lighting Company.
Lilia Limited, **17** 449
Lillian Vernon Corp., **12** **314–15**; **27** 429
Lillie Rubin, **30** 104–06
Lilliput Group plc, **11** 95; **15** 478
Lilly & Co. *See* Eli Lilly & Co.
Lilly Industries, **22** 437
Lillybrook Coal Co., **IV** 180
Lillywhites Ltd., **III** 105
Lily Tulip Co., **I** 609, 611; **8** 198
Limburger Fabrik und Hüttenverein, **IV** 103
Limhamns Golvindustri AB. *See* Tarkett Sommer AG.
The Limited, Inc., **V** **115–16**; **9** 142; **12** 280, 356; **15** 7, 9; **16** 219; **18** 193, 215, 217, 410; **20** **340–43 (upd.)**; **24** 237; **25** 120–21, 123; **28** 344
Limmer and Trinidad Ltd., **III** 752
LIN Broadcasting Corp., **II** 331; **6** 323; **9** **320–22**; **11** 330
Lin Data Corp., **11** 234
Linamar Corporation, **18** **308–10**
Lincoln American Life Insurance Co., **10** 246
Lincoln Automotive, **26** 363
Lincoln Benefit Life Company, **10** 51
Lincoln Electric Co., **II** 19; **13** **314–16**
Lincoln Electric Motor Works, **9** 439
Lincoln Federal Savings, **16** 106
Lincoln First Bank, **II** 248
Lincoln Income Life Insurance Co., **10** 246
Lincoln Liberty Life Insurance Co., **III** 254
Lincoln Marketing, Inc., **18** 518
Lincoln Motor Co., **I** 165
Lincoln National Corporation, **III** **274–77**; **6** 195; **10** 44; **22** 144; **25** **286–90 (upd.)**
Lincoln Property Company, **8** **326–28**
Lincoln Savings, **10** 340
Lincoln Savings & Loan, **9** 199
Lincoln Snacks Company, **24** **286–88**
Lincoln Telephone & Telegraph Company, **14** **311–13**
LinCom Corp., **8** 327
Lindal Cedar Homes, Inc., **29** **287–89**
Linde A.G., **I** 297–98, 315, **581–83**; **9** 16, 516; **10** 31–32; **11** 402–03; **25** 81
Lindemann's, **I** 220
Lindex, **II** 640
Lindsay Manufacturing Co., **20** **344–46**
Lindsay Parkinson & Co., **I** 567
Lindt & Sprüngli. *See* Chocoladefabriken Lindt & Sprüngli AG.
Lindustries, **III** 502; **7** 208
Linear Corp., **III** 643
Linear Technology, Inc., **16** **332–34**
Líneas Aéreas Postales Españolas, **6** 95
Linens 'n Things, Inc., **13** 81–82; **24** **289–92**
Linfood Cash & Carry, **13** 103
Linfood Holdings Ltd., **II** 628–29
Ling Products, **12** 25
Ling-Temco-Vought. *See* LTV Corporation.
Lingerie Time, **20** 143
Linjeflyg, **I** 120
Link House Publications PLC, **IV** 687
Link Motor Supply Company, **26** 347
Link-Belt Corp., **I** 443; **IV** 660
Linmark Westman International Limited, **25** 221–22
Linroz Manufacturing Company L.P., **25** 245
Lintas: Worldwide, **I** 18; **6** 30; **14** **314–16**
Lintott Engineering, Ltd., **10** 108
Linz, **16** 559
Lion Corporation, **III** **44–45**
Lion Manufacturing, **III** 430; **25** 40
Lion Match Company, **24** 450
Lion Oil, **I** 365
Lion's Head Brewery. *See* The Stroh Brewery Company.
Lionel L.L.C., **12** 494; **16** **335–38**; **18** 524
Lionex Corporation, **13** 46
Liontech, **16** 337–38
Lippincott & Margulies, **III** 283
Lippincott-Raven Publishers, **14** 556
Lipschutz Bros., Inc., **29** 511
Lipson Alport Glass & Associates, **27** 195
Lipton. *See* Thomas J. Lipton Company.
Liqui-Box Corporation, **16** **339–41**
Liquid Ag Systems Inc., **26** 494
Liquid Carbonic, **7** 74, 77
Liquor Barn, **II** 656
Liquorland, **V** 35
Liquorsave, **II** 609–10
LIRCA, **III** 48
Liris, **23** 212
Lisbon Coal and Oil Fuel Co., **IV** 504
Liscaya, **II** 196
Listening Library Inc., **31** 379
Lister, **21** 503
Litco Bancorp., **II** 192
LiTel Communications, Inc., **16** 318
Litho-Krome Corp., **IV** 621
LitleNet, **26** 441
Litronix, **III** 455; **21** 122
Littelfuse, Inc., **26** **266–69**
Little, Brown & Company, **IV** 675; **7** 528; **10** 355
Little Caesar Enterprises, Inc., **24** **293–96 (upd.)**; **27** 481
Little Caesar International, Inc., **7** **278–79**; **7** 278–79; **15** 344, 346; **16** 447; **25** 179, 227–28
Little Chef Ltd., **III** 105–06
Little General, **II** 620; **12** 179, 200
Little Giant Pump Company, **8** 515
Little League Baseball, Incorporated, **23** 450
Little Leather Library, **13** 105
Little, Royal, **I** 529–30; **8** 545; **13** 63
Little Switzerland, **19** 451
Little Tikes Co., **III** 614; **12** 169; **13** **317–19**
Littlewoods Financial Services, **30** 494
Littlewoods Organisation PLC, **V** **117–19**; **24** 316
Litton Industries Inc., **I** 85, 452, 476, **484–86**, 523–24; **II** 33; **III** 293, 473, 732; **IV** 253; **6** 599; **10** 520–21, 537; **11** **263–65 (upd.)**, 435; **12** 248, 271–72, 538–40; **15** 287; **17** 30; **19** 31, 110, 290; **21** 86; **22** 436
Litwin Engineers & Constructors, **8** 546
Livanos, **III** 516
LIVE Entertainment Inc., **18** 64, 66; **20** **347–49**; **24** 349
Liverpool and London and Globe Insurance Co., **III** 234, 350
Liverpool and London Fire and Life Insurance Co., **III** 349
Liverpool Fire and Life Insurance Co., **III** 350
Liverpool Mexico S.A., **16** 216
Livia, **I** 154; **10** 279
Living Centers of America, **13** 49
Living Videotext, **10** 508
Livingston Communications, **6** 313
Livingston, Fargo and Co., **II** 380, 395; **10** 59
LivingWell Inc., **12** 326
Liz Claiborne, Inc., **8** **329–31**; **16** 37, 61; **25** 258, **291–94 (upd.)**
LKB-Produkter AB, **I** 665
Lloyd A. Fry Roofing, **III** 721
Lloyd Adriatico S.p.A., **III** 377
Lloyd Aereo de Bolivia, **6** 97
Lloyd Creative Staffing, **27** 21
Lloyd George Management, **18** 152
Lloyd Instruments, Ltd., **29** 460–61
Lloyd Italico, **III** 351
Lloyd Thompson Group plc, **20** 313
Lloyd's Electronics, **14** 118
Lloyd's of London, **III** 234, **278–81**; **9** 297; **10** 38; **11** 533; **22** **315–19 (upd.)**
Lloyd-Truax Ltd., **21** 499
Lloyds Bank PLC, **II** **306–09** 319, 334, 358; **17** 324–25
Lloyds Chemists plc, **27** 177
Lloyds Life Assurance, **III** 351
LM Ericsson. *See* Telefonaktiebolaget LM Ericsson.
LMC Metals, **19** 380
LME. *See* Telefonaktiebolaget LM Ericsson.
LNG Co., **IV** 473–74
LNM Group, **30** 252
Lo-Cost, **II** 609
Lo-Vaca Gathering Co., **IV** 394; **7** 553
Loadometer Co., **III** 435
Lobitos Oilfields Ltd., **IV** 381–82
Loblaw Companies, **II** 631–32; **19** 116
Local Data, Inc., **10** 97
Locations, Inc., **IV** 727

Locke, Lancaster and W.W.&R. Johnson & Sons, **III** 680
Lockhart Catering, **III** 104
Lockhart Corporation, **12** 564
Lockheed Corporation, **I** 13, 41, 48, 50, 52, 54, 61, 63, **64–66**, 67–68, 71–72, 74, 76–77, 82, 84, 90, 92–94, 100, 102, 107, 110, 113, 121, 126, 195, 493–94, 529; **II** 19, 32–33; **III** 84, 539, 601; **IV** 15; **6** 71; **9** 12, 17–18, 272, 417, 458–60, 501; **10** 163, 262–63, 317, 536; **11** 164, 166, **266–69 (upd.)**, 278–79, 363–65; **12** 190; **13** 126, 128; **17** 306; **21** 140; **22** 506; **24** 84–85, 87, 311, 326, 375, 397; **25** 303, 316, 347
Lockheed Martin Corporation, **15 283–86 (upd.)**; **21** 86; **24** 88; **29** 409. *See also* Martin Marietta Corporation.
Lockwood Banc Group, Inc., **11** 306
Lockwood Greene Engineers, Inc., **17** 377
Lockwood National Bank, **25** 114
Lockwood Technology, Inc., **19** 179
Lockwoods Foods Ltd., **II** 513
Loctite Corporation, **8 332–34**; **30 289–91 (upd.)**
Lodding Engineering, **7** 521
Lodestar Group, **10** 19
Lodge Plus, Ltd., **25** 430
Lodge-Cottrell, **III** 472
LodgeNet Entertainment Corporation, **26** 441; **28 240–42**
Lodging Group, **12** 297
Loeb Rhoades, Hornblower & Co., **II** 450–51; **9** 469
Loehmann's Inc., **24 297–99**
Loening Aeronautical, **I** 61; **11** 164
Loew's Consolidated Enterprises, **II** 154
Loew's, Inc., **31** 99
The Loewen Group, Inc., **16 342–44**
Loewenstein Furniture Group, Inc., **21** 531–33
Loewi Financial Cos., **III** 270
Loews Corporation, **I** 245, **487–88**; **II** 134, 148–49, 169; **III** 228, 231; **12 316–18 (upd.)**, 418; **13** 120–21; **19** 362; **22** 73; **25** 177, 326–28
LOF Plastics, Inc. *See* Libbey-Owens-Ford.
Loffland Brothers Company, **9** 364
Loft Inc., **I** 276; **10** 451
Logan's Roadhouse, Inc., **19** 287–88; **22** 464; **29 290–92**
Logged Off Land Co., **IV** 355–56
Logic Modeling, **11** 491
Logica plc, **14 317–19**
Logicon Inc., **20 350–52**
Logility, **25** 20, 22
Logistics, **III** 431
Logistics Data Systems, **13** 4
Logistics Management Systems, Inc., **8** 33
Logitech International SA, **9** 116; **28 243–45**
Logo 7, Inc., **13** 533
Logon, Inc., **14** 377
Lojas Arapuã S.A., **22 320–22**
Loma Linda Foods, **14** 557–58
Lomak Petroleum, Inc., **24** 380
Lomas & Nettleton Financial Corporation, **III** 249; **11** 122
Lombard North Central, **II** 442
Lombard Orient Leasing Ltd., **II** 442
London & Hull, **III** 211
London & Leeds Development Corp., **II** 141
London & Midland Bank. *See* Midland Bank plc.
London & Rhodesia Mining & Land Company. *See* Lonrho Plc.
London and County Bank, **II** 334
London and Hanseatic Bank, **II** 256
London and Lancashire Insurance Co., **III** 350
London and Scottish Marine Oil, **11** 98
London and Westminster Bank, **II** 333–34
London Asiastic, **III** 699
London Assurance Corp., **III** 278, 369–71, 373
London Brick Co., **III** 502; **7** 208; **14** 249
London Brokers Ltd., **6** 290
London Buses Limited, **6** 406
London Cargo Group, **25** 82
London Central, **28** 155–56
London Chartered Bank of Australia, **II** 188
London Clermont Club, **III** 431
London County and Westminster Bank, **II** 334
London County Freehold & Leasehold Properties, **IV** 711
London East India Company, **12** 421
London, Edinburgh and Dublin Insurance Co., **III** 350
London Electricity, **12** 443
London Film Productions Ltd., **II** 157; **14** 399
London Fog Industries, Inc., **16** 61; **29 293–96**
London General Omnibus Company, **6** 406
London Guarantee and Accident Co., **III** 372
London Insurance Co., **III** 373
London Joint-Stock Bank, **II** 318, 388; **17** 324
London Life Assoc., **IV** 711
London Life Insurance Co., **II** 456–57
London, Provincial and South Western Bank, **II** 235
London Records, **23** 390
London Regional Transport, **6 406–08**
London South Partnership, **25** 497
London Transport, **19** 111
London Weekend Television, **IV** 650–51; **7** 389
Londontown Manufacturing Company. *See* London Fog Industries, Inc.
Lone Star and Crescent Oil Co., **IV** 548
Lone Star Brewing Co., **I** 255
Lone Star Gas Corp., **V** 609, 611
Lone Star Industries, **III** 718, 729, 753; **IV** 304; **23** 326; **28** 450
Lone Star Steakhouse, **21** 250
Lone Star Steel, **I** 440–41
Lone Star Technologies, Inc., **22** 3
Long Distance Discount Services, Inc., **8** 310; **27** 305
Long Distance/USA, **9** 479
Long Island Airways, **I** 115; **12** 379
Long Island Bancorp, Inc., **16 345–47**
Long Island Cable Communication Development Company, **7** 63
Long Island Daily Press Publishing Co., **IV** 582–83
Long Island Lighting Company, **V 652–54**; **6** 456; **27** 264
Long Island Power Authority, **27** 265
Long Island Trust Co., **II** 192, 218
Long John Silver's Restaurants Inc., **13 320–22**
Long Lac Mineral Exploration, **9** 282
Long Life Fish Food Products, **12** 230
Long Manufacturing Co., **III** 439; **14** 63
Long Valley Power Cooperative, **12** 265
Long-Airdox Co., **IV** 136
Long-Term Credit Bank of Japan, Ltd., **II** 301, **310–11**, 338, 369
The Longaberger Company, **12 319–21**
LongHorn Steaks Inc., **19** 341
Longines-Wittenauer Watch Co., **II** 121
Longman Group Ltd., **IV** 611, 658
Longmat Foods, **II** 494
Longs Drug Stores Corporation, **V 120**; **25 295–97 (upd.)**
Longview Fibre Company, **8 335–37**
Longwy, **IV** 227
Lonrho Plc, **IV** 651–52; **10** 170; **21 351–55**
Lonsdale Investment Trust, **II** 421
Lonvest Corp., **II** 456–57
Loomis, Sayles & Co., **III** 313
Loose Leaf Metals Co., Inc., **10** 314
Lor-Al, Inc., **17** 10
Loral Corporation, **II** 38; **7** 9; **8 338–40**; **9 323–25**; **13** 356; **15** 283, 285; **20** 262
Lord & Taylor, **13** 44; **14** 376; **15** 86; **18** 137, 372; **21** 302
Lord & Thomas, **I** 12–14; **IV** 660
Lord Baltimore Press, Inc., **IV** 286
Lord Chetwynd's Insurance, **III** 370
Lord Onslow's Insurance, **III** 370
L'Oréal, **II** 547; **III 46–49**, 62; **7** 382–83; **8** 129–31; **341–44 (upd.)**; **11** 41; **23** 238, 242; **31** 418
Lorenz, **I** 463
Lorillard Industries, **I** 488; **V** 396, 407, 417; **12** 317; **18** 416; **22** 73; **29** 195
Lorimar Telepictures, **II** 149, 177; **25** 90–91, 329
Loronix Inc., **24** 509
Lorraine-Escaut, **IV** 227
Lorvic Corp., **I** 679
Los Angeles Can Co., **I** 599
Los Angeles Drug Co., **12** 106
Los Angeles Gas and Electric Company, **V** 682; **25** 413
Los Angeles Steamship Co., **II** 490
Los Lagos Corp., **12** 175
Los Nietos Co., **IV** 570; **24** 520
Loss Prevention Inc., **24** 509
Lost Arrow Inc., **22 323–25**
Lothringer Bergwerks- und Hüttenverein Aumetz-Friede AG, **IV** 126
LOT$OFF Corporation, **24 300–01**
Lotus Cars Ltd., **14 320–22**
Lotus Development Corporation, **IV** 597; **6** 224–25, 227, **254–56**, 258–60, 270–71, 273; **9** 81, 140; **10** 24, 505; **12** 335; **16** 392, 394; **20** 238; **21** 86; **22** 161; **25 298–302 (upd.)**; **30** 251
Lotus Publishing Corporation, **7** 239; **25** 239
Lotus Radio, **I** 531
Louart Corporation, **29** 33–34
Loucks, Hoffman & Company, **8** 412
Loughead Aircraft Manufacturing Co., **I** 64
Louis Allis, **15** 288
Louis B. Mayer Productions, **II** 148; **25** 326–27
Louis C. Edwards, **II** 609
Louis Dreyfus Energy Corp., **28** 471
Louis Harris & Associates, Inc., **22** 188
Louis Kemp Seafood Company, **14** 515
Louis Marx Toys, **II** 559; **12** 410

Louis Rich, Inc., **II** 532; **12** 372
Louis Vuitton, **I** 272; **III** 48; **8** 343; **10 397–99**
Louisiana & Southern Life Insurance Co., **14** 460
Louisiana Bank & Trust, **11** 106
Louisiana Corporation, **19** 301
Louisiana Energy Services, **27** 130
The Louisiana Land and Exploration Company, **IV** 76, 365, 367; **7 280–83**
Louisiana-Pacific Corporation, **IV** 282, **304–05**; **9** 260; **16** 203; **22** 491; **31 314–317 (upd.)**
Louisville Cement Co., **IV** 409
Louisville Gas and Electric Company. *See* LG&E Energy Corporation.
Louisville Home Telephone Company, **14** 258
Loup River Public Power District, **29** 352
Louthan Manufacturing Company, **8** 178
LoVaca Gathering Company. *See* The Coastal Corporation.
Lovelace Truck Service, Inc., **14** 42
Loveman's, Inc., **19** 323
Lovering China Clays, **III** 690
Lowe Bros. Co., **III** 745
Lowe Group, **22** 294
Lowe's Companies, Inc., **V** 122–23; **11** 384; **12** 234, 345; **18** 239; **21** 324, **356–58 (upd.)**; **27** 416
Lowell Bearing Co., **IV** 136
Lowell Shoe, Inc., **13** 360
Löwenbräu, **I** 220, 257; **II** 240
Lowes Food Stores. *See* Alex Lee Inc.
Lowney/Moirs, **II** 512
Lowrance Electronics, Inc., **18 311–14**
Lowrey's Meat Specialties, Inc., **21** 156
Loyalty Group, **III** 241–43
LRL International, **II** 477
LSI. *See* Lear Siegler Inc.
LSI Logic Corporation, **13 323–25**; **18** 382
LTA Ltd., **IV** 22
LTU Group, **17** 325
The LTV Corporation, **I** 62–63, **489–91**; **7** 107–08; **8** 157, 315; **10** 419; **11** 166, 364; **12** 124; **17** 357; **18** 110, 378; **19** 466; **24 302–06 (upd.)**; **26** 406
Luberef, **IV** 538
The Lubrizol Corporation, **30 292–95 (upd.)**
Lubrizol Enterprises, Inc., **I 360–62**; **21** 385–87
Luby's Cafeteria's, Inc., **17 290–93**; **19** 301
Lucas Bols, **II** 642
Lucas Digital Ltd., **12** 322
Lucas Girling, **I** 157
Lucas Industries Plc, **III** 509, **554–57**; **27** 251
Lucas Ingredients, **27** 258
Lucas-Milhaupt, Inc., **23** 250
Lucasfilm Ltd., **9** 368, 472; **12 322–24**; **22** 459
LucasVarity plc, **27** 249, 251
Lucchini, **IV** 228
Lucent Technologies, **18** 154, 180; **20** 8; **22** 19; **26** 275, 277; **29** 44, 414
Lucky Brand Dungarees, **18** 85
Lucky Lager Brewing Co, **I** 268; **25** 280
Lucky Stores Inc., **II** 605, 653; **6** 355; **8** 474; **12** 48; **17** 369, 559; **22** 39; **27 290–93**
Lucky Strike, **II** 143
Lucky-Goldstar, **II 53–54**; **III** 457; **13** 574. *See also* Goldstar Co., Ltd.
Ludlow Corp., **III** 645
Ludovico, **25** 85
Lufkin Rule Co., **II** 16
Luftag, **I** 110
Lufthansa. *See* Deutsche Lufthansa Aktiengesellschaft.
The Luggage Company, **14** 224
Lukens Inc., **14 323–25**; **27** 65
Lukey Mufflers, **IV** 249
Lum's, **6** 199–200
Lumac B.V., **I** 387
Lumbermen's Investment Corp., **IV** 341
Lumbermens Mutual Casualty Co., **III** 269–71; **15** 257
Lumex, Inc., **17** 197
La Lumière Economique, **II** 79
Lummus Crest, **IV** 469; **26** 496
Lumonics Inc., **III** 635
Lunar Corporation, **29 297–99**
Luncheon Voucher, **27** 10
Lund Food Holdings, Inc., **22 326–28**
Lundstrom Jewelers, **24** 319
Lunenburg Sea Products Limited, **14** 339
Lunevale Products Ltd., **I** 341
L'Unite Hermetique S.A., **8** 515
Lunn Poly, **8** 525–26
Luotto-Pankki Oy, **II** 303
Lurgei, **6** 599
LURGI. *See* Metallurgische Gesellschaft Aktiengesellschaft.
Luria Bros. and Co., **I** 512–13; **6** 151
Lutèce, **20** 26
Luther's Bar-B-Q, **II** 556
Lutheran Brotherhood, **31 318–21**
Lux, **III** 478
Lux Mercantile Co., **II** 624
Luxor, **II** 69; **6** 205; **17** 353
Luxottica SpA, **17 294–96**; **23** 328
Luxury Linens, **13** 81–82
LVMH, **I** 272; **19** 86
LVMH Moët Hennessy Louis Vuitton S.A., **24** 137, 140
LVO Cable Inc., **IV** 596
LXE Inc., **21** 199–201
Lycos, **27** 517
Lydex, **I** 527
Lykes Corp., **I** 490–91; **24** 303
Lynde Company, **16** 269–71
Lynx Express Delivery, **6** 412, 414
Lyon & Healy, **IV** 660
Lyon's Technological Products Ltd., **III** 745
Lyondell Petrochemical Company, **IV** 377, **456–57**; **10** 110
Lyonnaise Communications, **10** 196; **25** 497
Lyonnaise des Eaux-Dumez, **I** 576; **V 655–57**; Eaux, **23** 332
Lyons. *See* J. Lyons & Co. Ltd.
LyphoMed Inc., **IV** 333; **17** 287
Oy Lypsyniemen Konepaja, **IV** 275–76
Lysaght, **24** 143
Lysaght's Canada, Ltd., **IV** 73
Lystads, **I** 333
Lytag Ltd., **31** 398–99

M and G Fund Management, **III** 699
M&J Diesel Locomotive Filter Co., **17** 106
M&M Limited, **7** 299
M and M Manufacturing Company, **23** 143
M&M/Mars, **14** 48; **15** 63–64; **21** 219
M & S Computing. *See* Intergraph Corporation.
M&T Capital Corporation, **11** 109
M/A Com Inc., **6** 336; **14** 26–27
M.A. Hanna Company, **8 345–47**; **12** 352
M.A.N., **III** 561–63; **IV** 86
M.B. McGerry, **21** 94
M-Cell Ltd., **31** 329
M.D.C., **11** 258
M.E.P.C. Ltd., **IV** 711
M.F. Patterson Dental Supply Co. *See* Patterson Dental Co.
M.G. Waldbaum Company, **25** 332–33
M. Guggenheim's Sons, **IV** 31
M.H. McLean Wholesaler Grocery Company, **8** 380
M. Hensoldt & Söhne Wetzlar Optische Werke AG, **III** 446
M-I Drilling Fluids Co., **III** 473; **15** 468
M.I. Schottenstein Homes Inc., **19** 125–26
M.J. Brock Corporation, **8** 460
M.J. Designs, Inc., **17** 360
M.L.C. Partners Limited Partnership, **22** 459
M. Loeb Ltd., **II** 652
M. Lowenstein Corp., **V** 379
M.M. Warburg. *See* SBC Warburg.
M.P. Burke PLC, **13** 485–86
M.P. Pumps, Inc., **8** 515
M. Polaner Inc., **10** 70
M-R Group plc, **31** 312–13
M. Samuel & Co., **II** 208
M. Sobol, Inc., **28** 12
M Stores Inc., **II** 664
M.T.G.I. Textile Manufacturers Group, **25** 121
M.W. Carr, **14** 245
M.W. Kellogg Co., **III** 470; **IV** 408, 534
M-Web Holdings Ltd., **31** 329–30
Ma. Ma-Macaroni Co., **II** 554
Maakauppiaitten Oy, **8** 293–94
Maakuntain Keskus-Pankki, **II** 303
MaasGlas, **III** 667
Maatschappij tot Exploitatie van de Onderneming Krasnapolsky. *See* Grand Hotel Krasnapolsky N.V.
Maatschappij tot Exploitatie van Steenfabrieken Udenhout, voorheen Weyers, **14** 249
MABAG Maschinen- und Apparatebau GmbH, **IV** 198
Mabley & Carew, **10** 282
Mac Frugal's Bargains - Closeouts Inc., **17 297–99**
Mac Publications LLC, **25** 240
Mac Tools, **III** 628
MacAndrews & Forbes Holdings Inc., **II** 679; **III** 56; **9** 129; **11** 334; **28 246–49**; **30** 138
Macau Telephone, **18** 114
Maccabees Life Insurance Co., **III** 350
MacCall Management, **19** 158
MacDonald Companies, **15** 87
MacDonald, Halsted, and Laybourne, **10** 127
Macdonald Hamilton & Co., **III** 522–23
Macey Furniture Co., **7** 493
Macfarlane Lang & Co., **II** 592–93
Macfield Inc., **12** 502
MacFrugal's Bargains Close-Outs Inc., **29** 312
MacGregor Sporting Goods Inc., **III** 443; **22** 115, 458; **23** 449
Mach Performance, Inc., **28** 147

Machine Vision International Inc., **10** 232
Macintosh. *See* Apple Computer, Inc.
Mack Trucks, Inc., I 147, **177–79; 9** 416; **12** 90; **22 329–32 (upd.)**
MacKay-Shields Financial Corp., **III** 316
MacKenzie & Co., **II** 361
Mackenzie Hill, **IV** 724
Mackenzie Mann & Co. Limited, **6** 360
Mackey Airways, **I** 102
Mackie Designs Inc., **30** 406
Mackinnon Mackenzie & Co., **III** 521–22
Maclaren Power and Paper Co., **IV** 165
Maclean Hunter Limited, III 65; **IV 638–40, 22** 442; **23** 98
Maclean Hunter Publishing Limited, 26 270–74 (upd.); 30 388
Maclin Co., **12** 127
MacMark Corp., **22** 459
MacMarr Stores, **II** 654
MacMillan Bloedel Limited, IV 165, 272, **306–09**, 721; **9** 391; **19** 444, 446; **25** 12; **26** 445
Macmillan, Inc., IV 637, 641–43; **7 284–86**, 311–12, 343; **9** 63; **12** 226; **13** 91, 93; **17** 399; **18** 329; **22** 441–42; **23** 350, 503; **25** 484; **27** 222–23
Macnaughton Blair, **III** 671
The MacNeal-Schwendler Corporation, 25 303–05
Macneill & Co., **III** 522
Macon Gas Company, **6** 447; **23** 28
Macon Kraft Co., **IV** 311; **11** 421; **19** 267
Maconochie Bros., **II** 569
Macrodata, **18** 87
Macwhyte Company, **27** 415
Macy's. *See* R.H. Macy & Co., Inc.
Macy's California, **21** 129
Mad Dog Athletics, **19** 385
Maddingley Brown Coal Pty Ltd., **IV** 249
Maddux Air Lines, **I** 125; **12** 487
Madge Networks N.V., 18 346; **26 275–77**
Madison & Sullivan, Inc., **10** 215
Madison Financial Corp., **16** 145
Madison Foods, **14** 557
Madison Furniture Industries, **14** 436
Madison Gas & Electric Company, **6** 605–06
Madison Resources, Inc., **13** 502
Madison Square Garden, **I** 452
MAEFORT Hungarian Air Transport Joint Stock Company, **24** 310
Maersk Lines, **22** 167
Maes Group Breweries, **II** 475
Maeva Group, **6** 206
Mafco Holdings, Inc., **28** 248
Magasins Armand Thiéry et Sigrand, **V** 11; **19** 308
Magazine and Book Services, **13** 48
Magazins Réal Stores, **II** 651
Magcobar, **III** 472
MagCorp, **28** 198
Magdeburg Insurance Group, **III** 377
Magdeburger Versicherungsgruppe, **III** 377
Magee Company, **31** 435–36
Magellan Corporation, **22** 403
Magic Chef Co., **III** 573; **8** 298; **22** 349
Magic City Food Products Company. *See* Golden Enterprises, Inc.
Magic Marker, **29** 372
Magic Pan, **II** 559–60; **12** 410
Magic Pantry Foods, **10** 382
Magicsilk, Inc., **22** 133
MagicSoft Inc., **10** 557
Magirus, **IV** 126
Maglificio di Ponzano Veneto dei Fratelli Benetton. *See* Benetton.
Magma Copper Company, 7 287–90, 385–87; **22** 107
Magma Power Company, 11 270–72
Magna Computer Corporation, **12** 149; **13** 97
Magnaflux, **III** 519; **22** 282
Magnavox Co., **13** 398; **19** 393
Magne Corp., **IV** 160
Magnesium Metal Co., **IV** 118
Magnet Cove Barium Corp., **III** 472
MagneTek, Inc., 15 287–89
Magnetic Controls Company, **10** 18
Magnetic Peripherals Inc., **19** 513–14
Magnivision, **22** 35
Magnolia Petroleum Co., **III** 497; **IV** 82, 464
Magnus Co., **I** 331; **13** 197
La Magona d'Italia, **IV** 228
Magor Railcar Co., **I** 170
MAGroup Inc., **11** 123
Mahalo Air, **22** 252; **24** 22
Maharam Fabric, **8** 455
Mahir, **I** 37
Mahou, **II** 474
Mai Nap Rt, **IV** 652; **7** 392
MAI PLC, **28** 504
MAI Systems Corporation, 10 242; **11 273–76; 26** 497, 499
Maidenform Worldwide Inc., 20 352–55
Mail Boxes Etc., 18 315–17; 25 500. *See also* U.S. Office Products Company.
Mail-Well, Inc., 25 184; **28 250–52**
Mailson Ferreira da Nobrega, **II** 200
Mailtek, Inc., **18** 518
MAIN. *See* Mid-American Interpool Network.
Main Event Management Corp., **III** 194
Main Plaza Corporation, **25** 115
Main Street Advertising USA, **IV** 597
Maine Central Railroad Company, 16 348–50
Mainline Industrial Distributors, Inc., **13** 79
Mainline Travel, **I** 114
Maison Bouygues, **I** 563
Maison de Schreiber and Aronson, **25** 283
Maison de Valérie, **19** 309
Maison Louis Jadot, 24 307–09
Maizuru Heavy Industries, **III** 514
Majestic Contractors Ltd., **8** 419–20
Majestic Wine Warehouses Ltd., **II** 656
Major League Baseball, **12** 457
Major Video Concepts, **6** 410
Major Video, Inc., **9** 74
MaK Maschinenbau GmbH, **IV** 88
Mak van Waay, **11** 453
Makepeace Preserving Co., **25** 365
Makhteshim Chemical Works Ltd., **II** 47; **25** 266–67
Makita Corporation, III 436; **20** 66; **22 333–35**
Makiyama, **I** 363
Makovsky & Company, **12** 394
Makro Inc., **18** 286
Malama Pacific Corporation, **9** 276
Malapai Resources, **6** 546
Malayan Breweries, **I** 256
Malayan Motor and General Underwriters, **III** 201
Malaysia LNG, **IV** 518–19
Malaysian Airlines System Berhad, 6 71, **100–02**, 117, 415; **29 300–03 (upd.)**
Malaysian International Shipping Co., **IV** 518
Malaysian Sheet Glass, **III** 715
Malbak Ltd., **IV** 92–93
Malcolm's Diary & Time-Table, **III** 256
Malcus Industri, **III** 624
Malden Mills Industries, Inc., 16 351–53
Malév Plc, 24 310–12; 27 474; **29** 17
Malheur Cooperative Electric Association, **12** 265
Malibu, **25** 141
Mallard Bay Drilling, Inc., **28** 347–48
Malleable Iron Works, **II** 34
Mallinckrodt Group Inc., III 16; **IV** 146; **8** 85; **19** 28, **251–53**
Malmö Flygindustri, **I** 198
Malmö Woodworking Factory. *See* Tarkett Sommer AG.
Malmsten & Bergvalls, **I** 664
Malone & Hyde, Inc., **II** 625, 670–71; **9** 52–53; **14** 147; **18** 506
Malrite Communications Group, **IV** 596
Malt-A-Milk Co., **II** 487
Malt-O-Meal Company, 15 189; **22 336–38**
Mameco International, **8** 455
Mammoet Transport B.V., 26 241, **278–80**
Man Aktiengesellschaft, III 301, **561–63**
MAN Gutehoffnungshütte AG, **15** 226
Management and Training Corporation, 28 253–56
Management Decision Systems, Inc., **10** 358
Management Engineering and Development Co., **IV** 310; **19** 266
Management Recruiters International, **6** 140
Management Science America, Inc., **11** 77; **25** 20
Manbré and Garton, **II** 582
Manchester and Liverpool District Banking Co., **II** 307, 333
Manchester Board and Paper Co., **19** 77
Manchester Commercial Buildings Co., **IV** 711
Manchester United Football Club plc, 30 296–98
Manco, Inc., **13** 166. *See also* Henkel Manco Inc.
Mancuso & Co., **22** 116
Mandabach & Simms, **6** 40
Mandarin Oriental Hotel Group International Ltd., **I** 471; **IV** 700; **20** 312
Mandel Bros., **IV** 660
Manetta Mills, Inc., **19** 304
Manhattan Card Co., **18** 114
Manhattan Co., **II** 217, 247
Manhattan Construction Company. *See* Rooney Brothers Co.
Manhattan Electrical Supply Co., **9** 517
Manhattan Fund, **I** 614
Manhattan International Limousine Network Ltd., **26** 62
Manhattan Trust Co., **II** 229
Manheim Auctions, Inc. *See* Cox Enterprises, Inc.
Manifatture Cotoniere Meridionali, **I** 466
Manischewitz Company. *See* B. Manischewitz Company.
Manistique Papers Inc., **17** 282
Manistique Pulp and Paper Co., **IV** 311; **19** 266

Manitoba Bridge and Engineering Works Ltd., **8** 544
Manitoba Paper Co., **IV** 245–46; **25** 10
Manitoba Rolling Mill Ltd., **8** 544
Manitou BF S.A., 27 294–96
Manitowoc Company, Inc., 18 318–21
Mann Egerton & Co., **III** 523
Mann Theatres Chain, **I** 245; **25** 177
Mann's Wine Company, Ltd., **14** 288
Manne Tossbergs Eftr., **II** 639
Mannesmann AG, I 411; **III 564–67**; **IV** 222, 469; **14 326–29 (upd.)**
Mannheimer Bank, **IV** 558
Manning, Selvage & Lee, **6** 22
Mannstaedt, **IV** 128
Manor Care, Inc., 6 187–90; **14** 105–07; **15** 522; **25 306–10 (upd.)**
Manor Healthcare Corporation, **26** 459
Manorfield Investments, **II** 158
Manos Enterprises, **14** 87
Manpower, Inc., 6 10, 140; **9 326–27**; **16** 48; **25** 432; **30 299–302 (upd.)**
Mantrec S.A., **27** 296
Mantua Metal Products. *See* Tyco Toys, Inc.
Manufactured Home Communities, Inc., 22 339–41
Manufacturers & Merchants Indemnity Co., **III** 191
Manufacturers and Traders Trust Company, **11** 108–09
Manufacturers Casualty Insurance Co., **26** 486
Manufacturers Fire Insurance Co., **26** 486
Manufacturers Hanover Corporation, II 230, 254, **312–14**, 403; **III** 194; **9** 124; **11** 16, 54, 415; **13** 536; **14** 103; **16** 207; **17** 559; **22** 406; **26** 453
Manufacturers National Bank of Brooklyn, **II** 312
Manufacturers National Bank of Detroit, **I** 165; **11** 137
Manufacturers Railway, **I** 219
Manufacturing Management Inc., **19** 381
Manus Nu-Pulse, **III** 420
Manville Corporation, III 706–09, 721; **7 291–95 (upd.)**; **10** 43, 45; **11** 420–22
Manweb plc, **19** 389–90
MAPCO Inc., IV 458–59; **26** 234; **31** 469, 471
Mapelli Brothers Food Distribution Co., **13** 350
Maple Leaf Mills, **II** 513–14
MAPP. *See* Mid-Continent Area Power Planner.
Mar-O-Bar Company, **7** 299
A.B. Marabou, **II** 511
Marantha! Music, **14** 499
Marantz Co., **14** 118
Marathon Insurance Co., **26** 486
Marathon Oil Co., **IV** 365, 454, 487, 572, 574; **7** 549, 551; **13** 458
Marathon Paper Products, **I** 612, 614
Marauder Company, **26** 433
Maraven, **IV** 508
Marblehead Communications, Inc., **23** 101
Marbodal, **12** 464
Marboro Books, Inc., **10** 136
Marbro Lamp Co., **III** 571; **20** 362
Marc's Big Boy. *See* The Marcus Corporation.
Marcade Group. *See* Aris Industries, Inc.
Marceau Investments, **II** 356
March of Dimes, 31 322–25
March-Davis Bicycle Company, **19** 383
Marchand, **13** 27
Marchland Holdings Ltd., **II** 649
Marchon Eyewear, **22** 123
Marciano Investments, Inc., **24** 157
Marcillat, **19** 49
Marcon Coating, Inc., **22** 347
Marconi Wireless Telegraph Co. of America, **II** 25, 88
Marconiphone, **I** 531
The Marcus Corporation, 21 359–63
Marcus Samuel & Co., **IV** 530
Marcy Fitness Products, Inc., **19** 142, 144
Mardon Packaging International, **I** 426–27
Mardorf, Peach and Co., **II** 466
Maremont Corporation, **8** 39–40
Margarete Steiff GmbH, 23 334–37
Margarine Unie N.V. *See* Unilever PLC (Unilever N.V.).
Marge Carson, Inc., **III** 571; **20** 362
Margo's La Mode, **10** 281–82
Marico Acquisition Corporation, **8** 448, 450
Marie Brizard & Roger International S.A., 22 342–44
Marie Callender's Restaurant & Bakery, Inc., 13 66; **28 257–59**
Marie-Claire Album, **III** 47
Marigold Foods Inc., **II** 528
Marinduque Mining & Industrial Corp., **IV** 146
Marine Bank and Trust Co., **11** 105
Marine Bank of Erie, **II** 342
Marine Computer Systems, **6** 242
Marine Diamond Corp., **IV** 66; **7** 123
Marine Group, **III** 444; **22** 116
Marine Harvest International, **13** 103
Marine Midland Corp., **I** 548; **II** 298; **9** 475–76; **11** 108; **17** 325
Marine Office of America, **III** 220, 241–42
Marine-Firminy, **IV** 227
Marinela, **19** 192–93
Marineland Amusements Corp., **IV** 623
MarineMax, Inc., 30 303–05
Marion Brick, **14** 249
Marion Foods, Inc., **17** 434
Marion Freight Lines, **6** 370
Marion Laboratories Inc., I 648–49; **8** 149; **9** 328–29; **16** 438
Marion Manufacturing, **9** 72
Marion Merrell Dow, Inc., 9 328–29 (upd.)
Marionet Corp., **IV** 680–81
Marisa Christina, Inc., 15 290–92; **25** 245
Maritime Electric Company, Limited, **15** 182
Mark Controls Corporation, **30** 157
Mark Cross, Inc., **17** 4–5
Mark Goldston, **8** 305
Mark Hopkins, **12** 316
Mark IV Industries, Inc., 7 296–98; **21** 418; **28 260–64 (upd.)**
Mark Travel Corporation, **30** 448
Mark Trouser, Inc., **17** 338
Markborough Properties, **II** 222; **V** 81; **8** 525; **25** 221
Market Growth Resources, **23** 480
Market Horizons, **6** 27
Market National Bank, **13** 465
Marketime, **V** 55
Marketing Data Systems, Inc., **18** 24
Marketing Equities International, **26** 136
Marketing Information Services, **6** 24
MarketSpan Corp. *See* KeySpan Energy Co.
Markham & Co., **I** 573–74
Marks and Spencer p.l.c., I 588; **II** 513, 678; **V 124–26**; **10** 442; **17** 42, 124; **22** 109, 111; **24** 268, 270; **313–17 (upd.)**, 474; **28** 96
Marks Brothers Jewelers, Inc., 24 318–20
Marks-Baer Inc., **11** 64
Marland Refining Co., **IV** 399–400
Marlene Industries Corp., **16** 36–37
MarLennan Corp., **III** 283
Marley Co., **19** 360
Marley Holdings, L.P., **19** 246
Marley Tile, **III** 735
Marlin-Rockwell Corp., **I** 539; **14** 510
Marlow Foods, **II** 565
Marman Products Company, **16** 8
The Marmon Group, III 97; **IV 135–38**; **16 354–57 (upd.)**
Marmon-Perry Light Company, **6** 508
Marolf Dakota Farms, Inc., **18** 14–15
Marotte, **21** 438
Marquam Commercial Brokerage Company, **21** 257
Marquardt Aircraft, **I** 380; **13** 379
Marquette Electronics, Inc., 13 326–28
Marquette Paper Corporation, **III** 766; **22** 545
Marquis Who's Who, **17** 398
Marriage Mailers, **6** 12
Marriner Group, **13** 175
Marriot Inc., **29** 442
Marriot Management Services, **29** 444
Marriott Corporation, II 173, 608; **III** 92, 94, 99–100, **102–03**, 248; **7** 474–75; **9** 95, 426; **15** 87; **17** 238; **18** 216; **19** 433–34; **21** 91, 364; **22** 131; **23** 436–38; **27** 334
Marriott International, Inc., 21 182, **364–67 (upd.)**; **29** 403, 406
Mars, Inc., II 510–11; **III** 114; **7 299–301**; **22** 298, 528
Marschke Manufacturing Co., **III** 435
Marsene Corp., **III** 440
Marsh & McLennan Companies, Inc., III 280, **282–84**; **10** 39; **14** 279; **22** 318
Marsh Supermarkets, Inc., 17 300–02
Marshalk Company, **I** 16; **22** 294
Marshall Die Casting, **13** 225
Marshall Field & Co., **I** 13, 426; **III** 329; **IV** 660; **V** 43–44; **8** 33; **9** 213; **12** 283; **15** 86; **18** 136–37, 488; **22** 72
Marshall Industries, **19** 311
Marshalls Incorporated, 13 329–31; **14** 62
Marsin Medical Supply Co., **III** 9
Marstellar, **13** 204
The Mart, **9** 120
Marten Transport, **27** 404
Martha, **IV** 486
Martha Lane Adams, **27** 428
Martha Stewart Living Omnimedia, L.L.C., 24 321–23
Martin & Pagenstecher GMBH, **24** 208
Martin Bros. Tobacco Co., **14** 19
Martin Collet, **19** 50
Martin Dennis Co., **IV** 409
Martin Electric Co., **III** 98
Martin Marietta Corporation, I 47, **67–69**, 71, 102, 112, 142–43, 184, 416; **II** 32, 67; **III** 671; **IV** 60, 163; **7** 356, 520; **8** 315; **9** 310; **10** 162, 199, 484; **11**

166, 277–78, 364; **12** 127, 290; **13** 327, 356; **15** 283; **17** 564; **18** 369; **19** 70; **22** 400; **28** 288. *See also* Lockheed Martin Corporation.
Martin Mathys, **8** 456
Martin Rooks & Co., **I** 95
Martin Sorrell, **6** 54
Martin Theaters, **14** 86
Martin Zippel Co., **16** 389
Martin's, **12** 221
Martin-Brower Corp., **II** 500; **III** 21; **17** 475
Martin-Senour Co., **III** 744
Martin-Yale Industries, Inc., **19** 142–44
Martindale-Hubbell, **17** 398
Martineau and Bland, **I** 293
Martini & Rossi, **18** 41
Martins Bank, **II** 236, 308
Martinus Nijhoff, **14** 555; **25** 85
Marubeni Corporation, 24 324–27 (upd.)
Marubeni K.K., I 432, **492–95**, 510; **II** 292, 391; **III** 760; **IV** 266, 525; **12** 147; **17** 556
Maruei & Co., **IV** 151; **24** 358
Maruetsu, **17** 124
Marufuku Co., Ltd., **III** 586; **7** 394
Marui Co. Ltd., V 127
Marukuni Kogyo Co., Ltd., **IV** 327
Marutaka Kinitsu Store Ltd., **V** 194
Maruzen Co., Limited, II 348; **IV** 403–04, 476, 554; **18 322–24**
Marvel Entertainment Group, Inc., 10 400–02; **18** 426, 520–21; **21** 404; **25** 141
Marvel Metal Products, **III** 570; **20** 361
Marvel-Schebler Carburetor Corp., **III** 438; **14** 63–64
Marvin & Leonard Advertising, **13** 511–12
Marvin H. Sugarman Productions Inc., **20** 48
Marvin Lumber & Cedar Company, 10 95; **22 345–47**
Marwick, Mitchell & Company, **10** 385
Marwitz & Hauser, **III** 446
Marx, **12** 494
Mary Ann Co. Ltd., **V** 89
Mary Ann Restivo, Inc., **8** 323
Mary Ellen's, Inc., **11** 211
Mary Kathleen Uranium, **IV** 59–60
Mary Kay Corporation, III 16; **9 330–32**; **12** 435; **15** 475, 477; **18** 67, 164; **21** 49, 51; **30 306–09 (upd.)**
Maryland Casualty Co., **III** 193, 412
Maryland Cup Company, **8** 197
Maryland Distillers, **I** 285
Maryland Medical Laboratory Inc., **26** 391
Maryland National Corp., **11** 287
Maryland National Mortgage Corporation, **11** 121
Maryland Shipbuilding and Drydock Co., **I** 170
Maryland Steel Co., **IV** 35; **7** 48
Marzotto S.p.A., 20 356–58
Masayoshi Son, **13** 481–82
Mascan Corp., **IV** 697
Maschinenbauanstalt Humboldt AG, **III** 541
Maschinenfabrik Augsburg-Nürnberg. *See* M.A.N.
Maschinenfabrik Deutschland, **IV** 103
Maschinenfabrik für den Bergbau von Sievers & Co., **III** 541
Maschinenfabrik Gebr. Meer, **III** 565
Maschinenfabrik Sürth, **I** 581
Masco Corporation, III 568–71; **11** 385, 534–35; **12** 129, 131, 344; **13** 338; **18** 68; **20 359–63 (upd.)**
Masco Optical, **13** 165
Mascon Toy Co., **III** 569; **20** 360
MASCOR, **14** 13
Mase Westpac Limited, **11** 418
Maserati. *See* Officine Alfieri Maserati S.p.A.
Masinfabriks A.B. Scania, **I** 197
MASkargo Ltd., **6** 101
Masland Corporation, 17 303–05; **19** 408
Mason & Hamlin, **III** 656
Mason Best Co., **IV** 343
Masonite Corp., **III** 764
Masonite Holdings, **III** 687
Mass Rapid Transit Corp., **19** 111
Massachusetts Bank, **II** 207
Massachusetts Capital Resources Corp., **III** 314
Massachusetts Mutual Life Insurance Company, III 110, **285–87**, 305; **14** 14; **25** 528
Massachusetts Technology Development Corporation, **18** 570
Massey Burch Investment Group, **23** 153
Massey-Ferguson, **II** 222, 245; **III** 439, 650–52; **13** 18. *See also* Varity Corporation.
Mast Holdings, **25** 120
Mast Industries, **V** 115–16
MasTec, Inc., 19 254–57
Master Boot Polish Co., **II** 566
Master Builders, **I** 673
Master Electric Company, **15** 134
Master Glass & Color, **24** 159–60
Master Pneumatic Tool Co., **III** 436
Master Processing, **19** 37
Master Products, **14** 162
Master Shield Inc., **7** 116
Master Tank and Welding Company, **7** 541
MasterBrand Industries Inc., **12** 344–45
MasterCard International, Inc., 9 333–35; **18** 337, 543; **25** 41; **26** 515
Mastercraft Homes, Inc., **11** 257
Mastercraft Industries Corp., **III** 654
Mastex Industries, **29** 132
Maszovlet. *See* Malév Plc.
Matador Records, **22** 194
Matairco, **9** 27
Matane Pulp & Paper Company, **17** 281
Matchbox Toys Ltd., **12** 168
Matco Tools, **7** 116
Material Management and Services Inc., **28** 61
Materials Services Corp., **I** 58
Mathematica, Inc., **22** 291
Mather & Crother Advertising Agency, **I** 25
Mather Co., **I** 159
Mather Metals, **III** 582
Matheson & Co., **IV** 189
Mathews Conveyor Co., **14** 43
Mathieson Chemical Corp., **I** 379–80, 695; **13** 379
Matra, **II** 38, 70; **IV** 617–19; **13** 356; **17** 354; **24** 88
Matra Aerospace Inc., **22** 402
Matra-Hachette S.A., 15 293–97 (upd.); **21** 267
Matria Healthcare, Inc., 17 306–09
Matrix Science Corp., **II** 8; **14** 27
Matson Navigation Company, Inc., **II** 490–91; **10** 40
Matsumoto Medical Instruments, Inc., **11** 476; **29** 455
Matsushita Electric Industrial Co., Ltd., II 5, **55–56**, 58, 61, 91–92, 102, 117–19, 361, 455; **III** 476, 710; **6** 36; **7** 163, 302; **10** 286, 389, 403, 432; **11** 487; **12** 448; **13** 398; **18** 18; **20** 81; **26** 511
Matsushita Electric Works, Ltd., III 710–11; **7 302–03 (upd.)**; **12** 454; **16** 167; **27** 342
Matsushita Kotobuki Electronics Industries, Ltd., **10** 458–59
Matsuura Trading Co., Ltd., **IV** 327
Matsuzakaya Company, V 129–31
Mattatuck Bank & Trust Co., **13** 467
Mattel, Inc., II 136; **III** 506; **7 304–07**; **12** 74, 168–69, 495; **13** 560–61; **15** 238; **16** 264, 428; **17** 243; **18** 520–21; **25 311–15 (upd.)**, 381, 488; **27** 20, 373, 375; **28** 159; **29** 74, 78
Matthes & Weber, **III** 32
Matthew Bender & Company, Inc., **IV** 677; **7** 94; **14** 97; **17** 486
Matthews International Corporation, 29 304–06
Matthews Paint Co., **22** 437
Maud Foster Mill, **II** 566
Maui Electric Company, **9** 276
Maui Land & Pineapple Company, Inc., 29 307–09
Mauna Kea Properties, **6** 129
Maurice H. Needham Co., **I** 31
Maus Frères, **19** 307
Maus-Nordmann, **V** 10; **19** 308
Max & Erma's Restaurants Inc., 19 258–60
Max Factor & Co., **III** 54, 56; **6** 51; **12** 314
Max Klein, Inc., **II** 572
Max Media Properties LLC, **25** 419
Max Television Co., **25** 418
Max-Grundig-Stiftung, **27** 190–91
Maxcell Telecom Plus, **6** 323
Maxco Inc., 17 310–11; **24** 159, 160
Maxell Corp., **I** 500; **14** 534
Maxi Vac, Inc., **9** 72
MAXI-Papier, **10** 498
Maxi-Papier-Markt, **24** 270
Maxicare Health Plans, Inc., III 84–86; **25 316–19 (upd.)**
Maxie's of America, **25** 389
The Maxim Group, 25 88, **320–22**
Maxim Integrated Products, Inc., 16 358–60
Maxis Software, **13** 115
Maxoptix Corporation, **10** 404
Maxpro Sports Inc., **22** 458
Maxpro Systems, **24** 509–10
Maxtor Corporation, 6 230; **10 403–05**, 459, 463–64
Maxus Energy Corporation, IV 410; **7 308–10**; **10** 191; **31** 456
Maxwell Communication Corporation plc, IV 605, 611, **641–43**; **7** 286, **311–13 (upd.)**, 343; **10** 288; **13** 91–93; **23** 350
Maxwell Morton Corp, **I** 144, 414
Maxwell Shoe Company, Inc., 30 310–12
MAXXAM Inc., IV 121, 123; **8 348–50**
Maxxim Medical Inc., 12 325–27
May and Baker, **I** 388
The May Department Stores Company, I 540; **II** 414; **V 132–35**; **8** 288; **11** 349;

12 55, 507–08; **13** 42, 361; **15** 275; **16** 62, 160, 206–07; **18** 414–15; **19 261–64 (upd.)**; **23** 345; **27** 61, 291, 346, 348
Maybelline, **I** 684
Mayer & Schweitzer, **26** 66
Mayfair Foods, **I** 438; **16** 314
Mayfield Dairy Farms, Inc., **7** 128
Mayflower Group Inc., 6 409–11; **15** 50
Mayne Nickless Ltd., **IV** 248
Mayo Foundation, 9 336–39; **13** 326
Maytag Corporation, III 572–73; **12** 252, 300; **21** 141; **22** 218, **348–51 (upd.)**; **23** 244
Mayville Metal Products Co., **I** 513
Mazda Motor Corporation, I 520; **II** 4, 361; **III** 603; **9 340–42**; **11** 86; **13** 414; **16** 322; **23 338–41 (upd.)**
Mazel Stores, Inc., 29 310–12
MB Group, **20** 108
MBB. *See* Messerschmitt-Bölkow-Blohm.
MBC. *See* Middle East Broadcasting Centre, Ltd.
MBNA Corporation, 11 123; **12 328–30**
MBPXL Corp., **II** 494
MCA Inc., II 143–45; **6** 162–63; **10** 286; **11** 557; **17** 317; **21** 23, 25–26; **22** 131, 194; **23** 125; **25** 411; **26** 151, 314
McAfee Associates. *See* Network Associates, Inc.
The McAlpin Company, **19** 272
McAndrew & Forbes Holdings Inc., **23** 407; **26** 119
McArthur Glen Realty, **10** 122
McCaffrey & McCall, **I** 33; **11** 496
McCain Feeds Ltd., **II** 484
McCall Pattern Company, **22** 512; **23** 99
McCall Printing Co., **14** 460
McCall's Corp., **23** 393
McCann-Erickson worldwide, **I** 10, 14, 16–17, 234; **6** 30; **10** 227; **14** 315; **16** 167; **18** 68; **22** 294
McCarthy Milling, **II** 631; **27** 245–47
McCaughan Dyson and Co., **II** 189
McCaw Cellular Communications, Inc., II 331; **6** 274, **322–24**; **7** 15; **9** 320–21; **10** 433; **15** 125, 196; **27** 341, 343–44; **29** 44, 61
McClanahan Oil Co., **I** 341; **14** 216
McClatchy Newspapers, Inc., 23 156, 158, **342–44**
McCleary, Wallin and Crouse, **19** 274
McClintic-Marshall, **IV** 36; **7** 49
The McCloskey Corporation, **8** 553
The McClure Syndicate, **25** 138
McColl-Frontenac Petroleum Inc., **IV** 439; **25** 232
McComb Manufacturing Co., **8** 287
McCormack & Dodge, **IV** 605; **11** 77
McCormick & Company, Incorporated, 7 314–16; **17** 104, 106; **21** 497; **27 297–300 (upd.)**
McCormick & Schmick's, **31** 41
McCormick Harvesting Machine Co., **I** 180; **II** 330
McCown De Leeuw & Co., **16** 510
McCracken Brooks, **23** 479; **25** 91
McCrory Stores, **II** 424; **9** 447–48; **13** 340
McCulloch Corp., **III** 436; **8** 348–49
McCullough Environmental Services, **12** 443
McDermott International, Inc., III 558–60
McDonald Glass Grocery Co. Inc., **II** 669
McDonald's Company (Japan) Ltd., **V** 205
McDonald's Corporation, I 23, 31, 129; **II** 500, 613–15 **646–48**; **III** 63, 94, 103; **6** 13; **7** 128, 266–67, 316, **317–19 (upd.)**, 435, 505–06; **8** 261–62, 564; **9** 74, 178, 290, 292, 305; **10** 122; **11** 82, 308; **12** 43, 180, 553; **13** 494; **14** 25, 32, 106, 195, 452–53; **16** 95–97, 289; **17** 69–71; **19** 85, 192, 214; **21** 25, 315, 362; **23** 505; **25** 179, 309, 387; **26 281–85 (upd.)**; **31** 278
McDonnell Douglas Corporation, I 41–43, 45, 48, 50–52, 54–56, 58–59, 61–62, 67–68, **70–72**, 76–77, 82, 84–85, 90, 105, 108, 111, 121–22, 321, 364, 490, 511; **II** 442; **III** 512, 654; **6** 68; **7** 456, 504; **8** 49–51, 315; **9** 18, 183, 206, 231, 271–72, 418, 458, 460; **10** 163–64, 317, 536; **11** 164–65, 267, **277–80 (upd.)**, 285, 363–65; **12** 190–91, 549; **13** 356; **15** 283; **16** 78, 94; **18** 368; **24** 84–85, 87; **28** 225
McDonough Co., **II** 16; **III** 502
McDougal, Littell & Company, **10** 357
McDowell Energy Center, **6** 543
McDowell Furniture Company, **10** 183
McDuff, **10** 305
McElligott Wright Morrison and White, **12** 511
McFadden Holdings L.P., **27** 41
McFadden Industries, **III** 21
McFadden Publishing, **6** 13
McGaughy, Marshall & McMillan, **6** 142
McGaw Inc., **11** 208
McGill Manufacturing, **III** 625
McGraw Electric Company. *See* Centel Corporation.
McGraw-Edison Co., **II** 17, 87
The McGraw-Hill Companies, Inc., II 398; **IV** 584, **634–37**, 643, 656, 674; **10** 62; **12** 359; **13** 417; **18 325–30 (upd.)**; **26** 79; **27** 360
McGregor Corporation, **6** 415; **26** 102
McGrew Color Graphics, **7** 430
MCI. *See* Manitou Costruzioni Industriali SRL. *or* Melamine Chemicals, Inc.
MCI Communications Corporation, II 408; **III** 13, 149, 684; **V 302–04**; **6** 51–52, 300, 322; **7** 118–19; **8** 310; **9** 171, 478–80; **10** 19, 80, 89, 97, 433, 500; **11** 59, 183, 185, 302, 409, 500; **12** 135–37; **13** 38; **14** 252–53, 260, 364; **15** 222; **16** 318; **18** 32, 112, 164–66, 569–70; **19** 255; **25** 358; **26** 102, 441; **27** 430; **29** 42
MCI WorldCom, Inc., 27 301–08 (upd.)
McIlhenny Company, 20 364–67
McIlwraith McEachern Limited, **27** 474
McJunkin Corp., **13** 79; **28** 61
McKee Foods Corporation, 7 320–21; **27 309–11 (upd.)**
McKenna Metals Company, **13** 295–96
McKesson Corporation, I 413, **496–98**, 713; **II** 652; **III** 10; **6** 279; **8** 464; **9** 532; **11** 91; **12 331–33 (upd.)**; **16** 43; **18** 97
McKesson General Medical, **29** 299
McKinsey & Company, Inc., I 108, 144, 437, 497; **III** 47, 85, 670; **9 343–45**; **10** 175; **13** 138; **18** 68; **25** 34, 317; **26** 161
McLain Grocery, **II** 625
McLane America, Inc., **29** 481
McLane Company, Inc., V 217; **8** 556; **13 332–34**
McLaren Consolidated Cone Corp., **II** 543; **7** 366
McLaughlin Motor Company of Canada, **I** 171; **10** 325
McLean Clinic, **11** 379
McLouth Steel Products, **13** 158
MCM Electronics, **9** 420
McMahan's Furniture Co., **14** 236
McMan Oil and Gas Co., **IV** 369
McManus, John & Adams, Inc., **6** 21
McMoCo, **IV** 82–83; **7** 187
McMoRan, **IV** 81–83; **V** 739; **7** 185, 187
McMullen & Yee Publishing, **22** 442
McMurtry Manufacturing, **8** 553
MCN Corporation, 6 519–22; **13** 416; **17** 21–23
McNeil Corporation, **26** 363
McNeil Laboratories, **III** 35–36; **8** 282–83
McNellan Resources Inc., **IV** 76
MCO Holdings Inc., **8** 348–49
MCorp, **10** 134; **11** 122
McPaper AG, **29** 152
McQuay International. *See* AAF-McQuay Incorporated.
McRae's, Inc., **19** 324–25
MCS, Inc., **10** 412
MCT Dairies, Inc., **18** 14–16
McTeigue & Co., **14** 502
McVitie & Price, **II** 592–93
McWhorter Inc., **8** 553; **27** 280
MD Distribution Inc., **15** 139
MD Pharmaceuticals, **III** 10
MDC. *See* Mead Data Central, Inc.
MDI Co., Ltd., **IV** 327
MDS/Bankmark, **10** 247
MDU Resources Group, Inc., 7 322–25
The Mead Corporation, IV 310–13, 327, 329, 342–43; **8** 267; **9** 261; **10** 406; **11** 421–22; **17** 399; **19 265–69 (upd.)**; **20** 18
Mead Cycle Co., **IV** 660
Mead Data Central, Inc., IV 312; **7** 581; **10 406–08**; **19** 268
Mead John & Co., **19** 103
Mead Johnson, **III** 17
Mead Packaging, **12** 151
Meade County Rural Electric Cooperative Corporation, **11** 37
Meadow Gold Dairies, Inc., **II** 473
Meadowcraft, Inc., 29 313–15
Means Services, Inc., **II** 607
Mears & Phillips, **II** 237
Measurex Corporation, **8** 243; **14** 56
Mebetoys, **25** 312
MEC - Hawaii, UK & USA, **IV** 714
MECA Software, Inc., **18** 363
Mecair, S.p.A., **17** 147
Mecca Leisure PLC, **I** 248; **12** 229
Mechanics Exchange Savings Bank, **9** 173
Mechanics Machine Co., **III** 438; **14** 63
Mecklermedia Corporation, 24 328–30; **26** 441; **27** 360, 362
Medal Distributing Co., **9** 542
Medallion Pictures Corp., **9** 320
Medar, Inc., **17** 310–11
Medco Containment Services Inc., 9 346–48; **11** 291; **12** 333
Medcom Inc., **I** 628
Medeco Security Locks, Inc., **10** 350
Medfield Corp., **III** 87
Medford, Inc., **19** 467–68
Medi Mart Drug Store Company. *See* The Stop & Shop Companies, Inc.
Media Exchange International, **25** 509
Media General, Inc., III 214; **7 326–28**; **18** 61; **23** 225

Media Groep West B.V., **23** 271
Media News Corporation, **25** 507
Media Play, **9** 360–61
Mediacom Inc., **25** 373
Mediamark Research, **28** 501, 504
Mediamatics, Inc., **26** 329
MediaOne Group Inc. *See* U S West, Inc.
MEDIC Computer Systems, **16** 94
Medical Care America, Inc., **15** 112, 114
Medical Development Corp. *See* Cordis Corp.
Medical Development Services, Inc., **25** 307
Medical Economics Data, **23** 211
Medical Expense Fund, **III** 245
Medical Indemnity of America, **10** 160
Medical Innovations Corporation, **21** 46
Medical Marketing Group Inc., **9** 348
Medical Service Assoc. of Pennsylvania, **III** 325–26
Medical Tribune Group, **IV** 591; **20** 53
Medicare-Glaser, **17** 167
Medicine Bow Coal Company, **7** 33–34
Medicine Shoppe International. *See* Cardinal Health, Inc.
Medicus Intercon International, **6** 22
Medifinancial Solutions, Inc., **18** 370
Mediobanca Banca di Credito Finanziario SpA, **II** 191, 271; **III** 208–09; **11** 205
The Mediplex Group, Inc., **III** 16; **11** 282
Medis Health and Pharmaceuticals Services Inc., **II** 653
Medite Corporation, **19** 467–68
Meditrust, 11 281–83
Medlabs Inc., **III** 73
Medtech, Ltd., **13** 60–62
Medtronic, Inc., 8 351–54; **11** 459; **18** 421; **19** 103; **22** 359–61; **26** 132; **30 313–17 (upd.)**
Medusa Corporation, 8 135; **24 331–33**; **30** 156
Mees & Hope, **II** 184
MEGA Natural Gas Company, **11** 28
Megafoods Stores Inc., 13 335–37; **17** 560
Megasource, Inc., **16** 94
MEI Diversified Inc., **18** 455
Mei Foo Investments Ltd., **IV** 718
Meier & Frank Co., 23 345–47
Meijer Incorporated, 7 329–31; **15** 449; **17** 302; **27 312–15 (upd.)**
Meiji Commerce Bank, **II** 291
Meiji Fire Insurance Co., **III** 384–85
Meiji Milk Products Company, Limited, II 538–39
Meiji Mutual Life Insurance Company, II 323; **III 288–89**
Meiji Seika Kaisha, Ltd., I 676; **II 540–41**
Meikosha Co., **II** 72
Meinecke Muffler Company, **III** 495; **10** 415
Meis of Illiana, **10** 282
Meisei Electric, **III** 742
Meisel. *See* Samuel Meisel & Co.
Meisenzahl Auto Parts, Inc., **24** 205
Meissner, Ackermann & Co., **IV** 463; **7** 351
Meister, Lucious and Company, **13** 262
Meiwa Manufacturing Co., **III** 758
N.V. Mekog, **IV** 531
Mel Farr Automotive Group, 20 368–70
Mel Klein and Partners, **III** 74
Melaleuca Inc., 31 326–28
Melamine Chemicals, Inc., 27 316–18
Melbourne Engineering Co., **23** 83
Melbur China Clay Co., **III** 690
Melco, **II** 58
Meldisco. *See* Footstar, Incorporated.
Melkunie-Holland, **II** 575
Mellbank Security Co., **II** 316
Mello Smello. *See* The Miner Group International.
Mellon Bank Corporation, I 67–68, 584; **II 315–17**, 342, 402; **III** 275; **9** 470; **13** 410–11; **18** 112
Mellon Indemnity Corp., **III** 258–59; **24** 177
Mellon-Stuart Co., I 584–85; **14** 334
Melmarkets, **24** 462
Mélotte, **III** 418
Meloy Laboratories, Inc., **11** 333
Melroe Company, **8** 115–16
Melville Corporation, V 136–38; **9** 192; **13** 82, 329–30; **14** 426; **15** 252–53;, **16** 390; **19** 449; **21** 526; **23** 176; **24** 167, 290
Melvin Simon and Associates, Inc., 8 355–57; **26** 262
Melwire Group, **III** 673
Memco, **12** 48
Memorex Corp., **III** 110, 166; **6** 282–83
The Men's Wearhouse, Inc., 17 312–15; **21** 311
Menasco Manufacturing Co., **I** 435; **III** 415
Menasha Corporation, 8 358–61
Menck, **8** 544
Mendelssohn & Co., **II** 241
Meneven, **IV** 508
Menka Gesellschaft, **IV** 150; **24** 357
The Mennen Company, **I** 19; **6** 26; **14** 122; **18** 69
Mental Health Programs Inc., **15** 122
Mentholatum Co., **IV** 722
Mentor Corporation, 26 286–88
Mentor Graphics Corporation, III 143; **8** 519; **11** 46–47, **284–86**, 490; **13** 128
MEPC plc, IV 710–12
Mepco/Electra Inc., **13** 398
MeraBank, **6** 546
Mercantile Agency, **IV** 604
Mercantile and General Reinsurance Co., **III** 335, 377
Mercantile Bank, **II** 298
Mercantile Bankshares Corp., 11 287–88
Mercantile Credit Co., **16** 13
Mercantile Estate and Property Corp. Ltd., **IV** 710
Mercantile Fire Insurance, **III** 234
Mercantile Mutual, **III** 310
Mercantile Property Corp. Ltd., **IV** 710
Mercantile Security Life, **III** 136
Mercantile Stores Company, Inc., V 139; **19 270–73 (upd.)**
Mercantile Trust Co., **II** 229, 247
Mercedes Benz. *See* Daimler-Benz A.G.
Mercedes Benz of North America, **22** 52
Merchant Bank Services, **18** 516, 518
Merchant Co., **III** 104
Merchant Distributors, Inc., **20** 306
Merchants & Farmers Bank of Ecru, **14** 40
Merchants Bank, **II** 213
Merchants Bank & Trust Co., **21** 524
Merchants Bank of Canada, **II** 210
Merchants Bank of Halifax, **II** 344
Merchants Dispatch, **II** 395–96; **10** 60
Merchants Distributors Inc. *See* Alex Lee Inc.
Merchants Fire Assurance Corp., **III** 396–97
Merchants Home Delivery Service, **6** 414
Merchants Indemnity Corp., **III** 396–97
Merchants Life Insurance Co., **III** 275
Merchants National Bank, **9** 228; **14** 528; **17** 135
Merchants National Bank of Boston, **II** 213
Merchants Union Express Co., **II** 396; **10** 60
Merchants' Assoc., **II** 261
Merchants' Loan and Trust, **II** 261; **III** 518
Merchants' Savings, Loan and Trust Co., **II** 261
Mercier, **I** 272
Merck & Co., Inc., I 640, 646, **650–52**, 683–84, 708; **II** 414; **III** 42, 60, 66, 299; **8** 154, 548; **10** 213; **11** 9, 90, **289–91 (upd.)**; **12** 325, 333; **14** 58, 422; **15** 154; **16** 440; **20** 39, 59; **26** 126
Mercury Air Group, Inc., 20 371–73
Mercury Asset Management (MAM), **14** 420
Mercury Communications, Ltd., V 280–82; **7 332–34**; **10** 456; **11** 547–48; **25** 101–02; **27** 365
Mercury General Corporation, 25 323–25
Mercury, Inc., **8** 311
Mercury Mail, Inc., **22** 519, 522
Mercury Records, **13** 397; **23** 389, 391
Mercury Telecommunications Limited, **15** 67, 69
Meredith and Drew, **II** 593
Meredith Corporation, IV 661–62; **11 292–94**; **17** 394; **18** 239; **23** 393; **29 316–19 (upd.)**
Meridian Bancorp, Inc., 11 295–97; **17** 111, 114
Meridian Emerging Markets Ltd., **25** 509
Meridian Healthcare, **18** 197
Meridian Insurance Co., **III** 332
Meridian Investment and Development Corp., **22** 189
Meridian Oil Inc., **10** 190–91
Meridian Publishing, Inc., **28** 254
Merillat Industries Inc., III 570; **13 338–39**; **20** 362
Merisel, Inc., 10 518–19; **12 334–36**; **13** 174, 176, 482
Merit Distribution Services, **13** 333
Merit Medical Systems, Inc., 29 320–22
Merit Tank Testing, Inc., **IV** 411
Meritage Corporation, 26 289–92
Merivienti Oy, **IV** 276
Merkur Direktwerbegesellschaft, **29** 152
Merla Manufacturing, **I** 524
Merlin Gérin, **II** 93–94; **18** 473; **19** 165
Merpati Nusantara Airlines, **6** 90–91
Merrell, **22** 173
Merrell Dow, **16** 438
Merrell Drug, **I** 325
Merrell-Soule Co., **II** 471
Merriam and Morgan Paraffine Co., **IV** 548
Merriam-Webster, Inc., **7** 165, 167; **23** 209–10
Merrill Corporation, 18 331–34
Merrill Gas Company, **9** 554
Merrill Lynch & Co., Inc., I 26, 339, 681, 683, 697; **II** 149, 257, 260, 268, 403, 407–08, 412, **424–26**, 441, 445,

449, 451, 456, 654–55, 680; **III** 119, 253, 340, 440; **6** 244; **7** 130; **8** 94; **9** 125, 187, 239, 301, 386; **11** 29, 122, 348, 557; **13** 44, 125, **340–43 (upd.)**, 448–49, 512; **14** 65; **15** 463; **16** 195; **17** 137; **21** 68–70, 145; **22** 404–06, 542; **23** 370; **25** 89–90, 329; **29** 295
Merrill, Pickard, Anderson & Eyre IV, **11** 490
Merrill Publishing, **IV** 643; **7** 312; **9** 63; **29** 57
Merry Group, **III** 673
Merry Maids, **6** 46; **23** 428, 430
Merry-Go-Round Enterprises, Inc., **8 362–64**; **24** 27
The Mersey Docks and Harbour Company, **30 318–20**
Mersey Paper Co., **IV** 258
Mersey White Lead Co., **III** 680
Merv Griffin Enterprises, **II** 137; **12** 75; **22** 431
Mervyn's, **V** 43–44; **10 409–10**; **13** 526; **18** 136–37; **27** 452
Mesa Airlines, Inc., **11 298–300**
Mesa Limited Partnership, **IV** 410, 523; **11** 441
Mesa Petroleum, **IV** 392, 571; **24** 521, 522; **27** 217
Mesaba Holdings, Inc., **I** 448; **22** 21; **28 265–67**
Messageries du Livre, **IV** 614
Messerschmitt-Bölkow-Blohm GmbH., **I** 41–42, 46, 51–52, 55, **73–75**, 111; **II** 242; **III** 539; **11** 267; **24** 86
Messner, Vetere, Berger, Carey, Schmetterer, **13** 204
Mesta Machine Co., **22** 415
Mestek, Inc., **10 411–13**
Met Food Corp. *See* White Rose Food Corp.
Met-Mex Penoles. *See* Industrias Penoles, S.A. de C.V.
Metabio-Joullie, **III** 47
Metaframe Corp., **25** 312
Metal Box plc, **I 604–06**; **20** 108
Metal Casting Technology, Inc., **23** 267, 269
Metal Closures, **I** 615
Metal Industries, **I** 531–32
Metal Manufactures, **III** 433–34
Metal Office Furniture Company, **7** 493
Metal-Cal. *See* Avery Dennison Corporation.
Metales y Contactos, **29** 461–62
Metaleurop S.A., **IV** 108–09; **21 368–71**
MetalExchange, **26** 530
Metall Mining Corp., **IV** 141; **27** 456
Metallgesellschaft AG, **IV** 17, **139–42**, 229; **16 361–66 (upd.)**
MetalOptics Inc., **19** 212
MetalPro, Inc., **IV** 168
Metals and Controls Corp., **II** 113
Metals Exploration, **IV** 82
Metalurgica Mexicana Penoles, S.A. *See* Industrias Penoles, S.A. de C.V.
Metaphase Technology, Inc., **10** 257
Metcalf & Eddy Companies, Inc., **6** 143, 441
Meteor Film Productions, **23** 391
Methane Development Corporation, **6** 457
Methanex Corp., **12** 365; **19** 155–56
Methode Electronics, Inc., **13 344–46**
Metinox Steel Ltd., **IV** 203
MetLife General Insurance Agency, **III** 293
MetMor Financial, Inc., **III** 293
MetPath, Inc., **III** 684; **26** 390
Metra Steel, **19** 381
Metric Constructors, Inc., **16** 286
Metric Systems, Inc., **18** 513
Metris Companies, **25** 41
Metro AG, **23** 311
Metro Distributors Inc., **14** 545
Metro Drug Corporation, **II** 649–50; **18** 181
Metro Glass, **II** 533
Metro Pacific, **18** 180, 182
Metro Southwest Construction. *See* CRSS Inc.
Metro Vermögensverwaltung GmbH & Co. of Dusseldorf, **V** 104
Metro-Goldwyn-Mayer Inc., **25** 173, 253, **326–30 (upd.)**. *See also* MGM/UA Communications Company.
Metro-Mark Integrated Systems Inc., **11** 469
Metro-Richelieu Inc., **II** 653
Metro-Verwegensverwaltung, **II** 257
Metrocall Inc., **18** 77
Metroland Printing, Publishing and Distributing Ltd., **29** 471
Metromail Corp., **IV** 661; **18** 170
Metromedia Companies, **II** 171; **6** 33, 168–69; **7** 91, **335–37**; **8** 311; **14** 107, **330–32 (upd.)**; **15** 362; **15** 363; **27** 306
Metromont Materials, **III** 740
MetroNet Communications Corp., **30** 391
Metroplitan and Great Western Dairies, **II** 586
Metropolitan Accident Co., **III** 228
Metropolitan Bank, **II** 221, 318; **III** 239; **IV** 644; **17** 323
Metropolitan Broadcasting Corporation, **7** 335
Metropolitan Clothing Co., **19** 362
Metropolitan Distributors, **9** 283
Metropolitan District Railway Company, **6** 406
Metropolitan Edison Company, **27** 182
Metropolitan Estate and Property Corp. Ltd., **IV** 710–11
Metropolitan Financial Corporation, **12** 165; **13 347–49**
Metropolitan Furniture Leasing, **14** 4
Metropolitan Gas Light Co., **6** 455
Metropolitan Housing Corp. Ltd., **IV** 710
Metropolitan Life Insurance Company, **II** 679; **III** 265–66, 272, **290–94**, 313, 329, 337, 339–40, 706; **IV** 283; **6** 256; **8** 326–27; **11** 482; **22** 266; **25** 300
Metropolitan National Bank, **II** 284
Metropolitan Petroleum Corp., **IV** 180–81; **19** 319
Metropolitan Railway, **6** 407
Metropolitan Railways Surplus Lands Co., **IV** 711
Metropolitan Reference Laboratories Inc., **26** 391
Metropolitan Tobacco Co., **15** 138
Metropolitan Vickers, **III** 670
METSA, Inc., **15** 363
Metsä-Serla Oy, **IV 314–16**, 318, 350
Metso Corporation, **30 321–25 (upd.)**
Mettler United States Inc., **9** 441
Mettler-Toledo International Inc., **30 326–28**
Metwest, **26** 391
Metzdorf Advertising Agency, **30** 80
Metzeler Kautschuk, **15** 354
Mexican Eagle Oil Co., **IV** 365, 531
Mexican Metal Co. *See* Industrias Penoles, S.A. de C.V.
Mexican Original Products, Inc., **II** 585; **14** 515
Mexofina, S.A. de C.V., **IV** 401
Meyer and Charlton, **IV** 90
Meyer Brothers Drug Company, **16** 212
Meyer Corporation, **27** 288
Meyerland Company, **19** 366
Meyers and Co., **III** 9
Meyers & Muldoon, **6** 40
Meyers Motor Supply, **26** 347
Meyers Parking, **18** 104
Meyrin, **I** 122
MFI, **II** 612
MFS Communications Company, Inc., **11 301–03**; **14** 253; **27** 301, 307
MG Holdings. *See* Mayflower Group Inc.
MG Ltd., **IV** 141
MG&E. *See* Madison Gas & Electric.
MGM. *See* McKesson General Medical.
MGM Grand Inc., **III** 431; **6** 210; **17 316–19**; **18** 336–37
MGM/UA Communications Company, **I** 286, 487; **II** 103, 135, **146–50**, 155, 161, 167, 169, 174–75, 408; **IV** 676; **6** 172–73; **12** 73, 316, 323, 455; **15** 84; **17** 316. *See also* Metro-Goldwyn-Mayer Inc.
MH Alshaya Group, **28** 96
mh Bausparkasse AG, **III** 377
MH Media Monitoring Limited, **26** 270
MHI Group, Inc., **13** 356; **16** 344
MHS Holding Corp., **26** 101
MHT. *See* Manufacturers Hanover Trust Co.
MI. *See* Masco Corporation.
Miami Power Corporation, **6** 466
Miami Subs Corp., **29** 342, 344
Micamold Electronics Manufacturing Corporation, **10** 319
Michael Anthony Jewelers, Inc., **24 334–36**
Michael Baker Corp., **14 333–35**
MICHAEL Business Systems Plc, **10** 257
Michael Foods, Inc., **25 331–34**
Michael Joseph, **IV** 659
Michael Reese Health Plan Inc., **III** 82
Michael's Fair-Mart Food Stores, Inc., **19** 479
Michaels Stores, Inc., **17 320–22**, 360; **25** 368
MichCon. *See* MCN Corporation.
Michelin, **III** 697; **7** 36–37; **8** 74; **11** 158, 473; **20** 261–62; **21** 72, 74; **28** 372
Michelin et Compagnie, **V** 236
Michiana Merchandising, **III** 10
Michie Co., **IV** 312; **19** 268
Michigan Automotive Compressor, Inc., **III** 593, 638–39
Michigan Automotive Research Corporation, **23** 183
Michigan Bell Telephone Co., **14 336–38**; **18** 30
Michigan Carpet Sweeper Company, **9** 70
Michigan Consolidated Gas Company. *See* MCN Corporation.
Michigan Fruit Canners, **II** 571
Michigan General, **II** 408
Michigan International Speedway, **V** 494
Michigan Motor Freight Lines, **14** 567

Michigan National Corporation, 11 304–06; **18** 517
Michigan Oil Company, **18** 494
Michigan Packaging Company, **15** 188
Michigan Plating and Stamping Co., **I** 451
Michigan Radiator & Iron Co., **III** 663
Michigan Shoe Makers. *See* Wolverine World Wide Inc.
Michigan Spring Company, **17** 106
Michigan State Life Insurance Co., **III** 274
Michigan Steel Corporation, **12** 352
Michigan Tag Company, **9** 72
Mick's Inc., **30** 329
Mickey Shorr Mobile Electronics, **10** 9–11
Micro D, Inc., **11** 194
Micro Decisionware, Inc., **10** 506
Micro Focus Inc., **27** 491
Micro Peripherals, Inc., **18** 138
Micro Power Systems Inc., **14** 183
Micro Switch, **14** 284
Micro Warehouse, Inc., 16 371–73
Micro-Circuit, Inc., **III** 645
Micro-Power Corp., **III** 643
Micro/Vest, **13** 175
MicroAge, Inc., 16 367–70; **29** 414
Microamerica, **12** 334
Microban Products Company, **27** 288
MicroBilt Corporation, **11** 112
Microcom, Inc., **26** 93
MicroComputer Accessories, **III** 614
Microcomputer Asset Management Services, **9** 168
Microcomputer Systems, **22** 389
Microdot Inc., I 440; **8 365–68**, 545
Microfal, **I** 341
Microform International Marketing Corp., **IV** 642; **7** 312
Microfral, **14** 216
Micromedex, **19** 268
Micron Technology, Inc., III 113; **11 307–09**; **29 323–26 (upd.)**
Micropolis Corp., **10** 403, 458, 463
MicroPro International Corp., **10** 556. *See also* The Learning Company Inc.
Microprocessor Systems, **13** 235
Microprose Inc., **24** 538
Micros Systems, Inc., 18 335–38
Microseal Corp., **I** 341
Microsoft Corporation, III 116; **6** 219–20, 224, 227, 231, 235, 254–56, **257–60**, 269–71; **9** 81, 140, 171, 195, 472; **10** 22, 34, 57, 87, 119, 237–38, 362–63, 408, 477, 484, 504, 557–58; **11** 59, 77–78, 306, 519–20; **12** 180, 335; **13** 115, 128, 147, 482, 509; **14** 262–64, 318; **15** 132–33, 321, 371, 483, 492, 511; **16** 4, 94, 367, 392, 394, 444; **18** 24, 64, 66, 306–7, 345, 349, 367, 541, 543; **19** 310; **20** 237; **21** 86; **24** 120, 233, 236, 371; **25** 21, 32, 34, 96, 117, 119, 184, 298–301, 498–99, 509; **26** 17, 294–95, 441, 520; **27 319–23 (upd.)**, 448, 517; **28** 245, 301; **29** 65, 439; **30** 391, 450
Microtek, Inc., **22** 413
Microtel Limited, **6** 309–10
Microware Surgical Instruments Corp., **IV** 137
Microwave Communications, Inc., **V** 302; **27** 302
Mid-America Capital Resources, Inc., **6** 508
Mid-America Dairymen, Inc., II 536; **7 338–40**; **11** 24; **21** 342; **22** 95; **26** 448
Mid-America Industries, **III** 495
Mid-America Interpool Network, **6** 506, 602
Mid-America Packaging, Inc., **8** 203
Mid-America Tag & Label, **8** 360
Mid-Central Fish and Frozen Foods Inc., **II** 675
Mid-Continent Area Power Planner, **V** 672
Mid-Continent Computer Services, **11** 111
Mid-Continent Life Insurance Co., **23** 200
Mid-Continent Telephone Corporation. *See* Alltel Corporation.
Mid-Georgia Gas Company, **6** 448
Mid-Illinois Gas Co., **6** 529
Mid-Pacific Airlines, **9** 271; **24** 21–22
Mid-Packaging Group Inc., **19** 78
Mid-South Towing, **6** 583
Mid-States Development, Inc., **18** 405
Mid-Texas Communications Systems, **6** 313
Mid-Valley Dairy, **14** 397
Mid-West Drive-In Theatres Inc., **I** 245
Mid-West Paper Ltd., **IV** 286
MidAmerican Communications Corporation, **8** 311
Midas International Corporation, I 457–58; **10 414–15**, 554; **24** 337
MIDCO, **III** 340
MidCon, **IV** 481; **25** 363
Middle East Broadcasting Centre, Ltd., **25** 506, 508
Middle East Tube Co. Ltd., **25** 266
Middle South Utilities, **V** 618–19
Middle West Corporation, **6** 469–70
Middle West Utilities Company, **V** 583–84; **6** 555–56, 604–05; **14** 227; **21** 468–69
Middle Wisconsin Power, **6** 604
Middleburg Steel and Alloys Group, **I** 423
The Middleby Corporation, 22 352–55
Middlesex Bank, **II** 334
Middleton Packaging, **12** 377
Middleton's Starch Works, **II** 566
Middletown Manufacturing Co., Inc., **16** 321
Middletown National Bank, **13** 467
Midhurst Corp., **IV** 658
Midial, **II** 478
Midland Bank plc, II 208, 236, 279, 295, 298, **318–20**, 334, 383; **9** 505; **12** 257; **14** 169; **17 323–26 (upd.)**; **19** 198; **26** 202
Midland Brick, **14** 250
Midland Cooperative, **II** 536
Midland Counties Dairies, **II** 587
Midland Electric Coal Co., **IV** 170
Midland Enterprises Inc., **6** 486–88
Midland Gravel Co., **III** 670
Midland Independent Newspaper plc, **23** 351
Midland Industrial Finishes Co., **I** 321
Midland Insurance, **I** 473
Midland International, **8** 56–57
Midland Investment Co., **II** 7
Midland Linseed Products Co., **I** 419
Midland National Bank, **11** 130
Midland Railway Co., **II** 306
Midland Southwest Corp., **8** 347
Midland Steel Products Co., **13** 305–06
Midland United, **6** 556; **25** 89
Midland Utilities Company, **6** 532
Midland-Ross Corporation, **14** 369
Midlands Electricity, **13** 485
Midlands Energy Co., **IV** 83; **7** 188
Midlantic Corp., **13** 411
Midrange Performance Group, **12** 149
Midrex Corp., **IV** 130
Midvale Steel and Ordnance Co., **IV** 35, 114; **7** 48
Midway Airlines, **6** 105, 120–21
Midway Games, Inc., 25 335–38
Midway Manufacturing Company, **III** 430; **15** 539
Midwest Agri-Commodities, **11** 15
Midwest Air Charter, **6** 345
Midwest Biscuit Company, **14** 306
Midwest Com of Indiana, Inc., **11** 112
Midwest Dairy Products, **II** 661
Midwest Express Airlines, **III** 40–41; **11** 299; **16** 302, 304
Midwest Federal Savings & Loan Association, **11** 162–63
Midwest Financial Group, Inc., **8** 188
Midwest Foundry Co., **IV** 137
Midwest Manufacturing Co., **12** 296
Midwest Realty Exchange, Inc., **21** 257
Midwest Refining Co., **IV** 368
Midwest Resources Inc., 6 523–25
Midwest Staffing Systems, **27** 21
Midwest Steel Corporation, **13** 157
Midwest Synthetics, **8** 553
Midwinter, **12** 529
Miele & Cie., **III** 418
MIG Realty Advisors, Inc., **25** 23, 25
Miguel Galas S.A., **17** 268
MIH Limited, 31 329–32
Mikasa, Inc., 28 268–70
Mike-Sell's Inc., 15 298–300
Mikemitch Realty Corp., **16** 36
Mikko, **II** 70
Mikko Kaloinen Oy, **IV** 349
Mikon, Ltd., **13** 345
Milac, **27** 259
Milani, **II** 556
Milbank Insurance Co., **III** 350
Milbank, Tweed, Hadley & McCloy, 27 324–27
Milbank, Tweed, Hope & Webb, **II** 471
Milcor Steel Co., **IV** 114
Miles Druce & Co., **III** 494
Miles Inc., **22** 148
Miles Kimball Co., **9** 393
Miles Laboratories, I 310, **653–55**, 674, 678; **6** 50; **13** 76; **14** 558
Miles Redfern, **I** 429
Milgo Electronic Corp., **II** 83; **11** 408
Milgram Food Stores Inc., **II** 682
Milgray Electronics, **19** 311
Milk Producers, Inc., **11** 24
Milk Specialties Co., **12** 199
Mill-Power Supply Company, **27** 129–30
Millbrook Press Inc., **IV** 616
Millennium Chemicals Inc., **30** 231
Miller Brewing Company, I 218–19, 236–37, 254–55, 257–58, **269–70**, 283, 290–91, 548; **10** 100; **11** 421; **12 337–39 (upd.)**, 372; **13** 10, 258; **15** 429; **17** 256; **18** 70, 72, 418, 499, 501; **21** 230; **22** 199, 422; **26** 303, 306; **27** 374; **28** 209–10
Miller Chemical & Fertilizer Corp., **I** 412
Miller Companies, **17** 182
Miller Container Corporation, **8** 102
Miller Freeman, Inc., **IV** 687; **27** 362; **28** 501, 504
Miller Group Ltd., **22** 282
Miller Industries, Inc., 26 293–95
Miller, Mason and Dickenson, **III** 204–05

Miller, Tabak, Hirsch & Co., **13** 394; **28** 164
Millet's Leisure, **V** 177–78
Millicom, **11** 547; **18** 254
Milliken & Co., V 366–68; **8** 270–71; **17 327–30 (upd.)**; **29** 246
Milliken, Tomlinson Co., **II** 682
Millipore Corporation, 9 396; **23** 284; **25 339–43**
Mills Clothing, Inc. *See* The Buckle, Inc.
Millstone Point Company, **V** 668–69
Millville Electric Light Company, **6** 449
Millway Foods, **25** 85
Milne Fruit Products, Inc., **25** 366
Milner, **III** 98
Milsco Manufacturing Co., **23** 299, 300
Milton Bradley Company, III 504–06; **16** 267; **17** 105; **21 372–75**; **25** 380
Milton Light & Power Company, **12** 45
Milton Roy Co., **8** 135
Milwaukee Cheese Co. Inc., **25** 517
Milwaukee Electric Manufacturing Co., **III** 534
Milwaukee Electric Railway and Light Company, **6** 601–02, 604–05
Milwaukee Electric Tool, **28** 40
Milwaukee Insurance Co., **III** 242
Milwaukee Mutual Fire Insurance Co., **III** 321
Minatome, **IV** 560
Mindport, **31** 329
Mine Safety Appliances Company, 31 333–35
Minemet Recherche, **IV** 108
The Miner Group International, 22 356–58
Mineral Point Public Service Company, **6** 604
Minerales y Metales, S.A. *See* Industrias Penoles, S.A. de C.V.
Minerals & Chemicals Philipp, **IV** 79–80
Minerals & Metals Trading Corporation of India Ltd., IV 143–44
Minerals and Resources Corporation Limited, **IV** 23; **13** 502. *See also* Minorco.
Minerals Technologies Inc., 11 310–12
Minerec Corporation, **9** 363
Minerva, **III** 359
Minerve, **6** 208
Mines et Usines du Nord et de l'Est, **IV** 226
Minet Group, **III** 357; **22** 494–95
Mini Stop, **V** 97
Mining and Technical Services, **IV** 67
Mining Corp. of Canada Ltd., **IV** 164
Mining Development Corp., **IV** 239–40
Mining Trust Ltd., **IV** 32
MiniScribe, Inc., **6** 230; **10** 404
Minister of Finance Inc., **IV** 519
Minitel, **21** 233
Minivator Ltd., **11** 486
Minneapolis General Electric of Minnesota, **V** 670
Minneapolis Heat Regulator Co., **II** 40–41; **12** 246
Minneapolis Millers Association, **10** 322
Minneapolis Steel and Machinery Company, **21** 502
Minneapolis-Honeywell Regulator Co., **II** 40–41, 86; **8** 21; **12** 247; **22** 427
Minnesota Cooperative Creamery Association, Inc., **II** 535; **21** 340
Minnesota Linseed Oil Co., **8** 552
Minnesota Mining & Manufacturing Company, I 28, 387, **499–501**; **II** 39; **III** 476, 487, 549; **IV** 251, 253–54; **6** 231; **7** 162; **8** 35, **369–71 (upd.)**; **11** 494; **13** 326; **17** 29–30; **22** 427; **25** 96, 372; **26 296–99 (upd.)**
Minnesota Paints, **8** 552–53
Minnesota Power & Light Company, 11 313–16
Minnesota Sugar Company, **11** 13
Minnesota Valley Canning Co., **I** 22
Minnetonka Corp., **II** 590; **III** 25; **22** 122–23
Minntech Corporation, 22 359–61
Minolta Camera Co., Ltd., III 574–76, 583–84
Minolta Co., Ltd., 18 93, 186, **339–42 (upd.)**
Minorco, **III** 503; **IV** 67–68, 84, 97; **16** 28, 293
Minstar Inc., **11** 397; **15** 49
The Minute Maid Company, I 234; **10** 227; **28 271–74**, 473
Minute Tapioca, **II** 531
Mippon Paper, **21** 546
MIPS Computer Systems, **II** 45; **11** 491
Miracle Food Mart, **16** 247, 249–50
Miracle-Gro Products, Inc., **22** 474
Miraflores Designs Inc., **18** 216
Mirage Resorts, Incorporated, 6 209–12; **15** 238; **28 275–79 (upd.)**; **29** 127
Miramar Hotel & Investment Co., **IV** 717
Mircali Asset Management, **III** 340
Mircor Inc., **12** 413
Mirrlees Blackstone, **III** 509
Mirror Group Newspapers plc, IV 641; **7** 244, 312, **341–43**; **23 348–51 (upd.)**
Mirror Printing and Binding House, **IV** 677
Misceramic Tile, Inc., **14** 42
Misr Airwork. *See* AirEgypt.
Misr Bank of Cairo, **27** 132
Misrair. *See* AirEgypt.
Miss Erika, Inc., **27** 346, 348
Miss Selfridge, **V** 177–78
Misset Publishers, **IV** 611
Mission Energy Company, **V** 715
Mission First Financial, **V** 715
Mission Group, **V** 715, 717
Mission Insurance Co., **III** 192
Mission Jewelers, **30** 408
Mississippi Chemical Corporation, **8** 183; **IV** 367; **27** 316
Mississippi Drug, **III** 10
Mississippi Gas Company, **6** 577
Mississippi Power & Light, **V** 619
Mississippi River Corporation, **10** 44
Mississippi River Recycling, **31** 47, 49
Missouri Book Co., **10** 136
Missouri Fur Company, **25** 220
Missouri Gaming Company, **21** 39
Missouri Gas & Electric Service Company, **6** 593
Missouri Pacific Railroad, **10** 43–44
Missouri Public Service Company. *See* UtiliCorp United Inc.
Missouri Utilities Company, **6** 580
Missouri-Kansas-Texas Railroad, **I** 472; **IV** 458
Mist Assist, Inc. *See* Ballard Medical Products.
Mistik Beverages, **18** 71
Mistral Plastics Pty Ltd., **IV** 295; **19** 225
Mitchel & King Skates Ltd., **17** 244
Mitchell Construction, **III** 753
Mitchell Energy and Development Corporation, 7 344–46
Mitchell Home Savings and Loan, **13** 347
Mitchell Hutchins, Inc., **II** 445; **22** 405–06
Mitchell International, **8** 526
Mitchells & Butler, **I** 223
Mitchum Co., **III** 55
Mitchum, Jones & Templeton, **II** 445; **22** 405
MiTek Industries Inc., **IV** 259
MiTek Wood Products, **IV** 305
Mitel Corporation, 15 131–32; **18 343–46**
MitNer Group, **7** 377
MITRE Corporation, 26 300–02
Mitre Sport U.K., **17** 204–05
Mitsubishi Aircraft Co., **III** 578; **7** 348; **9** 349; **11** 164
Mitsubishi Bank, Ltd., II 57, 273–74, 276, **321–22**, 323, 392, 459; **III** 289, 577–78; **7** 348; **15** 41; **16** 496, 498
Mitsubishi Chemical Industries Ltd., I 319, **363–64**, 398; **II** 57; **III** 666, 760; **11** 207
Mitsubishi Corporation, I 261, 431–32, 492, **502–04**, 505–06, 510, 515, 519–20; **II** 57, 59, 101, 118, 224, 292, 321–25, 374; **III** 577–78; **IV** 285, 518, 713; **6** 499; **7** 82, 233, 590; **9** 294; **12 340–43 (upd.)**; **17** 349, 556; **24** 325, 359; **27** 511
Mitsubishi Electric Corporation, II 53, **57–59**, 68, 73, 94, 122; **III** 577, 586; **7** 347, 394; **18** 18; **23** 52–53
Mitsubishi Estate Company, Limited, IV 713–14
Mitsubishi Foods, **24** 114
Mitsubishi Group, **V** 481–82; **7** 377; **21** 390
Mitsubishi Heavy Industries, Ltd., II 57, 75, 323, 440; **III** 452–53, 487, 532, 538, **577–79**, 685, 713; **IV** 184, 713; **7 347–50 (upd.)**; **8** 51; **9** 349–50; **10** 33; **13** 507; **15** 92; **24** 359
Mitsubishi International Corp., **16** 462
Mitsubishi Kasei Corp., **III** 47–48, 477; **8** 343; **14** 535
Mitsubishi Kasei Industry Co. Ltd., **IV** 476
Mitsubishi Marine, **III** 385
Mitsubishi Materials Corporation, III 712–13; **IV** 554
Mitsubishi Motors Corporation, III 516–17, 578–79; **6** 28; **7** 219, 348–49; **8** 72, 374; **9 349–51**; **23 352–55 (upd.)**
Mitsubishi Oil Co., Ltd., IV 460–62, 479, 492
Mitsubishi Paper Co., **III** 547
Mitsubishi Rayon Co. Ltd., I 330; **V 369–71**; **8** 153
Mitsubishi Sha Holdings, **IV** 554
Mitsubishi Shipbuilding Co. Ltd., **II** 57; **III** 513, 577–78; **7** 348; **9** 349
Mitsubishi Shokai, **III** 577; **IV** 713; **7** 347
Mitsubishi Trading Co., **IV** 460
Mitsubishi Trust & Banking Corporation, II 323–24; **III** 289
Mitsui & Co., Ltd., I 282; **IV** 18, 224, 432, 654–55; **V** 142; **6** 346; **7** 303; **13** 356; **24** 325, 488–89; **27** 337; **28 280–85 (upd.)**
Mitsui Bank, Ltd., II 273–74, 291, **325–27**, 328, 372; **III** 295–97; **IV** 147, 320; **V** 142; **17** 556

Mitsui Bussan K.K., **I** 363, 431–32, 469, 492, 502–04, **505–08**, 510, 515, 519, 533; **II** 57, 66, 101, 224, 292, 323, 325–28, 392; **III** 295–96, 717–18; **IV** 147, 431; **9** 352–53. *See also* Mitsui & Co., Ltd.
Mitsui Gomei Kaisha, **IV** 715
Mitsui Group, **9** 352; **16** 84; **20** 310; **21** 72
Mitsui House Code, **V** 142
Mitsui Light Metal Processing Co., **III** 758
Mitsui Marine and Fire Insurance Company, Limited, **III** 209, **295–96**, 297
Mitsui Mining & Smelting Co., Ltd., **IV** **145–46**, 147–48
Mitsui Mining Company, Limited, **IV** 145, **147–49**
Mitsui Mutual Life Insurance Company, **III** **297–98**
Mitsui O.S.K. Lines, Ltd., **I** 520; **IV** 383; **V** **473–76**; **6** 398; **26** 278–80
Mitsui Petrochemical Industries, Ltd., **I** 390, 516; **9** **352–54**
Mitsui Real Estate Development Co., Ltd., **IV** **715–16**
Mitsui Shipbuilding and Engineering Co., **III** 295, 513
Mitsui Toatsu, **9** 353–54
Mitsui Trading, **III** 636
Mitsui Trust & Banking Company, Ltd., **II** **328**; **III** 297
Mitsui-no-Mori Co., Ltd., **IV** 716
Mitsukoshi Ltd., **I** 508; **V** **142–44**; **14** 502
Mitsuya Foods Co., **I** 221
Mitteldeutsche Creditbank, **II** 256
Mitteldeutsche Energieversorgung AG, **V** 747
Mitteldeutsche Privatbank, **II** 256
Mitteldeutsche Stickstoff-Werke Ag, **IV** 229–30
Mitteldeutsches Kraftwerk, **IV** 229
Mixconcrete (Holdings), **III** 729
Miyoshi Electrical Manufacturing Co., **II** 6
Mizuno Corporation, **25** **344–46**
Mizushima Ethylene Co. Ltd., **IV** 476
MJB Coffee Co., **I** 28
MK-Ferguson Company, **7** 356
MLC Ltd., **IV** 709
MLH&P. *See* Montreal Light, Heat & Power Company.
MLT Vacations Inc., **30** 446
MMAR Group Inc., **19** 131
MML Investors Services, **III** 286
MMS America Corp., **26** 317
MNC Financial. *See* MBNA Corporation.
MNC Financial Corp., **11** 447
MND Drilling, **7** 345
MNet, **11** 122
Mo och Domsjö AB, **IV** 315, **317–19**, 340
Moa Bay Mining Co., **IV** 82; **7** 186
Mobay, **I** 310–11; **13** 76
Mobil Corporation, **I** 30, 34, 403, 478; **II** 379; **IV** 93, 295, 363, 386, 401, 403, 406, 423, 428, 454, **463–65**, 466, 472–74, 486, 492, 504–05, 515, 517, 522, 531, 538–39, 545, 554–55, 564, 570–71; **V** 147–48; **6** 530; **7** 171, **351–54 (upd.)**; **8** 552–53; **9** 546; **10** 440; **12** 348; **16** 489; **17** 363, 415; **19** 140, 225, 297; **21** **376–80 (upd.)**; **24** 496, 521; **25** 232, 445; **26** 369
Mobil Oil Australia, **24** 399
Mobile America Housing Corporation. *See* American Homestar Corporation.
Mobile and Ohio Railroad, **I** 456
Mobile Corporation, **25** 232
Mobile Mini, Inc., **21** 476
Mobile Telecommunications Technologies Corp., **V** 277–78; **6** 323; **16** 74; **18** **347–49**
Mobilefone, Inc., **25** 108
MobileStar Network Corp., **26** 429
Mobira, **II** 69; **17** 353
Mobley Chemical, **I** 342
Mobu Company, **6** 431
Mobujidosha Bus Company, **6** 431
MOÇACOR, **IV** 505
Mocatta and Goldsmid Ltd., **II** 357
Mochida Pharaceutical Co. Ltd., **II** 553
Moctezuma Copper Co., **IV** 176–77
Modar, **17** 279
Modell's Shoppers World, **16** 35–36
Modem Media, **23** 479
Modern Equipment Co., **I** 412
Modern Furniture Rentals Inc., **14** 4; **27** 163
Modern Handling Methods Ltd., **21** 499
Modern Maid Food Products, **II** 500
Modern Merchandising Inc., **19** 396
Modern Patterns and Plastics, **III** 641
Modernistic Industries Inc., **7** 589
Modine Manufacturing Company, **8** **372–75**
MoDo. *See* Mo och Domsjö AB.
MoDo Paper AB, **28** 446
Moen Incorporated, **12** **344–45**
Moët-Hennessy, **I** **271–72**; **10** 397–98; **23** 238, 240, 242
Mogul Corp., **I** 321; **17** 287
The Mogul Metal Company. *See* Federal-Mogul Corporation.
Mohasco Corporation, **15** 102; **26** 100–01
Mohawk & Hudson Railroad, **9** 369
Mohawk Airlines, **I** 131; **6** 131
Mohawk Carpet Corp., **26** 101
Mohawk Industries, Inc., **19** **274–76**; **31** 199
Mohawk Rubber Co. Ltd., **V** 256; **7** 116; **19** 508
Mohr-Value Stores, **8** 555
Moilliet and Sons, **II** 306
Mojave Foods Corporation, **27** 299
Mojo MDA Group Ltd., **11** 50–51
Mokta. *See* Compagnie de Mokta.
MOL. *See* Mitsui O.S.K. Lines, Ltd.
Molecular Biosystems, **III** 61
Molex Incorporated, **II** 8; **11** **317–19**; **14** 27
Moline National Bank, **III** 463; **21** 173
Molinera de México S.A. de C.V., **31** 236
Molinos de Puerto Rico, **II** 493
Molinos Nacionales C.A., **7** 242–43; **25** 241
Molins Co., **IV** 326
Molkerie-Zentrak Sud GmbH, **II** 575
Moll Plasticrafters, L.P., **17** 534
Molloy Manufacturing Co., **III** 569; **20** 360
Mölnlycke AB, **IV** 338–39; **28** 443–45
The Molson Companies Limited, **I** **273–75**, 333; **II** 210; **7** 183–84; **12** 338; **13** 150, 199; **21** 320; **23** 404; **25** 279; **26** **303–07 (upd.)**
Molycorp, **IV** 571; **24** 521
Mon-Dak Chemical Inc., **16** 270
Mon-Valley Transportation Company, **11** 194
MONACA. *See* Molinos Nacionales C.A.
Monaco Coach Corporation, **31** **336–38**
Monadnock Paper Mills, Inc., **21** **381–84**
Monarch Air Lines, **22** 219
Monarch Food Ltd., **II** 571
Monarch Foods, **26** 503
Monarch Marking Systems, **III** 157
MonArk Boat, **III** 444; **22** 116
Mond Nickel Co., **IV** 110–11
Mondadori. *See* Arnoldo Monadori Editore S.p.A.
Mondex International, **18** 543
Mondi Paper Co., **IV** 22
Monet Jewelry, **II** 502–03; **9** 156–57; **10** 323–24
Money Access Service Corp., **11** 467
Monfort, Inc., **13** **350–52**
Monheim Group, **II** 521
Monier Roof Tile, **III** 687, 735
Monis Wineries, **I** 288
Monitor Dynamics Inc., **24** 510
Monk-Austin Inc., **12** 110
Monmouth Pharmaceuticals Ltd., **16** 439
Monochem, **II** 472; **22** 93
Monogram Aerospace Fasteners, Inc., **11** 536
Monogram Models, **25** 312
Monogramme Confections, **6** 392
Monolithic Memories Inc., **6** 216; **16** 316–17, 549
Monon Corp., **13** 550
Monon Railroad, **I** 472
Monoprix, **V** 57–59
Monro Muffler Brake, Inc., **24** **337–40**
Monroe Auto Equipment, **I** 527
Monroe Calculating Machine Co., **I** 476, 484
Monroe Cheese Co., **II** 471
Monroe Savings Bank, **11** 109
Monrovia Aviation Corp., **I** 544
Monsanto Company, **I** 310, 363, **365–67**, 402, 631, 666, 686, 688; **III** 741; **IV** 290, 367, 379, 401; **8** 398; **9** 318, **355–57 (upd.)**, 466; **12** 186; **13** 76, 225; **16** 460–62; **17** 131; **18** 112; **22** 107; **23** 170–71; **26** 108; **29** **327–31 (upd.)**
Monsavon, **III** 46–47
Mont Blanc, **17** 5; **27** 487, 489
Montabert S.A., **15** 226
Montan TNT Pty Ltd., **27** 473
Montan Transport GmbH, **IV** 140
Montana Enterprises Inc., **I** 114
Montana Power Company, **6** 566; **7** 322; **11** **320–22**
Montana Refining Company, **12** 240–41
Montana Resources, Inc., **IV** 34
Montana-Dakota Utilities Co., **7** 322–23
Montaup Electric Co., **14** 125
MontBell America, Inc., **29** 279
Montecatini, **I** 368; **IV** 421, 470, 486
Montedison S.p.A., **I** **368–69**; **IV** 413, 421–22, 454, 499; **14** 17; **22** 262; **24** **341–44 (upd.)**; **26** 367
Montefibre, **I** 369
Montefina, **IV** 499; **26** 367
Montell N.V., **24** 343
Monterey Homes Corporation. *See* Meritage Corporation.
Monterey Mfg. Co., **12** 439
Monterey's Tex-Mex Cafes, **13** 473
Monterrey, Compania de Seguros sobre la Vida. *See* Seguros Monterrey.
Monterrey Group, **19** 10–11, 189
Montfort of Colorado, Inc., **II** 494
Montgomery Elevator Company, **27** 269

Montgomery Ward & Co., Incorporated, **III** 762; **IV** 465; **V 145–48**; **7** 353; **8** 509; **9** 210; **10** 10, 116, 172, 305, 391, 393, 490–91; **12** 48, 309, 315, 335, 430; **13** 165; **15** 330, 470; **17** 460; **18** 477; **20** 263, **374–79 (upd.)**, 433; **22** 535; **25** 144; **27** 428–30
Montiel Corporation, **17** 321
Montinex, **24** 270
Montreal Bank, **II** 210
Montreal Engineering Company, **6** 585
Montreal Light, Heat & Power Consolidated, **6** 501–02
Montreal Mining Co., **17** 357
Montres Rolex S.A., **8** 477; **13 353–55**; **19** 452
Montrose Chemical Company, **9** 118, 119
Montrose Chrome, **IV** 92
Monument Property Trust Ltd., **IV** 710
Monumental Corp., **III** 179
MONYCo., **III** 306
Moody's Investment Service, **IV** 605; **16** 506; **19** 133; **22** 189
Moog Inc., **13 356–58**
Moon-Hopkins Billing Machine, **III** 165
Mooney Chemicals, Inc. *See* OM Group, Inc.
Moonlight Mushrooms, Inc. *See* Sylvan, Inc.
Moonstone Mountaineering, Inc., **29** 181
Moore and McCormack Co. Inc., **19** 40
Moore Corporation Limited, **IV 644–46**, 679; **15** 473; **16** 450
Moore Gardner & Associates, **22** 88
The Moore Group Ltd., **20** 363
Moore McCormack Resources Inc., **14** 455
Moore Medical Corp., **17 331–33**
Moore-Handley Inc., **IV** 345–46
Moorhouse, **II** 477
Moran Group Inc., **II** 682
Moran Health Care Group Ltd., **25** 455
MoRan Oil & Gas Co., **IV** 82–83
Moran Towing Corporation, Inc., **15 301–03**
Morana, Inc., **9** 290
Moreland and Watson, **IV** 208
Moretti-Harrah Marble Co., **III** 691
Morgan & Banks Limited, **30** 460
Morgan & Cie International S.A., **II** 431
Morgan Construction Company, **8** 448
Morgan Edwards, **II** 609
Morgan Engineering Co., **8** 545
Morgan Grampian Group, **IV** 687
Morgan Grenfell Group PLC, **II** 280, 329, **427–29**; **IV** 21, 712
Morgan Guaranty International Banking Corp., **II** 331; **9** 124
Morgan Guaranty Trust Co. of New York, **I** 26; **II** 208, 254, 262, 329–32, 339, 428, 431, 448; **III** 80; **10** 150
Morgan Guaranty Trust Company, **11** 421; **13** 49, 448; **14** 297; **25** 541; **30** 261
Morgan, Harjes & Co., **II** 329
Morgan, J.P. & Co. Inc. *See* J.P. Morgan & Co. Incorporated.
Morgan, Lewis & Bockius LLP, **29 332–34**
Morgan, Lewis, Githens & Ahn, Inc., **6** 410
Morgan Mitsubishi Development, **IV** 714
Morgan Schiff & Co., **29** 205
Morgan Stanley Group, Inc., **I** 34; **II** 211, 330, 403, 406–08, 422, 428, **430–32**, 441; **IV** 295, 447, 714; **9** 386; **11** 258; **12** 529; **16 374–78 (upd.)**; **18** 448–49; **20** 60, 363; **22** 404, 407; **25** 542; **30** 353–55
Morgan Yacht Corp., **II** 468
Morgan's Brewery, **I** 287
Mori Bank, **II** 291
Moria Informatique, **6** 229
Morino Associates, **10** 394
Morita & Co., **II** 103
Mormac Marine Group, **15** 302
Morning Star Technologies Inc., **24** 49
Morning Sun, Inc., **23** 66
Morris Air, **24** 455
Morris Motors, **III** 256; **7** 459
Morris Travel Services L.L.C., **26 308–11**
Morrison Industries Ltd., **IV** 278; **19** 153
Morrison Knudsen Corporation, **IV** 55; **7 355–58**; **11** 401, 553; **28 286–90 (upd.)**
Morrison Machine Products Inc., **25** 193
Morrison Restaurants Inc., **11 323–25**; **18** 464
Morse Chain Co., **III** 439; **14** 63
Morse Equalizing Spring Company, **14** 63
Morse Industrial, **14** 64
Morse Shoe Inc., **13 359–61**
Morss and White, **III** 643
Morstan Development Co., Inc., **II** 432
Mortgage & Trust Co., **II** 251
Mortgage Associates, **9** 229
Mortgage Insurance Co. of Canada, **II** 222
Mortgage Resources, Inc., **10** 91
Morton Foods, Inc., **II** 502; **10** 323; **27** 258
Morton International Inc., **9 358–59 (upd.)**, 500–01; **16** 436; **22** 505–06
Morton Thiokol Inc., **I** 325, **370–72**; **19** 508; **28** 253–54. *See also* Thiokol Corporation.
Morton's Restaurant Group, Inc., **28** 401; **30 329–31**
Mos Magnetics, **18** 140
MOS Technology, **7** 95
Mosby-Year Book, Inc., **IV** 678; **17** 486
Moseley, Hallgarten, Estabrook, and Weeden, **III** 389
Mosher Steel Company, **7** 540
Mosinee Paper Corporation, **15 304–06**
Moskatel's, Inc., **17** 321
Mosler Safe Co., **III** 664–65; **7** 144, 146; **22** 184
Moss-Rouse Company, **15** 412
Mossgas, **IV** 93
Mossimo, Inc., **27 328–30**
Mostek Corp., **I** 85; **II** 64; **11** 307–08; **13** 191; **20** 175; **29** 323
Mostjet Ltd. *See* British World Airlines Ltd.
Móstoles Industrial S.A., **26** 129
Motel 6 Corporation, **10** 13; **13 362–64**. *See also* Accor SA
Mother Karen's, **10** 216
Mother's Oats, **II** 558–59; **12** 409
Mothercare Stores, Inc., **16** 466
Mothercare UK Ltd., **17** 42–43, **334–36**
Mothers Work, Inc., **18 350–52**
Motif Inc., **22** 288
Motion Designs, **11** 486
Motion Picture Corporation of America, **25** 326, 329
Moto-Truc Co., **13** 385
Motor Haulage Co., **IV** 181
Motor Parts Industries, Inc., **9** 363
Motor Transit Corp., **I** 448; **10** 72
Motor Wheel Corporation, **20** 261; **27** 202–04
Motoren-und-Turbinen-Union, **I** 151; **III** 563; **9** 418; **15** 142
Motoren-Werke Mannheim AG, **III** 544
Motorenfabrik Deutz AG, **III** 541
Motorenfabrik Oberursel, **III** 541
Motornetic Corp., **III** 590
Motorola, Inc., **I** 534; **II** 5, 34, 44–45, 56, **60–62**, 64; **III** 455; **6** 238; **7** 119, 494, 533; **8** 139; **9** 515; **10** 87, 365, 367, 431–33; **11** 45, 308, **326–29 (upd.)**, 381–82; **12** 136–37, 162; **13** 30, 356, 501; **17** 33, 193; **18** 18, 74, 76, 260, 382; **19** 391; **20** 8, 439; **21** 123; **22** 17, 19, 288, 542; **26** 431–32; **27** 20, 341–42, 344
Motown Records Company L.P., **II** 145; **22** 194; **23** 389, 391; **26 312–14**
Moulinex S.A., **22 362–65**
Mound Metalcraft. *See* Tonka Corporation.
Mount. *See also* Mt.
Mount Hood Credit Life Insurance Agency, **14** 529
Mount Isa Mines, **IV** 61
Mount Vernon Group, **8** 14
Mountain Fuel Supply Company. *See* Questar Corporation.
Mountain Fuel Supply Company, **6** 568–69
Mountain Pass Canning Co., **7** 429
Mountain Safety Research, **18** 445–46
Mountain State Telephone Company, **6** 300
Mountain States Mortgage Centers, Inc., **29 335–37**
Mountain States Power Company. *See* PacifiCorp.
Mountain States Telephone & Telegraph Co., **V** 341; **25** 495
Mountain States Wholesale, **II** 602; **30** 25
Mountleigh PLC, **16** 465
Mounts Wire Industries, **III** 673
Mountsorrel Granite Co., **III** 734
Movado Group, Inc., **28 291–94**
Movado-Zenith-Mondia Holding, **II** 124
Movie Gallery, Inc., **31 339–41**
Movie Star Inc., **17 337–39**
Movies To Go, Inc., **9** 74; **31** 57
Moving Co. Ltd., **V** 127
The Moving Picture Company, **15** 83
The Mowry Co., **23** 102
MPB Corporation, **8** 529, 531
MPM, **III** 735
Mr. Coffee, Inc., **14** 229–31; **15 307–09**; **17** 215; **27** 275
Mr. D's Food Centers, **12** 112
Mr. Donut, **21** 323
Mr. Gasket Inc., **11** 84; **15 310–12**
Mr. Gatti's, **15** 345
Mr. Goodbuys, **13** 545
Mr. How, **V** 191–92
Mr. M Food Stores, **7** 373
Mr. Maintenance, **25** 15
Mr. Payroll Corp., **20** 113
MRC Bearings, **III** 624
MRN Radio Network, **19** 223
Mrs. Baird's Bakeries, **29 338–41**
Mrs. Fields' Original Cookies, Inc., **27 331–35**
Mrs. Paul's Kitchens, **II** 480; **26** 57–58
Mrs. Smith's Frozen Foods, **II** 525; **13** 293–94
MS-Relais GmbH, **III** 710; **7** 302–03
MSAS Cargo International, **6** 415, 417

MSI Data Corp., **10** 523; **15** 482
MSL Industries, **10** 44
MSNBC, **28** 301
MSR. *See* Mountain Safety Research.
MSU. *See* Middle South Utilities.
Mt. *See also* Mount.
Mt. Beacon Insurance Co., **26** 486
Mt. Carmel Public Utility Company, **6** 506
Mt. Goldsworthy Mining Associates, **IV** 47
Mt. Lyell Investments, **III** 672–73
Mt. Summit Rural Telephone Company, **14** 258
Mt. Vernon Iron Works, **II** 14
MTC. *See* Management and Training Corporation.
MTC Pharmaceuticals, **II** 483
MTel. *See* Mobile Telecommunications Technologies Corp.
MTM Entertainment Inc., **13** 279, 281
MTV, **31** 239
MTV Asia, **23** 390
Mueller Co., **III** 645; **28** 485
Mueller Furniture Company, **8** 252
Mueller Industries, Inc., 7 359–61
Mujirushi Ryohin, **V** 188
Mukluk Freight Lines, **6** 383
Mule Battery Manufacturing Co., **III** 643
Mule-Hide Products Co., **22** 15
Mülheimer Bergwerksvereins, **I** 542
Mullen Advertising, **13** 513
Mullens & Co., **14** 419
Multex Systems, **21** 70
Multi Restaurants, **II** 664
Multibank Inc., **11** 281
Multicom Publishing Inc., **11** 294
Multilink, Inc., **27** 364–65
MultiMed, **11** 379
Multimedia, Inc., **IV** 591; **11 330–32**; **30** 217
Multiple Access Systems Corp., **III** 109
Multiple Properties, **I** 588
MultiScope Inc., **10** 508
Multitech International. *See* Acer Inc.
Multiview Cable, **24** 121
Münchener Rückversicherungs-Gesellschaft. *See* Munich Re.
Munford, Inc., **17** 499
Mungana Mines, **I** 438
Munich Re, **II** 239; **III** 183–84, 202, **299–301**, 400–01, 747
Municipal Assistance Corp., **II** 448
Munising Paper Co., **III** 40; **13** 156; **16** 303
Munising Woodenware Company, **13** 156
Munksjö, **19** 227
Munksund, **IV** 338
Munsingwear, Inc., **22** 427; **25** 90; **27** 443, 445. *See also* PremiumWear, Inc.
Munson Transportation Inc., **18** 227
Munster and Leinster Bank Ltd., **16** 13
Mura Corporation, **23** 209
Murdock Madaus Schwabe, **26 315–19**, 470
Murfin Inc., **8** 360
Murmic, Inc., **9** 120
Murphey Favre, Inc., **17** 528, 530
Murphy Family Farms Inc., **7** 477; **21** 503; **22 366–68**
Murphy Oil Corporation, **7 362–64**
Murphy-Phoenix Company, **14** 122
Murray Bay Paper Co., **IV** 246; **25** 10
Murray Corp. of America, **III** 443
Murray Goulburn Snow, **II** 575
Murray Inc., **19** 383
Murrayfield, **IV** 696
Murtaugh Light & Power Company, **12** 265
Musashino Railway Company, **V** 510
Muscatine Journal, **11** 251
Muscocho Explorations Ltd., **IV** 76
Muse Air Corporation, **6** 120; **24** 454
Music and Video Club, **24** 266, 270
Music Corporation of America. *See* MCA Inc.
Music Go Round, **18** 207–09
Music Man, Inc., **16** 202
Music Plus, **9** 75
Music-Appreciation Records, **13** 105
Musical America Publishing, Inc., **22** 441
Musician's Friend, **29** 221, 223
Musicland Stores Corporation, **9 360–62**; **11** 558; **19** 417
Musitek, **16** 202
Muskegon Gas Company. *See* MCN Corporation.
Musotte & Girard, **I** 553
Mutoh Industries, Ltd., **6** 247; **24** 234
Mutual Benefit Life Insurance Company, **III** 243, **302–04**
Mutual Broadcasting System, **23** 509
Mutual Gaslight Company. *See* MCN Corporation.
Mutual Life Insurance Co. of the State of Wisconsin, **III** 321
Mutual Life Insurance Company of New York, **II** 331; **III** 247, 290, **305–07**, 316, 321, 380
Mutual Medical Aid and Accident Insurance Co., **III** 331
Mutual of Omaha, **III** 365; **25** 89–90; **27** 47
Mutual Oil Co., **IV** 399
Mutual Papers Co., **14** 522
Mutual Safety Insurance Co., **III** 305
Mutual Savings & Loan Association, **III** 215; **18** 60
Mutualité Générale, **III** 210
Mutuelle d'Orléans, **III** 210
Mutuelle de l'Quest, **III** 211
Mutuelle Vie, **III** 210
Mutuelles Unies, **III** 211
Muzak, Inc., **7** 90–91; **18 353–56**
Muzzy-Lyon Company. *See* Federal-Mogul Corporation.
MVC. *See* Music and Video Club.
Mwinilunga Canneries Ltd., **IV** 241
MXL Industries, **13** 367
MY Holdings, **IV** 92
Myanmar Oil and Gas Enterprise, **IV** 519
MYCAL Group, **V** 154
Myco-Sci, Inc. *See* Sylvan, Inc.
Mycogen Corporation, **21 385–87**
Mycrom, **14** 36
Myer Emporium Ltd., **20** 156
Myers Industries, Inc., **19 277–79**
Mygind International, **8** 477
Mylan Laboratories Inc., **I 656–57**; **20 380–82 (upd.)**
Myllykoski Träsliperi AB, **IV** 347–48
Myokenya, **III** 757
Myrna Knitwear, Inc., **16** 231
Myson Group PLC, **III** 671
Mysore State Iron Works, **IV** 205

N.A. Otto & Cie., **III** 541
N.A. Woodworth, **III** 519; **22** 282
N. Boynton & Co., **16** 534
N.C. Cameron & Sons, Ltd., **11** 95
N.C. Monroe Construction Company, **14** 112
N.E.M., **23** 228
N.H. Geotech. *See* New Holland N.V.
N.K. Fairbank Co., **II** 497
N.L. Industries, **19** 212
N M Electronics, **II** 44
N.M. Rothschild & Sons, **IV** 64, 712; **24** 267
N.M.U. Transport Ltd., **II** 569
N.R.F. Gallimard, **IV** 618
N. Shure Company, **15** 477
N.V. *see under first word of company name*
N.W. Ayer & Son, **I** 36; **II** 542
N.Y.P. Holdings Inc., **12** 360
Na Pali, S.A. *See* Quiksilver, Inc.
Naamloze Vennootschap tot Exploitatie van het Café Krasnapolsky. *See* Grand Hotel Krasnapolsky N.V.
Nabisco, **24** 358
Nabisco Brands, Inc., **II** 475, 512, **542–44**; **7** 128, 365–67; **12** 167; **25** 366. *See also* RJR Nabisco.
Nabisco Foods Group, **7 365–68 (upd.)**; **9** 318; **14** 48
Nabisco Holdings Corporation, **25** 181
Nabisco Ltd., **24** 288
Nabors Industries, Inc., **9 363–65**
NACCO Industries, Inc., **7 369–71**; **17** 213–15, 246, 248
Nacional Financiera, **IV** 513
Nadler Sportswear. *See* Donnkenny, Inc.
NAFI Corp. *See* Chris-Craft Industries, Inc.
Nagano Seiyu Ltd., **V** 188
Nagasaki Shipyard, **I** 502
Nagasakiya Co., Ltd., **V 149–51**
Nagasco, Inc., **18** 366
Nagase & Company, Ltd., **8 376–78**
Nagase-Alfa, **III** 420
Nagel Meat Markets and Packing House, **II** 643
Nagoya Bank, **II** 373
Nagoya Electric Light Co., **IV** 62
NAI. *See* Network Associates, Inc.
Naigai Tsushin Hakuhodo, **6** 29
Naikoku Tsu-un Kabushiki Kaisha, **V** 477
Naiman Co., **25** 449
Nairn Linoleum Co., **18** 116
Nakai Shoten Ltd., **IV** 292
Nakano Vinegar Co. Ltd., **26** 58
Nalco Chemical Corporation, **I 373–75**; **12 346–48 (upd.)**
Nalfloc, **I** 374
Nalge Co., **14** 479–80
NAM. *See* Nederlandse Aardolie Maatschappij.
Namco, **III** 431
Namkwang Engineering & Construction Co. Ltd., **III** 749
Nampack, **I** 423
Nan Ya Plastics Corp., **14** 197–98
NANA Regional Corporation, **7** 558
Nankai Kogyo, **IV** 225; **24** 489
Nansei Sekiyu, **IV** 432
Nantucket Allserve, Inc., **22 369–71**
Nantucket Corporation, **6** 226
Nantucket Mills, **12** 285
Nanyo Bussan, **I** 493; **24** 326
NAPA. *See* National Automotive Parts Association.
NAPC. *See* North American Philips Corp.
Napier, **I** 194
NAPP Systems, Inc., **11** 253

Narmco Industries, **I** 544
NAS. *See* National Audubon Society.
NASA. *See* National Aeronautics and Space Administration.
Nash DeCamp Company, **23** 356–57
Nash Finch Company, **8 379–81**; **11** 43; **23 356–58 (upd.)**
Nash Motors Co., **I** 135; **8** 75
Nash-Kelvinator Corp., **I** 135; **12** 158
Nashaming Valley Information Processing, **III** 204
Nashua Corporation, **8 382–84**
The Nashville Network, **11** 153
Nassau Gas Light Co., **6** 455
NASTECH, **III** 590
Nasu Aluminium Manufacturing Co., **IV** 153
Natal Brewery Syndicate, **I** 287
Natco Corp., **I** 445
NaTec Ltd. *See* CRSS Inc.
Nathan's Famous, Inc., **29 342–44**
National, **10** 419
National Acme Company. *See* Acme-Cleveland Corp.
National Advanced Systems, **II** 64–65
National Advertising Company, **27** 280
National Aeronautics and Space Administration, **II** 139; **6** 227–29, 327; **11** 201, 408; **12** 489
National Air Transport Co., **I** 128; **6** 128; **9** 416; **11** 427
National Airlines, **I** 97, 116; **6** 388; **21** 141; **25** 146
National Allied Publications. *See* DC Comics Inc.
National Aluminate Corp., **I** 373; **12** 346
National Aluminum Company, **11** 38
National American Life Insurance Co. of California, **II** 181
National American Title Insurance Co., **II** 181
National Amusements Inc., **28 295–97**
National Aniline & Chemical Coompany, **I** 414; **22** 29
National Association of Securities Dealers, Inc., **10 416–18**
National Audubon Society, **26 320–23**
National Australia Bank, **III** 673
National Auto Credit, Inc., **16 379–81**
National Automobile and Casualty Insurance Co., **III** 270
National Automotive Fibers, Inc. *See* Chris-Craft Industries, Inc.
National Automotive Parts Association, **26** 348
National Aviation, **I** 117
National Baby Shop, **V** 203
National Bancard Corporation, **11** 111–13
National Bancorp of Arizona, **12** 565
National Bank, **II** 312
National Bank for Cooperatives, **8** 489–90
National Bank für Deutschland, **II** 270
National Bank of Belgium, **II** 294
National Bank of Commerce, **II** 331; **9** 536; **11** 105–06; **13** 467
National Bank of Commerce Trust & Savings Association, **15** 161
National Bank of Detroit, **I** 165. *See also* NBD Bancorp, Inc.
National Bank of Egypt, **II** 355
The National Bank of Jacksonville, **9** 58
National Bank of New Zealand, **II** 308; **19** 155
National Bank of North America, **II** 334
National Bank of South Africa Ltd., **II** 236
National Bank of the City of New York, **II** 312
National Bank of Turkey, **IV** 557
National Bank of Washington, **13** 440
National BankAmericard Inc. *See* Visa International.
National Bankers Express Co., **II** 396; **10** 60
National Basketball Association, **12** 457
National Bell Telephone Company, **V** 259
National Benefit and Casualty Co., **III** 228
National Benefit Co., **III** 228
National Beverage Corp., **26 324–26**
National Binding Company, **8** 382
National Biscuit Co., **IV** 152; **22** 336. *See also* Nabisco.
National Bridge Company of Canada, Ltd., **8** 544
National Broach & Machine Co., **I** 481–82
National Broadcasting Company, Inc., **II** 30, 88–90, 129–33, **151–53**, 170, 173, 487, 543; **III** 188, 329; **IV** 596, 608, 652; **6** 157–59, **164–66 (upd.)**; **10** 173; **17** 149–50; **19** 201, 210; **21** 24; **23** 120; **28** 69, **298–301 (upd.)**; **30** 99
National Building Society, **10** 6–7
National Cable & Manufacturing Co., **13** 369
National Cable Television Association, **18** 64
National Can Corp., **I** 601–02, **607–08**; **IV** 154; **13** 255
National Car Rental System, Inc., **I** 489; **II** 419–20, 445; **6** 348–49; **10** 373, **419–20**; **21** 284; **22** 406, 524; **24** 9; **25** 93, 143. *See also* Republic Industries, Inc.
National Carbon Co., Inc., **I** 400; **9** 516; **11** 402
National Carriers, **6** 413–14
National Cash Register Company. *See* NCR Corporation.
National Cheerleaders Association, **15** 516–18
National Chemsearch Corp. *See* NCH Corporation.
National Child Care Centers, Inc., **II** 607
National City Bank, **9** 475
National City Bank of New York, **I** 337, 462; **II** 253–54; **III** 380; **IV** 81
National City Co., **II** 254; **9** 124
National City Corp., **9** 475; **15 313–16**
National Cleaning Contractors, **II** 176
National Coal Board, **IV** 38–40
National Coal Development Corp., **IV** 48
National Comics Publications. *See* DC Comics Inc.
National Commercial Bank, **11** 108; **12** 422; **13** 476
National Components Industries, Inc., **13** 398
National Container Corp., **I** 609
National Convenience Stores Incorporated, **7 372–75**; **20** 140
National Cranberry Association. *See* Ocean Spray Cranberries, Inc.
National Credit Office, **IV** 604
National CSS, **IV** 605
National Dairy Products Corp., **II** 533; **7** 275; **14** 204
National Data Corporation, **24** 393
National Demographics & Lifestyles Inc., **10** 461
National Development Bank, **IV** 56
National Discount Brokers Group, Inc., **28 302–04**
National Disinfectant Company. *See* NCH Corporation.
National Distillers and Chemical Corporation, **I** 226, **376–78**; **IV** 11; **8** 439–41; **9** 231; **10** 181; **30** 441
National Drive-In Grocery Corporation, **7** 372
National Drug Ltd., **II** 652
National Economic Research Associates, **III** 283
National Education Association, **9** 367
National Educational Corporation, **26** 95
National Electric Company, **11** 388
National Electric Instruments Co., **IV** 78
National Electric Products Corp., **IV** 177
National Employers Life Assurance Co. Ltd., **13** 539
National Enquirer, **10** 287–88
National Executive Service. *See* Carey International, Inc.
National Express Laboratories, Inc., **10** 107
National Family Opinion. *See* NFO Worldwide, Inc.
National Fidelity Life Insurance Co., **10** 246
National Fidelity Life Insurance Co. of Kansas, **III** 194; **IV** 343
National Finance Corp., **IV** 22–23
National Fire & Marine Insurance Co., **III** 213–14
National Fire Insurance Co., **III** 229–30
National Football League, **12** 457; **29 345–47**
National Freight Corporation, **6** 412–13
National Fuel Gas Company, **6 526–28**
National Gateway Telecom, **6** 326–27
National General Corp., **III** 190–91
National Geographic Society, **9 366–68**; **30 332–35 (upd.)**
National Grape Co-operative Association, Inc., **20 383–85**
National Greyhound Racing Club, **II** 142
National Grid Company, **11** 399–400; **12** 349; **13** 484
National Grocers of Ontario, **II** 631
National Guardian Corp., **18** 33
National Gypsum Company, **8** 43; **10 421–24**; **13** 169; **22** 48, 170; **25** 535
National Health Enterprises, **III** 87
National Health Laboratories Incorporated, **11 333–35**
National Hockey League, **12** 457
National Hotel Co., **III** 91
National Housing Systems, Inc., **18** 27
National Hydrocarbon Corp., **IV** 543
National ICEE Corporation, **24** 242
National Import and Export Corp. Ltd., **IV** 240
National Indemnity Co., **III** 213–14
National India Rubber Company, **9** 228
National Industries, **I** 446
National Inking Appliance Company, **14** 52
National Instruments Corporation, **22 372–74**
National Integrity Life Insurance, **III** 249
National Intergroup, Inc., **IV** 237, 574; **V 152–53**; **12** 354; **16** 212; **26** 529. *See also* FoxMeyer Health Corporation.
National Iranian Oil Company, **III** 748; **IV** 370, 374, **466–68**, 484, 512, 535

National Key Company. *See* Cole National Corporation.
National Kinney Corp., **IV** 720; **9** 391
National Lead Co., **III** 681; **IV** 32; **21** 489
National Liability and Fire Insurance Co., **III** 214
National Liberty Corp., **III** 218–19
National Life and Accident Insurance Co., **III** 194
National Life Insurance Co., **III** 290
National Life Insurance Co. of Canada, **III** 243
National Living Centers, **13** 49
National Loss Control Service Corp., **III** 269
National Magazine Company Limited, **19** 201
National Manufacturing Co., **III** 150; **6** 264; **13** 6
National Marine Service, **6** 530
National Market System, **9** 369
National Media Corporation, 27 336–40
National Medical Care, **22** 360
National Medical Enterprises, Inc., III 79, **87–88**; **6** 188; **10** 252; **14** 233; **25** 307–08
National Minerals Development Corp., **IV** 143–44
National Mobility Corp., **30** 436
National Mortgage Agency of New Zealand Ltd., **IV** 278; **19** 153
National Mortgage Assoc. of Washington, **II** 410
The National Motor Bearing Company. *See* Federal-Mogul Corporation.
National Mutual Life Assurance of Australasia, **III** 249
National Office Furniture, **12** 297
National Oil Corp. *See* Libyan National Oil Corporation.
National Oil Distribution Co., **IV** 524
National Old Line Insurance Co., **III** 179
National Packaging, **IV** 333
National Paper Co., **8** 476
National Parks Transportation Company, **25** 420–22
National Patent Development Corporation, 7 45; **13 365–68**; **25** 54
National Periodical Publications. *See* DC Comics Inc.
National Permanent Mutual Benefit Building Society, **10** 6
National Petrochemical Co., **IV** 467
National Petroleum Publishing Co., **IV** 636
National Pharmacies, **9** 346
National Picture & Frame Company, 24 345–47
National Postal Meter Company, **14** 52
National Potash Co., **IV** 82; **7** 186
National Power PLC, 11 399–400; **12 349–51**; **13** 458, 484
National Presto Industries, Inc., 16 382–85
National Processing, Inc., **24** 394
National Propane Corporation, **8** 535–37
National Provident Institution for Mutual Life Assurance, **IV** 711
National Provincial Bank, **II** 319–20, 333–34; **IV** 722; **17** 324
National Public Radio, 19 280–82
National Quotation Bureau, Inc., **14** 96–97
National Railroad Passenger Corporation, 22 375–78
National Railways of Mexico, **IV** 512
National Record Mart, Inc., 29 348–50
National Register Publishing Co., **17** 399; **23** 442
National Regulator Co., **II** 41
National Reinsurance Corporation. *See* General Re Corporation.
National Rent-A-Car, **6** 392–93
National Research Corporation, **8** 397
National Revenue Corporation, **22** 181
National Rubber Machinery Corporation, **8** 298
National Sanitary Supply Co., 13 149–50; **16 386–87**
National Satellite Paging, **18** 348
National School Studios, **7** 255; **25** 252
National Science Foundation, **9** 266
National Sea Products Ltd., 14 339–41
National Seal, **I** 158
National Semiconductor Corporation, II 63–65; **III** 455, 618, 678; **6** 215, **261–63**; **9** 297; **11** 45–46, 308, 463; **16** 122, 332; **17** 418; **18** 18; **19** 312; **21** 123; **26 327–30 (upd.)**
National Service Industries, Inc., 11 336–38
National Shoe Products Corp., **16** 17
National Slicing Machine Company, **19** 359
National Stamping & Electric Works, **12** 159
National Standard Co., IV 137; **13 369–71**
National Star Brick & Tile Co., **III** 501; **7** 207
National Starch and Chemical Corp., **IV** 253; **17** 30
National Starch Manufacturing Co., **II** 496
National Steel and Shipbuilding Company, **7** 356
National Steel Car Corp., **IV** 73; **24** 143–44
National Steel Corporation, I 491; **IV** 74, 163, 236–37, 572; **V** 152–53; **7** 549; **8** 346, 479–80; **11** 315; **12 352–54**; **14** 191; **16** 212; **23** 445; **24** 144; **26** 527–29; **28** 325. *See also* FoxMeyer Health Corporation.
National Student Marketing Corporation, **10** 385–86
National Supply Co., **IV** 29
National Surety Co. of New York, **III** 395
National System Company, **9** 41; **11** 469
National Tanker Fleet, **IV** 502
National Tea, **II** 631–32
National Technical Laboratories, **14** 52
National Telecommunications of Austin, **8** 311
National Telephone and Telegraph Corporation. *See* British Columbia Telephone Company.
National Telephone Co., **III** 162; **7** 332, 508
National Theatres, Inc., **III** 190
National Trading Manufacturing, Inc., **22** 213
National Transcontinental, **6** 360
National Travelers' Insurance Co., **III** 290
National Trust Life Insurance Co., **III** 218
National Tube Co., **II** 330; **IV** 572; **7** 549
National Union Electric Corporation, **12** 159
National Union Fire Insurance Co. of Pittsburgh, Pa., **III** 195–97
National Union Life and Limb Insurance Co., **III** 290
National Utilities & Industries Corporation, **9** 363
National Westminster Bank PLC, II 237, **333–35**; **IV** 642; **13** 206
National-Ben Franklin Insurance Co., **III** 242
National-Southwire Aluminum Company, **11** 38; **12** 353
Nationalbank, **I** 409
Nationale Bank Vereeniging, **II** 185
Nationale-Nederlanden N.V., III 179, 200–01, **308–11**; **IV** 697
Nationar, **9** 174
NationsBank Corporation, 6 357; **10 425–27**; **11** 126; **13** 147; **18** 516, 518; **23** 455; **25** 91, 186; **26** 348, 453
NationsRent, **28** 388
Nationwide Cellular Service, Inc., **27** 305
Nationwide Credit, **11** 112
Nationwide Group, **25** 155
Nationwide Income Tax Service, **9** 326
Nationwide Logistics Corp., **14** 504
Nationwide Mutual Insurance Co., **26** 488
NATIOVIE, **II** 234
Native Plants, **III** 43
NATM Buying Corporation, **10** 9, 468
Natomas Co., **IV** 410; **6** 353–54; **7** 309; **11** 271
Natref, **IV** 535
Natronag, **IV** 325
Natronzellstoff-und Papierfabriken AG, **IV** 324
NatTeknik, **26** 333
Natudryl Manufacturing Company, **10** 271
Natural Gas Clearinghouse, **11** 355. *See also* NGC Corporation.
Natural Gas Corp., **19** 155
Natural Gas Pipeline Company, **6** 530, 543; **7** 344–45
Natural Gas Service of Arizona, **19** 411
Natural Wonders Inc., 14 342–44
NaturaLife International, **26** 470
The Nature Company, **10** 215–16; **14** 343; **26** 439; **27** 429; **28** 306
The Nature Conservancy, 26 323; **28 305–07**, 422
Nature's Sunshine Products, Inc., 15 317–19; **26** 470; **27** 353
Nature's Way Products Inc., **26** 315
Natuzzi Group. *See* Industrie Natuzzi S.p.A.
NatWest Bank, **22** 52. *See also* National Westminster Bank PLC.
Naugles, **7** 506
Nautica Enterprises, Inc., 16 61; **18 357–60**; **25** 258; **27** 60
Nautilus International, Inc., **III** 315–16; **13** 532; **25** 40; **30** 161
Nautor Ab, **IV** 302
Navaho Freight Line, **16** 41
Navajo Refining Company, **12** 240
Navale, **III** 209
Navarre Corporation, 22 536; **24 348–51**
Naviera Vizcaina, **IV** 528
Navigation Mixte, **III** 348
Navire Cargo Gear, **27** 269
Navistar International Corporation, I 152, 155, **180–82**, 186, 525, 527; **II** 330; **10** 280, **428–30 (upd.)**; **17** 327. *See also* International Harvester Co.
Navy Exchange Service Command, 31 342–45

Naxon Utilities Corp., **19** 359
Naylor, Hutchinson, Vickers & Company. *See* Vickers PLC.
NBC **24** 516–17. *See also* National Broadcasting Company, Inc.
NBC Bankshares, Inc., **21** 524
NBC/Computer Services Corporation, **15** 163
NBD Bancorp, Inc., 9 476; **11 339–41**, 466
NBTY, Inc., 31 346–48
NCA Corporation, **9** 36, 57, 171
NCB. *See* National City Bank of New York.
NCB Brickworks, **III** 501; **7** 207
NCC L.P., **15** 139
NCH Corporation, 8 385–87
Nchanga Consolidated Copper Mines, **IV** 239–40
NCNB Corporation, II 336–37; **12** 519; **26** 453
NCR Corporation, **I** 540–41; **III** 147–52, **150–53**, 157, 165–66; **IV** 298; **V** 263; **6** 250, **264–68 (upd.)**, 281–82; **9** 416; **11** 62, 151, 542; **12** 162, 148, 246, 484; **16** 65; **29** 44; **30 336–41 (upd.)**
NCS. *See* Norstan, Inc.
NCTI (Noise Cancellation Technologies Inc.), **19** 483–84
nCube Corp., **14** 15; **22** 293
ND Marston, **III** 593
NDB. *See* National Discount Brokers Group, Inc.
NDL. *See* Norddeutscher Lloyd.
NEA. *See* Newspaper Enterprise Association.
NEAC Inc., **I** 201–02
Nearly Me, **25** 313
Neatherlin Homes Inc., **22** 547
Nebraska Bell Company, **14** 311
Nebraska Cellular Telephone Company, **14** 312
Nebraska Consolidated Mills Company, **II** 493; **III** 52; **8** 433; **26** 383
Nebraska Furniture Mart, **III** 214–15; **18** 60–61, 63
Nebraska Light & Power Company, **6** 580
Nebraska Power Company, **25** 89
Nebraska Public Power District, 29 351–54
NEBS. *See* New England Business Services, Inc.
NEC Corporation, **I** 455, 520; **II** 40, 42, 45, 56–57, **66–68**, 73, 82, 91, 104, 361; **III** 122–23, 130, 140, 715; **6** 101, 231, 244, 287; **9** 42, 115; **10** 257, 366, 463, 500; **11** 46, 308, 490; **13** 482; **16** 139; **18** 382–83; **19** 391; **21 388–91 (upd.)**; **25** 82, 531
Neches Butane Products Co., **IV** 552
Neckermann Versand AG, **V** 100–02
Nedbank, **IV** 23
Nederland Line. *See* Stoomvaart Maatschappij Nederland.
Nederlander Organization, **24** 439
Nederlands Talen Institut, **13** 544
Nederlandsche Electriciteits Maatschappij. *See* N.E.M.
Nederlandsche Handel Maatschappij, **26** 242
Nederlandsche Heide Maatschappij, **III** 199
Nederlandsche Heidenmaatschappij. *See* Arcadis NV.
Nederlandsche Kunstzijdebariek, **13** 21
Nederlandsche Nieuw Guinea Petroleum Maatschappij, **IV** 491
Nederlandsche Stoomvart Maatschappij Oceaan, **6** 416
Nederlandse Cement Industrie, **III** 701
Nederlandse Credietbank N.V., **II** 248
Nederlandse Dagbladunie NV, **IV** 610
N.V. Nederlandse Gasunie, **I** 326; **V** 627, **658–61**
Nederlandse Handel Maatschappij, **II** 183, 527; **IV** 132–33
Nederlandse Vliegtuigenfabriek, **I** 54
Nedlloyd Group. *See* Koninklijke Nedlloyd N.V.
Nedsual, **IV** 23; **16** 28
Neeco, Inc., **9** 301
Needham Harper Worldwide, **I** 23, 28, 30–33; **13** 203; **14** 159
Needlecraft, **II** 560; **12** 410
Needleworks, Inc., **23** 66
Neenah Paper Co., **III** 40; **16** 303
Neenah Printing, **8** 360
NEES. *See* New England Electric System.
Negromex, **23** 171–72
Neighborhood Restaurants of America, **18** 241
Neilson/Cadbury, **II** 631
Neiman Bearings Co., **13** 78
Neiman-Marcus Co., **I** 246; **II** 478; **V** 10, 31; **12 355–57**; **15** 50, 86, 291; **17** 43; **21** 302; **25** 177–78; **27** 429
Neisler Laboratories, **I** 400
Neisner Brothers, Inc., **9** 20
Nekoosa Edwards Paper Co., **IV** 282; **9** 261
NEL Equity Services Co., **III** 314
Nelio Chemicals, Inc., **IV** 345
Nelson Bros., **14** 236
Nelson Publications, **22** 442
Nemuro Bank, **II** 291
Nenuco, **II** 567
Neodata, **11** 293
Neos, **21** 438
Neoterics Inc., **11** 65
Neozyme I Corp., **13** 240
Nepera, Inc., **I** 682; **16** 69
Neptun Maritime Oyj, **29** 431
Neptune, **22** 63
NER Auction Group, **23** 148
NERCO, Inc., **V** 689, **7 376–79**
Nesbitt Thomson, **II** 211
Nesco Inc., **28** 6, 8
Nescott, Inc., **16** 36
Nesher Israel Cement Enterprises Ltd., **II** 47; **25** 266
Neste Oy, **IV** 435, **469–71**, 519. *See also* Fortum Corporation
Nestlé S.A., **I** 15, 17, 251–52, 369, 605; **II** 379, 456, 478, 486–89, 521, **545–49**, 568–70; **III** 47–48; **6** 16; **7 380–84 (upd.)**; **8** 131, 342–44, 498–500; **10** 47, 324; **11** 15, 205; **12** 480–81; **13** 294; **14** 214; **15** 63; **16** 168; **19** 50–51; **21** 55–56, 219; **22** 78, 80; **23** 219; **24** 388; **25** 21, 85, 366; **28 308–13 (upd.)**
NetCom Systems AB, 26 331–33
Netherland Bank for Russian Trade, **II** 183
Netherlands Fire Insurance Co. of Tiel, **III** 308, 310
Netherlands India Steam Navigation Co., **III** 521
Netherlands Insurance Co., **III** 179, 308–10
Netherlands Trading Co. *See* Nederlandse Handel Maatschappij.
NetHold B.V., **31** 330
NetLabs, **25** 117
NetMarket Company, **16** 146
Netron, **II** 390
Netscape Communications Corporation, 15 320–22; **18** 541, 543; **19** 201; **20** 237; **25** 18, 21; **26** 19; **27** 518
NetStar Inc., **24** 49
Nettai Sangyo, **I** 507
Nettingsdorfer, **19** 227
Nettle Creek Corporation, **19** 304
Nettlefolds Ltd., **III** 493
Netto, **11** 240
NetWest Securities, **25** 450
Network Associates, Inc., **25** 119, **347–49**
Network Communications Associates, Inc., **11** 409
Neue Frankfurter Allgemeine Versicherungs-AG, **III** 184
Neue Holding AG, **III** 377
Neuenberger Versicherungs-Gruppe, **III** 404
Neuralgyline Co., **I** 698
Neuro Navigational Corporation, **21** 47
Neutrogena Corporation, 17 340–44
Nevada Bell Telephone Company, **V** 318–20; **14 345–47**
Nevada Community Bank, **11** 119
Nevada National Bank, **II** 381; **12** 534
Nevada Natural Gas Pipe Line Co., **19** 411
Nevada Power Company, **11 342–44**; **12** 265
Nevada Savings and Loan Association, **19** 412
Nevada Southern Gas Company, **19** 411
Neversink Dyeing Company, **9** 153
New America Publishing Inc., **10** 288
New Asahi Co., **I** 221
New Balance Athletic Shoe, Inc., **17** 245; **25 350–52**
New Bedford Gas & Edison Light Co., **14** 124–25
New Broken Hill Consolidated, **IV** 58–61
New Century Network, **13** 180; **19** 204, 285
New City Releasing, Inc., **25** 269
New Consolidated Canadian Exploration Co., **IV** 96
New Consolidated Gold Fields, **IV** 21, 95–96
New CORT Holdings Corporation. *See* CORT Business Services Corporation.
New Daido Steel Co., Ltd., **IV** 62–63
New Departure, **9** 17
New Departure Hyatt, **III** 590
New England Audio Company, Inc. *See* Tweeter Home Entertainment Group, Inc.
New England Business Services, Inc., 18 361–64
New England Confectionery Co., 15 323–25
New England CRInc, **8** 562
New England Electric System, V 662–64
New England Gas & Electric Association, **14** 124–25
New England Glass Co., **III** 640
New England Life Insurance Co., **III** 261
New England Merchants National Bank, **II** 213–14; **III** 313
New England Mutual Life Insurance Co., III 312–14

New England National Bank of Boston, **II** 213
New England Network, Inc., **12** 31
New England Nuclear Corporation, **I** 329; **8** 152
New England Power Association, **V** 662
New England Trust Co., **II** 213
New Fire Office, **III** 371
New Found Industries, Inc., **9** 465
New Galveston Company, Inc., **25** 116
New Guinea Goldfields, **IV** 95
New Halwyn China Clays, **III** 690
New Hampshire Gas & Electric Co., **14** 124
New Hampshire Insurance Co., **III** 196–97
New Hampshire Oak, **III** 512
New Hampton, Inc., **27** 429
New Haven District Telephone Company. *See* Southern New England Telecommunications Corporation.
New Haven Electric Co., **21** 512
New Hokkai Hotel Co., Ltd., **IV** 327
New Holland N.V., **22 379–81**
New Horizon Manufactured Homes, Ltd., **17** 83
New Hotel Showboat, Inc. *See* Showboat, Inc.
New Ireland, **III** 393
New Jersey Bell, **9** 321
New Jersey Hot Water Heating Company, **6** 449
New Jersey Shale, **14** 250
New Jersey Tobacco Co., **15** 138
New Jersey Zinc, **I** 451
New London City National Bank, **13** 467
New London Ship & Engine, **I** 57
New Mather Metals, **III** 582
New Mitsui Bussan, **I** 507; **III** 296
New Nippon Electric Co., **II** 67
New Orleans Canal and Banking Company, **11** 105
New Orleans Refining Co., **IV** 540
New Plan Realty Trust, **11 345–47**
New Process Company, **25** 76–77
New Process Cork Company Inc., **I** 601; **13** 188
New South Wales Health System, **16** 94
New Street Capital Inc., **8 388–90 (upd.)**. *See also* Drexel Burnham Lambert Incorporated.
New Sulzer Diesel, **III** 633
New Toyo Group, **19** 227
New Trading Company. *See* SBC Warburg.
New United Motor Manufacturing Inc., **I** 205
New UPI Inc., **25** 507
New Valley Corporation, **17 345–47**
New Vanden Borre, **24** 266–70
New World Communications Group, **22** 442; **28** 248
New World Development Company Ltd., **IV 717–19**; **8** 500
New World Entertainment, **17** 149
New World Hotel (Holdings) Ltd., **IV** 717; **13** 66
New York Air, **I** 90, 103, 118, 129; **6** 129
New York Airways, **I** 123–24
New York and Richmond Gas Company, **6** 456
New York and Suburban Savings and Loan Association, **10** 91
New York Biscuit Co., **II** 542
New York Central Railroad Company, **II** 329, 369; **IV** 181; **9** 228; **10** 43–44, 71–73; **17** 496
New York Chemical Manufacturing Co., **II** 250
New York City Transit Authority, **8** 75
New York Condensed Milk Co., **II** 470
New York Electric Corporation. *See* New York State Electric and Gas.
New York Evening Enquirer, **10** 287
New York Fabrics and Crafts, **16** 197
New York Gas Light Company. *See* Consolidated Edison Company of New York.
New York Glucose Co., **II** 496
New York Guaranty and Indemnity Co., **II** 331
New York Harlem Railroad Co., **II** 250
New York Improved Patents Corp., **I** 601; **13** 188
New York, Lake Erie & Western Railroad, **II** 395; **10** 59
New York Life Insurance Company, **II** 217–18, 330; **III** 291, 305, **315–17**, 332; **10** 382
New York Magazine Co., **IV** 651; **7** 390; **12** 359
New York Manufacturing Co., **II** 312
New York Marine Underwriters, **III** 220
New York Quinine and Chemical Works, **I** 496
New York Quotation Company, **9** 370
New York, Rio and Buenos Aires Airlines, **I** 115
New York State Board of Tourism, **6** 51
New York State Electric and Gas Corporation, **6 534–36**
New York Stock Exchange, Inc., **9 369–72**; **10** 416–17
New York Telephone Co., **9** 321
The New York Times Company, **III** 40; **IV 647–49**; **6** 13; **15** 54; **16** 302; **19 283–85 (upd.)**; **23** 158
New York Trust Co., **I** 378; **II** 251
New York, West Shore and Buffalo Railroad, **II** 329
New York Zoological Society. *See* Wildlife Conservation Society.
New York's Bankers Trust Co., **12** 107
New York-Newport Air Service Co., **I** 61
New Zealand Aluminum Smelters, **IV** 59
New Zealand Co., **II** 187
New Zealand Countrywide Banking Corporation, **10** 336
New Zealand Forest Products, **IV** 249–50
New Zealand Press Assoc., **IV** 669
New Zealand Sugar Co., **III** 686
New Zealand Wire Ltd., **IV** 279; **19** 154
Newark Electronics Co., **9** 420
Newco Waste Systems, **V** 750
Newcrest Mining Ltd., **IV** 47; **22** 107
Newell and Harrison Company. *See* Supervalu Inc.
Newell Co., **9 373–76**; **12** 216; **13** 40–41; **22** 35; **25** 22
Newey and Eyre, **I** 429
Newfoundland Brewery, **26** 304
Newfoundland Energy, Ltd., **17** 121
Newfoundland Light & Power Co. *See* Fortis, Inc.
Newfoundland Processing Ltd. *See* Newfoundland Energy, Ltd.
Newgateway PLC, **II** 629
Newhall Land and Farming Company, **14 348–50**
Newhouse Broadcasting, **6** 33
Newmark & Lewis Inc., **23** 373
Newmont Mining Corporation, **III** 248; **IV** 17, 20, 33, 171, 576; **7** 287–89, **385–88**; **12** 244; **16** 25; **23** 40
Newnes, **17** 397
Newport News Shipbuilding and Dry Dock Co., **I** 58, 527; **13 372–75**; **27** 36
News & Observer Publishing Company, **23** 343
News America Publishing Inc., **12 358–60**; **27** 42
News and Westminster Ltd., **IV** 685
News Corporation Limited, **II** 169; **IV 650–53**; **7 389–93 (upd.)**; **8** 551; **9** 429; **12** 358–60; **17** 398; **18** 211, 213, 254; **22** 194, 441; **23** 121; **24** 224; **25** 490; **26** 32; **27** 305, 473
News International Corp., **20** 79
Newsfoto Publishing Company, **12** 472
Newspaper Co-op Couponing, **8** 551
Newspaper Enterprise Association, **7** 157–58
Newspaper Proprietors' Assoc., **IV** 669
Newspaper Supply Co., **IV** 607
Newsweek, Inc., **IV** 688
Newth-Morris Box Co. *See* Rock-Tenn Company.
Newtherm Oil Burners, Ltd., **13** 286
Newton Yarn Mills, **19** 305
Newtown Gas Co., **6** 455
Nexar Technologies, Inc., **22** 409
NEXCOM. *See* Navy Exchange Service Command.
Next Inc., **III** 116, 121; **6** 219
NeXT Incorporated, **18** 93
Next plc, **6** 25; **29 355–57**
Nextel Communications, Inc., **10 431–33**; **21** 239; **26** 389; **27 341–45 (upd.)**
Neyveli Lignite Corp. Ltd., **IV** 49
NFC plc, **6 412–14**; **14** 547
NFL Properties, Inc., **22** 223
NFO Worldwide, Inc., **24 352–55**
NGC Corporation, **18 365–67**
NGI International Precious Metals, Ltd., **24** 335
NHK. *See* Japan Broadcasting Corporation.
NHK Spring Co., Ltd., **III 580–82**
NI Industries, **20** 362
Niagara Corporation, **28 314–16**
Niagara Fire Insurance Co., **III** 241–42
Niagara First Savings and Loan Association, **10** 91
Niagara Insurance Co. (Bermuda) Ltd., **III** 242
Niagara Mohawk Power Corporation, **V 665–67**; **6** 535; **25** 130
Niagara of Wisconsin, **26** 362–63
Niagara Silver Co., **IV** 644
Niagara Sprayer and Chemical Co., **I** 442
NIBRASCO, **IV** 55
Nicaro Nickel Co., **IV** 82, 111; **7** 186
Nice Day, Inc., **II** 539
Nice Systems, **11** 520
NiceCom Ltd., **11** 520
Nichi-Doku Shashinki Shoten, **III** 574
Nichia Steel, **IV** 159
Nichibo, **V** 387
Nichii Co., Ltd., **V 154–55**; **15** 470
Nichimen Corporation, **II** 442; **IV 150–52**, 154; **10** 439; **24 356–59 (upd.)**
Nichimo Sekiyu Co. Ltd., **IV** 555; **16** 490

Nicholas Kiwi Ltd., **II** 572; **15** 436
Nicholas Turkey Breeding Farms, **13** 103
Nicholas Ungar, **V** 156
Nichols & Company, **8** 561
Nichols Copper Co., **IV** 164, 177
Nichols Research Corporation, 18 368–70
Nichols-Homeshield, **22** 14
Nicholson File Co., **II** 16
Nicholson Graham & Jones, **28** 141
Le Nickel. *See* Société Le Nickel.
Nickelodeon, **25** 381
Nicolai Pavdinsky Co., **IV** 118
Nicolet Instrument Company, **11** 513
NICOR Inc., 6 529–31
Niederbayerische Celluloswerke, **IV** 324
Niederrheinische Hütte AG, **IV** 222
Niehler Maschinenfabrick, **III** 602
Nielsen, **10** 358
Nielsen & Petersen, **III** 417
Nielsen Marketing Research. *See* A.C. Nielsen Company.
Niemann Chemie, **8** 464
Niese & Coast Products Co., **II** 681
Niesmann & Bischoff, **22** 207
Nieuw Rotterdam, **27** 54
Nieuwe Eerste Nederlandsche, **III** 177–79
Nieuwe HAV-Bank of Schiedam, **III** 200
Nigeria Airways, **I** 107
Nigerian National Petroleum Corporation, IV 472–74
Nigerian Shipping Operations, **27** 473
Nihol Repol Corp., **III** 757
Nihon Denko, **II** 118
Nihon Keizai Shimbun, Inc., IV 654–56
Nihon Kensetsu Sangyo Ltd., **I** 520
Nihon Kohden Corporation, **13** 328
Nihon Lumber Land Co., **III** 758
Nihon Sangyo Co., **I** 183; **II** 118
Nihon Sugar, **I** 511
Nihon Synopsis, **11** 491
Nihon Teppan, **IV** 159
Nihon Timken K.K., **8** 530
Nihon Yusen Kaisha, **I** 503, 506; **III** 577, 712
Nihron Yupro Corp., **III** 756
NII. *See* National Intergroup, Inc.
Niitsu Oil, **IV** 542
Nike, Inc., V 372–74, 376; **8** 303–04, **391–94 (upd.)**; **9** 134–35, 437; **10** 525; **11** 50, 349; **13** 513; **14** 8; **15** 397; **16** 79, 81; **17** 244–45, 260–61; **18** 264, 266–67, 392; **22** 173; **25** 352; **27** 20; **29** 187–88; **31** 413–14
Nikka Oil Co., **IV** 150; **24** 357
Nikka Whisky Distilling Co., **I** 220
Nikkei. *See also* Nihon Keizai Shimbun, Inc.
Nikkei Aluminium Co., **IV** 153–55
Nikkei Shimbun Toei, **9** 29
Nikken Stainless Fittings Co., Ltd., **IV** 160
Nikko Copper Electrolyzing Refinery, **III** 490
Nikko International Hotels, **I** 106
Nikko Kido Company, **6** 431
Nikko Petrochemical Co. Ltd., **IV** 476
The Nikko Securities Company Limited, II 300, 323, 383, **433–35**; **9 377–79 (upd.)**; **12** 536
Nikko Trading Co., **I** 106
Nikolaiev, **19** 49, 51
Nikon Corporation, III 120–21, 575, **583–85**; **9** 251; **12** 340; **18** 93, 186, 340, 342
Nile Faucet Corp., **III** 569; **20** 360
Nillmij, **III** 177–79
Nilpeter, **26** 540, 542
Nimas Corp., **III** 570; **20** 362
Nimbus CD International, Inc., 20 386–90
9 Telecom, **24** 79
Nine West Group Inc., 11 348–49; **14** 441; **23** 330
Nineteen Hundred Washer Co., **III** 653; **12** 548
99¢ Only Stores, 25 353–55
Nintendo Co., Ltd., III 586–88; **7 394–96 (upd.)**; **10** 124–25, 284–86, 483–84; **13** 403; **15** 539; **16** 168, 331; **18** 520; **23** 26; **28 317–21 (upd.)**; **31** 237
Nintendo of America, **24** 4
NIOC. *See* National Iranian Oil Company.
Nippon ARC Co., **III** 715
Nippon Breweries Ltd. *See* Sapporo Breweries Ltd.
Nippon Broilers Co., **II** 550
Nippon Cable Company, **15** 235
Nippon Cargo Airlines, **6** 71
Nippon Chemical Industries, **I** 363
Nippon Credit Bank, II 310, **338–39**
Nippon Educational Television (NET). *See* Asahi National Broadcasting Company, Ltd.
Nippon Electric Company, Limited. *See* NEC Corporation.
Nippon Express Co., Ltd., II 273; **V 477–80**
Nippon Fruehauf Co., **IV** 154
Nippon Fukokin Kinyu Koku, **II** 300
Nippon Funtai Kogyo Co., **III** 714
Nippon Gakki Co., Ltd., **III** 656–58; **16** 554, 557
Nippon Ginko, **III** 408
Nippon Gyomo Sengu Co. Ltd., **IV** 555
Nippon Hatsujo Kabushikikaisha. *See* NHK Spring Co., Ltd.
Nippon Helicopter & Aeroplane Transport Co., Ltd., **6** 70
Nippon Hoso Kyokai. *See* Japan Broadcasting Corporation.
Nippon Idou Tsushin, **7** 119–20
Nippon International Container Services, **8** 278
Nippon Interrent, **10** 419–20
Nippon K.K. *See* Nippon Kokan K.K.
Nippon Kairiku Insurance Co., **III** 384
Nippon Kakoh Seishi, **IV** 293
Nippon Kogaku K.K., **III** 583–84
Nippon Kogyo Co. Ltd. *See* Nippon Mining Co. Ltd.
Nippon Kokan K.K., **IV** 161–63, 184, 212; **8** 449; **12** 354
Nippon Life Insurance Company, II 374, 451; **III** 273, 288, **318–20**; **IV** 727; **9** 469
Nippon Light Metal Company, Ltd., IV 153–55
Nippon Machinery Trading, **I** 507
Nippon Meat Packers, Inc., II 550–51
Nippon Menka Kaisha. *See* Nichimen Corporation.
Nippon Merck-Banyu, **I** 651; **11** 290
Nippon Mining Co., Ltd., III 759; **IV 475–77**; **14** 207
Nippon Motorola Manufacturing Co., **II** 62
Nippon New Zealand Trading Co. Ltd., **IV** 327
Nippon Oil Company, Limited, IV 434, 475–76, **478–79**, 554; **19** 74
Nippon Onkyo, **II** 118
Nippon Paint Co., Ltd, **11** 252
Nippon Pelnox Corp., **III** 715
Nippon Phonogram, **23** 390
Nippon Polaroid Kabushiki Kaisha, **III** 608; **7** 437; **18** 570
Nippon Pulp Industries, **IV** 321
Nippon Rayon, **V** 387
Nippon Sangyo Co., Ltd., **IV** 475
Nippon Sanso Corp., **I** 359; **16** 486, 488
Nippon Seiko K.K., III 589–90, 595
Nippon Sekiyu Co. *See* Nippon Oil Company, Limited.
Nippon Sheet Glass Company, Limited, III 714–16
Nippon Shinpan Company, Ltd., II 436–37, 442; **8** 118
Nippon Silica Kogyo Co., **III** 715
Nippon Soda, **II** 301
Nippon Soken, **III** 592
Nippon Steel Chemical Co., **10** 439
Nippon Steel Corporation, I 466, 493–94, 509; **II** 300, 391; **IV** 116, 130, **156–58**, 184, 212, 228, 298; **6** 274; **14** 369; **17 348–51 (upd.)**, 556; **19** 219; **24** 324–25, 370
Nippon Suisan Kaisha, Limited, II 552–53
Nippon Tar, **I** 363
Nippon Telegraph and Telephone Corporation, II 51, 62; **III** 139–40; **V 305–07**; **7** 118–20; **10** 119; **13** 482; **16** 224; **21** 330; **25** 301; **27** 327, 365
Nippon Television, **7** 249; **9** 29
Nippon Tire Co., Ltd. *See* Bridgestone Corporation.
Nippon Trust Bank Ltd., **II** 405; **15** 42
Nippon Typewriter, **II** 459
Nippon Victor (Europe) GmbH, **II** 119
Nippon Wiper Blade Co., Ltd., **III** 592
Nippon Yusen Kabushiki Kaisha, IV 713; **V 481–83**; **6** 398
Nippon Yusoki Company, Ltd., **13** 501
Nippon-Fisher, **13** 225
Nippondenso Co., Ltd., III 591–94, 637–38
NIPSCO Industries, Inc., 6 532–33
Nishi Taiyo Gyogyo Tosei K.K., **II** 578
Nishikawaya Co., Ltd., **V** 209
Nishimbo Industries Inc., **IV** 442
Nishizono Ironworks, **III** 595
Nissan Construction, **V** 154
Nissan Motor Acceptance Corporation, **22** 207
Nissan Motor Company, Ltd., I 9–10, **183–84**, 207, 494; **II** 118, 292–93, 391; **III** 485, 517, 536, 579, 591, 742, 750; **IV** 63; **7** 111, 120, 219; **9** 243, 340–42; **10** 353; **11** 50–51, **350–52 (upd.)**; **16** 167; **17** 556; **23** 338–40, 289; **24** 324; **27** 203
Nissan Trading Company, Ltd., **13** 533
Nisshin Chemical Industries, **I** 397
Nisshin Chemicals Co., **II** 554
Nisshin Flour Milling Company, Ltd., II 554
Nisshin Pharaceutical Co., **II** 554
Nisshin Steel Co., Ltd., I 432; **IV** 130, **159–60**; **7** 588
Nissho Iwai K.K., I 432, **509–11**; **IV** 160, 383; **V** 373; **6** 386; **8** 75, 392; **15** 373; **25** 449; **27** 107

Nissho Kosan Co., **III** 715
Nissui. *See* Nippon Suisan Kaisha.
Nitratos de Portugal, **IV** 505
Nitroglycerin AB, **13** 22
Nitroglycerin Ltd., **9** 380
Nittetsu Curtainwall Corp., **III** 758
Nittetsu Sash Sales Corp., **III** 758
Nitto Warehousing Co., **I** 507
Nittoku Metal Industries, Ltd., **III** 635
Nittsu. *See* Nippon Express Co., Ltd.
Niugini Mining Ltd., **23** 42
Nixdorf Computer AG, **I** 193; **II** 279; **III** 109, **154–55**; **12** 162; **14** 13, 169; **26** 497
Nixdorf-Krein Industries Inc. *See* Laclede Steel Company.
NKK Corporation, **IV** 74, **161–63**, 212–13; **V** 152; **24** 144; **28 322–26 (upd.)**
NL Industries, Inc., **III** 681; **10 434–36**; **19** 466–68
NLM City-Hopper, **I** 109
NLM Dutch Airlines, **I** 108
NLT Corp., **II** 122; **III** 194; **10** 66; **12** 546
NM Acquisition Corp., **27** 346
NMC Laboratories Inc., **12** 4
NMH Stahlwerke GmbH, **IV** 128
NMT. *See* Nordic Mobile Telephone.
No-Leak-O Piston Ring Company, **10** 492
No-Sag Spring Co., **16** 321
Noah's New York Bagels, **13** 494. *See also* Einstein/Noah Bagel Corporation.
Nobel Drilling Corporation, **26** 243
Nobel Industries AB, **I** 351; **9 380–82**; **16** 69. *See also* Akzo Nobel N.V.
Nobel-Bozel, **I** 669
Nobel-Hoechst Chimie, **I** 669
Noble Affiliates, Inc., **11 353–55**; **18** 366
Noble Broadcast Group, Inc., **23** 293
Noble Roman's Inc., **14 351–53**
Nobles Industries, **13** 501
Noblesville Telephone Company, **14** 258
Noblitt-Sparks Industries, Inc., **8** 37–38
Nocona Belt Company, **31** 435–36
Nocona Boot Co. *See* Justin Industries, Inc.
Noel Group, Inc., **24** 286–88
Noell, **IV** 201
Oy Nokia Ab, **19** 226
Nokia Corporation, **II 69–71**; **IV** 296; **6** 242; **15** 125; **17** 33, **352–54 (upd.)**; **18** 74, 76; **20** 439
Nolte Mastenfabriek B.V., **19** 472
Noma Industries, **11** 526
Nomai Inc., **18** 510
Nomura Securities Company, Limited, **II** 276, 326, 434, **438–41**; **9** 377, **383–86 (upd.)**
Nomura Toys Ltd., **16** 267
Non-Fiction Book Club, **13** 105
Non-Stop Fashions, Inc., **8** 323
Nonpareil Refining Co., **IV** 488
Noodle Kidoodle, **16 388–91**
Noordwinning Group, **IV** 134
NOP Research Group, **28** 501, 504
Nopco Chemical Co., **IV** 409; **7** 308
Nopri, **V** 63–65
Nor-Am Agricultural Products, **I** 682
Nor-Cal Engineering Co. GmbH, **18** 162
Nora Industrier A/S, **18** 395
NORAND, **9** 411
Noranda Inc., **IV 164–66**; **7 397–99 (upd.)**; **9** 282; **26** 363
Norandex, **16** 204
Norbro Corporation. *See* Stuart Entertainment Inc.
Norcast Manufacturing Ltd., **IV** 165
Norcen Energy Resources, Ltd., **8** 347
Norcliff Thayer, **III** 66
Norco Plastics, **8** 553
Norcon, Inc., **7** 558–59
Nord-Aviation, **I** 45, 74, 82, 195; **7** 10
Nordarmatur, **I** 198
Nordbanken, **9** 382
Norddeutsche Affinerie, **IV** 141
Norddeutsche Bank A.G., **II** 279
Norddeutscher-Lloyd, **I** 542; **6** 397–98
Nordfinanzbank, **II** 366
Nordic Bank Ltd., **II** 366
Nordic Joint Stock Bank, **II** 302
Nordic Mobile Telephone, **II** 70
Nordica, **10** 151; **15** 396–97
NordicTrack, **10** 215–17; **22 382–84**
Nordland Papier GmbH, **IV** 300, 302
Nordson Corporation, **11 356–58**
Nordstahl AG, **IV** 201
Nordstjernan, **I** 553–54
Nordstrom, Inc., **V 156–58**; **11** 349; **13** 494; **14** 376; **17** 313; **18 371–74 (upd.)**; **21** 302; **22** 173
Nordwestdeutsche Kraftwerke AG, **III** 466; **V** 698–700
Norelco, **17** 110
Norelco Consumer Products Co., **12** 439; **26 334–36**
Norelec, **27** 138
Norex Laboratories, **I** 699
Norex Leasing, Inc., **16** 397
Norfolk Carolina Telephone Company, **10** 202
Norfolk Southern Corporation, **V 484–86**; **6** 436, 487; **12** 278; **22** 167; **29 358–61 (upd.)**
Norfolk Steel, **13** 97
Norge Co., **III** 439–40; **18** 173–74
Norinchukin Bank, **II 340–41**
NORIS Bank GmbH, **V** 166
Norlin, **16** 238–39
Norma Cie., **III** 622
Norman BV, **9** 93
Norman J. Hurll Group, **III** 673
Normandy Mining Ltd., **23** 42
Normark Corporation. *See* Rapala-Normark Group, Ltd.
Normond/CMS, **7** 117
Norrell Corporation, **I** 696; **6** 46; **23** 431; **25 356–59**
Norris Cylinder Company, **11** 535
Norris Grain Co., **14** 537
Norsk Hydro A.S., **IV** 405–06, 525; **10 437–40**; **14** 494; **27** 317
Norstan, Inc., **16 392–94**
Norstar Bancorp, **9** 229
Nortek Inc., **I** 482; **14** 482; **22** 4; **26** 101
Nortex International, **7** 96; **19** 338
North & South Wales Bank, **II** 318; **17** 323
North Advertising, Inc., **6** 27
North African Petroleum Ltd., **IV** 455
North American Aviation, **I** 48, 71, 78, 81, 101; **7** 520; **9** 16; **10** 163; **11** 278, 427
North American Bancorp, **II** 192
North American Carbon, **19** 499
North American Cellular Network, **9** 322
North American Coal Corporation, **7** 369–71
North American Company, **6** 443, 552–53, 601–02
North American Dräger, **13** 328
North American Insurance Co., **II** 181
North American InTeleCom, Inc., **IV** 411
North American Life and Casualty Co., **III** 185, 306
North American Light & Power Company, **V** 609; **6** 504–05; **12** 541
North American Managers, Inc., **III** 196
North American Mogul Products Co. *See* Mogul Corp.
North American Philips Corporation, **II** 79–80; **19** 393; **21** 520
North American Printed Circuit Corp., **III** 643
North American Printing Ink Company, **13** 228
North American Reinsurance Corp., **III** 377
North American Rockwell Corp., **10** 173
North American Systems, **14** 230
North American Training Corporation. *See* Rollerblade, Inc.
North American Van Lines, **I** 278; **14** 37
North American Watch Company. *See* Movado Group, Inc.
North Atlantic Energy Corporation, **21** 411
North Atlantic Packing, **13** 243
North British Insurance Co., **III** 234–35
North British Rubber Company, **20** 258
North Broken Hill Peko, **IV** 61
North Carolina Motor Speedway, Inc., **19** 294
North Carolina National Bank Corporation, **II** 336; **10** 425–27; **18** 518
North Carolina Natural Gas Corporation, **6** 578
North Carolina Shipbuilding Co., **13** 373
North Central Airlines, **I** 132
North Central Finance, **II** 333
North Central Financial Corp., **9** 475
North Central Utilities, Inc., **18** 405
North Cornwall China Clay Co., **III** 690
North Eastern Bricks, **14** 249
North Eastern Coalfields Ltd., **IV** 48
The North Face, Inc., **8** 169; **18 375–77**; **25** 206
North Goonbarrow, **III** 690
North Holland Publishing Co., **IV** 610
North New York Savings Bank, **10** 91
North of Scotland Bank, **II** 318; **17** 324
North of Scotland Hydro-Electric Board, **19** 389
North Pacific Paper Corp., **IV** 298
North Pacific Railroad, **II** 330
North Sea Ferries, **26** 241, 243
North Sea Oil and Gas, **10** 337
North Sea Sun Oil Co. Ltd., **IV** 550
North Shore Gas Company, **6** 543–44
North Shore Land Co., **17** 357
North Shore Medical Centre Pty, Ltd., **IV** 708
North Star Egg Case Company, **12** 376
North Star Marketing Cooperative, **7** 338
North Star Mill, **12** 376
North Star Steel Company, **13** 138; **18 378–81**; **19** 380
North Star Universal, Inc., **25** 331, 333
North Supply, **27** 364
The North West Company, Inc., **12 361–63**; **25** 219–20
North West Water Group plc, **11 359–62**
North-West Telecommunications, **6** 327
Northamptonshire Union Bank, **II** 333
Northbrook Corporation, **24** 32

Northbrook Holdings, Inc., **22** 495
Northcliffe Newspapers, **IV** 685; **19** 118
Northeast Airlines Inc., **I** 99–100; **6** 81
Northeast Federal Corp., **13** 468
Northeast Petroleum Industries, Inc., **11** 194; **14** 461
Northeast Savings Bank, **12** 31; **13** 467–68
Northeast Utilities, **V 668–69**; **13** 182–84; **21** 408, 411
Northeastern Bancorp of Scranton, **II** 342
Northeastern New York Medical Service, Inc., **III** 246
Northern Aluminum Co. Ltd., **IV** 9–10
Northern and Employers Assurance, **III** 235
Northern Arizona Light & Power Co., **6** 545
Northern Border Pipeline Co., **V** 609–10
Northern California Savings, **10** 340
Northern Crown Bank, **II** 344
Northern Dairies, **10** 441
Northern Development Co., **IV** 282
Northern Drug Company, **14** 147
Northern Electric Company. *See* Northern Telecom Limited.
Northern Energy Resources Company. *See* NERCO, Inc.
Northern Engineering Industries Plc, **21** 436
Northern Fibre Products Co., **I** 202
Northern Foods PLC, **I** 248; **II** 587; **10 441–43**
Northern Illinois Gas Co., **6** 529–31
Northern Indiana Power Company, **6** 556
Northern Indiana Public Service Company, **6** 532–33
Northern Joint Stock Bank, **II** 303
Northern Light Electric Company, **18** 402–03
Northern National Bank, **14** 90
Northern Natural Gas Co., **V** 609–10
Northern Pacific Corp., **15** 274
Northern Pacific Railroad, **II** 278, 329; **III** 228, 282; **14** 168; **26** 451
Northern Paper, **I** 614
Northern Pipeline Construction Co., **19** 410, 412
Northern Star Co., **25** 332
Northern States Life Insurance Co., **III** 275
Northern States Power Company, **V 670–72**; **18** 404; **20 391–95 (upd.)**
Northern Stores, Inc., **12** 362
Northern Sugar Company, **11** 13
Northern Telecom Limited, **II** 70; **III** 143, 164; **V** 271; **V 308–10**; **6** 242, 307, 310; **9** 479; **10** 19, 432; **11** 69; **12** 162; **14** 259; **16** 392, 468; **17** 353; **18** 111; **20** 439; **22** 51; **25** 34; **27** 342
Northern Trust Company, **III** 518; **9 387–89**; **22** 280
Northfield Metal Products, **11** 256
Northgate Computer Corp., **16** 196
Northland. *See* Scott Fetzer Company.
Northland Publishing, **19** 231
NorthPrint International, **22** 356
Northrop Corporation, **I** 47, 49, 55, 59, **76–77**, 80, 84, 197, 525; **III** 84; **9** 416, 418; **10** 162; **11** 164, 166, 266, 269, **363–65 (upd.)**; **25** 316
Northrup King Co., **I** 672
NorthStar Computers, **10** 313
Northwest Airlines Inc., **I** 42, 64, 91, 97, 100, 104, **112–14**, 125, 127; **6** 66, 74, 82 **103–05 (upd.)**, 123; **9** 273; **11** 266, 315; **12** 191, 487; **21** 141, 143; **22** 252; **26 337–40 (upd.)**, 441; **27** 20; **28** 226, 265–66; **30** 447; **31** 419–20. *See also* Mesaba Holdings, Inc.
Northwest Benefit Assoc., **III** 228
Northwest Engineering, **21** 502
Northwest Engineering Co. *See* Terex Corporation.
Northwest Industries, **I** 342; **II** 468 **8** 367; **25** 165–66. *See also* Chicago and North Western Holdings Corporation.
Northwest Instruments, **8** 519
Northwest Linen Co., **16** 228
Northwest Outdoor, **27** 280
Northwest Paper Company, **8** 430
Northwest Steel Rolling Mills Inc., **13** 97
Northwest Telecommunications Inc., **6** 598
Northwestern Bell Telephone Co., **V** 341; **25** 495
Northwestern Benevolent Society, **III** 228
Northwestern Engraving, **12** 25
Northwestern Expanded Metal Co., **III** 763
Northwestern Financial Corporation, **11** 29
Northwestern Industries, **III** 263
Northwestern Manufacturing Company, **8** 133
Northwestern Mutual Life Insurance Company, **III 321–24**, 352; **IV** 333
Northwestern National Bank, **16** 71
Northwestern National Insurance Co., **IV** 29
Northwestern National Life Insurance Co., **14** 233
Northwestern Public Service Company, **6** 524
Northwestern States Portland Cement Co., **III** 702
Northwestern Telephone Systems, **6** 325, 328
Norton Company, **III** 678; **8 395–97**; **16** 122; **22** 68; **26** 70
Norton Healthcare Ltd., **11** 208
Norton McNaughton, Inc., **25** 245; **27 346–49**
Norton Opax PLC, **IV** 259
Norton Professional Books. *See* W.W. Norton & Company, Inc.
Norton Simon Industries, **I** 446; **IV** 672; **6** 356; **19** 404; **22** 513
Norwales Development Ltd., **11** 239
Norwalk Truck Lines, **14** 567
NORWEB plc, **13** 458; **24** 270
Norwegian Assurance, **III** 258
Norwegian Caribbean Line, **27** 90
Norwegian Globe, **III** 258
Norwegian Petroleum Consultants, **III** 499
Norweld Holding A.A., **13** 316
Norwest Bank, **19** 412
Norwest Corp., **16** 135
Norwest Mortgage Inc., **11** 29
Norwest Publishing, **IV** 661
Norwich Pharmaceuticals, **I** 370–71; **9** 358
Norwich Union Fire Insurance Society, Ltd., **III** 242, 273, 404; **IV** 705
Norwich Winterthur Group, **III** 404
Norwich-Eaton Pharmaceuticals, **III** 53; **8** 434; **26** 383
Norwood Company, **13** 168
Norwood Promotional Products, Inc., **26 341–43**
Nostell Brick & Tile, **14** 249
Notre Capital Ventures II, L.P., **24** 117
Nottingham Manufacturing Co., **V** 357
Nouvelle Compagnie Havraise Pénninsulaire, **27** 514
Nouvelles Galeries Réunies, **10** 205; **19** 308; **27** 95
Nouvelles Messageries de la Presse Parisienne, **IV** 618
Nova Corporation, **18** 365–67; **24** 395
Nova Corporation of Alberta, **V 673–75**; **12** 364–66
Nova Information Systems, **24** 393
Nova Pharmaceuticals, **14** 46
Nova Scotia Steel Company, **19** 186
NovaCare, Inc., **11 366–68**; **14** 233
Novacor Chemicals Ltd., **12 364–66**
Novagas Clearinghouse Ltd., **18** 367
Novalta Resources Inc., **11** 441
Novartis, **18** 51
Novell, Inc., **6** 255–56, 260, **269–71**; **9** 170–71; **10** 232, 363, 473–74, 558, 565; **11** 59, 519–20; **12** 335; **13** 482; **15** 131, 133, 373, 492; **16** 392, 394; **20** 237; **21** 133–34; **23 359–62 (upd.)**; **25** 50–51, 117, 300, 499
Novello and Co., **II** 139; **24** 193
Novellus Systems, Inc., **18 382–85**
Novo Industri A/S, **I 658–60**, 697
Novotel. *See* Accor SA.
NOVUM. *See* Industrie Natuzzi S.p.A.
Nowell Wholesale Grocery Co., **II** 681
Nowsco Well Services Ltd., **25** 73
Nox Ltd., **I** 588
Noxell Corporation, **III** 53; **8** 434; **26** 384
NPD Group, **13** 4
NPD Trading (USA), Inc., **13** 367
NPS Waste Technologies, **13** 366
NRG Energy, Inc., **11** 401
NS. *See* Norfolk Southern Corporation.
NS Group, **31** 287
NS Petites Inc., **8** 323
NSG Information System Co., **III** 715
NSK. *See* Nippon Seiko K.K.
NSK-Warner, **14** 64
NSMO. *See* Nederlandsche Stoomvart Maatschappij Oceaan.
NSN Network Services, **23** 292, 294
NSP. *See* Northern States Power Company.
NSU Werke, **10** 261
NTC Publishing Group, **22** 519, 522
NTCL. *See* Northern Telecom Limited.
NTN Corporation, **III 595–96**, 623; **28** 241
NTRON, **11** 486
NTT. *See* Nippon Telegraph and Telephone Corp.
NTTPC. *See* Nippon Telegraph and Telephone Public Corporation.
NU. *See* Northeast Utilities.
Nu Skin Enterprises, Inc., **27 350–53**; **31** 327
Nu-Era Gear, **14** 64
Nu-kote Holding, Inc., **18 386–89**
Nuclear Electric, **6** 453; **11** 399–401; **12** 349; **13** 484
Nuclear Power International, **19** 166
Nucoa Butter Co., **II** 497
Nucor Corporation, **7 400–02**; **13** 143, 423; **14** 156; **18** 378–80; **19** 380; **21 392–95 (upd.)**; **26** 407
Nucorp Energy, **II** 262, 620
NUG Optimus Lebensmittel-Einzelhandelgesellschaft mbH, **V** 74
Nugget Polish Co. Ltd., **II** 566
NUMAR Corporation, **25** 192
Numerax, Inc., **IV** 637

Nuovo Pignone, **IV** 420–22
NUR Touristic GmbH, **V** 100–02
Nurad, **III** 468
Nurotoco Inc. *See* Roto-Rooter Service Company.
Nursefinders, **6** 10
Nutmeg Industries, Inc., **17** 513
NutraSweet Company, **II** 463, 582; **8** **398–400**; **26** 108; **29** 331
Nutrena, **II** 617; **13** 137
Nutri-Foods International, **18** 467–68
Nutri/System Inc., **29** 258
Nutrilite Co., **III** 11–12
NutriSystem, **10** 383; **12** 531
Nutrition for Life International Inc., **22** **385–88**
Nuveen. *See* John Nuveen Company.
NV Dagblad De Telegraaf. *See* N.V. Holdingmaatschappij De Telegraaf.
NVR L.P., **8** **401–03**
NWA, Inc. *See* Northwest Airlines Corporation.
NWK. *See* Nordwestdeutsche Kraftwerke AG.
NWL Control Systems, **III** 512
NWS BANK plc, **10** 336–37
Nya AB Atlas, **III** 425–26
Nydqvist & Holm, **III** 426
Nyhamms Cellulosa, **IV** 338
NYK. *See* Nihon Yusen Kaisha, Nippon Yusen Kabushiki Kaisha *and* Nippon Yusen Kaisha.
Nyland Mattor, **25** 464
Nylex Corp., **I** 429
NYLife Care Health Plans, Inc., **17** 166
Nylon de Mexico, S.A., **19** 10, 12
Nyman & Schultz Affarsresbyraer A.B., **I** 120
Nymofil, Ltd., **16** 297
NYNEX Corporation, **V** **311–13**; **6** 340; **11** 19, 87; **13** 176; **25** 61–62, 102; **26** 520
Nyrop, **I** 113
Nysco Laboratories, **III** 55
NYSEG. *See* New York State Electric and Gas Corporation.
NZI Corp., **III** 257

O&K Rolltreppen, **27** 269
O&Y. *See* Olympia & York Developments Ltd.
O.B. McClintock Co., **7** 144–45
O.G. Wilson, **16** 560
O. Kraft & Sons, **12** 363
O.N.E. Color Communications L.L.C., **29** 306
O.S. Designs Inc., **15** 396
O.Y.L. Industries Berhad, **26** 3, 5
Oahu Railway & Land Co., **I** 565–66
Oak Farms Dairies, **II** 660
Oak Hill Investment Partners, **11** 490
Oak Hill Sportswear Corp., **17** 137–38
Oak Industries Inc., **III** 512; **21** **396–98**
Oak Technology, Inc., **22** **389–93**
Oakley, Inc., **18** **390–93**
OakStone Financial Corporation, **11** 448
Oaktree Capital Management, **30** 185
OakTree Health Plan Inc., **16** 404
Oakville, **7** 518
Oakwood Homes Corporation, **13** 155; **15** **326–28**
OASIS, **IV** 454
Oasis Group P.L.C., **10** 506
OASYS, Inc., **18** 112
ÖBB. *See* Österreichische Bundesbahnen GmbH.
Obbola Linerboard, **IV** 339
Oberheim Corporation, **16** 239
Oberland, **16** 122
Oberrheinische Bank, **II** 278
Oberschlesische Stickstoff-Werge AG, **IV** 229
Oberusel AG, **III** 541
Obi, **23** 231
Object Design, Inc., **15** 372
O'Boy Inc. *See* Happy Kids Inc.
O'Brien Kreitzberg, Inc., **25** 130
Obunsha, **9** 29
Occidental Bank, **16** 497
Occidental Chemical Corp., **19** 414
Occidental Insurance Co., **III** 251
Occidental Life Insurance Company, **I** 536–37; **13** 529; **26** 486–87
Occidental Overseas Ltd., **11** 97
Occidental Petroleum Corporation, **I** 527; **II** 432, 516; **IV** 264, 312, 392, 410, 417, 453–54, 467, **480–82**, 486, 515–16; **7** 376; **8** 526; **12** 100; **19** 268; **25** **360–63** **(upd.)**; **29** 113; **31** 115, 456
Occidental Petroleum Great Britain Inc., **21** 206
Océ N.V., **24** **360–63**
Ocean, **III** 234
Ocean Combustion Services, **9** 109
Ocean Drilling and Exploration Company. *See* ODECO.
Ocean Group plc, **6** **415–17**
Ocean Reef Management, **19** 242, 244
Ocean Salvage and Towage Co., **I** 592
Ocean Scientific, Inc., **15** 380
Ocean Specialty Tankers Corporation, **22** 275
Ocean Spray Cranberries, Inc., **7** **403–05**; **10** 525; **19** 278; **25** **364–67** **(upd.)**
Ocean Steam Ship Company. *See* Malaysian Airlines System BHD.
Ocean Systems Inc., **I** 400
Ocean Transport & Trading Ltd., **6** 417
Oceania Football Confederation, **27** 150
Oceanic Contractors, **III** 559
Oceanic Properties, **II** 491–92
Oceanic Steam Navigation Company, **19** 197; **23** 160
Oceans of Fun, **22** 130
Ocelet Industries Ltd., **25** 232
O'Charley's Inc., **19** **286–88**
OCL. *See* Overseas Containers Ltd.
Ocoma Foods, **II** 584
Octek, **13** 235
Octel Communications Corp., **III** 143; **14** 217, **354–56**; **16** 394
Octopus Publishing, **IV** 667; **17** 398
Oculinum, Inc., **10** 48
Odakyu Electric Railway Company Limited, **V** **487–89**
Odam's and Plaistow Wharves, **II** 580–81
Odd Job Trading Corp., **29** 311–12
Odd Lot Trading Company, **V** 172–73
Odda Smelteverk A/S, **25** 82
Odeco Drilling, Inc., **7** 362–64; **11** 522; **12** 318
Odegard Outdoor Advertising, L.L.C., **27** 280
Odeon Theatres Ltd., **II** 157–59
Odetics Inc., **14** **357–59**
Odhams Press Ltd., **IV** 259, 666–67; **7** 244, 342; **17** 397–98
ODM, **26** 490
ODME. *See* Toolex International N.V.
O'Donnell-Usen Fisheries, **II** 494
Odwalla, Inc., **31** **349–51**
Odyssey Holdings, Inc., **18** 376
Odyssey Partners Group, **II** 679; **V** 135; **12** 55; **13** 94; **17** 137; **28** 218
Odyssey Press, **13** 560
OEC Medical Systems, Inc., **27** **354–56**
Oelwerken Julias Schindler GmbH, **7** 141
OEN Connectors, **19** 166
Oertel Brewing Co., **I** 226; **10** 180
Oësterreichischer Phönix in Wien, **III** 376
Oetker Group, **I** 219
Off the Rax, **II** 667; **24** 461
Office Depot Incorporated, **8** **404–05**; **10** 235, 497; **12** 335; **13** 268; **15** 331; **18** 24, 388; **22** 154, 412–13; **23** **363–65** **(upd.)**; **27** 95
Office Mart Holdings Corporation, **10** 498
Office National du Crédit Agricole, **II** 264
Office Systems Inc., **15** 407
The Office Works, Inc., **13** 277; **25** 500
OfficeMax Inc., **8** 404; **15** **329–31**; **18** 286, 388; **20** 103; **22** 154; **23** 364–65
Official Airline Guides, Inc., **IV** 605, 643; **7** 312, 343; **17** 399
Officine Alfieri Maserati S.p.A., **11** 104; **13** 28, **376–78**
Offset Gerhard Kaiser GmbH, **IV** 325
Offshore Co., **III** 558; **6** 577
Offshore Food Services Inc., **I** 514
Offshore Transportation Corporation, **11** 523
Ogden Corporation, **I** **512–14**, 701; **6** **151–53**, 600; **7** 39; **25** 16; **27** 21, 196
Ogden Food Products, **7** 430
Ogden Gas Co., **6** 568
Ogilvie Flour Mills Co., **I** 268; **IV** 245; **25** 9, 281
Ogilvy & Mather, **22** 200
Ogilvy Group Inc., **I** 20, **25–27**, 31, 37, 244; **6** 53; **9** 180. *See also* WPP Group.
Oglebay Norton Company, **17** **355–58**
Oglethorpe Power Corporation, **6** **537–38**
O'Gorman and Cozens-Hardy, **III** 725
Ogura Oil, **IV** 479
Oh la la!, **14** 107
Ohbayashi Corporation, **I** 586–87
The Ohio Art Company, **14** **360–62**
Ohio Ball Bearing. *See* Bearings Inc.
Ohio Barge Lines, Inc., **11** 194
Ohio Bell Telephone Company, **14** **363–65**; **18** 30
Ohio Boxboard Company, **12** 376
Ohio Brass Co., **II** 2
Ohio Casualty Corp., **III** 190; **11** **369–70**
Ohio Crankshaft Co. *See* Park-Ohio Industries Inc.
Ohio Edison Company, **V** **676–78**
Ohio Electric Railway Co., **III** 388
Ohio Mattress Co., **12** 438–39
Ohio Oil Co., **IV** 365, 400, 574; **6** 568; **7** 551
Ohio Pizza Enterprises, Inc., **7** 152
Ohio Power Shovel, **21** 502
Ohio Pure Foods Group, **II** 528
Ohio River Company, **6** 487
Ohio Valley Electric Corporation, **6** 517
Ohio Ware Basket Company, **12** 319
Ohio-Sealy Mattress Mfg. Co., **12** 438–39
Ohlmeyer Communications, **I** 275; **26** 305

Ohlsson's Cape Breweries, **I** 287–88; **24** 449
OHM Corp., **17** 553
Ohmeda. *See* BOC Group plc.
Ohmite Manufacturing Co., **13** 397
Ohrbach's Department Store, **I** 30
Ohta Keibin Railway Company, **6** 430
ÖIAG, **IV** 234
Oil Acquisition Corp., **I** 611
Oil and Natural Gas Commission, IV 440–41, **483–84**
Oil and Solvent Process Company, **9** 109
Oil City Oil and Grease Co., **IV** 489
Oil Co. of Australia, **III** 673
Oil Distribution Public Corp., **IV** 434
Oil Drilling, Incorporated, **7** 344
Oil Equipment Manufacturing Company, **16** 8
Oil India Ltd., **IV** 440, 483–84
Oil Shale Corp., **IV** 522; **7** 537
Oil-Dri Corporation of America, 20 396–99
Oilfield Industrial Lines Inc., **I** 477
Oilfield Service Corp. of America, **I** 342
Oita Co., **III** 718
Oji Paper Co., Ltd., I 506, 508; **II** 326; **IV** 268, 284–85, 292–93, 297–98, **320–22**, 326–27
OK Bazaars, **I** 289; **24** 450
OK Turbines, Inc., **22** 311
Okadaya Co. Ltd., **V** 96
O'Keefe Marketing, **23** 102
Oki Electric Industry Company, Limited, II 68, **72–74**; **15** 125; **21** 390
Okidata, **9** 57; **18** 435
Okinoyama Coal Mine, **III** 759
Oklahoma Airmotive, **8** 349
Oklahoma Entertainment, Inc., **9** 74
Oklahoma Gas and Electric Company, 6 539–40; **7** 409–11
Oklahoma Oil Co., **I** 31
Oklahoma Publishing Company, **11** 152–53; **30** 84
Okonite, **I** 489
Okura & Co., Ltd., I 282; **IV 167–68**
Oland & Sons Limited, **25** 281
Olathe Manufacturing, **26** 494
OLC. *See* Orient Leasing Co., Ltd.
Olcott & McKesson, **I** 496
Old America Stores, Inc., 17 359–61
Old Colony Trust Co., **II** 207; **12** 30
Old Dominion Power Company, **6** 513, 515
Old El Paso, **I** 457; **14** 212; **24** 140–41
Old Harbor Candles, **18** 68
Old Kent Financial Corp., 11 371–72
Old Line Life Insurance Co., **III** 275
Old Mutual, **IV** 23, 535
Old National Bancorp, 14 529; **15 332–34**
Old Navy Clothing Company, **18** 193
Old Quaker Paint Company, **13** 471
Old Republic International Corp., 11 373–75
Old Spaghetti Factory International Inc., 24 364–66
Old Stone Trust Company, **13** 468
Oldach Window Corp., **19** 446
Oldham Estate, **IV** 712
Oldover Corp., **23** 225
Olds Motor Vehicle Co., **I** 171; **10** 325
Olds Oil Corp., **I** 341
Ole's Innovative Sports. *See* Rollerblade, Inc.
Olean Tile Co., **22** 170
Oleochim, **IV** 498–99
OLEX. *See* Deutsche BP Aktiengesellschaft.
Olex Cables Ltd., **10** 445
Olin Corporation, I 318, 330, **379–81**, 434, 695; **III** 667; **IV** 482; **8** 23, 153; **11** 420; **13 379–81 (upd.)**; **16** 68, 297
Olinkraft, Inc., **II** 432; **III** 708–09; **11** 420; **16** 376
Olins Rent-a-Car, **6** 348
Olinvest, **IV** 454
Olive Garden Italian Restaurants, **10** 322, 324; **16** 156–58; **19** 258
Oliver Rubber Company, **19** 454, 456
Olivetti. *See* Ing. C. Olivetti & C., S.p.A.
Olivine Industries, Inc., **II** 508; **11** 172
Olmstead Products Co., **23** 82
Olofsson, **I** 573
Olohana Corp., **I** 129; **6** 129
Olsen Dredging Co., **III** 558
Olson & Wright, **I** 120
Olsonite Corp., **I** 201
Olsten Corporation, 6 41–43; **9** 327; **29 362–65 (upd.)**
Olveh, **III** 177–79
Olympia & York Developments Ltd., IV 245, 247, 712, **720–21**; **6** 478; **8** 327; **9 390–92 (upd.)**; **25** 11–12; **30** 108
Olympia Arenas, Inc., **7** 278–79; **24** 294
Olympia Brewing, **I** 260; **11** 50
Olympia Floor & Tile Co., **IV** 720
Olympiaki, **III** 401
Olympic Airways, **II** 442
Olympic Courier Systems, Inc., **24** 126
Olympic Fastening Systems, **III** 722
Olympic Insurance Co., **26** 486
Olympic Packaging, **13** 443
Olympus Communications L.P., **17** 7
Olympus Optical Company, Ltd., **15** 483
Olympus Sport, **V** 177–78
Olympus Symbol, Inc., **15** 483
OM Group, Inc., 17 362–64
Omaha Cold Store Co., **II** 571
Omaha Public Power District, **29** 353
Oman Oil Refinery Co., **IV** 516
Omega Gas Company, **8** 349
Omega Gold Mines, **IV** 164
Omega Protein Corporation, **25** 546
Omex Corporation, **6** 272
OMI Corporation, **IV** 34; **9** 111–12; **22** 275
Omlon, **II** 75
Ommium Française de Pétroles, **IV** 559
Omnes, **17** 419
Omni Construction Company, Inc., **8** 112–13
Omni Hearing Aid Systems, **I** 667
Omni Hotels Corp., 12 367–69
Omni Products International, **II** 420
Omni-Pac, **12** 377
Omnibus Corporation, **9** 283
Omnicare, Inc., **13** 150
Omnicom Group Inc., I 28–32, 33, 36; **14** 160; **22 394–99 (upd.)**; **23** 478
Omnipoint Communications Inc., **18** 77
OmniSource Corporation, 14 366–67
Omron Corporation, 28 331–35 (upd.)
Omron Tateisi Electronics Company, II 75–77; **III** 549
ÖMV Aktiengesellschaft, IV 234, 454, **485–87**
On Assignment, Inc., 20 400–02
On Command Video Corp., **23** 135
On Cue, **9** 360
On-Line Software International Inc., **6** 225
On-Line Systems. *See* Sierra On-Line Inc.
Onan Corporation, **8** 72
Onbancorp Inc., **11** 110
Once Upon A Child, Inc., **18** 207–8
Oncogen, **III** 18
Ondal GmbH, **III** 69
Ondulato Imolese, **IV** 296; **19** 226
One Hundred Thirtieth National Bank, **II** 291
One Hundredth Bank, **II** 321
One Price Clothing Stores, Inc., 20 403–05
1-800-FLOWERS, Inc., 26 344–46; **28** 137
O'Neal, Jones & Feldman Inc., **11** 142
Oneida Bank & Trust Company, **9** 229
Oneida County Creameries Co., **7** 202
Oneida Gas Company, **9** 554
Oneida Ltd., 7 406–08; **31 352–355 (upd.)**
ONEOK Inc., 7 409–12
Onex Corporation, 16 395–97; **22** 513; **24** 498; **25** 282
OneZero Media, Inc., **31** 240
Onitsuka Tiger Co., **V** 372; **8** 391
Online Distributed Processing Corporation, **6** 201
Online Financial Communication Systems, **11** 112
Only One Dollar, Inc. *See* Dollar Tree Stores, Inc.
Onoda Cement Co., Ltd., I 508; **III 717–19**
Onomichi, **25** 469
Onsale Inc., **31** 177
Onstead Foods, **21** 501
Ontario Hydro, 6 541–42; **9** 461
Ontel Corporation, **6** 201
OnTrak Systems Inc., **31** 301
Oode Casting Iron Works, **III** 551
O'okiep Copper Company, Ltd., **7** 385–86
Opel. *See* Adam Opel AG.
Open Board of Brokers, **9** 369
Open Market, Inc., **22** 522
OpenTV, Inc., **31** 330–31
Operadora de Bolsa Serfin. *See* Grupo Financiero Serfin, S.A.
Opp and Micolas Mills, **15** 247–48
Oppenheimer. *See* Ernest Oppenheimer and Sons.
Oppenheimer & Co., **17** 137; **21** 235; **22** 405; **25** 450
Opryland USA, **11** 152–53; **25** 403
Optel Corp., **17** 331
OPTi Computer, **9** 116
Opti-Ray, Inc., **12** 215
Optical Radiation Corporation, **27** 57
Optilink Corporation, **12** 137
Optima Pharmacy Services, **17** 177
Optimum Financial Services Ltd., **II** 457
Opto-Electronics Corp., **15** 483
Optronics, Inc., **6** 247; **24** 234
Optus Communications, **25** 102
Optus Vision, **17** 150
OPW, **III** 467–68
Oracle Corporation, 24 367–71 (upd.); **25** 34, 96–97, 499
Oracle Systems Corporation, 6 272–74; **10** 361, 363, 505; **11** 78; **13** 483; **14** 16; **15** 492; **18** 541, 543; **19** 310; **21** 86; **22** 154, 293
Orange Julius, **10** 371, 373

Orange Line Bus Company, **6** 604
Orange PLC, **24** 89
Orb Books. *See* Tom Doherty Associates Inc.
Orbis Entertainment Co., **20** 6
Orbis Graphic Arts. *See* Anaheim Imaging.
Orbital Engine Corporation Ltd., **17** 24
Orbital Sciences Corporation, 22 400–03
Orchard Supply Hardware Stores Corporation, 17 365–67; 25 535
Orcofi, **III** 48
OrderTrust LLP, **26** 440
Ore and Chemical Corp., **IV** 140
Ore-Ida Foods Incorporated, II 508; **11** 172; **12** 531; **13 382–83**
Orebehoved Fanerfabrik, **25** 464
Oregon Ale and Beer Company, **18** 72
Oregon Craft & Floral Supply, **17** 322
Oregon Cutting Systems, **26** 119
Oregon Metallurgical Corporation, 20 406–08
Oregon Pacific and Eastern Railway, **13** 100
Oregon Steel Mills, Inc., 14 368–70; 19 380
O'Reilly Automotive, Inc., 26 347–49
Orford Copper Co., **IV** 110
Organon, **I** 665
Oriel Foods, **II** 609
Orient, **21** 122
Orient Express Hotels Inc., **29** 429–30
Orient Glass, **III** 715
Orient Leasing. *See* Orix Corporation.
Orient Overseas, **18** 254
Oriental Brewery Co., Ltd., **21** 320
Oriental Cotton Trading. *See* Tomen Corporation.
Oriental Land Co., Ltd., **IV** 715
Oriental Precision Company, **13** 213
Oriental Trading Corp., **22** 213
Oriental Yeast Co., **17** 288
Origin Systems Inc., **10** 285
Origin Technology, **14** 183
Original Arizona Jean Company, **18** 272
Original Cookie Co., **13** 166. *See also* Mrs. Fields' Original Cookies, Inc.
Original Musical Instrument Company (O.M.I.), **16** 239
Original Wassertragers Hummel, **II** 163
Origins Natural Resources Inc., **30** 190
Orinoco Oilfields, Ltd., **IV** 565
Orion, **III** 310
Orion Bank Ltd., **II** 271, 345, 385
Orion Healthcare Ltd., **11** 168
Orion Personal Insurances Ltd., **11** 168
Orion Pictures Corporation, II 147; **6 167–70; 7** 336; **14** 330, 332; **25** 326, 328–29; **31** 100
Orit Corp., **8** 219–20
Orix Corporation, II 442–43, 259, 348
Orkem, **IV** 547, 560; **21** 205
Orkin Pest Control, **11** 431–32, 434
Orkla A/S, 18 394–98; 25 205–07
Orm Bergold Chemie, **8** 464
Ormco Corporation, **14** 481
ÖROP, **IV** 485–86
Orowheat Baking Company, **10** 250
La Oroya, **22** 286
ORSCO, Inc., **26** 363
Ortho Diagnostic Systems, Inc., **10** 213; **22** 75
Ortho Pharmaceutical Corporation, **III** 35; **8** 281; **10** 79–80; **30** 59–60
Orthopedic Services, Inc., **11** 366
Orval Kent Food Company, Inc., **7** 430
Orville Redenbacher/Swiss Miss Foods Co., **17** 241
The Orvis Company, Inc., 28 336–39
Oryx Energy Company, IV 550; **7 413–15**
Osaka Aluminium Co., **IV** 153
Osaka Beer Brewing Co., **I** 220, 282; **20** 28
Osaka Electric Tramway, **V** 463
Osaka Gas Co., Ltd., V 679–81
Osaka General Bussan, **IV** 431
Osaka Iron Works, **III** 513
Osaka Marine and Fire Insurance Co., **III** 367
Osaka Nomura Bank, **II** 276, 438–39
Osaka North Harbor Co. Ltd., **I** 518
Osaka Shinyo Kumiai, **15** 495
Osaka Shosen Kaisha, **I** 503; **V** 473–74, 481–82
Osaka Spinning Company, **V** 387
Osaka Sumitomo Marine and Fire Insurance Co., Ltd., **III** 367
Osaka Textile Co., **I** 506
Osakeyhtiö Gustaf Cederberg & Co., **IV** 301
Osakeyhtiö T. & J. Salvesen, **IV** 301
Osborne Books, **IV** 637
Oscar Mayer Foods Corp., II 532; **7** 274, 276; **12** 123, **370–72**
Osco Drug, **II** 604–05
OSF Japan Ltd., **24** 365
Oshawa Group Limited, II 649–50
OshKosh B'Gosh, Inc., 9 393–95
Oshkosh Electric Power, **9** 553
Oshkosh Gas Light Company, **9** 553
Oshkosh Truck Corporation, 7 416–18; 14 458
Oshman's Sporting Goods, Inc., 16 560; **17 368–70; 27** 7
OSi Specialties, Inc., **16** 543
Osiris Holding Company, **16** 344
OSK. *See* Osaka Shosen Kaisha.
Osmonics, Inc., 18 399–401
Oster. *See* Sunbeam-Oster.
Österreichische Bundesbahnen GmbH, 6 418–20
Österreichische Creditanstalt-Wiener Bankverein, **IV** 230
Österreichische Elektrowerke, **IV** 230
Österreichische Industrieholding AG, **IV** 486–87
Österreichische Industriekredit AG, **IV** 230
Österreichische Länderbank, **II** 239; **23** 37
Österreichische Mineralölverwaltung AG, **IV** 485
Österreichische Post- und Telegraphenverwaltung, V 314–17
Österreichische Stickstoffswerke, **IV** 486
Ostschweizer Zementwerke, **III** 701
Osuuskunta Metsäliito, **IV** 316
Oswald Tillotson Ltd., **III** 501; **7** 207
Otagiri Mercantile Co., **11** 95
Otake Paper Manufacturing Co., **IV** 327
OTC, **10** 492
Other Options, **29** 400
Otis Company, **6** 579
Otis Elevator Company, Inc., I 85, **III** 467, 663; **13 384–86; 27** 267, 268; **29** 422
Otis Engineering Corp., **III** 498
Otis Spunkmeyer, Inc., 28 340–42
Otosan, **I** 167, 479–80
OTR Express, Inc., 25 368–70
Otsego Falls Paper Company, **8** 358
Ott and Brewer Company, **12** 312
Ottawa Fruit Supply Ltd., **II** 662
Ottaway Newspapers, Inc., 15 335–37
Otter Tail Power Company, 18 402–05
Otter-Westelaken, **16** 420
Otto Sumisho Inc., **V** 161
Otto Versand GmbH & Co., V 159–61; 10 489–90; **15 338–40 (upd.); 27** 427, 429; **31** 188
Otto-Epoka mbH, **15** 340
Ottumwa Daily Courier, **11** 251
Ourso Investment Corporation, **16** 344
Outback Steakhouse, Inc., 12 373–75
Outboard Marine Corporation, III 329, **597–600; 8** 71; **16** 383; **20 409–12 (upd.); 26** 494
Outdoor Systems, Inc., 25 371–73; 27 278–80
The Outdoorsman, Inc., **10** 216
Outlet, **6** 33
Outlet Retail Stores, Inc., **27** 286
Outlook Window Partnership, **19** 446
Outokumpu Metals Group. *See* OM Group, Inc.
Outokumpu Oy, **IV** 276
Ovako Oy, **III** 624
Ovation, **19** 285
OVC, Inc., **6** 313
Overhill Farms, **10** 382
Overland Energy Company, **14** 567
Overland Mail Co., **II** 380–81, 395; **10** 60; **12** 533
Overland Western Ltd., **27** 473
Overnite Transportation Co., 14 371–73; 28 492
Overseas Air Travel Ltd., **I** 95
Overseas Containers Ltd., **6** 398, 415–16
Overseas Petroleum and Investment Corp., **IV** 389
Overseas Shipholding Group, Inc., 11 376–77
Overseas Telecommunications Commission, **6** 341–42
Overseas Telecommunications, Inc., **27** 304
Owatonna Tool Co., **I** 200; **10** 493
Owen Steel Co. Inc., **15** 117
Owens & Minor, Inc., 10 143; **16 398–401**
Owens Corning Corporation, I 609; **III** 683, **720–23; 8** 177; **13** 169; **20 413–17 (upd.); 25** 535; **30** 283
Owens Yacht Company, **III** 443; **22** 115
Owens-Illinois Inc., I 609–11, 615; **II** 386; **III** 640, 720–21; **IV** 282, 343; **9** 261; **16** 123; **22** 254; **24** 92; **26 350–53 (upd.)**
Owensboro Municipal Utilities, **11** 37
Owosso Corporation, 29 366–68
Oxdon Investments, **II** 664
Oxfam America, **13** 13
Oxford Biscuit Fabrik, **II** 543
Oxford Bus Company, **28** 155–56
Oxford Chemical Corp., **II** 572
Oxford Financial Group, **22** 456
Oxford Health Plans, Inc., 16 402–04
Oxford Industries, Inc., 8 406–08; 24 158
Oxford Instruments, **III** 491
Oxford Paper Co., **I** 334–35; **10** 289
Oxford University Press, **23** 211
Oxford-AnsCo Development Co., **12** 18
Oxirane Chemical Co., **IV** 456
OXO International, **16** 234

Oxy Petrochemicals Inc., **IV** 481
Oxy Process Chemicals, **III** 33
OxyChem, **11** 160
Oxygen Media, **28** 175
Ozalid Corporation, **I** 337–38; **IV** 563; **22** 226
Ozark Airlines, **I** 127; **12** 489
Ozark Automotive Distributors, **26** 347–48
Ozark Pipe Line Corp., **IV** 540
Ozark Utility Company, **6** 593
OZM. *See* OneZero Media, Inc.

P&C Foods Inc., 8 409–11; 13 95, 394
P&F Technologies Ltd., **26** 363
P & M Manufacturing Company, **8** 386
P & O. *See* Peninsular & Oriental Steam Navigation Company.
P&O Nedlloyd, **26** 241, 243
P.A. Bergner & Company, **9** 142; **15** 87–88
P.A. Geier Company. *See* Royal Appliance Manufacturing Company.
P.A.J.W. Corporation, **9** 111–12
P.A. Rentrop-Hubbert & Wagner Fahrzeugausstattungen GmbH, **III** 582
P.C. Hanford Oil Co., **IV** 368
P.C. Richard & Son Corp., 23 372–74
P. D'Aoust Ltd., **II** 651
P.D. Associated Collieries Ltd., **31** 369
P.D. Kadi International, **I** 580
P.D. Magnetics, **I** 330; **8** 153
P.E.C. Israel Economic Corporation, **24** 429
P.G. Realty, **III** 340
P.H. Glatfelter Company, 8 412–14; 30 349–52 (upd.)
P.Ink Press, **24** 430
P.L. Porter Co., **III** 580
P.R. Mallory, **9** 179
P.S.L. Food Market, Inc., **22** 549
P. Sharples, **III** 418
P.T. Bridgeport Perkasa Machine Tools, **17** 54
P.T. Dai Nippon Printing Indonesia, **IV** 599
P.T. Darya-Varia Laboratoria, **18** 180
P.T. Gaya Motor, **23** 290
P.T. Muaratewe Spring, **III** 581
P.T. Semen Nusantara, **III** 718
P.W. Huntington & Company, **11** 180
Pabst, **I** 217, 255; **10** 99; **18** 502
PAC Insurance Services, **12** 175; **27** 258
Pac-Am Food Concepts, **10** 178
Pac-Fab, Inc., **18** 161
PACCAR Inc., I 155, **185–86; 10** 280; **26 354–56 (upd.)**
Pace Companies, **6** 149; **26** 221
Pace Express Pty. Ltd., **13** 20
Pace Foods Ltd., **26** 58
Pace Management Service Corp., **21** 91
PACE Membership Warehouse, Inc., **V** 112; **10** 107; **12** 50; **18** 286
Pace Pharmaceuticals, **16** 439
Pace-Arrow, Inc., **III** 484; **22** 206
Pacemaker Plastics, Inc., **7** 296
Pacer Tool and Mold, **17** 310
Pachena Industries Ltd., **6** 310
Pacific Aero Products Co., **I** 47; **10** 162
Pacific Air Freight, Incorporated, **6** 345
Pacific Air Transport, **I** 47, 128; **6** 128; **9** 416
Pacific Alaska Fuel Services, **6** 383
Pacific and European Telegraph Company, **25** 99
Pacific Bell, **V** 318–20; **11** 59; **12** 137; **21** 285; **22** 19
Pacific Brick Proprietary, **III** 673
Pacific Car & Foundry Company. *See* PACCAR Inc.
Pacific Cascade Land Co., **IV** 255
Pacific Coast Co., **IV** 165
Pacific Coast Condensed Milk Co., **II** 486
Pacific Coast Oil Co., **IV** 385
Pacific Communication Sciences, **11** 57
Pacific Dry Dock and Repair Co., **6** 382
Pacific Dunlop Limited, 10 444–46
Pacific Electric Heating Co., **II** 28; **12** 194
Pacific Electric Light Company, **6** 565
Pacific Enterprises, V 682–84; 12 477. *See also* Sempra Energy.
Pacific Express Co., **II** 381
Pacific Finance Corp., **I** 537; **9** 536; **13** 529; **26** 486
Pacific Fur Company, **25** 220
Pacific Gamble Robinson, **9** 39
Pacific Gas and Electric Company, I 96; **V 685–87; 11** 270; **12** 100, 106; **19** 411; **25** 415. *See also* PG&E Corporation.
Pacific Guardian Life Insurance Co., **III** 289
Pacific Health Beverage Co., **I** 292
Pacific Home Furnishings, **14** 436
Pacific Indemnity Corp., **III** 220; **14** 108, 110; **16** 204
Pacific Lighting Corp., **IV** 492; **V** 682–84; **12** 477; **16** 496. *See also* Sempra Energy.
Pacific Linens, **13** 81–82
Pacific Link Communication, **18** 180
Pacific Lumber Company, **III** 254; **8** 348–50
Pacific Magazines and Printing, **7** 392
Pacific Mail Steamship Company, **6** 353
Pacific Manifolding Book/Box Co., **IV** 644
Pacific Media K.K., **18** 101
Pacific Metal Bearing Co., **I** 159
Pacific Monolothics Inc., **11** 520
Pacific National Bank, **II** 349
Pacific National Insurance Co. *See* TIG Holdings, Inc.
Pacific Natural Gas Corp., **9** 102
Pacific Northern, **6** 66
Pacific Northwest Bell Telephone Co., **V** 341; **25** 495
Pacific Northwest Laboratories, **10** 139
Pacific Northwest Pipeline Corporation, **9** 102–104, 540; **12** 144
Pacific Northwest Power Company, **6** 597
Pacific Pearl, **I** 417
Pacific Petroleums Ltd., **IV** 494; **9** 102
Pacific Platers Ltd., **IV** 100
Pacific Power & Light Company. *See* PacifiCorp.
Pacific Pride Bakeries, **19** 192
Pacific Recycling Co. Inc., **IV** 296; **19** 226; **23** 225
Pacific Refining Co., **IV** 394–95
Pacific Resources Inc., **IV** 47; **22** 107
Pacific Sentinel Gold Corp., **27** 456
Pacific Silver Corp., **IV** 76
Pacific Southwest Airlines Inc., **I** 132; **6** 132
Pacific Steel Ltd., **IV** 279; **19** 154
Pacific Sunwear of California, Inc., 28 343–45
Pacific Telecom, Inc., V 689; **6 325–28; 25** 101
Pacific Telesis Group, V 318–20; 6 324; **9** 321; **11** 10–11; **14** 345, 347; **15** 125; **25** 499; **26** 520; **29** 387
Pacific Teletronics, Inc., **7** 15
Pacific Towboat. *See* Puget Sound Tug and Barge Company.
Pacific Trading Co., Ltd., **IV** 442
Pacific Trail Inc., **17** 462; **29** 293, 295–96
Pacific Western Extruded Plastics Company, **17** 441
Pacific Western Oil Co., **IV** 537
Pacific Wine Co., **18** 71
Pacific-Burt Co., Ltd., **IV** 644
Pacific-Sierra Research, **I** 155
PacifiCare Health Systems, Inc., III 85; **11 378–80; 25** 318
PacifiCorp, V 688–90; 6 325–26, 328; **7** 376–78; **26 357–60 (upd.); 27** 327, 483, 485
Package Products Company, Inc., **12** 150
Packaged Ice, Inc., **21** 338; **26** 449
Packaging Corporation of America, I 526; **12 376–78**, 397; **16** 191
Packard Bell Electronics, Inc., I 524; **II** 86; **10** 521, 564; **11** 413; **13 387–89**, 483; **21** 391; **23** 471
Packard Motor Co., **I** 81; **8** 74; **9** 17
Packer's Consolidated Press, **IV** 651
Packerland Packing Company, **7** 199, 201
Pacolet Manufacturing Company, **17** 327
PacTel. *See* Pacific Telesis Group.
Paddington Corp., **I** 248
PAFS. *See* Pacific Alaska Fuel Services.
Page, Bacon & Co., **II** 380; **12** 533
Page Boy Inc., **9** 320
PageAhead Software, **15** 492
Pageland Coca-Cola Bottling Works, **10** 222
PageMart Wireless, Inc., **18** 164, 166
Paging Network Inc., 11 381–83
Pagoda Trading Company, Inc., **V** 351, 353; **20** 86
Paid Prescriptions, **9** 346
Paige Publications, **18** 66
PaineWebber Group Inc., I 245; **II 444–46**, 449; **III** 409; **13** 449; **22** 352, **404–07 (upd.)**, 542; **25** 433
Painter Carpet Mills, **13** 169
Painton Co., **II** 81
La Paix, **III** 273
Pak Arab Fertilizers Ltd., **IV** 364
Pak Mail Centers, **18** 316
Pak Sak Industries, **17** 310; **24** 160
Pak-a-Sak, **II** 661
Pak-All Products, Inc., **IV** 345
Pak-Paino, **IV** 315
Pak-Well, **IV** 282; **9** 261
Pakhoed Holding, N.V., **9** 532; **26** 420
Pakkasakku Oy, **IV** 471
Paknet, **11** 548
Pakway Container Corporation, **8** 268
PAL. *See* Philippine Airlines, Inc.
Pal Plywood Co., Ltd., **IV** 327
Palace Station Hotel & Casino. *See* Station Casinos Inc.
Palais Royal, Inc., **24** 456
Palatine Insurance Co., **III** 234
Palco Industries, **19** 440
Pale Ski & Sports GmbH, **22** 461
Palestine Coca-Cola Bottling Co., **13** 163
Pall Corporation, 9 396–98
Palm Beach Holdings, **9** 157
Palm Shipping Inc., **25** 468–70
Palmafina, **IV** 498–99

Palmer Communications, **25** 418
Palmer G. Lewis Co., **8** 135
Palmer Tyre Ltd., **I** 428–29
Palmolive Co. *See* Colgate-Palmolive Company.
Palo Alto Brewing, **22** 421
Palo Alto Products International, Inc., **29** 6
Palo Alto Research Center, **10** 510
Palomar Medical Technologies, Inc., **22 408–10**; **31** 124
PAM Group, **27** 462
Pamida Holdings Corporation, **15 341–43**
Pamour Porcupine Mines, Ltd., **IV** 164
Pampa OTT, **27** 473
The Pampered Chef, Ltd., **18 406–08**
Pamplemousse, **14** 225
Pan American Banks, **II** 336
Pan American Petroleum & Transport Co., **IV** 368–70
Pan American World Airways, Inc., **I** 20, 31, 44, 64, 67, 89–90, 92, 99, 103–04, 112–13, **115–16**, 121, 124, 126, 129, 132, 248, 452, 530, 547–48; **III** 536; **6** 51, 65–66, 71, 74–76, 81–82, 103–05, 110–11, 123, 129–30; **9** 231, 417; **10** 561; **11** 266; **12** 191, **379–81 (upd.)**, 419; **13** 19; **14** 73; **24** 397; **29** 189
Pan European Publishing Co., **IV** 611
Pan Geo Atlas Corporation, **18** 513
Pan Ocean, **IV** 473
Pan Pacific Fisheries, **24** 114
Pan-Alberta Gas Ltd., **16** 11
Panacon Corporation, **III** 766; **22** 545
Panagra, **I** 547–48
Panama Refining and Petrochemical Co., **IV** 566
PanAmSat, **18** 211, 213
Panarctic Oils, **IV** 494
Panasonic, **9** 180; **10** 125; **12** 470
Panatech Research & Development Corp., **III** 160
Panavia Aircraft GmbH, **24** 84, 86–87
Panavia Consortium, **I** 74–75
Panavision Inc., **24 372–74**; **28** 249
PanCanadian Petroleum Ltd., **27** 217
Pandair, **13** 20
Pandel, Inc., **8** 271
Pandick Press Inc., **23** 63
PanEnergy Corporation, **27** 128, 131
Panerai, **27** 489
Panhandle Eastern Corporation, **I** 377, 569; **IV** 425; **V 691–92**; **10** 82–84; **11** 28; **14** 135; **17** 21
Panhandle Oil Corp., **IV** 498
Panhandle Power & Light Company, **6** 580
Panhard, **I** 194
Panhard-Levassor, **I** 149
Panificadora Bimbo, **19** 191
AB Pankakoski, **IV** 274
Panmure Gordon, **II** 337
Pannill Knitting Company, **13** 531
Panocean Storage & Transport, **6** 415, 417
Panola Pipeline Co., **7** 228
Panosh Place, **12** 168
Pansophic Systems Inc., **6** 225
Pantepec Oil Co., **IV** 559, 570; **24** 520
Pantera Energy Corporation, **11** 27
Pantheon Books, **13** 429; **31** 376
Panther, **III** 750
Panther Express International Company, **6** 346
Pantry Pride Inc., **I** 668; **II** 670, 674; **III** 56; **23** 407–08
Pants Corral, **II** 634
Papa John's International, Inc., **15 344–46**; **16** 447; **24** 295
Pape and Co., Ltd., **10** 441
Papelera Navarra, **IV** 295; **19** 226
Papeleria Calparsoro S.A., **IV** 325
Papeles Venezolanos C.A., **17** 281
The Paper Factory of Wisconsin, Inc., **12** 209
Paper Makers Chemical Corp., **I** 344
Paper Recycling International, **V** 754
Paper Software, Inc., **15** 322
Paper Stock Dealers, Inc., **8** 476
Paperituote Oy, **IV** 347–48
PaperMate, **III** 28; **23** 54
Paperwork Data-Comm Services Inc., **11** 64
Papeterie de Pont Sainte Maxence, **IV** 318
Papeteries Aussedat, **III** 122
Papeteries Boucher S.A., **IV** 300
Les Papeteries de la Chapelle-Darblay, **IV** 258–59, 302, 337
Papeteries de Lancey, **23 366–68**
Les Papeteries du Limousin, **19** 227
Papeteries Navarre, **III** 677; **16** 121
Papetti's Hy-Grade Egg Products, Inc., **25** 332–33
Papierfabrik Salach, **IV** 324
Papierwaren Fleischer, **IV** 325
Papierwerke Waldhof-Aschaffenburg AG, **IV** 323–24
Papyrus Design Group, **IV** 336; **15** 455
Para-Med Health Services, **6** 181–82
Parachute Press, **29** 426
Parade Gasoline Co., **7** 228
Paradise Creations, **29** 373
Paradise Island Resort and Casino. *See* Sun International Hotels Limited.
Paradyne, **22** 19
Paragon Corporate Holdings, Inc., **IV** 552; **28** 6, 8
Paramax, **6** 281–83
Parametric Technology Corp., **16 405–07**
Parametrics Corp., **25** 134
Paramount Communications Inc., **16** 338; **19** 403–04; **28** 296
Paramount Fire Insurance Co., **26** 486
Paramount Oil Company, **18** 467
Paramount Paper Products, **8** 383
Paramount Pictures Corporation, **I** 451–52; **II** 129, 135, 146–47, **154–56**, 171, 173, 175, 177; **IV** 671–72, 675; **7** 528; **9** 119, 428–29; **10** 175; **12** 73, 323; **19** 404; **21** 23–25; **23** 503; **24** 327; **25** 88, 311, 327–29, 418; **31** 99
Parasitix Corporation. *See* Mycogen Corporation.
Paravision International, **III** 48; **8** 343
Parcelforce, **V** 498
PARCO, **V** 184–85
Parcor, **I** 676
Parfums Chanel, **12** 57
Parfums Christian Dior, **I** 272
Parfums Rochas, **I** 670; **III** 68; **8** 452
Parfums Stern, **III** 16
Pargas, **I** 378
Paribas. *See* Compagnie Financiere de Paribas.
Paridoc and Giant, **12** 153
Paris Corporation, **22 411–13**
Paris Group, **17** 137
Paris Playground Equipment, **13** 319
Parisian, Inc., **14 374–76**; **19** 324–25
Park Consolidated Motels, Inc., **6** 187; **14** 105; **25** 306
Park Corp., **22 414–16**
Park Drop Forge Co. *See* Park-Ohio Industries Inc.
Park Hall Leisure, **II** 140; **24** 194
Park Inn International, **11** 178
Park Ridge Corporation, **9** 284
Park View Hospital, Inc., **III** 78
Park-Ohio Industries Inc., **17 371–73**
Parkdale State Bank, **25** 114
Parkdale Wines, **I** 268; **25** 281
Parke, Davis & Co. *See* Warner-Lambert Co.
Parke-Bernet, **11** 453
Parker, **III** 33
Parker Appliance Co., **III** 601–02
Parker Brothers, **II** 502; **III** 505; **10** 323; **16** 337; **21** 375; **25** 489
Parker Drilling Company, **28 346–48**
Parker Drilling Company of Canada, **9** 363
Parker Pen Corp., **III** 218; **9** 326
Parker's Pharmacy, Inc., **15** 524
Parker-Hannifin Corporation, **III 601–03**; **21** 108; **24 375–78 (upd.)**
Parkinson Cowan, **I** 531
Parkmount Hospitality Corp., **II** 142
Parks Box & Printing Co., **13** 442
Parks-Belk Co., **19** 324
Parkway Distributors, **17** 331
Parr's Bank, **II** 334; **III** 724
Parson and Hyman Co., Inc., **8** 112
The Parsons Corporation, **III** 749; **8 415–17**
Parsons International Trading Business, **27** 195
Parsons Place Apparel Company, **8** 289
Partech, **28** 346, 348
Partek Corporation, **11** 312
Partex, **IV** 515
Parthénon, **27** 10
Parthenon Insurance Co., **III** 79
Participating Annuity Life Insurance Co., **III** 182; **21** 14
La Participation, **III** 210
Partlow Corporation, **7** 116
Partnership Pacific Ltd., **II** 389
Parts Industries Corp., **III** 494–95
Parts Plus, **26** 348
PartyLite Gifts, Inc., **18** 67, 69
Pascagoula Lumber Company, **28** 306
Pascale & Associates, **12** 476
Paschen Contractors Inc., **I** 585
Pasha Pillows, **12** 393
Pasminco, **IV** 61
Pasqua Inc., **28** 64
Pass & Seymour, **21** 348–49
Patagonia, **16** 352; **18** 376; **21** 193; **25** 206. *See also* Lost Arrow Inc.
Patak Spices Ltd., **18** 247
Pataling Rubber Estates Syndicate, **III** 697, 699
Patch Rubber Co., **19** 277–78
Patchoque-Plymouth Co., **IV** 371
PATCO. *See* Philippine Airlines, Inc.
Patent Arms Manufacturing Company, **12** 70
Patent Nut & Bolt Co., **III** 493
Patent Slip and Dock Co., **I** 592
La Paternelle, **III** 210
Paternoster Stores plc, **V** 108; **24** 269
Paterson Candy Ltd., **22** 89

Paterson, Simons & Co., **I** 592
Path-Tek Laboratories, Inc., **6** 41
Pathé Cinéma, **6** 374
Pathe Communications Co., **IV** 676; **7** 529; **25** 329
Pathé Fréres, **IV** 626; **19** 203
Pathé SA, 29 369–71. *See also* Chargeurs International.
Pathmark Stores, Inc., II 672–74; **9** 173; **15** 260; **18** 6; **19** 479, 481; **23 369–71**
Patience & Nicholson, **III** 674
Patient Care, Inc., **13** 150
Patil Systems, **11** 56
Patina Oil & Gas Corporation, 24 379–81
Patino N.V., **17** 380
Patrick Industries, Inc., 30 342–45
Patricof & Company, **24** 45
Patriot American Hospitality, Inc., **21** 184
Patriot Co., **IV** 582
Patriot Life Insurance Co., **III** 193
Patterson Dental Co., 19 289–91
Patterson Industries, Inc., **14** 42
Pattison & Bowns, Inc., **IV** 180
Patton Electric Company, Inc., **19** 360
Patton Paint Company. *See* PPG Industries, Inc.
Paul A. Brands, **11** 19
Paul Boechat & Cie, **21** 515
Paul C. Dodge Company, **6** 579
Paul Davril, Inc., **25** 258
Paul H. Rose Corporation, **13** 445
Paul Harris Stores, Inc., 15 245; **18 409–12**
Paul, Hastings, Janofsky & Walker LLP, 27 357–59
Paul Koss Supply Co., **16** 387
Paul Marshall Products Inc., **16** 36
Paul Masson, **I** 285
The Paul Revere Corporation, 12 382–83
Paul Wahl & Co., **IV** 277
Paul Williams Copier Corp., **IV** 252; **17** 28
Paul Wurth, **IV** 25
Pauls Plc, **III** 699
Pavallier, **18** 35
Pavex Construction Company. *See* Granite Rock Company.
Pawnee Industries, Inc., **19** 415
Paxall, Inc., **8** 545
Pay 'N Pak Stores, Inc., 9 399–401; 16 186–88
Pay 'n Save Corp., **12** 477; **15** 274; **17** 366
Pay Less, **II** 601, 604
Paychex, Inc., 15 347–49
Payless Cashways, Inc., 11 384–86; 13 274
Payless DIY, **V** 17, 19
PayLess Drug Stores, **12** 477–78; **18** 286; **22** 39
Payless ShoeSource, Inc., V 132, 135; **13** 361; **18 413–15**; **26** 441
PBF Corp. *See* Paris Corporation.
PBL. *See* Publishing and Broadcasting Ltd.
PBS. *See* Public Broadcasting Stations.
PC Globe, Inc., **13** 114
PC Realty, Canada Ltd., **III** 340
PCA-Budafok Paperboard Ltd., **12** 377
PCI Acquisition, **11** 385
PCI/Mac-Pak Group, **IV** 261
PCI Services, Inc. *See* Cardinal Health, Inc.
PCL Industries Ltd., **IV** 296; **19** 226
PCO, **III** 685
PCS. *See* Potash Corp. of Saskatchewan Inc.
PCS Health Systems Inc., **12** 333
PDA Engineering, **25** 305
PDA Inc., **19** 290
PDO. *See* Petroleum Development Oman.
PDQ Transportation Inc., **18** 226
PDV America, Inc., **31** 113
PDVSA. *See* Petróleos de Venezuela S.A.
Peabody Coal Company, I 559; **III** 248; **IV** 47, 169–71, 576; **7** 387–88; **10 447–49**
Peabody Holding Company, Inc., IV 19, **169–72**; **6** 487; **7** 209
Peabody, Riggs & Co., **II** 427
Peaches Entertainment Corporation, **24** 502
Peachtree Doors, **10** 95
Peachtree Federal Savings and Loan Association of Atlanta, **10** 92
Peachtree Software Inc., **18** 364
Peak Oilfield Service Company, **9** 364
The Peak Technologies Group, Inc., 14 377–80
Peakstone, **III** 740
Peapod, Inc., 22 522; **30 346–48**
Pearce-Uible Co., **14** 460
Pearl Health Services, **I** 249
Pearl Package Co., Ltd., **IV** 327
Pearle Vision, Inc., I 688; **12** 188; **13 390–92**; **14** 214; **23** 329; **24** 140
Pearson plc, IV 611, 652, **657–59**; **14** 414; **25** 283, 285
Peasant Restaurants Inc., **30** 330
Peat Marwick. *See* KPMG Peat Marwick.
Peaudouce, **IV** 339
Peavey Electronics Corporation, II 494; **12** 81; **16 408–10**
Peavey Paper Mills, Inc., **26** 362
Pebble Beach Corp., **II** 170
PEC Plastics, **9** 92
Pechelbronn Oil Company, **III** 616; **17** 416–17
Pechiney S.A., I 190, 341; **IV** 12, 59, 108, **173–75**, 560; **V** 605; **12** 253–54; **14** 216; **26** 403; **31** 11
Péchiney-Saint-Gobain, **I** 389; **III** 677; **16** 121
PECO Energy Company, 11 387–90
Pediatric Services of America, Inc., 31 356–58
Pedigree Petfoods, **22** 298
Peebles Inc., 16 411–13
Peekskill Chemical Works. *See* Binney & Smith Inc.
Peel-Conner Telephone Works, **II** 24
Peerless, **III** 467; **8** 74; **11** 534
Peerless Gear & Machine Company, **8** 515
Peerless Industries, Inc., **III** 569; **20** 360
Peerless Paper Co., **IV** 310; **19** 266
Peerless Pump Co., **I** 442
Peerless Spinning Corporation, **13** 532
Peerless Systems, Inc., **17** 263
Peet's Coffee, **13** 493; **18** 37
Pegulan, **I** 426–27; **25** 464
PEI. *See* Process Engineering Inc.
Peine, **IV** 201
Pekema Oy, **IV** 470–71
Peko-Wallsend Ltd., **13** 97
Pel-Tex Oil Co., **IV** 84; **7** 188
Pelican and British Empire Life Office, **III** 372
Pelican Homestead and Savings, **11** 107
Pelican Insurance Co., **III** 349
Pelican Life Assurance, **III** 371–72
Pelikan Holding AG, **18** 388
Pella Corporation, 10 95; **12 384–86**; **22** 346
Pelto Oil Company, **14** 455
PEM International Ltd., **28** 350
Pemex. *See* Petróleos Mexicanos.
Peñarroya, **IV** 107–08
Penda Corp., **19** 415
Pendexcare Ltd., **6** 181
Pendle Travel Services Ltd. *See* Airtours Plc.
Pengrowth Gas Corp., **25** 232
Penguin Publishing Co. Ltd., **IV** 585, 659
Penhaligon's, **24** 237
Peninsula Stores, Ltd. *See* Lucky Stores, Inc.
Peninsular and Oriental Steam Navigation Company, II 296; **III** 521–22, 712; **V 490–93**; **22** 444; **26** 241, 243
Peninsular and Oriental Steam Navigation Company (Bovis Division), I 588–89
Peninsular Portland Cement, **III** 704
Peninsular Power, **6** 602
Peninsular Railroad Company, **17** 440
Penn Advertising, **27** 280
Penn Central Corp., **I** 435; **II** 255; **IV** 576; **10** 71, 73, 547; **17** 443
Penn Champ Co., **9** 72
Penn Controls, **III** 535–36; **26** 229
Penn Corp., **13** 561
Penn Cress Ice Cream, **13** 393
Penn Engineering & Manufacturing Corp., 28 349–51
Penn Fuel Co., **IV** 548
Penn Health, **III** 85
Penn Square Bank, **II** 248, 262
Penn Traffic Company, 8 409–10; **13** 95, **393–95**
Penn-American Refining Co., **IV** 489
Penn-Texas Corporation, **I** 434; **12** 71
Penn-Western Gas and Electric, **6** 524
Pennaco Hosiery, Inc., **12** 93
Pennington Drug, **III** 10
Pennroad Corp., **IV** 458
Pennsalt Chemical Corp., **I** 383
Pennsylvania Blue Shield, III 325–27
Pennsylvania Coal & Coke Corp., **I** 434
Pennsylvania Coal Co., **IV** 180
Pennsylvania Electric Company, **6** 535; **27** 182
Pennsylvania Farm Bureau Cooperative Association, **7** 17–18
Pennsylvania General Fire Insurance Assoc., **III** 257
Pennsylvania Glass Sand Co., **I** 464; **11** 198
Pennsylvania House, Inc., **10** 324; **12** 301
Pennsylvania International Raceway, **V** 494
Pennsylvania Life Insurance Company, **27** 47
Pennsylvania Power & Light Company, V 676, **693–94**; **11** 388
Pennsylvania Pump and Compressor Co., **II** 16
Pennsylvania Railroad, **I** 456, 472; **II** 329, 490; **6** 436; **10** 71–73; **26** 295
Pennsylvania Refining Co., **IV** 488–89
Pennsylvania Salt Manufacturing Co., **I** 383
Pennsylvania Steel Co., **IV** 35; **7** 48
Pennsylvania Water & Power Company, **25** 44

Pennwalt Corporation, **I 382–84**; **IV** 547; **12** 18; **21** 205
Penny Curtiss Baking Co., Inc., **13** 395
Pennzoil Company, **IV 488–90**, 551, 553; **10** 190; **14** 491, 493; **20 418–22 (upd.)**; **23** 40–41; **25** 443, 445
Penray, **I** 373
Penrod Drilling Corporation, **7** 228, 558
Pension Benefit Guaranty Corp., **III** 255; **12** 489
Penske Corporation, **V 494–95**; **19** 223, **292–94 (upd.)**; **20** 263
Penske Truck Rental, **24** 445
Pentair, Inc., **III** 715; **7 419–21**; **11** 315; **26 361–64 (upd.)**
Pental Insurance Company, Ltd., **11** 523
Pentane Partners, **7** 518
Pentastar Transportation Group, Inc. *See* Dollar Thrifty Automotive Group, Inc.
Pentaverken A.B., **I** 209
Pentech International, Inc., **14** 217; **29 372–74**
Pentes Play, Inc., **27** 370, 372
Pentland Group plc, **20 423–25**
Pentland Industries PLC, **V** 375; **26** 396–97
Penton Media, Inc., **9** 414; **27 360–62**
People Express Airlines Inc., **I** 90, 98, 103, **117–18**, 123–24, 129–30; **6** 129; **21** 142; **22** 220
People That Love (PTL) Television, **13** 279
People's Bank of Halifax, **II** 210
People's Bank of New Brunswick, **II** 210
People's Drug Store, **II** 604–05; **22** 37–38
People's Ice and Refrigeration Company, **9** 274
People's Insurance Co., **III** 368
People's Natural Gas, **IV** 548; **6** 593
People's Radio Network, **25** 508
People's Trust Co. of Brooklyn, **II** 254; **9** 124
Peoples, **24** 315–16
Peoples Bancorp, **14** 529
Peoples Bank, **13** 467; **17** 302
Peoples Bank & Trust Co., **31** 207
Peoples Bank of Youngstown, **9** 474
Peoples Energy Corporation, **6 543–44**
Peoples Finance Co., **II** 418
Peoples Gas Light & Coke Co., **IV** 169; **6** 529, 543–44
Peoples Gas Light Co., **6** 455; **25** 44
Peoples Jewelers of Canada, **16** 561
Peoples Life Insurance Co., **III** 218
Peoples Natural Gas Company of South Carolina, **6** 576
Peoples Restaurants, Inc., **17** 320–21
Peoples Savings of Monroe, **9** 482
Peoples Security Insurance Co., **III** 219
PeopleServe, Inc., **29** 401
PeopleSoft Inc., **11** 78; **14 381–83**
The Pep Boys–Manny, Moe & Jack, **11 391–93**; **16** 160; **26** 348
PEPCO. *See* Portland Electric Power Company *and* Potomac Electric Power Company.
Pepe Clothing Co., **18** 85
Pepperell Manufacturing Company, **16** 533–34
Pepperidge Farm, **I** 29; **II** 480–81; **7** 67–68; **26** 56–57, 59
PepsiCo, Inc., **I** 234, 244–46, 257, 269, **276–79**, 281, 291; **II** 103, 448, 477, 608; **III** 106, 116, 588; **7** 265, 267, 396, 404, 434–35, 466, 505–06; **8** 399; **9** 177, 343; **10** 130, 199, 227, 324, **450–54 (upd.)**; **11** 421, 450; **12** 337, 453; **13** 162, 284, 448, 494; **15** 72, 75, 380; **16** 96; **18** 65; **19** 114, 221; **21** 143, 313, 315–16, 362, 401, 405, 485–86; **22** 95, 353; **23** 418, 420; **25** 91, 177–78, 366, 411; **28** 271, 473, 476; **31** 243
Pepsodent Company, **I** 14; **9** 318
Perception Technology, **10** 500
Percy Bilton Investment Trust Ltd., **IV** 710
Percy Street Investments Ltd., **IV** 711
Perdue Farms Inc., **7 422–24**, 432; **23 375–78 (upd.)**
Perfect Circle Corp., **I** 152
Perfect Fit Industries, **17** 182–84
Perfect-Ventil GmbH, **9** 413
Performance Contracting, Inc., **III** 722; **20** 415
Performance Food Group Company, **31 359–62**
Performance Technologies, Inc., **10** 395
Perfumania, Inc., **22** 157
Pergamon Holdings, **15** 83
Pergamon Press, **IV** 611, 641–43, 687; **7** 311–12
Perini Corporation, **8 418–21**
Perisem, **I** 281
The Perkin-Elmer Corporation, **III** 455, 727; **7 425–27**; **9** 514; **13** 326; **21** 123
Perkins, **I** 147; **12** 90
Perkins Bacon & Co., **10** 267
Perkins Cake & Steak, **9** 425
Perkins Engines Ltd., **III** 545, 652; **10** 274; **11** 472; **19** 294; **27** 203
Perkins Family Restaurants, L.P., **22 417–19**
Perkins Oil Well Cementing Co., **III** 497
Perkins Products Co., **II** 531
Perl Pillow, **19** 304
Perland Environmental Technologies Inc., **8** 420
Permal Group, **27** 276, 513
Permaneer Corp., **IV** 281; **9** 259. *See also* Spartech Corporation.
Permanent General Companies, Inc., **11** 194
Permanent Pigments Inc., **25** 71
Permanente Cement Co., **I** 565
Permanente Metals Corp., **IV** 15, 121–22
Permian Corporation, **V** 152–53
PERMIGAN, **IV** 492
Permodalan, **III** 699
Pernod Ricard S.A., **I** 248, **280–81**; **21 399–401 (upd.)**
Pernvo Inc., **I** 387
Perot Systems Corporation, **13** 482; **29 375–78**
Perret-Olivier, **III** 676; **16** 120
Perrier, **19** 50
Perrier Corporation of America, **16** 341
Perrigo Company, **12** 218, **387–89**
Perrin, **IV** 614
Perrot Brake Co., **I** 141
Perrow Motor Freight Lines, **6** 370
Perry Brothers, Inc., **24** 149
Perry Capital Corp., **28** 138
Perry Drug Stores Inc., **12** 21; **26** 476
Perry Ellis, **16** 37
Perry Manufacturing Co., **16** 37
Perry Sports, **13** 545; **13** 545
Perry Tritech, **25** 103–05
Perry's Shoes Inc., **16** 36
Perscombinatie, **IV** 611
Pershing & Co., **22** 189
Personal Care Corp., **17** 235
Personal Performance Consultants, **9** 348
Personal Products Company, **III** 35; **8** 281, 511
Personnel Pool of America, **29** 224, 26–27
Perstorp A.B., **I 385–87**
PERTAMINA, **IV** 383, 461, **491–93**, 517, 567
Pertec Computer Corp., **17** 49; **18** 434
Pertech Computers Ltd., **18** 75
Perusahaan Minyak Republik Indonesia, **IV** 491
Peruvian Corp., **I** 547
Pet Food & Supply, **14** 385
Pet Incorporated, **I** 457; **II** 486–87; **7 428–31**; **10** 554; **12** 124; **13** 409; **14** 214; **24** 140; **27** 196
Petco Animal Supplies, Inc., **29 379–81**
Pete's Brewing Company, **18** 72, 502; **22 420–22**
Peter Bawden Drilling, **IV** 570; **24** 521
Peter, Cailler, Kohler, Chocolats Suisses S.A., **II** 546; **7** 381
Peter Cundill & Associates Ltd., **15** 504
Peter Gast Shipping GmbH, **7** 40
Peter J. Schmitt Co., **13** 394; **24** 444–45
Peter J. Schweitzer, Inc., **III** 40; **16** 303
Peter Jones, **V** 94
Peter Kiewit Sons' Inc., **I** 599–600; **III** 198; **8 422–24**; **15** 18; **25** 512, 514
Peter Norton Computing Group, **10** 508–09
Peter Paul/Cadbury, **II** 477, 512; **15** 221
Peterbilt Motors Co., **I** 185–86; **26** 355
Peters Shoe Co., **III** 528
Peters-Revington Corporation, **26** 100. *See also* Chromcraft Revington, Inc.
Petersen Publishing Company, **21 402–04**
Peterson, Howell & Heather, **V** 496
Peterson Soybean Seed Co., **9** 411
La Petite Academy, **13** 299
Petite Sophisticate, **V** 207–08
Petoseed Co. Inc., **29** 435
Petrie Stores Corporation, **8 425–27**
Petrini's, **II** 653
Petro/Chem Environmental Services, Inc., **IV** 411
Petro-Canada Limited, **IV** 367, **494–96**, 499; **13** 557
Petro-Coke Co. Ltd., **IV** 476
Petro-Lewis Corp., **IV** 84; **7** 188
Petroamazonas, **IV** 511
Petrobas, **21** 31
Petrobel, **IV** 412
Petrobrás. *See* Petróleo Brasileiro S.A.
Petrocarbona GmbH, **IV** 197–98
Petrocel, S.A., **19** 12
Petrochemical Industries Co., **IV** 451
Petrochemicals Company, **17** 90–91
Petrochemie Danubia GmbH, **IV** 486–87
Petrochim, **IV** 498
Petrocomercial, **IV** 511
Petrocorp. *See* Petroleum Company of New Zealand.
Petroecuador. *See* Petróleos del Ecuador.
Petrofertil, **IV** 501
PetroFina S.A., **IV** 455, 495, **497–500**, 576; **7** 179; **26 365–69 (upd.)**
Petrogal. *See* Petróleos de Portugal.
Petroindustria, **IV** 511
Petrol, **IV** 487
Petrol Ofisi Anonim Sirketi, **IV** 564
Petrolane Properties, **17** 558

Petróleo Brasileiro S.A., **IV** 424, **501–03**
Petróleo Mecânica Alfa, **IV** 505
Petróleos de Portugal S.A., **IV 504–06**
Petróleos de Venezuela S.A., **II** 661; **IV** 391–93, **507–09**, 571; **24** 522; **31** 113
Petróleos del Ecuador, **IV 510–11**
Petróleos Mexicanos, **IV 512–14**, 528; **19** 10, **295–98 (upd.)**
Petroleum and Chemical Corp., **III** 672
Petroleum Authority of Thailand, **IV** 519
Petroleum Company of New Zealand, **IV** 279; **19** 155
Petroleum Development (Qatar) Ltd., **IV** 524
Petroleum Development (Trucial States) Ltd., **IV** 363
Petroleum Development Corp. of the Republic of Korea, **IV** 455
Petroleum Development Oman LLC, **IV 515–16**
Petroleum Projects Co., **IV** 414
Petroleum Research and Engineering Co. Ltd., **IV** 473
Petrolgroup, Inc., **6** 441
Petroliam Nasional Bhd. *See* Petronas.
Petrolite Corporation, **15 350–52**
Petrolube, **IV** 538
Petromex. *See* Petróleos de Mexico S.A.
Petromin Lubricating Oil Co., **17** 415
Petronas, **IV 517–20**; **21** 501
Petronor, **IV** 514, 528
Petropeninsula, **IV** 511
Petroproduccion, **IV** 511
Petroquímica de Venezuela SA, **IV** 508
Petroquimica Española, **I** 402
Petroquisa, **IV** 501
PETROSUL, **IV** 504, 506
Petrotransporte, **IV** 511
PETsMART, Inc., **14 384–86**; **27** 95; **29** 379–80
Petstuff, Inc., **14** 386
Pettibone Corporation, **19** 365
Petzazz, **14** 386
Peugeot S.A., **I** 163, **187–88**; **II** 13; **III** 508; **11** 104; **26** 11. *See also* PSA Peugeot Citroen S.A.
Pfaff-Pegasus of U.S.A. Inc., **15** 385
The Pfaltzgraff Co. *See* Susquehanna Pfaltzgraff Company.
Pfaudler Vacuum Co., **I** 287
Pfauter-Maag Cutting Tools, **24** 186
PFCI. *See* Pulte Financial Companies, Inc.
PFI Acquisition Corp., **17** 184
Pfizer, Hoechst Celanese Corp., **8** 399
Pfizer Inc., **I** 301, 367, **661–63**, 668; **9** 356, **402–05 (upd.)**; **10** 53–54; **11** 207, 310–11, 459; **12** 4; **17** 131; **19** 105
Pflueger Corporation, **22** 483
PG&E Corporation, **26 370–73 (upd.)**; **27** 131. *See also* Portland General Electric.
PGH Bricks and Pipes, **III** 735
Phaostron Instruments and Electronic Co., **18** 497–98
Phar-Mor Inc., **12** 209, **390–92**, 477; **18** 507; **21** 459; **22** 157
Pharma Plus Drugmarts, **II** 649–50
Pharmacia & Upjohn Inc., **25** 22, **374–78 (upd.)**. *See also* Upjohn Company.
Pharmacia A.B., **I** 211, **664–65**
Pharmaco Dynamics Research, Inc., **10** 106–07
Pharmacom Systems Ltd., **II** 652
Pharmacy Corporation of America, **16** 57
PharmaKinetics Laboratories, Inc., **10** 106
Pharmanex, Inc., **27** 352
Pharmaprix Ltd., **II** 663
Pharmazell GmbH, **IV** 324
Pharmedix, **11** 207
Pharos, **9** 381
Phelan & Collender, **III** 442
Phelan Faust Paint, **8** 553
Phelps Dodge Corporation, **IV** 33, **176–79**, 216; **7** 261–63, 288; **19** 375; **28 352–57 (upd.)**
Phenix Bank, **II** 312
Phenix Cheese Corp., **II** 533
Phenix Insurance Co., **III** 240
Phenix Mills Ltd., **II** 662
PHF Life Insurance Co., **III** 263; **IV** 623
PHH Corporation, **V 496–97**; **6** 357; **22** 55
Phibro Corporation, **II** 447–48; **IV** 80; **13** 447–48; **21** 67
Philadelphia and Reading Corp., **I** 440; **II** 329; **6** 377; **25** 165
Philadelphia Carpet Company, **9** 465
Philadelphia Coke Company, **6** 487
Philadelphia Company, **6** 484, 493
Philadelphia Drug Exchange, **I** 692
Philadelphia Electric Company, **V 695–97**; **6** 450
Philadelphia Life, **I** 527
Philadelphia Smelting and Refining Co., **IV** 31
Philco Corp., **I** 167, 531; **II** 86; **III** 604; **13** 402
Philip Environmental Inc., **16 414–16**
Philip Morris Companies Inc., **I** 23, 269; **II** 530–34; **V** 397, 404, **405–07**, 409, 417; **6** 52; **7** 272, 274, 276, 548; **8** 53; **9** 180; **12** 337, 372; **13** 138, 517; **15** 64, 72–73, 137; **18** 72, **416–19 (upd.)**; **19** 112, 369; **20** 23; **22** 73, 338; **23** 427; **26** 249, 251; **29** 46–47
Philip Smith Theatrical Enterprises. *See* GC Companies, Inc.
Philipp Abm. Cohen, **IV** 139
Philipp Brothers Chemicals, Inc., **II** 447; **IV** 79–0; **25** 82
Philipp Holzmann AG, **II** 279, 386; **14** 169; **16** 284, 286; **17 374–77**
Philippine Aerospace Development Corporation, **27** 475
Philippine Airlines, Inc., **I** 107; **6 106–08**, 122–23; **23 379–82 (upd.)**; **27** 464
Philippine American Life Insurance Co., **III** 195
Philippine Sinter Corp., **IV** 125
Philips, **V** 339; **6** 101; **10** 269; **22** 194
Philips Electronics N.V., **8** 153; **9** 75; **10** 16; **12** 475, 549; **13** 396, **400–03 (upd.)**; **14** 446; **23** 389; **26** 334; **27** 190–92
Philips Electronics North America Corp., **13 396–99**; **26** 334
N.V. Philips Gloeilampenfabriken, **I** 107, 330; **II** 25, 56, 58, **78–80**, 99, 102, 117, 119; **III** 479, 654–55; **IV** 680; **12** 454. *See also* Philips Electronics N.V.
Philips Medical Systems, **29** 299
Phillip Hawkins, **III** 169; **6** 285
Phillip Securities, **16** 14
Phillippe of California, **8** 16
Phillips & Drew, **II** 379
Phillips & Jacobs, Inc., **14** 486
Phillips Cables, **III** 433
Phillips Carbon Black, **IV** 421
Phillips Colleges, **22** 442
Phillips Manufacturing Company, **8** 464
Phillips Petroleum Company, **I** 377; **II** 15, 408; **III** 752; **IV** 71, 290, 366, 405, 412, 414, 445, 453, 498, **521–23**, 567, 570–71, 575; **10** 84, 440; **11** 522; **13** 356, 485; **17** 422; **19** 176; **24** 521; **31** 457
Phillips Sheet and Tin Plate Co., **IV** 236
Phillips-Van Heusen Corporation, **24 382–85**
PHLCorp., **11** 261
PHM Corp., **8** 461
Phoenicia Glass, **25** 266–67
Phoenix Assurance Co., **III** 242, 257, 369, 370–74
Phoenix Financial Services, **11** 115
Phoenix Fire Office, **III** 234
Phoenix Insurance Co., **III** 389; **IV** 711
Phoenix Microsystems Inc., **13** 8
Phoenix Mutual Life Insurance, **16** 207
Phoenix Oil and Transport Co., **IV** 90
Phoenix State Bank and Trust Co., **II** 213
Phoenix Technologies Ltd., **13** 482
Phoenix-Rheinrohr AG, **IV** 222
Phone America of Carolina, **8** 311
Phonogram, **23** 389
Photocircuits Corp., **18** 291–93
PhotoDisc Inc., **31** 216, 218
PHP Healthcare Corporation, **22 423–25**
Phuket Air Catering Company Ltd., **6** 123–24; **27** 464
Physical Measurements Information, **31** 357
Physician Corporation of America, **24** 231
Physician Sales & Service, Inc., **14 387–89**
Physician's Weight Loss Center, **10** 383
Physicians Formula Cosmetics, **8** 512
Physicians Placement, **13** 49
Physio-Control International Corp., **18 420–23**; **30** 316
Physiotherapy Associates Inc., **29** 453
Piaget, **27** 487, 489
Piaggio & C. S.p.A., **17** 24; **20 426–29**
PIC International Group PLC, **24 386–88 (upd.)**
Pic 'N' Save, **17** 298–99
PIC Realty Corp., **III** 339
Picard Surgeles, **27** 93
Picault, **19** 50
Piccadilly Cafeterias, Inc., **19 299–302**
Pick, **III** 98
Pick-N-Pay, **II** 642; **9** 452
Pickands Mather, **13** 158
Picker International Corporation, **II** 25; **8** 352; **30** 314
Pickfords Ltd., **6** 412–14
Pickland Mather & Co., **IV** 409
PickOmatic Systems, **8** 135
Pickwick, **I** 613
Pickwick Dress Co., **III** 54
Pickwick International, **9** 360
Piclands Mather, **7** 308
Pico Ski Area Management Company, **28** 21
Picture Classified Network, **IV** 597
PictureTel Corp., **10 455–57**; **27 363–66 (upd.)**
Piece Goods Shops, **16** 198
Piedmont Airlines, Inc., **6** 132; **12** 490; **28** 507
Piedmont Coca-Cola Bottling Partnership, **10** 223

Piedmont Concrete, **III** 739
Piedmont Natural Gas Company, Inc., 27 367–69
Piedmont Pulp and Paper Co. *See* Westvaco Corporation.
Pier 1 Imports, Inc., 12 179, 200, **393–95**
Pierburg GmbH, **9** 445–46
Pierce, **IV** 478
Pierce Brothers, **6** 295
Pierce Leahy Corporation, 24 389–92
Pierce National Life, **22** 314
Pierce Steam Heating Co., **III** 663
Piercing Pagoda, Inc., 29 382–84
Pierre Foods, **29** 203
Pierre Frozen Foods Inc., **13** 270–72
Pierson, Heldring, and Pierson, **II** 185
Pietrafesa Corporation, **29** 208
Pietro's Pizza Parlors, **II** 480–81; **26** 56–57
Piezo Electric Product, Inc., **16** 239
Pig Improvement Co., **II** 500
Piggly Wiggly Southern, Inc., II 571, 624; **13** 251–52, **404–06**; **18** 6, 8; **21** 455; **22** 127; **26** 47; **27** 245; **31** 406, 408
Pignone, **IV** 420
Pike Adding Machine, **III** 165
Pike Corporation of America, **I** 570; **8** 191
Pikrose and Co. Ltd., **IV** 136
Pilgrim Curtain Co., **III** 213
Pilgrim's Pride Corporation, 7 432–33; 23 383–85 (upd.)
Pilkington plc, I 429; **II** 475; **III** 56, 641–42, 676–77, 714–15, **724–27**; **16** 7, 9, 120–21; **22** 434
Pillar Holdings, **IV** 191
Pilliod Furniture, Inc., **12** 300
Pillowtex Corporation, 19 303–05; **31** 200
Pillsbury Company, II 133, 414, 493–94, 511, **555–57**, 575, 613–15; **7** 106, 128, 277, 469, 547; **8** 53–54; **10** 147, 176; **11** 23; **12** 80, 510; **13 407–09 (upd.)**, 516; **14** 212, 214; **15** 64; **16** 71; **17** 70–71, 434; **22** 59, 426; **24** 140–41; **25** 179, 241; **27** 196, 287; **29** 433
Pillsbury Madison & Sutro LLP, 29 385–88
Pilot, **I** 531
Pilot Freight Carriers, **27** 474
Pilot Insurance Agency, **III** 204
Pinal-Dome Oil, **IV** 569; **24** 520
Pinault-Printemps-Redoute S.A., 15 386; **19 306–09 (upd.)**; **22** 362; **27** 513
Pincus & Co., **7** 305
Pine Tree Casting. *See* Sturm, Ruger & Company, Inc.
Pinecliff Publishing Company, **10** 357
Pinelands, Inc., **9** 119; **26** 33
Pineville Kraft Corp., **IV** 276
Pinewood Studios, **II** 157
Pininfarina, **I** 188
Pinkerton's Inc., 9 406–09; **13** 124–25; **14** 541; **16** 48
Pinnacle Art and Frame, **31** 436
Pinnacle Books, **25** 483
Pinnacle Fitness, **25** 42
Pinnacle West Capital Corporation, 6 545–47; **26** 359
Pinsetter Corp., **III** 443
Pinto Island Metals Company, **15** 116
Pioneer Airlines, **I** 96; **21** 141
Pioneer Asphalt Co., **I** 404
Pioneer Asphalts Pty. Ltd., **III** 728
Pioneer Concrete Services Ltd., **III** 728–29
Pioneer Cotton Mill, **12** 503
Pioneer Electronic Corporation, II 103; **III 604–06; 28 358–61 (upd.)**
Pioneer Federal Savings Bank, **10** 340; **11** 115
Pioneer Financial Corp., **11** 447
Pioneer Food Stores Co-op, **24** 528
Pioneer Hi-Bred International, Inc., 9 410–12; **17** 131; **21** 387
Pioneer International Limited, III 687, **728–30**; **28** 83
Pioneer Life Insurance Co., **III** 274
Pioneer Natural Gas Company, **10** 82
Pioneer Outdoor, **27** 280
Pioneer Plastics Corporation, **31** 399–400
Pioneer Readymixed Concrete and Mortar Proprietary Ltd., **III** 728
Pioneer Saws Ltd., **III** 598
Pioneer-Standard Electronics Inc., 13 47; **19 310–14**
Pipe Line Service Company. *See* Plexco.
Pipeline and Products Marketing Co., **IV** 473
Piper Aircraft Corp., **I** 482; **II** 403; **8** 49–50
Piper Jaffray Companies Inc., 22 426–30, 465
Pirelli S.p.A., IV 174, 420; **V 249–51**; **10** 319; **15 353–56 (upd.)**; **16** 318; **21** 73; **28** 262
Piscataquis Canal and Railroad Company, **16** 348
Pisces Inc., **13** 321
Pispalan Werhoomo Oy, **I** 387
The Piston Ring Company, **I** 199; **10** 492
Pitcairn Aviation, **I** 101
Pitney Bowes, Inc., III 156–58, 159; **19 315–18 (upd.)**
Pittman Company, **28** 350
Pittsburgh & Lake Angeline Iron Company, **13** 156
Pittsburgh & Lake Erie Railroad, **I** 472
Pittsburgh Aluminum Alloys Inc., **12** 353
Pittsburgh Brewing Co., **10** 169–70; **18** 70, 72
Pittsburgh Chemical Co., **IV** 573; **7** 551
Pittsburgh Consolidation Coal Co., **8** 346
Pittsburgh Corning Corp., **III** 683
Pittsburgh Life, **III** 274
Pittsburgh National Bank, **II** 317, 342; **22** 55
Pittsburgh National Corp., **II** 342
Pittsburgh Paint & Glass. *See* PPG Industries, Inc.
Pittsburgh Plate Glass Co. *See* PPG Industries, Inc.
Pittsburgh Railway Company, **9** 413
Pittsburgh Reduction Co., **II** 315; **IV** 9, 14
Pittsburgh Steel Company, **7** 587
Pittsburgh Trust and Savings, **II** 342
The Pittston Company, IV 180–82, 566; **10** 44; **19 319–22 (upd.)**
Pittway Corporation, 9 413–15; **27** 361–62; **28** 133–34
Pixel Semiconductor, **11** 57
Pizitz, Inc., **19** 324
Pizza Dispatch. *See* Dominos's Pizza, Inc.
Pizza Hut Inc., I 221, 278, 294; **II** 614; **7** 152–53, 267, **434–35**, 506; **10** 450; **11** 50; **12** 123; **13** 336, 516; **14** 107; **15** 344–46; **16** 446; **17** 71, 537; **21** 24–25, 315, **405–07 (upd.)**; **22** 353; **24** 295; **25** 179–80, 227; **28** 238
Pizza Inn, **16** 447; **25** 179
PizzaCo, Inc., **7** 152
Pizzeria Uno, **25** 178
PJS Publications, **22** 442
PKbanken, **II** 353
Place Two, **V** 156
Placer Cego Petroleum Ltd., **IV** 367
Placer Development Ltd., **IV** 19
Placer Dome Inc., IV 571; **20 430–33**; **24** 522
Placid Oil Co., **7** 228
Plaid Holdings Corp., **9** 157
Plain Jane Dress Company, **8** 169
Plainwell Paper Co., Inc., **8** 103
Planet Hollywood International, Inc., 18 424–26; **25** 387–88
Planet Insurance Co., **III** 343
Plank Road Brewery, **I** 269; **12** 337
Plankinton Packing Co., **III** 534
Plant Genetics Inc., **I** 266; **21** 320
Planters Company, **24** 287
Planters Lifesavers, **14** 274–75
Planters Nut & Chocolate Co., **I** 219; **II** 544
Plas-Techs, Inc., **15** 35
Plastic Coating Corporation, **IV** 330; **8** 483
Plastic Containers, Inc., **15** 129; **25** 512
Plastic Engineered Products Company. *See* Ballard Medical Products.
Plastic Parts, Inc., **19** 277
Plasticos Metalgrafica, **I** 231
Plastics, Inc., **13** 41
Plasto Bambola. *See* BRIO AB.
Plastrier. *See* Compagnie de Saint-Gobain S.A.
Plate Glass Group, **24** 450
Plateau Holdings, Inc., **12** 260; **13** 502
PLATINUM Technology, Inc., 14 390–92
Platt & Co., **I** 506
Platt Bros., **III** 636
Platt's Price Service, Inc., **IV** 636–37
Play by Play Toys & Novelties, Inc., 26 374–76
Play It Again Sports, **18** 207–08
Playboy Enterprises, Inc., 18 427–30
PlayCore, Inc., 27 370–72
Players International, Inc., 16 263, 275; **19** 402; **22 431–33**
Playland, **16** 389
Playmates Toys, 23 386–88
Playskool, Inc., III 504, 506; **12** 169; **13** 317; **16** 267; **25 379–81**
Playtex Products, Inc., II 448, 468; **8** 511; **13** 448; **15 357–60**; **24** 480
Playworld, **16** 389–90
Plaza Coloso S.A. de C.V., **10** 189
Plaza Medical Group, **6** 184
Plaza Securities, **I** 170
PLC. *See* Prescription Learning Corporation.
Pleasant Company, 25 314; **27 373–75**
Pleasurama PLC, **I** 248; **12** 228
Plessey Company, PLC, II 25, 39, **81–82**; **IV** 100; **6** 241
Plews Manufacturing Co., **III** 602
Plexco, **7** 30–31
Plezall Wipers, Inc., **15** 502
Plitt Theatres, Inc., **6** 162; **23** 126
Plon et Juillard, **IV** 614
Plough Inc., **I** 684
Plum Associates, **12** 270
Pluma, Inc., 27 376–78
Plumb Tool, **II** 16
Plus Development Corporation, **10** 458–59
Plus Mark, Inc., **7** 24

Plus System Inc., **9** 537
Plus-Ultra, **II** 196
Ply Gem Industries Inc., 12 396–98; 23 225
Plymouth County Electric Co., **14** 124
Plymouth Mills Inc., **23** 66
PMC Contract Research AB, **21** 425
PMC Specialties Group, **III** 745
PMI Corporation, **6** 140. *See also* Physical Measurements Information
PMI Mortgage Insurance Company, **10** 50
PMS Consolidated, **8** 347
PMT Services, Inc., 24 393–95
PN Pertambangan Minyak Dan Gas Bumi Negara, **IV** 492
PNC Bank Corp., 13 410–12 (upd.); 14 103; **18** 63
PNC Financial Corporation, II 317, **342–43; 9** 476; **17** 114
Pneumo Abex Corp., **I** 456–58; **III** 512; **10** 553–54
Pneumo Dynamics Corporation, **8** 409
PNL. *See* Pacific Northwest Laboratories.
PNM. *See* Public Service Company of New Mexico.
PNP. *See* Pacific Northwest Power Company.
POAS, **IV** 563
POB Polyolefine Burghausen GmbH, **IV** 487
Pocahontas Foods USA, **31** 359, 361
Pocket Books, Inc., **10** 480; **13** 559–60
Poclain Company, **10** 380
Pogo Producing, **I** 441
Pohang Iron and Steel Company Ltd., IV 183–85; 17 351
Pohjan Sellu Oy, **IV** 316
Pohjoismainen Osakepankki, **II** 302
Pohjola Voima Oy, **IV** 348
Pohjolan Osakepankki, **II** 303
Point Chehalis Packers, **13** 244
Polak & Schwarz Essencefabricken, **9** 290
Poland Spring Natural Spring Water Co., **31** 229
Polar Manufacturing Company, **16** 32
Polar Star Milling Company, **7** 241
Polaris Industries Inc., I 530; **12 399–402; 16** 31–32; **25** 16
Polaroid Corporation, I 30–31; **II** 412; **III** 475–77, 549, 584, **607–09; IV** 330; **7** 161–62, **436–39 (upd.); 12** 180; **28 362–66 (upd.)**
Polbeth Packaging Limited, **12** 377
Polenghi, **25** 84
Policy Management Systems Corporation, 11 394–95
Polioles, S.A. de C.V., **19** 10, 12
Politos, S.A. de C.V., **23** 171
Pollenex Corp., **19** 360
Polo Food Corporation, **10** 250
Polo/Ralph Lauren Corporation, 9 157; **12 403–05; 16** 61; **25** 48
Polser, **19** 49, 51
Poly P, Inc., **IV** 458
Poly Version, Inc., **III** 645
Poly-Glas Systems, Inc., **21** 65
Poly-Hi Corporation, **8** 359
Polyblend Corporation, **7** 4
Polycell Holdings, **IV** 666; **17** 397
Polydesign België, **16** 421
Polydesign Nederland, **16** 421
Polydor B.V., **23** 389
Polydor KK, **23** 390
Polydress Plastic GmbH, **7** 141
PolyGram N.V., 13 402; **22** 194; **23 389–92; 25** 411; **26** 152, 314, 394; **31** 269
Polyken Technologies, **11** 220
Polymer Technologies Corporation, **26** 287
Polysar Energy & Chemical Corporation of Toronto, **V** 674
Polysius AG, **IV** 89
Pomeroy's, **16** 61
Pommersche Papierfabrik Hohenkrug, **III** 692
Pommery et Greno, **II** 475
Ponderosa Steakhouse, 7 336; **12** 373; **14** 331; **15 361–64**
Ponderosa System Inc., **12** 199
Pont-à-Mousson S.A., **III** 675, 677–78, 704; **16** 119, 121–22; **21** 253
Pontiac, **III** 458; **10** 353
Pontificia, **III** 207
Ponto Frio Bonzao, **22** 321
Pony Express, **II** 380–81, 395
Poorman-Douglas Corporation, **13** 468
Pope and Talbot, Inc., 12 406–08
Pope Cable and Wire B.V., **19** 45
Pope Tin Plate Co., **IV** 236; **26** 527
Popeye's/Church's, **23** 115, 117
Popeyes Famous Fried Chicken and Biscuits, Inc., **7** 26–28
Pophitt Cereals, Inc., **22** 337
Poppe Tyson Inc., **23** 479; **25** 91
Poppin' Fresh Pies, Inc., **12** 510
Popsicle, **II** 573; **14** 205
Popular Aviation Company, **12** 560
Popular Club Plan, **12** 280
Popular Merchandise, Inc., **12** 280
Pori, **IV** 350
Poron Diffusion, **9** 394
Porsche AG, 13 28, 219, **413–15; 31 363–366 (upd.)**
Port Blakely Mill Company, **17** 438
Port Harcourt Refining Co., **IV** 473
Port Stockton Food Distributors, Inc., **16** 451, 453
Portage Industries Corp., **19** 415
Portals Water Treatment, **11** 510
Porter Chadburn plc, **28** 252
Porter Shoe Manufacturing Company, **13** 360
Porter-Cable Corporation, **26** 361–63
Portex, **25** 431
Portia Management Services Ltd., **30** 318
Portland General Corporation, 6 548–51
Portland Heavy Industries, **10** 369
Portland Plastics, **25** 430–31
Portland-Zementwerke Heidelberg A.G., **23** 326
Portnet, **6** 435
Portways, **9** 92
Poseidon Exploration Ltd., **IV** 84; **7** 188
Posey, Quest, Genova, **6** 48
Positive Response Television, Inc., **27** 337–38
Post Office Counters, **V** 496
Post Office Group, V 498–501
Post Properties, Inc., 26 377–79
PostBank, **II** 189
La Poste, V 470–72
Posti- Ja Telelaitos, 6 329–31
PostScript, **17** 177
Postum Cereal Company, **II** 497, 523, 530–31; **7** 272–73; **13** 291
Potash Corporation of Saskatchewan Inc., 18 51, **431–33; 27** 318
Potlatch Corporation, IV 282; **8 428–30; 9** 260; **19** 445
Potomac Electric Power Company, 6 552–54; 25 46
Potomac Insurance Co., **III** 257
Potomac Leasing, **III** 137
Potter & Brumfield Inc., 11 396–98
Pottery Barn, **13** 42; **17** 548–50
Potts, **IV** 58
Poulan/Weed Eater. *See* White Consolidated Industries Inc.
Poulsen Wireless, **II** 490
PowCon, Inc., **17** 534
Powell Duffryn plc, III 502; **IV** 38; **31 367–70**
Powell Energy Products, **8** 321
Powell River Co. Ltd., **IV** 306–07
Power Applications & Manufacturing Company, Inc., **6** 441
Power Financial Corp., **III** 260–61
Power Jets Ltd., **I** 81
Power Parts Co., **7** 358
Power Products, **8** 515
Power Specialty Company, **6** 145
Power Team, **10** 492
Powercor. *See* PacifiCorp.
PowerFone Holdings, **10** 433
PowerGen PLC, 11 399–401; 12 349; **13** 458, 484
Powerhouse Technologies, Inc., 13 485; **27 379–81**
Powers Accounting Machine Company, **6** 240
Powers Regulator, **III** 535
Powers-Samas, **6** 240
PowerSoft Corp., **11** 77; **15** 374
Pozzi-Renati Millwork Products, Inc., **8** 135
PP&L. *See* Pennsylvania Power & Light Company.
PPG Industries, Inc., I 330, 341–42; **III** 21, 641, 667, 676, 722, 725, **731–33; 8** 153, 222, 224; **16** 120–21; **20** 415; **21** 221, 223; **22** 147, **434–37 (upd.)**
PR Holdings, **23** 382
PR Newswire, **IV** 687; **28** 501, 504
Prac, **I** 281
Practical and Educational Books, **13** 105
Practical Business Solutions, Inc., **18** 112
Pragma Bio-Tech, Inc., **11** 424
Prairie Farmer Publishing Co., **II** 129
Prairie Holding Co., **IV** 571; **24** 522
Prairie Oil and Gas Co., **IV** 368
Prairielands Energy Marketing, Inc., **7** 322, 325
Prakla Seismos, **17** 419
Pratt & Whitney, I 47, 78, 82–85, 128, 434; **II** 48; **III** 482; **6** 128; **7** 456; **9** 14, 16–18, 244–46, **416–18; 10** 162; **11** 299, 427; **12** 71; **13** 386; **14** 564; **24** 312; **25** 267
Pratt Holding, Ltd., **IV** 312; **19** 268
Pratt Hotel Corporation, **21** 275; **22** 438
Pratt Properties Inc., **8** 349
Pratta Electronic Materials, Inc., **26** 425
Praxair, Inc., 11 402–04; 16 462
Praxis Biologics, **8** 26; **27** 115
Praxis Corporation, **30** 499
Pre-Fab Cushioning, **9** 93
Pre-Paid Legal Services, Inc., 20 434–37
Precious Metals Development, **IV** 79
Precise Imports Corp., **21** 516
Precision Castparts Corp., 15 365–67
Precision Games, **16** 471

Precision Husky Corporation, **26** 494
Precision Interconnect Corporation, **14** 27
Precision LensCrafters, **13** 391
Precision Moulds, Ltd., **25** 312
Precision Optical Co., **III** 120, 575
Precision Optical Industry Company, Ltd. *See* Canon Inc.
Precision Power, Inc., **21** 514
Precision Software Corp., **14** 319
Precision Studios, **12** 529
Precision Tube Formers, Inc., **17** 234
Precor, **III** 610–11
Predica, **II** 266
Predicasts Inc., **12** 562; **17** 254
Preferred Medical Products. *See* Ballard Medical Products.
Preferred Products, Inc., **II** 669; **18** 504
PREINCO Holdings, Inc., **11** 532
PREL&P. *See* Portland Railway Electric Light & Power Company.
Prelude Corp., **III** 643
Premark International, Inc., **II** 534; **III 610–12**; **14** 548; **28** 479–80
Premex A.G., **II** 369
Premier (Transvaal) Diamond Mining Co., **IV** 65–66
Premier & Potter Printing Press Co., Inc., **II** 37
Premier Brands Foods, **II** 514
Premier Consolidated Oilfields PLC, **IV** 383
Premier Cruise Lines, **6** 368; **27** 92
Premier Diamond Mining Company, **7** 122
Premier Health Alliance Inc., **10** 143
Premier Industrial Corporation, **9 419–21**; **19** 311
Premier Insurance Co., **26** 487
Premier Medical Services, **31** 357
Premier Milling Co., **II** 465
Premier Parks, Inc., **27 382–84**
Premier Radio Networks, Inc., **23** 292, 294
Premier Rehabilitation Centers, **29** 400
Premier Sport Group Inc., **23** 66
Premiere Products, **I** 403
Premisteres S.A., **II** 663
Premium Standard Farms, Inc., **30 353–55**
PremiumWear, Inc., **30 356–59**
Prémontré, **III** 676; **16** 120
Prentice Hall Computer Publishing, **10** 24
Prentice Hall Inc., **I** 453; **IV** 672; **19** 405; **23** 503
Prescott Ball & Turben, **III** 271; **12** 60
Prescott Investors, **14** 303
Prescription Learning Corporation, **7** 256; **25** 253
Présence, **III** 211
La Preservatrice, **III** 242
Preserves and Honey, Inc., **II** 497
President Casinos, Inc., **22 438–40**
President Riverboat Casino-Mississippi Inc., **21** 300
Presidential Airlines, **I** 117
Presidents Island Steel & Wire Company. *See* Laclede Steel Company.
Presidio Oil Co., **III** 197; **IV** 123
Press Associates, **IV** 669; **19** 334
Press Trust of India, **IV** 669
Presse Pocket, **IV** 614
Pressed Steel Car Co., **6** 395; **25** 169
Presses de la Cité, **IV** 614–15
Presstar Printing, **25** 183
Pressware International, **12** 377
Prest-O-Lite Co., Inc., **I** 399; **9** 16, 516; **11** 402
Prestige et Collections, **III** 48
Prestige Fragrance & Cosmetics, Inc., **22** 158
The Prestige Group plc., **19** 171
Prestige Leather Creations, **31** 435–36
Prestige Properties, **23** 388
Presto Products, Inc., **II** 609–10; **IV** 187; **19** 348
Preston Corporation, **6 421–23**; **14** 566, 568
Prestone Products Corp., **22** 32; **26** 349
Prestwick Mortgage Group, **25** 187
Pretty Good Privacy, Inc., **25** 349
Pretty Neat Corp., **12** 216
Pretty Paper Inc., **14** 499
Pretty Polly, **I** 429
Pretzel Time. *See* Mrs. Fields' Original Cookies, Inc.
Pretzelmaker. *See* Mrs. Fields' Original Cookies, Inc.
Pretzels Incorporated, **24** 241
Preussag AG, **I** 542–43; **II** 386; **IV** 109, 201, 231; **17 378–82**; **21** 370; **28** 454
Preussenelektra Aktiengesellschaft, **I** 542; **V 698–700**
Preval, **19** 49–50
Previews, Inc., **21** 96
Priam Corporation, **10** 458
Priba, **26** 158, 160
Pribina, **25** 85
Price Chopper Supermarkets. *See* The Golub Corporation.
Price Club, **V** 162–64
Price Company Ltd, **II** 664; **IV** 246–47; **V 162–64**; **14** 393–94; **25** 11
Price Enterprises, Inc., **14** 395
Price, McCormick & Co., **26** 451
Price Rite, **25** 67
Price Waterhouse LLP, **III** 84, 420, 527; **9 422–24**; **14** 245; **26** 439. *See also* PricewaterhouseCoopers
PriceCostco, Inc., **14 393–95**
Pricel, **6** 373; **21** 103
PricewaterhouseCoopers, **29 389–94 (upd.)**
Prichard and Constance, **III** 65
Pride & Clarke, **III** 523
Pride Petroleum Services. *See* DeKalb Genetics Corporation.
Priggen Steel Building Co., **8** 545
Primadonna Resorts Inc., **17** 318
Primark Corp., **10** 89–90; **13 416–18**
Prime Computer, Inc. *See* Computervision Corporation.
Prime Motor Inns Inc., **III** 103; **IV** 718; **11** 177; **17** 238
Prime Service, Inc., **28** 40
Prime Telecommunications Corporation, **8** 311
The Prime-Mover Co., **13** 267
PrimeAmerica, **III** 340
Primedex Health Systems, Inc., **25 382–85**
Primedia Inc., **7** 286; **12** 306; **21** 403–04; **22 441–43**; **23** 156, 158, 344, 417; **24** 274
Primerica Corporation, **I** 597, 599–602, 604, 607–09, **612–14**, 615; **II** 422; **III** 283 **8** 118; **9** 218–19, 360–61; **11** 29; **15** 464; **27** 47. *See also* American Can Co.
Primerica Financial Services, **30** 124
PriMerit Bank, **19** 412
Primes Régal Inc., **II** 651
PrimeSource, **26** 542
PRIMESTAR Partners L.P., **28** 241
Primex Fibre Ltd., **IV** 328
Primo Foods Ltd., **I** 457; **7** 430
Prince Co., **II** 473
Prince Gardner Company, **17** 465; **23** 21
Prince Golf International, Ltd., **23** 450
Prince Holding Corporation, **26** 231
Prince Motor Co. Ltd., **I** 184
Prince of Wales Hotels, PLC, **14** 106; **25** 308
Prince Sports Group, Inc., **15 368–70**
Prince Street Technologies, Ltd., **8** 271
Prince William Bank, **II** 337; **10** 425
Princess Cruise Lines, **IV** 256; **22 444–46**
Princess Dorothy Coal Co., **IV** 29
Princess Hotel Group, **21** 353
Princess Metropole, **21** 354
Princeton Gas Service Company, **6** 529
Princeton Laboratories Products Company, **8** 84
Princeton Review, **12** 142
Princeton Telecommunications Corporation, **26** 38
Princeville Airlines, **24** 22
Principal Mutual Life Insurance Company, **III 328–30**
Principles, **V** 21–22
Princor Financial Services Corp., **III** 329
Pringle Barge Line Co., **17** 357
Print Technologies, Inc., **22** 357
Printex Corporation, **9** 363
Printronix, Inc., **14** 377–78; **18 434–36**
Priority Records, **22** 194
Pripps Ringnes, **18** 394, 396–97
Prism Systems Inc., **6** 310
Prismo Universal, **III** 735
Prisunic SA, **V** 9–11; **19** 307–09
Prisunic-Uniprix, **26** 160
Pritchard Corporation. *See* Black & Veatch, Inc.
Pritzker & Pritzker, **III** 96–97
Privatbanken, **II** 352
Pro-Fac Cooperative, Inc., **7** 104–06; **21** 154–55, 157
Pro-Lawn, **19** 250
Pro-optik AG, **31** 203
Probe Exploration Inc., **25** 232
Process Engineering Inc., **21** 108
Process Systems International, **21** 108
Processing Technologies International. *See* Food Ingredients Technologies.
Procino-Rossi Corp., **II** 511
Procor Limited, **16** 357
Procordia Foods, **II** 478; **18** 396
Procter & Gamble Company, **I** 34, 129, 290, 331, 366; **II** 478, 493, 544, 590, 684, 616; **III** 20–25, 36–38, 40–41, 44, **50–53**; **IV** 282, 290, 329–30; **6** 26–27, 50–52, 129, 363; **7** 277, 300, 419; **8** 63, 106–07, 253, 282, 344, 399, **431–35 (upd.)**, 477, 511–12; **9** 260, 291, 317–19, 552; **10** 54, 288; **11** 41, 421; **12** 80, 126–27, 439; **13** 39, 197, 199, 215; **14** 121–22, 262, 275; **15** 357; **16** 302–04, 440; **18** 68, 147–49, 217, 229; **22** 146–47, 210; **26 380–85 (upd.)**
Proctor & Collier, **I** 19
Proctor & Schwartz, **17** 213
Proctor-Silex. *See* Hamilton Beach/Proctor-Silex Inc.

Prodigy, Inc., **10** 237–38; **12** 562; **13** 92; **27** 517
Product Components, Inc., **19** 415
Productos Ortiz, **II** 594
Produits Chimiques Ugine Kuhlmann, **I** 303; **IV** 547
Produits Jaeger, **27** 258
Profarmaco Nobel S.r.l., **16** 69
Professional Care Service, **6** 42
Professional Computer Resources, Inc., **10** 513
Professional Education Systems, Inc., **17** 272
Professional Health Care Management Inc., **14** 209
Professional Research, **III** 73
Proffitt's, Inc., 19 323–25, 510, 512. *See also* Saks Holdings, Inc.
Profile Extrusion Company, **22** 337
Profimatics, Inc., **11** 66
PROFITCo., **II** 231
Progil, **I** 389
Progress Development Organisation, **10** 169
Progress Software Corporation, 15 371–74
Progressive Bagel Concepts, Inc. *See* Einstein/Noah Bagel Corporation.
Progressive Corporation, 11 405–07; **29 395–98 (upd.)**
Progressive Distributors, **12** 220
Progressive Grocery Stores, **7** 202
Progresso, **I** 514; **14** 212
Project Carriers. *See* Hansa Linie.
Projexions Video Supply, Inc., **24** 96
Projiis, **II** 356
Prolabo, **I** 388
Proland, **12** 139
Proler International Corp., **13** 98; **19** 380–81
Promarkt Holding GmbH, **24** 266, 270
Promigas, **IV** 418
Promodès Group, **24** 475; **26** 158, 161
Promotional Graphics, **15** 474
Promstroybank, **II** 242
Promus Companies, Inc., **III** 95; **9 425–27**; **15** 46; **16** 263; **22** 537
Pronto Pacific, **II** 488
Prontophot Holding Limited, **6** 490
Prontor-Werk Alfred Gauthier GmbH, **III** 446
Propaganda Films, Inc., **23** 389, 391
Prophet Foods, **I** 449
Propwix, **IV** 605
Prosim, S.A., **IV** 409
ProSource Distribution Services, Inc., **16** 397; **17** 475
Prospect Farms, Inc., **II** 584; **14** 514
The Prospect Group, Inc., **11** 188
Prospect Provisions, Inc. *See* King Kullen Grocery Co., Inc.
Prospectors Airways, **IV** 165
Protan & Fagertun, **25** 464
Protective Closures, **7** 296–97
La Protectrice, **III** 346–47
Protek, **III** 633
Proto Industrial Tools, **III** 628
Protogene Laboratories Inc., **17** 288
Proventus A.B., **II** 303
Provi-Soir, **II** 652
Provi-Viande, **II** 652
Provibec, **II** 652
The Providence Journal Company, 28 367–69; **30** 15
La Providence, **III** 210–11
Providence National Bank, **9** 228
Providence Steam and Gas Pipe Co. *See* Grinnell Corp.
Providencia, **III** 208
Provident Bank, **III** 190
Provident Institution for Savings, **13** 467
Provident Life and Accident Insurance Company of America, III 331–33, 404
Provident National Bank, **II** 342
Provident Services, Inc., **6** 295
Provident Travelers Mortgage Securities Corp., **III** 389
Provigo Inc., II 651–53; **12** 413
Les Provinces Réunies, **III** 235
Provincetown-Boston Airlines, **I** 118
Provincial Bank of Ireland Ltd., **16** 13
Provincial Engineering Ltd, **8** 544
Provincial Gas Company, **6** 526
Provincial Insurance Co., **III** 373
Provincial Newspapers Ltd., **IV** 685–86; **28** 502
Provincial Traders Holding Ltd., **I** 437
Provinzial-Hülfskasse, **II** 385
Provost & Provost, **II** 651
PROWA, **22** 89
Proximity Technology, **23** 210
Prudential Assurance Company, **24** 314
Prudential Bache Securities, **9** 441
Prudential Corporation plc, II 319; **III 334–36; IV** 711; **8** 276–77
Prudential Insurance Company of America, I 19, 334, 402; **II** 103, 456; **III** 79, 92, 249, 259, 265–67, 273, 291–93, 313, 329, **337–41**; **IV** 410, 458; **10** 199; **11** 243; **12** 28, 453, 500; **13** 561; **14** 95, 561; **16** 135, 497; **17** 325; **22** 266; **23** 226; **25** 399; **30 360–64 (upd.)**
Prudential Oil & Gas, Inc., **6** 495–96
Prudential Refining Co., **IV** 400
Prudential Steel, **IV** 74; **24** 143–44
Prudential-Bache Trade Corporation, **II** 51; **21** 331
PSA. *See* Pacific Southwest Airlines.
PSA Peugeot Citroen S.A., **7** 35; **28 370–74 (upd.)**
PSCCo. *See* Public Service Company of Colorado.
PSE, Inc., **12** 100
PSF. *See* Premium Standard Farms, Inc.
PSI. *See* Process Systems International.
PSI Resources, 6 555–57
Psychiatric Institutes of America, **III** 87–88
Psychological Corp., **IV** 623; **12** 223
PT Components, **14** 43
PT PERMINA, **IV** 492, 517
PTI Communications, Inc. *See* Pacific Telecom, Inc.
PTT Nederland N.V., **27** 472; **30** 393–94
PTT Telecom BV, **V** 299–301; **6** 303
PTV. *See* Österreichische Post- und Telegraphenverwaltung.
Pubco Corporation, 17 383–85
Publi-Graphics, **16** 168
Public Broadcasting Stations, **29** 426
Public Home Trust Co., **III** 104
Public National Bank, **II** 230
Public Savings Insurance Co., **III** 219
Public Service Co., **14** 124
Public Service Company of Colorado, 6 558–60
Public Service Company of Indiana. *See* PSI Energy.
Public Service Company of New Hampshire, 21 408–12
Public Service Company of New Mexico, 6 561–64; **27** 486
Public Service Electric and Gas Company, **IV** 366; **V** 701–03; **11** 388
Public Service Enterprise Group, **V** 701–03
Public Service Market. *See* The Golub Corporation.
Public Storage, Inc., **21** 476
Public/Hacienda Resorts, Inc. *See* Santa Fe Gaming Corporation.
Publicis S.A., **13** 204; **19 329–32**; **21** 265–66; **23** 478, 480; **25** 91
Publicker Industries Inc., **I** 226; **10** 180
Publishers Clearing House, 23 393–95; **27** 20
Publishers Paper Co., **IV** 295, 677–78; **19** 225
Publishers Press Assoc., **IV** 607; **25** 506
Publishing and Broadcasting Ltd., **19** 400–01
Publix Super Markets Inc., **II** 155, 627; **7 440–42**; **9** 186; **20** 84, 306; **23** 261; **31 371–374 (upd.)**
Puck Lazaroff Inc. *See* The Wolfgang Puck Food Company, Inc.
Puente Oil, **IV** 385
Puerto Rican Aqueduct and Sewer Authority, **6** 441
Puerto Rican-American Insurance Co., **III** 242
Puget Mill Company, **12** 406–07
Puget Sound Alaska Van Lines. *See* Alaska Hydro-Train.
Puget Sound National Bank, **8** 469–70
Puget Sound Power And Light Company, 6 565–67
Puget Sound Pulp and Timber Co., **IV** 281; **9** 259
Puget Sound Tug and Barge Company, **6** 382
Pulitzer Publishing Company, 15 375–77
Pullman Co., **II** 403; **III** 94, 744
Pullman Savings and Loan Association, **17** 529
Pullman Standard, **7** 540
Pulsar Internacional S.A., 21 413–15
Pulse Engineering, Inc., **29** 461
Pulte Corporation, 8 436–38; **22** 205, 207
Puma, **14** 6–7; **17** 244
AB Pump-Separator, **III** 418–19
Punchcraft, Inc., **III** 569; **20** 360
Purdue Fredrick Company, **13** 367
Pure Milk Products Cooperative, **11** 24
Pure Oil Co., **III** 497; **IV** 570; **24** 521
Pure Packed Foods, **II** 525; **13** 293
Purex Corporation, **I** 450; **III** 21; **22** 146
Purex Pool Systems, **I** 13, 342; **18** 163
Purfina, **IV** 497
Puris Inc., **14** 316
Puritan Chemical Co., **I** 321
Puritan Fashions Corp., **22** 122
Puritan-Bennett Corporation, 13 419–21
Purity Stores, **I** 146
Purity Supreme, Inc., **II** 674; **24** 462
Purle Bros., **III** 735
Purnell & Sons Ltd., **IV** 642; **7** 312
Purodenso Co., **III** 593
Purolator Courier, Inc., **6** 345–46, 390; **16** 397; **18** 177; **25** 148

Purolator Products Company, **III** 593; **21 416–18**; **28** 263
Puros de Villa Gonzales, **23** 465
Puss 'n Boots, **II** 559
Putnam Investments Inc., **25** 387; **30** 355
Putnam Management Co., **III** 283
Putnam Reinsurance Co., **III** 198
Putt-Putt Golf Courses of America, Inc., **23 396–98**
PWA Group, **IV 323–25**; **28** 446
PWS Holding Corporation, **13** 406; **26** 47
PWT Projects Ltd., **22** 89
PWT Worldwide, **11** 510
PYA/Monarch, **II** 675; **26** 504
Pyramid Communications, Inc., **IV** 623
Pyramid Electric Company, **10** 319
Pyramid Electronics Supply, Inc., **17** 275
Pyramid Technology Corporation, **10** 504; **27** 448
Pytchley Autocar Co. Ltd., **IV** 722
Pyxis. *See* Cardinal Health, Inc.
Pyxis Resources Co., **IV** 182

Q Lube, Inc., **18** 145; **24** 339
Qantas Airways Limited, **I** 92–93; **6** 79, 91, 100, 105, **109–13**, 117; **14** 70, 73; **24 396–401 (upd.)**; **27** 466; **31** 104
Qatar General Petroleum Corporation, **IV 524–26**
Qintex Australia Ltd., **II** 150; **25** 329
QO Chemicals, Inc., **14** 217
QSP, Inc., **IV** 664
Quad/Graphics, Inc., **19 333–36**
Quail Oil Tools, **28** 347–48
Quaker Fabric Corp., **19 337–39**
Quaker Oats Company, **I** 30; **II 558–60**, 575, 684; **12** 167, 169, **409–12 (upd.)**; **13** 186; **22** 131, 337–38; **25** 90, 314; **27** 197; **30** 219; **31** 282
Quaker State Corporation, **7 443–45**; **21 419–22 (upd.)**; **25** 90; **26** 349
Qualcomm Inc., **20 438–41**; **26** 532
Qualicare, Inc., **6** 192
QualiTROL Corporation, **7** 116–17
Quality Bakers of America, **12** 170
Quality Care Inc., **I** 249
Quality Courts Motels, Inc., **14** 105. *See also* Choice Hotels International, Inc.
Quality Dining, Inc., **18 437–40**
Quality Food Centers, Inc., **17 386–88**; **22** 271, 273
Quality Importers, **I** 226; **10** 180
Quality Inns International, **13** 363; **14** 105. *See also* Choice Hotels International, Inc.
Quality Markets, Inc., **13** 393
Quality Oil Co., **II** 624–25
Quality Paperback Book Club (QPB), **13** 105–07
Quality Products, Inc., **18** 162
Qualtec, Inc., **V** 623
Quanex Corporation, **13 422–24**
Quantex Microsystems Inc., **24** 31
Quantum Chemical Corporation, **8 439–41**; **11** 441; **30** 231, 441
Quantum Computer Services, Inc. *See* America Online, Inc.
Quantum Corporation, **6** 230–31; **10** 56, 403, **458–59**, 463; **25** 530
Quantum Health Resources, **29** 364
Quantum Marketing International, Inc., **27** 336
Quantum Offshore Contractors, **25** 104
Quantum Overseas N.V., **7** 360
Quantum Restaurant Group, Inc., **30** 330
Quarex Industries, Inc. *See* Western Beef, Inc.
Quarrie Corporation, **12** 554
Quasi-Arc Co., **I** 315; **25** 80
Quebec Bank, **II** 344
Quebéc Hydro-Electric Commission. *See* Hydro-Quebéc.
Quebecor Inc., **12 412–14**; **19** 333; **26** 44; **29** 471
Queen Casuals, **III** 530
Queen Insurance Co., **III** 350
Queens Isetan Co., Ltd., **V** 87
Queensland Alumina, **IV** 59
Queensland and Northern Territories Air Service. *See* Qantas Airways Limited.
Queensland Mines Ltd., **III** 729
Queensland Oil Refineries, **III** 672
Queiroz Pereira, **IV** 504
Quelle Group, **V 165–67**
Quennessen, **IV** 118
Quesarias Ibéricas, **23** 219
Quesnel River Pulp Co., **IV** 269
Quest Aerospace Education, Inc., **18** 521
Quest Diagnostics Inc., **26 390–92**
Quest Pharmacies Inc., **25** 504–05
Questar Corporation, **6 568–70**; **10** 432; **26 386–89 (upd.)**
Questor Partners, **I** 332; **26** 185
The Quick & Reilly Group, Inc., **18** 552; **20 442–44**; **26** 65
QUICK Corp., **IV** 656
Quick-Shop, **II** 619
Quickie Designs, **11** 202, 487–88
Quik Stop Markets, Inc., **12** 112
Quiksilver, Inc., **18 441–43**; **27** 329
QuikWok Inc., **II** 556; **13** 408
Quill Corporation, **28 375–77**
Quillery, **27** 138
Quilter Goodison, **II** 260
Quimica Industrial Huels Do Brasil Ltda., **I** 350
Quimicos Industriales Penoles. *See* Industrias Penoles, S.A. de C.V.
Quincy Compressor Co., **I** 434–35
Quincy Family Steak House, **II** 679; **10** 331; **19** 287; **27** 17, 19
Quintana Roo, Inc., **17** 243, 245; **25** 42
Quintex Australia Limited, **25** 329
Quintiles Transnational Corporation, **21 423–25**
Quinton Hazell Automotive, **III** 495; **IV** 382–83
Quintron, Inc., **11** 475
Quintus Computer Systems, **6** 248
Quixote Corporation, **15 378–80**
Quixtar Inc., **30** 62
Quixx Corporation, **6** 580
Quoddy Products Inc., **17** 389, 390
Quotron Systems, Inc., **III** 119; **IV** 670; **9** 49, 125; **30** 127
QVC Network Inc., **9 428–29**; **10** 175; **12** 315; **18** 132; **20** 75; **24** 120, 123
Qwest Communications International, **25** 499; **26** 36

R & B Manufacturing Co., **III** 569; **20** 361
R&O Software-Technik GmbH, **27** 492
R. and W. Hawaii Wholesale, Inc., **22** 15
R.A. Waller & Co., **III** 282
R-B. *See* Arby's, Inc.
R. Buckland & Son Ltd., **IV** 119
R-Byte, **12** 162
R-C Holding Inc. *See* Air & Water Technologies Corporation.
R.C. Bigelow, **16** 90
R.C. Willey Home Furnishings, **18** 60
R. Cubed Composites Inc., **I** 387
R.E. Funsten Co., **7** 429
R.G. Barry Corp., **17 389–91**
R.G. Dun-Bradstreet Corp., **IV** 604–05
R. Griggs Group Limited, **23 399–402**; **31** 413–14
R.H. Macy & Co., Inc., **I** 30; **V 168–70**; **8 442–45 (upd.)**; **10** 282; **11** 349; **13** 42; **15** 281; **16** 206–07, 328, 388, 561; **23** 60; **27** 60, 481; **30 379–83 (upd.)**; **31** 190, 192–93
R.H. Squire, **III** 283
R.H. Stengel & Company, **13** 479
R. Hoe & Co., **I** 602; **13** 189
R. Hornibrook (NSW), **I** 592
R.J. Brown Co., **IV** 373
R.J. Reynolds, **I** 259, 261, 363; **II** 542, 544; **III** 16; **IV** 523; **V** 396, 404–05, 407–10, 413, 415, 417–18; **7** 130, 132, 267, 365, 367; **9** 533; **13** 490; **14** 78; **15** 72–73; **16** 242; **18** 416; **19** 369; **21** 315; **27** 125; **29** 195. *See also* RJR Nabisco.
R.J. Reynolds Tobacco Holdings, Inc., **30 384–87 (upd.)**
R.J. Tower Corporation. *See* Tower Automotive, Inc.
R.K. Brown, **14** 112
R.L. Crain Limited, **15** 473
R.L. Manning Company, **9** 363–64
R.L. Polk & Co., **10 460–62**
R.N. Coate, **I** 216
R.O. Hull Co., **I** 361
R.P.M., Inc., **25** 228
R.P. Scherer, **I 678–80**
R.R. Bowker Co., **17** 398; **23** 440
R.R. Donnelley & Sons Company, **IV 660–62**, 673; **9 430–32 (upd.)**; **11** 293; **12** 414, 557, 559; **18** 331; **19** 333
R.S.R. Corporation, **31** 48
R.S. Stokvis Company, **13** 499
R. Scott Associates, **11** 57
R. Stock AG, **IV** 198
R.T. French USA, **II** 567
R.T. Securities, **II** 457
R.W. Beck, **29** 353
R.W. Harmon & Sons, Inc., **6** 410
R.W. Sears Watch Company, **V** 180
RABA PLC, **10** 274
Rabbit Software Corp., **10** 474
Rabobank, **26** 419
Racal Electronics PLC, **II 83–84**; **11** 408, 547
Racal-Datacom Inc., **11 408–10**
Race Z, Inc. *See* Action Peformance Companies, Inc.
Racine Hardware Co., **III** 58
Racine Hidraulica, **21** 430
Racine Threshing Machine Works, **10** 377
Racing Champions. *See* Action Performance Companies, Inc.
Racing Collectables Club of America, Inc. *See* Action Performance Companies, Inc.
Rack Rite Distributors, **V** 174
Racket Store. *See* Duckwall-ALCO Stores, Inc.
Rada Corp., **IV** 250
Radiant Lamp Corp., **13** 398
Radiation Dynamics, **III** 634–35
Radiation, Inc., **II** 37–38
Radiation-Medical Products Corp., **I** 202

Radiator Specialty Co., **III** 570; **20** 362
Radio & Allied Industries, **II** 25
Radio & Television Equipment Company (Radio-Tel), **16** 200–01
Radio Austria A.G., **V** 314–16
Radio Cap Company. *See* Norwood Promotional Products, Inc.
Radio City Productions, **30** 102
Radio Corporation of America. *See* RCA Corporation.
Radio Receptor Company, Inc., **10** 319
Radio Shack, **II** 106–08; **12** 470; **13** 174
Radio Vertrieb Fürth. *See* Grundig AG.
Radio-Keith-Orpheum, **II** 32, 88, 135, 146–48, 175; **III** 428; **9** 247; **12** 73; **31** 99
Radiometer A/S, **17** 287
Radiometrics, Inc., **18** 369
RadioShack Canada Inc., **30** 391
Radiotelevision Española, **7** 511
Radisson Hotels Worldwide, **22** 126–27
Radium Pharmacy, **I** 704
Radius Inc., 16 417–19
Radix Group, Inc., **13** 20
RadNet Managed Imaging Services, Inc., **25** 382–84
Radnor Venture Partners, LP, **10** 474
Raf, Haarla Oy, **IV** 349
Raffinerie Tirlemontoise S.A., **27** 436
Raffineriegesellschaft Vohburg/Ingolstadt mbH, **7** 141
Rag Shops, Inc., 30 365–67
Ragan Outdoor, **27** 280
Ragazzi's, **10** 331
Ragnar Benson Inc., **8** 43–43
RAI, **I** 466
Rail Link, Inc., **27** 181
Railroad Enterprises, Inc., **27** 347
RailTex, Inc., 20 445–47
Railway Express Agency, **I** 456; **II** 382; **6** 388–89; **25** 146–48
Railway Maintenance Equipment Co., **14** 43
Railway Officials and Employees Accident Assoc., **III** 228
Railway Passengers Assurance Co., **III** 178, 410
Rainbow Crafts, **II** 502; **10** 323
Rainbow Home Shopping Ltd., **V** 160
Rainbow Production Corp., **I** 412
Rainbow Programming Holdings, **7** 63–64
Rainbow Resources, **IV** 576
RainbowBridge Communications, Inc., **25** 162
Rainer Pulp & Paper Company, **17** 439
Rainfair, Inc., **18** 298, 300
Rainforest Cafe, Inc., 25 386–88
Rainier Brewing Company, 23 403–05
Rainier Pulp and Paper Company. *See* Rayonier Inc.
Rainy River Forest Products, Inc., **26** 445
Rajastan Breweries, Ltd., **18** 502
Raky-Danubia, **IV** 485
Ralcorp Holdings, Inc., **13** 293, 425, 427; **15** 189, 235; **21** 53, 56; **22** 337. *See also* Ralston Purina Company.
Raley's Inc., 14 396–98
Ralli International, **III** 502; **IV** 259
Rally's Hamburgers, Inc., 25 389–91
Rally's Inc., **14** 452; **15** 345; **16** 96–97; **23** 225
Rallye S.A., **12** 154. *See also* Casino.
Ralph & Kacoo's. *See* Piccadilly Cafeterias, Inc.
Ralph Lauren. *See* Polo/Ralph Lauren Corportion.
The Ralph M. Parsons Company. *See* The Parsons Corporation.
Ralph Wilson Plastics, **III** 610–11
Ralph's Industries, **31** 191
Ralphs Grocery Co., **17** 558, 560–61; **28** 510
Ralston Purina Company, I 608, **II** 544, 560, **561–63**, 617; **III** 588; **6** 50–52; **7** 209, 396, 547, 556; **8** 180; **9** 180; **12** 276, 411, 510; **13** 137, 270, 293, **425–27 (upd.)**; **14** 194–95, 558; **18** 312; **21** 56; **23** 191. *See also* Ralcorp Holdings, Inc.
Ram dis Ticaret, **I** 479
Ram Golf Corp., **III** 24
Ram's Insurance, **III** 370
Ramada International Hotels & Resorts, **II** 142; **III** 99; **IV** 718; **9** 426; **11** 177; **13** 66; **21** 366; **25** 309; **28** 258
Ramazotti, **I** 281
Rambol, **25** 84
Ramo-Woolridge Corp., **I** 539; **14** 510
Ramón Areces Foundation, **V** 52
Ranbar Packing, Inc. *See* Western Beef, Inc.
Ranchers Packing Corp. *See* Western Beef, Inc.
Rand American Investments Limited, **IV** 79; **21** 211
Rand Drill Co., **III** 525
Rand Group, Inc., **6** 247; **24** 234
Rand McNally & Company, 28 378–81
Rand Mines Ltd., **I** 422; **IV** 22, 79, 94
Rand Selection Corp. Ltd., **IV** 79
Random House, Inc., II 90; **IV** 583–84, 637, 648; **13** 113, 115, 178, **428–30**; **14** 260; **18** 329; **19** 6, 285; **31 375–380 (upd.)**
Randstad Holding n.v., 16 420–22
Randsworth Trust P.L.C., **IV** 703
Rank Organisation PLC, II 139, 147, **157–59**; **III** 171; **IV** 698; **6** 288; **12** 229; **14 399–402 (upd.)**; **24** 194; **26** 543, 546
Ranks Hovis McDougall Limited, II 157, **564–65**; **28 382–85 (upd.)**
Ransburg Corporation, **22** 282
Ransom and Randolph Company, **10** 271
Ransomes America Corp., **III** 600
Rapala-Normark Group, Ltd., 30 368–71
Rapicom, **III** 159
Rapid American, **I** 440
Rapides Bank & Trust Company, **11** 107
Rapifax of Canada, **III** 160
Rare Hospitality International Inc., 19 340–42
RAS. *See* Riunione Adriatica di Sicurtà SpA.
Rascal House, **24** 243
Rassini Rheem, **III** 581
Rational GmbH, **22** 354
Rational Systems Inc., **6** 255; **25** 299
Ratti Vallensasca, **25** 312
Rauland Corp., **II** 124; **13** 573
Rauma-Repola Oy, **II** 302; **IV** 316, 340, 349–50. *See also* Metso Corporation
Rauscher Pierce Refsnes, Inc., **15** 233
Raven Press, **14** 555
Ravenhead, **16** 120
Ravenna Metal Products Corp., **12** 344
Ravenseft Properties Ltd., **IV** 696, 704–05
RAVIcad, **18** 20
Rawlings Sporting Goods Co., Inc., 7 177; **23** 449; **24 402–04**
Rawlplug Co. Ltd., **IV** 382–83
Rawls Brothers Co., **13** 369
Rawson, Holdsworth & Co., **I** 464
Ray Industries, **22** 116
Ray Simon, **24** 94
Ray Strauss Unlimited, **22** 123
Ray's Printing of Topeka, **II** 624
Raychem Corporation, III 492; **8 446–47**
Raycom Sports, **6** 33
Raymar Book Corporation, **11** 194
Raymond International Inc., **28** 201
Raymond, Jones & Co., **IV** 647
Raymond, Trice & Company, **14** 40
Raynet Corporation, **8** 447
Rayonese Textile, Inc., **29** 140
Rayonier Inc., 24 405–07
Rayovac Corporation, 13 431–34; **17** 105; **23** 497; **24** 480
Raytheon Company, I 463, 485, 544; **II** 41, 73, **85–87**; **III** 643; **8** 51, 157; **11** 197, **411–14 (upd.)**; **12** 46, 247; **14** 223; **17** 419, 553, 564; **21** 200; **23** 181; **24** 88; **25** 223
Razorback Acquisitions, **19** 455
RB&W Corp., **17** 372
RBC Dominion Securities, **25** 12
RCA Corporation, I 142, 454, 463; **II** 29–31, 34, 38, 56, 61, 85–86, **88–90**, 96, 102, 117–18, 120, 124, 129, 132–33, 151–52, 313, 609, 645; **III** 118, 122, 132, 149, 152, 165, 171, 569, 653–54; **IV** 252, 583, 594; **6** 164–66, 240, 266, 281, 288, 334; **7** 520; **8** 157; **9** 283; **10** 173; **11** 197, 318, 411; **12** 204, 208, 237, 454, 544, 548; **13** 106, 398, 429, 506, 573; **14** 357, 436; **16** 549; **17** 29; **20** 361; **21** 151; **22** 541; **23** 181; **26** 358, 511; **28** 349; **31** 376
RCA Global Communications, Inc., **27** 304
RCG International, Inc., **III** 344
RCN Corp., **25** 107
REA. *See* Railway Express Agency.
Rea & Derick, **II** 605
Rea Construction Company, **17** 377
Rea Magnet Wire Co., **IV** 15
React-Rite, Inc., **8** 271
Read, R.L., **II** 417
Read-Rite Corp., 10 403–04, **463–64**; **18** 250
The Reader's Digest Association, Inc., IV 663–64; **17 392–95 (upd.)**
Reader's Garden Inc., **22** 441
Reading and Bates, **III** 559
Reading Railroad, **9** 407
Ready Mixed Concrete, **III** 687, 737–40; **28** 82
Real Decisions, **21** 236
Real Estate Maintenance, **25** 15
Real Fresh, **25** 85
Real-Share, Inc., **18** 542
RealCom Communications Corporation, **15** 196
Reale Mutuale, **III** 273
The Really Useful Group, 23 390; **26 393–95**
Realty Development Co. *See* King Kullen Grocery Co., Inc.
Realty Investment Group, **25** 127
Realty Parking Properties II L.P., **18** 104
Réassurances, **III** 392
Recaro North America Inc., **26** 231

Reckitt & Colman plc, **II 566–67**; **15** 46, 360; **18** 556; **22** 148; **27** 69
Reconstruction Bank of Holland, **IV** 707
Reconstruction Finance Bank, **II** 292
Reconstruction Finance Corp., **I** 67, 203; **II** 261; **IV** 10, 333
Record Bar / Licorice Pizza, **9** 361
Record Merchandisers. *See* Entertainment UK.
Record World Inc., **9** 361
Recoton Corp., **15 381–83**
Recoupe Recycling Technologies, **8** 104
Recovery Centers of America, **III** 88
Recovery Engineering, Inc., **25 392–94**
Recreational Equipment, Inc., **18 444–47**; **22** 173
Recticel S.A., **III** 581; **17** 182–84
Rectigraph Co., **III** 171
Recycled Paper Greetings, Inc., **21 426–28**
Red & White, **II** 682
Red Ant Entertainment, **17** 14
Red Apple Group, Inc., **23 406–08**; **24** 528–29; **31** 231
Red Arrow, **II** 138
Red Ball, Inc., **18** 300
Red Brick Systems Inc., **30** 246
Red Bull, **31** 244
Red Food Stores, Inc., **19** 327–28
Red House Books Ltd., **29** 426
Red Kap, **V** 390–91
Red L Foods, **13** 244
Red Lion Entertainment, **29** 503
Red Lobster Inns of America, **16** 156–58
Red Lobster Restaurants, **II** 502–03; **6** 28; **10** 322–24; **19** 258
Red Owl Stores, Inc., **II** 670; **18** 506
Red Roof Inns, Inc., **13** 363; **18 448–49**; **21** 362
Red Rooster, **V** 35
Red Sea Insurance Co., **III** 251
Red Star Express, **14** 505
Red Star Milling Co., **II** 501; **6** 397; **10** 322
The Red Wing Co., Inc., **28** 382
Red Wing Shoe Company, Inc., **9 433–35**; **30 372–75 (upd.)**
Redactron, **III** 166; **6** 282
Redbook Florists Service, **28** 138
Redbook Publishing Co., **14** 460
Reddy Elevator Co., **III** 467
Reddy Ice, **II** 661
Redentza, **IV** 504
Redgate Communications, **26** 19
Redhill Tile Co., **III** 734
Redhook Ale Brewery, Inc., **31 381–84**
Redi, **IV** 610
Rediffusion, **II** 139; **24** 194
Reditab S.p.A., **12** 109
Redken Laboratories, **8** 131; **24** 251
Redland Plasterboard, **28** 83
Redland plc, **III** 495, 688, **734–36**; **14** 249, 739; **15** 154
Redlaw Industries Inc., **15** 247
Redman Industries, Inc., **17** 81, 83
Redmond & Co., **I** 376
La Redoute, S.A., **V** 11; **19** 306, 309
Redpath Industries, **II** 581–82
Redrow Group plc, **31 385–87**
Redwood Design Automation, **11** 47; **16** 520
Redwood Fire & Casualty Insurance Co., **III** 214
Reebok International Ltd., **V 375–77**; **8** 171, 303–04, 393; **9** 134–35, **436–38 (upd.)**; **11** 50–51, 349; **13** 513; **14** 8; **17** 244–45, 260; **18** 266; **19** 112; **22** 173; **25** 258, 352, 450; **26 396–400 (upd.)**
Reed & Ellis, **17** 439
Reed & Gamage, **13** 243
Reed Corrugated Containers, **IV** 249
Reed Elsevier plc, **19** 268; **23** 271, 273; **31 388–394 (upd.)**
Reed International PLC, **I** 423; **IV** 270, 642, **665–67**, 711; **7** 244–45, 343; **10** 407; **12** 359; **17 396–99 (upd.)**; **23** 350
Reed Tool Coompany, **III** 429; **22** 68
Reeder Light, Ice & Fuel Company, **6** 592
Reedpack, **IV** 339–40, 667; **28** 445
Reeds Jewelers, Inc., **22 447–49**
Reese Finer Foods, Inc., **7** 429
Reese Products, **III** 569; **11** 535; **20** 361
Reeves Banking and Trust Company, **11** 181
Reeves Brothers, **17** 182
Reeves Pulley Company, **9** 440
Refco, Inc., **10** 251; **22** 189
Reference Software International, **10** 558
Refined Sugars, **II** 582
Reflectone Inc., **24** 87
Reflex Winkelmann & Pannhoff GmbH, **18** 163
Reform Rt, **IV** 652; **7** 392
Refractarios Mexicanos, S.A. de C.V., **22** 285
Refrigeração Paraná S.A., **22** 27
Regal Drugs, **V** 171
Regal Inns, **13** 364
Regal Manufacturing Co., **15** 385
Regal-Beloit Corporation, **18 450–53**
Regency, **12** 316
Regency Electronics, **II** 101
Regency Health Services Inc., **25** 457
Regency International, **10** 196
Regenerative Environmental Equipment Company, Inc., **6** 441
Regeneron Pharmaceuticals Inc., **10** 80
Regent Canal Co., **III** 272
Regent Communications Inc., **23** 294
Regent Insurance Co., **III** 343
Regent International Hotels Limited, **9** 238; **29** 200
Régie Autonome des Pétroles, **IV** 544–46; **21** 202–04
Régie des Mines de la Sarre, **IV** 196
Régie des Télégraphes et Téléphones. *See* Belgacom.
Régie Nationale des Usines Renault, **I** 136, 145, 148, 178–79, 183, **189–91**, 207, 210; **II** 13; **III** 392, 523; **7** 566–67; **11** 104; **12** 91; **15** 514; **19** 50; **22** 331
Regina Verwaltungsgesellschaft, **II** 257
Regional Bell Operating Companies, **15** 125; **18** 111–12, 373
Regis Corporation, **18 454–56**; **22** 157; **26** 475, 477
Register & Tribune Co. *See* Cowles Media Company.
Registered Vitamin Company, **V** 171
Regnecentralen AS, **III** 164
Rego Supermarkets and American Seaway Foods, Inc., **9** 451; **13** 237
Rehab Hospital Services Corp., **III** 88; **10** 252
RehabClinics Inc., **11** 367
REI. *See* Recreational Equipment, Inc.
Reich, Landman and Berry, **18** 263
Reichart Furniture Corp., **14** 236
Reichhold Chemicals, Inc., **I** 386, 524; **8** 554; **10 465–67**
Reichs-Kredit-Gesellschaft mbH, **IV** 230
Reichs-Kredit- und Krontrollstelle GmbH, **IV** 230
Reichswerke AG für Berg- und Hüttenbetriebe Hermann Göring, **IV** 200
Reichswerke AG für Erzbergbau und Eisenhütten, **IV** 200
Reichswerke Hermann Göring, **IV** 233
Reid Bros. & Carr Proprietary, **III** 672–73
Reid Dominion Packaging Ltd., **IV** 645
Reid Ice Cream Corp., **II** 471
Reid, Murdoch and Co., **II** 571
Reid Press Ltd., **IV** 645
Reidsville Fashions, Inc., **13** 532
Reigel Products Corp., **IV** 289
Reimersholms, **31** 458–60
Reims Aviation, **8** 92; **27** 100
Rein Elektronik, **10** 459
Reinsurance Agency, **III** 204–05
Reisebüro Bangemann, **II** 164
Reisholz AG, **III** 693
Reisland GmbH, **15** 340
Reiue Nationale des Usines Renault, **7** 220
Rekkof Restart NV, **28** 327
Relational Courseware, Inc., **21** 235–36
Relational Database Systems Inc., **10** 361–62
Relational Technology Inc., **10** 361
Release Technologies, **8** 484
Reliable Stores Inc., **14** 236
Reliable Tool, **II** 488
Reliance Electric Company, **IV** 429; **9 439–42**
Reliance Group Holdings, Inc., **II** 173; **III 342–44**; **IV** 642
Reliance Life Insurance Co., **III** 275–76
Reliance National Indemnity Company, **18** 159
Reliance Steel & Aluminum Co., **19 343–45**
ReLife Inc., **14** 233
Relocation Central. *See* CORT Business Services Corporation.
Rembrandt Group, **I** 289; **IV** 91, 93, 97; **V** 411–13; **19** 367–69; **24** 449
RemedyTemp, Inc., **20 448–50**
Remgro, **IV** 97
Remington Arms Company, Inc., **I** 329; **8** 152; **12 415–17**; **26** 125
Remington Rand, **III** 122, 126, 148, 151, 165–66, 642; **6** 251, 265, 281–82; **10** 255; **12** 416; **19** 430; **30** 337
Remmele Engineering, Inc., **17** 534
Rémy Cointreau S.A., **20 451–53**
REN Corp. USA, Inc., **13** 161
Renaissance Communications Corp., **22** 522
Renaissance Connects, **16** 394
Renal Systems, Inc. *See* Minntech Corporation.
Renault. *See* Régie Nationale des Usines Renault.
Renault S.A., **26** 11, **401–04 (upd.)**
Rendeck International, **11** 66
Rendic International, **13** 228
René Garraud, **III** 68
Renfro Corp., **25** 167
Rengo Co., Ltd., **IV 326**
Rennies Consolidated Holdings, **I** 470; **20** 312
Reno Air Inc., **23 409–11**; **24** 400; **28** 25

Reno Technologies, **12** 124
Réno-Dépôt Inc., **26** 306
Rent-A-Center, **22** 194; **24** 485
Rental Service Corporation, 28 386–88
Rentz, **23** 219
Reo Products. *See* Lifetime Hoan Corporation.
Repco Ltd., **15** 246
REPESA, **IV** 528
Replacement Enterprises Inc., **16** 380
Repligen Inc., **13** 241
Repola Ltd., **19** 465; **30** 325
Repola Oy, **IV** 316, 347, 350
Repsol S.A., **IV** 396–97, 506, 514, **527–29**; **16 423–26 (upd.)**
Repubblica, **IV** 587
Republic Aircraft Co., **I** 89
Republic Airlines, **I** 113, 132; **6** 104; **25** 421; **28** 265
Republic Aviation Corporation, **I** 55; **9** 205–07
Republic Broadcasting Corp., **23** 292
Republic Corp., **I** 447
Republic Engineered Steels, Inc., 7 446–47 26 405–08 (upd.)
Republic Freight Systems, **14** 567
Republic Indemnity Co. of America, **III** 191
Republic Industries, Inc., **24** 12; **26 409–11**, 501
Republic Insurance, **III** 404
Republic National Bank, **19** 466
Republic New York Corporation, 11 415–19
Republic Pictures, **9** 75
Republic Powdered Metals, Inc., **8** 454
Republic Realty Mortgage Corp., **II** 289
Republic Rubber, **III** 641
Republic Steel Corp., **I** 491; **IV** 114; **7** 446; **12** 353; **13** 169, 157; **14** 155; **24** 304. *See also* Republic Engineered Steels, Inc.
Republic Supply Co. of California, **I** 570
Res-Care, Inc., 29 399–402
Research Analysis Corporation, **7** 15
Research Cottrell, Inc., **6** 441
Research Polymers International, **I** 321; **12** 103
Research Publications, **8** 526
Resem SpA, **I** 387
Reserve Mining Co., **17** 356
Reservoir Productions, **17** 150
Residence Inns, **III** 103; **9** 426
Residential Funding Corporation, **10** 92–93
Resin Exchange, **19** 414
Resinous Products, **I** 392
ResNet Communications Inc., **28** 241
Resolution Systems, Inc., **13** 201
Resolution Trust Corp., **10** 117, 134; **11** 371; **12** 368
Resorts International, Inc., **I** 452; **12 418–20**; **19** 402; **26** 462
Resource Associates of Alaska, Inc., **7** 376
Resource Electronics, **8** 385
Resource Group International, **25** 207
ReSource NE, Inc., **17** 553
reSOURCE PARTNER, INC., **22** 95
Response Oncology, Inc., 27 385–87
Rest Assured, **I** 429
The Restaurant Company, **22** 417
Restaurant Enterprises Group Inc., **14** 195
Restaurant Franchise Industries, **6** 200
Restaurant Property Master, **19** 468
Restaurants Les Pres Limitée, **II** 652
Restaurants Universal Espana S.A., **26** 374
Restaurants Unlimited, Inc., 13 435–37; **23** 127–29
Restoration Hardware, Inc., 30 376–78
Resurgens Communications Group, **7** 336; **8** 311; **27** 306
Retail Credit Company. *See* Equifax.
Retail Systems Consulting, Inc., **24** 395
Retail Ventures Inc., **14** 427; **24** 26
Retailers Commercial Agency, Inc., **6** 24
Retequattro, **19** 19
Retirement Care Associates Inc., **25** 457
Retirement Inns of America, Inc., **III** 16; **11** 282
Reuben H. Donnelley Corp., **IV** 605, 661; **19** 133
Reunion Properties, **I** 470; **20** 311–12
Reuters Holdings PLC, **IV** 259, 652, 654, 656, **668–70**; **10** 277, 407; **21** 68–70; **22 450–53 (upd.)**
Revco D.S., Inc., **II** 449; **III** 10; **V 171–73**; **9** 67, 187; **12** 4; **13** 449; **16** 560; **19** 357
Revell-Monogram Inc., **16 427–29**; **25** 71; **27** 14
Revere Copper and Brass Co., **IV** 32. *See also* The Paul Revere Corporation.
Revere Foil Containers, Inc., **12** 377
Revere Furniture and Equipment Company, **14** 105; **25** 307
Revere Ware Corporation, 22 454–56
Revlon Inc., **I** 29, 449, 620, 633, 668, 677, 693, 696; **II** 498, 679; **III** 29, 46, **54–57**, 727; **6** 27; **8** 131, 341; **9** 202–03, 291; **11** 8, 333–34; **12** 314; **16** 439; **17** 110, **400–04 (upd.)**; **18** 229; **22** 157; **25** 55; **26** 384; **28** 246–47; **30** 188–89
Revson Bros., **III** 54
Rewe-Liebbrand, **28** 152
Rex Pulp Products Company, **9** 304
REX Stores Corp., 10 468–69; **19** 362
Rexall Drug & Chemical Co., **II** 533–34; **III** 610; **13** 525; **14** 547
Rexel, Inc., 15 384–87
Rexene Products Co., **III** 760; **IV** 457
Rexham Inc., **IV** 259; **8** 483–84
Rexnord Corporation, **I** 524; **14** 43; **21 429–32**
Reydel Industries, **23** 95–96
Reyes Holdings, Inc., **24** 388
Reymer & Bros., Inc., **II** 508; **11** 172
Reymersholm, **II** 366
Reynolds and Reynolds Company, **17** 142, 144
Reynolds Electric Co., **22** 353
Reynolds Metals Company, **II** 421–22; **IV** 11–12, 15, 59, **186–88**; **IV** 122; **12** 278; **19 346–48 (upd.)**; **21** 218; **22** 455; **25** 22
RF Communications, **II** 38
RF Monolithics Inc., **13** 193
RHC Holding Corp., **10** 13; **13** 364; **27** 11
RHD Holdings, **23** 413
Rhee Syngman, **I** 516; **12** 293
Rheem Manufacturing, **25** 368
Rhein-Elbe Gelsenkirchener Bergwerks A.G., **IV** 25
Rheinelbe Union, **I** 542
Rheinisch Kalksteinwerke Wulfrath, **III** 738
Rheinisch Oelfinwerke, **I** 306
Rheinisch-Westfalische Bank A.G., **II** 279
Rheinisch-Westfälischer Sprengstoff AG, **III** 694
Rheinisch-Westfälisches Elektrizatätswerke AG, **I** 542–43; **III** 154; **IV** 231; **V** 744; **25** 102
Rheinische Aktiengesellschaft für Braunkohlenbergbau, **V** 708
Rheinische Creditbank, **II** 278
Rheinische Metallwaaren- und Maschinenfabrik AG, **9** 443–44
Rheinische Wasserglasfabrik, **III** 31
Rheinische Zuckerwarenfabrik GmbH, **27** 460
Rheinmetall Berlin AG, 9 443–46
Rheinsche Girozentrale und Provinzialbank, Düsseldorf, **II** 385
Rheinstahl AG, **IV** 222
Rheinstahl Union Brueckenbau, **8** 242
Rheintalische Zementfabrik, **III** 701
Rhenus-Weichelt AG, **6** 424, 426
RHI Entertainment Inc., **16** 257
Rhino Entertainment Company, 18 457–60; **21** 326
RHM. *See* Ranks Hovis McDougall.
Rhodes & Co., **8** 345
Rhodes Inc., 23 412–14
Rhodesian Anglo American Ltd., **IV** 21, 23; **16** 26
Rhodesian Development Corp., **I** 422
Rhodesian Selection Trust, Ltd., **IV** 17–18, 21
Rhodesian Sugar Refineries, **II** 581
Rhodiaceta, **I** 388–89
Rhokana Corp., **IV** 191
Rhône-Poulenc S.A., **I** 303–04, 371, **388–90**, 670, 672, 692; **III** 677; **IV** 174, 487, 547; **8** 153, 452; **9** 358; **10 470–72 (upd.)**; **16** 121, 438; **21** 466; **23** 194, 197
Rhymey Breweries, **I** 294
Rhymney Iron Company, **31** 369
Rhythm Watch Co., Ltd., **III** 454; **21** 121
La Riassicuratrice, **III** 346
Ricard, **I** 280
Riccar, **17** 124
Riccardo's Restaurant, **18** 538
Rice Broadcasting Co., Inc., **II** 166
Rice-Stix Dry Goods, **II** 414
Riceland Foods, Inc., **27** 390
Rich Products Corporation, 7 448–49
Rich's Inc., **9** 209; **10** 515; **31** 191
Richard A. Shaw, Inc., **7** 128
Richard D. Irwin Inc., **IV** 602–03, 678
Richard Hellman Co., **II** 497
Richard Manufacturing Co., **I** 667
Richard P. Simmons, **8** 19
Richard Shops, **III** 502
Richard Thomas & Baldwins, **IV** 42
Richards Bay Minerals, **IV** 91
Richardson Electronics, Ltd., 17 405–07
Richardson's, **21** 246
Richardson-Vicks Company, **III** 53; **8** 434; **26** 383
Richfield Oil Corp., **IV** 375–76, 456
Richfood Holdings, Inc., 7 450–51
Richland Co-op Creamery Company, **7** 592
Richland Gas Company, **8** 349
Richmon Hill & Queens County Gas Light Companies, **6** 455
Richmond American Homes of Florida, Inc., **11** 258
Richmond Carousel Corporation, **9** 120
Richmond Cedar Works Manufacturing Co., **12** 109; **19** 360

Richmond Corp., **I** 600; **15** 129
Richmond Paperboard Corp., **19** 78
Richmond Pulp and Paper Company, **17** 281
Richway, **10** 515
Richwood Building Products, Inc., **12** 397
Richwood Sewell Coal Co., **17** 357
Ricils, **III** 47
Rickards, Roloson & Company, **22** 427
Rickel Home Centers, **II** 673
Ricky Shaw's Oriental Express, **25** 181
Ricoh Company, Ltd., III 121, 157, **159–61**, 172, 454; **6** 289; **8** 278; **18** 386, 527; **19** 317; **21** 122; **24** 429
Ricolino, **19** 192
Riddell Sports Inc., 22 457–59; 23 449
Ridder Publications, **IV** 612–13, 629; **7** 191
Ride, Inc., 22 460–63
Ridge Tool Co., **II** 19
Ridgewell's Inc., **15** 87
Ridgewood Properties Inc., **12** 394
Ridgway Co., **23** 98
Ridgway Color, **13** 227–28
Rieck-McJunkin Dairy Co., **II** 533
Riedel-de Haën AG, **22** 32
Riegel Bag & Paper Co., **IV** 344
Rieke Corp., **III** 569; **11** 535; **20** 361
Rieter Machine Works, **III** 638
Rig Tenders Company, **6** 383
Riggin & Robbins, **13** 244
Riggs National Corporation, 13 438–40
Right Associates, **27** 21
Right Source, Inc., **24** 96
RightSide Up, Inc., **27** 21
Rijnhaave Information Systems, **25** 21
Rike's, **10** 282
Riken Corp., **IV** 160; **10** 493
Riken Kankoshi Co. Ltd., **III** 159
Riken Optical Co., **III** 159
Riklis Family Corp., 9 447–50; 12 87; **13** 453
Riku-un Moto Kaisha, **V** 477
La Rinascente, **12** 153
Ring King Visibles, Inc., **13** 269
Ringier America, **19** 333
Ringköpkedjan, **II** 640
Ringling Bros., Barnum & Bailey Circus, **25** 312–13
Ringnes Bryggeri, **18** 396
Rini Supermarkets, **9** 451; **13** 237
Rini-Rego Supermarkets Inc., **13** 238
Rinker Materials Corp., **III** 688
Rio Grande Industries, Inc., **12** 18–19
Rio Grande Oil Co., **IV** 375, 456
Rio Grande Servaas, S.A. de C.V., **23** 145
Rio Grande Valley Gas Co., **IV** 394
Rio Sul Airlines, **6** 133
Rio Tinto plc, 19 349–53 (upd.); 27 253
Rio Tinto-Zinc Corp., **II** 628; **IV** 56, 58–61, 189–91, 380; **21** 352
Rioblanco, **II** 477
Riordan Freeman & Spogli, **13** 406
Riordan Holdings Ltd., **I** 457; **10** 554
Riser Foods, Inc., 9 451–54; 13 237–38
Rising Sun Petroleum Co., **IV** 431, 460, 542
Risk Planners, **II** 669
Rit Dye Co., **II** 497
Rite Aid Corporation, V 174–76; 9 187, 346; **12** 221, 333; **16** 389; **18** 199, 286; **19 354–57 (upd.); 23** 407; **29** 213; **31** 232
Rite-Way Department Store, **II** 649
Riteway Distributor, **26** 183
Rittenhouse and Embree, **III** 269
Rittenhouse Financial Services, **22** 495
Ritter Co. *See* Sybron Corp.
Ritz Camera Centers Inc., **18** 186
Ritz Firma, **13** 512
Ritz-Carlton Hotel Company L.L.C., 9 455–57; 21 366; **29 403–06 (upd.)**
Riunione Adriatica di Sicurtà SpA, III 185, 206, **345–48**
The Rival Company, 17 215; **19 358–60**
Rivarossi, **16** 337
Rivaud Group, **29** 370
River Boat Casino, **9** 425–26
River City Broadcasting, **25** 418
River Steam Navigation Co., **III** 522
River Thames Insurance Co., Ltd., **26** 487
River-Raisin Paper Co., **IV** 345
Riverside Chemical Company, **13** 502
Riverside Furniture, **19** 455
Riverside Insurance Co. of America, **26** 487
Riverside Iron Works, Ltd., **8** 544
Riverside National Bank of Buffalo, **11** 108
Riverside Press, **10** 355–56
Riverwood International Corporation, 7 294; **11 420–23**
Riviana Foods, **III** 24, 25; **27 388–91**
Riyadh Armed Forces Hospital, **16** 94
Rizzoli Publishing, **IV** 586, 588; **19** 19; **23** 88
RJMJ, Inc., **16** 37
RJR Nabisco Holdings Corp., I 249, 259, 261; **II** 370, 426, 477–78, 542–44; **V 408–10, 415; 7** 130, 132, 277, 596; **9** 469; **12** 82, 559; **13** 342; **14** 214, 274; **17** 471; **22** 73, 95, 441; **23** 163; **24** 273; **30** 384. *See also* R.J Reynolds Tobacco Holdings Inc., Nabisco Brands, Inc. *and* R.J. Reynolds Industries, Inc.
RKO. *See* Radio-Keith-Orpheum.
RKO Radio Sales, **6** 33
RKO-General, Inc., **8** 207
RLA Polymers, **9** 92
RM Marketing, **6** 14
RMC Group p.l.c., III 734, **737–40**
RMF Inc., **I** 412
RMP International, Limited, **8** 417
Roadhouse Grill, Inc., 22 464–66
Roadline, **6** 413–14
Roadmaster Industries, Inc., 16 430–33; 22 116
Roadmaster Transport Company, **18** 27
RoadOne. *See* Miller Industries, Inc.
Roadway Express, Inc., 25 395–98 (upd.)
Roadway Services, Inc., V 502–03; 12 278, 309; **14** 567; **15** 111
Roaman's, **V** 115
Roan Selection Trust Ltd., **IV** 18, 239–40
Roanoke Capital Ltd., **27** 113–14
Roanoke Fashions Group, **13** 532
Robb Engineering Works, **8** 544
Robbins & Myers Inc., 13 273; **15 388–90**
Robbins Co., **III** 546
Robeco Group, **IV** 193; **26** 419–20
Roberds Inc., 19 361–63
Roberk Co., **III** 603
Robert Allen Companies, **III** 571; **20** 362
Robert Benson, Lonsdale & Co. Ltd., **II** 232, 421–22; **IV** 191
Robert Bosch GmbH, I 392–93, 411; **III** 554, 555, 591, 593; **13** 398; **16 434–37 (upd.); 22** 31
Robert E. McKee Corporation, **6** 150
Robert Fleming Holdings Ltd., **I** 471; **IV** 79; **11** 495
Robert Gair Co., **15** 128
Robert Garrett & Sons, Inc., **9** 363
Robert Grace Contracting Co., **I** 584
Robert Half International Inc., 18 461–63
Robert Hall Clothes, Inc., **13** 535
Robert Johnson, **8** 281–82
Robert McLane Company. *See* McLane Company, Inc.
Robert McNish & Company Limited, **14** 141
Robert Mondavi Corporation, 15 391–94
Robert R. Mullen & Co., **I** 20
Robert Stigwood Organization Ltd., **23** 390
Robert W. Baird & Co., **III** 324; **7** 495
Robert Warschauer and Co., **II** 270
Robert Watson & Co. Ltd., **I** 568
Roberts Express, **V** 503
Roberts, Johnson & Rand Shoe Co., **III** 528–29
Roberts Pharmaceutical Corporation, 16 438–40
Robertson Building Products, **8** 546
Robertson, Stephens & Co., **22** 465
Robertson-Ceco Corporation, 8 546; **19 364–66**
Robin Hood Flour Mills, Ltd., **7** 241–43; **25** 241
Robin International Inc., **24** 14
Robinair, **10** 492, 494
Robinson & Clark Hardware. *See* Clarcor Inc.
Robinson Clubs, **II** 163–64
Robinson Industries, **24** 425
Robinson Radio Rentals, **I** 531
Robinson Smith & Robert Haas, Inc., **13** 428
Robinson's Japan Co. Ltd., **V** 89
Robinson-Danforth Commission Co., **II** 561
Robinson-Humphrey, **II** 398; **10** 62
Robot Manufacturing Co., **16** 8
Robotic Vision Systems, Inc., **16** 68
ROC Communities, Inc., **I** 272; **22** 341
Roch, S.A., **23** 83
Roche Biomedical Laboratories, Inc., 8 209–10; **11 424–26**
Roche Bioscience, 14 403–06 (upd.)
Roche Holding AG, **30** 164
Roche Products Ltd., **I** 643
Rochester American Insurance Co., **III** 191
Rochester Gas And Electric Corporation, 6 571–73
Rochester German Insurance Co., **III** 191
Rochester Instrument Systems, Inc., **16** 357
Rochester Telephone Corporation, 6 332–34; 12 136; **16** 221
Röchling Industrie Verwaltung GmbH, **9** 443
Rock Bottom Restaurants, Inc., 25 399–401
Rock Island Oil & Refining Co., **IV** 448–49
Rock Island Plow Company, **10** 378
Rock Systems Inc., **18** 337
Rock-Tenn Company, IV 312; **13 441–43; 19** 268
Rockcor Inc., **I** 381; **13** 380

Rockcote Paint Company, **8** 552–53
Rockefeller & Andrews, **IV** 426; **7** 169
Rockefeller Group, **IV** 714
Rocket Chemical Company. *See* WD-40 Company.
Rockford Drilling Co., **III** 439
Rockland Corp., **8** 271
Rockland React-Rite, Inc., **8** 270
Rockmoor Grocery, **II** 683
Rockower of Canada Ltd., **II** 649
Rockport Company, **V** 376–77; **26** 397
Rockresorts, Inc., **22** 166
RockShox, Inc., 26 412–14
Rockwell International Corporation, I 71, **78–80**, 154–55, 186; **II** 3, 94, 379; **6** 263; **7** 420; **8** 165; **9** 10; **10** 279–80; **11** 268, 278, **427–30 (upd.)**, 473; **12** 135, 248, 506; **13** 228; **18** 369, 571; **22** 51, 53, 63–64
Rocky Mountain Bankcard, **24** 393
Rocky Mountain Financial Corporation, **13** 348
Rocky Mountain Pipe Line Co., **IV** 400
Rocky River Power Co. *See* Connecticut Light and Power Co.
Rocky Shoes & Boots, Inc., 26 415–18
Rodale Press, Inc., 22 443; **23 415–17**
Rodamco N.V., IV 698; **26 419–21**
Rodel, Inc., **26** 425
Rodeway Inns of America, **II** 142; **III** 94; **11** 242; **25** 309
Rodney Square Management Corp., **25** 542
Rodven Records, **23** 391
Roederstein GmbH, **21** 520
Roegelein Co., **13** 271
Roehr Products Co., **III** 443
Roermond, **IV** 276
Roessler & Hasslacher Chemical Co., **IV** 69
Roger Cleveland Golf Company, **15** 462
Roger Williams Foods, **II** 682
Rogers & Oling, Inc., **17** 533
Rogers Bros., **I** 672
Rogers Communications Inc., 30 388–92 (upd.). *See also* Maclean Hunter Publishing Limited.
Rohe Scientific Corp., **13** 398
Röhm and Haas Company, I 391–93; **14** 182–83; **26 422–26 (upd.)**
ROHN Industries, Inc., 22 467–69
Rohölgewinnungs AG, **IV** 485
Rohr Gruppe, **20** 100
Rohr Incorporated, I 62; **9 458–60**; **11** 165
Roja, **III** 47
Rokke Group, **16** 546
Rokuosha, **III** 547
Rol Oil, **IV** 451
Rola Group, **II** 81
Roland Murten A.G., 7 452–53
Rolex. *See* Montres Rolex S.A.
Rollalong, **III** 502; **7** 208
Rollerblade, Inc., 15 395–98; **22** 202–03
Rolling Stones Records, **23** 33
Rollins Burdick Hunter Co., **III** 204
Rollins Communications, **II** 161
Rollins, Inc., 11 431–34
Rollins Specialty Group, **III** 204
Rollo's, **16** 95
Rolls-Royce Allison, 29 407–09 (upd.)
Rolls-Royce Motors Ltd., I 25–26, 81–82, 166, **194–96**; **III** 652; **9** 16–18, 417–18; **11** 138, 403; **21** 435
Rolls-Royce plc, I 41, 55, 65, **81–83**, 481; **III** 507, 556; **7 454–57 (upd.)**; **9** 244; **11** 268; **12** 190; **13** 414; **21 433–37 (upd.)**; **24** 85; **27** 495–96
Rolm Corp., **II** 99; **III** 149; **18** 344; **22** 51
Rolodex Electronics, **23** 209, 212
Rolscreen. *See* Pella Corporation.
Rombas, **IV** 226
Rome Cable and Wire Co., **IV** 15
Rome Network, Inc., **24** 95
Romper Room Enterprises, Inc., **16** 267
Rompetrol, **IV** 454
Ron Nagle, **I** 247
Ronco, Inc., 15 399–401; **21** 327
Rondel's, Inc., **8** 135
Ronel, **13** 274
Roni-Linda Productions, Inc., **27** 347
Ronnebyredds Trävaru, **25** 463
Ronningen-Petter, **III** 468
Ronzoni Foods Corp., **15** 221
Roombar S.A., **28** 241
Rooms To Go Inc., 28 389–92
Rooney Brothers Co., 25 402–04
Roots Canada, **27** 194
Roots-Connersville Blower Corp., **III** 472
Roper Industries Inc., III 655; **12** 550; **15 402–04**; **25** 89
Ropert Group, **18** 67
RoProperty Services BV. *See* Rodamco N.V.
Rorer Group, I 666–68; **12** 4; **16** 438; **24** 257
Rosaen Co., **23** 82
Rosarita Food Company, **25** 278
Rose & Co., **26** 65
Rose Exterminator Company, **25** 15
Rose Foundation, **9** 348
Rose's Stores, Inc., 13 261, **444–46**; **23** 215
Rosebud Dolls Ltd., **25** 312
Rosefield Packing Co., **II** 497
Rosehaugh, **24** 269
RoseJohnson Incorporated, **14** 303
Rosemount Inc., II 20; **13** 226; **15 405–08**
Rosen Enterprises, Ltd., **10** 482
Rosenblads Patenter, **III** 419
Rosenbluth International Inc., 14 407–09
Rosenfeld Hat Company. *See* Columbia Hat Company.
Rosenmund-Guèdu, **31** 158
Rosenthal, **I** 347; **18** 236
Rosevear, **III** 690
Rosewood Financial, Inc., **24** 383
Roshco, Inc., **27** 288
Ross Carrier Company, **8** 115
Ross Clouston, **13** 244
Ross Gear & Tool Co., **I** 539; **14** 510
Ross Hall Corp., **I** 417
Ross Stores, Inc., 17 408–10
Rossendale Combining Company, **9** 92
Rossignol Ski Company, Inc. *See* Skis Rossignol S.A.
Rössing Uranium Ltd., **IV** 191
Rossville Union Distillery, **I** 285
Rostocker Brauerei VEB, **9** 87
Roswell Public Service Company, **6** 579
Rota Bolt Ltd., **III** 581
Rotadisk, **16** 7
Rotan Mosle Financial Corporation, **II** 445; **22** 406
Rotary International, 31 395–97
Rotary Lift, **III** 467–68
Rotax, **III** 555–56. *See also* Orbital Engine Corporation Ltd.
Rote. *See* Avery Dennison Corporation.
Rotelcom Data Inc., **6** 334; **16** 222
Rotex, **IV** 253
Roth Co., **16** 493
Roth Freres SA, **26** 231
Rothmans International p.l.c., I 438; **IV** 93; **V 411–13**; **27** 488
Rothmans UK Holdings Limited, 19 367–70 (upd.)
Rothschild Financial Corporation, **13** 347
Rothschild Group, **6** 206
Rothschild Investment Trust, **I** 248; **III** 699
Roto-Rooter Corp., 13 149–50; **15 409–11**; **16** 387
Rotodiesel, **III** 556
Rotor Tool Co., **II** 16
Rotterdam Bank, **II** 183–85
Rotterdam Beleggings (Investment) Consortium. *See* Robeco.
Rotterdam Lloyd, **6** 403–04; **26** 241–42
The Rottlund Company, Inc., 28 393–95
Rouge et Or, **IV** 614
Rouge Steel Company, 8 448–50
Roughdales Brickworks, **14** 249
Rougier. *See* Groupe Rougier, SA.
Round Hill Foods, **21** 535
Round Table, **16** 447
Roundup Wholesale Grocery Company, **V** 55
Roundy's Inc., 14 410–12
The Rouse Company, II 445; **15 412–15**; **22** 406
Roussel Uclaf, I 669–70; **8 451–53 (upd.)**; **18** 236; **19** 51; **25** 285
Rousselot, **I** 677
Routh Robbins Companies, **21** 96
Roux Séguéla Cayzac & Goudard. *See* Euro RSCG Worldwide S.A.
Rover Group Ltd., I 186; **7 458–60**; **11** 31, 33; **14** 36; **21 441–44 (upd.)**; **24** 87–88
Rowe & Pitman, **14** 419
Rowe Bros. & Co., **III** 680
Rowe Price-Fleming International, Inc., **11** 495
Rowell Welding Works, **26** 433
Rowntree and Co., **27** 104
Rowntree Mackintosh PLC, II 476, 511, 521, 548, **568–70**; **7** 383; **28** 311
Roxana Petroleum Co., **IV** 531, 540
Roxoil Drilling, **7** 344
Roy and Charles Moore Crane Company, **18** 319
Roy Farrell Import-Export Company, **6** 78
Roy Rogers, **III** 102
Royal Ahold. *See* Koninklijke Ahold N.V.
Royal Aluminium Ltd., **IV** 9
Royal Appliance Manufacturing Company, 15 416–18; **17** 233
Royal Baking Powder Co., **II** 544; **14** 17
Royal Bank of Australia, **II** 188
The Royal Bank of Canada, II 344–46; **21 445–48 (upd.)**
Royal Bank of Ireland Ltd., **16** 13
Royal Bank of Queensland, **II** 188
The Royal Bank of Scotland Group plc, II 298, 358; **10** 336–37; **12 421–23**
Royal Brewing Co., **I** 269; **12** 337
Royal Business Machines, **I** 207, 485; **III** 549
Royal Canada, **III** 349

Royal Caribbean Cruises Ltd., **6** 368; **22** 444–46; **470–73**; **27** 29, 91
Royal Copenhagen A/S, **9** 99
Royal Crown Company, Inc., **II** 468; **6** 21, 50; **8** 536–37; **14** 32–33; **23 418–20**
Royal Data, Inc. *See* King Kullen Grocery Co., Inc.
Royal Doulton Plc, **IV** 659; **14 413–15**
Royal Dutch Harbour Co., **IV** 707
Royal Dutch Paper Co., **IV** 307
Royal Dutch Petroleum Company, **IV 530–32**, 657; **24** 496. *See also* Shell Transport and Trading Company p.l.c.
Royal Dutch/Shell Group, **I** 368, 504; **III** 616; **IV** 132–33, 378, 406, 413, 429, 434, 453–54, 460, 491–92, 512, 515, 517–18, 530–32, 540–45, 557–58, 569; **7** 56–57, 172–73, 481–82; **17** 417; **19** 73, 75; **21** 203; **22** 237; **24** 520
Royal Electric Company, **6** 501
Royal Exchange Assurance Corp., **III** 233–34, 278, 349, 369–71, 373
Royal Farms, **24** 528
Royal Food Distributors, **II** 625
Royal Foods, **24** 528–29
Royal General Insurance Co., **III** 242
Royal Hawaiian Macadamia Nut Co., **II** 491
Royal Industries, Inc., **19** 371
Royal Insurance Holdings plc, **III 349–51**
Royal International, **II** 457; **III** 349
Royal Interocean Lines, **6** 404; **26** 243
Royal Jackson, **14** 236
Royal Jordanian, **6** 101
Royal KPN N.V., **30 393–95**, 461, 463
Royal London Mutual Insurance, **IV** 697
Royal Mail Group, **V** 498; **6** 416; **19** 198
Royal Nedlloyd. *See* Koninglijke Nedlloyd N.V.
Royal Netherlands Steamship Company. *See* KNSM.
Royal Orchid Holidays, **6** 122–23
Royal Ordnance plc, **13** 356; **24** 87–88
Royal Packaging Industries Van Leer N.V., **9** 305; **30 396–98**
Royal Pakhoed N.V., **9** 532
Royal PTT Post, **30** 463
Royal Re, **III** 349
Royal Sash Manufacturing Co., **III** 757
Royal Securities Company, **6** 585
Royal Securities Corp. of Canada, **II** 425
Royal Sporting House Pte. Ltd., **21** 483
Royal Trust Co., **II** 456–57; **V** 25
Royal Union Life Insurance Co., **III** 275
Royal USA, **III** 349
Royal Wessanen, **II** 527
Royale Belge, **III** 177, 200, 394
Royale Inns of America, **25** 307
Royalite, **I** 285
Royce Electronics, **III** 569; **18** 68; **20** 361
Royce Ltd., **I** 194
Royster-Clark, Inc., **13** 504
Rozes, **I** 272
RPC Industries, **III** 635
RPI. *See* Research Polymers International.
RPM Inc., **8 III** 598; **454–57**
RSC. *See* Rental Service Corporation.
RSI Corp., **8** 141–42; **30** 160
RSO Records, **23** 390
RSV, **26** 496
RTE Corp., **II** 17
RTL-Véeronique, **IV** 611
RTZ Corporation PLC, **IV 189–92**; **7** 261, 263; **27** 256
RTZ-CRA Group. *See* Rio Tinto plc.
Rubber Latex Limited, **9** 92
Rubbermaid Incorporated, **III 613–15**; **12** 168–69; **13** 317–18; **19** 407; **20** 262, **454–57 (upd.)**; **21** 293; **28** 479; **31** 160–61
Ruberoid Corporation, **I** 339; **22** 227
Rubloff Inc., **II** 442
Rubo Lederwaren, **14** 225
Rubry Owen, **I** 154
Ruby, **III** 47
Ruby Tuesday, Inc., **18 464–66**
Rubyco, Inc., **15** 386
La Ruche Meridionale, **12** 153
Ruddick Corporation, **23** 260
Rudisill Printing Co., **IV** 661
Rudolf Wolff & Co., **IV** 165
Rudolph Fluor & Brother, **I** 569
Ruff Hewn, **25** 48
Rug Corporation of America, **12** 393
The Rugby Group plc, **31 398–400**
Ruger Corporation, **19** 431
Ruhr-Zink, **IV** 141
Ruhrgas AG, **V 704–06**; **7** 141; **18** 50
Ruhrkohle AG, **III** 566; **IV** 26, 89, 105, **193–95**
Ruinart Père et Fils, **I** 272
Rumbelows, **I** 532
Runcorn White Lead Co., **III** 680
Runnymede Construction Co., **8** 544
Runo-Everth Treibstoff und Ol AG, **7** 141
Rural Bank, **IV** 279; **19** 155
Rural/Metro Corporation, **28 396–98**
Rurhkohle AG, **V** 747
Rush Laboratories, Inc., **6** 41
Russ Berrie and Company, Inc., **12 424–26**
Russell & Co., **II** 296
Russell Corporation, **8 458–59**; **12** 458; **30 399–401 (upd.)**
Russell Electric, **11** 412
Russell Electronics, **II** 85
Russell Kelly Office Services, Inc. *See* Kelly Services Inc.
Russell, Majors & Waddell, **II** 381
Russell Stover Candies Inc., **12 427–29**
Russwerke Dortmund GmbH, **IV** 70
Rust Craft Greeting Cards Incorporated, **12** 561
Rust International Inc., **V** 754; **6** 599–600; **11 435–36**
Rustenburg Platinum Co., **IV** 96, 118, 120
Rütgerswerke AG, **IV** 193; **8** 81
Ruth's Chris Steak House, **28 399–401**
Ruti Machinery Works, **III** 638
Rutland Plastics, **I** 321; **12** 103
RWE Group, **V 707–10**
RxAmerica, **22** 40; **25** 297
Ryan Aeronautical, **I** 525; **10** 522; **11** 428
Ryan Aircraft Company, **9** 458
Ryan Homes, Inc., **8** 401–02
Ryan Insurance Co., **III** 204
Ryan Milk Company of Kentucky, **7** 128
Ryan's Family Steak Houses, Inc., **15 419–21**; **19** 287; **22** 464
Rycade Corp., **IV** 365, 658
Rydelle-Lion, **III** 45
Ryder System, Inc., **V 504–06**; **13** 192; **19** 293; **24 408–11 (upd.)**; **25** 93, 144; **28** 3
Ryerson Tull, Inc., **19** 216
Rykoff-Sexton, Inc., **21** 497; **26** 503, 505
The Ryland Group, Inc., **8 460–61**; **19** 126
Ryobi Ltd., **I** 202
Rypper Corp., **16** 43
Rysher Entertainment, **22** 162; **25** 329
Ryukyu Cement, **III** 760
The Ryvita Company, **II** 466; **13** 52

S&A Restaurant Corp., **7** 336; **10** 176; **14** 331; **15** 363
S&C Electric Company, **15 422–24**
S&H. *See* Sperry and Hutchinson Co.
S&H Diving Corporation, **6** 578
S&K Famous Brands, Inc., **23 421–23**
S&V Screen Inks, **13** 227–28
S. & W. Berisford, **II** 514, 528
S&W Fine Foods, **12** 105
S+T Gesellschaft fur Reprotechnik mbH, **29** 306
S.A. CARFUEL, **12** 152
S.A. Cockerill Sambre. *See* Cockerill Sambre Group.
S.A. de C.V., **29** 461
S.A. des Ateliers d'Aviation Louis Breguet. *See* Groupe Dassault Aviation SA.
s.a. GB-Inno-BM. *See* GIB Group.
S.A. Greetings Corporation, **22** 35
S.A. Innovation—Bon Marché N.V., **26** 160
S.A. Schonbrunn & Co., **14** 18
S.B. Irving Trust Bank Corp., **II** 218
S.B. Penick & Co., **I** 708; **8** 548
S.C. Johnson & Son, Inc., **I** 14; **III** 45, **58–59**; **8** 130; **10** 173; **12** 126–28; **17** 215; **21** 386; **28** 215, **409–12 (upd.)**
S-C-S Box Company, **8** 173
S.D. Cohn & Company, **10** 455; **27** 364
S.D. Warren Co., **IV** 329–30
S-E Bank Group, **II** 351–53
S.E. Massengill, **III** 66
S.E. Rykoff & Co., **26** 503
S.F. Braun, **IV** 451
S.G. Warburg and Co., **II** 232, 259–60, 422, 629; **14** 419; **16** 377. *See also* SBC Warburg.
S. Grumbacher & Son. *See* The Bon-Ton Stores, Inc.
S.H. Benson Ltd., **I** 25–26
S.H. Kress & Co., **17** 203–04
S.I.P., Co., **8** 416
S-K-I Limited, **15 457–59**
S.K. Wellman, **14** 81
S. Kuhn & Sons, **13** 221
S.M.A. Corp., **I** 622
S Pearson & Son Ltd., **IV** 657–59
S.R. Dresser Manufacturing Co., **III** 470–71
S.S. Kresge Company. *See* Kmart Corporation.
S.S. White Dental Manufacturing Co., **I** 383
S. Smith & Sons. *See* Smiths Industries PLC.
S.T. Cooper & Sons, **12** 283
S.T. Dupont Company, **III** 28; **23** 55
S.W.M. Chard, **27** 259
SA Alliance Air, **28** 404
SA Express, **28** 404
Sa SFC NA, **18** 163
Sa SFC NV, **18** 162
SAA. *See* South African Airways.
SAA (Pty) Ltd., **28 402–04**
SAAB. *See* Svenska Aeroplan Aktiebolaget.

Saab-Scania A.B., I 197–98, 210; **III** 556; **V** 339; **10** 86; **11 437–39 (upd.)**; **16** 322
Saarberg-Konzern, IV 196–99
Saarstahl AG, **IV** 228
Saatchi & Saatchi plc, I 21, 28, **33–35**, 36; **6** 53, 229; **14** 49–50; **16** 72; **21** 236; **22** 296
SAB. *See* South African Breweries Ltd.
Sabah Timber Co., **III** 699
Saban Entertainment, **24** 171
SABENA, **6** 96; **18** 80
Saber Energy, Inc., **7** 553–54
Saber Software Corp., **25** 348
Sabi International Ltd., **22** 464
SABIM Sable, **12** 152
Sabine Corporation, **7** 229
Sabine Investment Co. of Texas, Inc., **IV** 341
SABO Maschinenfabrik AG, **21** 175
Sabratek Corporation, 29 410–12
SABRE Group Holdings, Inc., 25 144; **26 427–30**; **28** 22
Sacer, **31** 127–28
Sachs-Dolmer G.m.b.H., **22** 334
Sachsgruppe, **IV** 201
Sacilor, **IV** 174, 226–27
Sackett Plasterboard Co., **III** 762
Sacks Industries, **8** 561
OY Saco AB, **23** 268
SACOR, **IV** 250, 504–06
Sacramento Savings & Loan Association, **10** 43, 45
SAE Magnetics Ltd., **18** 250
Saeger Carbide Corp., **IV** 203
Saes, **III** 347
SAFECO Corporation, III 352–54; **10** 44
Safeguard Scientifics, Inc., 10 232–34, **473–75**; **27** 338
Safelite Glass Corp., 19 371–73
Safer, Inc., **21** 385–86
Safeskin Corporation, 18 467–70
Safety 1st, Inc., 24 412–15
Safety Fund Bank, **II** 207
Safety Rehab, **11** 486
Safety Savings and Loan, **10** 339
Safety-Kleen Corp., 8 462–65
Safeway Inc., II 424, 601, 604–05, 609–10, 628, 632, 637, **654–56**; **6** 364; **7** 61, 569; **9** 39; **10** 442; **11** 239, 241; **12** 113, 209, 559; **13** 90, 336, 340; **16** 64, 160, 249, 452; **22** 37, 126; **24** 273, **416–19 (upd.)**; **25** 296; **27** 292; **28** 510; **30** 24, 27
Safmarine, **IV** 22
SAFR. *See* Société Anonyme des Fermiers Reúnis.
Safrap, **IV** 472
Saga Communications, Inc., II 608; **III** 103; **IV** 406; **27** 226, **392–94**
Saga Corp.,
Sagebrush Sales, Inc., **12** 397
Sagebrush Steakhouse, **29** 201
Saginaw Dock & Terminal Co., **17** 357
Sagitta Arzneimittel, **18** 51
Sagittarius Productions Inc., **I** 286
Sahara Casino Partners L.P., **19** 379
Sahara Resorts. *See* Santa Fe Gaming Corporation.
SAI. *See* Stamos Associates Inc.
Sai Baba, **12** 228
Saia Motor Freight Line, Inc., **6** 421–23
Saibu Gas, **IV** 518–19
SAIC Velcorex, **12** 153; **27** 188
Saiccor, **IV** 92
Sainrapt et Brice, **9** 9
Sainsbury's. *See* J Sainsbury PLC.
St. Alban Boissons S.A., **22** 515
St. Alban's Sand and Gravel, **III** 739
St. Andrews Insurance, **III** 397
St. Charles Manufacturing Co., **III** 654
St. Clair Industries Inc., **I** 482
St. Clair Press, **IV** 570
St. Croix Paper Co., **IV** 281; **9** 259
St. George Reinsurance, **III** 397
St. Helens Crown Glass Co., **III** 724
The St. Joe Company, 31 422–25
St. Joe Gold, **23** 40
St. Joe Minerals Corp., **I** 569, 571; **8** 192
St. Joe Paper Company, 8 485–88
St. John Knits, Inc., 14 466–68
St. John's Wood Railway Company, **6** 406
St. Joseph Co., **I** 286, 684
St. Jude Medical, Inc., 6 345; **11 458–61**
St. Laurent Paperboard Inc., **30** 119
St. Lawrence Cement Inc., **III** 702; **8** 258–59
St. Lawrence Corp. Ltd., **IV** 272
St. Lawrence Steamboat Co., **I** 273; **26** 303
St. Louis and Illinois Belt Railway, **6** 504
Saint Louis Bread Company, **18** 35, 37
St. Louis Concessions Inc., **21** 39
St. Louis Refrigerator Car Co., **I** 219
St. Louis Troy and Eastern Railroad Company, **6** 504
St. Martin's Press, **25** 484–85
St. Paul Bank for Cooperatives, 8 489–90
The St. Paul Companies, **III 355–57**; **15** 257; **21** 305; **22** 154, **492–95 (upd.)**
St. Paul Fire and Marine Insurance Co., **III** 355–56
St. Regis Corp., **I** 153; **IV** 264, 282; **9** 260; **10** 265; **20** 129
St. Regis Paper Co., **IV** 289, 339; **12** 377; **22** 209
Saint-Gobain. *See* Compagnie de Saint Gobain S.A.
Saint-Quirin, **III** 676; **16** 120
Sainte Anne Paper Co., **IV** 245–46; **25** 10
Saipem, **IV** 420–22, 453
SAir Group, **29** 376
Saison Group, **V** 184–85, 187–89
Saito Ltd., **IV** 268
Saiwa, **II** 543
Saks Fifth Avenue, **I** 426; **15** 291; **18** 372; **21** 302; **22** 72; **25** 205; **27** 329
Saks Holdings, Inc., 24 420–23
Sakurai Co., **IV** 327
Salada Foods, **II** 525; **13** 293
Salant Corporation, 12 430–32; **27** 445
Sale Knitting Company, **12** 501. *See also* Tultex Corporation.
Salem Broadcasting, **25** 508
Salem Carpet Mills, Inc., **9** 467
Salem Sportswear, **25** 167
Salen Energy A.B., **IV** 563
Salick Health Care, Inc., **21** 544, 546
Salim Group, **18** 180–81
Sallie Mae. *See* SLM Holding Corp. *and* Student Loan Marketing Association.
Sally Beauty Company, Inc., **8** 15–17
Salmon Carriers, **6** 383
Salmon River Power & Light Company, **12** 265
Salomon Brothers Inc., **28** 164
Salomon Inc., I 630–31; **II** 268, 400, 403, 406, 426, 432, 434, 441, **447–49**; **III** 221, 215, 721; **IV** 80, 137; **7** 114; **9** 378–79, 386; **11** 35, 371; **13** 331, **447–50 (upd.)** Inc.; **18** 60, 62; **19** 293; **21** 67, 146; **22** 102; **23** 472–74; **25** 12, 125
Salomon Smith Barney, **30** 124
Salomon Worldwide, 20 458–60
Salora, **II** 69; **17** 353
Salsåkers Ångsågs, **IV** 338
Salt River Project, 19 374–76
Salton, Inc., 30 402–04
Saltos del Sil, **II** 197
Salvagnini Company, **22** 6
Salvation Army, **15** 510–11
Salzgitter AG, IV 128, 198, **200–01**; **17** 381
Sam & Libby Inc., **30** 311
Sam Ash Music Corporation, 30 405–07
Sam Goody, **I** 613; **9** 360–61
Sam's Clubs, **V** 216–17; **8** 555–57; **12** 221, 335; **13** 548; **14** 393; **15** 470; **16** 64; **25** 235
Samancor Ltd., **IV** 92–93
Samaritan Senior Services Inc., **25** 503
Sambo's, **12** 510
Sambre-et-Moselle, **IV** 52
Samcor Glass, **III** 685
Samedan Oil Corporation, **11** 353
Sames, S.A., **21** 65–66
Samim, **IV** 422
Samkong Fat Ltd. Co., **III** 747
Samna Corp., **6** 256; **25** 300
Sampson's, **12** 220–21
Samson Technologies Corp., **30** 406
Samsonite Corp., 6 50; **13** 311, **451–53**; **16** 20–21
Samsung Electronics Co., Ltd., 14 416–18; **18** 139, 260
Samsung Group, I 515–17; **II** 53–54; **III** 143, 457–58, 517, 749; **IV** 519; **7** 233; **12** 211–12; **13** 387; **18** 124; **29** 207–08
Samsung-Calex, **17** 483
Samuel Austin & Son Company, **8** 41
Samuel Meisel & Company, Inc., **11** 80–81; **29** 509, 511
Samuel Montagu & Co., **II** 319; **17** 324–25
Samuel Moore & Co., **I** 155
Samuel Samuel & Co., **IV** 530, 542
Samuel, Son & Co. Ltd., **24** 144
Samuels Jewelers Incorporated, 30 408–10
Samwha Paper Co., **III** 748
San Antonio Public Service Company, **6** 473
San Diego Gas & Electric Company, V 711–14; **6** 590; **11** 272; **25** 416
San Francisco Mines of Mexico Ltd., **22** 285
San Gabriel Light & Power Company, **16** 496
San Giorgio Macaroni Inc., **II** 511
San Miguel Corporation, I 221; **15 428–30**; **23** 379
SAN-MIC Trading Co., **IV** 327
Sanborn Co., **III** 142; **6** 237
Sanborn Hermanos, S.A., 20 461–63; **21** 259
Sanborn Manufacturing Company, **30** 138
Sandcastle 5 Productions, **25** 269–70
Sanders Associates, Inc., **9** 324; **13** 127–28
Sanderson & Porter, **I** 376
Sanderson Computers, **10** 500
Sanderson Farms, Inc., 15 425–27

Sandoz Ltd., **I** 632–33, **671–73**, 675; **7** 315, 452; **8** 108–09, 215; **10** 48, 199; **11** 173; **12** 388; **15** 139; **18** 51; **22** 475; **27** 299
Sandoz Nutrition Corp., **24** 286
SandPoint Corp., **12** 562; **17** 254
Sandusky Plastics, Inc., **17** 157
Sandusky Portland Cement Company, **24** 331
Sandvik AB, **III** 426–27; **IV 202–04**
Sandwell, Inc., **6** 491
Sandy's Pool Supply, Inc. *See* Leslie's Poolmart, Inc.
SANFLO Co., Ltd., **IV** 327
Sangu Express Company, **V** 463
Sanichem Manufacturing Company, **16** 386
Sanitary Farm Dairies, Inc., **7** 372
Sanitas Food Co., **II** 523
Sanitation Systems, Inc. *See* HMI Industries.
Sanjushi Bank, **II** 347
Sanka Coffee Corp., **II** 531
Sankin Kai Group, **II** 274
Sanko Kabushiki Kaisha. *See* Marubeni Corporation.
Sankyo Company Ltd., **I** 330, **674–75**; **III** 760; **8** 153
Sanlam, **IV** 91, 93, 535
Sano Railway Company, **6** 430
Sanofi Group, **I** 304, **676–77**; **III** 18; **IV** 546; **7** 484–85; **21** 205; **23** 236, 238, 242
Sanseisha Co., **IV** 326
Santa Ana Savings and Loan, **10** 339
Santa Ana Wholesale Company, **16** 451
Santa Cruz Operation, **6** 244
Santa Cruz Portland Cement, **II** 490
Santa Fe Gaming Corporation, **19 377–79**
Santa Fe Industries, **II** 448; **12** 19; **13** 448; **28** 498
Santa Fe International, **IV** 451–52
Santa Fe Pacific Corporation, **V 507–09**; **24** 98. *See also* Burlington Northern Santa Fe Corporation.
Santa Fe Railway, **12** 278; **18** 4
Santa Fe Southern Pacific Corp., **III** 512; **IV** 721; **6** 150, 599; **9** 391; **22** 491
Santa Rosa Savings and Loan, **10** 339
Santal, **26** 160
Santiam Lumber Co., **IV** 358
Santone Industries Inc., **16** 327
Sanus Corp. Health Systems, **III** 317
Sanwa Bank, Ltd., **II** 276, 326, **347–48**, 442, 511; **III** 188, 759; **IV** 150–51; **7** 119; **15** 43, **431–33 (upd.)**; **24** 356, 358
Sanyo Chemical Manufacturing Co., **III** 758
Sanyo Electric Company, Ltd., **I** 516; **II** 55–56, **91–92**; **III** 569, 654; **6** 101; **14** 535; **20** 361
Sanyo Ethylene Co. Ltd., **IV** 476
Sanyo Petrochemical Co. Ltd., **IV** 476
Sanyo Railway Co., **I** 506; **II** 325
Sanyo Semiconductor, **17** 33
Sanyo-Kokusaku Pulp Co., Ltd., **IV** 326, **327–28**
SAP AG, **11** 78; **16 441–44**; **25** 34: 496, 498 ...nats
Sapac, **I** 643
SAPAC. *See* Société Pa... Company. *See* en Commun.
Sapirstein Gree...ngs Corporation.
American...
Sappi Ltd., **IV** 91–93
Sapporo Breweries, Ltd., **I** 9, 220, 270, **282–83**, 508, 615; **II** 326; **13 454–56 (upd.)**; **20** 28–29; **21** 319–20
Sara Lee Corporation, **I** 15, 30; **II 571–73**, 675; **7** 113 **8** 262; **10** 219–20; **11** 15, 486; **12** 494, 502, 531; **15** 359, **434–37 (upd.)**, 507; **19** 192; **25** 91, 125, 166, 523; **26** 325, 503; **29** 132
Saracen's Head Brewery, **21** 245
Saratoga Partners, **24** 436
Sarawak Trading, **14** 448
Sargent & Lundy, **6** 556
Sarget S.A., **IV** 71
SARL, **12** 152
Sarma, **III** 623–24; **26** 159–61
Sarmag, **26** 161
Saros Corp., **15** 474
Sarotti A.G., **II** 546
Sarpe, **IV** 591
SAS. *See* Scandinavian Airlines System.
SAS Institute Inc., **10 476–78**
Saseba Heavy Industries, **II** 274
Saskatchewan Oil and Gas Corporation, **13** 556–57
Sasol Limited, **IV 533–35**
Sason Corporation, **V** 187
SAT. *See* Stockholms Allmänna Telefonaktiebolag.
Satellite Business Systems, **III** 182; **21** 14; **23** 135; **27** 304
Satellite Information Services, **II** 141
Satellite Software International, **10** 556
Satellite Television PLC, **IV** 652; **7** 391; **23** 135
Satellite Transmission and Reception Specialist Company, **11** 184
Säteri Oy, **IV** 349
Sato Yasusaburo, **I** 266
Saturday Evening Post Co., **II** 208; **9** 320
Saturn Corporation, **III** 593, 760; **7 461–64**; **21 449–53 (upd.)**; **22** 154
Saturn Industries, Inc., **23** 489
SATV. *See* Satellite Television PLC.
Saucona Iron Co., **IV** 35; **7** 48
Saucony Manufacturing Company, **17** 244
Sauder Woodworking Co., **12 433–34**
Saudi Arabian Airlines, **6** 84, **114–16**; **27** 132, **395–98 (upd.)**
Saudi Arabian Oil Company, **IV 536–39**; **17 411–15 (upd.)**. *See also* Arabian American Oil Co.
Saudi Arabian Parsons Limited, **8** 416
Saudi British Bank, **II** 298
Saudi Consolidated Electric Co., **IV** 538; **17** 414
Saudi Refining Inc., **IV** 539; **17** 258
Saudia. *See* Saudi Arabian A...
Sauer Motor Company. ...
Saul Lerner & Co., ...
Saunders Karp, **12** 477
Saunders, K...
Saunde...
Sa...oup, **20** 263
...vacentre Ltd., **II** 658; **13** 284
Savage, **19** 430
Savage Shoes, Ltd., **III** 529
Savannah Foods & Industries, Inc., **7 465–67**
Savannah Gas Company, **6** 448; **23** 29
Save & Prosper Group, **10** 277
Save Mart, **14** 397; **27** 292
Save-A-Lot, **II** 682; **11** 228
Savia S.A. de C.V., **29** 435
Saviem, **III** 543
Savin, **III** 159; **26** 497
Savings of America, **II** 182
Savio, **IV** 422
Oy Savo-Karjalan Tukkuliike, **8** 293
Savon Sellu Mills, **IV** 315
Savory Milln, **II** 369
Savoy Group, **I** 248; **IV** 705; **24** 195
Savoy Industries, **12** 495
Savoy Pictures Entertainment Inc., **25** 214
Sawdust Pencil Company, **29** 372
Sawyer Electrical Manufacturing Company, **11** 4
Sawyer Industries, Inc., **13** 532
Sawyer Research Products, Inc., **14** 81
Saxby, S.A., **13** 385
Saxon and Norman Cement Co., **III** 670
Saxon Oil, **11** 97
Saxon Petroleum, Inc., **19** 162
Sayama Sekiyu, **IV** 554
SBAR, Inc., **30** 4
Sbarro, Inc., **16 445–47**; **19** 435; **27** 146
SBC. *See* Southwestern Bell Corporation.
SBC Communications Inc., **25** 498–99; **29** 62
SBC Warburg, **II** 369; **14 419–21**; **15** 197
Sberbank, **II** 242
SBK Entertainment World, Inc., **22** 194; **24** 485; **26** 187
SBS Technologies, Inc., **25 405–07**
SCA. *See* Svenska Cellulosa Aktiebolaget.
SCA Services, Inc., **V** 754; **9** 109
Scaldia Paper BV, **15** 229
Scali, McCabe & Sloves, **I** 27; **22** 200
Scan Screen, **IV** 600
Scana Corporation, **6 574–76**; **19** 499
Scandinavian Airlines System, **I** 107, **119–20**, 121; **6** 96, 122; **25** 159; **26** 11... **27** 26, 463, 474; **31** 305
Scandinavian Bank, **II** 352
Scandinavian Trading Co., I...
ScanDust, **III** 625
Scania-Vabis. *See* S... Inc., **29**
ScanSource, I...
Scantron ...4, **715–17**; **6** 590
Scarb...es, Inc., **25** 420, 423
...graphic Designs, **21** 277
...chäfer, **31** 158
Schaffhausenschor Bankverein, **II** 281
Schaper Mfg. Co., **12** 168
Scharff-Koken Manufacturing Co., **IV** 286
Scharnow, **II** 163–64
Schaum Publishing Co., **IV** 636
Schauman Wood Oy, **IV** 277, 302
Schawk, Inc., **24 424–26**
Schein Pharmaceutical Inc., **13** 77
Schenker-Rhenus Ag, **6 424–26**
Schenley Industries Inc., **I** 226, 285; **9** 449; **10** 181; **24** 140
Scherer. *See* R.P. Scherer.
Schering A.G., **I 681–82**, 684, 701; **10** 214; **14** 60; **16** 543

Schering-Plough Corporation, **I** 682, **683–85**; **II** 590; **III** 45, 61; **11** 142, 207; **14** 58, 60, **422–25 (upd.)**
Schiavi Homes, Inc., **14** 138
Schibsted ASA, **31 401–05**
Schicht Co., **II** 588
Schick Shaving, **I** 711; **III** 55
Schieffelin & Co., **I** 272
Schindler Holding AG, **II** 122; **12** 546; **27** 267; **29 419–22**
Schlage Lock Co., **III** 526
Schleppschiffahrtsgesellschaft Unterweser, **IV** 140
Schlesischer Bankverein, **II** 278
Schlitz Brewing Co., **I** 218, 255, 268, 270, 291, 600; **10** 100; **12** 338; **18** 500; **23** 403
Schlumberger Limited, **III** 429, 499, **616–18**; **13** 323; **17 416–19 (upd.)**; **22** 64, 68; **25** 191
Schmalbach-Lubeca-Werke A.G., **15** 128
Schmid, **19** 166
Schmidt, **I** 255
Schneider Co., **III** 113
Schneider et Cie, **IV** 25; **22** 42
Schneider National Inc., **13** 550–51; **20** 439; **26** 533
Schneider S.A., **II 93–94**; **18 471–74 (upd.)**; **19** 165–66
Schneiderman's Furniture Inc., **28 405–08**
Schnitzer Steel Industries, Inc., **19 380–82**
Schnoll Foods, **24** 528
Schober Direktmarketing, **18** 170
Schocken Books, **13** 429
Schoeller & Hoesch Group, **30** 349, 352
Schoenfeld Industries, **16** 511
Scholastic Corporation, **10 479–81**; **29** 143, **423–27 (upd.)**
Scholl Inc., **I** 685; **14** 424
Schöller, **27** 436, 439
Scholz Homes Inc., **IV** 115
Schott Glaswerke, **III** 445–47
Schottenstein Stores Corp., **14 426–28**; **19** 108; **24** 26. *See also* American Eagle Outfitters, Inc.
Schrader Bellows, **III** 603
eiber Foods, **26** 432
Frères. *See* Groupe Les Echos.
Schumt Company, **13** 564
Schuler Choc Co., **II** 389
Schuller Internationa 345
III 204
Schultz Sav-O Stores, Inc., **31 406–08**
Schumacher Co., **II** 624
Schuykill Energy Resources, **12** 41
Schwabe-Verlag, **7** 42
Schwabel Corporation, **19** 453
Schwan's Sales Enterprises, Inc., **7 468–70**; **26 435–38 (upd.)**
Schwartz Iron & Metal Co., **13** 142
Schweitzer-Maudit International Inc., **16** 304
Schweiz Allgemeine, **III** 377
Schweiz Transport-Vericherungs-Gesellschaft, **III** 410
Schweizer Rück Holding AG, **III** 377
Schweizerische Bankgesellschaft AG, **II** 379; **V** 104
Schweizerische Kreditanstalt, **III** 375, 410; **6** 489
Schweizerische Nordostbahn, **6** 424
Schweizerische Post-, Telefon- und Telegrafen-Betriebe, **V 321–24**
Schweizerische Ruckversicherungs-Gesellschaft. *See* Swiss Reinsurance Company.
Schweizerische Unfallversicherungs-Actiengesellschaft in Winterthur, **III** 402
Schweizerische Unionbank, **II** 368
Schweizerischer Bankverein, **II** 368
Schweppe, Paul & Gosse, **II** 476
Schweppes Ltd. *See* Cadbury Schweppes PLC.
Schwinn Cycle and Fitness L.P., **16** 494; **19 383–85**; **26** 412
The Schwinn GT Co., **26** 185
Schwitzer, **II** 420
SCI. *See* Service Corporation International *or* Société Centrale d'Investissement.
SCI Systems, Inc., **9 463–64**; **12** 451
Scicon, **14** 317
SciCor Inc., **30** 152
Science Applications International Corporation, **15 438–40**
Scientific Communications, Inc., **10** 97
Scientific Data Systems, **II** 44; **III** 172; **6** 289; **10** 365
Scientific Games Holding Corp., **III** 431; **20** 48
Scientific Materials Company, **24** 162
Scientific-Atlanta, Inc., **6 335–37**
SciMed Life Systems, **III** 18–19
Scioto Bank, **9** 475
Scitex Corporation Ltd., **15** 148, 229; **24 427–32**; **26** 212
SCM Corp., **I** 29; **III** 502; **IV** 330; **7** 208; **8** 223–24; **17** 213
SCOA Industries, Inc., **13** 260
SCOR S.A., **III** 394; **20 464–66**
The Score Board, Inc., **19 386–88**
Scot Bowyers, **II** 587
Scot Lad Foods, **14** 411
Scotch House Ltd., **19** 181
Scotia Securities, **II** 223
Scotiabank. *See* The Bank of Nova Scotia.
Scotsman Industries, Inc., **II** 420; **16** 397; **20 467–69**
Scott Communications, Inc., **10** 97
Scott Fetzer Company, **III** 214; **12 435–37**, 554–55; **17** 233; **18** 60, 62–63
Scott, Foresman, **IV** 675
Scott Graphics, **IV** 289; **8** 483
Scott Health Care, **28** 445
tt Holdings, **19** 384
Scott hgow, **III** 516; **7** 232
Scott-Ballan **Company**, **III** 749; **IV** 258,
95, 327, **329–31**; **8** 483;
of Omaha, Inc. **18** 181; **19** 266; **22**
Scott-McDuff, **II** 107 **(upd.)**
Scotti Brothers, **20** 3
tyne
Scottish & Newcastle plc, **13** 458; **15 441–44**; **21** 229
Scottish Aviation, **I** 50; **24** 85–86
Scottish Brick, **14** 250
Scottish Electric, **6** 453
Scottish General Fire Assurance Corp., **III** 256
Scottish Hydro-Electric PLC, **13 457–59**
Scottish Inns of America, Inc., **13** 362
Scottish Land Development, **III** 501; **7** 207
Scottish Malt Distillers, **I** 240
Scottish Nuclear, Ltd., **19** 389
Scottish Sealand Oil Services Ltd., **25** 171
Scottish Union Co., **III** 358
ScottishPower plc, **19 389–91**; **27** 483, 486
ScottishTelecom plc, **19** 389
The Scotts Company, **22 474–76**
Scotts Stores, **I** 289
Scotty's, Inc., **12** 234; **22 477–80**; **26** 160–61
Scovill Fasteners Inc., **IV** 11; **22** 364; **24 433–36**
Scranton Corrugated Box Company, Inc., **8** 102
Scranton Plastics Laminating Corporation, **8** 359
Screen Gems, **II** 135–36; **12** 74; **22** 193
Screg Group, **I** 563; **24** 79; **31** 128
Scribbans-Kemp Ltd., **II** 594
Scriha & Deyhle, **10** 196
Scripps-Howard, Inc., **IV** 607–09, 628; **7** 64, 157–59. *See also* The E.W. Scripps Company.
Scrivner Inc., **17** 180
Scudder, Stevens & Clark, **II** 448; **13** 448
Scurlock Oil Co., **IV** 374
SD-Scicon plc, **24** 87
SDC Coatings, **III** 715
SDGE. *See* San Diego Gas & Electric Company.
SDK Health Care Information Systems, **16** 94
SDK Parks, **IV** 724
Sea Containers Ltd., **29 428–31**
Sea Diamonds Ltd., **IV** 66; **7** 123
Sea Far of Norway, **II** 484
Sea Insurance Co. Ltd., **III** 220
Sea Life Centre Aquariums, **10** 439
Sea Ray, **III** 444
Sea World, Inc., **IV** 623–24; **12** 224
Sea-Alaska Products, **II** 494
Sea-Land Service Inc., **I** 476; **9** 510–11; **22** 164, 166
Seabee Corp., **18** 276
Seaboard Air Line Railroad. *See* CSX Corporation.
Seaboard Finance Company, **13** 63
Seaboard Fire and Marine Insurance Co., **III** 242
Seaboard Life Insurance Co., **III** 193
Seaboard Lumber Sales, **IV** 307
Seaboard Oil Co., **IV** 552
Seaboard Surety Company, **III** 357; **22** 494
Seabourn Cruise Lines, **6** 368; **27** 90, 92
Seabrook Farms Co., **24** 527–28
Seabulk Offshore International. *See* Hvide Marine Incorporated.
Seabury & Smith, **III** 283
Seacat-Zapata Off-Shore Company, **18** 513
Seacoast Products, **III** 502
afield Capital Corporation, **27** 385, 387
Sea Estate and Consolidated
Inc. s Berhad, **14** 448
SeaFirst Corp., tle First National Bank,
462

Seagate Technology, Inc., **6** 230–31; **8** **466–68**; **9** 57; **10** 257, 403–04, 459; **11** 56, 234; **13** 483; **18** 250; **25** 530
The Seagram Company Ltd., **I** 26, 240, 244, **284–86**, 329, 403; **II** 456, 468; **IV** 401; **7** 155; **18** 72; **21** 26, 401; **22** 194; **23** 125; **25** 266, 268, 366, **408–12 (upd.)**; **26** 125, 127, 152; **28** 475; **29** 196; **31** 269
Seagull Energy Corporation, **11** **440–42**
Seal Products, Inc., **12** 264
Seal Sands Chemicals, **16** 69
Sealand Petroleum Co., **IV** 400
Sealectro, **III** 434
Sealed Air Corporation, **14** **429–31**
Sealed Power Corporation, **I** **199–200**; **10** 492–94
Sealright Co., Inc., **17** **420–23**
SealRite Windows, **19** 446
Sealtest, **14** 205
Sealy Inc., **12** **438–40**; **28** 416
Seaman's Home Furnishings, **28** 389
Seamless Rubber Co., **III** 613
Seaquist Manufacturing Corporation, **9** 413–14
Searle & Co. *See* G.D. Searle & Co.
Sears Canada Inc., **25** 221
Sears Logistics Services, **18** 225–26
Sears plc, **V** **177–79**
Sears, Roebuck and Co., **I** 26, 146, 516, 556; **II** 18, 60, 134, 331, 411, 414; **III** 259, 265, 340, 536, 598, 653–55; **V** **180–83**; **6** 12–13; **7** 166, 479; **8** 224, 287–89; **9** 44, 65–66 156, 210, 213, 219, 235–36, 430–31, 538; **10** 10, 50–52, 199, 236–37, 288, 304–05, 490–91; **11** 62, 349, 393, 498; **12** 54, 96–98, 309, 311, 315, 430–31, 439, 522, 548, 557; **13** 165, 260, 268, 277, 411, 545, 550, 562–63; **14** 62; **15** 402, 470; **16** 73, 75, 160, 327–28, 560; **17** 366, 460, 487; **18** 65, 168, 283, 445, **475–79 (upd.)**; **19** 143, 221, 309, 490; **20** 259, 263; **21** 73, 94, 96–97; **23** 23, 52, 210; **25** 221, 357, 535; **27** 30, 32, 163, 347–48, 416, 428–30
Sears Roebuck de México, S.A. de C.V., **20** **470–72**; **21** 259
Seashore Transportation Co., **13** 398
Season-all Industries, **III** 735
SEAT. *See* Sociedad Española de Automoviles de Turismo.
Seatrain International, **27** 474
Seattle Brewing and Malting Company. *See* Rainier Brewing Company.
Seattle Electric Company, **6** 565
Seattle FilmWorks, Inc., **20** **473–75**
Seattle First National Bank Inc., **8** **469–71**
Seattle Times Company, **15** **445–47**
Seaview Oil Co., **IV** 393
Seaway Express, **9** 510
Seaway Food Town, Inc., **9** 452; **15** **448–50**
SeaWest, **19** 390
SEB-Fastigheter A.B., **II** 352
Sebastiani Vineyards, Inc., **28** **413–15**
SECA, **IV** 401
SECDO, **III** 618
SECO Industries, **III** 614
Seco Products Corporation, **22** 354
Secon GmbH, **13** 160
Second Bank of the United States, **II** 213; **9** 369
Second Harvest, **29** **432–34**
Second National Bank, **II** 254
Second National Bank of Bucyrus, **9** 474
Second National Bank of Ravenna, **9** 474
Secoroc, **III** 427
Le Secours, **III** 211
SecPac. *See* Security Pacific Corporation.
Secure Horizons, **11** 378–79
Secure Networks, Inc., **25** 349
Securicor, **11** 547
Securitas Esperia, **III** 208
Securities Industry Automation Corporation, **9** 370
Securities International, Inc., **II** 440–41
Securities Management & Research, Inc., **27** 46
Security Bancorp, **25** 186–87
Security Capital Corporation, **17** **424–27**; **21** 476
Security Connecticut Life Insurance Co., **III** 276
Security Engineering, **III** 472
Security Express, **10** 269
Security First National Bank of Los Angeles, **II** 349
Security Life and Annuity Company, **11** 213
Security Management Company, **8** 535–36
Security National Bank, **II** 251, 336
Security National Corp., **10** 246
Security Pacific Corporation, **II** **349–50**, 422; **III** 366; **8** 45, 48; **11** 447; **17** 137
Security Trust Company, **9** 229, 388
Security Union Title Insurance Co., **10** 43–44
Sedat Eldem, **13** 475
SEDCO, **17** 418
Sedgwick Group PLC, **I** 427; **III** 280, 366; **10** 38; **22** 318
Sedgwick Sales, Inc., **29** 384
SEDTCO Pty., **13** 61
See's Candies, Inc., **III** 213; **18** 60–61; **30** **411–13**
Seeburg Corporation, **II** 22; **III** 430; **15** 538
Seed Restaurant Group Inc., **13** 321; **27** 145
Seed Solutions, Inc., **11** 491
Seeger Refrigerator Co., **III** 653; **12** 548
Seeger-Orbis, **III** 624
Seeman Brothers. *See* White Rose, Inc.
SEEQ Technology, Inc., **9** 114; **13** 47; **17** 32, 34
SEG, **I** 463
Sega Enterprises, Ltd., **28** 320
Sega of America, Inc., **7** 396; **10** 124–25, 284–86, **482–85**; **18** 520
Sega of Japan, **24** 4
Segespar, **II** 265
Sego Milk Products Company, **7** 428
Seguros Comercial America, **21** 413
Seguros El Corte Inglés, **V** 52
Seguros Monterrey, **19** 189
Seguros Serfin S.A., **25** 290
Seibels, Bruce & Co., **11** 394–95
Seiberling Rubber Company, **V** 244; **20** 259
Seibu Allstate Life Insurance Company, Ltd., **27** 31
Seibu Department Stores, Ltd., **II** 273; **V** **184–86**
Seibu Railway Co. Ltd., **V** 187, **510–11**, 526
Seibu Saison, **6** 207
Seijo Green Plaza Co., **I** 283
Seikatsu-Soko, **V** 210
Seiko Corporation, **I** 488; **III** 445, **619–21**; **11** 46; **12** 317; **13** 122; **16** 168, 549; **17** **428–31 (upd.)**; **21** 122–23; **22** 413
Seiko Instruments USA Inc., **23** 210
Seine, **III** 391
Seino Transportation Company, Ltd., **6** **427–29**
Seismograph Service Limited, **II** 86; **11** 413; **17** 419
Seita, **23** **424–27**
Seiwa Fudosan Co., **I** 283
Seiyu, Ltd., **V** **187–89**; **10** 389
Seizo-sha, **12** 483
Sekisui Chemical Co., Ltd., **III** **741–43**
SEL, **I** 193, 463
Selat Marine Services, **22** 276
Selden, **I** 164, 300
Select Theatres Corp. *See* Shubert Organization Inc.
Select-Line Industries, **9** 543
Selection Trust, **IV** 67, 380, 565
Selective Auto and Fire Insurance Co. of America, **III** 353
Selective Insurance Co., **III** 191
Selectronics Inc., **23** 210
Selenia, **I** 467; **II** 86
Self Auto, **23** 232
Self Service Restaurants, **II** 613
The Self-Locking Carton Company, **14** 163
Self-Service Drive Thru, Inc., **25** 389
Selfridge (Department Store), **V** 94, 177–78
Seligman & Latz, **18** 455
Selkirk Communications Ltd., **26** 273
Selleck Nicholls, **III** 691
The Selmer Company, Inc., **19** **392–94**, 426, 428
Seltel, **6** 33
Semarca, **11** 523
Sematech, **18** 384, 481
Sembler Company, **11** 346
Semet-Solvay, **22** 29
Semi-Tech Global, **30** 419–20
Seminis, Inc., **21** 413; **29** **435–37**
Seminole Electric Cooperative, **6** 583
Seminole Fertilizer, **7** 537–38
Semitool, Inc., **18** **480–82**
Sempra Energy, **25** **413–16 (upd.)**
Semrau and Sons, **II** 601
SEN AG, **IV** 128
Sencel Aero Engineering Corporation, **16** 483
Seneca Foods Corporation, **17** **432–34**
Senelle-Maubeuge, **IV** 227
Senior Corp., **11** 261
Senshusha, **I** 506
Sensi, Inc., **22** 173
Sensormatic Electronics Corp., **11** **443–45**
Sentinel Foam & Envelope Corporation, **14** 430
Sentinel Group, **6** 295
Sentinel Savings and Loan, **10** 339
Sentinel Technologies, **III** 38
Sentinel-Star Company, **IV** 683; **22** 521
Sentrust, **IV** 92
Sentry, **II** 624
Sentry Insurance Company, **10** 210
Senyo Kosakuki Kenkyujo, **III** 595
Seohan Development Co., **III** 516; **7** 232
Sepa, **II** 594

AB Separator, **III** 417–19
SEPECAT, **24** 86
SEPIC, **I** 330
Sept, **IV** 325
Sequa Corp., 13 460–63
Séquanaise, **III** 391–92
Sequent Computer Systems Inc., **10** 363
Sequoia Athletic Company, **25** 450
Sequoia Insurance, **III** 270
Sequoia Pharmacy Group, **13** 150
Sera-Tec Biologicals, Inc., **V** 175–76; **19** 355
Seraco Group, **V** 182
Serck Group, **I** 429
SEREB, **I** 45; **7** 10
Sereg Valves, S.A., **17** 147
Serewatt AG, **6** 491
Sergeant Drill Co., **III** 525
Sero-Genics, Inc., **V** 174–75
Serta, Inc., 28 416–18
Serval Marketing, **18** 393
Servam Corp., **7** 471–73
Servel Inc., **III** 479; **22** 25
Service America Corp., 7 471–73; 27 480–81
Service Bureau Corp., **III** 127
Service Control Corp. *See* Angelica Corporation.
Service Corporation International, 6 293–95; 16 343–44
Service Corporation of America, **17** 552
Service Games Company, **10** 482
Service Merchandise Company, Inc., V 190–92; 6 287; **9** 400; **19 395–99 (upd.)**
Service Partner, **I** 120
Service Pipe Line Co., **IV** 370
Service Q. General Service Co., **I** 109
Service Systems, **III** 103
ServiceMaster Inc., 23 428–31 (upd.)
Servicemaster Limited Partnership, 6 44–46; 13 199
Services Maritimes des Messageries Impériales. *See* Compagnie des Messageries Maritimes.
ServiceWare, Inc., **25** 118
Servicios Financieros Quadrum S.A., **14** 156
Servisco, **II** 608
ServiStar Coast to Coast Corporation. *See* TruServ Corporation.
ServoChem A.B., **I** 387
Servomation Corporation, **7** 472–73
Servomation Wilbur. *See* Service America Corp.
Servoplan, S.A., **8** 272
SES Staffing Solutions, **27** 21
Sesame Street Book Club, **13** 560
Sespe Oil, **IV** 569; **24** 519
Sessler Inc., **19** 381
SET, **I** 466
SETCAR, **14** 458
Settsu Marine and Fire Insurance Co., **III** 367
Seven Arts Limited, **25** 328
Seven Arts Productions, Ltd., **II** 147, 176
Seven Network Limited, **25** 329
7-Eleven. *See* The Southland Corporation.
Seven-Up Bottling Co. of Los Angeles, **II** 121
Seven-Up Co., **I** 245, 257; **II** 468, 477; **18** 418
Severn Trent PLC, 12 441–43
Seversky Aircraft Corporation, **9** 205
Sevin-Rosen Partners, **III** 124; **6** 221
Sewell Coal Co., **IV** 181
Sewell Plastics, Inc., **10** 222
Sextant In-Flight Systems, LLC, **30** 74
Seybold Machine Co., **II** 37; **6** 602
Seymour Electric Light Co., **13** 182
Seymour International Press Distributor Ltd., **IV** 619
Seymour Press, **IV** 619
Seymour Trust Co., **13** 467
SFNGR. *See* Nouvelles Galeries Réunies.
SFX Broadcasting Inc., **24** 107
SGC. *See* Supermarkets General Corporation.
SGI, 29 438–41 (upd.)
SGLG, Inc., **13** 367
SGS Corp., **II** 117; **11** 46
Shaffer Clarke, **II** 594
Shakespeare Company, 16 296; **22 481–84**
Shakey's Pizza, **16** 447
Shaklee Corporation, 12 444–46; 17 186
Shalco Systems, **13** 7
Shamrock Advisors, Inc., **8** 305
Shamrock Broadcasting Inc., **24** 107
Shamrock Capital L.P., **7** 81–82
Shamrock Holdings, **III** 609; **7** 438; **9** 75; **11** 556; **25** 268
Shamrock Oil & Gas Co., **I** 403–04; **IV** 409; **7** 308
Shan-Chih Business Association, **23** 469
Shanghai Crown Maling Packaging Co. Ltd., **13** 190
Shanghai Hotels Co., **IV** 717
Shanghai International Finance Company Limited, **15** 433
Shanghai Kyocera Electronics Co., Ltd., **21** 331
Shanghai Petrochemical Co., Ltd., 18 483–85; 21 83
Shangri-La Asia Ltd., **22** 305
Shannon Group, Inc., **18** 318, 320
Shansby Group, **27** 197
Share Drug plc, **24** 269
Shared Financial Systems, Inc., **10** 501
Shared Medical Systems Corporation, 14 432–34
Shared Technologies Inc., **12** 71
Shared Use Network Systems, Inc., **8** 311
Shari Lewis Enterprises, Inc., **28** 160
Sharon Steel Corp., **I** 497; **7** 360–61; **8** 536; **13** 158, 249
Sharon Tank Car Corporation, **6** 394; **25** 169
Sharp & Dohme, Incorporated, **I** 650; **11** 289, 494
Sharp Corporation, I 476; **II 95–96; III** 14, 428, 455, 480; **6** 217, 231; **11** 45; **12 447–49 (upd.); 13** 481; **16** 83; **21** 123; **22** 197
The Sharper Image Corporation, 10 486–88; 23 210; **26** 439; **27** 429
Sharples Co., **I** 383
Sharples Separator Co., **III** 418–20
Shasta Beverages. *See* National Beverage Corp.
Shaw Communications Inc., **26** 274
Shaw Industries, 9 465–67; 19 274, 276; **25** 320
Shaw's Supermarkets, Inc., **II** 658–59; **23** 169
Shawell Precast Products, **14** 248
Shawinigan Water and Power Company, **6** 501–02
Shawmut National Corporation, II 207; **12** 31; **13 464–68**
Shea's Winnipeg Brewery Ltd., **I** 268; **25** 280
Sheaffer Group, **23** 54, 57
Shearson Hammill & Company, **22** 405–06
Shearson Lehman Brothers Holdings Inc., I 202; **II** 398–99, 450, 478; **III** 319; **8** 118; **9 468–70 (upd.); 10** 62–63; **11** 418; **12** 459; **15** 124, 463–64
Shearson Lehman Hutton Holdings Inc., II 339, 445, **450–52; III** 119; **9** 125; **10** 59, 63; **17** 38–39
Shedd's Food Products Company, **9** 318
Sheepbridge Engineering, **III** 495
Sheffield Banking Co., **II** 333
Sheffield Exploration Company, **28** 470
Sheffield Motor Co., **I** 158; **10** 292
Sheffield Twist Drill & Steel Co., **III** 624
Shekou Container Terminals, **16** 481
Shelby Insurance Company, **10** 44–45
Shelby Steel Tube Co., **IV** 572; **7** 550
Shelby Williams Industries, Inc., 14 435–37
Shelco, **22** 146
Sheldahl Inc., 23 432–35
Shelf Life Inc. *See* King Kullen Grocery Co., Inc.
Shell. *See* Shell Transport and Trading Company p.l.c. *and* Shell Oil Company.
Shell Australia Ltd., **III** 728
Shell BV, **IV** 518
Shell Chemical Corporation, **IV** 410, 481, 531–32, 540; **8** 415; **24** 151
Shell Coal International, **IV** 532
Shell Forestry, **21** 546
Shell France, **12** 153
Shell Nederland BV, **V** 658–59
Shell Oil Company, I 20, 26, 569; **III** 559; **IV** 392, 400, 531, **540–41; 6** 382, 457; **8** 261–62; **11** 522; **14** 25, **438–40 (upd.); 17** 417; **19** 175–76; **21** 546; **22** 274; **24** 520; **25** 96, 232, 469; **26** 496
Shell Transport and Trading Company p.l.c., I 605; **II** 436, 459; **III** 522, 735; **IV** 363, 378–79, 381–82, 403, 412, 423, 425, 429, 440, 454, 466, 470, 472, 474, 484–86, 491, 505, 508, **530–32**, 564; **31** 127–28. *See also* Royal Dutch Petroleum Company *and* Royal Dutch/Shell.
Shell Western E & P, **7** 323
Shell Winning, **IV** 413–14
Sheller-Globe Corporation, I 201–02; 17 182
Shelly Brothers, Inc., **15** 65
Shenley Laboratories, **I** 699
Shepard Warner Elevator Co., **III** 467
Shepard's Citations, Inc., **IV** 636–37
Shepherd Hardware Products Ltd., **16** 357
Shepherd Neame Limited, 30 414–16
Shepherd Plating and Finishing Company, **13** 233
Shepler Equipment Co., **9** 512
Sheraton Corp. of America, **I** 463–64, 487; **III** 98–99; **11** 198; **13** 362–63; **21** 91
Sherborne Group Inc./NH Holding Inc., **17** 20
Sherbrooke Paper Products Ltd., **17** 281
Sheridan Bakery, **II** 633
Sheridan Catheter & Instrument Corp., **III** 443
Sherix Chemical, **I** 682
Sherr-Gold, **23** 40

Sherritt Gordon Mines, **7** 386–87; **12** 260
The Sherwin-Williams Company, III 744–46; **8** 222, 224; **11** 384; **12** 7; **13 469–71 (upd.)**; **19** 180; **24** 323; **30** 474
Sherwood Equity Group Ltd. *See* National Discount Brokers Group, Inc.
Sherwood Medical Group, **I** 624; **III** 443–44; **10** 70
SHI Resort Development Co., **III** 635
ShianFu Optical Fiber, **III** 491
Shibaura Seisakusho Works, **I** 533; **12** 483
Shieh Chi Industrial Co., **19** 508
Shields & Co., **9** 118
Shikoku Drinks Co., **IV** 297
Shikoku Electric Power Company, Inc., V 718–20
Shikoku Machinery Co., **III** 634
Shillito's, **31** 192
Shimotsuke Electric Railway Company, **6** 431
Shimura Kako, **IV** 63
Shin Nippon Machine Manufacturing, **III** 634
Shin-Nihon Glass Co., **I** 221
Shinano Bank, **II** 291
Shinko Electric Co., Ltd., **IV** 129
Shinko Rayon Ltd., **I** 363; **V** 369–70
Shinriken Kogyo, **IV** 63
Shintech, **11** 159–60
Shinwa Tsushinki Co., **III** 593
Shiomi Casting, **III** 551
Shionogi & Co., Ltd., I 646, 651; **III 60–61**; **11** 90, 290; **17 435–37 (upd.)**
Ship 'n Shore, **II** 503; **9** 156–57; **10** 324
Shipley Co. Inc., **26** 425
Shipowners and Merchants Tugboat Company, **6** 382
Shipper Group, **16** 344
Shipstad & Johnson's Ice Follies, **25** 313
Shiro Co., Ltd., **V** 96
Shirokiya Co., Ltd., **V** 199
Shiseido Company, Limited, II 273–74, 436; **III** 46, 48, **62–64**; **8** 341, 343; **22 485–88 (upd.)**
SHL Systemhouse Inc., **27** 305
Shochiku Company Ltd., **28** 461
Shockley Electronics, **20** 174
Shoe Carnival Inc., 14 441–43
Shoe Corp., **I** 289
Shoe Supply, Inc., **22** 213
Shoe Works Inc., **18** 415
Shoe-Town Inc., **23** 310
Shohin Kaihatsu Kenkyusho, **III** 595
Shoman Milk Co., **II** 538
Shonac Corp., **14** 427
Shonco, Inc., **18** 438
Shoney's, Inc., 7 474–76; **14** 453; **19** 286; **23 436–39 (upd.)**; **29** 290–91
Shop & Go, **II** 620
Shop 'n Bag, **II** 624
Shop 'n Save, **II** 669, 682; **12** 220–21
Shop Rite Foods Inc., **II** 672–74; **7** 105; **19** 479. *See also* Big V Supermarkets, Inc.
ShopKo Stores Inc., II 669–70; **18** 505–07; **21 457–59**
Shoppers Food Warehouse Corporation, **16** 159, 161
Shoppers World Stores, Inc. *See* LOT$OFF Corporation.
ShopRite, **24** 528. *See also* Foodarama Supermarkets, Inc.
Shopwell/Food Emporium, **II** 638; **16** 247, 249
Shore Manufacturing, **13** 165
Shorewood Packaging Corporation, 28 419–21
Short Aircraft Co., **I** 50, 55, 92
Short Brothers, **24** 85
Shoseido Co., **17** 110
Shoshi-Gaisha, **IV** 320
Shotton Paper Co. Ltd., **IV** 350
Showa Aircraft Industry Co., **I** 507–08
Showa Aluminum Corporation, **8** 374
Showa Bank, **II** 291–92
Showa Bearing Manufacturing Co., **III** 595
Showa Cotton Co., Ltd., **IV** 442
Showa Denko, **I** 493–94; **II** 292; **IV** 61; **24** 324–25
Showa Marutsutsu Co. Ltd., **8** 477
Showa Paper Co., **IV** 268
Showa Photo Industry, **III** 548
Showa Products Company, **8** 476
Showa Shell Sekiyu K.K., II 459; **IV 542–43**
ShowBiz Pizza Time, Inc., 12 123; **13 472–74**; **15** 73; **16** 447. *See also* CEC Entertainment, Inc.
Showboat, Inc., 19 400–02
Showcase of Fine Fabrics, **16** 197
Showerings, **I** 215
Showscan Film Corporation, **28** 206
Showtime, **II** 173; **7** 222–23; **9** 74; **23** 274–75, 391, 503; **25** 329–30
Shredded Wheat Co., **II** 543; **7** 366
Shreve and Company, **12** 312
Shreveport Refrigeration, **16** 74
Shrewsbury and Welshpool Old Bank, **II** 307
Shu Uemura, **III** 43
Shubert Organization Inc., 24 437–39
Shubrooks International Ltd., **11** 65
Shueisha, **IV** 598
Shuford Mills, Inc., **14** 430
Shugart Associates, **6** 230; **8** 466; **22** 189
Shull Lumber & Shingle Co., **IV** 306
Shulman Transport Enterprises Inc., **27** 473
Shun Fung Ironworks, **IV** 717
Shunan Shigyo Co., Ltd., **IV** 160
Shurgard Storage Centers of Seattle, **21** 476
Shuttleworth Brothers Company. *See* Mohawk Industries, Inc.
Shuwa Corp., **22** 101
SHV Holdings N.V., **IV** 383; **14** 156
SI Holdings Inc., **10** 481; **29** 425
SIAS, **19** 192
SIAS-MPA, **I** 281
SIATA S.p.A., **26** 363
Sibco Universal, S.A., **14** 429
Siboney Shoe Corp., **22** 213
SIBV/MS Holdings, **IV** 295; **19** 226
Sicard Inc., **I** 185
SICC. *See* Univision Communications Inc.
Sick's Brewery, **26** 304
Siclet, **25** 84
Siddeley Autocar Co., **III** 508
Sidel. *See* Groupe Sidel S.A.
Sidélor, **IV** 226
Siderbrás, **IV** 125
Sidermex, **III** 581
Sidérurgie Maritime, **IV** 26
SIDMAR NV, **IV** 128
Siebe plc, **13** 235. *See also* BTR Siebe plc.
Siebel Group, **13** 544–45
Siebel Marketing Group, **27** 195
Siegas, **III** 480; **22** 26
Siegler Heater Corp., **I** 481
Siemens AG, I 74, 192, 409–11, 462, 478, 542; **II** 22, 25, 38, 80–82, **97–100**, 122, 257, 279; **III** 139, 154–55, 466, 482, 516, 724; **6** 215–16; **7** 232; **9** 11, 32, 44; **10** 16, 363; **11** 59, 196, 235, 397–98, 460; **12** 546; **13** 402; **14** 169, **444–47 (upd.)**; **15** 125; **16** 392; **18** 32; **19** 166, 313; **20** 290; **22** 19, 373–74; **23** 389, 452, 494–95; **24** 88; **30** 11
The Sierra Club, 28 422–24
Sierra Designs, Inc., **10** 215–16
Sierra Health Services, Inc., 15 451–53
Sierra Leone External Telegraph Limited, **25** 100
Sierra Leone Selection Trust, **IV** 66
Sierra On-Line Inc., 13 92, 114; **14** 263; **15 454–56**; **16** 146; **29** 75
Sierra Pacific Industries, 22 489–91
Sierrita Resources, Inc., **6** 590
Sigma Alimentos, S.A. de C.V., **19** 11–12
Sigma Coatings, **IV** 499
Sigma Network Systems, **11** 464
Sigma-Aldrich, I 690–91
Sigmor Corp., **IV** 410; **31** 455
Signal Companies, Inc. *See* AlliedSignal Inc.
Signal Galaxies, **13** 127
Signal Oil & Gas Inc., **I** 71, 178; **IV** 382; **7** 537; **11** 278; **19** 175; **22** 331
Signalite, Inc., **10** 319
Signature Brands USA Inc., **28** 135; **30** 139
Signature Corporation, **22** 412–13
Signature Group, **V** 145
Signature Health Care Corp., **25** 504
Signet Banking Corporation, 11 446–48
Signet Communications Corp., **16** 195
Signetics Co., **III** 684; **11** 56; **18** 383
Signode Industries, **III** 519; **22** 282
Sika Finanz AG, **28** 195
SIKEL NV, **IV** 128
Sikes Corporation, **III** 612
Sikorsky Aircraft Corporation, I 47, 84, 115, 530; **III** 458, 602; **9** 416; **10** 162; **18** 125; **24 440–43**
SIL&P. *See* Southern Illinois Light & Power Company.
Silenka B.V., **III** 733; **22** 436
Silex. *See* Hamilton Beach/Proctor-Silex Inc.
Silgan Holdings Inc., **26** 59
Silicon Beach Software, **10** 35
Silicon Compiler Systems, **11** 285
Silicon Engineering, **18** 20
Silicon Graphics Inc., 9 471–73; **10** 119, 257; **12** 323; **15** 149, 320; **16** 137, 140; **20** 8; **25** 96; **28** 320. *See also* SGI.
Silicon Microstructures, Inc., **14** 183
Silicon Systems Inc., **II** 110
Silo Electronics, **16** 73, 75
Silo Holdings, **9** 65; **23** 52
Silo Inc., **V** 50; **10** 306, 468; **19** 123
Silver & Co., **I** 428
Silver Burdett Co., **IV** 672, 675; **7** 528; **19** 405
Silver City Airways. *See* British World Airlines Ltd.
Silver City Casino, **6** 204
Silver Dollar Mining Company, **20** 149
Silver Furniture Co., Inc., **15** 102, 104
Silver King Communications, **25** 213
Silver King Mines, **IV** 76
Silver Screen Partners, **II** 174

Silver's India Rubber Works & Telegraph Cable Co., **I** 428
Silverado Banking, **9** 199
Silverado Partners Acquisition Corp., **22** 80
Silverline, Inc., **16** 33
Silvermans Menswear, Inc., **24** 26
SilverPlatter Information Inc., **23 440–43**
Silvershoe Partners, **17** 245
Silverstar Ltd. S.p.A., **10** 113
Silvertown Rubber Co., **I** 428
Silvey Corp., **III** 350
Simca, **I** 154, 162; **11** 103
Sime Darby Berhad, **14 448–50**
Simeira Comercio e Industria Ltda., **22** 320
SIMEL S.A., **14** 27
Simer Pump Company, **19** 360
SIMEST, **24** 311
Simicon Co., **26** 153
Simkins Industries, Inc., **8** 174–75
Simms, **III** 556
Simon & Schuster Inc., **II** 155; **IV 671–72**; **13** 559; **19 403–05 (upd.)**; **23** 503; **28** 158
Simon Adhesive Products, **IV** 253; **17** 30
Simon de Wit, **II** 641
Simon DeBartolo Group Inc., **26** 146; **27** 401
Simon Engineering, **11** 510
Simon Marketing, Inc., **19** 112, 114
Simon Property Group, Inc., **27 399–402**
Simon Transportation Services Inc., **27 403–06**
Simonius'sche Cellulosefabriken AG, **IV** 324
Simonize, **I** 371
Simons Inc., **26** 412
AB Simpele, **IV** 347
Simple Shoes, Inc., **22** 173
Simplex Industries, Inc., **16** 296
Simplex Technologies Inc., **21 460–63**
Simplex Wire and Cable Co., **III** 643–45
Simplicity Pattern Company, **I** 447; **8** 349; **23** 98; **29** 134
Simpson Investment Company, **17 438–41**
Simpson Marketing, **12** 553
Simpson Thacher & Bartlett, **27** 327
Simpsons, **V** 80; **25** 221
Sims Telephone Company, **14** 258
Simsmetal USA Corporation, **19** 380
SimuFlite, **II** 10
Sinai Kosher Foods, **14** 537
Sincat, **IV** 453
Sinclair Broadcast Group, Inc., **25 417–19**
Sinclair Coal Co., **IV** 170; **10** 447–48
Sinclair Crude Oil Purchasing Co., **IV** 369
Sinclair Oil Corp., **I** 355, 569; **IV** 376, 394, 456–57, 512, 575
Sinclair Paint Company, **12** 219
Sinclair Petrochemicals Inc., **IV** 456
Sinclair Pipe Line Co., **IV** 368–69
Sinclair Research Ltd., **III** 113
Sindo Ricoh Co., **III** 160
Sing Tao Holdings Ltd., **29** 470–71
Singapore Airlines Ltd., **6** 100, **117–18**, 123; **12** 192; **20** 313; **24** 399; **26** 115; **27** 26, **407–09 (upd.)**, 464, 466; **29** 301
Singapore Alpine Electronics Asia Pte. Ltd., **13** 31
Singapore Candle Company, **12** 393
Singapore Cement, **III** 718
Singapore Petroleum Co., **IV** 452
Singapore Straits Steamship Company, **6** 117
Singapore Telecom, **18** 348
Singapour, **II** 556
Singareni Collieries Ltd., **IV** 48–49
Singer and Friedlander, **I** 592
Singer Company, **I** 540; **II** 9–11; **6** 27, 241; **9** 232; **11** 150; **13** 521–22; **19** 211; **22** 4; **26** 3; **29** 190. *See also* Bicoastal Corp.
The Singer Company N.V., **30 417–20 (upd.)**
Singer Controls, **I** 155
Singer Hardware & Supply Co., **9** 542
Singer Sewing Machine Co., **12** 46
Singer Supermarkets, **25** 235
Single Service Containers Inc., **IV** 286
Singleton Seafood, **II** 494
Singular Software, **9** 80
Sinkers Inc., **21** 68
Sinochem. *See* China National Chemicals Import and Export Corp.
Sintel, S.A., **19** 256
Sioux City Gas and Electric Company, **6** 523–24
SIP. *See* Società Italiana per L'Esercizio delle Telecommunicazioni p.A.
Siporex, S.A., **31** 253
Sir Speedy, Inc., **16 448–50**
SIRCOMA, **10** 375
SIREM, **23** 95
The Sirena Apparel Group Inc., **25** 245
Sirloin Stockade, **10** 331
Sirrine. *See* CRSS Inc.
Sirrine Environmental Consultants, **9** 110
Sirte Oil Co., **IV** 454
Sisters Chicken & Biscuits, **8** 564
Sisters of Bon Secours USA. *See* Bon Secours Health System, Inc.
SIT-Siemens. *See* Italtel.
Sitca Corporation, **16** 297
Sithe Energies, Inc., **24** 327
Sitmar Cruises, **22** 445
Sitzmann & Heinlein GmbH, **IV** 198–99
Six Companies, Inc., **IV** 121; **7** 355
Six Flags Theme Parks, Inc., **III** 431; **IV** 676; **17 442–44**
600 Fanuc Robotics, **III** 482–83
Six Industries, Inc., **26** 433
61 Going to the Game!, **14** 293
Sizes Unlimited, **V** 115
Sizzler International Inc., **15** 361–62
SJB Equities, Inc., **30** 53
The SK Equity Fund, L.P., **23** 177
Skånes Enskilda Bank, **II** 351
Skånska Ättiksfabriken, **I** 385
Skadden, Arps, Slate, Meagher & Flom, **10** 126–27; **18 486–88**; **27** 325, 327
Skaggs Companies, **22** 37
Skaggs Drug Centers, Inc., **II** 602–04; **7** 20; **27** 291; **30** 25–27
Skaggs-Albertson's Properties, **II** 604
Skagit Nuclear Power Plant, **6** 566
Skandia, **25** 85
Skandinaviska Enskilda Banken, **II 351–53**, 365–66; **IV** 203
Skanska AB, **IV** 204; **25** 463
Skanza Mammoet Transport Sdn Bhd, **26** 280
Skechers U.S.A. Inc., **31 413–15**
Skelly Oil Co., **IV** 575
Sketchley plc, **19** 124
SKF Industries Inc. *See* AB Volvo.
Skidmore, Owings & Merrill, **13 475–76**
Skil-Craft Playthings, Inc., **13** 560
Skillern, **16** 560
Skillware, **9** 326
Skinner Macaroni Co., **II** 511
Skis Rossignol S.A., **15 460–62**
Skönvik, **IV** 338
SKS Group, **20** 363
SKW Nature's Products, Inc., **25** 332
SKW-Trostberg AG, **IV** 232
Sky Channel, **IV** 652
Sky Chefs, Inc., **16** 397
Sky Climber Inc., **11** 436
Sky Courier, **6** 345
Sky Merchant, Inc., **V** 78
Sky Television, **IV** 652–53; **7** 391–92
Skyband, Inc., **IV** 652; **7** 391; **12** 359
SkyBox International Inc., **15** 72–73
Skylight, **25** 508
Skyline Corporation, **30 421–23**
Skyline Homes, **17** 82
SkyMall, Inc., **26 439–41**; **28** 241
Skypak, **27** 474
SkyTel Corp., **18** 349; **23** 212
Skywalker Sound, **12** 322
Skyway Airlines, **6** 78; **11** 299
SkyWest, Inc., **25 420–24**
SL Holdings. *See* Finlay Enterprises, Inc.
Slade Gorton & Company, **13** 243
Slater Co. Foods, **II** 607
Slater Electric, **21** 349
Slater Systems, Inc., **13** 48
Slick Airways, **6** 388; **25** 146
Slim Jim, Inc. *See* GoodMark Foods, Inc.
Slim-Fast Nutritional Foods International, Inc., **12** 531; **18 489–91**; **27** 196
Slingerland Drum Company, **16** 239
Slip-X Safety Treads, **9** 72
SLJFB Vedrenne, **22** 344
SLM Holding Corp., **25 425–28 (upd.)**
SLN-Peñarroya, **IV** 108
Sloan's Supermarkets Inc. *See* Gristede's Sloan's, Inc.
Sloman Neptun Schiffahrts, **26** 279
Slope Indicator Company, **26** 42
Sloss Industries Corporation, **22** 544
Slots-A-Fun, **6** 204
Slough Estates plc, **IV 722–25**
AB Small Business Investment Co., Inc., **13** 111–12
Small Tube Products, Inc., **23** 517
SMALLCO, **III** 340
Smalley Transportation Company, **6** 421–23
SMAN. *See* Societe Mecanique Automobile du Nord.
Smart & Final, Inc., **12** 153–54; **16 451–53**
Smart Communications, **18** 180, 182
Smart Shirts Ltd., **8** 288–89
Smart Talk Network, Inc., **16** 319
SmartCash, **18** 543
Smead Manufacturing Co., **17 445–48**
Smedley's, **II** 513
Smethwick Drop Forgings, **III** 494
SMH. *See* The Swatch Group SA.
SMI Industries, **25** 15
Smirnoff, **14** 212; **18** 41
Smit International, **26** 241
Smith & Butterfield Co., Inc., **28** 74
Smith & Hawken, **10** 215, 217
Smith & Nephew plc, **17 449–52**
Smith & Wesson Corporation, **30 424–27**

Smith & Weston, **19** 430
Smith Barney Inc., I 614; **III** 569; **6** 410; **10** 63; **13** 328; **15 463–65**; **19** 385; **20** 360; **22** 406
Smith Bros., **I** 711
Smith Corona Corp., III 502; **7** 209; **13 477–80**; **14** 76; **23** 210
Smith International, Inc., III 429; **15 466–68**
Smith Mackenzie & Co., **III** 522
Smith McDonell Stone and Co., **14** 97
Smith Meter Co., **11** 4
Smith New Court PLC, **13** 342
Smith Packaging Ltd., **14** 429
Smith Parts Co., **11** 3
Smith Transfer Corp., **II** 607–08; **13** 49
Smith's Food & Drug Centers, Inc., 8 472–74; **17** 558, 561; **24** 36; **26** 432
Smith's Stampings, **III** 494
Smith-Higgins, **III** 9–10
Smithfield Foods, Inc., 7 477–78, 524–25; **22** 509, 511
SmithKline Beckman Corporation, I 389, 636, 640, 644, 646, 657, **692–94**, 696; **II** 331; **III** 65–66; **14** 46, 53; **26** 391; **30** 29–31
SmithKline Beecham PLC, III 65–67; **8** 210; **9** 347; **10** 47, 471; **11** 9, 90, 337; **13** 77; **14** 58; **16** 438; **17** 287; **24** 88; **25** 82
Smiths Bank, **II** 333
Smiths Food Group, Ltd., **II** 502; **10** 323
Smiths Industries PLC, III 555; **25 429–31**
Smithsonian Institution, 27 410–13
Smitty's Super Valu Inc., **II** 663–64; **12** 391; **17** 560–61
SMP Clothing, Inc., **22** 462
SMS, **IV** 226; **7** 401
Smucker. *See* The J.M. Smucker Company.
Smurfit Companies. *See* Jefferson Smurfit Group plc.
Smurfit-Stone Container Corporation, 26 442–46 (upd.)
SN Repal. *See* Société Nationale de Recherche de Pétrole en Algérie.
Snack Ventures Europe, **10** 324
Snake River Sugar Company, **19** 468
Snam Montaggi, **IV** 420
Snam Progetti, **IV** 420, 422
Snap-On, Incorporated, 27 414–16 (upd.)
Snap-on Tools Corporation, III 628; **7 479–80**; **25** 34
Snapper, **I** 447
Snapple Beverage Corporation, 11 449–51; **12** 411; **24** 480; **27** 153; **31** 243
Snapps Drive-Thru, **25** 389
Snappy Car Rental, Inc., **6** 393; **25** 142–43. *See also* Republic Industries, Inc.
SNE Enterprises, Inc., **12** 397
SNEA. *See* Société Nationale Elf Aquitaine.
Snecma Group, **17** 482
Snell & Wilmer L.L.P., 28 425–28
Snell Acoustics, **22** 99
SNET. *See* Southern New England Telecommunications Corporation.
SNMC Management Corporation, **11** 121
Snoqualmie Falls Plant, **6** 565
Snow Brand Milk Products Company, Limited, II 574–75
Snow King Frozen Foods, **II** 480; **26** 57
Snow White Dairies Inc. *See* Dairy Mart Convenience Stores, Inc.
Snowy Mountains Hydroelectric Authority, **IV** 707; **13** 118
SNPA, **IV** 453
Snyder Oil Corporation, **24** 379–81
SnyderGeneral Corp., **8** 321. *See also* AAF-McQuay Incorporated.
Soap Opera Magazine, **10** 287
Sobrom, **I** 341
Sobu Railway Company, **6** 431
Socal. *See* Standard Oil Company (California).
SOCAR, **IV** 505
Sochiku, **9** 30
Sociade Intercontinental de Compressores Hermeticos SICOM, S.A., **8** 515
La Sociale di A. Mondadori & C., **IV** 585
La Sociale, **IV** 585
Sociedad Alfa-Laval, **III** 419
Sociedad Bilbaina General de Credito, **II** 194
Sociedad Española de Automobiles del Turismo S.A. (SEAT), **I** 207, 459–60; **6** 47–48; **11** 550
Sociedad Financiera Mexicana, **19** 189
Sociedade Anónima Concessionária de Refinacao em Portugal. *See* SACOR.
Sociedade de Lubrificantes e Combustiveis, **IV** 505
Sociedade Nacional de Petróleos, **IV** 504
Sociedade Portuguesa de Petroquimica, **IV** 505
Sociedade Portuguesa e Navios-Tanques. *See* SOPONATA.
Società Anonima Fabbrica Italiana di Automobili, **I** 161
Società Anonima Lombarda Fabbrica Automobili, **13** 27
Società Azionaria Imprese Perforazioni, **IV** 419–20
Società Concessioni e Costruzioni Autostrade, **I** 466
Società Edison, **II** 86
Societa Esercizio Fabbriche Automobili e Corse Ferrari, **13** 219
Società Finanziaria Idrocarburi, **IV** 421
Società Finanziaria Telefonica per Azioni, I 465–66; **V 325–27**
Società Generale di Credito Mobiliare, **II** 191
Società Idrolettrica Piemonte, **I** 465–66
Societa Industria Meccanica Stampaggio S.p.A., **24** 500
Societa Italiana Gestione Sistemi Multi Accesso, **6** 69
Società Italiana per L'Esercizio delle Telecommunicazioni p.A., **I** 466–67; **V** 325–27
Società Italiana per la Infrastrutture e l'Assetto del Territoria, **I** 466
Società Italiana Pirelli, **V** 249
Società Italiana Vetro, **IV** 421
Società Nazionale Metanodotti, **IV** 419–21
Società Ravennate Metano, **IV** 420
Società Reale Mutua, **III** 207
Société Africaine de Déroulage des Ets Rougier, **21** 439
Société Air France, 27 417–20 (upd.). *See also* Groupe Air France.
Société Alsacienne de Magasins SA, **19** 308
Societe Anonima Italiana Ing. Nicola Romeo & Company, **13** 27
Societe Anonomie Alfa Romeo, **13** 28
Societe Anonyme Automobiles Citroen, **7** 35–36. *See also* PSA Peugeot Citroen S.A.
Société Anonyme Belge des Magasins Prisunic-Uniprix, **26** 159
Société Anonyme de la Manufactures des Glaces et Produits Chimiques de Saint-Gobain, Chauny et Cirey. *See* Compagnie de Saint-Gobain S.A.
Société Anonyme des Ciments Luxembourgeois, **IV** 25
Société Anonyme des Fermiers Reúnis, **23** 219
Société Anonyme des Hauts Fourneaux et Aciéries de Differdange-St. Ingbert-Rumelange, **IV** 26
Société Anonyme des Hauts Fourneaux et Forges de Dudelange, **22** 42
Société Anonyme des Mines du Luxembourg et des Forges de Sarrebruck, **IV** 24; **22** 42
La Societe Anonyme Francaise Holophane, **19** 211
Societe Anonyme Francaise Timken, **8** 530
Société Anonyme Telecommunications, **III** 164
Société, Auxiliaire d'Entrepreses SA, **13** 206
Société Belge de Banque, **II** 294–95
Société BIC, S.A., **III** 29; **8** 60–61; **23** 55–57
Société Calédonia, **IV** 107
Société Centrale d'Investissement, **29** 48
Société Centrale Union des Assurances de Paris, **III** 391, 393
Société Chimiques des Usines du Rhône, **I** 388
Société Civile Valoptec, **21** 222
Societe Commerciale Citroen, **7** 36
Société Congolaise des Grands Magasins Au Bon Marché, **26** 159
Société d'Investissement de Travaux Publics, **31** 128
Société d'Ougrée-Marihaye, **IV** 51
Société de Collecte des Prodicteirs de Preval, **19** 50
Societe de Construction des Batignolles, **II** 93
Societé de Crédit Agricole, **II** 264
Société de Développements et d'Innovations des Marchés Agricoles et Alimentaires, **II** 576
Société de Diffusion de Marques, **II** 576
Société de Diffusion Internationale Agro-Alimentaire, **II** 577
Societé de garantie des Crédits à court terme, **II** 233
Société de l'Oléoduc de la Sarre a.r.l., **IV** 197
Société de Prospection Électrique, **III** 616; **17** 416
La Société de Traitement des Minerais de Nickel, Cobalt et Autres, **IV** 107
Société des Caves de Roquefort, **24** 444
Société des Caves et des Producteurs Reunis de Roquefort, **19** 49
Societé des Eaux d'Evian, **II** 474
Société des Etablissements Gaumont. *See* Gaumont SA.
Société des Forges d'Eich–Metz et Cie, **IV** 24
Société des Forges et Aciéries du Nord-Est, **IV** 226

Société des Forges et Fonderies de Montataire, **IV** 226
Société des Grandes Entreprises de Distribution, Inno-France, **V** 58
Société des Hauts Fourneaux et Forges de Denain-Anzin, **IV** 226
Société des Mines du Luxembourg et de Sarrebruck, **IV** 25
Société des Pétroles d'Afrique Equatoriale, **IV** 545; **7** 482
Société des Usines Chimiques des Laboratoires Français, **I** 669
Société des Vins de France, **I** 281
Société du Louvre, 27 421–23
Société Economique de Rennes, **19** 98
Société Électrométallurgique Francaise, **IV** 173
Société European de Semi-Remorques, **7** 513
Societé Européenne de Brasseries, **II** 474–75
Société Européenne de Production de L'avion E.C.A.T. *See* SEPECAT.
Société Financiére Européenne, **II** 202–03, 233
Societe Financiere pour l'Industrie au Mexique, **19** 188
Société Française de Transports Pétroliers, **27** 514
Société Française des Cables Electriques Bertrand-Borel, **9** 9
Société Française des Teintures Inoffensives pour Cheveux, **III** 46
Société Française pour l'Exploitation du Pétrole, **IV** 557
Société Gélis-Poudenx-Sans, **IV** 108
Société General de Banque, **17** 324
Société Générale, II 233, 266, 295, **354–56**; **9** 148; **13** 203, 206; **19** 51
Société Générale de Banque, **II** 279, 295, 319; **14** 169
Société Générale de Belgique S.A., **II** 270, 294–95; **IV** 26; **10** 13; **22** 44; **26** 368; **27** 11
Societé Générale du Telephones, **21** 231
Société Générale pour favoriser l'Industrie nationale, **II** 294
Société Industrielle Belge des Pétroles, **IV** 498–99
Société Internationale Pirelli S.A., **V** 250
Société Irano-Italienne des Pétroles, **IV** 466
Société Laitière Vendômoise, **23** 219
Société Le Nickel, **IV** 107–08, 110
Societe Mecanique Automobile de l'Est/du Nord, **7** 37
Société Métallurgique, **IV** 25–26, 227
Société Minière de Bakwanga, **IV** 67
Société Minière des Terres Rouges, **IV** 25–26
Société Nationale de Programmes de Télévision Française 1. *See* Télévision Française 1.
Société Nationale de Recherche de Pétrole en Algérie, **IV** 545, 559; **7** 482
Société Nationale de Transport et de Commercialisation des Hydrocarbures, **IV** 423
Société Nationale des Chemins de Fer Français, V 512–15
Société Nationale des Pétroles d'Aquitaine, **21** 203–05
Société Nationale Elf Aquitaine, I 303–04, 670, 676–77; **II** 260; **IV** 174, 397–98, 424, 451, 453–54, 472–74, 499, 506, 515–16, 518, 525, 535, **544–47**, 559–60; **V** 628; **7 481–85 (upd.)**; **8** 452; **11** 97; **12** 153
Société Nationale pour la Recherche, la Production, le Transport, la Transformation et la Commercialisation des Hydrocarbures, **IV** 423–24
Société Nord Africaine des Ciments Lafarge, **III** 703
Société Nouvelle d'Achat de Bijouterie, **16** 207
Société Nouvelle des Etablissements Gaumont. *See* Gaumont SA.
Société Parisienne d'Achats en Commun, **19** 307
Societe Parisienne pour l'Industrie Electrique, **II** 93
Société Parisienne Raveau-Cartier, **31** 128
Société pour l'Eportation de Grandes Marques, **I** 281
Société pour l'Étude et la Realisation d'Engins Balistiques. *See* SEREB.
Société pour L'Exploitation de la Cinquième Chaîne, **6** 374
Société pour le Financement de l'Industrie Laitière, **19** 51
Société Samos, **23** 219
Société Savoyarde des Fromagers du Reblochon, **25** 84
Société Succursaliste S.A. d'Approvisonnements Guyenne et Gascogne. *See* Guyenne et Gascogne.
Société Suisse de Microelectronique & d'Horlogerie. *See* The Swatch Group SA.
Societe Vendeenne des Embalages, **9** 305
Societe-Hydro-Air S.a.r.L., **9** 27
Society Corporation, 9 474–77
Society of Lloyd's, **III** 278–79
SOCO Chemical Inc., **8** 69
Socombel, **IV** 497
Socony. *See* Standard Oil Co. (New York).
Socony Mobil Oil Co., Inc., **IV** 465; **7** 353
Sodak Gaming, Inc., **9** 427
Sodastream Holdings, **II** 477
Sodexho Alliance SA, **23** 154; **29 442–44**
Sodiaal, **II** 577; **19** 50
SODIMA, II 576–77
Sodiso, **23** 247
Sodyeco, **I** 673
Soekor, **IV** 93
Soffo, **22** 365
Soficom, **27** 136
SOFIL. *See* Société pour le Financement de l'Industrie Laitière.
Sofimex. *See* Sociedad Financiera Mexicana.
Sofiran, **IV** 467
Sofitam, S.A., **21** 493, 495
Sofitels. *See* Accor SA.
Sofrem, **IV** 174
Soft Lenses Inc., **25** 55
Soft Sheen Products, Inc., 31 416–18
Soft*Switch, **25** 301
Softbank Corp., **12** 562; **13 481–83**; **16** 168; **27** 516, 518
SoftKat. *See* Baker & Taylor, Inc.
SoftKey Software Products Inc., **24** 276
Softsel Computer Products, **12** 334–35
SoftSolutions Technology Corporation, **10** 558
Software AG, **11** 18
Software Arts, **6** 254; **25** 299
Software Development Pty., Ltd., **15** 107
Software Dimensions, Inc. *See* ASK Group, Inc.
Software, Etc., **13** 545
The Software Group Inc., **23** 489, 491
Software International, **6** 224
Software Plus, Inc., **10** 514
Software Publishing Corp., **14** 262
Softwood Holdings Ltd., **III** 688
Sogara S.A., **23** 246–48
Sogebra S.A., **I** 257
Sogedis, **23** 219
Sogen International Corp., **II** 355
Sogexport, **II** 355
Soginnove, **II** 355–56
Sohio Chemical Company, **13** 502
Sohken Kako Co., Ltd., **IV** 327
Soil Teq, Inc., **17** 10
Soilserv, Inc. *See* Mycogen Corporation.
Soinlahti Sawmill and Brick Works, **IV** 300
Sola Holdings, **III** 727
Solair Inc., **14** 43
La Solana Corp., **IV** 726
Solar, **IV** 614
Solar Electric Corp., **13** 398
Solectron Corp., **12** 161–62, **450–52**
Solel Boneh Construction, **II** 47; **25** 266–67
Soletanche Co., **I** 586
Solid Beheer B.V., **10** 514
Solid State Dielectrics, **I** 329; **8** 152
Solite Corp., **23** 224–25
Sollac, **IV** 226–27; **24** 144; **25** 96
Solley's Delicatessen and Bakery, **24** 243
Solmer, **IV** 227
Solo Serve Corporation, **23** 177; **28 429–31**
Soloman Brothers, **17** 561
Solomon Smith Barney Inc., **22** 404
Solomon Valley Milling Company, **6** 592
Solon Automated Services, **II** 607
Solsound Industries, **16** 393
Soltam, **25** 266
Solutia Inc., **29** 330
Solvay & Cie S.A., **I** 303, **394–96**, 414–15; **III** 677; **IV** 300; **16** 121; **21** 254, **464–67 (upd.)**
Solvay Animal Health Inc., **12** 5
Solvent Resource Recovery, Inc., **9** 109
Solvents Recovery Service of New Jersey, Inc., **8** 464
SOMABRI, **12** 152
SOMACA, **12** 152
Somali Bank, **31** 220
Someal, **27** 513, 515
Somerville Electric Light Company, **12** 45
Somerville Packaging Group, **28** 420
Sommer-Allibert S.A., **19 406–09**; **22** 49; **25** 462, 464
Sommers Drug Stores, **9** 186
SONAP, **IV** 504–06
Sonat, Inc., **6 577–78**; **22** 68
Sonatrach. *See* Entreprise Nationale Sonatrach.
Sonecor Systems, **6** 340
Sonesson, **I** 211
Sonet Media AB, **23** 390
Sonic Corporation, **14 451–53**; **16** 387
Sonic Restaurants, **31** 279
Sonneborn Chemical and Refinery Co., **I** 405
Sonnen Basserman, **II** 475
SonnenBraune, **22** 460

Sonoco Products Company, **8 475–77**; **12** 150–51; **16** 340
The Sonoma Group, **25** 246
Sonoma Mortgage Corp., **II** 382
Sonometrics Inc., **I** 667
Sony Corporation, **I** 30, 534; **II** 56, 58, 91–92, **101–03**, 117–19, 124, 134, 137, 440; **III** 141, 143, 340, 658; **6** 30; **7** 118; **9** 385; **10** 86, 119, 403; **11** 46, 490–91, 557; **12** 75, 161, 448, **453–56 (upd.)**; **13** 399, 403, 482, 573; **14** 534; **16** 94; **17** 533; **18** 18; **19** 67; **20** 439; **21** 129; **22** 194; **24** 4; **25** 22; **26** 188, 433, 489, 511; **28** 241; **30** 18; **31** 239
Sonzogno, **IV** 585
Soo Line, **V** 429–30; **24** 533
Soo Line Mills, **II** 631
Sooner Trailer Manufacturing Co., **29** 367
Soparind, **25** 83–85
Sope Creek, **30** 457
SOPEAL, **III** 738
Sophia Jocoba GmbH, **IV** 193
SOPI, **IV** 401
Sopwith Aviation Co., **III** 507–08
Soravie, **II** 265
Sorbents Products Co.
Sorbus, **6** 242
Sorcim, **6** 224
Soreal, **8** 344
Sorg Paper Company. *See* Mosinee Paper Corporation.
Soros Fund Management LLC, **27** 198; **28 432–34**
Sorrento, Inc., **19** 51; **24 444–46**; **26** 505
SOS Co., **II** 531
SOS Staffing Services, **25 432–35**
Sosa, Bromley, Aguilar & Associates, **6** 22
Soterra, Inc., **15** 188
Sotheby's Holdings, Inc., **11 452–54**; **15** 98–100; **29 445–48 (upd.)**
Sound of Music Inc. *See* Best Buy Co., Inc.
Sound Trek, **16** 74
Sound Video Unlimited, **16** 46
Sound Warehouse, **9** 75
Souplantation Incorporated. *See* Garden Fresh Restaurant Corporation.
Source One Mortgage Services Corp., **12** 79
Source Perrier, **7** 383; **24** 444
Souriau, **19** 166
South African Airways Ltd., **6** 84, 433, 435; **27** 132
The South African Breweries Limited, **I 287–89**, 422; **24 447–51 (upd.)**; **26** 462
South African Coal, Oil and Gas Corp., **IV** 533
South African Railways, **6** 434–35
South African Torbanite Mining and Refining Co., **IV** 534
South African Transport Services, **6** 433, 435
South American Cable Co., **I** 428
South Asia Tyres, **20** 263
South Bend Toy Manufacturing Company, **25** 380
South Carolina Electric & Gas Company, **6** 574–76
South Carolina Industries, **IV** 333
South Carolina National Corporation, **16** 523, 526
South Central Bell Telephone Co. **V** 276–78
South Central Railroad Co., **14** 325
South China Morning Post (Holdings) Ltd., **II** 298; **IV** 652; **7** 392
South Coast Gas Compression Company, Inc., **11** 523
South Coast Terminals, Inc., **16** 475
South Dakota Public Service Company, **6** 524
South Fulton Light & Power Company, **6** 514
South Improvement Co., **IV** 427
South Manchuria Railroad Co. Ltd., **IV** 434
South of Scotland Electricity Board, **19** 389–90
South Penn Oil Co., **IV** 488–89
South Puerto Rico Sugar Co., **I** 452
South Puerto Rico Telephone Co., **I** 462
South Sea Textile, **III** 705
South Texas Stevedore Co., **IV** 81
South-Western Publishing Co., **8** 526–28
Southam Inc., **7 486–89**; **15** 265; **24** 223
Southco, **II** 602–03; **7** 20–21; **30** 26
Southcorp Holdings Ltd., **17** 373; **22** 350
Southdown, Inc., **14 454–56**
Southeast Bank of Florida, **11** 112
Southeast Banking Corp., **II** 252; **14** 103
Southeast Public Service Company, **8** 536
Southeastern Personnel. *See* Norrell Corporation.
Southeastern Power and Light Company, **6** 447; **23** 28
Southeastern Telephone Company, **6** 312
Southern and Phillips Gas Ltd., **13** 485
Southern Australia Airlines, **24** 396
Southern Bank, **10** 426
Southern Bearings Co., **13** 78
Southern Bell, **10** 202
Southern Biscuit Co., **II** 631
Southern Blvd. Supermarkets, Inc., **22** 549
Southern Box Corp., **13** 441
Southern California Edison Co., **II** 402; **V** 711, 713–15, 717; **11** 272; **12** 106
Southern California Financial Corporation, **27** 46
Southern California Fruit Growers Exchange. *See* Sunkist Growers, Inc.
Southern California Gas Co., **I** 569; **25** 413–14, 416
Southern Casualty Insurance Co., **III** 214
Southern Clay Products, **III** 691
Southern Clays Inc., **IV** 82
Southern Co., **24** 525
Southern Colorado Power Company, **6** 312
Southern Comfort Corp., **I** 227
Southern Connecticut Newspapers Inc., **IV** 677
Southern Cotton Co., **IV** 224; **24** 488
Southern Cotton Oil Co., **I** 421; **11** 23
Southern Discount Company of Atlanta, **9** 229
Southern Electric PLC, **13 484–86**
Southern Electric Supply Co., **15** 386
Southern Equipment & Supply Co., **19** 344
Southern Extract Co., **IV** 310; **19** 266
Southern Forest Products, Inc., **6** 577
Southern Gage, **III** 519; **22** 282
Southern Graphic Arts, **13** 405
Southern Guaranty Cos., **III** 404
Southern Idaho Water Power Company, **12** 265
Southern Illinois Light & Power Company, **6** 504
Southern Indiana Gas and Electric Company, **13 487–89**
Southern Japan Trust Bank, **V** 114
Southern Kraft Corp., **IV** 286
Southern Lumber Company, **8** 430
Southern Manufacturing Company, **8** 458
Southern National Bankshares of Atlanta, **II** 337; **10** 425
Southern Natural Gas Co., **III** 558; **6** 447–48, 577
Southern Nevada Power Company, **11** 343
Southern Nevada Telephone Company, **6** 313; **11** 343
Southern New England Telecommunications Corporation, **6 338–40**
Southern Nitrogen Co., **IV** 123
Southern Oregon Broadcasting Co., **7** 15
Southern Pacific Communications Corporation, **9** 478–79
Southern Pacific Rail Corp., **12** 18–20. *See also* Union Pacific Corporation.
Southern Pacific Railroad, **I** 13; **II** 329, 381, 448; **IV** 625; **19** 202
Southern Pacific Transportation Company, **V 516–18**; **12** 278; **26** 235
Southern Peru Copper Corp., **IV** 33
Southern Phenix Textiles Inc., **15** 247–48
Southern Pine Lumber Co., **IV** 341
Southern Power Company. *See* Duke Energy Corporation.
Southern Railway Company, **V** 484–85; **29** 359
Southern Science Applications, Inc., **22** 88
Southern States Cooperative, Inc., **26** 168
Southern States Trust Co., **II** 336
Southern Sun Hotel Corporation. *See* South African Breweries Ltd. and *Sun International Hotels Limited.*
Southern Surety Co., **III** 332
Southern Telephone Company, **14** 257
Southern Television Corp., **II** 158; **IV** 650; **7** 389
Southern Union Company, **12** 542; **27 424–26**
Southern Utah Fuel Co., **IV** 394
Southern Video Partnership, **9** 74
Southern Water plc, **19** 389–91
Southgate Medical Laboratory System, **26** 391
The Southland Corporation, **II** 449, 620, **660–61**; **IV** 392, 508; **V** 89; **7** 114, 374, **490–92 (upd.)**; **9** 178; **13** 333, 449, 525; **23** 406–07; **25** 125; **26** 447; **31** 115, 231
Southland Mobilcom Inc., **15** 196
Southland Paper, **13** 118
Southland Royal Company, **27** 86
Southland Royalty Co., **10** 190
Southlife Holding Co., **III** 218
Southmark, **11** 483
Southtrust Corporation, **11 455–57**
Southview Pulp Co., **IV** 329
Southwest Airlines Co., **I** 106; **6** 72–74, **119–21**; **21** 143; **22** 22; **24 452–55 (upd.)**; **25** 404; **26** 308, 439–40
Southwest Airmotive Co., **II** 16
Southwest Convenience Stores, LLC, **26** 368
Southwest Converting, **19** 414
Southwest Enterprise Associates, **13** 191
Southwest Forest Industries, **IV** 287, 289, 334
Southwest Gas Corporation, **19 410–12**
Southwest Hide Co., **16** 546
Southwest Potash Corp., **IV** 18; **6** 148–49

Southwestern Bell Corporation, V 328–30; **6** 324; **10** 431, 500; **14** 489; **17** 110; **18** 22
Southwestern Bell Publications, **26** 520
Southwestern Electric Power Co., 21 468–70
Southwestern Gas Pipeline, **7** 344
Southwestern Illinois Coal Company, **7** 33
Southwestern Life Insurance, **I** 527; **III** 136
Southwestern Pipe, **III** 498
Southwestern Public Service Company, 6 579–81
Southwestern Refining Company, Inc., **IV** 446; **22** 303
Southwestern Textile Company, **12** 393
Southwire Company, Inc., 8 478–80; **12** 353; **23 444–47 (upd.)**
Souvall Brothers, **8** 473
Sovereign Corp., **III** 221; **14** 109
Sovran Financial, **10** 425–26
SovTransavto, **6** 410
Soyland Power Cooperative, **6** 506
SP Reifenwerke, **V** 253
SP Tyres, **V** 253
Space Control GmbH, **28** 243–44
Space Craft Inc., **9** 463
Space Data Corporation, **22** 401
Space Systems Corporation. *See* Orbital Sciences Corporation.
Space Systems/Loral, **9** 325
Spacemakers Inc., **IV** 287
Spaghetti Warehouse, Inc., 25 436–38
Spagnesi, **18** 258
Spago. *See* The Wolfgang Puck Food Company, Inc.
Spalding & Evenflo, **24** 530
Spalding, Inc., **17** 243; **23** 449
Spanish International Communications Corp. *See* Univision Communications Inc.
Spanish River Pulp and Paper Mills, **IV** 246; **25** 10
Sparbanken Bank, **18** 543
SPARC International, **7** 499
Spare Change, **10** 282
Sparklets Ltd., **I** 315; **25** 80
Sparks Computerized Car Care Centers, **25** 445
Sparks Family Hospital, **6** 191
Sparks-Withington Company. *See* Sparton Corporation.
Sparrow Records, **22** 194
Sparta, Inc., **18** 369
Spartan Insurance Co., **26** 486
Spartan Motors Inc., 14 457–59
Spartan Stores Inc., I 127; **II** 679–80; **8 481–82**; **10** 302; **12** 489; **14** 412
Spartech Corporation, 9 92; **19 413–15**
Sparton Corporation, 18 492–95
SPCM, Inc., **14** 477
Spec's Music, Inc., 19 416–18
Spécia, **I** 388
Special Agent Investigators, Inc., **14** 541
Special Foods, **14** 557
Special Light Alloy Co., **IV** 153
Special Zone Limited, **26** 491
Specialized Bicycle Components Inc., **19** 384
Specialty Brands Inc., **25** 518
Specialty Coatings Inc., 8 483–84
Specialty Equipment Companies, Inc., 25 439–42
Specialty Foods Corporation, **29** 29, 31
Specialty Papers Co., **IV** 290
Specialty Products Co., **8** 386
Specialty Retailers, Inc., **24** 456
Spectra Star, Inc., **18** 521
Spectra-Physics AB, **9** 380–81
Spectradyne, **28** 241
Spectral Dynamics Corporation. *See* Scientific-Atlanta, Inc.
Spectron MicroSystems, **18** 143
Spectrum Club, **25** 448–50
Spectrum Communications Holdings International Limited, **24** 95
Spectrum Concepts, **10** 394–95
Spectrum Data Systems, Inc., **24** 96
Spectrum Dyed Yarns of New York, **8** 559
Spectrum Health Care Services, **13** 48
Spectrum Medical Technologies, Inc., **22** 409
Spectrum Technology Group, Inc., **7** 378; **18** 112
Spectrumedia, **21** 361
Speed-O-Lac Chemical, **8** 553
SpeeDee Marts, **II** 661
SpeeDee Oil Change and Tune-Up, 25 443–47
Speedy Auto Glass, **30** 501
Speedy Muffler King, **10** 415; **24** 337, 339
Speidel Newspaper Group, **IV** 612; **7** 191
Spelling Entertainment Group, Inc., 9 75; **14 460–62**; **23** 503; **28** 296
Spencer & Spencer Systems, Inc., **18** 112
Spencer Beef, **II** 536
Spencer Gifts, Inc., **II** 144; **15** 464
Spencer Stuart and Associates, Inc., 14 463–65
Spenco Medical Corp., **III** 41; **16** 303
Sperry & Hutchinson Co., **12** 299; **23** 243–44
Sperry Aerospace Group, **II** 40, 86; **6** 283; **12** 246, 248
Sperry Corporation, **I** 101, 167; **III** 165, 642; **6** 281–82; **8** 92; **11** 139; **12** 39; **13** 511; **18** 386, 542; **22** 379. *See also* Unisys Corporation.
Sperry Milling Co., **II** 501; **10** 322
Sperry New Holland. *See* New Holland N.V.
Sperry Rand Corp., **II** 63, 73; **III** 126, 129, 149, 166, 329, 642; **6** 241, 261, 281–82; **16** 137
Sphere Inc., **8** 526; **13** 92
Sphere SA, **27** 9
Spicer Manufacturing Co., **I** 152; **III** 568; **20** 359; **23** 170–71
Spie Batignolles SA, **I** 563; **II** 93–94; **13** 206; **18** 471–73; **24** 79
Spiegel, Inc., III 598; **V** 160; **8** 56–58; **10** 168, **489–91**; **11** 498; **9** 190, 219; **13** 179; **15** 339; **27 427–31 (upd.)**
Spillers, **II** 500
Spin Physics, **III** 475–76; **7** 163
Spinnaker Software Corp., **24** 276
SPIRE Corporation, **14** 477
Spire, Inc., **25** 183
Spirella Company of Great Britain Ltd., **V** 356
Spirit Airlines, Inc., 31 419–21
Spirit Cruises, **29** 442–43
Spliethoff, **26** 280
Spoerle Electronic, **10** 113
Spokane Falls Electric Light and Power Company. *See* Edison Electric Illuminating Company.
Spokane Falls Water Power Company, **6** 595
Spokane Gas and Fuel, **IV** 391
Spokane Natural Gas Company, **6** 597
Spokane Street Railway Company, **6** 595
Spokane Traction Company, **6** 596
Spom Japan, **IV** 600
Spoor Behrins Campbell and Young, **II** 289
Spoornet, **6** 435
Sporis, **27** 151
Sporloisirs S.A., **9** 157
Sport Chalet, Inc., 16 454–56
Sport Supply Group, Inc., 22 458–59; **23 448–50**; **30** 185
Sporting Dog Specialties, Inc., **14** 386
Sporting News Publishing Co., **IV** 677–78
Sportland, **26** 160
Sportmart, Inc., 15 469–71. *See also* Gart Sports Company.
Sports & Co. *See* Hibbett Sporting Goods, Inc.
Sports & Recreation, Inc., 15 470; **17 453–55**
The Sports Authority, Inc., 15 470; **16 457–59**; **17** 453; **18** 286; **24** 173
The Sports Club Company, 25 448–51
Sports Experts Inc., **II** 652
Sports Inc., **14** 8
Sports Traders, Inc., **18** 208
Sports-Tech Inc., **21** 300
Sportservice Corporation, **7** 133–35
Sportstown, Inc., **15** 470
Sportsystems Corporation, **7** 133, 135
Sprague Co., **I** 410
Sprague Devices, Inc., **11** 84
Sprague Electric Company, **6** 261
Sprague Electric Railway and Motor Co., **II** 27; **12** 193
Sprague Technologies, **21** 520
Sprague, Warner & Co., **II** 571
Spray-Rite, **I** 366
Sprayon Products, **III** 745
Spraysafe, **29** 98
Sprecher & Schub, **9** 10
Spring Co., **21** 96, 246
Spring Forge Mill, **8** 412
Spring Industries, Inc., V 378–79
Spring Valley Brewery. *See* Kirin Brewery Company, Limited.
Springbok Editions, **IV** 621
Springer Verlag GmbH & Co., **IV** 611, 641
Springfield Bank, **9** 474
Springhouse Corp., **IV** 610
Springhouse Financial Corp., **III** 204
Springmaid International, Inc., **19** 421
Springs Industries, Inc., 19 419–22 (upd.); **29** 132; **31** 199
Sprint Communications Company, L.P., 9 478–80; **10** 19, 57, 97, 201–03; **11** 183, 185, 500–01; **18** 32, 164–65, 569–70; **22** 19, 162; **24** 120, 122; **25** 102; **26** 17; **27** 365. *See also* US Sprint Communications.
Spruce Falls Power and Paper Co., **III** 40; **IV** 648; **16** 302, 304; **19** 284
SPS Technologies, Inc., 30 428–30
Spun Yarns, Inc., **12** 503
Spur Oil Co., **7** 362
SPX Corporation, 10 492–95
SPZ, Inc., **26** 257
SQ Software, Inc., **10** 505
SQL Solutions, Inc., **10** 505

Square D Company, **18** 473
Square Industries, **18** 103, 105
Squibb Beech-Nut. *See* Beech-Nut Nutrition Corp.
Squibb Corporation, **I** 380–81, 631, 651, 659, 675, **695–97**; **III** 17, 19, 67; **8** 166; **9** 6–7; **13** 379–80; **16** 438–39
Squire Fashions Inc. *See* Norton McNaughton of Squire, Inc.
SR. *See* Southern Railway.
SR Beteilgungen Aktiengesellschaft, **III** 377
SRI International, **10** 139
SRI Strategic Resources Inc., **6** 310
SS Cars, Ltd. *See* Jaguar Cars, Ltd.
SSA. *See* Stevedoring Services of America Inc.
Ssangyong Cement Industrial Co., Ltd., **III 747–50**; **IV** 536–37, 539
SSC&B-Lintas, **I** 16–17; **14** 315
SSDS, Inc., **18** 537
SSI Medical Services, Inc., **10** 350
SSMC Inc., **II** 10
SSP Company, Inc., **17** 434
St. *See under* Saint
Staal Bankiers, **13** 544
Stadia Colorado Corporation, **18** 140
Stadt Corporation, **26** 109
Städtische Elecktricitäts-Werke A.G., **I** 410
Staefa Control System Limited, **6** 490
StaffAmerica, Inc., **16** 50
Stafford Old Bank, **II** 307
Stafford-Lowdon, **31** 435
Stag Cañon Fuel Co., **IV** 177
Stage Stores, Inc., **24 456–59**
Stagecoach Holdings plc, **30 431–33**
Stags' Leap Winery, **22** 80
Stahl-Urban Company, **8** 287–88
Stahlwerke Peine-Salzgitter AG, **IV** 201
Stahlwerke Röchling AG, **III** 694–95
Stahlwerke Südwestfalen AG, **IV** 89
Stal-Astra GmbH, **III** 420
Staley Continental, **II** 582
Stamford Drug Group, **9** 68
Stamford FHI Acquisition Corp., **27** 117
Stamos Associates Inc., **29** 377
Stanadyne, Inc., **7** 336; **12** 344
Standard & Poor's Corp., **IV** 29, 482, 636–37; **12** 310; **25** 542
Standard Accident Co., **III** 332
Standard Aero, **III** 509
Standard Aircraft Equipment, **II** 16
Standard Alaska, **7** 559
Standard Bank, **17** 324
Standard Bank of Canada, **II** 244
Standard Box Co., **17** 357
Standard Brands, **I** 248; **II** 542, 544; **7** 365, 367; **18** 538
Standard Car Truck, **18** 5
Standard Chartered PLC, **II** 298, 309, 319, **357–59**, 386; **10** 170
Standard Chemical Products, **III** 33
Standard Commercial Corporation, **12** 110; **13 490–92**; **27** 126
Standard Drug Co., **V** 171
Standard Electric Time Company, **13** 233
Standard Electrica, **II** 13
Standard Elektrik Lorenz A.G., **II** 13, 70; **17** 353
Standard Equities Corp., **III** 98
Standard Federal Bank, **9 481–83**
Standard Fire Insurance Co., **III** 181–82
Standard Fruit and Steamship Co. of New Orleans, **II** 491; **31** 168
Standard Gauge Manufacturing Company, **13** 233
Standard General Insurance, **III** 208
Standard Gypsum Corp., **19** 77
Standard Industrial Group Ltd., **IV** 658
Standard Insert Co., **28** 350
Standard Insulation Co., **I** 321
Standard Insurance Co. of New York, **III** 385
Standard Investing Corp., **III** 98
Standard Kollsman Industries Inc., **13** 461
Standard Life & Accident Insurance Company, **27** 47–48
Standard Life Assurance Company, **III 358–61**; **IV** 696–98
Standard Life Insurance Company, **11** 481
Standard Magnesium & Chemical Co., **IV** 123
Standard Metals Corp., **IV** 76
Standard Microsystems Corporation, **11 462–64**
Standard Milling Co., **II** 497
Standard Motor Co., **III** 651
Standard of America Life Insurance Co., **III** 324
Standard of Georgia Insurance Agency, Inc., **10** 92
Standard Oil Co., **III** 470, 513; **IV** 46, 372, 399, 426–29, 434, 463, 478, 488–89, 530–31, 540, 542, 551, 574, 577–78, 657; **V** 590, 601; **6** 455; **7** 169–72, 263, 351, 414, 551; **8** 415; **10** 110, 289; **14** 21, 491–92; **25** 230; **27** 129
Standard Oil Co. (California), **II** 448; **IV** 18–19, 385–87, 403, 429, 464, 536–37, 545, 552, 560, 578; **6** 353; **7** 172, 352, 483; **13** 448
Standard Oil Co. (Illinois), **IV** 368
Standard Oil Co. (Indiana), **II** 262; **IV** 366, 368–71, 466–67; **7** 443; **10** 86; **14** 222
Standard Oil Co. (Minnesota), **IV** 368
Standard Oil Co. (New York), **IV** 428–29, 431, 460, 463–65, 485, 504, 537, 549, 558; **7** 171, 351–52
Standard Oil Co. of Iowa, **IV** 385
Standard Oil Co. of Kentucky, **IV** 387
Standard Oil Co. of New Jersey, **I** 334, 337, 370; **II** 16, 496; **IV** 378–79, 385–86, 400, 415–16, 419, 426–29, 431–33, 438, 460, 463–64, 488, 522, 531, 537–38, 544, 558, 565, 571; **V** 658–59; **7** 170–72, 253, 351; **13** 124; **17** 412–13; **24** 521
Standard Oil Co. of Ohio, **IV** 373, 379, 427, 452, 463, 522, 571; **7** 57, 171, 263; **12** 309; **21** 82; **24** 521
Standard Oil Development Co., **IV** 554
Standard Oil Trust, **IV** 31, 368, 375, 385–86, 427, 463
Standard Plastics, **25** 312
Standard Printing Company, **19** 333
Standard Process & Engraving, Inc., **26** 105
Standard Products Company, **19** 454
Standard Rate & Data Service, **IV** 639; **7** 286
Standard Register Co., **15 472–74**
Standard Sanitary, **III** 663–64
Standard Screw Co., **12** 344
Standard Shares, **9** 413–14
Standard Steel Propeller, **I** 47, 84; **9** 416; **10** 162
Standard Telephone and Radio, **II** 13
Standard Telephones and Cables, Ltd., **III** 162–63; **6** 242
Standard Tin Plate Co., **15** 127
Standard-Vacuum Oil Co., **IV** 431–32, 440, 460, 464, 491–92, 554–55; **7** 352
Standex International Corporation, **16** 470–71; **17 456–59**
Stanhome Inc., **9** 330; **11** 94–96; **15 475–78**
STANIC, **IV** 419, 421
Stanko Fanuc Service, **III** 483
Stanley Electric Manufacturing Co., **II** 28; **12** 194
Stanley Home Products, Incorporated. *See* Stanhome Inc.
Stanley Mining Services, Ltd., **19** 247
The Stanley Works, **III 626–29**; **7** 480; **9** 543; **13** 41; **20 476–80 (upd.)**
StanMont, Inc., **24** 425
Stanolind Oil & Gas Co., **III** 498; **IV** 365, 369–70
Stant Corporation, **15** 503, 505
Staples, Inc., **8** 404–05; **10 496–98**; **18** 24, 388; **20** 99; **22** 154; **23** 363, 365; **24** 270
Star, **10** 287–88
Star Air Service. *See* Alaska Air Group, Inc.
Star Alliance, **26** 113
Star Banc Corporation, **11 465–67**; **13** 222; **31** 206
Star Building Systems, Inc., **19** 366
Star Engraving, **12** 471
Star Enterprise, **IV** 536, 539, 553
Star Enterprises, Inc., **6** 457
Star Finishing Co., **9** 465
Star Laboratories Inc., **24** 251
Star Markets Company, Inc., **23** 169
Star Medical Technologies, Inc., **22** 409; **31** 124
Star Paper Ltd., **IV** 300
Star Paper Tube, Inc., **19** 76–78
Star Sportwear Manufacturing Corp., **29** 294
Star Video, Inc., **6** 313
Starber International, **12** 181
Starbucks Corporation, **13 493–94**; **18** 37; **22** 370; **25** 178, 501; **28** 63
Starcraft Corporation, **III** 444; **13** 113; **22** 116; **30 434–36**
Stardent Computer Inc., **III** 553; **26** 256
Starfish Software, **23** 212
Stark Record and Tape Service. *See* Camelot Music, Inc.
StarKist Foods, **II** 508; **11** 172
Starlawerken, **I** 527
Starlen Labs, Ltd., **31** 346
Starlight Networks, Inc., **27** 366
Starline Optical Corp., **22** 123
StarMed Staffing Corporation, **6** 10
Starpointe Savings Bank, **9** 173
Starrett Corporation, **21 471–74**
Star's Discount Department Stores, **16** 36
Startech Semiconductor Inc., **14** 183
Startel Corp., **15** 125
Starter Corp., **12 457–458**
Starwood Capital, **29** 508
State Bank of Albany, **9** 228
State Farm Insurance Companies, **27** 30; **29** 397
State Farm Mutual Automobile Insurance Company, **III 362–64**; **10** 50; **22** 266; **23** 286; **25** 155
State Finance and Thrift Company, **14** 529

State Leed, **13** 367
State Metal Works, **III** 647
State Savings Bank and Trust Co., **11** 180
State Street Boston Corporation, 8 491–93
State Trading Corp. of India Ltd., **IV** 143
State-o-Maine, **18** 357–59
State-Record Co., **IV** 630
Staten Island Advance Corp., **IV** 581–82; **19** 4
Stater Brothers, **17** 558
Statex Petroleum, Inc., **19** 70
Static, Inc., **14** 430
Station Casinos Inc., 25 452–54
Stationers Distributing Company, **14** 523
Stationers, Inc., **28** 74
Statler Hotel Co., **III** 92, 98; **19** 206
Statoil. *See* Den Norske Stats Oljeselskap AS.
StatScript Management Services, **26** 73
Statter, Inc., **6** 27
Staubli International, **II** 122; **12** 546
Stauffer Chemical Company, **8** 105–07; **21** 545
Stauffer-Meiji, **II** 540
Stax Records, **23** 32
STC PLC, III 141, **162–64**; **25** 497
Stead & Miller, **13** 169
Steag AG, **IV** 193
Steak & Ale, **II** 556–57; **7** 336; **12** 373; **13** 408–09
Steak n Shake, **14** 130–31
Steam and Gas Pipe Co., **III** 644
Steam Boiler Works, **18** 318
Steamboat Ski and Resort Corporation, **28** 21
Stearman, **I** 47, 84; **9** 416; **10** 162
Stearns & Foster, **12** 439
Stearns Catalytic World Corp., **II** 87; **11** 413
Stearns Coal & Lumber, **6** 514
Stearns Manufacturing Co., **16** 297
Steaua-Romana, **IV** 557
Steego Auto Paints, **24** 160
Steel and Tube Co. of America, **IV** 114
Steel Authority of India Ltd., IV 205–07
Steel Ceilings and Aluminum Works, **IV** 22
Steel Co. of Canada Ltd., **IV** 208
Steel Dynamics, Inc., **18** 380; **26** 530
Steel Mills Ltd., **III** 673
Steel Products Engineering Co., **I** 169
Steel Stamping Co., **III** 569; **20** 360
Steelcase Inc., 7 493–95; **8** 251–52, 255, 405; **25** 500; **27 432–35 (upd.)**
Steelmade Inc., **I** 513
Steely, **IV** 109
Steenfabriek De Ruiterwaard, **14** 249
Steenkolen Handelsvereniging, **IV** 132
Steering Aluminum, **I** 159
Stefany, **12** 152
Stegbar Pty Ltd., **31** 398–400
Steger Furniture Manufacturing Co., **18** 493
Steiff. *See* Margarete Steiff GmbH.
Steil, Inc., **8** 271
Stein Mart Inc., 19 423–25
Stein Printing Company, **25** 183
Stein Robaire Helm, **22** 173
Steinbach Inc., **IV** 226; **14** 427
Steinbach Stores, Inc., **19** 108
Steinberg Incorporated, II 652–53, **662–65**; **V** 163
Steinberger, **16** 239
Steinheil Optronik GmbH, **24** 87
Steinman & Grey, **6** 27
Steinmüller Verwaltungsgesellschaft, **V** 747
Steinway & Sons, **16** 201
Steinway Musical Properties, Inc., 19 392, 394, **426–29**
Stelco Inc., IV 208–10; **24** 144
Stella Bella Corporation, **19** 436
Stella D'Oro Company, **7** 367
Stellar Systems, Inc., **III** 553; **14** 542
Stellenbosch Farmers Winery, **I** 288
Stelux Manufacturing Company, **13** 121
Stena AB, **25** 105; **29** 429–30
Stensmölla Kemiska Tekniska Industri, **I** 385
Stentor Canadian Network Management, **6** 310
Stenval Sud, **19** 50
Stepan Company, 30 437–39
Stephen F. Whitman & Son, Inc., **7** 429
Stephens Inc., **III** 76; **16** 59; **18** 223
Stephenson Clarke and Company, **31** 368–69
Sterchi Bros. Co., **14** 236
STERIS Corporation, 29 449–52
Sterling Chemicals, Inc., 16 460–63; **27** 117
Sterling Drug Inc., I 309–10, **698–700**; **III** 477; **7** 163; **13** 76–77
Sterling Electronics Corp., 18 496–98; **19** 311
Sterling Engineered Products, **III** 640, 642; **16** 9
Sterling Forest Corp., **III** 264
Sterling Industries, **13** 166
Sterling Information Services, Ltd., **IV** 675; **7** 528
Sterling Manhattan, **7** 63
Sterling Oil, **I** 526
Sterling Oil & Development, **II** 490
Sterling Organics Ltd., **12** 351
Sterling Plastics, **III** 642
Sterling Plastics Inc., **16** 9
Sterling Products Inc., **I** 622; **10** 68
Sterling Remedy Co., **I** 698
Sterling Software, Inc., 11 468–70; **31** 296
Sterling Stores Co. Inc., **24** 148
Sterling Winthrop, **7** 164
Stern & Stern Textiles, **11** 261
Stern Bros. Investment Bank, **V** 362–65; **19** 359
Stern's, **9** 209
Stern-Auer Shoe Company, **V** 207
Sternco Industries, **12** 230–31
STET. *See* Società Finanziaria Telefonica per Azioni.
Steuben Glass, **III** 683
Stevcoknit Fabrics Company, **8** 141–43
Stevedoring Services of America Inc., 28 435–37
Stevens Linen Associates, Inc., **8** 272
Stevens Park Osteopathic Hospital, **6** 192
Stevens Sound Proofing Co., **III** 706; **7** 291
Stevens, Thompson & Runyan, Inc. *See* CRSS Inc.
Steve's Ice Cream, **16** 54–55
Steward Esplen and Greenhough, **II** 569
Stewards Foundation, **6** 191
Stewart & Stevenson Services Inc., 11 471–73
Stewart Bolling Co., **IV** 130
Stewart Cash Stores, **II** 465
Stewart Enterprises, Inc., 16 344; **20 481–83**
Stewart P. Orr Associates, **6** 224
Stewart Systems, Inc., **22** 352–53
Steyr Walzlager, **III** 625
Stichting Continuiteit AMEV, **III** 202
Stieber Rollkupplung GmbH, **14** 63
Stihl Inc. *See* Andreas Stihl.
Stilecraft, **24** 16
Stimson & Valentine, **8** 552
Stinnes AG, 6 424, 426; **8** 68–69, **494–97**; **23** 68–70, **451–54 (upd.)**
Stirling Readymix Concrete, **III** 737–38
STM Systems Corp., **11** 485
Stock, **IV** 617–18
Stock Clearing Corporation, **9** 370
Stockholder Systems Inc., **11** 485
Stockholm Southern Transportation Co., **I** 553
Stockholms Allmänna Telefonaktiebolag, **V** 334
Stockholms Enskilda Bank, **II** 1, 351, 365–66; **III** 419, 425–26
Stockholms Intecknings Garanti, **II** 366
Stockton and Hartlepool Railway, **III** 272
Stockton Wheel Co., **III** 450
Stoelting Brothers Company, **10** 371
Stokely Van Camp, **II** 560, 575; **12** 411; **22** 338
Stokvis/De Nederlandsche Kroon Rijwiefabrieken, **13** 499
Stone & Webster, Inc., 13 495–98
Stone and Kimball, **IV** 660
Stone Container Corporation, IV 332–34; **8** 203–04; **15** 129; **17** 106; **25** 12. *See also* Smurfit-Stone Container Corporation.
Stone Exploration Corp., **IV** 83; **7** 187
Stone Manufacturing Company, 14 469–71
Stone-Consolidated Corporation, **25** 9, 12
Stonega Coke & Coal Co. *See* Westmoreland Coal Company.
Stoner Associates. *See* Severn Trent PLC.
Stonewall Insurance Co., **III** 192
Stonington Partners, **19** 318
StonyBrook Services Inc., **24** 49
Stoody Co., **19** 440
Stoof, **26** 278–79
Stoomvaart Maatschappij Nederland, **6** 403–04; **26** 241
The Stop & Shop Companies, Inc., II 666–67; **9** 451, 453; **12** 48–49; **16** 160, 314; **23** 169; **24 460–62 (upd.)**
Stop N Go, **7** 373; **25** 126
Stoppenbauch Inc., **23** 202
Stora Kopparbergs Bergslags AB, III 693, 695; **IV 335–37**, 340; **12** 464; **28** 445–46
Storage Dimensions Inc., **10** 404
Storage Technology Corporation, III 110; **6 275–77**; **12** 148, 161; **16** 194; **28** 198
Storage USA, Inc., 21 475–77
Storebrand Insurance Co., **III** 122
Storehouse PLC, II 658; **13** 284; **16 464–66**; **17** 42–43, 335; **24** 75
Storer Communications, **II** 161; **IV** 596; **7** 91–92, 200–1; **24** 122
Storer Leasing Inc., **I** 99; **6** 81
Storm Technology, **28** 245
Storz Instruments Co., **I** 678; **25** 56; **27** 115

Stouffer Corp., **I** 485; **II** 489, 547; **6** 40; **7** 382; **8 498–501**
Stouffer Foods Corporation, **28** 238
Stout Air Services, **I** 128; **6** 128
Stout Airlines, **I** 47, 84; **9** 416; **10** 162
Stout Metal Airplane Co., **I** 165
Stowe Machine Co., Inc., **30** 283
Stowe Woodward, **I** 428–29
STP, **19** 223; **26** 349
STRAAM Engineers. *See* CRSS Inc.
Straits Steamship Co. *See* Malaysian Airlines System.
Stran, **8** 546
Strata Energy, Inc., **IV** 29
StrataCom, Inc., **11** 59; **16 467–69**
Stratford Corporation, **15** 103; **26** 100
Strathmore Consolidated Investments, **IV** 90
Stratos Boat Co., Ltd., **III** 600
Stratton Ski Corporation, **15** 235
Stratus Computer, Inc., **6** 279; **10 499–501**
Straus-Frank Company, **29** 86, 88
Strauss Turnbull and Co., **II** 355
Strawberries, **30** 465
Strawbridge & Clothier's, **6** 243
Street & Smith Publications, Inc., **IV** 583; **13** 178
Stride Rite Corporation, **8 502–04**; **9** 437
Stroehmann Bakeries, **II** 631
Stroh and Co., **IV** 486
The Stroh Brewery Company, **I** 32, 255, **290–92**; **13** 10–11, 455; **18** 72, **499–502 (upd.)**; **22** 422; **23** 403, 405
Strömberg, **IV** 300; **27** 267, 268
Stromberg Carburetor Co., **I** 141
Stromberg-Carlson, **II** 82
Stromeyer GmbH, **7** 141
Strong Brewery, **I** 294
Strong Electric Corporation, **19** 211
Strong International, **27** 57
Strother Drug, **III** 9–10
Structural Dynamics Research Corporation, **10** 257
Structural Fibers, Inc. *See* Essef Corporation.
Structural Iberica S.A., **18** 163
Struebel Group, **18** 170
Strydel, Inc., **14** 361
Stryker Corporation, **10** 351; **11 474–76**; **29 453–55 (upd.)**
Stuart Co., **I** 584
Stuart Entertainment Inc., **16 470–72**
Stuart Hall Co., **17** 445
Stuart Medical, Inc., **10** 143; **16** 400
Stuart Perlman, **6** 200
Stuckey's, Inc., **7** 429
Studebaker Co., **I** 141–42, 451; **8** 74; **9** 27
Studebaker Wagon Co., **IV** 660
Studebaker-Packard, **9** 118; **10** 261
Student Loan Marketing Association, **II 453–55**. *See also* SLM Holding Corp.
Studiengesellschaft, **I** 409
Studley Products Inc., **12** 396
Stuffit Co., **IV** 597
Sturbridge Yankee Workshop, Inc., **10** 216
Sturgeon Bay Shipbuilding and DryDock Company, **18** 320
Sturm, Ruger & Company, Inc., **19 430–32**
Stuttgart Gas Works, **I** 391
Stuttgarter Verein Versicherungs-AG, **III** 184
Stuyvesant Insurance Group, **II** 182
Stylus Writing Instruments, **27** 416
Stymer Oy, **IV** 470–71
SU214, **28** 27, 30
Suave Shoe Corporation. *See* French Fragrances, Inc.
Sub-Zero Freezer Co., Inc., **31 426–28**
Subaru, **6** 28; **23** 290
SubLogic, **15** 455
Submarine Boat Co., **I** 57
Submarine Signal Co., **II** 85–86; **11** 412
Suburban Cablevision, **IV** 640
Suburban Coastal Corporation, **10** 92
Suburban Cos., **IV** 575–76
Suburban Light and Power Company, **12** 45
Suburban Propane Partners, L.P., **I** 378; **30 440–42[ro**
Suburban Savings and Loan Association, **10** 92
Subway, **15** 56–57
Successories, Inc., **30 443–45[ro**
Suchard Co., **II** 520
Sud-Aviation, **I** 44–45; **7** 10; **8** 313
Sudbury Inc., **16 473–75**; **17** 373
Sudbury River Consulting Group, **31** 131
Suddeutsche Bank A.G., **II** 279
Süddeutsche Donau-Dampfschiffahrts-Gesellschaft, **6** 425
Süddeutsche Kalkstickstoffwerke AG, **IV** 229, 232
Sudler & Hennessey, **I** 37
Südpetrol, **IV** 421
Südzucker AG, **27 436–39**
Suez Bank, **IV** 108
Suez Canal Co., **IV** 530
Suez Oil Co., **IV** 413–14
Suffolk County Federal Savings and Loan Association, **16** 346
Sugar Land State Bank, **25** 114
Sugarland Industries. *See* Imperial Holly Corporation.
SugarLoaf Creations, Inc. *See* American Coin Merchandising, Inc.
Sugarloaf Mountain Corporation, **28** 21
Suita Brewery, **I** 220
Suito Sangyo Co., Ltd. *See* Seino Transportation Company, Ltd.
Suiza Foods Corporation, **25** 512, 514; **26 447–50**
Sukhoi Design Bureau Aviation Scientific-Industrial Complex, **24 463–65**
Sullair Co., **I** 435
Sullivan & Cromwell, **26 451–53**; **27** 327
Sullivan, Stauffer, Colwell & Bayles, **14** 314
Sullivan Systems, **III** 420
Sullivan-Schein Dental Products Inc., **31** 256
Sulpetro Limited, **25** 232
Sulphide Corp., **IV** 58
Sulzbach, **I** 409
Sulzer Brothers Limited, **III** 402, 516, **630–33**, 638
Sumergrade Corporation, **19** 304
Suminoe Textile Co., **8** 235
Sumisei Secpac Investment Advisors, **III** 366
Sumisho Electronics Co. Ltd., **18** 170
Sumitomo Bank, Limited, **I** 587; **II** 104, 224, 273–74, 347, **360–62**, 363, 392, 415; **IV** 269, 726; **9** 341–42; **18** 170; **23** 340; **26 454–57 (upd.)**
Sumitomo Chemical Company Ltd., **I** 363, **397–98**; **II** 361; **III** 715; **IV** 432
Sumitomo Corporation, **I** 431–32, 492, 502, 504–05, 510–11, 515, **518–20**; **III** 43, 365; **V** 161; **7** 357; **11 477–80 (upd.)**, 490; **15** 340; **17** 556; **18** 170; **24** 325; **28** 288
Sumitomo Electric Industries, **I** 105; **II 104–05**; **III** 490, 684; **IV** 179; **V** 252
Sumitomo Heavy Industries, Ltd., **III** 533, **634–35**; **10** 381
Sumitomo Life Insurance Co., **II** 104, 360, 422; **III** 288, **365–66**
Sumitomo Marine and Fire Insurance Company, Limited, **III 367–68**
Sumitomo Metal Industries, Ltd., **I** 390; **II** 104, 361; **IV** 130, **211–13**, 216; **10** 463–64; **11** 246; **24** 302
Sumitomo Metal Mining Co., Ltd., **IV 214–16**; **9** 340; **23** 338
Sumitomo Realty & Development Co., Ltd., **IV 726–27**
Sumitomo Rubber Industries, Ltd., **V 252–53**; **20** 263
Sumitomo Trust & Banking Company, Ltd., **II** 104, **363–64**; **IV** 726
Sumitomo Wire Company, **16** 555
Summa Corporation, **9** 266; **17** 317
Summer Paper Tube, **19** 78
Summers Group Inc., **15** 386
The Summit Bancorporation, **14 472–74**
Summit Constructors. *See* CRSS Inc.
Summit Engineering Corp., **I** 153
Summit Family Restaurants Inc., **19** 89, 92, **433–36**
Summit Gear Company, **16** 392–93
Summit Management Co., Inc., **17** 498
Summit Screen Inks, **13** 228
Summit Technology Inc., **30** 485
Sun Aire, **25** 421–22
Sun Alliance Group PLC, **III** 296, **369–74**, 400
Sun Chemical Corp. *See* Sequa Corp.
Sun Company, Inc., **I** 286, 631; **IV** 449, **548–50**; **7** 114, 414; **11** 484; **12** 459; **17** 537; **25** 126
Sun Country Airlines, **I** 114; **30 446–49**
Sun Distributors L.P., **12 459–461**
Sun Electric, **15** 288
Sun Electronics, **9** 116
Sun Equities Corporation, **15** 449
Sun Federal, **7** 498
Sun Federal Savings and Loan Association of Tallahassee, **10** 92
Sun Financial Group, Inc., **25** 171
Sun Fire Coal Company, **7** 281
Sun Fire Office, **III** 349, 369–71
Sun Foods, **12** 220–21
Sun Healthcare Group Inc., **25 455–58**
Sun International Hotels Limited, **12** 420; **26 462–65**
Sun Kyowa, **III** 43
Sun Life Assurance Co. of Canada, **IV** 165
Sun Life Group of America, **11** 482
Sun Mark, Inc., **21** 483
Sun Media, **27** 280; **29** 471–72
Sun Men's Shop Co., Ltd., **V** 150
Sun Microsystems, Inc., **II** 45, 62; **III** 125; **6** 222, 235, 238, 244; **7 498–501**; **9** 36, 471; **10** 118, 242, 257, 504; **11** 45–46, 490–91, 507; **12** 162; **14** 15–16, 268; **15** 321; **16** 140, 195, 418–19; **18** 537; **20** 175, 237; **21** 86; **22** 154; **23**

471; **25** 348, 499; **26** 19; **27** 448; **30** **450–54 (upd.)**
Sun Newspapers, **III** 213–14
Sun Oil Co., **III** 497; **IV** 371, 424, 548–50; **7** 413–14; **11** 35; **18** 233; **19** 162. *See also* Sunoco, Inc.
Sun Optical Co., Ltd., **V** 150
Sun Pharmaceuticals, **24** 480
Sun Shades 501 Ltd., **21** 483
Sun Ship, **IV** 549
Sun Sportswear, Inc., **17** **460–63**; **23** 65–66
Sun State Marine Services, Inc. *See* Hvide Marine Incorporated.
Sun Techno Services Co., Ltd., **V** 150
Sun Technology Enterprises, **7** 500
Sun Television & Appliances Inc., **10** **502–03**; **19** 362
Sun-Diamond Growers of California, **7** **496–97**
Sun-Fast Color, **13** 227
Sun-Maid Growers of California, **7** 496–97
Sun-Pat Products, **II** 569
SunAir, **11** 300
SunAmerica Inc., **11** **481–83**
Sunbeam-Oster Co., Inc., **9** **484–86**; **14** 230; **16** 488; **17** 215; **19** 305; **22** 3; **28** 135, 246; **30** 136
Sunbelt Coca-Cola, **10** 223
Sunbelt Nursery Group, Inc., **12** 179, 200, 394
Sunbird, **III** 600; **V** 150
Sunburst Hospitality Corporation, **26** **458–61**
Sunburst Yarns, Inc., **13** 532
Sunciti Manufacturers Ltd., **III** 454; **21** 122
Sunclipse Inc., **IV** 250
Sunco N.V., **22** 515
Suncoast Motion Picture Company, **9** 360
SunCor Development Company, **6** 546–47
Sundance Publishing, **IV** 609; **12** 559
Sunday Pictorial, **IV** 665–66; **17** 397
Sundheim & Doetsch, **IV** 189
Sunds Defibrator AG, **IV** 338–40, 350; **28** 444
Sundstrand Corporation, **7** **502–04**; **21** **478–81 (upd.)**
Sundt Corp., **24** **466–69**
SunGard Data Systems Inc., **11** **484–85**
Sunglass Hut International, Inc., **18** 393; **21** **482–84**
Sunglee Electronics Co. Ltd., **III** 748–49
Sunila Oy, **IV** 348–49
Sunkiss Thermoreactors, **21** 65
Sunkist Growers, Inc., **7** 496; **25** 366; **26** **466–69**
Sunkist Soft Drinks Inc., **I** 13
Sunkus Co. Ltd., **V** 150
Sunnybrook Farms, **25** 124
Sunoco, Inc., **28** **438–42 (upd.)**
SunQuest HealthCare Corp. *See* Unison HealthCare Corporation.
Sunray DX Oil Co., **IV** 550, 575; **7** 414
The Sunrider Corporation, **26** 316, **470–74**; **27** 353
Sunrise Medical Inc., **11** 202, **486–88**
Sunrise Test Systems, **11** 491
Sunsations Sunglass Company, **21** 483
Sunshine Bullion Co., **25** 542
Sunshine Jr. Stores, Inc., **17** 170
Sunshine Mining Company, **20** 149
SunSoft, **7** 500
Sunstate, **24** 396
Sunsweet Growers, **7** 496
Suntory Ltd., **13** 454; **21** 320
SunTrust Banks Inc., **23** **455–58**
Sunward Technologies, Inc., **10** 464
Supasnaps, **V** 50
Super Bazars, **26** 159
Super D Drugs, **9** 52
Super Dart. *See* Dart Group Corporation.
Super 8 Motels, Inc., **11** 178
Super Food Services, Inc., **15** **479–81**; **18** 8
Super Oil Seals & Gaskets Ltd., **16** 8
Super 1 Stores. *See* Brookshire Grocery Company.
Super Quick, Inc., **7** 372
Super Rite Foods, Inc., **V** 176; **19** 356
Super Sagless Spring Corp., **15** 103
Super Store Industries, **14** 397
Super Valu Stores, Inc., **II** 632, **668–71**; **6** 364; **7** 450; **8** 380; **14** 411; **17** 180; **22** 126; **23** 357–58. *See also* Supervalu Inc.
Super-Power Company, **6** 505
SuperAmerica Group, Inc., **IV** 374
Superbrix, **14** 248
Supercomputer Systems, Inc., **III** 130; **16** 138
Supercuts Inc., **26** **475–78**
Superdrug plc, **V** 175; **24** 266, 269–70
Superenvases Envalic, **I** 231
Superior Bearings Company. *See* Federal-Mogul Corporation.
Superior Healthcare Group, Inc., **11** 221
Superior Industries International, Inc., **8** **505–07**
Superior Oil Co., **III** 558; **IV** 400, 465, 524; **7** 353
Superior Recycled Fiber Industries, **26** 363
Superior Transfer, **12** 309
Superior Uniform Group, Inc., **30** **455–57**
SuperMac Technology Inc., **16** 419
Supermarchés GB, **26** 159
Supermarchés Montréal, **II** 662–63
Supermarkets General Holdings Corporation, **II** **672–74**; **16** 160; **23** 369–70
Supermart Books, **10** 136
Supersaver Wholesale Clubs, **8** 555
Supersnaps, **19** 124
SuperStation WTBS, **6** 171
Supertest Petroleum Corporation, **9** 490
Supervalu Inc., **18** **503–08 (upd.)**; **21** 457–57; **22** 327. *See also* Super Valu Stores, Inc.
Supervalue Corp., **13** 393
Supervised Investors Services, **III** 270
SupeRx, **II** 644
Suprema Specialties, Inc., **27** **440–42**
Supreme International Corporation, **27** **443–46**; **30** 358
Supreme Life Insurance Company of America, **28** 212
Supreme Sugar Co., **I** 421; **11** 23
Supron Energy Corp., **15** 129
Surety Life Insurance Company, **10** 51
SureWay Air Traffic Corporation, **24** 126
Surgical Health Corporation, **14** 233
Surgical Mechanical Research Inc., **I** 678
Surgical Plastics, **25** 430–31
Surgikos, Inc., **III** 35
Surgitool, **I** 628
Suroflex GmbH, **23** 300
Surpass Software Systems, Inc., **9** 81
Surplus Software, **31** 176
Survey Research Group, **10** 360
SurVivaLink, **18** 423
Susan Bristol, **16** 61
Susan Kay Cosmetics. *See* The Cosmetic Center, Inc.
Susie's Casuals, **14** 294
Susquehanna Pfaltzgraff Company, **8** **508–10**
Sussex Group, **15** 449
Sussex Trust Company, **25** 541
Sutherland Lumber Co., **19** 233
Sutter Corp., **15** 113
Sutter Health, **12** 175–76
Sutter Home Winery Inc., **16** **476–78**
Sutton & Towne, Inc., **21** 96
Sutton Laboratories, **22** 228
Suwa Seikosha, **III** 620
Suzaki Hajime, **V** 113–14
Suzannah Farms, **7** 524
Suze, **I** 280
Suzhou Elevator Company, **29** 420
Suzuki & Co., **I** 509–10; **IV** 129; **9** 341–42; **23** 340
Suzuki Motor Corporation, **III** 581, 657; **7** 110; **8** 72; **9** **487–89**; **23** 290, **459–62 (upd.)**
Suzuki Shoten Co., **V** 380, 457–58
Suzy Shier, **18** 562
Svea Choklad A.G., **II** 640
Svensk Fastighetskredit A.B., **II** 352
Svensk Golvindustri, **25** 463
Svenska A.B. Humber & Co., **I** 197
Svenska Aeroplan Aktiebolaget. *See* Saab-Scania AB.
Svenska Cellulosa Aktiebolaget SCA, **II** 365–66; **IV** 295–96, 325, 336, **338–40**, 667; **17** 398; **19** 225–26; **28** **443–46 (upd.)**
Svenska Centrifug AB, **III** 418
Svenska Elektron, **III** 478
A.B. Svenska Flaktfabriken, **II** 2; **22** 8
Svenska Flygmotor A.B., **I** 209; **26** 10
Svenska Handelsbanken, **II** 353, **365–67**; **IV** 338–39; **28** 443–44
Svenska Järnvagsverkstäderna A.B., **I** 197
Svenska Kullagerfabriken A.B., **I** 209; **III** 622; **7** 565; **26** 9. *See also* AB Volvo.
Svenska Oljeslageri AB, **IV** 318
Svenska Stålpressnings AB, **26** 11
Svenska Varv, **6** 367
Svenska Varv, **27** 91
Svenskt Stål AB, **IV** 336
Sverdrup Corporation, **14** **475–78**
Sverker Martin-Löf, **IV** 339
SVF. *See* Société des Vins de France.
SVIDO, **17** 250
Sviluppo Iniziative Stradali Italiene, **IV** 420
SVPW, **I** 215
Swallow Airplane Company, **8** 49; **27** 98
Swallow Sidecar and Coach Building Company, **13** 285
Swan, **10** 170
Swan Electric Light Co., **I** 410
Swan's Down Cake Flour, **II** 531
Swank Inc., **17** **464–66**
Swann Corp., **I** 366
The Swatch Group SA, **7** 532–33; **25** 481; **26** **479–81**
Swearingen Aircraft Company, **9** 207
SwedeChrome, **III** 625
Swedish Ericsson Group, **17** 353
Swedish Furniture Research Institute, **V** 82
Swedish Intercontinental Airlines, **I** 119

Swedish Match S.A., **IV** 336–37; **9** 381; **12 462–64**; **23** 55; **25** 464
Swedish Ordnance-FFV/Bofors AB, **9** 381–82
Swedish Telecom, V 331–33
Sweedor, **12** 464
Sweeney Specialty Restaurants, **14** 131
Sweeney's, **16** 559
Sweet & Maxwell, **8** 527
Sweet Life Foods Inc., **18** 507
Sweet Traditions LLC, **21** 323
Swett & Crawford Group, **III** 357; **22** 494
Swift & Co., **II** 447, 550; **13** 351, 448; **17** 124
Swift Adhesives, **10** 467
Swift Independent Packing Co., **II** 494; **13** 350, 352
Swift Textiles, Inc., **12** 118; **15** 247
Swift Transportation, **26** 533
Swift-Armour S.A., **II** 480
Swift-Armour S.A. Argentina, **25** 517; **26** 57
Swift-Eckrich, **II** 467
Swing-N-Slide, Inc. *See* PlayCore, Inc.
Swingline, Inc., **7** 3–5
Swire Pacific Ltd., **I** 469–70, **521–22**; **6** 78; **16 479–81 (upd.)**; **18** 114; **20** 310, 312
Swisher International Group Inc., **14** 17–19; **23 463–65**; **27** 139
Swiss Air Transport Company Ltd., **I** 107, 119, **121–22**; **24** 312; **27** 409
Swiss Banca de Gottardo, **26** 456
Swiss Banca della Svizzera Italiano, **II** 192
Swiss Bank Corporation, **II** 267, **368–70**, 378–79; **14** 419–20; **21** 145–46
Swiss Cement-Industrie-Gesellschaft, **III** 701
Swiss Colony Wines, **I** 377
Swiss Drilling Co., **IV** 372; **19** 22
Swiss Federal Railways (Schweizerische Bundesbahnen), V 519–22
Swiss General Chocolate Co., **II** 545–46; **7** 380–81
Swiss Locomotive and Machine Works, **III** 631–32
Swiss Oil Co., **IV** 372–73
Swiss Reinsurance Company, **III** 299, 301, 335, **375–78**; **15** 13; **21** 146
Swiss Time Australia Pty Ltd, **25** 461
Swiss Volksbank, **21** 146–47
Swiss-American Corporation, **II** 267; **21** 145
Swissair Associated Co., **I** 122; **6** 60, 96, 117
Switchboard Inc., **25** 52
SXI Limited, **17** 458
Sybase, Inc., **6** 255, 279; **10** 361, **504–06**; **11** 77–78; **15** 492; **25** 96, 299; **27 447–50 (upd.)**
SyberVision, **10** 216
Sybra, Inc., **19** 466–68
Sybron International Corp., **14 479–81**; **19** 289–90
SYCOM, Inc., **18** 363
Sydney Electricity, **12** 443
Sydney Paper Mills Ltd., **IV** 248
Sydney Ross Co., **I** 698–99
Syfrets Trust Co., **IV** 23
Sylacauga Calcium Products, **III** 691
Syllogic B.V., **29** 376
Sylvan, Inc., **22 496–99**
Sylvan Lake Telephone Company, **6** 334
Sylvan Learning Centers, **13** 299
Sylvania Companies, **I** 463; **II** 63; **III** 165, 475; **V** 295; **7** 161; **8** 157; **11** 197; **13** 402; **23** 181
Sylvia Paperboard Co., **IV** 310; **19** 266
Symantec Corporation, **10 507–09**; **25** 348–49
Symbios Logic Inc., **19** 312; **31** 5
Symbiosis Corp., **10** 70
Symbol Technologies, Inc., **10** 363, 523–24; **15 482–84**
Symington-Wayne, **III** 472
Symphony International, **14** 224
Syms Corporation, **29 456–58**
Symtronix Corporation, **18** 515
Syn-Optics, Inc., **29** 454
Synbiotics Corporation, **23** 284
Syncordia Corp., **15** 69
Syncrocom, Inc., **10** 513
Syncrude Canada Limited, **25** 232
Synercom Technology Inc., **14** 319
Synercon Corporation, **25** 538
Synergen Inc., **13** 241
Synergy Dataworks, Inc., **11** 285
Synergy Software Inc., **31** 131
Synetic, Inc., **16** 59
Synfloor SA, **25** 464
Synopsis, Inc., **11 489–92**; **18** 20
SynOptics Communications, Inc., **10** 194, **510–12**; **11** 475; **16** 392; **22** 52
Synovus Financial Corp., **12 465–67**; **18** 516–17
Syntax Ophthalmic Inc., **III** 727
Syntex Corporation, **I** 512, **701–03**; **III** 18, 53; **8** 216–17, 434, 548; **10** 53; **12** 322; **26** 384
Syntex Pharmaceuticals Ltd., **21** 425
Synthecolor S.A., **8** 347
Synthélabo, **III** 47–48
Synthetic Blood Corp., **15** 380
Synthetic Pillows, Inc., **19** 304
Syntron, Inc., **18** 513–15
SyQuest Technology, Inc., **18 509–12**
Syracuse China, **8** 510
Syratech Corp., **14 482–84**; **27** 288
Syrian Airways, **6** 85; **27** 133
Syroco, **14** 483–84
SYSCO Corporation, **II 675–76**; **9** 453; **16** 387; **18** 67; **24 470–72 (upd.)**, 528; **26** 504
Sysorex Information Systems, **11** 62
SysScan, **V** 339
Systech Environmental Corporation, **28** 228–29
System Designers plc. *See* SD-Scicon plc.
System Development Co., **III** 166; **6** 282
System Fuels, Inc., **11** 194
System Integrators, Inc., **6** 279
System Parking West, **25** 16
System Software Associates, Inc., **10 513–14**
Systematics Inc., **6** 301; **11** 131
Systembolaget, **31** 459–60
Systems & Computer Technology Corp., **19 437–39**
Systems and Services Company. *See* SYSCO Corporation.
Systems Center, Inc., **6** 279; **11** 469
Systems Construction Ltd., **II** 649
Systems Development Corp., **25** 117
Systems Engineering and Manufacturing Company, **11** 225
Systems Engineering Labs (SEL), **11** 45; **13** 201
Systems Exploration Inc., **10** 547
Systems Magnetic Co., **IV** 101
Systems Marketing Inc., **12** 78
Systronics, **13** 235
Syufy Enterprises. *See* Century Theatres, Inc.
Szabo, **II** 608

T. and J. Brocklebank Ltd., **23** 160
T&N PLC, **26** 141
T.G.I. Friday's, **10** 331; **19** 258; **20** 159; **21** 250; **22** 127
T.J. Falgout, **11** 523
T.J. Maxx, **V** 197–98; **13** 329–30; **14** 62
T. Kobayashi & Co., Ltd., **III** 44
T.L. Smith & Company, **21** 502
T/Maker, **9** 81
T. Mellon & Sons, **II** 315
T. Rowe Price Associates, Inc., **10** 89; **11 493–96**
T.S. Farley, Limited, **10** 319
T-Shirt Brokerage Services, Inc., **26** 257
T-Tech Industries, **26** 363
T. Wear Company S.r.l., **25** 121
TA Associates, **10** 382
TA Media AG, **15** 31
TAB Products Co., **17 467–69**
Tabacalera, S.A., **V 414–16**; **15** 139; **17 470–73 (upd.)**
Table Supply Stores, **II** 683
Tabulating Machine Company. *See* International Business Machines Corporation.
Taco Bell Corp., **I** 278; **7** 267, **505–07**; **9** 178; **10** 450; **13** 336, 494; **14** 453; **15** 486; **16** 96–97; **17** 537; **21** 315, **485–88 (upd.)**; **25** 178
Taco Cabana, Inc., **23 466–68**
Taco John's International Inc., **15 485–87**
Taco Kid, **7** 506
Tadiran Telecommunications Ltd., **II** 47; **25** 266–67
Taehan Cement, **III** 748
Taft Broadcasting Co. *See* Great American Broadcasting Inc.
TAG Heuer International SA, **7** 554; **25 459–61**
TAG Pharmaceuticals, **22** 501
Taguchi Automobile. *See* Seino Transportation Company, Ltd.
Taiba Corporation, **8** 250
Taiheiyo Bank, **15** 495
Taikoo Dockyard Co., **I** 521; **16** 480
Taikoo Sugar Refinery, **I** 521; **16** 480
Taio Paper Mfg. Co., Ltd. *See* Daio Paper Co., Ltd.
Taisho America, **III** 295
Taisho Marine and Fire Insurance Co., Ltd., **III** 209, 295–96
Taisho Pharmaceutical, **I** 676; **II** 361
Taittinger S.A., **27** 421
Taiwan Aerospace Corp., **11** 279; **24** 88
Taiwan Auto Glass, **III** 715
Taiwan Power Company, **22** 89
Taiwan Semiconductor Manufacturing Company Ltd., **18** 20; **22** 197
Taiway, **III** 596
Taiyo Bussan, **IV** 225; **24** 489
Taiyo Fishery Company, Limited, **II 578–79**
Taiyo Kobe Bank, Ltd., **II** 326, **371–72**
Taiyo Metal Manufacturing Co., **III** 757
Takada & Co., **IV** 151; **24** 358
Takara, **25** 488

Takaro Shuzo, **III** 42
Takashimaya Co., Limited, V 193–96
Takeda Chemical Industries Ltd., I 704–06; **III** 760
Takeda Riken, **11** 504
Takeuchi Mining Co., **III** 545
Takihyo, **15** 145
Takkyubin, **V** 537
Tako Oy, **IV** 314
The Talbots, Inc., II 503; **10** 324; **11 497–99**; **12** 280; **31 429–432 (upd.)**
Talcott National Corporation, **11** 260–61
Talegen Holdings Inc., **26** 546
Taliq Corp., **III** 715
Talisman Energy, 9 490–93
Talk Radio Network, Inc., **23** 294
Talley Industries, Inc., 10 386; **16 482–85**
Tally Corp., **18** 434
Talmadge Farms, Inc., **20** 105
TAM Ceramics, **III** 681
Tamar Bank, **II** 187
Tamarkin Co., **12** 390
Tambrands Inc., III 40; **8 511–13**; **12** 439; **15** 359–60, 501; **16** 303; **26** 384
Tamco, **12** 390; **19** 380
TAMET, **IV** 25
Tamglass Automotive OY, **22** 436
Tampa Electric Company, **6** 582–83
Tampax Inc. *See* Tambrands Inc.
Oy Tampella Ab, **II** 47; **III** 648; **IV** 276; **25** 266
Tampere Paper Board and Roofing Felt Mill, **IV** 314
Tampereen Osake-Pankki, **II** 303
Tampimex Oil, **11** 194
Tamura Kisan Co., **II** 552
Tanaka, **6** 71
Tanaka Kikinzoku Kogyo KK, **IV** 119
Tanaka Matthey KK, **IV** 119
Tandem Computers, Inc., 6 278–80; **10** 499; **11** 18; **14** 318; **26** 93; **29** 477–79
Tandon, **25** 531
Tandy Corporation, II 70, **106–08**; **6** 257–58; **9** 43, 115, 165; **10** 56–57, 166–67, 236; **12 468–70 (upd.)**; **13** 174; **14** 117; **16** 84; **17** 353–54; **24** 502; **25** 531; **26** 18
Tandycrafts, Inc., 31 433–37
Tangent Industries, **15** 83
Tangent Systems, **6** 247–48
Tangiers International. *See* Algo Group Inc.
Tangram Rehabilitation Network, Inc., **29** 401
Tanjong Pagar Dock Co., **I** 592
Tanks Oil and Gas, **11** 97
Tanne-Arden, Inc., **27** 291
Tanner-Brice Company, **13** 404
Tantalum Mining Corporation, **29** 81
TAP Air Portugal. *See* Transportes Aereos Portugueses.
Tapiola Insurance, **IV** 316
Tappan. *See* White Consolidated Industries Inc.
Tara Exploration and Development Ltd., **IV** 165
Tara Foods, **II** 645
Target Stores, V 35, 43–44; **10** 284, **515–17**; **12** 508; **13** 261, 274, 446; **14** 398; **15** 275; **16** 390; **17** 460–61; **18** 108, 137, 283, 286; **20** 155; **22** 328; **27** 315, **451–54 (upd.)**
Tarkett Sommer AG, 12 464; **25 462–64**
Tarmac plc, III 734, **751–54**; **14** 250; **28 447–51 (upd.)**
TarMacadam (Purnell Hooley's Patent) Syndicate Ltd., **III** 751
Tarragon Oil and Gas Ltd., **24** 522
Tarslag, **III** 752
TASC. *See* Analytical Sciences Corp.
Tashima Shoten, **III** 574
Tasman Pulp and Paper Co. Ltd. *See* Fletcher Challenge Ltd.
Tasman U.E.B., **IV** 249
Tasmanian Fibre Containers, **IV** 249
Tasty Baking Co., 14 485–87
TAT European Airlines, **14** 70, 73; **24** 400
Tata Airlines. *See* Air-India Limited.
Tata Enterprises, **III** 43
Tata Industries, **20** 313; **21** 74
Tata Iron and Steel Company Ltd., IV 48, 205–07, **217–19**
Tate & Lyle plc, II 514, **580–83; 7** 466–67; **13** 102; **26** 120
Tatebayashi Flour Milling Co., **II** 554
Tateisi Electric Manufacturing, **II** 75
Tateisi Medical Electronics Manufacturing Co., **II** 75
Tatham Corporation, **21** 169, 171
Tatham/RSCG, **13** 204
Tati SA, 25 465–67
Tatung Co., III 482; **13** 387; **23 469–71**
Taurus Exploration, **21** 208
Taurus Programming Services, **10** 196
Tax Management, Inc., **23** 92
Taylor Corp., **22** 358
Taylor Diving and Salvage Co., **III** 499
Taylor Made Golf Co., 23 270, **472–74**
Taylor Material Handling, **13** 499
Taylor Medical, **14** 388
Taylor Petroleum, Inc., **17** 170
Taylor Publishing Company, 12 471–73; **25** 254
Taylor Rental Corp., **III** 628
Taylor Wines Co., **I** 234; **10** 227
Taylor Woodrow plc, I 590–91; **III** 739; **13** 206
Taylor-Evans Seed Co., **IV** 409
Taylors and Lloyds, **II** 306
Tayto Ltd., **22** 515
Tazuke & Co., **IV** 151; **24** 358
TBC Corp., **20** 63
TBS. *See* Turner Broadcasting System, Inc.
TBWA Advertising, Inc., 6 47–49; **22** 394
TC Debica, **20** 264
TCA. *See* Air Canada.
TCBC. *See* Todays Computers Business Centers.
TCBY Enterprises Inc., 17 474–76
TCF Holdings, Inc., **II** 170–71
TCH Corporation, **12** 477
TCI. *See* Tele-Communications, Inc.
TCI Communications, **29** 39
TCPL. *See* TransCanada PipeLines Ltd.
TCS Management Group, Inc., **22** 53
TCW Capital, **19** 414–15
TDK Corporation, I 500; **II 109–11**; **IV** 680; **17 477–79 (upd.)**
TDS. *See* Telephone and Data Systems, Inc.
Teaberry Electronics Corp., **III** 569; **20** 361
Teachers Insurance and Annuity Association, III 379–82; **22** 268
Teachers Service Organization, Inc., **8** 9–10
Team America, **9** 435
Team Penske, **V** 494
Team Rental Group. *See* Budget Group, Inc.
Teamsters Central States Pension Fund, **19** 378
Teamsters Union, **13** 19
Tebel Maschinefabrieken, **III** 420
Tebel Pneumatiek, **III** 420
Tech Data Corporation, 10 518–19
Tech Pacific International, **18** 180
Tech Textiles, USA, **15** 247–48
Tech-Sym Corporation, 18 513–15
Techalloy Co., **IV** 228
Technair Packaging Laboratories, **18** 216
Technical Ceramics Laboratories, Inc., **13** 141
Technical Coatings Co., **13** 85
Technical Materials, Inc., **14** 81
Technical Publishing, **IV** 605
Technicare, **11** 200
Technicolor Inc., **28** 246
Technicon Instruments Corporation, **III** 56; **11** 333–34; **22** 75
Technifax, **8** 483
Techniques d'Avant-Garde. *See* TAG Heuer International SA.
Technisch Bureau Visser, **16** 421
Technitrol, Inc., 29 459–62
Techno-Success Company, **V** 719
AB Technology, **II** 466
Technology Management Group, Inc., **18** 112
Technology Resources International Ltd., **18** 76
Technology Venture Investors, **11** 490; **14** 263
Technophone Ltd., **17** 354
Teck Corporation, 9 282; **27 455–58**
Tecnamotor S.p.A., **8** 72, 515
Tecneco, **IV** 422
Tecnifax Corp., **IV** 330
Tecnipublicaciones, **14** 555
TECO Energy, Inc., 6 582–84
Tecom Industries, Inc., **18** 513–14
Tecstar, Inc., **30** 436
Tecumseh Products Company, 8 72, **514–16**
Ted Bates, Inc., **I** 33, 623; **10** 69; **16** 71–72
Teddy's Shoe Store. *See* Morse Shoe Inc.
Tedelex, **IV** 91–92
Teekay Shipping Corporation, 25 468–71
Tees and Hartlepool, **31** 367, 369
TEFSA, **17** 182
TEIC. *See* B.V. Tabak Export & Import Compagnie.
Teijin Limited, I 511; **V 380–82**
Teikoku Bank, **I** 507; **II** 273, 325–26
Teikoku Hormone, **I** 704
Teikoku Jinken. *See* Teijin Limited.
Teikoku Sekiyu Co. Ltd., **IV** 475
Teikoku Shiki, **IV** 326
Teito Electric Railway, **V** 461
Teito Transport Co. Ltd., **V** 536
Tekmunc A/S, **17** 288
Teknekron Infoswitch Corporation, **22** 51
Tekrad, Inc. *See* Tektronix, Inc.
Tekton Corp., **IV** 346
Tektronix, Inc., II 101; **8 517–21**; **10** 24; **11** 284–86; **12** 454
Tel-A-Data Limited, **11** 111
TelAutograph Corporation, **29** 33–34

Telcon. *See* Telegraph Construction and Maintenance Company.
Tele Consulte, **14** 555
Tele-Communications, Inc., II 160–62, 167; **10** 484, 506; **11** 479; **13** 280; **15** 264–65; **17** 148; **18** 64–66, 211, 213, 535; **19** 282; **21** 307, 309; **23** 121, 502; **24** 6, 120; **25** 213–14; **26** 33; **28** 241
Telebook, **25** 19
Telec Centre S.A., **19** 472
TeleCheck Services, **18** 542
TeleCheck Services, Inc., **11** 113
Teleclub, **IV** 590
Teleco Oilfield Services Inc., **6** 578; **22** 68
TeleColumbus, **11** 184
Telecom Australia, 6 341–42
Telecom Canada. *See* Stentor Canadian Network Management.
Telecom Eireann, 7 508–10. *See also* eircom plc.
Telecom Italia, **15** 355; **24** 79
Telecom New Zealand, **18** 33
Telecom One, Inc., **29** 252
Telecom*USA, **27** 304
Telecommunications of Jamaica Ltd., **25** 101
Telecomputing Corp., **I** 544
Telecredit, Inc., **6** 25
Telectronic Pacing Systems, **10** 445
Teledyne Inc., I 486, **523–25**; **II** 33, 44; **10** 262–63, 365, **520–22 (upd.)**; **11** 265; **13** 387; **17** 109; **18** 369; **29** 400
Teleflora Inc., **28** 1 8–90; **19** 12; **21** 259
Téléfrance, **25** 174
Telefunken Fernseh & Rundfunk GmbH., **I** 411; **II** 117
Telegate, **18** 155
Teleglobe Inc., **14** 512
Telegraph Condenser Co., **II** 81
Telegraph Construction and Maintenance Company, **25** 98–100
Telegraph Manufacturing Co., **III** 433
Telegraph Works, **III** 433
Telegraphic Service Company, **16** 166
Telekomunikacja S.A., **18** 33
Telelistas Editors Ltda., **26** 520
TeleMarketing Corporation of Louisiana, **8** 311
Telemarketing Investments, Ltd., **8** 311
Telematics International Inc., **18** 154, 156
Télémécanique, **II** 94; **18** 473; **19** 166
Telemundo Group, Inc., **III** 344; **24** 516
Telenet Communications, **18** 32
Telenor, **31** 221
Telenorma, **I** 193
Telenova, **III** 169; **6** 285
Teleos Communications Inc., **26** 277
Telephone and Data Systems, Inc., 9 494–96, 527–529; **31** 449
Telephone Company of Ireland, **7** 508
Telephone Exchange Company of Indianapolis, **14** 257
Telephone Management Corporation, **8** 310
Telephone Utilities, Inc. *See* Pacific Telecom, Inc.
Telephone Utilities of Washington, **6** 325, 328
Telepictures, **II** 177
Teleport Communications Group, **14** 253; **24** 122
Teleprompter Corp., **II** 122; **7** 222; **10** 210; **18** 355
Telerate Systems Inc., **IV** 603, 670; **10** 276–78; **21** 68
Teleregister Corp., **I** 512
Telerent Europe. *See* Granada Group PLC.
TeleRep, **IV** 596
Telesat Cable TV, Inc., **23** 293
Telesis Oil and Gas, **6** 478
Telesistema, **18** 212
Telesistema Mexico. *See* Grupo Televisa.
Telesphere Network, Inc., **8** 310
Telesystems SLW Inc., **10** 524
Telettra S.p.A., **V** 326; **9** 10; **11** 205
Tele2 AB, **26** 331–33
Teletype Corp., **14** 569
Televimex, S.A., **18** 212
Television de Mexico, S.A., **18** 212
Television Española, S.A., 7 511–12; **18** 211
Télévision Française 1, 23 475–77
Television Sales and Marketing Services Ltd., **7** 79–80
Teleway Japan, **7** 118–19; **13** 482
Telex Corporation, **II** 87; **13** 127
Telfin, **V** 339
Telia Mobitel, **11** 19; **26** 332
Telihoras Corporation, **10** 319
Telinfo, **6** 303
Telinq Inc., **10** 19
Telios Pharmaceuticals, Inc., **11** 460; **17** 288
Tellabs, Inc., 11 500–01
Telmex. *See* Teléfonos de México S.A. de C.V.
Telpar, Inc., **14** 377
Telport, **14** 260
Telrad Telecommunications Ltd., **II** 48; **25** 266–67
Telxon Corporation, 10 523–25
Tembec, Inc., **IV** 296; **19** 226
Temco Electronics and Missile Co., **I** 489
Temenggong of Jahore, **I** 592
Temerlin McClain, **23** 479; **25** 91
Temp Force, **16** 421–22
Temp World, Inc., **6** 10
Temple, Barker & Sloan/Strategic Planning Associates, **III** 283
Temple Frosted Foods, **25** 278
Temple Inks Company, **13** 227
Temple Press Ltd., **IV** 294–95; **19** 225
Temple-Inland Inc., IV 312, **341–43**, 675; **8** 267–69; **19** 268; **31 438–442 (upd.)**
Templeton, **II** 609
TEMPO Enterprises, **II** 162
Tempo-Team, **16** 420
Tempus Expeditions, **13** 358
TemTech Ltd., **13** 326
10 Sen Kinitsu Markets, **V** 194
Ten Speed Press, **27** 223
Tenacqco Bridge Partnership, **17** 170
Tenby Industries Limited, **21** 350
Tengelmann Group, II 636–38; **16** 249–50; **27 459–62**
Tengen Inc., **III** 587; **7** 395
Tennant Company, 13 499–501
Tenneco Inc., I 182, **526–28**; **IV** 76, 152, 283, 371, 499; **6** 531; **10** 379–80, 430, **526–28 (upd.)**; **11** 440; **12** 91, 376; **13** 372–73; **16** 191, 461; **19** 78, 483; **21** 170; **22** 275, 380; **24** 358
Tennessee Book Company, **11** 193
Tennessee Coal, Iron and Railroad Co., **IV** 573; **7** 550
Tennessee Eastman Corporation, **III** 475; **7** 161. *See also* Eastman Chemical Company.
Tennessee Electric Power Co., **III** 332
Tennessee Gas Pipeline Co., **14** 126
Tennessee Gas Transmission Co., **I** 526; **13** 496; **14** 125
Tennessee Insurance Company, **11** 193–94
Tennessee Paper Mills Inc. *See* Rock-Tenn Company.
Tennessee Restaurant Company, **9** 426; **30** 208–9
Tennessee River Pulp & Paper Co., **12** 376–77
Tennessee Trifting, **13** 169
Tennessee Valley Authority, **II** 2–3, 121; **IV** 181; **22** 10
Tennessee Woolen Mills, Inc., **19** 304
Tenngasco, **I** 527
Teollisuusosuuskunta Metsä-Saimaa, **IV** 315
TEP. *See* Tucson Electric Power Company.
Tequila Sauza, **31** 91
Tequilera de Los Altos, **31** 92
Teradata Corporation, **6** 267; **30** 339–40
Teradyne, Inc., 11 502–04
Terex Corporation, 7 513–15; **8** 116
Teril Stationers Inc., **16** 36
Terminal Transfer and Storage, Inc., **6** 371
Terminix International, **6** 45–46; **11** 433; **23** 428, 430; **25** 16
Terra Industries, Inc., 13 277, **502–04**
Terrace Park Dairies, **II** 536
Terracor, **11** 260–61
Terragrafics, **14** 245
Terre Haute Electric, **6** 555
Terre Lune, **25** 91
Territorial Hotel Co., **II** 490
Territory Ahead, Inc., **29** 279
Territory Enterprises Ltd., **IV** 59
Terry Coach Industries, Inc., **III** 484; **22** 206
Terry's of York, **II** 594
Tesa, S.A., **23** 82
TESC. *See* The European Software Company.
Tesco PLC, II 513, **677–78**; **10** 442; **11** 239, 241; **24 473–76 (upd.)**
Tesoro Bolivia Petroleum Company, **25** 546
Tesoro Petroleum Corporation, 7 516–19
Tesseract Corp., **11** 78
Tessman Seed, Inc., **16** 270–71
Testor Corporation, **8** 455
TETI, **I** 466
Tetley Inc., **I** 215; **14** 18
Tetra Plastics Inc., **V** 374; **8** 393
Tetra Tech, Inc., 29 463–65
Teutonia National Bank, **IV** 310; **19** 265
Teva Pharmaceutical Industries Ltd., 22 500–03
Tex-Star Oil & Gas Corp., **IV** 574; **7** 551
Texaco Canada Inc., **25** 232
Texaco Inc., I 21, 360; **II** 31, 313, 448; **III** 760; **IV** 386, 403, 418, 425, 429, 439, 461, 464, 466, 472–73, 479–80, 484, 488, 490, 510–11, 530–31, 536–39, 545, **551–53**, 560, 565–66, 570, 575; **7** 172, 280, 483; **9** 232; **10** 190; **12** 20; **13** 448; **14 491–94 (upd.)**; **17** 412; **18** 488; **19** 73, 75, 176; **24** 521; **27** 481; **28** 47
Texada Mines, Ltd., **IV** 123
Texas Air Corporation, I 97, 100, 103, 118, **123–24**, 127, 130; **6** 82, 129; **12** 489; **21** 142–43
Texas Almanac, **10** 3
Texas Bus Lines, **24** 118

Texas Butadiene and Chemical Corp., **IV** 456
Texas Co., **III** 497; **IV** 386, 400, 464, 536, 551–52; **7** 352
Texas Commerce Bankshares, **II** 252
Texas Eastern Corp., **6** 487; **11** 97, 354; **14** 126
Texas Eastern Transmission Company, **11** 28
Texas Eastman, **III** 475; **7** 161
Texas Electric Service Company, **V** 724
Texas Gas Resources Corporation, **IV** 395; **22** 166
Texas Gypsum, **IV** 341
Texas Homecare, **21** 335
Texas Industries, Inc., **8 522–24**; **13** 142–43
Texas Instruments Incorporated, **I** 315, 482, 523, 620; **II** 64, **112–15**; **III** 120, 124–25, 142, 499; **IV** 130, 365, 681; **6** 216, 221–22, 237, 241, 257, 259; **7** 531; **8** 157; **9** 43, 116, 310; **10** 22, 87, 307; **11** 61, 308, 490, 494, **505–08 (upd.)**; **12** 135, 238; **14** 42–43; **16** 4, 333; **17** 192; **18** 18, 436; **21** 123; **23** 181, 210; **25** 81, 96, 531
Texas International Airlines, **I** 117, 123; **II** 408; **IV** 413; **21** 142
Texas Life Insurance Co., **III** 293
Texas Metal Fabricating Company, **7** 540
Texas Oil & Gas Corp., **IV** 499, 572, 574; **7** 549, 551
Texas Overseas Petroleum Co., **IV** 552
Texas Pacific Coal and Oil Co., **I** 285–86
Texas Pacific Group, **22** 80; **23** 163, 166; **30** 171
Texas Pacific Oil Co., **IV** 550
Texas Pipe Line Co., **IV** 552
Texas Power & Light Company, **V** 724
Texas Public Utilities, **II** 660
Texas Super Duper Markets, Inc., **7** 372
Texas Trust Savings Bank, **8** 88
Texas United Insurance Co., **III** 214
Texas Utilities Company, **V 724–25**; **12** 99; **25 472–74 (upd.)**
Texas-New Mexico Utilities Company, **6** 580
Texasgulf Inc., **IV** 546–47; **13** 557; **18** 433
Texboard, **IV** 296; **19** 226
Texize, **I** 325, 371
Texkan Oil Co., **IV** 566
Texstar Petroleum Company, **7** 516
Texstyrene Corp., **IV** 331
Textile Diffusion, **25** 466
Textile Paper Tube Company, Ltd., **8** 475
Textile Rubber and Chemical Company, **15** 490
Textron Inc., **I** 186, **529–30**; **II** 420; **III** 66, 628; **8** 93, 157, 315, 545; **9** 497, 499; **11** 261; **12** 251, 382–83, 400–01; **13** 63–64; **17** 53; **21** 175; **22** 32; **27** 100
Textron Lycoming Turbine Engine, **9 497–99**
Texwood Industries, Inc., **20** 363
TF-I, **I** 563
TFN Group Communications, Inc., **8** 311
TF1 **24** 79. *See also* Télévision Française 1
TGEL&PCo. *See* Tucson Gas, Electric Light & Power Company.
Th. Pilter, **III** 417
TH:s Group, **10** 113
Thai Airways International Ltd., **I** 119; **II** 442; **6 122–24**
Thai Airways International Public Company Limited, **27 463–66 (upd.)**
Thai Aluminium Co. Ltd., **IV** 155
Thai Union International Inc., **24** 116
Thalassa International, **10** 14; **27** 11
Thalhimer Brothers, **V** 31
Thames Board Ltd., **IV** 318
Thames Television Ltd., **I** 532
Thames Trains, **28** 157
Thames Water plc, **11 509–11**; **22** 89
Thameslink, **28** 157
Tharsis Co., **IV** 189–90
Thatcher Glass, **I** 610
THAW. *See* Recreational Equipment, Inc.
Thayer Laboratories, **III** 55
Theatrical Syndicate, **24** 437
Theo H. Davies & Co., **I** 470; **20** 311
Theo Hamm Brewing Co., **I** 260
Théraplix, **I** 388
Therm-o-Disc, **II** 19
Therm-X Company, **8** 178
Thermacote Welco Company, **6** 146
Thermadyne Holding Corporation, **19 440–43**
Thermal Dynamics, **19** 441
Thermal Energies, Inc., **21** 514
Thermal Power Company, **11** 270
Thermal Snowboards, Inc., **22** 462
Thermal Transfer Ltd., **13** 485
Thermo BioAnalysis Corp., **25 475–78**
Thermo Electron Corporation, **7 520–22**; **11** 512–13; **13** 421; **24** 477; **25** 475–76
Thermo Fibertek, Inc., **24 477–79**
Thermo Instrument Systems Inc., **11 512–14**; **25** 475–77
Thermo King Corporation, **13 505–07**
Thermodynamics Corp., **III** 645
Thermoforming USA, **16** 339
Thermogas Co., **IV** 458–59
Thermolase Corporation, **22** 410
Thermoplast und Apparatebau GmbH, **IV** 198
Thermos Company, **16 486–88**
Thies Companies, **13** 270
Thiess, **III** 687
Thiess Dampier Mitsui, **IV** 47
Things Remembered, **13** 165–66
Think Entertainment, **II** 161
Think Technologies, **10** 508
Thiokol Corporation, **I** 370; **8** 472; **9** 358–59, **500–02 (upd.)**; **12** 68; **22 504–07 (upd.)**
Third National Bank. *See* Fifth Third Bancorp.
Third National Bank of Dayton, **9** 475
Third National Bank of New York, **II** 253
Third Wave Publishing Corp. *See* Acer Inc.
Thistle Group, **9** 365
Thom McAn, **V** 136–37; **11** 349
Thomas & Betts Corp., **II** 8; **11 515–17**; **14** 27
Thomas and Hochwalt, **I** 365
Thomas & Howard Co., **II** 682; **18** 8
Thomas and Judith Pyle, **13** 433
Thomas Barlow & Sons Ltd., **I** 288, 422; **IV** 22
Thomas Bros. Maps, **28** 380
Thomas Cook Group Ltd., **17** 325
Thomas Cook Travel Inc., **6** 84; **9 503–05**; **27** 133
Thomas Firth & Sons, **I** 573
Thomas H. Lee Co., **11** 156, 450; **14** 230–31; **15** 309; **19** 371, 373; **24 480–83**; **25** 67; **28** 134; **30** 219
Thomas Industries Inc., **29 466–69**
Thomas J. Lipton Company, **II** 609, 657; **11** 450; **14 495–97**; **16** 90
Thomas Jefferson Life Insurance Co., **III** 397
Thomas Linnell & Co. Ltd., **II** 628
Thomas Nationwide Transport. *See* TNT.
Thomas Nationwide Transport Limited. *See* TNT Post Group N.V.
Thomas Nelson Inc., **8** 526; **14 498–99**; **24** 548
Thomas Publishing Company, **26 482–85**
Thomas Tilling plc, **I** 429
Thomas Y. Crowell, **IV** 605
Thomaston Mills, Inc., **27 467–70**
Thomasville Furniture Industries, Inc., **III** 423; **12 474–76**; **22** 48; **28** 406; **31** 248
Thompson Aircraft Tire Corp., **14** 42
Thompson and Formby, **16** 44
Thompson Medical Company. *See* Slim-Fast Nutritional Foods International Inc.
Thompson PBE Inc., **24** 160–61
Thompson Products Co., **I** 539
Thompson-Hayward Chemical Co., **13** 397
Thompson-Ramo-Woolridge, **I** 539
Thompson-Werke, **III** 32
Thomson BankWatch Inc., **19** 34
The Thomson Corporation, **IV** 651, 686; **7** 390; **8 525–28**; **10** 407; **12** 361, 562; **17** 255; **22** 441
Thomson Multimedia, **18** 126
Thomson S.A., **I** 411; **II** 31, **116–17**; **7** 9; **13** 402
Thomson T-Line, **II** 142
Thomson Travel Group, **27** 27
Thomson-Bennett, **III** 554
Thomson-Brandt, **I** 411; **II** 13, 116–17; **9** 9
Thomson-CSF, **II** 116–17; **III** 556
Thomson-Houston Electric Co., **II** 27, 116, 330; **12** 193
Thomson-Jenson Energy Limited, **13** 558
Thomson-Lucas, **III** 556
Thomson-Ramo-Woolridge. *See* TRW Inc.
Thonet Industries Inc., **14** 435–36
Thorn Apple Valley, Inc., **7 523–25**; **12** 125; **22 508–11 (upd.)**; **23** 203
Thorn EMI plc, **I** 52, 411, **531–32**; **II** 117, 119; **III** 480; **19** 390; **22** 27, 192–94; **24** 87, 484–85; **26** 151. *See also* EMI Group plc.
Thorn plc, **24 484–87**
Thorncraft Inc., **25** 379
Thorndike, Doran, Paine and Lewis, Inc., **14** 530
Thornton, **III** 547
Thornton & Co., **II** 283
Thornton Stores, **14** 235
Thoroughgood, **II** 658
Thorsen Realtors, **21** 96
Thos. & Wm. Molson & Company. *See* The Molson Companies Limited.
Thousand Trails, Inc., **13** 494
Thousands Springs Power Company, **12** 265
Threadz, **25** 300
3 Guys, **II** 678, **V** 35
3 Maj, **25** 469
Three Rivers Pulp and Paper Company, **17** 281
Three Score, **23** 100
3 Suisses International, **12** 281

Three-Diamond Company. *See* Mitsubishi Shokai.
3-in-One Oil Co., **I** 622
3Com Corp., III 143; **6** 238, 269; **10** 237; **11 518–21**; **20** 8, 33; **26** 276
3DO Inc., **10** 286
3M. *See* Minnesota Mining & Manufacturing Co.
3S Systems Support Services Ltd., **6** 310
Threlfall Breweries, **I** 294
Threshold Entertainment, **25** 270
Thrif D Discount Center, **V** 174
Thrift Drug, **V** 92
Thrift Mart, **16** 65
ThriftiCheck Service Corporation, **7** 145
Thriftimart Inc., **12** 153; **16** 452
Thriftway Food Drug, **21** 530
Thriftway Foods, **II** 624
Thrifty Corporation, **25** 413, 415–16
Thrifty PayLess, Inc., **V** 682, 684; ; **12 477–79**; **18** 286; **19** 357; **25** 297
Thrifty Rent-A-Car, **6** 349; **24** 10. *See also* Dollar Thrifty Automotive Group, Inc.
Throwing Corporation of America, **12** 501
Thummel Schutze & Partner, **28** 141
Thuringia Insurance Co., **III** 299
Thurmond Chemicals, Inc., **27** 291
Thurston Motor Lines Inc., **12** 310
Thy-Marcinelle, **IV** 52
Thyssen AG, II 279; **III** 566; **IV** 195, **221–23**, 228; **8** 75–76; **14** 169, 328
Thyssen Krupp AG, 28 104, **452–60 (upd.)**
Thyssen-Krupp Stahl AG, **26** 83
TI. *See* Texas Instruments.
TI Corporation, **10** 44
TI Group plc, 17 480–83
Tianjin Agricultural Industry and Commerce Corp., **II** 577
Tianjin Automobile Industry Group, **21** 164
Tianjin Bohai Brewing Company, **21** 230
Tibbals Floring Co., **III** 611
Tiber Construction Company, **16** 286
Ticino S tle Insurance Co., **10** 45
Tidel Systems, **II** 661
Tidewater Inc., 11 522–24
Tidewater Oil Co., **IV** 434, 460, 489, 522
Tidi Wholesale, **13** 150
Tidy House Products Co., **II** 556
Tiel Utrecht Fire Insurance Co., **III** 309–10
Tien Wah Press (Pte.) Ltd., **IV** 600
Le Tierce S.A., **II** 141
Tierco Group, Inc., **27** 382
Tierney & Partners, **23** 480
Tiffany & Co., III 16; **12** 312; **14 500–03**; **15** 95; **19** 27; **26** 145; **27** 329
TIG Holdings, Inc., 26 486–88
Tiger Accessories, **18** 88
Tiger International, Inc., **17** 505; **18** 178
Tiger Management Associates, **13** 158, 256
Tiger Oats, **I** 424
Tigon Corporation, **V** 265–68
Tilcon, **I** 429
Tilden Interrent, **10** 419
Tile & Coal Company, **14** 248
Tilgate Pallets, **I** 592
Tillie Lewis Foods Inc., **I** 513–14
Tillotson Corp., 14 64; **15 488–90**
Tim Horton's Restaurants, **23** 507
Tim-Bar Corp., **IV** 312; **19** 267
Timber Realization Co., **IV** 305
The Timberland Company, 11 349; **13 511–14**; **17** 245; **19** 112; **22** 173; **25** 206
Timberline Software Corporation, 15 491–93
TIMCO. *See* Triad International Maintenance Corp.
Time Distribution Services, **13** 179
Time Electronics, **19** 311
Time Industries, **IV** 294; **19** 225; **26** 445
Time Saver Stores, Inc., **12** 112; **17** 170
Time Warner Inc., II 155, 161, 168, 175–177, 252, 452; **III** 245; **IV** 341–42, 636, **673–76**; **6** 293; **7** 63, 222–24, 396, **526–30 (upd.)**; **8** 267–68, 527; **9** 119, 469, 472; **10** 168, 286, 484, 488, 491; **12** 531; **13** 105–06, 399; **14** 260; **15** 51, 54; **16** 146, 223; **17** 148, 442–44; **18** 66, 535; **19** 6, 336; **22** 52, 194, 522; **23** 31, 33, 257, 274, 276, 393; **24** 321–22; **25** 141, 498–99; **26** 33, 151, 441; **27** 121, 429–30. *See also* Warner Communications Inc.
Time-Life Books, Inc. *See* Time Warner Inc.
Time-O-Stat Controls Corp., **II** 41; **12** 247
Time-Sharing Information, **10** 357
Timely Brands, **I** 259
Timeplex, **III** 166; **6** 283; **9** 32
Times Media Ltd., **IV** 22
The Times Mirror Company, I 90; **IV** 583, 630, **677–78**; **14** 97; **17 484–86 (upd.)**; **21** 404; **22** 162, 443; **26** 446
Times Newspapers, **8** 527
Times-Picayune Publishing Co., **IV** 583
TIMET. *See* Titanium Metals Corporation.
Timex Corporation, 25 479–82 (upd.)
Timex Enterprises Inc., III 455; **7 531–33**; **10** 152; **12** 317; **21** 123; **25** 22
The Timken Company, III 596; **7** 447; **8 529–31**; **15** 225
Timothy Whites, **24** 74
Timpte Industries, **II** 488
Tioxide Group PLC, **III** 680
Tip Corp., **I** 278
Tip Top Drugstores plc, **24** 269
Tip Top Tailors, **29** 162
TIPC Network. *See* Gateway 2000.
Tiphook PLC, **13** 530
Tipton Centers Inc., **V** 50; **19** 123
Tiroler Hauptbank, **II** 270
Tishman Realty and Construction, **III** 248
Tissue Papers Ltd., **IV** 260
Tissue Technologies, Inc., **22** 409
Titan Industries, **31** 52
Titan Manufacturing Company, **19** 359
Titanium Metals Corporation, 10 434; **21 489–92**
Titanium Technology Corporation, **13** 140
Titianium Enterprises, **IV** 345
TITISA, **9** 109
Title Guarantee & Trust Co., **II** 230
Titmus Optical Inc., **III** 446
Tivoli Systems, Inc., **14** 392
TJ International, Inc., 19 444–47
The TJX Companies, Inc., V 197–98; **13** 548; **14** 426; **19 448–50 (upd.)**; **29** 106
TKD Electronics Corp., **II** 109
TKM Foods, **II** 513
TKR Cable Co., **15** 264
TLC Associates, **11** 261
TLC Beatrice International Holdings, Inc., 22 512–15. *See also* Beatrice Co.
TLC Gift Company, **26** 375
TLC Group, **II** 468
TLO, **25** 82
TMB Industries, **24** 144
TMC Industries Ltd., **22** 352
TML Information Services Inc., **9** 95
TMP Worldwide Inc., 30 458–60
TMS, Inc., **7** 358
TMS Marketing, **26** 440
TMS Systems, Inc., **10** 18
TMT. *See* Trailer Marine Transport.
TN Technologies Inc., **23** 479
TNT Crust, Inc., **23** 203
TNT Freightways Corporation, IV 651; **14 504–06**
TNT Limited, V 523–25; **6** 346
TNT Post Group N.V., 27 471–76 (upd.); **30** 393, **461–63 (upd.)**
Toa Airlines, **I** 106; **6** 427
Toa Fire & Marine Reinsurance Co., **III** 385
Toa Kyoseki Co. Ltd., **IV** 476
Toa Medical Electronics Ltd., **22** 75
Toa Nenryo Kogyo, **IV** 432
Toa Oil Co. Ltd., **IV** 476, 543
Toa Tanker Co. Ltd., **IV** 555
Toasted Corn Flake Co., **II** 523; **13** 291
Toastmaster, **17** 215; **22** 353
Tobacco Group PLC, **30** 231
Tobacco Products Corporation, **18** 416
Tobata Imaon Co., **I** 183
Tobias, **16** 239
Tobler Co., **II** 520–21
Tobu Railway Co Ltd, 6 430–32
TOC Retail Inc., **17** 170
Tocom, Inc., **10** 320
Today's Man, Inc., 20 484–87; **21** 311
Todays Computers Business Centers, **6** 243–44
Todays Temporary, **6** 140
Todd Shipyards Corporation, IV 121; **7** 138; **14 507–09**
Todhunter International, Inc., 27 477–79
Todorovich Agency, **III** 204
Toei Co. Ltd., **9** 29–30; **28** 462
Tofas, **I** 479–80
Toggenburger Bank, **II** 378
Togo's Eatery, **29** 19
Toho Co., Ltd., I 363; **IV** 403; **24** 327; **28 461–63**
Tohoku Alps, **II** 5
Tohoku Pulp Co., **IV** 297
Tohokushinsha Film Corporation, **18** 429
Tohuku Electric Power Company, Inc., V 724, 732
Tojo Railway Company, **6** 430
Tokai Aircraft Co., Ltd., **III** 415
The Tokai Bank, Limited, II 373–74; **15 494–96 (upd.)**
Tokai Paper Industries, **IV** 679
Tokan Kogyo, **I** 615
Tokheim Corporation, 21 493–95
Tokio Marine and Fire Insurance Co., Ltd., II 323; **III** 248, 289, 295, **383–86**
Tokos Medical Corporation, **17** 306, 308–09
Tokushima Ham Co., **II** 550
Tokushima Meat Processing Factory, **II** 550
Tokushu Seiko, Ltd., **IV** 63
Tokuyama Soda, **I** 509
Tokuyama Teppan Kabushikigaisha, **IV** 159
Tokyo Broadcasting System, **7** 249; **9** 29; **16** 167
Tokyo Car Manufacturing Co., **I** 105
Tokyo Confectionery Co., **II** 538
Tokyo Corporation, **V** 199

Tokyo Dairy Industry, **II** 538
Tokyo Denki Kogaku Kogyo, **II** 109
Tokyo Dento Company, **6** 430
Tokyo Disneyland, **IV** 715; **6** 123, 176
Tokyo Electric Company, Ltd., **I** 533; **12** 483
Tokyo Electric Express Railway Co., **IV** 728
Tokyo Electric Light Co., **IV** 153
Tokyo Electric Power Company, **IV** 167, 518; **V 729–33**
Tokyo Electronic Corp., **11** 232
Tokyo Express Highway Co., Ltd., **IV** 713–14
Tokyo Express Railway Company, **V** 510, 526
Tokyo Fire Insurance Co. Ltd., **III** 405–06, 408
Tokyo Food Products, **I** 507
Tokyo Fuhansen Co., **I** 502, 506
Tokyo Gas and Electric Industrial Company, **9** 293
Tokyo Gas Co., Ltd., **IV** 518; **V 734–36**
Tokyo Ishikawajima Shipbuilding and Engineering Company, **III** 532; **9** 293
Tokyo Maritime Insurance Co., **III** 288
Tokyo Motors. *See* Isuzu Motors, Ltd.
Tokyo Sanyo Electric, **II** 91–92
Tokyo Shibaura Electric Company, Ltd., **I** 507, 533; **12** 483
Tokyo Steel Works Co., Ltd., **IV** 63
Tokyo Tanker Co., Ltd., **IV** 479
Tokyo Telecommunications Engineering Corp. *See* Tokyo Tsushin Kogyo K.K.
Tokyo Trust & Banking Co., **II** 328
Tokyo Tsushin Kogyo K.K., **II** 101, 103
Tokyo Yokohama Electric Railways Co., Ltd., **V** 199
Tokyu Corporation, **IV** 728; **V** 199, **526–28**
Toledo Edison Company. *See* Centerior Energy Corporation.
Toledo Milk Processing, Inc., **15** 449
Toledo Scale Corp., **9** 441; **30** 327
Toledo Seed & Oil Co., **I** 419
Toll Brothers Inc., **15 497–99**
Tom Bowling Lamp Works, **III** 554
Tom Doherty Associates Inc., **25 483–86**
Tom Huston Peanut Co., **II** 502; **10** 323
Tom Piper Ltd., **I** 437
Tom Snyder Productions, **29** 470, 472
Tom Thumb-Page, **16** 64
Tomakomai Paper Co., Ltd., **IV** 321
Toman Corporation, **19** 390
Tombstone Pizza Corporation, **13 515–17**
Tomei Fire and Marine Insurance Co., **III** 384–85
Tomen Corporation, **IV 224–25**; **19** 256;
Tomen Corporation, **24 488–91 (upd.)**
Tomen Transportgerate, **III** 638
Tomkins plc, **11 525–27**; **28** 382, 384; **30** 424, 426
Tomkins-Johnson Company, **16** 8
Tomlee Tool Company, **7** 535; **26** 493
Tommy Hilfiger Corporation, **16** 61; **20 488–90**; **25** 258
Tomoe Trading Co., **III** 595
Tonami Transportation Company, **6** 346
Tone Brothers, Inc., **21 496–98**
Tone Coca-Cola Bottling Company, Ltd., **14** 288
Tonen Corporation, **IV 554–56**; **16 489–92 (upd.)**
Tong Yang Group, **III** 304
Toni Co., **III** 28; **9** 413
Tonka Corporation, **12** 169; **14** 266; **16** 267; **25** 380, **487–89**
Tonkin, Inc., **19** 114
Tony Lama Company Inc., **19** 233
Tony Stone Images, **31** 216–17
Toohey, **10** 170
Toolex International N.V., **26 489–91**
Tootal Group, **V** 356–57
Tootsie Roll Industries Inc., **12 480–82**; **15** 323
Top End Wheelchair Sports, **11** 202
Top Green International, **17** 475
Top Man, **V** 21
Top Shop, **V** 21
Top Tool Company, Inc., **25** 75
Top Value Stamp Co., **II** 644–45; **6** 364; **22** 126
Topco Associates, **17** 78
Topkapi, **17** 101–03
Toppan Printing Co., Ltd., **IV** 598–99, **679–81**
Topps Company, Inc., **13 518–20**; **19** 386
Topps Markets, **16** 314
Tops Appliance City, Inc., **17 487–89**
Topy Industries, Limited, **8** 506–07
Tor Books. *See* Tom Doherty Associates Inc.
Toray Industries, Inc., **V** 380, **383**; **17** 287
Torbensen Gear & Axle Co., **I** 154
Torchmark Corporation, **III** 194; **9 506–08**; **10** 66; **11** 17; **22** 540–43
Torfeaco Industries Limited, **19** 304
Torise Ham Co., **II** 550
Tornator Osakeyhtiö, **IV** 275–76
Toro Assicurazioni, **III** 347
The Toro Company, **III** 600; **7 534–36**; **26 492–95 (upd.)**
Toromont Industries, Ltd., **21 499–501**
Toronto and Scarborough Electric Railway, **9** 461
Toronto Electric Light Company, **9** 461
Toronto-Dominion Bank, **II** 319, **375–77**, 456; **16** 13–14; **17** 324; **18** 551–53; **21** 447
Torpshammars, **IV** 338
Torrey Canyon Oil, **IV** 569; **24** 519
The Torrington Company, **III** 526, 589–90; **13 521–24**
Torrington National Bank & Trust Co., **13** 467
Torstar Corporation, **IV** 672; **7** 488–89; **19** 405; **29 470–73**
Tosa Electric Railway Co., **II** 458
Toscany Co., **13** 42
Tosco Corporation, **7 537–39**; **12** 240; **20** 138; **24** 522
Toshiba Corporation, **I** 221, 507–08, **533–35**; **II** 5, 56, 59, 62, 68, 73, 99, 102, 118, 122, 326, 440; **III** 298, 461, 533, 604; **6** 101, 231, 244, 287; **7** 529; **9** 7, 181; **10** 518–19; **11** 46, 328; **12** 454, **483–86 (upd.)**, 546; **13** 324, 399, 482; **14** 117, 446; **16** 5, 167; **17** 533; **18** 18, 260; **21** 390; **22** 193, 373; **23** 471
Toshin Kaihatsu Ltd., **V** 195
Toshin Paper Co., Ltd., **IV** 285
Tostem. *See* Toyo Sash Co., Ltd.
Total Audio Visual Services, **24** 95
Total Beverage Corporation, **16** 159, 161
Total Compagnie Française des Pétroles S.A., **I** 303; **II** 259; **III** 673; **IV** 363–64, 423–25, 466, 486, 498, 504, 515, 525, 544–47, **557–61**; **V** 628; **7** 481–84; **13** 557; **21** 203
Total Exploration S.A., **11** 537
Total Global Sourcing, Inc., **10** 498
Total Petroleum Corporation, **21** 500
TOTAL S.A., **24 492–97 (upd.)**, 522; **25** 104; **26** 369
Total System Services, Inc., **12** 465–66; **18** 168, 170, **516–18**
Totem Resources Corporation, **9 509–11**
Totino's Finer Foods, **II** 556; **13** 516; **26** 436
Toto Bank, **II** 326
TOTO LTD., **III 755–56**; **28 464–66 (upd.)**
Totsu Co., **I** 493; **24** 325
Touch-It Corp., **22** 413
Touche Remnant Holdings Ltd., **II** 356
Touche Ross. *See* Deloitte Touche Tohmatsu International.
Touchstone Films, **II** 172–74; **6** 174–76; **30** 487
Tour d'Argent, **II** 518
Tourang Limited, **7** 253
Touristik Union International GmbH. and Company K.G., **II 163–65**
Touron y Cia, **III** 419
Touropa, **II** 163–64
Toval Japon, **IV** 680
Towa Nenryo Kogyo Co. Ltd., **IV** 554–55
Tower Air, Inc., **28 467–69**
Tower Automotive, Inc., **24 498–500**
Tower Records, **9** 361; **10** 335; **11** 558; **30** 224
Towers, **II** 649
Towle Manufacturing Co., **14** 482–83; **18** 69
Town & City, **IV** 696
Town & Country Corporation, **7** 372; **16** 546; **19 451–53**; **25** 254
Town Investments, **IV** 711
Townsend Hook, **IV** 296, 650, 652; **19** 226
Toxicol Laboratories, Ltd., **21** 424
Toy Biz, Inc., **10** 402; **18 519–21**
Toy Liquidators, **13** 541–43
Toy Park, **16** 390
Toyad Corp., **7** 296
Toymax International, Inc., **29 474–76**
Toyo Bearing Manufacturing, **III** 595
Toyo Cotton Co., **IV** 224–25
Toyo Ink Manufacturing, **26** 213
Toyo Kogyo, **I** 167; **II** 361; **11** 139
Toyo Marine and Fire, **III** 385
Toyo Menka Kaisha Ltd. *See* Tomen Corporation.
Toyo Microsystems Corporation, **11** 464
Toyo Oil Co., **IV** 403
Toyo Pulp Co., **IV** 322
Toyo Rayon, **V** 381, 383
Toyo Sash Co., Ltd., **III 757–58**
Toyo Seikan Kaisha Ltd., **I 615–16**
Toyo Soda, **II** 301
Toyo Tire & Rubber Co., **V** 255–56; **9** 248
Toyo Toki Co., Ltd., **III** 755
Toyo Tozo Co., **I** 265; **21** 319
Toyo Trust and Banking Co., **II** 347, 371; **17** 349
Toyoda Automatic Loom Works, Ltd., **I** 203; **III** 591, 593, 632, **636–39**
Toyokawa Works, **I** 579
Toyoko Co., Ltd., **V** 199
Toyoko Kogyo, **V** 199
Toyomenka (America) Inc., **IV** 224

Toyomenka (Australia) Pty., Ltd., **IV** 224
Toyota Gossei, **I** 321
Toyota Industrial Equipment, **27** 294, 296
Toyota Motor Corporation, **I** 9–10, 174, 184, **203–05**, 507–08, 587; **II** 373; **III** 415, 495, 521, 523, 536, 579, 581, 591–93, 624, 636–38, 667, 715, 742; **IV** 702; **6** 514; **7** 111, 118, 212, 219–21; **8** 315; **9** 294, 340–42; **10** 353, 407; **11** 351, 377, 487, **528–31 (upd.)**; **14** 321; **15** 495; **21** 162, 273; **23** 289–90, 338–40; **25** 198
Toyota Tsusho America, Inc., **13** 371
Toys 'R' Us, Inc., **III** 588; **V 203–06**; **7** 396; **10** 235, 284, 484; **12** 178; **13** 166; **14** 61; **15** 469; **16** 389–90, 457; **18 522–25 (upd.)**; **24** 412; **25** 314; **31** 477–78
Tozer Kemsley & Milbourn, **II** 208
TPA. *See* Aloha Airlines Incorporated.
TPCR Corporation, **V** 163; **14** 394
TPG. *See* TNT Post Group N.V.
Trace International Holdings, Inc., **17** 182–83; **26** 502
Tracey Bros., **IV** 416
Tracey-Locke, **II** 660
Tracinda Corporation, **25** 329–30
Tracker Services, Inc., **9** 110
Traco International N.V., **8** 250
Tracor Inc., **10** 547; **17 490–92**; **26** 267
Tractebel S.A., **20 491–93**
Tractor Supply Corp., **I** 446
Tradax, **II** 617; **13** 137
Trade Assoc. of Bilbao, **II** 194
Trade Development Bank, **11** 415–17
Trade Waste Incineration, Inc., **9** 109
Trade Winds Campers, **III** 599
TradeARBED, **IV** 25
Trader Joe's Co., **13 525–27**
Trader Publications, Inc., **IV** 597
Trader Publishing Company, **12** 302
Traders & General Insurance, **III** 248
Traders Bank of Canada, **II** 344
Traders Group Ltd., **11** 258
Tradesmens National Bank of Philadelphia, **II** 342
The Trading Service, **10** 278
Traex Corporation, **8** 359
Trafalgar House Investments Ltd., **I** 248–49, 572–74; **IV** 259, 711; **20** 313; **23** 161; **24** 88
Trailer Marine Transport, **6** 383
Trailways, **I** 450; **9** 425
Trak Auto Corporation, **16** 159–62
TRAK Microwave Corporation, **18** 497, 513
Trammell Crow Company, **IV** 343; **8** 326–28, **532–34**
Tran Telecommunications Corp., **III** 110; **14** 14
Trane Company, **III** 663, 665; **10** 525; **21** 107; **22** 6; **26** 4; **30** 46, 48–49
Trans Air System, **6** 367; **27** 90
Trans Colorado, **11** 299
Trans Freight Lines, **27** 473–74
Trans International Airlines, **I** 537; **13** 529
Trans Ocean Products, **II** 578; **8** 510
Trans Rent-A-Car, **6** 348
Trans Union Corp., **IV** 137; **6** 25; **28** 119
Trans Western Publishing, **25** 496
Trans World Airlines, Inc., **I** 58, 70, 90, 97, 99–100, 102, 113, 121, 123–24, **125–27**, 132, 466; **II** 32–33, 142, 425, 679; **III** 92, 428; **6** 50, 68, 71, 74, 76–77, 81–82, 114, 130; **9** 17, 232; **10** 301–03, 316; **11** 277, 427; **12** 381, **487–90 (upd.)**; **13** 341; **14** 73; **15** 419; **21** 141–42; **22** 22, 219; **26** 439; **29** 190
Trans World Entertainment Corporation, **24 501–03**
Trans World International, **18** 262–63
Trans World Life Insurance Company, **27** 46–47
Trans World Music, **9** 361
Trans World Seafood, Inc., **13** 244
Trans-Arabian Pipe Line Co., **IV** 537, 552
Trans-Australia Airlines, **6** 110–12
Trans-Canada Air Lines. *See* Air Canada.
Trans-Continental Leaf Tobacco Company, (TCLTC), **13** 491
Trans-Natal Coal Corp., **IV** 93
Trans-Pacific Airlines, **22** 251. *See also* Aloha Airlines Incorporated.
Trans-Resources Inc., **13** 299
Trans-World Corp., **19** 456
Transaction Systems Architects, Inc., **29 477–79**
Transaction Technology, **12** 334
TransAlta Utilities Corporation, **6 585–87**
Transamerica Corporation, **I 536–38**; **II** 147–48, 227, 288–89, 422; **III** 332, 344; **7** 236–37; **8** 46; **11** 273, 533; **13 528–30 (upd.)**; **21** 285; **25** 328; **27** 230. *See also* TIG Holdings, Inc.
Transat. *See* Compagnie Générale Transatlantique (Transat).
Transatlantic Holdings, Inc., **III** 198; **11 532–33**; **15** 18
Transatlantische Dampfschiffahrts Gesellschaft, **6** 397
Transatlantische Gruppe, **III** 404
TransBrasil S/A Linhas Aéreas, **6** 134; **29** 495; **31 443–45**
TransCanada PipeLines Limited, **I** 264; **V** 270–71, **737–38**; **17** 22–23
Transco Energy Company, **IV** 367; **V** 739–40; **6** 143; **18** 366
Transcontinental Air Transport, **I** 125; **9** 17; **11** 427; **12** 487
Transcontinental and Western Air Lines, **9** 416; **12** 487
Transcontinental Gas Pipe Line Corporation, **V** 739; **6** 447
Transcontinental Pipeline Company, **6** 456–57
Transcontinental Services Group N.V., **16** 207
TransCor America, Inc., **23** 154
Transelco, Inc., **8** 178
TransEuropa, **II** 164
Transflash, **6** 404; **26** 243
Transfracht, **6** 426
Transinternational Life, **II** 422
Transit Mix Concrete and Materials Company, **7** 541
Transitions Optical Inc., **21** 221, 223
Transitron, **16** 332
Transking Inc. *See* King Kullen Grocery Co., Inc.
Transkrit Corp., **IV** 640; **26** 273
Translite, **III** 495
Transmanche-Link, **13** 206–08
Transmedia Network Inc., **20 494–97**
Transmisiones y Equipos Mecanicos, S.A. de C.V., **23** 171
Transmitter Equipment Manufacturing Co., **13** 385
TransMontaigne Inc., **28 470–72**
Transnet Ltd., **6 433–35**
TransOcean Oil, **III** 559
Transpac, **IV** 325
Transport Management Co., **III** 192
Transport- und Unfall-Versicherungs-Aktiengesellschaft Zürich, **III** 411
Transportacion Maritima Mexicana S.A. de C.V., **12** 279; **26** 236
Transportation Insurance Co., **III** 229
Transportes Aereos Portugueses, S.A., **6 125–27**
Transrack S.A., **26** 363
Transtar, **6** 120–21; **24** 454
Transue & Williams Steel Forging Corp., **13** 302
Transvaal Silver and Base Metals, **IV** 90
Transway International Corp., **10** 369
Transworld Corp., **14** 209
Transworld Drilling Company Limited. *See* Kerr-McGee Corporation.
The Tranzonic Cos., **8** 512; **15 500–02**
Trapper's, **19** 286
Trasgo, S.A. de C.V., **14** 516
Trausch Baking Co., **I** 255
Trävaru Svartvik, **IV** 338
Travel Air Manufacturing Company, **8** 49; **27** 97
Travel Automation Services Ltd., **I** 95
Travel Inc., **26** 309
Travel Information Group, **17** 398
Travel Ports of America, Inc., **17 493–95**
Travelers Bank & Trust Company, **13** 467
Travelers Book Club, **13** 105
Travelers Corporation, **I** 37, 545; **III** 313, 329, **387–90**, 707–08; **6** 12; **15** 463 124. *See also* Citigroup Inc.
Travelers/Aetna Property Casualty Corp., **21** 15
Traveller's Express, **I** 449
TraveLodge, **III** 94, 104–06
Travenol Laboratories, **I** 627–28; **10** 141–43
Travocéan, **25** 104
Trayco, **III** 570; **20** 362
Traylor Engineering & Manufacturing Company, **6** 395; **25** 169
TRC. *See* Tennessee Restaurant Company.
TRE Corp., **23** 225
Treadco, Inc., **16** 39; **19** 38, **454–56**
Treasure Chest Advertising, **21** 60
Treasure House Stores, Inc., **17** 322
Treatment Centers of America, **11** 379
Trebuhs Realty Co., **24** 438
Trechmann, Weekes and Co., **III** 669
Tredegar Industries, Inc., **10** 291
Tree of Life, Inc., **II** 528; **29 480–82**
Tree Sweet Products Corp., **12** 105; **26** 325
Tree Tavern, Inc., **27** 197
TrefilARBED, **IV** 26
Tréfimétaux, **IV** 174
Trefoil Capital Investors, L.P., **8** 305
Trek, **IV** 90, 92–93
Trek Bicycle Corporation, **16 493–95**; **19** 384–85
Trelleborg A.B., **III** 625; **IV** 166
Tremec. *See* Transmisiones y Equipos Mecanicos, S.A. de C.V.
Tremletts Ltd., **IV** 294; **19** 225
Tremont Corporation, **21** 490
Trend International Ltd., **13** 502
Trend-Lines, Inc., **22 516–18**
TrendWest, **12** 439
Trent Tube, **I** 435

Trenton Foods, **II** 488
TrentonWorks Limited. *See* The Greenbrier Companies.
Tresco, **8** 514
Trethowal China Clay Co., **III** 690
Tri-City Federal Savings and Loan Association, **10** 92
Tri-City Utilities Company, **6** 514
Tri-County National Bank, **9** 474
Tri-Marine International Inc., **24** 116
Tri-Miller Packing Company, **7** 524
Tri-Sonics, Inc., **16** 202
Tri-State Improvement Company, **6** 465–66
Tri-State Publishing & Communications, Inc., **22** 442
Tri-State Recycling Corporation, **15** 117
Tri-State Refining Co., **IV** 372
Tri-Union Seafoods LLC, **24** 116
Triad, **14** 224
Triad Artists Inc., **23** 514
Triad International Maintenance Corp., **13** 417
Triad Nitrogen, Inc., **27** 316, 318
Triangle Auto Springs Co., **IV** 136
The Triangle Group, **16** 357
Triangle Industries Inc., **I** 602, 607–08, 614; **II** 480–81; **14** 43
Triangle Manufacturing, **26** 57
Triangle Portfolio Associates, **II** 317
Triangle Publications, Inc., **IV** 652; **7** 391; **12** 359–60
Triangle Refineries, **IV** 446; **22** 302
Triarc Companies, Inc., 8 535–37; 13 322; **14** 32–33
Triathlon Leasing, **II** 457
Tribe Computer Works. *See* Zoom Telephonics.
Tribune Company, III 329; **IV 682–84; 10** 56; **11** 331; **22 519–23 (upd.); 26** 17
Trical Resources, **IV** 84
Tricity Cookers, **I** 531–32
Trick & Murray, **22** 153
Trico Products Corporation, I 186; **15 503–05**
Tricon Global Restaurants, Inc., **21** 313, 317, 405, 407, 485
Tridel Enterprises Inc., 9 512–13
Trident NGL Holdings Inc., **18** 365, 367
Trident Seafoods, **II** 494
Trifari, Krussman & Fishel, Inc., **9** 157
Trigen Energy Corp., **6** 512
Trigon Industries, **13** 195; **14** 431
Trilan Developments Ltd., **9** 512
Trilogy Fabrics, Inc., **16** 125
Trilon Financial Corporation, II 456–57; IV 721; **9** 391
Trimac Ltd., **25** 64
TriMas Corp., III 571; **11 534–36; 20** 359, 362
Trinidad and Tobago External Telecommunications Company, **25** 100
Trinidad Oil Co., **IV** 95, 552
Trinidad-Tesoro Petroleum Company Limited, **7** 516, 518
Trinity Beverage Corporation, **11** 451
Trinity Broadcasting, **13** 279
Trinity Capital Opportunity Corp., **17** 13
Trinity Distributors, **15** 139
Trinity Industries, Incorporated, 7 540–41
Trinkaus und Burkhardt, **II** 319; **17** 324
TRINOVA Corporation, III 640–42, 731; **13** 8; **16** 7, 9
Trintex, **6** 158
Triology Corp., **III** 110
Triple P N.V., 26 496–99
Triplex, **6** 279
Triplex (Northern) Ltd., **III** 725
Trippe Manufacturing Co., **10** 474; **24** 29
Triquet Paper Co., **IV** 282; **9** 261
TriStar Pictures, **I** 234; **II** 134, 136–37; **6** 158; **10** 227; **12** 75, 455; **23** 275; **28** 462. *See also* Columbia TriStar Motion Pictures Companies.
Triton Bioscience, **III** 53; **26** 384
Triton Energy Corporation, 11 537–39
Triton Group Ltd., **I** 447; **31** 287
Triton Oil, **IV** 519
Triton Systems Corp., **22** 186
Triumph American, Inc., **12** 199
Triumph Films, **25** 174
Triumph, Finlay, and Philips Petroleum, **11** 28
Triumph Group, Inc., 21 153; **31 446–48**
Triumph-Adler, **I** 485; **III** 145; **11** 265
Trivest, Inc., **II** 457; **21** 531–32
Trizec Corporation Ltd., 9 84–85; **10 529–32**
TRM Copy Centers Corporation, 18 526–28
Trojan, **III** 674
Troll, **13** 561
Trolley Barn Brewery Inc., **25** 401
Trona Corp., **IV** 95
Tropical Oil Co., **IV** 415–16
Tropical Shipping, Inc., **6** 529, 531
Tropicana Products, Inc., II 468, 525; **13** 293; **25** 366; **28** 271, **473–77**
Trotter-Yoder & Associates, **22** 88
Troxel Cycling, **16** 53
Troy & Nichols, Inc., **13** 147
Troy Metal Products. *See* KitchenAid.
Troyfel Ltd., **III** 699
TRT Communications, Inc., **6** 327; **11** 185
Tru-Run Inc., **16** 207
Tru-Stitch, **16** 545
Tru-Trac Therapy Products, **11** 486
Truck Components Inc., **23** 306
Trudeau Marketing Group, Inc., **22** 386
True Form Boot Co., **V** 177
True North Communications Inc., 23 478–80; 25 91
True Temper Hardware Co., **30** 241–42
True Value Hardware Stores, **V** 37–38; **30** 168. *See also* TruServ Corporation.
Trugg-Hansa Holding AB, **III** 264
TruGreen, **23** 428, 430
Truitt Bros., **10** 382
Truman Dunham Co., **III** 744
Truman Hanburg, **I** 247
Trumball Asphalt, **III** 721
Trümmer-Verwertungs-Gesellschaft, **IV** 140
Trump Organization, 16 262; **23 481–84**
Trunkline Gas Company, **6** 544; **14** 135
Trunkline LNG Co., **IV** 425
Trus Joist Corporation. *See* TJ International, Inc.
TruServ Corporation, 24 504–07
Trussdeck Corporation. *See* TJ International, Inc.
Trust Co. of the West, **19** 414
Trustcorp, Inc., **9** 475–76
Trusted Information Systems, Inc., **25** 349
Trustees, Executors and Agency Co. Ltd., **II** 189
Trusthouse Forte PLC, I 215; **III 104–06; 16** 446
TRW Inc., I 539–41; II 33; **6** 25; **8** 416; **9** 18, 359; **10** 293; **11** 68, **540–42 (upd.); 12** 238; **14 510–13 (upd.); 16** 484; **17** 372; **18** 275; **19** 184; **23** 134; **24** 480; **26** 141; **28** 119
Tryart Pty. Limited, **7** 253
TSA. *See* Transaction Systems Architects, Inc.
Tsai Management & Research Corp., **III** 230–31
TSB Group plc, 12 491–93; 16 14
TSI Soccer Corporation, **29** 142–43
TSO. *See* Teacher's Service Organization, Inc.
TSO Financial Corp., **II** 420; **8** 10
Tsogo Sun Gaming & Entertainment, **17** 318
TSP. *See* Tom Snyder Productions.
TSR Inc., **24** 538
Tsuang Hine Co., **III** 582
Tsubakimoto-Morse, **14** 64
Tsukumo Shokai, **I** 502; **III** 712
Tsumeb Corp., **IV** 17–18
Tsurumi Steelmaking and Shipbuilding Co., **IV** 162
Tsurusaki Pulp Co., Ltd., **IV** 285
Tsutsunaka Plastic Industry Co., **III** 714; **8** 359
TSYS. *See* Total System Services, Inc.
TTK. *See* Tokyo Tsushin Kogyo K.K.
TTX Company, 6 436–37
Tube Fab Ltd., **17** 234
Tube Forming, Inc., **23** 517
Tube Investments, **II** 422; **IV** 15
Tube Reducing Corp., **16** 321
Tube Service Co., **19** 344
Tubed Chemicals Corporation, **27** 299
Tuborg, **9** 99
Tucker, Lynch & Coldwell. *See* CB Commercial Real Estate Services Group, Inc.
TUCO, Inc., **8** 78
Tucson Electric Power Company, V 713; **6 588–91**
Tucson Gas & Electric, **19** 411–12
Tuesday Morning Corporation, 18 529–31
Tuff Stuff Publications, **23** 101
TUI. *See* Touristik Union International GmbH. and Company K.G.
Tuileries et Briqueteries d'Hennuyeres et de Wanlin, **14** 249
TUJA, **27** 21
Tultex Corporation, 13 531–33
Tunhems Industri A.B., **I** 387
Tupolev Aviation and Scientific Technical Complex, 24 58–60
Tupperware Corporation, I 29; **II** 534; **III** 610–12;, **15** 475, 477; **17** 186; **18** 67; **28 478–81**
Turbinbolaget, **III** 419
Turbine Engine Asset Management LLC, **28** 5
Turcot Paperboard Mills Ltd., **17** 281
Turkish Engineering, Consultancy and Contracting Corp., **IV** 563
Turkish Petroleum Co. *See* Türkiye Petrolleri Anonim Ortakliği.
Türkiye Garanti Bankasi, **I** 479
Türkiye Petrolleri Anonim Ortakliği, IV 464, 557–58, **562–64; 7** 352
Turnbull, **III** 468

Turner Broadcasting System, Inc., II 134, 149, 161 **166–68**; **IV** 676; **6 171–73 (upd.)**; **7** 64, 99, 306, 529; **23** 33, 257; **25** 313, 329, 498; **28** 71; **30** 100
The Turner Corporation, 8 538–40; **23 485–88 (upd.)**; **25** 402
Turner Entertainment Co., **18** 459
Turner Glass Company, **13** 40
Turner Network Television, **21** 24
Turner's Turkeys, **II** 587
TURPAS, **IV** 563
Turtle Wax, Inc., 15 506–09; **16** 43; **26** 349
Tuscarora Inc., 17 155; **29 483–85**
Tussauds Group Ltd., **IV** 659
Tutt Bryant Industries PLY Ltd., **26** 231
Tuttle, Oglebay and Company. *See* Oglebay Norton Company.
TV & Stereo Town, **10** 468
TV Asahi, **7** 249
TV Food Network, **22** 522
TVE. *See* Television Española, S.A.
TVE Holdings, **22** 307
TVH Acquisition Corp., **III** 262, 264
TVI, Inc., 15 510–12
TVS Entertainment PLC, **13** 281
TVW Enterprises, **7** 78
TVX, **II** 449; **13** 449
TW Kutter, **III** 420
TW Services, Inc., II 679–80; **10** 301–03
TWA. *See* Trans World Airlines *and* Transcontinental & Western Airways.
Tweco Co., **19** 441
Tweeds, **12** 280
Tweeter Home Entertainment Group, Inc., 30 464–66
Twen-Tours International, **II** 164
Twentieth Century Fox Film Corporation, II 133, 135, 146, 155–56, **169–71**, 175; **IV** 652; **7** 391–92; **12** 73, 322, 359; **15** 23, 25, 234; **25** 327, **490–94 (upd.)**
Twentsche Bank, **II** 183
21st Century Food Products. *See* Hain Food Group, Inc.
21st Century Mortgage, **18** 28
Twenty-Second National Bank, **II** 291
"21" International Holdings, **17** 182
21 Invest International Holdings Ltd., **14** 322
TWI. *See* Trans World International.
Twin City Wholesale Drug Company, **14** 147
Twin Disc, Inc., 21 502–04
Twining Crosfield Group, **II** 465; **13** 52
Twinings Tea, **II** 465; **III** 696
Twinings' Foods International, **II** 466
Twinpak, **IV** 250
Two Guys, **12** 49
2-in-1 Shinola Bixby Corp., **II** 497
TWW Plc, **26** 62
TXEN, Inc., **18** 370
TXL Oil Corp., **IV** 552
TXP Operation Co., **IV** 367
TxPort Inc., **13** 8
Ty-D-Bol, **III** 55
Tyco International Ltd., 21 462; **28 482–87 (upd.)**; **30** 157
Tyco Laboratories, Inc., III 643–46; **13** 245–47
Tyco Toys, Inc., 12 494–97; **13** 312, 319; **18** 520–21; **25** 314
Tyler Corporation, 23 489–91
Tymnet, **18** 542
Tyndall Fund-Unit Assurance Co., **III** 273
Typhoo Tea, **II** 477
Typpi Oy, **IV** 469
Tyrolean Airways, **9** 233
Tyrvään Oy, **IV** 348
Tyskie Brewery, **24** 450
Tyson Foods, Inc., II 584–85; **7** 422–23, 432; **14 514–16 (upd.)**; **21** 535; **23** 376, 384; **26** 168

U S West, Inc., V 341–43; **11** 12, 59, 547; **25** 101, **495–99 (upd.)**
U.C.L.A.F. *See* Roussel-Uclaf.
U-Haul International Inc. *See* Amerco.
U.K. Corrugated, **IV** 296; **19** 226
U.S. Appliances, **26** 336
U.S. Bancorp, 12 165; **14 527–29**
U.S. Bank of Washington, **14** 527
U.S. Banknote Company, **30** 43
U.S. Bearings Company. *See* Federal-Mogul Corporation.
U.S. Billing, Inc. *See* Billing Concepts Corp.
U.S. Biomedicals Corporation, **27** 69
U.S. Brass., **24** 151
U.S. Can Corporation, 30 474–76
U.S. Cellular Corporation, 31 449–452 (upd.)
U.S. Delivery Systems, Inc., 22 153, **531–33**
U.S. Electrical Motors, **II** 19
U.S. Elevator Corporation, **19** 109–11
U.S. Envelope, **19** 498
U.S. Food Products Co., **I** 376
U.S. Foodservice, 26 503–06
U.S.G. Co., **III** 762
U.S. Generating Company, **26** 373
U.S. Geological Survey, **9** 367
U.S. Graphite. *See* Wickes Inc.
U.S. Guarantee Co., **III** 220; **14** 108
U.S. Healthcare, Inc., 6 194–96; **21** 16
U.S. Home Corporation, 8 541–43
U.S. Industries, Inc., **7** 208; **18** 467; **23** 296; **24** 150; **27** 288
U.S. Intec, **22** 229
U.S. International Reinsurance, **III** 264
U.S. Land Co., **IV** 255
U.S. Lawns, **31** 182, 184
U.S. Life Insurance, **III** 194
U.S. Lines, **I** 476; **III** 459; **11** 194
U.S. Lock Corporation, **9** 543; **28** 50–52
U.S. Long Distance Corp. *See* Billing Concepts Corp.
U.S. Marine Corp., **III** 444
U.S. News and World Report Inc., 30 477–80
U.S. Office Products Company, 25 500–02
U.S. Overall Company, **14** 549
U.S. Plywood Corp. *See* United States Plywood Corp.
U.S. Realty and Improvement Co., **III** 98
U.S. RingBinder Corp., **10** 313–14
U.S. Robotics Inc., 9 514–15; **20** 8, 69; **22** 17; **24** 212
U.S. Rubber Company, **I** 478; **10** 388
U.S. Satellite Broadcasting Company, Inc., 20 505–07
U.S. Satellite Systems, **III** 169; **6** 285
U.S. Smelting Refining and Mining, **7** 360
U.S. Software Inc., **29** 479
U.S. Steel Corp. *See* United States Steel Corp.
U.S. Telephone Communications, **9** 478
U.S. Tile Co., **III** 674
U.S. Time Corporation, **13** 120
U.S. Trust Co. of New York, **II** 274
U.S. Trust Corp., 17 496–98
U.S. Vanadium Co., **9** 517
U.S. Venture Partners, **15** 204–05
U.S. Vitamin & Pharmaceutical Corp., **III** 55
U.S. Windpower, **11** 222–23
U.S. Xpress Enterprises, Inc., **18** 159
U-Tote'M, **II** 620; **7** 372
UA. *See* Metro- Goldwyn-Mayer Inc., MGM/UA Communications Company, *and* United Artists Corp.
UAA. *See* EgyptAir.
UAL, Inc. *See* United Airlines.
UAP. *See* Union des Assurances de Paris.
UARCO Inc., **15** 473–74
UAT. *See* UTA.
Ub Iwerks, **6** 174
Ube Industries, Ltd., III 759–61
Uberseebank A.G., **III** 197
Ubique Ltd, **25** 301
UBS. *See* Union Bank of Switzerland.
Ucabail, **II** 265
UCC-Communications Systems, Inc., **II** 38
Uccel, **6** 224
Uchiyama, **V** 727
UCI, **IV** 92; **25** 173
UCPMI, **IV** 226
Uddeholm and Bohler, **IV** 234
Udet Flugzeugwerke, **I** 73
Udo Fischer Co., **8** 477
UE Automotive Manufacturing, **III** 580
UETA Inc., **29** 510–11
Ugg Holdings, Inc., **22** 173
UGI. *See* United Gas Improvement.
UGI Corporation, 12 498–500
Ugine S.A., IV 174; **20 498–500**
Ugine Steels, **IV** 227
Ugine-Kuhlmann, **IV** 108, 174
Ugly Duckling Corporation, 22 524–27
Uhlmans Inc., **24** 458
UI International, **6** 444
UIB. *See* United Independent Broadcasters, Inc.
Uinta Co., **6** 568
Uintah National Corp., **11** 260
UIS Co., **13** 554–55; **15** 324
Uitgeversmaatschappij Elsevier, **IV** 610
Uitzendbureau Amstelveen. *See* Randstad Holding n.v.
UJB Financial Corp., **14** 473
UK Paper, **IV** 279; **19** 155
UKF. *See* Unie van Kunstmestfabrieken.
UL. *See* Underwriters Laboratories, Inc.
Ullrich Copper, Inc., **6** 146
Ullstein AV Produktions-und Vertriebsgesellschaft, **IV** 590
Ullstein Langen Müller, **IV** 591
Ullstein Tele Video, **IV** 590
ULN. *See* Union Laitière Normande.
ULPAC, **II** 576
Ulstein Holding ASA, **27** 494
Ulster Bank, **II** 334
Ultimate Electronics, Inc., 18 532–34; **21** 33; **24** 52, 269
Ultra Bancorp, **II** 334
Ultra High Pressure Units Ltd., **IV** 66; **7** 123
Ultra Mart, **16** 250
Ultra Pac, Inc., 24 512–14
Ultra Radio & Television, **I** 531

UltraCam. *See* Ultrak Inc.
UltraCare Products, **18** 148
Ultrak Inc., **24 508–11**
Ultralar, **13** 544
Ultramar Diamond Shamrock Corporation, **31 453–457 (upd.)**
Ultramar PLC, **IV 565–68**
Ultrametl Mfg. Co., **17** 234
Ultronic Systems Corp., **IV** 669
UM Technopolymer, **III** 760
Umacs of Canada Inc., **9** 513
Umberto's of New Hyde Park Pizzeria, **16** 447
UMI Company, **29** 58
Umm-al-Jawabi Oil Co., **IV** 454
Umpqua River Navigation Company, **13** 100
Unadulterated Food Products, Inc., **11** 449
UNAT, **III** 197–98
Unbrako Socket Screw Company Ltd., **30** 429
Uncas-Merchants National Bank, **13** 467
Uncle Ben's Inc., **22 528–30**
Under Sea Industries, **III** 59
Underground Group, **6** 407
Underwood, **III** 145; **24** 269
Underwriters Adjusting Co., **III** 242
Underwriters Laboratories, Inc., **30 467–70**
Underwriters Reinsurance Co., **10** 45
UNELCO. *See* Union Electrica de Canarias S.A.
Unelec, Inc., **13** 398
Unfall, **III** 207
Ungermann-Bass, Inc., **6** 279
Uni Europe, **III** 211
Uni-Cardan AG, **III** 494
Uni-Cast. *See* Sturm, Ruger & Company, Inc.
Uni-Charm, **III** 749
Uni-Marts, Inc., **17 499–502**
Uni-Sankyo, **I** 675
Unic, **V** 63
Unicapital, Inc., **15** 281
Unicare Health Facilities, **6** 182; **25** 525
Unicco Security Services, **27** 22
Unicer, **9** 100
Unichem, **25** 73
Unichema International, **13** 228
Unicoa, **I** 524
Unicom Corporation, **29 486–90 (upd.)**
Unicomi, **II** 265
Unicon Producing Co., **10** 191
Unicoolait, **19** 51
Unicord, **24** 115
Unicorn Shipping Lines, **IV** 91
UniCorp, **8** 228
Unicorp Financial, **III** 248
Unicredit, **II** 265
Uniden, **14** 117
UniDynamics Corporation, **8** 135
Unie van Kunstmestfabrieken, **I** 326
Uniface Holding B.V., **10** 245; **30** 142
Unifi, Inc., **12 501–03**
Unified Management Corp., **III** 306
Unified Western Grocers, **31** 25
UniFirst Corporation, **16** 228; **21** 115, **505–07**
Unigate PLC, **II 586–87**; **28 488–91 (upd.)**; **29** 150
Unigep Group, **III** 495
Unigesco Inc., **II** 653
Uniglory, **13** 211
Unigroup, **15** 50
UniHealth America, **11** 378–79
Unik S.A., **23** 170–171
Unilab Corp., **26** 391
Unilac Inc., **II** 547
Unilever PLC/Unilever N.V., **I** 369, 590, 605; **II** 547, **588–91**; **III** 31–32, 46, 52, 495; **IV** 532; **7** 382, **542–45 (upd.)**, 577; **8** 105–07, 166, 168, 341, 344; **9** 449; **11** 205, 421; **13** 243–44; **14** 204–05; **18** 395, 397; **19** 193; **21** 219; **22** 123; **23** 242; **26** 306; **28** 183, 185; **30** 396–97
Unilife Assurance Group, **III** 273
UniLife Insurance Co., **22** 149
UniMac Companies, **11** 413
Unimat, **II** 265
Unimation, **II** 122
Unimetal, **IV** 227; **30** 252
Uninsa, **I** 460
Union, **III** 391–93
Union & NHK Auto Parts, **III** 580
Union Acceptances Ltd., **IV** 23
Unión Aérea Española, **6** 95
Union Aéromaritime de Transport. *See* UTA.
Union Assurance, **III** 234
Union Bag–Camp Paper Corp., **IV** 344–45
Union Bancorp of California, **II** 358
Union Bank. *See* State Street Boston Corporation.
Union Bank of Australia, **II** 187–89
Union Bank of Birmingham, **II** 318; **17** 323
Union Bank of California, **16 496–98**
Union Bank of Canada, **II** 344
Union Bank of England, **II** 188
Union Bank of Finland, **II** 302, 352
Union Bank of Halifax, **II** 344
Union Bank of London, **II** 235
Union Bank of New London, **II** 213
Union Bank of New York, **9** 229
Union Bank of Prince Edward Island, **II** 220
Union Bank of Scotland, **10** 337
Union Bank of Switzerland, **II** 257, 267, 334, 369, 370, **378–79**; **21** 146
Union Battery Co., **III** 536
Union Bay Sportswear, **17** 460
Union Camp Corporation, **IV 344–46**; **8** 102
Union Carbide Corporation, **I** 334, 339, 347, 374, 390, **399–401**, 582, 666; **II** 103, 313, 562; **III** 742, 760; **IV** 92, 374, 379, 521; **7** 376; **8** 180, 182, 376; **9** 16, **516–20 (upd.)**; **10** 289, 472; **11** 402–03; **12** 46, 347; **13** 118; **14** 281–82; **16** 461; **17** 159; **18** 235; **22** 228, 235
Union Cervecera, **9** 100
Union Colliery Company, **V** 741
Union Commerce Corporation, **11** 181
Union Commerciale, **19** 98
Union Corporation. *See* Gencor Ltd.
Union d'Etudes et d'Investissements, **II** 265
Union des Assurances de Paris, **II** 234; **III** 201, **391–94**
Union des Coopératives Bressor, **25** 85
Union des Cooperatives Laitières. *See* Unicoolait.
Union des Transports Aériens. *See* UTA.
Union Electric Company, **V** 741–43; **6** 505–06; **26** 451
Union Electrica de Canarias S.A., **V** 607
Union Equity Co-Operative Exchange, **7** 175
Union et Prévoyance, **III** 403
Union Fertilizer, **I** 412
Union Fidelity Corp., **III** 204
Union Financiera, **19** 189
Union Gas & Electric Co., **6** 529
Union Générale de Savonnerie, **III** 33
l'Union Générale des Pétroles, **IV** 545–46, 560; **7** 482–83
Union Glass Co., **III** 683
Union Hardware, **III** 443; **22** 115
Union Hop Growers, **I** 287
Union Laitière Normande, **19** 50. *See also* Compagnie Laitière Européenne.
Union Levantina de Seguros, **III** 179
Union Light, Heat & Power Company, **6** 466
Union Marine, **III** 372
Union Mutual Life Insurance Company. *See* UNUM Corp.
Union National Bank, **II** 284; **10** 298
Union National Bank of Wilmington, **25** 540
Union of European Football Association, **27** 150
Union of Food Co-ops, **II** 622
Union of London, **II** 333
Union Oil Associates, **IV** 569
Union Oil Co., **9** 266
Union Oil Co. of California, **I** 13; **IV** 385, 400, 403, 434, 522, 531, 540, 569, 575; **11** 271. *See also* Unocal Corporation.
Union Pacific Corporation, **I** 473; **II** 381; **III** 229; **V 529–32**; **12** 18–20, 278; **14** 371–72; **28 492–500 (upd.)**
Union Pacific Tea Co., **7** 202
Union Paper Bag Machine Co., **IV** 344
Union Petroleum Corp., **IV** 394
L'Union pour le Developement Régional, **II** 265
Union Power Company, **12** 541
Union Rückversicherungs-Gesellschaft, **III** 377
Union Savings, **II** 316
Union Savings and Loan Association of Phoenix, **19** 412
Union Savings Bank, **9** 173
Union Savings Bank and Trust Company, **13** 221
Union Steam Ship Co., **IV** 279; **19** 154
Union Steamship Co. of New Zealand Ltd., **27** 473
Union Steel Co., **IV** 22, 572; **7** 550
Union Sugar, **II** 573
Union Sulphur Co., **IV** 81; **7** 185
Union Supply Co., **IV** 573; **7** 550
Union Tank Car Co., **IV** 137
Union Telephone Company, **14** 258
Union Texas Petroleum Holdings, Inc., **I** 415; **7** 379; **9 521–23**; **22** 31
Union Trust Co., **II** 284, 313, 315–16, 382; **9** 228; **13** 222
The Union Underwear Company, **I** 440–41; **8** 200–01; **25** 164–66
Union Wine, **I** 289
Union-Capitalisation, **III** 392
Union-Transport, **6** 404; **26** 243
Unionamerica, Inc., **16** 497
Unionamerica Insurance Group, **III** 243
UnionBay Sportswear Co., **27** 112
Unione Manifatture, S.p.A., **19** 338
Unique Casual Restaurants, Inc., **27 480–82**

Uniroy of Hempstead, Inc. *See* Aris Industries, Inc.
Uniroyal Corp., **I** 30–31; **II** 472; **V** 242; **8** 503; **11** 159; **20** 262
Uniroyal Holdings Ltd., **21** 73
Unishops, Inc. *See* Aris Industries, Inc.
Unison HealthCare Corporation, 25 503–05
Unisource, **I** 413
Unistar Radio Networks, **23** 510
Unisys Corporation, **II** 42; **III 165–67**; **6 281–83 (upd.)**; **8** 92; **9** 32, 59; **12** 149, 162; **17** 11, 262; **18** 345, 386, 434, 542; **21** 86
The Unit Companies, Inc., **6** 394, 396; **25** 170
Unit Group plc, **8** 477
Unitech plc, **27** 81
United Acquisitions, **7** 114; **25** 125
United Advertising Periodicals, **12** 231
United Agri Products, **II** 494
United AgriSeeds, Inc., **21** 387
United Air Express. *See* United Parcel Service of America Inc.
United Air Fleet, **23** 408
United Aircraft and Transportation Co., **I** 48, 76, 78, 85–86, 96, 441, 489; **9** 416, 418; **10** 162, 260; **12** 289; **21** 140
United Airlines, **I** 23, 47, 71, 84, 90, 97, 113, 116, 118, 124, **128–30**; **II** 142, 419, 680; **III** 225; **6** 71, 75–77, 104, 121, 123, **128–30 (upd.)**, 131, 388–89; **9** 271–72, 283, 416, 549; **10** 162, 199, 301, 561; **11** 299; **12** 192, 381; **14** 73; **21** 141; **22** 199, 220; **24** 21, 22; **25** 146, 148, 421–23; **26** 113, 338–39, 440; **27** 20; **29** 507
United Alaska Drilling, Inc., **7** 558
United Alkalai Co., **I** 351
United Alloy Steel Company, **26** 405
United American Insurance Company of Dallas, **9** 508
United American Lines, **6** 398
United Arab Airlines. *See* EgyptAir.
United Artists Corp., **I** 537; **II** 135, 146–48, 149, 157–58, 160, 167, 169; **III** 721; **IV** 676; **6** 167; **9** 74; **12** 13, 73; **13** 529; **14** 87, 399; **21** 362; **23** 389; **26** 487. *See also* MGM/UA Communications Company *and* Metro-Goldwyn-Mayer Inc.
United Auto Group, Inc., 26 500–02
United Bank of Arizona, **II** 358
United Biscuits (Holdings) PLC, **II** 466, 540, **592–94**; **III** 503; **26** 59
United Brands Company, **II 595–97**; **III** 28; **7** 84–85; **12** 215; **21** 110, 112; **25** 4
United Breweries Ltd. **I** 221, 223, 288; **24** 449. *See also* Carlsberg A/S.
United Broadcasting Corporation Public Company Ltd., **31** 330
United Cable Television Corporation, **II** 160; **9** 74; **18** 65
United California Bank, **II** 289
United Car, **I** 540; **14** 511
United Carbon Co., **IV** 373
United Central Oil Corporation, **7** 101
United Cigar Manufacturers Company, **II** 414. *See also* Culbro Corporation.
United City Property Trust, **IV** 705
United Co., **I** 70
United Communications Systems, Inc. **V** 346
United Computer Services, Inc., **11** 111
United Consolidated Industries, **24** 204
United Corp., **10** 44
United County Banks, **II** 235
United Dairies, **II** 586–87
United Dairy Farmers, **III** 190
United Defense, L.P., 30 471–73
United Distillers & Vintners. *See* Diageo plc.
United Dominion Corp., **III** 200
United Dominion Industries Limited, **IV** 288; **8 544–46**; **16 499–502 (upd.)**
United Drapery Stores, **III** 502; **7** 208
United Drug Co., **II** 533
United Electric Light and Water Co., **13** 182
United Engineering Steels, **III** 495
United Engineers & Constructors, **II** 86; **11** 413
United Express, **11** 299
United Factors Corp., **13** 534–35
United Features Syndicate, Inc., **IV** 607–08
United Federal Savings and Loan of Waycross, **10** 92
United Financial Corporation, **12** 353
United Financial Group, Inc., **8** 349
United 5 and 10 Cent Stores, **13** 444
United Foods, Inc., 21 508–11
United Fruit Co., **I** 529, 566; **II** 120, 595; **IV** 308; **7** 84–85; **21** 110–11
United Funds, Inc., **22** 540–41
United Gas and Electric Company of New Albany, **6** 555
United Gas and Improvement Co., **13** 182
United Gas Corp., **IV** 488–90
United Gas Improvement Co., **IV** 549; **V** 696; **6** 446, 523; **11** 388
United Gas Industries, **III** 502; **7** 208
United Gas Pipe Line Co., **IV** 489–90
United Geophysical Corp., **I** 142
United Graphics, **12** 25
United Grocers, **II** 625
United Guaranty Corp., **III** 197
United Health Maintenance, Inc., **6** 181–82
United HealthCare Corporation, 9 524–26; **24** 229, 231. *See also* Humana Inc.
The United Illuminating Company, 21 512–14
United Image Entertainment, **18** 64, 66
United Independent Broadcasters, Inc., **II** 132
United Industrial Syndicate, **8** 545
United Information Systems, Inc., **V** 346
United Insurance Co., **I** 523
Oy United International, **IV** 349
United International Holdings Inc., **28** 198
United International Pictures, **II** 155
United Investors Life, **22** 540
United Iron & Metal Co., **14** 156
United Kent Fire, **III** 350
United Kingdom Atomic Energy Authority, **6** 451–52
United Knitting, Inc., **21** 192, 194
United Liberty Life Insurance Co., **III** 190–92
United Life & Accident Insurance Co., **III** 220–21; **14** 109
United Life Insurance Company, **12** 541
United Light & Railway Co., **V** 609
United Light and Power, **6** 511
United Machinery Co., **15** 127
United Match Factories, **12** 462
United Media, **22** 442
United Medical Service, Inc., **III** 245–46
United Merchandising Corp., **12** 477
United Merchants & Manufacturers, Inc., 13 534–37; **31** 160
United Meridian Corporation, **8** 350
United Metals Selling Co., **IV** 31
United Microelectronics Corporation, **22** 197
United Micronesian, **I** 97; **21** 142
United Molasses, **II** 582
United Mortgage Servicing, **16** 133
United Natural Gas Company, **6** 526
United Netherlands Navigation Company. *See* Vereenigde Nederlandsche Scheepvaartmaatschappij.
United News & Media plc, 28 501–05 (upd.)
United Newspapers plc, IV 685–87
United of Omaha, **III** 365
United Office Products, **11** 64
United Oil Co., **IV** 399
United Optical, **10** 151
United Pacific Financial Services, **III** 344
United Pacific Insurance Co., **III** 343
United Pacific Life Insurance Co., **III** 343–44
United Pacific Reliance Life Insurance Co. of New York, **III** 343
United Packages, **IV** 249
United Paper Mills Ltd., **II** 302; **IV** 316, **347–50**
United Paramount Network, **25** 418–19; **26** 32; **31** 109
United Paramount Theatres, **II** 129
United Parcel Service of America Inc., **V 533–35**; **6** 345–46, 385–86, 390; **11** 11; **12** 309, 334; **13** 19, 416; **14** 517; **17 503–06 (upd.)**; **18** 82, 177, 315–17; **24** 22, 133; **25** 148, 150, 356; **27** 471, 475
United Pipeline Co., **IV** 394
United Power and Light Corporation, **6** 473; **12** 541
United Presidential Life Insurance Company, **12** 524, 526
United Press International, Inc., **IV** 607, 627, 669–70; **7** 158–59; **16** 166; **19** 203; **22** 453; **25 506–09**
United Railways & Electric Company, **25** 44
United Refining Co., **23** 406, 408
United Rentals Inc., **28** 386, 388
United Resources, Inc., **21** 514
United Retail Merchants Stores Inc., **9** 39
United Roasters, **III** 24; **14** 121
United Satellite Television, **10** 320
United Savings of Texas, **8** 349
United Servomation, **7** 471–72
United Shirt Shops, Inc. *See* Aris Industries, Inc.
United Skates of America, **8** 303
United Software Consultants Inc., **11** 65
United States Aluminum Co., **17** 213
United States Aviation Underwriters, Inc., **24** 176
United States Baking Co., **II** 542
United States Can Co., **15** 127, 129
United States Cellular Corporation, **9** 494–96, **527–29**. *See also* U.S. Cellular Corporation.
United States Department of Defense, **6** 327
United States Distributing Corp., **IV** 180–82
United States Electric and Gas Company, **6** 447

United States Electric Light and Power Company, **25** 44
The United States Electric Lighting Company, **11** 387
United States Export-Import Bank, **IV** 55
United States Express Co., **II** 381, 395–96; **10** 59–60; **12** 534
United States Fidelity and Guaranty Co., **III** 395
United States Filter Corporation, **I** 429; **IV** 374; **20 501–04**
United States Foil Co., **IV** 186; **19** 346
United States Football League, **29** 347
United States Glucose Co., **II** 496
United States Graphite Company, **V** 221–22
United States Gypsum Co., **III** 762–64
United States Health Care Systems, Inc. *See* U.S. Healthcare, Inc.
United States Independent Telephone Company, **6** 332
United States Leasing Corp., **II** 442
United States Mail Steamship Co., **23** 160
United States Medical Finance Corp., **18** 516, 518
United States Mortgage & Trust Company, **II** 251; **14** 102
United States National Bancshares, **25** 114
United States National Bank of Galveston. *See* Cullen/Frost Bankers, Inc.
United States National Bank of Oregon, **14** 527
The United States National Bank of Portland, **14** 527–28
United States National Bank of San Diego, **II** 355
United States Pipe and Foundry Co., **III** 766; **22** 544–45
United States Plywood Corp., **IV** 264, 282, 341; **9** 260; **13** 100; **20** 128
United States Postal Service, **10** 60; **14 517–20**
United States Realty-Sheraton Corp., **III** 98
United States Satellite Broadcasting Company Inc., **24** 226
United States Security Trust Co., **13** 466
United States Shoe Corporation, **V 207–08**; **17** 296, 390; **23** 328
United States Steel Corp., **I** 298, 491; **II** 129, 330; **III** 282, 326, 379; **IV** 35, 56, 110, 158, 572–74; **6** 514; **7** 48, 70–73, 401–02, 549–51; **10** 32; **11** 194; **12** 353–54; **17** 350, 356; **18** 378; **26** 405, 451. *See also* USX Corporation.
United States Sugar Refining Co., **II** 496
United States Surgical Corporation, **10 533–35**; **13** 365; **21** 119–20; **28** 486
United States Tobacco Company, **9** 533
United States Trucking Corp., **IV** 180–81
United States Trust Co. of New York. *See* U.S. Trust Corp.
United States Underseas Cable Corp., **IV** 178
United States Zinc Co., **IV** 32
United Stationers Inc., **14 521–23**; **25** 13
United Steel, **III** 494
United Steel Mills Ltd., **25** 266
United Supers, **II** 624
United Technologies Automotive Inc., **15 513–15**
United Technologies Corporation, **I** 68, **84–86**, 143, 411, 530, 559; **II** 64, 82; **III** 74; **9** 18, 418; **10 536–38 (upd.)**; **11** 308; **12** 289; **13** 191, 384–86; **22** 6
United Telecommunications, Inc., **V 344–47**; **8** 310; **9** 478–80; **10** 202; **12** 541
United Telephone Company, **7** 508; **14** 257
United Telephone Company of the Carolinas, **10** 202
United Telephone of Indiana, **14** 259
United Telephone System, Inc., **V** 346
United Telespectrum, **6** 314
United Television, Inc., **9** 119; **26** 32
United Television Programs, **II** 143
United Transportation Co., **6** 382
United Truck Lines, **14** 505
United Utilities, Inc., **V** 344; **10** 202
United Van Lines, **14** 37; **15** 50
United Verde Copper Co., **IV** 178
United Video Satellite Group, **18 535–37**
United Vintners, **I** 243, 260–61
United Westburne Inc., **19** 313
United Westphalia Electricity Co., **IV** 127
United-American Car, **13** 305
Unitek Corp., **III** 18
Unitel Communications, **6** 311
Unitika Ltd., **V 387–89**
Unitog Co., **16** 228; **19 457–60**; **21** 115
Unitransa, **27** 474
Unitrin Inc., **16 503–05**
Unitron Medical Communications, **29** 412
Unity Financial Corp., **19** 411
Unity Joint-Stock Bank, **II** 334
UNIVAC, **III** 133, 152, 313; **6** 233, 240, 266
Univar Corporation, **8** 99; **9 530–32**; **12** 333
Univas, **13** 203 **23** 171
Universal Adding Machine, **III** 165
Universal American, **I** 452
Universal Atlas Cement Co., **IV** 573–74; **7** 550–51
Universal Belo Productions, **10** 5
Universal Cheerleaders Association. *See* Varsity Spirit Corp.
Universal Cigar Corp., **14** 19
Universal Consumer Products Group, **30** 123
Universal Containers, **IV** 249
Universal Controls, Inc., **10** 319
Universal Cooler Corp., **8** 515
Universal Corporation, **V 417–18**
Universal Data Systems, **II** 61; **22** 17
Universal Foods Corporation, **7 546–48**; **21** 498
Universal Footcare Products Inc., **31** 255
Universal Forest Products Inc., **10 539–40**
Universal Frozen Foods, **23** 321
Universal Furniture, **III** 571; **20** 362
Universal Genève, **13** 121
Universal Guaranty Life Insurance Company, **11** 482
Universal Health Services, Inc., **6 191–93**
Universal Highways, **III** 735
Universal Industries, Inc., **10** 380; **13** 533
Universal Instruments Corp., **III** 468
Universal International, Inc., **25** 353, 355, **510–11**
Universal Juice Co., **21** 55
Universal Leaf Tobacco Company. *See* Universal Corporation.
Universal Manufacturing, **I** 440–41; **25** 167
Universal Marking Systems, **25** 331
Universal Match, **12** 464
Universal Matchbox Group, **12** 495
Universal Matthey Products Ltd., **IV** 119
Universal Music Group, **22** 194; **26** 152
Universal Paper Bag Co., **IV** 345
Universal Pictures, **II** 102, 135, 144, 154–55, 157; **10** 196; **14** 399; **25** 271. *See also* Universal Studios, Inc.
Universal Press Syndicate, **10** 4
Universal Records, **27** 123
Universal Resources Corporation, **6** 569; **26** 388
Universal Shoes, Inc., **22** 213
Universal Stamping Machine Co., **III** 156
Universal Studios Florida, **14** 399
Universal Studios, Inc., **II** 143–44; **12** 73; **21** 23–26; **25** 411
Universal Telephone, **9** 106
Universal Television, **II** 144
Universal Textured Yarns, **12** 501
Universal Transfers Co. Ltd., **IV** 119
University Computing Corp., **II** 38; **11** 468; **17** 320; **25** 87
University Microfilms, **III** 172; **6** 289
University of Phoenix, **24** 40
Univisa, **24** 516
Univision Communications Inc., **IV** 621; **18** 213; **24 515–18**
UNIX, **6** 225; **25** 20–21
UNM. *See* United News & Media plc.
Uno Restaurant Corporation, **16** 447; **18** 465, **538–40**
Uno-Ven, **IV** 571; **24** 522
Unocal Corporation, **IV** 508, **569–71**; **24 519–23 (upd.)**
UNR Industries, Inc. *See* ROHN Industries, Inc.
Unterberg Harris, **25** 433
UNUM Corp., **III** 236; **13 538–40**
Uny Co., Ltd., **II** 619; **V 209–10**, 154; **13** 545
UPI. *See* United Press International.
Upjohn Company, **I** 675, 684, 686, 700, **707–09**; **III** 18, 53; **6** 42; **8 547–49 (upd.)**; **10** 79; **12** 186; **13** 503; **14** 423; **16** 440; **29** 363. *See also* Pharmacia & Upjohn Inc.
UPM-Kymmene Corporation, **19 461–65**; **25** 12; **30** 325
UPN. *See* United Paramount Network.
UPS. *See* United Parcel Service of America Inc.
UPSHOT, **27** 195
Upton Machine Company, **12** 548
Uraga Dock Co., **II** 361; **III** 634
Uraga Heavy Industries, **III** 634
Urbaine, **III** 391–92
Urban Investment and Development Co., **IV** 703
Urban Outfitters, Inc., **14 524–26**
Urban Systems Development Corp., **II** 121
Urenco, **6** 452
Urwick Orr, **II** 609
US Airways Group, Inc., **28 506–09 (upd.)**
US Industrial Chemicals, Inc., **I** 377; **8** 440
US Industries Inc., **30** 231
US 1 Industries, **27** 404
US Order, Inc., **10** 560, 562
US Sprint Communications Company, **V** 295–96, 346–47; **6** 314; **8** 310; **9** 32; **10** 543; **11** 302; **12** 136, 541; **14** 252–53; **15** 196; **16** 318, 392; **25** 101; **29** 44. *See also* Sprint Communications Company, L.P.
US Telecom, **9** 478–79

US West Communications Services, Inc., **19** 255; **21** 285; **29** 39, 45, 478. *See also* Regional Bell Operating Companies.
USA Cafes, **14** 331
USA Floral Products Inc., **27** 126
USA Networks Inc., **25** 330, 411
USA Security Systems, Inc., **27** 21
USAA, 10 541–43
USAir Group, Inc., I 55, **131–32**; **III** 215; **6** 121, **131–32 (upd.)**; **11** 300; **14** 70, 73; **18** 62; **21** 143; **24** 400; **26** 429. *See also* US Airways Group, Inc.
USANA, Inc., 27 353; **29 491–93**
USCC. *See* United States Cellular Corporation.
USCP-WESCO Inc., **II** 682
USF&G Corporation, III 395–98; **11** 494–95; **19** 190
USFL. *See* United States Football League.
USFreightways, **27** 475
USG Corporation, III 762–64; **26 507–10 (upd.)**
Usines de l'Espérance, **IV** 226
Usines Métallurgiques de Hainaut, **IV** 52
Usinor Sacilor, IV 226–28; **22** 44; **24** 144; **26** 81, 84
USLD Communications Corp. *See* Billing Concepts Corp.
USLIFE, **III** 194
USM, **10** 44
USSC. *See* United States Surgical Corporation.
USSI. *See* U.S. Software Inc.
UST Inc., 9 533–35
USV Pharmaceutical Corporation, **11** 333
USX Corporation, I 466; **IV** 130, 228, **572–74**; **7** 193–94, **549–52 (upd.)**
UTA, **I** 119, 121; **6** 373–74, 93
Utag, **11** 510
Utah Construction & Mining Co., **I** 570; **IV** 146; **14** 296
Utah Federal Savings Bank, **17** 530
Utah Gas and Coke Company, **6** 568
Utah Group Health Plan, **6** 184
Utah International, **II** 30; **12** 196
Utah Medical Products Inc., **29** 320–21
Utah Mines Ltd., **IV** 47; **22** 107
Utah Oil Refining Co., **IV** 370
Utah Power and Light Company, 9 536; **12** 266; **27 483–86**. *See also* PacifiCorp.
UTI Energy Corp., **12** 500
Utilicom, **6** 572
Utilicorp United Inc., 6 592–94
Utilities Power & Light Corporation, **I** 512; **6** 508
Utility Constructors Incorporated, **6** 527
Utility Engineering Corporation, **6** 580
Utility Fuels, **7** 377
Utility Supply Co. *See* United Stationers Inc.
AB Utra Wood Co., **IV** 274
Utrecht Allerlei Risico's, **III** 200
UUNET WorldCom. *See* MCI WorldCom, Inc.
UV Industries, Inc., **7** 360; **9** 440

V & V Cos., **I** 412
V&S Variety Stores, **V** 37
V.A.W. of America Inc., **IV** 231
V.L. Churchill Group, **10** 493
Vabis, **I** 197
Vacheron Constantin, **27** 487, 489
Vaculator Division. *See* Lancer Corporation.
Vacuum Metallurgical Company, **11** 234
Vacuum Oil Co., **IV** 463–64, 504, 549; **7** 351–52
Vadic Corp., **II** 83
Vadoise Vie, **III** 273
Vagnfabriks A.B., **I** 197
Vail Associates, Inc., 11 543–46; **31** 65, 67
Val Corp., **24** 149
Val Royal LaSalle, **II** 652
Val-Pak Direct Marketing Systems, Inc., **22** 162
Valassis Communications, Inc., 8 550–51
Valcambi S.A., **II** 268; **21** 145
Valcom, **13** 176
ValCom Inc. *See* InaCom Corporation.
Valdi Foods Inc., **II** 663–64
Valdosta Drug Co., **III** 9–10
Vale Harmon Enterprises, Ltd., **25** 204
Vale Power Company, **12** 265
Valentine & Company, **8** 552–53
Valeo, III 593; **23 492–94**
Valero Energy Corporation, IV 394; **7 553–55**; **19** 140; **31** 119
Valhi, Inc., 10 435–36; **19 466–68**
Valid Logic Systems Inc., **11** 46, 284
Valio-Finnish Co-operative Dairies' Assoc., **II** 575
Valke Oy, **IV** 348
Valley Bank of Nevada, **19** 378
Valley Crest Tree Company, **31** 182–83
Valley Deli Inc., **24** 243
Valley East Medical Center, **6** 185
Valley Falls Co., **III** 213
Valley Fashions Corp., **16** 535
Valley Federal of California, **11** 163
Valley Fig Growers, **7** 496–97
Valley Forge Life Insurance Co., **III** 230
Valley National Bank, **II** 420
Valley Transport Co., **II** 569
Valley-Todeco, Inc., **13** 305–06
Valleyfair, **22** 130
Vallourec, **IV** 227
Valmac Industries, **II** 585
Valmet Corporation, I 198; **III 647–49**; **IV** 276, 350, 471
Valmet Oy. *See* Metso Corporation.
Valmont Industries, Inc., 13 276; **19** 50, **469–72**
Valores Industriales S.A., 19 10, 12, 189, **473–75**; **29** 219
The Valspar Corporation, 8 552–54
Valtec Industries, **III** 684
Valtek International, Inc., **17** 147
Valtur, **6** 207
Value America, **29** 312
Value City Department Stores, **29** 311
Value Foods Ltd., **11** 239
Value Giant Stores, **12** 478
Value House, **II** 673
Value Investors, **III** 330
Value Line, Inc., 16 506–08
Value Merchants Inc., 13 541–43
Value Rent-A-Car, **9** 350; **23** 354
Valueland, **8** 482
ValueVision International, Inc., 22 534–36; **27** 337
ValuJet, Inc. *See* AirTran Holdings, Inc.
Valvoline, Inc., **I** 291; **IV** 374
Valvtron, **11** 226
Van Ameringen-Haebler, Inc., **9** 290
Van Brunt Manufacturing Co., **III** 462; **21** 173
Van Camp Seafood Company, Inc., II 562–63; **7 556–57**; **13** 426. *See also* Chicken of the Sea International.
Van Cleef & Arpels Inc., **26** 145
Van de Kamp, **II** 556–57; **7** 430
Van den Bergh Foods, **II** 588; **9** 319
Van der Horst Corp. of America, **III** 471
Van Dorn Company, **13** 190
Van Dorn Electric Tool Co., **III** 435
Van Gend and Loos, **6** 404; **26** 241, 243
Van Houton, **II** 521
Van Kirk Chocolate, **7** 429
Van Kok-Ede, **II** 642
Van Leer Containers Inc., **30** 397
Van Leer Holding, Inc., **9** 303, 305
Van Leer N.V. *See* Royal Packaging Industries Van Leer N.V.
Van Mar, Inc., **18** 88
Van Munching & Company, Inc., **I** 256; **13** 257, 259
Van Nostrand Reinhold, **8** 526
Van Ryn Gold Mines Estate, **IV** 90
Van Schaardenburg, **II** 528
Van Sickle, **IV** 485
Van Waters & Rogers, **8** 99
Van Wezel, **26** 278–79
Van Wijcks Waalsteenfabrieken, **14** 249
Vanadium Alloys Steel Company (VASCO), **13** 295–96
Vanant Packaging Corporation, **8** 359
Vance International Airways, **8** 349
Vancouver Pacific Paper Co., **IV** 286
Vanderbilt Mortgage and Finance, **13** 154
Vanderlip-Swenson-Tilghman Syndicate, **IV** 81; **7** 185
Vanessa and Biffi, **11** 226
The Vanguard Group of Investment Companies, 9 239; **14 530–32**
Vanity Fair Mills, Inc., **V** 390–91
Vanity Fair Paper Mills, **IV** 281; **9** 259
Vans, Inc., 16 509–11; **17** 259–61
Vansickle Industries, **III** 603
Vanstar, **13** 176
Vantage Analysis Systems, Inc., **11** 490
Vantona Group Ltd., **V** 356
Vantress Pedigree, Inc., **II** 585
Vapor Corp., **III** 444
Varco-Pruden, Inc., **8** 544–46
Vare Corporation, **8** 366
Variable Annuity Life Insurance Co., **III** 193–94
Varian Associates Inc., 12 504–06
Varibus Corporation, **6** 495
Variform, Inc., **12** 397
VARIG S.A. (Viação Aérea Rio-Grandense), 6 133–35; **26** 113; **29 494–97 (upd.)**; **31** 443–45
Varity Corporation, III 650–52; **7** 258, 260; **19** 294; **27** 203, 251
Varlen Corporation, 16 512–14
Varney Air Lines, **I** 47, 128; **6** 128; **9** 416
Varney Speed Lines. *See* Continental Airlines, Inc.
Varo, **7** 235, 237
Varsity Spirit Corp., 15 516–18; **22** 459
Varta AG, III 536; **9** 180–81; **23 495–99**; **26** 230
Vasco Metals Corp., **I** 523; **10** 520, 522
Vascoloy-Ramet, **13** 295
VASP (Viaçao Aérea de Sao Paulo), **6** 134; **29** 495; **31** 444–45
Vasset, S.A., **17** 362–63
Vastar Resources, Inc., 24 524–26
Vaughan Harmon Systems Ltd., **25** 204

Vaughan Printers Inc., **23** 100
Vaungarde, Inc., **22** 175
Vauxhall, **19** 391
VAW Leichtmetall GmbH, **IV** 231
VBB Viag-Bayernwerk-Beteiligungs-Gesellschaft mbH, **IV** 232
VDM Nickel-Technologie AG, **IV** 89
VEB Londa, **III** 69
Veba A.G., **I** 349–50, **542–43**; **III** 695; **IV** 194–95, 199, 455, 508; **8** 69, 494–495; **15** **519–21 (upd.)**; **23** 69, 451, 453–54; **24** 79; **25** 102; **26** 423
VECO International, Inc., **7** **558–59**
Vector Automotive Corporation, **13** 61
Vector Casa de Bolsa, **21** 413
Vector Gas Ltd., **13** 458
Vector Video, Inc., **9** 74
Vedelectric, **13** 544
Vedior International, **13** 544–45
Veeder-Root Company, **7** 116–17
Vel-Tex Chemical, **16** 270
Velcarta S.p.A., **17** 281
Velcro Industries N.V., **19** **476–78**
Velda Farms, Inc., **26** 448
Vellumoid Co., **I** 159
VeloBind, Inc., **10** 314
Velsicol, **I** 342, 440
Velva-Sheen Manufacturing Co., **23** 66
Vemar, **7** 558
Vencemos, **20** 124
Vencor, Inc., **IV** 402; **14** 243; **16** **515–17**; **25** 456
Vendex International N.V., **10** 136–37; **13** **544–46**; **26** 160
Vendôme Luxury Group plc, **27** **487–89**; **29** 90, 92
Vendors Supply of America, Inc., **7** 241–42; **25** 241
Venevision, **24** 516, 517
Vennootschap Nederland, **III** 177–78
Ventura, **29** 356–57
Venture Out RV, **26** 193
Venture Stores Inc., **V** 134; **12** **507–09**
Venturi, Inc., **9** 72
Vepco. *See* Virginia Electric and Power Company.
Vera Cruz Electric Light, Power and Traction Co. Ltd., **IV** 658
Vera Imported Parts, **11** 84
Verafumos Ltd., **12** 109
Veragon Corporation. *See* Drypers Corporation.
Veratex Group, **13** 149–50
Veravision, **24** 510
Verbatim Corporation, **III** 477; **7** 163; **14** **533–35**
Verd-A-Fay, **13** 398
Vereenigde Nederlandsche Scheepvaartmaatschappij, **6** 404; **26** 242
Vereeniging Refractories, **IV** 22
Vereeniging Tiles, **III** 734
Verein für Chemische Industrie, **IV** 70
Vereinigte Aluminium Werke AG, **IV** 229–30, 232
Vereinigte Deutsche Metallwerke AG, **IV** 140
Vereinigte Elektrizitäts und Bergwerke A.G., **I** 542
Vereinigte Elektrizitätswerke Westfalen AG, **IV** 195; **V** **744–47**
Vereinigte Energiewerke AG, **V** 709
Vereinigte Flugtechnische Werke GmbH., **I** 42, 55, 74–75
Vereinigte Glanzstoff-Fabriken, **13** 21
Vereinigte Industrie-Unternehmungen Aktiengesellschaft, **IV** 229–30
Vereinigte Leichmetall-Werke GmbH, **IV** 231
Vereinigte Papierwarenfabriken GmbH, **IV** 323
Vereinigte Papierwerke Schickedanz AG, **26** 384
Vereinigte Stahlwerke AG, **III** 565; **IV** 87, 104–05, 132, 221; **14** 327
Vereinigte Versicherungsgruppe, **III** 377
Vereinigten Westdeutsche Waggonfabriken AG, **III** 542–43
Vereinsbank Wismar, **II** 256
Vereinte Versicherungen, **III** 377
Verenigde Bedrijven Bredero, **26** 280
N.V. Verenigde Fabrieken Wessanen and Laan, **II** 527
Verenigde Nederlandse Uitgeverijen. *See* VNU N.V.
Verenigde Spaarbank Groep. *See* VSB Groep.
Verienigte Schweizerbahnen, **6** 424
VeriFone, Inc., **15** 321; **18** **541–44**; **27** 219–21; **28** 191
Verilyte Gold, Inc., **19** 452
Veritas Capital Partners, **26** 408
Veritus Inc., **27** 208–09
Verlagsgruppe Georg von Holtzbrinck GmbH, **15** 158, 160; **25** 485
Vermeer Manufacturing Company, **17** **507–10**
Vermont Teddy Bear Company, **31** 479
Verneuil Holding Co, **21** 387
Vernitron Corporation, **18** 293
Vernon and Nelson Telephone Company. *See* British Columbia Telephone Company.
Vernon Graphics, **III** 499
Vernon Paving, **III** 674
Vernon Savings & Loan, **9** 199
Vernons, **IV** 651
Vernors, Inc., **25** 4
Vero, **III** 434
La Verrerie Souchon-Neuvesel, **II** 474
Verreries Champenoises, **II** 475
Versace. *See* Gianni Versace SpA.
Versatec Inc., **13** 128
Versatile Farm and Equipment Co., **22** 380
Versax, S.A. de C.V., **19** 12
Versicherungs-Verein, **III** 402, 410–11
Verson Allsteel Press Co., **21** 20, 22
Vert Baudet, **19** 309
Vertical Technology Industries, **14** 571
Verticom, **25** 531
Verve Records, **23** 389
Vessel Management Services, Inc., **28** 80
Vestek Systems, Inc., **13** 417
Vestro, **19** 309
Vesuvius Crucible Co., **III** 681
Vesuvius USA Corporation, **8** 179
Veszpremtej, **25** 85
Veterinary Cos. of America, **III** 25
VEW, **IV** 234
Vexlar, **18** 313
VF Corporation, **V** **390–92**; **12** 205; **13** 512; **17** 223, 225, **511–14 (upd.)**; **25** 22; **31** 261
VFW-Fokker B.V., **I** 41, 55, 74–75
VHA Long Term Care, **23** 431
VH1 Inc., **23** 503
VI-Jon Laboratories, Inc., **12** 388
VIA/Rhin et Moselle, **III** 185
Via-Générale de Transport et d'Industrie SA, **28** 155
Viacao Aerea Rio Grandense of South America. *See* VARIG, SA.
Viacom Enterprises, **6** 33; **7** 336
Viacom Inc., **23** 274–76, **500–03 (upd.)**; **24** 106, 327; **26** 32; **28** 295; **30** 101; **31** 59, 109. *See also* National Amusements Inc.
Viacom International Inc., **7** 222–24, 530, **560–62**; **9** 429; **10** 175; **19** 403
Viag AG, **IV** **229–32**, 323; **25** 332
Viajes El Corte Inglés, S.A., **26** 129
VIASA, **I** 107; **6** 97
Viasoft Inc., **27** **490–93**
Viatech Continental Can Company, Inc., **25** **512–15 (upd.)**
Vichy, **III** 46
Vickers Inc., **III** 640, 642; **13** 8; **23** 83
Vickers plc, **I** 194–95; **II** 3; **III** 555, 652, 725; **16** 9; **21** 435; **27** **494–97**
Vickers-Armstrong Ltd., **I** 50, 57, 82; **24** 85
Vicoreen Instrument Co., **I** 202
VICORP Restaurants, Inc., **12** **510–12**
Vicra Sterile Products, **I** 628
Vicsodrive Japan, **III** 495
Victor Company, **10** 483
Victor Company of Japan, Ltd., **I** 411; **II** 55–56, 91, 102, **118–19**; **III** 605; **IV** 599; **12** 454; **26** **511–13 (upd.)**
Victor Comptometer, **I** 676; **III** 154
Victor Equipment Co., **19** 440
Victor Manufacturing and Gasket Co., **I** 152
Victor Musical Industries Inc., **II** 119; **10** 285
Victor Talking Machine Co., **II** 88, 118
Victor Value, **II** 678
Victoria, **III** 308
Victoria & Legal & General, **III** 359
Victoria Coach Station, **6** 406
Victoria Creations Inc., **13** 536
VICTORIA Holding AG, **III** **399–401**
Victoria Paper Co., **IV** 286
Victoria Sugar Co., **III** 686
Victoria Wine Co., **I** 216
Victoria's Secret, **V** 115–16; **11** 498; **12** 557, 559; **16** 219; **18** 215; **24** 237; **25** 120–22, 521
Victorinox AG, **21** **515–17**
Victory Fire Insurance Co., **III** 343
Victory Insurance, **III** 273
Victory Oil Co., **IV** 550
Victory Refrigeration Company, **22** 355
Victory Savings and Loan, **10** 339
Victory Supermarket. *See* Big V Supermarkets, Inc.
Vidal Sassoon, **17** 110
Video Concepts, **9** 186
Video Independent Theatres, Inc., **14** 86
Video Library, Inc., **9** 74
Video News International, **19** 285
Video Superstores Master Limited Partnership, **9** 74
Videoconcepts, **II** 107
VideoFusion, Inc., **16** 419
Videotex Network Japan, **IV** 680
Videotron, **25** 102
VideV, **24** 509
La Vie Claire, **13** 103
Vielle Montaign, **22** 285
Vienna Sausage Manufacturing Co., **14** **536–37**

View-Master/Ideal Group, **12** 496
Viewdata Corp., **IV** 630; **15** 264
Viewer's Edge, **27** 429
Viewlogic, **11** 490
ViewStar Corp., **20** 103
Viewtel, **14** 36
Vigilance-Vie, **III** 393
Vigilant Insurance Co., **III** 220; **14** 108
Vigoro, **22** 340
Vigortone, **II** 582
Viiala Oy, **IV** 302
Viking, **II** 10; **IV** 659
Viking Brush, **III** 614
Viking Building Products, **22** 15
Viking Computer Services, Inc., **14** 147
Viking Consolidated Shipping Corp, **25** 470
Viking Direct Limited, **10** 545
Viking Foods, Inc., **8** 482; **14** 411
Viking Office Products, Inc., **10 544–46**
Viking Penguin, **IV** 611
Viking Press, **12** 25
Viking Pump Company, **21** 499–500
Viking Star Shipping, Inc. *See* Teekay Shipping Corporation.
Viktor Achter, **9** 92
Village Inn. *See* VICORP Restaurants, Inc.
Village Super Market, Inc., **7 563–64**
Villager, Inc., **11** 216
Villazon & Co., **27** 139
VILPAC, S.A., **26** 356
Vin & Spirit AB, **31 458–61**
Vinci B.V., **27** 54
Vine Products Ltd., **I** 215
Viner Bros., **16** 546
Vingaarden A/S, **9** 100
Vingresor A.B., **I** 120
Vining Industries, **12** 128
Viniprix SA, **10** 205; **19** 309; **27** 95
Vinland Web-Print, **8** 360
Vinson & Elkins L.L.P., **28** 48; **30 481–83**
Vinyl Maid, Inc., **IV** 401
Vipont Pharmaceutical, **III** 25; **14** 122
VIPS, **11** 113
Viratec Thin Films, Inc., **22** 347
Virco Manufacturing Corporation, **17 515–17**
Virgin Atlantic Airlines. *See* Virgin Group PLC.
Virgin Group PLC, **12 513–15**; **14** 73; **18** 80; **22** 194; **24** 486; **29** 302
The Virgin Islands Telephone Co., **19** 256
Virgin Retail, **9** 75, 361
Virginia Eastern Shore Sustainable Development Corporation, **28** 307
Virginia Electric and Power Company, **V** 596–98
Virginia Fibre Corporation, **15** 188
Virginia Folding Box Company, **IV** 352; **19** 497
Virginia Laminating, **10** 313
Virginia National Bankshares, **10** 426
Virginia Railway and Power Company (VR&P), **V** 596
Virginia Trading Corp., **II** 422
Viromedics, **25** 382
Visa. *See* Valores Industriales S.A.
Visa International, **II** 200; **9** 333–35, **536–38**; **18** 543; **20** 59; **26 514–17 (upd.)**
Visco Products Co., **I** 373; **12** 346
Viscodrive GmbH, **III** 495
Viscount Industries Limited, **6** 310
Vishay Intertechnology, Inc., **11** 516; **21 518–21**
VisiCorp, **6** 254; **25** 298
Vision Centers, **I** 688; **12** 188
Vision Technology Group Ltd., **19** 124
Visionworks, **9** 186
Viskase Corporation, **17** 157, 159
Visking Co., **I** 400
Visnews Ltd., **IV** 668, 670
VisQueen, **I** 334
Vista Bakery Inc., **14** 306
Vista Chemical Company, **I 402–03**; **V** 709
Vista Concepts, Inc., **11** 19
Vista Resources, Inc., **17** 195
Vistana, Inc., **22 537–39**; **26** 464
Visual Action Holdings plc, **24** 96, 374
Visual Information Technologies, **11** 57
Visual Technology, **6** 201
VISX, Incorporated, **30 484–86**
Vita Lebensversicherungs-Gesellschaft, **III** 412
Vita Liquid Polymers, **9** 92
Vita-Achter, **9** 92
Vitafoam Incorporated, **9** 93
Vital Health Corporation, **13** 150
Vital Processing Services LLC, **18** 516, 518
Vitalink Communications Corp., **11** 520
Vitalink Pharmacy Services, Inc., **15 522–24**; **25** 309–10
Vitamin World, **31** 346–48
Vitex Foods, **10** 382
Vitro Corp., **8** 178; **10 547–48**; **17** 492
Vitro S.A., **19** 189
VIVA, **23** 390
Viva Home Co., **III** 757
Vivendi, **29** 369, 371
Vivesvata Iron and Steel Ltd., **IV** 207
Viviane Woodard Cosmetic Corp., **II** 531
Vivra, Inc., **15** 119; **18 545–47**
VK Mason Construction Ltd., **II** 222
Vlasic Foods International Inc., **II** 480–81; **7** 67–68; **25 516–19**; **26** 56, 59
VLN Corp., **I** 201
VLSI Technology, Inc., **11** 246; **16 518–20**; **31** 300
VMG Products. *See* Drypers Corporation.
VMX Inc., **14** 355
VND, **III** 593
Vnesheconobank, **II** 242
VNS. *See* Vereenigde Nederlandsche Scheepvaartmaatschappij.
VNU N.V., **27** 361, **498–501**
VNU/Claritas, **6** 14
Vobis Microcomputer, **20** 103; **23** 311
VocalTec, Inc., **18** 143
Vodac, **11** 548
Vodafone Group plc, **II** 84; **11 547–48**
Vodapage, **11** 548
Vodata, **11** 548
Vodavi Technology Corporation, **13** 213
Voest-Alpine Stahl AG, **IV 233–35**; **31** 47–48
Vogel Peterson Furniture Company, **7** 4–5
Vogoro Corp., **13** 503
Voice Data Systems, **15** 125
Voice Powered Technology International, Inc., **23** 212
Voice Response, Inc., **11** 253
Voith, **II** 22
Vokes, **I** 429
Volkert Stampings, **III** 628
Volkswagen A.G., **I** 30, 32, 186, 192, **206–08**, 460; **II** 279; **IV** 231; **7** 8; **10** 14; **11** 104, **549–51 (upd.)**; **13** 413; **14** 169; **16** 322; **19** 484; **26** 12; **27** 11, 496; **31** 363–65
Volt Information Sciences Inc., **26 518–21**
Volta Aluminium Co., Ltd., **IV** 122
Volume Distributors. *See* Payless ShoeSource, Inc.
Volume Service Company. *See* Restaurants Unlimited, Inc.
Volume Shoe Corporation. *See* Payless ShoeSource,Inc.
Voluntary Hospitals of America, **6** 45
Volunteer Leather Company, **17** 202, 205
Volunteer State Life Insurance Co., **III** 221
AB Volvo, **I** 186, 192, 198, **209–11**; **II** 5, 366; **III** 543, 591, 623, 648; **IV** 336; **7 565–68 (upd.)**; **9** 283–84, 350, 381; **10** 274; **12** 68, 342; **13** 30, 356; **14** 321; **15** 226; **16** 322; **18** 394; **23** 354; **26 9–12 (upd.)**, 401, 403
Volvo-Penta, **21** 503
von Roll, **6** 599
Von Ruden Manufacturing Co., **17** 532
von Weise Gear Co., **III** 509
Von's Grocery Co., **II** 419; **8** 474; **17** 559
The Vons Companies, Incorporated, **II** 655; **7 569–71**; **12** 209; **24** 418; **28 510–13 (upd.)**
VOP Acquisition Corporation, **10** 544
Vornado Realty Trust, **20 508–10**
Voroba Hearing Systems, **25** 56
Vorwerk & Co., **27 502–04**
Votainer International, **13** 20
Vought Aircraft Co., **11** 364
Voxson, **I** 531; **22** 193
Voyage Conseil, **II** 265
Voyager Communications Inc., **24** 5
Voyager Energy, **IV** 84
Voyager Ltd., **12** 514
Voyager Petroleum Ltd., **IV** 83; **7** 188
Voyageur Travel Insurance Ltd., **21** 447
VR&P. *See* Virginia Railway and Power Company.
VRG International. *See* Roberts Pharmaceutical Corporation.
Vroom & Dreesmann, **13** 544–46
Vrumona B.V., **I** 257
VS Services, **13** 49
VSA. *See* Vendors Supply of America, Inc.
VSB Groep, **III** 199, 201
VSD Communications, Inc., **22** 443
VSEL, **24** 88
VSM. *See* Village Super Market, Inc.
VST. *See* Vision Technology Group Ltd.
Vtel Corporation, **10** 456; **27** 365
VTR Incorporated, **16** 46
Vulcan Materials Company, **7 572–75**; **12** 39; **25** 266
Vulcraft, **7** 400–02
VVM, **III** 200
VW&R. *See* Van Waters & Rogers.
VWR Textiles & Supplies, Inc., **11** 256
VWR United Company, **9** 531
Vycor Corporation, **25** 349
Vyvx, **31** 469

W. & G. Turnbull & Co., **IV** 278; **19** 153
W. & M. Duncan, **II** 569
W&A Manufacturing Co., LLC, **26** 530
W&F Fish Products, **13** 103
W.A. Bechtel Co., **I** 558

W.A. Harriman & Co., **III** 471
W.A. Krueger Co., **19** 333–35
W. Atlee Burpee & Co., II 532; **11** 198; **27 505–08**
W.B. Constructions, **III** 672
W.B. Doner & Company, **10** 420; **12** 208; **28** 138
W.B. Saunders Co., **IV** 623–24
W.C. Bradley Company, **18** 516
W.C.G. Sports Industries Ltd. *See* Canstar Sports Inc.
W.C. Heraeus GmbH, **IV** 100
W.C. Norris, **III** 467
W.C. Platt Co., **IV** 636
W.C. Ritchie & Co., **IV** 333
W.C. Smith & Company Limited, **14** 339
W. Duke & Sons, **V** 395, 600
W. Duke Sons & Company, **27** 128
W.E. Andrews Co., Inc., **25** 182
W.E. Dillon Company, Ltd., **21** 499
W.F. Linton Company, **9** 373
W. Gunson & Co., **IV** 278; **19** 153
W. Gutzeit & Co., **IV** 274–77
W.H. Brady Co., 17 518–21
W.H. Gunlocke Chair Co. *See* Gunlocke Company.
W.H. McElwain Co., **III** 528
W.H. Morton & Co., **II** 398; **10** 62
W.H. Smith & Son (Alacra) Ltd., **15** 473
W H Smith Group PLC, V 211–13
W.J. Noble and Sons, **IV** 294; **19** 225
W.L. Gore & Associates, Inc., 14 538–40; **26** 417
W.M. Bassett Furniture Co. *See* Bassett Furniture Industries, Inc.
W.M. Ritter Lumber Co., **IV** 281; **9** 259
W.O. Daley & Company, **10** 387
W.R. Bean & Son, **19** 335
W.R. Berkley Corp., III 248; **15 525–27**
W.R. Breen Company, **11** 486
W.R. Case & Sons Cutlery Company, **18** 567
W.R. Grace & Company, I 547–50; **III** 525, 695; **IV** 454; **11** 216; **12** 337; **13** 149, 502, 544; **14** 29; **16** 45–47; **17** 308, 365–66; **21** 213, 507, 526; **22** 188, 501; **25** 535
W. Rosenlew, **IV** 350
W.S. Barstow & Company, **6** 575
W.T. Grant Co., **16** 487
W.T. Rawleigh, **17** 105
W.T. Young Foods, **III** 52; **8** 433; **26** 383
W. Ullberg & Co., **I** 553
W.V. Bowater & Sons, Ltd., **IV** 257–58
W.W. Cargill and Brother, **II** 616; **13** 136
W.W. Grainger, Inc., V 214–15; **13** 297; **26 537–39 (upd.)**
W.W. Kimball Company, **12** 296; **18** 44
W.W. Norton & Company, Inc., 28 518–20
Waban Inc., V 198; **13 547–49**; **19** 449
Wabash National Corp., 13 550–52
Wabash Valley Power Association, **6** 556
Wabush Iron Co., **IV** 73; **24** 143
Wachbrit Insurance Agency, **21** 96
Wachovia Bank of Georgia, N.A., 16 521–23
Wachovia Bank of South Carolina, N.A., 16 524–26
Wachovia Corporation, II 336; **10** 425; **12** 16, **516–20**; **16** 521, 524, 526; **23** 455
The Wackenhut Corporation, 13 124–25; **14 541–43**; **28** 255
Wacker Oil Inc., **11** 441
Waco Aircraft Company, **27** 98
Wacoal Corp., 25 520–24
Waddell & Reed, Inc., 22 540–43
Wade Smith, **28** 27, 30
Wadsworth Inc., **8** 526
WaferTech, **18** 20
Waffle House Inc., 14 544–45
Wagenseller & Durst, **25** 249
The Wagner & Brown Investment Group, **9** 248
Wagner Castings Company, **16** 474–75
Wagner Litho Machinery Co., **13** 369–70
Wagner Spray Tech, **18** 555
Wagonlit Travel, **22** 128
Wagons-Lits, **27** 11; **29** 443
Wah Chang Corp., **I** 523–24; **10** 520–21
AB Wahlbecks, **25** 464
Wahlstrom & Co., **23** 480
Waialua Agricultural Co., **II** 491
Waitaki International Biosciences Co., **17** 288
Waite Amulet Mines Ltd., **IV** 164
Waitrose, **V** 94–95
Wakefern Cooperative, **II** 672; **18** 6
Wakefern Food Corp., **7** 563–64; **25** 66, 234–35; **28** 143
Wako Shoji Co. Ltd. *See* Wacoal Corp.
Wakodo Co., **I** 674
Wal-Mart Stores, Inc., II 108; **V 216–17**; **6** 287; **7** 61, 331; **8** 33, 295, **555–57 (upd.)**; **9** 187, 361; **10** 236, 284, 515–16, 524; **11** 292; **12** 48, 53–55, 63–64, 97, 208–09, 221, 277, 333, 477, 507–08; **13** 42, 215–17, 260–61, 274, 332–33, 444, 446; **14** 235; **15** 139, 275; **16** 61–62, 65, 390; **17** 297, 321, 460–61; **18** 108, 137, 186, 283, 286; **19** 511; **20** 263; **21** 457–58; **22** 224, 257, 328; **23** 214; **24** 148, 149, 334; **25** 221–22, 254, 314; **26 522–26 (upd.)**, 549; **27** 286, 313, 315, 416, 451; **29** 230, 314, 318
Walbro Corporation, 13 553–55
Walchenseewerk AG, **23** 44
Waldbaum, Inc., II 638; **15** 260; **16** 247, 249; **19 479–81**; **24** 528
Walden Book Company Inc., V 112; **10** 136–37; **16** 160; **17 522–24**; **25** 30
Waldes Truarc Inc., **III** 624
Oy Waldhof AB, **IV** 324
Wales & Company, **14** 257
Walgreen Co., V 218–20; **9** 346; **18** 199; **20 511–13 (upd.)**; **21** 186; **24** 263
Walk Haydel & Associates, Inc., **25** 130
Walk Softly, Inc., **25** 118
Walker & Lee, **10** 340
Walker Cain, **I** 215
Walker Dickson Group Limited, **26** 363
Walker Interactive Systems, **11** 78; **25** 86
Walker Manufacturing Company, I 527; **19 482–84**
Walker McDonald Manufacturing Co., **III** 569; **20** 361
Walkers Parker and Co., **III** 679–80
Walki GmbH, **IV** 349
AB Walkiakoski, **IV** 347
Walkins Manufacturing Corp., **III** 571; **20** 362
Walkup's Merchant Express Inc., **27** 473
Wall Paper Manufacturers, **IV** 666; **17** 397
Wall Street Leasing, **III** 137
Wallace and Tiernan, **I** 383; **11** 361
The Wallace Berrie Company. *See* Applause Inc.
Wallace Computer Services, Inc., **25** 182, 184
Wallace International Silversmiths, **I** 473; **14** 482–83
Wallace Murray Corp., **II** 420
Wallbergs Fabriks A.B., **8** 14
Wallens Dairy Co., **II** 586
Wallin & Nordstrom, **V** 156
Wallingford Bank and Trust Co., **II** 213
Wallis, **V** 177
Wallis Arnold Enterprises, Inc., **21** 483
Wallis Tin Stamping Co., **I** 605
Wallis Tractor Company, **21** 502
Walrus, Inc., **18** 446
Walsin-Lihwa, **13** 141
Walston & Co., **II** 450; **III** 137
Walt Disney Company, II 102, 122, 129, 156, **172–74**; **III** 142, 504, 586; **IV** 585, 675, 703; **6** 15, **174–77 (upd.)**, 368; **7** 305; **8** 160; **10** 420; **12** 168, 208, 229, 323, 495–96; **13** 551; **14** 260; **15** 197; **16** 143, 336; **17** 243, 317, 442–43; **21** 23–26, 360–61; **23** 257–58, 303, 335, 476, 514; **25** 172, 268, 312–13; **27** 92, 287; **30 487–91 (upd.)**
Walt Disney World, **6** 82, 175–76; **18** 290
Walter Baker's Chocolate, **II** 531
Walter Bau, **27** 136, 138
Walter E. Heller, **17** 324
Walter Herzog GmbH, **16** 514
Walter Industries, Inc., III 765–67; **22 544–47 (upd.)**
Walter Kidde & Co., **I** 475, 524; **27** 287
Walter Pierce Oil Co., **IV** 657
Walter Wright Mammoet, **26** 280
Walton Manufacturing, **11** 486
Walton Monroe Mills, Inc., 8 558–60
Wander Ltd., **I** 672
Wanderer Werke, **III** 154
Wang Laboratories, Inc., II 208; **III 168–70**; **6 284–87 (upd.)**; **8** 139; **9** 171; **10** 34; **11** 68, 274; **12** 183; **18** 138; **19** 40; **20** 237
Wanishi, **IV** 157; **17** 349
WAP, **26** 420
Waples-Platter Co., **II** 625
War Damage Corp., **III** 353, 356; **22** 493
War Emergency Tankers Inc., **IV** 552
War Production Board, **V** 676
Warburg, Pincus Capital Corp., **6** 13; **9** 524; **14** 42; **24** 373
Warburtons Bakery Cafe, Inc., **18** 37
Ward Manufacturing Inc., **IV** 101
Ward's Communications, **22** 441
Wardley Ltd., **II** 298
Wards. *See* Circuit City Stores, Inc.
Waring and LaRosa, **12** 167
The Warnaco Group Inc., 9 156; **12 521–23**; **22** 123; **25** 122, 523. *See also* Authentic Fitness Corp.
Warner & Swasey Co., **III** 168; **6** 284; **8** 545
Warner Brothers, **25** 327–28; **26** 102
Warner Communications Inc., II 88, 129, 135, 146–47, 154–55, 169–70, **175–77**, 208, 452; **III** 443, 505; **IV** 623, 673, 675–76; **7** 526, 528–30 **8** 527; **9** 44–45, 119, 469; **10** 196; **11** 557; **12** 73, 495–96; **17** 65, 149, 442–43; **21** 23–25, 360; **22** 519, 522; **23** 23–24, 390, 501; **24** 373; **25** 418–19, 498; **26** 151. *See also* Time Warner Inc.

Warner Cosmetics, **III** 48; **8** 129
Warner Gear Co., **III** 438–39; **14** 63–64
Warner Records, **II** 177
Warner Sugar Refining Co., **II** 496
Warner-Lambert Co., **I** 643, 674, 679, 696, **710–12**; **7** 596; **8** 62–63; **10** **549–52 (upd.)**; **12** 480, 482; **13** 366; **16** 439; **20** 23; **25** 55, 366
Warren Bank, **13** 464
Warren, Gorham & Lamont, **8** 526
Warren Oilfield Services, **9** 363
Warren Petroleum Company, **18** 365, 367
Warri Refining and Petrochemicals Co., **IV** 473
Warrick Industries, **31** 338
Warringah Brick, **III** 673
Warrington Products Ltd. *See* Canstar Sports Inc.
Warrior River Coal Company, **7** 281
Wartsila Marine Industries Inc., **III** 649
Warwick Chemicals, **13** 461
Warwick Electronics, **III** 654
Warwick International Ltd., **13** 462
Wasa, **I** 672–73
Wasag-Chemie AG, **III** 694
Wasatch Gas Co., **6** 568
Wascana Energy Inc., 13 556–58
Washburn Crosby Co., **II** 501, 555; **10** 322
Washburn Graphics Inc., **23** 100
Washington Duke Sons & Co., **12** 108
Washington Federal, Inc., 17 525–27
Washington Gas Light Company, **19** **485–88**
Washington Inventory Service, **30** 239
Washington Mills Company, **13** 532
Washington Mutual, Inc., 17 528–31
Washington National Corporation, **11** 482; **12** **524–26**
Washington Natural Gas Company, **9** **539–41**
The Washington Post Company, **III** 214; **IV** **688–90**; **6** 323; **11** 331; **18** 60, 61, 63; **20** **515–18 (upd.)**; **23** 157–58
Washington Railway and Electric Company, **6** 552–53
Washington Scientific Industries, Inc., **17** **532–34**
Washington Specialty Metals Corp., **14** 323, 325
Washington Steel Corp., **14** 323, 325
Washington Water Power Company, **6** 566, **595–98**
Washtenaw Gas Company. *See* MCN Corporation.
Wassall Plc, 18 548–50
Wasserstein Perella Partners, **II** 629; **III** 512, 530–31; **V** 223; **17** 366
Waste Control Specialists LLC, **19** 466, 468
Waste Management, Inc., **V** 749–51, **752–54**; **6** 46, 600; **9** 73, 108–09; **11** 435–36; **18** 10; **20** 90; **23** 430
Water Engineering, **11** 360
Water Pik, **I** 524–25
Water Products Group, **6** 487–88
Water Street Corporate Recovery Fund, **10** 423
The Waterbury Companies, **16** 482
Waterford Wedgwood Holdings PLC, **IV** 296; **12** **527–29**
Waterhouse Investor Services, Inc., **18** **551–53**
Waterloo Gasoline Engine Co., **III** 462; **21** 173
Waterlow and Sons, **10** 269
Waterman Marine Corporation, **27** 242
The Waterman Pen Company. *See* BIC Corporation.
WaterPro Supplies Corporation, **6** 486, 488
Waterstreet Inc., **17** 293
Watertown Insurance Co., **III** 370
Watkins Manufacturing Co., **I** 159
Watkins-Johnson Company, 15 528–30
Watkins-Strathmore Co., **13** 560
Watmough and Son Ltd., **II** 594
Watney Mann and Truman Brewers, **I** 228, 247; **9** 99
Watson Pharmaceuticals Inc., 16 527–29
Watson-Triangle, **16** 388, 390
Watson-Wilson Transportation System, **V** 540; **14** 567
Watt & Shand, **16** 61
Watt AG, **6** 491
Watt Electronic Products, Limited, **10** 319
The Watt Stopper, **21** 348, 350
Wattie Pict Ltd., **I** 437
Wattie's Ltd., 7 576–78; **11** 173
Watts Industries, Inc., 19 489–91
Watts/Silverstein, Inc., **24** 96
Waukesha Engine Servicenter, **6** 441
Waukesha Foundry Company, **11** 187
Waukesha Motor Co., **III** 472
Wausau Paper Mills, **15** 305
Wausau Sulphate Fibre Co. *See* Mosinee Paper Corporation.
Wavelength Corporate Communications Pty Limited, **24** 95
Waverly, Inc., **10** 135; **16** **530–32**; **19** 358
Waverly Oil Works, **I** 405
Waverly Pharmaceutical Limited, **11** 208
Wawa Inc., 17 535–37
Waxman Industries, Inc., **III** 570; **9** **542–44**; **20** 362; **28** 50–51
Wayco Foods, **14** 411
Waycross-Douglas Coca-Cola Bottling, **10** 222
Wayne Home Equipment. *See* Scott Fetzer Company.
Wayne Oakland Bank, **8** 188
WB. *See* Warner Communications Inc.
WCI Holdings Corporation, **V** 223; **13** 170
WCK, Inc., **14** 236
WCRS Group plc, **6** 15
WCT Live Communication Limited, **24** 95
WD-40 Company, **18** **554–57**
Wear-Ever, **17** 213
WearGuard, **13** 48
Wearne Brothers, **6** 117
The Weather Department, Ltd., **10** 89
Weather Guard, **IV** 305
Weathers-Lowin, Leeam, **11** 408
Weaver, **III** 468
Webb & Knapp, **10** 43
Webber Gage Co., **13** 302
WeBco International LLC, **26** 530
Weber, **16** 488
Weber Metal, **30** 283–84
Webers, **I** 409
Weblock, **I** 109
Webster Publishing Co., **IV** 636
Webtron Corp., **10** 313
Wedgwood. *See* Waterford Wedgewood Holdings PLC.
Week's Dairy, **II** 528
Wegert Verwaltungs-GmbH and Co. Beteiligungs-KG, **24** 270
Wegmans Food Markets, Inc., 9 545–46; **24** 445
Weidemann Brewing Co., **I** 254
Weider Nutrition International, Inc., 29 **498–501**
Weider Sporting Goods, **16** 80
Weifang Power Machine Fittings Ltd., **17** 106
Weight Watchers International Inc., **II** 508; **10** 383; **11** 172; **12** **530–32**; **13** 383; **27** 197
Weirton Steel Corporation, **I** 297; **IV** **236–38**; **7** 447, 598; **8** 346, 450; **10** 31–32; **12** 352, 354; **26** 407, **527–30** **(upd.)**
Weis Markets, Inc., 15 531–33
Welbecson, **III** 501
Welbilt Corp., 19 492–94; **27** 159
Welch's, **25** 366
Welcome Wagon International Inc., **III** 28; **16** 146
Weldless Steel Company, **8** 530
Welex Jet Services, **III** 498–99
Wella Group, III 68–70
Wellby Super Drug Stores, **12** 220
Wellcome Foundation Ltd., **I** 638, **713–15**; **8** 210, 452; **9** 265; **10** 551
Weller Electric Corp., **II** 16
Wellington, **II** 457
Wellington Management Company, **14** 530–31; **23** 226
Wellington Sears Co., **15** 247–48
Wellman, Inc., 8 561–62; **21** 193
Wellmark, Inc., **10** 89
Wellness Co., Ltd., **IV** 716
WellPoint Health Networks Inc., **25** **525–29**
Wells Aircraft, **12** 112
Wells Fargo & Company, **II** **380–84**, 319, 395; **III** 440; **10** 59–60; **12** 165, **533–37 (upd.)**; **17** 325; **18** 60, 543; **19** 411; **22** 542; **25** 434; **27** 292
Wells Fargo HSBC Trade Bank, **26** 203
Wells Lamont, **IV** 136
Wells Rich Greene BDDP, **6** 48, **50–52**
Wellspring Associates L.L.C., **16** 338
Welsbach Mantle, **6** 446
Welsh Associated Collieries Ltd., **31** 369
Weltkunst Verlag GmbH, **IV** 590
Wendy's International, Inc., **II** 614–15, 647; **7** 433; **8** **563–65**; **9** 178; **12** 553; **13** 494; **14** 453; **16** 95, 97; **17** 71, 124; **19** 215; **23** 384, **504–07 (upd.)**; **26** 284
Wenger S.A., **III** 419; **21** 515
Wenlock Brewery Co., **I** 223
Wenstroms & Granstoms Electriska Kraftbolag, **II** 1
Werkhof GmbH, **13** 491
Werknet, **16** 420
Werner Enterprises, Inc., 26 531–33
Werner International, **III** 344; **14** 225
Wernicke Co., **I** 201
Wertheim Schroder & Company, **17** 443
Weru Aktiengesellschaft, 18 558–61
Wesco Financial Corp., **III** 213, 215; **18** 62
Wesco Food Co., **II** 644
Wescot Decisison Systems, **6** 25
Weserflug, **I** 74
Wesper Co., **26** 4
Wesray and Management, **17** 213
Wesray Capital Corporation, **6** 357; **13** 41; **17** 443
Wesray Corporation, **22** 55
Wesray Holdings Corp., **13** 255
Wesray Transportation, Inc., **14** 38
Wessanen. *See* Koninklijke Wessanen N.V.

Wessanen and Laan, **II** 527
Wessanen Cacao, **II** 528
Wessanen USA, **II** 528; **29** 480
Wessanen's Koninklijke Fabrieken N.V., **II** 527
Wesson/Peter Pan Foods Co., **17** 241
West Australia Land Holdings, Limited, **10** 169
West Bend Co., **III** 610–11; **14 546–48**; **16** 384
West Coast Entertainment Corporation, **29 502–04**
West Coast Grocery Co., **II** 670; **18** 506
West Coast Machinery, **13** 385
West Coast of America Telegraph, **I** 428
West Coast Power Company, **12** 265
West Coast Restaurant Enterprises, **25** 390
West Coast Savings and Loan, **10** 339
West Coast Telecom, **III** 38
West End Family Pharmacy, Inc., **15** 523
West Fraser Timber Co. Ltd., **IV** 276; **17 538–40**
West Georgia Coca-Cola Bottlers, Inc., **13** 163
West Ham Gutta Percha Co., **I** 428
West Harrison Gas & Electric Company, **6** 466
West India Oil Co., **IV** 416, 428
West Japan Heavy Industries, **III** 578–79; **7** 348
West Jersey Electric Company, **6** 449
West Lynn Creamery, Inc., **26** 450
West Marine, Inc., **17 541–43**
West Missouri Power Company. *See* UtiliCorp United Inc.
West Newton Savings Bank, **13** 468
West Newton Telephone Company, **14** 258
West of England, **III** 690
West of England Sack Holdings, **III** 501; **7** 207
West One Bancorp, **11 552–55**
West Penn Electric. *See* Allegheny Power System, Inc.
West Point-Pepperell, Inc., **8 566–69**; **9** 466; **15** 247; **25** 20; **28** 218. *See also* WestPoint Stevens Inc. *and* JPS Textile Group, Inc.
West Publishing Co., **IV** 312; **7 579–81**; **10** 407; **19** 268
West Rand Consolidated Mines, **IV** 90
West Rand Investment Trust, **IV** 21; **16** 27
West Richfield Telephone Company, **6** 299
West Side Bank, **II** 312
West Side Printing Co., **13** 559
West Surrey Central Dairy Co. Ltd., **II** 586
West Texas Utilities Company, **6** 580
West Union Corporation, **22** 517
West Virginia Bearings, Inc., **13** 78
West Virginia Pulp and Paper Co. *See* Westvaco Corporation.
West Witwatersrand Areas Ltd., **IV** 94–96
West Yorkshire Bank, **II** 307
West's Holderness Corn Mill, **II** 564
WestAir Holding Inc., **11** 300; **25** 423
Westamerica Bancorporation, **17 544–47**
Westbrae Natural, Inc., **27** 197–98
Westburne Group of Companies, **9** 364
Westchester County Savings & Loan, **9** 173
Westchester Specialty Group, Inc., **26** 546
Westclox Seth Thomas, **16** 483
Westcott Communications Inc., **22** 442
Westdeutsche Landesbank Girozentrale, **II** 257–58, **385–87**
Westec Corporation. *See* Tech-Sym Corporation.
Western Aerospace Ltd., **14** 564
Western Air Express, **I** 125; **III** 225; **9** 17
Western Air Lines, **I** 98, 100, 106; **6** 82; **21** 142; **25** 421–23
Western Alaska Fisheries, **II** 578
Western American Bank, **II** 383
Western Assurance Co., **III** 350
Western Atlas Inc., **III** 473; **12 538–40**; **17** 419
Western Australian Specialty Alloys Proprietary Ltd., **14** 564
Western Auto, **19** 223
Western Auto Supply Co., **8** 56; **11** 392
Western Automatic Machine Screw Co., **12** 344
Western Bancorporation, **I** 536; **II** 288–89; **13** 529
Western Bank, **17** 530
Western Beef, Inc., **22 548–50**
Western Bingo, **16** 471
Western California Canners Inc., **I** 513
Western Canada Airways, **II** 376
Western Coalfields Ltd., **IV** 48–49
Western Company of North America, **15 534–36**; **25** 73, 75
Western Condensing Co., **II** 488
Western Copper Mills Ltd., **IV** 164
Western Corrugated Box Co., **IV** 358
Western Crude, **11** 27
Western Dairy Products, **I** 248
Western Data Products, Inc., **19** 110
Western Digital Corp., **10** 403, 463; **11** 56, 463; **25 530–32**
Western Edison, **6** 601
Western Electric Co., **II** 57, 66, 88, 101, 112; **III** 162–63, 440; **IV** 181, 660; **V** 259–64; **VII** 288; **11** 500–01; **12** 136; **13** 57
Western Empire Construction. *See* CRSS Inc.
Western Equities, Inc. *See* Tech-Sym Corporation.
Western Federal Savings & Loan, **9** 199
Western Fire Equipment Co., **9** 420
Western Geophysical, **I** 485; **11** 265; **12** 538–39
Western Glucose Co., **14** 17
Western Grocers, Inc., **II** 631, 670
Western Hotels Inc. *See* Westin Hotels and Resorts Worldwide.
Western Illinois Power Cooperative, **6** 506
Western Inland Lock Navigation Company, **9** 228
Western International Hotels, **I** 129; **6** 129
Western International Media, **22** 294
Western International University, **24** 40
Western Kraft Corp., **IV** 358; **8** 476
Western Life Insurance Co., **III** 356; **22** 494
Western Light & Telephone Company. *See* Western Power & Gas Company.
Western Light and Power. *See* Public Service Company of Colorado.
Western Massachusetts Co., **13** 183
Western Merchandise, Inc., **8** 556
Western Merchandisers, Inc., **29** 229–30
Western Mining Corp., **IV** 61, 95
Western Mortgage Corporation, **16** 497
Western National Life Company, **10** 246; **14** 473
Western Natural Gas Company, **7** 362
Western New York State Lines, Inc., **6** 370
Western Newell Manufacturing Company. *See* Newell Co.
Western Nuclear, Inc., **IV** 179
Western Offset Publishing, **6** 13
Western Offshore Drilling and Exploration Co., **I** 570
Western Pacific, **22** 220
Western Pacific Industries, **10** 357
Western Paper Box Co., **IV** 333
Western Pioneer, Inc., **18** 279
Western Piping and Engineering Co., **III** 535
Western Platinum, **21** 353
Western Playing Card Co., **13** 559
Western Powder Co., **I** 379; **13** 379
Western Power & Gas Company. *See* Centel Corporation.
Western Printing and Lithographing Company, **19** 404
Western Public Service Corporation, **6** 568
Western Publishing Group, Inc., **IV** 671; **13** 114, **559–61**; **15** 455; **25** 254, 313; **28** 159; **29** 76
Western Reserve Bank of Lake County, **9** 474
Western Reserve Telephone Company. *See* Alltel Corporation.
Western Reserves, **12** 442
Western Resources, Inc., **12 541–43**; **27** 425
Western Rosin Company, **8** 99
Western Sizzlin', **10** 331; **19** 288
Western Slope Gas, **6** 559
Western Steel Group, **26** 407
Western Steer Family Restaurant, **10** 331; **18** 8
Western Sugar Co., **II** 582
Western Telegraph Company, **25** 99
Western Telephone Company, **14** 257
Western Union Corporation, **I** 512; **III** 644; **6** 227–28, 338, 386; **9** 536; **10** 263; **12** 9; **14** 363; **15** 72; **17** 345–46; **21** 25; **24** 515
Western Union Insurance Co., **III** 310
Western Vending, **13** 48
Western Veneer and Plywood Co., **IV** 358
Western-Mobile, **III** 735
Westfair Foods Ltd., **II** 649
Westfalenbank of Bochum, **II** 239
Westfalia AG, **III** 418–19
Westfalia Dinnendahl Gröppel AG, **III** 543
Westfälische Transport AG, **6** 426
Westfälische Verbands-Elektrizitätswerk, **V** 744
Westgate House Investments Ltd., **IV** 711
Westimex, **II** 594
Westin Hotel Co., **I** 129–30; **6** 129; **9** 283, **547–49**; **21** 91
Westin Hotels and Resorts Worldwide, **29 505–08 (upd.)**
Westinghouse Air Brake Co., **III** 664
Westinghouse Brake & Signal, **III** 509
Westinghouse Cubic Ltd., **19** 111
Westinghouse Electric Corporation, **I** 4, 7, 19, 22, 28, 33, 82, 84–85, 524; **II** 57–58, 59, 80, 86, 88, 94, 98–99, **120–22**, 151; **III** 440, 467, 641; **IV** 59, 401; **6** 39, 164, 261, 452, 483, 556; **9** 12, 17, 128, 162, 245, 417, 439–40, 553; **10** 280, 536; **11** 318; **12** 194, **544–47 (upd.)**; **13** 230, 398, 402, 506–07; **14** 300–01; **16** 8; **17** 488; **18** 320, 335–37, 355; **19** 164–66, 210; **21**

43; **26** 102; **27** 269; **28** 69. *See also* CBS Corporation.
Westland Aircraft Ltd., **I** 50, 573; **IV** 658; **24** 85
WestLB. *See* Westdeutsche Landesbank Girozentrale.
Westmark Mortgage Corp., **13** 417
Westmark Realty Advisors, **21** 97
Westmark Systems, Inc., **26** 268
Westmill Foods, **II** 466
Westminster Bank Ltd., **II** 257, 319, 320, 333–34; **17** 324
Westminster Press Ltd., **IV** 658
Westminster Trust Ltd., **IV** 706
Westmoreland Coal Company, 7 582–85
Westmount Enterprises, **I** 286
Weston and Mead, **IV** 310
Weston Bakeries, **II** 631
Weston Foods Ltd., **II** 631
Weston Pharmaceuticals, **V** 49; **19** 122–23
Weston Resources, **II** 631–32
Westpac Banking Corporation, II 388–90; **17** 285
Westphalian Provinzialbank-Hülfskasse, **II** 385
WestPoint Stevens Inc., 16 533–36; **21** 194; **28** 219. *See also* JPS Textile Group, Inc.
Westport Woman, **24** 145
Westvaco Corporation, I 442; **IV 351–54**; **19 495–99 (upd.)**
The Westwood Group, **20** 54
Westwood One, Inc., 17 150; **23 508–11**
Westwood Pharmaceuticals, **III** 19
Westwools Holdings, **I** 438
Westworld Resources Inc., **23** 41
Westwynn Theatres, **14** 87
The Wet Seal, Inc., 18 562–64
Wetterau Incorporated, II 645, **681–82**; **7** 450; **18** 507
Wexpro Company, **6** 568–69
Weyerhaeuser Company, I 26; **IV** 266, 289, 298, 304, 308, **355–56**, 358; **8** 428, 434; **9 550–52 (upd.)**; **19** 445–46, 499; **22** 489; **26** 384; **28 514–17 (upd.)**; **31** 468
Weyman-Burton Co., **9** 533
Whalstrom & Co., **I** 14
Wharf Holdings Limited, **12** 367–68; **18** 114
Wheat, First Securities, **19** 304–05
Wheaton Industries, 8 570–73
Wheatsheaf Investment, **27** 94
Wheel Horse, **7** 535
Wheel Restaurants Inc., **14** 131
Wheelabrator Technologies, Inc., I 298; **II** 403; **III** 511–12; **V** 754; **6 599–600**; **10** 32; **11** 435
Wheeler Condenser & Engineering Company, **6** 145
Wheeler, Fisher & Co., **IV** 344
Wheeling-Pittsburgh Corp., 7 586–88
Wheelock Marden, **I** 470; **20** 312
Whemco, **22** 415
Whemo Denko, **I** 359
Wherehouse Entertainment Incorporated, 9 361; **11 556–58**; **29** 350
WHI Inc., **14** 545
Whippet Motor Lines Corporation, **6** 370
Whippoorwill Associates Inc., **28** 55
Whirl-A-Way Motors, **11** 4
Whirlpool Corporation, I 30; **II** 80; **III** 572, 573, **653–55**; **8** 298–99; **11** 318; **12** 252, 309, **548–50 (upd.)**; **13** 402–03, 563; **15** 403; **18** 225–26; **22** 218, 349; **23** 53; **25** 261
Whirlwind, Inc., **6** 233; **7** 535
Whiskey Trust, **I** 376
Whistler Corporation, **13** 195
Whitaker Health Services, **III** 389
Whitaker-Glessner Company, **7** 586
Whitall Tatum, **III** 423
Whitbread PLC, I 288, **293–94**; **18** 73; **20 519–22 (upd.)**; **29** 19
Whitby Pharmaceuticals, Inc., **10** 289
White Automotive, **10** 9, 11
White Brand, **V** 97
White Bus Line, **I** 448
White Castle Systems, Inc., 12 551–53
White Consolidated Industries Inc., II 122; **III** 480, 654, 573; **8** 298; **12** 252, 546; **13 562–64**; **22** 26–28, 216–17, 349
White Discount Department Stores, **16** 36
White Eagle Oil & Refining Co., **IV** 464; **7** 352
White Fuel Corp., **IV** 552
White Industrial Power, **II** 25
White Miller Construction Company, **14** 162
White Motor Co., **II** 16
White Mountain Freezers, **19** 360
White Oil Corporation, **7** 101
White Rock Corp., **I** 377; **27** 198
White Rose, Inc., 12 106; **24 527–29**
White Star Line, **23** 161
White Stores, **II** 419–20
White Swan Foodservice, **II** 625
White Tractor, **13** 17
White Weld, **II** 268; **21** 145
White-New Idea, **13** 18
White-Rodgers, **II** 19
White-Westinghouse. *See* White Consolidated Industries Inc.
Whiteaway Laidlaw, **V** 68
Whitehall Canadian Oils Ltd., **IV** 658
Whitehall Company Jewellers, **24** 319
Whitehall Electric Investments Ltd., **IV** 658
Whitehall Labs, **8** 63
Whitehall Petroleum Corp. Ltd., **IV** 657–58
Whitehall Securities Corp., **IV** 658
Whitehall Trust Ltd., **IV** 658
Whitewater Group, **10** 508
Whitewear Manufacturing Company. *See* Angelica Corporation.
Whitman Corporation, 7 430; **10** 414–15, **553–55 (upd.)**; **11** 188; **22** 353–54; **27** 196. *See also* IC Industries.
Whitman Publishing Co., **13** 559–60
Whitman's Chocolates, **I** 457; **7** 431; **12** 429
Whitmire Distribution. *See* Cardinal Health, Inc.
Whitney Communications Corp., **IV** 608
Whitney Holding Corporation, 21 522–24
Whitney National Bank, **12** 16
Whittaker Corporation, I 544–46; **III** 389, 444
Whittar Steel Strip Co., **IV** 74; **24** 143
Whitteways, **I** 215
Whittle Communications L.P., **IV** 675; **7** 528; **13** 403; **22** 442
Whitworth Brothers Company, **27** 360
Whole Foods Market, Inc., 19 501–02; **20 523–27**
Wholesale Cellular USA. *See* Brightpoint, Inc.
The Wholesale Club, Inc., **8** 556
Wholesale Depot, **13** 547
Wholesale Food Supply, Inc., **13** 333
Wholly Harvest, **19** 502
Whyte & Mackay Distillers Ltd., **V** 399; **19** 171
Wicat Systems, **7** 255–56; **25** 254
Wichita Industries, **11** 27
Wickes Companies, Inc., I 453, 483; **II** 262; **III** 580, 721; **V 221–23**; **10** 423; **13** 169–70; **15** 281; **17** 365–66; **19** 503–04; **20** 415
Wickes Inc., 25 533–36 (upd.)
Wickman-Wimet, **IV** 203
Widows and Orphans Friendly Society, **III** 337
Wielkopolski Bank Kredytowy, **16** 14
Wien Air Alaska, **II** 420
Wienerwald Holding, **17** 249
Wiesner, Inc., **22** 442
Wifstavarfs, **IV** 325
Wiggins Teape Ltd., **I** 426; **IV** 290
Wild by Nature. *See* King Cullen Grocery Co., Inc.
Wild Leitz G.m.b.H., **23** 83
Wild Oats Markets, Inc., 19 500–02; **29** 213
Wildlife Conservation Society, 31 462–64
Wildwater Kingdom, **22** 130
Wiles Group Ltd., **III** 501; **7** 207
Wiley Manufacturing Co., **8** 545
Oy Wilh. Schauman AB, **IV** 300–02; **19** 463
Wilhelm Fette GmbH, **IV** 198–99
Wilhelm Weber GmbH, **22** 95
Wilhelm Wilhelmsen Ltd., **7** 40
Wilkins Department Store, **19** 510
Wilkinson, Gaddis & Co., **24** 527
Wilkinson Sword Co., **III** 23, 28–29; **12** 464
Willamette Falls Electric Company. *See* Portland General Corporation.
Willamette Industries, Inc., IV 357–59; **13** 99, 101; **16** 340; **28** 517; **31 465–468 (upd.)**
Willcox & Gibbs Sewing Machine Co., **15** 384
Willetts Manufacturing Company, **12** 312
William A. Rogers Ltd., **IV** 644
William B. Tanner Co., **7** 327
William Barnet and Son, Inc., **III** 246
William Barry Co., **II** 566
William Benton Foundation, **7** 165, 167
William Bonnel Co., **I** 334; **10** 289
The William Brooks Shoe Company. *See* Rocky Shoes & Boots, Inc.
William Burdon, **III** 626
William Byrd Press Inc., **23** 100
William Carter Company, **17** 224
William Colgate and Co., **III** 23
William Collins & Sons, **II** 138; **IV** 651–52; **7** 390–91; **24** 193
William Cory & Son Ltd., **6** 417
William Crawford and Sons, **II** 593
William Douglas McAdams Inc., **I** 662; **9** 403
William Duff & Sons, **I** 509
William E. Pollack Government Securities, **II** 390
William E. Wright Company, **9** 375
William Esty Company, **16** 72
William Gaymer and Son Ltd., **I** 216

William Grant Company, **22** 343
William H. Rorer Inc., **I** 666
William Hancock & Co., **I** 223
William J. Hough Co., **8** 99–100
William Lyon Homes, **III** 664
William M. Mercer Inc., **III** 283
William Mackinnon & Co., **III** 522
William McDonald & Sons, **II** 593
William Morris Agency, Inc., III 554; **23 512–14**
William Morrow & Company, **19** 201
William Neilson, **II** 631
William Odhams Ltd., **7** 244
William Penn Cos., **III** 243, 273
William Penn Life Insurance Company of New York, **24** 285
William Press, **I** 568
William R. Warner & Co., **I** 710
William S. Kimball & Co., **12** 108
William Southam and Sons, **7** 487
William T. Blackwell & Company, **V** 395
William Underwood Co., **I** 246, 457; **7** 430
William Varcoe & Sons, **III** 690
William Zinsser & Co., **8** 456
Williams & Glyn's Bank Ltd., **12** 422
Williams & Wilkins. *See* Waverly, Inc.
Williams Brother Offshore Ltd., **I** 429
Williams Communications, **6** 340; **25** 499
The Williams Companies, Inc., III 248; **IV** 84, 171, **575–76**; **27** 307; **31 469–472 (upd.)**
Williams Deacon's Bank, **12** 422
Williams, Donnelley and Co., **IV** 660
Williams Electronics, **III** 431; **12** 419
Williams Electronics Games, Inc., **15** 539
Williams Gold Refining Co., **14** 81
The Williams Manufacturing Company, **19** 142–43
Williams Oil-O-Matic Heating Corporation, **12** 158; **21** 42
Williams Printing Company. *See* Graphic Industries Inc.
Williams/Nintendo Inc., **15** 537
Williams-Sonoma, Inc., 13 42; **15** 50; **17 548–50**; **27** 225, 429
Williamsburg Gas Light Co., **6** 455
Williamson-Dickie Manufacturing Company, 14 549–50
Willie G's, **15** 279
Willis Corroon Group plc, III 280, 747; **22** 318; **25 537–39**
Willis Stein & Partners, **21** 404
Williston Basin Interstate Pipeline Company, **7** 322, 324
Willor Manufacturing Corp., **9** 323
Willys-Overland, **I** 183; **8** 74
Wilmington Coca-Cola Bottling Works, Inc., **10** 223
Wilmington Trust Corporation, 25 540–43
Wilsdorf & Davis, **13** 353–54
Wilshire Real Estate Investment Trust Inc., **30** 223
Wilshire Restaurant Group Inc., **13** 66; **28** 258
Wilson & Co., **I** 490
Wilson Brothers, **8** 536
Wilson Foods Corp., **I** 489, 513; **II** 584–85; **12** 124; **14** 515; **22** 510
Wilson, H.W., Company. *See* H.W. Wilson Company.
Wilson Jones Company, **7** 4–5
Wilson Learning Group, **17** 272
Wilson Pharmaceuticals & Chemical, **I** 489
Wilson Sporting Goods Company, I 278, 489; **13** 317; **16** 52; **23** 449; **24** 403, **530–32**; **25** 167
Wilson's Motor Transit, **6** 370
Wilson's Supermarkets, **12** 220–21
Wilson-Maeulen Company, **13** 234
Wilsons The Leather Experts Inc., 21 525–27
WilTel Network Services, **27** 301, 307
Wilts and Dorset Banking Co., **II** 307
Wiltshire United Dairies, **II** 586
Wimpey International Ltd., **13** 206
Wimpey's plc, **I** 315, 556
Win Schuler Foods, **II** 480; **25** 517; **26** 57
Win-Chance Foods, **II** 508
Wincanton Group, **II** 586–87
Winchell's Donut Shops, **II** 680
Winchester Arms, **I** 379–81, 434; **13** 379
Windmere Corporation, 16 537–39
Windmere-Durable Holdings, Inc., **30** 404
WindowVisions, Inc., **29** 288
Windsor Manufacturing Company, **13** 6
Windsor Trust Co., **13** 467
Windstar Sail Cruises, **6** 368; **27** 90–91
Windsurfing International, **23** 55
Windward Capital Partners, **28** 152, 154
Wine World, Inc., **22** 78, 80
Wingate Partners, **14** 521, 523
Wings & Wheels, **13** 19
Wings Luggage, Inc., **10** 181
Winkelman Stores, Inc., **8** 425–26
Winkler-Grimm Wagon Co., **I** 141
Winlet Fashions, **22** 223
Winmar Co., **III** 353
Winn-Dixie Stores, Inc., II 626–27, 670, **683–84**; **7** 61; **11** 228; **15** 178; **16** 314; **18** 8; **21 528–30 (upd.)**
Winnebago Industries Inc., 7 589–91; **22** 207; **27 509–12 (upd.)**
Winners Apparel Ltd., **V** 197
Winning International, **21** 403
Winschermann group, **IV** 198
WinsLoew Furniture, Inc., 21 531–33
Winston & Newell Company. *See* Supervalu Inc.
Winston Furniture Company, Inc., **21** 531–33
Winston Group, **10** 333
Winston, Harper, Fisher Co., **II** 668
WinterBrook Corp., **26** 326
Wintershall, **I** 306; **IV** 485; **18** 49
Winterthur Insurance, **21** 144, 146–47
Winterthur Schweizerische Versicherungs-Gesellschaft, III 343, **402–04**
Winthrop Laboratories, **I** 698–99
Winthrop Lawrence Corporation, **25** 541
Winton Engines, **10** 273
Winton Motor Car Company, **V** 231
Wire and Cable Specialties Corporation, **17** 276
Wire and Plastic Products PLC. *See* WPP Group PLC.
Wireless Hong Kong. *See* Hong Kong Telecommunications Ltd.
Wireless LLC, **18** 77
Wireless Management Company, **11** 12
Wireless Speciality Co., **II** 120
Wirtz Productions Ltd., **15** 238
Wisaforest Oy AB, **IV** 302
Wisconsin Bell, Inc., 14 551–53; **18** 30
Wisconsin Central Transportation Corporation, 12 278; **24 533–36**
Wisconsin Dairies, 7 592–93
Wisconsin Energy Corporation, 6 601–03, 605
Wisconsin Gas Company, **17** 22–23
Wisconsin Knife Works, **III** 436
Wisconsin Power and Light, **22** 13
Wisconsin Public Service Corporation, 6 604–06; **9 553–54**
Wisconsin Steel, **10** 430; **17** 158–59
Wisconsin Tissue Mills Inc., **8** 103
Wisconsin Toy Company. *See* Value Merchants Inc.
Wisconsin Wire and Steel, **17** 310; **24** 160
Wise Foods, Inc., **22** 95
Wiser's De Luxe Whiskey, **14** 141
Wishnick-Tumpeer Chemical Co., **I** 403–05
Wispark Corporation, **6** 601, 603
Wisser Service Holdings AG, **18** 105
Wisvest Corporation, **6** 601, 603
Witco Corporation, I 403, **404–06**; **16 540–43 (upd.)**
Wite-Out Products, Inc., **23** 56–57
Witech Corporation, **6** 601, 603
Withington Company. *See* Sparton Corporation.
Wittington Investments Ltd., **13** 51
Wizards of the Coast Inc., 24 537–40
WizardWorks Group, Inc., **31** 238–39
WLR Foods, Inc., 14 516; **21 534–36**
Wm. Wrigley Jr. Company, 7 594–97
WMS Industries, Inc., III 431; **15 537–39**
WMX Technologies Inc., 11 435–36; **17 551–54**; **26** 409
Woermann and German East African Lines, **I** 542
Wöhlk, **III** 446
Wolf Furniture Enterprises, **14** 236
Wolfe & Associates, **25** 434
Wolfe Industries, Inc., **22** 255
Wolff Printing Co., **13** 559
The Wolfgang Puck Food Company, Inc., 26 534–36
Wolohan Lumber Co., 19 503–05; **25** 535
Wolters Kluwer NV, IV 611; **14 554–56**; **31** 389, 394
Wolvercote Paper Mill, **IV** 300
Wolverine Die Cast Group, **IV** 165
Wolverine Insurance Co., **26** 487
Wolverine Tube Inc., 23 515–17
Wolverine World Wide Inc., 16 544–47; **17** 390
Womack Development Company, **11** 257
Women's World, **15** 96
Wometco Coca-Cola Bottling Co., **10** 222
Wometco Coffee Time, **I** 514
Wometco Enterprises, **I** 246, 514
Wonderware Corp., **22** 374
Wong International Holdings, **16** 195
Wood Fiberboard Co., **IV** 358
Wood Gundy, **II** 345; **21** 447
Wood Hall Trust plc, I 438, **592–93**
Wood River Oil and Refining Company, **11** 193
Wood Shovel and Tool Company, **9** 71
Wood, Struthers & Winthrop, Inc., **22** 189
Wood Wyant Inc., **30** 496–98
Wood-Metal Industries, Inc. *See* Wood-Mode, Inc.
Wood-Mode, Inc., 23 518–20
Woodall Industries, **III** 641; **14** 303
Woodard-Walker Lumber Co., **IV** 358
Woodbury Co., **19** 380

Woodcock, Hess & Co., **9** 370
Woodfab, **IV** 295; **19** 225
Woodhaven Gas Light Co., **6** 455
Woodhill Chemical Sales Company, **8** 333
Woodlands, **7** 345–46
Woods and Co., **II** 235
Woodside Travel Trust, **26** 310
Woodville Appliances, Inc., **9** 121
Woodward Corp., **IV** 311; **19** 267
Woodward Governor Co., 13 565–68
Woodworkers Warehouse, **22** 517
Woolco Department Stores, **II** 634; **7** 444; **V** 107, 225–26; **14** 294; **22** 242
Woolverton Motors, **I** 183
The Woolwich plc, 30 492–95
Woolworth Corporation, **II** 414; **6** 344; **V** 106–09, **224–27**; **8** 509; **14** 293–95; **17** 42, 335; **20 528–32 (upd.)**; **25** 221
Woolworth Holdings, **II** 139; **V** 108; **19** 123; **24** 194
Woolworth's Ltd., **II** 656. *See also* Kingfisher plc.
Wooster Preserving Company, **11** 211
Wooster Rubber Co., **III** 613
Worcester City and County Bank, **II** 307
Worcester Gas Light Co., **14** 124
Worcester Wire Works, **13** 369
Word, Inc., **14** 499
Word Processors Personnel Service, **6** 10
WordPerfect Corporation, **6** 256; **10** 519, **556–59**; **12** 335; **25** 300
WordStar International, **15** 149. *See also* The Learning Company Inc.
Work Wear Corp., **II** 607; **16** 229
Working Title Films, **23** 389
World Air Network, Ltd., **6** 71
World Airways, **10** 560–62; **28** 404
World Book Group. *See* Scott Fetzer Company.
World Book, Inc., **IV** 622; **12 554–56**
World Color Press Inc., **12 557–59**; **19** 333; **21** 61
World Commerce Corporation, **25** 461
World Communications, Inc., **11** 184
World Duty Free Americas, Inc., **29 509–12 (upd.)**
World Film Studio, **24** 437
World Financial Network National Bank, **V** 116
World Flight Crew Services, **10** 560
World Foot Locker, **14** 293
World Gift Company, **9** 330
World International Holdings Limited, **12** 368
World Journal Tribune Inc., **IV** 608
World Publishing Co., **8** 423
World Savings and Loan, **19** 412
World Service Life Insurance Company, **27** 47
World Trade Corporation. *See* International Business Machines Corporation.
World Yacht Enterprises, **22** 438
World-Wide Shipping Group, **II** 298; **III** 517
WorldCom, Inc., **14** 330, 332; **18** 33, 164, 166; **29** 227. *See also* MCI WorldCom, Inc.
WorldCorp, Inc., **10 560–62**
WorldGames, **10** 560
Worlds of Fun, **22** 130
Worlds of Wonder, Inc., **25** 381; **26** 548
Worldview Systems Corporation, **26** 428
WorldWay Corporation, **16** 41
Worldwide Logistics, **17** 505
Worldwide Underwriters Insurance Co., **III** 218–19
Wormald International Ltd., **13** 245, 247
Worms et Cie, **27** 275–76, **513–15**
Wormser, **III** 760
Worth Corp., **27** 274
Wortham, Gus Sessions, **III** 193; **10** 65
Worthen Banking Corporation, **15** 60
Worthington & Co., **I** 223
Worthington Corp., **I** 142
Worthington Foods, Inc., **I** 653; **14 557–59**
Worthington Industries, Inc., **7 598–600**; **8** 450; **21 537–40 (upd.)**
Worthington Telephone Company, **6** 312
Woven Belting Co., **8** 13
WPL Holdings, **6 604–06**
WPM. *See* Wall Paper Manufacturers.
WPP Group plc, **I** 21; **6 53–54**; **22** 201, 296; **23** 480. *See also* Ogilvy Group Inc.
Wrather Corporation, **18** 354
Wrenn Furniture Company, **10** 184
WRG. *See* Wells Rich Greene BDDP.
Wright & Company Realtors, **21** 257
Wright Aeronautical, **9** 16
Wright Airplane Co., **III** 151; **6** 265
Wright and Son, **II** 593
Wright Company, **9** 416
Wright Engine Company, **11** 427
Wright Group, **22** 519, 522
Wright Manufacturing Company, **8** 407
Wright Plastic Products, **17** 310; **24** 160
Wright, Robertson & Co. *See* Fletcher Challenge Ltd.
Wright Stephenson & Co., **IV** 278
Wrightson Limited, **19** 155
Write Right Manufacturing Co., **IV** 345
WSGC Holdings, Inc., **24** 530
WSI Corporation, **10** 88–89
WSM Inc., **11** 152
WSMP, Inc., **29** 202
WTC Airlines, Inc., **IV** 182
WTD Industries, Inc., **20 533–36**
Wührer, **II** 474
Wunderlich Ltd., **III** 687
Wunderman, Ricotta & Kline, **I** 37
Wurlitzer Co., **17** 468; **18** 45
Württembergische Landes-Elektrizitäts AG, **IV** 230
WVPP. *See* Westvaco Corporation.
WWG Industries, Inc., **22** 352–53
WWTV, **18** 493
Wyandotte Chemicals Corporation, **18** 49
Wyandotte Corp., **I** 306
Wyant Corporation, **30 496–98**
Wycombe Bus Company, **28** 155–56
Wyeth Laboratories, **I** 623; **10** 69
Wyeth-Ayerst Laboratories, **25** 477; **27** 69
Wyle Electronics, **14 560–62**; **19** 311
Wyly Corporation, **11** 468
Wyman-Gordon Company, **14 563–65**; **30** 282–83
Wymore Oil Co., **IV** 394
Wynn's International Inc., **22** 458
Wynncor Ltd., **IV** 693
Wyoming Mineral Corp., **IV** 401
Wyse Technology, Inc., **10** 362; **15 540–42**

X-Acto, **12** 263
X-Chem Oil Field Chemicals, **8** 385
XA Systems Corporation, **10** 244
Xaos Tools, Inc., **10** 119
Xcelite, **II** 16
Xcor International, **III** 431; **15** 538
Xeikon NV, **26 540–42**
Xenia National Bank, **9** 474
Xenotech, **27** 58
Xerox Corporation, **I** 31–32, 338, 490, 693; **II** 10, 117, 157, 159, 412, 448; **III** 110, 116, 120–21, 157, 159, **171–73**, 475; **IV** 252, 703; **6** 244, **288–90 (upd.)**, 390; **7** 45, 161; **8** 164; **10** 22, 139, 430, 510–11; **11** 68, 494, 518; **13** 127, 448; **14** 399; **17** 28–29, 328–29; **18** 93, 111–12; **22** 411–12; **25** 54–55, 148, 152; **26** 213, 540, 542, **543–47 (upd.)**; **28** 115
Xilinx, Inc., **16** 317, **548–50**; **18** 17, 19; **19** 405
XP, **27** 474
Xpert Recruitment, Ltd., **26** 240
Xpress Automotive Group, Inc., **24** 339
XRAL Storage and Terminaling Co., **IV** 411
XTRA Corp., **18** 67
XTX Corp., **13** 127
Xynetics, **9** 251
Xytek Corp., **13** 127

Y & S Candies Inc., **II** 511
Yacimientos Petrolíferos Fiscales Sociedad Anónima, **IV** 578
Yageo Corporation, **16 551–53**
Yahoo! Inc., **25** 18; **27 516–19**
Yakovlev, **24** 60
Yale & Towne Manufacturing Co., **I** 154–55; **10** 279
Yamabun Oil Co., **IV** 403
Yamagata Enterprises, **26** 310
Yamaguchi Bank, **II** 347
Yamaha Corporation, **III** 366, 599, **656–59**; **11** 50; **12** 401; **16** 410, **554–58 (upd.)**; **17** 25; **18** 250; **19** 428; **22** 196
Yamaha Musical Instruments, **16** 202
Yamaichi Securities Company, Limited, **II** 300, 323, 434, **458–59**; **9** 377
Yamano Music, **16** 202
Yamanouchi Pharmaceutical, **12** 444–45
Yamatame Securities, **II** 326
Yamato Transport Co. Ltd., **V 536–38**
Yamazaki Baking Co., **II** 543; **IV** 152; **24** 358
Yanbian Industrial Technology Training Institute, **12** 294
Yankee Energy Gas System, Inc., **13** 184
Yankton Gas Company, **6** 524
Yarmouth Group, Inc., **17** 285
Yaryan, **I** 343
Yashica Co., Ltd., **II** 50–51; **21** 330
Yasuda Fire and Marine Insurance Company, Limited, **II** 292, 391; **III 405–07**, 408
Yasuda Mutual Life Insurance Company, **II** 292, 391, 446; **III** 288, 405, **408–09**; **22** 406–07
The Yasuda Trust and Banking Company, Limited, **II** 273, 291, **391–92**; **17 555–57 (upd.)**
Yates Circuit Foil, **IV** 26
Yates-Barco Ltd., **16** 8
Yawata Iron & Steel Co., Ltd., **I** 493, 509; **II** 300; **IV** 130, 157, 212; **17** 350; **24** 325
Year Book Medical Publishers, **IV** 677–78
Yearbooks, Inc., **12** 472
Yeargin Construction Co., **II** 87; **11** 413

Yellow Cab Co., **I** 125; **V** 539; **10** 370; **12** 487; **24** 118
Yellow Corporation, **14 566–68**
Yellow Freight System, Inc. of Deleware, **V** 503, **539–41**; **12** 278
Yeomans & Foote, **I** 13
Yeomans & Partners Ltd., **I** 588
YES! Entertainment Corporation, **10** 306; **26 548–50**
Yesco Audio Environments, **18** 353, 355
Yeti Cycles Inc., **19** 385
Yeung Chi Shing Estates, **IV** 717
YGK Inc., **6** 465, 467
Yhtyneet Paperitehtaat Oy. *See* United Paper Mills Ltd.
Yili Food Co., **II** 544
YKK, **19** 477
YMCA of the USA, **31 473–76**
Ymos A.G., **IV** 53; **26** 83
Yokado Clothing Store, **V** 88
Yokogawa Electric Corp., **III** 142–43, 536; **26** 230
Yokogawa Electric Works, Limited, **6** 237; **13** 234
Yokohama Bottle Plant, **21** 319
Yokohama Cooperative Wharf Co., **IV** 728
Yokohama Electric Cable Manufacturing Co., **III** 490
The Yokohama Rubber Co., Ltd., **V 254–56**; **19 506–09 (upd.)**
Yokohama Specie Bank, **I** 431; **II** 224
Yoosung Enterprise Co., Ltd., **23** 269
Yoplait S.A., **II** 576
York & London, **III** 359
The York Bank and Trust Company, **16** 14
York Corp., **III** 440
York Developments, **IV** 720
York International Corp., **13 569–71**; **22** 6
York Manufacturing Co., **13** 385
York Safe & Lock Company, **7** 144–45; **22** 184
York Steak House, **16** 157
York Wastewater Consultants, Inc., **6** 441
York-Benimaru, **V** 88
Yorkshire and Pacific Securities Ltd., **IV** 723
Yorkshire Insurance Co., **III** 241–42, 257
Yorkshire Paper Mills Ltd., **IV** 300
Yorkshire Post Newspapers, **IV** 686; **28** 503
Yorkshire Television Ltd., **IV** 659
Yorkshire-Tyne Tees Television, **24** 194
Yorkville Group, **IV** 640
Yosemite Park & Curry Co., **II** 144
Yoshikazu Taguchi, **6** 428
Yoshitomi Pharmaceutical, **I** 704
Young & Rubicam Inc., **I** 9–11, 25, **36–38**; **II** 129; **6** 14, 47; **9** 314; **13** 204; **16** 166–68; **22 551–54 (upd.)**
Young & Selden, **7** 145
Young & Son, **II** 334
Young Readers of America, **13** 105
Young's Engineering Co., **IV** 717
Youngblood Truck Lines, **16** 40
Youngs Drug Products Corporation, **8** 85
Youngstown, **IV** 114
Youngstown Pressed Steel Co., **III** 763
Youngstown Sheet & Tube, **I** 490–91; **13** 157
Younkers, Inc., **19** 324–25, **510–12**
Yount-Lee Oil Co., **IV** 369
Youth Centre Inc., **16** 36
Youth Services International, Inc., **21 541–43**; **30** 146
Youthtrack, Inc., **29** 399–400
Yoxall Instrument Company, **13** 234
Yoyoteiki Cargo Co., Ltd., **6** 428
YPF Sociedad Anónima, **IV 577–78**
Yside Investment Group, **16** 196
YTT. *See* Yorkshire-Tyne Tees Television.
Yuasa Battery Co., **III** 556
Yuba Heat Transfer Corp., **I** 514
Yucaipa Cos., **17 558–62**; **22** 39
Yukon Pacific Corporation, **22** 164, 166
Yurakucho Seibu Co., Ltd., **V** 185
Yutani Heavy Industries, Ltd., **IV** 130
Yves Rocher, **IV** 546
Yves Saint Laurent, **I** 697; **12** 37
Yves Soulié, **II** 266

Z.C. Mines, **IV** 61
Zaadunie B.V., **I** 672
Zahnfabrik Weinand Sohne & Co. G.m.b.H., **10** 271
Zahnradfabrik Friedrichshafen, **III** 415
Zale Corporation, **16** 206, **559–61**; **17** 369; **19** 452; **23** 60
Zambezi Saw Mills (1968) Ltd., **IV** 241
Zambia Breweries, **25** 281
Zambia Industrial and Mining Corporation Ltd., **IV 239–41**
Zander & Ingeström, **III** 419
Zanders Feinpapiere AG, **IV** 288; **15** 229
Zanussi, **III** 480; **22** 27
Zany Brainy, Inc., **31 477–79**
Zap, Inc., **25** 546
Zapata Corporation, **17** 157, 160; **25 544–46**
Zapata Drilling Co., **IV** 489
Zapata Gulf Marine Corporation, **11** 524
Zapata Offshore Co., **IV** 489
Zapata Petroleum Corp., **IV** 489
Zausner, **25** 83
Zayre Corp., **V** 197–98; **9** 20–21; **13** 547–48; **19** 448; **29** 106; **30** 55–56
Zealand Mines S.A., **23** 41
Zebco, **22** 115
Zebra Technologies Corporation, **14** 378, **569–71**
Zecco, Inc., **III** 443; **6** 441
Zehrmart, **II** 631
Zeiss Ikon AG, **III** 446
Zell Bros., **16** 559
Zell/Chilmark Fund LP, **12** 439; **19** 384
Zellers, **V** 80; **25** 221
Zellstoff AG, **III** 400
Zellstoffabrik Waldhof AG, **IV** 323–24
Zellweger Telecommunications AG, **9** 32
Zeneca Group PLC, **21 544–46**
Zenith Data Systems, Inc., **II** 124–25; **III** 123; **6** 231; **10 563–65**
Zenith Electronics Corporation, **II** 102, **123–25**; **10** 563; **11** 62, 318; **12** 183, 454; **13** 109, 398, **572–75 (upd.)**; **18** 421
Zentec Corp., **I** 482
Zentralsparkasse und Kommerzialbank Wien, **23** 37
Zentronics, **19** 313
Zero Corporation, **17 563–65**
Zero Plus Dialing, Inc. *See* Billing Concepts Corp.
Zetor s.p., **21** 175
Zeus Components, Inc., **10** 113
Zewawell AG, **IV** 324
Zhongbei Building Material Products Company, **26** 510
Ziebart International Corporation, **30 499–501**
The Ziegler Companies, Inc., **24 541–45**
Ziff Communications Company, **7** 239–40; **12** 359, **560–63**; **13** 483; **16** 371; **17** 152, 253; **25** 238, 240
Zijlker, **IV** 491
Zilber Ltd., **13** 541
Zilkha & Company, **12** 72
Zilog, Inc., **15 543–45**; **16** 548–49; **22** 390
Zimbabwe Sugar Refineries, **II** 581
Zimmer AG, **IV** 142
Zimmer Inc., **10** 156–57; **11** 475
Zimmer Manufacturing Co., **III** 18
Zinc Corp., **IV** 58–59, 61
Zinc Products Company, **30** 39
Zion Foods, **23** 408
Zions Bancorporation, **12 564–66**; **24** 395
Zippo Manufacturing Company, **18 565–68**
Zipps Drive-Thru, Inc., **25** 389
Zippy Mart, **7** 102
Zircotube, **IV** 174
Zivnostenska, **II** 282
Zody's Department Stores, **9** 120–22
Zoecon, **I** 673
Zoll Medical, **18** 423
Zondervan Publishing House, **14** 499; **24 546–49**
Zoom Telephonics, Inc., **18 569–71**
Zortech Inc., **10** 508
Zotos International, Inc., **III** 63; **17** 110; **22** 487
ZPT Radom, **23** 427
ZS Sun Limited Partnership, **10** 502
Zuid Nederlandsche Handelsbank, **II** 185
Zürcher Bankverein, **II** 368
Zurich Insurance Group, **15** 257; **25** 154, 156
Zürich Versicherungs-Gesellschaft, **III** 194, 402–03, **410–12**
Zurn Industries, Inc., **24** 150
Zwarovski, **16** 561
Zycad Corp., **11** 489–91
Zycon Corporation, **24** 201
Zymaise, **II** 582
ZyMOS Corp., **III** 458
Zytec Corporation, **19 513–15**

INDEX TO INDUSTRIES

Index to Industries

ACCOUNTING

Andersen Worldwide, 29 (upd.)
Deloitte & Touche, 9
Deloitte Touche Tohmatsu International, 29 (upd.)
Ernst & Young, 9; 29 (upd.)
L.S. Starrett Co., 13
McLane Company, Inc., 13
Price Waterhouse, 9
PricewaterhouseCoopers, 29 (upd.)
Univision Communications Inc., 24

ADVERTISING & OTHER BUSINESS SERVICES

A.C. Nielsen Company, 13
ABM Industries Incorporated, 25 (upd.)
Ackerley Communications, Inc., 9
Adia S.A., 6
Advo, Inc., 6
Aegis Group plc, 6
AHL Services, Inc., 27
American Building Maintenance Industries, Inc., 6
The American Society of Composers, Authors and Publishers (ASCAP), 29
Armor Holdings, Inc., 27
The Associated Press, 13
Barrett Business Services, Inc., 16
Bates Worldwide, Inc., 14
Bearings, Inc., 13
Berlitz International, Inc., 13
Big Flower Press Holdings, Inc., 21
Bozell Worldwide Inc., 25
Bright Horizons Family Solutions, Inc., 31
Broadcast Music Inc., 23
Burns International Security Services, 13
Campbell-Mithun-Esty, Inc., 16
Carmichael Lynch Inc., 28
Central Parking Corporation, 18
Chiat/Day Inc. Advertising, 11
Christie's International plc, 15
Cintas Corporation, 21
Computer Learning Centers, Inc., 26
CORT Business Services Corporation, 26
Cox Enterprises, Inc., 22 (upd.)
Cyrk Inc., 19
Dale Carnegie Training, Inc., 28
D'Arcy Masius Benton & Bowles, Inc., 6
DDB Needham Worldwide, 14
Deluxe Corporation, 22 (upd.)
Dentsu Inc., I; 16 (upd.)
Deutsche Post AG, 29
EBSCO Industries, Inc., 17
Employee Solutions, Inc., 18
Ennis Business Forms, Inc., 21
Equifax Inc., 6; 28 (upd.)
Equity Marketing, Inc., 26
ERLY Industries Inc., 17
Euro RSCG Worldwide S.A., 13
Fallon McElligott Inc., 22
FlightSafety International, Inc., 29 (upd.)
Florists' Transworld Delivery, Inc., 28
Foote, Cone & Belding Communications, Inc., I
Gage Marketing Group, 26
Grey Advertising, Inc., 6
Gwathmey Siegel & Associates Architects LLC, 26
Ha-Lo Industries, Inc., 27
Hakuhodo, Inc., 6
Handleman Company, 15
Hays Plc, 27
Heidrick & Struggles International, Inc., 28
Hildebrandt International, 29
International Management Group, 18
Interpublic Group Inc., I
The Interpublic Group of Companies, Inc., 22 (upd.)
Japan Leasing Corporation, 8
Jostens, Inc., 25 (upd.)
JWT Group Inc., I
Katz Communications, Inc., 6
Kelly Services Inc., 6; 26 (upd.)
Ketchum Communications Inc., 6
Kinko's Inc., 16
Labor Ready, Inc., 29
Lamar Advertising Company, 27
Learning Tree International Inc., 24
Leo Burnett Company Inc., I; 20 (upd.)
Lintas: Worldwide, 14
Mail Boxes Etc., 18
Manpower, Inc., 30 (upd.)
National Media Corporation, 27
New England Business Services, Inc., 18
New Valley Corporation, 17
NFO Worldwide, Inc., 24
Norrell Corporation, 25
Norwood Promotional Products, Inc., 26
The Ogilvy Group, Inc., I
Olsten Corporation, 6; 29 (upd.)
Omnicom Group, I; 22 (upd.)
On Assignment, Inc., 20
1-800-FLOWERS, Inc., 26
Outdoor Systems, Inc., 25
Paris Corporation, 22
Paychex, Inc., 15
Pierce Leahy Corporation, 24
Pinkerton's Inc., 9
PMT Services, Inc., 24
Publicis S.A., 19
Publishers Clearing House, 23
Randstad Holding n.v., 16
RemedyTemp, Inc., 20
Rental Service Corporation, 28
Robert Half International Inc., 18
Ronco, Inc., 15
Saatchi & Saatchi PLC, I
ServiceMaster Limited Partnership, 6
Shared Medical Systems Corporation, 14
Sir Speedy, Inc., 16
Skidmore, Owings & Merrill, 13
SOS Staffing Services, 25
Sotheby's Holdings, Inc., 11; 29 (upd.)
Spencer Stuart and Associates, Inc., 14
Superior Uniform Group, Inc., 30
TBWA Advertising, Inc., 6
Ticketmaster Corp., 13
TMP Worldwide Inc., 30
TNT Post Group N.V., 30
Transmedia Network Inc., 20
TRM Copy Centers Corporation, 18
True North Communications Inc., 23
Tyler Corporation, 23
U.S. Office Products Company, 25
UniFirst Corporation, 21
United News & Media plc, 28 (upd.)
Unitog Co., 19
The Wackenhut Corporation, 14
Wells Rich Greene BDDP, 6
William Morris Agency, Inc., 23
WPP Group plc, 6
Young & Rubicam, Inc., I; 22 (upd.)

AEROSPACE

A.S. Yakovlev Design Bureau, 15
The Aerospatiale Group, 7; 21 (upd.)
Alliant Techsystems Inc., 30 (upd.)
Aviacionny Nauchno-Tehnicheskii Komplex im. A.N. Tupoleva, 24
Avions Marcel Dassault-Breguet Aviation, I
B/E Aerospace, Inc., 30
Banner Aerospace, Inc., 14
Beech Aircraft Corporation, 8
The Boeing Company, I; 10 (upd.)
British Aerospace plc, I; 24 (upd.)
Canadair, Inc., 16
Cessna Aircraft Company, 8
Cobham plc, 30
Daimler-Benz Aerospace AG, 16
Ducommun Incorporated, 30
Fairchild Aircraft, Inc., 9
G.I.E. Airbus Industrie, I; 12 (upd.)
General Dynamics Corporation, I; 10 (upd.)
Groupe Dassault Aviation SA, 26 (upd.)
Grumman Corporation, I; 11 (upd.)
Gulfstream Aerospace Corporation, 7; 28 (upd.)
HEICO Corporation, 30
N.V. Koninklijke Nederlandse Vliegtuigenfabriek Fokker, I; 28 (upd.)
Learjet Inc., 8; 27 (upd.)
Lockheed Corporation, I; 11 (upd.)
Lockheed Martin Corporation, 15 (upd.)
Martin Marietta Corporation, I
McDonnell Douglas Corporation, I; 11 (upd.)
Messerschmitt-Bölkow-Blohm GmbH., I
Moog Inc., 13
Northrop Corporation, I; 11 (upd.)
Orbital Sciences Corporation, 22
Pratt & Whitney, 9
Rockwell International Corporation, I; 11 (upd.)
Rolls-Royce Allison, 29 (upd.)
Rolls-Royce plc, I; 7 (upd.); 21 (upd.)
Sequa Corp., 13
Sikorsky Aircraft Corporation, 24
Smiths Industries PLC, 25
Société Air France, 27 (upd.)
Sukhoi Design Bureau Aviation Scientific-Industrial Complex, 24
Sundstrand Corporation, 7; 21 (upd.)

Textron Lycoming Turbine Engine, 9
Thiokol Corporation, 9; 22 (upd.)
United Technologies Corporation, I; 10 (upd.)

AIRLINES

Aeroflot Soviet Airlines, 6
Aeroflot—Russian International Airlines, 29 (upd.)
Air Canada, 6; 23 (upd.)
Air New Zealand Limited, 14
Air-India Limited, 6; 27 (upd.)
AirTran Holdings, Inc., 22
Alaska Air Group, Inc., 6; 29 (upd.)
Alitalia-Linee Aeree Italiana, S.p.A., 6; 29 (upd.)
All Nippon Airways Company Limited, 6
Aloha Airlines, Incorporated, 24
America West Airlines, 6
American Airlines, I; 6 (upd.)
The American Society of Composers, Authors and Publishers (ASCAP), 29
AMR Corporation, 28 (upd.)
Aviacionny Nauchno-Tehnicheskii Komplex im. A.N. Tupoleva, 24
British Airways PLC, I; 14 (upd.)
British World Airlines Ltd., 18
Cathay Pacific Airways Limited, 6
China Eastern Airlines Co. Ltd., 31
Comair Holdings Inc., 13
Continental Airlines, Inc., I; 21 (upd.)
Corporación Internacional de Aviación, S.A. de C.V. (Cintra), 20
Delta Air Lines, Inc., I; 6 (upd.)
Deutsche Lufthansa Aktiengesellschaft, I; 26 (upd.)
Eastern Airlines, I
EgyptAir, 6; 27 (upd.)
El Al Israel Airlines Ltd., 23
Finnair Oy, 6; 25 (upd.)
Frontier Airlines, Inc., 22
Garuda Indonesia, 6
Groupe Air France, 6
HAL Inc., 9
Hawaiian Airlines, Inc., 22 (upd.)
Iberia Líneas Aéreas de España S.A., 6
Japan Air Lines Company Ltd., I
Kitty Hawk, Inc., 22
Kiwi International Airlines Inc., 20
Koninklijke Luchtvaart Maatschappij, N.V. (KLM Royal Dutch Airlines), I; 28 (upd.)
Korean Air Lines Co., Ltd., 6; 27 (upd.)
Lan Chile S.A., 31
Malév Plc, 24
Malaysian Airlines System Berhad, 29 (upd.)
Malaysian Airlines System BHD, 6
Mesa Airlines, Inc., 11
Mesaba Holdings, Inc., 28
Northwest Airlines Corporation, I; 6 (upd.); 26 (upd.)
Pan American World Airways, Inc., I; 12 (upd.)
People Express Airlines, Inc., I
Philippine Airlines, Inc., 6; 23 (upd.)
Qantas Airways Limited, 6; 24 (upd.)
Reno Air Inc., 23
SAA (Pty) Ltd., 28
Saudi Arabian Airlines, 6; 27 (upd.)
Scandinavian Airlines System, I
Singapore Airlines Ltd., 6; 27 (upd.)
SkyWest, Inc., 25
Southwest Airlines Co., 6; 24 (upd.)
Spirit Airlines, Inc., 31
Sun Country Airlines, 30
Swiss Air Transport Company, Ltd., I
Texas Air Corporation, I
Thai Airways International Public Company Limited, 6; 27 (upd.)
Tower Air, Inc., 28
Trans World Airlines, Inc., I; 12 (upd.)
TransBrasil S/A Linhas Aéreas, 31
Transportes Aereos Portugueses, S.A., 6
United Airlines, I; 6 (upd.)
US Airways Group, Inc., 28 (upd.)
USAir Group, Inc., I; 6 (upd.)
VARIG S.A. (Viação Aérea Rio-Grandense), 6; 29 (upd.)

AUTOMOTIVE

AB Volvo, I; 7 (upd.); 26 (upd.)
Adam Opel AG, 7; 21 (upd.)
Alfa Romeo, 13
American Motors Corporation, I
Arvin Industries, Inc., 8
Automobiles Citroen, 7
Automobili Lamborghini S.p.A., 13
Bayerische Motoren Werke A.G., I; 11 (upd.)
Bendix Corporation, I
Borg-Warner Automotive, Inc., 14
The Budd Company, 8
CARQUEST Corporation, 29
Chrysler Corporation, I; 11 (upd.)
Cummins Engine Co. Inc., I; 12 (upd.)
Custom Chrome, Inc., 16
Daihatsu Motor Company, Ltd., 7; 21 (upd.)
Daimler-Benz A.G., I; 15 (upd.)
Dana Corporation, I; 10 (upd.)
Douglas & Lomason Company, 16
Ducati Motor Holding S.p.A., 30
Eaton Corporation, I; 10 (upd.)
Echlin Inc., I; 11 (upd.)
Federal-Mogul Corporation, I; 10 (upd.); 26 (upd.)
Ferrari S.p.A., 13
Fiat S.p.A, I; 11 (upd.)
FinishMaster, Inc., 24
Ford Motor Company, I; 11 (upd.)
Ford Motor Company, S.A. de C.V., 20
Fruehauf Corporation, I
General Motors Corporation, I; 10 (upd.)
Gentex Corporation, 26
Genuine Parts Company, 9
Harley-Davidson Inc., 7; 25 (upd.)
Hayes Lemmerz International, Inc., 27
Hino Motors, Ltd., 7; 21 (upd.)
Honda Motor Company Limited, 29 (upd.)
Honda Motor Company Limited (Honda Giken Kogyo Kabushiki Kaisha), I; 10 (upd.)
Insurance Auto Auctions, Inc., 23
Isuzu Motors, Ltd., 9; 23 (upd.)
Kelsey-Hayes Group of Companies, 7; 27 (upd.)
Kia Motors Corporation, 12; 29 (upd.)
Lear Seating Corporation, 16
Lotus Cars Ltd., 14
Mack Trucks, Inc., I; 22 (upd.)
Masland Corporation, 17
Mazda Motor Corporation, 9; 23 (upd.)
Mel Farr Automotive Group, 20
Metso Corporation, 30 (upd.)
Midas International Corporation, 10
Mitsubishi Motors Corporation, 9; 23 (upd.)
Monaco Coach Corporation, 31
Monro Muffler Brake, Inc., 24
Navistar International Corporation, I; 10 (upd.)
Nissan Motor Company Ltd., I; 11 (upd.)
O'Reilly Automotive, Inc., 26
Officine Alfieri Maserati S.p.A., 13
Oshkosh Truck Corporation, 7
Paccar Inc., I
PACCAR Inc., 26 (upd.)
Pennzoil Company, 20 (upd.)
Penske Corporation, 19 (upd.)
The Pep Boys—Manny, Moe & Jack, 11
Peugeot S.A., I
Piaggio & C. S.p.A., 20
Porsche AG, 13; 31 (upd.)
PSA Peugeot Citroen S.A., 28 (upd.)
Regie Nationale des Usines Renault, I
Renault S.A., 26 (upd.)
Republic Industries, Inc., 26
Robert Bosch GmbH., I; 16 (upd.)
RockShox, Inc., 26
Rolls-Royce plc, I; 21 (upd.)
Rover Group Ltd., 7; 21 (upd.)
Saab-Scania A.B., I; 11 (upd.)
Safelite Glass Corp., 19
Saturn Corporation, 7; 21 (upd.)
Sealed Power Corporation, I
Sheller-Globe Corporation, I
Spartan Motors Inc., 14
SpeeDee Oil Change and Tune-Up, 25
SPX Corporation, 10
Superior Industries International, Inc., 8
Suzuki Motor Corporation, 9; 23 (upd.)
Tower Automotive, Inc., 24
Toyota Motor Corporation, I; 11 (upd.)
TRW Inc., 14 (upd.)
Ugly Duckling Corporation, 22
United Auto Group, Inc., 26
United Technologies Automotive Inc., 15
Valeo, 23
Volkswagen A.G., I; 11 (upd.)
Walker Manufacturing Company, 19
Winnebago Industries Inc., 7; 27 (upd.)
Ziebart International Corporation, 30

BEVERAGES

A & W Brands, Inc., 25
Adolph Coors Company, I; 13 (upd.)
Allied Domecq PLC, 29
Allied-Lyons PLC, I
Anheuser-Busch Companies, Inc., I; 10 (upd.)
Asahi Breweries, Ltd., I; 20 (upd.)
Bacardi Limited, 18
Bass PLC, I; 15 (upd.)
Beringer Wine Estates Holdings, Inc., 22
Boston Beer Company, 18
Brauerei Beck & Co., 9
Brown-Forman Corporation, I; 10 (upd.)
Canandaigua Wine Company, Inc., 13
Carlsberg A/S, 9; 29 (upd.)
Carlton and United Breweries Ltd., I
Casa Cuervo, S.A. de C.V., 31
Cerveceria Polar, I
Coca Cola Bottling Co. Consolidated, 10
The Coca-Cola Company, I; 10 (upd.)
Corby Distilleries Limited, 14
Dean Foods Company, 21 (upd.)
Distillers Company PLC, I
Dr Pepper/7Up Companies, Inc., 9
E. & J. Gallo Winery, I; 7 (upd.); 28 (upd.)
Ferolito, Vultaggio & Sons, 27
Foster's Brewing Group Ltd., 7; 21 (upd.)
G. Heileman Brewing Company Inc., I
General Cinema Corporation, I
Grand Metropolitan PLC, I
Green Mountain Coffee, Inc., 31
The Greenalls Group PLC, 21
Greene King plc, 31
Grupo Modelo, S.A. de C.V., 29
Guinness PLC, I
Hansen Natural Corporation, 31
Heineken N.V, I; 13 (upd.)

Heublein, Inc., I
Hiram Walker Resources, Ltd., I
Interbrew S.A., 17
Jacob Leinenkugel Brewing Company, 28
JD Wetherspoon plc, 30
Kendall-Jackson Winery, Ltd., 28
Kikkoman Corporation, 14
Kirin Brewery Company, Limited, I; 21 (upd.)
Labatt Brewing Company Limited, I; 25 (upd.)
Maison Louis Jadot, 24
Marie Brizard & Roger International S.A., 22
Miller Brewing Company, I; 12 (upd.)
The Minute Maid Company, 28
Moët-Hennessy, I
The Molson Companies Limited, I, 26 (upd.)
National Beverage Corp., 26
National Grape Cooperative Association, Inc., 20
Ocean Spray Cranberries, Inc., 25 (upd.)
Odwalla, Inc., 31
Pepsico, Inc., I; 10 (upd.)
Pernod Ricard S.A., I; 21 (upd.)
Pete's Brewing Company, 22
Philip Morris Companies Inc., 18 (upd.)
Rainier Brewing Company, 23
Redhook Ale Brewery, Inc., 31
Rémy Cointreau S.A., 20
Robert Mondavi Corporation, 15
Royal Crown Company, Inc., 23
Sapporo Breweries, Ltd., I; 13 (upd.)
Scottish & Newcastle plc, 15
The Seagram Company Ltd., I; 25 (upd.)
Sebastiani Vineyards, Inc., 28
Shepherd Neame Limited, 30
Snapple Beverage Corporation, 11
The South African Breweries Limited, I; 24 (upd.)
Starbucks Corporation, 13
The Stroh Brewery Company, 18 (upd.)
The Stroh Brewing Company, I
Sutter Home Winery Inc., 16
Todhunter International, Inc., 27
Vin & Spirit AB, 31
Whitbread and Company PLC, I

BIOTECHNOLOGY

Amgen, Inc., 10; 30 (upd.)
Biogen Inc., 14
Centocor Inc., 14
Chiron Corporation, 10
Covance Inc., 30
IDEXX Laboratories, Inc., 23
Immunex Corporation, 14
Life Technologies, Inc., 17
Medtronic, Inc., 30 (upd.)
Millipore Corporation, 25
Minntech Corporation, 22
Mycogen Corporation, 21
Quintiles Transnational Corporation, 21
Seminis, Inc., 29
STERIS Corporation, 29

CHEMICALS

A. Schulman, Inc., 8
Air Products and Chemicals, Inc., I; 10 (upd.)
Akzo Nobel N.V., 13
AlliedSignal Inc., 22 (upd.)
American Cyanamid, I; 8 (upd.)
ARCO Chemical Company, 10
Atochem S.A., I
Baker Hughes Incorporated, 22 (upd.)
BASF Aktiengesellschaft, I; 18 (upd.)
Bayer A.G., I; 13 (upd.)
Betz Laboratories, Inc., I; 10 (upd.)
The BFGoodrich Company, 19 (upd.)
BOC Group plc, I; 25 (upd.)
Brenntag AG, 8; 23 (upd.)
Burmah Castrol PLC, 30 (upd.)
Cabot Corporation, 8; 29 (upd.)
Cambrex Corporation, 16
Celanese Corporation, I
Chemcentral Corporation, 8
Chemi-Trol Chemical Co., 16
Church & Dwight Co., Inc., 29
Ciba-Geigy Ltd., I; 8 (upd.)
The Clorox Company, 22 (upd.)
Crompton & Knowles, 9
Cytec Industries Inc., 27
DeKalb Genetics Corporation, 17
The Dexter Corporation, I; 12 (upd.)
The Dow Chemical Company, I; 8 (upd.)
DSM, N.V, I
E.I. Du Pont de Nemours & Company, I; 8 (upd.); 26 (upd.)
Eastman Chemical Company, 14
Ecolab, Inc., I; 13 (upd.)
English China Clays plc, 15 (upd.)
ERLY Industries Inc., 17
Ethyl Corporation, I; 10 (upd.)
Ferro Corporation, 8
First Mississippi Corporation, 8
Formosa Plastics Corporation, 14
Fort James Corporation, 22 (upd.)
G.A.F., I
Georgia Gulf Corporation, 9
Great Lakes Chemical Corporation, I; 14 (upd.)
Hawkins Chemical, Inc., 16
Hercules Inc., I; 22 (upd.)
Hoechst A.G., I; 18 (upd.)
Hoechst Celanese Corporation, 13
Huls A.G., I
Huntsman Chemical Corporation, 8
IMC Fertilizer Group, Inc., 8
Imperial Chemical Industries PLC, I
International Flavors & Fragrances Inc., 9
Koppers Industries, Inc., I; 26 (upd.)
L'air Liquide, I
Lawter International Inc., 14
LeaRonal, Inc., 23
Loctite Corporation, 30 (upd.)
Lubrizol Corporation, I; 30 (upd.)
M.A. Hanna Company, 8
Mallinckrodt Group Inc., 19
Melamine Chemicals, Inc., 27
Mitsubishi Chemical Industries, Ltd., I
Mitsui Petrochemical Industries, Ltd., 9
Monsanto Company, I; 9 (upd.); 29 (upd.)
Montedison SpA, I
Morton International Inc., 9 (upd.)
Morton Thiokol, Inc., I
Nagase & Company, Ltd., 8
Nalco Chemical Corporation, I; 12 (upd.)
National Distillers and Chemical Corporation, I
National Sanitary Supply Co., 16
NCH Corporation, 8
NL Industries, Inc., 10
Nobel Industries AB, 9
Novacor Chemicals Ltd., 12
NutraSweet Company, 8
Olin Corporation, I; 13 (upd.)
OM Group, Inc., 17
Pennwalt Corporation, I
Perstorp A.B., I
Petrolite Corporation, 15
Praxair, Inc., 11
Quantum Chemical Corporation, 8
Reichhold Chemicals, Inc., 10
Rhône-Poulenc S.A., I; 10 (upd.)
Rohm and Haas Company, I; 26 (upd.)
Roussel Uclaf, I; 8 (upd.)
The Scotts Company, 22
Sequa Corp., 13
Shanghai Petrochemical Co., Ltd., 18
Solvay & Cie S.A., I; 21 (upd.)
Stepan Company, 30
Sterling Chemicals, Inc., 16
Sumitomo Chemical Company Ltd., I
Terra Industries, Inc., 13
Teva Pharmaceutical Industries Ltd., 22
TOTAL S.A., 24 (upd.)
Union Carbide Corporation, I; 9 (upd.)
Univar Corporation, 9
Vista Chemical Company, I
Witco Corporation, I; 16 (upd.)
Zeneca Group PLC, 21

CONGLOMERATES

Accor SA, 10; 27 (upd.)
AEG A.G., I
Alcatel Alsthom Compagnie Générale d'Electricité, 9
Alco Standard Corporation, I
Alfa, S.A. de C.V., 19
Allied Domecq PLC, 29
Allied-Signal Inc., I
AMFAC Inc., I
Aramark Corporation, 13
Archer-Daniels-Midland Company, I; 11 (upd.)
Arkansas Best Corporation, 16
Barlow Rand Ltd., I
Bat Industries PLC, I
Bond Corporation Holdings Limited, 10
BTR PLC, I
Bunzl plc, 31 (upd.)
Burlington Northern Santa Fe Corporation, 27 (upd.)
C. Itoh & Company Ltd., I
Cargill Inc., 13 (upd.)
CBI Industries, Inc., 7
Chemed Corporation, 13
Chesebrough-Pond's USA, Inc., 8
CITIC Pacific Ltd., 18
Colt Industries Inc., I
The Connell Company, 29
CSR Limited, 28 (upd.)
Daewoo Group, 18 (upd.)
De Dietrich & Cie., 31
Deere & Company, 21 (upd.)
Delaware North Companies Incorporated, 7
Desc, S.A. de C.V., 23
The Dial Corp., 8
El Corte Inglés Group, 26 (upd.)
Elders IXL Ltd., I
Engelhard Corporation, 21 (upd.)
Farley Northwest Industries, Inc., I
First Pacific Company Limited, 18
Fisher Companies, Inc., 15
Fletcher Challenge Ltd., 19 (upd.)
FMC Corporation, I; 11 (upd.)
Fortune Brands, Inc., 29 (upd.)
Fuqua Industries, Inc., I
GIB Group, 26 (upd.)
Gillett Holdings, Inc., 7
Grand Metropolitan PLC, 14 (upd.)
Great American Management and Investment, Inc., 8
Greyhound Corporation, I
Grupo Carso, S.A. de C.V., 21
Grupo Industrial Bimbo, 19
Gulf & Western Inc., I
Hankyu Corporation, 23 (upd.)
Hanson PLC, III; 7 (upd.)
Hitachi Ltd., I; 12 (upd.)
Hutchison Whampoa Ltd., 18

IC Industries, Inc., I
Inchcape plc, 16 (upd.)
Ingram Industries, Inc., 11
Instituto Nacional de Industria, I
International Controls Corporation, 10
International Telephone & Telegraph Corporation, I; 11 (upd.)
Istituto per la Ricostruzione Industriale, I
Jardine Matheson Holdings Limited, I; 20 (upd.)
Jason Incorporated, 23
Jefferson Smurfit Group plc, 19 (upd.)
Justin Industries, Inc., 19
Kanematsu Corporation, 24 (upd.)
Kao Corporation, 20 (upd.)
Katy Industries, Inc., I
Kesko Ltd. (Kesko Oy), 8; 27 (upd.)
Kidde, Inc., I
KOC Holding A.S., I
Koninklijke Nedlloyd N.V., 26 (upd.)
Koor Industries Ltd., 25 (upd.)
K2 Inc., 16
The L.L. Knickerbocker Co., Inc., 25
Lancaster Colony Corporation, 8
Larry H. Miller Group, 29
Lear Siegler, Inc., I
Lefrak Organization Inc., 26
Leucadia National Corporation, 11
Litton Industries, Inc., I; 11 (upd.)
Loews Corporation, I; 12 (upd.)
Loral Corporation, 8
LTV Corporation, I
Marubeni Corporation, 24 (upd.)
Marubeni K.K., I
MAXXAM Inc., 8
McKesson Corporation, I
Menasha Corporation, 8
Metallgesellschaft AG, 16 (upd.)
Metromedia Co., 7
Minnesota Mining & Manufacturing Company (3M), I; 8 (upd.); 26 (upd.)
Mitsubishi Corporation, I; 12 (upd.)
Mitsui & Co., Ltd., 28 (upd.)
Mitsui Bussan K.K., I
The Molson Companies Limited, I; 26 (upd.)
Montedison S.p.A., 24 (upd.)
NACCO Industries, Inc., 7
National Service Industries, Inc., 11
Nichimen Corporation, 24 (upd.)
Nissho Iwai K.K., I
Norsk Hydro A.S., 10
Ogden Corporation, I
Onex Corporation, 16
Orkla A/S, 18
Park-Ohio Industries Inc., 17
Pentair, Inc., 7
Powell Duffryn plc, 31
Preussag AG, 17
Pubco Corporation, 17
Pulsar Internacional S.A., 21
The Rank Organisation Plc, 14 (upd.)
Red Apple Group, Inc., 23
Rubbermaid Incorporated, 20 (upd.)
Samsung Group, I
San Miguel Corporation, 15
Sara Lee Corporation, 15 (upd.)
Schindler Holding AG, 29
Sea Containers Ltd., 29
ServiceMaster Inc., 23 (upd.)
Sime Darby Berhad, 14
Société du Louvre, 27
Standex International Corporation, 17
Stinnes AG, 23 (upd.)
Sudbury Inc., 16
Sumitomo Corporation, I; 11 (upd.)
Swire Pacific Ltd., I; 16 (upd.)
Talley Industries, Inc., 16
Tandycrafts, Inc., 31
Teledyne, Inc., I; 10 (upd.)
Tenneco Inc., I; 10 (upd.)
Textron Inc., I
Thomas H. Lee Co., 24
Thorn Emi PLC, I
Thorn plc, 24
TI Group plc, 17
Time Warner Inc., IV; 7 (upd.)
Tomen Corporation, 24 (upd.)
Tomkins plc, 11
Toshiba Corporation, I; 12 (upd.)
Tractebel S.A., 20
Transamerica Corporation, I; 13 (upd.)
The Tranzonic Cos., 15
Triarc Companies, Inc., 8
TRW Inc., I; 11 (upd.)
Unilever PLC, II; 7 (upd.)
Valhi, Inc., 19
Valores Industriales S.A., 19
Veba A.G., I; 15 (upd.)
Vendôme Luxury Group plc, 27
Viacom Inc., 23 (upd.)
Virgin Group PLC, 12
W.R. Grace & Company, I
Wheaton Industries, 8
Whitbread PLC, 20 (upd.)
Whitman Corporation, 10 (upd.)
Whittaker Corporation, I
WorldCorp, Inc., 10
Worms et Cie, 27

CONSTRUCTION

A. Johnson & Company H.B., I
ABC Supply Co., Inc., 22
Abrams Industries Inc., 23
AMREP Corporation, 21
The Austin Company, 8
Baratt Developments PLC, I
Beazer Homes USA, Inc., 17
Bechtel Group, Inc., I; 24 (upd.)
BFC Construction Corporation, 25
Bilfinger & Berger Bau A.G., I
Bird Corporation, 19
Black & Veatch LLP, 22
Bouygues S.A., I; 24 (upd.)
Brown & Root, Inc., 13
CalMat Co., 19
Centex Corporation, 8; 29 (upd.)
Cianbro Corporation, 14
The Clark Construction Group, Inc., 8
Colas S.A., 31
Day & Zimmermann, Inc., 31 (upd.)
Dillingham Corporation, I
Dominion Homes, Inc., 19
Eiffage, 27
Environmental Industries, Inc., 31
Eurotunnel PLC, 13
Fairclough Construction Group PLC, I
Fleetwood Enterprises, Inc., 22 (upd.)
Fluor Corporation, I; 8 (upd.)
George Wimpey PLC, 12
Granite Rock Company, 26
Hillsdown Holdings plc, 24 (upd.)
Horton Homes, Inc., 25
Hospitality Worldwide Services, Inc., 26
Hovnanian Enterprises, Inc., 29
J.A. Jones, Inc., 16
John Brown PLC, I
John Laing PLC, I
Kajima Corporation, I
Kaufman and Broad Home Corporation, 8
Kitchell Corporation, 14
The Koll Company, 8
Komatsu Ltd., 16 (upd.)
Kumagai Gumi Company, Ltd., I
L'Entreprise Jean Lefebvre, 23
Lennar Corporation, 11
Lincoln Property Company, 8
Lindal Cedar Homes, Inc., 29
Linde A.G., I
Mellon-Stuart Company, I
Michael Baker Corp., 14
Morrison Knudsen Corporation, 7; 28 (upd.)
New Holland N.V., 22
NVR L.P., 8
Ohbayashi Corporation, I
The Peninsular & Oriental Steam Navigation Company (Bovis Division), I
Perini Corporation, 8
Peter Kiewit Sons' Inc., 8
Philipp Holzmann AG, 17
Post Properties, Inc., 26
Pulte Corporation, 8
Redrow Group plc, 31
Rooney Brothers Co., 25
The Rottlund Company, Inc., 28
The Ryland Group, Inc., 8
Schuff Steel Company, 26
Shorewood Packaging Corporation, 28
Simon Property Group, Inc., 27
Sundt Corp., 24
Taylor Woodrow PLC, I
Thyssen Krupp AG, 28 (upd.)
Toll Brothers Inc., 15
Trammell Crow Company, 8
Tridel Enterprises Inc., 9
The Turner Corporation, 8; 23 (upd.)
U.S. Home Corporation, 8
Walter Industries, Inc., 22 (upd.)
Wood Hall Trust PLC, I

CONTAINERS

Ball Corporation, I; 10 (upd.)
BWAY Corporation, 24
Clarcor Inc., 17
Continental Can Co., Inc., 15
Continental Group Company, I
Crown, Cork & Seal Company, Inc., I; 13 (upd.)
Gaylord Container Corporation, 8
Golden Belt Manufacturing Co., 16
Greif Bros. Corporation, 15
Inland Container Corporation, 8
Kerr Group Inc., 24
Keyes Fibre Company, 9
Liqui-Box Corporation, 16
The Longaberger Company, 12
Longview Fibre Company, 8
The Mead Corporation, 19 (upd.)
Metal Box PLC, I
National Can Corporation, I
Owens-Illinois, Inc., I; 26 (upd.)
Primerica Corporation, I
Reynolds Metals Company, 19 (upd.)
Royal Packaging Industries Van Leer N.V., 30
Sealright Co., Inc., 17
Smurfit-Stone Container Corporation, 26 (upd.)
Sonoco Products Company, 8
Thermos Company, 16
Toyo Seikan Kaisha, Ltd., I
U.S. Can Corporation, 30
Ultra Pac, Inc., 24
Viatech Continental Can Company, Inc., 25 (upd.)

DRUGS/PHARMACEUTICALS

A.L. Pharma Inc., 12
Abbott Laboratories, I; 11 (upd.)
ALZA Corporation, 10
American Home Products, I; 10 (upd.)

Amgen, Inc., 10
Astra AB, I; 20 (upd.)
Barr Laboratories, Inc., 26
Bayer A.G., I; 13 (upd.)
Block Drug Company, Inc., 8
Bristol-Myers Squibb Company, III; 9 (upd.)
Carter-Wallace, Inc., 8
Chiron Corporation, 10
Ciba-Geigy Ltd., I; 8 (upd.)
D&K Wholesale Drug, Inc., 14
Eli Lilly & Company, I; 11 (upd.)
F. Hoffmann-Laroche & Company A.G., I
Fisons plc, 9; 23 (upd.)
FoxMeyer Health Corporation, 16
Fujisawa Pharmaceutical Company Ltd., I
G.D. Searle & Company, I; 12 (upd.)
GEHE AG, 27
Genentech, Inc., I; 8 (upd.)
Genetics Institute, Inc., 8
Genzyme Corporation, 13
Glaxo Holdings PLC, I; 9 (upd.)
Johnson & Johnson, III; 8 (upd.)
Jones Medical Industries, Inc., 24
Marion Merrell Dow, Inc., I; 9 (upd.)
McKesson Corporation, 12
Merck & Co., Inc., I; 11 (upd.)
Miles Laboratories, I
Monsanto Company, 29 (upd.)
Moore Medical Corp., 17
Murdock Madaus Schwabe, 26
Mylan Laboratories Inc., I; 20 (upd.)
National Patent Development Corporation, 13
Novo Industri A/S, I
Pfizer Inc., I; 9 (upd.)
Pharmacia & Upjohn Inc., 25 (upd.)
Pharmacia A.B., I
Quintiles Transnational Corporation, 21
R.P. Scherer, I
Roberts Pharmaceutical Corporation, 16
Roche Bioscience, 14 (upd.)
Rorer Group, I
Roussel Uclaf, I; 8 (upd.)
Sandoz Ltd., I
Sankyo Company, Ltd., I
Sanofi Group, I
Schering A.G., I
Schering-Plough Corporation, I; 14 (upd.)
Shionogi & Co., Ltd., 17 (upd.)
Sigma-Aldrich, I
SmithKline Beckman Corporation, I
Squibb Corporation, I
Sterling Drug, Inc., I
The Sunrider Corporation, 26
Syntex Corporation, I
Takeda Chemical Industries, Ltd., I
Teva Pharmaceutical Industries Ltd., 22
The Upjohn Company, I; 8 (upd.)
Vitalink Pharmacy Services, Inc., 15
Warner-Lambert Co., I; 10 (upd.)
Watson Pharmaceuticals Inc., 16
The Wellcome Foundation Ltd., I

ELECTRICAL & ELECTRONICS

ABB ASEA Brown Boveri Ltd., II; 22 (upd.)
Acer Inc., 16
Acuson Corporation, 10
ADC Telecommunications, Inc., 30 (upd.)
Adtran Inc., 22
Advanced Micro Devices, Inc., 30 (upd.)
Advanced Technology Laboratories, Inc., 9
Aiwa Co., Ltd., 30
Alliant Techsystems Inc., 30 (upd.)
AlliedSignal Inc., 22 (upd.)
Alpine Electronics, Inc., 13
Alps Electric Co., Ltd., II
Altera Corporation, 18
Altron Incorporated, 20
American Power Conversion Corporation, 24
AMP Incorporated, II; 14 (upd.)
Analog Devices, Inc., 10
Analogic Corporation, 23
Anam Group, 23
Andrew Corporation, 10
Arrow Electronics, Inc., 10
Ascend Communications, Inc., 24
Atari Corporation, 9; 23 (upd.)
Atmel Corporation, 17
Autodesk, Inc., 10
Avnet Inc., 9
Bicoastal Corporation, II
Bose Corporation, 13
Boston Acoustics, Inc., 22
Burr-Brown Corporation, 19
Cabletron Systems, Inc., 10
Canon Inc., 18 (upd.)
Casio Computer Co., Ltd., 16 (upd.)
Citizen Watch Co., Ltd., 21 (upd.)
Cobham plc, 30
Cobra Electronics Corporation, 14
Coherent, Inc., 31
Compagnie Générale d'Électricité, II
Cooper Industries, Inc., II
Cray Research, Inc., 16 (upd.)
Cubic Corporation, 19
Cypress Semiconductor Corporation, 20
Dallas Semiconductor Corporation, 13; 31 (upd.)
Dell Computer Corporation, 31 (upd.)
DH Technology, Inc., 18
Digi International Inc., 9
Discreet Logic Inc., 20
Dixons Group plc, 19 (upd.)
Dolby Laboratories Inc., 20
Dynatech Corporation, 13
E-Systems, Inc., 9
Electronics for Imaging, Inc., 15
Emerson Electric Co., II
Emerson Radio Corp., 30
ENCAD, Incorporated, 25
ESS Technology, Inc., 22
Everex Systems, Inc., 16
Exar Corp., 14
Exide Electronics Group, Inc., 20
Fluke Corporation, 15
Foxboro Company, 13
Fuji Electric Co., Ltd., II
Fujitsu Limited, 16 (upd.)
General Electric Company, II; 12 (upd.)
General Electric Company, PLC, II
General Instrument Corporation, 10
General Signal Corporation, 9
GenRad, Inc., 24
GM Hughes Electronics Corporation, II
Goldstar Co., Ltd., 12
Gould Electronics, Inc., 14
Grundig AG, 27
Hadco Corporation, 24
Hamilton Beach/Proctor-Silex Inc., 17
Harman International Industries Inc., 15
Harris Corporation, II; 20 (upd.)
Hayes Corporation, 24
Hewlett-Packard Company, 28 (upd.)
Holophane Corporation, 19
Honeywell Inc., II; 12 (upd.)
Hubbell Incorporated, 9; 31 (upd.)
Hughes Supply, Inc., 14
Hutchinson Technology Incorporated, 18
Hypercom Corporation, 27
Imax Corporation, 28
In Focus Systems, Inc., 22
Indigo NV, 26
Intel Corporation, II; 10 (upd.)
International Business Machines Corporation, 30 (upd.)
International Rectifier Corporation, 31
Itel Corporation, 9
Jaco Electronics, Inc., 30
Juno Lighting, Inc., 30
Keithley Instruments Inc., 16
Kemet Corp., 14
Kent Electronics Corporation, 17
Kenwood Corporation, 31
Kingston Technology Corporation, 20
KitchenAid, 8
KnowledgeWare Inc., 9
Kollmorgen Corporation, 18
Konica Corporation, 30 (upd.)
Koor Industries Ltd., II
Kyocera Corporation, II
Lattice Semiconductor Corp., 16
Legrand SA, 21
Linear Technology, Inc., 16
Littelfuse, Inc., 26
Loral Corporation, 9
Lowrance Electronics, Inc., 18
LSI Logic Corporation, 13
Lucky-Goldstar, II
Lunar Corporation, 29
MagneTek, Inc., 15
Marquette Electronics, Inc., 13
Matsushita Electric Industrial Co., Ltd., II
Maxim Integrated Products, Inc., 16
Methode Electronics, Inc., 13
Mitel Corporation, 18
MITRE Corporation, 26
Mitsubishi Electric Corporation, II
Motorola, Inc., II; 11 (upd.)
National Instruments Corporation, 22
National Presto Industries, Inc., 16
National Semiconductor Corporation, II; 26 (upd.)
NEC Corporation, II; 21 (upd.)
Nintendo Co., Ltd., 28 (upd.)
Nokia Corporation, II; 17 (upd.)
Oak Technology, Inc., 22
Oki Electric Industry Company, Limited, II
Omron Corporation, 28 (upd.)
Omron Tateisi Electronics Company, II
Otter Tail Power Company, 18
Palomar Medical Technologies, Inc., 22
The Peak Technologies Group, Inc., 14
Peavey Electronics Corporation, 16
Philips Electronics N.V., II; 13 (upd.)
Philips Electronics North America Corp., 13
Pioneer Electronic Corporation, 28 (upd.)
Pioneer-Standard Electronics Inc., 19
Pittway Corporation, 9
The Plessey Company, PLC, II
Potter & Brumfield Inc., 11
Premier Industrial Corporation, 9
Racal Electronics PLC, II
Radius Inc., 16
Raychem Corporation, 8
Rayovac Corporation, 13
Raytheon Company, II; 11 (upd.)
RCA Corporation, II
Read-Rite Corp., 10
Reliance Electric Company, 9
Rexel, Inc., 15
Richardson Electronics, Ltd., 17
The Rival Company, 19
S&C Electric Company, 15
Sam Ash Music Corporation, 30
Samsung Electronics Co., Ltd., 14
Sanyo Electric Company, Ltd., II
ScanSource, Inc., 29
Schneider S.A., II; 18 (upd.)
SCI Systems, Inc., 9

Scitex Corporation Ltd., 24
Sensormatic Electronics Corp., 11
SGI, 29 (upd.)
Sharp Corporation, II; 12 (upd.)
Sheldahl Inc., 23
Siemens A.G., II; 14 (upd.)
Silicon Graphics Incorporated, 9
Smiths Industries PLC, 25
Solectron Corp., 12
Sony Corporation, II; 12 (upd.)
Sterling Electronics Corp., 18
Sumitomo Electric Industries, Ltd., II
Sun Microsystems, Inc., 30 (upd.)
Sunbeam-Oster Co., Inc., 9
SyQuest Technology, Inc., 18
Tandy Corporation, II; 12 (upd.)
Tatung Co., 23
TDK Corporation, II; 17 (upd.)
Tech-Sym Corporation, 18
Technitrol, Inc., 29
Tektronix, Inc., 8
Telxon Corporation, 10
Teradyne, Inc., 11
Texas Instruments Incorporated, II; 11 (upd.)
Thomson S.A., II
Tops Appliance City, Inc., 17
Toromont Industries, Ltd., 21
Tweeter Home Entertainment Group, Inc., 30
Ultrak Inc., 24
Varian Associates Inc., 12
Victor Company of Japan, Limited, II; 26 (upd.)
Vishay Intertechnology, Inc., 21
Vitro Corp., 10
VLSI Technology, Inc., 16
Westinghouse Electric Corporation, II; 12 (upd.)
Wyle Electronics, 14
Yageo Corporation, 16
Zenith Data Systems, Inc., 10
Zenith Electronics Corporation, II; 13 (upd.)
Zoom Telephonics, Inc., 18
Zytec Corporation, 19

ENGINEERING & MANAGEMENT SERVICES

AAON, Inc., 22
Aavid Thermal Technologies, Inc., 29
Alliant Techsystems Inc., 30 (upd.)
Analytic Sciences Corporation, 10
Arcadis NV, 26
The Austin Company, 8
Brown & Root, Inc., 13
C.H. Heist Corporation, 24
CDI Corporation, 6
CH2M Hill Ltd., 22
Coflexip S.A., 25
Corrections Corporation of America, 23
CRSS Inc., 6
Dames & Moore, Inc., 25
DAW Technologies, Inc., 25
Day & Zimmermann Inc., 9; 31 (upd.)
Donaldson Co. Inc., 16
EG&G Incorporated, 8; 29 (upd.)
Eiffage, 27
Essef Corporation, 18
Foster Wheeler Corporation, 6; 23 (upd.)
Framatome SA, 19
Halliburton Company, 25 (upd.)
Harding Lawson Associates Group, Inc., 16
Harza Engineering Company, 14
ICF Kaiser International, Inc., 28
Jacobs Engineering Group Inc., 6; 26 (upd.)
JWP Inc., 9
Layne Christensen Company, 19
The MacNeal-Schwendler Corporation, 25
McKinsey & Company, Inc., 9
Ogden Corporation, 6
The Parsons Corporation, 8
Rosemount Inc., 15
Rust International Inc., 11
Science Applications International Corporation, 15
Stone & Webster, Inc., 13
Susquehanna Pfaltzgraff Company, 8
Sverdrup Corporation, 14
Tetra Tech, Inc., 29
Thyssen Krupp AG, 28 (upd.)
Tracor Inc., 17
Underwriters Laboratories, Inc., 30
United Dominion Industries Limited, 8; 16 (upd.)
VECO International, Inc., 7

ENTERTAINMENT & LEISURE

Acclaim Entertainment Inc., 24
Airtours Plc, 27
All American Communications Inc., 20
Alliance Entertainment Corp., 17
Amblin Entertainment, 21
AMC Entertainment Inc., 12
American Skiing Company, 28
Anchor Gaming, 24
Applause Inc., 24
Aprilia SpA, 17
Argosy Gaming Company, 21
The Art Institute of Chicago, 29
Asahi National Broadcasting Company, Ltd., 9
Aspen Skiing Company, 15
The Atlantic Group, 23
Autotote Corporation, 20
Aztar Corporation, 13
Baker & Taylor, Inc., 16
Bally Total Fitness Holding Corp., 25
Bertelsmann AG, 15 (upd.)
Bertucci's Inc., 16
Blockbuster Entertainment Corporation, 9
Blockbuster Inc., 31 (upd.)
Bonneville International Corporation, 29
Booth Creek Ski Holdings, Inc., 31
Boston Celtics Limited Partnership, 14
British Broadcasting Corporation Ltd., 7; 21 (upd.)
British Sky Broadcasting Group Plc, 20
Cablevision Systems Corporation, 7
Capital Cities/ABC Inc., II
Carlson Companies, Inc., 22 (upd.)
Carmike Cinemas, Inc., 14
Carnival Corporation, 27 (upd.)
Carnival Cruise Lines, Inc., 6
CBS Inc., II; 6 (upd.)
Cedar Fair, L.P., 22
Central Independent Television, 7; 23 (upd.)
Century Theatres, Inc., 31
Chris-Craft Industries, Inc., 31 (upd.)
Churchill Downs Incorporated, 29
Cineplex Odeon Corporation, 6; 23 (upd.)
Cirque du Soleil Inc., 29
Columbia Pictures Entertainment, Inc., II
Columbia TriStar Motion Pictures Companies, 12 (upd.)
Comcast Corporation, 7
Continental Cablevision, Inc., 7
Corporation for Public Broadcasting, 14
Cox Enterprises, Inc., 22 (upd.)
Cruise America Inc., 21
Cunard Line Ltd., 23
Death Row Records, 27
dick clark productions, inc., 16
E! Entertainment Television Inc., 17
Edwards Theatres Circuit, Inc., 31
Equity Marketing, Inc., 26
Euro Disneyland SCA, 20
Family Golf Centers, Inc., 29
Fédération Internationale de Football Association, 27
First Team Sports, Inc., 22
Fox Family Worldwide, Inc., 24
Gaumont SA, 25
Gaylord Entertainment Company, 11
GC Companies, Inc., 25
Geffen Records Inc., 26
Gibson Guitar Corp., 16
Granada Group PLC, II; 24 (upd.)
Grand Casinos, Inc., 20
Hanna-Barbera Cartoons Inc., 23
Harpo Entertainment Group, 28
Harrah's Entertainment, Inc., 16
Harveys Casino Resorts, 27
Hastings Entertainment, Inc., 29
Hollywood Casino Corporation, 21
Hollywood Entertainment Corporation, 25
Hollywood Park, Inc., 20
Home Box Office Inc., 7; 23 (upd.)
Imax Corporation, 28
International Family Entertainment Inc., 13
International Speedway Corporation, 19
Interscope Music Group, 31
The Intrawest Corporation, 15
Irvin Feld & Kenneth Feld Productions, Inc., 15
Jackpot Enterprises Inc., 21
Japan Broadcasting Corporation, 7
The Jim Henson Company, 23
King World Productions, Inc., 9; 30 (upd.)
Knott's Berry Farm, 18
The Kushner-Locke Company, 25
Ladbroke Group PLC, II; 21 (upd.)
Lego A/S, 13
Lionel L.L.C., 16
LIVE Entertainment Inc., 20
LodgeNet Entertainment Corporation, 28
Lucasfilm Ltd., 12
Manchester United Football Club plc, 30
The Marcus Corporation, 21
MCA Inc., II
Media General, Inc., 7
Metro-Goldwyn-Mayer Inc., 25 (upd.)
Metromedia Companies, 14
MGM Grand Inc., 17
MGM/UA Communications Company, II
Midway Games, Inc., 25
Mizuno Corporation, 25
Motown Records Company L.P., 26
Movie Gallery, Inc., 31
Muzak, Inc., 18
National Amusements Inc., 28
National Broadcasting Company, Inc., II; 6 (upd.)
National Football League, 29
National Public Radio, 19
Navarre Corporation, 24
Nintendo Co., Ltd., 28 (upd.)
O'Charley's Inc., 19
Orion Pictures Corporation, 6
Paramount Pictures Corporation, II
Pathé SA, 29
Play by Play Toys & Novelties, Inc., 26
Players International, Inc., 22
PolyGram N.V., 23
Powerhouse Technologies, Inc., 27
Premier Parks, Inc., 27
President Casinos, Inc., 22
Princess Cruise Lines, 22
Promus Companies, Inc., 9
Putt-Putt Golf Courses of America, Inc., 23

Rainforest Cafe, Inc., 25
Rank Organisation PLC, II
Rawlings Sporting Goods Co., Inc., 24
The Really Useful Group, 26
Rhino Entertainment Company, 18
Ride, Inc., 22
Royal Caribbean Cruises Ltd., 22
S-K-I Limited, 15
Salomon Worldwide, 20
Santa Fe Gaming Corporation, 19
Schwinn Cycle and Fitness L.P., 19
Seattle FilmWorks, Inc., 20
Sega of America, Inc., 10
Showboat, Inc., 19
Shubert Organization Inc., 24
Six Flags Theme Parks, Inc., 17
Smithsonian Institution, 27
Spelling Entertainment Group, Inc., 14
The Sports Club Company, 25
Station Casinos Inc., 25
Stuart Entertainment Inc., 16
Tele-Communications, Inc., II
Television Española, S.A., 7
Thomas Cook Travel Inc., 9
The Thomson Corporation, 8
Ticketmaster Corp., 13
Toho Co., Ltd., 28
Touristik Union International GmbH. and Company K.G., II
Toy Biz, Inc., 18
Trans World Entertainment Corporation, 24
Turner Broadcasting System, Inc., II; 6 (upd.)
Twentieth Century Fox Film Corporation, II; 25 (upd.)
Univision Communications Inc., 24
Vail Associates, Inc., 11
Viacom Inc., 7; 23 (upd.)
Walt Disney Company, II; 6 (upd.); 30 (upd.)
Warner Communications Inc., II
West Coast Entertainment Corporation, 29
Wherehouse Entertainment Incorporated, 11
Wildlife Conservation Society, 31
Wilson Sporting Goods Company, 24
Wizards of the Coast Inc., 24
YES! Entertainment Corporation, 26
YMCA of the USA, 31

FINANCIAL SERVICES: BANKS

Abbey National PLC, 10
Abigail Adams National Bancorp, Inc., 23
Algemene Bank Nederland N.V., II
Allied Irish Banks, plc, 16
American Residential Mortgage Corporation, 8
AmSouth Bancorporation, 12
Amsterdam-Rotterdam Bank N.V., II
Anchor Bancorp, Inc., 10
Australia and New Zealand Banking Group Ltd., II
Banc One Corporation, 10
Banca Commerciale Italiana SpA, II
Banco Bilbao Vizcaya, S.A., II
Banco Bradesco S.A., 13
Banco Central, II
Banco do Brasil S.A., II
Banco Espírito Santo e Comercial de Lisboa S.A., 15
Banco Itaú S.A., 19
Bank Austria AG, 23
Bank Brussels Lambert, II
Bank Hapoalim B.M., II
Bank of Boston Corporation, II
Bank of Mississippi, Inc., 14
Bank of Montreal, II
Bank of New England Corporation, II
The Bank of New York Company, Inc., II
The Bank of Nova Scotia, II
Bank of Tokyo, Ltd., II
Bank of Tokyo-Mitsubishi Ltd., 15 (upd.)
BankAmerica Corporation, II; 8 (upd.)
Bankers Trust New York Corporation, II
Banque Nationale de Paris S.A., II
Barclays PLC, II; 20 (upd.)
BarclaysAmerican Mortgage Corporation, 11
Barings PLC, 14
Barnett Banks, Inc., 9
BayBanks, Inc., 12
Bayerische Hypotheken- und Wechsel-Bank AG, II
Bayerische Vereinsbank A.G., II
Beneficial Corporation, 8
Boatmen's Bancshares Inc., 15
Canadian Imperial Bank of Commerce, II
Carolina First Corporation, 31
Casco Northern Bank, 14
The Chase Manhattan Corporation, II; 13 (upd.)
Chemical Banking Corporation, II; 14 (upd.)
Citicorp, II; 9 (upd.)
Citigroup Inc., 30 (upd.)
Commercial Credit Company, 8
Commercial Federal Corporation, 12
Commerzbank A.G., II
Compagnie Financiere de Paribas, II
Continental Bank Corporation, II
CoreStates Financial Corp, 17
Countrywide Credit Industries, Inc., 16
Crédit Agricole, II
Crédit Lyonnais, 9
Crédit National S.A., 9
Credit Suisse Group, II; 21 (upd.)
Credito Italiano, II
Cullen/Frost Bankers, Inc., 25
The Dai-Ichi Kangyo Bank Ltd., II
The Daiwa Bank, Ltd., II
Dauphin Deposit Corporation, 14
Deposit Guaranty Corporation, 17
Deutsche Bank A.G., II; 14 (upd.)
Dime Savings Bank of New York, F.S.B., 9
Donaldson, Lufkin & Jenrette, Inc., 22
Dresdner Bank A.G., II
Fifth Third Bancorp, 13; 31 (upd.)
First Bank System Inc., 12
First Chicago Corporation, II
First Commerce Bancshares, Inc., 15
First Commerce Corporation, 11
First Empire State Corporation, 11
First Fidelity Bank, N.A., New Jersey, 9
First Hawaiian, Inc., 11
First Interstate Bancorp, II
First Nationwide Bank, 14
First of America Bank Corporation, 8
First Security Corporation, 11
First Tennessee National Corporation, 11
First Union Corporation, 10
First Virginia Banks, Inc., 11
Firstar Corporation, 11
Fleet Financial Group, Inc., 9
Fourth Financial Corporation, 11
The Fuji Bank, Ltd., II
Generale Bank, II
The Governor and Company of the Bank of Scotland, 10
Grameen Bank, 31
Great Lakes Bancorp, 8
Great Western Financial Corporation, 10
GreenPoint Financial Corp., 28
Grupo Financiero Serfin, S.A., 19
H.F. Ahmanson & Company, II; 10 (upd.)
Habersham Bancorp, 25
Hancock Holding Company, 15
The Hongkong and Shanghai Banking Corporation Limited, II
HSBC Holdings plc, 12; 26 (upd.)
Huntington Bancshares Inc., 11
The Industrial Bank of Japan, Ltd., II
J.P. Morgan & Co. Incorporated, II; 30 (upd.)
Japan Leasing Corporation, 8
Kansallis-Osake-Pankki, II
KeyCorp, 8
Kredietbank N.V., II
Kreditanstalt für Wiederaufbau, 29
Lloyds Bank PLC, II
Long Island Bancorp, Inc., 16
Long-Term Credit Bank of Japan, Ltd., II
Manufacturers Hanover Corporation, II
MBNA Corporation, 12
Mellon Bank Corporation, II
Mercantile Bankshares Corp., 11
Meridian Bancorp, Inc., 11
Metropolitan Financial Corporation, 13
Michigan National Corporation, 11
Midland Bank PLC, II; 17 (upd.)
The Mitsubishi Bank, Ltd., II
The Mitsubishi Trust & Banking Corporation, II
The Mitsui Bank, Ltd., II
The Mitsui Trust & Banking Company, Ltd., II
National City Corp., 15
National Westminster Bank PLC, II
NationsBank Corporation, 10
NBD Bancorp, Inc., 11
NCNB Corporation, II
Nippon Credit Bank, II
Norinchukin Bank, II
Northern Trust Company, 9
NVR L.P., 8
Old Kent Financial Corp., 11
Old National Bancorp, 15
PNC Bank Corp., 13 (upd.)
PNC Financial Corporation, II
Pulte Corporation, 8
Republic New York Corporation, 11
Riggs National Corporation, 13
The Royal Bank of Canada, II; 21 (upd.)
The Royal Bank of Scotland Group plc, 12
The Ryland Group, Inc., 8
St. Paul Bank for Cooperatives, 8
The Sanwa Bank, Ltd., II; 15 (upd.)
SBC Warburg, 14
Seattle First National Bank Inc., 8
Security Capital Corporation, 17
Security Pacific Corporation, II
Shawmut National Corporation, 13
Signet Banking Corporation, 11
Skandinaviska Enskilda Banken, II
Société Générale, II
Society Corporation, 9
Southtrust Corporation, 11
Standard Chartered PLC, II
Standard Federal Bank, 9
Star Banc Corporation, 11
State Street Boston Corporation, 8
The Sumitomo Bank, Limited, II; 26 (upd.)
The Sumitomo Trust & Banking Company, Ltd., II
The Summit Bancorporation, 14
SunTrust Banks Inc., 23
Svenska Handelsbanken, II
Swiss Bank Corporation, II
Synovus Financial Corp., 12
The Taiyo Kobe Bank, Ltd., II
The Tokai Bank, Limited, II; 15 (upd.)
The Toronto-Dominion Bank, II
TSB Group plc, 12

U.S. Bancorp, 14
U.S. Trust Corp., 17
Union Bank of California, 16
Union Bank of Switzerland, II
Wachovia Bank of Georgia, N.A., 16
Wachovia Bank of South Carolina, N.A., 16
Wachovia Corporation, 12
Washington Mutual, Inc., 17
Wells Fargo & Company, II; 12 (upd.)
West One Bancorp, 11
Westamerica Bancorporation, 17
Westdeutsche Landesbank Girozentrale, II
Westpac Banking Corporation, II
Whitney Holding Corporation, 21
Wilmington Trust Corporation, 25
The Woolwich plc, 30
The Yasuda Trust and Banking Company, Ltd., II; 17 (upd.)
Zions Bancorporation, 12

FINANCIAL SERVICES: NON-BANKS

A.G. Edwards, Inc., 8
ADVANTA Corp., 8
American Express Company, II; 10 (upd.)
American General Finance Corp., 11
Arthur Andersen & Company, Société Coopérative, 10
Avco Financial Services Inc., 13
Bear Stearns Companies, Inc., II; 10 (upd.)
Bozzuto's, Inc., 13
Cash America International, Inc., 20
Cetelem S.A., 21
The Charles Schwab Corporation, 8; 26 (upd.)
Citfed Bancorp, Inc., 16
Commercial Financial Services, Inc., 26
Coopers & Lybrand, 9
Credit Acceptance Corporation, 18
CS First Boston Inc., II
Daiwa Securities Company, Limited, II
Dean Witter, Discover & Co., 12
Dow Jones Telerate, Inc., 10
Drexel Burnham Lambert Incorporated, II
E*Trade Group, Inc., 20
Eaton Vance Corporation, 18
Edward Jones, 30
Fair, Isaac and Company, 18
Federal National Mortgage Association, II
Fidelity Investments Inc., II; 14 (upd.)
First Data Corporation, 30 (upd.)
First USA, Inc., 11
FMR Corp., 8
Fortis, Inc., 15
Franklin Resources, Inc., 9
Gabelli Asset Management Inc., 30
Goldman, Sachs & Co., II; 20 (upd.)
Green Tree Financial Corporation, 11
Gruntal & Co., L.L.C., 20
H & R Block, Incorporated, 9; 29 (upd.)
Household International, Inc., II; 21 (upd.)
Inter-Regional Financial Group, Inc., 15
Istituto per la Ricostruzione Industriale S.p.A., 11
Jefferies Group, Inc., 25
The John Nuveen Company, 21
Kansas City Southern Industries, Inc., 26 (upd.)
Kleinwort Benson Group PLC, II
Kohlberg Kravis Roberts & Co., 24
KPMG Worldwide, 10
MacAndrews & Forbes Holdings Inc., 28
MasterCard International, Inc., 9
Merrill Lynch & Co., Inc., II; 13 (upd.)
Morgan Grenfell Group PLC, II
Morgan Stanley Group Inc., II; 16 (upd.)
Mountain States Mortgage Centers, Inc., 29
National Association of Securities Dealers, Inc., 10
National Auto Credit, Inc., 16
National Discount Brokers Group, Inc., 28
New Street Capital Inc., 8
New York Stock Exchange, Inc., 9
The Nikko Securities Company Limited, II; 9 (upd.)
Nippon Shinpan Company, Ltd., II
Nomura Securities Company, Limited, II; 9 (upd.)
Orix Corporation, II
PaineWebber Group Inc., II; 22 (upd.)
Piper Jaffray Companies Inc., 22
The Prudential Insurance Company of America, 30 (upd.)
The Quick & Reilly Group, Inc., 20
Safeguard Scientifics, Inc., 10
Salomon Inc., II; 13 (upd.)
SBC Warburg, 14
Shearson Lehman Brothers Holdings Inc., II; 9 (upd.)
SLM Holding Corp., 25 (upd.)
Smith Barney Inc., 15
Soros Fund Management LLC, 28
State Street Boston Corporation, 8
Student Loan Marketing Association, II
T. Rowe Price Associates, Inc., 11
Total System Services, Inc., 18
Trilon Financial Corporation, II
The Vanguard Group of Investment Companies, 14
VeriFone, Inc., 18
Visa International, 9; 26 (upd.)
Waddell & Reed, Inc., 22
Washington Federal, Inc., 17
Waterhouse Investor Services, Inc., 18
Yamaichi Securities Company, Limited, II
The Ziegler Companies, Inc., 24

FOOD PRODUCTS

Agway, Inc., 7
Ajinomoto Co., Inc., II; 28 (upd.)
Alberto-Culver Company, 8
Aldi Group, 13
Alpine Lace Brands, Inc., 18
American Crystal Sugar Company, 11
American Italian Pasta Company, 27
American Maize-Products Co., 14
Amfac/JMB Hawaii L.L.C., 24 (upd.)
Archway Cookies, Inc., 29
Associated British Foods PLC, II; 13 (upd.)
Associated Milk Producers, Inc., 11
The B. Manischewitz Company, LLC, 31
Barilla G. e R. Fratelli S.p.A., 17
Beatrice Company, II
Beech-Nut Nutrition Corporation, 21
Ben & Jerry's Homemade, Inc., 10
Besnier SA, 19
Bestfoods, 22 (upd.)
Blue Bell Creameries L.P., 30
Blue Diamond Growers, 28
Bongrain SA, 25
Booker PLC, 13; 31 (upd.)
Borden, Inc., II; 22 (upd.)
Brach and Brock Confections, Inc., 15
Bridgford Foods Corporation, 27
Brothers Gourmet Coffees, Inc., 20
Broughton Foods Co., 17
Brown & Haley, 23
BSN Groupe S.A., II
Burger King Corporation, 17 (upd.)
Bush Boake Allen Inc., 30
Cadbury Schweppes PLC, II
Cagle's, Inc., 20
Campbell Soup Company, II; 7 (upd.); 26 (upd.)
Canada Packers Inc., II
Cargill Inc., 13 (upd.)
Carnation Company, II
Castle & Cooke, Inc., II; 20 (upd.)
Cattleman's, Inc., 20
Celestial Seasonings, Inc., 16
Central Soya Company, Inc., 7
Chelsea Milling Company, 29
Chicken of the Sea International, 24 (upd.)
Chiquita Brands International, Inc., 7; 21 (upd.)
Chock Full o'Nuts Corp., 17
Chocoladefabriken Lindt & Sprüngli AG, 27
The Clorox Company, 22 (upd.)
Coca-Cola Enterprises, Inc., 13
Conagra, Inc., II; 12 (upd.)
The Connell Company, 29
Continental Grain Company, 10; 13 (upd.)
CPC International Inc., II
Cumberland Packing Corporation, 26
Curtice-Burns Foods, Inc., 7; 21 (upd.)
Dalgery, PLC, II
Dannon Co., Inc., 14
Darigold, Inc., 9
Dawn Food Products, Inc., 17
Dean Foods Company, 7; 21 (upd.)
DeKalb Genetics Corporation, 17
Del Monte Corporation, 7
Del Monte Foods Company, 23 (upd.)
Di Giorgio Corp., 12
Diageo plc, 24 (upd.)
Dole Food Company, Inc., 9; 31 (upd.)
Domino Sugar Corporation, 26
Doskocil Companies, Inc., 12
Dreyer's Grand Ice Cream, Inc., 17
Emge Packing Co., Inc., 11
ERLY Industries Inc., 17
Eskimo Pie Corporation, 21
Farmland Foods, Inc., 7
Fieldale Farms Corporation, 23
Fleer Corporation, 15
Flowers Industries, Inc., 12
FoodBrands America, Inc., 23
Fresh America Corporation, 20
Fresh Foods, Inc., 29
Fromageries Bel, 23
General Mills, Inc., II; 10 (upd.)
George A. Hormel and Company, II
Gerber Products Company, 7; 21 (upd.)
Ghirardelli Chocolate Company, 30
Gold Kist Inc., 17; 26 (upd.)
Golden Enterprises, Inc., 26
Good Humor-Breyers Ice Cream Company, 14
GoodMark Foods, Inc., 26
Gorton's, 13
Goya Foods Inc., 22
Grist Mill Company, 15
Gruma, S.A. de C.V., 31
H.J. Heinz Company, II; 11 (upd.)
Hain Food Group, Inc., 27
The Hartz Mountain Corporation, 12
Herman Goelitz, Inc., 28
Hershey Foods Corporation, II; 15 (upd.)
Hill's Pet Nutrition, Inc., 27
Hillsdown Holdings plc, II; 24 (upd.)
Hormel Foods Corporation, 18 (upd.)
Hudson Foods Inc., 13
Hunt-Wesson, Inc., 17
Iams Company, 26
IBP, Inc., II; 21 (upd.)
Imperial Holly Corporation, 12
International Multifoods Corporation, 7; 25 (upd.)
Interstate Bakeries Corporation, 12

Itoham Foods Inc., II
J & J Snack Foods Corporation, 24
The J.M. Smucker Company, 11
J.R. Simplot Company, 16
Jacobs Suchard A.G., II
Jim Beam Brands Co., 14
John B. Sanfilippo & Son, Inc., 14
Kal Kan Foods, Inc., 22
Kellogg Company, II; 13 (upd.)
Kerry Group plc, 27
Kikkoman Corporation, 14
The King Arthur Flour Company, 31
King Ranch, Inc., 14
Koninklijke Wessanen N.V., II
Kraft General Foods Inc., II; 7 (upd.)
Kraft Jacobs Suchard AG, 26 (upd.)
Krispy Kreme Doughnut Corporation, 21
La Choy Food Products Inc., 25
Lamb Weston, Inc., 23
Lance, Inc., 14
Land O'Lakes, Inc., II; 21 (upd.)
Leprino Foods Company, 28
Lincoln Snacks Company, 24
Malt-O-Meal Company, 22
Mars, Inc., 7
Maui Land & Pineapple Company, Inc., 29
McCormick & Company, Incorporated, 7; 27 (upd.)
McIlhenny Company, 20
McKee Foods Corporation, 7; 27 (upd.)
Meiji Milk Products Company, Limited, II
Meiji Seika Kaisha, Ltd., II
Michael Foods, Inc., 25
Mid-America Dairymen, Inc., 7
Mike-Sell's Inc., 15
Monfort, Inc., 13
Mrs. Baird's Bakeries, 29
Murphy Family Farms Inc., 22
Nabisco Foods Group, II; 7 (upd.)
Nantucket Allserve, Inc., 22
Nathan's Famous, Inc., 29
National Sea Products Ltd., 14
Nestlé S.A., II; 7 (upd.); 28 (upd.)
New England Confectionery Co., 15
Newhall Land and Farming Company, 14
Nippon Meat Packers, Inc., II
Nippon Suisan Kaisha, Limited, II
Nisshin Flour Milling Company, Ltd., II
Northern Foods PLC, 10
NutraSweet Company, 8
Ocean Spray Cranberries, Inc., 7; 25 (upd.)
Ore-Ida Foods Incorporated, 13
Oscar Mayer Foods Corp., 12
Otis Spunkmeyer, Inc., 28
Perdue Farms Inc., 7; 23 (upd.)
Pet Incorporated, 7
Philip Morris Companies Inc., 18 (upd.)
PIC International Group PLC, 24 (upd.)
Pilgrim's Pride Corporation, 7; 23 (upd.)
Pillsbury Company, II; 13 (upd.)
Pioneer Hi-Bred International, Inc., 9
Premium Standard Farms, Inc., 30
The Procter & Gamble Company, III; 8 (upd.); 26 (upd.)
Quaker Oats Company, II; 12 (upd.)
Ralston Purina Company, II; 13 (upd.)
Ranks Hovis McDougall Limited, II; 28 (upd.)
Reckitt & Colman PLC, II
Rich Products Corporation, 7
Riviana Foods Inc., 27
Roland Murten A.G., 7
Rowntree Mackintosh, II
Russell Stover Candies Inc., 12
Sanderson Farms, Inc., 15
Sara Lee Corporation, II; 15 (upd.)
Savannah Foods & Industries, Inc., 7
Schwan's Sales Enterprises, Inc., 7
See's Candies, Inc., 30
Seminis, Inc., 29
Smithfield Foods, Inc., 7
Snow Brand Milk Products Company, Limited, II
SODIMA, II
Sorrento, Inc., 24
Stouffer Corp., 8
Südzucker AG, 27
Suiza Foods Corporation, 26
Sun-Diamond Growers of California, 7
Sunkist Growers, Inc., 26
Supervalu Inc., 18 (upd.)
Suprema Specialties, Inc., 27
Sylvan, Inc., 22
Taiyo Fishery Company, Limited, II
Tasty Baking Co., 14
Tate & Lyle PLC, II
TCBY Enterprises Inc., 17
Thomas J. Lipton Company, 14
Thorn Apple Valley, Inc., 7; 22 (upd.)
TLC Beatrice International Holdings, Inc., 22
Tombstone Pizza Corporation, 13
Tone Brothers, Inc., 21
Tootsie Roll Industries Inc., 12
Tropicana Products, Inc., 28
Tyson Foods, Incorporated, II; 14 (upd.)
U.S. Foodservice, 26
Uncle Ben's Inc., 22
Unigate PLC, II; 28 (upd.)
United Biscuits (Holdings) PLC, II
United Brands Company, II
United Foods, Inc., 21
Universal Foods Corporation, 7
Van Camp Seafood Company, Inc., 7
Vienna Sausage Manufacturing Co., 14
Vlasic Foods International Inc., 25
Wattie's Ltd., 7
Wisconsin Dairies, 7
WLR Foods, Inc., 21
Wm. Wrigley Jr. Company, 7
Worthington Foods, Inc., 14

FOOD SERVICES & RETAILERS

Advantica Restaurant Group, Inc., 27 (upd.)
Albertson's Inc., II; 7 (upd.); 30 (upd.)
Aldi Group, 13
Alex Lee Inc., 18
America's Favorite Chicken Company, Inc., 7
American Stores Company, II
Applebee's International Inc., 14
ARA Services, II
Arby's Inc., 14
Arden Group, Inc., 29
Argyll Group PLC, II
Ark Restaurants Corp., 20
Asahi Breweries, Ltd., 20 (upd.)
Asda Group PLC, II
ASDA Group plc, 28 (upd.)
Associated Grocers, Incorporated, 9; 31 (upd.)
Au Bon Pain Co., Inc., 18
Avado Brands, Inc., 31
Back Bay Restaurant Group, Inc., 20
Benihana, Inc., 18
Big Bear Stores Co., 13
Big V Supermarkets, Inc., 25
Blimpie International, Inc., 15
Bob Evans Farms, Inc., 9
Boston Chicken, Inc., 12
Brinker International, Inc., 10
Brookshire Grocery Company, 16
Bruno's, Inc., 7; 26 (upd.)
Buffets, Inc., 10
Burger King Corporation, II
C.H. Robinson, Inc., 11
California Pizza Kitchen Inc., 15
Cargill, Inc., II
Caribou Coffee Company, Inc., 28
Carlson Companies, Inc., 22 (upd.)
Carr-Gottstein Foods Co., 17
Casey's General Stores, Inc., 19
CEC Entertainment, Inc., 31 (upd.)
Chart House Enterprises, Inc., 17
Checkers Drive-Up Restaurants Inc., 16
The Cheesecake Factory Inc., 17
Chi-Chi's Inc., 13
Chick-fil-A Inc., 23
Cinnabon Inc., 23
The Circle K Corporation, II
CKE Restaurants, Inc., 19
Coborn's, Inc., 30
Comptoirs Modernes S.A., 19
Consolidated Products Inc., 14
The Cooker Restaurant Corporation, 20
Cracker Barrel Old Country Store, Inc., 10
D'Agostino Supermarkets Inc., 19
Dairy Mart Convenience Stores, Inc., 7; 25 (upd.)
Darden Restaurants, Inc., 16
DeMoulas / Market Basket Inc., 23
DenAmerica Corporation, 29
Domino's Pizza, Inc., 7; 21 (upd.)
Edeka Zentrale A.G., II
Einstein/Noah Bagel Corporation, 29
El Chico Restaurants, Inc., 19
Embers America Restaurants, 30
Etablissements Economiques du Casino Guichard, Perrachon et Cie, S.C.A., 12
Fazoli's Systems, Inc., 27
Flagstar Companies, Inc., 10
Fleming Companies, Inc., II
Food Lion, Inc., II; 15 (upd.)
Foodarama Supermarkets, Inc., 28
Foodmaker, Inc., 14
The Fred W. Albrecht Grocery Co., 13
Fresh Choice, Inc., 20
Fresh Foods, Inc., 29
Friendly Ice Cream Corp., 30
Furr's Supermarkets, Inc., 28
Garden Fresh Restaurant Corporation, 31
The Gateway Corporation Ltd., II
George Weston Limited, II
Ghirardelli Chocolate Company, 30
Giant Food Inc., II; 22 (upd.)
Godfather's Pizza Incorporated, 25
Golden Corral Corporation, 10
The Golub Corporation, 26
Gordon Food Service Inc., 8
The Grand Union Company, 7; 28 (upd.)
The Great Atlantic & Pacific Tea Company, Inc., II; 16 (upd.)
Gristede's Sloan's, Inc., 31
Ground Round, Inc., 21
Groupe Promodès S.A., 19
Guyenne et Gascogne, 23
H.E. Butt Grocery Co., 13
Hannaford Bros. Co., 12
Hard Rock Cafe International, Inc., 12
Harris Teeter Inc., 23
Harry's Farmers Market Inc., 23
Hickory Farms, Inc., 17
Hooters of America, Inc., 18
Hughes Markets, Inc., 22
Hungry Howie's Pizza and Subs, Inc., 25
ICA AB, II
IHOP Corporation, 17
Il Fornaio (America) Corporation, 27
In-N-Out Burger, 19
Ingles Markets, Inc., 20
Inserra Supermarkets, 25
International Dairy Queen, Inc., 10

J Sainsbury PLC, II; 13 (upd.)
JD Wetherspoon plc, 30
Jerry's Famous Deli Inc., 24
Jitney-Jungle Stores of America, Inc., 27
Johnny Rockets Group, Inc., 31
KFC Corporation, 7; 21 (upd.)
King Kullen Grocery Co., Inc., 15
Koninklijke Ahold N.V. (Royal Ahold), II; 16 (upd.)
Koo Koo Roo, Inc., 25
The Kroger Company, II; 15 (upd.)
Kwik Save Group plc, 11
Landry's Seafood Restaurants, Inc., 15
Leeann Chin, Inc., 30
Levy Restaurants L.P., 26
Little Caesar Enterprises, Inc., 24 (upd.)
Little Caesars International, Inc., 7
Logan's Roadhouse, Inc., 29
Long John Silver's Restaurants Inc., 13
Luby's Cafeteria's, Inc., 17
Lucky Stores, Inc., 27
Lund Food Holdings, Inc., 22
Marie Callender's Restaurant & Bakery, Inc., 28
Marsh Supermarkets, Inc., 17
Max & Erma's Restaurants Inc., 19
McDonald's Corporation, II; 7 (upd.); 26 (upd.)
Megafoods Stores Inc., 13
Meijer Incorporated, 7
Metromedia Companies, 14
The Middleby Corporation, 22
Morrison Restaurants Inc., 11
Morton's Restaurant Group, Inc., 30
Mrs. Fields' Original Cookies, Inc., 27
Nash Finch Company, 8; 23 (upd.)
Nathan's Famous, Inc., 29
National Convenience Stores Incorporated, 7
Noble Roman's Inc., 14
O'Charley's Inc., 19
Old Spaghetti Factory International Inc., 24
The Oshawa Group Limited, II
Outback Steakhouse, Inc., 12
P&C Foods Inc., 8
Papa John's International, Inc., 15
Pathmark Stores, Inc., 23
Peapod, Inc., 30
Penn Traffic Company, 13
Performance Food Group Company, 31
Perkins Family Restaurants, L.P., 22
Piccadilly Cafeterias, Inc., 19
Piggly Wiggly Southern, Inc., 13
Pizza Hut Inc., 7; 21 (upd.)
Planet Hollywood International, Inc., 18
Players International, Inc., 22
Ponderosa Steakhouse, 15
Provigo Inc., II
Publix Super Markets Inc., 31 (upd.)
Publix Supermarkets Inc., 7
Quality Dining, Inc., 18
Quality Food Centers, Inc., 17
Rally's Hamburgers, Inc., 25
Rare Hospitality International Inc., 19
Restaurants Unlimited, Inc., 13
Richfood Holdings, Inc., 7
Riser Foods, Inc., 9
Roadhouse Grill, Inc., 22
Rock Bottom Restaurants, Inc., 25
Ruby Tuesday, Inc., 18
Ruth's Chris Steak House, 28
Ryan's Family Steak Houses, Inc., 15
Safeway Inc., 24 (upd.)
Safeway Stores Incorporated, II
Sbarro, Inc., 16
Schultz Sav-O Stores, Inc., 21
Schwan's Sales Enterprises, Inc., 26 (upd.)
Seaway Food Town, Inc., 15
Second Harvest, 29
See's Candies, Inc., 30
Seneca Foods Corporation, 17
Service America Corp., 7
Shoney's, Inc., 7; 23 (upd.)
ShowBiz Pizza Time, Inc., 13
Smart & Final, Inc., 16
Smith's Food & Drug Centers, Inc., 8
Sodexho Alliance SA, 29
Sonic Corporation, 14
The Southland Corporation, II; 7 (upd.)
Spaghetti Warehouse, Inc., 25
Spartan Stores Inc., 8
Steinberg Incorporated, II
The Stop & Shop Companies, Inc., II
Super Food Services, Inc., 15
Super Valu Stores, Inc., II
Supermarkets General Holdings Corporation, II
Supervalu Inc., 18 (upd.)
SYSCO Corporation, II; 24 (upd.)
Taco Bell Corp., 7; 21 (upd.)
Taco Cabana, Inc., 23
Taco John's International Inc., 15
Tesco PLC, II
Trader Joe's Co., 13
Travel Ports of America, Inc., 17
Tree of Life, Inc., 29
TW Services, Inc., II
Unique Casual Restaurants, Inc., 27
Uno Restaurant Corporation, 18
VICORP Restaurants, Inc., 12
Village Super Market, Inc., 7
The Vons Companies, Incorporated, 7; 28 (upd.)
Waffle House Inc., 14
Waldbaum, Inc., 19
Wawa Inc., 17
Wegmans Food Markets, Inc., 9
Weis Markets, Inc., 15
Wendy's International, Inc., 8; 23 (upd.)
Wetterau Incorporated, II
White Castle Systems, Inc., 12
White Rose, Inc., 24
Wild Oats Markets, Inc., 19
Winn-Dixie Stores, Inc., II; 21 (upd.)
The Wolfgang Puck Food Company, Inc., 26
Yucaipa Cos., 17

HEALTH & PERSONAL CARE PRODUCTS

Alberto-Culver Company, 8
Alco Health Services Corporation, III
Allergan, Inc., 10; 30 (upd.)
American Safety Razor Company, 20
American Stores Company, 22 (upd.)
Amway Corporation, III; 13 (upd.)
Aveda Corporation, 24
Avon Products Inc., III; 19 (upd.)
Bally Total Fitness Holding Corp., 25
Bausch & Lomb Inc., 7; 25 (upd.)
Baxter International Inc., I; 10 (upd.)
BeautiControl Cosmetics, Inc., 21
Becton, Dickinson & Company, I; 11 (upd.)
Beiersdorf AG, 29
Big B, Inc., 17
Bindley Western Industries, Inc., 9
Block Drug Company, Inc., 8; 27 (upd.)
The Boots Company PLC, 24 (upd.)
Bristol-Myers Squibb Company, III; 9 (upd.)
C.R. Bard Inc., 9
Cardinal Health, Inc., 18
Carson, Inc., 31
Carter-Wallace, Inc., 8
Chattem, Inc., 17
Chesebrough-Pond's USA, Inc., 8
Chronimed Inc., 26
The Clorox Company, III
CNS, Inc., 20
Colgate-Palmolive Company, III; 14 (upd.)
Conair Corp., 17
Cordis Corp., 19
Cosmair, Inc., 8
Del Laboratories, Inc., 28
Dentsply International Inc., 10
DEP Corporation, 20
DePuy, Inc., 30
The Dial Corp., 23 (upd.)
Drackett Professional Products, 12
Elizabeth Arden Co., 8
Empi, Inc., 26
The Estée Lauder Companies Inc., 9; 30 (upd.)
Ethicon, Inc., 23
Forest Laboratories, Inc., 11
Forever Living Products International Inc., 17
French Fragrances, Inc., 22
General Nutrition Companies, Inc., 11; 29 (upd.)
Genzyme Corporation, 13
The Gillette Company, III; 20 (upd.)
Groupe Yves Saint Laurent, 23
Guerlain, 23
Guest Supply, Inc., 18
Helen of Troy Corporation, 18
Helene Curtis Industries, Inc., 8; 28 (upd.)
Henkel KGaA, III
Henry Schein, Inc., 31
Herbalife International, Inc., 17
Invacare Corporation, 11
IVAX Corporation, 11
John Paul Mitchell Systems, 24
Johnson & Johnson, III; 8 (upd.)
Kao Corporation, III
Kendall International, Inc., 11
Kimberly-Clark Corporation, III; 16 (upd.)
Kyowa Hakko Kogyo Co., Ltd., III
L'Oreal, III; 8 (upd.)
Lever Brothers Company, 9
Lion Corporation, III
Luxottica SpA, 17
Mary Kay Corporation, 9; 30 (upd.)
Maxxim Medical Inc., 12
Medco Containment Services Inc., 9
Medtronic, Inc., 8
Melaleuca Inc., 31
Mentor Corporation, 26
Merit Medical Systems, Inc., 29
Nature's Sunshine Products, Inc., 15
NBTY, Inc., 31
Neutrogena Corporation, 17
Nutrition for Life International Inc., 22
OEC Medical Systems, Inc., 27
Patterson Dental Co., 19
Perrigo Company, 12
Physician Sales & Service, Inc., 14
Playtex Products, Inc., 15
The Procter & Gamble Company, III; 8 (upd.); 26 (upd.)
Revlon Group Inc., III
Revlon Inc., 17 (upd.)
Roche Biomedical Laboratories, Inc., 11
S.C. Johnson & Son, Inc., III
Safety 1st, Inc., 24
Schering-Plough Corporation, 14 (upd.)
Shionogi & Co., Ltd., III
Shiseido Company, Limited, III; 22 (upd.)
Slim-Fast Nutritional Foods International, Inc., 18
Smith & Nephew plc, 17
SmithKline Beecham PLC, III

Soft Sheen Products, Inc., 31
Sunrise Medical Inc., 11
Tambrands Inc., 8
Turtle Wax, Inc., 15
United States Surgical Corporation, 10
USANA, Inc., 29
VISX, Incorporated, 30
Weider Nutrition International, Inc., 29
Wella Group, III

HEALTH CARE SERVICES

The American Cancer Society, 24
American Medical International, Inc., III
Applied Bioscience International, Inc., 10
Beverly Enterprises, Inc., III; 16 (upd.)
Bon Secours Health System, Inc., 24
Caremark International Inc., 10
Chronimed Inc., 26
COBE Laboratories, Inc., 13
Columbia/HCA Healthcare Corporation, 15
Community Psychiatric Centers, 15
CompDent Corporation, 22
CompHealth Inc., 25
Comprehensive Care Corporation, 15
Continental Medical Systems, Inc., 10
Express Scripts Incorporated, 17
Extendicare Health Services, Inc., 6
FHP International Corporation, 6
Genesis Health Ventures, Inc., 18
GranCare, Inc., 14
Hazelden Foundation, 28
Health Care & Retirement Corporation, 22
Health Risk Management, Inc., 24
Health Systems International, Inc., 11
HealthSouth Rehabilitation Corporation, 14
Highmark Inc., 27
The Hillhaven Corporation, 14
Hooper Holmes, Inc., 22
Hospital Corporation of America, III
Humana Inc., III; 24 (upd.)
Intermountain Health Care, Inc., 27
Jenny Craig, Inc., 10; 29 (upd.)
Kinetic Concepts, Inc. (KCI), 20
Manor Care, Inc., 6; 25 (upd.)
March of Dimes, 31
Matria Healthcare, Inc., 17
Maxicare Health Plans, Inc., III; 25 (upd.)
Mayo Foundation, 9
Merit Medical Systems, Inc., 29
National Health Laboratories Incorporated, 11
National Medical Enterprises, Inc., III
NovaCare, Inc., 11
Oxford Health Plans, Inc., 16
PacifiCare Health Systems, Inc., 11
Palomar Medical Technologies, Inc., 22
Pediatric Services of America, Inc., 31
PHP Healthcare Corporation, 22
Primedex Health Systems, Inc., 25
Quest Diagnostics Inc., 26
Res-Care, Inc., 29
Response Oncology, Inc., 27
Rural/Metro Corporation, 28
Sabratek Corporation, 29
St. Jude Medical, Inc., 11
Sierra Health Services, Inc., 15
The Sports Club Company, 25
Sun Healthcare Group Inc., 25
U.S. Healthcare, Inc., 6
Unison HealthCare Corporation, 25
United HealthCare Corporation, 9
Universal Health Services, Inc., 6
Vencor, Inc., 16
VISX, Incorporated, 30
Vivra, Inc., 18
WellPoint Health Networks Inc., 25

HOTELS

Amerihost Properties, Inc., 30
Aztar Corporation, 13
Bristol Hotel Company, 23
The Broadmoor Hotel, 30
Caesars World, Inc., 6
Carlson Companies, Inc., 22 (upd.)
Castle & Cooke, Inc., 20 (upd.)
Cedar Fair, L.P., 22
Choice Hotels International Inc., 14
Circus Circus Enterprises, Inc., 6
Club Mediterranée S.A., 6; 21 (upd.)
Doubletree Corporation, 21
Fibreboard Corporation, 16
Four Seasons Hotels Inc., 9; 29 (upd.)
Granada Group PLC, 24 (upd.)
Grand Casinos, Inc., 20
Grand Hotel Krasnapolsky N.V., 23
Helmsley Enterprises, Inc., 9
Hilton Hotels Corporation, III; 19 (upd.)
Holiday Inns, Inc., III
Hospitality Franchise Systems, Inc., 11
Howard Johnson International, Inc., 17
Hyatt Corporation, III; 16 (upd.)
ITT Sheraton Corporation, III
JD Wetherspoon plc, 30
John Q. Hammons Hotels, Inc., 24
La Quinta Inns, Inc., 11
Ladbroke Group PLC, 21 (upd.)
Manor Care, Inc., 25 (upd.)
The Marcus Corporation, 21
Marriott International, Inc., III; 21 (upd.)
Mirage Resorts, Incorporated, 6; 28 (upd.)
Motel 6 Corporation, 13
Omni Hotels Corp., 12
Park Corp., 22
Players International, Inc., 22
Promus Companies, Inc., 9
Red Roof Inns, Inc., 18
Resorts International, Inc., 12
Ritz-Carlton Hotel Company L.L.C., 9; 29 (upd.)
Santa Fe Gaming Corporation, 19
Showboat, Inc., 19
Sun International Hotels Limited, 26
Sunburst Hospitality Corporation, 26
Trusthouse Forte PLC, III
The Walt Disney Company, 30 (upd.)
Westin Hotel Co., 9
Westin Hotels and Resorts Worldwide, 29 (upd.)

INFORMATION TECHNOLOGY

Adaptec, Inc., 31
Adobe Systems Incorporated, 10
Advanced Micro Devices, Inc., 6
Aldus Corporation, 10
Amdahl Corporation, III; 14 (upd.)
America Online, Inc., 10 ; 26 (upd.)
American Business Information, Inc., 18
American Management Systems, Inc., 11
American Software Inc., 25
Amstrad PLC, III
Analytic Sciences Corporation, 10
Apollo Group, Inc., 24
Apple Computer, Inc., III; 6 (upd.)
Asanté Technologies, Inc., 20
ASK Group, Inc., 9
AST Research Inc., 9
AT&T Bell Laboratories, Inc., 13
AT&T Corporation, 29 (upd.)
AT&T Istel Ltd., 14
Autologic Information International, Inc., 20
Automatic Data Processing, Inc., III; 9 (upd.)
Autotote Corporation, 20
Aydin Corp., 19
Baan Company, 25
Banyan Systems Inc., 25
Battelle Memorial Institute, Inc., 10
BBN Corp., 19
Bell and Howell Company, 9; 29 (upd.)
Billing Concepts Corp., 26
Bloomberg L.P., 21
Boole & Babbage, Inc., 25
Booz Allen & Hamilton Inc., 10
Borland International, Inc., 9
Bowne & Co., Inc., 23
Brite Voice Systems, Inc., 20
Broderbund Software, 29 (upd.)
Broderbund Software, Inc., 13
Business Objects S.A., 25
CACI International Inc., 21
Cadence Design Systems, Inc., 11
Caere Corporation, 20
CalComp Inc., 13
Canon Inc., III
Caribiner International, Inc., 24
Catalina Marketing Corporation, 18
CDW Computer Centers, Inc., 16
Cerner Corporation, 16
Cheyenne Software, Inc., 12
CHIPS and Technologies, Inc., 9
Ciber, Inc., 18
Cincom Systems Inc., 15
Cirrus Logic, Incorporated, 11
Cisco Systems, Inc., 11
Citizen Watch Co., Ltd., 21 (upd.)
Commodore International Ltd., 7
Compagnie des Machines Bull S.A., III
Compaq Computer Corporation, III; 6 (upd.); 26 (upd.)
Complete Business Solutions, Inc., 31
CompuAdd Computer Corporation, 11
CompuCom Systems, Inc., 10
CompuServe Incorporated, 10
CompuServe Interactive Services, Inc., 27 (upd.)
Computer Associates International, Inc., 6
Computer Data Systems, Inc., 14
Computer Sciences Corporation, 6
Computervision Corporation, 10
Compuware Corporation, 10; 30 (upd.)
Comshare Inc., 23
Conner Peripherals, Inc., 6
Control Data Corporation, III
Control Data Systems, Inc., 10
Corbis Corporation, 31
Corel Corporation, 15
Corporate Software Inc., 9
Cray Research, Inc., III
CTG, Inc., 11
Cybermedia, Inc., 25
Dassault Systèmes S.A., 25
Data Broadcasting Corporation, 31
Data General Corporation, 8
Datapoint Corporation, 11
Dell Computer Corp., 9
Dialogic Corporation, 18
Digital Equipment Corporation, III; 6 (upd.)
The Dun & Bradstreet Corporation, IV; 19 (upd.)
Dun & Bradstreet Software Services Inc., 11
ECS S.A, 12
Edmark Corporation, 14
Egghead Inc., 9
El Camino Resources International, Inc., 11
Electronic Arts Inc., 10
Electronic Data Systems Corporation, III; 28 (upd.)
EMC Corporation, 12
Encore Computer Corporation, 13

Evans & Sutherland Computer Corporation, 19
Exabyte Corporation, 12
First Financial Management Corporation, 11
Fiserv Inc., 11
FlightSafety International, Inc., 9
FORE Systems, Inc., 25
Franklin Electronic Publishers, Inc., 23
FTP Software, Inc., 20
Fujitsu Limited, III
Fujitsu-ICL Systems Inc., 11
Future Now, Inc., 12
Gartner Group, Inc., 21
Gateway 2000, Inc., 10
Gateway, Inc., 27 (upd.)
GT Interactive Software, 31
Hewlett-Packard Company, III; 6 (upd.)
Hyperion Software Corporation, 22
ICL plc, 6
Imation Corporation, 20
Information Access Company, 17
Information Builders, Inc., 22
Information Resources, Inc., 10
Informix Corporation, 10; 30 (upd.)
Ing. C. Olivetti & C., S.p.a., III
Inso Corporation, 26
Intelligent Electronics, Inc., 6
Intergraph Corporation, 6; 24 (upd.)
International Business Machines Corporation, III; 6 (upd.); 30 (upd.)
Intuit Inc., 14
Iomega Corporation, 21
J.D. Edwards & Company, 14
Jack Henry and Associates, Inc., 17
KLA Instruments Corporation, 11
KnowledgeWare Inc., 31 (upd.)
Komag, Inc., 11
Kronos, Inc., 18
Lam Research Corporation, 11
Lason, Inc., 31
The Learning Company Inc., 24
Learning Tree International Inc., 24
Legent Corporation, 10
Logica plc, 14
Logicon Inc., 20
Logitech International SA, 28
Lotus Development Corporation, 6; 25 (upd.)
The MacNeal-Schwendler Corporation, 25
Madge Networks N.V., 26
MAI Systems Corporation, 11
Maxtor Corporation, 10
Mead Data Central, Inc., 10
Mecklermedia Corporation, 24
Mentor Graphics Corporation, 11
Merisel, Inc., 12
Micro Warehouse, Inc., 16
Micron Technology, Inc., 11; 29 (upd.)
Micros Systems, Inc., 18
Microsoft Corporation, 6; 27 (upd.)
MITRE Corporation, 26
National Semiconductor Corporation, 6
Navarre Corporation, 24
NCR Corporation, III; 6 (upd.); 30 (upd.)
Netscape Communications Corporation, 15
Network Associates, Inc., 25
Nextel Communications, Inc., 10
NFO Worldwide, Inc., 24
Nichols Research Corporation, 18
Nimbus CD International, Inc., 20
Nixdorf Computer AG, III
Novell, Inc., 6; 23 (upd.)
Océ N.V., 24
Odetics Inc., 14
Oracle Corporation, 24 (upd.)
Oracle Systems Corporation, 6
Packard Bell Electronics, Inc., 13
Parametric Technology Corp., 16
PeopleSoft Inc., 14
Perot Systems Corporation, 29
Pitney Bowes Inc., III
PLATINUM Technology, Inc., 14
Policy Management Systems Corporation, 11
Primark Corp., 13
Printronix, Inc., 18
Progress Software Corporation, 15
Quantum Corporation, 10
Racal-Datacom Inc., 11
Reuters Holdings PLC, 22 (upd.)
Ricoh Company, Ltd., III
SABRE Group Holdings, Inc., 26
SAP AG, 16
SAS Institute Inc., 10
SBS Technologies, Inc., 25
SCB Computer Technology, Inc., 29
Schawk, Inc., 24
Seagate Technology, Inc., 8
Sierra On-Line Inc., 15
SilverPlatter Information Inc., 23
Softbank Corp., 13
Standard Microsystems Corporation, 11
STC PLC, III
Sterling Software, Inc., 11
Storage Technology Corporation, 6
Stratus Computer, Inc., 10
Sun Microsystems, Inc., 7; 30 (upd.)
SunGard Data Systems Inc., 11
Sybase, Inc., 10; 27 (upd.)
Symantec Corporation, 10
Symbol Technologies, Inc., 15
Synopsis, Inc., 11
System Software Associates, Inc., 10
Systems & Computer Technology Corp., 19
Tandem Computers, Inc., 6
3Com Corp., 11
Timberline Software Corporation, 15
Transaction Systems Architects, Inc., 29
Triple P N.V., 26
Unisys Corporation, III; 6 (upd.)
Verbatim Corporation, 14
VeriFone, Inc., 18
Viasoft Inc., 27
Volt Information Sciences Inc., 26
Wang Laboratories, Inc., III; 6 (upd.)
Western Digital Corp., 25
WordPerfect Corporation, 10
Wyse Technology, Inc., 15
Xerox Corporation, III; 6 (upd.); 26 (upd.)
Xilinx, Inc., 16
Yahoo! Inc., 27
Zapata Corporation, 25
Zilog, Inc., 15

INSURANCE

AEGON N.V., III
Aetna Life and Casualty Company, III
Aetna, Inc., 21 (upd.)
AFLAC Inc., 10 (upd.)
Alexander & Alexander Services Inc., 10
Alleghany Corporation, 10
Allianz Aktiengesellschaft Holding, III; 15 (upd.)
The Allstate Corporation, 10; 27 (upd.)
American Family Corporation, III
American Financial Corporation, III
American General Corporation, III; 10 (upd.)
American International Group, Inc., III; 15 (upd.)
American National Insurance Company, 8; 27 (upd.)
American Premier Underwriters, Inc., 10
American Re Corporation, 10
N.V. AMEV, III
Aon Corporation, III
Assicurazioni Generali SpA, III; 15 (upd.)
Axa, III
AXA Colonia Konzern AG, 27
B.A.T. Industries PLC, 22 (upd.)
Berkshire Hathaway Inc., III; 18 (upd.)
Blue Cross and Blue Shield Association, 10
Business Men's Assurance Company of America, 14
Capital Holding Corporation, III
Catholic Order of Foresters, 24
The Chubb Corporation, III; 14 (upd.)
CIGNA Corporation, III; 22 (upd.)
Cincinnati Financial Corporation, 16
CNA Financial Corporation, III
Commercial Union PLC, III
Connecticut Mutual Life Insurance Company, III
Conseco Inc., 10
The Continental Corporation, III
Empire Blue Cross and Blue Shield, III
The Equitable Life Assurance Society of the United States Fireman's Fund Insurance Company, III
Farmers Insurance Group of Companies, 25
First Executive Corporation, III
Foundation Health Corporation, 12
Gainsco, Inc., 22
GEICO Corporation, 10
General Accident PLC, III
General Re Corporation, III; 24 (upd.)
Great-West Lifeco Inc., III
Gryphon Holdings, Inc., 21
Guardian Royal Exchange Plc, 11
The Home Insurance Company, III
Horace Mann Educators Corporation, 22
Household International, Inc., 21 (upd.)
Jackson National Life Insurance Company, 8
Jefferson-Pilot Corporation, 11; 29 (upd.)
John Hancock Mutual Life Insurance Company, III
Johnson & Higgins, 14
Kemper Corporation, III; 15 (upd.)
Legal & General Group plc, III; 24 (upd.)
The Liberty Corporation, 22
Lincoln National Corporation, III; 25 (upd.)
Lloyd's of London, III; 22 (upd.)
Lutheran Brotherhood, 31
Marsh & McLennan Companies, Inc., III
Massachusetts Mutual Life Insurance Company, III
The Meiji Mutual Life Insurance Company, III
Mercury General Corporation, 25
Metropolitan Life Insurance Company, III
Mitsui Marine and Fire Insurance Company, Limited, III
Mitsui Mutual Life Insurance Company, III
Munich Re (Münchener Rückversicherungs-Gesellschaft), III
The Mutual Benefit Life Insurance Company, III
The Mutual Life Insurance Company of New York, III
Nationale-Nederlanden N.V., III
New England Mutual Life Insurance Company, III
New York Life Insurance Company, III
Nippon Life Insurance Company, III
Northwestern Mutual Life Insurance Company, III
Ohio Casualty Corp., 11
Old Republic International Corp., 11

The Paul Revere Corporation, 12
Pennsylvania Blue Shield, III
Principal Mutual Life Insurance Company, III
Progressive Corporation, 11
The Progressive Corporation, 29 (upd.)
Provident Life and Accident Insurance Company of America, III
Prudential Corporation PLC, III
The Prudential Insurance Company of America, III; 30 (upd.)
Reliance Group Holdings, Inc., III
Riunione Adriatica di Sicurtà SpA, III
Royal Insurance Holdings PLC, III
SAFECO Corporaton, III
The St. Paul Companies, Inc., III; 22 (upd.)
SCOR S.A., 20
The Standard Life Assurance Company, III
State Farm Mutual Automobile Insurance Company, III
Sumitomo Life Insurance Company, III
The Sumitomo Marine and Fire Insurance Company, Limited, III
Sun Alliance Group PLC, III
SunAmerica Inc., 11
Swiss Reinsurance Company (Schweizerische Rückversicherungs-Gesellschaft), III
Teachers Insurance and Annuity Association, III
Texas Industries, Inc., 8
TIG Holdings, Inc., 26
The Tokio Marine and Fire Insurance Co., Ltd., III
Torchmark Corporation, 9
Transatlantic Holdings, Inc., 11
The Travelers Corporation, III
Union des Assurances de Pans, III
Unitrin Inc., 16
UNUM Corp., 13
USAA, 10
USF&G Corporation, III
VICTORIA Holding AG, III
W.R. Berkley Corp., 15
Washington National Corporation, 12
Willis Corroon Group plc, 25
"Winterthur" Schweizerische Versicherungs-Gesellschaft, III
The Yasuda Fire and Marine Insurance Company, Limited, III
The Yasuda Mutual Life Insurance Company, Limited, III
"Zürich" Versicherungs-Gesellschaft, III

LEGAL SERVICES

Baker & McKenzie, 10
Baker and Botts, L.L.P., 28
Brobeck, Phleger & Harrison, LLP, 31
Coudert Brothers, 30
Foley & Lardner, 28
Hildebrandt International, 29
Holme Roberts & Owen LLP, 28
King & Spalding, 23
LeBoeuf, Lamb, Greene & MacRae, L.L.P., 29
Milbank, Tweed, Hadley & McCloy, 27
Morgan, Lewis & Bockius LLP, 29
Paul, Hastings, Janofsky & Walker LLP, 27
Pillsbury Madison & Sutro LLP, 29
Pre-Paid Legal Services, Inc., 20
Skadden, Arps, Slate, Meagher & Flom, 18
Snell & Wilmer L.L.P., 28
Sullivan & Cromwell, 26
Vinson & Elkins L.L.P., 30

MANUFACTURING

A.B.Dick Company, 28
A.O. Smith Corporation, 11
A.T. Cross Company, 17
AAF-McQuay Incorporated, 26
AAON, Inc., 22
AAR Corp., 28
ABC Rail Products Corporation, 18
ACCO World Corporation, 7
Acme-Cleveland Corp., 13
Ag-Chem Equipment Company, Inc., 17
AGCO Corp., 13
Aisin Seiki Co., Ltd., III
Aktiebolaget Electrolux, 22 (upd.)
Aktiebolaget SKF, III
Alfa-Laval AB, III
Alliant Techsystems Inc., 8; 30 (upd.)
Allied Healthcare Products, Inc., 24
Allied Products Corporation, 21
Allied Signal Engines, 9
AlliedSignal Inc., 22 (upd.)
Allison Gas Turbine Division, 9
Alltrista Corporation, 30
American Business Products, Inc., 20
American Homestar Corporation, 18
American Standard Companies Inc., 30 (upd.)
American Tourister, Inc., 16
American Woodmark Corporation, 31
Ameriwood Industries International Corp., 17
AMETEK, Inc., 9
Ampex Corporation, 17
Amway Corporation, 30 (upd.)
Analogic Corporation, 23
Anchor Hocking Glassware, 13
Andersen Corporation, 10
The Andersons, Inc., 31
Andreas Stihl, 16
Anthem Electronics, Inc., 13
Applied Materials, Inc., 10
Applied Power, Inc., 9
ARBED S.A., 22 (upd.)
Arctco, Inc., 16
Armor All Products Corp., 16
Armstrong World Industries, Inc., III; 22 (upd.)
Atlas Copco AB, III; 28 (upd.)
Avery Dennison Corporation, 17 (upd.)
Avondale Industries, Inc., 7
Badger Meter, Inc., 22
Baker Hughes Incorporated, III
Baldor Electric Company, 21
Baldwin Piano & Organ Company, 18
Baldwin Technology Company, Inc., 25
Ballantyne of Omaha, Inc., 27
Ballard Medical Products, 21
Bally Manufacturing Corporation, III
Barnes Group Inc., 13
Barry Callebaut AG, 29
Bassett Furniture Industries, Inc., 18
Bath Iron Works Corporation, 12
Beckman Coulter, Inc., 22
Beckman Instruments, Inc., 14
Beiersdorf AG, 29
Belden Inc., 19
Bell Sports Corporation, 16
Beloit Corporation, 14
Benjamin Moore and Co., 13
Berry Plastics Corporation, 21
BIC Corporation, 8; 23 (upd.)
BICC PLC, III
Binks Sames Corporation, 21
Binney & Smith Inc., 25
Biomet, Inc., 10
BISSELL Inc., 9; 30 (upd.)
The Black & Decker Corporation, III; 20 (upd.)
Blount, Inc., 12
Blyth Industries, Inc., 18
BMC Industries, Inc., 17
Borden, Inc., 22 (upd.)
Borg-Warner Automotive, Inc., 14
Borg-Warner Corporation, III
The Boyds Collection, Ltd., 29
Bridgeport Machines, Inc., 17
Briggs & Stratton Corporation, 8; 27 (upd.)
BRIO AB, 24
Brother Industries, Ltd., 14
Brown & Sharpe Manufacturing Co., 23
Broyhill Furniture Industries, Inc., 10
Brunswick Corporation, III; 22 (upd.)
BTR Siebe plc, 27
Bucyrus International, Inc., 17
Bugle Boy Industries, Inc., 18
Bulgari S.p.A., 20
Bulova Corporation, 13
Bundy Corporation, 17
Burelle S.A., 23
Burton Snowboards Inc., 22
Bush Boake Allen Inc., 30
Bush Industries, Inc., 20
Butler Manufacturing Co., 12
Callaway Golf Company, 15
Cannondale Corporation, 21
Caradon plc, 20 (upd.)
Carl-Zeiss-Stiftung, III
Carrier Corporation, 7
Casio Computer Co., Ltd., III
Caterpillar Inc., III; 15 (upd.)
Central Sprinkler Corporation, 29
Cessna Aircraft Company, 27 (upd.)
Champion Enterprises, Inc., 17
Chanel, 12
Chart Industries, Inc., 21
Chris-Craft Industries, Inc., 31 (upd.)
Chromcraft Revington, Inc., 15
Cincinnati Milacron Inc., 12
Circon Corporation, 21
Citizen Watch Co., Ltd., III
Clarcor Inc., 17
Clark Equipment Company, 8
Clayton Homes Incorporated, 13
The Clorox Company, 22 (upd.)
Cobra Golf Inc., 16
Cockerill Sambre Group, 26 (upd.)
Colas S.A., 31
The Coleman Company, Inc., 30 (upd.)
Colt's Manufacturing Company, Inc., 12
Columbia Sportswear Company, 19
Congoleum Corp., 18
Conso International Corporation, 29
Converse Inc., 9
Corrpro Companies, Inc., 20
Crane Co., 8; 30 (upd.)
Crown Equipment Corporation, 15
Cuisinart Corporation, 24
Culligan International Company, 12
Curtiss-Wright Corporation, 10
Cutter & Buck Inc., 27
Daewoo Group, III
Daikin Industries, Ltd., III
Danaher Corporation, 7
Daniel Industries, Inc., 16
Decora Industries, Inc., 31
Deere & Company, III
Defiance, Inc., 22
Department 56, Inc., 14
Detroit Diesel Corporation, 10
Deutsche Babcock A.G., III
Diebold, Incorporated, 7; 22 (upd.)
Dixon Industries, Inc., 26
Dixon Ticonderoga Company, 12
Donnelly Corporation, 12

Douglas & Lomason Company, 16
Dover Corporation, III; 28 (upd.)
Dresser Industries, Inc., III
Drew Industries Inc., 28
Drexel Heritage Furnishings Inc., 12
Drypers Corporation, 18
Ducommun Incorporated, 30
Duracell International Inc., 9
Durametallic, 21
Duriron Company Inc., 17
Eagle-Picher Industries, Inc., 8; 23 (upd.)
Eastman Kodak Company, III; 7 (upd.)
Eddie Bauer Inc., 9
EG&G Incorporated, 29 (upd.)
Ekco Group, Inc., 16
Elano Corporation, 14
Electrolux Group, III
Eljer Industries, Inc., 24
Elscint Ltd., 20
Enesco Corporation, 11
Escalade, Incorporated, 19
Essilor International, 21
Esterline Technologies Corp., 15
Ethan Allen Interiors, Inc., 12
The Eureka Company, 12
Fanuc Ltd., III; 17 (upd.)
Farah Incorporated, 24
Featherlite Inc., 28
Fedders Corp., 18
Federal Signal Corp., 10
Fellowes Manufacturing Company, 28
Fender Musical Instruments Company, 16
Figgie International Inc., 7
Firearms Training Systems, Inc., 27
First Alert, Inc., 28
First Brands Corporation, 8
Fisher Controls International, Inc., 13
Fisher Scientific International Inc., 24
Fisher-Price Inc., 12
Fisons plc, 9
Fleetwood Enterprises, Inc., III; 22 (upd.)
Flexsteel Industries Inc., 15
Florsheim Shoe Company, 9
Fort James Corporation, 22 (upd.)
Fountain Powerboats Industries, Inc., 28
Foxboro Company, 13
Framatome SA, 19
Frigidaire Home Products, 22
Frymaster Corporation, 27
FSI International, Inc., 17
Fuji Photo Film Co., Ltd., III; 18 (upd.)
Fuqua Enterprises, Inc., 17
Furon Company, 28
The Furukawa Electric Co., Ltd., III
G.S. Blodgett Corporation, 15
The Gates Corporation, 9
GE Aircraft Engines, 9
GEA AG, 27
Gehl Company, 19
GenCorp Inc., 8; 9 (upd.)
General Housewares Corporation, 16
Gerber Scientific, Inc., 12
Giddings & Lewis, Inc., 10
The Gillette Company, 20 (upd.)
GKN plc, III
Gleason Corporation, 24
The Glidden Company, 8
Goody Products, Inc., 12
The Gorman-Rupp Company, 18
Goulds Pumps Inc., 24
Graco Inc., 19
Grinnell Corp., 13
Groupe André, 17
Groupe Legis Industries, 23
Grow Group Inc., 12
The Gunlocke Company, 23
H.B. Fuller Company, 8
Hach Co., 18
Haemonetics Corporation, 20
Halliburton Company, III
Hanson PLC, 30 (upd.)
Hardinge Inc., 25
Harland and Wolff Holdings plc, 19
Harmon Industries, Inc., 25
Harnischfeger Industries, Inc., 8
Harsco Corporation, 8
Hasbro, Inc., III; 16 (upd.)
Hawker Siddeley Group Public Limited Company, III
Haworth Inc., 8
Health O Meter Products Inc., 14
Heekin Can Inc., 13
HEICO Corporation, 30
Henkel Manco Inc., 22
The Henley Group, Inc., III
Herman Miller, Inc., 8
Hillenbrand Industries, Inc., 10
Hillsdown Holdings plc, 24 (upd.)
Hitachi Zosen Corporation, III
Hitchiner Manufacturing Co., Inc., 23
HMI Industries, Inc., 17
Holnam Inc., 8
Holson Burnes Group, Inc., 14
HON INDUSTRIES Inc., 13
The Hoover Company, 12
Huffy Corporation, 7; 30 (upd.)
Hunt Manufacturing Company, 12
Hunter Fan Company, 13
Hyster Company, 17
Hyundai Group, III; 7 (upd.)
Igloo Products Corp., 21
Illinois Tool Works Inc., III; 22 (upd.)
IMI plc, 9
Imo Industries Inc., 7; 27 (upd.)
Inchcape PLC, III; 16 (upd.)
Industrie Natuzzi S.p.A., 18
Ingalls Shipbuilding, Inc., 12
Ingersoll-Rand Company, III; 15 (upd.)
Insilco Corporation, 16
Interco Incorporated, III
Interface, Inc., 8
The Interlake Corporation, 8
International Controls Corporation, 10
International Game Technology, 10
Irwin Toy Limited, 14
Ishikawajima-Harima Heavy Industries Co., Ltd., III
J.I. Case Company, 10
Jacuzzi Inc., 23
Jayco Inc., 13
Jervis B. Webb Company, 24
Johnson Controls, Inc., III; 26 (upd.)
Johnson Worldwide Associates, Inc., 28
Johnstown America Industries, Inc., 23
Jones Apparel Group, Inc., 11
Jostens, Inc., 7; 25 (upd.)
Kaman Corp., 12
Kawasaki Heavy Industries, Ltd., III
Kaydon Corporation, 18
Kerr Group Inc., 24
Kewaunee Scientific Corporation, 25
Key Tronic Corporation, 14
Keystone International, Inc., 11
KHD Konzern, III
Kimball International, Inc., 12
Kit Manufacturing Co., 18
Knape & Vogt Manufacturing Company, 17
Knoll Group Inc., 14
Kobe Steel, Ltd., IV; 19 (upd.)
Koch Enterprises, Inc., 29
Kohler Company, 7
Komatsu Ltd., III; 16 (upd.)
Kone Corporation, 27
Konica Corporation, III
Kubota Corporation, III; 26 (upd.)
Kuhlman Corporation, 20
Kyocera Corporation, 21 (upd.)
LADD Furniture, Inc., 12
Ladish Co., Inc., 30
Lafarge Corporation, 28
Lam Research Corporation, 31 (upd.)
Lamson & Sessions Co., 13
Lancer Corporation, 21
The Lane Co., Inc., 12
Leggett & Platt, Incorporated, 11
Lennox International Inc., 8; 28 (upd.)
Lenox, Inc., 12
Lexmark International, Inc., 18
Linamar Corporation, 18
Lincoln Electric Co., 13
Lindal Cedar Homes, Inc., 29
Lindsay Manufacturing Co., 20
Little Tikes Co., 13
Loctite Corporation, 8
Logitech International SA, 28
The Longaberger Company, 12
Louis Vuitton, 10
Lucas Industries PLC, III
MacAndrews & Forbes Holdings Inc., 28
Mail-Well, Inc., 28
Makita Corporation, 22
MAN Aktiengesellschaft, III
Manitou BF S.A., 27
Manitowoc Company, Inc., 18
Mannesmann AG, III; 14 (upd.)
Margarete Steiff GmbH, 23
Marisa Christina, Inc., 15
Mark IV Industries, Inc., 7; 28 (upd.)
The Marmon Group, 16 (upd.)
Marvin Lumber & Cedar Company, 22
Mary Kay, Inc., 30 (upd.)
Masco Corporation, III; 20 (upd.)
Mattel, Inc., 7; 25 (upd.)
Matthews International Corporation, 29
Maxco Inc., 17
Maxwell Shoe Company, Inc., 30
Maytag Corporation, III; 22 (upd.)
McDermott International, Inc., III
Meadowcraft, Inc., 29
Merillat Industries Inc., 13
Mestek Inc., 10
Metso Corporation, 30 (upd.)
Mettler-Toledo International Inc., 30
Michael Anthony Jewelers, Inc., 24
Microdot Inc., 8
Mikasa, Inc., 28
Miller Industries, Inc., 26
Milton Bradley Company, 21
Mine Safety Appliances Company, 31
Minolta Camera Co., Ltd., III
Minolta Co., Ltd., 18 (upd.)
Mitsubishi Heavy Industries, Ltd., III; 7 (upd.)
Modine Manufacturing Company, 8
Moen Incorporated, 12
Mohawk Industries, Inc., 19
Molex Incorporated, 11
Montres Rolex S.A., 13
Moulinex S.A., 22
Movado Group, Inc., 28
Mr. Coffee, Inc., 15
Mr. Gasket Inc., 15
Mueller Industries, Inc., 7
Nashua Corporation, 8
National Gypsum Company, 10
National Picture & Frame Company, 24
National Standard Co., 13
NCR Corporation, 30 (upd.)
New Balance Athletic Shoe, Inc., 25
New Holland N.V., 22
Newell Co., 9
Newport News Shipbuilding and Dry Dock Co., 13

NHK Spring Co., Ltd., III
Nikon Corporation, III
Nintendo Co., Ltd., III; 7 (upd.)
Nippon Seiko K.K., III
Nippondenso Co., Ltd., III
NKK Corporation, 28 (upd.)
NordicTrack, 22
Nordson Corporation, 11
Norton Company, 8
Norton McNaughton, Inc., 27
Novellus Systems, Inc., 18
NTN Corporation, III
Nu-kote Holding, Inc., 18
Oak Industries Inc., 21
Oakwood Homes Corporation, 15
The Ohio Art Company, 14
Oil-Dri Corporation of America, 20
Oneida Ltd., 7; 31 (upd.)
Osmonics, Inc., 18
Otis Elevator Company, Inc., 13
Outboard Marine Corporation, III; 20 (upd.)
Owens Corning Corporation, 20 (upd.)
Owosso Corporation, 29
Pacific Dunlop Limited, 10
Pall Corporation, 9
Panavision Inc., 24
Park Corp., 22
Parker-Hannifin Corporation, III; 24 (upd.)
Patrick Industries, Inc., 30
Pella Corporation, 12
Penn Engineering & Manufacturing Corp., 28
Pentair, Inc., 26 (upd.)
Pentech International, Inc., 29
The Perkin-Elmer Corporation, 7
Phillips-Van Heusen Corporation, 24
Physio-Control International Corp., 18
Pioneer Electronic Corporation, III
Pitney Bowes, Inc., 19
PlayCore, Inc., 27
Playmates Toys, 23
Playskool, Inc., 25
Pleasant Company, 27
Ply Gem Industries Inc., 12
Polaris Industries Inc., 12
Polaroid Corporation, III; 7 (upd.); 28 (upd.)
PPG Industries, Inc., 22 (upd.)
Precision Castparts Corp., 15
Premark International, Inc., III
Prince Sports Group, Inc., 15
Printronix, Inc., 18
Puritan-Bennett Corporation, 13
Purolator Products Company, 21
Quixote Corporation, 15
R. Griggs Group Limited, 23
Rapala-Normark Group, Ltd., 30
Raychem Corporation, 8
Recovery Engineering, Inc., 25
Red Wing Shoe Company, Inc., 9
Regal-Beloit Corporation, 18
Reichhold Chemicals, Inc., 10
Remington Arms Company, Inc., 12
Revell-Monogram Inc., 16
Revere Ware Corporation, 22
Rexnord Corporation, 21
Rheinmetall Berlin AG, 9
Riddell Sports Inc., 22
Roadmaster Industries, Inc., 16
Robbins & Myers Inc., 15
Robertson-Ceco Corporation, 19
RockShox, Inc., 26
ROHN Industries, Inc., 22
Rohr Incorporated, 9
Rollerblade, Inc., 15
Roper Industries Inc., 15
Royal Appliance Manufacturing Company, 15
Royal Doulton Plc, 14
RPM Inc., 8
Rubbermaid Incorporated, III
Russ Berrie and Company, Inc., 12
S.C. Johnson & Son, Inc., 28 (upd.)
Safeskin Corporation, 18
Salant Corporation, 12
Salton, Inc., 30
Samsonite Corp., 13
Sauder Woodworking Co., 12
Schindler Holding AG, 29
Schlumberger Limited, III
Scotsman Industries, Inc., 20
Scott Fetzer Company, 12
The Scotts Company, 22
Scovill Fasteners Inc., 24
Sealed Air Corporation, 14
Sealy Inc., 12
Seiko Corporation, III; 17 (upd.)
The Selmer Company, Inc., 19
Semitool, Inc., 18
Sequa Corp., 13
Serta, Inc., 28
Shakespeare Company, 22
Shelby Williams Industries, Inc., 14
Shorewood Packaging Corporation, 28
The Singer Company N.V., 30 (upd.)
Skis Rossignol S.A., 15
Skyline Corporation, 30
Smead Manufacturing Co., 17
Smith & Wesson Corporation, 30
Smith Corona Corp., 13
Smith International, Inc., 15
Smiths Industries PLC, 25
Snap-on Tools Corporation, 7
Snap-On, Incorporated, 27 (upd.)
Sparton Corporation, 18
Specialty Equipment Companies, Inc., 25
SPS Technologies, Inc., 30
Standex International Corporation, 17
The Stanley Works, III; 20 (upd.)
Steelcase, Inc., 7; 27 (upd.)
Steinway Musical Properties, Inc., 19
Stewart & Stevenson Services Inc., 11
Stryker Corporation, 11; 29 (upd.)
Sturm, Ruger & Company, Inc., 19
Sub-Zero Freezer Co., Inc., 31
Sudbury Inc., 16
Sulzer Brothers Limited (Gebruder Sulzer Aktiengesellschaft), III
Sumitomo Heavy Industries, Ltd., III
Susquehanna Pfaltzgraff Company, 8
Swank Inc., 17
The Swatch Group SA, 26
Swedish Match S.A., 12
Sybron International Corp., 14
Syratech Corp., 14
TAB Products Co., 17
TAG Heuer International SA, 25
Tarkett Sommer AG, 25
Taylor Made Golf Co., 23
Tecumseh Products Company, 8
Tektronix, Inc., 8
Tennant Company, 13
Terex Corporation, 7
Thermadyne Holding Corporation, 19
Thermo BioAnalysis Corp., 25
Thermo Electron Corporation, 7
Thermo Fibertek, Inc., 24
Thermo Instrument Systems Inc., 11
Thermo King Corporation, 13
Thiokol Corporation, 22 (upd.)
Thomas & Betts Corp., 11
Thomas Industries Inc., 29
Thomasville Furniture Industries, Inc., 12
Thyssen Krupp AG, 28 (upd.)
Timex Corporation, 25 (upd.)
Timex Enterprises Inc., 7
The Timken Company, 8
TJ International, Inc., 19
Todd Shipyards Corporation, 14
Tokheim Corporation, 21
Tonka Corporation, 25
Toolex International N.V., 26
Topps Company, Inc., 13
The Toro Company, 7; 26 (upd.)
The Torrington Company, 13
TOTO LTD., 28 (upd.)
Town & Country Corporation, 19
Toymax International, Inc., 29
Toyoda Automatic Loom Works, Ltd., III
Trek Bicycle Corporation, 16
Trico Products Corporation, 15
TriMas Corp., 11
Trinity Industries, Incorporated, 7
TRINOVA Corporation, III
Triumph Group, Inc., 31
Tultex Corporation, 13
Tupperware Corporation, 28
Twin Disc, Inc., 21
Tyco International Ltd., 28 (upd.)
Tyco Laboratories, Inc., III
Tyco Toys, Inc., 12
U.S. Robotics Inc., 9
United Defense, L.P., 30
United Dominion Industries Limited, 8; 16 (upd.)
United States Filter Corporation, 20
Unitog Co., 19
Valmet Corporation (Valmet Oy), III
Valmont Industries, Inc., 19
The Valspar Corporation, 8
Varity Corporation, III
Varlen Corporation, 16
Varta AG, 23
Velcro Industries N.V., 19
Vermeer Manufacturing Company, 17
Vickers plc, 27
Victorinox AG, 21
Virco Manufacturing Corporation, 17
Vorwerk & Co., 27
W.H. Brady Co., 17
W.L. Gore & Associates, Inc., 14
W.W. Grainger, Inc., 26 (upd.)
Wabash National Corp., 13
Walbro Corporation, 13
Washington Scientific Industries, Inc., 17
Wassall Plc, 18
Waterford Wedgwood Holdings PLC, 12
Watts Industries, Inc., 19
WD-40 Company, 18
Welbilt Corp., 19
Wellman, Inc., 8
Weru Aktiengesellschaft, 18
West Bend Co., 14
Western Digital Corp., 25
Whirlpool Corporation, III; 12 (upd.)
White Consolidated Industries Inc., 13
Wilson Sporting Goods Company, 24
Windmere Corporation, 16
WinsLoew Furniture, Inc., 21
WMS Industries, Inc., 15
Wolverine Tube Inc., 23
Wood-Mode, Inc., 23
Woodward Governor Co., 13
Wyant Corporation, 30
Wyman-Gordon Company, 14
Yamaha Corporation, III; 16 (upd.)
York International Corp., 13
Zero Corporation, 17
Zippo Manufacturing Company, 18

MATERIALS

AK Steel Holding Corporation, 19
American Biltrite Inc., 16
American Colloid Co., 13
American Standard Inc., III
Ameriwood Industries International Corp., 17
Apogee Enterprises, Inc., 8
Asahi Glass Company, Limited, III
Bairnco Corporation, 28
Bayou Steel Corporation, 31
Blessings Corp., 19
Blue Circle Industries PLC, III
Boral Limited, III
British Vita PLC, 9
Cameron & Barkley Company, 28
Carborundum Company, 15
Carlisle Companies Incorporated, 8
Cemex SA de CV, 20
Chargeurs International, 21 (upd.)
Compagnie de Saint-Gobain S.A., III; 16 (upd.)
Cookson Group plc, III
Corning Incorporated, III
CSR Limited, III
Dal-Tile International Inc., 22
The David J. Joseph Company, 14
The Dexter Corporation, 12 (upd.)
ECC Group plc, III
84 Lumber Company, 9
English China Clays plc, 15 (upd.)
Envirodyne Industries, Inc., 17
Feldmuhle Nobel A.G., III
Fibreboard Corporation, 16
Foamex International Inc., 17
Formica Corporation, 13
GAF Corporation, 22 (upd.)
The Geon Company, 11
Giant Cement Holding, Inc., 23
Granite Rock Company, 26
Groupe Sidel S.A., 21
Harbison-Walker Refractories Company, 24
Harrisons & Crosfield plc, III
Heidelberger Zement AG, 31
Hexcel Corporation, 28
"Holderbank" Financière Glaris Ltd., III
Howmet Corp., 12
Ibstock plc, 14
Joseph T. Ryerson & Son, Inc., 15
Lafarge Coppée S.A., III
Lafarge Corporation, 28
Lehigh Portland Cement Company, 23
Manville Corporation, III; 7 (upd.)
Matsushita Electric Works, Ltd., III; 7 (upd.)
Medusa Corporation, 24
Mitsubishi Materials Corporation, III
Nippon Sheet Glass Company, Limited, III
OmniSource Corporation, 14
Onoda Cement Co., Ltd., III
Owens-Corning Fiberglass Corporation, III
Pilkington plc, III
Pioneer International Limited, III
PPG Industries, Inc., III
Redland plc, III
RMC Group p.l.c., III
The Rugby Group plc, 31
Schuff Steel Company, 26
Sekisui Chemical Co., Ltd., III
Shaw Industries, 9
The Sherwin-Williams Company, III; 13 (upd.)
Simplex Technologies Inc., 21
Sommer-Allibert S.A., 19
Southdown, Inc., 14
Spartech Corporation, 19
Ssangyong Cement Industrial Co., Ltd., III
Sun Distributors L.P., 12
Tarmac PLC, III
Tarmac plc, 28 (upd.)
TOTO LTD., III; 28 (upd.)
Toyo Sash Co., Ltd., III
Tuscarora Inc., 29
Ube Industries, Ltd., III
USG Corporation, III; 26 (upd.)
Vulcan Materials Company, 7
Walter Industries, Inc., III
Waxman Industries, Inc., 9

MINING & METALS

A.M. Castle & Co., 25
Alcan Aluminium Limited, IV; 31 (upd.)
Alleghany Corporation, 10
Allegheny Ludlum Corporation, 8
Aluminum Company of America, IV; 20 (upd.)
AMAX Inc., IV
Amsted Industries Incorporated, 7
Anglo American Corporation of South Africa Limited, IV; 16 (upd.)
ARBED S.A., IV, 22 (upd.)
Arch Mineral Corporation, 7
Armco Inc., IV
ASARCO Incorporated, IV
Battle Mountain Gold Company, 23
Bethlehem Steel Corporation, IV; 7 (upd.); 27 (upd.)
Birmingham Steel Corporation, 13
Boart Longyear Company, 26
British Coal Corporation, IV
British Steel plc, IV; 19 (upd.)
Broken Hill Proprietary Company Ltd., IV, 22 (upd.)
Brush Wellman Inc., 14
Carpenter Technology Corporation, 13
Chaparral Steel Co., 13
Christensen Boyles Corporation, 26
Cleveland-Cliffs Inc., 13
Coal India Limited, IV
Cockerill Sambre Group, IV; 26 (upd.)
Coeur d'Alene Mines Corporation, 20
Cold Spring Granite Company, 16
Commercial Metals Company, 15
Companhia Vale do Rio Duce, IV
CRA Limited, IV
Cyprus Amax Minerals Company, 21
Cyprus Minerals Company, 7
Daido Steel Co., Ltd., IV
De Beers Consolidated Mines Limited/De Beers Centenary AG, IV; 7 (upd.); 28 (upd.)
Degussa Group, IV
Dofasco Inc., IV; 24 (upd.)
Echo Bay Mines Ltd., IV
Engelhard Corporation, IV
Fansteel Inc., 19
Freeport-McMoRan Inc., IV; 7 (upd.)
Fried. Krupp GmbH, IV
Gencor Ltd., IV, 22 (upd.)
Geneva Steel, 7
Gold Fields of South Africa Ltd., IV
Handy & Harman, 23
Hanson PLC, 30 (upd.)
Hecla Mining Company, 20
Hemlo Gold Mines Inc., 9
Heraeus Holding GmbH, IV
Hitachi Metals, Ltd., IV
Hoesch AG, IV
Homestake Mining Company, 12
The Hudson Bay Mining and Smelting Company, Limited, 12
Imetal S.A., IV
Inco Limited, IV
Industrias Penoles, S.A. de C.V., 22
Inland Steel Industries, Inc., IV; 19 (upd.)
Ispat International N.V., 30
Johnson Matthey PLC, IV; 16 (upd.)
Kaiser Aluminum & Chemical Corporation, IV
Kawasaki Steel Corporation, IV
Kennecott Corporation, 7; 27 (upd.)
Kentucky Electric Steel, Inc., 31
Kerr-McGee Corporation, 22 (upd.)
Klockner-Werke AG, IV
Kobe Steel, Ltd., IV; 19 (upd.)
Koninklijke Nederlandsche Hoogovens en Staalfabrieken NV, IV
Laclede Steel Company, 15
Layne Christensen Company, 19
Lonrho Plc, 21
The LTV Corporation, 24 (upd.)
Lukens Inc., 14
Magma Copper Company, 7
The Marmon Group, IV; 16 (upd.)
MAXXAM Inc., 8
Metaleurop S.A., 21
Metallgesellschaft AG, IV
Minerals and Metals Trading Corporation of India Ltd., IV
Minerals Technologies Inc., 11
Mitsui Mining & Smelting Co., Ltd., IV
Mitsui Mining Company, Limited, IV
National Steel Corporation, 12
NERCO, Inc., 7
Newmont Mining Corporation, 7
Niagara Corporation, 28
Nichimen Corporation, IV
Nippon Light Metal Company, Ltd., IV
Nippon Steel Corporation, IV; 17 (upd.)
Nisshin Steel Co., Ltd., IV
NKK Corporation, IV; 28 (upd.)
Noranda Inc., IV; 7 (upd.)
North Star Steel Company, 18
Nucor Corporation, 7; 21 (upd.)
Oglebay Norton Company, 17
Okura & Co., Ltd., IV
Oregon Metallurgical Corporation, 20
Oregon Steel Mills, Inc., 14
Park Corp., 22
Peabody Coal Company, 10
Peabody Holding Company, Inc., IV
Pechiney, IV
Peter Kiewit Sons' Inc., 8
Phelps Dodge Corporation, IV; 28 (upd.)
The Pittston Company, IV; 19 (upd.)
Placer Dome Inc., 20
Pohang Iron and Steel Company Ltd., IV
Potash Corporation of Saskatchewan Inc., 18
Quanex Corporation, 13
Reliance Steel & Aluminum Co., 19
Republic Engineered Steels, Inc., 7; 26 (upd.)
Reynolds Metals Company, IV
Rio Tinto plc, 19 (upd.)
Rouge Steel Company, 8
The RTZ Corporation PLC, IV
Ruhrkohle AG, IV
Saarberg-Konzern, IV
Salzgitter AG, IV
Sandvik AB, IV
Schnitzer Steel Industries, Inc., 19
Southwire Company, Inc., 8; 23 (upd.)
Steel Authority of India Ltd., IV
Stelco Inc., IV
Sumitomo Metal Industries, Ltd., IV
Sumitomo Metal Mining Co., Ltd., IV
Tata Iron and Steel Company Ltd., IV
Teck Corporation, 27
Texas Industries, Inc., 8
Thyssen AG, IV
The Timken Company, 8

Titanium Metals Corporation, 21
Tomen Corporation, IV
Ugine S.A., 20
Usinor Sacilor, IV
VIAG Aktiengesellschaft, IV
Voest-Alpine Stahl AG, IV
Walter Industries, Inc., 22 (upd.)
Weirton Steel Corporation, IV; 26 (upd.)
Westmoreland Coal Company, 7
Wheeling-Pittsburgh Corp., 7
Worthington Industries, Inc., 7; 21 (upd.)
Zambia Industrial and Mining Corporation Ltd., IV

PAPER & FORESTRY

Abitibi-Consolidated, Inc., 25 (upd.)
Abitibi-Price Inc., IV
Amcor Limited, IV; 19 (upd.)
American Pad & Paper Company, 20
Asplundh Tree Expert Co., 20
Avery Dennison Corporation, IV
Badger Paper Mills, Inc., 15
Beckett Papers, 23
Bemis Company, Inc., 8
Bohemia, Inc., 13
Boise Cascade Corporation, IV; 8 (upd.)
Bowater PLC, IV
Bunzl plc, IV
Caraustar Industries, Inc., 19
Champion International Corporation, IV; 20 (upd.)
Chesapeake Corporation, 8; 30 (upd.)
Consolidated Papers, Inc., 8
Crane & Co., Inc., 26
Crown Vantage Inc., 29
Daio Paper Corporation, IV
Daishowa Paper Manufacturing Co., Ltd., IV
Dillard Paper Company, 11
Domtar Inc., IV
Enso-Gutzeit Oy, IV
Esselte Pendaflex Corporation, 11
Federal Paper Board Company, Inc., 8
Fletcher Challenge Ltd., IV
Fort Howard Corporation, 8
Fort James Corporation, 22 (upd.)
Georgia-Pacific Corporation, IV; 9 (upd.)
Groupe Rougier SA, 21
Honshu Paper Co., Ltd., IV
International Paper Company, IV; 15 (upd.)
James River Corporation of Virginia, IV
Japan Pulp and Paper Company Limited, IV
Jefferson Smurfit Group plc, IV
Jujo Paper Co., Ltd., IV
Kimberly-Clark Corporation, 16 (upd.)
Kruger Inc., 17
Kymmene Corporation, IV
Longview Fibre Company, 8
Louisiana-Pacific Corporation, IV; 31 (upd.)
MacMillan Bloedel Limited, IV
The Mead Corporation, IV; 19 (upd.)
Metsa-Serla Oy, IV
Mo och Domsjö AB, IV
Monadnock Paper Mills, Inc., 21
Mosinee Paper Corporation, 15
Nashua Corporation, 8
NCH Corporation, 8
Oji Paper Co., Ltd., IV
P.H. Glatfelter Company, 8; 30 (upd.)
Packaging Corporation of America, 12
Papeteries de Lancey, 23
Pope and Talbot, Inc., 12
Potlatch Corporation, 8
PWA Group, IV
Rayonier Inc., 24
Rengo Co., Ltd., IV
Riverwood International Corporation, 11
Rock-Tenn Company, 13
St. Joe Paper Company, 8
Sanyo-Kokusaku Pulp Co., Ltd., IV
Scott Paper Company, IV; 31 (upd.)
Sealed Air Corporation, 14
Sierra Pacific Industries, 22
Simpson Investment Company, 17
Specialty Coatings Inc., 8
Stone Container Corporation, IV
Stora Kopparbergs Bergslags AB, IV
Svenska Cellulosa Aktiebolaget SCA, IV; 28 (upd.)
Temple-Inland Inc., IV; 31 (upd.)
TJ International, Inc., 19
Union Camp Corporation, IV
United Paper Mills Ltd. (Yhtyneet Paperitehtaat Oy), IV
Universal Forest Products Inc., 10
UPM-Kymmene Corporation, 19
West Fraser Timber Co. Ltd., 17
Westvaco Corporation, IV; 19 (upd.)
Weyerhaeuser Company, IV; 9 (upd.); 28 (upd.)
Wickes Inc., 25 (upd.)
Willamette Industries, Inc., IV; 31 (upd.)
WTD Industries, Inc., 20

PERSONAL SERVICES

AARP, 27
ADT Security Systems, Inc., 12
Correctional Services Corporation, 30
CUC International Inc., 16
DeVry Incorporated, 29
Educational Testing Service, 12
Franklin Quest Co., 11
Goodwill Industries International, Inc., 16
KinderCare Learning Centers, Inc., 13
The Loewen Group, Inc., 16
Management and Training Corporation, 28
Manpower, Inc., 9
Regis Corporation, 18
Rollins, Inc., 11
Rosenbluth International Inc., 14
Rotary International, 31
Service Corporation International, 6
SOS Staffing Services, 25
Stewart Enterprises, Inc., 20
Supercuts Inc., 26
Weight Watchers International Inc., 12
Youth Services International, Inc., 21

PETROLEUM

Abu Dhabi National Oil Company, IV
Agway, Inc., 21 (upd.)
Alberta Energy Company Ltd., 16
Amerada Hess Corporation, IV; 21 (upd.)
Amoco Corporation, IV; 14 (upd.)
Anadarko Petroleum Corporation, 10
ANR Pipeline Co., 17
Anschutz Corp., 12
Apache Corp., 10
Ashland Inc., 19
Ashland Oil, Inc., IV
Atlantic Richfield Company, IV; 31 (upd.)
Baker Hughes Incorporated, 22 (upd.)
BJ Services Company, 25
The British Petroleum Company plc, IV; 7 (upd.); 21 (upd.)
Broken Hill Proprietary Company Ltd., 22 (upd.)
Burlington Resources Inc., 10
Burmah Castrol PLC, IV; 30 (upd.)
Caltex Petroleum Corporation, 19
Chevron Corporation, IV; 19 (upd.)
Chiles Offshore Corporation, 9
Chinese Petroleum Corporation, IV; 31 (upd.)
CITGO Petroleum Corporation, IV; 31 (upd.)
The Coastal Corporation, IV; 31 (upd.)
Compañia Española de Petróleos S.A., IV
Conoco Inc., IV; 16 (upd.)
Cooper Cameron Corporation, 20 (upd.)
Cosmo Oil Co., Ltd., IV
Crown Central Petroleum Corporation, 7
DeepTech International Inc., 21
Den Norse Stats Oljeselskap AS, IV
Deutsche BP Aktiengesellschaft, 7
Diamond Shamrock, Inc., IV
Egyptian General Petroluem Corporation, IV
Elf Aquitaine SA, 21 (upd.)
Empresa Colombiana de Petróleos, IV
Energen Corporation, 21
Enron Corporation, 19
Ente Nazionale Idrocarburi, IV
Enterprise Oil plc, 11
Entreprise Nationale Sonatrach, IV
Exxon Corporation, IV; 7 (upd.)
FINA, Inc., 7
Flying J Inc., 19
Forest Oil Corporation, 19
General Sekiyu K.K., IV
Giant Industries, Inc., 19
Global Marine Inc., 9
Halliburton Company, 25 (upd.)
Helmerich & Payne, Inc., 18
Holly Corporation, 12
Hunt Consolidated, Inc., 27 (upd.)
Hunt Oil Company, 7
Idemitsu Kosan K.K., IV
Imperial Oil Limited, IV; 25 (upd.)
Indian Oil Corporation Ltd., IV
Kanematsu Corporation, IV
Kerr-McGee Corporation, IV; 22 (upd.)
King Ranch, Inc., 14
Koch Industries, Inc., IV; 20 (upd.)
Koppers Industries, Inc., 26 (upd.)
Kuwait Petroleum Corporation, IV
Libyan National Oil Corporation, IV
The Louisiana Land and Exploration Company, 7
Lyondell Petrochemical Company, IV
MAPCO Inc., IV
Maxus Energy Corporation, 7
Mitchell Energy and Development Corporation, 7
Mitsubishi Oil Co., Ltd., IV
Mobil Corporation, IV; 7 (upd.); 21 (upd.)
Murphy Oil Corporation, 7
Nabors Industries, Inc., 9
National Iranian Oil Company, IV
Neste Oy, IV
NGC Corporation, 18
Nigerian National Petroleum Corporation, IV
Nippon Oil Company, Limited, IV
Noble Affiliates, Inc., 11
Occidental Petroleum Corporation, IV; 25 (upd.)
Oil and Natural Gas Commission, IV
ÖMV Aktiengesellschaft, IV
Oryx Energy Company, 7
Parker Drilling Company, 28
Patina Oil & Gas Corporation, 24
Pennzoil Company, IV; 20 (upd.)
PERTAMINA, IV
Petro-Canada Limited, IV
PetroFina S.A., IV; 26 (upd.)
Petróleo Brasileiro S.A., IV
Petróleos de Portugal S.A., IV
Petróleos de Venezuela S.A., IV
Petróleos del Ecuador, IV

Petróleos Mexicanos, IV; 19 (upd.)
Petroleum Development Oman LLC, IV
Petronas, IV
Phillips Petroleum Company, IV
Qatar General Petroleum Corporation, IV
Quaker State Corporation, 7; 21 (upd.)
Repsol S.A., IV; 16 (upd.)
Royal Dutch Petroleum Company/ The "Shell" Transport and Trading Company p.l.c., IV
Sasol Limited, IV
Saudi Arabian Oil Company, IV; 17 (upd.)
Schlumberger Limited, 17 (upd.)
Seagull Energy Corporation, 11
Shanghai Petrochemical Co., Ltd., 18
Shell Oil Company, IV; 14 (upd.)
Showa Shell Sekiyu K.K., IV
Société Nationale Elf Aquitaine, IV; 7 (upd.)
Suburban Propane Partners, L.P., 30
Sun Company, Inc., IV
Sunoco, Inc., 28 (upd.)
Talisman Energy, 9
Tesoro Petroleum Corporation, 7
Texaco Inc., IV; 14 (upd.)
Tonen Corporation, IV; 16 (upd.)
Tosco Corporation, 7
Total Compagnie Française des Pétroles S.A., IV
TOTAL S.A., 24 (upd.)
TransMontaigne Inc., 28
Travel Ports of America, Inc., 17
Triton Energy Corporation, 11
Türkiye Petrolleri Anonim Ortakliği, IV
Ultramar Diamond Shamrock Corporation, 31 (upd.)
Ultramar PLC, IV
Union Texas Petroleum Holdings, Inc., 9
Unocal Corporation, IV; 24 (upd.)
USX Corporation, IV; 7 (upd.)
Valero Energy Corporation, 7
Vastar Resources, Inc., 24
Wascana Energy Inc., 13
Western Atlas Inc., 12
Western Company of North America, 15
The Williams Companies, Inc., IV; 31 (upd.)
YPF Sociedad Anonima, IV

PUBLISHING & PRINTING

A.B.Dick Company, 28
A.H. Belo Corporation, 10; 30 (upd.)
Advance Publications Inc., IV; 19 (upd.)
Affiliated Publications, Inc., 7
American Banknote Corporation, 30
American Greetings Corporation, 7, 22 (upd.)
American Media, Inc., 27
American Printing House for the Blind, 26
Arnoldo Mondadori Editore S.p.A., IV; 19 (upd.)
The Associated Press, 31 (upd.)
The Atlantic Group, 23
Axel Springer Verlag AG, IV; 20 (upd.)
Banta Corporation, 12
Bauer Publishing Group, 7
Berlitz International, Inc., 13
Bertelsmann A.G., IV; 15 (upd.)
Big Flower Press Holdings, Inc., 21
Blue Mountain Arts, Inc., 29
Book-of-the-Month Club, Inc., 13
Bowne & Co., Inc., 23
Broderbund Software, 29 (upd.)
Brown Printing Company, 26
Burda Holding GmbH. & Co., 23
The Bureau of National Affairs, Inc., 23
Butterick Co., Inc., 23
Cadmus Communications Corporation, 23
CCH Inc., 14
Central Newspapers, Inc., 10
Champion Industries, Inc., 28
The Chronicle Publishing Company, Inc., 23
CMP Media Inc., 26
Commerce Clearing House, Inc., 7
The Condé Nast Publications Inc., 13
Consumers Union, 26
The Copley Press, Inc., 23
Cowles Media Company, 23
Cox Enterprises, Inc., IV; 22 (upd.)
Crain Communications, Inc., 12
Dai Nippon Printing Co., Ltd., IV
Daily Mail and General Trust plc, 19
Day Runner, Inc., 14
DC Comics Inc., 25
De La Rue PLC, 10
Deluxe Corporation, 7; 22 (upd.)
Dorling Kindersley Holdings plc, 20
Dow Jones & Company, Inc., IV; 19 (upd.)
The Dun & Bradstreet Corporation, IV; 19 (upd.)
Duplex Products Inc., 17
The E.W. Scripps Company, IV; 7 (upd.); 28 (upd.)
Edmark Corporation, 14
Elsevier N.V., IV
EMI Group plc, 22 (upd.)
Encyclopedia Britannica, Inc., 7
Engraph, Inc., 12
Enquirer/Star Group, Inc., 10
Essence Communications, Inc., 24
Farrar, Straus and Giroux Inc., 15
Flint Ink Corporation, 13
Follett Corporation, 12
Forbes Inc., 30
Franklin Electronic Publishers, Inc., 23
Gannett Co., Inc., IV; 7 (upd.); 30 (upd.)
Gibson Greetings, Inc., 12
Golden Books Family Entertainment, Inc., 28
Graphic Industries Inc., 25
Gray Communications Systems, Inc., 24
Grolier Inc., 16
Groupe de la Cite, IV
Groupe Les Echos, 25
Hachette, IV
Hachette Filipacchi Medias S.A., 21
Hallmark Cards, Inc., IV; 16 (upd.)
Harcourt Brace and Co., 12
Harcourt Brace Jovanovich, Inc., IV
Harcourt General, Inc., 20 (upd.)
HarperCollins Publishers, 15
Harte-Hanks Communications, Inc., 17
Havas, SA, 10
Hazelden Foundation, 28
The Hearst Corporation, IV; 19 (upd.)
Her Majesty's Stationery Office, 7
N.V. Holdingmaatschappij De Telegraaf, 23
Hollinger International Inc., 24
Houghton Mifflin Company, 10
IDG Books Worldwide, Inc., 27
International Data Group, Inc., 7; 25 (upd.)
IPC Magazines Limited, 7
John Fairfax Holdings Limited, 7
John H. Harland Company, 17
John Wiley & Sons, Inc., 17
Johnson Publishing Company, Inc., 28
Jostens, Inc., 25 (upd.)
Journal Register Company, 29
Knight-Ridder, Inc., IV; 15 (upd.)
Kodansha Ltd., IV
Landmark Communications, Inc., 12
Larry Flynt Publishing Inc., 31
Lee Enterprises, Incorporated, 11
Maclean Hunter Publishing Limited, IV; 26 (upd.)
Macmillan, Inc., 7
Martha Stewart Living Omnimedia, L.L.C., 24
Marvel Entertainment Group, Inc., 10
Matra-Hachette S.A., 15 (upd.)
Maxwell Communication Corporation plc, IV; 7 (upd.)
McClatchy Newspapers, Inc., 23
The McGraw-Hill Companies, Inc., IV; 18 (upd.)
Mecklermedia Corporation, 24
Meredith Corporation, 11; 29 (upd.)
Merrill Corporation, 18
The Miner Group International, 22
Mirror Group Newspapers plc, 7; 23 (upd.)
Moore Corporation Limited, IV
Multimedia, Inc., 11
National Audubon Society, 26
National Geographic Society, 9; 30 (upd.)
The New York Times Company, IV; 19 (upd.)
News America Publishing Inc., 12
News Corporation Limited, IV; 7 (upd.)
Nihon Keizai Shimbun, Inc., IV
Ottaway Newspapers, Inc., 15
Pearson plc, IV
Penton Media, Inc., 27
Petersen Publishing Company, 21
Playboy Enterprises, Inc., 18
Pleasant Company, 27
Primedia Inc., 22
The Providence Journal Company, 28
Pulitzer Publishing Company, 15
Quad/Graphics, Inc., 19
Quebecor Inc., 12
R.L. Polk & Co., 10
R.R. Donnelley & Sons Company, IV; 9 (upd.)
Rand McNally & Company, 28
Random House Inc., 13; 31 (upd.)
The Reader's Digest Association, Inc., IV; 17 (upd.)
Recycled Paper Greetings, Inc., 21
Reed Elsevier plc, 31 (upd.)
Reed International PLC, IV; 17 (upd.)
Reuters Holdings PLC, IV; 22 (upd.)
Rodale Press, Inc., 23
Rogers Communications Inc., 30 (upd.)
Schawk, Inc., 24
Schibsted ASA, 31
Scholastic Corporation, 10; 29 (upd.)
Scott Fetzer Company, 12
Seattle Times Company, 15
The Sierra Club, 28
Simon & Schuster Inc., IV; 19 (upd.)
Sir Speedy, Inc., 16
SkyMall, Inc., 26
Softbank Corp., 13
Southam Inc., 7
Standard Register Co., 15
Taylor Publishing Company, 12
Thomas Nelson Inc., 14
Thomas Publishing Company, 26
The Thomson Corporation, 8
The Times Mirror Company, IV; 17 (upd.)
Tom Doherty Associates Inc., 25
Toppan Printing Co., Ltd., IV
Torstar Corporation, 29
Tribune Company, IV, 22 (upd.)
U.S. News and World Report Inc., 30
United News & Media plc, 28 (upd.)
United Newspapers plc, IV
United Press International, Inc., 25
Valassis Communications, Inc., 8
Value Line, Inc., 16
VNU N.V., 27

Volt Information Sciences Inc., 26
W.W. Norton & Company, Inc., 28
The Washington Post Company, IV; 20 (upd.)
Waverly, Inc., 16
West Publishing Co., 7
Western Publishing Group, Inc., 13
Wolters Kluwer NV, 14
World Book, Inc., 12
World Color Press Inc., 12
Xeikon NV, 26
Zebra Technologies Corporation, 14
Ziff Communications Company, 12
Zondervan Publishing House, 24

REAL ESTATE

Amfac/JMB Hawaii L.L.C., 24 (upd.)
Associated Estates Realty Corporation, 25
Boston Properties, Inc., 22
Bramalea Ltd., 9
Canary Wharf Group Plc, 30
CapStar Hotel Company, 21
Castle & Cooke, Inc., 20 (upd.)
Catellus Development Corporation, 24
CB Commercial Real Estate Services Group, Inc., 21
Cheung Kong (Holdings) Limited, IV; 20 (upd.)
Del Webb Corporation, 14
The Edward J. DeBartolo Corporation, 8
Forest City Enterprises, Inc., 16
Grubb & Ellis Company, 21
The Haminerson Property Investment and Development Corporation plc, IV
Harbert Corporation, 14
Hongkong Land Holdings Limited, IV
Hyatt Corporation, 16 (upd.)
JMB Realty Corporation, IV
Kaufman and Broad Home Corporation, 8
Kerry Properties Limited, 22
Kimco Realty Corporation, 11
The Koll Company, 8
Land Securities PLC, IV
Lefrak Organization Inc., 26
Lend Lease Corporation Limited, IV; 17 (upd.)
Lincoln Property Company, 8
Manufactured Home Communities, Inc., 22
Maui Land & Pineapple Company, Inc., 29
Maxco Inc., 17
Meditrust, 11
Melvin Simon and Associates, Inc., 8
MEPC plc, IV
Meritage Corporation, 26
Mitsubishi Estate Company, Limited, IV
Mitsui Real Estate Development Co., Ltd., IV
The Nature Conservancy, 28
New Plan Realty Trust, 11
New World Development Company Ltd., IV
Newhall Land and Farming Company, 14
Olympia & York Developments Ltd., IV; 9 (upd.)
Park Corp., 22
Perini Corporation, 8
Post Properties, Inc., 26
Rodamco N.V., 26
The Rouse Company, 15
Shubert Organization Inc., 24
The Sierra Club, 28
Slough Estates PLC, IV
Starrett Corporation, 21
Storage USA, Inc., 21
Sumitomo Realty & Development Co., Ltd., IV
Tokyu Land Corporation, IV
Trammell Crow Company, 8
Tridel Enterprises Inc., 9
Trizec Corporation Ltd., 10
Trump Organization, 23
Vistana, Inc., 22
Vornado Realty Trust, 20

RETAIL & WHOLESALE

A.C. Moore Arts & Crafts, Inc., 30
Aaron Rents, Inc., 14
ABC Appliance, Inc., 10
ABC Carpet & Home Co. Inc., 26
Abercrombie & Fitch Co., 15
Academy Sports & Outdoors, 27
Ace Hardware Corporation, 12
Action Performance Companies, Inc., 27
Alba-Waldensian, Inc., 30
Allou Health & Beauty Care, Inc., 28
Amazon.com, Inc., 25
American Coin Merchandising, Inc., 28
American Eagle Outfitters, Inc., 24
American Furniture Company, Inc., 21
American Stores Company, 22 (upd.)
Ames Department Stores, Inc., 9; 30 (upd.)
Amway Corporation, 13; 30 (upd.)
The Andersons, Inc., 31
Ann Taylor Stores Corporation, 13
Arbor Drugs Inc., 12
Arcadia Group plc, 28 (upd.)
Art Van Furniture, Inc., 28
ASDA Group plc, 28 (upd.)
Ashworth, Inc., 26
Au Printemps S.A., V
Audio King Corporation, 24
Authentic Fitness Corp., 20
Auto Value Associates, Inc., 25
AutoZone, Inc., 9; 31 (upd.)
Aveda Corporation, 24
B. Dalton Bookseller Inc., 25
Babbage's, Inc., 10
Baby Superstore, Inc., 15
Baccarat, 24
Bachman's Inc., 22
Banana Republic Inc., 25
Barnes & Noble, Inc., 10; 30 (upd.)
Barnett Inc., 28
Barney's, Inc., 28
Bearings, Inc., 13
bebe stores, inc., 31
Bed Bath & Beyond Inc., 13
Belk Stores Services, Inc., V; 19 (upd.)
Bergen Brunswig Corporation, V; 13 (upd.)
Bernard Chaus, Inc., 27
Best Buy Co., Inc., 9; 23 (upd.)
Bhs plc, 17
Big O Tires, Inc., 20
Black Box Corporation, 20
Blair Corporation, 25; 31 (upd.)
Bloomingdale's Inc., 12
Blyth Industries, Inc., 18
The Body Shop International PLC, 11
The Bombay Company, Inc., 10
The Bon Marché, Inc., 23
The Bon-Ton Stores, Inc., 16
Books-A-Million, Inc., 14
The Boots Company PLC, V; 24 (upd.)
Borders Group, Inc., 15
Boscov's Department Store, Inc., 31
Bozzuto's, Inc., 13
Bradlees Discount Department Store Company, 12
Brooks Brothers Inc., 22
Brookstone, Inc., 18
The Buckle, Inc., 18
Burlington Coat Factory Warehouse Corporation, 10
The Burton Group plc, V
Buttrey Food & Drug Stores Co., 18
C&A Brenninkmeyer KG, V
Cabela's Inc., 26
Cache Incorporated, 30
Caldor Inc., 12
Camelot Music, Inc., 26
Campeau Corporation, V
Campo Electronics, Appliances & Computers, Inc., 16
Carrefour SA, 10; 27 (upd.)
Carson Pirie Scott & Company, 15
Carter Hawley Hale Stores, Inc., V
Cartier Monde, 29
Catherines Stores Corporation, 15
Cato Corporation, 14
CDW Computer Centers, Inc., 16
Celebrity, Inc., 22
Central Garden & Pet Company, 23
Chadwick's of Boston, Ltd., 29
Cifra, S.A. de C.V., 12
The Circle K Company, 20 (upd.)
Circuit City Stores, Inc., 9; 29 (upd.)
The Clothestime, Inc., 20
CML Group, Inc., 10
Coborn's, Inc., 30
Coinmach Laundry Corporation, 20
Coldwater Creek Inc., 21
Cole National Corporation, 13
Coles Myer Ltd., V; 20 (upd.)
Comdisco, Inc., 9
CompUSA, Inc., 10
Computerland Corp., 13
Corby Distilleries Limited, 14
Corporate Express, Inc., 22
The Cosmetic Center, Inc., 22
Cost Plus, Inc., 27
Costco Wholesale Corporation, V
Cotter & Company, V
County Seat Stores Inc., 9
Crate and Barrel, 9
Crowley, Milner & Company, 19
Crown Books Corporation, 21
Cumberland Farms, Inc., 17
Daffy's Inc., 26
The Daiei, Inc., V; 17 (upd.)
The Daimaru, Inc., V
Dairy Mart Convenience Stores, Inc., 25 (upd.)
Daisytek International Corporation, 18
Damark International, Inc., 18
Dart Group Corporation, 16
Darty S.A., 27
Dayton Hudson Corporation, V; 18 (upd.)
Deb Shops, Inc., 16
Debenhams Plc, 28
dELiA*s Inc., 29
Designer Holdings Ltd., 20
Dillard Department Stores, Inc., V; 16 (upd.)
Dillon Companies Inc., 12
Discount Auto Parts, Inc., 18
Discount Drug Mart, Inc., 14
Dixons Group plc, V; 19 (upd.)
Do it Best Corporation, 30
Dollar Tree Stores, Inc., 23
The Dress Barn, Inc., 24
Drug Emporium, Inc., 12
Duane Reade Holding Corp., 21
Duckwall-ALCO Stores, Inc., 24
Duty Free International, Inc., 11
Dylex Limited, 29
E-Z Serve Corporation, 17
Eagle Hardware & Garden, Inc., 16
Eckerd Corporation, 9
Egghead.com, Inc., 31 (upd.)
El Corte Inglés Group, V
Elder-Beerman Stores Corporation, 10
Ellett Brothers, Inc., 17

EMI Group plc, 22 (upd.)
Euromarket Designs Inc., 31 (upd.)
Evans, Inc., 30
Family Dollar Stores, Inc., 13
Fastenal Company, 14
Fay's Inc., 17
Federated Department Stores, Inc., 9; 31 (upd.)
Fielmann AG, 31
Fila Holding S.p.A., 20
Fingerhut Companies, Inc., 9
The Finish Line, Inc., 29
Finlay Enterprises, Inc., 16
Fleming Companies, Inc., 17 (upd.)
Florsheim Shoe Company, 9
Florsheim Shoe Group Inc., 31 (upd.)
FNAC, 21
Follett Corporation, 12
Footstar, Incorporated, 24
Fortunoff Fine Jewelry and Silverware Inc., 26
Frank's Nursery & Crafts, Inc., 12
Fred Meyer, Inc., V; 20 (upd.)
Fred's, Inc., 23
Frederick Atkins Inc., 16
Fretter, Inc., 10
Friedman's Inc., 29
Funco, Inc., 20
G.I. Joe's, Inc., 30
Gadzooks, Inc., 18
Galeries Lafayette S.A., V; 23 (upd.)
Gander Mountain, Inc., 20
Gantos, Inc., 17
The Gap, Inc., V; 18 (upd.)
Garden Ridge Corporation, 27
Gart Sports Company, 24
GEHE AG, 27
General Binding Corporation, 10
General Host Corporation, 12
Genesco Inc., 17
Genovese Drug Stores, Inc., 18
Giant Food Inc., 22 (upd.)
GIB Group, V; 26 (upd.)
The Good Guys!, Inc., 10
The Good Guys, Inc., 30 (upd.)
Goodwill Industries International, Inc., 16
Goody's Family Clothing, Inc., 20
Gottschalks, Inc., 18
The Great Universal Stores plc, V; 19 (upd.)
Grossman's Inc., 13
Groupe Castorama-Dubois Investissements, 23
Groupe DMC (Dollfus Mieg & Cie), 27
Grow Biz International, Inc., 18
GT Bicycles, 26
Guccio Gucci, S.p.A., 15
Guitar Center, Inc., 29
Hahn Automotive Warehouse, Inc., 24
Hammacher Schlemmer & Company, 21
Hancock Fabrics, Inc., 18
Hankyu Department Stores, Inc., V
Harold's Stores, Inc., 22
Haverty Furniture Companies, Inc., 31
Hechinger Company, 12
Heilig-Meyers Co., 14
Hennes & Mauritz AB, 29
Hertie Waren- und Kaufhaus GmbH, V
Hibbett Sporting Goods, Inc., 26
Hills Stores Company, 13
Holiday RV Superstores, Incorporated, 26
The Home Depot, Inc., V; 18 (upd.)
Home Shopping Network, Inc., V; 25 (upd.)
House of Fabrics, Inc., 21
Hudson's Bay Company, V; 25 (upd.)
The IKEA Group, V
IKEA International A/S, 26 (upd.)
InaCom Corporation, 13
Insight Enterprises, Inc., 18
Intimate Brands, Inc., 24
Isetan Company Limited, V
Ito-Yokado Co., Ltd., V
J&R Electronics Inc., 26
J. Baker, Inc., 31
J.C. Penney Company, Inc., V; 18 (upd.)
Jack Schwartz Shoes, Inc., 18
Jacobson Stores Inc., 21
Jalate Inc., 25
Jay Jacobs, Inc., 15
Jennifer Convertibles, Inc., 31
JG Industries, Inc., 15
John Lewis Partnership PLC, V
JUSCO Co., Ltd., V
Just For Feet, Inc., 19
K & B Inc., 12
K & G Men's Center, Inc., 21
K-tel International, Inc., 21
Karstadt Aktiengesellschaft, V; 19 (upd.)
Kash n' Karry Food Stores, Inc., 20
Kaufhof Holding AG, V
Kaufhof Warenhaus AG, 23 (upd.)
Kay-Bee Toy Stores, 15
Kingfisher plc, V; 24 (upd.)
Kinney Shoe Corp., 14
Kmart Corporation, V; 18 (upd.)
Knoll Group Inc., 14
Kohl's Corporation, 9; 30 (upd.)
Kotobukiya Co., Ltd., V
Krause's Furniture, Inc., 27
L. Luria & Son, Inc., 19
L.A. T Sportswear, Inc., 26
La-Z-Boy Chair Company, 14
Lamonts Apparel, Inc., 15
Lands' End, Inc., 9; 29 (upd.)
Lazare Kaplan International Inc., 21
Lechmere Inc., 10
Lechters, Inc., 11
LensCrafters Inc., 23
Lesco Inc., 19
Leslie's Poolmart, Inc., 18
Levitz Furniture Inc., 15
Lewis Galoob Toys Inc., 16
Lifetime Hoan Corporation, 27
Lillian Vernon Corp., 12
The Limited, Inc., V; 20 (upd.)
Linens 'n Things, Inc., 24
The Littlewoods Organisation PLC, V
Liz Claiborne, Inc., 25 (upd.)
Loehmann's Inc., 24
Lojas Arapuã S.A., 22
Longs Drug Stores Corporation, V; 25 (upd.)
Lost Arrow Inc., 22
LOT$OFF Corporation, 24
Lowe's Companies, Inc., V; 21 (upd.)
Mac Frugal's Bargains - Closeouts Inc., 17
MarineMax, Inc., 30
Marks and Spencer p.l.c., V; 24 (upd.)
Marks Brothers Jewelers, Inc., 24
Marshalls Incorporated, 13
Marui Co., Ltd., V
Maruzen Co., Limited, 18
Mary Kay, Inc., 30 (upd.)
Matsuzakaya Company Limited, V
The Maxim Group, 25
The May Department Stores Company, V; 19 (upd.)
Mazel Stores, Inc., 29
McLane Company, Inc., 13
Meier & Frank Co., 23
Meijer Incorporated, 27 (upd.)
Melville Corporation, V
The Men's Wearhouse, Inc., 17
Mercantile Stores Company, Inc., V; 19 (upd.)
Merry-Go-Round Enterprises, Inc., 8
Mervyn's, 10
Michaels Stores, Inc., 17
Micro Warehouse, Inc., 16
MicroAge, Inc., 16
Mitsukoshi Ltd., V
Montgomery Ward & Co., Incorporated, V; 20 (upd.)
Morse Shoe Inc., 13
Mothers Work, Inc., 18
Musicland Stores Corporation, 9
Nagasakiya Co., Ltd., V
National Intergroup, Inc., V
National Record Mart, Inc., 29
Natural Wonders Inc., 14
Navy Exchange Service Command, 31
Neiman Marcus Co., 12
Next plc, 29
Nichii Co., Ltd., V
Nine West Group Inc., 11
99¢ Only Stores, 25
Noodle Kidoodle, 16
Nordstrom, Inc., V; 18 (upd.)
Norelco Consumer Products Co., 26
The North West Company, Inc., 12
Norton McNaughton, Inc., 27
Nu Skin Enterprises, Inc., 27
Office Depot Incorporated, 8; 23 (upd.)
OfficeMax Inc., 15
Old America Stores, Inc., 17
One Price Clothing Stores, Inc., 20
Orchard Supply Hardware Stores Corporation, 17
The Orvis Company, Inc., 28
Oshman's Sporting Goods, Inc., 17
Otto-Versand (GmbH & Co.), V; 15 (upd.)
Owens & Minor, Inc., 16
P.C. Richard & Son Corp., 23
Pamida Holdings Corporation, 15
The Pampered Chef, Ltd., 18
Parisian, Inc., 14
Paul Harris Stores, Inc., 18
Pay 'N Pak Stores, Inc., 9
Payless Cashways, Inc., 11
Payless ShoeSource, Inc., 18
Pearle Vision, Inc., 13
Peebles Inc., 16
Petco Animal Supplies, Inc., 29
Petrie Stores Corporation, 8
PETsMART, Inc., 14
Phar-Mor Inc., 12
Pier 1 Imports, Inc., 12
Piercing Pagoda, Inc., 29
Pinault-Printemps Redoute S.A., 19 (upd.)
The Price Company, V
PriceCostco, Inc., 14
Proffitt's, Inc., 19
Quelle Group, V
Quill Corporation, 28
R.H. Macy & Co., Inc., V; 8 (upd.); 30 (upd.)
Rag Shops, Inc., 30
Raley's Inc., 14
Rapala-Normark Group, Ltd., 30
Recoton Corp., 15
Recreational Equipment, Inc., 18
Reeds Jewelers, Inc., 22
Restoration Hardware, Inc., 30
Revco D.S., Inc., V
REX Stores Corp., 10
Rhodes Inc., 23
Riklis Family Corp., 9
Rite Aid Corporation, V; 19 (upd.)
Roberds Inc., 19
Rocky Shoes & Boots, Inc., 26
Rogers Communications Inc., 30 (upd.)
Rooms To Go Inc., 28
Rose's Stores, Inc., 13

Ross Stores, Inc., 17
Roundy's Inc., 14
S&K Famous Brands, Inc., 23
Saks Holdings, Inc., 24
Sam Ash Music Corporation, 30
Samuels Jewelers Incorporated, 30
Sanborn Hermanos, S.A., 20
Schneiderman's Furniture Inc., 28
Schottenstein Stores Corp., 14
Schultz Sav-O Stores, Inc., 31
The Score Board, Inc., 19
Scotty's, Inc., 22
Sears plc, V
Sears Roebuck de México, S.A. de C.V., 20
Sears, Roebuck and Co., V; 18 (upd.)
Seibu Department Stores, Ltd., V
The Seiyu, Ltd., V
Service Merchandise Company, Inc., V; 19 (upd.)
Shaklee Corporation, 12
The Sharper Image Corporation, 10
Shoe Carnival Inc., 14
ShopKo Stores Inc., 21
SkyMall, Inc., 26
Solo Serve Corporation, 28
Spec's Music, Inc., 19
Spiegel, Inc., 10; 27 (upd.)
Sport Chalet, Inc., 16
Sport Supply Group, Inc., 23
Sportmart, Inc., 15
Sports & Recreation, Inc., 17
The Sports Authority, Inc., 16
Stage Stores, Inc., 24
Stanhome Inc., 15
Staples, Inc., 10
Starcraft Corporation, 30
Stein Mart Inc., 19
Stinnes AG, 8
The Stop & Shop Companies, Inc., 24 (upd.)
Storehouse PLC, 16
Stride Rite Corporation, 8
Successories, Inc., 30
Sun Television & Appliances Inc., 10
Sunglass Hut International, Inc., 21
Supreme International Corporation, 27
Syms Corporation, 29
Takashimaya Co., Limited, V
The Talbots, Inc., 11; 31 (upd.)
Target Stores, 10; 27 (upd.)
Tati SA, 25
Tech Data Corporation, 10
Tengelmann Group, 27
Tesco PLC, 24 (upd.)
Thrifty PayLess, Inc., 12
Tiffany & Co., 14
The TJX Companies, Inc., V; 19 (upd.)
Today's Man, Inc., 20
Tokyu Department Store Co., Ltd., V
Tops Appliance City, Inc., 17
Toys "R" Us, Inc., V; 18 (upd.)
Trend-Lines, Inc., 22
TruServ Corporation, 24
Tuesday Morning Corporation, 18
Tupperware Corporation, 28
TVI, Inc., 15
Tweeter Home Entertainment Group, Inc., 30
Ultimate Electronics, Inc., 18
Ultramar Diamond Shamrock Corporation, 31 (upd.)
Uni-Marts, Inc., 17
The United States Shoe Corporation, V
United Stationers Inc., 14
Universal International, Inc., 25
Uny Co., Ltd., V
Urban Outfitters, Inc., 14
Value Merchants Inc., 13
ValueVision International, Inc., 22
Vendex International N.V., 13
Venture Stores Inc., 12
Viking Office Products, Inc., 10
Vorwerk & Co., 27
W. Atlee Burpee & Co., 27
W H Smith Group PLC, V
W.W. Grainger, Inc., V
Waban Inc., 13
Wacoal Corp., 25
Wal-Mart Stores, Inc., V; 8 (upd.); 26 (upd.)
Walden Book Company Inc., 17
Walgreen Co., V; 20 (upd.)
West Marine, Inc., 17
Western Beef, Inc., 22
The Wet Seal, Inc., 18
Whole Foods Market, Inc., 20
Wickes Inc., V; 25 (upd.)
Williams-Sonoma, Inc., 17
Wilsons The Leather Experts Inc., 21
Wolohan Lumber Co., 19
Woolworth Corporation, V; 20 (upd.)
World Duty Free Americas, Inc., 29 (upd.)
Younkers, Inc., 19
Zale Corporation, 16
Zany Brainy, Inc., 31
Ziebart International Corporation, 30

RUBBER & TIRE

Aeroquip Corporation, 16
Bandag, Inc., 19
The BFGoodrich Company, V
Bridgestone Corporation, V; 21 (upd.)
Carlisle Companies Incorporated, 8
Compagnie Générale des Établissements Michelin, V
Continental Aktiengesellschaft, V
Continental General Tire Corp., 23
Cooper Tire & Rubber Company, 8; 23 (upd.)
General Tire, Inc., 8
The Goodyear Tire & Rubber Company, V; 20 (upd.)
The Kelly-Springfield Tire Company, 8
Myers Industries, Inc., 19
Pirelli S.p.A., V; 15 (upd.)
Safeskin Corporation, 18
Sumitomo Rubber Industries, Ltd., V
Tillotson Corp., 15
Treadco, Inc., 19
The Yokohama Rubber Co., Ltd., V; 19 (upd.)

TELECOMMUNICATIONS

A.H. Belo Corporation, 30 (upd.)
Acme-Cleveland Corp., 13
ADC Telecommunications, Inc., 10
Adelphia Communications Corp., 17
Adtran Inc., 22
AirTouch Communications, 11
Alltel Corporation, 6
American Telephone and Telegraph Company, V
Ameritech Corporation, V; 18 (upd.)
Ascom AG, 9
Aspect Telecommunications Corporation, 22
AT&T Bell Laboratories, Inc., 13
AT&T Corporation, 29 (upd.)
BCE Inc., V
Belgacom, 6
Bell Atlantic Corporation, V; 25 (upd.)
Bell Canada, 6
BellSouth Corporation, V; 29 (upd.)
BET Holdings, Inc., 18
BHC Communications, Inc., 26
Bonneville International Corporation, 29
Bouygues S.A., 24 (upd.)
Brightpoint, Inc., 18
Brite Voice Systems, Inc., 20
British Columbia Telephone Company, 6
British Telecommunications plc, V; 15 (upd.)
Cable & Wireless HKT, 30 (upd.)
Cable and Wireless plc, V; 25 (upd.)
Cablevision Systems Corporation, 30 (upd.)
Canal Plus, 10
Carlton Communications plc, 15
Carolina Telephone and Telegraph Company, 10
CBS Corporation, 28 (upd.)
Centel Corporation, 6
Century Communications Corp., 10
Century Telephone Enterprises, Inc., 9
Chancellor Media Corporation, 24
Chris-Craft Industries, Inc., 9
Cincinnati Bell, Inc., 6
Clear Channel Communications, Inc., 23
Comcast Corporation, 24 (upd.)
Comdial Corporation, 21
Commonwealth Telephone Enterprises, Inc., 25
Comsat Corporation, 23
Comverse Technology, Inc., 15
DDI Corporation, 7
Deutsche Bundespost TELEKOM, V
Dialogic Corporation, 18
Directorate General of Telecommunications, 7
DSC Communications Corporation, 12
ECI Telecom Ltd., 18
eircom plc, 31 (upd.)
Electromagnetic Sciences Inc., 21
EXCEL Communications Inc., 18
Executone Information Systems, Inc., 13
Fox Family Worldwide, Inc., 24
France Télécom Group, V; 21 (upd.)
Frontier Corp., 16
Gannett Co., Inc., 30 (upd.)
General DataComm Industries, Inc., 14
Geotek Communications Inc., 21
Getty Images, Inc., 31
Gray Communications Systems, Inc., 24
Groupe Vidéotron Ltée., 20
Grupo Televisa, S.A., 18
GTE Corporation, V; 15 (upd.)
Havas, SA, 10
Hong Kong Telecommunications Ltd., 6
Hubbard Broadcasting Inc., 24
Hughes Electronics Corporation, 25
IDB Communications Group, Inc., 11
Illinois Bell Telephone Company, 14
Indiana Bell Telephone Company, Incorporated, 14
Infinity Broadcasting Corporation, 11
IXC Communications, Inc., 29
Jacor Communications, Inc., 23
Jones Intercable, Inc., 21
Koninklijke PTT Nederland NV, V
LCI International, Inc., 16
LDDS-Metro Communications, Inc., 8
LIN Broadcasting Corp., 9
Lincoln Telephone & Telegraph Company, 14
LodgeNet Entertainment Corporation, 28
Martha Stewart Living Omnimedia, L.L.C., 24
MasTec, Inc., 19
McCaw Cellular Communications, Inc., 6
MCI Communications Corporation, V
MCI WorldCom, Inc., 27 (upd.)
Mercury Communications, Ltd., 7
Metromedia Companies, 14

MFS Communications Company, Inc., 11
Michigan Bell Telephone Co., 14
MIH Limited, 31
MITRE Corporation, 26
Mobile Telecommunications Technologies Corp., 18
Multimedia, Inc., 11
National Broadcasting Company, Inc., 28 (upd.)
NCR Corporation, 30 (upd.)
NetCom Systems AB, 26
Nevada Bell Telephone Company, 14
New Valley Corporation, 17
Nextel Communications, Inc., 27 (upd.)
Nippon Telegraph and Telephone Corporation, V
Norstan, Inc., 16
Northern Telecom Limited, V
NYNEX Corporation, V
Octel Communications Corp., 14
Ohio Bell Telephone Company, 14
Österreichische Post- und Telegraphenverwaltung, V
Pacific Telecom, Inc., 6
Pacific Telesis Group, V
Paging Network Inc., 11
PictureTel Corp., 10; 27 (upd.)
Posti- ja Telelaitos, 6
Qualcomm Inc., 20
QVC Network Inc., 9
Rochester Telephone Corporation, 6
Rogers Communications Inc., 30 (upd.)
Royal KPN N.V., 30
Saga Communications, Inc., 27
Schweizerische Post-, Telefon- und Telegrafen-Betriebe, V
Scientific-Atlanta, Inc., 6
Sinclair Broadcast Group, Inc., 25
Società Finanziaria Telefonica per Azioni, V
Southern New England Telecommunications Corporation, 6
Southwestern Bell Corporation, V
Sprint Communications Company, L.P., 9
StrataCom, Inc., 16
Swedish Telecom, V
SynOptics Communications, Inc., 10
Telecom Australia, 6
Telecom Eireann, 7
Telefonaktiebolaget LM Ericsson, V
Telefónica de España, S.A., V
Telefonos de Mexico S.A. de C.V., 14
Telephone and Data Systems, Inc., 9
Télévision Française 1, 23
Tellabs, Inc., 11
U.S. Satellite Broadcasting Company, Inc., 20
U S West, Inc., V; 25 (upd.)
U.S. Cellular Corporation, 31 (upd.)
United States Cellular Corporation, 9
United Telecommunications, Inc., V
United Video Satellite Group, 18
Vodafone Group plc, 11
The Walt Disney Company, 30 (upd.)
Watkins-Johnson Company, 15
Westwood One, Inc., 23
The Williams Companies, Inc., 31 (upd.)
Wisconsin Bell, Inc., 14

TEXTILES & APPAREL

Adidas AG, 14
Alba-Waldensian, Inc., 30
Albany International Corp., 8
Algo Group Inc., 24
American Safety Razor Company, 20
Amoskeag Company, 8
Angelica Corporation, 15
AR Accessories Group, Inc., 23
Aris Industries, Inc., 16
Authentic Fitness Corp., 20
Banana Republic Inc., 25
Benetton Group S.p.A., 10
Birkenstock Footprint Sandals, Inc., 12
Blair Corporation, 25
Brazos Sportswear, Inc., 23
Brooks Brothers Inc., 22
Brown Group, Inc., V; 20 (upd.)
Bugle Boy Industries, Inc., 18
Burberrys Ltd., 17
Burlington Industries, Inc., V; 17 (upd.)
Calvin Klein, Inc., 22
Candie's, Inc., 31
Canstar Sports Inc., 16
Carhartt, Inc., 30
Cato Corporation, 14
Chargeurs International, 21 (upd.)
Charming Shoppes, Inc., 8
Cherokee Inc., 18
Chic by H.I.S, Inc., 20
Chorus Line Corporation, 30
Christian Dior S.A., 19
Claire's Stores, Inc., 17
Coach Leatherware, 10
Coats Viyella Plc, V
Collins & Aikman Corporation, 13
Columbia Sportswear Company, 19
Concord Fabrics, Inc., 16
Cone Mills Corporation, 8
Converse Inc., 31 (upd.)
Courtaulds plc, V; 17 (upd.)
Crown Crafts, Inc., 16
Crystal Brands, Inc., 9
Culp, Inc., 29
Cygne Designs, Inc., 25
Danskin, Inc., 12
Deckers Outdoor Corporation, 22
Delta Woodside Industries, Inc., 8; 30 (upd.)
Designer Holdings Ltd., 20
The Dixie Group, Inc., 20
Dominion Textile Inc., 12
Donna Karan Company, 15
Donnkenny, Inc., 17
Dyersburg Corporation, 21
Edison Brothers Stores, Inc., 9
Esprit de Corp., 8; 29 (upd.)
Evans, Inc., 30
Fab Industries, Inc., 27
Fabri-Centers of America Inc., 16
Fieldcrest Cannon, Inc., 9; 31 (upd.)
Fila Holding S.p.A., 20
Florsheim Shoe Group Inc., 31 (upd.)
Fossil, Inc., 17
Frederick's of Hollywood Inc., 16
Fruit of the Loom, Inc., 8; 25 (upd.)
Fubu, 29
G&K Services, Inc., 16
G-III Apparel Group, Ltd., 22
Galey & Lord, Inc., 20
Garan, Inc., 16
Gianni Versace SpA, 22
The Gitano Group, Inc. 8
Greenwood Mills, Inc., 14
Groupe DMC (Dollfus Mieg & Cie), 27
Groupe Yves Saint Laurent, 23
Guccio Gucci, S.p.A., 15
Guess, Inc., 15
Guilford Mills Inc., 8
Gymboree Corporation, 15
Haggar Corporation, 19
Hampton Industries, Inc., 20
Happy Kids Inc., 30
Hartmarx Corporation, 8
The Hartstone Group plc, 14
Healthtex, Inc., 17
Helly Hansen ASA, 25
Hermès S.A., 14
Hyde Athletic Industries, Inc., 17
I.C. Isaacs & Company, 31
Interface, Inc., 8; 29 (upd.)
Irwin Toy Limited, 14
Items International Airwalk Inc., 17
J. Crew Group Inc., 12
Jockey International, Inc., 12
Johnston Industries, Inc., 15
Jordache Enterprises, Inc., 23
Jos. A. Bank Clothiers, Inc., 31
JPS Textile Group, Inc., 28
Kellwood Company, 8
Kenneth Cole Productions, Inc., 25
Kinney Shoe Corp., 14
L.A. Gear, Inc., 8
L.L. Bean, Inc., 10
LaCrosse Footwear, Inc., 18
Laura Ashley Holdings plc, 13
Lee Apparel Company, Inc., 8
The Leslie Fay Companies, Inc., 8
Levi Strauss & Co., V; 16 (upd.)
Liz Claiborne, Inc., 8
London Fog Industries, Inc., 29
Lost Arrow Inc., 22
Maidenform Worldwide Inc., 20
Malden Mills Industries, Inc., 16
Marzotto S.p.A., 20
Milliken & Co., V; 17 (upd.)
Mitsubishi Rayon Co., Ltd., V
Mossimo, Inc., 27
Mothercare UK Ltd., 17
Movie Star Inc., 17
Nautica Enterprises, Inc., 18
New Balance Athletic Shoe, Inc., 25
Nike, Inc., V; 8 (upd.)
The North Face, Inc., 18
Oakley, Inc., 18
OshKosh B'Gosh, Inc., 9
Oxford Industries, Inc., 8
Pacific Sunwear of California, Inc., 28
Pentland Group plc, 20
Pillowtex Corporation, 19
Pluma, Inc., 27
Polo/Ralph Lauren Corporation, 12
PremiumWear, Inc., 30
Quaker Fabric Corp., 19
Quiksilver, Inc., 18
R.G. Barry Corp., 17
Recreational Equipment, Inc., 18
Red Wing Shoe Company, Inc., 30 (upd.)
Reebok International Ltd., V; 9 (upd.); 26 (upd.)
Rollerblade, Inc., 15
Russell Corporation, 8; 30 (upd.)
St. John Knits, Inc., 14
Shelby Williams Industries, Inc., 14
Skechers U.S.A. Inc., 31
Springs Industries, Inc., V; 19 (upd.)
Starter Corp., 12
Stone Manufacturing Company, 14
Stride Rite Corporation, 8
Sun Sportswear, Inc., 17
Superior Uniform Group, Inc., 30
Teijin Limited, V
Thomaston Mills, Inc., 27
The Timberland Company, 13
Tommy Hilfiger Corporation, 20
Toray Industries, Inc., V
Tultex Corporation, 13
Unifi, Inc., 12
United Merchants & Manufacturers, Inc., 13
Unitika Ltd., V
Vans, Inc., 16
Varsity Spirit Corp., 15
VF Corporation, V; 17 (upd.)

Walton Monroe Mills, Inc., 8
The Warnaco Group Inc., 12
Wellman, Inc., 8
West Point-Pepperell, Inc., 8
WestPoint Stevens Inc., 16
Williamson-Dickie Manufacturing Company, 14
Wolverine World Wide Inc., 16

TOBACCO

American Brands, Inc., V
B.A.T. Industries PLC, 22 (upd.)
Brooke Group Ltd., 15
Brown and Williamson Tobacco Corporation, 14
Culbro Corporation, 15
Dibrell Brothers, Incorporated, 12
DIMON Inc., 27
800-JR Cigar, Inc., 27
Gallaher Limited, V; 19 (upd.)
Imasco Limited, V
Japan Tobacco Incorporated, V
Philip Morris Companies Inc., V; 18 (upd.)
R.J. Reynolds Tobacco Holdings, Inc., 30 (upd.)
RJR Nabisco Holdings Corp., V
Rothmans International p.l.c., V
Rothmans UK Holdings Limited, 19 (upd.)
Seita, 23
Standard Commercial Corporation, 13
Swisher International Group Inc., 23
Tabacalera, S.A., V; 17 (upd.)
Universal Corporation, V
UST Inc., 9

TRANSPORT SERVICES

Air Express International Corporation, 13
Airborne Freight Corp., 6
Alamo Rent A Car, Inc., 6; 24 (upd.)
Alexander & Baldwin, Inc., 10
Amerco, 6
American Classic Voyages Company, 27
American President Companies Ltd., 6
Anschutz Corp., 12
Atlas Van Lines, Inc., 14
Avis Rent A Car, Inc., 22 (upd.)
Avis, Inc., 6
BAA plc, 10
Bekins Company, 15
British Railways Board, V
Broken Hill Proprietary Company Ltd., 22 (upd.)
Budget Group, Inc., 25
Budget Rent a Car Corporation, 9
Burlington Northern Inc., V
Burlington Northern Santa Fe Corporation, 27 (upd.)
Canadian National Railway System, 6
Canadian Pacific Limited, V
Carey International, Inc., 26
Carlson Companies, Inc., 6
Carolina Freight Corporation, 6
Celadon Group Inc., 30
Chargeurs, 6
Chicago and North Western Holdings Corporation, 6
Coach USA, Inc., 24
Coles Express Inc., 15
Compagnie Générale Maritime et Financière, 6
Consolidated Delivery & Logistics, Inc., 24
Consolidated Freightways Corporation, V; 21 (upd.)
Consolidated Rail Corporation, V
Crowley Maritime Corporation, 6; 28 (upd.)
CSX Corporation, V; 22 (upd.)
Danzas Group, V
Deutsche Bundesbahn, V
DHL Worldwide Express, 6; 24 (upd.)
Dollar Thrifty Automotive Group, Inc., 25
East Japan Railway Company, V
Emery Air Freight Corporation, 6
Emery Worldwide Airlines, Inc., 25 (upd.)
Enterprise Rent-A-Car Company, 6
Evergreen Marine Corporation Taiwan Ltd., 13
Expeditors International of Washington Inc., 17
Federal Express Corporation, V
FedEx Corporation, 18 (upd.)
Fritz Companies, Inc., 12
Frozen Food Express Industries, Inc., 20
GATX Corporation, 6; 25 (upd.)
Genesee & Wyoming Inc., 27
The Go-Ahead Group Plc, 28
The Greenbrier Companies, 19
Hankyu Corporation, V; 23 (upd.)
Hapag-Lloyd AG, 6
Harland and Wolff Holdings plc, 19
Harper Group Inc., 17
Heartland Express, Inc., 18
The Hertz Corporation, 9
Hospitality Worldwide Services, Inc., 26
Hvide Marine Incorporated, 22
Illinois Central Corporation, 11
International Shipholding Corporation, Inc., 27
J.B. Hunt Transport Services Inc., 12
Kansas City Southern Industries, Inc., 6; 26 (upd.)
Kawasaki Kisen Kaisha, Ltd., V
Keio Teito Electric Railway Company, V
Kinki Nippon Railway Company Ltd., V
Kirby Corporation, 18
Koninklijke Nedlloyd Groep N.V., 6
Kuhne & Nagel International A.G., V
La Poste, V
Leaseway Transportation Corp., 12
London Regional Transport, 6
Maine Central Railroad Company, 16
Mammoet Transport B.V., 26
Mayflower Group Inc., 6
Mercury Air Group, Inc., 20
The Mersey Docks and Harbour Company, 30
Miller Industries, Inc., 26
Mitsui O.S.K. Lines, Ltd., V
Moran Towing Corporation, Inc., 15
Morris Travel Services L.L.C., 26
National Car Rental System, Inc., 10
National Railroad Passenger Corporation, 22
NFC plc, 6
Nippon Express Co., Ltd., V
Nippon Yusen Kabushiki Kaisha, V
Norfolk Southern Corporation, V; 29 (upd.)
Ocean Group plc, 6
Odakyu Electric Railway Company Limited, V
Oglebay Norton Company, 17
Österreichische Bundesbahnen GmbH, 6
OTR Express, Inc., 25
Overnite Transportation Co., 14
Overseas Shipholding Group, Inc., 11
The Peninsular and Oriental Steam Navigation Company, V
Penske Corporation, V
PHH Corporation, V
Post Office Group, V
Preston Corporation, 6
RailTex, Inc., 20
Roadway Express, Inc., 25 (upd.)
Roadway Services, Inc., V
Ryder System, Inc., V; 24 (upd.)
Santa Fe Pacific Corporation, V
Schenker-Rhenus AG, 6
Seibu Railway Co. Ltd., V
Seino Transportation Company, Ltd., 6
Simon Transportation Services Inc., 27
Société Nationale des Chemins de Fer Français, V
Southern Pacific Transportation Company, V
Stagecoach Holdings plc, 30
Stevedoring Services of America Inc., 28
Stinnes AG, 8
Sunoco, Inc., 28 (upd.)
The Swiss Federal Railways (Schweizerische Bundesbahnen), V
Teekay Shipping Corporation, 25
Tidewater Inc., 11
TNT Freightways Corporation, 14
TNT Limited, V
TNT Post Group N.V., 27 (upd.); 30 (upd.)
Tobu Railway Co Ltd, 6
Tokyu Corporation, V
Totem Resources Corporation, 9
Transnet Ltd., 6
TTX Company, 6
U.S. Delivery Systems, Inc., 22
Union Pacific Corporation, V; 28 (upd.)
United Parcel Service of America Inc., V; 17 (upd.)
United States Postal Service, 14
Werner Enterprises, Inc., 26
Wisconsin Central Transportation Corporation, 24
Yamato Transport Co. Ltd., V
Yellow Corporation, 14
Yellow Freight System, Inc. of Delaware, V

UTILITIES

The AES Corporation, 10; 13 (upd.)
Air & Water Technologies Corporation, 6
Allegheny Power System, Inc., V
American Electric Power Company, Inc., V
American Water Works Company, 6
Arkla, Inc., V
Associated Natural Gas Corporation, 11
Atlanta Gas Light Company, 6; 23 (upd.)
Atlantic Energy, Inc., 6
Baltimore Gas and Electric Company, V; 25 (upd.)
Bayernwerk AG, V; 23 (upd.)
Big Rivers Electric Corporation, 11
Black Hills Corporation, 20
Boston Edison Company, 12
Bouygues S.A., 24 (upd.)
British Gas plc, V
British Nuclear Fuels plc, 6
Brooklyn Union Gas, 6
Canadian Utilities Limited, 13
Carolina Power & Light Company, V; 23 (upd.)
Cascade Natural Gas Corporation, 9
Centerior Energy Corporation, V
Central and South West Corporation, V
Central Hudson Gas and Electricity Corporation, 6
Central Maine Power, 6
Centrica plc, 29 (upd.)
Chubu Electric Power Company, Incorporated, V
Chugoku Electric Power Company Inc., V
Cincinnati Gas & Electric Company, 6
CIPSCO Inc., 6
Citizens Utilities Company, 7
City Public Service, 6
CMS Energy Corporation, V, 14
The Coastal Corporation, 31 (upd.)

Cogentrix Energy, Inc., 10
The Coleman Company, Inc., 9
The Columbia Gas System, Inc., V; 16 (upd.)
Commonwealth Edison Company, V
Commonwealth Energy System, 14
Connecticut Light and Power Co., 13
Consolidated Edison Company of New York, Inc., V
Consolidated Natural Gas Company, V; 19 (upd.)
Consumers Power Co., 14
Consumers Water Company, 14
Consumers' Gas Company Ltd., 6
Destec Energy, Inc., 12
The Detroit Edison Company, V
Dominion Resources, Inc., V
DPL Inc., 6
DQE, Inc., 6
DTE Energy Company, 20 (upd.)
Duke Energy Corporation, 27 (upd.)
Duke Power Company, V
Eastern Enterprises, 6
El Paso Electric Company, 21
El Paso Natural Gas Company, 12
Electricité de France, V
Elektrowatt AG, 6
ENDESA Group, V
Enron Corp., V
Enserch Corporation, V
Ente Nazionale per L'Energia Elettrica, V
Entergy Corporation, V
Equitable Resources, Inc., 6
Florida Progress Corporation, V; 23 (upd.)
Fortis, Inc., 15
Fortum Corporation, 30 (upd.)
FPL Group, Inc., V
Gaz de France, V
General Public Utilities Corporation, V
Générale des Eaux Group, V
GPU, Inc., 27 (upd.)
Gulf States Utilities Company, 6
Hawaiian Electric Industries, Inc., 9
Hokkaido Electric Power Company Inc., V
Hokuriku Electric Power Company, V
Hongkong Electric Holdings Ltd., 6; 23 (upd.)
Houston Industries Incorporated, V
Hydro-Québec, 6
Idaho Power Company, 12
Illinois Bell Telephone Company, 14
Illinois Power Company, 6
Indiana Energy, Inc., 27
IPALCO Enterprises, Inc., 6
The Kansai Electric Power Co., Inc., V
Kansas City Power & Light Company, 6
Kenetech Corporation, 11
Kentucky Utilities Company, 6
KeySpan Energy Co., 27
KU Energy Corporation, 11
Kyushu Electric Power Company Inc., V
LG&E Energy Corporation, 6
Long Island Lighting Company, V
Lyonnaise des Eaux-Dumez, V
Magma Power Company, 11
MCN Corporation, 6
MDU Resources Group, Inc., 7
Midwest Resources Inc., 6
Minnesota Power & Light Company, 11
Montana Power Company, 11
National Fuel Gas Company, 6
National Power PLC, 12
Nebraska Public Power District, 29
N.V. Nederlandse Gasunie, V
Nevada Power Company, 11
New England Electric System, V
New York State Electric and Gas, 6
Niagara Mohawk Power Corporation, V
NICOR Inc., 6
NIPSCO Industries, Inc., 6
North West Water Group plc, 11
Northeast Utilities, V
Northern States Power Company, V; 20 (upd.)
Nova Corporation of Alberta, V
Oglethorpe Power Corporation, 6
Ohio Edison Company, V
Oklahoma Gas and Electric Company, 6
ONEOK Inc., 7
Ontario Hydro, 6
Osaka Gas Co., Ltd., V
Otter Tail Power Company, 18
Pacific Enterprises, V
Pacific Gas and Electric Company, V
PacifiCorp, V; 26 (upd.)
Panhandle Eastern Corporation, V
PECO Energy Company, 11
Pennsylvania Power & Light Company, V
Peoples Energy Corporation, 6
PG&E Corporation, 26 (upd.)
Philadelphia Electric Company, V
Piedmont Natural Gas Company, Inc., 27
Pinnacle West Capital Corporation, 6
Portland General Corporation, 6
Potomac Electric Power Company, 6
PowerGen PLC, 11
PreussenElektra Aktiengesellschaft, V
PSI Resources, 6
Public Service Company of Colorado, 6
Public Service Company of New Hampshire, 21
Public Service Company of New Mexico, 6
Public Service Enterprise Group Incorporated, V
Puget Sound Power and Light Company, 6
Questar Corporation, 6; 26 (upd.)
Rochester Gas and Electric Corporation, 6
Ruhrgas A.G., V
RWE Group, V
Salt River Project, 19
San Diego Gas & Electric Company, V
SCANA Corporation, 6
Scarborough Public Utilities Commission, 9
SCEcorp, V
Scottish Hydro-Electric PLC, 13
ScottishPower plc, 19
Sempra Energy, 25 (upd.)
Severn Trent PLC, 12
Shikoku Electric Power Company, Inc., V
Sonat, Inc., 6
The Southern Company, V
Southern Electric PLC, 13
Southern Indiana Gas and Electric Company, 13
Southern Union Company, 27
Southwest Gas Corporation, 19
Southwestern Electric Power Co., 21
Southwestern Public Service Company, 6
TECO Energy, Inc., 6
Texas Utilities Company, V; 25 (upd.)
Thames Water plc, 11
Tohoku Electric Power Company, Inc., V
The Tokyo Electric Power Company, Incorporated, V
Tokyo Gas Co., Ltd., V
TransAlta Utilities Corporation, 6
TransCanada PipeLines Limited, V
Transco Energy Company, V
Tucson Electric Power Company, 6
UGI Corporation, 12
Unicom Corporation, 29 (upd.)
Union Electric Company, V
The United Illuminating Company, 21
Utah Power and Light Company, 27
UtiliCorp United Inc., 6
Vereinigte Elektrizitätswerke Westfalen AG, V
Washington Gas Light Company, 19
Washington Natural Gas Company, 9
Washington Water Power Company, 6
Western Resources, Inc., 12
Wheelabrator Technologies, Inc., 6
Wisconsin Energy Corporation, 6
Wisconsin Public Service Corporation, 9
WPL Holdings, Inc., 6

WASTE SERVICES

Allwaste, Inc., 18
Azcon Corporation, 23
Browning-Ferris Industries, Inc., V; 20 (upd.)
Chemical Waste Management, Inc., 9
Copart Inc., 23
Philip Environmental Inc., 16
Roto-Rooter Corp., 15
Safety-Kleen Corp., 8
Waste Management, Inc., V
WMX Technologies Inc., 17

NOTES ON CONTRIBUTORS

Notes on Contributors

BIANCO, David. Freelance writer, editor, and publishing consultant.

BISCONTINI, Tracey Vasil. Pennsylvania-based freelance writer, editor, and columnist.

BROWN, Susan Windisch. Freelance writer and editor.

BRYNILDSSEN, Shawna. Freelance writer and editor based in Bloomington, Indiana.

COHEN, M. L. Novelist and freelance writer living in Paris.

COVELL, Jeffrey L. Freelance writer and corporate history contractor.

DERDAK, Thomas. Freelance writer and adjunct professor of philosophy at Loyola University of Chicago.

FIERO, John. Freelance writer, researcher, and consultant.

FUJINAKA, MARIKO. Freelance writer and editor based in California.

HALASZ, Robert. Former editor in chief of *World Progress* and *Funk & Wagnalls New Encyclopedia Yearbook*; author, *The U.S. Marines* (Millbrook Press, 1993).

HAUSER, Evelyn. Freelance writer and marketing specialist based in Northern California.

INGRAM, Frederick C. South Carolina-based business writer who has contributed to *GSA Business, Appalachian Trailway News,* the *Encyclopedia of Business,* the *Encyclopedia of Global Industries,* the *Encyclopedia of Consumer Brands,* and other regional and trade publications.

LEMIEUX, Gloria A. Freelance writer and editor living in Nashua, New Hampshire.

MARTIN, Rachel. Denver-based freelance writer.

ROTHBURD, Carrie. Freelance technical writer and editor, specializing in corporate profiles, academic texts, and academic journal articles.

STANFEL, Rebecca. Freelance writer and editor.

TRADII, Mary. Freelance writer based in Denver, Colorado.

UHLE, Frank. Ann Arbor-based freelance writer; movie projectionist, disc jockey, and staff member of *Psychotronic Video* magazine.

WALDEN, David M. Freelance writer and historian in Salt Lake City; adjunct history instructor at Salt Lake City Community College.

WERNICK, Ellen. Freelance writer and editor.

WOODWARD, A. Freelance writer and editor.